GREAT LIVES of the CENTURY

GREAT LIVES of the CENTURY

As Reported by
The New York Times

Edited by
Arleen Keylin

AN ARNO PRESS BOOK

Times BOOKS

A Note to the Reader
Original copies of *The New York Times* were not available to the publisher. This volume, therefore, was created from 35mm microfilm.

 For information, address: Times Books, a division of Quadrangle/The New York Times Book Co., Inc., Three Park Avenue, New York, N.Y. 10016. Manufactured in the United States of America.

Library of Congress Cataloging in Publication Data
Main entry under title:
Great lives of the century.
1. Obituaries. 2. Biography—20th century.
I. Keylin, Arleen. II. New York Times.
CT120.P46 920'.02 76-55945
ISBN: 0-8129-0732-9

Assistant to the Editor: Suri Fleischer
Editorial Assistant: Sandra Jones

Book design by Stephanie Rhodes

Manufactured in the United States of America

CONTENTS

GREAT LIVES of the CENTURY

"All the News That's Fit to Print"

The New York Times

LATE CITY EDITION

Weather: Mostly sunny, hot today; fair tonight. Sunny tomorrow. Temp. range: today 71-90; Tuesday 69-91. Temp.-Hum. Index yesterday 81. Full U.S. report on Page 74.

VOL. CXX . . No. 41,437 NEW YORK, WEDNESDAY, JULY 7, 1971 15 CENTS

PRESIDENT ASKS THAT STEEL PACT BE 'CONSTRUCTIVE'

He Calls for an Accord to Strengthen U.S. Industry in the World Market

OFFERS NO GUIDELINES

He Confers at White House With Both Sides on Eve of Contract Bargaining

By PHILIP SHABECOFF
Special to The New York Times

WASHINGTON, July 6—Appealing to patriotism and enlightened self-interest, President Nixon admonished leaders of the steel union and the steel industry today to reach a "constructive" contract settlement.

As he brought the power of the Presidency to bear on the initial stages of a national bargaining process for the first time since he took office, Mr. Nixon summoned representatives of the major steel companies and the United Steelworkers to the Cabinet Room of the White House this morning.

He told them that the interests of labor, management and the nation would coincide in the negotiation of a new contract that would help the United States steel industry to become more competitive in the world market.

He Speaks to Editors

Later, stopping in Kansas City, Mo., to address a group of editors on his way to the summer White House in San Clemente, Calif., the President said that the nation would face heavy economic competition from four powers—the Soviet Union, China, Western Europe and Japan. He said this country would have to make internal reforms to meet the challenge.

George P. Shultz, director of the Office of Management and Budget, said at a news briefing that the President had not told the steel negotiators what to settle for or how to conduct their negotiations.

Union Firm on Aims

Mr. Shultz said that the chances of a strike when the three-year contract between the union and the major steel companies expired on Aug. 1 had receded considerably since the beginning of the year.

The union, which negotiates for more than 400,000 employes in the steel industry, has let it be known that it will not settle for less than the 31 per cent wage increase over three years won by the aluminum workers earlier this year.

Administration officials have said privately that it is "realistic" to expect a similar settlement in steel.

I. W. Abel, president of the United Steelworkers, and R. Heath Larry, vice chairman of the United States Steel Corporation and chief company negotiator, will go to the Shoreham

Continued on Page 17, Column 1

Associated Press

WHITE HOUSE CONFERENCE ON STEEL: George P. Shultz, left, head of Office of Management and Budget, and Joseph P. Malony, right, vice president of the United Steelworkers, at session yesterday. Across the table, from left: R. Heath Larry, vice chairman of United States Steel Corporation; President Nixon; I. W. Abel, president of the steel union, and Paul W. McCracken, who is the chairman of the President's Council of Economic Advisers.

Bar Group Bids Judges Set Example of Decorum

By LESLEY OELSNER

By unanimous voice vote of its 297-member policy-making unit, the American Bar Association adopted yesterday a set of courtroom guidelines that urged judges to set the tone for orderly proceedings by behaving well themselves.

The guidelines also listed the measures judges might use to handle disorderly defendants, lawyers and spectators, but they suggested that they use the "least severe sanction" appropriate to the situation.

The association, again by unanimous vote, also agreed to begin lobbying for "humanitarian treatment" of prisoners of war in Southeast Asia.

Repatriation Asked

The objectives of its war efforts, a resolution said, would include immediate "repatriation of all seriously wounded or sick" prisoners; repatriation or internment in a neutral country of those who had been held for more than 18 months; and, "at a minimum," a "full list" of all persons now detained.

"The American Bar Association calls upon all appropriate organizations of lawyers of all the countries of the world," the resolution said, to urge upon "their respective governments" any action that would obtain these objectives.

A committee report attached to the resolution — the first stand the A.B.A. has taken on the subject—indicated that the association's leadership would

Continued on Page 21, Column 1

2 Held Without Bail In Prostitution Case By an Angry Judge

By JUAN M. VASQUEZ

Two women charged with prostitution were held without bail yesterday in Manhattan Criminal Court by an irate judge who complained that "the midtown area is inundated with prostitution."

Judge Morris L. Schwalb took the action — which is without known precedent here in a prostitution case—after imposing increasingly stern measures to deal with what he said was an increasing load of such cases.

"They have created a hazard to the business, theater, restaurant and hotel interests," the judge said from the bench in the arraignment courtroom.

Only last week, the Police Department said harassment of visitors to the midtown area by prostitutes had become so frequent that it would begin taking Polaroid photographs of the women to supply evidence against them in court.

"We all know that venereal disease has reached epidemic proportions," Judge Schwalb said, "and streetwalking prostitutes contribute to disease in a large measure. They are responsible for serious crimes against persons and property."

The actions against the two women stood in sharp contrast to the routine fashion in which prostitution cases are handled.

The police often complain that they arrest prostitutes only to find them back out on the street and "on the job" within

Continued on Page 21, Column 4

2 SLUM REBUILDERS ACCUSED BY RUSKIN

Investigation Chief Asserts They Got $300,000 Excess From City Loan Setup

By EDITH EVANS ASBURY

City Investigation Commissioner Robert K. Ruskin charged yesterday that two men had pocketed a $300,000 windfall from an inflated mortgage from the city's Municipal Loan Program and suspended further payments for slum rehabilitation to the pair.

The two men, Herbert Zabell and David Leber, and various companies they control, are doing approximately $7-million worth of work on five rehabilitation jobs for the city, according to a spokesman for the Housing and Development Administration.

William D. Clarke, then deputy commissioner in charge of rehabilitation for the Housing and Development Administration, approved the inflated mortgage, and is also under investigation, Mr. Ruskin said.

The Municipal Loan Program, established in 1962 and since funded with a total of $136-million, is under supervision of the H.D.A. department that Mr. Clarke headed. He resigned last January.

The loan program was established to finance the rehabilitation of slum buildings by lending

Continued on Page 49, Column 4

Governor Signs Bill Allowing Purchase Of Stadium by City

By THOMAS P. RONAN
Special to The New York Times

ALBANY, July 6—Governor Rockefeller announced today the signing of a bill authorizing New York City to buy and modernize Yankee Stadium as a means of keeping the New York Yankees and the Football Giants in the city.

Mayor Lindsay promptly hailed the Governor's action as clearing the way for the city to implement its plans for the stadium "so that big-league baseball and football can flourish as never before in the Bronx."

The Governor also signed a bill authorizing the city to build what is expected to be the country's largest convention and exhibition center along the Hudson River north of 42d Street, and another bill requiring that the Board of Estimate approve all consultants' contracts over $10,000.

The 30-day period for the Governor to sign or veto bills passed by the Legislature ends at midnight and Mr. Rockefeller was in his New York City office completing action on about 200 measures left of the more than 1,500 sent to him. His decisions are expected to be announced tomorrow.

"The new Yankee Stadium and its surrounding facilities will meet every requirement of a modern sports complex," the Mayor said in a City Hall

Continued on Page 49, Column 2

29 LARGE BANKS RAISE PRIME RATE TO 6% FROM 5½%

But 3 Largest Do Not Follow Manufacturers Hanover's Lead in the Increase

By H. ERICH HEINEMANN

The nation's major banks—many of them carefully playing the role of reluctant dragon—began yesterday to raise their prime lending rates to 6 per cent from 5½ per cent.

The Manufacturers Hanover Trust Company, the third-largest bank in New York City and the fourth-largest bank in the country, announced its increase in this key minimum charge on loans to the most creditworthy businesses at about 9:45 yesterday morning.

By the end of the business day, at least 28 other large banks had joined in the increase, which had been widely anticipated for more than a month because of the upward sweep of interest rates in the open market.

However, of those banks setting a 6 per cent rate, only six were among the 20 largest banks in the country. Among those remaining at 5½ per cent were the three largest—Bank of America, San Francisco, and the First National City and Chase Manhattan banks in New York. The First Pennsylvania Banking & Trust Company, which set a 5¾ per cent rate in mid-June, increased its prime rate to 6 per cent yesterday.

Patman Seeks Rollback

Interest rates on home mortgages are already on the upgrade in response to the same money-market pressures that have helped to trigger the increase in the prime rate. This upward drift appeared yesterday likely to continue, but it seemed less probable that there would be near-term increases in other consumer lending charges—for example, on personal loans or loans to purchase autos or appliances.

In Washington, the Nixon Administration—a sharp critic of the increase in the prime rate to 5½ per cent from 5¼ per cent in April and of First Pennsylvania's action last month—had no comment yesterday.

But Representative Wright Patman, Texan, Democrat chairman of the House Banking Committee and longtime foe of high interest rates, had a very different reaction.

Mr. Patman called on President Nixon to use his existing credit-control authority to roll back the increase. The higher prime rate, he asserted, was "totally unnecessary and incon-

Continued on Page 49, Column 5

Associated Press

DISCUSSES PEACE PLAN: Le Duc Tho, member of Communist party's Politburo in North Vietnam.

U.S. MAY PUT OFF REPLY TO VIETCONG

Need for Further Study of Peace Plan Is Likely to Delay a Response

By TAD SZULC
Special to The New York Times

WASHINGTON, July 6—The United States is giving such serious study to the Vietcong peace plan submitted in Paris last Thursday that a formal response is likely to be delayed, senior Administration officials said today.

They added that subsequent Communist clarifications, given through private channels and in press interviews, were also contributing to making it unlikely that a reply would be delivered at the next scheduled session of the peace talks on Thursday.

Under a seven-point plan presented by Mrs. Nguyen Thi Binh, the chief Vietcong delegate, the Communists would gradually release all American prisoners of war this year if all United States troops were withdrawn from Vietnam in the same period of time.

'New Ground' Seen

But officials, speaking privately, noted that in an interview with The New York Times today, a high-level adviser to the North Vietnamese delegation, Le Duc Tho, may have "broken new ground" in suggesting that the prisoner question was "separable" from the other proposals, which apparently linked a cease-fire with the political settlement in Vietnam.

They also found it to be of interest that, whereas Mrs. Binh's seven-point plan had called for the formation of a new government in Saigon to negotiate a settlement with the Communists, Mr. Tho today spoke of talks with the existing South Vietnamese Government, except for President Nguyen Van Thieu.

"If he means what he is reported to have said, the Communist position indeed sounds interesting," an official familiar with peace-talk diplomacy said

Continued on Page 14, Column 7

HANOI AIDE SAYS P.O.W. AGREEMENT CAN BE SEPARATE

Political Questions Can Wait, Tho, a Politburo Member, Asserts in Interview

HE SEES A QUICK ACCORD

North Vietnamese Demands Removal of Thieu Before Any Subsequent Talks

Excerpts from the interview will be found on Page 14.

By ANTHONY LEWIS
Special to The New York Times

PARIS, July 6—A high-ranking North Vietnamese leader said today that the new Communist offer to return war prisoners if American forces are withdrawn by the end of 1971 was not dependent on a political settlement in South Vietnam.

Le Duc Tho, a member of the Politburo in Hanoi, said that the questions of prisoners and withdrawal could be negotiated separately now in the Paris peace talks, with future political arrangements to be discussed afterward.

In an interview, Mr. Tho said that if President Nixon agreed to set a final date for total American withdrawal, the "modalities" of withdrawal and of the release of prisoners could be "rapidly settled."

With 'the First Batch'

He said North Vietnam and the Vietcong would release some prisoners quickly after agreement on the withdrawal and on prisoners. When "the first batch of soldiers" leaves Vietnam after an agreement is reached, he added, "the first batch of prisoners will be released."

[Expressing the same views as Mr. Tho, Mrs. Nguyen Thi Binh, the Vietcong representative, said in an interview that the proposals were not made on a take-it-or-leave-it basis. Page 14.]

Mr. Tho's comments appeared to clarify an important question that American officials had raised privately about the seven-point peace plan proposed last Thursday by Mrs. Binh: Whether the various points were interdependent.

Difficult Political Issues

Point 1 set forth the new proposal on the prisoners and withdrawal. Then came suggestions for a coalition government in South Vietnam and other difficult political issues on which the negotiators have made no progress here in three years.

American officials here, informed of Mr. Tho's statement that Point 1 was separately negotiable, said it could be significant. They added, however, that there were still many potential difficulties in the language of the proposal itself.

The chief United States negotiator, David K. E. Bruce,

Continued on Page 14, Column 3

Louis Armstrong, Jazz Trumpeter and Singer, Dies

C.B.S./Tony Esparza, 1966

By ALBIN KREBS

Louis Armstrong, the celebrated jazz trumpeter and singer, died in his sleep yesterday morning at his home in the Corona section of Queens. He had observed his 71st birthday Sunday.

Death was attributed to a heart attack. Mr. Armstrong had been at home since mid-June, when he was discharged from Beth Israel Medical Center after 10 weeks of treatment for heart, liver and kidney disorders. He seemed in good health during an interview June 23, in which he played his trumpet and announced his intention to return to public performances.

President Nixon released this statement:

"Mrs. Nixon and I share the sorrow of millions of Americans at the death of Louis Armstrong. One of the architects of an American art form, a free and individual spirit, and an artist of worldwide fame, his great talents and magnificent spirit added richness and pleasure to all our lives."

Tributes to Mr. Armstrong also came from a number of leading musicians, including Duke Ellington, Gene Krupa, Benny Goodman, Al Hirt, Earl (Fatha) Hines, Tyree Glenn and Eddie Condon.

Mr. Ellington commented: "If anybody was Mr. Jazz it was Louis Armstrong. He was the epitome of jazz and always will be. He is what I call an American standard, an American original."

"He could play a trumpet like nobody else," Mr. Condon said, "then put it down and sing a song like no one else could."

Mr. Hines, who frequently said he had taken his piano style from Mr. Armstrong's trumpet style, remarked: "We were almost like brothers. I'm so heartbroken over this. The world has lost a champion."

In Washington, the State Department, noting that Mr. Armstrong had toured Africa, the Middle East and Latin America on its behalf, said:

"His memory will be enshrined in the archives of effective international communications. The Department of State, for which he traveled on tours to almost every corner

Continued on Page 41, Column 1

Reserve Aide Tells N.A.A.C.P. Blacks' Job Outlook Is Gloomy

By EARL CALDWELL
Special to The New York Times

MINNEAPOLIS, July 6 — A leading Negro economist predicted here today that it would be "quite some time" before there would be any improvement in the employment situation for black Americans.

Dr. Andrew F. Brimmer, the lone black member of the board of governors of the Federal Reserve System, said that the picture was now so bleak that many blacks had "given up" and no longer even bothered to enter the labor force.

He said it was essential that the Federal Government act immediately and suggested that the public payroll be used to provide immediate jobs.

"The main thing," he declared, "is that they do something."

Dr. Brimmer, in an address to the annual convention of the National Association for the Advancement of Colored People, said that, while the "vast proportion of black people still do not have marketable skills," others were doing "reasonably well."

"In fact," he went on, "they're doing a hell of a lot better than any of us thought they would do."

But he said that this troubled him.

"This is why I am afraid of a schism [among blacks] devel-

Continued on Page 23, Column 2

NEWS INDEX

Nation's Energy Crisis: Nuclear Future Looms

This is the second of three articles on the national energy crisis produced by the conflict between the need for more power and the desire to save the environment.

By JOHN NOBLE WILFORD

Slowly, reluctantly and fearfully, the United States is moving toward a nuclear-powered future. It is not that people have learned to love the atom; it is because few can think of any other acceptable answer to the nation's energy crisis.

Nuclear power is technically difficult, initially expensive, a source of thermal pollution and the subject of acrimonious controversy and widespread anxiety about possible radiation hazards.

And yet to a growing number of technologists, economists and political leaders, it is the only way within the traditional economic system to meet the ever rising consumer demand for a steady supply of reasonably inexpensive power without ravaging the environment.

Thus the Nixon Administration has made nuclear power the keystone of its "clean energy" plan for the decade. And future Administrations, barring unforeseen discoveries, can be expected to follow the same general policy.

For nuclear power, despite its drawbacks, is without doubt more plentiful, ultimately cheaper and relatively less damaging to the environment than other fuels. The alternatives, in other words, could be worse.

Coal, for example, is still

Continued on Page 24, Column 1

Louis Armstrong Dies in His Home at 71

Continued From Page 1, Col. 6

of the globe, mourns the passing of this great American."

The entertainer's final appearance was last February, when he played a two-week engagement at the Waldorf-Astoria Hotel.

Last month, noting that his legs were weak from his hospitalization, he said, "I'm going back to work when my treaders get in as good shape as my chops."

A master showman known to millions as Satchmo, Mr. Armstrong lived by a simple credo. Putting it into words a couple of years ago, he said:

"I never tried to prove nothing, just always wanted to give a good show. My life has been my music, it's always come first, but the music ain't worth nothing if you can't lay it on the public. The main thing is to live for that audience, 'cause what you're there for is to please the people."

Mr. Armstrong was first and most importantly a jazz trumpet player without peer, a virtuoso soloist who was one of the most vivid and influential forces in the development of American music.

But he was also known to delighted millions around the world for his ebulliently sandpapery singing voice, his merry mangling of the English language and his great wide grand-piano keyboard of a smile.

Jazz music, probably the only art form ever wholly originated in America, and Louis Armstrong grew up together in New Orleans. It was in a seamy slum there that Mr. Armstrong learned to love and play jazz in the company of gamblers, pimps and prostitutes.

But in time he was to play his trumpet and sing in command performances before royalty and, through his numerous worldwide tours, to become known unofficially as "America's ambassador of goodwill."

Recognized for Role

Jazz experts, even the purists who criticized Mr. Armstrong for his mugging and showmanship, more often than not agreed that it was he, more than any other individual, who took the raw, gutsy Negro folk music of the New Orleans funeral parades and honky-tonks and built it into a unique art form.

Over the years, his life and his artistry changed radically. He left New Orleans for Chicago in the early nineteen-twenties, when he was still playing the cornet, and before 1930 made some of his most memorable recordings — with his Hot Five or Hot Seven groups.

Mr. Armstrong won his initial fame playing an endless grind of one-night stands. Under constant pressure to put on a show that made the customers tap their feet and cry for more, he did not hesitate to exploit a remarkable flair for showmanship. His mugging, his wisecracking and most of all his willingness to constantly repeat programs that had gone over well in the past won him the cheers of his audiences, along with the disapproving clucks of some of his fellow musicians and jazz specialists.

The criticism that he no longer improvised enough, innovated enough, mattered little to Mr. Armstrong. He dismissed the more "progressive" jazz approved of by some leading critics as "jujitsu music."

He did not mind being called "commercial" because he followed popular music trends, and he deliberately introduced into his repertory crowd-pleasers such as "Mack the Knife" and "Hello, Dolly!," which put his recordings on the best-seller charts when he was in his 60's.

Like 'Sandpaper Calling'

As his ability to play his horn exceptionally well waned with the years, Mr. Armstrong supplanted his trumpet solos with his singing voice. An almost phenomenal instrument in its own right, it has been compared to iron filings and to "a piece of sandpaper calling to its mate."

Just watching an Armstrong performance could be an exhilarating experience. The man radiated a jollity that was infectious. Onstage he would bend back his stocky frame, point his trumpet to the heavens and joyfully blast out high C's. When he sang he fairly bubbled with pleasure. And as he swabbed away at the perspiration stirred up by his performing exertions, Satchmo grinned his famous toothy smile so incandescently that it seemed to light up the auditorium.

"I never did want to be no big star," Mr. Armstrong said in 1969, in an interview for this article. "It's been hard goddam work, man. Feel like I spent 20,000 years on the planes and railroads, like I blowed my chops off. Sure, Pops, I like the ovation, but when I'm low, beat down, wonder if maybe I hadn't of been better off staying home in New Orleans."

Mr. Armstrong's early years, spent in New Orleans, were marked by extreme poverty and squalor, but he emerged able to recall them without self-pity and even with good humor.

"I was a Southern Doodle Dandy, born on the Fourth of July, 1900," said Daniel Louis Armstrong. "My mother Mary Ann — we called her Mayann — was living in a two-room shack in James Alley, in the Back O' Town colored section of New Orleans. It was in a tough block, all them hustlers and their pimps and gamblers with their knives, between Gravier and Perdido Streets."

Mr. Armstrong's father, Willie Armstrong, who stoked furnaces in a turpentine factory, left Mrs. Armstrong when the boy was an infant. Leaving the child with his paternal grandmother, Mrs. Armstrong went to live in the Perdido-Liberty Street area, which was lined with prostitutes' cribs.

"Whether my mother did any hustling I can't say," Mr. Armstrong said. "If she did, she kept it out of my sight."

However, Louis, who rejoined his mother when he was 6 years old, recalled that for many years afterward there was always a "stepfather" on the premises and that before his mother "got religion and gave up men" around 1915, "I couldn't keep track of the stepdaddies, there must have been a dozen or so, 'cause all I had to do was turn my back and a new pappy would appear." Some of them, he added, "liked to beat on little Louis."

However, Mr. Armstrong was always intensely fond of his mother, and he cared for her until her death in the early nineteen-forties.

Dippermouth, as he was called as a child, and his friends often sang for pennies on the streets. To help support his mother and a sister, Barbara, Louis delivered coal to prostitutes' cribs and sold food plucked from hotel garbage cans.

The night of Dec. 31, 1913, Louis celebrated the New Year by running out on the street and firing a .38-caliber pistol that belonged to one of his "stepfathers." He was arrested and sent to the Colored Waifs Home for Boys.

"Pops, it sure was the greatest thing that ever happened to me," Mr. Armstrong said. "Me and music got married at the home."

Played in Home's Band

Peter Davis, an instructor at the home, taught Louis to play the bugle and the cornet. Soon the boy became a member of the home's brass band, which played at socials, picnics and funerals for a small fee. Louis was in the fifth grade when he was released from the home after spending 18 months there. He had no other formal education.

The youth worked as a junkman and sold coal, while grabbing every chance he could to play cornet in honky-tonk bands. The great jazz cornetist Joe (King) Oliver befriended him, gave him a cornet and tutored him.

"I was foolin' around with some tough ones," Mr. Armstrong recalled in 1969. "Get paid a little money, and a beeline for one of them gambling houses. Two hours, man, and I was a broke cat, broker than the Ten Commandments. Needed money so bad I even tried pimping, but my first client got jealous of me and we got to fussing about it and she stabbed me in the shoulder. Them was wild times."

In 1918, Mr. Armstrong married a 21-year-old prostitute named Daisy Parker. Since Daisy "wouldn't give up her line of work," Mr. Armstrong said, the marriage was both stormy and short-lived.

The same year he was married, Mr. Armstrong joined the Kid Ory band, replacing King Oliver, who had moved to Chicago. In the next three years he marched with Papa Celestin's brass band and worked on the riverboat Sidney with Fate Marable's band. Dave Jones, a mellophone player with the Marable band, gave him his first lessons in reading music.

By then Mr. Armstrong's fame was spreading among New Orleans musicians, many of whom were moving to Chicago. In 1922 King Oliver sent for his protégé. Mr. Armstrong became second cornetist in Mr. Oliver's by then famous Creole Jazz Band. The two-cornet team had one of the most formidably brilliant attacks ever heard in a jazz group. Mr. Armstrong's first recordings were made with the Oliver band in 1923.

The pianist in the band was Lilian Hardin, whom Mr. Armstrong married in 1924. Miss Hardin had had training as a classical musician, and she gave him some formal musical education.

Mrs. Armstrong, convinced that as long as her husband stayed in the Oliver band he would remain in the shadow of his popular mentor, persuaded him to leave the band in 1924 to play first cornet at the Dreamland Cafe. The same year he joined Fletcher Henderson's orchestra at the Roseland Ballroom in New York.

For the first time, Mr. Armstrong found himself in the company of musicians of an entirely different stripe from those he had known in New Orleans and Chicago who, like himself, had fought their way up out of the back alleys and were largely unschooled in music. From these men, many of whom had conservatory educations, he learned considerable musical discipline.

Moving back to Chicago in 1925, Mr. Armstrong again played at the Dreamland Cafe, where his wife, Lil, had her own band, and with Erskine Tate's "symphonic jazz" orchestra at the Vendome Theater. It was at that point that he gave up the cornet for the trumpet.

"I was hired to play them hot choruses when the curtain went up," Mr. Armstrong recalled. "They put a spotlight on me. Used to hit 40 or 50 high C's — go wild, screamin' on my horn. I was crazy, Pops, plain nuts."

Billed as 'World's Greatest'

During his second Chicago period, Mr. Armstrong doubled in Carroll Dickerson's Sunset Cabaret orchestra, with billing as the "World's Greatest Trumpeter." The proprietor of the Sunset was Joe Glaser, who became Mr. Armstrong's personal manager and acted in that capacity for the rest of his life. Mr. Glaser died on June 6, 1969.

In that Chicago period, Mr. Armstrong began to make records under his own name, the first being "My Heart," recorded Nov. 12, 1925. Louis Armstrong's Hot Five (and later Hot Seven) recorded, over a three-year span, a series of jazz classics, with Earl (Fatha) Hines on the piano. These records earned Mr. Armstrong a worldwide reputation, and by 1929, when he returned to New York, he had become an idol in the jazz world.

While playing at Connie's Inn in Harlem, Mr. Armstrong also appeared on Broadway in the all-Negro review "Hot Chocolates," in which he introduced Fats Waller's "Ain't Misbehavin,'" his first popular-song hit. (He later appeared as Bottom in "Swingin' the Dream," a short-lived travesty on "A Midsummer Night's Dream." Over the years he appeared in many movies, including "Pennies From Heaven," "A Song Is Born," "The Glenn Miller Story" and "High Society.")

For several years, Mr. Armstrong "fronted" big bands assembled for him by others. By 1932, the year he was divorced from Lil Hardin Armstrong, he had become so popular in Europe, via recordings, that he finally agreed to tour the Continent.

It was while he was starring at the London Palladium that Mr. Armstrong acquired the nickname Satchmo. A London music magazine editor inadvertently invented the name by garbling an earlier nickname, Satchelmouth.

While he was in London, Mr. Armstrong demonstrated memorably that he had little use for the niceties of diplomatic protocol.

During a command performance for King George V, Mr. Armstrong ignored the rule that performers are not supposed to refer to members of the Royal Family while playing before them and announced on the brink of a hot trumpet break, "This one's for you, Rex."

(Many years later, in 1956, Satchmo played before King George's granddaughter, Princess Margaret. "We're really gonna lay this one on for the Princess," he grinned, and launched into "Mahogany Hall Stomp," a sort of jazz elegy to a New Orleans bordello. The Princess loved it.)

One of Mr. Armstrong's pre-World War II European tours lasted 18 months. Over the years his tours took him to the Middle East and the Far East, to Africa and to South America. In Accra, Ghana, 100,000 natives went into a frenzied demonstration when he started to blow his horn, and in Léopoldville, tribesmen painted themselves ochre and violet and carried him into the city stadium on a canvas throne.

His 1960 African tour was denounced by the Moscow radio as a "capitalist distraction," which made Mr. Armstrong laugh.

"I feel at home in Africa," he said during the tour. "I'm African-descended down to the bone, and I dig the friendly ways these people go about things. I got quite a bit of African blood in me from my grandmammy on my mammy's side and from my grandpappy on my pappy's side."

Before the war, Mr. Armstrong worked with several big bands, including the Guy Lombardo orchestra, concentrating on New Orleans standards such as "Muskrat Ramble" and "When the Saints Go Marchin' In" and on novelties such as "I'll Be Glad When You're Dead, You Rascal You." He did duets with Ella Fitzgerald and he accompanied Bessie Smith.

After 1947 he usually performed as leader of a sextet, working with such musicians as Jack Teagarden, Earl Hines, Joe Bushkin and Cozy Cole. He was a favorite at all the jazz festivals, in this country and abroad.

The jolly Mr. Armstrong was quite inured to his fame as a jazz immortal. Not too many years ago, he was interviewed backstage by a disk jockey who began with the announcement, "And now we bring you a man who came all the way from New Orleans, the Crescent City, to become a Living American Legend." The Living American Legend, who was changing his clothes, dropped his trousers and began the interview with the observation, "Tee hee!"

Louis Armstrong appeared with Bing Crosby in the 1937 movie *Pennies From Heaven.*

"All the News That's Fit to Print"

The New York Times

LATE CITY EDITION

Weather: Some cloudiness today; rain likely tonight and tomorrow. Temp. range: today 54-36; Thursday 41-29. Full U.S. report on Page 94.

VOL. CXVIII . No. 40,501 — NEW YORK, FRIDAY, DECEMBER 13, 1968 — 10 CENTS

CITY HIGH SCHOOLS TO GIVE STUDENTS A VOICE IN POLICY

Donovan Sets Up a Panel to Recommend the Guidelines for Involving Youths

ADVISORY ROLE PLANNED

McCoy Defies State Order Removing Him and Goes to His Office as Usual

By JAMES P. STERBA

The Superintendent of New York City Schools announced yesterday the formation of a committee to recommend city-wide guidelines for enlisting high school students in helping to make administrative and policy decisions in their schools.

While some school officials dismissed suggestions that the committee was being formed in response to recent student outbreaks here, they said that they did recognize growing high school student unrest and that the committee might find ways of avoiding serious outbreaks of violence.

In another development involving the city's schools, Rhody A. McCoy ignored a state order removing him as administrator of the Ocean Hill-Brownsville district in Brooklyn. He went to his office yesterday morning as usual, but the district's state trustee said that Mr. McCoy would be barred—by the police if necessary—if he showed up today.

A Representative Panel

The 12-member committee, called the Committee on Student Participation in School Management, will be made up of four high school principals, three students, two teachers, two representatives of parent groups and a deputy superintendent of schools, said Superintendent Bernard E. Donovan.

"This committee has no boundaries on where it can go," he said in an interview.

Seelig L. Lester, deputy superintendent of schools in charge of instruction, stressed, however, that the committee would deal with involving students as advisers in the decision-making process. The principals would continue to have final authority.

Mr. Lester, who will head the committee, said it would explore the most effective ways of giving students a voice in all matters of school policy, including curriculum, student

Continued on Page 40, Column 7

Columbia Hecklers Bested by Lindsay In Moderation Plea

By RICHARD REEVES

Mayor Lindsay outlasted a dozen radical hecklers at Columbia University yesterday and won the applause of 1,500 other students with a warning that "obscene names" and "shouting down speakers" would stop the social revolution that the hecklers say they want.

While the hecklers from the campus chapter of Students for a Democratic Society shouted, "Cut it out, Johnny!" and a few less polite things, Mr. Lindsay answered one question by saying:

"If the forces of moderation are driven from the battlefield by these tactics and only the extremists are left, there will be no school decentralization, there will be no social change. You will defeat your own purpose."

The answer followed the theme of the Mayor's speech to the students who crowded

Continued on Page 41, Column 5

N.A.A.C.P. DEPLORES HARLEM 'TERROR'

Asks for Harsher Penalties, on Mugging Especially, and More Patrolmen

By MAURICE CARROLL

An immediate halt to "the reign of criminal terror in Harlem," with remedial measures to include a mandatory five-year prison sentence for muggers, was demanded yesterday by the New York branch of the National Association for the Advancement of Colored People.

Vincent Baker, chairman of the branch's anticrime committee, said that no doubt crime was the product of "vast social evils" that demand solution, "but with people here being beaten, robbed and murdered, something should be done about crime right now."

A six-page report, prepared from studies initiated in February and approved a week ago by the branch's executive committee, was made public at a news briefing in the branch headquarters at 261 West 125th Street.

The report said that "the attitude toward crime and criminals must change" in Harlem.

"There are people known to cheer when some offender rushes from a store" with his loot, Mr. Baker told newsmen. "They seem to have the idea that these are some sort of 20th century Robin Hoods. With the hoods, we agree."

Among the report's demands were these:

¶Added protection, including more policemen on Harlem beats and "armed guards in every house in all public housing projects."

¶Harsher sentences, including a 10-year minimum for narcotics sellers and at least 30 years for those convicted of first-degree murder. The report

Continued on Page 59, Column 3

CARNEGIE PANEL ASKS U.S. TO SEND POOR TO COLLEGE

Plan Similar to G.I. Bill Is Proposed—Cost Put at $13-Billion by 1976

Summary of recommendations is printed on Page 43.

By FRED M. HECHINGER

The Carnegie Commission on Higher Education proposed yesterday that a multi-billion-dollar Federal program be set up to aid students, subsidize colleges and universities and expand medical education.

The 14-member group, headed by Dr. Clark Kerr, former president of the University of California, and financed by the Carnegie Corporation of New York, called for a Civilian Bill of Educational Rights, comparable to the G.I. Bill of Rights, to assure that financial need would not prevent any qualified student from going to college.

"What the American nation now needs from higher education can be summed up in two words: quality and equality," the commission said in a 54-page report addressed to Congress and the new Administration. It warned that "these essential national needs will not be fully met unless the Federal Government assumes new levels of responsibility for higher education."

Start at $7-Billion

The unanimous recommendations by the commission, made up of leading educators, business executives and economists, would raise the Federal aid to colleges and universities from the present annual level of $3.5-billion to $7-billion in 1970 and to $13-billion by 1976.

But more important than the dollar amounts involved, Dr. Kerr said, would be the effect of giving students greater freedom in selecting the institutions they wish to attend. The colleges and universities that accept the Federally aided students would recieve a special cost-to-education allowance to be used at the institutions' discretion. Such aid to institutions would start at $1.13-billion in 1970 and rise to $2.71-billion by 1976.

In addition, the proposals would, within the next eight years, provide the capacity to train 75 per cent more physicians than now, to help meet the demand for more and different medical services.

"Today, a young man or

Continued on Page 43, Column 1

Associated Press

TOP-LEVEL CONFERENCE: President-elect Nixon and President Johnson during meeting at the White House yesterday

NIXON AGAIN PAYS CALL ON JOHNSON; TALK FAR-RANGING

Middle East, Vietnam and Missile Curb Parley With Soviet Are Discussed

CHAFEE WEIGHING OFFER

Post for Gov. Boe Indicated —President-Elect Meets With Cabinet Choices

By R. W. APPLE Jr.
Special to The New York Times

WASHINGTON, Dec. 12 — President-elect Richard M. Nixon discussed a wide range of foreign and domestic issues with President Johnson this evening in a White House meeting that lasted more than an hour and a half.

One question touched upon, according to qualified sources, was whether the Johnson Administration should begin negotiating with the Soviet Union on the limitation of nuclear missiles before it leaves office in 38 days.

Without the concurrence of Mr. Nixon, Mr. Johnson is believed to be unwilling to begin the long-delayed talks in any form. With concurrence, he would be ready to begin with a summit meeting if the Russians agreed.

Commitment Uncertain

It was not known whether the President-elect had given any commitment.

George Christian, the White House press secretary, said Mr. Nixon and Mr. Johnson had talked in the President's office about the Middle East, Vietnam "and other world problems," Mr. Johnson's forthcoming State of the Union and Budget Messages, and Mr. Nixon's Cabinet, as well as "housekeeping" matters.

Asked whether the subject of a possible summit meeting had been among the items discussed, Mr. Christian said, "I have no idea."

The meeting between the incoming and outgoing Presidents was the second since Election Day. They last talked at the White House on Nov. 11, and Mr. Nixon pledged then to allow Mr. Johnson to speak for both the old and the new Administrations on foreign policy until inauguration day.

Joined by Mrs. Nixon

Mr. Nixon took his wife, Patricia, and his elder daughter, Tricia, to the White House, and members of the new Presidential staff came along. While Mr. Nixon met privately with President Johnson, the families and staffs also talked.

The Nixon entourage arrived at 6:42 P.M., 12 minutes late. Mr. Johnson, who was coatless, stood at the south portico with Mrs. Johnson and their younger daughter, Mrs. Patrick J. Nugent, to welcome the visitors.

A source close to the President-elect reported, meanwhile, that Mr. Nixon had selected a retiring Governor to head the Office of Emergency Planning. He specifically ex-

Continued on Page 36, Column 1

Enemy's Build-Up In South Vietnam Stirs Washington

By WILLIAM BEECHER
Special to The New York Times

WASHINGTON, Dec. 12 — The Johnson Administration is concerned over reports of a new enemy build-up in South Vietnam.

Intelligence reports from the field tell of North Vietnamese and Vietcong regiments and battalions moving from border regions closer to populated areas north and northwest of Saigon, west of Danang and along the central coast west of Quinhon.

According to officials here, Gen. Creighton W. Abrams, the American commander in Vietnam, has alerted his forces to prepare for a new round of attacks. He is said to expect that an offensive may start within the next few days and continue until the Christmas cease-fire, starting Dec. 24, proposed by the Vietcong.

[Military sources in Saigon said that South Vietnamese soldiers and policemen were at a full alert in Saigon for the possibility of enemy attack. Page 7.]

Military and civilian officials at the Defense Department generally believe that, despite the

Continued on Page 4, Column 4

U.S. PLANE WITH 51 DOWN OFF CARACAS

Wreckage of 707 Jetliner Out of New York Sighted —'No Signs of Life'

Special to The New York Times

CARACAS, Venezuela, Friday, Dec. 13 — A Pan American jetliner carrying 51 persons on a flight here from New York crashed in the Caribbean last night on its approach to Maiquetía International Airport.

Venezuelan naval vessels and aircraft spotted the wreckage of the plane, a Boeing 707 on Flight 217, bobbing in the water some 10 miles from the airport runway.

The airport control tower and the port authority at the coastal city of La Guayra reported that "there are no signs of life" around the wreckage.

[A majority of the passengers were Venezuelan citizens, although two Cubans and several United States citizens were also believed to be aboard, The Associated Press reported.]

Radio Cut at 1,800 Feet

The plane, piloted by Capt. Sidney E. Stillwaugh of West Islip, L. I., left Kennedy International Airport at 4:40 P.M., New York time. It was due in Caracas at 9:05.

Spokesmen at the airport here said they lost contact with the 707 when it was 18 miles from the airport and flying at an altitude of 1,800 feet. By 9:50 the plane was officially reported missing and a search was ordered.

Venezuelan vessels went out into calm seas and planes flew in clear skies looking for signs of wreckage. These were not found until some two hours later.

A Venezuelan National Guard officer stationed at the airport,

Continued on Page 12, Column 1

Congress Support Voiced For Nixon Cabinet Choices

By JOHN W. FINNEY
Special to The New York Times

WASHINGTON, Dec. 12—With a team of moderate Republicans in his Cabinet, President-elect Richard M. Nixon appeared today to have laid the political foundations for bridging the sometimes stormy gap between Congress and the Executive branch on foreign and military policies.

Congressional reaction to the Nixon Cabinet was generally approving, even among Democratic liberals who can be expected to form the core of opposition to the new Republican Administration.

At least for the time being, Mr. Nixon seemed to have disarmed any Democratic opposition by picking a team of men whose personal credentials could not be challenged and whose policies were unknown.

Muskie's Reaction

In a reaction typical of many Democrats, Senator Edmund S. Muskie of Maine, the Democratic Vice-Presidential candidate, commented that the President-elect had picked "men of competence," with "a demonstrated ability in each field." But then, paraphrasing a comment of President Kennedy on seeing a new nephew, he said:

"It looks like a good baby, but we will know more later."

Congressional approval focused in particular upon probably the two most important Cabinet selections—William P. Rogers as Secretary of State and Melvin R. Laird as Secretary of Defense.

After years of squabbling with the State Department under the Johnson Administration, influential Democrats see a new era of good feeling developing between the Senate Foreign Relations Committee and the State Department under a Nixon Administration.

Personalities and Policies

The differences in the past have been as much over personalities as over policies, and if there is a change now it will be largely because of Mr. Rogers's personality rather than his policies.

Among Democrats as well as Republicans on the committee, Mr. Rogers is regarded as more tolerant of Congressional views than Secretary of State Dean Rusk and, perhaps, because he is not so well informed in foreign affairs, more receptive to Senate advice on foreign policy.

The first test of Mr. Rogers's success on Capitol Hill may well come with his reaction to a renewed assertion by the Senate of its constitutional prerog-

Continued on Page 36, Column 6

F.C.C. SAID TO PLAN CURB ON CABLE TV

Congressional Sources See Freeze on Applications— Pay Television Backed

Special to The New York Times

WASHINGTON, Dec. 12— The Federal Communications Commission was reported today to have agreed on proposals to restrict the expansion of cable television systems and to curtail their right to rebroadcast television programs.

At the same time, it was reported that the communications commission would authorize a go-ahead on pay television systems, which until now have been held to an experimental status.

In cable television systems, which have been expanding in New York and other metropolitan areas, programs are carried by coaxial cables into homes. A monthly charge, usually about $5, is paid for the service.

In pay television, by contrast, the programs are broadcast over the air in an encoded form. A person is then charged for the programs he chooses to see by using a special decoder on his television set.

Congressional sources reported that the commission would propose tomorrow a freeze on all new applications for cable television systems,

Continued on Page 34, Column 3

STATE APPROVES RYE-NASSAU SPAN

The New York Times Dec. 13, 1968

Route of proposed bridge

By JOSEPH C. INGRAHAM

J. Burch McMorran, the State Transportation Commissioner, yesterday announced approval of the controversial Long Island Sound bridge-causeway between Westchester and Nassau Counties.

He said the approach roads for the six-mile-long, $140-million span would be in Oyster Bay on the Nassau side and in the Rye-Portchester area in Westchester, but he did not specify any exact alignment.

However, the favored route would have the bridge touch Long Island at Bayville, in Oyster Bay Town.

Public hearings will start in January to help the department select the best corridors and alternative route locations, the Commissioner said. The hear-

Continued on Page 33, Column 3

New Drive Planned For Negro Self-Aid

By JOHN HERBERS
Special to The New York Times

WASHINGTON, Dec. 12 — Members of Congress, business leaders and Negro militants met here today to push a bipartisan "community self-determination" bill that fits Richard M. Nixon's campaign promises to give Negroes "a piece of the action."

Republican Senators assured the group that the bill would receive favorable consideration in the new Administration.

Roy Innis, national director of the Congress of Racial Equality and one of the originators of the bill, and Joseph C. Wilson, board chairman of Xerox Corporation, announced separate plans to mount a national campaign for the proposed legislation.

Opposition was registered

Continued on Page 38, Column 3

Tallulah Bankhead Dead at 65; Vibrant Stage and Screen Star

By MURRAY SCHUMACH

Tallulah Bankhead, the star whose offstage performances often rivaled her roles in the theater, film and television, died at St. Luke's Hospital yesterday of pneumonia, complicated by emphysema. She was 65 years old.

The actress, a member of one of the most famous political families of Alabama, was admitted to the hospital last Friday after contracting influenza. The influenza developed into penumonia.

With her when she died were her sister, Eugenia Bankhead, and a nephew, William Brockman Bankhead 2d. Her marriage to John Emery, an actor, ended in divorce in 1941.

The New York Times

Tallulah Bankhead

To admirers — and gossip mongers — for more than 40 years, Miss Bankhead was a personality as much as a star. Her vibrant energy, sultry voice, explosive speech and impetuous behavior seemed at times a phenomenon better suited for study by physicists than by journalists, who chronicled her antics with and without script.

The raw power and uninhibited style she discharged into even poor plays—and she had many—once prompted Arnold Bennett, the novelist, to write:

"I have seen Tallulah electrify the most idiotic, puerile plays into some sort of realistic coherence by her individual force."

The same force was described, from another point of view, by an awed observer who knew her socially, and said:

"A day away from Tallulah is like a month in the country."

One of Miss Bankhead's many feuds with producers resulted in a famous exchange with Billy Rose during rehearsals of "Clash by Night." She called him "a loathesome little bully," and he responded, "How can you bully Niagara Falls?"

Miss Bankhead's personal life had such flair that in recent years, when she did so little stage work, there was a tendency to underestimate her talent by a generation that had never seen her as the eternal

Continued on Page 42, Column 1

Hanoi Allows Gifts For Captive Pilots

By PETER GROSE
Special to The New York Times

WASHINGTON, Dec. 12 — North Vietnam agreed today to let captive American pilots receive Christmas packages from the United States for the first time in the Vietnam war.

The State Department announced that Ambassador W. Averell Harriman, chief United States negotiator in the Paris talks, had received a message from the North Vietnamese chief negotiator, Xuan Thuy, conveying Hanoi's authorization. The message said:

"On the occasion of Christmas, 1968, the Government of the Democratic Republic of Vietnam, acting in pursuit of humanitarian policies, authorizes United States pilots in

Continued on Page 6, Column 4

NEWS INDEX

Sybaris, Ancient City of Luxury, Believed Found in Southern Italy

By WALTER SULLIVAN

American and Italian archeologists believe they have found the long-sought site of Sybaris, the seat of proverbial luxury in the ancient world.

Its inhabitants, the Sybarites, were so attentive to their own comfort that, according to classic accounts, they built roofs over roads leading out of the city to provide shade for travelers.

Likewise, it is said that according to local law, invitations to public functions had to be issued a year in advance. This was to allow the ladies time to attire themselves in suitable opulence.

Hence the word sybarite has come to mean anyone devoted to a life of luxury.

The discovery of the city, which was destroyed in civil strife in 510 B.C. after flourishing for 200 years, was announced in Philadelphia last night at the University Museum of the University of Pennsylvania.

The find was described there by Dr. Froelich G. Rainey, director of the museum, and Prof. Giuseppe Foti, superintendent of antiquities of Calabria, in southern Italy.

Sybaris was situated in Calabria. Ancient writers placed it between the rivers Crathis (or Crati) and Sybaris (or Coscile), where they emptied into the sea.

In the 25 centuries that have passed since then the terrain has changed. The two rivers now meet before they reach the sea, and the ancient Greek col-

Continued on Page 2, Column 7

Tallulah Bankhead, the Vibrant and Tempestuous Stage and Screen Personality, Dies Here at 65

Continued From Page 1, Col. 4

prostitute, Sabrina, in Thornton Wilder's "The Skin of Our Teeth," or as the mercenary Regina in Lillian Hellman's "The Little Foxes."

The young were able to appraise her talent fairly only from revivals or television screenings of Alfred Hitchcock's "Lifeboat," in which, as the foreign correspondent, she won the best acting award in 1944 from the New York Film Critics.

In the latter phase of Miss Bankhead's hectic career, radio and television projected into millions of living rooms the personality more than the talent.

Better known to this vast new audience than any of the lines she uttered in plays was her throaty "Daaahling," with which she greeted friends and strangers. In the one word were blended her energy and sensuality, the Alabama drawl to which she was born and the London insouciance she acquired in the theater in the nineteen-twenties.

Always in Spotlight

Miss Bankhead's ability to consume liquor became a subject for public appraisal and her ownership of a lion cub, or flamboyant love of baseball became better known than the fact that she had won important critical awards.

Miss Bankhead's fondness for baseball was concentrated in a passion for the New York Giants. She owned a few shares of stock in the club, which she vowed she would never sell, even when the franchise moved to San Francisco.

Willie Mays, informed of her death, said: "A wonderful lady has died."

She did not need anyone to encourage her to step into the spotlight wherever she went.

At Yankee Stadium in 1938, for instance, when Joe Louis knocked out Max Schmeling in the first round, she wheeled upon four men behind her whom she suspected of pro-Nazi sympathies and her triumphant voice echoed back over the multitudes: "I told you so, you sons of bitches."

She never tried to deny her marathon carousing. But one point she was determined to set straight in her autobiography, "Tallulah," published in 1952.

"In all my years in the theater," she wrote, "I've never missed a performance because of alcoholic wounds."

Miss Bankhead's unabashed style emerged very often in interviews and press conferences, where she needed no help from publicity men to make startling comments. During one press gathering in 1964, she said:

"The last beau I had, let's see, someplace in California, I think. Well, this man said: 'Look here Tallulah, you don't need a man, you need a caddy.' That's the way I am honey. I have a lot of stuff I leave around, that's just the way I am. I just can't think in terms of remembering gloves and furs and things."

Acted in Williams Plays

Tennessee Williams saw her in a different light. He came to know her when she appeared in a revival of his "A Streetcar Named Desire," and a revised revival of "The Milk Train Doesn't Stop Here Anymore."

"Tallulah," he asserted, "is the strongest of all the hurt people I've ever known in my life."

He looked upon her as the result of "fantastic cross-breeding of a moth and a tiger." He extolled her "instinctive kindness to a person in whom she senses a vulnerability that is kin to her own."

Mr. Williams scoffed at Miss Bankhead's periodic comments—out of pique or frustration—that she hated the theater and did it solely "to keep out of debtor's prison."

"She loves it with so much of her heart," the playwright said, "that in order to protect her heart she has to say that she hates it. But we know better when we see her onstage."

But those she had hurt with her biting tongue and her aggressiveness did not look upon her with such sweetness. During rehearsals for "The Skin of Our Teeth" in 1942, Elia Kazan, who had not yet attained his later stature as a director, was subjected to tantrums and abuse he did not forget for many years. Before the play opened, the actress's behavior had put the producer, Michael Myerberg, in the hospital with nervous prostration.

Long Democratic Line

Disparaging comments about Miss Bankhead sometimes stemmed from ignorance or malice. Thus, those who spoofed her campaigning for Democratic candidates for the White House forgot that her father, William, had been Speaker of the House of Representatives and that a grandfather and an uncle had been United States Senators—all Democrats from Alabama.

There were many stories about Miss Bankhead's stormy friendships with men. Generally, she ignored comments about her morals. But once she summed up her attitude:

"I'd rather go on like I do than be like a lot of women I know who only look clean."

Another time she retorted:

"I'm as pure as the driven slush."

Indicative of her restrained behavior were her antics at parties. At one, she threw the shoes of the women guests into the street. At another, she did a strip tease.

On another occasion, when there had been an accumulation of tales about her behavior, or of her having given away a necklace worth thousands, or of her having gone for days without sleep as part of her dread of loneliness, she said, with a satiric flutter of eyelashes:

"I'm not the confidential type."

Contrary to widespread belief, the animal spirits of this actress were generated by a woman only 5 feet, 3 inches tall and weighing less than 130 pounds. In her prime, her beauty, with the blue eyes, voluptuous mouth, honey-colored hair that fell in waves to her shoulder, impelled Augustus John to do her portrait.

The New York Times

Tallulah Bankhead with the Augustus John portrait of herself in her London home, 1930.

The New York Times Studio

Miss Bankhead as Regina in "The Little Foxes," a 1939 play

Banks on Herself

As the wrinkles multiplied and the beauty faded, she sometimes turned some of her sharpest barbs against herself. One day, for instance, when she was preparing for a horror movie, she said:

"They used to shoot Shirley Temple through gauze. They should shoot me through linoleum."

When her acting days had become more a matter of summer stock and memory, her fame remained international because of her personality. Millions of women recalled that during the twenties they had copied her hair-do and had tried to imitate her throaty insolence.

She was one of the few people who was known throughout the world by her first name. When a major corporation named a hair cream "Tallulah," without asking her, the actress, who traditionally refused to give testimonials, sued and won.

Jokes were made of her name. Bugs Baer, the humorist, once wrote that the man who christened her must have been chewing bubble gum.

Actually, she was named for a paternal grandmother, who was named after Tallulah Falls, Ga.

Born into a wealthy Southern family, Miss Bankhead was reared by an aunt after the death of her mother.

As a child her tantrums were notorious among the Bankheads. Later, her sense of mischief and resentment of discipline caused her transfer through several finishing schools.

Not until she got a bit part in a Broadway show, in 1918, did Miss Bankhead find a constructive channel for her talent. However, New York showed no great enthusiasm for her during her first few years in the theater, when she appeared in "Squab Farm," "Footloose," "39 East," "Nice People," Everyday," "Danger," "Her Temporary Husband" and "The Exciters."

Won Fame Abroad

Impatient with her progress, Miss Bankhead left for London in 1923, where she became a sensation in "The Dancers."

Her fame spread throughout England and her clothes, her hair, her speech, became the rage with thousands of young girls as she drew acclaim in "The Green Hat," "Fallen Angels," "They Knew What They Wanted," "The Gold Diggers," "Her Cardboard Lover" and "The Lady of the Camellias."

Movies brought her back to the United States in 1931. But her films were not successful. She returned to Broadway in 1933 in "Forsaking All Others."

For a time, it seemed that Broadway would bring her nothing but bad luck, as she performed in "Dark Victory," "Reflected Glory," "I Am Different" and "The Circle."

She received some encouragement by doing Sadie Thompson, the prostitute, in a revival of "Rain." But she was derided for her Cleopatra in a revival of "Antony and Cleopatra."

In 1939, Miss Bankhead found the play that was worthy of her artistry, "The Little Foxes." In Miss Hellman's drama, she overwhelmed the critics with her performance of Regina Giddens, a woman of extraordinary selfishness and cruelty, who goads her husband to death for money.

Words like "superb" and "magic" were used to describe her performance.

For this role, and for her Sabina in "The Skin of Our Teeth," Miss Bankhead received the award of the New York Drama Critics Circle for the best acting of the season.

Her only claim to fame in the theater thereafter stemmed from her delivery of a 22-mintue monologue in "The Eagle Has Two Heads."

Some of those acquainted with Miss Bankhead's love of talk said this was not much of a strain on her. One writer said she was so fond of talking that she had led "a lifelong filibuster."

Miss Bankhead, however, had a different summary of her life.

"Live," she said, "in the moment."

"All the News That's Fit to Print"

The New York Times

LATE CITY EDITION
Weather: Sunny, cool today; clear tonight. Fair and mild tomorrow. Temp. range: today 30-46; Saturday 38-46. Additional details on Page 96.

SECTION ONE

VOL. CXXIII ... No. 42,316 NEW YORK, SUNDAY, DECEMBER 2, 1973

75¢ beyond 50-mile zone from New York City, except Long Island. Higher in air delivery cities.

50 CENTS

Ben-Gurion Is Dead at 87; Founding Father of Israel

Horst-Tappe

DAVID BEN-GURION

Special to The New York Times

TEL AVIV, Dec. 1 — David Ben-Gurion, a founding father of modern Israel and its first Premier, died today at the age of 87. He succumbed at 11:06 A.M. local time (4:06 A.M. New York time) to a brain hemorrhage that had struck him two weeks ago.

Because of the Sabbath the Government withheld an official announcement until sundown tonight. However, the news was reported unofficially earlier by the state radio.

Premier Golda Meir convened the Cabinet for a memorial meeting in Jerusalem tonight. Minister of Interior Yosef Burg ordered flags on all public buildings lowered to half-staff from tomorrow morning until Monday night.

Mr. Ben-Gurion will lay in state at the Knesset, or Parliament, building in Jerusalem from 10 A.M. tomorrow through the night until 7 A.M. Monday. The public will be able to pay

An obituary, Pages 76 and 77; tributes are on Page 77.

respects. Places of entertainment throughout the country will be closed tomorrow.

The start of a funeral service at 11 A.M. Monday will be marked by sirens throughout the country and two minutes of silence will be observed. In Jerusalem work will stop for an hour during the service.

The coffin will then be flown for burial to Sde Boker, the collective settlement in the Negev where Mr. Ben-Gurion made his home after he retired temporarily from the premier-

Continued on Page 77, Column 7

Ben-Gurion Is Mourned In City Sabbath Services

By ROBERT D. McFADDEN

The word of David Ben-Gurion's death was passed in whispers at Sabbath services in synagogues across the metropolitan area yesterday, and it evoked the prayers and tears of people who grieve at the loss of a great man.

In the midst of services at the East Midwood Jewish Center, one of the largest Conservative congregations in Brooklyn, a messenger arrived and approached Rabbi Harry Halpern, whispering the word into his ear.

The rabbi announced the death to 500 members of his congregation. "They gasped," he recalled later. "It was very emotional. People cried. They were very shocked."

Rabbi Halpern called then for a standing salute to Mr. Ben-Gurion, including a three-minute prayer. He said plans would be made during the week for special memorial services at the synagogue, at 1625 Ocean Avenue between Avenues K and L. The American and Israeli flags atop the synagogue were brought to half-staff after the services.

Because Orthodox Jews do

Continued on Page 77, Column 4

CAIRO ASKS SOVIET AND U.S. TO PRESS ISRAELIS ON TRUCE

Seeks Pullback of Forces to Oct. 22 Lines to Break Deadlock in Talks

By HENRY TANNER

Special to The New York Times

CAIRO, Dec. 1—Egypt has asked the United States and the Soviet Union to break the new deadlock in the Middle East by putting pressure on Israel to withdraw her forces to the cease-fire lines of Oct. 22.

The Egyptian request was made by Foreign Minister Ismail Fahmy last night in separate meetings with Ambassadors Hermann F. Eilts of the United States and Vladimir M. Vinogradov of the Soviet Union, official sources said.

The Egyptian Government said this morning that it would not return to the military talks on the Cairo-Suez road until Egypt was sure that Israeli "obstruction" there was ended.

[Premier Golda Meir of Israel conceded in a radio interview that the negotiations with Egypt had encountered a serious snag, but she said that she remained hopeful that further meetings would be held. Page 7.]

86 Violations Charged

The Egyptian Army today reported that Israeli forces had violated the truce 86 times since the cease-fire agreement negotiated by Secretary of State Kissinger was signed on Nov. 11.

Maj. Gen. Azzedin Mokhtar, speaking at a news conference, said that each of the violations had caused casualties.

"Israel yesterday said that she had lost one killed and one wounded, but in fact Israeli losses usually are much much higher than that," General Mokhtar said in answer to a question.

Egyptian officials today again said that Egypt was still considering what step to take next, and they hinted that her attendance at a peace conference in Geneva in December was hanging in the balance.

No Categorical Refusal

The officials were careful to avoid stating categorically that Egypt would refuse to attend the conference if there was no prior agreement on an Israeli withdrawal to the Oct. 22 cease-fire lines.

The thrust of all these Egyptian statements during the last 24 hours was to underline the danger that the Middle East might slip back into war if American and Soviet pressure does not bring about an initial Israeli withdrawal soon.

Egypt broke off the military talks on the Cairo-Suez highway Thursday when Maj. Gen. Mohammed Abdel Ghany el-Gamasy concluded that Israel was determined not to agree to an early withdrawal.

The authoritative daily Al Ahram of Cairo reported today that General Gamasy's last move at the conference table Thursday was to ask Maj. Gen. Ensio Siilasvuo of the United Nations to record that the Egyptian Army's crossing to the east side of the Suez Canal is "irrevocable and not negotiable." General Siilasvuo, a Finn who heads the United Nations Emergency Force, has been presiding at the meetings.

Foreign Minister Fahmy is understood to have told the

Continued on Page 8, Column 1

The New York Times/Joyce Dopkeen

At the Hess gasoline station on 10th Avenue and 44th Street the pumps were closed to cars yesterday afternoon. Neighborhood youngsters found room to play football under gaze of the station's private guard.

NIXON WILL CREATE AN ENERGY AGENCY IN MAJOR SHAKE-UP

Simon, a Treasury Official, Reported Picked to Head Cabinet-Level Office

HE WILL REPLACE LOVE

Current Aide Will Remain an Assistant to President but Lose Policy Role

By EDWARD COWAN

Special to The New York Times

WASHINGTON, Dec. 1—In a major executive-branch shake-up, President Nixon has decided to create a Federal Energy Administration, high Administration sources reported today. They said it would be headed by William E. Simon, the former Wall Street investment banker who has been Deputy Secretary of the Treasury for the last 11 months.

Mr. Simon, who will continue as deputy secretary, will get the additional rank of counselor to the President. The dual positions were seen here as a clear indication that Mr. Simon would be the President's senior energy policy adviser.

The designation as counselor to the President will elevate Mr. Simon to Cabinet rank and bring him into to the inner circle of Presidential advisers.

John A. Love, who resigned as Governor of Colorado last July to come to Washington as director of the newly created Energy Policy Office, will remain in the Administration as an assistant to the President, a collateral rank he has also held. However, Mr. Love will no longer be coordinating energy policy for the President. The fate of the Energy Policy Office was unclear tonight.

Widespread Dissatisfaction

There has been widespread dissatisfaction with Mr. Love's performance, both within the executive branch and on Capitol Hill. His personal integrity and commitment to the national interest were never called into question, but it was widely felt that he had failed to establish himself as the energy "czar" who would forge a disciplined, well-coordinated team out of the several agencies with responsibility in the energy sphere.

Informed sources said that the White House would announce the reorganization and the appointment of Mr. Simon on Monday. Mr. Simon's deputy in the new agency will be John C. Sawhill, 37 years old, who has been serving for nearly a year as an executive director of the Office of Management and Budget.

As Federal energy administrator, Mr. Simon, who turned 46 last Tuesday, will be in

Continued on Page 74, Column 3

HOUSE UNIT LOOKS TO IMPEACHMENT

Committee Will Act on Any Misdeed by Nixon Even if It Falls Short of Crime

By JAMES M. NAUGHTON

Special to The New York Times

WASHINGTON, Dec. 1—Members of the House Judiciary Committee are prepared, by a substantial majority, to recommend the impeachment of President Nixon if they find evidence of serious misconduct even if such misconduct falls short of criminal wrongdoing.

The Judiciary Committee will not get into the thick of its impeachment inquiry before next February, and it is not likely to reach a determination on Mr. Nixon's conduct in office before next spring.

But a New York Times check conducted this week among the 21 Democrats and 17 Republicans who serve on the committee produced a surprising consensus on the question that will be central to the outcome of the inquiry: What constitutes an impeachable offense under the Constitution?

Of 32 members of the Judiciary Committee who were

Continued on Page 54, Column 1

Senators Will Vote Today In Debt Ceiling Deadlock

By WARREN WEAVER Jr.

Special to The New York Times

WASHINGTON, Dec. 1—The Senate failed today to break a deadlock over campaign spending legislation that has forced the Federal Government to operate with a total debt about $63-billion over the legal ceiling.

The resulting fiscal problem, academic over the weekend but which could be real when business resumes on Monday, was serious enough for the Treasury Department to halt the sale of savings bonds, on the ground that the Government's credit had run out at midnight last night and no further borrowing could be permitted.

During two hours of fitful debate, the Senators were unable to summon up enough votes to send to conference with the House a bill increasing and extending the debt ceiling, which had been amended to provide for financing the 1976 Presidential election, at least in part, with tax revenues.

At the same time, conservative opponents of the campaign finance proposal could not produce enough votes to kill the funding plan and continued to stage an informal desultory filibuster designed to delay any action.

The Senate will convene for an unusual Sunday session tomorrow and vote at 11 A.M. on whether to cut off debate on the question of sending the combined debt ceiling-campaign finance measure to conference, where differences with a House-passed bill that deals only with the debt ceiling would be worked out.

Supporters of the campaign finance plan clearly had doubts

Continued on Page 53, Column 1

MOTORISTS LINE UP FOR GASOLINE HERE

Closing of Service Stations Is Anticipated by Drivers Across the Country

By DAVID A. ANDELMAN

Anticipating widespread voluntary closings of service stations today, motorists lined up at gasoline pumps throughout the New York area and across the United States yesterday to stock up on fuel.

Cars were three and four deep at the pumps as early as 7 A.M. yesterday, and by mid-afternoon, many of the nation's 220,000 service stations reported such a heavy run on their fuel stocks that they were already running low. Some began closing down well before the cutoff of 9 P.M. yesterday in an effort to assure themselves of some supplies Monday morning.

Many of the motorists were also confronted with higher prices—as much as 2 or 3 cents or more a gallon—at the pumps when they drove in yesterday morning. On Friday, three of the major national oil companies—Shell, Atlantic-Richfield and Sun Oil Company—announced major price increases and others indicated they would follow suit this week.

Surveys in the New York metropolitan area and other scattered regions of the country indicated that in most cases 90 per cent or more of the service-station operators intended to observe the voluntary closings from 9 P.M. yesterday to midnight tonight suggested by President Nixon as a means of conserving gasoline.

By 4 P.M., most stations in Manhattan had closed for the weekend and by early evening they were closing in other boroughs. The New York and New Jersey state police reported traffic generally lighter than usual for a Saturday in December, and, on Long Island, the state parkway police reported normal flows.

The New York Automobile Club reported that a telephone survey of 294 stations in the 14 southernmost counties of

Continued on Page 72, Column 4

Illegal Market in Pistols Found Flourishing Here

By MICHAEL T. KAUFMAN

Rings of gunrunners are selling thousands of cheap pistols here in a lucrative black market that, according to a recent study, is flourishing in bars and on street corners of the city.

The firearms are for the most part purchased in large lots in four Southern states at prices ranging from $15 to $25 each. They are sold in New York City, which has the most stringent gun laws in the country, for $90 to $150.

In an attempt to stop, or at least lessen, the flow of such illegal weapons, the Police Department four weeks ago established a special gun squad. Its undercover operatives are currently "making buys" on the streets, attempting to trace and break the small and apparently independent gunrunning bands.

The scale of the problems here is sketched out in the statistics of Project Identification, the just-completed study in which the Treasury Department's Bureau of Alcohol, Tobacco and Firearms traced the

Continued on Page 84, Column 3

Navy Routs Army, 51-0; Aussies Win Davis Cup

Navy crushed Army, 51-0, at Philadelphia yesterday. It was the widest margin in the 84-year-old football rivalry. Army did not win this year.

Australia recaptured the Davis Cup in tennis by trouncing the United States in the doubles for a 3-0 lead in the final at Cleveland.

Details in Section 5.

Europe Deeply Insecure Over U.S. Troop Plans

Some Pullout Expected

By SEYMOUR TOPPING

Special to The New York Times

BONN, Nov. 29 — The Governments of Britain, France and West Germany have become convinced that the United States is determined to withdraw some of its military forces from Europe. Conversations with senior officials in the capitals of the three countries convey a deep sense of insecurity about the future defense of the region.

A round of intensive consultations was concluded this week by leaders of the major West European nations with a decision to coordinate regional defense efforts more closely and to make a new approach to the United States. The Americans will be asked to delay any pullout of troops, in view of the heavy build-up of the Soviet armed forces that is continuing despite the talk of improved East-West relations.

This position will be put to Secretary of State Kissinger when he visits Brussels early next month for a meeting of the Ministerial Council of the North Atlantic Treaty Organi-

Continued on Page 32, Column 1

A NATO Nuclear Strategy

By JOHN W. FINNEY

Special to The New York Times

WASHINGTON, Dec. 1—The North Atlantic Treaty allies have agreed upon a strategy providing that any large-scale use of nuclear weapons by forces within Europe should be accompanied by strikes by United States forces stationed outside Europe, a report by the staff of the Senate Foreign Relations Committee disclosed today.

A clear implication of this NATO strategy is that "a general nuclear response" by the tactical forces of the European allies would not be limited to Europe, but would include strikes against the Soviet Union by United States missiles and planes.

The strategy thus forges a direct link between the so-called tactical nuclear weapons that the United States has in Europe to deter a conventional Soviet attack and the strategic weapons deployed around the world to deter a nuclear war between the United States and the Soviet Union.

As a result, the staff report

Continued on Page 34, Column 1

Hermitage Caper Cracked by Soviet

By CHRISTOPHER S. WREN

Special to The New York Times

MOSCOW, Dec. 1 — When embellishments began disappearing from the antique furniture and rare books inside the Hermitage Museum in Leningrad five years ago, officials thought that thieves were sneaking in with the millions of legitimate visitors.

But when crystal pendants and petals vanished from the chandeliers high overhead, the Leningrad police suspected an inside job.

They proceeded to crack a ring of four present or former museum electricians who, over the next eight months, were tried, convicted and

Continued on Page 18, Column 1

More Trouble Plaguing Con Ed A-Plant

The New York Times

Technicians at Con Edison's nuclear facility at Indian Point testing the bulging steel liner of nuclear plant. Bent shadow line, left, shows extent of the bulge.

By DAVID BIRD

The Consolidated Edison Company's new nuclear generating plant at Indian Point, which was shut down by an accident on Nov. 13, has more problems than those that were publicly announced, the utility's officials have conceded.

Con Edison had said after the accident that the only apparent problem was a cracked 18-inch water pipe and that the large 873-megawatt plant would be back in operation within several weeks.

But under questioning last Friday, the utility said there was another problem: the buckling and bulging of the steel liner in the reinforced-concrete dome in which the nuclear plant is housed. Con Edison officials said that there was no danger now because the plant was shut down, but that there might be problems of what to do to get the plant started up again.

No previous public mention of the buckling of the liner had

Continued on Page 70, Column 4

12 Cases Dismissed In City Loan Scandal

By JOSEPH P. FRIED

Criminal indictments have been dismissed in court against 12 of 14 persons who had been charged in a major scandal two years ago with fraudulently obtaining nearly a million dollars from the city's municipal loan program for rehabilitating slum housing.

Nine of the accused had their indictments dismissed at the prosecutor's recommendation, and the office of District Attorney Frank S. Hogan of Manhattan said it was also "in the process of evaluating" whether to recommend dropping the indictments against the remaining two defendants.

The office's recommendation

Continued on Page 26, Column 1

Today's Sections

Index to Subjects

Ben-Gurion Is Dead at Age 87; One of the Founders of Israel

Continued From Page 1, Col. 2

ship in 1953. The burial service will be private, attended only by members of the family and close associates.

An official announcement tonight said that public participation in the funeral would be restricted because of the emergency situation after the October war.

However, the service at the Knesset and the interment at Sde Boker will be broadcast live by Israel television and radio.

In accordance with Mr. Ben-Gurion's last will, there will be no eulogies at the funeral. However, President Ephraim Katzir broadcast a tribute tonight.

The President alluded to the current crisis over Israel's future and said that Mr. Ben-Gurion's credo should guide the people at this time. He said it was particularly timely to recall what Mr. Ben-Gurion wrote to his colleagues in the Zionist leadership in 1946 when the British rulers of Palestine "imprisoned Jewish leaders and tried to paralyze Jewish life in the country."

Mr. Ben-Gurion wrote: "No despair and no illusions. No Massada and no Vichy. While bitter and difficult struggles lie ahead of us we are not preparing for a final battle. Nor do we wish to die with the Philistines. On the other hand we must recognize that the moment we give in and bow our heads and lose our will to stand up fearlessly, we begin to roll down the slope which leads to the abyss."

President Katzir said that Mr. Ben-Gurion was the greatest Jewish leader of his generation.

Mr. Ben-Gurion had been in and out of the Sheba Medical Center of Tel Hashomer Hospital, near Tel Aviv, during the two months preceding his stroke. He was last released Nov. 14. The brain hemorrhage that struck him four days later had been unconnected with his earlier ailments, according to his physician, Dr. Boleslaw Goldman.

The stroke came in Mr. Ben-Gurion's home in Keren Kayemet Boulevard here. It paralyzed the right side of the body. He was conscious but unable to talk.

Doctors at the Sheba Medical Center reported an improvement in his condition during the week but last Saturday his blood pressure dropped, his temperature rose and he fell into semiconsciousness.

Shortly before 10 A.M. today a nurse noticed that his breathing had quickened and had become irregular. Physicians were alerted and Mr. Ben-Gurion's children summoned. His son Amos and his daughters Mrs. Renana Leshen and Mrs. Geula Ben-Elizier reached his bedside.

Government leaders later arrived at the hospital to pay their respects. Among them were Defense Minister Moshe Dayan and Minister of Transport Shimon Peres, Mr. Ben-Gurion's favorite political protégés.

Dr. Goldman said that Mr. Ben-Gurion had continued his vigorous walks until he was advised to discontinue them a few months ago. He had earlier stopped his yoga headstands. The doctor said that Mr. Ben-Gurion had never been an obedient patient but had complied with doctors' orders after he had received full explanations of the purposes.

In recent years Mr. Ben-Gurion concentrated on his literary work. At the time of his stroke, he was preparing his memoirs for the year 1937.

The former leader had been politically inactive since 1970 when he resigned his Knesset seat in midterm. He later composed his differences with former political opponents. An associate said that he had folllowed events after the outbreak of the war Oct. 6 but did not express opinions.

Ben-Gurion Is Mourned Here in Sabbath Services

Continued From Page 1, Col. 2

not listen to broadcasts or answer the telephone on the Sabbath, many of them were unaware yesterday of Mr. Ben-Gurion's death. Even many members of Conservative congregations had not heard the news before arriving at services yesterday morning.

Services were well under way at Temple Israel, in Great Neck, L. I., when a messenger arrived and whispered the news to Rabbi Mordecai Waxman, who made the announcement to 850 members of the congregation.

"They knew he had been very ill," Rabbi Waxman said later. "But you could sense the sadness running through the congregation."

He quoted from the 121st Psalm: "I will lift up mine eyes unto the mountains, from whence cometh my help. . . ." And he concluded with a portion of Ecclesiasticus, xliv, I: "Let us now praise famous men. . . ."

Rabbi Nathan Perilman, senior rabbi of Temple Emanu-El, made the announcement of Ben-Gurion's death to 600 members of his congregation at the conclusion of yesterday morning's services.

While the Kaddish, or mourning prayer, is customarily not recited until after burial, Rabbi Perilman asked the congregation to make an exception in memory of Mr. Ben-Gurion. The soft cadences of the doxology of sanctification followed, and in a short eulogy, Rabbi Perilman praised Mr. Ben-Gurion as "surely a man touched by greatness."

"We are all diminished somewhat when such a man dies," he said. "If there hadn't been one like him, the nation [of Israel] would not have survived."

Ben-Gurion, Symbol of the Tough State of Israel, Achieved a Lifelong Dream

By HOMER BIGART

David Ben-Gurion symbolized the tough little state of Israel. Short, round, with a nimbus of white hair flaring angrily from a massive head, "B-G," as he was known to many, attained world leadership by firmly concentrating on the achievement of a dream.

That dream, the birth and triumphant survival of a Jewish homeland amid a sea of hostile Arabs, led Mr. Ben-Gurion through a lifetime of turmoil.

He was chairman of the Jewish Agency, the executive body of the World Zionist Organization, through the critical years of rising Arab nationalism, of Nazism, of World War II and of the postwar diplomatic struggle between Britain and the Jews of Palestine. When Britain finally gave up the Palestine mandate, it was Mr. Ben-Gurion who proclaimed the Jewish state.

This was his moment of supreme test. For on that same day, May 14, 1948, the Arab armies began their invasion of the fledgling state. Jerusalem was besieged by Transjordan's Arab Legion. In the Judean hills and in Galilee, Jewish settlements were under attack by Syrian and Iraqi forces, while Egyptians invaded from the south.

Battle Dress at 62

Exhilarated by the challenge, the 62-year-old leader put on battle dress and assumed the direction of military operations. He was de facto Premier and Minister of Defense.

Some of his decisions were questionable. He ordered a costly and ineffective attack to drive the Arab Legion from Jerusalem. But he had surrounded himself with young and competent officers such as Yigal Yadin, Yigal Allon and Moshe Dayan. The Arabs, who lacked unity of command, were soon routed.

To Mr. Ben-Gurion fell most of the credit for having won the first Jewish campaign since that of Judas Maccabaeus 2,000 years before.

He became an almost mystical figure to many Zionists: the wise patriarch who embodied all the traditional virtues and who would ultimately lead Israel to triumph over the ring of Arab enemies.

But he embittered millions of others. He alarmed the United Nations and insured the continued hatred of the Arab states by adopting a policy of swift and ruthless retaliation for Arab raids on Israel. Although an armistice was arranged by the United Nations, technically Jordan, Lebanon, Syria and Egypt remained at war with Israel, and border incidents were frequent after the war of 1948-49.

Angered U.S. Jews

Mr. Ben-Gurion also alienated many American Jews by insisting that all true Zionists must live in Israel. Disturbed by the influx of Oriental Jews, which he feared would transform Israel into "just another Levantine state," Mr. Ben-Gurion dreamed of a vast migration of Jews from the Soviet Union and the United States.

In the early years only 5,000 American Jews were "ingathered," a scant migration that drew scornful reproaches from Mr. Ben-Gurion.

A feud between Mr. Ben-Gurion and a large segment of American Jewry dated from August, 1957, when he said at a Zionist ideological conference in Jerusalem that a sound Jewish life was not possible outside Israel.

"There seems to be a general agreement," he said, "that a Jew can live in America, speak and read English and bring up his children in America and still call himself a Zionist. If that is Zionism I want no part of it."

In subsequent speeches Mr. Ben-Gurion reiterated his belief that Jewish life in the outside world had a dim future. His dogmatism alienated potential friends of Israel among both Jews and gentiles. Non-Zionist Jews resented his insistence that Judaism was not a mere religion but a nationalistic ethos. Almost every Zionist faction in the United States joined the mounting protest.

Adamant on Israel's Role

Stubbornly, though, Mr. Ben-Gurion insisted that essentially Judaism was a nationality and Israel was the only sovereign spokesman for the world's Jews.

In June, 1962, he again infuriated American Jewish leaders at a Jerusalem conference by equating Judaism with nationality. Stanley H. Lowell, chairman of the New York City Commission on Intergroup Relations, retorted:

"You aren't the only answer to Jewish living, Jewish creativity and Jewish survival. This generation and the next generations to come shall and will remain part and parcel of the great American experience of democracy."

In later years, though, with the 1967 and 1973 wars and increased United States aid, the old man's idea of Zionism came to be the accepted one. The anti-Zionist organizations became virtually extinct; by 1970, American immigration to Israel was reaching 10,000 a year.

At home, Mr. Ben-Gurion managed to roll elements of the population, even members of his own Mapai party, by methods that often seemed autocratic. He never enjoyed sharing authority, and he chafed under Israel's system of proportional representation, which assures religious parties of representation in the government. These parties were often in bitter disagreement with Mr. Ben-Gurion, who opposed their dream of a theocracy.

The Mapai party, although dominant, was never able to win a clear majority in the Knesset, or Parliament; this was a cause of the formation of 11 coalition governments in Israel, including the provisional government that was set up in April, 1948. In March, 1949, Mr. Ben-Gurion became Premier in the first regularly constituted Government of Israel.

These political marriages into coalitions were usually brief and stormy. The Socialist Mapai had little in common with the small left-wing labor parties and religious groups that were persuaded to join coalitions in exchange for concessions in legislation or for a ministerial post or two.

Sometimes Mr. Ben-Gurion would become so frustrated that he would resign and retire to his four-room cottage in Sde Boker, a kibbutz that was his favorite retreat, in the stony Negev Desert.

Usually the mere threat of resignation was enough to force the concessions Mr. Ben-Gurion demanded. The only Israeli with enough stature to offer alternative leadership was Moshe Sharett, another Mapai stalwart. But Mr. Sharett was considered too cautious, too temporizing. Israelis thought they needed daring leadership to meet the growing threat brought on by Egypt's acquisition of Communist-bloc arms, by the nationalization of the Suez Canal and by the military alliance between Egypt and Syria.

Mr. Ben-Gurion resigned several times, but his retirements to Sde Boker were fleeting except for one interval: In December, 1953, he turned over his office and leadership to Mr. Sharett, explaining that he felt "tired, tired, tired."

For 14 months he stayed in Sde Boker compiling "Rebirth and Destiny of Israel," a collection of his addresses and essays, and working at agriculture in the kibbutz while his wife helped in the communal kitchen.

Even in retirement he cast his long shadow over the country: soon, in February, 1955, he was called to Jerusalem to resume the post of Minister of Defense, which he had held throughout his Premiership. He also assumed leadership of the Mapai and again became Premier in November, 1955.

Under Mr. Ben-Gurion, Israel adopted a policy that led to war. There had been a flurry of frontier incidents. Israel complained that the United Nations truce supervision teams were futile instruments for checking Arab commando raids. Mr. Ben-Gurion mounted large-scale retaliatory operations aimed at destroying what he called guerrilla bases across the frontier.

To United Nations observers the border incidents about which the Israelis complained often appeared hardly serious enough to warrant the thunderous retaliation visited upon the Arabs by the Israelis. In balance, at least five or six Arabs died for every Israeli killed.

Attack in Syria

In December, 1955, after Syrians had fired on Israeli fishing craft in the Sea of Galilee, Mr. Ben-Gurion ordered his army into Syrian territory. A network of Syrian coastal positions was blown up, and 50 Syrian soldiers were killed.

The raid was ill-timed politically. On that same day the temperate Mr. Sharett, then Foreign Minister, was waiting in Washington for an answer to his request for Western arms to offset Communist arms that were reaching Egypt. News of the raid shocked and vexed the State Department. Mr. Sharett returned empty-handed, furious with Mr. Ben-Gurion, whom he accused of having undermined his mission.

Mr. Ben-Gurion not only re-

(continued)

fused to modify his retaliation policy but also told Mr. Sharett that diplomacy was to be subordinated to security. In June, 1956, he ousted Mr. Sharett and chose as his new Foreign Minister Mrs. Golda Meir, a former Milwaukee teacher, whom he could trust to follow his line.

Tension rose during the summer of 1956, and in September a major retaliatory action led by General Dayan, then chief of the Israeli armed forces, resulted in the death of 37 Jordanians.

Nasser Termed Fascist

Such actions Mr. Ben-Gurion defended as "self-defense," and he told his Parliament that the greatest menace to Israel was an impending attack by "the Egyptian Fascist dictator," President Gamal Abdel Nasser. He proclaimed: "We will never start a war. We do not believe that wars provide comprehensive solutions to historic problems."

Two weeks after he had spoken those words Mr. Ben-Gurion, in complicity with France and Britain, launched a "preventive war" to knock out President Nasser's army. Israeli forces overran the Gaza Strip, the tiny corner of the old British Palestine mandate administered by Egypt, and plunged deep into Sinai.

Mr. Ben-Gurion's objective was the fall of President Nasser and the signing of a peace treaty with Egypt.

By prearrangement, Britain and France moved to seize the Suez Canal. Port Said fell to the British and French forces. The invasion by the three nations was on the verge of success.

Then the roof fell in. President Dwight D. Eisenhower was furious at Britain and France for having committed open aggression while the West was reaping moral capital over the Hungarian revolt. So the United States supported United Nations demands that the invading forces vacate Egypt promptly and unconditionally.

Confronted also by threats of Soviet intervention, Britain and France withdrew their forces in 27 days.

Israel balked. Mr. Ben-Gurion wanted to keep the Gaza Strip. He also wanted assurances that the Gulf of Aqaba, the northern arm of the Red Sea, would be open to Israeli shipping. The gulf had been denied to Israeli ships for six years by Egyptian guns commanding the narrow passage at Sharm el Sheik.

President Eisenhower insisted that no nation invading another in the face of United Nations disapproval should set conditions on its withdrawal. Aggression, he said, must not be rewarded.

Mr. Ben-Gurion defied the world for weeks, flouting six successive General Assembly orders to get out of Egypt. His Parliament had approved a defiant resolution committing Israel never to yield either the gulf or Gaza.

But when President Eisenhower cut short a vacation to warn of "pressure" if Israel failed to cooperate, the tough little Premier knew the game was up.

Pale and drawn from pneumonia contracted after a PT-boat ride in the Gulf of Aqaba, Mr. Ben-Gurion went before his Cabinet to propose more flexibility in Israel's position. Knesset politicians were insisting on all-out defiance.

'Noose Is Tightening'

"The noose is tightening around our neck," a bearded, skullcapped member cried.

"The devil with this," snapped Mr. Ben-Gurion. "The devil with the coalition." He threatened to quit and form a new government. Finally he got the leeway he needed.

Israel agreed to withdraw from Gaza and Sharm el Sheik on these "assumptions": that freedom of navigation would prevail on the Gulf of Aqaba; that the Gaza Strip would be administered by the United Nations pending a peace settlement between Egypt and Israel; and that Israel had the right, under the self-defense guarantee of the United Nations Charter, to send ships through the Gulf of Aqaba by armed force if there should be interference and to "defend its rights" in the Gaza Strip if raids were renewed.

The collapse of the Sinai adventure was the bleakest momoment in Mr. Ben-Gurion's career. That he survived it politically was considered a tribute to his toughness, his resilience, his ability to persuade most Israelis and a great segment of world Jews that his action was morally sound.

Again in 1960 Mr. Ben-Gurion risked alienating world opinion; he decided to try Adolf Eichmann, the Gestapo colonel who had shipped millions of Jews to death camps in World War II.

There was little or no sympathy for Eichmann, but there was widespread resentment over the way he was brought to justice. The Nazi was kidnapped in Argentina, put aboard an El Al Israel Airlines plane and eventually exposed to a show trial in a Jerusalem theater converted into a courtroom.

There were protests that Eichmann could not possibly have a fair trial in Jerusalem, that the case should be heard by a German court or an international tribunal. Many Jews assailed the "arrogance" of Mr. Ben-Gurion's contention that Israel, as the sovereign Jewish state, was "from a moral point of view" the only place where Eichmann could be tried.

The furor died quickly as the trial unfolded. The Israeli judges seemed impeccable in the hearing during the spring and summer of 1961. After they had condemned Eichmann to the gallows, Robert Servatius, his West German lawyer, conceded that the defendant had had a fairer trial than he would have got in West Germany.

The trial enhanced Mr. Ben-Gurion's exalted status in his own country. By bringing Eichmann to trial he had taught the new generation of Israelis that "Jews are not sheep to be slaughtered, but a people who can hit back—as Jews did in the War of Independence."

Born Green, a Pole

Israel's man of decision was born in Plonsk, Poland, on Oct. 16, 1886. His name was David Green, and his father was Avigdor Green, an unlicensed lawyer who wore a silk top hat and a frock coat rather than the fur hat and caftan traditionally worn by the men of his community. David was to adopt the pen name "Ben-Gurion" as a journalist in Jerusalem. He thought it had a resonant Old Testament ring—it was the name of one of the last defenders of Jerusalem against the Roman legions. The Hebrew word "Ben" means "Son of," and "Gurion" means "Lion Cub."

Mr. Ben-Gurion's mother, Sheindal, died during the birth of her 11th child. David, her sixth, was 10 years old at the time.

The tone of the family was vigorously intellectual. There were discussions of Socialism and the newly re-emerged Zionism advocated by the Viennese journalist Theodor Herzl at the historic Jewish conference at Basel, Switzerland, in 1897.

Standing beneath a portrait of Theodor Herzl, the founder of modern Zionism, David Ben-Gurion proclaimed the independence of Israel on May 14, 1948.

Mr. Ben-Gurion's formal education did not go much beyond the Plonsk Jewish schools, but he acquired an excellently stocked mind through wide reading, particularly in history. Possessed of tremendous concentration, he became in his lifetime a keen student of Greek and Eastern philosophies. He achieved a brilliant reputation as a linguist through his mastery of English, Russian, Greek, Yiddish, Turkish, French and German. He read but did not speak Arabic. He also studied Spanish.

Active Socialist Zionist

In Plonsk he was active in the Poale Zion movement, which combined Zionism and Socialism. Plonsk was in Russian Poland, and the revolutionary movement against the Czars was followed by pogroms there. Many Polish and Russian Jews emigrated. In 1906, kindled by Herzl's aim for a Jewish commonwealth, David Green was one of a group of young Plonsk Jews who went to Palestine.

Of his first night in Palestine he wrote in a letter to his father:

"I did not sleep. I was amid the rich smell of corn. I heard the braying of donkeys and the rustle of leaves in the orchards. Above were massed clusters of stars against the deep blue firmament. My heart overflowed with happiness."

But Mr. Ben-Gurion was repelled by the political apathy of the Jewish settlers — there were about 60,000 Jews in Palestine when he arrived. He joined the small Workers party, Poale Zion, which was to emerge as Mapei, and soon became one of its leading organizers and propagandists. Today Mapai is moderately Socialist, probably no more leftist than the British Labor party, and has little in common with doctrinaire Marxism.

One Meal a Day

Mr. Ben-Gurion worked for a time as a farm laborer for wages just sufficient to provide him with a room and one meal a day. He displayed a natural ability to negotiate in labor disputes, and he soon had considerable prestige among his fellow workers.

Articles signed Ben-Gurion began to appear in the Poale Zion party newspaper, and Mr. Ben-Gurion was elected to the three-man administrative presidium of the party at the 1907 Jaffa conference. At that conference he succeeded in having this platform plan adopted: "The party will strive for an independent state for the Jewish people in this country."

In that year, to prevent difficulties for his father in Plonsk, Mr. Ben-Gurion returned to Russia to do his military service. He served for one week, deserted and made his way back to Palestine.

The success of Enver Pashá's "Young Turk" movement in Turkey in 1908 led Mr. Ben-Gurion and many of his associates to believe that reasonable coexistence could be established between the new and supposedly liberal Turkish Government and the Jewish community in Palestine, which was in the Ottoman Empire. Mr. Ben-Gurion and several other Zionist leaders went to Constantiople to study Turkish law and administration, hoping to enter the Turkish Government as representatives of Jewish Palestine.

Early in World War I, Mr. Ben-Gurion wrote articles advocating the creation of a Jewish battalion in the Turkish Army. But the Turks suspected his motives and expelled him as subversive. With his chief collaborator, a young Ukranian Jew named Itzhak Ben-Zvi, who was to become the second President of Israel, Mr. Ben-Gurion made his way to the United States in 1915.

It was in New York that Mr. Ben-Gurion and Mr. Ben-Zvi founded Hechalutz (the Pioneers), which created Jewish settlements in Palestine between the world wars. And it was here that he met Paula Moonwess, daughter of an immigrant from Minsk. She was a student at the Brooklyn Jewish Training School for Nurses. They were married at City Hall in 1917.

Paula, a direct and uninhibited woman, was to become a legend in Israel. She is said to have startled Dag Hammarskjold, the late Secretary General of the United Nations, by saying to him, "Why don't you get married and leave the Jews and Arabs alone?" Mr. Hammarskjold remained a bachelor.

Served in Egypt

Until Russia had left the war and the United States had entered it, Mr. Ben-Gurion believed that the best interests of the Palestine Jews lay with Turkey. But by 1917 there were indications that the Turks might not be on the winning side. Mr. Ben-Gurion helped organize two Jewish battalions in the United States and Canada to serve with the British in the Middle East. He served as a corporal in one of the battalions, with the Royal Fusiliers in Egypt, but saw no action.

The Balfour Declaration of 1917 established the principle of a Jewish homeland in Palestine, and in 1922 the British were entrusted by the League of Nations with a mandate for Palestine.

Israel's future leader in World War I uniform. In U.S., he helped organize Jewish Legion to serve with British in Mideast, then saw duty in battalion of the Royal Fusiliers.

Dr. Chaim Weizmann, the intellectual who was to become the first President of Israel, headed the world Zionist movement mostly from London. Mr. Ben-Gurion preached Jewish working-class solidarity on the scene in Palestine.

To a group of Zionist delegates he once said:

"Let me inform you gentle-

Cont'd on Following Page

men that Zionism has no content if you do not constantly bear in mind the building of the Jewish state. And such a state is only possible on the basis of a maximum number of workers, and if you cannot understand that, woe to your Zionism."

The Jewish Legion had been formed too late to contribute much to the defeat of Turkey, but its existence provided Mr. Ben-Gurion with a fine channel for propaganda. He proselytized for the Poale Zion party among the 3,000 legionnaires. It was largely because of his initiative that Histadrut, the General Federation of Labor, was formed in 1920, with Mr. Ben-Gurion as Secretary General.

This powerful body, now quartered in a modern Tel Aviv skyscraper that enemies of Mr. Ben-Gurion called the Kremlin, expanded into banking, health plans, contracting, agriculture, marketing, education, insurance, transportation, employment agencies, collectives and cooperatives of every kind.

For the next five years Mr. Ben-Gurion campaigned for the union of Palestine's labor parties, and in 1930 the Mapai was formed. In 1935 he became chairman of the Jewish Agency, the executive body of Zionism.

Opposed by Many

Mr. Ben-Gurion had many opponents in the general Zionist movement. Vladimir Jabotinsky was one leader of a nationalist movement opposed to what many Zionists believed to be Mr. Ben-Gurion's strong Socialist views.

In 1936, Palestinian Arabs staged a bloody revolt against increasing Jewish influence, and the next year Mr. Ben-Gurion favored a partition of Palestine as recommended by a Royal Commission under Earl Peel. The Arabs rejected the proposal, and the British dropped the plan.

British policy became clearly pro-Arab, and in 1939 the British Government issued a White Paper that limited Jewish immigration to Palestine and land purchases there and was aimed at insuring a permanent minority status for the Jews there.

When Britain declared war on Germany, the Jews in Palestine pledged support against the common enemy but continued their resistance to the British policy, which they considered a threat to their existence.

Mr. Ben-Gurion put it this way: "We shall fight in the war against Hitler as if there were no White Paper, but we shall fight the White Paper as if there were no war."

During the war years he was preoccupied with these aims and internal matters in Palestine. And the mass extermination of German Jews intensified his desire to establish a Jewish homeland.

In 1945 he visited displaced-persons camps in Germany and the next year told a conference of survivors: "We shall not rest until the last one of you who so desires shall join us in the land of Israel to build the Jewish state together with us."

Mr. Ben-Gurion believed that if the Jews in Palestine could not defend themselves they would be driven out by the Arabs. From 1907, when he was with "Hashomer," the armed guard movement, while he was a labor leader in Sejera, a small isolated village in Galilee, he acted in the belief that the Palestinian Jews would have to protect themselves.

After the United Nations, on Nov. 29, 1947, resolved to partition Palestine into Jewish and Arab states, Mr. Ben-Gurion assumed the security portfolio of the Jewish Agency Executive.

He planned and supervised the transformation of the Haganah from an illegal underground military arm of the Jewish Agency into the Israel Defense Forces. He sent men to Europe to buy arms, including World War II surplus equipment, and to recruit Jewish war veterans to operate the planes, tanks and artillery with which the Haganah had had no experience.

Volunteers came from the United States, Canada, South Africa, South America and most European countries. Mr. Ben-Gurion obtained funds from Jews in the United States and bought machinery to establish an arms industry.

Cooperation With British

From time to time Mr. Ben-Gurion cooperated with the British against terrorists, and armed clashes were narrowly averted.

During the mandate the Irgun Zvai Leumi, an extreme nationalist group, had conducted terrorist activities against the British Government. Unlike the Haganah, it had spurned the authority of the official Jewish leadership.

During a United Nations truce, the Irgun ran the landing ship Altalena ashore at Tel Aviv with weapons and volunteers. Mr. Ben-Gurion ordered Haganah troops to fire at the ship, which blew up. Men were killed and wounded on both sides.

The Altalena affair was one of the most controversial events in Mr. Ben-Gurion's career as Premier. Many Israelis never forgave his order, which deprived Israel of badly needed weapons and nearly touched off a civil war. Others said it had been one of the most courageous and statesmanlike actions of his career. They believed that by handling the situation firmly in that crucial period Mr. Ben-Gurion had established once and for all that there was no authority in the state but the Government of Israel and in fact averted a civil war.

After the truce, renewed sharp fighting with the Arabs secured the Negev and central Galilee for Israel. Armistice agreements with Egypt, Lebanon, Syria and Jordan in 1949 ended the hot war for the time being.

Drastic Economic Steps

Because large-scale immigration had nearly doubled the population and it was still necessary to maintain military preparedness, the Israelis by 1951 found it necessary to take drastic steps to bolster the country's economy.

Premier Ben-Gurion came to the United States on a fund-raising drive. He was received with enthusiasm and initiated the sale of $500-million in Israeli Bonds.

At this time Israel abandoned her foreign policy of "non-identification" and openly aligned herself with the United States in the cold war. Previously, Israel, in her independence struggle, had bought arms from Soviet-bloc countries and had enjoyed good relations with the Soviet Union, one of the first nations to recognize the State of Israel.

At home Mr. Ben-Gurion wrestled with succeeding Cabinet crises until the day in 1953 when he decided that he had had enough for a while.

In an article written for The New York Times from his retreat at Sde Boker on his retirement, he said:

"No single person alone can determine the fate of a nation. No man is indispensable. In war there may be a commander or statesman on whom much or even all depends. Not so in time of peace. The fate of a country depends upon its own character, its ability, its capacity, its faith in itself, its sense of responsibility, both individual and collective. A statesman who sees himself as the determining factor in the fate of his country is harmful and dangerous."

The New York Times/Gertrude Samuels

During one of his periods of retirement, Mr. Ben-Gurion tills the soil at the kibbutz of Sde Boker in the Negev.

Yet for 15 years Mr. Ben-Gurion made most of the decisions for Israel, and the most fateful were to come after he had returned to Jerusalem in 1955 and had begun leading the nation on a more adventurous path.

Although his country was in reality a ward of the United States, absolutely dependent on financial aid from Washington and from American Jewish groups, Mr. Ben-Gurion refused to permit any outside meddling in her affairs.

He showed his freedom from American controls early by ignoring strong Washington pressure to put Israel's capital in Tel Aviv, rather than in Jerusalem, which the United Nations had proposed as an international city. (The United States has refused to move its embassy from Tel Aviv to Jerusalem.)

In domestic politics, Mr. Ben-Gurion also defied strong forces, notably the ultra-Orthodox religious groups. Once, during an interminable Knesset debate over whether swine—forbidden to Jews as food—should be bred in Israel, Mr. Ben-Gurion remarked that if the Lord had objected to pigs He wouldn't have led them to Noah's Ark.

At another time he shocked rabbis in the Knesset by announcing that after a study of Exodus he had concluded that only 600 Jews—not 600,000 as the Bible maintained — could have left Egypt and crossed the Sinai Desert.

Student of Bible

Mr. Ben-Gurion was a profound student of the Bible. His speeches were enriched with references to the heroes and Prophets of the Old Testament. He had had little formal education, but his intellectual curiosity led him, at 56, to learn Greek so he could read the Septuagint, the Greek version of the Old Testament. At 68 his interest turned to the Dialogues of Buddha, and he began learning Sanskrit to understand them fully.

He already knew enough yoga to stand on his head, and photos of Mr. Ben-Gurion in bathing trunks, inverted on the Mediterranean sands, invoked wry comment. Friends insisted however that Hazaken — the Old Man—as he was affectionately called, was sharper-witted upside down than most of his opponents right side up.

The most serious domestic challenge to Mr. Ben-Gurion's rule came as a result of the celebrated "Lavon affair."

A former protégé of Mr. Ben-Gurion, Pinhas Lavon, had risen in the Histadrut until his political influence was so considerable that he was regarded as a possible heir to the national leadership.

But Mr. Ben-Gurion fell out with Mr. Lavon and sought to destroy his power. A cloak-and-dagger fiasco, involving the collapse of an Israeli spy network in Egypt, gave Mr. Ben-Gurion the chance in 1955 to force Mr. Lavon's resignation as Defense Minister.

The scandal smoldered for six years. Few Israelis knew what the affair was about. The press was allowed to print only the state censor's approved phrase, "a security disaster in 1954." The Egyptian Government charged in 1954 that it had uncovered an Israeli spy ring that planned to blow up British and American consular offices to sabotage relations between Cairo and the Western powers.

Then, in December, 1960, the Lavon affair burst into the news again. Mr. Lavon was able to prove at a meeting of the Israeli Cabinet that forged papers had been part of the evidence that forced him from office. Mr. Ben-Gurion stormed from the room, but even this did not prevent his Cabinet from clearing Mr. Lavon of responsibility for the 1954 fiasco.

Mr. Ben-Gurion followed his usual tactic of bringing down the Government by resigning. But this time other members of his six-party coalition were so disturbed that they refused to join him in a new government. Hoping to silence his critics, Mr. Ben-Gurion called for new elections. The results, he conceded, were "a national disaster," for Mapai slipped from 47 seats to 42 in the 120-seat Knesset. After lengthy dickering, however, he formed a new Cabinet, and meanwhile the Mapai Central Committee had destroyed Mr. Lavon's base of power by ousting him as Secretary General of the Histadrut.

Eventually Mr. Ben-Gurion suffered the bitter fate that overtakes a statesman who has been around too long. He became a bore to his people, and they rejected him.

He resigned as Premier in June, 1963, because of "personal needs." He said later that he wanted to write a history of the Jews' return to their homeland. But in semiretirement he erupted sporadically, like a cooling volcano. He became increasingly critical of Levi Eshkol, the new Premier, and the estrangement between the two grew wider when Mr. Ben-Gurion proclaimed that Mr. Eshkol was "unfit to lead the nation."

He demanded a reopening of the Lavon affair. But the country was bored by the 10-year-old scandal, and Premier Eshkol refused a judicial inquiry into the almost-forgotten fiasco.

Mr. Ben-Gurion's efforts to return to active politics ended in humiliation. The Mapai Central Committee refused to put him on the party's list for the 1965 election. So he formed Rafi, a splinter party, taking with him a handful of younger politicians including General Dayan, the former Chief of Staff. The new party ran a poor fourth with less than 9 per cent of the vote, and won 10 seats in Parliament.

Mr. Ben-Gurion's wife died in 1968 and the old warrior spent much of his time thereafter in solitary contemplation. In 1968, after his small Rafi party decided to join the newly formed Israel Labor party, a number of Rafi members led by Mr. Ben-Gurion broke away. They formed the Independent National List and won four Knesset seats in 1969.

He remained in the Knesset until 1970, when he delivered a hand-written resignation note to the speaker, Reuven Barkatt and, dry-eyed, left the chamber for good.

Soon afterward, he told a visitor to Tel Aviv that he had found farm work more satisfying than politics. And he had this to say about Soviet intentions in the Middle East:

"They want to get the two oceans, the Atlantic and the Pacific. So first of all they must have the Mediterranean, and it is not easy to get that without the Arabs. They want the Arabs, I do not think they are interested in destroying Israel, because if they do, the Arabs will not need them."

Concerning the territories that Israel occupied in the 1967 Arab-Israeli war, Mr. Ben-Gurion took a relatively dovish position:

"I consider peace more important than territory," he said. "The area we had before the six-day war would be enough to take in all the Jews."

He continued: "For peace, I would be for giving back all the captured areas, with the exception of Jerusalem and the Golan heights."

Turning to his old theme of the need for further immigration, he said Israel still needed "another five or six million" Jews. But he observed wryly, "I don't believe that all Jews will settle in Israel—unless the Messiah comes."

"All the News That's Fit to Print"

The New York Times

LATE CITY EDITION

Weather: Partly cloudy today; cold tonight. Cloudy and cold tomorrow. Temperature range: today 35-48; Friday 33-40. Details on Page 44.

VOL.CXXIV...No.42,707 NEW YORK, SATURDAY, DECEMBER 28, 1974 Price higher in air delivery cities. 20 CENTS

3 Boston School Officials In Contempt Over Busing

Federal Judge Cites Foes of a Citywide Plan for Racial Desegregation

By JOHN KIFNER
Special to The New York Times

Associated Press
Judge W. Arthur Garrity Jr.

BOSTON, Dec. 27—Federal District Judge W. Arthur Garrity Jr. held three Boston School Committeemen in civil contempt of court today for refusing to approve a citywide busing plan for school desegregation.

The judge took under advisement until Monday what sanctions he might impose on the recalcitrant committee members.

Lawyers for the National Association for the Advancement of Colored People, the original plaintiffs, suggested that a proper sanction might be $500-a-day fines until the committeemen "purged" themselves of contempt by approving the plan. The judge has a wide range of options, including jail sentences, but appeared to be leaning toward avoiding harsh measures against the commit teemen.

Rejected 3 to 2

Judge Garrity had ordered the School Committee to draft a plan for next fall, approve it — he insisted on the approval—and submit it to him on Dec. 16. But minutes before the plan was due, the school committee voted 3 to 2 against approving it.

In the closing minutes of the day-long hearing today, Judge Garrity appeared to be proposing a solution in which the committee would somehow "submit" the plan as the official School Committee plan without "approving" it.

But only moments before, under the judge's questioning, the three committee members stubbornly repeated their opposition to the citywide plan drawn up by the School Department staff.

"I can't go for a plan that calls for a forced busing of schoolchildren," said Chairman John J. Kerrigan, who spoke of the city's blacks as a "hostile, militant community."

"I don't think it will work, your honor," said Committeeman John J. McDonough. "I disapprove of the plan because it's going to result in the destruction of the city and injury to people."

Pressed as to whether he would consider voting to "submit" the plan, Committeeman Paul J. Ellison complained: "It's like when you're a kid in a fight, when you're down and they're twisting your arm until you say, 'I give.' I voted my conscience."

In holding the School Committee members in civil con-

Continued on Page 8, Column 2

FORD AND 15 AIDES NARROW OPTIONS ON ENERGY POLICY

Nessen Says 'No Definitive Decisions Were Made,' but Calls Parley 'Intense'

By JOHN HERBERS
Special to The New York Times

VAIL, Colo., Dec. 27—President Ford met with 15 advisers today in an effort to formulate new policy proposals on energy that would increase the supply and restrict consumption.

Ron Nessen, the White House press secretary, who sat in on the day-long meeting in the private home where Mr. Ford is vacationing, described the session as "intense" with a clash of ideas, but one in which the "choices were narrowed but no definitive decisions were made."

He said the President had ordered that there be "no public discussion" of the options under consideration but added: "This is going to be a comprehensive program and it's going to deal with both increasing supply and it's going to deal with restricting consumption and it's going to deal with three time frames: the short term, which is between now and 1977; the mid-term, which is 1977 to 1985, and the long term, which is beyond 1985.

"It's going to deal with the impact of the energy policy on the domestic economy and it's going to deal with the impact on the international economy and on international relations."

'Practically No Clash'

Mr. Ford plans to announce his energy policy in his State of the Union Message to Congress on Jan. 20. Mr. Nessen said some of the proposals would be carried out through executive order and others submitted to Congress for enactment.

Environmental issues have figured in the discussions, Mr. Nessen said, but these have been "narrowed to where there was practically no clash on that this morning."

Those attending today's meeting in addition to Mr. Nessen were:

Rogers C. B. Morton, Secretary of the Interior and Chairman of the Energy Resources Council.

Frank G. Zarb, Administrator of the Federal Energy Administration.

William E. Simon, Secretary of the Treasury.

Alan Greenspan, Chairman of the Council of Economic Advisers.

William Seidman, Assistant to the President for Economic Affairs.

Eric Zausner and John Hill, officials of the Federal Energy Administration.

Donald Rumsfeld, White House Chief of Staff.

Roy L. Ash, Director of the Office of Management and Budget.

Thomas O. Enders, Assistant

Continued on Page 6, Column 5

United Press International

President Ford conferring with Rogers C. B. Morton, center, Secretary of the Interior, and Frank G. Zarb, the Federal energy chief, yesterday. The scene is Vail, Colo., where the Ford family is on holiday.

PROSECUTOR BIDS WATERGATE JURY CLOSE THE LEDGER

Neal Winds Up Arguments, Declaring 'People Must Be Called to Account'

SUMMATIONS ARE ENDED

Sirica Will Give Case to the Jurors on Monday After Instructions in Law

By LESLEY OELSNER
Special to The New York Times

WASHINGTON, Dec. 27—The prosecution wound up the final arguments at the Watergate cover-up trial today by telling the jurors that it was now up to them to "balance the accounts" and close the ledgers on Watergate.

The jurors are to begin their deliberations on Monday after instructions in the law by Federal Judge John J. Sirica.

"It's no fun casting stones," the chief prosecutor, James F. Neal, told the jury this afternoon. "This Government that's represented here does not cast stones with joy or happiness.

"But to keep society going, stones must be cast. People must be called to account."

Calling to Account

If Government officials commit crimes, Mr. Neal said, if they "cover up" their mistakes, or "strike foul blows," or "assault the temples of justice," then, "when these things occur, society must call those responsible to account."

"No one at this table," he said, gesturing toward the one where six assistant prosecutors were sitting, would suggest a verdict.

"But as representatives of the people in a free society, you are the ones who must now balance the accounts and close the ledger plates of Watergate."

The prosecutor said later that he had meant "ledger," not "ledger plates."

Mr. Neal's appeal, made in the final moments of his closing statement to the jury, concluded all but the final stage of the trial— the judge's instructions and the jurors' deliberations.

Often Emotional Day

It also capped a full and often emotional day, a day in which one of the defense lawyers, summing up the case before his client, wept openly and one of the prosecutors, summing up part of the Government's case, told of his pride that the country was "confident" and strong enough to have such a trial.

The defense lawyer, Jacob A. Stein, told the jury that his client, Kenneth Wells Parkinson, had been "deceived" and "abused" by an assortment of White House and campaign officials, including two of his co-defendants, former Attorney General John N. Mitchell and former Assistant Attorney General Robert C. Mardian.

This occurred, Mr. Stein said, when Mr. Parkinson, a Washington lawyer, was retained by the campaign committee for the re-election of former President Nixon in the summer of 1972 to handle the legal problems stemming from the break-in at Democratic national headquarters in the Watergate complex on June 17, 1972.

Mr. Stein began to weep when he told the jury, toward the end of his argument, of Mr. Parkinson's good reputation, built up over more than 20 years as a lawyer.

"What is good character worth?" he asked.

Is it to be "thrown away," he asked, "and cynically tossed out in favor of the testimony of confessed perjurers? ... Doesn't a lifetime where you built it up grain by grain weigh against that?"

Mr. Stein was followed to the lectern by Richard Ben-Veniste, who presented the Government's rebuttal to the closing

Continued on Page 9, Column 1

Family Court Judge Is Convicted on L.I. On Perjury Charge

By ROY R. SILVER
Special to The New York Times

MINEOLA, L.I., Dec. 27—Judge Martin Ginsberg of Family Court was found guilty today of one count of perjury for having denied before a grand jury that he had received money from two businessmen in exchange for promises to use his influence in their behalf.

The 44-year-old judge sat impassively in County Court as Judge Con G. Cholakis, who presided at the three-week nonjury trial, announced his verdict.

Judge Ginsberg was acquitted by Judge Cholakis, who is from Rensselaer County, of a second count of perjury, because Judge Cholakis said, there was "a serious question" of corroboration of the testimony by one of the prosecution witnesses.

Bribery Count Dropped

Earlier in the trial, after the state rested its case, Judge Cholakis dismissed extortion and bribery charges, which had been part of the indictment last April 26 by a Nassau County grand jury.

After Judge Cholakis issued his verdict, Judge Ginsberg leaned over to John J. Sutter, his lawyer, and said: "I don't believe it."

"Neither do I," Mr. Sutter responded.

After comforting her two daughters, Wendy, 20, and Susan, 18, who were weeping, Judge Ginsberg's wife, Joan, went up to her husband, held his head and said: "Relax, darling."

"My entire life and career is destroyed," the judge murmured to the lawyer.

Judge Ginsberg, who will be sentenced Feb. 14, faces a pris-

Continued on Page 16, Column 1

JUDGE HERE CURBS LAW SECRETARIES

Order to Prohibit Private Practice and Holding Office in Political Organizations

By MARY BREASTED

The presiding justice of the Appellate Division, Second Department of State Supreme Court, issued a directive yesterday barring law secretaries from holding office in political organizations and said he would enforce a court rule that bars them from practicing law except in rare cases.

Justice Frank A. Gulotta's directive strikes at the heart of what the bar associations and the special state prosecutor, Maurice H. Nadjari, have identified as the major areas of corruption and political patronage in the city's court system.

Although the directive did not spell out what penalties violators of Justice Gulotta's order would suffer, the judge said during an interview that he would ask violators to explain their behavior to the Appellate Division, and he strongly implied that those who did not adhere to the directive would be encouraged to resign.

Justice Gulotta's department, which takes in Brooklyn, Queens and Staten Island and Nassau, Suffolk, Westchester, Rockland, Putnam, Dutchess and Orange Counties, has been targeted in investigations by Mr. Nadjari's office as one of the worst areas of corruption and patronage involving law secretaries.

In addition, a survey by The New York Times conducted last week turned up several instances of political-patronage appointments of law secretaries and one instance of a law secretary who is a Democratic district leader in the Appellate Division, First Department, which takes in Manhattan and the Bronx.

The state's chief judge, Charles D. Breitel, said yesterday that in the upstate Appellate Division, Fourth Department, which

Continued on Page 11, Column 2

Connecticut School Taxing Is Ruled Unconstitutional

By LAWRENCE FELLOWS
Special to The New York Times

HARTFORD, Dec. 27—A Superior Court judge in Connecticut ruled today that the state's system of providing financial aid to public schools was unconstitutional.

Under the system, funds are distributed evenly to towns according to the number of pupils. In a decision that could add momentum to a developing national trend, the judge, Jay E. Rubinow, declared that this system did nothing to correct inequities arising from the disparate wealth of the towns.

Whether from rich communities or poor, schoolchildren are entitled to equal protection under the law, as guaranteed in Article I of Connecticut's Constitution, the judge ruled.

Article VIII provides that the General Assembly shall insure that there are laws to provide free public elementary and secondary schools.

"Hence, although the duty of educating children has been delegated by statute to municipalities, both the common law of this state and the Connecticut Constitution provide that the duty of educating Connecticut children is upon the state, as a whole, and not upon its municipalities," Judge Rubinow declared.

The Superior Court is the second highest in the state. Judge Rubinow's judgment was a declaratory one, made on the assumption that the state would appeal to the State Supreme Court.

Judge Rubinow gave no new plan for school financing and did not ask for one. Yet, he retained jurisdiction in the case until the state or the Supreme Court moves it a step farther.

"This is a landmark case," Attorney General Robert K. Killian said. "I think we will have to get a ruling from the highest authority. That's fairly obvious."

Judge Rubinow's decision falls closely in line with rulings

Continued on Page 29, Column 1

State Bars 197% Rate Rise For Malpractice Insurance

By DAVID A. ANDELMAN

The State Superintendent of Insurance yesterday suspended a 197 per cent rate increase sought by the Argonaut Insurance Company for malpractice insurance for physicians in the state, and ordered the company to continue covering the physicians until public hearings in January. The increase was to have taken effect on Jan. 10.

The actions were taken under the Unfair Insurance Practices Act, and the superintendent, Benjamin R. Schenck, said that "never before has any such order been issued."

The superintendent also ordered Argonaut to appear at two hearings, the first on Jan. 7, to show why it should not be forbidden to stop writing such insurance, and the second on Jan. 9, to justify its proposal to triple malpractice insurance rates.

In Washington today, Caspar W. Weinberger, the Secretary of Health, Education and Welfare, said that agency was working on emergency measures to make certain that the nation's physicians do not lose malpractice insurance. [Page 7.]

The orders by Mr. Schenck came within hours of the decision by the council of the Medical Society of the State of New York to refuse to agree to the rate increase. The council is the society's policy-making body. Without the increase, Argonaut said two weeks ago, it would refuse to continue to write insurance for the 27,000 of the state's 35,000 doctors who

Continued on Page 7, Column 1

House Unit Brands F.A.A. As Sluggish on Air Safety

By RICHARD WITKIN

A House committee that conducted a nine-month study of air hazards accused the Federal Aviation Administration yesterday of avoiding leadership and showing signs of "sluggishness which at times approaches an attitude of indifference to public safety."

The Special Subcommittee on Investigations said the agency had "needlessly and unjustifiably put at risk" thousands of lives by failing to deal properly with dangers of the DC-10 for almost two years.

The F.A.A. began adopting stronger measures only after a McDonnell Douglas DC-10 crashed near Paris last March following sudden loss of the rear cargo door. The death toll of 346 was the largest in aviation history. The committee called on the F.A.A. to reexamine the basic design of the door's much-modified locking system.

In a 245-page report, the House group also charged the Federal agency with "foot-dragging" in allowing a long delay before ordering airliners to be equipped with a cockpit warning device designed to prevent the most common type of accident—one in which the crew inadvertently flies a properly functioning plane into a hilltop or unpaved terrain short of the runway.

The most recent case was the crash Dec. 1 of a Boeing 727 into a hillside west of Washington. Ninety-two persons died in that crash. Four days later, the F.A.A. said that it would require installation of the warning device on all planes by next Dec. 1.

In a development yesterday, the head of the F.A.A., Alexander P. Butterfield, announced two actions, prompted primarily by the DC-10 and 727 tragedies.

The first action called for centralizing in Washington the jobs now done by field offices in certifying new planes as fit to fly and in overseeing design improvements later on.

The move was in line with a recommendation of an in-house F.A.A. inquiry board that

Continued on Page 44, Column 6

Jack Benny, 80, Dies of Cancer on Coast

By RICHARD F. SHEPARD

Jack Benny, whose brilliant gift for self-deprecating caricature brought laughter to the nation for 40 years, died late Thursday at his home in Beverly Hills, Calif. He was 80 years old.

Irving Fein, Mr. Benny's manager and associate for many years, said that the comedian died of cancer of the pancreas. The cancer was not discovered until it appeared on X-rays last Friday. Mr. Fein said that Mr. Benny's physician had said the case was inoperable.

After word Thursday that Mr. Benny had terminal cancer, Gov. Ronald Reagan, Frank Sinatra, Bob Hope, Danny Kaye and George Burns, who was Mr. Benny's friend for 50 years, visited the Benny home.

Funeral services have been scheduled for noon tomorrow at Hillside Memorial Cemetery in Culver City, Calif. Mr. Hope and Mr. Burns will deliver eulogies. A special tribute to Mr. Benny will be televised by CBS tomorrow from 7:30 to 8:30 P.M.

The pallbearers will be Mr. Fein; Mervyn Leroy; Hilliard Marks, his wife's brother; Gregory Peck; Mr. Sinatra; Mil-

Continued on Page 26, Column 1

1959

Jack Benny

Amy Vanderbilt, 66, Falls to Death Here

By JUDITH CUMMINGS

Amy Vanderbilt, the syndicated columnist on etiquette, fell or jumped to her death last night from a second-story window of her residence at 438 East 87th Street, the police said.

Miss Vanderbilt, who was 66 years old, was pronounced dead on arrival at Metropolitan Hospital shortly before 8 P.M., minutes after her body was found lying near the front steps of the four-story building by a passer-by.

Miss Vanderbilt sent her interpretation of proper manners and mores into millions of American homes through her column, called "Amy Vanderbilt's Etiquette" distributed beginning in 1954 by the United Features Syndicate and later by

Continued on Page 20, Column 7

Argentine Cattle Industry Is in Crisis

By JONATHAN KANDELL
Special to The New York Times

BUENOS AIRES, Dec. 27 — The sweet smell of roasting beef drifted through the muggy summer air in the downtown area. Parking-lot attendants, construction workers and street repairmen have once again taken to cooking slabs of prime sirloin on crude charcoal grills on top of empty paint cans.

When the Peronist Government came to power 18 months ago, it promised to put a price freeze on beef, the staple of the Argentine diet, and to raise yearly per-capita consumption to 165 pounds within a three-year period.

The Government has succeeded beyond its wildest dreams. Today, the average Argentine eats his way through 240 pounds of beef a year, about three times as much as Western European and twice as much as a citizen of the United States.

However, behind the prosperous veneer of crowded riverside beef restaurants and outdoor barbecues, the livestock industry has entered one of its most serious crises in recent years.

Agronomists and cattlemen agree that herds are being depleted at an alarming rate and that it is only a matter of time before there is another beef shortage — repeating the cycle that plagues the country's agriculture and explains the mysterious inability of Argentina to realize her vast agrarian potential.

"The cattle livestock industry is already in grave crisis and presents such a bleak panorama in the immediate future that urgent measures are necessary," says the Argentine Rural Society, the country's most prestigious agricultural association, in a year-end report.

The current livestock problems are partly the result of a decision earlier this year by the European Common Market countries to limit Argentine beef sharply in favor of European farmers. As a result, Argentina this year will export less than half the 556,000 tons she did in 1973.

Exports usually account for only about a third of beef production here, so it is little wonder that cattlemen have attacked the Government for the impact of its policies on the domestic market.

The freeze on meat prices was part of a general agreement negotiated by the Peronist Government between big business and labor to hold down prices and wages. But the farmers point out that the wage-

Continued on Page 2, Column 1

NEWS INDEX

Amy Vanderbilt Is Dead at 66 After a Plunge From Window

Continued From Page 1, Col. 1

The Los Angeles Times Syndicate.

She was a first cousin of Commodore Cornelius Vanderbilt, the railroad magnate, and claimed descent from America's first Vanderbilt, Jan Aoertsen van der Bilt.

The police said Miss Vanderbilt's husband, Curtis B. Kellar, and her son, who was identified by the police as Stephen Knopf, were in the residence when the fall occurred. Her body was taken to the Medical Examiner's office for an autopsy, the police said.

The police said Mr. Knopf, the youngest of Miss Vanderbilt's three sons, who was on a holiday from college, told them his mother had spent the evening working and occasionally lying down to rest in a second-floor study at the front of the town house. He said he had last talked with her within 20 minutes of her death.

Miss Vanderbilt's body was reported found near the front door of the town house close by three steps that lead to street level. She was dressed in a light-colored, flower-patterned dress, covered by a blue jacket-type housecoat. Police officer Alfred Swetokas, who responded to the call, said there had apparently been a heavy impact of the left side of the head against the pavement, causing what he thought was instantaneous death.

Detectives said a window was found open in the study. The metal frame of what had been an outer strom window, but which contained no glass, was in a bent state, but this appeared to have been a long-standing condition and was held unrelated to last night's incident, detectives added.

Associated Press

Amy Vanderbilt

Of Miss Vanderbilt's medical history, the police said it was immediately known only that she had been under treatment for diabetes. No drugs of any kind were found in the room where she was last seen alive, they said.

Etiquette's Arbiter

By ROBERT D. McFADDEN

To Amy Vanderbilt, etiquette was more than a set of social rules or a guide to gracious living. It was, rather, a panoramic view of the world that enabled her to see—and to comment extensively upon—the greatness and smallness of people.

For years, she was the nation's principal authority on the subject, the successor to Emily Post and the arbiter of manners in an increasingly classless society.

Miss Vanderbilt was a celebrity long before the 1952 publication of "Amy Vanderbilt's Complete Book of Etiquette," a 700-page source book of customs, mores and manners that reviewers of the day called a monumental tract for social historians of the future.

The book, revised a number of times in years since, sold millions of copies. Its advice ranged over the behavioral spectrum from the placement of a soup spoon to the running of a mansion full of servants.

She was a prolific writer. In addition to a half-dozen books, she wrote scores of articles for The New Yorker, McCall's, Collier's, This Week, Better Homes & Gardens, American Home and other magazines and wrote for newspapers for more than 30 years.

She was a columnist for the old International News Service in the nineteen-thirties, and from 1954 to 1968 her column for United Features Syndicate was published in more than 100 newspapers in the United States and abroad and had an audience of more than 40 million readers.

In more recent years, she wrote a column for The Los Angeles Times Syndicate, living, working and occasionally entertaining in her century-old brownstone in Manhattan.

Miss Vanderbilt was married four times and divorced three times and had three sons, Lincoln Gill Clark, Paul Vanderbilt Knopf and Stephen John Knopf.

Her marriages were to Robert S. Brinkerhoff in 1929, Morton G. Clark in 1935, Hans Knopf in 1945 and Curtis B. Kellar in 1968.

A strikingly cosmopolitan woman with gray eyes, Miss Vanderbilt enjoyed her craft and her celebrity. She drew up a code of courtesy for New York bus and subway riders about 10 years ago, and lectured a group of taxi drivers here a year ago.

Miss Vanderbilt was a direct descendant of Jan Aoertsen van der Bilt, who settled on Long Island in 1650, and of five generations of antecedents who lived on Staten Island starting in 1715. She was a cousin of Commodore Cornelius Vanderbilt, the shipping and railroad magnate; her great-great-grandfather was one of the founders of the Bank of Manhattan, and her grandfather, Joseph L. Vanderbilt, invented the figure-eight stitch on baseballs.

She was born on July 22, 1908, the daughter of Joseph Mortimer Vanderbilt, an insurance broker, and Mary Estelle Brooks Vanderbilt. While attending Curtis High School on Staten Island, she worked as a society and feature writer for The Staten Island Advance, beginning her journalism career at the age of 16.

Studied in Switzerland

After studies in Switzerland and at the Packer Collegiate Institute in Brooklyn, she entered New York University and studied journalism for two years. In the nineteen-thirties and forties, she worked in a variety of jobs, as an account executive in an advertising agency, the business manager of a literary magazine known as The American Spectator, and in public relations for several concerns.

It was in the late nineteen-forties that Doubleday, Inc., approached her to write a book about etiquette. She retired to "Daisyfields," her farm in Westport, Conn., and devoted about four years to the project that was to make her the national authority on the subject of etiquette.

At first, she told acquaintances that she thought it was "almost silly" to describe "such things as the traditional formal dinner for 34 with a butler and several footmen." But she warmed to the task and produced a massive volume that Leo Lerman, in a review for The New York Times, described as "monumental."

"In writing what is obviously the most comprehensive of current manners manuals," he said, "Amy Vanderbilt has, while codifying today's manners for those who wish information on usage, made a large contribution to the future social historian."

Miss Vanderbilt never talked of etiquette as mere rules, but rather as the basis of kindnesses among people. In recent years, she called traditional etiquette out of place in an era of social, philosophical and economic upheaval and war atrocities.

But she noted that formalized behavior had value in some situations, such as at funerals, where people need to mask their disquiet.

She eschewed the feminist "Ms." title, declaring: "Ms. is unbearable. Look it up in the dictionary. It means 'manuscript.'"

In addition to her literary efforts, Miss Vanderbilt also appeared often on Television and radio. From 1954 to 1960, she was the host of a television etiquette program called "It's in Good Taste," and from 1960 to 1962 she had a radio show called "The Right Thing to Do."

Miss Vanderbilt, an official etiquette consultant for a variety of organizations, including the World Book Encyclopedia and the State Department, traveled widely, lectured frequently and occasionally found time to tend a garden or fish in the Saugatuck River near her Connecticut farm.

She was often the hostess of parties at her town house here, but she once told an interviewer: "I hate big parties. I like simplicity in people and in entertaining. I have met all kinds of people; I like to talk to and hear them talk."

But, she added, "I have no use for people who exhibit manners."

Jack Benny, 80, Dies of Cancer in Beverly Hills

Continued From Page 1, Col. 2

ton Berle; Billy Wilder; Leonard Gershe; Fred Decordova and Armand Deutch.

Honorary pallbearers included Ray Stark, Jules Stein, Taft Schreiber, Lew Wasserman, Ned Miller, Robert Sarnoff, William S. Paley, Mayor Tom Bradley, Alfred Hart, George Murphy, Senator John Tunney, Irving Lazar, Dennis Day, Mel Blanc, Benny Rubin, Dr. Rex Kennamer, Mr. Reagan, Zubin Mehta, Isaac Stern, Mr. Kaye, Gregor Piatigorsky, Jack Lemmon, Walter Matthau, James Stewart, Johnny Carson, George Jessel, Phil Harris, Eddie Anderson and Don Wilson.

In a telegram to the comedian's widow, President Ford said, "If laughter is the music of the soul, Jack and his violin and his good humor have made life better for all men."

Jack Benny's very special talent for the comic was, according to his own analysis, an ability to mirror the failings people recognized in themselves or their acquaintances. Decades of insistence on the air that he was only 39 years old made the joke better rather than cornier; it was one of show business's most durable bits.

Other comedians told funnier jokes. Other comedians projected their own personalities into stage situations that made an audience laugh. Other comedians were much more effective in displaying their own ad lib wit. Where Mr. Benny told one joke, Bob Hope or Milton Berle could tell three in the same time.

Yet Mr. Benny was perhaps the most constantly funny of America's funny men. He was adored by the public and even the most sophisticated critics appreciated him as an outstanding comedian. The late President Kennedy once recalled that his father used to herd the family into their home's library every Sunday night to hear the Jack Benny show on radio. No one was ever excused from listening. So it was with much of America.

A Permanent Prop

A masterly sense of timing, worthy of the violin virtuoso he realized he would never be, made him the only performer who could evoke laughter from intervals of silence. He carefully developed a performing character as a tight-fisted, somewhat pompous fellow who walked with a mincing, almost effeminate gait, and often expressed exasperation merely by resting his chin in his hand and making his blue eyes stare, martyrlike, at his viewers. His violin became his most permanent prop, and he performed nicely for fund-raising with Isaac Stern, President Truman and the New York Philharmonic.

Just as Charlie Chaplin represented the "little fellow," Mr.

(continued)

The Jack Benny Show, November 30, 1948. From the left, Jack Benny, his wife Mary Livingstone, Don Wilson, Phil Harris and Dennis Day.

Jack Benny plays an impromptu duet with Vice President Harry S. Truman, 1945.

Jack Benny in the show *Broadway Melody of 1935.*

Benny also caught the frustrations of the average man, maybe a middle-class American, whose aspirations were always being leveled by family, friends and others.

One of his most famous bits had him being held up by a bandit who demanded "your money or your life." Silence. More silence. Silence punctuated with laughter from the audience. Then, desperately, "I'm thinking, I'm thinking."

Philosophy of Humor

It was not so much in his lines and in his delivery that he scored successes. His philosophy of humor shed little light on the art but it told something about the man.

It was not the words that brought the house down. It was the peerless execution of little things that became perpetually funny clichés, such as his piqued utterance of "hmmm," or his fussy, angered riposte to ribbing, "Now cut that out!"

"Never laugh at the other fellow; let him laugh at you," he said. "I try to make my character encompass about everything that is wrong with everybody. On the air, I have everybody's faults. All listeners know someone or have a relative who is a tightwad, show-off or something of that sort. Then in their minds I become a real character."

As a result, he was often the butt of his second bananas, who devastated him with their barbs. Eddie Anderson, as Rochester, his valet, lacked a shred of servility but always complained to the boss, man to man, about the Benny thrift. Mary Livingstone, his wife, Don Wilson, the announcer, and Phil Harris, the orchestra leader, also shared in the laugh lines. But Mr. Benny somehow came out ahead. Mel Blanc, the man of many voices, among them "Mr. Kitzel," and Sheldon Leonard had choice supporting parts.

Meticulous in Preparation

Mr. Benny was meticulous in preparation. Although it was widely known that he possessed a ready wit and a wonderful humor, which he often demonstrated in off-the-cuff observations on off-the-air occasions, he never—well, almost never—deviated from the script his highly paid writers had created for him.

"There is no tranquilizer like a prepared script," he once explained. For years he kept a good-humored "feud" running with Fred Allen, the humorist noted for his quick wit. Once when Mr. Allen had demolished him with a line, Mr. Benny blurted that if his scriptwriters had been there, Mr. Allen would never have gotten away with that.

He was absolutely serious about his work, in a way that many other comedians were not. At rehearsal, Mr. Benny would be sober-faced and worried about details. He was not a monster—it has always been impossible to find a colleague or even a former colleague to speak ill of him—but he was an

(continued)

A National Institution

To Millions in the 30's and 40's, Sunday Night at 7 Meant Jack Benny and Gang

By JOHN J. O'CONNOR

An Appraisal

Although he was successful on television, in nightclubs and even on the stage in "one-man" shows, Jack Benny was perhaps the most enduring and astonishingly shrewd creation of radio. For anyone growing up in the nineteen-thirties and forties, Sunday night at 7 o'clock meant Jack Benny and "the gang."

Week after week, the cast regulars went through a series of thoroughly predictable routines. Week after week, listeners at home laughed along with the studio audience. The brilliantly calculated Benny persona, offering magnanimous displays of the hilariously petty, was being fixed securely in the public's affection.

His radio years began in the Depression. Radio was concentrating on entertainment. There were very few regular news formats in those days. Not surprisingly, the center of the entertainment spotlight was held by veterans of vaudeville. In addition to Jack Benny, there were Eddie Cantor, George Burns and Gracie Allen, Al Jolson, Ed Wynn and Phil Baker.

A National Character

By 1937, Jack Benny had edged out Eddie Cantor for top position in the "Hooper-ratings." In 1950, a couple of years before the television explosion, he was still No. 1 in the ratings. Meantime, he had used radio to develop a national character of rare longevity.

The vehicle consisted of nothing but sound and, with the Benny sense of faultless timing, silence. The old Maxwell auto sputtered and coughed. The endless series of locks protecting the cellar bank vault squeaked and clanked. The pay telephone and cigarette machine in the living room noisily consumed coins. The immediately recognizable Benny family was created by a group of performers standing in front of microphones.

The effect was a combination of intimacy and elusiveness, a combination still unique to radio. The disembodied voices became personal friends, perhaps vaguely linked to faces in press photographs. The contexts and settings were constructed in the imaginations of the listener. The very lack of visual literalness expanded the possibilities for radio.

All of that changed, of course, with television. The new medium proved considerably more devouring than the old. Seeing the old Maxwell was not quite as funny as hearing it. Seeing it a second time was not nearly so funny as hearing it for the 100th time. The quality of elusiveness was lost.

'Blockbuster' Successes

The Benny program and other radio formats did have respectable runs on television, but the medium was bestowing its "blockbuster" successes on more "visual" material — Milton Berle's mugging, Sid Caesar's skits, the pandemonium of "Laugh-In." But the blockbusters, too, were eventually devoured. None were as long-lived as the old-time radio favorites.

The Benny persona, however, survived. It did not depend on one-line jokes or energetic physical routines. He could still show up on his own specials or as a guest star getting incredible mileage out of his penny-pinching routines or deadpan silences.

On one of his last television appearances, in an Anne Bancroft special called "Annie and the Hoods," he played a psychiatrist listening to the silly prattle of a patient. He didn't utter one word. He didn't have to. The radio character had become a national institution.

earnest, hard-working funny man.

This was an attitude born of experience.

'Timing Was The Key'

"I soon discovered that telling jokes was not a breeze, after all," he reminisced. "Sometimes you could throw a punch line away. Other times you had to ride it hard. A pause could set up a joke—or bury it. Timing was the key."

And there was, indeed, a sort of lucky timing that determined the course of the life of this comedian out of the Midwest, a timing that found him at the right age in the right age, an age of broadcasting that made reputations overnight, as against the age of vaudeville, when it took years.

Jack Benny was named Benjamin Kubelsky when he was born in Chicago on Valentine's Day, 1894. He grew up in Waukegan, Ill., where his father Meyer, had a store, and Mr. Benny often, for laughs, used to say that this was the town where he was born.

Meyer Kubelsky, a Jewish immigrant from Russia, loved music, and when his son was 8 the father gave him a $50 violin. The boy was soon giving concerts at the town's Barrison Theater.

Got Violin at 8

The young violinist quit school in the ninth grade and, at the age of 18, went into vaudeville. He worked with a woman pianist, Cora Salisbury, and soon teamed up with Lyman Woods, also a pianist. It was during an appearance with her that Mr. Benny, who then called himself Ben K. Benny, told a joke.

"The audience laughed," he later recalled. "The sound intoxicated me. That laughter ended my days as a musician, for I never again put the violin back where it belonged except as a gag."

Life became the customary round of one-night stands in the Midwest, and the young performer was not, at least not yet, the man to startle the vaudeville bookers. When World War I came along, he joined the Navy and was assigned to "The Great Lakes Review," a sailors' road show. Here his comic genius made an impression, and his decision to renounce music became irrevocable.

After the war, he embarked on the highly competitive career of the ad libber, where his greatest asset soon proved to be his instinct for proper timing. His silence was eloquent and his double-takes were the envy of his profession. By 1926, he had a part in a Broadway musical, "The Great Temptations."

Led Popularity Polls

This led to the most coveted assignment of all: master of ceremonies at the Palace Theater, citadel of the two-a-day. Soon he went on to Hollywood, and in 1932, he found his most durable niche: radio. It started with a guest shot on Ed Sullivan's radio show and before the year was out, he had his own program on the National Broadcasting Company network.

From 1934 through 1936 he was the champion of the radio popularity polls, and for many years he was always among the top 10 programs. His wife, Sadie Marks, whom he married in 1927, became Mary Livingstone, the wife of the radio Jack Benny, as he had been calling himself for a number of years.

'The Best Format'

He still sawed away at his violin, and his never-completed rendition of "Love in Bloom" became a hallmark of the show. His writers alone received a total of $250,000 a year. In 1948, Mr. Benny took his show from NBC to CBS. As part of the move, CBS paid $2,260,000 for Mr. Benny's Amusement Enterprises organization, as part of a capital gains deal. He got $1,356,000 of this but had to pay more than $1-million in income taxes when he was unable to sustain his argument that the money did, indeed, fall into the capital gains category.

Jack Benny with Phil Harris and Eddie "Rochester" Anderson.

Entertaining servicemen during World War II.

CBS kept the radio show until 1955, when, 23 years after Mr. Benny had done his first program, it went off the air. Even earlier, however, he had made the acquaintance of the new medium, television. He had been a bit wary of the tube, and his fears seemed to be substantiated by the critical reception of that first telecast, on Oct. 28, 1950.

The critics said the show had little visual attraction, that it relied too heavily on the radio tradition. But Mr. Benny made the grade with his third telecast the next April when he drastically altered his old routines and caused one critic to observe, "Mr. Benny has the best format, no format at all."

He stepped up his television schedule from irregularly scheduled shows, to semiweekly programs to weekly telecasts, which lasted from 1960 to 1965. When he "retired," he found himself almost as busy as ever, on television and in personal appearances. He appeared in many special telecasts. The last one, last Jan. 24, was billed as "Jack Benny's Second Farewell," because it came not many months after the first.

He began, more than ever, to play nightclubs, the Sahara in Las Vegas, the Waldorf-Astoria's Empire Room here. He worked the Palladium. He was tireless in performing at benefit concerts on behalf of musical causes, whether to save Carnegie Hall or to keep an orchestra afloat. In 1970, it was estimated that he had raised $5-million in 14 years.

Made Many Films

Viewers of late show or midday movies occasionally glimpse Mr. Benny in many of the films he made. Among them were "Hollywood Revue of 1929" (his first), "Chasing Rainbows," "The Medicine Man," "It's in the Air," "College Holiday," "Artists and Models," "Transatlantic Merry-Go-Round," "Buck Benny Rides Again," "Charley's Aunt," "To Be or Not to Be," "George Washington Slept Here," "The Meanest Man in the World" and "The Horn Blows at Midnight."

Several years ago, when an interviewer asked him why he was making television commercials, Mr. Benny replied: "Show business has changed. I'm changing with it. There's no more class in show business today. You do everything and anything."

But he had already done everything and done it well.

Mr. Benny, who died at 11:32 P.M. (2:32 A.M. Friday, New York time), is survived by his widow, an adopted daughter, Joan Blumoff, and several grandchildren.

"All the News That's Fit to Print"

The New York Times

LATE CITY EDITION

Weather: Fair, very cold today and tonight. Chance of snow tomorrow. Temp. range: today 24-14; Sunday 33-26. Full U.S. report on Page 30.

VOL. LXXII....No. 23,803. NEW YORK, TUESDAY, MARCH 27, 1923. TWO CENTS In Greater New York | THREE CENTS Within 200 Miles | FOUR CENTS Elsewhere

BERNHARDT DIES IN HER SON'S ARMS IN PARIS, AGED 78

Throng Sorrows at Her Door as She Succumbs After Comment on Long Agony.

LAST WORDS FOR AMERICA

"Greatest Actress" to Have a State Funeral — Flowers Cover Her Deathbed.

MOURNED IN MANY LANDS

The Theatre Here Pays Tribute—Career Began Sixty Years Ago—Triumphs in Many Roles.

PARIS, March 26 (Associated Press).—Sarah Bernhardt is dead. The "greatest actress" passed away at 7:50 P. M. in the arms of her son, Maurice, who had just entered the room at that moment. Death came in a large room on the second floor of her home with windows wide open on the Boulevard Pereire, the noise of trucks and the railroad keeping up a low roar to which she was long accustomed. It was the sudden closing of these windows, opened on the finest day of Spring, that gave the signal to those waiting and watching without that Bernhardt was dead.

Bernhardt's grandson, M. Grosse, brought the first flowers into the death chamber—mauve and white lilacs. Flowers came from many friends quickly, and soon the room was heaped with them, those from the family and dearest friends being placed on the bed. Then words and tokens of mourning came flowing in from many lands.

The whole world had seemed to be watching with the group of six doctors, hoping for recovery, but regretfully realizing that a great career was ending. Arthur Mayer, editor of La Gaulois, who had known Mme. Bernhardt for many years, was the last caller; he arrived five minutes before her death, but realizing what was happening, left without seeing her. Just as he departed, the windows of the bedchamber closed and a moment later Dr. Marot appeared and informed the newspapermen, who had been keeping watch day and night:

"Mme. Sarah Bernhardt has just expired in the arms of her son."

Knew End Was Near.

The actress's son, Maurice; her granddaughter, Lysiane (Mme. Collin du Bocage), and Mlle. Louise Abbema, sculptress and painter, who was known as Bernhardt's best friend, had remained close to the chamber in which the patient lay, for death had been momentarily expected for many hours.

Just one hour and fourteen minutes before her death the actress sent this last message to America, where she had so often triumphed and been feted:

"I am deeply touched with the sympathetic interest of my beloved American friends."

The message was given to the Associated Press at 6:45 o'clock by her secretary, Mme. Normand.

It is understood that Bernhardt will have a state funeral. The date has not yet been fixed, but it is thought that Thursday or Friday will be selected. In accordance with French custom, watch was kept throughout the night beside the body by members of the family, and tomorrow all who wish will be admitted for a last view of the artiste, who lies surrounded by flowers, with candles burning.

Bernhardt suffered greatly in her last illness, except perhaps in the closing hours, but, ever thoughtful of others, she concealed her pain from all but Dr. Marot. From time to time she became delirious and declaimed passages from the tragedy "Phedre" and "L'Aiglon," her two greatest triumphs.

Word of Bernhardt's death spread through Paris rapidly and caused universal sorrow. At the Théâtre Sarah Bernhardt, where "L'Aiglon" was playing, the announcement was made about the middle of the first act. The play was stopped and the audience filed out sorrowfully.

Announcement was made at the other theatres after the conclusion of the first act. In the meantime great crowds collected outside the residence on the Boulevard Pereire, gazing at the shuttered windows and watching the carriages and automobiles bringing celebrities of the literary and dramatic world.

Mme. Bernhardt was 78 years old. An acute uremic condition was the cause of death. The last lingering hope was abandoned shortly after noon when the patient lapsed into unconsciousness.

She Gets Last Rites.

In the afternoon she was kept constantly under the influence of hypodermic injections. At 3:10 in the afternoon, when she struggled into semi-consciousness for the last time, a priest, Father Riesler, came from the near by Church of St. Francis de Sales to administer Extreme Unction. His entrance into the Bernhardt home was taken by the watchers outside as visible evidence of the abandonment of hope. When Father Riesler emerged he said that she was sufficiently conscious to show, by movements of her hands and otherwise, that she understood the ceremony.

Throughout the day hundreds of the actress's friends were calling at the house in a steady stream, and the street was somtimes crowded with carriages and automobiles of those coming to pay their respects.

Early in the morning Bernhardt herself for the first time admitted that she was fighting a losing fight, and that the end was coming. Before she

Continued on Page Eight.

FROM © PHOTO BY UNDERWOOD & UNDERWOOD

SARAH BERNHARDT

The Great French Tragedienne Who Died Yesterday, As She Looked in Her Later Years.

SOVIET COURT DOOMS ARCHBISHOP TO DIE

But Clemency Is Expected for Roman Catholics Accused of Opposing the Government.

PRISON FOR 13 PRIESTS

Death for Vicar General—Women Scream as the Verdicts Are Announced.

Special Cable to THE NEW YORK TIMES.

MOSCOW, March 26.—In profound silence early this morning, Galkin, the Presiding Judge of the Soviet Supreme Court, read a verdict imposing the death sentence on Archbishop Zepliak, head of the Roman Catholic Church in Russia, and his Vicar General, Father Butchkavitsch, who have been on trial on the charge of opposing the Soviet Government.

A woman's scream rang out from the crowd. For the moment an icy cold of horror came over the scene, which previously had conveyed no deep impression of tragedy. The woman's emotion was contagious, and other screams burst forth, to which the silence and unmoved faces of the accused clerics showed a striking contrast.

The Archbishop made the sign of the cross as he heard the grim words, but his strong countenance betrayed neither excitement nor distress. As he stated in his final speech on the preceding day, his conscience was clear; he felt guiltless of any crime "against God or Caesar" and was ready to face with tranquillity "this court or the higher tribunal before which I may soon be called to appear."

Five accused priests were sentenced to ten years' imprisonment, eight to three years, and one prisoner, a choirboy, was acquitted.

After nearly eight hours of deliberation the Judges re-entered the long room packed with 500 or 600 people for the last act in the drama to which the attention of the Christian world has been attracted. Evidence had shown that the Pope had recently authorized Archbishop Zepliak to make an agreement with the Soviet Government, a factor which doubtless led strength to the appeal against the sentence which the attorney for the defense announced would be made to the Central Executive Committee, but which Prosecutor Krylenko said did not affect the actual decision of the case involving definite charges relating to the past conduct of the accused.

Following the reading of the sentence, Krylenko ordered that the room be cleared by soldiers, which was done rapidly and without difficulty.

The Central Executive Committee is expected to give its decision on the ap-

Continued on Page Six.

STINNES CONFERS WITH GARY IN ROME

Also Talks With Fred I. Kent and Other American Delegates to Commerce Congress.

FAVORS ECONOMIC PARLEY

Would Have It Held in United States, With Delegates Fully Empowered to Act.

ROME, March 26 (Associated Press)—Hugo Stinnes, Germany's great industrial figure, who, upon his arrival here yesterday, went to the hotel occupied by the American delegates to the Commerce Congress, interviewed today Elbert H. Gary, Chairman of the United States Steel Corporation, and Fred I. Kent, Vice President of the Bankers Trust Company of New York among others.

From these conversations it appears that he came to Rome when he heard of American proposals that a portion or all of the war debts owing to the United States would be remitted after the European States had given assurances they would put their finances in order.

He gave no notice of his coming. Even the German Ambassador knew nothing about it until he learned of the magnate's presence through the newspapers.

While Herr Stinnes refused to grant an interview today, saying he had no statement to make, it is learned that he is in favor of the American suggestion to call an international economic conference at which all the countries interested would be represented by delegates having full powers in order to be able definitely to solve the reparations, inter-allied debt and exchange stabilization questions.

He is represented as believing that the United States is the country best adapted for the conference, being outside Europe and unaffected by the influences of the contending parties.

Herr Stinnes was desirous of meeting Premier Mussolini, his purpose being, it was understood, to enlist Signor Mussolini's support in the hope that his influence might have a decisive effect on the attitude of most of the other countries.

The Giornale d'Italia says that Stinnes while in Rome had a conversation with Pope Pius and also saw Cardinal Gasparri, the Papal Secretary of State.

BERLIN, March 26 (Associated Press).—Industrial and financial circles in Berlin declared today they had no information regarding the nature of the visit of Hugo Stinnes is paying to Rome, although it is taken for granted that the meeting which dispatches say he is to have with Elbert H. Gary was prearranged.

At Herr Stinnes's private office it was said he had gone to Rome on purely private business.

George Gould Is Reported Sinking Rapidly; Pneumonia, Aggravated by Blood Pressure

Special to The New York Times.

LAKEWOOD, N. J., March 26.—Practically all hope for the recovery of George J. Gould, ill with pneumonia at Mentone, France, has been abandoned, according to a cable message received at Georgian Court by Mr. and Mrs. Carroll Wainwright today. Mr. Gould's condition, it was said, has been aggravated by high blood pressure.

Late tonight another cable message was received which said there had been no change for the better. Mrs. Wainwright, Mr. Gould's daughter, is looking forward to other messages early tomorrow, as so far but few details of her father's illness had been received. It is known that he is suffering from pleuro-pneumonia and has been ill about two weeks.

Mrs. Wainwright, it was said, left for New York City tonight. Her husband, however, remained here. The Wainwrights had been entertaining friends when word of the seriousness of Mr. Gould's illness was received. They have been occupying Georgian Court, for years the Gould residence here, since Mr. Gould sailed for Europe, where he was married to Mrs. Sinclair last Fall.

NICE, France, March 26.—According to the latest reports from Cap Martin, there is no change in the condition of George J. Gould.

Mr. Gould has been abroad since his marriage to Mrs. Guinevere Jeanne Sinclair on May 1, last year, a few months after the death of his former wife, Mrs. Edith Kingdon Gould. It had been rumored that Mr. and Mrs. Gould would not return to this country except for visits and that Georgian Court, long the home of the Goulds, would be sold.

When Mr. Gould and his bride first went abroad they leased Castle Grant, Grantown-on-Spey, the ancestral home of the Earls of Seafield. They had house parties there during the grouse and deer shooting seasons, and then traveled on the Continent.

SMITH ASKS POWER OVER FARM COUNCIL; HITS AT ASSEMBLY

Tells Legislature He Cannot Accept Responsibility for Department as Now Organized.

WANTS CONSUMERS GUARDED

Likens the Present System to the Establishment of an "Agricultural Soviet."

MACHOLD QUICK TO RETORT

Speaker Declares No Measure to Carry Out the Governor's Wish Will Pass Lower House.

Special to The New York Times.

ALBANY, March 26.—With the Republican Assembly engaged in slaughtering legislation advocated by him, Governor Smith sent a special message to the Legislature tonight in which he urged drastic reorganization of the Department of Farms and Markets, with a view of making it responsible to the Governor and not, as at present, to the Legislature.

Tonight's message was sent for the particular benefit of the hostile Assembly. The Democratic Senate already has passed and sent to the lower house a bill introduced by Senator Straus, which carries out the Governor's recommendations.

Speaker Machold of the Assembly was not slow in joining issue with the Chief Executive. When asked to comment on the message, he declared without any attempt at equivocation that any legislation along the lines of the Governor's message would be beaten in the Assembly.

Under the present law the Governor has practically no control over this important administrative department, except such as he can exercise indirectly through his veto power over bills and other measures affecting agriculture and distribution of agriculture products. During the Whitman régime the organization now in force was set up, with the department controlled by a farms and markets council composed of ten members elected by the Legislature on joint ballot, one from each Judicial District and one at large, and an additional member, the Commissioner of Markets of New York City. The council, not the Governor, names the executive head of the department, the Commissioner of Farms and Markets.

Governor Smith points out in his message that under the present system the machinery of the Farms and Markets Department virtually is dominated by the agricultural interests and its activities for that reason are one-sided. Little heed, the Governor says, is given to the just claims of the consumer in the management of the department. He adds that unless a change is made along lines recommended by him he must disclaim all responsibility for the manner in which the Farms and Markets Department is being conducted.

Text of the Governor's Message.

Governor Smith's message to the Legislature follows:

"To the Legislature:

"In accordance with the promise made in my annual message to communicate with you again in relation to the agricultural policy of the State, I have carefully considered the subject and sought to confer with the many interests involved. Thoroughly mindful of the important part our agricultural industries play in the prosperity of the State, I am at all times eager to serve them and also to promote the interests of the consumers.

"Everything connected with the subject in this State has had to undergo a slow process of eliminating confusion and gradually bringing many scattered powers into a unified department. It is significant that the whole history of the department points to a series of well-intentioned attempts to unify the activities comprehended in the production and distribution of food.

"After legislative investigation, the Department of Farms and Markets was set up in 1917 to deal with the production of food and its marketing. No attempt to discuss the subject of agriculture which confines itself to production exclusive of marketing could be adequate. In fact, the early organization of the department recognized this when it was divided into two parts, a Division of Agriculture and a Division of Foods and Markets.

"Somehow or other, the agricultural interests of the State have always seemed to believe that the functioning of this department belongs peculiarly and particularly to them, and persuaded the Legislature that there should be established over the department a regency similar to that which exists in the Department of Education. As a result, a Council of Farms and Markets was created, composed of eleven members elected by the Legislature and representing the nine judicial districts of the State. This council had administrative and executive functions. The attempt to keep all agricultural interests strictly under the control of their own representatives is almost like the establishment of an agricultural Soviet.

"An analogy to this condition might be found if the labor interests of the State were to assert that the Labor Department belonged exclusively to them and was established solely to protect their interests and was administered by a regency composed of representatives of the labor organizations and a Labor Commissioner chosen by and representing their organizations exclusively, or that we might erect a regency over the Banking and Insurance Departments of the State that would permit them to control the departments that regulate them.

"In the same degree as this would be resented by all of the other industrial interests of the State, it is my feeling that the Department of Farms and Mar-

Continued on Page Two.

13,000,000 Tons at Hamburg Leads All Ports on Continent

BERLIN, March 26.—Hamburg has regained her prewar position as the greatest shipping centre on the European Continent, according to the tonnage statistics for last year just published. These show that the Port of Hamburg handled more than 13,000,000 net tons, as compared with 12,750,000 for Antwerp and 12,250,000 for Rotterdam.

The German lines, whose operations before the war accounted for 67 per cent. of Hamburg's traffic, now handle only 29 per cent., being second to the British, whose percentage is 34. The Dutch are third and the Americans fourth.

The Hamburg-America Line, the figures show, now has 30 per cent. of its prewar tonnage, having reached this figure through new construction and repurchases of vessels from the Allies.

WILSON BRINGS OUT A SENATE CANDIDATE

Former President Asks Colorado Governor to Name Huston Thompson, an Old Friend.

CAUSES WASHINGTON STIR

Many Party Leaders in State Resent His Appeal as Being "Presumptuous."

Special to The New York Times.

WASHINGTON, March 26.—Woodrow Wilson, former President of the United States, has caused a political sensation in Washington by sending a telegram to Governor Sweet of Colorado asking him to appoint Huston Thompson to the Senate in place of Senator Samuel D. Nicholson, who died on Saturday. The receipt of the telegram was announced in Denver today.

Mr. Thompson is a member of the Federal Trade Commission, to which he was appointed by President Wilson. He said, when the former President's telegram to Governor Sweet was called to his attention, that it was news to him, as he had no personal knowledge of Mr. Wilson's action.

Mr. Thompson has been mentioned before as a possible Democratic candidate for Senator from Colorado. He has been a citizen of that State for twenty-four years. Born at Lewisburg, Pa., in 1875, he was graduated from Princeton studied law in the New York Law School and went to Denver in 1899 to practice law.

He was Assistant Attorney General of Colorado from 1907 to 1909. In April, 1913, President Wilson appointed him Assistant Attorney General of the United States while James C. McReynolds was Attorney General. He served in that capacity until December, 1918, when he became a Federal Trade Commissioner.

Mr. Thompson classifies himself as a Progressive Democrat, the designation used by Governor Sweet in stating his political affiliation. He is President of the Boy Scout Council of the District of Columbia and Chairman of the Ways and Means Committee of the National Parks Association. Mr. Thompson is highly regarded in Washington.

His First Request of the Kind.

No explanation of his action in asking Governor Sweet to appoint Mr. Thompson has come from Mr. Wilson. Since his term as President expired he has taken occasional public means of showing his interest in politics, but this is the first time, as far as is known, that he has asked any Governor to appoint a Senator.

There have been several instances in which Mr. Wilson has sought to defeat Democratic candidates for nomination in party primaries. His most recent effort of that character was directed against Senator James A. Reed of Missouri, when Mr. Reed was a candidate for renomination last year. Mr. Reed had voted against the Treaty of Versailles and the League of Nations Covenant and had opposed other measures of the Wilson Administration.

In publicly expressing the hope that Mr. Reed would not be renominated, Mr. Wilson advocated the selection of Breckinridge Long, who had been Third Assistant Secretary of State in the Wilson Administration. Mr. Reed was renominated and re-elected.

During his term as President and subsequently, Mr. Wilson openly opposed the nomination of Democrats who had declined to support policies of his Administration. One of those whom he singled out in this connection was former Senator James K. Vardaman, who was a candidate for nomination in the Mississippi Democratic Senatorial primaries. Vardaman was defeated.

James L. Sladen, who had served in Congress as a Democrat for many years from the San Antonio District of Texas, was also opposed for renomination by Mr. Wilson, and was defeated by Carlos A. Bee, brother-in-law of Albert S. Burleson, then Postmaster General in President Wilson's Cabinet.

Expected to Advise on Campaign.

In political circles the expectation exists that Mr. Wilson will take an active part in an advisory capacity in the Presidential campaign of next year, but nobody cares to predict whether he will have any participation in the pre-convention campaign for the selection of candidate for President. In 1920, when he was President, Mr. Wilson declined to show preference for any aspirant for the Democratic nomination, even for his son-in-law, William G. McAdoo, who was one of the leading contenders. His interest then was manifested in the platform declarations.

The action of Mr. Wilson in the Colorado Senatorship is taken to mean that he intends to continue to use his influence in political matters whenever he believes the occasion demands. His health is now better than it has been at

Continued on Page Two.

RED MEETING HERE MARCH 18 REVEALED AT TRIAL OF FOSTER

Prosecutor's Questions Suggest That Even Then Illegal Action Was Contemplated.

FEDERAL AGENT ATTENDED

Ruthenberg Admits That He Was Present and Translated Speech of the Soviet Envoy.

HE IS STILL ON THE STAND

State in Cross-Examination Fails to Make Him Commit Himself to Use of Violence.

Special to The New York Times.

ST. JOSEPH, Mich., March 26.—Testimony introduced at the Foster syndicalism trial today disclosed that the Government is still keeping an eye on every movement of the Communist leaders in the United States. "Under cover" agents are still in the radical ranks in the same capacity as Francis Morrow, the "K-97" of the Department of Justice, who attended the Red convention at Bridgman last August as a delegate. The new evidence showed that another Department of Justice agent within the Communist fold had furnished the Government with a complete report of a meeting of fifty leading Communists in New York City on March 18, after the Foster trial had started.

Charles W. Gore, who this afternoon cross-examined Charles E. Ruthenberg, the first witness for the defense, used a copy of the report in questioning Ruthenberg. A summary of the report, obtained after court had adjourned for the day, showed that the meeting had been held at 162 Madison Avenue, New York, and had lasted from 9 o'clock to 11:30 A. M. on March 18. The report referred to the meeting as the New York City convention of the Communist Party of America and named John Balan as Chairman and Sonya Diamond as Secretary, [illegible] of the thirty-two defendants in the Bridgman case.

Ruthenberg admitted he attended the New York meeting. He contended it was a private but not a secret meeting, and was held in a public hall, but admitted it was for members of the Workers' Party of America only. He denied that it was a convention of the Communist Party, saying that the Communist Party as such had gone out of existence after the Bridgeman raid. Ruthenberg was formerly Executive Secretary and member of the Central Executive Committee of the Communist Party, and now holds the same offices in the Workers' Party. He admitted today that the Workers Party is advocating the doctrines of communism, and that it hoped to resume the name of the Communist Party of America some time. The State contends that the Workers' Party is only a smoke screen to hide the further advocacy of a revolution by violence in this country.

Admits Connection With International.

Ruthenberg admitted that the Workers' Party still had a direct connection with the Communist International and that he himself had communicated several times recently with one Polacco, in Moscow, Secretary of the Executive Committee of the Communist International. He also admitted that the New York City meeting had taken up the question of whether Communist work here was to be carried on in the open hereafter, and that he had translated a lengthy speech delivered by a man named Pepper.

According to Ruthenberg, Pepper told the New York Communists that the leaders of the International in Moscow favored an open Communist movement in America because they believed the political situation here had changed enough to make it possible to advocate publicly a revolution and dictatorship by the proletariat. This change, the Russians said, had been brought about by the election of liberals to the Senate, the House of Representatives and other political bodies in the various States.

Reading from the Government report of the New York meeting, the Prosecutor asked the following question:

"Is it not a fact that you told the meeting that the apparatus of the Communist Party of America would consist of a very confidential committee, which would direct illegal work, such as sending men into the American Legion, the Ku Klux Klan, the army and the navy; and in the case of an uprising, this committee will take care of getting arms and distributing them, also to get the people to distribute illegal literature and do the general work of the party?"

"That is not true," Ruthenberg replied.

Ruthenberg said that the New York meeting adopted the "open" program

Continued on Page Three.

Two Roads Pay $25,000 Fines For Violations of Fuel Rules

CLEVELAND, Ohio, March 26.—Fines of $25,000 each, plus costs, were paid today in Federal court by the Newburg & South Shore Railroad and the Lake Terminal Company after both had confessed to fifty violations of the 1922 fuel priority rulings of the Interstate Commerce Commission. They paid $500 fines for each violation.

Both companies are alleged to have received fifty carloads of coal during the coal strike in the Summer of 1922 after claiming priorities as common carriers. Instead of converting this to its own use, the Terminal Company is said to have turned its consignment over to the National Tube Company in Lorain and the Newburg & South Shore its consignment to the Newburg plant of the American Steel and Wire Company.

All four concerns involved are said to be subsidiaries of the United States Steel Corporation.

PIGGLY RECORD TOLD BY STOCK EXCHANGE

All Stock Due From "Shorts" Delivered by 2:15 Yesterday, Statement Says.

SAUNDERS IS ASSAILED

He Says He Will Sue Brokers Who Failed to Deliver Within 24 Hours.

The New York Stock Exchange yesterday issued a statement reviewing the entire controversy over the alleged corner in shares of Piggly Wiggly Stores, Inc., in which it asserted that every move made by the Exchange was in accordance with its constitution and rules. It stated that all Piggly Wiggly stock deliverable to the Stock Clearing Corporation on security balance orders was delivered prior to 2:15 yesterday afternoon; that the total amount of shares short was only 11,200 instead of 25,000 as stated by Clarence Saunders, President of Piggly Wiggly, that Mr. Saunders failed to keep promises he had made to the Stock Exchange, and that trading in Piggly Wiggly stock was suspended on March 21 with the consent of Mr. Saunders's legal representative.

About the same time, in Memphis, Tenn., Mr. Saunders gave out a statement in which he said that he would enter suit against every broker who was in default in the delivery to him of Piggly Wiggly stock within 24 hours after the trade had been made. He also repeated his threat to sue the New York Stock Exchange for conspiracy.

The Stock Exchange, in its statement, said that one of the reasons for the suspension of trading in Piggly Wiggly stock was that Mr. Saunders was maintaining two markets at various prices, and thereby using the high prices that prevailed on the New York Stock Exchange to sell stock through advertisement on a time-payment plan throughout the United States.

The statement goes thoroughly into the history of the Piggly Wiggly stock since March 12, when a protest was made to Saunders against selling the stock through an advertising campaign at prices differing from those quoted on the New York Stock Exchange. On March 19 the Exchange was notified that the advertising campaign would be discontinued on March 21. Next on March 20 Mr. Saunders called for delivery to him of all stock held long for his account.

The Stock Exchange statement then continues:

"The observance of his instructions led to the calling of all loans of stock carried for accounts of Mr. Saunders and representatives of Mr. Saunders. The amount of stock involved far exceeded all the stock in the market other than that held for account of Mr. Saunders and other Directors of Piggly-Wiggly stores.

"The enforcement simultaneously of all contracts for the return of the stock would have forced the stock to any price that might be fixed by Mr. Saunders, and competitive bidding for the insufficient supply might have brought about conditions illustrated by other corners, notably the Northern Pacific corner in 1901. The demoralizing effects of such a situation are not limited to those directly affected by the contracts, but extends to the market involving widespread loss and injury."

The suspension of trading in the stock on March 20 by the Governing Committee after consultation with Saunders's attorney is cited. "The suspension of the rule requiring the delivery by 2:15 o'clock P. M. on March 21 of the Piggly Wiggly stock, deliverable through the Stock Clearing Corporation came next.

Continued on Page Nine.

New Police Whistle to Reduce Accidents; McAdoo Announces New Traffic Signals

Traffic policemen on duty at street crossings yesterday were equipped with a new model whistle provided by the Police Department Bureau of Public Safety at the suggestion of Chief City Magistrate William McAdoo, Chairman of the Mayor's Committee on Traffic, with a view to reducing accidents.

Chief Magistrate McAdoo issued a statement in regard to the use of the new whistles, in which he said:

"My attention has been called to the new whistle signals that were put in operation this morning by officers at crossings. Briefly, this is the basis of the new system: One blast on the whistle stops all the traffic. The vehicular traffic at right angles to the traffic just stopped shall not move until two short blasts followed by a long blast are given on the whistle by the policeman. Before giving the long blast, the police officer will blow two short blasts as a warning to pedestrians and drivers that he is about to allow traffic to start.

"In other words, the crossing man with the use of the whistle is to carry out the principle of the system now in operation with both lights and whistles on Fifth Avenue. As the two warning blasts on the whistle are equivalent to the red lights on the towers on that avenue, it is a warning that after an interval of six seconds, traffic will start.

"The success of this system of signals depends largely upon the pedestrians themselves, and therefore the pedestrian shall not cross until the whistle signal shows that vehicular traffic is open in the direction he wants to go. He should travel with the vehicles.

"Don't undertake to make a crossing until you know whether the warning signal of two blasts of the whistle, as stated above, has been given as a notice that the long blast is impending. There will be a pause of about six seconds between the two short blasts and the long blast."

$1,000 BOND, LAST GIFT BY MITCHELL TO GIRL, MISSING

Also Gave Dorothy Keenan Hundreds in Cash on Day Before She Was Killed.

WILL JOIN WIFE ON TRAIN

Starts South to Meet Private Car Bringing Mrs. Mitchell and Her Father, E. T. Stotesbury.

GUIMARES DEFIES POLICE

Demands They Arrest, Not Threaten Him—Says He Has Nothing Left but Fur Coat.

Frederick E. Goldsmith, attorney for Albert E. Guimares, a figure in the investigation of the murder of Dorothy Keenan, issued a statement last night challenging the District Attorney or the police to proceed against Guimares for either blackmail or murder. The statement was made on what appeared to be the lawyer's conviction that Guimares was the target of the officials.

"I don't like the idea of a smoke screen being thrown up to protect Mr. Mitchell," he said at one point, and at another he spoke of "star chamber proceedings" and pink teas between Mr. Pecora and Neilson Olcott, counsel to John H. Jackson, New York lawyer, and John Kearsley Mitchell, son-in-law of Edward T. Stotesbury, Philadelphia banker.

Prior to Goldsmith's statement the authorities had announced that some of the clothing missing from the West Fifty-seventh Street studio of Miss Keenan had been found in her mother's possession. Mrs. Keenan's explanation was that grief made her forget to tell the police. It also was disclosed that on Wednesday, March 14, the day before the girl was slain, Mitchell had presented her with a $1,000 Liberty bond, several hundred dollars in cash and a jade bracelet.

Mitchell Gift Bond Missing.

The $1,000 bond was among the things stolen from the room and Chief Assistant District Attorney Ferdinand Pecora, who made the fact known, admitted that it might prove to be one of the strongest clues in the solution of the murder. Another item expected to prove valuable is the chloroform bottle which detectives expect to trace.

No statement came during the day from Mitchell, Jackson or their counsel. Mr. Mitchell was reported on his way South to board the Florida Special of the Atlantic Coast Line. Mrs. Mitchell and her father are in a private car attached to this train. Mr. Pecora said he understands Mr. Mitchell wished to be the first to tell his wife of "the unfortunate affair."

"Guimares," said Goldsmith in his office at 1,540 Broadway, "is innocent and has nothing to fear. He has lavished as much money upon Dorothy Keenan as Mr. Mitchell. Mr. Guimares liked good times just as much as Mr. Mitchell and he paid just as much as Mr. Mitchell.

Says Guimares Is Available.

"Mr. Guimares doesn't like those insinuations made against him by Mr. Pecora, those veiled threats and silent thrusts. As far as Mr. Coughlin is concerned he doesn't need to send out fifteen detectives to find Guimares. He was in my office here for five hours today and no policeman was in sight. I'll produce Guimares any time they want him on a telephone call. Pecora and Coughlin are barking up the wrong tree. I don't like the idea of a smoke screen being thrown up to protect Mr. Mitchell.

"I reiterate what I have said before to the press and that is that inasmuch as Mr. Mitchell is a non-resident of this State, Section 618B of the Code of Criminal Procedure should apply, and that Mr. Mitchell should be placed under a bond to appear for any criminal proceeding, especially in view of the fact that he is a non-resident. The District Attorney of the County of New York, upon a short affidavit presented before a court of proper record, would have no difficulty in compelling Mr. Mitchell to enter into an undertaking to appear whenever wanted. The District Attorney of the County of New York has no right to take the word of a material witness or his attorney that he will appear, and once a material witness is without the State of New York he cannot be subpoenaed.

Fur Coat His Chief Asset.

"I do not think that in the furtherance of justice one law should apply to the rich and one to those who are less fortunate. My client today is practically destitute, outside of the fur coat which they made so much fuss about, and you couldn't 'hock' that fur coat for $30 in Simpson's.

"Mr. Pecora and Inspector Coughlin, if they feel that my client has been guilty of blackmail or murder, should not allow him to roam the streets of New York without being arrested on some more serious charge than a misdemeanor. I don't like these star chamber proceedings between Mr. Neilson Olcott and Mr. Pecora. I don't understand why I am not a guest at one of these functions.

"I am just as good an adviser and a friend of the public prosecutor as Mr. Olcott, and nothing would give me better enjoyment than to be at one of these pink tea parties. Mr. Guimares will make no further statements in this case, but he will do so at the proper time and the press will be present. We have nothing to hide or conceal or to be afraid of. The only trouble is that Mitchell was a hit-and-run man, while my client lingered and has to pay."

Goldsmith said that Inspector Coughlin had told him that the detectives had checked up Guimares's alibi on the

BERNHARDT DIES IN HER SON'S ARMS

Continued from Page 1, Column 1.

went to sleep under an opiate she exclaimed to the friends and members of the family gathered at the bedside:

"How very slow my death agony is!"

At times during the morning Bernhardt insisted on talking of her own funeral. She was anxious to know yesterday whether the rosewood coffin she bought thirty years ago was still preserved, saying that she wished to be buried in it.

Jests With Maurice.

As her son, deeply moved, mechanically crumpled up a scrap of paper and nervously threw it out of the window, the patient found strength to tell him jokingly to be careful or he would be called to account "for throwing things on the street," which is contrary to a city ordinance.

Shortly after 4 o'clock this morning Mme. Edmond Rostand, widow of the poet and playwright, whose "Chanticleer" was one of the famous pieces of Bernhardt's repertoire, arrived at the home of the dying woman. She entered the house weeping, supportd by her son, Maurice.

While this scene was going on, workmen were carrying from the house and loading into a van the equipment and setting for the last motion picture film made by Mme. Bernhardt, in which she played the part of a paralytic, until the onset of her last illness a few days ago. Bernhardt's last stage rôle, in Sacha Guitry's play "Un Sujet de Roman," was never filled. She insisted she would appear, but the doctors and her family interfered and prevented her. Her last appearance was in the motion picture made in her home, which remains unfinished.

BERNHARDT LIVED FOR WORK.

Began Her Career in 1862 and Held World Fame for Two Generations.

"I dream of dying, like the great Irving, in the harness," said Mme. Bernhardt in September, 1910. That one sentence sums up her whole life. Action was the one big essential of her existence; work was her fountain of youth. She was never idle; she never rested.

Sarah Bernhardt was the natural child of Julie Bernhardt and a merchant of Amsterdam, who died shortly after her birth, on Oct. 22, 1844. Little is known of her babyhood except that she was an unusually brilliant and willful child. At the age of 8 she was placed in Mme. Fressard's school at Auteuil, and two years later, in 1855, was a scholar at the Grandchamps Convent at Versailles. The religious atmosphere of the convent made a strong appeal to her emotional nature, and after being converted to the Catholic faith she decided to become a nun. Here also she appeared in her first play, one written by Mother Ste. Thérèse and called "Toby Recovering His Eyesight." This was a simple miracle play, and Mme. Bernhardt appeared, as she wrote in her "Memoirs," in "heavenly blue tarletan, with a blue sash around my waist to help confine the filmy drapery, and two paper wings fastened upon each shoulder for celestial atmosphere."

Her mother and relatives were much alarmed when she announced that she would become a nun and a family council was called. She was taken to the theatre every night, and though greatly overjoyed at this, she persisted in her wish to enter the nunnery. When 14 years old she was taken to a performance of "Britannicus" at the Théâtre Français, and was so moved and impressed that her family decided to make her an actress. Two years later she competed for the National Conservatoire and at the public trials recited a simple little fable of La Fontaine's, "The Two Pigeons." When her recitation was announced the jury of admission was not inclined to take her seriously, but her performance so astonished it that she was immediately and unanimously entered.

Provost and Sampson, who had trained the great Rachel, became her teachers, and in 1861 she won the second prize in tragedy and in 1862 the second prize for comedy. At the end of her first year, when it was understood that she would be forced to leave the Conservatoire, the cast of the Comédie Française, seeing her great progress and promise of future greatness, took up a collection that allowed her to spend another year with her teachers.

Her Professional Debut.

In 1862 Edmond Thierry called her to the Comédie Française and she made her professional début in a minor part in "Iphigenie," with small success, however. Then came four years of unremitting hard work done in obscurity and with small appreciation. It was during this period at a reception in honor of an anniversary of Molière that Mme. Bernhardt inadvertently offended Mme. Nathalie, one of the senior actresses of the company. The older woman became very angry and reproved her, and the altercation ended by the young actress slapping her face. There was a scandal, and Mme. Bernhardt announced her intention of buying a candy shop in the boulevards. However, when she saw the place its gloomy appearance discouraged her and she gave up the idea. When her savings were gone she entered the Gymnase de Montigny in 1866, where she was discovered by Doucet and made her first success. Doucet then recommended her to MM. Chilly and Duquesnel of the Odéon, but the former refused her because she was too thin. The latter, however, recognized her latent genius and engaged her, paying her first year's salary out of his own pocket. In 1867 Mme. Bernhardt made her début as Armande in "Les Femmes Savantes," and this appearance is considered as the real starting point of her wonderful career. As Cordelia in a translation of "King Lear," as the Queen in Victor Hugo's "Ruy Blas," but chiefly as Zanette in Francois Coppée's "Le Passant" she began to be famous by the end of 1869.

Becomes a War Nurse.

Then came the Franco-Prussian war, and with all the enthusiasm of her intense nature she became a nurse. She turned a Parisian theatre into a hospital and for more than a year gave herself up to the care of the wounded and dying. This action did much to increase her popularity.

In 1872 Mme. Bernhardt signed a contract to become a life member of the Comédie Française and scored great successes in "Phèdre," as Berthe in "La Fille de Roland," and as Posthumia in "Rome Vaincue." Three years later she was elected a "sociétaire," or a sharing life member of the Comédie Française.

Then came a period of clashes with M. Perrin, the managing director of the Comédie Française. Mme. Bernhardt received rôles that were uncongenial, and her rival in the company, Mlle. Croizette, whom she had known from childhood, seemed favored over her. The part of Clorinda in "L'Aventurière" was particularly distasteful to her, and one day, after remonstrating with M. Perrin for assigning this part to her, she burst out of his office like a tempest and gave up the stage.

Sculptor, Then Actress Again.

Mme. Bernhardt then took up sculpture, plunged into the work with all her soul and commenced her first piece, "After the Storm," which was accepted by the Salon when finished a few years later. The stage, however, called her too strongly, and she returned to the Comédie Française, under M. Perrin, only to break with him permanently shortly after. This last break was brought about by an incident typical of the Bernhardt temperament. She insisted on going up in a balloon—this was during the Exposition of 1878—and M. Perrin and the others of the company were sure she would break her engagement to play at the matinée that day. She landed just in time to keep the appointment, but Perrin was furious. He burst into denunciations of her eccentricities and finished by announcing that she was fined 1,000 francs for going on a journey without the permission of the administration, which meant himself.

Mme. Bernhardt immediately resigned, thereby breaking her contract, which ultimately cost her 100,000 francs, as the Comédie Française won the suit brought against her for not living up to her lifelong engagement.

She then played for the first time outside France, appearing in London with other members of the Comédie Française in "Phèdre," and as Mrs. Clarkson in "L'Etrangère," at the Gaiety Theatre, and achieved a great success.

"The English people," she said after this invasion, "first among all foreign nations welcomed me with such kindness that they made me believe in myself."

She returned to Paris for a time, and in May, 1880, returned to London and gave with great success "Frou Frou" and "Adrienne Lecouvreur." On Nov. 8, 1880, she made her first appearance in New York at Booth's Theatre under the management of Henry E. Abbey.

Her First American Tour.

Mme. Bernhardt's first American tour comprised 27 performances in this city and 156 in 50 other cities during a period of seven months. She played eight dramas, of which "La Dame aux Camelias" and "Frou Frou" were given most often.

Then came a tour of Russia and Denmark, and in 1882 she earned fresh triumphs at the Vaudeville in Paris. One year later she became the owner of the Porte Sainte-Martin Theatre and played in répertoire until 1886, when she made her second American tour. "Theodora" was first presented on this tour, and on the return to Paris Mme. Bernhardt gave "La Tosca" and "L'Aveu," an original drama written by herself. Her third American tour followed in 1888-1889, and she presented "Jeanne d'Arc," by Sardou in collaboration with Emile Moreau. Then in 1891-1893 Mme. Bernhardt made an extended tour covering the United States, South America and many of the capitals of Europe. On her return to Paris she undertook the management of the Théâtre de la Rénaissance and presented "Les Rois," "Izely," "Gismonda," "La Femme de Claude," "La Princesse Lointaine," and "Magda."

Mme. Bernhardt made her fifth American tour in 1896, and in December of that year was present at a great festival given in her honor in Paris. She was crowned queen of the drama before 600 artists, actors and authors, and poems in her honor were read by Coppée, Rostand, André Theuriet and Catulle Mendes. A determined effort was also made to obtain for her the Legion of Honor. In 1899 she obtained the Théâtre Municipal des Nations, and the Municipal Council of Paris changed its name, at a special session, to the Theatre Sarah Bernhardt. In the same year she played "Hamlet," and the discussion over her performance led to a duel, in which Catulle Mendes was one of the principals. In 1900 Mme. Bernhardt gave "L'Aiglon," by Rostand.

Her sixth American tour was made in 1901-02, and "Cyrano de Bergerac" was presented for the first time, with the support of Constant Coquelin. She made this tour under the management of Maurice Grau and gave 180 performances in the principal cities. Mme. Bernhardt returned to her playhouse in Paris and presented a number of new plays with brilliant success, and in 1905 made her seventh visit to this country under the management of the Shuberts.

Attacked by Mob in Quebec.

She played in both North and South America, and in Quebec, Canada, she went through an unpleasant experience. She was credited with making certain

Sarah Bernhardt

Mme. Bernhardt as Lady Macbeth

criticisms of French Canadians by the newspapers, and she and her company were attacked by a mob on their way to the station after the engagement.

Eggs, stones, sticks, and snowballs were thrown, and several members of the company received painful injuries. Mme. Bernhardt was unhurt, and shortly after received an official apology from Sir Wilfrid Laurier, the Premier, on behalf of the Canadian people. This tour was during the "theatrical war," and Mme. Bernhardt was playing in opposition to the so-called "trust." She played in halls, armories, skating rinks, churches, and tents, and in Texas, owing to the fact that no theatres could be obtained, she played in a Barnum & Bailey tent. There were 235 performances, including several in the Greek Theatre at Berkeley, Cal.

Mme. Bernhardt was now 63 years old, and on her return to this city was made an honorary member of the Cercle Française of Harvard University and received similar honors from Yale University, Johns Hopkins and Bowdoin College. On her return to Paris she gave a greater number of plays than ever before, and in 1910 returned to this country under the management of W. F. Connor for the first of her "farewell tours." In thirty-five weeks she gave 285 performances, among them being three new plays, one being "Judas," by John de Kay, the American author. "La Samaritaine" was also given and aroused much discussion on account of its portrayal of Christ. On this tour she several times played ten performances in one week.

Mme. Bernhardt returned to this country in December, 1912, for a vaudeville engagement that lasted until the Spring of the following year and took her to the principal cities of the United States. Her repertoire consisted of famous scenes from her great successes, and the tour was an unqualified success. It ended at the Palace Theatre in this city in May, 1913, and during her engagement there a laurel wreath in gold and silver was presented to her by the men and women of the American theatre.

Operation Costs Her Leg.

The closing years of the artiste's life were destined to be crowded with dramatic incidents, as was fitting for one whose whole career had been so picturesque. When the war came and the sons of her beloved France began pouring into Paris suffering with the wounds inflicted by the invaders she converted her theatre into a hospital, just as she had nearly a half-century before. Then in the midst of her ministrations she was stricken with inflammation of articulation of the right knee and had to undergo an operation which cost her her right leg. She had had trouble with the knee for a good many years, and on her visit to America in 1912-13 she was scarcely able to use that leg and never tried to walk on the stage without support.

The operation was successfully performed in February, 1915. That she was acting again at the end of six months was typical of her indomitable will. In August she took part in an entertainment in an open-air theatre near Bordeaux, and in November she returned to the Paris stage and acted in a dramatic sketch called "Les Cathedrales." In this the players represented the voices of the devastated cathedrals of France.

Mme. Bernhardt was the voice of the Cathedral of Strassburg, and when she recited the closing words, "Weep, Germans, weep; thy Prussian Eagles have fallen bleeding into the Rhine," the audience, one of the most notable ever assembled in France, became fairly wild with emotion.

A trip to the United States had been planned for that Fall, but the actress had not sufficiently recovered from the operation to make it advisable, and besides she was finding it difficult to manipulate her artificial leg. She did go to England, however, in January of 1916, and remained there for several months. Upon her return to France and shortly before she sailed for America she visited the French front and acted for the soldiers. She also posed for a motion picture, entitled "Mothers of France," which was recently exhibited here. The French Government extended unheard of privileges to the great artiste for the photographing of this picture, some of the scenes of which were taken in the very front-line trenches.

Mme. Bernhardt arrived on her last visit early in October, 1916, and after a preliminary tour played an engagement of several weeks at the Empire. Her repertoire was made up of playlets devised to conform to her inability to walk and of scenes from her old plays. During this engagement she acted her first English-speaking part.

She was operated upon in Mount Sinai Hospital April 17, 1917, for a kidney ailment and for a time was in a critical condition, her abundant vitality, as often before, pulling her through.

During the Summer she rested at Long Beach and then set off on one of the most arduous tours of her career, playing at first in legitimate theatres and then on the Keith vaudeville circuit. At the Palace in this city she invariably received an ovation, particularly for her performance as the young French officer in "Du Théâtre au Champ d'Honneur." She closed her season in Cleveland in October, 1918, and sailed for France. Since then she often expressed the intention of visiting us again.

Her appearance in Paris in April, 1920, in one of her great parts, Racine's "Athalie," aroused tremendous enthusiasm, the audience according her an unusually emotional reception. Critics stated that her old power in the rôle remained. The following Spring she presented "Daniel" in London, enacting a young man of 25. This production followed, too, her début in a Paris music hall the previous January in a one-act comedy as part of a typical vaudeville program. Further evidence of her undying energy was given in the Summer of 1921, when she published in the illustrated daily paper Excelsior her first novel, "La Petite Idole," wherein she made use of many eminent persons of her time but thinly disguised as characters. In October, 1921, she presented at her own theatre, "La Gloire," a play especially written for her by Maurice Rostand. Last Spring she acted "Regine Armand"—not to mention revivals of old successes.

Admitted to be the greatest actress of all time, Mme. Bernhardt also won distinction as a sculptor, writer, and artist. Her group, "After the Storm," received honorable mention at the Salon in 1878 and a number of her busts, notably those of Victorien Sardou, Canrobert, and Emile de Girardin are famous. Her book, "Dans les Nuages," written in 1878, describing her balloon ascension, was widely read, as were also her "Memoirs."

Married Greek Actor in 1882.

She was married in 1882 in London to Jacques Damala, a handsome Greek actor of her own company; but they parted after one year. Later, when he was dying of consumption, she removed him to her home and nursed him tenderly until the end.

For forty years Mme. Bernhardt's residence in Paris was the old house on the Boulevard Pereire. Her natural son, Maurice, lived with her there. Maurice and his wife and their unmarried daughter, Lysian, came over here in August, 1917, while Mme. Bernhardt was convalescing. The other daughter of Maurice is the wife of Louis Verneuil, a playwright, and is herself a parent. Consequently Bernhardt was a great-grandmother.

Some of her American tours netted as much as $500,000, and she always received half as her share. She spent money with a free hand, and lost heavily in backing unsuccessful productions at her own theatre. Her best work was done where she was able to display her powerful emotions. In her prime the emotional acting based on love, hate, and jealousy held the predominant place taken by character delineation in her later years. She was never surpassed and never will be, her critics say, in the emotional school. She played in more than two hundred parts and created most of them, being never content to act as others had interpreted them.

Mme. Bernhardt's crowning honor was the winning of the Cross of the Legion of Honor after thirty years of trying. In February last she was made an Officer. In 1912 the King of Spain gave her the Cross of Alfonso XII. She is the only member of the theatrical profession ever to receive the cross solely in recognition of her stage career, and it is said that it will never be conferred on any other. She received other honors without number. Public fêtes were given in London and Paris and other capitals for her, and in Vienna one night after playing "Hamlet" the audience tore the horses from her carriage and dragged her through the street shouting "Vive Bernhardt!"

SARAH BERNHARDT.

Two phenomena gave glory to the theatre in the closing decades of the nineteenth century, unimaginable, unforgetable, irreplaceable—the subtle masque of DUSE and the golden voice of BERNHARDT. One was instinct with the Italian sense of actuality in characterization; the other had the French genius for verbal expression, kindling to all the varied moods of eloquence. One was a mirror of what is most spiritual and suffering in womanhood; the other was organ of its supreme passions—love, triumph, despair.

Original BERNHARDT was as few artists of the stage have ever been, and with a will that seemed untamable; but she was loyal always to the spirit of her early training at the Conservatoire and the Comédie Française. There are devices that electrify the unknowing multitudes where sound art fails—vain posturings, mannerisms of empty charm, abrupt contrasts of voice or of tempo that have no relation to the scene in hand. She would have none of them. Her method was simple and unalloyed. It was by virtue of this fidelity that she commanded so wide a range of parts—from Cléopâtre to Hamlet, from Phèdre to Roxane—for she had no extraordinary gift in impersonation, no great range in extrinsic characterization. What she gave her public was not so much parts as plays, not so much great characters as great moods, great moments. The supreme organ was her voice. It was called golden—and so it was, as no other voice has ever been; but it could also be of velvet, of tempered steel, of the metal of a clarion. One word as she spoke it had a thousand inflections—the word that means love. It purred invitingly and delicately caressed; it languished, it exulted, it raged. In that one word as she spoke it lay the gamut of all her art.

Her career on the American stage bridged two widely different generations. In the '80s and early '90s good folk regarded her art as something forbidden, an alien evil. Young people did not tell their parents when they went to see her as Cléopâtre in the play of SARDOU. That scene in which the Serpent of Old Nile drew her coils round the throne of Marc Antony, circling ever nearer with the venom of her wiles, was a revelation of things scarcely to be whispered. It was a vastly altered public that saw her last—less naively impressionable perhaps, less easily swayed to the heights, but more human. It recognized not only the great artist but the great woman—who herself had suffered a change. The lure of youth was gone, its passions and despairs. All that was left was material abnegation and sacrifice. Physically maimed and defeated in all material things, she struggled on beneath the brave motto Quand Même, inscribed on her curtain. Only her art remained—the manner of great passions still authentic, the gold of her voice scarcely dimmed—and the public took her to its heart.

A rare character, too, indomitable in pride as in will. During her last stay here, at the time of the visit of Marshal JOFFRE, she was ill in hospital, and necessarily out of the public eye. One of her New York friends, who had attended her faithfully, excused an absence of some days on the plea that she had been busy on the Joffre reception committee. "JOFFRE?" asked BERNHARDT, knitting her eyebrows, "JOFFRE? Qui est-ce?"

"All the News That's Fit to Print"

The New York Times.

LATE CITY EDITION
Condensation of U.S. Weather Bureau forecast: Mostly fair and very cold today; snow flurries likely tonight.
Temperature range today: 22—5
Temperature range yesterday: 24—7.8
Full U. S. Weather Bureau Report, Page 56

© 1957, by The New York Times Company.

VOL. CVI. No. 36,151. Entered as Second-Class Matter, Post Office, New York, N. Y. NEW YORK, TUESDAY, JANUARY 15, 1957. Times Square, New York 36, N. Y. Telephone LAckawanna 4-1000 FIVE CENTS

PRESIDENT VISITS 4 DROUGHT STATES AND PLEDGES AID

Views Damage in Southwest and Promises 'Everyone Will Do His Best'

PEOPLE ARE OPTIMISTIC

Eisenhower Hails 'Chins-Up' Attitude—Flies to Tucson After Inspecting Farms

By W. H. LAWRENCE
Special to The New York Times.

TUCSON, Ariz., Jan. 14—President Eisenhower took a hard day-long look today at what searing sun and little or no rain have done to farms and ranches over a large section of the Southwest.

The President made inspection tours in the areas around San Angelo, Tex., Woodward, Okla., and Clovis, N. M., before flying into Tucson late this afternoon. Tomorrow he will visit Pueblo, Colo., and Garden City, Kan., before attending a fifteen-state drought conference in Wichita, Kan.

From automobiles and from a high-flying aircraft he saw burned-out crops and gaunt cattle, eloquent testimonials of the fearful economic cost of this natural disaster.

But the people he met were perpetual optimists, their spirit not unlike that of Brooklyn Dodger baseball fans in the lean years between National League pennants.

"Just wait until next year," was the refrain throughout the Southwest, just as it used to be in Brooklyn.

Praises Attitude

But, the experts say, these people require more than rain in the next crop season; they also need more generous short and long-term assistance than the Federal Government now is providing.

The President congratulated them for a "chins-up" attitude and said "everyone will do his best."

But it remained uncertain whether this signaled a reversal in current Administration policy against huge expenditures for more water conservation projects.

Everywhere President Eisenhower went he was confronted with pleas for Federal help in building new conservation projects that would trap flood waters in the spring to save them for the hot summer months.

Projects Are Urged

In Texas alone, projects totaling more than $1,000,000,000 were proposed on a self-liquidating basis over a fifty-year term. Gov. Raymond Gary of Oklahoma also turned in a sizable list of new reservoirs needed to re-establish agriculture in his state on a more normal basis to withstand the years when rains do not fall in normal quantities.

Nearly every local committee urged longer term loans at lower interest rates than the Government now is providing.

Although these droughts have persisted over many years and in some areas are the worst on record, the people the President visited remained determined to solve their problem.

An illustrated appeal on behalf of the Clovis area put the problem this way:

"When a crisis such as flood,

Continued on Page 22, Column 4

Humphrey Bogart, 57, Dies of Cancer

Special to The New York Times.

HOLLYWOOD, Calif., Jan. 14—Humphrey Bogart died in his sleep early this morning in the bedroom of his Holmby Hills home. The 57-year-old movie actor, an Academy Award winner, had been suffering for more than two years from cancer of the esophagus.

In the latter part of February, 1956, he underwent surgery at Good Samaritan Hospital for removal of a malignant growth. He recovered from the operation and gained back some of the weight he had lost. But, in November, 1956, he was admitted to St. John's Hospital in Santa Monica for treatment of nerve pressure caused by the growth of scar tissue on his throat.

Mr. Bogart leaves his wife, Lauren Bacall, actress, whom he married in 1945. The couple had two children, a son, Stephen Humphrey, born in 1949, and a

Continued on Page 29, Column 2

Associated Press Wirephoto

FIRST-HAND VIEW OF DROUGHT AREA: President Eisenhower looks out over the parched farm of Carl Peoples, left, in Woodward, Okla. Ezra Taft Benson, Secretary of Agriculture, who is accompanying the President on tour of Southwest, takes a closer look.

Six Months on Active Duty Required of All Guardsmen

By JACK RAYMOND
Special to The New York Times.

WASHINGTON, Jan. 14—Young men who join the National Guard or the Army Reserves will be required after April 1 to take at least six months' training on active duty.

The Army, in announcing this and other revisions in reserve training today, said the changes were "based on military considerations."

Until now only youths enlisting in the Army Reserve have been required to take six months' active duty training, followed by seven and one-half years in the Reserve. National Guardsmen had the option of volunteering for the six months active duty.

The new plan, it was said, would apply only to those who join the Guard or Reserve after April 1.

Under the new program, youths who volunteer for the six months' active duty training in the Guard or Reserves will be required to serve only four and one-half years in the Reserve instead of seven and one-half years. This provision will be retroactive to Aug. 9, 1955, when the National Reserve Act was passed.

The new order will allow enlistees between the ages of 18½ and 25 to take the six months' training duty with a subsequent Reserve duty obligation. This would enable them to escape the draft altogether. This had been open to youths between 17 and 18½ previously.

Youths who are drafted under the Selective Service Act will be required to serve only two years instead of three in the ready reserve after they have

Continued on Page 20, Column 5

LEGISLATORS' PAY EXPECTED TO RISE

Harriman Indicates He Would Not Veto an Increase—Urges Court Reform

By DOUGLAS DALES
Special to The New York Times.

ALBANY, Jan. 14—Governor Harriman has given state legislators reason to hope for a pay increase. The legislators now are talking in terms of a rise of $1,500, bringing the salaries of the 150 Assemblymen and fifty-eight Senators to $9,000 a year.

The subject came up at a Democratic caucus last week during a discussion by the Governor of the need for court reform, it was learned today.

The Governor made a strong bid for Democratic support of legislation simplifying and modernizing the court structure along lines proposed by the Temporary Commission on the Courts, headed by Harrison Tweed.

So far, no enthusiasm for court reform has been shown among legislators of either party. The only court measure for which there is optimism is a bill, still to be introduced, to increase the number of Supreme Court Justices by twenty-one.

Measures Vetoed

A similar measure was approved by the Legislature last year, along with a bill increasing the salaries of Supreme Court Justices by $2,000. They were vetoed, however, on the plea of Mayor Wagner that New York City did not have the funds to pay for its additional judges.

In expressing himself as friendly to a pay increase for legislators, there was no suggestion that the Governor's attitude was contingent upon approval of court-reform legislation.

The Governor said he understood that there was some opposition among the Democrats to changes in the court structure, but expressed the hope the reforms would have Democratic support. He also was reported to have suggested that legislators try to make more of a career out of the Legislature for longer periods.

At this point, a county leader interrupted to say that "they [the legislators] all want to become judges."

Mr. Harriman was reported to have replied that in that case perhaps an increase in pay would make the Legislature more attractive.

To this, the Assembly minority leader, Eugene F. Bannigan of Brooklyn, said that if the Governor were disposed favorably toward a pay increase, a bill would be forthcoming.

The Governor was said to have replied that if the bill came to him, he would not oppose it.

Any pay increase approved by the Legislature this year or next year could not become effective until 1959. The State Constitution bars Legislators from increasing their salaries for the

Continued on Page 26, Column 3

COLD SETS RECORD FOR SEASON HERE

Mercury Drops to 5°—High Today in 20's—Upstate Reading Is 50 Below

The temperature dropped to 5 degrees at 2 A. M. today, making it the coldest Jan. 15 on record. The previous low for the date was 6.3 degrees in 1927.

This morning's seasonal low was the coldest any day has been here since Feb. 3, 1955, when the mercury dropped to zero.

The Weather Bureau predicted temperatures this morning would descend to between 0 and 5 degrees in the city and zero inland.

The following record from the Weather Bureau shows hourly temperatures since 4 A. M. Monday:

4 A. M.	16	5 P. M.	21
5 A. M.	16	6 P. M.	20
6 A. M.	15	7 P. M.	17
7 A. M.	13	8 P. M.	15
8 A. M.	12	9 P. M.	12
9 A. M.	15	10 P. M.	10
10 A. M.	17	11 P. M.	9
11 A. M.	19	Midnight	8.3
12 Noon	22	Tuesday	
1 P. M.	23	1 A. M.	6
2 P. M.	24	2 A. M.	5
3 P. M.	24	3 A. M.	5
4 P. M.	23		

The Weather Bureau offered no hope for a warming trend in the predictable future. The forecast for today was for mostly fair weather with cloudiness developing in the afternoon and a chance of snow flurries at night. The high temperature today is expected to be between 20 and 25 degrees and the low will be between zero and 10 degrees. Clearing weather is ex-

Continued on Page 25, Column 4

CHOU IS ASSURING POLES OF SUPPORT IN LIBERAL TREND

In Return, Warsaw's Leaders Are Promising Not to Hurt Solidarity of Red Bloc

By SYDNEY GRUSON
Special to The New York Times.

WARSAW, Jan. 14—Premier Chou En-lai of Communist China has given assurances of continued support for efforts to evolve a more democratic form of communism in Poland.

In return the Polish Government has accepted the Chinese view—a view to which it was slowly coming around on its own—that nothing should be done by Poland to disturb the solidarity of the Communist camp.

Reliable Communist sources said these points were the essence of an understanding reached in the first three days of discussions between the Poles and Chinese. Premier Chou was in Wroclaw today and will return to Warsaw tomorrow for the conclusion of the talks.

Pole Pledges Amity

Welcoming Mr. Chou to Cracow yesterday, Premier Jozef Cyrankiewicz assured him that "we want to build socialism" in Poland and that "we want good relations with Socialist countries" on the basis of freedom and equality.

"Our talks with our Chinese friends revealed that they fully understand this, our road of reforming our life, and this pleases us very much," M. Cyrankiewicz said.

"The coexistence of nations should not be like the coexistence of various kinds of fish living in one big pond or lake, the bigger fish devouring the smaller ones," the Polish Premier added. "We are fighting against all forms of national oppression."

Warsaw Is Reassured

The Poles are now satisfied that Mr. Chou did not come here, as had been feared, to push them back into a satellite status. On the contrary, he was said to have shown sympathy for and understanding of Poland's insistence that she must be allowed to work out her internal problems in her own way.

The Chinese Communist leader apparently warned the Poles against trying to assume a role in international affairs similar to Yugoslavia's. The Chinese have described the Yugoslav position as divisive and a danger to the Communist world. The Poles have no illusions about their international position. As they see it, their geography and nothing else forbids the effort to emulate Yugoslavia.

According to the Poles their acceptance of the Chinese view of the necessity for solidarity of the Communist camp does not mean revision of their views on the Hungarian uprising, for example. It does mean, however,

Continued on Page 3, Column 5

Dulles Calls Mideast Peril 'Most Serious in 10 Years'

He Advises Senators That Eisenhower's Plan for Troops and Aid Funds Is Vital to Parry Red Threat

By WILLIAM S. WHITE
Special to The New York Times.

WASHINGTON, Jan. 14—John Foster Dulles declared today that in possible international Communist aggression in the Middle East lay "the most serious threat we have faced over the past ten years."

With this grave language the Secretary of State opened before

Texts of the Dulles and Green statements, Page 10.

the Senate Foreign Relations and Armed Services Committees the Administration's request for Congressional backing of a new policy involving:

¶The right of the President to use the United States armed forces as he might see fit to sustain peace in the Middle East.

¶Special Presidential authority to use in the area up to $200,000,000 of foreign aid funds, without existing restrictions, to combat economic disorder—and thus indirectly to combat Communist subversion.

Ultimately $400,000,000 more will be sought for the purpose, but that is not directly at issue now.

Secretary Dulles appeared before two of the Senate's most powerful committees.

He was hard-pressed on the economic aspect of the Administration's proposal. He agreed to some revision of the Administration's resolution that would make it plain that Congress was not committing itself to any long-range assistance. Another

Continued on Page 11, Column 3

Israel Plans to Hold Gaza, Report to U. N. Indicates

By KATHLEEN TELTSCH
Special to The New York Times.

UNITED NATIONS, N. Y., Jan. 14—The Israeli authorities have restored law and order in the Gaza Strip, a United Nations military officer said in a report today. He also gave the impression that Israel planned to occupy the area permanently.

The sandy Gaza Strip, with its crowded settlements of Pales-

Text of report on Gaza Strip appears on Page 14.

tinian Arab refugees, was taken over by Israeli troops invading Egypt last October.

[Israeli troops were blowing up Egyptian military installations at El Arish in the Sinai area Monday, according to a dispatch from headquarters of the United Nations Emergency Force. A spokesman for the Israeli delegation to the United Nations said the report was "unfounded".]

A somber and more critical account of conditions resulting from Israel's military actions in Gaza was given in a second report, also circulated today at the United Nations, from Henry R. Labouisse, head of the United Nations Relief and Works Agency for Palestine refugees.

Mr. Labouisse gave a report of the casualties among the refugees resulting from the Israeli troop action, which, he said, had caused fear and tension among the Arab population.

He said trustworthy sources had reported 386 dead in two major incidents, at Khan Yunis and Rafa. An additional sixty-

Continued on Page 14, Column 3

AID TO CAIRO TIED TO MIDEAST PLAN

U.S. Economic Help Depends, Officials Say, on Egypt's Cooperation on Issues

By DANA ADAMS SCHMIDT
Special to The New York Times.

WASHINGTON, Jan. 14—United States officials indicated today that future United States relations with Egypt in the economic field depended in large part on Egypt's cooperation in solving Middle East political problems.

Ambassador Ahmed Hussein of Egypt made another vain attempt to unfreeze the more than $40,000,000 worth of Egyptian assets in the United States.

This was the most specific point in the day's round of the general complaint the Egyptians have been making to the State Department in recent weeks, more or less as follows:

¶The United States has been at some pains since the invasion of Egypt to help the invaders, especially Britain, to weather the economic effects of their act; but it has not lifted a finger to help Egypt.

¶The Egyptian assets, which Egyptian sources say are valued as high as $80,000,000, were frozen after Egypt nationalized the Universal Suez Canal Company last July.

Americans' Interests

United States officials say the Egyptian assets were frozen to protect the interests of American holders of Suez Canal company stock and the action cannot be reversed until the Suez Canal problem is settled.

The Egyptian Ambassador conferred for forty-five minutes with William M. Rountree, Assistant Secretary of State for Near Eastern, South Asian and African Affairs, and Raymond A. Hare, United States Ambassador just back from his Cairo post.

In reply to questions as to Egypt's attitude toward President Eisenhower's Middle East plan, Ambassador Hussein said that his Government had decided not to make any official comment until after the plan had taken final form. He said he did not know anything about newspaper comment in Cairo, which, after a period of restraint, has turned sharply critical of President Eisenhower and his program.

The Egyptian Ambassador declined to comment on his talk with Mr. Rountree and Mr. Hare.

But United States officials other than Messrs. Rountree and Hare made it pretty clear that the future of United States economic relations with Egypt, in matters of aid, surplus sales, release of frozen assets and the like, depended very much on the degree of Egyptian cooperation in solving the political problems of the Middle East.

In denying a report that the United States had rebuffed an

Continued on Page 10, Column 5

U.S. GIVES THE U.N. NEW 5-POINT PLAN ON DISARMAMENT

It Urges Missile Control and Curbs on Experiments for War From Outer Space

SOVIET CONDEMNS MOVE

Kuznetsov Asks for Special Assembly Session to Deal With Arms Problem

Excerpts from speeches will be found on Page 4.

By LINDESAY PARROTT
Special to The New York Times.

UNITED NATIONS, N. Y., Jan. 14—The United States presented to the United Nations today a new five-point proposal for world disarmament. It included international control of intercontinental missiles and of experiments for warfare in new regions of space.

The program was explained before the United Nations Political Committee by Henry Cabot Lodge Jr., head of the United States delegation.

It immediately elicited a vigorous attack from the Soviet Union on the new Eisenhower policy for the Middle East, on British and French "aggression" in Egypt, and on the alleged intention of the West to profit from such incidents as "the revolutionary conspiracy in Hungary."

[In Moscow, the newspaper Pravda renewed the suggestion for a meeting of the Big Four and India to consider the problem of world disarmament.]

Larger Body Proposed

The Soviet spokesman, Vasily V. Kuznetsov, called on the powerful committee to recommend a special session of the General Assembly to deal exclusively with disarmament. He suggested also that the United Nations Disarmament Commission and its working subcommittee be enlarged, including states not in possession of atomic weapons.

Later, Mr. Lodge called Mr. Kuznetsov's speech "bitterly discouraging" and "contemptuous of the work of the United Nations."

The United States, the Soviet Union, Britain, France and Canada are the members of the subcommittee, which has considered all disarmament plans for the last several years. The full commission includes all members of the Security Council, as well as the major countries producing nuclear energy.

Special Body Is Suggested

The United States proposal again emphasized the necessity for a working system of inspection and control to eliminate the possibility of evasion of disarmament pledges.

In a new development, however, it suggested the formation of a special body to undertake this responsibility.

"The United States proposes that such an international agency for the regulation of armaments should be installed concurrently with the beginning of the [disarmament] program," Mr. Lodge told the committee. "It can constitute a nucleus of hope at the center of the grim implications which radiate from the

Continued on Page 5, Column 3

Fare Rises Spark Barcelona Violence

By BENJAMIN WELLES
Special to The New York Times.

MADRID, Jan. 14—Three policemen were injured and at least eight persons arrested today in violent demonstrations at Barcelona University.

The demonstrations were believed to have been held in connection with a city-wide boycott of public bus, street car and subway systems, called to protest higher fares.

Gen. Felipe Acedo, Civil Governor of Barcelona, issued two statements in which he charged that students of the city's university had demonstrated and had uttered shouts of a "subversive nature."

"The demonstrators were dispersed," he announced "and some arrests were made."

Earlier in the day, the Governor charged that a group of "students and unidentified persons" had gathered at the doors of the University and

Continued on Page 18, Column 3

The New York Times (by Edward Hausner)

NOT RUNNING: Low temperatures yesterday turned trickling water into ice on the spillway of Croton (N.Y.) Dam

Humphrey Bogart Is Dead at 57; Movie Star Had Throat Cancer

Continued From Page 1

daughter, Leslie, born in 1952. The actor is survived also by a sister, Frances Rose Bogart of New York.

Miss Bacall was Mr. Bogart's fourth wife. His previous marriages were also to actresses. He married Helen Menken in 1926 and divorced her a year later. His marriage to Mary Philips the next year lasted until 1937. In 1938 he took Mayo Methot as his third wife. The couple was divorced shortly before Mr. Bogart wed Miss Bacall.

Deflated Publicity Balloons

Mr. Bogart was one of the most paradoxical screen personalities in the recent annals of Hollywood. He often deflated the publicity balloons that keep many a screen star aloft, but he remained one of Hollywood's top box-office attractions for more than two decades.

On the screen he was most often the snarling, laconic gangster who let his gun do his talking. In private life, however, he could speak glibly and wittily on a wide range of subjects and make better copy off the cuff than the publicists could devise for him.

He had a large, seemingly permanent following among the mass audience. Yet he said he deplored "mass activities." Furthermore, he did everything he could to confound the popular image of a movie star.

Mr. Bogart received an Academy Award in 1952 for his performance in "The African Queen." Still, he made it clear he set little store by such fanfare. Earlier he had established a mock award for the best performance in a film by an animal, making sure that the bit of satire received full notice in the press.

Proud of Profession

But despite this show of frivolity, he was fiercely proud of his profession. "I am a professional," he said. "I have a respect for my profession. I worked hard at it."

Attesting to this are a number of highly interesting characterizations in such films as "The Petrified Forest" (1936), "High Sierra" (1941), "Casablanca" (1942), "To Have and Have Not" (1944), "Key Largo" (1948), "The Treasure of Sierra Madre" (1948), "The African Queen" (1951), "Sabrina," "The Caine Mutiny" (1954) and "The Desperate Hours" (1955). The actor's last film, "The Harder They Fall," was released last year.

Mr. Bogart's high sense of responsibility toward his profession may have stemmed from the fact that both his parents were highly successful professional persons. His mother was Maud Humphrey, a noted illustrator and artist. His father was Belmont DeForest Bogart, a prosperous surgeon. Their son, born on Christmas Day in 1899, was reared in fashionable New York society.

He attended Trinity School and Phillips Academy at Andover, Mass., but an early note of discord crept into this genteel strain when he was expelled from Andover for irreverence to a faculty member.

Mr. Bogart enlisted in the Navy in 1917 and crossed the Atlantic several times as a helmsman aboard a transport ship. As a civilian he was a tugboat inspector and saw brief service in an investment house.

Next, he had a job with World Films for a short while and then appeared as a stage manager for an acting group. It was an easy step to his first roles in the early Nineteen Twenties. His rise to fame over the next fifteen years, however, was a hard road, often lined with critical brickbats.

He appeared in "Swifty" and plugged on in drawing-room comedies, appearing in "Hell's Bells, "The Cradle Snatchers," "Its a Wise Child" and many others in which he usually played a callow juvenile or a romantic second lead.

He accepted a movie contract with Fox in 1931, but roles in a few Westerns failed to improve matters and soon he was back on Broadway, convinced that his hard-bitten face disqualified him in the close-ups as a matinee idol.

In 'Petrified Forest'

But toward the end of 1934 he used this granite-like face to rebuild, with enormous success, a new dramatic career. Having heard that Robert E. Sherwood's "The Petrified Forest" had a gangster role, he approached Mr. Sherwood for the important part. The playwright referred him to the director, who told Mr. Bogart to return in three days for a reading.

When Mr. Bogart reappeared before the director he had a three-day growth of beard and was wearing shabby clothes. His reading and appearance brought him the supporting role of Duke Mantee, his most memorable Broadway part. Leslie Howard was the star of the play. Mr. Bogart later did the same part for the movie to considerable critical acclaim.

This was the first of more than fifty pictures that Mr. Bogart made, most of them for Warner Brothers. A spate of crime dramas followed, including "Angels With Dirty Faces," "The Roaring Twenties," Bullets or Ballots," "Dead End," "San Quentin" and, finally, "High Sierra" in 1941.

Mr. Bogart then insisted on roles with more scope. They were forthcoming in such films as "Casablanca," "To Have and Have Not" and "Key Largo," wherein Mr. Bogart's notorious screen hardness was offset by a latent idealism that showed itself in the end.

Won New Followers

In "The Treasure of Sierra Madre," as a prospector driven to evil by a lust for gold, the range of his characterization won him new followers.

A further range of his talents was displayed also in "The African Queen," wherein his portrayal of a tropical tramp with a yen for gin and Katharine Hepburn won him an "Oscar." Another distinguished portrait was that of the neurotic Captain Queeg in the movie version of "The Caine Mutiny." His aptitude for romantic comedy became clear when he played the bitter business man who softens under the charms of Audrey Hepburn in "Sabrina." Mr. Bogart also appeared in "The Barefoot Contessa," made in 1954.

The movie actor made no secret of his nightclubbing. He was also a yachting enthusiast. At one point in his career he reportedly made $200,000 a film and he was for years among the top ten box-office attractions.

Mr. Bogart joined other actors in 1947 in a flight to Washington to protest the methods of the House Un-American Activities Committee, which was investigating communism in the movie colony. He was often a supporter of Democratic political causes.

The Maltese Falcon starring Bogart, Peter Lorre, Mary Astor and Sydney Greenstreet.

Bogart in his first major film role in *The Petrified Forest*.

Humphrey Bogart and Ida Lupino in a scene from *High Sierra*.

"All the News That's Fit to Print."

The New York Times.

LATE CITY EDITION
WEATHER—Showers today, cooler tonight; tomorrow fair.
Temperatures Yesterday—Max., 64; Min., 47

VOL. CXX..No. 41,489 NEW YORK, SATURDAY, AUGUST 28, 1971 15 CENTS

TRAVEL SNARLED BY 4.1-INCH RAIN; MORE DUE TODAY

Tropical Storm Doria Moves Toward Metropolitan Area —Emergency in Jersey

DOWNPOUR SETS MARK

Queens and Bronx Subways Halted, Creating Chaos During Evening Rush

By LAWRENCE VAN GELDER

Torrential rains created transportation chaos yesterday for hundreds of thousands of travelers in the metropolitan area.

Homebound commuters from Manhattan found themselves confronted with crippled subway and railroad systems and roads flooded by record rainfall and congested with stalled cars.

Last night the National Weather Service said that tropical storm Doria, moving up from the south, would affect the area from Manasquan, N. J., to Cape Ann, Mass., which includes New York City, Long Island and the south coast of Connecticut.

A hurricane watch was in effect for the region, though winds in the storm center were still below the 75 miles an hour needed for hurricane status.

The storm center was expected to pass offshore from New York City early today, bringing the city possibly two or three more inches of rain.

Yesterday the recorded 24-hour rainfall was 4.16 inches; the previous record for an Aug. 27 was 2.13 inches in 1967.

Heavier Rain in Jersey

In New Jersey the rains were even heavier than the city's downpour. The central part of the state received up to 6.5 inches during the 18-hour period ended at 5 P.M. States of emergency were declared in several communities, including Elizabeth, West Orange, Saddle Brook and Union Township.

In Elizabeth, electrical power was out in much of the city, and a number of persons were taken from cars and houses in rowboats as streets were flooded and water rose over the tops of autos.

In New York City, subway service was severely disrupted for Queens-bound commuters and Bronx riders, and traffic on virtually every major road in the city was slowed and often stalled by the downpour.

Lines at Phone Booths

While many commuters stood in line outside telephone booths in the station at 53d Street and Fifth Avenue, where no E or F trains were running yesterday evening, the Transit Authority announced that it was instituting bus service from Manhattan and Queens and the Bronx.

But most people affected by the disruptions at the end of the work day seemed unaware of these alternatives.

Mayor Lindsay criticized the Metropolitan Transporation Authority last night because, he said, it "overreacted" to the situation by "unnecessarily"

Continued on Page 11, Column 1

The New York Times/Neal Boenzi

IN NEW YORK: Cars splash through water on Belt Parkway in Brooklyn below Verrazano Bridge to Staten Island

Associated Press

IN NEW JERSEY: Families clean up debris after storm ripped through Cape May. Power was cut off for 11 hours.

STORM DRENCHES MARYLAND COAST

60 M.P.H. Winds Reported —Flash Flooding Occurs Along the Seaboard

By United Press International

OCEAN CITY, Md., Saturday, Aug. 28 — A tropical storm called Doria, with winds of near-hurricane force, moved northeastward along the Atlantic coast early today, dumping heavy rains and causing flash flooding in Maryland and Delaware.

Hurricane experts expected the tropical storm, the season's fourth, to make a second landfall on Long Island today after having touched land yesterday in North Carolina and in the Virginia Capes with flash floods and tornadoes.

Early today, the storm's center was near Lat. 38 degrees N., Long. 75.4 degrees W., or near Wallops Island, Va., and moving at 30 miles an hour.

The storm generated winds up to 60 miles an hour as it moved along in the Atlantic near this coastal resort city, causing heavy rains that left streets knee-deep in water.

The United States Coast Guard reported that the barometer was "falling like a rock."

The National Hurricane Center in Miami said the storm was reaching near-hurricane

Continued on Page 11, Column 2

Failure of Charter Flights Strands Many in Europe

By ROBERT LINDSEY

Hundreds of Americans, most of them college students, are stranded in Europe because charter airlines have refused to honor their return tickets.

Most of the tickets were bought at two New York travel agencies that are now defunct and under investigation for fraud.

Government officials said they feared the number of stranded young people could grow substantially between now and Labor Day, as more arrive at airports and discover their return tickets are worthless.

There was no way of determining last night how many persons were currently stranded in London and other European cities, but a Civil Aeronautics Board official estimated that there were probably 350.

According to state and Federal authorities, most of the worthless return-flight vouchers were sold by the University Students Association, which until recently had its offices at 1 Fifth Avenue, and the American Union of Students, which until recently was at 135 East 27th Street.

The two agencies had paid, through intermediaries, several European nonscheduled airlines to carry the youths from New York to Europe, but officials of the airlines have contended that they were not paid for the return trip, so they refused to honor the return-flight vouchers.

The offices of both travel agencies here were vacant yesterday, and employes of other businesses in the buildings said they did not know where the officials of the two agencies had gone.

In London, where some of the youths are looking for jobs

Continued on Page 52, Column 7

RUMANIA WORRIED BY SOVIET MOVES

Bucharest Reported Taking Precautions as a Result of Rising 'War of Nerves'

By TAD SZULC

Special to The New York Times

WASHINGTON, Aug. 27 — Rumania is displaying growing concern over what foreign diplomats describe as a Soviet "war of nerves" against the regime of President Nicolae Ceausescu that has been in progress since midsummer.

Reports reaching here from Bucharest portray Rumania as taking new political and diplomatic "precautions" in the light of Moscow's mounting pressure. This pressure appears to reflect the Soviet displeasure over Rumania's intimacy with China and her independence in economic policies.

Diplomats suggest that these reports from Bucharest, conveying the Rumanian views, may represent a diplomatic drive by Mr. Ceausescu to head off any Soviet moves by alerting the world to the possibility of trouble with Moscow.

Since June, when Mr. Ceausescu visited Peking, the Russians and their allies have been applying a form of psychological warfare against Rumania, ranging from a series of Warsaw Pact military maneuvers

Continued on Page 4, Column 3

LEGISLATIVE UNIT IN SAIGON ACCUSES THIEU OF RIGGING

Charges Many Irregularities in Upcoming Assembly and Presidential Elections

By IVER PETERSON

Special to The New York Times

SAIGON, South Vietnam, Aug. 27—A South Vietnamese legislative committee accused the Government of President Nguyen Van Thieu today of numerous instances of election rigging.

The committee, consisting of 22 anti-Government senators and deputies, asserted in an interim report that it had evidence of irregularities and rigging in connection with this Sunday's lower house election and the presidential election scheduled for Oct. 3.

It declared that its findings, together with a "secret document" purportedly containing Government orders to rig the elections, represented "a record of our bitter experiences with elections in this dark period of our country." This controversial document was made public by Duong Van Minh, a retired general, in withdrawing from the Presidential race last week.

Several Cases Cited

The legislative panel, known as the National Assembly Committee on Election Fraud, cited several cases in which opposition candidates for the lower house and their supporters were arrested, allegedly without pretext. The report said that after the committee had learned of the arrests and protested to the Government, most of those arrested were released.

[Senator Vu Van Mau, the committee chairman, said the President and his supporters tried to monopolize or hoard the endorsements needed by other presidential candidates to qualify for the ballot, The Associated Press reported. The senator noted that Mr. Thieu was required to get only 40 signatures from members of the National Assembly or 100 from members of provincial or city councils, but that he had obtained the backing of 87 deputies, 15 senators and 452 councilmen.]

Thieu Still Planning Election

In addition to General Minh, Vice President Nguyen Cao Ky has also dropped out of the presidential race on the ground that it is rigged in the President's favor. However, his name is still scheduled to appear on the ballot.

Mr. Thieu, although he has made no public statements on the situation, is reported to be determined to go ahead with the presidential election despite the absence of any real opponent and despite pressure from the United States to come up with a compromise that might persuade Mr. Ky to reverse his refusal to campaign.

Mr. Ky is reported to believe that public outrage over the election fraud issue will eventually force the President to yield. The Vice President has suggested that both he and Mr. Thieu resign and that an in-

Continued on Page 2, Column 7

JAPANESE ALLOW FLOATING OF YEN, BUT U.S. IS WARY

'STEP' WELCOMED

Treasury Sees More Realistic Aligning of Exchange Rate

By RICHARD HALLORAN

Special to The New York Times

WASHINGTON, Aug. 27—Officials of the Nixon Administration reacted warily today to the Japanese decision to allow the yen to float and let market forces determine its value.

The Treasury issued a restrained statement saying: "We welcome the decision of Japan as a further step toward a more realistic realignment of international exchange rates which the President envisioned in his address to the nation on Aug. 15."

In San Clemente, Calif., the White House press secretary, Ronald L. Ziegler, echoed that sentiment, saying: "We feel that this is a useful step toward constructive realignment of the exchange rate." Officials here emphasized the word "step" and said the Japanese move was no more than that.

Persuading the Japanese to revalue the yen and to reduce their barriers against American exports and investment in Japanese industry have been among the main objectives of the international aspects of President Nixon's new economic policy.

But officials here pointed out that the Japanese statement on freeing the yen cut two ways. They noted that the Japanese termed the float "temporary,"

Continued on Page 12, Column 4

LIMIT IS STRESSED

Action Follows Heavy Dollar Selling on Tokyo Market

By TAKASHI OKA

Special to The New York Times

TOKYO, Saturday, Aug. 28—After nearly two weeks of a stubborn and lonely effort to keep the yen pegged at 360 to the dollar, the Japanese Government announced that as of today the yen would be allowed to float within unspecified limits against the dollar. The Bank of Japan would intervene if the yen rose too high.

Finance Minister Mikio Mizuta made the dramatic, long-awaited announcement last night after a hectic day in which $1.25-billion was unloaded on the Tokyo exchange and the Bank of Japan had to buy almost all these dollars at 357.57 yen to the dollar to maintain the yen at close to its pegged rate.

The Japanese Government's decision brings Tokyo in line with West European capitals, which have been floating their currencies or, as in the case of France, adopting a two-tier system since reopening their exchange markets on Monday.

In New York, trading in the yen was halted yesterday in the foreign exchange market after the Japanese decision.

The Finance Minister, at a crowded news conference three hours after the foreign exchange had closed, said also that Japan would ask the United States to halt imposition of

Continued on Page 12, Column 2

HOW DOLLAR HAS DECLINED

Value of	Par	Friday	Change
In Pounds	.4[illegible]	.40	—2.8%
In French Francs	5.55	[illegible]39	—2.9%
In Marks	3.[illegible]	[illegible]40	—7.1%
In Yen	360	320	—11.1%

The New York Times Aug. 28, 1971

Friday values, from London market, are compared with the official values that existed before currencies were floated. Franc cited is used only in financial deals.

Europe Welcomes Move; Dollar Trading Is Mixed

By JOHN M. LEE

Special to The New York Times

LONDON, Aug. 27—The dollar reacted in mixed fashion against major European currencies today as foreign exchange dealers welcomed the Japanese decision to float the yen as a contribution to resolving the world currency crisis.

"It's what Nixon's wanted, isn't it?" a trader at a big British merchant bank said.

A common view in London was that the Japanese willingness to let the yen float up in value, not just against the dollar but against European and other currencies as well, could remove inhibitions against higher floating rates in Europe.

The reasoning is that European countries will be more amenable to accepting some competitive disadvantage through higher rates for their own currencies now that they know Japan will accept a similar handicap.

The Japanese move could thus accelerate the appreciation of foreign currencies and the depreciation of the dollar that President Nixon has sought through his new economic measures. The Administration's objective is said to be a 12 to 15 per cent dollar depreciation.

The yen was in short supply in London today for anyone wanting to trade after the Japanese announcement. But in a few deals that barely tested the water, the yen was traded here at 320 to the dollar. This rate

Continued on Page 12, Column 8

Mass Ousters of Black Students A Growing Integration Problem

By PAUL DELANEY

Special to The New York Times

COLUMBIA, S. C., Aug. 27—Last fall, when this city's schools underwent massive integration, 500 very poor black youngsters were assigned to A.C. Flora High, a 1,700-student institution nestled among tall pine trees in an all-white, upper-middle-class neighborhood.

By the end of the school year, a small army of them—from one-fifth to nearly one-half or more, depending on various estimates by school officials—had been suspended or expelled.

The prevailing view in the white community is that the reasons for the trouble were "cultural clash" and class differences, that an influx of poor white students with as little preparation and motivation for the move would have had the same effect. But a large number of people here, whites as well as blacks, blame simple racial discrimination.

What happened at Flora High has to one extent or another happened again and again over the last year as communities ranging in size and region from tiny Cross, S. C., to metropolitan Chicago went through the pains of school integration.

And with further massive integration taking place this week as the new school year gets under way in some parts of the nation, the problem of the "pushouts," as the youngsters are called by some educators and civil rights leaders,

Continued on Page 22, Column 1

Margaret Bourke-White, Photo-Journalist, Is Dead

By ALDEN WHITMAN

Margaret Bourke-White, one of the world's pre-eminent photographers, died yesterday morning at the Stamford (Conn.) Hospital from complications after a long battle with Parkinson's disease, a nerve disorder. She was 67 years old and lived in Darien, Conn.

Miss Bourke-White had been on the staff of Life magazine since its founding in 1936. She resigned two years ago, but had not contributed to the magazine for many years.

Paying tribute to her yesterday, Alfred Eisenstadt, a longtime friend and fellow photographer, said that Miss Bourke-White "was great because there was no assignment no picture, that was unimportant to her."

"She immersed herself in the smallest detail," he continued, "and everything she did was a challenge to her."

One of the first photo-journalists who told a news story in pictures and also wrote the text, Miss Bourke-White summed up the secret of her work a few years ago by saying:

"The camera is a remarkable instrument. Saturate yourself with your subject and the cam-

Continued on Page 28, Column 1

The New York Times

Margaret Bourke-White

Meany For Wage-Price Board That Would Set Its Own Rules

Labor's Postfreeze Plan

By PHILIP SHABECOFF

Special to The New York Times

WASHINGTON, Aug. 27 — George Meany, president of the A.F.L.-C.I.O., gave the first hint today of the economic machinery that organized labor will seek as a successor to the Nixon Administration's 90-day wage and price freeze.

Mr. Meany indicated at a meeting with reporters that he would favor the creation of a board representing labor, management and the public, similar to the War Labor Board of World War II, to deal with wage and price issues on a continuing basis after the freeze expires.

Such a board, he suggested, would be empowered not only

Continued on Page 12, Column 5

Romney Urges Curbs

By JOHN HERBERS

Special to The New York Times

WASHINGTON, Aug. 27 — George Romney, Secretary of Housing and Urban Development and a member of the Cost of Living Council, proposed today the establishment of a wage-price review board with power to curb inflationary practices of corporations and unions, effective when the 90-day freeze expires on Nov. 13.

The board would rely on enforcement by the Justice Department through the courts in much the same way that the antitrust laws are endorsed, Mr. Romney said.

And he said that whatever restraints followed the current

Continued on Page 12, Column 6

NEWS INDEX

Increased Earnings For A.T.&T. Backed

By CHRISTOPHER LYDON

Special to The New York Times

WASHINGTON, Aug. 27—A staff examiner for the Federal Communications Commission ruled today that the American Telephone and Telegraph Company should be allowed an 8¼ per cent rate of return on interstate service under today's financial conditions.

He also proposed a general range of 7.9 to 8.8 per cent as reasonable interstate earnings that A.T.&T. could expect to justify in the future.

In the unlikely event that the seven-member F.C.C. does not review the examiner's findings the proposed rate of return would become effective in 50 days, on Oct. 16. But, in any event, under the wage-price freeze, the telephone company

Continued on Page 39, Column 4

Margaret Bourke-White, Photo-Journalist, Dead at 67

Continued From Page 1, Col. 3

era will all but take you by the hand."

And indeed her camera took her through a life of high adventure that included wars, dust bowls, communal riots, death camps and floods. She was torpedoed off North Africa in World War II and ambushed in Korea. She flew on American bombing raids in Tunis and rode with an artillery spotter in Italy.

Aggressive and relentless in pursuit of pictures, Maggie, as Miss Bourke-White was generally known, had the knack of being at the right place at the right time. For example, she interviewed and photographed Mohandas K. Gandhi a few hours before his assassination in India. And she was the only American photographer in the Soviet Union in 1941 while the battle for Moscow raged.

Many of the world's notables sat for her shutter—President Franklin D. Roosevelt, Winston Churchill (who gave her just 12 minutes), Emperor Haile Selassie, Pope Pius XI and Stalin.

For her meeting with Stalin in the Kremlin in 1941, which was arranged by Harry Hopkins, Miss Bourke-White employed a stratagem to catch him off guard. Recalling the incident, she wrote:

"I made up my mind that I wouldn't leave without getting a picture of Stalin smiling. When I met him, his face looked as though it were carved out of stone, he wouldn't show any emotion at all. I went virtually berserk trying to make that 'great stone face' come alive.

"I got down on my hands and knees on the floor and tried out all kinds of crazy postures searching for a good camera angle. Stalin looked down at the way I was squirming and writhing and for the space of a lightning flash he smiled—and I got my picture. Probably, he had never seen a girl photographer before and my weird contortions amused him."

Miss Bourke-White often maintained that "a woman shouldn't trade on the fact that she is a woman." Nonetheless, several of her male colleagues were certain that her fetching looks—she was tall, slim, dark-haired and possessed of a beautiful face—were often employed to her advantage.

"Generals rushed to tote her cameras," Mr. Eisenstadt recalled, "and even Stalin insisted on carrying her bags."

'Truth is Essential'

"I feel that utter truth is essential," Miss Bourke-White said of her work, "and to get that truth may take a lot of searching and long hours."

In practice, this attitude resulted in pictures of starkness and simplicity, but that were withal infused with a sense of humanity. Her photographs of the American sharecroppers, presented in "You Have Seen Their Faces" captured the tragedy and desolation of the rural United States in the nineteen-thirties. The cracked and parched earth seemed one with the lined and weathered faces of the Depression's victims.

Miss Bourke-White became a photographer by necessity. Born in New York on June 14, 1904, she was the daughter of Joseph and Minnie Bourke White. Her father was a naturalist, engineer and inventor. She attended six colleges, winding up at Cornell. Meantime, her father had died and after a marriage at 19 had broken up, Miss Bourke-White was obliged to support herself.

She turned to taking pictures with a second-hand, $20 Ica

Photographs courtesy of Life

Mohandas K. Gandhi with his charka, or spinning wheel, in 1946. The spinning wheel became a symbol of India's struggle for independence, because it had made it possible for the Indians to sustain their boycott of British textiles by making their own cloth.

Reflex that had a crack straight through the lens. Her first painfully taken photographs, of Cornell's spectacular Ithaca campus, sold well enough to encourage her to become a professional photographer. She made her first reputation in Cleveland as an architectural and industrial photographer. Arriving in the Lake Erie city by boat, she said:

"I stood on the deck to watch the city come into view. As the skyline took form in the morning mist, I felt I was coming to my promised land—columns of machinery gaining height as we drew toward the pier, derricks swinging like living creatures. Deep inside I knew these were my subjects."

From 1927 to 1930, Miss Bourke-White (who had hyphenated her name on her divorce) made machinery beautiful, transforming, one critic said, "the American factory into a Gothic cathedral and [glorifying] the gears." Her pictures caught the eye of Henry Luce, who invited her to join the staff of his Fortune magazine.

For Fortune, she took notable pictures of a shoe-manufacturing plant in Lynn, Mass.; glass blowing in Corning, N.Y., and hog processing in Chicago. She also traveled to the Soviet Union, taking pictures of factory workers, iron puddlers and the Dneiper Dam. With the photographs left over from her magazine assignment, she published a photo-journalism book, "Eyes of Russia," a record of the Five Year Plan.

Back in the United States, she did a picture article in 1934 for Fortune of the dust bowl, journeying from the Dakotas to the Texas Panhandle for shots of the drought and its victims.

Two years later, Miss Bourke-White and Erskine Caldwell, the novelist, toured the rural South, photographing sharecroppers and tenant farmers. The result, "You Have Seen Their Faces," angered mill-owners and landlords, who charged that Miss Bourke-White and Mr. Caldwell had gone out of their way to portray gaunt cotton pickers and wan children. The book, however, has since become a classic of photographic realism.

In 1939, five years after their collaboration, the photographer and the writer were married. It was an unhappy union, and was dissolved by divorce in 1942.

Miss Bourke-White was an original member of the Life staff in 1936, for whose first issue she took pictures of the Fort Peck Dam in Montana. In other prewar issues of the magazine, she did photo-essays on the Arctic, on Central Europe and on the variety of life in the United States. And in the Soviet Union in 1941 she covered the fighting at Smolensk as well as the Nazi attack on Moscow.

In the spring of 1942, with the United States in the war, Miss Bourke-White, now returned to New York, was accredited to the Army Air Forces, the first woman thus assigned. She covered (and photographed) the fighting in North Africa and Italy, sending Life some of its most memorable war pictures.

One of her most awesome series of pictures was taken in 1945, when, attached to Lieut. Gen. George C. Patton's Third Army, she went through Buchenwald, the Nazi concentration camp. Her photos of stacks of naked dead bodies stirred world revulsion.

After the war, Life sent Miss Bourke-White to India, where she photographed the communal disorders between the Moslems and the Hindus. In 1949 and 1950 she was in South Africa to study labor conditions and racial problems. She photographed diamond and gold miners, and in the Orange Free State she was lowered 2,000 feet in a basket to take pictures of a gold mine while underground rain poured around her.

When the Korean conflict broke out, she went to the front with American troops. It was on her way home in 1952 that she noticed, according to her autobiography, "Portrait of Myself," a dull ache in her left leg and arm, the first symptoms of Parkinsonism. The disease went undiagnosed for several years while she undertook futile therapeutic exercises. Finally, in 1958, her condition was recognized and she underwent the first of two operations for the relief of her tremors and her awkward gait.

Her gallant struggle against the disease was recounted in a movie, "The Margaret Bourke-White Story," starring Eli Wallach and Teresa Wright. In recent years, however, the illness, which affected her muscles and her gait, recurred. She was hospitalized three weeks ago.

Miss Bourke-White's pictures are in a number of museums, including the Brooklyn Museum, the Cleveland Museum of Art and the Museum of Modern Art in New York.

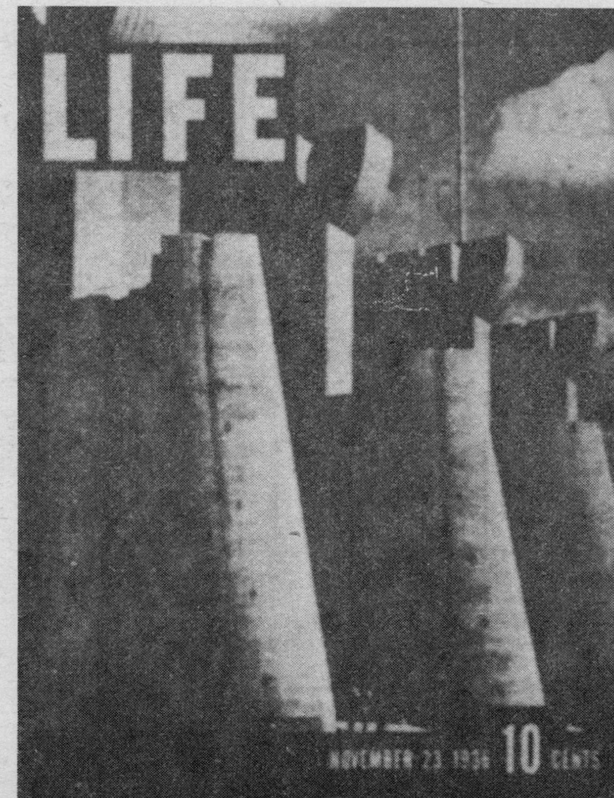

When Life made debut in 1936, Margaret Bourke-White's photograph of Fort Peck Dam in Montana was on cover.

This study of South African miners, taken in 1950, was Miss Bourke-White's favorite among all her photographs.

"All the News That's Fit to Print."

The New York Times.

LATE CITY EDITION
Partly cloudy, continued warm today followed by much cooler this afternoon. Tomorrow fair, cooler.
Temperatures Yesterday—Max., 90; Min., 72

Copyright, 1941, by The New York Times Company.

VOL. XCI..No. 30,571. Entered as Second-Class Matter, Postoffice, New York, N. Y. NEW YORK, MONDAY, OCTOBER 6, 1941. THREE CENTS NEW YORK CITY and Vicinity

YANKS WIN IN 9TH, FINAL 'OUT' TURNS INTO 4-RUN RALLY

Game-Ending Third Strike Gets Away From Dodger Catcher, Leading to 7-4 Victory

KELLER IS BATTING HERO

Double, His Fourth Safety, Puts New York in Front—Victors Now Lead in Series, 3-1

By JOHN DREBINGER

It couldn't, perhaps, have happened anywhere else on earth. But it did happen yesterday in Brooklyn, where in the short space of twenty-one minutes a dazed gathering of 33,813 at Ebbets Field saw a world series game miraculously flash two finishes before its eyes.

The first came at 4:35 of a sweltering afternoon, when, with two out and nobody aboard the bases in the top half of the ninth inning, Hugh Casey saw Tommy Henrich miss a sharp-breaking curve for a third strike that for a fleeting moment had the Dodgers defeating the Yankees, 4 to 3, in the fourth game of the current classic.

But before the first full-throated roar had a chance to acclaim this brilliant achievement there occurred one of those harrowing events that doubtless will live through all the ages of baseball like the Fred Snodgrass muff and the failure of Fred Merkle to touch second.

Makes Frantic Dash

Mickey Owen, topflight catcher of the Dodgers, let the ball slip away from him and, before he could retrieve it in a frantic dash in front of his own dugout, Henrich had safely crossed first base.

It was all the opening Joe McCarthy's mighty Bronx Bombers, shackled by this same Casey ever since the fifth inning, needed to turn defeat for themselves into an amazing victory which left a stunned foe crushed.

For in the wake of that excruciating error came a blazing single by Joe DiMaggio, a two-base smash against the right-field barrier by Charley Keller, a pass to Bill Dickey by the now thoroughly befuddled Casey and another two-base clout by the irrepressible Joe Gordon.

Flatbush's Darkest Hour

Four runs hurtled over the plate and, though the meteorological records may still contend that this was the brightest, sunniest and warmest day in world series history, it was easily the darkest hour that Flatbush ever has known.

For this astounding outburst gave the Yankees the game, 7 to 4, and with this victory McCarthy's miraculous maulers moved to within a single stride of another world championship. Their lead, as the series enters the fifth encounter at Ebbets Field today, now stands at three games to one, and the Bombers need to touch off only one more explosion to bring this epic interborough struggle to a close.

Almost from the moment Mayor La Guardia threw out the first ball this battle was one that had the crowd seething and sizzling under an emotional strain that at times threatened to burst out the sides of the arena in the heart of Flatbush.

Higbe First to Go

Neither of the starting pitchers, Kirby Higbe for the Dodgers and Atley Donald, survived the fierce fighting under the blistering midsummer sun. Kirby, twenty-two-game winner of the National League champions, making his delayed first appearance in the series, was the first to go. He was driven to cover in the fourth inning, by which time the Yanks had run up a lead of 3 to 0.

But this merely provided the setting for the making of a couple of Brooklyn heroes who last night would have been the toast of the borough had victory remained where it momentarily perched at 4:35 o'clock.

One was Jimmy Wasdell, who hit a pinch double in the last of the fourth to drive in two runs. The other was Pete Reiser, freshman star of the Dodgers, who, finally coming into his own, whacked a homer over the rightfield wall with Dixie Walker on base in the fifth inning to give the Brooklyn host its 4-to-3 lead.

That blow finished Donald and,

Continued on Page Twenty-one

Hurricane Pounds Bahamas, Roars On to Florida Coast

102-Mile-an-Hour Wind Hurls Boats on Shore and Darkens Nassau as Southern Resorts Put Up Boards in Preparation

By The United Press.

NASSAU, The Bahamas, Oct. 5—A 102-mile-an-hour hurricane swept past Nassau early tonight, leaving the town littered with the wreckage of boats blown out of the harbor, uprooted trees and disabled electric wires.

Buildings stood fast through the storm and no loss of life was reported.

One schooner, four sloops and a dozen smaller craft were lifted out of the water and dashed into Bay Street, Nassau's main thoroughfare. Two shipyard docks and one private dock were demolished.

A survey after the storm had passed showed considerable general damage, but there was no material damage to buildings in which the populace had taken refuge.

Waves smashed into Bay Street at the height of the storm and the street was littered with small debris. It was under a foot and a half of water two miles east of the town.

Uprooted trees littered roads in each direction from Nassau for at least three or four miles.

Government House, official residence of the Duke of Windsor, Governor of the Bahamas, was unharmed. It had been strongly boarded up. The Duke and Duchess are at his Canadian ranch.

The 102-mile-an-hour velocity

Continued on Page Ten

Record 90° Heat Drives Throngs to Beaches and Parks Here—Slow-Moving Cars Jam Roads—100,000 Visit Coney Island

Summer continued its last-ditch stand against Autumn yesterday as the temperature reached 90 degrees, setting a new record for the date, and hundreds of thousands of New Yorkers piled into cars and fled to beaches and woodlands, giving traffic policemen another dose of Sunday blues.

Yesterday was the first time since Sept. 23 that the temperature had touched 90. The low for the day was 72 degrees, which made the mean temperature 81 degrees, twenty more than normal for the date. The previous record for an Oct. 5 was 87 degrees, set in 1922.

The humidity started out at 6 A. M. with an 85, a good deal over par; fell off considerably as the temperature rose—a customary procedure—and was at 47 at sundown.

Today, the Weather Man said, will be partly cloudy and warm, growing much cooler this afternoon, and tomorrow will be fair and cooler.

Automobile traffic was particularly heavy yesterday along the Henry Hudson and West Side Highways, many of the arteries in Westchester, and in the vicinity of Coney Island and the Rockaways. At the latter resort automobiles formed solid lines along the Beach Channel Drive, Cross Bay Boule-

Continued on Page Ten

LABOR IS UNITING IN LA GUARDIA AID

Lyons Names an A. F. L. Group to Support Mayor—C. I. O. Left Wing to Act Wednesday

Mayor La Guardia seemed yesterday to be well on his way to obtaining support from both wings of organized labor in addition to that he derives as the nominee of the American Labor party.

Thomas J. Lyons, president of the New York State Federation of Labor, announced the opening of headquarters of the American Federation of Labor Non-Partisan Committee on the ninth floor of the County Trust Building, 265 West Fourteenth Street. As chairman of the committee, he said it intended to make the most intensive campaign among trade union voters in the city's history for the re-election of Mayor La Guardia.

The position of C. I. O. unions, exclusive of the Amalgamated Clothing Workers and other right-wing units that already have endorsed the Mayor, will be determined at a special meeting Wednesday night at the Fraternal Clubhouse, 110 West Forty-eighth Street.

Citizen Committee Heads

Appointment of the executive committee of the Citizens Committee for the Re-election of La Guardia, McGoldrick and Morris, composed of 550 members, including many prominent in the civic and business life of the city, was announced yesterday by William M. Chadbourne, campaign manager. Mr. Chadbourne said the membership of the general committee was more than 5,000 with many being added daily, and predicted that the people of the city would re-elect Mayor La Guardia and his running mates by a large majority.

Among the members of the executive committee are Winthrop W. Aldrich, A. A. Ballantine, James G. Blaine, Mrs. Sidney C. Borg, Henry Bruere, Dr. and Mrs. Nicholas Murray Butler, Eddie Cantor, Alfred A. Cook, Dr. Harry Woodburn Chase, David Dubinsky, Sidney Hillman, Frank L. Polk, Victor Ridder, Mrs. Kermit Roosevelt, Thomas D. Thacher, Charles H. Tuttle, Mr. and Mrs. Charles Evans Hughes Jr., Isidore Nagler, Attilio Picarelli, William M. Calder, Mrs. Alvah W. Burlingame, Mrs. Reuben L. Haskell, John Haynes Holmes, Mrs. Raymond V. Ingersoll, Duncan MacInnes, Lewis H. Pounds, Mrs. Jessie O'Brien, Manuel J. Johnson and Ernest C. Smith.

Mr. Lyons announced the appointment of Charles E. Sinnigen, secretary of the Central Union Label Council of Greater New York,

Continued on Page Twenty-five

FREEDOM RALLY THRILLS 17,000

Knudsen Pleads for Speed-Up in Defense Work—Willkie Scores Appeals to Bigotry

Bill Robinson, no Aryan, tapdanced on Adolf Hitler's coffin in Madison Square Garden last night before 17,000 persons, as the band played "When That Man Is Dead and Gone."

Bojangles, wearing gold pants, grinned happily through his taptap-tap a few minutes after the 17,000 onlookers had come close to having the wits scared out of them by a bombing and parachutist attack on the Garden, in the course of which thousands of soldiers descended from the vast ceiling. The Garden was in darkness for that stunt, but the darkness was broken by crisscrossing searchlights. A sound track provided real bombing raid racket.

It was a wholly realistic business—until the parachutes got within a few feet of the audience on the floor. They turned out to be about eight inches in diameter, and the soldiers they bore were of cardboard, five inches high.

Dramatization of Viewpoint

All this was part of the "Fun to Be Free" rally staged by Fight For Freedom, Inc., to dramatize its view that the United States already and necessarily is involved in the war and that the country immediately should take an active shooting part in it.

There were speakers for the occasion, among them being William S. Knudsen, director general of the Office of Production Management, who urgently called for a speed-up in the national defense program, and Wendell L. Willkie, who declared, referring to the recent speeches of Charles A. Lindbergh, that interjection of the racial issue into the American war debate had proved that the "opposition is becoming bankrupt of argument" and that the only chance of the 1942 Congressional elections being called off would result from national acceptance of the isolationist policy.

In addition to comedy, terror and oratory, the rally had considerable emotional appeal, notably when Ethel Merman called to the stage microphones a 10-year-old girl, dressed in white, her ash-blond hair caught by a bright red ribbon, and a 5-year-old boy, notable for an eager and wanting-to-be-helpful smile and for an expertly starched blue and white sailor suit.

"Where's your Mommie?" Miss Merman asked the girl.

"In London," she replied.

"Where's your Daddie?" Miss Merman asked the boy.

"In London," he said.

Continued on Page Seven

LOUIS D. BRANDEIS, RETIRED JUSTICE, DIES AT CAPITAL

Member of the Supreme Court for 23 Years Succumbs to Heart Attack at 84

LONG FAMOUS AS LIBERAL

Held People's Rule Should Mean Industrial Democracy as Well as Political

Special to The New York Times.

WASHINGTON, Oct. 5—Louis Dembitz Brandeis, retired Associate Justice of the Supreme Court and one of the greatest liberals in the history of that tribunal, died at his residence here at 7:15 o'clock this evening.

Justice Brandeis, whose name was often linked in dissents with that of the late Justice Oliver Wendell Holmes, would have been 85 years old on Nov. 13. He had a heart attack on Wednesday and had been in a coma for several hours before the end.

At his bedside were Mrs. Brandeis and their two daughters, Mrs. Elizabeth Brandeis Rauschenbusch of the faculty of the University of Wisconsin and Mrs. Susan Brandeis Gilbert, a judge in New York City.

Mrs. Brandeis received from President Roosevelt a message of condolence, which was not made public. It was stated for the family that the funeral would be private and that a memorial service would be held later.

Keen Despite Frail Health

In frail health even before his retirement, Justice Brandeis had been little heard of during the last two years, but his close friends in public and private life kept in touch with him constantly. Remaining almost all the time at his residence, he devoted himself largely to consideration of the problems of Jews, whose plight during the European war and under the Nazi persecutions affected him intensely.

More than 82 years old at the time of his retirement, Justice Brandeis was nevertheless marked for his logic, surprising intellectual energy, and extraordinary ability to obtain the basic facts in legal controversies. But his physical strength was decreasing, and after a siege of grippe in January, 1939, he decided to leave the bench where he had sat so long.

Three other former members of the Supreme Court survive Justice Brandeis, former Chief Justice Charles Evans Hughes, who retired July 1 of this year; Asso-

Continued on Page Nine

NEUTRALITY MOVE MAY BE LIMITED TO ARMING SHIPS

Roosevelt's Legal Aides Are Said to Hold He Has Power to Void Combat Zones

AND OPEN WAY TO SHIPPING

Congress Opponents Talk of Debating Change in Act as a Declaration of War

By FRANK L. KLUCKHOHN

Special to The New York Times.

HYDE PARK, N. Y., Oct. 5—All indications today were that Mr. Roosevelt was preparing for one of the busiest weeks Washington has seen for some time. At a bipartisan meeting with Senate leaders Tuesday morning at the White House, the Executive is expected to make a final decision as to whether repeal or modification of the Neutrality Act is to be asked of Congress. Later in the week he may send his message on modification of the Social Security Act to Capitol Hill.

The President will return to Washington with his hand strengthened by the knowledge that the persistent sinkings in the Atlantic of American-owned ships or ships traveling in the Pan-American "safety" belt have aroused the American public. The sinking of the American-owned tanker I. C. White within the neutrality zone, which Secretary Hull yesterday termed another "act of piracy," is expected to give another fillip to American opinion, which was reported in a Gallup survey published today to be 70 per cent convinced that it is more important to defeat Hitler than to keep the United States out of war.

May Merely Ask Arms for Ships

On the other hand, Mr. Roosevelt is reported to be anxious to avoid a two-months debate in Congress on the Neutrality Act, and that is why modification, rather than repeal, may be decided upon Tuesday, according to some informed sources.

Modification may even be restricted to removing the ban on arming American ships, according to reports in a few quarters. In this case, these reports say, the President, acting under his executive powers, would eliminate by proclamation those of the declared combat zones whose existence has most hampered shipment of war supplies to Britain and her Allies. Some of his legal aides are advising the Executive that he has the power to do the latter under

Continued on Page Four

The International Situation

MONDAY, OCTOBER 6, 1941

Russian troops are still on the offensive all along the line, Moscow declared yesterday. Counterattacks in the Ukraine were said to have made substantial gains and the Leningrad defenders were declared to be driving the Nazis back. Ridiculing Adolf Hitler's claim of Soviet losses, a Soviet spokesman put total Russian losses at 1,128,000 and those of the Germans at 3,000,000. [Page 1, Column 8.]

Berlin's reports confirmed the hard fighting of the Russians, particularly at the approach to the Crimean Peninsula. Minor successes and extensive air activity by the Nazis were reported. [Page 2, Column 2.] Stockholm heard a report that the Germans would abandon their attempt to reduce Leningrad as not worth the cost and would concentrate on other operations, possibly a drive on Moscow. [Follows the above.]

A Moscow broadcast declared that Russian planes had arrived in Yugoslavia to aid rebellious elements there. The Germans were said to be bombing centers of unrest with little effect. Guerrillas have taken more German hostages, it was reported, and have cut the Vienna-Trieste railway in fourteen places. [Page 1, Column 7.]

Moscow's reiteration of the Constitutional provisions in respect to freedom of worship and freedom of anti-religious activity appeared to have brought disappointment to United States Government quarters, where it was felt that an opportunity for real progress by the Soviet had been lost. [Page 1, Columns 6 and 7.]

A survey of British industries revealed that lease-lend materials—finished goods, raw materials and food—were now beginning to arrive in Britain. Misuse of them was vigorously denied. Schools for mechanics have been set up to improve the servicing of American planes. [Page 5, Column 1.]

Lack of a satisfactory reply from Germany continued to delay the exchange of British and German prisoners, but negotiations were continuing and the British believed that the exchange would be consummated shortly. [Page 2, Column 6.]

In Washington, President Roosevelt was expected to take up some move in respect to the Neutrality Act with Congressional leaders tomorrow. Modification rather than repeal was thought to be the likely Administration ground and there were signs that the Congressional opposition was preparing for a fight. [Page 1, Column 5.]

Reports of a naval engagement off the coast of Brazil persisted. Residents of the town of Maragogy said they had heard many shots and had seen one vessel move away under a smoke screen. No details were available in official quarters. [Page 1, Column 6.]

On the Far Eastern scene, conversations were concluded in Manila between Sir Robert Brooke-Popham, Britain's commander in the Orient, and United States defense officers there. A clarification of the United States and Philippine position was believed to have resulted. [Page 3, Column 1.]

RUSSIANS KEEP UP PRESSURE; PUT NAZI LOSSES AT 3,000,000 AND THEIR OWN AT 1,128,000

Moscow Statement on Religion Disappoints White House Circles

President Sees Taylor Tomorrow on Vatican Mission, Now Linked to Issue—Soviet's Stand 'Mockery,' Father Walsh Says

From a Staff Correspondent

HYDE PARK, N. Y., Oct. 5—President Roosevelt talked by telephone today with Myron C. Taylor, his personal representative to the Vatican, who arrived in New York by transatlantic clipper yesterday.

The President arranged to get a comprehensive report on Mr. Taylor's recent conferences with Pope Pius XII in a personal conversation at the White House in Washington Tuesday afternoon, soon after Mr. Roosevelt returns to the capital.

Mr. Taylor is expected on Tuesday to give the President full news on the Pope's attitude toward a diplomatic move seeking to induce Italy to declare a separate peace, and toward the world situation in general.

Mr. Taylor said yesterday in New York that he had information of "the utmost value" to give the President from the persons he talked with in Europe. He telephoned to Mr. Roosevelt this morning from his home at Locust Valley, L. I.

[Little doubt existed around the temporary White House, The Associated Press reported from Hyde Park, that the President wanted to consult Mr. Taylor on the latter's two audiences with Pope Pius, as well as on the animated controversy over freedom of religion in Russia.

[At a press conference in Washington on Friday Mr. Roosevelt left it an open question, pending Mr. Taylor's arrival home, whether he had asked his envoy to take up with the Pope the problem of freedom of worship in the Soviet Union.]

There was little question but that disappointment existed here today over the statement issued in Moscow yesterday by the official spokesman, S. A. Lozovsky, reiterating the guarantees of reli-

Continued on Page Four

HITLER IS DISPUTED

His Claims Cut in Half—Russians Report Gain Near Leningrad

GO 20 MILES IN UKRAINE

Counter-Offensive to Relieve Army in Crimea Is Said to Have Isolated Nazis

By C. L. SULZBERGER

Wireless to The New York Times.

MOSCOW, Oct. 5—The Red Army is continuing strong counterattacks in the Ukraine and in the vicinity of Leningrad. It was reported today that Soviet troops had advanced as much as twenty miles in the former region, reoccupying a strategically important enemy stronghold, and that Major Gen. Knokoff's army in the north had forced another river passage, capturing a strongly defended village and pushing on three more miles.

These fierce sallies on the part of the Russian forces are, perhaps, the best possible answer to Reichsfuehrer Hitler's claims as the sixteenth week of this slowed-up Blitzkrieg begins. However, Alexander Scherbakoff, director of the Soviet Information Bureau, published a lengthy rebuttal to Herr Hitler's boasts of two days ago. Mr. Scherbakoff not only denied the predictions of the Nazi leader, but also gave new estimates of the casualties suffered by the contending armies thus far.

According to these latest official statistics, Russia has lost 1,128,000 men—230,000 killed, 720,000 wounded and 178,000 missing—as well as 7,000 tanks, 8,900 cannon and 5,316 aircraft. The Nazi estimates of Soviet losses were about twice as high as these.

Estimate of Nazi Loss

On the other hand, Mr. Scherbakoff said, the Germans have now lost 3,000,000 men—killed, wounded or prisoners—and 11,000 tanks, 13,000 cannon and 9.000 aircraft.

[The Nazi High Command announced the capture of 12,000 Russians in recent actions in the Southern Ukraine. Extensive Nazi operations on the approaches to Crimea were reported, but it was indicated that the Russians were fighting hard.]

Mr. Scherbakoff's statement indicated not only that the drain on German reserves of man power and matériel was far greater than the drain on those of the U.S.S.R., but also that the disparity between the two was widening and that the Nazis had been losing in increasing proportions during the last two months of fighting. That is quite contrary to Herr Hitler's predictions. The Soviet not only is far from being defeated but is handing back blow for blow and recapturing territory on many salients, according to reports received in the last forty-eight hours.

The recapture of thirty villages in the Ukraine was reported yesterday, and it was asserted today that the Axis lines had been penetrated at several points and that the Russians, in one thrust, had driven nine miles to reoccupy the small town of "B," from which the Germans and Rumanians were driven after sharp street fighting.

Russians Report Pursuit

In two days of fighting for the town the Russians captured fifty-five field pieces and nine tanks and inflicted thousands of casualties, it was reported. The town was said to have been a key point in the enemy defensive system on that salient, as well as a concentration point for forces scheduled to advance. The Russians declared that their tanks were pursuing the retreating Axis units northward.

It is increasingly evident that the extreme length of the front is too much even for the enormous German Army, and more and more advices tell of the extensive use of Hungarian and Rumanian troops. Two Hungarian companies were reported to have been wiped out

Continued on Page Two

BATTLE REPORTED OFF TIP OF BRAZIL

Townspeople Tell of Gunfire by 2 Ships Friday and New Cannonading Saturday

By The Associated Press.

MARAGOGY, Alagoas State, Brazil, Oct. 5—Cannonading at sea accompanied by a display of searchlights last night was reported today by fishermen near Maceio, about sixty miles south of here, indicating possible continuation of a battle believed to have started between unidentified ships late Friday.

Fishermen at Pajussara Beach, near Maceio, said that the rolling thunder of what sounded like big guns came in from far out in the Atlantic.

The people of this coastal town seem firmly convinced that two unidentified ships engaged in a thirty-minute battle, exchanging thirty cannon shots, about twenty miles southeast of here last Friday evening.

Among the townspeople are many who say they saw the action. Almost every one heard the sounds that rumbled in from the sea, along the easternmost coast of Brazil.

"I haven't the slightest doubt that this was naval combat, as shots, characteristic of a cannonade, were heard clearly by all the populace," said Former Mayor Ayres Costa.

This correspondent arrived at Maragogy today to investigate rumors of the battle, which had been circulating widely in Rio de Janeiro since Saturday morning.

Among the first residents he talked with was José Bispo, a fisherman, who said that "after hearing the shots for some time I climbed a hill of about eighty meters (more than eighty yards), from where I saw a ship about twenty miles southeast, but I was unable to identify her as a warship or armored vessel."

"Another ship was more distant and I was able to see only the column of her smoke," he added.

Accounts agree that the sounds like cannonading started at 4:45 P. M. (2:45 P. M., Eastern standard time). About one detonation a minute for the succeeding half-hour was noted.

Mr. Bispo continued:

"When I reached the top of the hill the shooting ended. The nearest vessel was steaming southward and the other was visible only by her small column of smoke, and I was unable to determine if this one was fleeing or had halted to attack. Afterward the nearest ship disappeared over the horizon.

"It is not true, as reported, that lifeboats or wreckage were found on the beaches here or in the vicinity. The only thing seen was

Continued on Page Six

SOVIET FLIERS AID YUGOSLAV REBELS

Moscow Says Russian Planes Are Taking Part in Growing Guerrilla Warfare

By Telephone to The New York Times.

BERNE, Switzerland, Oct. 5—The Moscow radio announced today that "a certain number" of modern Russian bombers had arrived in Yugoslavia to aid the insurgents. Heavy German aerial attacks against several important centers in Hercegovina Province were said to have failed to do more than slight material damage.

The Moscow broadcast also said there had been heavy German troop movements on the eastern frontier of Yugoslavia as large forces were rushed from their Rumanian bases to cope with outbreaks. A battle, reported to have been under way on the Belgrade-Nish railroad during the last four days, was said to have made "considerable progress."

Reports to neutral foreign diplomatic quarters in Berne—mentioned also in the late Moscow radio bulletins but unconfirmed otherwise—indicate guerrilla warfare is widespread in Yugoslavia.

Last night's report that 650 German hostages were held by the Yugoslav guerrillas was amplified this evening by the statement that these hostages included German officers and soldiers.

Reports from Belgrade state that so far the Germans appear not to have carried out their threat to shell the capital "unless guerrilla resistance ceased immediately," presumably, according to a clandestine Yugoslav radio station, "because we hold so many hostages."

Serb Rebel Regime Active

By Telephone to The New York Times.

STOCKHOLM, Sweden, Oct. 5—The Berlin correspondent of the Aftonbladet reports today that an insurrectional Radical Socialist government has been established by Serbian patriots in the mountains of Montenegro and that the Germans are compelled to use dive-bombers to subdue the rebels.

The correspondent said:

"According to a Fascist newspaper, Our Fight, appearing in Belgrade, a Radical Socialist government had been built up in Montenegro under the presidency of a university professor. This government feels itself so firmly in the saddle that it issues passports and visas for those wanting to visit the inaccessible mountains of Montenegro."

The correspondent adds that the general headquarters of the rebels are established in Uzice and that officers of the former Yugoslav Army are commanding more than 10,000 men there.

"A few days ago the occupa-

Continued on Page Five

LOUIS D. BRANDEIS, EX-JUSTICE, 84, DIES

Continued From Page One

ciate Justice George Sutherland, who retired Jan. 5, 1938, and Mr. McReynolds, who left his seat Feb. 1 last. Each is in his eightieth year.

Of the present Supreme Court bench, Chief Justice Stone and Associate Justices Roberts, Black, Reed and Frankfurter were colleagues of Justice Brandeis.

HUGHES EXTOLS BRANDEIS

Ex-Chief Hails 'Imprint Upon Jurisprudence'—Other Tributes

Special to THE NEW YORK TIMES.

WASHINGTON, Oct. 5—Former Chief Justice Charles Evans Hughes tonight issued the following tribute to Justice Brandeis:

"I am profoundly grieved by the passing of Justice Brandeis, my friend of over fifty years. I worked with him in the early days at the bar and I deemed it a high privilege to be associated with him in the work of the court.

"He brought his wide experience and his extraordinary acumen to the service of the public interest and in a judicial career of the highest distinction left his permanent impress upon our national jurisprudence."

Another tribute was that of Judge Louis E. Levinthal of Philadelphia, president of the Zionist Organization of America, who said:

"I find it difficult to express what his loss means to the Zionist movement. He was its sage and mentor. He was the prophet and statesman. He was the kindly guide and friend. Zionists the world over will rededicate themselves at this moment to carry on his ideals and his name shall forever remain a source of hope and determination."

Dr. Solomon Goldman, vice president of the Zionist Organization, who is rabbi of the Anshe Emet Synagogue of Chicago, said:

"The free democratic world will mourn the loss of one of its greatest and most cherished prophets. Few men in our day were as much the embodiment and the symbol of the values most precious to civilized men as Louis Dembitz Brandeis."

B'Nai B'Rith, through its president, Henry Monsky, said that Justice Brandeis "did much by his intellectual integrity and the enduring quality of his judicial opinions to keep the torch of Americanism shining brightly."

SUPREME COURT HONORS BRANDEIS

Brief Session Is Devoted to Stone's Eulogy of Jurist 'of Prophetic Vision'

ROOSEVELT PAYS HOMAGE

Links 'Wisdom and Humanism' of the Justice—Tributes Are Spoken in Senate and House

Special to THE NEW YORK TIMES.

WASHINGTON, Oct. 6—In his first official act as presiding officer of the Supreme Court, Harlan F. Stone, Chief Justice of the United States, paid tribute from the bench today to the character and attainments of Louis Dembitz Brandeis, the 84-year-old retired Associate Justice who died last night.

Hearing the Chief Justice eulogize Justice Brandeis as one of "rare sagacity and wisdom, prophetic vision and integrity of character," the court, meeting for the first session of its 1941-42 term, deferred all of its routine business and in respect to the memory of Justice Brandeis, adjourned until next Monday.

The three-minute session was devoted almost entirely to the official notice of Mr. Brandeis's death.

After the nine Justices ascended the dais, Justice Roberts formally stated that Chief Justice Hughes had retired and President Roosevelt had appointed as his successor Mr. Stone, who had taken the necessary oaths. Mr. Stone made a similar statement concerning Associate Justices James F. Byrnes and Robert H. Jackson.

Tribute of the Supreme Court

Then announcing "with profound sorrow" the death of Justice Brandeis, Chief Justice Stone said:

"Learned in the law, with wide experience in the practice of his profession, he brought to the service of the court and of his country rare sagacity and wisdom, prophetic vision, and an influence which derived power from the integrity of his character and his ardent attachment to the highest interests of the court as the implement of government under a written constitution.

"His death brings to a close a career of high distinction, and life of tireless devotion to the public good.

"As mark of respect to Justice Brandeis's memory the court will adjourn without transacting further business."

Message from the President

President Roosevelt sent this telegram to Mrs. Brandeis from Hyde Park:

"My heart goes out to you and yours in the loss of a loved and loving husband and father who was my faithful friend through the long years. Mrs. Roosevelt joins me in this assurance of deepest sympathy.

"The whole nation will bow in reverence to the memory of one whose life in the law, both as advocate and judge, was guided by the finest attributes of mind and heart and soul. In his passing American jurisprudence has lost one whose years, whose wisdom and whose broad spirit of humanism made him a tower of strength."

Speeches in Senate and House

Eulogies of Justice Brandeis were delivered in the Senate and House.

Senator Walsh, recalling his early associations with Mr. Brandeis in Massachusetts, said that the jurist's "advocacy of liberal economic policy won the esteem, gratitude and affection of the masses."

Senator Barkley of Kentucky, majority leader, recalling the birth of Justice Brandeis in Louisville, praised the jurist as a "great humanitarian," who had been a "sort of Gulf Stream in the judicial history of the country."

In the House, Representative John W. McCormack of Massachusetts, majority leader, praised Justice Brandeis as "one of the greatest Americans of all time."

Memorials to Follow Funeral

A private funeral for Justice Brandeis will be held tomorrow in this city. The family requested that no flowers be sent. Arrangements for a memorial service, presumably in the Senate chamber, will be made later.

Judge Louis E. Levinthal, president of the Zionist Organization of America, stated that special memorial rites for Justice Brandeis will be held Nov. 2 in connection with observance of the twenty-fourth anniversary of the Balfour Declaration.

Miss Sylvia Brody, national president of Junior Hadassah, announced that in memory of Justice Brandeis it would plant 100 trees in Ein Hashofet (Well of the Judges), a cooperative agricultural colony in Palestine.

Louis D. Brandeis

BRANDEIS ESTATE PUT AT $3,200,000

Justice's 27-Page Will Sets Up Trust Funds for His Widow and Daughters

AID FOR 4 PHILANTHROPIES

Survey Associates, University of Louisville, Palestine Fund, Hadassah to Share

Special to THE NEW YORK TIMES.

WASHINGTON, Oct. 7—Louis D. Brandeis, the 84-year-old retired associate justice of the Supreme Court, who died Sunday night, left an estate of nearly $3,200,000, according to his will admitted to probate in the Federal District Court today.

The veteran of almost twenty-three years court service established trust funds for his wife and daughters and made arrangements whereby in certain circumstances, including the death of some beneficiaries, the trust funds would go one-quarter to Survey Associates "for the maintenance of civil liberty and the promotion of workers' education in the United States"; one-quarter to the University of Louisville for its library and law school, and the other one-half equally to Palestine Endowment and Hadassah for "the upbuilding of Palestine as a national home for the Jewish people."

In view of the great detail of the 27-page will, which included many contingencies, officials of the Federal court would not estimate the sum intended for the charities named but in other quarters it was said that at least $1,000,000 was intended for these purposes.

Private funeral services were held for Justice Brandeis at his late residence this afternoon. Chief Justice Stone, fromer Chief Justice Hughes and virtually every associate justice attended the simple ceremonies, at which Dean Acheson, Assistant Secretary of State, and Associate Justice Frankfurter delivered eulogies.

Among those who attended the ceremonies were Mrs. Woodrow Wilson, Mrs. Henry Wallace and Archibald MacLeish. As the funeral procession later passed the Supreme Court Building en route to a cemetery, the court guards stood at attention.

The Brandeis estate totaled $3,178,495.75, in addition to his Summer home at Chatham, Mass., assessed at $9,450. Of the estate, $2,875,356 was in bonds. The remainder was: Cash, $294,139; furniture and furnishings, at Chatham, $1,000; furniture and furnishings at Washington, $3,000; and an 1881 life insurance policy of $5,000. Debts were put at not more than $5,000.

Justice Brandeis came from a well-to-do Louisville, Ky., family and practiced corporation law in Boston before becoming a member of the Supreme Court.

Probate for the will was asked by the executors, Mrs. Brandeis, the former Alice Goldmark; Mrs. Susan Brandeis Gilbert of 1175 Park Avenue, New York City, and Mrs. Elizabeth Raushenbush of Madison, Wis., two daughters; Edward F. McClennen, Justice Brandeis's former law partner, and E. Louis Malloch, both of Cambridge, Mass.

Surplus for "Public Purposes"

In the lengthy document signed on Jan. 16, 1931, Justice Brandeis said:

"I have made for my wife and my daughters provision larger than will be required for that simple living which we have practiced from conviction and which I assume each will continue. I have done this because I desire that each of them shall have ample means to carry forward or otherwise aid the public work in which she may from ttime to time be interested. This course will, I believe, best insure the wise application of the surplus to public purposes."

Under the will, Mrs. Brandeis receives land, buildings and personal belongings. Of the "rest" of the estate, $400,000 or three-eighths or "whichever is larger goes to a trust fund for Mrs. Brandeis. She receives the income and may draw upon the principal. Trust funds each of $200,000 or three-sixteenths or whichever is larger are set up for the daughters who must receive at least $5,000 yearly and may use the principal.

Ages Average Under 56 in Supreme Court As It Convenes Today With Stone as Chief

By The Associated Press.

WASHINGTON, Oct. 5—A Supreme Court averaging slightly under 56 years in age, the youngest in many years, will reassemble tomorrow to plunge into the work of deciding far-reaching legal controversies that accumulated during the four-month Summer recess.

The principal attraction of the opening session of the new eight-month term will be the fact that a new Chief Justice, Harlan F. Stone, and two new Associate Justices, James F. Byrnes and Robert H. Jackson, will take their seats.

All three have taken the required oaths and no ceremony is expected by court attachés. However, high government officials plan to be present.

The appointment of Mr. Jackson, 49 years old, who had been Attorney General, and of Mr. Byrnes, 62, who had been one of President Roosevelt's Senate leaders, caused the average age to drop from slightly above 61. They were selected after the retirement of Chief Justice Charles Evans Hughes and Associate Justice James C. McReynolds, each 79.

Chief Justice Stone had been an Associate Justice since 1925, when he was appointed to succeed Mr. Hughes. Although a New England Republican, he has been one of the most consistent supporters of the Roosevelt Administration's legislation brought before the tribunal. He is 68 years old.

The average age of members of the court in 1937, when elderly members began to retire, was just under 72. That was when President Roosevelt called for "new bood."

Ages of the other present members of the tribunal are: Owen J. Roberts, 65; Hugo L. Black, 55; Stanley F. Reed, 56; Felix Frankfurter, 58; William O. Douglas, 42; Frank Murphy, 48.

Justice Roberts, a Pennsylvania Republican, is the only member of the nine-man tribunal who has not been appointed by President Roosevelt. However, Mr. Stone was originally appointed to the court by President Coolidge. Most of the decisions on New Deal legislation have been pro-Administration since the term that began in October, 1936.

The session tomorrow will be brief. Under present plans, the justices will march into the chamber, admit several attorneys to practice, receive a few motions, and then adjourn for a week.

During the week several conferences will be held to discuss the petitions on file and to determine what controversies will be reviewed. The decisions of the conferences will be announced on Oct. 13.

More than 650 cases already are pending, about 150 in excess of last year and a record for several years.

BRANDEIS TOOK HOLMES MANTLE

Tradition of Liberalism Long Shared With Colleague Maintained by Jurist to the Last

FOR REMOLDING ECONOMY

Concept of Democracy Widened in His Dissents—Lawyer for People Before Rise to Bench

When Justice Oliver Wendell Holmes died, in 1935, the mantle of judicial liberalism long since had been wrapped about the lean shoulders of Louis Dembitz Brandeis, like his mentor an outstanding apostle of dissent. He already had spent a long lifetime in pursuit of justice, both real and in the abstract, before he was appointed to the highest court of the land by Woodrow Wilson in 1916.

Throughout the years that followed he continued to pursue it, handing down decision after decision that sparkled with the integrity of his mind, the breadth of his learning and great human qualities which the exactitudes of legalism were never able to dull.

He had been appointed against the wishes of a united front which used every weapon at its command to keep him from donning the black silken robes of an associate justice of the Supreme Court of the United States. But when, ten years after he had passed man's allotted span, his aquiline face still peered down from the august bench, men and women in every walk of life, including some of his most bitter former enemies, joined in paying him tribute as one of America's best-loved citizens.

In one of his best-known dissenting opinions, Justice Brandeis expressed those qualities which endeared him even to those who, spurred on by President Roosevelt in 1937, felt that an age limit of 70 years should be imposed upon the members of the court. He read this decision in a quiet, almost colorless voice on March 21, 1932, while Herbert Hoover was still President and the New Deal had not been broached. It attracted less attention then than it did later, when its prophetic words had more direct meaning.

Urged Right to Experiment

"Some say that our present plight is due, in large measure, to the discouragement to which social and economic invention has been subjected," he said. "I cannot believe that the framers of the Fourteenth Amendment, or the States which ratified it, intended to leave us helpless to correct the evils of technological unemployment and excess productive capacity which the march of invention and discovery have entailed. There must be power in the States and the nation to remold through experimentation our economic practices to meet changing social and economic needs.

"To stay experimentation within the law in things social and economic is a grave responsibility. Denial of the right to such experimentation may be fraught with serious consequences to the nation. It is one of the happy incidences of the Federal system that a single courageous State may, if its citizens choose, serve as a laboratory; and try novel social and economic experiments without risk to the rest of the country. This court has the power to stay such experimentation. We may strike down the statute embodying it on the ground that, in our opinion, it is arbitrary, capricious or unreasonable; for the due-process clause has been held applicable to substantive law as well as to matters of procedure. But in the exercise of this power we should be ever on guard, lest we erect our prejudices into legal principles.

"If we would guide by the light of reason, we must let our minds be bold."

Behind these words lay, at that time, three-quarters of a century in which Mr. Justice Brandeis had steadfastly endeavored to guide by the light of reason and in which he had been characterized by the boldness of his mind. In his youthful encounters with the law as a corporation attorney in the Massachusetts courts he had gone through an intellectual struggle which had left him, at last, on the side of the consumer and opposed to the beliefs of his former clients.

Some of Causes He Espoused

He fought then, successfully, to keep Boston's transportation under the city's direct control; he reduced the consumer's cost of gas while working out a plan to enable the manufacturers to profit; he broke the industrial life-insurance monopoly—in his own mind his greatest contribution to society—by obtaining passage of a State law permitting savings banks to write policies; he defended the constitutionality of the Oregon ten-hour law for women workers, breaking legal precedent in the submission of his briefs.

He arbitrated the 1910 garment strike in New York, which affected 70,000 workers and $180,000,000 worth of business; he drove Secretary of the Interior Richard A. Ballinger from office in the Indian "land-grab" scandals of the Taft administration, and he fought zealously the battle of the small entrepreneur, summarizing his economic philosophy in the famous phrase, "the curse of bigness."

This was the phrase so long associated with Mr. Brandeis: a phrase as applicable to his philosophy under the New Deal as it was when Woodrow Wilson, daring a flood of gibes, appointed him to the Supreme Court bench. It was said of the Justice that he matured early and never had a chance to change his mind about the fundamentals. In 1905 he said:

"Democracy is only possible—industrial democracy—among people who think . . . and that thinking is not a heaven-born thing. It is a gift men make and women make for themselves. It is earned, and it is earned by effort."

Ten years later he was to write:

"The end for which we must strive is the attainment of rule by the people, and that involves industrial democracy as well as political democracy."

Years later others were to write entire books around this theme, especially after the depression had settled upon America to lend point to the prophetic words of the lawyer who spoke them on the eve of his appointment to the highest judicial court of the land. In 1928 he had carried this belief, expressed in the words "industrial democracy," a little further when he said that there were still "intelligent, informed, just-minded and civilized persons who believe that the growing aggregation of capital through corporations constitutes an insidious menace to the liberty of the citizen."

Hardly a decision was written or concurred in by Justice Brandeis involving this theory of industrial democracy that did not bear the stamp of his fundamental belief.

No change in his philosophy was forced by the New Deal. That which he liked in it he accepted as the cases came before the Supreme Court. That with which he differed he opposed. In 1937 it was estimated that he had voted in favor of the New Deal's viewpoint in twenty-one cases crucially affecting the Administration. In seven instances he had voted against it. He was against the National Recovery Act because—as might have been supposed—it aroused his fundamental dislike for "bigness."

Justice Brandeis upheld the minimum-wage law for women. He was with the unsuccessful minority in the instance of the New York State case; successful, with Justice Roberts, in the Washington State case. He was author of the majority opinion in a much-quoted anti-injunction suit in Wisconsin, a decision which upheld the right to picket, but which did not uphold the right to intimidate; and this caused one observer to write: "Judging by his record, Justice Brandeis would be as much opposed to an overbearing labor union as to an overbearing employer."

His latter-day decisions showed that his mind was unimpaired. Until the end he did his full share in the court, either of pleading or of the handing down of decisions. His famed teas, toward the end, saw him sitting down rather than greeting each guest at the door. Mrs. Brandeis watched him closely, saw that he did not overtax himself.

The Law Was a Window to Him

He was past 82 when one reporter wrote these descriptive words:

"Few judges have been so conversant with the framework of the law. Few have found the law less a prison. To him it was a window

On January 28, 1916, Brandeis was nominated by President Wilson to fill the vacancy in the Supreme Court caused by the death of Associate Justice Joseph R. Lamar.

through which he looked out upon the world—a wide window through which he can see men and women marching toward a far horizon of peace and justice."

Outside the legal sphere, this son of German exiles who fled their native land after the failure of the Revolution of 1848 achieved the respect of men of all faiths by his stern adherence to his own religious beliefs. Often called America's outstanding Jew, he became a leader of the Zionist movement, devoting time, energy and money to this cause.

Inestimable is the influence he had upon younger men, especially in the law. Annually, as did Justice Holmes before him, he had as secretary a selected Harvard law graduate of the preceding June. Many of them have reached distinction in their profession. Men in all walks of life sought advice from him, even after he had become a justice. His almost Spartan simplicity, which never verged on Puritanism, was a characteristic that set him apart in a capital where "the ostentation of democracy" is the rule.

His wide learning, revealed in more than one decision where his footnotes refer not only to scores of law texts, dozens of newspaper and magazine articles ranging from The Nation to The Nation's Business, but to a wide array of books both ancient and modern and, in one instance to a book still in manuscript, set him apart from his brethren on the bench.

Endeared Himself to Millions

Upon the occasion of his seventy-fifth birthday THE NEW YORK TIMES said of Mr. Justice Brandeis it was by his dissenting opinions involving the guarantees of the Bill of Rights that he had endeared himself to millions of citizens.

"But," the newspaper added, "like Mr. Justice Holmes, he is no respecter of persons. His eye is single only to what he believes the right interpretation of the Constitution to be."

After quoting two decisions—one was his opinion in the wire-tapping case during prohibition—which showed from opposite points of view the breadth of his mind, THE TIMES added, "* * * his logic, his learning, the lucid order of his reasoning, his extraordinary penetration of facts, his intellectual energy, have long marked him as one destined to be memorable in the front row of great judges. Too much has been made of his 'liberalism.' This simply means that * * * he regards the Constitution as no iron straitjacket, but as a garment that must fit each generation."

Justice Brandeis was born in Louisville, Ky., on Nov. 13, 1856. The spirit of Jackson and the frontier still hovered over the Kentucky in which this German-Jewish lad grew up in comfort derived from his father's grain business. His maternal grandfather had been a leader in a Polish revolution in 1830; an uncle helped nominate Lincoln for President in 1860; his father was an outspoken Union sympathizer in a hostile land, and his mother had risked her life to bring succor to Northern soldiers.

Thus both his ancestry and his background were such as might well have produced a noted man. His was a cultured family, well enough off financially to send him, after attendance at the Louisville public schools, to the University of Louisville, oldest of municipal colleges in the United States. Long years afterward he was to remember this institution by sending it seven large packets of his personal—and perhaps historically important—papers to be opened after his death.

When his parents took up residence abroad, he entered the Annen Realschule at Dresden, where he studied for three years. He returned to America and received his Bachelor of Laws degree from Harvard in 1877. For a year he practiced law in St. Louis. Then he returned to Boston, where he lived and had a wide law practice until his appointment to the highest bench in 1916.

Established Good Practice

He had made many friends at Harvard, especially among young men who were "going places" in Boston's commercial and legal worlds. Perhaps because at that time he had established no philosophy except how "best to steer his clients toward their chief goal, that of increasing dividends" (as Allen and Pearson, his biographers, put it in "The Nine Old Men") he had little difficulty in establishing a good practice.

His first partnership was in the firm of Brandeis & Warren, which was founded with the late Samuel D. Warren of Boston upon his return from St. Louis. This lasted until 1897, when the firm of Brandeis, Dunbar & Nutter was formed.

It was as a member of this firm that he became counsel for the powerful United Shoe Machinery Company, one of Boston's foremost industrial units. As its attorney and as a director he originated its leasing system whereby the United retained ownership of all the machinery it rented and its leases contained a "tying in" clause which compelled the renter to take all the machinery the United produced. Not only did Mr. Brandeis help organize this system, but he defended it before the State Legislature, maintaining that the leases were monopolies "fully as legal as patents."

Shortly, however, he looked upon this set-up in a different light and tried to revise the United's policy. Failing, he resigned as counsel and for several years refused offers to serve United's rivals as their attorneys. Sixteen years later, in 1911, he represented an alliance of small manufacturers, this time again appearing before the State Legislature to oppose as restraint of trade the system he once had defended.

In the interim, he had swung more and more toward the economic liberalism which found expression in his writings, dissents and occasional majority opinions. Between the years 1907 and 1916 he was active in his new rôle as crusading people's attorney and during this period built up the enmity which all but kept him from the Supreme Court.

Strike Turned Him to Labor

According to his own confession, made years later, it was the Homestead steel strike of 1892 that first set him thinking about the labor problem.

"I had been asked to deliver a series of lectures on common law at the Massachusetts Institute of Technology, but after the Homestead riots I saw that the common law was inadequate and I threw the lectures away," he said.

His first entrance into the lists was in 1897, when he went to Washington to "represent those who form a larger part of the people of this country than any who have found representation here." He spoke thus at his first appearance before the Ways and Means Committee of the House, then considering the Dingley Tariff Act. It was almost unprecedented that any one should appear in behalf of "the people"—the ultimate payers of the tariff costs. He was jeered and sneered at by the committee but he spoke his piece.

Next he attracted attention by his arduous fight against the proposed fifty-year lease of the Boston subway system. His efforts forced the Boston Elevated Railway Company to accept a twenty-year lease and upon conditions far more favorable to the city than the transit company had desired. This did not make him too many friends in high places on State Street.

At about this same time—between 1907 and 1913—he turned his attention to the Boston Gas Company and forced it to put a sliding-scale rate into effect. This, incidentally, served to raise dividends as rates were lowered, so that in the long run both sides of the deal profited. Then he turned to the New Haven Railroad.

Aided by some of the most distinguished barristers in Boston and New York, the New Haven was seeking a monopoly of the transportation systems of New England and was attempting to seize control of the Boston & Maine. Mr. Brandeis opposed this vigorously. Here he was beginning to show his philosophy of the "curse of bigness." "Size brings monopoly instead of competition; size submerges the talents of millions of people, and the wealth of the nation is gauged by the capacity of great numbers and not by the few."

His social consciousness was developing all the time, and, while his law practice was lucrative, he found time for matters that satisfied his conscience more than his pocketbook. He was "people's counsel" in behalf of the Oregon and Illinois women's ten-hour law, the California eight-hour law and the Oregon State minimum wage law between 1900 and 1907, all models of social legislation by the State. He fought the Oregon law through half a dozen courts with dogged persistence before he was successful.

Mr. Brandeis exposed during this period the manner in which the Equitable Life Assurance Society was, in his opinion, wasting its policyholders' money, and from this beginning manoeuvred the then unique Massachusetts State Insurance plan through the Legislature. This, too, stands as a model of its kind. Around its workings Mr.

Brandeis wrote many treatises on insurance, and he never tired of the subject, being a firm believer in State-managed insurance companies, a form vigorously fought by the large, private companies for many years. In 1936 he proudly pointed out a 30 per cent increase in savings bank insurance in the year's first quarter.

By this time Mr. Brandeis was looked upon with suspicion by many of his former friends, and was termed a traitor to his class—but he went ahead in his own way. In 1910 he represented Atlantic Coast trade organizations before the Interstate Commerce Commission in a memorable fight against railroad rate increases. He argued that the railroads could save $1,000,000 a day. These hearings gave him a national reputation as a man with a passion for facts and a superb ability to use them in grueling cross-examination which left many a witness limp by the end of the day. These hearings took place in 1910 and 1911 and again in 1913 and 1914.

In 1914 Mr. Brandeis served as special counsel for the government in the suit brought by the Riggs National Bank of Washington. The bank sought injunctions against Secretary William G. McAdoo, United States Treasurer Burke and Controller Williams, charging that these men had "conspired to wreck the bank."

Efforts were made to drive Mr. Brandeis from the case and at one time he threatened to withdraw but was prevailed upon by Samuel Untermyer to remain as counsel. He did, and was successful in proving the government's contention that the bank had speculated unlawfully and committed other illegal acts.

Defended Ousted Official

Another case which brought Mr. Brandeis to the attention of the country was his defense of Louis R. Glavis, who had been dismissed as investigator for the Department of the Interior in 1910. Mr. Glavis had revealed a "land-grab," and the scandal reflected upon the integrity of his chief, Secretary Ballinger. Mr. Brandeis's vehement cross-examination not only caused the resignation of Mr. Ballinger but caught President Taft in some uncomfortable positions because of his attempt to shield the Secretary of the Interior, his Cabinet appointee.

A storm broke out when, in 1913, Woodrow Wilson, who became President that year, selected Mr. Brandeis as his Attorney General, an appointment that was withdrawn when the cry of "radical" was raised against the Boston lawyer. This storm, however, was nothing to that which broke when, in 1916, Mr. Wilson named him to the Supreme Court. Mr. Wilson was accused of seeking the Jewish vote by his choice, feeling that it was necessary to offset the loss of certain of the conservative element, especially in New England, where the hatred against Mr. Brandeis was most vociferous.

Leaders of the bar raged. Mr. Taft, recalling the Ballinger episode, fought the appointment. Business men and public utilities representatives came to Washington to argue against the former "people's crusader," the man who knew the "curse of bigness." Arrayed against him were men of the school of social and economic thought later characterized by Franklin D. Roosevelt as the "economic royalists." Every former president of the American Bar Association stood against him.

The fight raged from January until June, but Mr. Brandeis was confirmed finally by the Senate after Oscar Underwood had spread the record of his opponents before the Senate, showing their lack of disinterestedness in fighting confirmation. Chief Justice Taft was later to admit to Mr. Brandeis that he had done him a great injustice. Senator Borah apologized. But no apology was forthcoming from many others.

As an associate justice, Mr. Brandeis's record was primarily as a jurist of a transitional society. His thought was geared to social change. Although he was often linked in the famous phrase, "Holmes and Brandeis dissenting," he was not merely the elder jurist's follower. Mr. Brandeis had his eyes fixed upon society's mutations; Mr. Holmes "delighted to observe the essential identities behind them." The elder jurist believed in the right of the people to experiment. Mr. Brandeis went further. Mr. Brandeis read economics; Mr Holmes reread Plato.

As a justice Mr. Brandeis did not revise his economic doctrines but, in the words of Max Lerner, he stood by his guns that "wherever monopoly has taken the place of former competitive units he wishes to restore and maintain competition; where, in a competitive situation, unfair practices threaten the competitive equilibrium he wishes to curb them and so maintain the plane of competition; where competition is impossible or undesirable, due to the nature of the industry, he wishes to pattern the system of control as closely as possible upon . . . putative competition."

Of the sixteen major New Deal laws which were brought before the Supreme Court for decision Justice Brandeis sided with the administration in ten instances. The first of the few New Deal legal victories was the gold devaluation case, in which the court split 5 to 4, Justices Hughes, Stone, Roberts and Cardozo voting with Mr. Brandeis to sustain.

In October, 1938, Justice Brandeis was stirred out of his judicial seclusion. He had begun his career as "the people's advocate," and toward the end he again became just that.

Forgetting the robes of office, because a high humanitarian cause in which he had always been interested called him, he turned his attention and thereby the attention of many other Americans to the plight of the Jews of the world.

Making one of his rare public appearances in the twenty-two years he had then been on the bench of the country's highest court, the venerable Brandeis, white of hair but still steady of gait and unflinching of mind, went to the White House.

There for more than two hours he was closeted with President Roosevelt. Neither announced what was discussed; none doubted that the question of Jewish refugees from Nazi Germany was the topic. Some commentators went as far as to suggest that Mr. Roosevelt's stand against Hitler after the Munich pact stemmed from this talk.

Although throughout his many years on the bench Justice Brandeis was intensely interested in Zionism, it was not until after 1910 that he became associated with this cause. Before that time, according to Jacob de Haas, one of his biographers, he had taken little or no interest in Jewish affairs. It undoubtedly was his close connection with the New York garment strike of that year which drew his attention to the plight of Jewry. Previously his life had not led him into contact with the working class of Jews.

Became Active in Zionism

Justice Brandeis's first public utterance on Zionism, which, if he had thought of it at all, had been merely as a subject of academic interest, was in the form of an interview in The Jewish Advocate, a Boston daily newspaper. There he set forth some of his principles as they applied to his own race. He began by stating that there was no room anywhere for "hyphenated Americans," and spoke of the obligations of Jews to American institutions. Under a complete democracy, he said, there should be an elimination of class distinction. The lawyer in him caused him to recall that racial discrimination is prohibited by the Constitution.

Three years later, at Boston's Plymouth Theatre, he made his first speech in behalf of Zionism. It was not until after the outbreak of the European war, which made necessary transfer of the conduct of Zionist affairs to the United States, that Justice Brandeis was persuaded to take an active part. When he did he conducted himself with his customary vigor and attention, devoting much of his time to the cause. In August, 1914, he was elected chairman of the Zionist Provisional Emergency Committee at an extraordinary meeting called at the Hotel Versailles in New York.

Thereafter and for several years he was considered one of the outstanding American advocates of Zionism. In June, 1915, he delivered an address before the Eastern Council of the Central Conference of Reform Rabbis which was historic. Entitled "The Jewish Problem: How to Solve It," it was later reprinted in pamphlet form and ran into more than five editions. In it he followed the theories previously suggested by Theodor Herzl. Its most striking portion was that in which he clearly defined the difference between nation and nationality, and set forth the rights of minority groups.

That year Mr. Brandeis presided at many sessions of the international Zionist convention held in Boston and delivered several addresses. It was there that the Jewish Congress movement began, in which both Mr. Brandeis and Dr. Cyrus Adler were active. The following June a mass meeting was held in New York's Carnegie Hall for the purpose of arousing public interest in the Congress and Mr. Brandeis was the principal speaker. The next four years saw him active, despite the fact that he was elevated to the Supreme Court during this period.

Break With Movement

Always Mr. Brandeis sought to approach the Jewish problem without abandoning the essential Americanism of his methods, as outlined even in his initial interview on the subject that for a decade had been close to his heart. When the Zionist leadership failed to agree with his methods he broke with Zionism and did not travel its path again until 1938, when the plight of the German Jews brought him, old but not infirm, back into the arena. Between 1920 and 1938 the jurist seemed content to confine his guidance to private consultations. He neither wrote nor spoke publicly on the subject.

Mr. Brandeis joined with seven other justices in affirming the Tennessee Valley Authority case over the lone dissent of Justice McReynolds. He also voted for the Arms Embargo Act for the Chaco War and in two other minor instances sustained the New Deal.

Mr. Brandeis did not always dissent in favor of the New Deal in its defeats. His own economic predilections kept him from dissenting in the National Recovery Act case, which lost, 9—0. He supported the Agricultural Adjustment Act, which lost, 6 to 3. He supported the wage and hour regulations of the Guffey Coal Act, but he voted against the Federal regulations of "hot oil." He sided with the full bench in finding the conversion of building and loan associations to Federal charters when opposed by the States to be unconstitutional. He did the same in the unanimous decision finding the dismissal of William E. Humphrey from the Federal Trade Commission to be an illegal act by President Roosevelt.

With Justices Hughes, Stone and Cardozo, he voted for the original Railway Pension Act which the majority disapproved, and with Justices Stone and Cardozo he believed, although six justices did not, that the Security Exchange Commission had a right to compel J. E. Jones of New York to testify about a stock issue proposed and withdrawn before the regulations became effective. He joined the minority of four to defend the Municipal Bankruptcy Act, but did not dissent from the AAA processing tax refunding case.

Letter of Resignation

On Monday, Feb. 13, 1939, Justice Brandeis sent the following brief letter to President Roosevelt:

Dear Mr. President:

Pursuant to the act of March 1, 1937, I retire this day from regular active service on the bench.

Cordially,
LOUIS D. BRANDEIS.

Thus laconically was ended the long service of the liberal justice. To his letter President Roosevelt replied:

My Dear Mr. Justice Brandeis:

One must perforce accept the inevitable. Ever since those days long ago when you first took your seat on the Supreme Court bench I have come to think of you as a necessary and very permanent part of the court—and since 1933 as one who would continue his fine service there until long after I had left Washington.

The country has needed you through all these years, and I hope you will realize, as all your old friends do, how unanimous the nation has been in its gratitude.

There is nothing I can do but accede to your retirement. But with this goes the knowledge that our long association will continue, and the hope that you will be spared for many long years to come to render additional services to mankind.

FRANKLIN D. ROOSEVELT.

Much speculation followed as to who would be selected by President Roosevelt as his successor. The post went to William Orville Douglas, then chairman of the Securities and Exchange Commission.

Age and failing health brought about the justice's sudden decision to retire, which was announced dramatically at the end of a day in which he had taken part in the work of the court. A week before he had returned to the bench after a month's absence caused by grippe and a disease of the heart.

He spent his last years in retirement working for the Zionist movement, reading, writing letters and talking with his friends.

On Nov. 13, 1940, when Justice Brandeis celebrated his eighty-fourth birthday, he received hundreds of congratulatory messages from all parts of the country and abroad. Zionists held special functions in Washington and in the Palestine colony of Ein Hashofet, which was established in his honor in 1937 by American Jewish boys of the Zionist colonizing group, Hashomer Hatzair.

In his private life Mr. Brandeis was simple, even austere. His Washington home was a model of unostentation and long the gathering place—despite the host's advanced years and the supposed inaccessibility of Supreme Court justices—of leaders in many realms of endeavor. Hosts of social workers, lawyers, executives knew and admired him and turned to him for advice and inspiration.

Justice Brandeis had a musty office above his living quarters, crowded with books, where his secretary worked. He himself worked downstairs, in a small, almost bare room. But he had a view of sprawling, low-lying Washington that was impressive. There he wrote, in pencil, his decisions, taking meticulous care. During 1936, when 80, he wrote sixteen decisions.

Mr. Brandeis married the former Alice Goldmark of New York on March 23, 1891. They had two daughters, Susan (Mrs. Jacob H. Gilbert) and Elizabeth (Mrs. Stephen Raushenbush).

Mr. Justice Brandeis and his wife on his 83rd birthday.

"All the News That's Fit to Print"

The New York Times.

LATE CITY EDITION
Partly cloudy today and tomorrow; somewhat warmer tomorrow.
Temperature Range Today-Max., 80; Min., 67
Temperatures Yesterday—Max., 74; Min., 69
Full U. S. Weather Bureau Report, Page 37

VOL. LXXIV...No. 24,656. NEW YORK, MONDAY, JULY 27, 1925. TWO CENTS In Greater New York | THREE CENTS Within 200 Miles | FOUR CENTS Elsewhere in the U. S.

ABD-EL-KRIM OFFERS TO NEGOTIATE PEACE; PETAIN TO RETURN

Marshal Expected Back in Paris to Confer on Deal With Moors.

RIFF CHIEF ASKS PLEDGE

Wants Assurance of His Country's Independence as Condition of Conference.

SELECTS TANGIER FOR IT

His Tribesmen Prepared to Kill Their Women and Children and Die Fighting, He Says.

Special Cable to THE NEW YORK TIMES.

PARIS, July 26.—The most significant development of the Moroccan situation today is an announcement of Marshal Pétain's intention of return to Paris within the next ten days. Entire direction of the operations in the field was given him only a few days ago and it is generally believed here that he would not be leaving the scene of action unless he felt the crisis had been resolved and the end of the war was definitely in sight.

In well-informed quarters the conviction even prevails that Marshal Pétain is not to present the Government with a plan of campaign when he returns, but with a peace plan which he has been able to develop as the result of his personal contact with the situation.

Abd-el-Krim Offers to Parley.

Special Cable to THE NEW YORK TIMES.

TANGIER, July 26.—Abd-el-Krim informs me that he has replied to the Franco-Spanish note which stated that the terms of peace which the French and Spanish Governments were prepared to offer him were at his disposal if he wished to consult them.

Abd-el-Krim [illegible] that he is prepared to [illegible] with France and Spain on condition that before the negotiations are opened he shall receive solemn assurance that the Riff will enjoy independence. In a separate communication he demands that the negotiations shall take place at Tangier.

I am informed that if France and Spain agree to these two stipulations Abd-el-Krim is prepared to cease hostilities and enter upon immediate negotiations for permanent peace.

The French and Spanish Governments will probably receive Abd-el-Krim's reply tomorrow.

It is not difficult to surmise the main lines of the peace terms which Spain and France are willing to offer Obd-el-Krim. These main lines are in a measure independence for the Riff under the sovereignty of the Sultan and under the authority of the Khalifa of the Spanish zone, with the proposed title of Emir for Abd-el-Krim; rectification of the French protectorate frontier by granting the Riffs facilities for procuring and growing grain and other foodstuffs, assistance in introducing home rule in the Riff and a semblance of disarmament of the tribes.

What Riff Chief Hopes For.

The press of Europe and Morocco has lately published very diverse accounts of what Abd-el-Krim himself demands, but as a matter of fact Abd-el-Krim has never stated any definite terms. He has from time to time as a measure of propaganda told journalists who visited him and has announced to the tribes that he will insist upon the cession of Tetuan Laraiche and Arsella, and only intends to leave in possession of the Spaniards Ceuta, Melilla and the smaller presidios.

At times his successes have almost made such demands possible, but that day has passed and even his most enthusiastic followers realize that all that today is beyond his reach. For some months it has been an open secret that Abd-el-Krim has abandoned all claim to Tetuan and other towns, the capture of which he had promised the Jabala as a means of procuring their assistance.

In return for the abandonment of Tetuan he speaks of demanding an indemnity of 25,000,000 Spanish pesetas. He bases his claim on the ground that when after the Spanish War in Morócco in 1859 the Spaniards consented to evacuate Tetuan they received an indemnity of that amount from the Sultan. The Riff leader argues that as the Spanish Government agreed by treaty to abandon Tetuan in perpetuity and since has reoccupied it he can justly demand the return of the sum extorted from his country on that occasion.

The difficult point in the peace negotiations must turn upon the measure of independence which Abd-el-Krim is to enjoy. It is not only difficult from his personal point of view, but still more so because it is the only subject on which he made definite promises to the Riff tribes. All other subjects of negotiation are for him and him alone to settle, but this question of independence is shared by all. He has definitely promised the tribesmen not to negotiate peace except on the understanding that independence of the Riff is assured. It was the only price by which he could obtain their full-hearted cooperation.

Realizes His Limitations.

Complete independence, however, is impossible, partly because of existing treaties but more from the fact that Abd-el-Krim and his Riffians are not

Continued on Page Five.

Treviso Statue Declared To Be by Michelangelo

TREVISO, Italy, July 26 (AP).—Officials of the Venetian Art Academy have announced that a terra cotta statue found some time ago by Eugenio Loschi, a public employe, is the work of Michaelangelo.

The statue is about 24 inches high. Loschi will present it to the Vatican through the local Bishop.

The recent discovery in the Vatican of seven terra cotta statuettes by Michelangelo led Loschi to request art experts to come to Treviso and examine the object he had found.

INQUIRY THREATENS PUBLIC LAND SCANDAL

Senate Committee Will Begin Delving Soon Into Alleged Maladministration.

WIDESPREAD CHARGES MADE

Allegations Against Park Service and Forestry Bureau to Have Full Airing.

Special to The New York Times.

WASHINGTON, July 26.—The Senate Committee on Public Lands, the committee which exposed the Teapot Dome and Elk Hills Naval Reserve Oil leases, is going hunting again. This time it is going to investigate the administration of the public domain, the Forestry Bureau and the national parks. According to some members of the committee the investigation is expected to develop a situation which will parallel in interest the sensational developments of the naval oil hearings. The committee will act under a Senate resolution passed near the close of the last Congress and its authority is virtually unlimited.

Governor Pinchot of Pennsylvania, a former Chief Forester of the Government, a few days ago gave out a statement warning the "friends of the forest service" that an assault against that Government bureau is about to start. The Governor did not mention the Senate, but it is known that he had the Public Lands Committee in mind. And the national forest question is going to be thoroughly investigated. For instance, Senator Cameron of Arizona is authority for the statement that of the more than 136,000,000 acres of public land in the Federal forest reserve more than 90,000,000 acres are treeless. There is one forest in Arizona, it is charged, 13,000,000 acres in extent, that never has had a tree on it since the beginning of the world.

The administration of the forest reserve, as well as the public domain, the latter 186,000,000 acres in extent, has, it is alleged by certain Western Senators, worked great injury to the stock raising business.

The cattle industry, it is asserted, has almost touched bottom, and one of the main subjects of the inquiry will be to find a way, if possible, to resuscitate this business.

In one Western town, it was pointed out, bank failures, due mainly to the crisis in the cattle industry, involved bank losses exceeding $10,000,000. There are scores of other towns, it is asserted, which have been proportionately hard hit for the same reason.

Cattlemen who a few years ago were reputed wealthy, some of them millionaires, are now poverty stricken, according to stories current in legislative circles. A case cited is that of a man who six years ago was said to be worth more than $1,000,000. Recently this man accepted a job as an assistant sergeant-at-arms of a Western State Legislature.

One other case is that of a cattleman who had been listed as among the wealthiest men in his community. He is now running a little adobe hotel in a town of less than 500 population.

Questions Midwest Company's Deals.

It is asserted that these are but samples of thousands of other cases involving men who were mainstays of the great cattle business a few years back.

The homesteading features of the public domain administration will be another phase of the inquiry, as will also the disposition of mineral and oil lands, other than those included in the naval reserves.

One feature of the oil part of the investigation is expected to involve the Salt Creek (Wyo.) holdings of the Midwest Refining Company, a subsidiary of the Standard of Indiana. Salt Creek adjoins Teapot Dome, but it is a vastly richer field than the Sinclair lease.

Senator Walsh of Montana, a member of the committee, said recently that there is no more important duty facing

Continued on Page Five.

SINNOTT FIRM HIRES MAX STEUER TO SUE ON BOND EXPOSURES

Lawyer Says Libel Actions Will Be Brought Against Craig, Kerrigan and Newspapers.

SEES "VENOM" IN CHARGES

Declares Recent Published Statements Require That Proceedings Be Brought.

WON'T HALT INVESTIGATION

"Let Them Go Ahead," Is Controller's Comment—Wants Chance to Get Hylan on the Stand.

Announcement that the bonding and insurance firm of Sinnott & Canty would bring libel actions against Controller Charles L. Craig, Deputy Controller Charles F. Kerrigan, and those newspapers which have published statements from either of them regarding the investigation of alleged relations between the firm and the Mayor's office, was made yesterday by Max D. Steuer, attorney for the members of the firm.

Mr. Steuer said that he had at first advised the members of the firm, the head of which, J. Paul Sinnott, is a brother of John F. Sinnott, Mayor Hylan's secretary and son-in-law, not to bring suit because he sought to keep them out of a political controversy into which he believed Mr. Craig and Mr. Kerrigan were seeking to force them. Mr. Steuer added that recent published statements by Mr. Craig and Mr. Kerrigan were "so much more veromous" that he had determined that the best interests of Sinnott & Canty required that an action be brought and that the facts be developed in court.

Mr. Craig and Mr. Kerrigan, neither of whom had been served with notice of any action yesterday, declared that no libel action would be permitted to interrupt their investigation. Mr. Craig declared that he would welcome the opportunity to have the members of the Sinnott & Canty firm and Mayor Hylan examined on the witness stand.

Steuer Issues Statement.

Mr. Steuer's statement, announcing the determination to bring libel actions, follows:

"When the articles instigated by Controller Craig and his deputy, Charles Kerrigan, first began to appear in the press, the firm of Sinnott & Canty conferred with me concerning their rights against the individuals who instigated them and the press that continued to publish them. I advised Messrs. Sinnott & Canty then that upon the facts as submitted by them, the articles were clearly libelous and that for the damage by them sustained each of the defendants could be compelled to answer.

"Nevertheless, I suggested that they abstain from commencing any actions because of the fact that the claim would immediately be put up that the suits were brought solely to aid the present City Administration in anticipation of the coming primaries and election.

"Solely because of my insistence, they abstained not only from commencing suits, but from demanding that criminal prosecutions be instituted. With each separate publication they submitted to me a statement of the facts as they claimed them to be and as investigation actually indicates they are. On each occasion, however, I adhered to the view that I first expressed, and although they became more and more desirous of putting their version before the public, I advised against it, seeking to keep them out of a political controversy that seemingly Mr. Craig, Mr. Kerrigan and others were attempting to force Sinnott & Canty into.

"The recent publications, however, are so much more venomous, encouraged very likely by the previous silence of these men, that I have finally determined that the best interests of Sinnott & Canty make necessary the immediate commencement of actions against Mr. Craig, Mr. Kerrigan and the various newspapers that have seen fit to publish these articles maliciously calculated to deceive the public and to grievously injure the firm as well as the individuals whose names figure therein.

"In consequence thereof, I have advised my assistants to immediately cause process to be served upon Mr. Craig, Mr. Kerrigan and each of the newspapers in which these articles appeared, and such process is now out for service.

"The only place, in my opinion, where the real facts can be developed satisfactorily is the courts, and at the earliest moment the plaintiffs will seek a

Continued on Page Five.

Palestine Explorers Find Chambers in Rock That May Prove to Be the Tomb of David

Special Cable to THE NEW YORK TIMES.

JERUSALEM, July 26.—Discovery of what it is hoped may prove to be the long-sought tomb of David was announced today by the Rev. J. Garrow Duncan of the Palestine Exploration Fund.

The Rev. Mr. Duncan states that the excavations at Ophel brought to light on the western side a series of underground rock-cut chambers comprising a large central room, with five smaller chambers, five feet square, branching from it. The southernmost room, which is fifteen by sixteen feet in size, leads into two rooms, each fifteen by eight feet. These again lead into similar narrow chambers, each with smaller chambers cut into its walls.

Toolmarks on the walls are of the Iron Age period and not earlier than 1000 B. C. There is a similar series of rock chambers and galleries on the eastern side of Ophel, entered from the face of a rock scarp under the Jebusite east city wall and closed by a curious stone door. It is considered not improbabl that this constitute David's tomb, and the probability is that both sets of parts constitute a series of royal tombs. Its series is much abused by later usage, first as an olive press and as store rooms in the Byzantine period, then as cisterns by Arabs.

Coolidges Take Little Space In North Shore 'Who's Who'

Special to The New York Times.

SWAMPSCOTT, Mass., July 26.—Very modest is the manner in which President and Mrs. Coolidge and their son John Coolidge are listed in the 1925 issue of Who's Who Along the North Shore, distributed yesterday. Their names appear under the Cs as follows:

Coolidge, President and Mrs. Calvin, Swampscott, Little's Point, White Court. Winter residence, Washington, D. C., the White House. President of the United States. (Mrs. Coolidge was Grace A. Goodhue.)

Coolidge, John, with President and Mrs. Coolidge (son), Swampscott. Student at Amherst College.

BUCKNER TO BARGAIN WITH DRY VIOLATORS

Prosecutor Will Ask for Fines for Small Offenders Who Plead Guilty.

JAIL FOR THOSE WHO FIGHT

Drive Planned to Clear Docket of 2,000 Cases for New Campaign in the Fall.

United States Attorney Emory R. Buckner will open his second drive on the overcrowded liquor calendar before Judge Edwin L. Garvin in the Federal Court today. This campaign, he said, would be in the nature of a bargain sale and those of the 2,000 petty offenders who pleaded guilty would be fined and those who stood trial and were convicted would be recommended for a jail term. He said he expected to clear up the 2,000 cases in the coming week, after which he would take up the fifty padlocking cases which were ready for presentation.

To accommodate the expected crowd of owners and employes of speakeasies Mr. Buckner cut departmental red tape and has had his own force remove the chairs and tables from the special court room. When Mr. Buckner undertook to have the custodian of the building remove the chairs and tables he found that the order would have to travel by a roundabout way to Washington for official sanction and then be returned for the further approval of a Judge.

"I have told Judge Garvin that I think it is in the public interest and in the interest of prohibition enforcement to clean up these 2,000 small cases on the basis of a July clearance bargain sale," he said. "I have recommended, and I hope he will approve, the imposition of fines running from $50 to $100 upon all who plead guilty, and jail sentences upon all who stand trial and are convicted.

No Bargains in the Fall.

"We want to clear ourselves of all stock of this character and we hope to open in the Fall with an entirely new line of prohibition goods. We shall discontinue the five and ten-cent counter in accordance with the policy which has been in effect since I took office, so far as new cases are concerned, and we will deal only, generally speaking, in the padlock for the retailer and jail sentences for the bootlegger, the wholesaler, the importer, the manufacturer, and the financial backer.

"Prohibition enforcement will get nowhere in this district until the owner of the retail establishment finds himself padlocked on the outside, and until the man who supplies him with liquor finds himself padlocked on the inside.

"The policy of stopping petty arrests and concentrating upon the men higher up and those actively engaged in the bootleg trade, which I put into effect five months ago, has been cordially approved by Gen. Lincoln C. Andrews.

"The thousands of petty arrests which have been made in this district during the past few years have so swamped Federal machinery as to render it impossible to wage a concentrated and sustained war against the rum-runners and bootleggers and manufacturers. The Federal officials have been trying to run a marathon on tanglefoot flypaper. The piling up of thousands of arrests and the collection of hundreds of thousands of dollars' worth of fines, calling them 'convictions,' make a very impressive 'record,' but from the standpoint of law enforcement are nothing but a farce.

Explains His Plans.

"This farce has been aggravated by the absolute necessity of dealing with these petty offenses only on a fine basis, as there has not been any remote possibility of trials before juries and jail sentences for the smallest fraction of them. It is a little short of compounding with crime for the Government to take this dirty money and call it rigid enforcement of the prohibition law.

"An arrest is the beginning and not the end of law enforcement. Until Federal officials look only at the end of a prosecution and not at the beginning of a prosecution, we shall make no headway in dealing with the formidable and vexatious problem of prohibition in this district.

"When Judge Garvin cleans up the 2,000 petty liquor cases to be brought before him this week there will be no more cases of that type, generally speaking, so long as I am in office. I am not picking and choosing prosecutions according to whim or caprice, or attempting to repeal the law in part and enforce it in part. I am simply picking and choosing prosecutions in accordance with the number of Judges, the number of assistants and the number of clerks which are provided by the Federal Government, and my oath of office not only justifies but actually compels me to employ this limited machinery in the manner which will peg out the greatest advance in the enforcement of the prohibition law, while at the same time enabling me to enforce other laws with equal regard.

"I cannot, in justice to the rest of my job, devote more than 25 per cent. of my equipment to the enforcement of the prohibition law, and I want to make this 25 per cent. produce the greatest results which it is capable of producing rather than merely to keep it conspicuously busy milling around with a mob of petty violators of the Volstead act."

W. J. BRYAN DIES IN HIS SLEEP AT DAYTON, WHILE RESTING IN EVOLUTION BATTLE; HAD SPOKEN CONTINUOUSLY SINCE TRIAL

LARGE EFFECT IN POLITICS

Democrats Divided as to How Bryan's Death Touches Party.

GREAT CREATOR OF ISSUES

Fear Had Arisen, However, That the Commoner Would Cause a Religious Schism.

HAD PREMONITION OF DEATH

Bryan Felt His Strength Was Waning at the Convention Here a Year Ago.

By RICHARD V. OULAHAN.
Special to The New York Times.

WASHINGTON, July 26.—Practically deserted during this heated season of those politically prominent, there were few in Washington this evening who had been associated with William Jennings Bryan or had known him during his active career since he came here a young Congressman from Nebraska in 1893, thirty-two years ago.

For that reason it cannot be said, in the sense of widespread knowledge of it, that Mr. Bryan's sudden death created a sensation in the national capital. But to the meagre number of those here tonight whose public life had brought them into close contact with the great Commoner the news of his passing came as a distinct shock. That was apparent from their exclamations when they were informed of the tragic happening in the little Tennessee town where he so recently fought his last battle for principles in which he believed and to the promotion and defense of which he devoted every bit of his abundant energy.

The death of Mr. Bryan was entirely unexpected in Washington, but that he was not in the best of physical condition and had feared for some time that his days were numbered was disclosed by a fellow Nebraskan, also a Democrat, Gilbert M. Hitchcock, former Senator, who was Chairman of the Senate Committee on Foreign Relations when Mr. Bryan was Secretary of State.

Spoke of Death at Convention.

Their official duties during the rather brief period of Mr. Bryan's tenure in the Cabinet interlocked, and years before then they had been on the most intimate professional and personal terms through the fact that Mr. Bryan was the editor of The Omaha World-Herald, owned by Mr. Hitchcock. But in more recent times they were bitter personal opponents in the leading rôles they played within the Democratic Party.

When he had recovered from the distinct shock that the news of Bryan's death caused him, the former Senator said that, on reflection, it was not so surprising, as he recalled that during the Democratic National Convention in Madison Square Garden last year Mr. Bryan had told his fellow members of the Committee on Resolutions, when they were engaged in the bitter contest over the matter of including a denunciation of the Ku Klux Klan in the party platform, or omitting reference to it, that he felt that his life was fast coming to an end.

"I think he had a premonition," said Mr. Hitchcock. "He could not any longer stand fatigue. I served with him on the Committee on Resolutions during the convention and he told us in committee that this would be the last convention he would attend. He seemed to have a feeling that he would not live. He had overtaxed himself so much. Evidently the struggle in Dayton during the hot weather was too much."

That the premonition of an early death had been in Mr. Bryan's mind prior to the Democratic convention a year ago was indicated by Mr. Davis, who disclosed that his former chief had written to him about two years ago with reference to obtaining a plot of ground in Arlington for the last resting place of Mrs. Bryan and himself. Mr. Davis at

Continued on Page Two.

© Underwood & Underwood.

WILLIAM JENNINGS BRYAN,
Who Died Suddenly Yesterday Afternoon at a Friend's Home in Dayton, Tenn.

BRYAN IS EULOGIZED, EVEN BY OPPONENTS

Leaders of Varying Political and Religious Beliefs Join in Tributes.

HONORED FOR SINCERITY

Governor Smith, Mayor Hylan and John W. Davis Among Many Praising Him.

Political friends and foes of William Jennings Bryan, Modernists and Fundamentalists, were shocked and saddened by the news of his death last night.

His immense vigor and activity during the last few weeks heightened the surprise caused by his death. He was thought to be hale and hearty enough to be the leading champion of the causes of Fundamentalism and prohibition for many years to come.

The political and religious enemies of the old crusader spoke with feeling last night in expressing their regret at his sudden death. Those who had fought him for three generations respected him as a foe for his sincerity and for his fighting qualities. His followers in religious and political battles were stunned by the news of his sudden death. The drys regarded him as the greatest living champion of prohibition and the Fundamentalists looked to him as their national chief and hoped that the man who played so great a part in putting prohibition into the Constitution would eventually succeed in safeguarding the literal word of the Bible by legislation.

Governor Alfred E. Smith said: "I heard of the death of Bryan with a great deal of regret. He was a vigorous American and even those who disagreed with his ideas had a great regard for him."

Mayor Hylan said: "I regret very much to hear of the death of Colonel Bryan. I have known Colonel Bryan for a great many years and always held him in high esteem. I believe that he has always been sincere in any cause he espoused."

John W. Davis, Democratic candidate for President at the last election, said at his home at Locust Valley, L. I.:

"The depressing news of Mr. Bryan's death must prove a great shock, not only to his friends but to the country at large. I am most deeply grieved by it.

Continued on Page Three.

ARLINGTON BURIAL ASKED FOR BRYAN

Military Service in Spanish War Entitles Him to Rest in Hallowed Soil.

HAD REMARKED ITS BEAUTY

Funeral Arrangements Will Be Made Today by Ben G. Davis, His Secretary for Many Years.

Special to The New York Times.

WASHINGTON, July 26.—Arrangements are being made for the burial of Colonel William J. Bryan in Arlington National Cemetery.

Immediately after the death of her husband at Dayton, this afternoon, Mrs. Bryan sent a telegram to Ben G. Davis of Takoma Park, Md., former chief clerk of the State Department and an intimate personal friend of Colonel Bryan, stating that the latter had died while asleep and requesting Mr. Davis to make arrangements for his interment at Arlington. Mr. Davis was unable to communicate tonight with Major Robert P. Harbold of the office of the Quartermaster General of the Army, who is in charge of the cemeterial division.

After conferring with the superintendent at Arlington and with attachés in Colonel Harbold's office, Mr. Davis sent a telegram to Mrs. Bryan asking for further particulars with respect to her wishes and informing her that he will take up the matter with the War Department tomorrow. Colonel and Mrs. Bryan are both entitled to burial at Arlington under the Federal law which permits interment there and in other national cemeteries of all who have served in the army, navy and marine corps, or the volunteer forces of the United States, and their wives.

Led Nebraska Infantry.

Colonel Bryan is entitled to burial at Arlington by reason of his service in the Spanish-American War. He raised the Third Regiment of Nebraska Volunteer Infantry in May, 1898, for service in the war with Spain and became its Colonel. After serving in that war, he came to Washington and made possible the ratification of the Treaty of Peace which had been negotiated by the American commission at Paris.

The treaty was in danger of being defeated by Democratic votes but Colonel Bryan exerted his influence and swung them into line so that he could make "imperialism" the issue in the subsequent national campaign. When laid away under the oaks at Arlington on the green Virginia hills with the placid Potomac below, Colonel Bryan will rest, after life's fitful fever, with many of the distinguished dead of the Nation. It is there that the American Unknown Soldier, now the mecca for distinguished visitors from all parts of the world, is buried.

Will Lie With Many Famous Dead.

On the slopes of the hill, near the old Lee Mansion, at Arlington, are the graves of Major L'Enfant, the French engineer who planned the City of Washington, General "Phil" Sheridan, Admirals Porter and Farragut, General Crook, the great Indian fighter, former Secretary of State Gresham, Generals Lawton, Wright, Hazen, Myers, Meigs, Belknap and many others. The latest distinguished army officer to be interred there was the late Major Gen. Nelson A. Miles.

Until recently Admiral George Dewey

Continued on Page Two.

APOPLEXY CAUSES HIS DEATH

Had Said He 'Never Felt Better' on His Return From Church.

SPOKE TO 50,000 SATURDAY

Full of Zeal to Take Cause to Country, He Was Thrilled by Crowds on Last Journey.

WIFE WAS APPREHENSIVE

Feared Anti-Evolution Fight Was Overtaxing His Strength, but Now Bears Loss Bravely.

Special to The New York Times.

DAYTON, Tenn., July 26.—William Jennings Bryan died suddenly of heart disease while he slept this afternoon at the residence of Richard Rodgers here.

Apparently in perfect health, full of plans to make a nation-wide fight for laws protecting the Bible against the teaching of evolution, Mr. Bryan went to his room for a nap after a hearty meal.

At 2 o'clock Mrs. Bryan's housekeeper, Mrs. C. Stevens, passed through Mr. Bryan's room and he said cheerfully: "I think I'm going to get a good sleep." Soon after 4 o'clock, Mrs. Bryan, who was in a wheelchair on the porch, became nervous over her husband's failure to awaken and asked William H. McCarney, the family chauffeur, to rouse him.

Mr. McCartney shook Mr. Bryan gently but got no response. He realized something was wrong and called a neighbor, A. B. Andrews, who summoned Dr. A. C. Broyles and Dr. W. F. Thomison. The doctors said that Mr. Bryan had been dead about twenty minutes. Death occurred about 4:45 o'clock. They said the cause was apoplexy, accompanied by a cerebral hemorrhage.

Dr. Broyles said that the clogging of veins in the neck indicated that death was not caused by heart dilation, the opinion of Dr. Wallace of Chattanooga, who examined Mr. Bryan on Friday. The Commoner was 65 years odl.

Physicians were then summoned. They found that Mr. Bryan had been dead for some minutes. Death occurred at about 4:45 o'clock.

Refused to Take Vacation.

His death came as the greatest possible shock because Mr. Bryan himself and every one else believed that he had passed through the Dayton ordeal without suffering the least detriment to his health through the heat, fatigue and excitement.

"I never felt better in my life," the veteran orator said time after time today and yesterday, when the friends he had made at Dayton called on him.

"The fight that we have made here will be transferred to a greater scope," he said, referring to movements in several Southern and Western States to enact anti-evolution or Bible-protecting legislation.

Mr. Bryan had lost weight during the trial and his face was pale and lined, but the zest of battle had been awakened in him and the ardent spirit of the old crusader did not permit him to consider the need of rest. Many of his friends advised the former Secretary of State and three times candidate for President to take a vacation and recruit his strength.

"No," he replied, "we must strike while the iron is hot." Following this principle, he had been speaking incessantly at Tennessee meetings since the conviction of Scopes. He planned further speeches in Tennessee, and had in mind a speaking tour of many States in behalf of this cause into which he threw his heart more fully than he had into any other.

His Last Triumphant Journey.

He told his friends during and after the Scopes trial that no cause has ever stirred him to the bottom of the heart like this one, not even the cause of peace before 1917 or the cause of free silver twenty-nine years ago.

Less than twenty-four hours before his death, the Commoner spoke to a great crowd at Winchester, Tenn. He was in fine form. He delivered a stirring speech and took delight in the applause and in the evident affection and admiration in which the crowd held him.

Returning from Winchester last night, Mr. Bryan's train was like his famous election special of 1896. From the rear platform he made speech after speech at each stop, and the crowds cheered him wildly and kept the train until its schedule was thoroughly disjointed.

At the town of Cowan Mr. Bryan spoke for twenty minutes. He electrified his hearers, as he has seldom failed to do in his public career of thirty years. He represented the conviction of Scopes as a great victory for the cause of Christianity, and a staggering blow to "the forces of darkness." Never had Christian and crusading zeal of the old warrior of the ancient faith burned more fiercely than during two or three days preceding his death.

His trip, which turned spontaneously into a rear platform speaking tour, covered more than 200 miles on Saturday. At 10 o'clock in the morning yesterday

Gladstones, Angered at Attack on Father, Call Capt. Wright "Liar, Coward and Fool"

Special Cable to THE NEW YORK TIMES.

LONDON, July 26. — Viscount Gladstone and Henry Neville Gladstone, sons of the late Liberal statesman W. E. Gladstone, have written to Captain Peter Wright, author, calling him "a liar, coward and fool."

Mr. Wright, in a recent volume of impressionist sketches entitled "Portraits and Criticisms," declared W. E. Gladstone "founded a great tradition since observed by many of his followers and successors with such pious fidelity—in public to speak the language of the highest and strictest principle and in private to pursue and possess every sort of woman."

Viscount Gladstone addressed a letter to Mr. Wright saying, "Your garbage about Mr. Gladstone in 'Portraits and Criticisms' has come to our knowledge. You are a liar. Because you slander a dead man you are a coward, and because you think the public will accept inventions from such as you, you are a fool.

The following line was added by H. N. Gladstone: "I associate myself with this letter."

Mr. Wright has replied to the Gladstones with a letter in which he repeats his charges against the late statesman. He says, among other things:

"I attributed to Mr. Gladstone the character of a hypocrite in matters of sex. I have evidence of his conduct as good as any that exists about events in the past. I wrote what I did write on the authority of the late Lord Milner.

"To use Milner's own phrase, Mr. Gladstone was 'governed by his seraglio.' This foible had considerable political effect. One affair turned Mr. Gladstone from being a friend of Turkey and an enemy of Russia, as he was in the '50s, into being a friend of Russia and an enemy of Turkey, as he was in the '80s.

he spoke at the town of Jasper. At 2:30 o'clock he spoke to more than 8,000 people at Fairgrounds. Altogether he spoke to nearly 50,000 people during the day.

Mrs. Bryan, whose health was a matter of great concern and anxiety to her husband a year ago, was with him at Dayton. On his return from his strenuous day she was worried lest he should be overdoing it.

But Mr. Bryan was in a happy and exulting mood, full of triumph and jubilance over the progress of the latest and, as he regarded it, the greatest of his causes. He had always enjoyed a health that was nearly perfect and he made light of any fears as to his physical condition.

Mrs. Bryan was in a wheel chair on the porch when she learned that her husband was dead. She was overcome with grief. According to their intimates, no more devoted couple ever lived. Up to the time of her illness Mrs. Bryan had made her one object in life the comfort and care of her husband, and since she has been an invalid Mr. Bryan's tenderness toward her had been most striking. Her consolation in his sudden death was that it was without pain and that it took place at a time when he was happiest.

Mrs. Bryan rallied after the first shock and showed outwardly her accustomed calm. She expressed a desire to those at the Rodgers residence that Mr. Bryan should be buried in the Arlington Cemetery, because he was a Colonel in the Spanish-American War and it was his wish that he should be buried in Arlington Cemetery.

No definite decision will be reached, however, until she has communicated with William Jennings Bryan Jr., who is in California.

Mrs. Bryan had arranged to start for Idaho tomorrow. Mr. Bryan was to join her at a time not yet fixed, but in the meantime he had agreed to make many speeches in Tennessee and elsewhere.

He was to leave Dayton on Tuesday for Knoxville, where he was to make two speeches on the Scopes trial and to outline his idea of a national campaign to arouse the people to the danger in which he believes the Christian religion stands today.

He was billed to speak in Nashville on the same topic. After that he was going to make a short trip to Florida, speaking on the way, and then to make a railroad trip to join Mrs. Bryan, stopping over for further anti-evolution speeches.

Natives Blame Stress of Trial.

The news of his death spread swiftly through the streets of Dayton, and the inhabitants were stunned to learn of the sudden taking of the man whom they had regarded as a sort of living patron saint and protector of the town.

The whole populace poured into the streets and formed groups discussing the tragic occurrence. It was made known that serious concern was felt for Mrs. Bryan because of the shock and her precarious health, and on that account there were very few visitors at the Rodgers home.

The townspeople were inclined to blame the rigors of the trial for the sudden death of their idol. Many of them had been surprised to find Bryan so white and thin when he first arrived. From the plumpness and color of a few years ago he had dwindled and faded. His face was deeply lined and the loose skin indicated recent loss of weight.

Throughout the trial he suffered intensely from the heat. Still, when he burst into action in the last few days his eyes snapped, his cheeks glowed and he appeared full of life and fire.

The joy of battle carried him easily through the trial and the excitement and enthusiasm of success inspired the great outburst of energy on his part which followed the trial and which in all probability cut short his life.

The fact that he had spent his strength and shortened his life in the defense of the sacred Book raised him to martyrdom in the eyes of Dayton. Some of his impressive sentences, his declarations of faith on the witness stand, his bitter characterizations of the "infidels," were recalled and given the weight of direct inspiration and Divine sanction.

Resting for Conference on College.

Dayton had adopted Bryan and Bryan had adopted Dayton. The idea of making Dayton the site of the proposed Bryan University, which was to be created at the great citadel of the old faith, had filled the mind of Mr. Bryan.

He was taking the nap, during which he died, to recruit his strength for a meeting at the Hotel Aqua with promoters of the Bryan University, in which plans for the financial arrangements and for the curriculum were to be discussed.

After the conference on the proposed Bryan School, he was to address a meeting at the Dayton Court House. This was planned as the final demonstration of Dayton in his honor before he left. Mr. Bryan had prepared a speech with great care, and the inhabitants for miles in all directions were coming to hear it.

The courthouse meeting was to have heard the famous undelivered speech which Mr. Bryan had prepared for the Scopes trial. The sudden collapse of that singular legal proceeding prevented its delivery at that time.

No greater blow could have fallen on those who were to compose his audience than the news of his sudden death. To many it was incredible.

Led in Prayer at Church.

Only four or five hours before the first report of his death, Mr. Bryan had been the centre of interest at the Southern Methodist Church, where he led the congregation in prayer and brought a chorus of fervent "Amens" from all parts of the church.

William Jennings Bryan in 1908.

His prayer, it was said, was the most beautiful and most affecting ever delivered in the church.

Mr. Bryan conferred later with C. Wesley Hicks, the choir director, on the music for the sermon on "What Shall I Do With Jesus?" which Mr. Bryan was to deliver tomorrow night. Mr. Bryan requested that two hymns be sung, "One Sweetly Solemn Thought" and "I'll Go Where You Want Me to Go."

"Don't sing the fancy, jumpy arrangement of 'One Sweetly Solemn Thought,'" Mr. Bryan said. "I want the sweet, old-time tune."

After the services, practically every member of the audience pressed around him to shake his hand and exchange a word with him. Mr. Bryan then returned to his temporary home and sat down at the dining table.

He remarked that his strenuous exertions of the past two days had given him an unusually hearty appetite. He ate heartily. After dinner, he was drowsy and went to this room for the nap from which he did not awaken.

EFFECT OF HIS DEATH ON THE DEMOCRATS

By RICHARD V. OULAHAN.

Continued from Page 1, Column 5.

that time ascertained all the information necessary for Mr. Bryan to make application for this burial place and sent it to Mr. Bryan. Whether Mr. Bryan selected the spot in Arlington in which he desired interment Mr. Davis said he did not know. But wherever his body is placed in the spacious cemetery its site will overlook the City of Washington, with the White House, the mecca of Mr. Bryan's desire for many years, a conspicuous object in the not-distant background.

The few of the political world now in Washington, and many others here who knew Mr. Bryan, were profoundly moved when they learned of his death this evening, for whatever controversial differences with the Commoner may have caused some of them to cherish a critical attitude toward his policies, he was personally much liked. From the viewpoint of the human side, Mr. Bryan was popular with his associates.

A Charming Companion.

Men who had rubbed elbows with him said this evening that when he was seen in his purely personal aspect, separated from the various political, religious and social crusades in which he engaged from the time be became the Democratic Party's nominee for President of the United States in 1896, he was a charming companion, full of the milk of human kindness and as entertaining a man as one would be likely to meet. He was especially happy in making after-dinner speeches when no politics was involved, and members of the Gridiron Club and guests at their notable functions have a lively memory of how he entered into the spirit of these occasions and how free from any bitterness he was in his interprandial remarks, based, as they necessarily were, on parodies of the activities in which Mr. Bryan had been or was engaged.

Effect on Politics Discussed.

Mr. Bryan's personality was so virile and his stamp on American political life so marked that it was inevitable that the news of his death this evening should be followed by intense discussion of the effect of his passing on national politics. Especially was there comment and surmise over the relation of his death to the fortunes of the Democratic party. While few Senators and Representatives of the Democratic faith are in Washington, there are many still here who have taken a keen interest in the trend of political affairs in the United States and are qualified to render judgment as to the probable meaning of the removal of the Commoner from those public activities in which he had played so notable and conspicuous a part.

It was strikingly apparent from what was said in political and near-political quarters that the recent participation of Mr. Bryan in the trial of John Thomas Scopes at Dayton, Tenn., the little town which now comes into additional prominence through the circumstance that it was here that the man who was the candidate of his party for President of the United States three times—and was three times defeated—a record equaled only by that of Henry Clay—had been cause for worry among leading men of the Democratic Party.

Feared Religious Dispute.

While Mr. Bryan had denied that he had declared in a Sunday talk in Dayton that he intended to organize a crusade "to put the Bible in the Constitution," his remarks on that occasion produced an uneasy feeling among some of the Democratic faith that he contemplated organizing a movement that would revive, in the next Democratic National Convention, the bitterness of religious controversy that marked the anti-evolution episode dramatized in the Tennessee hills.

Nothing had come to light in political circles since the trial of Scopes got into full swing to show that the issue involved in the court proceedings at Dayton would be injected into national politics. But it was apparent from comment that came to the surface this evening following the news of Mr. Bryan's death that the fear existed among well-wishers of the Democratic Party that the next Democratic Convention, to be held in 1928, might find itself confronted by a situation even more embarrassing than that produced by the injection of the Ku Klux Klan issue in its quadrennial gathering of 1924.

Mr. Bryan, it was recalled, usually had produced some new issue at successive national conventions of his party. In 1896 it was the issue of free silver, although Mr. Bryan was not primarily responsible for that. In 1900 it was "imperialism," based on the taking over of the Philippines, Porto Rico and Guam as possessions of the United States.

That year Mr. Bryan, as in 1896, was the candidate of his party for President.

Gave Parker Little Support.

In 1904 Mr. Bryan took little part in the Presidential campaign because Alton B. Parker, the Democratic nominee for President, was not to his liking, especially as he had declined to accept a platform declaration in line with Mr. Bryan's free silver views. In 1908, when Mr. Bryan again was the Democratic Presidential nominee, he stressed in his campaign a governmental guarantee of bank deposits and other principles which worried the more conservative element of his party.

At another time he had advocated Government ownership of railroads as a party declaration. In the Democratic convention of 1912, at Baltimore, he abandoned his instructions as a Nebraska delegate to support the candidacy of Champ Clark, and espoused the cause of Woodrow Wilson. In 1920 he sought to have a flat endorsement of the prohibition amendment inserted in the party platform but did not succeed, after a bitter oratorical duel with W. Bourke Cockran on the convention floor.

Generally he had been a stormy petrel in his party's affairs for thirty years, and had produced more worry to Democratic leaders than any man high in the party council.

A 1900 campaign poster

BRYAN IS EULOGIZED, EVEN BY OPPONENTS

Continued from Page 1, Column 6.

No other man of his generation has been so long identified with public questions or has been so universally known throughout the United States. Although many of the things put forward by him were not accepted, I think it is only fair to say few men, if any, have lived to see so many of the policies they advocated enacted into law.

"His incalculable influence upon public thought cannot be measured however, only by the standards of personal or political success. If he had done no more than furnish to the men of his day an outstanding example of unflinching moral courage he would have rendered a great service to his age. This virtue earned him the respect even of those who most profoundly disagreed with him. He was never content until he had discovered what he believed was the moral right or wrong of every public question. When this had been decided he was unwavering.

"The country is poorer for his loss."

United States Senator Royal S. Copeland said he had always recognized Mr. Bryan's great sincerity and persuasive power, although he had never followed him in politics.

"No man ever had greater power over an audience than William Jennings Bryan," said the Senator. "I talked to him many times about his religious convictions. He said that he felt his influence was greater than it ever could have been had he been President of the United States, because he felt that he had a greater personal following and personal influence than any President had had. I think he was right in that. Great numbers of people fere enthused and uplifted by him."

DARROW DEEPLY GRIEVED.

Scopes Counsel Says He Respected Bryan's Sincerity and Devotion.

ELKMONT, Tenn., July 26 (AP).—"I am pained to hear of the death of the Hon. William Jennings Bryan," Clarence Darrow, Chicago attorney and cross-examiner of the Commoner in the recent trial of John T. Scopes at Dayton, Tenn., last Monday, declared this evening when informed of the demise of the notable American by The Knoxville Journal.

"I had known Mr. Bryan since 1896 and supported him twice for the Presidency. He was a man of strong convictions and always espoused his cause with ability and courage," Mr. Darrow continued. "I differed with him on many questions, but always respected his sincerity and devotion. I am very sorry for his family and for his friends, who loved him."

Mr. Darrow, associated with John R. Neal, Dudley Field Malone and Arthur Garfield Hays in the defense of Mr. Scopes, who was on trial for the violation of the Tennessee Anti-Evolution act, is spending several days in the Great Smoky Mountains with Mrs. Darrow, his secretary, Dr. Neal and Knoxville citizens.

ARLINGTON CHOSEN FOR BRYAN BURIAL

Continued from Page 1, Column 7.

was buried at Arlington, but at the request of his widow, the Dewey remains were removed from Arlington and reinterred at the Protestant Episcipal National Cathedral at Mount St. Albans, where Woodrow Wilson rests.

Mr. Davis, who is handling funeral arrangements, was intimately associated with Colonel Bryan since the latter served in Congress. When Mr. Bryan entered the House Mr. Davis served with him, beginning in 1895, as private secretary. Later he was with him in his campaigns for the Presidency, and when Mr. Bryan became Secretary of State in the Wilson Administration he asked Mr. Davis to serve as his confidential secretary. Later Mr. Bryan appointed him chief clerk of the State Department, a position which he filled until a year ago.

Mr. Davis said he did not feel at liberty to make public Mrs. Bryan's telegram, but stated that Mrs. Bryan, after saying that Colonel Bryan had died while asleep, requested him to make arrangements for burial at Arlington.

PRESIDENT PAINED BY DEATH OF BRYAN

He Eulogizes Him in Telegram of Condolence to Widow.

DAWES SPEAKS AS FRIEND

Special to The New York Times.

SWAMPSCOTT, Mass., July 26.—President Coolidge learned tonight of the death of William Jennings Bryan with profound regret. The news of his end was communicated to him by THE NEW YORK TIMES correspondent.

An appreciation of Mr. Bryan as an American who had spent his life courageously fighting for causes he sincerely espoused will be sent by the President tomorrow in a telegram of condolence to Mrs. Bryan.

Mr. Bryan and President Coolidge were on the best of terms, and in his frequent visits to Washington the former always called at the White House offices, and was a frequent luncheon guest at the White House.

The news of Mr. Bryan's death so soon after his battle for Fundamentalism, which brought him again into national attention, was quickly communicated to the hotels, where the orchestras tonight were giving sacred concerts.

"Nearer, My God, to Thee" was played at the Ocean House, and the musical selections at the Hotel Preston were devoted to special hymns in memory of the dead defender of Fundamentalism.

Active, Political and Civic Career of W. J. Bryan

Lifted Into Nation-Wide Prominence by One Speech in National Convention.

UNIQUE IN PARTY POLITICS

He Dominated the Democratic Organization for Sixteen of His Sixty-five Years.

Lifted over night from comparative obscurity into nation-wide prominence by his "cross of gold" speech at the 1896 Democratic National Convention, which made him the party nominee for President, William Jennings Bryan occupied a unique position in the politics of the country for thirty years.

Thrice nominated for the Presidency and thrice defeated, Mr. Bryan practically dominated the Democratic Party in the nation for nearly sixteen years. With his political power waning, he was nevertheless strong enough to bring about the nomination of Woodrow Wilson for President in 1912, after Champ Clark, the latter's leading opponent, had obtained the vote of more than a majority of the delegates.

Opposed by powerful leaders of his own party, particularly in the East, Mr. Bryan was regarded as a disruptive force by many Democrats. By others he was considered as almost a second Moses divinely appointed to lead the people of the United States to righteousness and prosperity. No man in public life in the United States in recent years had more political enemies. For a time, at least, none had more devoted followers.

Storm Centre in Religion.

Mr. Bryan was a political storm centre in religion as well as politics. A Presbyterian Fundamentalist, he sought unsuccessfully election as Moderator of the Presbyterian General Assembly three years ago. Between political campaigns Mr. Bryan toured the country as a Chautauqua circuit lecturer, delivering a series of addresses, of which his "Prince of Peace" was the best known.

Years before the enactment of the Tennessee law, which resulted in the trial of John T. Scopes for teaching the evolutionary theory of the origin of man, at which he was one of the central figures, Mr. Bryan had preached against Darwinism in nearly every city and town in the country. The expression of his views of evolution, as given in his testimony at the Scopes trial, contained little that he had not said many times before.

The highest office ever held by Mr. Bryan was that of Secretary of State by appointment of President Wilson. There was a widespread public opinion that his talents were hardly of a nature to enable him to give a successsful administration of that office, particularly in the difficult days which preceded the entrance of the United States into the World War. His resignation, just before the final break with Germany, came as a result of a disagreement with President Wilson over the latter's notes to Germany, due to Mr. Bryan's desire for peace. He was subsequently subjected to much unfavorable criticism on a charge of aiding the propaganda of the Central Powers, unintentionally, by his speeches and writings.

Born in Illinois.

William Jennings Bryan was born in Salem, Ill., March 19, 1860. His father was Silas Lillard Bryan, a native of Culpeper County Va., a lawyer and a Judge. The son, after graduating from Illinois College in 1881, and from the Union College of Law, Chicago, in 1883, entered the law office of Lyman Trumbull, former United States Senator. Subsequently Mr. Bryan moved to Jacksonville, Ill., where he practiced law until 1887, when he settled in Lincoln, Neb.

During the Presidential campaign of 1888 Mr. Bryan's speeches in behalf of the Democratic national ticket attracted attention, and in 1890 he received the Democratic nomination for Representative in the First Nebraska Congressional District, a Republican stronghold. The nomination went to Mr. Bryan because no one else would have it and it was believed that no Democrat could win. Displaying the forensic power that later made him known nationally, Mr. Bryan made a personal canvass of the district and was elected. He served in Congress from 1891 to 1895, being made a member of the important Ways and Means Committee during his first term.

Two speeches during this period gave Mr. Bryan some degree of prominence. One, against the Republican policy of a protective tariff, was delivered on March 16, 1892, and the other, against the repeal of the silver purchase clause of the Sherman act, on Aug. 16, 1893. In the latter speech Mr. Bryan advocated "the free and unlimited coinage of silver, irrespective of international agreement, at the ratio of 16 to 1," a policy with which his name was afterward most prominently associated until he entered the Cabinet of President Wilson.

Beaten on Sound-Money Issue.

Mr. Bryan was beaten for a third term in the House on the sound-money issue, and also suffered defeat when he ran as the Democratic candidate for Senator against John M. Thurston, Republican, of Nebraska. Abandoning the law, Mr. Bryan became editor of the Omaha World-Herald and championed the cause of bi-metallism as vigorously with his pen as he had in his speeches. He was known through the Middle West as an outspoken advocate of "free silver" when the party national conventions were held in 1896.

The silver question was then rending both the major political parties, and in the Republican Party culminated in the split of the Free Silver Republicans, whose nominee for President, Senator Henry M. Teller of Colorado, threw his support to Mr. Bryan when the latter won the Democratic nomination at Chicago.

Mr. Bryan's first nomination for the Presidency, which was made on July 10, 1896, has been characterized as one of the "miracles" of American politics. His "cross of gold" speech, which has been quoted from perhaps more frequently than any other of his speeches and made him the oponent of William McKinley, head of the Republican national ticket, came at the close of a debate on the floor of the convention in advocacy of a free silver plank. Men nationally prominent in the party had preceded him and had opposed the adoption of a free silver plank unless bimetallism should be provided for by international agreement.

The situation was tense when Mr. Bryan, then only 36 years old—only a year more than the constitutional age requirement for a President—arose to speak.

The delegates and spectators were tired. Everybody seemed ready for a compromise, but there was no compromise in the mien of the young delegate and ex-Representative from Nebraska when he began his speech.

Famous "Cross of Gold" Speech.

"I would be présumptuous, indeed, to present myself against the distinguished gentlemen to whom you have listened if this were a mere measuring of abilities," he said, "but this is not a contest between persons. The humblest citizen in all the land, when clad in the armor of a righteous cause, is stronger than all the hosts of error. I came to speak to you in a cause as holy as that of liberty—the cause of humanity."

Then, charging the evils of the day, the idle mills, the low wages and the social unrest, to the scarcity of money and "the idle holders of idle money in Wall Street," he continued:

"The individual is but an atom; he is born; he acts; he dies; but his principles are eternal, and this has been a contest over a principle. Having behind us the producing masses of this nation and the world, supported by the commercial interests, the laboring interests ond the toilers everywhere, we will answer those who demand a single gold standard by saying:

"'You shall not press down upon the brow of labor this crown of thorns. You shall not crucify mankind upon a cross of gold.'"

Stampedes the Convention.

This daring metaphor, based on the crucifixion of the Saviour, stampeded the convention. He was nominated as the party candidate on the fifth ballot over eight other candidates, following a speech by a Georgia delegate who referred to Mr. Bryan as "a Saul come to lead the Israelites to battle." Later he also was made the nominee of the People's and National Silver Parties.

Mr. Bryan broke all political speechmaking records in his first campaign. He travelled more than 18,000 miles and made more than 600 speeches in twenty-seven states. Everywhere he appeared great crowds, in many cases larger than ever had greeted any other candidate, turned out to see and hear him. His speech in Madison Square Garden in this city during the Fall of that year, and to an overflow meeting outside, established a record for attendance at a political meeting here.

It was a different Bryan from the one known in the last twenty years who came into the East in 1896 in his first invasion of what he later called "the enemy's country." Vigorous, magnetic and virile at that time, Mr. Bryan spoke with the fire and the grace of a natural orator. He seemed to think naturally in oratorical phrases and his deep, powerful voice, with notes like those of a pipe organ, enabled him to reach without difficulty the most distant auditor in a crowd of thousands—a great advantage in the days before the use of voice-amplifying devices.

So successful on the surface was Mr. Bryan's campaign that the Republican campaign managers, headed by Mark Hanna, National Chairman, became greatly worried and for a time it seemed as if Mr. Bryan might sweep all before him through sheer power of his oratory. Roused to a sense of peril, the business interests of the country practically united against him and the nomination of the "gold Democratic" ticket of Palmer and Buckner took from him the votes of thousands of Democrats.

Defeated by McKinley.

Mr. Bryan polled a popular vote of 6,502,925 to 7,104,779 for McKinley and received 176 votes in the electoral college to 271 for his opponent.

Although defeated, Mr. Bryan remained the leader of the Democratic Party, despite opposition, mainly in the East.

At the outbreak of the Spanish-American war in 1898 Mr. Bryan entered the volunteer army and gained his title of Colonel as comander of the Third Nebraska Volunteer Infantry. The regiment never got out of training camp. After the war he oposed the permanent retention of the Philipines by the United States.

In 1900 Mr. Bryan was again nominated for the Presidency by the Democratic Party. He made "anti-imperialism" the "paramount issue" of his campaign, but refused to permit a specific declaration in favor of the free coinage of silver to be omitted from the party platform. He made another speaking campaign of the "whirlwind" variety, although not so sensational as his first tour. He was defeated this time by President McKinley by a popular vote of 7,207,923 to 6,358,133 and an electoral vote of 292 to 155.

After his second defeat Mr. Bryan returned to Lincoln and started the publication of a weekly newspaper, The Commoner. He had a strong following throughout the country, even though in the minority, and the financial success of the paper was almost immediate. It was during this period that Mr. Bryan first came into great demand as a public speaker and was criticized for accepting fees for his speeches, although it was said he never charged for a speech on a purely political topic.

In 1904 Mr. Bryan retired temporarily to the background, and Alton B. Parker, then Chief Judge of the Court of Appeals of New York State, was made the Democratic nominee for President as a "safe and sane" candidate to run against Theodore Roosevelt, who had succeeded to the Presidency on the assassination of President McKinley. Mr. Bryan was not actively a candidate at the Democratic National Convention, but vigorously opposed the Democracy's "conservative" attitude in naming Judge Parker.

The interval between 1904 and the next Presidential election in 1908 was occupied by Mr. Bryan, now styled by many of his followers "The Peerless Leader," in several enterprises which kept him in the public eye. Notable among these was a trip around the world, on which he started on Sept. 21, 1906. Accompanied by his wife, son and daughter, Mr. Bryan first went to Japan and China, where he was entertained and made many addresses, one of which, "The White Man's Burden," was commended by the Japanese-American Society. The Bryans were presented to the Emperor of Japan and everywhere were accorded honors due to foremost Americans.

Mr. Bryan and his party went to the Philippines, where his liberal views on Filipino independence were welcomed by the natives. During this visit the Moros of Mindanao Island made Mr. Bryan a "datto," or chief, of one of their tribes.

Mr. Bryan and his party afterward went to India, Palestine, Turkey, Austria-Hungary, Germany, Russia, Italy, Norway, Sweden and other European countries, and arrived in London on July 8, 1906. During his trip Mr. Bryan "interviewed" King Edward VII., the Czar of Russia and other rulers, and Count Leo Tolstoy, and made numerous speeches, practically all of which were reported in the American press. Democrats in the United States arranged for a great reception, which was held upon his return in September.

In a speech at Madison Square Garden on this occasion, Mr. Bryan threw a verbal bombshell among the Democrats by advocating the Government ownership of railroads. This intensified the opposition to him of many Eastern Democrats.

Urged World Disarmament.

Soon after his return Mr. Bryan came out for world disarmament, an ideal which is said to have prompted his drafting in 1913, after he had become Secretary of State, a particular form of treaty between the United States and foreign nations "by which all disputes were to be submitted to an impartial investigating tribunal for a year before hostilities could begin." Mr. Bryan regarded this as his greatest achievement, for thirty foreign nations, including the Central Powers and representing about three-fourths of the population of the world, became signatories. About a year

© Underwood & Underwood.

MR. BRYAN WITH HIS FAMILY, AT HIS FLORIDA HOME IN 1923.

Left to right: Miss Kitty Owen, granddaughter; Major Reginald Owen, son-in-law, and baby Helen Rudd Owen, granddaughter; Mrs. Bryan, Master Byran Owen, Mrs. Reginald Owen, daughter, and W. J. Bryan.

United News Pictures.

AT THE EVOLUTION TRIAL IN DAYTON.

later the World War began.

In 1908, despite strong opposition against what his foes within the party stigmatized as "the blight of Bryanism," Mr. Bryan was again named as the Democratic candidate for President against William H. Taft, the Republican nominee. For a third time he suffered defeat, polling 6,409,104 votes, to 7,678,908 for Taft, and receiving 162 electoral votes, to 321 for his opponent.

Mr. Bryan took his political defeats rather gracefully and was what is known as a "good loser." After the 1908 election he continued to edit his newspaper, and at the same time retained his hold upon a considerable section of his party.

The demand for him as a lecturer increased, and his income was augmented by writing for newspapers and magazines and by the authorship of several books. The latter included "The First Battle," a story of his first Presidential campaign; "The Old World and Its Ways," a result of his tour of the world, and "Heart to Heart Appeal."

During this period Mr. Bryan took to spending his Winters in the more favorable climate of the South, first at Asheville, N. C., and later in Miami, Fla., where he established a permanent residence.

A few months before the 1912 Democratic National Convention Mr. Bryan announced that he would not be a candidate for the nomination for President, and that he was "ready to enter upon a campaign in behalf of a true Democrat with even more vigor than that with which I have fought at any time on my own behalf."

Woodrow Wilson at that time was Governor of New Jersey and had attracted the favorable attention of Mr. Bryan by his "progressive" policies. When the convention met at Baltimore, Mr. Bryan, although suspected of ambition for a fourth nomination, aligned himself in support of Wilson.

His first attack upon the "interests" was an oratorical onslaught against Tammany, Charles F. Murphy, then its leader, and August Belmont and Thomas F. Ryan, delegates to the convention, whom he denounced as representatives of the "interests." Mr. Bryan made this attack, to which the late John B. Stanchfield replied the next day, in a speech opposing the selection of Alton B. Parker, whose nomination and platform he had opposed four years before, as temporary Chairman, and demanding the selection of a chairman who would sound a "progressive" keynote.

Thereafter, during the convention, Mr. Bryan battled to bring about the nomination of Mr. Wilson and to defeat Champ Clark, then Speaker of the House of Representatives. Mr. Clark led for twenty-seven ballots and once had a clear majority of nine, which ordinarily would have made him the party's candidate despite the rule requiring a two-thirds vote to nominate. The persistence of Mr. Bryan's opposition and his reiteration of a plea against the "domination of the party by Wall Street," finally broke the ranks of the Clark supporters and brought about the designation of Mr. Wilson.

The Republican Party already had been split by the fight between Taft and Roosevelt at Chicago, and the nomination of Roosevelt as the candidate of the National Progressive Party followed soon after the Baltimore convention. A sweeping victory for Mr. Wilson came at the November election.

Made Secretary of State.

President Wilson considered himself indebted to Mr. Bryan for his nomination and showed his appreciation by inviting him to head his Cabinet as Secretary of State. The two years of Mr. Bryan's incumbency of this office were years of difficulty. The trouble with Mexico, the Japanese alien land controversy in California and the correspondence with Germany and Austria-Hungary before the entrance of the United States into the World War caused the Secretary much anxiety.

During Mr. Bryan's term of office, because of an insult to the American flag and the refusal of Huerta, President or "dictator" of Mexico, to order a salute fired in apology, American troops were sent to Vera Cruz, which was captured April 21, 1914. Subsequently the troops and warships were withdrawn, Huerta was deposed and a constitutionalist Government under Venustiana Carranza was set up in his stead.

At the height of the alien land law controversy in California Mr. Bryan went to that State, had several conferences with its Governor and spoke before the Legislature. Strained relations with Japan were improved by the passage of another measure known as the Webb bill, which modified somewhat the restrictions against Japanese in California.

Quits Cabinet Suddenly.

Mr. Bryan's resignation from President Wilson's Cabinet, which occurred on June 9, 1915, came suddenly. It was known that there had been differences of opinion between the President and the head of the State Department, but it was not realized generally that the breach had gone beyond healing. Germany's aggressions and policy of ruthless submarine warfare seemed to be drawing the United States into the war, but Mr. Bryan appeared to be for peace in any event.

The time came when President Wilson's notes to Germany took on a stronger tone and the sinking of another American ship by a German submarine led to a more emphatic protest from the President. Mr. Bryan, who had previously declared that there was "nothing final between friends," sent a letter of resignation to the President. Mr. Wilson, deploring Mr. Bryan's resignation as a "personal loss," accepted his Secretary's withdrawal and said that they both sought the same end but by different methods.

Mr. Bryan's zeal to bring about world peace led him to enthusiasm in act and speech that subjected him to hostile criticism. Before the United States entered the war he pledged himself to accompany Henry Ford's "peace ship" expedition to Europe, "to get the boys out of the trenches by Christmas," but subsequently he changed his mind and decided not to go.

He was accused of aiding the propaganda of the Central Powers by his speeches and writings, and early in the war declared that it had been fomented by "profit seekers." In an address in San Francisco he said that for the United States to go to war with Germany would be "like challenging a madhouse."

Sought Service as a Private.

He also at one time opposed the United States making any loans to belligerents. When America entered the war, however, Mr. Bryan promptly declared that Germany must be "defeated at all costs," and offered his services to President Wilson as a private soldier.

During his two years as Secretary of State Mr. Bryan was criticized for his frequent abscences as a lecturer, and his appearances on the Chautauqua circuit became a matter for raillery in the public press. Mr. Bryan explained in a statement that the $12,000 salary he received as a Cabinet officer was too little to meet the ordinary household demands upon his pocketbook and that he felt obliged to supplement his income.

Mr. Bryan's practice of serving grape juice instead of alcoholic beverages when entertaining members of the diplomatic corps also was ridiculed. He said he did this as a matter of principle. His long advocacy of "teetotalism" was considered by many as having contributed greatly to the adoption of the Eighteenth Amendment to the Constitution, prohibiting the manufacture, sale or transportation of alcoholic beverages.

Mr. Bryan cut little figure in Democratic national politics in 1916. He was not a delegate to the National Convention at St. Louis, at which President Wilson was renominated, but attended as a newspaper man. His presence was recognized and he was called to the platform by demand of the delegates and spectators and made a speech.

Silent in Cox Campaign.

His position of power in the Democratic Party waned further in the 1920 convention at San Francisco. Although elected a delegate-at-large from Nebraska despite the opposition of the faction controlling the State organization, Mr. Bryan took little effective part in the convention proceedings. His attempt to get a "dry" plank in the platform was beaten. He could not support James M. Cox of Ohio, who was nominated for President, because he believed him to have "wet" tendencies, but he would not oppose him, it was said, because Mr. Cox had supported him each time he ran for President. He remained silent throughout the campaign, and it was said afterward that it was the first time in forty years that he had made no speeches for a Democratic candidate.

"My heart is in the grave with our cause," Mr. Bryan said, after the defeat of the proposed dry plank on the convention floor. "I must pause until it comes back to me."

Soon after the election of President Harding, Mr. Bryan suggested that President Wilson should resign because the people had voted against the entrance of the United States into the League of Nations. He proposed that President Wilson should turn over his office to Vice President Marshall and that the latter should appoint Mr. Harding Secretary of State and then resign, so that Mr. Harding might succeed him as President without waiting for the constitutional date of March 4. The suggestion was regarded as impractical, as was thought of many of Mr. Bryan's other suggestions and theories.

Makes His Home in Florida.

After 1920 Mr. Bryan became a legal resident of Miami, Fla., and was credited with having made a substantial sum by his investments in Florida real estate. He was elected from that State as a delegate to the Democratic National Convention of 1924, which met at Madison Square Garden in New York City. He took a prominent part in the proceedings, but his influence was much less than it had been at previous conventions.

Mr. Bryan opposed the adoption of a resolution denouncing the Ku Klux Klan and advocated the nomination of William G. McAdoo for President. He had no success in breaking the deadlock between Mr. McAdoo and Governor Alfred E. Smith of New York, which lasted for two weeks, until both these candidates released their delegates and John W. Davis was nominated, but it was his potential influence that caused his brother, Charles W. Bryan, Governor of Nebraska, to be nominated for Vice President. Mr. Bryan took a comparatively minor part in the campaign which resulted in the defeat of the Democratic national ticket and the election of President Coolidge.

In a discussion of the proposed Klan resolutions by the Committee on Resolutions of the convention, of which he was a member, Mr. Bryan dropped on one knee and urged the other members to join him in prayer that they might receive Divine guidance in acting on the resolution.

Mr. Bryan married Miss Mary E. Baird of Perry, Ill. They had three children, one son and two daughters.

Stimulated by Hostile Audiences.

No recent political speaker in the United States was accustomed to have more hostile audiences than Mr. Bryan, and there was no speaker on whom a hostile audience had so little effect. Opposition and interruptions seemed to stimulate him, and he frequently used antagonism to himself to draw his opponents into a trap.

In the argument before the Committee on Resolutions of the 1920 Democratic National Convention Mr. Bryan, acting as field marshal of the dry forces, had introduced each speaker, giving in every case the name of the organization represented as well as of the speaker. A well-known lawyer, marshal for the wet forces, introduced the first wet speaker without going through the formality of naming any organization. Mr. Bryan very courteously asked that the name of an organization be included.

"I would like to know whom the gentleman represents," he said.

"And I would like to know whom Mr. Bryan represents," the lawyer replied with the trace of a sneer.

"I represent the women and children of America whom your damnable traffic would slay," Mr. Bryan thundered, and he started a three-minute denunciation of the liquor traffic which left the lawyer speechless during the rest of the hearing.

Mr. Bryan started one of his speeches at the Madison Square Garden convention in sorrowful mood, with a gallery of spectators bitterly hostile to him, both on general principles and because of his opposition to the nomination of Governor Smith.

"This may be the last convention that I shall ever attend," Mr. Bryan began.

The galleries exploded instantly into ironical applause, which lasted several minutes. The light of battle came into Mr. Bryan's eyes. His pensive mood was displaced instantly by a fighting one. He stood with uplifted hand, as he had stood many times before, waiting for the demonstration, really a hostile one, to cease.

"Don't cheer," he exclaimed smiling, when he had restored silence. "I might change my mind."

BRYAN SAID HE HAD $500,000 LAST APRIL

Resenting Reports of His Great Wealth, He Gave These Figures to Editor in Tampa.

PROFITS IN REAL ESTATE

Denied He Was a Millionaire and and Declared He Never Would Be.

William Jennings Bryan's wealth, a matter of much speculation, particularly in the period of his Florida real estate investments, was announced by him April 27 last to be in the neighborhood of $500,000. He said he expected to have that amount to invest in bonds when he concluded his realty transactions.

This announcement by Mr. Bryan was made in a letter to E. D. Lambright, editor of The Tampa (Fla.) Morning Tribune, which was published in The World. Editorial articles commenting on his real estate deals had angered him and he said he selected Mr. Lambright's paper because of his fair attitude. Of the reports that he had become a millionaire, Mr. Bryan wrote:

"I am not a millionaire; I am far from it, and never shall be, but I have been fortunate in the matter of finances. There has never been a year since my first nomination in which I could not have made a million had I taken the side of privilege and favoritism.

"The unexpected profits that I have made in Miami real estate have so increased my savings that I now have the promise of an income that will as fully meet the new conditions as the income from my earnings alone would have met old conditions.

"I have sold nearly all my property, including my first home here (Tampa, Fla.), Villa Serena, except the new and less valuable home into which we moved last Fall. When the remainder of my property is turned into interest-bearing securities I can reasonably expect to have for the first time in my life an income sufficient for the needs of Mrs. Bryan and myself, even when I am no longer able to add to that income by literary work.

"When we moved from Nebraska we gave our home, valued by us at $50,000 and by those who received it at more than $75,000, to the Methodist Church for a hospital. The value of that gift alone was more than one-tenth of all the profits I have ever received from real estate. It is mor than one-tenth of the profits I ever will receive on real estate. Our subscriptions to churches in this State have amounted to more than $10,000 within the past year."

BRYAN ADVENTURES IN EAST

Crows in Ceylon Stole His Watch and Part of His Breakfast.

Mr. Bryan was known to fame in all the large cities of the world. At Rangoon, for instance, where he stopped on his trip around the world in 1905-06, he was surrounded by a host of admirers in the Strand Hotel, where he and his family were registered. Every one clamored to shake the hand of the "great Commoner." To a NEW YORK TIMES reporter there he spoke on subjects ranging from the condition of the people of India to the latest political news from home.

He expressed his belief that he would eventually be elected President of the United States. Mr. Bryan repeated this in the drawing room of the hotel when he was surrounded by American tourists after dinner who applauded him and the women begged him to autograph their books.

The Great Commoner showed considerable interest in the condition of the native of India and told those who called to see him that he would speak on their behalf when he returned home and also in England.

At that time the electric fans, now so common throughout the East Indies, were not in general use in Burman and guests in the hotel had canvas punkahs over their beds which boys called "punkahs wallas" wafted to and fro all night for twenty cents.

Mr. Bryan said it was a blot on the civilization of the twentieth century, that such a state of things should exist. He could not find any other means of keeping cool at night, however, and had to use a punkah walla the same as every one else.

Later at Colombo, Ceylon, when the reporter met him again, Mr. Bryan, while stopping at the Galle Face Hotel, had a quaint adventure with some crows which had their early morning rendezvous on the upper branches of some lofty palm trees just outside the window of his room.

Notices were posted in all the bedrooms on that side of the hotel warning the guests not to place any glistening objects like diamond rings, pendants, earrings or other articles of jewelry on the dressing table because the crows might fly in and steal them.

Mr. Bryan had left the shutter open because of the heat and was aroused by the bright sunlight streaming across his bed, as he sat up a big crow as black as pet flew into the room and seized his gold watch and chain that was lying on the dressing table and flew out with it.

The kitmagar, native servant, came in with his early morning breakfast at that time and saw what had occurred. He went to the window and shouted in Singalese to the crow and the bird dropped its glitterig loot on the sandy beach, under the palm trees.

When Mr. Bryan went to eat his breakfast two more crows, friends of the first black-feathered robber, flew into the room and started to steal the things on the painted wooden tray. One bird seized a banana and the other a slice of toast, while Mr. Bryan grabbed his bamboo cane and tried to beat them off. The native boy came back at that moment with the watch and chain and the crows flew out of the room holding the booty in their beaks.

SCOUT NEW VERSION OF WHY BRYAN QUIT

Officials Find No Confirmation of Wilson Interference on a Note Shown to Dumba.

LETTER GAVE HIS REASONS

Mr. Bryan Told the President He Could Not Sign the Lusitania Note to Germany.

Special to The New York Times.

WASHINGTON, July 29.—Investigation today failed to confirm the statement of Milton A. Miller of Portland, Ore., that a note to Austria, a copy of which was shown by William Jennings Bryan, then Secretary of State, to Count Dumba, at that time Austrian Ambassador, to the United States relative to plots by the Austrian Embassy and the German War Office to cripple American munition plants, had been obtained from the cable office and altered by President Wilson before being sent to Dr. Dumba's Government, and that this was the reason for Mr. Bryan's resignation from the Wilson Cabinet.

Then as now diplomatic notes sent from this Government to its representatives abroad to be delivered to foreign powers were not filed at the commercial telegraph offices but at the official cable office in the State, War and Navy Building, and it would have been most unusual for a President without consulting with or without the knowledge of a Secretary of State to send over to the operator on duty in the cable office of the State Department for a copy of a note which the Secretary of State had sent to the cable office to be sent.

It is true that Dr. Dumba's recall was requested on account of a communication he had sent to Count Burian of his own Government relative to crippling American munition plants, but this occurred after Secretary Bryan had resigned. The date of Secretary Bryan's resignation was June 8, 1915. It was not until Sept. 8, 1915, that the recall of Count Dumba, on the ground that he was no longer acceptable to the United States, was requested by Secretary Lansing in a note delivered to the Austrian Government through American Ambassador Penfield at Vienna.

Why Dumba Was Recalled.

Secretary Lansing asked for the recall of Count Dumba after the Ambassador had admitted that he proposed to his Government plans to instigate strikes in American factories engaged in the production of war munitions. Information to this effect reached the American Government through a copy of the letter from the Ambassador to his Government. The bearer of the letter to Count Burian was James J. Archibald, an American newspaper correspondent, to whom it had been entrusted and from whom it was taken upon his arrival at Falmouth, England. The Dumba letter was made public by Secretary Lansing after he had asked for the recall of Count Dumba. It was dated Aug. 20, 1915, more than two months after Mr. Bryan had resigned as Secretary of State.

At the time of the resignation of Mr. Bryan many conflicting reasons for the break between President Wilson and his Secretary of State were circulated. Mr. Bryan himself, in his letter of resignation, said he resigned because he could not in fairness to the cause nearest his heart—prevention of war—sign the new note to Germany on the subject of submarine warfare.

"Obedient to your sense of duty and actuated by the highest motives, you have prepared for transmission to the German Government," said Mr. Bryan's letter of resignation, "a note in which I cannot join without violating what I deem to be an obligation to my country, and the issue involved is of such moment that to remain a member of the Cabinet would be as unfair to you as it would be to the cause which is nearest my heart—namely, the prevention of war. I therefore respectfully tender my resignation to take effect when the note is sent, unless you prefer an earlier hour."

Bryan Explained His Reasons.

The note was sent on June 9, 1915, and Mr. Bryan issued a formal statement in which he said:

"My reason for resigning is clearly stated in my letter of resignation—namely, that I may employ as a private citizen the means which the President does not feel at liberty to employ. I honor him for doing what he believes to be right, and I am sure that he desires, as I do, to find a peaceful solution to the problem which has been created by the action of the submarines. Two of the points on which we differed, each conscientious in his conviction, are: First, as to the suggestion of an investigation by an international commission, and second, as to warning Americans against traveling on belligerent vessels or with cargoes of ammunition."

There was no allusion in any of Mr. Bryan's statements issued at the time of his resignation to any alteration by the President of a note alleged to have been delivered by Mr. Bryan to Dr. Dumba.

Following his resignation Mr. Bryan remained in Washington until June 27, when he left for San Francisco. Meanwhile there were widespread reports that he had informed Dr. Dumba that Mr. Wilson's first note to Germany after the Lusitania disaster was not to be taken seriously. Just before leaving Washington on June 27 Mr. Bryan issued a statement in which he took cognizance of these reports.

"I have noticed," he said, "that a number of jingo papers are publishing a statement to the effect that after the sending of the first note to Germany, I gave Ambassador Dumba the impression that the note was not to be taken seriously. I am not willing that the uninformed shall be misled by that portion of the press which is endeavoring to force this country into war. I reported to the President the conversation which I had with Ambassador Dumba and received his approval of what I had said. When we learned that the conversation had been misinterpreted in Berlin, I brought the matter to the attention of Ambassador Dumba, and secured from him a statement certifying to the correctness of the conversation which I had made to the President. Ambassador Dumba's statement was sent to our embassy at Berlin, and Ambassador Dumba also telegraphed the German Government affirming the correctness of my report of the interview and denying the construction that had been placed upon it. These are the facts in the case."

"All the News That's Fit to Print"

The New York Times

LATE CITY EDITION

Weather: Cloudy and mild, periods of rain likely through tomorrow. Temp. range: today 38-55; Tuesday 38-42. Full U.S. report on Page 85.

VOL. CXXII . . No. 42,046 NEW YORK, WEDNESDAY, MARCH 7, 1973 15 CENTS

Papp's Troupe to Replace Lincoln Repertory

Producer Will Stress New U.S. Plays in Major Policy Shift

By MEL GUSSOW

Joseph Papp's New York Shakespeare Festival, with Mr. Papp as producer and president, will replace the Repertory Theater of Lincoln Center. In a major change of artistic policy at the center, Mr. Papp will emphasize the production of new American plays instead of revivals at the Vivian Beaumont Theater and will turn the 299-seat Forum Theater into a year-round home for Shakespeare.

The announcement of the change in constituents was made yesterday by Amyas Ames, chairman of the board of Lincoln Center, Inc. It came after a two-month study by the Committee for Theater at Lincoln Center, which recommended that "Institutional Theater be brought to the highest level in New York."

Mr. Papp's company will join Lincoln Center at the end of the current season as a full constituent, to be called the New York Shakespeare Festival at Lincoln Center. At the same time, the Shakespeare Festival board will also replace the Repertory Theater board, in the past a target of criticism, much of it from Mr. Papp himself, for its failure to raise enough money to support its company.

Mr. Papp said that he would add new members to his board, perhaps choosing some from the Repertory board.

The New York Times/Jack Manning

Amyas Ames, at left, chairman of Lincoln Center's board, and Joseph Papp outside the Vivian Beaumont Theater, where Mr. Papp will produce plays.

In addition to the two Lincoln Center theaters, Mr. Papp will continue his usual Shakespeare Festival activities — his six theaters in the Public Theater, the Delacorte Theater summer season of Shakespeare in Central Park, and mobile theaters throughout New York City, as well as his work on Broadway and on television.

Such a concentration of power is unprecedented in modern theatrical history.

Mr. Papp said that his Lincoln Center policy of emphasizing new works instead of revivals was "exactly the same in every respect" as it had been at the Shakespeare Festival, but that it was the opposite of the policy of the Repertory Theater of Lincoln

Continued on Page 38, Column 1

Papp Play Off C.B.S.

A telecast of "Sticks and Bones," produced by Joseph Papp, has been postponed indefinitely by C.B.S. It said that the play, about the homecoming of a blinded Vietnam veteran, "might be unnecessarily abrasive . . . at a time when prisoners of war and other veterans" were returning home. Details, Page 87.

1972 CRIME TOTAL IN CITY FELL 18% AS VIOLENCE ROSE

Data for Reported Incidents Lowest Since '67—Rape, Murder and Assault Up

By DAVID BURNHAM

Police Commissioner Patrick V. Murphy announced yesterday an 18 per cent decline in serious crimes reported to the police last year, even though in some categories—murder, rape and felonious assault—the number showed an increase over 1971.

The decrease, which brought the over-all number of reported serious crimes to its lowest level since 1967, was accounted for by decreases in robbery, burglary, larceny involving $50 and over and auto theft.

Although Mr. Murphy said at a news conference that the reduction in reported crime in the city was no cause for complacency, he added that "overall we can conclude that the streets are a little safer than they were last year."

Certain of Accuracy

He flatly rejected a suggestion that the figures had been "engineered" by the Police Department. "It is my sincere belief that we have the most accurate and honest crime statistics in the history of the New York Police Department," he said.

Mr. Murphy's announcement, nevertheless, brought immediate expressions of disbelief. Representative Edward I. Koch, who has made crime the central issue of his candidacy for the Democratic nomination for Mayor, said: "I have been talking with people in each of the city's five boroughs and everywhere I go people say crime is rising."

Representative Mario Biaggi, a former New York policeman and another Democratic candidate for mayor, said he was "apprehensive about the accuracy of the figures."

'Favorable Numbers'

"As a former police officer and a member of that department for 20 years," he declared, "I am familiar with the administrative gimmickery that can be used to come up with more favorable numbers."

According to the Police Department, reports of three of the four crimes against the person increased: murder cases were up 15.3 per cent, to 1,691, rape was up 35.4 per cent, to 3,271 and aggravated assault was up 9.6 per cent, to 37,130. But robbery — which includes muggings, holdups and some purse-snatchings — was down

Continued on Page 67, Column 1

OIL AND GASOLINE PRICES PUT UNDER CONTROL AGAIN; FARM CURBS ALSO WEIGHED

MOVE IS SURPRISE

1% Over-All Limitation Placed on Rises of 23 Largest Companies

By EDWARD COWAN

Special to The New York Times

WASHINGTON, March 6—The Nixon Administration, in a surprise move, reimposed mandatory price controls today on the country's 23 biggest oil companies. Crude oil, gasoline, heating oil and other refinery products, but not natural gas, were covered.

Swinging the much-discussed "stick in the closet" for the first time since the third phase of the wage-price stabilization program began Jan. 11, the Cost of Living Council set a 1 per cent limit on the average increase in prices each company may make without Government approval.

A similar approach to controlling farm prices, which are now unregulated, is under consideration. The steady upward march of agricultural prices in recent months is a source of increasing frustration to the Administration and is viewed as threatening the prospects for persuading labor to accept pay increases that are noninflationary.

Similar Situations

The Administration has been emphatically opposed to applying price controls to farmers ever since the stabilization program began on Aug. 15, 1971. However, the situation in oil, where mandatory controls had not been expected, is described as similar to the farm situation in one key respect: Demand is outstripping supply and is thereby pulling up prices.

The council let stand, as justified by higher costs, the increases in heating oil prices posted by most companies in January and February after the termination of the mandatory price controls of the second phase.

Prices May Increase

The Cabinet-level council imposed no limit on the increase that may be made in the price of any single product so long as the average remains within the over-all 1 per cent limitation.

That may portend sharply higher prices for gasoline this summer in markets where supplies are tight. Such shortages have been predicted, but it is not clear how widespread or acute they will be or what the price consequences may be.

The new regulations were applied to the 23 oil companies with annual sales above $250-million each. The companies account for 95 per cent of the industry's $80-billion annual sales and are the price leaders

Continued on Page 23, Column 1

Counsel to Nixon Attended F.B.I. Watergate Quizzing

By JOHN M. CREWDSON

Special to The New York Times

WASHINGTON, March 6 — Acting F.B.I. Director L. Patrick Gray 3d said today that John W. Dean 3d, a Presidential counsel, had been present when White House employes were interviewed by F.B.I. agents about the Watergate bugging case. He called Mr. Dean's attendance "not normal procedure" and said that it had occurred against his personal wishes.

"I could have said, 'We will not conduct any investigation of White House personnel,'" Mr. Gray told the Senate Judiciary Committee, "and I jolly well could not make that decision, so I said, 'We will conduct the investigation with Mr. Dean sitting in.'"

Asked by Senator Edward M. Kennedy, Democrat of Massachusetts, whether he had communicated his displeasure to Mr. Dean, Mr. Gray replied that he was not certain, "but the probability is that I did."

Mr. Gray said that although "our preference is to interview individuals without an attorney present," the bureau consents to such interviews when they are requested.

Senator Kennedy then asked whether Mr. Dean had been present as attorney for those being questioned by Federal investigators, and Mr. Gray replied, "I was informed that he was here in his official capacity as counsel to the President of the United States."

Gerald L. Warren, the deputy White House press secretary, acknowledged today that Mr. Dean sat in on all of the interviews with White House officials during the F.B.I.'s in-

Continued on Page 21, Column 1

Senate, 47 to 38, Retains A Limit on Open Hearings

By DAVID E. ROSENBAUM

Special to The New York Times

WASHINGTON, March 6—The Senate, with its leadership in firm control, rejected today a proposal that would have made most critical committee meetings open to the public. The action placed the Senate in direct contrast with the House of Representatives, where reform forces appear to have the votes to place a sharp limitation on secrecy in committees.

The Senate did agree today to a modification of secrecy rules, but reformers contended the measure that was passed merely endorsed a "presumption of secrecy."

On the key vote, the Senate voted, 47 to 38, against a proposal that would have made every committee meeting open unless a majority of the committee voted at the beginning of the meeting to close the doors to outsiders.

Most junior Senators voted for the proposal, but the leaders and whips of both parties and all but one committee chairman went against it.

After defeating the move by reformers, the Senate agreed

Continued on Page 22, Column 7

A DEADLINE GIVEN TO PENN CENTRAL

Judge Allows Road Until July to Offer Reorganizing or Liquidation Plan

By ROBERT E. BEDINGFIELD

Judge John P. Fullam of the Federal District Court in Philadelphia yesterday gave the Penn Central Railroad's trustees until July 2 to file with him either a practicable plan of reorganization for the 20,000-mile system or a proposal for its liquidation.

Judge Fullam said that on the basis of the record to date—the Penn Central has been in bankruptcy since June 20, 1970—it appeared "highly doubtful" that the railroad could "properly be permitted to continue to operate on its present basis beyond Oct. 1."

Judge Fullam asked for a "feasible plan for reorganization or suitable proposals for liquidation or other disposition of the enterprise."

Meanwhile, Judge Fullam, who is in charge of the Penny's bankruptcy, was asked by the trustees of an-

Continued on Page 57, Column 1

Ellsberg Witness Asserts Military Falsified Reports

By MARTIN ARNOLD

Special to The New York Times

LOS ANGELES, March 6—A Central Intelligence Agency analyst testified today at the Pentagon papers trial that he had attended conferences, in Saigon and Hawaii and at the agency, in which the military purposely diminished estimates of enemy strength in Vietnam.

The witness, Samuel A. Adams, said that there were "political pressures in the military to display the enemy as weaker than he actually was."

He did not say why, but the defense contends that this was done to make it appear that the Army was winning the war.

Mr. Adams said that the monthly estimates of the enemy's military strength, called the order of battle, were prepared for the press and for the White House and that they were so inaccurate that after the enemy's Tet offensive in 1968, two official sets of estimates had to be put together each month, one by the Army, the other by the agency.

The Adams testimony pertains to a 1968 Joint Chiefs of Staff memorandum, eight pages of which are among the 20 "top secret - sensitive" documents in this case.

A Government witness, Lieut. Gen. William G. DePuy, assistant to the vice chief of staff of the Army, has testified that disclosure of those eight pages damaged the national defense, was of advantage to a foreign nation and could have helped Hanoi during the Vietnam war.

An example of the information that could have helped Hanoi, General DePuy said, was the American estimates of the enemy order of battle.

Mr. Adams said that he believed the memorandum, written after the early Tet offense in 1968, "would be virtually

Continued on Page 5, Column 1

9 SEWAGE PLANTS IN STATE GET AID

U.S. Provides $200-Million for Brooklyn, S.I. and Upstate Projects

By PETER KIHSS

Federal grants totaling $200,031,620 for nine sewage-treatment projects—one in Staten Island, one in Brooklyn and seven upstate—were announced yesterday, making possible early starts on the long-planned major plants that will treat by 1979 virtually the last of the city's raw sewage.

"It was a real cliff-hanger that kept us dangling to the last possible date," said Martin Lang, the city's Commissioner of Water Resources.

Official approval came just before a March 1 deadline, after which new Federal requirements would have forced redesign and resubmittal of the long-pending projects here and upstate.

The Oakwood Beach water-pollution control project in southeastern Staten Island, which was described by Mr. Lang as a "catalyst" for development in the borough, received a grant of $81,922,270 from the Federal Environmental Protection Agency. The facility is scheduled in its first stage to treat 40 million gallons of sewage a day now going into

Continued on Page 49, Column 1

1,200 Apartments To Be Cooperatives In Renovation Plan

By JOSEPH P. FRIED

Forty buildings containing nearly 1,200 apartments throughout the city will be rehabilitated and converted to tenant-owned cooperatives as part of a "major" new publicly assisted housing program announced by Mayor Lindsay yesterday.

Also, 54 buildings with more than 1,700 apartments are being considered for the program—which is designed for low-income and moderate-income families—and the inclusion of still more buildings is contemplated in the future, the Mayor said.

The purchase and renovation of the first 40 buildings are expected to cost more than $8-million, with the work on most of them scheduled to be completed by June 30, 1974, Mr. Lindsay said.

The program, which is the type of venture some experts have said is necessary to preserve existing housing, is partly intended to reduce housing decay and abandonment by putting slum-area buildings under the ownership of their tenants. Presumably, as owners, the people would have a greater incentive to keep up the properties.

But buildings not in slum areas will also be eligible for the program, according to Robert Schur, deputy commissioner

Continued on Page 51, Column 1

Sudan Says Fatah Official Helped Plan Embassy Raid

Accusation in Khartoum

By HENRY TANNER

Special to The New York Times

KHARTOUM, the Sudan, March 6—President Gaafar al-Nimeiry today accused the head of the Khartoum office of Al Fatah, the Palestinian commando organization, of having been the key planner of the attack by Black September terrorists on the Saudi Arabian Embassy in which three Western diplomats were slain.

In a grim speech on radio and television, he announced that the headquarters of all Palestinian organizations in the Sudan would be closed, and he vowed that the eight Black September guerrillas would be tried for murder under Sudanese law. The law provides the death penalty for murder.

The President said that the Fatah representative, Fawaz Yassin, had left the Sudan on a Libyan airliner a few hours before the Saudi Embassy was invaded by the terrorists last Thursday night.

He asked that Mr. Yassin be extradited by the "Arab country where he may now find himself." He asserted that before leaving the Sudan Mr. Yassin had received a message

Continued on Page 9, Column 1

Offer by King Hussein

By JUAN de ONIS

Special to The New York Times

BEIRUT, Lebanon, March 6—King Hussein of Jordan, responding to Arab appeals for clemency, offered today to suspend death sentences against 17 Palestinian commandos if their guerrilla organizations halted subversion against Jordan.

In making the offer, King Hussein said that the "Arab cause" against Israel was being undermined in world opinion by extremist actions by Black September, such as the killing of three diplomats—two Americans and a Belgian—in the Sudan last week.

The Americans, Cleo A. Noel Jr., the United States Ambassador to the Sudan, and the outgoing charge d'affaires, George C. Moore, as well as a Belgian diplomat, Guy Eid, were killed while being held hostage by Arab extremists whose de-

Continued on Page 8, Column 1

Deadlock on Prisoners Is Broken In Apparent Saigon Compromise

By CHARLES MOHR

Special to The New York Times

SAIGON, South Vietnam, Wednesday, March 7—An impasse on the exchange of Vietnamese prisoners of war was broken today with what appeared to be a South Vietnamese compromise.

An American spokesman said that at a meeting of the Four-Party Joint Military Commission this morning, South Vietnam offered to release 6,300 prisoners in its custody in the "second phase" of P.O.W. exchanges.

South Vietnam originally said it held 28,000 Communist prisoners, and it released about one fourth, or 7,000 of these last month in the first exchanges. In recent days, however, Saigon had scaled down the number to be exchanged next to 3,000 in an attempt to force the North Vietnamese and the Vietcong to admit they were holding far more than the 4,700 Government soldiers they have acknowledged.

The Communists hotly protested the Saigon move and on Monday threatened to boycott meetings of the military commission. The settlement, which was very close to the Communist demand, was apparently reached behind the scenes yesterday and accepted at a meeting of all four parties this morning.

The Communists will release somewhat more than 1,000 Government soldiers in the forthcoming second increment of exchanges and have promised to ascertain if they are holding more prisoners than have been listed so far, an informed source said.

No exact time for the new

Continued on Page 2, Column 4

Pearl Buck Is Dead at 80; Won Nobel Prize in 1938

Pearl S. Buck

By ALBIN KREBS

Pearl S. Buck, the author of more than 85 books and winner of the Nobel and Pulitzer Prizes in literature, died yesterday at her home in Danby, Vt., after a long illness.

Mrs. Buck, who was 80 years old, had recently completed a children's book and was at work on two novels, one of which, "The Red Earth," deals with the modern-day descendants of the characters in her best-known novel, "The Good Earth."

She was able to continue working despite failing health, which caused her to be hos-

Continued on Page 49, Column 1

Nixon's Presidency: A Nation Is Changed

This is the fourth and last of a series of articles on Richard M. Nixon's use of the powers of the Presidency and its effects on the Government and the national life.

By JOHN HERBERS

Special to The New York Times

WASHINGTON, March 6—For four years, Nixon Administration officials traveled the nation telling audiences that the Federal Government, over which they were presiding, was flawed in many ways as a means of delivering services to the public.

The standard argument, used by everyone from the President to deputy assistant secretaries, was that the Federal Government was "muscle-bound" under a "patronizing bureaucratic élite" and that local governments should be trusted and strengthened.

Now they are fulfilling their prophecy. Money and authority are flowing back to the states and the President and his men are dismantling programs built by four decades of Democratic government. Although it has just begun, this reversal of a long-term trend is one of the many ways in which the Nixon Presidency has had enormous impact on the national life.

Like all Presidents, Mr. Nixon is seeking to have an important impact on the nation. But he has undertaken to make fundamental changes in what kind of schools people attend, what kind of cities and communities they live in, what kind of news they watch on television and read in the papers, what taxes they pay and to whom, what system of justice they live under, what their employment and income opportunities will be and a host of other matters af-

Continued on Page 22, Column 1

NEWS INDEX

Pearl Buck, Author of 'Good Earth,' Who Won Nobel Prize, Dies

Continued From Page 1, Col. 6

pitalized several times in the last year and to undergo surgery for the removal of her gall bladder last September.

Mrs. Buck is survived by a daughter, Carol; nine adopted children, Janice, Richard, John, Edgar, Jean, Henriette, Theresa, Chieko and Johanna; a sister, Mrs. Grace Yaukey, and 12 grandchildren.

According to her wishes, the funeral service will be private.

In a tribute to Mrs. Buck, President Nixon said yesterday that she was "a human bridge between the civilizations of the East and West."

In a reference to the fact that Mrs. Buck spent almost all of the first 40 years of her life in China and devoted much of her writing to Chinese subjects, Mr. Nixon said:

"It is fitting that Pearl Buck lived to see two peoples she loved so much draw closer together during her last years. . . . With simple eloquence she translated her personal love for the people and culture of China into a rich literary heritage, treasured by Asians and Westerners alike. She lived a long, life as artist, wife, mother, and philanthropist."

Although Mrs. Buck's love for the Chinese people was enduring, she was persona non grata with that country's current leaders. Recently she was turned down in her efforts to be admitted to China because, Chinese authorities said, her works have "for a long time taken an attitude of distortion, smear and vilification toward the people of China and their leaders."

Mrs. Buck, who rarely minced words, was once asked by an interviewer, "Why do you write so many books?"

"Why not?" she replied, with a touch of irritation in her voice. "I'm a writer."

Wave of Resentment

For the strong-willed, highly opinionated Mrs. Buck, winner of a Pulitzer Prize and the only American woman Nobel Laureate for literature, the explanation was as simple as that. "When I say I'm a working writer, I accent 'working,'" she said.

Mrs. Buck was indeed a prolific writer. Her first novel, "East Wind: West Wind," was not published until 1930, when she was 38 years old, but by her 80th birthday in 1972 she had published more than 85 novels and collections of short stories and essays, and more than 25 volumes still awaited publication. She was the most translated of all American authors.

"Of course, one pays the price for being prolific," Mrs. Buck said in an interview for this article in 1969. "I sometimes feel quite guilty for being so, and Heaven knows the literary Establishment can't forgive me for it, nor for the fact that my books sell. With some people, that's suspect, you know."

Mrs. Buck referred, as she was often wont to do throughout her lengthy and profitable career, to the disdain with which many critics looked upon her. Most of them welcomed her second novel, "The Good Earth," which became one of the most phenomenally popular books of the century, but there was much resentment when it was awarded the Pulitzer Prize in 1931.

Her detractors argued that the Pulitzer is supposed to be given to a distinctly American work, by an American writer, and that "The Good Earth," about Chinese peasants, was written by a woman who had lived most of her life in China.

When Mrs. Buck was awarded the Nobel Prize in 1938, it was fashionable in literary circles to complain that if any American woman was entitled to a Nobel, it was Willa Cather, not Pearl Buck.

"Above all," Mrs. Buck said, "so many writers and critics have seemed to be jealous of me not simply because my books are popular, or that the Book-of-the-Month Club has distributed a dozen of them, but because I write them swiftly. It's true, I do. It took me just two months to write 'The Good Earth.' But what must not be forgotten is that those agony-filled two months were devoted to writing words on paper. The novel took shape in my mind over perhaps 10 years."

While busily turning out an average of two volumes a year, on an almost daily writing regime that began at 8 A.M. and ended at 1 P.M, Mrs. Buck managed to care for her mentally retarded daughter Carol and nine adopted children, while at the same time taking an active interest in projects for the aid of mentally retarded children, the placement for adoption of children of mixed blood, and the betterment of international relations.

Involved as she seemingly was in the lives of other people, Mrs. Buck possessed a certain air of detachment and, as she put it, she was "a solitary person, an intellectual loner." She said that she actually liked people, "but I prefer their company only in small doses; I have expected so much from so many people, and I have been so often disappointed."

If she viewed others with cool detachment, it was also true that Mrs. Buck believed the feeling was mutual. "Somehow I have always been an object, rather than a person," she said. "As a child, I was white with yellow hair and blue eyes in a country where everyone knew the proper color of eyes and hair was black, and skin was brown. can remember my Chinese friends bringing their friends to look at me because I was different. By the time I came to this country I was different again. I was already what people call famous. People came to see me as they would an object, not a person."

Mrs. Buck was the product of two cultures, which enabled her to become what she called "mentally bifocal." She loved China and the Chinese and came to be equally devoted to America and Americans although she never hesitated to criticize both cultures

Pearl Comfort Sydenstricker was born June 26, 1892, in Hillsboro, W. Va., the daughter of Absalom Andrew and Caroline Stulting Sydenstricker. Her Presbyterian missionary parents had been in China for 12 years, during which three of their four children had died in infancy of tropical diseases.Pearl Comfort was born during the Sydenstrickers' one-year home leave. When she was three months old, the family set out for home—Chinkiang, a city about 200 miles west off the mouth of the Yangtze River.

Billeted in Community

The Rev. Mr. Sydenstricker believed that in order to convert the Chinese to Christianity, he should live among them and gain their trust. For some years he wore Chinese garb and even grew a queue, and, against the wishes of his superiors on the Presbyterian Board of Missions, insisted that his family be billeted in the Chinese community instead of the comfortably isolated compound set aside for foreigners.

Pearl was taught her lessons by her mother in the morning, and was tutored by a Confucian scholar afternoons. "I learned to speak Chinese before I could speak English," she said. "I seldom saw white children. I played with the Chinese, visited in their homes, ate their food. I did not consider myself, as a child, different from the Chinese, a people I grew to love and have continued to love all my life."

But when she was 8 years old, Pearl Sydenstricker learned that she was indeed different from her darker-skinned playmates. The Empress Dowager Tzu Hsi, who had come under the influence of the Boxers, a fanatic secret society, decreed the death of every white man, woman and child in China. Following the slaughter of several missionary families in Shantung, Mr. Sydenstricker decided to send his wife and daughters, Pearl and Caroline, to Shanghai, which was considered safer. They did not return to Chinkiang until a year later, after the Boxer Rebellion had been put down by an international force. (Pearl's older brother, Clyde, was in school in the United States at the time.)

When she was 16, Pearl Sydenstricker returned to the United States to attend Randolph-Macon Women's College at Lynchburg, Va., where her brother lived. She was president of her graduating class in 1914, a Phi Beta Kappa, and winner of two literary prizes in her senior year. Invited to teach psychology at the college, she stayed on a semester but had to return to China to care for her mother, who had contracted sprue, a debilitating tropical disease.

Moved to Nanking

In 1917, Pearl Sydenstricker met and married John Lossing Buck, an agricultural missionary of whom her parents did not approve. "I had to live on my own," she said years later, "and I married a man I saw alone only four times before the ceremony. My parents were right and I was wrong. I married a handsome face, and who wants to live with just a handsome face?"

She, nevertheless, remained the wife of John Lossing Buck for 18 years. The Bucks spent five years in a small town in north China, where their daughter, Carol, was born in 1921. The following year they moved to Nanking, where Mrs. Buck taught English literature at the University of Nanking, Southeastern University and Chung Yang University. (During this period, she said many years later, she took a half-Chinese lover. She never revealed his name.)

In 1924 the Bucks came to the United States with their daughter to spend a year at Cornell University. While her husband studied agriculture, Mrs. Buck pursued a master's degree in English, which she received in 1926, along with the Laura Messenger Prize in history for an essay, "China and the West." The Bucks adopted an infant daughter, Janice, before returning to China.

Mrs. Buck had, since her childhood, when she began contributing short pieces to the children's page of The Shanghai Mercury, wanted to be a writer. She sold an article detailing life in China to The Atlantic in 1923 and in 1924 Forum Magazine published her essay, "Beauty in China." Her first work of fiction, "A Chinese Woman Speaks," was published by Asia Magazine in 1926.

She had completed the manuscript of a novel and a biography of her mother when, in March, 1927, the Bucks had to flee Nanking because it had been invaded by Communist revolutionary soldiers. After a year spent in Japan, the family returned, and Mrs. Buck found that the manuscript of "The Exile," her mother's biography (not published until 1936) was safe, but the novel had disappeared in the looting of her home. With her customary detachment, Mrs. Buck later said, "the novel probably wasn't good."

By 1928, Mrs. Buck had become tragically aware of a new reason why she must sell any writing that she could; she knew by then that her daughter, Carol, was hopelessly retarded, and would need special costly care.

She was unsophisticated in literary ways then, and having no agent, she wrote to two she found listed in an old copy of The Writer's Guide picked up in a bookshop in Shanghai. One declined to represent her on the ground that "no one wants to read stories about China." The other, David Lloyd, cautiously asked to see a sample of her work. She sent him "East Wind: West Wind," which was turned down by more than a dozen publishers before the John Day Company bought it for publication in 1930.

Meanwhile, in 1929, Mrs. Buck brought Carol to The Training School, in Vineland, N.J. (where she still lives). But it cost $1,000 a year for Carol to remain there, and Mrs. Buck desperately wanted two years free of teaching to write the novel that was already formed mentally, "The Good Earth." A doctor in New York spoke of her plight to Mrs. John H. Finley, wife of the former editor in chief of The New York Times, and Mrs. Finley anonymously lent her the needed $2,000. (The two women later became close friends.)

"The Good Earth" was an instant success, both critically and financially. It was on the best-seller lists for 21 months, was translated into more than 30 languages, received the 1931 Pulitzer Prize, was dramatized for Broadway and became a hit motion picture starring Paul Muni as Wang Lung the Chinese peasant whose rise from poverty and ignorance reflected the main currents of the development of modern China. Luise Rainer, who portrayed Wang's wife, O-lan, received an Academy Award for her performance in the film.

Money began to pour in. Mrs. Buck paid off her $2,000 debt, established two trust funds to ensure care for Carol for the rest of her life, and had a bathhouse built for the women in her Nanking neighborhood.

"Sons," published in 1932, and "A House Divided," (1935) completed the trilogy begun with "The Good Earth." (The trilogy was later published as one volume, "House of Earth.") In 1933, John Day published "All Men Are Brothers," Mrs. Buck's translation of the classic Chinese novel "Shui H Chuan," and in 1936, the biographies of her mother ("The Exile") and her father ("Fighting Angel").

In 1932, the Bucks returned to the United States and to Ithaca, N.Y., where her husband undertook further study at Cornell. Mrs. Buck, suddenly famous, was launched on a whirl of cocktail parties, luncheons, dinners and speaking engagements. She often lunched in New York with Richard J. Walsh, president of the John Day Company, "and slowly we fell in love," she said years later. He followed her to China in 1933 to try to persuade her to marry him. In 1934 she left her husband and sailed for the United States with her adopted daughter.

Both Mr. Walsh, who had children of his own, and Mrs. Buck secured divorces in Reno, Nev., on June 11, 1935, and were married there the same day. The publisher and his prize author moved into a Park Avenue apartment in New York, but spent their weekends on the 400-acre estate, Green Hills Farm, in Bucks County, Pa., which Mrs. Buck had bought shortly after she left China for the last time.

"My husband wanted children," Mrs. Buck said in 1969," but I really don't think I wanted to produce another child—even if I could have—because, we have to face it, I am not a maternal woman. I love children as human beings and I respect them from the moment they are born, but I am not primarily a mother."

The Walshes adopted two infant boys in 1936 and in the years to follow, six more children, among them three Americans and a girl whose mother was German and whose father was a black G.I. Caring for the children, maintaining an apartment, the place in Bucks County, and, later, a summer home in Vermont, took money. And, as Mrs. Buck was to say with her usual self-containment and candor: "I married two men in my lifetime who were unable to support me; I have always supported myself and my family, and it's been a large family."

Although she really didn't need an excuse to write, since she possessed a great compulsion to do so, the desire to keep money, and lots of it, constantly coming in helped wed Mrs. Buck to her typewriter. And the books seemed to roll effortlessly forth.

Some of her most successful novels were "Dragon Seed," "This Proud Heart," "Imperial Woman," "Come, My Beloved," "Command the Morning," "The Patriot," "Portrait of a Marriage," and "The Promise." There were six collections of short stories, 14 books for children, and more than a dozen works of nonfiction, including "The Child Who Never Grew," the movingly told story of her daughter, Carol.

Not a 'One-Book Writer'

Mrs. Buck's publisher-husband believed it would be unwise to issue more than one Pearl Buck novel a year and so, at one point, in the forties, the writer decided to adopt a pseudonym, "John Sedges," which appeared on five novels all with American locales. The most successful of these was "The Townsman," a 1945 best-seller and one of Mrs. Buck's favorite novels. (She was vastly amused when the reviewer for The Kansas City Star wrote of "The Townsman," which was set in Kansas, that "it could only have been written by someone who had spent a lifetime in Kansas.")

Despite the fact that she turned out an extraordinarily large number of books, covering a wide variety of subjects and themes, Mrs. Buck was usually identified by the public as "the author of 'The Good Earth' " and this she found extremely irksome. "I've heard so much about it I can't bear it," she said. "Sinclair Lewis said he never wanted to hear 'Main Street' mentioned again, and I can understand that perfectly. It is grossly unfair for anyone to consider either of us one-book writers."

"All the News That's Fit to Print."

The New York Times.

THE WEATHER.
Fair, slightly warmer Thursday; Friday, fair, warmer; moderate winds, becoming south.
For full weather report see Page 22.

VOL. CVI.. No. 36,207. Entered as Second-Class Matter, Post Office, New York, N. Y. NEW YORK, TUESDAY, MARCH 12, 1957. Times Square, New York 36, N. Y. Telephone Lackawanna 4-1000 FIVE CENTS

NASSER MOVING TO TAKE OVER GAZA; NAMES GOVERNOR, SCORES U. N. UNIT; HAMMARSKJOLD DEFERRING ACTION

JERSEY DECREES FULL-VALUE TAX ON LAND BY 1959

State Supreme Court Splits 4-3 on Grace Period to Obey Century-Old Law

CUT IN RATES EXPECTED

Ruling Is Made in Monmouth Case—Railroads Win on Lower Terminal Levies

By GEORGE CABLE WRIGHT
Special to The New York Times.

TRENTON, March 11—The State Supreme Court, in a long-awaited decision, ordered Middletown Township today to reassess all local property at its true market value by 1959.

The 4-to-3 ruling is expected to result in a revaluation and reassessment of virtually all real property throughout New Jersey.

Despite a century-old state statute requiring such assessments at true value, only one municipality, Princeton Township, assesses it this way. All of the 566 other communities in the state have traditionally ignored the law and based their property assessments on percentages of market value ranging from 7.7 to 77.

In Middletown the base varies between 14 and 18 per cent. This variance led to a taxpayer's suit that resulted in today's court action.

Railroad Gets Tax Equality

In a related decision, the Supreme Court unanimously ordered the state tax director, Aaron K. Neeld, to bring levies on nonmainline railroad property in line with imposts on real property. The ruling resulted from a suit instituted a year ago by the Delaware, Lackawanna and Western Railroad.

Similar suits were filed in a lower court last week by five other railroads. All contend that they are being discriminated against by tax collectors in seven municipalities.

Local property tax collections in New Jersey last year amounted to $580,000,000. With a revaluation and reassessment of all property at true value, they could conceivably exceed $1,500,000,000. In reality, however, they would in all probability be considerably less than the latter figure.

Sees No Sharp Rate Cut

Mr. Neeld stressed, nevertheless, that tax rates could not be expected to drop in proportion to the change in the assessment base. He explained that sharp increases in municipal budgets throughout the state made such a move impracticable.

The majority opinion in the Middletown case was written by Justice Harry Heher. Justices A. Dayton Oliphant and Albert E. Burling concurred. Chief Justice Arthur T. Vanderbilt and Justice Nathan L. Jacobs, in separate dissenting opinions, demanded that Middletown be forced to undertake the reassessment immediately. Justice William A. Wachenfeld wrote a fourth opinion terming the decison on reassessment a prerogative of the Legislature. Justice Joseph Weintraub, in a fifth opinion, concurred with Justice Heher.

The decision upheld but amended a verdict rendered by the

Continued on Page 29, Column 3

Admiral Byrd Dies at 68; Made 5 Polar Expeditions

The New York Times
Rear Admiral Richard E. Byrd in the Antarctic last year

By The Associated Press.

BOSTON, March 11—Rear Admiral Richard E. Byrd, U. S. N., retired, the first man to fly over the North and South Poles, died in his sleep tonight at his Brimmer Street home. He was 68 years old.

His death was attributed to a heart ailment brought on by overwork in connection with his many activities.

The polar explorer, who had been named head of the Navy's Operation Deep Freeze in Antarctica, had been ill for several months. This prevented him from assuming on-the-spot supervision of the polar expedition in the International Geophysical Year beginning July 1.

Admiral Byrd was decorated on Feb. 21 with the Defense Department's Medal of Freedom. The presentation was made quietly by Admiral Arleigh Burke, Chief of Naval Operations, who flew to Boston, made the award and returned immediately by air to Washington.

Admiral Byrd had been under

Continued on Page 18, Column 1

REPUBLICANS MAP 6 REGIONAL TALKS FOR '58 CAMPAIGN

Plan Early Start in Drive to Win Congress—President Hails 'Auspicious' Move

By W. H. LAWRENCE
Special to The New York Times.

WASHINGTON, March 11—The Republican high command scheduled today six regional fact-finding conferences to get the 1958 Congressional campaign under way months ahead of time.

President Eisenhower endorsed the plan, calling it "an auspicious start in the all-important task of electing a Republican Senate and Republican House of Representatives." The G. O. P. leaders met with the President at the White House after their conference.

Meade Alcorn, new party chairman, called it the earliest start on the most intensive Congressional campaign in history.

The announcement of the regional sessions came after a meeting of the Republican executive committee and the chairmen of the Senate and House campaign committees.

'56 Outcome Accents Task

The party's task of trying to regain Congressional control in the mid-term elections was emphasized by the 1956 election results. Last November, Democratic candidates for the House outpolled Republicans by more than 1,600,000 votes, although President Eisenhower was reelected by more than 9,600,000 votes.

In a letter to the conferees, the President said the regional meetings were essential to "assure that the voice of the people is truly the voice of the Republican party."

Mr. Alcorn, at a news conference, dodged questions about the intra-party struggle over General Eisenhower's effort to adopt more modern objectives. The President has said the Republicans lost Congress because a majority of the people did not feel that the party, as a whole, was firmly back of modern Republicanism.

Allusion to McCarthy

Mr. Alcorn said his group would take no part in selecting party candidates for the House and Senate, but would back any Republican who had been nominated.

He was told of "a couple of Senators up for re-election next year who have been described by the President as a drag on his program." The allusion apparently was to Senators Joseph R. McCarthy of Wisconsin and George Malone of Nevada.

Mr. Alcorn commented:

"Any Republican who is nominated through the regular processes and runs on the Republican ticket is entitled to our support and will have our help."

"Do you expect the White

Continued on Page 25, Column 6

BUNCHE REACHES EGYPT: Dr. Ralph J. Bunche, U. N. Under Secretary, confers at Abu Suweir in the Canal Zone with Maj. Gen. E. L. M. Burns, left, commander of U. N. Emergency Force. With them at meeting Sunday was Brig. Amin Helmi of Egyptian Army.
Associated Press Radiophoto

CAIRO MAKES BID

Seeks to Reduce Role of Gen. Burns' Force to Border Patrol

By HOMER BIGART
Special to The New York Times.

CAIRO, March 11—Egypt accused the United Nations Emergency Force today of exceeding its authority in Gaza and announced her intention of taking over the Gaza Strip immediately.

President Gamal Abdel Nasser named Gen. Hassan Abdel Latif as Governor of Gaza. The President intends to reduce the role of the United Nations force to mere supervision of the demarcation line between the Gaza Strip and Israel and of the Sinai frontier with Israel.

Taking advantage of the general confusion over the vague directives of the United Nations force, President Nasser took the action at the most embarrassing moment for the force. Last Thursday, following the Israeli withdrawal, Maj. Gen. E. L. M. Burns, United Nations Commander, announced that his troops were assuming responsibility for civil affairs in Gaza.

U. N. Named a Governor

General Burns appointed Col. Carl Engholm of Denmark as Military Governor. Municipal councils were formed in Gaza and three other towns in the Gaza Strip.

The United Nations Commander was acting on orders from Secretary General Dag Hammarskjold that the take-over of both military and civilian control from Israel would be "exclusively by the United Nations Emergency Force in the first instance." Mr. Hammarskjold never defined the duration of "the first instance."

Neither General Burns nor Dr. Ralph J. Bunche, an Under Secretary, who visited Gaza during the day, had any inkling that President Nasser would demand the end of United Nations rule now.

No Advance Warning

Dr. Bunche first learned of the Egyptian action on returning to Cairo tonight. He declined comment, but pointed out that the United Nations had "never questioned Egypt's legal rights in Gaza."

The United Nations had no intention to internationalize Gaza, he said.

Demonstrating once again his acute sense of timing, President Nasser waited until Gaza mobs had provoked a shooting incident before demanding the immediate restoration of Egyptian rule. The United Nations force seems to have no alternative but to yield to the Egyptian demand.

Col. Salah Gohar, director of the Egyptian Palestine Department, said tonight that Mr. Hammarskjold was expected in Cairo Saturday. Mr. Hammarskjold will be told that United Nations troops must leave the town of Gaza immediately and that they must be deployed only

Continued on Page 3, Column 1

MORHOUSE BACKS 1C 'GAS' TAX RISE

State G. O. P. Leader Splits With Party's Legislators—Fears Highway Delay

By LEO EGAN
Special to The New York Times.

ALBANY, March 11—The Republican state chairman publicly declared himself today in favor of increasing the gasoline tax 1 cent a gallon.

L. Judson Morhouse thereby put himself in open opposition to the position taken by Republican leaders of the Legislature. His attitude raised the possibility of a Republican legislative split on the issue.

Mr. Morhouse took his stand in favor of raising the gasoline tax at a Republican women's legislative conference. Afterwards he supplemented his statement in an interview.

Just before Mr. Morhouse addressed the women's group, Senator Austin W. Erwin, Republican of Genesee, had told them flatly that such a tax increase was not needed either this year or next to finance the enlarged highway construction program the state is contemplating.

Senator Erwin is chairman of the Senate Finance Committee and usually reflects the views of Senator Walter J. Mahoney, the Republican leader of the Senate, as well as his own.

"When they talk about a gaso-

Continued on Page 28, Column 6

New One-Way Plan Cuts Delay by 30% In Midtown Traffic

By JOSEPH C. INGRAHAM

Traffic gains outweighed the shortcomings of the new one-way avenue pattern in midtown yesterday.

Despite a six-hour bottleneck in the Herald Square area, travel on Broadway, Seventh Avenue and the Avenue of the Americas (Sixth Avenue) was 30 per cent faster than under the old two-way system.

More important, according to Traffic Commissioner T. T. Wiley, the transition accomplished the prime purpose of reducing crosstown delays. Test runs by Traffic Department engineers and independent checks by civic groups showed a 50 per cent drop in "sitting still" time.

Bus drivers and patrons complained of delays. Taxicab operators chafed at not being able to hurry along the avenues. There were some complaints of extra cruising to get to destinations. Street repairs clogged traffic, too.

Nevertheless, it was apparent that the general flow was better. This was pointedly borne out by a police decision to reduce the supervisory force that is assigned to minimize the confusion attendant on any new traffic program. This force will be reduced 30 per cent today.

The police detail to be withdrawn will all be north of Forty-second Street. This is near the midpoint in the new system,

Continued on Page 29, Column 1

COURT REINSTATES UNION INDICTMENT

Supreme Bench Refuses, 5-3, to Rule on U.A.W. Political Spending Before a Trial

By JOSEPH A. LOFTUS
Special to The New York Times.

WASHINGTON, March 11—The Supreme Court refused, 5 to 3, today to rule now on whether a law banning political spending by a union was constitutional. Such a decision was deferred at least until there had been a trial of the facts.

The decision reinstated an indictment against the United Auto Workers.

The majority opinion, written by Justice Felix Frankfurter, said in effect: If the union did as charged, it violated the laws, but the Court is not saying now whether Congress had a constitutional right to enact the law.

The union is expected to concede the central facts. Its position is that these facts violate no constitutional law.

Judge Frank A. Picard of the United States District Court in Detroit had held that Congress did not intend to forbid such expenditures as the indictment alleged so there was nothing to try

Continued on Page 19, Column 1

U.N. Chief Suggests Move Aims to Placate Egyptians

By THOMAS J. HAMILTON
Special to The New York Times.

UNITED NATIONS, N. Y., March 11—Dag Hammarskjold and his Advisory Committee on the Middle East adopted a wait-and-see attitude tonight toward the appointment of an Egyptian Governor of the Gaza Strip.

Although the Secretary General called a meeting of the committee to consider the news, he insisted that nothing should be done at this stage.

[United States officials in Washington were surprised and shocked at the action taken by Egypt. Some suggested that the assumption on which the United States had urged Israel to withdraw might prove false. This was that Egypt would waive her rights in the Gaza Strip under the 1949 Palestine Armistice Agreement.]

Slur at U. N. Force Seen

Some members of Mr. Hammarskjold's committee insisted that the appointment of a Governor was a sign that Gamal Abdel Nasser, President of Egypt, had decided to discredit the United Nations Emergency Force and to drive it out of the Gaza Strip.

They insisted that, as a minimum, Mr. Hammarskjold should ask President Nasser to explain his action. However, the Secretary General contended that such an inquiry would be attaching too much political importance to the appointment and indicated that it was merely in response to Egyptian public opinion.

At the close of the meeting, therefore, Mr. Hammarskjold said he would assume that all

Continued on Page 2, Column 3

ISRAEL HOLDS U.N. MUST GUARD GAZA

World Body's Responsibility Is to Keep Egyptians Out, Foreign Ministry Says

Special to The New York Times.

TEL AVIV, Israel, March 11—Walter Eytan, Director General of the Israeli Foreign Ministry, said today that the United Nations had the responsibility for preventing the Egyptians from returning to the Gaza Strip.

A few hours after he had spoken, it was announced in Cairo that Egypt had appointed a man as Governor of the Gaza Strip. [In Jerusalem, an Israeli Government spokesman expressed "grave concern" at this, The Associated Press reported.]

Mr. Eytan had said:

"A great responsibility now rests on the United Nations—the responsibility for asserting international rule in Gaza and making it impossible for Egypt to return to the area and resume the murderous activities which led up to the Sinai campaign last October."

Warns of Terrorism

He called for effective police action by the United Nations Emergency Force and warned: "If Egypt is allowed to spread terror in Gaza, she alone will be accountable for the consequences."

Mr. Eytan accused Egypt of what he termed "the campaign of terror unleashed in Gaza."

Mr. Eytan charged that Egypt had employed propagandists, agitators, strong-arm men and thugs.

"Every man in Gaza knows that if he does not turn out to demonstrate in the streets he will find himself on Egypt's blacklist, which means that he has every chance of being beaten up or killed," Mr. Eytan said.

Fedayeen Activities Charged

JERUSALEM, March 11 (AP)—Mr. Eytan said also that Egypt had resumed "sending fedayeen [guerrilla squads] once again to operate against life and property in Israel."

"Israel has made it perfectly clear she will not tolerate provocations of this kind," he added, saying "refugees from Gaza have started fleeing to Israel." He continued:

"Egypt's methods are familiar—they are methods by which

Continued on Page 3, Column 6

House Group Insists President Cut Budget

By The United Press.

WASHINGTON, March 11—The House Rules Committee overrode Republican protests today and approved a resolution calling on President Eisenhower to recommend cuts in his $71,800,000,000 budget for the 1958 fiscal year. The fiscal year begins July 1.

The measure will come before the House tomorrow for a vote. Democratic leaders said it would pass.

However, a partisan fight was in prospect. Republicans charged the action is designed to "pass the Federal economy buck to the President."

A Senate vote is not required.

William F. Knowland of California, Senate Republican leader, called for public support for a three-pronged drive to cut Government spending, trim the national debt, and "to lay a foundation for some tax reduction next year." Precival F.

Continued on Page 25, Column 2

Fried Resigns Post With Prisons Board

Special to The New York Times.

ALBANY, March 11—Governor Harriman accepted tonight the resignation of Henry Fried as a member of the State Correction Commission. Mr. Fried had been named in a New York City Council investigation into the fitness of Hugh Quinn to hold his seat on the Council.

In his letter of resignation, Mr. Fried said that he had given consideration to the events of the last few months and had "come to the decision to submit my resignation."

In accepting it, Governor Harriman said that reports from Thomas J. McHugh, Correction Commissioner, were that Mr. Fried had been a useful and conscientious member of the Commission of Correction.

Testimony in the Quinn inquiry has brought out the fact that Mr. Fried headed corpo-

Continued on Page 27, Column 7

Music Sleuth Finds Missing Haydn Mass

By JOHN MacCORMAC
Special to The New York Times.

VIENNA, March 11—One of Josef Haydn's two missing masses has been discovered in Austria in unusual circumstances by H. C. Robbins Landon, an American musicologist.

It was known that the mass existed, but since no score was found it has never been performed in modern times. Its history is one of vicissitudes. What has been found is not a conductor's score of the entire work but a complete set of manuscript parts for individual instruments and voices.

Someone who obviously thought he knew better crossed Haydn's name off the manuscript around 1800. It survived through all the wars in the library of Goettweig Monastery in Lower Austria. From there it was taken to another monastery in Altenburg, near the

Continued on Page 37, Column 6

The New York Times
NEW TRAFFIC PATTERN, which was initiated Sunday, is shown yesterday during its first weekday test. Both Broadway, left, and Avenue of the Americas, right, had carried two-way traffic until the change went into effect. Now Broadway is one way south and the old Sixth Avenue is one way north. Cross street in foreground is Thirty-third.

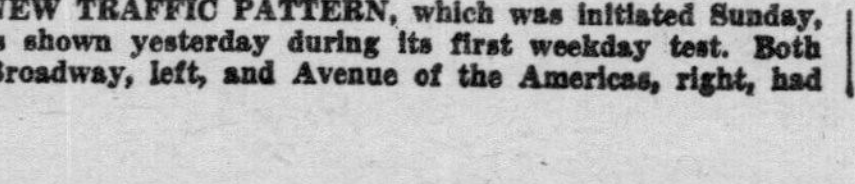

Admiral Flew Over Both Poles and Helped Establish Antarctic as a Continent

BYRD DIES AT 68; POLAR EXPLORER

5 Arctic and Antarctic Trips Provided Groundwork for U. S. Defense Concepts

Continued From Page 1

the care of Dr. William E. Greer and Dr. Paul Dudley White, heart specialist who was a consultant when President Eisenhower suffered a heart attack.

At Admiral Byrd's bedside when he died were his wife, the former Marie D. Ames, whom he married in 1915, and their four children, Lieut. Richard E. Byrd Jr. of the Navy, Mrs. William A. Clarke Jr. of Swarthmore, Pa., Mrs. Robert G. Breyer of Los Angeles and Mrs. Lawrence J. Stabler Jr. of Milmont Park, Pa., a suburb of Philadelphia.

The New York Times

HONORED: Admiral Byrd receiving special medal of National Geographic Society from President Hoover in 1930.

The New York Times

EXPLORING THE ANTARCTIC: The Admiral taking a sight during his expedition in 1929 at Little America I.

Associated Press

DECORATED: In January, 1945, President Roosevelt presented him the Legion of Merit for "outstanding services."

The New York Times

AFTER HISTORIC FLIGHT: Admiral Byrd, then a commander, being congratulated by Roald Amundsen after first flight over top of world in 1926. At right was Floyd Bennett.

Associated Press

LITTLE AMERICA REVISITED: In December of 1955 the explorer returned to site of the Antarctic camp. All but 8 feet of a 75-foot tower, behind him, was hidden by snow.

Frigid Testing Ground

America's strategic concept of polar defense is an outgrowth of Admiral Byrd's five exploration ventures into the Arctic and Antarctic.

After his 1946-47 expedition into the Antarctic, the lines of national defense moved to the polar regions. In addition to establishing the new defense lines, Admiral Byrd's explorations laid the groundwork for claims to potentially vast deposits of metals and other minerals. From the military standpoint they provided a testing-ground for various types of uniform and equipment in temperatures running far below zero.

When he was a boy, Admiral Byrd heard his geography teacher say that the Antarctic was an ocean. During his lifetime he was to play a leading part in establishing it as the Antarctic Continent, the world's last frontier.

The land beyond the horizon always had a fascination for Richard Evelyn Byrd. In pursuit of it he went around the world at the age of 12, flew over both the North and South Poles, across the North Atlantic and other thousands of miles in both the Arctic and Antarctic regions.

First Trip in 1928-29

The explorer's first expedition to Antarctica, in 1928-29, was highlighted by his flight to the South Pole and back on Nov. 29, 1929. His second expedition was from 1933 to 1935.

It was during a six-month vigil at an advance weather base, where he saw no other living thing and with the radio his only link with the outside world, that he received the inspiration for the peace work into which he threw his energies in 1936.

In line with this decision, Admiral Byrd accepted the honorary chairmanship of the No-Foreign-War Crusade sponsored by the Emergency Peace Campaign headed by Dr. Harry Emerson Fosdick.

The qualities of leadership that Admiral Byrd displayed even in early life were a natural heritage from distinguished ancestors. His family was one of the oldest in Virginia. An ancestor, William Byrd, landed at the then crown colony in 1674 to found the American branch of the family. The first Byrds owned large tracts of land, at one time holding title to more than 100,000 acres.

Born in Virginia

Richard E. Byrd was born in Winchester, Va., Oct. 25, 1888, in a household of tradition and affluence. His father was a lawyer. One brother, Harry, became Governor of Virginia and later United States Senator from Virginia. His mother once said that "Richard was born an adventurer and explorer, absolutely without fear."

Admiral Byrd graduated from the Naval Academy in 1912 and went to sea. An old injury continued to bother him, however. After five years, unable to carry his weight on the injured ankle for the long watches that Navy duties required, he was forced to retire.

Admiral Byrd was recalled to active duty in the Navy Department in World War I. Irked by desk duty, he requested assignment to flying school. Navy physicians told him that he was not well enough to learn to fly. He begged for a month in which to prove his ability to "come back."

He went to Pensacola for instruction and was there when a new flying boat was built by the Navy. It was the NC-1, prototype of one that later made the first crossing of the Atlantic. Admiral Byrd conceived the idea of flying it across the ocean to be delivered to the Navy for patrol work.

With Walter Hinton, who later made the flight, Admiral Byrd practiced navigation out of sight of land, and in July, 1918, he asked permission to pilot the NC-1 to Europe.

But instead of flying to Europe he was sent to Halifax, N. S., to take command of an air station there.

The war ended and found him still in Nova Scotia. When he got back to Washington he learned that the Atlantic flight was being taken up in earnest. Admiral Byrd was ordered to Pensacola, but managed to get the orders canceled so that he could help in the preliminary work of preparing the navigation instruments and data for the flight.

Opportunity was beginning to come nearer, although it did not come in the way he thought it would. He was assigned to work on a proposed flight of the dirigible Shenandoah over the North Pole in 1924. The flight was to have started in Alaska and ended in Spitsbergen, the group of Arctic Ocean islands between Greenland and Franz Josef Land, on the other side of the Canadian Arctic. This flight was called off by President Coolidge. But the idea of flying in the Arctic was firmly in Admiral Byrd's mind, and he went to work to make such a flight possible.

It was at this time that he was promoted to lieutenant commander by Congress, promotion having to come in this way to one on the retired list.

His new rank gave him the chance to ask for support for an Arctic flight. He wanted to reach the Pole by air. He obtained funds from Edsel Ford and from John D. Rockefeller Jr., who had backed him in all his ventures. Capt. Robert Bartlett, Admiral Robert E. Peary's ship captain, also raised some money.

Donald B. MacMillan, also a polar explorer and later a rear admiral, had asked the Navy Department for two planes and so had Admiral Byrd. As there were only three amphibians in the Navy, they had to join forces. With three planes and a picked group of mechanics and pilots, Admiral Byrd started off as the flying officer of the expedition. It was on this trip that he became acquainted with Floyd Bennett, who later flew with him over the Pole. Mr. Bennett was a Navy enlisted man who became one of the service's greatest aviators. A friendship began that lasted until Mr. Bennett's death in 1928.

With Mr. Bennett, Admiral Byrd made several notable flights over Greenland and as far north as Ellsmere Land. It was dangerous flying, accompanied by depressing toil of preparation. But it gave him his first taste of the North, and he liked it. The mystery and silence of the frozen land got into his blood. As a result of his experience, he and Mr. Bennett decided that a flight to the North Pole was possible. Admiral Byrd began to plan quietly to accomplish it.

It was not until 1926 that he could obtain leave for himself and Mr. Bennett. They decided to go alone and obtain the necessary money as best they could. They had to raise more than $100,000, and when he returned, Admiral Byrd was $30,000 in debt. He obtained a ship, the Chantier, from the Government, got together a crew of volunteers, and sailed for Spitsbergen in April.

From Spitsbergen they proceeded by plane. They reached the Pole on May 9, 1926. Sixteen hours after they had left their base at Kings Bay on the Arctic Ocean they were back after having flown 1,360 miles.

The news of the flight was received with enthusiasm all over the world.

When he returned to New York Admiral Byrd was welcomed as a hero. The Medal of Honor was bestowed on him. He was promoted to commander, while Mr. Bennett received the rank of warrant officer. Admiral Byrd's modesty and smiling courtesy added to his fame, and his popularity grew as much from his personal qualities as from what he had done.

Admiral Byrd took time out from polar exploration in 1927 to join in the air race across the Atlantic. The flight he and his crew made was one of several that prepared the way for regular trans-Atlantic airplane service. He soon returned to his effort to conquer the polar frontier.

When he returned to the United States in 1927 after a flight to France, Admiral Byrd was already full of plans for his next venture. He soon set in motion the machinery for the most expensive and, he hoped, the most complete expedition to the Antarctic. It was to cost $500,000, but before it started the money raised and materials offered to him amounted to $800,000.

The plan included not only a flight to the Pole but also, what was of greater scientific importance, exploration of a part of the vast continent of 5,000,000 square miles, which was almost unknown, except for a few places on the outer edge.

To supplement the exploration work of the planes Admiral Byrd took with him a scientific staff of twelve men, all kinds of instruments and dog sleds for laying down bases and doing some work of exploration. With this equipment he hoped to clear up many of the mysteries of the Antarctic. His flying was to be chiefly over King Edward VII Land and the country to the south and east, which was within easy striking distance of his base.

The expedition left Dunedin, New Zealand, on Dec. 2, 1928. The City of New York, a slow and heavily loaded auxiliary wooden bark, was towed to the ice pack about 2,000 miles south of New Zealand by the Eleanor Bolling. There the two ships joined the Larsen, a large Norwegian whaler, which towed the City of New York through the pack in eight days, despite unusually heavy ice conditions. On the other side of the pack, which was 240 miles wide that year, the City of New York left the Larsen and headed for the ice barrier, which was sighted on Christmas Day.

After a brief stay at Discovery inlet the ship went on to the Bay of Whales. Admiral Byrd found the bay filled with ice, which showed no signs of going out, as it had done when Roald Amundsen had wintered there. Unloading operations began at once, however, and the heavy load of shelters, food, gasoline, oil and other supplies was hauled distances of from eight to eleven miles to the base camp at the head of an ice inlet off the bay. These operations lasted more than a month and a half, and during this time Admiral Byrd did some flying to the eastward.

His four pilots were Bernt Balchen, a Navy aviator, who was chief; Dean Smith, a veteran of the airmail service; Alton Parker, who had been with him in the Arctic, and Harold June, a Navy flier of wide experience.

Flying to the east was always difficult because of the fog and clouds, which frequently came up rapidly and barred the way. But on the first short flight Admiral Byrd saw mountains that were later photographed and explored in detail and named the Rockefeller Mountains, after John D. Rockefeller Jr., one of the backers of the expedition.

The coastline was also traced eastward from the Bay of Whales farther than a ship had been able to penetrate by sea, and some distance beyond the nunataks — insular hills surrounded by ice sheets—discovered by the British explorer Robert F. Scott and named after him.

The geological party, headed by Dr. Laurence M. Gould, had gotten under way some time before Admiral Byrd was ready for the long flight to the South Pole. Dr. Gould's party was at the Queen Maud Mountains reporting on weather conditions. An airplane supply base had also been placed at the foot of these mountains by plane.

Besides Admiral Byrd, those in the plane were Mr. Balchen, pilot; Mr. June, co-pilot and radio operator, who also watched the fuel and took motion pictures, and Capt. Ashley McKinley, aerial photographer.

When it reached the vicinity of the Pole as definitely as could be determined, a radio message was sent back by Admiral Byrd and relayed in a few minutes to The New York Times. The radio played a dramatic part in the entire expedition, for not only did it serve to keep units of the expedition in touch at all times but also enabled the late Russell Owen, the correspondent of The Times with the expedition, to send back news with little interruption. It was the first time an Antarctic expedition had been in almost daily contact with home.

Polar Flight Eclipsed Work

The South Pole flight, because of the long preparations for it and the continuous radio news from the Antarctic, caused even more of a sensation than Byrd's North Pole flight. He was promoted to rear admiral by Congress, and a Congressional medal was struck to be presented to all the members of the expedition.

But the most important result of the expedition work was eclipsed by the polar flight. A few days later Admiral Byrd, with Mr. Parker as pilot instead of Mr. Balchen, made a flight to the northeast and for once was not stopped by clouds and fog. He traced the coast to its most northerly point in this sector of the Antarctic, reaching a region that had been and still is beyond the reach of ships by sea.

He also discovered the entire eastern boundary of the Ross Sea. He found that the sea ended on the east, as it did on the west, in a magnificent mountain range split by huge glaciers. It was the most important discovery of the expedition, but it went almost unnoticed. It was another instance of how frequently the spectacular in exploration triumphs over the scientific.

Admiral Byrd returned to the Antarctic in 1933. This expedition covered a greater territory than any other expedition that had been to the Antarctic.

Under Federal Auspices

In November, 1939, he sailed from Boston on an Antarctic expedition on which, among other things, he discovered more than 100,000 square miles of area.

A crowning recognition for Admiral Byrd's polar experience came in 1946, when he was placed in command of the Navy's Antarctic Developments Project 1947, the most ambitious polar expedition ever attempted. The Navy dispatched thirteen ships and their planes with a complement of 4,000 officers and men to the Antarctic on Operation High Jump. The operational commander was Rear Admiral Richard Harold Cruzen, who had been Byrd's second in command in the 1939-40 expedition.

In 1954, Admiral Byrd was named head of the Navy's Operation Deep Freeze, a huge polar expedition.

Aerial Navigation Aids Were Invented by Byrd

Aerial navigation attracted Admiral Byrd, and he made a special study of the instruments used in the science. He invented several that contributed to greater accuracy in air navigation.

One was a "bubble sextant," for obtaining an artificial horizon and calculating position in flight. Another was a "sun compass," which served as a check upon and substitute for the magnetic compass. He also devised a "drift indicator," for measuring departure from course.

Desperate Air Voyage Added to Byrd's Fame

1927 Flight Helped to Show Value of Safety Features

Richard E. Byrd was one of a group of leading aviators in the mid-Twenties who took part in a race to be the first to cross the Atlantic Ocean non-stop from west to east by airplane.

Admiral Byrd, then a commander, and his crew, came in third. Charles A. Lindbergh, flying alone, made it from New York to Paris on May 20-21, 1927. He covered 3,610 miles in thirty-three and a half hours. Then Clarence D. Chamberlain and Charles A. Levine flew from New York to Eisleben, Germany, on June 4-5, 1927. They covered 3,905 miles in forty-two and a half hours.

Admiral Byrd and his crew flew non-stop from New York to Ver-sur-Mer, France, on June 29-30, 1927. They covered 3,477 miles in 43 hours, 21 minutes. These and many other flights of the period demonstrated that the day of transoceanic and transcontinental non-stop flight was dawning.

The idea of taking part in the race came to Admiral Byrd while he was still in the Arctic after he had flown to the North Pole in 1926. While his expedition ship the Chantier was still at Kings Bay, Spitsbergen, Admiral Byrd stood on deck one day with Floyd Bennett, the Naval aviator, and other friends. They talked about the future.

"I'd like to fly the Atlantic now," said Admiral Byrd.

"So would I," said Mr. Bennett. "We can do it with that plane."

Admiral Byrd found an eager and enthusiastic backer in this venture in the late Rodman Wanamaker, who had long cherished an ambition to send a plane from America to Paris. Mr. Wanamaker had furnished the money for the construction of the America, the first big flying boat ever built and the prototype of the NC planes that finally made the first Atlantic flight.

However, when the plane was flown on its first test flight, in 1927, when it seemed certain that Admiral Byrd would be the first to get away on the Atlantic flight, it turned over in landing. Admiral Byrd's wrist was broken and Mr. Bennett was injured so badly that for a time it was thought he would not recover. The accident also damaged the plane so badly that Admiral Byrd was out of the race. Before the plane could be repaired, Charles A. Lindbergh made his epical solo flight to Paris on May 20-21, 1927.

Mr. Bennett's place was taken by Bert Acosta, and the others in the crew were Bernt Balchen and George O. Noville. On June 29, 1927, the weather seemed good enough for a take-off. The huge America rose slowly from the field and started for Paris with a circling escort of small planes. That was the beginning of one of the most desperate air voyages ever undertaken.

The weather was bad all the way. For hours they flew through fog, over clouds and past dark, towering masses of mist that would have inspired awe in the heart of the bravest man.

When they saw the coast of France it was the most welcome bit of coastline they had ever seen. But the worst conditions were at the end of the flight. They found north central France enveloped in a violent storm.

So the nose of the plane was turned again toward the sea. After another long battle with the storm they reached the coast and picked up the lighthouse near Ver-sur-Mer. Flares were dropped, and by their illumination Mr. Balchen brought the plane down. As it touched the waves the wheels were torn off. The America landed with a crash and filled with water. The crew made its way to land in a collapsible boat.

Admiral Byrd had not reached his objective, but he had given the world a more dramatic moment than if he had. The flight added greatly to his reputation. His care in preparing for the venture had been fully justified. Again the three-motored airplane had proved its safety, and the radio had enabled fliers to navigate when the earth and the sky and the sun were obscured. It was the first really scientific flight over the ocean, a flight in which safety was made a major objective.

EXPLORER SET UP OUTPOSTS FOR U. S.

As Head of Navy's Operation Deep Freeze He Established Year-Round Polar Bases

Admiral Richard E. Byrd's greatest polar expedition was achieved when he was in his late sixties. He was in over-all command of the Naval task force that, between 1955 and 1959, was to prepare, supply and maintain a series of scientific stations in the Antarctic. In addition, he was appointed the Government's chief Antarctic policy-maker.

It took him years of work to achieve Government sponsorship of the expedition.

In 1949 and again in 1953 Admiral Byrd made unsuccessful attempts to organize another South Polar expedition to get weather information and to afford training to Navy personnel for defense purposes.

His activity was successful in 1954, when the Government decided to sponsor his fifth expedition, Operation Deep Freeze of 1955-59, as part of its participation in the International Geophysical Year of 1957-58. This exercise is a cooperative effort of governments and scientific societies to develop information about the earth by simultaneous and coordinated observation.

The expedition was set up by the Navy to land men and equipment to build six scientific observation bases, one at the South Pole. The bases were for 148 civilian scientists.

1,800 Men Involved

In the first phase, 1955-56, seven ships and fourteen aircraft, with 1,800 men, were involved. They constructed the two largest year-round bases ever set up in the Antarctic. One was a seventy-three-man outpost in Kainan Bay at Little America. The other was a ninety-three-man outpost on Ross Island in McMurdo Sound.

They also established an air-operating facility at McMurdo Sound to support the construction of a manned station at the South Pole, 800 miles away. They stockpiled 500 tons of cargo at McMurdo Sound for the Pole station and 550 tons at Little America for a station to be built in Marie Byrd Land 500 miles away.

For work in the 1957 season, twelve ships, thirty-eight aircraft and 3,525 men were detailed. The second phase was to build the Pole and Marie Byrd Land stations, at least two more in the Knox Coast and Weddell Sea areas, and to resupply. The third phase, 1957-58, was to resupply all stations, and the fourth was to wind up the scientific program in 1958-59.

Admiral Byrd visited the Antarctic from Dec. 17, 1955, to Feb. 3, 1956. He flew over the Pole, as he had done in 1929 and 1947, on Jan. 8, 1956. The flight carried him deep into a region never seen before.

Almost at the outset the fifth expedition began yielding scientific discoveries. One was of a vast trough of ice, between Victoria Land and Wilkes Land, thousands of square miles in extent. In this chute the vilest weather in the world is spawned and through it glacial ice slides into the Indian Ocean.

Did Not Rejoin Expedition

Admiral Byrd, at 68, was to have left Jan. 15, 1957, to rejoin his expedition. But he was obliged to cancel his plans by declining health and the need to support legislation on the Antarctic program.

Besides being in over-all command of the expedition, he was placed by President Eisenhower in charge of all Antarctic activities of the United States. He was also adviser to the Operations Coordinating Board of the National Security Council on the preparation and execution of Antarctic policy. In addition, he was to coordinate the activities of governmental departments participating in the establishment of a "permanent unit for Antarctic activity."

This was a victory for his policy, which was aimed to achieve permanent settlement of the continent. When he headed home from the Antarctic in February, 1956, he had reiterated his desire to see the United States establish permanent stations in the remote continent—to him, as he scanned the vast white spaces, "a beautiful place."

EXPEDITION IN 1933 IMPAIRED HIS HEALTH

When Admiral Byrd returned to the Antarctic in 1933, he used two ships much larger than he had used on his first expedition.

During the winter period of this expedition Admiral Byrd isolated himself in a hut 125 miles south of Little America for the purpose of making meteorological observations to be checked against those at the northern base. Gas fumes from his stove, resulting from a clogged chimney, incapacitated him during the winter, so that he was sick and weak when a tractor party reached him early in the spring. His health was so impaired that he was able to go on only one of the airplane flights during the summer season of exploration, although he mapped out the work to be done.

This expedition obtained contours that showed a plateau of about 4,000 feet between the Edsel Ford Range and the Queen Maud Mountains. This disposed of the theory that there was a frozen strait, partly filled in, through this part of the Antarctic between the Ross and Weddell Seas.

Associated Press

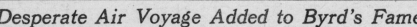

Commander Byrd's tri-motor plane in water off Ver-sur-Mer, France, after crash-landing

"All the News That's Fit to Print"

The New York Times

LATE CITY EDITION

Weather: Cloudy, colder today; cold tonight. Cloudy and cold tomorrow. Temperature range: today 30-40; Thursday 37-44. Details, page B4.

VOL. CXXVI .... No. 43,392 NEW YORK, FRIDAY, NOVEMBER 12, 1976

25 cents beyond 50-mile zone from New York City, except Long Island. Higher in air delivery cities. 20 CENTS

The New York Times

Alexander Calder

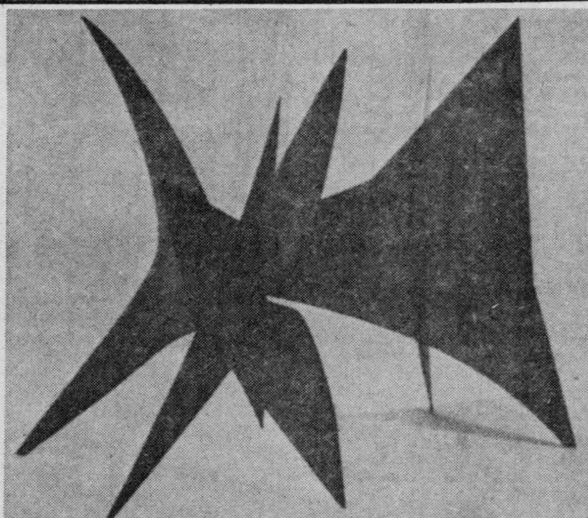

One of the artist's sheet metal stabiles, made around 1956

Alexander Calder, Leading U.S. Artist, Dies

By JOHN RUSSELL

Alexander Calder died in New York City yesterday of a heart attack at the home of his daughter, Mrs. Robert Howar. He was 78 years old.

More than any other American artist, Calder penetrated the awareness of the public at large. He was known initially for the mobile sculptures that hung in public buildings all over this country and in cities all over the world. Since the late 1950's, he had also become known for the "stabiles" — monumental and motionless structures in sheet metal or steel plate—which can be seen outdoors at Lincoln Center and the World Trade Center in New York, on the Empire State Plaza in Albany, in the Federal Center Plaza in Chicago, in a plaza in Great Plains, Mich., and in open spaces throughout Europe, Japan, Australia and South America.

Calder was a complete artist and a complete citizen. In his life, as in his art, he never prevaricated. It somehow got through to everyone, irrespective of age, nationality, color or crede, that Alexander Calder was all of a piece, and that for all the irresistible sense of fun which bubbled up in his work, he was a man who could be depended upon to know what was right and to act upon it.

Family of Artists

The current show of his work, "Calder's Universe," at the Whitney Museum had been organizd by Jean Lipman, who with her husband Howard Lipman, president of the museum, was one of Calder's oldest admirers. Even to those who thought they knew Calder best, the show came as a revelation; and yesterday, when the news of his death became known, it was thronged with a vast audience that came to mourn and stayed to smile.

Today, a private funeral service will be held in New York City.

Alexander Calder was born on July 22, 1898, in Lawnton, Pa., which is now part of Philadelphia. His father, Alexander Stirling Calder, and his grandfather, Alexander Milne Calder, were both distinguished sculptors. His grandfather was responsible for the 35-foot-high effigy of William Penn that stands on top of City Hall in Philadelphia. His mother, Nanette Lederer Calder, was a painter.

Much of Calder's youth was spent in California, where in 1913 his father was appointed acting chief of sculpture for the 1915 World's Fair in San Francisco. At an early age he began to make jewelry for his elder sister Peggy and toys and gadgets for himself.

After graduating from Lowell High School in Berkeley, Calif. Calder decided to become an engineer. At the Stevens Institute of Technology in Hoboken, N.J., he received the highest grades ever awarded for descriptive geometry. In June 1919, he graduated with a degree in mechanical engineering after writing on "Stationary Steam Turbines" as his senior thesis topic.

After several months' service in the

Continued on Page D14, Col. 1

NEW ZONING TO CURB PORNOGRAPHY PLACES SUBMITTED BY BEAME

Plan Would Prohibit All Outlets in Residential Areas and Cut Those in Commercial Districts

By CHARLES KAISER

New York City's array of "massage parlors," peepshows, "adult bookstores" and topless bars would be banned from residential areas and their numbers sharply reduced in commercial districts under proposed new zoning changes announced yesterday by Mayor Beame.

Confronted with an industry that has resisted every effort to date to stem its growth, including an abortive attempt to license the so-called massage parlors, the Beame administration's latest plan is modeled in part after tough zoning regulations in Detroit that were upheld last June by the United States Supreme Court.

If the new zoning regulations are approved and upheld by the courts, they would ban all pornographic establishments on Eighth Avenue and would limit to three the number of such establishments permitted on any single block of 42d Street, a City Planning Commission official said.

Hearing Set for Dec. 1

"This proposal, if enacted, will be a potent weapon to regulate so-called adult entertainment," Mayor Beame said.

The changes would require the approval of the City Planning Commission and the Board of Estimate. The Planning Commission has scheduled a hearing on the proposal for Dec. 1, and it could become law as soon as next January.

As the number of pornographic establishments in the Times Square area has mushroomed during the last decade, so has the controversy surrounding them. More recently, these highly profitable businesses have been put in more fashionable areas like Lexington Avenue, between 50th and 60th Streets, and in lower Manhattan and downtown Brooklyn.

Growth Resists Many Efforts

Countless efforts to limit their growth have been thwarted by everything from constitutional challenges in the courts based on the right to free speech to New York City police regulations that prohibit officers from disrobing in the presence of prostitutes, even when posing as clients.

City officials said yesterday that their hope for the success of this latest effort was partly based on the success of the Detroit effort. At the same time, they conceded that the New York proposals went far beyond the Detroit law upheld by the Supreme Court.

New so-called "adult establishments" would be banned from within 500 feet of areas of the city that are zoned exclusively for residential use.

In commercial districts, the number of

Continued on Page B3, Col. 1

Catholic Bishops Reaffirm Stands On Sexual Ethics

Pastoral Letter Meets Strong Opposition

By KENNETH A. BRIGGS

Special to The New York Times

WASHINGTON, Nov. 11—The Catholic bishops of the United States approved today by a vote of 172 to 25 a pastoral letter on morality that strongly reaffirms the Roman Catholic Church's traditional teachings on sexual ethics in the face of rising discontent within the church.

The letter repeats the moral stands in the Vatican's "Declaration on Sexual Ethics" issued earlier this year.

However, the letter ran into unexpectedly strong opposition from bishops who argued that the document lacked sufficient compassion for those Roman Catholics who experience difficulty obeying church proscriptions against artificial birth control, divorce and abortion.

Reject Pleas for Change

By upholding those prohibitions in the final day of their semiannual meeting, the bishops implicitly rejected pleas for changes in church law and mounting evidence that Roman Catholics are increasingly at variance with church principles.

The recent "Call to Action" conference in Detroit, which brought together a widely diverse gathering of Catholics under the auspices of the bishops, called for many alterations in church policy. They included removal of excommunication from divorced and remarried Catholics and emphasized the rights of couples to decide on birth control on the basis of conscience.

Spokesmen for the bishops emphasized that the pastoral letter was not a response to the Detroit proposals, having

Continued on Page A11, Col. 2

'Hidden' Subsidies In Housing Scored

By JOSEPH P. FRIED

John G. Heimann, who will shortly take over an expanded and more powerful office of New York State Housing Commissioner, yesterday urged an end to what he called "hidden subsidies"—the kind of tax relief and reduced borrowing costs for developers that have long been incentives for housing and other construction in New York and elsewhere.

Mr. Heimann said that unlike actual government appropriations for a project —"up front" subsidies, he called them— the so-called hidden subsidies could be financially destructive and that they kept the public from knowing how much it was actually paying for a project.

In his talk and in an interview afterward, Mr. Heimann, who will leave his current post as State Superintendent of Banks to take the housing job, said so-

Continued on Page A13, Col. 3

PROPOSALS TO SPUR ECONOMIC ACTIVITY OPPOSED BY BURNS

CARTER'S VIEWS ARE SHUNNED

Federal Reserve Chairman Warns Against Tax Cutting and Other Suggestions as Inflationary

By EILEEN SHANAHAN

Special to The New York Times

WASHINGTON, Nov. 11—Arthur F. Burns, the chairman of the Federal Reserve Board, warned today against the possible inflationary consequences of trying to stimulate the economy through tax cuts, increases in Government spending or a looser monetary policy.

These are the very policies that President-elect Jimmy Carter has said he would consider, in January, if the economic recovery still appeared to be slow.

In testimony before the Senate Banking Committee, Dr. Burns expressed his view that any stimulative steps would be unnecessary, as well as dangerous. That is because he believes that "all in all, it seems entirely reasonable to expect a pickup in the tempo of economic activity in the near future," without any special governmental action to create it.

'Course of Moderation'

For this reason, he said, the Federal Reserve would continue "to adhere to a course of moderation" in its actions that deal with regulating the supply of money that is available to fuel the nation's economy.

Dr. Burns's remarks did appear to be a clear warning to Mr. Carter that the Federal Reserve would refuse to go along with, and might even act to counter Carter Administration policies aimed at speeding the recovery from the recession.

The President-elect and the Federal Reserve chairman were not yet on a definite collision course, however, for at least two reasons.

The first was that Mr. Carter has stated that he has not yet made up his mind that stimulative policies are needed. He said that he would wait until he saw the economic statistics for November and December before he made any decisions on the matter.

Maintaining Vigilance

The second is that Mr. Burns tempered his remarks with the observation that Federal Reserve policy is "not frozen in concrete."

He pledged that he and his colleagues on the seven-member Federal Reserve board would remain "vigilant" to the need for change in the board's policies.

In addition, he conceded that "both here and abroad, the recovery from the deep recession of 1974-75 has been incomplete" and noted that there were still un-

Continued on Page D9, Col. 2

EXECUTION IN UTAH STAYED BY GOVERNOR

He Acts So State Board of Pardons Can Review Case Next Week

By GRACE LICHTENSTEIN

Special to The New York Times

SALT LAKE CITY, Nov. 11—Gov. Calvin L. Rampton today stayed the execution of Gary Mark Gilmore until after the State Board of Pardons meets Wednesday.

Mr. Gilmore, a convicted murderer, had asked to be shot by a firing squad on schedule Monday morning. The death penalty has not been carried out in the United States for more than nine years.

Governor Rampton's announcement came the morning after the Utah Supreme Court granted Mr. Gilmore's wish by voiding an earlier appeal for a stay. The 35-year-old convict, clean shaven and in leg irons, handcuffs and white prison denims, made his appeal before the five justices yesterday.

Governor Explains Stand

A great deal of confusion surrounds this case. Mr. Gilmore dismissed his two court-appointed attorneys because they would not heed his pleas for an early execution. His new attorneys, his former attorneys, the American Civil Liberties Union and the State Attorney General have all become involved.

Governor Rampton said in a letter to the Board of Pardons that he was stepping in because it was his duty to do so under the State Constitution. The Governor, who is retiring in January, made it clear that he was expressing no

Continued on Page A12, Col. 3

Experts Say New Campaign Law Had Major Impact on '76 Election

By WARREN WEAVER Jr.

Special to The New York Times

WASHINGTON, Nov. 11—The campaign law that Congress enacted in 1974 in the wake of the Watergate scandals had a profound impact on last week's election, although the political revolution it brought about was very nearly invisible to the voters.

Political veterans in both parties are in general agreement that the campaign law, in its first test, had the following significant results:

¶Establishment of Federal matching funds to help finance primary campaigns of Presidential candidates who demonstrated a reasonable level of national support enabled Jimmy Carter, an obscure former Governor of Georgia, to win the Democratic nomination despite an initially narrow base of geographical and financial support.

¶The same public subsidization of primary competition allowed Ronald Reagan, the former Governor of California, to make—and very nearly win—a challenge to the renomination of an incumbent President.

¶The first spending ceilings ever imposed on a Presidential general election—$21.8 million each for President Ford and Mr. Carter—almost certainly, in the light of the very close result, produced a Democratic victory. Without the limits, most politicians believe, millions of dollars more invested in the Republican campaign would probably have reversed the result.

¶The last power of wealthy individuals and well-financed special interest groups to buy a future interest in the activity of Presidential and Congressional candidates was reduced to a minimal level by new limits on the size of contributions.

The contest between Mr. Carter and Mr. Ford and the earlier, sharply contested primaries in both parties looked and sounded very much like past national campaigns, but they were conducted under a fundamentally different set of ground rules that almost certainly affected the outcome.

Changes Widely Accepted

Although many of the candidates and politicians involved complained about the restrictions and burdens that the new law imposed, the first blush of post-election reaction indicated that its basic radical changes in the electoral process had been widely accepted and were likely to remain intact for the foreseeable future, with only minor adjustments.

By setting limits of $1,000 on contribu-

Continued on Page A16, Col. 1

Teamster Fund to Cite Kleindienst As Defendant in Insurer Fraud Suit

By A. H. RASKIN

The principal welfare fund of the International Brotherhood of Teamsters decided yesterday to name Richard G. Kleindienst as an individual defendant in a $14 million damage suit that it filed last August alleging fraud by five life insurance companies.

The decision, disclosed by a spokesman for the Central States, Southeast and Southwest Areas Health and Welfare Fund in Chicago, followed unsuccessful efforts by the fund's attorneys to obtain voluntary return of a $250,000 fee shared by the former Attorney General and another Washington lawyer for helping steer millions of dollars in fund premiums to the companies involved in the alleged plot.

In testimony before the Securities and Exchange Commission on Sept. 3, Mr. Kleindienst reported that his role as middleman in the insurance transaction involved five to seven hours of work in late April and early May of this year.

This was three years after he left the Justice Department in the wake of the Watergate scandals, but the contacts on which his intercession was based were made during his service in the Nixon Administration.

According to the Kleindienst deposition, the fee-splitting deal was broached to him by Thomas Webb Jr., a lawyer, whom he had met originally at the Burning Tree Country Club near Washington when he was Deputy Attorney General.

Mr. Kleindienst's principal function was to make contact with Frank E. Fitzsimmons, president of the truck union, and tell him that he would "appreciate" any help that the union chief could give in swinging the fund's life insurance business.

In a civil suit filed in the Federal District Court in Washington six weeks ago, the S.E.C. charged that the result of the deal was an elaborate swindle under which four men switched permiums from the lead company in the combine—the Old Security Life Insurance Company of

Continued on Page D12, Col. 5

INSIDE

Israel Censured at U.N.

The United Nations Security Council unanimously deplored Israel's establishment of settlements in occupied Arab territories. Page A6.

Neo-Fascism Irks Spain

The Spanish Government's apparent inability to check neofascist "commandos" has become an embarrassing test of its democratic aims. Page A2.

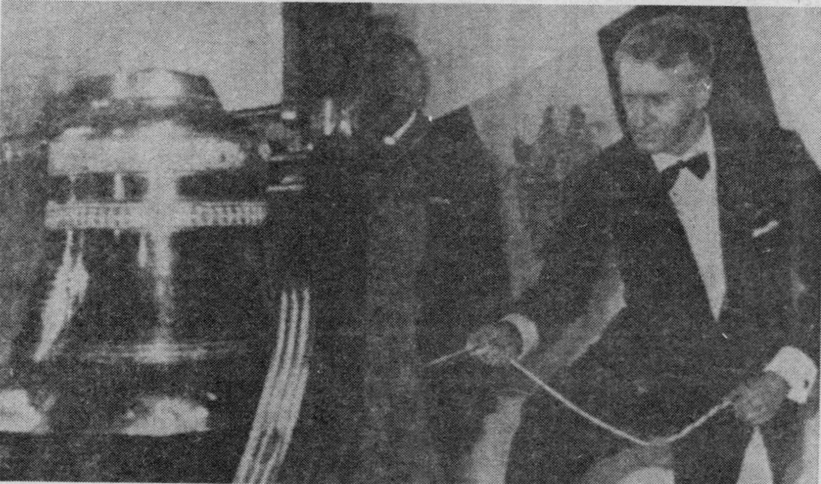

Associated Press

In Salisbury, Prime Minister Ian D. Smith rings in the 12th year of Rhodesian independence

Rhodesians Celebrate 11th Anniversary of Breakaway

By MICHAEL T. KAUFMAN

Special to The New York Times

SALISBURY, Rhodesia, Nov. 11—Just before midnight Prime Minister Ian D. Smith approached a polished brass bell at a tobacco auction hall here and solemnly rang in the 12th year of Rhodesian independence and defiance.

The bell, patterned after the American Liberty Bell, bore the inscription, "I toll for justice, civilization and Christianity."

As it pealed 12 times, the 750 people attending the independence ball stood still and quiet, the men in dinner clothes or regimental kilts, the women in lavish gowns. Mr. Smith raised a goblet of locally produced champagne, which if not a paean to the vintner's art is at least a credit to the ingenuity and adaptability of Rhodesia under sanctions.

"To Rhodesia," he proclaimed. The crowd, all white, all ardent supporters of Mr. Smith's ruling Rhodesian Front Party echoed, "To Rhodesia."

Before he rang the bell, Mr. Smith made a short speech. He said he was speaking in "a low key" because he did not want to make "any provocative statements" in view of the talks going on in Geneva. He asked for the crowd's understanding for not being more passionate in his remarks.

"It is an understatement when I say there are a few dark clouds on the horizon," the Prime Minister declared. "But there are also some light patches of blue sky and we are charting our course in that direction." He urged, however, that Rhodesia not be blind "to the realities of the world."

"The code of moral standards is continually being eroded. We live in an era when the big lie is accepted more and more as a fact of life which the world learns to live with, as it has accepted hijacking and terrorism."

Mr. Smith said it was regrettable that there seemed to be less resolve in "the free world than in the nonfree world."

"The free world is constantly backing down before Communist aggression," he said. "Rhodesia is one of the few exceptions to the trend of compromise

Continued on Page A9, Col. 1

Alexander Calder, Major Sculptor, Painter and Designer, Dies at 78

Continued from Page A1

Students' Army Training Corps, Naval Section, at the Stevens Institute, Calder led a vagabond life from 1919 to 1921, working in a wide variety of technical capacities, none of which engaged him very closely. In 1922, he worked in the boiler room of a passenger ship that plied between New York and San Francisco via the Panama Canal.

Studied Painting

From the fall of 1923 until 1926 he followed what by then had manifested itself as an imperious bent and studied painting at the Art Students League in New York, where his teachers included John Sloan, George Luks, Guy Pene du Bois, Thomas Hart Benton and Kenneth Hayes Miller. Like many a distinguished American artist at that time, he found parttime work as a commercial artist. In particular, he was a sports illustrator for the National Police Gazette. With the help of his Gazette pass, he developed his lifelong interest in the circus, and in 1925 he produced his first wire sculpture, a sundial in the form of a rooster on a vertical rod.

In 1926 Calder made a large number of drawings from animals in the Bronx and Central Park zoos. These formed the subject of his first book, "Animal Sketching." In the same crucial year, he had his first show of oil paintings at the Artists' Gallery on East 61st Street and sailed for Europe as a day laborer on a British freighter. Once in Paris, he soon established himself as an unusual and strikingly vigorous character.

Living in a tiny room on the Rue Daguerre, he made his first movable wood and wire animals, exhibited a bird made of bread and wire at the Salon des Independants, made a portrait in wire of Josephine Baker and began work on the miniature circus for which he later became famous. Through the English painter and engraver S.W. Hayter, he made friends with the sculptor Jose de Creeft; and though he still considered himself a painter, it quickly became clear that his main contribution was to be as a sculptor of an original and distinctive kind.

Chris Kutchera

Alexander Calder as he touched up decoration of the jet Braniff commissioned him to paint, in Paris last year

In 1927 Calder, returned to the United States, where the Gould Manufacturing Company wished to market the toys on which he had lavished an unsentimental fancy. A group of wire athletes earned for him his first four-figure check. "I was about 30," he said later, "and Hoover already had a million dollars by that time. Mine came much slower." Traveling back and forth between New York, Paris and Berlin, Calder pursued an active but not very lucrative career as miniature-circus manager, sculptor and jeweler.

On one of his trans-Atlantic journeys, he met and was captivated by Louisa Cushing James, a great-niece of Henry and William James. "Look out!" her father said to her, "There's an adventurer on every ship!" Undeterred, she responded to his ardent and sustained courtship and was married to him in January 1931, inaugurating a marriage that has a high place in the annals of monogamy. They had two daughters, Sandra Davidson and Mary Howar.

Calder maintained throughout his life an equilibrated French-American existence. Invited in 1930 by Edward Warburg to show with the Harvard Society for Contemporary Art, he was back in Paris in time to join the Abstraction-Création group, which included Van Doesburg, Mondrian, Arp, Delaunay, Pevsner and Hélion. His contacts at that time with Piet Mondrian, Fernand Léger and Joan Miró were fundamental to his development.

Léger wrote a preface for his show of sculptures, drawings and wire portraits at the Galerie Percier in Paris in 1931, and when Calder visited Mondrian in his studio, he told Mondrian that he admired his paintings but would prefer to see them oscillate. Unwelcome though this notion may have been to Mondrian, Calder went on to make motorized and hand-cranked sculptures in 1932. The term "mobiles" he owed to Marcel Duchamp, and the term "stabiles" to Jean Arp. When his moving sculptures were shown at the Julien Levy Gallery in New York in 1932, Calder said to a reporter: "Why must art be static? The next step in sculpture is in motion."

Connecticut Farmhouse

In 1933 the Calders bought an 18th-century farmhouse in Roxbury, Conn. He later described it as "our very first house, my first house, and I was 35." In the spring of 1934, Alfred Barr bought a motorized Calder mobile for the Museum of Modern Art, and the Calders decided to settle in the United States, working in Roxbury and each winter renting small shops on New York's Upper East Side for use as studios. Whitewashing the windows and choosing the west side of the street for the morning sun, Calder got a lot of work done in New York.

Calder in the 1930's impressed himself more and more as an artist who brought a poetic concision, an inimitable gaiety and an unmatched technical competence to all that he undertook. What he wanted to work, worked. If it was a set for Martha Graham in 1935, and again in 1936, it worked. If it was a fountain for the Paris World's Fair in 1937, it was the most popular thing in the place. James Johnson Sweeney was a most active advocate of his in the United States and his exhibitions at the Pierre Matisse gallery from 1934 to 1943 engrossed a steadily larger public (not many of whom were disposed to write out a check, however).

When the Museum of Modern Art moved to its new building on West 53d Street in 1939, it commissioned a large Calder mobile for its main stairwell. The museum also organized Calder's first major exhibition, in September 1943, and that year, the most discerning of dealers, Curt Valentin, became Calder's dealer and publisher. In 1945, when France was liberated, Calder happened to be making a long series of mobiles that were small enough to go into an envelope. Marcel Duchamp suggested to him that it was with these tiny words that he should return to Paris. His first postwar show in Europe was held in October 1946 at the Galerie Louis Carré in Paris. Jean-Paul Sartre wrote the catalogue's preface, Henri Matisse was among the first visitors, and Calder was welcomed as he deserved.

Once back in Europe, Calder entered with characteristic relish into French life. He cared little for Surrealism, but took part in "Surrealism in 1947" at the Galerie Maeght in Paris. He traveled to Brazil, Finland, England, Sweden and Germany. He won first prize for sculpture at the Venice Biennale in 1952 (James Johnson Sweeney did the installation and the catalogue). When Gérard Philipe was the most famous young actor in Europe, it was Calder who in 1952 made the sets for Henri Pichette's "Nucléa," in which Philipe was the star. In that same year, Calder broke entirely new ground with his acoustic ceiling for University City in Caracas, Venezuela. There seemed to be no country, no function, and no public for which Calder was not in demand.

In 1953, the Calders went for the first time to Saché, near Tours, in France, where their friend Jean Davidson, soon to become their son-in-law, urged them to buy an ancient house by the river Indre. It was barely more than an immensely evocative hole in the wall. They bought it, and thereafter Saché was, with Roxbury, their home. Fame and fortune by no means went together at that time; at one of Calder's beautiful shows in New York, in 1955, nothing whatever was sold.

Commissions Came In

But as of 1958 the big commissions began to come in: for the Brussels World's Fair, for what is now Kennedy International Airport, for the headquarters of the United Nations Education, Scientific and Cultural Organization in Paris. In that same year, Calder won first prize at the Carnegie International in Pittsburgh, and by 1960 he was saying that "I have a pleasant sensation of having arrived at a financial basis where I can do what I want." But it was only a year or two before that he had said to his new dealer in New York, Klaus Perls: "What! You think I could get a thousand dollars for a mobile?"

In time, Calder could do what he liked with an absolute assurance that almost too many people would want it. He could draw, he could paint, he could illustrate books, he could design tapestries and stage sets, he could make toys for his grandchildren. He had ideal collaborators in the craftsmen of the Etablissements Biémont, an ironworks in Tours, and he could prepare for retrospective exhibitions that turned into apotheoses, like the one at the Solomon R. Guggenheim Museum in New York in 1964.

Attentions of this sort amused and delighted him, but he and Mrs. Calder did not give into the narcissistic, world-ignoring state of mind that has tempted many another famous artist in his 60's. On Jan. 2, 1966, they placed a full-page advertisement in The New York Times to protest against the Vietnam war, calling for "an end to hypocrisy, self-righteousness, self-interest, expediency, distortion and fear, wherever they exist." "Our only hope," they concluded, "is in thoughtful Man. Reason is not treason." These sentiments at that time were not often expressed so forthrightly.

Not long after that, "La Grande Voile," a monumental stabile 40 feet high, weighing 25 tons and commissioned by I. M. Pei, was installed at the Massachusetts Institute of Technology in Cambridge, Mass. Major sculptures by Calder began to be installed in public places all over the world. Some were mobiles, in which Calder made deft, witty and continually imaginative use of materials that had previously been thought of as ponderous and inert.

Some were stabiles, in which sheet metal or steel plate took on the look of gigantic stalking creatures, part insect and part extravagant vegetable, that had made a momentary landfall in places that did not expect them.

Calder also produced a continuous stream of paintings and drawings in which his mischievous impulses found a ready outlet. He loved a challenge. If Braniff Airways asked him to paint an aircraft, he did it. If Bavarian Motor Works asked him to decorate a racing car, he did it. If the Jerusalem Foundation asked him to make a huge stabile for what may well be the most beautiful city in the world, he did it. Nothing defeated him, and he brought to every commission the same patient, resourceful and conscientious attention.

Nougat-Covered Stabile

Honors came his way continually. He was a member, for instance, of the American Academy of Arts and Letters, which in 1971 awarded him its gold medal. But he prized above all the affectionate manifestations that did not get into the history books: The occasion in Tours in 1967, for instance, when someone built him a stabile out of cardboard and covered it with nougat just in time for a visit by a group of officials.

In his 70's, and although his health gave cause for anxiety to everyone but himself, he multiplied his activity. He was here, there, and everywhere. He flew in the Braniff aircraft, and if he did not race in the BMW automobile, it was through no fault of his. He took hold of life and shook it, in his last years, and when the occasion called for a supreme effort, he was ready.

Sears Tower Sculpture

The occasion came in 1974, when he made a mechanized mural of gigantic size for the new Sears Tower in Chicago. (A reduced version of this is now on view at the Whitney Museum). His life's work was summed up in this enormous piece as it revolved, swung, turned as if on a spit, and generally activated itself in the full brilliance of Calder's favorite colors. Calder at that time was an old man, and a sick man, but no one could have guessed it.

The last weeks of Alexander Calder's life were spent in New York City, at the home of his daughter Mary Howar, in an atmosphere of universal jubilation. No one who was there will ever forget the party which was given for him last month at the Whitney Museum by Howard and Jean Lipman. His show had just opened to enormous acclaim; people had come from far and wide; Calder danced; Mrs. Calder called for her favorite samba; Georgia O'Keeffe and Norman Mailer and Louise Nevelson and John Cage and Merce Cunningham were on hand to greet one of the people who has best deserved the name of "American." He loved it, and we loved him, and we shall go on doing it for ever and ever.

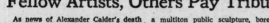

One of his mobiles—the term derived from Marcel Duchamp—made in 1960

This work, made of steel wire in 1929, was entitled "Acrobats" by the artist

Fellow Artists, Others Pay Tribute

As news of Alexander Calder's death spread through the art world yesterday, fellow artists, critics, museum people and admirers paused to reminisce and pay tribute to him both as a friend and an artist.

President Ford, who as a Congressman helped secure a Calder stabile, "La Grande Vitesse," for his home town of Grand Rapids, Mich., was among them. He said:

"It was with the deepest regret that I learned of the death of Alexander Calder, whose universally recognized creativity in art brought joy to millions.

"Mr. Calder's sculpture and innovative art forms helped evolve an entirely new state of consciousness and demonstrated what American improvisation could achieve.

"I am proud that a magnificent Calder is on display in my home town, Grand Rapids. It has won a place in the hearts of Michiganders just as the Calder artistry has enriched a world that became Calder's universe.

"Art has lost a genius and the United States has lost a great American who has contributed much to the civilization of the 20th century.

"Mrs. Ford joins me in sending her condolences to Mrs. Calder and the family."

Others paying tribute were the following:

HENRY MOORE, the sculptor, from his home in England: "It's very, very sad. I've known Sandy since the 1930's, when he was living in Paris and had shows in England. We've been great friends ever since, though our work was very different. He was so wonderfully innovative. And he had such a sense of humor—his work was so gay and happy; full of the happiness of life. And that's a tremendous contribution, isn't it?"

MARTHA GRAHAM, the choreographer: "I first met Sandy at Bennington College. A lovely story about him concerns a set he did for me of mobiles. We had no place to rehearse with them, so we rigged them up in the open field, stretched ropes from tree to tree, and learned to manipulate them to give the illusion of the world of fantasy that Sandy wanted and which enchanted me. The field bordered a public highway and by a loud blowing of horns we became aware that we had stopped traffic and people were caught up in this fantastic world of trees and meadow and yellow flowers and Sandy and mobiles and dancers. I thank him for that memory."

PHILIP JOHNSON, the architect: "I knew him from my days at Harvard in 1926, 1927. Lincoln Kirstein brought him there, and what his wonderful 'Circus' did to my eyes as a stupid undergraduate majoring in Greek! I'll never forget how he jumped that bear over the edge of the ring, how he pulled the strings in a way that showed how he knew the movements of bears! What an actor!"

JOHN CANADAY, former art critic for The New York Times: "His invention of the mobile opened a whole new era of 20th-century sculpture. No other artist I can think of combined so much wit with such unfailing esthetic discipline. Everything he did, from the kitchen forks he improvised for use at home to a multiton public sculpture, bore his very personal stamp."

LOUISE NEVELSON, the sculptor: "Calder is an original, the outstanding creative mind of the 20th century."

JEAN LIPMAN, organizer of "Calder's Universe," the current show at the Whitney Museum of American Art: "He died at what was absolutely the peak of his career. A lot of artists live into old age and we're very kind about them but the fact is that Sandy's work was greater year by year. 'Universe,' the motorized mural he did in 1974 for the Sears Tower in Chicago, was the great culminating masterpiece of ideas he'd been working on for 50 years."

TOM ARMSTRONG, director of the Whitney Museum: "We are now celebrating 50 years of his life's work and he died as the most acclaimed American artist, at the top of his powers."

JAMES JOHNSON SWEENEY, art historian, exhibition organizer and former director of the Solomon R. Guggenheim Museum: "What made him a great artist was his persistence in remaining himself. That's what we're going to miss."

WILLIAM RUBIN, director of the department of painting and sculpture at the Museum of Modern Art: "Alexander Calder was the first American modernist working in any medium to impose himself on the history of art as an artist of worldwide importance, and to be universally recognized as such."

MARTIN FRIEDMAN, director of the Walker Art Center in Minneapolis: "He was one of the greatest form-givers America has ever produced. His art is characterized by wit, invention and humanity. He not only dispelled the suspicion of abstraction, he actually made it seem a natural process. He was a gentle revolutionary — his concepts were clearly radical in the late 1920's and 30's, when sculpture was conceived to consist only of fixed forms. His introduction of motion as a crucial, formal component of art was an unprecedented event."

H. HARVARD ARNASON, art historian and author of two books on Calder's work: "It wasn't just that he created sculpture that moved. The objects were beautiful in themselves. His stabiles were some of the great monuments of the 20th century. He had a lightness of touch but at the same time could achieve architectural monumentality."

THOMAS HOVING: director of the Metropolitan Museum of Art: "Sandy Calder must be considered a virtual giant of the last two generations of American art. Iventive, joyful, yet powerful, and at the same time imbued with an excellence of craftsmanship, his diverse works of art will surely last, bringing a sense of celebration and lively lissussion for future generations."

HENRY BERG, deputy director of the Guggenheim Museum: "A genuine and original form-giver of the 20th century, he has literally populated the world with evidence of his unquenchable creative energy. To all those who have been touched by his genius, Cader's name is synononymous with the profound as well as the lighthearted in artistic expression. To hi friends, the world is a much dimmer place today."

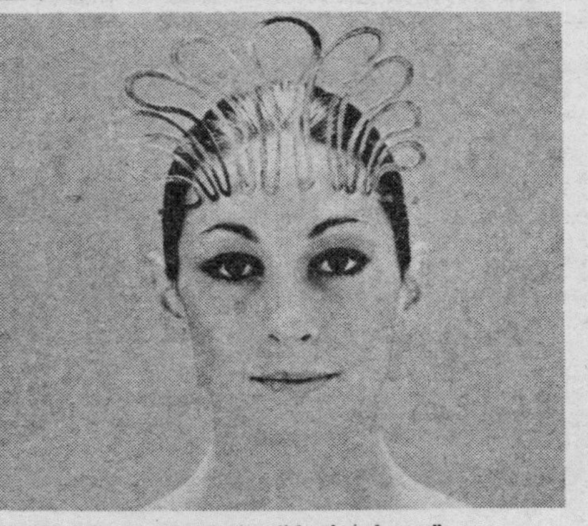

The Calder brass tiara: Altogether beautiful, and parody as well.

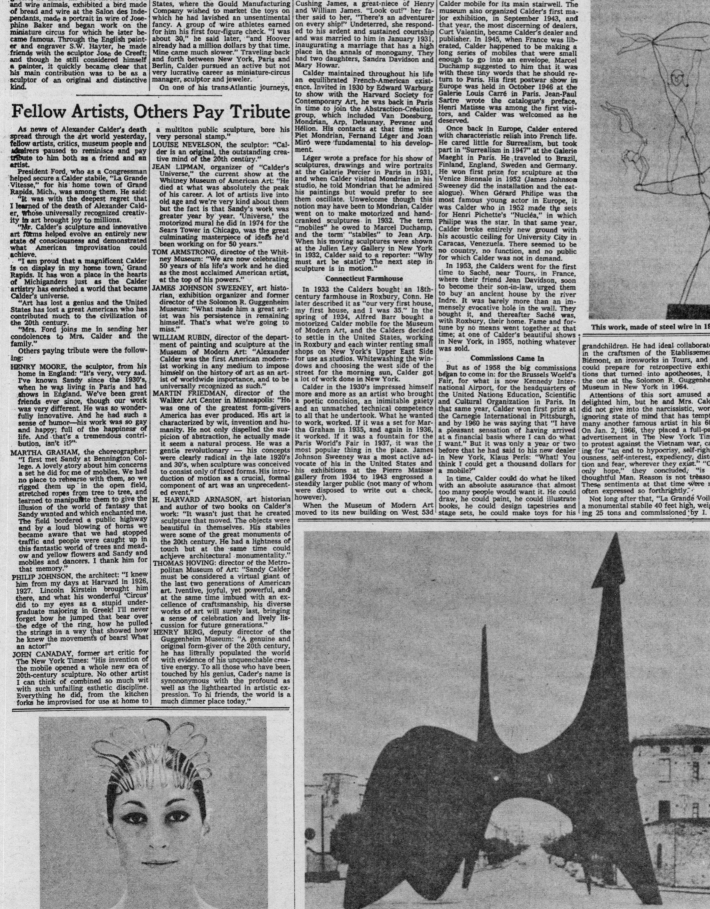

A stabile, 59 feet high, called "Teodelapio," of painted steel plate, was made in 1962. It is in Spoleto, Italy.

"All the News That's Fit to Print"

The New York Times.

LATE CITY EDITION
U.S. Weather Bureau Report (Page 77) forecasts: Showers, then clearing today; chance of showers tonight. Fair tomorrow.
Temp. Range: 71—53; yesterday: 59—53.

VOL. CXIII—No. 38,798. NEW YORK, WEDNESDAY, APRIL 15, 1964. TEN CENTS

MAYOR'S BUDGET ADDS $80 MILLION TO SCHOOL FUNDS

Community College Tuition Will Be Free — Wagner to Submit Data Today

HE STRESSES EDUCATION

Tells Scholastic Group City's Finances Must Be Austere Except for School Needs

By PETER KIHSS

A record-breaking increase of "well over $80 million" for educational costs in the city budget will be submitted to the City Council and Board of Estimate today, Mayor Wagner announced last night.

The increase, he said, will raise the city's spending for education at all levels and for school pension and debt costs to $985,962,000, or 29.4 per cent of the total city budget.

Calculations showed that such a percentage would make the over-all budget exceed $3.35 billion, a quarter-billion-dollar increase over the budget for the present fiscal year.

The Mayor said that $79,287,000 of the increase would go to grade and high schools. The Board of Education, which had an allotment of $802 million for the present year, had sought an increase of $121 million. The city provides funds in a lump sum for the board to apportion as it sees fit.

Free Community Colleges

Another increase, the Mayor reported, would be $2.1 million to defray the entire cost for 6,500 students at the city's two-year community colleges. Students have been paying $300 a year in tuition at three colleges. Two more will be opened in the fall.

In addition, the Mayor said he would recommend extra funds for the free four-year colleges to pay for more faculty members to handle a larger enrollment. He explained that more students would "become eligible for admission through the lowering by two points of the qualifying grade."

The Board of Higher Education said yesterday the Mayor had promised it $2 million last January to permit the admission of 1,700 more freshmen in the senior colleges and 500 more in the community colleges by easing entrance requirements. The senior colleges had 36,000 day students this year.

Mayor Wagner gave the unusual preview of data on the city budget at the annual dinner of the Mayor's Committee

Continued on Page 14, Column 1

Gross and School Board Near Showdown in Feud

Superintendent's Record as Leader Drawing Panel's Criticism

By LEONARD BUDER

Dr. Calvin E. Gross

A showdown is shaping up between Dr. Calvin E. Gross, the city's Superintendent of Schools, and the Board of Education.

It could come next Monday, when the board is to hold a private meeting to examine its organization and its working relationship with Dr. Gross.

The 45-year-old Superintendent, who today starts his second year in office, has already informed the members that if the board sets up committees and hires its own assistants, he will publicly voice his opposition.

The impending conflict is part of a widening split between the school board and the city's chief school administrator.

The new board set-up is being urged by James B. Donovan, the president, and is backed by several members. Mr. Donovan has said that if the board is to function effectively, it must establish special committees "to deal in depth with situations as they arise."

As for the need for research and administrative assistants, who would report directly to the members, Mr. Donovan asserted recently:"We need someone to evaluate the staff work. Otherwise we are totally dependent on the staff."

The "staff" refers to Dr. Gross and his assistants.

But Dr. Gross said these moves by the board would

Continued on Page 15, Column 3

SANITATION UNION BACKS 'STALL-IN,' WON'T TOW CARS

Aid to Police in a Fair Tie-Up Barred—CORE Unit Drops Plan to Open Faucets

By JUNIUS GRIFFIN

The head of the sanitation workers' union said yesterday that all 10,000 men in his local would stay home on April 22 if they were asked to tow away cars stalled in the proposed traffic tie-up on the opening day of the World's Fair.

John J. DeLury, president of Sanitation Men's Local 831 of the International Brotherhood of Teamsters, voiced the warning yesterday between telephone conversations with a police official and Sanitation Commissioner Frank J. Lucia.

The Brooklyn Chapter of the Congress of Racial Equality has said it will stage a "stall-in" to tie up traffic on routes to the World's Fair. The chapter has been suspended by the national organization for proposing such a demonstration.

[In Washington, New York's Senators criticized the stall-in and said it would injure the cause of civil rights.]

Fear of Fire Cited

Another Brooklyn CORE plan—to waste water by organizing a campaign to keep faucets open—was abandoned after a meeting with other civil rights groups Monday night.

Supporters of the stall-in said the open-faucet plan was too extreme, as it raised the risk of inadequate water pressure in the event of a tenement fire.

Mr. DeLury, pacing his wood-paneled office on the second floor of the union's headquarters at 428 Broadway, declared: "We're not going to scab on anyone fighting for freedom or civil rights. The police can have the 33 wreckers the Sanitation Department has and we'll have no objections."

Mr. DeLury called a Negro official of the union into his office, then went on to say that all 10,000 men in the local were employed by the city and were qualified to drive.

Rules Out Substitutions

"Consequently," he said, "if the city attempted to have regular drivers of wreckers remove the stalled cars and they refused, the city could turn to other sanitation men.

"So we'll all stay home if the city tries to do this."

The union indicated that no politics was involved in its policy, but rather that the local was simply supporting the fight for civil rights.

A Sanitation Department spokesman, commenting on Mr. DeLury's stand, pointed out

Continued on Page 20, Column 4

ROCKEFELLER SEEKS LIQUOR REVISIONS AT SESSION TODAY

Compromise Plan Includes Wholesale Prices as Low as Those in Any State

By DOUGLAS DALES
Special to The New York Times

ALBANY, April 14—A proposal that would require New York State wholesale liquor prices to be as low as those in any other state is among several compromise proposals that went before Republican Senate and Assembly conferences today.

The conferences met as the Legislature prepared to convene in special session at noon tomorrow to consider Governor Rockefeller's modified liquor reform program. The original program was rejected by the lawmakers last month.

The outlook for passage of the compromise program was still uncertain tonight.

Other Proposals Listed

Other proposed amendments to the original measure would do these things:

¶Bar liquor retail sales at below cost.

¶Require light foods to be available in taverns.

¶Permit cities and towns by referendum to ban tavern licenses.

¶Allow the State Liquor Authority to deny licenses to new package stores when public convenience would not be served.

Speaker Joseph F. Carlino said no effort was made to take a vote this afternoon at the Assembly conference which lasted nearly three hours.

The session tomorrow is expected to recess quickly to permit further conferences of the majority in an attempt to reach final decisions.

Although most of the Republicans were on hand for today's conference, 10 Republican Senators failed to arrive in time. The Democrats will not arrive until just before the session starts tomorrow.

Carlino 'Still Hopeful'

Asked whether he thought the Assembly would accept the revised liquor program, Mr. Carlino said: "I'm still hopeful we will pass it."

Senate Majority Leader Walter J. Mahoney predicted after the Senate conference today that "we will go out of this session with a good program of liquor reform."

But what shape the reform will take, he said, will not be known until after tomorrow's conference. He reported that "the biggest bone of contention

Continued on Page 44, Column 3

Hussein Confers With President

Associated Press Wirephoto

King Hussein of Jordan with the President at White House

By HEDRICK SMITH
Special to The New York Times

WASHINGTON, April 14—King Hussein of Jordan tonight ruled out the possibility of an international compromise on the Arab-Israeli dispute over Israel's plan to divert waters from the Jordan River. Arriving as a representative of the Arab world and the first Arab leader to visit President Johnson since the President took office last November, King Hussein said at a news conference that it was "too late" to revive an American plan to map out a

Continued on Page 3, Column 5

PENTAGON BARES FIGURES SHOWING ATOM ARMS LEAD

540 U.S. Bombers to 270 for Soviet and 750 ICBM's to 188 Are Listed

A REPLY TO GOLDWATER

McNamara and the Senator Renew Their Battle Over Missiles' Dependability

Special to The New York Times

WASHINGTON, April 14—The Administration published this evening an inventory of American and Soviet nuclear power to demonstrate the United States' increasing superiority and to head off another "missile gap" debate in the election.

Responding to new charges of military irresponsibility by Senator Barry Goldwater, the Defense Department distributed a listing of its missiles, bombers and missile-bearing nuclear submarines and compared them with Soviet strength in each category.

The Defense Department has been under attack by the Senator for what he calls an overemphasis on missiles for defense.

A Pentagon spokesman said that some of the information was being released for the first time. This included the official estimates of comparative strength.

Breakdown of Figures

The Pentagon gave the following breakdown of relative American and Soviet power:

¶The Air Force has 540 strategic or long-range bombers constantly on alert. The Soviet Union could send over the United States no more than about 120 heavy bombers and perhaps 150 medium bombers that could return home after dropping their bombs. The Soviet craft would be limited in range to targets in Alaska and the northwestern areas of the country.

¶The Air Force has on launchers about 750 intercontinental ballistic missiles. The Soviet Union has fewer than one-fourth that number, or 188, in operation.

¶The United States has 192 Polaris missiles deployed aboard nuclear-powered submarines. Each missile can be launched from beneath the water's surface and each has a range of 1,500 miles or more. The Soviet Union has "substantially fewer" missiles on submarines, only a small percentage of which are nuclear-powered. Each Soviet missile has a range of less than 500 miles and can

Continued on Page 6, Column 4

Goldwater Wins in Illinois; 27% Vote for Mrs. Smith

By AUSTIN C. WEHRWEIN
Special to The New York Times

CHICAGO, Wednesday, April 15—Senator Barry Goldwater of Arizona won the Illinois Republican Presidential primary last night, but Senator Margaret Chase Smith of Maine rolled up a surprising vote.

Mrs. Smith, who got less than 3 per cent of the vote in the Republican primary in New Hampshire and said she had spent less than $1,000 campaigning in Illinois, had about 27 per cent as the returns were counted last night.

Mrs. Smith said she had entered the race in a state that had been regarded as a Goldwater stronghold to give the voters a choice. Her name and Senator Goldwater's were the only ones on the ballot.

Former Vice President Richard M. Nixon and Ambassador Henry Cabot Lodge got lesser numbers of write-in votes. Both had asked their supporters in the state to refrain from conducting active campaigns in their behalf.

With 6,664 of the 10,256 precincts reporting, the vote was:

Goldwater	257,085
Smith	107,360
Lodge	21,839
Nixon	10,233

Percy Is Winner

Governor Rockefeller received 813 write-in votes, Gov. William W. Scranton of Pennsylvania 686, Gov. George Romney of Michigan 182 and Harold E. Stassen 34.

In the bitter Republican gubernatorial primary, Charles H. Percy, 44-year-old industrialist, who was chairman of the Platform Committee at the 1960 Republican National Convention, defeated William J. Scott, 37, state treasurer and a Goldwater supporter. Mr. Percy was uncommitted in the Presidential contest. Mr. Scott conceded his defeat.

With 7,671 of the 10,256 precincts reporting, the vote was:

Percy	335,758
Scott	200,422

Mr. Percy, who was accused by Mr. Scott's supporters of

Continued on Page 18, Column 3

U.S. SUES TO STOP HUMBLE OIL DEAL

Opposes Sale by Tidewater of West Coast Operations as Curb on Competition

By ANTHONY LEWIS
Special to The New York Times

WASHINGTON, April 14 — The Government brought suit tonight to keep the Humble Oil and Refining Company from acquiring the western operations of the Tidewater Oil Company.

The action, filed in Los Angeles and announced here, was one of the largest ever brought under Section 7 of the Clayton Act.

The section, known as the Celler-Kefauver Act since its amendment in 1950, prohibits mergers that might substantially lessen competition.

Humble agreed last Nov. 22 to buy all of Tidewater's western refining, marketing and transportation facilities for $329 million in cash. The sale is now scheduled to be closed on April 30.

The Justice Department charged that the acquisition would increase concentration in the oil industry and end actual and potential competition between Humble and Tidewater in the West.

The department asked the court to block the deal with a temporary injunction pending trial of the case.

In legal terms, the major import of the case lay in the significance the Justice Department saw in the size and economic power of Humble and its giant parent company, Standard Oil Company (New Jersey).

Jersey is the world's largest

Continued on Page 51, Column 2

British Budget Raises Tax On Cigarettes and Alcohol

By CLYDE H. FARNSWORTH
Special to The New York Times

LONDON, April 14—The Government presented today an election-year budget that forecasts a continued rise in spending and provides for a 10 per cent increase in taxes on tobacco and alcoholic drinks to help foot the bill.

The Chancellor of the Exchequer, Reginald Maudling, said the purpose of his 1964 budget was to "achieve a smooth transition from the recent exceptionally rapid rate of growth to the long-term growth rate of 4 per cent."

The danger, he said in his 85-minute budget speech to the House of Commons, is "overheating" of the economy. Economic growth is at a faster rate than can be sustained without the development of inflationary pressures, he explained.

His formula is to increase tax revenues by £103 million ($288 million) and thereby reduce pressures from consumer spending. The tax changes take effect tomorrow. Income taxes are not affected.

Milder Than Expected

The budget was milder than many had expected. Influential groups had urged that taxes be raised by £200 million.

Some doubts were expressed whether the measure would be strong enough. Mr. Maudling said he had to be careful not to go "so far as to give a definite check to expansion."

Harold Wilson, leader of the Opposition Labor party, called it a "lame-duck budget for a lame-duck Government . . . a tired budget in terms of the problems of the country, an irrelevant budget."

Rising after the Chancellor had finished, Mr. Wilson brought laughter to the packed house with this gibe: The budget itself showed a "marked inflationary tendency—there were far too many words chasing far too few ideas."

The reaction of the tobacco and liquor trades to the higher imposts was highly critical.

The taxes mean a little more than 4 cents added to the cost of a pack of cigarettes now selling for the equivalent of 56

Continued on Page 11, Column 1

U.S. WILL REVAMP ITS SAIGON FORCES

Advisory Group to Become Part of Military Command in Efficiency Measure

By JACQUES NEVARD
Special to The New York Times

SAIGON, South Vietnam, April 14—Senior American officers said here today that the United States Military Advisory Group would be merged into the Military Assistance Command in Vietnam.

The object is to reduce paperwork and duplication of effort and to make more efficient use of the nearly 16,000 United States servicemen in South Vietnam.

American sources said they expected a "slight increase" in the number of United States troops in South Vietnam soon, but they doubted that the total would reach 17,000.

There is no indication that the streamlining would alter the subordinate role of the Military Assistance Command to the United States Pacific Forces Command in Hawaii, military officials said. There have been rumors that the command in Vietnam would be made directly responsible to the Pentagon.

The merger of the Military Advisory Group into the Military Assistance Command is expected to reduce by 100 the 700 headquarters jobs in the two commands. It is believed that some of the posts that may be eliminated are held by generals. There are now 14 American

Continued on Page 4, Column 5

JOHNSON TO SLOW U.S. PROMOTIONS

Step to Curb Job Upgrading Is Part of Economy Drive

By EDWIN L. DALE Jr.
Special to The New York Times

WASHINGTON, April 14 — President Johnson, in an unannounced move in his drive to lower Government spending, has ordered a slowdown in the rate of promotion of Federal employes.

Under the President's orders, the Budget Bureau has sent a letter to every major Federal agency citing the "almost continuous rise in the average grade of Federal employes" as a "cause for concern."

The letter specifies the need to curb a "particularly large increase in the higher-grade jobs," with their higher rates of pay.

About two million civilian employes of the Government in all parts of the country are potentially affected by the move.

Under the civil service system, which covers most Federal employment, employes are graded from 1 to 18. The average grade is about 7.2.

If the average grade rose only one point, to 8.2, the cost to the Government would be about $1.5 billion a year. A rise of only one-tenth of one point in a year, as has been happening, costs about $150 million. These increases are apart from the

Continued on Page 19, Column 1

Cohn Conspiracy Count Voided; Case Will Go to Jury Tomorrow

By HOMER BIGART

The conspiracy charge in an indictment against Roy M. Cohn and Murray E. Gottesman was dismissed yesterday by Federal Judge Archie O. Dawson. But Judge Dawson refused to dismiss nine other counts alleging perjury and obstruction of justice.

He said he would give the case to the jury of 10 men and two women tomorrow morning after hearing summations today.

On the nine remaining counts, three cite Mr. Cohn for perjury, four cite him for obstruction of justice, and two charge Mr. Gottesman with perjury.

Mr. Cohn, former counsel to the late Senator Joseph R. McCarthy, could still receive a maximum jail sentence of 35 years. But the throwing out of the conspiracy count was considered a blow to the Government.

Now the Government must prove that the two defendants actually lied, rather than conspired to lie, to a 1962 Federal grand jury, and that Mr. Cohn actually threatened, rather than conspired to threaten, other grand jury witnesses.

The Government charged that Mr. Cohn and Mr. Gottesman lied in order to cover up their efforts in 1959 to enable four stock swindlers to escape indictment in a $5 million scandal involving United Dye and Chemical Corporation stock.

Two of the stock swindlers testified that a $50,000 payoff for "fixing" the indictment was split between Mr. Cohn and Morton S. Robson, former chief assistant United States Attor-

Continued on Page 47, Column 1

Rachel Carson Dies of Cancer; 'Silent Spring' Author Was 56

Magnum

Rachel Carson on field trip at Boothbay Harbor, Maine

Rachel Carson the biologist and writer on nature and science, whose book "Silent Spring" touched off a major controversy on the effects of pesticides, died yesterday in her home in Silver Spring, Md. She was 56 years old.

Her death was reported in New York by Marie Rodell, her literary agent. Miss Rodell said that Miss Carson had had cancer "for some years," and that she had been aware of her illness.

With the publication of "Silent Spring" in 1962, Rachel Louise Carson, the essence of gentle scholarship, set off a nationally publicized struggle between the proponents and opponents of the widespread use of poisonous chemicals to kill insects. Miss Carson was an opponent.

Some of Miss Carson's critics, admiringly and some not so admiringly, compared her to Carrie Nation, the hatchet-wielding temperance advocate.

This comparison was rejected quietly by Miss Carson, who in her very mild but firm manner refused to accept the identification of an emotional crusader.

Miss Carson's position, as a biologist, was simply that she was a natural scientist in search of truth and that the indiscriminate use of poisonous

Continued on Page 25, Column 1

Boy, 7, Coaxes Uncle Off Ledge As Crowd Jeers, 'Jump! Jump!'

Special to The New York Times

ALBANY, April 14—A 19-year-old youth who threatened to leap from a 12th-story hotel ledge last night was coaxed to safety by his 7-year-old nephew while onlookers below jeered "Jump! Jump! Jump!"

The youth, Richard Reinemann, who has been under psychiatric care in the Albany Medical Center, perched on the 36-inch-wide ledge for two hours, sometimes pacing unsteadily and staring down at the crowd that finally numbered 4,000 persons.

While spotlights played on the distraught youth and members of his family, several policemen and a Roman Catholic Bishop spoke to him softly from the roof of the De Witt Clinton Hotel. As the crowd gathered across the street on the lawn of the State Capitol, shouts of "Jump! Jump! Jump!" echoed.

"Aw, c'mon, you're chicken" one teen-ager shouted.

"Jump! What's the matter, ya yellow?" another shouted.

One word became a chant from a cluster in the crowd: "Jump—Jump—Jump!"

At times, it seemed the youth would obey the taunts. He chain-smoked, but threw half-finished cigarettes down at the crowd. Once he pulled an empty pint whisky bottle from his pocket, shook it, and hurled it to the street.

A girl, no more than 10 years old, climbed onto a five-foot-high monument base and teetered on its edge to mimic the youth. She flailed the air with her arms, and many in the crowd laughed.

"I'm gonna jump, I'm gon-

Continued on Page 80, Column 1

BRAZIL TO DETAIL PLOT BY LEFTISTS

Will Offer Proof of Plan to Win Power Under Goulart

By JUAN de ONIS
Special to The New York Times

RIO DE JANEIRO, April 14—Brazil's anti-Communist military leaders prepared today a documented exposé of a left-wing revolutionary plan to seize power under former President João Goulart.

The plan was confirmed in its general lines by some of Brazil's left-wing radicals who are in hiding or in asylum at embassies in Brazil.

According to these sources, it was the refusal of Mr. Goulart to arm several key union groups in Rio, in Brasilia, the capital, and in other centers that brought the collapse of the leftist plan and Mr. Goulart's subsequent flight to exile in Uruguay. The military seized power April 1 in an almost bloodless coup d'état.

Documents seized by military policemen and interrogation of hundreds of arrested labor leaders, Communists, political and

Continued on Page 9, Column 1

NEWS INDEX

Rachel Carson, Author of 'Silent Spring,' Is Dead of Cancer at 56

Continued From Page 1, Col. 5

chemical sprays called for public awareness of what was going on.

She emphasized that she was not opposed to the use of poisonous chemical sprays—only their "indiscriminate use," and, at a time when their potential was not truly known.

Quoting Jean Rostand, the French writer and biologist, she said: "The obligation to endure gives us the right to know."

On April 3, 1963, the Columbia Broadcasting System's television series "C.B.S. Reports" presented the program "The Silent Spring of Rachel Carson." In it, Miss Carson said:

"It is the public that is being asked to assume the risks that the insect controllers calculate. The public must decide whether it wishes to continue on the present road, and it can do so only when in full possession of the facts.

"We still talk in terms of conquest. We still haven't become mature enough to think of ourselves as only a tiny part of a vast and incredible universe. Man's attitude toward nature is today critically important simply because we have now acquired a fateful power to alter and destroy nature.

But man is a part of nature, and his war against nature is inevitably a war against himself. The rains have become an instrument to bring down from the atmosphere the deadly products of atomic explosions. Water, which is probably our most important natural resource, is now used and re-used with incredible recklessness.

"Now, I truly believe, that we in this generation, must come to terms with nature, and I think we're challenged as mankind has never been challenged before to prove our maturity and our mastery, not of nature, but of ourselves."

3 Earlier Works

Miss Carson, thanks to her remarkable knack for taking dull scientific facts and translating them into poetical and lyrical prose that enchanted the lay public, had a substantial public image before she rocked the American public and much of the world with "Silent Spring."

This was established by three books, "Under the Sea Wind," "The Sea Around Us," and "The Edge of the Sea." "The Sea Around Us" moved quickly into the national best-seller lists, where it remained for 86 weeks, 39 of them in first place. By 1962 it had been published in 30 languages.

"Silent Spring," four-and-a-half years in preparation and published in September of 1962, hit the affluent chemical industry and the general public with the devastating effect of a Biblical plague of locusts. The title came from an apocalyptic opening chapter, which pictured how an entire area could be destroyed by indiscriminate spraying.

Legislative bodies ranging from New England town meetings to the Congress joined in the discussion. President Kennedy, asked about the pesticide problem during a press conference, announced that Federal agencies were taking a closer look at the problem because of the public's concern.

The essence of the debate was: Are pesticides publicly dangerous or aren't they?

They Should Be Called Biocide

Miss Carson's position had been summarized this way:

"Chemicals are the sinister and little-recognized partners of radiation in changing the very nature of the world—the very nature of life.

"Since the mid-nineteen forties, over 200 basic chemicals have been created for use in killing insects, weeds, rodents and other organisms described in the modern vernacular as pests, and they are sold under several thousand different brand names.

"The sprays, dusts and aerosols are now applied almost universally to farms, gardens, forests and homes—non-selective chemicals that have the power to kill every insect, the good and the bad, to still the song of birds and the leaping of fish in the streams—to coat the leaves with a deadly film and to linger on in soil—all this, though the intended target may be only a few weeds or insects.

"Can anyone believe it is possible to lay down such a barrage of poisons on the surface of the earth without making it unfit for all life? They should not be called 'insecticides' but 'biocides'."

The chemical industry was quick to dispute this.

Dr. Robert White-Stevens, a spokesman for the industry, said:

"The major claims of Miss Rachel Carson's book, 'Silent Spring,' are gross distortions of the actual facts, completely unsupported by scientific, experimental evidence, and general practical experience in the field. Her suggestion that pesticides are in fact biocides destroying all life is obviously absurd in the light of the fact that without selective biologicals these compounds would be completely useless.

"The real threat, then, to the survival of man is not chemical but biological, in the shape of hordes of insects that can denude our forests, sweep over our crop lands, ravage our food supply and leave in their wake a train of destitution and hunger, conveying to an undernourished population the major diseases scourges of mankind."

The Monsanto Company, one of the nation's largest chemical concerns, used parody as a weapon in the counterattack against Miss Carson. Without mentioning her book, the company adopted her poetic style in an article labeled "The Desolate Year," which began: "Quietly, then, the desolate year began . . ." and wove its own apocalyptic word picture—but one that showed insects stripping the countryside and winning.

As the chemical industry continued to make her a target for criticism, Miss Carson remained calm.

"We must have insect control," she reiterated. "I do not favor turning nature over to insects. I favor the sparing, selective and intelligent use of chemicals. It is the indiscriminate, blanket spraying that I oppose."

Actually, chemical pest control has been practiced to some extent for centuries. However, it was not until 1942 that DDT, a synthetic compound, was introduced in the wake of experiments that included those with poison gas. Its long-term poisonous potency was augmented by its ability to kill some insects upon contact and without being ingested. This opened a new era in pest control and led to the development of additional new synthetic poisons far more effective even than DDT.

As the pesticide controversy grew into a national quarrel, support was quick in going to the side of Miss Carson.

Supreme Court Justice William O. Douglas, an ardent naturalist, declared, "We need a Bill of Rights against the 20th century poisoners of the human race."

Earlier, an editorial in The New York Times had said:

"If her series [then running in part in The New Yorker publication of the book] helps arouse public concern to immunize Government agencies against the blandishments of the hucksters and enforces adequate controls, the author will be as deserving of the Nobel Prize as was the inventor of DDT."

Presidential Report

In May 1963, after a long study, President Kennedy's Science Advisory Committee, issued its pesticide report.

It stressed that pesticides must be used to maintain the quality of the nation's food and health, but it warned against their indiscriminate use. It called for more research into potential health hazards in the interim, urged more judicious care in the use of pesticides in homes and in the field.

The committee chairman, Dr. Jerome B. Wiesner, said the uncontrolled use of poisonous chemicals, including pesticides, was "potentially a much greate hazard" than radioactive fallout.

Miss Carson appeared before the Senate Committee on Commerce, which was hearing testimony on the Chemical Pesticides Coordination Act, and a bill that would require labels to tell how to avert damage to fish and wildlife.

"I suggest," she said, "that the report by the President's Science Advisors has created a climate in which creation of a Pesticide Commission within the Executive Department might be considered."

One of the sparks that caused Miss Carson to undertake the task of writing the book (whose documentation alone fills a list of 55 pages of sources), was a letter she had received from old friends, Stuart and Olga Huckins. It told of the destruction that aerial spraying had caused to their two-acre private sanctuary at Powder Point in Duxbury, Mass.

Miss Carson, convinced that she must write about the situation and particularly about the effects of spraying on ecological factors, found an interested listener in Paul Brooks, editor in chief of the Houghton-Mifflin Company, the Boston publishing house that had brought out "The Edge of the Sea."

As to her own writing habits, Miss Carson once wrote for 20th Century Authors:

"I write slowly, often in longhand, with frequent revision. Being sensitive to interruption, I write most freely at night.

"As a writer, my interest is divided between the presentation of facts and the interpretation of their significance, with emphasis, I think toward the latter."

"Silent Spring" became a best seller even before its publication date because its release date was broken. It also became a best seller in England after its publication there in March, 1963.

One of Miss Carson's greatest fans, according to her agent, Marie Rodell, was her mother. Miss Rodell recalled that the mother, who died of pneumonia and a heart ailment in 1960, had sat in the family car in 1952 writing letters while Miss Carson and Miss Rodell explored the sea's edge near Boothbay Harbor. To passers-by the mother would say, pointing, "That's my daughter, Rachel Carson. She wrote "The Sea Around Us."

People remembered Miss Carson for her shyness and reserve as well as for her writing and scholarship. And so when she received a telephone call after the publication of "The Sea Around Us," asking her to speak in the Astor Hotel at a luncheon, she asked Miss Rodell what she should do.

The agent counseled her to concentrate on writing. Miss Carson nodded in agreement, went to the phone, and shortly came back and said somewhat helplessly: "I said I'd do it."

There were 1,500 persons at the luncheon, Miss Carson was "scared to death," but she plunged into the talk and acquitted herself. As part of her program she played a recording of the sounds of underseas, including the clicking of shrimp and the squeeks of dolphins and whales. With the ice broken as a public speaker, Miss Carson continued with others sporadically.

Did Research by Herself

Miss Carson had some preliminary help in researching "Silent Spring" but soon found that she could go faster by doing the work herself because she could skim past so much that she already knew.

Miss Carson had few materialistic leanings. When she found "The Sea Around Us" was a great financial success, her first extravagance was the purchase of a very fine binocular-microscope, which she had always wanted. Her second luxury was the summer cottage on the Maine coast.

Her agent said that Miss Carson's work was her hobby but that she was very fond of her flower garden at Silver Spring, Md., where she also loved to watch the birds that came to visit.

Miss Carson had two favorite birds, a member of the thrush family called the veery, and the tern, a small, black-capped gull-like bird with swallowlike forked tails.

She once told an interviewer that she was enchanted by the "hunting, mystical call" of the veery, which is found in moist woods and bottomlands from Newfoundland to southern Manitoba, and in mountains to northern Georgia.

In manner, Miss Carson was a small, solemn-looking woman with the steady forthright gaze of a type that is sometimes common to thoughtful children who prefer to listen rather than to talk. She was politely friendly but reserved and was not given to quick smiles or to encouraging conversation even with her fans.

The most recent flare-up in the continuing pesticide controversy occurred early this month when the Public Health Service announced that the periodic huge-scale deaths of fish on the lower Mississippi River had been traced over the last four years to toxic ingredients in three kinds of pesticides. Some persons believed that the pesticides drained into the river from neighboring farm lands.

A hearing by the Agriculture Department of the Public Health Service's charges ended a week ago with a spokesman for one of the pesticide manufacturers saying that any judgment should be delayed until more information was obtained.

Miss Carson was born May 27, 1907, in Springdale, Pa., the daughter of Robert Warden Carson and the former Maria McLean. She was brought up in Springdale and in nearby Parnassus.

She owed her love of nature in large measure to her mother, who once wrote in The Saturday Review of Literature, that she had taught her daughter "as a tiny child joy in the out-of-doors and the lore of birds, insects, and residents of streams and ponds." She was a rather solitary child. She never married.

After being graduated from Parnassus High School, she enrolled in the Pennsylvania College for Women at Pittsburgh with the intention of making a career of writing. First she specialized in English composition. Later biology fascinated her and she switched to that field, going on to graduate work at Johns Hopkins University.

She then taught for seven consecutive sessions at the Johns Hopkins Summer School. In 1931 she became a member of the zoology staff of the University of Maryland. She remained five years. Her Master of Arts degree was conferred by Johns Hopkins in 1932.

Meanwhile, a childhood curiosity about the sea stayed with her. She absorbed all that she could read about the biology of the sea and she undertook post-graduate work at the Marine Biological Laboratory in Woods Hole, Mass., at Cape Cod.

In 1936 she was offered a position as aquatic biologist with the Bureau of Fisheries in Washington. She continued with the bureau and its successor, the Fish and Wildlife Service. In 1937, an article, "Undersea," in Atlantic led to her first book, "Under the Sea Wind," in 1941, and this was followed by her appointment as editor in chief of the Fish and Wildlife. Service—blending her two worlds: biology and writing.

Tribute to Rachel Carson

Julian Huxley Salutes Her Work and Warns of Pesticide Danger

TO THE EDITOR:

May I, as a biologist and conservationist, pay tribute to the work of Rachel Carson [Editorial April 16] in so compellingly drawing attention to man's ecological predicament, and especially to the grave dangers of one-sided and ill-thought-out interference with nature: I am thinking particularly of the unregulated use of pesticides in the presumed interest of higher food production, without taking into account other equally important human interests such as conservation, amenity, scientific study and recreation.

I had the privilege of being invited to write the foreword to the English edition of "Silent Spring" and can testify to the scientific thoroughness with which Miss Carson documented her subject. I can also assure Americans that the situation in Britain at that time was as grave as in the United States. As a result of insecticides and herbicides, we are in the process of losing large numbers of our songbirds and birds of prey, our butterflies and bees, and our prized wild flowers.

When I told my brother Aldous the facts, he said, "We are destroying half the basis of English poetry." In addition, we have been busily destroying the balance of nature in Britain.

However, thanks largely to the stimulus of Rachel Carson's book, the problem is now being thoroughly investigated and the Government has already made stricter regulations as to the use of various pesticides.

The nub of the matter is that the notion of exterminating pests by chemical means is quite chimerical: a remnant will always escape; still worse, new pesticide-resistant types will always develop and spread. But meanwhile in this vain attempt we shall certainly bring about the extermination or near-extermination of a number of non-pests. We need to control and manage nature, not to conquer or mutilate her.

In any case, the unregulated use of pesticides is only one aspect of our unbalanced emphasis on material utility and immediate profitability. This is leading, among other things, to the wholesale pollution of our rivers, lakes and seashores. Sewage has made it unsafe to swim in the Swiss lakes and on many English beaches: and sewage plus various chemical effluents is destroying many rivers as habitats for fish. Indeed, our boasted affluent society is in danger of becoming an effluent society.

I note in your news article on Miss Carson that a spokesman for one of the pesticide manufacturers demanded that any judgment on the role of pesticides in the recent mass death of fish in the lower Mississippi should be delayed until more information had been obtained.

I should have thought that the more sensible course would have been to delay the mass use of known toxic substances liable to drain into the river until more information was available as to the probable consequences on fish and other aquatic life.

JULIAN HUXLEY.

New York, April 15, 1964.

"All the News That's Fit to Print."

The New York Times

THE WEATHER
Showers today; Thursday fair; not much change in temperature; moderate to fresh northwest winds.
☞ For weather report see next to last page.

VOL. LXX....No. 23,202. ••• NEW YORK, WEDNESDAY, AUGUST 3, 1921. TWO CENTS In Greater New York | THREE CENTS Within 200 Miles | FOUR CENTS Elsewhere

ENRICO CARUSO DIES IN NATIVE NAPLES; END CAME SUDDENLY

Famous Tenor Succumbs When Taken From Sorrento for New Operation.

NATIONAL MOURNING IN ITALY

Tenor, It Is Now Disclosed, Had Undergone Six Operations and Blood Transfusion.

COLLEAGUES PAY TRIBUTE

Called "Matchless Singer" by Those Who Sang With Him—Whole World Watched His Long Illness Here.

NAPLES, Italy, Aug. 2 (Associated Press).—Enrico Caruso died here today. The great singer, whose ultimate recovery had been hoped for under the benign influences of his own Neapolitan skies, passed away at 9 o'clock this morning at the Hotel Vesuvius in this city.

At his own request, Caruso's body will be embalmed and the funeral services will be held tomorrow. It is recalled that when he lay gravely stricken in New York, he had expressed the wish that he might die in Italy, and now all Italy is mourning that this sad wish has come true.

The feeling of Italians has always been one of pride that Caruso for so many years represented the musical genius of their race. And not only that, many of them had found a friend in the beloved singer in time of need.

Signor Caruso had been brought here hurriedly from Sorrento, on the Bay of Naples, where less than a week ago he avowed his returning strength and expressed the conviction that he would sing again as in the old days.

He had been able to visit the famous Sanctuary of Our Lady of Pompeii, giving a thank offering for his recovery. He went also to the wonderful Island of Capri, where he attended a luncheon in his honor. But soon afterward unfavorable symptoms, in the form of a high fever, manifested themselves, and his wife telegraphed to a Rome specialist to come to Sorrento. It was then discovered that a new internal abscess had developed.

Caruso's removal to Rome for an operation was advised, but he showed such weakness that it was impossible to transfer him further than Naples, where he arrived by sea Sunday evening. Four eminent physicians were called in consultation, and their examination showed the presence of a subphrenic abscess, accompanied by severe peritonitis.

An operation at noon today was decided upon, but the patient's condition became suddenly worse at 4:30 in the morning, and he died soon afterward. Prior to this, heart stimulation was resorted to hourly.

In order that Caruso should not tire himself, the attending physicians ordered him not to speak, so during his last night he uttered no word.

Of the members of his family present at the deathbed, the most pathetic was his father's widow, who had always clung obstinately to her little home, despite her stepson's efforts to accustom her to the material comforts of life.

Mrs. Caruso With Him to the Last.

Present also at the bedside were Caruso's wife, who was Dorothy, daughter of Park Benjamin of New York; their little daughter Gloria and Caruso's eldest son, Rodolfo, as well as the tenor's brother, Giovanni, several nephews, and Vincenzo Bellezza and Paolo Longone, two musicians.

For a time after his arrival in Italy Caruso showed improvement, his native air having a beneficial effect. Nevertheless, he conserved his strength, and for this reason was obliged to refuse a request to sing at a reception given by the Admiralty to Crown Prince Hirohito of Japan.

That his voice remained strong and clear was declared to have been evidenced when recently he sang before the soprano Hidalgo and the baritone Montesanto, who expressed their delight.

There was grave anxiety, however, when Caruso, only a few days ago, began to show signs of depression. The rising temperature, which had characterized previous attacks, recurred, and steadily his condition grew worse until Saturday, when he suffered from violent pains in the abdominal region.

The medical consultation followed, and it was apparent that the patient was not only suffering acute physical pain, but that his heart was weakening rapidly. Oxygen was administered and other measures were taken to prolong his vitality.

Caruso himself wanted to proceed immediately to Rome, but he was dissuaded from this because such a journey, it was pointed out, might prove fatal.

Found New Operation Necessary.

LONDON, Aug. 2 (Associated Press).—Caruso was prepared for an operation Sunday, over the results of which the surgeons were pessimistic, according to an Exchange Telegraph dispatch from Rome today, quoting a Naples message.

Caruso was said to have become extremely weak yesterday afternoon, the weakness of his heart necessitating injection of camphor every two hours.

The operation, the dispatch said, was for an abscess between the liver and the diaphragm, which caused acute peritonitis. Caruso's wife and his brother were at his bedside.

The tenor was until a week ago believed to be on the way to recovery from the long illness which began in New York last Winter early in the operatic season.

Then suddenly he had an unexpected

Continued on Page Six.

Ford Rate Cuts Too Rapid; Commerce Board Halts Him

WASHINGTON, Aug. 2.—Freight-rate reductions on Henry Ford's Toledo, Detroit & Ironton Railroad have been made too rapidly to comply with the regulations of the Interstate Commerce Commission. His application to file a tariff reducing by 20 per cent. the rate on stone from Sibley, Mich., to Detroit was for this reason denied today by the commission.

Mr. Ford put into effect a reduction on July 26 of 5 cents a hundred on this traffic, and under the regulations thirty days must elapse before additional reductions can be made on the same traffic.

CARUSO KEPT HOPING HE WOULD RETURN

What He Said in the Last Interview He Gave for American Friends.

WELL IN YEAR, HE THOUGHT

Told a Dream of Death, Showed Scars in His Chest—'Intense Pain' When He Sang.

Copyright, 1921, by The Chicago Tribune Co.

CHICAGO, Aug. 2.—The Chicago Tribune received today by mail what may have been the last interview given to a correspondent by Enrico Caruso. The interview took place at Sorrento on July 19.

"I shall sing when I wish, where I wish and what I wish," declared Caruso to the newspaper's representative, who called on him at the Hotel Vittoria. "No one is forcing me to sing at any specified time, and the moment when I shall sing again just depends upon when I think I have recovered sufficient strength after my illness. I am gaining strength and weight every day. Two weeks ago I was flabby. Now my muscles are firm. Those who say that I have sung my last on the operatic stage are wrong, for my voice is unimpaired."

The last time the reporter had seen Caruso had been in the opera "Aida," and the warrior costumes of the Radames of Verdi's masterpiece contrasted strangely with the garb Caruso wore on the present occasion. On his head he wore a loose duck bathing cap. A blue bathing suit, a pink and white bathrobe carelessly thrown over one shoulder, and a pair of white canvas beach shoes, completed Caruso's attire.

He was accompanied by Mrs. Caruso, formerly Miss Dorothy Benjamin of New York, and by his two intimate friends Signor Amedo Canessa, a collector and antiquarian of New York, Naples and Paris, and Dr. Raffele Nilao of Naples.

His Fight to Regain Strength.

Caruso was thinner and his walk a trifle shaky. He fully looked the man convalescing from a most serious illness. His good nature was the same, however, and his determination to recover his strength bespoke a great deal.

It was the bathing hour, and the aristocratic population of Italy's most beautiful seaside resort was making its way to the water's edge. From the hotel to the beach at the bottom of the cliff below, one has to descend in an elevator. Caruso was puffing vigorously on an Egyption cigarette and, when his smoking was remarked, he exclaimed:

"Of course I smoke. What do you think? That I am sick?"

Then he continued playing "rich man, poor man, beggar man" on the buttons of the elevator boy's coat, imitating the sound of a bell on each button, much to the surprise and rather the fearful apprehension of the lad, who smiled in a somewhat doubtful way.

Reaching the beach, Caruso was greeted on every side by cries of "Tanti auguri, Signor Commendatore"—(many good wishes, Signor Commander)—from his title of Commander of the Crown of Italy, an honor conferred by the King.

For it was St. Henry's Day, and the forty-eighth one that Enrico—or Henry—Caruso had passed. All Sorrento was eager to present its compliments to its famous guest on his Saint's Day—Santo Enrico.

"Per mille anni"—(for a thousand years)—added an old begrizzled sailor, holding forth to Caruso an enormous bouquet of flowers, while another old mariner started the phenograph in Caruso's yacht playing the Italian royal march.

Took Sun Baths for Lung Cure.

While Mrs. Caruso joined friends and went to bathe, Caruso, Signor Canessa, Dr. Niola and the reporter got into a little boat and were rowed out to a discreet distance from shore, when Caruso divested himself of the upper part of his bathing suit in order to let the fortifying rays of Italian sunshine as much as possible into his left side, where four ugly gashes, remaining from his operation for pleurisy, were witness to the seriousness of his illness.

"Every morning I have my sun bath," said he, "and every afternoon my

Continued on Page Six.

BRYCE SAYS TREATY SOWS SEEDS OF WAR; FEARS OUTBREAKS

Finds Danger of Conflict on the Rhine, in Tyrol, the Balkans, and Russia and Turkey.

PEACE NEEDED SUPERMEN

But Some of the Negotiators, He Says, Did Not Seem to Believe Principles They Professed.

HE ATTACKS DEEP SECRECY

In Williams Address He Laments That Victors Bear Resentment Like Vanquished.

Special to The New York Times.

WILLIAMSTOWN, Mass., Aug. 2.—It would have taken a group of supermen to have made a satisfactory peace treaty at Versailles, Viscount Bryce declared today in a lecture before the Institute of Politics at Williams College. As it was, he said, the work of the negotiators has received nothing but censure in Europe and has resulted in sowing the seeds of future wars.

"There is," declared Lord Bryce, "no blacker cloud pregnant with future storm hanging over Europe now than that which darkens the bank of the Rhine."

He said that Europe's sore spots are many, and predicted that the slightest irritation of any of them may lead to armed conflict. "The war has shown one unprecedented feature painful in the prospect it opens," he asserted. "The victors bear as much resentment against the vanquished as the vanquished do against the victors."

Reviews Problems of Versailles.

Discussing the peace treaty and the events that led up to it Lord Bryce said: "After the war came the settlement by the representatives of the victorious powers assembled at Paris; not a fortunate spot for the kind of deliberation needed. Of them and of the methods they employed this is not the place or the time to speak. Their work has received in Europe nothing but censure. Comparing the treaties they framed with those which were made by the congress at Vienna in 1814-1815, European critics observe that the men of Vienna, Alexander and Metternich, Talleyrand and Hardenberg and Castlereagh, may have had bad principles and employed despotic methods and misconceived the interests of their peoples, but they at least knew what they were doing and gave effect to their principles.

"Their work bestowed upon Europe a tolerable peace, which lasted for more than thirty years. But there is not one of the treaties of 1919-20 which is not now already admitted to need amendment, while some are seen to lead straight to future wars. One hears people say 'The sort of peace that those negotiations have given us is as bad as was the war.'

"With these and many other strictures you are doubtless familiar, and you can judge how far they are deserved. But against these severe judgments let us give consideration to the difficulties which faced the negotiators at Paris.

"The men of Vienna had a common ground in their faith in monarchical principles and in their reliance upon force to carry out their principles. They had only monarchs to consider, not the will of peoples, and could do what they thought best for the interest of those they served. But the negotiators at Paris differed in their principles and ideals, and at least some of them do not seem to have believed in the principles then professed. European critics have suggested that some of them may have thought they must play down to their own electorates, and regard not what ought to be done, but also what would help in their next electoral campaigns. Popular prejudices, popular passions and cupidities had to be humored or gratified.

"Moreover—and this is an excuse which must not be lightly brushed aside—the task before them was one of unprecedented difficulty. New States had to be created, territories redistributed, indemnities secured and all on a scale incomparably greater than any international congress ever before had attempted.

Says Supermen Were Needed.

"A task so great needed not politicians of the usual type, but persons of the class which we now call supermen; persons who possessed not only a profound and accurate knowledge of the facts they had to deal with, but also a wide vision, a grasp of fundamental

Continued on Page Five.

Found Starving Russian Children Bound To Keep Them From Cannibalism

Copyright, 1921, by The New York Times Company.
Special Cable to THE NEW YORK TIMES.

RIGA, Aug. 2.—A refugee from the Bashkir Republic, in the Ural region, relates that he came to a lone farm where he found an old man sitting before the door. He seemed half insane and unable to answer the other's questions as to the meaning of the strange howling that came from the interior. The stranger entered the house and found four children, whose ages ranged from 10 to 16, each tied up in a different corner. The two youngest bore open wounds on their arms and bodies, which were naked to the waist. They were so fastened as to prevent the elder pair from tearing the younger in pieces and devouring them.

Reports state that while there is a considerable flood of refugees toward Moscow, the majority is moving like a flight of locusts east and southwest. At the same time fears are expressed here that sooner or later there will be a wave of sufferers toward Latvia. The anxiety is real, for the authorities say they could not get the troops to fire on the helpless people, who would stream across the frontier unchecked, to ravage everything in their path.

SENATOR FRANCE ASSAILS COL. RYAN

Publicly Charges American Red Cross Officer With Having Fomented Kronstadt Revolt.

CREATES A SCENE IN RIGA

Shrieks Threats Against Ryan, Who Reproaches Him for Friendship With "Murderers."

By WALTER DURANTY.

Copyright, 1921, by The New York Times Company
Special Cable to THE NEW YORK TIMES.

RIGA, Aug. 2.—Senator France last night startled not only the American colony, but considerable numbers of natives—for the affair was public—by accusing in no moderate language Colonel Edward W. Ryan, head of the American Red Cross in the Baltic States, of having fomented the abortive Kronstadt revolution last Spring.

It appears that the Senator has undertaken the mission of championing his Moscow friends against a bitter and intolerant world. For he is preparing, so he declares, a campaign not only against the Red Cross, but against THE NEW YORK TIMES, which he called "the lying sheet that poisons the hearts of America towards the noble leaders of Russia."

The Senator's "discussion" with Colonel Ryan began in his room at the Hotel Petersburg, throughout which his angry voice soon began to ring. He opened his attack by warning Colonel Ryan that there was law in America, and that before that law he would be condemned. The Red Cross man was amazed by the outbreak but the Senator continued.

"You Started the Kronstadt Revolution"

"You needn't attempt a denial. We have got proofs against you. I know, and the world shall know also, that you are guilty of criminal interference in the affairs of a friendly State. It was you who started the Kronstadt revolution, and for that you shall be punished."

By this time the Senator's angry tones had gathered several other guests of the hotel. Colonel Ryan was heard to ask what were the proofs of which the Senator boasted.

"I will receive them shortly," he shouted, "but for me no written proof is necessary. I have been told of your dishonorable conduct by men whose word I take—honest men, men who wouldn't lie."

This was too much. Passionately Colonel Ryan questioned the Senator's right to accuse him on the bare assertion of Bolshevist rulers "whose hands are still dripping with the blood of murdered women and children."

"It shames me," Colonel Ryan cried, "to think that you, an elected representative of the American people, have taken those hands in friendship."

And so the altercation continued from the hotel to the street, from the street to the station, where the Senator declaimed with furious eloquence before a crowd of bewildered Letts. He "told the world," and told it loudly, that he would bring Ryan and the Red Cross before the pillory of the American Senate and show up their vices and corruption. It was an unedifying scene, deeply regretted by all the Americans present. It was not easy to tell a Lettish questioner that a wild-eyed, furious man, waving his arms and shrieking threats at the top of his voice, was indeed a member of the Senate of the United States.

Charge Made on Tchitcherin's word.

Aside from Senator France, who admitted that he had nothing but Tchitcherin's word as the basis of the charges he made, the latter seem to rest on the flimsiest foundation. But the Bolsheviki are so crazed by suspicion of all the world that they are ready to take up anything.

It appears, however, that a certain allied agent did penetrate Kronstadt—not before, but during the revolution—on the pretext that he belonged to the American Red Cross. Indeed, he bore a paper, procured without authority, with the letter-head of the Red Cross, stating that he was a member of that organization, which was untrue. As for Colonel Ryan, he was in Paris at the time.

The Red Cross further incurred the ire of the Soviet by feeding the 8,000 Russian refugees who crossed the ice from Kronstadt to Finland when the revolution was crushed.

In point of fact, the revolution itself was not a "White" affair, but a squabble between two groups of communists.

The Soviet leaders are, however, bitterly angry over the publication last year of a Red Cross report containing statements made by Colonel Ryan after his return from the interior of Russia.

The American authorities here will only say that Senator France's charges are grotesque, but it was easy to see that today's affair had created a most

Continued on Page Two.

RUM RUNNER CAUGHT; SEE 'STARTLING' PLOT

Schooner Under British Flag Taken Beyond Three-Mile Limit Without Legal Precedent.

MASTER AND MATE ESCAPE

Vessel Brought Here and Her Crew Detained as Officials Seek Heads of Conspiracy.

Following the seizure late Monday off Atlantic City of the Henry L. Marshall, a liquor laden schooner flying the British flag, she was towed into this port yesterday and Federal officials who questioned members of the crew announced that they had evidence of a gigantic rum-running plot involving many persons in cities along the Atlantic coast. Although declining to reveal the nature of their evidence, which they characterized as "startling," the Federal agents indicated that they were in a position to obtain valuable data regarding vessels which have been landing liquor.

The Marshall was captured four miles off the New Jersey resort by the Coast Guard cutter Seneca in charge of Commander Aaron L. Gamble, who recently had been detailed to watch for violations of the Volstead act in this section. Although the vessel was outside the three-mile limit the Federal authorities justified their action by saying that they had evidence of a conspiracy.

Discussing the legal features of the seizure, which it was admitted had no precedent, Assistant United States District Attorney Clark said:

"It is our position that we have a right to seize a vessel outside of the three-mile limit if there is evidence of a conspiracy to violate our customs laws and the Volstead act. While the actual sale of liquor outside of the three-mile limit is not in itself illegal, yet if it can be shown that persons from this country go out there to buy contraband, then conspiracy has been established."

No specific complaint has been lodged against the schooner, which, with her cargo of 1,500 cases of liquor, is being detained by the United States Marshal with armed guards aboard. A cook and three seamen are being held as material witnesses pending further investigation.

Threw Over Some Cargo.

The Seneca left this port a week ago to search for "floating bars" reported bobbing up mysteriously along the coast. Late Monday afternoon the Seneca sighted the Marshall, flying the British flag, and started in pursuit of the schooner, which was running under gasoline auxiliary engine.

When those aboard the Marshall saw that they were being run down, they began throwing overboard some of the cargo, according to officers of the Seneca. As the Government cutter drew nearer, a motor boat was put over the side of the schooner, and two men, the Captain and mate, entered it and sped away toward Atlantic City.

The seamen gave their names as Pike, Clarence King, M. Murphy and L. Maul. They said that the Captain was K. Klausen and the first mate E. Thompson. They also were reported to have told the Coast Guard officials that the vessel had loaded her cargo at a place five miles east of the Island of New Providence in the Bahamas.

Authorities Get Busy.

After completing an examination of the schooner, Commander Gamble placed seven of his men aboard and towed the craft to this port. A wireless message was sent to Captain Byron Reed, local superintendent of the Coast Guard Service, and he in turn notified United States Marshal Thomas McCarthy to have men waiting at Quarantine.

United States District Attorney Hayward assigned Assistant District Attorneys Cahill, Rothwell and Clark to the case and they went to the office of Collector of Customs Aldridge in the Custom House, where a preliminary hearing was held. Pike, the seaman, was said to have given the Federal agents leads to work on.

The Seneca, it was said, had been directed to keep an especial lookout for the Marshall, which the authorities understood already had made three voyages with liquor to this country. On one of these trips, it was said, the vessel had flown the American flag. It was reported that the schooner had changed to British registry within recent months, but as the crew was unable yesterday to give any supporting evidence this is being investigated.

Until a year ago, when sold to William McCoy of Daytona, Fla., the Marshall was used as a fishing craft out of Gloucester, Mass. It was said at the time of sale that she was to be used for trading in the West Indies. The vessel was built in 1916 and registered at seventy-eight tons. McCoy has not been seen in Gloucester since he took over the ship, nor is he known in that city.

Dispatches from Atlantic City last Thursday told how the Marshall had lingered outside the three-mile limit off that city, where motor boats went out to make purchases. It was said that the Captain, whose name was reported to be Enric Andersen, had boasted that he was "working for a crowd of wealthy men" and that "these Federal men can't do anything to me but make it uncomfortable."

Captain Andersen was quoted as having admitted making a prior trip to Montauk Point with a cargo of liquor. On this trip he had 2,900 cases of liquor, he was said to have sold wholesale.

WHITE SOX PLAYERS ARE ALL ACQUITTED BY CHICAGO JURY

Two Others, Indicted With Them, Are Also Declared Not Guilty.

WILD SCENES IN THE COURT

Cheers Greet Verdict and Jurors Lift the Freed Players to Their Shoulders.

JUDGE FRIEND IS PLEASED

Defense Lawyer Calls It Vindication of Most Maltreated Players—State Attorneys Silent.

CHICAGO, Aug. 2 (Associated Press).—The seven former Chicago White Sox baseball players and two others on trial for alleged conspiracy to defraud the public through throwing of the 1919 world series games were found not guilty by a jury tonight.

The jury took only one ballot.

The verdict was reached after two hours and forty-seven minutes of deliberation, but was not returned until forty minutes later, Judge Hugo M. Friend being out of court when the decision was reached.

Announcement of the verdict was greeted by cheers from the several hundred persons who remained in court for the final decision, with shouts of "Hooray for the clean Sox!"

Judge Friend congratulated the jury, saying he thought it a just verdict.

Eddie Cicotte was the first of the defendants to reach the jurors. He grabbed William Barrett by both hands, shouting his thanks.

Joe Jackson, Claude Williams and the others were close behind, and the jurors lifted them on to their shoulders, while flashlight photographs were taken.

Bailiffs vainly pounded for order and, finally noticing Judge Friend's smiles, joined in the whistling and cheering.

Hats sailed high in the air, papers were thrown around and the courtroom was the scene of the wildest confusion in any recent Cook County criminal case.

As the jurors filed out of the room they were slapped on the back, and the spectators shouted congratulatory words.

They Had Paced the Floor.

The defendants, on hearing the nine verdicts solemnly read by the Court Clerk, gave vent to their feelings in varied manners. Throughout the hours the jury deliberated the men on trial had paced up and down at times, gathered in little groups quietly to discuss the case or remained secluded.

When the three loud knocks on the jury room door were heard, indicating a verdict, every one jumped for the courtroom; but the excitement was momentary, it being some time before Judge Friend could be reached.

Buck Weaver and "Swede" Risberg were the most excited over the verdict, grabbing each other by the arms and shouting. Felsch and Williams merely smiled, while Joe Jackson took the decision very quietly. Gandil shook hands with a few friends and slipped from the courtroom.

"I'll give a sailor's farewell to Ban Johnson," said Gandil. "Good-bye, good luck and to —— with you."

"I knew I'd be cleared," said Weaver, "and I'm glad the public stood by me until the trial was over."

Williams termed the verdict a "true one," saying he was proud to have "come through clean."

Cicotte and Risberg rushed to telegraph offices to notify their wives.

David Zelcer will return to his home in Des Moines immediately and Carl Zork plans to leave for St. Louis tomorrow.

Henry Berger, defense counsel, termed the verdict a "complete vindication of the most mistreated ball players in history."

The State's attorneys were silent.

The case was placed in the hands of the jury at 7:52 o'clock in a special session of the court tonight, after Judge Hugo Friend had instructed the jury as to the numerous legal points involved.

Arguments Concluded in Afternoon.

The closing arguments were concluded this afternoon when George Gorman, Assistant State's Attorney in charge of the prosecution, in a brief closing address informed the jury that in his opinion the State had presented such a conclusive case that a long address was unnecessary.

Judge Friend in his instructions, which he spent most of the afternoon in pre-

Continued on Page Three.

Penrose Does Not See Why Any One Wants to Be an Envoy

Special to The New York Times.

WASHINGTON, Aug. 2.—Senator Penrose today had as one of his callers Cyrus E. Woods, former Secretary of the Commonwealth of Pennsylvania, who recently resigned that office to become Ambassador to Spain. Mr. Woods is here getting his final instructions from the State Department and will sail from New York on Saturday.

"I do not see why any one would want to give up an important political position to become Ambassador," said Mr. Penrose. "About all our Ambassadors and Consuls do is to get boarding places for American tourists and keep American visitors out of jail. And they have to pay for the honor of such a job."

MAIL ROBBER GANG HAD SINCLAIR BONDS

Stolen Securities of Oil Company in Chicago Vaults of Worthington Concern.

TOTAL LOOT OF $350,000

New York Man Is Arrested for Alleged Connection With Chicago Firm's Deals.

CHICAGO, Aug. 2.—Bonds of the Sinclair Oil Company, which recently disappeared in New York, and securities missing since the Toledo, Council Bluffs and the Dearborn Station, Chicago, mail robberies, were found today among the effects of the Central Securities Company, whose leaders, John W. Worthington and Owen T. Evans, were arrested here yesterday, according to announcement of Federal officials. The securities found total about $350,000.

Based upon these discoveries, additional indictments against the men were asked by John V. Clinnin, Assistant United States District Attorney.

Mr. Clinnin is directing the case, which is aimed also at twenty-six other persons indicted with Worthington and Evans.

The Federal investigators expect that the case will clear up mail robberies totaling nearly $6,000,000.

"We absolutely have the goods on Worthington," said Mr. Clinnin. He said that besides the Sinclair, Toledo and Dearborn station securities, there had been found War Savings stamps and cancelled Internal Revenue stamps "washed" by an illegal process for use a second time.

Worthington and Evans pleaded not guilty when arraigned before Judge Landis and their bonds were set at $50,000 each.

Warrants for five Chicagoans, two residents each of Cleveland and Pittsburgh, and one each of New York and Philadelphia residents, were issued today and postal inspectors departed for the East to serve the warrants.

Five of the persons wanted are known as J. C. Ellington, Louis Leonard, B. Kelly, J. J. Epps and Alva Harschmann. In addition Federal agents sent from Chicago, carried "John Doe" warrants on which to make arrests if necessary.

In the arrest of Arthur H. Goldsmith of New York City, Mr. Clinnin declares the New York headquarters of what the officials believe to be a gigantic "robbers' trust" has been uncovered.

Goldsmith's name was found on many letters and other documents captured in the raids on Worthington's office, and the New York authorities were at once asked to arrest him.

"Goldsmith in New York was what Worthington was in Chicago," said Mr. Clinnin.

Reports were received of the arrest in Detroit of "Lefty" Lewis, said to be another of Worthington's aids.

Arthur M. Goldsmith, proprietor of a commercial school at 165 East Seventy-second Street, known as the President Institute, was arrested yesterday on suspicion of being concerned in the mail thefts of $6,000,000, for which John W. Worthington of the Central Securities Company and others are in the hands of Federal authorities in Chicago. The arrest was made by Chief Hugh McQuillah of the Intelligence Bureau of the Treasury Department on instructions telegraphed here from the Federal officials in Chicago.

The arrest was made at Goldsmith's home in East Sixty-ninth Street by Special Agent Walter P. Murphy and Post Office Inspector Joseph Vick. He denied connection with the conspiracy, but admitted that in addition to operating his school, he had bought and sold Liberty bonds and War Savings stamps, and that some of these dealings were through the Central Securities Company.

Maxwell S. Mattuck told United States Commissioner Hitchcock that Goldsmith was indicted by a Grand Jury in Chicago with Worthington and others, and that the officials in Chicago considered Goldsmith an important figure in the alleged thefts. Inquiry showed that Goldsmith has been operating his school in Harlem for fifteen years. Bail was fixed at $10,000 for a hearing Tuesday.

HASKELL TOSSES HAT INTO RING AS FUSION DESIGNATES CURRAN

Conference Unanimously Names Borough President for Mayor, Lockwood for Controller.

TO FILL THIRD PLACE TODAY

Cyrus C. Miller of the Bronx Offered Designation—Others Discussed and Dropped.

CANDIDATES GIVE PLEDGES

All Say They Will Abide by the Primaries—Livingston Puzzles Republican Leaders.

By unanimous vote the anti-Tammany Conference Committee yesterday indorsed the recommendation of Republican and Coalition Committee leaders for the designation of Henry H. Curran, Borough President of Manhattan, for the nomination for Mayor and of Senator Charles C. Lockwood of Brooklyn for Controller. The selections, before becoming valid, must be ratified by the enrolled Republican voters in the primaries on Sept. 13. Circulation of petitions for the 1,500 signatures required to give the candidates a place on the primary ballot will be begun at once.

When the Conference Committee adjourned, to meet again at 2 P. M. today, the third place on the city slate remained vacant, although several candidates for the nomination for President of the Aldermanic Board had been discussed and dropped.

Republican and Coalition Committee leaders were trying last night to get into communication with Cyrus C. Miller, former Borough President of the Bronx and an independent Democrat. Mr. Miller is spending the Summer at Greensboro, Vt. At a late hour the leaders had not been able to reach him either by telephone or telegraph. Should he indicate willingness to become a candidate—of which there appears to be doubt—he is practically certain to be named when the committee resumes deliberations.

Haskell Formally Enters Race.

While members of the Conference Committee at the Commodore were listening to Curran and Lockwood "nominating" speeches, the entry of a fourth contender for the anti-Tammany Mayoralty nomination was heralded in a formal announcement by County Judge Reuben L. Haskell of Brooklyn that his hat was in the ring. Judge Haskell, with vitriolic denunciation of "Fusion," declared he had entered the fray as a "straight Republican" candidate.

Despite the crowding in of candidates and the bitterness that appears likely to mark the fight, the peril of a third ticket which four years ago brought political disaster to John Purroy Mitchel, the coalition candidate for Mayor, seems to have been averted. While both F. H. LaGuardia, President of the Board of Aldermen, and former Senator William M. Bennett, winner in the city primaries in 1917, announced that they were in the fight to stay, both said they would support the winner in the primary. Judge Haskell and Mr. Curran also announced they would be bound by the primary results.

Should the third place on the city ticket be filled this afternoon the Anti-Tammany Conference Committee will have carried out the greater part of its mission. Candidates for borough and county offices will be selected in the next few days by special committees appointed by the Republican organisations in their respective localities after consultation with similar local committees representing the Coalition Committee and other independent groups.

Platform Still to Be Drafted.

One task, however, remains for the conference committee—the drafting and promulgation of an anti-Tammany city platform. Some of the "best minds" in the Republican Party are said to be giving constructive thought to platform pronouncements and finding it a very ticklish job indeed.

The chief difficulty, according to all accounts, appears to be in drafting a traction plank, which, without giving offense to Governor Miller and advocates of his transit plan, will be in consonance with the views expressed by the two leading candidates. Borough President Curran has denounced the Governor's plan as a violation of home rule. Senator Lockwood spoke and voted against the Transit bill.

Republican leaders intend to defer the promulgation of a platform until just before the primaries. It has not been decided whether a pseudo city convention shall be held, but the Coalition Committee has already made public its own platform, embodying a straight-out declaration for the five-cent fare and opposition to the Miller plan, and a majority of the Republican conferees are not prepared to accept it in its present form.

Senator Lockwood remained at his Summer home in Long Beach yesterday. Borough President Curran attended a conference of Republican and coalition leaders in the National Republican Club.

Curran Issues Statement.

Before he departed he made public his first statement since the Coalition conferences have been under way.

"I deeply appreciate the honor," he said, "that the leaders of my party and the Independents and Democrats in the Coalition Committee have conferred upon me in recommending to the enrolled voters that I be nominated for the office of Mayor of the City of New York. This honor carries with it a responsibility, the seriousness of which I understand very well. There is no field in which greater service can be given to the people of our city today than in that of the city's Government. The power there, for good or evil, as I know

New Movie Censors, Shocked, Say 'No!' to Film In Which Artists' Models Are Displayed

The axe of the censor was wielded with deadly effect yesterday for the first time in the history of the motion-picture industry in this State. Although the censors—the newly created Motion Picture Commission, appointed by Governor Miller—have been on the job only two days, they served notice on producers that their slogan would be: "Hew to the line, let the chips fall where they may."

The first victim of censorial disapproval was not revealed.

Several new films ready for release as soon as they had been passed upon, were awaiting the action of the commissioners when they arrived at the new censorship headquarters in the Candler Building, 220 West Forty-second Street.

"Educational" and "current events" pictures—the kind that depict such scenes as "Icelandic Maidens Marketing Icicles" and "Pittsburgh, Pa.—Three Hundred Barrels of Liquor Dumped in Gutter"—were the first to be shown. There was nothing in them to arouse more than the censors' mild interest.

Then the "studio" picture was brought on. It began mildly. The women in the first part of the scene were so thoroughly dressed that it looked like a scene in 1891. One began to surmise that it would be a dull day for the censors. But the change was abrupt. More women entered into the picture, some of them representing artists' models. Finally a picture within the picture—description deleted by censor—was flashed. This one was too much. There was a chorus of "Out" or "Thumbs Down," or whatever censors say. The whole film was ruled "out of order" and the official "certificate of disapproval" was signed, sealed and mailed. The producer, probably will frame it for display in other States.

Body of Newark Lad, Killed in the Argonne, Left by Soldiers on Porch of Father's Home

An army truck drew up to 186 East Kinney Street, Newark, yesterday afternoon, and one of four soldiers in the truck shouted to several boys playing in front of the house: "Does Bufanio live here?" The boys told them, that Fortunato Bufanio lived in the house with his family, but that none of the family was at home at the time.

The soldiers then backed the truck to the curb and carried to the porch of the house a coffin draped with the American flag.

"What floor do they live on?" asked the spokesman of the soldiers.

"On the second," was the answer.

The coffin was carried into the ground floor hall, but when the soldiers found that the stairway presented difficulties one of them said: "Let's leave it on the porch. They can have it carried up stairs." They put the coffin out on the porch and hurried off in the truck.

Bufanio returned home about two hours later and found a crowd of neighbors angrily commenting on the behavior of the soldiers in their treatment of the body of his son, Silveno, who was killed while fighting with the 312th Infantry in the Argonne.

Bufanio was grief-stricken, and some of his neighbors volunteered to carry the coffin upstairs. There Bufanio told that several days ago he received word from the War Department that his son's body had arrived at the army pier at Hoboken, but that it was not ready for delivery to his father's home. The notice also stated, he said, that he would be notified a few days in advance. He added that he had received no further notice, and that he had gone down to the Hoboken pier yesterday to learn the cause of the delay.

Members of the American Legion in Newark were indignant last night when they learned of the action of the soldiers. They announced that a military funeral for Silveno, who was 22 years old when he was killed while serving with a Newark contingent, would be held today.

ENRICO CARUSO DIES IN NATIVE NAPLES

Continued from Page 1, Column 1.

relapse and was removed from Sorrento to Naples.

He arrived at Naples Sunday night, added the message, and the specialists who were called decided to operate immediately.

The burial of Caruso will take place today (Wednesday) amid national mourning, at the Church of Santa Maria Gracia, in Naples, according to the Daily Mail.

Crowds in Italy Watched Bulletins.

Special Cable to THE NEW YORK TIMES.

ROME, Aug. 2.—The news of Caruso's fatal relapse filled every one in Rome with the deepest consternation, as throughout Italy it had been hoped that the singer was definitely on the road to recovery. According to reports here, the greatest impression was caused in his native Naples, where a vast crowd in perfect silence waited all morning outside the clinic in order to hear how the patient was progressing. Some papers printed special editions, giving bulletins of Caruso's condition.

Hundreds of telegrams expressing sympathy, and others of encouragement up to the last, were received from all over Italy. The physicians did not disguise the gravity of the operation, for which they had prepared, especially in view of the weakened condition of the patient, but they had expressed even yesterday the strong hope of saving Caruso's life.

Late last night in Rome, knots of people had remained standing outside the newspaper offices to get the first news of the result of the operation. Instead came the news of his death this morning.

CARUSO KEPT HOPING HE WOULD RETURN

Continued from Page 1, Column 2.

massage. In a week or so I shall begin 'setting up' exercises, but am not quite up to it at present. In the afternoon I also do my correspondence, and in the evening, if there is nothing on at the little village theatre here in Sorrento, I go to bed early. Quite a normal life, you see. Doctor? I have no doctor. I take care of myself, or rather, Mrs. Caruso and my valet take perfect care of me."

Caruso was emphatic in his denial that his voice was lost, and was particularly assertive with regard to an alleged interview, which it was reported he had given to a certain Dr. Fulton, in which he was quoted as declaring that he would never sing again.

"Of course, these gashes you see on my left side are pretty deep, and the severed muscles are just knitting. Naturally, my diaphragm is weak, and at present it will hardly support the sustaining of a strong vocal note without intense pain. But I am gaining strength every day.

Said He Needed Year to Recover.

"Besides, one needs a year to recover completely from pleurisy. When my wounds are quite healed and my strength recovered I shall sing. For my voice and throat are the same as ever. I am my own master and shall not sing again until I feel completely able and recuperated."

Speaking of his illness, Caruso said he had a vision that he believed had been its turning point.

"One night I dreamed I was dead. It was when my illness was at its height. I seemed to be buried and, strangely enough, could at the same time see my bas-relief carved on the top of my tombstone. It seemed so calm and peaceful to be dead—no more suffering. A loud automobile horn in the street below brought me back to life, and I woke up to find Mrs. Caruso looking anxiously into my face. I told her one experience beyond the grave would be sufficient for me for some time, and from that moment I have been improving. It's very agreeable to be dead, but it's a great deal nicer to be alive."

By this time the rowboat had reached the pier again, and all went ashore. Caruso joined other friends down the beach and went into the water, the second time he had been in since his illness. He did not swim or stay in more than ten minutes, and, coming out basked in the sun a while and smoked a cigarette before going back to his apartments in the hotel, on the cliff above.

Just as he was about to leave the beach he espied the nurse girl with his little daughter, Gloria, 1½ years old. Caruso stopped to cover the little girl with kisses and to make her laugh by making funny noises.

"We shall stay in Sorrento about another month," said he, "and then go and see our cows, pigs, ducks and hens at our farm in the outskirts of Florence.

"When shall we go back to America? I don't know. That, too, shall be when I wish, for our plans are not made, and we shall merely follow our own convenience. We shall probably sail from France."

© Mishkin

Enrico Caruso, 1905.

MANY LAUD CARUSO AS MAN AND ARTIST

His Place Impossible to Fill, Says Farrar, and McCormack Calls Him Greatest Singer.

ITALIANS PLAN MEMORIAL

Want Theatre or Foundation for Operatic Students as Fitting Tribute for Great Tenor.

News of the death of Caruso called forth praise for "the greatest singer of the age," and tributes to him as a man of generous deeds. These came not alone from his associates in the world of music, but from those who had met him off the stage and loved him for his qualities.

This grief and feeling of loss extended to thousands of Italians, who praised him as one of the greatest man of their nationality. Several Italian organizations immediately initiated plans for a memorial in this city to the great singer. The Order of the Sons of Italy proposes a Caruso theatre here or a Caruso foundation for the training of young singers, and will hold a meeting today to further its aims.

Geraldine Farrar, who sang with Caruso in the Metropolitan for many seasons, said:

"Mr. Caruso's death came as a great shock to me, as the day before he sailed I went to see him and Mrs. Caruso and remarked his good spirits and hopeful mood. I certainly had no premonition of this sorrowful end and thought that he would return to us later in the season in all his former glory.

"As friend and comrade of fifteen years' standing I grieve and puzzle at the destiny that forced him to battle so long and valiantly for this finale undreamed of. His ardent wish to close his eyes in his native land was granted by a kind dispensation of fate.

"His great gift was unique. Its like will not be approached in our generation; his place is impossible to fill in our present-day musical world.

"His kindnesses and qualities as friend and comrade are too well known to detail. He was a universal figure, beloved and admired. May God rest his soul."

John McCormack, famous tenor and friend of Caruso, said at his home in Darien:

"I have lost one of my best friends and the public has lost its greatest artist, but the artists have lost a great pal. For the fourteen years I have known him I never knew him say an unkind word of or to a colleague. His epitaph might well be: 'He was the greatest singer God ever created.' I feel that the tenors of America, we of the younger generation, must in some way get up a memorial worthy of the great man and artist. I have lost a dear friend."

Antonio Scotti, lifelong friend and intimate of Caruso, who had sung with him for years, said:

"It takes half my life. What tribute could I pay to such a man—to such a heart? I would have given anything to save him, but, of course, there was nothing I could do."

Amelita Galli Curci, who sang with Caruso in South America, said:

"I am shocked and grieved to learn of the death of Enrico Caruso. Thus ends one of the most brilliant careers in musical history. All the world will remember him, not alone for his glorious voice and untiring devotion to art, but for his human qualities and big, generous heart, and, lastly, for his heroic struggle in his last long illness."

Rafael Diaz, Metropolitan Opera Company tenor, said:

"He always had a kind word and often a bit of priceless advice for younger singers. It is a pity that one who gave his whole as a sacrifice to his art could not live to enjoy it more. It can be said of him more than of any other person I ever knew that he lived for his work and for others, never for himself. But for his unsparing devotion to his art he might be alive today."

Stefano Miele, National Master of the Order of the Sons of Italy, said:

"Enrico Caruso did more for the Italian race in this country than any single individual, and the loss will strike deep into the hearts of all Italians and Americans of Italian birth or descent, as well as all lovers of the purest arts, no matter what their nationalities.

"Mindful of what Caruso has done to interpret the soul of Italy throughout the world, it is fitting that the order should take steps to perpetuate the memory of its most illustrious son. The Order of the Sons of Italy will feel it to be its duty to honor the memory of Caruso, and certainly nothing could be more in accord with the spirit of that great artist than to create a foundation which in the name of Caruso could extend a helping hand to promising young artists and help them toward the goal of their ambition—the operatic stage.

"In that way it may be possible to rear another Caruso, who will delight the hearts of future generations as Caruso's golden voice and art have delighted the hearts of the present generation."

The Lotos Club, whose members honored Caruso at a dinner several years ago, cabled to Mrs. Caruso:

"Our deepest sympthies in your great bereavement."

The Italy-America Society, of which the President is Paul D. Cravath, one of the Directors of the Metropolitan Opera Company, said in a note of tribute:

"All those who loved Caruso, who wished him well all the Winter when his life was in danger, hoped to have him back on the stage, to hear the beautiful clear voice fill the opera house like a rich wave of harmony. That beloved voice is silent forever, but Caruso's wish of ending his days in his native country has been accomplished."

ENRICO CARUSO.

The place of ENRICO CARUSO among famous singers of the world finds but halting comparison in his own time. There was no second. There is, there will be, no like successor. The Metropolitan Opera House, where for the unprecedented period of eighteen years he was king, has been called a graveyard of reputations; it may well be so, during years to come, for those tenor aspirants who elect to singe their wings by flight into the glowing empyrean of his remembered voice in his memorable rôles. The king is dead; but art is long, and opera is longer. Other times, other tenors—and the tenor who follows CARUSO will doubtless be the embodiment of a new age, as he was after those who reigned before him; a man of new type, individual timbre, distinctive répertoire.

It is mostly from plain folk that great tenors come. The reason, perhaps, is that which LINCOLN assigned for the Creator's seeming preference for common people, "because He made so many of them." In the humblest walk of life supreme genius and beauty of song may occur; it may be associated with any rank, even with a man of title, but such supremacy oftenest arises among the peasant stock. The voice of TAMAGNO was a heroic tenor of amazing power, one of the sort called tenori robusti, or more properly tenori di forza. It is yet said that MARIO was "the perfection of the tenor voice." RUBINI, a tenore di grazia, indulged in the vibrato, natural to him but abused by his imitators. ITALO CAMPANINI was a tenor of middle character between force and grace. Thus doubly gifted also was CARUSO, capable of a variety never achieved by DE RESZKE, king of the lyric stage before him, nor by BONCI, a living tenore di grazia today.

The voice itself was authentically one of the greatest voices of the period, and those who have heard it have a great memory to treasure. In the beginning a voice of light, almost lyric, quality, it gained greatly in power and weight, in golden purity and dramatic potency of late years. And Mr CARUSO possessed an artist's fine skill in the use of it, in the technical accomplishment by which a great voice is made to tell to its utmost, though all who hear it may not know how or why. He cannot be entirely acquitted of a fondness for pleasing those who are transported by the high note, the loud note, the long-sustained note, the lachrymose sob, and thereby making the judicious grieve. But these same judicious were as likely as not to be themselves transported the next moment or the next evening by a matchless exhibition of art of the finer sort: of sustained legato, of exquisite mezza voce, of a beautifully turned phrase or succession of phrases, all of a poignant quality that tugged hard at the heartstrings.

Of his growth in constancy to great ideals, of his steady development in serious parts, there has been since DE RESZKE no such example among singing men. Canio in "Pagliacci," the Duke in "Rigoletto," Nemorino in "L'Elisir d'Amore," Lionel in "Marta," remained favorites with his audiences long after he himself preferred to be taken at higher value in "Aïda," and latterly in "Samson," in "Le Prophète," or in "La Juive," the opera of his final Metropolitan appearance last Christmas Eve. He never lost, however, his great natural fund of humor; playful where the play allowed it, he held the audience's sympathy, met its quick response before the curtain, while always respectful of his companion artists and eager that the prima donna or the baritone should receive a due share of applause.

Mr. CARUSO's cartoons were everywhere famous. They were to thousands here as familiar as to millions the world over were the "records" of his voice. He drew his pencil sketches naturally, with the same impulse of a practical joker, the same animal spirits and vitality, that animated all he did or sang. To New York he was affectionately the "neighbor CARUSO" who lived for many seasons in the thick of things on theatrical Broadway. The city, like the American public at large, was proud of its large share in his career; he was an honorary member of its police and a recipient of its official flag in recognition of his services to its charities during the World War.

While the tenor's home and family at the last were here in New York, he never gave up his loyalty to his native land. By coincidence, he reached Naples to die in the city of his birth. Elsewhere, fourteen miles from the City of Florence, he maintained the chief of his estates, on which 200 persons gained their livelihood. His elder son, now a man grown, served with the Italian colors in the war. A younger lad he brought to be educated in the United States, and it was in New York that his infant daughter, GLORIA, was born, a CARUSO of American ancestry as well. The great tenor sent gifts to a poorer cousin's wedding in Paterson, N. J. He for years here had with him on the stage a friend singing small parts in opera, who when they were boys together about the Bay of Naples had been first to discover CARUSO's voice. These things it will be good to remember, not of the opera's lost star, but of CARUSO the man.

LITTLE ITALY IN TEARS OVER WORD OF DEATH

The first report of the death of Caruso was carried in news dispatches, and several cablegrams from Mrs. Caruso confirmed the news later in the day. These messages said briefly: "Enrico died this morning."

Crowds of Italians gathered around the bulletin boards of Italian newspapers, waiting for the details of the death of their idol and discussing his triumphs. Many wept.

Il Progresso, Italo-Americano, which usually devotes most of its front page to foreign news, gave the whole page today to Caruso.

Bruno Zirato, Caruso's secretary, refused at first to believe the news reports, and dispatched a cablegram to Italy, begging for some news which he hoped would be good and feared would be bad. He accepted the truth later in the day and for hours sat silently in the Caruso suite in the Hotel Vanderbilt, head in hands, weeping.

At the Metropolitan Opera House those preparing for the next season knocked off work for the day and stood around discussing the voice now silent. All of them loved Caruso.

Few of the directors of the opera company or the Directors were in the city. Otto H. Kahn, Chairman of the board, is in Europe. So is Gatti-Casazza, general manager, and many of the members. There was no one to express for the company the sorrow felt keenly by all.

The Rev. P. R. Mele of the Roman Catholic Church of the Blessed Sacrament in Passaic, N. J., received a cablegram with the news, and messages also came to five of Caruso's relatives in the Italian colony there. Father Mele was an intimate friend of the singer, visited him frequently during his illness and christened Gloria Caruso.

CAREER OF CARUSO A LONG CRESCENDO

Early Called "Baritone," "Failure," He Became Chief of Tenors, Ranging All Styles.

BORN AND DIED IN NAPLES

Mother's Death Made Him Run Away to Stage—His Life of Hard Work Amid Uncontested Supremacy.

Enrico Caruso was 48 years old having been born at Naples on Feb. 27, 1873. His origin was not so humble as it has been often represented. His father was a mechanic, but he was also an inventor and a man of considerable intelligence. Caruso himself had wit and brains, as well as a voice.

Caruso's early life was told by himself as follows:

"Had I followed the path that was chosen for me I should have been a mechanic, or possibly an engineer. My father was employed in Naples as a working mechanic and he had two sons—myself and a younger boy. I was a sad trial to my parents. I was very noisy and lively. I sang constantly and my voice then was pretty piercing.

"My father chastised me and tried to make me a sober, industrious mechanic, like himself. This did not attract me. I wanted to be a sailor and I haunted the docks for days. I swam there for hours at a time. I broke most of the rules and regulations at school and lived in constant disgrace.

"By the time I was 11 years old, I had developed a great love for singing and had, I believe, a fine contralto voice.

"One day the old organist of the Church of St. Anna, Naples, heard me singing some popular melody, and my youthful efforts delighted him so much that he engaged me to sing in his choir. And I received for my labors each Sunday the large sum of 10 pence weekly—the first money I ever earned.

"When I was 12 my schoolmaster sent me home in haste for refusing to obey certain rules. On the doorstep my father met me; chastisement followed as usual, after which he declared that I must be apprenticed at once to a mechanical engineer. I was, and I loathed my new work whole-heartedly. In fact, my only interest centred round mechanical drawing, and I promptly had dreams of being an artist—an ambition that finds an outlet to this hour in occasional caricatures.

Mother's Death Sent Him to Stage.

"The turning point in my life came at the age of 15, when my dear mother died. Had she lived it is probable that I should have continued my mechanical studies to please her. But her death seemed to me to justify an alteration in my career before it was too late. A mechanical career disgusted me; an artistic career appealed to me.

"Accordingly I announced my intention of devoting myself to art and music and left my father's house, following his furious ultimatum that I could 'be a mechanic or starve!'

"So I became a wanderer, with no weapons to help me in the fight for success but a remarkable physique and tremendous optimism, which — I thank heaven—has never failed me. Somehow I managed to pick up a poor livelihood by singing at church festivals and private houses.

"I was often hungry, but never unhappy; and thus I went on until, at the age of 18, I was faced by this fearful problem, 'Was I a tenor or a baritone?' My voice at that time was so thin that it resembled the 'wind' whistling through a gaping window, and my fellow students laughed at my hopes of an operatic career. Undisturbed I worked on until my studies were curtailed by military duty.

"The time came for me to serve my king and country, so away I went to be a soldato, registering a private vow that Naples should eventually acclaim me as 'El Tenore Caruso.' For a year I wore the uniform of the Thirteenth Regiment of Artillery, and practiced the 'goose step' at Rieti. One morning I was polishing the buttons on my tunic and singing for sheer joy, with an 'open throat.' I can picture the scene in my mind at this moment and see the glorious sunshine streaming in as I sat polishing vigorously. Suddenly Major Nagliati appeared, listened, and then inquired: 'What is your profession?' Stammering, I muttered: 'I aspire to sing in opera.'

"Without a word he left me, and I imagined he had not heard my mumbled reply. But that same evening he told me he had found me a singing master, and that during my remaining thirty-five days in Rieti I could continue my studies.

His First Failure in Opera.

A little later my kind Major arranged that my brother should take my place, and thus it happened that in 1895, at the age of 22, I made by début in a new opera at the Teatro Nuovo, Naples.

"I was not a success nor was the opera, for in Naples there is a group of chronic dissentients whose presence makes that city a bad place for a début. Disappointed singers or composers themselves, they quickly condemn new artists and new operas. Thus I failed; but, though discouraged, determined to win success one day.

"My master, Vergine, to whose unfailing sympathy and endless patience I owe my deepest gratitude, encouraged me to go on studying and singing at every opportunity in various theatres. In this way my voice improved in timbre, strength and tone, and at last my great day dawned—though I nearly spoiled my own success through obstinacy.

"Sonsogno, Manager of the Teatro Lirico, Milan, asked me if I would study the rôle of Marcello in 'La Bohème' to sing at his theatre. Accordingly, with Vergine's help, I began to study this rôle, but after a few days decided that it did not suit me and returned it with many regrets.

"A little later I visited Milan and there Sonsogno came to me with a request that I would change my mind and consent to study the rôle, as he was certain it would suit me and that I should make a success in it!

"Strange, was it not, that he should be convinced of my success when I felt confident of failure?

Makes Success in Milan.

"Spurred by his belief in me I learned the rôle, and on Tuesday, Nov. 8, 1898, appeared as Marcello at the Teatro Lirico, Milan and made, if I may say so in all humility, my first success.

"On Nov. 9 I awoke to find press and public in agreement that I had not mistaken my vocation, and I laughed aloud to think that if I had followed my own convictions I might have struggled on in obscurity for years. For, after all, it is 'opportunity' that every artist needs, and I had nearly let mine slip by unseen.

"Since that day I have been working constantly in every capital of the world and I hope for many years to continue the story of 'How I began'—which is, as you will know if your patience has lasted through my memories, a story of work, for which I am more than repaid in the kindness of my good friends the public."

Of his days in the Italian army, Caruso himself told many stories of how he started to unroll the red tape that should free him to devote himself to singing.

Singing for the Soldiers.

"My position became such in the course of time," he said, "that when a popular soldier was imprisoned for some slight offense I could obtain his freedom by volunteering to sing any song the officer on duty would care to hear. I well remember one lovely Easter day, when the officers gave a luncheon to the soldiers of the regiment. At one end of the table sat the commander, Major Nagliate. At the other end, facing him, I sat.

"After the luncheon it was proposed and universally seconded, that I should sing the 'Wine Song' of 'Cavalleria Rusticana' in honor of the Major. My song was greeted with most enthusiastic applause, and cries of encore. The Major silenced every one by raising his hand, and presently rose to make a speech.

"What was our surprise and chagrin when he delivered a very sharp lecture directed against the regiment in general and myself in particular, saying that it was unpardonable to compel me to sing at each beck and whim, and criminal to request it after a meal, and that I was a fool and didn't deserve the gift I held so lightly, and that if in the future there was a repetition he would not only put in irons the person, regardless of rank, who compelled me to sing, but he would punish me too.

"I was in the barracks for two months altogether, and released when my brother volunteered to serve out the time in my stead. On release I was engaged for a season of opera at Caserta, and from this time on my operatic career has simply been a case of being lifted from one round of the ladder to the next.

"After singing in one Italian city after another, I went to Egypt; from there back to Paris; and then to Berlin; thence to the Argentine. From there I went to Rio Janeiro, where I was honored by President Campos-Galles for singing at a gala performance given in honor of the President of Argentina, who was on an official visit to the city. From Rio I went to sing in London."

Caruso Becomes a New Yorker.

The late Maurice Grau made the contract that brought Caruso to America, but it was left to Grau's successor, Heinrich Conried, to introduce him here. He was an undoubted success in New York City from his first appearance at the opening of the season of 1903, winning the popular verdict finally three years later in the "opera war" of Conried and Hammerstein, and repeating with greater and greater successes in every season since. According to many admirers, Caruso and the opera season were one and the same thing. His first Metropolitan rôle was the Duke in "Rigoletto" Nov. 23, 1903; the Gilda was Mme. Sembrich.

One of the great artist's characteristics was a childlike love of praise and applause, a type of vanity entirely divorced from megalomania or the self-love which is mingled with envy and contempt for others. New York's unbounded admiration for him won his heart completely. Though an Italian patriot and a cosmopolitan, he eventually became fundamentally a New Yorker. He numbered his warm personal friends here by the thousands.

He spent most of his last eighteen years in Manhattan and married here. On one of his arrivals here he went through a pretty ceremony of picking up a handful of earth at the pier and kissing it, by way of saluting America. He was so thoroughly Manhattanized that in 1919 he accepted an appointment as Captain in the New York Police Reserves, got a fine tailor-made uniform, and wore the gold badge of authority on his breast.

"All the medals and documents bestowed on me in the past," said Caruso at the time, "are as nothing to this new authority I possess as a Captain of the police of New York. I will go right over to the Metropolitan Opera House and arrest somebody."

New York's regard for the great tenor was expressed in the ceremony at the Metropolitan Opera House in April of last year, when the flag of New York City and the thanks of the city were officially presented to him by Mayor Hylan—a very uncommon thing for the matter-of-fact old municipality and a tribute which sent Caruso into ecstacies. This was partly a tribute to the unique talent of the singer, partly to his good-natured and well-disposed personality, and partly to his repeated and generous dedication of his voice to good causes during the war days.

Some Penalties of Fame.

Heavy penalties went with his fame and success. He probably suffered more from the admiration he excited than from the envy. He could never appear in public without having every eye in range fixed on him. Crowds gathered around him on the streets, in railway stations, at theatre lobbies and wherever else he appeared outside of his own apartments. Souvenir hunters, hero-worshippers, cranks and interviewers haunted him.

Smothered by well-meant admiration on one side, he was beset all through the days of his greatness by those who envied his greatness and those who sought to take advantage of his past frailties for blackmail. The affairs of his youth were tediously exploited. Women popped into court every little while here and in Europe demanding a few hundred thousand dollars or so from Caruso. The most resounding of these episodes was that of the Central Park monkey house in 1906, which resulted in Caruso's being fined $10.

Caruso complained bitterly both of the admiration and spite which jointly laid siege to his peace of mind, and alleged in a lyrical outburst on one of his recent birthday interviews that he would rather be a laborer getting $2 a day than earning his vast income, which was then made up of his $2,500 a performance at the Metropolitan and his royalties from phonograph records and his wages as a motion picture actor.

How He Viewed His Success.

Once when he was asked for his own theory of his great success he said:

"This is how I have succeeded. I never refused an engagement and I have never been without work with the exception of two months in Naples after my second engagement. Then I went to Cairo and sang, and when I came back a small boat met the ship and brought me an offer. In that engagement I received 700 lire, then worth $140.

"I never refused to work. If one would come to me and say, 'Will you go to such and such a place for the Summer and sing?' I would ask, 'How much will you pay me?' The answer is '$2,000.' But I say, 'The price for that was $3,000.' 'Never mind,' they say, '$2,000 is all that can be paid this Summer,' and I refuse. 'Very well,' they say, 'we get So-and-so.' Then I make quick thoughts in my head"—Caruso described swift geometric problems on his forehead—"and I say, 'I will go.' Otherwise I lose the Summer and the experience. And the experience is everything. Always in that way I have had work, always since I came to America, and before."

Caruso would not admit that he had any favorite rôle in opera. "The singer who has a favorite rôle," he said, "is not an artist, but a specialist. It is the public that makes the favorite rôles. The public," he added, "was just in its estimates, and its musical taste was improving.

"But not enough," he added. "Of perhaps 80,000,000 men and women in the country 20,000,000 are cultivated. The remaining three-fourths are not inoculated with the spirit of the opera."

Feared for Voice in Later Years.

Next to court actions, scandal and gossip, Caruso was vexed most by the constant speculation as to his physical condition and by occasional croakings that his voice was not quite what it used to be, coupled with real or pretended anxiety lest it should be lost. In 1915, becoming vexed when a critic modestly expressed the opinion that he had not been at the top of his form on the preceding night, Caruso took a blue pencil and in colossal letters scrawled over the article:

"LIAR.

Enrico Caruso."

This he posted on the bulletin board at the Metropolitan Opera House.

Before his final season, however, legitimate alarm had been felt more than once about the condition of his throat. He was operated on in 1906, 1909 and 1911 for the removal from the larynx of polypi, or small growths, which have sometimes caused loss of voice.

Caruso was a heavy smoker, usually puffing a cigarette in a long mouthpiece. He would not admit that this hurt his voice. He was conscientious in not talking for some hours before a performance and in taking care of himself generally, but he would not take the precaution of dropping cigarettes. The publication Tobacco and other organs of the trade paid incessant honors to the great singer. For years he had been the cornerstone of the official defenses for the use of tobacco. The pro-tobacco publications have rung with challenges to anti-nicotine periodicals to come forward and attempt to explain the case of Caruso.

His Supremacy Long Maintained.

In one of his interviews Caruso said:

"Alas, people envy me without knowing all my cares, without realizing the efforts I have to make over and over again to remain on a level with my renown. I am the man who will never be pardoned for the slightest falling off! What an existence that inflicts on me. But I gain lots of money, you will say. But do you reckon as nothing the money I lose by not singing? For example, I set out for America with a splendid engagement, that's understood. I am ill. I don't sing, or I sing only a little, and I spend a lot of money over there while gaining very little. It might happen some day that I lose money this way, and that would be abominable. What do you think of it?

"No, the public don't think of these things, do they? You see I have my risks and uneasiness. I am not entirely happy."

Following the operation on Mr. Caruso's throat in 1909, Professor Vedova said to a correspondent of THE NEW YORK TIMES:

"When he came to me I was at first seriously alarmed, seeing that the range of his singing voice was impaired to a great extent. I was much relieved when, after a patient study, I came to the conclusion that the lowering of the range of his singing voice was caused by what we call here a vocal knot or a singer's knot, affecting first one and then the other of the vocal cords.

"The operation and the nursing were not easy, considering the responsibility of a voice which has the value and worldwide reputation of Caruso's and the character of the patient.

"The operation was so successful that if Caruso will be careful for a few months more, both in not forcing his voice too much and in leading a healthy and hygienic life, there will be in the volume and clearness of his singing a constant crescendo, which will reach its culmination in a few years from now, giving the world the sensation of vocal effects never heard before."

Tenor Never "Took It Easy."

During most of his career, nevertheless, Caruso had enjoyed robust health and on his last birthday he said that the secret of it was not his voice but his teeth.

"Samson's strength was in his hair. Mine is in my teeth," he said. "I have never had a toothache in my life. My perfect teeth have contributed greatly to my good health, and my good health has sustained me in my art. I really believe that when one of these teeth I have shown you goes I go. Caruso is finished. But they are strong yet."

In spite of his supreme power and skill as an operatic singer, Caruso never took it easy, and even in his last years went through each performance keyed up to an intense pitch.

"Each time I sing," he said, "I feel as if there were some one waiting to seize my position from me, to destroy Caruso, and I must fight, fight like a bull to hold my own."

In this interview, which took place less than a year ago, he said that he had been attacked by a sudden fit of stage fright just before a performance of "La Juive" in Brooklyn.

"But the moment I appeared on the stage and beheld the audience, among them Bonci, I realized that I had to sing, and there was no other way out of it," he said. "And then a miracle happened. Some one, some unseen power seemed to unlock the compartment within me that holds my voice, and I sang. I sang with all the voice and power within me. You see, we artists must struggle desperately to get to the top, and when once there we must hold on, hold on with all the strength we have. For, once we slip, the journey down is steep and fast. I frequently feel unable to sing until I arrive in my dressing room and put on my clothes. Once in the proper atmosphere my voice appears, and then it's up to me to make the most of it."

Two of Caruso's children are Rodolpho and Enrico, Jr., the sons of Signora Giachetti, who was for many years known as Mme. Caruso. Rodolpho was a soldier in the Italian Army during the war. The younger son, Enrico, Jr., came over in 1919 to a military academy in this country, where he was placed by his father.

Signora Giachetti and Caruso first met during a performance of "La Bohème," in which both took part. The woman was then the wife of Gino Botti, a singer who had taken up a banking business. As divorce is not sanctioned by Italian laws, Caruso afterward explained to friends that a ceremony was impossible.

After whatever kind of union it was Caruso and Mme. Giachetti purchased a palatial villa in Florence, where they made their home. Some years later Mme. Giachetti left Caruso's home. Caruso often said he spent more than $50,000 a year for his family, besides showering thousands of dollars' worth of rare jewels on the signora.

In August, 1918, the singer married Miss Dorothy Park Benjamin, daughter of Park Benjamin, a well-known lawyer of this city. Mrs. Caruso and the little daughter Gloria survive him.

After the marriage Caruso took a fine country home at East Hampton, L. I., which is well known as the scene of the great Caruso jewel robbery last July, when $400,000 worth of gems disappeared mysteriously. Mrs. Caruso and her child were at the country estate at the time. The singer was on a trip to Havana.

The roster of the rôles Caruso had sung, covering wide fields of operatic composition, added weight to what he said of personal and intelligent study. They told of more than twenty-five years of hard work, or at least a musician could find in them food for thought and discussion, particularly as Caruso emphatically declared that he never assumed a rôle that was not suited to his voice. Here or abroad, he was said to have sung as many as seventy different roles, including early efforts long forgotten.

In eighteen successive seasons at the Metropolitan he appeared in at least forty operas. Among these were Verdi's "Rigoletto," "Trovatore," "Traviata," "Forza del Destino," "Masked Ball" and "Aida"; Leoncavallo's "Pagliacci," Mascagni's "Cavalleria Rusticana," "Iris" and "Lodoletta"; Puccini's "Manan Lescaut," "La Bohème," "Tosca," "Madame Butterfly" and "Girl of the Golden West"; Poncielli's "La Gioconda," Donizetti's "Lucrezia Borgia," "Favorita," "Lucia" and "Elisir d'Amore"; Montemezzi's "Amore dei Tre Re," Giordano's "Fedora," Cilea's "Adriana Lecouvreur," Franchetti's "Germania," Gluck's "Armide" and Flotow's "Martha." In French he sang Gounod's "Faust," Bizet's "Carmen" and "Pearl Fishers," Saint Saëns's "Samson et Dalila," Massenet's "Manon," Meyerbeer's "Le Prophete," "Les Huguenots" and "L'Africaine," Charpentier's "Julien" and Halévy's "La Juive."

Greatest Voice of His Century.

Caruso came to be recognized by many critics as the "greatest voice of his century." He once confessed his success in America was not lightly won. "Of course," he remarked, "I had to fight with both the critics and the public—and even now I am fighting—because in 1903 there was a memory of 'another.' Every time I sang some of the critics would write: 'Yes, * * * a beautiful voice, wonderful quality, velvet, everything which is required in an Italian tenor voice, but * * * Jean.' He referred to Jean de Reszke, who had withdrawn from the Metropolitan a short time before, leaving a record no other tenor had previously approached.

"But I went on just the same," said Caruso, "because I could not forget that some years before this 'Jean' had said something in Salsomaggiore which made me very happy. It was in the presence of his brother that 'Jean' said, 'This is the boy who will some day turn the world upside down with his voice.'

"Nevertheless, for three years after I joined the Metropolitan it did not seem as if the part of the world in which New York lay would be turned upside down by my voice; some of the critics continued to write, 'A beautiful voice, but white, like an Italian * * * and we don't particularly like it.'"

"But you never sang with the 'white voice,'" remarked his interrogator.

"Oh, yes," replied Caruso. "I sang 'white' then. The voice, however, was growing rounder, getting more color, more of what you call body, a stronger voice, which is what the American public likes best."

Gatti-Casazza's Tribute.

Giulio Gatti-Casazza, his countryman, under whose management the greater part of his Metropolitan years were spent, was among his most outspoken admirers, and Mr. Gatti is commonly a silent man.

"I have heard all the great tenors of my time," said the Italian Director of thirteen seasons in New York, "over and over again. Many of them were wonderful artists, with exceptional voices; and all sang, I remember, some wonderful performances. Yet no one ever, in my judgment, sang any single rôle with the vocal or artistic consistency of Caruso, and certainly no other tenor I can think of remotely compares with Caruso in continuing to sing, week after week and season after season, with the same almost unvarying achievement of supremacy, a man who almost never disappointed an audience through physical inability to appear. He has been a unique artist, with whom none other compared; I doubt if we will ever have such another."

This was Gatti-Casazza's statement last season, the year that brought the tenor, in December, to a series of performances in which he sang with increasing difficulty, or as often sang not at all, before his illness.

SON GETS WORD ON TRAIN.

Enrico Caruso Jr. Says He Had No Word of Father's Critical Illness.

CULVER, Ind., Aug. 2.—Enrico Caruso Jr., son of the famous tenor, was en route to Chicago when informed of his father's death this morning. Young Caruso, who is a student at Culver Military Academy, left here early with a committee from the academy in charge of an exhibit the school is presenting at the Pageant of Progress being held in Chicago.

CARUSO RECORDS ARE IMPERISHABLE

Voice of the Master Tenor Preserved for Future Generations in the Phonograph.

HEIRS TO GET ROYALTIES

Contract Under Which He Was Singing Was to Have Run Until 1935.

The voice of Caruso in all his greatest rôles is preserved intact for the ages as long as singers wish to study his marvelous technique and to compare his tonal beauty with that of other great tenors yet to come, or as long as the public wishes to hear the arias of the greatest singer of his time.

The voice of the great Mario was stilled with his death, but the voice of Caruso is recorded in about 200 songs, arias, hymns and duets, in metal matrices that are virtually imperishable. Millions more of phonographic records may be added to the several millions already in existence without any deterioration in the metal disks that first took the impression of "the golden voice."

For twenty years Caruso has been making records in this country and in Europe, and his total income from this source alone since 1906 is estimated by experts at about $1,500,000. The largest sale of his records was in the last two years and his yearly income from royalties was said to be more than $150,000.

The voice of Caruso was heard all over town yesterday, many owners of records having put them on the machines, and many having purchased new records after his death. Dealers in records had many inquiries about the continuance of the records.

About 162 records of Caruso's already are in the catalogue of the Victor Talking Machine Company, for whom Caruso made records exclusively for about eighteen years, and it was learned that between twenty and thirty have not yet been released. These were made at the recording laboratories of the company in Camden, N. J., in June and September, 1920.

Caruso's Heirs to Get Royalties.

The contract under which Caruso was making records was made in 1911 and was to have run until 1935. Under its terms Caruso was to have a guarantee of a certain amount of royalties each year—it never went under the guarantee and some years nearly doubled it—and his heirs were to receive the same royalties on the records after his death and just as long as Caruso records were made. This royalty was 10 per cent. of the catalogue or selling price of each record.

Caruso's first records for this country were made in 1902, the year before he joined the Metropolitan Opera Company. They were taken by the Gramaphone Company in London, which at that time had a working agreement with the Victor company in this city. C. G. Child, now director of the recording laboratories of the Victor company, met Caruso that year in Europe, but it was not until 1903 that an arrangement was made for him to make records in this country for Victor dealers.

For these first years he worked on a cash basis for each record—how much has not been disclosed—but Mr. Child said yesterday that when he reported this arrangement to his company some of the officials told him that it would ruin the company. This arrangement was continued for about two years, and then a new contract was drawn which provided for royalties. It was the custom to run this contract for five-year periods until 1911, when Caruso informed the company that he desired to make a life contract. Twenty-five years was the period finally decided upon.

In 1911 Caruso had an offer from another company to make records for a large sum, and he delegated his intimate friend, Antonio Scotti, to tell the Victor Company about this and to ask whether it would be possible to make a few records for the second company. A representative of the Victor Company called upon Caruso, who asked what was permissible under the contract. The question of a new contract came up.

Offered $25,000 for New Contract.

"I will give you $25,000 cash just to sign a new contract," said the representative.

"When will you bring the money?" asked Caruso.

"It's Saturday now," was the reply, "and I cannot get it until Monday. I'll have it here Monday noon."

"Twenty-five thousands dollars just for a new contract," mused Caruso. And will you let me write my own contract? No? Well, see this contract."

Caruso pulled over a piece of paper and wrote: "For the rest of his life Caruso sings only for you."

"That wouldn't be a legal contract," said the representative. "It's indeterminate."

"Then fifty years," said Caruso.

"Twenty-five would be better," replied the representative.

"All right, twenty-five years," replied Caruso, "and never mind bringing that $25,000 check. Caruso has confidence in you."

Mr. Child, who has known Caruso intimately for nearly twenty years, said that it was typical of him to trust his friends implicity, and recalled that when the first contract was signed Caruso said:

"You say this is a good contract? Then I'll sign it now."

And he signed the contract, virtually without looking at it. Mr. Child said that there was never the slightest friction over any feature of the contract.

In a formal statement Mr. Child yesterday told of the great work of Caruso as a recorder of his voice and was loath to talk of the records because he feared that the public might believe he was "trying to exploit the calamity of our beloved friend." This feeling of delicacy has been so widely expressed among the officials of the company that there has been discussion of withholding a record listed for October sale.

Records Are Imperishable.

"The requests have been many that we should make some statement as to the records of Caruso's voice, their possible life and selections yet unlisted," said Mr. Child in his formal statement. "We had thought to evade replies to inquiries of this nature, as we did not wish any one to think we were commercializing Caruso's death, but it is the general opinion and expression of those with whom we have talked that the records of Caruso's voice are for the world in general and their future is of interest to every one who knew or had heard him.

"Records which have been made are preserved in such a way that they can be handed on from generation to generation without loss or deterioration. The master matrices are cared for in such a way that there is absolutely no loss or change, and new records can be made from these indefinitely for all time.

"The June record—Messe Solennelle-Domine Deus—was sung from a manuscript by Rossini, which Caruso found in Italy at his last visit there and was chosen by him as a 'Thanks to God' for what we believed at that time was his recovery. The records which will follow in later issues will be in the order chosen by Caruso himself for their appearance."

One of these new pieces from Caruso was Salvatore Rosa, a cansonetta, written originally for the violin and piano. Caruso himself wrote the words of a Neapolitan song to go with this music. Among the other preserved pieces are some of Caruso's best work, and the experts who record the human voice believe that he did his best work in the last few years.

Caruso was enthusiastic about his rec-

VOICE FOR 20 YEARS, TENOR TOLD FRIEND

In a Note From Sorrento, Dated July 17, Caruso Wrote That He Was in Good Health.

SULTANTO A TE, NEW RECORD

Composed for Tenor by His Accompanist, Salvatore Fucito, and Not Yet Released.

In a letter to Salvatore Fucito, Caruso's coach, accompanist and personal friend, written July 17 and received at Mr. Fucito's home at 2,025 Broadway on Monday, the tenor said that he was in good health and had "voice to sell for still a score of years."

This message, believed to be the last one to have reached here before cable messages from Naples brought the news of Caruso's death, was in Italian to "Maestro" Fucito and his wife. It came from Sorrento and was written on both sides of a post card picturing a bust of the singer, made by C. Cifariello, and translated reads as follows:

"To Salvatore and Bice Fucito: Infinite thanks for your welcome good wishes. I am in good health, thanks to the sun and the sea baths. I have voice to sell for still a score of years. Whatever I want to do, I do with great vigor. Cordial salutations. Enrico Caruso."

"I cannot believe it," said Mr. Fucito, who was in his studio with his wife, after the news had been telephoned to him by the tenor's secretary, Mr. Zirato. Mr. Fucito had in his hand one of the last phonograph records made by Caruso, "Sultanto a Te (Only to Thee)," which has not yet been released to the public. Mr. Fucito composed it especially for the tenor, and the words are by Riccardo Cordiferro. A literal translation follows:

If thou wert of this heart a queen,
As thou a queen of beauty art,
So I could write thee hymns of love.
How many songs I would like to send!
For these tresses of gold, than silk more soft,
I would become a poet as of ancient time,
And I would write thee old-time songs;
I would write songs only to thee.

Talking of Caruso Mr. Fucito disclosed the fact that he had wished to establish a conservatory of music in New York for men and women who had musical ability, but not the means to study under the great masters.

"On many occasions, before taking sick, and while he was confined to his room in the Vanderbilt," he said, "Caruso told me that some day after his return from Italy he was going to build a great conservatory in this city for poor persons.

"He had never made definite plans for carrying out his aspirations, putting it off until he returned to New York. In fact, so far as I know, he had decided on two things only—that he was to be the general manager of the conservatory and that I was to serve as artistic manager."

"I shall never forget the visits I made to the tenor's suite at the hotel when he was convalescing," continued Mr. Fucito. "I played on the piano in his room while he sang the songs he loved so much. Although his voice was not as powerful as it was when he was perfectly healthy, it was no less clear or lyrical. Caruso would still be the world's greatest singer at 60 if he had recovered from his illness. His voice was better last Winter than it was fifteen years ago, and it would have remained beautiful for twelve to fifteen years more. There is no one living who can take his place, and I doubt if there ever will be any one like him.

Mr. Fucito told of the manner in which Caruso learned a new rôle. The accompanist, he said, would play the score while Caruso, looking at the words, hummed. After going over it once, Caruso played solitaire, sketched, wrote a letter, or pasted postage stamps in an album, Mr. Fucito playing and singing the tenor's part in the interim. When the pianist had finished, Caruso stopped what he was doing, and went through the rôle without a word or note in front of him. The rapidity with which he mastered a rôle was remarkable, said Mr. Fucito.

It was not generally known that Caruso could mold in clay, but Mr. Fucito has a plaque made by the artist as "Eleanor."

Mr. Fucito's training in composition was received at the St. Cecilia School in Rome, and his chief master at the piano was the famous Sgambati. He was assistant conductor at the Metropolitan Opera House from 1915 to 1917. Some of the artists whom he coached were Crimi, Raisa, Romaine, Mellish and the late Luca Botta.

ENRICO CARUSO AS AN AMATEUR ARTIST

WOODROW WILSON

THEODORE ROOSEVELT

THE LATE J. P. MORGAN

CARUSO AS CANIO

KAISER WILHELM

GROVER CLEVELAND

"All the News That's Fit to Print"

The New York Times

LATE CITY EDITION

Weather: Mostly sunny today; clear tonight. Fair and warmer tomorrow. Temp. range: today 63-82; Saturday 67-83. Temp.-Hum. Index yesterday 77. Full U.S. report on Page 83.

SECTION ONE

VOL. CXX . No. 41,490

NEW YORK, SUNDAY, AUGUST 29, 1971

75c beyond 50-mile zone from New York City except Long Island. Higher in air delivery cities.

BQLI 50 CENTS

THIEU SAYS NATION WILL VOTE OCT. 3 ACCORDING TO PLAN

U.S. Officials Now Resigned to a One-Man Race for Vietnam's Top Post

OUTBURSTS EXPECTED

But President Is Believed Able to Maintain Order—House Elections Today

By ALVIN SHUSTER

Special to The New York Times

SAIGON, South Vietnam, Sunday, Aug. 29—President Nguyen Van Thieu said this morning that South Vietnam's presidential elections "will proceed as scheduled" on Oct. 3 even though only he would campaign.

Arriving at a schoolhouse to vote in the lower house elections, President Thieu also rejected the proposal by Vice President Nguyen Cao Ky, that both he and Mr. Ky resign so that the presidential elections could be postponed and reorganized to insure their honesty.

"I can tell you that I am not going to resign," the President said at the schoolhouse, about a block from the United States Embassy.

First Comment by Thieu

It was the first comment by Mr. Thieu himself since Vice President Ky pulled out of the presidential race last Monday, accusing Mr. Thieu of manipulating the elections and suggesting that other officials organize new ones.

The President's aides had previously indicated that the elections would go on.

United States officials see little chance of reaching a compromise in the election crisis and have reconciled themselves to the one-man candidacy of Mr. Thieu.

Informed diplomatic sources said today that President Thieu feels confident that he can maintain stability in South Vietnam if anti-Government demonstrations begin. The sources said that they expect such outbursts but not "in great magnitude."

Protests Are Muted

However, the sources said, if widespread urban violence developed in coming weeks, Mr. Thieu might be forced to postpone the October voting. But the sources believe that there is no reason yet to fear that such protests would reach that crescendo, particularly if opposition candidates do well in the elections today for the 159 seats in the lower house.

Informed sources did not rule out the possibility that Mr. Thieu would make some suggestion, such as the creation of a watchdog committee made up

Continued on Page 11, Column 1

United Press International

TENSION IN SAIGON: South Vietnamese soldiers in combat gear patrol the streets of the capital to insure order in today's election for National Assembly seats. About 2,000 troops arrived Friday to bolster security in the city.

Connally Feels Economy Will Keep Some Controls

In Interview He Predicts Some 'Parameters' for Labor and Business

By ROBERT B. SEMPLE Jr.

Special to The New York Times

WASHINGTON, Aug. 28—The second most influential man in the Nixon Administration leaned forward in his chair, took a small bite from the end of an unlit cigar, and said:

"We are at the end of an era in our economic policy. It will be the disposition of the American people to have as few constraints as possible after the 90-day freeze period, and if we can get voluntary compliance now we can avoid stringent controls later.

"But it would be unwise to think we can go back to where we were before. American business and labor may have to get used to the idea of living within certain parameters."

Chief Evangelist

The speaker was John Bowden Connally, the Secretary of the Treasury, and the occasion was an interview this week, a brief interlude wrenched from his duties as the chief evangelist and enforcer of Mr. Nixon's new economic program.

During the 50-minute session, Mr. Connally would not speculate in detail about what would happen after the freeze ended, and his general comments on the economic scene did not seem nearly so dramatic as the statement that day by the Secretary of Commerce, Maurice H. Stans, that any postfreeze program would have to include mandatory elements.

But coming from John Connally, the clear hint that it would be some time before the United States could return to an era free of some Government supervision of wages and prices carried considerable weight.

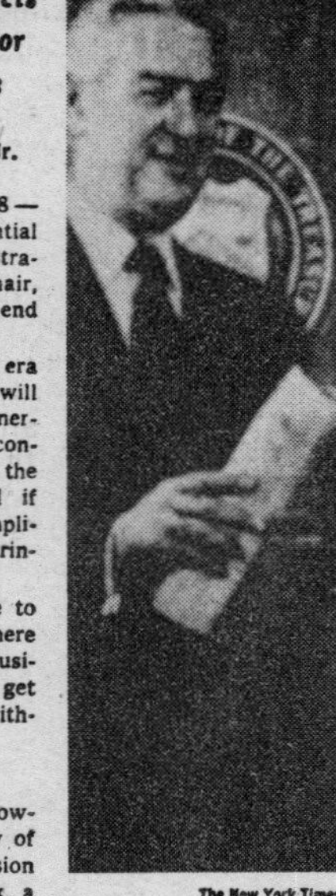

The New York Times

John B. Connally

For in his eight-month tenure as head of the Treasury Department, the tall, silver-haired Texas Democrat of impeccable dress and conservative views has become not only Mr. Nixon's chief economic spokesman but also—in a city that both admires and fears power, but mainly admires it—one of the two most powerful members of the Nixon Cabinet. He equals John N. Mitchell, the Attorney General, in influence while surpassing him in terms of the

Continued on Page 36, Column 6

COUNCIL TO ALLOW CAR PRICES TO TOP AUGUST DISCOUNTS

Permits Rises in Economic Areas Normally Subject to Seasonal Fluctuations

WAGES ALSO AFFECTED

Europeans Voice Doubt That World Powers Are Ready to Yield on Dollar Value

By JOHN HERBERS

Special to The New York Times

WASHINGTON, Aug. 28—The Cost of Living Council, in its latest move in President Nixon's program to bolster the economy, announced today how it will enforce controls over prices and wages that fluctuate seasonally.

The action will affect the purchase price of automobiles, a major product in the economy. President Nixon's order of Aug. 15 to freeze prices came at a time when many automobile dealers were selling 1971 models at discount prices to clear their showrooms for 1972 models.

Under the council ruling, dealers now selling 1971 cars at a discount will be able to charge more than the discount price for 1972 models, but not more than they asked for the 1971 models when they first came out last fall.

Tokyo Trading Calm

In reaction to the international aspects of the Nixon economic program, European observers expressed doubts today that Western European countries and Japan were yet ready to concede to the President all the advantages he seeks for the overvalued dollar.

Mr. Nixon, in an effort to reduce the value of the dollar against other currencies and make American exports more competitive, has imposed a 10 per cent surcharge on imports and suspended the dollar's convertibility into gold.

The Governor of the Bank of Japan described his notion as being embarked on "a voyage to unknown lands" after Tokyo's decision to join the European nations in allowing her currency to float, letting its value be set by market forces, within limits. In calm trading, $140-million changed hands as the dollar fell about 5 per cent from its old rate of 360 yen to the dollar today.

1,700 Complaints Received

In announcing the guidelines that will apply to seasonal variations of prices and wages, Arnold R. Weber, executive director of the Cost of Living Council, said it was too early to tell how well the public was abiding by the terms of the 90-day freeze.

He said that so far the Government has received about 1,700 complaints of violations. He said that agents for the Internal Revenue Service, which

Continued on Page 36, Column 1

25 DEAD AS FERRY BURNS OFF ITALY

Higher Toll Feared—Some 1,000 Saved, Many After Jumping Overboard

Special to The New York Times

BRINDISI, Italy, Aug. 28—At least 25 persons died and others may be missing after a Greek ferryboat carrying more than 1,000 people caught fire in the Adriatic Sea 25 miles from this port city today.

The vessel, the 11,232-ton Heleanna, was sailing from Patras, Greece, to Ancona, Italy, on its biweekly run.

Port authorities at Bari an-

The New York Times Aug. 29, 1971

nounced tonight that 1,096 persons had been recovered from the disaster, including 25 dead. They said that 243 of the survivors had been taken to hospitals for observation and that several were seriously injured.

The number of persons missing is still unknown because the Italian authorities have not yet received a complete list of those who boarded the ferry at Patras.

The Merchant Marine Ministry in Athens stated later today that the boat carried some 150 Italian tourists, some 200 Greeks and Frenchmen and several hundred German and Swiss tourists. The vessel also had some 200 autos aboard.

Some Panic Reported

Survivors said that there had been wild scenes of panic and fights for space on lifeboats on the burning ship.

Port officials here said that a distress signal was received from the ship at 6:20 A.M., apparently 50 minutes after crew members had detected a fire in a kitchen in the stern of the 17-year-old ship, a converted tanker.

Many passengers jumped overboard as scores of vessels—Italian warships and coast guard cutters, yachts, a Soviet freighter and a Lebanese tanker—reached the scene.

The ferryboat's 43-year-old captain, Demetrios Antypas, ordered the lifeboats lowered and at 8:30 A.M. gave the order to abandon ship.

Many of the survivors were in nightdress and said they had been in the water two hours or

Continued on Page 3, Column 3

Mayor, Barring a '73 Race, Says '8 Years Is Enough'

By RICHARD REEVES

Mayor Lindsay has decided not to run for re-election in 1973 because, he said, "Eight years is enough for me and for the city. It's time for a new face." But he quickly added that he would try to influence the selection of his successor in City Hall.

During a two-hour interview Friday night about his personal plans and political future after switching from the Republican to the Democratic party, Mr. Lindsay also predicted that almost every big-city mayor in the country would soon make the same decision to get out.

"Unless something happens and happens quick, none of them with the possible exception of Dick Daley in Chicago and Henry Maier in Milwaukee wants to sit there and take it much longer," he said of the 17 members of the Legislative Action Committee of the U.S. Conference of Mayors.

Unit Seeks Federal Aid

That committee, which includes the mayors of the nation's largest cities, has traveled the country together pleading for greater Federal commitment to urban problems.

That statement led to the question of whether he would run again. "No," he answered, "absolutely not. It's time for a change."

After a moment of reflection, he added: "I say no. Boom. Maybe that means very, very unlikely. But the city needs a new face. And I think I should, men should change what they do."

He continued that the realization that "I'll be a lame duck" would guarantee that "a long list" of mayoral candidates will emerge. In fact, at least a dozen politicians of some note are already considered 1973 candidates and they, and others, have assumed for some time Mr. Lindsay would never run again in the city.

Change of Mind Noted

Some of those assumptions were based on a September, 1970, news conference at which Mr. Lindsay said he was planning to retire from politics at the end of his term. He also talked that day about his reported switch to the Democratic party as "an event that's not going to happen."

Since then, however, Mr. Lindsay's political world has completely changed. Not only is he now a Democrat, he also is considering running for President next year and his staff believes he is in a better position to seek a third term in City Hall as a Democrat.

In Friday's interview, Mr. Lindsay added that he now had

Continued on Page 31, Column 1

RECORD RAINFALL WATERLOGS CITY

Suburbs Take Storm's Brunt and Suffer Power Failures and Flooded Streets

By PAUL L. MONTGOMERY

Tropical storm Doria, losing power as it left the sea, blustered over western Connecticut and Massachusetts yesterday, leaving behind broken power lines, flooded streets and basements and a waterlogged metropolitan area.

The center of the storm, its winds never quite reaching the 75 miles an hour required before it could be called a hurricane, passed between New York and Newark between 7 and 8 A.M., creating another record downpour of rain to augment Friday's deluge.

The tempest from the south was not gentle in its passage. Several hundred thousand households in New York, New Jersey and Connecticut suffered power interruptions; a spokesman for the Connecticut Light and Power Company said about one-third of its 478,000 customers were affected.

In Trenton, an overflowing creek cut off through Penn Central train service from New York to Philadelphia, stranding about 1,000 passengers. The Delaware River was reported five feet above normal. Tides

Continued on Page 52, Column 1

Army Softens Rigors Of Recruits' Training

By B. DRUMMOND AYRES Jr.

Special to The New York Times

FORT ORD, Calif., Aug. 28—The United States Army's campaign to make military life a more appealing and satisfying experience has had a revolutionary impact on one of its most traditional and hidebound devices—the eight-week basic training course.

While such things as the elimination of reveille, the shaved head and the screaming, abusive drill sergeant have received wide attention, there have been much more sweeping changes and they have reached down into the very substance of the training regimen itself.

Gone, for example, is the infiltration course, the test of nerve and grit with its live bullets buzzing overhead and its explosive charges scattering fear and dirt everywhere. Not very realistic, says the revised manual.

Gone, too, is the midnight inspection. Every trainee is now guaranteed eight hours of sleep every night—and if he does not get it he can complain to the "trainee council," an elected group of recruits in constant consultation with the company commander.

And gone are the long work days and work weeks. Recruits today often get off at 5:30 P.M. Mondays through Fridays and have weekends free, too, provided they have performed reasonably well during the week, paid attention to lectures about drugs and race relations and stayed awake during the new film on how to refuse illegal orders.

Old-Timers Shaken

Predictably enough, all of these changes have shaken the old-line troopers to the gleaming toes of their spit-shined boots. Many fear the morale and disciplinary problems already facing the Army as a result of the Vietnam war will only be aggravated.

But surprisingly, many recruits are not pleased either. Almost to a man they do not

Continued on Page 48, Column 3

Today's Sections

Index to Subjects

News and features of special interest in Brooklyn, Queens and Long Island, Pages 67 to 82.

Associated Press — The New York Times/Meyer Liebowitz

THE MORNING AFTER: In the wake of storm Doria, a power boat was swept aground in Larchmont, N. Y., and other boats were overturned. In Elmont, L. I., a large tree, uprooted by the wind, crashed on roof of a suburban home.

Bennett Cerf Dies; Publisher, Writer

By ALDEN WHITMAN

Bennett Cerf, one of the country's foremost book publishers, died late Friday night at his estate in Mount Kisco, N. Y. He was 73 years old.

The cause of death was not immediately determined, but Mr. Cerf had recently been discharged from Lenox Hill Hospital following surgery. Last December he underwent a major abdominal operation at the hospital.

Few book publishers were more widely known than Bennett Alfred Cerf, although he was more often identified as a television personality, raconteur, joke teller, author, lec-

Continued on Page 56, Column 5

United Press International

TELLS OF CONTROLS: Arnold R. Weber of Cost of Living Council discussing the wage-price freeze.

Bennett Cerf, Publisher and Writer, Is Dead at 73

Continued From Page 1, Col. 7

turer and partygoer than he was as the publisher of such disparate writers as James Joyce, John O'Hara and Charles Reich.

Indeed, the public side of his extroverted personality, which was exhibited for 16 years as a weekly panelist on the television parlor-game show "What's My Line?," tended to obscure his almost 50 years of less conspicuous activity as a powerful shaper of the country's literary and cultural life. Yet his importance was surely greater as a publisher than it was as a retailer of quips and puns, for it was his Random House that broke the Federal censorship ban on "Ulysses" in a landmark court case, published Marcel Proust and underwrote the career of William Faulkner.

With a flair for commerce and advertising promotion, Mr. Cerf was something of a blithe spirit in the book world—a man quite different from the staid, tweedy gentlemen-publishers who dominated American book houses prior to the nineteen-twenties. Whereas such publishers tended to insist that all their books contain literary merit, Mr. Cerf had a keen eye for the sales chart and the balance sheet. Thus it was that he published Plato and Franz Kafka and Eugene O'Neill along with many writers who catered to more transient public whims.

A National Celebrity

In other important respects Mr. Cerf also differed from both his ivory-tower predecessors and his contemporaries. One of these was his avid engagement in nonpublishing activities, chiefly "What's My Line?," on which he started in 1951. The show, in which panelists attempted to guess the occupations of various guests, made Mr. Cerf a national celebrity. "I have to remind people I'm a publisher," he once said as he was being sought out for his autograph.

Questioned a few years ago by Geoffrey Hellmann of The New Yorker about his desire for celebrity, Mr. Cerf explained:

"Everyone has a streak of pure unadulterated ham. Many won't admit it. I revel in it."

With fame, or at least attention, focused on him, the publisher appeared, usually without fee, in advertisements endorsing such products as Yuban coffee, L & M cigarettes, Bostonian shoes and Schiaparelli's Snuff, an after-shave lotion. In one ad endorsing Heublein's martinis, he was shown dueling with Moss Hart, the playwright. Reproved by his wife, who pointed out that he didn't need the money, Mr. Cerf replied:

"Everyone needs money. Besides, I like the publicity and I'm all dressed up in a dueling outfit in the ad."

At least one of Mr. Cerf's endorsements was sharply criticized in public, and that was his membership on "the Guiding Faculty" of the Famous Writers School of Westport, Conn., a mail-order concern that purports to teach writing. Jessica Mitford took the publisher to task in The Atlantic of July, 1970.

Joke Books Sold Widely

Another activity that set Mr. Cerf apart from his fellow book men was his subtrade as a jokesmith. Jokes concocted or recounted by him appeared in Saturday Review for many years and until his death in newspapers that bought his syndicated columns. His collected jokes also were printed in more than 20 books that had total sales of more than five million copies. His most recent book, published by Doubleday, was called "The Sound of Laughter" and he introduced it by saying in the foreword:

"It is aimed straight at your jocular vein, and I can only hope that detractors will be limited to a Boeing 747."

Mr. Cerf's jokes included these:

¶Have you heard about the sultan who left a call for seven in the morning?

¶A maker of eyeglasses has just moved his shop to an island off Alaska, and is now know as an optical Aleutian.

¶A wealthy manufacturer regarded the young man pleading for his daughter's hand with deep suspicion. "I wonder," he mused, "if you'd be so anxious to marry my Rosalie if I didn't have a penny?" "I think I'd love her twice as much," vowed the suitor fervently. "Get out," cried the manufacturer. "We've got enough idiots in the family already!"

On the Lecture Platform

The fame accruing to Mr. Cerf from his uncultural roles gave him yet another occupation—that as a lecture-platform personality. He appeared at colleges, clubs and conventions, speaking on such topics as "Modern Trends in Literature and Humor" and "Authors I Have Known." Describing the publisher at the lectern, Mr. Hellmann wrote in The New Yorker in 1959:

"He chats in a confidential nasal drawl, easy of stance, hands in pockets, feeding his audience puns, anecdotes and such teasing remarks as (in toto) 'John O'Hara was in our office the other day. I could tell you stories about him by the hour.'"

Tall, brown-eyed and bespectacled, flawlessly tailored, Mr. Cerf looked the dandy, but was saved from foppishness by his boyish, cheerful, unsophisticated manner. He, moreover, was genuinely warmhearted and likable and hard-working, and much of his display—his lavish houses, his devotion to Cadillacs, his dining at Toots Shor's, his self-publicity—was forgiven him. He was, after all, Bennett Cerf, and he made very few pretenses about his love of pleasure and fun.

Yet he was an extraordinarily industrious and shrewd publisher, who actually read many of the books he issued and who was liked and respected by most of his authors. He had the great ability for inspiring friendship, and he was, for example, on close terms equally with John Hersey and John O'Hara. Not to mention such unliterary types as Frank Sinatra.

"He was one of the great men of the literary world, who made New York City the leader in books, art and communications," Mayor Lindsay said yesterday.

Inherited $100,000 at 16

Friendships and a taste for writing brought Mr. Cerf into publishing. Born in Harlem on May 25, 1898, Bennett Cerf was the only child of Gustave Cerf, a lithographer and Fredericka Wise Cerf. The elder Cerf was a French Jew. Bennett's maternal grandfather was a wholesale tobacco distributor who bequeathed him a trust fund of $100,000, which came to him when he was 16 and an honors graduate of Townsend Harris High School, the public high school.

He entered Columbia in 1915 and became both a columnist for The Daily Spectator, the student newspaper, and editor of The Jester, the college humor magazine.

After receiving his degree along with a Phi Beta Kappa key, he got a job as a clerk in the Wall Street brokerage house of which he was a customer. At lunch one day in 1923 with Richard L. Simon, a Columbia contemporary who was on the staff of Boni & Liveright, the book publishers, Mr. Simon confided that he was about to leave his job and, with Max Schuster, set up a new publishing venture.

Mr. Cerf, who was bored with brokerage, quit his job by telephone and went to see Horace Liveright, who offered him a vice-presidency at $50 a week in return for a $10,000 investment in the firm. Two years later, on his 27th birthday, Mr. Cerf bought the Modern Library, a series of reprinted classics that Mr. Liveright had set up in 1918. His partner in the purchase was his best friend, Donald S. Klopfer, then 23. After getting Rockwell Kent and Elmer Adler to redesign the books and after binding them in cloth, the partners went out to peddle them, and with such success that by 1927 they had recouped their investment of $210,000.

50 Million Copies

The Modern Library series, one of the forerunners of the paperback, has since become a staple of Random House. Vastly expanded from its original 109 titles, it now includes 400 books. More than 50 million copies have been sold.

With Modern Library doing well, Mr. Cerf and Mr. Klopfer established a subsidiary to publish limited editions. And since its titles would be chosen at random, they called it Random House. Mr. Cerf was president, a post he held until 1965, when he became chairman of the board. He stepped down in December, 1970, and was succeeded by Mr. Klopfer.

Early Random House books included a Kent-illustrated "Candide" and a lavishly printed "Adventures of Tom Sawyer." But by 1933 the Depression put an end to the market for such luxuries, and Random House turned to trade books by acquiring the rights to Eugene O'Neill's plays and the works of Robinson Jeffers. Mr. Cerf sealed the O'Neill deal by flying to Sea Island, Ga., where the playwright was staying. The fact that the two had met worked in Mr. Cerf's favor.

Out of the O'Neill acquisition came the decision to hire Saxe Commins, who was Random House's chief editor until his death in 1958. With Mr. Commins's counsel and Mr. Cerf's instincts, Random House began to grow into one of the giants of the books business.

One of its early ventures—and among its most significant—was the publication, in 1934, of the unabridged "Ulysses." Mr. Cerf had to go to court to upset the Federal ban on the James Joyce masterpiece, which was officially regarded as obscene. With Morris Ernst as counsel, Mr. Cerf won a notable victory over Government censorship that benefited the entire publishing industry, and Mr. Cerf was much praised for the principled battle he waged for literary freedom.

In 1936, Random House brought up Robinson Smith & Robert Haas, Inc., a merger that added to Mr. Cerf's list William Faulkner, Isak Dinesen, Edgar Snow, Angela Thirkell and the "Babar" books. Over the years he added Sinclair Lewis, W. H. Auden, Gertrude Stein, William Saroyan, James Michener, John O'Hara, Robert Penn Warren, Truman Capote, Kathleen Winsor and Robert Jay Lifton. There was, as well, a roster of Broadway playwrights.

Show Business 'Branch'

Mr. Cerf assembled a corps of editors that included, in addition to Mr. Commins, Albert Erskine Jr. and Jason Epstein. He gave them pretty much free rein, while he took charge of major ad campaigns and financial dealings with the authors. He appeared to run a happy shop, which was housed, until 1969, in the palatial old Villard House, a landmark on Madison Avenue just behind St. Patrick's Cathedral. The company moved to 201 East 50th Street, where Mr. Cerf had a more functional, if less grand, office.

The fact that Mr. Cerf had the qualities of an impresario did not bother his co-workers. "Bennett runs Random House as a conservative branch of show business," Mr. Epstein conceded a few years ago. "The company is vulgar to a degree. But what makes the difference with Bennett is how important he feels it is to have Philip Roth and William Styron on the list. Some other publishers would know a thousand ways to get rich without having one author like that. Bennett Cerf doesn't."

One of Mr. Cerf's biggest projects was "The Random House Dictionary of the English Language," a 2,059-page volume issued in 1966 after a decade of preparation costing $3-million. It has sold more than 600,000 copies.

In the nineteen-fifties Mr. Cerf branched out into young people's books, publishing works on American and world history, nature and science. Under the title of Beginner Books, he published the works of Dr. Seuss.

Mr. Cerf's multiple activities, cultural and otherwise, brought him about $375,000 a year, much of which he spent on the full life. This included a townhouse on East 62d Street and his 42-acre estate in Mount Kisco. Many of his evenings were given over to dinner parties, either as a guest or as a host. "It's Bennett's theory," his wife said, "that if you're going to have two people for dinner you might as well have 40."

Purchased by R.C.A.

His offhand infectiousness could hardly have been in greater contrast to that of Alfred A. Knopf, whose manner and appearance resembled that of a Cossack sergeant. Yet, in 1960, Mr. Cerf bought out Mr. Knopf for about $3-million, and the two men got along well, with Mr. Knopf operating his fiefdom under Random House overlordship. This was followed six years later by the purchase of the Random House complex by the Radio Corporation of America for about $40-million. Mr. Cerf, in his turn, became a count with a fiefdom. If he minded the loss of his kingship, he kept it to himself.

In any event, the publisher was by then so prominent in the book world and so much the personification of Random House that a change of title was not a matter of consequence. And it did not diminish his delight in his job.

"I have enjoyed every moment of it," he said in an interview for this article. "I had a small talent, and it was fun to expand it to its maximum."

Liberal Sympathies

Mr. Cerf had liberal political sympathies. He was, for example, a defender of Loyalist Spain and visited that country during the Civil War. When he came to publish a book about the Federal Bureau of Investigation, its agents, without telling him until afterward, investigated his career, apparently lest he harbored what in the F.B.I.'s view might have been undesirable associations. It was one of the few experiences that made Mr. Cerf fume, even years later.

The publisher married twice. His first wife was Sylvia Sidney, the actress. They were married in 1935 after a lengthy and spectacular cross-country courtship, but the union lasted less than a year. His second wife was Helen Nichols, who, as a child actress, had changed her name to Phyllis Fraser. They were married in New York in 1940 with Mayor Fiorello H. La Guardia officiating. Mrs. Cerf became an editor of children's books at Random House.

Leonard Lautenberger

Regulars on "What's My Line?" in 1964 were, from left, Arlene Francis, Mr. Cerf and the late Dorothy Kilgallen, panelists, and John Daly, moderator. Show began in 1950.

"All the News That's Fit to Print"

The New York Times

LATE CITY EDITION

Weather: Mostly sunny, cool today; cloudy and cold tonight, tomorrow. Temp. range: today 41-31; Sunday 37-26. Full U.S. report on Page 45.

VOL. CXX ... No. 41,260 NEW YORK, MONDAY, JANUARY 11, 1971 15 CENTS

The New York Times

REPORT NEW GALAXIES: Dr. Nannielou Dieter, left, Dr. Ivan R. King and Dr. Hyron Spinrad, right, at University of California yesterday. Galaxies were named Maffei 1 and 2.

2 Galaxies Found Near Earth's

By SANDRA BLAKESLEE

Special to The New York Times

BERKELEY, Calif., Jan. 10—Two massive galaxies "next door" to the earth's own galaxy, the Milky Way, have been detected by California astronomers.

The galaxies have been overlooked up to now, the astronomers say, because they were obscured by a thick curtain of interstellar dust in the Milky Way.

The discovery is being reported in tomorrow's issue of The Astrophysical Journal. Astronomers from the University of California at Berkeley, the California Institute of Technology and the Carnegie Institution of Washington participated in the findings.

The existence of two "new" galaxies enlarges the membership of what astronomers call the "local group" or "local cluster." Galaxies, which are enormous revolving "islands" in the universe with as many as a million million stars in them along with vast amounts of dust and gases, tend to cluster together throughout the observable universe. Some clusters are quite large and may contain as many as 800 galaxies.

However, the local group, which houses the earth, is quite small. It includes the Milky Way (in which the sun is a minor star), the Andromeda galaxy, three small satellite galaxies and, with this recent discovery, two more large gal-

Continued on Page 45, Column 6

JOINT CHIEFS' HEAD TO VISIT CAMBODIA AND ASSESS CRISIS

Moorer Expected to Go and to Return to Saigon Today —Laird Orders Mission

By ALVIN SHUSTER

Special to The New York Times

SAIGON, South Vietnam, Jan. 10—Secretary of Defense Melvin R. Laird is sending the chairman of the Joint Chiefs of Staff to Pnompenh amid increasing concern here over the plight of the Cambodian Government.

Adm. Thomas H. Moorer, the chairman, who came to South Vietnam last week with Mr. Laird to assess the military situation in Indochina, will be the highest ranking military official to have visited Cambodia in the current crisis.

He is scheduled to go to Pnompenh tomorrow and return to Saigon a few hours later to report to Mr. Laird. The Secretary ends his four-day visit tomorrow night.

Take-Over Is Doubted

Shortly before he left Washington, Admiral Moorer expressed doubt that North Vietnam could take over Cambodia by force, even if it tried an all-out effort this spring. He added, however, that if the campaign succeeded, he believed South Vietnam could keep Cambodian ports closed to shipments of war supplies without direct American military involvement.

The Vietnamese Communists themselves have cut off Cambodia's only deepwater port, Kompong Som, from Pnompenh by controlling a key highway, Route 4. This has caused a critical fuel shortage in the capital.

Mr. Laird apparently wants Admiral Moorer to study the military picture in Cambodia and report back before the Secretary briefs President Nixon, who is now in San Clemente, Calif., preparing his State of the Union address.

8,000 Men in Cambodia

High-ranking officials here expect the main ground fighting in Indochina in the next few months to come in Cambodia, where Communist forces are reportedly trying to rebuild and establish supply areas. Serious difficulties in Cambodia could strain the South Vietnamese Army—which now has 8,000 men in the eastern provinces of Cambodia—and this, in turn, could affect the pace of American troop reductions here.

There had been speculation that Secretary Laird, who stopped in Paris and Bangkok before coming here, would make an unannounced trip to Cambodia, but he denied such a plan.

Mr. Laird continued his talks with American military and civilian officials, conferred with South Vietnamese military officers at the nearby base at Cuchi and visited a hamlet of 600 Vietnamese. He strolled down the main street, stopped in a small grocery store and chatted with local officials.

The hamlet, 22 miles south

Continued on Page 3, Column 6

United Press International

LAIRD GETS BRIEFING IN CUCHI: Secretary of Defense Melvin R. Laird talking with South Vietnamese Lieut. Gen. Do Cao Tri, regional military chief, at base camp near Saigon.

Vietnamese Face Vast Uprooting

Special to The New York Times

SAIGON, South Vietnam, Jan. 10 — South Vietnamese and American officials here have disclosed plans for what is expected to be the largest organized movement of peasants in the history of Vietnam.

The Saigon Government, with full American support, hopes to resettle the refugees in more sparsely populated provinces. The peasants are to be moved to the two southernmost military regions, called III Corps and IV Corps.

Estimates of the total number to be involved in the movement vary. American sources cite figures ranging from 200,000 to more than a million, depending on security and the willingness of the peasants. South Vietnamese officials, however, confirm that the movement could involve between two million and three million peasants throughout two military regions during the next three years.

It is an attempt by the South Vietnamese to solve chronic refugee problems in the northernmost military zone, called I Corps.

Some American officials here have expressed fear that the movement will create more physical and psychological stress than the peasants, already bewildered by the war, can handle. They add that the movement will add greatly to postwar social reconstruction problems.

South Vietnamese officials feel the vast movement will be acceptable to the refugees who have already broken ties with their ancestral plots, so important as centers of Vietnamese religious worship.

Some Vietnamese, sharply critical of the movement, say that the plan is a political move by the Government against the Vietnamese of the northernmost provinces, who have consistently resisted control by the Saigon Government.

The area has been traditionally sympathetic to the Communists and remains the poorest economic region in South Vietnam. By moving the peasants, these critics say, the Government would attempt to disperse its opposition at the cost of still more suffering.

The project, already approved in principle by the highest South Vietnamese and American officials, is now in its final planning stages and will be announced soon by Saigon. A new agency will be formed to handle the movement.

The project will be financed by the United States, according to Franklin Stewart, the director of the War Victims Program in Vietnam.

"We expect that this year's

Continued on Page 6, Column 3

N. VIETNAM
DMZ
Danang
THAILAND
LAOS
I CORPS
CAMBODIA
II CORPS
Pnompenh
III CORPS
Saigon
SOUTH VIETNAM
IV CORPS

The New York Times Jan. 11, 1971

PRESIDENT MOVES TO PARE BILLIONS IN BUSINESS TAXES

He Will Relax Depreciation Rule Without Waiting for Any Action by Congress

ANNOUNCEMENT TODAY

The Aim of Move Is to Spur Investment and Reverse Downturn in Economy

By EILEEN SHANAHAN

Special to The New York Times

WASHINGTON, Jan. 10 — The Nixon Administration, in the hope of reversing the current business downturn, is planning an immediate reduction of several billion dollars in the taxes paid by business—a reduction that it will put into effect without waiting for Congress to act.

The tax cut for business will come in the form of liberalization of the rules by which businesses write off the costs of their new machinery and equipment.

Announcement of the liberalized rules covering these depreciation write-offs will be made tomorrow by President Nixon from the California White House.

Two Key Elements

There will be at least two major elements in the depreciation liberalization.

¶The period of time over which businesses will be permitted to write off the cost of their machinery and equipment —that is, to deduct the cost from income before calculating their taxes—will be shortened by 20 per cent.

¶The depreciation allowance for equipment installed during any given year will be more generous. Businesses can now claim a half year's write-off for machinery that they have used for any fraction of a year. Under the new rule, they will be able to get a half year's depreciation for any use at all and a full year's depreciation for anything more than six months of use.

The liberalized depreciation rules will be put into effect without asking for Congressional approval under existing law, which merely requires that allowances for depreciation be "reasonable."

The Democrats, in 1962, also put a major liberalization of depreciation into effect without asking Congressional approval.

Criticism Possible

There may be some criticism from Democrats now, however, on the ground that the 20 per cent reduction in the established time periods for depreciation is not "reasonable" when compared with the period of time that businesses keep their equipment in use.

In an attempt to forestall such criticism, Secretary of the Treasury David M. Kennedy flew to Arkansas on Friday to inform the chairman of the House Ways and Means Committee, Wilbur D. Mills, of the impending action.

Faster depreciation write-offs have long been advocated by most businessmen and business-oriented economists, who believe that they provide a significant incentive for businesses to increase their investments in new machinery and equipment.

The incentive exists, it is believed, for two reasons. First, because larger depreciation write-offs mean lower taxes and, thus, make more cash available for investment. Second, because the faster write-

Continued on Page 16, Column 3

CITY SUSPENDS 4 IN TOMBS DEATH

Guard Reverses His Story of Beating of Prisoner and Accuses Fellow Officers

By PETER KIHSS

Four city correction officers were suspended yesterday after another guard reversed his story and accused them of beating a prisoner, who was later found hanged.

Correction Commissioner George F. McGrath said he had suspended the men after William J. vanden Heuvel, chairman of the Board of Correction, had told him that the guard had changed his testimony.

Mr. vanden Heuvel said later that the guard asked to talk to him last Thursday after being shaken by still another suicide at the same institution—the Manhattan House of Detention, also known as the Tombs.

Still another apparent suicide of a prisoner was reported yesterday, involving a 26-year-old Army veteran found hanging in a cell at 4:40 A.M. at the new 68th Precinct station house, 4302 Fourth Avenue, in the Bay Ridge section of Brooklyn. The man, Jose Lopez, had been arrested two hours earlier on a drunken-driving charge.

The suspension of the four correction officers grew out of the case of Raymond Lavon Moore, known also as Raymond Lavon, who had been held in the Tombs for 10 months on charges of assaulting a policeman but who was never brought to trial. He was found dead by hanging Nov. 3 and pronounced a suicide by the Medical Examiner's office.

Commissioner McGrath said that the four suspended guards and Mr. Blake had all originally

Continued on Page 36, Column 7

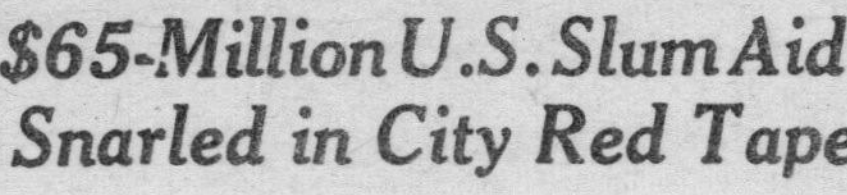

$65-Million U.S. Slum Aid Snarled in City Red Tape

By DAVID K. SHIPLER

Snarled for 19 months in its own red tape, New York City has been able to spend only half of its $65-million grant of Federal Model Cities funds. The city expects to have $32-million still unused at the end of this month.

Slum neighborhoods that are supposed to be the beneficiaries of the Model Cities program are receiving just under half the services originally scheduled to begin when the city received the Federal grant on July 1, 1969. Most of those services were started during the last few months.

This inability to use funds may have repercussions far beyond the Model Cities program. It comes at a time when Mayor Lindsay is appealing repeatedly for more Federal money. It is a time also when President Nixon is reported considering shifting funds from the Model Cities program to a revenue sharing plan that would allow cities to use the money in any way they choose.

The problems here have given Federal officials a rare glimpse of the unwieldy machinery of city government. And that may jeopardize future Federal funding in other programs as well as Model Cities.

For example, the bureaucracy has grown through the years to the point where it now takes 71 steps through 10 different agencies for the city to buy equipment such as a desk or a sanitation truck.

"Nobody wants to look at it," said Joseph B. Williams, a former Family Court judge who took over last February as New York's Model Cities Administrator. "Nobody wants to see

Continued on Page 36, Column 1

Chanel, the Couturier, Dead in Paris

Special to The New York Times

PARIS, Jan. 10—Gabrielle (Coco) Chanel, one of the greatest couturiers of the 20th century, died tonight in her apartment at the Ritz Hotel. She was 87 years old.

The death of Coco, as she was known the world over, was announced by close friends. They said that her death came peacefully and that nothing in recent days had indicated she was in bad health. The cause of death was not immediately known.

Her friends said that a chambermaid discovered that Coco was ill and called a physician.

Coco's death occurred as she was working on her collection to be presented in the spring fashion shows this month.

Her life story was turned into

Continued on Page 35, Column 1

The New York Times/Leombruno-Bodi

Gabrielle Chanel in one of her best known creations

NIXON CONSIDERS AGENCY SHAKE-UP

Overhaul Would Create Four Departments and Dissolve or Alter Some Others

By ROBERT B. SEMPLE Jr.

Special to The New York Times

SAN CLEMENTE, Calif., Jan. 10—A major overhaul of the executive branch of the Federal Government, including the creation of four new Government departments, has been proposed to President Nixon.

The idea, which also involves the dissolution of or radical changes in several existing agencies, is said to be under serious consideration at the White House.

Sources in Washington and in San Clemente, where the President is drafting his State of the Union Message, would not say whether Mr. Nixon had made a final decision to go ahead with the recommendations. The proposals are contained in various Presidential task force reports, including those provided last November by the President's Advisory Council on Executive Reorganization, headed by Roy L. Ash, chairman of Litton Industries.

Some of these sources said that the recommendations had received the most intense scrutiny and were regarded by the President as fully consistent with his desire to emphasize the theme of "improving the quality of government" in his State of the Union Message.

At the same time, the sources

Continued on Page 16, Column 6

Jewish Defense League Plans to Harass Russians

The head of the Jewish Defense League said yesterday that his group was forming teams to "follow, question and harass" Soviet diplomats in the city.

Rabbi Meir Kahane, the founder and leader of the militant Jewish organization, said the purpose of the harassment would be to provoke a crisis in Soviet-American relations that would stop the two countries from "building bridges over Jewish bodies."

"In short," he said, referring to his plan to harass Soviet personnel here, "the life of each Russian will be made miserable."

Speaks Outside Mission

Rabbi Kahane, surrounded by about 40 followers, spoke outside the headquarters of the Soviet mission to the United Nations at 136 East 67th Street.

United Press International reported that Rabbi Kahane had also said his group would "assault" Soviet diplomats. The rabbi, through the league's general counsel, Bertram Zweibon, denied last night that he had used that word.

Rabbi Kahane's remarks followed a series of recriminations, bombings and demonstrations that have exacerbated Soviet-American relations. In Moscow over the weekend the cars of three United States correspondents were vandalized on public streets, apparently in retaliation for harassment of Soviet representatives here and in Washington. [Page 15.]

During the day here, a few league members followed cars emerging from the mission. The cars had police escorts, and policemen blocked off 67th Street between Third and Lexington Avenues.

Members of the group said they also had spat on a bus belonging to the mission and on a Russian whose name they did not know.

The league, which was founded in 1968, claims a membership of 15,000. Most of the members seen in demonstrations and at the league's office here appear to be teen-aged.

Arkadi V. Gouk, first secretary at the Soviet mission, said last night: "Some of our people were followed by some unknown people with provocative

Continued on Page 15, Column 1

The New York Times

Rabbi Meir Kahane

NEWS INDEX

Transportation and Weather News Appears on Page 45.

Chanel: The Fashion Spirit of the 20th Century

1916: The first designer to use humble jersey cloth, Chanel put velvet ribbon on this sport suit. Her "poor-girl look" became chic shortly after World War I.

1926: She urged women to take off corsets, bob hair, wear tweed suits with jersey blouses, pearl strands.

1931: Chanel arrived in America clad in a coat that would not be out of style today. She defined "true luxe" as clothes that women could wear for years.

1937: A black jersey suit with red binding, sailor hat—some more Chanelisms. Also of this era, the dark dress with white collar and cuffs, ribbon bows for hair.

Mid-1940's: During her 15-year sabbatical from high fashion, she clung to tailored look and vivid jewelry that had started the lasting fad for costume baubles.

1954: A navy blue suit with white muslin shirt (it was Number 5, her lucky number) heralded her return as a designer wildly popular.

1964: Women stood in line to purchase copies of Chanel suit with a striped blouse at $165. Ohrbach's sold 200 of the suits in one day.

1970 (right): As hems fell, hers stayed near the knee, or were even shortened a fraction—a typical Chanel gesture of nonconformity.

Illustrations: 1916, 1926, 1937, 1954, Vogue © Condé Nast Publications, Inc.; 1931, Associated Press; 1940's, Studio Lipnitzki; 1964, The New York Times; 1970, sketch by Manina.

Continued From Page 1, Col. 2

a musical, "Coco," which ran on Broadway last year starring Katharine Hepburn in her first singing and dancing role. Miss Hepburn, 60 at the time the show opened, was termed "too old" for the part by the tart-tongued Coco, who was 86.

In addition to Chanel philosophy, the show featured many models parading in the popular fashions Chanel designed through her long career.

Chanel dominated the Paris fashion world in the nineteen-twenties and at the height of her career was running four business enterprises—a fashion house, a textile business, perfume laboratories and a workshop for costume jewelry—that altogether employed 3,500 workers.

It was perhaps her perfume more than her fashions that made the name Chanel famous around the world. Called simply "Chanel No. 5"—she had been told by a fortune-teller that five was her lucky number—it made Coco a millionaire.

Fashion Was Her Pulpit

By ENID NEMY

An intense woman with a scalding tongue, hair-trigger wit, unbounded immodesty and ineffable charm, Gabrielle Chanel was, throughout her life, a free spirit who used fashion as her pulpit. Her message was carried to millions through the medium of the Paris haute couture, a world over which she reigned, with arrogant self-assurance, for long stretches of almost six decades.

The darling of French society, a good friend of dukes and dandies, a confidante of the rich and famous, she was impatient of pretense, intolerant of restrictions, incapable of self-deception.

"There is no time for cut-and-dried monotony," she once said. "There is time for work. And time for love. That leaves no other time!"

Chanel was the fashion spirit of the 20th century, a Pied Piper who led women away from complicated, uncomfortable clothes to a bone-simple, uncluttered and casual look that eventually became synonymous with her name.

Without marching in a parade or campaigning for right, she emancipated her sex from the tyrannies of fashion. Her strong convictions and independent opinions, her unswerving belief in simplicity and elegance, freed women of unnecessary constrictions and what she called "ludicrous trimmings and fussy bits and pieces."

Slim and straight and dark-haired, with piercing black eyes and a generous if uncompromising mouth, Chanel always believed she was right, and often was. She was responsible for many of the timeless fashions that look as current today as they did when she first introduced them, in some cases more than half a century ago.

Among her innovations, most of them considered revolutionary at the time, were jersey dresses and suits, tweed suits with jersey blouses, bell-bottom trousers, trenchcoats, pea jackets, turtleneck sweaters, sailor hats, bobbed hair, costume jewelry and the little black dress, often collared and cuffed in white.

The omnipresent Chanel suit, with its collarless, braid-trimmed cardigan jacket and graceful skirt, has probably been copied more, in all price ranges, than any other single garment designed by a couturier.

Chanel's handbag — soft, quilted leather with a chain handle—was copied so widely that it became one of the most universal accessories of the nineteen-sixties. Other widespread Chanelisms were ropelike necklaces, sling-back pumps in her special colors—beige and black—and large, flat, tailored hair bows.

The copying of her designs never disturbed her. "Let them copy," she said. "My ideas belong to everyone. I refuse no one."

Perhaps the strongest tribute to her genius was that women of wealth, who took pride in exclusivity of design, did not mind being seen in the same clothes as working girls. Both groups wanted, and were willing to pay for, in varying degrees, the Chanel look.

The customers who went to the House of Chanel, a six-story building at 31 rue Cambon in Paris, included, at one time or another, Marlene Dietrich, Romy Schneider, Juliette Greco, Elsa Martinelli, Anouk Aimée, Bettina, Suzy Parker, Françoise Sagan, Colette, Mrs. Georges Pompidou, Princess Paola, wife of the younger brother of King Baudouin of the Belgians; Mrs. Hélène Gordon-Lazareff, editor of the French fashion magazine Elle; Mrs. Diana Vreeland, editor in chief of Vogue; the Rothschild baronesses and countless American socialites.

Chanel, who was said to have "a true affection" for money, dressed comparatively few members of royalty and nobility.

"Those princesses and duchesses . . . they never pay their bills," she was reported to have said. "Why should I give them something for nothing? No one ever gave me anything."

The well-known names, who could afford to pay her prices—about $1,000 for a suit—frequently added to the original Chanels in their wardrobes with line-for-line copies made by American manufacturers.

Chanel, despite her own taste for luxury and her patrician friends, was the constant democratizer of fashion. Her friend Picasso once said, "She is the most sensible woman in Europe," and her own definition of true luxe as "clothes they [women] can wear for years" confirmed the artist's description.

Award for Significance

For Chanel, the great changes in fashion stemmed from significant changes in the manner and requirements of daily life. She explained her philosophy in 1957 when she traveled to the United States to receive, from Neiman-Marcus in Dallas, an award as the most significant designer of the last 50 years.

She told a reporter from The New Yorker that she inspired women to take off their bone corsets and to cut their hair, in 1925, because they were just beginning to work in offices.

"Women drive autos, and this you cannot do with a crinoline skirt," she said.

"But the grand problem," she added, "the most important problem, is to rejuvenate women, to make women look young. Then their outlook on life changes. They feel more joyous."

During the period in the sixties when many women were feeling more joyous wearing miniskirts, Chanel never ceased her barrage of verbal thunderclaps against the fashion.

As autocratic and articulate as ever, the aging couturier did not take kindly to youth-oriented pop culture and fashion. "An exhibition of meat," was one of the phrases she used.

"I hate *les vieilles petites filles* [old little girls]," she said, railing against miniskirted women over 30.

"She's got horrible taste and she's responsible for spreading it all over America," Chanel said in 1967 of the then Mrs. John F. Kennedy. She was criticizing the white Courrèges dress that the President's widow had worn to Runnymede, England, at the dedication of a monument to him.

The selective memory Chanel employed on other occasions chose to forget that Mrs. Kennedy had worn a Chanel suit for her visit to Dallas on Nov. 22, 1963. Its raspberry wool was stained with her husband's blood.

When skirts were descending to midcalf in 1970, Chanel's hemlines remained more or less where they had always been, hovering near the knee. Some observers thought they might have been a fraction shorter than usual, a typical Chanel gesture of nonconformity.

In Chanel's 87th year, on Dec. 18, 1969, the name that illuminated fashion went up in lights on Broadway. Coco (Little Pet), the nickname bestowed on the couturier by her father, became the title of a musical show based on her life. Starring Katharine Hepburn, it was produced by Frederick Brisson, a longtime friend of Chanel's.

The show, with book and lyrics by Alan Jay Lerner, music by André Previn and Chanel-facsimile costumes by Cecil Beaton (263 in all), was one of the greatest fashion spectaculars ever mounted on a stage.

During her lifetime, Chanel created an empire. In the twenties, at a time when she employed 2,400 people in her workrooms, her personal fortune was rumored to be $15-million.

The financial basis of the empire was Chanel No. 5, a perfume that she introduced in 1922 and named after her lucky number. Created by a chemist on the Riviera, it was an unorthodox blend of fragrances and soon became the most familiar perfume in the world.

"Women are not flowers," she once said, commenting on the scent. "Why should they want to smell like flowers?"

Her newest perfume, a light and delicate scent named No. 19, was introduced in 1970.

In 1924, Chanel founded Les Parfums Chanel with Pierre and Paul Wertheimer, owners of the Bourjois perfume interests. They became the majority stockholders in the new company.

By 1934, Chanel had been removed as president and the next year the company, in which she had a 10 per cent interest, began to cede its rights to subsidiaries and to Bourjois.

Les Parfums Chanel became the parent company of a large perfume empire that operated in France, Britain and the United States.

In 1946, Chanel sued Les Parfums Chanel, charging that it had produced merchandise of an inferior quality. The suit asked that the French parent concern be ordered to cease manufacturing and selling all products and restore to her the ownership and sole rights over products, formulas and manufacturing processes.

The suit was unsuccessful, but the feud apparently healed because when Chanel returned to the fashion world in 1954, after an absence of about 15 years, she exchanged her substantial stock ownership for another system of compensation that involved royalties and commissions.

A legend in her own time, Chanel became increasingly temperamental, willful and, at times, vitriolic, as she grew older. Her parakeet voice never stopped speaking her mind and, although this was done at considerable length and with unabashed frequency, she left untouched the myths that swirled around her.

"What do I care what people write about me?" she once said. "Each year they will invent a new story. I will never sue."

Chanel herself added yearly, and with somewhat pixyish glee, to the tangle of dates, places and names.

Her age was never proved—"A woman has the age she deserves," she used to say—but it is generally accepted that she was born on Aug. 19, 1883. It is certain that she was born near Issoire in the Auvergne, a dour mountainous region of south central France. She was baptized Gabrielle Bonheur—Gabrielle Happiness.

When she was 6 years old, her mother died of tuberculosis and her father abandoned his four daughters. She went to live with two aunts, who were relentless disciplinarians. They raised horses to sell to the French Army, and Coco became an expert horsewoman at an early age. She also learned how to sew.

The 'Poor-Girl Look'

Before her 16th birthday, she showed signs of the determination and indomitable spirit that remained with her throughout her life. On a visit to her grandfather, a Vichy blacksmith, she escaped from her aunts by persuading a young cavalry officer to take her away.

The obliging officer provided not only a means of escape but also an entry into another world. Etienne Balsan was a member of a wealthy family of industrialists who owned fine stables, and it was during this liaison that Chanel learned the habits and tastes of the wealthy and rode some of the country's best horses.

It is believed that Chanel and Balsan were inseparable for the next 10 years, living in a family chateau outside Paris or following the horsey set through France. About 1911 she was selling hats in a haphazard fashion in a tiny shop in Paris.

The career that was to make her name began in the summer of 1913 in Deauville. She opened a tiny hat boutique. It was the heyday of elaborate and grotesque hats and she detested them.

"How can the brain function under those things?" she asked, and went on to provide millinery that offered nothing but simplicity and line. She took a fancy to turtleneck sweaters worn by English sailors in port, and sold a few of them.

The next year she returned to Paris and opened a shop at 31 rue Cambon, where she sold hats, then sweaters and a few clothes. Within five years, she was a force to be reckoned with in the world of fashion.

She began to impress wealthy, influential women with her originality. She was the first designer to use ordinary jersey for clothes; the September, 1917, issue of Vogue magazine referred to the Maison Chanel as "the jersey house." A little later, she started the "poor-girl look," and rich women playfully wore clothes based on the garments of the humble.

Despite World War I, her social life was brilliant and hectic. Balsan was succeeded in her life by Arthur Capel, who was nicknamed Boy, an immensely rich, polo-playing Englishman. His lavish presents started her astonishing collection of jewels.

The dashing aristocrat was also credited, perhaps apocryphally, with being the inspiration for one of Chanel's most famous fashions. Her boxy suit jacket, with its practical pockets, was said to have been born after she had borrowed Capel's blazer on chilly days at polo games.

Boy Capel, described by friends later as "the only man she really loved," was killed in an automobile accident.

In the mid-twenties, Chanel's name grew luminous. By 1924, well-dressed women on both sides of the Atlantic were taken with a Chanel costume of a beige jersey blouse worn with a single strand of pearls, and a tweed suit with a cardigan jacket. It is possible to appreciate the revolution she wrought only if one studies the ornate creations of the House of Worth and the pictures of pre-World War I Edwardian elegance.

Chanel's first period of professional pre-eminence, from the mid-twenties to the late thirties, coincided, in part, with her most famous alliance, with Hugh Richard Arthur Grosvenor, the second Duke of Westminster, one of Europe's wealthiest man, who was married four times and was divorced three times.

The Duke's devotion to Chanel was expressed in gifts of remarkably valuable jewels. She often had the gifts copied in fake stones.

"I couldn't wear my own real pearls without being stared at in the street, so I started the vogue of wearing false ones," she said.

She also designed real jewelry and for both she used big, chunky stones at a time when fashion called for small, quieter ones. A typical Chanel touch in the late twenties, still much in evidence, was a long necklace with colored stones forming a medallion.

Although she hated the sea, Chanel frequently accompanied the Duke aboard his yachts, one of them a converted destroyer manned by a crew of 180. One winter she came back from Cannes with bronzed skin; other women, who had always considered paleness a mark of a lady, began to imitate her.

Slacks With Jewelry

On a trip to Venice, Chanel ignited another revolution. She appeared wearing slightly bell-bottomed jersey slacks with a sweater and masses of jewelry. A friend contended later that the designer wore the trousers because she did not wish to show her famous legs to the gondolier. It seems more likely that Chanel bought the pants for the sake of comfort and sensation.

Although there was considerable speculation, both in Europe and the United States, that Chanel might marry the Duke, the volatile high priestess of couture preferred to retain her own identity.

"Everyone marries the Duke of Westminster," she reportedly said. "There are a lot of duchesses but only one Coco Chanel."

Chanel's friendship with the Duke ended by 1934. Years later, she professed to be nostalgic for Scotland — and especially for the Sundays, when she used to ride a horse on his estate.

She remained impressed by the clothes worn by Englishmen. When Randolph Churchill told her one day that he had been assigned to write an article for The Daily Mail on what women wore for the Derby, her reply was that the women were not worth writing about, that the men had all the distinction.

"My God," she said. "There is nothing more ugly than the way the women dress."

The founder of the House of Chanel in the thirties

One of the engineering secrets of the Chanel jacket was its high, tight armhole. It could have been tailored in Savile Row.

"The armhole was never high enough. She'd reset a sleeve six times," recalled Jackie Rogers, a Boston-born mannequin who modeled for Chanel in 1963 and now has her own New York boutique. "The high armhole gave the jacket the cleaner, closer fit she wanted. She wanted a tight sweater look.

'Suit Never Finished'

"But a suit was never finished ot her, even when the day came on which it was to be shown. Her designs were her children, never completed."

Unlike most couturiers, Chanel never made a drawing or toile—linen prototype—of her clothes. The only way she could work was by taking the material in her hands.

All her instincts and professional knowledge seemed to come from her fingers. She loved working with her hands. A few years ago she told a friend, "If I were not embarrassed to be seen, I would love to shoe a horse."

Chanel at one time entertained frequently at the splendid house she kept on the Faubourg St. Honoré. She also kept a small bedroom suite at the Ritz, where she often slept and dressed. She once said that the reason she slept at the Ritz was to escape the disorder in her house after a party.

The Ritz was the scene of one of the few verified episodes in her life. It resulted in the fashion for bobbed hair.

One night, some gas in the hot water heater exploded, spraying her with soot. An impatient woman, Chanel cut off her long black hair so there would be less to shampoo. She washed it quickly and tied a ribbon around it.

That night she appeared at the opera in a white dress and short hair. The effect was stunning and became an immediate fashion craze.

In her later years, Chanel was almost never seen without a hat. It was as much a part of her face as the false bangs she wore. The bangs were due to her antipathy to hairdressers. The hat was never taken off, she said, so that people she did not like would think she was on her way out.

Chanel's salon embraced the artistic world as well as the social. Jean Cocteau once wrote that she had the head of "a little black swan." And the heart, Colette added, of "a little black bull."

During the thirties, Chanel was reported engaged to Paul Iribe, a painter and decorator. He died while playing tennis at her villa in Roquebrune.

A story that has a choice place in the Chanel legend is that Sergei Diaghilev, desperate for funds for his ballet, got a huge check from Chanel on the day they met. Those who thought she had the flint of a French peasant doubted the story. Others, recalling her comment that the artistic White Russians in Paris "brought me everything I missed in my life," found the tale more believable.

She was a close friend of Grand Duke Dimitri of Russia, first cousin of Czar Nicholas II, and of the composer Stravinsky. Although she sometimes felt insecure in this milieu, she was fascinated by it.

In the late thirties, when the fashionable world deserted Chanel for Elsa Schiaparelli, the Italian designer, and World War II broke out, Chanel shut her couture house and went across the street to hibernate at the Ritz. The Nazis later took many rooms there but they never commandeered the hotel. Chanel remained there, then went on to Vichy and to Switzerland, but the record of her life for 15 years is more blurred than usual.

Chanel's comeback, on Feb. 5, 1954, was a major turning point in the fashion world although hardly anyone realized it.

She showed a suit in heavy navy jersey with two patch pockets, worn with a white tucked muslin blouse and a sailor hat. The critics' reaction was civil but not ecstatic; however, women bought it. It was the forerunner of a style that evolved year after year with increasing success.

Lukewarm Reception

The reception was equally lukewarm after her second collection in October of that year. Chanel had always been considered a rebel and people expected shocks. Instead, Chanel, as always, was simply extending and developing the shapes that satisfied her.

The suit that was in every city in America by 1964 was an evolution of the navy design of a decade earlier. Her own favorite was a beige tweed trimmed with red and dark-blue braid, with the patch pockets used as purses.

Chanel, in her 80's and perhaps at the peak of her career, continued to rule her salon like a royal court. People jostled for favors, almost fearing success and braced for reversal.

Anne Chamberlin, writing in The Ladies Home Journal in October, 1963, said, "The weeks preceding the opening of a new collection are, next to the Bastille Day fireworks, one of the great pyrotechnic spectacles in Paris, witnessed by only a privileged few."

Her account bore out the description:

"Mademoiselle takes up her station on one of the gold ballroom chairs in the big showroom, with a pair of scissors hanging from a rope around her neck and a box of straight pins on the chair beside her ("I want every single pin in this house changed, not one is long enough"), asks to see the first dress, and the fun begins.

"She suffers from rheumatism and arthritis. Yet she still literally attacks each fitting with her bare hands, clawing and pushing at the fabric, jamming in pins, tearing out seams, sending seamstresses off in tears behind the fitting screens, where they get revenge by jabbing pins into the models.

"While the pretty doe-eyed models in their white smocks wait on gold chairs for their turn at a fitting and an ancient lady in espadrilles sews the treads back on the stairs, a scene of frenzied activity unfolds, accompanied by a stream of Chanelesque advice. 'Look for the woman in the dress,' goes a constant theme. 'If there is no woman, there is no dress.'"

The mannequins, young and energetic, sagged with fatigue as the fittings went on, frequently up to six or eight hours without a break. Chanel was impervious, indefatigable and seemingly indestructible.

One of the few times that Chanel combined designing with other aspects of the couture business was, as she herself admitted, a disaster. She hired four prostitutes as mannequins, apparently thinking she would reform them. Her zeal was generally unappreciated. The prostitutes attempted to draft the other models into their profession, telling them how much more money they could earn on the streets.

"What a scandal!" Chanel recalled with some relish.

Nourished by Feuds

Her private quarters in her couture house—a salon with a wide suède sofa, a dining room, a small library, a kitchen and a huge bathroom—were open to only a few members of the staff, friends and clients who impressed her. For several years, she gave a dinner party in the dining room to mark the end of each couture season. The waiters wore white gloves, the guests drank Scotch and wine and Chanel made a little speech saying, in effect, that this had been her last collection. Everyone knew better.

Always nourished by feuds, she took obvious delight in baiting her fellow designers. "They consider me a sort of pestilence," she said.

A well-known designer who had once worked for her (the experience was so upsetting that he did not even refer to it in his autobiography) and provoked her, achieved fame designing for another house.

Chanel vengefully scheduled her opening one year at exactly the same time that his couture house did. Fashion reporters who peeked quickly at his clothes and then streaked to Chanel found themselves barred.

More recently, she endeared herself to another member of the couture by saying, "Saint Laurent has excellent taste. The more he copies me, the better taste he displays."

Chanel never reserved her rapierlike tongue for her foes, or even those she disliked. After the war, she expressed scorn for the New Look of her friend Christian Dior. A pinch-waisted silhouette with a long billowing skirt, it scored an enormous success with its rejection of all the limitations of wartime.

"I adore you," Chanel was reported to have said to Dior, "but you dress women like armchairs."

The last years of her life were relatively quiet, dedicated to the couture house (which was often operated at a loss, the deficit paid cheerfully by the parent company because the publicity helped the sales of every other Chanel product) and to acerbic comments and racing horses. Her stables in Chantilly included a well-known mare, Romantica.

Chanel outlived many of her closest friends and felt separated from others. She had never married, not because she preferred solitude but, according to one quotation, because she "never wanted to weigh more heavily on a man than a bird."

Her weight on fashion was immeasurable.

Cecil Beaton

Chanel in 1936

"All the News That's Fit to Print"

The New York Times

LATE CITY EDITION

Weather: Cloudy, rain likely today; partly cloudy tonight, tomorrow. Temp. range: today 29-46; Saturday 20-35. Full U.S. report on Page 63.

SECTION ONE

VOL. CXXI.. No. 41,616

NEW YORK, SUNDAY, JANUARY 2, 1972

75¢ beyond 50-mile zone from New York City, except Long Island. Higher in air delivery cities.

NJ 50 CENTS

SUPPLIES FLOWN TO BASE IN LAOS RINGED BY ENEMY

Ammunition Is Lifted Into Long Tieng After Planes Curb Foe's Artillery

TRAIL NET IS ATTACKED

U.S. Makes 200 Air Strikes Against Supply Routes of North Vietnamese

By Agence France-Presse

VIENTIANE, Laos, Jan. 1—Communist forces today eased their pressure on the vital and encircled Long Tieng base in northern Laos after two days of heavy shelling, enabling American planes to fly in ammunition to the allied garrison there.

A military source here said that the enemy's firepower had been cut when United States planes destroyed three or four 130-mm. cannons. The enemy forces were believed to be shifting their remaining four or five guns to new positions.

[American planes made more than 200 strikes against the Ho Chi Minh trail network of North Vietnamese supply lines in Laos and Cambodia, the Associated Press reported from Saigon.]

Evacuation Apparently Off

The evacuation of Long Tieng's 30,000-man garrison also appeared to have been put off. The commander of the Military Region II, Gen. Vang Pao, and his more than 30 American advisers remained at the base.

Although losses in men were reported light, the base has suffered considerable damage during the last two days.

Communist shells have destroyed the ammunition dump and radio transmission center as well as the headquarters of Military Region II and a joint operations center manned by the Laotians and the Americans.

While the net remained tight around Long Tieng, which lies across the line of Communist advance towards Vientiane, 73 miles to the south, the North Vietnamese and the Pathet Lao guerrillas mounted another offensive against Pakse, the country's second largest city.

Government troops have been driven back 11 miles and the main defense line is now 21 miles from Pakse.

Earlier today, 61 American

Continued on Page 3, Column 1

Sadat Raises New Arab Union Flag

Special to The New York Times

CAIRO, Jan. 1—President Anwar el-Sadat raised a new banner of Arab unity—the red, white and black flag with a golden hawk of the Federation of Arab Republics—over Cairo today amid the contrasting sounds of a 21-gun military salute and the fluttering of doves of peace.

The Egyptian leader kissed the flag during the ceremony.

Similar ceremonies were held at noon in Syria and Libya, which joined with Egypt in the loose federation after plebiscites on Sept. 1.

An eight-member federal Cabinet was chosen a week ago by President Sadat, President Hafez al-Assad of Syria and Col. Muammar el-Qaddafi, the Libyan leader.

The golden hawk in the federation's flag replaces as Egypt's official insigne the black eagle of Saladin, the 12th century Kurdish warrior who united the Arabs and defeated the Crusaders. The golden hawk was the emblem of the Koreish tribe of Mohammed, the founder of Islam.

United Press International

Flag of the Arab states flying over Government House in Cairo yesterday.

The New York Times/Donal F. Holway

ANNOUNCING TRANSIT PACT yesterday were, from left, Matthew Guinan, president of Transport Workers Union; Vincent D. McDonnell, mediator, and Dr. William J. Ronan, head of Metropolitan Transportation Authority. At right is Michael I. Sovern, another mediator. Behind Mr. McDonnell is Douglas L. MacMahon, union executive.

150-MILLION PACT AVERTS WALKOUT ON TRANSIT LINES

But Fare of at Least 35c Is Certain if Legislature Approves City Package

ACCEPTANCE PREDICTED

T.W.U. and 5 Private Bus Companies Later Reach a Similar Settlement

By DAMON STETSON

A new transit labor agreement costing an estimated total of $150-million averted a bus and subway strike in the city yesterday, but an early fare increase of at least 5 cents is certain.

The new labor costs and a previous operating deficit calculated at $152,972,825 for the current fiscal year accentuated the Transit Authority's financial plight, leaving no doubt that the fare would be raised soon—to 35 cents if the State Legislature approves a proposed transit package.

The new agreements with the Transport Workers Union and the Amalgamated Transit Union were announced shortly before 3 A.M., well ahead of the 5 A.M. deadline set for a strike if no settlement had been achieved. In 1970, the agreement was not announced until three hours after the deadline.

Referendum by Mail

Matthew Guinan, president of the Transport Workers Union, representing 38,000 bus and subway workers, described the settlement as "fair and reasonable"—and forecast approval by his membership in a mail referendum. The Amalgamated Transit Union represents 2,000 bus drivers in Queens and on Staten Island.

Dr. William J. Ronan, chairman of the Metropolitan Transportation Authority, noted that the Transit Authority, which operates under the M.T.A., was assured of improved performance by its personnel under the new contract. He also said that officials of the Transit Authority were convinced that the settlement met Federal guidelines, which generally call for a limitation to about 5.5 per cent in annual increases.

Terms of Accord

Last night, the T.W.U. reached a settlement with five private bus lines in the city that was virtually identical to the earlier accord with the Transit Authority. [Page 57.]

Both settlements provide for 18 per cent in pay increases over 27 months, in contrast to the two-year contracts that have prevailed for years. This means an end, at least for a time, to the cliff-hanging nego-

Continued on Page 57, Column 4

Sharp Rise in Immigration Expected by Israel in '72

By PETER GROSE

Special to The New York Times

JERUSALEM, Jan. 1—An exhilarating but quite unexpected challenge is confronting Israel in 1972: the absorption of a great stream of new immigrants in numbers expected to be comparable to the new arrivals in the heady first years of statehood beginning in 1948.

Israeli authorities received clear indications in the last weeks of 1971 that the trickle of Jews arriving here from the Soviet Union was rapidly increasing.

At the same time, a record immigration is expected in 1972 from the United States and other Western countries, building on the momentum that started with the 1967 Arab-Israeli war.

At its last Cabinet meeting of 1971, the Government revised its estimate of 1972 immigration upward by nearly 50 per cent to 70,000 people. Until three weeks ago, economic and social planning was based on the probable need to absorb about 45,000 immigrants.

Welcomed though it is, this influx brings financial, social and psychological problems far more awesome than even those in the normally complex process of absorbing newcomers into an established society.

Fully half the newcomers in 1972 are expected to come from the Soviet Union, according to

Continued on Page 14, Column 1

U.S. Now Big Landlord In Decaying Inner City

By JOHN HERBERS

Special to The New York Times

WASHINGTON, Jan. 1—A new and ominous chapter has opened in the decline of the central cities: The Federal Government has begun to come into ownership or control of a large portion of faltering or abandoned inner-city housing.

Many of the subsidized projects built or rehabilitated in recent years with the intent of renewing the cities are in default of mortgage payments or in deep financial trouble; and in one way or another the Government is assuming the losses incurred by urban decay and the excesses and mistakes of developers.

The development has important implications. It is an indicator of accelerated decline for the cities; it is a blow to the mushrooming housing subsidy programs, which have increasingly become a subject of national controversy, and it raises the possibility of the central Government's holding large land reservations in some of the central cities.

Washington officials involved acknowledged that the housing programs have encountered great difficulties in the cities, but said they were being brought under control. In some of the cities, however, there was much less optimism.

In Philadelphia, the name of

Continued on Page 26, Column 1

Transit Fare Situation

The 30-cent fare on the city's subways and buses will be increased this week to at least 35 cents and possibly as high as 45 cents as a result of the new transit contract.

The extent of the increase will be determined by the size of the tax package to help the Transit Authority that is to be adopted when the State Legislature resumes its special session tomorrow in Albany.

The 11-member board of the Metropolitan Transportation Authority, which supervises the Transit Authority, will have to approve the fare increase. The increase will also require approval by the Federal Price Commission.

Passengers were limited yesterday to the purchase of three tokens a person. Some subway turnstiles were being altered, but the Transit Authority declined to say whether the old small tokens that were in use when the fare was 20 cents or the present larger ones would be used when the fare was increased.

Governor Holding Fiscal Talks Today

By JAMES F. CLARITY

Governor Rockefeller scheduled a meeting with the four top leaders of the Legislature for today to try to rebuild a coalition of bipartisan support for his battered emergency fiscal program.

Gerald McLaughlin, Mr. Rockefeller's assistant press secretary, said the Governor discussed the program with the leaders by telephone yesterday. But, Mr. McLaughlin said, details of the conversations would not be disclosed.

In calling today's meeting, the Governor gave the leaders only one day's rest from conferences on the fiscal crisis. Support for the program crumbled in Albany on Friday, after a week of negotiations produced a delicately structured compromise package of tax increases and cuts and delays in state aid.

The Governor's revised program is designed to bridge a budget gap of $1.5-billion for the 15-month period that began yesterday. The failure of the program to win approval on time will have no immediate effect on state finances, state officials said.

The legislature, which began meeting in special session last Monday, failed to pass the program when the Republican majority in the Assembly balked. About 35 to 40 Democratic Assemblymen had agreed to vote for the program, but withdrew their support when they learned of the Republican recalcitrance.

The Republicans control the Assembly by 79 to 71, but without Democratic help they did not have 76 votes needed to pass legislation. In the Republican-controlled Senate, the program was considered virtually certain of passage by a coalition of Democrats and Republicans.

Before he left Albany Friday, Mr. Rockefeller said agreement on the package would be reached over the weekend. Senate Majority Leader Earl W. Brydges of Niagara Falls and Joseph Zaretzki of Manhattan, the Democratic minority leader, agreed with him. Assemblyman Stanley Steingut of Brooklyn, the Democratic leader, said he would work toward such agreement. Assembly Speaker Perry B. Duryea of Montauk, L. I., remained noncommittal.

While the Governor and the four leaders spent New Year's

Continued on Page 46, Column 4

The New York Times

NEW ORLEANS PAGEANTRY: Tennessee float rolling into Sugar Bowl Stadium in half-time show yesterday. Floats representing many Southern states joined parade.

The Bowl Games

ORANGE—Nebraska, sparked by a 77-yard punt return by Johnny Rodgers and the aggressive defensive play of Rich Glover, reaffirmed its claim to the mythical national championship by overwhelming Alabama, 38-6, before a crowd of 78,151 at Miami.

COTTON—Penn State rallied from a 6-3 half-time deficit to trounce Texas, 30-6 before a crowd of 72,000 at Dallas. A 1-yard touchdown plunge by Lydell Mitchell early in the third quarter gave Penn State a 10-6 lead. The Nittany Lions increased their advantage to 17-6 moments later on a 65-yard scoring pass from John Hufnagel to Scott Skarzynski.

ROSE—Rod Garcia kicked a 31-yard field goal with 12 seconds to play to give Stanford a 13-12 upset triumph over Michigan. A crowd of 103,154 at Pasadena, Calif., saw the 155-pound kicking specialist give the Wolverines their first setback of the season.

SUGAR—Oklahoma with Jack Mildren scoring three touchdowns, rolled to a 40-22 triumph over Auburn before 84,031 at New Orleans. The Sooners, the third-ranked college team, scored five touchdowns in the first half, a Sugar Bowl record.

Details in Section 5

At Half Time in Football, A Big and Costly Show

By STEVEN V. ROBERTS

Special to The New York Times

PASADENA, Calif., Jan. 1—In 1869, when Rutgers defeated Princeton in the first college football game, reports do not indicate what happened between halves of the game. Probably there was a lot of gasping for breath. But there is a record of the first college football cheer: "Siss Boom Bah, Prince-ton!"

One hundred and two years of fumbles and fractures later, football is a national institution. So is half time, 20 minutes of pep or pageantry (depending on one's viewpoint), fast-stepping marchers and high-kicking majorettes, gaggles of twirlers and gobs of tradition, the essential hole in the doughnut of football.

Half-time shows are a big and expensive business. The total cost of the extravaganzas at the four major bowl games today—Rose, Orange, Sugar and Cotton—probably approaches $500,000.

But that is only a tiny fraction of what is spent annually at thousands of shows from the high school to the professional level. Just the

Continued on Page 50, Column 1

Maurice Chevalier Dead; Singer and Actor Was 83

Special to The New York Times

PARIS, Jan. 1—Maurice Chevalier, probably the most popular and best-known entertainer that France has produced this century, died here tonight. He was 83 years old.

The singer and actor, whose stage and screen career covered well over half a century, entered Necker Hospital Dec. 13 in critical condition from kidney failure. Despite several false alarms he amazed both doctors and the public with his vitality. Yesterday morning a hospital bulletin was still able to talk of "his good general condition."

The thousands of messages that he received at the hospital attested to the fact that although he belonged to another generation he was still remembered and still popular.

According to an official hospital communiqué, the cause of death was heart failure. After his death the body was taken to his home at Marnes-la-Coquette, west of Paris. His impresario, François Vals, said, that though many admirers of Mr. Chevalier had already appeared at the house hoping to pay their last respects, the funeral would be "extremely discreet" in keeping with his wishes.

Camera Press

Maurice Chevalier

The Elegant Boulevardier

By ALDEN WHITMAN

No French entertainer was so jaunty, so debonair, so burnished yet so saucy, so much the elegant boulevardier of an idealized Paris as Maurice Chevalier.

Attired in a one-button, dark blue suit, sporting a springtime boater and singing and talking in his magical Gallic accent, he was America's No. 1 Frenchman, the bubbling personification of a glass of champagne. He was also France's No. 1 chanteur, whose renditions of "Ma Louise," "Mimi," "Valen-

Continued on Page 54, Column 3

Study Finds Black Market Developing in Methadone

By JAMES M. MARKHAM

The drug methadone, which is gaining popularity as a clinically administered alternative to heroin, is gradually joining heroin and other drugs on the streets of urban America as a black-market commodity.

A survey by The New York Times of 14 major American cities that have methadone maintenance programs has found that in all of them there is some trafficking in the synthetic, addictive drug.

The precise fluctuations of supply and demand in the methadone black market, which is much smaller than its better-organized heroin counterpart, are hard to gauge. But both supply and demand appear to be growing.

Supply has several origins: outpatients on methadone maintenance programs who sell part of their allotted dose to purchase heroin, barbiturates, amphetamines or alcohol; thefts of methadone from pharmacies and maintenance programs, by addicts and employes, and a small but disturbing number of private physicians who prescribe or dispense overgenerous quantities of the drug, which then finds its way into the black market.

Two years ago, agents from the Federal Bureau of Narcotics and Dangerous Drugs arrested a chemist in Tupelo, Miss., and seized 22 pounds of pure methadone that he had allegedly manufactured for distribution by underworld elements on the East Coast. But since then the bureau has had no evidence that organized crime has found

Continued on Page 52, Column 1

Today's Sections

Today's Sections

Because of a revised printing schedule, The Week in Review section is folded inside the Financial section.

Maurice Chevalier, Singer and Actor, Is Dead in Paris

Continued From Page 1, Col. 5

tine," "Ma Pomme," "Ca Va, Ca Va," "Place Pigalle" and "Paris Oui Oui" reflected the bittersweet of life and the careless rapture of the nineteen-twenties and thirties.

Mr. Chevalier was, moreover, ageless: a headliner at the Folies-Bergère in 1909, he was still without a peer as a revue artist almost 60 years later.

"Le Grand Maurice" he was called in the fall of 1966 when he appeared, full of zest in his 79th year, in the Empire Room of the Waldorf-Astoria Hotel. Although the years had etched his once-smooth face into a faint resemblance of Will Rogers, Mr. Chevalier, once he started to perform, became in the twinkling of an eye a well-preserved man of no more than 55. His voice was full and strong, his step was spry and his light blue eyes shimmered.

His way with an audience, an observer noted, was unaffected and unforced. He enchanted them by being their Maurice, and when he departed waving his boater after an hour of songs and gentle patter about the joys of senescence it was to a spontaneous standing ovation.

Discussing his artistic longevity, Mr. Chevalier once remarked:

"I believe in the rosy side of life. I know that life has many, many dark sides for everybody. It has been for me at many moments of my life. But I believe in bringing to the people the encouragement of living, and I think I am lasting so long in the interest of the people through something that comes out of my personality and out of my work, which is just to be sort of a sunshine person, see."

$20,000-a-Week Star

At his best in songs and skits, in which his joie de vivre and personality bedazzled, Mr. Chevalier was only somewhat less renowned as a motion picture actor. In the thirties he starred at $20,000 a week in such Hollywood romantic classics as "The Love Parade" and "The Merry Widow," which were directed by Ernst Lubitsch. In these he was the gay, sophisticated and irresistible lover, the leading man to such actresses as Jeanette MacDonald, Claudette Colbert and Evelyn Brent.

There was a 10-year hiatus in his film career that ended with the French movie "Le Silence Est d'Or" in 1947, which won the grand prize at the Brussels World Film Festival. His comeback in American films — now as a dramatic and character actor — occurred in 1957 in "Love in the Afternoon." And playing with Leslie Caron in 1958, he stole the show as the aging ladies' man in "Gigi," a film that added the song "Thank Heaven for Little Girls" to his repertory. His performance won him an honorary Oscar. There followed character roles in "Can-Can," "Fanny," "Jessica" and "The Castaways" that gained him additional acclaim.

In all Mr. Chevalier appeared in 40 films, the first released in 1914, and achieved an international reputation. He was a hard and self-centered worker. "I could never say that working with him was anything more than agreeable," Miss MacDonald remarked of their association. "All he cared about was his career and his mother."

Once when Mr. Chevalier was in Hollywood he was a house guest of Mary Pickford. "He would go out on the lawn every day with his straw hat and rehearse his entire music-hall act," the actress recalled. "He leaves nothing to chance."

Although he made a lot of money in the movies and reached a world audience through them, Mr. Chevalier's métier was the revue and the one-man show. In these he mesmerized his listeners, who were transfixed by his long underlip, dancing eyes and roguish smile. American and English audiences might suspect that his fractured English was a shade too carefully preserved and that his accent was too perfect, but such skepticism melted before his warmth. Indeed, his appeal was so irresistible that he once got the august Charles de Gaulle, President of France, to join him at a charity ball in a refrain of "Ma Pomme."

As a singer Mr. Chevalier was no great shakes. He could carry an uncomplicated tune, phrase a line and be sly at the proper time, but that was about all. By unending practice, however, he converted his vocal deficiencies into assets.

"Thank God, it was my good luck not to have any voice," he said. "If I had, I would have tried to be a singer who sings ballads in a voice like a velvet fog, but since I am barely able to half-talk and half-sing a song, it made me look for something to make me different from a hundred other crooners who are neither good nor bad. If I had any voice, I would have been content to rest on my voice and learn nothing else. Since I had no voice, I had to find something that would hold the interest of the public."

"Any third-rate chanteur de charme [a crooner] has a better voice than I," he said on another occasion. "But they sing from the throat while I sing from the heart."

Mr. Chevalier's handling of a song, as well as the songs themselves, contributed to the spell he cast on the stage or in supper clubs. A favorite was "Ma Louise," written for him in the twenties; another was "Ca Va, Ca Va," which he wrote for himself in the forties. Still another was "Valentine." It is the story of a girl who was so little and so sweet. The years go by and Valentine is encountered again, but she is no longer petite and she has a double chin into the bargain.

"It is a very human story," he said of the song, and by accenting that quality he gave it a special character. Audiences never seemed to tire of it.

As an entertainer Mr. Chevalier considered himself in the tradition of Sir Harry Lauder, the Scottish balladeer, and Al Jolson, the American song-and-dance man. He admired both for the intimacy they established with their audiences and for their artistic intensity.

A similar intensity appeared to account for Mr. Chevalier's reluctance to retire. "Often people ask me how it feels to be 78," he said shortly after he reached that age. "And I say wonderful, considering the alternatives."

"I'm traveling through old age without being unhappy, without being forgotten," he said another time, adding:

"I get my energy from the audience."

Energy, ambition and drive for stage success characterized Mr. Chevalier from early childhood. Born Sept. 12, 1888, in the impoverished Paris working-class quarter of Ménilmontant, he was the youngest of nine children of Victor Charles and Josephine Bossche Chevalier. His father was a ne'er-do-well house painter who deserted the family when Maurice was 8, and his mother was a lacemaker, to whom he was devoted throughout her life. Her death, in 1932, was a severe emotional blow, but he kept her memory alive by naming his Paris villa La Louque, a nickname he had given his mother.

Maurice ended his formal schooling at the age of 10, when he was apprenticed to an engraver, and he later worked briefly in a tack factory. But he wanted to be an entertainer, first as an acrobat with his brother, Paul, and then as a singer. An accident nipped his acrobatics, and he made his vocal debut in a neighborhood cafe on amateur night. It was un grand succès d'hilarité, for he was laughed off the stage for singing in a different key from that of the pianist.

Unfazed, the Chaplinesque ragamuffin persisted, and he began to sing in the hurly-burly variety halls and cafés-concert in Paris and in the provinces. His comic efforts were based on his youth, his extravagant attire and earthy songs. When he was 15 he began to play in the boulevard revues as a singing comedian. He was billed as "Le Petit Jesus" ("The Wonder Boy") and he started to make an impression.

"Records and radio and movies did not exist at that time," Mr. Chevalier later said of those hansom-cab-and-gaslight days. "It took years of traveling and playing to a few hundred people a night to build a reputation."

Partner of Mistinguett

His big break came in 1909, when he was 21: He was hired by the Folies-Bergère to be the legendary Mistinguett's partner in a revue. Mistinguett began life as a flower girl and achieved fame on account of her pungent personality, her slender, sexy legs and a song called "Mon Homme." When Mr. Chevalier met her she was 36 and at the top of her career.

The two did something called "The Flooring Waltz," in which they rolled themselves up in a carpet, fell to the stage, rose and unrolled. One evening early in the revue's run, they were a little slower than usual in unrolling, and they emerged from the tapestry in love.

"She was very attractive and I loved her madly," Mr. Chevalier said later of their liaison. "People have said that she made me a star. That is not true. I was already a star of the younger generation. However, I learned much from her because she was a great artiste. She also brought me the dearest and biggest love a man can have."

Called up for compulsory military duty in late 1913, Mr. Chevalier was at Mélun when World War I broke out. In the German invasion, he was hit in the right lung by shrapnel and was captured. After 26 months in a prisoner-of-war camp in Germany, during which he learned English from a fellow inmate, he was released in a prisoner exchange and went home to Mistinguett and to a Croix de Guerre.

Overcoming his lung wound, he played at the Olympia in Paris, returned to the Folies-Bergère and appeared at the Théâtre Femina and the Casino de Paris. After his first trip to London, in 1919, he adopted a dress suit, top hat and white gloves to accentuate his new smoothness as a singer and comedian.

"Then one day in London I saw a young fellow in a tuxedo and a straw hat," he later recalled. "He looked so smart that I thought, 'I do not need to look farther. There is my hat. It's a man's hat. It's a gay hat. It's the hat to go with a tuxedo.' From that moment I was never without a straw boater if I could help it, even when those hats went out of fashion."

Back in Paris, he played in a musical, did a further stint at the Folies-Bergère with Mistinguett, then appeared in a song-and-dance revue with Yvonne Vallée, to whom he was subsequently married for about six years. After playing the lead in the operetta "Dédé," Mr. Chevalier was brought to the United States by Charles B. Dillingham, the New York producer, but he was too frightened or too awed to perform and was released from his contract.

His first working visit to this country was in 1928, and in the following seven years he made 12 films. This film stint ended in 1935 when Irving Thalberg, the producer, wanted to give Grace Moore top billing in a Chevalier picture.

"I told Thalberg I had never been second on any bill since I was 20," Mr. Chevalier said. "I left for Paris. It was the end of my first American movie career."

New York Debut

Between pictures, however, he had made his New York debut at the New Amsterdam Roof Garden and played the Fulton Theater. His song repertory even then captivated New Yorkers.

Returning to Paris, Mr. Chevalier was again a hit in the music halls. He entertained King George VI and Queen Elizabeth on their state visit to France in 1938 and was decorated as a Chevalier of the Legion of Honor. By 1940, when World War II embroiled France, he was a friend of Nita Raya, a young actress. Fearing Nazi persecution because Miss Raya was Jewish, the couple moved to Mr. Chevalier's villa at Cannes, in the Free French Zone.

His conduct during the war suggested a degree of collaboration with the Nazis, as the recent documentary film, "Le Chagrin et la Pitié," demonstrated. In it he could be seen and heard in a sequence in which he defended his performing during the Nazi occupation. He contended that he never sang for the Germans, never in Germany and only before German-held French prisoners. The incidents were investigated at the time, and his collaboration was deemed not serious enough to merit special punishment. He returned to the Paris stage without a noticeable decline in his popularity.

After touring Belgium, the Netherlands, Switzerland and the Scandinavian countries, Mr. Chevalier brought his one-man show to New York in 1947. Critical acclaim was undiminished, and he toured the United States and Canada for almost a year.

Mr. Chevalier planned to return to the United States in 1951, but he was refused a visa because he had signed the Stockholm Appeal, a plea against the use of thermonuclear weapons. On the ground that Communists had been energetic in circulating the appeal, the State Department adjudged the entertainer potentially dangerous to the security of the United States. The matter was considered of such moment at the time that Secretary of State Dean Acheson sought to justify the visa ban. The barrier was not lifted until 1954 despite Mr. Chevalier's protest that he had signed the appeal out of a sense of humanity.

After that he was in the country several times, either to make films or to play theater and club dates. He also appeared on a number of television shows, none of lasting note.

Off stage Mr. Chevalier lived a relatively quiet and unostentatious life. In his early years he liked to box and sparred from time to time with Georges Carpentier, the French pugilist and a close friend. He kept his 5-foot-11½-inch figure in trim with calisthenics and by playing golf.

With advancing years he also practiced moderation. "Until the age of 50," he remarked to a friend, "I lived from the belt down to the heels; since then I have oriented myself toward the part that lies between the belt and the head."

Three years ago, Mr. Chevalier gave another "last" recital at the Théâtre des Champs-Elysées in Paris. In a short speech he said it had been his aim to "pay homage to Paris . . . after 68 years of good and loyal services" to its glory.

In 1970, he published one more book of thoughts about things, "Les Pensées de Momo" ("Momo's Thoughts" — Momo being a Parisian abbreviation for Maurice). This followed the completion of his memoirs, "Ma Route et Mes Chansons" ("My Road and My Songs").

His most recent activity was the recording of the theme song for the French version of the Walt Disney production "The Aristocats."

In the last couple of years, he also occasionally put out a record containing a few new songs. He could occasionally be seen at an opening night, theater or movie. And he would attend the major horse racing events, striking people by his impeccable dress, looking jaunty and fit as ever with his red cheeks and seeming no more than a well-preserved 60.

In the nineteen-fifties Mr. Chevalier donated his Cannes villa to the French Society of Authors and Composers, and lived in a long, low, white house at Marnes-la-Coquette, near Paris. With him on the 2½-acre estate was Janie Michels, a young, red-haired painter who was his protégée.

The house itself contained a museum of his show-business souvenirs, including photographs of friends and associates. One of Marlene Dietrich, signed "Marlinou," said, "I have always known you were the greatest. But since I have invaded your profession I am on my knees."

There were also paintings—a Utrillo scene of Ménilmontant and oils by Cézanne, Matisse, Dufy and Picasso. Statuettes of himself in various stage poses stood against the walls, and metal ash trays shaped and colored like his straw hat were much in evidence.

Mr. Chevalier's egocentricity was not, however, so overpowering as it might have seemed. A few years ago a film publicity writer had occasion to drive from Marseilles to Paris with him. For much of the distance Mr. Chevalier entertained his guest with a nonstop song recital, and the writer was completely charmed. And Mr. Chevalier was doing what he liked best—entertaining. It was this characteristic that led Jean Cocteau to call him "le grand sympathique."

"All the News That's Fit to Print"

The New York Times

LATE CITY EDITION

Weather: Fair, very cold today and tonight. Chance of snow tomorrow. Temp. range: today 24-14; Sunday 33-26. Full U.S. report on Page 30.

VOL. CXXIV . No. 42,806 NEW YORK, SUNDAY, APRIL 6, 1975

$1.00 beyond 50-mile zone from New York City, except Long Island. Higher in air delivery cities.

60 CENTS

SUBWAY RIDERSHIP LOWEST SINCE '18; OFF 20% IN DECADE

Rising Fare and Service Cut Cited as Principal Causes —Bus Situation Similar

DECLINE IS CONTINUING

Patronage Dips 4% in First 2 Months of '75—M.T.A. Changing Its Priorities

By EDWARD C. BURKS

Subway ridership in the city has plunged to the lowest level since 1918, when the city had 2.5 million fewer residents.

In the last decade alone, the subways have lost a million daily riders, or more than 20 per cent, as the fare rose in stages from 15 cents to the current 35 cents.

Bus routes under the Metropolitan Transportation Authority, have shown a similar sharp ridership decline in the 10-year period, according to newly available figures from the agency.

Despite the continuing decline in subway riders, the authority is going ahead with construction of a $1.5-billion line between Central Park and Jamaica, Queens, via 63d Street. The line, the agency's only major new construction at present, will generally parallel the IND Queens Boulevard route, which has had a 14 per cent loss in ridership since 1962.

Funds Committed

The city and the agency decided to continue it because $207-million has already been committed, and the Queens Boulevard line, the city's most overcrowded route during rush hours, operates at 177 per cent of capacity in the peak 20 minutes in the morning.

The agency figures show that average daily subway ridership has dropped from 5.5 million shortly after World War II to 4.7 million in 1964 and to 3.7 million for the 1974 fiscal year, which ended last June 30.

Yearly subway ridership has not been below a billion since World War I. For a few years after World War II, it topped two billion. But for fiscal 1974 the total was down to 1.096-billion. The 1918 count was 1.029-billion on a much smaller system.

Decline Continues

The downward trend is continuing this year, with David L. Yunich, the Metropolitan Transportation Authority chairman, reporting a further 4 per cent drop in the average daily ridership in January and February.

After taking control of the transit system in 1968, the authority began an ambitious program of re-equipping and extending the lines. More than 1,800 new subway cars have been delivered or are on order. The total fleet consists of 6,700 cars.

The "new lines" program was designed to tap new markets and ease rush-hour overcrowding primarily on the Lexington Avenue IRT and the

Continued on Page 48, Column 1

Chiang Kai-shek Is Dead in Taipei at 87; Last of Allied Big Four of World War II

Special to The New York Times

TAIPEI, Taiwan, Sunday, April 6—Chiang Kai-shek, the President of Nationalist China and the last survivor of the Big Four Allied leaders of World War II, died of a heart attack here last night. He was 87 years old.

An announcement by the Government said Generalissimo Chiang suffered a heart attack at 10:20 P.M. and was taken to the Taipei Central Hospital, where he died at 11:50 P.M. (10:50 A.M., New York time). His wife and his eldest son, Premier Chiang Ching-kuo, were at his bedside.

A state funeral will be held, but no plans were announced immediately.

General Chiang will be succeeded automatically as President by Vice President C.K. Yen, but the real power in the Government is expected to remain in the hands of Premier Chiang, 65, who assumed control when his father fell ill and was incapacitated nearly three years ago.

Chiang Kai-shek and Mme. Chiang

Two hours after his death, the Government made public a political testament of General Chiang. Dated March 29, 1975, it called on his supporters to recapture the mainland from the Communists, a dream he had long cherished in vain.

The testament said:

"Just at the time when we are getting stronger, my colleagues and my countrymen, you should not forget our sorrow and our hope because of my death. My spirit will be always with my colleagues and my countrymen to fulfill the three people's principles, to recover the mainland and to restore our national culture."

The three principles mentioned are nationalism, democracy and social well-being.

"In the past more than 20 years we are becoming stronger and stronger in this citadel of freedom and we have been fighting the Communist evils on the China mainland, engaging in political warfare against them," the testament said.

"Our anti-Communist and national rehabilitation [programs] are being carried out. My compatriots and all the members of my party should not feel depressed because of my passing away."

With Roosevelt, Churchill

Continued on Page 47. Column 1

FORD MEETS JET FLYING CHILDREN OUT OF VIETNAM

President Boards Craft and Takes Off Infant—900 Flown From Saigon

By The Associated Press

SAN FRANCISCO, April 5—President Ford boarded a chartered plane that brought 325 South Vietnamese children to the United States tonight and carried an infant girl from the jumbo jet. They were among 900 flown from Saigon by United States planes today.

As Red Cross attendants watched, the President walked down a boarding ramp and to a waiting bus with the child, clad in pajamas and wrapped in a blanket to protect her from a heavy rain.

The President and Mrs. Ford flew here from Palm Springs, Calif., where they are vacationing, to greet the aircraft when it landed at San Francisco International Airport after a flight from Saigon, with a stop at Yakota, Japan.

Mrs. Ford was forbidden to go near the children because her post-cancer chemotherapy has destroyed her immunity to such diseases as chicken pox and measles, it was announced.

Taken to Army Base

Officials said that the plane carried 40 children who survived Friday's crash near Saigon of a giant C-5A carrying more than 240 homeless Vietnamese children.

Stationed near the Boeing 747, chartered from Pan American World Airways, were 20 buses, each with a team consisting of a doctor, a nurse, a Government official to register the children for entry into this country and 20 Red Cross volunteers to carry the children to the buses.

After being loaded onto the buses, the children were to be driven to medical facility at the Presidio, the Army base here, for medical examinations.

Businessman's Aid

The Fords arrived about 15 minutes before the plane touched down and were met at the airport by physicians from the Society for the Protection of Vietnamese Orphans and Robert Macaulay of New Canaan, Conn., a businessman who financed the flight. [Page 28.]

The society, involving civic groups, doctors, the Red Cross and various adoption agencies, is meeting the children when they come into the United States, providing medical attention and then transporting them to their adoptive parents throughout the country.

Mr. Macauley said that after the crash of the C-5A flight from Saigon, he got in touch with the society to arrange the flight that arrived tonight.

Continued on Page 28, Column 4

HANOI STEPS UP ATTACKS IN AREA SOUTH OF SAIGON; U.S. REASSESSING POLICY

United Press International

In Palm Springs, Calif., the Army Chief of Staff, Gen. Frederick C. Weyand, reported on his trip to South Vietnam to President Ford and Secretary of State Kissinger.

Attica Jury Convicts One Of Murder, 2d of Assault

By MICHAEL T. KAUFMAN

Special to The New York Times

BUFFALO, April 5—The jury in the trial of two former Attica inmates convicted both defendants here tonight—John Hill of murder and Charles Joseph Pernasilice of attempted assault—for their roles in the death of a prison guard during the September, 1971, rebellion at the prison.

When the jury, which had been deliberating for more than 25 hours, returned at 9:15 P.M., Genevieve Klug, the court clerk, asked the foreman of the jury, Rosa Moore, whether a verdict had been reached.

'I Want My Wife'

"Yes, ma'am," replied Mrs. Moore, a 44-year-old clerical worker.

"In the case of the People versus John Hill, what is the verdict?" Mrs. Klug asked.

"Murder, guilty," the foreman replied.

Mr. Hill, the 23-year-old defendant, who had maintained his composure through most of his trial on charges of killing correction officer William E. Quinn, stood up. A court officer asked him to sit down

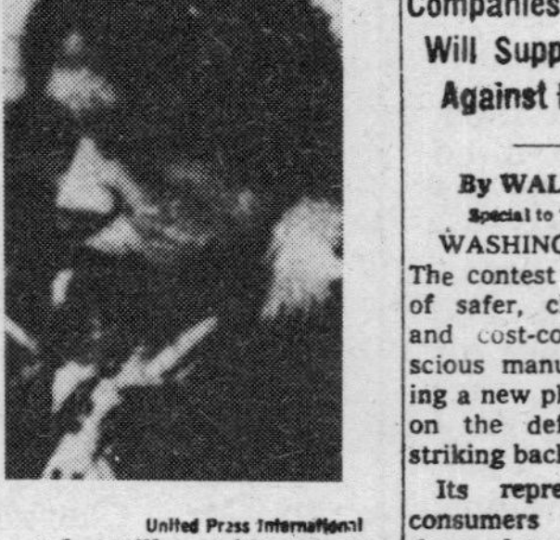

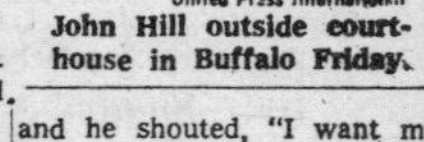

United Press International

John Hill outside courthouse in Buffalo Friday.

and he shouted, "I want my wife."

Three women, sitting among some 20 supporters of the defendants, began to sob. Meanwhile, Mrs. Klug continued to ask Mrs. Moore what the jury had found in the case of "the People versus Charles Joseph Pernasilice."

The foreman replied that

Continued on Page 30, Column 1

INDUSTRY RESISTS CAR-SAFETY COSTS

Companies Feel Consumers Will Support Their Fight Against New Standards

By WALTER RUGABER

Special to The New York Times

WASHINGTON, April 5 — The contest between advocates of safer, cleaner automobiles and cost-conscious, style-conscious manufacturers is entering a new phase. After 10 years on the defensive, Detroit is striking back.

Its representatives believe consumers are less attached these days, when many are less affluent and more cost-conscious, to improvements such as strong bumpers, complex braking systems and sophisticated antipollution gear.

The car companies—arguing that Federal guidelines are helping drive up prices at a time of economic hardship—are demanding relief from some existing Government regulations together with a five-year moratorium on any new safety

Continued on Page 42, Column 4

Congress to Hear Decision On Saigon in Ford Speech

By JOHN HERBERS

Special to The New York Times

PALM SPRINGS, Calif., April 5—Secretary of State Kissinger said today that the United States would review its policies toward the Saigon Government next week following an assessment of the situation by Gen. Frederick C Weyand, the Army Chief of Staff.

After a 90-minute meeting this morning, in which General Weyand reported on his mission to President Ford and the Secretary of State, Mr. Kissinger said various options would be discussed by the National Security Council in Washington on Tuesday or Wednesday.

Secretary Kissinger added that President Ford would disclose his decision in his speech before Congress on the state of the world, scheduled for 9 p.m. on Thursday.

In a news conference at the International Hotel, Mr. Kissinger left the impression that the Government did not know what to do about the deteriorating military situation, which Mr. Kissinger described as serious. The tone of his remarks was pessimistic.

Mr. Kissinger said the crucial issue was whether the Saigon Government would be able to defend its remaining territory.

"There is a possibility for the South Vietnamese military forces to stabilize the situation," he said. "The next question is for what length of time and against what level of attack.

"Then, there is also the moral question for the United States, whether when an ally with which it has been associated for 10 years wishes to defend itself, whether it is the United States that should make the decision for it, by withholding supplies, that it should no longer defend itself. These are all questions that are involved in the examination that is now going on."

He said that the President believed the United States had no legal commitment to support Saigon but that "he is

Continued on Page 29, Column 1

NEW FRONT IS SEEN

But Pressure Eases Around Tay Ninh North of Capital

By FOX BUTTERFIELD

Special to The New York Times

SAIGON, South Vietnam, Sunday, April 6—North Vietnamese troops increased their probing attacks in the Mekong Delta area yesterday, and Western intelligence officials said it appeared that the Communists might now be trying to open a new front on Saigon's southern flank.

Clashes were reported in a number of provinces across the delta, with the principal fighting apparently occurring in Kien Giang along the Gulf of Siam. The Saigon command said that its troops there had killed 77 Communist soldiers while losing five killed and eight wounded. It also said that 39 Communist soldiers had been killed in fighting in five other provinces during the day.

Meanwhile, Communist pressure appeared to have eased northwest of Saigon in the Tay Ninh area, which the Government had heavily reinforced. Western officials said a North Vietnamese division that had been threatening to cut a major highway in the area had been moving south through the Parrot's Beak of Cambodia into the Mekong Delta to bolster Communist forces operating there.

May Have Changed Plans

It appeared, officials suggested, that the North Vietnamese might have decided that a battle in the Tay Ninh area now might be too costly. Last week, many South Vietnamese and Western officials said that the North Vietnamese appeared poised for an attack on Tay Ninh as a first step in an assault on Saigon.

Action in the Mekong Delta during the day included the shelling of Tan An Luong, a village in Vinh Long Province. The Communists were reported to have fired 300 mortar rounds into the headquarters there and to have wounded 15 South Vietnamese militiamen. Twenty homes were said to have been destroyed.

In another development favorable to the Saigon Government, South Vietnamese mili-

Continued on Page 26, Column 1

Thieu Is Reported Ready to Act On Generals Who Gave Ground

By MALCOLM W. BROWNE

Special to The New York Times

SAIGON, South Vietnam, April 5—President Nguyen Van Thieu is reported planning action against a number of his officers, on the ground that they were personally responsible for the loss of two-thirds of the nation's territory in the last few weeks.

[In Paris, the French Government called for the carrying out of a "process" that would bring a political settlement in South Vietnam. There was no explanation of what the Government had decided to do. Page 29.]

Informants said measures were expected to be taken against Lieut. Gen. Ngo Quang Truong, commander of Military Region I, Maj. Gen. Pham Van Phu, commander of Military Region II, and Maj. Gen. Bui The Lan, commander of the Marine Division.

Military Regions I and II were lost to the Communists in a matter of days as Government units collapsed, with little or no fighting anywhere. Thousands of Government troops remained behind with the Communists after getting rid of their uniforms, and others threw away vast amounts of equipment and weapons in fleeing.

General Phu and General Truong are both reported at present in a hospital in Saigon recovering from what is described in French as a "crise des nerves."

President Thieu has been having growing difficulties with most of his generals lately, including the Army Chief of Staff, Gen. Cao Van Vien. The General Staff, according to informants, has repeatedly urged Mr. Thieu to step down.

But informants also deny the spate of rumors during the last few days to the effect that President Thieu had been given an ultimatum by his generals and that a military coup was being planned.

"There is always the possibil-

Continued on Page 28, Column 1

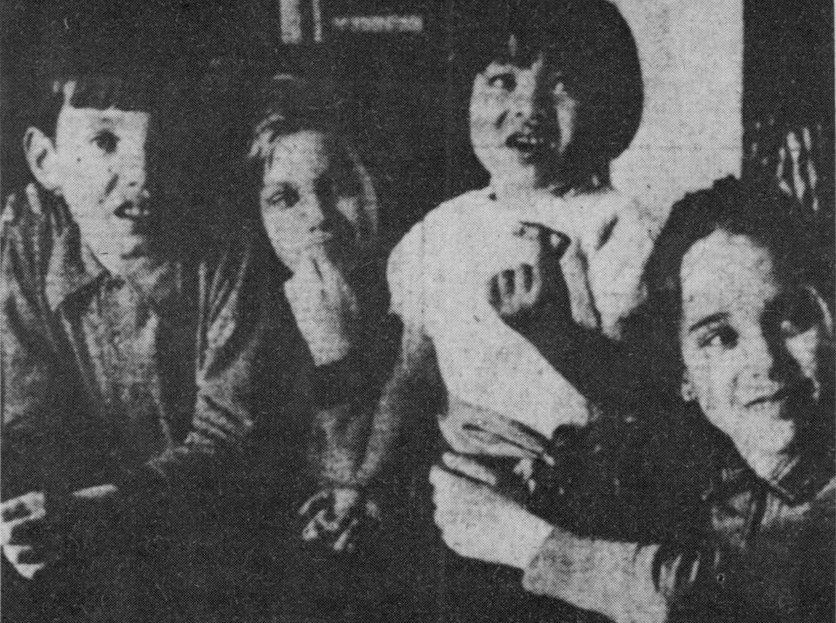

Associated Press

Nguyen Thi Thu Cuc, a 3-year-old Vietnamese orphan adopted by Robert and Josepha Flanigan, after arriving at her new home in Edison, N.J. The other Flanigan children are Robert, 7, James, 5, and, at right, Caroline, 9.

Today's Sections

Index to Subjects

CHIANG KAI-SHEK IS DEAD IN TAIPEI

Continued From Page 1, Col. 4

and Stalin, Chiang was known in World War II as one of the Big Four leaders of the Allies in the war against Germany, Italy and Japan.

His Nationalist Government was driven from the mainland by the Communists in 1949 and has been in exile here since then.

The death of General Chiang is not expected to have any significant impact on the policies of the Nationalist Chinese Government or on the political morale of the people here.

The President had not taken an active role in governmental affairs for nearly three years, and was seen in public only rarely after he fell ill with pneumonia in the summer of 1972.

Most people in Taiwan felt that the political succession had already taken place. His elder son became Premier in May, 1972, and since then has consolidated his position as the undisputed leader of the Government.

While the death of General Chiang is an emotional shock to many here, particularly those who followed him to Taiwan from the Chinese mainland, it is unlikely to have a demoralizing effect on the people.

The major reason is the emergence of his son as a strong leader who has seemed to gain the confidence of most of the population. Although General Chiang had groomed his son for leadership, moving him through a succession of increasingly important positions, he was not well known in his own right until he became Premier.

Once out of the shadow of his father and the circle of senior advisers, the Premier surprised most observers of Taiwan politics by the sense of assurance with which he took over the Government and the swiftness with which he stamped his own style on the administration.

In particular, his frequent inspection trips to construction sites and talks with farmers, his concentration on economic problems and his appointment of a Cabinet including native Taiwanese gave him a reputation as a more modern and practical politician than was his father.

Taiwan's economic and internal political stability in recent years, despite diplomatic reversals, has contributed to an increased sense of confidence.

Although the last four years have seen the United States begin a process of détente with the People's Republic of China, Taiwan's loss of its United Nations seat and decisions by more than 30 countries to break relations with Taiwan and to recognize Peking, daily life in Taiwan for most people has been little affected.

Until the recent world economic recession hurt Taiwan's export markets, the years since the expulsion from the United Nations had brought the biggest economic boom the island had ever know. Despite a decline in the growth rate, the economy is still considered basically sound.

No-Compromise Policy

The majority opinion here is that President Chiang's death will not lead the Government to alter any of its basic policies, including a frequently proclaimed determination never to compromise with the Communists on the mainland.

But some political observers, both Chinese and foreign, believe the passing of the President will set the stage for a de-emphasis of the declared obligation to recover the mainland, and an increasing stress on Taiwan as an entity separate from China.

Most such observers expect that such a development will be gradual and doubt that it will involve an open declaration of the establishment of a Republic of Taiwan with no political ties to or claims on the mainland.

Such a declaration is considered improbable for both external and domestic reasons. It might serve only as a provocation to Peking, which insists that Taiwan is China's territory, and it might weaken the hold of the basically "mainlander" leadership by stirring demands among native Taiwanese for a greater share of authority.

Hardly anyone in Taiwan expects General Chiang's death to make the Nationalist Government any more likely to consider an accord with the Communists. Officials maintain that this position does not represent stubbornness, but rather adherence to basic principles and confidence that Taiwan has the strength and internal stability to survive.

The Life of Chiang Kai-shek: A Leader Who Was Thrust Aside by Revolution

By ALDEN WHITMAN

Twenty-two years after rising to the leadership of China in a bloody coup against the Communists in 1927, Chiang Kai-shek lost the mantle he had so dearly gained and so precariously maintained to a triumphant Communist revolution. Thrust aside at the age of 62 by the convulsion that shook half a billion people and an ancient culture, he spun out his long life on the small island of Taiwan in the East China Sea 110 miles from the mainland.

There he presided sternly over a martial group of 2 million Nationalist refugees and about 11 million Taiwanese. At first he talked aggressively of returning to the mainland by force; but as that possibility faded he waited hopefully for the Communist regime to collapse of its own inner tensions and for the Chinese to welcome back a faithful statesman.

That did not take place either. On the contrary, the People's Republic of China grew in internal strength and international might, displacing Chiang's regime in the United Nations in 1971 and winning diplomatic recognition by 1972 from all the major powers except the United States. And even this country, as a result of President Nixon's visit to Peking in 1972, all but dropped Chiang diplomatically. His bitterness in his last years was enormous.

During his years as China's leader, Chiang ruled an uneasy and restive country, beset by intractable domestic strife as well as by armed conflict with Japanese invaders. Although China had a national government for these two decades, there was so much political, social and economic turmoil, so much Japanese aggression to cope with—it started in 1931 in Manchuria and intensified in 1937—that national unity was more fiction that reality.

Nonetheless, Chiang was the visible symbol of China; a member, with Franklin D. Roosevelt, Winston Churchill and Josef Stalin, of the Big Four; his nation's supreme commander in World War II; and the principal architect of a domestic policy that aimed, however unsuccessfully, at internal stability.

To the world, Chiang's lean, trim, erect figure bespoke resoluteness and determination. His asceticism and personal austerity seemed to befit a man of dedication to the ideal of a China resurgent against insuperable odds.

Faced Herculean Tasks

Having emerged to power in a country the victim of a quarter-century and more of political decay, Chiang faced Herculean tasks once his National Government at Nanking was recognized by the Western powers in November, 1928. With the nation in fragments, he chose to seek political unification by force of arms in precedence to attacking fundamental social and economic problems, especially those centering on agriculture, in which the great bulk of the population was engaged. Only later, and under enormous pressure, did he turn his attention to rebuffing the Japanese.

The choice proved unwise, for his campaigns and his battles with local satraps permitted the Communists to befriend the peasantry, harness the forces of social revolution that had been gathering since 1911 and, ultimately, to align themselves with a nascent nationalism in the anti-Japanese war.

Had China been more than a geographical expression in the nineteen-twenties, Chiang might have imposed a viable government on it. But the weaknesses of the social system were such that his regime was quickly enmeshed in corruption and guile. Despite Chiang's personal probity, he could not contain the rapaciousness of others, with the result that his policies were sapped from the start.

Compounding this state of affairs, the Chinese family system, once a force for stability, proved unsuited to modern nationalism. Many officials thought more of bettering their families than they did of furthering the national interest, a concept difficult in any case for many Buddhist- and Confucian-oriented Chinese to grasp and apply. One result was that widespread nepotism, from which not even Chiang himself was entirely immune, enfeebled the Government and its bureaucracy.

To many Americans Chiang was a heroic and embattled figure, the embodiment of a "new" China struggling to adapt politically and culturally to the 20th century. He was widely pictured as indomitable and as a bulwark against Communism in Asia.

From the nineteen-forties onward, Chiang's chief promoters and partisans were collectively known as the China Lobby. According to W. A. Swanberg, the historian and biographer, "the China Lobby was an amorphous group, preponderantly Republican, boosting Chiang for reasons of anti-Communism and also as an issue against the Democrats." It included such persons as Alfred Kohlberg, an importer of Chinese lace; Representative Walter H. Judd, Republican of Minnesota; Senator William F. Knowland, Republican of California; Mrs. Claire Chennault, widow of the Flying Tiger leader; Thomas Corcoran, the Washington lawyer; Senator Styles Bridges, Republican of New Hampshire; William Loeb, the New Hampshire publisher; and Henry R. Luce, the publisher of Time, Life and Fortune.

Because of an emotional and ideological commitment to Chiang and his command of three national magazines, Mr. Luce was among the lobby's most powerful members. His periodicals published eulogistic articles about Chiang and optimistic assessments of the situation in China.

From 1945 to 1949, the lobby tirelessly pressured Congress and the Administration for military and economic aid to Chiang, at least $30-million of which was reported to have been pocketed by his generals. In all, about $3-billion in arms and aid was given Chiang, Seymour Topping estimated in his book "Journey Between Two Chinas." Much of the military equipment, he added, wound up in the hands of the Communists.

At the same time Gen. David Barr, chief of the American military advisers to Chiang, reported to Washington that there was "complete ineptness of military leaders and widespread corruption and dishonesty throughout the armed forces."

Such was the influence of the China Lobby, however, that this somber evaluation of Chiang's leadership was submerged. The notion was advanced that abandonment of the generalissimo would be an act of surrender to Communism.

After the Nationalist debacle, which had been foreseen by General Barr and many other Americans on the scene, the China Lobby helped to savage a number of Foreign Service officers in China who had long warned of Chiang's fatal shortcomings. In the McCarthyite atmosphere of the early fifties, such diplomats as John Paton Davies and John Carter Vincent were accused of

(continued)

Chiang and Mao Tse-tung at a 1945 meeting set up by the United States.

having "lost" China to the Communists. Even Dean Acheson, President Harry S. Truman's Secretary of State, and Gen. George C. Marshall, who had headed a fruitless mission to China just after the war, were not immune from attacks, although both were stanch anti-Communists.

Indeed, in the early fifties, the myth was widely propagated that Chiang was more the victim of State Department "subversives" than of his own weaknesses.

Even in exile in Taiwan, Chiang retained a remarkable image in the United States. The China Lobby and Mr. Luce continued to praise him and to urge American financial and military support of him; but into the bargain Chiang fitted into the Communist-containment policy of the Eisenhower Administration, a circumstance that helped to fortify his position militarily and diplomatically. A pro-Chiang policy carried over into the nineteen-sixties also.

Policy Widely Supported

Although it seemed evident to many that his Taiwan regime was not a world power, it retained not only its membership in the United Nations but also its seat as a permanent member of the Security Council until 1971. The United States consistently voted against the admission of the People's Republic to the United Nations, and it was widely supported in this policy by Americans who saw desertion of Chiang as a betrayal of an old ally and as a concession to the forces of Communism. As recently as October, 1972, Chinag's partisans, describing him as a "brilliant leader," publicly deplored his Government's ouster from the United Nations.

Another aspect of Chiang that appealed to many in this country was his conversion to Protestantism—he joined the Methodist Church in 1931—and his professed devotion to New Testament ideals. Missionaries portrayed the generalissimo in a favorable light, citing his protection of their activities and his comprehension of Christian ethics. Some of the more visionary of his admirers hoped that he would lead the way to the Christianization of China.

Chiang, however, was not a missionary ruler, despite his creation of the New Life Movement, a politico-spiritual program containing elements of Christianity. Deeply imbued with Confucius' thought, he believed with the pre-Christian philosopher, "If the ruler is virtuous, the people will also be virtuous." He also believed in rigorous self-examination of his moral actions, and he kept a diary in which he set down every week the results of his introspection. This gave him both an inner certainty and an insularity to criticism.

Scolding his subordinates, he seemed like a Savonarola, an impression reinforced by his drawn, monklike face with its severe cropped mustache and his shaven pate. And, like a monk, he set aside a time for daily meditation and Bible reading. Moreover, he regularly attended Sunday religious services.

Unlike some of his associates, Chiang Kai-shek, whose given name can be rendered in English as "Firm Rock," led an austere and frugal life, albeit in surroundings of imperial opulence. He made a point of eating simply and sparingly, drinking powdered milk or weak green tea. He did not smoke, gamble or indulge in recreations more frivolous than walking.

He dressed customarily in a natty but otherwise undistinguished brown high-necked tunic and matching trousers. But relaxing at home he would wear a traditional long gown and skull cap. He spoke a rough Mandarin for state occasions, although his conversational tongue was the Ningpo dialect.

Another aspect of Chiang's traditionalism was his belief in a system of personal loyalty, in which the subject was loyal to the ruler, the son to the father, the younger to older. This led to situations where he imputed disloyalty to his critics; it also led to his reliance on a very small circle of advisers, only a few of whom felt they could speak up to him with impunity.

Added to this was a shortness of temper that exhibited itself in bizarre ways. Once, for example, Chiang was witnessing a movie at home that contained a scene displeasing to him. He stalked out and ordered the hapless projectionist thrashed soundly. And, on a more con-

Generalissimo Chiang Kai-shek and Madame Chiang, to whom many Chinese looked for leadership.

sequential level, he was capable of jailing or otherwise punishing those who crossed him.

Chiang was very much a product of the breakup of the Manchu Dynasty and the conditions of near-anarchy that ensued. He was born in the waning years of the dynasty—on Oct. 31, 1887, at Fenghua, Chekiang Province, 100 miles south of Shanghai. The son of a petty salt merchant and his "second wife," or concubine, he had a grim boyhood. On his 50th birthday he recalled:

"My father died when I was 9 years old. The miserable condition of my family at that time is beyond description. My family, solitary and without influence, became at once the target of much insult and abuse.

"It was entirely due to my mother [a devout Buddhist] and her kindness and perseverance that the family was saved from utter ruin. For a period of 17 years—from the age of 9 until I was 25 years old—my mother never spent a day free from domestic difficulties."

Meeting With Dr. Sun

The events of his youth are obscure, but somehow he was able in 1906 to enter the Paoting Military Academy, where he did well enough to be sent to Japan in 1907 for two years of advanced instruction. There he became acquainted with a number of Chinese revolutionaries, including, it is said, Dr. Sun Yat-sen, one of the principal founders of modern China.

Chiang joined the Tung Meng Hui, a secret society that was the forerunner of the Kuomintang, the Nationalist party, which he dominated after Dr. Sun's death in March, 1925. When revolts broke out in China in October, 1911, Chiang resigned from the Japanese Army (he had signed up as an officer), returned to the mainland and took the field against the Manchu forces. A capable commander, he led a successful attack on Hangchow and later held military positions in the Shanghai area.

In the next 10 years, however, his fortunes were mixed, and it is believed that at one point he quarreled with Dr. Sun. According to O. Edmund Clubb's "Twentieth Century China," Chiang "made his [temporary] exit from the political scene in 1913 and engaged in brokerage in Shanghai for nearly a decade."

"It was during that period," the book said, "that he established connections with the powerful political and financial figures in Shanghai that were to have so important an influence on his later orientation."

By 1921-22 Chiang returned to military-political life as chief of staff of Dr. Sun's Canton-based regime. Rickety and in constant clash with warlords and with the shadowy official government in Peking, this regime fortuitously sought and received military and political help from the newly established Soviet Union.

Chiang was sent to Moscow to help organize this assistance, meeting many of the top Soviet revolutionaries in the process. One result of his mission was that scores of Soviet advisers went to China and became influential in the Kuomintang, attempting to give it a left-wing orientation. Indeed, members of the new Chinese Communist party were encouraged to join it. Chiang, as another consequence of the mission, organized the Whampoa Military Academy, which trained officers for the Kuomintang army.

With Dr. Sun's death the bond between the Communists and Chiang's more conservative group in the Kuomintang dissolved; and in a tragedy of plot and counterplot Chiang slaughtered thousands of Communists and workers in Canton and Shanghai and, in 1927-28, organized his own National Government at Nanking.

According to some China specialists, Chiang was materially helped by Shanghai financial interests and wealthy landowners.

"The bankers and industrialists of Shanghai, led by the brilliant Soong-Kung Family group, had now come to terms with Chiang," George H. Kerr wrote in "Formosa Betrayed," adding: "Apparently, Chiang made a bargain. In return for financial support on a large scale he agreed to exclude left-wing elements and Communists from the new 'National Revolutionary Government.'

"The bargain was cemented by a marriage between Chiang and an 'unclaimed jewel' of the Soong family, the beautiful Soong Mei-ling, aged 26, the youngest sister of T. V. Soong [the powerful banker]."

The marriage with the American-educated and Christianized Miss Soong was clouded at the outset by disputes over Chiang's divorce from a previous wife. His subsequent baptism, however, mollified his missionary critics, who became his most persistent and influential advocates among Americans.

Over the years Mrs. Chiang was not only a close confidante of her husband but also his best link with the economic power structure. Members of her family held key Government and party posts and dealt also in diplomacy.

With the coup that brought Chiang to power, the Chinese Communist party was shattered. Its leaders and some members fled the coastal cities and found refuge in the Chingkang Mountains of Kiangsi. Over the next few years Chiang, with the expert advice of imported Nazi generals, sought to eliminate the Communists; but despite several proclamations of success the Communists proved elusive. In fact, they battened on campaigns against them and, after breaking free of an attempt to trap them in Kiangsi, conducted the epic Long March through the wilderness of western China and reached safety in Yenan in the northwest.

Meantime, Chiang's regime failed to achieve unification of China. True, there was a national currency and a national legislative apparatus; but what passed for a national administration at Nanking was in fact only one of many regional factions of limited authority and influence. Instead of subduing the more powerful northern warlords, Chiang preferred to make deals; if they would accept him as titular head of state, he in return would respect their local sovereignty.

Thus the Nationalist regime became a loose coalition of military chieftains bound to Chiang by pledges of personal loyalty. This situation was exacerbated by the diversion of Nationalist energy and money into futile pacification drives against the Communists.

What made these campaigns so vain was that social and land reform under the Nationalists was largely a matter of rhetoric. The Communists, meanwhile, were winning the peasantry by putting their reforms into effect.

Despite his aloofness, Chiang was aware that he governed a volatile country; but his ideological recipe was vague and moralistic, whereas that of the Communists was precise and empirical. The New Life Movement, for example, encouraged the young to lead lives of Christian piety and Confucian virtue, while the Communists, in addition to promising an exciting new world, took active steps to improve living conditions in the here and now.

To students and patriots of virtually every political stripe, Chiang's tepid program seemed all the more irrelevant in the face of Japanese aggression. The Japanese threat was unmistakable from 1931 onward, but Chiang's "pacification" projects only postponed a confrontation with the Japanese while permitting them to gobble up Manchuria and convert it into a puppet state.

Alarmed by the possibility that the Japanese would strike southward, the northern warlords rebelled in 1936. In theory up to then these warlords, principally Marshal Chang Hsueh-Liang, were battling the Communists in Shensi; but, in fact, agitation for a united front against the Japanese was so effective that little blood was being shed. Chiang arrived in Sian, Marshal Chiang's capital in December, 1936, to investigate, and was promptly arrested on Chang's orders. The generalissimo, attempting to flee in his nightgown, was easily captured.

Chang, known as the Young Marshal, presented his superior with a series of demands that included immediate cessation of the civil war against the Communists in favor of a general policy of armed resistance to Japan in cooperation with the Communists.

Some insurgents wanted to execute Chiang, but he was saved by the timely intervention of the Communist leader Chou En-lai, who traveled to Sian to support the national united front program. In weird negotiations involving the Communists, the Chang dissidents and high officials from Nanking, Chiang capitulated and was released. The shotgun alliance also had one notable side-

(continued)

effect—a decision by the Soviet Union to bolster Chiang with air power and military advisers.

Role in World War II

The Japanese, perturbed at the prospect of a unified China, struck south from Peking in 1937-38. The ferocity of the onslaught, while it held the united front together for a time, drove Chinese troops out of key coastal cities and obliged the Government to shift its capital from Nanking to the smaller interior city of Chungking. However, when the Japanese armies stalled and the war entered a seven-year period of attrition, the Chiang-Communist alliance disintegrated under the impact of mutual suspicions and political intrigue.

With United States entry into World War II in late 1941, American strategists saw China as a potentially effective front against Japan, and military and economic aid was dispatched there. However, Chiang's relations with Americans sent to help him were less than cordial, especially those with Gen. Joseph W. (Vinegar Joe) Stilwell, who was sent to Chungking in 1942 as Chiang's chief of staff.

Meantime, to overcome what Mr. Clubb described as Chiang's "pronounced reluctance to take the field" against Japan, the generalissimo was invited, toward the close of 1943, to confer with President Roosevelt and Prime Minister Churchill at Cairo. There he obtained a promise for the postwar return to China of Manchuria and of Formosa (Taiwan), which had been under Japanese rule since 1895. A plan for joint Allied action in Burma was also agreed upon.

General Stilwell, who loved the Chinese and spoke their language, was President Roosevelt's choice to be commander in chief of Chinese and American forces in China. But Chiang and the outspoken general fell out. In his report to the War Department, General Stilwell said that Chiang sought to "dominate rather than unify and lead" China against Japan.

Confiding to his diary, the general was even more blunt. He wrote:

"I never have heard Chiang Kai-shek say a single thing that indicated gratitude to the President or to our country for the help we were extending to him. Invariably, when anything was promised, he would want more.

"He would make comparisons between the huge amounts of Lend-Lease supplies going to Great Britain and Russia with the meager trickle going to China. He would complain that the Chinese had been fighting for six or seven years and yet we gave them practically nothing.

"It would have of course been undiplomatic to go into the nature of the military effort Chiang Kai-shek had made since 1938. It was practically zero."

By 1944, with the military situation in China in disarray save in the Communist-controlled areas, the United States proposed that General Stilwell be given command of the Nationalist troops. "With further delay, it may be too late to avert a military catastrophe tragic both to China and to our Allied plans for the early overthrow of Japan," President Roosevelt cabled Chiang.

However, according to "Stilwell and the American Experience in China" by Barbara Tuchman, Chiang "thoroughly intended in his own mind to stay out of the war . . . no matter how much of east China was lost, until the Allies should defeat Japan and he could emerge on the winning side." Nonetheless, Mrs. Tuchman said, the generalissimo proved devious, giving General Stilwell the impression in an interview in September, 1944, that he was indeed commander of the Chinese Army.

At the same time, Chiang interposed conditions, among them control of millions in American Lend-Lease supplies lest any arms get into the hands of the Communists, whose efficient troops General Stilwell wanted to use against the Japanese. The Communists, Mrs. Tuchman wrote, were willing to fight under the general, but not under Chiang.

Chiang's backing and filling infuriated General Stilwell. He often referred to the generalissimo in private as "the Peanut," and now his diary contained such phrases as "that hickory nut he uses for a head." "He is impossible," the general wrote at one point.

In addition to Lend-Lease control, Chiang wanted effective authority over the general in the matter of strategy and tactics. In attempting to reach an understanding with Chiang through the wily T.V. Soong, the general remarked that what Chiang wanted in a commander was "an over-all stooge."

In the face of Chiang's calculated reluctance to place General Stilwell in full command, President Roosevelt sent the generalissimo a strong, almost peremptory, cable, saying, in part:

"It appears plainly evident to all of us here that all your and our efforts to save China are to be lost by further delays."

General Stilwell himself handed the message to Chiang, writing afterward that the "harpoon" hit the generalissimo "in the solar plexus and went right through him." Shocked though he was by the President's bluntness, Chiang almost immediately rose to heights of wrath. According to Mrs. Tuchman, "He knew he could not accept the American demand . . . without opening the way to his own discard. If the Americans succeeded in imposing Stilwell on him against his will, they might do likewise in the matter of the Communists."

The result was Chiang's formal demand for General Stilwell's recall, an action to which a weary President Roosevelt acceded. He was not prepared "to impose an American commander against the express wishes of a chief of state," Mrs. Tuchman said. The general's reaction was succinct and prescient:

"If Old Softy gives in on this as he apparently has, the Peanut will be out of control from now on."

The general's leavetaking had overtones of comic opera. Chiang offered him the Special Grand Cordon of the Blue Sky and White Sun, a decoration that was refused. There was, though, a final tea. Describing it, Mrs. Tuchman said:

"Chiang Kai-shek, with T.V. Soong at his elbow, was gracious. He regretted all this very much, it was only due to differences of personality, he hoped Stilwell would continue to be China's friend. . . . The guest was laconic."

In a news article on the Stilwell ouster, Brooks Atkinson, a New York Times correspondent in China, wrote that the action represented the "political triumph of a moribund antidemocratic regime."

Chiang's hold on the Nationalist leadership was prolonged, at least temporarily, by mounting American successes against Japan in the Pacific in 1945 that culminated in that country's unconditional surrender in August.

In December, 1945, after the close of the war, President Truman sent Gen. George C. Marshall to China with orders to unify and pacify the country. He exerted enormous pressure on Chiang and the Communists to end the civil strife that had erupted afresh with the defeat of Japan. On Jan. 10, 1946, a cease-fire accord was signed; but the truce was quickly breached and before long open civil war raged through the nation.

With three million troops to Mao Tse-tung's one million, Chiang gained the upper hand in the first few months of the war; but once the Communists felt strong enough to mount an offensive in the spring of 1947, it was clear where the initiative lay.

As Communist forces were overrunning the country, the United States issued a 1,054-page White Paper, writing off Nationalist China and attributing Communist successes to Chiang's military and political errors. Published in the summer of 1949, the State Department document dourly recounted Chiang's dissipation of the more than $3-billion in American aid his regime had received between August, 1945, and the middle of 1948.

Details of White Paper

In asserting the futility of additional help to Chiang, Secretary of State Acheson said in the White Paper:

"A large proportion of the military supplies furnished the Chinese armies by the United States since V-J Day has fallen into the hands of the Chinese Communists through the military ineptitude of the Nationalist leaders, their defections and surrenders, and the absence among their forces of the will to fight.

"It has been urged that relatively small amounts of additional aid—military and economic—to the National Government would have enabled it to destroy Communism in China. The most trustworthy military, economic and political information available to our Government does not bear out this view.

"A realistic appraisal of conditions in China, past and present, leads to the conclusion that the only alternative open to the United States was full-scale intervention in behalf of a Government which had lost the confidence of its own troops and its own people."

Earlier, as Nationalist defeats turned into a rout and the Communists were pressing for the arrest of Chiang and his wife as war criminals, the generalissimo issued a statement of resignation as President of the Republic on Jan. 1, 1949. Three weeks later, he paid a ceremonial farewell in Nanking by driving in his Cadillac to the Sun Yat-sen Mausoleum. After bowing three times before a marble statue of the preeminent founder of modern China, he retired to his birthplace to prepare his retreat to Taiwan.

Air and naval units were transferred to the island along with gold and silver bullion reserves. "The generalissimo also clamped tighter military and police control over the restive Taiwanese," Mr. Topping wrote in "Journey Between Two Chinas." The island had been returned to Chinese sovereignty after Japan's surrender, and some Nationalist forces had been sent there in 1945.

"The Nationalist troops . . . looted and stripped the island, which had been developed with Japanese capital [since 1895]," the book reported. Many Kuomintang officials expropriated land from the Taiwanese for themselves. In February and March, 1947, the Taiwanese demonstrated against the sacking of their island, demanding that the Nationalist governor, Chen Yi, reform his corrupt, dictatorial administration.

"Chen Yi's response was to bring in additional troops from the mainland and put down the demonstration in an orgy of killing in which between 10,000 and 20,000 Taiwanese were massacred, including several thousand of the island's political and economic leaders and intellectual élite.

"On the generalissimo's orders, Chen Yi eventually was shot for his excesses but the population of the island . . . remained hostile to the mainlanders."

In December, 1949, Chiang came out of retirement and flew to Taiwan, declaring Taipei to be the temporary capital of China, a status it still retains, according to the Nationalists. On March 1, 1950, Chiang announced that he had resumed the Presidency of China.

In the next two decades he received hundreds of millions in American military aid that permitted him to build a smartly turned out armed force. Over the same period, private American capital flowed into the island and built up a network of light industry, chiefly in the textile and electronics fields. Low labor costs—Chiang was not tolerant of trade unions—contributed to creation of an economic boom. Thriving industry, however, was accompanied by repressive military rule.

Simultaneously, the Nationalists introduced land reforms and scientific agricultural practices that permitted the island abundant crops, some of them for export.

Chiang Kai-shek at the 100th birthday celebration of Sun Yat-sen, founder of the Republic of China, in 1965.

In the bitterness of exile and defeat, Chiang said:

"I must put the blame on myself. The disastrous military reverses on the mainland were not due to the overwhelming strength of the Communists, but due to the organizational collapse, loose discipline and low spirits of the [Nationalist] party members."

Outbreak of Korean Conflict

At that moment the generalissimo seemed destined to fade away in a shower of rhetoric. He was rescued, however, by an unforeseen international event—the outbreak of the Korean conflict in June, 1950, and the participation of the Soviet Union on the side of the North Koreans.

The United States assigned its Seventh Fleet to the Strait of Taiwan and began to bolster Chiang as a counterweight to Communism in Asia. Political, economic and military assistance was poured into Taiwan. In May, 1951, an American mission began to equip and train a new Nationalist army, which eventually totaled 600,000 men and ate up the bulk of the island's budget. Moreover, in 1954, the United States and the Chinese regime concluded a mutual defense treaty.

Chiang, for his part, became emboldened to think of returning in triumph to the mainland. Inaugurated for a fourth term as President in 1966, he called himself an "undiscouraged old soldier," and vowed that he "would exterminate Mao Tse-tung and his cohorts, liberate our mainland compatriots and establish on the ruins a new country of unity and freedom."

In private, however, Chiang was less sanguine about his chances. He hoped for a return, of course, but he expected that it would follow a political collapse on the mainland. Meantime, he engaged himself in keeping his army on the ready and in improving the economy of Taiwan. Paradoxically, as the island became more prosperous, many among his followers grew more concerned with benefiting from Taiwan's wealth and less eager to embark on uncertain military ventures.

With the years, Chiang's hold on the political stucture of Taiwan tightened. Part of this owed to the deference that Chinese customarily pay to age and part to the vigilance of his secret police and the repressions of the regime. Below the surface, however, there was a discreet restiveness among the younger sons and daughters of the mainland refugees who wanted a freer political and cultural life than Chiang's regime was willing to accord them. This yearning was joined by many Taiwanese, who never ceased to resent Chiang's intrusion in 1949 and who were still bitter over the massacre of thousands of them by Nationalist troops.

Chiang's official international stature began to erode seriously in the early nineteen-sixties, when support for the admission of the People's Republic of China to the United Nations gained an increasing number of votes with each session of the General Assembly.

Finally, in 1971, the Communists were voted into the world organization. This recognition of the realities of global politics was followed in February, 1972, by President Richard M. Nixon's visit to Peking and the establishment of an entente of sorts between Peking and Washington. The United States, however, did not immediately recognize the People's Republic and thus continued diplomatic relations with Chiang. Later in 1972 Japan recognized Peking, further isolating Chiang in the world community.

In 1972 Chiang was sworn in for his fifth six-year term as head of state, but soon afterward he fell ill and tacitly surrendered control to his elder son, Chiang Ching-kuo, the child of his first marriage, who had been named Deputy Premier. Chiang and his second wife were childless; another acknowledged son, Chiang Wei-kuo, shunned political life.

Though enfeebled toward the close of his life, Chiang never admitted defeat. Last December, the 25th anniversary of his arrival on Taiwan, passed as an all-but-forgotten occasion. There were no speeches, editorials or public commemoration. Indeed, it was more than two year since the generalissimo had appeared in public, and there has been no new photograph of him in more than a year.

WINSTON CHURCHILL'S LIFE: A SPECIAL SECTION APPEARS IN TODAY'S ISSUE

"All the News That's Fit to Print"

The New York Times

LATE CITY EDITION

Weather: Fair, very cold today and tonight. Chance of snow tomorrow. Temp. range: today 24-14; Sunday 33-26. Full U.S. report on Page 30.

VOL. CXIV..No. 39,083. | NEW YORK, MONDAY, JANUARY 25, 1965. | TEN CENTS

CHURCHILL IS DEAD AT 90; THE WORLD MOURNS HIM; STATE FUNERAL SATURDAY

Karsh, Ottawa

SIR WINSTON CHURCHILL

MAYOR ACCUSES 'KENNEDY BLOC' OF POWER PLAY

Says Chiefs at Albany Are 'More Concerned With '66 and '68 Than 1965'

FIRM OPPOSITION URGED

Wagner Hails Opponents of Steingut and Bronston in Leadership Struggle

By CLAYTON KNOWLES

Mayor Wagner charged yesterday that a power play by political bosses "more concerned with 1966 and 1968 than with 1965" had produced the Democratic leadership deadlock in the Legislature.

A high City Hall spokesman said the Mayor's two-page statement was aimed at the "Kennedy bloc of leaders" who, he said, were viewing the election of an Assembly Speaker and Senate majority leader chiefly in terms of power it would give them in the gubernatorial race in 1966 and the Presidential election in 1968.

As the Mayor struck back at critics, William H. McKeon, Democratic state chairman, was receiving a resounding vote of confidence from county leaders at an Albany meeting. The Mayor charged a week ago that Mr. McKeon had offered committee chairmanships and "lulus"—payments in lieu of itemized expenses—in an attempt to turn the leadership election.

Public Hearings Near

The Mayor got a report on the Albany developments, but he had no comment. Members of his staff said they were "temporarily out of touch" with him.

Public hearings on the Mayor's charge against Mr. McKeon will be held Wednesday and Thursday by the State Investigation Commission. Jacob Grumet, the committee's chairman, said the purpose was to let the public judge for itself whether the allegations had been sustained.

Mr. Wagner will be the first witness as the hearings open at 10 A.M. Wednesday in the commission offices at 270 Broadway. Mr. McKeon and other representatives of the "Kennedy bloc" will be among the other eight high Democratic officials who will be heard.

In interpreting Mr. Wagner's latest statement, the City Hall aide stressed that no personal criticism was intended of United States Senator Robert F. Kennedy. He sought the Vice-Pres-

Continued on Page 17, Column 4

New Math Is Replacing Third 'R'

School Pupils Learn Ideas Once Taught Chiefly in College

Some Experts Fear Haste in Change Is Hurting Teaching

By HARRY SCHWARTZ

Warning to elementary and high school students, parents and teachers: Brace yourselves. The "new mathematics" of today may be followed by an even newer and stranger mathematics. You may look back on the present as "the good old days."

And yet, there are those who say the new mathematics already introduced has been thrown into the curriculum, in many cases, too hastily. They contend that the mathematics revolution has sometimes taken place so rapidly that teachers have not received adequate training to teach it.

The new mathematics is an attempt to introduce into elementary and high school teaching some of the ideas and points of view that have dominated mathematics research for more than a century. The aim is to help children to understand mathematics as well as to do it.

It is a good deal more advanced than the "old mathematics," which, say the proponents of the new, was little more than rote memorization.

One warning of possible things to come is contained in a published proposal that tomorrow's junior high school youngsters study derivatives, Diophantine equations and iterative procedures, and that high school students explore such other esoteric fields as the topology of the complex plane and the matrices of a transformation.

The proposal is in a report of the 1963 Cambridge Conference on School Mathematics, held at Cambridge, Mass.

New Reforms Urged

One influential elder statesman among American mathematicians thinks that even this proposal does not go far enough. He recently submitted to the Carnegie Corporation a memorandum calling for even more radical revision of the curriculum below college level.

The reforms now being introduced, he said, are "timid and patently inadequate." The corporation asked that his name be withheld.

The United States Commissioner of Education, Francis Keppel, has declared that the schools must aim toward the more advanced curriculums that have been proposed. But he warned that not only would most teachers "be completely incapable of teaching much of the mathematics" set forth in the Cambridge proposal but also "most teachers would be hard put to comprehend it."

One of the voices raised against the speed of the mathematics teaching revolution in the elementary and high schools has been that of Dr. Max Beberman, the noted University of Illinois pioneer in the field.

Dr. Beberman, a stocky man, whose enthusiasm is infectious, told mathematics teachers in Montreal last month that "a major national scandal" may be in the making because of hasty introduction of the new mathematics in the elementary

Continued on Page 18, Column 1

PRESIDENT HOPES TO GO TO LONDON; HEALTH IMPROVES

Statement Praises Churchill—Johnson and His Wife Both Rally From Colds

By CHARLES MOHR

Special to The New York Times

WASHINGTON, Jan. 24—President Johnson, still in a hospital bed with a bad cold, said today that he wanted to attend the funeral of Sir Winston Churchill and that he would do so if his health permitted.

If he goes to London for Sir Winston's funeral and informed sources said he surely would it will be the first trip abroad by Mr. Johnson since he became President on Nov. 22, 1963.

The President appeared to be recovering rapidly from the painful cough and tracheitis—or sore throat for which he was admitted to the United States Naval Hospital at Bethesda, Md. at 2:50 A.M. yesterday.

"The improvement is considerable," said the White House press secretary, George E. Reedy. "The harsh, racking cough is gone. It is an extremely light cough."

Mrs. Johnson, who was admitted to the same hospital with a head cold yesterday afternoon, was also improved and "resting comfortably," Mr. Reedy said.

Mr. Johnson was told of Sir Winston's death at 3:50 A.M. by a Navy chief pharmacist mate, Thomas Mills, Mr. Reedy said. He had asked to be told at once if Sir Winston died.

'He Is History's Child'

At 10:08 A.M., Mr. Reedy released a statement by the President on Sir Winston's death, which said:

"He is history's child, and what he said and what he did will never die."

In the afternoon the President signed an Executive order instructing that the American flag be flown at half-staff in the United States and at all the United States installations abroad through Saturday, the day Sir Winston will be buried. Flags will fly at half-mast on all United States ships.

Four newsmen, representing the many reporters covering the President's illness at the Naval Hospital, were allowed to see him for eight minutes today, and they asked if he would attend Sir Winston's funeral.

"I want very much to go," Mr. Johnson said. "It all depends on how I feel."

Propped on four pillows and wearing green pajamas with

Continued on Page 14, Column 3

Saigon Generals Wavering In Backing Premier Huong

By SEYMOUR TOPPING

Special to The New York Times

SAIGON, South Vietnam, Jan. 24—Military leaders of South Vietnam wavered today in their support of Premier Tran Van Huong in the face of large-scale Buddhist agitation for his Government's resignation.

After intensive discussions with civilian leaders of the Government and United States Embassy officials, most of the top generals were understood to have indicated that they would continue to back the Premier.

However, no firm decision was taken on the future of the Government or on measures to be adopted to counter the Buddhist demonstrations in the main cities. These demonstrations are aimed at both the Premier and the United States, which is being denounced for supporting him.

[Paratroopers occupied a Buddhist school in Saigon Monday after they had fired tear gas into classrooms at students shouting anti-Government slogans, The Associated Press reported. About 70 persons, including 12 Buddhist monks, were arrested. Page 6.]

Buddhist leaders called at midnight a 48-hour "noncooperation strike" in the central Vietnamese cities of Hue and Quangtri, during which Americans were not to be served by shops, restaurants or other commercial establishments. The

Continued on Page 6, Column 5

FRANCO RECEIVES JEWS' SPOKESMEN

Last Such Talk by Spanish Head of State Was in 1492—Legal Status Discussed

By PAUL HOFMANN

Special to The New York Times

MADRID, Jan. 24—Generalissimo Francisco Franco has received the heads of the Jewish communities in Madrid and Barcelona and has discussed with them the status of Jews in Spain.

A participant in the unpublicized meeting, which was held Wednesday, said today that it probably was the first time that a Spanish head of state had officially seen representatives of the nation's Jews since King Ferdinand and Queen Isabella expelled thousands of Jews from Spain in 1492.

Max Mazin and Alberto Levi, representing the Jews of Madrid and Barcelona, asked Generalissimo Franco for legal recognition of Spanish Jewish communities.

The chief of state promised to examine the request. Mr. Mazin said the audience at the Pardo Palace, General Franco's residence, had been cordial. Mr. Mazin said: "Now we are waiting for a reply to our requests."

The number of Jews in Spain is put at 5,000. Most live in Barcelona; fewer than 2,000

Continued on Page 4, Column 4

BLASTS RUIN HALF OF LAOS AIR FORCE

Fighter-Bombers Destroyed at Vientiane—Explosions Believed Accidental

Special to The New York Times

VIENTIANE, Laos, Jan. 24—A series of explosions this morning demolished half the fighter-bomber strength of the Laotian Air Force and completely destroyed Vientiane's military airport.

Probably nine fighter-bombers were destroyed, as well as a Cessna reconnaissance plane, and at least two transports were damaged. A maintenance hangar was wrecked and trailers, equipment and ammunition lost.

At 9:30 A.M. a series of six loud explosions shook Vientiane. Smoke poured from the airport, .30 and .50 caliber machine-gun ammunition exploded, flames leaped from a hangar and soldiers rushed to get arms and ammunition to safety.

Guns Strewn on Field

All that remained of the T-28 fighter-bombers were propellers and engine cowlings. Machine guns were strewn all around.

Parts of the military parking area were torn up and 500-pound bombs lay around.

The explosions were believed to have been accidental, but the possibility of sabotage was not ruled out.

Airport sources said there was no attack on the airport.

A widely accepted version was that the circuit in one of the machine guns on a T-28 shorted, firing a bullet that hit

Continued on Page 6, Column 3

COUNTY LEADERS SUPPORT M'KEON

Binding Caucuses Favored—Compromise Discussed

By JOHN SIBLEY

Special to The New York Times

ALBANY, Jan. 24—Democratic county leaders gave State Chairman William H. McKeon an overwhelming vote of confidence today in his struggle with Mayor Wagner over the selection of the Legislature's leaders.

The meeting also backed a proposal to let the leadership fight be settled by binding caucuses in which the Democratic Senators and Assemblymen would vote secretly.

There appeared little hope that the action in itself would bring about an early settlement of the battle, which has left the Legislature paralyzed without a Senate majority leader and an Assembly Speaker.

Immediately after the meeting, however, Moses Weinstein, the Queens County leader and a Wagner man, conferred at an Albany restaurant with leaders of the McKeon group.

The Mayor's allies were reported ready to support Stanley Steingut of Brooklyn for Assembly Speaker if Mr. McKeon's coalition would support Thomas J. Mackell of Queens for Senate majority leader. This would be a compromise, as the McKeon group has been supporting Mr. Steingut, and the Mayor's group, Mr. Mackell.

Under such an arrangement, the majority leadership of the

Continued on Page 17, Column 3

Chou Asks New U.N. In Backing Jakarta

By The Associated Press

TOKYO, Jan. 24 — Premier Chou En-lai of Communist China called today for the creation of a new United Nations, free of "the manipulation of United States imperialism."

Mr. Chou said the United Nations had made "too many mistakes" and had "utterly disappointed" the new nations of Africa and Asia.

His denunciation of the world body, which has repeatedly barred his country from membership, came during a speech in Peking in honor of the Indonesian Foreign Minister, Dr. Subandrio, and his delegation. The remarks were monitored in a broadcast from Peking by Hsinhua, the Chinese press agency.

Praising the Jakarta regime's withdrawal from the United

Continued on Page 10, Column 5

Sleet and Rain Turn Streets Into Rivers of Slush

The New York Times (by Patrick A. Burns)

Plow clears snow from Fifth Avenue at 37th Street. Slush was piled up at many corners.

By PHILIP BENJAMIN

A warm-up is expected today, making the skies bright and the streets full of water. Foot and motor travel was hazardous yesterday after a night and day of snow and sleet. After the sleet storm ended here yesterday morning, a freezing drizzle began, turning into a freezing rain in the afternoon. In all, three inches of sleet or snow accumulated over the weekend, the fourth in a row in which it has rained or snowed. The Weather Bureau, in its forecast for today, said that skies would clear by this afternoon and that temperatures would begin rising. A high reading in the low 40's was predicted. Alternate-side parking regulations were suspended for today. Sanitation Commissioner Frank J. Lucia called on motorists to leave their cars home or, if they drove, to

Continued on Page 19, Column 4

CONGRESS TO GET '66 BUDGET TODAY

Total Expected to Be Kept Below $100 Billion—Byrd Urges Balancing Books

By MARJORIE HUNTER

Special to The New York Times

WASHINGTON, Jan. 24 — President Johnson's new budget estimates, expected to be just shy of the magic $100 billion mark, will go to Congress tomorrow.

Described as a "bare-bones" budget by sources close to the White House, it represents months of Presidential trimming of existing programs to finance new plans for the Great Society.

"I don't think the President will leave much fat for us to cut away," said George H. Mahon, the Texas Democrat who heads the House Appropriations Committee.

Less than two months ago President Johnson said at a news conference at his LBJ Ranch that he "rather doubted" that he could hold the budget under $100 billion. The nation's budget has never reached that figure.

However, by trimming here and there—including orders to close some naval yards, military bases, veterans hospitals and Veterans Administration regional offices he is believed to have kept the budget just under $100 billion.

The budget sent to Congress

Continued on Page 15, Column 3

Mrs. Cafritz Robbed Of $265,000 in Gems

By The Associated Press

WASHINGTON, Jan. 24—Mrs. Gwen Cafritz, one of Washington's best-known hostesses, was robbed at knifepoint early today of jewels insured for $265,000.

The police said four men broke into her home on fashionable Foxhall Road at 12:45 A.M., shortly after she had turned out the lights. They entered through a second-floor balcony door.

One of the men held a knife at her throat. When the 54-year-old Mrs. Cafritz started to call out, the man said: "Another word out of you and I will kill you. Where is your money?"

Mrs. Cafritz, the widow of Morris Cafritz, a builder and financier, was forced to open a bedroom wall safe and hand

Continued on Page 16, Column 5

De Gaulle in Tribute To Comrade in Arms As 'Greatest' of Era

By DREW MIDDLETON

Special to The New York Times

PARIS, Jan. 24—France mourned Sir Winston Churchill tonight as though he had been one of her sons. To the French, he was the author of victory in World War II.

President de Gaulle, who will attend the funeral of his old comrade in arms, set the tone for France's sorrow with a stately and moving tribute.

"France feels profoundly the grief which has stricken Britain," he said in a message to Queen Elizabeth II.

"For all in my country and for myself, Sir Winston is, and will forever remain, the one who, in directing to final victory the admirable effort of Great Britain, contributed powerfully to the salvation of the French people and to the liberty of the world.

"In the great drama, he was the greatest.

"I pray that Your Majesty will accept my very respectful and very saddened homage."

'From the Bottom of the Heart'

To Lady Churchill, General de Gaulle sent a message "from the bottom of the heart" telling her that the news of Sir Winston's death had aroused the greatest sorrow in France.

"For myself," he said, "I see the departure in the person of so great a man, my wartime companion and my friend."

At President de Gaulle's order, the French flag will fly at half staff for 24 hours to honor the memory of Sir Winston.

From every quarter of France and from every political party, except the Communist, came tributes to this Englishman who had been France's friend, counselor and ally in two World Wars.

One of the most poignant came from another celebrated Englishman, W. Somerset Maugham, who will celebrate his 91st birthday tomorrow.

"We have lost the greatest

Continued on Page 13, Column 5

COMMONS TO MEET

It Will Authorize Rites in St. Paul's—Burial to Be in Country

By ANTHONY LEWIS

Special to The New York Times

LONDON, Jan. 24—Winston Churchill's struggle for life ended this morning, and the people he had cherished and inspired and led through darkness mourned him as they have no other in this age.

Sir Winston died just after 8 o'clock, in the 10th day of public anxiety over his condition after a stroke. He was in his 91st year.

Britons small and great—village curate, Prime Minister and Queen—paid him tribute through the day and this evening. Statesmen around the world joined in homage to the statesman they acknowledge as the greatest of the age.

Londoners, during the last struggle, had come to accept Sir Winston's death as inevitable. There was little of the shock and horror seen in the reaction to President Kennedy's death.

Many Difficult Moments

Nevertheless, even those who consider themselves unsentimental found that they had difficult moments as they were reminded of the great Churchillian days.

The radio followed the announcement of the death with Beethoven's Symphony No. 5. The opening theme symbolizing the knock of victory—three short notes and a long note—evoked memories of Churchill's wartime gesture, two fingers held aloft in a "V for Victory."

Parliament will meet tomorrow to authorize a state funeral, the first held for a commoner in this century. For the rest of the week public affairs will be slowed almost to a stop.

The body will lie in state Wednesday, Thursday and Friday in Westminster Hall, the lofty medieval chamber adjoining Sir Winston's real home, the House of Commons.

On Saturday a state funeral service will be held at St. Paul's Cathedral. Burial will be in the country churchyard at Bladon

Continued on Page 12, Column 1

NEWS INDEX

The News Summary and Index appear today on Page 2.

The Economy Of Africa

The annual special trade and financial review of Africa begins today on Page 47.

Churchill Dies at 90

Continued From Page 1, Col. 8

village, near Blenheim Palace, the ancestral castle where Sir Winston was born. Queen Elizabeth will attend the state funeral.

Sir Winston had been failing for some years. His last public appearance was Nov. 30, his 90th birthday, when he waved to a crowd from the window of his town house. He seemed in good spirits but feeble.

The end was signaled this morning when Sir Winston's doctor and old friend, Lord Moran, arrived at the town house at 7:18. He gave the death announcement to the Press Association at 8:35, after informing Queen Elizabeth and the Prime Minister. [News of Sir Winston's death was published in the final edition of Sunday's New York Times.]

He Died 'Without Pain'

A spokesman said: "Sir Winston died in peace and without pain."

At the bedside were Lady Churchill and three living children—Randolph, Sarah and Mary.

At St. Paul's this morning the state bell, "Great Tom," tolled. It is usually rung only for the death of royalty, certain clergymen or the Lord Mayor of London.

Tonight the lights in Piccadilly Circus were out. The advertisers whose garish signs are for many a symbol of London decided to pay their respects with darkness tonight and again Saturday after the funeral.

Another change in London tradition was made in tribute to Sir Winson tonight. The Times of London broke its deeply established custom of carrying classified advertisements, not news, on the first page.

In Monday's edition, the first page is given over to pictures of Sir Winston and the start of an obituary. The classified ads were moved to Page 3 for the first time since World War I. The paper also printed a 16-page supplement on Churchill's career.

British politics, which just came to a point of fierce tension, will be frozen this week.

Conservatives, emboldened by a by-election gain, had expected to move to the attack in the House of Commons.

But all that is off for the moment. Parliament is expected to adjourn for the week or deal only with nonpartisan matters.

The Voice Heard Again

The radio today carried the Churchill voice — recordings of speeches that aroused a people to deeds of valor in a grim time.

"We shall never surrender." It was such Churchillian words as these—and the conviction with which he spokes them—that many believe saved Britain and her allies from defeat and subjection to Hitler.

The weekly journal The Spectator said:

"We are a free people because a man called Winston Churchill lived."

It is as the great wartime Prime Minister that he will above all be recorded. But those who mourned him today were moved by more than that.

WINSTON CHURCHILL: HIS LIFE AND TIMES

Architect of Allied Victory In World War II Fashioned Grand Alliance Against Axis

"YOU have sat here too long for any good you have been doing. Depart, I say, and let us have done with you. In the name of God, go!" The date was May 8, 1940. The words were those Oliver Cromwell used in dismissing the Long Parliament in 1653. The man who repeated them, with an accusatory finger pointed at Prime Minister Neville Chamberlain, was a fellow Conservative, Leopold Amery. The occasion was a bitter debate in Commons over Britain's mounting peril in the faltering, bumbling conduct of the war with Hitler's Germany.

Amery's harsh injunction echoed the country's gloomy frustrations, its demand for vigorous war leadership. For two days Chamberlain, the man who had returned from Munich in 1938 after the rape of Czechoslovakia clutching an umbrella and a piece of paper that he said guaranteed "peace in our time," tried to stave off the inevitable. But events forced his hand.

At dawn May 10, Hitler flung his proud and unbeaten forces against the Low Countries and toward France and the Channel ports. At that moment Mussolini, joined his Axis partner in the war. The hour of Britain's greatest peril since the Spanish Armada loomed.

Chamberlain stepped down, and King George VI called upon Winston Leonard Spencer Churchill, 66-year-old First Lord of the Admiralty, to prosecute the war he had for so long foreseen, and for which his life, up to that point, might be said to have been but a prelude to the greatness of leadership that carried Britain and her allies to triumph in 1945.

He struck the note of his leadership in his first report to Commons May 13 as the Nazi Panzer divisions were heading into France. It was a note he sustained with his countrymen throughout the war—candor that kindled national unity, inspirited the faltering, inspired the brave, forged the will to fight, fashioned the certainty of victory.

What Is Our Policy?

His theme was, as he put it later, "no one can guarantee success in war, but only deserve it."

"I would say to the House, as I said to those who have joined this Government: 'I have nothing to offer but blood, toil, tears and sweat.'

"We have before us an ordeal of the most grievous kind. We have before us many, many long months of struggle and of suffering.

"You ask, what is our policy? I will say: It is to wage war, by sea, land and air, with all our might and with all the strength that God can give us: to wage war against a monstrous tyranny, never surpassed in the dark, lamentable catalogue of human crime. That is our policy.

"You ask, what is our aim? I can answer in one word: Victory, victory at all costs, victory in spite of all terror, victory, however long and hard the road may be; for without victory, there is no survival. Let that be realized: no survival for the British Empire; no survival for all that the British Empire has stood for; no survival for the urge and impulse of the ages, that mankind will move forward towards its goal.

"But I take up my task with buoyancy and hope. I feel sure that our cause will not be suffered to fail among men. At this time I feel entitled to claim the aid of all, and I say, 'Come, then, let us go forward together.'"

For Britain and for Churchill that was the beginning of "their finest hour."

Churchill described his own feelings on becoming Prime Minister in the first volume of his history of the war:

"During these last crowded days of the political crisis my pulse had not quickened at any moment. I took it all as it came. But I cannot conceal from the reader in this truthful account that as I went to bed about 3 A.M. I was conscious of a profound sense of relief.

"At last I had the authority to give directions over the whole scene. I felt as if I were walking with Destiny, and that all my past life had been but a preparation for this hour and for this trial. Eleven years in the political wilderness had freed me from ordinary party antagonisms. My warnings over the last six years had been so numerous, so detailed, and were now so terribly vindicated, that no one could gainsay me. I could not be reproached either for making the war or with want of preparation for it. I thought I knew a good deal about it all, and I was sure I should not fail. Therefore, although impatient for the morning, I slept soundly and had no need for cheering dreams. Facts are better than dreams."

The man through whose mind these confident thoughts flowed knew also that his nation now stood virtually alone and at the mercy of Germany and Italy. Indeed, Britain was not to win her first solid victory until the Battle of El Alamein ended Nov. 4, 1942. But to his Herculean tasks he brought Herculean energy, Herculean determination, Herculean tact. With them he fashioned the Grand Alliance of 26 nations. With them he became a giant of his epoch.

To his tasks, too, he brought all his imposing gifts as a master of the language of Shakespeare, Milton, Gibbon and Macaulay, his skill and wit as an orator. As the late President Kennedy said, "He mobilized the English language and sent it into battle."

Sometimes in a business suit but more often in black jacket and gray striped trousers, he made an imposing figure whether seated on the Treasury bench in Commons with his chin resting on his chest or standing, gripping the upper lapels of his jacket to address the House.

Portly and solid in appearance, he often seemed like a kindly aging schoolmaster peering over his half spectacles.

His voice lacked volume and he had trouble with the letter S, but this gave style to his delivery. He was a master of the tempting pause before the utterance of a noble phrase. Emphasis was added by a rising inflection and at a half-growl at the end of his most truculent challenges, which produced a cadenced speech of transcendent rhetorical effect.

Churchill was an aristocrat, an imperialist and a royalist who at the same time trusted the people. It is no contradiction to describe him as a Tory democrat. To the multitudes he was "Winnie."

He was both arrogant and humble, courteous and rude. None could question his courage, yet he was unashamed of tears when deeply moved. He was resourceful, inventive, a master at improvisation, a genius at handling detail.

His many hats, the bow tie, the cigar clenched tightly between his teeth, his walking stick and the V sign became a personification of Britain.

"It was the British that had the lion's heart," he said on his 80th birthday. "I had the luck to be called upon to give the roar." He was too modest: his personality kept the heart beating.

Nonetheless, until he reached the pinnacle of power he had been regarded by some as too clever, too daring to be trusted. The disaster of the Dardanelles, the costly futile attempt to break the deadlock in World War I, dogged his career.

On becoming Prime Minister, Churchill brought Liberal and Labor members into his Cabinet to create a national government. He created a War Council of five. With Parliament's approval, he established a Ministry of Defense with himself as its head. He brought in Gen. Hastings Ismay to advise him. In effect, Churchill became commander in chief.

Nation's Mood Rises

There was a mood of relief among the British people that now at last they could "get on with it" under a leader who knew his goal and who was determined to attain it. No one but themselves could let them down. The long weekend vanished. People called for harder tasks, greater sacrifices.

Only 16 days after speaking to Parliament, Churchill was confronted by Dunkirk. The British Expeditionary Force in France, faced with envelopment by the Wehrmacht and dive-bombed by the Luftwaffe, was being driven into the sea.

On May 28 Churchill informed the House that King Leopold of the Belgians had surrendered. This melancholy news was followed by week later by his announcement the bulk of the British Expeditionary Force, driven into the sea, had been brought safely home. Many hailed this as a miracle.

More than 1,000 ships from small to large, he told the House, "carried over 335,000 men, French and British, out of the jaws of death and shame, to their native land and to the tasks which lie ahead."

"We must be very careful not to assign to this deliverance the attributes of a victory," he cautioned. "Wars are not won by evacuations."

The ships were protected by the Royal Air Force, which engaged the main force of the Luftwaffe, inflicting losses of 4 to 1.

To the British, the escape of so many husbands and fathers called for thanksgiving, if not for cheers.

Nevertheless, 30,000 were left behind, dead, wounded or prisoners. The cost in matériel was great.

Indomitable as ever in adversity, Churchill closed his Dunkirk report with these words:

"We shall not flag or fail. We shall go on to the end, we shall fight in France, we shall fight on the seas and oceans, we shall fight with growing confidence and growing strength in the air, we shall defend our island, whatever the cost may be, we shall fight on the beaches, we shall fight on the landing grounds, we shall fight in the fields and in the streets, we shall fight in the hills; we shall never surrender, and even if, which I do not for a moment believe, this island or a large part of it were subjugated and starving, then our Empire beyond the seas, armed and guarded by the British Fleet, would carry on the struggle, until, in God's good time, the new world, with all its power and might, steps forth to the rescue and the liberation of the old."

Churchill now realized that Britain alone could never win the war. He aimed at getting help from the most likely source, the United States. Although that country was neutral, President Roosevelt was willing to give "all aid short of war."

Quickly Roosevelt made available to Britain an array of light and heavy weapons, all that could be spared from the leftovers of World War I. There followed the exchange of 50 over-age destroyers for 99-year leases on British bases in the Western Hemisphere.

Later, with Roosevelt's prodding, the Lend-Lease Act was passed in 1941. "Give us the tools, and we will finish the job," Churchill said.

After Dunkirk, disaster followed disaster. Churchill made a desperate attempt to keep France in the war by offering a Franco-British union with common citizenship, a joint Parliament and a shared military command. It was too late. France surrendered June 21.

Pledge to Fight On

Anticipating the surrender, Churchill had told his people four days earlier:

"We have become the sole champions now in arms to defend the world cause. We shall do our best to be worthy of this high honor. We shall defend our island home and with the British Empire we shall fight on unconquerable until the curse of Hitler is lifted from the brows of mankind."

Churchill faced a bitter choice. By his order commanders of the French naval vessels were given the option of coming over to the British, sailing to ports safe from the enemy, or being sunk by British guns.

The commanders hesitated. So, in an action at the French naval base near Oran, in North Africa, one of two French battle cruisers was damaged and beached and one battleship was sunk. Another was badly damaged and two destroyers and an aircraft carrier were sunk or burned.

As the summer, bright and warm, advanced, fears of invasion rose. Businessmen drilled with wooden guns and pikestaffs. The

(continued)

beaches and coasts bristled with improvised obstacles and antique weapons.

Churchill warned of the coming ordeal:

"I expect that the battle of Britain is about to begin. Upon this battle depends the survival of Christian civilization. Upon it depends our own British life, and the long continuity of our institutions and our Empire. The whole fury and might of the enemy must very soon be turned on us.

"Hitler knows that he will have to break us in this island or lose the war. If we can stand up to him, all Europe may be free and the life of the world may move forward into broad, sunlit uplands. But if we fail, then the whole world, including the United States, including all that we have known and cared for, will sink into the abyss of a new dark age made more sinister, and perhaps more protracted, by the lights of perverted science.

"Let us therefore brace ourselves to our duties, and so bear ourselves that, if the British Empire and its Commonwealth last for a thousand years, men will still say, 'This was their finest hour.' "

The "finest hour" became the agony of the Battle of Britain, waged in the splendor of the September skies. Although Churchill neither planned nor supervised the battle, he invoked the nation's fortitude that inspired the airmen to their magnificent and sleepless struggle that eventually saved the island kingdom.

In the early days of the battle hundreds of Hurricanes and Spitfires were put out of action; a fourth of the fighter pilots were killed or wounded; thousands of civilians perished.

The raids went on day and night. The banshee howls of the sirens sent people scuttling in and out of shelters. The terror that struck by night was the worst. Finally, as youngsters in flight training took the place of their dead comrades, the Germans found daylight raids too costly, even on the foggiest days of autumn. Thenceforth the bombers came and went at dusk and dawn.

For days and weeks there was a late afternoon march of weary men, women and children, carrying their bedclothes, trundling baby carriages, heading for the underground stations where thousands slept nightly. But there was no real safety.

Tribute to Airmen

For the first nights there was no reply to the rain of bombs. Then, all at once, the antiaircraft batteries in the parks and on the outskirts opened up with a resounding and reassuring roar. Bursts even rattled from a Bofors gun atop the Admiralty Arch.

The fire from the ground did little damage to the Germans. The ammunition could hardly be spared. But it did much good for morale to see a bomber pinpointed by searchlights diving and squirming to avoid, not always successfully, bursts of flak.

The tribute Churchill paid to the Royal Air Force just before the bombardment of London began took on a deeper meaning.

"Never in the field of human conflict," he said, "was so much owed by so many to so few."

The people had been told that the ringing of church bells would signal a German invasion. On Sept. 11, Churchill said in a broadcast that if the invasion were going to be tried at all it would not be long delayed.

But British bombers attacked the invasion fleet gathered in ports from Boulogne to Antwerp. On the 17th Hitler postponed and later canceled Operation Sea Lion, his invasion plan.

During those days Churchill spent much time at 10 Downing Street, or the underground war room, usually in what he called his siren suit, the zipper front of which delighted him. On weekends he went to Chequers, the country home of Prime Ministers.

Addressing the crew of H.M.S. *Exeter* on their return from the sinking of the *Graf Spee*.

It was his custom to awaken at 8 o'clock. For the next couple of hours he read dispatches and sent off memos in all directions, usually beginning with "Pray see to it . . ." or "Pray find out . . .", to his generals or colleagues. By midmorning he was working full blast in his office.

Luncheon, for which he usually had guests, was followed by an hour's nap. Then came more work. In the evening there were generally dinner guests. The meal was followed by a session of idea swapping that often went far into the early morning, with Churchill pouring out an endless flow of suggestions. His constant companions were General Ismay and Brendan Bracken, Minister of Information, who were said to be the only ones who could stay the course.

London, meanwhile, had become the seat of eight governments in exile: Belgium, the Netherlands, Free France, Norway, Czechoslovakia, Poland, Greece and Yugoslavia. The Government of the Grand Duchy of Luxembourg was in Canada.

With these governments, Churchill busied himself welding the Grand Alliance, often putting the damper on petty squabbles and adjudicating trivial rivalries and smoothing the easily ruffled feathers of Charles de Gaulle, the Free French leader.

"We all have our crosses to bear," he once said. "Mine was the Cross of Lorraine."

Always on the Go

As the war became global after the entry of the Soviet Union and the United States, China and Japan, Churchill's travels in keeping the Alliance glued together were ceaseless. He journeyed to Newfoundland, three times to Washington, twice to Quebec, twice to Moscow, once to Ottawa, to Athens, to Casablanca, to Cairo (to confer with Roosevelt and Chiang Kai-shek), to Teheran and to Yalta (for conferences with Roosevelt and Stalin) and to Potsdam (to meet with Truman and Stalin). In all, he saw Roosevelt nine times and exchanged 1,700 communications with him.

On Aug. 9, 1941, Churchill and Roosevelt had their first rendezvous in Placentia Bay, Newfoundland, the President having arrived aboard the cruiser Augusta and the Prime Minister on the battleship Prince of Wales.

Supported by the arm of his son, Elliott, the President received Churchill aboard the Augusta while the national anthems of the United States and Britain were played. The next day, Sunday, the President returned Churchill's visit and attended divine services on the battleship's quarter deck.

The Atlantic Charter

Churchill described the scene later:

"This service was felt by all of us to be a deeply moving expression of the unity of faith of our two peoples and none who took part in it will forget the spectacle presented that sunlit morning on the crowded quarter deck—the symbolism of the Union Jack and the Stars and Stripes draped side by side on the pulpit; the American and British chaplains sharing in the reading of the prayers; the highest naval, military and air officers of Britain grouped in one body behind the President and me; the close-packed ranks of British and American sailors completely intermingled, sharing the same books and joining fervently together in the prayers and hymns familiar to both."

Out of that meeting at sea came the Atlantic Charter, a statement of principles that was later, in substance, to be incorporated in the aims of the United Nations.

The charter rejected any aspirations for aggrandizement, territorial or otherwise; declared British and American opposition to territorial changes not in accord with the wishes of the peoples concerned, and affirmed the right of peoples to choose their own form of government.

Of importance, too, were the staff talks that took place and the concord reached on the division of supplies from the United States between Russia and Britain.

Although the United States was still neutral, Roosevelt also agreed that the American Navy would take over patrol of the American-Iceland segment of the Atlantic, thus relieving the hard-pressed British of some of their convoy duties.

Held to a standstill against Britain, Hitler turned eastward, striking in June, 1941, at the Soviet Union, his partner in the nonaggression pact of August, 1939. Churchill had warned Stalin that Hitler was about to strike. Now he pledged aid to the Soviet cause.

In a radio broadcast June 22, 1941, he said:

"At 4 o'clock this morning, Hitler attacked and invaded Russia. All his usual formalities of perfidy were observed with scrupulous technique. A nonaggression treaty had been solemnly signed and was in force between the two countries. No complaint had been made by Germany of its nonfulfillment. Under its cloak of false confidence, the German armies drew up in immense strength along a line which stretches from the White Sea to the Black Sea; and their air fleets and armored divisions slowly and methodically took their stations. Then, suddenly, without declaration of war, without even an ultimatum, German bombs rained down from the air upon the Russian cities, the German troops violated the frontiers; and an hour later the German Ambassador, who till the night before was lavishing his assurances of friendship, almost of alliance, upon the Russians, called upon the Russian Foreign Minister to tell him that a state of war existed between Germany and Russia."

Churchill heaped invective on Hitler—"a monster of wickedness," "a bloodthirsty guttersnipe"—and upon his "accomplice and jackal Mussolini."

"But," he said, "all this fades away before the spectacle which is now unfolding. Any man or State who fights on against Nazidom will have our aid. Any man or State who marches with Hitler is our foe."

Throughout the war Churchill's relations with Stalin were blunt and forthright. With Roosevelt they were softened because of friendship. Roosevelt tended to see the war in military terms whereas Churchill directed his mind as much to political considerations.

It was this that in 1942 caused Churchill to lose his enthusiasm for the planned supporting attack on the south of France in favor of a thrust from Italy to stem the advance of Russia into Europe. Churchill did not have his way, and he argued afterward that had his views been adopted postwar Europe would not have been so dark.

U. S. Enters the War

With the Germans gaining in Russia, battering at the gates of Leningrad and Moscow and thrusting into southern Russia, Japan, Hitler's Axis partner in the Far East, entered the war with an air attack on United States air and naval bases at Pearl Harbor Dec. 7, 1941. This brought the United States into the war in Europe, too, for Germany and Italy, as part of the Axis pact, declared war on the United States. Churchill was quick to see that Pearl Harbor was the beginning of the end for Hitler, Mussolini and Hirohito. As he wrote in his memoirs:

"Once again in our long island history we should emerge, however mauled or mutilated, safe and victorious. We should not be wiped out. Our history would not come to an end. We might not even have to die as individuals. Hitler's fate was sealed. Mussolini's fate was sealed. As for the Japanese, they would be ground to powder."

True to a promise given Roosevelt earlier, to declare war "within the hour" if Japan attacked, Churchill called his Cabinet and then notified the Japanese Ambassador that a state of war existed between his country and Britain.

On the day of Pearl Harbor, the Japanese also landed on the Malayan Coast and bombed Singapore and Hong Kong. And before they were driven back, they were to sink the Prince of Wales and the Repulse, to overrun Malaya, Thailand and Burma and to cost Churchill challenges in Parliament to his leadership.

Visit With Roosevelt

At the outset Churchill went to the United States to concert with Roosevelt on the conduct of the war. He had fears, later disclosed, over these conferences.

"We feared lest the true proportion of the war as a whole might not be understood. We were conscious of a serious danger that the United States might pursue the war against Japan in the Pacific and leave us to fight Germany and Italy in Europe, Africa, and in the Middle East.

"Hitherto, as a nonbelligerent, the President had been able and willing to divert large supplies of equipment from the American armed forces, since these were not engaged. Should we be able to persuade the President and the American Service chiefs that the defeat of Japan would not spell the defeat of Hitler, but that the defeat of Hitler made the finishing-off of Japan merely a matter of time and trouble?"

It was on this visit, on Dec. 26, that Churchill delivered the first of two wartime speeches to Congress. The second was under happier circumstances on May 19, 1943, when the outlook was brighter.

Meantime, things were going badly for the British in North Africa. In a decision, the wisdom of which was later questioned, troops were moved from Africa to Crete and Greece when Germany struck into the Balkans. It was seemingly as a consequence of this step that Rommel and his Afrika Corps were able, in the summer of 1942, to capture Tobruk. The victory, although preceded by severe reverses in the desert, came as a shock. In Commons, it brought on a no-confidence vote, but Churchill survived it, 475 to 25.

The loss of Tobruk was softened somewhat when Roosevelt offered American tanks for the African front. The tide was eventually reversed and Rommel humbled at El Alamein, but that was not until November, 1942. Although winning the Battle of Britain had been a strategic victory of great significance, it was at El Alamein that there was tangible military victory, and that was what, in a dark hour, showed the British people the glimmer on the horizon.

The Soviet Union, too, in this period suffered badly, and in May, 1942, Molotov visited London with an urgent request for an Anglo-American second front on the Continent to draw off some of the German forces from the east.

The project, at first suggested by Roosevelt, was postponed for a large-scale operation in Africa.

It was Churchill's lot to break the news to Stalin in Moscow. He asked Roosevelt to let W. Averell Harriman accompany him because "I have a somewhat raw job."

Talks With Stalin

As Churchill outlined the change in plans, Stalin "looked very glum and seemed unconvinced." He said there was "not a single German division in France that was of any value."

Churchill replied that there were 25, of which nine were of the first line. He agreed that it would be possible to land six divisions but that it could be more harmful to future operations than helpful for the present.

Stalin, now restless and impatient, declared that "a man who was not prepared to take risks could not win a war."

But he became somewhat mollified as Churchill unfolded the North African plan to "threaten the belly of Hitler's Europe."

"To illustrate my point," Churchill recalled, "I had meanwhile drawn a picture of a crocodile and explained to Stalin with the help of this picture how it was our intention to attack the soft belly of the crocodile as he attacked his hard snout."

Stalin seemed to grasp the idea, but the next day, with Stalin and Molotov, there "began a most unpleasant discussion."

"We argued for about two hours during which he [Stalin] said a great many disagreeable things, especially about our being too much afraid of fighting the Germans and if we tried it like the Russians we should not find it so bad."

On the African front, a British-American force under Eisenhower landed Nov. 7, 1942 at Casablanca, Algiers and Oran.

A jubilant but cautious Churchill proclaimed the good news at the Mansion House Nov. 10. "We have

(*continued*)

victory—a remarkable and definite victory. The bright gleam has caught the helmets of our soldiers, and warmed and cheered all our hearts. Now this is not the end. It is not even the beginning of the end. But it is, perhaps, the end of the beginning."

Victory in Africa

It was indeed the end of the beginning. From this point on Allied pressure on the Axis was relentlessly applied on land and sea and in the air. By May 13, 1943, General Alexander reported that the Tunisian campaign was over, that "we are masters of the North African shores." One continent had been freed of the enemy.

Thenceforth Allied fortunes improved. Using Sicily as a stepping stone, United States and British troops liberated Italy and regained a foothold on Europe.

The following June the supreme effort, the culmination of all the planning that had gone before, came when the greatest amphibious force ever assembled swarmed ashore on the Normandy Beaches and began the long, slow march through France, Belgium, the Netherlands and Germany to the Elbe, where it met the Soviet Army advancing from the east.

On May 8 Churchill broadcast the news of Germany's unconditional surrender, but warned that Japan "remains unsubdued."

Churchill recalled that night in his memoirs:

"The unconditional surrender of our enemies was the signal for the greatest outburst of joy in the history of mankind. The Second World War had indeed been fought to the bitter end in Europe. The vanquished as well as the victors felt inexpressible relief.

"But for us in Britain and the British Empire, who had alone been in the struggle from the first day to the last and staked our existence on the result, there was a meaning beyond what even our most powerful and valiant Allies could feel. Weary and worn, impoverished but undaunted and now triumphant, we had a moment that was sublime. We gave thanks to God for the noblest of all His blessings, the sense that we had done our duty."

The Potsdam Meeting

Unconditional surrender insisted upon by Roosevelt at Casablanca and reluctantly accepted by Churchill was regarded by some in Britain as an obstacle to an early end of the war. After Roosevelt's death the concept caused some heart searching at the Potsdam conference when Stalin disclosed that he had received an offer of surrender from the Emperor of Japan through his Ambassador in Moscow.

The message indicated that Japan could not accept unconditional surrender but might be prepared to settle on softer terms.

Churchill, in talks with Truman, dwelt upon the enormous loss of life that might be entailed, if nothing less than complete surrender was required. He suggested giving the Japanese "some way of saving their military honor and some assurance of their national existence." To this Truman replied that he did not believe the Japanese "had any military honor after Pearl Harbor."

It was then agreed to send an ultimatum bidding Japan surrender unconditionally or face total destruction. The ultimatum, published July 26, 1945, was followed by the dropping of leaflets over Japan warning of the impending danger, but not mentioning the nature of the weapon about to be dropped on Hiroshima and Nagasaki.

Churchill had been informed that an atomic device had been detonated in New Mexico. He saw in the weapon a means to speed the end to the war in the Far East and to eliminate the necessity of asking favors from Stalin.

With the ultimate weapon at hand, Churchill wrote in his memoirs, he had never any doubt that Truman would use it, "nor have I ever doubted since that he was right."

Defends Atom Bomb

"To quell the Japanese resistance man by man and conquer the country yard by yard might well require the loss of a million American lives and half that number of British — or more if we could get them there: for we were resolved to share the agony. Now all this nightmare picture vanished."

Just before Potsdam an election had been scheduled. Churchill hoped to keep his Government in power at least until Japan had been defeated, but the Labor party, now that the peril in Europe was over, was impatient for a test of domestic strength.

The campaign was not Churchill's most admirable, filled as it was with invective against his Laborite wartime colleagues. This dismayed many of his admirers.

On election day, July 25, he returned to London for the results, satisfied that "the British people would wish me to continue my work."

"However, just before dawn [of the 26th]", he recalls in his memoirs, "I awoke suddenly with a sudden sharp stab of almost physical pain. A hitherto unconscious conviction that we were beaten broke forth and dominated my mind. All the pressure of great events on and against which I had mentally so long maintained my 'flying speed' would cease and I should fall. The power to shape the future would be denied me."

So it was for almost six years.

A Statesman's Growth: 40 Years of Public Life

WINSTON CHURCHILL descended from John Churchill, first Duke of Marlborough (1650-1722), a great captain of history who never fought a battle he did not win nor beseiged a city he did not take.

In his four-volume biography of Marlborough, Churchill drew a brilliant portrait of this great but devious character. The statesman and moral man of the world of the 20th century cast a keen but understanding eye on the statesman and amoral man of the world of the 18th century.

Churchill's Marlborough was first of all a military genius and a skillful diplomat. He was handsome, charming, courageous and self-possessed a loving and dutiful husband after rakish earlier years; a man capable of humanity and kindness. He was also politically treacherous, avaricious; a solicitor and taker of bribes, large and small, who peculated on his soldiers' supplies.

Churchill showed him against the background of his times. For example, he took some of the sting out of the story that John Churchill got his start in the army because his sister, Arabella, was a mistress of the Duke of York.

"In those youthful days," he wrote "John gained no office or promotion that might not have come to any young gentleman accepted at court. Nor shall we join the meretricious disputing about whether John received his commission before or after Arabella became the Duke's mistress. The Guards gained a good recruit officer in normal course."

Marlborough's most celebrated military victory was over the French at Blenheim, Bavaria, Aug. 13, 1704. A grateful Queen Anne had built for him a residence at Woodstock, near Oxford.

Gloomy Blenheim

This ponderous and gloomy pile, Blenheim Palace, has depressed a long succession of Marlborough women, including Winston Churchill's mother. Marlborough left no male heir; his title passed in the female line through his daughters —first Henriette and then Anne, wife of Charles, Lord Spencer. Winston Churchill's full name was Winston Leonard Spencer Churchill.

Down the years the Spencer Churchill family made certain contributions to British history. But no firm tone was set until the appearance of Lord Randolph Churchill (1849-1895). He was the second surviving son of the seventh Duke of Marlborough and the father of Winston Churchill.

Lord Randolph was Chancellor of the Exchequer in 1886 and seemed on his way to becoming Prime Minister. He possessed intuitive knowledge of politics but his wit left scars.

Lord Randolph was a rugged debater in Commons. There he led a small Conservative party "ginger group." His specialty was baiting the somber Gladstone, leader of the Liberal party opposition and sometimes Prime Minister.

When Lord Randolph became Chancellor of the Exchequer, it was evident that his views were considerably more advanced in social reform than those of Lord Salisbury, the Prime Minister.

"The final collision occurred over a comparatively trivial point [the budget's military and naval estimates]. He resigned on the eve of Christmas 1886 at the wrong time, on the wrong issue, and he made no attempt to rally support," his son wrote of the end of his father's political career.

Brunette Jennie

Lord Randolph's political career lay far ahead of him at the moment when, at the age of 24 he met the future mother of Winston Churchill. A scintillating member of London's society (despite one or two disapproving frowns from Queen Victoria and a quarrel with the Prince of Wales) Lord Randolph missed few of the occasions of his day.

He was attending the Royal Yacht Squadron regatta at Cowes in August, 1873, when he first saw Jennie Jerome of New York at a ball. A brunette beauty with sparkling dark eyes, she was a daughter of Leonard Walter Jerome, a New York financier and turfman.

Randolph proposed a day or two after the meeting. He was accepted. To his father he wrote, that "she is nice, as lovable, and amiable and charming in every way as she is beautiful, and by her education and bringing-up she is in every way qualified to fill any position."

The Duke reacted brusquely:

"From what you tell me & what I have heard this Mr. J. seems to be a sporting, and I should think, vulgar sort of man. I hear he & his two brothers are stockbrokers, one of them bears a *bad* reputation in commercial judgment in *this* county. I do not know, but it is evident that he is in a class of speculators; he has been bankrupt once, & may be so again."

Randolph finally won over his father and mother. He agreed to meet his father's stipulation that he would settle down and stand for Parliament. There was a bit of a fuss over the dowry. Although Jerome had run into hard luck on the market, he settled £50,000, about $250,000, on the couple. All the income was to go to Randolph, who promised to give his wife £1,000 a year.

Winston Churchill wrote in his biography of his father:

"On April 15, 1874, the marriage was celebrated at the British Embassy in Paris and after a tour—not too prolonged—upon the Continent, Lord Randolph returned in triumph with his bride to receive the dutiful laudations of the Borough of Woodstock and enjoy the leafy glories of Blenheim in the spring."

On Dec. 3, 1874, The Times of London printed the following among its birth announcements:

"On 30th November at Blenheim Palace, the Lady Randolph Churchill, prematurely, of a son."

Born in a Palace

Winston Churchill was already a young man in a hurry. A ball (presumably attended by his mother) was held at Blenheim Nov. 30 and Winston was born in a first-floor room of the palace called Dean Jones's Room, in use at the time as a ladies' cloakroom.

At Blenheim, the child played soldier in the vast and draughty halls. He was undersized, sometimes shy, sometimes overassertive. He seemed to be able to learn nothing at school. He adored his brilliant father, who, however, was convinced by his son's school failures that the boy was retarded.

Few homes of the British aristocracy are child-oriented and Winston saw little of his mother.

"My mother made a brilliant impression upon my childhood life," he said in his memoirs. "She shone for me like the evening star. I loved her dearly but at a distance. She always seemed to me like a fairy princess."

The boy became deeply attached to his nanny, Mrs. Everest. As he put it, "My nurse was my confidante and nearest and most intimate friend."

When he became one of the grand figures of his age, it was Mrs. Everest's picture that was over his desk.

Churchill's brother, John Strange Spencer-Churchill (the form of the Churchill name that he used) was born in February, 1880. He was an amiable figure often known as Jack Churchill. He served with some distinction in South Africa and in World War I.

In 1908 he married Lady Gwendoline Theresa Mary Bertie, daughter of the seventh Earl of Abingdon. A daughter, Anne Clarissa, was married to Sir Anthony Eden. Spencer-Churchill died in 1947.

At 7 Winston was sent to a school at Ascot. He was a sore trial to his masters. He would neither learn nor behave and he was caned regularly. Caught stealing sugar from the pantry, he received the usual birching. This was repeated when, in revenge, he kicked the headmaster's straw hat to pieces. Sent to another school at Brighton, he discovered books and read everything he could get his hands on.

In 1888 he entered Harrow. When the boys filed past the headmaster in order of their academic standing, he was often at the end of the line. He became used to hearing visitors exclaim, "Why that's Randolph Churchill's boy and he's last!"

Gradually the more perceptive of his teachers began to sense that Winston was far from stupid. He could not come to grips with Latin and Greek and mathematics but he was the school's star in general knowledge. Nonetheless, he never got out of the lower form.

"However, by being so long in the lowest form, I gained an immense advantage over the cleverer boys," he recalled. "They all went on to learn Latin and Greek and splendid things like that. But I was taught English. I got into my bones the essential structure of an ordinary English sentence—which is a noble thing."

Winston was four and a half years at Harrow, and after three examination failures and prodigious cramming, he was finally admitted, in June, 1893, to the Royal Military College, now the Royal Military Academy, at Sandhurst. Once there, he did well. He stood eighth in his class of 150 at the end of the courses.

Two years later he was commissioned a lieutenant and joined the Fourth Hussars at Aldershot. There seemed little immediate prospect of active service.

"All my money had been spent on polo ponies," he wrote. "I searched the world for some scene of adventure or excitement."

His eye lighted on Cuba and the fighting between the independence forces and the Spanish. Family connections helped him get clearance of the Spanish Government. Lord Randolph had written for The Daily Graphic and his son made use of this to get an assignment to report on the Cuban fighting. He was to get £5 an article.

In Cuba, near Trocham, on Nov. 29, 1895, the eve of his 21st birthday, Winston Churchill came under fire for the first time.

"On this day when we halted for breakfast every man sat by his horse and ate what he had in his pocket," he wrote later. "I had been provided with half a skinny chicken. I was engaged in gnawing the drumstick when suddenly, close at hand, almost in our faces it seemed, a ragged volley rang out from the edge of the forest. So at any rate I had been under fire. That was something."

After he returned to Britain his regiment was ordered to India and he went into garrison at Bangalore. He played polo and read seriously, stocking his mind by memorizing large sections of Bartlett's "Familiar Quotations."

But he became restless. Through Gen. Sir Bindon Blood, a family friend, he found his way to the headquarters of the Malakand Field Force on the Northwest Frontier. There was action there, and he wrote of an encounter with a Pathan:

"I wore my cavalry sword well sharpened. After all, I had the public school fencing medal. The savage saw me coming. He picked up a big stone and hurled it at me with his left hand, and then awaited me, brandishing his sword. There were others waiting behind him and I changed my mind about the cold steel."

Churchill fired his pistol and took off.

A contemporary described him as "a slight, red-headed, freckled snub-nosed young subaltern, vehement, moody, quickly responsive, easily hurt, taciturn at times and at times quite opinionative with a tumbling flow of argument, confident to the point of complacency, but capable of generous self-sacrifice, proud but no snob."

After writing a book—it was his first — that was less than gently critical of the expedition's management, he turned to fiction. The result was his only novel, "Savrola. A Tale of the Revolution in Laurania."

Savrola is a dashing young man —an understanding liberal who is nonetheless a traditionalist at heart. He bears a striking resemblance to Churchill's conception of himself.

Novelist Sees Himself

"Would you rise in the world?" said Savrola. "You must work while others amuse themselves. Are you desirous of a reputation for courage? You must risk your life. Would you be strong morally or physically? You must resist temptations. All this is paying in advance; that is prospective finance. Observe the other side of the picture; the bad things are paid for afterward."

The novel issued in 1900 was a moderate success and it was re-

(continued)

printed in 1956. The author had second thoughts about its literary merit, however. "I have consistently urged friends not to read it," he wrote later.

Having acquired a taste for battle, Churchill sought more, this time in Egypt where Kitchener was leading a British force slowly up the Nile into the Sudan. Churchill's reputation for aiming journalistic barbs at generals had preceded him and Kitchener would have none of him.

Churchill invoked his mother's influence in London. "Many were the pleasant luncheons and dinners attended by the powers in those days which occupied two months of strenuous negotiations."

Finally, Prime Minister Salisbury yielded and asked Kitchener to let Churchill join his force. He was classed as a supernumerary officer and he was also a correspondent for The Morning Post.

In Cavalry Charge

Having agreed to foot his own hospital and burial expenses, he was assigned to the 21st Lancers in time for the Battle of Omdurman on Sept. 2, 1898. He was up early that day.

"Talk of fun! Where will you beat this! On horseback at daybreak, within shot of an advancing enemy and seeing everything."

He charged with his Lancers, pistol in hand (a shoulder injury prevented his wielding a saber), and went through the slashing, stabbing struggle.

The British victory virtually ended the war.

At loose ends after the Sudan, Churchill considered going to Oxford, but he lacked sufficient Latin and Greek. Instead, he opted for India, where he served briefly. He then resigned his commission and determined to enter politics.

The year was 1899. When he applied to the Conservative party for a Commons seat to contest, he was not widely known and had only about enough spare money to pay his election expenses.

He was assigned to contest a vacancy in Oldham, a dreary Manchester industrial suburb. He lost—the first of five defeats as against 19 victories—but he was not disheartened.

"Live and learn!" he wrote later. "I think I might say without conceit that I was in those days a pretty good candidate. However, when the votes were counted, we were well beaten."

It took another war, however, for Churchill to fix himself firmly in British politics. This was the Boer War, brought on when the Boers in South Africa ordered British troops away from their frontiers and the British refused.

"The Boer ultimatum had not ticked out on the tape machine for an hour when Oliver Borthwick [editor of The Morning Post] came to offer me an appointment as principal War Correspondent. £250 a month, all expenses paid," he wrote.

Churchill had scarcely reached Natal when he suffered the ignominy of being captured on an armored train and put, a prisoner of war, in the State Model Schools in Pretoria. After four weeks, however, he escaped by climbing a wall.

Wanted at £25

"I said to myself," he recalled, "'*toujours de l'audace*,' put my hat on my head, strode into the middle of the garden, walked past the windows of the house without any attempt at concealment, and so went through the gate. I passed the sentry at less than five yards."

Free with £74 in his pocket and four slabs of chocolate, he hopped a freight train without any notion of where it was heading. In the morning he left it (and the coal sacks on which he had slept) at Witbank, in the Transvaal, to seek food and shelter. To a householder at whose door he knocked, he said he was a Boer lost from his command, but the tale didn't wash, "so I took the plunge and threw all I had upon the board."

"I am Winston Churchill, war correspondent of The Morning Post," he confessed. "I escaped last night from Pretoria. I have plenty of money. Will you help me?"

Fortunately, the man, Frank Howard, manager of the Transvaal Collieries, proved sympathetic. He took Churchill down into a coal mine, leaving him with some candles, a bottle of whisky and a box of cigars.

Meanwhile, his Pretoria escape was discovered, and the Boers sent out a circular offering £25 for his apprehension. He had, the notice said, "a small, hardly noticeable mustache, talks through his nose and cannot pronounce the letter S properly."

After a couple of days in the mine, Howard got the bedraggled correspondent onto another freight train where he hid between two bales of wool until it reached neutral Portuguese East Africa and the city of Lourenço Marques, whence, after getting help from the British consul, he went to Durban.

An astonishing acclaim greeted him. "I reached Durban to find myself a popular hero. I was received as if I had won a great victory. I was nearly torn to pieces by enthusiastic kindness. Sheaves of telegrams from all parts of the world poured in on me."

However, it was with reluctance that the British military permitted him to continue as a correspondent as well as a temporary lieutenant in the South African Light Horse, an irregular force. He was thus on hand for the relief of Ladysmith, the battles in the Orange Free State and hard skirmishing in the Transvaal, he returned to London in the late summer of 1900.

His plan was to re-enter politics, but first there was a quick lecture trip in the United States under the sponsorship of Mark Twain. Churchill and Mark Twain had never met and it was suggested that they should confer in private for an hour or so before dinner to become acquainted. Both men would rather talk than listen and each liked to dominate the conversation. Friends waiting for the Churchill-Mark Twain causerie to end were making bets on who would outtalk the other.

Mark Twain Bemused

Mark Twain was the first to emerge. He looked bemused and beaten and Churchill was at his heels with, "As I was saying, sir. . . ."

Churchill made $10,000 and expenses on this tour, the first of several in America. He gave most of the $10,000 to his banker friend, Sir Ernest Cassel, to invest for him.

In the election of 1900 a total of 11 Parliamentary constituencies offered Churchill a chance to contest them, but with typical stubbornness he chose Oldham, the scene of his earlier defeat. He was asked by many leaders of his party to speak in their districts.

The campaign in Oldham became so raucous that it attracted national attention. Churchill's Boer War adventures were told and retold. "Soldiers of the Queen" had been a popular song and it became Churchill's theme song. The bands played either this or "See, the Conquering Hero Comes!" Girls wore blue sashes emblazoned "God Bless Churchill, England's Noblest Hero."

T. E. Dunville, the music-hall comedian, reminded audiences:

You've heard of Winston Churchill:
That is all I need to say—
He's the latest and the greatest
Correspondent of the day.

However, despite Churchill's martial allure, he just scraped in; and at the age of 26 he entered the House of Commons, Jan. 23, 1901, part of the 134-vote majority of the Conservative party.

Churchill with his mother and younger brother John.

Great interest centered on the new M.P. His father was well remembered and everyone wondered what his son would do. A fellow M.P. said that "Churchill had not been in the Commons for five minutes until he was seen to lean back, tip his top hat over his forehead, cross his legs, bury his hands in his pockets and survey the scene as if he were the oldest, not the youngest member."

New members were not supposed to speak until they had been on hand at least a month but Churchill got the Speaker's eye and was on his feet four days after he had been sworn in. The Boer War was still on—it was not to end until June, 1902—and reference to it in debate gave Churchill a chance to speak.

His Maiden Speech

He stood, lean and red-haired in a long frock coat with satin lapels. Whether by design or naturally, his gestures recalled his father's. Like his hero, Savrola, "he showed or perhaps he feigned, some nervousness at first, and here and there in his sentences he paused as if searching for a word."

However, he had prepared his speech and had memorized it.

Early in his speech he made a gallant reference to the men he had fought in South Africa by saying, "If I were a Boer fighting in the field—and if I were a Boer I hope I should be fighting in the field— . . ."

Then he went on:

"I earnestly hope that the Colonial Secretary will leave nothing undone to bring home to those brave and unhappy men who are still fighting in the field that whenever they are prepared to recognize that their small independence must be merged in the larger liberties of the British Empire, there will be a full guarantee for the security of their property and religion."

The brisk give-and-take of Commons was the breath of life to Churchill. He once called Aneurin Bevan a "squalid nuisance" and referred to the politically supple Ramsay MacDonald as "the boneless wonder."

One of Churchill's most vigorous and durable feuds was with the American-born Lady Astor. There is a story that the exchange between them once became so sulphurous that Lady Astor burst out:

"If you were my husband, I'd put poison in your coffee."

"If you were my wife, I'd drink it," Churchill shot back.

Churchill's speeches in Parliament and elsewhere seemed to many to have been delivered extemporaneously. However, according to Lord Birkenhead, Churchill "spent the best years of his life writing his impromptu speeches."

Never a blind follower, Churchill progressively became a problem to his party leaders. His views were somewhat advanced on social reform, and he was soon a leading light in a "ginger group," called the Hughlighans, after one of their number, Lord Hugh Cecil. He began to take pot shots at Balfour, the Prime Minister, and his position as a Conservative grew untenable.

In a dramatic scene May 31, 1903, Churchill entered the House, glanced at the Conservative bench, bowed to the Speaker and "crossed the floor" amid Tory catcalls to join the Liberal party amid their cheers.

His reward came in the election of 1905, when the Liberals swept into power with a 356-seat majority and he was appointed Under Secretary for the Colonies. Two years later, at the age of 32, he was made a Privy Councillor.

Characteristically, the new Under Secretary toured the colonies, arranging to write magazine articles about his travels. Lacking a private fortune, he supported himself by such articles and by lecturing. Indeed, he needed the money, for he liked London's social life, good food, the best brandy and cigars, polo and the turf.

Standing for the first time as Liberal in the election of 1906, Churchill ran in Manchester Northwest and won, although assailed as a Conservative turncoat. Two years later, however, things went badly for him over the issue of woman suffrage. He opposed it; his opponent was for it. With the lusty help of the suffragettes, including, naturally, Sylvia Pankhurst, Churchill lost.

This was by no means his last encounter with that determined band of women. Later, in 1910, when he was Home Secretary with general supervision of the London police, he was involved in the suffragette "Black Friday" when a riotous group of women surrounded Prime Minister Asquith near 10 Downing Street, and the police, only with difficulty, hustled him to safety in a taxicab.

Wins Dundee Election

Churchill was stationed nearby, watching the fray and ordering the police, at one point, to drive a woman away. On several occasions thereafter he was attacked by women wielding umbrellas, but he managed to escape unscathed, except politically, for the Tories taunted him in the House over "Black Friday."

Meanwhile, after his defeat in Manchester Northwest, Churchill bounced back by winning a by-election in Dundee, which caused his colleagues in Commons to greet him with the cry of "Marmalade!"—the well-known product of that constituency.

Under Asquith, Churchill received a full Cabinet post, President of the Board of Trade.

It so happened that the Countess of Airlie who had made herself useful to Churchill in Dundee had a very attractive granddaughter, Clementine Ogilvy Hozier. Miss Hozier was a daughter of Sir Henry Montague Hozier and Lady Henrietta Blanche Hozier, daughter of the seventh Earl of Airlie.

Churchill and Miss Hozier were married at St. Margaret's, Westminster, Sept. 12, 1908. He had been a full Cabinet minister since April and the wedding was a considerable social event. King Edward VII and Queen Alexandra and members of the Cabinet sent presents. Lord Hugh Cecil, Churchill's colleague in the Hughlighans, was his best man.

After a few days at Blenheim and a brief trip to Lake Maggiore, the Churchills took up residence in a house in Queens Gate, London. Churchill called his wife Clemmie and she was standing at his side at the window of their home on his 90th birthday.

In October, 1910, Asquith offered Churchill the post of Secretary for Ireland, but, as more than one politician had ended his career in this job, Churchill neatly side-stepped. Asquith made him Home Secretary instead. This was one of the key Cabinet offices—often a step toward the Prime Ministership.

A coal miners' strike in Wales posed difficulties. After several incidents Churchill had troops sent before local authorities requested for them, a move for which he was widely criticized, although the intervention restored order without casualties.

At this time bomb-throwing anarchists were spreading terror in Europe, and some of them were known to be in London.

Sidney Street Battle

On the morning of Jan. 3, 1911, Churchill was summoned to the telephone from his bath. Girt with a towel, he heard that suspected anarchists were exchanging shots with the police from a house in Sidney Street.

After ordering a battalion of the Scots Guards and two field guns to the scene, Churchill dressed and appeared in Sidney Street in a silk hat and fur-collared overcoat. Several photographers recorded the scene. A desultory exchange of shots ended when the building caught fire. Two bodies, one of a man killed by bullet wounds and the other of a man who had suffo-

(continued)

cated, were found inside.

The episode produced laughter from the Opposition in Commons. It was charged that the Home Secretary had turned a simple police action into something resembling war.

In later years Churchill gained so exalted a position in the admiration and affection of his countrymen that it is hard to remember that he was not always so regarded. At various times in his career, he was widely suspected and disliked. When he was a war correspondent and soldier, for instance, he was called a medal-snatcher and glory hunter.

In politics, the Conservatives considered him an opportunist for deserting the party of his father. Some of the Liberals regarded him as a Johnny-come-lately in the cause of social reform. He was thought, too, as too facile and glib. Stanley Baldwin once referred to "Winston's 100-horse-power mind."

On Oct. 23, 1911, Churchill became First Lord of the Admiralty, the Cabinet head of the navy. Having been acquainted with Britain's naval problems, he took steps to spur the modernization of her ships and organization. His prescience was responsible for the fact that naval units were at their posts and battle-ready when World War I opened. Recalling the war's beginning, Churchill wrote:

"It was 11 o'clock at night—12 by German time [Aug. 4, 1914] when the [British] ultimatum expired. The windows of the Admiralty were thrown wide open in the warm night air. Under the roof from which Nelson had received his orders were gathered a small group of admirals and captains and a cluster of clerks, pencils in hand, waiting.

"Along the Mall from the direction of [Buckingham] palace the sound of an immense concourse singing 'God Save the King' floated in. On this deep wave there broke the chimes of Big Ben and, as the first stroke of the hour boomed out, a rustle of movement swept across the room. The war telegram, which meant 'Commence hostilities against Germany', was flashed to the ships and establishments under the White Ensign all over the world.

Rupert Brooke Poem

"I walked across the Horse Guards Parade to the Cabinet Room and reported to the Prime Minister and the Ministers who were assembled there that the deed was done."

When the war began Churchill was besieged by friends or friends of friends who wanted commissions in the Naval Division. Bernard Freyberg who had been a dental mechanic in San Francisco told Churchill a tall tale about having fought in Mexico with Pancho Villa and got a commission. He became one of the best natural military commanders of his day, won a Victoria Cross, became a full general and was elevated to the peerage as Baron Freyberg for his World War II services.

The young Cambridge poet, Rupert Brooke, was also a friend and he was commissioned in the Naval Division. He wrote "The Soldier," which so well summed up British feeling in 1914. It begins:

If I should die, think only this
of me:
That there's some corner of a
foreign field
That is forever England . . .

When the bugles of battle sounded it was agony for Churchill to be out of the fighting. He accompanied the Naval Division on the expedition to relieve Antwerp, but he was a civilian and had no military uniform. Instead, he wore that of an Elder Brother of Trinity House, a venerable guild of lighthouse inspectors. This gave rise to a report in Antwerp that the elder brother of the Trinity had come to the city's aid. He pleaded for a commission and to

After graduating from Sandhurst in December 1894, Churchill was commissioned a lieutenant in the Queen's Fourth Hussars in March 1895.

command the expedition, but in vain, and he returned to the Admiralty in London.

As a naval strategist, he was convinced that the considerable British sea power reserve could be utilized to relieve pressure on the main ground war fronts on the Continent while at the same time finding and exploiting the flanks of the Central Powers.

The possibility of action in the Mediterranean, so stimulating to Nelson and Napoleon, caught Churchill's imagination, too. The operation that seemed to offer the greatest possibilities was the forcing of the Dardanelles.

The Strait of the Dardanelles unites the Aegean with the Sea of Marmora and controls the approaches to Istanbul, then called Constantinople, and entrance into the Black Sea. The European side of the strait is formed by the Gallipoli Peninsula, a tongue of land 63 miles long. Its possession assures control of the Dardanelles.

A twofold result might be gained from the opening of the Dardanelles. A helping hand could be extended through the Black Sea to Russia and it might be possible to raise the Balkans in the rear of Austria-Hungary and Germany. As it happened though, the Dardanelles nearly ended Churchill's political career.

On March 18, 1915, a combined British and French fleet attempted to force the Dardanelles with disastrous results and heavy losses in ships and lives. The first infantry units fought their way onto the Gallipoli Peninsula April 25. Other landings followed and there were months of desperate fighting. Incompetence and ill luck dogged the British efforts. A British general got his men ashore and instead of moving immediately to seize commanding heights overlooking the beach, let his men go swimming. The Turks managed to get men on the heights during the night and the British attack the next day failed.

It was moments like this that were anguish to Churchill in the London Admiralty headquarters. He knew he was right, but the atmosphere about him began to cool.

Soon the Dardanelles campaign reached a sort of befuddled standstill. "From this slough I was not able to lift the operation. All the negative forces began to band themselves together," he wrote. "The 'No' principle had become established in men's minds and nothing could ever eradicate it."

Churchill recalled that a War Council meeting May 14, 1915, was "sulphurous."

"Lord Kitchener began in a strain of solemn and formidable complaint . . . when he had finished, the Council turned to me—almost on me."

Resigns Cabinet Post

The ground was cut from under Churchill on the Dardanelles when he was deserted by his chief technical adviser, Admiral Lord Fisher.

A munitions shortage and general dissatisfaction with the conduct of the war forced Asquith to form a coalition Government a few days later. Churchill was succeeded at the Admiralty by Arthur Balfour, a Conservative. It was probably the lowest point in his career. He was subsequently cleared by a board of inquiry of sole responsibility for the Dardanelles failure but that was much later and the damage had been done.

Churchill remained in the Government as Chancellor of the Duchy of Lancaster, a sinecure. Within five months he resigned from the Cabinet.

He thereupon got a major's commission and went to the front in France for a refresher course with a battalion of the Grenadier Guards.

There was little or no fighting in that sector and after he got his battalion smartened up, Churchill spent some time in his dugout in France in an old blue civilian raincoat listening to classical records on a gramaphone.

Meantime, Lloyd George managed to bring down the Asquith Government and became Prime Minister Dec. 6, 1916. He wanted Churchill in his Cabinet but dared not include him because of the uproar over the Dardanelles. However, he did manage to get him in as Minister of Munitions in July, 1917.

He was in that post when the Armistice was signed Nov. 11, 1918.

"On the night of the Armistice I dined with the Prime Minister at Downing Street," Churchill wrote. "We were alone in the large room from whose walls the portraits of Pitt and Fox, of Nelson and Wellington, and—perhaps somewhat incongruously—of Washington then looked down. My own mood was divided between anxiety for the future and desire to help the fallen foe. From outside the songs and cheers of the multitudes could be remotely heard like the surf on the shore."

After the general election of 1918 Lloyd George reorganized his Cabinet and Churchill became Secretary for War. No more thankless task could have been given to anybody at that moment.

There were mutinies in France and Britain. Riding in Hyde Park, King George V was surrounded by a disorderly crowd of soldiers and an attempt was made to pull him from his horse. Churchill had to use detachments of Guards to restore order among the more than 3,000 soldiers on the Horse Guards Parade.

Meantime, the specter that had been haunting Europe since 1848 materialized in Imperial Russia when Lenin's Communists seized power in November, 1917. Once the outlines of the new regime became evident, Churchill grew alarmed. Trustful of the common man though he was, he was not prepared to trust Lenin's version of the same abstraction. Of the Russian Revolution, he wrote:

"Meanwhile the German hammer broke down the front and Lenin blew up the rear. Could any man have made head at once against this double assault? All broke, all collapsed, all liquefied in the universal bubble and approaching cannonade, and out of this anarchy emerged the one coherent, frightful entity and fact—the Bolshevik punch!"

Churchill was convinced of the need for armed intervention to aid the White Russian counter-revolutionaries. Small forces under British command, composed chiefly of British and American troops, did occupy Murmansk and Archangel, but the Red Army in the end prevailed. These expeditions, and Churchill's role in them, were still sharp in the memories of Soviet leaders 20 years afterward, and they contributed to Russian suspicions of Churchill in World War II.

Liberals Defended

Politics gave Churchill a breathing spell in 1922. Lloyd George was toppled by the Conservatives under Bonar Law. For the first time since 1900 Churchill was without a seat in Commons.

Vastly annoyed, he contested the Leicester West Division in 1923, but lost.

A bitter moment in Churchill's career came in 1924. He had been twice beaten for a Commons seat. He then posed his candidature in the Abbey Division of Westminster, in which the Houses of Parliament are situated, and one considered safely Conservative.

Churchill ran as an Independent and exerted himself to the utmost to win. Many of his Tory friends helped him. But when the votes were counted he had lost by 43 votes out of 22,778 cast.

Meantime, he was edging his way back toward the Conservative party and he had run as an Independent.

By 1924 Churchill believed that the Liberal party had become so infiltrated by Socialists that it could no longer afford him a spiritual home. Moreover, it was going into eclipse because of factional strife.

The same year Churchill stood in the general election from the Epping Division of Essex as a Constitutionalist. There was a Conservative sweep and Churchill won. He did not expect to be asked to join the Baldwin Government. However, Baldwin called him to his office and said:

"Will you take the Chancellor?"

(continued)

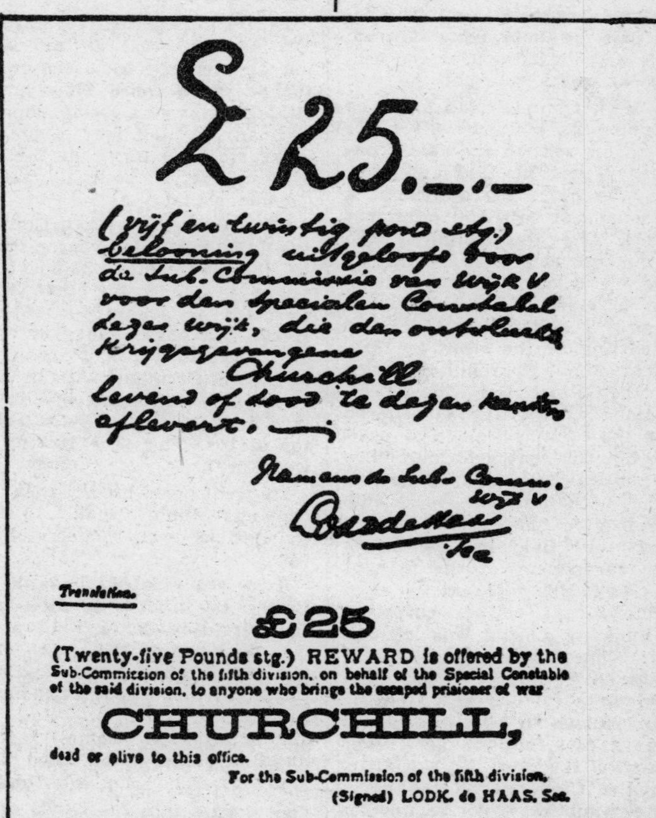

£25.—.—

(vijf en twintig pond stg.)
belooning uitgeloofd door
de Sub-Commissie van Wijk V
voor den specialen Constabel
dezer wijk, die den ontvluchte
Krijgsgevangene
Churchill
levend of dood te dezen kantore
aflevert.

Namens de Sub-Comm.
Wijk V
Lodk. de Haas
Sec.

Translation.

£25

(Twenty-five Pounds stg.) REWARD is offered by the Sub-Commission of the fifth division, on behalf of the Special Constable of the said division, to anyone who brings the escaped prisoner of war

CHURCHILL,

dead or alive to this office.

For the Sub-Commission of the fifth division,
(Signed) LODK. de HAAS, Sec.

The young adventurer, his taste for combat whetted in Cuba, India and Africa, sailed for the Boer War in 1899 as a correspondent. He was captured, then escaped, the Boers setting the price of £25 on his head. The dangerous situation was not unfamiliar to him. The year before, he rode with the 21st Lancers against the dervishes in the Battle of Omdurman. This was among the last of the great cavalry charges.

Churchill was married to Clementine Hozier in 1908.

Thinking it was the general utility post of Chancellor of the Duchy of Lancaster, Churchill said:

"Of the Duchy?"

"No," Baldwin replied, "Chancellor of the Exchequer."

Churchill was well and truly out of the political wilderness.

He went home and dug out the robes of office worn by his father as Chancellor of the Exchequer in 1886. They did him very well on the rare occasions that he had to wear them.

Churchill obtained the backing of Baldwin in restoring the pound to its prewar value. Britain had gone off the gold standard as a war measure. Churchill's act temporarily strengthened Britain's credit but it hurt the country's export trade.

In the coal mining industry the return to the gold standard threatened to price coal out of the export market. Prices had to be cut and the mine owners, in turn, cut wages.

Editor in the Strike

This was one of the chief causes of the great General Strike of 1926. It was touched off when printers of The Daily Mail refused to set an editorial headed "For King and Country" condemning the threatened strike. Three million British workers quit their jobs May 3 to protest pay cuts for the miners.

Many of the newspapers were shut down. Churchill was assigned to put out an emergency newspaper, The British Gazette. He took over the building of the old Morning Post just off the Strand, installed himself as editor and laid hands on as much newsprint as he could find.

It became the fashionable thing to do late at night to go down to The Post building and watch and listen to Churchill put out The British Gazette. It made no pretense of printing anything but the Government's side of the strike.

The British Gazette ran for seven issues before the General Strike was ended. Its circulation reached 1,801,400 before it was discontinued.

The most highly publicized duty of the Chancellor of the Exchequer is to present, or "open," the budget in Commons. Churchill presented five budgets in all. The advice that he followed was from highly orthodox financial and economic sources.

In 1924, Churchill ran and won in Epping as a Conservative. He held to his seat in the same constituency in 1929, 1931 and 1935.

He was never again without a Commons seat until his retirement in 1964. After the election of 1935 he was returned from the nearby Woodford Division in 1945, 1950, 1951, 1955 and 1959.

Churchill and Baldwin reached the parting of the ways in 1929, and in June Churchill resigned from the Cabinet. Baldwin was riding along with what was believed to be the country's mood of pacifism, but this was not Churchill's. His political luck held. If he had stayed with Baldwin, he would have had to share some of the criticism of Baldwin's failure to seek rearmament in the face of the rising Hitler threat.

"But I was neither surprised nor unhappy when I was left out of it," Churchill recalled. "What I should have done if I had been asked to stay I cannot tell. It is superfluous to discuss doubtful temptations that have never existed."

In the Churchill of the early nineteen-thirties — portly, middle-aged and at times somewhat pugnacious — dignity joined with a youthful spirit to mold the figure the world was to know in World War II. Someone said of him then that he was "Half Pitt and half Puck."

King Edward VIII ascended the throne on Jan. 30, 1936, on the death of his father, George V. It soon became known that Edward wished to marry Mrs. Wallis Warfield Simpson, a divorced American with one former husband living and a second divorce in prospect. Baldwin told the King that attempts to obtain Parliamentary consent to a marriage might result in a general election, with the monarch's private life the main issue. Edward was dismayed and confused.

Churchill had always held the monarchy in great respect and esteem. He championed the King's cause in Commons and sought more time for him to decide, and in one tumultuous session underwent the unusual experience of being shouted down. After Edward had abdicated on Dec. 10, 1936, Churchill recalled that as Home Secretary he had proclaimed Edward's title as Prince of Wales.

"I should have been ashamed if, in my independent and unofficial position, I had not cast about for every lawful means, even the most forlorn, to keep him on the throne of his fathers."

Rise of Hitlerism

During this period it was generally assumed that Britain would not be menaced by a major war for years to come. However, by 1932 Hitler was a rising power in Germany, calling for rearmament to reverse the terms of the Versailles Treaty. Churchill said in Commons that year:

"The demand is that Germany should be allowed to rearm. Do not let the Government delude themselves by supposing that which Germany is asking for is equal status. All these bands of splendid Teutonic youth marching to and fro in Germany, with the light of desire to suffer for their fatherland in their eyes, are not looking for status. They are looking for weapons."

He went on to predict that their demands would "shake to their foundations every country in the world."

Two years later Churchill attacked the limited funds allowed for increasing Britain's air power.

"We are, it is admitted, the fifth air power only—if that. Germany is arming fast and no one is going to stop her. She is going to arm; she is doing it. I dread the day when the means of threatening the heart of the British Empire should pass into the hands of the present rulers of Germany."

On May 3, 1935, Commons was told that Germany had reached at least theoretical air parity with Britain. Soon after this the Baldwin Government proposed increases in the country's air capability. Churchill regarded the proposal as inadequate, and asked:

"Why, then, not fight for something that will give us safety? Why, then, not insist that the provision for the air force should be adequate?"

Describing his attitude, he recalled:

"Although the House listened to me with close attention, I felt a sensation of despair. To be so entirely convinced and vindicated in a matter of life and death to one's country, and not to be able to make Parliament and the nation heed the warning, or bow to the proof by taking action was an experience most painful."

Nor did he confine his warnings to his countrymen. In 1937 he had an interview with Ribbentrop, the German Ambassador to the Court of St. James's. Ribbentrop told him that Germany wanted a free hand in eastern Europe. She must have living space for her increasing population. All that Germany asked of the British Commonwealth and Empire was not to interfere. Churchill made clear his belief that Britain would give no such assurances. To this Ribbentrop replied:

"In that case, war is inevitable."

Ribbentrop Told Off

Churchill retorted:

"When you talk of war, which, no doubt, would be a general war, you must not underrate England. She is a curious country and few foreigners can understand her mind. Do not judge by the attitude of the present Administration. Once a great cause is presented to the people, all kinds of unexpected actions might be taken by this very Government and by the British nation.

"Do not underrate England. She is very clever. If you plunge us all into another great war, she will bring the whole world against you like the last time."

Meanwhile, Hitler reoccupied the Rhineland in March, 1936, and two years later to the month took over Austria.

To Churchill the peril to his country was ever more real.

"All this time the vast degeneration of the forces of Parliamentary democracy will be proceeding throughout Europe. Every six weeks another corps will be added to the German army. All this time important countries, great rail and river communications will pass under the control of the German General Staff.

"All this time populations will be continually reduced to the rigors of Nazi domination and assimilated to that system. All this time the forces of conquest and intimidation will be consolidated, towering up soon in real and not make-believe strength and superiority.

"For five years I have talked to the House on these matters—not with very great success. I have watched this famous island descending incontinently, fecklessly, the stairway which leads to a dark gulf. It is a fine broad stairway at the beginning, but after a bit the carpet ends. A little farther on there are only flagstones, and a little farther on still these break under your feet.

Punic Wars Recalled

"Look back upon the last five years—since, that is to say, Germany began to rearm in earnest and openly to seek revenge. If we study the history of Rome and Carthage, we can understand what happened and why. It is not difficult to understand and form an intelligent view about the three Punic Wars; but if mortal catastrophe should overtake the British nation and the British Empire, historians a thousand years hence will still be baffled by the mystery of our affairs.

"They will never understand how it was that a victorious nation, with everything in hand, suffered themselves to be brought low, and to cast away all they had gained by measureless sacrifice and absolute victory — 'gone with the wind!'

"Now the victors are the vanquished, and those who threw down their arms in the field and sued for an armistice are striding on to world mastery. That is the position—that is the terrible transformation that has taken place bit by bit."

In 1938 British and French appeasement of Hitler resulted in the partition of Czechoslovakia. Churchill was distraught, seeing with frightening clarity the war in its chrysalis:

"The partition of Czechoslovakia under pressure from England and France amounts to the complete surrender of the Western democracies to the Nazi threat of force. Such a collapse will bring peace or security neither to England nor to France. On the contrary it will place these two nations in an ever-weaker and more dangerous situation.

"The belief that security can be obtained by throwing a small state to the wolves is a fatal delusion."

Again in April, 1939, with Europe on the brink of war, he sounded one of his final and most eloquent warning.

"The danger is now very near. A great part of Europe is to a very large extent mobilized. Millions of men are being prepared for war. Everywhere the frontier defenses are manned. Everywhere it is felt that some new stroke is impending. If it should fall, can there be any doubt but that we shall be involved? We are no longer where we were two or three months ago. We have committed ourselves in every direction, rightly in my opinion, having regard to all that has happened.

"Surely then, when we aspire to lead all Europe back from the verge of the abyss on to the uplands of law and peace, we must ourselves set the highest example. We must keep nothing back. How can we bear to continue to lead our comfortable easy life here at home, unwilling even to pronounce the word 'compulsion,' unwilling even to take the necessary measure by which the armies that we have promised can alone be recruited?

"How can we continue—let me say it with particular frankness and sincerity—with less than the full force of the nation incorporated in the governing instrument?"

'Winston Is Back'

The World War began Sept. 1, 1939. After some light prodding by Churchill, Chamberlain named him First Lord of the Admiralty, a post he assumed on Sept. 3.

"I therefore sent word to the Admiralty that I would take charge forthwith. On this, the board were kind enough to signal to the Fleet, 'Winston is back.'

"So it was that I came again to the room I had quitted in pain and sorrow almost exactly a quarter of a century before."

His removal from the Admiralty in 1915 over the Gallipoli incident had left such scars that when he was First Lord once more, he had passing moments of self-doubt and fear. Such a moment came when was returning to London after a visit to the fleet in Scotland. He had just learned that the navy had lost the aircraft carrier Courageous.

"We had a picnic lunch on the way by a stream," he wrote later. "I felt oppressed with my memories.

"No one had ever been over such a terrible course twice with such an interval between. No one had felt its dangers and responsibilities from the summit as I had or, to descend to a small point, understood how First Lords of the Admiralty are treated when great ships are sunk and things go wrong. If we were in fact going over the same cycle a second time, should I once again have to endure the pangs of dismissal?"

Chamberlain Resigns

As First Lord he had the responsibility for dispatching sea and land forces to check the German thrust into Norway. The British undertaking was unsuccessful, a fact made all the more galling because at its beginning Chamberlain had assured the nation that "Hitler has missed the bus."

When the early passive phases of the war ended in the spring of 1940, and the Germans invaded the Netherlands, Belgium and France, Chamberlain submitted his resignation.

In his recollections of May 10, Churchill wrote:

"Presently a message arrived summoning me to [Buckingham] Palace. It only takes two minutes to drive from the Admiralty along the Mall. Although I suppose the evening papers must have been full of the terrific news from the Continent, nothing had been mentioned about a Cabinet crisis. The public had not had time to take in what was happening either abroad or at home, and there was no crowd about the Palace gate.

"I was taken immediately to the King. His Majesty received me most graciously and bade me sit down. He looked at me searchingly and quizzically for some moments, and then said: 'I suppose you don't know why I have sent for you?' Adopting his mood, I replied: 'Sir, I simply couldn't imagine why.' He laughed and said: 'I want to ask you to form a Government.' I said I would certainly do so."

That is how Churchill became Prime Minister.

(continued)

In Opposition: Counselor to the West, Foe of Communism, Historian, Painter

"IN defeat: defiance." This apothegm of his own devising Churchill put to practice when war-weary British voters turned him out of the Prime Ministership within 80 days of the apotheosis of his career, the surrender of Germany.

Stunned, unbelieving at first, the 71-year-old war leader toyed with retirement from politics to bask as an elder statesman, to paint, to write, to live benignly with his wife at Chartwell, his estate in his beloved Kent. At first too, he took his defeat with ill humor, declining King George VI's offer of the Order of the Garter and peevishly denouncing Labor's victory as "one of the greatest disasters that has smitten us in our long and checkered history."

To quit the combat and sulk, however, had never been his characteristic, nor was it now, and in October he was telling his fellow Conservatives:

"I have naturally considered very carefully what is my own duty in these times. It would be easy for me to retire gracefully in an odor of civic freedom, and this plan crossed my mind frequently some months ago. I feel now, however, that the situation is so serious and what may have to come so grave that I am resolved to go forward carrying the flag as long as I have the necessary strength and energy and have your confidence."

Domestic politics aside, there was another, and perhaps weightier, reason that impelled him to carry on. Explaining it in 1951, he said:

"If I remain in public life at this juncture, it is because, rightly or wrongly, but sincerely, I believe that I may be able to make an important contribution to the prevention of a third world war and to bring nearer that lasting peace settlement which the masses of people of every race and in every land so fervently desire."

Thus, Churchill was soon back in the political fray he loved so much, combating Socialism at home and Communism in the world with an energy scarce diminished by the toll of his wartime exertions.

The Fulton Speech

Less than a year after he became Leader of the Opposition, he appeared, as the guest of Truman, at obscure Westminister College in an even obscurer Fulton, Mo., "to give true and faithful counsel" to the West. His words on that budding March 5 spring day exploded around the world, heralding the Arctic chill of the cold war.

Speaking as the war's Grand Alliance, so painfully carpentered, lay virtually shattered by recrudescent Soviet ambitions and by the unleashing of the universe's basic force at Hiroshima, Churchill's words resembled those of a sibylline oracle.

"From Stettin on the Baltic to Trieste in the Adriatic an iron curtain has descended across the Continent. Behind that line lie all the capitals of the ancient states of Central and Eastern Europe – Warsaw, Berlin, Prague, Vienna, Budapest, Belgrade, Bucharest and Sofia—all these famous cities and the populations around them lie in what I must call the Soviet sphere and are all subject in one form or another not only to Soviet influence but to a very high and in many cases increasing measure of control from Moscow."

"On the other hand I repulse the idea that a new war is inevitable; still more that it is imminent. It is because I am sure that our fortunes are still in our own hands and that we hold the power to save the future that I feel the duty to speak out now that I have the occasion and the opportunity to do so. I do not believe that Soviet Russia desires war. What they desire is the fruits of war and the indefinite expansion of their power and doctrines.

"Our difficulties and dangers will not be removed by closing our eyes to them. They will not be removed by mere waiting to see what happens, nor will they be removed by a policy of appeasement. What is needed is a settlement, and the longer this is delayed, the more difficult it will be, and the greater our dangers will become.

"From what I have seen of our Russian friends and allies during the war, I am convinced there is nothing they admire so much as strength, and there is nothing for which they have less respect than for weakness, especially military weakness."

In place of a "quivering, precarious balance of power to offer its temptation to ambition or adventure," he proposed a partnership of the English-speaking peoples in the United States and the British Commonwealth that would be "an overwhelming assurance of security." If the English-speaking peoples and the European democracies stood together in adherence to the principles of the United Nations, no one was likely to molest them. If they failed or faltered "catastrophe may overwhelm us all."

"Last time I saw it all coming and cried aloud to my own fellow countrymen and to the world, but no one paid any attention. Up till the year 1933 or even 1935 Germany might have been saved from the awful fate which has overtaken her and we might all have been spared the miseries Hitler let loose upon mankind. There never was a war in all history easier to prevent by timely action than the one which has just desolated such great areas of the globe."

The Soviet drive for expansion of Communist power and doctrines that Churchill divined soon came to pass. There was strife in Greece, but she was saved for the West, as was Turkey, by timely American aid. The West began to coalesce, to shape a policy of help for freedom-loving nations, to draw the lines of containment, to concert military plans for the common defense.

Before these were consolidated, however, Czechoslovakia passed into the Muscovite orbit and the teeming millions of China came under Communist rule. The French were tumbled from Indochina, and Korea was only half saved. In less than 10 years after the war the world was riven—East and West. Where peace should have dwelt, armies patrolled; where victory's harmony had hinted goodwill among men, emotions of Armageddon prevailed.

Churchill echoed the fears and feelings of many in the West in those years in a speech in 1949.

"We are now confronted with something quite as wicked but in some ways more formidable than Hitler because Hitler had only the Herrenvolk pride and the anti-Semitic hatred to exploit. He had no fundamental theme. But these 13 men in the Kremlin have their hierarchy and a church of Communist adepts, whose missionaries are in every country as a fifth column, obscure people, but awaiting the day when they hope to be absolute masters of their fellow countrymen and pay off old scores.

"They have their anti-God religion and their Communist doctrine of the absolute subjugation of the individual to the state, and behind this stands the largest army in the world in the hands of a government pursuing imperialist aggression as no Czar or Kaiser has ever done."

Earlier, Churchill placed the force of his prestige behind the creation of a new European unity, with Franco-German amity its cornerstone and with a leading role for Britain. His wartime hate had cooled with the surrender of the Nazis, and, indeed, he chose for the motto of his war memoirs an inscription he once proposed for a monument in France. It was:

"In War: Resolution
"In Defeat: Defiance
"In Victory: Magnanimity
"In Peace: Goodwill."

A "kind of United States of Europe" aligned with the English-speaking people — Churchill's proposed "sovereign remedy" for the containment of Soviet power—did not come off, save in the form of the North Atlantic Treaty Organization.

In these years, Churchill gave appearance of youthful vigor. Bald save for a thatch of hair on the back of his head, his rotund, cherubic face was still well fleshed and hardly wrinkled. With his seldom smiling, mostly solemn mien, he moved slowly, as an elephant pushing through underbrush, his massive head with its lowering eyebrows almost resting on his chest from his strong, short neck. Only his natural stoop was more marked.

Voters who turned out to hear him noticed that he often let tears roll down his ruddy cheeks when political meetings wound up with the singing of "Land of Hope and Glory."

All the while, Churchill was busy with his private enterprises, pursuits and amusements. Chartwell was enlarged by 500 acres and he became a gentleman farmer. In 1948 he started a stable of horses, to his profit unlike so many others.

One of his horses, a gray three-year-old named Colonist II, romped in a winner at Ascot in 1949 and in 1950 ran up a string of 13 victories. In all Colonist II won £13,000 for his owner.

He spent much of his time at Chartwell puttering, laying bricks and painting. He painted whenever he had an idle moment; while these were few, canvases were many. Hundreds of his landscapes piled up in spare rooms.

Dominating all of his activities was his writing. In this period he worked on his four-volume "History of the English Speaking Peoples."

Even more astounding was his compilation of a six-volume history of World War II as seen through his eyes and recorded in memorandums, letters, cables, diaries and official records.

These volumes were "The Gathering Storm," "Their Finest Hour," "The Grand Alliance," "The Hinge of Fate," "Closing the Ring," and "Triumph and Tragedy." All were published between 1948 and 1954.

For this Gargantuan task, Churchill gathered an assemblage of scholars, historians, technical experts, researchers and, of course, enough secretaries to keep up with the endless torrent of words that Churchill poured into recording machines. Sometimes the secretaries worked in shifts so that they could keep going while Churchill slept. He often dictated 8,000 words in a day.

The sorting, selection, the rejection of material, the endless winnowing and typing sometimes went on through the night. The words and the choice of phrase were Churchill's; and, despite the committee method of production of a work of more than 1.5 million words, the style is unmistakably, majestically Churchillian.

Literary Output

This was the crown of his literary achievements. His other books included "The Story of the Malakand Field Force" (1898); "The River War: An Historical Account of the Reconquest of the Soudan" (two volumes 1899); "Savrola" (1900); "Ian Hamilton's March" (1900; "Mr. Broderick's Army" (1903); "Lord Randolph Churchill" (two volumes, 1906); "My African Journey" (1908); "The World Crisis" (five volumes, 1923-31); "My Early Life" (1930); "Thoughts and Adventures" (1932); "Marlborough: His Life and Times" (four volumes, 1933-38); "Great Contemporaries" (1937); "Painting as a Pastime" (1948); and "A History of the English Speaking Peoples" (four volumes, 1956).

Throughout the years he was in Opposition, Churchill, while continuing to stress the menace of Communism, found time to give the Socialists little peace at home. He attacked them constantly for policies toward the Empire, the parlous economic situation in Britain and for nationalization policies in coal mining, railroads and especially steel.

In 1947 and 1948 Churchill delivered 52 major speeches on a variety of subjects from Indian independence—he was against it—to nationalization, to devaluation of the pound from its pegged rate of $4.82 to $2.80. He was also against that.

"When I am abroad I always make it a rule never to criticize or attack the Government of my own country," he told the House in April, 1947. "I make up for lost time when I come home."

In July, 1949, Churchill made a pronouncement of Conservative intentions before 40,000 at an outdoor gathering in Wolverhampton. It was based largely on policy devised by R. A. Butler, who had been entrusted with formulating a campaign program after the Conservative defeat of 1945. It conceded that the Welfare State—Churchill had been one of its early authors, with Lloyd George—had come to stay.

Churchill almost made his come back in the election of 1950, pinning his campaign on opposition to Labor's Socialism, but Attlee squeaked by. Labor maintained its precarious hold until October, 1951. In this period, the Conservatives' war of attrition in Parliament harried the Laborites; troubles mounted for the Government at home as living costs rose and consumer goods grew scarcer; abroad, the situation was sticky, especially in the ever-troublesome Middle East where traditional British influence was dwindling with the rise of Nasser of Egypt; and in Africa the colonies were restive, not always beneath the surface.

The campaign was venomous. "Vote Tory and Reach for a Rifle," one handbill read. Weakness and vacillation, retorted the Conservatives. From this Churchill's party emerged with a small, but workable majority in Commons.

In the early evening of Oct. 26, 1951, Winston Leonard Spencer Churchill, a month from his 77th birthday, was invested by King George VI with the seals of office. Doughty still, he undertook the onerous duties of Prime Minister for a second time.

(continued)

On a painting holiday in 1950.

Prime Minister for Second Time

Queen Confers A Knighthood

BACK in power after six years in Opposition, Winston Churchill gave himself with his old-time vigor to the three great tasks he had set himself after the victory in World War II.

These were to remove the shadow of a new tyranny by reaching an accord with the Soviet Union for a just and lasting peace, security of the West through the closest association of a united Europe with the British Commonwealth and the United States, and, at home, an unscrambling of the Socialist omelet.

It is a measure of the stature he had attained throughout the world that even when he was merely the leader of a minority in the House his pronouncements on world affairs had been received with the attention reserved usually for the head of a government. Now he spoke as the leader of the British nation, not so great as in the Victorian Age of his youth but still a major power.

This time he had not been called to leadership at a time of crisis and cataclysm but through the deliberate choice of voters who, having given Socialism a six-year trial, had decided they wanted a change in the hope of a better and richer life. In four years Churchill sought to give it to them.

India Independent

They were years mixed with success and failure, of satisfaction mixed with sorrow and disappointment. He who had said he did not "become the King's First Minister to preside over the liquidation of the British Empire" had to watch the beginning of its disintegration from the sidelines and its further weakening by events which even he could not control.

India was gone but Churchill found a measure of satisfaction that in granting independence to the great subcontinent, the communal massacres he had feared were averted by a provision for a Muslim Pakistan separate from India. He never had believed that independence was itself a cure for social injustice but the tides of nationalism were stronger than any man could breast.

His hopes for a United States of Europe—never precisely or clearly defined—did not materialize. A stroke of fate prevented his hoped-for confrontation of Malenkov in the brief period he led the Soviet Union after Stalin's death.

Although he lost no time in attacking Socialism in calling for the repeal of the act nationalizing the steel industry in his first session of Parliament, he never succeeded in entirely undoing the work of the Labor party. Indeed, in the 13 years the Conservatives remained in power after 1951 they embraced the basic principles of the Welfare State.

Retained His Wit

The wit and wry humor that spiced so many of the grimmest of his wartime speeches was still with him through this Indian summer of his life.

Speaking at the rebuilt Guildhall, which had been partly destroyed by German bombs, Churchill said:

"When I should have been here as Prime Minister [the first time] the Guildhall was blown up and before it was repaired I was blown out."

Churchill's durability and continued capacity to work hard and relax zestfully was the wonder of his friends. He had not been a robust youth and he had had pneumonia several times, but he recovered quickly from these bouts of illness as he did from his accidents.

He once told Pearson, the Prime Minister of Canada, that one of his secrets was "never stand when you can sit down and never sit if you can lie down."

In one of his books he wrote that he "always went to bed at least for one hour as early as possible in the afternoon and exploited to the full my happy gift of falling almost immediately into deep sleep." By "this means I was able to press a day and a half's work into one."

The first Parliamentary sessions after Churchill's return to power were not notable for legislative achievements. It was a time for conciliation of party strife and a consolidation of a new Government. Nevertheless the Government was blessed by an end of the conflict in Korea and a truce in Indochina. Vietnam was partitioned and Laos and Cambodia neutralized. Britain's economic position began to improve.

Call for a Summit

In a progress report to Parliament he asked that his Government's achievements be seen in relation to its inheritance from Labor's "six-year record of extravagance and waste, of overspending and living upon American money."

He declared that at the time of the election Britain was spending £800 million a year more than it was earning from exports. If drastic measures had not been taken by his Government and followed by the Commonwealth, he said, "the whole reserve of gold and dollars would have been exhausted by the summer's end." These measures, he noted, had reduced purchases abroad by £600 million.

In that speech he also referred to his call in 1950 for a conference between the heads of government and declared that he and Eden still held to "the idea of a supreme effort to bridge the gulf between the two worlds so that each can live its life, if not in friendship at least without the fear, the hatreds and the frightful waste of the 'cold war.'"

On Feb. 6, 1952, a grief stricken nation learned that King George VI, who had survived an operation for lung cancer some months before had died in his sleep at Sandringham, a royal country residence. Churchill, devoted to the Crown as a symbol and to King George as a friend and collaborator, delivered one of his most moving tributes to the institution of monarchy and the King himself in a radio broadcast the next day.

"The last few months of King George's life with all the pain and physical stresses that he endured—his life hanging by a thread from day to day—and he all the time cheerful and undaunted—stricken in body but quite undisturbed and even unaffected in spirit — these have made a profound and enduring impression and should be a help to all.

"During these last months the King walked with death, as if death were a companion, an acquaintance whom he recognized and did not fear. In the end death came as a friend, and after a happy day of sunshine and sport, and after a 'good night' to those who loved him best, he fell asleep, as every man or woman who strives to fear God and nothing else in the world may do."

He concluded with a tribute to the Queens of England, now about to have another.

"Famous have been the reigns of our queens. Some of the great periods in our history have unfolded under their scepters. Now that we have the second Queen Elizabeth also ascending the throne in her 26th year our thoughts are carried back nearly 400 years to the magnificent figures who presided over and in many ways embodied and inspired the grandeur and genius of the Elizabethan age.

"I, whose youth was passed in the august, unchallenged and tranquil glories of the Victorian era, may well feel a thrill in invoking once more, the prayer and anthem:

"God Save the Queen."

Death of Stalin

On March 5, 1953, the day that Stalin died, Churchill thought the time propitious to repeat his call for a "summit meeting." He wanted to "take the measure of the new man in the Kremlin," he told a friend.

The sole survivor of the three who led the Grand Alliance sent no personal message of condolence when Stalin died. This was in marked contrast to his action when Roosevelt died April 12, 1945, when he mourned the ending of "a dear and cherished friendship forged in the fires of war."

A spokesman for the Prime Minister explained that the British Government had expressed sympathy "and that is all that is required under normal diplomatic procedure."

"Mr. Churchill will do no more and no less," the spokesman said.

On first learning that Stalin was ill, Churchill had sent a secretary to the Soviet Embassy to ask to be kept informed of Stalin's condition.

It was not until 1955 that Churchill, who had always maintained that successful negotiations with Russia could be held only by those with equal or superior strength, explained why the opportunity of 1953 for high-level talks had been allowed to pass.

It came with the announcement to a stilled House that the Government had decided to proceed with the manufacture of a hydrogen bomb.

Before Russia caught up with the United States in atomic weapons he had believed that the secret of this dreadful "deterrent" was best left to the United States.

Now, he informed the House of his conviction that only possession of the hydrogen bomb, the means of its delivery and a determination to use it, if necessary, was the prerequisite to a "conference where these matters can be put plainly and bluntly."

He would have liked to have arranged such a conference after Malenkov took power, he said, and intended to try to convince Eisenhower of the desirability of such a meeting.

"However, I was struck down by a very sudden illness which paralyzed me completely physically and I had to put it all off and it was not found possible to persuade President Eisenhower to join in the process."

The German Problem

He was referring to June 10, 1953, when he, then in his 77th year, suffered a paralytic stroke that incapacitated him to some extent for several months.

A month previously, he had spoken of the change of attitude and mood in the Kremlin.

"The dominant problem is, of course, Germany. If our advice had been taken by the United States after the Armistice with Germany the Western Allies would not have withdrawn from the line which their armies had reached to the agreed occupation lines until and unless agreement had been reached with Soviet Russia on the many points of difference about the occupation of enemy territories, of which the occupation of Germany was, of course, only a part. Our view was not accepted and a wide area of Germany was handed over to the Soviet occupation without any general settlement among the three victorious powers."

In 1953 Queen Elizabeth II knighted Churchill and invested him with the insignia of a Knight Companion of the Most Noble Order of the Garter.

On April 24 of that year, the Queen made Churchill a Knight Companion of the Most Noble Order of the Garter, the highest order of chivalry to which a Briton can attain and still be eligible to sit in the House of Commons. Thus, the child of the House of Commons, who always said that the letters he cherished most after his name were M. P., became Sir Winston.

The same year the Nobel Prize for Literature was awarded him. With it went a citation for his oratory.

Churchill was the first statesman and the seventh of his countrymen to receive the world's highest award for literature.

After expressing the hope that the judges had not erred in their assessment, he said:

"I notice that the first Englishman to receive the Nobel Prize was Rudyard Kipling and that another equally rewarded was Mr. Bernard Shaw. I certainly cannot attempt to compete with either of those. I knew them both quite well and my thought was much more in accord with Mr. Rudyard Kipling than with Mr. Bernard Shaw. On the other hand, Mr. Rudyard Kipling never thought much of me, whereas Mr. Bernard Shaw often expressed himself in most flattering terms."

At the Coronation

London in April was already aflutter with bunting, flags and decorations in preparation for the coronation ceremony of June 2. It was a time of jubilation in a city long immersed in the gloom of war and an austere peace. Newspapers picked up the theme of the dawn of a new Elizabethan age and spirits rose higher than they had been at any time since the German surrender.

When the great day came, however, it was pouring rain and the temperature was in the lower forties. In the old Abbey transformed for the ritual, half religious and half secular, Churchill sat in his robes as a Knight of the Garter among the crowned heads of many lands, the peers in their robes trimmed with ermine and their ladies wearing glittering tiaras. He who had served as a soldier of the Queen in Victoria's reign saw the Archbishop of Canterbury place the old imperial crown upon the girlish head of her great granddaughter.

After his stroke there were rumors that he was preparing to retire. He scotched them at a party conference.

"If I stay on for the time being, bearing the burden at my age, it is not because of love or power or office. I have had an ample feast of both. If I stay it is because I have the feeling that I may, through things that have happened, have an influence on what I care about above all else—the building of a sure and lasting peace."

By December, Churchill was well enough to journey to Washington to see Eisenhower just before the latter's inauguration. Again in the summer of 1954 he was in Washington to sign the Potomac Charter reaffirming the principles of the Atlantic Charter.

To a question at a news conference here about when he planned to retire, he replied:

"Not until I am a great deal worse and the Empire is a great deal better."

His Step Less Firm

He was asked whether death held any terror for him, and he replied:

"I am prepared to meet my Maker. Whether my Maker is prepared for the great ordeal of meeting me is another matter."

Meanwhile, in Commons it was noticed that Churchill showed signs of slowing down. He walked with a more pronounced stoop. His step was less firm. He appeared tired and sometimes did not seem able to follow the proceedings. This was perhaps due to increasing deafness, for he wore his hearing aid only sporadically and reluctantly in public.

Churchill passed his 80th birthday on Nov. 30, 1954, still Prime Minister and still the master of Britain's destiny. Only Palmerston and Gladstone had held that office beyond that age. To mark the occasion, members of the House of Commons and the House of Lords gathered in Westminster Hall to do him honor.

There were messages of goodwill from the great and lesser peoples of his own and many other lands. Churchill's acknowledgment was perfunctory and brief.

The speech on Britain's nuclear plans was delivered March 1, 1955. Just a month later he and Lady Churchill entertained Queen Elizabeth II and Prince Philip at 10 Downing Street. As it turned out, it was the Prime Minister's farewell to the sixth monarch he served.

On April 5 he resigned. Ironically, there was a newspaper strike in London and the event that marked the end of a noble era of British statesmanship went unrecorded immediately in London, but it was carried to people across the land and throughout the world by radio.

(continued)

The Declining Years

U.S. Votes Sir Winston An Honorary Citizenship

FREED of the burdens of office, Churchill now entered the twilight of his life, illumined, however, with honors and distinctions that continued to fall upon him.

Even so, he was not ready to relinquish his membership in that most exclusive club, the House of Commons, of which he had been a member more than half a century. He stood for his old constituency of Woodford and won in the election of 1955 and again in 1959.

No longer was he seated on the front bench as he had been for years with the members of the Government and as Leader of the Opposition. Instead, he sat among the back benchers as a private member.

Serenely benign, and for long periods aloof and withdrawn, he took little part in the debates and none in the thrust and parry of Parliamentary procedure. His appearances in the House and his presence in his favorite corner of the Members Lounge became less and less frequent.

Churchill had made two visits to the United States after his retirement as Prime Minister, one in May, 1959, when he visited Eisenhower at the White House and again in April, 1961, when he sailed to Miami and New York aboard a friend's yacht.

His sense of humor did not desert him as the years marched on. On his 82d birthday, when a photographer expressed the hope that he might take another picture of him at the age of 90, Churchill regarded him solemnly and said:

"I see no reason why you shouldn't, young man. You look hale and hearty enough."

He spent more and more time at Chartwell surrounded by his family, his grandchildren, his dogs, his racing stable. He puttered and lived the life of a country squire. Much time was spent in painting.

To Paint, Be Daring

As a painter—mostly in oils—he favored landscapes and interiors rather than the portraits that Eisenhower seemed to prefer. Hitler had tried to paint, too, but his work was marked by the hard straight line whereas Churchill's style was softer. His work was characterized by bold colors and an impressionist approach that sought to convey a mood or feeling as well as a pictorial representation. An exhibition of 62 of his paintings at Burlington House in 1959 drew more than 140,000 persons.

"Audacity," he said "is a very great part of the art of painting."

He wrote a book, "Painting as a Pastime," that contained this passage revelatory of the man and his work:

"Just to paint is great fun. The colors are lovely to look at and delicious to squeeze out. Matching them, however crudely, with what you see is fascinating and absolutely absorbing. Try it if you have not done so—before you die.

"As one slowly begins to escape from the difficulties of choosing the right colors and laying them in the right places and in the right way, wider considerations come into view.

"One begins to see, for instance, that painting a picture is like fighting a battle; and trying to paint a picture is, I suppose, like trying to fight a battle. It is, if anything, more exciting than fighting it successfully. But the principle is the same.

"When we look at the larger Turners—canvases yards wide and tall—and observe that they are all done in one piece and represent one single second of time, and that every innumerable detail, however small, however distant, however subordinate, is set forth naturally and in its true proportion and relation, without effort, without failure, we must feel in the presence of an intellectual manifestation the equal in quality and intensity of the finest achievements of warlike action, of forensic argument or of scientific or philosophical adjudication."

Even in retirement he could not repress the will to speak on world affairs when occasion offered. One such presented itself a year after his resignation as Prime Minister when he went to Aachen in Germany to receive the Charlemagne Prize for services to Europe. There he reverted to his theme of a united Europe in which Russia must play a part as a guarantor of peace. Thus, he said, the reunification of Germany might be accomplished more easily—a statement not well-received by the Bonn Government.

He never relinquished the idea that at the moment of peace victory was lost and for this he felt that Roosevelt's confidence that he could "handle" Stalin was at fault. In the last volume of his memoirs he wrote:

"The United States stood on the scene of victory, master of world fortunes, but without a true and coherent design. Britain, though still very powerful, could not act decisively alone. I could at this stage only warn and plead.

"I moved through cheering crowds or sat at a table adorned with congratulations and blessings with an aching heart and a mind oppressed by forebodings."

As a Knight Companion of the Garter, he was a member along with those of royal blood and the peerage of the highest order of chivalry his Queen could bestow upon him. It had been offered him in 1945 by King George VI but he declined. At that time selections for membership in the order were made by the sovereign on the recommendation of the Prime Minister. The fact that Attlee was Prime Minister may have had something to do with Churchill's decision. Subsequently, the older system was restored, making selection the prerogative of the sovereign.

Most Prized Honor

He also held the Order of Merit, which is limited to 24 members at any one time and that is awarded for outstanding excellence in the arts, letters and sciences. He was the first non-American to be given the Freedom Award. De Gaulle decorated him with the Cross of Liberation in 1958.

He was a Freeman of more than 50 towns and cities in his own country and abroad and the holder of honorary degrees from more than 20 universities.

Of all his foreign honors, including the Nobel Prize, Churchill prized most highly his honorary citizenship of the United States conferred upon him by Kennedy on April 9, 1963. The proposal to do what Congress had never done for a foreign national was first offered by Representative Francis B. Walter, Democrat of Pennsylvania, April 1, 1958.

At that time Churchill informed Mr. Walter that "after most careful consideration, I think that I should decline it rather than have an official seal put on the affection and high regard in which I hold your country."

Mr. Walter renewed his proposal in 1963 and, on Jan. 24, Kennedy told a news conference that he believed that a declaration of honorary citizenship or high esteem for Churchill "would be a gracious act."

Churchill then informed Mr. Walter through the British Embassy that "due to the changed situation from 1958" he would "be delighted to be so honored." He did not elaborate on the cryptic "the changed situation."

H.R. 4374, the bill to confer citizenship on the Briton whose mother was American-born, was passed by the House of Representatives March 12, 1963, and by the Senate April 2.

The conferral ceremony was held in the White House Rose Garden April 9. Unable to be present, Churchill was represented by his son, Randolph, but he watched and heard it all on a television broadcast carried across the Atlantic by a communications satellite. He was deeply moved.

In remarks before reading the proclamation he had signed, Kennedy said:

"Whenever and wherever tyranny threatened he has always championed liberty. Facing firmly toward the future he has never forgotten the past. Serving six sovereigns of his native Great Britain, he has served all men's freedom and dignity.

"Now his stately ship of life, having weathered the serverest storms of a troubled century, is anchored in tranquil waters, proof that courage and faith and zest for freedom are truly indestructible. The record of his triumphant passage will inspire free hearts all over the globe."

George Ball, Acting Secretary of State, then handed Randolph an honorary citizen's passport enclosed in a walnut box with a brass clasp, calling it "the only document of its kind in the world and a unique document for a unique citizen."

Randolph then read his father's acceptance.

"It is a remarkable comment on our affairs that the former Prime Minister of a great sovereign state should thus be received as an honorary citizen of another.

"I say 'great sovereign state' with design and emphasis, for I reject the view that Britain and the Commonwealth should now be relegated to a tame and minor role in the world. Our past is the key to our future, which I firmly trust and believe will be no less fertile and glorious. Let no man underrate our energies, our potentialities and our abiding power for good."

With his election to Parliament in 1959 he had contested 20 elections and been successful in 15 of them. He had held every cabinet post except that of Foreign Minister. Having represented Woodford successively since 1924, he was the "Father of the House of Commons" from 1959 until the dissolution of Parliament for the election of 1964 when, nearing 90, he announced that he would not stand again for Parliament.

On July 28, just before dissolution, the House adopted a motion putting on record "its unbounded admiration and gratitude for his services to Parliament, to the nation and to the world."

As his 90th birthday drew near, Churchill disengaged himself completely from public affairs and lived at Chartwell and at Hyde Park Gate with his wife. His mind remained clear but his health was frail and he tired easily. He saw only such old and close friends as Gen. Hastings Ismay and Lord Montgomery of Alamein.

Sir Winston and Lady Churchill had five children. The third child, Marigold, died in childhood. Diana, who was the wife of Duncan Sandys, was born in 1909 and died in 1963.

Three of their children are living. Randolph, his son, is a journalist who has edited and published several volumes of his father's speeches. He is working on the collected papers and preparing a biography.

Sarah Churchill is an actress and Mary, the youngest, is the wife of Christopher Soames.

His hand, at 90, was too unsteady to paint but he could still light his own cigars. He was permitted an occasional nip of brandy.

He lived expansively, however, and insisted on surrounding himself with a retinue of retainers and a larger secretariat than he needed.

In the final period Churchill became more and more withdrawn and uninterested in public affairs. He showed little curiosity, for example, over the outcome of the election of 1964 in which Labor returned to power after 13 years.

Like many other elderly folk, he loved to reminisce about his youth, and this he did with his few visitors and with members of his family.

He had outlived most of his contemporaries and he had seen the world change vastly from the horse-and-carriage era to the age of space vehicles. The old great empires of his youth had fallen and the new world that was emerging could hardly have been attractive to the constitutional traditionalist he was.

Although during the war Churchill held the powers of a dictator with the approval of Parliament, he never forgot, or let others forget, that it was in the province of Parliament to dismiss him at its pleasure. Recalling one of his meetings with Stalin and Roosevelt, he wrote:

"It was with some pride that I reminded my two great comrades on more than one occasion that I was the only one of our trinity who could at any moment be dismissed from power by the vote of a House of Commons freely elected on universal franchise, or could be controlled from day to day by the opinion of a war cabinet representing all parties in the State.

"The President's term of office was fixed and his powers not only as President but as Commander in Chief were almost absolute under the American Constitution. Stalin appeared to be, and at this moment certainly was, all-powerful in Russia. They could order; I had to convince and persuade. I was glad that this should be so. The process was laborious, but I had no reason to complain of the way it worked."

At 90 he was photographed with his wife of 56 happy years. He was standing at the window of his home at Hyde Park Gate looking wistfully out and evidently near tears at the crowd gathered to cheer the man who had so gallantly led them with the powers of a wartime autocrat and who had then stepped down leaving them free citizens of a democratic nation. That itself was not the least of his contributions to his times and to his fellow Britons.

Queen Elizabeth II being received by Sir Winston and Lady Churchill at 10 Downing Street on April 4, 1955, for a dinner to mark his retirement.

"All the News That's Fit to Print"

The New York Times

LATE CITY EDITION

Weather: Mostly cloudy, cold today and tonight. Rain likely tomorrow. Temperature range: today 21-37; Monday 23-35. Details on Page 66.

VOL. CXXV . . No. 43,088 | NEW YORK, TUESDAY, JANUARY 13, 1976 | 20 CENTS

25 cents beyond 50-mile zone from New York City, except Long Island. Higher in air delivery cities.

U.S. Finds Nation Healthy But Hurt by Living Habits

Study Notes Fewer Infant Deaths and Other Gains but Sees Peril in Alcohol and Tobacco and Lack of Exercise

By NANCY HICKS
Special to The New York Times

WASHINGTON, Jan. 12 — The Federal Government said today in its first comprehensive report on the state of health of Americans that the population was generally healthy but the American life style continued to be a major health hazard.

"The data suggest that much improvement in health status could come from individual action," said Dr. Theodore Cooper, Assistant Secretary for Health, whose staff prepared the report.

Excessive use of alcohol and tobacco and the lack of proper exercise and diet contribute heavily to cancer, heart and respiratory ailments, kidney and liver disease and accidents (a major killer among young people), according to the figures gathered by the Department of Health, Education and Welfare.

The infant mortality rate declined from 29.2 per 1,000 live births in 1950 to an estimated 16.5 in 1974, the report said. Even with the drop in the United States, there still are 14 other countries with lower infant death rates.

Deaths from heart disease are falling, the report said, and life expectancy has risen by almost four years since 1950.

At the same time, cancer deaths and chronic and venereal diseases are on the rise, according to the report.

The three-volume report, entitled "Health, United States, 1975," was required by law. This first annual report to Congress and the President attempted to merge health statistics with figures on population trends and health costs so that planners and policymakers could make decisions with some knowledge of potential impact.

While the trends for particular diseases may not be new—infant mortality rates have been falling for years—their presentation together gave a more complete view of health and how well the health care system functions.

"The report shows considerable achievement as well as need for improvement," Dr. Cooper said.

"Virtually every area touched upon is marked with contrasts. For example, the death rate for heart disease among persons

Continued on Page 22, Column 1

Carey Changes His Mind, Will Not Seek Taxes Now

By STEVEN R. WEISMAN
Special to The New York Times

ALBANY, Jan. 12—Governor Carey has changed his mind and has decided not to seek new taxes to balance the 1976-77 budget he will submit to the Legislature next week, according to well-informed aides.

"The Governor will go the cut route first," one aide said today. "He has moved from a belief in the need for new taxes to an intense concern about the state's economy, and he feels that continual taxation is not the answer."

Instead of the new taxes that he said two weeks ago would be unavoidable, the Governor will seek to balance the budget through a combination of new revenues, including a revamped lottery and a continuation of the present 2.5 percent income-tax surcharge; speeded-up collection of current revenues, and cuts in state programs deeper by about $175 million than the $600 million in cuts he has already requested.

One aide said the Governor was "trying desperately" to bring the new budget in without any increase in state spending. The current budget is about $10.7 billion, and the state is obliged to increase its spending by about $175 million for debt service, Social Security and employee pensions.

The Governor's strategy apparently will be to make some new taxes appear preferable to the deep cuts in state programs and local assistance by the time the Legislature adopts the new budget in late March. He signaled this approach in his annual message last week, when he declared that "to the extent that we do not close the gap through reductions, the only alternative is to increase our revenues."

The Republican leadership of both houses has vowed to resist additional taxes beyond the $600 million package of increased business taxes the Legislature enacted last month.

A budget without new tax

Continued on Page 29, Column 3

HIGH COURT VOIDS NEW YORK RULES FOR FAIR CAMPAIGN

Justices Unanimously Back View That Curbs Infringe on Freedom of Speech

By LESLEY OELSNER
Special to The New York Times

WASHINGTON, Jan. 12—The Supreme Court ruled unanimously today that major portions of New York State's fair campaign practices plan — including portions that forbid a candidate to make racial attacks on another candidate or to misrepresent an opponent's qualifications deliberately—are unconstitutional under the First Amendment.

The Court's decision came in the case of challenges originally filed by three candidates for the State Assembly in the 1974 elections, each of whom was charged by an opponent with violating the state's fair campaign code.

In another case, the Court rejected pleas from the school authorities and a group representing Chicanos that it take a second look at segregation in the public schools of Denver. [Page 22.]

In an Oklahoma case, it agreed to decide whether it is constitutional for a state to allow women to buy beer at a younger age than men. [Page 23.]

Affirmed Old Ruling

In the New York campaign case, the Court acted without hearing arguments and delivered no opinion. Instead, it simply affirmed the ruling of a three-judge Federal court that had considered the case last summer and had held, "The challenge sections of the code and of the statute are repugnant to the right of freedom of speech guaranteed by the First Amendment and are unconstitutional on their face."

The Supreme Court, by affirming that ruling without comment, makes the lower court's ruling, though not necessarily its reasoning, the decision of the high court.

The high court's judgment is immediately applicable only to the New York plan—to a portion of the state election law

Continued on Page 23, Column 5

Stocks Climb Again

The Dow Jones industrial average rose 11.26 points yesterday to close at 922.39, its highest level in 26 months, as trading on the New York Stock Exchange continued active. Volume on the exchange, at 30.44 million shares, was the 10th-heaviest in history. Page 45.

The New York Times/Larry Morris

Farouk Kaddoumi, Palestine Liberation Organization representative, taking his seat after Security Council vote

BRITAIN PLANNING NEW ULSTER TALKS

Leaders of Protestant and Catholic Parties Would Again Seek Formula

By BERNARD WEINRAUB
Special to The New York Times

LONDON, Jan. 12—The British Government announced plans tonight to bring together Roman Catholic and Protestant politicians of Northern Ireland in another attempt to work out a political settlement for the province.

In making the announcement to the House of Commons, Merlyn Rees, the British administrator for Northern Ireland, made it plain that the Government remained hopeful that a fragile agreement could be reached. There has been a wave of religious killings in the last two weeks in Northern Ireland.

Privately, Government officials as well as Catholics and Protestants in Northern Ireland held out scant hope that the Government's plan for resumption of a convention of Catholics and Protestants could achieve a breakthrough on the issue of power-sharing. Leading members of Ulster's majority community of Protestants have drawn up plans for a campaign of civil disruption if any form of power-sharing is introduced.

A Hint to Try Again

Previous attempts at power-sharing have collapsed. In May 1974, Protestant workers staged a crippling strike that led to the collapse of a Catholic-Protestant provincial executive body led by Brian Faulkner as chief minister.

A convention charged last year with proposing another solution was dominated by Protestants and urged a return to Protestant control in the province, now directly governed by the British. Mr. Rees insisted today that this was objectionable and,

Continued on Page 5, Column 1

Parley on Angola Ends Without Decision

By MICHAEL T. KAUFMAN
Special to The New York Times

ADDIS ABABA, Ethiopia, Tuesday, Jan. 13—The Organization of African Unity ended its special session on Angola at 5:30 A.M. today after the heads of state and government failed to agree on a single point.

"There has been nothing and now we are going home," said Daniel Arap Moi, the Vice President of Kenya, who headed his nation's delegation. "Neither side would move. It is a pity. Angola has been failed."

He referred to the even split that divided the delegations almost since the extraordinary session was convened three days ago.

One faction insisted on the recognition of the Popular Movement for the Liberation of Angola, which has Soviet and Cuban support, as the sole representative of Angola within the O.A.U. The other faction was opposed to the recognition of either of the two governments at war in Angola.

Other issues separated the groups, such as whether to condemn the Russians, Cubans and Americans for intervening in Angola, as well as the South Africans.

After almost 25 hours of discussion it had appeared for a while that some small face-saving compromise might be agreed on that would simply assert the solidarity of the Organization of African Unity and shelve the question of Angola for further consideration. But this, too, apparently failed.

In a communiqué issued after the end of the session Peter Onu, a spokesman for the organization, said:

"After seriously considering the Angolan problem from the 10th to the 13th of January, the assembly of heads of state and government decided to adjourn and request the bureau of the 12th summit to continue to follow the Angolan problem closely."

Yesterday delegates for the first time began to openly concede that a substantial compromise—one that could resolve the fighting between the Popular Movement and the rival coalition of the National Front for the Liberation of Angola and the National Union for the Total Independence of

Continued on Page 4, Column 2

Thai Prime Minister Quits, Blaming Foes

By DAVID A. ANDELMAN
Special to The New York Times

BANGKOK, Thailand, Jan. 12—Thailand's coalition Cabinet collapsed tonight as Prime Minister Kukrit Pramoj resigned and the King dissolved Parliament and called for new national elections in April.

In a nationwide radio and television address, the Prime Minister, who agreed to stay on as a caretaker until the elections could be held, appealed for calm.

The speech was broadcast tonight at 10 P.M. in an unusual bulletin, but taped this afternoon after he met with King Phumiphol Aduldet. Prime Minister Kukrit blamed the opposition's "pressuring the Government" for his decision to dissolve the Cabinet and request the dissolution of Parliament.

"The Government must have stability in order to decide how to run the country," Mr. Kukrit said.

The actions ended the first democratically elected government in Thailand's history and came less than two days before a special session of Parliament was scheduled—a session that, it began to appear late today, would have voted no confidence in the Kukrit Government.

The conservative Thai military establishment, which has given grudging support to Mr. Kukrit's centrist regime, reportedly approved tonight's dissolution principally as a way to prevent a leftist coalition from taking power in the wake of a no-confidence vote.

What Mr. Kukrit and other supporters of his Government are clearly hoping for is that, in the new elections, his own Social Action Party or another single major party will receive a majority and be able to govern alone or at least in a more stable combination with only one or two others.

In the election last year, more than 40 parties sponsored candidates throughout the kingdom or in various regions and some 22 political parties were represented in the 269-seat Parliament. The coalition consisted of eight parties.

The opposition consists of 14 parties, each of which has its

Continued on Page 2, Column 4

SECURITY COUNCIL VOTES 11-1 TO SEAT P.L.O. FOR DEBATE

Group Gets Member's Rights in Mideast Talks—U.S. Is Alone in Opposition

ISRAELIS ARE ASSAILED

Palestinian Scores Zionism, Rejects Key Resolutions as Basis for Settlement

By BERNARD GWERTZMAN
Special to The New York Times

UNITED NATIONS, N.Y., Jan. 12 — The Security Council opened its debate on the Middle East today by voting overwhelmingly to allow the Palestine Liberation Organization to participate with the rights of a United Nations member nation despite a vehement objection by the United States that such action "eroded the influence and authority" of the Council.

The vote was 11 to 1, with the United States voting against the proposal. Britain, France and Italy abstained.

Egypt, Jordan, Syria, Qatar and the United Arab Emirates will also be allowed to sit in the chamber. There were no objections raised to the presence of those countries.

In the debate, the United States was unable to use its veto because a veto is possible only on substantive resolutions and not in procedural debates such as those on agenda or participation.

Israel, anticipating that the P.L.O. would be seated, had already announced that it would not ask to take part in the debate, which is expected to go on over the next two weeks. Its delegate, Chaim Herzog, spoke at a meeting across from the United Nations this morning and warned that the Council was laying the groundwork for a new Middle East war.

Moynihan Assails Council

Although the vote to admit the P.L.O. had been expected as a result of previous actions in the United Nations in November and December, Daniel P. Moynihan, the chief United States delegate, bitterly assailed what he called a rise of "totalitarianism" in the Council, and sharply rebuked the P.L.O. for its refusal to recognize the existence of Israel.

The two-hour debate that preceded the vote on the P.L.O.'s seating had been anticipated in a behind-the-scenes dispute this morning when the Council met to discuss the procedures to be followed.

Yakov A. Malik, the chief

Continued on Page 6, Column 3

Agatha Christie, Creator of Poirot, Dies

By MAX LOWENTHAL

Lord Snowdon, Camera Press

Dame Agatha Christie

Dame Agatha Christie, the English writer who created two of the most distinctive sleuths of detective fiction—Jane Marple and Hercole Poirot—as the central characters in a hugely successful series of mystery stories for half a century, died yesterday at her home in Wallingford, England, 47 miles west of London. She was 85 years old.

The sheer volume of Dame Agatha's writing since 1920, when "The Mysterious Affair at Styles" appeared, was enough to stagger even the most incurable addict of detective fiction. The "sausage machine," as she once called herself, produced some 60 detective novels alone, and her books went through reprint after reprint and sold hundreds of million of copies. When its usually superior quality was taken into account, her output appeared to be nothing less than prodigious.

The creator of the dapper, relentless Monsieur Poirot, the shrewd, garrulous Miss Marple and a half-dozen other energetic fictional sleuths was herself a shy, self-effacing but regal person who set out to be an opera singer. Instead, starting to write in response to a challenge from her sister, she became a virtuoso performer in the fine art of the detective story who often devised her plots while lolling in the bathtub.

Dame Agatha turned out more than 100 works—the full-scale detective stories, 6 psychological or romantic novels published under the name Mary Westmacott, 19 volumes of short mystery stories, 14 plays based on detective themes (among them "The Mousetrap," which has broken just about every theatrical record since 1952 and is still running in London), 2 works of nonfiction and a book of verse.

In addition, most of her books were translated into almost every major language, and several of her plots were adapted for the stage, in a number of foreign tongues as well as English, or made into movies.

On two occasions, though briefly, three Christie plays were on the London stage at

Continued on Page 40, Column 1

2 Held Here as Confidence Men; Victims' Loss Put at $400,000

By ROBERT D. McFADDEN

Detectives seized two alleged confidence men here yesterday and said they were believed to have fleeced rich widows and other women who live alone of more than $400,000 over the last six months in a low-risk, big-money swindle called "The Bank Examiner Game."

In this, con men posing as policemen working for the State Bank Examiner tell the victims by phone that their savings accounts and safe-deposit boxes are being looted by crooked bank clerks.

To help catch the culprits and get a reward, the victims are asked to withdraw cash and other valuables, ostensibly because they bear the crooked clerks' fingerprints. This "evidence"—which the victims are told is destined for the police laboratory—is then picked up by a "detective," who furnishes a signed receipt and vanishes.

The suspects, Fred Walker, a 37-year-old former Atlantic City police officer, and George Walker, 50, of Los Angeles, no relation, were arrested by detectives of the pickpocket and confidence squad at noon in the lobby of the Euclid Hall Hotel, 2345 Broadway, near 86th Street.

The arresting officers said

Continued on Page 20, Column 1

NEWS INDEX

3 Bombs With a Timer Found Near U.N.

By PETER KIHSS

The New York Times/Paul Hosefros

Members of the Police Department bomb section placing pipe bombs found near the U.N. in bomb-proofed truck.

Three pipe bombs were found packed in a paper bag in an underground passageway next to the United Nations headquarters on 42d Street east of First Avenue yesterday.

The police and United Nations officials said one had been timed to explode at 3 P.M., which would have been a half hour before the scheduled start of the expected stormy Middle East debate in the Security Council.

After tests at the police firing range at Rodmans Neck in the Bronx, Officer Charles Wells, of the bomb section, estimated late yesterday that the bombs, a mixture of explosive powders, could have inflicted injuries in a radius of 50 feet.

Early today, the police found and disarmed another bomb, this one made of two propane cylinders and a timing device, that had been placed in an alley next to the Iraqi mission to the United Nation, at 14 East 79th Street, near Fifth Avenue. The police said the propane bomb had been timed to go off early this morning and that damage would have been extensive to the mission, several miles from the United Nations building.

An anonymous telephone caller told CBS Channel 2 and The Associated Press late last night that the propane bomb

Continued on Page 7, Column 1

Agatha Christie Dies at 85; Wrote Mysteries 50 Years

Continued From Page 1, Col. 3

one time.

Dame Agatha's forte was, supremely adroit plotting and sharp, believable characterization (even the names she used usually rang true). Her style and rhetoric were not remarkable; her writing was almost invariably sound and workmanlike, without pretense or flourish. Her characters were likely to be of the middle-middle or upper-middle class, and there were certain archetypes, such as the crass American or the stuffy retired army officer now in his anecdotage.

However familiar all this might be, the reader would turn the pages mesmerized as unexpected twist piled on unexpected twist until, in the end, he was taken by surprise and realized that he had stupidly ignored the vital clue casually introduced on Page 123. There was simply no outguessing Poirot or Miss Marple — or Agatha Christie.

A few Christies — "The Murder of Roger Ackroyd," a controversial book because of its unorthodoxy since its publication in 1926, is a pre-eminent example—were both extremely well-written and extremely skillfully plotted and ranked with the best of Simenon, S. S. Van Dine and perhaps even Conan Doyle.

On the other hand, when Dame Agatha went into situations requiring more expressive writing, the results were often less than satisfactory and, indeed, were sometimes a little painful. Her love scenes in particular tended to be a bit soppy.

'Extraordinary Ability'

Margery Allingham, also a mystery writer of wide reputation, said of Dame Agatha in an article in The New York Times Book Review in 1950:

"The impression she leaves is that she is a woman of extraordinary ability who could have done anything she chose to do. What she has done is to entertain more people for more hours at a time than almost any other writer of her generation."

This appraisal was not universally shared, however. Robert Graves, another prodigious author, albeit of more serious works, writing of detective fiction in The Book Review in 1957, asked: "Will the 21st-century English literature course include Agatha Christie—statistically the most popular detective-writer today?" His reply was negative, although he acknowledged her popularity, especially on the stage.

"Though she knows the Devonshire countryside well and is not only a qualified pharmacist, an enthusiastic gardener, but a capable archeological worker," he said, "nobody could promise Agatha immortality as a novelist. Her English is school-girlish, her situations for the most part artificial, her detail faulty."

Father Was New Yorker

Dame Agatha was born Agatha Mary Clarissa Miller in Torquay, England, on Sept. 15, 1890, the second of two children of Frederick A. Miller, a native of New York of independent means—his father had been a successful merchant—and of an English mother. The parents had moved in 1882 to the popular seaside resort, which eventually figured in a number of Christies.

Her biographical sketch which required nearly five inches in the British "Who's Who" to make room for all the titles of her works, reflected her lifelong insistence on privacy by giving the barest of details. It noted that she was made a Commander of the Order of the British Empire in 1956, that she was a fellow of the Royal Society of Letters and that she had an honorary doctorate in literature. Since she was the wife of Sir Max Mallowan, she could choose to be called either Dame Agatha or Lady Mallowan. After the word "education" there appeared the word "home"; like many young women of good family at that time, she was largely educated by her mother, to whom she was intensely devoted.

J. Hedsecoe Ltd.

Dame Agatha with husband, Sir Max Mallowan, the archeologist, in 1967.

Abandoned Singing

Musically gifted and having a good voice, she started on a singing career and went to Paris to study, but her shyness led her to abandon the venture.

In 1914, after a two-year engagement, she was married to a British air officer, Col. Archibald Christie, whose name she retained for professional purposes after their divorce in 1928. They had a daughter, Rosalind, whose first husband died in war and who later became Mrs. Anthony Hicks. Colonel Christie died in 1962.

During World War I, Dame Agatha volunteered for hospital work, becoming a nurse and then a pharmacist and gaining expertise on poisons. (She did the same sort of volunteer work in World War II.) It was during this period that her sister challenged her to write a detective story. "The Mysterious Affair at Styles," partly based on her wartime work, took several years to write and was turned down by so many publishers that she had nearly given up when it was accepted by the Bodley Head.

"Styles" was successful but no earthshaker. Its importance lay in the introduction of the grandly mustachioed Belgian egotist Poirot, his creator's favorite detective.

Producing books at the rate of about one a year in that period, Dame Agatha soon established herself as among the most successful and entertaining authors of detective fiction.

In December 1926, shortly after "Roger Ackroyd" was published, the writer of mysteries offered the public a mystery of her own—she disappeared for 10 days. The incident resulted in reams of stories in Britain and elsewhere, and it was widely believed at the time to be a stunt, but a principal clue—a name—showed this theory to be erroneous.

Upset over the recent loss of her mother, sensing that her marriage was breaking up and perhaps not in the best of health, Dame Agatha apparently had an attack of amnesia. Whatever the reason, she abandoned her car and vanished, only to be found—after an intensive land, sea and air search involving thousands of policemen, soldiers and amateur sleuths—at a Yorkshire hotel, where she was registered under the name of the woman who was to become Colonel Christie's second wife.

Sales of her books spurted and they were serialized in the press. She and her husband were reunited, but in April 1928 she filed for divorce in an action that was undefended.

She then began to travel, concentrating on the Middle East. There, in 1930, she met a British archeologist and scholar, Max E. L. Mallowan (now Sir Max), who was making one of his recurrent forays into the mysteries of Nineveh and Ur. They were married that September and she accompanied him on his annual trips, becoming something of an archeology buff, incorporating the milieu into her mysteries and later writing a book, "Come, Tell Me How You Live," describing expedition life.

At Peak in 1930's

The 1930's saw Dame Agatha reach her peak output—in 1934-35 she published six novels—and, at the same time, gratify her taste for buying, decorating and furnishing houses, often with fine antiques. At one time the Mallowans owned eight properties. Their principal residence in recent years were in Wallingford, Berkshire, in Churston Ferrers, South Devon, and at Oxford.

With the outbreak of World War II, Professor Mallowan, who is an honorary fellow of the Metropolitan Museum of Art in New York, became an adviser to the British Government and his wife went back to the study of poisons and the dispensing of drugs. This did not interfere with the detective business, for a book or two appeared every year during the war.

Among them was a revival of a team of amateurs, Tommy and Tuppence Baresford, who as a young couple were involved with espionage activities in World War I (in "The Secret Adversary") and then, with grown children of their own, were concerned with Nazi infiltration. One of Dame Agatha's talents was the ability to keep up with the times.

After the war Dame Agatha's reputation and audience grew even greater, and her sales, particularly in paperback editions, skyrocketed. It was not unusual for a paperback—Pocket Books and Dell were her American publishers in that form—to go into a 10th or 15th printing. Pocket Books has had sales of 5 million copies in a year, and Penguin Books, the British paperback house, listed Christies as the best sellers it has had. "The Murder of Roger Ackroyd" alone sold more than a million copies.

The stories and characters infiltrated from stage and screen onto radio and television. Perhaps the high point in this was in 1947, when the British Broadcasting Corporation presented a radio tribute to Queen Mary for her 80th birthday. She asked that an Agatha Christie be included, and the delighted author did "Three Blind Mice"—on which "The Mousetrap" was later based—to order for the occasion.

Dame Agatha also scored tremendously on the stage, although her record there was far more uneven than in books. "The Mousetrap," whose stage title was taken from a line in another hit play, "Hamlet," has broken every record for regular theatrical productions since it opened in 1952 to mixed reviews at the Ambassador Theater in London. It wears out cast, staff and furniture but goes on and on, perhaps on its own momentum. Last night's performance was No. 9,612, and London theaters dimmed their lights in tribute to the writer.

With such a success on her hands, and with taxes what they were Dame Agatha eventually decided to turn the rights to "The Mousetrap" over to her grandson, Mathew C. T. Prichard, who was born in 1943. Its earnings have enabled him to live in the grand style.

Her first stage venture, "Alibi," based on "Roger Ackroyd," was highly successful in London and in New York, where it opened in 1932. Charles Laughton depicted Poirot; years later he starred with Marlene Dietrich in the film version of another highly successful Christie play, "Witness for the Prosecution." Named the best foreign play of the 1954-55 New York season, it, in turn, was based on a rather undistinguished Christie short story.

Another work that was a hit in several forms is known to Americans as "Ten Little Indians" or "And Then There Were None" (and also as "The Nursery Rhyme Murders"). A particularly ingenious piece of plotting, it was based, like many by the author, on a familiar nursery rhyme (the rhyme in the American versions was quite different from that in the originals). First published as a novel in 1939, the work was dramatized by Dame Agatha in 1943 and made into a movie in 1945 with Barry Fitzgerald and Walter Huston and in 1965 with Wilfrid Hyde White and Stanley Holloway. A third film version in 1975 starred Oliver Reed and Elke Sommer.

Popular in Last Years

Her popularity — never exactly at a low point even though some of her postwar books received less-than-enthusiastic notices—rose remarkably in the last two years of her life, because of the release of the motion picture "Murder on the Orient Express" (based on her book "Murder on the Calais Coach") and to the publication of "Curtain," in which Poirot dies.

"Curtain" was one of the books written decades earlier that Dame Agatha designated for publication after her death. But she evidently relented and decided to release it earlier. The book did exceedingly well, appearing on the best-seller lists almost immediately on publication last Oct. 15. It was No. 1 on The New York Times Book Review best-seller charts last week. More than 200,000 copies of "Curtain" are in print.

With "Murder on the Orient Express," Dame Agatha set a box-office high. Directed by Sidney Lumet, it had an all-star cast that included Albert Finney as Poirot, and Lauren Bacall, Ingrid Bergman, Sean Connery, John Gielgud, Wendy Hiller, Anthony Perkins, Richard Widmark, Michael York, Vanessa Redgrave and Rachel Roberts.

8th Highest Money Maker

The film, released here by Paramount, returned $17.8 million in rentals to Paramount. It thus became the eighth highest money maker of last year. This represents receipts in the United States and Canada. Its earnings elsewhere in the world could equal or surpass that total.

Agatha Christie, a tallish, white-haired "presence" who was always well-turned out, insisted that she was not to be found in her books. Her shyness, which gave way to graciousness in her later years, made that idea credible enough. But it might be that Miss Marple, an aging "lady" with conservative tastes and somewhat old-fashioned ideas but, nevertheless, with an acute awareness of what was going on about her, was the closest to Dame Agatha.

Discussing the murderer after the solution of the crime in "A Murder Is Announced," Miss Marple, who figured in about 15 novels and helped her creator get through periods of boredom with Poirot, said:

"People with a grudge against the world are always dangerous. They seem to think life owes them something. I've known many an invalid who has suffered far worse and been cut off from life much more than Charlotte Blacklock—and they've managed to lead happy, contented lives. It's what's in yourself that makes you happy or unhappy."

Poirot, also a talkative fellow, who remarked (in "The A.B.C. Murders") that "there is nothing so dangerous for anyone who has something to hide as conversation," frequently made trenchant comments about crime and criminals. In "Evil Under the Sun," he said:

"There is no such thing as a plain fact of murder. Murder springs, 9 times out of 10, out of the character and circumstances of the murdered person. Because the victim was the kind of person he or she was, therefore was he or she murdered!"

Following Dame Agatha through the years, readers received a clear picture of certain segments of life, particularly that in the upper middle class in the English village. While sandwiching in contemporary elements, so that her writings were a light-hearted social history, Dame Agatha managed to respond to a continuity of reader tastes.

Escapist and superficial though detective stories may be, those by skilled professionals like Dame Agatha provided first-rate intellectual fare. On the other hand, the typical mystery does not really play fair with the reader because there are certain elements of which he is kept unaware. Dame Agatha maintained that she never cheated, but she confessed that she wrote ambiguously. Miss Marple, who became a movie character in the person of Margaret Rutherford, was known to acknowledge that she had information that others, including the reader, did not possess. Furthermore, the writer frequently resorted to coincidental meetings as a vital plot device.

Even if she had cheated it would not have mattered much, for her fans were devotedly loyal. One of them, a Florentine, wrote a book in Italian in 1957 entitled "Love Letters to Agatha Christie."

"All the News That's Fit to Print"

The New York Times

LATE CITY EDITION

Weather: Breezy, cool today; cold tonight. Cloudy and cool tomorrow. Temperature range: today 43-56; yesterday 47-52. Details, page 47.

VOL.CXXVII....No.43,729 © 1977 The New York Times Company NEW YORK, SATURDAY, OCTOBER 15, 1977 35 cents beyond 50-mile zone from New York City. Higher in air delivery cities. 20 CENTS

The New York Times/Larry Morris

Bing Crosby during appearance at Avery Fisher Hall last December.

Bing Crosby, 73, Dies in Madrid On Golf Course

Special to The New York Times

MADRID, Oct. 14—Bing Crosby, the singer and actor whose breezy baritone voice charmed popular music listeners for 50 years and made him one of the most successful personalities of American show business, died of an apparent heart attack today while playing golf at a course outside Madrid. He was 73 years old.

The singer, an avid golfer, collapsed at the 17th hole of La Moraleja Golf Course while playing a round with several Spanish champions, Manuel Piñero, Valentín Barrios and César de Zulueta.

Mr. Crosby had arrived in Spain yesterday, primarily to relax and play golf, after having completed an enthusiastically received tour of Britain, including a sold-out engagement at the Palladium in London. He had planned a golfing trip to the Spanish island of Majorca before returning to his home near San Francisco.

Invited By Mrs. Carter

A spokesman at the White House said that Rosalynn Carter only yesterday had sent Mr. Crosby a letter asking him to sing next December at the traditional White House Christmas party.

Bob Hope, whose running gag feud with Mr. Crosby was a trademark of both their careers, was "too devastated" to comment on the death of his old friend, according to a spokesman. Mr. Hope, who was in New York City, canceled a benefit appearance at the Governor Morris Inn in Morristown, N.J., and flew home to California.

William S. Paley, chairman of CBS Inc., who signed Mr. Crosby to a national radio contract in 1931, called his death "a great loss to the entertainment world," and said in a statement, "He will be remembered as one of the best-loved and most highly respected figures in theatrical history."

A Star Almost 5 Decades

Harry Lillis Crosby parlayed a burbling baritone voice, a relaxed manner and a sense of business acumen into millions of dollars and a place in the front rank of world-famous entertainers.

A star performer for almost five decades, he delighted millions on radio, tele-

Continued on Page 11, Column 1

FORMER REP. HANNA INDICTED FOR FRAUD IN KOREAN SCANDAL

40 Felony Charges Also Include Bribery and Conspiracy to Influence Congress

By NICHOLAS M. HORROCK

Special to The New York Times

WASHINGTON, Oct. 14—A Federal grand jury indicted former Representative Richard T. Hanna of California here today on 40 felony charges stemming from an investigation of alleged bribery and influence peddling by members of the South Korean Central Intelligence Agency.

Mr. Hanna is the first present or former member of Congress to be criminally charged in the two-and-a-half-year-old investigation. Tongsun Park, until recently a Washington businessman, and Hancho C. Kim, a Korean-American living in Maryland, were indicted earlier this year in connection with the case.

The grand jury charged Mr. Hanna with conspiring with Mr. Park and two former directors of the South Korean C.I.A. to manipulate the actions of the United States Government and the United States Congress. It also charged him with three counts of seeking some $100,000 in bribes in exchange for his official actions and for influencing fellow members of Congress.

Mail Fraud Also Charged

The indictment also charged Mr. Hanna with failing to register as an agent of a foreign government and with 35 counts of mail fraud.

If convicted on all counts, Mr. Hanna, a Democrat, could face 217 years in prison and $105,000 in fines. Charles McNelis, a Washington lawyer who represents Mr. Hanna in the case, said, "We are preparing a defense against these charges."

Mr. Hanna could not be reached for comment. Last November, he told The New York Times in an interview that he did not believe there was anything illegal about his relationship with Mr. Park.

2 Co-Conspirators Named

Today's indictment involves the same case under which Mr. Park was indicted last June. As it was handed up, Benjamin Civiletti, Assistant Attorney General in charge of the criminal division, and Paul Michel, the chief prosecutor in the case, were on their way to South Korea to try to work out terms for questioning Mr. Park.

The long and detailed indictment charged that Mr. Hanna had conspired to "defraud the United States of America and the Congress of the United States" by allegedly interfering with both Congressional and executive branch deliberations on United States policy toward the Republic of South Korea.

It named Kim Hyung Wook, a former chief of the Seoul C.I.A. and now a resident of the United States, and Lee Hu Rak, another former Korean C.I.A. head,

Continued on Page 17, Column 4

Associated Press

One of the hijackers of a Lufthansa jetliner examining a catering van at Dubai airport yesterday. In addition to food and water, the hijackers were given an air conditioner; temperature on tarmac was about 95 degrees.

CARTER AND TORRIJOS AGREE ON U.S. RIGHT TO DEFEND THE CANAL

GIVE STATEMENT AFTER MEETING

Military Force Could Be Used to Keep the Waterway Open, but Not to Intervene in Internal Affairs

By BERNARD GWERTZMAN

Special to The New York Times

WASHINGTON, Oct. 14—In an effort to facilitate approval of the Panama Canal treaty in both the United States and Panama, President Carter and Brig. Gen. Omar Torrijos Herrera said today that the United States had the right "to act against any aggression or threat directed against the Canal."

In a "statement of understanding" issued after the two leaders had met at the White House for an hour and 40 minutes, the United States and Panama also affirmed that the right of the United States to use military force to keep the Panama Canal open did not mean that the United States would intervene in "the internal affairs of Panama."

"Any United States action will be directed at insuring that the Canal will remain open, secure and accessible, and shall never be directed against the territorial integrity or political independence of Panama," said the statement, which was released here and in Panama.

Goal Is to Ease Apprehension

The joint statement was issued in order to ease apprehension that had arisen in the Senate, even among supporters of the treaties. The wording in parts of the treaty dealing with how the canal would be operated after Panama takes full control by the year 2000 was ambiguous. This led to varying interpretations by commentators and officials in both this country and Panama and to calls for clarification. At his news conference yesterday, President Carter said, "I think the clarification is crucial."

A plebiscite on the treaties is scheduled in Panama on Oct. 23, and both sides wanted to insure that there was agreement on controversial points before the voting occurred. Presumably today's statement goes some distance toward meeting that objective.

In addition the brief statement said that the Neutrality Treaty, one of the two canal documents signed by the two leaders in Washington on Sept. 7, provides that military ships of the United States would be entitled to transit the canal "expeditiously."

Linowitz Briefs Senate Leaders

The clarifying statement said that this term was intended to mean that in case of an emergency American warships could "go to the head of the line of vessels in order to transit the Canal rapidly."

Sol M. Linowitz, who had been one of the American negotiators of the treaties, immediately briefed Senate leaders this afternoon after Mr. Carter and General Torrijos, the Panamanian head of Government, had completed their meeting.

Mr. Linowitz told reporters at an early evening briefing at the White House that he was "pleased" by a statement made by Senator John J. Sparkman, chairman

Continued on Page 8, Column 1

SENATE PANEL BACKS NEW ENERGY TAX BILL

Plan Would Spur Oil Savings but Cost U.S. $32 Billion in 8 Years

By STEVEN RATTNER

Special to The New York Times

WASHINGTON, Oct. 14—The Senate Finance Committee, which earlier rejected President Carter's major energy tax proposals, approved a revised program today that would save substantial amounts of oil but would cost the Treasury $32 billion over the next eight years.

After a final review in about a week, the bill goes before the full Senate, where it faces an uncertain fate.

The bill differs from the President's proposal by using tax credits—dollar-for-dollar reductions of taxes—and incentives to achieve more energy production and conversion to plentiful fuels. The President has suggested using new taxes and limited incentives to spur conversion and conservation.

However, the provisions approved by the Senate Finance Committee will reduce imports of oil by about 2.24 million barrels a day, according to staff estimates, compared to a range of 1.7 million to 2.5 million barrels a day for the tax provisions approved by the House of Representatives in early August.

The most important provision of the revised bill is a tax credit for purchase of "alternative energy property" such as

Continued on Page 35, Column 1

Hijacking of Jet With 91 to Dubai Linked With German Kidnapping

By Reuters

DUBAI, United Arab Emirates, Saturday, Oct. 15—The hijackers of a West German airliner with 91 people on board were promised fuel for their hijacked aircraft today in exchange for some of their hostages, including some believed to be ill.

The hijackers, who diverted the plane here from Europe yesterday, have threatened to kill their hostages unless 13 terrorists are freed from West German and Turkish jails by tomorrow.

While the talks dragged on, it became clear that the hijacking of the Lufthansa Boeing 737 yesterday over the Mediterranean was linked with the kidnapping on Sept. 5 of Hanns-Martin Schleyer, the West German industrialist.

Demand 11 Tons of Fuel

The Defense Minister of the United Arab Emirates, Sheik Mohammed bin Rashid al-Maktum, said the hijackers had demanded 11 tons of fuel. Experts said this would be enough for about four hours of flight.

The Defense Minister said he was continuing consultations at the airport control tower with a West German delegation headed by Minister of State Hans Jurgen Wischnewski, which arrived here on board a special Lufthansa aircraft shortly after midnight.

Mr. Wischnewski immediately conferred with the West German Ambassador, Hans Joachim Neumann, who has been negotiating with the hijackers.

Ultimatums received by the West German Government in Bonn from the Schleyer kidnappers and those from the hijackers set Sunday deadlines for the release of 11 German guerrillas detained in West German prisons and two Palestinians held in Turkish jails. West Germany was told that failure to comply would mean death for Mr. Schleyer.

West Germany indicated it would consider the hijackers' demands, but the Turkish Government said it would not release the two Palestinians.

The Government spokesman in Bonn, Klaus Bölling, said that there were four hijackers, two men and two women, and that they were armed with pistols and hand grenades.

Dubai officials said yesterday that there

Continued on Page 26, Column 3

Briton, Swede Get Nobel Prize For Economics

By ROBERT D. HERSHEY Jr.

Special to The New York Times

STOCKHOLM, Oct. 14 — Two pioneers in international trade theory, one Swedish and the other British, won the 1977 Nobel Memorial Prize in Economic Science, it was announced here today.

They are Bertil Ohlin, 78 years old, once an academic prodigy and later leader of the Swedish Liberal Party, and James E. Meade, 70, a former professor at Cambridge University.

They were cited for their "pathbreaking contributions to the theory of international trade and international capital movements," a field that had not been recognized in the eight preceding economics prizes.

The Royal Swedish Academy observed that both men attracted wide attention when their main works appeared in the 1930's and 1950's and that others have used their theories as the basis for extensive empirical research.

"The breadth and importance of Ohlin's and Meade's contributions have, however,

Continued on Page 33, Column 3

Hectic Week for the Dollar: Uncertainties Drive It Down

By ANN CRITTENDEN

One of the most hectic weeks in foreign exchange trading in some years came to an end yesterday with the dollar at lows or near-lows against almost all the world's major currencies. The movement of funds was unusually heavy.

"It has been a chaotic week, with an unusually quick depreciation of the dollar," said Ernst Brutsche, a senior vice president of Citibank and a foreign exchange expert.

He said the dollar would have fallen even more if the world's central banks had not moved into the markets to support the United States currency with a level of intervention not seen in two years.

Behind the decline, Mr. Brutsche and other traders said, was a continuing concern over a number of economic factors, particularly the record American trade deficit and the uncertainty about the fate of the Administration's tax and energy programs, both of which will affect the American trade position.

Other factors include world pressure on nations with strong economies (notably Japan, West Germany and Switzerland) to let their currencies rise in value to discourage their exports and encourage growth by other nations. Dollars are thus being sold to buy these stronger currencies.

Bankers and businessmen all over the world react to these factors when they buy and sell foreign currencies for trade and investment purposes. Under world

Continued on Page 35, Column 3

INSIDE

Minimum Wage Rise

House and Senate conferees agreed to legislation raising the minimum wage to $3.35 by 1981, an increase of $1.05 over the current rate. Page 10.

Exhumation in Gem Case

Puerto Rico's police ordered a murder victim's burned body exhumed to determine if it is that of a missing New York gem salesman. Page 36.

Mrs. Onassis Resigns Editing Post

By DEIRDRE CARMODY

Jacqueline Kennedy Onassis has resigned as a consulting editor at the Viking Press because of its publication of a novel that depicts Senator Edward M. Kennedy, her brother-in-law, as the target of an assassination attempt.

Several months ago, Mrs. Onassis was informed by her long-time friend, Thomas Guinzburg, the president of Viking, that the publishing house planned to sign a contract to publish the novel "Shall We Tell the President?" by a British author and former member of Parliament, Jeffrey Archer.

At the time, Mrs. Onassis reportedly did not attempt to dissuade Mr. Guinzburg from acquiring the book. However, she apparently became "extremely upset" this week when an article in The Boston Globe and the review of the book in The New York Times seemed to suggest that she was connected with publication of the book.

"Last spring, when told of the book, I tried to separate my lives as a Viking employee and a Kennedy relative," Mrs. Onassis was quoted by Nancy Tuckerman, her spokesman as having said.

"But this fall, when it was suggested that I had had something to do with acquiring the book and that I was not distressed by its publication. I felt I had to resign," Mrs. Onassis said, according to Miss Tuckerman.

Late Thursday afternoon, Mrs. Onassis sent a hand-written letter of resignation to Mr. Guinzberg. Neither Miss Tucker-

Continued on Page 36, Column 2

Associated Press

Reggie Jackson being congratulated by Billy Martin, the Yankees' manager, after scoring in the first inning

Yanks Win, 5-3, and Take 2-1 Edge in Series

By JOSEPH DURSO

Special to The New York Times

LOS ANGELES, Oct. 14—Surrounded by the joys and comforts of California culture and by the sound and fury of their own family feud, the New York Yankees overpowered the Los Angeles Dodgers by 5-3 tonight and took a lead of two games to one in the 74th World Series.

They did it methodically, too, with no signs of revolt or retreat. Mike Torrez pitched a solid seven-hitter that kept the Dodgers relatively tame while the Yankee bats went to work early with three runs in the first inning, just when people were suggesting that brawling in public would bring the New York team to no good end.

As the transcontinental rivals opened their weekend in Dodger Stadium, nearly 3,000 miles west of the week's first battleground, they were flanked by a sellout crowd of 55,992 fans and a national television audience. And in the center of the glittering stage stood the two men pitching to break the deadlock in the Series: Mike Torrez of Topeka, Kan., a 31-year-old right-hander who won 17 games this summer, and Tommy John of Terre Haute, Ind.,

Continued on Page 13, Column 3

Bing Crosby Is Dead at 73; a Star for 5 Decades

Continued From Page 1

vision, and in motion pictures and near World War II battlefields, where he entertained countless servicemen. His records sold worldwide by the millions, and his earnings from his performances and investments well exceeded a million dollars a year for many years.

In all, Mr. Crosby sold more than 300 million records and in his later years, when he stopped making movies, he continued nonetheless to attract enormous public attention with appearances on television and at the Bing Crosby Pro-Amateur Golf Tournament in Pebble Beach, Calif.

His domestic life was, in many ways, as vigorous and fruitful as his professional career. His four sons by his first wife, Dixie Lee, who died in 1952, followed their father as professional entertainers.

In 1957, Mr. Crosby, then 53 years old, married 23-year-old Kathryn Grant, a brown-eyed actress from Texas, and they had two sons, Harry and Nathaniel, and a daughter, Mary Frances. They all appeared together on television in occasional Christmas specials and commercials.

Liks Rudy Vallee a few years earlier and Frank Sinatra a little later, Bing Crosby burst on the American scene in 1931 as a practitioner of crooning, which was then setting teenagers and many older audiences into ecstasies. His mellow rendition of "When the Blue of the Night Meets the Gold of the Day," with his distinctive bu-bu-bu-buing between phrases, made him an overnight sensation.

Instead of fading into a footnote on the musical fare of that decade, Mr. Crosby went on to become an institution. Some historians of the Great Depression era have maintained that what carried him to expanding poplarity was his espousal in song of the "don't worry" philosophy.

Instead of concentrating on the woes of unrequited love, he brightened the idle moments of an impoverished or worried generation with songs about not needing a bundle of money to make life sunny or about pennies from heaven. Over the radio, on records, in motion picture houses, the masses here, and later abroad, were entranced by his smooth and seemingly effortless singing, which gradually dropped its more extreme mannerisms like the bu-bu-bu-bus.

Subtlety and Depth

Mr. Crosby won a movie Oscar in 1944 as the year's best actor for his role as a priest in "Going My Way." Among the most popular of his half a hundred films were the "Road" comedies —"The Road to Singapore," "The Road to Zanzibar" and others—with Bob Hope and Dorothy Lamour.

His acting style was an embellishment, in a sense, of Mr. Crosby's own personality as a performer—relaxed, low-key and quietly charming. He almost never played a heavy, even as the spineless alcoholic husband opposite Grace Kelly in the film of Clifford Odets's "The Country Girl," released in 1954, in which Mr. Crosby gave one of his most compelling performances.

Again in 1966, he played an alcoholic sort, this time, the sodden, unshaven doctor in a remake of the classic western, "Stagecoach." And again, it seemed to reviewers that his innate likability came across to produce a performance of subtlety and depth.

Indeed, Mr. Crosby once recognized his own screen personality when he told an interviewer how he had recently turned down the role of Scrooge for a Hollywood film.

"I don't think I would have been believable as Scrooge for a minute," he said. "Everybody knows I'm just a big good-natured slob."

Bing Crosby, of the blue eyes and brown hair, made no secret of having to wear a toupee in pictures. Off screen he usually wore a hat to cover his baldness.

The easy-going humor and the bizarrely loud sport shirts that were his trademarks through the years were in evidence off stage as well as before the cameras or microphones. But they did not encompass the whole man, who knew trouble and anguish, too.

Mr. Crosby and Barry Fitzgerald won Oscars for their roles as priests in the 1944 film "Going My Way," which also won the award for best picture.

Discipline for His Sons

His first marriage had much heartbreak. Some of the unhappiness between him and Dixie Lee stemmed from his iron-handed disciplining of their sons—Gary, the twins Phillip and Dennis, and Lindsay —who got into more than a modicum of trouble as young men and one of whom was estranged from his father until a later reconciliation.

The future performing star acquired the nickname Bing when he was 7 or 8 years old because of his fondness for a comic strip called "The Bingville Bugle." As a boy he was called Bing-o, but the "o" got lost along the way.

Another version of the name's origin, however, involved young Crosby annoying one of his grade school teachers with a wooden gun, which he would fire, shouting, "Bing! Bing!" She started calling him "Bing-bing," this version went, and the name stuck.

He became a regular on the Columbia Broadcasting System's radio networks in 1932. He resisted many blandishments to appear on television until June 1952, when he made his TV debut on a telethon with Bob Hope to raise money for the United States Olympic Fund. This appearance made the public want more. Jack Gould, reviewing his debut in The New York Times, wrote: "Bing's relaxed style and easygoing ways were made to order for home viewing."

'Silent Night' the Favorite

Mr. Crosby made occasional spot appearances on television, but continued to shy away from a regular TV spot until 1958, when he signed a five-year radio and television contract with the Americon Broadcasting Company.

Of more than a score of his recordings that sold above the million-disk mark, the most popular was "Silent Night," with "White Christmas" second. It has been said that there was not a moment during the year that the Crosby voice was not being heard somewhere in the world—on radio, phonograph or jukebox.

Mr. Crosby's autobiography, published in 1953, had the modest title, "Call Me Lucky." Written in collaboration with Pete Martin of the Saturday Evening Post, it appeared serially in that magazine and was published in book form by Simon & Schuster.

Mr. Crosby made wise investments of most of the earnings his talent for entertainment brought him. Even his stable of race horses, of whose slowness audiences were often reminded, paid off in the form of gags concocted by his script writers. He also bred horses, and in the mid-1930's he helped to establish and became president of the Del Mar race track in California. He sold his interest in the track in 1946 for nearly half a million dollars.

When fire destroyed his home in 1943, he poked through the ashes and retrieved $2,000 in horse-race winnings from a shoe. His interest in sports led him at one time to buy 15 percent of the Pittsburgh Pirates baseball team and later about 5 percent of the Detroit Tigers.

Exhibitions Aided Charities

His exhibition golf matches with Bob Hope, his great friend with whom he also engaged in bantering exchanges of insults, raised thousands of dollars for charities. In World War II, after each match, they auctioned their clubs and golf togs to buyers of war bonds. An expert, playing in the low 70's, Mr. Crosby was given the William D. Richardson Memorial Trophy in 1950 for his contributions to the game. He played with President Kennedy at Palm Beach in 1961. He was also an enthusiastic hunter and fisherman.

Early in his career, Bing made his brother Everett his business manager. A network of business enterprises included Bing Crosby Ltd., the Crosby Investment Company, Crosby Productions Inc., and the Crosby Research Foundation.

Some of the crooner's earnings, after enormous taxes, were invested in oil wells, frozen orange juice, real estate, a West Coast television station and the operation of large cattle ranches.

Sports and Travel

In his later years, Mr. Crosby led the life style of a man of wealth without much flamboyance. He continued his favorite hobbies—golf, fishing and hunting—and traveled frequently with his family on safaris in Africa.

The Bing Crosby Pro-Amateur Tournament and Pebble Beach, known popularly as the Crosby Clambake, became one of the major golf classics as the pros came to dominate the amateurs and capture prize money that swelled to more than $200,000.

Although he sold his interest in Minute Maid orange juice, Mr. Crosby continued to appear on commercials that featured his family. And he spent time at his ranch in Baja California and his rambling home in Hillsborough, a well-to-do suburb south of San Francisco.

He emerged from semiretirement last year to mark his 50 years in show business with a series of concerts and shows to benefit various charities. He appeared at the Los Angeles Music Center in March, and in June and July made a successful tour that included the Palladium in London, other theaters in Ireland and Scotland and more appearances in the United States, singing medleys of his oldies.

In November, he and members of his family went on the CBS television network for a "White Christmas Special." In a more ambitious run, he brought "Bing Crosby and Friends" into the Uris Theater on Broadway from Dec. 7 to Dec. 19, a dozen evenings of nostalgia that were appreciatively received by critics and theatergoers alike. Clive Barnes of The New York Times wrote:

"The man is fantastic. He is still a great singer, with a sweet, accomplished voice. I loved the performance. He had come back with all that certain charm and, really, all of that gorgeous voice."

Last March 3 Mr. Crosby suffered a ruptured disk in his lower back when he fell 20 feet from a stage into an orchestra pit at a theater in Pasadena, Calif., where he was videotaping a television special. He lost his footing while acknowledging a standing ovation from the audience. The injury left him hospitalized for more than a month. Though still suffering from the effects of the fall, he completed his concert tour of Britain.

Bing Crosby was born in Tacoma, Wash., on May 2, 1904, the fourth of seven children of Harry Lowe Crosby, a brewery bookkeeper, and the former Kate Harrigan. Most of his siblings later became associated with one or another of his enterprises. His youngest brother, Bob, became well-known as a singer and bandleader.

Left Law for Music

Bing attended Gonzaga University in Spokane, Wash., where he studied law but was more interested in a local band, with which he played drums and sang at dances and in a Spokane theatre. He worked part-time in a local law firm, but the entertainment world lured him from that and from his law studies.

In 1925, Bing and Al Rinker, the band's piano player, left Spokane for Los Angeles, where Mr. Rinker's sister, Mildred Bailey, was a successful singer. The "Two Boys and a Piano," as they were billed, played engagements along the West Coast. Paul Whiteman, who caught their act in 1927 at the Metropolitan Theater in Los Angeles, hired them as a singing act for his band. Later, Harry Barris joined them to form the Rhythm Boys. They toured the Keith-Orpheum vaudeville circuit and played in Mr. Whitman's picture, "The King of Jazz."

Bing's casual attitude did not go well with Mr. Whiteman, who dismissed him for not being serious enough about his work. The other members of the trio left with him. They played the Montmartre Cafe and the Cocoanut Grove in Los Angeles.

At the Montmartre, Bing met Wilma Winifred Wyatt, a rising young film star known professionally as Dixie Lee. They were married on Sept. 29, 1930. At the Cocoanut Grove, the next year, Mr. Crosby sang for the first time on the radio, with Gus Arnheim's orchestra on a two-hour nightly outlet.

Shortly thereafter, Everett Crosby sent a record of Bing's crooning of "I Surrender, Dear" to William S. Paley, CBS president. The singer was put on the network from New York and became an immediate sensation. He appeared in 1932 at the Paramount Theater for a record run of twenty consecutive weeks.

The success of his program led Paramount Pictures to include him in "The Big Broadcast of 1932," a film featuring radio favorites. From then on, his public life as one success after another.

Bob Hope and Bing Crosby in 1940

"All the News That's Fit to Print"

The New York Times.

LATE CITY EDITION
U. S. Weather Bureau Report (Page 93) forecasts:
Becoming cloudy today through tonight. Fair, seasonable tomorrow.
Temp. Range: 40—27; yesterday: 38—31.

VOL. CXVI..No. 39,773.

NEW YORK, FRIDAY, DECEMBER 16, 1966. 10 CENTS

DEMOCRATS GAIN CONVENTION RULE IN STATE CANVASS

Conservatives Obtain Third Line on the Ballot When They Outpoll Liberals

HARRINGTON IS CRITICAL

Court Fight Is Possible on Democrats' 102-84 Edge in Constitutional Parley

By RICHARD L. MADDEN
Special to The New York Times

ALBANY, Dec. 15—Five men sat around a conference table here today and signed a stack of tally sheets giving the Democrats control of the 1967 Constitutional Convention and the Conservative party the third line on the voting machines for the next four years.

The five-member State Board of Canvassers certified the results of the Nov. 8 election, which showed that Democratic delegates would outnumber the Republicans, 102 to 84, at the Constitutional Convention when it convenes here next April 4.

The official canvass gave the Democrats 89 district delegates to the convention, and the Republicans 82.

In addition, Democratic-Liberal candidates won 13 of the 15 places as delegates at large, elected on a statewide basis. Two Republicans running with Conservative support won the remaining at-large seats.

Challenge Still Possible

The head of the Republican at-large slate, Senator Jacob K. Javits, who also had Liberal endorsement, fell about 14,000 votes short of election.

Today's canvass was the first definitive tally of the election of delegates, but the possibility of a court suit remained because of the tangled count of write-in votes for the at-large delegates.

The canvass also verified earlier reports that the four-year-old Conservative party had displaced the 22-year-old Liberal Party as the state's third-ranking political party.

The Conservatives won the right to Line C on future ballots when their candidate for Governor, Dr. Paul L. Adams, edged the Liberal candidate, Franklin D. Roosevelt Jr., by 2,789 votes.

The canvass, which was based on final tabulations by county boards of elections, showed 510,023 votes for Dr. Adams and 507,234 for Mr. Roosevelt. Unofficial tallies on election night had given Mr. Roosevelt a slight lead over Dr. Adams.

Police Board a Factor

Surprisingly, the Conservatives outpolled the Liberals in New York City, but trailed them in upstate New York, where Conservative sentiment tends to be strong.

The vote for Governor in New York City was put at 234,590 for the Conservatives and 218,740 for the Liberals. Outside the city, the vote was 288,494 for Dr. Adams and 275,433 for Mr. Roosevelt.

Politicians attributed the relatively strong Conservative showing within New York City to the Conservative-supported campaign to defeat the Police Department Civilian Complaint Review Board in a local referendum on Nov. 8.

Questioning the differences in the official canvass and the unofficial tallies on election night,

Continued on Page 55, Column 1

Museum May Name Hoving as Director

The New York Times

Thomas P. F. Hoving

By RICHARD F. SHEPARD

Thomas P. F. Hoving is expected to be named next week as the new director of the Metropolitan Museum of Art.

The appointment of New York's administrator of recreational and cultural affairs to the post will, it is understood, be announced Tuesday, when the museum's board of trustees considers the recommendation of a selection committee for a successor to James J. Rorimer, who died May 11.

Mayor Lindsay, replying to

Continued on Page 56, Column 1

A SLOWER GROWTH OF ECONOMY SEEN FOR NEXT 3 YEARS

Labor Department Lays Cut From 5.5% a Year to 4 to Low Jobless Figure

By EDWIN L. DALE Jr.
Special to The New York Times

WASHINGTON, Dec. 15—The American economy can grow no faster than about 4 per cent a year between now and 1970, a Labor Department study concluded today.

This is a sharp reduction from the growth rates of 5.5 per cent of 1964, 1965 and 1966. The chief reason for the difference is that faster growth in the last three years has been possible because there was still unemployed labor that could be absorbed.

With unemployment now below 4 per cent of the labor force, growth in the future will have to depend on new entries into the labor force.

A slower rate of growth would still permit an increase in the general standard of living of the population, including wage increases. But one major effect would be a less rapid rise in the Government's revenues than has been the case in the last three years, meaning less money to devote to Government programs or to tax reductions.

Today's 4 per cent growth figure is well below estimates made by some private and Government economists, but coincides with the relatively conservative figure used by the President's Council of Economic Advisers.

How Growth Is Measured

Economic growth is measured by the rise in the gross national product, or total output of goods and services. Today's report was concerned only with "real" growth—that is, growth after the effect of higher prices is subtracted.

The report was aimed primarily at projecting the probable composition of available jobs in 1970 on the basis of various assumptions about the state of the economy at that time.

But to do this, the survey first had to project the potential output of the economy at full employment, variously defined as either 4 per cent or 3 per cent unemployed.

This potential depends on these things:

¶The growth of the labor force, which can be projected with some precision on the basis of the number of persons already born. Today's report put labor force growth at 1.9 per cent to 2 per cent a year between 1965 and 1970.

¶The growth of productivity, which means output for each manhour. This is the most difficult projection to make. To-

Continued on Page 80, Column 2

Coppolino Acquitted of Murdering Farber

But Still Faces Trial in Death of First Wife

By RONALD SULLIVAN
Special to The New York Times

FREEHOLD, N. J., Dec. 15—Dr. Carl A. Coppolino was acquitted today of the charge that he murdered Lieut. Col. William E. Farber.

The verdict caused a sharp uproar in the courtroom here, and the pale, 34-year-old defendant broke into tears.

As Judge Elvin Simmill warned from the bench, "There will be no demonstration," the doctor's 39-year-old wife, Mary, and his mother, Anna, clutching a rosary, rushed forward into his arms.

"My prayers have saved you, my poor boy," the doctor's mother sobbed.

The defendant and his wife, tears streaming down their cheeks, held each other tightly.

Then, to each other they said, "I love you."

Despite the verdict, Dr. Coppolino did not go free tonight. He has been indicted for murder in the death of his first wife, Carmela, who died in Sarasota, Fla., on Aug. 28, 1965.

Dr. Coppolino was accused here of strangling Colonel Farber, his friend and next-door neighbor in nearby Middletown, on July 30, 1963.

Gov. Richard J. Hughes of New Jersey, in gaining the doctor's extradition to stand trial here, promised Gov. Haydon Burns of Florida to return the anesthesiologist and hypnotist for a trial in Sarasota.

Since Sarasota authorities have already accepted a $15,000 bond for Dr. Coppolino's freedom, the doctor is expected to be released on bail when he returns there. Even Judge Simmill said he agreed that F. Lee Bailey, Dr. Coppolino's defense lawyer, had presented good reasons for freeing the doctor now. These would include his acquittal here and his bond in Florida.

The judge said, however, that he was bound by the agreement between the two Governors.

"What happens to him in Florida, I don't know," the judge said.

John Gawler, chief of county detectives here, said tonight that he would take Dr. Coppolino under guard to Florida tomorrow.

Frank Schaub, a Florida state attorney who attended the trial

Continued on Page 54, Column 5

Associated Press Wirephoto

Dr. Carl A. Coppolino gives his happy reaction after his acquittal in Freehold, N. J.

U.S. SAIGON AIDES ASSERT NO BOMBS FELL INSIDE HANOI

Westmoreland's Office Says Raids This Week Struck Only Military Targets

PILOT REPORTS STUDIED

Washington Produces Map to Show What Was Hit—Mistake Still Possibility

By The Associated Press

SAIGON, South Vietnam, Friday, Dec. 16—United States military headquarters in Saigon said today that no United States bombs fell in the city of Hanoi in the American raids on the Hanoi area Tuesday and Wednesday.

A special announcement from the headquarters of Gen. William C. Westmoreland, the United States commander in Vietnam, said:

"A complete review of pilot reports and photographs of the 13-14 December air strikes on the Vandien truck depot and the Yenvien railroad classification yard showed that all ordnance expended by U.S. strike aircraft was in the military target areas.

"None fell in the city of Hanoi.

"On December 14th, pilots reported seeing a SAM missile hit a North Vietnamese junk."

The reference to the Soviet-built surface-to-air missile was not further explained, but there has been speculation here that antiaircraft weapons fired by the North Vietnamese might accidentally have dropped shells inside Hanoi.

Two Targets Hit

The chief targets of the American raids Tuesday and again Wednesday were the Vandien depot five miles south of Hanoi and the Yenvien yards six miles northeast of the Communist capital.

The vehicle depot is a sprawling complex of more than 30 maintenance buildings, garages and storage structures as well as a motor pool area. Before the first raid in early December, the depot was reported to have contained 500 vehicles.

The rail yard northeast of Hanoi is a major junction of three rail lines, two of which link North Vietnam with Communist China.

Both installations were described by United States pilots as heavily damaged in this week's raids.

The North Vietnamese and Communist newsmen in Hanoi repeatedly claimed that Hanoi itself was bombed. Dispatches from Hanoi asserted that there were numerous civilian casualties and that a workers' residential quarter was bombed.

Raids Defended by U.S.

By HEDRICK SMITH
Special to The New York Times

WASHINGTON, Dec. 15—The Administration today defended American air raids on targets in the Hanoi region and produced a map to show that none of those targets was inside the city limits.

Officials confirmed reports that there had been damage to civilian areas inside Hanoi during raids this week, but the question of whether American planes might have been accidentally responsible was not fully resolved here.

Some officials had said yesterday that targets hit by American planes could be considered, in the parlance of the man in the street, as within metropolitan Hanoi. Other officials insisted today that this was not the case.

The map made available by the Administration indicated the political limits of Hanoi and showed villages and built-up areas adjacent to several target areas raided recently. Officials said boundaries had been drawn on a 1965 United States Army map on the basis of North Viet-

Continued on Page 2, Column 4

GOVERNORS LINK LOSS TO JOHNSON

Democrats at Parley Agree Election Setback Reflects Rising National Hostility

By WARREN WEAVER Jr.
Special to The New York Times

WHITE SULPHUR SPRINGS, W. Va., Friday, Dec. 16—Angry resentment against the political leadership of President Johnson broke into the open early today among the nation's Democratic Governors.

All but two of nearly 20 Governors who met privately for three hours last night agreed that Democratic losses in the 1966 election were directly attributable to a growing national hostility toward the Johnson Administration.

The Governors are here for the National Governors Conference.

Gov. Harold E. Hughes of Iowa, chairman of the Democratic Governors' caucus, said that the state leaders were convinced they would have to play a greater part in developing party policy.

Governor Hughes said that the Democratic Governors were largely agreed that the Great Society was moving toward realization too rapidly.

He was particularly critical

Continued on Page 25, Column 1

Falling Slab Blocks East River Drive; Huge Jams Follow

Massive traffic tie-ups on the East Side harried drivers in both the morning and evening rush hours yesterday following the fall of a 20-foot slab of concrete on the Franklin D. Roosevelt Drive. The slab hit two cars and injured two persons.

The tie-ups may continue into today. The Traffic Department announced it was closing the northbound lanes of the Drive from Houston Street to 62d Street until its engineers could assess the safety of the elevated roadway from which the concrete slab fell.

Tie-ups resulted from the diversion of thousands of cars that normally use the highway onto such holiday-clogged northbound arteries as First, Third and Park Avenues.

Extra details of the Police Department's Safety Division, reinforced by platoons of probationary patrolmen, were stationed along the avenues last night to keep the cars moving.

At 7:30 P.M., an hour after rush-hour traffic on First Avenue usually thins out, a tenant in 870 United Nations Plaza looked out his floor-to-ceiling living room window and reported that "cars and trucks are blocked up as far south as I can see."

The drive carries an average

Continued on Page 72, Column 6

TRADING OF SKILLS SUGGESTED BY U.S.

McGeorge Bundy, Acting for President, Will Sound Out Soviet and Other Lands

By MAX FRANKEL
Special to The New York Times

WASHINGTON, Dec. 15—President Johnson has asked McGeorge Bundy, the president of the Ford Foundation, to explore the possibilities of establishing a permanent forum for the exchange of management knowledge with the Soviet Union and all other advanced societies.

Mr. Bundy, a former special assistant to the President for international security affairs, will work and travel as Mr. Johnson's personal representative to arouse interest in the idea among both governmental and private institutions.

The hope in the Administration is that students and practitioners of management in industrial societies will agree to share their research and experiences in the problems of running factories, cities, transportation systems, hospitals, large farms and similar enterprises.

Origin of Idea

The idea arose during the search for new steps that might be taken in improving contacts with the Soviet Union and other European Communist nations. From there, it grew into the Bundy mission to see whether the nations of Western Europe, plus Japan and a few others, would also be interested.

Mr. Bundy, who will be working in an individual capacity and not as a representative of the Ford Foundation, came to the White House today to discuss the idea with Mr. Johnson and two of the President's assistants, Walt W. Rostow and Francis Bator.

Mr. Bundy and Mr. Bator disclosed the plan to newsmen, stressing that they would engage in only quiet exploration

Continued on Page 12, Column 5

Kennedy Book Fight Prompting Feelers To Avoid Court Test

By JOHN CORRY

Efforts are under way to avoid a court fight in Mrs. John F. Kennedy's battle to prevent the publication of "Death of a President," William Manchester's book on the assassination of her husband.

One source said, "There is a lot of maneuvering going on." Another said that "you might say there is a lot of talking back and forth."

There were reports that Senator Robert F. Kennedy was eager to avoid a public confrontation between Mrs. Kennedy and Mr. Manchester, Harper & Row, Publishers, Inc., and Look magazine, which plans to serialize the book.

Senator Kennedy, one reliable report said, had opposed Mrs. Kennedy when she decided last Friday to bring legal action. Mrs. Kennedy has stated that publication of the book violates "accepted standards of propriety."

Senator Kennedy was said to believe that court action was impractical, that it simply was not worth the effort.

One source said that the Senator once had rejected a suggestion that he sue Mr. Manchester, and that this offered some indication of Mr. Kennedy's feelings.

However, a spokesman for the Kennedy family insisted that "there is an absolute identity of views between Bob and Mrs. Kennedy."

"This absolute identity of

Continued on Page 41, Column 1

SOVIET INCREASES DEFENSE SPENDING

Rise for '67, Second in Two Years, Is Linked to Cost of Arms for Hanoi

By RAYMOND H. ANDERSON
Special to The New York Times

MOSCOW, Dec. 15—The Soviet Government announced today that its military spending next year would be increased by 1.1 billion rubles, or 8.2 per cent over this year's arms budget of 13.4 billion rubles ($14.8 billion).

Finance Minister Vasily F. Garbuzov declared in a report to the Supreme Soviet that the increase was necessary because "the aggressive monopolist circles of the United States have recently sharpened international tensions and increased the danger of a new world war."

Simultaneously, the Government issued a sharp statement denouncing United States bombing raids on Hanoi, the capital of North Vietnam. Moscow pledged to continue assistance to the North Vietnamese and renewed a warning that it was prepared to send "volunteers" to Vietnam.

Observers in Moscow had expected an increase in the military budget for next year to cover growing Soviet assistance to North Vietnam. Moscow has not made public the extent of its military aid to Hanoi, but substantial deliveries of costly antiaircraft missiles and other

Continued on Page 5, Column 4

Portion of Highway Roofing Drops on Passing Cars

Policemen inspect area of Franklin D. Roosevelt Drive at 61st Street where accident occurred. A 20-foot slab of concrete—pieces of which are still on the road—dropped eight feet from upper level of the highway during the height of the morning rush hour.

The New York Times (by Neal Boenzi)

The slab crushed one automobile (above) and damaged another, injuring two motorists

Consumer Council Calls for Reforms

By WILLIAM M. BLAIR
Special to The New York Times

WASHINGTON, Dec. 15—Consumers, through "confusion and ignorance, some deception and even fraud," often fail to get their money's worth in the market place, a consumer panel said today.

The Consumer Advisory Council, in a long-delayed report to President Johnson, proposed reforms in a number of areas, including the automobile industry, health care, credit and home maintenance and repair.

The report was completed last June 12 and was submitted to the President a few days later. It was released today by the council with no explanation for the delay of nearly six months.

Some sources attributed the delay to the President's desire for a "consensus" report, al-

Continued on Page 82, Column 3

28 Indicted Here In Wiretap Inquiry

By JACK ROTH

A secret 27-month investigation by District Attorney Frank S. Hogan's office into illegal wiretapping and illegal electronic eavesdropping resulted yesterday in 11 indictments against 28 persons charged with various crimes dealing with invasion of privacy.

Mr. Hogan said he was amazed that there had been no leak to those under surveillance in the lengthy inquiry since those indicted were, in the main, private investigators, employes of detective agencies and electronics experts.

Alfred J. Scotti, chief assistant district attorney, who has been in charge of the investigation with the assistance of two aides, Peter D. Andreoli and David T. Austern, said those named as defendants were involved in

Continued on Page 36, Column 1

Walt Disney, 65, Dies on Coast; Founded an Empire on a Mouse

Walt Disney

Mickey Mouse

Special to The New York Times

LOS ANGELES, Dec. 15—Walt Disney, who built his whimsical cartoon world of Mickey Mouse, Donald Duck and Snow White and the Seven Dwarfs into a $100-million-a-year entertainment empire, died in St. Joseph's Hospital here this morning. He was 65 years old.

His death, at 9:35 A.M., was attributed to acute circulatory collapse. He had undergone surgery at the hospital a month ago for the removal of a lung tumor that was discovered after he entered the hospital for treatment of an old neck injury received in a polo match. On Nov. 30 he re-entered the hospital for a "post-operative checkup."

Just before his last illness, Mr. Disney was supervising the construction of a new Disneyland in Florida, a ski resort in Sequoia National Forest and the renovation of the 10-year-old Disneyland at Anaheim. His motion-picture studio was turning out six new productions and several television shows and he was spearheading the development of the vast University of the Arts, called Cal Art, now under construction here.

Although Mr. Disney held no

Continued on Page 40, Column 1

NEWS INDEX

Walt Disney, Who Built Entertainment Empire on a Mouse, Dies

Continued From Page 1, Col. 7

formal title at Walt Disney Productions, he was in direct charge of the company and was deeply involved in all its operations. Indeed, with the recent decision of Jack L. Warner to sell his interest in the Warner Brothers studio, Mr. Disney was the last of Hollywood's veteran moviemakers who remained in personal control of a major studio.

Roy Disney, Walt Disney's 74-year-old brother, who is president and chairman of Walt Disney Productions and who directs its financial operations, said:

"We will continue to operate Walt's company in the way that he had established and guided it. All of the plans for the future that Walt had begun will continue to move ahead."

Besides his brother, Mr. Disney is survived by his widow, Lillian, two daughters, Mrs. Ron Miller and Mrs. Robert Brown.

A private funeral service will be held at a time to be announced.

Weaver of Fantasies

From his fertile imagination and industrious factory of drawing boards, Walt Elias Disney fashioned the most popular movie stars ever to come from Hollywood and created one of the most fantastic entertainment empires in history.

In return for the happiness he supplied, the world lavished wealth and tributes upon him. He was probably the only man in Hollywood to have been praised by both the American Legion and the Soviet Union.

Where any other Hollywood producer would have been happy to get one Academy Award—the highest honor in American movies—Mr. Disney smashed all records by accumulating 29 Oscars.

"We're selling corn," Mr. Disney once told a reporter, "and I like corn."

David Low, the late British political cartoonist, called him "the most significant figure in graphic arts since Leonardo."

Mr. Disney went from seven-minute animated cartoons to become the first man to mix animation with live action, and he pioneered in making feature-length cartoons. His nature films were almost as popular as his cartoons, and eventually he expanded into feature-length movies using only live actors.

The most successful of his non-animated productions, "Mary Poppins," released in 1964, has already grossed close to $50-million. It also won an Oscar for Julie Andrews in the title role.

From a small garage-studio, the Disney enterprise grew into one of the most modern movie studios in the world, with four sound stages on 51 acres. Mr. Disney acquired a 420-acre ranch that was used for shooting exterior shots for his movies and television productions. Among the lucrative by-products of his output were many comic scripts and enormous royalties paid to him by toy-makers who used his characters.

Mr. Disney's restless mind created one of the nation's greatest tourist attractions, Disneyland, a 300-acre tract of amusement rides, fantasy spectacles and re-created Americana that cost $50.1-million.

By last year, when Disneyland observed its 10th birthday, it had been visited by some 50 million people. Its international fame was emphasized in 1959 by the then Soviet Premier, Nikita S. Khrushchev, who protested, when visiting Hollywood, that he had been unable to see Disneyland. Security arrangements could not be made in time for Mr. Khrushchev's visit.

Even after Disneyland had proven itself, Mr. Disney declined to consider suggestions that he had better leave well enough alone:

"Disneyland will never be completed as long as there is imagination left in the world."

Repeatedly, as Mr. Disney came up with new ideas he encountered considerable skepticism. For Mickey Mouse, the foundation of his realm, Mr. Disney had to pawn and sell almost everything because most exhibitors looked upon it as just another cartoon. But when the public had a chance to speak, the noble-hearted mouse with the high-pitched voice, red pants, yellow shoes and white gloves became the most beloved of Hollywood stars.

When Mr. Disney decided to make the first feature-length cartoon—"Snow White and the Seven Dwarfs"—many Hollywood experts scoffed that no audience would sit through such a long animation. It became one of the biggest money-makers in movie history.

Mr. Disney was thought a fool when he became the first important movie producer to make films for television. His detractors, once again were proven wrong.

Mr. Disney's television fame was built on such shows as "Disneyland," "The Mickey Mouse Club," "Zorro," "Davy Crockett" and the current "Walt Disney's Wonderful World of Color."

He was, however, the only major movie producer who refused to release his movies to television. He contended, with a good deal of profitable evidence, that each seven years there would be another generation that would flock to the movie theaters to see his old films.

Mickey Mouse would have been fame enough for most men. In France he was known as Michel Souris; in Italy, Topolino; in Japan, Miki Kuchi; in Spain, Miguel Ratoncito; in Latin America, El Raton Miguelito; in Sweden, Muse Pigg, and in Russia, Mikki Maus. On D-Day during World War II Mickey Mouse was the pass-word of Allied Supreme Headquarters in Europe.

But Mickey Mouse was not enough for Mr. Disney. He created Donald Duck, Pluto and Goofy. He dug into books for Dumbo, Bambi, Peter Pan, The Three Little Pigs, Ferdinand the Bull, Cinderella, the Sleeping Beauty, Brer Rabbit, Pinocchio. In "Fantasia," he blended cartoon stories with classical music.

Though Mr. Disney's cartoon characters differed markedly, they were all alike in two respects: they were lovable and unsophisticated. Most popular were big-eared Mickey of the piping voice; choleric Donald Duck of the unintelligible quacking; Pluto, that most amiable of clumsy dogs, and the seven dwarfs, who stole the show from Snow White: Dopey, Grumpy, Bashful, Sneezy, Happy, Sleepy and Doc.

His cartoon creatures were often surrounded with lovely songs. Thus, Snow White had "Some Day My Prince Will Come" and the dwarfs had "Whistle While You Work." From his version of "The Three Little Pigs," his most successful cartoon short, came another international hit, "Who's Afraid of the Big Bad Wolf?" Cliff Edwards as Jiminy Cricket sang "When You Wish Upon a Star" for "Pinocchio." More recently, "Mary Poppins" introduced "Supercalifragilisticexpialidocious."

Exhibition at Museum

Mr. Disney seemed to have had an almost superstitious fear of considering his movies as art, though an exhibition of some of his leading cartoon characters was once held in the Metropolitan Museum of Art in New York. "I've never called this art," he said. "It's show business."

One day, when Mr. Disney was approaching 60 and his black hair and neatly trimmed mustache were gray, he was asked to reduce his success to a formula. His brown eyes became alternately intense and dreamy. He fingered an ashtray as he gazed around an office so cluttered with trophies that it looked like a pawn shop.

"I don't really know," he said. "I guess I'm an optimist. I'm not in business to make unhappy pictures. I love comedy too much. I've always loved comedy. Another thing. Maybe it's because I can still be amazed at the wonders of the world.

"Sometimes I've tried to figure out why Mickey appealed to the whole world. Everybody's tried to figure it out. So far as I know, nobody has. He's a pretty nice fellow who never does anybody any harm, who gets into scrapes through no fault of his own, but always manages to come up grinning. Why Mickey's even been faithful to one girl, Minnie, all his life. Mickey is so simple and uncomplicated, so easy to understand that you can't help liking him."

But when Dwight D. Eisenhower was President, he found words for Mr. Disney. He called him a "genius as a creator of folklore" and said his "sympathetic attitude toward life has helped our children develop a clean and cheerful view of humanity, with all its frailties and possibilities for good."

When France gave to Mr. Disney its highest artistic decoration as Officier d'Académie, he was cited for his "contribution to education and knowledge" with such nature-study films as "Seal Island," "Beaver Valley," "Nature's Half Acre" and "The Living Desert."

From Harvard and Yale, this stocky, industrious man who had never graduated from high school received honorary degrees. He was honored by Yale the same day as it honored Thomas Mann, the Nobel Prize-winning novelist. Prof. William Lyon Phelps of Yale said of Mr. Disney:

"He has accomplished something that has defied all the efforts and experiments of the laboratories in zoology and biology. He has given animals souls."

By the end of his career, the list of 700 awards and honors that Mr. Disney received from many nations filled 29 typewritten pages, and included 29 Oscars, four Emmys and the Presidential Freedom Medal.

There were tributes of a different nature. Toys in the shape of Disney characters sold by the many millions. Paris couturiers and expensive jewelers both used Disney patterns. One of the most astounding exhibitions of popular devotion came in the wake of Mr. Disney's films about Davy Crockett. In a matter of months, youngsters all over the country who would balk at wearing a hat in winter, were adorned in 'coonskin caps in midsummer.

In some ways Mr. Disney resembled the movie pioneers of a generation before him. He was not afraid of risk. One day, when all the world thought of him as a fabulous success, he told an acquaintance, "I'm in great shape, I now owe the bank only eight million."

A friend of 20 years recalled that he once said, "A buck is something to be spent creating." Early in 1960 he declared, "It's not what you have, but how much you can borrow that's important in business."

Mr. Disney had no trouble borrowing money in his later years. Bankers, in fact, sought him out. Last year Walt Disney Productions grossed $110-million. His family owns 38 per cent of this publicly held corporation, and all of Retlaw, a company that controls the use of Mr. Disney's name.

Mr. Disney's contract with Walt Disney Productions gave him a basic salary of $182,000 a year and a deferred salary of $2,500 a week, with options to buy up to a 25 per cent interest in each of his live-action features. It is understood that he began exercising these options in 1961, but only up to 10 per cent. These interests alone would have made him a multimillionaire.

Famous Disney characters are, clockwise from top left, Donald Duck, Pinocchio and Pluto.

Mr. Disney, like earlier movie executives, insisted on absolute authority. He was savage in rebuking a subordinate. An associate of many years said the boss "could make you feel one-inch tall, but he wouldn't let anybody else do it. That was his privilege."

Once in a bargaining dispute with a union of artists, a strike at the Disney studios went on for two months and was settled only after Government mediation.

This attitude by Mr. Disney was one of the reasons some artists disparaged him. Another was that he did none of the drawings of his most famous cartoons. Mickey Mouse, for instance, was drawn by Ubbe Iwerks, who was with Mr. Disney almost from the beginning.

However, Mr. Iwerks insisted that Disney could have done the drawings, but was too busy. Mr. Disney did, however, furnish Mickey's voice for all cartoons. He also sat in on all story conferences.

Although Mr. Disney's power and wealth multiplied with his achievements, his manner remained that of some prosperous Midwestern storekeeper. Except when imbued with some new Disneyland project or movie idea, he was inclined to be phlegmatic. His nasal speech, delivered slowly, was rarely accompanied by gestures. His phlegmatic manner often masked his independence and tenacity.

Walt Disney was born in Chicago on Dec. 5, 1901. His family moved to Marceline, Mo., when he was a child and he spent most of his boyhood on a farm.

He recalled that he enjoyed sketching animals on the farm. Later, when his family moved back to Chicago, he went to high school and studied cartoon drawing at night at the Academy of Fine Arts. He did illustrations for the school paper.

When the United States entered World War I he was turned down by the Army and Navy because he was too young. So he went to France as an ambulance driver for the Red Cross. He decorated the sides of his ambulance with cartoons and had his work published in Stars and Stripes.

After the war the young man worked as a cartoonist for advertising agencies. But he was always looking for something better.

When Mr. Disney got a job doing cartoons for advertisements that were shown in theaters between movies, he was determined that that was to be his future. He would say to friends, "This is the most marvelous thing that has ever happened."

In 1920 he organized his own company to make cartoons about fairy tales. He made about a dozen but could not sell them. He was so determined to continue in this field that at times he had no money for food and lived with Mr. Iwerks.

In 1923 Mr. Disney decided to leave Kansas City. He went to Hollywood, where he formed a small company and did a series of film cartoons called "Alice in Cartoonland."

After two years of "Alice in Cartoonland," Mr. Disney dropped it in favor of a series about "Oswald the Rabbit." In 1928 most of his artists decided to break with him and do their own Oswald. Mr. Disney went to New York to try to keep the series but failed. When he returned, he, his wife, his brother Roy and Mr. Iwerks tried to think of a character for a new series, but failed. They decided on a mouse. Mrs. Disney named it Mickey.

The first Mickey Mouse cartoon, "Plane Crazy," was taken to New York by Mr. Disney. But the distributors were apathetic. "Felix, the Cat" was ruler of the cartoon field, and they saw nothing unusual in a mouse.

When Mr. Disney returned from New York he decided that sound had a future in movies. He made a second Mickey Mouse, this one with sound, called "Steamboat Bill." In October, 1928, the cartoon opened at the Colony Theater in New York. Success was immediate and the Disney empire began.

"All the News That's Fit to Print."

The New York Times.

THE WEATHER
Fair today and tomorrow; little change in temperature.
Temperature yesterday—Max., 84; min., 67.
U. S. Weather Forecast—For details see Page 42.

Copyright, 1930, by The New York Times Company.

VOL. LXXIX....No. 26,463. NEW YORK, TUESDAY, JULY 8, 1930. TWO CENTS in Greater New York | THREE CENTS Within 200 Miles | FOUR CENTS Elsewhere Except 7th and 8th Postal Zones

EWALD INDICTED WITH FIVE FOR FRAUD IN MINE PROJECT; TO BE ASKED TO QUIT BENCH

PLOT LAID TO MAGISTRATE

$400,000 Said to Have Been Lost in Sales of Cotter Butte Stock.

TUTTLE SEES COURT FAVORS

Asserts He Has Letters From Politicians to Ewald and Ignored Summonses.

INDIRECT BANKING CHARGED

Jurist's Commissions Paid to Woman, Bill Holds—Corrigan to Meet Accused Today.

Magistrate George F. Ewald, until last Fall a director in the Cotter Butte Mines, Inc., was indicted yesterday with five others by a Federal grand jury which charged use of the United States mails in a scheme to defraud, and conspiracy to use the mails for that purpose. There were twenty-four counts in the mail fraud indictment, and one in the conspiracy indictment.

The others named in the indictment are Dr. Louis Anton Ewald, brother of Magistrate Ewald and vice president of the Cotter Butte Mines, the properties of which were characterized [illegible] by United States Attorney Tuttle as "a hole in the ground"; [illegible] Cotter, from whom the properties of the company were taken over by the corporation; Frank E. Mitterlechner, secretary; Francis M. Schirp, another promoter of the enterprise, in which at least $400,000 has been lost, according to Mr. Tuttle, and Frank M. Bins, mine manager of the company. The indictment also named the corporation itself.

Magistrate Ewald is scheduled to appear in Federal court at 10:30 this morning for arraignment, probably before Federal Judge Robert P. Patterson, to whom the indictments were returned. Before that, however, at 10 o'clock, he has an appointment with Chief Magistrate Joseph Corrigan.

Expected to Leave Bench.

Although Mr. Corrigan said yesterday he had no power to remove, or even suspend Magistrate Ewald, he admitted that he had the right to ask Magistrate Ewald to step off the bench temporarily, pending trial. This, it was predicted yesterday, will be the course that will be followed. Magistrate Ewald can ask to be relieved of his duties. The magistrate declined to be interviewed last night, and referred questioners to his counsel, former Judge Alfred J. Talley. Mr. Talley said he had no statement to make.

Federal Attorney Tuttle added to Magistrate Ewald's troubles last night by announcing that he was sending certain papers to District Attorney Crain, to Magistrate Corrigan and to the Bar Association. These papers, only photostatic copies of which will be sent, are in three classes, Mr. Tuttle explained.

The first, he said, is a series of letters from politicians, asking for leniency in traffic court cases from Magistrate Ewald. The second is a sort of unofficial docket, Mr. Tuttle said, containing the list of persons for whom favors were sought, with the names of the politicians interested, and the third, he declared, is a stack of traffic court summonses. The latter might have been expected to be found in court records, not in a private house, Mr. Tuttle said.

Although the name of "J. Walker" was reported to be on the list, Mayor Walker at City Hall yesterday said that he had not seen Magistrate Ewald since the day he swore him in and had never asked any favors of him.

Assignment of Shares Alleged.

The corporate agreement under which the Cotter Butte Mines was formed called for giving 1,050,000 of the 2,500,000 shares to Cotter, the indictment of the grand jury revealed. In connection with this, Mr. Tuttle charged last night that Cotter some eight months ago had assigned 100,000 of these shares to Magistrate Ewald without visible consideration.

"Whether the use of the magistrate's name had or did not have anything to do with the conveyance is something to receive consideration at the trial," Mr. Tuttle added.

The grand jury indictment alleged that while the corporation received only 25 cents a share for each of the 800,000 shares of treasury stock an

Continued on Page Twelve.

Detroit Mayor Fighting Recall Loses in State's High Court

Special to The New York Times.

DETROIT, Mich., July 7.—The State Supreme Court today denied the petition of Mayor Charles Bowles to further delay a recall election in Detroit by ordering Circuit Court action on alleged frauds. Five members of the court sitting at Lansing simply wrote the one word "denied" across the face of the petition.

Counsel for the recall committee immediately announced that they would go before Judge Robert M. Toms of Circuit Court at 10 A. M., tomorrow to ask dissolution of a new restraining order obtained by Mayor Bowles's attorneys today. The order, returnable Friday, is all that stands in the way of a recall election.

BALDWIN SEEKS FALL OF LABOR ON TARIFF

Prepares Censure Motion, Hoping to Split Government and Force Autumn Election.

DROPS REFERENDUM IDEA

Demands Home Safeguards and Empire Free Trade—Debate Likely on Thursday.

Special Cable to THE NEW YORK TIMES.

LONDON, July 7.—The now famous resolution by a group of bankers in favor of empire free trade and tariffs against all other nations was fashioned tonight by leaders of the Conservative party into a motion of censure of the MacDonald Government. It is in form a wedge which they hope to drive into the Labor party between that iron-bound free trader, Philip Snowden, Chancellor of the Exchequer, and J. H. Thomas, Minister of Dominions, who is believed to be leaning toward tariffs with a large following.

The Conservatives have no hope of carrying the motion, which appears in the names of former Prime Minister Stanley Baldwin and Neville Chamberlain, his chief lieutenant, for they realize they cannot rely on Liberal support in a matter where tariffs are concerned.

Mr. Baldwin's resolution suggests that a return to prosperity can best be promoted "by safeguarding the home market against unfair foreign competition and by expanding the export market by reciprocal agreements with the empire overseas." It censures the government for havin "reversed the policy of safeguarding instead of extending it," and adds that the government has "arbitrarily excluded from consideration the imposition of duties on foreign foodstuffs devised to obtain equivalent advantages for British manufactures and agriculture in empire markets and elsewhere."

Expect Motion Thursday.

It is expected that the motion will be forced on Thursday, as the Conservatives are eager, as soon as possible, to discover whether the government is going into the imperial conference with unfettered hands as regards tariffs, as Mr. Thomas has suggested, and whether it will be possible to discuss the whole question of imperial preference with the Dominions.

The motion was construed in political circles tonight as an admission that the proposed referendum on food taxes finally would be dropped from the Conservative program and that the Baldwin party would be perfectly prepared to fight the next election on any concrete scheme which may emerge from the imperial conference.

There was considerable conjecture tonight as to how long the MacDonald government can keep its ship afloat in the present sea of troubles. Labor members are waiting with considerable anxiety the resumption of the committee stages of the finance bill on Wednesday. At a meeting of the Liberal party tonight it was decided to press the new clause which proposes that the reserves of a company which are definitely used for reconditioning plant and machinery shall be exempted from income tax. There is little likelihood of Mr. Snowden accepting this amendment, and the Conservatives are being whipped up to attend the debate in force.

Discord in Labor Party.

Behind the scenes the government will be attacked by its own backbenchers at party meetings Tuesday and on the new naval shipbuilding program Wednesday. Then, after the statement at Simla Wednesday of the Viceroy, Lord Irwin, Wedgewood Been, Secretary for India in the MacDonald Cabinet, will be called upon in the House of Commons to say whether the Simon report will be shelved at the forthcoming round-table conference. If he implies it will be shelved, both Conservatives and Liberals will be against him.

LINDBERGH ADVISES GENEVA ON AVIATION; ASKS UNIFORM LAWS

In a Detailed Outline, He Urges Standard Markings, Signals and Rules for Clearing.

SEEKS RADIO WEATHER DATA

Cooperation of Entire World Is Necessary to Develop Air Transport, He Says.

CONFERENCE OPENS TODAY

Representatives of 15 Nations Will Meet in First International Session on Flying.

By CLARENCE K. STREIT.
Wireless to THE NEW YORK TIMES.

GENEVA, July 7.—The importance and necessity of aviation were emphasized by Colonel Charles A. Lindbergh in a statement to the League of Nations Transit Section received by cable from him today. The League recently invited him to give his views on the general subject of what governments could do to aid international aviation for the benefit of its first international conference on commercial aviation, opening here tomorrow.

League circles are delighted that Colonel Lindbergh did not confine himself to generalities, but gave a list of detailed suggestions of what could be done to help aviation. He urges standardization of airways, a uniform system of markings and signals, the establishment of a comprehensive meteorological and radio reporting system, uniform regulations for clearing and other formalities of international air transit, which now are complicated and confusing. His cabled statement follows:

Aviation must be considered from an international standpoint; the ability to cover great distances in a relatively short time makes it a leading factor in world intercourse.

Every advance in transportation has stimulated commerce and brought people into closer contact with each other. One after another, the fears and prejudices of isolation have been overcome as methods of communication and transport have improved.

Would Remove Restrictions.

Aviation, with its great speed and freedom of movement, is too powerful an instrument of progress to be long confined by the remaining artificial restrictions left over from an age of provincialism. Constructive thought is turning more and more toward international cooperation and nothing is of more importance in this field than the simplification of communication and intercourse at the present time. While the world's airlines are in a formative stage in their development, much can be done to encourage their progress and avoid unnecessary complications in the future.

There is great need for international cooperation in the standardization of airways. A uniform system of markings and signals should be decided upon and a comprehensive meteorological and radio reporting system established.

Adoption of uniform regulations is of the utmost importance. In some countries today, aircraft are placed in the same class as ocean steamers and must go through similar procedure in clearing. As a result the clearance charges are high and delays are often comparatively long in relation to the time spent in actual travel.

There are instances where only aircraft registered within a country and carrying its markings are allowed to operate; others where it is required that a native pilot be carried; in certain countries a visiting pilot must qualify for a license before he is permitted to fly.

Lack of Uniformity Great.

Numerous and complicated papers are often required where a careful study would make most of them unnecessary. The lack of uniformity is so great that it is at times impossible for a private flier to obtain accurate information regarding the regulations he will encounter on an international trip without an unreasonable report delay.

Intelligent consideration of these and many other problems confronting aviation at the present time would be of untold assistance in the development of international air commerce.

Aviation does not concern one nation alone. Its ultimate value lies in the bringing of the various countries of the earth into closer contact. It is not possible to develop air transport and communication in its broadest aspect without the cooperation of the entire world.

Statements on the same subject by Dr. Hugo Eckener and by the Italian Air Minister, General Italo Balbo, who is a flyer himself, will be released tomorrow and others are ex-

Continued on Page Ten.

Vesuvius Pours Out Lava; Flow Over Slopes Unlikely

By The Associated Press.

NAPLES, July 7.—Mount Vesuvius today burst into a state of active eruption, developing three fountains of burning lava that invaded the whole northwest section of the vast platform of its crater. The eruptive cone fell ninety-five feet down into the crater.

Alessandro Malladra, director of the Vesuvius Observatory, said the eruptive activity would continue for several weeks, but the lava would probably solidify in the crater and in the Valley of the Inferno. He thought it would not pour over the neighboring fertile slopes.

CONAN DOYLE DEAD FROM HEART ATTACK

Spiritist, Novelist and Creator of Famous Fiction Detective Ill Two Months—Was 71.

FAMILY AWAITS 'MESSAGE'

Son Is Confident Father Will Confirm Spirit Existence, in Which He Believed.

Wireless to THE NEW YORK TIMES.

LONDON, July 7.—Sir Arthur Conan Doyle, creator of Sherlock Holmes and a noted spiritist, died today at his home, Windlesham, in Crowborough, Sussex. He was 71 years old.

Sir Arthur had been ill from heart trouble for two months, but was making good progress against the malady until last Saturday, when a return of the heart attacks prostrated him.

At his bedside when he died were Lady Doyle, his two sons and one daughter. Sir Arthur's illness was attributed to his work in Scandinavia last October, when he gave a series of lectures on spiritism.

Although Sir Arthur had been in failing health for some time, that did not deter him from his work. Up to the end his enthusiasm for psychic investigation was unflagging. Only last March he caused a sensation by resigning from the Society for Psychical Research, of which he had been a leading member for thirty-six years. His letter of resignation was written from his sickbed.

Told of Spirit Talks.

Sir Arthur claimed to have had conversations with the spirits of many great men, including Cecil Rhodes, Earl Haig, Joseph Conrad and others. Adrian Conan Doyle, the novelist's son, said today the whole family believed Sir Arthur would continue to keep in touch with them.

"I know perfectly well I am going to have conversations with my father," he said.

In his later years Sir Arthur often expressed a wish that he should be remembered for his psychic work rather than for his novels. When he celebrated his seventy-first birthday on May 22 he confessed he was tired of hearing about his celebrated character, Sherlock Holmes.

"Holmes is dead," he said. "I have done with him." Ten of Sir Arthur's sixty books are about spiritism.

For years Lady Doyle was his constant companion, accompanying him on all his travels. It was to her the dying novelist spoke his last words.

"You are wonderful," he said with a smile.

He died peacefully. Lady Doyle had nursed him through his illness to the end.

Family Awaits a Message.

LONDON, July 7 (AP).—The family of Sir Arthur Conan Doyle today expressed the belief he would communicate with them from the spirit world, as he had promised.

Adrian Conan Doyle, son of the novelist and spiritist, asked if his father had spoken of communicating

Continued on Page Nine.

DRY CHIEFS CALLED TO PLAN CAMPAIGN OF 'STEADY PRESSURE'

Woodcock Summons Administrators to Capital From All Twelve Districts.

CALLS FOR DAILY REPORTS

New Forms Are Supplied to Inform Headquarters Promptly of Raids and Court Action.

PADLOCK SUITS PROMISED

New Director Will Use Them Freely, but He Does Not Seek Spectacular Drives.

Special to The New York Times.

WASHINGTON, July 7.—Prohibition administrators, having charge of all twelve districts in the United States, have been summoned to meet in Washington on July 30 and 31 to plan with Amos W. W. Woodcock, new prohibition director in the Department of Justice, a campaign of "steady pressure" to reduce illicit liquor and bootlegging activities throughout the country.

This meeting will be the first major stroke by Mr. Woodcock in his task of prohibition enforcement. Later, probably about Sept. 1, he will make a personal tour of each district and its subsections, to observe at first hand the actual conditions.

Mr. Woodcock has devised a plan to spur activities in enforcement, which is soon to be put into effect. This calls for daily reports by every administrator and deputy administrator of their accomplishments. Charts on which the reports are to be made to the central office here have been mailed out and this particular device will be put into operation right away.

Mr. Woodcock feels that with the information to be furnished by these reports he will be better able to direct the fight against bootleg liquor from Washington, and also that with the necessity of having to report daily the field operatives themselves will be more active.

Will Use Steady Pressure.

Through these reports Mr. Woodcock hopes to be able to keep an accurate general record of prohibition activities, both in detection and legal phases. The charts are sufficiently comprehensive to show what happens in raids and court actions, both as to criminal proceedings and injunction or "padlock" suits, which the new director is expected to use quite freely.

Mr. Woodcock made it plain today that he does not intend to rely on spectacular drives here and there, but rather on a "steady, earnest and lawful" pressure. It had been stated that Mr. Woodcock would attempt to administer the law in a more popular way than formerly, but it was made clear today that any question of popularity had little to do with his plan. He feels that a surer way to clamp down the lid is to use continuous pressure, and asserted that he will follow such a policy for the sake of effectiveness and not for any popular accord.

Has Set Up New Quarters.

The new Prohibition Bureau created at the recent session of Congress is setting up quarters in the old Southern Railway Building. So far the offices have few pieces of furniture and are undergoing redecoration. Down below, in the same building, is the Industrial Alcohol Bureau of the treasury, one of the few remnants of the prohibition administration left in that department, in charge of Dr. James M. Doran, former Prohibition Commissioner.

Mr. Woodcock will spend some time during the next two weeks at Fort

Continued on Page Six.

Mrs. Edison Calls Women Back to the Home; Lose Prestige in Business, She Says on Radio

Mrs. Thomas A. Edison, wife of the inventor and daughter of Lewis Miller, co-founder of Chautauqua Institution, in a radio talk yesterday afternoon from Station WJZ urged women to return to home-making and to pay less heed to the allurements of professional and business careers.

Because the art of home-making has declined so much in recent years, due to trends originating in woman suffrage and the World War, according to Mrs. Edison, the country is facing a situation of widespread restlessness. Men no longer find satisfaction in their homes, she explained.

"Unless the women of America make a decided effort to return to the business of home-making, the most vital institution of the country is threatened," she said. "America is essentially a nation of homes. The woman who doesn't want to make a home is undermining our nation."

There was an aversion to housekeeping, Mrs. Edison admitted, on the ground that there was too much drudgery connected with it, but "every business and everything in life is 98 per cent drudgery," she said.

As a matter of fact, she asserted, a good home-maker must have executive ability and be a good purchasing agent, an economist, something of a chemist to supervise the diet of her family and a gracious hostess. She also should be versed in music, art and literature to have a proper background and to be able to entertain herself, her husband and her friends, according to Mrs. Edison.

A college education is invaluable for such a home-maker, she continued, adding that if the family finances make it necessary to choose between sending a boy or a girl to college, the girl should be the one selected. The boy can get his broadening contacts in business and elsewhere, Mrs. Edison declared.

The college woman, however, must realize that home-making is her highest goal and that it is a full-time proposition which is as much of a business as running an office, she said. Her opinion was that in flocking into outside business, women had lost their prestige in their own field without making up for it by accomplishment on a par with that of men in business.

"Deep down in her heart every woman wants a home, and most women want children," Mrs. Edison said. She spoke under the auspices of the Chautauqua, which is offering a series of radio talks on adult education.

HOOVER MESSAGE OPENS TREATY FIGHT; OPPOSITION CALLS FOR SECRET DOCUMENTS; 58 SENATORS SIT IN SPECIAL SESSION

Nearly a Dozen Absentee Senators Expected Soon, But Many in Capital Are Uneasy and Want to Go.

Special to The New York Times.

WASHINGTON, July 7.—Thirty-eight Senators were absent when the special session of the upper house, called by the President to ratify the London Naval Treaty, was called to order at noon today.

The absentees were:

REPUBLICANS—Baird, Blaine, Brookhart, Cutting, Deneen, Frazier, Glenn, Goff, Gould, Greene, Grundy, Hatfield, Kean, McMaster, Norbeck, Pine, Robsion, Schall, Smoot, Steiwer, Waterman—21.

DEMOCRATS—Ashurst, Blease, Bratton, Brock, Broussard, Copeland, Dill, Hawes, Heflin, Ransdell, Robinson (Ark.), Smith, Steck, Tydings, Wagner, Wheeler—16.

FARMER-LABOR—Shipstead—1.

The Senators who answered to their names at today's roll-call were:

REPUBLICANS—Allen, Bingham, Borah, Capper, Couzens, Dale, Fess, Gillett, Goldsborough, Hale, Hastings, Hebert, Howell, Johnson, Jones, Keyes, La Follette, McCulloch, McNary, Metcalf, Moses, Norris, Nye, Oddie, Patterson, Phipps, Reed, Robinson (Ind.), Shortridge, Sullivan, Thomas (Idaho), Townsend, Vandenberg, Walcott, Watson—35.

DEMOCRATS—Barkley, Black, Caraway, Connally, Fletcher, George, Glass, Harris, Harrison, Hayden, Kendrick, King, McKellar, Overman, Pittman, Sheppard, Simmons, Stephens, Swanson, Thomas (Okla.), Trammell, Walsh (Mass.), Walsh (Mont.)—23.

Of the absentees, Senators Smoot and Baird are on their honeymoons, the former in the West and the latter in Europe. They have notified the President that they are returning immediately to Washington. Others expected here in the next two or three days are Senators Copeland, Tydings, Glenn, Goff, Grundy, Kean, Broussard, Ransdell and Wagner. On the other hand, some who are here are anxious to go home to look after their political fences. This group is now causing the treaty leaders anxious moments.

BRITISH HEIR ON RADIO LAUDS ROCKEFELLER

Calls Him Model Philanthropist in London Speech Rebroadcast Throughout This Country.

APPEALS FOR STUDENTS

Urges Aid to National Union Such as Has Been Given by American Financier.

The Prince of Wales pointed to John D. Rockefeller as a model philanthropist whom wealthy Englishmen might well emulate, in an address delivered last night in London, flashed across the ocean by short-wave radio, and rebroadcast throughout the United States.

The heir to the British throne delivered his tribute to Mr. Rockefeller in the midst of an appeal for a fund of £30,000 to establish a home for the National Union of Students and otherwise help the union to carry on effectively its work of assisting and entertaining students from other parts of the Empire and from foreign countries visiting in England, and of sending English students to other countries.

This work, said the Prince, was enormously important in giving students from other lands a true insight into British culture and character. In this connection he told of the students' houses in New York and other cities erected through "the munificence of one to whom we in this country have great cause to be thankful."

"It is possible the British prototype of Mr. Rockefeller is among us tonight," said the Prince, to the accompaniment of laughter among those standing in the studio with him. "If he is not. I hope it will not be long before the National Union finds him."

Address Clearly Heard Here.

The Prince delivered his address in the Savoy Hotel at a dinner of the National Union of Students, and it was received with such clarity in this country that hardly a word was missed. The speech was greeted with considerable applause from the British audience, and this also was plainly heard over the radio on this side of the Atlantic. The Prince began speaking at 4:25 P. M., New York Daylight Time, and finished at 4:50.

The Prince's address, as taken by stenographers at the headquarters of the National Broadcasting Company in New York, was as follows:

Mr. Chairman, My Lords, Ladies and Gentlemen: I thank you sincerely for the kind way in which you have received me. I can assure you that I am glad to be here tonight to speak of a cause which is interesting because it is perhaps somewhat out of the ordinary. It is a cause concerned not with the sick, nor the aged, but with young people — young people who are sound enough in mind and limb and who appeal to you not directly on their own behalf, but for your support to a piece of educational machinery which they themselves are creating in the belief that it will provide them with experience and knowledge necessary to the full assumption of citizenship. It

Continued on Page Four.

HUSTON SEES HOOVER AND WON'T QUIT NOW

White House Conference With Chairman on His Status Lasts an Hour and a Half.

SENATE FOES PERPLEXED

Capital Hears National Committee Plans $1,000,000 Fund for Fall Campaign.

Special to The New York Times.

WASHINGTON, July 7.—President Hoover and Claudius H. Huston, chairman of the Republican National Committee, had a conference of an hour and a half at the White House last night concerning the latter's status as head of the party organization. When the fact that the meeting had taken place became known today, no definite information concerning it was obtainable at the White House or from Chairman Huston.

It was learned from authoritative sources, however, that the President did not ask Mr. Huston to retire from the chairmanship in view of the testimony before the Senate lobby committee with regard to Mr. Huston's alleged lobbying activities, and the transactions by which money contributed to the Tennessee River Improvement Association, interested in legislation concerning the government's power plant at Muscle Shoals, was deposited to Mr. Huston's private trading account with a New York stock brokerage house before being transmitted to the association.

At the White House the only information obtainable was that Mr. Huston had called on the President and had remained an hour and a half.

All that Mr. Huston would say was:

"I conferred with the President, but have no statement to make."

No Intention of Resigning.

The attitude of Mr. Huston, according to some of his friends, is that he has done nothing to disqualify him as chairman, and that he has no present intention of relinquishing his post. In his opinion, the demand for his resignation comes chiefly from the "Young Guard" Senate group, and since the President has not asked him to resign he feels, it was said, there is no reason why he should be moved to retire because of the hostility of certain Senators and some members of the Republican National Committee.

Associates of Mr. Huston were authority for the statement that he would give up his office if the President publicly requested him to do so. In that event, it was explained, Mr. Huston would make a public answer to the President. Today's developments all went to indicate that Mr. Huston has no intention at present of resigning voluntarily, and that there is no movement supported by the administration to oust him.

Senators who have been active in advising President Hoover with respect to choosing a new chairman were greatly surprised that the effort was not brought to a head at the White House conference. They had fully expected that the President would suggest that Mr. Huston

Continued on Page Three.

PACT URGED AS PEACE STEP

President Asks for Ratification as Sole Means to Arms Limitation.

HE CRITICIZES MILITARISTS

McKellar at Once Moves to Get London Parley Papers—Reed Offers Them in Confidence.

JOHNSON SPURNS PROPOSAL

Opening Quorum Pleases the Backers of Accord, but Foes Tactics May Delay Debate.

Special to The New York Times.

WASHINGTON, July 7.—The battle over ratification of the London naval treaty started today when the Senate convened in extra session and listened to a message from the White House in which President Hoover asserted that rejection of the pact would mean "that the world will be again plunged backward from its progress toward peace."

Forebodings of Senator Watson, the Republican leader, who on Saturday doubted that a quorum would be present when the Senate convened, were unfounded. Fifty-eight Senators, nine more than a quorum, answered when the roll was called.

The reading of the President's message and of the treaty itself occupied most of the hour and a half's sitting. But there were signs in plenty that the treaty may not reach a vote with the speed some ardent advocates of ratification have been insisting would be the case.

At the very start the controversy over the refusal of the Executive to make public all documents bearing on the negotiation of the treaty was revived. Senator McKellar, Democrat, of Tennessee, introduced a resolution requesting the President to send to the Senate "all letters, cablegrams, minutes, memoranda, instructions and dispatches and all records" bearing on the London conference.

McKellar Acts Quickly.

Mr. McKellar, immediately following the conclusion of the reading of the President's message, gained recognition and put the resolution calling for the documents before the Senate.

The resolution went to the table, and it is expected Mr. McKellar will move to consider it tomorrow. There is no chance of its adoption, but it can be debated without limit, thereby slowing up consideration of the treaty itself. Several Senators, among them Senator Norris of Nebraska, who will vote to ratify, will probably support the McKellar resolution.

The galleries were crowded half an hour before the Senate was called to order. Senators Johnson, Moses and McKellar, leaders of the opposition, were the first Senators to enter the chamber. A few minutes later Mr. Watson and Senator Swanson of Virginia, ranking Democrat on the Foreign Relations Committee, who tomorrow will make the opening speech in favor of ratification, came in arm and arm. Senator Robinson, Democrat, of Arkansas, who with Senator Reed, Republican, of Pennsylvania, is to lead in the fight for ratification of the compact they helped as members of the London delegation to negotiate, was not at the session. Mr. Robinson was reported on his way from Arkansas and may be in his seat tomorrow.

The first business was reading of the President's message, to which the Senators present gave close attention. There had been no advance copies of the message.

President Hits at Treaty Foes.

Pro-treaty Senators smiled at Senators Johnson, Moses and McKellar when the clerk read a reference by the President to opponents of the treaty as those "who believe in unrestricted military strength as an objective of the American nation." It was a treaty, asserted the President, the ratification of which was in the interest of the United States, a treaty fair to all the signatory powers.

"We have only to look at the state of Europe in 1914 to find ample evidence of the futility and danger of competition in arms," he said.

From the standpoint of national defense, the President said, no critic of the treaty had been willing to go so far as to assert that, under the terms of the pact, the United States could not defend itself against outside aggression. On the basis of the naval limitation sought in the futile Geneva conference of 1927, the savings to this country, Great Britain

CONAN DOYLE DEAD FROM HEART ATTACK

Continued from Page 1, Column 4.

with his family after his death, said:

"Why, of course, my father fully believed that when he passed over he would continue to keep in touch with us. All his family believe so, too.

"There is no question that my father will often speak to us, just as he did before he passed over. We will always know when he is speaking, but one has to be careful because there are practical jokers on the other side, as there are here.

"It is quite possible that these jokers may attempt to impersonate him. But there are tests which my mother knows, such as little mannerisms of speech which cannot be impersonated and which will tell us it is my father himself who is speaking."

Adrian paid tribute to his celebrated father. He said: "He was a great man and a splendid father and he was loved—and was happy because he knew it—by all of us.

"My mother's and father's devotion to each other at all times was one of the most wonderful things I have ever known. She nursed him right through his illness to the end.

Smiled in His Suffering.

"His last words were to her, and they show just how much he thought of her. He simply smiled up at her and said, 'You are wonderful.' He was in too much pain to say a lot. His breathing was very bad, and what he said was during a brief flash of consciousness. I never have seen any one take anything more gamely in all my life. Even when we all knew he was suffering great pain he always managed during times when he was conscious to keep a smile on his face for us."

Sir Arthur during the latter part of his life presented an heroic and at the same time somewhat tragic figure. For the past few years he had devoted virtually all his time to the propagation of spiritism, and was recognized as one of the great leaders of the world in that belief. Because of his association with this crusade which he himself characterized as an unpopular one, he gradually lost some of his old-time literary friends who saw no virtue in spiritism and were inclined to look upon him as an eccentric.

Sir Arthur was grieved because his friends could not see eye to eye with him, but he never wavered in his pursuit of the cause in which he believed. He even opened a "psychic bookshop" and spiritist museum in Victoria Street in the shadow of Westminster Abbey. Here he created a centre for spiritistic literature and distributed much of it throughout the world.

Spent Thousands on Venture.

Sir Arthur once told the writer that he spent thousands of dollars of his own money to keep the shop and the museum open. Still this adventure did not worry him. "I am in a position to do it," he said with a smile. "I might play with a steam yacht or own race horses. I prefer to do this."

There was no doubt in Sir Arthur's mind about the existence of spirits. One of his proofs that spirits exist was a huge photograph of himself which depicted the face of his dead son looking over his shoulder. He showed this picture to the correspondent and remarked, simply:

"I handled the plate for that picture myself. Nobody else touched it. How can people doubt when they have such proof as that?"

Not long ago Sir Arthur said:

"I pledge my honor that spiritism is true, and I know that spiritism is infinitely more important than literature, art, politics, or in fact anything in the world."

Twice Revived Sherlock Holmes.

Sir Arthur Conan Doyle gained universal fame as one of the greatest writers of detective stories through the criminological feats of his master sleuth, Sherlock Holmes. Perhaps Holmes himself was even better known than his creator and the fictional address of the former's chambers on Baker Street in London have been sought out by countless visitors to London who were bitterly disappointed when they were informed that Sherlock Holmes had never existed in the flesh.

Twice after his career had been definitely terminated by his author, Sherlock Holmes was brought back to fictional life, so avid was the appetite of the public for the narratives of the solution of crime by minute deductive reasoning. The first time was in 1904, with "The Return of Sherlock Holmes," after he had apparently been killed in the last preceding tale;, and the second was with the publication of "The Case Book of Sherlock Holmes," in 1927. On the latter occasion Sir Arthur announced that under no circumstances would the great detective ever appear again.

Although Sherlock Holmes was the source of Sir Arthur's world-wide fame and the name of the detective became a by-word throughout the world, these stories, of which there were a total of sixty-eight, were never considered the most important part of his work by the author himself. Furthermore, they did not win immediate recognition, and although the first Sherlock Holmes volume appeared in 1887, it was through "Micah Clarke," a historical novel which appeared the following year, that he gained his first literary recognition.

Historical novels Sir Arthur always regarded as a more serious part of his work, and he was the author of several others, including "Sir Nigel" and "The White Company," the latter considered his finest work of the kind. He also devoted much energy to work of a journalistic character, including two books explaining England's position in the Boer War, for which he received his knighthood, and a quantity of work of similar character during the World War. But of all his varied labors, Sir Arthur himself regarded his devotion to spiritism, which occupied most of his time after the war, as the most important effort of his life.

Sir Arthur was born in Edinburgh in 1859. His father, grandfather, and uncle were all artists and caricaturists of considerable note. He was interested in writing almost from infancy, despite the fact that he was educated as a physician and practiced for several years.

First Book at Age of Six.

His first book was written at the age of six and illustrated by the author. After that there was apparently less written material, but throughout his school years he was known among his fellows as a great story teller. He would invent a character at the beginning of a term, and keep up a marvelous list of adventures which would hold his character on the stage until vacation arrived. His first published story was during his years as a medical student, and the three guineas he received for it gave him the necessary conviction that he could write things which people would pay for.

With such a promising background as a narrator, his youth passed with little more direct development in that direction. It was not until he was a practicing physician at Southsea that he turned seriously and industriously to writing in the unwelcome leisure of a young physician at the outset of his practice. But the half dozen preceding years had produced much experience which was to prove valuable to him as an author.

In the first place, they had brought him into close contact with the man who became the prototype of Sherlock Holmes. This was Dr. Joseph Bell, a distinguished Scotch surgeon and Sir Arthur's professor in the Edinburgh University medical school. Dr. Bell had remarkable powers of observation and deduction, through which he was able to diagnose almost on sight. It was these same abilities, turned to crime, that later produced Sherlock Holmes.

Sir Arthur's family did not have abundant funds, and the young medical student worked as an assistant during his Summers to help defray the cost of his professional medical education. Work in the slums of large cities brought diversified contacts which all proved fodder for the author's imagination later. A trip as surgeon on a whaling ship during one Summer and a trip to Africa as a ship's surgeon after he had taken his medical degree, contributed further broadening.

Began Writing in Spare Time.

Settled at Southsea, with few patients in his first days of practice, Sir Arthur went at writing seriously. Short stories anonymously published proved no royal road to literary fame, but kept all his leisure well occupied. This period produced the first Sherlock Holmes stories, published in book form as "A Study in Scarlet," in 1887. It culminated the following year with the publication of "Micah Clarke," which was refused by several publishers before Andrew Lang read it as reader for Longmans.

The career of a physician, in which he was gaining some success, was abandoned for the next two years, which were devoted to the writing of "The White Company." After its completion he turned around and abandoned literature for medicine, devoting some time to further study to equip himself as an eye specialist, and establishing himself in London.

Leisure time, however, found him writing again and his health soon began to suffer under the severe regimen of mornings of private practice, afternoons of hospital work, and nights, or a good part of them, devoted to writing. Accordingly, he was again faced with the dilemma of choosing between two promising careers, and he definitely abandoned medicine. His only return thereafter was during the Boer War, when he served as the head of a British hospital.

On two occasions Sir Arthur carried his proclivities for crime detection into the world of realities. In both cases his purpose was to right a miscarriage of justice, and in both instances he succeeded in exonerating a man who had been convicted and sentenced to a long term at hard labor. The beneficiaries were Adolph Beck, a Swede by birth, whose conviction for swindling resulted from mistaken identity, and George Edalji, a young lawyer whose father was an East Indian, whose conviction for maiming animals was apparently brought about through manufactured evidence inspired by the local unpopularity of the victim.

Sir Arthur was first married to Louise Hawkins of Minsterworth in 1885. She died in 1906, leaving a son and a daughter. He was married again to Miss Jean Leckie of Blackheath in 1907 and the couple had three children. His son by his first wife was killed in the World War, and it was this tragedy which was largely responsible for Sir Arthur's almost exclusive interest in spiritism during his later years.

Times Wide World Photo.

SIR ARTHUR CONAN DOYLE,
Who Died in England Yesterday at Age of 71.

LAUD CONAN DOYLE, A PIONEER SPIRITIST

Psychic Investigators Extol His Sincerity, Enthusiasm and 'Utility as an Advocate.'

DETECTIVES PAY TRIBUTE

Heads of Large Agencies Say Ideas of "Sherlock Holmes's" Creator Were Effective in Practice.

Sir Arthur Conan Doyle, in his dual capacity as the world's most widely known advocate of spiritism and the creator of the character of Sherlock Holmes, had tribute paid to his memory yesterday by leading spiritists and detectives in this city.

Frederick Bligh Bond, editor of Psychic Research, official publication of the American Society for Psychical Research, Inc., at 15 Lexington Avenue, when told of Sir Arthur's death commented as follows:

"Sir Arthur was eminently the great plowman in our field of work. From the very forcefulness of his work and the enthusiasm of his faith in its verity he was prone to pay little heed to those principles of scientific discrimination and critical watchfulness which are held as vital to the work of psychical research. Hence, beyond that measure of respect and sympathy which would be the universal tribute accorded to him and the recognition of his great utility as an advocate and publicist, his activities lay in a great measure outside the scope of philosophic inquiry for which the official societies stand. For this reason the relation between himself and the American Society for Psychical Research would be based on a cordial and friendly appreciation rather than on any intimacy of work or ideals.

His Belief "a Religion."

"With Sir Arthur, belief in the continuity of human life and intercourse with the other world was a religion, and his fervent spirit would scarcely tolerate another view. Spiritualism was, for him, the great tree of which all the notable world-religions were but the branches. His experience led him to some extent to 'prove all things and hold fast that which is true,' but the scientific method he probably never grasped in its entirety; and his lifelong training as a writer of romantic fiction inevitably created in him an imaginative mentality liable to unfit him as a recorder of statistical fact or as an assayer of evidential values. But when all is said and done, his work was essential in its own sphere and its conscientious thoroughness cannot be denied."

Hereward Carrington, psychic investigator and writer, spoke in a similar vein:

"There is a great difference," he said, "between the attitude assumed by Sir Arthur and that of the average scientific psychical researcher Conan Doyle was a spiritualist and regarded it as a religion, whereas the psychic investigator regards this subject as a science. Sir Arthur was in a sense a bishop of a church, and he represented it just as any other bishop would represent any other church.

"Personally Sir Arthur was a most delightful and charming man, very sincere and quite incapable of understanding the fact that one-half of humanity is out to fool the other half. In other words, his own nature was in a sense his own worst enemy.

Says Sir Arthur Erred.

"Believing as I do in the reality of psychic phenomena, I do not doubt that he witnessed many genuine manifestations. At the same time he undoubtedly endorsed many mediums who were unquestionably fraudulent. For example, his endorsement of the fairy photographs was, from our point of view, a very foolish stand for him to take. However, I do not doubt he gave help and encouragement to thousands of people in their distress, by reason of his supreme confidence in the reality of a spiritual world. He was a most charming personality and a delightful friend, and his loss will be keenly felt by all those who had the privilege of knowing him."

Raymond J. Burns, president of the William J. Burns International Detective Agency, said he considered "Sherlock Holmes" "the greatest of all fiction detectives."

"We all knew Sir Arthur very well," said Mr. Burns. "My father, William J. Burns, had been one of his intimate friends for twenty-five years, and they always had many interesting discussions together about the detection of crime. I met him for the first time about twenty years ago, when my father took us all for a visit to Sing Sing.

"In his day the methods employed by 'Sherlock Holmes' were the most advanced ever developed. Of course detective work today is on a more scientific basis, but the work in general profited greatly by the methods of Sir Arthur's fiction detective. Of all the detectives in fiction 'Sherlock Holmes' still remains the greatest."

Gerard M. Flynn, head of the William J. Flynn Detective Agency, and son of William J. Flynn, said Sir Arthur possessed "one of the greatest detective minds of all time."

"My father and I have read his works," he said, "and enjoyed them as well as profited by them. I derived from them practical suggestions on several occasions, and I believe that detectives the world over have been helped by them quite a lot. Sherlock Holmes's methods were not merely workable in fiction; they could have been used in actual practice."

Gillette Feels Loss of a Friend.

William Gillette, who created the stage rôle of Sherlock Holmes and played it intermittently for nearly half a century, until his retirement last year, asked to be excused from commenting on the death of his friend of long standing, according to The Associated Press. Mr. Gillette is now at his Summer home in Deep River, Conn.

However, Mr. Gillette stated that he could speak of Sir Arthur only in the very highest terms and that his long years of friendship with him had been most pleasant ones.

Spiritists in Rochester, N. Y., the city Sir Arthur termed "the birthplace and world centre of spiritualism," planned to pay a tribute to his memory at the Hydesville Memorial, the international shrine of spiritism, which stands on the lawn of the Plymouth Spiritualist Church. Sir Arthur made the first subscription to the memorial, $500, when he visited Rochester on April 14, 1923, for the purpose of talking to the Fox sisters, whose mediumistic activities were attracting wide attention at the time.

Bernard M. L. Ernst, attorney at 25 West Forty-third Street, legal representative of Sir Arthur in this country for many years, yesterday made public a letter written to him by his client and friend, dated Nov. 20, 1929, in wihch Sir Arthur referred to the alleged spirit message of Houdini and indicated his awareness of the nearness of death.

"I write this in bed," the letter reads, "as I have broken down badly and have developed angina pectoris, so there is just a chance that I may talk it all over with Houdini himself before so very long. I view the prospect with perfect equanimity. That is one thing that psychic knowledge does. It removes all fears of the future."

Houdini and Sir Arthur differed violently over spiritism, but the two remained close friends until Houdini published what amounted to a personal attack on Sir Arthur in his "Magician Among the Spirits." However, when Houdini died in 1926, Sir Arthur wrote his widow that Houdini was "the most remarkable man he had ever met."

SALE OF DOYLE BOOKS HIGH

Last Two Fiction Volumes Reached Well Over 1,000,000 Copies Here.

The detective stories of Sir Arthur Conan Doyle were among the most widely sold of contemporary books. Throughout the years they have proved steady sellers, and even those which came out originally forty years ago are still popular. The total sale of his books in this country could not be learned yesterday, since they were issued by various publishers, were reprinted and on some the copyright had run out.

His most recent publishers estimated that "The Hound of the Baskervilles" and "The Return of Sherlock Holmes" had each sold well over 1,000,000 copies in this country. Although Sir Arthur was not so prolific a writer as some other contemporary authors of detective fiction, his sales per volume ranked high.

One of Sir Arthur's last literary acts, according to his publishers, was to autograph pages for a twenty-four volume collected edition of his works. His literary labors continued until the end, according to Frederick Bligh Bond, editor of Psychic Research, who said that Sir Arthur left an unpublished work, "The Edge of the Unknown." Sir Arthur's detective stories, according to one publishing house here yesterday, are still the models by which all others are judged.

Section 1

"All the News That's Fit to Print."

The New York Times.

LATE CITY EDITION
POSTSCRIPT
THE WEATHER—Fair, continued cool today; tomorrow fair, rising temperature.
Temperatures yesterday—Max. 56, min. 48.
U. S. Weather Forecast—Page 12, Section 10.

Section 1

Copyright, 1931, by The New York Times Company.

VOL. LXXXI....No. 26,930. NEW YORK, SUNDAY, OCTOBER 18, 1931. Including Rotogravure Picture Section in two parts—Magazine and Book Sections in Rotogravure. TEN CENTS

BRAZIL SUSPENDS PAYMENTS IN CASH ON $500,000,000 DEBT

To Pay Interest in Scrip for 3 Years Owing to Decline in Exchange Value of Milreis.

$152,800,000 IN BONDS HERE

Bulk of External Obligations Held in England—Service Kept Up on Three Issues.

BANKERS APPROVE TERMS

Brazil Announcement Follows Word From New York and London Financiers.

Cash interest payments on the equivalent of about $500,000,000 of the external debt of the United States of Brazil have been suspended, Sebastiao Sampaio, Brazilian Consul General in New York, announced last night. Sinking fund obligations were suspended on Sept. 1.

Payments on the suspended obligations will be made during a period of three years in special scrip bearing interest at 5 per cent. The service on only three of the twenty-five external issues of the government will be met in cash on the due dates. These are the 5 per cent funding loan of 1898, amounting to £7,065,180; the 5 per cent funding loan of 1914, aggregating £14,278,960, and the 1922 7½ per cent coffee security loan, totaling £8,209,200.

Of the entire external debt affected by Brazil's action $152,800,000 is payable in dollars and most of it presumably is held in this country. All of the interest on such bonds is now to be paid in scrip. The total debt payable in sterling is £106,988,593 ($518,000,000 at the gold parity), but from this is to be deducted £29,054,000 ($141,000,000 at par), covering the three issues on which interest payments in cash are to be continued. The amount payable in French currency is 333,577,000 francs, on all of which the interest payments are to be made in scrip.

Brazil's Explanation of Action.

According to the Consul General's announcement, the action of his government was due to the "impossibility of acquiring foreign exchange for the transfer of funds to the markets where the coupons of the external debt are payable." "The Brazilian Federal Government, after placing before their bankers all facts regarding the position of the country," the statement continued, "is reluctantly obliged to authorize them to communicate to the holders of Brazilian bonds that they are only in a position to pay in full in cash, on the dates stipulated in the contract, the interest and sinking fund" on the three issues described.

"Interest on all other loans," the announcement said, "will be paid on their respective due dates during a period of three years in special scrip, bearing interest at 5 per cent per annum and divided into two series; the first series, redeemable in twenty years, will be in respect of the bonds issued against the following loans: Brazil 1903 5 per cent sterling bonds, Brazil 1909 5 per cent French franc bonds, Brazil 1921 8 per cent gold dollar bonds, Brazil 1922 7 per cent gold dollar bonds, Brazil 1926 6½ per cent gold dollar bonds, Brazil 1927 6½ per cent sterling and gold dollar bonds.

"The second series, redeemable in forty years, will be in respect of all other existing Brazilian Federal Government foreign loans.

"The Brazilian Federal Government undertakes to review the situation at the end of the first and second years with a view to extending cash payments should circumstances permit. The sums in milreis at the rate of exchange last fixed for stabilization, namely, 6 pence, corresponding to the interest not being remitted, will be deposited in an approved bank in the city of Rio de Janeiro and applied in the purchase of bills of exchange, provided that the market can supply them. Such remittances would be sent to the government's bankers and applied to the redemption of the new scrip, either by purchase if below par or by means of drawing if at par. The scrip of the series redeemable in twenty years will be dealt with first. Should the market not supply the necessary foreign exchange, the government will acquire bonds of the internal debt, which will be held in trust until such time as exchange can be obtained.

"The Brazilian Federal Government will pay the interest and the sinking fund on the new scrip in cash on their due dates. The sums in milreis earmarked for the payment of the suspended sinking fund, which are being deposited and which

Continued on Page Twenty-eight.

First German-American Battle In 1917 to Be Marked Saturday

The fourteenth anniversary of the first conflict between American and German troops in the World War will be observed on Saturday, when the First Division will hold its thirteenth annual reunion at Fort Hamilton, Brooklyn, now the division's headquarters. Brig. Gen. Lucius R. Holbrook, commander of the division, announced yesterday that General Charles P. Summerall, retired Chief of Staff, and Lieut-Gen. Robert Lee Bullard, both former battle commanders of the division, would attend.

From all sections of the country veterans of the division will assemble. At least 1,000 officers and men are expected. Major Gen. Hanson E. Ely, who led the Twenty-eighth Infantry of the First Division at Cantigny, will attend, as will Major Gen. Stephen O. Fuqua, one of the division's wartime chiefs of staff.

SHERWOOD DENIES WALKER PHONED HIM

"Disgusted With Entire Affair," His Only Comment on Call From Here to Mexico City.

PUBLIC INQUIRY FOR OLVANY

Legal Fight Expected on Move to Force Ex-Head of Tammany to Reveal His Clients.

Special Cable to The New York Times.

MEXICO CITY, Oct. 17.—"I'm disgusted with the entire affair," was the only comment Russell T. Sherwood, personal accountant to Mayor Walker, would make today when he was questioned regarding a telephone call he had received from New York. He denied, however, that the call had come from Mayor Walker.

Sherwood is honeymooning in Mexico City with his bride, the former Eleanor Rumpf of Brooklyn, to whom he was married on Oct. 6. The records show that Miss Rumpf was divorced from Eugene Conner of New York in Cuernavaca on Sept. 5.

The Sherwoods spent most of their time today sightseeing with Mr. and Mrs. Burton Wilson of New York. Among other places they visited the Pachuca and the scenic mountain village of El Chico. Efforts to interview Sherwood when he had luncheon at Pachuca were as unsuccessful as on other occasions. He refused to say whether or not he planned to return to New York to tell the Hofstadter committee about his business relations with Mayor Walker, and launched into a long tirade against tabloid newspapers and the reports they had carried regarding him.

MEXICO CITY, Oct. 17 (AP).—Informed that efforts were being made in New York to find a way to bring about his return there, Russell T. Sherwood did not seem greatly concerned. He said he was aware of his legal position while here.

He repeated he had planned to remain in Mexico indefinitely, and that he had hoped to enjoy a honeymoon here, but that since he had been discovered by the press, his stay was anything but pleasant and he might change his plans.

"I detest publicity and I will not consent to have my photograph taken on that account," he said.

Seabury to Question Olvany.

With little prospect of being able to bring Russell T. Sherwood, Mayor Walker's accountant, back from Mexico City in the next few weeks, Samuel Seabury, counsel of the Hof-

Continued on Page Twenty-two.

CAPONE CONVICTED OF DODGING TAXES; MAY GET 17 YEARS

Jury Finds Him Guilty on Two Misdemeanor and Three Felony Counts.

IT IS OUT FOR 8 HOURS

Tuesday Set for Hearing Defense Motion for New Trial, Before Sentence Is Passed.

VERDICT PUZZLES COUNSEL

But Prosecutor Accepts It After Conference—"Not Guilty" on 18 Counts Pleases Gang Chief.

By MEYER BERGER.

Staff Correspondent of The New York Times.

CHICAGO, Oct. 17.—Al Capone was found guilty here tonight on five of the twenty-three counts contained in the two indictments brought against him by the Federal Government for income tax evasion from 1924 to 1929.

Two of the five counts are misdemeanors, failure to file income tax in 1924 and 1928, each carrying possible maximum sentence of one year imprisonment and $10,000 fine. The other counts on which he was found guilty are felonies and each carries a maximum penalty of five years' imprisonment and $10,000 fine for "attempt to evade and defeat" the income tax in 1925, 1926 and 1927.

Judge Wilkerson set Tuesday morning for hearing on motions by defense counsel for arrest of judgment and for a new trial.

The verdict, returned eight hours and ten minutes after the jury filed out at 2:40 P. M., was a puzzling one to all in the court room.

Capone grinned as though he felt he had gotten off easily. His counsel asked that the verdict be re-read that they might grasp it.

Jacob I. Grossman, Assistant United States Attorney, mumbled that he thought the finding "inconsistent" and asked for time to confer with the other members of the prosecutor's staff.

Government Accepts Verdict.

Ten minutes later Mr. Grossman was back in the room. He announced that the government has decided that there was no inconsistency and that it was willing to have the verdict entered. Albert Fink of defense counsel then made a motion for arrest of judgment.

"I will not hold your motion for arrest of judgment," said Judge Wilkerson. "I think you will make another motion."

"You mean a motion for a new trial?" said Mr. Fink. "Do I waive my motion for a new trial if I make a motion for arrest of judgment?"

The court did not answer.

Capone faces a maximum of seventeen years' imprisonment and $50,000 fine. He did not seem to realize that. He kept grinning at all and sundry in the court room, his bulky figure in a screaming green suit (one of the $135 ones) drawing all eyes toward him.

As soon as the verdict was entered, he got out of his seat and virtually ran from the room. He rushed on lumbering feet across the dim corridor, stepped into the elevator and as soon as it touched the rotunda floor he ran out to the street to a waiting automobile. No one interviewed him.

The jury was ready with the verdict at 10:50 P. M., but Capone was not there when the knock on the

Continued on Page Nineteen.

Thomas Edison Dies in Coma at 84; Family With Him as the End Comes

THOMAS ALVA EDISON,
From the Painting by Ellis M. Silvette.

Inventor Succumbs at 3:24 A. M. After Fight for Life Since He Was Stricken on Aug. 1—World-Wide Tribute Is Paid to Him as a Benefactor of Mankind.

From a Staff Correspondent of The New York Times.

WEST ORANGE, N. J., Sunday, Oct. 18.—Thomas Alva Edison died at 3:24 o'clock this morning at his home, Glenmont, in the Llewellyn Park section of this city. The great inventor, the fruits of whose genius so magically transformed the everyday world, was 84 years and 8 months old.

Announcement of Mr. Edison's passing was made at 3:37 A. M. by Arthur L. Walsh, vice president of the Thomas A. Edison Industries, Inc., who had acted as spokesman for the family during the night.

The end came almost imperceptibly as the sick man's ebbing strength, sapped by long months of struggle against a complication of ailments, gradually receded until his heart ceased beating. He had suffered no pain through the later stages of his illness, his attendants said.

With him when death came were his entire immediate family and Dr. Hubert S. Howe of New York, his personal physician. His wife, who was Miss Mina Miller before their marriage in 1886, had been almost constantly at his bedside since his illness became acute early this month.

Their children, Mrs. John Eyre Sloane and Charles and Theodore Edison, all live near by and have been at Glenmont daily through that period, as has Thomas A. Edison Jr., a son of the inventor's first marriage. Mrs. Marion Oser of Norwalk, Conn., and William L. Edison of Wilmington, Del., the other children by the first marriage, had been summoned when it became apparent that the end was near.

Mr. Edison never roused from the coma into which he lapsed last Thursday. Through the last hours of his long and fruitful life he lay in what seemed like deep and restful slumber. He had been unable to take any nourishment since last Sunday or any liquids in almost two weeks.

Through the long days before that when he calmly, cheerfully awaited the inevitable, amazing evidences of the world's affectionate concern for one of its most useful citizens were plentiful. Pope Pius XI, President Hoover, Henry Ford and a host of others kept in daily touch with his condition.

Anxiety for the man whose creative genius gave the world the electric light, the phonograph, the motion picture camera and a thousand of other inventions ranging through all the various fields of science had been general since he collapsed in the living room of his home on Aug. 1.

The obituary of Mr. Edison and a page of pictures of outstanding events in his life in Section II.

DEBT SLASH BY HALF IS URGED IN PARIS AS LAVAL'S AIM HERE

Le Matin Gives French 'Unofficial Opinion' as Basis of Coming Talks With Hoover.

LONGER MORATORIUM HIT

Policies on Arms Reduction, Reparations and Banking Credits Suggested in Outline.

PREMIER CONFERS AT SEA

He and His Seven Experts Prepare for Conversations, Studying Our Point of View.

By P. J. PHILIP.

Special Cable to The New York Times.

PARIS, Oct. 17.—While Premier Laval is taking to Washington no rigid plan and no fixed doctrine as to how calm, credit and confidence can be brought back to the world, he is taking with him what may be called an "official opinion" on all questions which are likely to arise. What that "official opinion" is, is set forth in an article in Le Matin of today, which confirms at every point the outline of the French position as described in a dispatch to The New York Times ten days ago.

While emphasizing that the outline of the French position which it prints does not constitute a definite program, Le Matin says that the suggestions contained in it are those which Premier Laval will contribute in the Washington conversations with President Hoover.

Against Extending Moratorium.

Le Matin's article reads:

"First, the intergovernmental debts: "While America inclines toward an extension of the moratorium, France believes that this method has grave inconveniences, because it holds the threat of accumulated payments over Germany and other countries which are in financial difficulties.

"In place of the moratorium, debt reduction representing inevitable sacrifices and reaching as high as 50 per cent is regarded as the only real help in the world situation. If the United States should consent, it would have to bear a loss, even though only a theoretic loss, of about $200,000,000 yearly.

"Germany's payments would be reduced by that amount, and during a certain period the remaining payments by Germany might be made to the Bank for International Settlements, but instead of being transferred abroad, and finally to the United States, might be reloaned in Germany and other countries which are in financial difficulties.

As to Action in Disarmament.

"Second, disarmament:

"France in compensation for the sacrifice asked from the United States is disposed to embark on a program of progressive disarmament which will be of a kind to help the American budgetary position. This, however, is on two conditions: first, that disarmament shall be sought by a reduction of the present budgets and not by the equalization of armaments; secondly, that the Kellogg pact shall be completed by one or two articles stipulating that in the case of a threat of or the outbreak of a conflict the United States shall act in concert and without delay with the other powers, and once the

Continued on Page Five.

Americans in Japan Suffer As Chinese Cooks Start Home

By The Associated Press.

TOKYO, Oct. 17.—The Sino-Japanese controversy has produced an echo in the kitchens of Americans and others in Japan who employ Chinese cooks. Seventy-two Chinese chefs today decided to inform their employers they would pack their bags and depart for China as a result of the international dispute, and, consequently thirty Chinese restaurants in Tokyo and several in Yokohama, Osaka and Kobe may have to close.

In addition, the kitchens of numerous private families face the loss of their culinary experts, most of whom are from Canton.

JAPAN WILL AWAIT LEAGUE PROPOSALS

Tokyo Accepts Move on China Calmly, Foreseeing Delay, but Continues Protest.

RUSSIAN RIGHTS ARE CITED

Japanese Point Out That Soviet, and 50 Others Also Signed Briand-Kellogg Pact.

By HUGH BYAS.

Special Cable to The New York Times.

TOKYO, Oct. 17.—The government has accepted the creation of a "united front" at Geneva regarding Manchuria with complete calmness, and displays no intention either of quitting the League or of obstructing the efforts of the enlarged Council.

The attendance of Kenkichi Yoshizawa at the session yesterday at which the American representative, Prentiss Gilbert, was present, is accepted as a matter of course, and he will continue to attend, though his government is still not convinced that the Council acted constitutionally and will press for a decision on the legal points involved.

By instructing Mr. Yoshizawa to repeat its protest regarding the legality of the move, the government is simply marking time until Geneva reaches the stage of practical proposals.

One possibility of obstruction hitherto overlooked, which the League's action opens, is that Russia, as a signatory of the Briand-Kellogg pact also, and with vast interests in Manchuria, might likewise ask to participate. Probably, as Japan is now taking as much care to avoid infringing the Russian sphere as Russia took in 1929 to avoid Japan's sphere, Russia will copy Japan's 1929 attitude of non-interference, but it seems to Japan that by opening the door to America the League also has opened it to Russia, which, conceivably, might seek entirely different results.

Japan Sees Expediency.

In Japan's view, the League was influenced by expediency, and if the covenant is to be interpreted in terms of opportunism at every varying situation, the position of all members is affected. Withdrawal from the League, however, is an unlikely possibility which no responsible persons are as yet considering.

Minister of War Minami gave out a violently worded interview last evening in which he spoke of the League exposing its weakness by inviting America, and America provoking the Japanese people's feelings by attending the League, but his remarks need not be taken too seriously.

The Foreign Office has been furnished with a copy of Prentiss Gilbert's instructions, which empower

Continued on Page Two.

LEAGUE INVOKES THE KELLOGG PACT; ASKS NATIONS' AID

Council Drafts Identical Notes Reminding China and Japan of Peace Obligations.

FURTHER ACTION PLANNED

Session Today Will Seek Ways for Japanese Evacuation and Safety in China.

JAPAN TO WIDEN DEMANDS

Tries to Revive Rights Given Up at Washington Parley—Her Delegation Resentful.

By LANSING WARREN.

Special Cable to The New York Times.

GENEVA, Oct. 17.—As a result of two secret sessions of the League of Nations Council today, at which the American representative, Prentiss B. Gilbert, took part on a basis of full equality, an entirely new force has been brought into play to bring a peaceful settlement of the Manchurian conflict between China and Japan, the only two members of the Council not present at these meetings.

This force, new so far as League action is concerned, is the moral force of the Briand-Kellogg pact, which until America's entry into the League Council sittings had remained inoperative while the League was attempting separate action through the machinery of the League covenants.

The Council decided tonight after long discussions that the Briand-Kellogg pact (known officially as the Pact of Paris) could best be coordinated with the League's action if the countries represented on the League Council would send identical cablegrams to the Nanking and Tokyo Governments reminding them of their obligations under Article 2 of the pact to settle their differences by pacific means.

Some Messages Are Sent.

While all the members of the Council are signatories to the Pact of Paris, only those represented by Foreign Ministers with full powers in the matter were able to dispatch these messages from Geneva tonight. Representatives who were bound to consult their governments notified their Foreign Offices of the action suggested by the Council, with recommendations that like action be taken without delay.

But the decision went further, aiming to make other League members outside the Council and even non-members of the League who are signatories to the Briand-Kellogg pact. To all of these, including Russia, the League tonight dispatched telegrams informing them of the Council's decision and urging that they join in putting the pressure of their authority under the treaty into the service of world peace. Mr. Gilbert, as United States representative with the Council, tonight formally sent an identical appeal to Secretary of State Stimson at Washington to join with the other nations in dispatch to China and Japan.

This will be the second time the American Government has had occasion to invoke the Pact of Paris, the first time curiously enough having also been in a conflict in Manchuria, which took place between the Chinese and the Russians. Tonight's action, however, having been initiated through the collaboration of the League, the United States has been relieved of the responsibility for instigating a movement which is shared alike by all nations represented on the Council. In participating, the United States stands exactly in the same position as other non-member States who will decide to take the same action.

Stimson's Action Forecast.

On the basis of a long transatlantic telephone conversation, which is known to have taken place last night between Mr. Stimson and Mr. Gilbert, it is taken for granted that the United States will take part in this move. How many other States will join is not known to the Secretariat. There is particular doubt as to exactly what position will be taken by Russia, which perhaps is the most directly interested non-member in the Manchurian dispute.

Regardless of how the action may be viewed by the governments of Japan and China, it is felt that the recital of obligations from governments in all parts of the world cannot but exert a powerful impression. Not only will they serve to draw the attention of Tokyo and Nanking to world opinion, which is so interested in the peaceful settlement of the struggle, but they will bring the problem into prominence in practically every country in the world. Each country thus aroused, it is presumed, will henceforth feel a direct interest in a peaceful settlement, and a moral force not easily neglected will have been set in force.

The Briand-Kellogg pact, without

Results in Major Sports Yesterday.

FOOTBALL—Local gridirons produced one of the big upsets yesterday when Columbia defeated Dartmouth, 19 to 6, at Baker Field. Fordham tied Holy Cross, 6—6, at the Polo Grounds. The N. Y. U. team beat Rutgers, 27 to 7, at the Yankee Stadium. A determined rally in the second period gave Harvard a victory over Army at West Point, 14 to 13, Army scoring its points in the first period. Celebrating the fortieth anniversary of A. A. Stagg as football coach, Yale on her first trip to the mid-West conquered Chicago, 27 to 0. Cornell downed Princeton, 33 to 0; Pennsylvania vanquished Lehigh, 32 to 0; Navy beat Delaware, 12 to 7, and at Troy, R. P. I. defeated C. C. N. Y., 13 to 3. Other gridiron scores were Colgate 33, Manhattan 0; Brown 38, Tufts 12; Syracuse 33, Florida 12; Villanova 12, Boston College 6; Lafayette 22, St. John's of Annapolis 0; Pittsburgh 32, Western Reserve 0; Ohio State 20, Michigan 7; Notre Dame 63, Drake 0; Wisconsin 21, Purdue 14; Illinois 20, Bradley 0; Northwestern 19, University of California (L. A.) 0; Tennessee 25, Alabama 0; Tulane 19, Vanderbilt 0; Georgia 32, North Carolina 7; Stanford 25, Oregon State 7; Southern California 53, Oregon 0; Washington 39, Idaho 7; California 13, Washington State 7.

RACING—William Woodward's Ormesby won the Pierrepont Handicap, one of the feature events of the closing day at Jamaica, finishing the mile and a furlong over a slow track a length and a half ahead of A La Carte, the favorite. Mrs. George Harris's Cambal won the Remsen Handicap, for 2-year-olds, by a head from H. C. Phipps's Regula Baddun, with John J. Robinson's Lucky Tom, the favorite, third. At Laurel, the Linton Farms' Flagstone, an outsider, won the Laurel Stakes, with $10,000 added, beating Clock Tower by a head. Mr. Sponge and Curate were among the also ran. At Latonia R. S. Clark's Kakapo won the $15,000 added Kentucky Jockey Club Stakes by three lengths from Pompeius. Air Pilot was third.

Complete Details of These and Other Sports Events in Sports Section.

PETAIN DECLARES YORKTOWN DEBT PAID

Marshal Praises America's Part in War and Ideals to Maintain Peace.

From a Staff Correspondent of The New York Times.

YORKTOWN, Va., Oct. 17.—The frills and furbelows of an age that is gone graced the ancient streets of this little village today as the second day of the sesquicentennial celebration of the Battle of Yorktown passed into history.

Silks and satins styled in the modes of another era, flounced crinolines and billowing taffetas, powdered wigs and silver buckles, pigtails and perukes flashed against the old brick walls of Yorktown's ancient homes to vie in incongruous but pleasing contrast with the bright uniforms of the soldiers and sailors of today, with the silk hats and frock coats of diplomatic dignitaries, with the neat khaki of General Pershing and the horizon blue of Marshal Petain and with the sombre business suits of political leaders, business executives and plain citizens.

It was "Revolutionary Day" in this town that had its birth in 1691, when fifty acres of land for the establishment of "Ye Towne of Yorke" were sold for 10,000 pounds of tobacco. Crisp Fall weather and bright, searching sunshine; pageants of the

Continued on Page Sixteen.

WAGNER TREASURES COMING TO AMERICA

Mrs. Mary Bok Buys the Famous Burrell Collection Throwing New Light on Composer.

Announcement of world-wide importance to music lovers and Wagner students is made in Overtones, the monthly musical magazine of the Curtis Institute of Music, issued yesterday in Philadelphia, that Mrs. Mary Louise Curtis Bok, founder of the institute, is the purchaser and sole owner of the Burrell collection of Wagnerians.

This collection was discovered under highly dramatic circumstances two years ago in England. Very little of its contents has been made public, but enough of its material is known for it to be certain that their publication will necessitate drastic revisions of many chapters in long accepted biographies of the master and in establishing the true place of many shadowy and enigmatic characters in history.

The Burrell collection, of which the existence was known only to a few scholars, and of which the whereabouts was completely unknown, was discovered two years ago in an English country house by two Americans, Messrs. Hurn and Root, who were in Europe seeking material for a drama on Wagner. The priceless collection was discovered reposing in

Continued on Page Thirty-one.

Hitlerites Battle Foes in Brunswick Streets; 10 Sent to Hospital on Eve of 'Nazi' Review

By The Associated Press.

BRUNSWICK, Germany, Oct. 17.—Serious street fights between Hitlerites and anti-Hitlerites occurred here today on the eve of the National Socialist [Nazis] field day, at which Adolf Hitler, the "Nazi" leader, will review forces drawn from all parts of the Reich. Ten persons required hospital treatment and several others received less serious knife wounds.

An automobile containing twenty-seven "Nazis" en route to Brunswick overturned near Wurzen. One of the occupants was killed and all the others were injured.

Thousands of Herr Hitler's followers thundered down the streets here to the accompaniment of martial music as a curtain-raiser to tomorrow's events.

Squad after squad of them, carrying flaming torches, tramped past Herr Hitler, who stood in an automobile and smilingly acknowledged the greeting of "Hoch!" from the legions, responding by raising his arm in the Fascist salute.

"Nazi" headquarters predicted that at least 75,000 of the Hitlerite "storm troops" would be on hand tomorrow, as well as an equal number of civilians. Those arriving on trains tonight already had donned the mustard-colored uniforms which are not permitted in Prussia and some other States. The uniforms were put on as soon as the Brunswick border had been crossed.

Adolf Hitler's "Nazis," Dr. Alfred Hugenberg's Nationalists and the Peasants' League joined forces in a military rally at Bad Harzburg last Sunday and formed the National Opposition, whose immediate aim was the overthrow of the Bruening Government.

Chancellor Bruening, however, succeeded in obtaining a vote of confidence from the Reichstag on Friday by 295 to 270, the Communists and People's party joining the Nationalists in voting against him, with the Socialists, the Centrists and other middle parties and smaller groups enabling him to gain the victory. The Reichstag then voted to adjourn until Feb. 23.

Edison Began Experiments as Boy and Won Fame Early; Long Career Boon to World

PROSPERO IS DEAD.

EDISON the light-bearer has gone into darkness. The master of the waves of sound is silent. Round him had gathered an atmosphere of respect, admiration and affection such as surrounded no other American of our time. His victories over iron fortune, his long years of almost superhuman labor, the splendor and scope of his inventions, took strong hold of the popular imagination; the national pride, too. Ours was this wondersmith of the world. He might have wrought all these marvels and remained apart, solitary in his laboratory. His companionable and social nature, its fine simplicities and boyishness, endeared the man, set up his essential human image in millions of minds. He was not only honored, but loved.

It seems at first as though some mighty and creative force had ended. It is not ended. It is continued and transmitted immortally. As he profited by his predecessors, so will his successors profit by him. If nothing can take the place of or soften the regret for a warm human presence, let us think what an earthly immortality is his. Every incandescent light is his remembrancer. Every power house is his monument. Wherever there is a phonograph or radio, wherever there is a moving picture, mute or speaking, EDISON lives. Of him and no man else may it be truly said that "his fame folds in this orb o' the earth."

The Eskimo on Bering Strait, the Kirghiz of the steppes, East Indians in remote villages, Moors of the town and Bedouins of the desert, east, west, north, south, all the tribes of men, owe a harmless pleasure, a quickening of the imaginative pulse, to the incomparable magician. He is the god of safety to seamen and riders of the air. He is the universal lamplighter. Multitudinous homes and buildings and streets shine every night in his praise. He has illuminated and broadened the use and wont of life. How many men and women he has set to work in the industries sprung from his brain is beyond estimation. Between the time of our grandfathers and our own he has transformed the world. He has added immeasurably to the comfort, enjoyment and productivity of mankind.

The farewell of regret to the eager, friendly, so profoundly living and seeking man will change insensibly into a hymn of triumph, undying hope and everlastingness. If in the body EDISON is to vanish from us, he survives in the subtle and mysterious powers he made his servants. He is ever living in electricity, sound, light. Prospero is not dead because the wand has dropped from his hand. He reigns still in his viewless empery.

EDISON THE INVENTOR.

To Americans EDISON was always the "wizard"; to European peasants a half-legendary figure—technical ingenuity incarnate. But to the social philosopher he is as much the symbol of a culture as LEONARDO.

No figure so completely satisfied the popular conception of what an inventor should be. Here was a solitary genius revolutionizing the world and making an invisible force do his bidding—a genius that conquered conservatism, garlanded cities in light and created wonders that transcended the predictions of Utopian poets. Moreover, he was ideally practical. Everything that he invented worked; everything filled a human need.

We think of him working in a fine frenzy, guided by flashes of inspiration. There were, in fact, whole days when he and his assistant slept on benches, with resistance-boxes for pillows, and lived on food passed through windows. But his successes must be attributed more to an extraordinary technical imagination, driving force and a fierce tenacity. There was the desire for perfection, too—a desire that urged him, for example, to test no fewer than 6,000 materials before he discovered a satisfactory lamp filament. But the lamp had to be brought into the home. So he built and equipped the first power-house and provided a distribution system, junction-boxes, sockets, meters—the whole paraphernalia of a public utility. At a bound he became the first electrical engineer.

Few inventors succeed in transforming society as EDISON did in his own lifetime, or leaving their impress on a whole period. This electrical age is largely of his creation. He found a world that hardly knew what a piece of insulated wire was, burning kerosene and gas; he left it sending several telegrams over one wire in accordance with his invention, viewing motion pictures which he made practical, painting with his electric light and listening to the notes of great singers and orchestras embalmed by his phonograph. With him passes perhaps the last of the heroic inventors and the greatest of the line. The future probably belongs to the corporation research laboratory, with trained engineers and chemists directed by a scientific captain. EDISON saw the change coming. Yet he must have realized that the electrical forces he had unleashed were too formidable for a lone Titan to master.

EDISON BELIEVED IN 'SUPREME MIND'

Belonged to Freethinkers, but He Was Neither an Atheist Nor an Agnostic.

HE DOUBTED IMMORTALITY

But in the Last Few Years His Attitude Shifted Toward the Presumption of a Hereafter.

Considerable confusion exists concerning Edison's religious beliefs. When it was proposed in Elmira, N. Y., two years ago, for instance, to call a new high school the Thomas A. Edison High School, a protest was addressed to the city officials against naming an educational institution for "an avowed unbeliever in God and a life hereafter."

An examination of the many public declarations of Edison on the subject, however, shows an unchanging profession of belief in what he called "a supreme intelligence." As to his own personal continuance after death, he remained uncertain but more inclined in later years to consider it likely.

He never at any time occupied the position of atheist, and was even less of an agnostic than a freethinker. For years he and the late Luther Burbank were the most important figures in the Freethinkers Society, rejecting ecclesiastical authority and traditions but retaining the idea of a "supreme intelligence."

Edison did not devote much thought, however, either to God or to the possibility of his own hereafter, until he had passed seventy years of age. Even then there was no indication of any personal need of God, or of the mystic yearning which forms the basis of religion. He disposed of organized churches in the United States in 1928, on his eighty-first birthday, by saying, "People are drifting away from superstition and bunk; increase in scientific knowledge is responsible."

His Views on Spiritualism.

His mind first turned to the problem of a hereafter in 1920, at the age of 73, during a great wave of spiritualism here and abroad, when the ouija-board took possession of popular attention. Edison said he did not believe psychic research could be based on such an unscientific piece of apparatus and set out to devise something more likely to facilitate communication with departed spirits, if any existed.

This spirit apparatus never developed, but during the search for it Edison pondered over the problem of life and death. In an interview in The Scientific American, Oct. 30, 1920, he said: "I cannot conceive of such a thing as a spirit. Imagine something which has no weight, no material form, no mass, in a word, imagine nothing."

Three years later, in the Sunday Magazine of THE NEW YORK TIMES, he presented a theory of "entities." "I believe," Mr. Edison said, "that the human body is vivified, made to function mentally and physically by myriads of infinitesimal entities, each in itself a unit of life, living in the body cells but not visible even to the ultramicroscope. These entities are life. I do not believe that the human being has a soul—unless you want to call these entities soul—nor that a human being has a conscious life after death in any form, spiritual or physical."

His belief in "a supreme intelligence" remained undisturbed. In January, 1924, he said "No intelligent man denies the existence of a supreme intelligence."

In 1925, Edison was one of the leaders in founding a memorial museum at New Rochelle, N. Y., in honor of Thomas Paine. In an interview in July, 1925, Edison said that he had begun to read Paine's works when he was thirteen years of age. "Paine suffers from the misinterpretations of others," Edison wrote. "He has been called an atheist, but he was not. Paine believed in a supreme intelligence as representing the idea which other men often express by the name of deity."

Edison was vice president of the Thomas Paine National Historical Association in 1927, when, on his eightieth birthday, he submitted to the annual interview on all subjects, particularly the immortality of the soul.

Deplored Lack of Data.

"We really haven't got any very great amount of data on this subject," he said, "and without data how can we reach definite conclusions? All we have, everything, favors the idea of what religionists call the 'hereafter.' Science, if it ever learns the facts, probably will find another and more definitely descriptive term."

It was during this 1927 interview that Edison was asked "What does the word God mean to you?" and he replied, "Nothing." A storm of criticism arose over this apparent profession of final unbelief. Mrs. Edison later explained that her husband's answer referred to the word "God" and not to the idea it represented, and that he simply preferred to use the term "supreme intelligence."

Edison's attitude toward immortality shifted gradually during the last few years from a rejection of the prospect of a hereafter to the presumption of his survival. His latest declaration, before his health began to fail, was that his belief in some sort of life after death was "fifty-fifty—one way or the other." When he was asked how he expected to spend his life after death, if any, he chuckled and said: "Experimenting."

Edison at work.

WORLD FOLLOWED NEWS OF HIS ILLNESS

WEST ORANGE, Oct. 17. (AP).—With the interest and sympathy which it reserves only for its great, the entire world followed the illness and passing of Thomas Alva Edison. Throughout the long weeks of his illness, the old-fashioned Victorian home in Llewellyn Park, where the enfeebled white-haired inventor awaited death, was the focal point of universal solicitude.

Daily hundreds of inquiries on Mr. Edison's condition came to the inventor's house and to members of his family. They came from others of the world's great—from President Hoover, Pope Pius XI, Henry Ford and Harvey Firestone. And they came from the anonymous public whom Mr. Edison had served by his 1,300 inventions.

First Vigil Began Aug. 1.

When Mr. Edison suffered his first collapse on Aug. 1, reporters and special writers from newspapers and press associations descended upon his estate to flash the news of his condition to a nation and a world filled with anxiety.

The ten-car garage near the Edison home was speedily transformed into a press headquarters. Telephone linemen, called out in the middle of the night, worked through till dawn, stringing up emergency telephone lines. Tables were set up in the garage to serve as writing desks, and makeshift wooden benches were hurriedly put together.

Then began the first vigil, which lasted ten days. For the newspaper men it was a twenty-four-hour-a-day assignment, and they snatched what little sleep they could in the back seats of the eight Edison automobiles.

Three times a day Dr. Hubert Howe, the inventor's personal physician, and Charles Edison, the inventor's son, issued bulletins on Edison's condition, which were rushed to a waiting public by newspapers and radio stations.

As if in sympathetic response to these reports, a tide of nation-wide inquiry flowed back to the inventor's West Orange estate. Henry Ford and Harvey Firestone and others of Mr. Edison's friends called by long distance telephone for news of his condition. During the serious phases of the inventor's illness, they kept in constant communication with his home.

Legion of Admirers.

There were other friends, not as intimate as the men who have been called Mr. Edison's "cronies," and a legion of admirers of his genius. From these came numerous letters of encouragement and sympathy and telegrams of inquiry.

Mr. Edison's first collapse occurred on a Saturday. The next day his home in the thickly wooded Llewellyn Park was the destination of many Sunday tourists. The roads about the grounds were lined with their parked automobiles, while the passengers stood about timidly, half uncertain how to express the sympathy and interest that had prompted them to make the journey. The West Orange police detailed two detachments of eight policemen to patrol the estate day and night to guard the sick man against unnecessary commotion or unwelcome intrusion.

It was not the first time some of the patrolmen had served Mr. Edison—they had been there in 1928 when President Hoover visited "the wizard of Menlo Park," and again last Spring when the King of Siam came to meet the inventor.

EDISON, AT 10, BEGAN CAREER AS INVENTOR

Regarded Dull in School Days at Milan, Ohio, He Early Showed His Genius.

EDUCATED BY HIS MOTHER

He Started Fortune by Devices Revolutionizing the Telegraph Business While an Operator.

PROLIFIC IN NEW IDEAS

Reached Height of Career Early With Development of Trolleys, Electric Light, Phonograph, Kinetoscope.

Thomas Alva Edison was born at Milan, Ohio, on Feb. 11, 1847. He came of vigorous and independent-minded stock, originally coming to America from the Zayder Zee. His great-grandfather was Thomas Edison, a New York banker of prominence on the Tory side during the Revolutionary War. So much of a Loyalist was he that when the Colonies won their independence he went to Canada to live under the British flag. There his grandson, Samuel, became a rebel against the King, rose to the rank of Captain in Papineau's insurgent army in 1837 and fled to the States with a price on his head.

Samuel Edison settled at Milan, Ohio, where his son, Thomas Alva Edison, was born. Edison got most of his schooling there. He was always, as he remembered it later, at the foot of his class. In interviews he recalled his mother's indignation when one of his teachers told him that he was "addled," a fighting adjective in country districts. His mother, who had been a teacher, took him out of school and educated him herself. His early reading, like that of Abraham Lincoln, consisted of what the village afforded. At the age of 9 he had read or his mother had read to him "The Penn Encyclopedia," "Hume's History of England," a history of the Reformation; Gibbons's "Decline and Fall of the Roman Empire," and Sear's "History of the World."

Started Experimenting Early.

But the books which put the backward schoolboy of the tiny canal village on the way to become one of the greatest men of his time were popular works on electricity and chemistry. He and his mother performed some of the simple chemical experiments they found described in the books. That started Edison on his career as an experimenter, investigator and scientist. The first steps of his career are described as follows in a condensed biography by William H. Meadowcroft, for many years Edison's private secretary:

"At about 10 or 11 years of age Edison became greatly interested in chemistry, and, having procured some books on the subject, persuaded his mother to allow him a space in her cellar for a laboratory. Here he experimented with such chemicals as he could procure at the local drug stores with his limited pocket money. He had gathered together about 200 bottles of various sizes and shapes to contain his chemicals, and labeled them all with the word 'Poison,' so that they would not be disturbed. At that early age, as later, he doubted the statements in books until he had proved them by experiment.

"Edison continued his chemical studies at home until he was between 12 and 13 years old, and then, finding that his pocket money was inadequate to purchase all the apparatus and chemicals he wanted, persuaded his father and mother to allow him to become a railroad newsboy, in order that he might earn money for his experiments. He received the necessary permission and thus came to sell newspapers, magazines, candy, &c., on one of the trains of the Grand Trunk Railway running between Port Huron and Detroit. Part of the baggage car was allowed him for his stock of goods, and into this space he moved his laboratory from his home on to the train and there continued to experiment, but on an enlarged scale. He also bought a printing press and some type and published on the train a weekly newspaper which he called The Weekly Herald, of which he was proprietor, publisher, editor, compositor, pressman and distributor. The paper contained local, market and railway news, and had as many as 400 paid subscribers at one time. So far as is known, this was the first newspaper ever printed on a moving train, and by the youngest known editor in the world.

Conductor Boxed His Ears.

Edison continued along these lines of work between two and three years until one day a bottle containing phosphorus fell off a shelf and broke upon the floor. The phosphorus set fire to the car, which was with some difficulty saved from burning up, and the conductor put the boy and his belongings off the train and boxed his ears so soundly as to cause the beginning of the deafness with which he has ever since been afflicted.

"Some little time before this Edison had saved from death the child of a station agent along the line of the railway, and the father, in gratitude, offered to teach the boy telegraphy. This offer was eagerly accepted, and since that time Edison had assiduously studied the art, besides continuing his chemical and other studies. His career as a train newsboy being ended after the incident above related, he now sought and obtained employment as telegraph operator, and at about 15 years of age entered upon this phase of his career. He plunged into the art with great enthusiasm and worked as an operator in various telegraph offices in different parts of the United States. Having the ability of living with but a very few hours of sleep, he worked nearly twenty hours a day, and not only continued his chemical studies but also applied himself very closely to the study of electricity and the art of telegraphy. He was always willing to take the place of a skilled press operator and work through the night after working all day, in order to perfect his speed, and succeeded so well that he became one of the most rapid and efficient telegraphers of his day, and advanced to the position and pay of a first-class operator."

One of his first inventions caused his discharge from his job. Young Edison had his mind so full of inventions and science that he did not have time to put in his full hours as operator. The circuit manager, suspecting that Edison might wander away from his telegraph instruments for an hour or so, required him to send the signal "six" every half hour while he was on duty. The outcome was the invention of a wheel with notches in it which automatically ticked off the required signal. The signals were given with such remarkable precision that suspicion was aroused. He was investigated, found out, and let it go. The invention was the forerunner of the modern messenger boy "call box."

Edison had worked in a dozen cities before he became of age and had achieved a reputation as the operator who couldn't keep a job. He lost his job because his mind was too full of "duplex transmission," which has since revolutionized the telegraph business.

He invented in those early days a "repeater," which automatically picks up a feeble message at the end of a long wire.

He drifted to New York, but there were no jobs for him. He turned up at the offices of the Law Gold Reporting Company one afternoon when the crude ticker service they were operating for market reports had broken down. He repaired it and promptly got a mechanican's job at $300 a month. He was about 22 years old then, and from that time fortune began to smile on him. He worked out improvements in stock tickers and telegraph appliances and got $50,000 for one invention of a ticker.

It was this money that gave him the means to extend his experiments. During this period he had developed the multiple telegraph appliance into a six-fold transmission system, the carbon telephone transmitter, the microtasimeter for measuring the smallest changes in temperature, the megaphone, the incandescent lamp, the phonograph, the kinetoscope, the alkaline storage battery, the magnetic ore separator and the trolley car.

Questionnaire Became Famous.

Almost entirely self-educated, Edison never had the opportunity or the leisure to make himself a profound student of physics, mathematics and theoretical chemistry, but he had a rich equipment for an inventor. To an enormous practical grasp of physics and electricity he joined wide general experience, reading and intellectual activity. The scattering and unsystematic book learning which he had gathered as a boy at home he developed in the same discursive way throughout the rest of his life. He read books of every kind. He was a believer in vast and miscellaneous general information, as he demonstrated in 1921, when the Edison questionnaire became famous. He gave to his prospective employes the kind of an examination which he himself could have passed when he was a youth. He wanted to find men of his own type, men of intellectual curiosity and general knowledge. He recognized the necessity for specialists but he insisted that a great specialist needed a diffused intellectual background.

In talking about the questionnaire Edison's secretary said that his chief, then nearly 75, was still an omnivorous reader and devoured the whole magazine field from The Police Gazette to The Astrophysical Journal. His general experience and knowledge fed the inventor with ideas. His practical scientific knowledge, his original, penetrating mind and his invincible industry gave him the greatest output of invention of any living man.

An Invention Every Two Weeks.

In 1914 it was announced that the patent records at Washington showed that Edison had patented new ideas at the rate of one every two weeks for nearly forty years. He knew more about what the world needed and how to supply it than any other man of his time, if not of all time. Many of his inventions were failures. Some were good enough as inventions, but not commercial successes. Asked in one of his interviews what was his first electrical invention Edison replied:

"What was my first electrical invention? You would never guess. It was a machine to record votes in Congress. It was a mighty good invention. I had a lot of iron type, each member's name being set up in a line, and these lines were controlled by push buttons and electromagnets, so that each man could bring his name upon the 'yea' side or the 'nay' side as he pleased. I used chemically sensitized paper to record them, and the thing worked fine. A brother telegraph operator named Sam—I have forgotten the rest of his name—and myself were dead sure that we were going to make $50,000 out of it. He took the thing before a Congressional committee, and the first thing they told him was that if there was anything on earth the members of Congress did not want it was just that kind of thing, because the only right the minority had was to delay the game! After that experience, which was in 1869, I knew enough not to invent anything again until I was sure it was wanted."

Moves to Larger Shop.

When Edison was only 26 years old, in 1873, he made an agreement with the Western Union Telegraph Company to give them an option on all telegraph inventions that came out of his head. He then moved to Newark, N. J., into a bigger shop than his Manhattan working place. He completed an automatic telegraph, making possible the transmission of 1,000 words a minute, in all conditions of weather, between points as far distant as Washington and New York. He devised a Roman letter system of chemical telegraphy.

At the age of 29 Edison had become so famous that curious people crowded his workshop at Newark and he could not work satisfactorily. He moved further away from New York, to Menlo Park, N. J. At that time he had made $400,000 from his inventions.

Before that time he had already experimented on an incandescent electric light that would compare in size and expense with the ordinary gas jet and that might be handled as easily as gas. At the time the arc lamp was already in existence in public squares in this city. Backed by a syndicate with a capital of $300,000, including men such as J. Pierpont Morgan, J. Hood Wright, Henry Villard, Grosvenor P. Lowery and Edward D. Adams, Edison extended his experiments.

His first accomplishment was a lamp with a platinum burner protected by a high vacuum in a glass globe. He continued his experiments with other substances and finally, in 1879, he made the discovery which made the incandescent light a success. The incident was described as follows in a New York newspaper article, the accuracy of which was vouched for by Edison himself:

(continued)

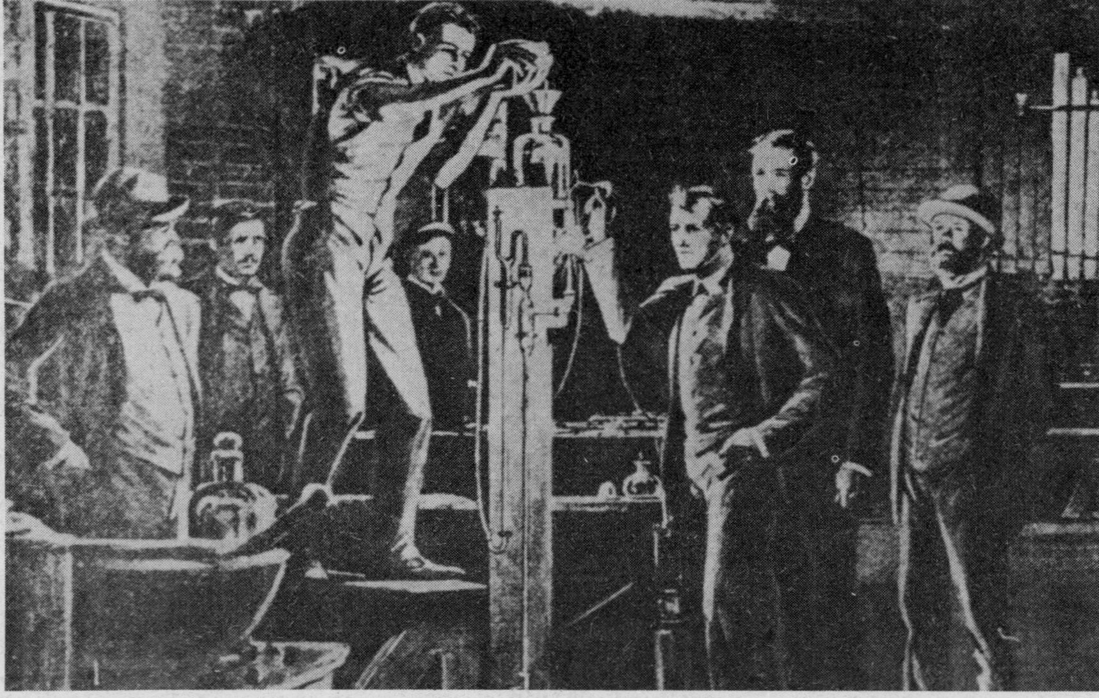

The scene in 1879 in the first Edison laboratory when the young inventor, third from right, demonstrated the incandescent lamp to skeptics at Menlo Park, N.J.

The great inventor at the age of 41, when, on June 16, 1888, after five days and nights of continuous work, he perfected the cylinder type of phonograph.

"Sitting one night in his laboratory, reflecting on some of the unfinished details, Edison began abstractedly rolling between his fingers a piece of compressed lampblack mixed with tar for use in his telephone. For several minutes his thoughts wandered far away, his fingers in the meantime mechanically rolling out the little piece of tarred lampblack until it became a slender filament. Happening to glance at it, the idea occurred to him that it might give good results as a burner if it were made incandescent. A few minutes later the experiment was tried, and to the inventor's gratification satisfactory though not surprising results were obtained. Further experiments were made with altered forms and compositions of the substance, each experiment demonstrating that the inventor was on the right track.

"A spool of cotton thread lay on the table in the laboratory. The inventor cut off a small piece, put it in a groove between two clamps of iron and placed the latter in the furnace. At the expiration of an hour he removed the iron mold containing the thread from the furnace and took out the delicate carbon framework of the thread—all that was left of it after its fiery ordeal. This slender filament he placed in a globe and connected it with the wires leading to the machine generating the electric current. Then he extracted the air from the globe and turned on the electricity.

Brilliant Light His Reward.

"Presto! A beautiful light greeted his eyes. He turned on more current, expecting the fragile filament immediately to fuse; but no. The only change was a more brilliant light. He turned on more current and still more, but the delicate thread remained intact. Then, with characteristic impetuosity, and wondering and marveling at the strength of the little filament, he turned on the full power of the machine and eagerly watched the consequences. For a minute or more the tender thread seemed to struggle with the intense heat passing through it—heat that would melt the diamond itself Then at last it succumbed and all was darkness. The powerful current had broken it in twain, but not before it had emitted a light of several gas jets.

"Night and day, with scarcely rest enough to eat a hearty meal or to catch a brief repose, the inventor kept up his experiments, and from carbonizing pieces of thread he went to splinters of wood, straw, paper and many other substances never before used for that purpose. The result of his experiments showed that the substance best adapted for carbonization and the giving out of incandescent light was paper, preferably thick, like cardboard, but giving good results even when very thin."

Edison's discovery was embodied in Patent 223,898, filed Nov. 4, 1879. Improvements have since been made in the method of making the filament, but the incandescent lamps that light the world are like the lamps described in Patent 223,898. On Jan 1, 1880, the public was invited to go to Menlo Park and see the operation of the first lighting plant. Electricians, many of them, insisted that there was some trickery in the exhibition, but almost simultaneously the Edison lighting system spread all over civilization. Syndicates were formed all over the world.

Invention of Phonograph.

The fiftieth anniversary of the phonograph was celebrated at Edison's laboratories in 1927. It was invented by Edison in 1877 and publicly demonstrated in 1878. This invention came easy to him. An accident attracted his attention. His daring imagination and vast store of knowledge were instantly focussed on the accident, and the phonograph was born in his mind almost instantaneously. His story of the phonograph, told in the North American Review ten years after the invention, was as follows:

"To make the idea of the recording of sound more clear, let me remark one or two points. We have all been struck by the precision with which even the faintest sea waves impress upon the surface of the beach, the fine sinuous line which is formed by the rippling edge of their advance. Almost as familiar is the fact that grains of sand sprinkled on a smooth surface of glass or wood near a piano sift themselves into various lines and curves according to the vibrations of the melody played on the piano keys. These things indicate how easily the particles of solid matter may receive an imparted motion, or take an impression from delicate liquid waves, air waves, or waves of sound. Yet, well known though these phenomena were, they apparently never suggested until within a few years that the sound waves set going by human voice might be so directed as to trace an impression upon some solid substance with a nicety equal to that of the tide recording its flow upon the beach.

Discovery an Accident.

"My own discovery that this could be done came to me almost accidentally while I was busy with experiments having a different object in view. I was engaged upon a machine intended to repeat Morse characters which were recorded on paper by indentations that transferred their message to another circuit automatically when passed under a tracing point connected with a circuit-closing apparatus. In manipulating this machine I found that when the cylinder carrying the indented paper was turned with great swiftness, it gave off a humming noise from the indentations—a musical, rhythmic sound resembling that of human talk heard indistinctly. This led me to try fitting a diaphragm to the machine which would receive the vibrations or sound waves made by my voice when I talked to it and register these vibrations upon an impressible material placed on the cylinder.

"The material selected for immediate use was paraffined paper, and the results obtained were excellent. The indentations on the cylinder, when rapidly revolved, caused a repetition of the original vibrations to reach the ear through a recorder, just as if the machine itself was speaking. I saw at once that the problem of registering human speech so that it could be repeated by mechanical means as often as might be desired was solved."

The actual story of the making of the first phonograph is told in Francis Arthur Jones's biography of Edison as follows:

"When Edison had conceived the phonograph, he called Krusei to him, showed him a rough sketch of the proposed machine and asked him to build the model as quickly as he could. In those days Edison's model makers worked by the piece, and it was customary to mark the price on each model. In this instance, the cost agreed upon was $8. Krusei was asked how long it would take him to complete the model and he replied that he couldn't tell, but he promised that he wouldn't rest until it was finished. This was in the Menlo Park days, when Edison was looked upon as a sleepless wonder. He was accustomed to his chief assistants working for him for two or three days without a rest, and no man showed more tireless energy than Krusei. He could do with as little repose as the inventor himself, and would become so absorbed in his work that fatigue was unfelt and time forgotten. The principles of the phonograph he absorbed with lightning rapidity, but it took him thirty hours to make the model—thirty hours without rest and very little food. At the end of that time he brought to Edison the historic machine which is now preserved in the South Kensington Museum. It was a large, clumsy affair; tinfoil was used as the material on which the indentations were to be made and the cylinder was revolved by hand.

"If Edison was in any way excited on receiving the first model of his invention for recording human speech, he did not show it, and those who were with him on that memorable occasion affirm that he regarded it at the time more in the light of a queer toy than that of a machine which would create any great sensation. Among those who were present when Krusei brought in his model was Carman, the foreman of the machine shop; and this man, unable to believe what he had been told, bet Edison a box of cigars that the machine wouldn't work. The inventor, with much good humor, accepted the wager and then, with a smile, born of absolute faith in his deductions, slowly turned the handle of the machine and spoke into the receiver the first verse of 'Mary Had a Little Lamb.' Then the cylinder was returned to the starting point and faint but distinct came back the words of that juvenile classic faithfully repeated in Edison's familiar tones. Those present were awed rather than astonished, and the tension was not broken until Carman, in accents of pretended disappointment and with assumed disgust, exclaimed, 'Well, I guess I've lost.'"

Edison invented the motion picture machine in 1887. The Zoetrope and other machines were then in existence for throwing pictures from transparencies on a screen one after another and giving the effect of action. It occurred to Edison that pictures could be taken in rapid succession by the camera and later used to synthesize motion. The question who was first in this field is a mooted one. Terry Ramsaye, after an exhaustive investigation, gives the credit to Edison, holding that he was first to produce the motion picture camera and to find a method of flashing the pictures successively on the

Thomas Alva Edison and Mrs. Edison

eye so that they fused into a representation of the original action. Edison put his pictures on the market in the form of a peep-show. Put a nickel in the slot and you could see dances, prizefights, fencing matches and other bits of action.

Failed as a Prophet.

Here Edison, for all his powers of forecasting the future, made his major failure as a prophet. He did not foresee the future of the motion pictures. Open-minded as he often was, he could not be argued into believing that they had any future. For a long time he opposed the idea of projecting pictures on the screen. He thought that it would ruin the nickel-in-the-slot peepshow business. In spite of his creative imagination and his comprehensive genius, Edison seemed to have been lacking in showmanship. The one thing absent from his varied life was some contact with the stage or with the advertising business. He allowed others to anticipate him in actually throwing motion pictures on the screen.

Edison had the talking pictures in mind from the first. To put it more exactly, he regarded the motion picture as something which would be useful for illustrating the phonograph. Mr. Ramsaye records the statement of old employes of Mr. Edison that, back in 1888, when he returned from a trip to Europe, phonograph and motion pictures were brought into synchronization, so that a man stepped forward and bowed on the picture screen, while the voice on the phonograph croaked, "Welcome home, Mr. Edison," or a greeting to that effect. The inventor worked on the idea of talking pictures and sought to introduce them commercially in 1913, but they were a failure, because the phonograph had not then reached its present perfection.

Edison worked for a while on the airplane. James Gordon Bennett Jr. had offered a prize for the first flying machine. Edison had the idea of a helicopter. He tried to make an engine by using ticker tape soaked in dynamite. This tape was fed into the engine piecemeal and exploded. Something went wrong with the machine and a workman was nearly killed. The inventor decided that the dynamite-driven engine would not do.

His Contribution to Radio.

One of Edison's chance discoveries is the basis of radio. This is the so-called Edison effect. It was the discovery that a current of electricity is produced when a filament is heated in a vacuum. For many years this was a laboratory novelty. But at length other scientists found various uses for it. It is the basis of the radio tube of De Forest and the whole radio industry is founded on it. In the field of pure science, as apart from the field of applied science, the discovery of the Edison effect remains the inventor's greatest achievement.

During the latter years of his life Edison worked on many improvements on the phonograph, on improvements on batteries and other electrical equipment.

Edison was married twice, in 1873 to Miss Mary G. Stillwell, by whom he had three children, Marion Estelle, Thomas A. and William L. Edison, and in 1886 to Miss Mina Miller, who is the mother of Madeleine, Charles and Theodore Edison. The elder daughter is now Mrs. Marion Oser of Norwalk, Conn., and the younger is Mrs. John Eyre Sloane of West Orange.

Edison a Freethinker.

Edison was a freethinker and, with Luther Burbank, one of the stars of the Freethinkers' Society. He shifted his ground from time to time on the question of immortality, and one of his last pronouncements on the subject was a statement that the evidence did not preclude the possibility that man had an immortal soul. In 1920 he caused something of a sensation by announcing that he was at work on a machine to be used in communicating with the spirits of the dead. This caused a controversy which raged for a long time. Many thought that Edison was not the hard-headed thinker that he used to be. The inventor refused to contribute anything further to the controversy. Years after he told a friend:

"This is how that happened. One very cold day a nice young fellow came out to my laboratory and told me that he wanted a story. I had nothing to tell him, but he was bluenosed and shivering, and I wanted to make his trip worth while, so on the spur of the moment I cooked up the story about a machine to communicate with the dead. It was all a hoax."

He would not let down the young man, who had accepted the tale in good faith, and he therefore declined to say anything, one way or the other, while the controversy was still a live issue.

In 1921 he caused another great stir with his questionnaire. This was a set of 150 questions which he submitted to young college men who were candidates for employment in his plant. The inventor said that his questions revealed a state of incredible ignorance in the average college graduate. He gave the XYZ mark to more than 90 per cent. of them. With his vast range of knowledge, he had no patience with the ill-informed man, especially with the ill-informed man who presented a college degree.

Relaxed in the South.

Mr. Edison relaxed a little in the latter years of his life. He spent his Winters at Fort Myers, Fla., where he experimented with a miniature rubber plantation and tried out several thousand varieties of plants which he thought might produce rubber or textiles or some other valuable product. In spite of his deafness, which was a heavy cross for a man of his sociable and inquisitive temperament, he remained sunny and genial till the end of his days. Honors came to him from all sides. Every nation recognized him as one of the greatest geniuses of his time and the greatest material benefactor of mankind. Edison's career was brilliantly summed up by Arthur Williams, Vice President of the New York Edison Company, who said:

"Entering this building [the Hotel Astor] tonight, we passed through that extraordinary area of publicity by light, often called the brightest spot on earth—Times Square. Standing there, thinking of Edison and his work, we may well remember the inscription on the tomb of Sir Christopher Wren in St. Paul's, London, 'If you would see his monument, look around.'"

"Light's Golden Jubilee."

Edison was showered with worldwide tributes in connection with "Light's Golden Jubilee," or the fiftieth anniversary of his development of the incandescent lamp, on Oct. 22, 1929. The jubilee centred at Dearborn, Mich., where Henry Ford had installed in his historical museum the little frame hut, and even the soil on which it stood at Parsippany, N. J., in which Edison concluded that experiment. Edison re-enacted the experiment. Ford had just characterized Edison as "the happiest man in the world."

President and Mrs. Hoover joined in the celebration, as did Harvey Firestone, rubber tire manufacturer, and Mrs. Firestone, and George Eastman, kodak manufacturer. In the Edison museum, on which Ford is said to have spent $5,000,000, there is also a crying doll which Edison made in 1889. The friendship of Edison, Ford, Firestone, Eastman and the late John Burroughs took them on many camping expeditions together.

Returning from Dearborn on a special train with President and Mrs. Hoover and other guests, Mr. Edison re-enacted the part of a butcher boy, hawking candies and fruits from car to car and selling a peach to the President.

In June, 1929, the State of Ohio offered to buy and preserve as a museum the birthplace of Edison at Milan, but the veteran inventor, for sentimental reasons, refused to sell his birthplace. He made a counter offer, proposing to grant the State a protectorate over it.

Scholarship for Brightest Boy.

In the Spring of 1929 Edison announced his scholarship contests for the brightest boy to be picked in each State by the Governor, and in the District of Columbia by its commissioners. William B. Huston, 16, of Seattle, son of Bishop S. Arthur Huston of the Episcopal Diocese of Olympia, was the winner of the contest and the college education provided by Mr. Edison. The second contest in 1930 was won by 16-year-old Arthur O. Williams, a messenger of the Rhode Island Hospital Trust Company at Providence. Both winners became students at Massachusetts Institute of Technology. The contest cost Mr. Edison about $25,000 each, and owing to continued business depression, was abandoned in 1931.

In August, 1929, Mr. Edison contracted a cold which developed into pneumonia, and it is believed that he never entirely regained his strength after that illness.

Mr. Edison was an advocate of prohibition. He believed that the surface had only been scratched in scientific subjects. He maintained that man was still efficient at 80, and that the secret of success lay in ambition to work.

Mr. Edison said that of all his inventions the greatest thrill came to him with the perfection of the phonograph. His favorite flowers were the heliotrope, dahlia and (for its rubber) the goldenrod.

"All the News That's Fit to Print"

The New York Times.

LATE CITY EDITION
Considerable cloudiness today.
Fair and warmer tomorrow.
Temperature Range Today—Max., 69; Min., 50
Temperature Yesterday—Max., 62; Min., 44
Full U. S. Weather Bureau Report, Page 43

VOL. CIV No. 35,514. Entered as Second-Class Matter, Post Office, New York, N. Y. NEW YORK, TUESDAY, APRIL 19, 1955. Times Square, New York 36, N. Y. Telephone LAckawanna 4-1000 FIVE CENTS

TRANSPORT PANEL URGES FREER REIN FOR COMPETITION

Eisenhower Advisory Group Asks Lessening of Power to Regulate Rates

RAILS WOULD BE HELPED

Weeks Sees Public Benefits Pattern Established to Spur Rivalry

By WILLIAM M. BLAIR
Special to The New York Times.

WASHINGTON, April 18—President Eisenhower's Advisory Committee on Transportation urged today fewer Government controls in the transportation industry.

The Cabinet-level group recommended a limitation on Federal powers to regulate rates. It suggested other broad revisions of Federal law to promote "dynamic competition." Many provisions, it said, had become outmoded in the "transportation revolution of the last thirty years."

As drawn, the recommendations were interpreted as giving railroads a better chance to compete in the growing and varied rivalry of trucks, airplanes and water carriers.

The Secretary of Commerce, Sinclair Weeks, chairman of the committee, said he believed that the "comprehensive review sets a pattern for better and less expensive transportation for the American people."

"Archaic regulations and practices are imposing large and unnecessary costs upon carriers, shippers, travelers and the ultimate consuming public," he said in a statement.

Extensive Revisions Made

It was understood that all seven members of the advisory committee had approved the long-delayed report. The report has made at least two round trips between the Commerce Department and the White House where it was due last Dec. 1.

The report had undergone considerable revision after motor trucking and other non-railroad groups protested some early suggestions. These interests contended then that the report would specifically aid railroads although its language was broad enough to cover all forms of transportation.

It was understood that the report had been discussed with Democratic and Republican Congressional leaders and that legislation to carry out the report would be forthcoming soon.

A major recommendation would restrict the Interstate Commerce Commission to determination of reasonable minimum and maximum rates. A similar provision is in the present law but the committee said that in "practical effect, the I. C. C. may prescribe precise rates."

Repeal of the present provision, the committee asserted, "would remove one of the most objectionable features of rate regulation." This, it said, was the "necessity that the commission substitute its own judgment for that of carrier management" as to the effect of the rates on the movement of traffic.

In outlining how the transportation industry had grown from a virtual monopoly by railroads to one of "pervasive competition," the committee said:

"During this same period, Gov-

Continued on Page 17, Column 3

Dr. Albert Einstein Dies in Sleep at 76; World Mourns Loss of Great Scientist

Rupture of Aorta Causes Death—Body Cremated —Memorial Here Set

Special to The New York Times.

PRINCETON, N. J., April 18—Dr. Albert Einstein, one of the great thinkers of the ages, died in his sleep here early today.

A rupture of the aorta, main artery of the body, brought death to the 76-year-old master physicist and mathematician and practicing humanitarian.

Dr. Einstein died at 1:15 A. M. in Princeton Hospital, where he had been a patient since last Friday. Announcement was not made until 8 A. M., when hospital aides notified local newspapers and news services.

The last words of the intellectual giant were lost to the world. The only person at his deathbed, Mrs. Alberta Rozsel, the night nurse, said he mumbled in his sleep several words in German that she did not understand.

The shy professor's exit was as unostentatious as the life he had led for many years in the New Jersey village, where he was attached to the Institute for Advanced Study.

The body was cremated without ceremony at 4:30 P. M. at Ewing Cemetery in Trenton after the removal, for scientific study, of vital organs, among them the brain that had worked out the theory of relativity and made possible the development of nuclear fission.

The immediate cremation was in accordance with Dr. Einstein's wishes.

Announcement of Dr. Einstein's death brought mourning around the world. President Eisenhower declared that "no other man contributed so much to the vast expansion of twentieth century knowledge." Eminent scientists and heads of state sent tributes from many nations, including Israel, whose establishment as a state he had championed.

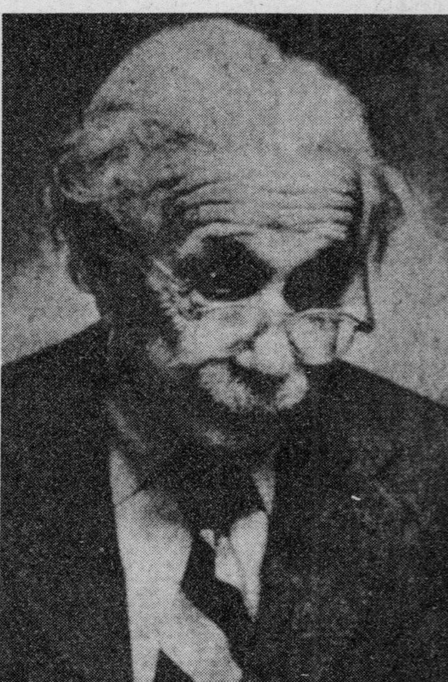
The New York Times (by Patrick A. Burns, 1953).
DR. ALBERT EINSTEIN

Continued on Page 25, Column 7

TRUMAN ASKS U. S. TO TAKE THREATS TO PEACE TO U. N.

Tells Senate Group World Organization Has Averted 'Unlimited' Warfare

Prepared testimony given by Mr. Truman is on Page 8.

By WILLIAM S. WHITE
Special to The New York Times.

WASHINGTON, April 18—Former President Truman suggested today that the United States take to the United Nations General Assembly "the current threats to world peace."

He declined, before the Senate Foreign Relations Committee, to identify the sources of those "threats." The principal one is viewed as the situation in the Formosa Strait.

Testifying before the committee in its study of whether the United States ought to seek fundamental revisions in the United Nations Charter, Mr. Truman urged that only the most cautious steps be taken in that direction.

The debate resulting from a serious effort at Charter revision, he said, might well end only in emphasizing the "defects" of the United Nations and obscuring its great value.

Without the United Nations, he said, the world would have fallen again into "unlimited" warfare.

An appeal to the General Assembly on the question of Formosa, stronghold of the Nationalist Government of Chiang Kai-shek, had been proposed on April 11 by Adlai E. Stevenson, the 1952 Democratic Presidential candidate. The Communist Chinese claim Formosa as part of the integral territory of China.

Urged U. S. to Call on Assembly

Mr. Stevenson had recommended that the United States and its Allies call on the Assembly "to condemn any effort to alter the present status of Formosa by force."

He also had come out against using United States forces to defend the Nationalist-held islands of Quemoy and Matsu, just off the Chinese Communist mainland, as part of the strategy of defending Formosa itself.

The Eisenhower Administration has not excluded the possibility of military intervention in some circumstances to hold the offshore islands. Mr. Truman said nothing of any of this.

Moreover, in discussing possible United Nations action, he avoided any detailed proposal, just as he avoided any criticism of any aspect of the foreign policy of the Eisenhower Administration.

Asked by Senator Homer E. Capehart, Republican of Indiana, whether he cared to amplify his reference to threats to peace, the former President replied: "I am not in position to do so in this dignified meeting. Some day, when I am making a political speech, I'll do it."

Senator Capehart, who had already saluted Mr. Truman's continued "sense of humor," ob-

Continued on Page 9, Column 1

Jordan and Israel Set Up Jerusalem Security Zone

Arrangement to Prevent Hostile Actions Follows Slaying of American

By HARRY GILROY
Special to The New York Times.

JERUSALEM, April 18—Israel and Jordan established today an arrangement designed to prevent firing and other hostile acts in the Jerusalem area and to halt any armed clashes.

The arrangement was agreed to at a meeting between Col. Abdul Halim al-Saket of Jordan and Col. Chaim Herzog of Israel this morning at the offices of the United Nations Mixed Armistice Commission in No Man's Land near the Mandelbaum Gate. These two officers are in charge of all military and police forces in their sectors of Jerusalem.

The officers will meet again tomorrow to work out details for a telephone line to connect the two headquarters.

The arrangement covers a rectangular area four miles east and west and six and a half miles north and south. The area centers on the railroad station in the Israeli sector.

No treaty was signed. However each nation has informed the United Nations truce organization that it agrees to the arrangement. Maj. Gen. E. L. M. Burns of Canada, United Nations Chief of Staff, attended today's meeting.

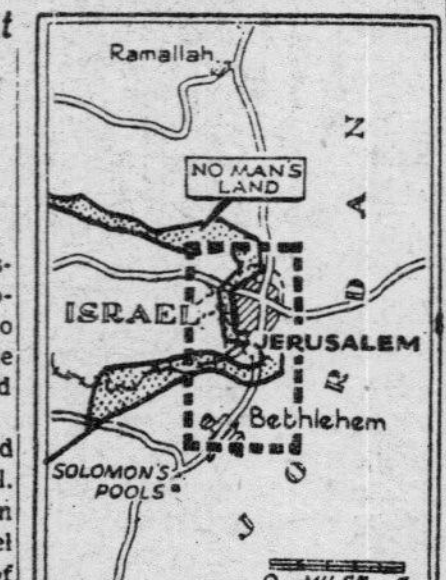

The New York Times April 19, 1955
Broken lines indicate area covered by the agreement.

The arrangement covers the following points:

¶Only disciplined military and police will occupy first-line defensive positions.

¶Guards will have orders not to fire without order of a commissioned officer unless in danger of attack by superior numbers.

¶The designated senior offi-

Continued on Page 10, Column 3

REBUFFS TO REDS AND NEHRU BRING BANDUNG DISCORD

Asian-African Parley's Even Course Is Being Disrupted by Procedural Disputes

WEST RECEIVES SUPPORT

Iraqi Denounces Colonialism, Zionism and Communism—Cambodia Joins Neutrals

By TILLMAN DURDIN
Special to The New York Times.

BANDUNG, Indonesia, Tuesday, April 19—The Asian-African conference entered its second day with controversies and ruffled tempers threatening to disrupt and delay its progress.

The even course planned for the twenty-nine-nation conference was considerably disturbed by developments yesterday, and efforts to keep differences from growing were begun today.

A distinct breakaway from the leadership of Jawaharlal Nehru, Indian Prime Minister, has developed on a number of procedural matters.

In addition, yesterday's session heard a vigorous anti-Communist attack by Dr. Fadhil al-Jamali, Minister of State of Iraq and leader of his delegation, and expressions of affinity with the United States and the West by the acting Iranian delegate, Dr. Djalal Abdoh.

[Prince Wan Waithayakon, speaking for Thailand, called on the Communists Tuesday to prove their intention to live up to the spirit and letter of "peaceful organization because it was threatened by Red subversion and possible aggression," The United Press said. For that reason, he asserted, Thailand wants to know what the Reds mean by "coexistence." Reuters said Prime Minister Mohammed Ali of Pakistan defended the right of self-defense "exercised singly or collectively."]

Chou Plans Address

When the conference opened this morning for a public session, Chou En-lai, Premier of Communist China, told newsmen that he had come to the gathering to make friends, not to quarrel. However, he added that he was planning to make a speech at this afternoon's session.

It had been reported earlier that Mr. Chou would not make a public address. Autograph hunters and photographers crowded around the Chinese leader as he took his seat.

Competent sources reported this morning that Mr. Nehru tried after yesterday's speech by Dr. al-Jamali to mollify conference tempers and urge that indulgence in recriminatory speeches be avoided. Whether Mr. Chou's speech, which he announced this morning he would give, would observe this Nehru attitude is not known.

Dr. al-Jamali named colonialism, Zionism and communism as evils that disturbed world peace and harmony. He scored communism as a "subversive religion" that bred hatred among classes and peoples. He reviewed the history of Communist aggression in Eastern Europe and Central Asia and said the Communists "confront the world with a new form of colonialism much deadlier than the old."

An emphatic speaker, Dr. al-Jamali faced Mr. Chou when he said: "Today the Communist

Continued on Page 2, Column 3

HUNGARIANS NAME HEGEDUS PREMIER

One of Top Reds Succeeds Nagy, Ousted Advocate of Consumer Goods

By JOHN MacCORMAC
Special to The New York Times.

VIENNA, April 18—Andras Hegedus, former Minister of Agriculture and Deputy Premier of Hungary, was elected Premier at a special session of the Parliament at Budapest today.

He succeeds Imre Nagy, father of Hungary's now discredited "new course," which favored consumer goods production. Mr. Nagy's dismissal was announced early this morning.

Mihaly Farkas has also been dropped from his post as Second Secretary of the Central Committee of the Hungarian Workers (Communist) party and membership in the party's ruling Political Committee. Mr. Nagy also has been expelled from the party leadership.

Neither the demotion of Mr. Nagy nor his replacement by Mr. Hegedus was a surprise. Both shifts had been considered certain since the celebration of the tenth anniversary of Hungary's "liberation" by the Soviet army two weeks ago. At that time Soviet Marshal Kliment E. Voroshilov demonstrated his support for Matyas Rakosi, Hungarian Communist leader and opponent of Mr. Nagy.

The uncertainty centered not on Mr. Nagy's dismissal but why it was so long delayed since the end of the "new course."

Mr. Nagy had pursued an eco-

Continued on Page 6, Column 1

REBELS OPEN FIRE ON VIETNAM FORCE

Truce Imperiled by Saigon Clashes—Collins Is Called Back to Washington

By A. M. ROSENTHAL
Special to The New York Times.

SAIGON, Vietnam, April 18—Rebel machine-gunners opened fire today on soldiers of South Vietnam's national army. French and United States officers were working in an attempt to prevent Saigon's shaky truce from collapsing.

The fighting was sporadic, and seemed to have been touched off by nervous trigger-fingers rather than by any planned campaign to bring war again to Saigon's streets. But as reports of the incidents came in, the French at least made it plain they were afraid that, unless both sides maintained the tightest discipline, this capital of South Vietnam was in for more bloodshed.

[The State Department announced Monday that Gen. J. Lawton Collins, President Eisenhower's special representative in South Vietnam, had been recalled to Washington for consultation.]

At Independence Palace, where Premier Ngo Dinh Diem lives and works, a spokesman had a calming word. He said that the army wanted to take action but added that the Premier was keeping the military in check and urging patience.

One soldier of the Vietnamese Army was killed during the day and others were kidnapped by the Binh Xuyen, a private army

Continued on Page 3, Column 2

City Seeking More Vaccine; President Asks Salk Honor

Guarantees Refused

By PETER KIHSS

Drug manufacturers refused yesterday to guarantee New York City enough vaccine for proposed free inoculation of all 5-to-9-year-old children against poliomyelitis before schools close this June.

Checks on limited supplies of the Salk vaccine raised strong doubts that the city would go through with a program announced Saturday for free inoculation of all persons 1 through 19 years of age.

There are 2,210,000 youngsters in this age bracket. Of these, 540,000 in kindergarten through the fourth grade are to get first priority.

Free vaccine already contracted for by the National Foundation for Infantile Paralysis would protect 281,000 of these lowest-graders. But the rest, even in this group, would need 518,000 cubic centimeters of city and state supplies. None of this has yet been acquired. The vaccine was licensed only last Tuesday.

Joseph V. Spagna, Purchase Commissioner, opened bids yesterday at the Municipal Building on 500,000 cubic centimeters, which the city proposed to buy before June 30. Two companies offered highly conditional promises of any supply. A third said it would supply vaccine only after June 30. The remaining three vaccine manufacturers declined bids.

Throughout the nation, the National Foundation has 18,000,000 cubic centimeters under contract to inoculate 9,000,000 children free with two doses of

Continued on Page 16, Column 2

New Medal Proposed

By FELIX BELAIR Jr.
Special to The New York Times.

AUGUSTA, Ga., April 18—President Eisenhower wants Dr. Jonas E. Salk to be the first recipient of the Congressional Medal for Distinguished Civilian Achievement.

James C. Hagerty, White House press secretary, made this known today. He said the President also was hopeful that the new award would be authorized by Congress in time for his Friday appointment in Washington with the developer of polio vaccine.

With or without the medal of achievement, General Eisenhower plans to extend his personal congratulations to the research scientist. Sharing in the Presidential commendation will be Basil O'Connor, president of the National Foundation for Infantile Paralysis, which financed Dr. Salk's work.

Nearing the end of his work-and-play holiday from White House routine, President Eisenhower planned a full morning session tomorrow with Harold E. Stassen. The President will confer with the Foreign Operations Administrator on the special message he will send Congress Wednesday on the Administration's $3,530,000,000 foreign aid program for the fiscal year 1956, which starts July 1.

Stassen in Augusta

Mr. Stassen arrived by Air Force plane late today. He was accompanied by Kevin McCann, chief of the White House writing staff.

In making known the President's Friday appointment with Dr. Salk, Mr. Hagerty recalled that General Eisenhower in his January Message on the State of the Union had proposed a new "award for distinguished civilian achievement."

The award would go to civilians who make outstanding contributions toward the advancement of civilization and of the nation. It was the President's understanding that legislation to authorize the award would be introduced in the Senate and House of Representatives this week, according to Mr. Hagerty.

It was further the White House understanding that the authorizing legislation would have several prominent sponsors on either side of the aisles—Republican and Democratic.

It would be a "nice thing," as Mr. Hagerty put it, if Congress could act in time to permit presentation of the award by the President to Dr. Salk on Friday. But in any case, President Eisenhower thinks the polio vaccine developer should be the first to receive the medal—whenever it may become available, Mr. Hagerty said. The Administration already has earmarked more

Continued on Page 16, Column 4

FULBRIGHT WARNS OF MARKET FEVER

Senator Sees the Beginning of Excessive Speculation in Latest Stock Gains

The stock market has again entered a period of dangerous speculative activity, Senator J. William Fulbright, chairman of the Senate Banking and Currency Committee, warned last night.

After a brief respite during the Senate hearings on the stock market last month, he said, stocks have resumed their movement into a boom-and-bust cycle.

Prices on the New York Stock Exchange yesterday scored their sharpest gains in nine consecutive days of advance. The New York Times industrial average made a new historic high, and the combined average hit the highest point since Oct. 18, 1929.

Senator Fulbright, Democrat of Arkansas, addressed a dinner of the Economic Club of New York in the Sheraton-Astor Hotel. He pleaded for private as well as public leaders to "break the hypnotic spell cast over them by the rise in stock prices."

Senator Fulbright drew a sharp distinction between the level of stocks and the rate of advance. It was the rate of advance, especially in the two final months of 1954, that brought about the hearings. There seemed a good chance, to some observers then, that the boom might carry prices far beyond the ability of the economy to support them.

But the Senator did not find

Continued on Page 40, Column 4

Fight on Postal Pay Again Due in House

By C. P. TRUSSELL
Special to The New York Times.

WASHINGTON, April 18—The House Rules Committee decided today on a second showdown on the floor for a bill to raise postal workers' pay.

Last month the House turned it down. Its increases were held to be too small. Procedures then prevented any changes.

Today the Rules Committee sent the bill to the floor under conditions that might provoke a Presidential veto. The House appeared to be in a mood to take this chance. Yet, it was argued, the President had made one compromise—for a rise from 6 per cent to about 7½ per cent—and will might not make another. The Senate voted for a 10 per cent increase.

Floor debate may start

Continued on Page 18, Column 5

Plan for Unifying 4 City Colleges Under Chancellor Voted by Board

By LEONARD BUDER

The Board of Higher Education late last night created the position of chancellor of the municipal college system.

The post would unify the four municipal colleges—City, Hunter, Queens and Brooklyn—under a single chief administrator, and would, in effect, create a city-wide university system.

The establishment of the post of chancellor had been recommended by various city and board studies. The new post would carry the same salary, of $20,000 a year, that the four college presidents now receive. The college presidents would continue to function in much the same fashion as they now do, except that there would be an administrative officer over them.

The board's action was announced at 12:05 A. M. today by Mrs. Ella D. Streator, chairman of the executive committee. The meeting, which began at 8 o'clock last night, was held at Hunter College, 695 Park Avenue.

Implementation of the plan, Mrs. Streator emphasized, depended upon whether the board could obtain the necessary funds from the city government.

The resolution adopted by the board also authorized its chairman, Dr. Joseph B. Cavallaro, to ask the city for $75,000. In addition to covering the salary of the chancellor, the sum would provide for "two or three top-level assistants," as well as for secretarial and clerical help.

When the new set-up goes into effect, the present Board of Higher Education, which occupies space in Hunter College, will be transferred to the Office of the Administrator. Mrs. Pearl N. Max, who is administrator of the board, will be "designated

Continued on Page 26, Column 7

Associated Press

FAMILIAR SCENE: Former President Truman meets with Democratic Senators at luncheon in the Capitol. Members of Mr. Truman's onetime Senate team are, from left, Lyndon B. Johnson of Texas, Thomas C. Hennings Jr. of Missouri and Stuart Symington of Missouri.

U. S. Still Hopeful On China Captives

Special to The New York Times.

WASHINGTON, April 18—State and Defense Department officials reported in a closed Senate committee session today on the plight of 500 American prisoners held by Communist China.

The State Department was reported as being "still optimistic" that the Reds would release the prisoners. Eleven of them are United States airmen accused of being "spies." About forty are civilians. The status of the others is uncertain.

Originally the estimate of the Americans held in Communist China was 944. This had been cut down to 481 military and forty civilians. The list dwindled because of estimates of the number who disappeared in captivity.

Senator John L. McClellan, Democrat of Arkansas, was cautious in his report of the

Continued on Page 3, Column 3

DR. EINSTEIN DIES IN HIS SLEEP AT 76

Continued From Page 1

pioned, and Germany, which he had left forever in 1932 because of nazism's rising threat against individual liberty and Jewish life.

In Moscow, the Soviet news agency Tass carried a brief report on the death of Dr. Einstein, calling him "one of the world's greatest scientists and physicists."

Daniel Gutman, counsel to Governor Harriman, announced that a public memorial to Dr. Einstein would be held May 22 at Carnegie Hall. Mr. Gutman is chairman of the sponsoring committee of the American Jewish Literary Committee.

Dr. Irving M. Levey, rabbi of the Hillel Foundation, a Princeton campus organization, announced that "friends of mine and of Dr. Einstein" had decided to hold a memorial service in Whig Hall at 8 P. M. Friday.

Became Ill Last Wednesday

Dr. Einstein, who had suffered intermittent attacks of pain from a gall bladder ailment over several years, had an unusually severe seizure last Wednesday at home. He lived at 112 Mercer Street in a two-and-one-half-story yellow frame house with his daughter Margot and Miss Helene Dukas, his secretary-housekeeper of many years.

The scientist's physician, Dr. Guy K. Dean, said he had found him with pains in the back and lower abdomen worse than he had ever experienced before and with severe nausea. Dr. Dean said his patient was "very stoical about pain" and was "his usual kind, shy self" under stress of intense pain.

Dr. Dean found also that the scientist, who had been developing progressive hardening of the arteries, had a small leakage of blood from the hardened aorta. The physician eased his patient's pain with a sedative.

Later that night, two New York physicians, Dr. Rudolf Ehrmann and Dr. Gustav Bucky, a radiologist, were called to Princeton. Dr. Dean said they had come as old friends of Dr. Einstein and discussed with the attending physician and the scientist his ailment "at great length."

Patient Opposed Surgery

On Thursday, Dr. Frank Glenn, cardiac and aortic surgeon of New York Hospital, came down for consultation. Dr. Dean said that Dr. Einstein "knew with full clarity what faced him" and was "violently opposed" to having surgery. A complication of the old gall bladder condition had developed by this time, increasing his pain.

Dr. Einstein was taken to the hospital Friday so that glucose and saline solution could be given him intravenously. This was necessary because he was then unable to take fluid by mouth.

The scientist's condition improved so that on Saturday and Sunday he had several visitors, including a son, Hans Albert Einstein, who arrived Saturday from the University of California, where he is Professor of Engineering.

In attendance on the case with Dr. Dean were two other Princeton physicians, Dr. Ralph J. Belford and Dr. W. G. Painey.

Dr. Dean said that Dr. Einstein's condition appeared so favorable by Sunday afternoon that "we hoped the leak would cease." The scientist felt considerable pain a few hours later and a hypodermic was given. When Dr. Dean looked in at 11 P. M. Sunday his patient was sleeping peacefully.

Mrs. Rozsel, the nurse, noticed at 1:10 A. M. that Dr. Einstein was breathing differently than he had been up to then. She summoned another nurse, who helped her roll up the head of the bed. Right after the other nurse left Dr. Einstein mumbled in German. Then, as Mrs. Rozsel put it, "he gave two deep breaths and expired."

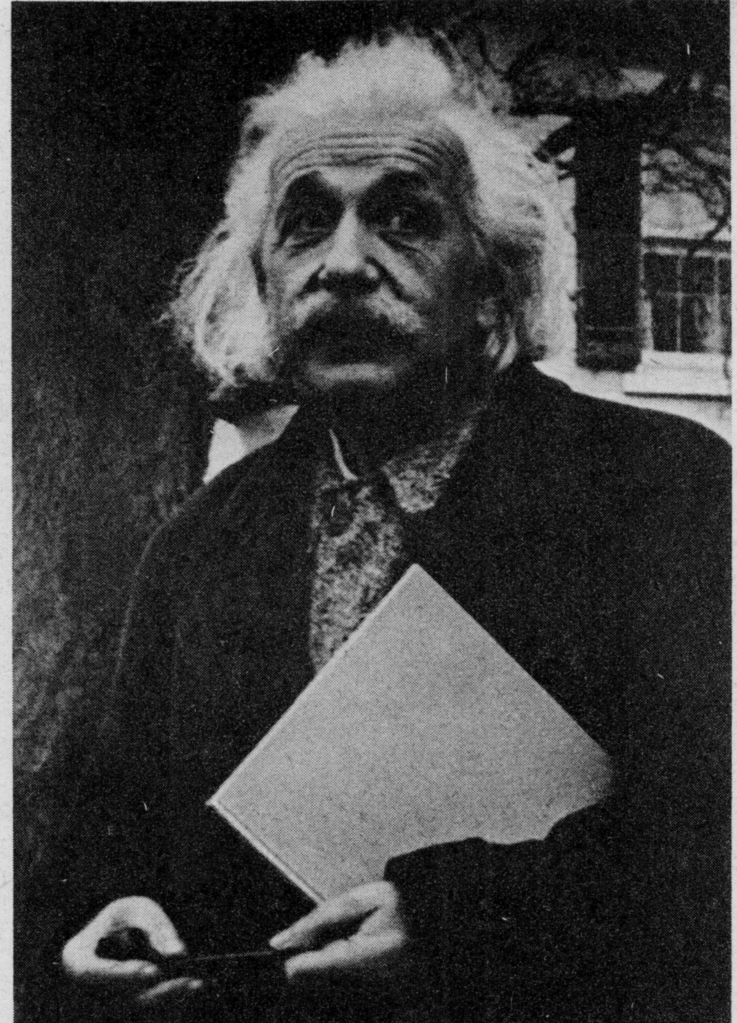

Dr. Albert Einstein

PAPERS IN HIS 20'S WON RECOGNITION

Many Nations Conferred on Scientist Awards Lauding His Spectacular Work

EXILE FROM NAZIS IN '33

Einstein Reacted Strongly to Hitlerism—German Home Sacked by Brown Shirts

Albert Einstein was born at Ulm, Wuerttemberg, Germany, on March 14, 1879. His boyhood was spent in Munich, where his father, who owned electro-technical works, had settled. The family migrated to Italy in 1894, and Albert was sent to a cantonal school at Aarau in Switzerland. He attended lectures while supporting himself by teaching mathematics and physics at the Polytechnic School at Zurich until 1900. Finally, after a year as tutor at Schaffthausen, he was appointed examiner of patents at the Patent Office at Bern where, having become a Swiss citizen, he remained until 1909.

It was in this period that he obtained his Ph. D. degree at the University of Zurich and published his first papers on physical subjects.

These were so highly esteemed that in 1909 he was appointed Extraordinary Professor of Theoretical Physics at the University of Zurich. In 1911 he accepted the Chair of Physics at Prague, only to be induced to return to his own Polytechnic School at Zurich as full professor the next year. In 1913 a special position was created for him in Berlin as director of the Kaiser Wilhelm Physical Institute. He was elected a member of the Royal Prussian Academy of Sciences and received a stipend sufficient to enable him to devote all his time to research without any restrictions or routine duties.

He was elected a foreign member of the Royal Society in 1921, having also been made previously a member of the Amsterdam and Copenhagen Academies, while the Universities of Geneva, Manchester, Rostock and Princeton conferred honorary degrees on him. In 1925 he received the Copley Medal of the Royal Society and in 1926 the Gold Medal of the Royal Astronomical Society in recognition of his theory of relativity. He received a Nobel Prize in 1921.

Honors continued to be conferred on him. He was made a member of the Institute de France, one of the few foreigners ever to achieve such a distinction. Other great universities throughout the world, including Oxford, Cambridge, Paris, Madrid, Buenos Aires, Zurich, Yeshiva, Harvard, London and Brussels, awarded honorary doctorates to him.

One of the highest American scientific honors, the Franklin Institute Medal, came to him in 1935, when he startled the scientific world by failing to deliver more than a mere "thank-you" in lieu of the scientific address customary on such occasions. He made up for it later by contributing an important paper to the Journal of the Franklin Institute dealing with ideas, he explained, that were not quite ripe at the time he received the medal.

Dr. Einstein married Mileva Marec, a fellow-student in Switzerland, in 1901. They had two sons, Albert Einstein Jr., an electrical engineer who also came to this country, and Eduard. The marriage ended in divorce. He married again, in 1917, this time his cousin, Elsa Einstein, a widow with two daughters. She died in Princeton in 1936.

To Institute at Princeton in '32

When the Institute for Advanced Study was organized in 1932 Dr. Einstein was offered, and accepted, the place of Professor of Mathematics and Theoretical Physics, and served, also, as the head of the Mathematics Department. The institute was situated at Princeton, N. J., and Dr. Einstein made plans to live there about half of each year.

These plans were changed suddenly. Adolf Hitler rose to power in Germany and essential human liberty, even for Jews with world reputations like Dr. Einstein, became impossible in Germany. He announced that he would not return to Berlin, sailed for Europe and went to Belgium.

Immediately many nations invited him to make his home in their lands. In the late spring of 1933 Dr. Einstein learned, in Belgium, that his two step-daughters had been forced to flee Germany.

Not long after that he was notified through the press that he had been ousted from the supervising board of the German Bureau of Standards. His home at Caputh was sacked by Hitler Brown Shirts on the allegation that the world-renowned physicist and pacifist had a vast store of arms hidden there.

The Prussian Academy of Science expelled him and also attacked him for having made statements regarding Hitler atrocities. His reply was this:

"I do not want to remain in a state where individuals are not conceded equal rights before the law for freedom of speech and doctrine."

In September of 1933 he fled from Belgium and went into seclusion on the coast of England, fearful that the Nazis had plans upon his life. Then he journeyed to Princeton and made his home there. He bought a home in Princeton and settled down to pass his remaining years there. In 1940 he became a citizen of the United States.

Einstein Noted as an Iconoclast In Research, Politics and Religion

In 1904, Albert Einstein, then an obscure young man of 25, could be seen daily in the late afternoon wheeling a baby carriage on the streets of Bern, Switzerland, halting now and then, unmindful of the traffic around him, to scribble down some mathematical symbols in a notebook that shared the carriage with his infant son, also named Albert.

Out of those symbols came the most explosive ideas in the age-old strivings of man to fathom the mystery of his universe. Out of them, incidentally, came the atomic bomb, which, viewed from the long-range perspective of mankind's intellectual and spiritual history may turn out, Einstein fervently hoped, to have been just a minor by-product.

With those symbols Dr. Einstein was building his theory of relativity. In that baby carriage with his infant son was Dr. Einstein's universe-in-the-making, a vast, finite-infinite four-dimensional universe, in which the conventional universe—existing in absolute three-dimensional space and in absolute three-dimensional time of past, present and future—vanished into a mere subjective shadow.

Dr. Einstein was then building his universe in his spare time, on the completion of his day's routine work as a humble, $600-a-year examiner in the Government Patent Office in Bern.

A few months later, in 1905, the entries in the notebook were published in four epoch-making scientific papers. In the first he described a method for determining molecular dimensions. In the second he explained the photoelectric effect, the basis of electronics, for which he won the Nobel Prize in 1921. In the third, he presented a molecular kinetic theory of heat. The fourth and last paper that year, entitled "Electrodynamics of Moving Bodies," a short article of thirty-one pages, was the first presentation of what became known as the Special Relativity Theory.

Three of the papers were published, one at a time, in Volume 17 of the German scientific journal, Annalen der Physik, leading journal of physics in the world at the time. The fourth was printed in Volume 18. Neither Dr. Einstein, nor the world he lived in, nor man's concept of his material universe, were ever the same again.

Many other scientific papers, of startling originality and intellectual boldness, were published by Dr. Einstein in the succeeding years. The scientific fraternity in the world of physics, particularly the leaders of the group, recognized from the beginning that a new star of the first magnitude had appeared on their firmament. But with the passing of time his fame spread to other circles, and by 1920 the name of Einstein had become synonymous with relativity, a theory universally regarded as so profound that only twelve men in the entire world were believed able to fathom its depths.

Paradoxically, as the years passed, the figure of Einstein the man became more and more remote, while that of Einstein the legend came ever nearer to the masses of mankind. They grew to know him not as a universe-maker whose theories they could not hope to understand but as a world citizen, one of the outstanding spiritual leaders of his generation, a symbol of the human spirit and its highest aspirations.

"The world around Einstein has changed very much since he published his first discoveries * * * but his attitude to the world around him has not changed," wrote Dr. Philipp Frank, Dr. Einstein's biographer, in 1947. "He has remained an individualist who prefers to be unencumbered by social relations, and at the same time a fighter for social equality and human fraternity.

"Many famous scholars live in the distinguished university town," [Princeton] Dr. Frank continues, "but no inhabitant will simply number Einstein as one among many other famous people. For the people of Princeton in particular and for the world at large he is not just a great scholar, but rather one of the legendary figures of the twentieth century. Einstein's acts and words are not simply noted and judged as facts; instead each has its symbolic significance * * *"

"Saintly," "noble" and "lovable" were the words used to describe him by those who knew him even casually. He radiated humor, warmth and kindliness. He loved jokes and laughed easily.

Princeton residents would see him walk in their midst, a familiar figure, yet a stranger, a close neighbor, yet at the same time a visitor from another world. And as he grew older his otherworldliness became more pronounced, yet his human warmth did not diminish.

Outward appearance meant nothing to him. Princetonians, old and young, soon got used to the long-haired figure in pullover sweater and unpressed slacks wandering in their midst, a knitted stocking cap covering his head in winter.

"My passionate interest in social justice and social responsibility," he wrote, "has always stood in curious contrast to a marked lack of desire for direct association with men and women. I am a horse for single harness, not cut out for tandem or team work. I have never belonged wholeheartedly to country or state, to my circle of friends, or even to my own family. These ties have always been accompanied by a vague aloofness, and the wish to withdraw into myself increases with the years.

"Such isolation is sometimes bitter, but I do not regret being cut off from the understanding and sympathy of other men. I lose something by it, to be sure, but I am compensated for it in being rendered independent of the customs, opinions and prejudices of others, and am not tempted to rest my peace of mind upon such shiftless foundations."

It was this independence that made Dr. Einstein on occasions the center of controversy, as the result of his championship of some highly unpopular causes. He declared himself a stanch pacifist in Germany during Worl War I and brought down upon his head a storm of violent criticism from all sides. When outstanding representatives of German art and science signed, following the German invasion of Belgium in violation of treaty, the "Manifesto of Ninety-two German Intellectuals," asserting that "German culture and German militarism are identical," Dr. Einstein refused to sign and again faced ostracism and the wrath of the multitudes.

Father of Relativity and Outstanding Pacifist Inspired U. S. to Make Atomic Bomb

WARNING STIRRED PRESIDENT TO ACT

Einstein Relativity Theory, One of History's Boldest, Proved by Nuclear Fission

HE SOUGHT COSMIC LAW

Devoted His Life to Develop All-Embracing Equations of Forces in Universe

By WILLIAM L. LAURENCE

When the atom bomb exploded with a blinding flash over Japan it did more than bring the greatest war in history to a triumphant end. It flashed to the minds of men the most spectacular proof of the Einstein Theory of Relativity, which provided the key to the vast treasure house of energy within the atom.

It was the Einstein Special Theory of Relativity, a short scientific paper consisting largely of abstruse mathematical formulas, published in 1905, that contained what has since become the world's most famous mathematical equation — $E=mc^2$ — in which E stands for energy, m for mass and c^2 for the square the velocity of light.

This equation, so simple that a student in high school could work it out, represented one of the boldest intellectual concepts in history—that matter and energy, up to then believed to be totally separate and distinct entities, were actually different manifestations of one and the same reality, matter being frozen energy, while energy was fluid matter.

More specifically, the formula revealed that a mass (m) of one gram has locked up within itself in a frozen state an energy (E) equivalent in ergs (energy units) to the square of the velocity of light in centimeters a second. Since light travels with a velocity of thirty billion centimeters a second, one gram of matter contains in the frozen state an energy of 900 billion billion ergs, or 25,000,000 kilowatt - hours. This is equivalent to Coulee Dam working at full capacity for twelve and one-half hours.

First substantiation of the correctness of the formula, suggested by Einstein himself, came from the apparently inexhaustible energy emanated from the then newly discovered radioactive elements—radium and polonium. The formula formed one of the keystones in the construction of the modern concept of the atom, which led to the knowledge that most of the energy of the universe is locked up within the atomic nucleus.

Greatest Proof Was Bomb

But the greatest proof of all, the most spectacular confirmation ever given to an intellectual concept, came first on the morning of July 16, 1945, when the first atomic bomb exploded on the desert of New Mexico. To the world at large it came three weeks later with the destruction of Hiroshima and Nagasaki.

For the explosion of the atomic bomb marked for the first time the grand-scale conversion on earth of matter into energy. In each of the atom bombs a small amount of matter (uranium 235 or plutonium) was "unfrozen" and made "fluid." The total amount of matter so converted was in the vicinity of one gram, about two-fifths the mass of a dime, but the energy thus released was the equivalent of more than 20,000 tons of TNT.

By one of the strangest ironies in history, it was Einstein, the outstanding pacifist of his age, who initiated the move that started the United States on the project that led to the development of the atomic bomb. On learning that the Nazis were engaged in large-scale research on the development of such a weapon, which would have enabled them to realize their design for world domination, Einstein wrote a letter to President Roosevelt on Aug. 2, 1939, in which he informed the President of the danger confronting the free world and the need for "quick action on the part of the Administration."

"In the course of the last four months," Dr. Einstein wrote in that now historic letter, "it has been made probable through the work of Joliot [Frederic Joliot-Curie] in France, as well as Enrico Fermi and Leo Szilard in America—that it may become possible to set up a nuclear chain reaction in a large mass of uranium by which vast amounts of power and large quantities of radium-like elements would be generated. Now it appears this could be achieved in the immediate future.

"This new phenomenon would also lead to the construction of bombs, and it is conceivable, though much less certain—that extremely powerful bombs of a new type may thus be constructed. A single bomb of this type, carried by boat and exploded in a port, might very well destroy the whole port, together with some of the surrounding territory. However, such bombs might very well prove too heavy for transportation by air."

When the letter was written the B-29 was not yet in existence.

'This Requires Action'

On reading the Einstein letter, President Roosevelt called in the late Brig. Gen. Edwin M. Watson, his military secretary, known as Pa Watson.

"Pa," said the President, "this requires action!" With these four words the atomic bomb project, which was to cost $2,000,000,000, got under way. It is doubtful whether any other man except Einstein could have moved the President to pay any attention to a matter that at the time sounded more fantastic than anything in Jules Verne, H. G. Wells or any comic strip.

To no other man in his lifetime had come the universal acclaim that had been accorded Albert Einstein. From an unknown patent clerk in Switzerland he suddenly streaked, meteor-like, across the intellectual firmament of his day, and was at once recognized by the scientific elite as one of the all-time giants in the history of human thought.

Einstein was only 26 years old when he first announced to the world his special theory of relativity, which revolutionized man's concepts of space and time, of matter, energy and light, and gave him an entirely new and much more profound understanding of his universe. He was 36 when he announced his general theory of relativity, which vastly expanded the scope of the special theory and provided a revolutionary new concept of gravitation. But these were by no means the only great contributions he made in those years to human knowledge.

Developed Quantum Theory

Modern science has made its tremendous strides during the last fifty years because of two transcendent concepts. One of these is the theory of relativity. The other is the quantum theory, which deals with the fundamental nature of matter and radiation and their interaction. While Max Planck was the founder of the quantum theory, which revealed that radiation, instead of being continuous, comes in discrete packages, or quanta, it was Einstein who developed the theory into one of the fundamental pillars of modern science and laid the foundation for the modern concept of the forces that bind the universe together.

It was also Einstein who provided the first explanation of what is known as the photoelectric effect, the principle underlying the photo tubes that made possible the long - distance telephone, talking motion pictures, radio, television, the electron microscope and many other great modern inventions. It was he also who first explained the phenomenon known as Brownian motion, which provided the best "direct" proof of the existence of the molecule and enabled man to observe accurately for the first time the motions of molecules and to determine their number in any given unit of volume.

Dr. Einstein's theory of relativity, wrote Bertrand Russell in 1924, "is probably the greatest synthetic achievement of the human intellect up to the present time. It sums up the mathematical and physical labors of more than 2,000 years. Pure geometry from Pythagoras to Riemann, the dynamics and astronomy of Galileo and Newton, the theory of electromagnetism as it resulted from the researches of Faraday, Maxwell and their successors, are all absorbed, with the necessary modifications, in the theories of Einstein."

Mankind's progress has in large measure been determined by the intellectual synthesis of what had formerly been unrelated concepts. The synthesis by Faraday of magnetism and electricity into a unified concept of electromagnetism led to his discovery of the principle of electromagnetic induction, basic principle of the dynamo, which ushered in the age of electricity. Maxwell's synthesis by pure mathematics of electromagnetism and light led to the discovery of electromagnetic waves and thus to the age of radio and television. Similarly, Einstein's formulas that united space and time, matter and energy, brought into being the atomic age while at the same time they gave man a new vision of his universe.

One of 'Universe Makers'

In the entire course of man's recorded civilization, according to George Bernard Shaw, only eight men—Pythagoras, Aristotle, Ptolemy, Copernicus, Galileo, Kepler, Newton and Einstein—succeeded in synthesizing the sum total of the knowledge of their day and age into a new vision of the universe, vaster than the one encompassed in the visions of their predecessors.

"Even among these eight men," Shaw added, "I must make a distinction. I have called them 'Makers of the Universe,' but some of them were only repairers. Only three of them made universes." While he did not name the three, it was made clear at the time that Einstein was one of the trinity of Universe Makers, Pythagoras and Newton, presumably, being the two others.

Einstein dwelt all his life on a lonely scientific Sinai from which he descended from time to time with new and more comprehensive sets of laws to explain the workings of the cosmos. In his quest for new understanding of the fundamental laws governing the universe, he searched for simple unifying principles underlying the multifarious phenomena in which the cosmos manifests itself. In his Special and General theories of relativity, published in 1905 and 1916, respectively, which brought about the greatest intellectual revolution since Newton, he unified the concepts of space and time, matter and energy, gravitation and inertia—all considered at the time as independent, absolute entities—into one all-embracing cosmic concept.

In 1931, Dr. Einstein visited Mount Wilson Observatory at Pasadena, California, where he wrote the equation for the density of the Milky Way.

But having achieved what Russell described as "the greatest synthetic achievement of the human intellect," Einstein still found himself confronted with what was to him the profoundly disturbing fact that the universe, as revealed to him through relativity, appeared to flow in two seemingly parallel streams, or "fields"—the gravitational and electromagnetic fields—of which only the first could be traced directly to its source in the geometry of the world: the curvature of the four-dimensional space-time continuum. Convinced that both streams must have a common source in a larger cosmic geometrical design still hidden from him, Einstein dedicated his life from 1916 until the end to find the common origin of the two main cosmic streams, seeking, in the words of Omar Khayyam, the "single Alif" that may lead "to the Treasure-House, and, peradventure, to the Master, too."

What he was seeking with the consecrated devotion of a high priest for more than half his life was a simple set of logically coherent laws, embodied in mathematical formulas, that would unify the field of gravitation with the field of electromagnetism, a synthesis he called a "Unified Field Theory." In doing so, he hoped to reduce the physical universe in its totality to a few simple fundamental concepts that would unify all its multifarious and seemingly unrelated manifestations into one all-embracing intellectual synthesis.

But the big prize at the end of his scientific rainbow kept eluding him like a will-o'-the-wisp and gradually led to his intellectual isolation from his fellows. He first believed he had achieved his goal in 1929, after thirteen years of concentrated effort, only to find it illusory on closer examination. In 1950 he thought he almost had it within his grasp, having overcome "all the obstacles but one." In March, 1953, he felt convinced that he had at last overcome that lone obstacle and thus had attained the crowning achievement of his life's work. Yet even then he ruefully admitted that he had "not yet found a practical way to confront the theory with experimental evidence," the crucial test for any theory.

Even more serious, his field theory failed to find room in the universe for the atom and its component particles (electrons, protons, neutrons, mesons), which appeared to be "singularities in the field," like flies in the cosmic ointment. Despite these drawbacks, he never wavered in his confidence that the concept of the "pure field," free from "singularities" (i. e., the particle concept of the atom and the atomic character of energy) was the only true approach to a well-ordered universe, and that eventually "the field" would find room in it for the "enfant terrible" of the cosmos—the atom and the vast forces within it.

Schism Behind His Quest

Behind the Einstein quest for a Unified Field Theory—actually a quest to find a uniform set of cosmic laws for the universe of the stars and galaxies, and the universe of the atom, of which the stars and galaxies are constituted—lay one of the greatest intellectual schisms in the history of human thought, involving fundamental questions that had divided philosophers throughout the ages—monism vs. dualism, continuity vs. discontinuity, causality vs. chance, free will vs. determinism.

Einstein believed the physical universe was one continuous field, governed by one logical set of laws, in which every individual event is inexorably determined by immutable laws of causality. On the other hand, the vast majority of modern-day physicists champion the quantum theory, which leads to a discontinuous universe, made up of discrete particles and quanta (atoms) of energy, in which probability takes the place of causality and determinism is supplanted by chance.

According to the quantum theory, of which Einstein himself was one of the principal founders, the physical universe is dual in nature, everything in it partaking of the nature of both particle and wave. The theory, which applies to the atom while relativity applies to the universe at large, has as one of its keystones the Heisenberg Uncertainty Principle, according to which it is impossible to predict individual events, so that all knowledge is based on probability and thus at best can be only statistical in nature. The Uncertainty Principle has, furthermore, led to the universal acceptance by present-day physicists (with the exception of Einstein) that there was no causality or determinism in nature.

Einstein alone stood in majestic solitude against all these concepts of the quantum theory. Granting that it had had brilliant successes in explaining many of the mysteries of the atom and the phenomena of radiation, which no other theory had succeeded in explaining, he nevertheless insisted that a theory of discontinuity and uncertainty, of duality of particle and wave, and of a universe not governed by cause and effect, was an "incomplete theory"; that eventually laws would be found showing a continuous, unitary universe, governed by immutable laws in which every individual event was predictable.

In 1930, Dr. Einstein and his wife arrived in New York enroute to California where he planned to work in cooperation with scientists at the California Institute of Technology.

Chance Led to the Association Of Einstein With U. S. Institute

Dr. Flexner Tells of Meeting the Scientist in 1932—Says Rise of Hitler Kept Him in This Country

Chance played a substantial part in bringing Dr. Albert Einstein to the United States, and the accession of Adolf Hitler served to keep him here.

Dr. Abraham Flexner, whose unplanned meeting with the great scientist in 1932 resulted in Dr. Einstein's coming to Princeton, N. J., the next year, recalled the incident yesterday. He was interviewed in his office at 522 Fifth Avenue.

Louis Bamberger and his sister, the late Mrs. Felix Fuld, had entrusted to Dr. Flexner the task of setting up the Institute for Advanced Study. With an initial endowment of $5,000,000, he was to establish a small, flexible haven where accomplished scholars might have time, opportunity and complete freedom from pressure for their pursuit of their studies.

In 1932 Dr. Flexner was carrying out conferences with educators on the plans for the institute. Dr. Einstein was spending the early months of that year at the California Institute of Technology in Pasadena. He was there when Dr. Flexner made a visit to that institution.

"But I didn't go there to see him," Dr. Flexner said yesterday. "I hadn't thought of him for a place at the institute. I made no effort to see him. But on the day I was going to leave, Prof. John Hunt Morgan telephoned and said he thought Dr. Einstein would be glad to see me."

Institute Idea Fascinated Him

Dr. Flexner was introduced to the scientist, who was fascinated on hearing of the plans for the institute. The two arranged to meet again at Oxford, England, where both were planning to visit soon afterward. There they talked again at length. Next Professor Einstein invited Dr. Flexner to his beloved summer home at Caputh, near Potsdam. At that meeting, Dr. Einstein set the conditions on which he would come to Princeton, Dr. Flexner said.

"First, he wanted Dr. Walther Mayer as his assistant, and second, he said, he wanted $3,000 a year," Dr. Flexner recalled. "He asked, 'Could I live on less?' and I said, 'You couldn't live on that. Let Mrs. Einstein and me arrange it.' His salary was $16,000 a year and remained at that after he retired."

At first Dr. Einstein planned to spend only half his working time at Princeton. The rest was to be given to Germany. He was to take up his duties in the fall of 1933.

While the scientist was making his plans, however, the Hitler broth was brewing. Young Nazi students were agitating against the presence of Jewish students and teachers in the German universities. Still, Dr. Einstein was able to join in protests against Fascism and against anti-semitism.

Lost His Hope for Germany

On Dec. 10, 1932, the professor and his wife sailed from Bremen for California. Even after his arrival early in January he remained hopeful that Germany might retain her senses. But as Hitler and his brown-shirted followers gained strength, Dr. Einstein lost his hopefulness. He determined not to return to a Fascist Germany. In March, 1933, having gone to Belgium, he moved to renounce his Prussian citizenship.

Yet, Dr. Flexner said, it was solely his enthusiasm for the nature of the Institute for Advanced Study that had led Dr. Einstein to agree to come there.

"Hitler was never mentioned by either of us when we were discussing the institute and his coming to it," Dr. Flexner said. "I knew, of course, that he would have to flee, but I didn't tell him that."

Dr. Flexner said he considered Dr. Einstein "a great American and one of the great men of the world," yet "as simple and unpretentious as any child, and as easy to get along with as any good child."

"Of course," he added with a smile, "I can't understand anything he wrote."

GREAT OF SCIENCE PAID HIGH TRIBUTE

Einstein's Achievements Put Him in the Forefront of World's Intellects

Dr. Albert Einstein was respected above all others by scientists the world over as the outstanding intellect in modern times.

Prof. Arthur H. Compton, former chancellor of Washington University and a Nobel Prize winner in physics, said of Dr. Einstein on his seventieth birthday:

"Einstein is great because he has shown us our world in truer perspective and has helped us to understand a little more clearly how we are related to the universe around us.

"He has made it possible for man to see himself in his truer proportions. His concept of light quanta [atoms of light] has helped us understand the atoms that make up the world of which we are part. In his special theory of relativity he taught us that we must think in terms of objects that we see, not in terms of some imagined framework of space.

"By his general theory of relativity he unified our laws of motion and our law of gravitation, and opened the way for us to see with new clarity our universe, finite now in extent, but vaster far than had been dreamed before his thoughts stimulated the imagination of the scientific world."

A similar tribute was paid to Einstein by Prof. Niels Bohr of Denmark, also a Nobel Prize-winning physicist and one of the world's top scientists. Professor Bohr wrote:

"Through Albert Einstein's work, the horizon of mankind has been immeasurably widened, at the same time as our world picture has attained [through Einstein's work] a unity and harmony never dreamed of before. The background for such achievement was created by preceding generations of the world-wide community of scientists, and its full consequences will only be revealed to coming generations.

"The gifts of Einstein to humanity are in no way confined to the sphere of science. Indeed, his recognition of hitherto unheeded assumptions in even our most elementary and accustomed concepts means to all people a new encouragement in tracing and combating the deep-rooted prejudices and complacencies inherent in every national culture."

Many others of the elite in the world of science and philosophy gave their estimates of Einstein as a scientist, and of his contributions to world thought in Volume 7 of the Library of Living Philosophers, published in 1949 on the occasion of his 70th birthday under the title "Albert Einstein: Philosopher-Scientist." The volume consists of twenty-five descriptive and critical essays on Einstein's work by outstanding physicists and philosophers, including six Nobel Laureates in physics. It also includes an autobiography of Dr. Einstein and his comments on the essays.

Noted Scientists Pay Tribute

Following are excerpts from some of the essays:

ARNOLD SOMMERFELD

University of Munich

With the great work of Einstein of 1905 the mutual distrust, which existed during the last century between philosophy and physics, has disappeared. Einstein at this point touches upon the old basic questions of space and time, and proceeding from the most general results of physics, gives them a new content.

*** * * It is the relation between material motion and the universal speed of light which has led Einstein to the new analysis of space and time; that is to say, to their indissoluble connection. Not the relativizing of the perceptions of length and duration are the chief point for him, but the independence of natural laws from the standpoint of the observer.**

*** * * The marvelous thing which we experienced [after Einstein published his general relativity theory in 1916] was that now the paths of the planets could be calculated as "shortest lines" in the structurally modified [four-dimensional, curved] space, analogous to the straight lines in Euclidean space.**

The experimental verification was not to be long delayed. In the year 1918 a British solar eclipse expedition to the Tropics had photographed the surroundings of the eclipsed sun and compared the positions of the fixed stars nearest to the sun with their normal positions [seen at night]. They showed deviations from these latter to the extent of the effect predicted by Einstein [who postulated that the light-rays of stars passing close by the edge of the sun are deflected by a definite amount predicted by the theory].

LOUIS DE BROGLIE

French Nobel Laureate in Physics

The name of Albert Einstein calls to mind the intellectual effort and genius which overturned the most traditional notions of physics and culminated in the establishment of the relativity of the notions of space and time, the inertia of energy, and an interpretation of gravitational forces which is in some sort purely geometrical.

Therein lies a magnificent achievement comparable to the greatest that may be found in the history of the sciences; comparable, for example, to the achievements of Newton.

This alone would have sufficed to assure its author imperishable fame. But, great as it was, this achievement must not cause us to forget that Albert Einstein also rendered decisive contributions to other important advances in contemporary physics. * * * We could not fail to take note of the tremendous import of his research upon a developing quantum theory * * * Thus, Einstein became the source of an entire movement of ideas.

MAX BORN

Nobel Laureate in Physics

One of the most remarkable volumes in the whole of scientific literature seems to me Vol. 17 (4th series) of Annalen der Physik, 1905. It contains three papers by Einstein, each dealing with a different subject, and each today acknowledged to be a masterpiece, the source of a new branch of physics. These three subjects, in order of pages, are: theory of photons [atoms of light]; Brownian motion, and relativity.

Relativity is the last one, and this shows that Einstein's mind at that time was not completely absorbed by ideas on space-time * * * In my opinion he would be one of the greatest theoretical physicists of all time even if he had not written a single line on relativity—an assumption for which I have to apologize, as it is rather absurd. For Einstein's conception of the physical world cannot be divided into watertight compartments, and it is impossible to imagine that he should have by-passed one of the fundamental problems of the time.

Tributes in Yeshiva Volume

Many others among the elite in science and philosophy contributed to a celebration volume (Festschrift), presented to Dr. Einstein on the occasion of his seventy-fifth birthday last year by a delegation of the Albert Einstein College of Medicine of Yeshiva University. The volume included letters from fifteen Nobel Prize winners in physics, chemistry, medicine and physiology, literature and peace. Extracts from some of these follow:

ARNE TISELIUS

Nobel Laureate in Chemistry, Sweden

Albert Einstein has laid the foundation of many of our modern views of nature. He has discovered new basic laws which, to an exceptionally high degree, have helped us to understand better the world around us.

At the same time, his discoveries have demonstrated how a clear concept of the limitation of human thought may lead to the establishment of new and unexpected relationships, which have given results of the highest importance to mankind.

VICTOR F. LENZEN

University of California

The achievements of Albert Einstein in theoretical physics constitute a monument to the creative power of reason. For it has been his historic role to bring to completion, in principle, the classical era of physics, and to participate in laying the groundwork for the physical theories of a new era.

* * * As one reviews Einstein's contributions * * * a characteristic rationality stands out. His work has been the product of a creative reason guided by general principles; his goal has been the attainment of rational insight into the nature of reality; his efforts have been sustained by an unswerving faith in the ultimate rationality of the universe.

Einstein's reliance upon the power of reason prompts me to compare him with another great figure in the history of Western thought, the philosopher Spinoza. With the example of Platonic rationalism as embodied in Greek geometry before him, Spinoza constructed a metaphysical theory of substance which arranges the events of mind and nature in a cosmic order.

It was a principle of Spinoza's system that the order and connection of ideas is the order and connection of things. May we not find an expression of this same principle in the view of Einstein that reason is able to know the structure of the real? In Albert Einstein we have an exemplification of that rational insight which was expressed by Spinoza as the intellectual love of God.

ALBERT SZENT-GYORGYI

Nobel Laureate in Medicine and Physiology

Science, as an art of measuring, is said to have little to do with the humanities. Einstein has taught us that science is more than this: It is the art of understanding, the highest expression of man's craving to understand the universe in its entirety.

HENRY MARGENAU

Yale University

The question arises in the minds of many who have benefited from Einstein's work: "Wherein lies the singular quality of his greatness?" Some will say it is in the scope of his discoveries, in the unlimited sweep of his genius, and they are right. Some will say it resides in Einstein's miraculous ability to sense the importance of a problem, to drive to the heart of a difficulty and to succeed in conserving his energy for crucial matters. Others praise him for his intellectual daring. Surely, all these pronouncements relate to components of his scientific stature.

Yet, it seems to me, there is one quality of mind that transcends them all. It is a philosophic temper almost unique in our time, an inheritance from the scientific giants of another century developed to magnificent proportions. More than any modern thinker Einstein is imbued with a conviction of the fundamental orderliness and beauty of the cosmos, a conviction that leads him to demand a high measure of elegance and simplicity in his own conjectures and makes his scientific creations partake of the elements of the highest art.

This basic attitude, which sees in the workings of nature not merely secrets to be discovered but pattern and design to be explored, is obviously the living stratum which contains the wellsprings of his manifold successes.

"All the News That's Fit to Print"

The New York Times

LATE CITY EDITION

Weather: Chance of showers today. Cloudy, colder tonight, tomorrow. Temp. range: today 53-39; Friday 52-33. Full U.S. report on Page 70.

VOL. CXVIII . No. 40,607

NEW YORK, SATURDAY, MARCH 29, 1969

10 CENTS

EISENHOWER DEAD AT 78 AS AILING HEART FAILS; RITES WILL START TODAY

END IS PEACEFUL

De Gaulle Will Attend Funeral of the 34th President Monday

An obituary of Eisenhower appears as a slip-out section, Pages 17-20

By FELIX BELAIR Jr.
Special to The New York Times

WASHINGTON, March 28—Dwight David Eisenhower, 34th President of the United States, died peacefully at 12:25 P.M. today at Walter Reed General Hospital after a long fight against coronary heart disease. He was 78 years old.

Death came to the five-star General of the Army and hero of World War II as members of his immediate family stood at his bedside.

The end had been foreshadowed in a midmorning medical bulletin that said the general's condition "continues almost imperceptibly downhill." It added that Mrs. Eisenhower was at his side.

The former President's doctors gave no immediate cause of death, presumably because they considered this unnecessary. His damaged heart—scarred by seven attacks and weakened by recent episodes of congestive heart failure—finally gave out despite the best efforts of medical science to prolong his life.

A Popular Leader

In all corners of the earth where the name Eisenhower was associated with victory in war and a tireless crusade for peace, great men and small were moved by the passing of the man whose rise from a farm boy in Kansas to supreme Allied commander and conqueror of the Axis powers and President of the United States was a story of devotion to duty.

Trained to command, he welded together the greatest military coalition in history by the tactic of conciliation. After he became President in 1952 he ended the war in Korea, and he refused to give fighter planes to the French forces in Vietnam because he was fearful the United States might become directly involved as a result.

As President he governed effectively through the sheer force of his popularity among average Americans of both major parties, and it was the average American who was the real source of his power.

Record Pluralities

His critics at home accused him of playing too much golf and of garbling syntax at his news conferences. But the voters loved him and twice elected him President by the largest pluralities ever recorded at the time.

In his infectious grin and his highly expressive face, most Americans thought they saw in "Ike" a dim reflection of themselves.

In Paris, it was announced today that President de Gaulle, leader of the Free French forces when General Eisenhower was supreme Allied commander in Europe during World War II, would come to Washington for the funeral ceremonies on Monday.

From London, there was word that Lord Mountbatten, supreme Allied commander in Southeast Asia during the war, would attend as the personal representative of Queen Elizabeth.

The announcement of General Eisenhower's death, read to reporters by Brig. Gen. Frederic J. Hughes, commandant of Walter Reed, said:

"General of the Army Dwight D. Eisenhower, 34th President of the United States, died quietly at 12:25 this noon after a long and heroic battle against

Continued on Page 16, Column 1

The New York Times (by George Tames)

DWIGHT DAVID EISENHOWER, 1890-1969

BURIAL IN KANSAS

President Will Deliver Eulogy Tomorrow in Capitol's Rotunda

By WILLIAM M. BLAIR
Special to The New York Times

WASHINGTON, March 28—A three-day state funeral will be held for General of the Army Dwight D. Eisenhower in the nation's capital.

Tomorrow the former President's body will be removed from a private funeral home to the Bethlehem Chapel of the Washington Cathedral Church of SS. Peter and Paul, also known as the Washington Cathedral.

The body will lie in state for 28 hours before being borne to the Rotunda of the Capitol Sunday afternoon. There the public will be permitted to pay its last respects.

At the Capitol, President Nixon, who was Vice President under President Eisenhower, will deliver the eulogy. It was believed that this would be the first time a President had delivered the funeral eulogy for another President.

Service in Cathedral

On Monday afternoon, the body will be returned to the Washington Cathedral for the funeral service. Late Monday afternoon, the coffin will be taken to Union Station for the long journey to the World War II commander's boyhood home in Abilene, Kan. Burial services will be held Wednesday in the Eisenhower Center Chapel there.

The Presbyterian Book of Common Worship will be used for the service in the cathedral. General Eisenhower joined the Presbyterian church in 1953.

The funeral will be carried out under a plan drawn up in 1966 and approved by General Eisenhower. The times of each ceremony and the departure for Abilene were inserted into it this afternoon after consultation with members of the family and President Nixon.

A 54-page document, drafted by the Military District of Washington, specifies what is to be done nearly every moment of the three days. It details when soldiers shall present arms, the pace at which the cortege up Constitution Avenue to the Capitol shall move, when 21-gun-salutes shall be fired and when military bands will play.

Chose Kansas Burial

Although he approved the general plans for his funeral, General Eisenhower did not leave detailed instructions, as had his great friend, Sir Winston Churchill, with whom he shared the victory of World War II.

By contrast, General Eisenhower's funeral will be in the tradition of American democracy and according to a general outline held in readiness for Presidents by the military district.

The funeral will parallel that of President Kennedy in 1963, except for one notable exception. Mrs. Kennedy revised the plans to include a procession on foot from the White House to services in the Roman Catholic St. Mathew's Cathedral. She headed the procession that included President de Gaulle, King Haile Selassie of Ethiopia and other chiefs of state and heads of governments.

General Eisenhower also

Continued on Page 21, Column 1

Nixon Hails 'Great Leader' For His 'Moral Authority'

By ROBERT B. SEMPLE Jr.
Special to The New York Times

WASHINGTON, March 28—President Nixon led the nation in mourning for former President Dwight D. Eisenhower today, describing him as a wise and decent man "who spoke with a moral authority seldom equaled in American public life."

The President issued three tributes to the man who above all others was responsible for

President's statements on the death of Eisenhower, Page 16.

Mr. Nixon's own rise to the incomparable powers of the Presidency.

In a statement issued by the White House shortly after General Eisenhower's death, the President declared:

"General Eisenhower held a unique place in America's history, and in its heart, and in the hearts of people the world over.

"For a quarter of a century he spoke with a moral authority seldom equaled in American public life. This was not only because he held the nation's highest military rank and its highest civilian office, but more importantly because of the kind of man he was.

"He was a man of great strength, wisdom, and compassion. But it always seemed to me that two qualities stood out above all in both his public and private life: One was an unwavering sense of duty; the other was that whatever he did, he did because he believed it was right."

Separately, Mr. Nixon also dispatched a brief statement formally notifying Congress of the loss of "a great leader, a great friend, and a great man."

And the President issued a proclamation naming next Monday as a national day of mourning and ordering flags flown at half-staff on all Federal buildings and military installations at home and abroad for the next 30 days.

Mr. Nixon learned of the death while he was sitting at his desk in the Oval Office with Defense Secretary Melvin R. Laird. The two men had just emerged from a National Security Council meeting. The President sum-

Continued on Page 16, Column 6

Wife and Family With General As Death Ends 10-Month Vigil

By NAN ROBERTSON
Special to The New York Times

WASHINGTON, March 28—Mamie Doud Eisenhower was at her husband's bedside as he sank into a peaceful death shortly after noon on this fair day. It was the end of her vigil through 10 anxious months.

Since May 14, 1968, when General Eisenhower was admitted to Walter Reed General Hospital after his fourth heart attack, his wife of 52 years had lived in a suite just down the hall from the 34th President of the United States.

Her first job, she had said, was "looking after Ike." On at least one occasion during his last illness she had gone without sleep for 30 hours. She is 72 years old.

The minister who came to comfort Mrs. Eisenhower minutes after her husband's death said of her:

"She has been a great source of strength, a strong person in every way, a great Christian." The minister, the Rev. Edward L. R. Elson, is pastor of the Presbyterian church at which the general worshiped when he was President.

The Eisenhowers' only son John, and his wife, Barbara, were in the hospital room at the end. In the same third-floor suite waited General Eisenhower's only grandson and namesake, 20-year-old Dwight David, and his bride of three months, Julie Nixon Eisenhower.

The young couple broke off a vacation in Key Biscayne, Fla., last night and flew to Washington upon hearing of the general's deteriorating condition. At 10:30 this morning, after medical bulletins described him as "considerably" worse, his course continuing

Continued on Page 21, Column 3

STATE SALES TAX INCREASED 1 CENT BY G.O.P. IN ALBANY

Levy Up to 3%, Making Rate in City 6%—Legislators Seek to Pass Budget

RISE IN EFFECT TUESDAY

Price of Upstate Backing Is Still Deeper Cut in the Medicaid Program

By SYDNEY H. SCHANBERG
Special to The New York Times

ALBANY, March 28—The Republican majorities in the Legislature tonight passed a one-cent increase in the state sales tax as the first step in their approval of Governor Rockefeller's $6.4-billion budget.

Both the Senate and the Assembly then turned to the rest of the more than 20 budget bills that the Republican leaders intend to pass over the opposition of the Democratic minority. One more measure was forced through tonight—the "state purposes" bill appropriating the money for operating the state government—before the leaders adjourned until tomorrow morning to pass the rest of the budget package.

Defectors in Both Parties

The sales-tax measure—which the Governor is expected to sign—raises the state levy to 3 per cent from 2 per cent next Tuesday, making the total 6 per cent in communities such as New York City, which have a local 3 per cent tax.

It was passed first in the Senate, shortly before 8 P.M., by a vote of 33 to 24, along straight party lines.

However, the Democratic front was not so solid in the Assembly, when that house passed the tax increase about a half-hour later, 78 to 70.

Two upstate Democrats bolted to vote for the tax—in return for patronage and favors from the Governor and the G.O.P. legislative leaders, according to other legislators.

The defectors were Charles F. Stockmeister of Rochester and Albert J. Hausbeck of Buffalo.

The Republicans also had two defectors — conservatives who refused to vote for the tax rise. They were John T. Gallagher of Queens and John H. Terry of Syracuse.

Because the Republicans have a 78-to-72 margin in the Assembly and because the defec-

Continued on Page 24, Column 1

PENTAGON CURBS RELIGIOUS TALKS

Congressional Anger Then Prompts Review by Laird

By The Associated Press

WASHINGTON, March 28—Secretary of Defense Melvin R. Laird ordered today a high-level Pentagon review of Army plans to eliminate references to God and religious philosophy in character guidance courses that are given to soldiers.

The new Army policy, drawn up after a complaint last year by the American Civil Liberties Union, angered some members of Congress.

The liberties union contended that the mandatory lectures, which are intended to instill a sense of moral responsibility in soldiers, were being used as religious indoctrination.

Mr. Laird issued a statement today saying that he had just learned about the Army's planned revisions in the character guidance program and that he wanted the matter examined more clearly.

He assigned the Assistant Secretary of Defense for Manpower, Roger T. Kelley, and the Pentagon's general counsel to review the situation "since this is a matter which affects all the services."

"As Secretary of Defense I

Continued on Page 4, Column 3

Pope Names 33 Cardinals; Cooke Among 4 From U.S.

Sacred College at Peak Strength of 134 With Record Total of Appointments —Pittsburgh Bishop Elevated

By ROBERT C. DOTY
Special to The New York Times

ROME, March 29—Pope Paul VI nominated 33 Cardinals today, including four from the United States, to bring the membership of the College of Cardinals to 134, the largest ever.

The Pontiff's selections appeared to be mostly middle-of-the-road prelates, neither notably progressive nor notably conservative.

The four United States prelates, whose selection raises the number of American Cardinals to the record total of 10, are the Most Rev. Terence J. Cooke, 48 years old, Archbishop of New York; the Most Rev. John F. Dearden, 61, Archbishop of Detroit and president of the National Conference of Catholic Bishops; the Most Rev. John J. Carberry, 64, Archbishop of St. Louis, and the Most Rev. John J. Wright, 59, Bishop of Pittsburgh.

Pope Paul's list of nominations also represented the greatest number of Cardinals ever created at one time. Thirty-two prelates were given the red hat by Pius XII in his first postwar consistory, on Feb. 18, 1946.

The new princes of the church will be approved by a secret consistory of most of the 101 present Cardinals in the Vatican Palace on April 28 and installed in public ceremonies a day or two later.

The Pontiff also named two other prelates, whose identity is known only to him, to be Cardinals "in pectore" — that is, "in the heart." This is a sel-

Continued on Page 12, Column 7

Fulbright Derides ABM As a 'Political Gimmick'

By WARREN WEAVER Jr.
Special to The New York Times

WASHINGTON, March 28 — Senator J. W. Fulbright charged today that the Nixon Administration had made "no serious scientific review" of the antiballistic missile program and that its Safeguard system was "purely a political gimmick."

"The Defense Department doesn't take this committee of the Congress seriously," the chairman of the Senate Foreign Relations Committee protested. "They think they can pull the wool over our eyes."

Mr. Fulbright's outburst was prompted by testimony from Dr. Wolfgang K. H. Panofsky, a physicist at Stanford University, who was named two days ago by Deputy Defense Secretary David R. Packard as having participated in the Administration's review of the antimissile system.

'Did Not Participate'

Dr. Panofsky's was the only name that Mr. Packard produced when the Foreign Relations Disarmament Subcommittee, which held today's hearing as well as Wednesday's, pressed him to name a science adviser on the Safeguard plan who was not connected with the Pentagon.

"To clarify the record," Dr. Panofsky said as he opened his morning statement, "I would like to state that I did not

Continued on Page 2, Column 7

PERROTTA ADDED TO LINDSAY SLATE

Finance Chief Is Named by Mayor to Run for Controller —G.O.P. Backs Ticket

By RICHARD REEVES

Mayor Lindsay finished putting together his Republican-Democrat-Republican ticket yesterday morning by announcing that city Finance Administrator Fioravante G. Perrotta, a 37-year-old liberal Republican, would be his running mate for Controller.

Ten hours later, the citywide Republican executive committee endorsed the slate by a vote of 132 to 5 at a miniature convention, which was boycotted by about 30 committee members supporting State Senator John J. Marchi for the mayoral nomination.

The special meeting of the committee was called because state election laws require executive committee approval for candidates to run in the primary election of a party in which they are not registered—and Mr. Lindsay's choice for City Council President is a registered Democrat, Sanford D. Garelik, former chief inspector of the Police Department.

Garelik Main Issue

Mr. Garelik was actually granted permission to run in the June 17 primary by a unanimous voice vote, but Richard A. Bolton, Staten Island Republican leader, and four other committee members objected to endorsement of the ticket on the ground that the meeting was called only to consider the Garelik matter.

Mr. Bolton, who along with the Bronx leader, A. Joseph Ribustello, is supporting Mr. Marchi, said he had been authorized to speak for missing Staten Island and Bronx committee members.

"For us this meeting has no purpose," he told the crowd in the peeling gold-and-coral splendor of the roof garden of the St. George Hotel in Brooklyn. "We are going our own route this year with a completely Republican team."

That was the only dissident note of the hour-long session as other county leaders—John Crews of Brooklyn, Sidney Hein of Queens and Vincent F. Albano of the Bronx—heaped praise on the Lindsay-Garelik-Perrotta ticket.

Finally, Mr. Crews introduced "Captain Courageous John V. Lindsay" to standing applause and the Mayor introduced "my

Continued on Page 24, Column 3

QUICK BIG 4 MOVE ON MIDEAST PEACE IS SOUGHT IN U.N.

Britain and France Caution Council—Plan to Begin the Talks Thursday Reported

By JUAN de ONIS
Special to The New York Times

UNITED NATIONS, N. Y., March 28—Britain and France said in the Security Council today that the "highly dangerous" and "deteriorating" situation in the Middle East required a prompt peace initiative by the major powers.

A diplomatic source, not from one of the Big Four nations, said that the representatives of the United States, the Soviet Union, Britain and France had decided to hold their first four-sided talks on the Middle East Thursday.

Charles W. Yost, the United States delegate, said yesterday that the four-power consultations in an effort to prompt a Middle East peace agreement were in the "not-too-distant future."

U. S. Won't Confirm Date

United States sources said that the first meeting could take place next week, but refused to confirm any date. Charles W. Yost, the American delegate, said that efforts by the major powers toward a Middle East peace were "about to be renewed with fresh vigor."

The reluctance of United States sources to mention a firm date was part of a decision not to give the four-power contacts high visibility and a desire to preserve a degree of privacy for these consultations, which will probably go on for months in a confidential manner.

"We don't want to create a conference atmosphere," a United States diplomat said.

Promptness Stressed

Addressing the Council today, Sir Leslie Glass, the deputy British representative, said: "The outside world cannot afford to stand by and treat this as a local quarrel," adding that "the parties have had long enough to try and resolve it on their own."

Britain, which has a particular interest in the reopening of the Suez Canal, has been active in pushing for an early start on full-scale Big Four talks on the Middle East. Preliminary two-nation contracts have been under way for some time.

Sir Leslie spoke on the second day of the Security Council debate on complaints from Jordan and Israel over violations of the 1967 cease-fire.

Armand Bérard, the French

Continued on Page 8, Column 3

U.S. Backs Negro Suit to Recoup 'Blockbusting' Profit in Chicago

By FRED P. GRAHAM
Special to The New York Times

WASHINGTON, March 28—The Justice Department threw its weight behind the efforts of a group of Chicago Negroes seeking to make "blockbusting" real estate speculators pay back high profits they have made from Negro home purchasers.

In a friend-of-court brief filed in Federal District Court in Chicago, the Government asked the court to rule that a civil rights law passed in 1866 gave Negroes a legal right to recover overcharges gained from "blockbusting."

At a press briefing, Jerris Leonard, Assistant Attorney General in charge of the Civil Rights Division, called the overcharges a "race tax." He said that the Federal Government was considering attacks on similar speculation in other cities. Detroit was mentioned as the most likely second target.

"Blockbusting" is a tactic by which speculators sell one or two homes in a white neighborhood to Negroes and then persuade the remaining white homeowners to sell at low prices under the threat that the influx of Negroes would depress property prices. The speculators then resell the homes to Negroes at premium prices.

The practice was initially attacked in Chicago by the Contract Buyers League, a group on Chicago's West Side since 1958. The league sued about 50 investment companies, mortgage bankers, lending institutions, real estate agents and individual speculators, contending that the sales violated the Federal Constitution and various Federal civil rights statutes.

The defendants have asked for dismissal of the suit, contending that none of these provisions apply to the alleged blockbusting. Federal District Judge Hubert L. Will is to hear arguments on the dismissal motion next Thursday.

Mr. Leonard explained today that the Justice Department considered the case important because it could establish a precedent that would discourage blockbusting. "Anybody who rakes off a profit based on racial discrimination should have to pay it back with interest," he said.

However, he said the Civil Rights Division had not joined the suit as a plaintiff because its resources of attorneys would have been overtaxed. He indicated that the Government would make another legal move next week in Chicago with regard to Negroes' access to home financing.

Because the Negro purchasers in Chicago could not obtain mortgage financing, they bought their houses through

Continued on Page 23, Column 6

NEWS INDEX

Eisenhower, the 34th President and World War II Commander, Dies Peacefully at 78

De Gaulle Plans to Attend The Funeral on Monday

Continued From Page 1, Col. 8

overwhelming illness. His passing was peaceful, and he experienced no distress.

"Mrs. Eisenhower and the immediate family were near by. President Nixon, former Presidents Truman and Johnson, and General Eisenhower's brothers have been notified. The commanding general, Military District of Washington, is responsible for all arrangements for the state funeral.

"It is the wish of the family that, in lieu of flowers, friends will recall charities of their choice, or those of prime interest to General Eisenhower during his lifetime."

Visibly moved by the news he had to impart, General Hughes brushed aside an inquiry on whether there would be a medical briefing.

"No," he replied. "This is a period of mouring, not of medical discussion."

President Nixon, who had been notified of the death of his former chief moments after the event, left the White House at 12:50 P.M. and was sped to the hospital behind a motorcycle escort. He was accompanied by Mrs. Nixon and their eldest daughter, Tricia.

Proclamation by Nixon

The President, before leaving his office, signed a proclamation calling for a day of mourning on Monday and ordering that the flag be flown at half-staff on all Government buildings and other Government facilities at home and around the world for 30 days. The White House will be closed to visitors through Wednesday.

Mr. Nixon also sent a brief message to both houses of Congress notifying members officially of his action. Government offices were closed almost immediately, and Federal employes were sent home. The offices will remain closed through Monday.

Postmaster General Winton M. Blount announced there would be no mail deliveries on Monday and all post offices would be closed. Chief Justice Earl Warren announced that the Supreme Court would formally convene at 10 A.M. on Monday but would adjourn promptly without transacting any business.

General Eisenhower's brother Milton S. of Baltimore, former president of John Hopkins University, arrived at the hospital just ahead of the Presidential party. The other surviving brother, Edgar N., lives in Tacoma, Wash.

Behind the President's limousine followed one with Secretary of State William P. Rogers, Secretary of Defense Melvin R. Laird, Henry A. Kissinger, special Presidential assistant for national security affairs, and Bryce Harlow, White House legislative liaison chief, who had held the same post under President Eisenhower.

They joined the Eisenhower family in Mrs. Eisenhower's third-floor suite, adjoining that of General Eisenhower.

The family included David Eisenhower, the general's grandson, and his wife, the former Julie Nixon, daughter of the President. They had remained in an anteroom while the former President's wife, Mamie, his son, John, and the latter's wife, Barbara, remained at his bedside until the end.

Tributes to General Eisenhower were numerous. President Nixon said of the man with whom he worked for eight years as Vice President that "he spoke with a moral authority seldom equaled in American public life.

"Dwight Eisenhower was selfless," the President said. "He was devoted to the common cause of humanity, to his beloved country, and to his family and friends. He was both a great man and a good man. To millions the world over he was a symbol of decency and hope."

In his proclamation President Nixon said, "General Eisenhower's life will shape the future as it shaped our time."

"As long as free men cherish their freedom," he said, "Dwight Eisenhower will stand with them, as he stood during war and peace; strong, confident and courageous. Even in death he has left us a great spirit that will never die."

The President emerged from the hospital red-eyed and silent, entering his waiting limousine and returning to the Executive Mansion. He canceled all appointments for the next five days and left by helicopter for Camp David at Catoctin, Md., accompanied only by an aide.

In his eulogy of General Eisenhower, President Nixon offered as a key to his character a statement the general had prepared in event the Normandy invasion during World War II ended in disaster. It read:

"Our landings in the Cherbourg-Havre area have failed to gain a satisfactory foothold and I have withdrawn the troops. My decision to attack at this time was based upon the best information available. The troops, the air and Navy did all that bravery and devotion to duty could do. If any blame or fault attaches to the attempt it is mine alone."

Mr. Nixon said the statement was filed away and never used because the landings had been successful.

"But that was a man ready to take the consequences of decision," the President said. "That was Eisenhower."

To Lie in State

Plans for the state funeral and interment of the former President at Abilene, Kan., were approved by General Eisenhower himself in 1966. They will be put into effect starting just before 11 A.M. tomorrow when his body is taken from a funeral home here and conveyed by hearse to the Washington Cathedral.

The body will remain there until midafternoon Sunday, when it will be placed on a caisson, and a procession will go from the cathedral to the Capitol. There the body will lie in state from 5:30 P.M. Sunday until 1:30 P.M. Monday, on the same black-draped catafalque that supported the body of Lincoln in 1865.

Just before 4 P.M. on Monday the body will be returned by hearse to the Washington Cathedral for a formal funeral ceremony at about 4:30 P.M. At about 6 P.M. it will be placed aboard a special funeral train, also carrying old friends, for the trip to Abilene, taking about 40 hours, and burial on Wednesday.

The former President—he preferred to be addressed as General Eisenhower—had been a patient at Walter Reed since last May 14. He was flown here from March Air Force Base in Southern California, where he had been hospitalized temporarily after his fourth heart attack, on April 29.

There were three more attacks on June 14, Aug. 6 and Aug. 16. All but the last one was diagnosed as a myocardial infarction—severe damage to the myocardium, or main pumping muscle of the heart. The sixth attack was diagnosed as equaling in severity his first massive infarct, in Denver in 1955.

The seventh attack, although less damaging than the others, marked the onset of ventricular fibrillating, or fluttering of the lower left pumping chamber of the heart. On at least four occasions he had to be "defibrillated" by massive electric shock, restoring his normal heart rhythm.

In each of these episodes the old warrior lost consciousness, and there were times when his doctors despaired of his life. But, after being listed in "critical" condition for several weeks, he rallied.

All went well until Feb. 21, when it was discovered that General Eisenhower had developed intestinal adhesions as a result of earlier abdominal surgery. His doctors had no choice but to operate to remove the blockage or risk his death as a result of gangrene.

The General, as well as Mrs. Eisenhower, accepted the doctors' decision to operate "with equanimity," according to a hospital bulletin the next day. Equanimity mixed with light humor came to be recognized as the General's hallmark during his last days in the hosptial.

When told of the need for surgery, his immediate reaction was a wry smile.

He was heard to remark:

"Okay, if that's the way it has to be. But I don't want anybody waking me up at 2 in the morning to stick another needle in me and carting me off to the operating room. If there's going to be another invasion, I want to know about it in advance and that it's coming off on schedule."

Remarkable Recovery

Two days later Walter Reed doctors talked about the former President's "remarkable recovery." Less than seven months earlier, on Aug. 16, Lieut. Gen. Leonard Heaton, Surgeon General of the Army, talked openly about General Eisenhower's "miraculous recovery" from his seventh heart attack.

Since his last major heart attack, his doctors knew that death might strike at any time. General Eisenhower knew it, too. He had known since his second and third attacks, on Nov. 9 and 11, 1965, for which he was hospitalized at Fort Gordon, Ga., that he was living on borrowed time.

The general's doctors kept no secrets from him about his condition. He was aware that his cardiac disease was progressive and that he might just as readily die in a rocking chair at his Gettysburg, Pa., farm as on the golf course at Palm Desert in Southern California.

But General Eisenhower never seemed distressed at the thought. In August of 1968, after his sixth heart attack, he spoke of death to a long-time friend as preferable to life as a bed-ridden cripple and a burden to his family.

Associated Press

PAY THEIR RESPECTS: President and Mrs. Nixon, accompanied by their daughter Tricia, arriving at the hospital shortly after the death of General Eisenhower was announced.

The Hospital Statement

Special to The New York Times

WASHINGTON, March 28—Following is the text of the announcement of the death of former President Eisenhower read at Walter Reed General Hospital by Brig. Gen. Frederic J. Hughes Jr., commanding general of the hospital:

General of the Army Dwight David Eisenhower, 34th President of the United States, died quietly at 12:25 this noon after a long and heroic battle against overwhelming illness. His passing was peaceful and he experienced no distress.

United Press International

Brig. Gen. Frederic J. Hughes, commander of Walter Reed General Hospital.

Mrs. Eisenhower and the immediate family were nearby. President Nixon, former Presidents Truman and Johnson, and General Eisenhower's brothers have been notified.

The commanding general, Military District of Washington, is responsible for all arrangements for the state funeral.

It is the wish of the family that, in lieu of flowers, friends will recall charities of prime interest to General Eisenhower during his lifetime.

A listing of these charities follows:

Eisenhower Exchange Fellowships, Inc.

Eisenhower College, Senaca Falls, N. Y.

People-to-People.

Freedoms Foundation at Valley Forge.

D. D. Eisenhower Research Fund for Cerebral Palsy.

President's Proclamation

Special to The New York Times

WASHINGTON, March 28—Following is the text of a proclamation by President Nixon announcing the death of former President Dwight D. Eisenhower:

The White House

By the President of the United States of America

A Proclamation

To the people of the United States:

I have the sad duty to announce officially the death of Dwight David Eisenhower, the 34th President of the United States, on Friday, March 28, 1969.

In London, in 1945, the great soldier received the freedom of the City of London. At that time, he said: ". . . We should turn to those inner things, call them what you will—I mean those intangibles that are the real treasures free men possess."

As a soldier, he was guided by those inner things. As a President he was strengthened by their wisdom and by the knowledge that the ancient virtues, intangible but unconquerable, could offer comfort and solace even during the darkest hours.

And so it should be with us who today mourn his death. The memory of his greatness is now one of those "real treasures free men possess"; it belongs now to all Americans, and in its simplicity, its devotion, its courage, and its compassion, his life will shape the future as it shaped our time.

As long as free men cherish their freedom, Dwight Eisenhower will stand with them, as he stood during war and peace; strong, confident and courageous. Even in death he has left us a great spirit that will never die.

NOW, THEREFORE, I, Richard M. Nixon, President of the United States of America, in honor and tribute to the memory of this great and good man, and as an expression of public sorrow, do hereby direct that the flag of the United States be displayed at half-staff at the White House and on all buildings, grounds, and naval vessels of the United States for a period of 30 days from the day of death.

I also direct that for the same length of time the representatives of the United States in foreign countries shall make similar arrangements for the display of the flag at half staff over their embassies, legations, and other facilities abroad, including all military facilities and stations.

I HEREBY ORDER that suitable honors be rendered by units of the armed forces under orders of the Secretary of Defense on the day of the funeral.

I ALSO DO APPOINT Monday, March 31, 1969, to be a national day of mourning throughout the United States. I earnestly recommend that the people assemble on that day in their respective places of divine worship, there to bow down in submission to the will of the Almighty God, and to pay their homage of love and reverence to the memory of President Eisenhower. I invite the people of the world who share our grief to join us in this day of mourning and rededication.

IN WITNESS WHEREOF, I have hereunto set my hand this 28th day of March in the year of our Lord nineteen hundred and sixty-nine and of the independence of the United States of America the one hundred and ninety-third.

RICHARD M. NIXON

By the President:
WILLIAM P. ROGERS,
Secretary of State

Flags in Washington Fly at Half-Staff, Honoring the Former President

The Capitol, where General Eisenhower's body will lie in state from Sunday afternoon until Monday afternoon.

Associated Press

The White House. Looking toward the South Portico, the lawn in foreground is the putting green the General used.

Nixon Hails General as Moral Leader

Continued From Page 1, Col. 7

moned his wife, his daughter Tricia, and five associates—Mr. Laird; his press secretary, Ronald L. Ziegler; Secretary of State William P. Rogers; his legislative assistant, Bryce Harlow, who had served President Eisenhower in the White House, and Dr. Henry A. Kissinger, adviser on national security affairs.

The group then rushed to Walter Reed Army Medical Hospital. Mr. Nixon spent a half-hour with members of the general's family on the third floor of the hospital's east wing.

In mid-afternoon, accompanied by a single aide, he flew to the Presidential retreat at Camp David, Md., where General Eisenhower had spent many weekends during his eight years as President. Mr. Nixon will attend funeral rites here on Sunday and Monday, and fly to Abilene, Kan., for the burial Wednesday.

Mr. Nixon was a junior Senator from California with a controversial national reputation as an opponent of domestic Communism when General Eisenhower selected him as a running mate in 1952. General Eisenhower did not know Mr. Nixon well but trusted the judgment of Thomas E. Dewey and Herbert Brownell.

It was, in retrospect, Mr. Nixon's greatest political break, but in the years to come the general made other gestures that did much to help Mr. Nixon's career.

Once elected, General Eisenhower sought to make sure that the Vice-Presidency, so often a blind alley for aspiring politicians, would become for Mr. Nixon an avenue of influence and prestige. His first order was that Mr. Nixon was to be kept fully informed and was to participate in policy-making discussions at the Cabinet level.

Close to the Center

Mr. Nixon took full advantage of the mandate. He presided over 19 Cabinet meetings and 26 meetings of the National Security Council, attended weekly meetings with the Congressional leadership, was given access to much classified information, served on a number of the Presidential commissions, assumed some of the ceremonial burdens of the Presidency and traveled over 160,000 miles to 56 countries as the President's representative.

In exchange for the visibility thus provided, Mr. Nixon undertook many of the political chores for which he possessed a natural facility but for which General Eisenhower possessed only a profound distaste.

Mr. Nixon's official intimacy with the White House was not, however, matched by personal intimacy with the President.

In part because of the opportunities to educate himself in the mysteries of Government that General Eisenhower had given him, Mr. Nixon acquitted himself well during the general's three illnesses—the heart attack of 1955, the abdominal ailments of 1956, and the stroke in 1957.

"There is no man in the history of America who has had such careful preparation . . . for carrying out the duties of the Presidency," General Eisenhower declared after he had recovered from his 1955 heart attack.

Yet the relationship between the famous general and the California politician was filled with awkward episodes, periods of stress, and, particularly for Mr. Nixon, moments of acute embarrassment.

Little Support in 1952

The "slush fund" scandal of the 1952 campaign was a case in point. Accused of receiving illegal expense money from California businessmen, Mr. Nixon argued otherwise but received little support from General Eisenhower's associates, some of whom suggested that he be dropped from the ticket.

Mr. Nixon went on television to protest his innocence in the famous "Checkers" speech. Even then, however, General Eisenhower refused to absolve and embrace Mr. Nixon until the Vice-Presidential candidate had made a long and, in the view of his aides, humiliating pilgrimage to Wheeling, W. Va., where the general was making a campaign speech. Mr. Nixon has since attributed his public embarrassment to the "indecisiveness" of some of the "amateurs" around General Eisenhower, and not the general himself, but the episode left a lasting scar.

Mr. Nixon was similarly dismayed by the President's refusal to endorse him outright for the 1956 Vice-Presidential nomination, and by his own testimony he was often excluded from the inner circle of Eisenhower political advisers.

Embarrassed by Remark

General Eisenhower endorsed Mr. Nixon for the Presidency in 1960, but the latter was haunted throughout the campaign by a remark his chief made at a news conference in August of that year.

In an effort to praise the Vice President, General Eisenhower pointed out that Mr. Nixon had joined in all important discussions in his Administration. But when a reporter asked for a Nixon idea that General Eisenhower had adopted, the President replied:

"If you give me a week I might think of one. I don't remember."

The general said later that he regretted the remark, explaining that the question had taken him by surprise.

Last year, as Mr. Nixon made what might have been his last bid for the Presidency had he lost, the general supported his candidacy unreservedly.

In July, for example, two weeks before the Republican National Convention, General Eisenhower broke a long-standing practice of avoiding pre-convention endorsements and publicly backed Mr. Nixon's bid. He issued a laudatory statement and then, in a brief news conference, added these comments, which may have been the most useful of all to Mr. Nixon:

"Many people have mistakenly thought that I never really liked or supported or really believed in Nixon. This is a mere misapprehension. I just want the country to know that I have admired and respected this man and liked the man ever since I met him in 1952."

Text of Two Statements by Nixon

Special to The New York Times

WASHINGTON, March 28—Following are the texts of a statement issued by President Nixon on the death of former President Dwight D. Eisenhower and a statement announcing the death to Congress:

Statement by President

General Eisenhower held a unique place in America's history, and in its heart, and in the hearts of people the world over.

For a quarter of a century he spoke with a moral authority seldom equaled in American public life. This was not only because he held the nation's highest military rank and its highest civilian office but more importantly because of the kind of a man he was.

He was a man of great strength, wisdom and compassion. But it always seemed to me that two qualities stood out above all in both his public and his private life: One was an unwavering sense of duty; the other was that whatever he did, he did because he believed it was right.

The measure of Dwight Eisenhower's place in history is that we have to reach back two centuries, to the first days of our republic, to find another American who was "a citizen, first in war, first in peace, first in the hearts of his countrymen."

One key to the character of General Eisenhower was revealed in a message he prepared but never had to deliver. Just before D Day, he wrote a statement in the event of disaster:

"Our landings in the Cherbourg Havre area have failed to gain a satisfactory foothold and I have withdrawn the troops. My decision to attack at this time and place was based upon the best information available. The troops, the Air Force and the Navy did all that bravery and devotion to duty could do. If any blame or fault attaches to the attempt it is mine alone."

The landing was successful, and the message filed away. But that was a man ready to take the consequences of decision. That was Eisenhower.

Dwight Eisenhower was selfless. He was devoted to the common cause of humanity, to his beloved country, and to his family and friends. He was both a great man and a good man. To millions the world over, he was a symbol of decency and hope.

As President, I salute him for his services as a soldier, statesman and peacemaker. As one who was privileged to serve for eight years as his Vice President, I pay tribute to him as an inspiring leader and a great teacher.

As a person who is proud to have been his friend, and who has happily seen our families united, I join with my fellow Americans in mourning his death and in offering my condolences.

A grateful nation stands in his debt, and those of us who knew him, or who shared this period of history with him, will always warmly cherish his memory.

Message to Congress

It is may sad duty to inform you officially of the death of Dwight David Eisenhower, the 34th President of the United States.

We have lost a great leader, a great friend and a great man. I know there are many members of the Congress who had the privilege of serving under his military leadership, and who later, during his eight years as President, shared with him in the building of a better America.

He had a profound respect for the traditions, the institutions and the instruments of our nation. He leaves to the Congress and to all Americans the spirit of patriotism and statesmanship beyond party which marked his entire career.

As we grieve at his death, we all will recall that spirit, which can guide and sustain us in our tasks ahead. He had been an inspiration to us all, and ours is a better government because he walked among us.

Mourning for Eisenhower

Among the institutions and organizations in this area that will be affected by the mourning period for former President Dwight D. Eisenhower are the following:

SCHOOLS

The following will close: All of the schools and offices under the city's Board of Education; Columbia University, where General Eisenhower was president from June, 1948, until the end of 1950; the Brooklyn Center of Long Island University; all campuses of New York University; the new School for Social Research; all campuses of Fairleigh Dickinson University in New Jersey; Stevens Institute of Technology in Hoboken.

Other schools closing for the day include Princeton University, Yeshiva University, Pace College, both the Brooklyn and Farmingdale campuses of Polytechnic Institute of Brooklyn, and Fordham University.

Roman Catholic schools in the dioceses of Brooklyn and New York will remain open, but memorial tributes are scheduled.

EXCHANGES

All stock exchanges and commodities exchanges will close. Auctions of Treasury paper and Federal National Mortgage Association commitments will wait until Tuesday.

GOVERNMENT OFFICES

All post offices, Federal offices and banks will be closed. There will be no regular mail delivery. The Social Security Administration extended to Tuesday the deadline for persons 65 and over to sign up for doctors' bill insurance under Medicare.

All city offices and installations will be closed after 1 P.M. Monday except for emergency operations, including Health, Police and Fire departments.

THEATERS

The League of New York Theaters has recommended to all 24 Broadway stage shows that a minute of silence be observed before Monday evening's curtain; Off Broadway productions also are expected to have tributes Monday.

Dwight David Eisenhower: A Leader in War and Peace

MILITARY leadership of the victorious Allied forces in Western Europe during World War II invested Dwight David Eisenhower with an immense popularity, almost amounting to devotion, that twice elected him President of the United States. His enormous political success was largely personal, for he was not basically a politician dealing in partisan issues and party maneuvers. What he possessed was a superb talent for gaining the respect and affection of the voters as the man suited to guide the nation through cold war confrontations with Soviet power around the world and to lead the country to domestic prosperity.

Eisenhower's gift for inspiring confidence in himself perplexed some analysts because he was not a dashing battlefield general nor a masterly military tactician; apparently what counted most in his generalship also impressed the voters most: an ability to harmonize diverse groups and disparate personalities into a smoothly functioning coalition.

Thus Eisenhower's two terms in the White House were a personal triumph in which he transcended the persons and forces around him. About his bewitching, benign and smiling figure there grew an aura of certain success that weathered shifts in his personal popularity and began to wane only in the years after he left the Presidency.

Of all his unquestioned great moments, two stand out as landmarks. One is May 7, 1945, when Gen. Alfred Jodl, chief of the German Armed Forces Operations Staff, surrendered unconditionally to the Allies at a schoolhouse in Rheims, France, culminating the European phase of a terrible conflict that had nearly consumed the world.

The other is Nov. 6, 1956, when Eisenhower was elected to a second term as President by one of the largest votes ever rolled up by a candidate of any party. His vote of 35.5 million has since been eclipsed, but it was a stunning performance at the time.

The New York Times

INAUGURATED: General Eisenhower takes the oath, administered by Fred M. Vinson, the Chief Justice, in 1953.

Adviser to Presidents

In the years that followed his military and Presidential victories, he retired to the role of elder statesman, counseling his successors in the White House when they sought his advice and working to help unify (but never to lead) the Republican party along moderate lines. In the campaign of 1964, however, he declined to use his prestige to block the nomination of Senator Barry Goldwater of Arizona. Moderates backing Gov. William W. Scranton of Pennsylvania were disturbed and disheartened.

The sources of Eisenhower's qualities of leadership were far different from those of other contemporary statesmen Franklin D. Roosevelt was a patrician with a master's manner in handling men; Sir Winston Churchill was an aristocrat born to command; Josef Stalin was a tyrant who ruled by ruthless craft; Nikita S. Khrushchev was a peasant's son given to hearty bluster; Harry S. Truman was a commoner who led because he was stubborn.

Eisenhower's political appeal, apart from the glory conferred by his military accomplishments, lay in his background and his expression of it. He was a product of Abilene, Kan., a small Middle Western town that did not have a paved street until 1910 — the year after his graduation from high school. He was also the product of a close-knit Mennonite German family that passed on to him the simple pieties of 19th-century agricultural America.

Insulated all of his adult life from the rise of industrialism and the anxieties of the job world by the institutional security of Army life, Eisenhower preserved these homilies virtually intact: God helps those who help themselves; the devil finds mischief for idle hands; do justice and you will receive justice; prosperity is a sign of divine blessing; a change of heart expiates sin.

The heart-warming sincerity with which he uttered these beliefs and their obvious role in fashioning his life created around him an atmosphere of uncomplicated goodness and uprightness. It disarmed his critics and confounded his enemies.

A Man to Be Trusted

Eisenhower's scrubbed face, his dimpled, infectious grin, his exuberance, his quick Jovian anger (and his equally swift return to calm), his paternal manner, all fused into a personality that the American public responded to and heeded. Cloaked with the power to command, he preferred to persuade and conciliate; he seemed to radiate goodwill and diplomacy. He was, in short, a man to be trusted, a man to make the complex simple, to do the job.

For these characteristics much was overlooked: his vacations from the White House, his endless golf, his frequent bridge games, his fondness for cowboy stories, his bumbling syntax; for he exemplified the homespun, folksy virtues that many Americans liked to think they themselves possessed, or should ideally possess.

Eisenhower's entrance into politics was reluctant. Before the end of World War II Dr. Douglas Southall Freeman, the historian, suggested that he consider public office, and his reply was, "God forbid!"

In the glow of the war's end, President Harry S. Truman offered to assist the general if he wanted to seek the Presidency in 1948. "Mr. President," he said, "I don't know who will be your opponent for the Presidency, but it will not be I."

Pressure built up to draft Eisenhower for the race in 1948. Both Democrats and Republicans had hopes of snaring him because there was nothing in the public record to indicate which party, if either, held his favor.

The general squelched talk of a draft for the nomination. "I am not available for and could not accept nomination for high public office," he wrote in a letter. At the time he was on leave from the presidency of Columbia University to serve as commander of the North Atlantic Treaty Organization forces in Europe.

Despite Eisenhower's disclaimer, leading Republicans in the East kept their eye on him. In 1950, when the party seemed resurgent in Congress, Thomas E. Dewey of New York, the titular leader, proposed Eisenhower as the nominee for 1952. Soon there was a well-beaten path to Rocquencourt, outside Paris, where the general made his headquarters; it was trod by politicians and businessmen, many of whom assured him, with adroit flattery, of the public clamor for him back home and of the ease with which he could get the nomination.

Having indicated that he would accept the party's designation, however, Eisenhower soon discovered that it was not quite his for the asking. Pitted against him was Senator Robert A. Taft of Ohio, the "Mr. Republican" of the party's conservative wing. The decisive issue between them, as the general saw it, was isolationism. Indeed, Eisenhower agreed to run after he was convinced that Taft would not commit himself to the principles of NATO.

The struggle was close, and the general was obliged to do some campaigning. Up to the convention in July, 1952, the outcome was unresolved. With the party machinery in Taft's hands, the issue hinged on how delegate contests in Texas, Louisiana and Georgia would be decided. In a maneuver that outwitted and discomfited the opposition, the Eisenhower forces, masterminded by Dewey, put across a "fair play" amendment to the rules that restricted voting by contested delegations already seated. It swung control of the convention away from Taft and led to Eisenhower's nomination.

Victory Over Taft

The victory came after the regular order of the first roll-call, when Minnesota switched 19 votes and gave the general the 604 votes he required for nomination. Other shifts eventually brought his total to 845 votes, while Taft slipped from a high of 500 to 280.

As a Vice-Presidential candidate the convention chose Senator Richard M. Nixon of California, a man known then for his conservative views.

Eisenhower quickly moved to attain party unity by calling on Taft at his convention offices. Later the two had a dramatic breakfast meeting at Columbia University that brought Taft followers into line, for both agreed, in a communiqué, that they sought similar foreign and domestic objectives.

In the broadest terms, Eisenhower campaigned against his Democratic opponent, Gov. Adlai E. Stevenson of Illinois, on a pledge to clean up "the mess in Washington" and to balance the budget. Shortly before the election he promised he would personally go to Korea and try to end the war there. In its day-to-day unfolding, however, the campaign was much akin to a popularity contest. The country was covered with "I Like Ike" buttons, placards and posters; "All the Way With Adlai" was a fervent, but forlorn, cry.

Eisenhower's concepts of loyalty and integrity were tested twice in the campaign, once with Senator Nixon and once with Senator Joseph R. McCarthy, Republican of Wisconsin.

The Nixon case began with the disclosure that a group of California supporters had placed an $18,000 fund at his disposal while he was in the Senate. In a dramatic television appeal to the nation, Nixon made a sweeping denial of wrongdoing, satisfying Eisenhower's insistence that his running mate be "clean as a hound's tooth." Accepting Nixon's version of the fund, Eisenhower exclaimed: "That's my boy."

In the McCarthy episode, the general was persuaded to delete from a campaign speech a defense of General of the Army George C. Marshall, his Army mentor, whom Senator McCarthy had impugned as a traitor. Political advisers had told Eisenhower that he needed McCarthy's support to win the election.

These incidents seem not to have aroused adverse voter reaction, for Eisenhower polled 33,936,252 popular votes and 442 votes in the Electoral College; Stevenson received 27,314,992 popular votes and 89 electoral votes.

Significantly, Eisenhower's "crusade" (as he called it) carried four states of the Old Confederacy, a Democratic stronghold for generations. But the vote there, as elsewhere, was a personal tribute. The Republican edge in Congress was slight, and it vanished altogether in 1954 and 1956, indicating how far, in the voters' minds, the general stood above party.

Eisenhower began his first term in January, 1953, as a symbol of international goodwill as well as of national high purpose. He had traveled to Korea, where a truce was soon effected, bringing back thousands of servicemen. At home the government climate was benign and the press was friendly, even protective, as a seeming new era opened.

Even the political opposition struck at the men around the President rather than at Eisenhower himself. John Foster Dulles in the State Department and Ezra Taft Benson in Agriculture were popular targets between 1953 and 1957.

Oddly, Old Guard Republicans, long entrenched in Congress, were among the most vocal critics, because the first Republican Administration in 20 years did not make a clean break with the New and Fair Deals. The Old Guard objected when the Administration eased credit, abandoned efforts to balance the budget and, in addition to letting $5-billion in Korean War taxes lapse, sanctioned a further tax reduction of $2.4-billion. On top of this, the Administration put through an extension of insurance coverage under Social Security and accepted a minimum wage of $1 an hour, up from 75 cents.

It was the Democrats who gave Eisenhower the votes he required to pass key legislation.

In his conduct of the White House the new President introduced the staff concept, under which the workload was distributed among associates. Sherman Adams, a former New Hampshire Governor, headed the staff with the title "The Assistant to the President." Despite some initial creaking, the system worked smoothly, especially late in the first term when the President was twice stricken with serious illness.

Eisenhower attached great importance to business success, a fact evident from the many representatives of big business named to his Cabinet and other key posts. It was a standing joke that his first Cabinet was composed of "eight millionaires and a plumber." Perhaps significantly, the first to depart was the plumber, Martin P. Durkin, who resigned within a year as Secretary of Labor. He said the President had reneged on a promise to press for revision of the Taft-Hartley Act, which restricted the union shop.

At least three businessmen named to Cabinet-level posts—Charles E. Wilson, George M. Humphrey and Harold E. Talbott—were subjected to Senatorial questioning on their investments and on possible conflicts of interest between their official and business lives. Talbott, Secretary of the Air Force, later resigned over such charges.

What's Good for Business

Throughout, the President was irritated by suggestions that his policies favored business at the expense of other segments of the population. He firmly believed that what was good for business was good for the nation.

His contention seemed borne out by the economic boom that began in mid-1954 and continued through the rest of the first term. Because prosperous times followed a mild recession in 1953, tax concessions to business seemed all the more vindicated.

Under Eisenhower, the nation maintained its international leadership even if, at times, its course seemed uncertain and erratic. The Administration had high hopes that, with the Korean truce, psychological warfare would give the West an ascendancy in the battle of ideologies. But when Stalin died in 1953, and again when revolt flared three years later in Hungary and elsewhere behind the Iron Curtain, there was no master plan ready to capitalize on developments.

Yet Eisenhower's atoms-for-peace proposal, made before the United Nations in 1953, and his open skies inspection plan, presented at the summit conference in Geneva in 1955, contributed markedly toward relaxation of world tensions and a more hopeful outlook.

Although the promise of the Geneva conference, attended by Eisenhower, Soviet Premier Nikolai A. Bulganin, French Premier Edgar Fauré and British Prime Minister Anthony Eden, never fully materialized, the meeting did produce a tacit understanding that nuclear war would be avoided.

The neutral and nonaligned powers, notably India, liked Eisenhower's thinking in these areas. This was significant because other policies of this nation perturbed the neutrals. They did not agree that the cause of peace was being served by the ring of defensive alliances drawn around the Soviet bloc on the United States initiative. Among these was the Southeast Asia Treaty Organization, an alliance set up late in 1954 upon French withdrawal from Indochina.

A Pledge to Vietnam

At that time Eisenhower also wrote a letter to the Diem Government of South Vietnam, vaguely pledging United States economic and arms assistance. That letter, scarcely noticed at the time, was later used to justify massive American military involvement in Vietnam.

Although an uneasy détente existed in Europe, tension prevailed in the Orient, especially between the Peoples Republic of China and the Nationalist regime on Taiwan. This reached a high point in 1955, when the Communists seemed ready to strike at the offshore island. In a dramatic step, Eisenhower asked Congress to underwrite his authority to use American armed force "if necessary to assure the security" of Taiwan.

Many believed that the resolution, overwhelmingly approved, kept Communist China from moving against Quemoy and Matsu, Nationalist-held islands off China, because of uncertainty as to how the United States would react.

Karsh, Ottawa

OTHER HONORS AHEAD: Popular as the Allied leader in World War II, he went on to win the Presidency.

In some areas the United States found itself in trade-and-aid competition with the Soviet Union. Middle East developments in 1955 pointed up the extent of this rivalry. The West, jolted by an Egyptian arms purchase from the Soviet bloc, was drawn into the bidding to finance the Aswan High Dam that the United Arab Republic wanted to build on the Nile. Midway in 1956 the West pulled out of the bidding and in a matter of days the U.A.R. seized the Suez Canal.

Tensions mounted as negotiations failed to produce a formula for operation of the waterway, and by fall events were moving swiftly. After Israeli forces entered Egypt, Britain and France threatened on Oct. 30, 1956, to intervene if the fighting was not halted promptly. With world attention divided between the Mideast and Hungary, in the throes of upheaval, the U.A.R. balked, and Anglo-French forces took action. The conflict was speedily taken to the United Nations, where, in the voting for a cease-fire, the United States sided with the Soviet Union against France and Britain.

The U.A.R. came out of the struggle triumphant. Invasion forces were obliged to withdraw under United Nations pressure; the U.A.R. retained the Suez Canal, and financing for the Aswan Dam was arranged with the Soviet Union.

To many Americans, however, events abroad seemed remote in those years. Anxieties centered rather on the President, who suffered two major illnesses toward the end of his first term.

The first, on Sept. 24, 1955, was diagnosed as a coronary thrombosis, a clot in the artery of the heart. It sent the President to the hospital for seven weeks. The second occurred eight and a half months later, on June 8, 1956, and was diagnosed as ileitis, an inflammation of the lower part of the small intestine. Eisenhower underwent a successful operation the next day to bypass the ileum, which was obstructing the intestinal tract.

The President was on vacation in Denver when his heart attack occurred. He had just returned to the home of his mother-in-law, Mrs. John S. Doud, from a four-day fishing trip in the Rockies. After complaining of indigestion and intense chest pain, he was taken to the Fitzsimmons Army Hospital in Denver. Heart specialists were called in, including Dr. Paul Dudley White of Boston, who described the attack as "moderate." The patient was cleared to leave the hospital Nov. 10, and he flew to Washington the following day, "happy that the doctors have given me a parole if not a pardon."

Throughout the illness the public was kept minutely informed of the President's progress and of the fact that, with his staff, he continued to direct affairs of state. In these tasks he was aided by Vice President Nixon as well as by Sherman Adams. Despite the smoothness with which the President made decisions and despite the general uneventfulness of his recovery, speculation arose on his availability for a second term.

After being pronounced medically fit by Dr. White, the President consulted earnestly with his closest advisers. They unanimously favored a second term, telling him it was his duty to continue working for peace if his health permitted. This advice led to Eisenhower's announcement on Feb. 29, 1956, that he would run again.

The ileitis attack, coming in June, cast momentary doubt on Eisenhower's candidacy, but a routine recovery from three-hour surgery at the Walter Reed Army Medical Center in Washington relieved public apprehensions. The Republicans renominated him along with Nixon as his running mate.

A Limited Campaign

Eisenhower, at the peak of his popularity, conducted a restricted campaign in which he stood on his record of peace and prosperity. He made a limited number of radio and television speeches and undertook only two campaign swings that kept him away from the capital overnight.

Stevenson, again the Democratic choice, hammered away at the "breakdown of leadership," at domestic and foreign policies that were "stalled on dead center" and at a "part-time President." He inveighed against a Cabinet representative of "the larger interests" and, with references to "the heir apparent," sought to increase the misgivings of some about Nixon.

"Why this anguished cry of some politicians that we have no peace?" Eisenhower asked in the face of attacks on his foreign policy. Countering the charge of undue big-business influence, he demanded to know whether government affairs should be entrusted to "some failure . . . or a successful businessman." He insisted that his Administration had brought "sense and order" to Washington.

Developments in the Middle East in October, touched off by the Israeli march into Egypt and the Anglo-French thrust at Suez, unquestionably helped Eisenhower with the voters, for his quick response to those events put the United States on the side of peace.

The election results gave him 35,582,236 votes, a record up to that time, and 457 electoral votes, including those of five Southern states. Stevenson's popular vote was 26,031,322, his electoral total 73.

Difficult and fateful problems at home, abroad and in space confronted Eisenhower in his second term.

Economic Troubles

There was mob violence over school integration in the South, and in September, 1957, the President was obliged to send troops to Little Rock, Ark., to enforce court-ordered school desegregation.

Business slumped sharply in the winter of 1957-58, and only slowly recovered. By July, 1959, when a steel strike dealt the economy another stinging blow, employment still had not recovered. The national debt climbed higher than ever.

The Soviet Union achieved a stunning scientific success, with strong military implications, when it orbited the first man-made earth satellite in October, 1957.

With the collapse of the second summit conference, in May, 1960, the perilous stalemate between the Soviet Union and the West over Berlin continued.

Tensions in the Far East reached a peak a month later when the President, in the middle of a trip through the area, was forced to cancel a visit to Japan because of anti-American rioting there.

The widening rift between Cuba and the United States brought economic reprisals on both sides and a threat of Soviet intervention that led Eisenhower to declare that he would never "permit the establishment of a regime dominated by international Communism in the Western Hemisphere."

And in the Middle East a policy designed to promote stability did not prevent the decline of Western influence through civil war in Lebanon and revolution in Iraq.

The demands of the times would have taxed the energy of the healthiest of men, and they were especially heavy for Eisenhower on account of his heart attack and his bout of ileitis. His health was further compromised Nov. 25, 1957, when he suffered an occlusion of a small branch of the middle cerebral artery on the left side. He was left with a mild aphasia (difficulty in speaking) and he was not pronounced recovered from the stroke until March 1, 1958.

Eisenhower sought to preserve his strength and health by daily rests, week-

Associated Press

CANDIDATE: His great personal political success was manifest in the triumphant reception accorded him in Detroit in 1952, when he appeared as the Republican Presidential candidate. The button became a byword.

ends at his farm at Gettysburg, Pa., and periodic golfing holidays. Although public concern over his physical condition was intense, the President's popularity, as measured by public-opinion polls, began a perceptible decline soon after he took his second oath of office in January, 1957.

Large sections of the Republican party's conservative wing were alienated early in 1957 when Eisenhower submitted a $71.8-billion budget, the largest in peacetime history. One of the first to protest was George M. Humphrey, the industrialist who was Secretary of the Treasury. He retired six months later and was succeeded by Robert B. Anderson, a former deputy secretary of defense.

Congress, under Democratic leadership in both houses despite Eisenhower's sweep, did not hesitate to revise the President's legislative program, although it avoided, as had other Congresses, narrow partisanship.

It agreed with Eisenhower on the essentials of foreign aid and extension of the reciprocal trade program; it differed on Defense Department reorganization, and it took the initiative in measures to meet the recession of 1957-58 and the Soviet space challenge.

After Russia orbited its first satellite, a Senate committee under Lyndon B. Johnson of Texas, the Democratic leader, called for a speed-up of United States space programs; but it was not until Feb. 1, 1958, that the President was able to announce the launching of an American satellite, a puny device compared to the Russians' sputnik. In the years that followed, with the illusion of American technological superiority shattered, there was growing criticism of the United States space program.

On the domestic scene the President faced a direct challenge to Federal authority that grew out of resistance to the Supreme Court's ruling, in 1954, that racial segregation in the public schools was unconstitutional.

Riots in Little Rock

Gov. Orval E. Faubus of Arkansas called out the Arkansas National Guard in September, 1957, to prevent Negro students from entering the Little Rock Central High School. When a Federal District Court injunction forced him to withdraw the Guard, rioting broke out and the Negroes had to leave school.

Eisenhower ordered Federal troops to Little Rock, where they restored order. In this crisis Eisenhower spoke up for obedience to Federal law and the courts, but he avoided a direct commitment to the morality of integration.

During 1957, however, he signed the first major bill since Reconstruction to protect the constitutional rights of minorities. The bill created a Civil Rights Commission to investigate denials of minority rights.

Although the President's handling of the explosive Little Rock situation was applauded in the North and West, his prestige generally dropped with the downturn in the national economy. Starting late in 1957 and accelerating in 1958, the slump brought to an end the period of high employment and prosperity that marked Eisenhower's first term.

Some observers attributed the decline of Eisenhower's influence to his being the first President whose tenure was limited to two terms by the 22d Amendment. Others felt that the President was delegating too many of his functions to subordinates.

This view appeared to be reinforced in the summer of 1958 when Adams, the stern Assistant to the President who presided over the White House offices, came under investigation for alleged intervention with Federal agencies in behalf of his friends.

The New York Times

WITH KHRUSHCHEV: The President greeting Soviet Premier in 1959.

Much of the disenchantment that had been building up against the Administration seemed to culminate in criticism of Adams, one of Eisenhower's closest friends and associates. The President tried to ignore the criticism, insisting that Adams would remain on his staff because "I need him." But Adams resigned anyway on Sept. 22, 1958.

In the elections that November the Republicans lost 47 House seats and 13 of 21 contested Senate seats. The Democrats controlled Congress by the widest margins since the Roosevelt landslide of 1936.

Few realized it until well afterward, but the elections were the nadir of Eisenhower's political fortunes. The turning point had been the resignation of Adams, for thereafter the President began to take an ever-increasing role in national affairs. By the spring of 1959 some observers were talking about "the new Ike," while others insisted that it was only the re-emergence of the old Ike who had so fired the country's imagination in 1952.

One evidence of this change was a firmer attitude toward Congress. In September, 1959, he vetoed a $1.2-billion public works bill, citing a need for Federal economy. The veto was overridden, as was his veto of a bill to raise Federal employes' pay in the summer of 1960. The issue here was also economy. The essence of "the new Ike" was that he took a position and defended it with some vigor.

A second evidence of change was in the field of personal diplomacy and involved a visit to the United States by Premier Nikita S. Khrushchev of the Soviet Union in September, 1959. Although in later years Eisenhower disclosed that the Khrushchev visit had been authorized through a misunderstanding of his instructions by the State Department, he made the most of it at the time by inviting the Russian leader to the White House and to Camp David, the President's weekend retreat in Maryland. These informal talks resulted in what was termed "the spirit of Camp David," a thaw in the cold war between the United States and Russia in which peaceful coexistence was to replace bellicosity.

The Camp David spirit persisted until May, 1960, when a summit meeting in Paris was blasted by the disclosure that the United States was using a U-2 photo-reconnaissance plane over the Soviet Union.

Ten days before the summit meeting was to convene on May 5, Khrushchev announced that an American plane had been shot down over the Soviet Union. He withheld details. That night, in Washington, the National Aeronautics and Space Administration said that the pilot of a weather plane missing since May 1 had reported oxygen difficulties about an hour after takeoff. This, according to the agency, might have caused the Pakistan-based plane to stray over the Russian border.

The following day the Soviet Union said that the U-2 had been shot down by "a remarkable rocket." Meanwhile, the State Department unequivocally denied any "deliberate attempt to violate Soviet air space."

This denial had scarcely been made when the Russians produced Francis Gary Powers, the U-2 pilot, and the confession that he had been on a spying mission across Russian territory from Pakistan to Norway.

Moscow's revelations forced Washington to admit that it had engaged in U-2 espionage for the last four years. For this Eisenhower took full responsibility.

The upshot of the episode was to reflect on the President and his sincerity as a partner in the Camp David spirit. Thus, when he reached Paris May 15, he was on the defensive. but sought to make the most of it. "Far too much is at stake," he said, "to indulge the passions of the moment or to engage in profitless bickering."

His appeal was in vain, for Khrushchev demanded that the United States end its U-2 project, ban future flights and punish those "directly guilty." Angered by the Soviet leader's heavy-handedness, Eisenhower made only one concession, saying the espionage flights had been suspended and "are not to be resumed."

Collapse at the Summit

The summit meeting died the next day, as Khrushchev continued his attacks on the United States and refused to take part in a meeting with Eisenhower. His unrelenting recalcitrance tended, however, to shift sympathy to Eisenhower.

It was clear, nevertheless, that the last chance had gone for the President, in the final months of his term, to strengthen hopes for peace in line with the spirit of the first summit meeting at Geneva in 1955 and the Khrushchev visit to America in 1959.

Although Eisenhower regained a measure of popularity in the campaign of 1960 and spoke for the candidacy of Nixon, his Vice President, it was not enough to carry the country. The Eisenhower "magic" was his alone, and Senator John F. Kennedy of Massachusetts ended the eight-year Republican rule of the White House. Eisenhower stepped down Jan. 20, 1961.

Three days earlier, Eisenhower delivered a televised farewell address to the American people that contained a warning that has echoed down through the years.

Noting that a vast military establishment and a huge arms industry had developed in the United States, Eisenhower said:

"In the councils of government, we must guard against the acquisition of unwarranted influence, whether sought or unsought, by the military-industrial complex. The potential for the disastrous rise of misplaced power exists and will persist."

United Press International

RE-ELECTION: At the peak of his popularity in 1956, he won easily. Here, he cheered the victory in Washington with his wife and Vice President and Mrs. Richard M. Nixon.

A Farm Boy Becomes a General

DWIGHT D. EISENHOWER was born in Denison, Tex., on Oct. 14, 1890. He was of German descent. His ancestors belonged to evangelical groups from which evolved the Mennonite sect. Subjected to religious persecution, some of the family had emigrated from Bavaria to Switzerland in the 17th century.

The first Eisenhowers came to America from Switzerland in 1732. They settled in Pennsylvania, first at York and later at Elizabethville, near Harrisburg. They helped establish a Mennonite branch called Brethren of Christ. It also was known as the River Brethren because its members lived near the Susquehanna.

As Mennonites the Eisenhowers believed in plainness of dress, nonresistance and nonjuring. However, they put on the uniform of the Continental Army in the Revolutionary War and the Union Army in the Civil War.

In 1878 the Rev. Jacob Eisenhower, farmer and merchant, with other River Brethren, followed the covered-wagon trail west to Kansas. He settled on a 160-acre farm near Abilene. His son David, who was born in Elizabethville, Pa., was married in 1885 to Ida Elizabeth Stover of Mount Sydney, Va., in the United Brethren Church at Lecompton, Kan. In later life she joined Jehovah's Witnesses, another religious denomination.

David Eisenhower failed in grocery and banking ventures in Kansas. He then moved to Texas, where he got a job as mechanic in the Cotton Belt Railroad shops at Denison. With him went his wife and the first two of their seven sons.

The future President, their third son, was born in a house near the railroad yards. He was christened David Dwight Eisenhower and is so listed in the family Bible. His mother, however, reversed the order and called him Dwight David. This was partly to distinguish him from David his father and partly to avoid the nickname "Dave."

In 1892, when Dwight was 2 years old, the family returned to Abilene. The father got a job in a creamery and moved his family into a small house on East Fourth Street, with an adjoining two-and-one-half-acre farm.

One of Dwight's brothers died in infancy. The six remaining boys took turns getting up at dawn to build the kitchen fire and get breakfast started. They took care of the chickens and the garden. They milked the cow and sold farm products from door to door. They did odd jobs, and sometimes worked at the creamery with their father.

Even in grade school, Dwight's teachers were impressed with the engaging grin that became his political trademark. At high school, from which he was graduated in 1909, he showed a liking for history, military history and biography, mathematics and athletics.

After high school he at first had no definite idea of what he wanted to do. He worked in the creamery and at other jobs. These included hauling ice and loading wagons. He played semi-professional baseball, too.

His father could not afford to send him to college. The youth, however, took competitive examinations for both the United States Military Academy at West Point and the Naval Academy at Annapolis.

He finished first in the Annapolis and second in the West Point examinations. He received an appointment to Annapolis only to discover that he would be several months past the age limit of 20 when the next academy year started. But the high man on the West Point list was unable to accept his appointment and it went to Dwight. He entered the Military Academy on July 1, 1911.

At West Point, Cadet Eisenhower won his Army "A" in baseball and football. He was regarded as one of the most promising backs in the East until his playing career was halted after he wrenched his knee badly in a game with Tufts College and then, soon afterwards, twisted it again riding horseback.

He was graduated with a standing of 61st in a class of 164. Neither his scholastic record nor his deportment was of the best, though he was in the upper half of the class scholastically. A steady shower of demerits had rained down on him throughout his entire four years at the Point.

He was graduated with a "clean sleeve," being neither a cadet officer nor noncommissioned officer.

His first assignment, as a second lieutenant, was with the 19th Infantry at Fort Sam Houston, San Antonio, Tex. At a dinner-dance there in October, 1915, he met Mamie Geneva Doud, daughter of Mr. and Mrs. John Doud of Denver, who was visiting friends.

A Persistent Suitor

Lieutenant Eisenhower asked for a date and was told to call back in a month. Instead, he began calling the next day, every 15 minutes. He got a date that evening and appeared four hours early. By December they were engaged. The couple were married in Denver July 1, 1916.

The Eisenhowers had two sons, the first dying in infancy. The second son, John Sheldon Doud Eisenhower, was born in 1922. He went to West Point and became an Army officer. He saw service in Europe in World War II and later in Korea. He married Barbara Jean Thompson. They gave the Eisenhowers four grandchildren—Dwight David 2d, born in 1948; Barbara Anne, 1949; Susan Elaine, 1951, and Mary Jean, 1955.

The future President served at Fort Sam Houston from Sept. 13, 1915, until May 28, 1917.

He did not get overseas in World War I. From Fort Sam Houston he went to the 57th Infantry at Leon Springs, Tex., as regimental supply officer. He served there until Sept. 18, 1917.

He was promoted to captain May 15, 1917; to the temporary rank of major June 17, 1918, and to the temporary rank of lieutenant colonel Oct. 14, 1918.

After leaving the 57th Infantry he served as an instructor at the Officers Training Camp at Fort Oglethorpe, Ga., to Dec. 12, 1917, and as instructor at the Army Service Schools, Fort Leavenworth, Kan., to Feb. 28, 1918.

He organized the 65th Battalion Engineers at Camp Meade, Md., and remained there until March 24, 1918; commanded the Camp Colt tank training center at Gettysburg, Pa., until Nov. 18, 1918; commanded Tank Corps troops at Camp Dix, N. J., to Dec. 22, 1918, and at Fort Benning, Ga., to March 15, 1919.

For his World War I services he received the Distinguished Service Medal.

After the war he was reduced to the permanent rank of captain on June 30, 1920, but was promoted to the permanent rank of major July 2.

From Fort Benning he was ordered to Fort Meade, Md. There he was graduated from Infantry Tank School.

First in His Class

He then sailed for the Panama Canal Zone. There he served as executive officer at Camp Gaillard to Sept. 19, 1924.

He was recruiting officer at Fort Logan, Colo., until Aug. 19, 1925. Then came an opportunity that helped transform an ordinary military career into a distinguished one. He was sent to the Army's Command and General Staff School at Fort Leavenworth. He completed the course with honors in June, 1926, standing first among 275 selected Army officers.

Next he joined the 24th Infantry at Fort Benning Aug. 15, 1926. He was transferred to Washington Jan. 15, 1927, for service with the American Battle Monuments Commission until Aug. 15, 1927.

He was graduated from the Army War College in Washington June 30, 1928, and returned to duty with the American Battle Monuments Commission.

From Nov. 8, 1929, to Feb. 20, 1933, he was assistant executive officer of the Assistant Secretary of War in Washington. In that period he was graduated from the Army Industrial College.

In 1930 an official paper he wrote attracted the attention of Gen. Douglas MacArthur, then the Army's Chief of Staff.

The future President served in the Chief of Staff's office in Washington until Sept. 24, 1935, and then sailed to Manila as a member of the American Military Mission and assistant to General MacArthur as military adviser of the Commonwealth Government of the Philippine Islands.

On July 1, 1936, Major Eisenhower was promoted to the permanent rank of lieutenant colonel. He returned to the United States in 1939, after the outbreak of World War II in Europe.

He joined the 15th Infantry at Fort Ord, Calif., in February, 1940, and a few weeks later accompanied this regiment to Fort Lewis, Wash.

On March 11, 1941, he was promoted to the temporary rank of colonel. He was assigned as chief of staff to the Third Army, San Antonio, Tex., on June 24, 1941. He was promoted to the temporary rank of brigadier general on Sept. 29, 1941.

On Dec. 14, 1941, seven days after the Japanese attacked Pearl Harbor, Gen. George C. Marshall, then the Army's Chief of Staff, called Eisenhower to Washington.

Although he had never commanded troops in battle, he was recognized as a specialist in operations planning and organization. He also had made a reputation as a tactician in the large-scale Louisiana maneuvers of 1941. In this capacity, as well as in others, he impressed General Marshall, who sponsored his Army advancements.

Eisenhower was named Chief of the War Plans Division, General Staff, Feb. 16, 1942. When the division was reorganized and renamed he became Chief of Operations for the Army. He was promoted to the temporary rank of major general on March 27, 1942.

In the spring of 1942 he was sent to London to make a survey and recommendations on organization and development of United States forces in the European Theater of Operations. On returning to Washington, he submitted a draft directive for the Commanding General, E.T.O., and recommended another general to carry it out.

General Marshall approved the directive but named Eisenhower to the E.T.O. command to put his own plan into effect. On June 25, 1942, Eisenhower was designated Commanding General, E.T.O., with headquarters in London.

He flew to London, set up headquarters at Norfolk House and in July began planning the invasion of French North Africa. He was promoted to the temporary rank of lieutenant general July 7, 1942.

One of his chief objectives was to encourage harmony among British, French and United States officers at headquarters. Relations with the British and French had to be handled delicately. A story widely circulated at the time emphasized his determination to achieve this aim.

A United States colonel became involved in a quarrel with a British general. The colonel was called on the carpet before Eisenhower, who told him:

"I think you have the right of the argument. You called the general a so-and-so and I can understand that, too. But unfortunately you called him a British so-and-so, and for that I am sending you home."

On the eve of the North African invasion Eisenhower flew to Gibraltar, a central command post, to direct the troop landings at Casablanca, Oran and Algiers on Nov. 7. The following day he was named Allied Commander in Chief, North Africa, commanding British, French and United States forces. On Nov. 22 he transferred his headquarters to Algiers.

There he found that Gen. Henri-Honoré Giraud, tentative choice to command the French forces, was being ignored by French military commanders and colonial administrators. They were

Associated Press

MARRIAGE: Lieutenant Eisenhower and his bride, the former Mamie Doud, shortly after wedding July 1, 1916. The ceremony was held at the Doud home in Denver.

Monkmeyer

IN THE FAMILY GROUP: The future President Dwight Eisenhower was 10 years old when he posed, left, with his parents and brothers. Between Mr. and Mrs. David Eisenhower were Milton, with curls, and Earl. In the rear row, from the left: Edgar, Arthur and Roy. At this time the Eisenhowers were living on a small farm in Abilene, Kan., where the family had moved from Denison, Tex., Dwight's birthplace. His mother was the former Ida Stover.

Associated Press

FAMOUS SON: General Eisenhower, back from victory in Europe, with his mother at her Abilene home in 1945.

maintaining loyalty to Adm. Jean François Darlan.

Admiral Darlan had been in command of all French naval forces at the start of the war. After the collapse of French military resistance, he became Vice Premier of the Vichy regime that ruled France as a puppet of Nazi Germany.

Vichy named him Commander in Chief of all French forces, and he was in North Africa at the time of the invasion. Captured in Algiers, he ordered French forces in Algeria and Morocco to cease resistance. He was then recognized by the Allies as High Commissioner of French North Africa.

This arrangement brought criticism upon Eisenhower. He took full responsibility for it and defended it as a military necessity. He emphasized that it avoided fighting between Anglo-American and French forces, spared thousands of lives, and insured the success of the landings.

Support at the Top

President Franklin D. Roosevelt and Prime Minister Winston Churchill upheld Eisenhower. The incident, however, provoked a worldwide controversy. In the midst of it Admiral Darlan was assassinated by a French youth in Algiers on Christmas Eve, 1942.

The fighting in North Africa at first went badly for the Allies. Field Marshal Bernard Law Montgomery was backing the German general, Erwin Rommel, and his dreaded Afrika Korps across Libya into Tunisia, but Allied dispositions for a quick victory by attacking the rear of the retreating foes were faulty. United States troops were green and their commanders untried.

After the Allied defeat at Kasserine Pass, Eisenhower relieved Maj. Gen. Lloyd R. Fredenall, ranking United States commander in the field.

Eisenhower was promoted to the temporary rank of full general on Feb. 11, 1943. But until the end of the campaign he was uncertain whether he himself might not be replaced. In his book, "Crusade in Europe," after relating the removal of General Fredenall in July, he added: "Several others, myself included, shared responsibility for our week of reverses."

But the tide turned. In May, 1943, the mass surrender of German and Italian forces in Tunisia brought Eisenhower's first military campaign to a successful end. The Afrika Korps was routed and North Africa was liberated.

Eisenhower then directed the invasions of Sicily and Italy. Though the invasion of Italy did not force the Germans out of Italy, it did force the Italians out of the war. Eisenhower was promoted to the permanent rank of brigadier general and major general both on the same day, Aug. 30, 1943. He received the Oak Leaf Cluster to be added to the Distinguished Service Medal he had won in World War I.

Fall of Sicily and Italy

In a sustained campaign of 38 days, Eisenhower directed the combined operations leading to the conquest of Sicily and reduced Italy to a state of military impotence.

President Roosevelt personally decorated him with the medal of the Legion of Merit. Announcing Eisenhower's selection in December, 1943, as Supreme Allied Commander for the invasion of Western Europe, President Roosevelt said:

"The performances in Africa, Sicily and Italy have been brilliant. He knows by practical and successful experience the way to coordinate air, sea and land power."

On Dec. 10, 1943, Eisenhower first learned that he was to be chosen to command the invasion of Western Europe. On June 6, 1944, he directed the landings on the Normandy beaches in France. In between, he had devoted every waking moment to planning the long-awaited second front.

In his planning he had to make two vital decisions. The first dealt with an airborne operation to precede the landings. He planned to drop two United States divisions in a massed paratroop and glider assault onto the Cherbourg Peninsula in the early morning of D-Day.

Their task was to support the assault forces who were to cross the English Channel by boat and land on the Normandy beaches.

Two days before D-Day, at Eisenhower's advance command post near Portsmouth, the great British naval base by the English Channel, his air adviser, Air Chief Marshal Sir Trafford Leigh-Mallory, strongly urged against the airborne operation. He held that it could not succeed and might invite a massacre.

Eisenhower, in "Crusade in Europe," related what an ordeal it was to have to make this decision.

"It would be difficult to conceive of a more soul-racking problem," he wrote. "If my technical expert was correct, then the planned operation was worse than stubborn folly, because even at the enormous cost predicted we could not gain the principal object. . . . I took the problem to no one else. Professional advice and counsel could do no more. I went to my tent alone and sat down to think."

His decision was to take the calculated risk. Although the two divisions were badly mauled, and many of the troops were dropped by mistake into a marsh, the operation was credited with creating confusion behind German lines at the time the invasion forces were landing.

After the war, Eisenhower was asked what he considered the greatest moment of his military career. He replied, "When I got word that the 82d and 101st Airborne Divisions had landed on the Cherbourg Peninsula."

Gamble on the Weather

The second great decision that Eisenhower alone had to make was whether to postpone the invasion because of bad weather. It already had been postponed once.

First scheduled for June 5, it was delayed for 24 hours because of a weather forecast of an approaching storm. The weather prediction still looked bad for June 6, and some of Eisenhower's advisers recommended another postponement until the weather was favorable.

But Eisenhower had studied meteorology to learn how to interpret weather reports himself. He decided to go ahead. The silent travail he underwent in making this decision has been described by Lieut. Gen. Walter Bedell Smith, then his chief of staff. Writing in The Saturday Evening Post after the war, General Smith related:

"The silence lasted for five full minutes while General Eisenhower sat on a sofa before a bookcase that filled the end of the room. I never realized before the loneliness and isolation of a commander at a time when a momentous decision has to be taken, with full knowledge that the failure or success rests on his judgment alone. He sat there quietly, not getting up to pace with quick strides as he often does. He was tense, weighing every consideration. . . . Finally he looked up and tension was gone from his face. He said briskly, 'Well, we'll go.'"

It turned out that Eisenhower had selected the right day and hour for the invasion from a weather standpoint. Weather conditions still were far from favorable as the assault craft shoved off. Heavy swells on the Channel beset the troops with seasickness. Yet they were able to complete the landings.

On the night before the invasion, Eisenhower spent much of his time with the troops. He walked among them from

Associated Press

AT MacARTHUR'S RECALL: General Eisenhower was in Germany in 1951 when he heard that President Truman had relieved General Douglas MacArthur in Korea.

group to group, talking with them and patting them on the back.

Eisenhower rapidly built up reserves of troops, ammunition, armor and supplies in France. On July 25, the United States First Army under Lieut. Gen. Omar N. Bradley achieved the St. Lo breakthrough from the beachheads.

This success allowed Lieut. Gen. George S. Patton's Third Army to get loose for its spectacular drive inland. Between them, the First and Third Armies destroyed a major part of Field Marshal Guenther von Kluge's Seventh Army. This was ground to pieces in the Falaise pocket.

As the Allied forces swept the Germans out of France, Paris was liberated. On Aug. 27 Eisenhower flew there behind the liberating forces of the French general Jacques Le Clerc. He then moved his own headquarters from London to Versailles, near Paris.

On German Soil

Eisenhower, meanwhile, planned and directed the invasion of Southern France, beginning two months after D-Day in Normandy.

By September the Allied invasion from the west had reached German soil and was battering against the strongly fortified Siegfried Line.

Eisenhower was elevated by President Roosevelt to the temporary rank of General of the Army on Dec. 20, 1944. This five-star rank was established by Congress in World War II.

About this time the Allied campaign met a serious but temporary reverse. Just before Christmas, 1944, Field Marshal Karl von Rundstedt opened a surprise counteroffensive into Belgium and Luxembourg. In their last desperate drive, the German troops broke through a weak point in the United States lines and plunged deep into the Ardennes Forest. This became known as the Battle of the Bulge.

Eisenhower then was faced with a difficult decision comparable to those of D-Day. Field Marshal Montgomery, commanding the British forces north of the Bulge, was separated by it from General Bradley, commanding United States forces to the south.

Though Eisenhower knew his decision would be unpopular with his American subordinates, he unhesitatingly placed Field Marshal Montgomery in temporary command of all troops in the northern part of the Bulge, including American forces that had been under Bradley's command.

The Nazis then were gradually beaten back and the Bulge was wiped out.

The end followed quickly on the German defeat in the Bulge. Eisenhower rallied his armies and sent them crashing across the Rhine for the final campaign. In the spring of 1945 his troops took 317,000 prisoners and broke the back of German resistance in the Ruhr.

March 7, 1945, was a day always remembered by Eisenhower as "one of the happiest of my life." On that day General Bradley telephoned him that German bungling in their failure to blow up the Ludendorf Bridge over the Rhine at Remagen, in the United States sector of the front, had resulted in its capture intact.

The capture of the bridge was one of the turning points in the latter phase of the war. To exploit it Eisenhower quickly changed his plans. He decided to make his first thrust across the Rhine there instead of in the British sector. He ordered General Bradley to rush every available man and gun across the bridge before the Germans could destroy it.

On April 23, United States troops met the Russians in the Torgau area on the Elbe River. The Allies smashing from the west and the Russians from the east had crushed Hitler's once mighty legions. They also had reduced German cities to rubble by air and artillery bombardment.

The unconditional surrender of Germany was accepted by Eisenhower on May 7, 1945. When Gen. Alfred Jodl of the German Army arrived at Allied advance headquarters in a schoolhouse at Rheims, France, Eisenhower put General Smith in charge of the ceremonies and absented himself from the room.

Jodl signed the surrender document before General Smith and other Allied officers. He then was led down the hall to Eisenhower's office.

The German entered the room, clicked his heels and raised his field marshal's baton in salute. In "Crusade in Europe," Eisenhower wrote of this scene:

"I asked him through the interpreter if he thoroughly understood all provisions of the document he had signed.

"He answered, 'Ja.'

"I said, 'You will, officially and personally, be held responsible if the terms of this surrender are violated, including its provisions for German commanders to appear in Berlin at the moment set by the Russian High Command to accomplish formal surrender to that Government. That is all.'

"He saluted and left."

An Associated Press correspondent described the scene as follows:

"General Eisenhower's famous smile was absent. There was a moment of heavy silence. Then General Eisenhower spoke.

"He was brief and terse as always. His voice was cold and hard. In a few clipped sentences he made it plain that Germany was a defeated nation and that henceforth all orders to the German people would come from the Allies. He said they would be obeyed.

"Then the Germans filed out. It was over. Nazi Germany had ceased to exist. The war had ended."

Within a few weeks of the German surrender, Eisenhower was invited to Moscow by Premier Josef Stalin and he reviewed a victory parade from the top of Lenin's tomb.

He received Russia's highest award, the jeweled Order of Victory. This never before had been presented to a non-Russian. Only seven Russians ever had received it. He also was the first foreign general to receive Russia's highest military decoration, the Order of Suvarov.

The other Allied nations also heaped honors upon him. In London, at Buckingham Palace, King George VI invested him with the Order of Merit. He was the first United States soldier ever to receive this decoration.

In Paris more than one million persons thronged the streets through which he rode in a triumphal procession. In a ceremony before the Tomb of the Unknown Soldier, Gen. Charles de Gaulle, leader of the French Resistance against the Nazis, conferred upon him the title "Fellow of the Liberation."

The general received a series of enthusiastic welcomes in the United States. At Washington on June 18 more than one million persons turned out in the streets for him. Congress praised him in joint session.

The next day New York gave him a roaring welcome, with ticker-tape parade, a reception at City Hall and a dinner at the Waldorf-Astoria Hotel. The police estimated that four million persons had lined the streets to see him.

At West Point there was another hearty welcome for the general. The celebrations ended with ceremonies in Abilene, Kan., where he had spent his boyhood.

Eisenhower then returned to Europe for a short tour of duty as commander of the United States occupation forces and Military Governor of the United States-occupied zone in Germany, with headquarters at Frankfurt. He was recalled to the United States to succeed Gen. George C. Marshall on Nov. 20, 1945, as the Army's Chief of Staff.

On April 11, 1946, Eisenhower was promoted to the permanent five-star rank of General of the Army. He served as Chief of Staff until Feb. 7, 1948. He retired from the Army on May 2 of that year, taking what he believed to be his farewell salute.

In and Out at Columbia

On June 7, 1948, he became president of Columbia University. While there, however, he was called back into uniform on several occasions. The general served as temporary chairman of the Joint Chiefs of Staff under the unification program.

Eisenhower's final leave of absence from Columbia came in 1950. By that time the threat of aggression from the Soviet Union had become so obvious that nations of the North Atlantic area had formed the North Atlantic Treaty Organization to prepare defense armaments.

On Dec. 19, 1950, the 12 nations that had formed NATO unanimously asked President Truman to let Eisenhower command its military forces. The President consented.

Eisenhower once more put on his military uniform, for the second time as Supreme Commander, Allied Powers, Europe. His mission was to keep the peace in Europe.

The commander established headquarters first at the Hotel Astoria, Paris, and later at Rocquencourt, near Paris. He remained there until the spring of 1952. After a farewell tour of NATO countries, he resigned his command post. On May 30 he turned it over to Gen. Matthew B. Ridgway. At the same time he resigned from the Army.

This resignation was withdrawn in 1961 after his retirement from the Presidency. At his own request, his successor, President John F. Kennedy, asked Congress that his rank as General of the Army be restored. This was done and on March 22, 1961, Eisenhower again became a general of the line.

U. S. Army Air Force

Imperial War Museum

IN DISTINGUISHED COMPANY: As Commanding General of the European Theater of Operations, General Eisenhower accompanied President Franklin D. Roosevelt to a council of war in Sicily. He met with Prime Minister Winston Churchill at the front during 1945.

The Man as General: A Military Appraisal

By HANSON W. BALDWIN

DWIGHT D. EISENHOWER was born in an age when personal generalship at high command was a thing of the past. He could not command from horseback, as Napoleon did, nor could he plan in a tent, like Ulysses S. Grant and Robert E. Lee.

General Eisenhower's career spanned an age when the big battalions had been dethroned by the big factories as the arbiters of battle. And he was to live to see the "big bang" replace industrial output as the primary factor of a nation's military strength.

The development of nuclear weapons, with their awful power to devastate great areas, turned the military clock back during President Eisenhower's lifetime, not to superior numbers, not to superior mobilization potential, but to instantly ready professional forces capable of manning the ramparts of the sky. These were forces far different, indeed, from the traditional cavalry and infantry of General Eisenhower's youth.

General Eisenhower, therefore, was born into the age of technological revolution in war—an age when general management, rather than personal generalship, and an ability to capitalize on new technical developments were the hallmarks of military success. He also rose to power in a coalition war, with the need for the qualities of conciliation and patience in a supreme commander.

As an officer General Eisenhower had these qualities in abundance. His great achievement in World War II was as mediator, adjudicator and manager. He fashioned the often discordant elements of many nations into a fighting team that was, perhaps, the most successful combat coalition in history.

Personal generalship, in the old sense, had little to do with this success. But personal leadership did. His straightforward good humor, charm, reasonableness and the ability to make friends had a great deal to do with his military success. He was able to win over even some of his most difficult subordinates. This was not always done without strain on General Eisenhower. He might blow his top privately, but rarely publicly. In March, 1943, he told this writer in North Africa:

"Damn it, I can get along with anybody but Monty!"

He was referring to Field Marshal Montgomery, then commanding the British Eighth Army.

But General Eisenhower, mainly because of his warm and friendly personality, did get along with Field Marshal Montgomery. Despite many differences, the Briton became one of General Eisenhower's warmest admirers.

General Eisenhower had two other great qualities as a leader. He was able to pick good assistants and he had the knack of getting to the heart of a problem quickly, even though the subject matter might be unfamiliar to him. And when the chips were down, he did not lack decisiveness.

The Easiest Way

His decision to go ahead with the Normandy invasion in June, 1944, despite dubious weather prospects has perhaps been both overpublicized and overpraised. It was the correct decision but it was also the easiest and most logical one at that stage of preparations.

Less known, but requiring greater resolution at that early period of the war when his fame was not so firmly established, was General Eisenhower's decision to assault the Italian-held island of Pantelleria in the Mediterranean. This was a prelude to the invasion of Sicily.

The assault plan was so strongly opposed by one of his British subordinates that the differences were carried to Winston Churchill. The British officer held that the island was so heavily fortified that an assault would risk great loss and repulse. General Eisenhower maintained his stand despite great pressure. After heavy preliminary bombing and bombardment Pantelleria surrendered before the first assault wave had reached its shores.

General Eisenhower also demonstrated moral courage and independence of mind. When he was under heavy criticism because of early military setbacks at Kasserine Pass and elsewhere in North Africa and because of some Allied political dealings with Frenchmen described as "Vichyites," he is said to have sent a humorous but frank message to President Roosevelt.

Standing Up to F. D. R.

"Tell him," he said, "that I am the best damn lieutenant colonel in the U. S. Army."

His permanent Army rank at the time was lieutenant colonel. He held the temporary rank of general. The message implied that if the President did not like his leadership General Eisenhower would be glad to assume the rank and duties of lieutenant colonel.

General Eisenhower was in no way an intellectual soldier, but he had a native shrewdness and common sense. When he was assigned to high command in North Africa, these traits and his ability to pick good subordinates and get along with people helped him to compensate for his somewhat narrow general knowledge and his limited experience.

In some ways he was at that time still the Midwestern farm boy; in a conversation with this writer in Algiers he mis-

U.S. Army

INVASION: On June 5, 1944—D-Day Minus One—he spent much time with troops. Here, he talked to paratroops of 101st Airborne Division who were to be dropped behind enemy lines.

VICTORY: As the Supreme Allied Commander in Europe, he reacted to a tumultuous welcome in Kansas City on his triumphal return with a gesture that was to become very familiar.

pronounced the title Viscount as "Viz-count."

But he learned quickly, and he was never abashed in the company of the great and the near-great.

General Eisenhower's commanding roles in World War II did not test him as a tactician; tactics were essentially the province of his division and corps commanders. But he contributed to new tactical thought. The weight of his authority added to the emphasis on air power and its proper utilization on the battlefield and he became an exponent of the armored personnel carrier to increase the mobility of the infantry man.

As a strategist, history will probably judge General Eisenhower charitably but not as a planner of brilliance.

He had, as a matter of fact, little opportunity to display strategic talents. The strategy of World War II was not born from any one brain; it was a composite of plans developed by many men, and approved in the final analysis by the Joint and Combined Chiefs of Staff, Winston Churchill and President Roosevelt. General Eisenhower in World War II was really more the executor of strategy than the maker of it.

But his ideas influenced the composite result—and this influence was generally in favor of the so-called "blow to the heart"—the most direct attack possible against Germany and the quickest possible end of the fighting.

He was opposed by Winston Churchill, who wished to cancel the invasion of Southern France in the summer of 1944 and possibly substitute a Balkan drive.

(General Eisenhower told this writer after the war that his opposition to Churchill's proposed Balkan offensive had been wrong, politically.)

Compromise Strategy

General Eisenhower compromised on the single-thrust versus broad-front approach to Germany. He gave Field Marshal Montgomery heavy backing for his crossing of the Rhine in the north but also continued the attack with American armies in the south.

General Eisenhower was much criticized for not concentrating forces for a smashing blow into the heart of Germany. Yet the broad-front strategy was militarily successful; Germany and Italy were defeated, probably as quickly as possible.

In one major respect, however, the verdict of history will cast a shadow across General Eisenhower's final World War II victories. The halt at the Elbe River, the failure to drive for Berlin and the orders to Gen. George Patton to halt short of Prague are now generally viewed as mistakes—political rather than military.

United States or British capture of Berlin and Prague before the Russians reached those cities might have changed to some extent the postwar political complexion of Europe and would have strengthened the West's hand in its postwar conflict with Communism.

The capture of Berlin prior to Russian conquest was perhaps possible, but not certain. General Eisenhower was undoubtedly persuaded not to attempt it by two factors: the then current but fallacious belief that the Nazis would attempt to continue indefinite resistance from a "national redoubt" in the Alps, and the estimate of Gen. Omar Bradley, commander of the 12th Army Group, that the capture of Berlin might cost 100,000 casualties. Prague could admittedly have been taken without much difficulty well before the advancing Soviet armies reached it.

These "might-have-beens" of history troubled General Eisenhower later. But his defense of his actions was based on the premise that Berlin and Prague were not military objectives and that his concern was to wipe out as quickly as possible organized German resistance.

He, like Gen. George C. Marshall, Army Chief of Staff, then had a kind of political astigmatism, and the unconditional-surrender concept had in it no place for military operations that had essentially political goals.

Associated Press

PATRIARCH: Christmas at the White House in 1955 with their son, John, and his family. Grandchildren were Dwight David 2d, 7; Susan Elaine, 3, and Barbara Anne, 6. Another granddaughter, Mary Jean, was born during that year.

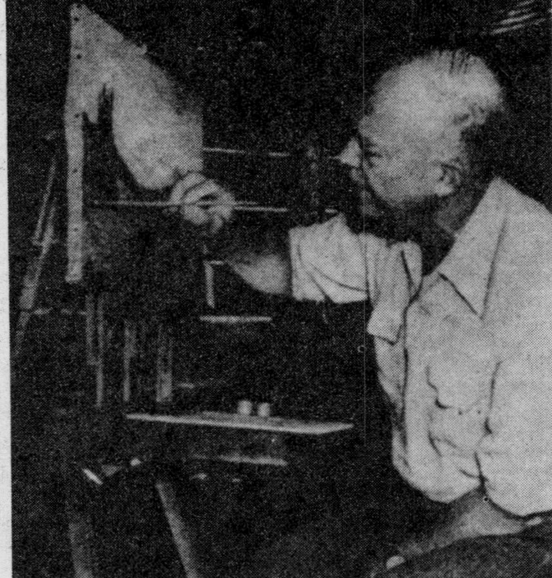

Associated Press

HOBBY: Painting for years was a source of relaxation and pleasure for him. Here he was on a Western holiday.

United Press International

FOND GRANDFATHER: President Eisenhower exchanged greetings with David Eisenhower in 1953 at Augusta links.

A Return, Off Duty, to Simplicity

UPON leaving the White House, Dwight D. Eisenhower went to live on his farm at Gettysburg, Pa., the first real home he had had since entering the Army in 1915. He had bought the farm in 1950 for $23,000. He liked the quiet, rolling Pennsylvania countryside and the opportunities that his new leisure afforded him to golf at the nearby Gettysburg Country Club and to paint in oils.

He maintained a small office on the second floor of the former residence of the president of Gettysburg College. There he wrote and painstakingly revised his two-volume memoirs, "The White House Years," and "At Ease: Stories I Tell My Friends," which was published in 1967. There he also saw many visitors and answered letters. The office was sparsely furnished—a desk, an American flag and a picture of Lincoln behind it, a bookcase, some Steuben glass, four chairs and a pinkish rug.

Although Eisenhower lived on a farm, he was so far from being a farmer that he once grabbed a bull's tail to move it for a visitor. He often complained that he was supporting the farm, rather than the farm supporting him, because his cattle business was not profitable. Actually, of course, he and his wife did not spend all their time in Gettysburg; they wintered at Palm Desert, Calif., and frequently vacationed in Georgia, where the former President golfed at the Augusta National Golf Club.

In retirement, Eisenhower had to do a number of things that had always been done for him. He thought, for example, that he ought to learn to drive an automobile, but a couple of times behind the wheel convinced him he was better off chauffeured, and a Negro sergeant drove him around most of the time. He also discovered that he sometimes had to buy train tickets for himself or dial telephone calls. These were irksome chores for a man who had been waited on most of his mature life.

Busier Than Ever

He felt keenly that he was busier in retirement than he had been as President, yet he also felt a strong responsibility to history to be a model public figure. For this reason he lent his name to such worthy causes as the English-Speaking Union; made speeches to Republican party gatherings, wrote his memoirs and responded to calls for advice from President Kennedy and President Johnson.

He was careful, however, to avoid public roles that might embarrass his successors in the White House. In line with this, he declined an invitation to visit the Soviet Union as a guest of the Kremlin. He did not feel the same hesitation, however, in visiting Western Europe. In July and August of 1962 he and his wife and several of their grandchildren toured Paris, Copenhagen, Stockholm, Cologne and London. He met with Chancellor Konrad Adenauer of West Germany and Sir Winston Churchill.

He revisited Europe the following year when he appeared in a television film on the Normandy invasion.

Later that year, "Mandate for Change," the first volume of his Presidential memoirs, was published. Prepared with the help of his son, John, Eisenhower's book recounted the events of his first term. The second volume, "Waging Peace, 1956-1960," was published in 1965 and covered his second term.

It was after his first retirement from the Army that Eisenhower wrote "Crusade in Europe," the story of his career as Allied commander. For the book he was paid $636,000, with a net return of $476,250 after taxes.

In the give-and-take of conversation, Eisenhower was never a syntactical talker. He was sensitive about this both in the White House and in retirement. He brought the matter up in an informal interview late in 1965, and explained to a reporter that he was "a man of ideas," not of talk, and that when he saw that his listeners understood what he was in the midst of saying he switched to the next point.

Eisenhower conversed with animation. Sometimes he would pace the floor as he talked; he would pound his desk for emphasis, or fling out both arms to suggest the magnitude of some problem. As an aftereffect of his stroke, he had difficulty pronouncing some words, but this impediment was not obtrusive.

A certain mellowness was evident in Eisenhower's conduct after he left the White House, but this involved conscious effort. He realized toward the end of his second Administration that he could not afford to let himself become angry, and he rather docilely yielded to intimates who sought to calm him down.

Once he topped a tee shot at Augusta and flared up in such anger that Richard Flohr, his Secret Service guard, grew alarmed. Mr. Flohr ran to the general and, in the manner of a top sergeant talking to a buck private, shouted: "Now you just cut that out right now, Mr. President. And I mean cut it out, or I'm going to put you in that cart and take you right back to the cottage and lock you in." Eisenhower was abashed and quieted down.

Always considerate of his wife, Mamie, Eisenhower traveled much by train in retirement because Mrs. Eisenhower was uncomfortable on airplanes. On many occasions he went out of his way to demonstrate his affection.

Not long before his 75th birthday he was presented with a large bouquet of white carnations at a public ceremony. He put one in his lapel and remarked, "The rest of these are for my sweetheart." To interviewers in his final years he liked to say that "the luckiest thing that ever happened to me was the girl I married."

All his life Eisenhower was influenced by the moralism of his Mennonite forebears, and it seemed only natural to him to consider social, economic and political questions in a moral environment. The Bible was the ultimate source of inspiration and consolation for his parents, and Eisenhower turned to it more and more after he left the Presidency.

In the living room of his Gettysburg farm was a well-thumbed Bible bound in soft black morocco. An interviewer asked him about it, and he replied:

"I wouldn't want to be portrayed as anything like a student of the Bible, let alone a Biblical scholar. But since leaving the White House I have found myself turning to it more and more. I suppose it's just that I have more time for reading what I please than was possible in White House years.

"My favorite passages? Well, that's not easy to answer. But mostly I like to read from the Prophets. In the midst of wars and rumors of wars, I don't know anything more helpful to straighten out your thinking. They had a way of putting first things first, and it has seemed to me that some of this quality must rub off on a man who reads them with a purpose.

"Then, too, they had a certain dignity of expression—an ennobling quality, if you will—that I have always liked. To me a reading from the Prophets is a reminder of the dignity of man and the essential worthwhileness of the individual."

As an elder statesman after he left the White House, Eisenhower was frequently consulted on national affairs by President Johnson. His advice was sought in particular on American military involvement in Vietnam, which he firmly supported. He suggested that patriotism required united public backing for a victory policy lest United States resolution in Southeast Asia be found wanting by the Communists.

As a revered figure in his party, the general was courted by Republican politicians eager for his endorsement. He professed greater concern, however, for party unity than for personalities; but he broke his rule in 1968 to endorse Richard M. Nixon for the Republican Presidential nomination. He cited Nixon's devotion to the party and his experience in government.

In the 1962 midterm election, he campaigned for a party united on moderate stands. Despite pressure from moderates at the 1964 Republican National Convention, he declined to endorse Gov. William W. Scranton of Pennsylvania or oppose Senator Barry Goldwater of Arizona, fearing a party rift.

"We must learn," he said, "that when a Republican concerns himself too much in condemning this or that faction of decent people in the party, he is hurting himself and the party."

Four years later, in a valedictory address to the party convention, he again stressed party solidarity, but devoted most of his talk to rallying the delegates to meet foreign and domestic challenges to the nation. Warning of Communist peril, he said:

"At every level of government we must . . . seek out candid and capable leaders. We need people who can point the way to sound progress, serenity and confidence at home, and respect for America throughout the world."

General Eisenhower had endorsed Nixon on July 18, lauding his "experience, decisiveness and intelligence." At the Walter Reed Army Medical Center in Washington, recuperating from his heart attacks, he received Nixon and other candidates before the November election.

Late in October, he wrote Nixon a "Dear Dick" letter, calling him better equipped for the Presidency "than any other political figure I have seen or heard."

Eisenhower's final years were beset by illness. He suffered two mild heart attacks in late 1965; he was operated on for a gall bladder condition in 1966 and was hospitalized three times the following year, twice for stomach ailments and once for an enlarged prostate gland. He suffered another heart attack in April, a fifth one in June and a sixth on Aug. 6, a few hours after addressing the party convention from his hospital room. His seventh heart attack occurred last Aug. 16.

Toward the close of his life Eisenhower was asked to tick off what he considered his greatest achievements and disappointments during his Presidency.

Referring to achievements, he told Walter Cronkite of the Columbia Broadcasting System:

"When I came to the Presidency, the country was rather in an unhappy state. There was bitterness and there was quarreling and so on. I tried to create an atmosphere of greater serenity and mutual confidence, and I think that it was noticeable over those eight years that that was brought about."

In "Waging Peace" he said that the defeat of Richard Nixon in 1960 was "my principal political disappointment." "I cannot ascribe any rational cause for the outcome," he wrote, "for I still believe, as I did then, that any objective comparison of the relative capacities and qualifications of the two opposing candidates would have resulted in an overwhelming judgment in Nixon's favor."

Eisenhower's major regret was "that as we left the White House I had to admit to little success in making progress in global disarmament or in reducing the bitterness of the East-West struggle." The "bleak record," he said in his book, was not owing to "any lack of striving on our part." "The difficulty was the frozen position of hostility with which the Communists greeted every Western proposal for enforceable, mutual disarmament or for any removal of the causes of tensions that so plague the world."

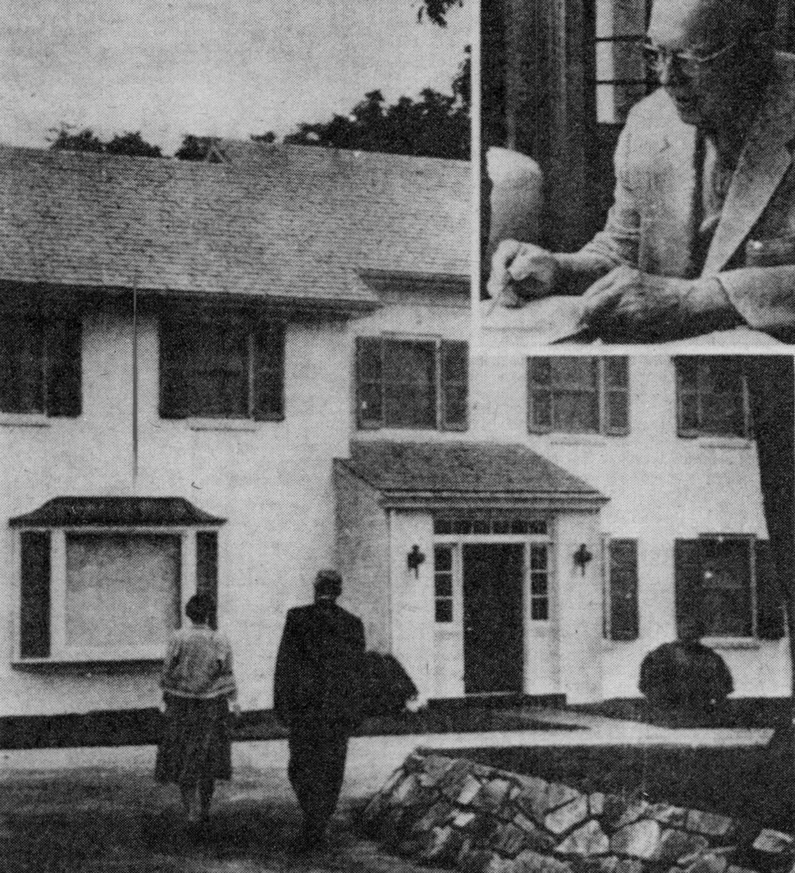

The New York Times (by Sam Falk), George Cserna

ELDER STATESMAN: General Eisenhower and Mrs. Eisenhower at their farm in Gettysburg, Pa. He maintained a small office in the town, where he wrote and revised his memoirs.

"All the News That's Fit to Print"

The New York Times

LATE CITY EDITION

Weather: Fair, very cold today and tonight. Chance of snow tomorrow. Temp. range: today 24-14; Sunday 33-26. Full U.S. report on Page 30.

VOL. CXXIII ... No. 42,490 © 1974 The New York Times Company NEW YORK, SATURDAY, MAY 25, 1974 20c beyond 50-mile radius of New York City, except Long Island. Higher in air delivery cities. 15 CENTS

SOVIET REPORTED RESUMING SUPPLY OF ARMS TO EGYPT

Move Is Seen Part of Effort by the Two Countries to End Strain in Relations

RUSSIAN ENVOY ARRIVES

Weapons and Spare Parts Are Said to Be the First Shipped in 6 Months

Special to The New York Times

CAIRO, May 24—The Soviet Union has resumed limited shipments of arms and spare parts to Egypt as part of an effort by both countries to improve their recently strained relations, informed foreign diplomats said today. The shipments are understood to be the first in about six months.

The Soviet gesture coincided with the arrival of the new Soviet Ambassador, Vladimir Polyakov, who brought with him last week a message from Chairman Leonid I. Brezhnev to President Anwar el-Sadat.

Mr. Sadat told his Cabinet Sunday that the Soviet message was "friendly" in tone and reflected a positive new phase in Soviet-Egyptian relations. He added that Egypt wanted to pursue a policy of nonalignment between the two superpowers.

Hope for Some Ties

Foreign diplomats regard the reported Soviet decision to resume arms shipments as a sign that Moscow has not written off Egypt in spite of Mr. Sadat's new friendship with the United States, rather that the Russians want to preserve correct and if possible warm relations with Cairo.

It was noted that the Soviet gesture also coincided with a week-long visit to Moscow by Maj. Abdul Salam Jalloud, the Libyan Premier.

The lengthy and apparently warm talks between the Soviet leaders and Mr. Jalloud, the representative of a fiercely anti-Communist regime, had been interpreted as a Soviet effort to find new friends in the Arab world to compensate for the Moscow-Cairo estrangement. That split followed Mr. Sadat's decision to resume relations with the United States and to rely exclusively on the mediation of Secretary of State Kissinger to help bring about a settlement with Israel.

Steps on Many Fronts

The Soviet Union, it is said here, is moving on many fronts to shore up its declining influence in the Middle East.

Diplomats here believe that the deepening rift between Egypt and Libya has caused the Libyan regime to mitigate her anti-Communism and seek closer relations with the Soviet Union.

Mr. Jalloud's visit to Moscow led to a trade agreement involving deliveries of Libyan oil produced by nationalized companies previously owned by American concerns.

The Soviet Union is believed to have agreed to supply Libya with certain types of Soviet arms.

The Russians used the occasion to criticize Mr. Kissinger indirectly by denouncing "partial solutions." They also went

Continued on Page 2, Column 4

Associated Press

ISRAELIS SEEK POSSIBLE INFILTRATORS: Aided by copter and bulldozer, soldiers work near Lebanese border to guard against the presence of Arab guerrillas and block new raids. Reports from Mideast, Pages 2 and 3.

British Bar Negotiations With the Ulster Strikers

By ALVIN SHUSTER

Special to The New York Times

BELFAST, Northern Ireland, May 24—The British Government decided today against making concessions to the Protestant extremist groups that are crippling Northern Ireland in a strike that is now 10 days old.

After a meeting of nearly five hours with leaders of the Ulster provincial government, who had flown to London, Prime Minister Wilson said there would be no negotiations with the Ulster Workers' Council, which is spearheading the Protestant loyalists' resistance movement. The strikers are trying to bring down the provincial government with a demand for new elections.

Mr. Wilson, who called an urgent Cabinet meeting after his talks with Northern Ireland's politicians at his country home, Chequers, reaffirmed his support for the province's executive, which includes Protestants and Roman Catholics. A statement from 10 Downing Street ruled out any negotiations with the workers' council, saying that the existing government structure here is the "only basis for the peace, order and good government of Northern Ireland."

A spokesman for the hard-line Protestants, Harry Murray, chairman of the council, promptly said: "We are not going to let up."

"We believe they will talk before we are finished," he added.

The question now is just what the British Government will do to meet the challenge of the strike, which has threatened the basis of British policy for the sharing of politi-

Continued on Page 2, Column 1

Inquiry at Cancer Center Finds Fraud in Research

By JANE E. BRODY

A scientific investigating committee at the Memorial Sloan-Kettering Cancer Center has concluded that a scientist deliberately falsified and misrepresented research results and has recommended that his affiliation with the center be terminated.

As a result of the findings the scientist, Dr. William T. Summerlin, 35 years old, has been given up to a one-year medical leave of absence with pay while he undergoes psychiatric care for an emotional illness, Dr. Lewis Thomas, president of the cancer center, said yesterday. Dr. Thomas told a news conference that in his opinion "the fraud in this work is a result of mental illness" but that even if he recovers, Dr. Summerlin would not return to the center.

According to the committee's long report, which was released at the news conference, Dr. Summerlin admitted to the committee that he had darkened the skin of two white mice with a pen to make it appear that the mice had accepted skin grafts from genetically different animals, and that on four occasions he had misrepresented the results of experimental transplants of human corneas into rabbit eyes.

Dr. Summerlin was attempting to prove in these and other experiments that, by keeping tissues in laboratory culture for several weeks, they could be successfully transplanted to genetically different animals without the use of dangerous drugs to suppress rejection. Such an achievement would have great practical importance

Continued on Page 10, Column 4

KENNETH RUSH SET FOR ECONOMIC JOB

Nixon May Appoint Him to Handle Inflation Problems And Squabbling Aides

By DAVID BINDER

Special to The New York Times

WASHINGTON, May 24 — President Nixon will name Kenneth Rush, the Deputy Secretary of State, as his chief economic coordinator tomorrow in an effort to deal with deepening inflation problems and squabbling between other economic aides, high Administration officials said today.

Mr. Rush, who is 64 years old, has pinch-hit for Mr. Nixon in other high Government posts since he left private business in 1969. He is now the second-ranking man in the State Department, having served previously as Deputy Secretary of Defense and Ambassador to West Germany.

Mr. Nixon was described by aides as being increasingly gloomy about negative economic developments, chiefly the domestic inflation rate of about 10 per cent and worldwide inflationary trends.

The aides also said the President was concerned about frictions that had developed between his newly appointed Secretary of the Treasury, William E. Simon, and Roy L. Ash, the director of the Office of Management and Budget.

Mr. Nixon was said to have intervened several times in recent weeks to smooth rela-

Continued on Page 7, Column 2

Kheel Gives Details On Innovative Pact Of Papers and Union

By DAMON STETSON

The newspaper-industry contract agreement reached Thursday will give the publishers of The New York Times and The Daily News the unrestricted right to use automated processes in exchange for lifetime guarantees of employment to regular and substitute printers and six-month paid sabbaticals as incentives to retirement.

Details of the innovative agreement, running to March 30, 1984, were explained yesterday by Theodore W. Kheel, mediator in the negotiations, at a news conference at Automation House, 49 East 68th Street.

"This marks an occasion in the history of collective bargaining of tremendous importance," Mr. Kheel said. "This settlement is a classical example of how collective bargaining works in solving a most difficult industrial problem.

"The publishers and the union each got 100 per cent. The publishers got 100 per cent unlimited productivity. The union got 100 per cent unqualified job security."

The tentative settlement between Typographical Union No. 6 and The Daily News and The New York Times is still subject to ratification by the local's membership, but the referendum vote is not expected for two or three weeks, according to Bertram A. Powers, Local 6 president, who said that parts of the agreement still had to be put into writing.

The agreement was described

Continued on Page 41, Column 3

Judge Denies U.S. Security Justified Ellsberg Break-In

Gesell Rules the President Has No Right to Authorize a Warrantless Search Even in Foreign Intelligence Peril

By SEYMOUR M. HERSH

Special to The New York Times

WASHINGTON, May 24 — The Federal judge in the White House "plumbers" case ruled today that the President has no constitutional right to authorize break-in and search without a warrant even when national security and foreign intelligence are involved.

In the ruling, Judge Gerhard A. Gesell of the United States District Court declared:

The text of Gesell decision is printed on Page 13.

"The Fourth Amendment protects the privacy of citizens against unreasonable and unrestrained intrusion by Government officials and their agents. It is not theoretical. It lies at the heart of our free society."

Judge Gesell also said that defendants were not entitled to cite "national security" as a legal justification for their participation in the break-in of the office of Dr. Daniel Ellsberg's former psychiatrist in 1971.

Hotly Disputed Area

Legal experts said that Judge Gesell's ruling on the Fourth Amendment, which is subject to appeal, could, if upheld, be a landmark in that it placed a specific prohibition on the powers of the President in foreign intelligence and foreign affairs —a legal area now hotly disputed.

Although, as Judge Gesell noted in his ruling, there was no evidence indicating that President Nixon had specifically authorized the break-in, the issue arose when the defendants contended that the President had delegated that authority to members of the "plumbers" unit.

"Whatever accommodation is required between the guarantees of the Fourth Amendment and the conduct of foreign affairs," Judge Gesell said, "it cannot justify a casual, ill-defined assignment to White House aides and part-time employes granting them an uncontrolled discretion to select,

Continued on Page 13, Column 1

United Press International

Judge Gerhard A. Gesell

Rodino Said to Ask Release Of Evidence on Watergate

By JAMES M. NAUGHTON

Special to The New York Times

WASHINGTON, May 24 — The chairman of the House Judiciary Committee will propose next week that the panel make public most, and perhaps all, of the Watergate evidence it has been examining in closed impeachment hearings, well-placed Congressional officials said today.

According to the officials, the chairman, Representative Peter W. Rodino Jr., Democrat of New Jersey, told senior colleagues on the committee yesterday that he favored releasing the material as soon as possible.

The officials said that Mr. Rodino would first seek clearance from the special Watergate prosecutor and officials of several other Congressional committees that provided confidential materials to the impeachment inquiry.

The following related developments occurred today in the impeachment controversy:

¶A spokesman for the Internal Revenue Service confirmed reports that the agency had refused to give the Judiciary Committee an audit of the President's income tax returns pending a Justice Department ruling on the legality of such a disclosure.

¶A Democratic member of the committee, Representative John Conyers Jr. of Michigan, declared at a news conference that President Nixon "may be continuing the cover-up" of the Watergate scandal by withholding tape recordings and other evidence from the impeachment inquiry and the courts.

Although technically a side issue in the investigation of Mr. Nixon's official conduct, the dispute over the collection and disposition of evidence has dominated the recent public dialogue over impeachment.

Gerald L. Warren, the deputy White House press secretary, objected again today to what he called "selective leaks" of information from the closed

Continued on Page 12, Column 7

HIGH COURT GETS JAWORSKI APPEAL ON NIXON TAPES

Watergate Prosecutor Asks Whether Privilege Exceeds His Need for Evidence

CONSPIRACY IS ALLEGED

White House Deliberations Termed Possible Effort to Obstruct Justice

By ANTHONY RIPLEY

Special to The New York Times

WASHINGTON, May 24 — Leon Jaworski, the special Watergate prosecutor, appealed to the United States Supreme Court today for access to 64 recorded White House conversations.

The President participated in all but one of the conversations, which, Mr. Jaworski said in his petition to the Court, occurred in the course of "the criminal conspiracy" charged against the seven defendants in the Watergate cover-up case.

Text of Jaworski's appeal appears on Page 12.

In the petition, Mr. Jaworski asked the Court to decide the following question:

"Whether a claim of executive privilege based on the generalized interest in the confidentiality of Government deliberations can block the prosecution's access to evidence material and important to the trial of charges of criminal misconduct by high Government officials who participated in those deliberations, particularly where there is a prima facie showing that the deliberations occurred in the course of the criminal conspiracy charged in the indictment."

Obstruction of Justice

The conspiracy charged in the indictment includes the obstruction of justice.

The Jaworski petition does not mention President Nixon as one of the alleged co-conspirators. What it says is that the prosecution has evidence indicating that conversations in which Mr. Nixon participated were "deliberations" that were carried out in the course of the conspiracy.

Mr. Jaworski has already made it clear that he feels a sitting President should not be indicted. The law is so unclear, he has indicated, that an indictment of a President would be challenged in the courts as improper, and the resulting litigation on the issue could cause delay and confusion.

Today's action marked the first time in the almost two-year-old Watergate affair that a case was taken to the Supreme Court.

Mr. Jaworski's action jumps over the United States Court of Appeals and asks the Supreme Court to consider the matter in its current term, using typewritten briefs if necessary.

Quick Action Urged

Mr. Jaworski said that the issues at stake were of "imperative public importance" and should be "resolved as quickly as possible to permit the trial in the Watergate cover-up case . . . to proceed as scheduled on Sept. 9, 1974."

Otherwise, he argued, the trial could not be brought before the spring of 1975 on issues "exceedingly important" to the nation.

Today's action began on April 16 when Mr. Jaworski requested the tapes to prepare the case for trial and to provide any information possible on the possible innocence of those charged in the March 1 indictment.

On May 20, Judge Sirica ordered the conversations turned over.

At the 4 P.M. deadline today for appealing the case, the

Continued on Page 12, Column 1

China Ousting 6-Man U.S. Marine Unit

By JOSEPH LELYVELD

Special to The New York Times

HONG KONG, May 24 — The United States Marines are being ousted from China—all six of them—apparently on suspicion of carousing.

The marines, who arrived in Peking at about this time last year to guard the new United States liaison office there, will be leaving in the next two or three weeks at the request of the Chinese authorities.

American diplomatic sources here declined to comment when asked why the Chinese had changed their minds about allowing the marine detachment to come to Peking. A marine guard is traditional at United States embassies, but the liaison office is not an embassy, for Peking and Washington have yet to establish normal diplomatic relations.

Some analysts may be tempted to interpret the departure of the marines as evidence of a cooler Chinese attitude to the United States. But foreign residents in Peking will probably conclude, instead, that the occasional levity and boisterousness of six marines were simply more than the puritanical Chinese capital could contain.

In their one year in Peking, the marines furnished the isolated and self-conscious diplomatic community there with a topic of conversation second only in popularity to the inevitable speculation about the pecking order in the Politburo of the Communist party.

Early in their stay, the marines opened a small clubhouse, as they do in most foreign capitals. The Chinese authorities soon objected that the club had become an unseemly source of noise and that it had been selling liquor without a license. At their request, it was closed down.

Another instance of reverse culture shock occurred when the marines ordered a cake at a bakery for the traditional ball held at foreign missions to commemorate the founding of the corps.

The design they submitted

Continued on Page 6, Column 6

Duke Ellington, a Master of Music, Dies at 75

Edward Kennedy Ellington, called Duke since childhood

By JOHN S. WILSON

Duke Ellington, who expanded the literature of American music with compositions and performances that drew international critical praise and brought listening and dancing pleasure to two generations, died here yesterday at the age of 75.

He entered the Columbia Presbyterian Medical Center's Harkness Pavilion at the end of March for treatment of cancer of both lungs, a condition that was complicated last Wednesday when he developed pneumonia.

At his death, the phrase "beyond category," which Edward Kennedy Ellington had used as his highest form of praise for others, could quite literally be applied to the Duke himself, whose works were played and praised in settings as diverse as the old Cotton Club, Carnegie Hall and Westminster Abbey.

The noted jazz critic and historian Ralph J. Gleason called Mr. Ellington "America's most important composer . . . the greatest composer this American society has produced," and summed him up as a "master musician, master psychologist, master choreographer."

"Ellington has created his own musical world which has transcended every attempt to impose category upon it and has emerged as a solid body of work unequalled in American music," Mr. Gleason wrote.

"His songs have become a standard part of the cultural heritage, his longer compositions a part of the finest art of our time and his concerts and personal appearances among the most satisfying for an audience of those of any artist. Every music honor this country can bestow is little enough for such a musical giant as this man. In reality, he has already won them and more by his imprint on the minds of all who have heard him."

Mr. Ellington, whose innate elegance of manner won him his nickname of Duke while he was still a schoolboy in Washington, was a tall, debonair, urbane man with a vitalizing sense of the dramatic and an ironic wit that often served as a protective shield.

Amid the protests voiced in 1965 when a unanimous recommendation by the Pulitzer Prize music jury that Mr. El-

Continued on Page 32, Column 1

NEWS INDEX

Duke Ellington Dies; A Master of Music

Continued From Page 1, Col. 7

lington be given a special citation was rejected by the Pulitzer advisory board, the only comment by the composer, pianist and orchestra leader was, "Fate is being kind to me. Fate doesn't want me to be famous too young." He was then 66 years old.

But beneath a suave, unruffled exterior, Mr. Ellington had a fiery appreciation of his worth and his style. When he was conducting a public rehearsal of his orchestra at the University of Wisconsin in 1972, he took his musicians through a first attempt at his latest composition.

"Letter E," he said to indicate where they were to start playing. But when only half the band began at the proper place, he shouted, "No! E! E as in Ellington! E! E as in Edward! E! E as in Ellington! E as in excellence! E as in elegance! as in Edward and Ellington! E E! E as in all good things! Edward ... Ellington ... excellence ... elegance! E!"

Mr. Ellington combined his musical talents, his excellence and his elegance in a manner that transcended the usual connotations of "jazz," a word that he consistently rejected in relation to his work.

"In the nineteen-twenties I used to try to convince Fletcher Henderson that we ought to call what we're doing 'Negro music,'" Mr. Ellington said in 1965. "But it's too late for that now. The music has become so integrated that you can't tell one part from the other so far as color is concerned. Well, I don't have time to worry about it. I've got too much music on my mind."

As a composer and arranger, Mr. Ellington created an unusual and (as many other orchestra leaders found) inimitable style by building his works on the individualistic sounds of the brilliant instrumentalists he gathered around him—the growling trumpets of Bubber Miley, Cootie Williams and Ray Nance, the virtuoso plunger mute effects of the trombonist Tricky Sam Nanton, the rich, mellow clarinet of Barney Bigard, the exquisite alto saxophone of Johnny Hodges, the huge, sturdy drive of Harry Carney's baritone saxophone. Billy Strayhorn, who was Mr. Ellington's musical right arm, his co-composer and co-arranger from 1939 until his death in 1967, explained that "Ellington plays the piano but his real instrument is his band."

Elusive to Others

The basis of the Ellington sound eluded other musicians. In the late nineteen-twenties, when Mr. Ellington's star was just beginning to rise and Paul Whiteman was the "King of Jazz," Mr. Whiteman and his arranger, Ferde Grofé, spent nights on end at the Cotton Club listening to the Ellington orchestra but, so legend has it, eventually abandoned their efforts to try to notate what the Duke's musicians were playing.

More recently Andre Previn, who is as familiar with the classical side of music as he is with jazz, shook his head in amazement as he noted that "Stan Kenton can stand in front of a thousand fiddles and a thousand brass and make a dramatic gesture and every studio arranger can nod his head and say, 'Oh, yes, that's done like this.' But Duke merely lifts his finger, three horns make a sound and I don't know what it is."

Although Mr. Ellington's basic working materials were almost invariably the blues and the voicelike manner in which a jazz musician plays his instrument, classically oriented musicians often found a relationship to Debussy, Delius and Ravel in his work. Constant Lambert wrote in 1934 that there is "nothing in Ravel so dexterous in treatment as the varied solos in the middle of the ebullient 'Hot and Bothered' [an Ellington variation on 'Tiger Rag'] and nothing in Stravinsky more dynamic than the final section."

Mr. Ellington was a pioneer in extending jazz composition beyond the customary chorus of 12 or 32 bars. His "Reminiscing in Tempo," written in 1934, was a 12-minute work. Four years later, Paul Whiteman commissioned him to write a concert piece, "Blue Belles of Harlem," for the Whiteman orchestra. Mr. Ellington's first major effort at an extended composition came in 1943, when he wrote "Black, Brown and Beige," which ran for 50 minutes when it was introduced at an Ellington concert in Carnegie Hall.

This was the first of what became an annual series of concerts in the forties at Carnegie Hall, for each of which Mr. Ellington prepared such works as "New World a-Comin,'" "The Deep South Suite" and "The Perfume Suite." Later, on commission from the Liberian Government, he wrote "The Liberian Suite" and, more recently for Togo, "Togo Brava."

His extended compositions also included "Harlem"; "Night Creatures," introduced by the Ellington band and the Symphony of the Air at Carnegie Hall in 1955; "Suite Thursday," inspired by John Steinbeck's book "Sweet Thursday" and commissioned by the Monterey Jazz Festival in 1960, and a Shakespeare suite, "Such Sweet Thunder," inspired by a Shakespeare Festival in Stratford, Ontario, in 1957.

In 1965, Mr. Ellington moved into a new musical field, presenting a Concert of Sacred Music of his own composition in Grace Cathedral in San Francisco. The performance, starting with the Biblical paraphrase "In the beginning, God . . .", was developed in typical Ellingtonian style with a company that included his full orchestra, three choirs, a dancer and several guest vocalists.

Mr. Ellington considered the concert "the most important thing I've ever done." It was repeated twice in New York at the Fifth Avenue Presbyterian Church in the same year. Three years later he introduced a Second Sacred Concert here at the Cathedral Church of St. John the Divine and, in 1973, a Third Sacred Concert was performed for the first time, in London at Westminster Abbey.

Repertory Standards

But before Mr. Ellington became involved in extended composition, his songs, which included "Solitude," "Sophisticated Lady," "In a Sentimental Mood," "I Let a Song Go Out of My Heart" and "I Got It Bad," had become standards in the popular repertory. In addition, his short instrumental pieces — such as "Black and Tan Fantasy," "The Mooche" "Creole Love Call" and "Mood Indigo" — were established as part of the jazz repertory.

Despite Mr. Ellington's prolific output as a composer—he wrote more than 6,000 pieces of varying length — one of the tunes most closely associated with him, "Take the 'A' Train," which he used as a signature theme for many years, was not written by him. It was composed by his close associate, Mr. Strayhorn.

Other theme tunes used by his band at various times included "East St. Louis Toodle-Oo" and "I Let a Song Go Out of My Heart," both composed by Mr. Ellington, and "Things Ain't What They Used to Be," composed by his son, Mercer.

Early Interest in Art

Mr. Ellington was born in Washington on April 29, 1899, the son of James Edward Ellington and the former Daisy Kennedy. His father was a blueprint maker for the Navy Department, who also worked occasionally as a butler, sometimes at the White House.

In high school, the Duke, whose nickname was given to him by an admiring neighborhood friend when he was 8 years old, was torn between his interests in painting and in music. He won a poster contest sponsored by the National Association for the Advancement of Colored People and in 1917 was offered a scholarship by the Pratt Institute of Applied Art. He turned it down, however, to devote himself to music.

He wrote his first composition, "Soda Fountain Rag," while he was working after school as a soda jerk at the Poodle Dog Cafe. Some piano lessons he had received at the age of 7 comprised the only formal musical education he had. He learned by listening to the "two-fisted piano players" of the period, paying particular attention to Sticky Mack, Doc Perry, James P. Johnson and Willie (The Lion) Smith.

By the time he was 20 he was making $150 a week playing with his small band at parties and dances. In this year, 1919, Sonny Greer became Mr. Ellington's drummer and remained with him until 1950, setting a pattern of longevity that was to be followed by many Ellington sidemen.

In 1922 Wilbur Sweatman, then a successful bandleader, asked Mr. Greer to join his band in New York. Mr. Ellington and three other members of the group went along, too, but jobs in New York were so scarce that soon they were all back in Washington. However, the visit gave Mr. Ellington an opportunity to hear the Harlem pianists who became a prime influence on his own playing — Willie (The Lion) Smith, James P. Johnson and Johnson's protégé Fats Waller.

At Mr. Waller's urging, Duke Ellington and his men returned to New York in 1923. This time they got a job playing at Barron's in Harlem with Elmer Snowden, the group's banjoist, as nominal leader. When they moved downtown to the Hollywood Club (later known as the Kentucky Club) at Broadway and 49th Street, Mr. Snowden left the group and Mr. Ellington assumed the leadership.

Call From Cotton Club

During the four and a half years that Ellington's Washingtonians remained at the Kentucky Club, the group made its first records and did its first radio broadcasts. Late in 1927, when the band had expanded to 10 men, the Cotton Club, a gaudy Harlem showplace, found itself in sudden need of an orchestra when King Oliver, whose band was scheduled to open there, decided he had not been offered enough money.

Mr. Ellington got the booking, but first he had to be released from a theater engagement in Philadelphia. This was arranged when the operators of the Cotton Club asked some

Ellington was the guest of honor at a White House party given in his honor on his 70th birthday. He was presented with the Presidential Medal of Freedom, the nation's highest civilian honor, by President Nixon.

associates in Philadelphia to call on the theater manager with a proposition: "Be big or you'll be dead." He was big and Duke Ellington began a five-year association with the Cotton Club.

A crucial factor in spreading the fame of the Ellington band was a nightly radio broadcast from the Cotton Club that was heard across the country, introduced by the Ellington signature theme "East St. Louis Toodle-Oo," with Bubber Miley's growling trumpet setting the mood for the stomping and often exotic music that followed. Mr. Ellington's unique use of growling brass (identified as his "jungle" style) and the rich variety of tonal colors that he drew from his band brought musicians of all schools to the Cotton Club.

In 1930 the Ellington band appeared in its first feature-length movie, "Check and Double Check," and in 1933 it went overseas for the first time, to Britain and Europe. During the thirties, the band appeared in several more films —"Murder at the Vanities," "Belle of the Nineties" and The Hit Parade" — and made a second European tour in 1939.

A Peak After Swing Era

When the furor over swing bands rose in the late thirties, the Ellington band was overshadowed by the glare of publicity that fell on the bands of Benny Goodman, Artie Shaw and Glenn Miller. But as the swing era faded, the Ellington band hit one of its peaks in 1941 and 1942, years when all the greatest of Mr. Ellington's star sidemen (except Bubber Miley) were together in the band and when Mr. Ellington himself was in an extraordinarily creative period as a composer.

By 1943, however, he was leaving the early phases of his career behind him and turning to the extended compositions and concert presentations that would be an increasingly important part of his work.

In the fifties, when interest in big bands dropped so low that all but a handful gave up completely or worked on a part-time basis, Mr. Ellington kept his band together even when the economic basis became very shaky.

"It's a matter of whether you want to play music or make money," he said. "I like to keep a band so I can write and hear the music next day. The only way you can do that is to pay the band and keep it on tap 52 weeks a year. If you want to make a real profit, you go out for four months, lay off for four and come back for another four. Of course, you can't hold a band together that way and I like the cats we've got. So, by various little twists and turns, we manage to stay in business and make a musical profit. And a musical profit can put you way ahead of a financial loss."

Dancing in the Aisles

The fortunes of the Ellington band started to rise again in 1956 when, at the Newport Jazz Festival, a performance of a composition Mr. Ellington had written 20 years before, "Diminuendo and Crescendo in Blue," propelled by a 27-chorus solo by the tenor saxophonist Paul Gonsalves, set off dancing in the aisles that reminded observers of the joyous excitement that Benny Goodman had generated at New York's Paramount Theater in the thirties.

During the next 15 years, Mr. Ellington's orchestra was heard in all areas of the world, touring the Middle East, the Far East and the Soviet Union under the auspices of the State Department, playing in Africa, South America and Europe. Mr. Ellington wrote scores for five films — "Paris Blues," "Anatomy of a Murder," "Assault on a Queen," "Change of Mind" and a German picture, "Janus."

Honors were heaped on him. In 1969, at a celebration of his 70th birthday at the White House, President Nixon awarded him the Presidential Medal of Freedom. President Georges Pompidou of France in 1973 gave him the Legion of Honor. The Royal Swedish Academy of Music elected him a member in 1971. Two African countries, Chad and Togo, issued postage stamps bearing his picture. In 1972, Yale University established the Duke Ellington Fellowship Fund "to preserve and perpetuate the Afro - American musical tradition."

Through all this, Mr. Ellington kept up the steady pace of composing and performing and traveling that he had maintained since the late nineteen-twenties. Everywhere he went, his electric piano went with him, for there was scarcely a day in his life when he did not compose something.

"You know how it is," he said. "You go home expecting to go right to bed. But then, on the way, you go past the piano and there's a flirtation. It flirts with you. So, you sit down and try out a couple of chords and when you look up, it's 7 A.M."

Quite logically Mr. Ellington called his autobiography, published in 1973, "Music Is My Mistress."

"Music is my mistress," he wrote, "and she plays second fiddle to no one."

"All the News That's Fit to Print"

The New York Times.

LATE CITY EDITION
U. S. Weather Bureau Report (Page 42) Forecast: Fair with some cloudiness today and tonight. Partly cloudy tomorrow.
Temp. range: 82-65; yesterday: 81-63.
Temp.-Hum. Index: mid 70's; yesterday: 74.

VOL. CXI..No. 38,150. NEW YORK, SATURDAY, JULY 7, 1962. FIVE CENTS

10 cents beyond 50-mile zone from New York City except on Long Island. Higher in air delivery cities.

2 SENATE GROUPS WILL INVESTIGATE FOREIGN LOBBIES

Extra-Diplomatic Activities Are to Be the Subject of a Foreign Relations Study

SUGAR BILL SPURS MOVES

Dodd Heads Judiciary Group for Inquiry Centering on Pressures for Quotas

By TAD SZULC
Special to The New York Times.

WASHINGTON, July 6—Two Senate committees have decided to conduct full-scale investigations into the activities of lobbyists for foreign governments, with special emphasis on the sugar bill.

The Senate Foreign Relations Committee voted today to authorize a "full and complete study" and public disclosure of what its resolution described as "the nondiplomatic activities of representatives of foreign governments and the extent to which they attempt to influence United States policies."

The Senate Judiciary Committee announced earlier that one of its subcommittees would undertake an investigation of sugar lobbying. This year the operation reached new heights of intensity and of remuneration for the lobbyists fighting to obtain quotas for foreign clients under this year's sugar legislation, still being fashioned in Congress.

Dodd to Head Inquiry

Heading the Judiciary group will be Senator Thomas J. Dodd, Democrat of Connecticut, who in 1957 and 1958 was a registered foreign agent for the Government of Guatemala. He received a total of $66,666.58 in fees, according to statements he filed with the Department of Justice.

Although Mr. Dodd was not a member of Congress at the time and his activities specifically excluded sugar lobbying, his former partner, Sheldon Z. Kaplan, has been engaged since 1960 in seeking a sugar quota for Guatemala.

Mr. Kaplan's file at the Justice Department contains copies of letters to Representative Harold D. Cooley, the North Carolina Democrat who is chairman of the House Agriculture Committee, pleading for a 20,000-ton quota for Guatemala in the premium-bearing United States market.

Representative Cooley was the initiator of this year's controversial sugar legislation and his award of the 20,000-ton quota to Guatemala — the first time that country had received a permanent allocation — was upheld in the House-Senate conference.

The Foreign Relations Committee indicated earlier this week that it had started a staff

Continued on Page 4, Column 2

William Faulkner Is Dead In Mississippi Home Town

The New York Times

William Faulkner during a visit to West Point last April

By United Press International.

OXFORD, Miss., July 6 — William Faulkner died of a heart attack today in this Mississippi town that he made famous in literature.

The author, who was 64 years old, died at 2 A. M. in a hospital with his wife, Estelle, at his bedside.

In recent years Mr. Faulkner had spent much of his time at the University of Virginia, where he was a lecturer on American literature. He and his wife returned last May to Oxford, a community of about 8,000 that Mr. Faulkner used as home base throughout his career.

President Kennedy, leading the nation in tributes to the author, said:

"Since Henry James, no writer has left behind such a vast and enduring monument to the strength of American literature."

Mr. Faulkner won the Nobel Prize for 1949 for a series of novels in which he created his own Yoknapatawpha County in northern Mississippi. There he

Continued on Page 6, Column 7

2 U.S. FARM AIDES ADMIT RECEIVING CASH FROM ESTES

Oklahomans Got $820 Each but Deny Improper Aid—Department Ousts Them

By PETER BRAESTRUP
Special to The New York Times.

WASHINGTON, July 6—Two Federal farm officials from Oklahoma admitted to a Senate subcommittee today that they had each accepted $820 in cash from Billie Sol Estes.

The officials were Arthur D. Stone, 55 years old, and his superior, Louis N. Dumas, 56, full-time Federal employes paid by the Department of Agriculture. They had been appointed by the locally elected Agricultural Stabilization and Conservation Committee in McIntosh County.

Both men denied giving improper aid to Mr. Estes' cotton dealings in McIntosh County.

But they conceded that they had lied to Federal investigators in denying they had received the Estes money. Mr. Stone, near tears, declared:

"I was simply scared and didn't know what to do. It had been bothering me quite a bit."

Punishment Called Harsher

The two men said that they had resigned, effective Monday. But the Agriculture Department said later that it would not accept their resignations and was suspending them both immediately.

The department said that suspension was harsher punishment than acceptance of the resignations because the officials would now be ineligible for re-employment by the department.

Mr. Stone and Mr. Dumas appeared in shirtsleeves before the Senate Permanent Investigations Subcommittee, headed by Senator John L. McClellan, Democrat of Arkansas.

The panel began hearings June 27 on the Department of Agriculture's handling of Mr. Estes' disputed transfers of cotton acreage allotments to West Texas from Oklahoma and other states.

Rejects Check Suggestion

Mr. Dumas, as county office manager, made $7,275 a year. His deputy, Mr. Stone, earned $5,070. Both men had held various field positions with the Agriculture Department since the early Nineteen Thirties.

The admissions of the two Oklahomans were prepared in advance. They came after the subcommittee heard preparatory testimony from Alphonse F. Calabrese, its chief staff investigator in Texas, and from Parnell E. Biggerstaff, a former Estes land agent. Mr. Biggerstaff said that he gave the two farm officials $1,640.80 in a plain envelope last fall.

Mr. Biggerstaff said that the payment to the two Oklahoma officials had been decided on by Mr. Estes' brothers and business partners, Bobby Frank and Word Estes.

"Bobby Frank said that if it was cotton-picking time, why, they could charge it to cotton picking, but it was a little too

Continued on Page 8, Column 3

Hydrogen Explosion Set Off Underground in Nevada

Associated Press Wirephoto

Nuclear device, exploded 650 feet underground at Nevada testing ground, raises a cloud

By United Press International.

NEVADA TEST SITE, July 6 — The mightiest nuclear blast within the United States and the first known detonation of any hydrogen type of explosive in this country was set off underground today. It tore a great open-faced crater in the desert floor. The thermonuclear blast was the first in a concentrated series of atomic tests. It is scheduled to be followed tomorrow by the first atmospheric nuclear shots here in four years. Today's explosion created a crater about 300 feet deep and a third of a mile wide in rocky, sandy soil. A huge, dirty cloud also rose into the clear sky. The cloud—visible

Continued on Page 5, Column 2

ALGERIA CHARGES MOROCCANS SEIZE A POST IN SAHARA

Reports 15-Mile Incursion —Says 'Press Campaign' Aims at Another Region

RABAT DENIES INVASION

French Forces Again Patrol in European Sectors of Oran After Fatal Clashes

By THOMAS F. BRADY
Special to The New York Times.

ALGIERS, July 6—The Algerian Provisional Government's official press service said today that Moroccan troops had occupied the Saharan post of Saf-Saf, fifteen miles within Algerian territory, in the region of Colomb-Béchar.

The Algerian press service article said also that a "press campaign" had been organized concerning Tindouf, a village and Saharan oasis in westernmost Algeria near the border of the Spanish Sahara.

The article criticized "the attitude of certain subaltern civil servants on the frontier, which has disquieted the Algerian authorities." It said that the occupation of Saf-Saf had been accompanied by a Moroccan troop concentration.

[In Rabat, Moroccan official quarters firmly denied reports that Moroccans had invaded the Colomb-Béchar region. Meanwhile, in the western Algerian city of Oran, French security forces again assumed control of the European section in cooperation with the Algerian National Liberation Army after Thursday's clashes had taken close to 100 lives.]

The Moroccan Claims

Morocco has demanded Saharan frontier revision for the last five years, and the regions concerned in the charges today are among those claimed by Moroccan irredentists.

The Moroccan press has recently given much attention to a delegation of "chiefs" from the region of Tindouf who have arrived in Rabat, the Moroccan capital, to swear allegiance to King Hassan II.

Through the article published today the Algerian Provisional Government made known its preoccupation "with the Saharan frontier situation that certain Moroccan circles are seeking to create."

Meanwhile, as the Provisional Government, weakened by its dispute with Vice Premier Mohammed Ben Bella, drew attention to the Saharan frontier, political difficulties appeared to be increasing.

Dispatches from Rabat declared that Mohammed Khider, an ally of Mr. Ben Bella who has resigned from the Provisional Government, had called the ministers in Algiers "rebels"

Continued on Page 3, Column 5

G.O.P. CARE BILL LOSES IN SENATE

Billion a Year to Aid Private Insurance for the Aged Is Beaten by Voice Vote

Special to The New York Times.

WASHINGTON, July 6—The Senate rejected today a billion-dollar medical care plan offered by Senator Thruston B. Morton, Republican of Kentucky.

Mr. Morton, a former Republican National Chairman, offered the proposal as an amendment to a public welfare bill. The Senate turned it down by voice vote after several hours of torpid debate. About twenty Senators were present.

Still pending as the Senate recessed for the week-end was an amendment embodying provisions of the Administration's medical care bill, with modifications designed to attract liberal Republican support. This amendment is sponsored by Senators Clinton P. Anderson, Democrat of New Mexico; Jacob K. Javits, Republican of New York, and twenty-one others.

The Morton amendment called for annual Federal subsidies of more than $1,200,000,000 to finance private health insurance for persons over 65 years old. The type of benefits would have been determined by the states.

The Senate is expected to approve the Anderson - Javits amendment, possibly next week, but there is still no prospect of House action this session.

The amendment would provide the same limited hospitalization, nursing care and clinical serv-

Continued on Page 5, Column 6

Rail Unions Reject Rules Arbitration; Showdown Nearing

By JOHN D. POMFRET
Special to The New York Times.

WASHINGTON, July 6 —The labor dispute between the nation's railroads and the five train-operating unions moved inexorably toward crisis today.

Move and counter-move followed with the precision and predictability of a minuet as the carriers sought to hurry a showdown and the unions sought to hold it off.

Today's moves were these:

¶The unions announced in Cleveland that they had rejected the National Mediation Board's request that the long work-rules controversy be submitted to arbitration.

¶The railroads said that they would serve notice, probably next week, that they would put into effect thirty days thereafter the sweeping changes in work rules and pay structures recommended by the Presidential Railroad Commission.

This does not mean that the showdown will come in about thirty days, however. President Kennedy can head it off for sixty more by naming an emergency board to look into the dispute and make recommendations.

In an exchange of statements, the unions accused the railroads of trying to precipitate a transportation crisis and of refusing to bargain in good faith. The five unions represent 200,000 employes. About 40,000 jobs are at stake in the work-rules change.

The railroads charged that the unions' rejection of arbitration was "in keeping with their continued refusal to face up to their public responsibilities and their

Continued on Page 48, Column 1

JETLINER WITH 94 LOST OVER INDIA

Italian DC-8 Vanishes Near Bombay in Rainstorm—Wide Search Begins

By The Associated Press.

BOMBAY, India, Saturday, July 7—An Italian airliner carrying ninety-four persons made contact with Bombay's Santa Cruz Airport six minutes before it was due to land and then vanished early today in a heavy rainstorm.

Hours later there was no trace of the plane and a widespread search was under way.

Alitalia Airlines said the flight had originated in Sydney, Australia, stopped at Darwin, Singapore and Bangkok, and was destined for Rome.

It was in the Santa Cruz area that a Dutch K. L. M. plane crashed into a hillside thirteen years ago this month, killing thirteen American news correspondents and editors who had been on a Dutch-sponsored tour of Indonesia.

Search Is Begun

The Italian plane, with a crew of nine among the ninety-four reported aboard, was due here at 12:05 A. M. The airport lies two miles from the water's edge on the Arabian sea. Hills lie beyond it.

Airport officials alerted crash services and police in a fifty-mile radius to begin searching.

The course of the Alitalia jet lay across the Bay of Bengal and then across the Indian peninsula over Hyderabad to Bombay.

The plane, a DC-8, normally carries 105 passengers on long intercontinental hauls, but can carry many more.

The rain that fell heavily through the night eased off just

Continued on Page 4, Column 7

U.S. Lifts Curb on Travel For Visitors From Soviet

By MAX FRANKEL
Special to The New York Times.

WASHINGTON, July 6—Soviet tourists, delegations and performers were exempted today from a severe restriction on travel in the United States. The State Department, in taking the action, called on the Soviet Government to ease its curbs on travel by Americans and to negotiate for a further easing of travel rules.

The State Department notified the Soviet Ambassador, Anatoly F. Dobrynin, that rules barring a long list of areas, counties and cities to Soviet citizens would henceforth apply only to diplomats, journalists and other temporary residents. The restrictions will no longer apply to Soviet visitors under the cultural exchange program.

Text of the United States note to Soviet is on Page 2.

Itineraries of the visitors will still have to be registered and in many cases negotiated with the department, but, in theory at least, the entire country will be open to them.

The closed areas, amounting to 26 per cent of the territory of the United States, were established in 1955 in retaliation for a similar system imposed on Americans in the Soviet Union. Both countries have modified the list of closed areas from time to time.

Soviet Reaction Awaited

How liberally Soviet visitors will now be admitted to the former closed areas, officials indicated, will depend to a considerable extent on how flexible Moscow becomes in opening some of its closed sites.

One of the purposes of today's move was to goad the Russians into easing all travel restrictions. But it had been under consideration for some time primarily as a convenience for the United States to make the cultural exchange program more effective.

For instance, until now a delegation of Soviet steel experts has been automatically barred from Pittsburgh, a city in one of the closed areas. Future delegations will be able to

Continued on Page 2, Column 2

LAOS CHIEF'S PLAN DISAPPOINTS WEST

Draft by Souvanna Phouma at Geneva Falls Short of Allied Neutrality Hopes

By SYDNEY GRUSON
Special to The New York Times.

GENEVA, July 6—The West was bitterly disappointed in the draft declaration of neutrality submitted today to the co-chairmen of the international conference on Laos by Prince Souvanna Phouma, the newly installed neutralist Premier.

The draft failed to meet the West's hopes on the two remaining issues of the fifteen-month-old conference.

Apart from the contents of the draft declaration, Prince Souvanna Phouma's tactics angered the Western delegation.

He asked the two co-chairmen to distribute his draft immediately to the other delegations and to have it taken up in a full session of the fourteen-nation conference.

Malcolm MacDonald, the British co-chairman, returned the draft to Prince Souvanna Phouma, and was reported to have told him to circulate it privately if he wanted to do so. The anger among Western delegates arose from what they considered to be Prince Souvanna Phouma's effort to get the co-chairman's endorsement on the document.

The draft that the Prince gave to Mr. MacDonald and to Georgi M. Pushkin of the Soviet Union did not even mention the molding of the rival Laotian armies into a single national force.

Instead, Prince Souvanna Phouma proposed that he make

Continued on Page 2, Column 4

SOBLEN REQUESTS HAVEN IN BRITAIN

Spy Jailed Pending Hearing on Habeas Corpus

By SETH S. KING
Special to The New York Times.

LONDON, July 6 — Dr. Robert A. Soblen applied for political asylum in Britain today after a writ of habeas corpus had blocked his return to the United States.

Tonight he was moved by stretcher from Hillingdon Hospital to Brixton Prison. If the habeas corpus action is upheld he will be free to go wherever he chooses.

Early this morning, Justice Alan Abraham Mocatta of the High Court let Soblen's lawyers obtain the writ. He set July 16 as the date for a hearing. This was later amended to July 17.

The issuance of the writ will bar the British Home Office from placing the spy aboard a New York - bound plane until a High Court ruling is given.

Soblen's request for political asylum in Britain will be considered by the Home Office, probably before the High Court hearing.

An extradition treaty is in force between Britain and the United States. But espionage is not an extraditable crime under this treaty.

Soblen's lawyers waited until the early morning hours of the

Continued on Page 2, Column 6

VOTING MACHINES ORDERED BY CITY

Purchase of 2,750 Assures Use in Primary Sept. 6

By CHARLES G. BENNETT

The use of voting machines in the primary election Sept. 6 was assured by the Board of Estimate yesterday.

At a special meeting the board voted to purchase 2,750 machines without public bidding for $3,998,000 from the Shoup Voting Machine Corporation here.

In 1961 voting machines were used only in the Democratic party's primary. This will be the first year in which machines will be used for all political parties in a primary.

The Board of Elections had warned that if a decision on the purchase were put off any longer, paper ballots would have to be used. After yesterday's meeting, James M. Power, president of the elections board, said the use of machines only on Sept. 6 was now assured.

Months of delay and indecision preceded the Estimate Board's action yesterday. The vote was taken after officials of the Automatic Voting Machine division of the Rockwell Manufacturing Company of

Continued on Page 48, Column 4

U. S. Official Says Calorie Book Was a Promotion for Capsules

By MARJORIE HUNTER
Special to The New York Times.

WASHINGTON, July 6—A Government official charged today that the best-selling book "Calories Don't Count" was deliberately created and used to promote sales of "worthless safflower oil capsules."

The charge was made by George P. Larrick, Commissioner of the Food and Drug Administration.

"Calories Don't Count" was published by Simon & Schuster, Inc., of New York as the work of Dr. Herman Taller. Nearly 2,000,000 copies have been printed.

[In New York, Simon & Schuster denied the Federal agency's charge as "vicious and irresponsible." It said that it had not published the book to promote a food product.]

A statement issued by the Food and Drug Administration of the Department of Health, Education and Welfare said that "a default decree entered by the United States District Court in Brooklyn has established that 'Calories Don't Count' capsules are misbranded by false and misleading health and diet claims" made in the book.

Judge George Rosling signed an order, filed by United States Attorney Joseph P. Hoey, condemning more than 280 cases of capsules with copies of the book that had been seized last January by United States marshals, the statement said.

Mr. Larrick said in his statement that "the freedom to publish 'health' books is a constitutional guarantee."

"But," he said, "the courts

Continued on Page 15, Column 4

Associated Press Wirephoto

ADMIT LINK TO ESTES: Arthur D. Stone, at left, and Louis N. Dumas, former Agriculture Department employes from Eufaula, Okla., appear before the Senate Investigations subcommittee inquiry into cotton allotments.

$168,675 More Found in Jersey, A Block From 2.4 Million Hoard

Special to The New York Times.

JERSEY CITY, July 6 — A police search of garages uncovered another cache of money here today. A total of $168,675.52 was hidden in an empty one-car garage a block from where $2,421,850 was found last Tuesday in the trunk of an abandoned car.

The new batch of money, in bills ranging from five to one hundred dollars, as well as $115.52 in coins, was in two shopping bags. They were found behind about twenty other bags stacked in the rear of the garage.

The authorities said the money, like the original find, was the property of Joseph Vincent (Newsboy) Moriarty, a 52-year-old gambler now serving a two-to-three-year term for the possession of policy slips.

The gambler, in Trenton State Prison, continued to refuse to confirm or deny that he owned any of the money.

During the day, Federal tax officials filed liens that would make Moriarty liable for the entire original cache, plus another million dollars.

Jersey city officials indicated that the city would move to claim today's $168,675, if it could not be proved to belong

Continued on Page 44, Column 4

NEWS INDEX

Faulkner's Home, Family and Heritage Were Genesis of Yoknapatawpha County

AUTHOR RECEIVED LEADING PRIZES

Novels Praised as Powerful Tragedy and Scorned as Raw Slabs of Depravity

The storm of literary controversy that beat about William Faulkner is not likely to diminish with his death. Many of the most firmly established critics of literature were deeply impressed by the stark and somber power of his writing. Yet many commentators were repelled by his themes and his prose style.

To the sympathetic critics Mr. Falkner dealt with the dark journey and the final doom of man in terms that recalled the Greek tragedians. They found symbolism in the frequently unrelieved brutality of the yokels of Yoknapatawpha County, the imaginary Deep South region from which Mr. Faulkner drew the persons and scenes of his most characteristic novels and short stories.

Actually Yoknapatawpha was Lafayette County and Jefferson town was the Oxford on the red-hill section of northern Mississippi where William Faulkner was reared and where his family had been deeply rooted for generations. The author once told a class at the University of Virginia that it was pronounced Yok-na-pa-TAW-pha and that it was a Chickasaw Indian term that meant "water passes slowly through flatlands."

While admitting that Mr. Faulkner's prose sometimes lurched and sprawled, his admirers could point out an undeniable golden sharpness of characterization and description.

'In the Image of the Land'

Of Mr. Faulkner's power to create living and deeply moving characters, Malcolm Cowley wrote:

"And Faulkner loved these people created in the image of the land. After a second reading of his novels, you continue to be impressed by his villains, Popeye and Jason and Joe Christmas and Flem Snopes: but this time you find more place in your memory for other figures standing a little in the background yet presented by the author with quiet affection: old ladies like Miss Jenny DuPré, with their sharp-tongued benevolence; shrewd but kindly bargainers like Ratliff, the sewing machine agent, and Will Varner, with his cotton gin and general store. . . ."

Mr. Faulkner was an acknowledged master of the vivid descriptive phrase. Popeye had eyes that "looked like rubber knobs." He had a face that "just went away, like the face of a wax doll set too near the fire and forgotten."

The apt phrases that Mr. Faulkner found for the weather and the changing seasons were cited by his admirers. There was the "hot pine-winey silence of the August afternoon." Or "the moonless September dust, the trees not rising soaring as trees should but squatting like huge fowl." Also, "those windless Mississippi December days which are a sort of Indian summer's Indian summer."

Some Saw Little Merit

Many critics contended that Mr. Faulkner served up raw slabs of pseudorealism that had relatively little merit as serious writing. They said that Mr. Faulkner's writings showed an obsession with murder, rape, incest, suicide, greed and general depravity that did not exist anywhere but in the author's mind in anything like the proportions that these subjects assumed in his novels and short stories.

A favorite device of the detractors of Mr. Faulkner's writings was to produce a condensed and completely deadpan description of his plots. The result was often a horrendous compilation of wickedness and jibbering. As for Mr. Faulkner, he seldom argued about his work.

For most of his literary life he detested talk about literature. He said that when one of his books was about to be published he had to remind himself that strangers were going to read it.

Mr. Faulkner was the fourth American to receive the Nobel Prize for Literature. The previous winners were Sinclair Lewis (1930), Eugene O'Neill (1936) and Pearl S. Buck (1938). Ernest Hemingway became the fifth American in 1954. The 1954 Pulitzer Prize for fiction was awarded to Mr. Faulkner for his novel "A Fable."

William Faulkner was born in New Albany, Miss., on Sept. 25, 1897. In the sharply stratified society that preoccupied Mr. Faulkner in his writings it could be said that he came from an upper middle - class family — one not quite of the old feudal cotton aristocracy.

The first Falkners — the "u" is a recent restoration by William Faulkner — came to Mississippi in the Eighteen Forties. The family is replete with colonels, one of whom was assassinated on the street by a business rival. William Faulkner was the oldest child of Murray Falkner and Maude Butler Falkner. Murray Falkner at one time ran a livery stable in Oxford and later became business manager of the University of Mississippi at Oxford.

In William Faulkner's fiction the Sartoris clan is the Falkner family. The Sartorises are forced to make humiliating compromises with the members of the grasping and upstart Snopes family.

"General Johnston or General Forrest wouldn't have took a Snopes into his army at all," a character says.

William Faulkner played quarterback on the Oxford high School football team and suffered a broken nose. He failed to graduate. Later he wrote: "Quit school to work in grandfather's bank. Learned medicinal value of his liquor. Grandfather thought it was the janitor. Hard on the janitor. . . ."

Oxford, where Mr. Faulkner grew up, is a typical Deep-South town. It has the traditional courthouse square flanked with statues of Confederate soldiers. and a quiet main street lined by one-story buildings and stores.

It is in Lafayette County in the northern part of Mississippi, about sixty miles southeast of Memphis. It is the seat of the University of Mississippi.

The 1949 motion picture "Intruder in the Dust," based on Mr. Faulkner's novel of that name, was filmed by Metro-Goldwyn-Mayer in Oxford. It was directed by Clarence Brown and its cast included Juano Hernandez, Claude Jarman Jr. and Elizabeth Patterson.

The film depicted racial intolerance and bigotry in a small Southern community but had a "happy ending" in which an elderly, proud Negro accused of murder—played by Mr. Hernandez—is saved from lynching by a white Southern lawyer with the help of a white boy and an elderly white woman. The movie was called "great" by Bosley Crowther, The New York Times critic. It made The Times' list of the year's ten best films, but it did not make money.

In an interview in 1958, Mr. Faulkner was asked for his reaction to the movie version of "Intruder in the Dust." He said:

"I'm not much of a moviegoer, but I did see that one. I thought it was a fine job. That Juano Hernandez is a fine actor —and man, too."

He also said he had written about a dozen movie scripts for Hollywood after his popular novel "Sanctuary" was published. He said that most of the scripts were done for Howard Hawks, his friend, and added:

"He sent for me later to help adapt what Ernest Hemingway said was the worst book he ever wrote, 'To Have and Have Not.' Then I did another one, from that book by Raymond Chandler, 'The Big Sleep.' I also did a war picture, one I liked doing, 'The Road to Glory,' with Fredric March and Lionel Barrymore. I made me some money and I had me some fun."

Private flying and World War I service as a Royal Canadian Air Force pilot gave Mr. Faulkner material for such tales as 'Pylon," a story of daredevil barnstorming pilots. Back home, he was a special student at the University of Mississippi for a few months and became postmaster at the hamlet of University near Oxford. He was dismissed for reading and playing bridge when he should have been distributing mail.

One who knew Mr. Faulkner as a student at the University of Mississippi is George W. Healy Jr., editor of The New Orleans Times-Picayune. In a telephone interview yesterday, Mr. Healy said that most Mississippians who knew Mr. Faulkner well loved him, but that the author was not an easy man to know.

"I first knew Bill when he was postmaster at the University of Mississippi post office in 1922," Mr. Healy said. "He was fresh back from World War I after having served as a pilot in the Canadian Air Force and after having done a little private flying. His father, whose first name was Murray, was business manager of the university and Bill went there to study law.

"But Bill got fired as postmaster because he used the post office as a kind of men's club. One day a post office inspector came in while a bridge game was in progress and a little while later Bill told us he was leaving."

Preferred Cartoons

Mr. Healy related that when he was editor of the university's humor magazine, The Scream, Mr. Faulkner approached him with some poetry he had written.

"Bill also had some cartoons that he had drawn and I liked the cartoons better than the poetry," Mr. Healy said.

The editor recalled that Mr. Faulkner later did some house-painting jobs in Oxford and then went to New Orleans where he "holed up while writing his first novel, 'Soldier's Pay.'" This is the story of a disfigured flier's return after World War I. It was published in 1926 by Liveright. A reviewer in The Times said it showed a "deft hand."

Mr. Healy noted that while he was writing the novel, Mr. Faulkner also wrote for The Times-Picayune "Mirrors of Chartres Street," a column of street scenes and vignettes.

Mr. Faulkner's period of literary apprenticeship included a foray into New York literary circles that ended in a brief and unhappy interlude as a clerk in the book department of Lord & Taylor. He was briefly a newspaper reporter in New Orleans where he saw something of Sherwood Anderson, who gave him valuable counsel.

'Marble Faun' in 1924

"The Marble Faun," a book of poems by Mr. Faulkner, appeared in 1924. Reviewers found the poems somewhat derivative.

With the publication of "The Sound and the Fury" in 1929, Mr. Faulkner gave strong indications of being a major writer. The critics found in it something of the word-intoxication of James Joyce and the long, lasso - like sentences of Henry James.

"Sanctuary," published in 1931, was Mr. Faulkner's most popular and best-selling novel. His friends did not believe him when he said that he had written it only for money.

It is a novel about the harrowing experiences of a sensitive Southern girl, Temple Drake, who, like many of Faulkner's characters, reappears in another book—in this case "Requiem for a Nun." One of Mr. Faulkner's most memorable characters, Popeye, was created for "Sanctuary."

Among Mr. Faulkner's other natable books were "The Sound and the Fury" and "As I Lay Dying."

The former, described by one critic as "noe of the few original efforts at experimental writing in America," is told partly through the mind of an idiot named Benjy.

Mr. Faulkner lived and did most of his writing in Oxford in a beautiful old colonial house that he bought in 1930. He was a slightly built man who carried himself somewhat tensely and when he was bothered or bored he could exhibit quick anger. He had thick iron - gray hair and a dark mustache and aquiline nose. When he felt like it he could be charming and his manners were impeccable. His accent was the easy drawl of the Deep South. One observer found in his manner "something old - fashioned, even archaic." In his Southern mansion he usually wanted to be left alone and there were explosive incidents when persons sought to intrude upon him.

When the Nobel Prize for literature for 1949 was awarded to Mr. Faulkner it was with considerable difficulty that members of his family persuaded him to go to Stockholm, Sweden, to receive the award.

He wore white tie and tails for the first time. The cash prize amounted to $30,000, which Mr. Faulkner set up as a fund for good works in his home town.

The clash of opinion over the question of desegregation in the public schools drew Mr. Faulkner somewhat out of his general aloofness to public problems. In 1956 he was interviewed and wrote on the problem of the Negro in the South. His writing on the subject showed a somewhat agonized attempt to understand several points of view on the question.

On June 20, 1929, Mr. Faulkner married Mrs. Estelle Oldham Franklin, who had two children by a previous marriage. One daughter, Jill, was born to the marriage of Mr. Faulkner and Mrs. Franklin.

William Faulkner was not the only novelist in his immediate family. A younger brother, John Faulkner, wrote several novels, including "Men Working," (1941), a story of Southern farmers who discovered a modern miracle they called "the WP & A," and "Chooky," (1950), a tale of a Southern boy who leads two Negro playmates through a series of adventures.

William Faulkner was among the Nobel Prize laureates invited by President Kennedy to a White House dinner this year. At the time the novelist was with the University of Virginia and was living at Charlottesville. He declined, saying: "Why that's a hundred miles away. That's a long way to go just to eat."

In 1957, when Mr. Faulkner first arrived at the University of Virginia, he was quoted as saying:

"I like Virginians because Virginians are all snobs and I like snobs. A snob has to spend so much time being a snob that he has little time left to meddle with you."

On another occasion, Bennett Cerf, head of Random House, Mr. Faulkner's publisher, had taken the bourbon-sipping author to task for not answering his mail. Mr. Faulkner was said to have replied:

"Mr. Cerf, when I get a letter from you, I open it and shake it and if a check doesn't fall out I tend to forget it."

Mr. Faulkner accepted an invitation in April to the United States Military Academy to hold informal discussions with the cadets on literary topics. Thirty young women from Vassar College also attended the seminar.

Mr. Faulkner held the cadets rapt as he discussed the destiny of man in a "ramshackle world." The Nobel Prize-winning author said a writer should "cut his throat and quit" whenever he felt satisfied with a book he had written.

He also told the cadets that "The Sound and the Fury" was the book closest to his heart because it had caused him the most anguish. He said that it was to him what a crippled child was to its mother.

Mr. Faulkner also discussed his latest novel, "The Reivers," with the cadets.

"The Reivers" was published by Random House on June 4 and was widely acclaimed by critics. For example, Orville Prescott in his review of the novel in The New York Times wrote:

"The good news about "The Reivers" is that it is one of the best novels Mr. Faulkner has written and much the most direct, simple and readily comprehensible. All his familiar mannerisms are present, but so muted and restrained that they cause no difficulty.

"In the past. Mr. Faulkner's humor has tended to be cruel or even grotesque. In "The Reivers' it is not exactly hilarious, but it is gay, engaging and kindly."

Associated Press

TRIUMPH: The author received the 1949 Nobel Prize for literature from King Gustaf VI Adolf of Sweden at Stockholm in 1950. Award was for Yoknapatawpha County books.

A Literary Personality

Faulkner's Legacy Is Found in His Diverse Uses of Talent and Power

By ORVILLE PRESCOTT

THE death of William Faulkner yesterday is a major loss to American letters. Critical opinions and personal reactions to Faulkner's many books may range from ecstatic admiration to ignorant denunciation, but one fact about the controversial chronicler of Yoknapatawpha County is beyond dispute: no novelist of Faulkner's time so successfully imposed his own vision of life upon his readers and none possessed so strikingly individual a literary personality.

Ernest Hemingway's literary personality was striking also, but it was Hemingway's nonliterary personality—the aura of sports, hunting, fishing, bullfighting and well-publicized heroics—that made him celebrated among millions who never read his books. All his life Faulkner shunned publicity and let his books speak for themselves. Just what they said is a matter of some conjecture.

"I'm just a writer, not a literary man," Faulkner once said. "I write about the people around Oxford. I know them and they know me."

This seemingly modest statement wasn't quite so. Faulkner did write about the people of Oxford in the present and back through four or five generations. But by the time he had finished writing about them most of them were no longer recognizable as people. They had become archetypes, legendary heroes and villains, symbolical figures and grossly caricatured figures.

Contradictory Aspects

It is true that Faulkner wrote about them with glittering brilliance, with flashes of demonic power, with frequent spasms of cruel and gusty humor and with compassion for the suffering of mortal men. He was probably as near to a genius as can be found among American writers. But Faulkner was also a sad example of literary self-indulgence, of a disastrous contempt for artistic self-discipline and of a kind of arrogance.

He scorned to write as well as he could. He refused not only to prune and clarify his labyrinthine style, which made many pages in many of his books almost impenetrable; he refused even to edit his novels so that they fitted together. Characters with the same names seem like different people in different books. Dates are confused. Anecdotes are repeated and contradict each other.

This kind of sloppiness irritated many non-Faulknerians. But their chief objections were two. The famous Faulkner style was more than many could put up with. Its marathon sentences, its peculiar words used peculiarly, its turgid incoherence and its thick viscosity repelled. Faulkner himself in his last three novels, "The Town," "The Mansion" and "The Reivers," seemed to be shifting to a much simpler and more readily comprehensible prose.

The other most often heard charge against Faulkner's novels is that in many of them there is an excessive emphasis on one kind of human behavior, the basest. Violence, murder and madness are almost normal in Faulkner's most powerful and impressive books, and sexual crimes and misdemeanors of astounding variety abound. Faulkner's most ardent admirers do not mind the agonized style, which undeniably achieves much emotional power, and they take the assorted horrors in their stride.

Surviving on Balance

And it is certainly true that even at his most clumsy and obscure William Faulkner was challenging, that his distorted vision of the South was arresting and that many of his characters are unforgettable. Faulkner was no minor writer. He was always an interesting one. He failed of greatness, but he proved that he at least had it in him to be great. And of how many novelists can this be said?

It remains to say something about his influence. Faulkner is internationally admired. He is often imitated by lesser writers who can surpass him in violence although they cannot rival his insights or his poetic power. And academic critics have written more about Faulkner than about any other contemporary American novelist. They find irresistible the opportunity to put order into confusion, to explain symbolical mysteries and to interpret obscurities. Consequently, young people with an interest in literature are indoctrinated early. Faulkner, for them, is the greatest of American novelists.

He isn't and will not always be so regarded. But he is worth reading and worth studying. His books can stir the emotions, challenge the mind and offer object lessons in good and in bad writing.

Ralph Thompson

SAGE: An Emily Clark Balch lecturer in American literature, he spent much time in recent years at the University of Virginia at Charlottesville, the home of his daughter.

Samples of the Writing

Following, as examples of William Faulkner's writing style, are a lengthy sentence from the short story, "The Bear," and a passage from his most recent work, "The Reïvers," a novel. They are copyrighted and reprinted by permission of Random House, Inc.

The Bear

This was chronicled in a harsher book, and McCaslin, fourteen and fifteen and sixteen, had seen it and the boy himself had inherited it as Noah's grandchildren had inherited the Flood although they had not been there to see the deluge: that dark corrupt and bloody time while three separate peoples had tried to adjust not only to one another but to the new land which they had created and inherited too and must live in for the reason that those who had lost it were no less free to quit it than those who had gained it were:—those upon whom freedom and equality had been dumped overnight and without warning or preparation or any training in how to employ it or even just endure it and who misused it, not as children would nor yet because they had been so long in bondage and then so suddenly freed, but misused it as human beings always misuse freedom, so that he thought *Apparently there is a wisdom beyond even that learned through suffering necessary for a man to distinguish between liberty and license;* those who had fought for four years and lost to preserve a condition under which that franchisement was anomaly and paradox, not because they were opposed to freedom as freedom but for the old reasons for which man (not the generals and politicians but man) has always fought and died in wars: to preserve a status quo or to establish a better future one to endure for his children: and lastly, as if that were not enough for bitterness and hatred and fear, that third race even more alien to the people whom they resembled in pigment and in whom even the same blood ran, than to the people whom they did not.—that race threefold in one and alien even among themselves save for a single fierce will for rapine and pillage, composed of the sons of middleaged Quartermaster lieutenants and Army sutlers and contractors in military blankets and shoes and transport mules, who followed the battles they themselves had not fought and inherited the conquest they themselves had not helped to gain, sanctioned and protected even if not blessed, and left their bones and in another generation would be engaged in a fierce economic competition of small sloven farms with the black men they were supposed to have freed and the white descendants of fathers who had owned no slaves anyway whom they were supposed to have disinherited, and in the third generation would be back once more in the little lost county seats as barbers and garage mechanics and deputy sheriffs and mill- and gin-hands and power-plant firemen, leading, first in mufti then later in an actual formalized regalia of hooded sheets and passwords and fiery Christian symbols, lynching mobs against the race their ancestors had come to save: and of all that other nameless horde of speculators in human misery, manipulators of money and politics and land, who follow catastrophe and are their own protection as grasshoppers are and need no blessing and sweat no plow or axe-helve and batten and vanish and leave no bones, just as they derived apparently from no ancestry, no mortal flesh, no act even of passion or even of lust: and the Jew who came without protection too, since after two thousand years he had got out of the habit of being or needing it, and solitary, without even the solidarity of the locusts, and in this a sort of courage since he had come thinking not in terms of simple pillage but in terms of his great-grandchildren, seeking yet some place to establish them to endure even though forever alien: and unblessed: a pariah about the face of the Western earth which twenty centuries later was still taking revenge on him for the fairy tale with which he had conquered it.

The Reivers

Ned had seen it too. He had already had one hard look at the mudhole. Now he looked at the already geared-up mules standing there swishing and slapping at mosquitoes while they waited for us. "Now, that's what I calls convenient—" he said.

"Shut up," Boon said in a fierce murmur. "Not a word. Dont make a sound." He spoke in a tense controlled fury, propping his muddy pole against the car and hauling out the block and tackle and the barbed wire and the axe and spade. He said Son of a bitch three times. Then he said to me: "You too."

"Me?" I said.

"But look at them mules," Ned said. "He even got a log chain already hooked to that doubletree—"

"Didn't you hear me say shut up?" Boon said in that fierce, quite courteous murmur. "If I didn't speak plain enough, excuse me. What I'm trying to say is, shut up."

"Only, what in the world do he want with the middle-buster?" Ned said. "And it muddy clean up to the handles too. Like he been—You mean to say he gets in here with that team and works this place like a patch just to keep it boggy?" Boon had the spade, axe and block and tackle all three in his hands. For a second I thought he would strike Ned with any one or maybe all three of them.

FAULKNER IS DEAD IN OXFORD AT 64

Continued From Page 1, Col. 3

set his Gothic saga of decadent sophisticates, greedy landlords, and shrewd and brutal tenant farmers.

Mr. Faulkner won a Pulitzer prize for his 1954 novel, "The Fable," and was awarded the National Book of Gold Medal in 1950 for his volume, "Collected Stories of William Faulkner."

His most famous novels were "Absalom, Absalom!" "Sartoris," "The Sound and the Fury," "As I Lay Dying," "Sanctuary" and "Light in August" and the trilogy "The Hamlet," "The Town" and "The Mansion." His most recent novel, "The Reivers," was published June 4 to wide critical acclaim.

In addition to his widow, other survivors include his daughter, Mrs. Paul Summer of Charlottesville, Va., his brothers, John and Murray, and three grandchildren.

His death followed by just a little more than a year the passing of another American literary giant—Ernest Hemingway, who died July 2, 1961.

A key to Mr. Faulkner's genius was the faculty he possessed of thinking and writing in the vernacular of poor whites and Negroes of his section.

The tales of Yoknapatawpha, interwoven with rape, violence and sadism, repelled some readers to the extent that recognition in his homeland had to await acclaim from abroad.

He once remarked somewhat bitterly: "The writer in America isn't part of the culture of this country. He's like a fine dog. People like him around, but he's of no use."

When he was named to receive the Nobel prize, Mr. Faulkner was reluctant to travel to Europe.

"I feel that what remains after thirty years of work is not worth carrying from Mississippi to Sweden," he said.

However, he went, explaining that his daughter should see Paris.

Mr. Faulkner was a familiar figure on the University of Virginia campus in Charlottesville. sauntering along with a curved pipe in his mouth. He occasionally spoke to an acquaintaince, but his mind was usually elsewhere and he has passed some of his best friends without seeing them

Mr. Faulkner, a bourbon-sipping Southern gentleman who frequently rode to the hounds, fell from his horse in the woods near his home about three years ago.

His collarbone was broken in the fall from a horse but thirty minutes after the accident, his neck in a brace, he was drinking bourbon with friends. He said then, "It didn't hurt no worse than a hangnail."

Burial to Be in Oxford

OXFORD, July 6 (AP)—The Rev. Duncan Gray, rector of the Oxford Episcopal Church, will preside at funeral services at 2 P. M. tomorrow at the Faulkner family home. Burial will be in St. Peter's Cemetery, Oxford.

THE NOBEL SPEECH: MAN WILL PREVAIL

Poet's Duty Is to Help Him Endure, Author Declared

William Faulkner's address of acceptance of the Nobel Prize for letters in Stockholm, Sweden, drew wide interest in literary circles.

On the day he gave it—Dec. 10, 1950—the Nobel ceremony was overshadowed by news of the heavy fighting in the Korean War. But subsequently Mr. Faulkner's speech attracted considerable comment. The text follows:

I feel that this award was not made to me as a man, but to my work—a life's work in the agony and sweat of the human spirit, not for glory and least of all for profit, but to create out of the materials of the human spirit something which did not exist before.

So this award is only mine in trust. It will not be difficult to find a dedication for the money part of it commensurate with the purpose and significance of its origin. But I would like to do the same with the acclaim too, by using this moment as a pinnacle from which I might be listened to by the young men and women already dedicated to the same anguish and travail, among whom is already that one who will some day stand here where I am standing.

One Question Left

Our tragedy today is a general and universal physical fear so long sustained by now that we can even bear it. There are no longer problems of spirit. There is only the question: When will I be blown up? Because of this, the young man or woman writing today has forgotten the problems of the human heart in conflict with itself which alone can make good writing because only that is worth writing about, worth the agony and the sweat.

He must learn them again. He must teach himself that the basest of all things is to be afraid; and, teaching himself that, forget it forever, leaving no room in his workshop for anything but the old verities and truths of the heart, the old universal truths lacking which any story is ephemeral and doomed—love and honor and pity and pride and compassion and sacrifice. Until he does so, he labors under a curse. He writes not of love but of lust, of defeats in which nobody loses anything of value, of victories without hope and, worst of all, without pity or compassion. His griefs grieve on no universal bones, leaving no scars. He writes not of the heart but of the glands.

Calls Man Immortal

Until he relearns these things, he will write as though he stood among and watched the end of man.

I decline to accept the end of man. It is easy enough to say that man is immortal simply because he will endure: that when the last ding-dong of doom has clanged and faded from the last worthless rock hanging tideless in the last red and dying evening, that even then there will be one more sound: that of his puny, inexhaustible voice, still talking.

I refuse to accept this. I believe that man will not merely endure: he will prevail. He is immortal, not because he alone among creatures has an inexhaustible voice, but because he has a soul, a spirit capable of compassion and sacrifice and endurance.

The poet's, the writer's, duty is to write about these things. It is his privilege to help man endure by lifting up his heart, by reminding him of the courage and honor and hope and pride and compassion and pity and sacrifice which have been the glory of his past.

The poet's voice need not merely be the record of man, it can be one of the props, the pillars to help him endure and prevail.

Chief Faulkner Works From 1924 to 1962

William Faulkner's principal works include the following:

"The Marble Faun" (poems), 1924; "Soldier's Pay," 1926; "Mosquitoes," 1927; "Sartoris," 1929; "The Sound and the Fury," 1929; "As I Lay Dying," 1930; "Sanctuary," 1931; "These Thirteen" (short stories), 1931; "Idyll in the Desert," 1931; "Light In August," 1932; "A Green Bough" (poems), 1933; "Doctor Martino," 1934; "Pylon," 1935; "Absalom, Absalom!" 1936, and "The Unvanquished."

Also, "The Wild Palms," 1939; "The Hamlet," 1940; "Go Down, Moses, and Other Stories," 1942; "Intruder in the Dust," 1948; "Knight's Gambit," 1949; "Collected Stories of William Faulkner," 1950, "Requiem for a Nun," 1951; "A Fable," 1954; "Big Woods," 1955; "The Town," 1957; "The Mansion," 1959, and "The Reivers," 1962.

"All the News That's Fit to Print"

The New York Times

LATE CITY EDITION

Weather: Sunny, mild today; fair tonight. Fair, mild tomorrow. Temp. range: today 69-45; Tues. 66-43. Full U. S. report on Page 94.

VOL. CXVII...No. 40,261 · NEW YORK, WEDNESDAY, APRIL 17, 1968 · 10 CENTS

NATION'S PRODUCT HAD RECORD GAIN IN FIRST QUARTER

Industrial Output, Spurred by Rise in Assemblies of Autos, Also Sets Mark

BUT HAZARDS ARE NOTED

U.S. Officials Fear a Boom in Economy Will Weaken Balance of Payments

By H. J. MAIDENBERG

Special to The New York Times

WASHINGTON, April 16—A record $20-billion increase in the gross national product in the first quarter and the setting of a new mark in industrial production last month were reported today by the Department of Commerce and the Federal Reserve System.

The gains in the key economic indicators, though conforming to the accelerating pace of the nation's economy, also reinforced concern among Administration officials. A booming economy, they fear, will further stimulate imports at a time when the country's balance-of-payments situation is deteriorating and inflationary clouds are thickening.

However, the speed-up in the rate of economic expansion is providing additional ammunition for the Administration's efforts to obtain a tax surcharge from the Congress for use in braking the adverse trends.

Dollar Yardstick

The gross national product—the dollar yardstick of the nation's total output of goods and services — climbed by $20-billion in the first three months of the year, to a seasonally adjusted annual rate of $827.3-billion, also a record, the Commerce Department said in its preliminary report.

This represented an increase of 2.5 per cent in the rate of economic expansion from the last quarter of 1967, when the gross product rose $16-billion, to an annual rate of $807.3-billion.

Consumer spending accounted for some $16-billion of the rise for the quarter, reflecting the high rate of employment and disposable income as well as the common factors of population increase and rising prices.

Annual Basis

As for prices, the Commerce Department said the 2.5 per cent increase in gross product consisted of 1 per cent for over-all higher prices and 1.5 per cent for the rise in physical volume of output. Projected on an annual basis, this would indicate that prices are rising at the rate of 4 per cent a year.

Many economists consider this rate too low and talk in terms of 5 per cent as more realistic for this year, if the present economic expansion continues apace. They also add a percentage point to last year's official figures showing price rise in the order of 3 per cent.

In any event, consumers spent about half the $16-billion recorded in that category on food and clothing, further support-

Continued on Page 70, Column 8

Lindsay Puts Life Ahead of Property In Curbing Looters

By RICHARD REEVES

Mayor Lindsay summed up the city's philosophy and strategy of dealing with racial violence yesterday in these words:

"We happen to think that protection of life, particularly innocent life, is more important than protecting property or anything else. . . . We are not going to turn disorder into chaos through the unprincipled use of armed force. In short, we are not going to shoot children in New York City."

The Mayor contrasted his thinking with the orders of Mayor Richard J. Daley of Chicago to shoot rioters—orders that were also criticized yesterday by Gov. Richard J. Hughes of New Jersey and former Mayor Robert F. Wagner.

Mr. Lindsay was showered with questions about the orders to Chicago police during a City Hall news conference. Mayor Daley had an-

Continued on Page 29, Column 1

C. A. B. EXAMINER URGES EXPANDING PACIFIC FLIGHTS

Vast Route Overhaul Would Admit Eastern, T.W.A. and Western to Area

By EVERT CLARK

Special to The New York Times

WASHINGTON, April 16 — A vast expansion of airline service to Hawaii, the South Pacific and the Orient was recommended today by a Civil Aeronautics Board examiner.

Urging the first overhaul of Pacific route structures in 20 years, Robert L. Park proposed that Eastern Air Lines, Trans World Airlines and Western Air Lines be admitted to the rapidly expanding Pacific market.

The new candidates would join Pan American, Northwest and United. Those three lines would be granted some new or improved routes. In addition, Flying Tiger would become the first American cargo line with Pacific authority, on a five-year experimental basis.

[In trading on the New York Stock Exchange, shares of the airlines recommended for new Pacific service registered price gains. Page 63.]

First Major Step

One effect of today's proposals would be to make Pan American and T.W.A. true round-the-world carriers of the American flag. T.W.A. now flies east from California to Hong Kong but no farther. Pan Am basically has no domestic routes, but recently got interim permission to link its West Coast terminals with New York.

The recommendation is the first major step in the biggest case in C.A.B. history. It must be reviewed by the board itself—perhaps by mid-June—and then by the President.

Mr. Parks's recommendation would increase competition in almost every area of the Pacific and give many inland and East Coast cities direct service to Hawaii and beyond.

Would Start in 70's

New and improved services proposed today would begin early in the nineteen-seventies. Six foreign-flag carriers now compete against the three American carriers in the Pacific.

The importance of the so-called Trans-Pacific Route Investigation was reflected in this statement by Mr. Parks:

"One cannot peruse the facts in this record without being deeply impressed by the nature and extent of the involvement of this nation in the Pacific. From every point of view — defense, economic, trade, tourism — the interests of the United States are being drawn inexorably toward the countries of the Pacific basin."

Seventy-two parties have introduced evidence in the case

Continued on Page 70, Column 4

United Press International

JOHNSON CONFERS WITH MILITARY LEADERS: The President and members of his party with leaders of services at headquarters in Hawaii. From the left: Gen. John D. Ryan, Air Force; Gen. Earle G. Wheeler, Chairman of the Joint Chiefs of Staff; Mr. Johnson; Adm. U. S. Grant Sharp; Cyrus R. Vance, Presidential aide; Gen. Dwight E. Beach, Army, and William P. Bundy, Assistant Secretary of State for Far Eastern Affairs. Meeting lasted three hours.

U.S. OPEN TO MOVE BY A THIRD PARTY ON SITE FOR TALKS

Officials Assert They Would Welcome Idea to Help End the Impasse With Hanoi

COMPROMISE IS SOUGHT

Diplomats Say Paris Might Be Proposed as a Capital Acceptable to Both Sides

By HEDRICK SMITH

Special to The New York Times

WASHINGTON, April 16—The United States would welcome suggestions from third parties to help break the current impasse with North Vietnam over the site for their preliminary talks, State Department officials said today.

Some officials expressed concern that, for reasons of face, Hanoi might be unwilling to accept any of the five sites proposed by the United States.

"It may be that some third parties can come up with a site which both sides can agree to without anybody losing face," an official said. "We're not trying to save face. We're trying to save South Vietnam."

Other officials said that proposals by third parties might be useful in breaking the deadlock.

Neutrality Stressed

But these officials, talking at a national foreign policy conference at the State Department, emphasized that the United States was insisting on a neutral site, at least partly to insure that it would be able to keep South Vietnam and its other allies in the war abreast of the negotiating process.

Privately, officials indicated that some proposals might be forthcoming from Secretary General Thant, who talked recently with Mai Van Bo, the North Vietnamese representative in Paris, and met today with Arthur J. Goldberg, the chief United States delegate to the United Nations.

Paris is the capital most prominently mentioned in diplomatic speculation as a possible compromise between American and North Vietnamese suggestions.

A Proposal Foreseen

Washington has proposed Geneva; New Delhi; Rangoon, Burma; Vientiane, Laos, and Jakarta, Indonesia. Hanoi has suggested Warsaw and Pnompenh, Cambodia. While neither side has flatly rejected the other's proposals, they have expressed strong objections to each other's suggestions.

Speculation has centered recently on Paris largely as a result of statements by a North Vietnamese press agency representative in a British television interview nearly two weeks ago. He said that the talks would probably be held in Warsaw, Pnompenh or Paris. Since Hanoi has already proposed the first two capitals, some officials foresee that it will now propose the third.

Robert J. McCloskey, the State Department spokesman, said today that the United

Continued on Page 4, Column 5

SANITATION STRIKE IN MEMPHIS ENDS

Employes Win Recognition of Union, Dues Checkoff and Raise of 15 Cents

By EARL CALDWELL

Special to The New York Times

MEMPHIS, April 16—The bitter sanitationmen's strike that had brought the Rev. Dr. Martin Luther King Jr. to Memphis and his death from a sniper's bullet ended today.

As outlined by Jerry Wurf, international president of the striking union, the agreement insured the sanitationmen of union recognition, including dues checkoff, promotions on the basis of seniority, and a 10-cent-an-hour wage increase on May 1 plus a 5-cent increase on Sept. 1.

Settlement Ratified

The union said that before the strike began two months ago the men had been earning $1.60 and $2.25 an hour.

The settlement was ratified quickly by the workers and then approved by the City Council with one dissenting vote.

The agreement was widely acclaimed by the city's Negro community, which had lined up solidly behind the garbage collectors. Most of the workers are Negroes.

"We won," a thin, aging Negro collector said, recalling Dr. King, "but we lost a good man along the way."

Dr. King had interrupted his plans for a Poor People's Cam-

Continued on Page 24, Column 3

Nonsectarian Panel Is Named to Study Parochial Schools

By M. A. FARBER

The Most Rev. Terence J. Cooke, Archbishop of New York, yesterday appointed a nonsectarian committee of leaders in education, finance, industry and civic affairs to conduct a comprehensive study of the archdiocese's 432 schools.

The committee, which is to recommend improvements in such areas as financing, managing and staffing, will begin its work Monday. Its 16 members include five college and university presidents.

Archbishop Cooke said that the archdiocesan schools "were confronting very serious problems" and that the committee would provide "a solid basis for action" to meet those difficulties.

Money a Problem

"Money, very frankly, is a problem," he added.

Other difficulties, the Archbishop noted, involve updating the curriculum, employing adequately trained teachers and "the role of the schools in disadvantaged" neighborhoods.

At a time when many members of the religious and laity are questioning whether parochial schools should be expanded or curtailed, Archbishop Cooke declared:

"I reaffirm my dedication to our educational endeavors. We must be certain that we move to strengthen and broaden these endeavors."

The Committee on Catholic Education is headed by T. Murray McDonnell, president and chairman of the board of Mc-

Continued on Page 52, Column 1

PROTESTS PAUSE IN WEST GERMANY

Students Hold Off Drive on Publisher to Examine the Recent Violence

Special to The New York Times

BONN, April 16—West Germany's radical student leaders, exhausted by five days of continual demonstrations, called today for a pause to reflect on the gains and losses of their violent protest.

Frank Wolf, a national leader of the Socialist German Student League in Frankfurt, said no actions were foreseen this evening against the conservative Axel Springer publishing chain.

Since last Thursday, when the student leader Rudi Dutschke was gravely wounded by an admirer of Hitler, Josef Bachmann, thousands of left-wing students have focused their protest demonstrations against Springer newspapers.

Papers Are Accused

The left-wing organization argues that the Springer papers, with 40 per cent of the national daily circulation, have "manipulated public opinion against basic democracy" in general and students in particular.

The students cite as an example a headline in Springer's Bild Zeitung: "Truncheons Out—Against Students!"

The Springer papers display a generally conservative editorial policy. They oppose neo-Nazis, but support nationalists. They deplore the war in Vietnam, but sympathize with the United States.

In the Springer view, German reunification should be achieved only by free elections in East Germany. East-West tensions, the papers contend, should be resolved by unilateral concessions from Communist countries, mainly the Soviet Union and Poland.

The tally after four nights

Continued on Page 11, Column 1

Johnson Briefed in Hawaii On Vietnam Deployments

By MAX FRANKEL

Special to The New York Times

HONOLULU, April 16—President Johnson spent more than three hours with his military commanders in the Pacific here today. He was told about the deployment of enemy and allied forces since the start of efforts to arrange negotiations between the United States and North Vietnam.

Reports from Vietnam had suggested a lull in the ground fighting, and presumably the President heard in detail about this. But no one in the Administration seems to relate the relative quiet on the battlefield to the attempts to establish ambassadorial contacts between Washington and Hanoi.

In fact, recent statements by Administration officials have suggested that the enemy has been forced to avoid contact because of severe casualties inflicted both by allied ground operations and by massive air assaults such as the bombings around Khesanh, the Marine outpost until recently besieged by the North Vietnamese.

No Word From Hanoi

While attending the briefing and awaiting the arrival of President Chung Hee Park of South Korea, Mr. Johnson was also keeping an eye on the continuing duel with Hanoi over arrangements for the first meeting of ambassadors. Members of his party reported that they had received no further messages from the North Vietnamese capital.

President Johnson asked yesterday for a direct reply to his proposal that the meetings take place in one of four neutral countries in which both North Vietnam and the United States maintain diplomatic missions and to which they have good communications. These countries are India, Burma, Indonesia and Laos.

2 Suggestions Received

North Vietnam, in two official messages received by Washington, suggested Cambodia or Poland. They are deemed unsuitable by the Johnson Administration, either because of poor communications or because of a presumed lack of access to the negotiations in a Communist country by officials and newsmen of allied countries such as South Vietnam and South Korea.

North Vietnam, in turn, said in a Foreign Ministry statement on Saturday that it found the sites proposed by the United States "not adequate."

The President's meetings at the headquarters of the Pacific command brought him in touch with officers who have been the most ardent advocates of

Continued on Page 4, Column 3

4 U.S. PLANES LOST IN NORTH VIETNAM

2 of Jets Collide After Raid —Flak Is Heaviest Since Limited Bombing Began

By JOSEPH B. TREASTER

Special to The New York Times

SAIGON, South Vietnam, April 16—The United States lost four jet fighter-bombers in North Vietnam yesterday as pilots twisted through the heaviest antiaircraft fire sent up since the start of President Johnson's bombing curtailment.

Two Air Force F-105 Thunderchiefs were shot down in the vicinity of Donghoi. Two Navy F-4 Phantoms collided as they pulled off a target south of Vinh and headed for their carrier in the Gulf of Tonkin.

Except for the pilot of one of the Thunderchiefs, who was reported missing, all the airmen bailed out and were rescued at sea.

American military sources said that the heavy fire indicated that the North Vietnamese had moved some of their antiaircraft weapons from Hanoi and Haiphong, where bombing has been forbidden, to the lower third of the country, where United States air power is concentrating.

Eighty-eight missions were flown over North Vietnam yesterday. The number for Sunday was 143. Informed military sources said that the decrease was due largely to foul

Continued on Page 2, Column 4

Edna Ferber, Novelist, 82, Dies

Edna Ferber, who celebrated American life in novels, short stories and plays, died yesterday after a long illness at her home, 730 Park Avenue. She was 82 years old.

With a love and enthusiasm that gained her world fame, Miss Ferber wrote about the United States for four decades. Her novels became minor classics and earned her a fortune as well as many honors. "So Big," among the earliest of her 12 larger-than-life portrayals of the national scene, sold more than 300,000 copies on publication in 1924 and became required reading in schools and universities.

"So Big," the story of a woman on a truck farm outside Chicago, was a part of a drama of America from shore to shore. Miss Ferber depicted show business life on the Mississippi in "Show Boat," frontier Oklahoma in "Cimarron," Connecticut in "American Beauty," New York in "Saratoga Trunk," Texas in "Giant," and Alaska in "Ice Palace."

Her books were not profound, but they were vivid and had a sound sociological basis. She was among the best-read novelists in the nation, and critics of the nineteen-twenties and thirties did not hesitate to call her the greatest American woman novelist of her day.

Fred Plaut, 1953

Edna Ferber

She peopled her work with men and women of the lower-middle and middle class because, she said, they interested her more than any other American stratum. Her stories concerned department store clerks and buyers, friends with whom she had grown up, madams seeking to become respectable. The conversation of a truck driver, she maintained, she always found more vigorous and stimulating than the conversation of a Cadillac owner.

Her novels about ordinary men and women, living ordinary lives, were written easily and gracefully in the American idiom. They went into many editions and hundreds of thousands of copies. Her short stories brought the highest rates. Plays on which she collaborated, or which were adapted from her work, enjoyed long runs and frequent revivals. Motion pictures based on her books were box-office hits.

Critics called her novels "gripping" and "romantic." They added "penetrating" when describing "So Big," which was the Pulitzer Prize-winning novel of 1924.

Miss Ferber was a dramatic writer with a keen eye for a story, a wholesome respect for the color and harmony of words and a precise ability at portraiture. She laid much of this to her early journalistic training as a reporter.

She was born in Kalamazoo,

Continued on Page 32, Column 4

Griswold Upholds Moral Dissent Right

Special to The New York Times

NEW ORLEANS, April 16—Erwin N. Griswold, Solicitor General of the United States, upheld today the moral right of dissenters to disobey laws they believe in conscience to be unjust.

But he denied that there was a legal right to disobey any laws, no matter how unjust they might seem. He declared that those who adopted the civil disobedience tactic of disobeying the law should be prepared to go to jail.

The statements were made in a speech delivered tonight at Tulane Law School.

In his first major address since October, when he became the Government's chief appellate advocate, the former dean of the Harvard Law School stressed the need for restraint

Continued on Page 16, Column 4

Sale of L.I.U. Site Opposed by Mayor

By LEONARD BUDER

Mayor Lindsay announced yesterday his opposition to the proposed sale of Long Island University's Brooklyn Center to the City University.

The City University had earlier expressed interest in the property, which reportedly carried a $32-million price tag, as a possible site for its Bernard M. Baruch College.

Students, alumni and many faculty members at the center have bitterly opposed its sale.

In a letter to Dr. R. Gordon Hoxie, the L.I.U. chancellor, Mr. Lindsay said the Brooklyn Center provided "a unique service" to its students and to the general community and should be continued.

The Mayor offered to work with the private university—he

Continued on Page 74, Column 4

NEWS INDEX

Czech Party Paper Links Death Of Masaryk to Beria 'Gorillas'

By RICHARD EDER

Special to The New York Times

PRAGUE, April 16 — The Czechoslovak Communist party newspaper, Rude Pravo, suggested today for the first time that Soviet agents might have been responsible for the death of Foreign Minister Jan Masaryk in 1948.

In what has become a series of increasingly sharp press comments about the Soviet Union and other Eastern European neighbors of Czechoslovakia, Rude Pravo gave official, if hedged, support to the theory not only that Dr. Masaryk had been murdered but that it might have been the Soviet secret police, under Lavrenti P. Beria, who ordered and carried out the killing.

The Czechoslovak party newspaper raised the question of what role "Beria's gorillas" might have played in the Masaryk case. It expressed the hope that "our Soviet friends" would provide assistance in the inquiry into the circumstances of the Foreign Minister's death.

In another aspect of liberalization, Bishop Frantisek Tomasek, acting leader of Czechoslovakia's Roman Catholics, said that a representative of the Vatican would come to Prague to discuss church questions with the Government.

Praising the current reforms, Bishop Tomasek said the Government was restoring freedom not only for men but for the "word of God." [Page 16.]

The press campaign against Czechoslovakia's allies that developed here over the weekend

Continued on Page 15, Column 1

Edna Ferber, Novelist Who Chronicled America, Is Dead at 82

Continued From Page 1, Col. 4

Mich., on Aug. 15, 1885, the daughter of Jacob Charles Ferber, a moderately successful Hungarian-born Jewish small-businessman, and his Milwaukee-born wife, the former Julia Neumann. She was always proud of her Jewish heritage.

When the time came for Edna to attend college, the family was hard put to manage it. She had dreamed of a career on the stage and had hoped to attend Northwestern University's School of Elocution, but she went to work, instead, at 17, as a reporter on The Appleton (Wis.) Daily Crescent.

She always remembered her newspaper career, which later took her to The Milwaukee Journal, with nostalgia and affection. Reporting, she maintained, developed in her a supercamera eye, a sense of the dramatic and a "vast storehouse of practical and psychological knowledge" that proved invaluable in her creative writing.

It was as a reporter, too, that she made contact with the railroad-crossing guards, farmers, motormen, mill workers and mechanics who were later to fill her novels.

Sent Home for a Rest

During her Milwaukee reporting days she drove herself ceaselessly, developed anemia and was sent home to Appleton to recuperate. It was then—wobbly and weak, but longing to do something — that she wrote her first novel, "Dawn O'Hara," the story of a newspaperwoman in Milwaukee.

As she remembered later she had had no idea what it was she would try to write when she bought a second-hand typewriter for $17 and set it up in a "sort of lean-to off the dining room."

"But the typewriter kept grinning up at me with time-stained teeth," she added. So she bought some yellow copy paper and began a novel. Then she wrote a short story about a homely girl who weighed 200 pounds but had "the soul of a willow wand." She sent the story to Everybody's magazine and a few days later it was accepted. She never returned to journalism.

Nationwide fame first came to her with her Emma McChesney stories of a traveling saleswoman who sold underskirts. American magazine bought the first (and what was supposed to be the last) of the McChesney stories, but Emma McChesney was such a sensation that magazines began to vie with each other for the next McChesney adventure. Before Miss Ferber refused to do any more, she had written 30 of these stories, and they were remembered long after she wished they had been forgotten.

When President Theodore Roosevelt met Miss Ferber at the 1904 Republican National Convention, at which he was nominated for the Presidency, he inquired, "What are you going to do about Emma McChesney?"

Ideas From Conversation

Like all good reporters, Miss Ferber was indefatigably curious. The ideas for many of her novels came from snatches of conversation that piqued her interest. The germ for the novel "Show Boat," which in turn engendered the hit musical of the same name, came just that way.

It was during the New London tryout of her play "Minick," written with George S. Kaufman. The weary playwrights, cast and production crews were gathered in the hotel suite of the producer, Winthrop Ames. No one was very happy about the show.

"Never mind, boys and girls," Mr. Ames said, "next time we won't bother with tryouts. We'll all charter a show boat and we'll just drift down the rivers, playing the towns as we come to them."

"What's a show boat?" Miss Ferber inquired. Mr. Ames told her that it was a floating theater and that such boats used to ply Southern rivers, giving performances in port after port.

"I had been slumped, a disconsolate heap, on a cushion on the floor," Miss Ferber recounted later in her first autobiography, "A Peculiar Treasure," published in 1939 (the second, "A Kind of Magic," came out in 1963). "Now I sat up and up and up like a cobra uncoiling. . . . Here was news of a dramatic and romantic America of which I'd never heard or dreamed."

It was not long before she was off on a chase to North Carolina after show boats.

The resulting novel, which was published in 1926, was turned into a musical comedy, with Oscar Hammerstein 2d doing the book and Jerome Kern the music. After the first Florenz Ziegfeld production, it was revived three times on Broadway, and three separate motion pictures were made of it.

Visit to Oklahoma

The curiosity that led Miss Ferber to research and write "Show Boat" was likewise stimulated by William Allen White, the Kansas newspaper editor. He recounted to her a trip he had made to Oklahoma, where Indians drove around in Pierce-Arrows on lands that only 50 years earlier had been buffalo mudwallow. Straight off she paid a visit to the area and started work on "Cimarron."

It was not to research, but to her love of the United States (which she found "varied, dazzling and unique") and to a somewhat uncanny ability to project herself into any environment that she attributed her success in writing so vividly of so many different places. If a character, an emotion or a situation sufficiently captured her fancy, she insisted, she need never have experienced, seen or read about it in order to write of it.

"I have never been on the Mississippi or in the Deep South," she explained. "I wrote 'Show Boat.' I know nothing of farms or farming, which forms the background of 'So Big.' I wrote 'Cimarron' after spending 10 days in Oklahoma."

She spent more time in Texas and her novel about that state and its citizens infuriated many of them. "Giant," which appeared in 1952, sold three million copies and became a film with James Dean, Elizabeth Taylor and Rock Hudson.

Miss Ferber spoke frequently of how much she enjoyed both life and her work. Her childhood love of the theater never left her and her plays, among them, "Dinner at Eight," "The Royal Family" and "Stage Door," all written with George S. Kaufman, were popular with more than one generation. Critics praised a humane quality in them, which they attributed to Miss Ferber.

"Life," she said, "can't ever really defeat a writer who is in love with writing, for life itself is a writer's lover until death — fascinating, cruel, lavish, warm, cold, treacherous, constant; the more varied the moods the richer the experience. I've learned to value every stab of pain and disappointment."

Although she toyed with marriage several times, Miss Ferber remained single. In a magazine article in 1967, she said:

Edna Ferber and Louis Bromfield at St.-Jean-de-Luz in France in 1926. That was the year Miss Ferber's "Show Boat" and Mr. Bromfield's "Early Autumn" were published.

"As a young woman, there was the alternative: either write or marry-and-live-happily-ever-after — but without the satisfactions of writing. . . . It is wonderful to be a writer. I couldn't be anything else."

For years, she wrote more than 1,000 words a day, 350 days a year. She had a tenacity that permitted no deviation from each day's appointed task.

"The entire output of my particular job depends on me," she said, after she had reached the pinnacle of popular acclaim in the nineteen-thirties and forties.

"By that I mean that when I put the cover on my typewriter, the works are closed. The office equipment consists of one flat table, a sheaf of yellow paper and one of white. All the wheels, belts, wires, bolts, files, tools—the whole manufacturing process—has got to be contained in the space between my chin and my topmost hairpin. And my one horror is that some morning I'll wake up and find that space vacant, and the works closed down, with a metal sign over the front door reading: 'For rent, fine, large, empty head: inquire within.' Still, even if that should happen, I would probably turn over and say, 'Well, what a grand time I have had.'"

'A White Paper Cocoon'

Although she wrote prodigiously, she fashioned her books with care. She called the start of a novel a terrifying experience. Once a book had been started, she maintained, nothing but death could separate her from it.

"Clothes are unimportant. Teeth go unfilled," she recounted. "Your idea of bliss is to wake up on a Monday morning knowing that you haven't a single engagement for the entire week. You are cradled in a white paper cocoon tied up with typewriter ribbon."

Appreciation pleased her. She was touched when she learned that members of the staff of Doubleday & Co., her publisher, had cried at reading her manuscript for "So Big." She took quiet pride in the fact that it had been printed in more than a half-dozen languages, that two films had been made of it and that it was on the required reading list of many schools.

She enjoyed fan mail, and two of the letters about her work that she valued most—although one of them was not written directly to her — were from Rudyard Kipling and James M. Barrie. The Kipling letter, which was not addressed to her, but which she saw, said that it was probable that she would not be appreciated in her own country or her own time.

But not all letters were so complimentary. Frequently, her works stirred up a storm of protest from the inhabitants of the region about which she had written. When "Giant" — a story of Texas manners, money and mores — appeared, furious letters poured in from the Lone Star State. There were even some suggestions made, but not seriously, that Miss Ferber be shot or lynched. "Cimarron" raised Oklahoma dander. But, invariably, the anger subsided as tourists began to flock to the sites Miss Ferber had described.

In "Giant," she pictured Texas and the Texans through the eyes of a bride from Virginia:

". . . Biggest ranch. Biggest steer. Biggest houses. Biggest hat. Biggest state. A mania for bigness. What littleness did it hide? . . . They lived against the climate in unconscious defiance of this tropical land. They built their houses with front porches on which they never could sit, with front yards forever grassless, they planted Northern trees that perished under the sun and drought, they planted lilacs and peonies and larkspur and roses and stock and lilies-of-the-valley and these died at birth. Arrogantly, in defiance of their Mexican compatriots, they wore Northern clothes, these good solid citizens, the men sweating in good cloth pants and coats, the women corseted, high-heeled, marcelled, hatted. We're the white Americans, we're the big men, we eat the beef and drink the bourbon, we don't take siestas, we don't feel the sun, the heat or the cold the wind or the rain, we're Texans."

She described a cattle camp:

"Cattle. So close-packed that it seemed you could walk on their backs for a mile—for miles as far as the eye could see. From the little sand hills, from the mesquite motts and the cactus came the living streams, a river here a river there, a river of moving flesh wherever the eye rested, and these sluggish lines were added to the great central pool until it became a Mississippi of cattle fed by its smaller tributaries."

Gracious and Thoughtful

The author was a small, dark-eyed woman, with hair that, in later years, was a silver shade. As a child, she had felt that she lacked beauty. She was always self-conscious about what she considered a too-large nose. Others, however, found her a handsome woman, with a low voice, a gracious elegance and a thoughtful manner.

Ferber, as her friends called her, had a mind both sparking and sparkling. All her life in New York was spent in close association with the city's witty and penetrating observers — Alexander Woollcott, Harold Ross, Russel Crouse, Anita Loos, George S. Kaufman, Noël Coward, the Howard Lindsays, the Richard Rodgerses, S. N. Behrman, Marc Connelly, Frank Sullivan, Kitty Carlisle and Moss Hart, among scores of other friends.

Miss Ferber was not much of a gadabout, so that her extensive social and salon life was carried on at dinner parties, frequently in her apartment, or in quiet evenings of heady conversation.

She was notable for her generosity. She said she never really cared about owning things.

"I prefer spending on 'live' pictures — people — rather than to load my rooms with paintings," she said. "I would rather surprise someone with theater tickets, a needed television set or perhaps a college education than to fill the secret drawer of my desk with jewelry."

She always remained close to her family — her sister, Fannie; her nieces, and her mother, for whom she made a home in her later years until the latter's death at the age of 89.

Miss Ferber lived in many places — Michigan, Iowa, Wisconsin, Illinois, Europe, Connecticut, New York. She said she loved New York, but not the garbage in the streets or the dirt in the air. She was active in efforts to keep the city clean.

In everything she undertook, whether civic improvement, books, plays, causes against prejudice, she had burning determination. Certainly, this was part of what took her to the top. But there was also her sense of awe — not at all unlike that of "So Big's" Selina De Jong, of whom Miss Ferber wrote:

"Always to her, red and green cabbages were to be jade and burgundy, chrysoprase and porphyry. Life has no weapons against a woman like that."

Miss Ferber is survived by her sister and two nieces, Mina Fox Klein and Mrs. Janet Goldsmith.

A funeral service will be held tomorrow at 1 P.M. at Frank E. Campbell's, Madison Avenue and 81st Street.

"All the News That's Fit to Print"

The New York Times.

LATE CITY EDITION
Mostly sunny and cool today. Partly cloudy, warmer tomorrow.
Temperatures Yesterday—Max.,67; Min.,46
Sunrise today, 5:29 A. M.; Sunset, 6:27 P. M.
Full U. S. Weather Bureau Report, Page 56

VOL. XCVI No. 32,581. Entered as Second-Class Matter, Postoffice, New York, N. Y. NEW YORK, TUESDAY, APRIL 8, 1947. THREE CENTS IN NEW YORK CITY

DISTANCE, TOLL PHONES CRIPPLED, DIAL SERVICE NORMAL IN STRIKE; CONGRESS MOVES TO CURB TIE-UPS

HENRY FORD IS DEAD AT 83 IN DEARBORN

PIONEER IN AUTOS

Leader in Production Founded Vast Empire in Motors in 1903

HE HAD RETIRED IN 1945

Began Company With Capital of $28,000 Invested by His Friends and Neighbors

By The Associated Press.

DETROIT, April 7—Henry Ford, noted automotive pioneer, died at 11:40 tonight at the age of 83. He had retired a little more than a year and a half ago from active direction of the great industrial empire he founded in 1903.

When he retired Mr. Ford was in excellent health, but turned over the management of the vast empire to his grandson, Henry Ford 2d, because, he said, he wanted to devote more time to personal interests.

Death came to the famed industrialist at his estate in Fairlane, in suburban Dearborn, not far from where he was born in 1863. At the Ford Company news bureau offices it was said that the exact cause of death would not be known until Henry Ford 2d, his grandson, could reach the family home, perhaps within an hour.

Mr. Ford was reported to have been in excellent health when he returned only a week ago from his annual winter visit to the Ford estate in Georgia.

Kept Interest in Research

The automobile industry leader dropped completely out of the management of the far-flung Ford Company when he resigned as president late in 1945. He had been able to spend some time each week at the Ford engineering laboratory, where he maintained a private office and workshop, but was rarely seen about the administration building, where affairs of the big company were directed.

There were many reports that the elder Ford had given up his leadership of the Ford interests at the insistence of other members of his family, particularly the widow of his only son, the late Edsel B. Ford. Although never confirmed officially, reports had it that she was dissatisfied with the course of company affairs.

He leaves a widow, the former Clara Bryant, whom he married in 1887, and two grandsons, Henry 2d and Benson.

Father of Mass Production

Henry Ford was the founder of modern American industrial mass production methods, built on the assembly line and the belt conveyor system, which no less an authority than Marshal Josef Stalin testified were the indispensable foundation for an Allied military victory in the Second World War.

Mr. Ford had many other distinctions. As the founder and unchallenged master of an industrial empire with assets of more than a billion dollars, he was one of the richest men in the world. He was the apostle of an economic philosophy of high wages and short hours that had immense repercussions on American thinking. He was a patron of American folkways and in later years acquired a reputation as a shrewd, kindly sage. But these were all relatively minor compared with the revolutionary importance of his contribution to modern productive processes.

His career was one of the most astonishing in industrial history. Nearing the age of 40 he was looked upon as a failure by his acquaintances — as a day-dreaming mechanic who preferred to tinker with odd machines than to work steadily at a responsible job. Yet within a dozen years he was internationally famous, and his Model T automobile was effecting changes in the American way of life of profound importance.

He lived to see the Ford Motor Company, which he founded with an initial investment of $28,000 put up by a few friends and neighbors who had faith in him, produce more than 29,000,000 automobiles before the war forced the conversion of its gigantic production fa-

Continued on Page 32, Column 1

Reds Poll Only 1% In Japanese Voting

Special to The New York Times.

TOKYO, April 7—Only 1 per cent of the votes cast in Japan's nation-wide mayoralty elections yesterday went to the Communists, tabulations revealed today.

Because the Democratic and Liberal parties generally refrained from nominating candidates against incumbents who ran as independents, no measure of their strength was possible. The Socialists polled 24.1 per cent of the total vote against 17.8 per cent last year.

GERMAN PLEBISCITE BARRED IN BIG FOUR

Soviet Plan for Picking Form of Government Is Peril to Peace, Says Marshall

By DREW MIDDLETON
Special to The New York Times.

MOSCOW, April 7—A Soviet proposal that the German people decide by a plebiscite whether their future state have a centralized or a federal government was rejected today by the United States, Britain and France.

Secretary of State Marshall described Soviet Foreign Minister Molotov's suggestion before the Council of Foreign Ministers as "highly dangerous to peace."

Russia's desire for a centralised government in Germany also was strongly opposed by Secretary Marshall, who declared that such a government "might eventually be transformed into an autocratic government dangerous to the peace of the world."

Today's meeting, the twenty-third since the opening of this session of the Council, centered on this key political problem—whether Germany is to have a strong central government, as the Russians desire, or a federal government such as the Americans, British and French agree upon in principle if not in detail.

Starts Bitter Argument

Secretary Marshall emphasized the United States' wish to consult the German people. This gave Mr. Molotov the opportunity he desired. He immediately proposed a plebiscite, and his proposal precipitated a long and bitter argument.

At the end of the argument the Foreign Ministers had accomplished nothing. Foreign Secretary Bevin of Britain, asked what he wished to discuss tomorrow, revealed a sense of futility.

"I do not really care," he said. "We have been here four weeks now without accomplishing anything."

Foreign Minister Bidault of France wearily agreed, saying that it was "tiring to do nothing."

The conflict over the form of the future German government arose when Mr. Molotov was discussing the functions of the proposed German advisory council on the basis of the report of the Foreign Ministers' coordinating committee, which was placed before them today.

This advisory council, under the Allied Control Council, would gov-

Continued on Page 10, Column 3

SOVIET CHARGES U.S. HURTS U.N. BY PLAN FOR GREECE, TURKEY

Gromyko in Security Council Asks for a Commission to Supervise Help to Athens

CALLS ANKARA INSINCERE

He Asserts It Deserves No Aid —Urges the Atom Bomb Be Destroyed Ahead of Control

The text of Gromyko's statement is on Page 4.

By THOMAS J. HAMILTON
Special to The New York Times.

LAKE SUCCESS, N. Y., April 7—Andrei A. Gromyko, Soviet Deputy Foreign Minister, charged today that the United States aid program for Greece constituted intervention in Greek internal affairs. He demanded that the United Nations Security Council establish a commission to see to it that United States help for Greece was administered exclusively for the benefit of the Greek people.

Although he praised the courage of the Greek people in fighting the Axis, he pointed out to the Security Council that Turkey did not enter the war on the side of the Allies until a few days before VE-Day. He asserted that Turkey had "profiteered" during the war by selling raw materials to Germany and was not entitled to assistance.

The Soviet Union's formal reply to the Truman proposals was delivered before an audience that jammed the Security Council chamber. Mr. Gromyko accused the United States of having seriously undermined the authority of the United Nations, and of having produced distrust among its members

Done in Professorial Way

Mr. Gromyko, who was wearing a sober blue suit, made his 2,500-word statement in the manner of a professor reading a dissertation. However, he warmed up afterward when Warren R. Austin, the United States representative, formally proposed that the Security Council direct its Balkan frontier commission to keep representatives in the area while it was drafting its report.

This, Mr. Gromyko asserted, was an attempt to put up a "screen" bearing the initials "U. N." to "hide the activities of the United States, which are not in the interests of the United Nations, if only because they constitute an effort to intervene in the internal affairs of Greece."

Mr. Gromyko's criticisms of the United States program were supported by the representatives of Bulgaria and Yugoslavia, which, though not members of the Security Council, were admitted to the discussions because the Balkan commission is investigating incidents on Greece's northern frontier.

On the other hand, Australia endorsed the statement by Mr. Austin of March 28, which notified the Security Council of the American program. Vasili Dendramis, the Greek representative, contented himself with thanking the representatives of the United States, Australia and the Soviet Union for their tribute to the heroism of the Greek people during the war.

All in all, today was the most spectacular day in Mr. Gromyko's career, and the overflow audience stayed on almost until the final wrangling over the date when the Security Council would consider the clashing United States and Soviet proposals.

Interestingly enough, Mr. Gro-

Continued on Page 3, Column 5

Time, Weather Calls Casualties of Strike

Two of the most popular telephone numbers in New York were dialed in vain yesterday. A call to MEridian 7-1212 or WEather 6-1212 brought the following recorded notice:

"Time and weather services have been discontinued temporarily because of the strike. There will be no charge for this call."

A spokesman for the New York Telephone Company said the time service had been operated on a continuous, twenty-four-hour-a-day basis since it was started on Aug. 15, 1928. The weather service was begun just eight years ago today. The daily average is 75,000 calls for the MEridian number and 45,000 for the WEather exchange.

WALKOUT TIES UP WESTERN ELECTRIC

60,000 of 81,000 Workers Quit as Off-Shoot of Strike by Telephone Employes

The manufacture, installation and distribution of Western Electric Company products were crippled yesterday in an off-shoot of the nation-wide telephone strike. Seventeen thousand workers were out at the company's main plant in Kearny, N. J., and at smaller plants in Clifton, Newark, Passaic, Bayonne and at 529 West Forty-second Street here.

A spokesman for the management said 60,000 of the company's 81,000 hourly rated employes here and in other sections of the country had joined the walkout, with demands similar to those of the telephone workers on wages and other conditions.

Mass picketing at the Kearny plant between 7 A. M. and 9 A. M. yesterday was generally orderly, but the police reported three strikers arrested for disorderly conduct.

J. Candiani, 29 years old, of 236

Continued on Page 16, Column 8

80,000 GO OUT HERE

Local Service Kept Up in City, Emergency Calls in Suburbs

PARLEYS CONTINUE TODAY

Jersey Seizes Lines but Few Union Workers Obey Driscoll Plea to Stay on the Job

By A. H. RASKIN

From 80,000 to 90,000 Bell System workers in the metropolitan area stayed away from their jobs yesterday. However, maintenance of normal dial service kept the telephone strike from bearing too heavily on 90 per cent of New York telephone users and 40 per cent of the New Jersey subscribers.

Long-distance calls were on an emergency basis and dropped to one-fifth of the normal volume. In suburban districts, where manually operated phone exchanges predominate, little service could be provided except for callers with emergency messages. These calls were handled without delay by supervisory employes.

Commissioner J. R. Mandelbaum of the United States Conciliation Service, who had met up to the 6 A. M. strike deadline with officials of the New York Telephone Company and four unions representing 35,000 employes in this city, Long Island and Westchester County, renewed his settlement efforts yesterday afternoon, but with no immediate success.

The conciliator conferred with company executives for two hours and announced that he would meet this morning with heads of the four unions. He said he was trying to arrive at "some working arrangement which may help to solve the existing problem and settle the local strike" as a preliminary to calling a new joint meeting of management and the unions.

That Mr. Mandelbaum's talk with the company had failed to

Continued on Page 16, Column 2

Enjoining of Great Strikes Favored by Senate Group

Taft Says Majority in Labor Committee Agrees on Letting Government Act if Health, Safety Are Menaced

By WILLIAM S. WHITE
Special to The New York Times.

WASHINGTON, April 7—A majority of the Senate Labor Committee agreed informally today upon proposed legislation to put down by Government injunction great strikes, such as that now silencing many telephones, where national health or safety was deemed imperilled.

This was disclosed by the chairman, Senator Robert A. Taft, Republican, of Ohio, in making public an otherwise wholly tentative print of a proposed omnibus bill for reform over the whole field of labor.

The plan to arm the Government with injunctive power in "national paralysis" walkouts was added over the week-end to the thick text of this general measure. Only upon this urgent phase of the bill, Mr. Taft emphasized, had there been anything approaching majority concurrence.

This concurrence was one of principle, rather than detail, and Senator Taft described it as a "consensus" of the seven members of the committee's total membership of thirteen who were present today. No formal vote was taken.

Meantime, it was learned that a bill now in final form before the Republican members of the House Labor Committee, and classified as secret, would carry this action by injunction beyond the point contemplated by the Senate.

The Senate plan would limit the life of any such restraining order to seventy-five days. The House approach, to which an effective committee majority was said to be in effect pledged, would make no provision for dissolving such an injunction.

These developments indicated strongly that the Republican leaders of Congress had formed a determination, after much deliberation, to risk hard, direct and quick legislation against national strikes, if and when "paralysis" was

Continued on Page 18, Column 1

U.S. to Ask $3,500,000 Fine Be Re-Levied on Mine Union

By JAY WALZ
Special to The New York Times.

WASHINGTON, April 7—The Government plans to ask Federal Justice T. Alan Goldsborough on Thursday to restore, in view of stoppages in the coal mines, the full $3,500,000 fine against the United Mine Workers, it was learned today. The $3,500,000 was set by the justice last December in the contempt case.

Lawyers of the Department of Justice will accuse John L. Lewis and the miners' union of "bad faith" and "subterfuge" in calling off the Krug-Lewis contract termination notice as ordered a month ago by the Supreme Court. The union is not, therefore, entitled to have the original fine reduced to $700,000 as the high tribunal provided, it will be argued.

Lewis' Tactics a Factor

It will also be pointed out that Mr. Lewis, in testimony last Thursday before a House committee, spoke of applying a "rule of reason" to the mines' safety problem, but did not carry it out next day when he asked J. A. Krug, Secretary of the Interior, to close all soft-coal mines, except two, for safety reasons.

Justice Department lawyers remained in conference today with the legal advisers of Mr. Krug and officials of the Coal Administration, headed by Capt. N. H. Collisson. They said they were watching the situation "very closely" but indicated that they would have no "official" statement before the scheduled meeting with Justice Goldsborough on Thursday.

John F. Sonnett, Assistant Attorney General, who handled the contempt case for the Government, is expected to appear for the

Continued on Page 20, Column 1

PROGRESS IS MADE IN STRIKE TALKS

Warren Reports Some Steps After 31-Hour Conference, but Outlook Is Gloomy

Special to The New York Times.

WASHINGTON, April 7—Progress toward settlement of the long lines telephone dispute was reported by the Labor Department tonight in the unprecedented national strike of telephone workers.

The progress announcement, made shortly before 5 P. M., came from Edgar L. Warren, chief of the United States Conciliation Service. Unshaven and haggard from his thirty-one-hour conference with the parties, Mr. Warren still was able to smile hopefully.

After reporting to Lewis Schwellenbach, Secretary of Labor, and taking a brief rest, he reopened conferences with Joseph A. Beirne, president of the National Federation of Telephone Workers, and several union officials later in the evening. But the outlook for quick settlement of the strike was reported as not hopeful.

About 10 P. M. conferences were interrupted to allow "all parties

Continued on Page 17, Column 7

300,000 QUIT POSTS

Strike in All Except Nine States in First Such Walkout in Nation

LONG LINE CALLS CUT 80%

But Company Says 20 Million Phones Provide Local Service —Report Peaceful Picketing

By FRANK S. ADAMS

Between 300,000 and 350,000 telephone workers walked out yesterday in the first country-wide strike in the industry's history. Workers in all except nine of the forty-eight states took part in the stoppage.

The American Telephone and Telegraph Company, against which the strike was directed, asserted at the close of the business day that substantially normal local service was being provided for more than 20,000,000 of the Bell System's 26,000,000 telephones.

It acknowledged that long distance and toll calls had been cut to an estimated 20 per cent of the normal volume of 5,361,000 daily. All such calls as well as local calls in areas where manually operated telephones remain in service were put through only on an emergency basis.

The A. T. & T. said, however, that the ranks of the supervisory personnel who had been manning the switchboards since the strike started at 6 A. M. were steadily reinforced during the day by the appearance of from 10 to 15 per cent of the nonsupervisory workers, with the result that the number of switchboard positions rose to an estimated 40 per cent at 5 P. M. here.

120,000 Strike in East

Officials of the National Federation of Telephone Workerr which called the strike in conjunction with a number of local unions, estimated in mid-afternoon that a minimum of 294,000 telephone workers had joined the strike. With reports incomplete, they said, 120,000 had walked out in Eastern states, 88,000 in Central states, 58,000 in the South and 28,000 in the West.

Henry Mayer, counsel for fifteen of the telephone unions involved in the strike, put the number participating even higher. He said last evening that 345,000 telephone workers were out. He added that 230,000 of these were women, the largest number of that sex to take part in a strike in history.

The NFTW, which claims a membership of 287,000 of the 615,000 A. T. & T. employes, asserted that craftsmen and technical workers were cooperating by refusing to cross its picket lines. It said that the strike was receiving "fair but spotty" support from unions unaffiliated with it.

New England Slightly Hit

The six New England states, where the telephone employes are not affiliated with the NFTW, were only slightly affected by the strike. Long-lines operators in Boston and local operators in Greenwich, Conn., which is served by the New York Telephone Company, walked out, but elsewhere in Maine, New Hampshire, Vermont, Massachusetts, Connecticut and Rhode Island service was virtually normal.

Montana was likewise not affected because the telephone workers there are not affiliated with the national union, and the A. T. & T. stated that in up-state New York and in eastern and central Pennsylvania enough operators and maintenance workers reported to enable the continuance of normal service.

In Virginia and Indiana, telephone employes remained at their jobs because of new statutes on the books of the two states, which were receiving their first major tests. The Indiana law calls for compulsory arbitration of labor disputes in public utilities, while that in Virginia provides five weeks' notice must be given before utility workers can strike.

New Jersey seized the telephone system in that state in accordance with the anti-utility strike law passed by the Legislature. Governor Alfred E. Driscoll publicly appealed to the employes to stay

Continued on Page 17, Column 5

Paris Gets Off With Year in Prison For Aiding Other 'Fix' Convictions

Alvin J. Paris, whose testimony as principal state witness was responsible for the imprisonment of the three "higher-ups" in the football "fix" scheme, was sentenced yesterday by General Sessions Judge Saul S. Streit to a one-year penitentiary term.

The suave, 28-year-old gambler, first to be convicted under a statute making the offer of a bribe to an athlete a felony, instead of a misdemeanor, had faced a maximum of five years in state prison. A plea for "utmost clemency" was made, however, by District Attorney Frank S. Hogan.

Paris, it was said, has a good chance of regaining freedom by August, as he has been in the Tombs since his arrest on Dec. 15, and because the law allows the reduction of one-third of each year of sentence if the prisoner's behavior is exemplary.

The final scene of the movie-like plot that began at a cocktail party last November in the Paris apartment, 56 West Fifty-sixth Street, was brief. Only a few spectators were in the courtroom—among them Paris' father Sidney.

The "fix" scheme was to have culminated in a clean-up of thousands of dollars by the gamblers, who had planned to bring about through bribery the victory of the Chicago Bears over the New York Giants in the Dec. 15 professional championship football game.

That the scheme failed, trial testimony showed, was due to the police becoming suspicious of the Paris residence and "tapping" the telephone wires on the assumption

Continued on page 30, Column 7

World News Summarized

TUESDAY, APRIL 8, 1947

More than 300,000 telephone workers in all but nine states walked out at 6 A. M. yesterday in the industry's first nation-wide strike. Manual service, long-distance and trans-ocean calls were crippled, but dial service operated normally. [1:8.]

Reports from all over the country showed the strike to be almost universally effective [17:4], and, in addition, Western Electric equipment employes joined the walkout. [1:4.]

Nearly 90,000 workers were out in metropolitan New York and New Jersey, where the state seized the telephone system but was unable to do anything because the law provided no penalties for refusing to work. [1:5.] Suburban areas and some local exchanges dependent upon manual operation were without service, except for emergency calls handled by supervisory workers, but the dial kept calls in this city on a near-normal basis. [17:1]

Labor Department conciliators reported some progress during a thirty-one-hour session toward arriving at a formula for settling the strike, but no agreement was foreseen for several days. [1:7.]

The walkout, the first major industrial dispute in nearly a year, combined with the soft-coal "safety strike" and clouds over the steel and automobile industries to cause concern at the White House. [1:6-7.]

Leaders in the steel union are expected next week to authorize a strike when current extended contracts expire on April 30. Negotiations with the companies have made no progress. [21:2.]

The telephone tie-up prevented an accurate check on the number of soft-coal miners who refused to enter the pits, but one source estimated that 281,000 men out of 400,000 were idle. [21:4.] Government attorneys, holding that John L. Lewis and the union had acted in "bad faith" and had called by "subterfuge" a strike that had been enjoined, plan to ask the court to reimpose the full $3,500,000 fine levied against the union. [1:6-7.]

A majority of the Senate Labor Committee was said to favor permitting the Government to halt by injunction strikes deemed to be threatening "national paralysis." [1:6-7.]

The Supreme Court ruled, 6 to 3, that the National Labor Relations Act was paramount to state "Little Wagner" acts in labor disputes. [20:1.]

Henry Ford, pioneer automobile manufacturer, died at his home in Dearborn, Mich., at the age of 83. [1:1.]

Russia opposes President Truman's program of aid to Greece because it "seriously undermines the authority of the United Nations" and is against any aid to Turkey, Andrei A. Gromyko informed the Security Council. In stating Moscow's attitude officially for the first time, he said distrust among member nations was encouraged by such action. [1:3.]

Senator Vandenberg moved to eliminate a "joker" in his amendment to the bill implementing the "Truman Doctrine." Senate debate on the bill is to begin today. [5:1.]

In Moscow, the three Western Powers lined up solidly against Foreign Minister Molotov's proposal to let the German people decide between a centralized and a federalized Germany. [1:2.]

Former President de Gaulle disavowed personal ambition in urging the French to rally around national "renewal" so that France could act as an "element of equilibirum" between the United States and Russia. [15:1.]

Don Juan, pretender to the Spanish throne, rejected Generalissimo Franco's proposed succession law. [14:2.]

Chinese Nationalists were reported set for a drive to clear the Communists from the vital Tientsin-Pukow railroad. [23:4, with map.]

Shattering of Labor Front Quiet Spurs Drive for Restrictive Laws

By LOUIS STARK
Special to The New York Times.

WASHINGTON, April 7—After nearly one year free of major disputes the industrial front was shattered today by two unprecedented major strikes. The White House was reported to be deeply concerned over the sudden change in the labor relations picture and its possible effects on the national economy and on international economic relations.

For the first time in the history of the coal industry a majority of the nation's coal diggers went on a "safety strike" today, imperiling the reserves now above ground and the supply required to help rebuild a war-torn Europe.

The national telephone strike—the first ever called—marked the "coming of age" of a "new" union led by young men and women in their twenties and thirties.

Developments on the labor sector today were scanned by negotiators in the steel and automobile industries.

While the network of telephone companies was hoping to stave off possible wage increases until the United States Steel Corporation had shown what it would do on the issue, other influences were at work to hasten price reductions as an offset to wage-increase demands.

Automobile manufacturers hoped for a moratorium on wage advances through reduction in steel prices. They declared that the best way to spread consumer buy-

Continued on Page 16, Column 6

Henry Ford Is Dead; Founder of Vast Automotive Empire and Leader in Mass Production

Continued From Page 1

cilities to weapons of war. Then he directed its production of more than 8,000 four-motored Liberator bombers, as well as tanks, tank destroyers, jeeps and amphibious jeeps, transport gliders, trucks, engines and much other equipment.

Struck a cruel blow shortly before his eightieth birthday by the death of his only son, Edsel Ford, on May 26, 1943, Mr. Ford unfalteringly returned to the presidency of the Ford Motor Company, which he had yielded to his son twenty-four years previously. He remained at its helm as it reached the peak of its gigantic war production, directing the war-expanded force of 190,000 workers.

Mr. Ford was born on July 30, 1863, on a farm near Dearborn, nine miles west of Detroit. He was the eldest of six children. His mother died when he was 12 years of age. He went to school until he was 15. Throughout his schooldays he worked on the farm after school hours and during vacations.

His mechanical bent first showed itself in an intense interest in the mechanism of watches. When he was 13 he took a watch apart and put it together again so that it would work. He had to do this work secretly at night, after he had finished his chores on the farm, because his father wanted to discourage his mechanical ambitions. His tools were home-made and were limited to a screwdriver and a pair of tweezers, fashioned respectively from a knitting needle and an old watch spring.

In 1879, at the age of 16, he took the step that foreshadowed his remarkable career. He ran away from home. Walking all the way to Detroit, almost penniless, he went to work as an apprentice in a machine shop. He did this in order to learn all he could of the making of machinery. He received $2.50 a week for ten hours a day, six days a week—a far cry from the wages paid in the Ford factories today. As he had to pay $3.50 a week for board and lodging, he took another job, working from 7 to 11 o'clock every night for a jeweler, for $2 more a week.

Built a Steam Tractor

Returning to his father's farm to live, he spent his spare time for several years endeavoring to evolve a practical farm tractor of relatively small size and cost. He succeeded in building a steam tractor with a one-cylinder engine, but was unable to devise a boiler light enough to make the tractor practicable. For several years he confined himself to cutting the timber on forty acres his father had given him; operating a sawmill and repairing farm machinery for his neighbors.

Convinced that the steam engine was unsuited to light vehicles, he turned to the internal combustion engine, which he had read about in English scientific periodicals, as a means of locomotion for the "horseless carriage" of which he and other automobile inventors had dreamed. For several years he spent most of his spare time reading about and experimenting with the gasoline engine.

In 1890 he got a job as engineer and machinist with the Detroit Edison Company at $45 a month, and moved to Detroit. He set up a workshop in his backyard and continued his experiments after hours. He completed his first "gasoline buggy" in 1892. It had a two-cylinder engine, which developed about four horsepower, and he drove it 1,000 miles. The first, and for a long time the only automobile in Detroit, it was too heavy to suit Mr. Ford, who sold it in 1896 for $200, to get funds to experiment on a lighter car. Later, when he became successful, he repurchased his first car for $100 as a memento of his early days.

Henry Ford in his office, 1909.

Named Chief Engineer

Meanwhile, he had become chief engineer of the electric company at $125 a month, but his superiors had no more use for his gas engine experiments than had his father. They offered to make him general superintendent of the company, but only on condition that he give up gasoline and devote himself entirely to electricity. He had the courage of his convictions, and he quit his job at the age of 36, on Aug. 15, 1899—a most important date, in view of later developments, in the automotive industry.

Mr. Ford had no money, but he persuaded a group of men to organize the Detroit Automobile Company to manufacture his car. The company made and sold a few cars on his original model, but after two years Mr. Ford broke with his associates over a fundamental question of policy. He already had envisioned the mass production of cars which could be sold in large quantities at small profits, while his backers were convinced that the automobile was a luxury, to be produced in small quantities at large profits per unit.

RENTED ONE-STORY SHED

Built Car for Barney Oldfield Which Won All Its Races

Renting a one-story brick shed in Detroit, Mr. Ford spent the year 1902 experimenting with two-cylinder and four-cylinder motors. By that time the public had become interested in the speed possibilities of the automobile, which was no longer regarded as a freak. To capitalize on this interest, he built two racing cars, the "999" and the "Arrow," each with a four-cylinder engine developing eighty horsepower. The "999," with the celebrated Barney Oldfield at its wheel, won every race in which it was entered.

The resulting publicity helped Mr. Ford to organize the Ford Motor Company, which was capitalized at $100,000, although actually only $28,000 in stock was subscribed. From the beginning Mr. Ford held majority control of this company. In 1919 he and his son, Edsel, became its sole owners, when they bought out the minority stockholders for $70,000,000.

In 1903 the Ford Motor Company sold 1,708 two-cylinder, eight horsepower automobiles. Its operations were soon threatened, however, by a suit for patent infringement brought against it by the Licensed Association of Automobile Manufacturers, who held the rights to a patent obtained by George B. Selden of Rochester, N. Y., in 1895, covering the combination of a gasoline engine and a road locomotive. After protracted litigation, Mr. Ford won the suit when the Supreme Court held that the Selden patent was invalid.

From the beginning of his industrial career, Mr. Ford had in mind the mass production of a car which he could produce and sell at large quantity and low cost, but he was balked for several years by the lack of a steel sufficiently light and strong for his purpose. By chance one day, picking up the pieces of a French racing car that had been wrecked at Palm Beach, he discovered vanadium steel, which had not been manufactured in the United States up to that time.

With this material he began the new era of mass production. He concentrated on a single type of chassis, the celebrated Model T, and specified that "any customer can have a car painted any color he wants, so long as it is black." On Oct. 1, 1908, he began the production of Model T, which sold for $850. The next year he sold 10,600 cars of this model. Cheap and reliable, the car had a tremendous success. In seven years he built and sold 1,000,000 Fords; by 1925 he was producing them at the rate of almost 2,000,000 a year.

He established two cardinal economic policies during this tremendous expansion: the continued cutting of the cost of the product as improved methods of production made it possible, and the payment of higher wages to his employes. By 1926 the cost of the Model T had been cut to $310, although it was vastly superior to the 1908 model. In January, 1914, he established a minimum pay rate of $5 a day for an eight-hour day, thereby creating a national sensation. Up to that time the average wage throughout his works had been $2.40 for a nine-hour day.

DEVISED CONVEYOR LINE

Each Workman Performed One Specialized Operation

These policies were made feasible by the revolutionary organization of production devised by Mr. Ford. Under the old factory system, a single workman constructed an entire spring, using several different tools and performing many different operations in the process. Mr. Ford substituted an arrangement under which each worker performed a single specialized operation, which was simplified to the utmost by scientific study.

To make a single leaf of a spring, for instance, eleven workmen stood in line, each using a single tool. A moving conveyor belt carried the steel from which the leaf was made along the line, at waist-high level. The workers never had to stoop or move to get anything, and the speed at which they worked was controlled by the speed of the conveyor rather than the desires of the workmen.

Every part of the automobile had its own conveyor line, carefully integrated to bring the various parts to completion in the proper ratio. In later years Mr. Ford found it wasteful to assemble the cars at the great River Rouge plant in Dearborn, Mich., which instead was limited to the manufacture of parts. These were shipped to assembly plants scattered throughout the United States and in many foreign countries.

Bought Own Mines and Forests

In order to reduce costs and eliminate intermediate profits on raw materials and transportation, Mr. Ford purchased his own coal mines, iron mines and forests, his own railways and his own lake and ocean steamships, all of which he operated on the Ford system of high wages, high production and low cost. Ownership of these collateral industries enabled Mr. Ford to keep down waste in men, time and material.

At the River Rouge plant, for example, iron from the furnace goes directly into the foundries and is poured without reheating. The slag from the furnace is used in a cement plant and all the steel scrap is converted by a combination of electric furnaces and a large rolling mill. In the Ford sawmills the parts are sawed directly from the logs, instead of converting the logs into lumber first. All the wood-working is done at the forest mill, the waste goes to a wood-distillation plant, and there is no waste in shipment.

The phenomenal success of the new system of production made Mr. Ford not only fabulously rich, but internationally famous, within a comparatively few years. His own very positive and often unusual opinions added to his renown. In the winter of 1915-16 he was convinced by a group of pacifists, of whom Rozika Schwimmer was the best known, that the warring nations in Europe were ready for peace and that a dramatic gesture would be enough to end the war.

Chartered Peace Liners

Mr. Ford chartered an ocean liner, the Oskar II, with the avowed purpose of "getting the boys out of the trenches by Christmas," and sailed from New York on Dec. 4, 1915, with a curiously assorted group of companions. The mission was ridiculed and failed to achieve anything. Mr. Ford himself left the party at Christiania, now Oslo, and returned home.

"We learn more from our failures than from our successes," was his comment.

When the United States declared war on Germany in April, 1917, Mr. Ford placed the industrial facilities of his plants at the disposal of the Government, although he had previously refused orders from belligerent countries. During the war he produced large quantities of automobiles, trucks, ambulances, Liberty airplane motors, munitions, whippet tanks and Eagle submarine chasers.

President Wilson persuaded Mr. Ford to become a candidate for United States Senator in 1918, although the manufacturer had never before displayed any particular interest in party politics. Going before the voters in the primaries on

(continued)

both the Democratic and Republican tickets, he received the Democratic nomination, but was defeated in the election by Truman H. Newberry, Republican, whose majority was reduced from 7,567 to 4,000 in a Senate recount. Previously Michigan had normally returned a Republican majority of 100,000, so that the closeness of the 1918 election showed Mr. Ford's personal popularity with the voters.

Mr. Ford retired as active head of the Ford Motor Company in 1918, at the age of 55, turning over the presidency to his son, Edsel, and announcing his intention of devoting himself thereafter to the development of his farm tractor, the Fordson, and to the publication of his weekly journal, The Dearborn Independent.

Sued Chicago Tribune

In 1919 Mr. Ford sued The Chicago Tribune for $1,000,000 on the ground of libel, because of an editorial which was headed "Ford is an Anarchist," and which accused him of having been pro-German during the war. The jury awarded him a verdict of 6 cents, but only after counsel for the defense had subjected him to a pitiless cross-examination which revealed him to be almost without knowledge of subjects outside his own field.

His activities as publisher of The Dearborn Independent involved him in another highly publicized libel suit. The weekly published a series of articles, which were widely criticized as anti-Semitic. Aaron Sapiro, a Chicago lawyer, brought suit for $1,000,000 on the ground that his reputation as an organizer of farmers' cooperative marketing organizations had been damaged by articles which charged that a Jewish conspiracy was seeking to win control of American agriculture.

On the witness stand Mr. Ford disclaimed animosity toward the Jews. It was brought out that, although a column in the paper was labeled as his, he did not write it nor did he read the publication. The editor wrote articles expounding Mr. Ford's economic and social ideas after consulting with him. Mr. Ford settled the suit without disclosing the terms of settlement and discontinued the paper. He appeased his critics by making a public apology, in which he explained he had discovered the articles were doing harm by the prejudice they created.

WEATHERED 1921 CRISIS

Refused Assistance of Bankers And Proved Resourcefulness

The 1921 business depression brought the Ford Motor Company its most severe financial crisis, and served to demonstrate both Mr. Ford's antipathy to bankers, and his resourcefulness. When it became acute the company had obligations of $58,000,000 due between Jan. 1 and April 18, and only $20,000,000 with which to meet them.

Investment bankers were convinced that he would have to go to them "hat in hand," and an officer of one large New York bank journeyed to Detroit to offer Mr. Ford a large loan on the condition that a representative of the bankers be appointed treasurer of the Ford Motor Company with full control over its finances. Mr. Ford silently handed him his hat.

He loaded up Ford dealers throughout the country with all the cars they could possibly handle and compelled them to pay cash, thereby adding nearly $25,000,000 to the funds in hand. Then, by purchasing a railroad of his own, the Detroit, Toledo & Ironton, and by other economies, he cut one-third from the time his raw materials and finished products were in transit. Thereby he was able to decrease by one-third the inventory of goods he needed on hand for uninterrupted production, and to release $28,000,000 from capital funds to ready cash.

Raised More than Needed

In addition he realized nearly $8,000,000 from the sale of Liberty bonds, nearly $4,000,000 from the sale of by-products and $3,000,000 in collections from Ford agents in foreign countries.

On April 1, consequently he had more than $87,000,000 in cash, or $27,000,000 more than he needed to wipe out all the indebtedness. Furthermore, by rigid economies of labor and materials hitherto thought impossible, he cut the overhead cost on each car from $146 to $93.

The crisis over, Mr. Ford severed all connections with the banks, except as a depositor. In fact, he became a competitor of the banks, frequently loaning several millions on call in the New York money market. He made a practice of carrying tremendous amounts on deposit in banks throughout the United States and in other countries. Bankers reported that he invariably drove a hard bargain in placing these funds. He often exacted a special rate of interest when his balance was to be above a certain amount for a certain time.

During the calm and increasingly prosperous years of the middle Nineteen Twenties Mr. Ford's business continued to grow, but more and more of his energies were devoted to his outside interests. He attempted in vain to interest the younger generation in old-fashioned dances and fiddlers. In 1923 he purchased the Wayside Inn at South Sudbury, Mass., which had been the subject of Longfellow's "Tales of a Wayside Inn," and restored it.

Mr. Ford startled the country late in 1926 by announcing the permanent adoption of the five-day week for his factories, after trying it out for some time. He declared that the five-day week would open the way to greater prosperity than that which the country then enjoyed and which he attributed to the eight-hour day and high wages, because they gave people time and money to consume the goods they produced. Without the five-day week, he said, the country would not be able to absorb the results of mass production and remain prosperous.

DEVELOPED MODEL A

Met Chevrolet Competition by Turning Out New Car

Late that same year Mr. Ford met his greatest industrial crisis. In 1924 the Ford company had manufactured about two-thirds of all the automobiles produced in this country, but by 1926 the Chevrolet car, manufactured by the General Motors Corporation, had become a serious competitor. Its production mounted from 25,000 in January, 1926, to 77,000 in November, while Ford sales dropped.

Mr. Ford closed his plants late in 1926 while he experimented with a six-cylinder model. He finally abandoned the Model T the next year, substituting the Model A, which became almost as well known. To produce the new model Mr. Ford had to make over almost his entire system of production, retooling his plants and retraining his workers, a feat of industrial renovation which many experts had contended would prove impossible.

The new model proved popular with the buying public, and the Ford Motor Company continued to expand. In 1928 Mr. Ford organized the British Ford Company, and subsequently began operations in other European countries. In Germany the German Ford Company was organized with the German dye trust as one of its principal stockholders.

Aided Soviet Industrialization

Mr. Ford had long regarded Soviet Russia as a potential market of great importance. By agreeing to aid in the construction of an automobile factory at Nizhni-Novgorod, and by providing technological assistance in the development of the automobile industry in the Soviet Union, Mr. Ford sold $30,000,000 worth of products to Russia, and, incidentally, gave added impetus to the industrialization of that country, which was to prove of such importance in later years.

When the stock market collapse of October, 1929, precipitated the great depression, Mr. Ford was one of the business and industrial leaders who were summoned to the White House by President Hoover. Unlike some industrialists who favored deflation of wages, Mr. Ford argued that the maintenance of purchasing power was of paramount importance.

Henry Ford and his first car, June 4, 1896.

Although the Ford Motor Company lost as much as $68,000,000 in a single depression year, Mr. Ford maintained his wage policy until the autumn of 1932, when it announced a readjustment from "the highest executive down to the ordinary laborer," including a new minimum wage scale of $4 a day, $1 less than that which he had put into effect eighteen years before. As the depression waned, however, he reverted to his high-wage policy and in 1935 established a minimum of $6 a day.

Mr. Ford was a central figure in the banking crisis which led to the closing of the Detroit banks in February, 1933, which in turn precipitated the chain of events that resulted in the national bank holiday when President Roosevelt was inaugurated the next month. When the collapse came the Ford Motor Company had about $32,500,000 on deposit in various banks of the Guardian Detroit Union group, and Edsel Ford personally and the Ford Motor Company had made loans of about $12,000,000 in cash and securities to try to stave off the closing.

How much the Ford interests lost because of the closing was never publicly revealed, but Edsel Ford subsequently helped to organize and capitalize a new national bank, the Manufacturers National Bank of Detroit, which took over most of the assets and obligations of the Guardian National group. Meanwhile the General Motors Company, Mr. Ford's closest business rival, aided by the Reconstruction Finance Corporation, opened another new bank, the National Bank of Detroit.

Early Foe of New Deal

Mr. Ford, who had supported Herbert Hoover for re-election in 1932, was regarded as one of the leading foes of the New Deal in the early days of President Roosevelt's Administration, and he refused to sign the automobile code of the National Recovery Administration, which stipulated that employes had a right to organize. In 1936 he supported Gov. Alf M. Landon, stating that the election would "determine if labor and industry in this country can continue under a system of free enterprise."

Despite Mr. Roosevelt's triumphant re-election with the strong support of the Committee for Industrial Organization, then headed by John L. Lewis, Mr. Ford remained outspokenly antagonistic to unions. In an interview on Feb. 19, 1937, he advised all workers to "stay out of unions." At the same time he declared that no group of strikers would ever take over a Ford plant.

The United Automobile Workers, a CIO union, began a vigorous drive to organize the workers in the Ford plants. The opening blow was a sit-down strike in the Ford plant at Kansas City, ended only by the promise of officials there to treat with the union, a step the Ford company had never taken before. Other sporadic strikes occurred in Ford plants in other sections of the country.

Mr. Ford fought back with the argument that his policy of high wages and short hours was satisfactory to the bulk of the workers in his plants. He charged that a group of international financiers had gained control of the unions and were utilizing their power to exploit labor and management alike.

HIS TROUBLE WITH UNION

UAW Won 70% Votes After NLRB Ordered Election

On May 26, 1937, a group of UAW organizers, including Richard T. Frankensteen and Walter Reuther, were distributing organizing literature outside the gate of the Ford plant at River Rouge, when they were set upon and badly beaten. The union charged that the beatings were administered by Ford company police. The Ford Motor Company denied this.

After lengthy hearings the National Labor Relations Board found the Ford Motor Company guilty of unfair labor practices. The Ford company fought the issue through the courts to the United States Supreme Court, which, in effect, upheld the finding by refusing to review it. In April, 1941, the UAW called a strike in the Ford plants and the NLRB held an election under the Wagner Act to determine the collective bargaining spokesman for the employes.

When the votes were counted in June, 1941, the UAW was found to have won about 70 per cent of them. With characteristic vigor, Mr. Ford, long looked upon as perhaps the strongest foe of unionism, did a complete about face. He signed a contract with the union which gave them virtually everything for which they had asked, including a union shop and a dues check-off system.

In the early days of the second World War, Mr. Ford opposed our entry into it and, true to his pacifist convictions, refused to manufacture airplane motors for Great Britain. He compelled the cancellation of a contract made by his son, Edsel, calling for the production of 6,000 Rolls-Royce engines for Great Britain, and 3,000 of the same type for the United States.

To support his contention that the United States was in no danger Mr. Ford, in May, 1940, stated that if it should become necessary the Ford Motor Company could "under our own supervision, and without meddling by Government agencies, swing into the production of a thousand airplanes of standard design a day." As the pressure for re-armament became greater, Mr. Ford was compelled by public opinion to agree to build planes for the United States.

The net result was the celebrated Willow Run plant for the construction of four-motored bombers. At its construction it was the largest single manufacturing establishment in the world, occupying a building 3,200 feet long and 1,280 feet wide, with 2,547,000 feet of floor space. In addition there were hangars with another 1,200,000 feet of floor space, and an adjacent air field larger than La Guardia Field in this city.

PRODUCED 8,000 B-24'S

Plant at Willow Run Turned Out One Bomber an Hour

Ground was broken for the plant on April 18, 1941, and the first of the thirty-ton B-24-E bombers came off its assembly line a little more than a year later, in May, 1942. For a time the plant was under severe criticism on the ground that it was not producing at the rate that had been anticipated, but this was eventually stilled when the gigantic factory began turning out bombers at the rate of one an hour, twenty-four hours a day.

By the spring of 1945, when the War Department announced that the production of Liberator bombers would be discontinued, Willow Run had produced more than 8,000 of them. In May, 1945, a spokesman for the company revealed that it had no plans for the post-war utilization of the gigantic factory, and that it planned to turn it back to the Defense Plant Corporation, the Government agency which had put up the $100,000,000 it cost.

When Mr. Ford resumed the active management of the company, after the unexpected death of his son, Edsel, he began a series of changes in its high officials. In March, 1944, Charles E. Sorenson, who had been considered for years as its greatest production expert, announced his retirement from the company. Not long after that Mr. Ford's personal secretary, Ernest G. Liebold, was dismissed, after having been one of the company's top executives for many years.

The Ford Company asked for and obtained the release of Henry Ford 2d, son of Edsel Ford, from the Navy, in which he had served for two and a half years and had risen to the rank of lieutenant, on the ground that he was needed in the executive end of the business. Mr. Ford let it be known that he was grooming his grandson and namesake, then 26 years old, for the eventual leadership of the business.

From time to time Mr. Ford gave interviews in which he emphasized his favorite beliefs: the folly of war, the need for world federation, the decentralization of industry, the advantages of hard work, utilitarian education, abstemiousness and simple pleasures. He was opposed to the use of tobacco and liquor, and he hated idling.

In a characteristic interview in September, 1944, he made known his adherence to his old doctrine of high wages for his employes. Declaring his intention of raising the wages of his workers as soon as the Government would allow him to do so, Mr. Ford said:

"As long as I live I want to pay the highest wages in the automobile industry. If the men in our plants will give a full day's work for a full day's pay, there is no reason why we can't always do it. Every man should make enough money to own a home, a piece of land and a car."

Mr. Ford was an ardent collector of Americana. In 1928 he established, and endowed with $5,000,000, a museum at Dearborn to commemorate the inventions of his old friend, Thomas A. Edison. The Menlo Park Laboratory, in which Mr. Edison perfected the electric light, was completely restored in the museum.

Mr. Ford also built Greenfield Village, a reproduction of the community in which Mrs. Ford, who was Clara Bryant before their marriage in 1887, was born. There he brought the original log cabin in which McGuffey, author of the celebrated reader, was born; the court house in which Abraham Lincoln first practiced law, and the home of Stephen Foster's parents, as well as momentos of his own youth.

One of his lifelong interests was in the training of youths to earn a livelihood, and he established various vocational schools for the purpose. He also made it a policy to employ a fixed proportion of blind persons and other handicapped individuals in his plants, and took a keen interest in the rehabilitation of wounded war veterans. At its convention in September, 1944, the American Legion awarded to him its Distinguished Service Medal for his efforts in behalf of disabled veterans of both world wars.

LONDON PAYS TRIBUTE

'He Brought Revolution in Way of Life,' Says The Times

Special to The New York Times.

LONDON, April 8—Editorials in British newspapers today paid tribute to Henry Ford as "the man who brought revolution in the world's way of life."

In Ford the man, the newspaper saw a figure who neither understood nor sympathized with the children of the machine age that he promoted; who reerected on his estate an English village that was the antithesis of the era he created. The London Times said: "The mainspring of Henry Ford's life and work was a personal philosophy about which he had no doubt whatever. He believed that he had the key to human progress. Inevitably his single-mindedness led him into paths which a more prudent and less dogmatic man might have avoided.

"His long-sustained opposition to 'iron collar' of trade unionism coupled with liberal treatment of Ford workers reflected his belief in benevolent depotism."

A Ford production line, 1916.

The last Model T was produced in 1927. The Model A (above) was its replacement.

World Leaders in Tribute

In the capitals of the world yesterday, as in the humble homes of the country, the passing of Henry Ford was sincerely mourned. British newspapers carried the story of Mr. Ford's death with streamer headlines, pointing out that the English Ford Company now employs many thousands in a huge plant outside London.

In Amsterdam, the Netherlands, the flag above the big plant of the Netherlands Ford Company was flown at half staff. In Rio de Janeiro, Brazil, all evening papers carried Mr. Ford's picture, calling him "world benefactor."

Among the tributes were:

President Sends Message

President TRUMAN—In a message to Mr. Ford's widow and family: In the sorrow which has come with such sudden and unexpected force I offer to you and to all who mourn with you this assurance of deepest sympathy.

ALFRED P. SLOAN Jr., Chairman of the Board of General Motors—The impact of Henry Ford's inventive and productive genius on the well-being of America is incalculable. He typified the best in American enterprise. He pioneered mass production, which has become the keystone of American economy. He contributed directly and by example to our high living standards. The nation's debt to him is large and enduring.

C. E. WILSON, President of General Motors—His life and example will continue to be an inspiration to the youth of America. His perseverance in overcoming heavy odds at a time when things he worked at were considered impractical provides an outstanding example of what can be done in America.

ORVILLE WRIGHT, airplane pioneer—He did more to promote the welfare of the American people, and particularly the working class, than any man who ever lived in this country. The present great wealth of this country has come indirectly from Mr. Ford through his development of mass production.

MRS. THOMAS A. EDISON, widow of the inventor—We have lost a friend and one near and dear to all of us.

CHARLES EDISON, former Governor of New Jersey, son of the inventor—I am grieved and shocked. My father was devoted to him and admired him enormously. His contributions to civilization have been beyond measure. He was my friend and no one ever had a better one.

Called Industrial Genius

THOMAS E. DEWEY, Governor of New York State—Our nation has suffered the loss of one of the great men of our times. His industrial genius contributed mightily to the development of our country. His philanthropic activities did much to bring our people educational, social and cultural gifts.

Senator ARTHUR H. VANDENBERG of Michigan—His death ends one of the greatest and most thrilling careers in the life of his country. It is the vivid epitome of what a man can do for himself and his fellow-men under our system of American freedom through his own irresistible genius and courage. He not only rose from humble obscurity to fame and fortune but founded a new national economy of mass production which blessed his hundreds of thousands of employes with high wages and his millions of customers with low prices.

Representative GEORGE A. DONDERO of Michigan—A great man, who brought transportation within the reach of the average man. An ordinary American, he was willing to work, and through his work and concentration of effort he rose to the top.

B. E. HUTCHINSON, vice president of the Chrysler Corporation—He conceived and dramatized to his country and the world the possibility of the mass production of material goods for the benefit of all people. A great vision faithfully adhered to.

GEORGE ROMNEY, general manager of the Automobile Manufacturers Association—The greatness of the American automotive industry is largely the result of others applying his methods and ideals.

GEORGE MASON, president of the Automobile Manufacturers Association—One of the greatest creative forces of our time. He joined Edison, Pasteur and other immortals. His Model T car has become a symbol of an era.

Praise from Britain

Sir MILES THOMAS, Vice Chairman of the Nuffield Organization, One of Britain's Largest Automobile Companies—Everyone who uses a motor car ought to pay tribute to his pioneer work, because it was he who first put motoring within the reach of the ordinary man. He was a mechanic with a profound sympathy for metals. Many of the engineering principles of his Model T car have stood the test of time.

HARVEY S. FIRESTONE, President of the Firestone Tire and Rubber Company—It was a great privilege to have known him, and I feel a deep sense of personal loss in his passing. Few men in history have made so profound a contribution to the advancement of civilization and the welfare of mankind. Through his genius, personal transportation has brought a higher standard of living to millions. He exemplified the virtues of hard work, vision and service which made this country great, and sought to preserve these virtues through his philanthopy so that the human, simple, pioneering spirit of America might be perpetuated.

Count GIANCARIO CAMARINI, Vice President of the Fiat Automobile Company of Rome, Italy—His death made a very deep impression on the executives of my company, which is a little Ford of Italy. It was especially shocking as it occurred only eighteen months after that of Giovanni Agnelli, founder of Fiat, who was closely attached to Mr. Ford.

WILLIAM S. KNUDSEN, chairman of the board of the Hupp Motor Car Corporation—A great teacher, and a great inspiration to all of us in American industry. He will be forever remembered for the things he has done and the beautiful example of his personal life.

PAUL H. GRIFFITH, National Commander, American Legion—His spirit will ever remain an inspiration for those who admired him.

EDDIE RICKENBACKER, president, Eastern Airlines—Deeply regret the untimely passing of my good friend, Mr. Ford, and hasten offer my condolences and deepest sympathy to you and other members of the family.

JOSEPHUS DANIELS, former Secretary of the Navy—I wish he could have lived to see the world peace that was near his heart.

"All the News That's Fit to Print"

The New York Times

LATE CITY EDITION

Weather: Mostly sunny today; cool tonight. Chance of rain tomorrow. Temperature range: today 46-66; Wednesday 52-59. Details, Page 82.

VOL. CXXV..No. 43,034

NEW YORK, THURSDAY, NOVEMBER 20, 1975

25 cents beyond 50-mile zone from New York City, except Long Island. Higher in air delivery cities.

20 CENTS

BRITAIN PLEDGES SCOTS AND WELSH SOME HOME RULE

Plan, Disclosed in Speech by Queen, Would Be Greatest Charter Change in Years

LONG DEBATE IS LIKELY

Wilson Plans to Introduce White Paper on Subject to New Parliament Nov. 27

By ROBERT B. SEMPLE Jr.

Special to The New York Times

LONDON, Nov. 19—Prime Minister Harold Wilson's Labor Party Government formally announced today its intention to provide Scotland and Wales with some form of home rule—a move that would represent the most profound constitutional change in the United Kingdom in many years.

The Government's intentions were disclosed in a single paragraph in Queen Elizabeth's traditional speech opening the new session of Parliament:

"My Government," the Queen said, speaking from an ornate throne in the House of Lords, "will bring forward legislative proposals for the establishment of Scottish and Welsh assemblies to exercise wide governmental responsibilities within the framework of the United Kingdom."

Only the Beginning

But as Mr. Wilson himself conceded in the House of Commons late this afternoon, the generalities in the Queen's speech—which is written for her by the Government in power, and is intended to be merely a general outline of the legislative business before a new Parliament—marked only the beginning of what will be an emotional and lengthy national debate.

The Government, Mr. Wilson said, planned to introduce a white paper on the subject of devolution—meaning the devolving of powers on to other parts of the United Kingdom—on Nov. 27. But unlike most white papers, this one would not represent the Government's final views on the subject. Mr. Wilson said he wanted "an extended debate" in Parliament and throughout the United Kingdom, after which he would submit a detailed bill.

The Government's proposal to at least present the issue to Parliament is in response to a pledge in last fall's election as well as to the growing sentiments in both Scotland and Wales for some form of autonomy. The independence movement in Scotland has become more intense because the new North Sea oil fields lie off the Scottish coast.

Other major sections of the Queen's speech said the Government would:

¶Ask for a new antiterrorist

Continued on Page 5, Column 3

Franco Is Dead in Madrid at 82

Juan Carlos to Take the Oath as King Within 48 Hours

By HENRY GINIGER

Special to The New York Times

MADRID, Thursday, Nov. 20—Generalissimo Francisco Franco died early today after 36 years of dictatorial rule over Spain. He was 82 years old.

The death of the Chief of State, who led rightist military forces to victory in the Spanish

An obituary article will be found on Page 34.

Civil War that ended in 1939, came at 4:30 A.M. at the La Paz Hospital on the northern edge of Madrid. He had been rushed there on Nov. 7 from the Pardo Palace for surgery to stop internal bleeding.

Although his designated successor, Prince Juan Carlos de Borbón, 37, had been acting Chief of State since Oct. 30, interim power upon the general's death passed formally to the three-member Council of the Regency, headed by Alejandro Rodríguez de Valcárcel, the Speaker of Parliament.

The panel will swear in Juan Carlos as King of Spain before a joint session of Parliament and the Council of the Realm within 48 hours, and as King, Juan Carlos will preside over the funeral of General Franco.

It was considered almost certain that General Franco would be buried in the Valley of the Fallen, a huge monument carved out of a mountain some 40 miles northwest of Madrid, which is a memorial to the dead of the Civil War.

General Franco's death came while most Spaniards were sleeping and few were aware of the event for several hours. The death was ascribed to toxic shock produced by peritonitis. The official announcement was delayed, presumably to allow time to inform the Franco family and the Prince. Mrs. Franco was at the official residence in

Continued on Page 35, Column 1

Camera Press

Generalissimo Francisco Franco

COLBY ASKS PANEL TO DROP 12 NAMES FROM PLOT REPORT

Says He Fears Retaliation —Data on Assassinations May Be Released Today

By JOHN M. CREWDSON

Special to The New York Times

WASHINGTON, Nov. 19—William E. Colby, the Director of Central Intelligence, appealed today to a Senate committee not to make public the names of 12 individuals, some of them agency officials, who were allegedly involved in C.I.A. plots against the lives of foreign heads of state.

In a rare news conference at the Central Intelligence Agency's suburban Virginia headquarters, Mr. Colby said that he feared that the individuals, if named in a committee report expected to be released tomorrow, might be subject to retaliation from "unstable and extremist groups."

Letters Are Sent

He said that while he opposed "in principle" publication of the report on C.I.A. assassination plots, which must be approved by the full Senate in order to be released, his immediate concern was to protect "the safety and livelihoods of the individuals involved" in those matters and also "the future of American intelligence."

[Senate and Administration sources said that Mr. Colby had sent letters stating his position to Senator John C. Stennis, Democrat of Mississippi, the Armed Services Committee chairman, and Senator John L. McClellan, Democrat of Arkansas, chairman of the Intelligence Operations Subcommittee, The Associated Press reported.]

Mr. Colby's unusual appeal, which seemed to have been addressed as much to the full Senate as to the 11 members of the Select Committee on Intelligence, which has voted unanimously to approve the report's release, marked an all-out effort by the Ford Administration to block disclosure of the document on the Senate floor.

The Senate is scheduled to begin a closed debate at 9 A.M. tomorrow on whether to approve or forbid the release of the assassination report, a document of nearly 400 pages that is based on a five-month investigation by the select committee.

Senator Frank Church, the committee's chairman, said that his panel had considered carefully the C.I.A.'s arguments for

Continued on Page 17, Column 1

Senate Eases Restrictions On Construction Picketing

Bill Would Allow Acts Against Entire Site in Dispute With One Employer— Issue Debated for 25 Years

By The Associated Press

WASHINGTON, Nov. 19—The Senate passed tonight by a vote of 52 to 45 a long-disputed bill greatly broadening the authority of building trades unions to picket at construction sites.

The Senate vote appeared to virtually end the 25-year controversy in Congress over the legislation, which would allow a union to try to picket, and thus close down, an entire construction site, even though it had a dispute with only one subcontractor. This is called "common situs" picketing.

The measure was sent back to the House for an expected conference in December after the Congressional Thanksgiving recess. There are only minor differences between the two versions.

The Senate adopted by a vote of 78 to 20 a last-minute amendment by Senator James B. Allen, Democrat of Alabama, stating that the bill's provisions would not apply to a project on which work began by last Saturday.

Earlier today, the Senate adopted, by a vote of 77 to 18, an amendment by Senator J. Glenn Beall, Republican of Maryland, exempting construction of homes with three or fewer floors from the bill's provisions.

Also adopted, by a vote of 93 to 0, was an amendment by Senator Jennings Randolph, Democrat of West Virginia, to ban picketing at a common site if this was intended to force a contractor not to use or install a particular product.

But an amendment by Senator Jesse Helms, Republican of North Carolina, to exempt from the bill all construction sites involving Federal or state government projects was defeated by a vote of 63 to 33.

Tied to the bill is a second major provision to set up new machinery to try to bring quicker and less inflationary settlement of labor disputes in the construction industry.

President Ford has said he will sign both proposals if they reach him at the same time.

But he has made clear he will not approve the picketing legislation unless the measure seeking to improve collective bar-

Continued on Page 33, Column 1

PRESIDENT AWAITS CITY-STATE MOVE BEFORE GIVING AID

Balks at Help to New York Now, but Will Reconsider After 'Concrete Action'

NEW REVENUES NEEDED

Albany Legislative Leaders Trying for a Tax Package to Raise $200 Million

By MARTIN TOLCHIN

Special to The New York Times

WASHINGTON, Nov. 19—President Ford said today that he would not now support Federal financial aid to prevent a New York City default, but would reconsider his position next week if the city and state took "further concrete actions."

In a five-paragraph, generally conciliatory statement that contrasted with his caustic Oct.

Text of the President's statement is on Page 46.

29 speech before the National Press Club, the President did not specify what steps he felt were needed.

His economic advisers said, however, that he would require Governor Carey to fulfill a pledge of legislative action to find $200 million in new revenues for the city, although they said increased taxes, per se, would not be insisted on.

New Taxes Planned

Legislative leaders of both parties met with the Governor in Albany tonight to try to fashion a package of revenues that would be acceptable on both sides of the aisle. The Republicans, who control the Senate, opposed income-tax rises that would fall on commuters; the Assembly Democrats fought any increase in sales taxes.

And fiscal experts in Albany maintained that the city was now $60 million short of cash that it will need next Tuesday. They said that only enactment of new city taxes and a favorable word from the President could help the city borrow enough to pay its bills next week. [Page 46.]

Temporary Assistance

Although the President's delay dismayed supporters of financial aid legislation, who had hoped for Congressional action today, some noted that the President had said for the first time that he might find predefault aid for the city "appropriate."

White House sources repeated, moreover, that if the Legislature acted, the likelihood was that Mr. Ford would support short-term financial aid of $2.5 billion.

These funds would be available to meet the city's temporary revenue shortfalls—times during the year when the city cannot temporarily meet its obligations, which are often followed by periods when the city

Continued on Page 46, Column 1

F.B.I. Aide Terms Effort To Vilify Dr. King Illegal

By NICHOLAS M. HORROCK

Special to The New York Times

WASHINGTON, Nov. 19—A top official of the Federal Bureau of Investigation said today that there was no "statutory basis or justification" for some 25 separate incidents of bureau harassment of the Rev. Dr. Martin Luther King Jr. during a six-year campaign to discredit the civil rights leader.

James B. Adams, assistant deputy director of the F.B.I., also told members of the Senate Select Committee on Intelligence that he could confirm that the F.B.I. mailed Dr. King a tape recording in late 1964. Mr. Adams said he "assumed" that an anonymous threatening letter, found in bureau files, had accompanied the tape.

According to evidence given the committee, Dr. King regarded the tape recording and unsigned letter as an effort to drive him to suicide. Mr. Adams said, however, that he had read the letter but could not conclude that its purpose was to force a suicide.

"As I read it, I don't know what it meant," he said.

Evidence concerning the letter and tape recording was given to the committee yesterday.

The letter read: "King, there is only one thing left for you to do. You know what it is. You have just 34 days in which to do it. (This exact number has been selected for a specific reason.) It has definite practical significance. You are done. There is but one way out for you."

The letter was found in F.B.I. files that had belonged to William Sullivan, former chief of the bureau's counterintelligence operation. Mr. Sullivan told committee investigators that he

Continued on Page 30, Column 4

Town's Boom Halted By a Strip Mine Ban

By GRACE LICHTENSTEIN

Special to The New York Times

GILLETTE, Wyo. — An antelope was grazing on the revegetated hillside above the Rawhide strip mine's new administration building. It was the only thing moving on the entire site. Several hundred yards away, the skeletons of two half-finished large coal silos stood out against the rolling, mustard-colored grass lands.

"We've got some people sitting on pins and needles," said Charles E. Smith Jr., president of the Carter Mining Company, a subsidiary of Exxon, which owns the coal mine. "They're chomping at the bit, ready to go."

Rawhide is one of four important strip mines in the Powder River Basin near Gillette in eastern Wyoming, the nation's richest coal region, whose development has been halted since January by a Federal court injunction, the result of an environmental lawsuit.

The suit, known as Sierra Club v. Morton, is now before the United States Supreme Court. In it, environmentalists argue that the Federal Government is required by law to study the impact of the projected coal boom on the entire tristate coal region, not just individual mines, before the mines become active.

The lawsuit could delay

Continued on Page 59, Column 3

DEMOCRATS KILL ANTIBUSING PLAN

Vote Proposal Down, 172-96 —House Caucus Opened to Public for First Time

By RICHARD L. MADDEN

Special to The New York Times

WASHINGTON, Nov. 19—House Democrats turned back today an effort to force an antibusing amendment to the Constitution out of the House Judiciary Committee.

The Democrats, opening their caucus to the public for the first time, tabled—and thus killed—a resolution sought by two Representatives from Texas, Olin E. Teague and Dale Milford. The vote was 172 to 96.

The defeated proposal would have directed Democrats on the Judiciary Committee to send to the House floor within 30 days a constitutional amendment "that would guarantee each child the right to attend the primary and secondary schools nearest his own home within his respective school district."

The caucus action was a victory for the Speaker, Representative Carl Albert of Oklahoma, and Representative Peter W. Rodino Jr. of New Jersey, who is chairman of the Judiciary Committee. Both men had appealed to their colleagues to reject such an amendment. The vote also indicated that a two-thirds vote to approve such an amendment could not be mustered now.

It was the first time under recently revised caucus rules that the public and press were admitted to the galleries to

Continued on Page 27, Column 4

Liquor Labeling Plan

The Food and Drug Administration said it would soon order the alcoholic beverage industry to list on labels the ingredients in all domestic and imported beer, wine and liquor. The Treasury Department recently rejected such a plan. Page 29.

New Haven Schools Shut as Unions Call For General Strike

By LAWRENCE FELLOWS

Special to The New York Times

NEW HAVEN, Nov. 19—Public schools in New Haven were ordered closed this afternoon in the face of a general strike that was threatened as a protest against the jailing of 90 teachers and union leaders.

Before the schools were ordered shut, the Greater New Haven Central Labor Council called a strike meeting for Friday night, determined, according to council leaders, to urge the 30,000 workers in its 92 affiliated unions in the New Haven area to walk out in support of the striking teachers.

Today, nearly a thousand janitors, cafeteria workers and other employees joined the school strike. The 700 teachers who remained on the picket lines suspended their strike for the rest of the week so that talks coulde be resumed over the issue of pay raises. School board officials would not negotiate during the strike; walkouts by teachers are illegal in Connecticut.

The 46 public schools in New Haven were open this morning, as they have been throughout the strike, which began Nov. 10, with classes being run by 400 nonstriking teachers, sub-

Continued on Page 49, Column 1

ALBANY MEETINGS SEEK AID ACCORD

Governor and Legislature's Chiefs Try to End Impasse on a Package for City

By LINDA GREENHOUSE

Special to The New York Times

ALBANY, Thursday, Nov. 20—The Republican and Democratic leadership was meeting this morning to try to break the partisan deadlock over a $200 million New York City revenue package that both sides agree is a prerequisite to President Ford's approval of loan-guarantee legislation for the city.

Governor Carey and Mayor Beame fielded questions from Democratic legislators for nearly three hours last night, at an unusual party conference that participants described as a "gripe session" and "group therapy." The session ended with the legislators applauding a rousing speech by Mr. Carey, in which he said that the city taxes were necessary to prevent a default.

But the Governor did not indicate what form the taxes would take. Earlier, the Democratic majority in the Assembly abandoned a plan to push through the Assembly a package of higher income taxes for residents and commuters, sought by Mayor Beame.

This bill would face almost

Continued on Page 47, Column 1

Jets Dismiss Coach

The New York Jets football team, which has lost six straight games, dismissed Charley Winner as head coach yesterday. Ken Shipp, an assistant, was named interim coach. Page 55.

A Pollution Emergency Curtails Steel Output in Pittsburgh Area

Special to The New York Times

PITTSBURGH, Nov. 19 — As many as 30 industrial plants in the Pittsburgh area were forced to curtail operations today as a weather inversion caused air pollution levels to soar to the highest levels since the establishment of Allegheny County's monitoring system.

The worst episode centered on the Monongahela and Youghiogheny River Valleys, heart of the area's steel industry, where air pollution readings reached a level of 249 on a scale of 300 in midafternoon, with the expectation the level could rise.

An air pollution emergency was declared by the Allegheny County commissioners in eight communities with a total population of 53,250, the first time such a step has been taken since stringent air-pollution laws were adopted here in 1971.

As a result of the emergency, the State Department of Environmental Resources ordered the United States Steel Corporation to shut down its giant Clairton Coke Works, The Associated Press reported. The order came several hours after county officials ordered that the plant operations be curtailed.

County public health officials warned persons with respiratory or heart conditions to remain indoors, avoid undue phy-

Continued on Page 35, Column 5

NEWS INDEX

Court Backs Cutting Of School Day Here

By LEONARD BUDER

A State Supreme Court Justice yesterday upheld the City Board of Education's right to shorten the school day of pupils, the most controversial element of the settlement that ended last September's teachers' strike.

Almost immediately after the ruling, School Chancellor Irving Anker announced that he was ordering 13 previously defiant community school boards to submit by Monday evening formal plans for shortening their school days. He added that he would give the districts "reasonable time," but no more than a few weeks, to implement their plans.

Boards that do not submit

Continued on Page 50, Column 2

The New York Times/Jonas Mohan

New Haven teachers, confined for refusing to return to their classes, show their pleasure at seeing fellow strikers who went to the Air Force National Guard camp where they are held. The visitors were kept outside.

FRANCO IS DEAD IN MADRID AT 82

Continued From Page 1, Col. 4

the Pardo Palace, where his body will be brought later this morning to lie in state. Tomorrow it will be taken to the royal palace in Madrid for a public lying-in-state, and burial is expected Saturday after the swearing in of Juan Carlos as King.

Camera Press

Prince Juan Carlos

Franco, 81, was photographed with his wife as he entered the hospital.

The official announcement of the death was made over the state-owned radio network by León Herrera Esteban, the Minister of Information, who asked the country to pray for General Franco's soul, to be grateful for his labors for Spain and to have a special thought for his family, 'which today is in the vanguard of the immense national sadness." Prime Minister Carlos Arias Navarro will address the country on radio and television later in the morning.

Aside from doctors and nurses working the night shift a few newsmen and members of the military and civilian staff there were no high officials or members of his family present when the general died. Mr. Arias Navarro arrived an hour later followed by the Minister of Justice, Jose María Sánchez-Ventura, who signed the official death certificate.

One of the doctors was the general's son-in-law, Cristóbal Martínez Bordiú, who left the hospital by the emergency entrance to inform Mrs. Franco and other members of the family at the Pardo.

Military security forces were expected to be deployed around Madrid and other possible disturbances. The over-all plan also sets elaborate military plans for the funeral. All schools, commercial establishments and official offices are expected to close Friday and Saturday.

General Franco's death coincided with the 39th anniversary of the death of José Antonio Primo de Rivera, one of the spiritual founders of his regime, who was executed by the Spanish Republic on Nov. 20, 1936. José Antonio, as he is always called here, is the principal figure buried in the Valley of the Fallen.

General Franco, stricken on Oct. 21 by acute heart disease, withstood a long series of crises complicated by kidney failure and severe bleeding from multiple ulcers.

In his final days, his fight for physical survival was linked in the minds of many Spaniards to the political survival of the authoritarian regime he founded. Even before his death, the Spanish political world was focusing discussion on what the post-Franco era under Juan Carlos might be like.

Out of the Crucible of Civil War, Franco's Iron Hand Forged a Modern Spain

By ALDEN WHITMAN

One of the most durable, canny and empirical of modern dictators, Francisco Paulino Hermenegildo Teódulo Franco y Bahamonde became master of Spain as a result of a military conspiracy, a dash of luck, timely help from foreign corporations, the influence of the Roman Catholic hierarchy and crucial armed assistance from Hitler and Mussolini.

He became dictator in 1939 in the culmination of a three-year civil war. He was aided in winning the war by the internal weaknesses of the incumbent Government, principally its inability to achieve political unity among its disparate parties and factions.

Although the Government put up a valiant defense, it had fatal difficulty in buying arms abroad. Its armed forces, moreover, were beset by the same sort of disunity that hobbled the Cabinet.

At the close of his long and sternly authoritarian rule, Generalissimo Franco could look back on 36 years of an imposed stability that rested on a policy of suppression of fundamental democratic rights. But it was also a stability that gave Spain a rising standard of living, industrial growth and an important alliance with the United States.

His regime, exceedingly harsh at the outset, was moderated somewhat from the middle of the nineteen-fifties into a condition of relative calm that persisted to the end of his rule. Contributing to this was the memory of the Civil War, a renewal of which none of his organized opponents wanted to provoke. There were outbursts against Franco—from the Basque nationalists, from among students—but these were put down.

5 Terrorists Executed

One of the last such episodes, which revealed an increasing impatience with Franco, occurred in September, 1975, when five convicted terrorists were executed despite protests from most of Western Europe and appeals for clemency from Pope Paul VI. The Vatican statement symbolized an about-face for the church, which for most of Franco's years had endorsed his policies. In the last five years, however, the church had been increasingly murmurous toward him.

The incident pointed up, moreover, a crumbling of support for Franco among some of his hitherto strong supporters. The church, members of the Falange, monarchists and the financial-industrial community were all restive for an orderly transfer of power from the hands of an aging ruler.

Coming to power after victory in a civil war that had devastated Spain, Franco clinched his grip on an impoverished and backward country by systematic terror. Then, by clever diplomacy, he took Spain through World War II as a nonbelligerent while averring his attachment to the Fascist powers. Exercising patience, he waited out years of international ostracism after the war, from which he was rescued by a United States decision in 1950 to acquire military bases in the country as a move in the cold war with the Soviet Union.

Now esteemed by the West, he was able in 1955 to have his nation admitted to the United Nations, which had expressly barred Spain in 1946 in a resolution asserting that "in origin, nature, structure and general conduct, the Franco regime is a Fascist regime patterned on, and established largely as a result of aid received from Hitler's Nazi Germany and Mussolini's Fascist Italy."

After his diplomatic resurrection, Franco began to loosen the rigors of dictatorship. Foreign investment was encouraged, tourism was promoted, wage levels inched upward. By 1962 per capita income for the nation's 33 million people reached $300 a year and then quadrupled by 1972.

Most authoritarian restrictions remained. There was no press freedom; no trade unions were permitted; only one political party was allowed; the armed forces were omnipresent.

The technique of his rule up to 1969 was to spread power among rival factions—big business and its technocrats, landowners, the church, the Falange, the army—and to control their respective gains and losses of strength. He was thus the indispensable arbiter of all major decisions.

In late 1969, however, Franco briefly tipped the balance in a Cabinet reshuffle that gave business and finance, through the technocrats and Opus Dei, a Catholic lay group, an advantage. The changes displaced the Falange as a powerful political force. The Falange, which had earlier been absorbed into the National Movement, was Franco's mass bulwark in the Civil War and afterward.

Four years later, when Franco was 80, he relinquished some of his administrative duties by naming a faithful aide, Adm. Luis Carrero Blanco, as Premier. His uneasy regime came to a violent end in December, 1973, when he was assassinated in an ambush attributed to Basque separatists. Evincing renewed firmness, Franco named Carlos Arias Navarro, the Interior Minister, as Premier.

A fresh round of repression began and was further fueled in 1974 by the winds of the Portuguese revolution. Part of Franco's problem was that Spain's relative economic boom engendered a libertarian backlash. Tourism brought in not only vital foreign exchange but also tourists who personified the rewards of the democratic countries from which they came. In addition, almost a million Spaniards went abroad to work in the sixties. They sent home cash and brought home rudimentary ideas of democratic freedoms and worker-controlled trade unions.

Product of 19th Century

Franco was very much the product of 19th-century Spain and the tradition that sons of military officers should follow the father's profession. He was born Dec. 4, 1892, at El Ferrol, on the Galician coast, the son of Nicolás Franco, a naval officer, and Pilar Bahamonde Franco. It is widely believed,

(continued)

although skirted officially, that Sephardic Jews were among his ancestors.

Franco was ticketed for a naval career, but, because of the loss of the navy in the Spanish-American War, there were no examinations for the Academia de Marina in 1907. So instead he entered the Academia de Infantería in Toledo, from which he was commissioned a second lieutenant in the army in 1910.

Posted to North Africa in 1912, he took part in engagements against rebellious tribesmen and became in rapid succession the youngest captain, major, colonel and general in the army. He developed a reputation for personal valor, for exacting discipline and for excellence as an organizer. He was deputy commander of the Spanish Foreign Legion from 1920 to 1923 and commander in chief from then until 1927. He was credited with master-minding the final defeat of the Riff chieftain, Abd-el-Krim.

During 1926 Franco studied at the Ecole Militaire in France under Marshal Henri-Philippe Pétain, with whom he struck up a warm friendship.

Returning to Spain, he was director of the Academia General Militar at Saragossa from 1927 until 1931. In that year the incompetent monarchy of King Alfonso XIII fell. He fled the country and a republic was established. The Saragossa academy was dissolved on the ground that it was promonarchist and Franco was posted to the Balearic Islands as captain-general. He was brought back in 1933, when the Spanish Republic moved to the right, and he was entrusted, in 1934, with the suppression of the Asturian miners' revolt. The following year he was named chief of the army general staff.

In February, 1936, Spain elected a Popular Front government, which was dominated by moderates and Socialists. The Communists held only 17 of 473 seats in the Cortes, or parliament, and the party's membership throughout the country was estimated at less than 10,000. Later, Communist influence in the Government rose, but the party never dominated the regime.

As soon as the election returns were posted, a generals' plot against the Republic took shape and was led by Gen. José Sanjurjo, in exile in Portugal since the failure of a previous conspiracy in 1932. He visited Germany in February, 1936, and saw Adm. Wilhelm Canaris, chief of German military intelligence. According to "The Spanish Civil War" by Hugh Thomas:

"While Sanjurjo did not actually make any purchases of arms (since he supposed that his conspiracy would be immediately successful) he presumably assured himself that German military aid, if it should be necessary to secure the success of the rising, would be contemplated by Canaris at least."

In addition to General Sanjurjo, other principal plotters were Gen. Emilio Mola Vidal, Gen. José Enrique Varela Iglesias, and Gen. Gonzalo Queipo de Llano. Also taking part was José Antonio Primo de Rivera, the Falangist leader and son of Gen. Miguel Primo de Rivera, the former dictator. Franco, after some initial hesitation, joined the conspiracy.

Between March and July 18, 1936, the day of the rising, the plotters perfected their plans. A private British plane was hired that carried Franco from the Canaries to Teután in Spanish Morocco, where he was to take command of Moorish and Spanish troops. Meantime, according to "The Spanish Republic and the Civil War" by Prof. Gabriel Jackson, "the American colonel who headed the Telephone Company had placed private lines at the disposal of the Madrid plotters for their conversations with Generals Mola and Franco."

Goering Is Consulted

Once in Morocco, Franco had to get his troops to Spain, and he accepted the offer of Johannes Bernhardt, a Nazi businessman, to supply Junker transports. Of this incident Professor Jackson wrote:

"On July 21 General Franco accepted Bernhardt's offer. The latter interviewed Hitler on July 26 at Bayreuth, where the Chancellor was attending the Wagner Festival.

"After consultation with Hermann Goering, chief of the German Air Force, Hitler authorized the immediate dispatch of some 20 JU-52 heavy transports. They were to be flown, unarmed, by German crews. As of July 28 these planes had established an air ferry between Teután and Seville. . . . By Aug. 5 the Insurgents were thus able to place some 15,000 troops in Seville despite the Republican naval blockade."

At the same time Mussolini also began to commit planes and men to the conspirators, and the flow of this support continued throughout the Civil War. Munitions and men were also sent to Franco's forces in great quantities by Hitler.

From the outset the rebels received important support from some elements of American business. The American-owned Vacuum Oil Company in Tangier, for example, refused to sell to Republican ships, according to Professor Jackson. And the Texas Oil Company, his book asserts, supplied gasoline on credit to Franco until the war's end.

The plotters had expected a quick success, but the first days of their revolt were disappointing. Indeed, it seemed for a time that they might fail. They had set themselves up as a Nationalist Government at Burgos in the monarchist heartland of Castile in northern Spain, but General Sanjurjo died when his plane, reportedly overloaded with suitcases of his dress uniforms, crashed on take-off in Portugal.

General Mola also died in a plane crash, and Gen. Manuel Goded was captured and executed by the Spanish Government.

New Title Bestowed

All three outranked Franco, but as a result of their deaths he became the Nationalist leader and was so invested in October, 1936. At that time he also received the title of Generalissimo of the Army. His regime was quickly recognized by Germany and Italy.

The Civil War lasted two years and 254 days before the fall of Madrid to the Franco forces on March 28, 1939. The conflict was waged on both sides with great ferocity, but Franco's side had the preponderance of foreign aid. The Spanish Government, for its part, was able to get some arms from France and the Soviet Union. Despite repeated requests, it received none from the United States. Individual Americans, with men from other nations, fought for the Government in the International Brigades, and the Government cause was the emotional rallying point for thousands of anti-Fascists the world over. Some of these, however, became disillusioned after witnessing the factionalism and terror among the groups, including the Communists, that supported the Government.

In the war one of history's most publicized experiments in calculated terror occurred. That was the bombing of Guernica on market day, April 26, 1937, by the Nazi Condor Legion. It was a Basque town without defenses and without military significance. The aviators, in complicity with the Nationalist command, first dropped high-explosive bombs on the townspeople, then machine-gunned them in flight and finally fired the town with incendiary bombs. A total of 1,654 persons were killed and 889 wounded in raids lasting 2 hours 45 minutes.

When the fighting ended in 1939, Franco ordered shot nearly all captured Republican officers, and his prisons contained thousands of so-called "Reds," many of whom were also executed. The United States recognized the new Government on April 1, 1939, and the same month Franco signed the Anti-Comintern Pact, formally allying Spain with Germany, Italy and Japan. Pope Pius XII, at about the same time, commended Franco for having brought "mercy and justice" to his country. World War II, which began in the fall of 1939, put Franco in a difficult position. His sympathies were with Hitler and Mussolini, but his nation was too desolated to join the fighting.

Key details of Franco's relations with Berlin and Rome came to light with the release of captured enemy documents after the war. Some of these documents, published by the State Department in 1946 under the title "The Spanish Government and the Axis," revealed his plans to enter the war against the Allies at an opportune moment and to obtain Gibraltar and French Morocco for his prizes.

'Identity of Views'

When Hitler conquered France in the spring of 1940, Franco sent him this message:

"In the moment when the German armies under your leadership are bringing the greatest battle of history victoriously to an end, I should like to deliver to you the expression of my enthusiasm and admiration as well as that of my people. . ."

Hitler thereupon awarded Franco the cross of the Order of the German Eagle.

Meeting with Mussolini in Italy in February, 1941, Franco affirmed an "identity of views" between Spain and Italy. Later that month he wrote Hitler:

"I consider as you do yourself that the destiny of history has united you with myself and with the Duce in an indissoluble way."

However, he resisted German demands to use Spain as a stopping point on military flights to Africa. But he did permit German tankers to use Spanish coastal waters in the refueling of submarines, and he relayed to the Axis information of Allied convoys passing through the Strait of Gibraltar. He also helped recruit the Spanish Blue Division, which joined German troops in the Soviet Union.

In the meantime, Franco was hedging his bets. A British-Spanish trade accord was signed in March, 1940, which was extended to other Allied powers. The dictator made it plain that he was a nonbelligerent.

Shortly after the American troop landings in North Africa in November, 1942, President Franklin D. Roosevelt told Franco that the Allies harbored no aggressive intentions toward Spain. In reply, Franco cited the "relations of friendship which unite our people and which should be preserved." He

(continued)

Generalissimo Franco in 1936 — the leader of the attack on Madrid and head of the anti-government forces.

also removed his brother-in-law, Ramón Serrano Suñer, an avowed Axis man, as Foreign Minister.

When the fortunes of the Axis declined, Franco's vigilant neutrality increased, although he made at least one effort to promote peace between Germany and Britain so that the two countries could undertake "common action" against "the Bolshevik danger."

After the war, nonetheless, the Allies put Franco temporarily beyond the pale, and the United States and many other nations withdrew their ambassadors or ministers from Madrid, but kept a chargé d'affaires there. The diplomatic boycott of Franco Spain ended in fact if not in name in November, 1950—a consequence of the cold war between the United States and the Soviet Union, in which Spain occupied a geographically important place.

$62.5-Million Loan

Several months before the boycott was lifted, Congress approved a $62.5-million loan to Spain. And in February, 1951, Stanton Griffis became the United States Ambassador to Madrid. That July the late Adm. Forrest P. Sherman opened talks with Franco about a defense agreement.

Franco realized that this was a turning point for his country, and in January, 1952, he told the Council of the Realm:

"Thanks both to God and the tenacity of Spaniards, the sun of our hopes begins to shine in the world."

Later that year he declared "Spain is now sought after by those who in years past scorned our offer to cooperate against Communism."

A formal agreement with the United States on bases was concluded in September, 1953. Under it Spain gave this country the right to use "a number of Spanish air and naval bases for the defense of Western Europe and the Mediterranean."

The United States agreed to put up $226-million to implement the accord. In 10 years the United States poured into Spain more than $1.5-billion in economic assistance and more than $500-million in military help. The pact was renewed in 1963, and again in 1970.

Spain's isolation from world affairs came to a ceremonial end in 1955, when she was admitted to United Nations membership. This entrance into the community of nations was further signalized in December, 1959, when President Eisenhower went to Madrid to confer with Franco.

As the dictator aged, he began to prepare for a succession. After seeming to favor Don Juan, son of Alfonso XIII, who fled the throne in 1931, he finally settled on Juan Carlos, Don Juan's son. In presenting him to the Cortes in 1969, Franco said:

"Conscious of my responsibility before God and history and taking into account the qualities to be found in the person of Prince Juan Carlos de Borbón who has been perfectly trained to take up the high mission to which he might be called, I have decided to propose him to the nation as my successor."

The Cortes obediently endorsed the Prince, who then swore loyalty to Franco.

For all the pervasiveness of his power, the Caudillo, "by the Grace of God," and Generalissimo of the Armies of Land, Sea and Air, and Chief of State for life, was among the least majestic of modern rulers.

Standing but 5 feet 3 inches tall, Franco looked gnomish even in his general's gold-trimmed, olive drab uniform with red silk sash. Unlike Hitler or Mussolini, he never harangued multitudes or stirred them to fervor. He spoke publicly no more then three or four times a year, in a high voice with a slight lisp. His face was so expressionless that when he gave his annual New Year's Eve address on television, the state network showed him for only a few minutes and flashed newsreel clips against his narration the rest of the time.

On ceremonial occasions he adopted an august role. Riding in his black Rolls-Royce, which carried the national coat of arms in place of license plates, he was preceded by an open car filled with burly red-bereted bodyguards and his route was flanked by policemen stationed 10 yards apart. He demanded the homage reserved for royalty, walking under a canopy, for example, at religious rites.

In 1942 Hitler greeted Premier Franco, whom he helped gain power.

Wednesday Audiences

His round, mustached face was immobile and his brown eyes were appraising and chill. This hauteur was evident at his Wednesday audiences for Spanish and foreign civilians and Spanish military men. Strictly according to protocol, they approached Franco, singly or in groups. There was a brief formal greeting and that was all.

Remote in his personality, the dictator nonetheless appeared often in public. He attended openings of everything from theaters to industrial exhibits. On these occasions, he waved in his stiff, almost timid manner and forced a smile here and there; but there seemed to be almost no rapport between him and the population. Crowds regarded him as more of an institution than as a person.

Franco lived and worked at El Pardo, a former royal hunting lodge on the outskirts of Madrid. His spacious office was furnished with Aubusson carpets, velvet draperies and gilt-inlaid furniture. The photographs on the walls changed over the years. Once there were inscribed portraits of Hitler and Mussolini; later there was one of President Eisenhower; and that was replaced by one of Pope Paul VI.

Franco's ormolu-mounted desk and a nearby table were piled with reports and memorandums, virtually all of them unread. "When the piles become too high," he once told Prince Juan Carlos, "I have everything taken out from the bottom and burned." Franco was reported to have chuckled at his own remark. He was, however, enormously well-informed, for he listened to his ministers and subordinates and visitors, and he read newspapers with care.

Some of this listening was done at semimonthly Cabinet meetings, over which he presided with great imperturbability. These sessions began at 9 A.M. and often continued all day and through the night, for they dealt not only with major matters but also with such trivia as a medal for a minor civil servant. Ministers might argue or step outside for a smoke (Franco forbade smoking in his presence), but the dictator was never known to get up from his chair or to relax the stiffness of his posture. Nor did he often interrupt his ministers or decide questions precipitously.

Franco was celebrated for his secretiveness. "Not even his collar knows what he is thinking," an associate once remarked. Thus, it was difficult to read his mind, and it was not uncommon for a subordinate, even a minister, to leave an audience convinced that he had made a splendid impression and the next morning to receive a letter from Franco thanking him for his services and informing him that he had been replaced.

Flattered in News Media

Franco was much flattered by the controlled press, radio and television. It was not unusual for him to be ranked above Augustus, Charles V and Napoleon. About 50 towns caught the spirit of this sycophancy and added his name.

He also had constructed a Pharaonic tomb, in which he wanted to be buried. Called the Valley of the Fallen and dedicated to the Civil War dead, it is situated close to the Escorial, near Madrid. Carved out of living rock, the interior is a basilica, one of the world's largest, and is surmounted by a cross 500 feet tall. Franco took a detailed interest in its construction, which covered 15 years and cost millions. Irreverent Spaniards called it "Franco's folly," but it became a major tourist attraction.

An avid sportsman, the dictator liked to shoot mountain goats, deer, rabbits and partridges. His bag of these birds sometimes reached 300 a day.

Franco's cruelty was that of the centurion, impersonal and efficient. Once, inspecting troops as a colonel of the Spanish Foreign Legion, he had food thrown in his face by a legionnaire protesting its quality. It spattered his uniform, but his facial expression did not change, nor did he say a word. He merely took out his handkerchief, wiped off the food and continued the inspection. Returning to his office, he calmly called an officer, pointed out the offender and said:

"Take that soldier out and execute him."

He exhibited the same methodical cruelty in 1934 when he imported legionnaires and Moors to crush an Asturian miners' uprising. At least 2,000 miners were rounded up and executed, many of them in the Oviedo bullring. Some officers reportedly sought to halt the slaughter, but Franco sent word that the officers must continue or face execution themselves.

Virtually a Teetotaler

Franco's home life was simple. He dined with his family as often as possible, and lightly to keep his girth down. He was virtually a teetotaler, limiting himself to a glass of wine or beer at a meal. There was no hint of personal scandal in his private life. He had married Carmen Polo y Martínez Valdés, a young woman of good Asturian family, in 1923.

If Franco felt any reaction to criticism or had any self-doubt, it was not observable. Indeed, he had a Moslem-like fatalism, the "maktoob" ("It is written") of the Moroccan rifleman. Horses were shot beneath him. Once a bullet struck a flask from which he was drinking. Leading an assault in 1916, he was shot through the abdomen, but recovered uneventfully. In 1961, the barrel of his gun exploded in his left hand as he was shooting pigeons, but his hand was saved.

A similar fatalism, or impassivity, seemed to attend Franco in moments of domestic tension as, for example, when five convicted Basque terrorists were executed in September, 1975. Although the Vatican and most Western European countries protested or asked for clemency, he had the sentences carried out.

The executions also led to speeches at the United Nations and to threatened economic sanctions by the Common Market. The regime, however, did not appear to be swayed.

"All the News That's Fit to Print."

The New York Times.

LATE CITY EDITION
Mostly cloudy, showers today, much cooler in afternoon. Tomorrow fair, temperature unchanged.
Temperatures Yesterday—Max.,77; Min.,57

Section 1

NEWS INDEX, PAGE 48, THIS SECTION

Copyright, 1939, by The New York Times Company.

VOL. LXXXIX....No. 29,828. Entered as Second-Class Matter, Postoffice, New York, N. Y. NEW YORK, SUNDAY, SEPTEMBER 24, 1939. PPP Including Rotogravure Picture, Magazine and Book Review. TEN CENTS | TWELVE CENTS Beyond 200 Miles Except in 7th and 8th Postal Zones.

FRENCH REPEL 3 COUNTER-ATTACKS; ADVANCE A MILE IN SIERCK SECTOR; MUSSOLINI WOULD HALT WAR NOW

SENATORS PREPARE FIRST DRAFT OF BILL TO KILL ARMS BAN

Proposal for 90-Day Credits Instead of 'Cash' Discussed by Committee Majority

SHARP CURB ON SHIPPING

Measure Would Bar War Trade in Our Vessels—Opponents Plan Radio Campaign

By CHARLES W. HURD

Special to THE NEW YORK TIMES.

WASHINGTON, Sept. 23—Fourteen Democratic members of the Senate Foreign Relations Committee, a majority headed by Senator Pittman, began writing behind locked doors today a bill to repeal the embargo on shipments of arms and munitions to belligerents. They expect to complete the draft for consideration by the full committee on Monday morning.

These members, all of whom are more or less convinced of the desirability of recall of the embargo, met at the invitation of Senator Pittman, and were called to meet again tomorrow afternoon.

In the meantime, the Republican members of the committee and Senator Clark of Missouri, lone dissident Democrat, were neither invited to express their views nor shown a copy of a confidential "working draft" which Senator Pittman had printed last night after he and Senators Connally and Thomas of Utah, working as a drafting committee, completed their work on it at midnight.

"I don't think they would be interested," Senator Pittman said.

Opponents of Bill Confer

While this section of the committee thus attempted to expedite action on legislation which constituted the purpose of President Roosevelt's action calling Congress into special session, the Senate group working to maintain the embargo held three strategy meetings, at which they discussed ways and means to be taken inside and outside of Congress to stop enactment of the proposed legislation.

All of those participating in the bill-drafting meeting today were reticent to an extreme degree, but it was learned that a long time was taken up by serious discussion as to the probable public reaction to a proposal actually to eliminate the "cash" from the so-called "cash-and-carry" program.

It has been suggested that while belligerents, under the proposed law, would have to take title to purchases in this country and transport goods in their own ships, they might have the benefit of commercial credits.

As a talking point the bill drafters considered ninety-day credits instead of spot cash on munitions shipments and longer ones on other commodities of a non-military nature, according to authoritative reports. But several members expressed fears that such action would arouse a public reaction which would add to the opposition to repeal of the embargo.

Pittman Silent on Credits

When Senator Pittman was asked about this phase of the committee deliberation, he replied, "I will not discuss that."

The fourteen Democratic members sat from 10:30 A. M. until 1 P. M. In the afternoon the trio consisting of Senators Pittman, Connally and Thomas met to pencil further the preliminary draft. The entire fourteen were invited to meet again tomorrow. The other eleven in the larger group are Senator Barkley, the majority leader, and Senators Wagner, Gillette, Reynolds, Murray, Green, Schwellenbach, George, Pepper, Guffey and Van Nuys.

This constituted the Democratic membership, along with Senator Clark of Missouri and Senator Harrison. The latter is absent on account of illness. Of those who met today, all are expected to help report out a bill, although not all are definitely pledged to support one on the floor.

Only Senator Murray made a statement for quotation after the meeting, aside from Chairman Pittman's remarks at a press conference. Mr. Murray told reporters, "I do not even know what they were talking about."

Heavy Penalties Are Planned

Chairman Pittman, while reticent in his statements in reply to inquiries, affirmed that the proposed new bill was similar to a bill he introduced last March as a substitute for the old cash-and-carry provision of the current Neutrality Law which expired on May 1.

He emphasized, however, that the new measure would reduce the President's discretion, enlarge penalties for violation of trade rules by

Continued on Page Twenty-seven

New Yorkers Gain Hour As Daylight Saving Ends

New Yorkers, in common with millions of others throughout the nation, set their clocks and watches back one hour last night before retiring in preparation for the end of daylight saving time at 2 A. M. today.

Observed in many cities and towns throughout the country during the Summer months, daylight saving affected the lives of about 30,000,000 persons, or about one-fourth of the nation's population, according to statistics compiled by the Merchants Association of New York.

Railroad, bus and air lines are changing their schedules to conform to the return of Eastern standard time. Clocks on public buildings will be changed, and the Fire Department will make the shift a matter of official business by sending out a preliminary warning of the change on the secondary alarm circuits at 1:59 A. M.

DR. SIGMUND FREUD DIES IN EXILE AT 83

Founder of Psychoanalysis Theory Succumbs at His Home Near London

Special Cable to THE NEW YORK TIMES.

LONDON, Sept. 23—Dr. Sigmund Freud, originator of the theory of psychoanalysis, died shortly before midnight tonight at his son's home in Hampstead at the age of 83.

Dr. Freud fled from Austria last year when the country was invaded by Germany and had been living with his son, Dr. Ernst Freud, ever since. He had been in ill health for more than a year and yesterday he passed into a coma from which he never rallied.

His Methods Widely Discussed

One of the most widely discussed scientists of the present day and originator of countless new ideas in the field of psychology, Dr. Sigmund Freud was a man who never compromised but often modified. In his long and stormy career he set the entire world talking about psychoanalysis, the method which he originated and in which he dramatized for mankind the hampering force of inhibitions.

"The mind is an iceberg—it floats with only one-seventh of its bulk above water," was one of his metaphorical statements on the vast preponderance of the subconscious element in human life. Another was, "The conscious mind may be compared to a fountain playing in the sun and falling back into the great subterranean pool of the subconscious from which it rises."

Probably the most radical departure from the old psychology introduced in Dr. Freud's science of psychoanalysis was that man is a willing rather than a thinking animal. Previous to his time psychology had been overwhelmingly "intellectual," regarding images, perceptions and ideas as the fundamental factors in mental life. But Dr. Freud, not satisfied with this non-progressing view of man's actions, laid the main stress of his system on the element of will or desire, relegating intellect to the background.

Brought New Words to Science

It was under this new system that Dr. Freud was able to explain many of the old "mysteries" of life, particularly regarding the fantasies and delusions of the deranged mind, and to shed a ray of light on the significance of dreams. It was also natural that, with this new basis of desire, sex should occupy the focal point of the system and that a new vocabulary of "Freudian" words should arise, among them "complex, inhibition, neurosis, psychosis, repression, resistance and transference."

The early critics of Freud's theories were filled with violent prejudice and moral indignation and sought to tear to pieces his entire system. The later critics, among whom are many present-day psychologists and scientists, acknowledged many of his theories to be valuable and devoted themselves to critical studies of his plan with a view to perfection rather than destruction. Dr. Freud himself believed that his ideas were harmed by their excessive popularity, which led to a reckless use of his theory and an exaggeration of his doctrines.

Although known as a Viennese, Dr. Freud was a Moravian by birth. He was born in this old Austro-Hungarian province on May 6, 1856, in the town of Freiberg. His parents moved to Vienna while he was still young and he received his education there, taking his degree of Doctor of Medicine at the university there in 1881. His parents had hoped he would follow a literary career, finding ability as a poet in him, but once he chose science he renounced all thought of literary aspirations. After his graduation he served in turn as demonstrator in the physiological institute, Vienna; assistant physician in the general hospital and lecturer on nervous diseases.

Studied in Charcot School.

After becoming intensely interested in psychiatry he went to Paris in 1885 to study in the famous

Continued on Page Forty-four

SAYS SOVIET PAYS PROPAGANDA COSTS WITH OUR DOLLARS

Dubrowsky Tells Dies Group Total Raised From 'Rackets' Here Runs Into Millions

FILMS BOOST THE TOTAL

Witness Asserts Estates Here Left to Russian Heirs 'Go Into Coffers of Stalin'

By LOUIS STARK

Special to THE NEW YORK TIMES.

WASHINGTON, Sept. 23 — Dr. David H. Dubrowsky of New York, former director of the Soviet Red Cross in the United States and friend of many early Bolshevik leaders, told the House Committee on Un-American Activities today that through "rackets" organized by the Soviet Government in the United States Americans had paid millions of dollars to finance propaganda aimed at themselves.

Dr. Dubrowsky, who said he was once an ardent Communist party member but had been disillusioned because "Stalin transformed what was once an idealistic movement into political gangsterism," also asserted that the Soviet Government virtually confiscated estates of Americans of Russian birth, paying a few "valueless" rubles to relatives of the deceased.

He declared that estates of American soldiers of Russian birth, left to relatives in Russia, also were confiscated by the Soviet Government. He estimated that the total reached $5,000,000 in 1935, when he resigned as the Russian Red Cross representative in this country. So far as Dr. Dubrowsky knew, he said, the American Government was still transmitting large sums to Russia for the relatives of deceased American soldiers and this money was being confiscated by the Russian Government.

The handling of these cases, said Dr. Dubrowsky in a letter to General Frank T. Hines of the Veterans Administration, was in the hands of "a Soviet official, whose loyalty is necessarily pledged to the Russian Communist party, of which he is a member, and to the Soviet Government, of which he is a citizen."

Names Lawyer as Stalin Agent

According to Mr. Dubrowsky the Soviet Government compels heirs of Russians dying in this country to sign powers of attorney over to Charles Recht of New York, a lawyer in Soviet employ, who arranges for the deposit of the funds to the credit of a Russian organization in New York, whence they may be drawn upon by the Soviet Embassy or by the Amtorg Trading Company for any purpose.

From this sum the Soviet authorities benefit up to $1,000,000 a year, said Dr. Dubrowsky. Mr. Recht, he said, has an "absolute monopoly" of the collection of these estates in the United States, the money going into the coffers of Stalin."

Dr. Dubrowsky accused Mr. Recht of deliberately lying when he told the committee yesterday he could not recall any connection he had

Continued on Page Twenty-two

Cutting Dikes for Defense Is in Experimental Stage

By The Associated Press.

BRUSSELS, Sept. 23—Belgian defense officials said today that the opening of the Albert Canal dikes to flood an area of Belgium as a protection to Antwerp would be unjustified under the present circumstances.

PARIS, Sept. 23 (UP)—The Netherlands and Belgium have begun experimental preliminary flooding of their frontier lands as a notice to warring powers that they are determined to defend their inviolability at any cost, it was understood today.

It was confirmed from Amsterdam that the Netherlands Government had flooded a small part of Utrecht Province, protecting the vital Amsterdam zone.

NAZI AIMS DECRIED AT PANAMA SESSION

Arosemena Urges Americas to Keep Clear of War as Aid in Serving Humanity

By HAROLD B. HINTON

Special Cable to THE NEW YORK TIMES.

PANAMA, Sept. 23—The world's attention was called to the fact that twenty-one Pan-American Foreign Ministers are assembled here with no thought to "destroy, enslave or dismember any nation," and with no secret treaties to negotiate, by President Juan Demostenes Arosemena of Panama in welcoming the delegations at the formal opening of the neutrality consultations here last today.

He added that the Foreign Ministers would not have to consider plans to "proscribe any race or attack any religion" and suggested as a motto, "America for Humanity," to recall to the delegates' minds the probability that their ability to finds ways and means of keeping the Western Hemisphere clear of the European war would have effects reaching beyond continental borders.

Meet in Plenary Session

Acting under machinery provided by the Buenos Aires convention of 1936 and the Lima declaration of 1938, the Foreign Ministers of all American republics or their personal representatives met for the first time in plenary session in the National University, which was hastily remodeled to accommodate the delegations.

The President's opening speech went so far in disassociating the Americas from totalitarianism as to include the explanation that the frequent South American dictatorships have been patriarchal manifestations springing from the inability of certain classes to govern

Continued on Page Forty

ROME SILENCE ENDS

Premier in Speech Gives Affirmation to Italian Policy of Neutrality

CALLS CONFLICT USELESS

Poland Gone, Allies Are Not Fighting Russia, He Asserts—Cuts Dodecanese Garrison

By HERBERT L. MATTHEWS

By Telephone to THE NEW YORK TIMES.

ROME, Sept. 23—Premier Mussolini broke his long period of silence today to reaffirm Italy's determination to remain neutral unless attacked. In a mildly pro-German speech, he flatly accused the Allies of abandoning their moral justification for the war by not taking measures against Russia. A further conflict could therefore be avoided, Signor Mussolini said.

He also took this occasion for a diatribe against Masons, Jews and anti-Fascist sympathizers, which seemed to forecast a "purge" that would include a new anti-Semitic drive.

He proclaimed three "watchwords" for Italy—military preparedness, help for any peace move and that the nation work vigilantly and in silence.

Premier Mussolini's speech coincided with news that Italian troops were being withdrawn from the Dodecanese Islands, reducing the garrisons to normal. Thus Chancellor Hitler got the fair word, but Britain and Turkey benefited by the deed.

First Speech Since May 20

The speech ended the "silence of Cuneo," maintained since May 20, when the Premier made an address at that beach town. It did not pronounce any great decision or change of policy. That will come "if and when"—as he said—Signor Mussolini appears on the balcony of the Palazzo Venezia and addresses the Italian people. At that time, one may guess, the historic decision of war or peace on one side or another will be announced.

Meanwhile it has to be stated that Signor Mussolini's words now add no new factor to what is already known of Italian policy, although they are nonetheless important in reaffirming that policy at a time when Russia and Germany seem to have divided Poland without making a Polish State and when the war threatens to involve the Balkans. Indeed, it seems almost certain now that the Premier wrote some if not all of the editorials in the Popolo d'Italia of recent days, for his speech takes exactly the same line.

It was made to the party hierarchy of Bologna, the first of a number of such contacts with party leaders that will embrace the whole country.

The Bologna Fascisti under the leadership of Achille Starace, secretary general of the party, have always taken a strong line of policy, bellicose, anti-Semitic and pro-German, and the speech was calculated to please them.

Foes of Fascism Scored

One hundred and thirty men and women Fascisti were gathered in the Hall of Battles of the Palazzo Venezia in the morning, when the Premier greeted them.

After praising the Bologna Fascisti, Signor Mussolini launched into a tirade against what he called the "miserable human dregs who have been reduced to living in slums, hidden places and dark corners." This "riffraff" he blamed for the rumors that had been circulating, especially against himself.

He said fascism must "clean up the human residue living in dark corners where Masonic and Jewish riffraff and anti-Fascist foreign sympathizers have taken refuge."

"My policy was fixed in the declaration of Sept. 1 [the Ministerial Council's statement that Italy would remain neutral unless attacked] and there is no reason to change it," said Signor Mussolini in the most important passage of his speech.

"This answers to our national interests, to our political pacts and the desire of all peoples, including the Germans. The policy is that of at least localizing the conflict.

"For the rest, with Poland liquidated, Europe is not yet actually at war. The masses of the armies have not yet clashed. The clash can be avoided by recognizing that it is a vain illusion to try to maintain, or worse still to reconstitute, positions

Continued on Page Forty-two

Russia Orders Troops to Remain Mobilized; Move Is Believed to Portend New Action

By G. E. R. GEDYE

Wireless to THE NEW YORK TIMES.

MOSCOW, Sept. 23 — Another grave element in the general situation so far as the Soviet Union is concerned was added late tonight when the Moscow radio broadcast a ukase signed by Mikhail Kalinin, Chairman of the Presidium of Supreme Soviet, ordering reservists recently called up to remain with the colors indefinitely.

It had not been assumed that these men were called up for a week-end in camp, but the definite announcement of their retention is regarded as a prelude to some graver announcement for which the present ukase is intended to prepare the Soviet population. The ukase says:

"Those members commanding and the rank and file personnel of the Red Army called up for service on Sept. 1 by special orders of the Moscow, Kalinin, Leningrad, White Russian, Kiev, Kharkov and Orel military areas on account of a special situation are mobilized until such time as another special order is given."

Regulations were issued for the paying of these men by the factories where they worked, the retention of their rooms and the issuance of special allowances for their families. For the latter purpose special commissions are to be established immediately in each district, which are ordered to decide upon the allowances within three days. The burden of the payments is to be borne by the Soviet budget.

All recruits' positions are to be held open, according to the orders.

The Soviet General Staff's summary of operations, made public today, stated that Bialystok and Brest-Litovsk were occupied yesterday and that the Red army was mopping up remnants of the Polish army in the Augustov forests northward of Grodno. It said the Western Ukraine and Sarny area were "cleansed of Polish officer groups," and that General Langer, with six divisions and two complete rifle regiments, surrendered to the Red army in the Lwow district. The summary added that up to Sept. 21 120,000 prisoners, 380 guns and 1,400 machine guns had been taken.

The contents of a leaflet issued to the Red army during the crossing of the Polish frontier was published in the army organ, Red Star. The leaflet informed the troops that the Poles constantly ill-treated Ukrainians and White Russians and declared that generals and other officers of the Polish army had fled. The leaflet purported to be an appeal from Ukrainians and White Russians to Soviet troops to free the former.

Pravda publishes a story of the capture of Vilna, which Russian troops are said to have entered after two hours of fighting between Polish artillery and Soviet tank detachments. When the city was entered, this account says, only scat-

Continued on Page Forty-two

The International Situation

German infantry raids under cover of continued heavy artillery fire marked the end of the third week of war on the Western Front yesterday. At one point in the middle of the Saar sector the French reported having thrown back three attacks. At the western end of this sector the French were said to have advanced a mile in the neighborhood of Sierck. [Page 1.]

In the East the Germans said their campaign was closed with the surrender of Lwow and Reich forces were withdrawing everywhere to the demarcation line announced on Friday by the German and Russian authorities. But Warsaw was still unconquered and even in Berlin it was conceded that a semblance of an organized army still existed northwest of the capital. [Page 1; text of a Berlin communiqué reviewing the war in Poland on Page 41.]

A major casualty in the Polish fighting was the death of Colonel General von Fritsch, former Commander in Chief of the German Army, who had been "purged" into retirement in February, 1938. Berlin announced that he had fallen during "an offensive reconnaissance patrol before Warsaw," but did not explain why a chief of regiment should have been on such a patrol instead of behind the lines. [Page 1.]

In the Russian half of Poland Soviet troops pushed their mopping-up activities and for them, too, the fighting seemed to be about over, yet Moscow announced that all troops mobilized since Sept. 7 would be kept under arms indefinitely. [Page 1.]

With the Red Army on her frontier, Hungary hastened to revive diplomatic relations with Russia. [Page 40.] And Bulgaria was said to be about to negotiate a trade pact with the Soviet. [Follows the above.]

Accompanying the virtual ending of military operations in Poland, Premier Mussolini broke a four-month silence to point out that elsewhere armies had not yet clashed and to urge that such a clash was unnecessary. He also took occasion to reaffirm Italy's intention to remain neutral and to attack Masons, Jews and anti-Fascist sympathizers. [Page 1; text of the Mussolini address, Page 42.]

German submarines added two Finnish ships to their toll, and, mysteriously, a British patrol boat struck a mine in the English Channel, virtually home waters. [Page 33.] Innocent victims of the war at sea, forty refugees from Germany, were stranded, probably for the duration of the war, at Vigo, Spain, on one of more than thirty German ships sheltering there. [Page 39.]

The nations of this hemisphere opened their neutrality consultations in Panama and heard President Arosemena of Panama condemn by implication Nazi aims. [Page 1; text of the Arosemena speech, Page 40.]

In Washington a bill to repeal the arms embargo was put into the drafting stage by fourteen Democratic members of the Senate Foreign Relations Committee. Tentatively the bill drafters were considering ninety-day credits to belligerent arms buyers in place of the cash in the cash-and-carry idea. [Page 1.]

FINAL VICTORY WON IN EAST, NAZIS SAY

Lwow Claimed, They Withdraw for 'Further Duties'—Poles Still Hold Out in Warsaw

By PERCY KNAUTH

Wireless to THE NEW YORK TIMES.

BERLIN, Sept. 23—Although Polish forces are still holding out at Warsaw, Modlin and on the Hela Peninsula, it was announced by the German High Command tonight that "the campaign in Poland is ended."

A long communiqué reviewing the operations in Poland said 450,000 prisoners had been captured thus far and that it was not possible to calculate "even approximately" the amount of war materiel seized.

It was announced earlier that the German troops withdrawing from Southeastern Poland to the Soviet-German military demarcation line had won a final victory late yesterday afternoon when the city of Lwow surrendered. The formalities of occupation, it was said, were transferred to Russian forces which had already partly taken over the German positions in the Lwow area. [Moscow had reported earlier in the week that Lwow had been occupied by Russian troops.]

This final victory marked the end of the German campaign in Central and Eastern Poland. The campaign began eight days ago when, with the southern and northern armies joined before Warsaw, German forces thrust their first long steel fingers across the Vistula toward Brest-Litovsk and Lwow.

The result of the drive is probably different from the outcome pictured at that time, for now German troops are withdrawing all along the line after a series of spectacular advances as swift and as successful as the first lightning drive into Western Poland three weeks ago.

Warsaw and the fortress town of Modlin, hitherto encircled by one ring of German soldiers, stood today under separate sieges after a German break-through along the south bank of the Vistula between the two places, it was announced. An army communiqué laconically reported that "the break-through succeeded after heavy fighting with a desperately resisting enemy."

The advance, it was said, was made by troops south of the Vistula, who have now established contact with the armies on the north. "Several thousand prisoners were taken," the communiqué said.

Polish troops such as those north

Continued on Page Forty-one

VON FRITSCH KILLED ON WARSAW FRONT

Ex-Commander in Chief of the German Army Was Leading a Reconnaissance Patrol

Wireless to THE NEW YORK TIMES.

BERLIN, Sept. 23—The death of Col. Gen. Werner von Fritsch, former Commander in Chief of the German Army, in the front line of his honorary regiment, the Twelfth Artillery, before Warsaw, was announced in a death notice issued by Col. Gen. Walther von Brauchitsch in his capacity as Commander in Chief of the Germany Army. It read:

"On the 22d of September, in the course of an offensive reconnaissance patrol before Warsaw, Col. Gen. Werner von Fritsch, chief of the Twelfth Regiment of Artillery, was killed in action.

"Marching from the first day at the side of his regiment, his life was an example for his army, for which he has now fallen in unconditional sacrifice.

"Deeply moved in all sorrow—yet full of great pride—the army stands at the bier of this great soldier.

"Von Brauchitsch, Colonel General, Commander in Chief of the army."

Beyond these few lines nothing is known of the circumstances of the death of the man who commanded the German Army throughout the period of its most spectacular rise until his retirement in the army purge of Feb. 4, 1938. His participation in a reconnaissance patrol, when in his capacity as chief of regiment he should have been behind the lines with his staff, remains unexplained.

Chancellor Hitler has ordered a state funeral for the former Commander in Chief of his army.

BERLIN, Sept. 23 (AP)—Col. Gen. Baron Werner von Fritsch, former Commander in Chief of the German Army, has been killed in action on the Warsaw front while fighting in a comparatively minor post.

First word of the death came from Chancellor Hitler's headquarters.

It was made clear that he held no army command nor any other post corresponding to his rank of colonel general, just below that of field marshal.

General von Fritsch, who resigned

Continued on Page Thirty-five

Dispatches from Europe and the Far East are now subject to censorship.

NAZIS HURLED BACK

Tank Assault East of Saarbruecken Fails to Regain Ground

ARTILLERY DUEL GOES ON

Allies Advance on Borg, Near Luxembourg Border, to Take Important Crossroads

By G. H. ARCHAMBAULT

Wireless to THE NEW YORK TIMES.

PARIS, Sept. 23—The end of the third week of the war is marked by German activity along the entire 120-mile front between the Rhine and the Moselle, but especially in sectors on the French right, which had been quiescent since the beginning of the operations.

This is activity that, in the French view, might be more correctly described as "nervous agitation."

During the past forty-eight hours it has taken the form of a series of infantry raids, some of which have been on a larger scale than any hitherto. Artillery fire has been virtually unceasing.

Some significance is being attached to the sudden flare-up on that part of the front adjoining the Rhine which has been calm since the French occupied a forest called Bienwald early in September. Here the German forces made several raids, all of which remained fruitless.

Simultaneously the Germans began a number of minor actions at various points along the line running some forty miles west of Wissembourg. In that sector they attempted to regain possession of several small woods through which the French infantry in recent days had seeped into their outposts.

Three Attacks Fail

One such wood near the village of Wittersheim on the main road from Saareguemines to Zweibruecken was attacked three times. Each time the German assault was halted by machine gun and artillery fire. In this action the Germans tried to advance on a battalion front.

The French announce that all this activity has left the respective positions absolutely unchanged.

Today War Office communiqués told something of this action. This morning's bulletin, Communiqué 39, said:

"Late yesterday afternoon the enemy made several attempts against the positions taken by us east of the Saar River; they were repulsed."

"During the night there was great activity on the front, especially between the Saar River and the region southeast of Zweibruecken and also on the Lauter River."

Tonight's message, Communiqué 40, reported:

"There was localized activity on the part of the artillery and the first line elements."

During this week artillery fire has increased considerably in volume on both sides and the number of batteries in action now is reported to be very great. The French in particular have been able to bring up heavy guns within a relatively short distance of front lines. In this connection any German large scale attack should prove very costly.

Unwonted activity on the right of the French lines, it is suggested in some quarters, may be a feint to distract attention from preparations elsewhere, notably in the Aachen zone. However that may be, it is known here that the Belgians continue to watch such preparations closely.

French Gain Reported

PARIS, Sept. 23 (UP)—French troops were reported to have thrown back a powerful German counter-attack along a nine-mile sector of the Saar front today and then swept forward about a mile along the Luxembourg border to seize an important hill northeast of Perl.

German troops rushed westward from the Polish front, under direction of Col. Gen. Walther von Brauchitsch, made three mass counter-thrusts at the French Saar lines with swift little midget tanks, big heavily armored tanks and infantry

A War Office communiqué said that all attacks were thrown back and unofficial French dispatches estimated that the Nazis had lost

Continued on Page Thirty-nine

DR. SIGMUND FREUD DIES IN EXILE AT 83

Continued From Page One

school of Charcot and Janet, known as the virtual founders of modern abnormal psychology. The influence of his masters, however, was largely one of provoking thought on his own part. He plunged into a wholly new investigation of neurotic disorders and delevoped a method so new that he made Janet one of his bitterest professional enemies, being accused by him of introducing unwarranted assumptions into the orthodox doctrine. Several of Dr. Freud's pupils in turn, among them C. G. Jung and Alfred Adler, diverged from him as widely as he did from his own teachers.

In forming his ideas about psychoanalysis Freud proceeded with an independence and uncompromising attitude which served either to alienate his associates completely or to win them over as virtual disciples.

After remaining in Paris a year he returned to Vienna, where he became a Professor Extraordinary of Neurology in 1902. He also used his apartment in Berggasse as a clinic and received daily many patients who came to him with all types and varieties of mental ailments. Later in life, age and illness forced him to cut down the number of his patients to a minimum and to make but few public appearances, but he continued to develop his theories and to write treatises on his chosen subject.

Deeply Interested in Soviet Russia.

The Communist experiment in Russia was of great interest to the psychoanalyst, but the United States failed to attract him, even though he had visited this country in 1909, when he received an honorary LL. D degree from Clark University. Probably the only American whom he held in high esteem was William James, who he said was "one of the most charming men I have ever met." Professor James, however, was to him the one exception in a country which has produced only "an unthinking optimism and a shallow philosophy of activity."

The United States, on the other hand, was scarcely more tolerant in many ways toward Dr. Freud, and many of Dr. Freud's conceptions of this country were based on exaggerated or burlesqued writings on his principles. "America is vulgarizing too extensively," he once said. "The newspapers seem too prone to popularize the lewd instead of the intellectual fact." Probably the most predominant criticism in America of the Freudian theory is that the element of sex is grossly overplayed in his explanations of human actions and reactions.

Even the defenders of Dr. Freud have from time to time admitted that, like most specialists, he had carried many of his ideas too far and that he saw sex, where its presence was debatable or even completely absent. They have also deplored the development of the original therapeutic system into one of philosophy and almost religion, placing the responsibility for this more on Dr. Freud's followers and rivals than on Dr. Freud himself.

Was a Prolific Writer.

Dr. Freud was a prolific writer. His books have won popularity in many countries and have put before the world his wealth of ideas, startling and even sensational during the pre-war conservatism. His works on hysteria and the interpretation of dreams were probably his most widely known writings. In these he brought out the theory that hysteria is the result of a nervous shock, emotional and usually sexual in nature, and that the ideas involved have been suppressed or inhibited until they can no longer be recalled. By a use of the principle of psychoanalysis and the employment of the patient's free-will associations these ideas can be recalled, he wrote, and the cause of the hysteria removed.

One of his outstanding works was an incidental writing which appeared near the close of the war, entitled "Reflections on War and Death."

"The history of the world is essentially a series of race murders," he wrote. "The individual does not believe in his own death. On the other hand, we recognize the death of strangers and of enemies, and sentence them to it just as willingly and unhesitatingly as primitive man did. In our unconscious mind we daily and hourly do away with all those who stand in our way, all those who have insulted or harmed us."

In August, 1930, Freud received the Goethe prize for the year, awarded by the city of Frankfort,

SIGMUND FREUD

Associated Press, 1937

Germany. The prize at that time was the greatest scientific and literary distinction in Germany. Illness prevented his accepting the honor in person.

Despite the ravages of cancer and infirmities of age, Dr. Freud continued active until after his eightieth birthday on May 6, 1936.

At that time, declining a request for an interview, he wrote: "What I had to tell the world I have told. I place the last period after my work."

Many who had been the bitterest critics of his psychoanalysis theories gathered in Vienna on his eightieth birthday to do him honor. He himself was not there, but his wife and family were, and they wept as Dr. Julius Wagneur-Jauregg, president of the Viennese Psychiatrists Association, said in opening the meeting:

"Viennese psychiatrists followed the trail blazed by Freud to worldwide fame and greatness. We are proud and happy to congratulate him as one of the great figures of the Viennese school of medicine."

One of Dr. Freud's last writings was a revision in 1936 of an article for the Psychiatric Almanac. A year earlier he had completed and published his "Autobiography," and three years before he had issued a small book, "A New Series of Introductory Lectures on Psychoanalysis."

He still received a few patients after 1930, but most of the questioning was done by his daughter Anna, whom he recognized as his successor, the aged, bearded, stoop-shouldered doctor merely nodding agreement from time to time. He made no public appearances and received only a few old friends, who called on Wednesday nights to talk and on Fridays to play cards.

To the last he remained intolerant of criticism or disagreement with his theories and he could not understand why he should be censured for his bitterness.

"What claims are to be made on us in the name of tolerance?" he wrote in his 1932 lectures. "That when somebody has expressed an opinion that we consider fundamentally false we should say, 'Thanks for the contradiction.'"

His last years also were disturbed by the pogroms against the Jews. When his books were burned by the Nazis in the bonfire which also consumed the works of Heine and other non-Aryan authors he remarked, "Well, at least I have been burned in good company."

Although egotistical in his professional contacts—he told the story himself that a peasant woman had told his mother when he was born that she had given birth to a great man—Freud was described by his family and his friends as gentle and considerate, a delightful companion when not talking "shop."

Soon after his eighty-first birthday, when he was suffering not only from cancer but also from a painful heart malady, he said despairingly, "It is tragic when a man outlives his body."

Dark Days Under the Nazis

During his last years, when he was to taste the bitterness of exile, Dr. Freud had been in retirement, engaged upon writing books to which all his research and study would have been but a preliminary. He had completed his last work in the development of his theory and now only a few patients were admitted to him.

He had retired into his library and was seeking, in the few years left to him, to make a pioneering study of the nature of religion. As the annexation of Austria appeared more and more a menace, he was urged by his friends to seek refuge abroad, but he refused to go. If the Nazis invaded the refuge of his library, he told them, he was prepared to kill himself.

He was ill, a shadow of his former self at 82, when Nazi Germany moved her army into Austria and absorbed his homeland and he was not at once told about it. His family was obliged to burn a whole truckload of his books they had sent to Switzerland. He was virtually penniless and the news came as a great shock to him.

He remained in seclusion in his five-room apartment, "dreading insults if he emerged—because he is a Jew," friends said. A delegation of Netherlands admirers went to Vienna to offer him the hospitality of their country, but the authorities forbade him to go, refusing him a passport. Soon the reason was disclosed. Not satisfied with having destroyed his income, as well as his family firm's stock of books, the Nazis were demanding that he be ransomed.

Huge Fund Raised for Passport

A fund had been raised quietly by American admirers to pay his and his family's living expenses once they left Vienna, but it was sadly inadequate to meet the demand. Princess George of Greece, who as Princess Marie Bonaparte had studied under Freud, induced the Nazi authorities after lengthy negotiations to accept a quarter million of Austrian schillings she had on deposit in Vienna to restore his passport. The American, British and French Psychoanalytical Associations and scientists all over the world brought pressure to aid her.

In June, 1938, he was able to leave with his family and some personal books and papers. He went to Paris and then to London, the Nazi press sending after him a parting gibe, calling his school a "pornographic Jewish specialty." A condition of his release was that he keep silence, and he was not able to tell how frequently Nazi officials upbraided him in the months before. Settling in London, he finished a book, "Moses and Monotheism" (published here last June), a study of the Moses legend and its relation to the development of Judaism and Christianity.

The book, a first effort to use his psychoanalytic system to explain the origins of the institution of religion, origins shrouded in the obscurity of ages, aroused a storm of controversy. Although he had long wanted to make such an investigation of the Bible, he had delayed its completion while in Vienna, he explained in an accompanying manuscript, because he had not wanted to affront the religious sensibilities of the Catholic authorities, who had treated him well and had protected his fellow-Jews.

Bulwark Against Barbarism

"Catholic Austria seemed the last bulwark against an impending danger," he wrote, "and even those who are opposed to the results of Catholicism have learned to submit to the lesser evil."

The book was bitterly attacked, no less for such beliefs as that Moses was an Egyptian, than for such suggestions as that ethical monotheism was not a cultural achievement evolved in the course of the spiritual development of the Jews but rather an amplification of the idea of one God Moses brought to the Jewish people from the religion of an Egyptian king, Ikhnaton.

But it also found admirers. Thomas Mann hailed it as showing that the Freudian theory had become "a world movement embracing every possible field of learning and science," as, for future generations, one of the most important foundation stones for "the dwelling of a freer and wiser humanity."

In London he spent a contented year in a house a few hundred yards north of Regent's Park. Leaving further development of his psychological theories to his daughter, Anna, and his disciples, he concentrated on his monumental study of the Old Testament, which he estimated would take him five years to complete, a work of which "Moses and Monotheism" was only to have been the first fruit.

He had stated its theme, that all religions only reflect the hopes and fears of man's own deepest nature, in "Totem and Taboo" twenty-five years before, but now he sought to buttress his speculations with supporting evidence. This work, which he believed would have a far-reaching effect on religion, is now left uncompleted, it is believed.

Dr. Freud at home, 1931.

Dr. Freud and his daughter Anna in 1938.

"All the News That's Fit to Print."

The New York Times.

LATE CITY EDITION
POSTSCRIPT
THE WEATHER—Generally fair and continued warm today and tomorrow.
Temperatures Yesterday—Max. 34; Min. 26.
U. S. Weather Forecast—See map in last page.

VOL. CXII....No. 38,357. © 1963 by The New York Times Company. NEW YORK, WEDNESDAY, JANUARY 30, 1963. Air delivery in Alaska & Hawaii 25 cents. Air delivery in Canada & Mexico 15 cents. TEN CENTS

COMMON MARKET TALKS WRECKED AS FRANCE VETOES BRITISH ENTRY; BLOW TO EUROPEAN UNITY IS SEEN

PRESIDENT ASKS BROAD PROGRAM TO AID EDUCATION

Message to Congress Calls for Package Bill Costing 1.2 Billion First Year

TOTAL PUT AT 6 BILLION

Funds Would Help States in Building Schools and Raising Teachers' Pay

Excerpts from Kennedy message on education, Page 4.

By MARJORIE HUNTER
Special to The New York Times.

WASHINGTON, Jan. 29 — President Kennedy asked Congress today for a new education program that he promised would have something in it for potentially every American.

In a special message to Congress, the President called for passage of a single bill that would put $1,215,000,000 of Federal money into the nation's schools and colleges in the fiscal year beginning July 1.

Some of the programs would extend for four years. According to one estimate the total cost would be up to $6,000,000,000.

"Instead of a general aid approach that could at best create a small wave in a huge ocean," the President said, "our efforts should be selective and stimulative, encouraging the states to redouble their efforts under a plan that would phase out Federal aid over a four-year period."

Single-Package Plan

The single package represented a departure from earlier Administration efforts to aid various levels of education. During the last two years, numerous bills dealing with separate educational programs were defeated.

Administration leaders said the new bill attempted to head off the church-state fight that defeated earlier general aid measures.

However, the President did not retreat from his position that general aid on the elementary and secondary levels should be limited to public schools.

The new proposals call for funds to aid states in constructing public school buildings or improving salaries of public school teachers.

Aid to private institutions is limited to the college and university levels through student loans and matching funds for construction of academic buildings.

Items in Proposal

The bill also provides construction grants for public junior colleges; seeks to improve teacher quality through institutes and other programs; provides aid to libraries and expands vocational education and special education programs.

However, provisions for improving the quality of education, through institutes and teacher preparation programs, would be available to teachers of both public and private schools.

The President explained he was seeking a single educational package "because education cannot easily or wisely be divided into separate parts. Each part is linked to the other."

An educational official put it

Continued on Page 4, Column 7

Robert Frost Dies at 88; Kennedy Leads in Tribute

Poet Won Four Pulitzer Prizes—Took Part in 1961 Inauguration

By The Associated Press.

BOSTON, Jan. 29 — Robert Frost, dean of American poets, died today at the age of 88.

He was pronounced dead at Peter Bent Brigham hospital at 1:50 A.M.

The poet's general condition began deteriorating two days ago.

His attending physician, Dr. Roger B. Hickler, said Mr. Frost died shortly after complaining of severe chest pains and a shortness of breath. The cause of death was listed as "probably a pulmonary embolism," or blood clot in the lungs.

Dr. Hickler said that a few hours before the fatal attack Mr. Frost was "talkative and comfortable."

Not long before his death, Mr. Frost had been dictating an article on Ezra Pound from his hospital bed when he fell asleep, according to his daughter, Leslie Frost.

President Kennedy was among

Associated Press
Robert Frost

Government and literary figures who paid tribute to Mr. Frost.

The poet entered the hospital Dec. 3 and underwent an operation on Dec. 10 for removal of a urinary obstruction.

Subsequently he had a heart

Continued on Page 5, Column 1

Long-Distance Rate in U.S. Cut to $1 Top After 9 P.M.

By ANTHONY LEWIS
Special to The New York Times.

WASHINGTON, Jan. 29—The Bell Telephone System agreed today to cut rates sharply on long distance calls made between 9 P.M. and 4:30 A.M. Starting about April 1, it will cost a maximum of $1 to telephone anywhere in the United States for three minutes during those hours. That will be the rate for a station-to-station call —one to a telephone number rather than a particular party.

The $1 ceiling will mean cuts up to 43 per cent below the minimum present rates, those for after 6 P.M. and on Sundays. In addition, there will be proportionate reductions below the $1 level.

The rate between New York and Los Angeles is now $1.75—nights and Sundays. It will be $1 after 9 P.M.

The New York—Chicago rate will drop from $1.15 to 70 cents after 9 P.M. and the San Francisco-Portland, Ore., rate from $1 to 65 cents.

The lower rates will begin at 9 P.M. local time in the city where the call originates.

Offsetting Reduction

Under the lower rate schedules, the charges for overtime will also be less, since they are based on a percentage of the initial three-minute charge. For example, at present a caller pays 45 cents for each extra minute on a $1.75 call between New York and Los Angeles. The new rate will be 25 cents for each extra minute on the $1.00 call.

The Federal Communications Commission announced the new rates today. It has been pressing the American Telephone and Telegraph Company and its Bell operating subsidiaries for some time to reduce the cost of long-distance tolls.

Under an agreement between the commission and the companies, they will file tariffs, effective "about April 1," incorporating what the F. C. C. called "after 9 reduced rates."

Positions Set Forth

The new tariffs will also include some small compensating increases in person-to-person rates, raising them 5 or 10 cents on calls up to 800 miles. The F. C. C. said these relatively short calls had not borne their share of costs.

Based on 1962 traffic volumes, the lower nighttime rates are expected to cost A. T. & T. $55,000,000 in revenue. The company will get $25,000,000 of that back in the person-to-person increases, for a net reduction of $30,000,000.

The commission said A.T.&T. would be able "to maintain a level of earnings on investments within the range realized by it since the last rate reduction [on interstate calls] in 1959."

In a statement issued here, A. T. & T. said: "The Bell companies are disappointed that the commission failed to recognize

Continued on Page 18, Column 3

U.S. TO INCREASE FEES FOR GRAZING

Will Use Money to Restore Lands in West—Strong Protest Expected

By WILLIAM M. BLAIR
Special to The New York Times.

WASHINGTON, Jan. 29 — The Interior Department will increase soon the fees it charges livestock producers for cattle and sheep grazing on the public domain in 10 Western states. The increase has a twofold purpose.

First, it would yield more money to help rehabilitate millions of acres of public range, which a recent study found in a "shocking condition." Range fees produced only $3,000,000 last year while the Federal Government spent nearly $12,000,000 for maintenance and management.

Second, it would establish the principle that people who use the public domain should help pay the costs whether for grazing or for recreation. The Administration will soon ask Congress to authorize new user fees to create a land conservation fund to be used to acquire and develop outdoor recreational facilities.

Cattle and sheep producers in the Western states now pay 19 cents per head of livestock per month on public rangeland established under the Taylor Grazing Act and administered by the Bureau of Land Management. The Interior Department, under a new formula, would nearly double the present fee.

This would yield a total of

Continued on Page 18, Column 2

U.N. CHIEF INVITES NATIONS TO GIVE CONGO DIRECT AID

Thant Report on Bilateral Help Attributed to World Body's Lack of Funds

By THOMAS J. HAMILTON
Special to The New York Times.

UNITED NATIONS, N. Y., Jan. 29—Secretary General U Thant said today that the United States and other countries were now free to supply bilateral assistance to the Congo, without going through the United Nations.

Mr. Thant's statement seemed to invite such assistance. It appeared to have been prompted by the realization that the United Nations, which is near bankruptcy, cannot provide the large sums needed for the rehabilitation of the Congo.

Harlan Cleveland, Assistant Secretary of State for International Organization Affairs, said yesterday that the Congolese Central Government would have a deficit of $100,000,000 this year.

According to Mr. Thant's statement, the United Nations would have no objection if the Soviet Union resumed direct aid to the Congo, provided it was requested by the Congolese Government.

Soviet Aid Recalled

The Soviet Union provided transport aircraft and supplies for the Congo in the summer of 1960 when the late Patrice Lumumba, a leftist, was in power. Soviet aid stopped, however, after Mr. Lumumba was ousted.

In any case, Mr. Thant's statement apparently foreshadows increased direct United States aid to the Congo. A mission, headed by Mr. Cleveland, left for Leopoldville today to discuss the Congo's needs with Premier Cyrille Adoula.

Previous United Nations resolutions had requested all states to channel their assistance to the Congo through the organization. Mr. Thant said in his statement, however, that the Congo, like any other independent state, had a right to accept bilateral assistance from any country if it wished to do so.

Military Phase Over

Mr. Thant commented that with the occupation of Elisabethville, Jadotville, and other Katanga centers. "it may be said with reasonable confidence that the phase of active military involvement by United Nations forces in the Congo is about over."

The Secretary General added that the United Nations Congo force, which now has a strength of 19,000, would be reduced to between 12,000 and 13,000 by the end of March. But he indicated that the United Nations force would have to be maintained at reduced strength for some time to help the Central Government cope with tribal disputes and to maintain law and order.

The Secretary General did not reply when a reporter asked

Continued on Page 2, Column 2

BRITON IS BITTER

Heath Says One Man's Will Has Thwarted Hopes of Many

Special to The New York Times.

BRUSSELS, Jan. 29—Edward Heath, Britain's chief negotiator in her effort to join the Common Market, said tonight that the end of negotiations was a "blow to the cause of that wider unity for which we have been striving."

In a bitter reference to President de Gaulle, who blocked British entry, Mr. Heath said at a news conference:

"The high hopes of so many have thus been thwarted for political reasons by the will of one man."

"We entered these negotiations 16 months ago in good faith, and have endeavored strenuously to reach a successful conclusion," Mr. Heath declared. "Five members of the Community and the Commission have said publicly that all the remaining problems were capable of solution. I share that view."

Some Gains Are Seen

Mr. Heath said that, as a result of the negotiations, the countries had a better understanding of one another's problems. He added that there was a "deeper recognition" in Europe of the nature of the British Commonwealth.

"We shall continue to work with all our friends in Europe," to make the Commonwealth "stronger and more prosperous," he said.

British sources of the highest authority disclosed three elements of British policy in the aftermath of the crisis:

¶There will be no policy of reprisal, economic or otherwise, against France.

¶Britain is not contemplating some form of "association" with the Common Market. An offer of association has been made by General de Gaulle but has not been made by the Community as such, which would have to make the offer for it to be valid.

¶There are unlikely to be any dramatic changes in British domestic policy.

A Heavy Blow to London

By SYDNEY GRUSON
Special to The New York Times.

LONDON, Jan. 29—The collapse of Britain's Common Market negotiations, though no surprise, came as a heavy blow here today. But the tenor of British reaction was that the country now must face up to

Continued on Page 3, Column 6

Washington Is Concerned; Moscow Welcomes Split

De Gaulle Aims Studied

By MAX FRANKEL
Special to The New York Times.

WASHINGTON, Jan. 29 — Administration officials declared today that President de Gaulle's veto of British membership in the Common Market had merely postponed the inevitable.

They told reporters and diplomats that history was on the side of allied unity, and that Washington intended to press ahead with economic and military policies to promote such unity.

But also discernible were an attitude of great disappointment and frustration and a foreboding of serious trouble for the Western alliance as a result of the collapse of negotiations at Brussels.

Privately, officials wondered about General de Gaulle's "real" objectives and some foresaw a French drive to cut down United States influence in Europe. They feared open economic and political competition within the alliance and acknowledged some suspicions of

Continued on Page 3, Column 2

Discord Pleases Soviet

Special to The New York Times.

MOSCOW, Jan. 29 — The Soviet Union, plagued by its quarrels with Communist China, welcomed today with unconcealed satisfaction the disarray among the Atlantic alliance.

The rift in the West has come at a time when Moscow has adopted a cautious foreign policy because of the ideological dispute with Peking, the Cuban reversal and internal economic difficulties.

Western diplomatic observers said it was unlikely that the Kremlin would attempt immediately to exploit the Western differences by provoking a crisis because the Soviet leaders have learned that pressure only tends to unify the Western allies. Soviet Government propaganda hailed the "breakdown" of the negotiations at Brussels for the entry of Britain into the Common Market. Wide prominence was given to the differences between President Kennedy and President de Gaulle.

Pravda, the Communist

Continued on Page 3, Column 3

BRUSSELS BREAK DEPRESSES BONN

Germans Fear They Will Be Chief Loser From Failure of Britain's Market Bid

By ARTHUR J. OLSEN
Special to The New York Times.

BONN, Jan. 29—News of the breakdown of the Brussels talks was received in West Germany tonight with discouragement and foreboding.

The feeling is general in official and private quarters that Bonn may turn out to be the big loser from the failure of the effort to bring Britain into the European Common Market. The adverse reaction in the United States, West Germany's indispensable ally, represents the dominating worry here.

Government comment was withheld until tomorrow, but a spokesman of Chancellor Adenauer's Christian Democratic party said that the policy of European unity had been thrust into "serious danger."

Comment by Ollenhauer

"The consequences cannot yet be foreseen." said Kurt Schmucker, spokesman of the Christian Democratic parliamentary group.

Erich Ollenhauer, chairman of the Opposition Social Democratic party, said collapse of the Brussels talks had dealt "a heavy blow to European unification and Atlantic solidarity."

Another party chief, Dr. Erich Mende of the Free Democrats, said France's act in Brussels was "bound to affect" West Germany's attitude toward its new treaty of cooperation with France. The treaty, signed last week, will soon be submitted to Parliament for ratification.

The leader of the Free Democrats, who are the junior partners in the governing coalition, said the treaty should not be permitted to become "the end station of European cooperation."

Preventive Action Urged

"A greater Europe without Britain and the Scandinavian countries is impossible in the long run," Dr. Mende said.

West German politicians and press commentators were quick to name President de Gaulle as the villain of the drama and Premier Khrushchev as the clear winner. The Hamburg newspaper Die Welt will sum up this bitter judgment this way in its leading editorial tomorrow:

"De Gaulle is responsible for the breakdown of the talks. This must be stated squarely in the light of attempts at putting the blame on the five other Common Market partners.... The winner of the day, a black day for both Europe and Western cooperation, is Khrushchev."

Continued on Page 3, Column 7

BRITAIN MAY CUT HER NATO FORCE

Reduction in Army of Rhine Likely to Follow Nation's Failure to Enter Market

By DREW MIDDLETON
Special to The New York Times.

PARIS, Jan. 29—The forward strategy of the North Atlantic Alliance in defense of Europe has been seriously threatened by France's exclusion of Britain from the European Economic Community, qualified sources declared tonight.

This strategy depends on the concentration as far east as possible of allied divisions. One consequence of Britain's exclusion from the economic community is expected to be the reduction, for economic reasons, of the British Army of the Rhine, a pivotal force on the northern flank in Europe.

Coupled with the failure of France to assign two badly needed divisions to the forward NATO forces, this is expected to force a re-examination and perhaps a revision of the alliance's forward strategy.

NATO, however, conscious that it is now the last stronghold in Europe of trans-Atlantic unity, intends to intensify its efforts to create a nuclear force.

The gloom that hung over the political and military offices in NATO as a result of the breakdown of the Brussels negotiations is matched by the forebodings of some French politicians.

Some, normally faithful to President de Gaulle's policies,

Continued on Page 3, Column 5

DE GAULLE IS FIRM

Erhard Says Britain's Exclusion Is 'Black Day for Europe'

By EDWIN L. DALE Jr.
Special to The New York Times.

BRUSSELS, Jan. 29 — Sixteen months of negotiations for British entry into the European Common Market ended today in failure and bitterness.

The end came at the demand of France. Britain and France's five Common Market partners wanted the talks continued, but France's right of veto made continuation without her useless. There is no move for a revival.

The end of the talks not only meant the wreckage of the historic move by Britain to cast her lot with continental Europe; it also left a heavy cloud over the future of the Common Market itself. Ludwig Erhard, West German Vice Chancellor and Minister of the Economy, said:

"This is a black day for Europe. The Common Market is now only a mechanism and no longer a living thing."

Kennedy Plan Shattered

Today's collapse also left in ruins, for the foreseeable future, President Kennedy's policy of an "equal partnership" between the United States on one hand and an enlarged Common Market including Britain on the other.

It was widely regarded as the worst political crisis in Europe since World War II, surpassing in its consequences that created by France's rejection in 1954 of the European defense community. All of the leading figures today blamed the crisis squarely on French President de Gaulle.

But General de Gaulle was evidently willing to take the blame in his stride. A French spokesman remarked: "France's shoulders are broad enough to bear the burden of responsibility."

Briton Is Summoned

The final act of the drama was played out today in an atmosphere of deep pessimism. Firm to the end, France's five Common Market partners — West Germany, Italy, Belgium, the Netherlands and Luxembourg — reached agreement on a concrete proposal for keeping negotiations going by giving a special mandate to the Common Market Executive Commission to make a three-week study of the outstanding problems and suggest solutions.

Maurice Couve de Murville, the French Foreign Minister, doggedly persisted in his refusal to accept this proposal because it would imply a continuation of the negotiations. In mid-afternoon, Edward Heath, Lord Privy Seal, the chief British negotiator, was called in to hear the result that he already knew.

Although Mr. Heath met briefly afterward with the foreign ministers of "the five,"

Continued on Page 3, Column 1

Major Fight on Mental Illness Urged on Congress by Kennedy

By ROBERT C. TOTH
Special to The New York Times.

WASHINGTON, Jan. 29 — President Kennedy will send to Congress within the next few days an ambitious national program to fight mental illnesses that afflict an estimated total of 22,000,000 Americans.

The program of prevention, care and rehabilitation would cost more than $400,000,000 over four to five years, in addition to the $1,000,000,000 annual Federal outlay for mental health today.

About three-fourths of the new funds would be directed at the psychological disorders grouped under mental diseases, while the rest would aim at the intelligence deficiencies that characterize the mentally retarded. This 3-1 ratio reflects the number of Americans institutionalized for these illnesses, roughly 700,000 and 200,000, respectively.

Beyond the Government effort, however, some officials hope the President's message will mobilize a national attack on mental illnesses much as Franklin D. Roosevelt's support of the March of Dimes sparked the fight against polio 25 years ago.

Behind the proposals on mental disease is an exhaustive, 10-volume report by the Joint Commission on Mental Illness and Health, which was set up by Congress. The commission's report, published in 1961 after six years of study, called for radical reforms in the public care of mentally ill at Federal, state and local levels.

It urged that the monolithic, prison-like mental institutions be replaced by intensive treatment hospitals, community clinics and emergency mental wards in general hospitals. It recommended Federal funds for making those changes, and for training specialists in mental health fields.

Political steam to implement the report has been building up, largely through the 80 specialized organizations who helped in the commission study, including the National Association for Mental Health with its 3,000 local chapters.

Mr. Kenedy was expected to propose Federal assistance for building and operating community centers that can treat patients either within the institution or on an out-patient basis. In both cases the ill would be treated as much as

Continued on Page 4, Column 8

Kennedy to Open Tax Returns Of Foreign Agents to Senate

By TAD SZULC
Special to The New York Times.

WASHINGTON, Jan. 29 — President Kennedy signed an Executive Order today allowing the Senate Foreign Relations Committee to inspect the tax returns of all non-diplomatic representatives of foreign governments in the United States.

The committee is investigating the activities of lobbyists and agents of foreign nations here to determine the extent of violations of the Foreign Agents Registration Act of 1938.

The study, which has the personal attention of Senator J. W. Fulbright, Arkansas Democrat who is committee chairman, is expected to lead to Congressional action tightening the law. This is necessary, he believes, to stop serious abuses and improper attempts to influence the conduct of United States foreign policy.

The committee expects to open formal hearings next week following seven months of inquiries by its investigators.

Under Secretary of State George W. Ball is scheduled to be the first Administration witness in open hearings. Subsequently, the committee plans to concentrate on executive sessions, questioning lobbyists and foreign agents in connection with material gathered here and abroad by its investigators.

The Presidential order provides for inspection by the committee of "any income, excess-profits, estate or gift tax returns for the years 1950 to 1962, inclusive" until next June 30, when the committee's investigation is to be completed.

Involved are returns that may

Continued on Page 2, Column 6

Thant Sees a Threat in Borneo That May Require U.N. Action

By ARNOLD H. LUBASCH
Special to The New York Times.

UNITED NATIONS, N. Y., Jan. 29—Secretary General U Thant warned today that the Borneo area in Southeast Asia could become a major trouble spot that would require United Nations action.

Surveying world problems in an hour-long news conference, Mr. Thant singled out the British protectorate of Brunei as posing a potentially "very serious problem." The Secretary General added that he might try to devise a formula to help ease tensions in the Borneo area.

Britain announced yesterday that an infantry brigade had been alerted to go to the Far East because of possible "outside interference" in Brunei, a rich oil-producing enclave on the island of Borneo. British forces there put down a brief rebellion last month.

Reports have circulated in London that 10,000 Soviet-equipped Indonesian troops were massed on the border for an effort to occupy Brunei. The reports were denied yesterday by Indonesia.

The situation in the South China Sea area has been further complicated because of the Philippine's claim to North Borneo. North Borneo and Sarawak are both British colonies and are scheduled to join Malaya and Singapore in forming the federation of Malaysia by Aug. 31.

Brunei, a British-protected sultanate, is also expected to join the federation.

Mr. Thant's warning on Borneo was regarded as implying that the situation there was

Continued on Page 2, Column 3

NEWS INDEX

Robert Frost, Four-Time Winner of the Pulitzer Prize, Dies in Boston at Age of 88

POET WAS SYMBOL OF INDIVIDUALITY

Work Rejected at First, He Later Moved Among World Leaders

Continued from Page 1, Col. 3

attack and blood clots settled in his lungs. In an attempt to ease the blood clots, doctors operated on both legs earlier this month to tie the veins.

Funeral Tomorrow

Special to The New York Times.

NEW YORK.

A private funeral service, to be attended by members of the family, will be held for Mr. Frost tomorrow. Burial will be in the family plot in Old Bennington, Vt. On Sunday, Feb. 17, at 2 P.M. a public memorial service will be held at Amherst College, Amherst, Mass.

The Frost family suggested that instead of flowers contributions may be made to a Robert Frost fund to establish special chairs for high school teachers. A number of such chairs have already been created in the poet's name, and the project was one in which he was deeply interested. Contributions should be sent to Mr. Frost's publisher, A. C. Edwards of Holt, Rinehart & Winston, 383 Madison Avenue, New York 17, N.Y.

Remarkable in Many Ways

Robert Frost was beyond doubt the only American poet to play a touching personal role at a Presidential inauguration; to report a casual remark of a Soviet dictator that stung officials in Washington, and to twit the Russians about the barrier to Berlin by reading to them, on their own ground, his celebrated poem about another kind of wall.

But it would be much more to the point to say he was also without question the only poet to win four Pulitzer Prizes and, in his ninth decade, to symbolize the rough-hewn individuality of the American creative spirit more than any other man.

Finally, it might have been even more appropriate to link his uniqueness to his breathtaking sense of exactitude in the use of metaphors based on direct observations ("I don't like to write anything I don't see," he told an interviewer in Cambridge, Mass., two days before his 88th birthday.)

Thus he recorded timelessly (by matching the sharpest observation with the most exact word) how the swimming buck pushed the "crumpled" water; how the wagon's wheels "freshly sliced" the April mire; how the ice crystals from the frozen birch snapped off and went "avalanching" on the snowy crust.

And to show that this phase of his gift did not blur with age, there was in his last book, published in 1962 by Holt, Rinehart & Winston, a piece called "Pod of the Milkweed." It told of the butterflies clustered on the blossoms so avidly that "They knocked the dyestuff off each others' wings."

He had seen the particular butterflies, most of them Monarchs, just outside his "boating" home at Ripton, Vt., a few years before.

Inauguration Incident

The incident of Jan. 20, 1961—when John F. Kennedy took the oath as President—was perhaps the most dramatic of Mr. Frost's "public" life.

Invited to write a poem for the occasion, he rose to read it. But the blur of the sun and the edge of the wind hampered him; his brief plight was so moving that a photograph of former President Dwight D. Eisenhower, Mrs. Kennedy and Mrs. Lyndon Johnson watching him won a prize because of the deep apprehension in their faces.

But Frost was not daunted. Aware of the problem, he simply put aside the new poem and recited from memory an old favorite, "The Gift Outright," dating to the nineteen-thirties. It fit the circumstances as snugly as a glove.

Later he took the unread "new" poem, which had been called "The Preface," expanded it from 42 to 77 lines, retitled it "For John F. Kennedy: His Inaugural"—and presented it to the President in March, 1962.

Later that year, Mr. Frost accompanied Stewart L. Udall, Secretary of the Interior, on a visit to Moscow.

A first encounter with Soviet children, studying English, did not encourage the poet. He recognized the problem posed by the language; it was painfully ironic, because he had said years before that poetry was what was "lost in translation." And in Moscow, his first hearers clearly did not understand well in English.

But a few days later, he read "Mending Wall" at a Moscow literary evening. "Something there is that doesn't love a wall," the poem begins. The Russians may not have got the subsequent nuances. But the idea quickly spread that the choice of the poem was not unrelated to the wall partitioning Berlin.

On Sept. 7, the poet had a long talk with Premier Khrushchev. He described the Soviet leader as "no fathead"; as smart, big and "not a coward."

"He's not afraid of us and we're not afraid of him," he added.

Subsequently, Frost reported that Mr. Khrushchev had said the United States was "too liberal to fight." It was this remark that caused a considerable stir in Washington.

Thus in the late years of his life, Frost moved among the mighty. He was a public personage to thousands of persons who had never read his works. But to countless others, loyal and loving to the point of idolatry, he remained not only a poet but the poet of his day.

During the first years of the Kennedy Administration, Frost was unquestionably a kind of celebrity-poet around Washington. His face was seen smiling in the background — and frequently the foreground — of news photographs from the Capitol, and quite often he appeared in public with Democratic politicians.

President Kennedy, when asked why he had requested that Frost speak at the inauguration, praised the "courage, the towering skill and daring" of his fellow New Englander.

Among the many things that both shared was the high esteem of a poet's place in American society.

"There is a story that some years ago an interested mother wrote to a principal of a school, 'Don't teach my boy poetry, he's going to run for Congress,'" President Kennedy said. "I've never taken the view that the world of politics and the world of poetry are so far apart. I think politicians and poets share at least one thing, and that is their greatness depends upon the courage with which they face the challenges of life."

He was echoing a cry that Frost had long made—the higher role of the poet in a business society. In fact, in 1960, Mr. Frost had urged Congress to declare poets the equal of big business, and received a standing ovation from spectators when he supported a bill to create a National Academy of Culture.

"I have long thought of something like this," Mr. Frost told a Senate education subcommittee. "Everyone comes down to Washington to get equal with someone else. I want our poets to be declared equal to—what shall I say?—the scientists. No, to big business."

Many years before, but several years after he had achieved recognition for his work, Frost had slouched characteristically before an audience of young writers gathered under Bread Loaf Mountains at Middlebury, Vt. He said:

"Every artist must have two fears—the fear of God and the fear of man—fear of God that his creation will ultimately be found unworthy and the fear of man that he will be misunderstood by his fellows."

These two fears were ever present in Robert Frost, with the result that his published verses were of the highest order and completely understood by thousands of Americans in whom they struck a ready response. To countless persons who had never seen New Hampshire birches in the snow or caressed a perfect ax he exemplified a great American tradition with his superb, almost angular verses written out of the New England scene.

Not since Whittier in "Snowbound" had captured the penetrating chill of New England's brief December day had any American poet more exactly caught the atmosphere north of Boston or the thin philosophy of its fence-mending inhabitants.

His pictures of an abandoned cord of wood warming "the frozen swamp as best it could with the slow smokeless burning of decay" or of how "two roads diverged in a wood, and I took the one less traveled by, and that has made all the difference," with their Yankee economy of words, moved his readers nostalgically and filled the back pastures of their mind with memories of a shrewd and quiet way of life.

Strangely enough, Frost spent 20 years writing his verses on stone walls and brown earth, blue butterflies and tall, slim trees without winning any recognition in America. When he sent them to The Atlantic Monthly they were returned with this note:

"We regret that The Atlantic has no place for your vigorous verse."

It was not until "A Boy's Will" was published in England and Ezra Pound publicized it that Robert Frost was recognized as the indigenous American poet that he was.

After that the way was not so hard, and in the years that followed he was to win the Pulitzer Prize four times, be honored by many institutions of higher learning and find it possible for a poet, who would write of things that were "common in experience, uncommon in writing," to earn enough money so that he would not have to teach or farm or make shoes or write for newspapers—all things he had done in his early days.

Raymond Holden, poet and critic, pointed out in a "profile" in The New Yorker magazine that there was more than the ordinary amount of paradox in the personality and career of Frost. Essentially a New England poet in a day when there were few poets in that region, he was born in San Francisco; fundamentally a Yankee, he was the son of an ardent Democrat whose belief in the Confederacy led him to name his son Robert Lee; a farmer in New Hampshire, he preferred to sit on a fence and watch others work; a teacher, he despised the rigors of the educational process as practiced in the institutions where he taught.

Like many another Yankee individualist, Robert Frost was a rebel. So was his father, William Frost, who had run away from Amherst, Mass., to go West. His mother, born in Edinburgh, Scotland, emigrated to Philadelphia when she was a girl.

His father died when Robert, who was born March 26, 1874, was about 11. The boy and his mother, the former Isabelle Moody, went to live at Lawrence, Mass., with William Prescott Frost, Robert's grandfather, who gave the boy a good schooling. Influenced by the poems of Edgar Allan Poe, Robert wanted to be a poet before he went to Dartmouth College, where he stayed only through the year 1892.

In the next several years he worked as a bobbin boy in the Lawrence mills, was a shoemaker and for a short while a reporter for The Lawrence Sentinel. He attended Harvard in 1897-98, then became a farmer at Derry, N. H., and taught there. In 1905 he married Elinor White, also a teacher, by whom he had five children. In 1912 Mr. Frost sold the farm and the family went to England.

He came home to find the editor of The Atlantic Monthly asking for poems. He sent along the very ones that had previously been rejected, and they were published. The Frosts went to Franconia, N. H., to live in a farm house Mr. Frost had bought for $1,000. His poetry brought him some money, and in 1916 he again became a teacher. He was a professor of English, then "poet in residence" for more than 20 years at Amherst College and he spent two years in a similar capacity at the University of Michigan. Later Frost lectured and taught at The New School in New York.

In 1938 he retired temporarily as a teacher. Mrs. Frost died that year in Florida. Afterward, he taught intermittently at Harvard, Amherst and Dartmouth.

In 1916 Frost, who had then been a poet for 20 years, was made a member of the National Institute of Arts and Letters; in 1930, of the American Academy. His books, "New Hampshire: A Poem With Notes And Gracenotes," won him the Pulitzer Prize in 1924. When his "Corrected Poems" were published in 1931, he again won that prize. The Pulitzer committee honored him a third time in 1937 for his book, "A Further Range," and again in 1943 for "A Witness Tree."

Frost won many honorary degrees, from master of arts at Amherst in 1917 to doctor of humane letters at the University of Vermont in 1923, and others followed from Harvard, Yale and other institutions.

The issuing in 1949 of "The Complete Poems of Robert Frost," a 642-page volume, was the signal for another series of broad critical appraisals studded with phrases like "lasting significance."

The Limited Editions Club awarded Frost its Gold Medal, and in the following October poets, scholars and editors gathered to do him honor at the Kenyon College Conference. In Washington the Senate adopted a resolution to send him greetings on his 75th birthday.

On that occasion he said that 20 acres of land for every man "would be the answer to all the world's problems" noting that life on the farm would show men "their burdens as well as their privileges."

The only existing copy of Frost's first book, "Twilight and Other Poems," was auctioned here that December for $3,000, a price thought to be the highest paid for a work by a contemporary American author. "It had no success and deserved none," the poet commented.

In later years, Frost, who once wrote:

I bid you to a one-man revolution — The only revolution that is coming,

became interested in politics, and some of his later verses were on this theme. His lectures, at Harvard, where he was Charles Eliot Norton lecturer in 1936 and 1939, and elsewhere, were less about poetry and more about the moral values of life. But it was less to these than to his earlier works that readers turned for satisfaction; to such lines as these on the "Hired Man":

Nothing to look backward to with pride
Nothing to look forward to with hope . . .

While critics heaped belated praise on his earthy, Yankee, birchbark-clear poems, there were also finely fashioned lyrics in which the man of the soil flashed fire with intellect. Such a poem was "Reluctance" with its nostalgic ending:

Ah, when to the heart of man
Was it ever less than treason
To go with the drift of things,
To yield with a grace to reason,
And bow and accept the end
Of a love or a season?

Or:

Some say the world will end in fire,
Some say in ice.
From what I've tasted of desire
I hold with those who favor fire.
But if I had to perish twice,
I think I know enough of hate
To say that for destruction ice
Is also great
And would suffice.

Even critics who found a harshness sometimes in his work credited Mr. Frost with being a great poet. They appreciated his philosophy of simplicity, perhaps more in later years than during the "renaissance" of American poetry in the nineteen-twenties. For they knew it was a part of Robert Frost, whose innate philosophy of unchangeableness he once expressed, when he wrote:

They would not find me changed from him they knew
Only more sure of all I thought was true. . . .

At an annual joint ceremonial in May 1950, of the American Academy and the National Institute, he read a poem entitled "How Hard It Is to Keep From Being King, When It's in You and in the Situation."

Asked about his method of writing a poem, Frost said: "I have worried quite a number of them into existence, but any sneaking preference [I have had] remains for the ones I have carried through like the stroke of a racquet, club or headsman's ax."

In an interview with Harvey Breit of The New York Times Book Review, he observed:

"If poetry isn't understanding all, the whole word, then it isn't worth anything. Young poets forget that poetry must include the mind as well as the emotions. Too many poets delude themselves by thinking the mind is dangerous and must be left out. Well, the mind is dangerous and must be left in."

"All the News That's Fit to Print"

The New York Times.

LATE CITY EDITION

U. S. Weather Bureau Report (Page 72) forecasts: Mostly fair, not as warm today; fair, cold tonight. Fair, mild tomorrow. Temp. range: 55—45; yesterday: 62.2—52.1.

VOL. CX.. No. 37,553.

NEW YORK, THURSDAY, NOVEMBER 17, 1960.

10 cents beyond 50-mile zone from New York City except on Long Island. Higher in air delivery cities.

FIVE CENTS

U.S. WILL REDUCE SPENDING ABROAD BY A BILLION TO STEM GOLD DRAIN; DEPENDENTS AT BASES TO BE CUT

CALIFORNIA IS PUT IN NIXON'S COLUMN BY ABSENTEE VOTE

But Kennedy Is Still Assured of Presidency With Total of 300 Electoral Ballots

POPULAR MARGIN SLIM

President-Elect Is in Texas to Hold Conference With Johnson and Rayburn

By The Associated Press.

SAN FRANCISCO, Nov. 16—Vice President Nixon captured California's thirty-two electoral votes from President-elect Kennedy tonight on unofficial returns from absentee ballots.

Senator Kennedy led in the tally of regular ballots with a majority of 34,568, but the absentee returns changed the picture.

Mr. Nixon's lead rose to 13,160 with about 20,000 absentee ballots still to be counted. Most of these are in Republican areas.

The absentee returns gave Mr. Nixon 132,168 to Mr. Kennedy's 84,458.

State-wide, absentee and resident, the count was: Mr. Nixon, 3,219,211; Mr. Kennedy, 3,206,051.

An official canvass, due by Nov. 28, will give the final result, but it appeared that only a gross error at the county level could upset Mr. Nixon.

Kennedy Not Imperiled

Senator Kennedy's election was not jeopardized by the California switch, but his margin was reduced and Mr. Nixon's prestige in his home state was strengthened.

The loss of California brought Mr. Kennedy's electoral total to 300.

[Senator Kennedy flew to Johnson City, Tex., Wednesday for a major policy conference at the ranch home of Vice President-elect Lyndon B. Johnson near-by. They will be joined by House Speaker Sam Rayburn.]

Los Angeles County, which had most of the remaining absentee votes, was giving Mr. Nixon a consistent edge of better than 63 per cent.

Los Angeles expects its absentee ballots to total about 80,000. About 200 observers from Republican and Democratic party organizations are watching the count.

Mr. Nixon has consistently

Continued on Page 28, Column 3

CLASH IN NEW ORLEANS: Policemen in motorcycle cars move in to help put down a demonstration against the admittance of Negro children to public schools in the city.

United Press International Telephoto

Governor Will Ask Rebate Of 10% on Taxes at Session

Special to The New York Times.

ALBANY, Nov. 16—Governor Rockefeller said today he would ask next year's Legislature to approve a 10 per cent rebate in 1960 personal income taxes. The Governor thus confirmed a proposal he made on June 14, when he said he would recommend a 10 per cent rebate if state revenues maintained their high levels.

A statement issued here today listed three factors that Mr. Rockefeller said made the rebate possible: savings achieved through greater efficiency and economy in the state government, increased tax collections as a result of the withholding system, and a relatively high level of business activity that produced more revenue than expected.

The state expects to have a surplus of about $120,000,000 when the fiscal year ends next March 31. Of that amount, $30,000,000 will go into the capital reserve fund. The tax refund proposed by the Governor will cost about $90,000,000.

Annual Message Due

Mr. Rockefeller said his recommendation would be included in his annual message to the Legislature, which convenes here Jan. 4. Taxpayers subject to withholding will receive their refunds after their 1960 personal income tax returns are processed, the Governor said. About 6,000,000 persons in the state file tax returns, which are due next April 15.

Senate Majority Leader Walter J. Mahoney said the Governor's recommendation would receive "most sympathetic consideration" from Republicans in the upper house. He added, however, that the Legislature would decide the amount and form of tax relief.

Most of the Republican Senators favor an across-the-board percentage cut, Mr. Mahoney said.

Last June 13, the day before Governor Rockefeller suggested the possibility of a tax refund, Republican Senators, meeting in New York City, adopted a resolution urging such relief. The resolution did not mention any specific plan.

Senator Mahoney advocated a tax cut at this year's session of the Legislature. When this failed, he blocked Governor

Continued on Page 31, Column 5

3 ON PORT BOARD TO BE PROSECUTED

But Celler Assails Justice Department Plan Not to Seek Indictments

By ANTHONY LEWIS

Special to The New York Times.

WASHINGTON, Nov. 16—The Department of Justice will proceed soon to prosecute three high officers of the Port of New York Authority for contempt of Congress.

The decision was disclosed today when a major dispute erupted between the department and Representative Emanuel Celler, Brooklyn Democrat, over the contempt cases. The controversy concerned the method that should be used to start the prosecutions.

Mr. Celler demanded that the department proceed by asking a grand jury to indict the three officials. But a Deputy Attorney General, Lawrence E. Walsh, decided instead to file an information which requires no action by a grand jury.

Refuse to Supply Data

The three Port Authority officers are S. Sloan Colt, the chairman; Austin J. Tobin, executive director, and Joseph G. Carty, secretary. In June they refused to supply records to a House Judiciary subcommittee, of which Mr. Celler is chairman. On Aug. 25 the House voted by large margins to cite all three for contempt.

Mr. Celler used strong language in denouncing Mr. Walsh and the department for its decision to proceed by information. He called it "preferential treatment" for the Port Authority officers and accused Mr. Walsh of "unwarranted intercession."

However, it was not immediately clear what, if any, significant difference it would make whether indictment or information was used.

Contribution Is Cited

The Constitution says that no person may be prosecuted in the Federal courts for a felony except by indictment. It also requires a grand jury indictment for any felony prosecution in the Federal courts unless the defendant waives the right to be indicted. Misdemeanors—crimes punishable by a year in jail or less—do not require indictment.

Contempt of Congress is a misdemeanor, punishable by a fine of not more than $1,000 and up to a year in jail. But there is a special statute that says that any contempt of Congress shall be reported to the "appropriate United States Attorney, whose duty it shall be to bring the matter before the grand jury for its action."

Representative Celler argued that this statute required initiation of a case by a grand jury through an indictment. He said the purpose of the law was "to remove all discretion from the United States Attorney," and he added:

"It was intended that deci-

Continued on Page 72, Column 6

POLICE HEAD RIPS P.B.A. CARD IN TWO

But Cassese Says Ouster Move Will Continue

By GUY PASSANT

In view of reporters and television cameras yesterday, Police Commissioner Stephen P. Kennedy tore up his membership card in the Patrolmen's Benevolent Association and dropped it into an ash tray.

"It seems to me that this whole business is somewhat ridiculous," he said with a smile.

"Does this mean that you are resigning from the P. B. A.?" he was asked.

"The act speaks for itself," he replied. "You can read into it any meaning you wish."

Later, with the two halves of the torn card taped back together, Commissioner Kennedy repeated his performance for television cameramen and photographers who had arrived late.

Patrolman John J. Cassese, president of the association, said that the group nevertheless would go ahead with a move to oust the Commissioner as a member.

"The Commissioner can do anything he wants with the card," Patrolman Cassese said. "That's his business.

"But, in keeping with the rules and by-laws of the association, and carrying out the mandate of the membership, he will be served with charges and specifications within a week, and at the next meeting he can plead his case.

"He will get a fair hearing at the next meeting. Of course he can lose by default."

On Tuesday night at a membership meeting in the base-

Continued on Page 32, Column 4

2,000 YOUTHS RIOT IN NEW ORLEANS

Police Arrest 50 and Subdue Anti-Integration Mobs—Fights Go On at Night

By CLAUDE SITTON

Special to The New York Times.

NEW ORLEANS, Nov. 16—Marauding youths surged through New Orleans streets today in demonstrations against school integration that were marked by sporadic rioting, assaults and vandalism.

An undetermined number of Negroes were attacked by whites and four were taken to hospitals. The police arrested more than fifty persons.

Estimates of the number who participated in the demonstrations ranged upward from 2,000. There was some property damage, mostly to automobiles, windows and neon signs.

The police used motorcycles and mounted patrolmen to clear the streets. When these measures proved ineffective, they brought up two fire trucks and turned hoses on the jeering demonstrators.

Violence Continues

The violence continued tonight, erupting in scattered areas of the city in attacks on one race by another. The police reported numerous incidents of Negroes throwing rocks, bricks and bottles at passing automobiles and buses.

A policeman at a district headquarters said that a number of Negro juveniles had been arrested for possession of "Molotov Cocktails"—bottles filled with gasoline and stoppered with cloth wicks.

Some 200 whites were reportedly halting cars outside a meeting called to organize a

Continued on Page 30, Column 3

Clark Gable Dies in Hollywood Of Heart Ailment at Age of 59

'King' of Film Capital Was One of Ten Top Boxoffice Attractions for Years

By The Associated Press.

HOLLYWOOD, Calif., Nov. 16—Clark Gable, for thirty years "king" of Hollywood actors, died tonight of a heart ailment that first struck him Nov. 6. He was 59 years old.

The film star died at 11 P. M. Pacific Coast Time (2 A. M. New York time) at Hollywood Presbyterian Hospital.

His wife, Kay, and his physician, Dr. Fred V. Cerini, were with him when he died.

Leader for Two Decades

As the "King of Hollywood" for more than two decades, Mr. Gable was one of the most popular actors in the world.

He held the affection of moviegoers longer than most other stars. For many years he was among the ten top boxoffice attractions. Theatre marquees would announce simply, "This week: Clark Gable."

To millions the tall, handsome man with the mustache, broad shoulders, brown hair and gray eyes was the symbol of masculinity, "naughty but nice."

He did not think he was a great actor. "I can't emote worth a damn," he said. "When I die they'll put on my tombstone, 'He was lucky—and he knew it.'"

When he was earning $7,500 a

Clark Gable

week he hung in his dressing room reminders of the days when he was a struggling actor or piling lumber in Oregon for $3.20 a day. Across the mementos he wrote: "Just to remind you, Gable."

There were many Gable legends. One was that in "It Happened One Night" (1934) he had sabotaged the undershirt industry overnight by peeling off his shirt in the picture and revealing nothing under his shirt but himself.

"I didn't know what I was do-

Continued on Page 37, Column 4

City to Bid Sinatra Testify on Cabarets

By LAYHMOND ROBINSON

Frank Sinatra and other star entertainers may testify in the city's widening investigation into charges of police corruption in the issuance of performers' cabaret permits.

This possibility arose yesterday when Investigation Commissioner Louis I. Kaplain said at a news conference that he intended to call in Mr. Sinatra and other entertainers if his search of nightclub records showed they had performed without permits from the city police.

Noting that Mr. Sinatra, who lives in California, was outside the jurisdiction of his office, Mr. Kaplan said: "I'll telephone him. I think he will respond. I think he's that public spirited."

The singer said through a spokesman on Tuesday that he

Continued on Page 32, Column 5

ALLIES AFFECTED

Impact to Hit Europe and Japan but Not Poorer Countries

By RICHARD E. MOONEY

Special to The New York Times.

WASHINGTON, Nov. 16—The principal impact of President Eisenhower's order to cut the Government's spending overseas will fall on Western Europe and Japan, officials said today.

Under-developed countries will feel it less, both by the nature of the measures that the President has ordered and by specific efforts to avoid hurting their economies.

The two biggest elements in the dramatic announcement from Augusta were the reduction of dependents overseas and the reduction of procurement abroad by the International Cooperation Administration.

In the case of dependents, more than half are in Europe and Japan. In the case of procurement, officials indicated that buying in under-developed lands would continue.

No Cuts Planned in Aid

Officials said no thought was being given to cutting foreign aid.

The President's directive allows for greater spending in instances in which purchases in this country would be more expensive than abroad.

At the Pentagon, officials said that the order on dependents would probably mean shorter overseas tours of duty for men who go abroad without their families and longer tours for those who go over with families. The details remain to be worked out by each of the military services.

Pentagon officials said the reduction in military dependents abroad would be accomplished largely by stopping new movements of families overseas, not by bringing home dependents already abroad.

The Army accounts for approximately half of the 484,000 overseas dependents of military men, the Air Force for 200,000 and the Navy and Marine Corps the remainder.

There are almost 200,000 dependents in West Germany, 100,000 in Britain, France, Spain and Italy combined, and 56,500 in Japan.

Thomas S. Gates Jr., the Secretary of Defense, dealt with the question of impact on morale in a statement saying: "Our people are accus-

Continued on Page 11, Column 2

Vote in France on Algeria Set for 1961 by de Gaulle

President Plans Referendum on Policy of Giving Moslems Choice of Links With Paris or Independence

By ROBERT C. DOTY

Special to The New York Times.

PARIS, Nov. 16—President de Gaulle will ask France to approve by referendum, probably early in January, his plans for letting the Algerians make their own choice between independence and continued association with France.

Formal announcement of the referendum plan after a Cabinet meeting today constituted a crossing of the Rubicon by the President, in the opinion of most observers here.

The forces opposing the President, here and in Algeria, in the name of continued French sovereignty thus were put on notice that unless they acted to block General de Gaulle's program before it obtained probably massive backing in metropolitan France they must resign themselves to defeat.

In political circles it was held that the next ten days would prove to be decisive. If the "activists" among the Europeans of Algiers plan a new insurrectional movement such as those in May, 1958, and January of this year, it will probably come to a climax in that period, according to this view.

In any new emergency, as in the previous two, the attitude of the French Army in Algeria probably would be decisive. Government circles in Paris were hopeful, if not confident, that the army as a whole would refuse to follow the minority of career officers that has made common cause with the dissident civilians in the past.

There were authoritative reports that up to 80 per cent of the officers were shocked and alarmed by General de Gaulle's Nov. 4 speech in which he fore-

Continued on Page 18, Column 2

HELP FOR DOLLAR

Directive of President Curtails Families of Troops by 284,000

Statement, directive and news conference, Page 10.

By FELIX BELAIR Jr.

Special to The New York Times.

AUGUSTA, Ga., Nov. 16—President Eisenhower ordered all Federal agencies today to cut their foreign spending to the bone to stem the increasing deficit in the United States' balance of payments and the consequent drain on the nation's gold reserves.

The President said the moves were necessary to prevent other nations from becoming fearful that the dollar was weakening.

It was estimated that his directives would save at least $1,000,000,000 a year. The balance-of-payments deficit is currently running at an annual rate of almost $3,800,000,000 and the President said it might reach $4,000,000,000.

A principal directive, which would produce almost half the total savings, provides a mandatory reduction in the total of dependents of military personnel abroad. General Eisenhower ordered the Secretary of Defense to reduce the dependents abroad from the current level of 484,000 to 200,000 at the rate of 15,000 a month, beginning Jan. 1.

C. I. A. Also Affected

The State Department, the Central Intelligence Agency and the International Cooperation Administration as well as the Defense Department were ordered to reduce civilian staffs wherever possible.

Referring to allied nations that have gained strength as a result of United States assistance, the President remarked: "We should insist that they carry their part of the economic programs and help to meet the payments which we find so burdensome."

To emphasize the importance he attached to the continued deficit in the nation's balance of international payments, President Eisenhower put in an unexpected appearance at the Richmond Hotel in downtown Augusta to talk with White House newsmen about his directives. The President is vacationing here.

At his news conference, summoned on half an hour's notice, the President hinted strongly that a reduction in troop

Continued on Page 10, Column 1

Congo Chief Seizes Ghanaian Diplomat As Figure in a Plot

By PAUL HOFMANN

Special to The New York Times.

LEOPOLDVILLE, the Congo, Nov. 16—Col. Joseph D. Mobutu's army regime disclosed today that it had arrested a secretary of the Ghanaian Embassy near the residence of Patrice Lumumba, deposed Premier.

The diplomat, it was stated, was found to have a considerable amount of money destined for Mr. Lumumba and documents concerning a projected invasion of secessionist Katanga Province by Lumumba forces.

[Meanwhile at the United Nations, the departure of a fifteen-nation conciliation committee for the Congo was postponed from Saturday until Tuesday in the hope that President Joseph Kasavubu could be persuaded to accept the committee.]

New Province Proposed

The name of the Ghanaian diplomat, who was detained last night, was given as Lovelace Mensah. He was held at Camp Leopold II, a military compound on the outskirts of the capital.

The alleged invasion plan was linked with the proposed establishment of a new Congolese province to be known as Lualaba after the Lualaba River in Katanga. The province would consist of the districts of Kamina, Albertville and Kolwezi, covering two-thirds of the province.

Manono is mentioned as the capital of the projected province. The Lualaba movement is promoted by a group of Lumumba followers headed by

Continued on Page 8, Column 1

U. S. TO REASSURE NATO ON ATOM USE

Plans to Tell Allies It Would Fight an Attack in Europe With Nuclear Weapons

By JACK RAYMOND

Special to The New York Times.

WASHINGTON, Nov. 16—The United States is planning to reassure the North Atlantic Treaty Organization that it will not hesitate to use nuclear weapons to fight aggression in Europe.

The belief that such reassurance is needed is understood to be the basis of United States proposals for a possible reorganization of the military structure of the Atlantic pact. This would include an international striking force armed with nuclear weapons and under NATO command.

By placing a nuclear striking force under command of the alliance, the United States would be sharing with the fourteen other members of the pact a veto power over a specific military unit. It would not be relinquishing its own veto. Nor would such an arrangement affect United States control of its own strategic forces.

Herter to Give Plan

Secretary of State Christian A. Herter, Secretary of Defense Thomas S. Gates and other officials will outline the United States proposals at the meeting of Atlantic pact ministers in Paris Dec. 16-18. The proposals will be part of a discussion of the organization's needs for the next ten years.

Secretary Gates said tonight that discussions were still going on in the Government on the position the United States would take. He said also that President Eisenhower had not finally reviewed all proposals.

West European sources have raised the question of whether the United States would go through with its plan to use nuclear weapons if United States soil was not under attack. The United States is not committed to use nuclear forces in Europe under any existing treaty.

The statements that the United States plans to make before the NATO meeting are being fashioned to deal with the suspicion that Washington

Continued on Page 4, Column 5

Churchill Suffers Back Injury in Fall

Special to The New York Times.

LONDON, Nov. 16—Sir Winston Churchill fell yesterday and broke a small bone in his back.

Anthony Montagu Brown, Sir Winston's secretary, said tonight "there is no cause for anxiety" after disclosing news of the injury. Sir Winston was described as "quite cheerful" and resting comfortably.

The former Prime Minister will have to remain in bed for some days, however. Sir Winston will be 86 years old Nov. 30. Since his return to London Oct. 25 from a vacation in the south of France he has appeared livelier than he had been for some time.

Lord Moran, who has been Sir Winston's personal physician since before World War II, visited his patient at his home at Hyde Park Gate this afternoon.

Continued on Page 6, Column 4

MAYOR QUESTIONS CITY TUITION PLAN

Wants Proof of Need to End Free Higher Education

Mayor Wagner declared yesterday that both he and the people of the city would have to be convinced of the "wisdom and necessity" of charging tuition and extending state supervision in the city's free municipal colleges.

These steps had been recommended Tuesday in a report to Governor Rockefeller by his three-man Committee on Higher Education, headed by Dr. Henry T. Heald, president of the Ford Foundation and a former chancellor of New York University.

The suggestion that tuition-free higher education be ended brought sharp protests from alumni groups and students at the city's colleges, and plans were announced to carry their opposition to Albany.

The Heald report, which called for a long-range program to revamp higher education in the state, proposed tuition "rebates" to students with limited incomes. It also urged state aid for all institutions of higher learning, public and private, including church-related colleges.

Mayor Wagner commended the proposal for a strengthened state university, "not the sprawling substitute for it that the Legislature gave to us a

Continued on Page 32, Column 6

NEWS INDEX

Clark Gable Dies in Hollywood Of Heart Ailment at Age of 59

Continued From Page 1, Col. 5

ing to the undershirt people," he recalled. "That was just the way I lived. I hadn't worn an undershirt since I started to school."

Some said that his ears had been pinned back when he became a star. His reply: "Never." Early in his career, however, he was turned down by one top studio. He quoted an executive as saying: "Gable won't do. Look at his big ears." The executive later hired him.

Associated Press

Clark Gable

A Native of Ohio

William Clark Gable (he dropped his first name after he entered the theatre) was born in Cadiz, Ohio, on Feb. 1, 1901. His father was an oil contractor. His mother died before he was 1 year old.

At 15, after his father had remarried, the family moved to Ravenna, Ohio. His father quit oil drilling for farming. Young Gable forked hay and fed hogs wanted to be a physician.

With a friend he went to Akron. While taking premedical courses in the evening he worked for a tire company molding treads on tires. He saw his first play and decided to be an actor. He got a job as a callboy at a theatre—running errands and doing assorted jobs. He received no salary—just tips.

At 16, after his stepmother died, he and his father went to the Oklahoma oil fields. After working as a tool dresser, he got a job with a troupe that played everything from "Uncle Tom's Cabin" to "Her False Step."

When the company closed in Montana, he took a freight train to Oregon. He worked in a lumber company, sold neckties, and was a telephone company linesman.

In 1924 Mr. Gable joined a theatre company in Portland. He made his first appearance on the screen in a silent film starring Pola Negri. He appeared in two Los Angeles stage productions and then headed for Broadway.

Portrayer of Villains

In three years, he portrayed mostly villains. Then he returned to Los Angeles, where was a hit in the role of Killer Mears in "The Last Mile."

This led to a movie role again as a heavy, in "The Painted Desert," with William Boyd for Pathé in 1930. The story is that Mr. Gable was interviewed and asked if he could ride a horse. He said he could, and got the job; then he went out and learned how to ride.

His effort won him a contract with Metro-Goldwyn-Mayer. He first became a leading man in "Dance, Fools, Dance," with Joan Crawford. His first big hit was "A Free Soul," in which he slapped Norma Shearer.

Women by the thousands wrote in that they, too, would like to be slapped around by Mr. Gable. "For two years I pulled guns on people or hit women in the face," he later recalled.

He was a workhorse. His pictures included "Hell Divers," "Susan Lennox," Polly of the Circus," "Strange Interlude," "Red Dust," "No Man of Her Own," "The White Sister," "Hold Your Man," "Night Flight," and "Dancing Lady."

Mr. Gable's roster of leading ladies included Greta Garbo, Jean Harlow, Carole Lombard and Helen Hayes.

In 1934, overwork led to his being hospitalized. M-G-M decided he was evading a picture. When he got out, he was sent to Columbia Pictures on loan, supposedly as a punishment.

Won Oscar in Columbia Film

Columbia starred him in a comedy—"It Happened One Night." Claudette Colbert played a runaway heiress, and Mr. Gable a newspaperman, traveling by bus from Miami to New York. Both won Academy Awards for the best performances of the year.

Mr. Gable had broken out of a type-casting rut.

The next year, he played Fletcher Christian in "Mutiny on the Bounty," which won an Academy Award as the best film of the year.

In the next seven years, Mr. Gable appeared in more than twenty-five films, including "China Seas," "San Francisco," "Saratoga," "Test Pilot," "Idiot's Delight," "Gone With the Wind," "Boom Town," "They Met in Bombay" and "Somewhere I'll Find You."

From 1932 through 1943, he was listed among the first ten money-making stars in the yearly surveys by The Motion Picture Herald. After time out for military duty, he regained that ranking in 1947, 1948, 1949 and 1955.

Observers believe his films have grossed more than $100,000,000, including $50,000,000 for "Gone With The Wind". He had roles in at least sixty pictures.

After his third wife, Miss Lombard, was killed in a plane crash during a bond tour in World War II in 1942, Mr. Gable enlisted in the Army Air Forces as a private. He was then 41.

He rose to major, took part in several hazardous bomber missions over Europe, filmed a combat movie on aerial gunnery and won the Distinguished Flying Cross and the Air Medal.

Metro Hails Veteran's Return

After the war, he returned to Hollywood, and a Metro slogan, "Gable is back and Garson's got him" spread across the country. He starred with Greer Garson in "Adventure."

Then followed such films as "The Hucksters," "Mogambo," "The King and Four Queens," "The Tall Men," "Soldier of Fortune," "Teacher's Pet," "Run Silent, Run Deep," and "But Not for Me." He had been a freelancer since leaving Metro in 1954.

"It Started in Naples," a comedy with Mr. Gable and Sophia Loren, opened in New York in September, 1960. The film concentrated on the voluptuous attractions of Miss Loren, and a review in The New York Times said "the screen play has him shaded from the outset."

In July, 1960, Mr. Gable had begun work with Marilyn Monroe on "The Misfits." The film, reportedly budgeted at $3,500,000, was interrupted when Miss Monroe became ill five weeks later, but resumed in the fall.

Mr. Gable married five times. His first two marriages — to Josephine Dillon and Rhea Langham—ended in divorces in 1930 and 1939. Mr. Gable next married Miss Lombard. His fourth marriage, to the former Lady Sylvia Ashley, resulted in divorce in 1952.

In 1955, he married Mrs. Kay Williams Spreckels, former model and screen actress. Last Sept. 30, Mr. Gable announced that she was to have a child in the spring making Mr. Gable a father for the first time. She had had two children by her marriage to Adolph Spreckels 2d.

Hollywood Mourns Death of Veteran Star at 59— Colleagues Pay Tribute

HOLLYWOOD, Calif., Nov. 17 (AP)—A private funeral service for Clark Gable will be held at 9 A. M. Saturday in the Church of the Recesional at Forest Lawn Memorial Park in near-by Glendale. The veteran star died last night of a heart attack in Hollywood Presbyterian Hospital. He was 59 years old.

As the movie world mourned one of its most popular figures, tributes to Mr. Gable began arriving from fellow actors and colleagues in the film industry. Among them were:

Joseph R. Vogel, president of Metro-Goldwyn-Mayer, to which Mr. Gable was under contract for twenty-three years—"In a sense Gable and the studio reached success together. His contributions to motion pictures and the happiness he gave to millions of moviegoers throughout the world as one of the screen's greatest stars can never be estimated. Clark Gable was a star as a human being as well as of films."

Gary Cooper—"He had a fine career and did well with his life. He was a fine representative of Hollywood and all of us were proud to know him."

Marilyn Monroe, Mr. Gable's last leading lady—"He was an excellent guy to work with and a decent human being. I have sent by regrets to his wife."

John Wayne—"He was one who brought great stature to our industry. Grief at his death will be universal."

Vivien Leigh, Mr. Gable's co-star in "Gone With The Wind" —"I heard the terrible news this morning, and I was sadder than I can tell."

In London, United States Ambassador John Hay Whitney said:

"I am saddened by the news of my friend Clark Gable's death. To me he will always be Rhett Butler of 'Gone With the Wind.' For this is the way he was: kind, considerate, with powerful charm and truly modest—everybody's gentleman."

Gable appeared for the last time without a mustache when he starred as Fletcher Christian in *Mutiny on the Bounty* in 1935.

Clark Gable and Claudette Colbert in a scene from *It Happened One Night*, for which they both won Academy Awards.

Clark Gable as Rhett Butler and Vivian Leigh as Scarlett O'Hara in *Gone With the Wind.*

"All the News That's Fit to Print"

The New York Times.

LATE CITY EDITION
Increasing cloudiness, cold today. Snow, not so cold tomorrow.
Temperature Range Today—Max., 18; Min., 0
Temperatures Yesterday—Max., 24; Min., 5.5
Full U. S. Weather Bureau Report, Page 31

VOL. XCVII No. 32,879. Entered as Second-Class Matter, Postoffice, New York, N. Y. NEW YORK, SATURDAY, JANUARY 31, 1948. THREE CENTS IN NEW YORK CITY

MANY HOMES WITHOUT HEAT AS ZERO COLD IS DUE HERE; U. S. CUTS OIL EXPORTS 18½%

FUEL CRISIS GROWS

Hundreds of Families Reported Suffering in City Area

BAY STATE SEIZES PLANT

Bradford Acts When Walkout Threatens Boston Gas—Oil Diversion Denied Here

By WILL LISSNER

Hundreds of families in the city were reported by their landlords to be in cold homes for lack of fuel oil last night as temperatures dropped toward zero in Manhattan and toward subzero levels in the suburbs.

At 3 A. M. today the temperature dropped to 2.2 degrees, establishing a new low record for the season. The previous record was 5 degrees, registered last Saturday.

The winter's coldest weather gripped not only New York but the whole Northwest. The Midwest and South, however, got some relief yesterday from the protracted cold spell. The fuel situation was reported acute in many cities throughout the East.

Temperatures, after falling to points between zero and 5 degrees above in Manhattan and zero and 10 degrees below in the suburbs, are expected to rise today to 20 degrees. The cold is due to continue, according to the United States Weather Bureau, but whereas yesterday was sunny, increasing cloudiness was expected today. More snow is threatened tomorrow. The lowest temperature yesterday was 5.5 degrees at 9:50 A. M.

Yesterday's hourly temperatures were:

1 A. M.	23	2 P. M.	12
2 A. M.	23	3 P. M.	15
3 A. M.	22	4 P. M.	14
4 A. M.	18	5 P. M.	12
5 A. M.	13	6 P. M.	12
6 A. M.	9	7 P. M.	11
7 A. M.	8	8 P. M.	9
8 A. M.	7	9 P. M.	8
9 A. M.	6	10 P. M.	7
9:50 A. M.	5.5	11 P. M.	7
10 A. M.	6	12 M.	6
11 A. M.	7	1 A. M.	5
Noon	9	2 A. M.	4
1 P. M.	10	3 A. M.	2.2

Petroleum Exports Cut

As the fuel shortage produced critical conditions for many apartment and home owners in this and other cities, officials took steps to relieve the situation.

The Commerce Department announced in Washington that it had ordered exports of petroleum products cut 18½ per cent from 11,850,000 to 9,650,000 barrels during the first quarter of the year. Oil exports to Japan and the Ryukyus were cut from 1,600,000 barrels to 100,000. Exports will be allowed only from areas where fuel can be spared best, the department said.

In Massachusetts Gov. Robert F. Bradford ordered the seizure of a gas plant in Everett where a walkout of 900 workers was threatened that would have affected service to sixty-four hospitals and 1,500,000 residents of Greater Boston. After seizure and issuance of a temporary injunction, union leaders ordered their followers to remain at work.

In Tennessee, Governor James McCord proclaimed a state of emergency and announced a voluntary fuel conservation program.

In Rochester, Sheriff's deputies and city policemen were organized to make emergency deliveries of fuel oil in extreme cases.

In Endicott, Mayor E. Raymond Lee declared an emergency due to the gas shortage and urged residents to conserve fuel. Many homes there and in Binghamton and Johnson City were without heat and residents sought emergency shelter.

Philadelphians Warned

Residents of Philadelphia were warned of a gas shortage caused by the oil shortage and were urged to restrict use of gas to the absolute minimum.

Police Commissioner Arthur W. Wallander of this city, regional fuel coordinator, sent telegrams asking eighty-six terminal dealers here to remain open today and tomorrow, because of the expected severe cold, to supply fuel oil to hardship cases.

Mayor O'Dwyer declared during the afternoon that it was not necessary at this time to proclaim a state of emergency and to divert

Continued on Page 12, Column 5

Petroleum Shipment Abroad Is Curbed to Ease Shortage

Department of Commerce Orders Quotas Reduced From 11,850,000 to 9,650,000 Barrels for Quarter—Slashes Japan

Special to The New York Times.

WASHINGTON, Jan. 30—The Department of Commerce announced today that "in view of the serious shortage of fuel oils," in this country it had ordered an 18½ per cent cut in exports of petroleum products during the first quarter of this year. Its action will reduce from 11,850,000 to 9,650,000 the barrels of petroleum designated for overseas.

The Department also announced that it would limit licenses for export of petroleum products to shipments for those areas of the United States where the fuel can best be spared during the emergency.

In addition, it was disclosed that a separate quota of gas oil and distillate fuel oil had been established for the first quarter for shipments to Japan and the Ryukyus, drastically cutting their supply from 1,600,000 barrels to 100,000. The Department said that the difference would be met from oil producing areas outside the United States.

Proposals had been made in Congress to stop all shipments abroad except those going to American military forces. Bills designed to accomplish this end have been introduced in the House and the Senate.

Walter S. Hallanan, chairman of the National Petroleum Council, said today that the petroleum industry had taken "prompt and forthright action to alleviate the shortages of some petroleum products which have been rendered acute in certain sections by the severe cold weather." The industry "takes pride in the fact that it was the first to develop a voluntary agreement under the recent authorization of Congress," he added.

Canada Is Not Affected

WASHINGTON, Jan. 30 (AP)—The action today of the Depart-

Continued on Page 11, Column 4

Hope Wanes in Sea Search For 28 Aboard Lost Airliner

By FREDERICK GRAHAM

The Atlantic area northeast of Bermuda was being searched last night for survivors of a British South American Airways plane that disappeared in the area early yesterday morning with a crew of six and at least twenty-two passengers, but hope had almost been abandoned.

The thirty-two-passenger plane, which listed among those aboard Air Marshal Sir Arthur Coningham, Royal Air Force, who commanded the Second Tactical Air Force of the Allies at the invasion of Normandy, was out of London and on the Azores-to-Bermuda leg of the flight when last heard from about 1 A. M. (EST) yesterday.

At least fifteen United States Air Force, Navy and Coast Guard planes plus three Coast Guard cutters, two commercial steamers and a British South American Airways plane worked over a large area about 400 miles northeast of Bermuda without success. More aircraft are scheduled to continue the search today.

The plane, a converted Lancaster bomber of the type used by the RAF for saturation bombing of Germany, had stopped in Santa Maria in the Azores to refuel. An Associated Press dispatch from Bermuda said the plane, believed to have been commanded by Capt. David Colby, radioed to Bermuda that it would arrive there at midnight Thursday, an hour and a half late. One hour later it reported to Bermuda again, saying it was 440 miles northeast of Bermuda, that there was a moderate sea swell and that it was bucking strong headwinds. Nothing more has been heard from the plane.

The only other report that might

Continued on Page 10, Column 2

ORVILLE WRIGHT, 76, IS DEAD IN DAYTON

Co-Inventor With His Brother, Wilbur, of the Airplane Was Pilot in First Flight

Special to The New York Times

DAYTON, Ohio, Jan. 30—Orville Wright, who with his brother, the late Wilbur Wright, invented the airplane, died here tonight at 10:40 in Miami Valley Hospital. He was 76 years old.

Mr. Wright, who had been confined to a hospital in October, collapsed in his office on Tuesday. He was suffering from lung congestion and coronary arteriosclerosis.

At the bedside when Mr. Wright died were Horace A. Wright, a nephew; Mrs. H. S. Miller, a niece, and Delyle Myers, a nurse.

The announcement of his death was made by Dr. A. B. Brower, family physician.

Engrossing Amusement

In the early fall of 1900 fishermen and Coast Guardsmen dwelling on that lonely and desolated spot of sand dividing Albemarle Sound from the Atlantic Ocean on the coast of North Carolina called

Continued on Page 12, Column 2

Arms Get Atomic Energy Priority In Policy Set by Congress Group

By WILLIAM S. WHITE
Special to The New York Times.

WASHINGTON, Jan. 30—The Joint Committee on Atomic Energy laid down today a firm policy that the production of atomic weapons, rather than work on peacetime applications of atomic energy, must be the "vital business" of the United States for the foreseeable future.

It declared also that "uninterrupted operation" of the "critical," or military, facilities of the Atomic Energy Commission was so essential to national security that an investigation was in motion to find a formula to assure "continuity of work" under all labor eventualities.

In its first report to Congress, the committee indicated some dissatisfaction "in a number of cases" with certain aspects of the handling of internal security within the personnel of the Atomic Energy Commission.

"In certain of these cases," the report went on, "the committee has requested that the commission outline in detail its security policy as applied to these specific instances."

"In the majority of these cases," it was added, the men in question had been employed while atomic energy still was under Army control.

As to the essential policy to be followed in atomic development, the committee declared:

"Until such time as an effective, enforceable and reliable program for the international control of atomic energy is in successful operation, the most vital business of the Atomic Energy Commission must be the meeting of the atomic requirements of national defense.

"The joint committee has been assured that those charged with these responsibilities are keenly aware thereof. This phase of the atomic energy program is of para-

Continued on Page 4, Column 5

Record 799-Million Budget Is Asked by Dewey for State

He Estimates Actual Outlay at 753 Millions for Next Fiscal Year, but Says No Rise in Taxes Is Needed—Warns on Inflation

By LEO EGAN
Special to The New York Times.

ALBANY, Jan. 30—Governor Dewey submitted another record-breaking budget to the Legislature tonight, calling for appropriations of $799,600,000, including deficiencies for the current year, but estimating expenditures in the new budget year at a figure of $753,500,000. The Governor regards the lower figure as his "budget" total.

Appropriations recommended are $128,200,000 higher than those carried in last year's budget message but, because of supplemental grants for teacher pay, veterans' housing, college housing, central schools and rent control, only $53,400,000 higher than actual appropriations, which were $746,200,000.

The expenditures of $753,500,000 contemplated in Mr. Dewey's message compare with an actual total of $707,500,000 in the current year, according to revised estimates. The revised figure reflects increased relief contributions and higher food prices for inmates of state institutions which are being provided for in deficiency appropriations.

Allowing for continuance of the reductions made in 1946, which he recommended, the Governor estimated that existing regular taxes would produce $758,600,000 in the new budget year, enough to balance expenditures and leave a $5,000,000 surplus.

The regular tax structure does not include the additional one-cent-a-package levy on cigarettes or the 20 per cent increase in existing income tax rates which were voted to finance the $400,000,000 veterans' bonus. If the present return from these special levies continued, Mr. Dewey said, the bonus bonds might be retired in eight or

Continued on Page 9, Column 1

Text of Gov. Dewey's budget message will be found on pages 8 and 9.

REALTY VALUATIONS RISE $745,775,468 IN CITY FOR 1948-49

Higher Accrued Value Is Chief Factor in $17,684,240,921 Total, Biggest Since '33

By LEE E. COOPER

New York's land and buildings, regarded as the richest segment of real estate in the world, have risen in value to $17,684,240,921 on the city's tax books for the coming fiscal year.

Municipal assessors have chalked up a tentative increase of $745,775,468 over current figures on taxable properties for the year beginning July 1, 1948, to carry the aggregate valuations to the highest level since 1933.

A report submitted to Mayor O'Dwyer yesterday by Harry B. Chambers, president of the Tax Commission, showed an average rise of about 4½ per cent for the five boroughs, accounted for largely by an upswing in "accrued value" rather than by addition of new construction to the assessment rolls.

The report set the following ten-

Continued on Page 11, Column 3

GOP GROUP SHAPES SHARP ERP REVISION WITH FUND REDUCED

A Proposal to Sell U. S. Goods to Latin America for Food for Europe Wins Favor

By FELIX BELAIR Jr.
Special to The New York Times.

WASHINGTON, Jan. 30—A fighting nucleus of eighteen Senate Republicans agreed late tonight to press for important changes in the Administration's European Recovery Program as the party's legislative leaders brushed aside President Truman's demand for approval of the full $6,800,000,000 asked for the first fifteen months of operations.

The group of eighteen Senators, in which Westerners predominated, called for a complete shift in emphasis of the Marshall Plan "from the underwriting of trade deficits to the support of specific production programs" in which financial aid would be contingent on increased output of food, coal, steel and transportation facilities.

Senator Joseph H. Ball of Minnesota said the principles agreed

Continued on Page 6, Column 2

World News Summarized

SATURDAY, JANUARY 31, 1948

Mohandas K. Gandhi, 78-year-old spiritual leader of hundreds of millions of Indians, was shot in New Delhi yesterday as he walked toward a pergola to lead 1,000 of his followers in evening prayer. He died twenty-five minutes later. His assassin, a Hindu, was seized after he had fired three quick shots into the frail leader, who only recently had ended a hunger strike in protest against communal strife. [1:8.]

News of the tragedy shocked the world. In Bombay, it ignited a new outburst of rioting. [2:3.] United Nations officials at Lake Success feared this might be the beginning of a new wave of violence throughout India. [2:4-5.] President Truman said the whole world would mourn and expressed hope that the assassination would "not retard the peace of India and the world." [2:1.] Similar expressions of regret were voiced in London, where the King and the Queen and Prime Minister Attlee were among the many leaders to pay tribute to Mr. Gandhi. [1:6-7.]

The French National Assembly approved, 308 to 242, the Government's program to establish a free gold market and to allow Frenchmen to repatriate foreign assets by paying a tax. The Socialists reversed their previous stand and voted for the program. [1:6-7.]

Two recent Russian notes protesting the reopening for American use of an airfield in Tripolitania and the presence of American naval craft in Italian ports will be rejected by the State Department. [6:5.] The Navy announced that another 1,000 marines would go to the Mediterranean soon to replace an equal number now serving in that area. [6:4-5.]

The United States consulate in Jerusalem declared American citizens participating in the fighting would lose their passports and right to protection. [1:7.] Britain announced at Lake Success before the Palestine Commission that she could not allow the formation of any armed militia in Palestine before her mandate ends. [4:3.]

In Washington a group of eighteen Senate Republicans urged a change in the European Recovery Program to support specific production goals and brushed aside the Administration's request for approval of the full initial fund of $6,800,000,000. [1:5.]

An 18½ per cent reduction in exports of petroleum products was ordered by the Commerce Department "in view of the serious shortage" of oil in this country. [1:2-3.]

Also in Washington, the Joint Committee on Atomic Energy declared this nation must concentrate for the foreseeable future on the "uninterrupted" production of atomic weapons in preference to the peaceful utilization of atomic energy. [1:2-3.]

Governor Dewey asked the Legislature to appropriate $799,600,000 as he submitted another record-breaking budget. Appropriations last year totaled $746,200,000. [1:4-5.]

Winter's coldest weather hit the metropolitan area, with the thermometer hovering near zero in the city. In the suburbs the temperature was expected to fall to sub-zero levels during the night. Some homes suffered from a shortage of fuel oil. [1:1.]

A thirty-two passenger British plane was feared lost on its way to Bermuda. [1:2-3.]

Orville Wright, air pioneer, died in Dayton, Ohio, at 76. [1:2.]

GANDHI IS KILLED BY A HINDU; INDIA SHAKEN, WORLD MOURNS; 15 DIE IN RIOTING IN BOMBAY

MOHANDAS K. GANDHI
The New York Times

THREE SHOTS FIRED

Slayer Is Seized, Beaten After Felling Victim on Way to Prayer

DOMINION IS BEWILDERED

Nehru Appeals to the Nation to Keep Peace—U. S. Consul Assisted in Capture

By ROBERT TRUMBULL
Special to The New York Times.

NEW DELHI, India, Jan. 30—Mohandas K. Gandhi was killed by an assassin's bullet today. The assassin was a Hindu who fired three shots from a pistol at a range of three feet.

The 78-year-old Gandhi, who was the one person who held discordant elements together and kept some sort of unity in this turbulent land, was shot down at 5:15 P. M. as he was proceeding through the Birla House gardens to the pergola from which he was to deliver his daily prayer meeting message.

The assassin was immediately seized.

He later identified himself as Nathuran Vinayak Godse, 36, a Hindu of the Mahratta tribes in Poona. This has been a center of resistance to Gandhi's ideology.

Mr. Gandhi died twenty-five minutes later. His death left all India stunned and bewildered as to the direction that this newly independent nation would take without its "Mahatma" (Great Teacher).

The loss of Mr. Gandhi brings this country of 300,000,000 abruptly to a crossroads. Mingled with the sadness in this capital tonight was an undercurrent of fear and uncertainty, for now the strongest influence for peace in India that this generation has known is gone.

[Communal riots quickly swept Bombay when news of Mr. Gandhi's death was received. The Associated Press reported that fifteen persons were killed and more than fifty injured before an uneasy peace was established.]

Appeal Made By Nehru

Prime Minister Pandit Jawaharlal Nehru, in a voice choked with emotion, appealed in a radio address tonight for a sane approach to the future. He asked that India's path be turned away from violence in memory of the great peacemaker who had departed.

Mr. Gandhi's body will be cremated in the orthodox Hindu fashion according to his often expressed wishes. His body will be carried from his New Delhi residence on a simple wooden cot covered with a sheet at 11:30 tomorrow morning. The funeral procession will wind through every principal street of the two cities of New and Old Delhi and reach the burning ghats on the bank of the sacred Jumna River at about 4 P. M. There the remains of the greatest Indian since Gautama Buddha will be wrapped in a sheet, laid on a pyre of wood and burned. His ashes will be scattered on the Jumna's waters, eventually to mingle with the Ganges where the two holy rivers meet at the temple city of Allahabad.

These simple ceremonies were announced tonight by Pandit Nehru in respect to Mr. Gandhi's wishes, although many of the leaders desired that his body be embalmed and exhibited in state. India will see the last of Mr. Gandhi as it saw him when he lived—a humble and unassuming Hindu.

News Spreads Quickly

News of the assassination of Mr. Gandhi—only a few days after he had finished a five-day fast to bring about communal friendship—spread quickly through New Delhi. Immediately there was spontaneous movement of thousands to Birla House, home of G. D. Birla, the millionaire industrialist, where Mr. Gandhi and his six secretaries had been guests since he came to New Delhi in the midst of the disturbances in India's capital.

While walking through the gardens to this evening's prayer meeting Mr. Gandhi had just reached the top of a short flight of brick steps, his slender brown arms

Continued on Page 3, Column 6

All Britain Honors Gandhi; Truman Deplores Tragedy

By HERBERT L. MATTHEWS
Special to The New York Times.

LONDON, Jan. 30—Mohandas K. Gandhi, in death, has won the unanimous tribute of Britons—something he never hoped for or expected during his life. Nowhere outside of India has the shock of his assassination contained the feelings and emotions evident here today because Britain and Mr. Gandhi have been linked for good or evil over the last forty years.

In a special broadcast to the British people tonight the Prime Minister said:

"The voice which pleaded for peace and brotherhood has been silenced, but I am certain that his spirit will continue to animate his fellow countrymen and will plead for peace and concord."

[President Truman and Secretary Marshall expressed their grief and condolences in messages to India. Members of Congress were apprehensive. Leaders of many other lands joined in paying tribute and in deploring the manner of Mr. Gandhi's death.]

The sincerity of today's expressions of regret, which came from the King and Queen, the Prime Minister, the political parties—even the Communist—and from many humble Londoners who filed silently into India House this afternoon to pay tribute, cannot be doubted.

Those many quarrels when Mr. Gandhi fought with his passive resistance against the imperial power of Britain are truly things of the past. Mr. Gandhi himself paid high tribute to Britain for her policy of freeing India and of trying to help to keep the two dominions at peace with each other.

The British, on their side, have

Continued on Page 2, Column 2

U. S. WARNS CITIZENS IN PALESTINE FIGHT

Consulate General Says They Face Loss of Passports and All Protective Rights

By SAM POPE BREWER
Special to The New York Times.

JERUSALEM, Jan. 30—United States citizens fighting in the armed services of the Jews or the Arabs will lose their passports and their right to protection, the United States Consulate General warned Americans in Palestine tonight. Furthermore, naturalized citizens, it was said, would lose their American nationality if they fought for a foreign power.

[Zionist hopes for getting United Nations help in arming a Jewish militia in Palestine were dimmed by the statement of Sir Alexander Cadogan, chief British representative, that the British Government would not allow formation of such forces before the end of the mandate.]

The consular warning is being twisted by Arab sources into a promise that those fighting for the Jews may have their passports back when the fighting ends. The relevant passage reads: "American passports valid only for direct

Continued on Page 4, Column 4

France Votes Free Gold Market, Legalizes Hidden Assets by a Tax

By HAROLD CALLENDER
Special to The New York Times.

PARIS, Jan. 30—Parliamentary sanction was given today for the Government's devaluation of the franc and its accompanying monetary policy.

By a vote of 308 to 242, the National Assembly passed the Government's bill to create a free gold market and to legalize the hitherto illegal possession of foreign securities held by Frenchmen, if those assets were repatriated and the owners paid a special tax of 25 per cent of the assets' value.

As a comparatively free market in dollars had already been established by decree—although its opening was delayed by the freezing of bank notes of 5,000 francs—today's vote by the Assembly completed the series of measures framed by the Government to derive maximum benefit from devaluation by getting possession of privately owned foreign securities and hoarded gold.

Estimates of the total of these illegal securities have been in the neighborhood of $300,000,000 in the United States alone, while official guesses have placed the value of the hidden gold in France at $2,000,000,000.

Apparently placated by the freezing of the bank notes, the Socialists once again switched their position and voted today for the gold market bill, which they had opposed bitterly Wednesday, although their Ministers had apparently accepted it in the Cabinet meeting last Saturday. They were not reluctant to switch, for they did not desire to upset the Government and wreck the "Third Force," hostile though they were to the Government's departure from a planned economy.

The freezing measure, taken when the Socialists had precipitated a Cabinet crisis by balking at the gold market, was considered mainly a political move. But René Mayer, Finance Minister, told the

Continued on Page 5, Column 2

GANDHI IS KILLED BY A HINDU YOUTH

Continued From Page 1

around the shoulders of his granddaughters, Manu, 17, and Ava, 20.

Someone spoke to him and he turned from his granddaughters and gave the appealing Hindu salute—palms together and the points of the fingers brought to the chin as in a Christian attitude of prayer.

At once a youngish Indian stepped from the crowd—which had opened to form a pathway for Mr. Gandhi's walk to the pergola—and fired the fatal shots from a European-made pistol. One bullet struck Mr. Gandhi in the chest and two in the abdomen on the right side. He seemed to lean forward and then crumpled to the ground. His two granddaughters fell beside him in tears.

Crowd Is Stunned

A crowd of about 500, according to witnesses, was stunned. There was no outcry or excitement for a second or two. Then the onlookers began to push the assassin more as if in bewilderment than in anger.

The assassin was seized by Tom Reiner of Lancaster, Mass., a vice consul attached to the American Embassy and a recent arrival in India. He was attending Mr. Gandhi's prayer meeting out of curiosity, as most visitors to New Delhi do at least once.

Mr. Reiner grasped the assailant by the shoulders and shoved him toward several police guards. Only then did the crowd begin to grasp what had happened and a forest of fists belabored the assassin as he was dragged toward the pergola where Mr. Gandhi was to have prayed. He left a trail of blood.

Mr. Gandhi was picked up by attendants and carried rapidly back to the unpretentious bedroom where he had passed most of his working and sleeping hours. As he was taken through the door Hindu onlookers who could see him began to wail and beat their breasts.

Less than half an hour later a member of Mr. Gandhi's entourage came out of the room and said to those about the door:

"Bapu (father) is finished."

But it was not until Mr. Gandhi's death was announced by All India Radio at 6 P. M. that the word spread widely.

Assassin Taken Away

Meanwhile the assassin was taken to a police station. He identified himself as coming from Poona.

It was remarked that the first of three attempts on Mr. Gandhi's life was made in Poona on June 25, 1934, when a bomb was thrown at a car believed to be Mr. Gandhi's. Poona is a center of the extremist anti-Gandhi orthodox Hindu Mahasabha (Great Society).

The second possible attempt to assassinate Mr. Gandhi was by means of a crude bomb planted on his garden wall on Jan. 20 of this year.

The only statement known to have been made by the assassin was his remark to a foreign correspondent: "I am not at all sorry."

He is large for a Hindu and was dressed in gray slacks, blue pullover and khaki bush jacket. His pistol, which was snatched from him immediately after the shooting by Royal Indian Air Force Flight Sergeant D. R. Singh, contained four undischarged cartridges.

Lying on a wooden cot in his bedroom, Mr. Gandhi said no word before his death except once to ask for water. Most of the time he was unconscious. When he was pronounced dead by his physician weeping members of his staff covered the lower half of his face with a sheet in the Hindu fashion and the women present sat on the floor and chanted verses from the sacred scriptures of the Hindus. Those who could see these ceremonies through the windows knew then that Mr. Gandhi had expired.

Pandit Nehru arrived at about 6 o'clock. Silently and with burning eyes he inspected the spot where Mr. Gandhi was shot and then went into the house without a word. Later he stood high on the front gate of Birla House and related the tentative funeral arrangements to several thousand persons gathered in the street and blocking all traffic. His voice shook with grief and hundreds in the crowd were weeping uncontrollably.

Several thousand mourners formed orderly and quiet queues at all doors leading into Birla House and for a time they were permitted to file past the body. Later when it became evident that only a small fraction of the gathering would be able to view Mr. Gandhi's remains tonight, the body was taken to a second-floor balcony and placed on a cot tilted under a floodlamp so all in the grounds would see their departed leader.

His head was illuminated by a lamp with five wicks representing the five elements—air, light, water, earth and fire—and also to light his soul to eternity according to Hindu belief.

Pandit Nehru delivered Mr. Gandhi's valedictory in his radio address late this evening. In a quivering voice he said:

"Gandhi has gone out of our lives and there is darkness everywhere. * * * The father of our nation is no more—no longer will we run to him for advice and solace. * * * This is a terrible blow to millions and millions in this country. * * *

"Our light has gone out, but the light that shone in this country was no ordinary light. For a thousand years that light will be seen in this country and the world will see it * * * Oh, that this has happened to us! There was so much more to do."

Referring to the assassin Pandit Nehru said:

"I can only call him a madman."

He pleaded for a renewed spirit of peace, which had been Mr. Gandhi's last project, saying:

"His spirit looks upon us—nothing would displease him more than to see us indulge in violence. All our petty conflicts and difficulties must be ended in the face of this great disaster * * * In his death he has reminded us of the big things in life."

Enmity Incurred

Mr. Gandhi's pleas for tolerance since the far-reaching communal warfare of last August and September had earned him the enmity of extremist elements, notably the Hindu Mahasabha which condemned his fast for inter-religious unity and whose leaders refused to sign his peace pledge. There was also a widespread condemnation of Mr. Gandhi's forgiving attitude among the refugees who had suffered deeply at Moslem hands in the West Punjab.

More serious to India perhaps than loss of Mr. Gandhi's restraining influence on fanatic passions may be the political implications of his death. Though he held no office he was the central figure of India's dominant Congress party and the last of the "old guard" in the long struggle for liberation from foreign rule.

Some Indian observers were predicting tonight that Mr. Gandhi's death would inevitably be followed by a fission in the Congress party and the emergence of a new political pattern after a period of deep confusion.

ALL BRITONS UNITE TO ACCLAIM GANDHI

Continued From Page 1

been full of admiration for Mr. Gandhi's successful efforts at Calcutta and recently at Delhi to bring about a better communal feeling through fasting.

That is why the tributes come first and they mean what they say. They are tributes to the character and career of Mr. Gandhi but almost all of them express the fervent hope that his death will lead to a sense of common Hindu-Moslem loss and will bring a reaction of a favorable nature to soothe communal feeling.

There was a frank sigh of relief when it was learned that the assassin was a Hindu, not a Moslem. It is realized that before the common people everywhere get to understand this fact there is going to be some trouble but it should die down soon, according to calculations here.

Prime Minister Attlee's message on behalf of the British Government, for instance, after a personal tribute to Mr. Gandhi, ended with these words:

"During the last months of his life he exerted with success his powerful influence to restrain communal bitterness and to promote the cooperation of all Indians for the common good. It is the earnest hope of the British Government in the United Kingdom that this example will be followed and that his moral influence will continue to guide men in the paths of peace."

Royalty Joins in Tribute

The message of the King, sent to Earl Mountbatten, Governor-General of India, said:

"The Queen and I are deeply shocked by the news of the death of Mr. Gandhi. Will you please convey to the people of India our sincere sympathy in the irreparable loss which they and indeed mankind suffered."

Winston Churchill, Opposition leader, said: "I am shocked at this wicked crime."

Sir Stafford Cripps, Chancellor of the Exchequer, was one of the many personal friends of Mr. Gandhi who pointed out that this loss will be deplored throughout the world.

The Earl of Halifax, who as Viceroy from 1926 to 1931, was closer to Mr. Gandhi and more respected by him than any Governor General of this century, also expressed the hope that the "effect of his tragic death may be to bring all his countrymen to understand and practice the principles he so constantly and faithfully preached."

Lord Pethick-Lawrence said: "I know there is one wish he would have made—that his death should not be revenged or made the occasion for further bloodshed but that it should lead to reconciliation among all the peoples of the subcontinent of Asia."

WASHINGTON FEELS CONCERN FOR INDIA

Truman Calls Gandhi's Death an 'International Tragedy,' Issues Formal Statement

MARSHALL SENDS A NOTE

Addresses Himself to Nehru—Members of Congress Hear of Bombay Disturbance

Special to THE NEW YORK TIMES.

WASHINGTON, Jan. 30—The assassination of Mohandas K. Gandhi shocked the capital today. Fears were expressed that it might lead to serious complications in India.

In an immediate reaction released through Charles G. Ross, Presidential press secretary, President Truman said it was "a tragic loss to the whole world," adding:

"I regard the assassination as a great international tragedy. Notwithstanding the great sorrow this will cause the world I sincerely hope it will not retard the peace of India and the world."

Later in a formal statement Mr. Truman declared that all peoples would be inspired by "his sacrifice" to work with increased vigor toward the peace and brotherhood which he symbolized.

Message from Marshall

Secretary of State George C. Marshall in a message to Pandit Jawaharlal Nehru, Prime Minister and Foreign Minister of the Dominion of India, said:

"The United States has been shocked by the tragic news of the passing of Mahatma Gandhi, and shares with India a heavy burden of sorrow and loss. In his devotion to tolerance and the brotherhood of man, the Mahatma was one of those rare spokesmen for the conscience of all mankind. The sense of bereavement felt in this country evidences the close ties between the peoples of the United States and India."

The Indian Embassy placed its flag at half staff in token of sorrow.

Official opinion here as to the possible consequences of the assassination were reserved, pending further development. The State Department delayed any detailed comment until reports have been received from its diplomatic representatives in the area.

Statement by Truman

In his formal statement President Truman said:

This morning when I heard the tragic news of the assassination of Mahatma Gandhi I sent a message to Earl Mountbatten, the Governor General of India, expressing my condolences to him and to the people of India.

Gandhi was a great Indian nationalist, but at the same time was a leader of international stature. His teachings and his actions have left a deep impression on millions of people.

He was and is revered by the people of India and his influence was felt not only in affairs of government but also in the realm of the spirit. Unhappily he did not live to witness the full realization of those ideals for which he struggled. But his life and his work will be, through the years to come, the greatest monument to him. His selfless struggle for the betterment of his people, will, I am sure, endure as an example of India's leaders, many of whom are his disciples.

I know not only the peoples of India, but all peoples will be inspired by his sacrifice to work with increased vigor toward the brotherhood and peace which the Mahatma symbolized.

Note to Mountbatten

In a message to Earl Mountbatten, the President said:

I am deeply grieved by the news of the assassination of Mohandas K. Gandhi, and I send you and the Government and people of India my sincere condolences. As a teacher and leader, his influence made itself felt not only in India but everywhere in the world, and his death brings great sorrow to all peace loving people. Another giant among men has fallen in the cause of brotherhood and peace. I know that the peoples of Asia will be inspired by his tragic death to strive with increased determination to achieve the goals of cooperation and mutual trust for which the Mahatma has now given his life.

U. N. Renders Tribute to Gandhi; Apprehension Felt at His Death

By A. M. ROSENTHAL

Special to THE NEW YORK TIMES.

LAKE SUCCESS, N. Y., Jan. 30—The uneasy fear that the death of Mohandas K. Gandhi would bring bloodshed and new disaster to India ran today like a thread through a day of gloom at the United Nations.

The Indian delegate unhappily told the Security Council that it was impossible to say what might happen in his country now that its "man of the great soul" was dead. And the Pakistani delegate looked around the Council table and said all India must unite or the assassination of the Mahatma would be just a taste of horror to come.

For weeks, India and Pakistan—the two Dominions that Mr. Gandhi wanted undivided—have appeared before the Council to quarrel over the future of the Princely State of Kashmir, to accuse each other of mass murder and systematic aggression. Today, however, there was no debate. The Council put aside the business of Kashmir to mourn for the Mahatma.

Delegates from every one of the eleven members of the Council spoke before a filled, quiet chamber to give condolences to India. They called the Mahatma a martyr, a symbol of peace, an apostle of brotherhood. They said hopefully that his death must bring India and Pakistan closer to the unity he represented. And then for the first time in the Council's history they stood in silence for thirty seconds.

Underlying Fear Felt

The assassination of Mr. Gandhi was felt outside the Council chamber, in the offices and corridors and delegates' lounge. Always, the underlying fear was that new riots would be touched off. Delegates and Secretariat members kept an ear to radios for word from India, and all through the day there were calls to newspaper offices with the same question:

"Is there rioting?"

For the Indian delegation, the day of mourning began at 7:45 A. M. when a reporter called their hotel to tell them the news. The delegate who first heard the story could not believe it, asked for a repeat, then hung up slowly and went to tell the others.

The United Nations went into mourning at the beginning of the work day. Acting Secretary General Byron Price ordered the white-on-blue flag of the world organization hung at half-mast for three days here, in New York and Geneva. None of the national flags of the fifty-seven United Nations will be raised for those three days.

At first there was talk that the Council would cancel its meeting out of respect for Mr. Gandhi but Fernand van Langenhove of Belgium, Council President, decided to hold a memorial session.

The delegates' lounge, where premeeting caucuses and informal talks take place, was a subdued room, with none of the usual high-pitched chatter and laughter. Sir Mohammed Zafrullah Khan, Pakistan's Foreign Minister, was the first delegate to enter and he waited by himself at first.

Other delegates entered and waited—Andrei A. Gromyko of the Soviet Union, Warren R. Austin of the United States, Philip J. Noel-Baker of the United Kingdom. They talked quietly of the news.

The Indian delegation entered the room. It was led by N. Gopalaswami Ayyangar. His throat was wrapped in a muffler and he looked tired. First Sir Zafrullah and then the other delegates walked over and said how sorry they were and what a loss it was.

When the meeting started, the press galleries, photographers, newsreel and radio booths were filled. Most of the audience who heard the eulogies to the 78-year-old Mahatma were youngsters from Long Island and New York high schools.

The delegates from Pakistan and India spoke last, but everything else seemed like prelude. Everybody in the room knew that the actions of those two Governments would decide what would happen to the people of the subcontinent.

Sir Zafrullah told the Council that the death of the Indian leader meant as much to Pakistan as to India.

"He was the keystone of the arch that is now subject to many stresses," he said.

In plain language, then, the Pakistan Foreign Minister said that the "catastrophe" of Mr. Gandhi's death might "become the forerunner of great disaster in many fields."

"It is devoutly to be prayed for that in this hour of grief and distress leaders of all communities in India will unite to devote every effort toward averting these disasters," he went on.

Hopes For Improvement

Mr. Ayyangar, who had received a condolence call from Sir Zafrullah earlier in the day, seemed optimistic before the meeting. He was asked whether Mr. Gandhi's death would further complicate the already complicated Kashmir case and he said he hoped it would have an "opposite effect."

MILLIONS ESTEEMED GANDHI AS A SAINT

Political Opinions About Him Differed, but His Enormous Influence Was Recognized

CAREER ALWAYS STORMY

Techniques of Fasting, Civil Disobedience Played Part in Work for Independence

Mohandas Karamchand Gandhi, Hindu reformer and nationalist leader, was looked upon as a saint by millions of his followers, who bestowed upon him the admiring appellation of "Mahatma," literally "the great-souled one."

As was perhaps inevitable in the case of one who was the center of violent controversies for more than half a century, there were others who had very different views about the Indian leader, even contending that he was no better than a scheming demagogue. But, whatever view history may eventually take, there can be no contradiction of the statement that the emaciated little man in shawl and loin cloth made himself the living symbol of India in the minds of most Americans.

He was born on Oct. 2, 1869, at Porbandar, on the Kathiawar peninsula of India, and came of a Bania family with official traditions. His father had been Prime Minister of the little native state. He was officially betrothed three times before he was old enough to realize it. His first two fiancees died; the third engagement, resulting in a marriage that lasted more than sixty years, came when he was only 7. The marriage took place when he was 13.

"I can see no moral argument in support of such a preposterous early marriage as mine," he wrote in his memoirs.

At the age of 19 Gandhi went to London, where he studied at University College and was called to the bar by the Inner Temple. He had a difficult time in London. Too proud to struggle against the snubs not only of white people but also of Brahmins, he retired to cheap lodgings, where he cooked his own vegetarian meals and lived for next to nothing.

Worked in South Africa

Returning to India Gandhi practiced law for a short time in the Bombay High Court, but in 1893 he was called to South Africa on professional business. There he became engrossed in a long struggle for the liberties of Indians who had migrated to that country, which was his principal occupation for more than twenty years. Both in Natal and the Transvaal race feeling against the Indian settlers was strong and discriminations were many.

When, in 1896, after a brief visit to India, Gandhi returned to Durban, he was attacked and badly beaten for his agitations. The South Africans had become incensed at a pamphlet he wrote in India on the conditions of the Indians in South Africa. It was then that his conception of passive nonviolent resistance developed. He relinquished his large income as a lawyer and founded a colony, the Tolstoy Farm, near Durban. It was along the lines of the Russian philosopher's estate at Yasnaya Polyana.

He was often imprisoned and more often subjected to indignities, but this neither checked his energies nor deterred him from rendering service of marked loyalty to the British Government.

In 1914, soon after a commission had removed some of the worst sources of injustice to the Indians living in South Africa, Gandhi returned to his native land and threw himself into support of the home rule movement. By 1918 he was busy organizing his Satyagraha (literally "insistence upon truth") movement, which he defined as follows:

"Satyagraha differs from passive resistance as the North Pole from the South. The latter has been conceived as a weapon for the weak and does not exclude the use of physical force or violence for the purpose of gaining one's end, whereas the former has been conceived as a weapon of the strongest and excludes the use of violence in any shape or form."

In the following year the British Government published the Rowlatt Acts, giving the government emergency powers for dealing with revolutionary crimes and conspiracies. Gandhi declared them to be an insult and denounced the bills as "instruments of oppression." His Satyagraha campaign spread with great rapidity throughout India.

Non-Cooperation Movement

Finally, in June, 1920, he formed his celebrated non-violent, non-cooperation movement. The main points of his campaign were the boycott of Government service, of the new Legislatures and of the courts of law; the surrender of all public offices and the withdrawal of children from Government schools. To this was subsequently added the militant boycott of foreign goods, the fighting of the liquor and opium trade, and the furtherance of Hindu-Moslem friendship.

Gandhi adopted the spinning wheel as a sort of symbol of economic independence. He advocated the home manufacture of khaddar, or homespun cloth, to replace the imported goods from the cotton mills of Lancashire. Hartals, or local strikes, were called and there were many burnings of stacks of foreign-made cloth. The general boycott was accompanied by rioting, looting of shops and unrest throughout India.

Partly by his eloquence, partly by his reputation as an ascetic, Gandhi had won enormous prestige in India by this time. The Indian Congress party delegated its full authority to him and empowered him to appoint his own successor. But the non-cooperation movement continued to be accompanied by outbursts of violence, many of them of a racial character.

In March, 1922, Gandhi was arrested and placed on trial on a charge of conspiring to spread disaffection with a view to overthrowing the Government. He pleaded guilty and took full blame.

His Sentence Remitted

He was condemned to six years' imprisonment but was released in January, 1924, after he had undergone an operation for appendicitis, and the rest of his sentence was unconditionally remitted. In 1925 he announced that he would retire from the world for a year. There followed a long period in which he was the apostle of the spinning wheel, and agitated with much energy for the uplifting of the "untouchables," the Hindu pariah caste.

Early in 1930 Gandhi proclaimed his intention of refusing to pay all Government taxes, and particularly the salt tax. On April 5 he set out with a group of followers to march from Ahmedabad to the sea, where they collected salt water in earthen jars, then obtained salt by evaporation of the water. On May 5 Gandhi was arrested at Surat and spirited away to Poona, charged with having been the leader of plans to seize the Government salt depots.

He was still languishing in prison when the first Indian Round-Table Conference began to gather in London. On Jan. 26, 1931, Gandhi was released by order of the Viceroy, Lord Irwin, who later became Viscount Halifax.

There was much criticism in England of Lord Irwin's action.

However, the following month Lord Irwin invited Gandhi to a series of conversations at Delhi which resulted in the Delhi Pact of March, 1931, by which the Viceroy lifted the ban on the Indian Congress party and Gandhi in turn called off the civil disobedience campaign.

As the representative of the Congress party, Gandhi went to London to participate in the roundtable conference. After much hesitation he undertook the mission, traveling steerage, clad in his shawl and loin cloth, and taking with him two goats. He was a guest, loin cloth and all, of King George V and Queen Mary in London, lunched with Lady Astor, and waited in vain for Mayor James J. Walker of New York to keep a date with him.

Debating the future of India at a roundtable conference at St. James Palace in 1931. Lord Sankey (in high-back chair) was chairman of the meeting.
The New York Times (London Bureau)

As a law student in London
The New York Times

Lived in London Slums

In London, he lived in the slums, familiarizing himself with the condition of the poor. He also visited the Lancashire mill districts, where he was both cheered and booed.

On his way home he stopped in Rome and had a conversation with Premier Mussolini, but because of his scanty costume he was not permitted an interview with the Pope.

He lost no time in instituting a new civil disobedience campaign on Jan. 4, 1932, and was promptly sent back to his old Yerovda Jail. From there he sent out the announcement that he would starve himself to death unless the Government reversed its decision to grant separate political representation for seventy years to the Untouchables.

His fast ended after six days, however, when he was told that the British Government had accepted "with great satisfaction" the principal terms of the settlement between the higher caste Indians and the Untouchables. But in April, 1933, he announced that he would fast for twenty-one days to call attention to the situation of the Untouchables. Despite almost unanimous medical opinion that that he could not stand such a strain, he refrained from food from May 8 to May 29, and soon regained his health.

Released from jail at the time he began his fast, Gandhi was rearrested with his wife and thirty followers on July 31, 1933, when he began a new "individual civil disobedience" campaign. He was sentenced to a year in jail as an ordinary political prisoner without the privileges that had formerly been accorded him. A week later he began a new fast to obtain privileges that would enable him to carry on his fight in behalf of the Untouchables.

In April, 1934, Gandhi instructed his followers to abandon civil disobedience and campaign for the forthcoming elections for the Legislative Assembly. Meanwhile the British had been preparing a new Constitution for India, which Gandhi had announced he would give a trial. On April 26 of that year he was attacked and narrowly escaped a beating by a mob of Indians who resented his attitude on the question of the Untouchables.

When the new Constitution was promulgated the following August, Gandhi was bitterly disappointed in it. Although he had been succeeded as leader of the Congress party by Jawaharlal Nehru, he remained active behind the scenes, helping to direct the opposition to the new form of government. He drafted certain conditions regarding the carrying out of the provisions of the India act, and his tactics hamstrung the workings of the new act until July, 1937, when a compromise was reached.

In the spring of 1939, five years after his ostensible retirement from politics, Gandhi openly returned to activity because the Congress party had elected a president whom he did not want, Subhas Chandra Bose. He began the sixth of his famous fasts to force certain reforms from the Thakore Saheb, autocratic ruler of the tiny principality of Rajkot, in northwestern India.

Apprehension swept India. Eight of the eleven autonomous Indian Governments established in the Provinces resigned and hamstrung the Government of India Act, which had been in operation only two years. Markets closed in Bombay. Trade was at a standstill. The mounting public unrest forced the British Viceroy, the Marquess of Linlithgow, to cut short a tour of northern India and return to the capital at New Delhi to protect the interests of the Crown. He informed Mr. Gandhi that the ruler of Rajkot would be forced to grant the reforms.

Gandhi broke his four-day fast with a glass of orange juice, and his millions of followers rejoiced.

The Congress party promptly committed its new president, Mr. Bose, to the guidance of Gandhi, and Mr. Bose resigned. Gandhi's follower, Dr. Rajendra Prasad, was elected to succeed him.

When the second World War broke out, the Viceroy declared India to be a participant in it without consulting the Congress party leaders. Gandhi, although a strong critic of Nazi Germany, demanded the complete independence of India as the price of Indian cooperation.

There followed three months of conversations between Gandhi and the Viceroy. In the last war, Gandhi pointed out, Britain had promised India "self-governing institutions" after victory. He wanted the promise kept by freeing India at once; Indians could not fight for democracy while it was denied to them. Lord Linlithgow answered for the British Government that any constitutional changes must be deferred until after the war and then Dominion status would be gradually extended to India. He said Gandhi must first solve the everlasting problem of protecting the Moslem and other minorities before they were turned over to the Hindus, who outnumbered them three to one—all creeds and sects hating one another. Gandhi insisted that freedom came first; the minorities would then become a domestic problem of no concern to Britain. There the conversations became deadlocked.

Hated Nazis More

For almost three years during the early part of the war Gandhi, in complete control of the Congress party, pursued a cautious policy of enlarging his support among the Hindu millions, and constantly seeking independence from the British.

In March, 1940, the Congress party voted Gandhi full power to direct its future policy and conduct its program. Under his control, the Working Committee, which is the executive body of the party, made a tentative offer of military aid to Britain in June, but withdrew it two months later when Gandhi declared he was convinced Britain had no intention of recognizing Indian independence.

In October, on his seventy-first birthday, he announced that he had no ill-will toward Britain and that there would be no civil disobedience campaign. Two weeks later he announced that there would be a campaign, but in order not to embarrass the British war effort it would be conducted by a few individuals in a symbolic rather than a massive way.

He instructed two members of the Congress party to break the Defense of India Act prohibiting speeches directed to impede the

(continued)

conduct of the war. One of them was his personal servant. The other was the former president of the Congress party, Pandit Nehru. They made speeches urging disregard of the laws and courts, non-cooperation with munitions manufacture, non-contribution of funds and not enlistment. They were jailed forthwith. Pandit Nehru was sentenced to four years.

Thereupon the Working Committee of the party ordered 1,500 individuals to invite arrest in the same way. The jails filled. Gandhi suspended his weekly paper, Harijan, when he was forbidden to publish accounts of the speeches and the arrests. He now kept out of jail, which he had never avoided previously, in order to direct the fight. In August, 1941, Gandhi said that the purpose was "not to force Britain but to convert her."

With the entry of Japan into the war in December, 1941, Gandhi, on Dec. 30, asked the Working Committee of the party to relieve him from leadership. He explained that sympathy for the Axis-overrun countries, rather than for Britain, dictated his second retirement. But he continued to run the Congress party from behind the scenes.

With the threat of Japanese invasion growing daily, Britain made a great effort in the spring of 1942 to unite the Indian factions behind a common policy of defense. Prime Minister Churchill dispatched Sir Stafford Cripps on a special mission to India to try to compose the difficulties of the parties there. He officially offered complete independence and equality for India in the British Commonwealth of Nations as soon as the war was won, with the right of ultimate secession.

Although this was the largest voluntary disbursement of power that Great Britain had ever offered, the warring groups within India refused it. The Moslems and other minority groups rejected it because of their fear of their status under a Hindu majority. The Congress party rejected it because it was not immediate. Gandhi, in April, introduced a resolution closing the door to further negotiations with the British on the issue. In May, Gandhi called upon the British to quit India.

Terms for an Ally

Shortly thereafter he laid a resolution before the Working Committee of the Congress party giving Britain a last choice: India would be her war ally if immediate freedom was granted; otherwise "full powers to lead a civil disobedience movement against Britain would be given to Mohandas K. Gandhi." The Working Committee adopted it unhesitatingly, and only ratification by the All-India Congress party's general assembly was required to launch "open non-violent rebellion."

Campaigning in behalf of the move, Gandhi said that he would not flinch at calling a general strike. He said that there was increasing ill will against Britain in India, and growing satisfaction at Japanese victories. He warned that India might welcome a Japanese invasion, even as many of the people of Burma had done.

In New Delhi, the British directed Government of India made public a copy of a memorandum seized in a raid on the headquarters of the Congress party, which purported to show that Gandhi had proposed conversations with the Japanese four months earlier. The Government charged that he and his followers were appeasers.

On Aug. 9 the Congress party assembly, in plenary session, voted to throw his strength behind the "non-violent rebellion" and the Government announced its intention "to use force as the necessities of the situation might require." Gandhi and some fifty of his followers were arrested as widespread rioting began. As he was taken to jail he left the slogan: "Either we get freedom or we die."

He was imprisoned in the Victorian palace of the Aga Khan in Poona, but the Government's action was not followed by as widespread unrest as had been predicted by some observers. There were demonstrations and acts of sabotage, but the Government's policy was successful in keeping the heavy war industries running.

Gandhi wrote the Viceroy, disclaiming the responsibility of the Congress party for the acts of violence that were occurring, and threatening to begin a new fast, his ninth, unless he was liberated. The Government, which published the correspondence, refused to yield, terming the hunger strike "political blackmail, for which there can be no moral justification."

Gandhi began his fast on Feb. 10, 1943. He announced that it would not be a "fast unto death," but that he would subsist for twenty-one days on a diet of citrus juice mixed with water. There were some disturbances among the Hindu community, but on the fifth day after the fast began THE NEW YORK TIMES correspondent in New Delhi wrote that "it was evident that his move would probably misfire."

Fears were felt for the life of the fasting man for several days, but he astonished the doctors by surviving, even though he was too weak to lift a glass of orange juice. American correspondents in India, pointing out that this was the first time he had failed to win at least a partial victory by a fast, said that his failure seemed to have disappointed and discouraged him.

Disorders marked the first anniversary of Gandhi's arrest, and agitation for his release was continued both in India and abroad. On Feb. 17, 1944, however, Viscount Wavell, who had assumed the position as Viceroy, declared that he and his associates would be held until they showed "some signs" of cooperation.

Mrs. Gandhi, his frail companion through a married life of more than sixty years, died late in February. She had faithfully followed her husband to jail more than once. He was released on parole for a week, and, sitting in the shade of a tamarind tree, he watched the cremation of her remains. Then he went back to prison.

On May 6, after twenty-one months as a prisoner, Gandhi was released by the Government because of his failing health. The official doctors had considered giving him blood transfusions but Gandhi was said to have frowned on the idea, maintaining that the essential life stream of one human should not be used to extend the life of another. Viscount Wavell was praised for his decision to release the Hindu leader.

Calling at 10 Downing Street for a conference with Ramsay MacDonald, then Prime Minister.

The New York Times (London Bureau)

Leaving his residence in New Delhi last October with granddaughters Manu (left) and Ava.

The New York Times

In a proposal designed to break the political deadlock over India's independence Gandhi in September, 1944, agreed to discuss with Mohammed Ali Jinnah, head of the Moslem League, the Moslem's long-standing demand that India be partitioned into separate Hindu and Moslem states. It was this basic plan that was finally agreed upon in 1947 when India won her long-sought independence, but Gandhi's conversations with Mr. Jinnah were fruitless.

Gandhi had some time previously made an offer to withdraw his civil disobedience campaign for the duration of the war. By this time the Japanese drive toward India had been turned back and to most observers the cooperation pledge from the Hindu leader seemed a little gratuitous. Nevertheless, Gandhi was hailed for his conciliatory attitude.

A White Paper issued in London in June, 1945, made a new attempt to break the deadlock in India, and Gandhi announced that he would ask Congress party leaders to accept it. The British offer, looking toward Dominion status for India, proposed setting up of a Viceroy's Council to be composed "in equal portions of Moslems and caste Hindus."

Eight months later Prime Minister Clement Attlee offered to India the right to full independence, and a Cabinet mission was dispatched to work out the procedure. Gandhi appealed to his people to be patient and to give the mission a chance, but warned against "fake promises." When the mission had drafted its plan for Indian self-government, Gandhi at first said he regarded it as "seed to convert this land of sorrow into one without sorrow and suffering."

By June, although the proposal had not been altered to any degree, Gandhi, for reasons that remained obscure, developed "vague misgivings," but the Congress party, which he once controlled, accepted the plan, as had the Moslem League.

In the ensuing months it became clear that other political leaders had taken the stage in India, but Gandhi remained the national Government's core and he told a NEW YORK TIMES correspondent that he intended to remain in politics for many years. Asked if he still expected to live to the age of 125, Gandhi, on the eve of his seventy-seventh birthday replied "Yes," in order to serve his people.

In early 1947 the British plan was to quit India by June, 1948, earlier if the Hindu and Moslem communities would compose their differences. Gandhi, in an open break with the Congress party, reversed himself and balked at a Hindu-Moslem partition and the formation of Pakistan as a separate state for the Moslem majority regions of India.

The Gandhi viewpoint was that whether it caused chaos or not, the British must leave India on the promised date and let India work out its own fate. By this time the British were convinced that partition was the only solution that would be accepted and finally Gandhi reluctantly went along, declaring: "Partition is bad. But whatever is past is past. We have only to look to the future."

When, on Aug. 15, 1947, India achieved her independence, Viscount Mountbatten, Viceroy of India, hailed Gandhi as the "architect of India's freedom through non-violence."

Gandhi did not participate in the independence observances held throughout India. At the moment of victory he sat on a wooden cot in a Calcutta hut, scorning the result of his decades of labor and fast. He announced his intention of living with the Hindu minority in Pakistan, the predominantly Moslem state created by partition.

Riots swept across much of India, with scores killed and injured in communal clashes. Gandhi started in Calcutta his first fast in independent India. It would end, he said, only when Calcutta "returned to sanity."

After he had been assured that there would be no more rioting in Calcutta, Gandhi broke his fast. He was credited with having restored peace to India's largest city. Crowds of Moslems and Hindus made their way to his camp and surrendered guns, swords and ammunition they had used in the riots.

"If the peace is broken again I will come back and undertake a fast unto death and die if necessary," he said.

He went to New Delhi, where he continued his efforts to end the communal strife, which had broken out more violently than ever along the Punjab border and in Delhi itself. Daily he exhorted all non-Moslems to accept Moslem neighbors as friends and brothers.

However, on Sept. 16 he told the Hindu Youth Organization that "if the Dominion of Pakistan persists in wrongdoing there is bound to be war between India and Pakistan."

On Oct. 2 he celebrated his seventy-ninth birthday (Hindus are counted a year old at birth), which had been declared a national holiday by the Government of India.

He started a new fast on Jan. 12, 1948, declaring that he would continue until greater unity between Hindu, Sikh and Moslem communities was achieved. This fast was ended after five days, when Hindus and Moslems in Delhi agreed to live in peace.

Christianity Was a Force In Life, Career of Gandhi

By The Associated Press.

LONDON, Jan. 30—Christianity was a potent force in the life of Mohandas K. Gandhi for more than sixty-five years.

From Christ, he said, he learned passive resistance and non-violence.

From Tolstoy he learned non-cooperation.

From Thoreau, he said, he learned disobedience.

"Prayer has saved my life," he wrote once. "Without it I should have been a lunatic long ago. Prayer came out of sheer necessity. The more my faith in Good increased, the more irresistible became the yearning for prayer. Life seems to be dull and vacant without it."

SMUTS EXPRESSES GRIEF OVER GANDHI

By G. H. ARCHAMBAULT

Special to THE NEW YORK TIMES.

CAPE TOWN, South Africa, Jan. 30—Prime Minister Jan Christiaan Smuts, an old adversary of Mohandas K. Gandhi, expressed today his personal condolences and those of South Africa, where Mr. Gandhi embarked on his political career. For twenty-one years Mr. Gandhi fought for the granting of full rights of citizenship to Indians in South Africa—an issue that is still alive here today.

It was in South Africa that Mr. Gandhi devised his technique of passive resistance, and for twenty-one years he was a thorn in the side of various Ministers, notably General Smuts as Colonial Secretary. Prime Minister Smuts forgot the past today in saying:

"I have heard of the assassination of Mr. Gandhi with the deepest grief, which, I am sure, will be shared all over the world. Mr. Gandhi was one of the great men of my time and my acquaintance with him over a period of more than thirty years has only deepened my high respect for him, however much we differed in our views and methods. A prince among men has passed away and we grieve with India in her irreparable loss."

Almost simultaneously with the news of the murder it was learned here that one of Mr. Gandhi's last pronouncements related to the differences between India and South Africa. Mr. Gandhi had said:

"I request the South African Government to treat Indians well and to maintain friendly relations with the Government of India. India and South Africa now enjoy equal independent status in the British Commonwealth. The fact that one party is white and the other brown should not be the cause of any dispute."

Among the Indian community of 250,000, settled mostly in Natal Province, public manifestations of grief are being organized.

Mr. Gandhi is recalled here as one of the few men who successfully flouted governmental authority. He came to Durban several years before the close of the last century as an attorney to defend a prominent Indian. When he found that in this country he was considered as a "coolie"—thrown off trains although holding a first-class ticket and arrested after sundown because he should have had a pass—it dawned upon him that he had work to do on behalf of his compatriots. He remained here twenty-two years.

"All the News That's Fit to Print"

The New York Times

LATE CITY EDITION

Weather: Possible showers today. Showers likely tonight, tomorrow. Temp. range: today 83-65; Sunday 80-62. Temp.-Hum. Index yesterday 71. Complete U.S. report on Page 78.

VOL. CXVIII...No. 40,693 | © 1969 The New York Times Company. | NEW YORK, MONDAY, JUNE 23, 1969 | 10 CENTS

POWELL DECLINES ELECTION SUPPORT FOR PROCACCINO

Hails Lindsay as Probably Only Man Able to Calm the Troubled Waters

'DEAL' ON PAY IS DENIED

Representative Says Court Studies Congress Issue—Mayor Asks Coalition

By WILLIAM E. FARRELL

Representative Adam Clayton Powell, the Harlem Democrat, said yesterday that he would not support Mario A. Procaccino, his party's candidate for Mayor, and that Mayor Lindsay was "probably the only man who can pour oil on the troubled waters of this city."

The minister and politician, asked at a news conference at the Abyssinian Baptist Church if he would support Mr. Procaccino, replied: "I wouldn't like to say yes or no, but I will say no."

Although he did not formally endorse Mr. Lindsay, who is seeking re-election as the Liberal party's candidate and as the nominee of another party that has not yet been formed, Mr. Powell said:

"Mayor Lindsay and I have not agreed on many things, but he's a very decent man."

Mayor Issues Statement

Told of Representative Powell's comments, Mr. Lindsay issued the following statement from Gracie Mansion through a spokesman:

"I would be gratified by the support of any New Yorker who feels as I do that the progressive moderate forces of the city must come together in a coalition for the good of all the people."

Mr. Powell called his news conference to deny a report in The New York Post that he had agreed not to demand $55,000 in back pay in return for reinstatement of his 22 years of seniority in the House of Representatives.

Last Monday, the Supreme Court ruled that the House had violated the Constitution when it excluded Mr. Powell from the 90th Congress on the ground that he had misused public funds and was contemptuous of New York courts and Congressional committees.

Mr. Powell said that the mat-

Continued on Page 28, Column 6

Cairo, Ill., Divided By Racial Conflict; City Fears Future

By DONALD JANSON

Special to The New York Times

CAIRO, Ill., June 22—"Our image has been devastated, our economy is crippled and our future, if there is one, is dark."

For a Chamber of Commerce, hardly a glowing assessment. Yet this is the conclusion of "The Cairo Story," written and published by the local chamber two months ago.

Nothing has happened since to brighten the image. This former capital of water and rail commerce at the confluence of the Mississippi and Ohio Rivers has regressed enough in recent years to recall the impression of "this dismal Cairo" by Charles Dickens after an 1842 visit: "an ugly sepulchre, a grave uncheered by any gleam of promise."

Cairo (pronounced CARE-o) has more problems than most cities its size, but compounding them is a racial polarization that has divided the town of 8,800 persons into two separate communities, with each race at the other's throat.

The latest chapter in Cairo's racial trouble began today when the Rev. Jesse L. Jackson of the Southern Christian Leadership Conference arrived from Chicago for a rally and a march on the city hall to protest local practices in law enforcement and employment. He also plans to lead protests on Tuesday and Wednesday against hunger among blacks.

Arriving separately today

Continued on Page 29, Column 1

Warren Era Ending Today After 16 Years of Reform

Ron Nelson for The New York Times

Chief Justice Earl Warren

The New York Times

Warren E. Burger

Burger's Seating to Close a Time of Controversy and Mixed Results

By FRED P. GRAHAM

Special to The New York Times

WASHINGTON, June 22—The Warren era ends at the Supreme Court tomorrow, after 16 years of bold reforms that have brought raging controversy and mixed results.

When Chief Justice Earl Warren turns over the Court's center seat to his successor, Warren E. Burger, one of the most ambitious and active eras in the Court's history will end.

Mr. Warren intends to disappear from the public scene for several months, going first on a fishing trip to Alaska and then on an autumn jaunt to the Far East, where he will attend a conference in New Delhi on World Peace Through Law.

He will depart on a strong note after having issued a historic opinion last Monday in the Adam Clayton Powell case.

In declaring that the House of Representatives acted unconstitutionally in 1967 when it refused to seat the Harlem Democrat, the 78-year-old Chief Justice asserted for the first time that the Supreme Court had jurisdiction to settle constitutional questions involving internal Congressional matters.

Results of Decisions

It is too soon to tell whether this will result in a damaging conflict between Congress and the Court or if Congress will accept the Court's judgment.

But even if a donnybrook is avoided over the Powell case, Earl Warren will step down as a controversial figure. The John Birch Society's "impeach Earl Warren" campaign was dropped several years ago, but the genial, strong-willed Chief Justice has remained as a symbol of judicial liberalism that sets conservative teeth on edge.

The controversy over the liberal Warren Court fed on opposition—mostly from political conservatives—against decisions that hobbled government loyalty-security programs, banned prayer and Bible reading in the public schools, outlawed segregation and malapportionment and limited police action.

Thus, much of the outcry over the Warren Court has been a measure of whose ox has been gored.

Conservatives have tended to denounce the Court (President Eisenhower was said to have called his appointment of Mr. Warren the "biggest damfool mistake I ever made"), while only liberals would be expected to agree with Lyndon B. Johnson's assessment of Mr. Warren as "the greatest Chief Justice of them all."

Yet one complaint about the

Continued on Page 24, Column 1

DRUGGISTS START MEDICAID BOYCOTT

State Refuses to Negotiate, Leader Says—City Aide Calls Complaints Valid

By DAVID BIRD

About 400 pharmacists, angered over cutbacks in their fees, yesterday began a boycott of the state's Medicaid program, which provides medical care for the poor.

Cheering and loud applause broke out at a meeting in the Hotel Manhattan as the chairman, Bernard Weitzman, said he expected "an almost complete cessation of Medicaid business" starting this morning.

About half the state's 5,000 drug stores handle Medicaid prescriptions, but it was uncertain yesterday just how many would join the boycott.

Mr. Weitzman, co-chairman of the Emergency Medicaid Committee of the Pharmaceutical Society of the State of New York, told the druggists at the meeting that the state had refused to negotiate any of the economy cutbacks of payments made to them under Medicaid.

Part of General Cut

The cutbacks were part of a 20 per cent across-the-board reduction—including payments to doctors and dentists—made effective June 1 to lower the cost of the financially troubled program.

The cutbacks have met general opposition but the druggists say they are especially hard hit because the reduced payments apply not only to their services but also to things they must pay for—the drugs they dispense.

Dr. Lowell Bellin, the acting first deputy commissioner of the city's Health Department, which handles Medicaid here, said the druggists' complaint against the state was "quite valid." He said the reductions put a "difficult economic hard-

Continued on Page 27, Column 3

NEWS INDEX

Joe Daniels for The New York Times

AMONG ABORIGINES: Charles A. Lindbergh during a helicopter visit to the Batangan, an aboriginal people who live on Mindoro in the Philippines. Such peoples, Mr. Lindbergh believes, "can help us retain contact with the roots of life."

Lindbergh Traveling Widely as Conservationist

By ALDEN WHITMAN

Special to The New York Times

MANILA—Charles Augustus Lindbergh, whose life for the last 40 years has been devoted to aviation, has taken on a new role—that of a passionate and articulate spokesman for conservation.

Profoundly convinced that civilization is imperiled by modern man's reckless disregard for important wildlife species, for primitive peoples, for irreplaceable timberlands and for unique marine life, he is spending a substantial part of his time and energies as a conservationist.

"We are in grave danger of losing forever not just millions of years of evolution on earth, but the eons of change that have produced man and his natural environment," he has said.

In the process of his involvement in conservation, Mr. Lindbergh has become willing—"where I can accomplish a purpose"—to lift briefly the cloak of inviolable privacy he has maintained since the kidnapping and murder of his first son, Charles Jr., in 1932.

The man who captured the world's imagination in 1927 by his solo flight from New York to Paris in the Spirit of St. Louis relaxed his privacy rule last month when he allowed a reporter and a photographer to join him on a strenuous round of activities here. He did so because, as he put it, "the Philippines are one of the last frontiers of conservation" and because he felt he could spur its fledgling conservation efforts.

Mr. Lindbergh's concern with the Philippines is recent. His attention was drawn to the archipelago last year by Prof. Tom Harrisson of Cornell, who alerted him to the plight of the tamarau, a deer-like animal regarded as a national symbol, and the monkey-eating eagle, reputedly the world's largest. Both are nearly extinct.

Mr. Lindbergh visited the islands briefly in January to scout the conservation situa-

Continued on Page 26, Column 1

ABM Opposition Waning In Senate as Vote Nears

By JOHN W. FINNEY

Special to The New York Times

WASHINGTON, June 22—As the Senate approaches a vote on the Administration's Safeguard missile defense system, the once-dominant opposition shows signs of losing some of its momentum and unity.

For the first time since the antiballistic missile debate started a year ago, the bipartisan opposition in the Senate is psychologically on the defensive. This turn of events is privately conceded by leaders of the opposition, who are now holding strategy sessions on how to recapture the initiative in the battle with the Administration.

What remains unclear is whether the opposition has lost strength to the degree that it no longer has the votes to block deployment of the $10.8-billion Safeguard system. At this point, the Administration and the opposition offer conflicting head counts, each designed to bolster its respective political position.

At his news conference last Thursday, President Nixon said the Administration had made such significant inroads on opposition strength that he was ready to assert: "We will win the fight on Safeguard." The President said the latest White House count showed 50 or 51 Senators supporting the Safeguard system, 46 opposed, and 3 or 4 Senators undecided.

The ABM opposition believes the White House is misreading Senate sentiment. The latest opposition count shows 49 Senators opposed, 46 favoring the Safeguard system and 5 uncommitted but with 3 of the

Continued on Page 13, Column 1

ISRAELI JETS RAID JORDANIAN SITES

Commandos Cross Border in Second Attack on Arab Positions in 24 Hours

Special to The New York Times

TEL AVIV, Monday, June 23—Israeli jets struck at Jordan last night, continuing a series of violent incidents that marked the weekend in the Middle East.

Early this morning, Israeli forces invaded Arab territory for the second time in 24 hours. Jordanian army positions east of the Yarmuk River were attacked and the Asor Canal was sabotaged, according to an official Israel Army announcement.

A few hours earlier, Israel had disclosed that an Egyptian commando group crossed the Suez Canal on Saturday, wounded four men and laid mines in an Israeli-held area. And Cairo disputed the Israeli account of an Israeli raid on an Egyptian installation last night.

Cairo said that five Egyptians had been killed and seven had been wounded in the Israeli raid across the canal at Ras Adabiya and that four Israelis had been killed and seven had been wounded. The Israeli account said that 15 Egyptian soldiers had been killed and two Israeli commandos had been injured in the raid, six miles south of Port Suez.

Buildings Bombed

The Israelis' target at Ras Adabiya was originally announced as a radar station. Yesterday, however, the Egyptians denied that any such station had been struck. The Israelis said intelligence had spotted the radar facility a few days ago but conceded it might have been moved before the raid.

According to the Israeli spokesmen, 30 Egyptian soldiers armed with light weapons guarded the base, which consisted of five one-story buildings. How the commandos reached the target was not revealed.

Some Egyptians racing toward the sea were also attacked by the raiders, the spokesmen said. The raiders said later they did not know how many Egyptians got away but that at least half the unit was left dead. Demolition squads then set charges to the

Continued on Page 9, Column 1

Rockefeller Ends Third Latin Trip; He Is 'Heartened'

By United Press International

MONTEVIDEO, Uruguay, June 22—Governor Rockefeller ended the third of his four fact-finding trips in Latin America for President Nixon today. He said he was heartened by the trip and hopeful that he could still visit the three nations that had asked him to stay away.

Mr. Rockefeller and his aides left Carrasco Airport, just outside Montevideo, after a short flight from the seaside resort of Punta del Este, 87 miles to the east.

[The Governor's plane landed at Kennedy International Airport at 9:30 P.M., Sunday.]

Threats and acts of anti-American violence in Montevideo forced Uruguay's Presi-

Continued on Page 6, Column 3

Judy Garland, 47, Found Dead

Frank Donato from Imapct

Judy Garland during an appearance at the Palace in 1967

Special to The New York Times

LONDON, June 22 — Judy Garland, whose successes on stage and screen were later overshadowed by the pathos of her personal life, was found dead in her home here today.

The cause of death of the 47-year-old singer was not immediately established, and an autopsy was scheduled. [Reuters reported that police sources said a preliminary investigation revealed nothing to suggest that Miss Garland had taken her own life.]

Miss Garland's personal life often seemed a fruitless search for the happiness promised in "Over the Rainbow," the song she made famous in the movie "The Wizard of Oz."

Her father died when she was 12 years old; the pressures of adolescent stardom sent her to a psychiatrist at the age of 18; she was married five times; she was frequently ill; her singing voice faltered, and she suffered from the effects of drugs she once said were prescribed either to invigorate or tranquilize her.

She came here at the end of last year to play a cabaret in another of the "comeback" performances that dotted her last 15 years.

Three months ago she married Mickey Deans, a discothèque manager. It was Mr. Deans, her fifth husband, who

Continued on Page 31, Column 1

SCHUMANN NAMED FOREIGN MINISTER, REPLACING DEBRE

Pompidou Picks Advocate of European Unity Despite Gaullist Objections

BIG CABINET APPOINTED

Giscard, Who Backs British Bid to Join Market, Gets French Finance Post

By HENRY TANNER

Special to The New York Times

PARIS, June 22 — President Pompidou today removed Michel Debré from the Foreign Ministry and replaced him with Maurice Schumann, a European-minded internationalist.

The shift of Foreign Ministers, made against the strong objections of orthodox Gaullists, was the most spectacular feature in the announcement of a new French Cabinet that comprises an unusually large total of 18 ministers and 20 secretaries of state. Mr. Debré was named Defense Minister.

Mr. Schumann, a prominent member of the Gaullist Resistance during World War II, became a close associate of Premier Robert Schuman, the "father of Europe," after the war.

The two men were among the leaders of the Popular Republican Movement, the Roman Catholic party that led the fight for European unity together with the West German and Italian Catholic leaders of the time, Chancellor Konrad Adenauer and Premier Alcide de Gasperi.

Giscard in Finance Post

Maurice Schumann is not expected to be a "strong" Foreign Minister but to take his orders from the President.

The "European" tendency in the Cabinet was reinforced by the choice of Valéry Giscard d'Estaing as Minister of Economy and Finance. Mr. Giscard d'Estaing recently joined the Action Committee for the United States of Europe, an international group headed by Jean Monnet that favors not only British membership in the Common Market but also political integration of Europe—both positions that are rejected by former President Charles de Gaulle.

In financial affairs, Mr. Giscard d'Estaing is known as a conservative who does not share General de Gaulle's trust in gold. He is expected to press for acceptance of the Special Drawing Rights, the new international reserve unit proposed by the world's major financial nations. [Page 55.]

At home he carried out a

Continued on Page 3, Column 1

United Press International

NAMED TO NEW CABINET POST: Michel Debré declining to talk with newsmen after conferring yesterday with Georges Pompidou, French President. Mr. Debré, who had been Foreign Minister, was shifted to Defense Minister.

Judy Garland, 47, Star of Stage and Screen, Is Found Dead

Continued From Page 1, Col. 5

found Miss Garland dead on the bathroom floor in their home in the Belgravia district.

Also surviving are three children, Liza Minnelli, the singer and actress, and Lorna and Joseph Luft.

Funeral arrangements were incomplete tonight.

Moved by Compulsion

Judy Garland's career was marked by a compulsive quality that displayed itself even during her first performance at the age of 30 months at the New Grand Theater in Grand Rapids, Minn. Here, the story is told, Frances Gumm—both her parents were vaudeville players—sang "Jingle Bells" on a Christmas program. She responded so favorably to the footlights that her father was forced to remove her after she had repeated the song seven times.

The other side of the compulsively vibrant, exhausting performances that were her stage hallmark was a seemingly unquenchable need for her audiences to respond with acclaim and affection. And often they did, screaming, "We love you, Judy—we love you."

She made more than 35 films, once set a New York vaudeville record with an engagement of 19 weeks and 184 performances, cut numerous records and in recent years made frequent television appearances.

Her other films include, "Every Sunday," "Babes In Arms," "Little Nellie Kelly," "For Me and My Gal," "The Harvey Girls," "Meet Me in St. Louis," "The Pirate," "Easter Parade," "A Star Is Born," "Judgment at Nuremberg," and "A Child Is Waiting."

Miss Garland's early success was firmly rooted in an extraordinary talent. She was an instinctive actress and comédienne with a sweet singing voice that had a kind of brassy edge to it, which made her something of an anachronism: a music hall performer in an era in which music halls were obsolete.

In an earlier era, or in another society, she might have grown up slowly, developing her talent as she disciplined it, and gone on like other, tougher performers to enjoy a long and profitable career.

Discipline Not Required

Instead, Judy became a star at 15 in the relentless world of motion pictures. Movies—which are put together in bits and pieces—do not particularly require rigid discipline, and she therefore never had a chance to acquire the quality that could have sustained her talent over the years.

Perhaps the most remarkable thing about the career of Judy Garland was that she was able to continue as long as she did — long after her voice had failed and long after her physical reserves had been spent in various illnesses that might have left a less tenacious woman an invalid.

She was the kind of movie personality whose private life defined much of her public response. Whenever she stepped out on a stage in recent years, she brought with her, whether she welcomed it or not, all the well-publicized phantoms of her emotional breakdowns, her career collapses and her comebacks.

The pressures of performing began for her at an early age. When she was 18 and Louis B. Mayer's favorite at Metro-Goldyn-Mayer Studios making $150,000 a picture, she was already seeing a psychiatrist.

She wrote about the experience years later: "No wonder I was strange. Imagine whipping out of bed, dashing over to the doctor's office, lying down on a torn leather couch, telling my troubles to an old man who couldn't hear, who answered with an accent I couldn't understand, and then dashing to Metro to make movie love to Mickey Rooney."

It was during this period that she also began taking stimulants and depressants. "They'd give us pep pills," she wrote. "Then they'd take us to the studio hospital and knock us cold with sleeping pills . . . after four hours they'd wake us up and give us the pep pills again . . .

"That's the way we worked, and that's the way we got thin. That's the way we got mixed up. And that's the way we lost contact."

Less than 10 years after these experiences, at the age of 28, the singer attempted suicide.

The unhappiness that plagued her during the last few years alone included the breakup of her 13-year marriage to Sid Luft, a film director and the third of her five husbands; a subsequent bitter custody fight over their children, Lorna and Joseph, with Mr. Luft accusing her of having attempted suicide on at least 20 occasions; sudden hospitalizations for causes ranging from paralysis to unconsciousness after a fall in a hotel room, and the breaking of her voice during appearances in several cities.

Miss Garland was born in Grand Rapids on June 10, 1922, the youngest of three daughters of Frank Avent and Ethel Marian Gumm. Her parents billed themselves in vaudeville as Jack and Virginia Lee.

After her debut with "Jingle Bells," she performed with her sisters, Suzanne and Virginia, until, according to theatrical legend, their act was erroneously billed at a Chicago theater as "The Glum Sisters."

Garland was her mother's maiden name. When the family arrived in Hollywood in 1936, the 14-year-old singer, who made her feature film debut in "Pigskin Parade," was billed as Judy Garland.

She made a short subject with another adolescent singer, Deanna Durbin. Louis B. Mayer was impressed, and when he learned that M-G-M had allowed Miss Durbin's contract to lapse and lost her to a rival studio, he determined to give Miss Garland a major build-up.

She sang "Dear Mr. Gable" in "Broadway Melody of 1938." Then she made a bigger hit as a gawky adolescent with a crush on Mickey Rooney in "Love Finds Andy Hardy."

In "Dear Mr. Gable" she confessed her hopeless adolescent love for an idealized movie star in special lyrics added to the ballad "You Made Me Love You."

At 17, playing the pig-tailed girl in "The Wizard of Oz," she sang the song that became her trademark, "Over the Rainbow" —a wistful pursuit of happiness that seemed, to her, unattainable.

In 1939, "The Wizard of Oz" earned her a special Oscar.

Ray Bolger, the dancer, actor and singer, who played the Scarecrow in "The Wizard," made it plain yesterday that Miss Garland's charisma was notable even when they made that film.

Three months after she had signed the contract with M-G-M, Judy's father died of spinal meningitis. In a newspaper article in 1964, Miss Garland wrote that her father's death "was the most terrible thing that ever happened to me in my life." "I can say that now," she went on, "because I'm more secure than I was then."

"But the terrible thing about it," she wrote, "was that I couldn't cry at my father's funeral. I'd never been to a funeral. I was ashamed because I couldn't cry, so I feigned it. But I just couldn't cry for eight days, and then I locked myself in a bathroom and cried for 14 hours.

"I wasn't close to my father, but I wanted to be all my life. He had a funny sense of humor, and he laughed all the time—good and loud, like I do. He was a gay Irish gentleman and very good-looking. And he wanted to be close to me, too, but we never had much time together."

Passed Awkward Age

By 1942, Miss Garland had passed the awkward age through a popular series of musical comedies with Mr. Rooney, and was playing love scenes with Gene Kelly in "For Me and My Gal." She was already one of the top box-office stars at the most celebrated star studio in Hollywood.

Her personal troubles had already begun. She was married to the composer-pianist David Rose in 1941. They were divorced three years later. The next year she was married to her director, the gifted musical specialist, Vincente Minnelli.

Under her husband's guidance, her career flourished. She sang "The Trolley Song" in "Meet Me in St. Louis" and was praised for her first nonsinging dramatic performance, in "The Clock."

By 1948, when Miss Garland played with Gene Kelly in "The Pirate," and Fred Astaire in "Easter Parade," she was indisputably the leading musical star in films.

The next year she failed to report for work on three successive films and was reported to be suffering from a nervous breakdown. The one film she did finish in this period, "Summer Stock," attracted much comment because of her increased weight.

It was during the next year, 1950, that she slashed her wrists after M-G-M suspended her contract. She and Mr. Minnelli were divorced the next year.

In 1951 Miss Garland returned to the stage in England, doing a solo singing show with great success. She had another success with a vaudeville engagement at the New York Palace.

Frequently, however, she complained of laryngitis, and critics noted that her voice had lost some of its quality. At the same time they noted that her personality retained its full impact.

In reviewing a later performance at the Palace, Vincent Canby wrote in The New York Times of Aug. 1, 1967, that "that the voice—as of last night's performance, anyway—is now a memory seems almost beside the point." He concluded that all the performers on the bill were good, "but it is Judy who is great. And let's not worry about her voice."

Another writer called a typical Garland appearance "more than a concert . . . it is a tribal celebration." The crowds often screamed during her frenzied finales for "More! More!" and began the ritual chants of "We Love You, Judy!"

When she left the stage for intermission, Miss Garland often staggered to her dressing room, sometimes gasping, panting that she could not possibly finish the show, that she was exhausted or that her throat ached. But back she went.

Judy Garland with frequent co-star, Mickey Rooney.

Miss Garland described her feelings toward the audience for a magazine interviewer in 1961:

"A really great reception makes me feel like I have a great big warm heating pad all over me. People en masse have always been wonderful to me. I truly have a great love for an audience, and I used to want to prove it to them by giving them blood. But I have a funny new thing now, a real determination to make people enjoy the show. I want to give them two hours of just pow."

Return Impressive

The performer made an impressive return to films in 1954 with "A Star Is Born," with James Mason. But her erratic work habits had caused the production to take months longer than planned, at great expense. A commercial disappointment, the film represented a personal triumph for her.

Her best song in "A Star Is Born," a torch ballad called "The Man That Got Away," joined "Over the Rainbow" as a Garland trademark. She was expected to win an Academy Award for her performance, but Grace Kelly won it instead, for "The Country Girl."

For the next few years Miss Garland was plagued by throat troubles and marital difficulties. She was overweight for a star, consistently ill and more temperamental than ever. Hollywood would not risk employing her.

By the autumn of 1959 she was unable to work at all. She felt sick, frightened and mentally confused. In late November she was admitted to a New York hospital, where doctors found she was suffering from hepatitis.

They said she might have had the illness for as long as three years and that the hepatitis was attributed at least in part, to the combined effects of certain tranquilizers and diet pills that previous doctors, treating earlier breakdowns, had prescribed for her.

Miss Garland admitted at the time to having taken a great many drugs over the last 15 years, including sleeping pills, pep pills, diet medicines and nerve tonics.

Then, in 1960, she came back again. During a concert at London's Palladium, she was more successful than ever. She followed it with a spectacular, sobbing performance at Carnegie Hall.

Miss Garland signed for a weekly television series, with much fanfare, in 1963, but it was a failure. The carefully nurtured emotional impact that made each of her performances a special event was lost in the weekly program.

The Columbia Broadcasting System dropped the show after one season, amid loud complaints from the voluble legion of Garland fans.

Seemingly undaunted, she set out for Australia on another concert tour. Again she was plagued by "laryngitis."

When Miss Garland left Australia, she spoke wistfully about retiring and devoting herself to her three children, Liza Minnelli, 18, Lorna Luft, 11, and Joseph Luft, 9.

After her divorce from Mr. Luft, Miss Garland admitted to friends that she sometimes felt "like I'm living in a blizzard."

In 1965 she married Mark Herron, an actor. Two years later, they were divorced.

She went to London at the end of 1968 for a five-week cabaret appearance and announced she would marry Mr. Deans.

Looking slim and relaxed, Miss Garland won a standing ovation at her first London appearance. But then she began to appear late for performances, and one night walked off the stage when she was heckled by the audience, whom she had kept waiting for an hour and 20 minutes.

A few days later it was announced she was ill and would not finish the last week of the run. Unpredictable as ever, Miss Garland appeared on the stage that night, gave a smash performance and announced that she had married Mr. Deans three weeks earlier in a secret church ceremony.

The confusion from which Miss Garland often seemed to suffer in her personal life apparently extended to her performance in "The Wizard of Oz." Harold Arlen, who composed the score for the film, said she felt most deeply about the song "Over the Rainbow."

He quoted yesterday from a letter he said he had received from Miss Garland. She wrote: "As for my feelings toward 'Over the Rainbow,' it's become part of my life. It is so symbolic of all my dreams and wishes that I'm sure that's why people sometimes get tears in their eyes when they hear it."

But recently recalling her role in "The Wizard" in another context, she said, "I was really little tortured Tillie in the whole damn thing."

"All the News That's Fit to Print"

The New York Times

LATE CITY EDITION

Weather: Chance of light rain or drizzle today, tonight, tomorrow. Temp. range: today 59-44; Tuesday 60-51. Full U.S. report on Page 86.

VOL. CXX..No. 41,199 © 1970 The New York Times Company. NEW YORK, WEDNESDAY, NOVEMBER 11, 1970 15 CENTS

FRANCE MOURNS DE GAULLE; WORLD LEADERS TO ATTEND A SERVICE AT NOTRE DAME

Magnum (by Bruno Barbey)

CHARLES de GAULLE

A SIMPLE FUNERAL

Pompidou Tells Nation 'France Is a Widow' —Rites Tomorrow

Special to The New York Times

PARIS, Nov. 10—"General de Gaulle is dead. France is a widow."

With those words, delivered in a trembling voice, President Pompidou announced on radio and television this morning that Charles de Gaulle died last night at his country retreat in Colombey-les-Deux-Eglises. He would have been 80 years old Nov. 22.

Death came to the wartime leader and peacetime Premier and President while he was playing a game of solitaire on a little card table in the quiet of his living room. Stricken with a heart attack, he collapsed at 7:30 P.M. and is believed to have died of a ruptured aorta soon afterward.

No State Funeral

President Pompidou, who succeeded the general as chief of state on June 20, 1969, was immediately informed, as were other high officials, but public announcement was held up until 9:41 o'clock this morning. The Cabinet met hurriedly in a somber atmosphere, and the President made his broadcast at 1 P.M.

No explanation was given for the delay overnight in the announcement of the death, but it was believed that Mrs. de Gaulle wanted to be undisturbed in the hours immediately afterward.

According to the general's wishes, no state funeral will be held. General de Gaulle is to be buried Thursday morning in the churchyard of Colombey-les-Deux-Eglises in an "extremely simple" ceremony.

A memorial service will be held at the same hour — 11 A.M. — in Notre Dame Cathedral, and it is there that President Pompidou and other French leaders are to join with some 80 chiefs of foreign states or heads of government—among them President Nixon, Premier Aleksei N. Kosygin of the Soviet Union, Prime Minister Heath of Britain—for last homage to the soldier-statesman.

Nation in Mourning

Other leaders expected to attend include Chancellor Willy Brandt of West Germany, Emperor Haile Selassie of Ethiopia, Queen Juliana of the Netherlands and President Giuseppe Saragat of Italy.

National mourning until the end of the month has been proclaimed, and all flags have been placed at half-staff.

As the mourning began, the French National Assembly adjourned its session. The regular Thursday meeting of the Vietnam peace talks was postponed

Continued on Page 18, Column 1

Nixon Going to Paris Rites With Rogers and Kissinger

By ROBERT B. SEMPLE Jr.

Special to The New York Times

KEY BISCAYNE, Fla., Nov. 10—President Nixon will attend memorial services for Charles de Gaulle, the White House announced today. Mr. Nixon will leave Washington tomorrow morning with a small official delegation, attend the service at Notre Dame Cathedral in Paris on Thursday, and return to Washington late Thursday night.

The White House staff, in Florida, emphasized that Mr. Nixon was going "for the sole purpose of paying his respects to the memory of General de Gaulle," and would conduct no official business during his brief stay in Paris. [Mr. Nixon returned to Washington from Florida at 9:30 P.M. Tuesday.]

Hopes to See Pompidou

The White House press secretary, Ronald L. Ziegler, said the President hoped while in Paris to pay a brief "courtesy call" on President Pompidou, and White House sources said he might pay a similar call on Ambassador David K. E. Bruce, the chief American negotiator at the Paris peace talks.

In addition, there remained the possibility that Mr. Nixon might also meet Premier Aleksei N. Kosygin at the memorial services or elsewhere, but Mr. Ziegler emphasized repeatedly that no official meeting with any head of state had been planned.

Mr. Nixon will be accompanied to Paris by Secretary of State William P. Rogers, his national security adviser, Henry A. Kissinger, and Arthur K. Watson, Ambassador to Paris.

Continued on Page 18, Column 8

De Gaulle Foresaw Amity With the U.S.

By C. L. SULZBERGER

Special to The New York Times

PARIS, Nov. 10—Although Charles de Gaulle had a long record of disagreements with the United States and made no secret of his fear that American hegemony threatened to dominate the world, he came to believe by the end of his long political career that major differences between Washington and Paris were near an end.

On Feb. 14, 1969, two months before his resignation, he had his last long talk as chief of state with this correspondent. Until now the content of the conversation has been held in confidence—it was off the record—although he gave permission to take extensive notes.

He looked fit, better than ever, although several times during a talk of almost an hour he had small spasms of coughing. Even if he had a cold, it did not seem serious. His skin was ivory pale but healthy. His eyes had a piercing, wicked, shrewd look. He took off his glasses, but his eyes bored right into his visitor.

He seemed to have lost some weight—he was definitely less turnip shaped around the middle. He was really an ugly old man but had a very winning way and he talked with immense self-assurance.

As always he was keeping all his options open. He took no trouble to disguise his growing feelings against West Germany and was clearly frightened by the increase in German power. He thought it had been a mistake for France to join the Americans and British in supporting Bonn's desire to hold elections in West Berlin.

De Gaulle talked swiftly, with great concentration, persuasively and with a complete mastery of what he had in mind, as he shifted from topic to topic.

President Nixon was due to arrive on his only state visit to de Gaulle. Asked whether he felt that a new Administration in Washington would make it easier to improve French United States relations the general replied:

"I think this process had already begun before President

Continued on Page 18, Column 3

NEWS INDEX

GOVERNOR INVITES BLOC IN CONGRESS TO FISCAL PARLEY

State Delegation Is Urged to Unify on Getting More Money Back From U.S.

SESSION NOV. 23 CALLED

Rockefeller Says Limit Has Been Reached on Taxing —Cites Rising Demands

By WILLIAM E. FARRELL

Special to The New York Times

ALBANY, Nov. 10—Governor Rockefeller today invited the entire New York State Congressional delegation to meet with him on the state's "critical fiscal situation" and to try to create a unified effort to "get more of our money back from Washington."

The Governor also talked on the telephone with President Nixon today and arranged to meet him sometime next week in Washington.

In his first news conference since his re-election last week to a fourth term, Mr. Rockefeller sounded a theme he has uttered in the past but that he is expected to press with renewed vigor as he enters his 13th year in office faced with the possible prospect of having to increase taxes.

Gets 11 Cents on Dollar

In brief, his theme goes like this: New York State has just about taxed itself to the limits conducive to keeping existing industry and attracting new industry and jobs to the state. Two-thirds of the tax money collected here, or $23.5-billion, is sent to Washington, but the state receives only $2.5-billion, or 11 cents on the dollar, in return.

This, Mr. Rockefeller says, is inadequate if the state is to meet the ever-increasing demands of localities, which are themselves overtaxed and underfinanced.

"With the tremendous pressure on local government and state government to meet people's needs in this changing society," Mr. Rockefeller told newsmen assembled in the State Capitol, "we have got to have the full cooperation of the entire delegation, the largest delegation in the Congress, working for their constituents back home."

A spokesman for the Governor said later that the invitation to meet with Mr. Rockefeller at the St. Regis Hotel in New York at 11 A.M. on Nov. 23 had been extended to both

Continued on Page 51, Column 4

2 U.S. Generals in Ankara After Detention in Soviet

United Press International

From the front are: Maj. Gen. Edward C. D. Scherrer, Brig. Gen. Claude M. McQuarrie Jr. and Col. Cevdat Deneli of Turkey as they arrived by plane yesterday at Ankara.

By The Associated Press

ANKARA, Turkey, Nov. 10—Two United States Army generals and a Turkish colonel returned to Turkey from Soviet Armenia today three weeks after their light plane landed 12 miles on the other side of the border and they were interned.

One of the Americans, Maj. Gen. Edward C. D. Scherrer, chief of the United States military-aid mission in Turkey, said on his arrival at Etimesgut military airfield here: "The long trip was not pleasant, but we were very well treated."

The two other men are Brig. Gen. Claude M. McQuarrie Jr., head of the military-aid mission's army section, and Col. Cevdat Deneli, a liaison officer. The Turkish Foreign Ministry said that all three were "healthy and in good shape."

Later a three-man Turkish crew flew the twin-engine, six-seat United States Army plane and its American pilot, Maj. James P. Russell, back across the border to Kars, its original destination on the flight that ended in Soviet territory.

A Foreign Ministry source said that Turkish and Soviet generals and civilian officials had negotiated at the border

Continued on Page 10, Column 1

LAIRD AUTHORIZES MORE GUARD ARMS AND RIOT DRILLING

Request for $20-Million for Protection Stems From the Kent State Case

By DANA ADAMS SCHMIDT

Special to The New York Times

WASHINGTON, Nov. 10—Secretary of Defense Melvin R. Laird authorized additional training and weapons for the National Guard today to make riot control more effective and minimize injuries to guardsmen and the public.

While the program will go ahead immediately with existing stocks of weapons, Mr. Laird asked Congress for $20-million to cover the cost of 140,000 face shields and batons, 120,000 protective vests and additional training for new guardsmen and those dealing with civil disturbances.

Other items to be furnished to the Guard in larger quantities, Jerry W. Friedheim, the Pentagon spokesman, said, are shotguns, public address systems, floodlights, radios, anti-sniper rifles and chemical agent dispensers. These are available from existing Army stocks, he said.

Kent 'Heightened Concern'

Asked whether these actions had been taken as a result of the clash between National Guardsmen and students at Kent State University in Ohio last May 4, in which four students were killed, Mr. Friedheim replied that the incident "obviously heightened the concern for the protection of the guardsmen."

Increased training, greater bodily protection from stones and other projectiles, and weapons of lower velocity than a combat rifle will reduce the chances of guardsmen firing into a crowd out of fear, he observed.

Mr. Friedheim estimated that the added training would about double the time now devoted by National Guard units to riot control training.

Mr. Laird's actions were in line with recommendations made on Sept. 26 by the President's Commission on Campus Unrest, headed by William W. Scranton, former Governor of Pennsylvania. The commission urged that National Guardsmen, who have in the last three years been called upon more than 200 times to intervene in civil disorders, be given "much more training."

Although there has been no formal response by the Administration to the commission's findings, the report became an

Continued on Page 14, Column 2

250,000 Subway Riders Stalled for Up to 5 Hours

By MICHAEL KNIGHT

More than 250,000 subway riders were delayed in a five-hour period through the evening rush hour yesterday when riders pulled emergency cords, automatically stopping trains and causing an almost complete shutdown of service in Queens and major delays throughout the system.

The delays were further complicated when several thousand frustrated and panicky passengers abandoned the trains and wandered on the tracks, forcing the Transit Authority to cut off the power.

City police and Transit Authority police officials said last night that they would begin investigations into the possibility of a plot to disrupt the city's subway system.

Trains were halted at least five times when passengers pulled emergency cords. A motorman on an N train in Brooklyn found his path blocked by a pipe laid across the tracks. Passengers in Queens broke car windows as they fled the halted trains and wandered on the tracks, forcing the Transit Authority to cut off power.

More than 20 people were treated for heat prostration, exhaustion and oxygen deficiency at an emergency first-aid center

Continued on Page 89, Column 1

6 RESERVE BANKS CUT LENDING RATE

Reduction From 6 to 5¾% in Discount Level Called 'Technical' by Board

By EDWIN L. DALE Jr.

Special to The New York Times

WASHINGTON, Nov. 10 — The Federal Reserve Board announced today a small reduction in the discount rate, in response to the recent sharp decline in other short-term interest rates.

The reduction from 6 to 5¾ per cent is in the rate charged by the Reserve to banks temporarily short of funds, and it may or may not affect interest rates charged to business and personal borrowers. By itself, it would not spur the economy, and a spokesman termed the move "purely technical."

[Reaction among New York bankers was largely one of disappointment that the reduction was not by a full half point, the amount that the markets seemed to have been anticipating.]

The precedents for changes in the discount rate affecting other rates are mixed, though the discount rate has considerable symbolic importance. In current circumstances the move may add to other pressures in the direction of a reduction in the "prime" lending rate of banks to their best corporate customers, already reduced

Continued on Page 63, Column 5

SUFFOLK FORBIDS DETERGENTS' SALE

Action, Believed the Nation's First, Is Taken to Keep Drinking Water Pure

By CARTER B. HORSLEY

Special to The New York Times

HAUPPAUGE, L. I., Nov. 10—The Suffolk County Legislature unanimously approved today a ban on the sale of virtually all detergents in the county. The only exceptions are those used in such relatively minor products as dishwashing powder, shampoos and tooth paste.

The action, which was believed to be the first of its kind taken by any local government in the country, will take effect next March 1, following the expected approval of County Executive H. Lee Dennison.

The law bars the sale of most laundry detergent products, including many national brands, in Suffolk, a county of 1.1 million people.

The Suffolk County Board of Health and the Suffolk County Water Authority had warned that continued widespread use of the detergents would seriously pollute the county's underground water supply and

Continued on Page 40, Column 1

Calley Jury to Hear Witnesses Barred In First Mylai Trial

By HOMER BIGART

Special to The New York Times

FORT BENNING, Ga., Nov. 10—The military judge in the murder trial of First Lieut. William L. Calley Jr. opened the way today for testimony by key prosecution witnesses who were barred from taking the stand at the trial of another defendant in the alleged massacre of South Vietnamese civilians at Mylai.

It was a serious legal setback for Lieutenant Calley, whose counsel had hoped that the judge, Col. Reid W. Kennedy, would follow the ruling last month of Col. George R. Robinson in the trial of Staff Sgt. David Mitchell at Fort Hood, Tex.

When a House Armed Services subcommittee refused to release testimony given at closed hearings on the incident in South Vietnam, Colonel Robinson ruled out testimony by any witnesses who had appeared at those hearings.

Colonel Robinson based his ruling on a 1957 law, the Jencks Act, permitting defense counsel to search for inconsistencies between a witness's

Continued on Page 5, Column 3

DRUG WAREHOUSE IS RAIDED ON L.I.

Dealer Accused of Selling Dangerous Pills to All

By MORRIS KAPLAN

A wholesale drug distributor was arrested yesterday on charges of selling thousands of doses of stimulants and depressants to virtually anyone who ordered them, ignoring requirements for prescriptions.

Law-enforcement authorities said it was the first time that such an action had been taken against a wholesale distributor in this area.

The distributor, Raymond Howard of 61 Shade Tree Lane, Roslyn Heights, L. I., was accused of having openly promoted sale of the drugs in widely distributed printed color brochures, soliciting purchases by the general public.

In a raid yesterday on one of his company warehouses in Plainview, L. I., Federal agents seized pills that they said would be worth $1-million in street sales.

In another drug case yesterday, a 34-year-old Cuban refugee was sentenced to up to life imprisonment for possession of narcotics, becoming the first person to receive the maximum penalty under a new state law. [Story on Page 54.]

Edward R. Neaher, United

Continued on Page 54, Column 6

Veterans Day

Today is Veterans Day. Following is a list of services that are affected:

Public and parochial schools —Closed.

Parking — Alternate-side-of-the-street regulations suspended. Other regulations in effect.

Post Office — Closed except for special delivery and perishables.

Stores—Most retail stores open.

Banks—Closed.

Stock Exchanges—Open.

Sanitation—No regular refuse collection.

Libraries — Main reading room of the Library at Fifth Avenue and 42d Street open from 9 A.M. to 10 P.M.; special rooms open from 1 to 6 P.M. All neighborhood branches closed except for Young Adult Library, 20 West 53d Street, open from noon to 10 P.M.

E. M. Forster Homosexual Novel Due

By ANTHONY LEWIS

Special to The New York Times

LONDON, Nov. 10 — A novel by E. M. Forster, withheld at his request for 55 years because of its homosexual theme, is now to be published.

The manuscript was found among Forster's papers after his death last June at the age of 91. Across the top he had written: "Publishable—but is it worth it?"

The novel, entitled "Maurice," was written between 1913 and 1915. Forster told his London publisher, Edward Arnold, about it years ago but said he did not want it to appear during his lifetime.

The publisher now hopes to bring it out by next fall. The exact date will depend on completion of legal formalities under the will, and preparation of the manuscript by Forster's literary executor, Prof. W. J. H. Sprott, of Nottingham University, and authorized biographer, P. N. Furbank.

Although universally regarded as a major figure in English fiction of this century, Forster wrote only five novels. The publication of a new one will be a major literary event.

The last was "A Passage to India," in 1924. Forster published numerous essays after that date, but his decades of silence as a novelist helped to make him a man of fascination and mystery in literary history.

Collection of Evert Barger

E. M. Forster in a portrait painted in 1911 by Roger Fry

The publication of "Maurice" will also throw more light on Forster's own homosexuality, and on changing British attitudes toward homosexuality in this century.

Forster's writing was so restrained and his public personality so reticent that many admirers probably never wondered about his sexuality. But since his death the question has been candidly discussed in Britain.

Lord Annan, intellectual historian and provost of University College, London, said last July in a British Broad-

Continued on Page 42, Column 6

France Mourns de Gaulle; World Leaders Will Attend Memorial at Notre Dame

Pompidou Tells People That 'France Is Widow'

Continued From Page 1, Col. 8

for a week and the general conference of the United Nations Educational, Scientific and Cultural Organization met and recessed.

The funeral arrangements were made in accord with what Mr. Pompidou read when he opened an envelope, on which was written "For My Funeral," that was handed to him on Jan. 16, 1952.

Ruling out a national funeral, the general had said that only the French armed forces could participate officially, but in modest numbers. There was to be no eulogy in Colombey or elsewhere, and no places were to be reserved except for the family, members of the Colombey Municipal Council and companions of the Order of Liberation—those who were the first to join de Gaulle in 1940, when he called on France to continue the war against Nazi Germany.

But the general added:

"The men and women of France and of other countries of the world may, if they wish, do my memory the honor of accompanying my body to its last resting place, but it is in silence that I wish it to be conducted."

Special trains and buses were to take the thousands of people expected Thursday in Colombey, and the National Federation of Road Transport asked trucks to stay off the roads leading to the Haute-Marne Department, where the village of a few hundred people is situated, about 120 miles east of Paris.

The body lay in the living room of the Colombey house dressed in a brigadier general's uniform with the French tricolor draped across it. At the feet was the Cross of Lorraine, symbol of the wartime Fighting French, and in the general's hands was a rosary given him by Pope Paul VI.

Debré Is First Visitor

Around him were his wife, their daughter Elizabeth, and her husband, Gen. Alain de Boissieu, and the de Gaulles' son, Philippe, a navy captain, and his wife. There are seven grandchildren.

The first Government member to arrive was Defense Minister Michel Debré, the general's first Premier and one of his most ardent supporters. Unable to go to the funeral because the general did not wish them to, President Pompidou and Premier Jacques Chaban-Delmas are expected to visit tomorrow.

It became known today that de Gaulle lapsed into unconsciousness on his collapse. His wife, who was with him, called a physician and a Roman Catholic priest, Canon Claude Jaugey, and they arrived as he was at the point of death.

Mr. Pompidou, in his television appearance, looked and talked like a man profoundly affected by the death of the man who had brought him into public life and paved his way to supreme power. After saying "France is a widow," Mr. Pompidou declared:

"In 1940 de Gaulle saved honor. In 1944 he led us to liberation and to victory. In 1958 he spared us civil war. He gave today's France her institutions, her independence and her place in the world.

"In this hour of mourning for the fatherland, let us bow before the sorrow of Mrs. de Gaulle, her children and her grandchildren. Let us measure the duties that gratitude imposes upon us. Let us promise to France to be worthy of the lessons given us, and in the national soul let de Gaulle live eternally."

Theaters to be Closed

As part of the national mourning, radio and television stations abandoned their regular programs in favor of those with a solemn cast. Ordinary Frenchmen went about their business as usual, however.

The country is to begin dropping its normal routine tomorrow with the Armistice Day holiday. On Thursday all movie and legitimate theaters are to be closed, as are schools and government offices.

In the National Assembly, many legislators heard the news only after their arrival for a budget debate, which was canceled.

Marc Jaquet, head of the Gaullist group, called out to his associates "Children, Father is dead!" After de Gaulle's departure from power last year, the Gaullist deputies were often called "de Gaulle's orphans."

The Communist party, in a double-edged statement, recalled the general's wartime role and said, "His death could leave no Frenchman indifferent." It added that he returned to power in 1958 at the head of "an authoritarian regime" in accordance with "the aspirations of big capital."

While most comments of public figures were eulogies, a similar distinction between the liberator of 1944 and the statesman of 1958-69 was drawn by the Socialist Daniel Mayer. Guy Mollet, the former Premier who fought de Gaulle during the last decade, said that it was the wrong moment to discuss his place in history.

On the Avenue de Breteuil, behind Les Invalides, hundreds of Parisians waited patiently in a light drizzle to sign a remembrance book in the hallway of de Gaulle's modest apartment-office.

The man they mourned, a leader who in war and peace refused to accept defeat or second-class status for France, had been out of power and virtually out of sight since April 28, 1969.

On the previous day, a Sunday, the French had rejected in a referendum one of the last of the great reforms he had contemplated; a decentralization of power by forming regions and making over the composition of the Senate to reflect the new regional arrangement.

He had said he would resign if the proposals were rejected and toward midnight, as the result became certain, he announced that he would cease to exercise his functions as of noon the next day.

First Memoir Appeared

So far as the public was concerned, he was never heard from again until last month, when the first of what was to be a three-volume set of memoirs appeared. He made no public appearances, except as a tourist, and no public statements. Offices were set up for him in Paris but he refused to occupy them.

When the election to choose his successor was held, he went to Ireland.

He dwelt on the past, and those who watched him work on the memoirs reported that he did so with the intensity of a man who was afraid death might catch him before he could finish. Only two chapters of the volume are complete, it is said. The first has seven chapters.

The second volume had been awaited with at least as much curiosity as the first because it covered a period in which Mr. Pompidou played a role of the first rank as Premier for six years. The general barely mentioned his successor in the first volume.

Last Day Was a Usual One

COLOMBEY - LES - DEUX - EGLISES, France, Nov. 10 (AP)—De Gaulle's last day, according to members of his family, was a normal one—going through his mail and writing, in the strong penmanship that rarely needed erasure or correction.

He began work at 9:30 A.M., two chapters into the text of the work on his final presidential years. He ate lunch with his wife and they walked in the woods, part of their routine.

He worked on his manuscript again in the afternoon. Around 7 P.M. he began a game of solitaire while waiting for the evening news.

Canon Jaugey related later that Mrs. de Gaulle said her husband put both hands below his waist and cried out: "Oh, how it hurts!"

When the priest arrived de Gaulle was unconscious and "was suffering terribly."

De Gaulle had attended mass as usual the day before. "He seemed normal," the priest said. "There were no signs of fatigue or apparent illness. Everyone was surprised."

Nixon Goes To Services Tomorrow

Continued From Page 1, Col. 7

In addition, Mr. Ziegler said the President has invited General de Gaulle's grandson Charles de Gaulle to accompany him to Paris aboard Air Force One. The grandson has been in New York since last week.

Earlier today, the White House released the following statement from the President:

"The passing of General de Gaulle reminds us of the qualities that make men and nations great. His was the quality of character that enables men to surmount all obstacles, to call up reserves of courage, to turn adversity into triumph.

"His was the quality of vision that could see the grand sweep of history at a time when others focused on the events of the moment. He provided inspiration to an age in danger of being overwhelmed by the commonplace and, therefore, his passing is a loss not only for the French nation but for all mankind."

Sends Letter in Addition

The President expressed many of the same sentiments in a letter to President Pompidou, in which he said he had been "shocked and grieved at the passing" of a man whom he described as a "steadfast ally in war and a true friend in peace."

"Greatness," the President continued in the letter, "knows no national boundaries, and therefore France's loss is the loss of mankind."

Mr. Nixon's decision to attend the memorial services forced him to curtail a "working vacation" here and postpone a luncheon for Luis Echeverría Alvarez, President-elect of Mexico, scheduled for Thursday. The luncheon has been rescheduled for Friday at the White House.

Mr. Nixon met de Gaulle several times and their relations were cordial. The warmest meeting was on Feb. 28, 1969, when the two men had a long, friendly talk during a visit in Paris by Mr. Nixon. De Gaulle subsequently told his Cabinet that the visit had deepened their personal and political relations.

While Vice President, Mr. Nixon met de Gaulle and in his book "Six Crises" recalls a talk in April, 1960, in which de Gaulle "commented philosophically on the fact that he was one of those rare individuals who was seeing some of his greatest days late in life."

Mr. Nixon while a private citizen visited de Gaulle occasionally in the sixties and during that period de Gaulle was quoted as predicting that Mr. Nixon was a "man with a great future."

In 1969 de Gaulle Foresaw Renewal of Amicable Relations With U.S.

Continued From Page 1, Col. 8

Johnson left office. Our relations were starting to get better during the last months of his Administration, and for natural reasons. But right now it is even easier to further this tendency because of developments. It is not a question of Presidents but of the problems posed.

"For us the principal question between our countries was NATO. But now that is all over. Now it is no longer a subject for discussion as far as we are concerned. There is no NATO for us French so there is no reason to have a problem on this with Washington." By this de Gaulle meant that France was no longer in the NATO "organization" although it remained a partner in the North Atlantic Treaty.

'It Will Lead to Peace'

"Then there was Vietnam," he continued, "but President Johnson started negotiations while he was still in office. The negotiation is bound to go on for a very long time. That is inevitable. But it has started and, in the end, it will lead to peace.

"There is no reason for major differences between us now. Our problems are on the road to solution. Of course, there is the question of the Middle East. We have not been in accord with you on this since 1967, but you should remember that this is merely a reverse of the previous situation.

"With the Fourth Republic there was also disagreement. You were against France and Israel in 1956 at the time of the Suez invasion for reasons that are just the contrary of our differences now. Now the United States is with Israel, which wishes to take the Suez Canal. The United States has changed its policy—and so has France.

"We agree that Israel should exist and should be a state—but not in an exaggerated way. The situation in the Middle East is not good today and it is not soluble along the lines Israel wishes. On this subject perhaps Nixon can draw closer to our policy."

Reverting to a possible improvement in United States-French relations, de Gaulle said:

"There is another aspect to the whole problem—namely relations with Russia. Little by little you are becoming more like us in your view of this problem.

"Like us you do not want to have them submerge Europe. But you are beginning to see that it is useful to develop practical contacts such as those we started. You will follow the same path that we have been following because that is the practical approach."

Long U. S.-French Amity

With regard to the two superpowers he said:

"We have always favored the United States. Historically, we have always been friends. We have been rivals before. Remember, in the past you were in Africa, in Asia or even in Europe.

"Also you should remember that we have old reasons for being friends of Russia. For us, in Europe, this Russian friendship has always been necessary as counterweight to Germany. Constantly in history we have sought to be on good terms with Russia, with the Czars, with the Soviets, as a counterweight to Germany. We have been old friends with America and old allies of Russia.

"Today we have no reason to renounce friendship with the United States. Nor, especially now that Germany re-emerges, have we any reason to break off with Russia."

"And another thing," he went on, "something you should never forget, is that one must always remember what France was historically, just after the war and what it is today. France is as it is and the French are as they are. If the French do not think of France, it disappears. But you cannot think of France if you lose a sense of independence. The friendship of the French for the United States requires no American hegemony.

"The same is true of Russia. It is for that reason that the Communists have never succeeded here; for national reasons, not for social reasons."

"As for Britain," he said, "Britain has renounced its independence. It has sold it off for advantages of all sorts. And Italy counts for very little."

Asked if the ultimate aim of his policy was to neutralize the Mediterranean, expelling both the American and Soviet fleets, he replied:

"The Mediterranean is open to everyone but we think that the concentration of a big United States fleet and the appearance of a big Soviet fleet do not

(continued)

constitute anything good for peace.

"However, if an international détente can be brought about, there will no longer be any reason for a permanent United States fleet stationed in the Mediterranean. And at that point that would reduce the reason for the presence of a Soviet fleet."

On the question how long American troops should remain in Europe, he said: "Until there is a real East-West détente, it is obviously normal to keep American troops in Germany. But if there is a *real* détente, there would be no more reason for such detachments except for symbolic units. But the fact that you have troops in Germany now does not irritate us; so have we."

Conversation in Moscow

The general was reminded that the official Soviet account of his conversations with Stalin in December, 1944, quoted him as saying: "French policy compels Frenchmen to desire first of all mutual-assistance pact with the Soviet Union." Asked if that was still true, he answered:

"When Germany is a danger, yes. If there is a German danger, we would have to have an alliance. You must remember how much both Russia and France suffered from Germany. If Germany were to become a big power militarily, economically and in a nuclear sense, we would have to have an alliance. Neither of us can accept a dangerous Germany."

Asked if he thought it feasible to work out a compromise revision of the world monetary system, he spoke for a few moments in a way that suggested that he was getting just bit beyond his depth. He confessed rather disarmingly: "Of course, you know, I am not a great expert on these things."

Nevertheless, he plunged ahead, speaking of gold as the world criterion for the balance of payments between states and saying that a common value must be agreed upon. Obviously, he added, its value has to be increased.

Neutral Stance in Mideast

Again discussing the Middle East, he indicated that the French considered themselves neutral as between the Israelis and the Arabs, in the sense that they would support either side if attacked by the other. "In 1967 I told Israel not to attack," he recalled. "I also told the same to the Arabs. We told both sides that we would hold either one responsible if it attacked the other."

A question about Nigeria and the Biafran civil war, then going on, led to a discussion of Canada.

"There is a French people there," he said. "They do not want to be anything else. There is also an English people, and in the West there is a people that is almost American.

"They must make up their own union on the basis of reciprocal engagements on such things as defense or currency. But to pretend to make English law on the backs of the French in Quebec cannot work. It is not just. It would be better to accept a state of Quebec in a union of Canada."

In Colombey, General Was Remote Figure

By ANDREAS FREUND

Special to The New York Times

COLOMBEY - LES - DEUX - EGLISES, France, Nov. 10 — A middle-aged man in a blue woolen sweater said, yes, he knew de Gaulle by sight, he had always seen him Sundays, at mass, and thus last Sunday. "He looked the same as usual, he looked in good health," he said.

A little blond girl in a red dress said shyly she, too, had seen the general, but not last Sunday, because she missed mass that day.

But none in this lovely hilltop village overlooking the autumnal splendor of the rolling countryside of Champagne where it borders on Lorraine ever seemed to have seen the general on days other than Sundays and places other than church.

"He was well liked, but he was remote," a waitress said.

They Learn on Radio

The man in the blue sweater offered an explanation for that remoteness: "He could never go out alone. Always he was escorted by half a dozen bodyguards, as if he were a prisoner. It must have been protocol but embarrassing to him. So he stayed home."

The people of Colombey, of whom there are 395, mostly learned of the death of their neighbor as the rest of France did: from the radio. But two of them knew before. One was the parish priest, Canon Claude Jaugey, called during the evening as the general was dying. He said that when he arrived at La Boisserie, the stately residence of the de Gaulles, "The general was still alive, although not conscious."

But the canon added that at one point when he administered the last sacraments, the general moved his eyelids slightly indicating awareness.

The other citizen informed slightly ahead of everyone this morning was the Mayor, Jean Raullet, who appeared somewhat helpless in the face of sudden prominence.

He did his best to answer questions from reporters, "several hundreds" of whom came to this town 120 miles east of Paris, according to the police.

Reporters were barred from La Boisserie, where only members of the family and two particular friends were admitted, as far as could be immediately ascertained. The two were Defense Minister Michel Debré, and a retired general, Jacques Massu.

In the morning, the Prefect of the Marne Department was also admitted briefly. The Prefect, Paul Dijoud, said the general's body, in the uniform of his military rank and covered with a tricolor, was lying in state in a salon adjacent to La Boisserie's main entrance.

House Hidden in Trees

La Boisserie, at one of the outer limits of the village, was invisible behind its ancient trees and thick stone walls. The estate was silent, its gate guarded by gendarmes.

By contrast, the square around the village church was busy with cars arriving and departing, and photographers aiming cameras at the church, which is the only one in the village, despite the implications of its name. It is a small, solid, Romanesque church in gray stone with a steep roof over its square tower. Adjoining is the cemetery where de Gaulle asked to be buried.

It is a small cemetery, with not many over a hundred family graves. The tombstones bear such local names as Leboeuf and Renard. From the cemetery, full of brown, yellow and violet chrysanthemums, the view is much as from La Boisserie, across the countryside below.

The grave of the de Gaulles' daughter Anne, next to whom he will be buried, is in a far corner. It is of ordinary whitish stone, surmounted by a cross. The inscription says only "à Anne de Gaulle."

General's Long Career: He Left Indelible Mark on Nation During 10 Years as President

By HENRY GINIGER

Special to The New York Times

PARIS, Nov. 10—Was Charles de Gaulle merely a moment in the history of France? Now that he is dead, has the moment passed?

An Appraisal

At a dinner once at the Elysée Palace, where de Gaulle reigned and ruled for 10 years, someone remarked that nothing would be better for Europe than to put an end to the centuries of enmity between France and Germany. "I have been saying that for a thousand years," de Gaulle commented.

It was his way of identifying himself with France. His fellow Frenchmen did not become aware of that incarnation until 1940, when, after France's worst military defeat, he appealed to her from British soil to fight on. For the next 30 years, in and out of power, he spread the idea by his words and actions that he really was France and that, through him, it was France that was speaking and acting.

"Everyone has been, is or will be a Gaullist," he once said, meaning that at some time or another every Frenchman could accept him. But at no particular time were his countrymen unanimous about him and the role he ought to play. He never achieved the unity he so cherished, but in this profoundly divided and opiniated country no French leader before him had ever achieved unanimity except for short intervals.

What is left of all the changes he wrought, which were so bitterly fought during his lifetime?

He radically transformed France's political structures with a Constitution that subdued Parliament, making the President pre-eminent in formulating and executing policy and making the Government an emanation of the presidency rather than of the National Assembly.

He did so with the support of a majority of the people but, as in 1945, he found the old political class arrayed against him. Some could not accept the way in which the Fourth Republic was brought to its knees by a civil and military uprising in Algiers, accompanied by the threat of a military attack on Paris, and they held de Gaulle responsible for what had occurred. Others objected to the power given one man, particularly when, in 1962, de Gaulle had the Constitution modified by popular referendum to provide for popular election of the President.

In foreign affairs de Gaulle proclaimed French independence, denounced the division of the world into two hegemonies, American and Soviet, and asserted France's claim to a position in the front rank of nations.

To back his words, he built up an independent atomic force as the only military force that really counted, pulled French troops from the American-dominated military organization of the North Atlantic Alliance, restored the franc to the position of a strong and stable currency, paralyzed moves toward political integration in Europe and traveled far to preach the doctrine of national sovereignty and nonintervention in other people's affairs.

He became a kind of spokesman for all the little nations that did not want to be lined up automatically in one camp or another. He was able to do so because France had ended most of her own hegemony overseas and, for the first time since 1939, was at peace with the world.

In this field, too, he was contested. There were those who found his aspirations to independence empty and even dangerous pretension — dangerous because, they said, France could not really go it alone and empty because France was in an undeveloped state and had neither the industrial nor the commercial strength to match the brave words.

The first major test of the institutions the general established came in 1969 when, after his sudden resignation upon his defeat in a referendum, new presidential elections were held. Even those who thought presidential power was dangerous participated fully.

The institutions did face a serious crisis in 1968 during the student and worker disorders. De Gaulle's force of character and the fear of something worse helped to preserve them.

The transition to President Pompidou was smooth, without the chaos, disorder and confusion that some had predicted.

In the ranks of the Gaullists some uncertainty and some suspicion of Mr. Pompidou's orthodoxy were evident. But in Parliament, as in the country, the movement stayed behind the President. Formed around a man, Gaullism has continued to live as an effort to perpetuate the institutions and philosophy of the man.

A Diluted Philosophy

The majority in the country and in Parliament is no longer purely Gaullist, so the philosophy has become a bit diluted. Other elements, mostly conservative, have joined to widen the political base of the regime. Part of the cohesion of this group, which includes people who opposed de Gaulle at one time or another, is forged by the conviction that only such a majority is capable of preserving France from a Communist-dominated government.

Abroad, France is speaking with a quieter and, some say, a more realistic voice. But there are some things Mr. Pompidou will not go back on. The atomic force is being built up and France will not submit it or any of her other military strength to the North Atlantic Treaty Organization.

Educated to a Gaullist way of thinking, Mr. Pompidou has done little to upset the general lines of Gaullist policy, though they may be followed in a less assertive way. A balance between the United States and the Soviet Union is being kept, although a warmer atmosphere between Paris and Washington has been established.

In Western Europe France continues to move cautiously in the direction of political unity but has ended the boycott on British entry into the Common Market—a move de Gaulle was expected to make himself.

A major element of de Gaulle's assertion of leadership among the nonaligned nations was his attempt to rebuild French positions among the Arabs, which led him into a clash with Israel. Mr. Pompidou has, if anything, tried to reinforce the policy, but it has run into difficulties.

De Gaulle's successor has been more attentive to weaknesses at home—outmoded industry, the lack of good roads, the telephones that do not work, the shortages of housing, hospitals and schools. De Gaulle's strong franc proved remarkably vulnerable and Pompidou had to devalue it —something de Gaulle had refused to do—before starting financial recovery.

There is greater awareness of French limitations and more prudence in asserting French power. It is a more mundane approach, and the people seem satisfied with it. But few are likely to forget soon the heady moments of Gaullist rule.

Last year, after the shock and bitterness of defeat, de Gaulle contemplated French ingratitude and became philosophical about it.

"One has to understand — and I do understand—that the march toward and on the heights cannot last without some respite" he wrote to a follower. "Here we are therefore, on the road down. But I am sure that the heights will regain their prestige if only there are the right circumstances and the men of character to exploit them."

If the French are operating at a less rarified level, it is still considerably higher than when de Gaulle came on the scene. That much at least, they remember and seem grateful for even those who fought him.

In Paris, Some Tears And Business as Usual

Special to The New York Times

PARIS, Nov. 10—There were some reddened eyes and a few unashamed tears, but the visible reaction of most Frenchmen to the death of Charles de Gaulle seemed to range from grave reflection to outward indifference.

In Paris, which had hailed de Gaulle as liberator and hooted him as autocrat, the crowds went about their business as usual. Stores and beauty parlors were crowded on the eve of the Armistice Day holiday and bars and restaurants served their normal trade. Few talked about the event to strangers.

On the Avenue de Breteuil behind Les Invalides, hundreds waited patiently under a light drizzle to sign a remembrance book in the hallway of de Gaulle's modest apartment-office. Most were middle-aged or older and appeared to be of the lower middle class.

De Gaulle Rallied France in War and Strove to Lead Her to Greatness

By ALDEN WHITMAN

"Your reply is going to determine the destiny of France," an intense, solemn yet aged voice told the French people on April 25, 1969, "because if I am disavowed by the majority of you, my present task as chief of state would obviously become impossible [and] I would immediately stop exercising my functions."

That curiously aloof yet paternal voice, which in 1940 had exhorted a prostrate nation to rise from defeat and fight still against a merciless and omnipresent enemy, and which in the years after 1958 had rallied a country to grandeur and glory beyond her size and resources, had now lost the compelling eloquence that, less than a year earlier, had seemed invincible. Thus it was that two days after his appeal for confidence over a relatively minor issue, Charles de Gaulle was repudiated by 53 per cent of the voters. And within 12 hours he departed the splendorous Elysée Palace on the banks of the Seine in Paris, his residence for almost 11 years, for his plain home in the tiny village of Colombey-les-Deux-Eglises. More than the end of a singular political reign, it was the end of an era.

That era started virtually unobserved on June 18, 1940, when an obscure temporary brigadier general, having escaped to London from a battered and disorganized France about to capitulate to Nazi Germany, exhorted his countrymen to continue in a war that he perceived would evolve into a world conflict.

"But has the last word been said?" the 49-year-old officer asked in his pungent speech in a British Broadcasting Corporation studio. "Must we abandon all hope? Is our defeat final and irremediable? To those questions I answer—No!

"For remember this, France is not alone. She is not alone. She is not alone. Behind her is a vast empire, and she can make common cause with the British Empire, which commands the seas and is continuing the struggle."

He concluded with these characteristically self-confident words:

"I, General de Gaulle, now in London, invite French officers and men who are at present in British soil, or may be in the future, with or without their arms; I invite engineers and skilled workmen from the armaments factories who are at present on British soil, or may be in the future, to get in touch with me.

"Whatever happens, the flame of French resistance must not and shall not die."

Very few Frenchmen heard that impromptu broadcast; and at first very few hearkened to it. In Britain, too, de Gaulle was unknown except by a few Cabinet ministers and Prime Minister Winston Churchill. Churchill, however, had an intuitive confidence in him, having already addressed him as "l'homme du destin."

"He carried with him in his small airplane the honor of France," Churchill wrote later of the general's flight to Britain.

Although it seemed ludicrous to some that de Gaulle, with a mere 100,000 francs and a handful of volunteers, could put together a Free French cause, the general exuded total faith in himself.

"When leaders fail," he wrote, "new leaders are projected upward out of the eternal spirit of France: from Charlemagne to Joan of Arc to Napoleon, Poincaré and Clemenceau. Perhaps this time I am one of those thrust into leadership by the failure of others."

And alluding to his self-conceived mission he wrote in "The Call to Honor," the first of his three-volume war memoirs:

"What I was determined to save was the French Nation and the French State. What I had to bring back into the war was not just Frenchmen, but France."

In a tone that appeared to derive from Louis XIV, he added:

"C'était à moi d'assumer la France." ("It was up to me to take responsibility for France.")

This merger of identities — in which de Gaulle believed himself to be the incarnation of the nation standing superior to factions — accounted for many of his actions, just as it roiled his critics. His certainty that he was France ("Je suis la France," he declared in 1940) sustained him thorough many mutations of fortune before the country's liberation in mid-1944; and it emboldened him when he was shaping the Fifth Republic, decolonizing the empire, freeing Algeria, creating a nuclear capability and fashioning a foreign policy designed to give France an independent world stature. His certainty, which some saw as hubris, or arrogance, also contributed to his downfall — to his blindness to the domestic economic disaffections that turned public opinion against him.

As he emerged in 1940, de Gaulle appeared tailored to the role of a man of destiny. Describing him after his initial broadcast, Pierre Bourdan wrote:

"I saw a man of another age. Very tall [he was 6 feet 4 inches], he was wearing a uniform and leggings and held himself extremely straight. But this erectness, accentuated by his thrown-back head and by his arms, which followed exactly the line of his body, seemed a natural and comfortable position for him.

A Preordained Look

"The bearing of his head, so very remote, and the expression of his face showed his intransigence.

"The chief characteristic of his eyes was that they were oblivious of the outer world. Their expression could not change to suit the mood of the people around him. Their look seemed preordained!"

It was this hauteur that permitted him to stride into the pantheon of heroes in August, 1944, as he led a Paris liberation parade from the Arch of Triumph to Notre Dame. Cheered by two million people in an explosion of national fervor, he experienced his finest hour, his apotheosis.

It was this hauteur, too, that exasperated Allied leaders during the war. "The Cross of Lorraine [de Gaulle's emblem] was the heaviest cross I have ever had to bear," Churchill once bristled, although he conceded in another context, "Never mind, he defied all. . ."

The general's fervid nationalism ("France cannot be France without greatness") impressed Stalin, and it seemed to him that this idiosyncratic conception of France explained de Gaulle.

De Gaulle as a Saint-Cyr cadet, class of '11.

"He is not a complicated man," Stalin remarked at the Yalta Conference in 1945. He thought that giving France an occupation zone in Germany was a courtesy gesture, not a right she had won in the war.

President Franklin D. Roosevelt's relations with de Gaulle were hostile from the outset. Suspicious of the general, Roosevelt saw him as "more and more unbearable," as petty, vainglorious and, potentially, a dictator. These attitudes, reinforced by gossip from French exiles in the United States and by adverse reports from the State Department and from pro-Vichy diplomats, involved the United States in a search for alternatives to de Gaulle up to the liberation of Paris.

"De Gaulle may be a good man," Roosevelt told Churchill in 1943, "but he has a messianic complex." One result of the President's mistrust was to foster in the hypersensitive de Gaulle an animosity toward the United States. He never forgot that the United States tried to maneuver him into turning over Free French leadership to Gen. Henri-Honoré Giraud in 1943; that the United States did not recognize the French National Committee until mid-1944, and then only grudgingly; and that Roosevelt had blackballed him from Yalta.

Although impersonal factors undoubtedly entered into the general's American policy, he was convinced on the basis of his own experience that the United States, in the war and later, was seeking "to settle Europe's future in France's absence." This sentiment hardened, and in the nineteen-sixties he believed the evidence of world events showed that the United States was aggressive, was engaging in "a dirty little war in Vietnam" and was a menace of great magnitude to European and world stability.

This estimate undoubtedly underlay his efforts to scuttle the North Atlantic Treaty Organization and American arming of West Germany. It also was in part responsible for his diplomatic initiatives in Latin America, Africa, the Soviet bloc, China and Southeast Asia. Tweaking the eagle's beak was not only a calculated sport; it was also a constituent of French glory.

Although much was made of de Gaulle's aloofness and his sibylline utterances, the founder and first President of the Fifth Republic was less of a mystery to those who had read his philosophy of leadership, as set down in "Le fil de l'épée" ("The Edge of the Sword") in 1932.

'The Mark of Grandeur'

Doctrine, character and prestige, he wrote, are the indispensable ingredients in a leader. "It is essential that the plan on which the leader has concentrated all his faculties shall bear the mark of grandeur," he wrote. And on another page he said, "First and foremost there can be no prestige without mystery, for familiarity breeds contempt."

As another precept, he spoke of calculating the effect of an action. "The great leaders have always carefully stage-managed their effects," he noted. Summing up, he said:

"The statesman must concentrate all his efforts on captivating men's minds. He has to know when to dissemble, when to be frank. He must pose as the servant of the public in order to be its master. He must outbid his rivals in self-confidence, and only after a thousand intrigues and solemn undertakings will he find himself entrusted with full power."

In the first years of the Fifth Republic de Gaulle did indeed seem to "concentrate all his efforts" on establishing his authority and his personality. In large matters, such as liquidating the Algerian war, he served as a unifier by casting what amounted to a spell over metropolitan France. This was nurtured by episodes of personal courage in hostile crowds: He was shot at but never hit; plots against him failed.

In small matters, too, de Gaulle made certain that he projected perfection. Every detail of a trip, a speech, a news conference was worked out in advance; whatever appeared to be a spur-of-the-moment gesture was a well-rehearsed bit of stage business. For television he took lessons from an actor; he practiced before a mirror; he learned his texts by heart.

Equally carefully prepared were his hand-shaking excursions into crowds. However, because he was near-sighted and disliked to wear glasses, he often shook hands with members of his own security guard along with those of the public. In each case, though, there was a stately personal greeting: "Bonjour, madame"; "bonjour, monsieur"; "bonjour, mon petit."

Groundwork for Visit

When it came to generating goodwill abroad, de Gaulle was indefatigable. For his 12-day trip to the Soviet Union in 1966, for example, he read up on all the places he was to visit and worked references to them into his speeches. Moreover, he took the trouble to conclude every toast with a few words in Russian, even once using a Pushkin quotation.

Although de Gaulle liked to invest every event with as much pomp as it could wear, he skimped on his state banquets. A rapid eater, he set the pace for his guests, who often had their plates snatched away three-quarters full. These repasts were cheeseless (de Gaulle did not fancy the smell) and fruitless (he thought fruit took too long to peel). An entire banquet rarely lasted more than an hour.

The fact that de Gaulle stood on his dignity so markedly in public gave rise to reports that he was equally ceremonial in private. One such story had de Gaulle's wife, Yvonne, returning to the Elysée from shopping, slumping into a chair and exclaiming, "God, I am tired." Her husband is supposed to have replied, "I have often told you, my dear, it was sufficient in private if you addressed me as 'Monsieur le Président.'

Actually, de Gaulle was quite unformidable in his private moments. After dinner, he and his wife, a self-effacing woman who was popularly known as Tante Yvonne, spent many evenings watching television, especially the light programs. On Thursday afternoons, a school holiday in France, their grandchildren often came to tea at the Elysée. De Gaulle had two surviving children, Philippe, a naval officer on his father's staff; and Elizabeth, the wife of Gen. Alain de Boissieu. Another daughter, Anne, was born a Mongoloid and died when she was 20.

Of his decision in 1940 to try to build a resistance movement at the bleakest moment of the war, de Gaulle wrote: "I felt within myself a life coming to an end—the life I had lived within the framework of a solid France and an indivisible army." And indeed the first 49 years of his life were solidly conventional.

Charles André Joseph Marie de Gaulle was born Nov. 22, 1890, in Lille. Members of the lesser nobility, conservative and stanchly Roman Catholic, the de Gaulle family had furnished soldiers, lawyers and writers to France since at least 1210.

Henri, Charles's father, was lay headmaster of the Jesuit College of the Immaculate Conception in Paris when his son was born. He also taught Latin, Greek, philosophy and literature there and at his own school after the Society of Jesus was expelled from France in 1907. Charles's mother, Jeanne Maillot-Delannoy, was his father's cousin, and, like her husband, she was intensely patriotic and conservative.

In childhood, Charles was much exposed to family conversations about the Franco-Prussian War of 1870, in which his father had been wounded. Talk centered on France's ignominious loss of Alsace-Lorraine and the abject defeat of the French Army.

Indoctrinated to believe that the army was the quintessence of France, the

(continued)

young man had little choice but to be a soldier, and in 1910 he entered Saint-Cyr, the officer-training academy. Graduated two years later, he joined the 33d Infantry Regiment at Arras commanded by Col. Henri-Philippe Pétain.

The lives of the two men became ironically entwined. Early in World War II, when de Gaulle founded the Resistance, his old Arras colonel, then a Marshal of France and head of the collaborationist Vichy regime, had him condemned to death for desertion. When the tables were turned after the war, Pétain was condemned to death for treason, and de Gaulle, the provisional President-Premier of France, commuted his sentence to life imprisonment.

In World War I, de Gaulle, who was wounded three times and captured by the Germans at Verdun, won a Legion of Honor and achieved the rank of captain. Afterward he taught briefly in a Polish military college, then at Saint-Cyr; then, becoming a protégé and close friend of Pétain—who was godfather to de Gaulle's son, Philippe—he spent two years at the army staff college.

Post on Defense Council

In 1925 Pétain attached his friend to his secretariat in the Supreme War Council. Two years later he became a major and served for two years in the occupation army in the Rhineland and two years in the Middle East. De Gaulle returned to France in 1932, became a lieutenant colonel and, at Pétain's intervention, was named secretary to the High Council of National Defense, a post that he held for five years and that brought him into everyday touch with the country's military leaders.

The job also gave him his first close-up view of parliamentary politics, by which he was not favorably impressed, for in five years no fewer than 14 Cabinets chased one another in and out of the swinging doors of the Chamber of Deputies in the Palais Bourbon.

De Gaulle's career up to this point had not been brilliant, despite Pétain's patronage. One reason was the officer's spit-and-polish personality; another was his scholarly but unorthodox book, "Vers l'armée de métier" ("Toward a Modern Army"), published in 1934.

Scornful of several pet army doctrines, including conscription, the book also disparaged the Maginot Line, a supposedly impregnable fortress system along the French-German border. Equally upsetting to the reigning military minds was de Gaulle's proposal for a modernized army with an élite mobile tank force at its head. This striking force, he argued, could overrun and disorganize enemy territory, which later could be occupied by foot soldiers.

When World War II broke out, de Gaulle was a colonel in command of a tank regiment in Metz. When Hitler, after chewing up Poland, turned on France, the debacle that de Gaulle had foreseen took place: The Maginot Line was turned and northern France was overrun by Nazi tanks. In the sweep de Gaulle, with his meager force, gave a good account of himself and was made a temporary brigadier general—the youngest in the army at that time. Premier Paul Reynaud brought him into the Cabinet June 5, 1940, as Under Secretary of Defense. In this capacity he met Churchill for the first time on a visit to London June 9.

It was about then that he came to his momentous decision—that events made it evident that Britain would remain in the war, that it would become worldwide and that he would try to organize French resistance based on the colonies. A few days afterward, in France, he sat next to Churchill at dinner. "Our conversation confirmed in me my confidence in Churchill," de Gaulle recalled. "And no doubt he also grasped that de Gaulle, though helpless at the moment, was as full of resolve as himself."

Epic Task Undertaken

After the discomfited French Government fled to Bordeaux and prepared to sue for an armistice, de Gaulle took flight to London. Assuming there the epic task of organizing a resistance, he was recognized June 28 by the British Government "as the leader of all the Free French, wherever they may be, who will rally to him in defense of the Allied cause."

With a mystique already sprouting around him, de Gaulle was able, by claiming to embody France (and no one challenged him then), to draw into his cause the governors of French Equatorial Africa, the Chad and the French Cameroons. This gave de Gaulle a territorial base that, however far removed from the war theaters, was at least more imposing than his office in Carlton Gardens.

Some of the edge was taken off his first successes when his small naval expedition to Dakar was easily repulsed by the Vichy garrison. Although he set up a Council for the Defense of the Empire in Brazzaville, the French Congo, and raised the Cross of Lorraine there, the Dakar failure made American recognition of the Vichy regime seem plausible.

The setback also held down his following inside France. A further setback in Syria in May, 1941, when Free French troops failed to win over Vichyite soldiers, almost made de Gaulle a chanticleer without a flock.

But a month later, in June, 1941, the Soviet Union's entrance into the war dramatically altered de Gaulle's fortunes by producing two important developments: direct Free French contact with the Russians and the start of an active Resistance in France, now organized by the energetic French Communist party. Ultimately, in July, 1942, the Soviet Union set its seal upon de Gaulle as the Resistance leader. By then the underground war in France was a flourishing armed enterprise of men and women of many political convictions.

Meanwhile, de Gaulle took astute political advantage of the Soviet Union's entry into the war by organizing, in September, 1941, the French National Committee, a virtual government in exile, with himself as chairman. The general, however, was far from receiving United States recognition and cooperation. On the contrary, Roosevelt, urged on by Adm. William D. Leahy, his envoy to Vichy, and by Robert W. Murphy, his representative in Algiers, sought an alternative to de Gaulle, someone more complaisant.

The Americans' choice fell on General Giraud, a Pétainist who was taken out of France to North Africa, where he was appointed French commander in chief in late 1942. At about the same time Adm. François Darlan, a Vichy man who thought the time had come to jump on the Allied bandwagon, arrived in Algiers. A deal was concluded whereby he became the chief French authority in North Africa, but his tenure was cut short by his assassination under mysterious circumstances on Christmas Day. General Giraud was then appointed civil and military commander.

In these murky dealings de Gaulle could not be ignored completely, for he had support in the colonies and in France; and in a complicated series of maneuvers Roosevelt and Churchill brought de Gaulle and General Giraud together at a conference at Anfa, near Casablanca, in late January, 1943. A fragile alliance was fabricated, symbolized by a handshake for cameramen. But General Giraud, with his conservative associations and his political ineptitude, was sacked as co-chairman of the Committee of National Liberation within a year.

Even in control of the committee, however, de Gaulle did not have the confidence of the Americans as the man to govern France after the war. W. Averell Harriman, the diplomat, summed up official feeling when he wrote:

"Unfortunately de Gaulle is thinking more of how he is going to rule France than of ways of liberating her. That is his great flaw. Also, he is extremely vain and imagines himself a sort of Joan of Arc, and that makes work with him difficult."

The hunt for a more pliable leader led to proposals to keep de Gaulle out of France after the Normandy landings in June, 1944. It also accounted in part for the fact that only a token French force went ashore on D-Day. This so irked de Gaulle that 20 years later he refused to attend commemorative rites at the Normandy beaches. "The Anglo-Saxons," he wrote, "never really treated us as real allies."

Circumventing Britain and the United States, the de Gaulle committee declared itself the Provisional Government of France; and then, on June 13, the general and a tiny group of aides made a quick, almost stealthy, trip to Bayeux, where he received a hearty welcome and where he appointed a Gaullist governor for Normandy.

De Gaulle did not return to France until Aug. 20, having met meanwhile with Roosevelt in Washington and established a superficially cordial relationship. One result was Washington's recognition of his committee as "qualified to exercise the administration of France." He went on to establish his personal authority in fact in a tremendous outburst of emotional frenzy that convulsed Paris when he led a triumphal march from the Arch of Triumph to the Cathedral of Notre Dame on Aug. 26, 1944.

Paris had been liberated the day before by the combined efforts of armed Parisians, Gen. Jacques Leclerc's Second Armored Division and American troops. But de Gaulle, tall, smartly turned out in his military best, was the one person on whom the hero's mantle seemed to fall. If he at this moment was not France, who was?

General de Gaulle leading the parade in celebration of the liberation of Paris in August 1944. A crowd of two million cheered the march from the Arch of Triumph to the Cathedral of Notre Dame.

14 Fitful Months

In the days that followed, de Gaulle created a moderate Government of National Unanimity, which lasted for 14 fitful months. During its tenure, he took pains to cold-shoulder leftist groups in the Resistance and to disarm their paramilitary units. Even so, he did not satisfy President Harry S. Truman, who told him bluntly on a trip to Washington in August, 1945, not to expect much American financial help unless he threw out the few Communists in his Cabinet.

In October, 1945, the French, disavowing the Third Republic, elected a Constituent Assembly. With its convocation, which foreshadowed the Fourth Republic, de Gaulle became a parliamentary executive, a role for which he had no liking. So, giving the excuse that the "regime of parties" had again emerged, he resigned in January, 1946. His sojourn, though, was brief, for he emerged from "retirement" in April, 1947, to call for formation of a Rally of the French People (Rassemblement du Peuple Français)—a party against parties. It was a venture that the general's admirers were later to play down.

At first he attracted thousands to the Rally as, in a bid for centrist and rightist backing, he inveighed against the Communists and the trade unions. The Rally had a grand success in the municipal elections of 1947, gathering nearly 40 per cent of the votes. But de Gaulle overplayed his hand by issuing a virtual ultimatum to the National Assembly that sought an immediate general election. The demand agitated the Assembly and dismayed many in the Rally's rank-and-file who still thought a bad republic preferable to a good tyranny. Moreover, the paramilitary character of Rally meetings disquieted public opinion, as did de Gaulle's friendly references to Dr. Konrad Adenauer, the West German leader.

No U.S. Backing

In any event, the Rally did not obtain significant big-business support and it failed also to attract the United States, which placed its confidence and its Marshall Plan money in such politicians as Robert Schuman and Jules Moch. De Gaulle seemed too unreliable.

By 1954, when his Rally was in disarray, de Gaulle's spirits were so buffeted that he could say, "J'étais la France" ("I was France"). And in July, 1955, he announced his retirement from public life: "I say farewell to you," he told newsmen. "We shall not meet again until the tempest again looses itself on France." He was nearing his 65th birthday.

From then until the middle of 1958, he lived at Colombey, where he completed "The War Memoirs of Charles de Gaulle." He also traveled to the French West Indies and the Pacific. More important, he received politicians at Colombey and journeyed to Paris once a week for political chats in his office on Rue Solférino.

The "tempest" that brought de Gaulle openly back to public life, and to power, was the war in Algeria, under way since 1954. The Fourth Republic, already stung by the loss of Indochina and the defeat at Dienbienphu, was bedeviled by the conflict against the Algerian Nationalists. By 1958 some 35,000 French troops were in Algeria attempting to contain 15,000 insurgents.

(continued)

The brutal war was unpopular in France, where its costs were cutting into a spreading prosperity; but no Cabinet knew how to liquidate it without risking an army coup. The crisis came in May, 1958, when hysterical Europeans in Algeria seized Government offices with the aid of army officers. There was talk of a rightist coup in Paris. Almost automatically attention swung to de Gaulle, and he was ready—with a statement that said:

"In the past, the country from its very depth entrusted me with the task of leading it to salvation. Today, with new ordeals facing it, let the country know that I am ready to assume the powers of the Republic."

After two weeks of frenetic political dealing he was invested as Premier of France on June 1 and given decree powers for six months with the right within that time to submit a new Constitution. He was accepted by the army in the belief that a general would surely support the war.

Abandoning demagoguery and proceeding with caution and adroit double talk, he moved to dismantle the French Algerians' Committees of Public Safety while appearing to place confidence in Gen. Raoul Salan as the Government representative in Algiers. With the immediate crisis muffled, a Constitution for the Fifth Republic was drafted that placed effective power in a President rather than in Parliament. It was ratified by an 80 per cent majority of the voters, and in December de Gaulle was elected President for a seven-year term that began Jan. 8, 1959.

Certain of his position in France, de Gaulle removed General Salan and, over a year, transferred to France 1,500 army officers associated with the French Algerian diehards. Nevertheless, in January, 1960, there was an army-led insurrection in Algiers, which was contained with the arrest of the ringleaders and the cashiering of some rightist generals.

In November of that year de Gaulle suggested an independent Algeria, a proposal that was endorsed in a referendum in France and Algeria in January, 1961. Orderly progression to independence was thwarted, however, by the rise of the Secret Army Organization and by the obduracy of many French Algerians. Terrorism spread into France, while the unrest and violence in Algeria culminated in rebellion there in April, 1961.

De Gaulle acted with firmness and energy. The revolt collapsed, and three of its four leaders went into hiding while the fourth was jailed.

Independence for Algeria

Finally, in September, 1962, an independent Algerian regime was established and within a year about 750,000 French Algerians emigrated to metropolitan France. All this was accomplished in the face of Secret Army terrorism that included two attempts to assassinate the President. In the second attempt, in August, 1962, a bullet missed his skull by an inch. Turning to his bodyguard, he remarked:

"This is getting to be dangerous. Fortunately, those gentlemen are poor shots."

Once the Algerian problem was solved, de Gaulle was able to flex French muscle in Europe and around the world. A mighty ingredient of the "new" France was her development of an atomic bomb, which came about in 1960, when a device was exploded in the Sahara. Further tests indicated a considerable military potential.

De Gaulle's European policy was aimed at restoring France to a position of greatness. This involved, on the one hand, an entente with the Soviet Union and, on the other, an effort to keep Britain and the United States at a distance. The Russian phase of his policy entailed a dramatic trip to the Soviet Union in mid-1966 and visits to other Eastern European nations.

His relations with Britain, never comfortable, seemed to reflect a belief that she was an American satellite. This was said to account for his veto of Britain's bids (the first rebuff was in 1963) to join the Common Market, a six-nation economic group composed of France, West Germany, Italy, Belgium, the Netherlands and Luxembourg.

De Gaulle profoundly disagreed with United States policy in Europe, and he eventually decided to withdraw France from NATO. He barred American nuclear warheads from French territory and denied French rocket sites to the United States. At the same time he sharpened his attitude toward West Germany, calling that country at one point "America's Foreign Legion in Europe." In addition, he established diplomatic relations with Peking and nettled Washington by condemning the Vietnam war.

His policy toward West Germany, however, proved ambiguous. On the one hand, de Gaulle was alert to the potential dangers of militarism across the Rhine. On the other hand, he sought to mute the hatreds generated by World War II. In this spirit, he toured West Germany and invited German officials to Paris. He seemed to realize that European stability could not be achieved unless the government in Bonn played its part in the economic and political life of Western Europe.

An Alternative Sought

He also strove to exert leadership in the nonaligned world by trying to create an alternative to the dual hegemonies of the United States and the Soviet Union. Polarization of the world into two antithetical camps, he believed, tended to increase global tensions. French nuclear development, he felt, helped to overcome an American-Soviet atomic monopoly.

At the same time, he could not resist shocking American opinion. He encouraged French-Canadian separatism. He courted Latin America, a United States preserve. In the Middle East, he leaned to the Arab cause against the Israelis by cutting off the flow of French arms to Israel.

Indeed, de Gaulle generated strong resentments among many Americans, some of whom even refused to visit France or purchase French-made goods while he was in power.

De Gaulle's first term as President of the Fifth Republic expired in January, 1966. He was elected to a second term, but only after a runoff in which he received 55 per cent of the votes. The principal attack on him came from the Left, temporarily united under François Mitterrand, on account of his essentially conservative domestic policies. Inflation and wage restraints bore heavily on the working class.

It was domestic discontent that eventually brought him down. Grandeur—membership in the nuclear "club," foreign aid in Africa (including support of Biafra) and elsewhere, stockpiling of gold reserves, pioneering in supersonic air travel — cost millions of francs. This meant austerity at home at a time when a nation of chiefly small shopkeepers and farmers was struggling to transform itself into a more modern country.

The transition brought with it tensions in virtually every segment of society. There were dislocations in the countryside as corporate farming increased; in the cities supermarkets began to appear, dooming the neighborhood grocery and meat stores. And more and more industrial workers were employed in larger and larger enterprises.

In education, more students than ever before crowded the universities and studied under curriculums and pedagogical practices that were clearly irrelevant to the times. In an effort to accommodate the influx of students, satellites of older universities were set up, as at Nanterre, just outside Paris.

It was at Nanterre that open rebellion against de Gaulle broke out in the spring of 1968. The issue was reform of education. Students at the graceless concrete school occupied a classroom on March 22, and were routed by the police, who used steel rods as spears. The number of militant students — many of them commuters from Paris—grew and the authorities closed the university in early May. Thereupon a group from Nanterre met with a Sorbonne group to plan a joint protest.

From this mild beginning sprang "the events of May," a month-long clash of social, economic and political forces that generated a near-revolution. The Sorbonne students went on strike, and were clubbed and buffeted by the police. The turmoil spread to the provinces, and soon the relatively prosperous sons and daughters of bourgeois parents were battling not just oppressive education but government itself.

General and Mrs. de Gaulle in their garden at Colombey-les-Deux Eglises.

Meanwhile, the students' spirit of audacity spread to the workers, who had their own discontents, and soon there were factory sit-ins. These grew despite efforts of union leaders to calm the situation, and all France seemed engaged in crisis demonstrations and strikes.

At first aloof to the disorders, de Gaulle passed the early days of the turmoil in writing out in longhand the speeches he was going to deliver in Rumania. And, indeed, he visited that country later in the month.

When he returned to Paris he found that the situation was nearly out of hand; and, after a quick conference with army leaders, then in Germany, to obtain assurances of their support, he began to resolve the crisis, first by acting to pacify the 10 million striking workers with pay increases and then by cracking down further on the students.

Finally, on May 30, he dissolved the National Assembly and warned the country in an emotional radio speech (the Government-run television system was on strike) that he would restore law and order with all the means at his disposal. There was an implied threat that 30,000 French troops might be on their way back to France from Germany. De Gaulle feared, he said, the possibility of a Communist "dictatorship."

Immediately after he spoke, hundreds of thousands of his adherents thronged the Place de la Concorde in Paris to voice their support. This segment of society, apprehensive over the possibility of a social revolution, proved to be his temporary bulwark. Leftist elements, including the Communists, backed down from the barricades, deciding to take their chances in the National Assembly elections made necessary by de Gaulle's dissolution of that body. The "days of May" were over.

Posing a choice between chaos and himself, de Gaulle won a big victory in the elections. He seemed more in control than ever, and strong enough to bar devaluation of the franc in the fall of 1968, when most signs pointed to the necessity for such action. However, as Georges Pompidou, then the Premier, remarked shortly after the student-worker insurgency, "Things would never be quite the same again."

What had taken place during May constituted a fatal undermining of the contention that de Gaulle was the incarnation of France. He might win a National Assembly victory, but it was clear that his policies did not correspond to the aspirations of either French college youths or the workers.

The proof that de Gaulle had lost the adherence of his people even as he had won their votes in June, 1968, came over a relatively minor issue—the future regional structure of France and the role of its Senate. The matter was to be settled in a referendum in April, 1969, which at first created only slight interest.

Then de Gaulle injected himself. The result of the voting was to be a test of public confidence. Precisely why he chose to make the referendum a personal matter is conjectural. As an autocrat he may have felt that he required the extra bolstering that victory would bring him. Perhaps he felt, too, that he could again discomfit his domestic enemies on the Left. Perhaps also the megalomania that often accompanies old age may have been a factor in his decision.

In any event he gambled on what he was convinced would be an assured success. His tactics of May and June, 1958, were used again: the attempt to frighten the electors with the threat of Communism and chaos should the voting be adverse. Where would they be without de Gaulle? he asked.

The general was unprepared for the results. He was persuaded, until the returns were indubitable, that he would triumph. He left office still dazed.

Retiring once more to Colombey with a secretary, a bodyguard, a chauffeur and his $35,000 pension, he set to writing his memoirs, dating from 1958. "The Renewal," the first of a projected three-volume "Memoirs of Hope," was published last month. Such was the magic of his name and interest in the events recounted that 250,000 copies were sold in a few days.

At Colombey, though, he vanished into political silence. When he retired in 1969, the long personalist epoch of Charles de Gaulle was over.

"All the News That's Fit to Print."

The New York Times.

LATE CITY EDITION
WEATHER—Partly cloudy, slightly cooler today; tomorrow fair.
Temperatures Yesterday—Max., 77; Min., 67.

Copyright, 1941, by The New York Times Company.

VOL. XC. No. 30,446. Entered as Second-Class Matter, Postoffice, New York, N. Y. NEW YORK, TUESDAY, JUNE 3, 1941. THREE CENTS NEW YORK CITY and Vicinity

HUGHES, 79, RETIRES FROM HIGH COURT; 2 VACANCIES NOW

PRESIDENT ACCEPTS

Tells Chief Justice His Decision Is a 'Great Shock' to Nation

JURIST CITES HEALTH, AGE

He Found Duties Increasingly Difficult—Wide Speculation as to Successor

By FRANK L. KLUCKHOHN
Special to THE NEW YORK TIMES.

HYDE PARK, N. Y., June 2—Charles Evans Hughes announced his retirement, effective July 1, as Chief Justice of the United States in a letter sent to President Roosevelt today. He gave as his reasons "health and age." The President, in accepting his retirement by telegraph, expressed deep distress, and added that he was sure the announcement would come as a shock to the country.

The Chief Justice offered his retirement under the law permitting members of the nation's highest court to retire on full pay after they pass the age of 70, which was the outcome of the Supreme Court battle in Congress in 1937. His letter was dated today and the Executive's telegram of reply accepting the resignation was transmitted immediately.

The text of the two messages read as follows:

Hughes to the President

Supreme Court of the United States, June 2, 1941.

My dear Mr. President:

Considerations of health and age make it necessary that I should be relieved of the duties which I have been discharging with increased difficulty. For that reason I avail myself of the right and privilege granted by the Act of March 1, 1937, 28 United States Code, Section 375b, and retire from regular active service on the bench as Chief Justice of the United States, this retirement to be effective on and after July 1, 1941.

I have the honor to remain,
Respectfully yours,
CHARLES EVANS HUGHES.

The President's Reply

June 2, 1941.

The Honorable The Chief Justice of the United States,
2223 R Street, N. W.,
Washington, D. C.

My dear Mr. Chief Justice:

I am deeply distressed by your letter of June 2 telling me of your retirement on July 1 from active service as Chief Justice of the United States. This comes to me, as I know it will to the whole nation, as a great shock for all of us had counted on your continuing your splendid service for many years to come.

My every inclination is to beg you to remain; but my deep concern for your health and strength must be paramount. I shall hope to see you this coming week in Washington.

Sincerely and affectionately yours,
FRANKLIN D. ROOSEVELT.

The resignation of Mr. Hughes, who has been ill a great deal this Winter and absent from high court sessions for long periods, came as no surprise, since it had been generally understood that he would retire at the termination of this session of the Supreme Court.

Speculation immediately developed as to who would succeed him. Among those mentioned were Robert H. Jackson of New York, Mr. Roosevelt's Attorney General, who this Spring accompanied the Executive as a guest on a fishing cruise in Florida waters; Associate Justice Harlan F. Stone, Associate Justice Frank Murphy and Associate Justice Stanley Reed and Secretary Hull.

Jackson Rumored as Possibility

Special to THE NEW YORK TIMES.

WASHINGTON, June 2—The retirement of Chief Justice Hughes gives President Roosevelt the opportunity to appoint two new members of the highest court, making his total larger than any other Executive except George Washington.

With the resignation of Mr. Hughes there are now two vacancies. For months the supposition has been that Robert H. Jackson, now Attorney General, would be an appointee if Mr. Hughes resigned and would be named not only to the bench but to the Chief Justiceship by President Roosevelt.

Mr. Roosevelt has not yet appointed a successor to Associate Justice James C. McReynolds, who left the bench in February. It is presumed that Senator James F.

Continued on Page Nineteen

Supreme Court Changes Made Since March 4, '33

By The United Press.

WASHINGTON, June 2—Here, in chronological order, are the changes in the Supreme Court since President Roosevelt took office on March 4, 1933:

Willis Van Devanter retired June 2, 1937; succeeded by Hugo L. Black.

George Sutherland, retired Jan. 18, 1938; succeeded by Stanley F. Reed.

Benjamin N. Cardozo died July 9, 1938; succeeded by Felix Frankfurter.

Louis D. Brandeis retired Feb. 13, 1939; succeeded by William O. Douglas.

Pierce Butler died Nov. 16, 1939; succeeded by Frank Murphy.

James C. McReynolds retired Feb. 1, 1941; vacancy unfilled.

Charles Evans Hughes retired effective July 1, 1941.

ORDERS REARGUING OF CONTEMPT CASES

Supreme Court Acts on Bridges and Los Angeles Times 'Free Speech' Stand

By LEWIS WOOD
Special to THE NEW YORK TIMES.

WASHINGTON, June 2—After more than seven and one-half months of consideration the Supreme Court gave orders today that the contempt cases of Harry Bridges and The Los Angeles Times should be reargued in October, to which date the tribunal took a recess.

The "free speech" issue was invoked by the defendants in these cases after they had been convicted of contempt of court for comment on cases before the court prior to final judgement.

Rarely has so long a period intervened between an argument and an order as in these cases which were heard last October. In the absence of definite information the general opinion is that the eight justices are hopelessly split and must await the appointment of a ninth before making a final decision. Both defendants are accused of contempt of the California courts.

Gov. Phillips Loses Case

In one of the four opinions handed down on the last day of the term the court rejected the efforts of Governor Phillips of Oklahoma to stop work on the government dam, to cost $54,000,000, across the Red River between Texas and Oklahoma near Denison, Texas. Through a ruling by Justice Douglas, the court extended the power of flood control to include tributaries of navigable streams and held constitutional the construction of the dam.

Governor Phillips had protested that 100,000 acres of Oklahoma would be inundated, much of it being valuable oil and farm land; that Oklahoma's boundary would be obliterated for forty miles and that State subdivisions would lose $40,000 in annual taxes. The court in quoting a recent decision regarding the regulatory power of the Federal Government over navigable streams, remarked:

"We now add that the power of flood control extends to the tributaries of navigable streams. For just as control over the non-navigable parts of a river may be essential or desirable in the interests of the navigable portions, so may the key to flood control on a navigable stream be found in whole or in part in flood control on its tributaries.

"We are of the view that the Denison Dam and Reservoir project is a valid exercise of the commerce powers of Congress."

Rules Against Kansas

Dividing four to three, the court sustained an injunction preventing Kansas City, Kan. and the Union Pacific Railroad from making payments to induce produce merchants of Kansas City, Mo., to move into a new food market in Kansas. Justice Reed wrote the majority opinion, while Justice Roberts submitted a dissent in which Justices Black and Douglas joined. Justice Murphy did not participate.

The majority held that the action of Kansas City, Kan., in "giving cash and rental credits" and other inducements, violated the Elkins act prohibiting rebates, concessions and discriminations respecting railroad transportation of property in interstate commerce.

Justice Roberts scouted this conclusion, saying the Elkins law was never intended to cover such a case and that members of Congress would be surprised to learn that

Continued on Page Fifteen

GEHRIG, 'IRON MAN' OF BASEBALL, DIES AT THE AGE OF 37

Rare Disease Forced Famous Batter to Retire in 1939—Played 2,130 Games in Row

SET MANY HITTING MARKS

Native of New York, He Became Star of Yankees—Idol of Fans Throughout Nation

Lou Gehrig, former first baseman of the New York Yankees and one of the outstanding batsmen baseball has known, died at his home, 5204 Delafield Avenue, in the Fieldston section of the Bronx, last night. Death came to the erstwhile "Iron Man" at 10:10 o'clock. He would have been 38 years old on June 19.

Regarded by some observers as the greatest player ever to grace the diamond, Gehrig, after playing in 2,130 consecutive championship contests, was forced to end his career in 1939 when an ailment that had been hindering his efforts was diagnosed as a form of paralysis.

The disease was chronic, and for the last month Gehrig had been confined to his home. He lost weight steadily during the final weeks and was reported twenty-five pounds under weight shortly before he died.

Member of Parole Board

Until his illness became more serious Gehrig went to his office regularly to perform his duties as a member of the New York City Parole Commission, a post he had held for a year and a half following his retirement from baseball. Ever hopeful that he would be able to conquer the rare disease—amyotrophic lateral sclerosis, a hardening of the spinal cord—although the ailment was considered incurable by many, Gehrig stopped going to his desk about a month ago to conserve his strength.

Two weeks ago he was confined to his bed, and from that time until his death his condition grew steadily worse. He was conscious until just before the end. At the bedside when he died were his wife, the former Eleanor Twitchell of Chicago; his parents, Mr. and Mrs. Henry Gehrig; his wife's mother, Mrs. Nellie Twitchell, and Dr. Caldwell B. Esselstyn.

It was said last night that funeral services would be private and would be held tomorrow morning at 10 o'clock in the Christ Episcopal Church in Riverdale. The Rev. Gerald V. Barry will officiate.

The body was taken this morning to the E. Willis Scott Funeral Parlor at 4 West Seventy-sixth Street.

Record Spanned Fifteen Years

When Gehrig stepped into the batter's box as a pinch hitter for the Yankees on June 1, 1925, he started a record that many believe will never be equaled in baseball. From that day on he never missed a championship game until April 30, 1939—fifteen seasons of Yankee box scores with the name of Gehrig always in the line-up. He announced on May 2, 1939, that he would not play that day, and thus his streak came to an end.

But as brilliant as was his career, Lou will be remembered for more than his endurance record. He was a superb batter in his heyday and a prodigious clouter of home runs. The record book is liberally strewn with his feats at the plate.

Only in his first season, 1925, and in his last full campaign, 1938, did he fail to go over the .300 mark. Once he led the American League in hitting with .363, but on three occasions he went over that with-

Continued on Page Twenty-six

New Zealanders in Crete Turned Signals on Nazis

By The Canadian Press.

LONDON, June 2—New Zealand troops in Crete, who discovered the light signals used by invading German parachute troops, used the knowledge to advantage and even eliminated a troop carrying plane, Chester Wilmott, correspondent of the Australian Broadcasting Corporation with the forces in the Middle East, said in an account of the fighting broadcast today by the British Broadcasting Corporation.

Officers from Crete landed at a "Middle East Port" told Mr. Wilmott how the New Zealanders would use the light signals to ask for ammunition and supplies from the German planes above. The supplies were dropped following the signals which led the Nazi aviators to believe their own men were below.

"They even signaled for a troop carrier which landed successfully and then was successfully dealt with," Mr. Wilmott said.

SAYS SPIES INFEST FORTS IN CITY AREA

Thomas of New Jersey Asks Stimson Act on Reds, Nazis Who 'Could Wreck Defense'

By HENRY N. DORRIS
Special to THE NEW YORK TIMES.

WASHINGTON, June 2—The presence of subversive agents at key positions at Army posts and cantonments in the New York and New Jersey area who "could wreck the entire defense of the New York area," was charged today by Representative J. Parnell Thomas, Republican of New Jersey, who has just returned from an inspection tour in that region.

Mr. Thomas wrote to Colonel Henry L. Stimson, Secretary of War, praising the morale of the officers and men, but criticizing what he said was a serious lack of certain types of ammunition and an almost complete absence of antiaircraft defenses. He also protested the sending of large coast defense guns to the new bases in Newfoundland and Bermuda until they could be replaced.

Asserting that Nazis and Communists had penetrated into the "nerve centers" of the Army in the area, Mr. Thomas recommended that draft induction boards use care in sending men of known Axis or communistic leanings to Forts Dix, Hancock, Monmouth and Tilden.

Army Assignments Cited

Mr. Thomas said that an officer who had a "close family relation with a well-known Nazi organization" had been assigned to an important gun position at Fort Hancock, but was later shifted to a "less strategic" position at Fort Tilden.

Known Communist sympathizers were employed in the laboratory at Fort Monmouth, he said, and while protection against sabotage within the laboratory appeared to be good, safeguards against outsiders entering the premises for possible sabotage were inadequate.

Although a civilian employe at Fort Monmouth was discovered sending vital defense information in code to a Communist leader, Mr. Thomas said, he had not been discharged, presumably because of "red tape" in the War Department and the Civil Service Commission.

He recommended that the Army be authorized to discharge civilian personnel without regard to any ruling of the Civil Service Commission.

At Fort Dix, Mr. Thomas said, there was a "deplorable state" in that there was no reserve supply of ammunition and not enough small arms ammunition to deal with an internal disorder. He charged that

Continued on Page Ten

Roosevelt Signs Mandatory Priorities Bill; Will Confer With Winant on Britain Today

Special to THE NEW YORK TIMES.

HYDE PARK, N. Y., June 2—President Roosevelt prepared today for conferences in Washington tomorrow which likely will be of far-reaching importance.

Meanwhile he signed two defense measures, one imposing mandatory priorities of wartime scope on industry. The other permits Canadian ships to carry ore between American Great Lakes ports during the 1941 transportation season and is intended to assure an adequate supply of steel.

Mr. Roosevelt will confer tomorrow with John G. Winant, Ambassador to Great Britain; Secretary Hull and, probably, his military and naval staff chiefs. He spent much time today in telephone conversation with Washington, according to William D. Hassett, Presidential secretary.

"No comment," said Mr. Hassett when reporters told him of rumors that Adolf Hitler and Benito Mussolini had discussed possible peace negotiations in their meeting at the Brenner Pass today. Speculation that the Axis leaders had considered countering any moves by the United States met with silence.

Before the new Priorities Law became effective with the President's signature, the government could give mandatory priorities only to contracts placed by the Army or Navy. Now the government also has authority to establish the order in which materials and machines are to be delivered for all planes, tanks, ships and other war equipment being produced under the Lease-Lend Act for Britain and other countries resisting the Axis.

Thus the government acquired the right to decide in all cases what production should come first, whether in the armaments or domestic civilian supply field.

The President already had delegated the priority power to the priority division of the Office of Production Management, which is headed by Edward R. Stettinius Jr., for-

Continued on Page Eight

GOVERNMENT BACKS A BILL FOR SEIZING DEFENSE PROPERTY

Sweeping Power Requested of Congress to Take Any Private Holdings in Emergency

ON FULL WORLD WAR LINES

President in Message Asks for $125,000,000 to Build Roads Into Military Areas

By TURNER CATLEDGE
Special to THE NEW YORK TIMES.

WASHINGTON, June 2—Following the proclamation of an unlimited national emergency by President Roosevelt Tuesday night, the Administration asked Congress today for authority to requisition, for just compensation, any private property, real or personal, which may be deemed in the interest of defense during the emergency.

A bill to carry the authority into effect was sent to the Capitol by the War Department, but it also bore the approval of the President, the Navy Department and the Office of Production Management. It was introduced immediately by Senator Reynolds, Democrat of North Carolina, chairman of the Military Affairs Committee.

The measure was a distillate of twenty-odd laws of similar purport enacted during the World War, but in its sweep was considered the broadest grant of Federal power over private property ever proposed in times of peace.

Under the bill's terms, as interpreted here, the President, by paying just compensation which he himself would be authorized to fix, temporarily or permanently, could take over any interest in any private property, from housewives' pots and pans to public utilities systems and railroads, when he considered it in the interest of national defense to do so.

The provisions could hardly be put more simply than in the language of the bill, as prepared in the office of Robert P. Patterson, Under Secretary of War.

TEXT OF THE MEASURE

The text of the bill was as follows:

A bill to authorize the President of the United States to requisition certain property for the use of or disposition by the United States.

Be it enacted by the Senate and House of Representatives of the United States of America in Congress assembled, that, during any period of national emergency proclaimed by the President, the President is authorized, when he deems it in the interest of national defense, (a) to requisition and take over, either temporarily or permanently, property of any kind or character, whether real or personal, tangible or intangible, or any part thereof, or any right or interest therein or with respect thereto, whether by virtue of contract, patent, license or otherwise, which itself or through its exercise or control can be used or is adaptable for use directly or indirectly in any way for national defense or in the construction, manufacture, production, transportation, repair, testing or storage of military or naval supplies or other articles, commodities, materials, machinery or equipment for national defense, and (b) to use and, on such terms as he shall deem satisfactory, to sell or otherwise dispose of, either temporarily or permanently, any property, right or interest requisitioned or taken over pursuant to the provisions of this act.

Provides for Compensation

Section 2—Whenever the President shall requisition and take over any property pursuant to the provisions of this act, the person or persons having right, title or interest therein shall be paid as compensation therefor such sum as the President shall determine to be fair and just.

If any such person or persons entitled to receive it are unwilling to accept as full and complete compensation for such property the sum so determined by the President, such person or persons shall be paid 75 percentum of the sum so determined by the President and shall be entitled to sue the United States for such additional sum as when added to the sum already received shall be deetrmined as fair and just compensation for such property in the manner provided for by Section 24, paragraph 20, and Section 145 of the Judicial Code (U. S. Code, Title 28, Section 41, paragraph 20, and Section 250), but no recovery shall be allowed against the United States in any such action unless the action be brought within two years after the date on which notice shall have been given of the determination by the President of the amount to be paid as compensation.

Section 3—Appropriations available for the acquisition of prop-

Continued on Page Eight

HITLER AND MUSSOLINI CHART WAR MOVES IN 5-HOUR TALK; BRITISH MASS AROUND SYRIA

The International Situation

TUESDAY, JUNE 3, 1941

Reichsfuehrer Hitler and Premier Mussolini met at Brenner Pass yesterday for another of their secret war councils that in the past have usually preceded new moves in Axis war operations. The dictators were accompanied this time not only by their Foreign Ministers and chiefs of staff, but also by an unusually large number of other military and political advisers. They conferred for more than five hours and it was generally believed that they discussed future operations in the Eastern Mediterranean, the Middle East and Africa, and the position of the United States in the light of President Roosevelt's recent speech. [Page 1, Column 8.]

The conquest of Crete was described by Reich Marshal Goering, in a special order of the day praising the work of the Luftwaffe, as proof that there was "no unconquerable island" so far as Germany was concerned. The German High Command, meanwhile, increased to 13,000 the number of Allied prisoners it claimed had been captured in Crete, and said that another British destroyer had been sunk. [Page 1, Column 6.]

In Iraq the German air-borne units that had been landed at Mosul were reported to have quit that oil center, although it was not determined whether other German forces remained at Kirkuk, the Iraqi terminal of the pipeline to Haifa. British prestige among the Arabs was reported to have increased as a result of Rashid Ali el Gailani's flight to Iran. [Page 4, Column 2.]

It was toward French-mandated Syria, however, that the eyes of the Middle East turned. With the Nazis reported in virtual control of the administration of Syria and Lebanon, diplomatic quarters believed a struggle between Germany and Britain to occupy the territories was coming soon. The British were said to be gathering their forces in Iraq and Palestine. Hundreds of German technicians have arrived in Syria, food supplies have been shipped there, and Nazi agents are stirring up trouble between the Moslem and Christian population, according to Ankara reports. [Page 1, Column 7; Map, Page 4.]

General Weygand, Commander-in-Chief of France's colonial empire, flew to Vichy and had a two-hour talk with Marshal Pétain, presumably on the swiftly developing situation affecting French interests in the Near East and Africa. No official explanation was made, however, concerning the surprise visit. [Page 4, Column 3.]

Italy's High Command hinted that the next major move might be an Axis attempt to drive the British out of besieged Tobruk on the Libyan coast, and said that German and Italian dive bombers had made heavy attacks on Tobruk's defenses. The British reported evidences of new activity by Axis forces at the Libyan-Egyptian border. [Page 4, Column 6.]

Berlin was attacked by British bombers last night and civilians were killed and injured, Nazi spokesmen reported early today. They claimed the destruction of three of the raiders. The British reported attacks on industrial targets in the Ruhr. London disclosed, meanwhile, that the English city blasted by Nazi raiders Sunday night was Manchester, where great devastation and many casualties were indicated. [Page 2, Column 2.]

In Washington the Administration placed before Congress a far-reaching proposal for the requisitioning by the President for defense purposes of private property of any kind and amount—from housewives' pots and pans to railroads and public utilities systems. The bill would authorise the President to fix compensation for the requisitioned property. [Page 1, Column 5.]

GOERING DECLARES NO ISLE INVINCIBLE

Says Crete Proves Hitler's Words—Nazis Claim 13,000 Captured, Destroyer Sunk

By The United Press.

BERLIN, June 2—Hinting at a possible air-borne invasion of Cyprus or a frontal assault or the British Isles, Reich Marshal Hermann Goering boasted tonight that the swift conquest of Crete "proves that there is no unconquerable island" for the German Air Force.

Marshal Goering's statement was contained in a special order of the day addressed to "Crete fighters, Comrades!" in which he said:

"A great and glorious deed in the history of our young weapon is completed. Our flags of victory wave over Crete. You, my parachutists and air-borne troops, you, my aviators, jointly with your army comrades under proved leaders of all ranks have completed a singular achievement.

"Unendingly proud and happy, I report to the Fuehrer the consummation of his order. You before the entire world have proved the Fuehrer's words. 'There is no unconquerable island.'"

"Thus," the statement said, "this first and audacious operation over the sea has crushed the enemy like a thunderstorm within a few days."

The statement also paid tribute to "the Italian Navy, formations of the Italian Air Force and troops of the Italian Army" for their part in the conquest of Crete.

Telling of "superhuman deeds accomplished by individual fighters under burning sun and on rocky ground," Marshal Goering added:

"In a hail of bombs from our bomber formations the enemy's guns were struck dumb; the enemy fled from fortified positions, and British warships and merchantmen that tried to bring aid were sunk and burned.

"In an old comradeship of arms from the great days of Narvik, aviators and mountain troops conquered the island and thereby threw England out of an important position in the Eastern Mediterranean.

"Comrades! The entire German people feels the deepest wonder and

Continued on Page Three

BRITISH SET LINES FOR SYRIAN MOVE

Poised for Drive to Checkmate Germans in French Area—Nazi Landing Reported

By C. L. SULZBERGER
Special Broadcast to THE NEW YORK TIMES.

ANKARA, Turkey, June 2—British forces were reported to be consolidating their positions in Western Iraq and Northern Palestine today as the Middle East in general awaited developments in the tense Syrian situation and responsible diplomatic quarters on both sides of the belligerent front concurred that it was a military necessity for Britain to try to occupy the French-mandated territories.

Rumors that German troops in uniform have been landed in Syrian ports are believed to be untrue or, at best, premature, but the Nazis have virtually taken over the administration of Syria and Lebanon and are understood to be working hard to develop bad feeling between the Christian and Moslem populations. Radio Beirut this evening published an official denial that any German troops were in the mandated territories.

[One such rumor, reported by The Associated Press from Ankara, was that German motorized infantry, with mobile field guns, had been landed at the Syrian port of Latakia. In Cyprus the British rushed defense preparations, anticipating an early Axis attack, removed women and children to Egypt and sent native families to the hills. The German radio reported that a state of siege had been declared for Eastern Syria, but The United Press said Vichy had no confirmation of this.]

The exiled Mufti of Jerusalem, who had sought to abet Premier Rashid Ali el Gailani's cause in Iraq, has fled from Baghdad and is rumored to have crossed the Syrian frontier, where presumably he will attempt to spread more anti-British sentiment among the Arabs.

[Rashid Ali's arrival in Teheran, Iran, was reported by The United Press.]

It is clear from the latest information received here that the Germans have established formidable

Continued on Page Four

U. S. BELIEVED TOPIC

Brenner Meeting Seen Laying Plans to Offset Our Expected Entry

ATLANTIC IS ONE PROBLEM

Nazis Stress Military Aspect of Parley—Mediterranean Drive Forecast in Rome

By CAMILLE M. CIANFARRA
By Telephone to THE NEW YORK TIMES.

ROME, June 2—With the Axis forces in possession of Crete, Reichsfuehrer Hitler and Premier Mussolini met today at the Brenner Pass for five hours to decide upon their next military and political moves.

A communiqué issued after the conference said that the two dictators and their Foreign Ministers had discussed "the political situation" for several hours. The conversation, it was stated, was held "in the spirit of the most cordial friendship and ended in complete agreement."

While it is impossible at present to have even an inkling of what the two dictators discussed specifically—the utmost reserve is being kept in Italian and German official quarters — the general opinion among the Italians is that the discussion touched on the three closely interlocked main problems facing the Axis. These are United States intervention in the war, which, after President Roosevelt's most recent speech, every one here believes to be only a matter of weeks; the Battle of the Mediterranean and the Battle of the Atlantic.

Longer War Is a Problem

In event of United States intervention, neutral diplomatic quarters say, the Axis, despite its chain of military successes, will be faced with a prolongation of the war for a period that not even Signor Mussolini and Herr Hitler are in a position to estimate. The two leaders, it is stressed, must therefore devise means to minimize as far as possible the weight of armed United States assistance to Britain and win positions that will enable them to cope for an indefinite period with a new strategic and political situation.

It is a safe guess, it is held, that the Axis will aim at transforming Europe and North Africa into a veritable fortress, making them impregnable, as far as possible, against Anglo-American attack, both militarily and economically.

To do this, it is generally believed, some countries that are still outside the direct influence of the Axis will be "induced" in one way or another to "collaborate." Italy's assistance on this point of the program is necessary, since one of the future Axis moves will, according to today's press, take place in the Mediterranean, where the Italian Navy and mercantile fleet will be useful.

"The result and the consequences of the new Axis victory in Crete," writes Virginio Gayda, "will soon be seen in the new developments in the Mediterranean war."

Role of Russia Is a Factor

In this connection Axis spokesmen have been saying for some time that a clarification of German-Russian relations will have to take place soon. Russia is said to be needed not only because her economic resources are valuable to the Axis, but also because of her political influence over Turkey. If Russia were "induced" to fight with the Axis, Turkey, it is held here, would have to conform and the Axis drive to the Middle East would be immeasurably facilitated.

Moreover, while the operations in the Eastern Mediterranean will probably be intensified, the situation in the Western Mediterranean is held by the Italians to be no less important to the Axis, since it is closely connected with the Battle of the Atlantic. It is insisted that the war will be won in the Atlantic.

Signor Mussolini and Herr Hitler cannot, therefore, have failed to discuss what they can expect from France and Spain, since those two Mediterranean countries have a geographical position as well as African possessions that would be extremely vaulable to the Axis.

The announcement of the Hitler-Mussolini meeting came as a distinct surprise in both diplomatic and journalistic quarters here. Arrangements for it were made in the strictest secrecy and only a few per-

Continued on Page Six

GEHRIG, 'IRON MAN' OF BASEBALL, DIES

Continued From Page One

out winning the batting crown—.373, .374 and .379.

But baseball has had other great hitters before and other great all-around players. It was the durability of Gehrig combined with his other qualities that lifted him above the ordinary players and in a class all his own.

An odd little incident gave Gehrig his start and an even stranger disease, one almost totally unknown for a robust athlete, brought it to an end. Columbia Lou's string of consecutive games began, innocently enough, when the late Miller Huggins sent him up to bat for Peewee Wanninger on June 1, 1925. The husky 22-year old promptly singled.

Huggins was impressed by the way Gehrig had delivered, but according to the tale that is told he had no notion of using him as a first baseman. The Yankees had a star at the initial sack in those days, Wally Pipp. But Pipp was troubled with frequent headaches.

On June 2 he was bothered by pains in his head.

"Has any one an aspirin tablet?" asked Pipp.

Huggins overheard him and, on a sheer hunch, decided to use the "kid"—Gehrig—at first base. He never left the line-up again until his voluntary resignation fourteen years later. Perhaps that story is not cut from the whole cloth. Gehrig has denied it, but Pipp insists just as vehemently that it is true. At any rate, it is an interesting sidelight on how a spectacular career was begun.

Slipped in 1938

The beginning of the Gehrig playing days was abrupt but the ending was a much slower process. In 1937 the Iron Horse batted .351, his twelfth successive season over the .300 mark. But in 1938 the Yankee captain slipped to .295, the same figure he had established in his 1925 campaign.

Not only his hitting but his fielding had lost much of its crispness. Batted balls that the Gehrig of old had gobbled up easily skidded past him for base hits. In fact, the situation had developed to such an extent that there was continual talk in Spring training in 1939 that the endurance record was approaching its completion.

This became even more obvious in the early games of the campaign. Yankee followers were amazed to see how badly Gehrig had fallen from the peak. He was anchored firmly near first base and only the fielding wizardry of Joe Gordon to his right saved Gehrig from looking very bad. The second sacker overshifted to cover the hole between him and his captain. Lou couldn't go to his right any more.

At bat Gehrig was not even a pale shadow of his former self. Once he had the outfielders backing up to the fences when he stepped to the plate. But this time he could hardly raise the ball out of the infield. On one occasion when he caromed a looping single to left—a certain double for even a slow runner—Gehrig was thrown out at second, standing up.

Last Game Against Senators

That day he saw the handwriting on the wall. And on April 30, 1939, he played his last big league game against the Washington Senators. The Bombers lost and Gehrig realized that he was a detriment to his team. When the Yanks took to the field again in Detroit on May 2, Gehrig—his batting average down to .143—withdrew from the line-up, his first missed game after 2,130 straight.

He acted as nonplaying captain from that point on. On June 12, when the Yankees engaged in an exhibition game in Kansas City, Lou played the last three innings, did nothing and promptly left for the Mayo Clinic. He was there a week, determined to discover just what was the matter with him. That something was wrong he was certain.

On June 21 the diagnosis was made. It was that he had a mild attack of paralysis. His career thus was brought to an abrupt conclusion. And an amazing career it had been.

Tribute by 61,808 at Retirement

The public's reaction to Gehrig's swift retirement gave rise to one of the most inspiring and dramatic episodes in sport when on July 4, in ceremonies preceding the afternoon's holiday double-header, a crowd of 61,808 joined in the Lou

Lou Gehrig

Gehrig Appreciation Day exercises at the Yankee Stadium and thundered a "hail and farewell' to baseball's stricken Iron Horse.

Players, officials, writers and employes at the park showered Lou with gifts, the climax of the spectacle coming when the Yankees themselves paraded on the field their world championship team of 1927. From far and wide these diamond stalwarts had returned to join in the tribute to their former team-mate, who had managed to carry on long after their own retirement from the game.

The group included such Yankee immortals as Babe Ruth, Waite Hoyt, Bob Meusel, Herb Pennock, Joe Dugan, Tony Lazzeri, Mark Koenig, Benny Bengough, Wally Schang, Everett Scott, Wally Pipp, George Pipgras and Bob Shawkey.

Overcome by this spontaneous reception, Gehrig finally mastered his emotions, and, in perhaps the most remarkable valedictory ever delivered in a sport arena, literally poured his heart out to his great throng of listeners, thanking them for their appreciation and assuring them, with characteristic pluck, that he still considered himself "the luckiest fellow on earth, with much to live for."

From then until the end of the season Gehrig stuck by his guns as retired field captain, and spent every day on the bench. He accompanied the club on all its road trips, and at the finish sat through all four of the 1939 world series games in which his colleagues crushed another National League rival.

With the close of the campaign, Lou retired himself within a small circle of close friends, spent much time in fishing, a sport second only to baseball in its fascination for him, and on Oct. 11 figured in another surprise move when Mayor La Guardia announced his appointment to a ten-year term as a member of the three-man Municipal Parole Commission at a salary of $5,700 a year. He tackled with considerable enthusiasm this newest job that was to launch him upon a new chapter in his astounding career.

In Spotlight Again

Although anxious to go quietly about his new task and remain as mush as possible in complete retirement, Gehrig was catapulted prominently into the spotlight again in mid-August of the 1940 pennant campaign when a New York newspaper, in a featured article, intimated that the extraordinary collapse of the four-time world champion Yankees might be attributable to the possibility that some of the players may have become infected with Gehrig's disease.

The story brought vehement protests from the Yankee players, who insisted they were suffering from no physical ailments and then, as if in final rebuttal to the charge, the Yanks, within a few days after publication of the article, launched their spectacular drive which was to lift them from fifth place into the thick of the flag race throughout the month of September.

In the meantime, Gehrig had papers served for a $1,000,000 libel action, while the publication printed an apology to Gehrig, stating that thorough investigation revealed that Lou's ailment was not communicable. No legal action was taken after this.

Gehrig was born in New York on June 19, 1903.

His career began unobtrusively enough when, as a husky youngster, he reported for the High School of Commerce nine in New York. He was tried in the outfield, where he was no Joe DiMaggio at catching fly balls. He was tried as pitcher but was as wild. He was tried as a first baseman and clicked. In later years Lou explained that, with his ever ready grin, by saying "We were mighty short on infielders in those days."

In his first season on the Commerce team he batted .170. Then he started hitting until he cracked the headlines with a crash in 1920. Commerce, the New York schoolboy champions, played Lane Tech of Chicago in a scholastic "world series." The single game was played at Wrigley Field and Gehrig was awed by his surroundings. But he was not too awed. In the ninth inning with Commerce one run behind and the bases full he drove a home run over the right field fence.

Columbia All-Around Player

Buster Gehrig was beginning to take shape. He matriculated at Columbia, pitching, outfielding and playing first base. He was a good enough college pitcher but did have the knack of hitting home runs. For one year there he also tried football, but that sport did not have the same appeal that baseball bore.

The diamond game carried such a zest for him that he quit before he had been long at Morningside Heights, joining the Yankees in 1923. He played thirteen games before Huggins decided that he was not yet ready for major league ball. Farmed out to Hartford in the Eastern League, he batted .304 for the rest of the season. Back with the Yanks the next campaign he followed the identical procedure. He took part in ten games and then it was a return trip to Hartford, where he began to belabor the fences in the circuit, hitting .369. That figure was an eye-opener to Huggins, who recalled him the following season.

That was in 1925. Gehrig batted .295 in 126 games and then he began to rocket through the baseball firmament. His first full season showed him with .313, but after that his successive batting averages were .373, .374, .300, .379, .341, .349, .334, .363, .329, .354, .351 and finally he was back to .295 in his last full campaign. The .363 average gave him the batting championship in 1934, but signal honors had come to him before that. In 1927, his second full campaign with the Yankees, he was voted the most valuable player in the American League.

Seven times he participated in world series and, oddly enough, was a star on the Yankees of 1926-27-28 and with the all-star contingent of 1936-37-38. Each of these groups has its supporters as the greatest baseball team of all time. Ruth-Gehrig-Meusel, the famed "Murderers' Row," or DiMaggio-Gehrig-Dickey? Those were the batting fulcrums around which the teams revolved. Columbia Lou was the lone tie between the two.

His series deeds have been awe-inspiring. His lifetime average in world series games was .361—his full regular average .340—and twice he hit over the fantastic mark of .500, with .545 in 1928 and .529 in 1932. Babe Ruth, however, holds the series record of .625 in 1928.

That is an oddity in itself, Gehrig with two terrific averages but still behind the Babe. Yet for the better part of his career the Iron Horse was to be in the shadow of Ruth. Lou entered baseball when the Babe was riding high, straddling the sport such as no man has straddled it before or since.

Gehrig never left that shadow. His all-time home run production was 494, a figure topped by only two men, Ruth and Jimmy Foxx, who at the end of 1940 had reached a 500 total. For many years Lou gave the Babe his closest pursuit in the home-run derby, but he never caught him until the Babe's last year as a Yankee. Only when the King was on the decline did the Crown Prince win the home-run championship of the league, 49 in 1934.

For one thing, Gehrig did not have the flamboyant Ruth personality. They were team-mates but far apart, one quiet, reserved and efficient and the other boisterous, friendly and efficient. Let it not be deduced that the Iron Horse was not of the friendly type. He was pleasant at all times, but unlike Ruth he never considered the world at large as his particular friend. Whereas the Babe would greet all and sundry with a booming "Hiya, kid?" Lou's was a more personalized welcome.

They were sharp contrasts, those two, both hulking men but as far apart as the two poles. Ruth was Gehrig's boyhood idol, and with the passing years Lou never lost that respect for the Home Run King. And in spite of his own tremendous record, Gehrig was always subordinated to Ruth.

What a pair they made at the plate, coming up to bat in order! Each was likely to drive the ball out of the park. Frequently either or both did just that. In fact, one of the many records that Lou set was that of hitting the most home runs with the bases filled, a startling twenty-three. Another was of four homers in one game.

The Ruthian association affected Gehrig's salary in two respects. In one way the heavy blow that Ruth struck at the payroll kept Lou from getting a compensation as close to the Babe's as their relative batting averages would indicate. Yet, on the other hand, the Bambino lifted the scale so high that Gehrig probably received more than he would have had there been no Ruth to blaze the trail.

Made Fortune in Game

Like most payrolls, the Yankee one is not open to the public gaze, but is more public property than an ordinary business. So the amount of money that Gehrig received each season is part guess and part accurate knowledge, especially in the more recent years when the Federal income tax rolls ceased being secret.

The general estimate is that the Iron Horse received a total of $361,500 in salary from the Yankees. Since he participated in seven world series where the share always was heavy his total income from baseball is estimated at $400,000.

Gehrig received $3,750 in his first season, $6,500 in his second year. This advanced $1,000 in 1927 and then the Iron Horse moved into the big-money class. He never dropped out of five figures for the rest of his career.

For the next five years he received $25,000 and then he dropped to $23,000 for 1933 and 1934, after which he received $31,000 in 1935 and 1936, $36,750 in 1937, $39,000 in 1938 and $35,000 for 1939, a campaign in which he played only eight games.

Baseball contracts are peculiar things, strictly one way. The club has the upper hand at all times and can sever any contract at will. Had they so desired the Yanks could have dropped Gehrig the day the report from the Mayo Clinic arrived. But he was kept on full salary for the remainder of the year.

So firm was his place in the Yankee scheme of things that Manager Joe McCarthy refused to break the Gehrig string even when there was a clamor to the effect that the Iron Horse himself would benefit from it. Marse Joe shook his head to that. "Gehrig plays as long as he wants to play," he said. Not many ball players would be granted such a privilege.

But in this respect McCarthy knew his man and knew him well. He realized that once Lou discovered his form had departed and that he was hindering the progress of the team he would call it quits. And that is what happened.

The day before he entered the Mayo Clinic for the examination baseball celebrated its centennial at Cooperstown and the Hall of Fame was dedicated. Ruth already had been elected to it and within a short time another bronze plaque joined the Babe's as Henry Louis Gehrig took his proper place among the all-time greats that this sport had produced.

For though Baseball's Hall of Fame committee decided to hold no elections for new candidates in 1939, it chose, upon recommendation of the Baseball Writers Association of America, to make an exception and name Gehrig as the lone Hall of Fame award for the year.

Gehrig got a fond reception from the most famous of his former team-mates, Babe Ruth.

"All the News That's Fit to Print."

The New York Times.

LATE CITY EDITION
Partly cloudy, showers, little change in temperature today. Tomorrow cooler, probably showers.
Temperatures Yesterday—Max., 88; Min., 70.

Copyright, 1937, by The New York Times Company.

VOL. LXXXVI....No. 29,024. Entered as Second-Class Matter, Postoffice, New York, N. Y. NEW YORK, MONDAY, JULY 12, 1937. PP TWO CENTS In New York City. | THREE CENTS Within 200 Miles. | FOUR CENTS Elsewhere Except in 7th and 8th Postal Zones.

RIOTING BREAKS OUT AT MASSILLON MILL; 1 DEAD; 6 WOUNDED

Police Battle Republic Steel Strikers at Union Hall After an Officer Is Stoned

INDIANA WORKS TO OPEN

C.I.O. Acts to Withdraw Pickets on Basis of 'Agreement' With Governor Townsend

HE DENIES SIGNED PACT

Youngstown Sheet and Tube Spurns Any Deal With S.W.O.C. but Union Hails 'Victory'

Day's Labor Developments

Strike rioting broke out at gates of Republic Steel plant at Massillon Ohio. Police fought rioters with tear gas. One man was reported killed. Page 1.

Youngstown Sheet and Tube's Indiana plant will be reopened today or tomorrow. S. W. O. C. moved to withdraw pickets. Company denied any agreement, but Governor Townsend said he had an "understanding" that ended the strike. Page 1.

Strike at Aluminum Company's Alcoa plant was ended by union on recommendation of representative of William Green. Page 4.

Republic Steel prepared to reopen more plants; Ohio will answer in Federal court today the C. I. O. suit to bar use of troops in strike. Page 4.

The Maritime Commission declared it would seek to end shipping strikes by setting new wage scales and training seamen. Page 4.

Agreements ending cloak trade stoppage will be signed today and 35,000 workers will return to 1,500 shops tomorrow. Page 5.

Subway motormen on the B. M. T. threatened to strike rather than submit to the referendum demanded by the Transport Workers Union, a C. I. O. affiliate Page 5.

Rioting in Ohio

By The Associated Press.

MASSILLON, Ohio, Monday July 12.—One man was killed and at least six others wounded late last night in an encounter between city police and striking steel workers and sympathizers at a union hall near Republic Steel Corporation's Central Alloy division here.

City Patrolman Leo Kelley said the rioting broke out when Major H. O. Curley, former army officer named by Police Chief Stanley Switter to assist him during the C. I. O. steel strike, was stoned in front of the union local's headquarters.

Doctors pronounced an unidentified man in civilian clothes dead upon arrival at City Hospital.

Six others were rushed to the hospital, five of them suffering from bullet wounds and one a victim of tear gas.

Troops Rushed to Scene

Ohio National Guardsmen, Company I, 166th Infantry, arrived from near-by Canton as the Massillon police and police reinforcements from Canton massed at the scene.

Participants in the fierce fighting were estimated at 150 to 200.

Among the identified wounded were: Nick Vadias, 45, shot in abdomen and hip, condition critical; Jim Decan, 47, bullet wounds; Bill Netras, bullet wounds, and Ted George, buckshot wounds in right side.

The battle lasted for nearly an hour. The National Guardsmen from Canton arrived soon after order was restored. They were deployed about the mill area immediately.

Patrolman Kelley said that between sixty-five and seventy men were assembled in or near the steel union's "New Deal" lodge headquarters, 500 feet from the main entrance to Republic's property.

Curley, he added, was in charge of forty regular and special police assigned to the area. An automobile stopped in front of the hall and an occupant played a spotlight on the crowd of strikers or sympathizers.

"Curley walked toward the machine and the strikers began to stone him," the policeman said. "Then one man stepped out of the union hall doorway and fired five shots. The police then returned the fire."

Sheet and Tube to Reopen

Special to THE NEW YORK TIMES.

CHICAGO, July 11.—Officials of the Youngstown Sheet and Tube Company announced tonight that they would reopen the company's

Continued on Page Four

Italy to Put $6,000,000 Into an Airport at Genoa

By The Associated Press.

GENOA, Italy, July 11.—Announcement was made today that Premier Benito Mussolini had approved plans for the construction of Italy's greatest combined seaplane and airport here, costing $6,000,000. The plans call for a long breakwater for the protection of shipyards and refueling docks along the waterfront.

A great air base at Genoa will be a danger to France. That port is only eighty miles from the French frontier and is only 200 miles from Marseilles.

This port is the chief French base for traffic with North Africa, and, according to present arrangements, most of the troops from Africa, on which France largely depends for defense, would be disembarked there.

3 RUSSIANS BEGIN NEW FLIGHT TO U.S.

Pilot Gromoff and 2 Comrades Take Off From Moscow for San Francisco via Pole

POOR WEATHER FORECAST

But Airmen Fear Worse Later and Start Second Record Attempt in Three Weeks

By HAROLD DENNY

Special Cable to THE NEW YORK TIMES.

MOSCOW, Monday, July 12.—In the face of bad weather forecasts another Soviet airplane took off from Moscow at 3:23 this morning [8:23 P. M. Sunday, New York time] on the adventurous route over the North Pole.

The object of this ship is understood to be to set a world distance record and at the same time add another Polar victory for Soviet aviation. Although no announcement was made here, the plane's objective was said to be San Francisco.

It was also said unofficially that a third Soviet plane piloted by Sigismund Levanevsky would take off for the United States within the next month if the weather permitted.

Mikhail Gromoff, another of the Soviet's galaxy of "superfliers," was at the controls of the plane that took to the air this morning. He is the finest type of aviator—tall, handsome, quiet and calm.

His two associates in the plane are also unusually likable men. They are Andrei Yumacheff and Sergei Danilin. Danilin, besides being an expert navigator, is a sculptor, and Yumacheff is a painter.

Sister Ship of Other Plane

The plane in which they are now plunging toward the North Pole is a sister ship of the one in which Valeri Chkaloff, Georgi Baidukoff and Alexander Beliakoff thrilled the United States by their flight to Vancouver, Wash., three weeks ago. It is marked ANT 25-1. It is a single-motored monoplane with a slim fuselage and long tapering wings painted red—a huge dragonfly.

The plane took off from the mile-long concrete runway at the Sholkovo military airdrome twenty-five

Continued on Page Two

O'MAHONEY SCORES 'DEBATE THROTTLE' ON COURT MEASURE

'First Time' He Ever Saw Attempt to Pass a Major Bill 'Without Any Explanation'

BOTH SIDES UNYIELDING

Senate's 'Fight to a Finish' Dooms Other Legislation This Session, Some Hold

Special to THE NEW YORK TIMES.

WASHINGTON, July 11.—The debate on the compromise Judiciary Reorganization Bill will enter its second week in the Senate tomorrow with both sides as determined to 'fight to a finish' as when they started. Senator O'Mahoney of Wyoming, who as a member of the Judiciary Committee opposed the President's original bill and who was one of the subcommittee of three which framed the majority's adverse report, expects to take the floor tomorrow morning to speak against the compromise measure.

Senator O'Mahoney said today that he did not expect to devote much of his argument to the political phases of the court situation, which have been emphasized by speakers during the past week, or to the majority report, which has brought the charge from administration supporters that it was as much an attack on the President himself as it was on the proposed legislation.

Will Discuss Bill Itself

The measure's opponents appear to be taking the attitude that Senators Wheeler and McCarran have answered pretty thoroughly the political arguments of the President's supporters and seek now to bring the discussion back to the merits or demerits of the measure itself.

"This is the first time in my experience that a major bill has been brought up and attempts made to pass it without a word of explanation," Senator O'Mahoney said today. "The measure itself hasn't been discussed by anybody yet, and that is what I am going to try to do."

Plainly irked by the administration strategy in invoking rules long in disuse to hinder a filibuster, Senator O'Mahoney said that it was "pretty hard to predict" what he would be allowed to do.

"It is difficult to predict what we can do," he said, "under these rules, which are obviously designed to throttle debate, but we will do what we can."

Bailey Ready to Take Place

On Saturday Senator O'Mahoney was ready to take the floor but could not speak because a cold had affected his voice. He is much improved today and expects to talk tomorrow.

If, however, Senator O'Mahoney's voice is still affected, Senator Bailey of North Carolina, who has been an opponent of both the original measure and any form of compromise since the plan was first broached by the President more than five months ago, plans to enter the debate. Senator Bailey likewise does not propose to touch on the political aspects, he said today.

"I shall address myself strictly to the merits of the proposals we are considering," he said. "My talk will

Continued on Page Two

Fifth Day of Heat Wave Kills 38 Before Thunderstorm Cools City

Heavy Rain Sends Mercury Down to 70° After It Had Reached High of 88°, but Only Temporary Relief Is Likely Before Thursday—295 Dead in Nation

A driving thunderstorm sent the mercury tumbling 12 degrees between 8:30 and 9 o'clock last night, giving the heat-oppressed the first real relief since the start of the five-day torrid wave that has scorched the nation from the West Coast to the Atlantic seaboard.

Thirty-eight persons died and thirty-three were prostrated in the metropolitan area alone on the fifth day. The death toll in the nation for the five days mounted to at least 295, many of them drownings, The Associated Press reported.

The temperature started dropping in the city as the storm approached, from 84 at 7 P. M. to 83 at 8, then to 82 at 8:30. As huge raindrops pelted the streets after 8:30 the mercury fell precipitately, touching 70 at 9 P. M.

The showers, the Weather Bureau said, would give only temporary relief. There was a possibility that there would be more showers today, but these, too, would give slight relief. Today's forecast is for partly cloudy weather with little change in temperature, except from possible showers. Tomorrow, however, is expected to be slightly cooler.

The Weather Bureau said it did not expect the heat wave to abate much before Thursday, adding, "even then the seasonal temperatures at that time will be rather warm." By the latter half of this week the government meteorologist thought New York City should come under the influence of a high-pressure area over the Middle West and Central Canada and possibly a low-pressure area off the Atlantic Coast. The combined effect should bring northerly winds and a consequent lowering of temperature.

The cumulative influence of the heat was shown by the twenty-five deaths on Saturday and the high number again yesterday. The death toll for the five-day period has risen to sixty-six.

Although the temperature yesterday was not as high as on the preceding four days, the humidity was higher. The lowest percentage of moisture content in the atmosphere up until 6 o'clock last night was 56. This contrasted with an average of 38 and 40 per cent for the preceding four days.

The humidity, the Weather Bureau said, was about 20 per cent too high for the temperature. Hence the more acute physical discomfort.

Instead of being down to 35 per

Continued on Page Three

GEORGE GERSHWIN, COMPOSER, IS DEAD

Master of Jazz Succumbs in Hollywood at 38 After Operation for Brain Tumor

WROTE 'RHAPSODY IN BLUE'

Also Composed 'Porgy and Bess,' 'Of Thee I Sing' and Many Musical Comedies

Special to THE NEW YORK TIMES.

HOLLYWOOD, Calif., July 11.—George Gershwin, 38-year-old composer, died today at 10:35 A. M. at the Cedars of Lebanon Hospital. He succumbed five hours after being operated on for removal of a brain tumor. The operation was decided upon when the composer's condition became critical at midnight.

Dr. Gabriel Segall of Los Angeles and Dr. Howard Nafsiger, University of California Professor of Surgery, performed the operation at 5 o'clock this morning.

Dr. Walter E. Dandy, Baltimore brain surgeon, turned back at Newark today upon learning that Mr. Gershwin's condition had changed suddenly and he would be operated on at once. Dr. Dandy had been summoned from Chesapeake Bay, where he was cruising over the week-end with Governor Harry W. Nice of Maryland.

Ira Gershwin, who wrote lyrics for his brother's music, was at his side when he died.

Two weeks ago Mr. Gershwin collapsed at the Samuel Goldwyn studios, where he had been working on nine compositions for "The Goldwyn Follies." He had completed five songs before his breakdown. Taken to the hospital for observation, the composer, when released last week, was in an extremely nervous condition. Yesterday he was returned to the hospital in a coma.

Also surviving are his mother, Mrs. Rose Gershwin; a sister, Mrs. Leopold Godowsky Jr. and another brother, Arthur.

He was a member of the American Society of Composers and Publishers, the Lambs Club and the Bohemians.

Child of the Jazz Age

George Gershwin was a composer of his generation. What he wanted to do most, he said, was to interpret the soul of the American people. Thus in the tempo of jazz he jabbed at the dignities of American life, while he won the plaudits of the musical elite with the classic qualities of "A Rhapsody in Blue." With his brother Ira and that master of gentle satire George S. Kaufman he set the nation laughing at the foibles of its government; but, in more serious mood, he found time to write music that the great conductors of the world were glad to present.

Mr. Gershwin was a child of the Twenties, the Age of Jazz. In the fast two-step time of the years after the war he was to music what F. Scott Fitzgerald was to prose. Four years after that mad decade began, Paul Whiteman sent the strains of his Rhapsody cascading far beyond Broadway and the music they called Jazz had come of age. Serge Koussevitzky of the Boston Symphony Orchestra played his work and the capitals of Europe called for more.

For the musical comedy stage, the vaudeville act, the Hollywood lot, he made his music. He had

Continued on Page Twenty

REPUBLICANS VIEW MAYOR AS NOMINEE

Leaders to Start Hunt This Week for a Rival, but Do Not Expect to Find One

'GO ALONG' RELUCTANTLY

Find Rank and File Resentful Toward La Guardia, but Hope for Fight Wanes

Republican leaders of the five counties are expected to start conferences this week on whether they should designate Mayor La Guardia as the party's candidate for re-election. It was considered unlikely that a decision would be made for another two weeks, however.

Republican leaders still are hopeful that a strong conservative Democrat, such as George V. McLaughlin, can be persuaded to make the race as the official Republican candidate, but they now do not really expect that to happen, and the redesignation of Mayor La Guardia by default is considered to be a probability.

It is possible that the Brooklyn and Queens organizations will decline to go along with Kenneth F. Simpson's New York County organization, should New York County swing in line for the Mayor, and in that event any one running against the Mayor in the primaries would have organization support in some districts, but not in others.

Friends of the Mayor claim a majority of the members of the Kings County Executive Committee, but this is disputed by friends of John R. Crews, Republican leader of Brooklyn.

Find Republicans Resentful

Republican leaders now disposed to "go along" with the Mayor declared yesterday that at the same time they were convinced that the sentiment of the rank and file of the organization was against the Mayor's renomination. He may be a good Mayor, and he may be reelected, one leader declared, but the Republicans do not like his policies.

It is regarded as possible that the Republican leaders may pass the responsibility for designating or rejecting the Mayor to the members of the county committee. Mr. Crews has indicated that he intends to have the matter taken up at such a meeting, and the same may be done in Queens, where the county committee will meet on July 29. Leaders in the other boroughs may follow suit.

A definite decision by the Republican leaders probably will await a decision by the Democrats on their candidate. Nomination of either Jeremiah T. Mahoney or Samuel Levy by the Democrats probably would insure the Republican nomination for Mr. La Guardia, it was said, but if the Democrats nominated Senator Royal S. Copeland or James A. Foley the Republicans would be inclined to endorse the Democratic nominee.

The third course of action the Republicans had considered, the nomination of a third candidate, a conservative, died with the withdrawal of Senator Robert F. Wagner from the race, it was said. Had Senator Wagner been the Democratic nominee and Mayor La Guardia the Labor candidate, nomination of a third candidate, run-

Continued on Page Five

LOYALISTS TRIUMPH ANEW NEAR MADRID AS DRIVE IS PUSHED

Occupy Villanueva del Pardillo in Their Biggest Offensive and Seize 600 Prisoners

WAR IS IN CRUCIAL PERIOD

Great Open Battle in View as Government Adds to Gains—Rebels Dispute Foe's Claims

By HERBERT L. MATTHEWS

Wireless to THE NEW YORK TIMES.

MADRID, July 11.—Spanish Government troops early today occupied Villanueva del Pardillo, about twelve miles west of Madrid, and took 600 more prisoners. This operation widened their salient and carried one step further the greatest government offensive of the civil war.

Since Monday the Loyalist forces have been making wide gains in a supreme effort to break the siege of Madrid, and this drive is regarded here as even stronger than the Rebel offensive against Bilbao. It is, therefore, no exaggeration to say that the war has reached its most crucial period.

It is hoped by the Loyalists that the race against time that the Negrin Government lost in the case of Bilbao will be won for Santander and Asturias.

In less than two months the government has worked a complete reorganization of the army and air forces, speeded up the war industries, made heavy purchases abroad and built up a great fighting machine. For weeks men, guns and materials of all sorts have been pouring up, choking roads with thousands of trucks. Planes by the dozens are filing the air over the Rebel lines, bombing towns, concentrations and trenches at will and again demonstrating that in Central Spain the Loyalists still dominate the air.

Equipment Is Extensive

Details of equipment cannot, of course, be given, but it can be said that there are many tanks, many guns and more troops than have yet been employed in this conflict.

The government is playing for the greatest of stakes, since, if it wins, the siege of Madrid will have been lifted. It is too soon to make any predictions. The Insurgents are naturally preparing a counter-offensive and, since the action is now in open territory, one must suppose that the first great open battle of the war will occur soon.

The offensive, whose first phase has ended with the capture of Villanueva del Pardillo, is conceded by foreign military experts here to be of particularly brilliant conception. Apparently the whole general staff worked it out, and those of us who have been watching its development see no reason to doubt that its direction has been entrusted to two Spanish officers—General José Miaja and Lieut. Col. Vicente Rojo, chief of the general staff.

The plan of campaign was and still is an intricate one. Its first part was successfully kept secret until it was launched, and its further development remains a mystery, except that it can clearly be seen from the map that the main thrust is in the direction of Navalcarnero, eighteen miles southwest of Madrid, and presumably intended to cut the Estremadura Road,

Continued on Page Six

Hero of Shanghai Fight Ready for Call to War

By The Associated Press.

MANILA, July 11.—General Tsai Ting-kai, former commander of the Chinese Nineteenth Route Army, which withstood a Japanese attack at Shanghai in 1932, said today he was preparing to return to China because of the tense Chino-Japanese situation. He said China was almost unanimous for war against Japan.

"Chinese nationalism," he said, "is now strong enough to resist Japanese aggression."

He said Generalissimo Chiang Kai-shek would urge immediate resistance should the Japanese "force China's hand." He added that his country was confident of its ability to repulse Japanese in Chinese territory.

SYRIAN ARABS RIOT FOR NEW MANDATE

Between 6 and 20 Are Slain in Upper Jezireh Area in Clash of Natives and Troops

DISTRICT GOVERNOR KILLED

Premier of Iraq Demands That All Moslems Combat Plan to Partition Palestine

By The Associated Press.

JERUSALEM, July 11.—Between six and twenty persons were killed and wounded in the upper Jezireh district Friday in a clash between troops and demonstrators demanding a separate mandate and dissociation from the Syrian Republic, advices reaching here today said.

The reports, received from Damascus, said troops attempted to break up demonstrations held in mosques.

The mosques were emptied as crowds stormed government offices. The district governor was believed to have been killed. Troops were forced to fire into the crowd to break up the attack.

In Jerusalem, the Arab National Defense party issued a manifesto tonight severely condemning the recommendations of the British Royal Commission for splitting Palestine into separate Arab and Jewish States and the creation of a new British mandate controlling the holy cities of Jerusalem, Bethlehem and Nazareth.

Iraq Expresses Sympathy

Bagheb Bey Nashashibi, former Mayor of Jerusalem, presided at an executive party meeting. The manifesto said his party was interested in a "noble Arab nation" and could not see the partition scheme as a solution. The proposal has been supported by Emir Abdullah of Trans-Jordan and opposed by the Muftist party.

More than 500 telegrams of protest were received from various societies and religious committees by the Arab High Committee.

Hikmet Suleiman, Premier of Iraq, also cabled the High Committee, asserting his sympathy for Palestine Arabs in opposition to partition.

The High Committee will meet here tomorrow to discuss replies from Arab princes and kings on future policies.

Nashashibi's party is holding a conference later this week.

Provisional distribution candidates elected from Palestine Jewry to the Zionist Congress to be held in Switzerland in August indicated

Continued on Page Nine

HOSTILITIES RAGE ON PEIPING'S EDGE; CHINA WARNS FOES

Nanking Rules Out Increase of Tokyo Troops in North—Insists Fighting End

NANKING MOVES FOR WAR

Clash Is Believed Part of Plan to Seize Hopei Province for 'Another Manchukuo'

TOKYO SENDS MORE MEN

Japanese Foreign Office Sees Peace on Basis of Revised Demands to Chinese

The Chinese Situation

SHANGHAI—China warned Japan she would not tolerate increase of alien troops on her soil and infringement of her sovereignty, saying such actions would cause her to take "defensive measures." Large contingents of troops were moved northward. Page 1.

TOKYO—While war preparations were hastened the Foreign Office announced Japan's demands for settlement of the Peiping fighting had been revised and it hoped the matter would be confined to a local incident. Previously, after many councils of governmental army and navy chiefs, determination had been expressed to enforce a showdown on anti-Japanese agitations in North China. Page 8.

PEIPING—Fighting was renewed west of the city. Previously Chinese and Japanese had told of a settlement of the affair, but the Twenty-ninth Army was believed to have rejected its terms. Heavy Chinese guards were posted in the city, and its streets were prepared for defense. Page 8.

HEAVY FIGHTING RENEWED

Special Cable to THE NEW YORK TIMES.

SHANGHAI, Monday, July 12.—The heaviest Chino-Japanese fighting since the initial outbreak last Wednesday began this morning on the outskirts of Peiping, according to telegrams received at the Chinese Government offices here.

TOKYO, Monday, July 12 (AP).—The Japanese War Office announced today that the vanguard of a Chinese army advancing from the south had opened fire on Japanese positions west of Peiping.

By HALLETT ABEND

Wireless to THE NEW YORK TIMES.

SHANGHAI, Monday, July 12.—Japan was officially warned yesterday that China would not tolerate any foreign nation's arbitrarily increasing its garrison on Chinese soil and infringing on China's territorial sovereignty.

In a vigorous oral protest to the Japanese Chargé d'Affaires at Nanking, the Vice Minister for Foreign Affairs asserted that if such acts continued, China would be forced to take defensive measures. The Chinese official demanded that the Chargé immediately cable Tokyo to tell the government to cease the concentration of Japanese military activities in the Peiping area.

The Chinese Government is reported to have telegraphed three orders to the Hopei-Chahar Political Council at Peiping:

First, the council must not accept the demands of the Japanese.

Second, the Twenty-ninth Army must not be permitted to retreat in any sectors.

Third, if necessary any and all sacrifices must be made to repel Japanese attacks.

The Hopei-Chahar Council in reply sent a telegram to the Nanking government emphatically denying having signed any agreement with the slightest political implications, although the Japanese Embassy in Peiping claims to have received a signed document accepting four terms at 8 o'clock last night.

Likened to 1932 Crisis

"The situation has assumed proportions more serious than anything that has arisen between China and Japan since the Shanghai hostilities early in 1932," said a high government spokesman in Shanghai. "Even the invasion and seizure of Jehol, previous incursions into North China, the fighting which resulted in the Tangku truce and last year's Suiyuan clash did not begin to approach in gravity today's crisis."

The Japanese report that several large contingents of Chinese troops, including some Central Government units, are moving northward. One force, commanded by General Wan Fu-lin, is advancing from

Continued on Page Eight

Fliers Quit Phoenix Hunt for Miss Earhart; Chance of Saving Her Held One in Million

By The Associated Press

HONOLULU, July 11.—Aviators from the battleship Colorado tonight abandoned hope of finding Amelia Earhart and her navigator, Captain Frederick J. Noonan, in the Phoenix Island area after four days of scanning the islands from their three catapult planes.

As Captain Wilhelm H. Friedell of the Colorado tentatively ended the ship's search of the Phoenix area and left the island group astern to head for a rendezvous with the destroyers Drayton, Lamptson and Cushing about 350 miles northeast of Howland Islands, however, navy fliers aboard the aircraft carrier Lexington prepared for a spectacular effort.

Heading in the approximate direction of Howland Islands but with their exact destination undetermined, the Lexington's 1,299 officers and men concentrated their immediate energies on detailed plans for a high speed 200,000-square mile aerial sweep of the Equatorial Pacific. The ship has sixty-two planes.

"There is only a chance in a million for a rescue," said naval officers directing the search.

They declared the main possibility remaining was that Miss Earhart's globe-girdling plane had alighted in the water and was still floating, in on which case it could be sighted from the Lexington's air fleet.

The Lexington's armada was expected to begin the search tomorrow afternoon or Tuesday, probably first scouting west and south of Howland Island and extending the search to the Gilbert Islands, toward which the equatorial currents in that area run.

Searchers said, however, that there was only an outside chance that the lost plane had succeeded as far short of Howland Island, its goal, as the Gilbert Islands, 600 miles east of Howland.

Until the Colorado's fliers confessed that they had lost hope, the Phoenix group had been regarded as the most likely place of finding Miss Earhart, missing since July 2.

The Colorado still was in position to send out her planes, however, and it was said they might make a final flight Monday.

The planes searched virtually the whole Phoenix area, but found nothing to bolster hopes for the missing fliers' safety. One of the planes, flying over Sydney Island in the group, reported sighting letters scooped in the sand spelling dozens of Polynesian words. The navy aviators, however, said there was no sign of life and they discounted the possibility that the markings in the sand could have related to the lost plane.

Mussolini Expels Austrian Soccer Team; Vienna, Match Banned, to Protest to Rome

Wireless to THE NEW YORK TIMES.

VIENNA, July 11.—A diplomatic protest will be made to Italy concerning the expulsion of an Austrian soccer team from that country, this correspondent learns.

The incident is a sequel to the free-for-all fight last Sunday in the Vienna Stadium between the Austrian Admira team and the Genoa eleven, which were competing for the Central European Cup. Four Italians were severely hurt.

The match, which ended in a tie, was to have been replayed in Genoa today, and the Admira team left Vienna Thursday, but Friday it was learned that the Italian soccer authorities refused to allow the match to take place.

The Admira players returned to Vienna tonight, announcing that they had been expelled from Italy by order of Premier Benito Mussolini.

"We telegraphed Il Duce yesterday," a member of the team declared, "to ask him to intervene with the Italian football authorities and allow the match to occur. Mussolini's reply was to order us to leave Italy within twenty-four hours. We wished to stay on in Venice to appeal to the committee of the Central European Cup contests, which is meeting tomorrow."

Dr. Geroe, the president of the Vienna Football Association, left tonight for Venice to enter an energetic protest at the meeting. One representative each of Italy, Austria, Czechoslovakia and Switzerland constitute the committee under a Hungarian president.

Baron Hornbostel, permanent head of the Austrian Foreign Office, tonight telephoned the Italian Minister of the Interior to ask for an explanation of the expulsion. He also spoke with Francesco Salata, the Italian Minister to Austria.

The Austrian Minister in Rome, Egon Berger-Waldenegg, has been instructed to make representations to the Italian Government.

A fight among the players, carried on to the accompaniment of shouts of defiance from spectators who were held in check by strong police cordons, marked the closing moments of play in the European Soccer Cup match between the Genoa team and the Austrian Admira team at Vienna July 4, according to cabled dispatches.

The free-for-all began after a young Austrian player, who had tied the score by conversion of a penalty, thumbed his nose at his opponents, and was knocked down by one of the Italian players.

GEORGE GERSHWIN, COMPOSER, IS DEAD

Continued From Page One

grown up on the streets of Brooklyn and he had served his apprenticeship in Tin Pan Alley. He had turned out tunes with all the tricks of the dove that rhymed with love. He had woven the cadences of Broadway into his songs and he had given America the plaintive Negro music of Porgy and Bess.

What he wrote was always provocative, often distinctive. Some have doubted that his inspiration and craftsmanship kept up with his ambition to use the forms of jazz in the classical manner. Some have claimed that his real contributions were his saucy, tuneful dance and musical comedy tunes. But upon one thing all are agreed—from the scholarly Philip Hale to the man in the street—that his music will not soon be forgotten.

Mr. Gershwin was born in Brooklyn, Sept. 26, 1898. His early boyhood gave no indication of a bent toward music, nor was his own attitude toward his music-practicing playmates anything more than contempt. "Little Maggies," he called them.

But when he was 12 years old two things happened that were to awaken a fateful unrest in the boy's mind. First, his mother bought a piano; second, he heard the violinist, Max Rosen, give a recital at school. This started young George on his musical career. The piano proved such an attraction that his parents arranged instruction with a young woman teacher of the neighborhood. In the next few years he turned to several teachers until he met Charles Hambitzer, who is credited by some as having "discovered" Gershwin.

Mr. Hambitzer, teacher of piano, violin and 'cello, versatile orchestra musician and composer of light music, found his new pupil a genius. It was Mr. Hambitzer who gave Mr. Gershwin his first rudiments of harmony, and initiated him to the wonder of the classics. At a crucial point in the boy's studies Mr. Hambitzer died. Mr. Gershwin was later to study piano with Ernest Hutcheson, and some composition and orchestration with Edward Kilenyi and Rubin Goldmark.

Worked as a 'Plugger'

Mr. Gershwin's real learning came from experience, and his course therein started at Remick's music-publishing house. The boy was 16 then, and had passed two years in the High School of Commerce. His new position was that of "plugger," and it netted him $15 a week. His duties, like those of a corps of other "pluggers," were to tour the haunts of Tin Pan Alley as a floor pianist to a song-and-dance performer, in order to note which songs were best received. For his future work it was invaluable experience.

It was about this time that, sensing his limitations as a concert pianist, he began to write tunes of his own. After two years at Remick's he left to make his first contact with the theatre. It was a job as rehearsal pianist for "Miss 1917," by Victor Herbert and Jerome Kern. His ability was evident immediately and he was retained after the opening of the show by Ned Wayburn at a salary of $35 a week. It was at one of the Sunday concerts that were part of the run of "Miss 1917" that some of Gershwin's songs had first important hearings, for Vivienne Segal sang "You—Just You" and "There's More to a Kiss."

Then followed a rapid succession of events. He went on the Keith Vaudeville Circuit as accompanist to Louise Dresser; he was hired by the publishing firm of Harms as staff composer; he toured as pianist with Nora Bayes, and, his muse becoming more and more fertile, his songs were being heard in revues and other shows.

Wrote "Scandals" Music

When he was 20 he received his first musical comedy commission from Alex Aarons. The product was "La La Lucille," given in 1919. He was then introduced to George White, with the result that Gershwin wrote the music for the "Scandals" of five successive years, beginning in 1920.

His renown spread rapidly. In the next decade he was to turn out such musical comedy hits as "Our Nell" (1922), "Sweet Little Devil" (1923), "Lady Be Good," "Primrose" (1924), "Tip Toes," "Song of the Flame" (1925), "Oh, Kay!" (1926), "Strike Up the Band," "Funny Face," "Shake Your Feet"

Times Wide World Photo.
GEORGE GERSHWIN

(1927), "Rosalie," "Treasure Girl" (1928), "Show Girl" (1929), "Girl Crazy" (1930), "Of Thee I Sing" (1931) "Pardon My English" (1932), "Let 'Em Eat Cake" (1933).

America was ripe for "Of Thee I Sing" when its characters cavorted across a Boston stage for the first time just before Christmas, 1931. Washington had become a stuffy place in the past few years and the Messrs. Kaufman and Gershwin hit upon the exact psychological moment to present Alexander Throttlebottom and the dancing graybeards of the Supreme Court.

To this gay satire of love in the White House, George Gershwin contributed the catchy tunes. His brother, Ira, wrote the lyrics, and many felt that it had at last developed the Gilbert and Sullivan of the new age. The music, especially that of the finale: "Of thee I sing—baby!" caught the spirit of the book exactly.

To some extent, Mr. Gershwin recaptured the vibrancy of this play in "Let 'Em Eat Cake," its successor, but critics felt, in the words of Mr. Brooks Atkinson, that there was more style than thought. Both scores, however, were hailed as masterpieces of modern light opera composition.

But he brought the artistic haut monde to his feet with the "Rhapsody in Blue," for piano and orchestra. It was written at the suggestion of Paul Whiteman and was first performed in the first concert of jazz music given by Mr. Whiteman's band Feb. 12, 1924, in Aeolian Hall. Mr. Gershwin himself played the solo part.

The next large work was the orchestral piece "An American in Paris," first heard at the hands of the Philharmonic-Symphony, under Dr. Damrosch, in Carnegie Hall. Serge Koussevitzky and the Boston Symphony Orchestra, with Gershwin as soloist, introduced the Second Rhapsody in January, 1932.

Mr. Gershwin often appeared at the Lewisohn Stadium concerts of the Philharmonic-Symphony, as soloist, composer and conductor. One program devoted entirely to his own works, given Aug. 16, 1932, attracted an audience that set a record for the stadium. He appeared with all the leading orchestras in this country and with many in Europe.

Perhaps his most ambitious work was the opera "Porgy and Bess," based on the dramatized novel of Dubose Heyward. Lyrics were by Ira Gershwin and Mr. Heyward. Described as something "between grand opera and musical comedy," it made a sensation at its world première performance in Boston, Sept. 30, 1935, by the Theatre Guild.

It reached the Alvin Theatre in New York Oct. 10 of the same year, and repeated its triumph.

A new light comedy by the Gershwin brothers and Mr. Kaufman had been briefly in the making a short time before the composer died. After going to Hollywood to write the score for the projected "Goldwyn Follies"—on which he was at work when he died—Mr. Gershwin, his brother and Mr. Kaufman had spent about a fortnight on their projected piece.

It was to have been a typical satire, not on government this time, but upon that world they all knew so well—"show business." They were forced to halt operations, however, because of the exacting nature of composing songs for Mr. Goldwyn. Into this work Mr. Gershwin threw himself whole heartedly and advance reports were that those of his tunes already completed for the motion picture were quite in his best manner.

Mr. Gershwin was a talented painter, and some of his works were placed on exhibition. He was also an enthusiastic collector of art objects and his apartment on Riverside Drive contained some notable items.

GERSHWIN CAUSED NEW JAZZ VALUES

His Place in American Music Is Held Unique Due to His Gifts and Circumstances

DID NOT IMITATE MASTERS

Struck Vein of His Own Which Was Fresh, New and Natural in Characteristic Scores

By OLIN DOWNES

Special to THE NEW YORK TIMES.

ASBURY PARK, N. J., July 11.—George Gershwin had a unique position in American music, one due in part to his wholly exceptional gifts and in part to a special set of circumstances which raised him in less than five years from the rank of a song plugger in Tin Pan Alley to that of a composer whose works invaded symphony concert programs and operatic auditoriums and made him internationally famous.

In some respects, and partly by virtue of the immense amount of publicity he received, his value may have been exaggerated. It remains that the composer of the "Rhapsody in Blue" and certain other representative compositions gave jazz itself a new importance and consideration as a musical medium, and proved that significant creation was possible in the terms of this popular national idiom.

Gershwin was not the first to realize these possibilities. Serious American composers such as Henry F. Gilbert, John Alden Carpenter and Aaron Copland of the younger generation had employed jazz motives in ways of their own in symphonies and symphonic poems. But Gershwin, in the first place, had the popular ear. In the second place, while he never was an intellectual composer, he had an extraordinary musical instinct and capacity for assimilation.

Composer of Limitations

He naturally grafted upon his own Broadway style harmonies and progressions he had heard in the works of classic masters. He did not imitate these masters, but naturally absorbed what he wanted of their expression, in a way to make his own richer and more significant than otherwise would have been the case, and without becoming unnaturally "high brow" or slavishly imitative.

He never passed a certain point as a "serious" composer. It was not in him to do what Dvorak did for Bohemian music, or even for America in the "New World" symphony, or what Grieg did for Norway in his art. Gershwin had too limited a technic for that, and the greater forms, because of his beginnings, were never really natural to him.

But in his most characteristic scores he struck out a vein of his own, sufficiently fresh, new, natural, and racy to command wide attention and to refresh enormously the ears in a period which offers little that is new and original in musical creation.

Some would see in his rise a manifestation of a certain phase of democracy and American opportunity. His emergence from the stage of a highly promising purveyor of popular entertainment to the higher realms of his art began when one day the singer Eva Gauthier walked into Harms Music Shop and asked the young Gershwin if he would play her accompaniment while she sang some American popular songs by him in Boston and New York, offering him for this special service something more than his accustomed $2 an hour.

Gershwin's Playing Effective

At first the young man at the piano did not understand the proposition, but he finally accepted, and soon was famous. The songs, by their swing, their wit, their original rhythmic and harmonic settings of the texts, made an absolutely novel sensation when they fell on ears habituated to, but also perhaps fatigued by, overintellectualized products of certain cerebral modern European composers. It may be added that no small part of the effect was furnished by Gershwin's playing.

Those who have not heard him accompany his songs do not suspect their full flavor. These accompaniments have never been fully written down. They cannot be. Gershwin had a tone, a touch and a rhythm not easily described. The accompaniments were themselves tone-pictures, however trivial or merely topical the character of the song might be. And they possessed one of the most distinctive characteristics of our American jazz—the element of improvisation. They also constituted an extraordinary commentary on Ira Gershwin's texts. These texts have not received their proper praise. They were made for George's special musical gift as George had precisely the style to set off the verses of Ira.

This was the beginning of Gershwin's reputation. Then came a greater success. It occurred when Paul Whiteman played the "Rhapsody in Blue" at the concert of "Ten Years of Jazz" which took place in Aeolian Hall in the early part of 1924.

Then Dr. Walter Damrosch invited Mr. Gershwin to compose a concerto in three movements for first performance by the New York Symphony Society. This was done. For a concerto by a man who had only passed the day before from successful popular song and operettas to a medium which required extensive technical knowledge of composition the piece made a very good showing.

It solidified the composer's position, at the same time that it showed his limitations. Gershwin added to these laurels with his orchestral "American in Paris," a work of a humorous sort which came later, but he never equaled in sheer creativeness the originality and the unprecedented confidence and gusto of the rascally theme which opens the "Rhapsody in Blue" and the best of the pages that follow.

Sometimes it seems that Gershwin was given too great a responsibility by musicians and critics so eager to see a real school of American composition developed that they encouraged him to more serious paths than those he was born to follow. But certainly he pointed the way, even though the first act of "Of Thee I Sing," and passages from his best light operas will rank much higher than any part of his attempted "folk opera" "Porgy"; and though some of his topical or risqué little songs carry a lilt of melody and a wealth of innuendo that outshine more serious attempts in real life and individuality.

A new step was taken by Gershwin for American music, a step that more pretentious composers were unable to execute. The sum of his achievement will make him live long in the record of American music.

George and Ira Gershwin in 1932. George composed the music and Ira provided the lyrics and the public was guaranteed the finest in musical comedy.

"All the News That's Fit to Print"

The New York Times

LATE CITY EDITION

Weather: Sunny, warm today; clear tonight. Sunny and warm tomorrow. Temperature range: today 59-83; Saturday 53-78. Details on page 43.

SECTION ONE

VOL. CXXV—No. 43,2333

NEW YORK, SUNDAY, JUNE 6, 1976

$1.00 beyond 50-mile zone from New York City, except Long Island. Higher in air delivery cities.

75 CENTS

FORD, IN AD SHIFT, DESCRIBES REAGAN AS PEACE THREAT

Commercials in California Attempt to Capitalize on Rhodesia Remarks

CHALLENGER IS ANGERED

Aide Calls New Radio and TV Spots "Dirty Trick" and Asks Their Withdrawal

By JON NORDHEIMER

Special to The New York Times

LOS ANGELES, June 5—In a sudden switch of tactics three days before the crucial California primary, President Ford's forces in the state scrapped a new advertising campaign and replaced it with radio and television spots depicting Ronald Reagan as a threat to peace.

The ads sought to capitalize on some murky remarks the former California Governor made when asked about possible use of American troops in Rhodesia. The Reagan camp reacted quickly and vehemently, and the clash added heat to the Presidential campaign with only Tuesday's primaries—in Ohio and New Jersey as well as California—left before the party conventions.

"Last Wednesday," a voice in the new spots intones, "Ronald Reagan said that he would send American troops to Rhodesia. On Thursday he clarified that. He said that they could be observers, or advisers. What does he think happened in Vietnam?"

The spots end with the warning: "When you vote Tuesday, remember, Governor Ronald Reagan couldn't start a war. President Ronald Reagan could."

Lyn Nofziger, the challenger's campaign manager in California, sent a telegram to President Ford, calling the ad-

Continued on Page 31, Column 3

Associated Press

Carl Albert, right, the Speaker of the House, meeting with Mike Mansfield, Senate majority leader, in the Rose Garden of the White House on Friday. Senator Mansfield has already announced that he will retire from the Senate at the end of this year.

ALBERT TO RETIRE; O'NEILL FAVORED AS NEW SPEAKER

Oklahoma Democrat to Quit House at End of Year—Leadership Fight Begun

By RICHARD L. MADDEN

Special to The New York Times

WASHINGTON, June 5—Carl Bert Albert, the speaker of the House of Representatives for the last five and a half years, announced today that he would retire from Congress when his current term expires at the end of this year.

The announcement by the 68-year-old Oklahoma Democrat will add to the wholesale reshuffling of top Congressional leadership posts that will take place when the 95th Congress convenes in January.

The Senate's two party leaders—Mike Mansfield, Democrat of Montana, who is majority leader, and Hugh Scott, Republican of Pennsylvania, who is minority leader—have already announced that they will not seek re-election.

O'Neill May Move Up

With the departure of Mr. Albert, Representative Thomas P. O'Neill Jr., a liberal, 63-year-old Massachusetts Democrat who has been majority leader since the beginning of 1971, is expected to be elected Speaker, perhaps without opposition, assuming the Democrats retain control of the House.

However, many House Democrats expect that there will be a bitter, three-way fight to succeed Mr. O'Neill as Democratic leader. The Democratic contenders, who are already quietly maneuvering for support, are Representative John J. McFall of California, the majority whip; Phillip Burton of California, chairman of the Democratic caucus, and Richard Bolling of Missouri, a senior member of the House Rules Committee.

If the Democrats again win control of the House in the November election, as is widely expected, the new Speaker and majority leader will be chosen by a majority vote of the Democratic caucus of re-elected and newly elected representatives. The Speaker presides over the full House of

Continued on Page 28, Column 1

J. Paul Getty Dead at 83; Amassed Billions From Oil

He Controlled Nearly 200 Concerns and Wielded Worldwide Influence

By ALDEN WHITMAN

J. Paul Getty, a symbol of oil, wealth and power, died early today at his country mansion near London. He was 83 years old. The cause of death was reported to be heart failure.

An American by birth, Mr. Getty had lived in Britain for nearly 25 years. He had been in failing health for several months.

Business associates who announced Mr. Getty's death said that the directors of the Getty Oil Company, of which Mr. Getty was still president, had already provided for the delegation of authority within the company and that normal business operations would continue.

The precise extent of Mr. Getty's wealth was difficult to compute, but in 1974 business associates put his fortune at from $2 billion to $4 billion. He had a majority or controlling interest in the Getty

Camera Press

J. Paul Getty

Oil Company and nearly 200 other concerns.

Mr. Getty tended to be reclusive in his last years. He spoke several times of wanting to return to Southern California, where he had lived for many years—but he never did. On his 80th birthday, dukes and

Continued on Page 38, Column 1

CHRISTIAN RIGHT IN LEBANON BACKS SYRIAN INCURSION

Franjieh and Other Officials Laud Military Intervention for Restoring of 'Stability'

BEIRUT HAS QUIET DAY

Egypt Withdraws Diplomats From Damascus—Orders It to Close Cairo Embassy

By JAMES M. MARKHAM

Special to The New York Times

BEIRUT, Lebanon, Sunday, June 6—Lebanon's right-wing Christian leadership acted yesterday to endorse Syria's military intervention in Lebanon, and Syrian armor reportedly remained in an uneasy standoff with Palestinian guerrillas and their Lebanese leftist allies in the eastern part of the country.

"It is only natural that we should support any measure that would lead to the stability of Lebanon," said a statement issued in the small village of Zouk Mikhael, which has become the headquarters of President Suleiman Franjieh. "We appreciate what sister Syria is doing for Lebanon in spite of the difficulties it is facing in Lebanon and elsewhere."

Explanations Cited

The statement by the right-wing leadership—consisting of Mr. Franjieh, Interior Minister Camille Chamoun, the Phalangist Party's chief, Pierre Gemayel, and the Rev. Charbel Kassis, head of the Order of Maronite Monks—said that the decision to support Syria's military moves had been made in light of "explanations" given by two Syrian colonels.

[In Cairo, Egypt announced that it was withdrawing its diplomatic mission from Damascus and that it was closing the Syrian Embassy in Cairo and asking the Syrian diplomats to leave the country. Page 22.]

Lately, there were signs of division within the Phalangist movement, the main rightist fighting group, with younger members apparently reluctant to endorse the Syrian takeover of much of eastern Lebanon.

The Phalangists consider themselves the torchbearers of Lebanese nationalism and, though the Syrians have lately ranged themselves on their side, it is painful for some of them to accept such overt foreign interference.

Beirut had one of its quietest days in months—with shoppers and curiosity seekers thronging

Continued on Page 21, Column 1

Chicago Latest to Feel Impact of Urban Crisis

By PAUL DELANEY

Special to The New York Times

CHICAGO, June 5—In this metropolis of more than three-million people, widely acclaimed as the city that works, something seems to be going awry.

Chicagoans up till now have felt fairly comfortable that Mayor Richard J. Daley was the medicine man with the cure-all to fix any ailment; that unlike other mayors, New York's in particular, he could wave a magic wand and make everything all right in Chicagoland.

But it seems that time is catching up with Chicago. Financial woes are such that not even Mayor Daley seems able to stave them off. Chicago, it is beginning to appear, is no better or worse off than New York or Philadelphia or a score of big cities facing the urban crisis, especially a severe money pinch.

Wide Range of Woes

Critics say that at best Mayor Daley has failed to circumvent the problems that seem to be piling up and that at worst he is to blame for some, if not most, of them. Additionally, they say, he is failing to face the problems realistically. Some of the problems are the following:

¶The city was forced to close schools on Thursday, 16 days early, because of a $47.4 million deficit that resulted from settlement of a 11-day teacher strike last fall, a settlement urged upon the school board by Mayor Daley. Unless the State Legislature waives the law to exempt the city from a penalty for the early closing, city schools will lose $56 million more in September.

¶Mayor Daley seems to be losing some of the clout he possessed as boss of the Chicago Democratic machine. He pushed for settlement of the teacher strike because he felt he could persuade the Legislature to pass three education bills that included financing for the schools. Although he

Continued on Page 58, Column 2

IDAHO DAM BURSTS; 30,000 EVACUATED

Six Rural Towns Flooded in Snake River Valley—No Deaths Are Reported

By United Press International

IDAHO FALLS, June 5—A corner of the new Teton Dam crumbled today, spreading water over 300 square miles in the upper Snake River Valley and forcing about 30,000 persons from their homes in six agricultural communities.

John Bender, the Idaho Director of Law Enforcement, said late tonight that none of the police agencies in the disaster zone had turned up any fatalities.

The hardest-hit of the six evacuated communities was Rexburg with a population of 10,000. Police Chief B. K. Siepert said a few persons in Rexburg were missing and some fishermen who had been below the dam might have been drowned by the wall of water. Most of the residents were

Continued on Page 36, Column 1

O.A.S. Aide Cautions Chile On 'Norm of Human Rights'

By JUAN de ONIS

Special to The New York Times

SANTIAGO, Chile, June 5—Foreign Minister Dudley Thompson of Jamaica told President Augusto Pinochet of Chile today that all American republics, including military dictatorships, should respect "a common international norm of human rights."

Mr. Thompson, who had a private luncheon meeting with Chile's military ruler, is one of the leaders of the movement among the foreign ministers of the Organization of American States, now assembled here, to improve human rights conditions in the hemisphere.

Accounts of Torture

"Every country has the primary responsibility to maintain law and order, and in a state of emergency or war this can limit human rights," Mr. Thompson said at a news conference. "But we make a distinction between an emergency and a permanent condition of a police state."

In a restricted study on violations of human rights in Chile circulated to delegations here by the human rights commission of the organization, detailed accounts of torture, prison deaths, and widespread arrests without judicial order by the security agencies, were presented.

"Absolutely bloodcurdling charges have been made," Mr. Thompson said. "If these are true, we should denounce it before the world and do something to stop it. If they are a lie, we should clear Chile's name."

Mr. Thompson, who is a lawyer, said he would press for "an investigation to the fullest extent," and he rejected the view of "those who say you can't find out what is going

Continued on Page 12, Column 3

Carter Woos Jewish Vote; Some Gain in North Cited

By ROY REED

Jimmy Carter has been fervently courting Jewish voters in the North, and his suit seems to be paying off. Several Jewish leaders report a small but definite movement toward the former Georgia Governor during recent weeks.

Considerable coolness remains. But political, religious and organizational leaders who are in touch with large numbers of Jews in the Northeast predict that Mr. Carter will receive a substantial majority of Jewish votes if he becomes the Democratic Presidential nominee.

Mr. Carter has begun to advertise heavily in Jewish publications. He is meeting with Jewish leaders in each primary state and is sending Jewish supporters from the South to plead his case in the populous Jewish community of New York.

He and his people are attacking what they perceive as an anti-Southern bias among Northern Jews, a fear (acknowledged by some Jews in New York) that his evangelical Christianity threatens Jews and an increasingly widespread impression that he is "fuzzy" on such issues as the security of Israel.

The Carter effort has been helped by the candidate's endorsement by Mayor Beame, the first Jewish Mayor of New York, and by such New York Jewish leaders as Howard Samuels, the prominent Democrat, and Morris B. Abram, the former president of Brandeis University and honorary president of the American Jewish Committee. Mr. Abram was reared in Georgia.

In addition, some Jewish reli-

Continued on Page 32, Column 5

The Search Begins at Loch Ness

By JOHN NOBLE WILFORD

Special to The New York Times

DRUMNADROCHIT, Scotland, June 5—The search for the Loch Ness monster has begun.

The Academy of Applied Science/New York Times Loch Ness expedition has already obtained 8,000 color pictures from one camera submerged in the murky waters of the Scottish lake. But until the film is processed some time next week it will not be known whether anything of significance revealed itself.

Late this afternoon, the engineers and scientists established a lakeside operations station. A television monitor and remote controls for underwater cameras were installed and tested. Only a late rain prevented them from deploying the television rig into the dark waters, at a planned depth of 40 feet. That move is now set for tomorrow.

Two zoologists in the party settled in for an all-night vigil on the Malaran, the expedition's 33-foot cabin cruiser. From a mooring on the loch, they will lower a side-scan sonar instrument into the water and watch for any patterns of returned sound signals that suggest large moving objects below.

Declaring the expedition "operational," Dr. Robert H. Rines of Boston, the leader, said:

"We have maximized our chances for success. We have some of the world's best experts, not only to design and build our equipment, but also to help us here install and operate it. We think we have what it will take to get the kind of information zoologists and others need to identify what these moving objects in the loch really are."

This summer's search for

Continued on Page 10, Column 4

Stones Sets Jump Mark

Dwight Stones of Long Beach State set a world record of 7 feet 7 inches in the high jump yesterday at the 55th annual National Collegiate track and field championships in Philadelphia. Details are in Section 5.

Loans to Communists

Communist countries' borrowing in the West is rising so much that the lending banks in this country and Western Europe are stiffening their terms and some American banks are said to be nearing their legal lending limits. Details, Section 3.

Consumer Unit Zeroes In On Gift Shops in Midtown

By FRANCES CERRA

In anticipation of the Democratic National Convention and the Bicentennial, and the unusual number of visitors both events will bring to the city, the New York City Department of Consumer Affairs has begun a law enforcement campaign against dishonest souvenir gift shops that are concentrated in Times Square and along Fifth Avenue.

According to David Saxe, consumer advocate for the department, one abuse the campaign will seek to eliminate is the use by these shops of fictitious prices that are actually the starting point for a bargaining process as lively as any in a Mexican market or a Turkish bazaar.

In addition, the department will be looking particularly for signs and advertising of discounts and sales that do not really exist, and for stores that sell merchandise for more than the manufacturer's list price without disclosing that fact.

In another action against some of the undesirable aspects of New York City, policemen and Federal immigration officers raided midtown brothels and so-called massage parlors, arresting 20 persons and detaining 28 as illegal aliens. Page 40.

A check of nearly a dozen of the souvenir gift shops by a reporter for The New York Times found misleading signs and pricing practices, one case of outright misrepresentation of the merchandise and repeated failures by sales personnel to give customer receipts. There is no law in the state requiring that receipts be given, but a buyer who does not get one and later finds something wrong with a purchase will have no way of proving his case.

Officials estimate that there are about 50 souvenir gift shops in the Times Square and Fifth Avenue areas that deal in portable, popular items like minicomputers, cameras, cheap watches, china figures, souvenir ash trays and the like, and, sometimes, Oriental rugs. They also frequently have signs in their windows that give the impression that they are about to go out of business, but they never do. In fact, some of these

Continued on Page 55, Column 1

Today's Sections

Index to Subjects

The New York Times

WINS BELMONT: Angel Cordero looking behind at the field as he heads into the homestretch aboard Bold Forbes. Section 5.

The New York Times/Paul Hosefros

Dr. Robert H. Rines, left, leader of expedition; Charles W. Wyckoff, center, photo analyst, and Dr. Harold E. Edgerton, the chief of photography, conduct a sonar sounding of Loch Ness to measure depth at various points.

Getty, the Restless Oil Billionaire, Filled Homes With Art and Life With Travel

Cautious With Cash, He Installed Pay Phone in Mansion in England

Continued From Page 1

duchesses, counts and countesses, bankers, business leaders and dressmakers turned up for a London party at which Margaret, Duchess of Argyll, was the hostess. A vocalist summed it all up by singing to the Cole Porter tune:

You're the top, you are J. Paul Getty

You're the top, and your cash ain't petty.

In 1957, when Fortune magazine first suggested that Jean Paul Getty was probably the world's richest private citizen, he was asked the inevitable question: how much would he really get in cash if he were to sell his oil, realty, art and other holdings? A note of gone-are-the-better-days crept into his response. "I would hope to realize several billions," he said. But, remember, a billion dollars isn't worth what it used to be."

Hardships of Fame

Mr. Getty, of course, did not sell out, and seven or eight years later, when his fortune had very much and very visibly increased, he was complaining of the hardships of wealth and the fame that accompanied it. The fame, it appeared, had generated the hardships. But these were not so great as to make them unbearable, nor to render fame less desirable than obscurity.

Before 1957 Mr. Getty cultivated his wealth in the relative shadows of the oil business here and abroad. He was also known by some newspaper readers for his purchase of the Pierre Hotel in New York and for his five marriages and an equal number of divorces. Once, however, the awesome vastness of his riches was made generally known he acquired celebrity. This he burnished by writing articles in mass-circulation magazines and by putting his name to two books.

For Young Executives

One was "My Life and Fortunes," published in 1963 by Duell, Sloan & Pearce. The other was "How to Be Rich," issued in 1965 by Playboy Press and consisting, in part, of articles Mr. Getty had composed, he said, for the "young executives and college students," who read Playboy magazine. He also permitted himself to be the subject of a biography, "The Richest American," by Ralph Hewins, which was published by Dutton in 1960.

The oilman's grandson, J. Paul Getty 3d, was kidnapped in Italy in 1973, and the oilman was asked to pay a $16 million ransom. He balked on the ground that "I have 14 other grandchildren and if I pay one penny now, then I'll have 14 kidnapped grandchildren." Eventually, however, the Getty family did pay $2.8 million, but how much Mr. Getty contributed was never disclosed.

A List of Grievances

Mr. Getty's principal grievances about being very rich were these:

¶People beseeched him for money.

¶People overcharged him or expected him to tip generously.

¶He could never be certain that he was liked for himself.

Most people, the oilman said he had discovered after 1957, were "so economically illiterate that they assume most of my fortune is in cash," whereas in fact all the folding money he had was a million dollars; and that was so parsimoniously budgeted by his accountants that he rarely carried more than $25 in his pockets.

The result of this lamentable public ignorance was that he received, he said, 3,000 letters a month from strangers, all seeking money. Recounting his plight in a magazine article entitled "It's Tough to Be a Billionaire," Mr. Getty said that "I never give money to individuals" because "it's unrewarding and wrong."

Returning to this theme in 1965 in a Saturday Evening Post article entitled "The World Is Mean to Millionaires" (why he had diminished his wealth status since 1958 was not explained), Mr. Getty said:

"If I were convinced that by giving away my fortune I could make a real contribution toward solving the problems of world poverty, I'd give away 99.5 percent of all I have immediately. But a hard-eyed appraisal of the situation convinces me this is not the case."

"However admirable the work of the best charitable foundation, it would accustom people to the passive acceptance of money," he added. This, he believed, was corrupting.

Always Handed the Bill

As for being gouged, Mr. Getty said that at luncheon or dinner with friends waiters automatically handed him the bill. "It's not the money I object to, it's the principle of the thing that bothers me—to say nothing of the monotony of it," he wrote.

"Even the simple, everyday matter of tipping can become a major problem," he continued. "If I tip well, someone is certain to accuse me of showing off. If I don't overtip, that someone will be the first to sneer 'penny-pincher!'"

Mr. Getty said he found himself lonely because so many people liked him for his bank balance while ignoring his other virtues. "Time is the only yardstick by which I can judge who are—and who aren't—really friends," he said, adding significantly:

"I've known many people for years who have never asked me for anything."

Providing Incentives

Was being so rich worth all the trouble? Mr. Getty was asked when he attained the age of 73. "Though our rewards may be small," he said of himself and his fellow Midases, "we are, if our society is to remain in its present form, essential to the nation's prosperity. We provide others with incentives which would not exist if we were to disappear."

Although the oilman obviously liked to talk about his money, he insisted that it was all rather vulgar. "I don't think there is any glory in being known as a moneybags," he asserted in his Oklahoma drawl. "I'd rather be considered a businessman."

Indeed, business was Mr. Getty's life. One of his former wives once remarked, perhaps astringently, that business was his "first love" and that wealth was merely a byproduct.

Describing how he often worked 16 and 18 hours a day to handle the complex transactions of his multifarious business dealings, Mr. Getty seemed to agree. "I can't remember a single day of vacation in the last 45 years that was not somehow interrupted by a cable, telegram or telephone call that made me tend to business for at least a few hours," he wrote in 1965. "Such work schedules and the need for devoting the majority of my time to business have taken a heavy toll of my personal life."

Boss of His Businesses

He made a point of being the boss of all of his businesses, even at one time making his executives stand at attention in his presence. When the head of one of his companies ventured a proposal, Mr. Getty cut him off. "Who does that fellow think he is?" he said. "Why, he's nothing but a damned office boy."

In a less irritated moment, he said of properties that included Tidewater Oil, Skelly Oil and Getty Oil, "I own my own companies. How many others do? There are just a few like me left."

Mr. Getty seemed to alternate between expressing pride over his undoubted entreprenurial genius and boasting about his penny-saving habits. He liked to recount, for example, how he had once waited with a party of friends to get into a dog show at a reduced price. "I've always watched things like that," he said. He also liked to be thrifty in other ways—washing his own socks, for one thing. "I have done it and I'll probably do it again," he told one interviewer.

Mr. Getty was seated at the time in the cushioned comfort of a Sheraton armchair in Sutton Place, his elegant 72-room mansion near Guildford, Surrey, 35 miles from London. This was one of several homes, the others being a place at Malibu Beach, Calif.; a spot at Mina Saud on the Persian Gulf, and a 15th-century palace and nearby castle at Ladispoli, on the coast northwest of Rome. He first began to occupy his Italian estate in 1966, when the rigors of British winters drove him from London.

Bought Residence From Duke

After 1959 the oilman's principal residence was in Britain. Previously he had led a restless life, running his business for many years from hotel suites. After World War II, he virtually expatriated himself from the United States. He could usually be found in those years at the George V in Paris or the Ritz in London.

He bought the 400-year-old Sutton Place in 1959 from the Duke of Sutherland for about $840,000 because it was convenient for his Middle East oil enterprise and because, he said, it was cheaper in the long run than living in a hotel.

Typically, one of Mr. Getty's first renovations was the installation of oil central heating. He also substituted a highly mechanized team of four gardeners for the previous 24 who had tended the 700-acre, two-swimming-pool estate, on which there were also 30 cottages and lodges, tennis courts and a trout stream.

Sutton Place was soon made into a garrison in conformity to Mr. Getty's penchant for privacy. An elaborate security system was installed, and every room, including the 14 bathrooms (one of them with gold fixtures), was wired. Windows and doors were barred, too; and 'No Trespass' signs were erected to warn visitors of the giant Alsatian dogs that had the run of the place.

Mr. Getty transferred part of his art collection to Sutton Place. Valued at more than $4 million, it included works by Tintoretto, Titian, Gainsborough, Romney, Rubens, Renoir, Dégas and Monet.

Perhaps the most talked-about feature of the mansion, however, was the pay telephone booth that Mr. Getty had installed so that his guests, as he explained it, did not need to feel they were imposing on their host.

He constantly worried about the state of his health. He ate health foods, chewing each mouthful 33 times; munched maple sugar candy between meals, worked at Bernarr Macfadden body-building exercises and walked two miles a day wearing a pedometer to calculate his mileage.

He liked to pretend to poverty by wearing rumpled suits and sweaters out at the elbow. He also liked to practice the prerogatives of wealth by attending splendid social gatherings and by escorting comely women many years his junior to parties. He was a friend of the Duke and Duchess of Windsor and of many correspondingly notable and fashionable people here and abroad.

He thought of himself as a man who yearned for privacy. Yet certainly after Fortune emblazoned his wealth, he courted publicity.

His appearances in the British press were quite frequent, both as contributor ("How to Make a Million Dollars") and as a subject, in which capacity he was photographed contemplating masterpieces in the Hanover Gallery; being fitted for a hat at Lock's; getting a haircut in St. James's; driving a Lotus racing car at 85 miles an hour around the Goodwood Circuit; posing with Ringo Starr, the Beatle, at a birthday luncheon at Trader Vic's in the London Hilton; masticating at a Foyles literary luncheon and grappling with the twist at a party in his Sutton Place for children from a Church of England home.

Mr. Getty was an art collector of note who wrote about his hobby in a book, "The Joys of Collecting" (1965), and who explained some of his expertise in another book, "Europe in the Eighteenth Century" (1949).

His collection, of more than 600 items, was housed partly in Sutton Place and partly in a gallery of his ranch home at Malibu. Mr. Getty started his collection in the nineteen-thirties. He purchased the house and 60-acre ranch near Los Angeles in 1943, and later added the gallery wing. At that time he placed the estate under a trust fund as the J. Paul Getty Museum, which was opened to the public in 1954. Some art objects were given to the Los Angeles County Museum. These included the legendary Ardabil Persian Carpet that had been made on the royal looms of Tabriz in 1535 and Rembrandt's "Martin Looten."

Other Malibu items included he Persian "Coronation Carpet," 18th-century Beauvais tapestries, 18th-century French and English furniture, rock crystal chandeliers and fine examples of Greek and Roman sculptures. There was also a somewhat less fine bust of the donor.

'Born at Right Time'

All this, and additional acquisitions, were housed after 1973 in a Roman villa-style museum on Mr. Getty's Malibu property. The building, fashioned after one found in the ruins of a town near Pompeii, was often criticized by art professionals, but it delighted the public, which clamored for tickets of admission.

Mr. Getty credited his global oil empire (and the riches it gushed for him) to his father's foresight and his own luck and ingenuity.

"In building a large fortune," he once said, "it pays to be born at the right time. I was born at a very favorable time. If I had been born earlier or later, I would have missed the great business opportunities that existed in World War I and later.

"I suppose it takes a long time and it takes extraordinary circumstances to be born at the right time, be there at the right time and have cash money available at the right time. I was fortunate due to my father's foresight and my good luck. In the Depression I did what the experts said one should not do. I was a very big buyer of oil company stocks."

Born in Minneapolis Dec. 15, 1892, Jean Paul Getty was the son of George Franklin Getty, a lawyer who went into the oil business in Oklahoma in 1903 and two years later moved to California. There Paul was reared.

He attended Harvard Military Academy and Polytechnic High School, both in Los Angeles, graduating in 1909. In the next two years he studied at the University of Southern California at Los Angeles and the University of California at Berkeley. Then he went to Oxford for two years where, in 1914, he took his diploma in politics and economics.

At 21 he arrived in Tulsa Okla., ready for work and determined to make a million in two years. This was the site of his millionaire father's Minnehoma Oil Company.

"I started in September, 1914, to buy [oil] leases in the so-called red-beds area of Oklahoma," Paul Getty said afterward. "The surface was red dirt and it was considered impossible there was any oil there. My father and I did not agree and we got many leases for very little money which later turned out to be rich leases."

By buying and selling oil leases with his father's backing, young Getty made his million by June, 1916, and retired to Los Angeles, where he lived a gaudy, girl-filled life for two years. In 1919 he returned to business with his father in buying and selling leases and drilling wildcat wells. More money rolled in.

In 1923, when he was 30, Mr. Getty married Jeannette Dumont, 18. She was the mother of his first child, George Franklin Getty 2d, and the first of his five wives. The others, also all younger than himself, were Allene Ashby, a Texas rancher's daughter, whom he married in 1925; Adolphine Helmle, a German girl, whom he married in 1928 and who was the mother of his second son, Jean Ronald; Ann Rork, a film starlet, whom he married in 1932 and who was the mother of two sons, Eugene Paul and Gordon Peter; and Louise Dudley Lynch, a debutante and cabaret singer, whom he married in 1939 and who was the mother of a son, Timothy, who died at the age of 12. His parents were divorced in 1958.

Most of Mr. Getty's former wives had a good word for him and he for them. He also expressed regrets for all his divorces "because I don't like anything to be unsuccessful."

Section 1

"All the News That's Fit to Print."

The New York Times.

THE WEATHER
Partly cloudy, much colder today; fair tomorrow, continued cold.

Section 1

VOL. LXXIV....No. 24,431.

NEW YORK, SUNDAY, DECEMBER 14, 1924.

FIVE CENTS

SAMUEL GOMPERS DIES IN SAN ANTONIO, BLESSING 'OUR GREAT INSTITUTIONS;' NATION MOURNS THE GREAT LABOR CHIEF

END COMES ON HOME SOIL

His Last Wish Granted, He Cheers Sorrowing Labor Colleagues.

STATE HONORS ARE OFFERED

Funeral Train, With Body in Bronze Casket, Starts for Washington and New York.

FUNERAL HERE THURSDAY

Body Will Lie in State in Two Cities—Burial at Sleepy Hollow.

SAN ANTONIO, Texas, Dec. 13 (Associated Press).—Samuel Gompers, for more than forty years President and active leader of the American Federation of Labor, died here this morning after a futile but gallant fight against the weaknesses that come with age and general disorders, from which he had suffered for many months. Mr. Gompers was 74 years old. He died upon American soil, realizing his last hope.

Since Saturday a week ago, when the fatal illness came upon him in Mexico City, where he had gone to attend the convention of the Pan-American Federation of Labor, Mr. Gompers's life was all but despaired of by labor leaders and friends who had accompanied him on this last trip of his career. Fighting death valiantly, but with a greatly weakened heart, due to the rigors of the Mexican trip and the higher altitudes there, he was placed aboard a special train and rushed to the United States, arriving in San Antonio last night.

The labor chieftain died surrounded by his comrades, many of whom had fought beside him, shoulder to shoulder, for a generation in behalf of the economic principles he expounded.

The end came in a hotel eleven hours after his arrival from Mexico City. His last words were spoken to his nurse about an hour before he died—a prayer for the American people and American institutions. Realizing that he was losing the battle so stubbornly fought, he turned to her and whispered:

"Nurse, this is the end. God bless our American institutions. May they grow better day by day."

Shortly before he lapsed into the unconsciousness which presaged the end, President Gompers gave a few simple directions for his funeral and bade a few life-long friends farewell.

Body Borne on Gun Carriage.

Tonight the body of the labor chieftain, sleeping in a massive bronze casket similar to that in which President Harding was laid to rest, was started on its long journey to the nation's capital, accompanied by his friends and associates. The funeral train left at 11:07. There were no services at the mortuary where the body reposed today.

A cosmopolitan throng all day long filed past the body, and tonight the city paid its respects to the stricken labor leader as his body was borne to the station for the beginning of its last journey, mounted on an artillery caisson, surrounded by a military escort and accompanied by delegations representing the city and the labor organizations here.

Up almost to the hour of departure, the crowds thronged about the little frame house that had been turned into a mortuary.

As the hour approached for the start of the cortège to the Missouri, Kansas & Texas Railroad station, streets along the line of march were roped off, while the city was hushed for a moment for the passing visitor.

The cosmopolitan metropolis of the Alamo, with its soldiers, its sojourners from all States and its adopted sons from the land below the border—all ceased their Saturday night diversions to give a many-voiced adieu to a gallant man.

Two special coaches on a regular M., K. & T. train waited at the station for their noted passenger and for the labor officials who had been Mr. Gompers's official council in life and were now his chief mourners in death.

The rear observation coach was made ready to receive the casket, while members of the labor group were to occupy a sleeping car just ahead. Two beds were placed in the funeral car, near the casket, for the labor officials, who will act as the watch and guard on the journey. Plans were made to have at least two comrades of the dead leader on watch at all times.

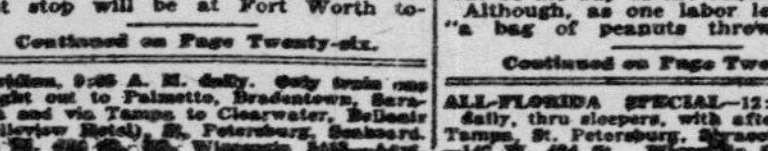

Members of the Executive Council of the Federation have been requested by telegraph to board the train at points on the route nearest their homes, so that the full council may escort the fallen President to his home in Washington.

Sixteen stops are listed on the train's itinerary as it goes to Washington. The first stop will be at Fort Worth to-

Continued on Page Twenty-six.

THE LATE SAMUEL GOMPERS,
President of the American Federation of Labor.

DUNCAN IS LIKELY TO SUCCEED GOMPERS

Vice President of Federation Will Probably Be Named for Office Thursday.

COMMITTEE TO MEET THEN

New Executive's Term Will Hardly Extend Beyond Next October's Convention.

A successor to Samuel Gompers as President of the American Federation of Labor will be chosen at a meeting of the Executive Council, probably next Thursday in New York, following the funeral.

Present indications are that the successor will be James Duncan, First Vice President and former President of the Granite Cutters' Union. Other contenders, in the order of possibility, are Matthew Woll, Sixth Vice President, and for fifteen years head of the Photo Engravers' Union; William Green, Third Vice President, who is Treasurer of the United Mine Workers, and T. A. Rickert, President of the United Garment Workers.

It is believed that had he been able to designate his successor Mr. Gompers would have named Matthew Woll, who in recent years was the confidant of the labor chief.

It is not thought in labor circles that an immediate successor to Mr. Gompers will be difficult for the Executive Council to choose. Whoever he is, it is likely that he will not remain in office longer than the convention of the Federation next October in Atlantic City.

Short Term Expected.

The contending factions in the Federation virtually will make it impossible for the immediate successor of Mr. Gompers to remain long on the uncertain seat provided for him. Those who say that Mr. Duncan probably will be chosen are of the opinion that, because of his age, Mr. Duncan will not aspire to continue in office after October. In deference, therefore, to his contributions to the labor movement, and also because of his lifelong friendship for the late leader, it is considered more than likely that he will be chosen.

The Acting President of the A. F. of L. today is Frank Morrison, its Secretary. The constitution provides that in case of a vacancy in the office of President the Secretary shall perform its duties until his successor is chosen.

"In that event," the constitution says, "it shall be the duty of the Secretary to issue within six days of the date of vacancy a call for a meeting of the Executive Council at headquarters for the purpose of electing a President to fill said vacancy."

As the members of the Executive Council have been away from their homes for a month, the first opportunity for them to meet and name a successor will be the day of the funeral.

Although, as one labor leader put it, "a bag of peanuts thrown into the

Continued on Page Twenty-six.

WOULD BAN BRINDELL 100 MILES FROM CITY

Untermyer Proposes a Geographical Limit on Labor Leader After Release.

WANTS HIM OUT OF UNIONS

Lawyer Renews Attack on Parole Board and Suggests Restrictions on Freedom.

Special to The New York Times.

OSSINING, Dec. 13.—Samuel Untermyer, who convicted wealthy Robert P. Brindell, grafting labor leader, wrote the State Board of Parole today condemning its methods and suggesting how Brindell be curbed when he is let out of prison on Dec. 26.

Several letters and telegrams exchanged between Mr. Untermyer, as Special Attorney General in the Brindell case, and members of the Parole Board, were made public today for the first time.

Mr. Untermyer recommends the following plan of restricting Brindell:

"First, that until the expiration of the maximum term of the sentence Brindell should take up his residence not less than 100 miles from the City of New York, or

"Second, that his parole be conditioned on his being and remaining during that term, directly or indirectly, disassociated from employment by interest in or relations with any labor union."

Mr. Untermyer's correspondence also discloses he wrote to Governor Smith last Summer recommending he be released then, because his sons contended their mother was seriously ill, but assumed that Brindell would be kept out of the labor unions.

Mr. Untermyer's correspondence also

Continued on Page Twenty.

Ralston Urges Democrats to Get Together; Asserts Party Will Live Despite Leaders

CHICAGO, Dec. 13 (Associated Press).—Senator Samuel M. Ralston of Indiana, who withdrew his name from the Democratic National Convention in New York last July when he appeared far in the lead for the Presidential nomination, in a public statement made here today, called upon Democrats to "pull themselves together, marshal their forces" and carry on.

Senator Ralston came to the city to speak before the annual dinner of the Indiana Society of Chicago.

In calling for new leadership in the ranks of democracy, the Senator said:

"As to the future of the Democratic Party, I have no doubt. It will live.

"It will live, not because of many of its present so-called leaders, but in spite of them. If they were all to meet and unitedly resolve that the party of Jefferson, of Jackson, of Cleveland and of Wilson should cease to be, their resolution would add strength and hope to that party.

"I can see that the Democratic Party can be crippled from within, but it cannot be killed, even from within.

"When the rule of democracy fails in this country chaos in the affairs of Government will, in my judgment, soon prevail everywhere; and it is my sincere belief that the life-giving force of American democracy has its source in the basic principles of the Democratic Party; and while they may be blurred for a time, they cannot be extinguished and our Government remain virile.

"It is therefore the patriotic duty of Democrats the country over to pull themselves together and marshal their forces, for the party will, where prevailing wrongs are uprooted, be just to all the people."

$110,000,000 A YEAR TO KEEP NAVY RATIO URGED BY WILBUR

That Amount Is Needed for New Ships Annually for Twenty Years, He Says.

COMMITTEE DENIES ALARM

Says Our Prestige Is Not Waning—Reports Out Supply Bill of $290,485,578.

Special to The New York Times.

WASHINGTON, Dec. 13.—America should spend $110,000,000 annually for the next twenty years on new construction for the navy, if its fleets are to be maintained on an equality with Great Britain's in all its branches, and superior to Japan's, thus carrying out the 5-5-3 ratio, Secretary Wilbur testified recently before the House Subcommittee on Naval Appropriations.

Secretary Wilbur's testimony became public today when the Naval Appropriation bill was reported to the House by the Appropriations Committee. The measure carries a total of $290,485,578, or only $938,350 less than recommended by the budget. While the sum allowed by the Appropriations Committee is not much below the budget it is $14,289,882 less than was approved for the current fiscal year.

An announcement by the subcommittee which drafted the bill declared that the country need not be alarmed by reports that American naval prestige was rapidly waning. Only those qualified to know had possession of intimate information concerning the navy, the committee said, and thus the authorship of the reports should be considered when opinions were formed.

Secretary Wilbur was quoted as follows:

"I am utterly out of sympathy with the newspaper criticisms and scare heads on the condition of the navy. I believe that we have the best navy we have ever had."

The Secretary insisted to the subcommittee, however, that the modernization program recently approved was necessary to place the navy on a parity with Great Britain's, and that continuing appropriations were essential to keep the fleet up to standard.

Secretary Wilbur's Building Estimate.

"The cost of building and replacements required for the next twenty years to build up and maintain the same ratio in all combatant ships and aircraft, as is provided in the treaty for capital ships (5-5-3) and based on the present strength of the treaty powers' navies, built, building and authorized (unless there is some further limitation of armament), will, if promptly made, average about $92,000,000 per annum for ships and about $18,000,000 for aircraft, total $110,000,000," Secretary Wilbur said.

When asked by the subcommittee about the eighteen battleships which this country possesses, the Secretary declared:

"All the ships are in condition to fight tomorrow, and the Florida could, with the limitations that I referred to."

The Secretary's allusion was to the needed repairs on the Florida, which have been authorized by Congress in the modernization bill just passed.

"There are repairs which we class as urgent," he said, "and the repairs

Continued on Page Twenty-four.

NATION'S DRYS SEEK TO COMPEL FEDERAL INQUIRY IN JERSEY

Attorney General Stone Has Been Asked to Detail Special Bootleg Investigator.

POLITICS ENTER SITUATION

Leaders Fear That "Rum Bottle May Replace Teapot as Emblem of Graft."

All the influence that the organized prohibition forces of the country can muster will be brought to bear on Attorney General Stone, it was learned yesterday, to induce him to send a special Assistant Attorney General to New Jersey to assume charge of the investigation and prosecution of the bootleg disclosures. Twelve men already have been indicted by the Hudson County Grand Jury as a result of charges of wholesale bribing of officials and politicians to furnish protection for the landing of millions of dollars' worth of liquor.

Political considerations also have become factors in the revelations, and it was said in Newark last night that "politicians fear the rum bottle may take the place of the teapot as an emblem of graft."

May Appeal to President.

If Attorney General Stone declines to accede to the request, already placed before him by Samuel Wilson, Assistant Superintendent of the Anti-Saloon League of New Jersey, the matter, it was said here last night, would be taken directly to President Coolidge. It will be argued that the scandal has become a matter for nation-wide concern. While no charges involving the personal integrity of Walter G. Winne, Federal District Attorney for New Jersey, are made, the dry leaders say that he is a wet, and that his appointment was due to the political influence of Senator Walter E. Edge, also a wet.

"I have no expectation that the real big men in Hudson County, who are financing and protecting rum-runners, will be brought to book by any Grand Jury in this county," said Mr. Wilson yesterday. "If Attorney General Stone and Mrs. Mabel Willebrandt, Assistant Attorney General, will commission a special Attorney General to work here, he will turn up enough evidence to rock the country. I have strongly recommended that kind of action, but what I communicated to the Attorney General must be kept private until I get a reply.

Winne May Be Called Off.

Mr. Winne's comment last night was: "I wouldn't be surprised if I were called off by Washington, but I haven't heard anything yet."

Senator Edge, in Washington, announced his intention to see the Attorney General tomorrow to learn exactly how Mr. Winne stood with the Department of Justice and whether there was a basis for recent reports that Mr. Winne's resignation would be welcomed because of wet sympathies.

"I believe that Winne is thoroughly honest and able," Senator Edge said. "I have every reason to hold him in the highest esteem and I believe he is as conscientious as any official in the public service.

"I think it is time to resent the assumption of superior virtue by the Anti-Saloon League and similar people in view of the actions of their own appointees.

"It is pretty nearly time they were made to answer for the character of the persons they have put in office. I well realize that I cannot give a blanket insurance policy on all of my own appointments, but I am sick and tired of hearing these people proclaim that they are the only honest people in New Jersey.

"Every one, of course, realizes the bitter disappointment in certain quarters as a result of the last campaign. Notwithstanding the repudiation given by the voters to the Anti-Saloon League, they now, apparently, want to make my appointments."

Federal Jury to Get Evidence.

Despite his doubt that he would be permitted by Washington to continue prosecutions, Mr. Winne was busily engaged yesterday with preparations for presenting all the evidence that has come into his possession to the Federal Grand Jury next Tuesday. He spent most of the day, he said, in framing the indictments which will be asked for. Al-

Continued on Page Two.

Sharp Border Patrol and Bad Weather Cuts Christmas Supply of Canadian Liquor Here

OGDENSBURG, N. Y., Dec. 13 (Associated Press).—The word has gone out from points along the northern boundary of the State that down-State residents and those living in metropolitan New York will have to be content with a limited amount of holiday liquor from the Northland this year. The movement of "refreshments" across the Northland New York line has been slow and is inadequate to supply the demand, customs and prohibition forces say.

The reason is declared to be the united efforts of augmented forces of customs agents and border patrolmen. The weather, causing bad roads and storms on the lakes, aided the Government forces.

Blizzards and storms such as raged today on Lake Ontario have been prevalent for some time, thus causing the marine rum-runners much trouble. Snow held off later than usual, also, and there was much warm weather, rendering the roads deep and soggy. Many a liquor-laden car has mired just long enough to permit troopers or prohibition agents to capture rum-runners and their cargoes.

The main highways across the line have been so closely guarded recently that the smugglers have been forced to seek the old, out of the way roads, hence lengthening their journeys. According to prohibition agents, any high-grade liquors that reach New York this holiday season will have crossed the line by the marine route.

Prohibition agents also say that January will witness the most intensive drive against liquor smuggling ever attempted in this region. It will be directed against the marine sector, with the border patrol leading the attack.

Approximately 1,000 barrels of liquor have been taken by the customs men since July 1 in Northern New York, along with about 400 automobiles. In addition, more than $1,000,000 worth of drugs has been seized. About 500 arrests on smuggling charges have been made in this period.

CANADIAN COURT ORDERS H. S. OSLER TO TELL INVESTIGATORS FROM THIS GOVERNMENT OF FALL'S CONNECTION WITH SINCLAIR DEAL

EX. SEC. ALBERT B. FALL — HARRY SINCLAIR

J. E. O'NEIL — H. M. BLACKMER

PRINCIPAL FIGURES IN THE GOVERNMENT'S ATTEMPT IN CANADA TO TRACE SINCLAIR PAYMENT IN LIBERTY BONDS TO ALBERT B. FALL.

WITNESS IS NOW IN AFRICA

Formed a Trading Company for Sinclair and Paid Profits in Liberty Bonds.

$2,000,000 IN ONE DEAL

Judge Calls Company a "Fake" and Sweeps Away Objections to Testifying.

OTHER WITNESSES ABROAD

O'Neil and Blackmer in France—Teapot Dome Trial Off Awaiting Their Testimony.

Special to The New York Times.

TORONTO, Dec. 13.—Justice Riddell of the Supreme Court of Ontario handed down a sweeping decision today in connection with the Teapot Dome oil case in the United States.

He directs Henry Smith Osler, former President of the defunct Continental Trading Company, Ltd., to appear here before United States Consul Shantz as commissioner and answer questions put to him by Newton C. Rowell and E. G. McMillan of Toronto, counsel for the United States Government, who are endeavoring to trace $90,000 worth of Liberty bonds alleged to have been paid Albert B. Fall, former American Secretary of the Interior, by the Continental Company in the form of a dividend.

For several months Mr. Osler, who is a King's Counselor, has fought against giving testimony. He and other witnesses who previously had appeared for examination refused to answer certain questions, whereupon the present motion was made to commit them for contempt of court. Mr. Osler claimed the privileges of attorney and client in the matter, but two high court Judges here had already decided that he must give the information.

There are big difficulties, however, in the way of getting an immediate answer to the questions. One is an expected appeal to the Appellate Division of the Supreme Court and the other is that Mr. Osler is away with a large party of friends hunting elephants in the interior of Africa and will not be back for some time. Nothing is said in the judgment as to any urgent necessity for his return.

The other day when the case was up in court Wallace Nesbit, a former Judge of the Supreme Court of Canada and counsel for Mr. Osler, said he would have to assume half of the responsibility for Mr. Osler being now out of the jurisdiction of the Court. He admitted that he advised his client that it would be all right for him to go on the hunting expedition, arrangements for which had been made a long time ago, he said. Whether or not any of the other persons mentioned in the present proceeding are with Mr. Osler has not been disclosed in court.

Justice Riddell's Decision.

Justice Riddell, in his decision handed down today, said that "this motion arises out of the notorious Teapot Dome transactions which have agitated the United States for some time" and that the charge was that Albert B. Fall and Harry F. Sinclair, the latter acting on behalf of the Mammoth Oil Company, entered into a conspiracy to defraud the United States by bringing about the lease of the Teapot Dome property.

"It is quite plain," goes on Justice Riddell, "that the sole object of this motion is to obtain the name of the person for whom the Continental Company was acting and the name of the persons to whom the very substantial sums which accrued to the Continental Company were paid, this for the very obvious purpose of connecting such principal and such payees with the scheme of fraud alleged."

Following the quotation of a statement by Mr. Osler, Justice Riddell continued:

"This being boiled down reduces to about the following:

"1. Mr. Osler met a gentleman in New York, whom for convenience I shall call Mr. X. How it does not appear, but the meeting could scarcely have been casual.

"2. He seems to have known Mr. X before. At all events he does not say or suggest that he met him for the first time, and did not know his name upon that occasion.

"3. Mr. X told Mr. Osler that he had a scheme requiring secrecy and he stipulated that his name was not to be disclosed.

"4. There was an implied promise on the part of Mr. Osler not to disclose the name. This, however, was necessarily subject to the implied [illegible] that if the law called upon him to disclose the name it should be [illegible].

"5. The scheme was in some [illegible] by some persons formulated.

"6. Mr. Osler, in order to [illegible] the scheme, formed a company [illegible] would, in the parlance of the [illegible] called a 'fake' company, [illegible] carry on business as a company [illegible] reality to do what Mr. Osler [illegible] would have done to [illegible]

DE FORD TO AID CITY IN TRANSIT INQUIRY

He Will Assist Edmund L. Mooney in Representing Transportation Board.

FIRST SESSION TOMORROW

No Indication Given as to Probable Procedure—Hylan to Start Subway Work on Heights.

The City Administration's array of counsel for the transit investigation, which will begin tomorrow morning at 10:30 before Justice John V. McAvoy in the large meeting room of the New York City Bar Association, received further additions yesterday when the Board of Transportation designated William A. De Ford, the only lawyer member of the commission, to attend the hearings as its official representative. Mr. De Ford will be assisted by his Secretary, John F. X. McGohey, who is a lawyer.

The selection of Mr. De Ford, who was formerly an attorney for William Randolph Hearst, was announced after a conference of the members of the Board of Transportation, at which John H. Delaney, Chairman, Daniel L. Ryan, Mr. De Ford, Edmund L. Mooney, special counsel of the board, and William G. Fullen, its counsel, attended. It was explained that the selection of Mr. De Ford to attend the hearings was entirely because he was a lawyer, and had no other significance.

In addition to Mr. De Ford and Mr. McGohey the lawyers who are expected to attend the opening hearing before Justice McAvoy as legal representatives of some branch of the City Government are:

Max D. Steuer and Harry A. Gordon, special counsel to the Board of Estimate; Edmund L. Mooney, special counsel to the Board of Tranportation; Corporation Counsel George P. Nicholson and Louis Lande, Special Assistant Corporation Counsel in the transit inquiry. The Transit Commission will be represented by former Justice Clarence J. Shearn, its special counsel.

Delaney Denies Seeing Smith.

Mr. Delaney denied a report that he had been to Albany to see Governor Smith in relation to the coming inquiry. Mr. Delaney has been credited with having brought about a change of attitude on the part of the City Administration.

In the absence of any information from Justice McAvoy or Henry L. Sherman, his counsel, the officials interested in the inquiry indulged in considerable speculation concerning the matters likely to be considered first. The belief at the offices of both the Transit Commission and the Board of Transportation was that the first day's program would depend largely upon the time Justice McAvoy might allow to counsel, and that it was quite likely that a start would be made at the first session on consideration of the charges brought by the Board of Estimate against the three Transit Commissioners.

In support of this view it was said that the proceeding before Justice McAvoy would technically be "an investigation into the management and affairs of the Transit Commission," and that

Continued on Page Eighteen.

MILLS URGES FUSION AT 'VICTORY' DINNER

Tells Republicans Hylanism Can Be Beaten Only by Aid of Independents.

SOUNDS PARTY RALLY CRY

Snell Says G. O. P. Here Must Mend Its Ways—Wadsworth Wants More Liberalism.

A rallying cry for next year's Mayoralty contest was sounded by Representative Ogden L. Mills and other speakers at the Victory Dinner given last night at the National Republican Club to the successful party candidates in the recent State campaign. Representative Mills said that if the Republican city organizations would stand together and make a winning appeal to the independents, Hylanism would become a thing of the past in New York City.

Mr. Mills boldly opposed some of the most influential leaders in the Republican State organization who would have the Republicans "go it alone" in the coming campaign. He believed Tammany could be defeated and Hylanism wiped out only by a concerted stand by Republicans and independents combined. He stood for fusion. He warned against opportunism that might mislead his part into attempting "the same kind of appeal" to the voters as the Tammany opposition and said that to win the Republicans must appeal to the conscience and intellect of the electorate.

Calder Wields the Gavel.

Former United States Senator William M. Calder, as President of the National Republican Club, wielded the gavel when the after-dinner oratory commenced. Seated with him at the speakers' table were Senator Wadsworth, Chairman Morris, Charles D. Hilles, Vice Chairman of the Republican National Committee; Colonel Theodore Roosevelt, defeated Republican candidate for Governor; Mrs. Florence E. S. Knapp, Secretary of State-elect; Representative Mills, Seymor Lowman, Lieut. Governor-elect, and Representative Bertrand H. Snell, Chairman of the Rules Committee of the House of Representatives. At a long table running at right angles with the speakers' table sat a majority of the other successful candidates for State offices and seats in Congress.

Senator Calder in his introductory remarks ascribed the defeat of Colonel Roosevelt mainly to the Republican stand against modification of the Volstead law. The Colonel said that, in view of the victory won by all the other candidates on the State ticket, he felt reconciled to his own defeat, inasmuch as he realized that the Republican Party leaders had done all in their power to uphold him in his contest with his popular Democratic opponent.

Representative Mills prefaced his speech with a defense of the Republican organizations in New York, which have been criticised by party leaders up-State as a result of the big plurality rolled up by Governor Smith here. While admitting that the party was not as efficient as it might be in New York City, he declared the up-State Republicans were in part responsible for the condition

Continued on Page Twenty-three.

Nation-Wide Tributes Are Paid to Dead Leader of American Union Labor

Continued from Page 1, Column 1.

morrow morning at 7:45 o'clock. From then on the stops in order will be: Denison, Texas; McAlester, Oklahoma City, Muskogee, Vinita, Okla.; Parsons, Kan.; Sedalia, St. Louis, Mo.; Vincennes, Mitchell, Ind.; North Vernon, Cincinnati, Midland City, Ohio; Parkersburg, Grafton, W. Va.; Cumberland, Md., and then to Washington.

Services are to be held in Washington, and the body is to be taken to New York on Wednesday morning, where further services probably will be held and a funeral oration delivered by some one to be selected. Burial will be in Sleepy Hollow Cemetery at Tarrytown, N. Y.

On the afternoon and night of Tuesday Mr. Gompers's body will lie in state at the Labor Federation headquarters in the national capital.

Knew His End Was Near.

From the moment of his collapse in Mexico City on Saturday a week ago, it was seen by those in attendance that Mr. Gompers's condition was extremely critical, and though he improved slightly as the train bearing him from the Mexican capital reached lower altitudes on its journey to American territory, there was little hope of his ultimate recovery.

During last night Mr. Gompers had a little sleep at two or three periods, but a change for the worse occurred at 2:30 this morning, and his heart began to fail, refusing to respond to drugs.

He was conscious much of the time and was able to talk to his physicians about administering a hypodermic. Apparently he knew the end was near, and called some of his closest friends to his bedside, with whom he talked over his own funeral arrangements. As William D. Mahon of Detroit, President of the Amalgamated Association of Street and Electric Railway Employes, came to his bedside he reached for his hand, calling him "Bill" and to his handclasp responded with a feeble effort.

James Duncan, a Vice President of the American Federation of Labor, who had known Mr. Gompers for forty-four years, was another close friend who was among the first to be summoned.

All officials of the Federation who were members of Mr. Gompers's party on the trip from Mexico City were present when he died.

Mr. Gompers's faithful nurse, Miss Mathilda May of New York, and a San Antonio woman nurse were left with the body.

Labor Leaders Say Good-bye.

It was apparent at 2:30 A. M. that Mr. Gompers was going, and an hour later Dr. Lee Rice told him that he was in a critical condition and might not live out the night. The dying man breathed more heavily for a moment, but there was no other response.

Dr. Rice sketched the patient's medical history after his arrival in San Antonio briefly as follows:

"The heart rate on arrival was 160, but under the influence of digitalis it had slowed down to 140 at 11 P. M. From this time he was improving until a sudden collapse occurred at 2:30 A. M., when his heart refused to respond to stimulation.

"Epinephrin was used and he was bled a pint and a half of blood to relieve congestion of his lungs. After each procedure he rallied for a few minutes, but almost at once collapsed.

"I was told he had been suffering from diabetes. Two specimens taken during the evening were free from sugar, and this disease did not participate in the final attack.

"The heart was fibrillating (absolute irregularity) when he arrived, but it is not known how long this condition had existed.

"I told Mr. Gompers at 3:30 that he was in a critical condition and might not pass through the night. He understood, but did not respond, his heavy breathing preventing any spoken words."

When the doctor announced that the end had come labor officials gathered about the bed and each laid an affectionate hand on the brow of the head of their leader and each in turn said "Good-bye, Sam."

Army Offers Tribute.

Colonel John C. McArthur, representing Major Gen. Charles P. Summerall, commanding Fort Sam Houston, tendered the respects of services of the United States Army.

"The army considers it has suffered a serious loss," said Colonel McArthur, as he stood in the room where the members of the Executive Council were gathered. "We consider him one of the greatest men the country has produced. He was a loyal American and a great citizen. He is a friend gone."

Mr. Duncan told of how Mr. Gompers had stood beside Field Marshall Haig, the British commander on the French front in the World War, while the bullets whizzed about him, "like snow flakes in Winter."

The great casket in which Mr. Gompers's body lies is the same style the late President Harding was buried in. It is of the massive state type, weighing 1,200 pounds.

On the nameplate was inscribed:

SAMUEL GOMPERS. 1850-1924.

Representatives of the many lodges of which Mr. Gompers was a member paid their respects today. He was a Scottish Rite Mason, a Shriner, a member of the Odd Fellows, Woodmen of the World, Knights of Pythias, Eagles and Moose.

Mayor Tobin of San Antonio issued this proclamation today:

"In the sad death of Samuel Gompers mankind has lost a great exponent of human rights and one whose name will live through the ages.

"San Antonio mourns him with a sorrow made more acute by his sad passing away in our midst.

"Let our people meet at the railroad station this evening at 11 o'clock, when his remains will start on their journey home, to testify to their respect for this great and good man, who commanded the admiration of the world and whose life is an inspiration to all."

Mr. Gompers is survived by three sons and his wife. The sons are Albert Gompers of New York, Henry Gompers of Washington and Samuel Gompers Jr., chief clerk in the Department of Labor, at Washington.

GOMPERS DEVOTED LONG LIFE TO LABOR

Beginning at the Age of 15, He Was a Founder and 41 Years President of Federation.

Loyalty to the United States during the World War, his part in bringing organized labor to practically solid support of the Government and its armed forces and his subsequent successful resistance to attempted inroads of Bolshevism and extreme radicalism in the labor unions of the country were probably the outstanding achievements of Samuel Gompers, dean of American labor leaders.

During his career of forty-one years as President of the American Federation of Labor, Mr. Gompers performed many important services to the cause to which he devoted his life, but in the crisis of the war and the difficult period following it, he seemed to rise superior to what in his case may have been a proper and natural class feeling. His services then were to the whole American people instead of to the organized workers of the country, of whom he was so long the head.

"Win the war for freedom!" Mr. Gompers said in his Labor Day speech in 1918, outlining the war policy of organized labor in America. "That is the Labor Day thought of America's workers and that will be their thought until the war for freedom is won.

"We count it our most sacred duty to win safety for our freedom and our democracy, for only when they are safe can life give us its opportunities and its value. Win the war for freedom! To that proposition we dedicate our labor and our lives as Americans and workers. It is the supreme purpose of our lives on this Labor Day."

Discouraged Strikes During War.

During the war Mr. Gompers put the foregoing preachment into practice. While looking out for the interests of labor, he discouraged strikes while the war was in progress, and pacifists or German sympathizers in the labor ranks made little progress because of his firm and wise leadership.

The conflict ended, he went to Paris, where he helped to organize the International Labor Congress. Five of its tenets were incorporated into the peace treaty. They were declarations that labor is not a commodity, for an international eight-hour day, for a standard and adequate living wage, for equal pay for men and women for equal work and for the prohibition of child labor.

Mr. Gompers was subject to considerable criticism after the war for endeavoring to keep wages up to the high standards of the war period. He undoubtedly believed it to be his duty to do this, and his insistence in this respect undoubtedly helped him to repel the attacks made upon him by the more radical members of the labor unions. The attack upon him culminated in the candidacy of John L. Lewis, head of the United Mine Workers, for President of the American Federation of Labor at its national convention in 1921. Mr. Gompers was elected by a vote of 25,022 to 12,324 for Mr. Lewis.

Mr. Gompers was one of the founders of the American Federation of Labor, which he saw grow from a group of small locals to a national organization with a membership of millions. In a career filled with efforts to improve the condition of workers from his fifteenth year, he became a unique figure in American public life.

Outspoken in his views on public questions, Mr. Gompers made many bitter critics as well as stanch supporters. He did not hesitate to criticise the United States Supreme Court when he thought its decisions were adverse to labor or to say what he thought of any other court or public official.

He charged German labor with having precipitated the World War, blamed prohibition for causing "unrest" in the United States, urged a labor union of the two Americas, denounced a United States Senate investigation of Mexico as "prussianism," assailed the open shop program of the United States Chamber of Commerce, demanded that Asiatics be kept out of the United States, pleaded for the release of all war-time and political prisoners, including Eugene V. Debs; opposed the establishment by the present Federal Administration of a Department of Welfare, praised President Harding's limitation of armament efforts and approved America's plan to aid famine-stricken Russia, although he consistently opposed any recognition of its Soviet Government.

Mr. Gompers early in his career refused to accept political office. He always opposed the establishment of a labor party and developed the policy of labor "punishing its enemies and rewarding its friends." In recent years, particularly in this State, Mr. Gompers's influence had been generally for the Democratic candidates, but this was explained by the fact that the Democratic platform declarations were more nearly what organized labor desired than the Republican.

Friend of Five Presidents.

Mr. Gompers was the friend of five American Presidents, McKinley, Roosevelt, Taft, Wilson and Harding. He was often called into consultation with them. Settlement of a number of industrial disputes which threatened to reach nation-wide proportions were attributed to his wise leadership, his conservatism and the trust reposed in him by the rank and file of American labor.

In the world-wide unrest which followed the World War Mr. Gompers took a leading part in resisting its spread in American industry.

"There has always been a radical element in the labor movement that has tried to destroy the very forces which have protected it all these years," he said in an interview explaining the menace of Bolshevism.

"It is this element which makes it so hard for organized labor to make its demands effective. These American Bolshevists have earned for labor countless enemies and have represented us in an unfavorable light."

Six months after these words were spoken, it was shown that of 300 strikes in various parts of the United States, only 62 were "authorized" by the American Federation of Labor. These "outlaw" strikes continued for a time and their gradual decrease was attributed largely to Mr. Gompers's influence.

When Albert Thomas, the French labor leader, was in Washington in January, 1923, in the interest of the International Labor Office at Geneva, a branch of the League of Nations, of which Mr. Thomas is the director, Mr. Gompers devoted much of his time in assisting Mr. Thomas in interesting people in this country in the Geneva organization, expressed regret that the United States had not become a member and indicated that he intended to work for American participation.

While Mr. Gompers had attended regularly to his duties as President of the American Federation of Labor and editor of The Federation, for which he wrote frequently, he had not exerted himself lately as a labor leader to the same degree as in the past. His hold upon the organized labor movement during the last year or two of his life was regarded by some as due more to the sentimental attachment of the rank and file of union labor than to any practical influence exerted by him. In the coal and railroad strikes of 1922 he issued occasional statements backing up the strikers, but did not assume any particular prominence in connection with the strikes, except by his opposition to an injunction against the striking railroad shopmen and his attack upon Attorney General Harry S. Daugherty for obtaining it. In this State Mr. Gompers opposed a bill to require the incorporation of labor unions, supported by Samuel Untermyer, counsel of the Lockwood committee.

Although Mr. Gompers had lessened his former activities as labor leader, it should not be inferred that he did not continue to lead. As big questions came up from time to time he made his views known and his influence felt, and he constantly traveled about the country on errands of unionism. As an instance of his habitual industry, during the four months ended Feb. 1 of this year he traveled 15,000 miles, delivered 210 addresses, presided at 300 conferences and wrote thousands of letters and statements.

At the time of the New York newspaper pressmen's strike in September, 1923, he emphatically condemned the strike, describing it as an "awful blunder." He presided at the exciting Federation meeting the following month at Portland, Ore., when the Communist leader, Dunne, was expelled, the incident calling down on Gompers the wrath of William Z. Foster. Earlier in life a pacifist, a believer that war is unnecessary, Mr. Gompers changed his views during the World War and announced his advocacy of thorough preparedness, particularly urging a strong navy. Last December, in The American Federationist, he reiterated his belief in the League of Nations as the only possible continuous forum without which "international bankers are sure to control international relations."

Active in Last Campaign.

For the last year, up to the opening of the political campaign, Mr. Gompers was comparatively quiet, although from time to time he issued statements assailing the workings of the Transportation act and the issuance of injunctions by the courts in strikes.

When the Democratic National Convention was held in New York City Mr. Gompers went before its Platform Committee to urge the inclusion of planks desired by the Federation.

Though in previous years he had advised labor and the unions to avoid allying themselves with any party, he threw aside this caution to endorse La Follette and advised labor to aid the Progressive Party with both money and votes.

He threw himself into the La Follette-Wheeler campaign with a vigor that had characterized his work in waging battle in behalf of labor in his more robust days. He had been chiefly instrumental in having labor take an active hand in the Presidential campaign as far back as Jan. 1, 1924, even declaring in a New Year's greeting, delivered in Washington, that labor not alone would stay in politics until the counting of the Presidential vote in the following November, "but in the selection of candidates in the primary elections everywhere."

His greeting contained many suggestions as to amending the laws of the country, such as were proposed in the subsequent La Follette-Wheeler platform, including restriction of the powers of Judges and amendments of the Constitution to eliminate child labor.

On his arrival in the following July at the meeting of the Executive Council of the Federation in Atlantic City Mr. Gompers issued a statement, however, in which he declared that the organization would not endorse any candidate for the Presidency, "but would abide by its time-tried policy of non-partisan action."

Later, after the nomination of Senator La Follette, Mr. Gompers openly came out in advocacy of his election, and two days before the election issued a final appeal to the trades unions of the country to support the Third Party ticket at the polls.

Describing the election as "more important than any since the election of Abraham Lincoln," Mr. Gompers added:

"There is a clear distinction between reaction and progress, and the voters of America have a most momentous decision to make."

On Oct. 12 he issued a circular to organized workers urging them to bring about the election of eighty candidates for Congress, on the ground that they were favorable to labor unionism. The election of these men, he pointed out, would give to labor a majority in the House.

A few days before the election he issued a statement attacking local labor leaders for their sudden switch from the La Follette-Wheeler ticket to John W. Davis and the entire Democratic ticket.

Father of Much Legislation.

Before the founding of the American Federation of Labor in 1881, the labor movement was in the hands of comparatively small, individual unions in various States, working without much real cooperation, and of the Knights of Labor, headed by Terence V. Powderly. Upon the formation of the Federation, Mr. Gompers, elected its President, welded the labor movement into a compact unit which has grown to be a power in the political, commercial and industrial life of the country.

Among the laws framed, supported or originated by Mr. Gompers were the eight-hour law for Government employes, the various State laws fixing hours of labor, laws establishing Labor Day as a holiday, the Federal Workmen's Compensation law and similar laws in various States, the law exempting labor unions from prosecution as combinations in restraint of trade and the law regulating punishment for contempt of court. He also was responsible for the law creating the Department of Labor as a separate department of the Federal Government with a Cabinet member at its head.

The legislation exempting trade unions from the anti-trust laws, regulating punishment for contempt and limiting the use of the injunction, which was included in the Clayton anti-trust law passed by the Sixty-third Congress, grew out of litigation against trade unions and their officials with which Mr. Gompers was directly concerned. The contempt section of the Clayton act was framed to meet conditions which arose through the conviction of Gompers, John Mitchell and Frank Morrison, officers of the American Federation of Labor, for contempt of court in 1908. Justice Daniel Thew Wright of the Supreme Court of the District of Columbia sentenced the three labor leaders to jail for violation of an injunction prohibiting the Federation from boycotting the Bucks Stove and Range Company of St. Louis. An appeal to the United States Supreme Court set aside the conviction on technical grounds and new contempt proceedings were instituted. Another conviction and sentence in the lower courts was set aside by the Supreme Court on the ground that the statute of limitation had expired before the second proceedings were begun.

During the seven years that his case was in litigation Mr. Gompers exerted his influence to change injunction and contempt procedure. Court decisions that trade unions could be prosecuted as combinations in restraint of trade under the Sherman anti-trust law prompted him to demand a specific exemption for labor organizations from anti-trust prosecutions.

His Campaign Against U. S. Steel.

Throughout the twenty years of anti-trust agitation which followed the enactment of the Sherman law Mr. Gompers was active in urging legislation and litigation against the big combinations of capital that had grown up in American industry. He conducted a campaign against the United States Steel Corporation which culminated in an investigation by a committee of the House of Representatives.

During his long administration of the American Federation of Labor Mr. Gompers was called upon constantly to avert threatened schisms and to bring together various factions. Compromise after compromise was effected by his efforts and the unity of the Federation was maintained. He was a stanch supporter of the "trade union" system of organization rather than the scheme of "one big union," and his efforts and those of his followers directed the American labor movement along that line. He was frequently called upon by unions affiliated with the Federation to arbitrate labor disputes and probably settled more strikes by his own efforts than any other man in labor history.

Mr. Gompers was born in London, Jan. 21, 1850. His father was a cigarmaker and Samuel was the eldest of eight children. His mother was a woman of excellent education and through her influence he was led to study, although he began at the age of 10 to help his father support the family. He went to school from his sixth to his tenth year and was then apprenticed to a shoemaker. He did not like this trade and worked with his father as a cigarmaker for three years, during which time he attended evening school.

A Cigarmaker at 13.

Mr. Gompers came to the United States when he was 13 years old and worked as a cigarmaker in New York City. He first became identified with the labor movement in 1864, when only 14 years old, and helped to organize the Cigarmakers' International Union. He became Secretary and President of the union, which became a large and successful organization, and also edited its publication, The Picket.

It was in connection with this work that he became interested in a national association of trade unions that would preserve the autonomy of local organizations. Under his leadership the Cigarmakers' Union fought the Knights of Labor on this principle. He served as President of the New York State Federation for two years and in 1881 took a leading part in the formation of the American Federation of Labor, serving as President for the first two years without compensation.

Mr. Gompers declined several opportunities for public office early in his career. He refused to run for the State Senate in New York, although offered both Republican and Democratic nominations. He declined a Republican nomination for Congress. Governor Hill offered him appointment on the New York State Board of Arbitration and President McKinley offered him a place on the Industrial Commission, but he declined both.

Notwithstanding strong opposition in union labor circles, Mr. Gompers took an active part in the organization of the National Civic Federation to establish better relations between capital and labor, and was its Vice President. He was affiliated with the Society for Ethical Culture, established in New York City by Dr. Felix Adler. He remained an active member of the Cigarmakers' Union and was also a member of the Masons, the Odd Fellows and the Elks.

Mr. Gompers was married twice. His first wife, Sophia Julian of New York, died in 1919, shortly after the celebration of their fiftieth anniversary. They had three sons and a daughter. The latter, a nurse in France, died during the war. On April 15, 1921, Mr. Gompers, then 71 years old, married Mrs. Gertrude A. G. Neuscheler, 38 years old, a music teacher, who survives him.

Besides his wife Mr. Gompers is survived by three sons, Alexander, an employe of the Compensation Bureau of the State Industrial Department, and Henry and Charles, residents of Washington; three brothers, Alexander Gompers of 99 Harrison Avenue, Brooklyn; Henry Gompers of 2,164 Grand Avenue, the Bronx, and Simon Gompers of East Norwalk, Conn., and two sisters, Hattie Gompers Isaacs and Bella Gompers Isaacs, both of Boston.

"All the News That's Fit to Print"

The New York Times.

LATE CITY EDITION
U. S. Weather Bureau Report (Page 30) forecasts:
Early thunderstorms, clearing today; fair, pleasant tonight and tomorrow.
Temp. range: 85—72; yesterday: 95—72.
Temp.-Hum. Index: mid 70's; yesterday: 82.

VOL. CX..No. 37,781. NEW YORK, MONDAY, JULY 3, 1961. 10 cents beyond 50-mile zone from New York City except on Long Island. Higher in air delivery cities. FIVE CENTS

BRITAIN'S FORCES IN KUWAIT MOVED TO IRAQ FRONTIER

Commandos and Infantry Dig in Along Desert Ridge—Reinforcements Land

SAUDI TROOPS FLOWN IN

Also, Artillerymen Arrive From England—Sheik's Unit in Border Guard

By DANA ADAMS SCHMIDT
Special to The New York Times.

KUWAIT, July 2—British Marine commandos backed by Centurion tanks moved out into the Kuwaiti desert toward the Iraqi frontier today to protect this Persian Gulf sheikdom from Iraq's threat of annexation.

Behind them, surging through continuing dust storms, came armored cars of the Eleventh Hussars, two companies of Coldstream Guards, other infantry of the Twenty-fourth Infantry Brigade and technicians of the Royal Electrical and Mechanical Engineers.

The Kuwaiti Government announced that Saudi Arabian troops had arrived in Kuwait by air to aid in the sheikdom's defense. Their location could not be established. A British spokesman said, however, that the "Saudi troops are here."

Troops Dig In on Ridge

The British troops dug in along a high sand ridge well back from the frontier along with Centurion tank units of the Kuwaiti army.

The British forces, which began arriving yesterday, are in Kuwait at the request of her ruler, Sheik Abdullah al-Salim al-Sabah. The Sheik asked for Britain's help under the terms of an agreement last month by which Kuwait took over the conduct of her own foreign affairs after having been a British protectorate for sixty-two years.

A week ago Premier Abdul Karim Kassim of Iraq declared that Kuwait was an "integral part of Iraq."

Unit Flies From Britain

Royal Air Force transports brought to Kuwait today the first unit to come directly from Britain. It was an airborne mortar unit known as the Parachute Battery of the Royal Horse Artillery.

The big transport planes flew over the landing strip of an unfinished airfield ten miles south of the town of Kuwait most of the night, unable to land because of swirling sand. At 3 A. M. the weather cleared enough for landings to begin.

A chartered plane brought in reinforcements from Nairobi, Kenya, during the morning.

Brig. Derek G. Horsford, in command of the Kuwait operation, inspected the British positions today, followed by Maj.

Continued on Page 2, Column 1

Kuwait Is Discussed at the U. N.

The New York Times

Dr. Adnan M. Pachachi of Iraq tells of Iraq's position on Kuwaiti question.

Sir Patrick Dean of the United Kingdom as he addressed Security Council.

Iraq Urges U. N. to Order British Units Out of Kuwait

By RICHARD EDER
Special to The New York Times.

UNITED NATIONS, N. Y., July 2—Iraq asked the Security Council today to order the withdrawal of British forces from the sheikdom of Kuwait. However, her delegate did not ask for immediate action by the United Nations.

Speaking in an unusual Sunday session of the Security Council, the Iraqi, Dr. Adnan M. Pachachi, said he would defer detailed discussion of British actions in Kuwait to a later meeting.

Excerpts from the British and Iraqi speeches, Page 2.

What appeared to be the first clear indication that the Soviet Union would support Iraq's claim to the former British protectorate, which was recently given its independence, came during a procedural wrangle at the start of the meeting.

Kuwait Backed by Cairo

Such support would align the Russians not only against Britain but also against a number of Arab states, led by the United Arab Republic, that support Kuwait's independence.

In a discussion on adoption of the agenda, the Soviet delegate, Valerian A. Zorin, referred to Kuwait as "the Kuwait area" instead of calling it a "state" or "nation."

Mr. Zorin also gave backing to Iraq's contention that the Council could not discuss a complaint directly from Kuwait but only as submitted by Britain, since Kuwait was not a country.

This morning's session, which

Continued on Page 2, Column 7

EAST BERLIN HELD ILLEGALLY ARMED

Bonn Survey Lists Military and Espionage Violations of Four-Power Accord

Special to The New York Times.

BONN, Germany, July 2—A West German Government survey shows that East Berlin is a center of Communist military and espionage activity in violation of the four-power agreement on Berlin's status.

Sources close to the West German Defense Ministry said today that the survey, expected to be made public soon, showed that East Germany even manufactured arms in East Berlin—also a violation of the agreement. One of the Communist charges against West Berlin is that it is a Western "hotbed of militarism."

The Soviet Union is demanding that West Berlin be made a demilitarized free city.

Military Forces Barred

Under the special Berlin agreement signed by the United States, Britain, France and the Soviet Union, neither West nor East Germany is allowed to maintain a military establishment in the divided city. Bonn has observed this restriction, the sources said, but the Communist East German Regime has not.

While no East German combat forces are stationed in the Eastern sector of the city, the survey showed that special "police" troops equipped with light and heavy weapons and armored cars were trained to function there as an army unit, the sources said.

The Bonn survey lists one regiment—4,500 men—of "alert police" as stationed in the suburb of Adlerhof. It is equipped with armored cars.

Police Units Armed

There is also a special unit of 3,700 "people's policemen" who live in barracks and have light and heavy infantry weapons, the survey found. The troops are under the direct command of East Berlin's police headquarters.

These forces can be augmented on short notice by 30,000 militiamen, it said. The militia is divided into regiments and battalions according to the survey, and is assigned to East Berlin's county governments.

Other units, in company and battle group strength, are trained to protect rail and street traffic, the survey showed. It found that these troops, though mostly equipped with light weapons, are trained to handle light tanks in street fighting.

The survey also lists a training center for political officers

Continued on Page 3, Column 6

LAOTIAN PREMIER IS CALLED LOSER

Cambodian Asserts Rightist Capitulated in Crisis

Special to The New York Times.

GENEVA, July 2—Prince Norodom Sihanouk, Cambodian head of state, said tonight a joint statement issued recently by the three rival Laotian leaders represented a "capitulation" by Prince Boun Oum, the Rightist Premier.

The Laotians' statement, issued in Zurich June 22, announced a vague accord to conciliate differences and form a neutral, independent and unified government. It did not say who would head the proposed regime.

Prince Sihanouk said the "winners" in the Laotian power struggle, judging by the statement, were Prince Souvanna Phouma, the neutralist leader, and his half-brother, Prince Souphanouvong, who heads the pro-Communist Pathet Lao forces.

These two Laotians signed the Zurich statement, along with Prince Boun Oum, whose Government is recognized by the United States.

The Cambodian leader played a key role in getting the three Laotian leaders together and was in Zurich when they met.

Speaking informally at a reception he gave for newsmen,

Continued on Page 3, Column 3

SOVIET WILL OPEN RESEARCH AREAS TO U. S. STUDENTS

Policy for Exchanges to Be Relaxed This Fall in New Display of Cooperation

By FRED M. HECHINGER

Soviet education authorities for the first time have opened their country's Research Institutes to American exchange scholars.

In a move toward greater cooperation, the Soviet Ministry of Higher Education is extending to American graduate students academic privileges that have been withheld from the exchange scholars since the Russian-American program began in 1958.

The Soviet move, coupled with a Russian call for an expansion of the exchange, contrasts with the deteriorating political relations between the two countries. American university spokesmen, who have negotiated the exchanges since 1958, expressed yesterday their satisfaction over the new Soviet readiness to eliminate red tape and delay.

They consider the opening of the Research Institutes a major milestone in academic relations. The new ruling will be effective in the fall.

New Soviet Attitude

Previously, the Ministry of Higher Education had declared these important research centers off limits to American students. American university spokesmen consider the new move a vital step toward the normalization of academic relations with the Soviet Union.

These observers, after checking this year's list of Russian students, believe that the Soviet authorities now have made scholarship rather than politics the key criterion for the exchange.

Another important indication of a new Soviet attitude toward the exchange program has been a suggestion initiated by Soviet negotiators. They proposed that they and the Inter-University Committee on Travel Grants, the American nongovernmental agency in charge of the program, exchange messages at regular intervals so that flaws in the operation of the exchange of scholars can be speedily rectified. The American committee is headed by Prof. Robert F. Byrnes of Indiana University.

68 Scholars Sent Here

In contrast to tardy or unpredictable arrival of Soviet students in the past, the Russians offered to have all their scholars arrive on Aug. 20. They also asked the American university authorities to offer an orientation course on American academic life.

Stephen Viederman, deputy chairman of the American committee, said this would probably be arranged. It was further agreed that closer contact be established between the stu-

Continued on Page 3, Column 6

Hemingway Dead of Shotgun Wound; Wife Says He Was Cleaning Weapon

Body Is Found in Home in Idaho—Novelist, 61, Won the Nobel Prize

Special to The New York Times.

KETCHUM, Idaho, July 2—Ernest Hemingway was found dead of a shotgun wound in the head at his home here today.

His wife, Mary, said that he had killed himself accidentally while cleaning the weapon.

Mr. Hemingway, whose writings won him a Nobel Prize and a Pulitzer Prize, would have been 62 years old July 21.

Frank Hewitt, the Blaine County Sheriff, said after a preliminary investigation that the death "looks like an accident." He said, "There is no evidence of foul play."

The body of the bearded, barrel-chested writer, clad in a robe and pajamas, was found by his wife in the foyer of their modern concrete house.

A double-barreled, 12-gauge shotgun lay beside him with one chamber discharged.

Mrs. Hemingway, the author's fourth wife, whom he married in 1946, issued this statement:

"Mr. Hemingway accidentally killed himself while cleaning a gun this morning at 7:30 A. M. No time has been set for the funeral services, which will be private."

Associated Press

Ernest Hemingway

Mrs. Hemingway was placed under sedation.

Coroner Ray McGoldrick said tonight that he would decide tomorrow, after speaking to Mrs. Hemingway, whether to hold an inquest.

The writer was discharged

Continued on Page 6, Column 5

U.S. FUNDS TO AID 3 LATIN NATIONS

Alliance for Progress Plan Approves First Projects —$3,780,000 Granted

Special to The New York Times.

WASHINGTON, July 2—The United States announced today the approval of the first Alliance for Progress projects under President Kennedy's special aid program in Latin America.

The projects will provide social welfare funds, totaling $3,780,000 for Panama, Guatemala and Argentina. These will be the first outlays from a $100,000,000 fund that has been set aside in the $600,000,000 Latin American aid program the President signed into law May 27.

An announcement by the State Department, on behalf of the International Cooperation Administration, did not indicate the cost of the special projects in each country. Their purpose was described as "improving the living conditions of millions of Latin Americans."

In Panama, the money will be used to help the Government increase the educational level of the people. A program will be undertaken to help build and equip approximately 200 schoolrooms in rural areas.

Panama, with a population of 1,053,110, has compulsory

Continued on Page 4, Column 5

95° Day Crowds Beaches; Holiday Traffic Toll Rises

By WALTER CARLSON

A day that began as if it were going to be a real scorcher turned out just that way yesterday. Temperatures that stayed in the nineties most of the day—and reached a high of 95 degrees at 3:05 P. M.—beckoned millions to the highways, many to their deaths.

The National Safety Council reported that traffic fatalities across the nation on the second day of the four-day holiday were running more than 25 per cent ahead of an ordinary week-end.

Early today The Associated Press reported 283 persons had died in traffic accidents. The National Safety Council has predicted a toll of 450 persons over the long week-end.

The high temperature for the day was just one degree below the high for the year, which was recorded on June 13. The record high for July 2, 100 degrees, was set in 1901 and the low, 56, in 1888. Comparative readings were as follows:

	Sun.	Sat.		Sun.	Sat.
1 A.M.	79	76	3 P.M.	94	88
2 A.M.	79	74	3:05P.M.	95	..
3 A.M.	76	70	4 P.M.	94	89
4 A.M.	74	70	5 P.M.	94	90
5 A.M.	74	68	6 P.M.	93	89
6 A.M.	76	67	7 P.M.	92	87
7 A.M.	76	68	8 P.M.	90	85
8 A.M.	77	70	9 P.M.	80	83
9 A.M.	80	75	10 P.M.	77	82
10 A.M.	83	77	11 P.M.	79	82
11 A.M.	87	80	Midn't	78	81
Noon	90	83		Mon.	Sun.
1 P.M.	92	84	1 A.M.	77	79
2 P.M.	93	86	2 A.M.	77	79

The ten-degree temperature drop between 8 and 9 P. M. was a result of brief, scattered showers in the metropolitan area.

Earlier, the Weather Bureau had issued tornado warnings for an area from the Southern Adirondacks to the Central Hudson Valley. Some thunderstorms were reported in the area, but none caused serious damage. At 9:15 P. M. the bureau issued an all-clear on tornadoes but said scattered thunder showers would continue through the night.

Skies to Clear

The forecast for today in the New York City area is for some early scattered thunderstorms followed by clearing, with temperatures in the mid-eighties.

Beaches in the metropolitan area reported their biggest crowds so far this year. There were more than 1,500,000 persons at Coney Island, more than 1,000,000 at the Rockaways, 200,000 at Jones Beach, 90,000 at Atlantic Beach, 90,000 at Riis Park, 55,000 at Manhattan Beach and 130,000 at Orchard Beach.

The story was similar in New Jersey, with resort centers reporting their greatest crowds in years. At Asbury Park, Mayor Thomas F. Shebell estimated the throng at more than 85,000, and most hotels and motels said they were doing capacity business.

Two young men, both nonswimmers, were lost in Paerdegat Basin, which empties into

Continued on Page 7, Column 2

SEAMEN'S FIGHTS EVICT U. S. PANEL

Hotel Asks Fact-Finders to Go After 3 Union Brawls—Battles Erupt on 9th Ave.

By GAY TALESE

The Presidential fact-finding board in the shipping strike was asked to leave the Edison Hotel and had to continue its meetings elsewhere yesterday after boisterous seamen swung fists and hurled objects in a series of skirmishes in the lobby.

Before the day was over seamen who differ on how to end the three-week-old strike had fought there some ten times and thrown eggs twice.

Four fights broke out during the afternoon on Ninth Avenue.

The three other fights, erupting after 1 A. M. in the Edison lobby, so upset the hotel's management that it evicted the board, which is also trying to mediate the strike. However, the hotel discussions were permitted to go on until they were halted for the night after 3 A.M.

The members of the board are David L. Cole, James J. Healy and Samuel I. Rosenman.

'Looked Like Waterfront'

"It looked like the waterfront around here at 1 A. M. when I arrived," a hotel official said yesterday, hours after the noise had ceased in the Edison, which is off Broadway between Forty-sixth and Forty-seventh Streets.

"One guy was lying flat, and about seventy were packed around him. After a discussion with Federal mediators, I suggested they adjourn and find other accommodations."

Though no one was arrested for fighting, several seamen were cut and bruised. One had his forehead cut by a flying ash tray at the Edison. He later received four stitches.

By and large, the fights seemed to be between members of two unions—Joseph Curran's National Maritime Union and Paul Hall's Seafarers International Union. The unions have been at odds over approaches in seeking contracts with the shipowners.

Both Mr. Curran and Mr. Hall

Continued on Page 32, Column 4

NEWS INDEX

News Summary and Index, Page 17

GULF COAST PACT FREES 250 SHIPS; U.S. READY TO ACT

71 More Also Get Contracts —Kennedy Orders Court Papers on Remainder

HE GETS REPORT TODAY

If Security Is Found to Be in Danger, Strike Will Be Halted 80 Days

By EDWARD A. MORROW

Agreements were signed yesterday freeing more than one-third of the nation's strike-bound merchant marine as President Kennedy prepared to seek an injunction to free the rest of the fleet.

A group of Gulf Coast shipowners, representing 250 vessels, signed contracts with four unions that encompass all of the types of manpower needed to sail the ships. Seventy-one other ships were freed when three owners signed the necessary contracts.

President Kennedy ordered the Attorney General's office to draw up the papers needed to begin court action for an injunction to force the remaining strikers back to work for an eighty-day cooling-off period.

Panel in the City

However, the court actions could not begin until today after the Government received a report on the seventeen-day strike from its three-man fact-finding panel.

The panel has been here studying the strike to see if the national security is endangered. Such a finding is needed before an injunction can be sought under the Taft-Hartley Act. The panel, headed by David L. Cole, also decided on its own to act as a mediator among the five unions and four management groups involved.

Although the panel's report was secret, there was considerable doubt among the parties in the dispute that the report would say that the national security was in danger.

Half Is Available

These sources pointed out that with more than 300 ships freed in the last forty-eight hours, plus the 130 that have not been affected, nearly half the nation's privately owned fleet was available for emergency shipments.

However, some emphasized that the President would make his own interpretation of the term emergency and of what could affect the nation's prestige. One Government source said, "You know, once they get the paperwork rolling at these levels, and it is rolling, it is hard to stop."

An injunction would mainly hit the Marine Engineers Beneficial Association, which has not settled with a large owners' group here, and the Masters,

Continued on Page 32, Column 5

GOLDWATER BUSY BOLSTERING G.O.P.

In Speeches Across Country, He Forges Party Links

By CABELL PHILLIPS
Special to The New York Times

WASHINGTON, June 30—During June the United States Senate was in session nineteen days. In the same month, Senator Barry Goldwater, Republican of Arizona, made twenty-three speeches away from Washington. Yet, he managed to appear at eleven of those Senate sessions in June, and to be recorded on fourteen roll-call votes.

This feat of political logistics has been matched in recent times by only one other member of the Senate, John F. Kennedy, who was a Senator from Massachusetts during the campaign year of 1960. It is the view of a good many observers here that both men have been agitated by the same virus — Presidential fever.

Many observers also assert that, next to the President, Senator Goldwater is the most exciting and provocative figure on the political landscape today.

As the leading apostle of a hard-boiled, unapologetic conservatism, he has filled the vacuum left by the late Robert A. Taft—and filled it with more dash and political appeal than

Continued on Page 16, Column 1

Artists May Strike to Save Lofts

1,000 Polled in City in Fight to Live in Old Factory Quarters

By McCANDLISH PHILLIPS

A vigorous campaign has begun to organize a strike of artists starting Sept. 11.

An artists' group, grieved by the apparent inhospitality of city laws, is polling 1,000 artists to test their readiness to take action to draw world-wide attention to their housing troubles.

According to the plan, participating artists would withhold their works from galleries and museums for as long as it takes the city to change its laws—or at least its mind—about letting them live and work in lofts.

Since February, the group says, life in lofts has been made uncertain, first by a wave of visits from Fire Department inspectors and more recently by a series of crackdowns by Building Department inspectors. Evictions have followed some visits.

If the strike move is successful, artists would keep their new works from galleries and museums here and would seek to withdraw works already on exhibition. Artists in other cities and in other nations would be urged to respect the New York picket lines.

But the proposal is broader

Continued on Page 31, Column 1

The New York Times

Disputed loft studios provide room and light for artists

Hemingway's Prize-Winning Works Reflected Preoccupation With Life and Death

'54 NOBEL AWARD HONORED CAREER

Novelist Was Identified With Bullfighting and Warfare —Noted Game Hunter

United Press International

HUNTER: The writer with a leopard that he killed in 1954 during a hunting expedition to Uganda, East Africa.

Associated Press

FISHERMAN: Ernest Hemingway with a 14-foot marlin he caught in 1956 off Peru. It weighed more than 1,000 pounds.

Ernest Hemingway achieved world-wide fame and influence as a writer by a combination of great emotional power and a highly individual style that could be parodied but never successfully imitated.

His lean and sinewy prose; his mastery of a kind of laconic, understated dialogue; his insistent use of repetition, often of a single word, or name—built up and transmitted an inner excitement to thousands of his readers. In his best work, the effect was accumulative; it was as if the creative voltage increased as the pages turned.

Not all readers agreed on Mr. Hemingway; and his "best" single work will be the subject of literary debate for generations. But possibly "The Old Man and the Sea," published in 1952, had the essence of the uncluttered force that drove his other stories. In it, character stands hard and clear, indomitable in failure. Man—an ordinary although an unusual man—is a victim of, and yet rises above, the elemental harshness of nature.

Won the Nobel Prize

The short novel won the Pulitzer Prize in 1953; it unquestionably moved the judges who awarded Mr. Hemingway the Nobel Prize for Literature the following year. And it was an occasion for relief and joy among those devotees of the novelist to whom "Across the River and Into the Trees," in 1950, had marked a low point in his career.

A great deal of Mr. Hemingway's work showed a preoccupation—frequently called obsessive—with violence and death. He loved guns; he was one of the great aficionados of the bullfight. He identified with the deadly adventures of partisan warfare; he swung a burp-gun in guerrilla fighting.

He wrote a great deal of hunting, fishing, prizefighting; with directness and vigor; with the accuracy of a man who has handled the artifacts of a sport, taken them apart, loved them. He was at times a hard liver and a hard drinker. But in a sense this was all part of his being a hard and constant worker—at his profession of observing life and recording it faithfully as he saw it.

Barb From Max Eastman

Mr. Hemingway's fascination with the calibers of cartridges, and exactly what each could do to a living target, and physical conflict generally, brought a barb from Max Eastman in 1937. Mr. Eastman, a writer who had flexed his own muscles in Marxist dialectics rather than in battle or in the hunt, wrote:

"Come out from behind that false hair on your chest, Ernest. We all know you."

When Mr. Hemingway and Mr. Eastman met in the New York offices of Charles Scribner's Sons, blows were exchanged as Mr. Hemingway bared his chest to prove that the hair was not false. In the later part of his life, Mr. Hemingway wore a beard, coarse and grizzled. It became one of the most famous beards in the world, and a kind of symbol of the man himself.

After Mr. Hemingway became a successful writer, much effort was made by psychologists, amateur and professional, to discover why he wrote as he did. In spite of much rummaging around in his childhood and in his days as a young man in Paris, many of the conclusions about him were contradictory. Mainly by trial and error, he had taught himself to write limpid English prose.

Apprentice as a Writer

Of his apprentice days as a writer in Paris, he wrote this:

"I was trying to write then and I found the greatest difficulty, aside from knowing what you really felt, rather than what you were supposed to feel, was to put down what really happened in action: what the actual things were which produced the emotions that you experienced * * * the real thing, the sequence of motion and fact which made the emotion * * * I was trying to learn to write, commencing with the simpiest things."

"All I want to do is write well," he once said.

Mr. Hemingway had a deadpan wit to which he gave many a special twist, as when he translated Spanish literally. Santiago, the man character in "The Old Man and the Sea," is a great American baseball fan and engages in the following dialogue:

"The Yankees cannot lose."

"But I fear the Indians of Cleveland."

"Have faith in the Yankees, my son. Think of the great Di Maggio."

"I fear both the Tigers of Detroit and the Indians of Cleveland."

"Be careful or you will fear even the Reds of Cincinnati and the White Sox of Chicago."

The man who could thus put the nuances of American baseball into the Spanish locutions of a humble fisherman; who rarely lost his sense of the humor that he found was as much a part of war and disaster as was courage itself, was born in Oak Park, Ill., a middle-class suburb of Chicago.

The date was July 21, 1899. Ernest Miller Hemingway was the second child of a family of six children; there were four sisters and a younger brother. His father was Dr. Clarence Edmonds Hemingway, a large bearded physician who was more devoted to hunting and fishing than to his practice.

His mother was Grace Hall Hemingway, a religious-minded woman who sang in the choir of the First Congregational Church. She gave her son a 'cello, and for a year made him practice on it. But the boy's father had greater lures. He gave the boy a fishing rod when he was 3 and a shot-gun when he was 10.

Ambulance Driver

With his graduation from Oak Park High, he completed his formal education. He read widely, however, and had a natural facility for languages.

It was wartime, and torment for a spirited young man not to be in the fighting. Finally he managed to get to Italy, where he wangled his way into the fighting as a Red Cross ambulance driver with the Italian Army. Although he arrived too late for the great Italian rout at Caporetto, he learned all about it and described it brilliantly in "A Farewell to Arms," published in 1929.

On July 8, 1918, while he was passing out chocolate candy to frontline troops at Fossalta di Piave, Mr. Hemingway was badly wounded in the leg by an Austrian mortar shell and was hospitalized for many weeks. He received the Medaglia d'Argento al Valore Militare, a high Italian military decoration.

He returned to Chicago, suffering from chronic insomnia. For a while, he edited the house organ of the Cooperative Society of America. But, inexorably, he drifted to the expatriate Left Bank world of Paris. He had a letter from Sherwood Anderson to Gertrude Stein, and he was soon one of the group of writers who frequented the bookstore of Sylvia Beach — Shakespeare & Co., at 18 Rue de l'Odéon. Here he met, among many others, André Gide and James Joyce.

Mr. Joyce and Mr. Hemingway did a certain amount of drinking together. The author of "Ulysses" was a thin, wispy and unmuscled man with defective eyesight. When they were making the rounds of the cafes and Mr. Joyce became embroiled with a brawler, as he frequently did, he would slip behind his hefty companion and cry, "Deal with him, Hemingway! Deal with him."

It was in Paris that Mr. Hemingway began to write seriously. He was greatly aided by the advice of the austere and sometimes curmudgeonish Miss Stein, whose unadorned style of writing influenced him greatly. If she was exacting, she was also sympathetic, although she was inclined to deride Mr. Hemingway's mania for firearms and thereby often hurt his feelings.

After several trips back to the United States, Mr. Hemingway settled in Europe. But instead of sitting his life away at the Café des Deux Magots, as many of his contemporaries did, he worked hard at his writing.

He wrote with discernment about the persons around him. They were his expatriate countrymen, together with the "Lost Generation" British and general European post-war strays, and he limned them with deadly precision.

Underwent Privations

Before he was established as a writer, Mr. Hemingway underwent the privations that were almost standard for young men of letters in Paris. He lived in a tiny room and often subsisted on a few cents worth of fried potatoes a day. With the publication in 1926 of "The Sun Also Rises" after three years of indifferent response to his work, he achieved sudden fame.

In "The Sun Also Rises," Mr. Hemingway showed the felicity for titles that characterized his work. The title is from the book of Ecclesiastes in the Bible and is in a passage that showed the seemingly meaningless coming and going of the sun, the tides and the winds as the lives of his characters seemed to the author to come and go pointlessly.

A concise biography of Mr. Hemingway that focused on his Paris years was written by his friend, Archibald MacLeish:

Veteran out of the wars before he was twenty;
Famous at twenty-five: thirty a master—
Whittled a style for his time from a walnut stick
In a carpenter's loft in a street of that April city.

In 1928, Mr. Hemingway returned to the United States, where he lived for the next ten years, mostly in Florida. He hated New York City and its literary life and kept away from it as much as he could. He was still only 30 when he published his highly successful "A Farewell to Arms."

When "Death in the Afternoon" was published in 1932, Mr. Hemingway said he had seen 1,500 bulls killed. The great success of the book established its author as one of the great popularizers of bullfighting.

For several years Mr. Hemingway hunted big game in Africa and did much shooting and fishing in different parts of the world. "Winner Take Nothing" was published in 1933 and "The Green Hills of Africa" in 1935.

The latter was one of the best contemporary accounts of the complex relationships between the hunter, the hunted and the African natives who are essential to the ritual of their confrontation. At the same time, the book told as much of Hemingway, the writer's writer, as of Hemingway, the big game hunter. For example:

"* * * the feeling comes when you write well and truly of something and know impersonally you have written it that way and those who are paid to read it and report on it do not like the subject so they say it is all a fake, yet you know its value absolutely * * *"

Like many American intellectuals, Mr. Hemingway offered some degree of support to Left-Wing movements during the Nineteen Thirties. In at least one of his books, "To Have and Have Not" (1937)—his only full-length novel with an American setting—one critic found he had spoken favorably of "social consciousness," and to another he had sounded "vaguely Socialist."

Action and Tragedy

But more readers will remember the work as a tale of action and tragedy in the Florida Keys. They will recall not so much the social aspects of Harry Morgan's career, but probably the remarkable love affair between the doomed boatman and his slatternly wife. Mr. Hemingway might stir the "social consciousness" of individual readers; but if so, he did it by exact characterization, never by didactics.

Nor had Mr. Hemingway ever joined the cafe-sitters who cheered on the progress of the Left. In 1936, with characteristic directness, he went to Spain. He covered the war for the North American Newspaper Alliance. And in 1940 his novel of the Spanish Civil War, "For Whom the Bell Tolls," showed both that his own deepest sympathies were with the Loyalists, and that he was agonizingly aware of the destructive effect upon their cause of the Comnuist commissars.

Indeed, the novel was in the broadest sense a lament for everyone involved in the conflict. Its striking title came from John Donne, who had reminded that no man is an island, and had written (in his seventeenth "Devotion"):

"* * * never send to know for whom the bell tolls;
it tolls for thee."

In the year World War II broke out, Mr. Hemingway took up residence in Cuba. But soon he was back in action in Europe, resuming thes combat correspondence he had begun in Spain.

Mr. Hemingway was with the first of the Allied armed forces to enter Paris, where, as he put it, he "liberated the Ritz" Hotel. Later he was with the Fourth United States Infantry Division in an assault in the Huertgen Forest. The Bronze Star was awarded to him for his semi-military services in this action.

In 1950, "Across the River and Into the Trees—the story of a frustrated and generally "beat up" United States infantry colonel who goes to Venice to philosophize, make love and die — disappointed critics. It touched off "Across the Street and Into the Grill," by E. B. White in The New Yorker. This was probably the supreme parody of Hemingway.

In 1950, The New Yorker also published a multi-part profile of Mr. Hemingway by Lillian Ross, who had spent several days with him in New York. It was a brilliant but savage series; it stirred much controversy and appears to have made more friends for Mr. Hemingway than for Miss Ross. But the most impressive riposte came from the novelist himself. When the profile was published in hard covers, Mr. Hemingway in The New York Herald Tribune listed it among the three books he had found most interesting that year.

"The Old Man and the Sea," two years later, pleased virtually everyone. It relied on the elemental drama of a fisherman who catches the greatest marlin of his life—only to have it eaten to the skeleton by sharks before he can get it to port.

Hurt in Air Crash

The 1954 Nobel Prize citation from the Swedish Academy said in part:

"For his powerful, style-forming mastery of the art of modern narration, as most recently evinced in 'The Old Man and the Sea.'"

On Jan. 23, 1954, the writer and the fourth Mrs. Hemingway, the former Mary Welsh (whom he called Miss Mary) figured in a double crash in Uganda, British East Africa. First reports said both had been killed.

Actually, after one light plane crashed, a second had picked up the couple unhurt. Both Mr. Hemingway and his wife suffered injuries in the crack-up of the rescue plane; and a friend who visited them in Havana soon after found that the novelist's injuries had been more severe than was generally supposed.

Mr. Hemingway's other published writings include "Three Stories and Ten Poems," 1923; "In Our Time," 1925; "The Torrents of Spring," 1926; "Men Without Women," 1927, and "The Fifth Column and First-Forty-nine Stories," in 1938.

Mr. Hemingway earned millions of dollars from his work; for one thing, a great many of his stories and novels were adapted to the screen and television. These included "The Killers," an early gangster story, celebrated for its dialogue; "The Snows of Kilimanjaro" and "The Short Happy Life of Francis Macomber," both set in East Africa; "The Sun Also Rises," "A Farewell to Arms," "For Whom the Bell Tolls" and "The Old Man and the Sea."

Mr. Hemingway's first wife was a boyhood sweetheart, the former Hadley Richardson, whom he married in 1919. She accompanied him on one of his early trips to Paris. They were divorced in 1926.

The next year Mr. Hemingway married Pauline Pfeiffer. This marriage was terminated by divorce in 1940 and in that year Mr. Hemingway married a novelist, Martha Gellhorn. After their divorce Mr. Hemingway married Miss Welsh.

A son, John, was born to Mr. Hemingway and his first wife. Two other sons, Patrick and Gregory, were born to the author and his second wife.

Associated Press

NOBEL PRIZE WINNER: Mr. Hemingway with his wife, Mary, in 1954 after learning he had won literature prize.

HEMINGWAY DIES OF A GUN WOUND

Continued From Page 1, Col. 7

from Mayo Clinic in Rochester, Minn., last Monday after two months of treatment for hypertension (high blood pressure) and what a Mayo spokesman called a "very old" case of hepatitis.

He had been treated there last year for the same conditions and had been released Jan. 23 after fifty-six days.

About a month ago, Mr. Hemingway's physician at the clinic described his health as "excellent."

The author had been worried about his weight, 200 pounds. He was six feet tall.

Mr. Hemingway and his wife, who drove from Rochester, arrived Friday night at this village on the outskirts of Sun Valley.

Chuck Atkinson, a Ketchum motel owner who has been a friend of Mr. Hemingway for twenty years, was with him yesterday. He said, "He seemed to be in good spirits. We didn't talk about anything in particular. I think he spent last night at home."

However, Marshal Les Jankow, another friend and the first law officer to reach the scene, said residents had told him that Mr. Hemingway had "looked thinner and acted depressed."

At the time of the shooting, Mrs. Hemingway, the only other person in the house, lay asleep in a bedroom upstairs. The shot woke her and she went down the stairs to find her husband's body near a gun rack in the foyer.

Mrs. Hemingway told friends that she had been unable to find any note.

Expert on Firearms

Mr. Hemingway was an ardent hunter and an expert on firearms.

His father, Dr. Clarence E. Hemingway, was also devoted to hunting. He shot himself to death at his home in Oak Park, Ill., in 1928 at the age of 57, despondent over a diabetic condition. The death weapon was a Civil War pistol that had been owned by the physician's father.

The theme of a father's suicide cropped up frequently in Mr. Hemingway's short stories and at least one novel, "For Whom the Bell Tolls."

Mr. Hemingway was given his first shotgun at the age of 10.

As an adult, he sought out danger. He was wounded by mortar shells in Italy in World War I and narrowly escaped death in the Spanish Civil War when three shells plunged into his hotel room.

In World War II, he was injured in a taxi accident that took place in a blackout. The author nearly died of blood poisoning on one African safari; he and his wife walked away from an airplane crash in 1954 on another big-game hunt.

Mr. Hemingway, who owned two estates in Cuba and a home in Key West, Fla., started coming to Ketchum twenty years ago. He bought his home here from Robert Topping about three years ago.

It is a large, ultramodern concrete structure that sits on a hillside near the banks of the Wood River. The windows give upon a panoramic view of the Sawtooth Mountains.

To Be Buried in Ketchum

"The funeral and burial will be in Ketchum," Mr. McGoldrick said. "This was Mr. Hemingway's home, he loved it here."

Under a new Idaho law that took effect yesterday, the chief law-enforcement officer must make an investigation into every case of violent death and determine the cause. He may hold an inquest if he wishes, but it is not mandatory.

Late in the day, Mr. McGoldrick said about the shooting:

"I can only say at this stage that the wound was self-inflicted. The wound was in the head. I couldn't say it was accidental and I couldn't say it was suicide. There wasn't anybody there."

The coroner said that the Sheriff did not have to hand in his report on the death "for several days."

"If anything comes up indicating foul play, he may hold an inquest," he said. "I don't think he'll hold an inquest but, based on new evidence, it could be called at any time."

He added: "He doesn't have to state on his report whether it was accidental or suicide."

Confers With Friends

"Mary felt it was accidental and I hope that's the way it will go out," Mr. Atkinson said. "But maybe we will have to change our plans and hold an inquest. I know that 'Papa' [Mr. Hemingway's nickname] wouldn't give a damn how it came out in the papers."

Previously, Mr. Atkinson had been busy trying to reach members of Mr. Hemingway's immediate family. He telephoned Mrs. Jasper J. Jepson, the novelist's sister, who said that she would fly to Ketchum immediately.

The author's 28-year-old son Gregory, a University of Miami medical student, will fly here from Miami tomorrow. Another son, Patrick, according to Mr. Atkinson, is on a safari in Africa and a third, John, is fishing in Oregon.

Mourned by Kennedy

HYANNIS PORT, Mass., July 2 (UPI)—President Kennedy mourned tonight the death of Ernest Hemingway, whom he called one of America's greatest authors and "one of the great citizens of the world."

The President, who is spending the Fourth of July weekend here with his family, issued a statement after hearing of Mr. Hemingway's death.

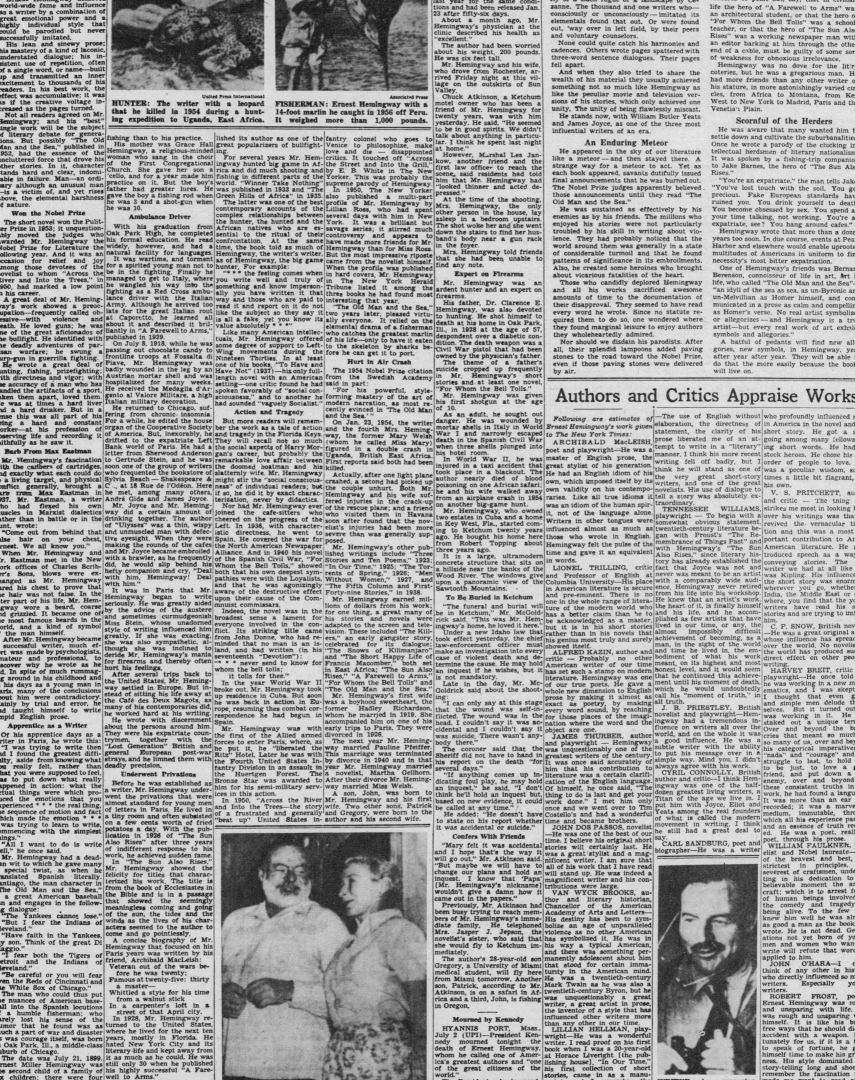

Books: Hemingway

By CHARLLS POORE

"PROSE is architecture, not interior decoration," Hemingway once said, "and the baroque is over."

In a way lucky for him, the baroque was not over. Against its weary, ornamented excesses the spareness of his style stood out. With that style he did something to change the course of storytelling in our century.

If it was a simple style it had the simplicity of a Bach fugue or a landscape by Cézanne. The thousand and one writers who—consciously or unconsciously—imitated its elementals found that out. Or were found out, 'way over in left field, by their peers and voluntary counselors.

None could quite catch his harmonies and cadences. Others wrote pages spattered with three-word sentence dialogues. Their pages fell apart.

And when they also tried to share the wealth of his material they usually achieved something not so much like Hemingway as like the peculiar movie and television versions of his stories, which only achieved one unity. The unity of being flawlessly miscast.

He stands now, with William Butler Yeats and James Joyce, as one of the three most influential writers of an era.

An Enduring Meteor

He appeared in the sky of our literature like a meteor — and then stayed there. A strange way for a meteor to act. Yet as each book appeared, savants dutifully issued final announcements that he was burned out. The Nobel Prize judges apparently believed those announcements until they read "The Old Man and the Sea."

He was sustained as effectively by his enemies as by his friends. The millions who enjoyed his stories were not particularly troubled by his skill in writing about violence. They had probably noticed that the world around them was generally in a state of considerable turmoil and that he found patterns of significance in its embroilments. Also, he created some heroines who brought about vicarious fatalities of the heart.

Those who candidly deplored Hemingway and all his works sacrificed awesome amounts of time to the documentation of their disapproval. They seemed to have read every word he wrote. Since no statute required them to do so, one wondered where they found marginal leisure to enjoy authors they wholeheartedly admired.

Nor should we disdain his parodists. After all, their splendid lampoons added paving stones to the road toward the Nobel Prize, even if those paving stones were delivered by air.

There is an unassailable mytholo*y about any writer's themes and characters. In Hemingway's case the salient idea is that he wrote about big-gamesters, pugs, thugs, girls with long legs and tawny hair, soldiers of fortune and misfortune.

And that's right, isn't it? Anyone who ventures to point out, say, that in civilian life the hero of "A Farewell to Arms" was an architectural student, or that the hero of "For Whom the Bell Tolls" was a schoolteacher, or that the hero of "The Sun Also Rises" was a working newspaper man with an editor barking at him through the other end of a cable, must be guilty of some sort of weakness for obnoxious irrelevance.

Hemingway was no dove for the lit'ry coteries, but he was a gregarious man. He had more friends than any other writer of his stature, in more astonishingly varied circles, from Africa to Montana, from Key West to New York to Madrid, Paris and the Venetian Plain.

Scornful of the Herders

He was aware that many wanted him to settle down and cultivate the suburbanalities. Once he wrote a parody of the clucking intellectual herdsmen of literary nationalism. It was spoken by a fishing-trip companion to Jake Barnes, the hero of "The Sun Also Rises."

"You're an expatriate," the man tells Jake. "You've lost touch with the soil. You get precious. Fake European standards have ruined you. You drink yourself to death. You become obsessed by sex. You spend all your time talking, not working. You're an expatriate, see? You hang around cafes."

Hemingway wrote that more than a dozen years too soon. In due course, events at Pearl Harbor and elsewhere would enable uprooted multitudes of Americans in uniform to find necessity's most bitter expatriation.

One of Hemingway's friends was Bernard Berenson, connoisseur of life in art, art in life, who called "The Old Man and the Sea"—"an idyll of the sea as sea, as un-Byronic and un-Melvillian as Homer himself, and communicated in a prose as calm and compelling as Homer's verse. No real artist symbolizes or allegorizes — and Hemingway is a true artist—but every real work of art exhales symbols and allegories."

A hatful of pedants will find new allegories, new symbols, in Hemingway, year after year after year. They will be able to do that the more easily because the books will live on.

Authors and Critics Appraise Works

Following are estimates of Ernest Hemingway's work given to The New York Times:

ARCHIBALD MacLEISH, poet and playwright—He was a master of English prose, the great stylist of his generation. He had an English idiom of his own, which imposed itself by its own validity on his contemporaries. Like all true idioms it was an idiom of the human spirit, not of the language alone. Writers in other tongues were influenced almost as much as those who wrote in English. Hemingway felt the pulse of the time and gave it an equivalent in words.

LIONEL TRILLING, critic and Professor of English at Columbia University—His place in American literature is secure and pre-eminent. There is no one in the whole range of literature of the modern world who has a better claim than he to be acknowledged as a master, but it is in his short stories rather than in his novels that his genius most truly and surely showed itself.

ALFRED KAZIN, author and critic — Probably no other American writer of our time has set such a stamp on modern literature. Hemingway was one of our true poets. He gave a whole new dimension to English prose by making it almost as exact as poetry, by making every word sound, by reaching for those places of the imagination where the word and the object are one.

JAMES THURBER, author and playwright — Hemingway was unquestionably one of the greatest writers of the century. It was once said accurately of him that his contribution to literature was a certain clarification of the English language. Of himself, he once said, "The thing to do is last and get your work done." I met him only once and we went over to Tim Costello's and had a wonderful time and became brothers.

JOHN DOS PASSOS, novelist—He was one of the best of our time. I believe his original short stories will certainly last. He was a great stylist and a magnificent writer. I am sure that all of his work that I have read will stand up. He was indeed a magnificent writer and his contributions were large.

VAN WYCK BROOKS, author and literary historian, Chancellor of the American Academy of Arts and Letters—His destiny has been to symbolize an age of unparalleled violence as no other American has symbolized it. He was in his way a typical American, and there was something permanently adolescent about him that stood for certain immaturity in the American mind. He was a twentieth-century Mark Twain as he was also a twentieth-century Byron, but he was unquestionably a great writer, a great artist in prose, the inventor of a style that has influenced other writers more than any other in our time.

LILLIAN HELLMAN, playwright—He was a wonderful writer. I read proof on his first book when I was a 20-year-old at Horace Liveright [the publishing house]. "In Our Time," his first collection of short stories, came in as a manuscript, and I remember the great joy of taking it home that first night. I still think it was his best book.

OLIVER LaFARGE, novelist—The use of English without elaboration, the directness of statement, the clarity of his prose liberated me of an attempt to write in a "literary" manner. I think his more recent writing fell off badly, but I think he will stand as one of the very great short-story writers, and one of the great novelists. His use of dialogue to tell a story was absolutely extraordinary.

TENNESSEE WILLIAMS, playwright — To begin with a somewhat obvious statement, twentieth-century literature began with Proust's "The Remembrance of Things Past" and with Hemingway's "The Sun Also Rises," since literary history has already established the fact that Joyce was not and never was meant to be an artist with a comparably wide audience. Hemingway never retired from his life into his workshop. He knew that an artist's work, the heart of it, is finally himself and his life, and he accomplished as few artists that have lived in our time, or any, the almost impossibly difficult achievement of becoming, as a man, in the sight of the world and time he lived in, the embodiment of what his work meant, on its highest and most honest level, and it would seem that he continued this achievement until his moment of death, which he would undoubtedly call his "moment of truth," in all truth.

J. B. PRIESTLEY, British novelist and playwright—Hemingway had a tremendous influence on writers all over the world, and on the whole it was a good influence. He was a subtle writer with the ability to put his message over in a simple way. Mind you, I didn't always agree with his work.

CYRIL CONNOLLY, British author and critic—I think Hemingway was one of the half-dozen greatest living writers, a Titan of the age we live in. I put him with Joyce, Eliot and Yeats among the real founders of what is called the modern movement in writing. I think he still had a great deal to say.

CARL SANDBURG, poet and biographer—He was a writer who profoundly influenced style in America in the novel and the short story. He got a style going among many fellows using short words. He had no stock heroes. He chose his own order of people to love. His was a peculiar wisdom, sometimes a little bit flagrant, but his own.

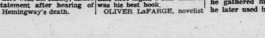

WRITER: As a reporter during Spanish Civil War, he gathered material that he later used in his books.

V. S. PRITCHETT, author and critic — The thing that strikes me most in looking back over his writings was that he revived the vernacular tradition and this was a most important contribution to Anglo-American literature. He reintroduced speech as a way of conveying stories. The only writer we had at all like him was Kipling. His influence on the short story was enormous, wherever you go, whether in India, the Middle East or elsewhere, you find that the young writers have read his short stories and are trying to imitate him.

C. P. SNOW, British novelist—He was a great original artist whose influence has spread all over the world. No novelist in the world has produced such a direct effect on other people's writing.

HARVEY BREIT, critic and playwright—He once told me he was working in a new mathematics, and I was skeptical. I thought that even great and simple men delude themselves. But it turned out he was working in it. He had staked out a unique terrain. Over and beyond the battle cries that meant so much to so many of us, over and beyond his categorical imperatives of "nada" and "courage" and the struggle to last, to hold out, to be just, to love a good friend, and put down a bad enemy, over and beyond all these consistent truths in his work, he had found a language. It was more than an ear that recorded; it was a marvelous medium, immutable, through which all his experience passed, and an essence of truth resulted. He was a poet, really a poet, through his prose.

WILLIAM FAULKNER, novelist and Nobel laureate—One of the bravest and best, the strictest in principles, the severest of craftsmen, undeviating in his dedication to his believable moment the antics craft; which is to arrest for a of human beings involved in the comedy and tragedy of being alive. To the few who knew him well he was almost as good a man as the books he wrote. He is not dead. Generations not yet born of young men and women who want to write will refute that word as applied to him.

JOHN O'HARA—I can't think of any other in history who directly influenced so many writers. Especially young writers.

ROBERT FROST, poet—Ernest Hemingway was rough and unsparing with life. He was rough and unsparing with himself. It is like his brave free ways that he should die by accident with a weapon. Fortunately for us, if it is a time to speak of fortune, he gave himself time to make his greatness. His style dominated our story-telling long and short. I remember the fascination that made me want to read aloud "The Killers" to everybody that came along. He was a friend I shall miss. The country is in mourning.

"All the News That's Fit to Print"

The New York Times.

LATE CITY EDITION
Clearing and warmer today. Cloudy with moderate winds tomorrow.
Temperatures Yesterday—Max., 51; Min., 44
Sunrise today, 5:54 A. M.; Sunset, 7:53 P. M.

Copyright, 1945, by The New York Times Company.

VOL. XCIV..No. 31,875. Entered as Second-Class Matter, Postoffice, New York, N. Y. NEW YORK, WEDNESDAY, MAY 2, 1945. THREE CENTS IN NEW YORK CITY

HITLER DEAD IN CHANCELLERY, NAZIS SAY; DOENITZ, SUCCESSOR, ORDERS WAR TO GO ON; BERLIN ALMOST WON; U. S. ARMIES ADVANCE

MOLOTOFF EASES PARLEY TENSION; NEW MOVES BEGUN

Russian Says Country Will Cooperate in World Plan Despite Argentine Issue

4 COMMISSIONS SET UP

They Will Deal With Council, Assembly, Court and Some General Problems

By JAMES B. RESTON
Special to THE NEW YORK TIMES.

SAN FRANCISCO, May 1—The United Nations Conference on International Organization has survived its first basic crisis and after six days of political maneuvering on secondary issues, it began to move at rapid tempo today toward its primary task—the creation of a world organization which would stop what Field Marshal Jan Christiaan Smuts called "this pilgrimage of death."

The test came last night. Rebuffed by the conference on his attempts to keep Argentina out of the conference and bring the Warsaw Poles in, Soviet Foreign Commissar Vyacheslaff M. Molotoff went late last night to Secretary Stettinius' penthouse at the Fairmont Hotel. He immediately made his position clear.

He still disapproved the conference actions on the Poles and the Argentine, but he wanted the conference to succeed; he would cooperate in its labors, and while he was under urgent pressure by the events in Europe to return to Moscow, he would remain at least for a few days until the major issues on the charter were thrashed out among the four sponsor powers. Then, he said, he would have to leave, probably at the week-end or early next week.

"Friendly Meeting" Is Held

Immediately, in what the Foreign Ministers of the United States, Great Britain and China described to their colleagues as "the most friendly meeting of the conference," the big four approved the formation of the working commissions and committees of the conference, and other committees began discussing, not the personalities or procedures of the conference, but the basic questions of creating an organization which would win the support, with the power, of the great nations without violating the rights and principles of all nations.

The three main developments of the day were as follows:

First, the conference approved four commissions to deal with the security council of the proposed organization, the general assembly, the judicial agency and general problems, and established twelve committees to study specific problems under these four commissions.

The heads of the four commissions were: Trygve Lie of Norway, Security Council; Field Marshal Smuts, General Assembly; Carraciolo Parra Rez of Venezuela, judicial organization; and Paul Henri Spaak of Belgium, general provisions.

Second, Field Marshal Smuts called on the four major powers to accept the special responsibilities which flow from the special authority given them under the Dumbarton Oaks proposals and urged all the nations here to pay more attention to the spiritual and economic aspects of the new charter than they had in the past.

Third, the Russians began studying in some detail the sixteen amendments to the Dumbarton Oaks proposals which were submitted by the United States. The other delegations started circulating amendments and exchanging views on proposals already circulated.

The facts on the crisis among the Big Three over Poland, Argentina, White Russia and the Ukraine can now be put down with assur-

Continued on Page 13, Column 6

Allies Invade North Borneo; Fighting Fierce, Tokyo Says

Australia Informed of Landing by Treasury Minister—MacArthur Reports Only Air Attacks and New Gains on Luzon

By The United Press.

MANILA, Wednesday, May 2—An official Australian announcement said yesterday that Allied troops had invaded Borneo, the world's third largest island, but Gen. Douglas MacArthur's communiqué early today reported only that heavy bombers were neutralizing enemy bases and airdromes on the oil-rich island.

Tokyo also reported the landings and said they had been made on the ten-square-mile island of Tarakan on the northeast coast, a region rich in oil wells, which the Netherlanders destroyed before the Japanese captured them in 1942. The enemy broadcast said "fierce fighting" was in progress.

[A later Japanese broadcast, picked up in San Francisco, reported that Allied units had landed on Tarakan Island at 6:30 A. M., Tuesday, Tokyo time. The broadcast said "the enemy had been bombarding the island since April 27, and on Monday morning began approaching the island in their landing attempts." It reported the landing force consisted of "about 5,000 soldiers" and said Japanese forces on the island "are holding secure their positions, obstructing the enemy's advance."]

General MacArthur announced that heavy bombers in attacks on Borneo had struck Kuching, Macassar and Kendari, while medium units and fighters had attacked Japanese gun positions on Tarakan.

General MacArthur announced that on Mindano Island the Twenty-fourth Division, in another swift drive, had advanced eleven miles

Continued on Page 16, Column 2

NEW CIGARETTES FACE PRICE INQUIRY

OPA Calls on Manufacturers of 21-Cent Brands to Prove Quality Merits Charge

By JAMES E. POWERS

Manufacturers of hitherto unheard of brands of cigarettes that have appeared on the market in recent weeks and are being retailed at four or more cents a package higher than ceiling prices for scarce popular brands will be called upon by the Office of Price Administration to show that the new products are of a quality rating the prices charged, it became known yesterday.

Daniel P. Woolley, regional OPA administrator, said an investigation was in progress as a result of complaints by smokers who said they had paid 21 cents a package for cigarettes "they had previously never heard of."

The United Wholesale Tobacco and Cigarette Distributors Association, a sub-jobbers' group, in a telegram to Senator William Langer of North Dakota, who recently introduced a resolution to set up a committee to look into the "black market" in cigarettes, demanded an immediate investigation of the entire cigarette shortage.

Mr. Woolley declared that as a result of OPA prosecution of violators of price ceilings, the black-market condition largely had been corrected here. He said he was centering on the pricing of the new cigarette brands.

Mr. Woolley added that studies were being made to determine

Continued on Page 40, Column 4

HARD COAL 'HOLIDAY' BRINGS WLB BAN

New Order by Board Asserts Output Is Urgent—Seizure Action Is Postponed

By JOSEPH A. LOFTUS
Special to THE NEW YORK TIMES.

WASHINGTON, May 1—The War Labor Board issued a new order tonight to the United Mine Workers and the operators to resume the production of hard coal. To give the UMW leaders an opportunity to act on the order it decided to defer for twenty-four to forty-eight hours a recommendation to President Truman for Government seizure of the mines.

The miners went on a holiday today after expiration of their contract at midnight.

Dr. George W. Taylor, WLB chairman, in a telegram to both parties took cognizance of the miners' traditional "no contract, no work" policy.

"The board's order provides for a continuing contract," he said. "It is urgent that production should be immediately resumed."

As in acting on the soft coal dispute a month ago, the WLB provided in the new order that any legal wage adjustment agreed upon or finally ordered be retroactive to the expiration date of the old contract.

Union spokesmen told the WLB at a brief hearing that the Tri-District Scale Committee had voted to advise the miners to return to work when the operators accepted the settlement proposal made by Secretary of Labor Perkins.

Dr. Taylor, in questioning John Owens of the UMW, noted that

Continued on Page 40, Column 3

Eisenhower Halted Forces at Elbe; Ninth Had Hoped to Storm Berlin

By The Associated Press.

WITH THE UNITED STATES NINTH ARMY, in Germany, April 26 (Delayed by Censorship)—A direct order from Supreme Allied Headquarters halted the United States Ninth Army's drive to Berlin at the Elbe River at a time when the most pessimistic officers were predicting that Lieut. Gen. William H. Simpson's forces could reach the German capital in ten days, "even if the Germans fought hard."

General Eisenhower's order said the Ninth would halt on the Elbe and await the arrival of Russian forces from the east, thereby leaving the capture of the capital to the Red Army. It also was understood that the American First and Third and British and Canadian armies received similar orders to halt at the Elbe.

It was not clear whether General Eisenhower's order was dictated by political policy agreed upon by the Great Powers or in a belief that it was a military necessity.

It was felt by high staff officers in the field, however, that the Ninth and other American forces could push on to the capital without great difficulty. While the order disappointed some staff officers, it was not altogether unexpected. It was known that the Ninth Army had pushed past the eventual British-American occupation area when it crossed the Weser River.

While the staff officers were disappointed; the American doughboys and tankmen who had to do the fighting and dying to get to Berlin expressed no regret. Almost to a man, they felt they could do with-

Continued on Page 4, Column 4

REDOUBTS ASSAILED

U. S. 3d, 7th and French 1st Armies Charging Into Alpine Hideout

NEAR BRENNER PASS

British in North Close About Hamburg—Poles Gain in Emden Area

Von Rundstedt Caught

By The Associated Press.

WITH UNITED STATES SEVENTH ARMY, Wednesday, May 2—Field Marshal Karl von Rundstedt has been captured by United States Seventh Army troops.

The Seventh Army caught the former German commander in the west in its drive into the Nazis' southeastern redoubt area.

By DREW MIDDLETON
By Wireless to THE NEW YORK TIMES.

PARIS, May 1—The last defenses of the Third Reich were crumbling as Allied tanks and infantry swept almost unopposed into the northern and southern redoubts.

Gen. George S. Patton's United States Third Army has resumed its offensive into Austria, crashing to within twenty miles of Linz, and is only fifty-four miles from Amstetten, where Marshal Fedor I. Tolbukhin's Third Ukrainian Army was last reported. According to reports from the front, radio contact has been established between tanks of the United States Eleventh Armored Division and the vanguard of the Soviet armies.

Other armored columns of the

Continued on Page 14, Column 1

NAZI CORE STORMED

Russians Drive Toward Chancellery Fortress, Narrowing Noose

BRANDENBURG TAKEN

Stralsund Port Swept Up in New Baltic Gains—Vah Valley Cleared

By C. L. SULZBERGER
By Wireless to THE NEW YORK TIMES.

MOSCOW, Wednesday, May 2—Street battles within smoldering Berlin today entered their twelfth day since the Russians first broke into the city, with Nazi die-hards still holding grimly to the central part of the town, whittled down by yesterday's fighting, in which Marshal Gregory K. Zhukoff's First White Russian Army group completely occupied Charlottenburg and Schoeneberg and more than 100 blocks in the capital's central region.

Some 14,000 prisoners were taken within the city on Monday, the Russians announced. At the same time, the remnants of a hold-out group south of Berlin, part of which had been annihilated at Wendisch Buchholtz, was split in two and the survivors are being ground to death by Marshal Zhukoff's men.

Curiously enough, the midnight communiqué does not mention Marshal Ivan S. Koneff's First Ukrainian Army group, which has been working from the southwestern sector of the city toward the desperately defended Tiergarten.

Marshal Zhukoff's forward spearheads meanwhile struck deep into Brandenburg Province, capturing the city of Brandenburg, halfway to Magdeburg from Berlin.

While Gen. Andrei I. Yeremenko proceeded apace in his lightning

Continued on Page 3, Column 3

War News Summarized

WEDNESDAY, MAY 2, 1945

Hitler is dead, according to the Hamburg radio, and on Monday, the day before he allegedly fell at his command post in the Chancellery in Berlin, he appointed Admiral Karl Doenitz to be the new Fuehrer. The head of the German Navy, who had made his mark directing the enemy's U-boats campaign, pledged continuance of the war. [1:8.]

Washington received the news, as did London, with some skepticism and a desire to see the body. Selection of Admiral Doenitz was considered logical in view of his strong Nazi feelings. [1:7.]

The new development was interpreted in London as a move to counteract Himmler's reported peace bids, but Prime Minister Churchill broadly intimated in the Commons that he might have "information of exceptional importance" to impart before Saturday. Peace will probably come before all enemy forces have surrendered, he said. [1:6-7.] Germany was reported to have begun evacuation of Denmark and to be ready to leave Norway. Count Bernadotte said in Sweden he had no new Himmler proposals, and the Nazis' Scandinavian withdrawals were related there to a prospective general capitulation. [11:1.]

Meanwhile, general Allied progress on the battlefields against slight resistance continued. The United States Third Army, on the day Hitler was declared to have died, captured Braunau, his birthplace. The drive into Austria was resumed and had reached to within twenty miles of Linz and fifty-four of the last known Russian position. The Seventh Army smashed through the Tyrol on a broad front and cleared Munich. The British Second Army, by-passing Hamburg, raced to within eighteen miles of the Baltic port of Luebeck. [1:4; map P. 14.]

General Eisenhower, it was revealed, personally ordered the halt of the Allied drive on Berlin from the west to permit the Russians to take the capital. [1:2-3.]

The Russians greatly cut down the German holding in Berlin, capturing the districts of Charlottenburg and Schoeneberg. West of the city they occupied Brandenburg and along the Baltic they seized Stralsund. [1:5; maps Pages 2 and 14.]

New Zealand troops in Italy made contact with Yugoslav Partisans at Monfalcone near Trieste and the British entered Udine. While the Eighth Army was closing a trap along the Swiss border, the Fifth neared France. [1:6-7; map P. 14.]

Mussolini and his mistress were buried in unmarked paupers' graves in Milan. [13:1.] Admiral Horthy, former Regent of Hungary, was captured. [4:3.]

Invasion of Borneo was officially disclosed in Australia, although no word of the break into the Japanese-held Netherlands East Indies had come from General MacArthur. On Mindanao in the Philippines, Americans were within six miles of the city of Davao. [1:2-3; map P.16.]

Seventh Division troops on Okinawa resumed their southward advance, entering the village of Kuhazu. [15:1.] More than 400 starved, naked Allied prisoners of war were liberated by the British as they drove on Rangoon in Burma. [15:3.]

Good progress was made at the San Francisco Conference. Foreign Commissar Molotoff, after assuring Secretary of State Stettinius of his desire that the conference succeed, announced that pressure of events would compel his return to Moscow within a few days. [1:1.]

ADOLF HITLER The New York Times, 1935

Clark's Troops Meet Tito's In General Advance in Italy

By VIRGINIA LEE WARREN
By Wireless to THE NEW YORK TIMES.

AT ADVANCED ALLIED HEADQUARTERS, in Italy, May 1—After advancing fifty-five miles in less than a day along the coastal road rimming the Gulf of Venice, units of one division of the Fifteenth Army Group made contact this afternoon with Marshal Tito's forces at Monfalcone while other troops under Gen. Mark W. Clark continued to sweep German remnants from the valleys of north Italy and to seal off the few remaining escape routes through the Alps.

No details of the meeting at the small seaport northwest of Trieste between Marshal Tito's men, who had driven fourteen miles from Trieste, and leading elements of the Eighth Army's Second New Zealand Division were given in tonight's communiqué.

On the other side of Italy another historic meeting was imminent as Fifth Army troops, continuing their drive along the Gulf of Genoa, advanced on the Aurelian Way to within sixty miles of the French border, which has already been crossed by French troops headed this way.

General Clark announced yesterday that the military power of Germany had virtually collapsed, but there still are drives for his two armies to make and engagements still to be won. The Germans, trying to regroup for their flight across the Alps, were deprived of two key road junctions leading to mountain passes west of Brenner when Belluno and Udine were occupied this afternoon by units of the Eighth Army.

Udine, which was taken by the British Sixth Armored Division, is twenty-eight miles southwest of Caporetto, the scene of the Italian disaster in World War I. The forces that entered Belluno went on five miles to Ponte nell 'Alpi, guardian of the approach to Italy's

Continued on Page 13, Column 5

DOENITZ' ACCESSION VIEWED AS A BLIND

Capital Lays His Designation to General Ignorance of His Allegiance to Party

By The Associated Press.

WASHINGTON, May 1—If Adolf Hitler really designated Grand Admiral Karl Doenitz his successor, military men here believe, he did so for the following reasons:

1. Doenitz is a Nazi supporter who could be counted on to keep German resistance going if possible.

2. But he is not associated in the Allies' minds with German atrocities and the extreme policies of the Nazi party. Therefore, Hitler probably figured that he might be able to get better treatment from the Allies when the hour of surrender came.

3. He is immensely popular with the German people.

There was a disposition here tonight to look for continued organized resistance whose core would now be centered in the Baltic and North Sea port areas. Those places are the homes of the German Navy and especially of the U-boat fleet that Doenitz commanded from 1936 until he succeeded Grand Admiral Erich

Continued on Page 5, Column 1

Churchill Hints Peace This Week; 2-Day Celebration Is Authorized

By CLIFTON DANIEL
By Wireless to THE NEW YORK TIMES.

LONDON, May 1—The general belief that peace with Germany will be announced this week persisted in Britain today, encouraged by Prime Minister Churchill himself and by Grand Admiral Karl Doenitz's announcement of the death of Adolf Hitler.

The War Cabinet again held a session tonight but so far as was known did not have any concrete proposal to consider. The chances that Heinrich Himmler ultimately will deliver an acceptable peace are now held in some official quarters to be only "fifty-fifty."

Nevertheless the buoyant Prime Minister told the House of Commons today that he might have "information of importance" to announce before Saturday.

The public's hopes were raised still further by a long Home Office circular giving the Government's views on how Britain should observe V-E Day, which the British, it appears, will be expected to celebrate strictly according to form.

[Stockholm reported, with the return there of Count Bernadotte, the "imminent liberation" of Denmark and Norway—already taking effect locally in Denmark—as a phase of a prospective general German capitulation that must be acceptable to the Allies' military commands.]

The hurrahing will begin with the announcement of the cessation of hostilities by Mr. Churchill over a nation-wide radio network. The King will speak at 9 o'clock that evening. And throughout that day

Continued on Page 10, Column 4

ADMIRAL IN CHARGE

Proclaims Designation to Rule—Appeals to People and Army

RAISES 'RED MENACE'

Britain to Insist Germans Show Hitler's Body When War Ends

By SYDNEY GRUSON
By Cable to THE NEW YORK TIMES.

LONDON, May 1—Adolf Hitler died this afternoon, the Hamburg radio announced tonight, and Grand Admiral Karl Doenitz, proclaiming himself the new Fuehrer by Hitler's appointment, said that the war would continue.

Crowning days of rumors about Hitler's health and whereabouts, the Hamburg radio said that he had fallen in the battle of Berlin at his command post in the Chancellery just three days after Benito Mussolini, the first of the dictators, had been killed by Italian Partisans. Doenitz, a 53-year-old U-boat specialist, broadcast an address to the German people and the surviving armed forces immediately after the announcer had given the news of Hitler's death.

[The British Foreign Office said that it would demand the production of Hitler's body after the end of hostilities, The Associated Press reported.]

First addressing the German people, Doenitz said that they would continue to fight only to save themselves from the Russians but that they would oppose the western Allies as long as they helped the Russians. In an order of the day to the German forces he repeated his thinly veiled attempt to split the Allies.

Radio Prepares Germans

Early this evening the Germans were told that an important announcement would be broadcast to them. There was no hint of what was coming. The stand-by announcement was repeated at 9:40 P. M., followed by the playing of excerpts from Wagner's "Goetterdaemmerung."

A few minutes later the announcer said: "Achtung! Achtung! In a few moments you will hear a

Continued on Page 5, Column 4

Copenhagen Writer Again Phones Story

By Cable to THE NEW YORK TIMES.

STOCKHOLM, Sweden, May 1—For the first time in more than five years THE NEW YORK TIMES correspondent in Copenhagen, Svend Carstensen, tonight telephoned a story from the Danish capital. The Nazi-imposed censorship there has been lifted. Mr. Carstensen said:

"The Danes are overjoyed at their imminent liberation, but it is not noticeable on the Copenhagen streets.

"Anxious to avoid trouble on May Day, Copenhageners have been staying indoors. The blackout is still enforced and it is pitch dark in Copenhagen tonight. All Copenhageners are glued to radios listening to broadcasts on Hitler's death.

"We expect King Christian will resume his functions and name a new Cabinet any day now. In the meantime the strictest discipline is being observed so as not to give the Germans any excuses for starting more trouble."

On April 9, 1940, Mr. Carstensen was the first to give the world the news of the German invasion of Denmark in a wireless dispatch to THE NEW YORK TIMES. His dispatch was cleared less than an hour before the Nazis seized the radio station and was the last to be sent.

DEATH OF HITLER ANNOUNCED BY FOE

Continued From Page 1

serious and important message to the German people." Then the news was given to the Germans and the world after the playing of the slow movement from Bruckner's Seventh Symphony, commemorating Wagner's death.

Appeals for Cooperation

Appealing to the German people for help, order and discipline, Doenitz eulogized Hitler as the hero of a lifetime of service to the nation whose "fight against the Bolshevik storm flood concerned not only Europe but the entire civilized world * * * It is my first task," Doenitz added, "to save Germany from destruction by the advancing Bolshevist enemy. For this aim alone the military struggle continues."

Clinging to the line of all recent German propaganda, reflected in Heinrich Himmler's reported offer to surrender to the western Allies but not to Russia, Doenitz said that the British and Americans were fighting not for their own interests but for the spreading of Bolshevism. He demanded of the armed forces the same allegiance that they had pledged to Hitler and he assured them that he took supreme command "resolved to continue the struggle against the Bolsheviks until the fighting men, until the hundreds of thousands of German families of the German east are saved from bondage and extermination." To the armed forces he described Hitler as "one of the greatest heroes of German history," who "gave his life and met a hero's death."

News tickers in the House of Commons lobby carried the news of Hitler's death just before the House rose tonight. The reaction of members and of the general public was much the same. Some doubted the truth of the announcement altogether, while others argued that there would have been no sense of making it if it were not true, since Hitler was perhaps the last person around whom the Germans still in unconquered territory would rally.

But there was an almost complete lack of excitement here. Those who believed the report seemed to accept it as a matter of course that Hitler would die. There was no official reaction.

The last reference to Hitler before tonight's announcement came in this afternoon's German communiqué, which said that the Berlin garrison had "gathered around the Fuehrer and, herded together in a very narrow space, is defending itself heroically." When Himmler offered his surrender to the Americans and British, it is reported, he told Count Folke Bernadotte, his Swedish emissary, that Hitler was dying of a cerebral hemorrhage. During the past week, Hitler was variously reported dead, dying or insane in Berlin, Salzburg or the Bavarian mountains.

Doenitz' self-proclaimed accession was believed in some quarters here to bear out reports of a recent split in the German hierarchy between the supporters of an immediate peace gathered around Himmler and the die-hard clique clinging to Hitler and his determination to fight to the very end.

It was noted that Doenitz commanded the last arm of the German military machine that could cause the Allies major difficulties, and his ability as an expert on submarine tactics is not belittled here.

He was one of the first military men to join the Nazis and his loyalty to the party and its ideology never wavered. Known as one of the most ruthless men in Germany, he has been a bitter enemy of Britain since his imprisonment during World War I, when he was confined to a Manchester asylum as a lunatic.

"Ghost" Interrupts Doenitz

LONDON, May 1 (AP)—When Doenitz declared on the radio that Hitler had died "a hero's death," a ghost voice immediately interrupted, shouting: "This is a lie!"

[The British Broadcasting Corporation subsequently reported that Hitler had actually died of a stroke, rather than in battle against the Russians, the National Broadcasting Company said.]

Hitler, who was 56 years old on April 20, was lauded by Doenitz as "one of the greatest heroes in German history." Here the ghost voice broke in: "The greatest of all fascists!"

"With proud respect and mourning, we lower our standards," Doenitz continued. "His death calls on us to act," the ghost voice interrupted. "Strike now!"

Doenitz launched into a pep talk to the German people and troops, only to be interrupted again by the ghost voice, crying: "Rise against Doenitz. The struggle is not worth while if crime wins."

Haw-Haw Repeats Message

After Doenitz had broadcast his message the Hamburg station played "Deutschland Ueber Alles" and the "Horst Wessel Lied." This was followed by three minutes of silence, then by a formal order of the day from Doenitz to the military services and then by funeral music. Then Lord Haw-Haw repeated the broadcast, including Doenitz' order of the day, in English.

The Foreign Office said that it believed that Hitler was dead, but it declined to comment on the accuracy of the Hamburg radio's report of how he died.

NAZI RUSE IS SEEN IN HITLER 'DEATH'

Writer Suggests the Report Is an Effort to Hide the Whereabouts of Leader

By LOUIS P. LOCHNER
Chief of the Former Associated Press Bureau in Berlin

WITH THE UNITED STATES SEVENTH ARMY, May 1 (AP)—I have just listened to the shortwave broadcast of Admiral Karl Doenitz' speech as the new Fuehrer of Germany, but I still find it difficult to believe that Hitler is really dead or that he remained in Berlin during the Russian assault.

The whole melodramatic buildup, beginning with Propaganda Minister Joseph Goebbels' announcement days ago that Hitler was personally conducting the defense of the capital, now reaching its climax in the claim that he met death in the Chancellery, of all places, looks like an effort to make good the Fuehrer's oft-repeated assertion: "I will never capitulate." Hitler could not afford to accept unconditional surrender, so what may prove to be the legend of his meeting a hero's death had to be staged.

Hitler may or may not be dead. If he is dead, it seems extremely unlikely that he died as the German radio says that he did. Having spent the past days in the very section of the country where Hitler rose to power, wrote "Mein Kampf" and conducted affairs of intrigue with the whole world from Munich, I still cannot escape the feeling that Hitler is some place where nobody expects him to be. From time to time people will claim to have seen him.

Doenitz' announcement by no means ends our troubles with Hitler. They may have only begun. There may be a state funeral for him, and photographers may have the opportunity to produce pictures of a dead man labeled Hitler. Then, some day much later, a "resurrected" Hitler may again stir the world.

The appointment of Doenitz as Hitler's successor indicates that the German leadership desires someone as chief of state who can possibly negotiate with the Allies. Doenitz had no experience in government and has no real hold on the affections of the German people. His appointment was obviously a political maneuver.

The course of the war is unlikely to be affected by his appointment.

FUEHRER ASCETIC IN PERSONAL LIFE

Celibate and a Vegetarian, He Neither Smoked Tobacco Nor Drank Liquor

Adolf Hitler was an ascetic, a celibate and a vegetarian and he neither smoked nor drank. From his early youth he was an eccentric. At the age of 16 he suffered from lung trouble and his passionate ambition to become a great historic figure impelled him to take good care of himself. Careful diet was his deliberately chosen method.

He led a simple life even after he had attained to the dizzy heights of Fuehrer and Chancellor. He had three residences: the official residence in the Chancellor's Palace in Berlin, a modest apartment in Munich and his châlet near Berchtesgaden.

In Berlin he maintained only five servants, carefully chosen from among old party comrades. One of these, Brigadier Schreck, was his chauffeur. The others included his chef, picked for the post because he knew how to cook Hitler's favorite vegetarian dishes and could be relied upon to guard against poisoning; his major-domo and aide-de-camp.

The Fuehrer liked to drive fast in an open automobile and was an aviation enthusiast. When driving he preferred to sit in front with the chauffeur.

Had a Passion for Neatness

His favorite costume consisted of black trousers, khaki coat and neat tie. His only decoration was the Iron Cross he won in the First World War. He disliked jewelry but had a passion for being neat.

Hitler never went shopping and had all the things he wanted to purchase sent to him at the Chancellery.

He suffered from insomnia, and for this reason had no regular hours for going to bed or rising. Luncheon was always promptly at 2 P. M., however. He entertained modestly, the guests usually being party officials and leaders from the provinces. He did not expect his guests to eat his vegetarian food, however, and served their favorite meat and fish dishes. Hitler disliked festive banquets but enjoyed eating out frequently, particularly when in Munich, where he had several haunts. He loved onion soup, prepared according to his own recipe.

When in Nuremberg, attending the spectacular Nazi party congresses, he stayed in a modest apartment at the Deutscher Hof, a second-rate hostelry. He shrewdly eschewed personal extravagance as politically unwise.

He was fond of films and liked to give private showings of favorite screen productions before guests at the Chancellery after dinner. He enjoyed looking at newsreels of himself and entertained his guests also with some foreign films. On such occasion he would seat himself on the floor in the dark and appeared to be having a good time.

Although he became the idol of many millions he had no talent for real friendship or intimacy. He had few women friends. His feminine associates, too, were chosen for political purposes. His only passion was politics.

Women of the people did not rally to him until after he had achieved a large degree of prominence. He never became a hero to his valet because he did not have any. Long before housemaids flocked to his support, his feminine supporters were women of the upper class. But he could be very charming to women when he chose and, after achieving power, even learned the art of kissing their hands in the salon manner. He was not without humor but of a rather heavy sort.

Although he had acquired considerable poise, he was violent in argument.

Hitler made what may be called his social debut in the earlier days of his career in the drawing room of Frau Katherine Hanfstaengl in Munich, but his greatest woman friend was Frau Victoria von Dirksen, widow of a millionaire who built the Berlin subway. She spent a large portion of her husband's fortune in helping to finance Hitler's propaganda. Although in later years she fell out with the party, he continued to regard her as a favorite and for a long time regularly took tea with her at her Berlin home every fortnight.

As a youth Hitler developed a passion for Wagnerian music. In Munich, where he laid the foundations of his movement, he met Frau Winifred Wagner, widow of Siegfried Wagner, the composer's son. Frau Wagner became an enthusiastic Hitlerite and this, together with Hitler's devotion to Wagner, made them fast friends. At one time there were reports that they would marry, but these were denied. Perhaps because of these reports Hitler drew away from her. To Frau Wagner, however, he owed much of his early financial aid. She was not wealthy, but because of her social position she was able to raise considerable sums for the Nazi movement when Hitler most needed money.

Another woman who had his favor was Leni Riefenstahl, a former movie actress, whom he entrusted with the task of editing the propaganda film "The Triumph of Will," the photographing of the 1935 Olympic Games in Berlin and various Nazi meetings and spectacles.

English Women His Friends

There were also two English women who were his friends, the daughters of Lord Redesdale—the Hon. Diana Freeman-Mitford, a supporter of Sir Oswald Mosley's Blackshirts in England, and the Hon. Unity Freeman-Mitford. The latter was Hitler's favorite and they often lunched together in Munich.

Frau Viorica Ursuleac, a member of the Berlin Opera, also enjoyed Hitler's friendship.

Hitler liked well-dressed women and admired French styles. On one occasion he scotched a movement launched by Frau Joseph Goebbels, wife of the Minister of Propaganda and Enlightenment, for a boycott on French dress models.

Hitler detested evening clothes and wore full dress only on rare visits to the opera.

Though merciless to political opponents, he was kind to animals. A militarist, he was sickened by the sight of blood. A Wagnerian mystic, he loved spectacles of heroics and death. He was simple. Spartan and vain to the point of megalomania. While he took good care of his loyal lieutenants he had no real loyalty to anyone, and in his party he knew how to thwart opposition by setting friends against one another. His enemies he suppressed ruthlessly.

While endowed with vast energy, he was a procrastinator in minor matters and was given to hasty decisions on important things. He talked with great rapidity. An interviewer usually found that it was himself who was being interviewed. While pretending to listen to advice, Hitler always made his own decisions.

He read little, although he possessed a library of 6,000 volumes. His outbursts of furious energy would be preceded by long periods of indolence. When roused to anger he became dangerous, even for his close associates. He brooked no contradiction. His neurasthenia frequently drove him to tears and hysterics.

Hitler was truly devoted to music not only as an art but as a tonic for his nerves. His favorites were Schubert, Beethoven and Wagner.

One of the many disappointments of his youth was his rejection by the Vienna Academy when he applied for admittance to study art and architecture. He found satisfaction for this rebuff as leader of the Nazi party when he supervised the plans for the Brown House in Munich, party headquarters. He also interfered much in the designing of new museums and Government buildings. To show his appreciation of things beautiful he liked to make gifts of expensively bound books and objects of art.

When the Chancellor's Palace in Berlin was being redecorated for him he superintended the work in several modernistic rooms and paid special attention to the installation of Nordic mythological tapestries depicting Wotan creating the world.

His Munich flat, which he redecorated in 1935 in his favorite baroque blue, white and gold, was in an unfashionable section of the Prinzregentenstrasse. To this flat he would retire when he wanted privacy. Munich was his favorite city, not only because of its architectural beauty but because it was there that his career was launched. The apartment was run by a half-sister, Frau Angella Raubal, who, until her marriage to a Professor Martin Hammizch, also supervised Haus Wachenfeld, Hitler's mountain retreat at Berchtesgaden overlooking a magnificent vista in the Bavarian Alps, at a point from which the Fuehrer could look across into his native Austria.

Hitler with Mussolini in June 1934.

"All the News That's Fit to Print"

The New York Times

LATE CITY EDITION

Weather: Chance of showers today, tonight. Cloudy tomorrow. Temp. range: today 76-65; Wed. 74-68. Temp.-Hum. Index yesterday 71. Complete U.S. report Page 93.

VOL. CXVIII..No. 40,766

NEW YORK, THURSDAY, SEPTEMBER 4, 1969 — 10 CENTS

HO CHI MINH DEAD AT 79; NORTH VIETNAM EXPECTED TO HOLD TO WAR POLICIES

HAS HEART ATTACK

He Won Independence for Nation and Led War Against U.S.

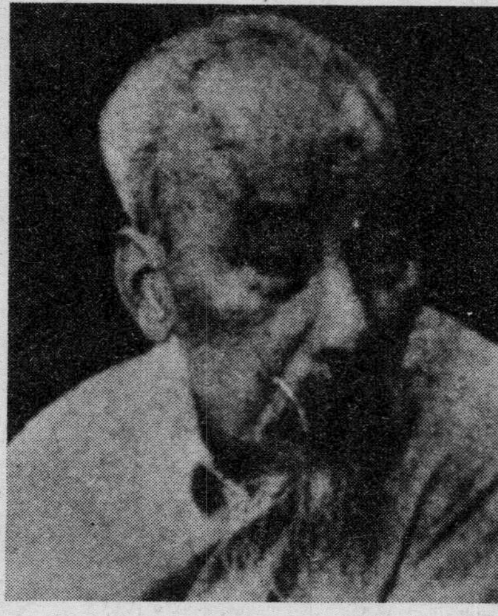

Camera Press-Pix

Ho Chi Minh

Text of Hanoi announcement of Ho's death, Page 16.

By TILLMAN DURDIN

Special to The New York Times

HONG KONG, Thursday, Sept. 4—President Ho Chi Minh of North Vietnam died yesterday morning in Hanoi at the age of 79.

A Hanoi radio report at 7 A.M. this morning announced that he succumbed at 9:47 A.M. Hanoi time yesterday "after a very sudden, serious heart at tack."

The radio disclosed only at 4 A.M. yesterday that President Ho had been gravely ill for several weeks and was under emergency treatment day and night by "a collective of professors and medical doctors."

There was no explanation for the delay of almost 24 hours in announcing the President's death.

White House Silent

Under the North Vietnamese Constitution, the Vice President take over if the President dies or is incapacitated, pending a new election. The Vice President is an obscure figure, Ton Duc Thang, 81.

[In San Clemente, Calif., the Western White House said that President Nixon would have no comment on Mr. Ho's death.]

The Hanoi announcement, in the form of a communiqué issued in the name of the Central Committee of the Vietnam Workers (Communist) party, the Standing Committee of the National Assembly and the Council of Ministers, said:

"We feel boundless grief in informing the entire party and the entire Vietnamese people that Comrade Ho Chi Minh, President of the Central Committee of the Vietnam Workers party and President of the Democratic Republic of Vietnam, passed away at 9:47, Sept. 3, 1969, after a very sudden, serious heart attack at the age of 79.

"Everybody has done his best, determined to cure the President at all costs. But due to his advanced age President Ho Chi Minh has departed from us." After the first announce-

Continued on Page 16, Column 1

STENNIS CHARGES ARMS FUND CUTS ENDANGER NATION

Answers Pentagon Critics as Senate Resumes Its Debate After Recess

FEARS 2D RATE STATUS

Senator's Defense of New Giant Transport Plane Challenged by Proxmire

By WARREN WEAVER Jr.

Special to The New York Times

WASHINGTON, Sept. 3 — Senate defenders of the Pentagon opened a strong counterattack today on the bipartisan bloc that has been successfully trimming the defense budget and is now questioning the necessity of major new weapons.

Senator John C. Stennis, chairman of the Armed Services Committee, charged that "the safety of the American people will be placed in jeopardy" if a series of moves to limit tank, carrier and aircraft development wins Senate approval over the next few weeks of debate.

In the prepared text of his remarks, he also declared that approval of the anti-Pentagon amendments would be "tantamount to a partial unilateral disarmament," but he dropped this paragraph in delivery.

Praised by Thurmond

The accusation will show up in the record anyway, for a few moments later Senator Strom Thurmond of South Carolina rose to congratulate Senator Stennis and singled out the "unilateral disarmament" charge for particular praise.

Reopening of the two-month Senate debate on the $20-billion military authorization bill was the principal activity on Capitol Hill as Congress returned from a three-week summer vacation to face an imposing accumulation of unprocessed legislation.

In the week before the Senate recessed Aug. 13, a coalition of liberal critics of the Pentagon and economizers succeeded in passing a series of restrictive amendments to the military bill or, alternatively, forcing its sponsors to accept compromises.

Senator Stennis, trying to halt the momentum of the military critics, maintained that if their pending proposals were approved "we will be a second-rate nation by 1975, and this fact shall become well known long before that time."

"I do not want this Senate to be in the position of saying to these young men [in the armed services] that this Gov-

Continued on Page 19, Column 1

Marine Commandant Acts To Ease Racial Tensions

Associated Press

Gen. Leonard F. Chapman Jr. at Washington news session

By WILLIAM BEECHER

Special to The New York Times

WASHINGTON, Sept. 3—The Marine Corps commandant issued an order today calling for an end to racial violence in the corps and outlining steps to eliminate discrimination against Negroes.

The commandant, Gen. Leonard F. Chapman Jr., appeared willing to bend traditional Marine rules a bit in an effort to be conciliatory toward the attitudes of some black marines.

Text of General Chapman's statement is on Page 39.

For example, he said that the Afro haircut would be permitted if it conformed with Marine regulations—that is, if it was neatly trimmed on the sides and in back and stood no more than three inches high on top.

General Chapman's order came in the wake of racial incidents at Camp Lejeune, N.C., and other marine garrisons in

Continued on Page 39, Column 1

WATER POLLUTERS WHO FAIL TO ACT FACE FEDERAL SUIT

Hickel Orders New Drive by Government to Identify and Prosecute Violators

Special to The New York Times

WASHINGTON, Sept. 3—The Interior Department plans to speed up its drive against water pollution by suing individual polluters if necessary.

Announcing a Government drive to "prosecute those who pollute," Interior Secretary Walter J. Hickel today ordered hearings before the Federal Water Pollution Control Administration. The City of Toledo, Ohio, four steel companies and a mining company have been charged by the Government with pollution, and their representatives will appear at the hearings.

The steel companies are the United States Steel Corporation, the Republic Steel Corporation, the Interlake Steel Company, and Jones & Laughlin Steel Company. The mining company is Eagle-Picher Industries, Inc., of Baxter Springs, Kan.

Those charged with water pollution are not required to attend the hearings, but they were sent official notification of the charges yesterday, according to an Interior Department official. If they are found guilty of the charges, and fail to take steps to eliminate pollution within 180 days, the Interior Department plans to bring suit.

Until today, states have had the responsibility for initiating court action against water polluters. Interior officials, however, feel that state court actions have been too slow in coming. The new drive at the Interior Department is designed to accelerate the cleaning up of the nation's waterways.

Act of 1965 Cited

In a statement, Secretary Hickel said: "This is just a beginning. We intend to continue the identification of polluters for prompt cleanup and pollution elimination."

Carl L. Klein, Assistant Secretary for water quality and research, said in a telephone interview that the Government for the first time would use the "abatement proceedings" provision of the Federal Water Pollution Control Act of 1965, which defined water pollution standards in various bodies of water.

Mr. Klein said the Interior Department's campaign procedure started with "fact finding" by scientists and engineers and called for voluntary hearings involving companies, municipalities or others charged with pollution.

Mr. Klein stressed that those found to be polluting water-

Continued on Page 24, Column 3

U.S. WOULD ALTER CURRENCY ABROAD LITTLE BUT OFTEN

Reform in Global Monetary System Deemed Necessary —Dollar to Stay Fixed

By EDWIN L. DALE Jr.

Special to The New York Times

WASHINGTON, Sept. 3 — The United States Government has concluded at the highest level that the international monetary system needs reform to provide more flexibility in exchange rates among currencies.

The method of flexibility favored is some version of a "crawling peg," under which exchange rates would make small but frequent changes, up or down. The change need not be universal but could be adopted only for a limited number of currencies, though that question is still left open.

The dollar would not be affected. Its exchange rate—expressed in terms of gold at $35 an ounce—would remain the "fixed star" of the system. Other currencies would move up or down against the dollar.

The United States will not make a formal proposal for introduction of this major reform at the International Monetary Fund's annual meeting later this month, according to authoritative sources.

Suggestion Likely

However, it is probable that the Secretary of the Treasury, David M. Kennedy, will suggest that the matter be formally studied by the I.M.F. or by the Group of Ten major financial powers or by both.

Even this would be a major step. It would signal to the world that the United States now looks sympathetically upon the next step in monetary reform, widely advocated outside Government circles, and it could lead to the placing of exchange-rate flexibility formally on an international agenda for the first time—a necessary first step in any reform.

The decision to back reform emerged from months of study by a group of high officials that began shortly after the Nixon Administration took office.

The reason for the United States decision is growing awareness of a flaw in the otherwise highly successful 25-year-old postwar monetary system. The keystone of the system has been fixed exchange rates, supported by government intervention in daily trading in the foreign-exchange markets.

The system always allowed for changes in exchange rates—devaluations or upward revaluations—for cases when a nation's economy, its rate of inflation or its foreign trade drift

Continued on Page 70, Column 4

Episcopal Leaders Vote $200,000 in 'Reparations'

By SETH S. KING

Special to The New York Times

SOUTH BEND, Ind., Sept. 3—After two days of emotional debate, the Episcopal Church indirectly allocated today $200,000 for the Black Economic Development Conference.

The Episcopalians thus became the first major denomination to offer money or recognition to the Negro group that promulgated the Black Manifesto.

The House of Deputies reversed its previous ban and voted this morning to provide the $200,000 demanded by the group, organized under the leadership of James Forman. This was to be the Episcopal Church's share of $500-million in "reparations" Mr. Forman demanded from the nation's churches and synagogues for their "racist oppression" of Negroes.

Both Houses Pass Measure

The House of Bishops, which shares the responsibility of directing the Episcopal Church, endorsed the House of Deputies' decision tonight.

The 600-man House of Deputies, consisting of clergymen and laymen, declared that it rejected much of the ideology expressed in the Black Manifesto. But it recognized the Black Economic Development Conference as a movement for organizing the "self-determination" of the black community.

The funds would not go directly to the Forman group. Instead they would be allocated to the interdenominational National Committee of Black Churchmen.

"But we expect the Black Economic Development Conference to be the ultimate recipient," said the Rev. Robert P. Varley, chairman of the committee that produced the

Continued on Page 38, Column 7

N.A.A.C.P. IS SUING ON BUILDING JOBS

Asks Halt in Construction Financed by Government Unless Negroes Are Hired

By DAMON STETSON

The National Association for the Advancement of Colored People announced yesterday a series of legal actions aimed at stopping work on Government-financed construction unless qualified Negroes were employed on the projects.

The legal moves are part of a stepped-up national drive to eliminate discrimination in building trades unions and to insure compliance on public construction with Federal laws.

At a news conference here, Roy Wilkins, executive director of the association, described the building trades unions as the "last bastion against employment of Negro workers as a policy" and asserted that the blacks of the nation wanted a just share of the $80-billion budgeted for construction this year by the building industry.

Asked about the effect of the 75 per cent cutbacks in Federal construction reportedly planned by the Nixon Administration, Mr. Wilkins replied that such a move would make things

Continued on Page 40, Column 4

FRANCE INVOKING MORE AUSTERITY

Government Exhorts Public to Help Save the Franc—Cuts Budget Sharply

By HENRY GINIGER

Special to The New York Times

PARIS, Sept. 3 — The French Government adopted new austerity measures today and appealed to the country to join in a battle to save the franc.

The battle plan includes major cuts in public spending this year, a balanced budget in 1970, immediate tax relief for low income groups only, restrictions on credit and prices, and spurs to savings.

After the Cabinet had adopted the economic-recovery program for the rest of this year and 1970, its details were presented by Premier Jacques Chaban-Delmas and the Finance Minister, Valéry Giscard d'Estaing.

'Our Fates Are Linked'

The state, the individual and the corporation were all enlisted in the fight.

"In this battle our fates are linked," Mr. Giscard d'Estaing declared at a news conference.

"It is not the ambition of the Government on one side and the well-being of Frenchmen on the other. The stake is the same for all."

The Finance Minister outlined the measures to the Finance Committee of the National Assembly, which has been called into special session for Sept. 16. Then, under hot floodlights at the Ministry of Finance, in a wing of the Louvre Palace, he spoke to several hundred reporters and, by radio and television, to the nation.

Tonight Premier Chaban-Del-

Continued on Page 6, Column 1

NO EFFECT IS SEEN ON TALKS IN PARIS

U.S. Officials Say Death of Mystical Leader Won't Alter Peace Outlook

By RICHARD HALLORAN

Special to The New York Times

WASHINGTON, Sept. 3 — United States officials said here tonight that the death of Ho Chi Minh meant the loss of an almost mystical leader but that it was not likely to change the course of the war in South Vietnam or to affect the prospects of reaching a settlement in the peace negotiations in Paris.

Sources close to the Vietnam situation said here that the most immediate impact would be the loss of leadership that has been embodied in Ho Chi Minh, the nationalist, the fighter for Vietnamese independence and the poetic revolutionary.

He has been such a figure for many of the Vietnamese for a half-century since he appeared at the Versailles Peace Conference in 1919 to seek more rights for his countrymen, who were then living under French colonial rule.

No Outstanding Figure

In the North, no other member of the inner circle of Communist leaders, some of whom have served with him for more than 30 years, enjoys anything like the stature of President Ho.

His quality of leadership cannot be passed on, it is thought here, and thus the future cohesion of North Vietnamese leadership is in some doubt. It is thought probable that a collective leadership, as in the Soviet Union after the death of Stalin, will emerge.

In the South, it is thought, the National Liberation Front,

Continued on Page 18, Column 1

HARTFORD POLICE MAINTAIN CURFEW

71 Are Arrested as Heavy Guard Patrols Streets

By JOHN DARNTON

Special to The New York Times

HARTFORD, Sept. 3—Overseeing a citywide curfew, the state and local police arrested at least 71 persons here tonight, but there was no repetition of the widespread racial disorders that swept this city's predominantly Negro and Puerto Rican North End for two successive days.

Most of tonight's arrest were for violations of the curfew. As heavy contingents of policemen patrolled the streets of the North End, they encountered only a few instances of bottle- and firecracker-throwing and one or two firebombs.

On one occasion, the police fired four tear gas canisters onto the roof of a four-story tenement in the North End where they said they had seen a man hurling bottles. Within seconds, seven patrol cars had rushed to the scene from all directions, but the man on the roof escaped.

The police described the situation in the 40-block riot area as quiet, despite large crowds drawn earlier in the day on

Continued on Page 28, Column 1

Con Edison Cable Failure Halts Stock Trading for Half an Hour

By PETER MILLONES

The New York Stock Exchange suspended trading for 30 minutes yesterday after a Consolidated Edison electric cable failed and the exchange's computers were knocked out of service.

Shouts of "power failure" echoed across the floor of the exchange at 12:28 P.M. when light bulbs flickered and the stock ticker, its tape projected on screens there and in brokerage houses, came to an abrupt halt.

The lights remained on, however, and many traders, undaunted, continued to buy and sell until the hastily convened floor governors of the exchange rang a bell signaling the suspension of trading at 12:35.

Trading and the ticker resumed at 1:05 P.M. and the interruption—allowing a few traders to snatch sandwiches—had no apparent effect on stock prices, which had been lower and remained so. The Dow-Jones industrial average, a barometer of blue chip stocks, closed 2.11 points lower at 835.67, in slightly heavier trading than the previous day.

Con Edison at $28.50 a share, only a few dimes above its 11-year low, was not affected by this latest problem in what has been a long hot summer of difficulties for the giant utility.

Faced almost daily with complaints from some of its three million customers, Con Edison contended that if the New York Exchange had had a better safety device on its computers, yesterday's problem would not have been serious.

An Exchange spokesman

Continued on Page 47, Column 3

Burns Moves Into City Campaign To Coordinate Procaccino's Race

By CLAYTON KNOWLES

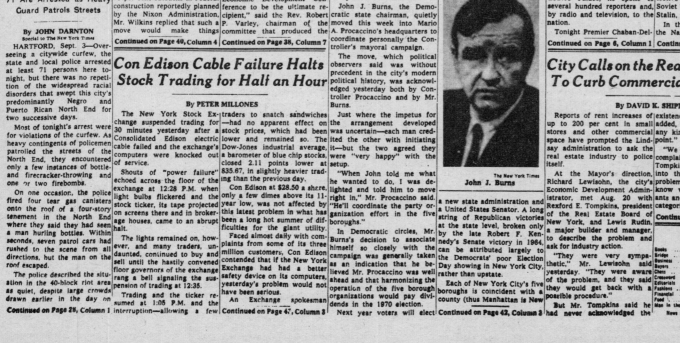

John J. Burns, the Democratic state chairman, quietly moved this week into Mario A. Procaccino's headquarters to coordinate personally the Controller's mayoral campaign.

The move, which political observers said was without precedent in the city's modern political history, was acknowledged yesterday both by Controller Procaccino and by Mr. Burns.

Just where the impetus for the arrangement developed was uncertain—each man credited the other with initiating it—but the two agreed they were "very happy" with the setup.

"When John told me what he wanted to do, I was delighted and told him to move right in," Mr. Procaccino said. "He'll coordinate the party organization effort in the five boroughs."

In Democratic circles, Mr. Burns's decision to associate himself so closely with the campaign was generally taken as an indication that he believed Mr. Procaccino was well ahead and that harmonizing the operation of the five borough organizations would pay dividends in the 1970 election.

Next year voters will elect

The New York Times

John J. Burns

a new state administration and a United States Senator. A long string of Republican victories at the state level, broken only by the late Robert F. Kennedy's Senate victory in 1964, can be attributed largely to the Democrats' poor Election Day showing in New York City, rather than upstate.

Each of New York City's five boroughs is coincident with a county (thus Manhattan is New

Continued on Page 42, Column 3

City Calls on the Realty Industry To Curb Commercial Rent Rises

By DAVID K. SHIPLER

Reports of rent increases of up to 200 per cent in small stores and other commercial space have prompted the Lindsay administration to ask the real estate industry to police itself.

At the Mayor's direction, Richard Lewisohn, the city's Economic Development Administrator, met Aug. 20 with Rexford E. Tompkins, president of the Real Estate Board of New York, and Lewis Rudin, a major builder and manager, to describe the problem and ask for industry action.

"They were very sympathetic," Mr. Lewisohn said yesterday. "They were aware of the problem, and they said they would get back with a possible procedure."

But Mr. Tompkins said he had never acknowledged the existence of a problem, and added, "We're not volunteering any kind of procedure at this point."

"We said we would take the complaints they had," Mr. Tompkins continued, "and look into them and see what the problem is. We're curious to know who are the complainants and whether they fall into categories and how many they

Continued on Page 53, Column 1

U.S. TELLS KOREANS IT WILL APOLOGIZE

But Pyongyang Rejects Plan to Free 3 on Copter

Special to The New York Times

PANMUNJOM, Korea, Thursday, Sept. 4—The American-led United Nations Command told North Korea today that it was prepared to submit a document of apology admitting that it had violated North Korean airspace if North Korea would, at the same time, release the three crewmen of an American OH-23 helicopter shot down over North Korea on Aug. 17.

The North Korean delegation at the Military Armistice Commission meeting here rejected the proposal.

Maj. Gen. Arthur H. Adams, the senior delegate of the United Nations Command, said that the proposed document would say that the helicopter "was on a military mission, it became lost and therefore flew into your territory."

He added that the document "would contain an expression of regret and statement that measures will be taken to prevent recurrences of an incident of this kind. It is preposterous to think that a three-man, unarmed helicopter would have

Continued on Page 19, Column 1

NEWS INDEX

HO CHI MINH DEAD OF HEART ATTACK

Continued From Page 1, Col. 8

ment of Mr. Ho's death, the Hanoi radio was being organized "with the most solemn rites of our country" and that a period of mourning from today until next Wednesday had been fixed.

A further special communiqué recapitulated the account of the death and described Mr. Ho as "the great, beloved leader of our Vietnamese working class and nation who all his life devotedly served the revolution, the people and the fatherland."

A thin, gaunt and stooped bachelor with a mustache and wispy beard, Mr. Ho was the prime mover of revolution in Vietnam for almost half a century and enjoyed enormous prestige even among anti-Communist Vietnamese.

He was titular head of the North Vietnamese Government and President as well of the Central Committee of the party, and though ill health in recent years impaired his functioning, he was the symbol of unity and continued struggle over South Vietnam.

Called for Sacrifices

Observers do not believe he had been making the day-to-day decisions for the Vietnamese Communists for the last year or two, but he frequently visited troops and made numerous declarations exhorting all Vietnamese to the maximum effort and sacrifice in the war.

There has long been thought to be a cleavage in Hanoi between a faction headed by Truong Chinh, a Politburo member and chairman of the National Assembly, and a second believed to include Le Duan, party First Secretary, and Gen. Vo Nguyen Giap, Politburo member, Vice Premier and Minister of National Defense.

Mr. Ho is believed to have played a decisive role in keeping the divisive tendencies from disrupting Vietnamese Communist unity.

Since his role in this respect has been so significant, it is believed that his death may lead to disputes and rivalries that may weaken the Communist war effort. The basic issue on which disruption might occur is whether concessions should be made to achieve peace in the near future or whether there should be a militant policy of continuing the war in an effort to win complete victory.

Chinese Send Message

Mr. Ho's death came as the North Vietnamese regime was celebrating the 24th anniversary of the proclamation of independence for Vietnam from French rule made by the Communist-led Vietminh government in 1945.

For the occasion, greetings were sent from Communist China signed by the party chairman, Mao Tse-tung, his chief deputy, Lin Piao, and Premier Chou En-lai.

The message denounced "the Soviet revisionist renegade clique" as having "worked hand-in-glove with United States imperialism to undermine the Vietnamese people's war."

Significantly, the message was not publicized from Hanoi. Possibly as an indication of Hanoi's neutral stand in the Peking-Moscow dispute, Hanoi carried a long article Tuesday paying tribute to the Russians for their long struggle against "Hitlerites and other fascists in Europe and Asia."

Body to Lie in State

HONG KONG, Thursday, Sept. 4 (Reuters) — The body of President Ho Chi Minh will lie in state in Ba Dinh Hall, in Hanoi, the Hanoi radio said today.

In a Vietnamese-language broadcast, it added that people from all walks of life would file past the body to pay their last respects. The broadcast added that the funeral ceremony would take place in Ba Dinh Square.

Public buildings throughout Hanoi were flying a black flag today as a mark of respect, and civil servants were wearing dark mourning bands on their left arms, the radio said.

All broadcasts of revolutionary music and cultural performances have been suspended, the radio added.

Duan to Head Funeral Group

SAIGON, South Vietnam, Thursday, Sept. 4 (AP) — A Hanoi broadcast heard in Saigon reporting the death of President Ho Chi Minh said today that Le Duan, First Secretary of the Vietnamese Communist party, had been named to head a special 26-man committee to take charge of the funeral.

The second name on the list was that of Vice President Ton, followed by Truong Chinh, the outspoken chief rival of Mr. Duan for leadership, and Pham Van Dong, Premier and outwardly the heir apparent to Mr. Ho.

Gen. Vo Nguyen Giap, the military leader who masterminded the victory over France in 1954, was listed as seventh on the funeral committee immediately after Le Duc Tho who heads Hanoi's delegation to the Paris peace talks. In fifth place is Pham Hung, a Vice Premier and member of the nine-member Politburo, which holds effective executive power.

Ho Chi Minh in May 1941 when he founded the Viet Minh.

Reflections and Opinions of President Ho Chi Minh

Ho Chi Minh conveyed his thoughts on issues of the day in letters, articles and speeches throughout his career. Some were expressed while he was an underground revolutionary, but most of them were voiced after 1945 as the leader of the Democratic Republic of Vietnam. Following are excerpts from his statements:

Revolutionary Beginnings

After World War I, I made a living in Paris, now as a retoucher at a photographer's, now as a painter of 'Chinese antiquities' (made in France!).

Heated discussions were then taking place in the branches of the Socialist party, about the question whether the Socialist party should remain in the Second International [a Socialist grouping founded in 1889], should a second-and-a-half International be founded, or should the Socialist party join Lenin's Third International [the Communist International founded in 1919.]

What I wanted most to know was: Which International sides with the peoples of colonial countries? [Written in 1960.]

*

A Poem From Prison

In the morning, the sun
climbs the wall
and comes knocking on the
door; the door stays shut;
night still tarries in the
depths of the prison . . .
Being chained is a luxury to
compete for.
The chained have somewhere
to sleep,
the unchained haven't . . .
The State treats me to its
rice, I lodge in its palaces,
its guards take turns escorting me.
Really the honor is too great.
. . .

[Written in Chinese Nationalist prison, 1942.]

*

After Dienbienphu

This victory is big, but it is only the beginning. We must not be self-complacent and subjective and underestimate the enemy. We are determined to fight for independence, national unity, democracy and peace. A struggle, whether military or diplomatic, must be long and hard before complete victory can be achieved. [Written after French defeat in 1954.]

*

On Unification of Country

During the armistice, our army is regrouped in the North; the French troops are regrouped in the South. . . . This is a necessity. North, Central and South Vietnam are territories of ours. Our country will certainly be unified, our entire people will surely be liberated. [After Geneva agreement of 1954.]

Texts of the Announcements by Hanoi

Following, as carried by The Associated Press, are the texts of two North Vietnamese communiqués issued Wednesday morning before the death of President Ho Chi Minh was announced, and a third issued Thursday morning announcing his death.

4 A. M. COMMUNIQUE

Over the past few weeks, President Ho Chi Minh has not been well.

Our party and state have been concentrating all capabilities and means to care for him. A collective of professors and medical doctors have been attending to him day and night.

We hereby inform our compatriots about the President's condition.

8 A. M. COMMUNIQUE

President Ho Chi Minh's condition is not stable. His illness is developing and is somewhat grave.

Our doctors are doing all they can to care for him.

Our party and state consider the task of curing his illness as an important and urgent task at present.

ANNOUNCEMENT OF DEATH

The Central Committee of the Vietnam Workers party, the Standing Committee of the National Assembly, the State Council of the Democratic Republic of Vietnam, the Presidium of the Vietnam Fatherland Front are extremely sorry and pained to announce to the party and to the entire Vietnam people that:

Comrade Ho Chi Minh, Chairman of the Central Committee of the Workers party and President of the Democratic Republic of Vietnam, died at 0947 hours, Sept. 3, 1969, after a grave and sudden heart attack.

During the time President Ho was sick, our party and Government leaders were attending him night and day and appointed a team of skilled medical professors and doctors with all modern equipment at their disposal to pursue all possible ways and methods to save and heal him.

Everyone tried his utmost and gave of his best to save him at any price, but because of his advanced age and the seriousness of the sudden severe heart attack, President Ho has left us forever.

President Ho is the great, respected and beloved leader of the working class and of the Vietnamese people.

He devoted all his life to the revolution for independence of our nation and our people, and to the people themselves, and to the fatherland.

He founded the Indochina Communist party, which now is the Vietnam Workers party. He founded the National Unified Front and the Vietnam People's Army.

He organized and victoriously led the August, 1945, revolution and established the DRVN.

He led our people in the victorious fight against the French colonialists before and now to fight against the United States imperialists to liberate the South, defend the North, and carry us forward toward the peaceful reunification of our entire country.

He obtained great and glorious victories in the struggle for national independence, for the peoples' democracy, and for socialism. President Ho was a firm and resolute and outstanding fighter for international Communism.

He was the dear friend to and of all the many various peoples in the world who are struggling for their own independence and freedom.

For over half of this century, the name, the virtue, the revolutionary tasks, and the revolutionary great achievements of President Ho have been closely and tightly linked to the life and the struggle of the Vietnamese people.

His death is an extremely great loss of our people and our party.

In order to show our loving remembrance and our everlasting gratitude to our beloved President Ho, a special meeting of the Central Committee of the Vietnam Workers party, the Standing Committee of the National Assembly, the State Council of the Democratic Republic of Vietnam, and the Presidium of the Vietnam Fatherland Front has decided to:

1. Organize the most solemn ceremonial state funeral of our nation.

2. The entire party, and all the people, and the entire army of Vietnam will mourn President Ho for seven days, from Sept. 4 to 11, 1969.

3. The Central Committee of the party, the Standing Committee of the National Assembly, the State Council, and the Presidium of the Fatherland Front will together organize the solemn mourning period and state funeral ceremony for President Ho.

4. They will appoint a state funeral committee consisting of one comrade leader of the highest rank in the party, the government, the Fatherland Front, and the various groups of patriotic people to be in charge of the state funeral ceremony.

Ho Chi Minh Was Noted for Success in Blending Nationalism and Communism

From Youth He Pursued A Goal of Independence

By ALDEN WHITMAN

Among 20th-century statesmen, Ho Chi Minh was remarkable both for the tenacity and patience with which he pursued his goal of Vietnamese independence and for his success in blending Communism with nationalism.

From his youth Ho espoused freedom for the French colony of Vietnam. He persevered through years when his chances of attaining his objective were so minuscule as to seem ridiculous. Ultimately, he organized the defeat of the French in 1954 in the historic battle of Dienbienphu. This battle, a triumph of guerrilla strategy, came nine years after he was named President of the Democratic Republic of Vietnam.

After the supposed temporary division of Vietnam at the 17th parallel by the Geneva Agreement of 1954 and after that division became hardened by United States support of Ngo Dinh Diem in the South, Ho led his countrymen in the North against the onslaughts of American military might. In the war, Ho's capital of Hanoi, among other cities, was repeatedly bombed by American planes.

At the same time Ho was an inspiration for the National Liberation Front, or Vietcong, which operated in South Vietnam in the long, bloody and costly conflict against the Saigon regime and its American allies.

In the war, in which the United States became increasingly involved, especially after 1964, Ho maintained an exquisite balance in his relations with the Soviet Union and the People's Republic of China. These Communist countries, at ideological sword's points, were Ho's principal suppliers of foodstuffs and war goods. It was a measure of his diplomacy that he kept on friendly terms with each.

Small and Frail

To the 19 million people north of the 17th parallel and to other millions below it, the small, frail, ivorylike figure of Ho, with its long ascetic face, straggly goatee, sunken cheeks and luminous eyes, was that of a patriarch, the George Washington of his nation. Although his name was not attached to public squares, buildings, factories, airports or monuments, his magnetism was undoubted, as was the affection that the average citizen had for him.

He was universally called "Uncle Ho," a sobriquet also used in the North Vietnamese press. Before the exigencies of war confined him to official duties, Ho regularly visited villages and towns. Simply clad, he was especially fond of dropping into schools and chatting with the children. Westerners who knew him were convinced that, whatever his guile in larger political matters, there was no pose in his expressions of feeling for the common people.

Indeed, Ho's personal popularity was such that it was generally conceded, even by many of his political foes, that Vietnam would have been unified under his leadership had the countrywide elections pledged at Geneva taken place. As it was, major segments of South Vietnam were effectively controlled by the National Liberation Front despite the presence of hundreds of thousands of American troops.

Intelligent, resourceful and dedicated, though ruthless, Ho created a favorable impression on many of those who dealt with him. One such was Harry Ashmore of the Center for the Study of Democratic Institutions and former editor of The Arkansas Gazette.

Mr. Ashmore and the late William C. Baggs, editor of The Miami News, were among the last Americans to talk with Ho at length when they visited Hanoi in early 1967.

"Ho was a courtly, urbane, highly sophisticated man with a gentle manner and without personal venom," Mr. Ashmore recalled in a recent interview. At the meeting Ho was dressed in his characteristic high-necked white pajama type of garment, called a cu-nao, and he wore open-toed rubber sandals. He chain-smoked cigarettes, American-made Salems.

Adept in English

Their hour-long conversation started out in Vietnamese with an interpreter, Mr. Ashmore said, but soon shifted to English. Ho astonished Mr. Ashmore by his adeptness in English, which was one of several languages—the principal others were Chinese, French, German and Russian—in which he was fluent.

At one point Ho reminded Mr. Ashmore and Mr. Baggs that he had once been in the United States. "I think I know the American people," Ho said, "and I don't understand how they can support their involvement in this war. Is the Statue of Liberty standing on her head?"

This was a rhetorical question that Ho also posed to other Americans in an effort to point up what to his mind was an inconsistency: a colonial people who had gained independence in a revolution were fighting to suppress the independence of another colonial people.

Ho's knowledge of American history was keen, and he put it to advantage in the summer of 1945 when he was writing the Declaration of Independence of the Democratic Republic of Vietnam. He remembered the contents of the American Declaration of Independence, but not its precise wording. From an American military mission then working with him he tried in vain to obtain a copy of the document, and when none could supply it Ho paraphrased it out of his recollections.

Thus his Declaration begins, "All men are created equal; they are endowed by their Creator with certain inalienable Rights; among these are Life, Liberty, and the pursuit of Happiness." After explaining that this meant that "all the peoples on the earth are equal from birth, all the peoples have a right to live, to be happy and free," Ho went on to enumerate, in the manner of the American Declaration, the grievances of his people and to proclaim their independence.

'Likable and Friendly'

Apart from Americans, Ho struck a spark with many others who came in contact with him over the years. "Extraordinarily likable and friendly" was the description of Jawaharlal Nehru, the Indian leader. Paul Mus, the French Orientalist who conducted delicate talks with Ho in 1946 and 1947, found him an "intransigent and incorruptible revolutionary, à la Saint Just."

A French naval commander who observed the slender Vietnamese for the three weeks he was a ship's passenger concluded that Ho was an "intelligent and charming man who is also a passionate idealist entirely devoted to the cause he has espoused" and a person with "naive faith in the politico-social slogans of our times and, generally, in everything that is printed."

Ho was an enormously pragmatic Communist, a doer rather than a theoretician. His speeches and articles were brought together in a four-volume "Selected Works of Ho Chi Minh" issued in Hanoi between 1960 and 1962. The late Bernard B. Fall, an American authority on Vietnam, published a collection of these in English in 1967 under the title "Ho Chi Minh on Revolution." They are simply and clearly worded documents, most of them agitational or polemical in nature and hardly likely to add to the body of Marxist doctrine.

Like Mao Tse-tung, a fellow Communist leader, Ho composed poetry, some of it considered quite affecting. One of his poems, written when he was a prisoner of the Chinese Nationalists in 1942-43, is called "Autumn Night" and reads in translation by Aileen Palmer:

In front of the gate, the guard
stands with his rifle.
Above, untidy clouds are
carrying away the moon.
The bedbugs are swarming
around like army tanks on
maneuvers,
While the mosquitoes form
squadrons, attacking like
fighter planes.
My heart travels a thousand li
toward my native land.
My dream intertwines with
sadness like a skein of a
thousand threads.
Innocent, I have now endured a
whole year in prison.
Using my tears for ink, I turn
my thoughts into verses.

Ho's rise to power and world eminence was not a fully documented story. On the contrary, its details at some crucial points are imprecise. This led at one time to the suspicion that there were two Hos, a notion that was discounted by the French Sûreté when it compared photographs of the early and the late Ho.

One explanation for the confusion is that Ho used about a dozen aliases, of which Ho Chi Minh (which can be translated as Ho, the Shedder of Light) was but one. Another was Ho's own reluctance to disclose biographical information. "You know, I am an old man, and an old man likes to hold on to his little mysteries," he told Mr. Fall. With a twinkle, he continued, "Wait until I'm dead. Then you can write about me all you want."

Nonetheless, Mr. Fall reported, before he left Hanoi he received a brief, unsigned summary of Ho's life "obviously delivered on the old man's instructions."

Despite Ho's apparent self-effacement, he did have a touch of personal vanity. Mr. Fall recalled having shown the Vietnamese leader a sketch of him by Mrs. Fall. "Yes, that is very good. That looks very much like me," Ho exclaimed. He took a bouquet of flowers from a nearby table and, handing it to Mr. Fall, said:

"Tell her for me that the drawing is very good and give her the bouquet and kiss her on both cheeks for me."

Although there is some uncertainty over Ho's birth date, the most reliable evidence indicates he was born May 19, 1890, in Kimlien, a village in Nghe-An Province in central Vietnam. Many sources give his true name as Nguyen Ai Quoc, or Nguyen the Patriot. However, Wilfred Burchett, an Australian-born correspondent who knew Ho well, believes (and it is now generally accepted) that Ho's birth name was Nguyen Tat Thanh.

He was said to be the youngest of three children. His father was only slightly better off than the rice peasants of the area, but he was apparently a man of some determination, for by rote learning he passed examinations that gave him a job in the imperial administration just when the French rule was beginning.

An ardent nationalist, Ho's father refused to learn French, the language of the conquerors of his country, and joined anti-French secret societies. Young Ho got his first underground experience as his father's messenger in the anti-French network. Shortly, the father lost his Government job and became a healer, dispensing traditional Oriental potions.

Ho's mother was believed to have been of peasant origin, but he never spoke of her.

Attended Lycée

Ho received his basic education from his father and from the village school, going on to a few years of high school at the Lycée Quoc-Hoc in the old imperial capital of Hue. This institution, founded by the father of Ngo Dinh Diem, was designed to perpetuate Vietnamese national traditions. It had a distinguished roster of graduates that included Vo Nguyen Giap, the brilliant guerrilla general, and Pham Van Dong, the current Premier of North Vietnam.

Ho left the school in 1910 without a diploma and taught briefly at a private institution in a South Annam fishing town. It was while he was there, according to now accepted sources, that he decided to go to Europe. As a step toward that goal, he went to a trade school in Saigon in the summer of 1911 where he learned the duties of a kitchen boy and pastry cook's helper, skills in demand by Europeans of that day.

His training gave Ho a gourmet's palate, which he liked to indulge, and an ability to whip up a tasty dish, which he delighted to do when he could.

For the immediate moment, though, his training enabled him to sign aboard the Latouche-Treville as a kitchen boy, a job so menial that he worked under the alias Ba. In his travels, he visited Marseilles and ports in Africa and North America. Explaining the crucial significance of these voyages for Ho's education as a revolutionary, Mr. Fall wrote in "The Two Vietnams":

"His contacts with the white colonizers on their home grounds shattered any of his illusions as to their 'superiority,' and his association with sailors from Brittany, Cornwall and the Frisian Islands — as illiterate and superstitious as the most backward Vietnamese rice farmer — did the rest.

"Ho still likes to tell the story of the arrival of his ship at an African port where, he claims, natives were compelled to jump into the shark-infested waters to secure the moorings of the vessel and were killed by the sharks under the indifferent eyes of passengers and crew.

"But his contacts with Europe also brought him the revelation of his own personal worth and dignity; when he went ashore in Europe in a Western suit, whites, for the first time in his life, addressed him as 'monsieur,' instead of using the deprecating 'tu,' reserved in France for children but used in Indochina by Frenchmen when addressing natives, no matter how educated."

In his years at sea, Ho read widely — Shakespeare, Tolstoy, Marx, Zola. He was even then, according to later accounts, an ascetic and something of a puritan, who was offended when prostitutes clambered aboard his ship in Marseilles. "Why don't the French civilize their own people before they pretend to civilize us?" he is said to have remarked.

(Ho, incidentally, is believed to have been a bachelor, although the record on this point is far from clear.)

With the advent of World War I, Ho went to live in London, where he worked as a snow shoveler and as a cook's helper under Escoffier, the master chef, at the Carlton Hotel. Escoffier, it is said, promoted Ho to a job in the pastry kitchen and wanted to teach him the art of cuisine. However that may be, the 24-year-old Vietnamese was more interested in politics. He joined the Overseas Workers Association, composed mostly of Asians, and agitated, among other things, for Irish independence.

Sometime during the war, Ho gave up the Carlton's kitchen for the sea and journeyed to the United States. He is believed to have lived in Harlem for a while. Ho himself often referred to his American visit, although he was hazy about the details. According to his close associate, Pham Van Dong, what impressed Ho in the United States were "the barbarities and ugliness of American capitalism, the Ku Klux Klan mobs, the lynching of Negroes."

Out of Ho's American experiences came a pamphlet, issued in Moscow in 1924, called "La Race Noire" ("The Black Race"), which assailed racial practices in America and Europe.

About 1918 Ho returned to France and lived in a tiny flat in the Montmartre section of Paris, eking out a living by retouching photos under the name of Nguyen Ai Quoc.

At the Versailles Peace Conference of 1919 Ho emerged as a self-appointed spokesman for his native land. Seeing in Woodrow Wilson's proposal for self-determination of the peoples the possibility of Vietnam's independence, Ho, dressed in a hired black suit and bowler hat, traveled to the Palace of Versailles to present his case. He was, of course, not received, although he offered a program for Vietnam. Its proposals did not include independence, but basic freedoms and equality between the French rulers and the native population.

Whatever hopes Ho may have held for French liberation of Vietnam were destroyed in his mind by the failure of the Versailles Conference to settle colonial issues. His faith was now transferred to Socialist action. Indeed, his first recorded speech was at a congress of the French Socialist party in 1920, and it was a plea not for world revolution but

(continued)

"against the imperialists who have committed abhorrent crimes on my native land." He bid the party "act practically to support the oppressed natives."

Immediately afterward Ho became, fatefully, a founding member of the French Communist party because he considered that the Socialists were equivocating on the colonial issue whereas the Communists were willing to promote national liberation.

"I don't understand a thing about strategy, tactics and all the other big words you use," he told the delegates, "but I understand well one single thing: The Third International concerns itself a great deal with the colonial question. Its delegates promise to help the oppressed colonial peoples to regain their liberty and independence. The adherents of the Second International have not said a word about the fate of the colonial areas."

Edited Weekly Paper

With his decision to join the Communists, Ho's career took a marked turn. For one thing, he became the French party's resident expert on colonial affairs and edited Le Paria (The Outcast), the weekly paper of the Intercolonial Union, which he was instrumental in founding in 1921. This group was a conglomeration of restless Algerian, Senegalese, West Indian and Asian exiles in Paris who were united by a fervid nationalism and, to a lesser extent, by a common commitment to Communism.

For another thing, the fragile-looking Ho became an orator of sorts, traveling about France to speak to throngs of Vietnamese soldiers and war workers who were awaiting repatriation.

In addition, Ho gravitated to Moscow, then the nerve center of world Communism. He went there first in 1922 for the Fourth Comintern Congress, where he met Lenin and became a member of the Comintern's Southeast Asia Bureau. By all accounts, Ho was vocal and energetic, meeting all the reigning Communists and helping to organize the Krestintern, or Peasant International, for revolutionary work among colonial peoples.

After a brief sojourn in France, Ho was back in Moscow, his base for many years thereafter. He attended the University of the Toilers of the East, receiving formal training in Marxism and the techniques of agitation and propaganda.

Following his studies in Moscow, Ho was dispatched to Canton, China, in 1925 as an interpreter for Michael Borodin, one of the leaders of the Soviet mission to help Chiang Kai-shek, then in Communist favor as an heir of Sun Yat-sen. Once in Canton, Ho set about to spread the spirit of revolution in the Far East. He organized Vietnamese refugees into the Vietnam Revolutionary Youth Association and set up the League of Oppressed Peoples of Asia, which soon became the South Seas Communist party, the forerunner of various national Communist groups, including Ho's own Indochinese Communist party of 1930.

For two years, until July, 1927, when Chiang turned on his Communist allies, Ho sent apt Vietnamese to Chiang's military school at Whampoa while conducting a crash training course in political agitation for his compatriots.

Fled to Moscow

After the Chiang-Communist break, Ho fled to Moscow by way of the Gobi. His life immediately thereafter is not clear, but it is believed that he lived in Berlin for a time and traveled in Belgium, Switzerland and Italy, using a variety of aliases and passports.

After 1928 Ho turned up in eastern Thailand, disguised as a shaven-headed Buddhist monk. He traveled among Vietnamese exiles and organized political groups and published newspapers that were smuggled over the border into Vietnam.

In 1930, on advice from the Comintern, Ho was instrumental in settling the vexatious disputes that had arisen among Communists in Indochina and in organizing the Indochinese Communist party, which later became the Vietnamese Communist party and, still later, the Vietnamese Workers party.

In that same year a peasant rebellion erupted in Vietnam, which the Communists backed. On its suppression by the French, Ho was sentenced to death in absentia. At the time he was in a British jail in Hong Kong, having been arrested there in 1931 for subversive activities.

The French sought his extradition, but Ho argued that he was a political refugee and not subject to extradition. The case, which was handled in London by Sir Stafford Cripps in a plea to the Privy Council, was decided for Ho. He was released, and fled Hong Kong in disguise (this time as a Chinese merchant) and made his way back to Moscow.

There he attended Communist schools — the Institute for National and Colonial Questions and the celebrated Lenin School. He was, however, back in China in 1938, now as a communications operator with Mao Tse-tung's renowned Eighth Route Army. Subsequently, he found his way south and entered Vietnam in 1940 for the first time in 30 years.

A Master Stroke

The timing was a master stroke, for the Japanese, virtually unopposed, had taken effective control of the Indochinese Peninsula and the French administrators, most of them Vichy adherents, agreed to cooperate with the Japanese. With great daring and imagination, Ho took advantage of World War II to piece together a coalition of Vietnamese nationalists and Communists into what was called the Vietminh, or Independence Front.

The Vietminh created a 10,000-man guerrilla force, "Men in Black," that battled the Japanese in the jungles with notable success.

Ho's actions projected him onto the world scene as the leading Vietnamese nationalist and as an ally of the United States against the Japanese. "I was a Communist," he said then, "but I am no longer one. I am a member of the Vietnamese family, nothing else."

In 1942 Ho was sent to Kunming, reportedly at the request of his American military aides. He was arrested there by Chiang Kai-shek's men and jailed until September, 1943, when he was released, it has been said, by American request.

On his release, according to Mr. Fall, Ho cooperated with a Chinese Nationalist general in forming a wide Vietnamese freedom group. One result of this was that in 1944 Ho accepted a portfolio in the Provisional Republican Government of Vietnam. That Government was largely a paper affair, but it permitted Ho to court vigorously the American Office of Strategic Services. Thus when Ho's Vietminh took over Hanoi in 1945, senior American military officials were in his entourage. It was in this period that he took the name of Ho Chi Minh.

Independence Proclaimed

With the end of World War II, Ho proclaimed the independence of Vietnam, but it took nine years for his declaration to become an effective fact.

First, under the Big Three Agreement at Potsdam, the Chinese Nationalists occupied Hanoi and the northern sector of Vietnam. Second, the French (in British ships) arrived to reclaim Saigon and the southern segment of the country. And third, Ho's nationalist coalition was strained under pressure of these events.

Forming a new guerrilla force around the Vietminh, Ho and his colleagues, according to most accounts, dealt summarily with dissidents unwilling to fight in Ho's fashion for independence. Assassinations were frequently reported. Meantime, as the Chinese withdrew from the north and the French advanced from the south, Ho negotiated with the French to save his nationalist regime.

In a compromise that Ho worked out in Paris in 1946, he agreed to let the Democratic Republic of Vietnam become a part of the French Union as a free state within the Indochina federation. The French recognized Ho as chief of state and promised a plebiscite in the South on the question of a unified Vietnam under Ho.

By the start of 1947, the agreement had broken down, and Ho's men were fighting the French Army. The Vietminh guerrillas held the jungles and the villages, the French the cities. For seven years the war raged as Ho's forces gathered strength, squeezing the French more and more. For most of this time, Ho was diplomatically isolated, for he was not recognized by Communist China or the Soviet Union until his victory over the French was virtually assured.

In an effort to shore up their political forces, the French resurrected Bao Dai, the puppet of the Japanese who held title as Emperor. Corrupt and pleasure-loving, he soon moved with his mistresses to France, leaving a weak and splintered regime in Saigon.

This, of course, proved no support for the French Army, which was also sapped by General Giap's guerrilla tactics. Finally, on May 8, 1954, the French forces were decisively defeated at Dienbienphu. The Indochina war ended officially in July at a cost to the French of 172,000 casualties and to the Vietminh of perhaps three times that many.

The cease-fire accord was signed in Geneva July 21, 1954, and it represented far less than Ho's hopes. But by that time the United States was involved in Vietnam on the French side through $800-million a year in economic aid. Fear of Communist expansion in Asia dominated Washington, with Vice President Richard M. Nixon saying, "If, to avoid further Communist expansion in Asia, we must take the risk of putting our boys in, I think the Executive Branch has to do it."

The Geneva Accord, however, divided Vietnam at the 17th parallel, creating a North and a South Vietnam. It removed the French administration from the peninsula and provided for all-Vietnam elections in 1956 as a means of unifying the country.

Although a party to the Geneva Accord, the United States declined to sign it. South Vietnam, also a nonsignatory, refused to hold the elections. Meantime, the United States built up its military mission in Saigon and its support of the regime of President Ngo Dinh Diem as a counter to continued guerrilla activity of the National Liberation Front, which became pronounced after 1956.

The front, technically independent of Ho Chi Minh in the North, increased its sway into the nineteen-sixties. It supplied itself from captured American arms and from materiel that came through from the North. Beginning in 1964, thousands of American troops were poured into South Vietnam to battle the Vietcong and then to bomb North Vietnam.

The halt of American bombing in 1968 finally led to the peace negotiations in Paris, but in the meantime the fighting in South Vietnam continued.

Confident of Victory

Throughout, Ho was confident of victory. In 1962, when the war was still a localized conflict between the South Vietnamese forces and 11,000 American advisers on the one hand and a smaller guerrilla force on the other, he told a French visitor:

"It took us eight years of bitter fighting to defeat you French, and you knew the country and had some old friendships here. Now the South Vietnamese regime is well-armed and helped by the Americans.

"The Americans are much stronger than the French, though they know us less well. So it perhaps may take 10 years to do it, but our heroic compatriots in the South will defeat them in the end."

Ho was still confident in early 1967, when he talked with Mr. Ashmore and Mr. Baggs. "We have been fighting for our independence for more than 25 years," he told them, "and of course we cherish peace, but we will never surrender our independence to purchase a peace with the United States or any party."

At the close of his conversation, he clenched his right fist and said emotionally, "You must know of our resolution. Not even your nuclear weapons would force us to surrender after so long and violent a struggle for the independence of our country."

Associated Press

In a happy mood at a Hanoi rally. Jawaharlal Nehru, the Indian leader, described him as "likable and friendly."

Marc Riboud—Magnum

With Mr. Dong, whom he called his "favorite nephew," in garden of the former palace of French Governors, Hanoi.

"All the News That's Fit to Print."

The New York Times.

LATE CITY EDITION
POSTSCRIPT
WEATHER—Cloudy, light rains today; tomorrow cloudy, colder.
Temperatures Yesterday—Max., 46; Min., 36
Detailed Weather Report, Page 41.

Copyright, 1935, by The New York Times Company.

VOL. LXXXIV....No. 28,165. Entered as Second-Class Matter, Postoffice, New York, N. Y. NEW YORK, WEDNESDAY, MARCH 6, 1935. TWO CENTS In New York City. | THREE CENTS Within 200 Miles | FOUR CENTS Elsewhere Except in 7th and 8th Postal Zones.

LONG DENOUNCED BY PARTY LEADER ON SENATE FLOOR

Senator Robinson Demands Stop Be Put on His Ravings and Arrogance.

HUEY'S 'GUARD' SEARCHED

Previously Louisianian, in Rage, Had Assailed Johnson, Baruch and the President.

TWO PRIESTS HERE DIFFER

Mgr. Belford Upholds Attack on Coughlin—Father J. A. Daly Calls It 'Maladroit.'

Long a Storm Centre.

Senator Long, following General Johnson's attack on him Monday, was the storm centre of discussion in Washington and New York yesterday.

In the Senate, after Senator Long had assailed General Johnson, Bernard Baruch and President Roosevelt, Senator Robinson, the Democratic leader, arraigned the Louisiana Senator and his tactics in one of the most scathing denunciations ever heard in the Senate.

General Johnson was both rebuked and praised in New York City by two priests who discussed his attack on Father Coughlin and Senator Long.

In Detroit Father Charles E. Coughlin said he would not reply to General Hugh Johnson's radio speech, denouncing him as a demagogue, until he had read the text of the address.

Debate in the Senate.

Special to THE NEW YORK TIMES.

WASHINGTON, March 5.—One of the most scathing denunciations in the history of the Senate was delivered today by Senator Robinson, the Democratic leader, who, following an attack on General Hugh S. Johnson, Bernard M. Baruch and President Roosevelt, by Senator Long, declared that the Louisiana Senator was "egotistical, arrogant and ignorant" and had just uttered the "ravings of a madman."

"It is about time that the manhood in the Senate assert itself here; it is about time that he should be made to know and take his place in a body composed for the most part of gentlemen," cried Senator Robinson in a speech marked with bitterness from end to end, and bringing applause from the crowded gallery.

"Innuendoes, insinuations and threats cannot prevail in the Senate of the United States, unless we have descended to the level of mediocre degenerates," Mr. Robinson shouted.

At the end of the exciting scene, Chester W. Jurney, Senate sergeant-at-arms, vainly searched for weapons a Louisianian who sits daily in the gallery and is described as "Long's chief bodyguard."

Long Not a Listener.

Senator Long was not in the chamber when the leader's remarks were made but he was obviously disconcerted and placed on the defensive by Mr. Robinson's sudden attack, regarded tonight as the start of a determined administration drive against him. He returned to the chamber a little later to reply in a speech which never really answered the most caustic parts of Senator Robinson's verbal castigation.

The "Kingfish" brought the severe rebuke upon himself by earlier taking up the biting radio speech in which the outspoken General Johnson last night, talking in New York, criticized Senator Long and Father Charles E. Coughlin of Detroit. It seemed obvious that General Johnson's phrases had stung the Louisianian, for he alluded little to the General's arraignment. For the most part he devoted himself to a denunciation of Mr. Baruch, who, he said, "sent Johnson here to organize the NRA" and who had "run" the White House in three Presidential régimes.

Hurling "ain'ts" and dropping g's," Mr. Long alluded to the scourge of Baruch and Johnson"; sarcastically alluded to Franklin De-La-No Roosevelt; declared that "they" had convinced General Johnson that he could be elected Senator from Oklahoma, and "warned" Senator Robinson to change his political program, lest he be defeated.

Asked About Armed Guard.

Senator Long strode out of the chamber before Senator Robinson leaped to his feet. When the Louisianian returned and began his reply, Senator Bailey at one point exclaimed:

"I would not take your word for that, or anything else."

At this Mr. Long flamed into

Continued on Page Six.

Justice Holmes Succumbs To Pneumonia at Age of 93

© Harris & Ewing.

The noted jurist on his ninetieth birthday, March 8, 1931, when he was the senior member of the United States Supreme Court.

End Comes in Washington Home of Retired Jurist—Civil War Soldier Was Chief Liberal of Supreme Bench for 29 Years.

Special to THE NEW YORK TIMES.

WASHINGTON, Wednesday, March 6.—Oliver Wendell Holmes, retired Associate Justice of the Supreme Court of the United States, where he served for twenty-nine years, and son of the author of "The Autocrat of the Breakfast Table," died this morning at his Washington home of bronchial pneumonia. His death was announced by Mark Howe, his former secretary.

Death came at 2:15 o'clock to the great liberal of the Supreme Court and soldier of the Union, who would have been 94 years old Friday. His service on the bench began on Dec. 4, 1902, and ended on Jan. 12, 1932.

He had been ill only since last Thursday.

It was announced that the funeral would be held at All Souls Church here at noon Friday, the former Justice's birthday, with a private military burial in Arlington Cemetery.

Honorary pallbearers will be the Chief Justice and the Associate Justices of the Supreme Court.

Justice Holmes was a tradition

Continued on Page Sixteen.

WILLIAMS RESIGNS AS NIRB CHAIRMAN

Reynolds Tobacco Official Had Been Under Persistent Attack by Labor.

Special to THE NEW YORK TIMES.

WASHINGTON, March 5.—Resignation of S. Clay Williams, chairman of the National Industrial Recovery Board, who has been under attack by organized labor for months, was announced by the White House tonight.

The announcement came as the date for a Congressional inquiry into the NRA was under discussion. It was learned that Mr. Williams had decided to resign after he had consulted important industrialists on the possible course of the Congressional inquiry. He decided to be in the position of a private citizen rather than official head of the NRA when he was called before the Congressional committee.

Mr. Williams was appointed Sept. 27, 1934, when President Roosevelt reorganized the NRA to eliminate the one-man rule under General Johnson. It was understood at the time that he would remain for sixty or ninety days and then return to the R. J. Reynolds Tobacco Company. He was chairman of the executive committee of the Peynolds company.

The resignation was accepted by Mr. Roosevelt in a letter made public with other official correspondence concerning the step by Mr. Williams. The President requested that Mr. Williams remain for at least two weeks. White House officials said that no successor to Mr. Williams has been designated.

William Green, president of the American Federation of Labor, said tonight:

"Now that Mr. Williams has resigned, I hope a reorganization of the NIRB may take place and that in the reorganization labor may have equal representation with industry."

The service of Mr. Williams as

Continued on Page Five.

SCHACKNO NRA ACT DECLARED INVALID

Appellate Division Rules the Legislature Lacked Power to Delegate Authority.

The Appellate Judges' opinions voiding Schackno act, Page 15.

Special to THE NEW YORK TIMES.

ALBANY, March 5.—The Schackno Act delegating legislative authority to the State Divisional Code Authority for the solid fuel industry was declared unconstitutional by the Appellate Division, Third Department, today. The court unanimously affirmed the two orders of Justice McNaught of Binghamton in a test case brought by Gustave C. Darweger of that city.

The Schackno Act was designed to make effective in intrastate business the general aims of the Federal National Industrial Recovery Act. It provided that the regulations of the NIRA shall apply to intrastate commerce and granted rights of code enforcement to the divisional Code Authorities.

The Appellate Division held that the Legislature had no power to delegate such power to an Authority. The adoption, administration and enforcement of any code, it ruled, are sought to be effected not by agencies of the State, subject to State control, but by the President, acting under the Federal law.

The court affirmed the order of Justice McNaught of Binghamton, in which the Code Authority moved to dismiss Mr. Darweger's complaint and affirmed the order granting an injunction preventing the Code Authority from interfering with Mr. Darweger in selling coal intrastate at prices other than that fixed by the Authority.

The case is to be taken at once to the Court of Appeals. The appeal will be conducted by Hinman, Straub & Hughes of Albany, acting for the Divisional Code Authority.

Attorney General Bennett will ap-

Continued on Page Fifteen.

HITLER, ILL, DEFERS TALK WITH SIMON; CHARGES IRK REICH

Fuehrer Suffers From Cold Caught in Saar—No Date Set for Conversations.

WHITE PAPER IS RESENTED

Germans Brand British Attack as 'Untimely,' 'Biased' and 'Greatly Exaggerated.'

By FREDERICK T. BIRCHALL.

Special Cable to THE NEW YORK TIMES.

LONDON, March 5.—The British Government, through Sir Eric Phipps, its Ambassador in Berlin, was requested today to postpone the official visit of Foreign Secretary Sir John Simon to the German capital on the ground of Reichsfuehrer Adolf Hitler's indisposition.

Herr Hitler, so Foreign Minister Constantin von Neurath informed Sir Eric, was suffering from a slight cold, coupled with severe hoarseness, contracted during his visit to the Saar. His doctors were said to have advised that conversations arranged for the immediate future should be canceled in order to spare his voice.

Sir Eric, instructed by London, expressed his government's regret at Herr Hitler's indisposition and its hope for his speedy recovery.

So Sir John Simon and Captain Anthony Eden will not fly to Berlin Thursday. It is uncertain when they will go, if at all.

Illness Seen as Diplomatic.

This uncertainty is due to the feeling that pervades virtually every quarter here that the Reichsfuehrer's indisposition is in some degree a diplomatic one, to which yesterday's White Paper on British defenses probably contributed. It is noted that Herr Hitler's cold is accompanied by an outburst of anger over the White Paper throughout the entire German press, an outburst not unexpected by impartial British commentators after reading it.

It is further noted here that Sunday afternoon was spent by Herr Hitler at the Berlin motor show in interested conversation over the exhibits. Indeed, German newspapers received here this morning display prominently a photograph of him taken there, bareheaded and wearing only his customary thin raincoat, talking cheerfully with one of the officials. So his cold must have developed very quickly. He returned from the Saar Saturday morning.

However, there is no doubt as to the cold. Friday afternoon Herr Hitler stood for an hour and a quarter, hatless and coatless, through an intermittent drizzle, reviewing the incoming parade of his Storm Troopers. His voice was hoarse when he spoke that evening.

On the other hand, German indignation over the British White Paper's references to German rearmament is equally unfeigned. They are described to British correspondents in Berlin as "unfriendly," and "ill-timed" and as "an attempt to intimidate the Reich" on the eve of negotiations and generally as misapprehending altogether the motives for Germany's actions.

Since the British Prime Minister seems responsible for at least this part of the document, having proclaimed his responsibility by affixing his initials, this has given a new opening to Mr. MacDonald's enemies. But he cannot answer them, for he, also, has a cold; but he is in bed. This announcement

Continued on Page Nine.

SENATE AGAIN GETS RELIEF BILL, SHORN OF WAGES CLAUSE

Types of Projects Specified, Swinging Two Vermont Senators to President's Side.

VOTE TODAY OR TOMORROW

Administration Leaders Feel They Now Have Strength to Put Measure Through.

Special to THE NEW YORK TIMES.

WASHINGTON, March 5.—Shorn of the "prevailing wage" amendment which caused its withdrawal from the Senate a week ago Friday, President Roosevelt's $4,880,000,000 work relief resolution was sent back to the floor today with a "rush order" for adoption.

As the measure resumed its legislative course, administration leaders counted at least three shifts in the Senate line-up which, they felt, would assure its passage in a form desired by the President.

The price of these shifts was an amendment, approved by the President and incorporated in the resolution by the Appropriations Committee today, breaking down the work relief program into eight general classifications of projects.

The resolution was reported to the Senate late this afternoon by Senator Glass and placed in position to be called up immediately after the War Department appropriation bill is disposed of tomorrow or Thursday. It was ordered reported after less than two hours of committee consideration this morning.

Senator McCarran, author of the "prevailing wage" amendment, said he would resume his fight on the floor. He expressed no great surprise that the committee had rejected the proposal today, which it did by a 12-to-12 tie. The same commitee had voted two weeks ago 14 to 9 for the Russell substitute, which later was rejected on the floor in favor of the McCarran amendment.

The committee report automatically carried the Russell amendment specifying that the President may fix wages under the resolution, but that if he finds that relief wages in any locality are likely to affect adversely private wage scales, then he shall prescribe payment of prevailing wages.

Senator McCarran said he hoped that the Senate would repeat its previous performance when it adopted his amendment 44 to 43. Reports were current, however, that at least two Republican Senators, Austin and Gibson of Vermont, and an unnamed Democrat would desert the original 44 and vote with the President.

The vote in committee on the McCarran amendment was as follows:

For the Amendment—Copeland, Thomas of Oklahoma, Adams, McCarran, Overton (by proxy), O'Mahoney and Truman, Democrats; Nye (by proxy), Steiwer, Dickinson, Townsend and Carey, Republicans, a total of 12.

Against the Amendment—Glass, McKellar, Hayden, Byrnes, Tydings, Russell, Coolidge, Bankhead (by proxy) and McAdoo, Democrats; Hale, Keyes and Norbeck, Republicans, a total of 12.

Way Funds Are Allocated.

The administration amendment allocating funds was offered in committee by Senator Glass and was adopted, 14 to 6. It provided for a breakdown of expenditures

Continued on Page Four.

Bankruptcy Notice Served Upon Walker After Debt Judgment, London Paper Says

By The Associated Press.

LONDON, Wednesday, March 6.—The Daily Express said today a bankruptcy notice had been served upon James J. Walker, former Mayor of New York, requiring him to make out and submit to a receiver a statement of the "nature and value of his assets."

The order was issued yesterday, the newspaper said, in Croydon County in connection with a judgment obtained against Mr. Walker in the New York courts. The Home Secretary, Sir John Gilmour, revealed that inquiry was being made to ascertain Mr. Walker's status as an alien.

Former Mayor Walker appeared last week in Chancery Court in London to answer two judgments against him for bills alleged to have been incurred here by him and his former wife.

The action, brought jointly by Sommers, Inc., and the 60 East Sixty-fifth Street Corporation, drew from Mr. Walker on the stand the answer that he had "no means."

Mr. Walker explained that the $25,000 yearly salary he drew as Mayor had not gone far—he gave $15,000 of it, he said, to his former wife.

The only personal income he was earning, he said, was $102 weekly for a London newspaper column. This money, he said, "represents my only earnings of any sort since 1933."

His financial condition was such, he told the court, that his present wife, the former Betty Compton, stage and screen star, had to pay the traveling expenses for a recent trip to Spain, made because of her health. Mrs. Walker paid for the trip, he said, out of her savings.

The Sommers, Inc., action is for $1,641 due on an original bill of $2,742 for shoes and handbags for the first Mrs. Walker. The 60 East Sixty-fifth Street Corporation suit is for rent, food and other items totaling $7,413 incurred at the Mayfair House, owned by the plaintiff.

240 IN VICE SQUADS SHIFTED TO SPUR RACKET CAMPAIGN; COURTS AID, SET HIGH BAIL

Dodge Rebuffs Mayor on Marcus's Powers, Lawyer Says He Is Satisfied With Status

Samuel Marcus, counsel to the Society for the Prevention of Crime, announced yesterday that he was satisfied with his status as a Special Assistant District Attorney, although it does not permit him to appear before the grand jury and present the evidence he has gathered on the policy racket.

He said that he had confidence in District Attorney Dodge and the regular assistants, and had been assured that he would have a voice in deciding what evidence went before the grand jury.

Mr. Dodge sharply rejected Mayor La Guardia's suggestion that the District Attorney ask the Board of Estimate for a $100 appropriation so that Mr. Marcus could be added to the payroll as a regular assistant. This would permit him under the law to present evidence to the grand jury. As a special assistant, Mr. Marcus is a $1-a-year man.

"I was elected District Attorney of New York County and in view of the oath I took following my election I owe a duty to the citizenry of New York County," said Mr. Dodge. "I need no instructions from any one else.

"I have a competent staff and I have assigned Assistant District Attorneys Albert B. Unger, Maurice Wahl and Lyon Boston to cooperate with Mr. Marcus. Until it is shown that these three are not competent and not to be trusted, I cannot see why any one else should present evidence before the grand jury.

"All I want is evidence. If I do not present the evidence after it is given to me I am subject to removal by the Governor."

Mr. Dodge added that Mr. Marcus was working in perfect harmony with the prosecution staff and had not made any request to be allowed to go before the grand jury.

Mr. Marcus spent the day in the office of Mr. Unger, to which he has been assigned until a separate office can be prepared for him. He devoted his efforts to preparing evidence on the policy racket, which will be presented to the grand jury after it finishes hearing the evidence in bail-bond cases involving alleged perjury and subornation of perjury, now being presented to it.

ALL BOROUGHS AFFECTED

Valentine Also Sets Up Picked Squad Headed by Lieut. Finn.

RAID TRAPS POLLY ADLER

Figure in the Seabury Inquiry Seized as Keeper of House Off 5th Av. With 3 Others.

RETIRED POLICEMAN BALKY

Won't Quit Jersey to Testify —Policy Banker Is Reported Ready to Reveal Leaders.

Police Commissioner Lewis J. Valentine ordered the transfer of 220 to 240 plainclothes detectives attached to borough headquarters and inspection districts throughout the city yesterday in the campaign against the policy racket, commercialized vice and allied evils.

The transfers began last night and will continue with shifts of detectives from one borough to another, and one inspection district to another, so that the racketeers in each locality will have "new faces" to contend with.

The Police Commissioner also announced the organization of a new special squad of eleven picked detectives to work directly under his supervision on the policy investigation. Its duties will include checking on the work of other detectives, including the "undercover squad" of fifteen men headed by Captain Michael Murphy, which is already working on policy, vice and other rackets.

Finn to Head Squad.

The new squad will be headed by Lieutenant James J. Finn, who had charge of the Lindbergh kidnapping investigation for the New York police until the arrest of Bruno Richard Hauptmann.

The shift of detectives, involving practically all the men on "vice squads" in all boroughs and in all sixteen inspection districts, became known after a conference of borough commanders called at police headquarters late yesterday afternoon by Chief Inspector John J. Seery, on Commissioner Valentine's orders.

At the conference, besides Seery, were the following deputy chief inspectors: David J. McAuliffe, commanding Manhattan; Joseph Reynolds, the Bronx; Edward A. Bracken, Brooklyn and Richmond, and Michael A. Lyons, Queens.

"Routine police duty," was the way Commissioner Valentine and Chief Inspector Seery described the purpose of the conference, but its real object was learned later from a high police official. This official said that Commissioner Valentine wanted to send "new men" into the "hot spots" of the policy racket so that they could seize the "higher-ups" in the racket before they could themselves be identified by the racketeers.

Seeks to Break Up Connections.

Another object of the transfers, it was explained, was to break up any connections that may exist in certain districts between racketeers and detectives known to them. It was pointed out that former Police Commissioner Edward P. Mulrooney used to transfer detectives on these details every six months, and that former Commissioner Grover Whalen made a practice of frequently transferring inspectors in command of inspection districts.

In a radio address last night the Rev. George Drew Egbert, president of the Society for the Prevention of Crime and pastor of the First Congregational Church in Flushing, called upon the city authorities to "turn the police loose" to clean up the city and smash the rackets.

He urged District Attorney William C. Dodge, who has said that he did not intend to engage in any "fishing expeditions," to "reverse himself" and follow up every lead.

Estimating the annual toll of the policy racket at $400,000,000, Mr. Egbert said that most of it comes from the poor and all is diverted from legitimate trade. If this drain on the city were stopped, he argued, relief funds and the sales tax would be unnecessary.

Louis F. Goodyear, a retired pa-

Continued on Page Two.

NEIGHBORS ARMING AS GREEKS BATTLE

Bulgaria, Reinforcing Border, Hopes Turkish Concentration Is Not Directed Against Her.

ATHENS LISTS VICTORIES

Loyal Forces Split the Rebels in Macedonia as Flanking Movement Is Successful.

Wireless to THE NEW YORK TIMES.

ATHENS, March 5.—From the confusion resulting from interrupted communications and government censorship the fact emerged that the government of Premier Panayoti Tsaldaris still held the upper hand in the Greek civil war today but was undoubtedly hard pressed, while the concentration of troops by Greece's neighbors on their frontiers gave the situation a graver aspect than the purely local revolts Greece has had in the past.

[In Sofia the Bulgarian Foreign Minister expressed alarm lest a large concentration of Turkish troops on the Bulgaro-Turkish border might be directed against Bulgaria, which has also heavily reinforced her frontier garrisons.]

For the government the danger points are Thrace, Macedonia and of course Crete, where the supporters of former Premier Eleutherios Venizelos are in full control. The government is making every possible effort to convince the rebels that they have lost the day.

Victories were reported all along the line by the government, but the reports failed to carry full conviction. Athens was quiet for the most part and the government canceled decrees limiting the repayment of deposits by the banks, but there were riots between Venizelist and Tsaldarist students, which caused Athens University to be closed indefinitely. Saloniki harbor has been protected by mines against rebel ships.

To Arrest Rebels' Relatives.

The government today ordered the arrest of all male and female relatives of rebels and their internment in concentration camps in order to compel the rebels to surrender.

Unconfirmed reports say that an artillery battle near Drama today ended in the rebels' favor.

Reports from Crete say that M. Venizelos is still confident of final victory and is planning to capture the Cyclades Islands preliminary to an attack on Athens and Southern Greece.

With General George Kondylis, the Minister of War, commanding, loyal troops crossed the Struma River in Macedonia early this afternoon. The cooperation of General Kondylis with the loyal General Yalistras resulted, according to an announcement from the government, in a completely successful

Continued on Page Three.

NEW ORDER CURBS LIQUOR LICENSES

Mulrooney Says None For On Premises Use This Year Will Be Issued After April 1.

BURKE BILL IS REPORTED

Measure Authorizing Combined Beer and Whisky Permits Opposed by Board.

Special to THE NEW YORK TIMES.

ALBANY, March 5.—The State Liquor Authority, in a surprise move today, announced that after April 1 no more licenses for the sale of beer and liquor in establishments where they are to be consumed on the premises would be issued by the State.

Edward P. Mulrooney, chairman of the Authority, made the announcement of the complete shutdown on license issuance and declared that it was based on the belief that the beer and liquor needs of the State were already being served by the existing restaurants.

The chairman's announcement, however, indicated that the suspension would be only temporary and that when, due to usual business shifts, a need for new or more licenses was made evident, the Authority would take up the question again.

"It is the opinion of the Liquor Authority," said Mr. Mulrooney's announcement, "that the social needs of the people of the State of New York are being adequately served with the number of existing on-premises licenses now in effect.

"In accordance with this opinion, on and after April 1, 1935, no new annual licenses for the on-premises consumption of alcoholic beverages in hotels, clubs, restaurants and eating places will be issued, subject to further determination by the Liquor Authority."

Power Rests With Board.

Under the terms of the law creating the State Liquor Authority that body has the power to limit the number of licenses on the basis of public necessity and social requirements.

The Authority filed last night with the Legislature its annual report, in which it revealed that in the State at present are 8,951 restaurants and 1,470 hotels where liquor is sold, 26,161 places licensed to sell beer alone, and 1,382 holding special wine licenses.

The Assembly Excise Committee reported favorably a bill strongly opposed by Chairman Mulrooney.

This was the Burke bill, which would establish a single license for sale on the premises of both beer and liquor and fix the fee at $800. At present a liquor license costs $1,200 in New York City and a beer license $200.

Spokesmen for liquor groups at the public hearing declared that

Continued on Page Twelve.

JUSTICE HOLMES DIES AT AGE OF 93

Continued From Page One.

even in the Federal city where street after street is tinged with history. He had been here so long, was so well known, so distinguished, such an integral part of Washington that, even at his great age, the actuality of his death was hard to comprehend.

When news of his last illness became known on Thursday a Washingtonian said:

"I thought he was immortal."

Last Years of Calm Waiting.

Since he retired from the Supreme Court bench, in January, 1932, Justice Holmes had spent nearly all of his days in the unostentatious little red brick house at 1,720 I Street where he died. There, in a mellow study running nearly from front to back of the dwelling, its walls lined with books, he read, dictated letters and received intimate friends who dropped in from time to time.

Amid these surroundings he had waited for an end he knew was inevitable, but waited, his friends said, without fear or without melancholy, but with never failing good nature.

A salient wit was one of Justice Holmes's chief characteristics and it never left him. As recently as ten days ago, informing a friend that he was reading a book he "did not like," he commented that a New England conscience drove him to finish the volume, once he had begun it.

Even with his whimsical outlook, the venerable justice was a realist, and knew that he could live only a few years at most. When he left the bench he told his associates that "for such little time as may be left" he would treasure their friendship as "adding gold to the sunset."

On his ninetieth birthday he quoted these words of a Latin poet:

"Death plucks my ears and says, 'Live. I am coming.'"

Keen and Vigorous at Great Age.

Nevertheless, the old Civil War soldier carried on from day to day with little change in his existence and with that keen sense of humor that contrasted with his austere countenance.

One day was very like another. Friends who saw him, even during the last year, marveled at his keenness and his curiosity about the world's doings. They could see a few signs of a very old age, such as failure to remember names and dates, but, all in all, his mind was splendidly active. A woman who talked with him two weeks ago said:

"He was just as charming and delightful as he ever was."

AMERICAN LEGEND IN LIFE OF HOLMES

Soldier, Jurist and Philosopher, He Sprang From New England's Cultural Dominance.

RARE GENIUS FOR THE LAW

'A Deserving Fame Never Dimmed and Always Growing,' Said Justice Hughes.

As Justice Holmes grew old he became a figure for legend. Eager young students of history and the law, with no possibility of an introduction to him, made pilgrimages to Washington merely that they might remember at least the sight of him on the bench of the Supreme Court. Others so fortunate as to be invited to his home were apt to consider themselves thereafter as men set apart. Their el-

© Harris & Ewing.

Out for a stroll on his eighty-fifth birthday with Chief Justice William Howard Taft.

ders, far from discouraging this attitude, strengthened it.

A group of leading jurists and liberals filled a volume of essays in praise of him, and on the occasion of its presentation Chief Justice Hughes said:

"The most beautiful and the rarest thing in the world is a complete human life, unmarred, unified by intelligent purpose and uninterrupted accomplishment, blessed by great talent employed in the worthiest activities, with a deserving fame never dimmed and always growing. Such a rarely beautiful life is that of Mr. Justice Holmes."

Born in Boston in 1841.

He was born on March 8, 1841, in Boston. The cultural dominance of New England was at its height. The West was raw, great parts of it wilderness as yet only sketchily explored. A majority of the nation's citizens still considered the enslavement of Negroes as the operation of a law of God, and Darwin had not yet published his "Origin of Species."

The circumstances of his birth were fortunate. His father, Dr. Oliver Wendell Holmes, was of New England's ruling caste and the atmosphere of his home was at once brahminical, scientific and literary. The boy was to start each day at that "autocratic" breakfast table where a bright saying won a child a second helping of marmalade.

The boy was prepared for Harvard by E. S. Dixwell of Cambridge. He was fortunate again in this. Well-tutored, he made an excellent record in college. His intimacy with Mr. Dixwell's household was very close. His tutor's daughter, Fanny Dixwell, and he fell in love with each other and later they were married.

Fort Sumter was fired on and President Lincoln called for 75,000 volunteers. Young Holmes, 20 years old and shortly to be graduated from Harvard with the class of '61, walked down Beacon Hill with an open Hobbe's "Leviathan" in his hand and learned that he was commissioned in the Twentieth Massachusetts Volunteers.

The regiment, largely officered by young Harvard men and later to be known as the "Harvard Regiment," was ordered South and into action at Ball's Bluff. There were grave tactical errors and the Union troops were driven down the cliff on the Virginia shore and into the Potomac. Men trying to swim to safety were killed and wounded men were drowned.

Lieutenant Holmes, with a bullet through his breast, was placed in a boat with dying men and ferried through saving darkness to the Maryland shore.

His wound was serious, but the sufferer was young and strong. For convalescence he was returned to Boston. On his recovery he returned to the front.

At Antietam a bullet pierced his neck and again his condition was critical. Dr. Holmes, on learning the news, set out to search for his son. The search lasted many worried days and brought the father close to the lines at several points. He found his son already convalescent and brought him back to Boston, where he wrote his experiences under the title, "My Hunt for the Captain," an article that was enthusiastically received as bringing home to Boston a first-hand picture of the trials of war directly behind the lines.

Wounded a Third Time.

Back at the front, the young officer was again wounded. A bullet cut through tendons and lodged in his heel. This wound was long in healing and Holmes was retired to Boston with the brevet ranks of Colonel and Major.

The emergency of war over, his life was his own again. There was the question, then, of what to do with it. Writing appealed to him. He had been class poet and prize essayist in college. But he finally turned to law, although it was long before he was sure that he had taken the best course.

"It cost me some years of doubt and unhappiness," he said later, "before I could say to myself: 'The law is part of the universe—if the universe can be thought about, one part must reveal it as much as another to one who can see that part. It is only a question if you have the eyes.'"

Philosophy and William James helped him find his legal eyes while he studied in Harvard Law School and James, a year younger, was studying medicine. Through long nights they discussed their "dilapidated old friend the Kosmos." James later was to write in affectionate reminiscence of "your whitely lit-up room, drinking in your profound wisdom, your golden jibes, your costly imagery, listening to your shuddering laughter."

But while James went on, continuing in Germany his search for the meanings of the universe, Holmes decided that "maybe the universe is too great a swell to have a meaning," that his task was to "make his own universe livable," and he drove deep into the study of the law.

He took his LL. B. in 1866 and went to Europe to climb some mountains. Early in 1867 he was admitted to the bar and James noted that "Wendell is working too hard." The hard work brought results. In 1870 he was made editor of the American Law Review.

Two years later, on June 17, 1872, he married Fanny Bowditch Dixwell and in March of the next year became a member of the law firm of Shattuck, Holmes & Munroe, resigning his editorship but continuing to write articles for The Review. In that same year, 1873, his important edition of Kent's Commentaries appeared.

His papers, particularly one on English equity, which bristled with citations in Latin and German, showed that he was a master scholar where mastery meant labor and penetration. It was into these early papers that he put the fundamentals of an exposition of the law that he was later to deliver in Lowell Lectures at Harvard and to publish under the title, "The Common Law." In this book, to quote Benjamin N. Cardozo, he "packed a whole philosophy of legal method into a fragment of a paragraph."

The part to which Judge Cardozo referred reads:

"The life of the law has not been logic; it has been experience. The felt necessities of the time, the prevalent moral and political theories, intuitions of public policy avowed or unconscious, even with the prejudices which judges share with their fellow-men, have had a great deal more to do than the syllogism in determining the rules by which men should be governed. The law embodies the story of a nation's development through many centuries, and it cannot be dealt with as if it contained only the axioms and corollaries of a book of mathematics."

Judge Cardozo, commenting on this, wrote:

"The student of juristic method, bewildered in a maze of precedents, feels the thrill of a new apocalypse in the flash of this revealing insight. Here is the text to be unfolded. All that is to come will be development and commentary. Flashes there are like this in his earlier manner as in his latest, yet the flashes grow more frequent, the thunder peals more resonant, with the movement of the years."

Makes His Début as Judge.

Holmes was only 39 years old when Harvard called him back to teach in her Law School and 41 when he became an Associate Justice on the Massachusetts Supreme Court bench.

So in that great period when Joseph H. Choate could call a Federal income tax "sheer communism," the young Massachusetts justice could, with no bias, write dozens of dissenting opinions in which he expressed views that since have been molded into law.

He was Chief Justice on the Commonwealth bench when, in 1901, Theodore Roosevelt noted that Holmes's "labor decisions" were criticized by "some of the big railroad men and other members of large corporations." Oddly enough the successor of William McKinley thought that was "a strong point in Judge Holmes's favor."

In reference to this the President wrote to Henry Cabot Lodge:

"The ablest lawyers and greatest judges are men whose past has naturally brought them into close relationship with the wealthiest and most powerful clients and I am glad when I can find a judge who has been able to preserve his aloofness of mind so as to keep his broad humanity of feeling and his sympathy for the class from which he has not drawn clients."

In further expression of this approval he in 1902 appointed Judge Holmes to the Supreme Court of the United States, an appointment that was confirmed by the Senate immediately and unanimously.

In a dissenting opinion written early in his career on the Supreme bench Justice Holmes bluntly told his associates that the case in hand had been decided by the majority on an economic theory which a large part of the country did not entertain, that general principles do not decide concrete cases, that the outcome depends on a judgment or institution more subtle than any articulate major premise.

A great struggle between the forces of Theodore Roosevelt and the elder J. P. Morgan began on March 10, 1902, when the government filed suit in the United States Circuit Court for the district of Minnesota charging that the Great Northern Securities Company was "a virtual consolidation of two competing transcontinental lines" whereby not only would "monopoly of the interstate and foreign commerce, formerly carried on by them as competitors, be created," but, through use of the same machinery, "the entire railway systems of the country may be absorbed, merged, and consolidated."

In April, 1903, the lower court decided for the government and 8,000 pages of records and briefs went to the United States Supreme Court for final review. On March 14, 1904, the high court found for the government, with Justice Holmes writing in dissent.

He held that the Sherman act did not prescribe the rule of "free competition among those engaged in interstate commerce," as the majority held. It merely forbade "restraint of trade or commerce." He asserted that the phrases "restraint of competition" and "restraint of trade" did not have the same meaning; that "restraint of trade," which had "a definite and well-established significance in the common law, means and had always been understood to mean, a combination made by men engaged in a certain business for the purpose of keeping other men out of that business * * *."

The objection to trusts was not the union of former competitors, but the sinister power exercised, or supposed to be exercised, by the combination in keeping rivals out of the business, he said. It was the ferocious extreme of competition with others, not the cessation of competition among the partners, which was the evil feared.

"Much trouble," he continued, "is made by substituting other phrases, assumed to be equivalent, which are then argued from as if they were in the act. The court below argued as if maintaining competition were the express purpose of the act. The act says nothing about competition."

It was at this time that John Morley visited America and returned to England with the affirmation that in Justice Holmes America possessed the greatest judge of the English-speaking world. Time has reinforced the emphasis. In his years on the Supreme Court bench he had done more to mold the texture of the Constitution than any man since John Marshall revealed to the American people what their new Constitution might imply.

Matthew Arnold, in his essay on the study of poetry, says that the best way to separate the gold from the alloy in the coinage of the poets is by the test of a few lines carried in the thoughts.

Excerpts From Holmes's Writings.

From the opinions and other writings of Justice Holmes the following lines are some that might be used for this test:

"When men have realized that time has upset many fighting faiths, they may come to believe even more than they believe the very foundations of their own conduct that the ultimate good desired is better reached by free trade in ideas—that the best test of truth is the power of the thought to get itself accepted in the competition of the market, and that truth is the only ground upon which their wishes can be carried out. That, at any rate, is the theory of our Constitution. It is an experiment, as all life is an experiment."

"In the organic relations of modern society it may sometimes be hard to draw the line that is supposed to limit the authority of the Legislature to exercise or delegate the power of eminent domain. But to gather the streams from waste and to draw from them energy, labor without brains, and so to save mankind from toil that it can be spared, is to supply what, next to intellect, is the very foundation of all our achievements and all our welfare. If that purpose is not public, we should be at a loss to say what is."

"The Fourteenth Amendment does not enact Mr. Herbert Spencer's social statics."

"While the courts must exercise a judgment of their own, it by no means is true that every law is void which may seem to the judges who pass upon it, excessive, unsuited to its ostensible end, or based upon conceptions of morality with which they disagree. Considerable latitude must be allowed for difference of view as well as for possible peculiar conditions which this court can know but imperfectly, if at all. Otherwise a Constitution, instead of embodying only relatively fundamental rules of right, as generally understood by all English-speaking communities, would become the partisan of a particular set of ethical or economic opinions, which by no means are held semper ubique et ab omnibus."

His contribution to American life was not limited to the law. He lived as he advised others to live, in the "grand manner." He sought quality rather than quantity of experience and knowledge of his success in living helped others to find it, too.

On his ninetieth birthday he delivered a short radio speech in reply to tributes from Chief Justice Hughes and other leaders of the American bar.

From a Latin poet he quoted the words:

"Death plucks my ears and says, 'Live—I am coming.'"

And in one line he gave the core of a life philosophy:

"To live is to function; that is all there is to living."

Justice Holmes resigned on Jan. 12, 1932. "The time has now come and I bow to the inevitable," he wrote to the President. He left, amid national regret, almost thirty years after he had been appointed to the Supreme Court bench.

Soon after that, in a message to the Federal Bar Association, Justice Holmes wrote:

"I cannot say farewell to life and you in formal words. Life seems to me like a Japanese picture which our imagination does not allow to end with the margin. We aim at the infinite, and when our arrow falls to earth it is in flames."

"At times the ambitious ends of life have made it seem to me lonely, but it has not been. You have given me the companionship of dear friends who have helped to keep alive the fire in my heart. If I could think that I had sent a spark to those who come after, I should be ready to say good-bye."

Justice Holmes was an honorary member of the Honourable Society of Lincoln's Inn, London, to which also belonged such men as Oliver Cromwell, William Pitt, Benjamin Disraeli and William Ewart Gladstone.

Soon after retiring, his salary was cut in two by reason of the economy law. It was restored to $20,000 a year a few months later, however, by special action of the Senate.

"All the News That's Fit to Print"

The New York Times

LATE CITY EDITION

Weather: Showers likely today and tonight. Partly cloudy tomorrow. Temp. range: today 63-75; Tuesday 60-75. Full U.S. report on Page 94.

VOL.CXXI.No.41,738 NEW YORK, WEDNESDAY, MAY 3, 1972 15 CENTS

Story of Joe Gallo's Murder: 5 in Colombo Gang Implicated

Informant, in Fear, Goes to the F.B.I.

By NICHOLAS GAGE

An associate of the Mafia family of Joseph A. Colombo Sr. has turned himself in to the Federal Bureau of Investigation and said that he and four other men carried out the killing of Joseph Gallo on April 7, according to law-enforcement officials.

An investigation by The New York Times has established that the informant, who is now in police custody, is Joseph Luparelli, a close associate of Joseph Yacovelli, now the acting head of the Colombo family and the man who officials believe sanctioned the Gallo murder.

The New York Times

Joseph Yacovelli after he appeared in the Brooklyn Federal Court last year.

The officials said that over the last three weeks Luparelli had given Federal authorities and the New York police the following account of the events surrounding the shooting of Gallo, a Colombo rival, at Umberto's Clam House on Mulberry Street:

At about 4:30 A.M. on April 7, Luparelli happened to be sitting at the clam bar in Umberto's with a friend. Ten minutes later Joseph Gallo, who was celebrating his 43d birthday, entered with a jovial group—his bride of three weeks, her 10-year-old daughter, Gallo's sister, his bodyguard Peter Diapoulas, 42, and the latter's date.

When he saw Gallo, who for several months had been marked for execution by the Colombo family, Luparelli dropped his spoon and hurried out of the restaurant.

He walked two blocks to another restaurant nearby frequented by Colombo men. Luparelli asked for Yacovelli, act-

Suspects Abandon Hideout in Nyack

ing head of the family since Colombo was gravely wounded last year at a Columbus Circle rally of the Italian-American Civil Rights League. He was told that Yacovelli was not around.

Then Luparelli related what he had seen to Philip Gambino, a Colombo man, and Carmine Di Biase, a former member of the family of the late Vito Genovese who had reportedly shifted to the Colombo group.

The two of them telephoned Yacovelli and were told to arm themselves, according to Luparelli. Gambino and Di Biase left the restaurant briefly and returned about 5:15 with several guns.

Luparelli, two men believed to be brothers whom Luparelli has not as yet identified, Gambino and Di Biase then drove two cars down Mulberry Street and parked not far from Umberto's. One of the cars was to serve as a "crash" car to intercept any car that tried to thwart the getaway.

All but one of the five entered Umberto's through the back door. Luparelli says he stayed at the wheel of one of the cars.

As the four gunmen casually

Continued on Page 39, Column 1

Yoichi Okamoto/Rapho Guillumette

J. Edgar Hoover

J. Edgar Hoover, 77, Dies; Will Lie in State in Capitol

By FRED P. GRAHAM

Special to The New York Times

WASHINGTON, May 2—J. Edgar Hoover, who directed the Federal Bureau of Investigation for 48 years and built it into a dominant and controversial force in American law enforcement, died during the night from the effects of high blood pressure.

Mr. Hoover, who at 77 years of age still held the F.B.I. firmly within his control, died in his bedroom after working a full day in his office yesterday. He was found by his housekeeper at 8:30 this morning, slumped on the floor beside his bed.

His home is near Rock Creek Park in the northwest section of Washington.

Dr. James L. Luke, Washington's Medical Examiner, attributed the death to "hypertensive cardio-vascular disease." He said that Mr. Hoover had been suffering from a heart ailment for some time but gave no details.

He said that death could have been caused by heart failure associated with high blood pressure, but that no autopsy would be performed because the death was known to be due to natural causes.

Acting Attorney General Richard G. Kleindienst announced the death at 11 A.M., after F.B.I. offices around the world had been given the news and reports of it began to circulate here. Congress promptly voted its permission for his body to lie in state in the Capitol Rotunda—an honor accorded to only 21 persons before, of whom eight were Presidents or former Presidents.

Mr. Hoover's body will be taken to the Rotunda tomorrow morning and will lie in state until shortly before the funeral Thursday. Arrangements for the funeral were incomplete today, but it was learned that President Nixon would deliver the eulogy at 11 A.M. Thursday at the National Presbyterian

Continued on Page 53, Column 1

BASES NEAR HUE ATTACKED; SOUTH VIETNAMESE TROOPS FLEE QUANGTRI IN DISORDER

Retreat Leaves Small Unit Of Marines Facing Enemy

By SYDNEY H. SCHANBERG

Special to The New York Times

HUE, South Vietnam, May 2—Thousands of panicking South Vietnamese soldiers—most of whom did not appear to have made much contact with the advancing North Vietnamese—fled in confusion from Quangtri Province today, streaming south down Route 1 like a rabble out of control.

Commandeering civilian vehicles at rifle point, feigning nonexistent injuries, carrying away C rations but not their ammunition, and hurling rocks at Western news photographers taking pictures of their flight, the Government troops of the Third Infantry Division ran from the fighting in one of the biggest retreats of the war.

No one tried to stop them: their officers were running too.

The battlefront north of Hue was thus left solely to a brigade of a few thousand South Vietnamese marines.

The Third Division had fallen back before, at the beginning of the enemy offensive a month ago, but the commander, Brig. Gen. Vu Van Giai, had managed to scrape it together again and put it back on the line around Quangtri until yesterday.

But today, according to American advisers, virtually the entire division—about 10,000 infantrymen plus 1,000 rangers—was in rout, not even stopping at the checkpoints where military policemen were supposed to halt runaways and turn them around.

It was the force that was supposed to have defended the city of Quangtri, which was abandoned yesterday and which had been the northernmost town held by the Government.

There does not seem to be much now between the North Vietnamese and their next and more important objective,

Continued on Page 20, Column 4

NEW ASSAULT DUE

U.S. General Expects Enemy Step-Up in Next Few Days

By HENRY KAMM

Special to The New York Times

SAIGON, South Vietnam, Wednesday, May 3—With the city of Quangtri lost, two South Vietnamese fire bases on the approaches to the former imperial capital of Hue were reported under enemy attack yesterday.

Hue itself, 32 miles southeast of the fallen capital of Quangtri Province, was bracing for a North Vietnamese onslaught.

Serious attacks could be expected in the next few days, newsmen in Hue were told last night by Brig. Gen. Thomas W. Bowen, senior adviser to the regional commander. United States intelligence sources estimated that it would take the enemy forces six to eight days to prepare for the assault.

Artillery Batters Base

United States military sources said last night that Fire Base Nancy, the northernmost position held by the South Vietnamese and their last one in Quangtri Province, was battered by enemy artillery. [United Press International, quoting officers in the field, said enemy soldiers attacking with the support of tanks had seized part of the outpost.]

The base, which is 20 miles northwest of Hue, lies a little west of Route 1, South Vietnam's main north-south highway, and on the boundary between Quangtri and Thuathien Provinces. Hue is the capital of Thuathien Province.

Heightening the threat to Hue, North Vietnamese troops nearing the city from the southwest reportedly struck at Fire Base Birmingham, 13 miles from the city. The base was subjected to heavy artillery fire.

[Meanwhile, the United States aircraft carrier Midway arrived off Vietnam to help support South Vietnamese forces, The Associated Press reported. With her arrival, the United States had five carriers operating in the area for the first time in t'e war.]

In the center of South Vietnam, Landing Zone English, the last Government position in the northern part of the coastal province of Binhdinh, was reportedly abandoned last night after several days of heavy enemy pressure. American advisers were evacuated from the base Monday, indicating that the base had been effectively written off.

American military sources reported that South Vietnam's 40th Infantry Regiment pulled out of Landing Zone English, north of the fallen district town

Continued on Page 20, Column 1

Humphrey Indiana Victor; Jackson Quits Primaries

Wallace Defeat Narrow

By SETH S. KING

Special to The New York Times

INDIANAPOLIS, May 2—Senator Hubert H. Humphrey of Minnesota won a narrow victory tonight over Gov. George C. Wallace of Alabama in the Indiana Presidential primary.

The Senator's edge in the statewide total, plus a lead in five Congressional Districts, indicated that he would have 49 of Indiana's 76 first-ballot votes at the Democratic National Convention. Mr. Wallace was leading in six districts, which would give him 27 delegates.

With 88 per cent of 4,480 precincts reporting, the tally was:

Humphrey	286,850 (47%)
Wallace	255,593 (41%)
Muskie	74,307 (12%)

In the Alabama primary today, Governor Wallace appeared to be assured of winning the majority of the state's 29 delegates. In the District of Columbia, a favorite-son slate pledged to the Rev. Walter E. Fauntroy won at least 13 of the district's 15 Democratic delegate votes [Details, Page 32.]

In Indiana, the Alabama Governor's percentage of the total

Continued on Page 32, Column 1

Race in Ohio Is Close

By DOUGLAS E. KNEELAND

Special to The New York Times

COLUMBUS, Ohio, Wednesday, May 3—Senators Hubert H. Humphrey of Minnesota and George McGovern of South Dakota were locked in a tight race early today in the Ohio Presidential primary.

Senator Henry M. Jackson of Washington who was trailing badly, announced shortly before midnight that, while he would remain a candidate, he would campaign in no more primaries. [Details on Page 32.]

There was no Presidential preference vote as such, but 38 of the 153 Democratic delegates were selected at large, providing a measure of popular sentiment statewide. The voter turnout was large.

With 5,592 of the 12,648 precincts reporting, the tally on at-large slates was:

Hmphrey	188,467 (41%)
McGovern	174,589 (38%)
Muskie	45,796 (10%)
Jackson	37,789 (8%)
McCarthy	10,950 (2%)

Far behind were Senator Edmund S. Muskie of Maine, who had withdrawn from active campaigning, and former Senator Eugene J. McCarthy of

Continued on Page 32, Column 4

24 POLICE INDICTED IN A BRIBERY CASE

Accused of Taking $250,000 Annually in Brooklyn to Protect Gamblers

By MORRIS KAPLAN

Three police sergeants, 20 patrolmen and one patrolwoman were arrested and suspended from the Police Department yesterday after they were indicted and accused of taking a quarter of a million dollars annually in payoffs to protect gamblers linked to the Mafia.

The arrests under what was called the largest single indictment ever handed up here against members of the police force followed by a day the suicide of a police lieutenant who was also under investigation in the case. He shot himself in the head in a rented hotel room.

The lieutenant, Fletcher Hueston, had been second in command of the Public Morals Squad of the 13th Division in Brooklyn — the unit to which each of the individuals named in the indictment had been assigned during some portion of the last 18 months.

Deputy Police Commissioner William P. McCarthy indicated that additional investigations were being made in several of the 17 other public morals units. At least two policemen and possibly some gamblers were used as undercover agents in the investigation, police sources said.

The Knapp Commission's

Continued on Page 51, Column 1

Pessimism in Saigon

Army's Inability to Defend the South Puts Government in a Perilous Stage

By CRAIG R. WHITNEY

Special to The New York Times

SAIGON, South Vietnam, May 2—The loss of South Vietnam's northernmost province and the collapse of two of its combat divisions in the last week have brought the Government of President Nguyen Van Thieu to a perilous stage.

News Analysis

Both American and Vietnamese officials here and elsewhere are deeply pessimistic — for the first time in years — about the country's prospects of pulling through.

The growing consensus among Americans here is that the South Vietnamese armed forces, in their country's hour of greatest danger, have unexpectedly proved unequal to the task of defending it. The principal reason is that the commanders, never before tested so rigorously, are not spurring the troops to resist the three-front North Vietnamese onslaught with the vigor and determination that would be required to repel rather than stalemate it.

Vietnamese observers in Hue described the scene in the former imperial capital today as "an agony," with the streets full of soldiers running aimlessly about.

The road from Hue south to Danang, Vietnam's second largest city, is jammed with refugees and with soldiers who appear to be deserters, trying to make their way to safety.

A senior American official in Danang said tonight that the

Continued on Page 21, Column 3

Washington Aides, Discouraged, Hint At Wider Bombings

By WILLIAM BEECHER

Special to The New York Times

WASHINGTON, May 2 — Administration officials tried publicly today to put a brave face on their reaction to news of the battle in South Vietnam, but throughout the Government there were widespread signs of growing pessimism.

Well-placed sources in the Nixon Administration hinted that unless the promise of positive results emerged later this week from public or secret peace talks, the United States would soon resume heavy bombing in the Hanoi and Haiphong areas of North Vietnam.

As officials at the White House, the State Department and the Defense Department studied reports of enemy advances in the south, there were these developments:

¶Pentagon officials said American field commanders were being given increasing latitude in conducting air strikes in the southern part of North Vietnam.

¶Diplomatic and Government

Continued on Page 20, Column 7

Canada Announces Plans To Curb Foreign Business

By JAY WALZ

Special to The New York Times

OTTAWA, May 2—Canada announced her long-awaited plans today to tighten controls over take-overs of Canadian businesses by foreign interests.

Under proposed legislation, which is expected to pass, the Government would screen take-overs involving Canadian businesses worth $250,000 or more and whose annual revenues exceeded $3-million.

A prospective buyer would be judged on the basis of

Text of minister's statement is printed on Page 74.

Cabinet-level findings that his purchase "will result in significant benefit to Canada."

"Our policy," Revenue Minister Herbert E. Gray told the House of Commons "is designed to insure that this country continues to develop as rapidly as possible in a way which is consistent with Canadian needs and aspirations and which safeguards our vital interests."

Mr. Gray's statement summarized the Government's decision to hold a closer rein on the country's industrial development. Over the last 40 years industry has fallen increasingly into the hands of foreign investors and managers, mostly Americans.

Attending legislation was immediately criticized by the Government's Political Opponents. They maintained that a plan to oversee foreign take-overs was not enough to meet the challenge to Canada's control of her economy.

Jean-Luc Pepin, Industry Minister who would administer the program under the proposed law, said at a news conference that the plan should be considered in the context of existing laws—on taxation, investment and Canadian-content. The proposal, he suggest-

Continued on Page 74, Column 2

NEWS INDEX

Bill to Stop Forest Hills Project Gets Final Passage in Assembly

By ALFONSO A. NARVAEZ

Special to The New York Times

ALBANY, May 2—The Assembly gave final passage today to a bill designed to kill the controversial Forest Hills low-income housing project.

The bill, passed by a vote of 101 to 35, provides that where projects planned by a housing authority have not progressed beyond the foundation stage within five years of the approval by the local legislative body they would have to be resubmitted for review and further determination as to their approval or disapproval.

The bill takes effect immediately. However, it provides that it is deemed to have been in effect since Sept. 1, 1971. The Forest Hills project was approved in the latter part of 1966, putting it within the five-year provision of the bill.

If the Forest Hills issue comes before the Board of Estimate the board is expected to vote it down and kill the plan for three 24-story buildings on the site in the middle-class community.

In other action, the Senate voted to amend the State Constitution to permit the legalization of new forms of gambling that are now illicit. The measure now goes to the Assembly, where the sponsors are hopeful of passage.

In another action, the Assembly Codes Committee released a bill to repeal the state's liberalized abortion law, even though Governor Rockefeller has said he would veto it. (Details on Page 18.)

The housing bill now goes to the Governor, who has not indicated what action he will take. However, during a news conference in March he noted that he was against scatter-site housing, which places low-income projects in the heart of middle income areas. The Governor said that he favored rehabilitating deteriorating communities to provide areas where integrated living could be accomplished.

"I think myself for the long pull that you would avoid exactly the kind of conflict which exists now," the Governor said at that time. "The community is faced with a very unfortunate, intense situation and I can't believe this is going

Continued on Page 17, Column 1

5 Dead, 77 Missing In Idaho Mine Fire

By The Associated Press

KELLOGG, Idaho, May 2 — Fire swept through the nation's deepest and richest silver mine today, killing at least five miners and leaving 77 unaccounted for in the rugged hills of northern Idaho.

Wallace Wilson, vice president of the Sunshine Silver Mine, said only five bodies had been counted and that company officials did not know the condition of the 77 missing men. He said 108 men were brought from the mine after the fire started.

Mr. Wilson held out hope for the missing miners. "There is fresh air as well as smoke-filled areas," he said.

Officials said an electrical failure may have been the cause of the fire.

Miners from other mines in

Continued on Page 22, Column 1

Associated Press

FORCED OUT OF QUANGTRI: South Vietnamese soldiers nearing friendly lines near Hue, to the south, yesterday

J. Edgar Hoover Is Dead at 77; to Lie in State in Capitol

Continued From Page 1, Col. 5

Church. As the only director that the F.B.I. ever had, the strong-willed and demanding bachelor molded the bureau in his own image—efficient, incorruptible and rigid.

He presided over it from the day—May 14, 1924—when he took over a small, politics-ridden bureau, through the eras of its most famous exploits. These included the solution of the Lindbergh kidnapping, the battles against gangsters like John Dillinger in the nineteen-thirties when "G-man" became a byword, the capture of spies in World War II and the campaign against Communists in the postwar period.

Yet toward the end of his reign, he became the target of critics from both the left and the right, from those who thought he rode roughshod over civil liberties and those who thought he was slighting the old F.B.I. role of spy-catching.

His death is expected to touch off a major political debate about the proper purposes and functioning of the agency, which has been accused by critics on the political left in recent years of devoting too much effort to pursuing radicals and alleged subversives, and too little to combating organized crime and white-collar offenders.

For this reason, there was speculation today that President Nixon might not name a successor until after the November elections or at least not until the current Senate struggle over Mr. Kleindienst's nomination has ended.

It was learned that an acting director would be named tomorrow, suggesting that no nomination would be sent to Capitol Hill for some time. Clyde A. Tolson, the 71-year-old associate director, who was said by Justice Department spokesmen to have assumed command of the F.B.I. today as its second-ranking official, is understood not to be in line to become acting director.

In 1968, Congress made the directorship of the F.B.I. subject to Senate confirmation. This will offer the Senate Judiciary Committee an opportunity when it holds hearings on the nominee, to delve into such festering issues as the agency's secret dossiers on individuals, its surveillance of the radical left and its new computerized criminal record data bank.

At least a score of persons were mentioned today as possible successors to Mr. Hoover. Most of then were veteran law enforcement figures, such as Evelle J. Younger, Attorney General of California, Peter J Pitchess, sheriff of Los Angeles County; Jerry Wilson, chief of police of the Distrct of Columbia, and Cartha Deloach, former Assistant Director of the F.B.I.

Supreme Court Justice Bryon R. White's name has been suggested frequently, but he has given no indication that he would accept the position.

The mandatory retirement age for F.B.I. directors is 70, but President Johnson waived it and so did President Nixon. Mr. Hoover had frequently given the impression that he hoped to remain on the job as long as he lived, or at least until the huge new F.B.I. building across Pennsylvania Avenue from the Justice Department was completed.

It is scheduled to be finished in three years.

In recent years, Mr. Hoover had come under periodic pressure to resign, usually after some widely publicized public quarrel with figures on the political left. He exchanged insults with the late Rev. Dr. Martin Luther King Jr., accused the late Senator Robert F. Kennedy of ultimate responsibility for the F.B.I.'s wiretapping when he was Attorney General and called former Attorney General Ramsey Clark "a jellyfish."

His most recent controversy grew out of his charge that the Rev. Philip F. Berrigan and other antiwar activists were plotting to kidnap Henry A. Kissinger, the President's top foreign policy adviser.

When a jury in Harrisburg, Pa., found no conspiracy, there were renewed demands that Mr. Hoover retire. But he weathered the criticism. When he testified recently before the House Appropriations subcommittee, he was showered with the usual compliments, and in the ensuing exchange he assured the Congressmen that the F.B.I. contained no activists, "gay or otherwise."

Mr. Hoover appeared also to be in the good graces of the Nixon Administration, although there was talk that he would be urged to step down if Mr. Nixon won re-election.

President Nixon went to the White House press room this morning to comment on Mr. Hoover's "unparalleled devotion and ability and dedication." Major figures across the political spectrum joined in a virtually unanimous chorus of admiration.

Representative Hale Boggs, Democrat of Louisiana, who last year accused the F.B.I. of having tapped his telephones, made a speech on the floor today declaring that he had never criticized Mr. Hoover personally. "I said then, and I say now, that no man has served his country with greater love and dedication," he said.

Dr. Benjamin Spock, the antiwar activist who is the people's party's candidate for President, called Mr. Hoover's death "a great relief, especially if his replacement is a man who better understands democratic institutions and the American process."

Gus Hall, general secretary of the Communist party, U.S.A., called Mr. Hoover "a servant of racism, reaction and repression" and a "political pervert whose mashochistic passion drove him to savage assaults upon the principles of the Bill of Rights."

He charged that the F.B.I. under Mr. Hoover had hunted down Communists but failed to bring to justice "a single lyncher of 5,000 black Americans."

J. Edgar Hoover Made the F.B.I. Formidable With Politics, Publicity and Results

By CHRISTOPHER LYDON
Special to The New York Times

WASHINGTON, May 2 — When J. Edgar Hoover ambled through the Mayflower Hotel after one of his ritual fruit-salad-and-coffee lunches late last year, he passed almost unnoticed.

The once ruddy face was puffy and pale. The brushed-back, gray-brown hair was straight and thin—not the wiry dark curls of a few years ago. He walked stiffly, although his figure was trim and erect. Behind his glasses, his dark brown eyes looked fixed, and he seemed to be daydreaming.

At the age of 77, the legendary G-man—in his 48th year as director of the Federal Bureau of Investigation—the most enduring and perhaps, if there is such a thing as a cumulative total, the most powerful official in the long span of the American Government—looked deceptively like any other old gentleman in the hotel lobby.

In one of his rare reflections on mortality a few years ago, Mr. Hoover told a reporter, "The greatest enemy is time." Time's advances against this seemingly indestructible official had become obvious. But then, Mr. Hoover was always more human than he or the myth admitted.

Mr. Hoover's power was a compound of performance and politics, publicity and personality. At the base of it all, however, was an extraordinary record of innovation and modernization in law enforcement — most of it in the first decade or so of his tenure.

The centralized fingerprint file (the print total passed the 200-million mark this year) at the Identification Division (1925) and the crime laboratory (1932) are landmarks in the gradual application of science to police work. The National Police Academy (1935) has trained the leadership élite of local forces throughout the country. Mr. Hoover's recruitment of lawyers and accountants, although they now make up only 32 per cent of the special agent corps, set a world standard of professionalism.

The National Crime Information Center enables 4,000 local law enforcement agencies to enter records and get questions answered on a network of 35 computer systems, with its headquarters at the F.B.I. office here.

From the start, Mr. Hoover got results. His bureau rounded up the gangsters in the nineteen-thirties. It made the once epidemic crime of kidnapping a rarity ("virtually extinct," as the director's friends like to say). It arrested German saboteurs within days after their submarines landed them on the Atlantic Coast. And, in one of its most sensational coups, the F.B.I. seized the slayers of Mrs. Viola Gregg Liuzzo only hours after the civil rights worker's shotgun death in Alabama in 1965.

The F.B.I. does not catch everybody, and it is sometimes many months before any of its "most wanted" suspects are arrested. But Mr. Hoover executed enough seemingly miraculous swoops to make any specific criticism perilous.

Mr. Hoover always understood the subtle currents of power among officials in Washington better than anyone know him. Not a New Dealer at heart, he had nonetheless dazzled President Franklin D. Roosevelt with his celebrated success against kidnappers.

J. Edgar Hoover in his office, 1934.

The more awesome Mr. Hoover's power grew, the more plainly he would state, for the record, that there was nothing "political" about it, that the F.B.I. was simply a "fact-finding agency" that "never makes recommendations or draws conclusions." The most pointed such declaration, coming in the furor about Harry Dexter White in 1953, was, paradoxically, one of Mr. Hoover's most political acts.

In a speech in Chicago, Herbert Brownell, President Eisenhower's Attorney General, said that Mr. White, who had served as Assistant Secretary of the Treasury under Roosevelt, was named in 1946 as the United States executive director of the International Monetary Fund even though President Truman had been told that Mr. White was a Soviet spy. Mr. Truman, in retirement, replied that the F.B.I. had contributed to the judgment that it would be safer to keep Mr. White in office, under observation, than to dismiss him.

Rushing before Senate investigators, Mr. Hoover did not question the "conclusion" that Mr. White was a spy — although the F.B.I.'s evidence had not been enough to persuade a grand jury to indict Mr. White before he died in 1948. As for Mr. White's promotion to the International Monetary Fund, Mr. Hoover stated emphatically that, while he knew of Mr. Truman's reasoning, he had not been in on the decision nor had he approved it.

At a time when the Republican party chairman was promising to make Communism in government the central issue of the 1954 Congressional campaign, Mr. Hoover's eager testimony was taken by some to be a boldly partisan move.

House Speaker Sam Rayburn was one of many Democrats who never forgave Mr. Hoover and encouraged speculation that a Democratic President would find a new F.B.I. director.

But Mr. Hoover's reappointment was virtually the first decision John F. Kennedy announced on the day after his election to the Presidency in 1960.

Despite its acrimonious endings the Hoover-Kennedy relationship started out cordially, based apparently on Mr. Hoover's long acquaintance with the President's father, the late Joseph P. Kennedy.

Robert Kennedy had urged the President-elect to retain Mr. Hoover; and when John Kennedy weighed assignments for his brother, Mr. Hoover urged him to follow his instinct and make Robert the Attorney General.

He Got Results

Roosevelt liked him; he slapped the F.B.I. director's back and laughed when Mr. Hoover confessed that an agent had been caught in the act of illegal wiretapping, and he was amused at the bureau's temerity in putting a spy on Harry Hopkins, Roosevelt's counselor, in London. Roosevelt's assignment of counter-espionage duties to the F.B.I. as war loomed in 1936 expanded the bureau's size and heightened Mr. Hoover's prestige.

But, when the Republicans won the White House again in 1952, Mr. Hoover's loyalty swung immediately to the new team.

(continued)

Later Robert Kennedy and Mr. Hoover fought a long tug-of-war over the assignment of agents to civil rights and organized crime cases. Mr. Hoover was not used to having an immediate boss who could block his access to the White House. He was annoyed when the Attorney General installed a "hot line" between their Justice Department offices, and was even more annoyed when Robert Kennedy had the F.B.I. phone moved from the desk of Helen Gandy, Mr. Hoover's long-time secretary, to the director's desk.

Robert Kennedy never forgave Mr. Hoover for the cold telephone call that brought the first word of his brother's assassination. Mr. Hoover's voice, Robert Kennedy told William Manchester, the author, was "not quite as excited as if he were reporting the fact that he had found a Communist on the faculty of Howard University."

Later, according to William W. Turner, a former agent who wrote an unflattering book on "Hoover's F.B.I.," Robert Kennedy called back on the hot line. "Hoover was in his office with several aides," Mr. Turner wrote, "when it rang . . . and rang . . . and rang. When it stopped ringing, the director snapped to an aide, 'Now get that phone back on Miss Gandy's desk.' "

Although Robert Kennedy remained Attorney General until the summer of 1964, he and Mr. Hoover never spoke again after the President's assassination.

Until Representative Hale Boggs of Louisiana, the House majority leader, criticized Mr. Hoover in the House last spring as a "feudal baron" and a wiretapper, the F.B.I. director had been sacrosanct in Congress' deference. The case of former Senator Edward V. Long, a Missouri Democrat who denounced government wiretapping and was quickly undone by Life magazine's disclosure, leaked from the F.B.I., that he was splitting legal fees with a teamster lawyer in St. Louis, is often cited as an example of the director's tactics.

Mr. Hoover insisted that he did not tap the phones or "bug" the offices of Congressmen, and Mr. Boggs failed notably to prove the contrary. But Mr. Hoover always had other ways to keep critics in line anyway.

The late Senator Kenneth D. McKellar, a Tennessee Democrat and chairman of the Senate Appropriations Committee, harassed Mr. Hoover from time to time in the nineteen-thirties, and in the spring of 1936 drew the blushing testimony that the director of the F.B.I. had never made an arrest.

Less than a month later, as if by magic, Mr. Hoover led a raid in New Orleans that captured Alvin (Kreepy) Karpis, a star of the Ma Barker mob.

By his own account, Mr. Hoover rushed up to the unsuspecting Karpis as he sat in a car, threatened him with a gun, then snapped out the order to other agents: "Put the cuffs on him, boys." In his recently published memoirs, Karpis contends that Mr. Hoover "hid until I was safely covered by many guns. He waited until he was told the coast was clear. Then he came out to reap the glory."

Karpis's account is obviously suspect, and about 35 years too late to undo Senator McKellar's embarrassment. When Senator McKellar tried to cut $225,000 out of the F.B.I. budget that year, Senator Arthur H. Vandenberg of Michigan denounced him, according to one report of the Senate debate, "as a miser whose parsimony would cause the threat of kidnapping to hang once more over every cradle in America." Mr. Hoover's full budget request was then passed by a resounding voice vote. Since that time, the Senate has never questioned the F.B.I. budget as reported by the House.

The Kennedy years.

And in the House, the veteran chairman of the Appropriations subcommittee that theoretically reviews the bureau's spending, Representative John J. Rooney, Democrat of Brooklyn, said that "I have never cut [Mr. Hoover's] budget and I never expect to."

As some of the men closest to him volunteer, Mr. Hoover's primary genius might well have been publicity. He had some famous fights with other police agencies — notably after the capture of Bruno Hauptmann, the Lindbergh kidnapper, in 1933 — to secure public credit for his bureau, but Mr. Hoover was no ordinary headline grabber.

The real foundations of his legend are built on more solid stuff than press relations; certainly his image was never dependent on the goodwill of newspapermen, to whom Mr. Hoover was normally inaccessible.

Mr. Hoover never held a news conference. The closest thing to a mouthpiece in the press was not a political pundit or a crime reporter but the late Walter Winchell, the Broadway gossip columnist, who traveled with an F.B.I. escotr and carried an item about "G-man Hoover" almost every day.

The making of the Hoover folk hero, in which Mr. Winchell played a large part, was undertaken purposefully in the early thirties — long atfer the director's quiet administrative mastery had established him securely.

Speakeasies were the fashion. Gangsterism ravaged the land, capturing headlines and, in a sense, the public fancy. For Mr. Hoover, the last straw was the Kansas City massacre of June 17, 1933, in which Charles (Pretty Boy) Floyd and his gang killed five men, including an F.B.I. agent and three local policemen. "If there is going to be publicity," the director raged, "let it be on the side of law and order."

Looking about for a symbol, Mr. Hoover found himself, and proceeded to orchestrate a dazzling range of movies, books, radio dramas and comic strips.

Mr. Hoover understood pop culture and its evolution. He promoted "junior G-man" clubs for boys, and sold two and a half million copies of "Masters of Deceit," a book on Communism. His "ten most wanted" list made a lot of seedy drifters into headline material. In the age of television, he shrewdly reserved the right to select the actor (Efrem Zimbalist Jr.) who would represent the F.B.I. in millions of living room in a popular television series.

The late Senator George Norris of Nebraska called Mr. Hoover "the greatest hound for publicity on the American continent." Even Chief Justice Harlan Fiske Stone, who had appointed the F.B.I. director in 1924, observed critically that "one of the great secrets of Scotland Yard has been that its movements are never advertised."

Popularity Was High

But Mr. Hoover, once committed to a public fight on crime, played the role with all his fierce energy. He unquestionably made a brilliant success of it. Even after political pot-shots at the director became fashionable in recent years, a Gallup Pol for Newsweek magazine last spring showed that 80 per cent of those who had any opinion about Mr. Hoover rated his performance "good" or "excellent."

Any general accounting of the F.B.I. director's power must also take note of the fact that his personality, as well as his office, has always inspired fear. Francis Biddle, President Roosevelt's Attorney General in the early nineteen-forties, sensed that, behind Mr. Hoover's "absolute self-control" was "a temper that might show great violence if he did not hold it on leash, subject to the domination of a will that is the master of his temperament."

There were hints of that temper in his passionate criticisms — favorite phrases such as "mental halitosis," and the "jellyfish" tag he put on former Attorney General Ramsey Clark. And Mr. Hoover had a hair-trigger sensitivity to criticism.

When the Warren commission was investigating President Kennedy's assassination and said that the F.B.I. had not shared its intelligence fully with the Secret Service, Mr. Hoover lashed out at what he called "a classic example of Monday morning quarterbacking," a charge that gravely displeased President Johnson.

And when the Rev. Dr. Martin Luther King Jr. said that Southern blacks could not turn to their local F.B.I. offices with any assurance of sympathy or zeal for civil rights, Mr. Hoover called Dr. King "the most notorious liar in the country." Later, Mr. Hoover had his staff invite newsmen to hear the taped record of F.B.I. bugs in Dr. King's hotel rooms as evidence that "moral degenerates," as Mr. Hoover put it, were leading the civil rights movement. This was a rare extension of Mr. Hoover's lifelong practice of entertaining Attorneys General and Presidents with spicy details about the secret lives of famous people.

Critics within the F.B.I. were crushed summarily, and men who were thought to have been good friends of the director reveal deeper levels of hostility in casual conversations. "I'm afraid of him," said a former aide who would seem to have been secure in a new and completely different pubilc career. "I can't imagine what he'd do to me, but I'd rather not mess with him."

John Edgar Hoover was born in Washington on New Year's Day in 1895, the youngest of three children of Dickerson N. Hoover, an easy-going Federal official, and the former Annie M. Scheitlin, the granddaughter of Switzerland's first Consul General in America.

The Hoovers' stucco house on Seward Square has been torn down, but Mr. Hoover's birthplace is memorialized in a stained glass window of the Presbyterian church that stands on the site of the house.

Mrs. Hoover, who has been described as "old-world strict," instilled in her son an intense discipline and stern sensitivity to moral issues. By all accounts, she was the dominant influence on his character.

As a boy, he was known as "Speed"—a reference, apparently, to his agile mind, rattling speech and efficiency as a grocery delivery boy in the Capitol Hill section of Washington.

Admirers have compared his physique to Babe Ruth's—heavy torso, spindly legs — and indeed, his flattened nose was the result of a hard-hit baseball. But Mr. Hoover was never an athlete. Remembering a day in 1909 when the football coach at Central High School rejected the puny volunteer brought twinges ever after.

In his disappointment, young Hoover turned all the more intensely to the school's military drill team, of which he became captain, and to public speaking. According to one biographer, he never had a regular girl friend in high school; friends teased him, wrote Mildred H. Comfort, "and accused him of being in love with Company A," an institutional attachment foreshadowing his marriage to the F.B.I.

J. Edgar Hoover at age 4.

As a debater, young Hoover argued "The Fallacies of Women Suffrage" with gusto and competitive success. He was valedictorian of his class and was described in the school yearbook as "a gentleman of dauntless courage and stainless honor." In his high school days, he also was a choir boy and Sunday school instructor.

Lessons on Indexing

Although the University of Virginia offered him a liberal arts scholarship, Mr. Hoover feared that his living expenses would be a burden on his father. Instead, he took a $30-a-month clerk's job at the Library of Congress (he would apply indexing lessons to law enforcement later), and enrolled at George Washington University, where he was able to win his law degree in three years.

With a master's degree in 1917, Mr. Hoover passed the bar and moved into a $1,200-a-year job at the Department of Justice — his only employer over a stretch that exceeded 55 years.

From the start, according to Jack Alexander's 1937 profile of Mr. Hoover in The New Yorker, he stood out from the other young lawyers around him.

"He dressed better than most, a bit on the dandyish side," Mr. Alexander wrote. "He had an exceptional capacity for detail work, and he handled small chores with enthusiasm and thoroughness. He constantly sought new responsibilities to shoulder, and welcomed chances to work overtime. When he was in conference with an official of his department, his manner was that of a young man who confidently expected to rise."

Mr. Hoover's first assignment in "counter-radical activities" left a profound mark. This was at the end of President Wilson's second term, the era of the "Red raids" under Attorney General A. Mitchell Palmer. Evidently caught up in the official agitation about bombs and Bolshevism, Mr. Hoover took charge of assembling a card file on 450,000 "radicals," and built his first informer nework — a controversial tool of police work that he used with dramatic results later against the Communist party and the Ku Klux Klan.

Many years later, Mr. Hoover said he had always "deplored" the hysterical dragnet arrests of thousands of innocent aliens in 1919 and 1920, but the record is also clear that, as the head of the new General Intelligence Division at the Justice Department, he was responsible for planning the raids, if not their execution.

A still darker era followed under President Harding. Within the Justice Department, according to Alpheus T. Mason, the historian, the Bureau of Investigation "had become a private secret service for corrupt forces within the Government." Mr. Hoover nearly quit in disgust.

When Harlan Fiske Stone became Attorney General under President Coolidge in 1924, he determined to rebuild the bureau after the image of Scotland Yard and sought, as his director, a man experienced in police work but free of the "more usual police tradition that it takes a crook to catch a crook and that lawlessness and brutality are more to be relied upon than skill and special training."

Secretary of Commerce Herbert Hoover, an untainted holdover from the Harding Administration, recommended J. Edgar (no relation) as "a lawyer of uncommon ability and character."

Attorney General Stone, who held the appointive power, offered him the job. But Mr. Hoover, who was then only 29 years old, did not leap at what

(continued)

was unmistakably the chance of a lifetime.

With confidence and cunning that were very much in character, he said he would accept the assignment only if appointments to the bureau were divorced entirely from outside politics and if he would have sole control over merit promotions. Mr. Stone replied that he would not allow Mr. Hoover to take the job under any other conditions. And thus in 1924 the modern bureau — renamed the Federal Bureau of Investigation in 1935—was born.

Organizing Principle

From the start, Mr. Hoover's personal grip on all the important strings was the organizing principle at the bureau. It had everything to do with discipline and morale; Mr. Hoover made Siberia assignments and the compassionate transfers. It had a lot to do with the agency's efficiency and its incomparable record of probity. Under the Hoover inspection system, there were no secrets and no independent power centers in the F.B.I. In recent years, the system also seemed to have inhibited the bureau from taking worthwhile risks. "The first rule," according to one former agent, was: "Do not embarrass the director."

The insulation from outside politics meant free play for Hoover politics. The 15,000 F.B.I. employes had neither the Civil Service nor a union to inhibit the director's whims. He shaped the bureau in his own Victorian image, and changed in the process himself.

Personal affairs were strictly regulated at the bureau. Women were not allowed to smoke on the job. No one got a coffee break. A clerk was once dismissed for playing with a yo-yo in the halls. In a case that went to court in 1967, a 26-year-old clerk was dismissed for keeping a girl friend in his apartment overnight. Agents have been reprimanded for reading Playboy magazine and transferred for being overweight.

Mr. Hoover wore custom-made, Brooks Brothers shirts and suits, and he ordered his agents to dress carefully, like young businessmen. The unofficial uniform for an agent includes a white shirt, dark suit, snap-brim hat and a handkerchief in the jacket pocket.

One-man rule also bred sycophancy. Flattery worked

Associated Press

Mr. Hoover aiming a submachine gun in an F.B.I. target range in 1935. He built skills not only of his men but also of many other officers of the law.

wonders around Mr. Hoover, according to an inside student of the director's office. "Let's say you're an agent," he said. "Go in there and tell him he looks better than ever, that you are inspired by his leadership, that he's saving America and you hope he lives forever. As soon as you leave there will be a memo from the director saying, 'This man has executive ability.' A lot of agents have caught on."

Agents admittedly quaked at the thought of the director's disapproval, expressed typically in the bright blue ink of Mr. Hoover's stub pen in the margins of their memorandums. His language was vehement ("This is asinine!"); the filling of all four borders around a typewritten sheet was known as a "four-bagger." Once, it is said, when an assistant's memorandum so filled the page that Mr. Hoover barely had room for a comment, he wrote, "Watch the borders," and his puzzled but obedient aides dispatched agents to patrol the Canadian and Mexican borders for a week.

Friends and detractors all agree that the system has mirrored and fed a colossal ego. In the office, for instance, Mr. Hoover never circulated; people came to him. He sat amid flags behind a raised, polished mahogany desk at the end of a 35-foot office. Visitors, if they sat, sank into deep leather chairs and inevitably looked up to the throned director.

A day in the life of J. Edgar Hoover testified to his unflagging energy and to the power of habit. The few changes in his rountine were forced on him: His friend Clyde Tolson, the F.B.I.'s associate director, was not well enough to walk the last few blocks to the office in recent days, so their morning strolls along Constitution Avenue were abandoned. The old Harvey's Restaurant was razed, so Mr. Hoover and Mr. Tolson had lunch instead at the Mayflower Hotel next door on Connecticut Avenue.

Old patterns persisted. The chauffeur picked up Mr. Hoover and then Mr. Tolson, about 9 o'clock every morning, and delivered them to the offive about 9:30.

At the end the director was still the complete master of the bureau's huge flow of paper work. He did little sleuthing himself, but he kept abreast of the F.B.I.'s major cases. Certain categories of business were handled by Mr. Hoover alone, including high-level personnel decisions, liaison in other than routine matters with Congress, the Attorney General and the White House, and anything that brought unfavorable publicity on the bureau.

He left for lunch at 11:30 A.M., returned by 12:45 P.M. and usually took work home with him when he left for the day at 4:30.

There were things he did not do anymore. He outlived the Stork Club in New York where he long enjoyed café society's attention and the friendship of Sherman Billingsley, the owner. He no longer tended the azaleas around his house. He had to give up his favorite angel food cake and chocolate cream pie to keep his weight down. Once an avid walker, he said that "conditions in this city," presumably a reference to the crime rate, kept him out of Rock Creek Park, formerly a favorite stamping ground near his house.

Some Continuities

Still, the continuities in his life were as noticeable as the changes: the Jack Daniel's whiskey before dinner; the Miami vacation during the last two weeks of December and the July break and physical check-up in La Jolla, Calif., the passion for horse racing; and above all, the friendship with Mr. Tolson, a fellow bachelor with whom Mr. Hoover had lunch and dinner six days a week since the late nineteen-twenties.

Mr. Tolson, who always stayed a respectful step behind Mr. Hoover in their famous walks together, lagged severely after two strokes and open-heart surgery. But the friendship was as fast as ever, and, through a special personnel device that Mr. Hoover engineered to get around Mr. Tolson's physical disability, Mr. Tolson remains the bureau's second-ranking officer.

Together they frequented the racetracks around Washington, as well as Gulfstream in Miami and Delmar in La Jolla. Mr. Hoover, who applied the same analytical imagination to the racing charts that he once used on kidnapping rings, was still bothered by touts who recognized him and wanted to tip him on a sure thing. But he bet only $2 on each race and would leave in disgust if his losses went over $10. Friends say it was Mr. Tolson, not Mr. Hoover, who sent junior F.B.I. agents around to the $50 and $100 windows with heavy side bets.

Mr. Hoover's humor usually ran to heavy-handed practical jokes. The late Julius Lulley, the restaurateur who always kept a special table set for Mr. Hoover and Mr. Tolson at Harvey's, once found his Maryland farm dotted with F.B.I. "wanted" posters bearing Mr. Lulley's picture.

Years ago, when Guy Hottel, a Hoover bodyguard and friend, got married, the F.B.I. director found out where Mr. Hottel was going on his honeymoon and conspired with the Virginia State Police to have the newlyweds picked up and held overnight on a fake charge.

Mr. Hoover was not always quick to appreciate other people's jokes. In his saloon-going days in New York, it was said that he avoided Toots Shor's restaurant because of the insults that were Mr. Shor's trademark.

However, there always was a droll undercurrent in many of Mr. Hoover's utterances—as in the W. C. Fields-like defense of racetracks as an outlet for people's emotions, "which, if they weren't at the track, they might use for less laudable escapades."

And Mr. Hoover recently took to public kidding about himself—the clearest sign of his rejuvenation under President Nixon and Attorney General John N. Mitchell.

Why Did He Stay?

At a party for Mr. Mitchell's wife Martha last summer, Mr. Hoover brought the house down with an impromptu speech. Referring to a recent Life magazine cover that featured a marble bust of his bulldog face and the headline, "Emperor of the F.B.I.," Mr. Hoover apologized to those who did not recognize him in a tuxedo.

"We emperors have our problems," he said. "My Roman toga was not returned from the cleaners."

Perhaps the most widely asked question about Mr. Hoover recently was why he stayed on the job, but that, too, had been around a while. Even in the nineteen-thirties his long tenure was considered remarkable. During the forties, a former aide recalls, "every year he'd ask for a computation of his retirement and there'd be a rumor that the old boy was stepping down." The inside gossip in the fifties was that Mr. Hoover had approved plans for the construction of his retirement villa at La Jolla.

After John Kennedy reappointed Mr. Hoover in 1960, it was thought he would bow out around the mandatory retirement age of 70, which would have come on New Year's Day, 1965. But as early as May, 1964, President Johnson waived the retirement law. The next obvious milestone was his 75th birthday in January, 1971, but that passed without incident, like all the rest.

Some people say that Mr. Hoover wanted to see the completion of the new $102-million F.B.I. building on Pennsylvania Avenue — sometime in 1974. Mr. Hoover says he will stay on the job as long as his physical condition permitted. But why? "I've always been against retiring a man by age," he said. "The longer a man is with us, the more valuable he becomes."

The men around Mr. Hoover pointed to his egotism—a sense of his own indispensability—and to the lack of family and interests that consoled other men in retirement. "For him the bureau is everything," said a friend.

Nixon Leads Officials in Paying Tribute to the Director of F.B.I.

Following are tributes to J. Edgar Hoover that were expressed yesterday:

PRESIDENT NIXON—All Americans today mourn the death of J. Edgar Hoover. He served his nation as Director of the F.B.I. for 48 years under eight American Presidents with total loyalty, unparalleled ability and supreme dedication. It can truly be said of him that he was a legend in his own lifetime. For millions he was the symbol and embodiment of the values he cherished most: courage, patriotism, dedication to his country and a granite-like honesty and integrity. In times of controversy, Mr. Hoover was never a man to run from a fight. His magnificent contribution to making this a great and good nation will be remembered by the American people long after the petty carpings and vicious criticisms of his detractors are forgotten. The F.B.I. he literally created and built is today universally regarded as the finest law-enforcement agency in the world. The F.B.I. is the eternal monument honoring this great American.

VICE PRESIDENT AGNEW—J. Edgar Hoover stood steadfast against the political assaults and personal vilification that sought to undermine his stature late in his career. . . . They disliked him for the qualities that endeared him to all other Americans, his total dedication to principle and his complete incorruptibility.

CHIEF JUSTICE OF THE UNITED STATES WARREN E. BURGER — The country has lost one of the great public servants in all of its history. He has justly been and will be an American legend. In dedicating his life to building the F.B.I., J. Edgar Hoover did so without impinging on the liberties guaranteed by the Constitution and by our traditions.

SENATOR JAMES O. EASTLAND, Chairman of the Senate Judiciary Committee—The modern tradition of law enforcement in America was built around J. Edgar Hoover. His courage, integrity and character was a model for all men who would dedicate themselves to the protection of the lives and property of their fellow citizens.

REPRSENTATIVE EMANUEL CELLER, Chairman of the House Judiciary Committee—I disagreed with him on the questions of civil rights and personal liberties, but that did not mar our cordial relations. . . . His was a life of personal achievement, but I believe his passing marks an end of an era.

REPRESENTATIVE CARL ALBERT, Speaker of the House—The bureau will forever bear the imprint of this dedicated and patriotic man.

SECRETARY OF THE TREASURY JOHN B. CONNALLY—His leadership, his cooperation with other agencies and his campaign to professionalize anticrime efforts at local, state and national levels will be long remembered.

SENATOR EDWARD M. KENNEDY—The nation has lost a dedicated and loyal public servant. . . . Even those who differed with him always had the highest respect for his honesty, integrity, and his desire to do what he thought was best for the country.

JOHN N. MITCHELL, former Attorney General — All of America is indebted to him for his construction of the F.B.I. and for its outstanding operation over the years. Anybody that would say anything against J. Edgar Hoover, his integrity, his honesty and his ability was absolutely maligning him.

SENATOR HUBERT H. HUMPHREY—J. Edgar Hoover has been for better than 40 years one of the central figures of our time—a man of unquestioned ability, personal integrity and professional competence.

SENATOR EDMUND S. MUSKIE—J. Edgar Hoover devoted his entire life to the service of his country. Some of us may have questioned some of his approaches in recent years, but no one could question his loyalty or dedication to his country. The nation owes Mr. Hoover its gratitude and respect.

SENATOR GEORGE McGOVERN—I think we can only be sad over the passing of an American, any citizen, any mortal. I am sad at his passing.

GOV. GEORGE C. WALLACE—He was a great American and put his love of country above everything else.

SENATOR HENRY M. JACKSON—In the final analysis, it is the personal qualities of J. Edgar Hoover, his courage, his integrity, his self-discipline, that live on today in the great institution he leaves behind.

RAMSEY CLARK, former Attorney General—He was a major figure on the American scene. This is hardly the time to talk about differences—right now we mourn his death.

ROBERT MORSE, United States Attorney, Eastern District—The death of J. Edgar Hoover is a loss to every American.

JOHN E. INGERSOLL, director of the Bureau of Narcotics and Dangerous Drugs—As an American and particularly as a law enforcement man, I feel a profound sense of loss.

LEON JAWORSKI, president of the American Bar Association—I know of no man in modern history who contributed more to law enforcement in our nation than J. Edgar Hoover.

GEORGE MURPHY, president of the International Association of Chiefs of Police—He created an outstanding law enforcement agency which made an outstanding contribution to the nation's fight against crime and the upgrading of law enforcement

"All the News That's Fit to Print."

The New York Times.

THE WEATHER.
Fair, slightly warmer Thursday; Friday, fair, warmer; moderate winds, becoming south.
For full weather report see Page 23.

VOL. LXXVI....No. 25,118. NEW YORK, MONDAY, NOVEMBER 1, 1926. TWO CENTS In Greater New York | THREE CENTS Within 200 Miles | FOUR CENTS Elsewhere in the U. S.

SHOT FIRED AT MUSSOLINI RIPS COAT, BUT HE ESCAPES; MOB KILLS BOY ASSAILANT

SIXTH ATTEMPT ON HIS LIFE

Youth Fires Point Blank at Premier as He Leaves Congress in Bologna.

MAYOR'S SLEEVE PIERCED

Duce Is Calm, but Crowd, at First Stunned, Turns Furious and Stabs Boy to Death.

PREMIER GOES TO REVIEW

He Inspects Guards of Honor at Station and Then Leaves for Home in Forli.

Special Cable to THE NEW YORK TIMES.

BOLOGNA, Oct. 31.—Premier Mussolini escaped assassination today by a fraction of an inch when a bullet fired point-blank at him by an 18-year-old boy cut in two the sash of the Order of St. Lazarus which he was wearing and pierced his coat. The bullet left the Premier unscathed.

The infuriated crowd fell upon the would-be assassin and killed him before the police could interfere.

The attempt on Mussolini's life was made near the end of several big celebrations here dur. Mussolini's visit to commemorate t fourth anniversary of the Fascist revolution. The Premier at the time was leaving the main square of the city, which was packed solidly with more than 100,000 people, and his car was just entering the Via Independenzia, leading to the railway station, when the crowd, in its anxiety to get near him, broke through the cordon of troops which lined the route to the station and surged up to the automobile.

Premier Bows to Throng.

The Premier appeared pleased. He smiled and bowed his appreciation of the crowd's enthusiasm and rose to his feet in the motor car as if to say a word to the crowd. Suddenly the sharp report of a revolver rang out. Mussolini heard it, and turned his head rapidly, to find himself confronted with the leveled pistol. Before the would-be assassin could press the trigger again, however, those standing near him knocked the youth to the ground.

Mussolini, as in previous attempts on his life, seemed to be the coolest and most unconcerned in all the vast throng, and in the momentary hesitation of the crowd he motioned to his chauffeur to proceed. Immediately the automobile speeded away toward the station.

Meanwhile indescribable scenes were witnessed in the square. Those on the outskirts of the crowd who did not know what had happened, but sensed some grave occurrence, tried to force their way into the already overcrowded piazza, shouting and adding to the intense confusion.

Cries, imprecations and calls for help were heard on all sides as the vast multitude surged like a sea in a storm. Many were crushed in the tremendous congestion.

Mussolini Appears Calm.

Mussolini meanwhile had arrived at the station, where it was found that the bullet, in addition to cutting the Premier's sash and piercing his coat, had also passed through the sleeve of the Mayor of Bologna, who was sitting beside him. The bullet had buried itself in the upholstery of the car.

Mussolini appeared quite calm. He coolly reviewed the guards of honor drawn up at the station and then boarded the train waiting to take him to his home town of Forli.

The Premier's family was waiting for him in the train, and he calmly told them of what had happened, treating the affair as though it were of little importance.

After chatting with his family for a few moments he leaned out the car window and smilingly acknowledged the cheers of the crowd which had assembled at the station to bid him farewell. A few minutes later, amid thunderous applause, the Premier was on his way to Forli.

Bologna Deeply Indignant.

The excitement in Bologna was enormous. The city, which in a certain sense was the birthplace of Fascism, owing to the tremendous riots which culminated in the killing of the Fascist City Councilor Giordani in 1921, and which ever since has been one of the most rapidly Fascist regions of Italy, seemed mad with indignation that the Premier's life should have been attempted here of all places. Small parades of Fascisti, obviously in an ugly mood, formed and went through the streets shouting their cries and looking for trouble. But the deploring of the attempted assassination was so unanimous and sincere that no incidents of great importance happened.

Who Mussolini's assailant was is not yet known. No one could identify him, but he appeared to be no more than 18 years old. The police immediately began an intensive investigation to find out who the boy was, where he came from and whether he acted on

Continued on Page Four.

Skies Rain Mud and Sand, Warming Spots in Cold France

Special Cable to THE NEW YORK TIMES.

PARIS, Oct. 31.—Several French towns report heavy rainfalls, accompanied by mud and sand, especially in the region about Marseilles and Château Chinon, near Nevers.

In the first-named region balls of mud the size of raindrops fell, while further north fine yellow sand similar to the desert sand of North Africa came down in minute particles. The fall was so heavy that Château Chinon housetops were colored yellow.

The phenomenon was accompanied by sultry warmth while the rest of France was freezing.

HARRY HOUDINI DIES AFTER OPERATIONS

Magician, Conscious to Last, Loses Fight for Life in Detroit Hospital.

DEATH DUE TO POISONING

Playful Blow Given by Montreal Student as Test Caused Appendix to Break.

Special to The New York Times.

DETROIT, Oct. 31.—Harry Houdini, world famous as a magician, a defier of locks and sealed chests and an exposer of spiritualistic frauds, died here this afternoon after a week's struggle for life, in which he underwent two operations.

Death was due to peritonitis, which followed the first operation, that for appendicitis. The second operation was performed last Friday. Like a newly discovered serum, used for the first time in Houdini's case, it was of no avail.

The chapter of accidents which ended fatally for the man who so often had seemed to thousands to be cheating the very jaws of death began early in October at Albany, N. Y. On the opening night of his engagement at a theatre there a piece of apparatus used in his "water torture cell" trick was overturned and struck him on the foot. Houdini called a physician from the audience, had his foot examined and then completed his performance. Afterward he went to a hospital and had the injured foot X-rayed.

Appendicitis Follows Blow.

A bone was found to be partly fractured and Houdini was advised to discontinue his tour a few days and give prompt attention and plenty of rest to the injured foot. He declined to cancel his engagements, however, and did not miss a show.

From Albany he and his company went to Schenectady. Houdini was suffering continuous pain and returned to Albany for several treatments. By the time he left Schenectady for Montreal his whole system was in a weakened condition.

On Tuesday, Oct. 19, while in Montreal he addressed a class of students on spiritualistic tricks. During a reception following the address he commented on the strength of his stomach muscles and their ability to withstand hard blows without injury.

One of the students without warning or giving time for Houdini to prepare struck him twice immediately over his appendix. He suffered no distress at the time but after he had boarded a train for Detroit he complained of pain. At first he attributed it to something he had eaten but as it increased he called in the company's nurse, who in turn arranged by wire to have a physician meet the magician in Detroit.

Dr. Leo Kretzka, a prominent physician, made a hurried examination and told the patient there were symptoms of appendicitis. He left it to Houdini to decide whether it would be advisable for him to appear that evening at the Garrick Theatre for the opening night of the show. Houdini would not disappoint his admirers.

Looking back on that last performance, the large audience now realizes that the famous magician did his tricks under a great strain. He felt the grip of bonds he had never tested, the snap of a lock not forged by human hands. He was worried for one of the few times in his career and was plainly not up to his best form in some of his tricks.

Conscious Until Death.

At his hotel after the performance the pain increased. The house physician and the best Detroit could furnish were called. Houdini was taken to Gray Hospital and the following afternoon underwent an operation for appendicitis. His removal from the hotel to the hospital was made at the suggestion of his family physician, William Stone of New York City, who had been notified by telephone of his friend's condition.

Until his death Houdini was conscious and his mind was keen and alert. The physicians who attended him say he was the best patient they ever had, and he helped them wonderfully. His mental attitude, combined with his unusual stamina, did much to prolong his life.

According to statements made by the physicians, the playful punches he received in Montreal were the direct

Continued on Page Six.

"KILLER" CUNNIFFE IS SLAIN IN DETROIT; THREE OTHERS DEAD

Bandit, Woman, Pal and Policeman Die in Row and Raid Following It.

TWO OTHERS ARE WOUNDED

$10,000 in Bills, Believed to Be Loot From Robberies, Is Found on Table in Room.

WANTED IN NEW JERSEY

Cunniffe Was Identified as Aiding "Bum" Rodgers in $300,000 Mail Hold-Up.

Special to The New York Times.

DETROIT, Mich., Oct. 31.—James ("Killer") Cunniffe, wanted for the murder of Frank Kearney and his son Robert, near New Brunswick, N. J., early in October, and the $300,000 robbery of a mail truck and the murder of the driver at Elizabeth a few days later, was killed early this morning in an apartment here after a row over the division of money.

Three other persons, one a woman and one a policeman, were killed in the fight and when the police broke in to investigate the shooting.

Cunniffe, known here as J. B. Quinn but identified by his fingerprints, was wanted for the New Jersey killings with "Bum" Rodgers, and also for a part in the Bellmore, L. I., bank hold-up in 1924 which resulted in the death of Ernest L. Whitman, a bond salesman.

On a table in the apartment was found nearly $10,000 in $10 and $100 bills, which the police believe was part of the proceeds of the Elizabeth robbery, in which more than $150,000 in cash was taken.

Seven Shots Fired Into His Body.

The fact that Cunniffe was apparently killed by William James Olsen, late killed by a policeman, after a fight over the money, indicates to the police that it might have been Olsen who was implicated with Cunniffe in the Elizabeth robbery instead of "Bum" Rodgers. Cunniffe was positively identified as one of the robbers, but the identification of Rodgers was never certain.

At first Olsen was believed to be "Bum" Rodgers, but his measurements failed to tally with those of Rodgers on file with the police here. Olsen is thought to have been a confederate in the New Jersey hold-ups and murders, however, and the police made inquiries of Eastern authorities tonight regarding his identity.

There was apparently intense hatred between Cunniffe and Olsen, for seven shots were fired into Cunniffe's body.

In addition to Cunniffe and Olsen, the dead are Patrolman Ernest Jones, 35 years old, patrol wagon driver of the Highland Park Police Department, and an unidentified woman, believed to have been Cunniffe's companion.

Two others were wounded, Patrolman Ephraim Rancour, minute man of the Highland Park Police Department, shot in the right shoulder, and Earl Burns, who occupied an apartment next to Cunniffe's, shot in the left cheek.

Olsen Struggles to the End.

The police heard that shots had been fired in the Highland Court apartments, 257 Highland Avenue, early this morning, and Patrolmen Jones and Rancour, with a tenant, Jesse Wickham, a former police officer, and Elmer Redman, city constable, set out to investigate. Jones knocked at the door of apartment 20, which was opened by Olsen, dressed in underwear and a bathrobe.

"What's the trouble, buddy," said Jones as he and the others crowded into the lobby of the apartment.

"Nothing at all," said Olsen, who had held his right hand behind him.

"What's all this shooting about?" said Jones.

"It's about this," snapped Olsen, pulling his right arm from behind him and shooting Jones through the forehead. As Jones collapsed, face down, Olsen fired twice at the others, hitting Rancour in the shoulder and Burns in the face.

Again Olsen pulled the trigger, but his pistol jammed and he ran to a dresser to get another gun. As he reached it Rancour fired at him and in his rage poured six bullets into the prostrate man, but until the last Olsen crept toward the dresser where the other gun lay.

Gun Battle in Narrow Passage.

The lobby in which the shooting took place is a narrow passage, at one end of which is a living room and at the other end a bedroom. In the centre are a bath room and a kitchen. After the first three shots, Olsen retreated to the bedroom, while Redman made for the living room. Rancour and Burns were in the bath room, firing around the corner.

When Olsen lay dead on the floor, Rancour entered the bedroom and found, sprawled on the bed there, the bodies of a man and a woman, both in underclothing. The woman had been shot twice and the man seven times. Both were dead.

Jones was taken to Highland Park General Hospital, where he died an hour after admission. He was a married man with no children. He joined the Highland Park Police Department in 1919, after serving overseas in the army. He was recognized as one of the most efficient officers on the force.

On a table in the centre of the room was a sum of money estimated as being between $7,000 and $10,000. The

Continued on Page Seven.

Royal Artist Coming to Paint Our Most Beautiful Woman

By Wireless to THE NEW YORK TIMES.

BERLIN, Oct. 31.—Nicholas Vadasz, Hungarian artist, who is known as the "painter of queens," is going to America in the near future incognito.

The reason for this is that he is a painter not only of crowned heads, including former Empress Zita and the Queen of Spain, but also of beautiful women in general. Vadasz, whose home is in Budapest, wants to discover and paint the most beautiful woman in America, and in order that he may not be influenced in his selection, he has decided to keep his identity hidden.

MISS EMERY TO WED GRAND DUKE DMITRI

New York Girl Now in France Engaged to Former Russian Nobleman.

SURPRISE TO FRIENDS HERE

Dmitry the Representative of Grand Duke Cyril, Claimant to the Czar's Throne.

Miss Audrey Emery, youngest daughter of Mrs. Alfred Anson of 5 East Sixty-eighth Street, is to marry the Grand Duke Dmitri of Russia. This was learned here yesterday following cable messages to relatives from France, where Miss Emery and her parents have been spending some time.

One of these messages was sent by Miss Emery to the housekeeper at the Anson town home here, who was formerly her nurse. Another was sent to Mrs. Benjamin Moore, her sister, whose home is in Syosset, L. I.

The announcement of the engagement came as a surprise to New York friends of the family, who, it was said, did not even know that Miss Emery and the Grand Duke were acquainted.

Miss Emery is one of the five children of the late John J. Emery of Cincinnati and Mrs. Anson, who married Mr. Anson, a brother of the Earl of Lichfield, four years after Mr. Emery's death.

John Emery, a brother of Miss Emery, who is in her early twenties, was married on Aug. 31 to Mrs. Irene Gibson Post, a daughter of Charles Dana Gibson and a niece of Lady Astor.

Representative for Cyril.

The Grand Duke Dmitri Paulovitch who has made his home in Paris since the Russian revolution, has been acting as the personal representative of Grand Duke Cyril since Cyril issued a proclamation announcing himself as Cyril I, Emperor of Russia.

He is one of two children of Alexander III's youngest brother, the Grand Duke Paul. He was brought up by his aunt, the widowed Grand Duchess Sergius, sister of the former Czarina, as his mother died soon after his birth. Because of an escapade in his younger days he was banished from Russia for four months just prior to the outbreak of the World War.

With Prince Felix Youssoupoff he is popularly believed to have been responsible for the death of Rasputin, the monk, and as a result was extremely popular with the Russian people, who had resented Rasputin's strange influence over the royal family. When a council of prominent exiled Russian noblemen was held in Paris several years ago to decide on who should be considered the logical claimant to the Russian throne should the Bolshevist régime be wiped out, Grand Duke Dmitri was one of those considered for the honor. That council, however, selected the Grand Duke Nicholas.

In connection with the death of Rasputin it was reported that the monk had spoken in a slighting manner of Dmitri's sister and the Grand Duke was determined to avenge her. With his regimental comrade and kinsman, Prince Youssoupoff, the monk was induced to visit a house where the noblemen were concealed.

Then, it was reported, Dmitri offered Rasputin a chance to fight for his life. He proposed a duel where both would have an equal chance. Rasputin, however, it was said, seized the revolver that was handed to him and before the Grand Duke had an opportunity to pick up his own weapon, fired at him. Having aimed his weapon too high, the bullet flew over Dmitri's head and before Rasputin could fire a second shot, he was shot dead by Prince Youssoupoff.

75 PAID 1924 TAX ON INCOMES LARGER THAN $1,000,000

Two in Michigan and One in New York Reported Net Receipts of $5,000,000.

THREE PAID ON $4,000,000

Treasury Books Show That 39 New Yorkers Had Incomes of $1,000,000 or More.

7,787,209 RETURNS FILED

Of These 417,421 Were Turned In by Corporations and the Rest Were Individual.

Special to The New York Times.

WASHINGTON, Oct. 31.—Seventy-five persons, twenty-one of them credited to the State of New York, reported net incomes of $1,000,000 or over for the calendar year 1924, and paid their taxes on that basis to the Federal Government, according to statistics given out by the Internal Revenue Bureau today. Three of those had net incomes of $5,000,000 and more, while three others reported net incomes ranging between $4,000,000 and $5,000,000, and fifteen had net incomes of between $2,000,000 and $3,000,000.

No official identification of those in this exclusive "blue ribbon" list of wealthy Americans is ever revealed by the Treasury Department, but it is possible to speculate fairly accurately as to who some of them are.

The trio reporting net incomes in excess of $5,000,000 each are credited to two States, two to Michigan and one to New York. The Michigan men are assumed to be Henry Ford and his son, Edsel. The one from New York probably is John D. Rockefeller Jr.

The three who reported incomes of between $4,000,000 and $5,000,000 each are credited one each to New Jersey, New York and Pennsylvania. The Pennsylvanian is believed to be Andrew Mellon, Secretary of the Treasury.

Distribution of Big Incomes.

The distribution of the seventy-five persons enjoying 1924 net incomes of $1,000,000 or more was as follows:

Over $5,000,000—Two in Michigan, one in New York.

$4,000,000 to $5,000,000—One in New Jersey; one in New York; one in Pennsylvania.

$3,000,000 to $4,000,000—One in California; two in New York; one in Pennsylvania.

$2,000,000 to $3,000,000—Two in Illinois; one in Michigan, nine in New York; one in Ohio; one in Pennsylvania, and one in Wisconsin.

$1,500,000 to $2,000,000—One in California; two in Massachusetts; one in Michigan; five in New York; one in Ohio; three in Pennsylvania.

$1,000,000 to $1,500,000—One in California; five in Illinois; one in Maryland; two in New Jersey; 21 in New York; five in Ohio; one in Pennsylvania; one in Rhode Island.

These 75 persons reported an aggregate net income of $155,974,475 after making general deductions of $31,362,793. The total net income reported by all Federal income taxpayers for the calendar year 1924, the year on whose income they paid their taxes in the calendar year 1925, was $25,656,153,454. The net income reported by the 75 persons in the millionaire class was 13.26 per cent. of the total net income reported by all taxpayers.

Sources of Incomes.

The gross income of the 75 millionaires was $190,337,268, divided as follows:

Wages and salaries	$4,033,484
Business	1,249,700
Partnership	10,331,445
Profits from real estate, stocks and bonds other than assets held for more than two years	2,951,746
Capital net gain from sale of assets held for more than two years	50,660,650
Rents and royalties	4,603,474
Interest and investment income	10,588,987
Interest on Government obligations wholly exempt from tax	681,396
Dividends	102,738,[illegible]
Fiduciary income	2,497,844

The net tax on individual income credited to the seventy-five persons was $47,207,203. It was distributed by income tax classes as follows:

Class.	Net Tax.	Av. Am't per Return.
$1,000,000 to $1,500,000	$12,738,840	$344,292.97
$1,500,000 to $2,000,000	5,261,011	404,693.15
$2,000,000 to $3,000,000	10,265,143	684,342.87
$3,000,000 to $4,000,000	3,607,087	901,021.7[illegible]
$4,000,000 to $5,000,000	4,274,317	1,424,772.33
$5,000,000 and over	11,060,205	3,686,735.00

The net incomes and dividend exemp-

Continued on Page Eight.

Carpentier Knocks Out Swindler in Paris; Lands Right to the Jaw; Retrieves $182 'Loan'

By Wireless to THE NEW YORK TIMES.

PARIS, Oct. 31.—Georges Carpentier just missed being the victim of a confidence man two days ago in a Paris bar, but he got his own back up and landed a right-hand swing to the chin of the would-be defrauder before he called a policeman and recovered his money.

Georges was fairly taken in by an elegant young man who claimed half a dozen mutual acquaintances. There was talk of big business and an invitation to dinner.

On the way, the young man had a payment to make and, being just a little short, touched Georges for $182. They drove to the Crillon Hotel, where the young man was staying. If Georges would be so patient as to wait in the cab, his host would refill his pocketbook.

But Georges did not wait in the cab. He got out and walked to the corner of the Place de la Concorde just in time to see his young friend slipping out by a door of the hotel into Rue Boissy d'Anglais.

Georges can still run and he is not above fighting for $182. He caught his man in a snappy sprint, and, just to teach him better manners and to prevent any kind of trouble, gave him one to the jaw. Then he called a policeman, explained that it was not his usual habit to fight in the street and asked the man of the law to search the pockets of his victim. Thereupon the "loan" was promptly repaid.

SMITH AND MILLS BOTH PREDICT VICTORY; GOVERNOR SEES SWEEP BY WHOLE TICKET; MILLS SETS HIS PLURALITY AT 125,000

EXPECTS TAMMANY LOSSES

Mills Says He Will Not Be Defeated Here by More Than 275,000.

CLAIMS 400,000 UP-STATE

Finds Farmers Aroused Over Milk—Charges Betting Odds Are 'Rigged.'

FEELS PROUD OF CAMPAIGN

Smith's Saying There Are No Issues Doesn't Wipe Them Out, He Declares.

Indicating by his tone and bearing complete belief that his campaign had been successful, Representative Ogden L. Mills, Republican nominee for Governor, predicted his own election by at least 125,000 in an interview at his home, 4 East Sixty-ninth Street, yesterday.

"So far as I am concerned, the election is won," he said.

"I have just received a telegram from George K. Morris, Chairman of the Republican State Committee, indicating that I will come to the Bronx with a plurality of 400,000, an estimate which is fully borne out by telegrams that I have personally received from every County Chairman.

"One of the most remarkable facts in connection with the telegrams is the emphasis which is placed upon the milk scandal in the dairy counties. They say that the farmers everywhere are thoroughly aroused. They see at last someone who is prepared to fight for their interests and they are 'determined to elect Mills' to get at the bottom of what is wrong with the milk industry.

Expects 275,000 Loss in City.

"Analysis of all the figures indicates that I will reach the Bronx with more than 400,000 plurality and that I will not lose New York City by more than 275,000.

"Tammany has not given out its inside figures. They don't dare to, because if the actual figures submitted by their leaders were made known, instead of only meaning defeat for Smith, they would bring about a landslide.

"Their efforts for the next two days will be to conceal the real situation and they are trying the old and time-worn trick of rigging the betting odds. Their attitude in this connection reminds me of what happened two years ago when I was a candidate for Congress. I picked up a newspaper the Sunday before election and read that Darnell & Co. had $15,000 to bet against $10,000 that I would not be elected. As soon as their office opened on Monday I offered to take that bet but was told that it was not available. I then offered to bet $10,000 to $5,000 that I would be elected, but I could not even get a bet of $100 at odds of 2 to 1.

"The truth is that during the last five weeks the people have awakened to the fact that there are real issues confronting them at Tuesday's election. It is an interesting fact that Governor Smith in his speech last night devoted more than an hour in an endeavor to tell the people that there were no issues. His saying so cannot wipe them out of existence.

"The people fully realize that there can be no economical administration under Smith and confidently believe that they will receive one from me. The people have come to realize that it is all wrong to keep plastering mortgages on the State. They don't want the credit of the State to be brought to the same pass that Tammany Hall has brought the credit of the city.

"Smith's water power plan means Government operation. He would be beaten on that issue alone.

Says People Seek Truth on Milk.

"The people are determined to know the truth about the milk situation. That goes not only for the consumers in New York City but for the farmers up-State. They cannot understand Governor Smith's determination not to have an impartial investigation. They know that my election means that they will know the truth. If everything is all right, then nothing will be lost by an investigation. If it is not all right, the people are determined that the people guilty of the meanest and most contemptible kind of graft shall be punished.

"Smith made a colossal blunder when he said he wouldn't turn on the light. Frankly, while I have had a great deal of experience in public life and have read a great deal of political history, I do not recall a single other time when a public official, where charges of corruption were made, would not permit them to be investigated.

"Certainly, every one who has studied the political history of New York City and State, particularly that of the city, knows that there is a periodical revolt against Tammany Hall. It usually comes when Tammany is so swollen with pride and confidence that outraged public senti-

Continued on Page Two.

Coolidge Appeals to Voters To Exercise Rights at Polls

Special to The New York Times.

WASHINGTON, Oct. 31.—President Coolidge tonight issued an appeal to the voters of the nation to participate in Tuesday's election, the most important held in his Administration, with control of the Senate in doubt and the Democratic leaders claiming a sweep in the election of members of the House.

His appeal reads:

Let no voters abdicate their sovereign right of self-government at the election on Tuesday by failing to vote.

CALVIN COOLIDGE.

The White House,
Nov. 1, 1926.

LOCAL ISSUES RULE AT POLLS TOMORROW

And They Are So Jumbled That the National Leaders Cannot Figure the General Trend.

SILENT VOTERS A PROBLEM

Their Number Is Unusually Large, and Each Party Simply Claims Their Support.

WASHINGTON, Oct. 31 (AP).—As the pre-election guessing by campaign managers entered its last fanciful stage today the usual forecasts of sweeping victory came from every camp. Behind the militant claims made by the leaders, there were, however, certain quite evident convictions. There was no doubt that many Democratic managers were convinced they had a fighting chance to capture control of at least one branch of Congress, or that the Republican leaders were just as sure that serious threat of such a result had been removed.

So far as the State campaigns were concerned, the issues had become so badly jumbled that those entrusted with national management of the parties were unable to make any general estimate of how the land might lay. Each contented himself with hopefully predicting that his party would hold its own in the net returns the country over.

By virtue of referendums in eight States bearing in one way or another on the prohibition question, wet and dry leaders joined the ranks of the victory-claimers. The States that are to vote either on a State enforcement code or on some other feature of the wet and dry problem are New York, Illinois, Wisconsin, Colorado, California, Nevada, Missouri and Montana.

Puzzled by Silent Voters.

But if there was a certain element of actual confidence manifest on both sides of all these contests, there also was apparent a certain offsetting apprehension and uncertainty, growing out of the wide-spread inability of political canvassers to ascertain what the voters really were thinking.

Unusually large numbers of the electorate have been altogether silent, while others have given only half hints of how they intend to vote or vote at all. Although in the aggregate the number who qualified this year in party registrations was disproportionately large, many reports to campaign headquarters from widely scattered sections have described a popular condition bordering on apathy.

This situation has given a great impetus this year to party and non-partisan get-out-the-vote crusades. To the drive for a big vote President Coolidge contributed tonight, when he appealed to citizens in a one-sentence message to vote on Tuesday. The President will go to Northampton, Mass., to vote for Senator Butler and Governor Fuller, whom he has publicly endorsed.

Of the forecasts issued tonight from the national party headquarters, those of the Democrats were the more sweeping. The party leaders claimed nothing less than a Democratic landslide—not simply the ordinary off-year rebuke to the Administration, but an actual revolution against Republican rule.

These statements the Republicans dismissed as nothing but a Democratic hallucination that would disappear on election day.

Democratic Hopes of the Senate.

Democratic hopes of winning a majority of the Senate hinge on a group of widely scattered States, where Democratic campaign ammunition has been spent most freely during the Summer. These States are Arizona, Colorado, Idaho, Illinois, Indiana, Kentucky, Maryland, Massachusetts, Missouri, Nevada, New York, Ohio, Oklahoma, Oregon, Utah and Washington.

Of these seats, all held now by Republicans, the Democrats must win nine to have a clear Senatorial majority. Even the most sanguine partisans do not hope to capture all, but the leaders count three or four as certain to fall into the Democratic column

Continued on Page Three.

SMITH SAYS IT'S ALL OVER

Does Not Expect Mills to Lead by Over 90,000 Up-State.

SURE CITY WILL STAND UP

Predicts Justice Wagner Will Come to the Harlem Ahead of Wadsworth.

LEHMAN MORE OPTIMISTIC

Declares Governor Will Win by the Record of 400,000 in the State.

Governor Smith said last night that he did not expect his opponent, Ogden L. Mills, to get more than about 90,000 plurality up the State, and he believed that the whole Democratic State ticket would be elected, while his manager, Colonel Herbert H. Lehman, asserted in a statement that the Governor would get the unprecedented plurality of 400,000 in the State, basing this on the Miller plurality up-State four years ago, which was the 90,000 Governor Smith referred to, and contending that in this city Smith will get close to 500,000.

The Governor's prophecy was made in the course of an interview at the Biltmore. He had previously said he would have some figures before the campaign closed. When asked for them he said:

"Colonel Lehman will talk figures to you."

The two had just been together. The Governor was then asked what he thought his own plurality would be and he replied:

"There is no way of talking about it except to predicate it upon the past. I don't know that there is any way to do it. I don't see any difference between this and four years ago. At best it is what everybody themselves want to make out of it. I can't understand Mills coming to the Bronx line with anything better than Miller got, 90,000; I don't see where he is going to get the votes."

"But what about the vote down here?" he was asked.

Sure Wagner Will Win.

"I think it is going to stand up. There is one thing I do feel satisfied about—and that is on the Senatorship. I am satisfied that Wagner will be elected. I haven't reduced it to figures but I am satisfied from what I hear of the up-State situation with regard to Cristman—the disaffection from the regular Republican vote in the country sections of the State that he (Wadsworth) cannot come down to the Harlem Bridge or the Bronx line with anything like Wagner is going to roll up. I don't know any reason why Wagner should not run right alongside of me in the city. He can drop down a little if there is any considerable hope of so-called Smith-Republicans who don't see anybody else but me in the Democratic party, he can lose some of them, but will still have enough to be able to carry him across, and I think comfortably.

"If I didn't predicate it on anything else," went on the Governor, "I would do it on the campaign that the Republican Party has waged in this State. It has been senseless—there isn't any background to it—they haven't impressed anybody with anything they said from the start to the finish.

"I am satisfied the election is all finished. I am satisfied that Wagner is going to win. My advice from up-State is that neither one of the candidates on the Republican ticket, I'll say none of the candidates on the Republican ticket—the whole ticket—can come to the Bronx line, to the Westchester line, with sufficient to overcome New York. It can't be done."

"Do you think the entire Democratic ticket will be elected?"

"Yes. There is nothing to indicate that any of these fellows can do any better than Governor Miller, who was an up-State man," he replied.

The Governor would make no guess as to the Assembly. He recalled that even in 1922 the Democrats did not win that. "That's a peculiar situation. I don't know anything about it. That's the honest answer to that," he said.

He also said he had no advices regarding the five Senate districts in the State supposed to be close, and which might mean a gain for the Democrats in the State Senate in case of a sweep.

Lehman Gives Figures.

Colonel Lehman has been chary about giving out figures during the last week, though it was clear he was becoming more and more optimistic. His figure of last night, however, was a complete surprise, as it is the highest recorded guess as to Smith's plurality. He said:

"Congressman Mills's campaign has collapsed so completely both in the city and in the up-State counties that it is my confident prediction that Governor Smith will carry the State by the unprecedented plurality of at least 400,000. His plurality in New York City will be not less than 500,000, while there is absolutely nothing to indicate that Congressman Mills will come down to

HARRY HOUDINI DIES AFTER OPERATIONS

Continued from Page 1, Column 2.

cause of Houdini's death, for one of the blows caused the appendix to burst, saturating his system with poison.

Streptococcus peritonitis, which developed soon after the operation last Monday, seriously complicated the case. This is a particularly virulent form of poisoning, and few cases are known to the medical profession where persons suffering from it have recovered.

The body will leave Detroit for New York in a special car Monday evening, arrive in New York Tuesday morning about 9 o'clock.

STAGE PAYS ITS TRIBUTES.

Praises Houdini as Magician, Man and Friend.

The stage and the world of magic and magicians joined yesterday in paying tribute to Houdini, not only as the leader in his particular field of entertainment but as a unique figure whose like will probably not be seen again for some time. The following tributes were voiced by persons with whom he had been intimately associated:

B. M. L. ERNST, Vice President of the Society of American Magicians—"He was the greatest magician of his time and maybe of all times. He was absolutely unique, as his stunts were his own and not redecorated from something some one else had done. Whether it was a trick or an artifice, he had an ability to escape from various sorts of objects which no one else has been able to duplicate and which may die with him. He was head of the principal magic organization of England as well as of this country. He was the leading authority on magic literature and had the largest magic library in the world."

E. F. ALBEE, President of the Keith-Albee Circuit of Theatres—"Houdini was more than a national character; he was known and has appeared throughout the world. I had the great honor of being his first manager some thirty years ago when his work was as wonderful as during these past years when he became recognized as the peer among mystifiers and magicians. He was a man of extraordinary intelligence and tremendous physical strength. His whole life was ideal and his habits moderate, except with regard to his own work. He was always thoughtful and sensitive of fellow artists and a loyal member of the National Vaudeville Artists. We have never known any one who could equal him in his methods of theatrical presentations. I don't believe there will ever be another just like Houdini. He was a prince of showmen. We shall all feel his loss."

MARK A. LUESCHER, Former Manager of the New York Hippodrome—"Houdini was the greatest acting showman of this generation. He appreciated the value of publicity but he always obtained his publicity through legitimate and well thought out methods. He was a student, a philosopher, a model husband and an enduring friend.

HENRY CHESTERFIELD, Secretary of the National Vaudeville Artists Club—"The theatrical profession has lost a showman whom it will be impossible to duplicate. He had an uncanny ability of selling his tricks in a way that made them appear entirely different from the tricks done by any one else, and for that reason he was of great value to his business."

ED WYNN—"On the theory that amusement is probably the most essential thing for the contentment of a community, Houdini's death must be taken as one of the greatest losses of recent times. During our friendship of some twenty years, I have always found him a man whose ambition was solely to entertain the masses. He was fearless and undoubtedly the greatest master of magic."

R. H. BURNSIDE—'As a man he was a fine upstanding character. He would go out of his way to do things not expected of him to make his entertainment a success. I regret to hear of his death because the stage has lost a brilliant performer."

SAILING BARUCH—"Houdini was a very remarkable man and a very fine man. I am very sorry to hear of his death. We shall miss him very much."

Professional tribute to the memory of Houdini will be paid tonight by the council of his organization, The Society of American Magicians, which has been called together for a special meeting at the offices of B. M. L. Ernst, 23 West Forty-third Street.

Harry Houdini, the famous magician, who died yesterday in Detroit.

Houdini and his wife Beatrice. She worked with him early in his career in "Metamorphosis," the sack and trunk substitution illusion.

SYRACUSE, N. Y., Oct. 31 (AP).—Howard Thurston, magician and for many years friend of Harry Houdini, in a statement made today, declared that in "the passing of Houdini, the world has lost a great mystifier and a useful, forceful character.

"We were friends for thirty-five years, starting at the bottom together and climbing toward the top," the statement said. "As a showman he was in a class with Barnum, in force of character he resembled Roosevelt."

HOUDINI WORLD FAMOUS.

No Locks Could Hold Him—Foe of Mediums.

Whatever the methods by which Harry Houdini deceived a large part of the world for nearly four decades, his career stamped him as one of the greatest showmen of modern times. In his special field of entertainment he stood alone. With a few minor exceptions, he invented all his tricks and illusions, and in certain instances only his four intimate helpers knew the solution. In one or two very important cases Houdini, himself, alone knew the whole secret.

Houdini was born on April 6, 1874. His name originally was Eric Weiss and he was the son of a rabbi. He did not take the name Harry Houdini until he had been a performer for many years. Legend has it that he opened his first lock when he wanted a piece of pie in the kitchen closet. It is certain that when scarcely more than a baby he showed skill as an acrobat and contortionist, and both these talents helped his start in the show business and his later development as an "escape king."

Joined Circus at 9.

At the age of 9 Houdini joined a traveling circus, touring Wisconsin as a contortionist and trapeze performer. The Davenport brothers were then famous, doing the first spiritualist work ever seen in this country. They would ring bells while bound inside a cabinet and would agree to free themselves from any bonds. This inspired Houdini to a somewhat similar performance. Standing in the middle of the ring, he would invite any one to tie him with ropes and would then free himself inside the cabinet.

In the ring at Coffeyville, Kan., a Sheriff tied him and then produced a pair of handcuffs with the taunt:

"If I put these on you, you'll never get loose."

Houdini, still only a boy, told him to go ahead. After a much longer stay in the cabinet then usual, the performer emerged, carrying the handcuffs in his free hands. That was the beginning of his long series of escapes from every known sort of manacle. For years he called himself the Handcuff King, a title discarded as he extended and elevated the range of his performances.

From 1885 to 1900 he played all over the United States, in museums, music halls, circuses and medicine shows, gradually improving his technique and giving up his purely contortionistic and acrobatic feats. In 1900 he made his first visit abroad, and in London his sensational escapes from handcuffs at Scotland Yard won him a six months' engagement at the Alhambra. This was the first instance of his cleverly obtaining notoriety by a public or semi-public exhibition outside the theatre. No other showman, unless it was Barnum, knew better how to arouse the curiosity and amazement of the public in this manner.

Escaped From Dozens of Prisons.

During a six-year tour of the Continent he escaped from dozens of famous prisons. In the Krupp plant at Essen he met the challenge of the workmen and freed himself from expertly constructed shackles before 70,000 persons. He returned to America to find his fame greatly increased and a newly organized vaudeville ready to pay him many times his old salary. He continued his prison escapes over here and in January, 1902, broke from Cell 2 in the Federal prison at Washington, the cell in which Guiteau, President Garfield's assassin, had been confined.

In 1908 Houdini dropped the handcuff tricks for more dangerous and dramatic escapes, including one from an air-tight galvanized vessel, filled with water, locked in an iron-bound chest. And he would free himself from the so-called torture cell, his own invention. In this he was suspended, head down, in a tank of water. To thrill the general public he would hang from the roof of a skycraper, bound in a strait-jacket, from which he would wriggle free to the applause of the crowd in the street below. Thrown from a boat or bridge into a river, bound hand and foot and locked and nailed in a box, doomed to certain death by drowning or suffocation, he would emerge in a minute or so, a free man, swimming vigorously to safety.

In the last twenty years Houdini made many long tours, playing in nearly every important city in Europe, Asia, Africa and Australia. Occasionally others would attempt to imitate him, but his supremacy never was remotely threatened. An evidence of the deep impression his work made on the public mind is the fact that the Standard Dictionary now contains a verb, "houdinize," meaning "to release or extricate oneself (from confinement, bonds, or the like), as by wriggling out." A slang dictionary probably would list the expression, 'do a Houdini," with a similar meaning.

Owned Valuable Library.

During the last few years Houdini had become internationally known as a tireless enemy and exposer of fraudulent mediums and all false claims in the field of spiritualism. He was a member of The Scientific American committee that investigated Margery, the Boston medium, whom he denounced in vigorous language. He was the author of "Spooks and Spiritualism," "The Unmasking of Robert Houdin," "Handcuff Secrets," and "Rope Ties and Escapes." At his home, 278 West 113th Street, he possessed a remarkable library, chiefly devoted to works on the theatre, to magic and the black arts. The collection has been valued at $500,000 and was insured for $350,000. Most of it has been willed to the National Museum at Washington.

In July, 1926, Houdini was elected for the ninth successive time President of the Society of American Magicians. He also was President of the Magicians' Club of London and a life member of the Authors' Club of London. He married in 1894 Wilhelmina Rahner of Brooklyn. He was a member of St. Cecile Lodge No. 568, F. & A. M.

BIZARRE EXPERIENCES TOLD BY HOUDINI

Tricked Roosevelt on River of Doubt—Had Four "Close-Ups With Death."

Few men could relate more interesting anecdotes and experiences than Harry Houdini. He was fond of telling how he beguiled the late Theodore Roosevelt and the late Victor Herbert on a voyage to Europe aboard the Imperator. Colonel Roosevelt had just returned from his exploration of the River of Doubt in Brazil.

"I was asked to give an entertainment," Houdini would relate, "and the subject of spirit writing came up. A number of other well-known men were present, all of them having intelligence of a high order. Certainly it was not a credulous audience. I offered to summon the spirits and have them answer any questions that might be asked.

"Roosevelt wanted to know if they could tell him where he had spent Christmas Day. I had a slate with the usual covering and in a few moments brought forth a map, done in a dozen different colors of chalk, which indicated the spot where he had been on the famous River of Doubt. That map was an exact duplicate of one that was to appear in his book which had not been published. I had never seen the map and, to make my case stronger, the name of W. T. Stead, the English spiritualist and writer who lost his life on the Titanic, was signed below the map in a handwriting which one man present instantly recognized as that of Stead. And I might add that I was unfamiliar with Stead's signature.

Colonel Roosevelt Dumfounded.

"Roosevelt was dumfounded.

"'Is it really spirit writing?' he asked.

"'Yes,' I replied with a wink."

Of course, Houdini never explained how the trick was done, at least to the public.

The magician tried his hand at the medium business in his early days in Kansas and used to tell in this wise how he prepared for one of his first seances:

"I had gone around to the cemeteries and read all of the inscriptions on tombstones, looked over a few birth and death records and acquired a lot of information from the gossips. When the time arrived for my act I puzzled the crowd by giving particulars of births and deaths in half of the families of the town. Gradually I worked up to a climax, exclaiming:

"'Now what do I see? What is this coming before me? Why, it is a man—a black man. He's lame—and his throat is cut from ear to ear. Who is this man?—why, I know him; he is Efram—Efram Alexander.' The negroes at the meeting deserted in a body with shrieks because they recognized a negro who had been killed recently."

For thirty-three years Houdini tried to solve the mysteries of spiritism. He told friends he was ready to believe. was anxious to believe, because he would find joy in proof that he could communicate with his father, mother and friends who had passed on. He had agreed with friends and acquaintances, numbering hundreds, that the first to die was to try to communicate from the spirit world to the world of reality. Fourteen of those friends had died, but none had ever given a sign, he said.

Anxious for Spirit Messages.

"One of those pledges," Houdini once told, "was with my secretary, John W. Sargent, one of those who exposed Palladino in this city. Our relations were most intimate. He died and I have not heard from him. Such an agreement I made with both my parents. They died and I have not heard from them. I thought once I saw my mother in a vision, but I now believe it was imagination.

"Another thing that seemed almost supernatural to me occurred at the death of William Berol, a mystifier and close friend of mine. We had worked together on the stage and had a private telegraphic code for signaling messages. We made a compact that the first who died should use that code to communicate with the other. At his deathbed I held Berol's hand. He had been unconscious for some time. He showed no outward signs of a return to consciousness. His eyes remained closed. But just as he passed away I could feel his hand making a faint pressure upon mine. That was repeated at intervals and I could recognize that the man who seemed unconscious and at death's door was talking to me in code. I received and understood his message. But I hold it sacred and have never repeated it."

Houdini counted that he had had "four close-ups with death" in his career of more than thirty years as a mystifier. The closest was in California, where he risked his life on a bet and not as a public performance. Seven years ago in Los Angeles he made a wager that he could free himself from a six-foot grave into which he was to be buried after being manacled. He had first accustomed himself to the sensation of burial by more shallow interments.

Scare Nearly Cost Life.

"The knowledge that I was six feet under the sod gave me the first thrill of horror I had ever experienced," Houdini was wont to say in telling of his hair-raising escaps. "The momentary scare, the irretrievable mistake of all daredevils, nearly cost me my life, for it caused me to waste a fraction of breath when every fraction was needed to pull through. I had kept the sand loose about my body so that I could work dexterously. I did. But as I clawed and kneed the earth my strength began to fail. Then I made another mistake. I yelled. Or, at least, I attempted to, and the last remnants of my self-possession left me. Then instinct stepped in to the rescue. With my last reserve strength I fought through, more sand than air entering my nostrils. The sunlight came like a blinding blessing, and my friends about the grave said that, chalky pale and wild-eyed as I was, I presented a perfect imitation of a dead man rising.

"The next time I am buried it will not be alive if I can help it."

But Houdini did later permit himself to be "buried alive" in a hermetically sealed casket of zinc which was submerged in a pool at a New York hotel. He remained there for more than an hour and a half, bettering the record of the Egyptian fakir, Rahmin Bey.

When there was talk of a "return" submergence contest between the magician and the fakir, Houdini made preparations to defend his title with all the care that he was wont to exercise in working up his baffling feats. He began to cancel engagements that conflicted with a period of training he mapped out for himself.

"I can't dine with you this afternoon at 6 o'clock because I have to go down at 5," said Houdini to a friend. Houdini went "down" or submerged in his sealed casket for half an hour daily.

Friends of the showman said yesterday that he had developed a dislike for being called by his first name, Harry. He always wished to be called Houdini and disliked the prefix, Mr.

"All the News That's Fit to Print"

The New York Times

LATE CITY EDITION

Weather: Partly sunny today; cold tonight. Sunny and cool tomorrow. Temperature range: today 40-60; Monday 35-59. Details on page 69.

VOL. CXXV . . No. 43,172 NEW YORK, TUESDAY, APRIL 6, 1976 — 25 cents beyond 50-mile zone from New York City, except Long Island. Higher in air delivery cities. — 20 CENTS

Howard Hughes Dies at 70 On Flight to Texas Hospital

Stroke Given as Cause of Billionaire's Death —Security Is Tight

United Press International

Howard Hughes years ago

By JAMES P. STERBA

Special to The New York Times

HOUSTON, April 5—Howard R. Hughes died today as mysteriously as he had lived.

The reclusive 70-year-old billionaire was on the way from Acapulco, Mexico, to the Methodist Hospital here for emergency medical treatment. A physician accompanying him told hospital officials that Mr. Hughes died at 1:27 P.M. in a chartered Lear jet flying over south Texas.

The body was taken by ambulance to the hospital, where tight security was imposed. Four armed Houston policemen stood guard outside the hospital's pathology laboratory, in the basement, where the body lay.

Hospital officials declined to discuss any medical details. They referred all questions to a Hughes spokesman in Los Angeles.

A spokesman for the Summa Corporation, the heart of the Hughes empire, said tonight, "Howard R. Hughes is dead."

A Hughes spokesman in Los Angeles said the cause of death was a "cerebral vascular accident." This is otherwise known as a stroke.

Mr. Hughes left an estate estimated to be worth $1.5 billion or more.

Mr. Hughes's wishes for the disposition of his holdings were as completely shrouded in secrecy as his life had been in recent years. His movements were always the subject of rumors but the rumors were rarely confirmed.

Larry Mathis, a Methodist Hospital vice president, reported that a Hughes aide telephoned hospital officials about 9 A.M. and said Mr. Hughes would be arriving this afternoon.

"We were aware it was an emergency, but we did not know what the nature of the problem was and we still don't know," Mr. Mathis said at 7:30 tonight.

The Harris County medical examiner, Dr. Joseph A. Jachimczyk, consulted with hospital officials tonight but refused to be interviewed afterward.

A spokesman for the Baylor College of Medicine, of which Methodist Hospital is a teaching affiliate, said that a Hughes aide telephoned Dr. Henry D. MacIntosh, the chairman of its department of internal medicine, this morning and requested that arrangements be made for an examination and treat-

Continued on Page 59, Column 4

A Modified Soviet Bloc Is Avowed as U.S. Policy

By DAVID BINDER

Special to The New York Times

WASHINGTON, April 5—Helmut Sonnenfeldt, Secretary of State Henry A. Kissinger's chief adviser, told American ambassadors in Europe that it is in the long-term interest of the United States to encourage East European countries to develop "a more natural and organic" relationship with the Soviet Union, according to an official but nonverbatim summary of his remarks.

The summary, made available today to The New York Times, has been the subject of controversy for two weeks as a result of various versions disclosed by the press.

Summary of the Sonnenfeldt remarks is on Page 14.

It was drafted when Mr. Sonnenfeldt, the State Department counselor, addressed a London meeting of ambassadors in mid-December and was distributed to them in the form of a cablegram from Washington as a memorandum last Feb. 12.

"With regard to Eastern Europe," the memorandum says, "it must be in our long-term interest to influence events in this area—because of the present unnatural relationship with the Soviet Union—so that they will not sooner or later explode, causing World War III. This inorganic, unnatural relationship is a far greater danger to world peace than the conflict between East and West."

He then entered a qualification, saying that if Western Europe turned inward in preoccupation with economic and social problems, it could cause a shift in the power balance inimical to American interests. Continuing on the East European theme, the summary said:

"So, our policy must be a policy of responding to the clearly visible aspirations in Eastern Europe for a more autonomous existence within

Continued on Page 14, Column 4

DEMOCRATS SEEK NEW YORK BACKING IN PRIMARY TODAY

Jackson, Udall and Carter Wind Up Campaigning— Wisconsin Also Voting

By FRANK LYNN

The three major candidates for the Democratic Presidential nomination wound up their drives for today's New York primary with diverse campaigning yesterday that reflected their political priorities and strategy.

Senator Henry M. Jackson of Washington, who must win decisively here to regain momentum in the Presidential race, campaigned across the state from Buffalo to Staten Island.

Representative Morris K. Udall of Arizona, who has tried to divide his effort between New York and Wisconsin, which also votes today, made a perfunctory appearance designed to attract as much news attention as possible.

Jimmy Carter, former Governor of Georgia, who spent the day in Wisconsin, campaigned in absentia in New York with mimeographed announcements of endorsements.

Wisconsin Campaigning

Meanwhile, in Wisconsin, Mr. Carter and Representative Udall were tying up loose ends in their campaigns. The two men, who are considered the front runners in Wisconsin, scurried across the state in a last-minute hunt for support.

Former Senator Fred R. Harris of Oklahoma, who had virtually abandoned his campaign here, made rare appearances in the city and upstate to try to salvage some delegates.

The polls in New York City will be open from 6 A.M. to 9 P.M. and outside the city from noon to 9 P.M. A total of 856 Democrats are vying for 206 national convention delegate berths in the state's 39 Congressional districts.

9 Percent of Delegates

The district delegates and 68 delegates at large to be appointed by the Democratic state committee and apportioned to each candidate on the basis of his showing today represent 9 percent of the 3,008 delegates who will convene July 12 at Madison Square Garden.

Senator Jackson has repeatedly predicted—and he did so again yesterday—that he will win a majority of the delegates. He has also made a major commitment of manpower, money and his own

Continued on Page 22, Column 1

Seaver Accepts Pact

Tom Seaver agreed last night to a three-year contract with the New York Mets that will pay the pitcher more than $200,000 a year. Seaver had two meetings with the Mets' board chairman, M. Donald Grant, before agreeing to terms. Details, Page 43.

Callaghan, Party's Choice, Is Prime Minister of Britain

Associated Press

James Callaghan, Britain's Foreign Secretary, arrives at Labor Party headquarters in London with his wife, Audrey.

Special to The New York Times

LONDON, April 5—James Callaghan, the Foreign Secretary, was chosen today as Britain's new Prime Minister. He promptly called on the divided factions of his party to unify behind efforts to rescue Britain from its long-term economic decline.

The Labor Party members of the House of Commons gave Mr. Callaghan, 64 years old, the party's leadership and this country's top government post by a comfortable margin in the third round of a balloting process that began on March 16, when Harold Wilson unexpectedly announced his resignation from office.

Mr. Callaghan received 176 votes today. Michael Foot, the Secretary of State for Employment and champion of the party's left wing, won 137 votes. They were the only nominees to survive the earlier rounds.

Technically, the most the members could confer on Mr. Callaghan was the leadership of the Labor Party. But since Mr. Wilson resigned as Prime Minister midway through the Labor Party Government's five-year term of office, his successor as party leader automatically became Prime Minister.

Although the vote made Mr. Callaghan's succession certain, he observed the time-honored ritual of presenting himself to Queen Elizabeth II before formally taking office.

Mr. Wilson arrived at Buckingham Palace at 5:26 to hand in his resignation and told the Queen of his and his party's "advice." Mr. Callaghan arrived

Continued on Page 16, Column 3

City U. Board Acts To Save John Jay; Students in Protest

By JUDITH CUMMINGS

Acting on its controversial austerity program to restructure the City University, the Board of Higher Education voted last night to close or merge several of its colleges but accepted a modification that would allow John Jay College to remain open with a diminished enrollment.

At the end of a seven-hour meeting in which the board's vice chancellor resigned to protest the cuts, Alfred A. Giardino, the board's chairman, declared that the board would not impose tuition.

The board voted, 6 to 1 with one abstention, to eliminate liberal arts majors from John Jay's curriculum, but to retain its criminal justice and "fire science" courses, effective Sept. 1, 1976.

On the Medgar Evers issue, the board voted, 6 to 3, to downgrade the curriculum, effective in June, 1978.

Earlier, the board approved plans to merge Richmond College with Staten Island Community College and to join Hostos Community College with Bronx Community College.

The board acted after a day in which student demonstrations erupted briefly into fights between the police and supporters of the colleges.

Some demonstrators marched to the East River Drive at 77th

Continued on Page 69, Column 1

HIGH COURT DENIES APPEAL BY CALLEY

Refuses, Without Comment, to Review His Conviction in 22 Slayings at My Lai

By LESLEY OELSNER

Special to The New York Times

WASHINGTON, April 5—The Supreme Court refused today to review the court-martial conviction of former Army Lieut. William L. Calley Jr. for the murder of 22 civilians in the South Vietnamese hamlet of My Lai in 1968.

The Court's action, announced without comment or explanation, closes one of the most bitter chapters of the Vietnam War.

It ends for all practical purposes the long legal aftermath of the My Lai episode, in which 25 Army officers and enlisted personnel were charged with various offenses growing out of the slayings; only six of those 25 were tried, and only Mr. Calley was convicted.

Mr. Calley, who has been free on bail pending appeal since late 1974, after serving a little more than three years of what was originally a life sentence, will not be returned to confinement.

The Army announced this afternoon that, in accord with earlier Army decisions and pronouncements on the case,

Continued on Page 25, Column 1

U.S. Assays Peking Strife As Move Against Radicals

By BERNARD GWERTZMAN

Special to The New York Times

WASHINGTON, April 5—United States Government officials said today that the violent demonstrations in Peking appeared to represent a major counterattack by supporters of a moderate political policy against radicals who had appeared in the ascendency in China since Prime Minister Chou En-lai's death in January.

Because of the importance of the months-long political struggle in China, the demonstrations have received close attention here. Specialists in various agencies are comparing notes and reading the latest news dispatches and cables from the United States Liaison Office in Peking.

There was disagreement among the China-watchers on the degree of spontaneity of the demonstrations that followed the discovery that wreaths laid in Mr. Chou's honor had been removed. But even those who gave more weight to the spontaneity agreed that there had to be direction and manipulation from influential figures in Peking sympathetic to the moderate cause.

According to a view in top Government circles here, Mr. Chou's death prompted the radicals to make a significant effort to seize as much power as they could.

They were able to prevent Mr. Chou's hand-picked successor, Teng Hsiao-ping, from tak-

Continued on Page 9, Column 1

Hair Codes for Policemen Upheld by Supreme Court

By PRANAY GUPTE

The United States Supreme Court ruled yesterday that police departments had the right to order police officers to wear their hair short and not to wear beards.

In a 6-to-2 vote, the Court reversed a decision by the United States Court of Appeals in New York that said policemen had the constitutional right to wear their hair any way they wished and also to be hirsute if they so chose.

Delivering the majority opinion, Associate Justice William H. Rehnquist said that people who worked for government agencies had "no absolute constitutional right" to wear any hair style. Police departments, he said, could enforce grooming codes if there was a "rational basis" for such regulations.

The Supreme Court's ruling was on a case involving the Suffolk County Police Department and the Suffolk Patrolmen's Benevolent Association, in which police officers of the Long Island county had protested against their department's regulation concerning beards and hair lengths.

Although there is temporarily no grooming code in the Suffolk Police Department, policemen were forbidden to wear beards and maintain hair that touched the ears or shirt collar when the class-action suit first went to Federal Court in 1972.

The majority opinion of the

Continued on Page 25, Column 1

PEKING IS RACKED BY A DAY OF RIOTS; MILITIA STEPS IN

Crowds, Put at 30,000, Set Cars on Fire and Try to Storm the Great Hall

BACKING FOR CHOU SEEN

Demonstrations Appear to Be Backlash to Campaign Against 'Rightists'

By Reuters

PEKING, Tuesday, April 6—Violent demonstrations, apparently in support of former Prime Minister Chou En-lai and his associates, were staged through the day yesterday in Peking's Tien An Men Square, and few attempts were made to stop them.

After a day of incidents in which demonstrators estimated to total 30,000 tried to break into the Great Hall of the People and many set cars and a nearby building afire, militiamen armed with wooden staves cleared the area. Long orderly lines of militamen were seen escorting people, apparently demonstrators, into the ancient Forbidden City, and late last night quiet appeared to have been restored.

Struggle for Power

The demonstrations appeared to be a backlash against the so-called antirightist campaign begun as part of the power struggle in the Chinese leadership after Mr. Chou died in January.

Peking's Mayor, Wu Ten, linked the demonstrations to that struggle as he appealed in late afternoon for the crowds to disperse. In a message broadcast through loudspeakers, he charged that the riots were aimed at Chairman Mao Tse-tung and the Central Committee of the Chinese Communist Party and that behind them were persons who supported the "capitalist road."

This was an allusion principally to Deputy Prime Minister Teng Hsiao-ping, an associate of Mr. Chou who had been expected to become Prime Minister and who has been main target of the antirightist campaign.

Teng Had Been in Disgrace

Mr. Teng, who was denounced during the Cultural Revolution of the late 1960's, was brought back from disgrace by Mr. Chou and given the posts of senior Deputy Prime Minister, Deputy Chairman of the party and acting Chief of Staff of the army in apparent preparation for taking over as head of the government. He has not appeared in public since the Chou funeral and has been increasingly accused of stressing material incentives over political awareness and thus trying to bring back capitalism.

The post of Acting Prime Minister that he was expected to get went instead to Hua Kuo-feng, a Deputy Prime Minister and Minister of Public Security.

Yesterday, throughout the day in Tien An Men Square, unarmed troops and militiamen tried to maintain order but were careful to avoid clashes. Authorities made no attempt to break up the crowds and appeared to

Continued on Page 8, Column 4

Oil Prospects Off Jersey 'Encouraging'

By MARTIN WALDRON

The prospect of finding oil and gas under offshore sites in the Atlantic Ocean is "very encouraging," according to the first reports from an exploratory well sunk by a consortium of petroleum companies 80 miles off the New Jersey coast.

The companies have declined to comment on the results, citing their proprietary interests, but New Jersey officials yesterday confirmed that core samples brought up in the test drilling suggest the presence of large oil and natural-gas deposits.

The test well was drilled three miles deep on the edge of the Baltimore Canyon, a trough that stretches from just south of Long Island to the Delaware-Maryland state line.

Initial tests, which ended on March 28, found "core samplings which followed exactly what could be expected from the indications of earlier seismic tests," a state official with access to the reports said.

On the basis of seismic tests and geologic studies, the Interior Department has estimated that two to four billion barrels of oil and five to 14 trillion cubic feet of gas lie under the Continental Shelf from Maine to Florida.

No offshore wells have been sunk to substantiate the presence of oil and gas reserves under the Continental Shelf.

The exploratory well was drilled to test the geological strata of what was believed to be a promising site. The mud, sand and rock brought up by the rig at the site suggested only that conditions for oil pooling and gas accumula-

Continued on Page 32, Column 6

NEWS INDEX

The New York Times/Don Hogan Charles

Students from Medgar Evers College of City University block traffic on the East River Drive at 77th Street as part of their protest

HOWARD HUGHES IS DEAD ON PLANE

Continued From Page 1, Col. 2

ment for Mr Hughes. The spokesman declined to discuss specifics. Dr. MacIntosh is the hospital's chief of internal medicine.

The jet carrying Mr. Hughes's body arrived at Houston's Intercontinental Airport at 1:50 P.M. from Acapulco, where he was reported to have been living at the Princess Hotel. The plane was chartered this morning in Fort Lauderdale, Fla., to fly to Acapulco and pick up Mr. Hughes.

At the airport, the plane was met by an unmarked ambulance and, according to reports, by Dr. MacIntosh. Marie Denton, a Customs inspector, said the body was carried on a stretcher, covered with a blanket, to the ambulance. She said she did not inspect the body, though she made a routine check of the jet and was shown a birth certificate with Mr. Hughes's name on it.

Besides the two crewmen and Mr. Hughes, the plane carried two physicians and an administrative aide.

The ambulance carried the body 28 miles from the airport to Methodist Hospital, which is in the Texas Medical Center complex.

A policeman outside the pathology laboratory said that Dr. Michael DeBakey, the heart surgeon who is president of Baylor College of Medicine, entered and stayed about 30 minutes earlier tonight.

In Los Angeles, Arlo Sederberg, a public relations man for Mr. Hughes, said that funeral services "probably would be decided by business associates of the late multimillionaire Tuesday."

Mr. Sederberg said that he was not aware of any relatives who would inherit the Hughes fortune, which he estimated at $2 billion.

Mr. Hughes had not been in poor health lately, Mr. Sederberg said.

The owner of a local funeral home said that unidentified representatives had been in touch with him about Hughes arrangements for disposition of the body, United Press International reported.

George Lewis Jr. told reporters that there would be an autopsy at 1 P.M. tomorrow and added, "We expect to get the body at 3 P.M.," the news service said.

There is reportedly a Hughes family plot in a small Houston cemetery where the billionaire's mother and father are buried.

Secrecy Shrouds Hughes Empire's Fate

By WALLACE TURNER
Special to The New York Times

SAN FRANCISCO, April 5—As the death of Howard R. Hughes was disclosed tonight, the ultimate disposition of his vast wealth was as big a secret as his personal life had been during his last years.

Someone somewhere knows what he owned. Somewhere someone knows what he wants done with it now that he is dead. The odds are that no one person holds all this information, and that when it is pieced together, disagreement will ensue.

Mr. Hughes left an empire worth upward of $1.5 billion. The best guess is that he also left a will that provides that his estate, and his wishes for disposition of it, be administered by three people.

These are Chester C. Davis of New York, a lawyer for Mr. Hughes for about two decades and chief counsel of the Summat Corporation; F. W. Gay of Encino, Calif., executive vice president of Summa, and Nadine Henley of Los Angeles, who started as Mr. Hughes's secretary 30 years ago and is now senior vice president of Summa.

The heart of Mr. Hughes's holdings was the Summa Corporation, which was his personal holding company. Once it had been the Hughes Tool Company, the concern that his father left to him and that was the foundation of his fortune.

But Mr. Hughes liquidated that company, selling it to a group of his major employees in 1972. The stock was passed along to the public and brought Mr. Hughes about $140 million, financial circles estimated at the time.

Mr. Hughes was a sole owner and so issued no stockholders' reports or balance sheets. An estimate, based on some inside knowledge, put the $1.5 billion figure on his wealth when he died.

This does not include the $800 million Hughes Aircraft Company, which he gave to a charitable trust in 1954. There has been much criticism of the enforcement by the Internal Revenue Service of tax laws as they apply to the conduct of the Howard R. Hughes Medical Foundation, owner of the Hughes Aircraft Company, but that does not change the fact that when Mr. Hughes died, he did not have title to the aircraft company.

Thus Mr. Hughes had disposed of about $1 billion of his property either through sale of the tool company or through creation of the charitable trust.

His gambling empire, built seemingly on a whim, was the largest in Nevada. He owned a string of hotels on the Las Vegas Strip—the Desert Inn, the Frontier, the Landmark, the Sands, Castaways, and the Silver Slipper Casino. He also owned Harold's Club in Reno.

These casinos had a gambling business that made Mr. Hughes the biggest gambler in Nevada, the only state to license casinos.

Yet, when he tired of this, he turned his back on the games, the hotels and the politics of Nevada to move away one night to live in the Bahamas, in London, in Managua, Nicaragua, and, finally in Acapulco, Mexico, where he went just a few months ago.

When he left Grand Bahama Island, his retreat for several years, he left a hotel he had purchased and where he occupied the penthouse.

Headquarters in Las Vegas

But the Hughes headquarters is still in Las Vegas. There officers of the Summa Corporation administer the gambling-hotel investments as well as Mr. Hughes's extensive land holdings.

He has a 520-acre ranch near Las Vegas, and he also has owned for decades a 40-square-mile block of land and another $75 million to $100 million in undeveloped land around Las Vegas.

Mr. Hughes owned KLAS-TV in Las Vegas, a CBS outlet, which he bought from Hank Greenspun, owner of the Las Vegas Sun. The story told at the time of the purchase was that Mr. Hughes wanted movies all night and when he could not get them, he bought the television station.

The Hughes helicopter manufacturing company in Culver City, Calif., is controlled by the holding company, Summa, as is Hughes Air West, a regional airline.

Some of his actions in the airline acquisition caused him to be indicted in 1974 on charges of violation of the Securities and Exchange Act. But the charges were dismissed on motions before trial.

There are odd bits and pieces scattered through the Hughes empire. For example, he owned Archisystems, an architecture and design company in Van Nuys, Calif. He also owend a sports television network.

And he owns scores of old, abandoned gold mines scattered around the West. He acquired these mines during his Las Vegas period, which lasted from November 1966, until November 1970.

Millions of dollars were spent by Mr. Hughes to acquire those gold mines, and by all accounts they were worthless.

The key to Mr. Hughes's spectacular wealth always seemed to be his ability to get government contracts, and to hold them despite the myriad problems he encountered.

Last December The Philadelphia Inquirer published the results of a long study of Mr. Hughes's relationships with Federal agencies. The newspaper estimated that companies controlled by Mr. Hughes had contracts with Federal agencies for $6 billion from 1965 to 1974.

The scope of the problem in guessing about what Mr. Hughes would do with his empire is best illustrated by a story told by Noah Dietrich, who for more than 30 years was Mr. Hughes's major domo.

Mr. Dietrich said that Mr. Hughes had once decided that he should have a will, since he risked death in his airplane flights. The industrialist had different secretaries type different pages, and had several different versions typed.

"Then he could go in a closet, shuffle the pages together from different versions and burn the pages he didn't want to use, and nobody would have the slightest idea what he wanted to do with his money," Mr. Dietrich said.

Philip Hannifin, chairman of the Nevada Gaming Control Board, said that state officials expected Mr. Hughes's casinos to continue to operate as they have. He pointed out that Mr. Hughes had had his principal executives listed as operators of the casinos. This covers any short-term problem, Mr. Hannifin said.

"In the long term, we will have to wait until his estate is probated to see what will happen," Mr. Hannifin said.

Three years ago Mr. Hughes gave up one of his most prized possessions — his privacy—to protect the licenses of his gambling establishments.

He actually showed himself to two outsiders. Gov. Mike O'Callaghan of Nevada and Mr. Hannifin. That meeting resulted from Mr. Hughes's involvement in a bitter fight with Robert A. Maheu, who had been his principal employee from about 1968 until Mr. Hughes fled Las Vegas in 1970.

Mr. Hughes agreed at the urging of aides to see the Governor and the head of the Gaming Control Board. However, they had to travel to London for the meeting, which they did in March 1973.

They were met by a gracious man who talked with them for a long time, they said, and listened to their replies by aiming a hearing aid microphone toward the speaker. He was described as wearing a Vandyke beard, well trimmed, as being terribly thin, but mentally alert and showing great strength of personality.

Hughes Seen By 2 Pilots As Worn Out

FORT LAUDERDALE, Fla., April 5 (AP)—When Howard R. Hughes was put aboard an air ambulance in Acapulco, Mexico, today, he looked "wasted" and "like a tired, worn-out old person," according to Jeff Abrams, the copilot of the jet.

Mr. Hughes died on the plane while being flown to Houston.

Roger Sutton, pilot of the Graf Jet air-ambulance charter service of Fort Lauderdale, described Mr. Hughes as being emaciated, with a thin beard and long, grayish hair.

"He was very wasted," Mr. Sutton said. "He was very, very pale."

Mr. Sutton, 30 years old, and Mr. Abrams, 22, were interviewed after returning home. They said that their jet had been chartered late Sunday by a South Florida physician whom they did not identify. They left Fort Lauderdale at 5 A.M. Eastern Standard Time today and reached Acapulco four hours later.

The pilots said that they did not know until near the end of a five-hour wait in Acapulco that their ambulance passenger was to be Mr. Hughes. But they said that they had a strong hunch it would be.

Mr. Sutton and Mr. Abrams said that they saw Mr. Hughes, wearing what appeared to be bed clothes, when he was loaded aboard their jet on a stretcher.

The pilots described the two-hour flight to Houston as "very routine." Mr. Abrams said that they did not know until after landing that Mr. Hughes had died on the flight.

Associated Press

Howard Hughes at the controls of a plane during demonstration of radar device in 1947

Life of Howard Hughes Was Marked by a Series of Bizarre and Dramatic Events

Two years ago one of Howard R. Hughes's many lawyers appeared before a Federal judge in Los Angeles in one of the many court cases involving the reclusive billionaire.

Asked to explain the failure of his client to appear, the attorney, Norbert Schlei, said Mr. Hughes was "a man to whom you cannot apply the same standards as you can to you and me."

He got no dispute on that point from judge or jury, although the case ended in one of the few setbacks Mr. Hughes ever encountered in court—a $2,823,333 defamation award to his former aide Robert A. Maheu.

Neither that development nor the sequence of dramatic events that continued until his death ever persuaded him to appear in public. Shy, suspicious and obsessed with privacy, he traveled by night in private planes, almost never emerged from his international network of aeries, rarely received even his closest business associates and from day to day was seen only by a handful of men who served as combination secretaries, nurses, cooks, bodyguards and messengers to the outside world.

Perhaps the most bizarre outcome of a Hughes effort emerged a year ago when it became known that he and the Central Intelligence Agency had teamed up in a science-fiction escapade to recover a sunken Soviet submarine from the Pacific Ocean floor.

Ship Constructed

The submarine, which sank 750 miles northwest of Hawaii in 1968, held nuclear warheads and code books, and Mr. Hughes, at the behest of the C.I.A., commissioned the construction of a ship called the Glomar Explorer and a mammoth barge to retrieve the vessel. The entire project was conducted under the ruse of being a deep-sea mining research venture.

The notoriety attending that adventure followed by less than a year a series of disclosures suggesting that part of a $100,000 Hughes "contribution" to former President Richard M. Nixon was included in some $50,000 that Charles G. Rebozo is alleged to have spent for Mr. Nixon's benefit.

A persistent theory is that the Watergate break-in and the cover-up plot that followed it stemmed from a White House effort to suppress public knowledge of the payment from Mr. Hughes to Mr. Nixon.

The Irving Affair

Controversial and headline-making as these incidents and numbers of others in Mr. Hughes's life were, none galvanized the attention of the world like the extraordinary sequence of events stemming from the announcement by McGraw-Hill and Life magazine on Dec. 7, 1971, that they planned to publish an "autobiography" of Mr. Hughes, as told to a little-known expatriate American writer named Clifford Irving.

Many writers had attempted to get Mr. Hughes to tell his story, but none had ever gained his cooperation. Then Mr. Irving, falsely claiming to have met secretly with his subject more than 100 times for tape-recorded discussions about his life, came forward with a 230-000-word manuscript entitled "The Autobiography of Howard Hughes."

McGraw-Hill gave him $750,000 for it—a $100,000 advance on book sales and $650,000 in checks made out to "H. R. Hughes," as payment to Mr. Hughes for his "cooperation."

Mr. Irving's wife, Edith, using the name Helga R. Hughes, deposited the checks in a Swiss bank. McGraw-Hill sold excerpt rights to Life.

Mr. Hughes promptly denounced the work as a hoax in an extraordinary telephone news conference, filed a lawsuit to halt publication and promised to prove Mr. Irving was a fake. (He also charged that his aide, Mr. Maheu, "stole me blind," leading to the defamation decision two years later.) The publishers rallied to Mr. Irving's defense—and the battle was joined.

For a nation preoccupied with the seemingly insolvable complexities of Vietnam, the Middle East and other problems, the Irving-Hughes fight was a fascinating mystery, fraught with intriguing ambiguities but sure to be unraveled in the end.

For weeks, the struggle was played out across the front pages and broadcast outlets of the country with claims and counterclaims by the principals, disputes among handwriting experts over the "H. R. Hughes" check endorsements and almost daily new revelations by investigative reporters.

Gradually, however, the tide began to turn against Mr. Irving. Edith Irving was exposed as the "Helga R. Hughes" who appeared in Switzerland. Evidence mounted that Mr. Irving's manuscript resembled published and unpublished materials produced by others.

In mid-February of 1972, Life and McGraw-Hill conceded the work was a hoax and canceled publication plans. Mr. Irving and his wife pleaded guilty and both served jail sentences for their deception.

After the Irving affair, during which he remained secluded in a hotel in the Bahamas, Mr. Hughes spent what was for him a busy year of moving around. Caught between political factions in a dispute over his presence in Nassau, he quit his penthouse at the Britannia Beach Hotel.

But he did not return to Las Vegas, where he had lived at the Desert Inn penthouse. Instead he went to Managua, Nicaragua, then to Vancouver, British Columbia, and back to Managua. Dislodged but unhurt in the earthquake that struck the country soon after that, he left and went to London, taking the penthouse suite at the Park Hotel.

No matter where he was, Mr. Hughes's five close-lipped male attendants served him around the clock, in shifts. All but one were Mormons, whom he favored because they did not smoke or drink. The fifth was married to a Mormon.

Other than these men, Mr. Hughes rarely saw anyone but his wife, Jean Peters, the actress he married in 1957. They were divorced in 1971 after a lengthy separation.

The difficulty of seeing Mr. Hughes was once summed up by his uncle, Rupert Hughes, the novelist, who said, "I can get through to the Almighty by dropping to my knees, but I don't know how to get in touch with Howard."

It wasn't always that way. Back in the nineteen-thirties when he was setting air speed records and was the maverick Hollywood producer of "Hell's Angels," "Scarface" and "The Outlaw," the newspapers were laden with photographs of a lean and smiling Mr. Hughes posing with Jane Russell, Lana Turner, Ava Gardner and other film and cafe society beauties. A fictive version of those Hollywood years was reputedly contained in Harold Robbins's novel "The Carpetbaggers."

Won Congressional Medal

As a daring pilot, he set several air speed records and in 1938 flew around the world in 91 hours—a feat for which he was voted a Congressional medal. He never bothered to pick it up, however, and years later President Harry S. Truman found it in a White House desk and mailed it to him.

In public welcomes and ticker-tape parades that honored his flying exploits — including one in New York — the lanky Mr. Hughes was a smiling hero. "He had the face of a poet and the shyness of a schoolboy," according to The New York Times account of his City Hall reception.

But even when Mr. Hughes was a public figure, there were elements of mystery and enigma to him. His comings and goings were cloaked in secretiveness; his business dealings were consummated at odd hours and at places as uncommon as a men's room in the Waldorf-Astoria Hotel.

Those who met Mr. Hughes in the early fifties, before he had secluded himself to the point where Fortune magazine spoke of him as "the spook of American capitalism," said that he customarily materialized for business conferences in tennis sneakers, jeans and a shirt open at the collar. There were a number of explanations for his reclusiveness: the desire of a billionaire to avoid importunate friends; his deafness; his shyness, which had been evident since young manhood; and a hypochondriacal fear of germs, which extended to separate refrigerators for himself and his wife, separate copies of magazines and newspapers and an unwillingness to shake hands.

One man who knew him well recalled:

"I went to shake hands and he said, 'I'm sorry, I've been eating a sandwich and I got mustard on my hand.' That's all right, I said. 'Well,' said Mr. Hughes, 'I cut my hand when I was shaving; I have both mustard and blood on my hand.' "

A Governor's Request

After Mr. Hughes had settled in Nevada in 1966 and had invested more than $125-million in casinos and real estate, Gov. Paul Laxalt let it be known that he would at least like to speak with his state's benefactor. Shortly thereafter Mr. Hughes —or a voice that identified itself as his—telephoned the Governor. Shrewd in politics, especially after his buffeting in Washington, Mr. Hughes, according to Mr. Laxalt, was an occasional telephoner, and the two men sometimes conversed for an hour.

About 25 years ago Mr. Hughes denied, in an interview, that there was anything especially eccentric about himself. He said:

"I am not a man of mystery. These stories grow like Greek myths. Every time I hear them, they're more fantastic. I run several businesses, and the people associated with me read those stories and do not understand them.

"There is nothing mysterious about me. I have no taste for expensive clothes. Clothes are something to wear and automobiles are transportation. If they merely cover me up and get me there, that's sufficient."

Eccentric or not, Mr. Hughes went to Nevada in 1966 under unusual circumstances, arriving at Las Vegas in the dead of night in a private railroad train from Boston. He had journeyed to Boston from his home in Bel Air, Calif., for, depending on which report was accurate, an operation to relieve his deafness or to scout ways to invest the $566-million he had recently received for his 78 per cent holding in Trans World Airlines. It was believed to be the largest sum ever to come into the hands of one man at one time.

Recuperated at Ranch

Mr. Hughes and his entourage installed themselves on the ninth (and top) floor of the Desert Inn, one of the most renowned of the Las Vegas hostelries. So far as is known, he left his quarters only for trips to his nearby ranch. Reports were that he often worked around the clock for four days at a stretch and then, exhausted, recuperated at the ranch.

Work, for Mr. Hughes, often consisted of one telephone call after another, associates said. However, he rarely made night calls to persons who did not work for him. Once, when an aide complained after he had been aroused by calls for the third time after midnight, Mr. Hughes told him:

"Look, the bankers and others I have to call during the day. But you work for me. I can call you any time."

Shortly after his arrival in Las Vegas, Mr. Hughes bought the operating contracts of the Desert Inn for $13.25-million, and later the property as well. One story was that he had acted when the owners requested him to leave his $250-a-day suite to make way for already-booked guests. Another explanation was that this was the first in a series of shrewdly calculated investments by which Mr. Hughes could multiply his millions with relative tax freedom. "There are very few places in America he could afford to get caught dead in," an aide remarked, alluding to Nevada's absence of state income or inheritance taxes.

A third, and perhaps complementary, explanation was provided by Mr. Hughes through Mr. Maheu in 1967 after the hermit entrepreneur had extended his Las Vegas holdings to desert acreage outside the city. This was that Mr. Hughes had in mind a huge regional airport for supersonic jets and subsonic jumbo jets that would

(continued)

The New York Times

The "World's Fair of 1939," a Howard Hughes plane landing at Floyd Bennett Field, Brooklyn, in July of 1938 after establishing a record of three days, 19 hours and 14 minutes in a round-the-world flight.

Associated Press

The Hughes flying boat at Long Beach, Calif., on Nov. 2, 1947 during its first and only test flight. The plane, with Mr. Hughes at the controls, got 70 feet off the water for a one-mile run. The Government put $18 million into the plane, and Mr. Hughes said he invested $23 million of his funds.

transform Las Vegas into a terminal for the Southwest and California.

"A whole new concept of airport versus city location may take place," the Hughes statement said. "For instance, there may be one SST and jumbo-jet airport to serve the entirety of southern Nevada, California and Arizona. From this terminus, passengers may be flown by regular jet aircraft to any normally located present-day airport."

However visionary this statement may have been, reaction to it in Las Vegas was optimistic. "Everybody's punchy, especially the real estate brokers," one businessman said at the time. Others built a castle of dreams in which the hot desert area bloomed with industry. And Hank Greenspun, publisher of The Las Vegas Sun, began to compare Mr. Hughes, quite favorably, to Sir Isaac Newton.

In all, up to the close of 1969, Mr. Hughes had invested about $150 million in Las Vegas properties. His chief holdings, in addition to the Desert Inn, were the Sands, the Frontier and the Castaways hotels, all containing gambling casinos; the Silver Slipper, a supper club and casino; the Landmark Hotel, as yet to be opened; the 520-acre Krupp ranch; and the North Las Vegas Airport.

Besides this, Mr. Hughes was the purchaser of Air West, with 9,000 route miles in eight Western states, Canada and Mexico. The acquisition was subject to approval of the Civil Aeronautics Board and the President. The line cost Mr. Hughes $150-million, but it put him back in the air travel business, which he had left when he sold his controlling interests in Trans World and Northeast.

Former F.B.I. Agent

Reputed to be an exceedingly shrewd businessman, albeit an unconventional one, Mr. Hughes operated through Mr. Maheu, a strapping, middle-age former agent for the Federal Bureau of Investigation, and scores of subordinates, most of whom never saw him.

The anchor of Mr. Hughes's fortune was his wholly owned Hughes Tool Company, situated in Texas, which manufactures and leases rock and oil drills. It also is the owner of a number of his other properties. He owned, moreover, the Hughes Aircraft Company in California, which manufactures electronic devices as well as planes and holds many Government contracts. This concern was nominally owned by the Howard Hughes Medical Institute. Furthermore, he controlled Sports Network, Inc., a company that syndicates live and taped coverage of sports events to television stations.

Not everything that Mr. Hughes sought was he able to acquire. In 1968, for example, he failed in a bid for the American Broadcasting Company network of television and radio outlets. And a deal for at least one Las Vegas casino fell through.

Befitting a man with a passion for privacy, Mr. Hughes tried to suppress books about himself. He was not totally successful, however. Before the Irving affair, one biography in progress was bought up from the writer; but two others persevered — Albert Gerber, who wrote "Bashful Billionaire" for Lyle Stuart, and John Keats, who did "Howard Hughes" for Random House. From these and other sources Mr. Hughes's life has been fairly well documented.

Howard Robard Hughes Jr. was born on Christmas Eve, 1905, in Houston. He was shy and serious as a boy and showed mechanical aptitude early. He attended two preparatory schools, the Fessenden School at West Newton, Mass., and the Thacher School at Ojai, Calif. He also took courses at Rice Institute in Houston and the California Institute of Technology, Pasadena. It is not clear how long he remained at either place. He held no degree.

Mr. Hughes's father was a mining engineer who developed the first successful rotary bit for drilling oil wells through rock. In 1909 the Hughes Tool Company was organized to manufacture and lease the patented rock bits. This was the beginning of the Hughes fortune.

The Hughes Tool Company had almost a monopoly in this field and consequently accumulated enormous revenues and profits. Even after the expiration of key patents in the nineteen-thirties and fifties, it continued to dominate the market.

When his mother died in 1922, Howard Hughes inherited 50 per cent of the company. On his father's death in 1924, he received 25 per cent. The family business was then appraised at $650,000. Mr. Hughes assumed personal direction of the company at the age of 18. Two years later, he bought out the remaining family interest.

When 19, Mr. Hughes married Ella Rice, a Houston social figure and member of the family that founded Rice Institute. This marriage lasted four and a half years. Mrs. Hughes obtained a divorce on the grounds of cruelty.

A Flop and a Hit

Meanwhile, Mr. Hughes had shifted his interest to Hollywood, where he set forth, characteristically, in lone-wolf style, to become a movie producer. His first film was called "Swell Hogan" and it was so bad it was never released.

But then came "Hell's Angels," starring the late Jean Harlow, the picture that made Miss Harlow a rising star and was a spectacular success all around. Filmed in 1930 at a cost of $4-million, it was then the most expensive movie ever made. Much of the cost resulted when the picture was made over for sound, which had come into general use when it was half finished. Mr. Hughes wrote, produced and directed this film, which grossed $8-million.

There followed other successes, including "Scarface" with Paul Muni and George Raft and "Front Page" with Pat O'Brien. As an independent producer, Mr. Hughes turned out about a dozen pictures in the late twenties and early thirties.

By then, Mr. Hughes had been intrigued with the still-young field of aviation. He learned to fly during the filming of "Hell's Angels" and was seriously injured when his plane, of World War I vintage, crashed.

There were to be other narrow escapes. In May, 1943, he was injured again when an experimental two-engined flying boat crashed and sank in Lake Mead near Boulder Dam, Nev. His most critical injuries occurred in 1946, when he crashed on the first flight of his XF-11, a high-speed, long-range airplane.

On the last occasion, Mr. Hughes tried to pancake the plane onto a golf course but hit three houses and a garage instead. His chest and left lung were crushed; he also suffered a skull fracture and had nine broken ribs. Physicians gave him little chance to live. During his recovery, he designed a new type of hospital bed.

Throughout the nineteen-thirties when he was designing, building and flying his own planes, Mr. Hughes was one of the gallery of spectacular names in flying. Between 1935 and 1938 he set three major speed records and twice won the Harmon Trophy.

These achievements, now a distant memory, were overshadowed in more recent years by a notable failure—that of the Hughes flying boat. This mammoth, eight-engine seaplane, built of plywood, was conceived by Mr. Hughes during World War II when a shortage of metal dictated the use of alternate materials. The Spruce Goose, as it was dubbed by the press, was designed to carry hundreds of troops to Europe safely above the mauraud-ing German submarines in the Atlantic. It had a wing spread of 320 feet, a hull three stories high and tail assembly eight stories tall.

The Government put $18-million into the plane, and Mr. Hughes said he had invested $23-million of his own funds. The giant craft flew only once—on Nov. 2, 1947, when, with Mr. Hughes at the controls, it got about 70 feet off the water for a one-mile run. At last report, the Spruce Goose was in a guarded hangar in Long Beach, Calif.

Before the war was over, Mr. Hughes had returned to independent motion-picture production. The occasion was a film that proved to be his most controversial venture. It was "The Outlaw," starring Mr. Hughes's personal discovery, Jane Russell.

This western movie was filmed in 1941-42, but it was denied a seal of approval by the Motion Picture Association of America because of greater exposure of Miss Russell than was customary.

The picture was released anyway and was shown in San Francisco in 1943. It ran into a storm of protest and censorship and was temporarily withdrawn. In 1946 "The Outlaw" was put into general distribution, with Mr. Hughes reaping both profits and publicity.

Two years later, Mr. Hughes made a more determined return to the motion-picture business by buying a controlling interest in the Radio-Keith-Orpheum Corporation, then Hollywood's fifth largest studio, for $8,-825,000.

During the erratic Hughes regime, R.K.O. was constantly in the red, losing more than $20-million, while other studios made money. In Mr. Hughes's last two years at the studio, R.K.O. made only five pictures, although it invested in others. Mr. Hughes was accused in one of the many stockholder suits of running the studio with "caprice, pique and whim."

On March 31, 1954, he wrote a personal check for $23,489,-478 and bought up the outstanding stock of R.K.O. He thus became the first person to own a major movie studio. The deal was the biggest personal transaction in Hollywood history.

But by July, 1955, Mr. Hughes was tired of the movies. He had been busy working on a jet liner with Convair and T.W.A. He sold the R.K.O. Radio Pictures Corporation, the motion picture subsidiary of R.K.O. Pictures, then a holding company, to the General Tire and Rubber Company for $25-million.

In the fall he merged the remaining R.K.O. company into the Atlas Corporation in return for an 11 per cent stock interest in Atlas. He was forced to put that stock in a trusteeship because of Atlas's stock control of Northeast Airlines. He later divested himself of his interest in Northeast.

All the while, Mr. Hughes was engaged in one of the most spectacular corporate battles in recent years. It involved control of Trans World Airlines and resulted in a complex mass of litigation.

Although retaining his nominally controlling interest in T.W.A., Mr. Hughes lost operating control of the airline to a group of Wall Street banks and financial institutions that had financed the purchase of jet planes for the line. That was in 1961 when Mr. Hughes was forced to put his majority stock interest in a voting trust for 10 years.

Thereafter, both sides — the new trustee management and the Hughes interests — sued each other more than $500-million. Repeated court hearings were held, although Mr. Hughes refused to appear at any of them.

Then on April 9, 1966, came the abrupt and surprising news that Mr. Hughes was putting his 78 per cent interest in T.W.A. up for sale.

Characteristically, Mr. Hughes had no comment, nor were his aides able to offer any explanation for the decision to sell.

Selling it out did not end the court fight, but Mr. Hughes ultimately won it in the Supreme Court.

United Press International

Howard Hughes with Ava Gardner in 1946

"All the News That's Fit to Print"

The New York Times

LATE CITY EDITION

Weather: Partly sunny, mild today; fair tonight. Sunny, mild tomorrow. Temp. range: today 45-59; Monday 35-54. Full U.S. report on Page 76.

VOL. CXXII . No. 42,003 | NEW YORK, TUESDAY, JANUARY 23, 1973 | 15 CENTS

LYNDON JOHNSON, 36TH PRESIDENT, IS DEAD; WAS ARCHITECT OF 'GREAT SOCIETY' PROGRAM

High Court Rules Abortions Legal the First 3 Months

State Bans Ruled Out Until Last 10 Weeks

National Guidelines Set by 7-to-2 Vote

By WARREN WEAVER Jr.

Special to The New York Times

WASHINGTON, Jan. 22 — The Supreme Court overruled today all state laws that prohibit or restrict a woman's right to obtain an abortion during her first three months of pregnancy. The vote was 7 to 2.

In a historic resolution of a fiercely controversial issue, the Court drafted a new set of

Excerpts from opinion and dissent are on Page 20.

national guidelines that will result in broadly liberalized anti-abortion laws in 46 states but will not abolish restrictions altogether.

Establishing an unusually detailed timetable for the relative legal rights of pregnant women and the states that would control their acts, the majority specified the following:

¶For the first three months of pregnancy the decision to have an abortion lies with the woman and her doctor, and the state's interest in her welfare is not "compelling" enough to warrant any interference.

¶For the next six months of pregnancy a state may "regulate the abortion procedure in ways that are reasonably related to maternal health," such as licensing and regulating the persons and facilities involved.

¶For the last 10 weeks of pregnancy, the period during which the fetus is judged to be capable of surviving if born, any state may prohibit

Continued on Page 20, Column 5

Cardinals Shocked —Reaction Mixed

By LAWRENCE VAN GELDER

Reaction to the Supreme Court decision on abortion fragmented yesterday along predictable lines, as leaders of the Roman Catholic Church assailed the ruling while birth control and women's rights activists praised it.

In the forefront of Catholic reaction were Cardinal Cooke of New York and Cardinal Krol of Philadelphia, who is also

Statements by Cooke and Krol appear on Page 20.

the president of the National Conference of Catholic Bishops.

Cardinal Cooke issued a statement calling the Court's action yesterday "shocking" and "horrifying." Cardinal Krol called the decision "an unspeakable tragedy for this nation."

But William Baird, a crusader for birth control and abortion, called the decision "a triumph" that culminated a long struggle.

"I'm delighted to see that our position—that women have the right to control their own bodies—has been vindicated," he said.

Dr. Alan F. Guttmacher, president of the Planned Parenthood Federation of America, called the decision "a wise and courageous stroke for the right to privacy, and for the protection of a woman's physical and emotional health."

"By this act," he said, "hundreds of thousands of American women every year will be

Continued on Page 20, Column 1

Ruling Seems to Forestall Abortion Debate in Albany

By WILLIAM E. FARRELL

Special to The New York Times

ALBANY, Jan. 22—The United States Supreme Court's abortion decision today appeared to quash the hopes of Right to Life and other anti-abortion groups for a full-scale debate in the Legislature again this year on repealing the state's liberalized abortion law.

"No way," replied Assemblyman Constance E. Cook, a Republican of Ithaca and a sponsor of the liberalized abortion law, when asked if the issue of restoring the old state statute would be seriously discussed again.

The liberalized state law permits a woman to have an abortion on demand until the 24th week of pregnancy. The old law permitted abortions only when a woman's life was in jeopardy.

Rendered 'Useless'

The Supreme Court's 7-to-2 ruling, Mrs. Cook said, rendered efforts by antiabortion lobbyists to force it to the floors of the Senate and Assembly "a useless show of strength."

Similarly, Assembly Speaker Perry B. Duryea, Republican of Montauk, said he felt it would be "futile" to bring repeal legislation up for debate again.

Well-organized opponents of the liberalized abortion law succeeded in having it repealed in both houses last year despite a pledge by Governor Rockefeller that he would veto a repeal measure. The Governor kept his promise.

Mr. Rockefeller, who did not comment on the court decision today pending a review of it by his legal staff, reaffirmed that he would again veto a repeal measure this year, but the antiabortion groups were undaunted.

Today, the comments of abortion opponents contained some of the emotional comments that the issue has always elicited here.

From his newly opened lobbying office near the Capitol, Edward J. Golden, chairman of the New York State Right to Life Committee, said, "virtually all protection under law has

Continued on Page 22, Column 1

3.7 MILLION CARS RECALLED BY G.M. TO CORRECT FLAW

Shields Will Be Installed to Prevent Entry of Gravel Into Steering System

By JERRY M. FLINT

Special to The New York Times

DETROIT, Jan. 22 — The General Motors Corporation recalled today 3.7 million 1971 and 1972 cars, its full-size Chevrolet, Pontiac, Buick and Oldsmobile models.

G.M. said it would install a shield at the bottom of the car to keep gravel from bouncing into the steering mechanism, which could jam the steering.

The automaker insisted that the trouble was rare, and rejected the idea of a recall on this problem last year. But at the same time the company said it had received reports of 96 incidents allegedly tied to the trouble, with 23 turned into accidents in which 12 injuries were reported.

Criticism by Nader

The recall is one of the largest but does not match the recall for correction of safety defects of 6.7 million G.M. cars in 1971 or 4.4 million Fords last June.

Ralph Nader, the auto industry's major critic, has criticized G.M. for its failure to recall cars to correct this problem, and last August the Government's safety agency issued a consumer warning bulletin on the problem.

At that time, General Motors said that it did not believe the safety hazard was serious but offered to repair the cars without charge. Reports of the trouble kept appearing and the company has changed its position.

Steering May Jam

The condition, General Motors said, can become a problem only if a car "is driven over loose gravel, on extremely rutted roads at speeds which caused the car to pitch excessively." If the front frame cross-member, a cross bar similar to a step on a ladder, dips so low to the ground that it scoops up loose stones or gravel "it then is possible that stones of a certain size and shape may lodge between the steering coupling and the frame." The stones fall out of the car if turned to the right, G.M. said, but the steering may

Continued on Page 78, Column 2

KISSINGER IN PARIS; CEREMONIAL SITE CHOSEN FOR TALKS

Use of Conference Center Indicates Both Sides View Truce Round as Vital

By FLORA LEWIS

Special to The New York Times

PARIS, Jan. 22 — Henry A. Kissinger arrived here tonight, and it was announced that his talks tomorrow with Le Duc Tho of North Vietnam would be moved to the ceremonial setting of the International Conference Center.

Hanoi and Washington announced jointly last week that this next round of negotiations would complete a cease-fire agreement for Vietnam. Today there was still no official word on how long that task would take, but the choice of location — after months of meetings in secluded private quarters — suggested that the two sides considered tomorrow's session important.

The announcement that the talks would be moved to the center was made by the North Vietnamese here tonight, then confirmed by the American delegation.

The conference center is the old Hotel Majestic, on the Avenue Kléber, site of the formal four-sided Paris peace conference for over four years.

At the airport Mr. Kissinger said nothing more than "I am glad to be here." He went directly to the residence of the South Vietnamese Forign Minister, Tran Van Lam, though it was nearly midnight and he had left Washington early in the morning.

That was apparently a proto-

Continued on Page 6, Column 4

NATION IS SHOCKED

Citizens Join Leaders in Voicing Sorrow and Paying Tribute

By ROBERT D. McFADDEN

Shock, sorrow and the sense of a historic leader lost were the mourning themes of public officials and private citizens across the nation last night as word spread that Lyndon Baines Johnson was dead.

From the White House and the halls of Congress where he had served, and in cities and towns across the land where he had campaigned and made his policies felt, there was an outpouring of tribute to the former President, Senator and Representative from Texas.

Statement by Nixon

Many recalled Mr. Johnson's efforts to promote racial equality, to fight poverty and to improve education; others said that his deep commitment to the war in Indochina had prevented him from achieving all his domestic goals.

President Nixon, in a statement, declared: "To President Johnson, the 'American Dream' was not a catch phrase—it was a reality of his own life. He believed in America, in what America could mean to all its citizens and what America could mean to the world. In the service of that faith, he gave himself completely."

Mr. Nixon noted that in more than three decades of public life, Mr. Johnson "knew times of triumph and times of despair—he knew controversy and adulation. Yet, no matter what the mood of the moment, at the center of his public life—and at the center of his spirit—was an unshakeable convic-

Continued on Page 25, Column 1

The New York Times/George Tames

LYNDON BAINES JOHNSON, 1908—1973

STRICKEN AT HOME

Apparent Heart Attack Comes as Country Mourns Truman

Special to The New York Times

SAN ANTONIO, Tex., Jan. 22 —Lyndon Baines Johnson, 36th President of the United States, died today of an apparent heart attack suffered at his ranch in Johnson City, Tex.

The 64-year-old Mr. Johnson, whose history of heart illness began in 1955, was pronounced dead on arrival at 4:33 P.M. central time at San Antonio International Airport, where he

An obituary article appears on Pages 26 through 29; an appraisal, Page 25.

had been flown in a family plane on the way to Brooke Army Medical Center here.

A spokesman at Austin said that Mr. Johnson's funeral would probably be held Thursday at the National City Christian Church in Washington. He said the body would lie in state at the Johnson Library in Austin from noon tomorrow until 8 A.M. Wednesday, with an honor guard, and then would be taken to Washington, where it will lie in state at the Capitol rotunda until the funeral. Mr. Johnson will be buried at the L.B.J. Ranch.

Death came to the nation's only surviving former President as the nation observed a period of mourning proclaimed less than a month ago for former President Harry S. Truman.

A Legacy of Progress

Although his vision of a Great Society dissolved in the morass of war in Vietnam, Mr. Johnson left to the nation a legacy of progress and innovation in civil rights, Social Security, education, housing and other programs attesting to his fundamental affection for his fellow Americans.

At Fort Sam Houston, where Brooke Army Medical Center is situated, flags were hoisted to full staff and then immediately lowered again in respect for the Texan who was thrust into the Presidency on Nov. 22, 1963, when an assassin's bullet took the life of President Kennedy in Dallas.

Ironically, Mr. Johnson died in what appeared to be the waning days of the Vietnam war. The man who won election in 1964 to a full term as President with the greatest voting majority ever accorded a candidate was transformed by that war into the leader of a divided nation.

Amid rising personal unpopularity, in the face of the lingering war and racial strife at home, Mr. Johnson surprised the nation on March 31, 1968, with a television speech in which he announced, "I shall not seek and I will not accept the nomination of my party as your President."

Stage Set for Defeat

He thus renounced an opportunity to cap with a second full term a career in public life that began in 1937 with his election to Congress as an ardent New Dealer and led to the majority leadership of the Senate and to the Vice-Presidency and the Presidency. His renunciation set the stage for Democratic defeat at the polls in 1968.

Two days before Mr. Johnson's death, Richard M. Nixon, the Republican who was elected in 1968, took the oath of office for his second term as President. Mr. Nixon telephoned Mrs. Johnson today at the hospital here to express his sympathy.

At a news briefing tonight in Austin at KTBC, the Johnson family's television and ra-

Continued on Page 25, Column 5

Foreman Stops Frazier In 2d Round, Wins Title

By RED SMITH

Special to The New York Times

KINGSTON, Jamaica, Jan. 22 —Under Caribbean skies that had never witnessed anything remotely like it, big George Foreman smashed Joe Frazier to the floor six times tonight and won the heavyweight championship of the world in 4 minutes 35 seconds.

Arthur Mercante, the referee from New York, stopped the uneven match with Frazier on his feet but hardly in the contest.

A crowd of 36,000 paying $412,000, substantially more than had been expected, saw one of the most startling upsets in two and a half centuries of heavyweight title matches. Frazier, in his 10th defense of the title New York State conferred on him in 1968 and his third since he whipped the former champion, Muhammad Ali, in 1971, had been favored at 1 to 3 in the betting shops here.

Foreman, unbeaten in 37 fights and author of 34 knockouts since he won the Olympic heavyweight title in 1968, had been recognized as Joe's most formidable opponent since Ali but most boxing men doubted that he could stand up under the ceaseless pressure of a characteristic Frazier attack.

They'll never know now whether they were right or wrong, for Joe never got a chance to apply pressure. Looking rather thick in the middle at 214 pounds, the champion tried to "come out smoking" but Foreman used his greater size and longer reach to smother the fire. At 6 feet 3 inches, the challenger had three and a half inches in height and a five-inch advantage in reach.

Reaching out with both hands, he fended off Frazier's early rushes, turning the challenge aside. Then he sank a hook deep into Joe's body, and the crowd had the first hint of what was in store. In a moment Foreman was moving forward, using both hands with authority. Even so, there was an instant of shocked silence when an uppercut sent Joe sprawling.

The champion got to his feet immediately and resumed his jigging style, both hands high,

Continued on Page 33, Column 6

Black Muslims Accused By Rival Sect in 7 Killings

Leader of Hanafis Calls for Muhammad Ouster

By PAUL DELANEY

Special to The New York Times

WASHINGTON, Jan. 22 — The leader of the Hanafi community of Moslems here today blamed the Black Muslims for the slaying last Thursday of seven of his followers, including three of his children, and he, in effect, declared war on the Black Muslims.

The leader, Hamaas Abdul Khaalis, called on other Moslem groups in this country and abroad to assist in deposing the Black Muslims and their leader, Elijah Muhammad.

The slayings and Mr. Hamaas's statement at a news conference evoked apprehension among law enforcement authorities and Islamic experts that more bloodshed would come.

Meanwhile, a team of Washington detectives went to New York today to investigate the possibility of a connection between the Moslem feud and the attempted robbery of a Brooklyn gun store that resulted in a 47-hour siege over the weekend. The belief is that the aborted robbery, which came one day after the mass killings here, was an attempt to obtain arms for the pending battle.

The slayings occurred at the headquarters of the Hanafi, a three-story stone mansion in the interracial "Gold Coast" section, where many of the city's black middle-class citizens reside. The seven victims included five children, four of whom were drowned, ranging in age from 9 days to 10 years old.

Mr. Hamaas revealed some

Continued on Page 77, Column 2

Four Held for Murder in Brooklyn Siege

By PETER KIHSS

The four men seized in the 47-hour weekend siege and shootout at a Brooklyn sporting goods store were held without bail yesterday on charges of murdering a policeman—which could lead to a death penalty—and of kidnapping 10 hostages.

Three were arraigned in Kings County Criminal Court with the proceedings virtually walled off by a tight guard of a dozen uniformed court officers ranged in front of the court railing.

The fourth was arraigned in Kings County Hospital, where he had undergone surgery for a bullet wound in the stomach.

District Attorney Eugene Gold told Judge Robert M. Haft that two of the defendants each had a previous arrest — one in 1964 and one in 1966. Both apparently were then about 16 years old, and Gerald Lefcourt, a defense lawyer, said the men told him the charges had been dismissed.

Outside of court, Robert M. McKiernan, president of the Patrolmen's Benevolent Association, demanded prosecution that could lead to electrocution for the fatal shooting of Patrol-

Continued on Page 77, Column 3

Pilgrims' Jet Crashes in Nigeria; 180 Are Feared Dead, a Record

By THOMAS A. JOHNSON

Special to The New York Times

LAGOS, Nigeria, Jan. 22 — A chartered jetliner carrying Nigerian Moslems home from a pilgrimage to Mecca crashed and burned today while landing in fog in northern Nigeria, and it was feared that 180 people had been killed.

Twenty-two of the 202 aboard survived, among them the pilot and several other crew members, according to reports from the airport at Kano, 525 miles north of here.

A death toll of 180 would make the crash the worst air disaster in history. Previously, the crash of a Soviet airliner near Moscow on Oct. 13, in which 176 people died, had been listed as the worst. The chartered jet, a Boeing 707 that belonged to Royal Jordanian Airways, was one of many planes involved in transporting Nigerian Moslems, as about

Continued on Page 10, Column 4

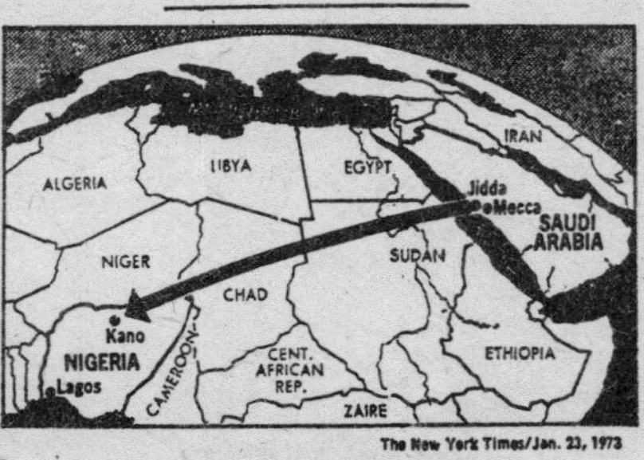

The New York Times/Jan. 23, 1973

Iceland Evacuates 7,000 on Isle After an Ancient Volcano Erupts

By The Associated Press

REYKJAVIK, Iceland, Tuesday, Jan. 23—Seven thousand people were being evacuated from an offshore Icelandic island early today as a volcano that had been quiet for more than a thousand years erupted.

Police authorities on the tiny island of Heimaey, one of a group off the south coast of Iceland, said boats and planes were being used to get the inhabitants of the town of Vestmannaeyjar to safety on the mainland.

But, they said, a hail of ash from the belching volcano of Helgafell was making operations from the island's airstrip difficult. They said a stream of molten lava also threatened to seal off the harbor, trapping boats.

Telephoned reports to Reykjavik—70 miles northwest of Heimaey—said a fissure 2,000 to 3,000 yards long opened and was spewing out lava and ash.

Fiery explosions were hurtling molten debris more than 1,500 feet into the air.

One side of Vestmannaeyjar is only 150 yards from Helgafell.

The police said the lava was flowing away from the town and into the Atlantic, but they said this could change at any time.

Women and children were being evacuated by air along with patients from the town's hospitals.

Others were boarding boats in the harbor. Iceland's big fishing fleet, Coast Guard vessels and other merchant ships were ordered to the island, the police said.

The United States Air Force base at Keflavik promised to

Continued on Page 10, Column 3

0 Miles 100 · Arctic Circle · ICELAND · Reykjavik · Vestmannaeyjar · Heimaey · Atlantic Ocean

The New York Times/Jan. 23, 1973

NEWS INDEX

Lyndon Johnson, 36th President, Is Dead

Continued From Page 1, Col. 8

dio station, Tom Johnson, executive vice president of the station, who was also a long-time aide to Mr. Johnson, gave the following account of the former President's death:

At 3:50 P.M., while in his bedroom for his regular afternoon nap, Mr. Johnson called the ranch switchboard and asked for Mike Howard, the head of his Secret Service detail, who was out in a car.

Bill Morrow, the switchboard operator, tried to call Mr. Howard and other Secret Service agents.

The first agents he reached were Ed Nowland and Harry Harris. They raced to the bedroom with a portable oxygen unit.

They found Mr. Johnson lying beside his bed. They said later he had already turned dark blue and appeared to be dead.

Nevertheless, they began trying to revive him. Mr. Nowland administered mouth-to-mouth resuscitation.

Two physicians were telephoned, Col. George McGranahan of Brooke Hospital and Dr. David J. Abbott of nearby Johnson City.

Placed Aboard Plane

Mr. Howard reached the bedroom at 3:55 P.M. and began an external heart massage.

At 4:05 P.M., Mrs. Johnson was called while riding in a car about a block from the L.B.J. Library in Austin, where she has an office. She flew by helicopter from the library to San Antonio.

At 4:19 P.M., Mr. Johnson was placed aboard a family plane, a Beech King Air. Also aboard the twin-engined plane were Dr. Abbott; Mr. Nowland; Mr. Harris; Mrs. Dale Malechek, wife of the ranch foreman, and the pilot, Barney Hulett.

The plane arrived at 4:33 in San Antonio, where Dr. Abbott pronounced the former President dead. At 4:45 P.M., Mrs. Johnson arrived from Austin, about 70 miles away. The ranch is about 45 miles from San Antonio.

At about the same time, Colonel McGranahan arrived at the airport and confirmed the death.

Mrs. Johnson, the former Claudia Alta Taylor, known as Lady Bird, returned to Austin in the company of Mr. Howard, arriving at 6:45 P.M. local time and going to her penthouse apartment at the family broadcasting station.

A short time later, she was joined by Brig. Gen. James Cross, Air Force, retired, a family friend and former pilot of the Presidential plane, Air Force One.

The Johnsons' two daughters, Mrs. Patrick J. Nugent and Mrs. Charles S. Robb, accompanied by their husbands, later met their mother at the ranch. Also present was J. C. Kellam, the general manager of the family business interests.

While they discussed funeral plans, the body of the former President was taken from Brooke Army Medical Center to Austin by the Weed-Corley Funeral Home of Austin.

Mr. Johnson had always made it clear that he wanted to be buried on the family ranch in Johnson City, in a small, walled burial plot about 400 yards from the ranch house, where his father, mother and other relatives had been laid to rest.

Colonel McGranahan said tonight that the former President's death was apparently caused by a coronary thrombosis.

An autopsy performed by Col. L. R. Hieger, chief of pathology at Brooke General Hospital, showed that Mr. Johnson had been suffering from severe coronary arterial disease. Two of three major arteries supplying the heart were completely occluded, Colonel Heiger said, and the third artery was 60 per cent occluded. Further evaluation will be made later, he said.

At a news briefing tonight Tom Johnson said Mrs. Johnson had told him that the former President's health had not altered recently, although she mentioned that he had been quieter than usual.

One of Mr. Johnson's last formal appearances took place last Tuesday in Austin, where he attended the inauguration of Gov. Dolph Briscoe and Lieut. Gov. William P. Hobby. On the ceremonial platform outside the capitol, Mr. Johnson, looking thin, seemed to be enjoying an opportunity to see old friends and shake hands with well-wishers who flocked around him.

Later that day, he took Walter Heller, the former chairman of his Council of Economic Advisers, to Southwest Texas State University, Mr. Johnson's alma mater, in San Marcos, for a talk to a group of students.

During the question-and-answer session, Mr. Johnson said to the audience, "Come on, now, make your questions quicker, and Walter, you make your answers shorter."

In a discussion of food and meat prices, Mr. Heller predicted a rise of 6 to 7 per cent in meat prices.

"I can tell you what's happening with cattle," Mr. Johnson said. "I paid my dealer $92 a ton for feed."
the bill went to $110 a ton and now its costing me $156 a ton for food."

Last Saturday, joining Mrs. Johnson in her beautification work, the former President went to Ranch Road 1, which runs across the Pedernales River from the L.B.J. Ranch, and planted a redbud tree, a Texas tree that blooms with red flowers. The tree was the first of 100 to be planted along the road.

On that occasion, Mr. Johnson told a friend that he was not feeling very well and said that that was why he had not gone to Washington for the inauguration of President Nixon.

Death Is Greeted With Shock And an Outpouring of Tributes

Continued From Page 1, Col. 5

tion in the essential rightness of the American experience."

The President called Mr. Johnson "a dynamic leader, a unique personality and a man of great ability and unshakeable courage," and said: "No man had greater dreams for America than Lyndon Johnson. Even as we mourn his death, we are grateful for his life, which did so much to make those dreams into reality. And we know that so long as this nation lives, so will his dreams and his accomplishments."

Senator George McGovern said in a statement in London, where he is visiting:

"Lyndon Johnson did more to advance public support for education and civil justice than any other President in our national history. His public career was marked by a deep sense of compassion for his fellow citizens. I deeply regret his death."

'Somehow Unbelievable'

Vice President Agnew, despite Mr. Johnson's recent illnesses, called news of his death "somehow unbelievable."

"I valued his counsel, admired his courage, respected his integrity and was privileged to be his friend," the Vice President said.

Senator Hubert H. Humphrey of Minnesota, who was Vice President under Mr. Johnson, said he would be remembered as "a strong man who cared for the weak and the sick," adding: "He was a school teacher who dedicated his public life to the cause of education, a man of compassion for the elderly and of concern for the young; he was a President who saw America as the guardian of freedom and he acted accordingly."

Chief Justice Warren E. Burger asserted that history "will appraise Lyndon B. Johnson as a strong President in a critical period when strength and courage were desperately needed."

At the United Nations, Secretary General Waldheim expressed shock and sorrow at the news of Mr. Johnson's death. "President Johnson's life," he said, "was dedicated to the service of his country and to the creating of a great and just society."

Mrs. Coretta Scott King, the widow of the Rev. Dr. Martin Luther King Jr., said the Vietnam war had clouded Mr. Johnson's domestic achievements. "It would be hypocritical to pretend one can forget a war that still goes on," she said, but added that "most comprehensive and effective legislation on civil rights was enacted" during the Johnson Administration.

Senator Edmund S. Muskie, Democrat of Maine, praised Mr. Johnson for his role in civil rights, education and other domestic programs, but said, "His tragedy—and ours—was the war." He added: "I will always think of him as a man of great achievement and great tragedy. Only history can write the final balance sheet."

Senator Mike Mansfield, the Montanan who is the Senate majority leader, said: "I am deeply saddened by his passage. He was the greatest President. The Great Society will be his monument in history."

Carl Albert, the Speaker of the House of Representatives, said he had "never been closer to anyone in high political office in my entire life," and declared: "I have lost a very dear friend and I am very greatly shocked."

Senator Barry Goldwater, the Arizona Republican who was defeated by Mr. Johnson in the 1964 Presidential election, said: "The country has lost a great political leader, a dedicated American, and I have lost a friend—the memory of whose friendship I will cherish."

Senator Edward M. Kennedy of Massachusetts asserted: "He was a loyal Vice President and he had the respect and affection of John Kennedy. As President, his brilliant leadership on the Civil Rights Act of 1964 and the Voting Rights Act of 1965 earned him a place in the history of civil rights alongside Abraham Lincoln."

In a joint statement, Bayard Rustin and A. Philip Randolph, the civil rights leaders, said that "with the exception of Lincoln, who freed the slaves, no single President contributed as much to the cause of racial equality as did Lyndon Johnson."

A Personal Politician

Johnson Pressed for Great Society And the War in a Face-to-Face Style

By MAX FRANKEL

He was larger than life, almost a caricature of the Texas caricature that he could never shake, but he never lost his humanity, because with Lyndon Johnson everything was really personal.

The war that overwhelmed his years in the White House was personal—a test of endurance against Ho Chi Minh, which he acknowledged having lost in the end, no matter who actually won the spoils of battle.

An Appraisal

The Great Society was personal, because a lackluster education in his own life had saved him from shiftlessness and he deemed learning of any kind to be forever more the way to get ahead in this world.

The civil rights laws that he wanted as his monument were, in the end, highly personal, because they were drawn on the testimony of his Negro cook and her humilitations whenever she traveled without reliable food or lodging between Washington and the Texas ranch.

Personal Politics

And even politics, the business in which he excelled and in which he took such great pride, was to him only a personal, face-to-face thing. If he had talked George Meany into acquiescence on a point, he thought he had won over all of American labor. If he had conquered Richard Russell on a budget matter, he thought he had won over the Southland.

In this fashion, he had been able to encompass every issue and every center of power in his years as majority leader of the Senate. But from the White House, even his huge reach fell short and his incredibly hard work and keen mind felt often overwhelmed.

Insecure despite his size and force, L.B.J. felt from the moment of John Kennedy's death in Dallas that the nation would never accept his Southern speech and rural manners as a replacement for the slain prince.

Clung to Kennedy Men

So he clung to the Kennedy men and boasted of their Ph.D. degrees and he was afraid, even after his landslide election in 1964, to bring his own men to the capital.

And he could not comprehend, to the moment of death, how so many Kennedy partisans around the country could turn against him because of a war in which he felt he had taken the counsel of his predecessor's Cabinet and aides.

So he took it personally. He thought he saw a plot to promote yet another Kennedy and he thought he saw his fate as being merely the caretaker between two Kennedy administrations and he hated the thought and all who made it seem so real.

In his own mind, he felt certain that history would bring vindication:

¶A Southerner, who brought the blacks to the ultimate legal equality, with their own seat on the Supreme Court and a Court that ruled in their cause.

¶A conservative kept alive in politics by conservative votes for Texas interests, who made war on poverty an elaborate concern of the Federal Government.

¶A wartime leader who was governed to the end by respect and occasionally even compassion for his "enemy," who really wanted to extend the Great Society to the Mekong River and who systematically refused to whip the nation into an anti-Communist frenzy.

¶A backwoods boy of modest learning, who gave what seemed to him the disrespectful Establishment figures of the East the scope and mandate for great social works.

That is how he saw himself and how he expected to be seen in history. He confronted antagonists to the end, always hoping that reason and short ideals and long conversations—really monologues—could find a compromise for every conflict.

Hated Conflict

Although overcome by a bitter war and the hatreds that it spawned throughout the country, Lyndon Johnson remained a man who hated conflict and who feared confrontation for himself and his country.

He made the Joint Chiefs of Staff testify in writing that he should really stand at the siege of Khe San.

He made all his diplomatic advisers commit themselves in writing to the advice that he really go to meet Soviet Premier Kosygin at Glassboro, N. J.

He won from his wife, Ladybird, a written recommendation that he ride into battle against Barry Goldwater in 1964 and that he should buck the battle for re-election in 1968. He never did want to stand alone.

"Well, Max," he asked an acquaintance on the morning after the surprise announcement of his intended retirement in 1968, "do you still believe in the First Amendment?" He thought free speech and free assembly had destroyed him, but he went on to confess that he believed in the First Amendment.

He wanted everyone with him all the time and when they weren't, it broke his heart.

Mr. Frankel, the Sunday editor of The New York Times, was chief of the Washington bureau and covered Mr. Johnson.

No Ex-President Alive For 6th Time in History

Former President Lyndon B. Johnson's death leaves the nation without a living former President for the sixth time in its history.

George Washington died on Dec. 14, 1799, more than a year before his successor, John Adams, completed his term. One or more former Presidents were always living after Adams left office until eight months before the end of Ulysses S. Grant's second term in 1877, when Andrew Johnson died.

Rutherford B. Hayes's death early in 1893 led to a two-month haitus at the end of Benjamin Harrison's term. Following Grover Cleveland's death in June of 1908 there was no living former President until Theodore Roosevelt left office on March 3, 1909. The death of Calvin Coolidge two months before Herbert Hoover relinquished office began the most recent period when no former Presidents were living.

Lyndon Johnson: Controversial President

By ALBIN KREBS

"I SHALL not seek, and I will not accept, the nomination of my party for another term as your President," Lyndon Baines Johnson told a startled nationwide television audience the night of March 31, 1968.

Despite the fact that the nation was frustrated and angry about the war in Vietnam, troubled by racial strife, and caught up in inflation, most Americans had more or less assumed that Mr. Johnson, the highly political and mightily proud 36th President of the United States, would run for re-election in 1968.

But in his televised speech, Mr. Johnson first gave the long-awaited word that he had ordered a major reduction in the bombing of Communist North Vietnam and called for peace talks.

Then, after acknowledging that there was "division in the American house," Mr. Johnson added his withdrawal statement, which had not been in his prepared text:

"What we won when all of our people were united must not now be lost in suspicion, distrust, selfishness and politics among our people," he said. "Believing this as I do, I have concluded that I should not permit the Presidency to become involved in the partisan divisions that are developing in this political year."

Then he said he would not be a candidate for another term.

With those electrifying words, Mr. Johnson in effect admitted the shattering of a dream he had cherished, since Nov. 22, 1963, when a madman's bullet killed his predecessor and made him President, that he would restore peace and serenity to the American people.

He set forth those goals in a ringing speech before a joint session of Congress on March 15, 1965. "This is the richest and most powerful country which ever occupied this globe," he said. "The might of past empires is little compared to ours. But I do not want to be the President who built empires, or sought grandeur, or extended dominion.

"I want to be the President who educated young children to the wonders of their world.

"I want to be the President who helped to feed the hungry and to prepare them to be taxpayers instead of tax-eaters.

"I want to be the President who helped the poor to find their own way and who protected the right of every citizen to vote in every election.

"I want to be the President who helped to end hatred among his fellow men and who promoted love among the people of all races, all regions and all parties.

"I want to be the President who helped to end war among the brothers of this earth."

These were Lyndon Johnson's aims, but few of them were to be achieved. Less than two years after that fateful day in Dallas when John F. Kennedy was shot, and less than a year after he had been chosen President in his own right, Mr. Johnson found himself trapped in a remote, bloody and incredibly costly war that, it seemed, would never end.

Progressively the budgets of his Administration were mortgaged to that war, and its unpopularity drained his political strength.

Moreover, the cities of America were ravaged by decay and racial dissension, and the white majority responded with anger, fear and vindictiveness.

By the time he left office on Jan. 20, 1969, his nation's reputation for violence, far from having diminished, had grown abroad to monstrous proportions.

The name of Lyndon Johnson, like that of the other three Democratic Presidents who served full terms in this century, had become inextricably linked with war and its consequences.

By all indications, the war in Vietnam was the least popular of the nation's wars in this century and Mr. Johnson became by far the most controversial wartime leader. Bitter controversy born of the war swirled about the President and drowned the memory of his good legislative works.

White House Photograph

CHIEF EXECUTIVE: *Lyndon Baines Johnson, 36th President of the United States, in the Cabinet Room at the White House*

Historians will long debate how and why he took the nation into the Vietnam quagmire. His contemporaries, unwilling to await that judgment, berated him from all sides, not only for getting involved in the first place, but also for his military and diplomatic tactics throughout.

But Mr. Johnson tried always to steer deftly to a middle course between the extremes of public opinion. He held grimly to the conviction that the course he had chosen was one of honor and national interest, and that the ordeal simply had to be borne, as Lincoln had borne his in the Civil War, and Franklin D. Roosevelt, to whom he wanted most to be compared, had borne his in this century.

In doing so, he knew that he had sacrificed not only popularity and the people's love, for which he lusted, but also the great domestic accomplishments that once had seemed within his grasp. For a man with a gargantuan appetite for achievement, this was a bitter pill to swallow.

Convinced as he was that he had pursued the right, even the just, course, by mid-1968 Lyndon Johnson made it plain that he was a deeply disillusioned and frustrated man, ready to shake off the shackles the Presidency by then represented.

Those who knew him knew this, but they would also remember that the essential Lyndon Johnson, forged in the political fires over a period of some 40 years, was an intense dynamo of a man, a mover, a shaker, a doer.

He was a man who slept little and worked himself and those around him like Texas field hands. He was constantly on the telephone, ordering, wheedling, threatening, wheeling and dealing, striving always to keep astride of every matter that affected the interests of the United States— and Lyndon Johnson.

He was a zestful man who brought to the Presidency a genuine love of politics, of the infighting and conniving and the sense of public interest that are all part of that most exacting and most vexing game.

He was sometimes inordinately loyal to his friends, and he was a forgiving man, a kind man. He was also often a cruel man, capable of great rages and monumental castigations of anyone who dared cross him. His vanity was legend, his compassion for a friend in trouble limitless. He was incredibly thin-skinned when criticized by the press, yet he held few grudges long. And he could shrug off attacks with the homily, "My Daddy told me that if you don't want to get shot at, stay off the firing line."

But by the time he had decided to leave the Presidency, Mr. Johnson had apparently concluded that he no longer wanted to be on the firing line.

The man who had been fond of saying, "Let us reason together," and "I want to be President of all the people," had found fewer and fewer of his fellow Americans reasoning along his lines, and vast numbers of the people wanted someone else to be their President.

However, Lyndon Johnson left office convinced still that a small war against "Communist aggression" in Asia would spare the world from another global war in the future, and he seemed confident that in time his policies would be vindicated in history.

A Texas Boy 'Born Into Politics'

ALTHOUGH it was often said that Lyndon Baines Johnson was born for the Presidency, it seemed quite unlikely that he would ever attain it.

For one thing, Mr. Johnson was not a revered theorist of government or the proponent of great change and innovation. Nor was he a polished orator, a magnetic personality, a powerful factional leader.

His personal and political career had been clouded by charges of vulgarism and provincialism, of opportunism and "wheeling and dealing," by his disputed election to the Senate in 1948, his ownership of lucrative, Government-regulated television broadcasting rights, and by the tangled affairs of his protégé, Robert G. Baker, who was secretary to the Democratic majority in the Senate during Mr. Johnson's most influential years there.

Moreover, Mr. Johnson was a Southerner, and there had been no Southerner in the White House since Woodrow Wilson, a Virginian, had left it in 1921.

All these factors contributed to the unlikelihood that Mr. Johnson would ever become President, short of the sort of accident that indeed gave him that high office. But the fact that he would go into politics seemed certain from the start.

Mr. Johnson's father, his father's father and his mother's father all served in the Texas Legislature. He was, as he put it, "born into politics."

It was said that on Aug. 27, 1908, Mr. Johnson's rancher grandfather, Sam Johnson Sr., rode on horseback around Johnson City, Tex., proclaiming that "a United States Senator was born this morning—my grandson."

Lyndon Johnson was born in the three-room Johnson home at Hye, near the small villages of Stonewall and Johnson City, in the sere hills of southwest Texas. He was the eldest of five children, the others being Rebekah, Josefa, Sam Houston and Lucia.

The Johnson family was extremely poor. Money was scarce in the back-country hills, cattle-raising was risky at best and the oil boom had not yet come to Texas. Water was a problem, and since the land was mesquite-choked, arid and sulphurous, farming was not, as the future President was to put it, "worth a cotton-pickin' damn."

Close to His Parents

Growing up in the "jackrabbit country" along the Pedernales River, Mr. Johnson was extremely close to his parents. He recalled in later years that his father, Samuel Ealy Johnson Jr., having high hopes for his first-born, would shake the boy awake mornings with the cry, "Son, get up! Every boy in town has a two-hour start on you." (In his Senate office years later, an adage of his father's hung on Mr. Johnson's wall: "When you're talkin', you ain't learnin' nothin'.")

From his mother, Rebekah Baines Johnson, Lyndon gained a lifetime respect for the value of an education although at first he balked at going to college. Mrs. Johnson had worked her own way through college and had taught "expression" in rural schools, and she taught her son the alphabet with A-B-C blocks.

Mrs. Johnson also taught Lyndon how to read; first with Mother Goose rhymes, then with lines from Longfellow and Tennyson, which the child did not enjoy. Then, and for the rest of his life, Mr. Johnson abhorred fiction. When his mother read to him, he would ask insistently, "But Ma, is it real? Did it really happen?"

YOUNG TEXAN: *The future President in a "pensive mood," his mother wrote in family album.*

Lyndon could read by the time he was 4 and he was in school at the age of 5. He rode to classes on a donkey and was thus the butt of many jokes. Fistfights with schoolmates were not uncommon, but the youth managed to be popular. Although he was not bookish and his grades were mediocre, he was president of his high school graduating class of seven students as well as of the debate team.

The team made it to the state debate finals. When Lyndon lost his match, he recalled later, "I went to the bathroom and was sick." Then, as in later years, Lyndon Johnson hated to lose—and even to associate with losers or what he called "cain't-doers."

Out of school at 15, Lyndon resisted parental suggestions that he go to college; instead he hitchhiked to California with five other boys. They split up there and, according to Mr. Johnson, "Up and down the Pacific Coast I tramped, washing dishes, waiting on tables, doing farm work and growing thinner and more homesick."

He returned to Texas, but college still struck him as a loathsome prospect, and for a time he worked on a road gang. Finally, he told his parents he was "sick of working with my hands," and with $75 borrowed on his own signature, in February, 1927, he entered Southwest Texas State Teachers College at San Marcos.

There he worked as a janitor, housepainter and secretary to the college president. He was a star debater and editor of the school paper. Already a reservoir of cyclonic energy, not to mention supreme self-confidence, Lyndon had no intention of "wasting" four years getting a degree. And even though he had to complete three months of pre-college work plus the regular course, he was graduated in three years at the age of 22.

His first full-time job was teaching public speaking and English at Sam Houston High School in Houston. Many Mexican-Americans attended the school, and there was discrimination against them there and in the community. Mr. Johnson encouraged the children to learn English so they could get along better in society.

Mr. Johnson obviously liked the Mexican-Americans. He learned to speak with them in a relaxed pidgin Spanish and, in the years to come, in their company he could unashamedly return affectionate abrazo for abrazo. In Houston he laid the groundwork for what was to become, in Texas politics, a reputation as the special friend and champion of the state's Mexican-American minority. As that minority grew in influence and affluence, Lyndon Johnson reaped considerable political benefits.

While still teaching in Houston, Mr. Johnson went to work as a volunteer in the 1931 Congressional campaign of Richard M. Kleberg Sr., one of the owners of the mammoth King Ranch and a friend of his father. Mr. Kleberg won the special election for a House seat. The tall, gangling Mr. Johnson, then 22, went to Washington with him as his legislative assistant.

Lyndon Johnson hit Capitol Hill in those Depression days like a Texas tornado. He called persistently on Federal bureaus, seeking drought relief, unemployment relief, civil service jobs, anything that was available for the folks back home. In those early days in Washington, Mr. Johnson had the not inconsiderable help of Sam Rayburn, soon to become the powerful Speaker of the House. Mr. Rayburn had been an old friend of Lyndon's father, Sam, with whom he had served in the Texas House of Representatives.

By 1934, young Mr. Johnson was a man-about-Washington, with friends in nearly every office in the capital.

A Whirlwind Courtship

He shuttled between Washington and Texas, tending Mr. Kleberg's political fences. It was on such a flying trip to Austin, in September, 1934, that he met Claudia Alta Taylor, who had been nicknamed Lady Bird by a nurse when she was a child. Their whirlwind courtship began three minutes after they met, when Mr. Johnson asked Lady Bird for a date. She declined. But Miss Taylor—the daughter of a well-to-do East Texan and fresh out of the University of Texas—was barraged by telegrams and telephone calls from Washington, all from a very determined young man who was intent on having his way. He did, and they were married on Nov. 17, 1934. (They had two daughters, Lynda Bird, now Mrs. Charles S. Robb, born in 1944, and Luci Baines, now Mrs. Patrick J. Nugent, born in 1947.)

Back in Washington, Mr. Johnson attended Law School at George Washington University, but in 1935, not yet 27 years old and still short of his law degree, he was—at Sam Rayburn's behest—appointed Texas state director of the National Youth Administration.

The job gave Mr. Johnson a splendid opportunity. By then he had firmly decided to get into the political big leagues, and so his new post was superbly designed to give him grass-roots links with young Texans just coming of voting age. He whirled around the state, making friends, passing out favors and getting his name into the newspapers.

His chance to run for office came in 1937. The United States Representative from his district, James P. Buchanan, died, and a special election to fill out the term was called. Mr. Johnson was one of 10 candidates in a no-primary, no-runoff, winner-take-all race.

In that election, Mr. Johnson showed the acute political sense that was to become his trademark. He needed a gimmick to distinguish his candidacy from those of his rivals, and he found it in support of the New Deal, which had fallen into disfavor with conservatives and businessmen in Texas. President Roosevelt's plan to "pack" the Supreme Court served to harden their resistance.

OFF TO CONGRESS: *Mr. Johnson's first election was to the House of Representatives in 1937. A supporter of Franklin D. Roosevelt, he won the President's friendship.*

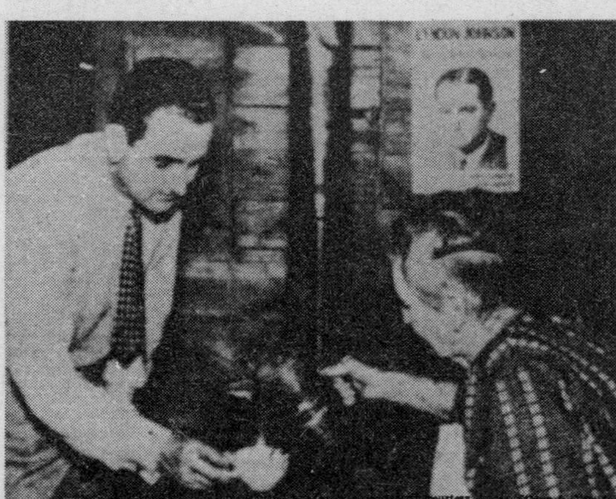

ON CAMPAIGN TRAIL: *He was unsuccessful in his first bid for the Senate, in 1941 (above). He stayed in Congress, served in World War II and won his Senate seat in 1948.*

It happened that Mr. Johnson was an admirer of Mr. Roosevelt's, and that he approved of the New Deal without reservation. He took a firm stand in support of the President, particularly his proposal to increase the membership of the Supreme Court. The tactic served to force his rivals to gang up on him—and put him into the limelight. He was no longer an unknown.

The result was that when the ballots were counted, Lyndon Johnson had piled up twice as many votes as his nearest opponent. He had won the first of his six House terms handily, along with the delight and gratitude of Franklin Delano Roosevelt. The President, who chanced to be cruising in the Gulf of Mexico off Galveston on Election Day, invited young Mr. Johnson aboard ship, and a mutually beneficial friendship blossomed. (When Mr. Roosevelt died, Mr. Johnson said mournfully: "He was like a Daddy to me.")

Mr. Johnson was sworn in as a member of Congress on May 14, 1937. The President, convinced that he was a "comer," with the cooperation of Mr. Rayburn, wangled him a coveted assignment to the Naval Affairs Committee, an unusual piece of luck for a junior Congressman, who would normally have to be content with a lackluster position on a minor committee.

The late nineteen-thirties was the high water mark of the "Texas era" in Washington, with such natives as Mr. Rayburn, John Nance Garner (Mr. Roosevelt's first Vice President), Tom Connally and Jesse Jones riding high. Mr. Johnson fitted well into that galaxy, benefited from its favors and in time shone with a light all his own.

He won re-election easily in 1938, and in 1940 he breezed through to a second full term without formal opposition. The same year his House Democratic colleagues recognized his political talents by electing him chairman of their Campaign Committee.

Meanwhile, Mr. Johnson kept his political fences in Texas in good repair by obtaining more than his share of conservation and public works projects for his district. Among these was a flood-control and electricity-generating dam-and-spillway system for the Pedernales River, which runs through what is now the LBJ Ranch at Johnson City.

In 1941 Mr. Johnson had to take a step back on the political ladder he was fast climbing. After the death of Senator Morris Sheppard, he called on his friend, Mr. Roosevelt, and then announced, on the steps of the White House, that he planned to run, with the President's support, for the vacant Senate seat.

But this was a different year and a different kind of race from his first one. Mr. Roosevelt was in supreme disfavor in Texas by then, and so it was probably a mistake for Mr. Johnson to have the President openly "telling Texas how to vote," as the cry across the state had it. Mr. Johnson lost the race, by 1,311 votes, to the colorful former Gov. W. Lee (Pappy) O'Daniel, a reactionary self-styled hillbilly. It was the only defeat he ever suffered at the hands of the electorate.

Fortunately for Mr. Johnson, he did not have to relinquish his House seat to participate in the special election, and he returned to his duties in Washington. One of these duties was to vote, in December, 1941, for a declaration of war against Japan. Three days after Pearl Harbor was attacked by the Japanese, he was commissioned a lieutenant commander in the Navy and dispatched to the Pacific on a three-man team to make a personal survey of battle conditions for the President.

It was a noncombat assignment, but Mr. Johnson did fly on some missions as an observer, surviving crash-landings on two occasions. General Douglas MacArthur awarded him the Silver Star for gallantry in action. Seven months after he went into uniform, Mr. Johnson's naval career ended, when President Roosevelt ordered all members of Congress in military service to return to their duties on Capitol Hill.

Wife Maintained Office

During his absence, Mr. Johnson's Congressional office was maintained by his wife. Upon his return to Washington in July, 1942, he found his political affairs in excellent shape.

At this time the Johnsons made a private decision that was to have an important bearing on the future. A virtually bankrupt radio station in Austin, one that blanketed all seven counties of Mr. Johnson's 10th District and some others besides, came up for sale. It was an unpromising investment, since in 1942 it had lost $7,000 on revenues of more than $26,000, but the Johnsons looked upon the station as a useful tool for his political career.

Mrs. Johnson had recently inherited about $65,000 from her grandmother. After much deliberation, she and her husband decided to risk a bid on the broadcasting property. They did, at $17,500, and the station, debts and all, became theirs.

The station, KTBC, and later KTBC-TV, became Mrs. Johnson's particular preoccupation while her husband carried on in the realm of politics. Its fortunes spiraled upward under her canny management, and by 1964 the station's assets were listed at $3.2-million. At that time the Johnsons put their holdings in a family trust, in which they remained until Mr. Johnson left the White House in 1969.

In the late nineteen-forties, Mr. Johnson's liberal New Deal voting record began showing lapses. The man who had voted enthusiastically for the Wagner

Act of 1935—"labor's Magna Carta," as it was called—in 1946 voted also for the Taft-Hartley Act, denounced by some of his colleagues as "a slave labor bill." (Mr. Johnson, as a Senator, also was lukewarm, at best, on civil rights proposals urged upon the Republican-controlled 80th Congress by President Harry S. Truman.)

By 1948, Mr. Johnson was ready for another try at the Senate. Mr. O'Daniel, who had defeated him in 1941, had decided not to run again, but he faced a formidable opponent in former Gov. Coke Stevenson, who was widely popular and soundly conservative. In the Democratic primary — in which there were a total of 11 candidates — Mr. Stevenson outpolled Mr. Johnson, 477,077 to 405,617, but neither had a clear majority and there had to be a runoff.

Mr. Johnson campaigned in a helicopter and by plane, something new and exciting in those days, and concentrated on the metropolitan areas where Mr. Stevenson had shown the most strength. In the runoff, Mr. Johnson squeaked to victory by a margin of only 87 votes of 988,295 cast.

'Landslide Lyndon'

There were accusations of ballot-box irregularities—particularly in south Texas, Mr. Johnson's Mexican-American stronghold. Mr. Stevenson filed suits in county, state and Federal courts; but Mr. Johnson, blithely filing countersuits, won all down the line. The state Democratic Executive Committee finally certified his primary election, and in the general election he defeated his Republican opponent by a 2-to-1 margin.

But for years afterward, Mr. Johnson was derisively called "Landslide Lyndon" and there were persistent charges that the election had been "fixed." During the 1964 Presidential race, extreme rightwingers, who loathed Mr. Johnson monumentally, charged that the 1948 election was the platform for his alleged "tower of illegitimate power."

Mr. Johnson's career in the Senate matched in vigor and ambition his career in the House, but it was marked also by maturity and a growing sophistication.

While observing the unwritten rule that freshman Senators should be seen and not heard, Mr. Johnson cultivated the veteran Senator Richard Russell of Georgia, a member of the Senate's "inner club" and chairman of the powerful Armed Services Committee. After the outbreak of the Korean War, he won a seat on that committee. And after he charged that the country had demobilized too swiftly after World War II and embarked on a "delay-defeat-retreat" policy, he found himself appointed chairman of a new Senate Armed Forces preparedness subcommittee.

Despite his criticism of the nation's defense policies, Mr. Johnson stood firmly with President Truman on Korean policy. When the Republicans and many Democrats blamed the war on Mr. Truman, he said with characteristic bluntness and simplicity:

"The Communists, not President Truman, were responsible for the invasion of South Korea. The quicker we direct our hostility to the enemy instead of to our leaders the quicker we will get the job done."

In 1951 Mr. Johnson was elected majority whip, a testament to his growing capacity to make friends and wield influence. His choice for the 1952 Democratic nomination for President was his friend Mr. Russell, but he gave his full support to Adlai E. Stevenson when the Illinois Governor captured the nomination.

The Democrats lost majority control in the Senate in the 1952 election, which brought Dwight D. Eisenhower into the White House. Mr. Johnson became Democratic minority leader. At 44, he was the youngest man ever to hold that position.

The Republicans lost control of both houses of Congress in 1954 and Mr. Johnson became majority leader in the Senate. Again, he was the youngest ever to hold such a position.

In the years that followed, Mr. Johnson was to gain the gratitude of Mr. Eisenhower for his active cooperation with the Republican branch on legislative matters, along with the scarcely disguised dislike and distrust of many liberals in his own party, who believed he was too conservative and was carrying bipartisanship too far.

His achievements as Senate majority leader became something of a legend in Washington. He was said by many to have been the most proficient of any who ever held the post, for, without resorting to bombast or open exhibitions of punishment or reward, he adroitly got temperamental and independent-minded Senators to see things his way.

Mr. Johnson exhibited an uncanny ability to count noses, to know precisely, long before a vote was taken, what chances a given bill had for passage. He gave patronage favors in return for voting favors, and, according to one admiring colleague, "Lyndon had a mind like a ledger — accounts payable, accounts receivable — and every transaction he ever made with any of us was recorded in it."

During those years Mr. Johnson, always a powerhouse, moved so fast and so furiously and with such blinding effect that, it was said, when someone once asked a page boy if he had seen Senator Johnson, the youth replied: "I haven't seen anything but a burning bush."

Hard-working Lyndon Johnson very nearly burned himself out. In July, 1955, he suffered a massive heart attack — "about as bad as a man can have and still live," as he described it—that put him on the sidelines for six months. As a friend put it, "he organized his recovery like one of his political campaigns." He gave up the chili dishes he favored and also his three-pack-a-day cigarette habit, trimmed down from 220 to 180 pounds and cut his normal working day from 18 to 14 hours.

In January, 1956, Mr. Johnson returned to his Senate post and within weeks his colleagues were worriedly complaining that, again, his tremendous energy might be endangering his health. But he seemed to thrive on hard work.

Presidential Speculation

The heart attack put a temporary damper on speculation that Mr. Johnson was a leading contender for his party's Presidential nomination. The speculation had arisen as Mr. Johnson seemed to be trying to divest himself of the image that he was a straight-down-the-line "Southern Senator," meaning a segregationist.

As early as 1954, Mr. Johnson had acted independently of his fellow Southerners, when he refused to sign the "Southern Manifesto" that all other Senators from the South did sign, denouncing the Supreme Court decision on desegregation of public schools. He was openly proud of having piloted through the Senate, in 1957, the first civil rights bill since Reconstruction, and in 1960 he helped beat back a filibuster aimed at blocking an expanded civil rights measure.

Mr. Johnson's decision to seek the Presidential nomination in 1960 was handled as cagily as he handled most political decisions in his life. He allowed friends to mount an unofficial campaign for him as early as December, 1959, but withheld his own announcement until the following July, shortly before the opening of the 1960 convention.

Many observers contended that he never seriously believed he could take the prize away from Senator John F. Kennedy, starting as late as he did to win delegates. Mr. Kennedy went into the convention at Los Angeles with impressive primary victories, plus the solid results of hard work and sharp dealing with state conventions by his

The New York Times

MAJORITY LEADER: His achievements as head of the Senate majority became something of a legend in Washington. Here he met, in 1959, with Speaker of the House Sam Rayburn, a Johnson mentor; President Dwight D. Eisenhower and Vice President Richard M. Nixon.

The New York Times

VICE PRESIDENT: When his bid for the 1960 Presidential nomination failed, Mr. Johnson became the running mate of John F. Kennedy and played active role in his Administration.

staff and most notably by his younger brother Robert.

Mr. Kennedy had the nomination clinched before the completion of the first roll call. His selection of Mr. Johnson as his Vice Presidential running mate came as a distinct surprise. So did Mr. Johnson's acceptance. His old friend, Mr. Rayburn, who had placed his name in nomination to lead the ticket, tearfully pleaded with him not to be "fool enough" to surrender his powerful Senate leadership in favor of the largely ceremonial position of Vice-President.

But having accepted the Kennedy offer willingly, even eagerly, Mr. Johnson said shortly after the convention:

"I recognized that there were only two offices in the land in which all the people had a choice. And I felt it offered a good opportunity, that it would be quite a challenge, and that it would be good for the party and the country."

It was common knowledge at the time that there was no love lost between Mr. Kennedy and Mr. Johnson, but Mr. Kennedy could obviously benefit from Mr. Johnson's considerable presence on his ticket. As a Roman Catholic Easterner, Mr. Kennedy's position in the Southern Bible Belt, traditionally regarded as a temple of anti-Catholicism, was not strong. He was also on shaky ground in the West. The Johnson image of a Texan, a Westerner, and a bit of a conservative would be helpful.

Mr. Johnson's campaign train, from which emanated almost constantly the strains of his favorite song, "Yellow Rose of Texas," took the Johnsons across the heart, width and breadth of the Old Confederacy, making whistlestops from Washington to New Orleans and on up to Memphis.

Besides making speeches, the candidate talked in private with hundreds of local, district and state politicians. A close associate said he reminded his listeners in these talks that, as Senate majority leader, he had done more for the modern South and its politicians than any other man. And indeed he had done much for them, in obtaining dams, rural electrification, defense installations, government contracts and other so-called "pork-barrel" favors.

Mr. Kennedy was, like Mr. Johnson, a formidable campaigner, yet the Democratic ticket finally triumphed over the Republican team of Richard M. Nixon and Henry Cabot Lodge by the smallest vote margin in this century. Of the 69 million votes cast, the Democrats won by approximately 113,000 votes. The electoral vote was 303 to 219.

Mr. Kennedy credited Mr. Johnson with cutting down the anticipated Nixon-Lodge vote in the South and West. In Texas, vote analysts agreed that Mr. Johnson's Mexican-American constituency was responsible for swinging the state into the Democratic column.

Early in his Vice Presidency, Mr. Johnson found it difficult to accustom himself to living in the shade traditionally reserved for holders of his office. Before long, however, Mr. Kennedy, who was said to have developed a warm personal regard for Mr. Johnson during and immediately following the campaign, took steps to make Mr. Johnson the most active Vice President in history.

The President sent him on missions to 33 countries. Many of the missions were ceremonial, but not all. Mr. Johnson could indeed reap snickers by befriending a camel driver in Karachi, Pakistan, and entertaining him in the United States. But he also flew to beleaguered West Berlin in August, 1961, and said: "This city can never be bullied into the surrender of its freedom."

Eye on Space Program

Mr. Johnson was brought into some of the inner circles of the Kennedy Administration. He sat in on National Security Council meeting, was placed in charge of the President's program to eliminate job discrimination at plants doing business with the Government and assigned the responsibility of keeping the Administration's eye on the nation's space program—which, as a Senator, he had been instrumental in getting off the ground.

Still, there were persistent rumors in 1963 that Mr. Kennedy was going to "dump" Mr. Johnson from his ticket in 1964. At his last news conference, held less than a month before the Dallas tragedy, the President emphatically stated that Mr. Johnson would be his running mate in 1964.

Mr. Kennedy also acceded to Mr. Johnson's request that he accompany him to Texas on a political fence-mending trip. In Texas, pro- and anti-Johnson, liberal and conservative, Democratic factions had been feuding for years. The President of the United States might be just the man to patch up the feud, to give the party a united cast as it headed for the next year's elections.

And so John F. Kennedy went with Lyndon Johnson to Texas on Nov. 21, 1963. The following day, Mr. Johnson and his wife rode in a motorcade through the sunlit streets of Dallas, behind an open limousine bearing John and Jacqueline Kennedy and Gov. John Connally of Texas.

Lee Harvey Oswald fired three shots from a window of the Texas Book Depository, and a President was dead.

Lyndon Johnson, a Texas ranch boy who had fought his way up the political ladder to become Vice President of his country, became the 36th President of the United States, at the age of 55.

Millions of Americans, stunned and frightened by the violence at Dallas, found consolation in the fact that, whether they liked him or not, Lyndon Johnson, propelled by chance into the Presidency, was as well equipped by experience for his task as any man in history.

After a Time of Tragedy, a Beginning Toward the 'Great Society'

VICE PRESIDENT JOHNSON and his wife had planned to entertain President and Mrs. Kennedy at their ranch in Johnson City, Tex., the night of Nov. 22, 1963.

But that afternoon, while he rode in a motorcade through the streets of Dallas, President Kennedy was killed by a sniper.

The Johnsons were riding in the third car of the motorcade. A Secret Service agent heard the assassin's shots and, as Mr. Johnson later recalled it, the agent "vaulted across the front seat . . . pushed me to the floor and shielded my body with his own body, ready to sacrifice his life for mine."

At Parkland Memorial Hospital, while President Kennedy lay dying, the frightened man who was to succeed him in only a few minutes stood in a hallway, muttering over and over, "The international Communists did it . . . The international Communists did it."

At 1:13 P.M., 43 minutes after he had been shot, John Fitzgerald Kennedy, the young and dashing 35th President of the United States, was pronounced dead.

Thirteen minutes later, Mr. Johnson was hustled into an unmarked police car to be driven at breakneck speed to Love Field, where Air Force One, the Presidential jet, was waiting. Fearing possible conspirators of the assassin, Mr. Johnson made the trip crouched on the floor of the police car.

The somber-faced Texan took the oath of office as President of the United States in the cramped executive suite of Air Force One. At his right stood his wife, Lady Bird, to his left the numbed and grief-stricken Jacqueline Kennedy, who still wore a pink wool suit spattered with her husband's blood. Instead of a Bible, Federal District Judge Sarah T. Hughes used a Roman Catholic missal to administer the oath to Mr. Johnson.

Air Force One, carrying the new President and his predecessor's body, took off immediately for Washington.

Dusk had fallen over Andrews Air Force Base, near Washington, when the jet rolled to a halt. A nationwide television audience watched, stunned, as Mr. Kennedy's casket was taken off the plane.

Then, under the harsh glare of the arc lights that flooded the plane, Mr. Johnson stepped forward and read the nation 57 words of reassurance from a white card:

"This is a sad time for all people. We have suffered a loss that cannot be weighed. For me, it is a deep personal tragedy. I know the world shares the sorrow that Mrs. Kennedy and her family bear. I will do my best. That is all I can do. I ask for your help—and God's."

Under the gravest of circumstances, the torch of leadership had been passed on. The new Chief Executive did not publicly take it up until five days after the assassination, when he stood before a joint session of Congress and said, "Let us continue."

Then he quickly made it apparent that what he meant was passage of Mr. Kennedy's entire legislative program, including civil rights laws and an unorthodox tax reduction to stimulate the economy.

In his rich Southern drawl, Mr. Johnson told Congress:

"We have talked long enough in this country about equal rights. We have talked for 100 years or more. It is time now to write it in the books of law."

He made it clear that he intended to keep the Kennedy vision for the world and pronounced it with unexpected force and eloquence:

"We will be unceasing in our search for peace, resourceful in our pursuit of areas of agreement even with those with whom we differ, and generous and loyal to those who join us in common cause."

For a few months, Mr. Johnson kept the staff of President Kennedy beside his own in the White House, as for years he was to retain the services of many of the key members of the Kennedy Cabinet, notably Secretary of State Dean Rusk and Secretary of Defense Robert McNamara. He even kept on, for more than a year, Attorney General Robert F. Kennedy, the late President's brother, despite the fact that he loathed him and the feeling was mutual.

Capt. Cecil Stoughton, White House Photographer

SUCCESSION TO PRESIDENCY: After the assassination of Mr. Kennedy in Dallas on Nov. 22, 1963, Mr. Johnson was sworn in aboard the Presidential plane as his wife, left, and Mrs. Kennedy watched. On returning to Washington, he gave reassurance to a stunned nation and quickly took up the Kennedy legislative program, telling Congress, "Let us continue."

It was in his first 15 months in office that Mr. Johnson best demonstrated the qualities for which he hoped to be remembered — by masterly managing the transition of power from the slain President to himself, by breaking legislative logjams of decades' duration, by restoring faith in the viability of the American system of divided legislative and executive powers, by proving the nation's capacity to withstand the horror of assassination and by persuading the world of the strength and continuity of American institutions.

In putting his own brand on the Presidency, he brought to the office a profound respect for the balancing force of Congress. He restored communications between the executive and legislative branches of government to such an extent that the 1964 Congresssional record was described as the most fruitful in a decade.

Shrewd management of his relations with Congress brought about quick action on a tax-cut bill only weeks after Mr. Johnson became President. He paved the way for the $11-billion cut by slashing the budget $900-million, which apparently impressed the economy blocs.

In July, 1964, Mr. Johnson proudly signed into law the most sweeping civil rights bill since Reconstruction days. The measure had been submitted to Congress in June, 1963, by Mr. Kennedy, and Mr. Johnson had pushed hard for its enactment from the time he became President.

The bill passed the Senate after a 13-week Southern filibuster. It outlawed discrimination in places of public accommodation, publicly owned facilities, employment and union membership, as well as in Federally-aided programs. A major feature of the legislation was the new power it gave the Attorney General to speed school desegregation and to enforce the Negro's right to vote.

To get the legislation he wanted, the President used with great success what came to be known in Washington as "the Johnson treatment."

The treatment consisted of a combination of cajolery, flattery, concession, arm-twisting threats and outright wooing, all applied by Mr. Johnson with an endless succession of telephone calls, bourbon-and-scotch lunches, barnyard jokes, the squeezing of elbows, the friendly arm around the shoulder, the cold stare when crossed. The technique was aimed at finding and touching the most sensitive nerve in Mr. Johnson's target—and, he said, "most often, that was the target's self-interest."

He used variations of the treatment to win a victory that had eluded the Administrations of both Dwight D. Eisenhower and John F. Kennedy over a period of more than five years. That was the settlement of the so-called "featherbedding" dispute over work-rule changes between the nation's railroads and the railroad unions.

Called to White House

When a nationwide rail strike was called by the unions for April 10, 1964, Mr. Johnson invited railroad and union leaders to the White House on April 9. The two sides agreed there would be no strike before April 25 and promised they would once more try to reach a settlement.

On April 21, labor fell in line for a settlement and the President turned the treatment on the nine management representatives. He popped in and out of their meetings, sent special emissaries to persuade them that they must agree to settle, and ate and drank with them. Finally, when he sensed it was a do-or-die proposition, he sat down with the management men, thinking, he confided to an aide, they were probably 7-to-2 against him.

When one management representative began the meeting with "I'm just an old country boy . . .," old country boy Lyndon Johnson imperiously shushed him.

"Hold it," he snapped, "stop right there. When I hear that around this town, I put my hand on my billfold. Don't start that with me."

The astonished butt of the Presidential dressing-down joined the laughter and said, "By God, I was just going to say that I'm ready to sign up." Mr. Johnson said later that he believed "that broke the deadlock, but of course I'll never know what he was going to say when I broke in."

The business community's initial reaction to Mr. Johnson was most favorable, in contrast to its attitude toward Mr. Kennedy, who was looked upon with suspicion by business after his crackdown on the steel industry over a price increase early in his Administration.

Mr. Johnson courted business in an hour-long, off-the-cuff speech before the United States Chamber of Commerce in 1964. Combining Texas blarney, homespun wit and candor ("Jettison your martyr complex . . . Stop obstructing the Government . . . Join with labor to help us hold down inflation . . ."), he won a standing ovation.

Henry Ford 2d, who admitted he had never voted for a Democrat for President, pronounced Mr. Johnson "terrific" and said he intended to vote for him in 1964.

There were occasions, of course, when business was less than enchanted with Mr. Johnson. In the latter part of 1965, for example, when the aluminum and copper industries announced price rises that the Administration felt were inflationary, the Government threatened to release some of its stockpiles of the metals to keep prices down.

Early in his Administration, the President declared what he called a "war on poverty." With Mrs. Johnson he made two trips to the distressed Appalachia area to dramatize the need for an antipoverty drive for which he asked Congress to appropriate $1-billion.

He first spoke of the Great Society, the catch-phrase with which he sought to to identify his Administration—as the New Deal did for Franklin D. Roosevelt's and the New Frontier for Mr. Kennedy's—in a commencement address at the University of Michigan on May 22, 1964. He repeated the call six days later in New York.

"I ask you to march with me along the road to the future," he said, "the road that leads to the Great Society, where no child will go unfed and no youngster will go unschooled . . . where every human being has dignity and every worker has a job; where education is blind to color and unemployment is unaware of race; where decency prevails and courage abounds . . ."

The Great Society became the slogan of Mr. Johnson's 1964 campaign to win a full four-year term in office, and well into that term he often promised that America could indeed become the great society. But he used the tag less and less as the nation became embroiled in racial strife, civil disorders and the ruinous war in Vietnam.

As the 1964 Democratic convention drew near, however, Mr. Johnson seemed to enjoy great popularity, and there was general approval of his handling of domestic problems and programs He was also praised, during that period, for his cautious approach to foreign crises.

After rioting broke out in the Panama Canal Zone on Jan. 9, 1964, in the outgrowth of a schoolboy dispute over the flying of United States and Panamanian flags in the Zone, Panama suspended diplomatic relations with the United States and demanded revision of the 1903 Canal Zone treaty.

Working through the Organization of American States, Mr. Johnson finally persuaded the Panamanians to resume relations with this country, and eventually the United States granted Panama concessions in the Zone. Throughout, Mr. Johnson appeared to proceed with a steady hand.

He was equally unruffled in February, 1964, when Premier Fidel Castro cut off the water supply for the United States Navy base at Guantánamo Bay, Cuba. He ordered water shipped to the base in tankers, and set in motion a crash program to build a desalinization plant at Guantánamo, making the base no longer dependent on the Castro regime for its water.

Choice of Running Mate

Mr. Johnson's record in the months after Mr. Kennedy's assassination, in addition to his previously unconcealed Presidential ambitions, left no doubts in the minds of Democrats and Republicans alike that he would be his party's nominee in the 1964 election. The only real question was who would be his running mate.

Robert F. Kennedy, still Attorney General, was believed to want the nomination, but Mr. Johnson quickly ruled him out by laying down the rule that no member of his Cabinet would be his candidate. He then began to leak the names of several other possible candidates, including Sen. Eugene J. McCarthy, who four years later was to become one of the President's most severe Vietnam war critics.

Finally, after what some called his "phony" manipulations had achieved the desired effect—suspense and titillation—Mr. Johnson broke precedent and flew up to Atlantic City to personally tell the delegates to the Democratic convention that he had chosen Sen. Hubert H. Humphrey of Minnesota.

An incident connected with that flight illustrates how Mr. Johnson sometimes treated the men who worked for him. To his subordinates at the White House, he was a driving taskmaster who could blaze with anger at incompetence and negligence. He respected and even liked his aides, but on occasion, such as the one involving the flight to Atlantic City, he was entirely capable of insulting them publicly.

United Press International

CIVIL RIGHTS MILESTONE: As President he pressed for passage of the most sweeping civil rights bill since Reconstruction. At the signing in 1964 were, from left, front row, Attorney General Robert F. Kennedy, Senator Everett McK. Dirksen and Senator Hubert H. Humphrey; and, at far right, second row, the Rev. Dr. Martin Luther King Jr.

The idea to fly to Atlantic City had been supplied by Pierre Salinger, Mr. Kennedy's press secretary, who had stayed on in the same capacity for Mr. Johnson before resigning to run unsuccessfully for the Senate in California. Mr. Johnson so liked the idea that he couldn't resist the temptation to turn to George Reedy, his new press secretary, and tell him scornfully, in the presence of newsmen, "Why don't you ever have good ideas like Pierre?" A shaken Mr. Reedy wrote out his resignation, but later tore it up after Mr. Johnson apologized, in private, for his offhand cruelty.

In the campaign Mr. Johnson advocated big Government programs that he called vital to the nation's welfare. His Republican opponent, Barry Goldwater, the conservative Senator from Arizona, called for cuts in Government spending and less "Washington control" of the affairs of individuals and business.

Much campaign oratory was given over to arguments as to whether Mr. Goldwater had an "itchy finger" that might, if he became President, press the button that could plunge the nation into atomic holocaust. The Democrats charged that a President Goldwater might feel constrained to escalate the United States participation in the fighting in Vietnam, while Mr. Johnson would do no such thing and indeed would seek peace in Southeast Asia.

Senator Goldwater's campaign was in marked contrast to Mr. Johnson's. The Senator held himself aloof and seldom mingled with the crowds, while Mr. Johnson kept his Secret Service guards constantly in jitters by breaking away and joining the throngs, shaking dozens of outstretched hands.

"Come on down to the speakin'," he would call through a bullhorn as his custom-built, bubble-top, armor-plated limousine cruised into a town. "Y'all don't need to dress up. It's not formal. Bring the kids and the dogs and come on down to the speakin'."

On both sides, the campaign was a relatively clean one. Mr. Johnson's supporters had few episodes verging on the scandalous that had to be explained to the voters.

One involved Robert G. Baker, a good and loyal friend of Mr. Johnson, who had served as secretary to the Senate Democratic majority at the time Mr. Johnson was majority leader. Just before the assassination of Mr. Kennedy, it was disclosed that Bobby Baker had used official influence to amass for himself a sizable fortune.

A Senate subcommittee investigation disclosed that Mr. Baker had arranged a deal between an insurance man and the LBJ Company, the Johnson family communications concern in Austin, collecting a considerable fee on it. Mr. Baker, it was testified, showed his gratitude to the then Vice President by giving him an $800 stereophonic system.

The Baker investigation never officially linked Mr. Johnson to Mr. Baker's alleged unethical practices, but the whole affair remained a source of embarrassment for the President. (In 1967, Mr. Baker was convicted of income tax evasion, theft and conspiracy to defraud the Government, but Mr. Johnson was not involved in the case.)

During the campaign, the Johnson family fortune, which included the LBJ Company and its television and radio stations, plus real estate in Texas, Missouri, Alabama and Louisiana, became a political issue that led to release of a reputable accounting firm's audit of the family interests. The official worth was put at $3.2-million, but this was the value of the properties and assets at cost. Actually, the selling value of the Johnson assets was estimated at about $15-million.

In revealing his financial statement, Mr. Johnson pointed out that exactly a week after he became President, the family stock and property had been put into the hands of trustees who had the power to sell and reinvest and were under instructions to furnish the Johnsons only with information needed to complete their tax returns. The properties did, of course, revert to the Johnsons when Mr. Johnson left the White House in 1969.

On Election Day, 1964, the Johnsons were at their ranch house in Johnson City, the unofficial White House during the Johnson Administration. The house was the old family homestead, much added to, replete with piped-in Muzak tunes in every room and a heated swimming pool. The President voted, then spent the day riding around his lavish spread, dotted with herds of Herefords and pure-bred Angus cattle nibbling at sweeping expanses of grass.

That night, as the votes were counted across the nation, it became quickly apparent that tens of thousands of Republicans had deserted their party to vote for Mr. Johnson. The people rewarded him with a record-breaking majority of 61 per cent of the popular vote.

Mr. Johnson called the result a "mandate for unity."

A President's Dream Grows Dim Under the Shadow of Vietnam

MRS. LYNDON B. JOHNSON held the Bible on which her husband's left hand rested as Chief Justice Earl Warren administered the oath of office to Mr. Johnson at his inauguration to his full term in the Presidency on Jan. 20, 1965.

Mr. Johnson wore an ordinary business suit, in contrast to the formal clothes worn by most of his predecessors at their inaugurations. His 1,500-word inaugural address was one of the shortest in history. In it he said:

"In a land of great wealth, families must not live in hopeless poverty. In a land rich in harvest, children must not go hungry. In a land of healing miracles, neighbors must not suffer and die untended. In a great land of learning and scholars, young people must be taught to read and write."

To the world Mr. Johnson said, "We aspire to nothing that belongs to others. We seek no dominion over our fellowman, but man's dominion over tyranny and misery."

The President had good reason to believe that many of his dreams for a better America could become reality, for the voters, while putting him into office in a landslide, had given him a Congress dominated by 295 Democrats against 140 Republicans in the House of Representatives and 68 Democrats against 32 Republicans in the Senate.

What the President called "the fabulous 89th" Congress soon began to enact far-reaching programs that had been bogged down in the legislative body for up to 30 years. Suddenly, they began to breeze through for signature by an exultant Chief Executive. The Congress passed 86 Administration measures, despite the fact that the Republicans called much of the legislation unwise and charged that it was rammed through by the Johnson Administration by means of sheer political power and with insufficient debate.

Among the measures that would have the most far-reaching effect on the quality of American life in the future was the bill to provide virtually free medical and hospital care for the aged under Social Security.

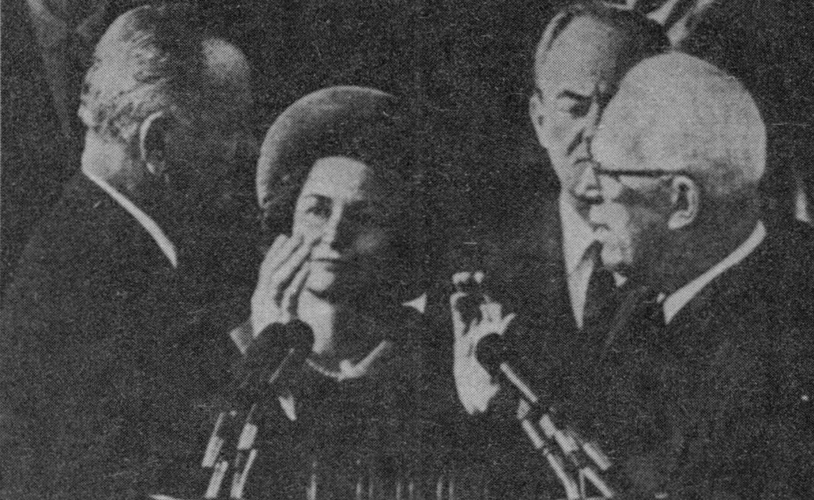

Associated Press

START OF FULL TERM: Campaigning on his theme of the Great Society, Mr. Johnson won a resounding victory in 1964. At the inauguration Jan. 20, 1965, Chief Justice Earl Warren gave the oath, Mrs. Johnson held the Bible and Vice President Humphrey looked on.

The measure, popularly known as the Medicare bill, was signed into law by the President on July 30, 1965, in the presence of former President Harry S. Truman. Mr. Johnson chose the Truman Library in Independence, Mo., as the site of the signing of the bill in tribute to Mr. Truman, who had unsuccessfully sought Medicare legislation during his own Administration.

Among Mr. Johnson's other notable successes during those first euphoric months of his full term in office were a massive program of Federal aid to elementary and secondary schools as well as greatly expanded help to colleges and college students; new safeguards for Negro voting rights; reform of the immigration laws; grants for the "model cities" development program and a program of rent subsidies for poor tenants; a higher minimum wage; increased funds for the antipoverty program; a series of measures to protect the consumer from fraudulent packaging and advertising; and a substantial start on efforts to rid the air and streams of pollution.

All these and tax cuts too were realized by the President, with the help of the 89th Congress, as were new health programs, greater support for the arts and humanities, a constitutional amendment to clarify the chain of executive command in case of Presidential disability, and two more Cabinet offices, Secretary of Transportation and Secretary of Housing and Urban Development.

To the latter post he named Robert C. Weaver, the first Negro to hold Cabinet rank. The President also appointed the first Negro ever to sit on the Supreme Court, Thurgood Marshall, who had won fame as a brilliant trial lawyer for Negro rights before Mr. Johnson appointed him Solicitor General of the United States.

He appointed other Negroes to high office and championed their cause, so that, he said, "now, maybe, every Negro kid in the United States could think, 'Goddamn it, maybe I can be a judge some day — or President.' I never thought I could be President. I want to put some incentive in them."

On many occasions, Mr. Johnson lent his prestigious Southern accent to the cry of nonviolent Negro demonstrations that "we shall overcome," and on one such occasion he used that phrase — the anthem of the civil rights movement — in urging Congress to enact strong voting rights legislation. On March 16, 1965, he told Congress:

"It is not just Negroes but really it is all of us who must overcome the crippling legacy of bigotry and injustice. And we shall overcome."

By habit and training, Mr. Johnson was a child of Congress, and the passing of legislation and the shaping of Federal programs were to him the essence of government. It appeared that, ideally, he would have liked to cut off the world at both oceans to let America put her own house in order and to help all Americans arrange for their welfare through normal political processes.

But events were not to allow him to take that course.

Since he had, over the years, been acknowledged as something of a master at handling domestic problems that lent themselves to the legislative process, perhaps Mr. Johnson could have smoothly handled the purely domestic perplexities that were soon to besiege him — had he not become embroiled in seemingly insoluble, highly explosive situations abroad.

As early as April, 1965, Mr. Johnson was severely criticized for his handling of a political crisis in the Dominican Republic. He rushed two divisions of American troops there — too swiftly and without proper notification to the Organization of American States, his critics charged — on the suspicion that Communists and Castroites were about to seize power there.

The troops helped put down the leftist forces in the Dominican Republic, amid many cries throughout the Western Hemisphere that Uncle Sam had abandoned his so-called good neighbor policy and was once more wielding the big stick.

Having foiled the leftists in Santo Domingo, the President, using typical Johnson wheeler-dealer tactics, it was charged, applied his political and economic influence to bar the extreme right, as well as the left, from power, and to arrange an election that gave control to moderate rightists.

Two years later, Mr. Johnson was able to bind up some of the wounds inflicted in the hemisphere by his management of the Dominican crisis, when he summoned a meeting of all the Latin-American heads of state. The conference, at Punta del Este, Uruguay, was called to demonstrate his more positive interests in the hemisphere's economic development.

However, throughout his Administration, a great shadow was cast over all his efforts abroad. It was the shadow of war, of the tragic, ugly, bloody, seemingly endless war in Vietnam.

Even Mr. Johnson's most severe critics would agree that in substantial measure the President inherited the problem of Vietnam.

South Vietnam, carved out of what had been French Indochina after France lost that colony with the fall of Dienbienphu in 1954, had plagued both President Dwight D. Eisenhower and President John F. Kennedy. They sent military advisers to help organize the South Vietnamese army to combat the guerrilla tactics of the Communist rebels, the Vietcong, who were aided and armed by Communist North Vietnam. But it was President Johnson's fate to commit American troops to a long and costly land war in South Vietnam.

The stage for his escalation of the war was actually set in August, 1964, after Communist PT boats had attacked United States destroyers in the Gulf of Tonkin. Mr. Johnson obtained Congressional approval of a resolution granting him full support for "all necessary action to protect our armed forces." (It was not until many months later, in bitter wrangling before the Senate Foreign Relations Committee, that doubt was cast on the intelligence information concerning the Tonkin incident that impelled Congress to give Mr. Johnson "a blank check to escalate the war," as some critics charged.)

In February, 1965, there were about 20,000 American servicemen in South Vietnam, functioning in the limited capacity of advising and giving logistic support to the weakening native forces.

Grim News From Saigon

At that time, there came to Mr. Johnson the grim news that the Saigon Government, which the United States had repeatedly promised to defend, stood in imminent danger of collapse, that the Vietcong insurgents were on the march, and that together with North Vienamese army units smuggled into the south they had begun a final and feasible drive for victory.

The choice to the President seemed to be either a great infusion of American military power or defeat and withdrawal as the Vietcong and Communists gradually took over. Feeling committed to the defense of South Vietnam by his predecessors; resolved, perhaps, not to start his full term of office with an international defeat; and led by his military and diplomatic advisers to believe that only a few months of direct military action would settle the matter, Mr. Johnson plunged ahead.

He authorized what soon became the daily, although selective, air bombardment of North Vietnam, which he blamed for planning and supplying the campaign of the Vietcong in South Vietnam. By July, 1965, Mr. Johnson had sent 75,000 American troops into the war zone and was planning an increase to 125,000. By November there were 160,000 American troops there.

Every few months, the President's advisers calculated that just a bit more strength would tip the scales and turn Vietnam into a victory. But three years after the escalation had begun, and Mr. Johnson approached the end of his White House tenure, the number of troops in Vietnam soared past a half million, and there was still no end in sight. The severity of the internal debates and doubts over escalation of the war was disclosed in the Pentagon papers, published in late 1971.

What was more tragic, more and more lives were being sacrificed to the Vietnam quagmire. By the end of January, 1969, some two weeks after Mr. Johnson left office, more than 31,000 Americans had been killed in Vietnam and nearly 435,000 had been hospitalized with wounds.

In financial terms, the cost of the war became staggering. It went from $103-million in 1965, the year Mr. Johnson began the escalation, to $5.8-billion in 1966, to more than $20-billion the following year, to $26.5-billion in 1968, and finally, for the 1969 fiscal year, an estimated $28.8-billion.

Despite the expenditure of lives and dollars, however, most of the increased American effort was offset by more men and supplies from North Vietnam.

Too, Communist China and the Soviet Union, themselves competing for authority in the Communist world, supplied the North Vietnamese and effectively protected them from total devastation or invasion with the implied threat to the United States of their own involvement, directly, in the war.

Associated Press

MEDICARE ACHIEVED: Among his Administration's most notable measures was Medicare. Mr. Johnson signed bill in 1965, in the presence of former President Harry S. Truman.

Associated Press

SUMMIT AT GLASSBORO: The President and Soviet Premier Aleksei N. Kosygin parting after talks in 1967. Their meeting helped to ease tensions between the two countries.

White House Photograph

United Press International

Associated Press

***THE VIETNAM WAR:** Escalation of the bloody, costly conflict in Southeast Asia embroiled Mr. Johnson in mounting controversy at home. He visited GI's on battlefield to assure them of support (left) and he flew to Honolulu to confer with South Vietnamese leaders (such as Vice President Nguyen Cao Ky, right), but opposition intensified greatly as 1968 election approached.*

Often, as criticism of his war policies grew both at home and abroad, the President pleaded for understanding. "We will never be second in the search for . . . a peaceful settlement in Vietnam," he said. "We remain ready for unconditional discussions."

From time to time, he stopped or reduced the bombing of North Vietnam to reinforce his calls for negotiation. Late in 1965, for example, during a truce, he set in motion a massive "peace offensive" in which Ambassador at Large W. Averell Harriman, Vice President Hubert H. Humphrey and many other officials flew to capitals on both sides of the Iron Curtain to enlist support for a Johnson peace plan.

Hanoi, Peking and Moscow denounced the peace offensive as a fraud designed as a smokescreen for further escalation of the war.

The Issue of Control

Despite such disappointments, the President continued to hammer home what he conceived as the central issue of the war, which was, simply, who is to control Vietnam?

The Vietcong, and their political arm, the Communist-backed National Liberation Front, claimed to be the only legitimate governing force in South Vietnam. So did the United States-backed Saigon Government, controlled largely by leaders of the South Vietnam armed forces.

Mr. Johnson steadfastly refused to pursue a settlement that would give the Liberation Front too great a share of political power in Saigon, fearing that total power was the Front's long-range aim. The other side refused to settle for anything less.

But, as the President said in his State of the Union Address on Jan. 12, 1966, "There are no arbitrary limits to our search for peace . . . We will meet at any conference table; we will discuss any proposals—4 points or 14 or 40—and we will work . . . for a ceasefire now or once discussions have begun. We'll respond if others reduce their use of force. . . ."

On all except this central issue, Mr. Johnson tried to be conciliatory, even generous. He refused to whip up hate for the enemy and he offered to spend, after the war, billions to help rebuild Vietnam and to help develop the economies of both the north and south.

But beyond charity, Mr. Johnson believed, the dominant issue was whether the United States would keep its word and prevent the forcible overthrow or conquest of a country it had promised to defend. The violation of such a promise, he insisted, would imperil dozens of other nations—especially those on the periphery of Communist China—and hence the peace of the world.

Many Americans agreed, and they also went along with Mr. Johnson's contention that promises and commitments, once made, could be violated only at the nation's peril. His stance won the approval of such diverse Republicans as General Eisenhower, Richard M. Nixon and Barry Goldwater.

However a large and highly vocal minority of Americans disagreed, sometimes violently, with Mr. Johnson's pursuit of the war in Vietnam. Some came to hate him and the war so passionately that they doubted he had any purpose in continuing the conflict except what they saw as a jingoist refusal to accept defeat or to admit mistakes.

Hawks and Doves Emerge

Americans gradually divided themselves into hawks and doves—those who would take even more vigorous military action than Mr. Johnson did to end the fighting, and those who would fight less and negotiate some face-saving end of the ordeal.

Partly because of displeasure with the war, a critical Congress and especially its Senate Foreign Relations Committee tore to shreds even Mr. Johnson's modest foreign aid programs for the hemisphere and other regions. And in a series of damaging public hearings in 1966, conducted by Mr. Johnson's fellow Democrat, Sen. J. William Fulbright, the Foreign Relations Committee challenged all the assumptions of the President's policies in Vietnam, toward Communist China and even Western Europe.

More carefully than many of his critics, however, Mr. Johnson sought to compartmentalize his foreign policies against the effects of Vietnam.

He constantly prodded the Soviet Union for a wider measure of agreement, and although Moscow refused while the war lasted to be conspicuously friendly, it did negotiate on some issues. Notably, it came to terms with Washington on treaties to limit the spread of nuclear weapons and to limit the use of such weapons in outer space.

The arms race continued, however, and the Russians nearly caught up to the United States in the number of land-based long-range missiles. Both sides began work on antimissile missile defenses. Their arms sales, linked with political deals with their friends, stimulated conflict in several regions, particularly the Middle East.

One such conflict erupted into a brief but dangerous war in which Israel was pitted against her Arab neighbors in June, 1967. Mr. Johnson dexterously maneuvered the Russians into agreeing that both Moscow and Washington would stay out of the conflict, which both knew to mean a deal to assure victory to the Israelis.

The war in the Mideast resulted in an emergency session of the United Nations, which brought Soviet Premier Aleksei N. Kosygin to New York to explain the Russian view of the crisis. After much delicate diplomacy, it was decided that the Premier and the President would hold a summit meeting in the small college town of Glassboro, N.J.

Nothing really concrete came out of the Glassboro talks, but they produced what came to be known as "the spirit of Glassboro," a subtle easing of tensions between the two great superpowers of the Soviet Union and the United States that Mr. Johnson said made the world "a little less dangerous."

The East-West confrontation across the heart of Europe remained quiet throughout the Johnson years, although the political sands continued to shift on both sides of the line. The European Common Market flourished, but at the price of accepting French President Charles de Gaulle's exclusion of Britain from the market and his imperious strictures against American influence. Thus the North Atlantic Treaty Organization foundered, becoming only a formal excuse for the retention of six American divisions in West Germany.

In Communist Europe, there was rebellion against Soviet dominance, particularly in Czechoslovakia, where liberalization of the Communist regime was crushed by Soviet and Soviet-bloc troops. There was also a gradual movement in the Communist sphere toward political arrangements that would promote economic development through cooperation with the West. Mr. Johnson had hoped to influence this trend through a major campaign for trade with the European Communist bloc of nations, but Congress, while criticizing his Vietnam war policies on the one hand, refused to cooperate with him on the other by "rewarding" North Vietnam's friends and allies with trade concessions.

Trouble in the Cities

Everywhere he turned, at home and abroad, it seemed, Lyndon Johnson ran headlong into the limitations set for him by the war, which sapped not only money but also governmental energy and priority. And, sadly, the war distracted the nation and its leader from what under any circumstances would have been a monumental problem, the decay of the cities and the revolt of the Negroes in the ghettos.

Only a week after Mr. Johnson had triumphantly signed the Voting Rights Act of 1965, the nation was vividly reminded that the race problem was far from reconciled. Wild rioting engulfed the Watts Negro ghetto of Los Angeles.

In succeeding summers, the looting and arson and shooting spread from city to city, ghetto to ghetto. Newark, Detroit and other cities were in open rebellion for several days in 1967, and after the assassination in April, 1968, of the Rev. Dr. Martin Luther King Jr., the moderate, nonviolent civil rights leader, dozens of cities across the nation were the scenes of frightening rioting.

Much of this occurred even while new civil rights laws, tardy relief programs and antisegregation orders were being put into effect, but the Negro, weary of having waited for generations for equality of opportunity and the end of racism in America, continued to press his revolt.

Mr. Johnson did what he could with limited resources for more education and job training and job opportunity, but he had to contend with a fearful and often angry white community that demanded repression of the rioters and rebelled against still more Federal spending to "reward" them.

Behind the riots lay the decay of the cores of the nation's major cities and the pervasive patterns of discrimination that kept poor Negroes imprisoned there. And behind the angry white response lay the deterioration of much of the quality of life in middle-class America, despite a booming economy and, for most of the people, an unparalleled prosperity.

Transportation systems were clogged,

The New York Times

***NOT A CANDIDATE:** On television March 31, 1968, Mr. Johnson announced new U.S. efforts for peace in Vietnam and told a startled nation he would not run for re-election.*

the air and water were polluted, public services were strained. Crime rates soared. To their elders, the young seemed embarked on a new permissive pursuit of an irresponsible life-style based on drugs, sex and rebellion against authority.

Mr. Johnson kept urging the nation to think positively, to remember what was "right with America." He regarded its problems as challenges, not defeats, and he tried to devise programs to deal with them.

During his five years in office, he doubled the size of the Federal budget to nearly $200-billion and tripled the amounts spent for education and health. His budgets tripled the amount of money spent on aid to the poor. He designed significant programs to attack urban blight, crime and pollution.

Yet Congress, no doubt reflecting the mood of the nation, long resisted his proposals to raise taxes even modestly to prevent the war in Vietnam from gutting all domestic programs. And, despite prosperity, the nation's military commitments abroad produced a net outflow of dollars and hence a constant drain on American gold reserves.

Thus Mr. Johnson was forced to devote much of his time to managing and manipulating the economy, to reducing the deficit in international payments, to holding Federal spending to the barest minimum and to keeping down wages and prices.

As Commander in Chief, Mr. Johnson exhibited a complex mixture of admiration for his generals and admirals with suspicion and fear of the advice they gave him. He eventually became a virtual prisoner of the military logic that plotted strategy in Vietnam, but he never ceased to question the professional military men to a degree that some of them resented.

Although nominally head of his party, Mr. Johnson never worked easily with the Democratic National Committee or its affiliates. He did try, desultorily, in 1966 to help party candidates win reelection to Congress but, sensing a doomed cause, backed away. The Democrats lost eight state houses, three Senate seats and 47 House seats.

Political friendship caused the President to appoint Abe Fortas a Supreme Court Justice—much to Mr. Johnson's ultimate sorrow. In 1969 Mr. Fortas had to resign amid criticism of his financial dealings.

At the outset of his Presidency, Mr. Johnson was admired by many, if not precisely loved. He showed what many considered likable traits of rustic humor, earthiness, folksiness, sentimentality and old-fashioned patriotism. Later, however, many who had supported him came to loathe him because of his war policies, and they came to consider him vulgar, tasteless and insular.

Mr. Johnson brought to the White House the manners of the raucous West, more forcibly than any President since Andrew Jackson. White House visitors were taken by him on exhaustive tours of what Mr. Johnson liked to call "your house," and specially favored guests were given a glimpse of his bedroom and bathroom as well.

With his lust for life and action, Mr. Johnson was perhaps naturally undisciplined in some of his personal habits. He ate hugely and had to suffer through periodic diets to take off the 20 or 30 additional pounds that would easily creep upon his 200-pound frame.

Mr. Johnson's language around men could be excessively profane, but in the presence of women he had an exaggerated sense of courtly decorum. He usually addressed them as "M'am."

The tall Texan liked expensive, elaborately tailored clothes, suits with narrow lapels and outsized shirt collars, all to give a streamined appearance to his somewhat ungainly form. He placed a cowboy's high premium on highly polished shoes or leather of any kind.

Colorful Host at Ranch

On his frequent retreats to the LBJ Ranch, Mr. Johnson was a colorful and solicitous host. He once held a news conference on the banks of the Pedenales River, with a bale of hay for a rostrum, and ending it by riding off on a Tennessee walking horse. Dignified diplomats were entertained at barbecues.

While touring the ranch, Mr. Johnson once took a Secret Service agent's pistol and blazed away at an armadillo. On another occasion the President drove a group of reporters on a wild, 90-mile-an-hour ride on a highway near the ranch, a bottle of beer on his dashboard.

He was widely criticized for that beer-drinking ride. On another occasion, the nation's dog lovers set up a considerable howl after they saw news photographs of the President holding up his beagles, Him and Her, by their ears "to make them bark—it's good for them," as he put it.

Another round of criticism was stirred by his public display of an operation scar. While recuperating in October, 1965, from an operation to remove a benign polyp from his abdomen, the President impulsively pulled up his shirttail to let newsmen see his incision. The photographs that resulted were splashed across hundreds of front pages, and the White House received hundreds of letters expressing shock and disgust that a President could be, as some said, "so coarse."

Mr. Johnson was never at ease in press conferences, especially large televised ones, for he knew he did not come off well on television. Newsmen were invited to his office at a moment's notice for informal conferences. He held one while strolling on the White House grounds, and to another he invited the newsmen's wives and children and served them cookies and punch.

The President seemed genuinely to want to be liked, even loved. Yet, as the nation sank deeper and deeper into the horror of Vietnam, his popularity continued to wane. The intellectual community, which in general had supported his election, found him vulgar and tiresome and untrustworthy. Much of the press treated him as crude and temperamental.

The impression spread that Mr. Johnson suffered from what was euphemistically called a "credibility gap"—a tendency to misstate and misrepresent issues and facts to the country.

In many respects, this was merely a new phrase for an old complaint about the self-serving nature of official propaganda; "managing the news" was an earlier one. But here again, many of the worst suspicions about Mr. Johnson were traceable to the war. The President had appeared to promise to avoid such a war in the 1964 campaign, and on many occasions thereafter he mistakenly represented it as going well.

As the time grew near for him to decide whether he would run for re-election in 1968, Mr. Johnson found himself being berated by hawks and doves alike on the war, by both whites and blacks on race relations.

The opposition to him became so great, so bitter, and often unfair, that he had reason to fear moving among the people, something that in happier days he enjoyed and did effectively and well.

In his own party, opponents of the Vietnam war and critics of his domestic failures were getting more and more attention. Two Democratic Senators, Eugene J. McCarthy of Minnesota and Robert F. Kennedy of New York (who was assassinated in June, 1968), had gone to the electorate in state primaries to challenge his right to renomination.

The national opinion polls showed that the public's confidence in the President's handling of his office had plunged so low that there was serious doubt he could win the November election against the Republican front-runner, Richard M. Nixon, even should he receive the Democratic nomination.

When, on March 31, 1968, he announced he would not run for re-election, Mr. Johnson said he was withdrawing from politics in the name of national unity and for the "ultimate strength of our country." He did not sound bitter; rather, there was a note of relief in his voice.

Mr. Johnson coupled his declaration with an announcement that he had ordered the bombing of North Vietnam restricted to the area below the 19th parallel, and he called for peace talks. Three days later the North Vietnamese agreed to preliminary discussions, and by mid-May, negotiations had begun.

On Dec. 22, 1968, a month before he left office, Mr. Johnson could note with pride that North Korea had released 82 crew members of the United States intelligence ship Pueblo, who had been imprisoned since Jan. 23, 1968, when their ship was captured by the Communists. At the time he had resisted Congressional and popular demands that force be used to effect the return of the ship.

On Jan. 20, 1969, Mr. Johnson turned over the Presidency to Mr. Nixon, the Republican who defeated Vice President Hubert H. Humphrey in the 1968 election. He left Washington the same day, going home to Texas to write his memoirs for the record price of $1.5-million.

Back home, he seemed relaxed and happy, surprising many who believed he could derive little pleasure from life out of the limelight and unnourished by politics. For the first time in years, no demanding schedule determined the course of his days. He had no set time to rise or sleep. He enjoyed his family and his ranch; he went to football games, attended to his correspondence, saw old friends and worked on his book.

In May, 1971, the $18.6-million Lyndon Baines Johnson Library complex in Austin on the University of Texas campus was dedicated in nationally televised ceremonies that drew 3,000 guests, including President Nixon. The library was designed to house 31 million pages of documents, 500,000 photographs and memorabilia.

Mr. Johnson's memoirs, "The Vantage Point: Perspectives of the Presidency, 1963-1969," were published Nov. 1, 1971, by Holt, Rinehart & Winston.

In The New York Times Book Review, David Halberstam said: "The real story of the Johnsonian Presidency is not to be found in this book. It is his story as he would have it, his view of how he would like things to be."

Lyndon Johnson had sought greatness but at the time he gave up the Presidency, many Americans would not say he had achieved it. Many more had chosen to forget the good he had done because they so despised his handling of the war in Vietnam.

Historian's Judgment

One of the first judgments of him, by a historian, came from Dr. Eric F. Goldman, a Princeton University professor who had served Mr. Johnson as a special consultant in the White House. Dr. Goldman's relationship with Mr. Johnson had been stormy, but, looking back, the historian took a compassionate view of the President.

In his book "The Tragedy of Lyndon Johnson," Dr. Goldman wrote:

"Lyndon Johnson could win votes, enact laws, maneuver mountains. He could not acquire that something beyond, which cannot be won, enacted or maneuvered but must be freely given . . . that respect, affection and rapport which alone permit an American President genuinely to lead. In his periods of triumph and of downsweep, in peace as in war, he stood the tragic figure of an extraordinarily gifted President who was the wrong man from the wrong place at the wrong time under the wrong circumstances."

Mr. Johnson's view of what he achieved might be summed up in a homily he once delivered to a group of young people.

"To hunger for use and to go unused is the worst hunger of all," he said. "Few men have the power by a single act or by a single lifetime to shape history for themselves. Presidents, for example, quickly realize that while a single act might destroy the world they live in, no one single decision can make life suddenly better or can turn history around for the good."

Associated Press

***FAMILY MAN:** He joined with his wife and daughters, Luci Nugent, left, and Lynda Bird Robb, and his grandson, Patrick Lyndon Nugent, for a Thanksgiving portrait in 1968.*

Associated Press

***BACK IN TEXAS:** During his Presidency he spent frequent vacations at the LBJ Ranch, to which he retired in 1969.*

"All the News That's Fit to Print"

The New York Times

LATE CITY EDITION

Weather: Chance of showers today, tonight. Fair and warmer tomorrow. Temp. range: today 70-60; Sat. 77-55. Full report on Page 91.

SECTION ONE

VOL. CXVII . No. 40,307

NEW YORK, SUNDAY, JUNE 2, 1968

60¢ beyond 50-mile zone from New York City, except Long Island. 75¢ beyond 200-mile radius. Higher in air delivery cities.

50 CENTS

KENNEDY DISPUTES M'CARTHY ON WAR IN TV DISCUSSION

Rivals Differ Over Whether Peace Parleys Should Urge a Coalition Government

AGREE ON MOST ISSUES

High-Level Confrontation Is First of Their Campaign for Democratic Nomination

Excerpts from the McCarthy and Kennedy debate, Page 64.

By R. W. APPLE Jr.

Senators Robert F. Kennedy and Eugene J. McCarthy met last night in the first face-to-face confrontation of their campaign for the Democratic Presidential nomination. It was a high-level discussion of issues in which they rarely disagreed.

The two Senators disputed one key point relating to the Vietnam peace negotiations. Mr. McCarthy urged the Administration to state now that it would accept a coalition Government in Saigon while Mr. Kennedy opposed such a declaration at this time.

After the Minnesotan had made his point, Senator Kennedy said he opposed "what I understand [to be] Senator McCarthy's position of forcing a coalition Government on the Government of Saigon, a coalition with the Communists."

Subtle Disagreements

Mr. McCarthy replied that that was not what he meant. He said that "if the South Vietnamese want to continue the fight, work out their own negotiation, that's well and good," but that the United States should take a stand.

There were other subtle disagreements in the hour-long discussion, which was nationally televised by the American Broadcasting Company from a studio in San Francisco. But the two contenders for the nomination agreed on a wide range of political, economic, civil rights and foreign policy questions.

Senator McCarthy mounted an unusually strong attack on Secretary of State Dean Rusk, whom he has said he would oust. Mr. Kennedy said he would prefer not to indulge in personalities, but, as the discussion progressed, he commented that he would not be likely to retain Mr. Rusk if elected President in view of their sharp differences of opinion on Vietnam.

"I happen to disagree with

Continued on Page 64, Column 3

Helen Keller, 87, Dies

Blind and Deaf Since Infancy, She Became Symbol of Courage

Special to The New York Times

WESTPORT, Conn., June 1—Helen Keller, who overcame blindness and deafness to become a symbol of the indomitable human spirit, died this afternoon in her home here. She was 87 years old.

American Foundation for the Blind

Helen Keller

"She drifted off in her sleep," said Mrs. Winifred Corbally, Miss Keller's companion for the last 11 years, who was at her bedside. "She died gently." Death came at 3:35 P.M.

She is survived by a brother, Phillips B. Keller of Dallas, and a sister, Mrs. Mildred Tyson of Montgomery, Ala.

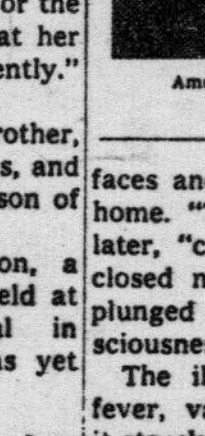

After private cremation, a funeral service will be held at the National Cathedral in Washington. No date has yet been set.

Triumph Out of Tragedy

By ALDEN WHITMAN

For the first 18 months of her life Helen Keller was a normal infant who cooed and cried, learned to recognize the voices of her father and mother and took joy in looking at their faces and at objects about her home. "Then," as she recalled later, "came the illness which closed my eyes and ears and plunged me into the unconsciousness of a newborn baby."

The illness, perhaps scarlet fever, vanished as quickly as it struck, but it erased not only the child's vision and hearing but also, as a result, her powers of articulate speech.

Her life thereafter, as a girl and as a woman, became a triumph over crushing adversity

Continued on Page 76, Column 1

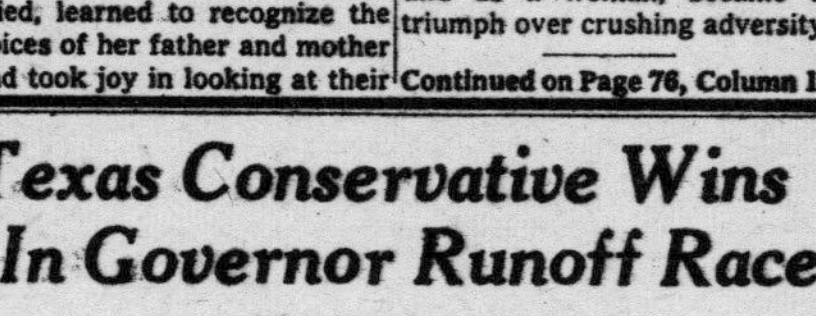

Texas Conservative Wins In Governor Runoff Race

By MARTIN WALDRON

Special to The New York Times

HOUSTON, June 1—Texas Democrats nominated for Governor tonight a nonconformist conservative, Preston A. Smith, rejecting for the third time a liberal candidate, Donald H. Yarborough. Mr. Smith, the Lieutenant Governor for six years, who is not a full-fledged member of the Texas political establishment, won handily in the runoff primary.

He piled up a large majority throughout the state without the help of the incumbent, Gov. John B. Connally Jr.

Mr. Yarborough conceded the election shortly before midnight, saying that his supporters had put up a "brave and courageous fight" but had been defeated by the conservative forces of Texas.

Mr. Yarborough had been favored, but he faltered in the four-week-long runoff campaign after Mr. Smith had proposed new state laws to crack down on "crime in the streets," including stiffer penalties for looting and street rioting. Mr. Yarborough is not related to Senator Ralph W. Yarborough.

80 Per Cent of Vote

Mr. Smith, who is 56 years old, is from Lubbock in the plains district in the north central part of the state.

With more than 80 per cent of the vote counted unofficially, the tally was:

Smith	732,962
Yarborough	595,555

The votes are counted by the Texas Election Bureau, a private organization that is financed by newspapers, television stations and the wire services.

The extent of Lieutenant Governor Smith's victory was reflected in Houston, normally a strong liberal stronghold and Mr. Yarborough's hometown.

With complete returns from Houston, Mr. Smith came with-

Continued on Page 28, Column 1

HUMPHREY BLUNT IN MICHIGAN BID

In a Tough Speech, He Asks State Delegation for Help in Getting Nomination

By ROY REED

Special to The New York Times

DETROIT, June 1—This may be remembered as the day Hubert Humphrey got tough. Speaking here this morning in an effort to collect some political I.O.U.'s, he reminded Michigan Democrats of the many times in the last 25 years he had traveled to their state to help build a liberal Democratic party.

"When you needed my help I was here," he told the State Democratic Convention at Cobo Hall, "in the dark days, in the difficult days."

Now, he said, he needs their help. The 96-vote Michigan delegation will be chosen tomorrow.

Mr. Humphrey's unaccustomed bluntness was an acknowledgement that the fight for convention delegates at Chicago had begun in earnest.

All over the nation, his operatives and those of his opponents are attending state party conventions such as the one in Detroit, and more intimate gatherings as well, to try to obtain delegates to the national convention at Chicago in August.

The Humphrey people were

Continued on Page 34, Column 3

VIETCONG CLINGING TO TWO FOOTHOLDS IN SAIGON REGION

Bombers Hammer Suburbs —Foe's Shells Kill Three in Center of the Capital

By JOSEPH B. TREASTER

Special to The New York Times

SAIGON, South Vietnam, Sunday, June 2 — The Vietcong shelled central Saigon this morning as they clung to positions in the heart of the Chinese quarter and on the city's northeastern fringe.

The United States command said that 11 rounds of "indirect fire"—presumably from rocket launchers or mortars—exploded in the streets between 1:40 and 3:27 A.M.

Two of the enemy shells struck within a mile of the presidential palace at the center of Saigon, about four blocks from the main business district.

According to early reports, 3 South Vietnamese civilians were killed and 10 wounded.

Blasts Rattle Windows

No shooting was reported this morning in the two pockets of the city held through the night by enemy infiltrators, but loud explosions rattled windows as allied bombers hammered the position to the northeast.

Sniper shots echoed late into the night through Cholon, the congested Chinese section, and there were reports that 300 of the enemy were skirmishing with South Vietnamese marines and paratroopers in the suburbs.

Fires set off by Vietcong rockets and allied recoilless rifles and grenades tore through two blocks in Cholon, and two large blazes on the edge of town lit the evening sky.

After analyzing the eight days of action in and around the South Vietnamese capital, senior American officers remained convinced that the enemy was bent on maintaining tension on the city rather than trying to penetrate or overrun it.

Link With Peace Talks

Allied commanders have said they believe the enemy's recent aggressiveness is intended to strengthen his position during the talks in Paris between the United States and North Vietnam. At a news conference last week, Lieut. Col. Phan Mau, identified as a Vietcong defector, substantiated that line of thought.

"The Communist plan consists of a very long schedule, composed of many offensives, all aimed at supporting the talks being held at Paris," Colonel Mau said.

The South Vietnamese command announced that 300 enemy dead had been counted in metropolitan Saigon since Thursday.

The United States command reported renewed action in the country's northernmost provinces.

In two battles near Khesanh, United States marines reported having killed 127 of the enemy. American paratroops operating seven miles east of Hue said

Continued on Page 7, Column 1

United Press International

FLEES EMBATTLED AREA IN SAIGON: A woman, on the verge of hysteria, carrying her belongings past a South Vietnamese marine as fighting continued in the Cholon area.

Two Tense Days in Elysee Palace

Pompidou Challenge to de Gaulle's Plan in Crisis Disclosed

By HENRY TANNER

Special to The New York Times

PARIS, June 1—Before flying to West Germany last Wednesday and seeking new strength in conversations with French Army officers there, President de Gaulle faced a grim personal challenge from his Premier, Georges Pompidou, and the possible defection of many Gaullist politicians.

The drama of the two previous days, as described by authoritative sources, includes a bitter confrontation at the Elysée Palace Tuesday night between the 77-year-old general and Mr. Pompidou, his chosen heir apparent.

The Premier, convinced that the country was sinking into chaos and dismayed by the President's silence and remoteness, is understood to have said that the general had only two choices: to call a new general election or to resign.

He is understood to have argued that a June referendum, which President de Gaulle announced five days earlier, was a totally inadequate response to the country's mood of rebellion.

The confrontation included a highly personal exchange in which the President accused his Premier of having betrayed him, according to the sources, who are not necessarily aligned with Mr. Pompidou.

The next morning President de Gaulle took the unusual step of leaving French territory, at the height of a national emergency. With his wife he flew to the airport in Baden-Baden, headquarters of French Army forces stationed in West Germany, where he was reported to have conferred with generals regarding the growing French rebelliousness of students and workers.

Having felt the reins of his control over the country slipping gradually from his hands during the preceding weeks and being faced with a challenge even from the head of his Government, the President had to know where the army stood. He found it obedient and ready to help, if necessary, with all the means at its disposal.

In the evening, the President flew to his country estate in Colombey - les - deux - Eglises. After a night of reflection there, he returned to Paris to tell the nation that "after having considered without exception all the possibilities," he would not retire.

The confrontation between the general and the Premier was a result of a deep malaise that had pervaded the

Continued on Page 41, Column 3

Drought Intensifies Misery in Ecuador

By PAUL L. MONTGOMERY

Special to The New York Times

MACARA, Ecuador, May 30—All through the valley of the Casanga, in drought-ridden southern Ecuador, vultures squat in the baked farmyards waiting for animals to die. On the roads, ragged bands of refugees press north, where there is water.

The New York Times June 2, 1968

Ecuador's drought is most severe in the area between the three underlined towns.

In the courtyard of a refugee center in Loja, the provincial capital, Juana Inez Narváez, from nearby Sabiango, tended a charcoal fire. Three of her eight children, wide-eyed, clung to her skirts. More than a hundred children played in the dust of the yard.

"The drought left us nothing," she said. "We planted and nothing grew. The animals had no strength; they fell over. I tell you there is nothing in Sabiango, nothing. We sold the bed, the house and land. We just left."

Mrs. Narváez did not know where her husband and other five children were. There was money enough only for her and the three youngest to come north.

"He went with the others to look for work," she said. "Perhaps in Macará, perhaps elsewhere," she added, referring to this Ecuadorian border town, where the Pan-American Highway crosses into Peru.

"There is one thing," she said. "God has been good to us. Others have died."

Much of southern Ecuador has been bone dry this year. Normal rainfall on the coast during the wet season, January through March, is 60 inches. This year it was 15 inches. In many of the inland valleys there was virtually no rain.

Current estimates are that the nation will lose 90 per cent of its cotton crop, 80 per cent of its upland rice, most of its corn and a good part of its cattle production.

Ecuador's total production of rice, which is the staple food of the coast, was 130 million pounds last year. This year it is expected to be 36.5 million pounds.

The Government has already attached 20 per cent of all rice currently in the mills. This will be put under army control for use in emergencies. Plans are also under way to import rice.

The situation is highly prejudicial to the entire economy of this nation of six million people. Ecuador has chosen to earn her foreign exchange almost exclusively from agriculture, primarily bananas. Imports of foodstuffs would upset the balance of trade and threaten the currency, which has been one of the most stable in Latin America.

The drought has received little attention from the Government, which is preoccupied with the national election to be held Sunday.

Some Ecuadorians say, however, that the Government has purposely underestimated the situation. Their reasoning is that any meaningful disaster relief would have to be financed by new taxes on foreign enterprises and luxury items. This would hurt foreign business, primarily North American, and the rich merchant class, to which President Otto Arosemena Gómez belongs.

So far, there have been

Continued on Page 2, Column 3

GAULLISTS OPEN DRIVE FOR VOTES; APPEAL FOR CALM

Pledge Voice for Workers in Industry and for Students in the Universities

MORE RETURN TO WORK

But Extreme Leftist Youths Demonstrate in Protest Against Elections

By JOHN L. HESS

Special to The New York Times

PARIS, June 1 — The Gaullist Government opened its re-election campaign today with an unusual formal appeal by the new Cabinet for votes for "progress, independence and peace."

It promised higher wages and a broader voice in the economy to the workers, participation and autonomy in universities to the students, and freedom from totalitarianism to the nation as a whole.

The declaration, adopted at a special meeting of the Government's new, sharply reorganized Cabinet, in effect summarized the platform on which Gaullists will run in the two-round legislative elections on June 23 and 30.

Exodus for Holiday

President de Gaulle announced the dissolution of the National Assembly Thursday in a tough speech that brought a dramatic turnabout in the upheaval and strikes that gripped France through the month of May.

The back-to-work movement that began yesterday continued, although it was slowed by a nationwide exodus from the cities for the three-day Whitsun holiday.

There was a good prospect that Paris subway and bus operations would resume Monday. Workers voted today on a 12 per cent wage increase as part of a package including a graduated reduction in hours. Many industries and individual plants are expected to resume work Tuesday and Wednesday, although strikes in other areas may linger for some time.

Reforms Are Unclear

Thousands of extreme leftist students marched through the Left Bank area today in protest against the Government's tactics and the elections. Daniel Cohn-Bendit, the young anarchist leader who was expelled from France and returned surreptitiously, marched at their head.

But it seemed a final gesture of the student uprising that set off the crisis. In principle, the students have won assurance that reforms will be made, but they never reached agreement among themselves on what the reforms should be, and no negotiations have yet been scheduled.

While etxremists among

Continued on Page 41, Column 1

GREENTREE COLT TAKES BELMONT

Stage Door Johnny Beats Forward Pass in Stakes

Greentree Stable's Stage Door Johnny, ridden by Heliodoro Gustines, rallied in the stretch to defeat heavily favored Forward Pass by a length and a quarter yesterday in the 100th running of the Belmont Stakes. The winner, who came from far back in the field of nine to take the lead near the eighth pole, returned $10.80, $4.40 and $2.60 for $2 across the board.

Forward Pass, the even-money favorite, thus failed in an attempt to become the first horse in 20 years to win the Triple Crown for 3-year-olds. Call Me Prince was the third-place finisher. First place in the $161,450 race was worth $117,700. Stage Door Johnny covered the mile and a half in 2 minutes 27 1/5 seconds before a crowd of 54,654.

TRACK AND FIELD

Dave Patrick of Villanova turned in the fastest outdoor mile ever run in the East as he covered the distance in 3 minutes 56.8 seconds at the 92d annual Intercollegiate Association of Amateur Athletes of America meet in Philadelphia. Patrick snapped his meet record of 4:04.9.

Details in Section 5.

California Primary: A Political Test of 'Newness'

Contrasts and Conflicts of a 'Make-Believe' Land Add Doubts to Campaign

By CHARLOTTE CURTIS

Special to The New York Times

LOS ANGELES, June 1 — When suave, perennially tanned Gov. Ronald Reagan is in the mood, he reels off statistics indicating that if California were a separate country, it would rank sixth among the nations of the world in total output.

Or, as suave, equally tanned Mayor Joseph L. Alioto of San Francisco put it, "California has more commercial clout than France or Italy — maybe even West Germany."

But for all its clout; its status as the nation's most populous state; its accomplishments in science, education, agriculture, electronics and aerospace; and what one elderly Santa Barbara real estate developer calls "the sun-kissed, ocean-washed, mountain-girded, island-guarded motif," California on the verge of its Presidential primary is perhaps the least sociologically structured and the most politically disorganized of the 50 states.

Except for aristocratic San Francisco, where afternoon tea is served and it is all right to have had ancestors who rode covered wagons across the plains for gold in 1849, or bucolic Santa Barbara, where the oldest families are descended from the Spanish conquistadores, only such groups as the America Indians, the Basque sheepherders, the Chinese whose grandfathers built the railroads, and the Swiss and Italian vintners have been around for very long. Virtually everybody else is new.

It is this newness, refreshed at the rate of some 1,300 new residents every day, combined with what's left of the frontier urge to experiment and the simultaneous desire for security, that has produced a new society and a new politic.

This imaginative state that popularized freeways, supermarkets, swimming pools, drive-ins, backyard barbecues, the bare midriff, house trailers, Capri pants, hot rods, sports shirts, split-level houses and tract living has a former B-movie actor in the Governor's chair at Sacramento, a fertile community as well known for its rice as its State Capitol.

In Governor Reagan, the only candidate in the Republican primary, the citizens have a Re-

Continued on Page 63, Column 1

Today's Sections

Index to Subjects

Helen Keller, Blind and Deaf Writer, Is Dead at 87

Continued From Page 1, Col. 3

and shattering affliction. In time, Miss Keller learned to circumvent her blindness, deafness and mutness; she could "see" and "hear" with exceptional acuity; she even learned to talk passably and to dance in time to a fox trot or a waltz. Her remarkable mind unfolded, and she was in and of the world, a full and happy participant in life.

What set Miss Keller apart was that no similarly afflicted person before had done more than acquire the simplest skills.

But she was graduated from Radcliffe; she became an artful and subtle writer; she led a vigorous life; she developed into a crusading humanitarian who espoused Socialism; and she energized movements that revolutionized help for the blind and the deaf.

Teacher's Devotion

Her tremendous accomplishments and the force of assertive personality that underlay them were released through the devotion and skill of Anne Sullivan Macy, her teacher through whom in large degree she expressed herself. Mrs. Macy was succeeded, at her death in 1936, by Polly Thomson, who died in 1960. Since then Miss Keller's companion had been Mrs. Winifred Corbally.

Miss Keller's life was so long and so crowded with improbable feats — from riding horseback to learning Greek — and she was so serene yet so determined in her advocacy of beneficent causes that she became a great legend. She always seemed to be standing before the world as an example of unquenchable will.

Many who observed her—and to some she was a curiosity and a publicity-seeker — found it difficult to believe that a person so handicapped could acquire the profound knowledge and the sensitive perception and writing talent that she exhibited when she was mature. Yet no substantial proof was ever adduced that Miss Keller was anything less than she appeared — a person whose character impelled her to perform the seemingly impossible. With the years, the skepticism, once overt, dwindled as her stature as a heroic woman increased.

Miss Keller always insisted that there was nothing mysterious or miraculous about her achievements. All that she was and did, she said, could be explained directly and without reference to a "sixth sense." Her dark and silent world was held in her hand and shaped with her mind. Concededly, her sense of smell was exceedingly keen, and she could orient herself by the aroma from many objects. On the other hand, her sense of touch was less finely developed than in many other blind people.

Tall, handsome, gracious, poised, Miss Keller had a sparkling humor and a warm handclasp that won her friends easily. She exuded vitality and optimism. "My life has been happy because I have had wonderful friends and plenty of interesting work to do," she once remarked, adding:

"I seldom think about my limitations, and they never make me sad. Perhaps there is just a touch of yearning at times, but it is vague, like a breeze among flowers. The wind passes, and the flowers are content."

This equanimity was scarcely foreshadowed in her early years. Helen Adams Keller was born on June 27, 1880, on a farm near Tuscumbia, Ala. Her father was Arthur Keller, an intermittently prosperous country gentleman who had served in the Confederate Army. Her mother was the former Kate Adams.

After Helen's illness, her infancy and early childhood were a succession of days of frustration, manifest by outbursts of anger and fractious behavior. "A wild, unruly child" who kicked, scratched and screamed was how she afterward described herself.

Her distracted parents were without hope until Mrs. Keller came across a passage in Charles Dickens's "American Notes" describing the training of the blind Laura Bridgman, who had been taught to be a sewing teacher by Dr. Samuel Gridley Howe of the Perkins Institution in Boston. Dr. Howe, husband of the author of "The Battle Hymn of the Republic," was a pioneer teacher of the blind and the mute.

Examined by Bell

Shortly thereafter the Kellers heard of a Baltimore eye physician who was interested in the blind, and they took their daughter to him. He said that Helen could be educated and put her parents in touch with Alexander Graham Bell, the inventor of the telephone and an authority on teaching speech to the deaf. After examining the child, Bell advised the Kellers to ask his son-in-law, Michael Anagnos, director of the Perkins Institution, about obtaining a teacher for Helen.

The teacher Mr. Anagnos selected was 20-year-old Anne Mansfield Sullivan, who was called Annie. Partly blind, Miss Sullivan had learned at Perkins how to communicate with the deaf and blind through a hand alphabet signaled by touch into the patient's palm.

"The most important day I remember in all my life is the one on which my teacher came to me," Miss Keller wrote later. "It was the third of March, 1887, three months before I was 7 years old.

"I stood on the porch, dumb, expectant. I guessed vaguely from my mother's signs and from the hurrying to and fro in the house that something unusual was about to happen, so I went to the door and waited on the steps."

Helen, her brown hair tumbled, her pinafore soiled, her black shoes tied with white string, jerked Miss Sullivan's bag away from her, rummaged in it for candy and, finding none, flew into a rage.

It was days before Miss Sullivan, whom Miss Keller throughout her life called "Teacher," could calm the rages and fears of the child and begin to spell words into her hand. The problem was of associating words and objects or actions: What was a doll, what was water? Miss Sullivan's solution was a stroke of genius. Recounting it, Miss Keller wrote:

"We walked down the path to the well-house, attracted by the fragrance of the honeysuckle with which it was covered. Someone was drawing water and my teacher placed my hand under the spout.

"As the cool stream gushed over one hand she spelled into the other the word water, first slowly, then rapidly. I stood still, my whole attention fixed upon the motions of her fingers. Suddenly I felt a misty consciousness as of something forgotten — a thrill of returning thought; and somehow the mystery of language was revealed to me.

"I knew then that 'w-a-t-e-r' meant the wonderful cool something that was flowing over my hand. That living word awakened my soul, gave it light, hope, joy, set it free. There were barriers still, it is true, but barriers that in time could be swept away."

Miss Sullivan had been told at Perkins that if she wished to teach Helen she must not spoil her. As a result, she was soon locked in physical combat with her pupil. This struggle was to thrill theater and film audiences later when it was portrayed in "The Miracle Worker" by Anne Bancroft as Annie Sullivan and Patty Duke as Helen.

Once Helen became more socialized and once she began to learn, her hunger for knowledge was insatiable. In a few hours one April day she added 30 words to her vocabulary. Abstractions—the meaning of the word "love," for example—proved difficult, but her teacher's patience and ingenuity prevailed.

Learning to Read

Helen's next opening into the world was learning to read. "As soon as I could spell a few words my teacher gave me slips of cardboard on which were printed words in raised letters," she recalled. "I quickly learned that each printed word stood for an object, an act or a quality.

"I had a frame in which I could arrange the words in little sentences; but before I ever put sentences in the frame I used to make them in objects. I found the slips of paper which represented, for example, 'doll,' 'is,' 'on,' 'bed' and placed each name on its object;then I put my doll on the bed with the words *is, on, bed* arranged beside the doll, thus making a sentence of the words, and at the same time carrying out the idea of the sentence with the things themselves."

Helen read her first connected story in May, 1887, and from that time "devoured everything in the shape of a printed page that has come with the reach of my hungry fingertips."

After three months with her pupil, Miss Sullivan wrote to Mr. Anagnos: "Something tells me that I am going to succeed beyond all my dreams."

Helen's progress was so rapid that in May, 1888, she made her first trip to the Perkins Institution in Boston, where she learned to read Braille and to mix with other afflicted children. For several years she spent the winters in the North and the summers with her family. It was in the spring of 1890 that Helen was taught to speak by Sarah Fuller of the Horace Mann School.

'Eager to Imitate'

"Miss Fuller's method was this," Miss Keller recalled. "She passed my hand lightly over her face, and let me feel the position of her tongue and lips when she made a sound. I was eager to imitate every motion and in an hour had learned six elements of speech: M, P, A, S, T, I. I shall never forget the surprise and delight I felt when I uttered my first connected sentence: 'It is warm.'"

Even so, it took a long time for the child to put her rushing thoughts into words. Most often Miss Sullivan or Miss Thomson was obliged to translate the sounds, for it took a trained ear to distinguish them accurately. When Miss Keller spoke very slowly and employed monosyllabic words, she was fairly readily understandable.

At the same time the child learned to lip-read by placing her fingers on the lips and throat of those who talked with her. But one had to talk slowly with her, articulating each word carefully. Nonetheless, her crude speech and her lip-reading facility further opened her mind and enlarged her experience.

When she was 14, in 1894, Miss Keller undertook formal schooling, first at the Wright-Humason School for the Deaf in New York and then at the Cambridge (Mass.) School for Young Ladies. With Miss Sullivan at her side and spelling into her hand, Miss Keller prepared herself for admission to Radcliffe, which she entered in the fall of 1900. It was indeed an amazing feat, for the examinations she took were those given to unhandicapped applicants, but no more astonishing than her graduation cum laude in 1904, with honors in German and English. Miss Sullivan was with her when she received her diploma, which she obtained by sheer stubborness and determination.

Helen Keller held her fingers at Anne Sullivan's nose, lips and throat in order to read her lips.

"I slip back many times," she wrote of her college years. "I fall, I stand still. I run against the edge of hidden obstacles. I lose my temper and find it again, and keep it better. I trudge on, I gain a little. I feel encouraged. I get more eager and climb higher and begin to see widening horizons."

While still in Radcliffe, Miss Keller wrote, on her Hammond typewriter, her first autobiography. "The Story of My Life" was published serially in The Ladies Home Journal and, in 1902, as a book. It consisted largely of themes written for an English composition course conducted by Prof. Charles Townsend Copeland, Harvard's celebrated "Copey."

After college Miss Keller continued to write, publishing "The World I Live In" in 1908, "The Song of the Stone Wall" in 1910 and "Out of the Dark" in 1913. Her writings, mostly inspirational articles, also appeared in national magazines of the time. And with Miss Sullivan at her side she took to the lecture platform.

After her formal talks—these were interpreted sentence by sentence by Miss Sullivan — Miss Keller answered questions, such as "Do you close your eyes when you go to sleep?" Her stock response was, "I never stayed awake to see."

Meantime, Miss Keller was developing a largeness of spirit on social issues, partly as a result of walks through industrial slums, partly because of her special interest in the high incidence of blindness among the poor and partly because of her conversations with John Macy, Miss Sullivan's husband, a social critic. She was further impelled toward Socialism in 1908 when she read H. G. Wells's "New Worlds for Old."

Although Miss Keller's Socialist activities diminished after 1921, when she decided that her chief life work was to raise funds for the American Foundation for the Blind, she was always responsive to Socialist and Communist appeals for help in causes involving oppression or exploitation of labor. As late as 1957 she sent a warm greeting to Elizabeth Gurley Flynn, the Communist leader, then in jail on charges of violating the Smith Act.

When literary tastes changed after World War I, Miss Keller's income from her writings dwindled, and, to make money, she ventured into vaudeville. She, with Miss Sullivan, was astonishingly successful; no Radcliffe graduate ever did better in variety than she. Harry and Herman Weber, the variety entrepreneurs, presented her in a 20-minute act that toured the country between 1920 and 1924. (Although some of her friends were scandalized, Miss Keller enjoyed herself enormously and argued that her appearances helped the cause of the blind.)

In the twenties, Miss Keller, Miss Sullivan and her husband and Miss Thomson (who had joined the household in 1914) moved from Wrentham, Mass., to Forest Hills, Queens, in New York. Miss Keller used this home as a base for her extensive fund-raising tours for the American Foundation for the Blind, of which she was counselor until her death. In this effort she talked in churches, synagogues and town halls. She not only collected money, but also sought to alleviate the living and working conditions of the blind. In those years the blind were frequently ill-educated and maintained in asylums; her endeavors were a major factor in changing these conditions.

Although she did not refer to it conspicuously Miss Keller was religious, but not a churchgoer. While quite young she was converted to the mystic New Church doctrines of Emanuel Swedenborg. The object of his doctrine was to make Christianity a living reality on earth through divine love, a theology that fitted Miss Keller's sense of social mission.

Although Miss Keller's serenity was buttressed by her religious faith, she was subjected in adulthood to criticisms and crises that sometimes unsettled her. Other people, she discovered, were attempting to run her life, and she was helpless to counter them. The most frustrating such episode occurred in 1916 during an illness of Miss Sullivan.

Miss Keller, then 36, fell in love with Peter Fagan, a 29-year-old Socialist and newspaperman who was her temporary secretary. The couple took out a marriage license, intending a secret wedding. But a Boston reporter found out about the license, and his witless article on the romance horrified the stern Mrs. Keller, who ordered Mr. Fagan out of the house and broke up the love affair.

"The love which had come, unseen and unexpected, departed with tempest on his wings," Miss Keller wrote in sadness, adding that the love remained with her as "a little island of joy surrounded by dark waters."

For years her spinsterhood was a chief disappointment. "If I could see," she said bitterly, "I would marry first of all."

With Miss Sullivan's death in 1936, Miss Keller and Miss Thomson moved from New York to Westport, Conn., Miss Keller's home for the rest of her life. At Westport she made friends with its artists (Jo Davidson executed a sculpture of her) and its writers (Van Wyck Brooks wrote a biographical sketch).

With Mr. and Mrs. Davidson, Miss Keller and Miss Thomson toured France and Italy in 1950, where Miss Keller saw great sculptures with her fingers under Mr. Davidson's tutelage. "What a privilege it has been," Mrs. Davidson remarked to a friend, "to live with Helen and Polly. Every day Helen delights us more and more—her noble simplicity, her ability to drink in the feel of things, and that spring of joyousness that bubbles up to the surface at the slightest pressure."

"All the News That's Fit to Print"

The New York Times.

LATE CITY EDITION
U. S. Weather Bureau Report (Page 58) forecasts: Cloudy, windy, chance of showers today and tonight. Cold tomorrow.
Temp. Range: 62—54; yesterday: 64—51.

VOL. CXIII...No. 38,654.

NEW YORK, SATURDAY, NOVEMBER 23, 1963. TEN CENTS

KENNEDY IS KILLED BY SNIPER AS HE RIDES IN CAR IN DALLAS; JOHNSON SWORN IN ON PLANE

TEXAN ASKS UNITY

Congressional Chiefs of Both Parties Promise Aid

By FELIX BELAIR Jr.
Special to The New York Times

WASHINGTON, Nov. 22—Lyndon B. Johnson returned to a stunned capital shortly after 6 P.M. today to assume the duties of the Presidency.

The new President asked for and received from Congressional leaders of both parties their "united support in the face of the tragedy which has befallen our country." He said it was "more essential that ever before that this country be united."

Partisan differences disappeared in the chorus of assurances with which the Congressional leaders responded.

Mr. Johnson was described by those who talked with him as "stunned and shaken" by the assassination of President Kennedy.

Discusses U.S. Security

But he moved quickly from problems of national security and foreign policy to funeral arrangements for Mr. Kennedy.

Across the street from the West Wing of the White House, the President conferred with officials in his old Vice-Presidential offices in the Executive Office Building.

Senator George A. Smathers, Democrat of Florida, a personal friend of the dead President, was one of those who described Mr. Johnson as shaken.

"Everyone is," he added. "But the President is the more so because he was right there when the tragedy occurred."

While flying to Washington aboard the Presidential plane, Mr. Johnson arranged for a meeting with Cabinet members to ask that they remain at their posts. He made the same request of staff members in the executive office.

Meets With Harriman

"Calm and contained" was the way Senator J. W. Fulbright described the President's manner during a discussion of foreign-policy matters with Under Secretary of State W. Averell Harriman. The Arkansas Senator said the President had been working on "what looked like a statement"—presumably an assurance of continuity of the nation's foreign policy.

The new President's first conference was aboard the helicopter that flew him the 15 miles from Andrews Air Force Base

Continued on Page 11, Column 3

Henry Grossman

"This is a sad time for all people. We have suffered a loss that cannot be weighed. For me it is a deep personal tragedy. I know the world shares the sorrow that Mrs. Kennedy and her family bear. I will do my best. That is all I can do. I ask for your help—and God's."—President Lyndon Baines Johnson.

PRESIDENT'S BODY WILL LIE IN STATE

Funeral Mass to Be Monday in Capital After Homage Is Paid by Public

By JACK RAYMOND
Special to The New York Times

WASHINGTON, Nov. 22—The body of John F. Kennedy will lie in state in the rotunda of the Capitol Sunday and then will be borne to St. Matthew's Roman Catholic Cathedral for a pontifical requiem mass at noon Monday.

The President's body was returned to Washington today in the same Air Force jet that carried him to Texas. The airliner, with Mrs. Kennedy, the new President, Lyndon B. Johnson, and Mrs. Johnson aboard, arrived at Andrews Air Force Base at 5:58 P.M.

It was announced later that Mr. Kennedy's body would lie in the White House tomorrow from 10 A.M. to 6 P.M., during which time Government and diplomatic officials will pay their respects.

The coffin will be taken from the White House to the Capitol rotunda Sunday morning, where

Continued on Page 9, Column 3

PARTIES' OUTLOOK FOR '64 CONFUSED

Republican Prospects Rise—Johnson Faces Possible Fight Against Liberals

By WARREN WEAVER Jr.
Special to The New York Times

WASHINGTON, Nov. 22—President Kennedy's assassination threw the American political scene into turmoil today.

It removed at a single blow the man who would have been renominated for a second term in the White House by acclamation nine months from now.

It elevated into the Presidency and the leadership of the Democratic party an older, more conservative man still emerging from his Southern heritage.

It increased immeasurably for the leaders of the Republican party prospects of electing a President next November.

The shock of the President's death stilled the official voices of politics in the capital. But so profound was the potential effect on the government and leadership that private consideration could not be silenced.

Before, there had been facts and strong probabilities on the

Continued on Page 6, Column 3

LEFTIST ACCUSED

Figure in a Pro-Castro Group Is Charged—Policeman Slain

By GLADWIN HILL
Special to The New York Times

DALLAS, Tex., Nov. 22—The Dallas police and Federal officers issued a charge of murder late tonight in the assassination of President Kennedy.

The accused is Lee Harvey Oswald, a 24-year-old former marine, who went to live in the Soviet Union in 1959 and returned to Texas last year.

Capt. Will Fritz, head of the Dallas police homicide bureau, identified Oswald as an adherent of the left-wing Fair Play for Cuba Committee.

Oswald was arrested about two hours after the shooting, in a movie theater three miles away, shortly after he allegedly shot and killed a policeman on a street nearby.

He was arraigned tonight on a charge of murdering the police officer. The charge related to the Kennedy killing was made later.

Appears in Line-Up

After the arraignment, the suspect, a slight, dark-haired man, was taken downstairs to appear in a line-up, presumably before witnesses of the Kennedy assassination.

While being escorted, handcuffed, through a police building corridor, he shouted: "I haven't shot anybody."

Captain Fritz said Oswald was employed—the exact job was unknown—at the Texas School Book Depository, a warehouse from which the assassin's bullets came. The captain said some witnesses had placed Oswald in the building at the time of the assassination.

The sequence of events leading to his arrest was as follows:

As a citywide manhunt began during the hour following the assassination, an unidentified man notified police headquarters, over a police-car radio, that the car's officer had been

Continued on Page 4, Column 1

NEWS INDEX

Henry Grossman

John Fitzgerald Kennedy
1917-1963

Why America Weeps

Kennedy Victim of Violent Streak He Sought to Curb in the Nation

By JAMES RESTON
Special to The New York Times

WASHINGTON, Nov. 22—America wept tonight, not alone for its dead young President, but for itself. The grief was general, for somehow the worst in the nation had prevailed over the best. The indictment extended beyond the assassin, for something in the nation itself, some strain of madness and violence, had destroyed the highest symbol of law and order.

Speaker John McCormack, now 71 and, by the peculiarities of our politics, next in line of succession after the Vice President, expressed this sense of national dismay and self-criticism:

"My God! My God! What are we coming to?"

The irony of the President's death is that his short Administration was devoted almost entirely to various attempts to curb this very streak of violence in the American character.

When the historians get around to assessing his three years in office, it is very likely that they will be impressed with just this: his efforts to restrain those who wanted to be more violent in the cold war overseas and those who wanted to be

Continued on Page 7, Column 6

The City Goes Dark

By ROBERT C. DOTY

The center of New York, the restless night city, wore darkness and went in near silence after the murder of President Kennedy last night.

In and around Times Square, the normal, frenetic Friday night pulse slowed as near to a halt as it ever comes. Most legitimate and movie theaters, night clubs and dance halls closed their doors and darkened their marquees.

As dusk came, automatic devices turned on the huge, gaudy display signs that normally blot out the night. Then, one by one, the lights blinked out, turning the great carnival strip into what was almost a mourning band.

There were exceptions, of course. Restaurants, by decision of their trade associations, remained lighted and open as a

Continued on Page 5, Column 2

Gov. Connally Shot; Mrs. Kennedy Safe

President Is Struck Down by a Rifle Shot From Building on Motorcade Route—Johnson, Riding Behind, Is Unhurt

By TOM WICKER
Special to The New York Times

DALLAS, Nov. 22—President John Fitzgerald Kennedy was shot and killed by an assassin today.

He died of a wound in the brain caused by a rifle bullet that was fired at him as he was riding through downtown Dallas in a motorcade.

Vice President Lyndon Baines Johnson, who was riding in the third car behind Mr. Kennedy's, was sworn in as the 36th President of the United States 99 minutes after Mr. Kennedy's death.

Mr. Johnson is 55 years old; Mr. Kennedy was 46.

Shortly after the assassination, Lee H. Oswald, described as a one-time defector to the Soviet Union, active in the Fair Play for Cuba Committee, was arrested by the Dallas police. Tonight he was accused of the killing.

Suspect Captured After Scuffle

Oswald, 24 years old, was also accused of slaying a policeman who had approached him in the street. Oswald was subdued after a scuffle with a second policeman in a nearby theater.

The shooting took place at 12:30 P.M., Central standard time (1:30 P.M., New York time). Mr. Kennedy was pronounced dead at 1 P.M. and Mr. Johnson was sworn in at 2:39 P.M.

Mr. Johnson, who was uninjured in the shooting, took his oath in the Presidential jet plane as it stood on the runway at Love Field. The body of the President was aboard. Immediately after the oath-taking, the plane took off for Washington.

Standing beside the new President as Mr. Johnson took the oath of office was Mrs. John F. Kennedy. Her stocking was saturated with her husband's blood.

Gov. John B. Connally Jr. of Texas, who was riding in the same car with Mr. Kennedy, was severely wounded in the chest, ribs and arm. His condition was serious, but not critical.

The killer fired the rifle from a building just off the motorcade route. Mr. Kennedy,

Continued on Page 2,

Capt. Cecil Stoughton via United Press International

THE NEW PRESIDENT: Lyndon B. Johnson takes oath before Judge Sarah T. Hughes in plane at Dallas. Mrs. Kennedy and Representative Jack Brooks are at right. To left are Mrs. Johnson and Representative Albert Thomas.

Associated Press

WHEN THE BULLETS STRUCK: Mrs. Kennedy moving to the aid of the President after he was hit by a sniper yesterday in Dallas. A guard mounts rear bumper. Gov. John B. Connally Jr. of Texas, also in the car, was wounded.

Kennedy Killed by Sniper as He Rides in Car in Dallas; Johnson Sworn In on Plane

Continued From Page 1

Governor Connally and Mr. Johnson had just received an enthusiastic welcome from a large crowd in downtown Dallas.

Mr. Kennedy apparently was hit by the first of what witnesses believed were three shots. He was driven at high speed to Dallas's Parkland Hospital. There, in an emergency operating room, with only physicians and nurses in attendance, he died without regaining consciousness.

Mrs. Kennedy, Mrs. Connally and a Secret Service agent were in the car with Mrs. Kennedy and Governor Connally. Two Secret Service agents flanked the car. Other than Mr. Connally, none of this group was injured in the shooting. Mrs. Kennedy cried, "Oh no!" immediately after her husband was struck.

Mrs. Kennedy was in the hospital near her husband when he died, but not in the operating room. When the body was taken from the hospital in a bronze coffin about 2 P.M., Mrs. Kennedy walked beside it.

Her face was sorrowful. She looked steadily at the floor. She still wore the raspberry-colored suit in which she had greeted welcoming crowds in Fort Worth and Dallas. But she had taken off the matching pillbox hat she wore earlier in the day, and her dark hair was windblown and tangled. Her hand rested lightly on her husband's coffin as it was taken to a waiting hearse.

Mrs. Kennedy climbed in beside the coffin. Then the ambulance drove to Love Field, and Mr. Kennedy's body was placed aboard the Presidential jet. Mrs. Kennedy then attended the swearing-in ceremony for Mr. Johnson.

As Mr. Kennedy's body left Parkland Hospital, a few stunned persons stood outside. Nurses and doctors, whispering among themselves, looked from the window. A larger crowd that had gathered earlier, before it was known that the President was dead, had been dispersed by Secret Service men and policemen.

Priests Administer Last Rites

Two priests administered last rites to Mr. Kennedy, a Roman Catholic. They were the Very Rev. Oscar Huber, the pastor of Holy Trinity Church in Dallas, and the Rev. James Thompson.

Mr. Johnson was sworn in as President by Federal Judge Sarah T. Hughes of the Northern District of Texas. She was appointed to the judgeship by Mr. Kennedy in October, 1961.

The ceremony, delayed about five minutes for Mrs. Kennedy's arrival, took place in the private Presidential cabin in the rear of the plane.

About 25 to 30 persons—members of the late President's staff, members of Congress who had been accompanying the President on a two-day tour of Texas cities and a few reporters—crowded into the little room.

No accurate listing of those present could be obtained. Mrs. Kennedy stood at the left of Mr. Johnson, her eyes and face showing the signs of weeping that had apparently shaken her since she left the hospital not long before.

Mrs. Johnson, wearing a beige dress, stood at her husband's right.

As Judge Hughes read the brief oath of office, her eyes, too, were red from weeping. Mr. Johnson's hands rested on a black, leather-bound Bible as Judge Hughes read and he repeated:

"I do solemnly swear that I will perform the duties of the President of the United States to the best of my ability and defend, protect and preserve the Constitution of the United States."

Those 34 words made Lyndon Baines Johnson, one-time farmboy and schoolteacher of Johnson City, the President.

Johnson Embraces Mrs. Kennedy

Mr. Johnson made no statement. He embraced Mrs. Kennedy and she held his hand for a long moment. He also embraced Mrs. Johnson and Mrs. Evelyn Lincoln, Mr. Kennedy's private secretary.

"O.K.," Mr. Johnson said. "Lets get this plane back to Washington."

At 2:46 P.M., seven minutes after he had become President, 106 minutes after Mr. Kennedy had become the fourth American President to succumb to an assassin's wounds, the white and red jet took off for Washington.

In the cabin when Mr. Johnson took the oath was Cecil Stoughton, an armed forces photographer assigned to the White House.

Mr. Kennedy's staff members appeared stunned and bewildered. Lawrence F. O'Brien, the Congressional liaison officer, and P. Kenneth O'Donnell, the appointment secretary, both long associates of Mr. Kennedy, showed evidences of weeping. None had anything to say.

Other staff members believed to be in the cabin for the swearing-in included David F. Powers, the White House receptionist; Miss Pamela Turnure, Mrs. Kennedy's press secretary, and Malcolm Kilduff, the assistant White House press secretary.

Mr. Kilduff announced the President's death, with choked voice and red-rimmed eyes, at about 1:36 P.M.

"President John F. Kennedy died at approximately 1 o'clock Central standard time today here in Dallas," Mr. Kilduff said at the hospital. "He died of a gunshot wound in the brain. I have no other details regarding the assassination of the President."

Mr. Kilduff also announced that Governor Connally had been hit by a bullet or bullets and that Mr. Johnson, who had not yet been sworn in, was safe in the protective custody of the Secret Service at an unannounced place, presumably the airplane at Love Field.

Mr. Kilduff indicated that the President had been shot once. Later medical reports raised the possibility that there had been two wounds. But the death was caused, as far as could be learned, by a massive wound in the brain.

Later in the afternoon, Dr. Malcolm Perry, an attending surgeon, and Dr. Kemp Clark, chief of neurosurgery at Parkland Hospital, gave more details.

Mr. Kennedy was hit by a bullet in the throat, just below the Adam's apple, they said. This wound had the appearance of a bullet's entry.

Mr. Kennedy also had a massive, gaping wound in the back and one on the right side of the head. However, the doctors said it was impossible to determine immediately whether the wounds had been caused by on bullet or two.

Resuscitation Attempted

Dr. Perry, the first physician to treat the President, said a number of resuscitative measures had been attempted, including oxygen, anesthesia, an indotracheal tube, a tracheotomy, blood and fluids. An electrocardiogram monitor was attached to measure Mr. Kennedy's heart beats.

Dr. Clark was summoned and arrived in a minute or two. By then, Dr. Perry said, Mr. Kennedy was "critically ill and moribund," or near death.

Dr. Clark said that on his first sight of the President, he had concluded immediately that Mr. Kennedy could not live.

"It was apparent that the President had sustained a lethal wound," he said. "A missile had gone in and out of the back of his head causing external lacerations and loss of brain tissue."

Shortly after he arrived, Dr. Clark said, "the President lost his heart action by the electrocardiogram." A closed-chest cardiograph massage was attempted, as were other emergency resuscitation measures.

Dr. Clark said these had produced "palpable pulses" for a short time, but all were "to no avail."

In Operating Room 40 Minutes

The President was on the emergency table at the hospital for about 40 minutes, the doctors said. At the end, perhaps eight physicians were in Operating Room No. 1, where Mr. Kennedy remained until his death. Dr. Clark said it was difficult to determine the exact moment of death, but the doctors said officially that it occurred at 1 P.M.

Later, there were unofficial reports that Mr. Kennedy had been killed instantly. The source of these reports, Dr. Tom Shires, chief surgeon at the hospital and professor of surgery at the University of Texas Southwest Medical School, issued this statement tonight:

"Medically, it was apparent the President was not alive when he was brought in. There was no spontaneous respiration. He had dilated, fixed pupils. It was obvious he had a lethal head wound.

"Technically, however, by using vigorous resuscitation, intravenous tubes and all the usual supportive measures, we were able to raise a semblance of a heartbeat."

Dr. Shires said he was "positive it was impossible" that President Kennedy could have spoken after being shot. "I am absolutely sure he never knew what hit him," Dr. Shires said.

Dr. Shires was not present when Mr. Kennedy was being treated at Parkland Hospital. He issued his statement, however, after lengthy conferences with the doctors who had attended the President.

Mr. Johnson remained in the hospital about 30 minutes after Mr. Kennedy died.

The details of what happened when shots first rang out, as the President's car moved along at about 25 miles an hour, were sketchy. Secret Service agents, who might have given more details, were unavailable to the press at first, and then returned to Washington with President Johnson.

Kennedys Hailed at B[illegible]kfast

Mr. Kennedy had opened his day in Fort Worth, first with a speech in a parking lot and then at a Chamber of Commerce breakfast. The breakfast appearance was a particular triumph for Mrs. Kennedy, who entered late and was given an ovation.

Then the Presidential party, including Governor and Mrs. Connally, flew on to Dallas, an eight-minute flight. Mr. Johnson, as is customary, flew in a separate plane. The President and the Vice President do not travel together, out of fear of a double tragedy.

At Love Field, Mr. and Mrs. Kennedy lingered for 10 minutes, shaking hands with an enthusiastic group lining the fence. The group called itself "Grassroots Democrats."

Mr. Kennedy then entered his open Lincoln convertible at the head of the motorcade. He sat in the rear seat on the right-hand side. Mrs. Kennedy, who appeared to be enjoying one of the first political outings she had ever made with her husband, sat at his left.

In the "jump" seat, directly ahead of Mr. Kennedy, sat Governor Connally, with Mrs. Connally at his left in another "jump" seat. A Secret Service agent was driving and the two others ran alongside.

Behind the President's limousine was an open sedan carrying a number of Secret Service agents. Behind them, in an open convertible, rode Mr. and Mrs. Johnson and Texas's senior Senator, Ralph W. Yarborough, a Democrat.

The motorcade proceeded uneventfully along a 10-mile route through downtown Dallas, aiming for the Merchandise Mart. Mr. Kennedy was to address a group of the city's leading citizens at a luncheon in his honor.

In downtown Dallas, crowds were thick, enthusiastic and cheering. The turnout was somewhat unusual for this center of conservatism, where only a month ago Adlai E. Stevenson was attacked by a rightist crowd. It was also in Dallas, during the 1960 campaign, that Senator Lyndon B. Johnson and his wife were nearly mobbed in the lobby of the Baker Hotel.

As the motorcade neared its end and the President's car moved out of the thick crowds onto Stennonds Freeway near the Merchandise Mart, Mrs. Connally recalled later, "we were all very pleased with the reception in downtown Dallas."

Approaching 3-Street Underpass

Behind the three leading cars were a string of others carrying Texas and Dallas dignitaries, two buses of reporters, several open cars carrying photographers and other reporters, and a bus for White House staff members.

As Mrs. Connally recalled later, the President's car was almost ready to go underneath a "triple underpass" beneath three streets—Elm, Commerce and Main—when the first shot was fired.

That shot apparently struck Mr. Kennedy. Governor Connally turned in his seat at the sound and appeared immediately to be hit in the chest.

Mrs. Mary Norman of Dallas was standing at the curb and at that moment was aiming her camera at the President. She saw him slump forward, then slide down in the seat.

"My God," Mrs. Norman screamed, as she recalled it later, "he's shot!"

Mrs. Connally said that Mrs. Kennedy had reached and "grabbed" her husband. Mrs. Connally put her arms around the Governor. Mrs. Connally said that she and Mrs. Kennedy had then ducked low in the car as it sped off.

Mrs. Connally's recollections were reported by Julian Reade, an aide to the Governor.

Most reporters in the press buses were too far back to see the shootings, but they observed some quick scurrying by motor policemen accompanying the motorcade. It was noted that the President's car had picked up speed and raced away, but reporters were not aware that anything serious had occurred until they reached the Merchandise Mart two or three minutes later.

Rumors Spread at Trade Mart

Rumors of the shooting already were spreading through the luncheon crowd of hundreds, which was having the first course. No White House officials or Secret Service agents were present, but the reporters were taken quickly to Parkland Hospital on the strength of the rumors.

There they encountered Senator Yarborough, white, shaken and horrified.

The shots, he said, seemed to have come from the right and the rear of the car in which he was riding, the third in the motorcade. Another eyewitness, Mel Crouch, a Dallas television reporter, reported that as the shots rang out he saw a rifle extended and then withdrawn from a window on the "fifth or sixth floor" of the Texas Public School Book Depository. This is a leased state building on Elm Street, to the right of the motorcade route.

Senator Yarborough said there had been a slight pause between the first two shots and a longer pause between the second and third. A Secret Service man riding in the Senator's car, the Senator said, immediately ordered Mr. and Mrs. Johnson to get down below the level of the doors. They did so, and Senator Yarborough also got down.

The leading cars of the motorcade then pulled away at high speed toward Parkland Hospital, which was not far away, by the fast highway.

"We knew by the speed that something was terribly wrong," Senator Yarborough reported. When he put his head up, he said, he saw a Secret Service man in the car ahead beating his fists against the trunk deck of the car in which he was riding, apparently in frustration and anguish.

Mrs. Kennedy's Reaction

Only White House staff members spoke with Mrs. Kennedy. A Dallas medical student, David Edwards, saw her in Parkland Hospital while she was waiting for news of her husband. He gave this description:

"The look in her eyes was like an animal that had been trapped, like a little rabbit—brave, but fear was in the eyes."

Dr. Clark was reported to have informed Mrs. Kennedy of her husband's death.

No witnesses reported seeing or hearing any of the Secret Service agents or policemen fire back. One agent was seen to brandish a machine gun as the cars sped away. Mr. Crouch observed a policeman falling to the ground and pulling a weapon. But the events had occurred so quickly that there was apparently nothing for the men to shoot at.

Mr. Crouch said he saw two women, standing at a curb to watch the motorcade pass, fall to the ground when the shots rang out. He also saw a man snatch up his little girl and run along the road. Policemen, he said, immediately chased this man under the impression he had been involved in the shooting, but Mr. Crouch said he had been a fleeing spectator.

Mr. Kennedy's limousine—license No. GG300 under District of Columbia registry—pulled up at the emergency entrance of Parkland Hospital. Senator Yarborough said the President had been carried inside on a stretcher.

By the time reporters arrived at the hospital, the police were guarding the Presidential car closely. They would allow no one to approach it. A bucket of water stood by the car, suggesting that the back seat had been scrubbed out.

Robert Clark of the American Broadcasting Company, who had been riding near the front of the motorcade, said Mr. Kennedy was motionless when he was carried inside. There was a great amount of blood on Mr. Kennedy's suit and shirtfront and the front of his body, Mr. Clark said.

Mrs. Kennedy was leaning over her husband when the car stopped, Mr. Clark said, and walked beside the wheeled stretcher into the hospital. Mr. Connally sat with his hands holding his stomach, his head bent over. He, too, was moved into the hospital in a stretcher, with Mrs. Connally at his side.

Robert McNeill of the National Broadcasting Company, who also was in the reporters' pool car, jumped out at the scene of the shooting. He said the police had taken two eyewitnesses into custody—an 8-year-old Negro boy and a white man—for informational purposes.

Many of these reports could not be verified immediately.

Eyewitness Describes Shooting

An unidentified Dallas man, interviewed on television here, said he had been waving at the President when the shots were fired. His belief was that Mr. Kennedy had been struck twice—once, as Mrs. Norman recalled, when he slumped in his seat; again when he slid down in it.

"It seemed to just knock him down," the man said.

Governor Connally's condition was reported as "satisfactory" tonight after four hours in surgery at Parkland Hospital.

Dr. Robert R. Shaw, a thoracic surgeon, operated on the Governor to repair damage to his left chest.

Later, Dr. Shaw said Governor Connally had been hit in the back just below the shoulder blade, and that the bullet had gone completely through the Governor's chest, taking out part of the fifth rib.

After leaving the body, he said, the bullet struck the Governor's right wrist, causing a compound fracture. It then lodged in the left thigh.

The thigh wound, Dr. Shaw said, was trivial. He said the compound fracture would heal.

Dr. Shaw said it would be unwise for Governor Connally to be moved in the next 10 to 14 days. Mrs. Connally was remaining at his side tonight.

Tour by Mrs. Kennedy Unusual

Mrs. Kennedy's presence near her husband's bedside at his death resulted from somewhat unusual circumstances. She had rarely accompanied him on his trips about the country and had almost never made political trips with him.

The tour on which Mr. Kennedy was engaged yesterday and today was only quasi-political; the only open political activity was to have been a speech tonight to a fund-raising dinner at the state capitol in Austin.

In visiting Texas, Mr. Kennedy was seeking to improve his political fortunes in a pivotal state that he barely won in 1960. He was also hoping to patch a bitter internal dispute among Texas's Democrats.

At 8:45 A.M., when Mr. Kennedy left the Texas Hotel in Fort Worth, where he spent his last night, to address the parking lot crowd across the street, Mrs. Kennedy was not with him. There appeared to be some disappointment.

"Mrs. Kennedy is organizing herself," the President said good-naturedly. "It takes longer, but, of course, she looks better than we do when she does it."

Later, Mrs. Kennedy appeared late at the Chamber of Commerce breakfast in Fort Worth.

Again, Mr. Kennedy took note of her presence. "Two years ago," he said, "I introduced myself in Paris by saying that I was the man who had accompanied Mrs. Kennedy to Paris. I am getting somewhat that same sensation as I travel around Texas. Nobody wonders what Lyndon and I wear."

The speech Mr. Kennedy never delivered at the Merchandise Mart luncheon contained a passage commenting on a recent preoccupation of his, and a subject of much interest in this city, where right-wing conservatism is the rule rather than the exception.

Voices are being heard in the land, he said, "voices preaching doctrines wholly unrelated to reality, wholly unsuited to the sixties, doctrines which apparently assume that words will suffice without weapons, that vituperation is as good as victory and that peace is a sign of weakness."

The speech went on: "At a time when the national debt is steadily being reduced in terms of its burden on our economy, they see that debt as the greatest threat to our security. At a time when we are steadily reducing the number of Federal employes serving every thousand citizens, they fear those supposed hordes of civil servants far more than the actual hordes of opposing armies.

"We cannot expect that everyone, to use the phrase of a decade ago, will 'talk sense to the American people.' But we can hope that fewer people will listen to nonsense. And the notion that this nation is headed for defeat through deficit, or that strength is but a matter of slogans, is nothing but just plain nonsense."

Kennedy Boyhood and Youth Were Often a Tale of Sharp Rivalry of 2 Brothers

JOSEPH JR. RULED JOHN WITH FISTS

Future President Offered Few Signs Then of His Interest in Politics

John Fitzgerald Kennedy grew up under the shadow of his brother Joseph. It laid a mark on his character. In later life, some persons were to see in the rivalry of the two Kennedy boys at least one reason for the success of the surviving brother.

But during the years of growing up it did not seem exactly that way to John. Joseph was not only two years older than John. He was also taller, heavier, stronger.

In the absence of the boys' father, young Joseph took on some of his authority. In the big family it was Joseph Jr. who laid down the law. He had a quick temper and he tended to enforce his rulings with his fists.

All through childhood and early adolescence Joseph Jr. and John fought. The outcome was inevitable—John was smaller, slimmer and less developed than his brother. But still the boys fought. Their younger brother, Robert, remembered years later how he and his sisters had cowered in an upstairs room while the two boys fought below.

The rivalry was not confined to the physical. Joseph Jr. was an able, aggressive, outgoing youngster.

John Kennedy gave few signs in his youth that he might some day head for the Presidency.

He was born on May 29, 1917, in Brookline, a Boston suburb. His first years were spent in Brookline at 83 Beals Street, a comfortable white frame house in a pleasant upper middle-class neighborhood.

Attended Private School

In Brookline, John started his education at the Dexter school, a private school rather than a parochial institution.

By 1926 Joseph Kennedy's business interests were concentrated in New York and he decided to uproot his family from the Boston milieu.

John went to fourth, fifth and sixth grades in the Riverdale Country Day School. Years later he was dimly remembered by his teachers as a likable youngster, moderately studious, polite and hot-tempered.

The family then moved to near-by Bronxville where Joseph Kennedy had purchased an 11-bedroom red brick house.

Only one year of John's education was spent in a Catholic institution. This was Canterbury, a preparatory school at New Milford, Mass., where John went for a year at the age of 13.

The next fall he shifted to Choate at Wallingford, Conn. Choate was a rather exclusive boys' school with a strong Protestant Episcopal orientation. His brother, Joseph Jr., had gone to the school two years ahead of John and was a leader.

There was nothing brilliant about John Kennedy's record at Choate. To his teachers he gave no outward sign of special ability. His grades were average.

At Choate John made friends with Lemoyne Billings, a boy from Baltimore. This was one of the earliest of his school friendships that were to endure and grow as his political career began to gather headway.

John Kennedy was graduated from Choate in 1935, when he was 18. He was tall, thin, wiry, good-looking and energetic.

John had decided to break with family tradition and go to Princeton rather than Harvard, where his father had studied, and where Joseph Jr. was already cutting out an important career.

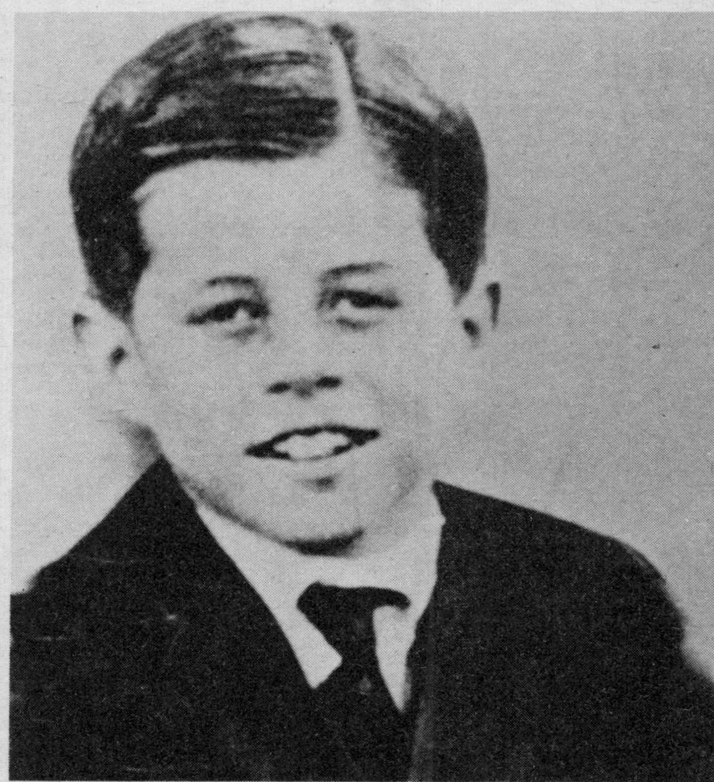

John F. Kennedy at Dexter School at the age of nine.

However, John had a recurrence of jaundice in December and left Princeton. In the autumn of 1936 he entered Harvard.

His first two years at Harvard were undistinguished. He got slightly better than a C average as a freshman and about the same as a sophomore.

John went out for freshman football but was too light to make the team. He suffered a back injury that was to plague him seriously later on. But football gave him another of his lifetime friends. This was Torbert H. Macdonald.

The turning point in John's college career probably was a trip to Europe that he made in the summer of 1937 with Billings.

John had an audience with the Pope and met Cardinal Pacelli, who was to become Pope Pius XII.

'Quite a Fellow'

"He is quite a fellow," John wrote his parents. John also admired the Fascist system in Italy "as everyone seemed to like it," but took a balanced view of the civil war in Spain.

Toward the close of 1937 his father was named Ambassador to the Court of St. James's by President Roosevelt.

Ambassador Kennedy was in the thick of the controversy over United States policy. He took the side of the supporters of Prime Minister Neville Chamberlain, backed the Munich agreement and, in general, expressed views regarded by his critics as those of isolationism and appeasement.

John Kennedy's interest in foreign affairs was further stimulated when he obtained permission from Harvard to spend the second semester of his junior year in Europe.

As a Harvard undergraduate, Kennedy was a member of the varsity swimming team. In this 1938 photograph, he prepares to dive during a practice session.

John's final year at Harvard was by far the best of his educational career.

For the first time he demonstrated intellectual drive and vigor. He was determined to be graduated with honors and took extra work in political science toward this end. His grades improved to a B average.

But his principal achievement of the year was the writing of a thesis, "Appeasement at Munich." In it, his basic point was:

Most of the critics have been firing at the wrong target. The Munich Pact itself should not be the object of criticism but rather the underlying factors such as the state of British opinion and the condition of Britain's armaments which made "surrender" inevitable.

"To blame one man, such as Baldwin, for the unpreparedness of British armaments is illogical and unfair, given the condition of democratic government."

In June, 1940, John Kennedy was graduated cum laude in political science. His thesis had won a magna cum laude.

Coconut Shell in the White House Recalled Rescue in World War II

On John F. Kennedy's desk in the White House a scarred and battered coconut shell held a place of honor.

On its rough bark was scratched this message:

"Native knows posit he can pilot 11 alive need small boat kennedy."

This crude memento was a souvenir of as close a brush with death as John Kennedy—or any other man—was likely to experience and live to talk about. It also marked the climax of his brief but daring and courageous military career.

Mr. Kennedy was graduated from Harvard in June, 1940, just after the so-called "phony war" had ended in Europe.

With World War II more and more dominating the world's headlines and the thoughts of men, Mr. Kennedy found it impossible to settle down to civilian existence.

He had talked of entering Yale Law School in the fall of 1940. But he changed his mind at the last moment and enrolled at the Stanford University business school for graduate work.

Wanted Military Service

He was restless, however, and left school to make a long tour of South America. By the time he got back he had but one interest—to get into the armed forces.

He undertook a rigorous course of conditioning and exercises and managed to pass a Navy physical in September, 1941.

He was assigned at first to a desk in Naval intelligence in Washington, preparing a news digest for the Navy Chief of Staff.

This was not to his liking. He invoked his father's influence and managed to get transferred to the torpedo boat training station at Melville, R. I., where a number of his friends, including his Harvard roommate, Torbert H. Macdonald, were already stationed.

In March, Lieutenant (j. g.) Kennedy had command of PT-109, a boat that was part of a PT squadron based at Rendova, south of New Georgia.

Not long after midnight Aug. 2, 1943, PT-109 was on patrol in Blackett Strait in the Solomon Islands, about forty miles from the Rendova base. The 26-year-old Lieutenant Kennedy was in charge, leading three other PT boats.

His first officer, George Ross, a Princeton graduate, was at the wheel.

(continued)

The Kennedy children (from left to right) are Jean, Robert, Patricia, Eunice, Kathleen, Rosemary, John (12) and Joseph Jr.

Suddenly out of the murk the Japanese destroyer, Amagiri, bore down on them at 30 knots. It rammed the boat squarely, cutting it in two and steamed on without loss of speed.

2 Crewmen Killed

Two members of the PT crew were killed outright. Lieutenant Kennedy was hurled onto the deck, falling on his back.

But he was not killed. Nor was his craft sunk. The after half of the PT remained afloat although the sea was covered with burning gasoline. Although his back had been injured by his fall, Lieutenant Kennedy and several of his crew members managed to aid two men who were badly hurt—Patrick H. McMahon, the engineer who was severely burned, and Harris, a fellow Bostonian who had hurt his leg.

The men hoped for an early rescue but no help came. Apparently the other PT boats had assumed all men were lost.

The next night the hull capsized and Lieutenant Kennedy led his party to a small island. Most of the way he swam, breast-stroke, pulling the injured Mr. McMahon by life preserver straps that he clasped in his teeth.

Lieutenant Kennedy left his exhausted mates on the atoll and swam on further to Ferguson Passage through which PT boats frequently operated. He carried with him a heavy ship's lantern for signaling.

All night long he swam and drifted in the Ferguson Passage, hoping a PT boat would come along. Sometimes he dozed in the water. No PT boats appeared. In early morning he swam back to the reef where his comrades waited and sank exhausted and sick on the sand.

The next night Mr. Ross swam to Ferguson Passage but had no more luck.

The next day Lieutenant Kennedy moved his men to another island closer to Ferguson Passage. All were hungry and thirsty. Some were ill.

On the fourth day Mr. Kennedy and Mr. Ross swam to Cross Island, even closer to Ferguson Passage. Here they made a great find—a keg of water and a box of biscuits and hard candy left behind by the Japanese. They also found a native dugout canoe. Mr. Kennedy left Mr. Ross on Cross and paddled back to his crew with food and water.

On the fifth day he returned to Cross, but on the way a storm swamped the canoe. But, in imminent peril of drowning, he was sighted by a group of Solomon Islanders in a large canoe. They took him to Cross and Mr. Ross. Here they led the Americans to a larger canoe concealed on the island.

Mr. Kennedy took a coconut, scratched on it the message:

"Native knows posit he can pilot 11 alive need small boat kennedy." He told the natives again and again "Rendova, Rendova." They paddled away.

That night he and Mr. Ross again went out to Ferguson Passage. Again their canoe was capsized and they nearly drowned. They made it back to Cross and sank on the beach in exhausted slumber.

But on that morning — the sixth since the disaster — Mr. Kennedy and Mr. Ross were awakened by four natives, one of whom spoke excellent English and said:

"I have a letter for you, sir."

More than seventeen years later, after Lieutenant Kennedy had become President Kennedy, the man who received the message and summoned help was identified as A. R. Evans, an Australian serving in his country's Naval Reserve. Mr. Evans was now an accountant at Sydney.

Within a matter of hours the PT survivors had all been rounded up and were back at their base, the worse for wear and tear, but happily alive.

The commander of the destroyer Amagiri Kohei Hanami, now a farmer in Japan, sent Mr. Kennedy congratulations on his election. Mr. Kennedy sent him a bronze medal commemorating the ceremony.

Lieutenant Kennedy's conduct won him the Purple Heart and the Navy and Marine Corps Medal with a citation from Adm. William F. Halsey that paid tribute to "his courage, endurance and excellent leadership in keeping with the highest traditions of the United States Naval Service."

But his career with the PT boats quickly ended. He contracted malaria. His weight dropped to 125 pounds. He was suffering some pain from the aggravation of his old back injury.

In December, 1943, he was sent back to the United States.

Mr. Kennedy still hoped for more active duty and thought he might be sent to the Mediterranean. But he was not well and late in the spring of 1944 he entered Chelsea Naval Hospital, near Boston.

Almost a year to the day after his adventure in the South Pacific the Kennedy family was gathered at Hyannis Port when two priests appeared and asked to see Joseph P. Kennedy Sr.

Joseph Jr. had been reported missing in action. Beginning in September, 1943, Joseph had flown combat duty with a Liberator bomber squadron attached to the British Coastal Command.

By July, 1944, after a second tour of duty, Joseph had orders to go home when he learned about and volunteered for an experimental mission called "Project Anvil."

The plan was to load a Liberator with 22,000 pounds of TNT, take it into the air with a pilot and co-pilot and then fix its flight controls on a course for the German V-2 rocket bases. The pilot and co-pilot would then parachute to safety.

On Aug. 12, 1944, Joseph Jr. and Lieut. Wilford J. Willy of Fort Worth, took off in the robot plane with two control planes accompanying them. About 6:20 P. M., as the plane coast, it blew up. The two pilots were instantly killed.

The death of Joseph Jr. at the age of 29 was but the first of a series of tragedies to strike the Kennedys. Less than four weeks later, on Sept. 10, 1944, the British War Office announced the death in action in France of Lord Hartington. He was the husband of Kathleen, oldest of the Kennedy girls and the only member of the family to marry outside the Roman Catholic Church.

Kathleen and Lord Hartington were married at the Chelsea Registry Office, London, in early May, 1944. She herself became the second member of the Kennedy family to die when, in May, 1948, she was killed in the crash of a small private plane in France.

John Kennedy remained in the hospital near Boston for a disk operation on his back. Finally, thin and in far from robust health, he appeared before a Navy board and was mustered out of service. His military career was at an end. His civilian life opened ahead of him.

Ambassador to Great Britain Joseph P. Kennedy and his two oldest sons, John (L) and Joseph Jr., in England in 1938.

Death of Brother in War Thrust Kennedy Into Career of Politics

"Just as I went into politics because Joe died, if anything happened to me tomorrow, my brother Bobby would run for my seat in the Senate. And if Bobby died Teddy would take over for him." So John F. Kennedy once described his decision to enter politics.

Early in 1945, John Kennedy was working for The International News Service as a special correspondent. He covered some important events, including the Potsdam Conference and the founding conference of the United Nations in San Francisco.

But he did not appear to have made up his mind about his career. By this time, however, he was seriously considering entering politics.

For this decision his father, Joseph P. Kennedy Sr., has taken full credit. He told an interviewer in 1957:

"I got Jack into politics. I was the one. I told him Joe was dead and that it was therefore his responsibility to run for Congress. He didn't want to do it. He felt he didn't have the ability and he still feels that way. But I told him he had to do it."

Journalism 'Too Passive'

That was not the way President Kennedy remembered it. He said he had been attracted strongly to journalism, but finally concluded that "it was too passive."

"We all liked politics," he said, "but Joe seemed a natural to run for office. Obviously, you can't have a whole mess of Kennedys asking for votes. So when Joe was denied his chance, I wanted to run and was glad I could."

By a quirk of political fortune, James Michael Curley, long a dominant figure in Boston politics, was vacating the Congressional seat in the Eleventh District in 1946. Mr. Curley, a political enemy of both of John Kennedy's grandfathers—Patrick J. Kennedy and John F Fitzgerald—was about to become Mayor of Boston.

Thus, it was in the old Eleventh District that John Kennedy first tried his political fortunes.

The district included East Boston, where John Kennedy's father was born. It included the North End, where his mother, Rose, and her father, John F. Fitzgerald, had been born. It included Cambridge, where the Kennedys had gone to Harvard.

It was a great district for a young Kennedy to run in—except for one thing.

No Roots in Boston

John Kennedy had no roots there, or hardly any roots in Boston. He had been born and spent a few childhood years in Brookline. He had gone to college at Harvard. He had summered at Hyannis Port on Cape Cod.

But he was not a genuine Bostonian. He had kept a Boston address—the Bellevue Hotel, next door to the State House, where his grandfather maintained rooms.

Regardless of any handicaps, John Kennedy got into the race with all he had. He was still yellow from the atabrine he had taken to combat malaria picked up in war service in the South Pacific. He was only 28 years old and looked about 21. He was scrawny and he was shy about meeting people.

But he had determination. He had the Kennedy name and the Kennedy money. He also had a rapidly growing group of fervent supporters, built around his family and his friends of prep school, college and Navy days.

Mr. Kennedy started campaigning early in the year for the June primary. If he was inept about treating the boys in the East Boston saloons he proved to be one of the most energetic campaigners the Eleventh District had ever seen.

And his organization began to grow, turning his headquarters at 122 Bowdoin Street into a bustling political center.

War Record Cited

Mr. Kennedy ran largely on his war record. Reprints of articles about his exploits in the South Pacific were widely circulated.

On election Day, Mr. Kennedy swamped his opponents.

His political career was now fairly launched and he won the final election without difficulty in November. In January, 1947 he presented himself at the House of Representatives.

He was 29 years old but so boyish in appearance that he was often mistaken for a college student. He had a shy smile, a great shock of hair and a thin but wiry frame.

Mr. Kennedy served three terms in the House. His record was not spectacular but his votes usually were on the liberal side.

He demonstrated flashes of independence, such as in his refusal to kowtow to Representative John W. McCormack, long-time leader of the Massachusetts Democratic delegation.

He also fought the American Legion for its opposition to housing projects, declaring that Legion "hasn't had a constructive thought since 1918."

Meantime, Mr. Kennedy was beginning to focus his eye on wider horizons. He had considered running for the Senate in 1948 against Leverett Saltonstall, but, after weighing the prospects, decided against it.

His chance came in 1952 when Gov. Paul A. Dever decided not to run for the Senate against Henry Cabot Lodge. Senator Lodge was a redoubtable candidate.

Once more the Kennedy family turned out in force to campaign. John Kennedy's brother, Robert, 27, was his campaign director. His sisters, Jean, Eunice and Patricia, went from door to door, poured tea and presided over coffee hours. His mother also took a leading part.

During the later part of the campaign an old back injury bothered Mr. Kennedy and he was forced to make appearances on crutches. But there was always a Kennedy to substitute for another Kennedy.

Confident of Victory

The year 1952 was the year of the Eisenhower landslide. But Mr. Kennedy felt confident of victory.

His confidence was well founded. He defeated Mr. Lodge by 1,211,984 votes to 1,141,247—a margin of 70,000—while the Republican Presidential ticket won in Massachusetts by 208,800 votes.

It was 36 years since John Kennedy's grandfather, Mr. Fitzgerald, had been defeated by Henry Cabot Lodge's grandfather of the same name, in the United States Senatorial election.

Mr. Kennedy's first years in the Senate were marked by three major events—one personal, one political and one physical.

The personal event was his marriage. In 1951 he first met Jacqueline Lee Bouvier, then 21 and a student at George Washington University. She was the daughter of Mr. and Mrs. John V. Bouvier 3d, who were divorced. She was brought up in New York and Washington, attended Vassar College and the Sorbonne in Paris and was a Roman Catholic.

Miss Bouvier was a striking young woman with soft, abundant hair, modulated voice and an independent, inquisitive mind.

Although Mr. Kennedy was instantly attracted to the dark slender girl, it was months before he saw much of her. They met just on the eve of his Senate campaign. Not until he returned to Washington in 1953 as a Senator did the courtship begin in earnest.

They were married on Sept. 12, 1953, at St. Mary's Roman Catholic Church in Newport. The Most Reverend Richard J. Cushing, then Archbishop of the Archdiocese of Boston and later a Cardinal, performed the ceremony.

Meanwhile, Mr. Kennedy's back was giving him new difficulty. The trouble grew worse. On Oct. 21, 1954, he entered Manhattan's Hospital for Special Surgery and underwent a double fusion of spinal discs in a long, difficult operation.

The operation was not altogether successful. He was in the hospital until late December. After a brief vacation, he had another operation in mid-February, 1955.

The most frequent rumor was that he suffered from Addison's disease, a serious malfunctioning of the adrenal glands. He had experienced some malfunctioning of the adrenals because of his wartime malaria. But after his critical back operations his health soon built back to the typically vigorous Kennedy level.

Against the background of these personal events a major political crisis occurred. This was once again on the subject of McCarthyism, a word given to the activities of Senator Joseph R. McCarthy of Wisconsin, a crusader against communism.

Senator Kennedy had, in effect, evaded the McCarthy issue

(continued)

The President and his bride, the former Jacqueline Bouvier, leave a Newport, R.I., church following their marriage in 1953.

in his campaign of 1952 But now as the Wisconsin Senator's activities impinged more and more on the national scene and sentiment rose in the Senate for curbing Mr. McCarthy's activities, the question of Mr. Kennedy's position came to the fore.

As the issue was drawn tighter Senator Kennedy continued to steer a cautious course in correspondence with his constituents and in public speeches.

Senator Kennedy did vote against Mr. McCarthy on certain issues. He voted for confirmation of James B. Conant as Ambassador to West Germany and Charles E. Bohlen as Ambassador to the Soviet Union, two appointments opposed by Mr. McCarthy

But the direct issue of Senate censure of Mr. McCarthy was building up rapidly. Mr. Kennedy decided to vote for censure—but on the narrow technical ground that Mr. McCarthy had jeopardized the dignity and honor of the Senate.

Senator Kennedy prepared a speech outlining his views. But he never delivered it and he was not in the Senate when the censure issue arose. When the vote on the censure was taken on Dec. 2, 1954, and Mr. McCarthy's power was checked by a 67-to-22 vote of the Senate, Mr. Kennedy was "absent by leave of the Senate because of illness." He was still recuperating from back surgery.

This was not the end of the matter, however. The question of Mr. Kennedy's attitude toward Mr. McCarthy and McCarthyism was to persist through his broadening political career. As late as 1959., the satirists of the Washington Press Club sang at a Gridiron dinner:

"Where you were, John,
Where were you, John,
When the Senate censored
Joe?"

VOLUME WRITTEN DURING '55 ILLNESS

The precise moment when John Fitzgerald Kennedy determined to run for the Presidency of the United States may never be determined.

Some historians feel that a campaign for the Presidency was implicit in John Kennedy's decision late in 1945 to embark upon a political career.

They point out that he took over, in effect, the projected ambitions of his late brother, Joseph P. Kennedy Jr., whose intention to try for the Presidency had been explicit as early as his college days at Harvard.

To some, the Kennedy ambition for the Presidency stemmed from a frustrated drive originally possessed by Joseph P. Kennedy Sr., and transmitted by him first to his son Joe and then to his son Jack.

Whatever the influence of these psychological factors may have been upon John Kennedy, it seems certain that his decision to make a bid for the highest American political honors stemmed from his own year of deep crisis, 1954 to 1955.

He spent most of that period in and out of hospital beds. He underwent surgery several times at grave risk of his life to correct his chronic and painful back injury.

During almost the whole period he was away from Washington, he was out of the mainstream of political life, isolated from ordinary affairs and in a position to think deeply about himself and about questions of human and political philosophy.

John Kennedy did not spend his months of illness and recuperation in idleness. He turned his mind and his interest to a task that intimately linked his personal and political interests. This was the writing of the book that he published in 1956 under the title "Profiles in Courage."

Before he picked up the political mantle of his brother Joe, John Kennedy had been headed for a career as a writer. He had dabbled in journalism and had written many articles for periodicals. And on the eve of World War II he had turned his college political science thesis into a widely read book called "Why England Slept." This was an analysis of the Baldwin-Chamberlain era that led England down the Munich staircase into World War II.

Wrote Studies in Courage

Then, just as the surgeons fused the injured discs of his spine, so he fused his literary and political aspirations and produced a study of notable examples of political courage in America. John Quincy Adams, Daniel Webster, Edmund Ross, George W. Norris, Sam Houston, Thomas Hart Benton, Robert A. Taft—these were some of the men whose lives Mr. Kennedy incorporated in his study.

Many vehicles have launched public men onto the stage of national politics. But seldom has the instrument been a best-selling collection of historical biographies. But such was the case with John Kennedy.

"Profiles in Courage" lifted him into a special category—a category of statesmanship and scholarship beyond the reach of most men in politics. It served a more subtle purpose as well. For in the process of writing about the great and brave men of American politics Mr. Kennedy acquired a stature and fiber of political philosophy that he had not had before.

His book won a Pulitzer Prize in biography in 1957. And this honor helped lift him, in public-opinion polls, into a leading position among Presidential possibilities.

There was one discordant note connected with the book. Rumors circulated that it had been ghost-written by his close friend and intimate political aide, Theodore C. Sorenson. Warnings by Senator Kennedy that he would sue for libel and slander finally halted the circulation of the rumors.

He returned to Washington on May 23, 1955, not completely recuperated from his operations. It was early 1956 before he moved into the clear as a national figure.

In view of his age and the general political situation—the renomination of Adlai E. Stevenson as the Democratic Presidential nominee was virtually certain—Senator Kennedy set his sights for the Vice-Presidential nomination.

Actually, this was merely a gambit toward a possible Presidential nomination four years hence. He wanted the advertising and political experience of a bid for a Vice-Presidential nomination. He would have liked the nomination but a brisk fight for it was almost as useful to his purposes.

In the end, after numerous ups and downs and a few moments of coming close, Senator Kennedy did not make it. He took the spotlight at the Democratic convention, placing Mr. Stevenson in nomination.

Mr. Stevenson then threw the race for the Vice Presidency open. There was a scramble between Senators Kennedy and Estes Kefauver of Tennessee. On the second ballot, Mr. Kennedy led 618 to 551½. But on the third ballot Mr. Kefauver swamped Mr. Kennedy.

Four years of intensive political activity and organization lay ahead of Senator Kennedy before his Presidential ambitions could be achieved.

Mr. Kennedy turned full time attention to Presidential politics. He stumped 26 states for Mr. Stevenson in 1956.

Then, in 1957, he began to build a national legislative record. He criticized the level of ambassadorial appointments of the Eisenhower Administration. He backed aid for Poland and for India. He called for the independence of Algeria. He published incisive critiques of United States foreign policy in the quarterly "Foreign Affairs." He warned of a missile gap.

Domestic Course Difficult

In domestic policy he steered a difficult course. He compromised on features of civil rights legislation, drawing criticism from the left. He backed better budgeting and fiscal housekeeping. He fought for moderate labor reform.

And he tucked away an indispensable demonstration of his live political appeal. In 1958 he ran for a second term for the United States Senate. It was a rough, tough campaign in which Mr. Kennedy first had to clear away some minor roadblocks put in his path by dissident Democrats in Massachusetts.

The biggest winning margin ever to be piled up by a candidate in Massachusetts had been achieved by Leverett Saltonstall in 1944. He won his Senate race that year with a majority of 561,668 votes.

Mr. Kennedy's enthusiasts hoped that he might make as good a showing. He did—and a good deal better. His margin was 874,608, the biggest in history and the biggest margin any Senatorial candidate in the United States won by in 1958.

From that time forward Presidential politics seemed almost completely to preoccupy Senator Kennedy. He was constantly on the go, appearing in every part of the country.

Aided by Seasoned Staff

Behind him he had a small but well organized and seasoned political staff. It was built around the Kennedy family. John was running for the Presidency. But it was still a clan operation.

Always there were some Kennedys traveling with him on the plane. His brother Robert was campaign manager. His principal aides were the old team—the group of close friends and associates he had gathered over the years, dating back to preparatory school days, plus a few acquired in his Washington years.

The key members of his organization were Lawrence F. O'Brien, experienced in Boston political battles; Kenneth P. O'Donnell, a Harvard football star and Boston political pro; Mr. Sorenson, who had become virtually a Kennedy alter ego in the years of his Senate service; Timothy J. Reardon Jr., who had roomed with Joseph Kennedy Jr., at Harvard; Torbert H. MacDonald, by now a United States Representative from Massachusetts; Francis X. Morrissey, another Boston pro, and others of this type.

A suite of offices was rented in the Esso Building in Washington, just under the brow of Capitol Hill—and the Kennedy campaign was moving fast.

The first task was to obtain the nomination. Senator Kennedy chose to go after that by competing in the primaries. This pitted him in two major contests with Senator Hubert H. Humphrey of Minnesota—first in Wisconsin in February and then in West Virginia in April.

Senators Kennedy and Humphrey campaigned in Wisconsin for a month, running up and down the state through bitter cold and winter snowstorms.

Mr. Kennedy won the state but Mr. Humphrey put up a good showing—good enough so that the coalescing opposition to Mr. Kennedy within the Democratic party could raise questions about his vote-getting ability in the Middle West.

Religious Issue Grew

Senator Kennedy had picked the Wisconsin primary boldly. He wanted to demonstrate two things—his ability to run well in the agricultural Middle West and his ability to overcome the "Catholic issue."

Although Mr. Kennedy had been in political life for nearly fifteen years, the issue of his religion loomed larger than ever when he entered openly upon his Presidential course. For overhanging the prospects of a Roman Catholic candidate was the long memory of the religious turmoil raised by the candidacy of Alfred E. Smith, a Catholic Democrat, who ran a disastrous race against Herbert Hoover in 1928.

Senator Kennedy was determined to meet the religious issue head-on. Indeed, he seemed to seek opportunities to emphasize his belief in the traditional separation of church and state and of the right of a Catholic to political equality with a non-Catholic.

Victory Over Humphrey

With the indecisiveness of the Wisconsin primary leaving these questions somewhat unsettled, Senators Kennedy and Humphrey were rematched in the West Virginia primary. Here for the first time Mr. Kennedy fought the religious issue out from one end of the state to another. And here he encountered voters who were hard-bitten in their opposition to any candidate of the Catholic faith.

There were many predictions that Mr. Kennedy might be defeated because of anti-Catholic prejudice among the voters or that he might just squeak through. But to the surprise of his own staff he won a big victory—a commanding success that drove Mr. Humphrey out of the Presidential competition and was hailed by the Kennedy supporters as conclusive evidence that the omen of the Al Smith defeat in 1928 no longer overhung his campaign chances.

From that time on the Kennedy bandwagon picked up overwhelming momentum.

By the time the Democratic National Convention opened in Los Angeles in July, experienced political observers were certain that Mr. Kennedy had put together a winning combination even though Senator Lyndon B. Johnson of Texas was still openly in the field against him and Mr. Stevenson still hoped for a third nomination.

But the hopes of Mr. Johnson and Mr. Stevenson were dependent upon holding the line with sufficient favorite-son candidates to prevent the Kennedy nomination on the first ballot. It was a hopeless task.

The big Democratic states had begun to line up behind Senator Kennedy. Gov. David L. Lawrence of Pennsylvania, Mayor Richard S. Daley of Chicago and most of the New York State delegation swung in behind Mr. Kennedy. He won easily on the first ballot. Senator Kennedy moved swiftly to heal the breaches in the party. He asked and got Mr. Johnson's acceptance as his running mate. Mr. Stevenson introduced Mr. Kennedy for the acceptance speech. The stage was set for the final drive for the Presidency.

From the moment that Vice President Richard M. Nixon was made the Republican candidate, it was apparent that he and Mr. Kennedy would wage vigorous campaigns. Each proposed to utilize all of the technological devices of the new age to present themselves to the electorate.

Each scheduled heavy programs of television time. Each utilized the jet airplane to carry out dazzling schedules, which whisked him from one end of the country to another. For the first time, with the admission of Hawaii and Alaska into the Union, the candidates had 50 rather than 48 states to campaign in.

The major innovation of the campaign, however, was not the jet airplane. It was the national television debate of the Presidential candidates.

During the West Virginia Presidential primary Mr. Kennedy and Mr. Humphrey met in a television debate and as early as the Wisconsin primary the Kennedy strategists had discussed the possibility of national television debates if the Senator won the nomination.

However, the initiative for the Presidential campaign debates came from the national television networks, which had long been interested in trying such a procedure. After considerable consultation by the broadcasters and representatives of each candidate, a series of four debates was agreed upon.

The first of the four debates, conducted on Sept. 26 in Chicago, proved, in retrospect, to be by far the most important. Indeed, when the election was over many observers felt that this encounter had been the turning point of the campaign.

It was not so much a clash of issues at the first debates as a contrast of personalities.

Kennedy partisans credited this debate with clearing away two major issues that had been raised against their candidate. The first was the issue of youth, inexperience and immaturity, which the Republicans had planned to make a cornerstone of their campaign.

But after the first and subsequent debates, the Republicans conceded, the issue lost most of its bite because Senator Kennedy presented himself to the national audience as an assured,

(continued)

John F. Kennedy, then Presidential candidate, with his brother, Robert F., (center), his campaign manager, and Edward M., his youngest brother. Robert became Attorney General. Edward later won the President's vacated Senate seat.

mature figure with a wealth of specific information about government and policy at his finger tips.

The second handicap removed by the television debates was the fact that Mr. Kennedy was less widely known than Mr. Nixon.

Nixon Seemed Nervous

The Vice President had been on the national stage continuously for eight years. Mr. Kennedy had been campaigning vigorously for four, but there was no doubt that he still lagged behind in the public awareness. After the debates, this disadvantage was eliminated.

There was a third factor of major consequence involved in the initial television appearance. In this debate, Mr. Nixon appeared thin, tired, nervous. He looked below par physically. In contrast, Mr. Kennedy was ebullient and self-confident and radiated health and energy.

The religious issue refused to be put down in the campaign. Mr. Kennedy was compelled to return to it again and again.

However, the climax of these efforts occurred early in the campaign when he appeared before a group of Protestant ministers in Houston, Tex.

The group was notably hostile to him and apparently convinced that a Catholic could not act with independence and freedom in the White House.

Mr. Kennedy confronted his accusers in a dramatic hour-long session, which was televised nationally and rerun again and again in areas in which religious prejudices were known to be high.

The high point of his presentation was a declaration that he would resign the office of the Presidency if he ever thought that his religious beliefs would not permit him to make a decision in the national interest.

Mr. Kennedy relied upon virtually ceaseless physical activity. He campaigned all day long by airplane in long trips from one coast to another. Then he set up late night campaign meetings and tours that sometimes seemed to turn night into day—as in the case of a notable foray into Connecticut, which began at 12:30 A.M. and went on until until nearly to 4 A. M. the following day.

By Nov. 8, Election Day, each candidate had traveled more thousands of miles than any of his predecessors in American political history. Each had spoken more times and to more millions of people than any candidate before.

Await the Returns

Mr. Kennedy wound up his campaign on home territory. He spent the Monday before election in a whirlwind tour of New England, culminating in a rally in his old Boston territory. He was up early in the morning to vote in Boston and then went to his home in Hyannis Port, Mass. to wait for results.

In Hyannis Port the whole Kennedy family was gathered—Mr. Kennedy's wife, awaiting the birth of their second child (the youngster, John F. Kennedy Jr., was born Nov. 25), his parents, his brother Robert and all the rest of the brothers, sisters, in-laws and children.

As they awaited for the returns to come in, the family, in the old tradition, played touch football on the lawn and demonstrated that not all the Kennedy energy had been exhausted in the election campaign. That is, all played football, except for the Senator's wife, Jacqueline. She went for a long walk, alone, along the sandy beach.

Twenty-four hours later, on the morning of Nov. 9, Mr. Nixon conceded the election to Mr. Kennedy after one of the closest votes in recent national history.

Irish Wards of Boston Forged Kennedy's Political Weapons

Not since the days of the Roosevelts has so numerous, so vigorous and so political a family as the Kennedys appeared on the national political horizon.

In energy, animal spirits and physical exuberance the Kennedys displayed closer affinity to Theodore Roosevelt and his dictum of "the strenuous life" than the more commonly evoked images of the Franklin D. Roosevelt family.

And, in numbers, the Kennedy family set a record, unmatched in modern White House annals.

The family is a product of and has long been a principal component of one of America's greatest political forging grounds—the Irish wards of old Boston.

The head is Joseph P. Kennedy, father of the thirty-fifth President. The matriarch is his wife Rose, beautiful, gracious and energetic in her seventh decade.

Family Closely United

The relationship of the Kennedy children, the Kennedy in-laws, the Kennedy grandchildren, the Kennedy connections to one another have little counterpart in contemporary American society.

It is marked by loyalty, affection and cohesiveness so intense that an observer once remarked:

"When an outsider threatens to thwart the ambitions of any-one of them, the whole family forms a close-packed ring, horns lowered, like a head of bison beset by wolves."

What is the origin of the Kennedy clan?

In the present generation it has been formed by the union of two Boston Irish political families, the Kennedys and the Fitzgeralds. Before that union, there had been a minimum of love and a maximum of hard-bitten antagonism between the two families.

The Kennedys were products of County Wexford. One day in 1947 John F. Kennedy, then a 30-year-old Massachusetts Congressman, made a sentimental pilgrimage back to County Kilkenny. He repeated the visit this year.

He went to Lismore Castle on the River Blackstone and then drove across the green countryside to the market town of New Ross on the Barrow River, where the Kennedy ancestral home had been. It was still standing—a thatch cottage with dirt floor and white-washed wall.

It was from this place that Patrick Kennedy set out to venture in America soon after 1845, at the height of the dreadful potato famine.

Like thousands of other emigrants, Patrick paid his $20 for steerage passage on a Cunard ship and landed on Noddle's Island in East Boston, across a narrow arm of land from Boston Harbor.

By 1850 Patrick Kennedy was working as a cooper. He married and had four children. The last of them, named Patrick J., was born in January, 1862. A little later the original Patrick died.

Patrick J. Kennedy began his working life as a dock roustabout and longshoreman. He was 5 feet 10 inches tall, had a sandy complexion, bright blue eyes and a handsome flowing moustache. He was quiet-spoken, industrious, ambitious.

Soon Patrick J. had founded a saloon across from the East Boston shipyard. He prospered. He added a retail liquor business, then more saloons. Eventually he had a coal company, a wholesale liquor company and a bank, the Columbia Trust Company. He had moved up a long way from the roustabout days on the docks.

Deeply Involved in Politics

But more important, perhaps, than any of these activities, he had gone into politics, deeply, skillfully and intensively.

By the Eighteen Eighties he was a man of influence. Five times he ran for State Representative—and always won. He tried for the State Senate and won. He was Fire Commissioner, Street Commissioner, Election Commissioner. Whatever he went after, he got.

He became a member of the famous "Board of Strategy"—the inner circle of Boston Irish ward leaders who met daily in Room 8 of the Old Quincy House on Brattle Street near Scollay Square. The "Board" decided all of Boston's political business in informal caucus.

Side by side with Patrick J. Kennedy's growth in political influence, wealth and community standing another political figure was making his way forward. He was John F. Fitzgerald — known as "Honey Fitz," "Little Nap" or "The Little General."

John F. Fitzgerald, third oldest in a family of nine, grew up in an eight-family tenement in Lower Hanover Street. By the time he was 16 he had lost both his parents. Soon he had a job as clerk in the Custom House under Leverett Saltonstall, grandfather of the present-day Governor and Senator from Massachusetts.

Honey Fitz was 5 feet 2 inches tall. He was as outgoing as Patrick J Kennedy was retiring

Mr. Fitzgerald bounced around Boston like a rubber ball. He wore a boutonnière in his coat. He was merry, ebullient, garrulous. His eyes sparkled, his sandy hair was parted down the middle and when he sang his campaign song, "Sweet Adeline," he rolled his eyes toward heaven

Honey Fitz was elected councilman, alderman and state legislator. He ran successfully twice for the United States House of Representatives and later was Boston's Mayor.

Patrick J. and Honey Fitz were fellow workers in Boston politics but not much more. Patrick J. found Honey Fitz insufferable. The feeling seems to have been mutual.

It was the next generation, however, that produced the merging of these two vigorous strains of Boston political stock.

In 1914, Joseph P. Kennedy, Patrick J's eldest son, married Rose Fitzgerald, daughter of Honey Fitz.

Joseph P. Kennedy began almost immediately to make money prodigiously. And his wife had babies at a fast rate—five in six years, nine in all. Seven of the children survived.

One of the Richest Men

Few men in their lifetime have amassed as much wealth as Joseph P. Kennedy. His fortune by 1960 was estimated from $200,000,000 to $400,000,000. He was rated as one of the world's most wealthy men.

He displayed financial shrewdness from the start. He persuaded his political father and father-in-law to get him a job as state bank examiner at $1,500 a year. He worked a few months, long enough to learn the banking situation from the inside.

The next move was to become, at 25, the president of the family-owned bank, the Columbia Trust, and to put his inside knowledge to work. World War I found him associated with the late Charles M. Schwab, the self-made millionaire head of Bethlehem Steel.

At war's end Mr. Kennedy plunged into Wall Street.

Enterprises Were Varied

He started out in the amusement industry, piling up millions in various film and theatre operations. He ran stock pools. He branched out into liquor and, with the repeal of Prohibition, got a firm grip on the import to the United States of scotch whiskies. He spread out into real estate.

As his fortune grew, Mr. Kennedy turned the drive and perfectionism of his character toward his clan-like family, inculcating it with a fierce kind of intra-family competitiveness and combativeness against the outside world.

The slogan of the Kennedy family was, "Second Best is a Loser." To encourage independence in his family, Mr. Kennedy settled on each of the children a $1,000,000 trust fund. As Mr. Kennedy put it, he wanted each child to be able to look at him—if he wished—and tell him to go to hell, that he would follow his own way.

First of the Kennedy children was Joseph P. Jr., born in 1915. He died in a crash of his plane over Europe in World War II.

John F. Kennedy was born on May 29, 1917.

Four girls followed. They were:

Rosemary, born in 1919; Kathleen, born in 1920, who married the Marquess of Hartington in 1944, was widowed the same year and died in a plane crash in 1948; Eunice, born in 1921, wife of Sargent Shriver, a business man who became head of the Peace Corps; Patricia, born in 1924, wife of Peter Lawford, British actor.

Robert F., manager of his brother's Presidential campaign, was born in 1926. He now is head of a household that numbers eight children.

Finally, came Jean, born in 1928, who is the wife of Stephen Smith, executive of Kennedy real estate interests in New York, and Edward (Teddy), born in 1932.

There has been endless speculation about the source of the political drives that have possessed the Kennedy family. On the surface the drive seems to have skipped from the generation of Grandfather Kennedy and Grandfather Fitzgerald to the generation of Joseph and John and Robert.

But other observers are not so certain of this.

Once Joseph P. Kennedy had begun to accumulate his millions, he moved more and more into the political sphere, although he never ran for elective office.

He was an early backer of Franklin D. Roosevelt. He worked energetically in the campaign of 1932, and was in the thick of the early New Deal.

He was named to several important offices in that period. The most important was the chairmanship of the Securities Exchange Commission. He was its first head.

His next Federal post was the chairmanship of the United States Maritime Commission. He backed President Roosevelt for a second term in 1936. Then, he was named Ambassador to the Court of St. James's.

About this time, and closely connected with the rising threat of World War II in Europe, Mr. Kennedy's views and those of President Roosevelt began to diverge. At the same time Washington political observers noted signs that they believed indicated that Mr Kennedy was nourishing major political ambitions himself.

However, the speculations about Mr. Kennedy's political ambitions were never to be tested.

With the war already on in Europe, Mr. Roosevelt decided to run for a third term, thus ending any hopes Mr. Kennedy might have had of running himself.

President and Mrs. Kennedy and their children, John F. Jr. and Caroline during their vacation in Palm Beach, Fla., on Easter Sunday in 1963.

"All the News That's Fit to Print"

The New York Times

LATE CITY EDITION

Weather: Sunny, warm today; fair, continued warm tonight, tomorrow. Temp. range: today 88-62; Wed. 83-59. Temp.-Hum. Index 75; Wed. 74. Full U.S. report on Page 94.

VOL. CXVII..No. 40,311

NEW YORK, THURSDAY, JUNE 6, 1968

10 CENTS

KENNEDY IS DEAD, VICTIM OF ASSASSIN; SUSPECT, ARAB IMMIGRANT, ARRAIGNED; JOHNSON APPOINTS PANEL ON VIOLENCE

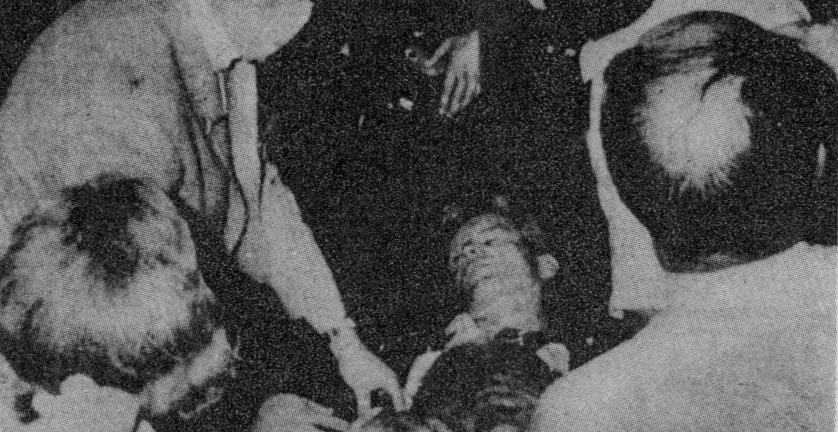

AFTER THE SHOOTING: Senator Kennedy's wife, Ethel, bends over him as a man checks pulse to determine condition

SURGERY IN VAIN

President Calls Death Tragedy, Proclaims a Day of Mourning

Texts of the medical reports appear on Page 22.

By GLADWIN HILL
Special to The New York Times

LOS ANGELES, Thursday, June 6—Senator Robert F. Kennedy, the brother of a murdered President, died at 1:44 A.M. today of an assassin's shots.

The New York Senator was wounded more than 20 hours earlier, moments after he had made his victory statement in the California primary.

At his side when he died today in Good Samaritan Hospital were his wife, Ethel; his sisters, Mrs. Stephen Smith and Mrs. Patricia Lawford; his brother-in-law, Stephen Smith; and his sister-in-law, Mrs. John F. Kennedy, whose husband was assassinated 4½ years ago in Dallas.

In Washington, President Johnson issued a statement calling the death a tragedy. He proclaimed next Sunday a national day of mourning.

The Final Report

Hopes had risen slightly when more than eight hours went by without a new medical bulletin on the stricken Senator, but the grimness of the final announcement was signaled when Frank Mankiewicz, Mr. Kennedy's press secretary, walked slowly down the street in front of the hospital toward the littered gymnasium that served as press headquarters.

Mr. Mankiewicz bit his lip. His shoulders slumped.

He stepped to a lectern in front of a green-tinted chalkboard and bowed his head for a moment while the television lights snapped on.

Then, at one minute before 2 A.M., he told of the death of Mr. Kennedy.

Following is the text of the statement from Mr. Mankiewicz:

"I have a short announcement to read which I will read at this time. Senator Robert Francis Kennedy died at 1:44 A.M. today, June 6, 1968. With

Continued on Page 20, Column 1

MARCUS TESTIFIES DE SAPIO HAD ROLE IN A CON ED DEAL

Says Itkin Sought Delay of Permit to Aid Own Scheme With Ex-Tammany Head

By BARNARD L. COLLIER

Former Water Commissioner James L. Marcus testified yesterday that he had been asked to delay approval of a permit to Consolidated Edison while the former Tammany Hall leader, Carmine G. De Sapio, was trying to make a deal with the utility company.

Marcus testified that the request came last September from his business partner, Herbert Itkin, who was in turn trying to negotiate a deal with Mr. De Sapio.

The testimony was elicited from Marcus under cross-examination on the third day of a Federal bribery conspiracy trial that has been marked by the mention in Marcus's testimony of several prominent members of both the Republican and Democratic parties.

Marcus was asked if there was a time when he, as Commissioner of Water Supply, Gas and Electricity, had "done business" with Con Edison. His answer was yes.

Says Itkin Asked Delay

"Itkin came to me," he said, "and said that Con Ed wanted a permit to increase the voltage on one of their power lines for 20 miles." He added that his approval as Commissioner was needed.

"Itkin said I should hold up for a while because he was negotiating with Carmine De Sapio, who was negotiating with Con Ed."

Marcus said that Mr. Itkin asked him to delay the approval for "a few weeks."

At that point in the trial, which came at about 4:40 P.M., Herman Zoloto, a lawyer representing Henry Fried, a contractor, and Mr. Fried's company, S. T. Grand, Inc., shouted:

"You're way ahead of your story, Mr. Marcus!"

Judge Edward Weinfeld broke in and scolded Mr. Zoloto for "a highly improper re-

Continued on Page 41, Column 1

France Will Meet Tariff Deadline; Strikes Dwindling

By HENRY TANNER
Special to The New York Times

PARIS, June 5 — Maurice Couve de Murville told France's partners in the Common Market today that despite the nationwide strike now coming to a close, the Government would honor the July 1 deadline for the abolition of remaining tariffs in the European trade bloc.

Today workers in the nationalized railroad company, the Paris transit system, the post and telegraph offices and other public administrations voted to go back to work. Trains are expected to start running tomorrow on several major national lines and the Paris subways.

By the end of the week, it is expected, the nationwide strike, now in its 18th day, will be all but ended.

Mr. Couve de Murville, who is the new Minister of Economy and Finance, also reassured his countrymen

Continued on Page 15, Column 1

6 IN RACE GUARDED

Secret Service Given Campaign Security Task by President

Text of the Johnson speech is printed on Page 23.

By MAX FRANKEL
Special to The New York Times

WASHINGTON, June 5—For the second time in five years, Lyndon B. Johnson undertook today, amid national shock and outrage, to offer protection, prayer, comfort and assistance to his political rivals in the Kennedy family and then to try to heal the country's political and psychological wounds.

The President's first reaction to the shooting of Senator Robert F. Kennedy this morning was that "there are no words equal to the horror of this tragedy."

But tonight, in an emotional and at times even angry statement on television, he pleaded with all Americans to end the violence in their midst once and for all, to tolerate neither hatred nor the preaching of violence and to resolve to live under the law.

A Guard for Candidates

Mr. Johnson said he was appointing a commission of distinguished citizens to investigate both the circumstances and the causes of physical violence of all kinds in the United States, in the hope that the nation can learn "how we can stop it".

Earlier he had moved swiftly to provide protective Secret Service details to the six announced Presidential candidates of major parties, other than Vice President Humphrey, who already has such protection because of his office.

Meanwhile, in the House of Representatives, a vote of 317 to 60 cleared the way for the House to accept the Senate version of an anticrime bill, including controls over the interstate sale of hand guns. The vote rejected a move to send the legislation to a Senate-House conference.

Members of Commission

To the commission Mr. Johnson named Milton Eisenhower, former president of Johns Hopkins University; Archbishop Terence J. Cooke of New York; Albert Jenner, Chicago lawyer who worked for the commission that investigated the assassination of President Kennedy; former Ambassador Patricia Harris; Eric Hoffer, the longshoreman-turned-philosopher; Senators Philip Hart, Democrat of Michigan, and Roman L. Hruska, Republican of Nebraska; Representative Hale Boggs, Democrat of Louisiana, majority whip in the House; Representative William M. McCulloch, Republican of Ohio, and Federal Judge Leon Higginbotham of Philadelphia.

The President described himself as shocked, dismayed and deeply disturbed, as he knew all Americans were, by the shooting, which he described as the "latest spectacular example" of lawlessness and violence.

"So let us, for God's sake, re-

Continued on Page 23, Column 1

JERUSALEM POLICE CLASH WITH ARABS

Israelis Halt Procession on Anniversary of War—U.N. Council Meets on Fighting

Special to The New York Times

JERUSALEM, June 5—A silent Arab procession commemorating the first anniversary of the Arab-Israeli war erupted into a violent clash today when Isareli policemen intercepted the marchers at the edge of the walled Old City of Jerusalem.

The clash was the most violent aspect of a widespread protest in which Arabs shuttered shops and other businesses here and elsewhere on the west bank of the Jordan and in the occupied Gaza Strip. It came after a day-long battle yesterday across the Jordan between the Israelis and Jordanians, in which aircraft and artillery were used.

[The United Nations Security Council met Wednesday at the urgent request of Israel and Jordan to consider recurrent hostilities along their cease-fire line. It postponed debate, probably until Thursday. Page 3.]

In the west-bank towns of Nablus, Jenin and Tulkarm, all centers of Arab nationalism, the general strike was 100 per cent effective. All stores, cafes and offices were closed, public transportation ceased and the streets were virtually devoid of traffic and pedestrians.

Schools throughout the west bank and Gaza Strip had no

Continued on Page 2, Column 4

HANOI INSISTS U.S. HALT ITS BOMBING

Aides Call Talks Response to Johnson—Suspicion Voiced of a Plot Against Kennedy

By HEDRICK SMITH
Special to The New York Times

PARIS, June 5—North Vietnamese negotiators contended today that Hanoi had responded to President Johnson's restriction of American air attacks on the north by entering official talks here. They asserted that the next move, a total halt in bombing, was up to the United States.

The North Vietnamese argument, put forward in the seventh negotiating session between the two sides since May 13, produced one of the sharpest exchanges since the Vietnam talks began here.

The North Vietnamese made no direct comment on the shooting of Senator Robert F. Kennedy, but circles close to the delegation voiced suspicions in private, asking if the attack was not part of a conspiracy by the Johnson Administration. [Page 33.]

Near the end of today's session at the former Majestic Hotel, Hanoi's chief representative, Xuan Thuy, leaned across the negotiating table and asked the American delegates bluntly:

"When will the United States unconditionally cease the bombing and all other acts of war against the Democratic Republic of Vietnam so that other questions can be discussed?"

In response, W. Averell Har-

Continued on Page 8, Column 4

The New York Times (by George Tames)

ROBERT F. KENNEDY

NOTES ON KENNEDY IN SUSPECT'S HOME

Cite 'Necessity' to Murder Senator Before June 5, Anniversary of War

By PETER KIHSS

A notebook found in the Pasadena home of Sirhan Bishara Sirhan had "a direct reference to the necessity to assassinate Senator Kennedy before June 5, 1968," Mayor Samuel W. Yorty of Los Angeles said last night.

The date was the first anniversary of the six-day war, in which Israeli forces smashed those of the United Arab Republic, Syria and Jordan.

Sirhan, a 24-year-old Christian Arab, who has described himself as a Jerusalem-born Jordanian, is being held in the shooting of the New York Senator.

Justice Department records indicated that Sirhan came to the United States with his family in January of 1957 as immigrants, less than three months after the Suez war in 1956. Sirhan was 12 at the time.

The family quickly broke up in discord, the father staying in New York to work as a plumber and then going back to their former Palestine home, the mother taking five children to California, where a sixth child immigrated later.

Sirhan was described yesterday by Police Chief Thomas Reddin of Los Angeles as "very cool, very calm, very stable and quite lucid."

He was quoted as having said,

Continued on Page 21, Column 6

KUCHEL UNSEATED AS RAFFERTY WINS

Conservative Beats Senator in California's Primary

By LAWRENCE E. DAVIES
Special to The New York Times

LOS ANGELES, June 5—Dr. Max Rafferty, State Superintendent of Public Instruction, defeated Senator Thomas H. Kuchel in the Republican Senatorial primary in California yesterday, cutting short Mr. Kuchel's 15-year career in the Senate.

Returns from 20,714 of 21,-301 precincts gave:

Rafferty . . .	1,056,038	50%
Kuchel	985,097	47%

As the vote count continued today, it became apparent that the conservative Republicanism of Southern California had carried Dr. Rafferty to victory over the heretofore unbeatable Republican whip in the Senate.

Mr. Kuchel, an outspoken liberal-moderate who had made political extremists such as John Birch Society members his targets in recent years, was beaten by the voters in Los Angeles, San Diego and Orange Counties, after having led Dr. Rafferty last night and early today.

Dr. Rafferty, who has become

Continued on Page 28, Column 3

A Pall Over Politics

Murder Raises Grave Questions for Presidency Races Now and in Future

By TOM WICKER
Special to The New York Times

News Analysis

WASHINGTON, Thursday, June 6—The murder of Robert F. Kennedy shattered the 1968 Presidential campaign and lowered a pall of uncertainty over American politics now and in the years to come. For the immediate future, it may well have assured the nominations by the Democrats and Republicans of the present front-running candidates — Vice President Humphrey and Richard Nixon. It raised grave questions, however, about the personal dangers of political campaigning in the United States. It added a tragic new dimension to the near-martyrdom of the Kennedy family, which has now lost two sons to assassins' bullets.

It removed forever one of the most promising young political leaders in recent American history, one with particular appeal for the poor, the downtrodden and the alienated inhabitants of the Negro slums. That appeal had been proved in all of Robert Kennedy's primary victories this year.

These elements of society also revered the Senator's brother, President Kennedy, who was assassinated on Nov. 22, 1963. How they would react to Robert Kennedy's murder—both in the immediate future and for the long political pull—was a crucial question.

The murder added sorrowful emphasis to one of Robert Kennedy's major political themes—the necessity for orderly and just redress of grievances, in place of violent action.

Ultimately, Mr. Kennedy's death—the first assassination of an American Presidential candidate—might lead to changes in campaigning practices, even to the fundamental manner in which the nation chooses its President.

The most immediate effect, however, was that for the third—and most harrowing—time a shock wave of unexpected events had completely altered the shape of the 1968 campaign.

The first came on March 12 when Senator Eugene J. McCarthy of Minnesota won 42 per cent of the Democratic vote in the New Hampshire primary, and Mr. Kennedy immediately thereafter became an active candidate.

The second transformation

Continued on Page 25, Column 6

TRANSIT PACKAGE SUBMITTED TO CITY

M.T.A. Seeks Approval of 8 New Subway Routes

By EMANUEL PERLMUTTER

A $1.27-billion package of subway and commuter railroad additions and improvements was submitted to the Board of Estimate and Mayor Lindsay yesterday.

The program was presented by the Metropolitan Transportation Authority and the New York City Transit Authority with a request for speedy city agreement on the new routes and engineering designs.

The over-all plan, which would take 10 years to complete, consists of eight new subway routes, including a Second Avenue subway, and Long Island Rail Road connections to the East Side of Manhattan and to Kennedy International Airport.

City approval of the routes and designs is a first step before application can be made for $60-million set aside by the Legislature for the engineering design of the mass transportation program presented by the Metropolitan Transportation

Continued on Page 55, Column 1

Italy's Cabinet Quits As Parliament Opens

By ROBERT C. DOTY
Special to The New York Times

ROME, June 5—Premier Aldo Moro and his center-left coalition Government, which has ruled Italy for four and a half years, resigned tonight with the convening of the new parliament, the fifth since World War II.

President Giuseppe Saragat asked Mr. Moro and his ministers to remain in office as a caretaker government while the search for a new government, which may be arduous, goes on.

Resignation of the government with the convening of a new parliament is automatic. But any hope that the Moro

Continued on Page 14, Column 3

NEWS INDEX

Big Board Weighs 4 Special Closings

By VARTANIG G. VARTAN

A securities industry panel recommended yesterday that the New York Stock Exchange, the American Stock Exchange and the over-the-counter market close down for four days over the next month to cope with the deluge of paperwork in brokerage offices.

The panel proposed closing the securities markets for three Wednesdays—June 12, 19 and 26—as well as Friday, July 5.

The board of governors of the New York Stock Exchange will meet this afternoon to consider the proposal. Wall Street sources said that in view of the critical situation the governors are expected to accept the pro-

Continued on Page 73, Column 1

Father of Suspect 'Sickened' by News

By TERENCE SMITH
Special to The New York Times

ET TAIYIBA, Israeli-Occupied Jordan, Thursday, June 6—Bishara Sirhan's hands trembled as he talked about his son Sirhan Bishara Sirhan, the accused assailant of Senator Robert F. Kennedy.

Mr. Sirhan dwelled on the tragedy of the shooting. He became angry as he talked, and finally said: "This news made me sick when I heard it. If my son has done this dirty thing, then let them hang him."

Mr. Sirhan's memories of his five sons are those of 10 years ago, when he last saw them and their mother. After years of fierce family quarrels, Bishara

Continued on Page 21, Column 4

Kennedy Dies, Victim of Assassin, After Doctors Perform 3-Hour Brain Operation

ARAB ARRAIGNED; $250,000 BAIL SET

Revolver Traced to Suspect —Senator, 42, Failed to Regain Consciousness

Continued From Page 1, Col. 8

Senator Kennedy at the time of his death was his wife, Ethel; his sisters, Mrs. Patricia Lawford and Mrs. Stephen Smith; his brother-in-law, Stephen Smith, and his sister-in-law, Mrs. John F. Kennedy.

"He was 42 years old."

Senator Kennedy's body will be taken to New York this morning and then to Washington.

The man accused of shooting Mr. Kennedy early yesterday in a pantry of the Ambassador Hotel was identified as Sirhan Bishara Sirhan, 24 years old, who was born in Palestinian Jerusalem of Arab parentage and had lived in the Los Angeles area since 1957. Sirhan had been a clerk.

$250,000 Bail

Yesterday, he was hurried through an early-morning court arraignment and held in lieu of $250,000 bail.

Sirhan was charged with six counts of assault with intent to murder, an offense involving a prison term of 1 to 14 years.

Five other persons in addition to the 42-year-old Senator were wounded by the eight bullets from a .22-caliber revolver fired at almost point-blank range into a throng of Democratic rally celebrants surging between ballrooms in the hotel. The shots came moments after Senator Kennedy had made a speech celebrating his victory in yesterday's Democratic Presidential primary in California.

The defendant, seized moments after the shooting, refused to give the police any information about himself. He was arraigned as "John Doe."

Three hours later, Mayor Samuel W. Yorty announced at a news conference at police headquarters that the defendant had been identified as Sirhan. He said the identity had been confirmed by Sirhan's brother and a second individual.

Senator Kennedy, accompanied by his wife, Ethel, was wheeled into the Good Samaritan Hospital shortly after 1 A.M. yesterday after a brief stop at the Central Receiving Hospital. A score of the Senator's campaign aides swarmed around the scene.

Grim Reminder

Less than five years back many of them had experienced the similar tragedy that ended the life of President John F. Kennedy.

At 2:22 A.M., Senator Kennedy's campaign press secretary, Frank Mankiewicz, came out of the hospital into a throng of hundreds of news people to announce that the Senator would be taken into surgery "in five or ten minutes" for an operation of "45 minutes or an hour."

One bullet had gone into the Senator's brain past the mastoid bone back of the right ear, with some fragments going near the brain stem. Another bullet lodged in the back of the neck. A third and minor wound was an abrasion on the forehead.

It was after 7 A.M. when Mr. Mankiewicz reported that more than three hours of surgery had been completed, and all but one fragment of the upper bullet had been removed. The neck bullet was not removed but "is not regarded as a major problem," Mr. Mankiewicz said.

He also reported that the Senator's vital signs remained about as they had been, except that he was now breathing on his own, which he had not been doing before the surgery. Then Mr. Mankiewicz said:

"There may have been an impairment of the blood supply to the mid-brain, which the doctors explained as governing certain of the vital signs—heart, eye track, level of consciousness—although not directly the thinking process."

Senator Kennedy was taken from surgery to an intensive-care unit

At 2:15 P.M. Mr. Mankiewicz announced that Senator Kennedy had not regained consciousness and that a series of medical tests had been "inconclusive and don't show measurable improvement in Senator Kennedy's condition."

"His condition as of 1:30 P.M. remains extremely critical," the spokesman continued. "His life forces — pulse, temperature, blood pressure and heart—remain good, and he continues to show the ability to breathe on his own, although he is being assisted by a resuscitator."

The tests included X-rays and electroencephalograms.

Mrs. Kennedy remained at the hospital.

Mrs. John F. Kennedy arrived at the hospital at 7:30 P.M. yesterday, after a chartered plane flight from New York.

A team of surgeons treating Senator Kennedy included Dr. James Poppen, head of neurosurgery at the Lahey Clinic in Boston. He was rushed to Los Angeles in an Air Force plane on instructions from Vice President Humphrey.

Mr. Humphrey and Senator Eugene J. McCarthy of Minnesota have been Senator Kennedy's rivals in the Democratic Presidential competition.

Mayor Yorty said the defendant's identification had come through a brother, Adel Sirhan, after the police had traced the ownership of the .22-caliber revolver involved in the shooting to a third brother, Munir Bishari Salameh Sirhan, also known as Joe Sirhan.

The weapon was traced through three owners, one in suburban Alhambra, the next in Marin County, adjacent to San Francisco, and back to an 18-year-old youth in suburban Pasadena. The youth said he had sold it to "a busny-haired guy named Joe" whom he knew only as an employe of a Pasadena department store.

Detectives identified the bushy haired man as Munir Sirhan. From him, the trail led to the two other brothers, who have been living together in Pasadena.

The snubnosed .22-caliber Iver Johnson Cadet model revolver seized after the shooting was described as having been picked out of a list of 2.5 million weapons registered in California in "just seconds" after the disclosure of its serial number. This was done by a new computer used by the State Bureau of Criminal Investigation and Identification in Sacramento, according to State Attorney General Thomas Lynch.

The defendant was arraigned at 7 A.M., unusually early, before Municipal Judge Joan Dempsey Klein, on a complaint issued by District Attorney Evelle Younger after all-night consultation with the police.

Deputy District Attorney William Ritzi said the case would be presented to the county grand jury on Friday.

The other victims of the shooting were Paul Schrade, 43 years old, a regional director of the United Automobile and Aerospace Workers Union, a prominent Kennedy campaigner; William Weisel, 30, a unit manager for the American Broadcasting Company; Ira Goldstein, 19, an employe of Continental News Service at nearby Sherman Oaks; Mrs. Elizabeth Evans, 43, of Sangus, in Los Angeles County, and Irwin Stroll, 17.

Mr. Weisel was reported in good condition after removal of a bullet from his abdomen.

The court complaint against Sirhan charged that "on or about the fifth day of June, 1968, at and in the county of Los Angeles a felony was committed by John Doe, who at the time and place aforesaid, did willfully, unlawfully and feloniously commit an assault with a deadly weapon upon Robert Francis Kennedy, a human being, with the intent then and there wilfully, unlawfully, feloniously and with malice aforethought to kill and murder the said Robert Francis Kennedy."

Sirhan was represented at the arraignment by the chief public defender, Richard S. Buckley. He asked Mr. Buckley to get in touch with the American Civil Liberties Union about getting private counsel for him.

Special to The New York Times

WASHINGTON, Thursday, June 6—President Johnson issued the following statement:

"This is a time of tragedy and loss. Senator Robert F. Kennedy is dead.

"Robert Kennedy affirmed this country—affirmed the essential decency of its people, their longing for peace, their desire to improve conditions of life for all.

"During his life, he knew far more than his share of personal tragedy. Yet he never abandoned his faith in America. He never lost his confidence in the spiritual strength of ordinary men and women.

"He believed in the capacity of the young for excellence and in the right of the old and poor to a life of dignity.

"Our public life is diminished by his loss.

"Mrs. Johnson and I extend our deepest sympathy to Mrs. Kennedy and his family.

"I have issued a proclamation calling upon our nation to observe a day of mourning for Robert Kennedy."

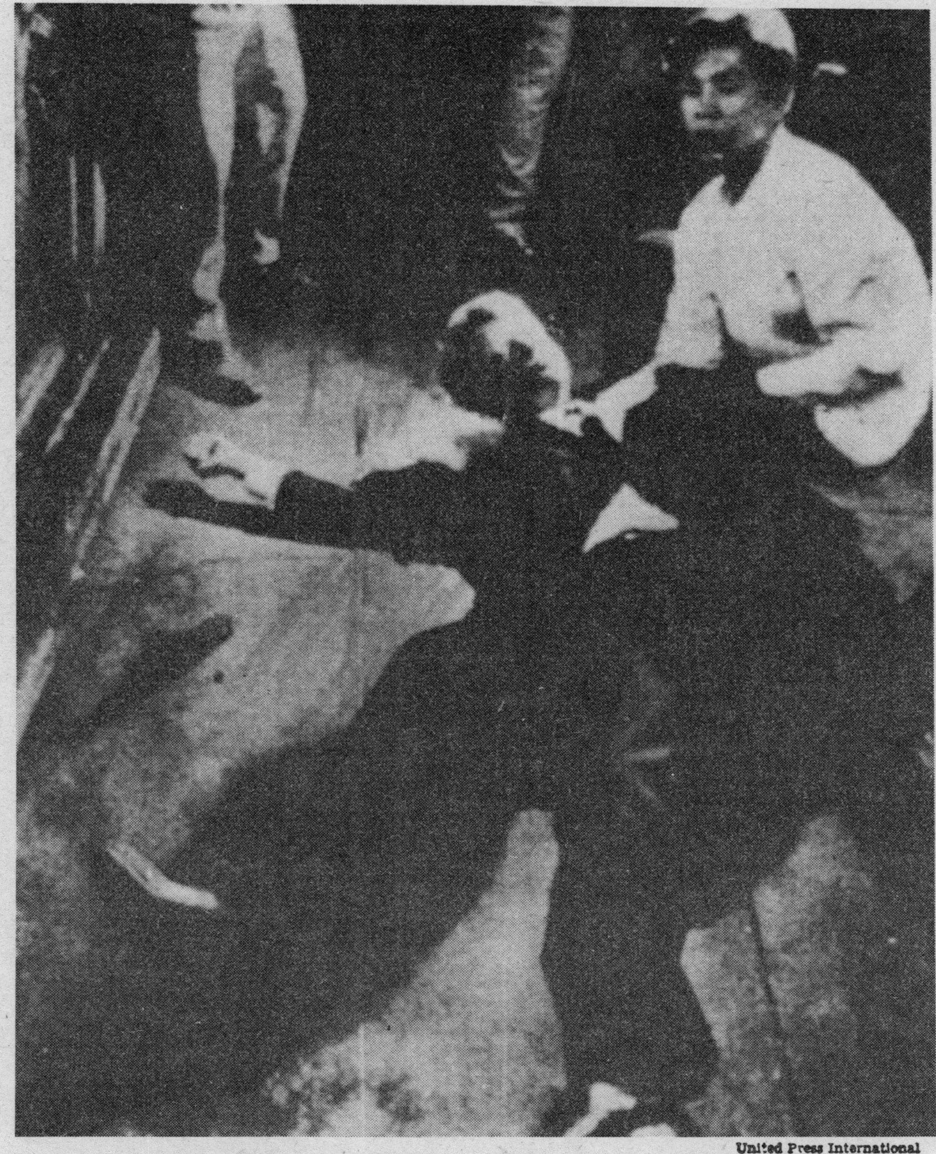

United Press International

FELLED: Senator Kennedy lying in a kitchen area of the Ambassador Hotel in Los Angeles after being wounded fatally by assassin. A hotel worker tries to give assistance.

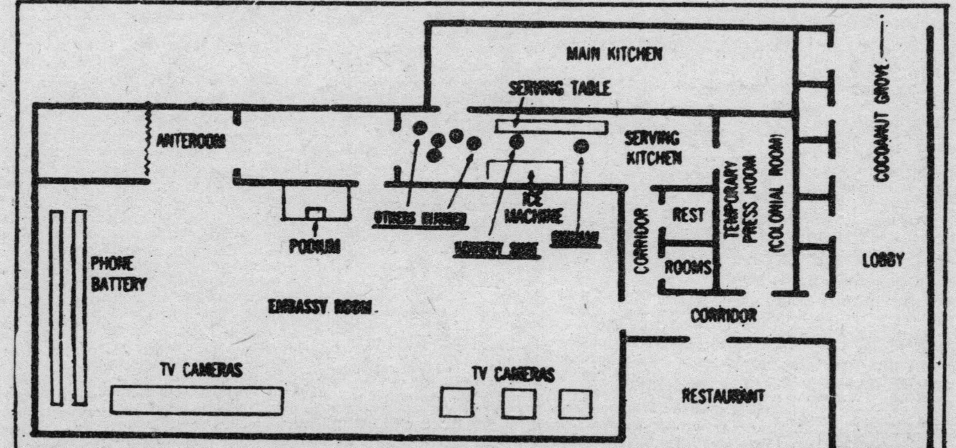

Associated Press

Diagram of Embassy Room of the Ambassador Hotel in Los Angeles and adjoining rooms

Robert Francis Kennedy: Attorney General, Senator and Heir of the New Frontier

By ALDEN WHITMAN

In his brief but extraordinary political career, the 42-year-old, Massachusetts-born Robert Francis Kennedy was Attorney General of the United States under two Presidents and Senator from New York. In those high offices he exerted an enormous influence on the nation's domestic and foreign affairs, first as the closest confidant of his brother, President John F. Kennedy, and then, after Mr. Kennedy's assassination in 1963, as the immediate heir to his New Frontier policies.

The Kennedy name, which John had made magical, devolved on Robert, enabling him to win a Senate seat from a state in which he had little or no previous association. The Kennedy aura also permitted him to campaign this year for the Democratic Presidential nomination and to gain important victories in the preference primaries. Wherever he went he drew crowds by evoking, through his Boston accent, his gestures and his physical appearance, a remarkable and nostalgic likeness to his elder brother.

At the same time Mr. Kennedy called forth sharply opposed evaluations of himself. For those who found him charming, brilliant and sincerely devoted to the welfare of his country there were others who vehemently asserted that he was calculating, overly ambitious and ruthless.

Those who praised him regarded his candidacy for his party's Presidential nomination this year as proof of his selflessness. They quoted with approval his announcement on March 16, in which he said:

"I do not run for the Presidency merely to oppose any man but to propose new policies. I run because I am convinced that this country is on a perilous course and because I have such strong feelings about what must be done, and I feel that I'm obliged to do all I can."

On the other hand, those who questioned his motives pointed out that his candidacy was posed only four days after the New Hampshire primary, in which Senator Eugene J. McCarthy had demonstrated the political vulnerability of President Johnson. Further, Mr. Kennedy's critics said, he had declared only as recently as Jan. 30:

"I have told friends and supporters who are urging me to run that I would not oppose President Johnson under any foreseeable circumstances."

Sure He'd Do 'the Right Thing'

Mr. Kennedy's partisans tended to ignore his inconsistencies or to belittle them. And even many voters who expressed reservations about him were certain that, in public office, he would do "the right thing." This belief was underlined, especially among Negroes and the poor, because of the earnestness with which he pleaded their cause.

Describing the reaction of one ghetto throng in California, Tom Wicker wrote in The New York Times of June 2:

"The crowds surge in alarmingly; children leap and shriek and grown men risk the wheels of Kennedy's car just to pound his arm or grasp his hand. Moving through the sleazy back streets of Oakland, he repeatedly stopped traffic; for six blocks along East 14th Street, his car could barely creep along."

Contrasting with such frenzied warmth was what Fortune magazine called last March "the implacable hostility toward him in the business community." The magazine quoted one Dallas businessman, a leading Democrat, as saying:

"I had great respect for his brother Jack, but I would not vote for Bobby."

The business community, according to Fortune, condemned Mr. Kennedy as immature and irresponsible. Business, it was said, was disquieted "by the reputation for radicalism that he has developed."

To criticism he could respond with asperity or angry chilliness. To the fervor and adulation of his supporters he seemed curiously aloof, exhibiting neither pleasure nor fright. Those close to Mr. Kennedy noticed that his eyes rarely sparkled, but, instead, were sad and withdrawn and that his manner, despite a grin, was unemotional.

Mr. Kennedy's campaign speeches (as well as those he delivered in the Senate) were, for the most part, devoid of oratorical fire and flourish. He spoke in an even baritone; there were no crescendos and little outward expansiveness. His only gestures were to chop the air with his right hand for emphasis or to brush back his shaggy forelock when it slipped down over his forehead.

His campaign humor was self-deprecating, an effort to divert criticism to his account. For example, he recently asked a rally in Fort Wayne, Ind., whether the city would vote for him. Otherwise, he went on, he and Ethel and all of their children would have to go on relief. "It'll be less expensive," he continued, deadpan, "just to send us to the White House. We'll arrange it so all 10 kids won't be there at once, and we won't need to expand the place. I'll send some of them away to school — and I'll make one of them Attorney General."

Mr. Kennedy was an indefatigable campaigner, able to put in a 16-hour day of stress and tension and then sleep briefly before going through another equally strenuous day. Indeed, he seldom seemed to relax, whether he was campaigning or not, for he played with as much concentration as he worked. He was, for instance, a vigorous touch football participant, a hardy skier, a pace-setting mountain climber and a swimmer who did not mind plunging into the cold Pacific surf on an Oregon beach, an exploit few in that state ever attempted.

Mr. Kennedy was so constantly in motion that he prompted some observers to say that he fled introspection, that he did not sit down with himself and figure out what he truly was and what he wanted to achieve. Commenting on this public and private extroversion in "The Heir Apparent," William V. Shannon wrote in 1967:

"In his compulsive athleticism, his reckless risk-taking, his aggressiveness, he seems to be driven by something not accounted for by the realities which engage him and not compatible with the high seriousness of his public ambitions."

'You Have to Struggle'

Mr. Kennedy was, of course, aware of what was said about him, for he not only read omnivorously but he also employed a large staff of experts and advisers to brief and counsel him. He often conceded that he was aggressive, explaining semihumorously:

"I was the seventh of nine children. And when you come from that far down, you have to struggle to survive."

Robert Kennedy was born Nov. 20, 1925, in Brookline, Mass., a fashionable suburb of Boston, the son of Joseph and Rose Fitzgerald Kennedy. His father, the son of poor South Boston parents, was then already amassing a fortune in the stock market and associated speculative enterprises.

Home only at intervals (the family moved in 1926 to Riverdale and then to Bronxville, N. Y.), he left the day-to-day management of the family to his capable wife, who was the daughter of John F. (Honey Fitz) Fitzgerald, who served three terms in the House of Representatives and was Mayor of Boston.

When Robert was born, his brother Joseph Jr. was 10 and John was 8. (Edward was born in 1932.) Thus Robert passed his early years as the little brother, with two older brothers and five young sisters — Rosemary, Kathleen, Eunice, Patricia and Jean. "He was the smallest and thinnest, and we feared he might grow up puny and girlish," his mother recalled, adding: "We soon realized there was no fear of that."

Not only were Robert's sisters tomboyish, but he was also prodded to competitiveness by his father and by Joseph Jr., who served as a surrogate father to his siblings.

"Joe taught me to sail, to swim, to play football and baseball," he remembered. Moreover, Robert's father laid down strict rules of conduct: Never take second best; when the going gets tough, the tough get going; passivity is intolerable.

Although Robert as a youth was overshadowed by his older brothers, he displayed grim determination to succeed. A classmate at Milton Academy, where he prepared for Harvard, said: "It was much tougher in school for him than the others—socially, in football, with studies." Nonetheless, Robert kept up.

He was a Harvard sophomore when Joseph Jr., on whom the family had pinned its political hopes, was killed in a Navy plane over the English Channel in 1944. Deeply affected, Robert traveled to Washington on his own several months later and persuaded Secretary of the Navy James Forrestal to assign him as a seaman to a destroyer newly named for his brother.

Robert spent the remainder of the war in the Caribbean, returning to Harvard in 1946. There his tenacity gained him a place as end on the football team, although he weighed only 160 pounds and stood 5 feet 9 inches tall. After graduation in 1948, he went to law school at the University of Virginia, where he took his degree in 1951.

That same year, after admission to the Massachusetts bar, he joined the criminal division of the Department of Justice in Washington and spent two years prosecuting a somewhat dreary succession of graft and income tax evasion cases without notable splash.

Resigned to Run Campaign

He resigned in 1952 to manage the campaign of his brother John for United States Senator from Massachusetts. The most impressive features of that race were the Kennedy organization's painstaking attention to detail and the vast amount of money it spent. Both later became hallmarks of Robert Kennedy's campaign methods.

Mr. Kennedy's first (and ultimately most controversial) venture into the public limelight occurred in 1953, when he was named one of 15 assistant counsel to the Senate Permanent Subcommittee on Investigations.

His immediate superior was Roy M. Cohn, the group's chief counsel. Above them both was Senator Joseph R. Mc-

(continued)

The Kennedy family photographed at the U.S. Ambassador's residence in London in 1938. Standing (from left): Kathleen (killed in 1948), Joseph Jr. (killed in 1944), Jean, Eunice, Joseph, Rosemary and John. Seated: Patricia, Teddy, Robert and Rose.

Carthy, Republican of Wisconsin, whose name was soon attached to the committee. It rapidly acquired a malodorous reputation among liberals, intellectuals and civil libertarians for its chivvying of witnesses in its investigations of asserted Communist conspiracies and plots in the Government. Robert had obtained his job through his father, who had contributed money to Senator McCarthy's anti-Communist campaign. He got along well with the Senator, a circumstance that plagued Mr. Kennedy when he became, years later, a professing liberal.

After a dispute with Mr. Cohn over the committee staff, Mr. Kennedy resigned his post in mid-1953, but rejoined it in February, 1954, as counsel to the Democratic minority. The following year — after the Army-McCarthy hearings — he succeeded Mr. Cohn as chief counsel and staff director when Senator John L. McClellan, Democrat of Arkansas, became committee chairman. In that post he pursued investigations into alleged Communist influence and helped develop some of the conflict-of-interest cases involving personalities in the Eisenhower Administration. Senator McClellan liked him, for he was a persistent questioner of witnesses and a resolute investigator.

One result was that the Senator chose Mr. Kennedy as chief counsel of the Senate Select Committee on Improper Activities in the Labor or Management Field when it was organized in January, 1957. Mr. Kennedy immediately began a headline-making inquiry into the affairs of the International Brotherhood of Teamsters, then under the presidency of Dave Beck. Beck was later imprisoned for filing false income tax returns.

Accused of Antilabor Views

Mr. Kennedy's sharp questioning of Beck before the Senate Rackets Committee, as the McClellan group was generally known, drew down on him the accusation that he was antilabor at worst and unsympathetic to the working man at best. This charge was compounded when he investigated James R. Hoffa, Beck's successor, in 1958.

Hoffa, who was eventually convicted and jailed for jury tampering and misuse of union funds, disliked Mr. Kennedy, calling him "a young, dim-witted, curly-headed smart-aleck" and "a ruthless monster." Calm and polite as the committee's counsel, Mr. Kennedy nevertheless did not conceal his disdain for Hoffa. His reaction to an involved and obscure answer was often a sarcastic and disbelieving: "Oh."

Later, when he was Attorney General, Mr. Kennedy continued his investigation of the 1,700,000-member teamsters union, causing Hoffa to charge that he was engaged in vendetta. Officials of other unions were also prosecuted by Mr. Kennedy, generating a coolness of organized labor toward him that was still evident when he was campaigning for the Democratic Presidential nomination in 1968. The attitude of the trade union hierarchy, however, did not permeate to the rank and file, who generally voted for him.

Mr. Kennedy left the rackets committee in 1959 to manage his brother's campaign for the Presidency. Describing the primary races of 1960, Lawrence J. Quirk, in "Robert Francis Kennedy," wrote:

"Bobby kept his card file constantly replenished with information on every local leader, every county VIP, every 'bit' player in every key town. And he bore down most heavily on the states where the primary battles looked hottest: New Hampshire, Indiana, West Virginia and Wisconsin (already marked for the kill), Oregon and Nebraska.

"But Bobby's strong-arm methods were not just limited to the states where the primaries were crucial. Gov. [Michael] Di Salle of Ohio, who had hoped to run as a favorite-son candidate, was soon finding himself unremittingly pressured by Bobby to endorse Jack Kennedy. The two little fighting words 'or else' hung in the air. With a primary fight against the Kennedys — a fight he stood to lose — a distinct possibility, Di Salle finally capitulated. 'The Kennedys play rough and they play for keeps,' he later said."

As his brother's vizier, Robert Kennedy never bothered to hide his political muscle in 1960. Answering one politician's complaint, he said blandly:

"I'm not running a popularity contest. It doesn't matter if they [the politicians] like me or not. Jack can be nice to them. I don't try to antagonize people but somebody has to be able to say no. If people are not getting off their behinds and working enough, how do you say that nicely? Every time you make a decision in this business you make somebody mad."

Senator and Mrs. Kennedy and eight of their ten children.

In the election campaign that followed, against Richard M. Nixon, the Republican candidate, Mr. Kennedy proved as drivingly perfectionist as he had been during the primary races. He traveled the country, tightening up the party organization, settling squabbles and dismissing incompetents. He even silenced Frank Sinatra, the singer, and Walter Reuther, head of the United Auto Workers, whom he considered liabilities to his brother.

In addition to these tasks, Mr. Kennedy advised his brother on tactics. He was also responsible, according to Mr. Quirk's book, for John Kennedy's intervention in the Martin Luther King case. As Mr. Quirk related it, this is what happened:

"The Rev. Martin Luther King was arrested for staging a sit-in at a department store in Atlanta, and was forthwith sentenced to four months of hard labor in a Georgia pentitentiary. This event occurred a scant week before the election.

Prompted Call to Mrs. King

"Bobby saw to it that J.F.K. called Mrs. King to offer comfort. Then Bobby called the judge who had sentenced Dr. King. Shortly afterward, the Negro leader was freed on bail, and a member of the King family declared, 'I've got a suitcase of votes, and I'm going to take them to Mr. Kennedy and dump them in his lap.'"

After John Kennedy defeated Mr. Nixon — the popular vote margin was 119,000 out of 68 million cast — he appointed his brother Attorney General. Robert Kennedy was reluctant at first, saying, "Everything I do will rub off on the President." He was also sensitive to the likely charge that the appointment was nepotic.

John Kennedy, however, wanted his brother in the Cabinet as an absolutely loyal and dependable confidant. In public, when criticism of the appointment mounted, the President explained his choice almost flippantly. "I can't see that it's wrong to give him a little legal experience before he goes out to practice law," he said.

Mr. Kennedy's term as Attorney General touched many sensitive areas of the nation's life — civil rights, immigration, crime, labor legislation, defense of the poor, pardons, economic monopoly, juvenile delinquency and the Federal judiciary.

In the opinion of his staff — and he recruited a brilliant group that included Byron R. White, now a Supreme Court justice, and Nicholas deB. Katzenbach, now Deputy Secretary of State — Mr. Kennedy was imaginative and inspiring. His relationship with J. Edgar Hoover, director of the Federal Bureau of Investigation, was reportedly more formal than cordial after Mr. Kennedy made it known that he was Mr. Hoover's superior in fact as well as in theory.

Conspicuously active in civil rights, Mr. Kennedy, among other achievements, exerted the Federal force that permitted James H. Meredith, a black student, to enroll in the University of Mississippi in 1962.

And owing to his relationship with the President, he had a hand in virtually every phase of the Administration. "Call Bobby, get together with him and come back with an idea on this," was a frequent White House order.

In foreign affairs, he was an especially close adviser. He investigated the Central Intelligence Agency after the Cuban Bay of Pigs fiasco in 1961. In the Cuban missile crisis the next year he opposed a pre-emptive air strike on Cuba and advocated the policy of restrained toughness that allowed the Soviet Union to retreat gracefully.

Mr. Kennedy was lunching at his home in McLean, Va., on Nov. 22, 1963, when he was informed of his brother's assassination in Dallas. Stunned, his shoulders drooping, his face solemn, he was at the airport when the Presidential plane landed in Washington with the President's body, his widow, Jacqueline, and the new President, Lyndon B. Johnson. During the public rites that preceded the funeral, he never left his sister-in-law's side. In the long, slow procession from the White House to St. Matthew's Cathedral, he and his brother Edward, a Senator from Massachusetts, walked on either side of her. And at Arlington National Cemetery both brothers helped her light an eternal flame over the grave.

Plunged Into Deep Grief

The assassination plunged Mr. Kennedy into a deep grief that amounted virtually to melancholy. His face was a mask; sadness enveloped his eyes; he seemed to have shrunk physically, and he often walked alone, his hands dug into his jacket pockets. And for the remainder of his life he lived with thoughts of his dead brother never far from the surface of his mind. When Dr. King was assassinated earlier this year, Mr. Kennedy was speaking at a political rally. Almost by reflex action he offered the family his condolences and remarked that he could understand their feeling of sudden loss because he himself had undergone a similar shock over his brother.

When his lassitude lifted, he set out to replan his political life. For a time in 1964 there was speculation that he might be President Johnson's running mate that fall. Whatever hopes he had, however, were dispelled when Mr. Johnson ruled out all Cabinet members as Vice-Presidential material. Displeased, Mr. Kennedy resigned to run for the Senate from New York; and, establishing residence, he put into operation the political structure he had erected for his brother in 1960 and won the nomination without difficulty.

His opponent was Senator Kenneth B. Keating, the incumbent Republican, who sought to picture Mr. Kennedy as a grasping carpetbagger. "Isn't the basic question 'Who can best represent the State of New York?'" Mr. Kennedy retorted. And to the charge of being sinister, he replied:

"I like to be involved in politics. I like to be involved in government. I've been in politics all my life. I would like to remain in government. I don't think that's so sinister."

He defeated Mr. Keating by 800,000 votes in a campaign that demonstrated the visceral appeal he had for voters. In the Senate (and a national figure in his own right) he forged a position slightly to the left of Mr. Johnson on the problems of the poor and the cities. He also sought to develop moderately "dovish" views on the war in Vietnam, but his opposition to Mr. Johnson on this issue always remained cautious.

It was so restrained, indeed, that he held back from contesting for the Presidential nomination of 1968 until after the New Hampshire primary on March 12 showed the extent of voter disaffection with the war.

Thereafter, however, he fought keenly for the nomination, winning major primaries in Indiana, Nebraska and California.

Campaigning with him was his wife, the former Miss Ethel Skakel of Greenwich, Conn., to whom he was married in 1950. Mrs. Kennedy is expecting their 11th child in January.

Their other children are Kathleen Harrington, 16; Joseph Patrick, 15; Robert Francis, 15; David Anthony, 12; Mary Courtney, 11; Michael Lemoyne, 10; Mary Kerry, 8; Christopher George, 4; Matthew Maxwell, 3, and Douglas Harriman, 14 months.

Robert Kennedy with his brother, President John F. Kennedy, in Washington in 1963.

"All the News That's Fit to Print"

The New York Times

LATE CITY EDITION

Weather: Cloudy, rain likely today, tonight. Partly cloudy tomorrow. Temp. range: today 71-77; Saturday 72-77. Full U.S. report on Page 95.

SECTION ONE

VOL. CXX . No. 41,504 · © 1971 The New York Times Company · NEW YORK, SUNDAY, SEPTEMBER 12, 1971 · 75¢ beyond 50-mile zone from New York City, except Long Island. Higher in air delivery cities. · BQLI · 50 CENTS

The New York Times/William E. Sauro

PANTHER LEADER ARRIVES AT ATTICA: Bobby G. Seale, in dark jacket, and Van Taylor, hurrying past state troopers into the troubled state prison late last night.

TO OUR READERS

Today The New York Times begins a separate section, 1-A, on Brooklyn, Queens and Long Island. It contains news and features of interest to readers in these areas and appears in copies distributed in Brooklyn, Queens and Nassau and Suffolk Counties.

Amnesty Demand Is Called Snag in Attica Prison Talks

By FRED FERRETTI

Special to The New York Times

ATTICA, N. Y., Sept. 11—State correction authorities were described today as being willing to grant most of the demands made by the more than 1,000 inmates who have controlled the interior compound of the Attica Correctional Facility and have held 33 guards hostage since Thursday morning.

In describing negotiations under way, however, William M. Kunstler, the lawyer, said state authorities were unwilling to grant complete amnesty from criminal charges that might stem from the three-day uprising, which has wrecked parts of the interior of this maximum-security prison.

The prisoners were adamant in their demand for amnesty, Mr. Kunstler said. Other observers with the lawyer, who asked not to be named, said they agreed with his assessment.

But the question of complete amnesty may have been cast into doubt late last night when it was disclosed that a guard who had been a hostage and who had reportedly been thrown by convicts from a second-floor cellblock window in Thursday's rioting had died in a Rochester hospital.

And the arrival at night of Bobby G. Seale, the chairman of the Black Panther party, added to the complicated negotiating process.

Seale spent two hours in the prison before he departed at 10:30, saying he would return in the morning. Other negotiators left soon afterward. They, too, will return, but they will remain on call during the night as the inmates discuss the demands and offers.

The dead guard had been one of 12 guards hospitalized from injuries received during the take-over. Six have been released.

A delegation from among an observer team invited to the prison by the inmates met with the Wyoming County District Attorney, Louis James, in an effort to determine just what degree of amnesty could be given the prisoners. The inmates earlier had rejected several promises of "administrative" amnesty from State Correction Commissioner Russell G. Oswald and a Federal Court injunction guaranteeing such amnesty.

The delegation, part of a 24-man observer team that spent many hours in the Cellblock

Continued on Page 72, Column 1

LUNA 18'S SIGNAL IS LOST ON MOON

'Unlucky Landing' by Soviet Unmanned Craft Ends a Mission of Nine Days

Special to The New York Times

MOSCOW, Sept. 11—The Soviet Union's latest effort to explore the moon's surface with an unmanned spacecraft ended in failure today as Luna 18 lost contact with the earth upon landing.

A brief Tass dispatch said that Luna 18, which was launched nine days ago, had planned to put down in a mountainous area near the Sea of Fertility but that the "moon landing in these difficult topographical conditions was unlucky."

According to the Soviet press agency, communications with the craft stopped at 10:48 A.M., Moscow time (3:48 A.M., New York time). This was believed to be the time it landed.

The Tass description left the impression that the impact on the lunar surface had knocked the sensitive equipment out of service. But it was impossible to determine whether the craft had crashed onto the moon or had simply hit it at a wrong angle.

No details on the objectives of the Luna mission have been made public, in keeping with the usual Soviet secrecy about its space launchings. Western scientific specialists in Moscow had speculated that Luna 18 was supposed to follow up the

Continued on Page 30, Column 1

THIEU PROMISES TO QUIT IF HE FAILS TO WIN MAJORITY

On TV, He Opens Unopposed Campaign for President as a Confidence Test

By ALVIN SHUSTER

Special to The New York Times

SAIGON, South Vietnam, Sept. 11 — President Nguyen Van Thieu officially opened his unopposed Presidential campaign tonight by saying that he would resign from office if he received less than 50 per cent of the votes cast on Oct. 3.

The voters who oppose him, he said in a television speech, could cast "irregular" ballots, which he would consider as votes of nonconfidence. But he did not explain to the South Vietnamese how they could render their ballots "irregular."

Other officials have said, however, that a voter could do so only by mutilating the ballot or by throwing it away and putting an empty envelope in the ballot box.

Not Easy to Understand

"As I want everything to be clear-cut," Mr. Thieu said in his speech. "I will consider an irregular ballot a ballot expressing nonconfidence. Therefore, at the counting of the votes, I will consider all regular ballots as expressing confidence and all irregular ballots as expressing nonconfidence. This will be a clear way for me to assess your confidence or nonconfidence."

This distinction will not be easy to understand for most South Vietnamese, who are relative newcomers to elections.

Accordingly, most observers and diplomats expect Mr. Thieu to have no trouble in meeting his percentage goal and gaining re-election to another four-year term, barring unforeseen events, such as a coup d'état, between now and election day.

A spokesman for the American Embassy, which tried to bring about a contest in the presidential election, said tonight it "was studying" Mr. Thieu's speech.

Bunker Meets With Thieu

Ambassador Ellsworth Bunker apparently received a copy this morning when he called on Mr. Thieu.

Sources suggested that Mr. Bunker also discussed with Mr. Thieu the speech in Washington yesterday by Senator Henry M. Jackson, long a supporter of the Vietnam war, who demanded that a "genuine" election be held here instead of what he called a "meaningless one-man referendum."

Senator Jackson, Democrat of Washington, indicated he would withdraw his support for military and economic aid to South

Continued on Page 3, Column 2

Khrushchev Is Dead at 77

By BERNARD GWERTZMAN

Special to the New York Times

MOSCOW, Sept. 11—Nikita S. Khruschchev, who ruled the Soviet Union with a dramatic flair for more than a decade before his ouster seven years ago by the current, more conservative Kremlin leaders, died today of a heart attack. He was 77 years old.

Associated Press

Nikita S. Khrushchev about to vote in national elections in Moscow on June 13 during his last public appearance.

Word of Mr. Khrushchev's death in a Kremlin hospital about noon was relayed to Western newsmen by friends of his family and confirmed informally by the Foreign Ministry in reply to queries.

As of 9 P.M. Moscow time—some nine hours later—there had been no official announcement of the death of the stocky man who became the head of the Soviet Communist party after Stalin's death in 1953 and who spent the next 11 years seeking to blacken the reputation and expose the crimes of the former dictator.

Stricken 4 Days Ago

Friends said that Mr. Khrushchev, who had a sclerotic condition for many years and who had been in and out of hospitals recently, suffered a heart attack about four days ago. He apparently was feeling better this morning, but about noon died in his sleep, the friends said.

His wife, Nina, and one of his daughters, Rada, were at his bedside, the friends said.

Because of the news blackout, ordinary Russians had no knowledge of the death of the man who made "peaceful coexistence" part of the world vocabulary. When told by newsmen, the reaction was much the same.

One woman said, "My God," but then continued on her business. Another woman said, "That's sad." In 24 hours, the word, however, will have spread throughout Moscow as people with short-wave radios tell their friends the news being reported from abroad.

The family said through friends that Mr. Khrushchev would be buried Monday in the Novodevichy Cemetery in Moscow, where many famous Russians, including Stalin's wife, have been interred.

As a former party and Government leader, Mr. Khrushchev would have been eligible for a full-scale state funeral, including a ceremony in Red Square and interment in the Kremlin wall.

After his forced resignation in what amounted to a Kremlin coup in October, 1964, Mr. Khrushchev lived in virtual

Continued on Page 77, Column 1

WAGE-PRICE UNIT TOLD TO PREPARE A 2D-STAGE PLAN

Nixon Seeks a Mid-October Decision—Connally Gives No Hint of New Steps

U.A.W. FOR REVIEW PANEL

Trade Pact Group Asserts U.S. Imports Surcharge Is Violation of Rules

By EDWIN L. DALE Jr.

Special to the New York Times

WASHINGTON, Sept. 11—President Nixon instructed his Cost of Living Council today to produce recommendations by Sept. 30 for the second phase of the wage-price stabilization program so that a decision can be made by mid-October.

The instructions were disclosed by Secretary of the Treasury John B. Connally after a meeting of the President and the council at the White House. Mr. Connally is chairman of the council.

In other sectors the following reactions to the President's new economic program were registered:

¶In Detroit, Leonard Woodcock, president of the United Automobile Workers, said that a major drive would be made in Congress next week for the establishment of a review board, representing labor, business and the public, to control wages and profits without governmental interference after the current freeze.

¶In Geneva, a special working group submitted a report to the Council of Representatives of the General Agreement on Tariffs and Trade stating that the United States surcharge on imports violated the organization's regulations and that GATT signatories were entitled to take counteraction against the United States.

¶In Miami Beach, Walter W. Heller, an economic adviser to President Johnson, told Democratic state chairmen and Governors that, while the Nixon economic program constituted "a bold initiative," it also represented "in a sense, a declaration of bankruptcy." Mr. Heller said the policy favored corporations over consumers.

Mr. Connally gave few indications of what his group might recommend. He said both the council and the President would continue to hold "consultations" with various private persons and groups during the decision-making period.

The Administration does not "anticipate" that it will need new legislation from Congress, "at least at this session," Mr. Connally said. The President's

Continued on Page 37, Column 1

Open Admission Dropouts Double Usual City U. Rate

By M. A. FARBER

The percentage of day freshmen who dropped out of the City University's senior colleges after the fall term in 1970 was nearly twice as high—12.4 per cent—among open-admissions freshmen as it was for their classmates.

The first official statistics, obtained as the university prepares to resume classes tomorrow for 200,000 students, show that 6.5 per cent of the freshmen who would have qualified for the senior colleges without the open admissions policy dropped out after the fall term in 1970.

No figures were available on the spring semester ending last May. Usually the dropout rate is 2 to 4 per cent higher in the spring term than in the fall semester.

The open-admissions plan, which assures a place in the university to any high school graduate in the city regardless of his grades, began in 1970. In the fall of 1969, a total of 7.7 per cent of the senior college freshmen dropped out; in the fall of 1968, the figure was 6.8 per cent.

Other new statistics, based on tests given by the university last spring to 28,000 volunteers among the 60,000 applicants for freshmen admission in 1971, indicate that more freshmen will need remedial work this year than last year.

Top officials of the university said yesterday that it was too early to gauge accurately the progress of open admissions during its first year.

"We're two months pregnant, in effect," said Dr. Timothy S. Healy, vice chancellor for academic affairs, "and every-

Dr. Timothy S. Healy

body wants to know if the baby has his daddy's bald spot. Well, we don't know yet."

Last May, however, university officials assessed the implementation of open admissions and their report, obtained yesterday, indicates that the

Continued on Page 34, Column 1

MISSISSIPPI CHIEF CUTS SCHOOL AID

Governor Slashes Funds for Jackson Over Compliance With a Busing Order

Special to The New York Times

JACKSON, Miss., Sept. 11—Gov. John Bell Williams of Mississippi challenged a Federal court-ordered busing plan today and issued an Executive order cutting off all state funds to the Jackson city schools.

Governor Williams said the move was intended to precipitate a legal showdown to eliminate all busing in the state of Mississippi and return to the neighborhood school concept.

His action was based on a 1953 state law that forbids the busing of students within a city or municipality.

[In Washington, a Justice Department source said the Nixon Administration was likely to seek a court order requiring Mississippi to show why it should not be forced to release school funds to Jackson.]

Fred Banks, a staff member of the N.A.A.C.P. Legal Defense and Educational Fund, Inc., which concurred in the Federal court plan providing busing in Jackson, said today that the Supreme Court "long ago de-

Continued on Page 25, Column 1

Today's Sections

*Included in all copies distributed in New York City and its suburban area.

**Included in all copies distributed in New York City and suburban area, except Manhattan.

Index to Subjects

Dorothea Lange

Dust-bowl refugees arriving in California, the Promised-Land-on-the-Pacific, in 1936. Last year, for the first time in century, about as many people moved out of as moved in. In mid-sixties it drew thousands of migrants a day.

Many Californians Leaving as Glamour Wanes

By STEVEN V. ROBERTS

Special to The New York Times

LOS ANGELES, Sept. 11—Thirteen years ago, Ardis Evans came to California when her father was transferred here from Minneapolis. In time she got married and had three children. Her husband's dental laboratory thrived and they bought a four-bedroom house in the suburbs.

But they did not live happily ever after. Now, Donald and Ardis Evans are moving to Yakima, Wash. They have had it with California. Mrs. Evans explained why:

"There are several things—smog, six million people, and the fact that when we wanted to go out for recreation we either had to drive two or three hours to get there, or go 20 minutes to Disneyland and spend a fortune. We're more of the outdoor type; we like hunting and fishing and camping, and that's what the Yakima area will be able to give us."

The Evanses are not alone. Last year, for the first time in this century, about as many people moved out of California as moved in. Estimates differ—some economists say there was actually a net loss from migration—but the situation is clear. The Golden State, which drew 1,000 net migrants a day in the mid-sixties, has grown tarnished. Like an aging movie star, the Promised-Land-on-the-Pacific has lost its allure.

"California always had some great attraction, something glamorous about," said James Lewis, director of research for

Continued on Page 66, Column 1

Minimum Wages Elude U.S. Farm Help

By DONALD JANSON

Special to The New York Times

EARLE, Ark., Sept. 8—Five years after Federal minimum wage legislation was extended to agriculture, thousands of farm workers still labor for pay well below the legal minimum of $1.30 an hour.

From the cotton plantations of the South to the cherry orchards of Michigan, from the blueberry fields of North Carolina to the apple ranches of the West, illegally low pay scales are not hard to find.

Here in the rich soil of the Mississippi River delta, a housewife weeds soybeans for 55 cents an hour.

In a large California prune orchard, migrants get the equivalent of a dollar an hour at piece rates.

In Michigan, members of a Texas crew toil for 70 cents an hour in the strawberry fields.

All were on farms large enough to be covered by the minimum wage law. On smaller farms, which employ two-thirds of all hired farm labor and are not covered by the law, the pay is usually even less.

At the Michael Moran apple ranch at Sebastopol, Calif., for example, Alex Lopez and his family recently averaged 37 cents an hour each for stooping to gather yellow Gravensteins from the ground.

A Senate Labor subcommittee will hold hearings Wednesday on proposed legislation to raise the minimum and tighten provisions in the existing law that exempt all but 2 per cent of the country's farms.

But to make even the present law wholly effective, Federal officials concede, enforcement would have to be strengthened.

The Labor Department provides few investigators to check up on covered farms. Few harvesters complain of il-

Continued on Page 54, Column 1

The New York Times

A girl carrying apples on farm on West Coast.

Khrushchev Dies at 77 of a Heart Attack

Continued From Page 1, Col. 7

isolation and was rarely mentioned in Soviet publications His record was often criticized by current leaders who found him too erratic in his work and too domineering in his style of leadership.

He lived most of the last seven years in a fenced-in estate at Petrovo-Dalneye, a pine-studded village some 15 miles west of Moscow. He also maintained an apartment in an old part of the capital But in recent years, because of his poor health, he rarely came into the city.

His living expenses were paid by the state, and he had a full retinue of security guards. His actions were limited and he was not usually permitted to go freely into public places.

The last time he was seen by Western newsmen was on June 13, when he and his wife arrived at their polling place in Moscow to cast their obligatory votes for the local candidate to the Supreme Soviet of the Russian Republic. Asked how he felt, he replied, "Good." Asked what he was doing these days. he said:

"I'm a pensioner. What do pensioners do?"

His death poses something of a problem to Leonid I. Brezhnev, who replaced him as party leader; Aleksei N. Kosygin, who took over as Premier, and the other members of the 15-man Politburo.

They must decide whether to allow Mr. Khrushchev to be eulogized for his past work or to maintain their virtual silence about him. The plans for a private funeral indicate that the current leaders have decided against any radical move to rehabilitate him.

Moreover, Mr. Khrushchev lived under something of a cloud after the publication abroad last year of "Khrushchev Remembers," which is said to contain Mr. Khrushchev's own recollections about certain incidents in his life. The Soviet Union has officially repudiated the book, and Mr. Khrushchev last November was obliged to sign a statement terming it "a fabrication."

The appearance of that book, however, forced authorities here to lift temporarily the ban on the use of Mr. Khrushchev's name in the press and on the air. Tass, the Soviet press agency, distributed his short statement, and the Moscow radio broadcast it—the first time his name had been heard in a broadcast since his ouster.

But Mr. Khrushchev's name has not been eliminated completely. Official party histories still note that "N. S. Khrushchev" was First Secretary from 1953 to 1964. Records of World War II take note of his participation in the Ukrainian front.

He is still regarded ambiguously by Soviet intellectuals. They praise him for his anti-Stalin campaign and his efforts to rehabilitate those wrongly condemned. But they criticized him for vulgarity boorishness, and meddling in the arts and sciences, which were considered beyond his competence.

When he was ousted in 1964, many liberal intellectuals believed that the new leadership would improve the climate. But since Mr. Brezhnev has partly rehabilitated Stalin as a wartime leader and has not given intellectuals the freedom they sought, Mr. Khrushchev in retrospect has gained more respect.

Khrushchev: Shift in Soviet Path

By HARRISON E. SALISBURY

An Appraisal

A young Russian émigré — a leader of underground dissidents—said a few days in New York: "Russia owes more to Nikita Sergeyevich than to any other man of our time. But of course no one will say it until he's dead."

What he meant was that Nikita S. Khrushchev, with all his faults, his fiery temper, his gambler's instinct, his braggadocio, had taken the "seven seals" off the Pandora's box that was Stalin's legacy to the Soviet Union. And no one, the young émigré felt, would ever be able to put them back again.

Some may doubt the permanency of the Soviet Union's turn from the oppression of the Stalin era. But few in or out of the Soviet Union can doubt the magnitude of Khrushchev's feat in putting his country on a new course.

It is nearly seven years since Khrushchev fell. His fall, like his rise, was melodramatic. He was toppled by the same close associates who helped him to high office. During the seven years his successors have slowly inched away from the free wheeling and erratic, but essentially liberalizing, tendency of the one-time peasant boy from Kalinovka.

What Khrushchev did for his country was no easy thing He said in the course of one of his endless disquisitions: "You have no idea how hard it is to be a politician. It is the hardest job in the world." Perhaps nowhere was it harder than in Russia, with its unbroken tradition—from czars to commissars—of arbitrary rule, palace intrigue and untrammeled exercise of power.

What Khrushchev did during the decade in which he was first among equals in the post-Stalin collective leadership is easier to relate than why he did it. In part surely it was a pent-up personal drive for power, accentuated by the years under Stalin when he was compelled to humble himself, playing the poor Ukrainian fool and, as he once said, to "dance the gopak."

But there was more to it. He was a man of insatiable curiosity and endless energy. He could not sit still. He could not stand still. He could not stop talking. And his small eyes bored into everything he saw. What he saw, he wanted for his country—whether it was pigeons in the streets of Moscow (as he had seen in London); helicopters to transport the Kremlin leaders (as his friend, as he called President Eisenhower, had), or more meat in the goulash, as he once told the Hungarians.

And he did not care what rules, what traditions, what precedents he broke in the process. He counted himself a thorough Marxist a prime believer in the Communist system, and he was everlastingly, childishly, naively determined that the Soviet Union was going to outpace the world.

He had come up the hard way—almost the hardest of ways—and he never lost the direct peasant habits of his boyhood. No world statesman but Khrushchev would have spent his first hour with Vice President Nixon in a countryboy bragging contest as to who had shoveled the most and worst kinds of manure as a barefoot farm boy No world statesman would have felt such utter disappointment at not going to Disneyland that great tears formed in the corners of his eyes. Nor is it likely that any other world statesman would have publicly threatened Jovian retaliation of missiles if Henry Cabot Lodge did not manage to treat him with a bit more politeness.

Why did he denounce Stalin —and denounce him in such a way that for all the endeavor of a thousand bureaucrats the Communist party's Central Committee has not been able to put Stalin even halfway back on the pedestal again? After his fall, Khrushchev talked about that to his intimates. It had to be done, he said. It had to be done if the Soviet Union was ever to compete in the modern world. And, of course, although he never said so, he probably thought that it would give him not only a winning edge over his rivals but a permanent one.

He could not make it permanent because for all his boldness, his rashness—and genuine cruelty in carrying out Stalin's orders—he was not himself a killer. He would not kill his rivals. Nor would he put them into prison. There were victims after Stalin, but those who were killed were policemen, Lavrenti P. Beria and his henchmen.

Since he would not kill, Khrushchev was vulnerable. He began to lose power long before it was publicly apparent. He told a questioner only two years ago that the critical moment was the U-2 incident in May, 1960. That incident torpedoed his fondest dream—the visit of President Eisenhower to the Soviet Union and, as he hoped, establishment of a Soviet-American condominium in the world. He had everything arranged for the President's trip, down to a secretly constructed golf course in the Crimea and special villas to entertain him in Siberia. There may even have been a Soviet version of Disneyland.

All that went down the drain with the U-2. From then on he fought and fought, but he never got back his power base.

He has bequeathed to his country the heritage of dimensions that only his death will begin to make visible. Much of his philosophy, many of his ideas for the Soviet Union's future—particularly for a freer, more humane, more contemporary, more liberal land—were encompassed in a curious volume published a few months ago, "Khrushchev Remembers." There almost certainly is a more specific, more detailed, more reliable testament left behind for his countrymen to read.

But greater than this is the testament he left to the world: A Soviet Union that for all its backsliding is not Stalin's terror state and a world that has perceived that it is possible to live and work and cooperate with the Soviet Union, regardless of ideology.

Khrushchev thought much about the future and about how the world would regard him. He once planned a pantheon in which to bury all the great Communists of the world. Later he succeeded in removing Stalin from beside Lenin in the Red Square mausoleum. The day may come when his countrymen will sense that if interment is a recognition of national leadership then Khrushchev has won a place close to—if not beside—Lenin.

Mrs. Khrushchev a Familiar Figure

The New York Times

Mrs. Khrushchev in a visit to Beltsville, Md., in 1959

Mrs. Nina Petrovna Khrushchev was at her husband's bedside when he died, remaining close to him, as she had ever since their marriage in 1924.

The 71-year-old wife of the former Soviet Premier, unlike the wives of other Soviet officials, emerged from the obscurity of the Stalin era to become a public figure in her own right.

She frequently accompanied her husband on diplomatic missions abroad, culminating in their trip to the United States in September, 1959.

While they were here, they were seen everywhere together, crammed into the back seat of a limousine with President Eisenhower, meeting each other unexpectedly in a supermarket aisle, placing a wreath on the grave of President Roosevelt.

Her devotion to her husband was unostentatious but evident. They exchanged lingering glances in Hollywood as they listened to Frank Sinatra singing a love song. She interrupted a formal news conference at Blair House to say good-by to Mr. Khrushchev when he left for Camp David, Md.

At first, she was somewhat reserved in the face of personal questions from clamoring Western reporters, but she gradually warmed up to reveal a vivacious, witty, and self - possessed personality that won the hearts of Americans.

While Mrs. Khrushchev was here, she told reporters that she had met her husband in the city of Yuzovka, in the Ukraine, when his two children by his first marriage —a daughter, Yulia, and a son, Leonid, subsequently killed in the war—were 6 and 8 years old. His first wife, she said, died "during the famine," referring apparently to the famines early in the nineteen twenties.

Three children—two daughters, Rada and Yelena, and a son, Sergei, were her own, she said.

Rada's husband, Aleksei I. Adzuhbei, was editor of the Government newspaper Izvestia and a powerful figure in the Soviet Union until he lost his post in 1964 when Mr. Khrushchev was deposed.

Red Parties Report the Death, But With Almost No Comment

In the first comment from any Communist source on the death of Nikita S. Khrushchev, a mass-circulation newspaper owned by the Italian Communist party said that his down-grading of Stalin had "unleashed Democratic forces of dissent with the old paternalistic and repressive methods that re-emerged also in the practice of the Khrushchev era."

The newspaper, Paesa Sera, printed a long biography by a former Moscow correspondent who wrote that Mr. Khrushchev's "vision was correct, but the means of applying them in practice, domestic and internationally, were outdated."

In Yugoslavia, the Belgrade press paid warm tribute to the former Soviet Leader.

The official newspaper, Borba, and the leading Belgrade daily, Politika, in early editions of Sunday's issues carried front-page reports of his death with pictures and extensive biographical notes and affectionate reminiscences on inside pages. Borba said in front page eulogy that Mr. Khrushchev had been a friend of Yugoslaves even though he sometimes offended them by displaying unjustified anger at them.

"Humanities Dimanche, the Sunday issue of the French Communist party newspaper, carried a two-column obituary on inside page. The obituary was devoted mainly to Mr. Khrushchev's youthful career. Mr. Khrushchev's years as Soviet leader was covered in nine lines of type.

There was no other comment from other Communist parties, governments or newspapers.

Khrushchev's Human Dimensions Brought Him to Power and to His Downfall

Sovfoto

Nikita S. Khrushchev, third from right, was among Soviet leaders at Stalin's bier in 1953. Others, from left: Vyacheslav M. Molotov, Kliment Y. Voroshilov, Lavrenti P. Beria, Georgi M. Malenkov, Nikolai A. Bulganin, Lazar M. Kaganovich and Anastas I. Mikoyan. Mr. Khrushchev's denunciation of Stalin as a tyrant was a turning point in Soviet history.

By ALDEN WHITMAN

LATE in the afternoon of Friday, Feb. 24, 1956, a short, rotund, round-headed, gleamingly bald, baggy-suited man stepped to the microphone at the concluding session of the 20th Congress of the Communist party of the Soviet Union, from which all foreign delegates and reporters had been excluded. "Comrades," he began in his somewhat harsh-hoarse deliberate voice, "in the report of the Central Committee of the party . . . in a number of speeches by delegates to [this] congress . . . quite a lot has been said about the cult of the individual and about its harmful consequences."

It was well after midnight when the session adjourned, and what the delegates had heard in Nikita Sergeyevich Khrushchev's 20,000-word speech was nothing less than a documented, count-by-count indictment of Josef Stalin, then dead about three years and who for a quarter-century had been held up to the Soviet people, Communist and non-Communist, and to Communists throughout the world as the infallible genius-leader of his country who had advanced it unerringly toward Socialism.

What some delegates may have suspected but refused to credence, Mr. Khrushchev, the First Secretary (chief) of the Soviet party, laid bare with whiplash candor — that Stalin, starting with the terrible purge years of the thirties, had brought about the deaths of thousands of innocent persons; that he had ruled the party and the country by terror and torture; that he had been pusillanimous in World War II; that he had become increasingly vainglorious to the point even of writing his own encomiums, and that he had set up "serious obstacle[s] in the path of Soviet social development." Some of the details were overdrawn, but the portrait was unmistakably horrifying.

Thus, the burden of the speech was to put the blame for the evils of Stalinism on Stalin's personal shortcomings, while seeking to make clear that the dictator's associates, including many of those on the congress podium — and the speaker himself — had been powerless alter those terrible events.

Speech Widely Circulated

Although this extraordinary speech was never printed in the Soviet press, it was circulated to an astonished public through the Communist party apparatus and marked the start of a 10-year de-Stalinization of Soviet life. The speech was widely published in the West (the United States State Department obtained a copy from Yugoslav sources and made it available to newspapers) and it started a chain reaction in the reassessment of Soviet Communism.

In speaking out with such uncompromising bluntness, Mr. Khrushchev exhibited some of the brash daring that characterized his 10 years (from 1954 to 1964) as one of the world's most powerful men. The risk was obvious: Could Stalin's reputation be denigrated without destroying the structure of the system that had made him possible? Mr. Khrushchev gambled that it could — and he won, although many observers doubted that he had calculated all the implications of his bravura speech.

Apart from presiding over the vast changes in Soviet and Communist policy that flowed from de-Stalinization (no less profound for the comparatively quiet manner in which they were carried out), Mr. Khrushchev put new emphasis on the bread-and-butter goals of Communism. ("And what sort of Communist society is it that has no sausage?" he often asked.)

Moreover, under the compulsions of the hydrogen bomb, he championed a policy of peaceful coexistence (symbolized in the 1963 nuclear test ban treaty) between Socialist and capitalist states, questioning the popular dictum that war between them was probably inevitable. (He was certain that Communism could provide more abundance than capitalism and would triumph in a peaceful world on account of its material attractions.)

Mr. Khrushchev also accepted some national differences among Socialist countries, as in the mixed economies of Poland and Yugoslavia; but not in Hungary, where he dealt with attempted revolt in 1956 as counterrevolution. Outside the Soviet sphere in Eastern Europe, he was less flexible. He tolerated Castroism for Cuba, but not as a model for South American revolutions. He had much less use for the Chinese way to Socialism and exacerbated the split in the Communist world in an acidulous quarrel with Peking over economic aid, the proper strategy against American "imperialism" and the Sino-Soviet borders.

Mr. Khrushchev introduced a new style into Soviet politics. Whereas Stalin was reclusive, his successor was a tireless traveler and speaker who became intimately acquainted with the cities, towns and villages of his country. Moreover, he obliged his deskbound associates to get out of their offices, admonishing them not to be afraid "to get mud on your boots." In creating a personal sense of hustle and sweat, he was practicing what he preached when he told a Communist leader that the way to success was "Be popular."

Just as he journeyed about his own country and Eastern Europe, so he traveled extensively in the world outside. As a traveling salesman for Soviet policy (and by implication for Communism) he initiated a personal diplomacy that took him to China, India, Britain, France, Switzerland, Austria and the United States. In two visits to this country, he conferred with President Dwight D. Eisenhower in 1959, trekked to California, shucked corn in Iowa, appeared on television; and in the fall of 1960 he was here for a meeting of the United Nations Assembly, at which, in a fit of pique, he took off his right shoe and banged it vigorously on his desk.

Behind these travels was not only his voracity for firsthand knowledge of people and events but also a belief that

Associated Press

Mr. Khrushchev was greeted by Mao Tse-tung in Peking in 1954. Their quarrels became increasingly bitter and worsened split in the Communist world.

statesmen could and should deal with one another face to face. It was in that vein that he cooperated in the establishing of a "hot line" between the White House and the Kremlin in President John F. Kennedy's Administration.

Some of the very extrovert traits that gave Mr. Khrushchev his human dimensions accounted for his downfall. By nature an impatient and impulsive man, he promised his people more than he could deliver. With two excellent harvests in 1956 and 1958, he pledged in 1959 that in seven years the per capita real income of Soviet citizens would rise by 40 per cent and that the minimum wage would be doubled. There would also be a 40-hour week. And by 1970, agriculture and industry would be producing more than their American counterparts. The Soviet Union was embarking on a new stage of its history — the "full-scale construction of Communist society."

One of the keys to the new era of plenty was a gigantic stride in meat and grain production. But try and improvise as he might, he could not achieve an output to match his grandiose expectations. He flew in the face of experts by trying to grow corn in unsuitable areas, in opening up so-called virgin lands in Siberia and in too-hasty reorganization of the cumbersome farm and industrial bureaucracy. The result was that economic and bureaucratic dislocation contributed heavily to his ouster. And not the least of those who turned against him were the bureaucrats whose traditional ways and power relationships he threatened.

Another ingredient in Mr. Khrushchev's ouster was the failure of his gamble in the Cuban missile crisis of 1962 to pay off. Although he claimed at the time to have obtained what he wanted — an American pledge not to attack Cuba — many in the Kremlin believed that the affair was a first-class miscalculation.

He was damaged also by the American U-2 spy plane incident in 1960 and the subsequent breakup of a Paris summit meeting with President Eisenhower. After Mr. Khrushchev's first visit to the United States, he insisted to his colleagues that President Eisenhower was a reasonable man and that statesmen could promote international amity through personal understandings. This homespun theory, part of his impatience to mute the cold war, was severely strained when the U-2 was shot down over the Soviet Union and President Eisenhower took the responsibility.

For a fourth thing, his bumptious conduct then and on other occasions, such as the shoe-banging at the United Nations, embarrassed some of his associates who felt that more dignity befitted the leader of a great superpower. Some of them, too, had been bullied by their leader in explosions of temper and were delighted to vote his ouster.

Ranged against him, too, were powerful voices in the army. To allocate capital for agricultural supplies and machinery, he was obliged to cut down on spending for heavy industry and defense. The army, which had earlier supported him, was dismayed by his schemes to achieve defense at the lowest possible cost and elements of the officer corps, whose jobs were threatened, joined in the pressure against him.

Mr. Khrushchev also caused alarm by the escalation of his quarrel with Mao Tse-tung, the Chinese leader. It had long been a shibboleth of Marxist thinking that the Communist world was necessarily a single entity since it derived from a single doctrine, and the Soviet leader's China policy seemed to many Soviet and other Communists to threaten the fraternal spirit of world Communism. His handling of the Mao situation was cited specifically in his ouster.

An additional count against him was his action in splitting the Communist party into industrial and agricultural sections, to enhance party control of all aspects of the economy. The party, in effect, was to concentrate on economic, not political, tasks. The step was taken precipitately in 1962. According to Mark Frankland, a British expert on Mr. Khrushchev's fall, "the plan was bound to upset just those party officials on whom Khrushchev had to a large extent built his own power."

"In particular," Mr. Frankland noted, "it threatened the interests of the regional party bosses by splitting their domains in two and so reducing their status and influence."

Finally, there was Mr. Khrushchev's willfulness as well as what seemed an increasing tendency to take the spotlight. His enemies accused him of both lack of foresight and building a cult of personality. He did indeed push his plans through the Politburo and was unwilling to accept frustration of his ideas. And he did seem to insist on adulation.

The combination of all his shortcomings came to more than outweigh his virtues in the eyes of his colleagues, and he was pensioned off in October, 1964. But it was a measure of the changes he had wrought that he was voted out of office, not shot, and that some of his key policies, such as peaceful coexistence and arms limitation and emphasis on Soviet consumer needs, were taken up by his successors, albeit in a less flamboyant fashion.

Part of Mr. Khrushchev's success as a Soviet leader was his idiosyncratic style — his easy and infectious smile that showed the marked gap between two front teeth, his thundering anger, his earthy wit, his use of old Russian proverbs, his capacity for strong drink, his rapport with workers and farmers. When he talked he jabbed his chubby fingers at the chest of the person listening to him, and he could say some impolitic things, such as telling Western diplomats at the Kremlin, "History is on our side—we will bury you." Or telling an envoy from a Mediterranean country, "Get out of NATO or we will drop a nuclear bomb on you." When the ambassador protested that "you are such a big country and we are such a small country," Mr. Khrushchev replied, "That's all right. For you we will use only a teeny tiny nuclear bomb."

Impatient With Theory

He was uncomfortable with intellectuals and impatient with abstract theory —both attitudes that reflected his own life—and his Marxism was one described as a set of rather simple maxims in which he believed deeply.

This uneasiness with speculation for its own sake enabled him to concentrate on practicality, but it also led into situations in which he relied overmuch on theoreticians. For example, he gave his blessing to publication of Aleksandr Solzhenitsyn's "One Day in the Life of Ivan Denisovich," a book that let some air into Soviet writing about life under Stalin. But he also went along with the 1958 conservative ideological attack on Boris Pasternak for his novel "Doctor Zhivago," which portrayed scenes of the Bolshevik Revolution.

Later, however, in retirement, Mr. Khrushchev found time to read the book and told a Soviet friend that he did not understand what the fuss had been all about. "We could have published that book," he said. "Maybe 200 words were questionable — that's all."

It was as a practical man that Mr. Khrushchev rose from lowly beginnings to the top in the Communist hierarchy. He was born April 17, 1894, in the mud hut of his grandfather in Kalinovka, a poor village in Kursk Province, where Great Russia borders on the Ukraine.

"My grandfather was a serf, the property of a landlord who could sell him if he wished, or trade him for a hunting dog," Mr. Khrushchev once recalled.

"My father was a farmer who worked in the [coal] mines in the winter in the hope that he would some day earn enough money to buy a horse, so that he could raise enough cabbage and potatoes to feed his family.

"As for myself, I began working as soon as I could walk. I herded calves, then sheep, and finally the landlord's cows, until I was 15. Then I went with my father to the coalfields of the Donbas to work in the shops and mines. I worked at a factory owned by the Germans, at coal pits owned by Frenchmen and at a chemical plant owned by Belgians. There I discovered something about capitalists. They are all alike, whatever their nationality. All they wanted from me was the most work for the least money that would keep me alive.

"So I became a Communist . . . I was not born a Communist . . . But life is a great school. It thrashes and bangs and teaches you."

In his brief account of his early years, Mr. Khrushchev omitted to mention that he had not joined the Bolshevik party until 1918, about a year after the outbreak of the Russian Revolution. He had escaped conscription during World War I because he was a skilled worker and he had helped to organize strikes among the Donbas miners. Once the Revolution began in the late winter of 1917, Mr. Khrushchev was active in practical measures in its defense and was a member of the Rutchenkovo Soviet.

In the civil war Mr. Khrushchev fought as a member of the Red Guards, working in the political department of the Ninth Army in the Ukraine. His job was to form Communist units among the troops. Having joined the party from practical rather than theoretical considerations, he was well suited to recruit others who saw the party chiefly as the defender of "their" revolution.

On his 1959 visit to the United States Mr. Khrushchev illuminated his feelings in those early years by recalling one of his first meetings with intellectuals "when I still had coal on my hands." One of them, a woman, twitted him about the ballet. "And I must admit that at that time," he reminisced, "I not only had never seen a ballet; I had never seen a ballerina. So I did not know what it — what sort of a dish it was and what you ate it with.

"And I said, 'Wait, it will all come. If she were to have asked me then what it was that would come, I could not have given her any reply—I did not know what would come. But I did know that the new and the good happy life would come."

When the civil war ended, Mr. Khrushchev returned to Rutchenkovo as a party organizer. His first wife, whom he married in 1916, died, it is said, in the famine of 1921, but this aspect of his life was obscure. His climb up the party ladder began in earnest in 1922, when he was sent to the Don Technical College at Yuzovka to remedy his lack of formal education and to become acquainted with Marxism.

At the college he was named party secretary, a post of considerable importance that he held for three years. He also remarried. His wife, Nina, who accompanied him to the United States, was a schoolteacher and is believed to have smoothed some of his rough edges.

On graduation, Mr. Khrushchev was appointed party secretary at Petrovo-Marinsky, a mining district in the Ukraine, where he distinguished himself for his bustling, first-hand knowledge of the mines. He was then under the patronage of Lazar M. Kaganovich, Stalin's man in the Ukraine, and as such attended his first party congress—the 14th—in Moscow in 1925.

Stalin was then consolidating his hold on the party—Lenin had died in 1924 —and was moving against his political enemies. Mr. Khrushchev, the records show, supported Stalin without apparent reservations, and in a speech at the Ukrainian party congress in 1926 endorsed the notion of "repressive measures" against Leon Trotsky, Grigory Zinovyev and Lev Kamenev.

Meantime, he moved up in the party apparatus, first to Kharkov and then to Kiev. Finally, in 1929 he was called to Moscow as a student at the Academy of Heavy Industry.

Still backed by Mr. Kaganovich, he was named party secretary at the academy and then, after a year, secretary of the district in which the academy was located. His rise was meteoric: second in command of the Moscow city party in 1933; its chief in 1934; membership in the party's Central Committee the same year, making him one of a hundred or so most powerful men in the Soviet Union, and in 1935 party leader for the entire Moscow region.

Mr. Khrushchev's principal job was in the modernization of Moscow and especially in the construction of its subway, for which he received his first Order of Lenin. No detail seemed too small for him—seeing to the cement supply, advising on the proper height for laying bricks, suggesting changes in subway-car design. His definition then of a "real Communist" was one "whose work is organized, whose machinery works and doesn't lie abandoned under all kinds of rubbish" and who "each day, each hour controls matters effectively."

Mr. Khrushchev's exertions in Moscow coincided with what has been called the Soviet Union's "Iron Age"—a period when heavy industry and industrial construction were stressed as part of Stalin's goal to build Socialism in one country, which meant making the Soviet Union as strong as possible in as brief a time as possible. It was also a period of forced collectivization of agriculture, in which hundreds of thousands of peasants died, and of the "show trials" in which Stalin's opponents were obliged to confess to horrendous crimes before they were executed. Of the 139 members of the Central Committee elected with Mr. Khrushchev in 1934, about 100 were arrested and shot by 1938.

Not a Stalin Intimate

Mr. Khrushchev appears to have been as extravagant in his praise for Stalin during the purges as any party leader, but he was not then a Stalin intimate. Of his activities and thoughts during the purges, he was extremely guarded. Indeed, he was later to suggest that he was ignorant of Stalin's murder of innocent Communists. Speaking in 1963, he said:

"It is asked, did the leading cadres of the party know of, let us say, the arrests of people at the time? Yes, they knew. But did they know that people who were innocent of any wrongdoing were arrested? No. This they did not know. They believed Stalin and did not admit the thought that repression could be applied to honest people devoted to our cause."

Having survived the worst of the purges, Mr. Khrushchev was elected to the Politburo in 1938 and dispatched to the Ukraine as first secretary of the party there. The party leadership in the Ukraine was replaced and a membership purge undertaken. Mr. Khrushchev was both Stalin's scourge and the one who helped rebuild a shattered party. His toughness is said to have been unrelenting also in managing the Ukrainian economy.

The Ukraine gave Mr. Khrushchev his first concentrated experience with agriculture, for that country was (and is) one of the Soviet Union's chief grain areas. Improving the harvests provided scope for his initiative and administrative talents. He got out among the farmers and in his unsubtle but effective fashion stirred the party to such activity that the grain yield rose. And although he was away from Moscow, he came to

Associated Press

On visit to U.S. in 1959, the Soviet Premier admired corn on Iowa farm of Roswell Garst. One of his key problems was inadequate Soviet food production.

A Kitchen Debate With a Future President, Coexistence and a Visit to America

be regarded as a farm expert and his speeches were reprinted in Pravda, the party newspaper.

The Nazi invasion of the Soviet Union in June, 1941 hit hard at the Ukraine — and at Mr. Khrushchev. According to Mr. Frankland's biography. "The shock of the first disastrous months of the war had its impact, too, on Khrushchev's relations with Stalin."

"Up to the war," Mr. Frankland wrote, "there is no evidence that Khrushchev ever questioned his leader, but this simple relationship was destroyed by the war, and was never re-established. It is possible that Khrushchev's belief in Stalin's infallibility was first shaken at the very start of the war."

During the war, Mr. Khrushchev not only represented the party at the front but also directed partisan warfare behind the German lines. He took part in the initial severe setbacks of the Soviet Army in the Ukraine and in the triumphant stand at Stalingrad in 1942. For his efforts at Stalingrad, one of the principal hinges of the war in the Soviet Union, he was made a lieutenant general, and he marched with the Red Army as it retook the Ukraine in 1943.

After the war Mr. Khrushchev was in charge of rebuilding the Ukraine, the most damaged of any area in Europe. Americans with the United Nations Relief and Rehabilitation Agency who saw him there remarked about his concern for the tiniest detail of his jobs—he was Premier as well as party leader—and his bounciness. Milovan Djilas, the Yugoslav Communist, found him using folk proverbs and sayings to rally his associates and reported that Mr. Khrushchev "delved into details, into the daily life of the Communist rank and file and the ordinary people."

Improvement, Not Change

"He did not do this with the aim of changing the system," Mr. Djilas continued, "but of strengthening and improving things under the existing system."

Rivalries at the top of the Soviet Communist party in 1946 almost did Mr. Khrushchev in. He came into conflict with Georgi M. Malenkov over the asserted low level of "ideological work" in the Ukraine and with Stalin over spring wheat, which the dictator favored.

Mr. Kaganovich was sent into the Ukraine to run the party, while Mr. Khrushchev was left as Premier. This episode is unclear in detail, but apparently Mr. Khrushchev worked his way out of disgrace, although there were reports later that he had almost been purged by Stalin. In any event, after a year, Mr. Khrushchev improved his situation (his differences with Mr. Malenkov continued, however) and at the end of 1949 he was brought to Moscow as head of the party organization and as one of the Central Committee secretariat, which ran the party day by day.

Until Stalin's death in 1953, Mr. Khrushchev lived a somewhat precarious existence, he indicated in his secret speech of 1956. On other occasions he related that Stalin had forced him to dance a peasant dance and to sit in a puddle of beer. More seriously, the two differed about agriculture. Whereas Stalin was content to sweat the peasants, Mr. Khrushchev seemed genuinely concerned to increase party control over the farms, to create more efficient production units and to raise the standards of living.

One instance of this was his proposal in 1950 and 1951 to create "agrotowns" — grand villages that would be centers of farm life. Under criticism he called them "collective farm settlements," but this failed to save him from Mr. Malenkov and others who chided him in public in 1952. More to the point, he was relieved of supervision over farming.

At this time Stalin's paranoia was growing — a plot of distinguished Jewish doctors to kill Soviet leaders was concocted in his brain — and. Mr. Khrushchev suggested in his 1956 speech, even those closest to the dictator felt apprehensive for their safety. In these circumstances Stalin's death as the result of a stroke was timely. "I wept," Mr. Khrushchev later told W. Averell Harriman, the American diplomat. "After all, we were his pupils and owed him everything. Like Peter the Great, Stalin fought barbarism with barbarism but he was a great man."

The chubby Mr. Malenkov was Stalin's immediate successor, but in the wheeling and dealing he was either forced or persuaded to drop his job as principal party secretary while retaining the Soviet Premiership. This step gave Mr. Khrushchev his opening, for he took over virtual control of the party organization — machinery that he knew best of all. Moreover, shortly after Stalin's death, he came to the fore in a critique of agriculture, with an implied promise of a better life for all.

With the elimination by shooting of Lavrenti P. Beria, the state security chief, Mr. Khrushchev and Mr. Malenkov engaged in a duel for power with agriculture one of the main points of difference. Mr. Khrushchev's theme was the low state of farm production and the cry that "Communist society cannot be built without an abundance of bread, meat, milk, butter, vegetables and other agricultural products." And to encourage farmers, he was willing to increase money incentives and to chastise Moscow bureaucrats. When the 1953 harvest fell short of predictions, he had increased leverage against Mr. Malenkov.

At his urging, an area equal to the entire cropland of Canada — some 75 million acres — of virgin and fallow land in Siberia and the Urals was plowed and sown to grain by an army of young people sent out from the cities of European Russia. Also he called for widespread corn-planting, gaining the nickname of Nikita Kukuruznik (Nikita the Corn Man). Although these measures were denounced by some of his colleagues as gambles, they paid off heavily in 1956 and 1958, when abundant rainfall permitted the virgin lands to contribute a record grain crop. His corn proposal was less successful, chiefly because large areas of the Soviet Union were climatically unsuited for it.

By early 1955 Mr. Khrushchev had strengthened his position sufficiently to strike down Mr. Malenkov. He accomplished this in part by getting army support (he pleaded that the Soviet hydrogen bomb detonated in 1953 required stronger defenses), and in the new alignment Marshal Nikolai A. Bulganin was Premier and Mr. Khrushchev was the party leader. Together they were known as "B & K."

The maneuver that disposed of Mr. Malenkov (whose policies Mr. Khrushchev was to adopt) was one step in the development of a post-Stalin consensus. Another was dismissal of Vyacheslav M. Molotov, Stalin's longtime Foreign Minister, which culminated in his removal from power in 1957 in the so-called "antiparty" affair.

Meantime, in 1955 "B & K" made three journeys abroad. in which Mr. Khrushchev displayed his energies and his extroversions to an astonished world. One of the most important of these trips was to Belgrade, where he apologized to Marshal Tito, the Yugoslav Communist leader, for Stalin's expulsion of him from the Communist world in 1948. The reconciliation was never complete, but there was a general accommodation.

Later, "B & K" went to Geneva, where they met President Eisenhower and the leaders of France and Britain and reiterated Soviet commitment to a policy of peaceful coexistence. "Vigorous, downright and stubborn but prepared to laugh" was British Prime Minister Anthony Eden's comment on Mr. Khrushchev at Geneva.

Foothold in Mideast

One of the greatest foreign policy victories was in the Mideast. In the summer of 1955 he arranged an arms deal with Egypt that opened the way for large-scale expansion of Soviet influence among the Arab peoples. He was also successful in wooing such countries as India, which he visited, and Indonesia, praising their third-world policy of neutralism and their struggles to rise from colonial status. As a salesman for Communism, he made three points: Peaceful coexistence and economic competition; war between East and West could be avoided, and there could be different paths to Socialism, including a parliamentary one.

Although Mr. Khrushchev was clearly the chief Soviet leader from 1954, when Mr. Malenkov went into effective eclipse, his position was vastly enhanced by his "secret speech" at the party congress in 1956. Its theme—that Stalin had abused his power—skipped lightly over Mr. Khrushchev's own role and that of his principal associates. However, by emphasizing the corrective steps the party had taken since 1953 and was prepared to take, the speech cast Mr. Khrushchev in a favorable light: He was now to pursue a policy of fairness and strict legality.

And there was in fact a thaw. Thousands of Stalin's victims were posthumously rehabilitated. Criticism of Stalin appeared in print. Some of the fears in Soviet life were muted. The authority of the party, as a collective group, was strengthened, and with it the principle of collegiality. And eventually, the speech contributed to the routing of Mr. Molotov and other hard-liners inside and outside the Soviet Union.

Restiveness first showed itself in Poland in October, 1956, when the Poles proposed to install as party leader Wladislaw Gomulka, a "nationalist" Communist whom Stalin had jailed. Mr. Khrushchev flew to Warsaw and confronted Mr. Gomulka and his associates in a considerable rage, threatening the use of force to prevent a Polish defection. Mr. Gomulka, however, stood his ground and won out after pledging to keep Poland within the Moscow bloc.

Immediately thereafter trouble broke out in Hungary. A de-Stalinized government under Imre Nagy announced that Hungary would leave the Warsaw Pact, the Eastern counterpart of the North Atlantic Treaty Organization.

This, to Mr. Khrushchev's mind, amounted to counterrevolution, and the Nagy regime was crushed with Soviet tanks and replaced with a more amenable government. The difference between Poland and Hungary appeared to be that the Poles were willing to remain within the Soviet orbit, whereas the Hungarians were not.

Mr. Khrushchev's triumph over his foes was complete in 1957, when Mr. Malenkov, Mr. Kaganovich and Mr. Molotov were outvoted in the Central Committee after winning an apparent victory in the Politburo. The three men were removed from their posts and expelled from the Central Committee, along with Dmitri Shepilov. Mr. Khrushchev had the help of Marshal Georgi K. Zhukov, who, however, was shortly ditched as was Marshal Bulganin, leaving Mr. Khrushchev as both Premier and party leader — the same dual role occupied by Stalin.

The New York Times/by George Tames

Mr. Khrushchev's meeting in 1959 with President Dwight D. Eisenhower at Camp David, Md., led to a period of seemingly improved U.S.-Soviet relations.

For more than six years he would rule without serious challenge. He grew cocky and domineering with his colleagues, unable to believe, until it was too late, that he could be deposed.

In these six years, the jaunty and irrepressible Mr. Khrushchev had his diplomatic ups and downs with the United States. One of the ups was his visit to the United States in September, 1959, which followed a "debate" with Vice President Richard M. Nixon in Moscow over the relative merits of capitalism and Communism. The impromptu exchange took place in a model kitchen at the American Exhibition there.

Arriving in the United States in a giant Tu-114 airliner, the Soviet leader got a decidedly mixed reception. He was thought of as "the butcher of Hungary," and there was hostility on the part of the press as well as from Roman Catholic prelates. He was, moreover, a Soviet Communist, a man many Americans had been conditioned to believe was a mortal enemy to the Republic. Mr. Khrushchev, however, came bearing olive branches, saying if "the two biggest countries in the world" could develop amicable relations "peace on earth will be more stable and durable."

He barnstormed the country from coast to coast, appeared on television, engaged in off-the-cuff colloquies, visited Roswell Garst's cornfields in Iowa, everywhere promoting the idea of a Soviet-American détente. The most important result of the tour was an easing of world tensions — over Berlin, which had erupted in 1958, and over nuclear testing — that was symbolized in an Eisenhower-Khrushchev conference at Camp David, Md.

Cordial relations gave way to harshness in May, 1960, when the Soviet Union shot down an American U-2 reconnaissance plane and could display the wreckage of the craft as well as its pilot. The wrangle over the episode caused the collapse of a projected Eisenhower-Khrushchev summit meeting in Paris, but it did not seriously deflect Mr. Khrushchev's policy of peaceful coexistence, although it did weaken the confidence of some Soviet leaders in the virtues of personal diplomacy.

Mr. Khrushchev returned to the United States in September, 1960, as chief of the Soviet delegation to the United Nations General Assembly. There was no official welcome and he was restricted to Manhattan and to weekend visits to Long Island. His presence provoked demonstrations—and incredulity, too. While Harold Macmillan, the British Prime Minister, was addressing the Assembly, Mr. Khrushchev interrupted him with heckling shouts and table-thumping.

Oblivious to decorum, he took off his right shoe, brandished it at one speaker and then pounded it on his desk. And he referred to a Philippine delegate as a stooge and a jerk. After 25 days, he returned home. His performance failed to please either the American public or his Soviet colleagues.

When John F. Kennedy became President in 1961, Mr. Khrushchev went to confer with him in Vienna. The purpose was to test each other's intentions, and Mr. Khrushchev is said to have come away with the belief that Mr. Kennedy lacked a certain nerve.

That impression may have contributed to Mr. Khrushchev's willingness to place missiles in Cuba in 1962, following the American Bay of Pigs invasion debacle in 1961. There appear to have been several motivations—to strengthen Fidel Castro's Socialism, to achieve an easy missile parity with the United States and, perhaps, to precipitate a situation that would lead to a Soviet-American summit session.

"If he could place Soviet medium-range missiles in Cuba," according to Frankland's book, "the main Soviet deficiency—in long-range ICBM's—would to a considerable extent be overcome. The heavy pressure on him to concentrate all available resources on the defense industries would be largely relieved."

Other commentators, however, insist that the missiles were intended to provoke a crisis that would inevitably lead to a climactic summit.

But Mr. Khrushchev reckoned without Mr. Kennedy and the threat the President discerned to the United States. A crisis was on, which was resolved late in October when the Soviet Union agreed to withdraw its missiles in return for a Kennedy pledge not to attack Cuba. In retrospect, there appears to have been a greater sense of crisis in the United States than in the Soviet Union, where Mr. Khrushchev made pointed public appearances, including a chat with an American singer. There is little evidence that he was preparing for war — and later he insisted that he had obtained what he wanted — the pledge on Cuba.

Last month, a Soviet article based on official archives asserted that Mr. Khrushchev had agreed to withdraw the Soviet missiles from Cuba after receiving private assurances from Robert F. Kennedy that the United States would pull its missiles out of Turkey.

The Cuban adventure cost Mr. Khrushchev dearly in his worsening quarrel with Mao Tse-tung, who saw it as yet another example of his inability to deal with American "imperialism." Differences with the Chinese Communists went back many years, but began to be acute with Mao's victory over Chiang Kai-shek in 1949.

After 1949 Mao turned to the Soviet Union for material help, seeking long-term credits and substantial quantities of capital goods. He received some assistance, but not nearly so much as he believed one Socialist country should render to another. Mao also did not get the credit he felt he deserved for his Marxist sagacity in accomplishing the Chinese revolution. Nor did he make any headway in his proposals for "border rectifications" with the Soviet Union — changes that would have returned some Chinese territory taken away under the Czars.

Moreover, Mao adopted a strong world revolutionary line, with American "imperialism" as its chief target. Taking into account the American setbacks in Korea in 1953, Soviet nuclear gains and the Soviet sputnik in 1957, he said — at the 40th anniversary of the Russian Revolution — that "the east wind now prevails over the west wind."

Offensive Urged by Mao

The world situation, Mao was convinced, had reached a turning point at which "the Socialist forces are overwhelmingly superior to the imperialist forces." The time was now, he indicated, to go on the offensive. But that was exactly what Mr. Khrushchev and his Soviet colleagues were unwilling to do. They preferred, they said, to "conquer capitalism with a high level of work and a higher standard of living" rather than to engage in warfare, although Mao offered his millions of Chinese as troops.

From 1957 onward, Mr. Khrushchev's quarrels with Mao went from bad to worse. China did not get Soviet nuclear help, credits were discouraged, technicians were withdrawn and by 1964 the exchange of polemics threatened to sever bonds between the two countries and the two Communisms.

As bitterness with China escalated, Mr. Khrushchev was faced with discontent at home. The virgin lands and the corn program faltered; harvests were poor; grain had to be imported from the United States, and in 1962 meat and butter prices were raised. Instead of the Khrushchev promises of a rapid advance to plenty, the economy was creaking.

All of these things came to a head in October, 1964, when members of the Politburo were quietly called to a meeting, with Leonid I. Brezhnev in the chair. Mr. Khrushchev was on holiday at his villa on the Black Sea. The vote went against him both in the Politburo and in the Central Committee. It was all over quickly and without fanfare.

Although Mr. Khrushchev had wrought tremendous changes, there was no popular outcry for him. His unfulfilled promises of consumer goods, his rough treatment of intellectuals — especially in 1962-63—and his attempts to reduce defense spending left him with few devoted followers. He was officially "relieved" of his posts and all but vanished.

The fourth volume of the new 30-volume Soviet Encyclopedia, published this April, even omitted Mr. Khrushchev from its listing of prominent political commissars of World War II.

From all reports, he was a lonely man in his last years. Relatively well treated as a high-ranking pensioner, with a town apartment and a country villa, he himself chose to be secluded. Friends said that he never got over the shame of his fallen stature.

Every year, on election day, Mr. Khrushchev did his civic duty and went to the polls in Moscow. His gait was slow and his smile dimmed, even when a few bystanders might greet him.

In December, 1970, Little, Brown & Co. published a 639-page book—and Life magazine published excerpts—entitled "Khrushchev Remembers" that purported to be his reminiscences made up of material emanating from "various circumstances."

Khrushchev issued a statement dissociating himself from the reminiscences, in which he said of the material, "This is a fabrication and I am indignant at this." The statement marked the first time his name had been mentioned on Soviet radio since he was deposed in 1964.

Even at his death, it had not been established whether the book was authentic, but the weight of expert opinion was that much, if not all, of it was compiled from authentic material.

Associated Press

In a model kitchen at American Exhibition in Moscow in 1959, Mr. Khrushchev and Richard M. Nixon, then Vice President, conducted an impromptu debate over the merits of capitalism and Communism in front of newsmen and government officials.

Premier Expressed Himself in Earthy Phrases

"Whether you like it or not, history is on our side. We will bury you!"—At a Kremlin reception in November, 1956.

"Someone tried to poke his snout into our affairs and we clobbered his snout—so that he now certainly knows where the border is."—At a news conference on the U-2 incident of May, 1960.

"Humanity's face is more beautiful than her backside."—After viewing can-can dancers in Hollywood, September, 1959.

"Those who wait for the Soviet Union to abandon Communism will wait until a shrimp learns to whistle."—To correspondents in Yugoslavia, 1963.

"He flagrantly flouted the Leninist principles of leadership and committed arbitrary actions and abuses of power. Stalin could look at a comrade sitting at the same table with him and say: 'Your eyes are shifting today!'"—Speech to the 20th party congress in February, 1956.

"We shall never take up arms to force the ideas of Communism upon anybody. Our ideas will capture the minds of mankind."—At a reception in Albania, April, 1957.

"If you have to keep a goat in your house, you can get used to its smell and live. Let us regard imperialism as a goat and our house as the whole planet. What the devil do we need war for? It is better to live with a goat and bear its unpleasant smell. But, as the saying goes, don't let it into the kitchen garden."—Speech in his birthplace in 1962.

"We have beaten you to the moon, but you have beaten us in sausage-making."—In Iowa, September, 1959, after tasting his first hot dog.

Associated Press

Mr. Khrushchev met President John F. Kennedy at Vienna in 1961. In U.S.-Soviet crisis the following year, the Premier withdrew missiles from Cuba.

"All the News That's Fit to Print"

The New York Times

LATE CITY EDITION

Weather: Clearing today, turning cold tonight. Fair, cool tomorrow. Temp. range: today 62-44; Thurs. 73-52. Full U.S. report on Page 92.

VOL. CXVII . No. 40,249 | NEW YORK, FRIDAY, APRIL 5, 1968 | 10 CENTS

MARTIN LUTHER KING IS SLAIN IN MEMPHIS; A WHITE IS SUSPECTED; JOHNSON URGES CALM

JOHNSON DELAYS TRIP TO HAWAII; MAY LEAVE TODAY

President Spends a Hectic Day Here and in Capital —Sees Thant at the U.N.

By MAX FRANKEL
Special to The New York Times

WASHINGTON, April 4 — President Johnson postponed his trip to Hawaii at least until tomorrow after he heard of the death of the Rev. Dr. Martin Luther King Jr. tonight.

The news, which visibly shocked the President, came at the end of one of the most extraordinary days in perhaps the most extraordinary week of his Administration.

Mr. Johnson was to have flown from Washington at about midnight for a weekend of strategy conferences with his military and diplomatic leaders stationed in South Vietnam. On the way, he had planned a breakfast meeting in California with former President Dwight D. Eisenhower.

Instead, the President telephoned Mrs. King in Atlanta, made a brief appeal for calm on television and went to his office to follow the reports of unrest and disturbance given him periodically by Attorney General Ramsey Clark.

Cancels Dinner Appearance

Mr. Johnson also canceled an appearance before a Democratic party fund-raising dinner here —the final event of a hectic schedule that became ever more hectic as the day unfolded.

The President began the day by making final arrangements for the Hawaii meeting. It had been tentatively planned before his order Sunday to curtail the bombing of North Vietnam and the news yesterday that Hanoi was interested in establishing direct contact.

[The new United States peace moves are producing a quiet but bitter reaction in the South Vietnamese Government that is causing increasing concern among United States officials in **Saigon. Page 14.**]

But the diplomatic development, though not the principal subject of the Honolulu meetings, added special weight to his conversations with Gen. Wiliam C. Westmoreland, the American commander in South Vietnam, and other officials.

Mr. Johnson was careful not to arouse false hopes of peace, but he appeared encouraged and in buoyant spirt as he decided before noon to fly first to New York to attend the investiture of the Most Rev. Terence J. Cooke as Archbishop of New York.

Then, while in New York,

Continued on Page 12, Column 1

Hanoi Charges U.S. Raid Far North of 20th Parallel

By EVERT CLARK
Special to The New York Times

WASHINGTON, April 4 — North Vietnam charged in a broadcast today that United States planes had bombed a "populated area" in northwestern Vietnam far north of the 20th parallel. The Defense Department said it knew of no such raid but was investigating.

President Johnson has ordered that there be no attacks on North Vietnam north of the 20th Parallel as a step toward de-escalating the war.

[In South Vietnam, United States marines beat off an attack by about 400 North Vietnamese soldiers charging up a hill near Khesanh, killing 93, The Associated Press reported. Meanwhile, an American relief column was nearing the besieged base. Page 15.]

The Hanoi radio, in a broadcast monitored and translated here, said three waves of United States planes dropped more than 50 bombs on a "populated area" about 30 miles west of Laichau, capital of Laichau Province, this morning.

The nearest village to that

Continued on Page 15, Column 1

The New York Times April 5, 1968
Hanoi said that area near Laichau (cross) was target.

HUMPHREY HINTS HE'LL ENTER RACE

Tells Unionists in Pittsburgh He Will Act Soon—Abel and Wirtz Back Him

By ROY REED
Special to The New York Times

PITTSBURGH, April 4—Two thousand labor representatives, including the head of the United Steel Workers union, clamorously urged Vice President Humphrey today to run for President.

The Vice President left little doubt that he would oblige them, but he indicated that he would wait until President Johnson returned from his Hawaii conference before making an announcement.

"I know what your request is, and I know what your thoughts are," he told the delegates to the Pennsylvania A.F.L.-C.I.O. convention. "I am most grateful. I am not one to walk away from a decision, and a decision will come in due time."

But nothing he does should interfere with President Johnson's peace mission, he said.

Several other political leaders urged Mr. Humphrey today to enter the race for the Democratic Presidential nomination. The most prominent among them was Secretary of Labor W. Willard Wirtz, who was addressing a union convention at Miami Beach.

I. W. Abel, president of the steelworkers Union, rose as Mr.

Continued on Page 32, Column 1

Johnson Shuns Role Of '68 'Lame Duck,' Kennedy Was Told

By JOHN HERBERS
Special to The New York Times

WASHINGTON, April 4—In his meeting with Senator Robert F. Kennedy yesterday President Johnson said he would remain out of the political fight this year because he did not believe it was appropriate for a "lame duck" President to try to pick his successor.

This and other details of the Johnson-Kennedy meeting were learned today from knowledgeable sources.

The meeting, which Senator Kennedy had requested in the interest of "national unity," was described as an extraordinarily friendly one, with both the Senator and the President speaking in a conciliatory manner.

President Johnson was pictured as the "elder statesman" of the party who had decided to remain aloof from this year's scramble for the Presidency in an effort to keep the party as strong as possible and retain his own dignity and effectiveness as President.

At one point, it was reported, the President said he did not want to make a spectacle of himself as a lame duck President attempting to dictate to the party who should be nominated at the national convention.

In this regard, he pointed out that in 1956 former President Harry S. Truman went to the

Continued on Page 31, Column 4

DISMAY IN NATION

Negroes Urge Others to Carry on Spirit of Nonviolence

By LAWRENCE VAN GELDER

Dismay, shame, anger and foreboding marked the nation's reaction last night to the Rev. Dr. Martin Luther King Jr.'s murder.

From the high offices of state to the man in the street, news of the moderate civil rights leader's violent death in Memphis yesterday drew, for the most part, stunned and sober statements.

Most major Negro organizations and Negro leaders, lamenting Dr. King's death, expressed hope that it serve as a spur to others to carry on in his spirit of nonviolence. But some Negro militants responded with bitterness and anger.

Roy Wilkins, executive director of the National Association for the Advancement of Colored People, said his organization was "shocked and deeply grieved by the dastardly murder of Dr. Martin Luther King."

"His murderer or murderers must be promptly apprehended and brought to justice," Mr. Wilkins said.

'A Man of Peace'

"Dr. King was a symbol of the nonviolent civil rights protest movement. He was a man of peace, of dedication, of great courage. His senseless assassination solves nothing. It will not stay the civil rights movement; it will instead spur it to greater activity."

Whitney M. Young Jr., executive director of the National Urban League, said:

"We are unspeakably shocked by the murder of Martin Luther King, one of the greatest leaders of our time. This is a bitter reflection on America. We fear for our country.

"The only possible answer now is for the nation to act immediately on what Dr. King has been fighting for—passage of the civil rights and antipoverty bills and a true and just equality for all men. Those of us who have remained loyal to his concept of nonviolence have been dealt a mortal blow."

Mayor Richard G. Hatcher of Gary, Ind., a Negro, termed the death of Dr. King "every man's loss."

"Men who care for humankind and struggle for its salvation through reason and faith have lost a leader of monumental stature," he said. "A man of his magnitude will not soon pass this way again."

At his home in Stamford, Conn., the former baseball star Jackie Robinson called the

Continued on Page 26, Column 1

PRESIDENT'S PLEA

On TV, He Deplores 'Brutal' Murder of Negro Leader

Statements by Johnson and Humphrey are on Page 24.

Special to The New York Times

WASHINGTON, April 4— President Johnson deplored tonight in a brief television address to the nation the "brutal slaying" of the Rev. Dr. Martin Luther King Jr.

He asked "every citizen to reject the blind violence that has struck Dr. King, who lived by nonviolence."

Mr. Johnson said he was postponing his scheduled departure tonight for a Honolulu conference on Vietnam and that instead he would leave tomorrow.

The President spoke from the White House. At the Washington Hilton Hotel, where Democratic members of Congress had gathered to honor the President and the Vice President, Mr. Humphrey, his voice strained with emotion, said:

"Martin Luther King stands with our other American martyrs in the cause of freedom and justice. His death is a terrible tragedy."

The dinner was canceled 10 to 15 minutes after the Vice President spoke. Mr. Johnson, who was scheduled to appear at the dinner, canceled his plans to attend.

F.B.I. Inquiry Ordered

Attorney General Ramsey Clark ordered an immediate inquiry by the Federal Bureau of Investigation into the shooting of Dr. King in Memphis.

He said the purpose of the investigation would be to determine whether any Federal law had been violated.

One provision of the law that could be invoked makes it a crime to engage in a conspiracy to deprive a person of his civil rights.

In addition to F.B.I. agents, Department of Justice civil rights representatives were on the scene in Memphis and were in touch with the Attorney General.

Military sources said that no National Guard units had yet been Federalized and no Regular Army troops had been alerted yet for possible movement to cities where violence had broken out.

National Guard troops, such as the 4,000 men who have been called into Memphis, remain under state control until the responsible Governor requests help and the President

Continued on Page 24, Column 7

Associated Press

THE REV. DR. MARTIN LUTHER KING Jr.

Scattered Violence Occurs In Harlem and Brooklyn

12 Are Arrested Here

By THOMAS A. JOHNSON

Sporadic violence erupted in Harlem and Brooklyn's Bedford-Stuyvesant section last night after news of Dr. Martin Luther King's assassination spread in the two predominantly Negro communities.

Mayor Lindsay, who went to Harlem in an effort to quiet the outbreaks, was caught in the midst of an unruly crowd and had to be hustled into a limousine by bodyguards.

Police reinforcements, including elements of the riot-trained Tactical Patrol Force, were rushed into both communities.

Two arrests were reported in Brooklyn and 10 in Harlem. A television crewman was said to have been injured by flying glass.

There were numerous instances of rock-throwing, looting and arson reported both in Brooklyn and in Harlem, starting around 11 P.M. and continuing early today.

Gangs of youth in both areas were reported roaming through the streets, now and then taunting policemen and firemen on duty.

The police fired several volleys of shots in the air to disperse crowds along Brooklyn's Fulton Street and Harlem's

Continued on Page 26, Column 2

Widespread Disorders

Disorders broke out in scattered parts of the nation last night after the slaying of the Rev. Dr. Martin Luther King Jr. The National Guard was called out or alerted in several cities.

In Washington, scattered but persistent looting and vandalism erupted, led for a time by Stokely Carmichael, former head of the Student Nonviolent Coordinating Commitee. All available policemen were being called to duty.

About 4,000 Tennessee National Guardsmen were ordered to duty in Nashville because of disorders.

In North Carolina, Gov. Dan K. Moore alerted the Guard in Greensboro at the request of Mayor Carson Bain. State Highway patrolmen were dispatched to Raleigh.

There were riotous outbursts

Continued on Page 26, Column 5

NEWS INDEX

GUARD CALLED OUT

Curfew Is Ordered in Memphis, but Fires and Looting Erupt

By EARL CALDWELL
Special to The New York Times

MEMPHIS, Friday, April 5— The Rev. Dr. Martin Luther King Jr., who preached nonviolence and racial brotherhood, was fatally shot here last night by a distant gunman who then raced away and escaped.

Four thousand National Guard troops were ordered into Memphis by Gov. Buford Ellington after the 39-year-old Nobel Prize-winning civil rights leader died.

A curfew was imposed on the shocked city of 550,000 inhabitants, 40 per cent of whom are Negro.

But the police said the tragedy had been followed by incidents that included sporadic shooting, fires, bricks and bottles thrown at policemen, and looting that started in Negro districts and then spread over the city.

White Car Sought

Police Director Frank Holloman said the assassin might have been a white man who was "50 to 100 yards away in a flophouse."

Chief of Detectives W. P. Huston said a late model white Mustang was believed to have been the killer's getaway car. Its occupant was described as a bareheaded white man in his 30's, wearing a black suit and black tie.

The detective chief said the police had chased two cars near the motel where Dr. King was shot and had halted one that had two out-of-town men as occupants. The men were questioned but seemed to have nothing to do with the killing, he said.

Rifle Found Nearby

A high-powered 30.06-caliber rifle was found about a block from the scene of the shooting, on South Main Street. "We think it's the gun," Chief Huston said, reporting it would be turned over to the Federal Bureau of Investigation.

Dr. King was shot while he leaned over a second-floor railing outside his room at the Lorraine Motel. He was chatting with two friends just before starting for dinner.

One of the friends was a musician, and Dr. King had just asked him to play a Negro spiritual, "Precious Lord, Take My Hand," at a rally that was to have been held two hours later in support of striking Memphis sanitationmen.

Paul Hess, assistant adminis-

Continued on Page 24, Column 1

Archbishop Cooke Installed; President Looks On

By EDWARD B. FISKE

The Most Rev. Terence J. Cooke was installed as the seventh Roman Catholic Archbishop of New York yesterday in a historic pageant attended by the President of the United States and highlighted by prayers for the success of his peace efforts in Vietnam.

"Let us pray with all our hearts that God will inspire our President," the 47-year-old Archbishop said in his homily at St. Patrick's Cathedral.

"In the last few days, we have all admired his heroic efforts in the search for peace in Vietnam. We ask God to bless his efforts with success. May God inspire not only our President, but also other leaders and the leaders of all nations of the world to find a way to peace."

Then the Archbishop, speaking from a white marble pulpit and surrounded by a blaze of purple, gold and scarlet robes, addressed himself directly to Mr. Johnson, who sat below him in a front pew.

The President, sitting with his hands clasped and his legs crossed, listened with obvious intensity to the Archbishop's words.

"Mr. President," he said, "our hearts, our hopes, our continued prayers go with you."

Mr. Johnson, accompanied by his daughter, Mrs. Patrick J. Nugent, led a festive congregation of about 5,000 cardinals, bishops, priests, laymen, nuns, civic leaders

Continued on Page 38, Column 1

The New York Times (by Neal Boenzi)

President Johnson and his daughter, Mrs. Patrick J. Nugent, right, listening during yesterday's ceremonies. At left are Mrs. John F. Kennedy and Lieut. Gov. Malcolm Wilson. Security personnel are in the row between them.

Archbishop Luigi Raimondi, Apostolic Delegate to the U.S., speaking after Archbishop Terence J. Cooke was enthroned

Martin Luther King Is Shot to Death in Memphis

4,000 GUARDSMEN ARE ORDERED OUT

Curfew Is Imposed on City, but Windows Are Broken and Policemen Stoned

Continued From Page 1, Col. 8

trator at St. Joseph's Hospital, where Dr. King died despite emergency surgery, said the minister had "received a gunshot wound on the right side of the neck, at the root of the neck, a gaping wound."

"He was pronounced dead at 7:05 P.M. Central standard time (8:05 P.M. New York time) by staff doctors," Mr. Hess said. "They did everything humanly possible."

Dr. King's mourning associates sought to calm the people they met by recalling his messages of peace, but there was widespread concern by law enforcement officers here and elsewhere over potential reactions.

In a television broadcast after the curfew was ordered here, Mr. Holloman said, "rioting has broken out in parts of the city" and "looting is rampant."

Dr. King had come back to Memphis Wednesday morning to organize support once again for 1,300 sanitation workers who have been striking since Lincoln's Birthday. Just a week ago yesterday he led a march in the strikers' cause that ended in violence. A 16-year-old Negros was killed, 62 persons were injured and 200 were arrested.

Yesterday Dr. King had been in his second-floor room—Number 306—throughout the day. Just about 6 P.M. he emerged, wearing a silkish-looking black suit and white shirt.

Solomon Jones Jr., his driver, had been waiting to take him by car to the home of the Rev. Samuel Kyles of Memphis for dinner. Mr. Jones said later he had observed, "It's cold outside, put your topcoat on," and Dr. King had replied, "O. K., I will."

Two Men in Courtyard

Dr. King, an open-faced, genial man, leaned over a green iron railing to chat with an associate, Jesse Jackson, standing just below him in a courtyard parking lot.

"Do you know Ben?" Mr. Jackson asked, introducing Ben Branch of Chicago, a musician who was to play at the night's rally.

"Yes, that's my man!" Dr. King glowed.

The two men recalled Dr. King's asking for the playing of the spiritual. "I really want you to play that tonight," Dr. King said, enthusiastically.

The Rev. Ralph W. Abernathy, perhaps Dr. King's closest friend, was just about to come out of the motel room when the sudden loud noise burst out.

Dr. King toppled to the concrete second-floor walkway. Blood gushed from the right jaw and neck area. His necktie had been ripped off by the blast.

"He had just bent over," Mr. Jackson recalled later. "If he had been standing up, he wouldn't have been hit in the face."

Policemen 'All Over'

"When I turned around," Mr. Jackson went on, bitterly, "I saw police coming from everywhere. They said, 'where did it come from?' And I said, 'behind you.' The police were

Flip Schulke-Black Star

LED MARCH ON WASHINGTON: Dr. King speaking to the marchers from steps of Lincoln Memorial on Aug. 28, 1963.

coming from where the shot came."

Mr. Branch asserted that the shot had come from "the hill on the other side of the street."

"When I looked up, the police and the sheriff's deputies were running all around," Mr. Branch declared.

"We didn't need to call the police," Mr. Jackson said. "They were here all over the place."

Mr. Kyles said Dr. King had stood in the open "about three minutes."

Mr. Jones, the driver, said that a squad car with four policemen in it drove down the street only moments before the gunshot. The police had been circulating throughout the motel area on precautionary patrols.

After the shot, Mr. Jones said, he saw a man "with something white on his face" creep away from a thicket across the street.

Someone rushed up with a towel to stem the flow of Dr. King's blood. Mr. Kyles said he put a blanket over Dr. King, but "I knew he was gone." He ran down the stairs and tried to telephone from the motel office for an ambulance.

Mr. Abernathy hurried up with a second larger towel.

Police With Helmets

Policemen were pouring into the motel area, carrying rifles and shotguns and wearing riot helmets.

But the King aides said it seemed to be 10 or 15 minutes before a Fire Department ambulance arrived.

Dr. King was apparently still living when he reached the St. Joseph's Hospital operating room for emergency surgery. He was borne in on a stretcher, the bloody towel over his head.

It was the same emergency room to which James H. Meredith, first Negro enrolled at the University of Mississippi, was taken after he was ambushed and shot in June, 1965, at Hernando, Miss., a few miles south of Memphis. Mr. Meredith was not seriously hurt.

Outside the emergency room some of Dr. King's aides waited in forlorn hope. One was Chauncey Eskridge, his legal adviser. He broke into sobs when Dr. King's death was announced.

"A man full of life, full of love and he was shot," Mr. Eskridge said. "He had always lived with that expectation—but nobody ever expected it to happen."

But the Rev. Andrew Young, executive director of Dr. King's Southern Christian Leadership Conference, recalled there had been some talk Wednesday night about possible harm to Dr. King in Memphis.

Mr. Young recalled: "He said he had reached the pinnacle of fulfillment with his non-violent movement, and these reports did not bother him."

Mr. Young believed that the fatal shot might have been fired from a passing car. "It sounded like a firecracker," he said.

In a nearby building, a newsman who had been watching a television program thought, however, that "it was a tremendous blast that sounded like a bomb."

There were perhaps 15 persons in the motel courtyard area when Dr. King was shot, all believed to be Negroes and Dr. King's associates.

Past the courtyard is a small empty swimming pool. Then comes Mulberry Street, a short street only three blocks away from storied Beale Street on the fringe of downtown Memphis.

Fire Station Nearby

On the other side of the street is a six-foot brick restraining wall, with bushes and grass atop it and a hillside going on to a patch of trees. Behind the trees is a rusty wire fence enclosing backyards of two-story brick and frame houses.

At the corner at Butler Street is a newish-looking white brick fire station.

Police were reported to have chased a late-model blue or white car through Memphis and north to Millington. A civilian in another car that had a citizens band radio was also reported to have pursued the fleeing car and to have opened fire on it.

The police first cordoned off an area of about five blocks around the Lorraine Motel, chosen by Dr. King for his stay here because it is Negro-owned. The two-story motel is an addition to a small two-story hotel in a largely Negro area.

Mayor Henry Loeb had ordered a curfew here after last week's disorder, and National Guard units had been on duty for five days until they were deactivated Wednesday.

Last night the Mayor reinstated the curfew at 6:35 and declared:

"After the tragedy which has happened in Memphis tonight, for the protection of all our citizens, we are putting the curfew back in effect. All movement is restricted except for health or emergency reasons."

Governor Ellington, calling out the National Guard and pledging all necessary action by the state to prevent disorder, announced:

"For the second time in recent days, I most earnestly ask the people of Memphis and Shelby County to remain calm. I do so aagin tonight in the face of this most regrettable incident.

"Every possible action is being taken to apprehend the person or persons responsible for committing this act.

"We are also taking precautionary steps to prevent any acts of disorder. I can fully appreciate the feelings and emotions which this crime has aroused, but for the benefit of everyone, all of our citizens must exercise restraint, caution and good judgment."

National Guard planes flew over the state to bring in contingents of riot-trained highway patrolmen. Units of the Arkansas State Patrol were deputized and brought into Memphis.

Assistant Chief Bartholomew early this morning said that unidentified persons had shot from rooftops and windows at policemen eight or 10 times. He said bullets had shattered one police car's windshield, wounding two policemen with flying glass. They were treated at the same hospital where Dr. King died.

Sixty arrests were made for looting, burglary and disorderly conduct, chief Bartholomew said.

Numerous minor injuries were reported in four hours of clashes between civilians and law enforcement officers. But any serious disorders were under control by 11:15 P.M., Chief Bartholomew said. Early this morning streets were virtually empty except for patrol cars riding without headlights on.

Once Stabbed in Harlem

In his career Dr. King had suffered beatings and blows. Once—on Sept. 20, 1958—he was stabbed in a Harlem department store in New York by a Negro woman later adjudged insane.

That time he underwent a four-hour operation to remove a steel letter opener that had been plunged into his upper left chest. For a time he was on the critical list, but he told his wife, while in the hospital, "I don't hold any bitterness toward this woman."

In Memphis, Dr. King's chief associates met in his room after he died. They included Mr. Young, Mr. Abernathy, Mr. Jackson, the Rev. James Bevel and Hosea Williams.

They had to step across a drying pool of Dr. King's blood to enter. Someone had thrown a crumpled pack of cigarettes into the blood.

After 15 minutes they emerged. Mr. Jackson looked at the blood. He embraced Mr. Abernathy.

"Stand tall!" somebody exhorted.

"Murder! Murder!" Mr. Bevel groaned. "Doc said that's not the way."

"Doc" was what they often called Dr. King.

Then the murdered leader's aides said they would go on to the hall where tonight's rally was to have been held. They wanted to urge calm upon the mourners.

Some policemen sought to dissuade them.

But eventually the group did start out, with a police escort.

At the Federal Bureau of Investigation office here, Robert Jensen, special agent in charge, said the F. B. I. had entered the murder investigation at the request of Attorney General Ramsey Clark.

Last night Dr. King's body was taken to the Shelby County morgue, according to the police. They said it would be up to Dr. Derry Francisco, county medical examiner, to order further disposition.

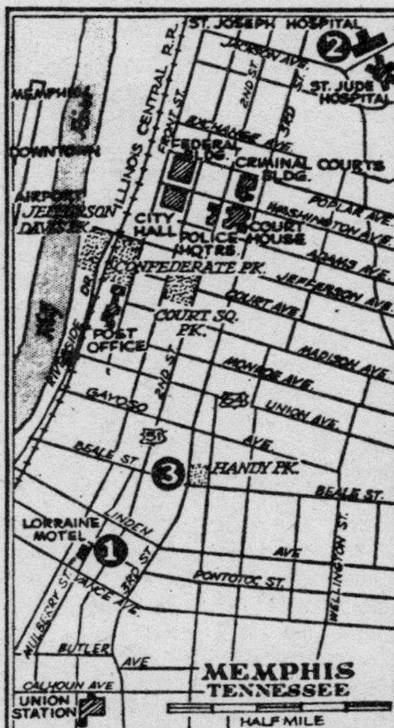

The New York Times April 5, 1968

AREA OF THE MURDER: (1) Motel where the shooting occurred; (2) hospital where Dr. King died, and (3) famed Beale Street, scene of demonstrations.

Washington Is Shaken; Leaders Call for Calm

WASHINGTON, April 4 (UPI)—Not since John F. Kennedy was assassinated on Nov. 22, 1963, has the capital been so shaken by a murder. Washington was plunged into gloom and feared the repercussions of the slaying of the Rev. Dr. Martin Luther King Jr.

Leaders called for calm. Some in Congress said open housing legislation should now be passed as a memorial to the man who marched for it.

Dr. King, said Speaker of the House, John McCormack, "was a martyr to a cause—and that cause will be strengthened if the House concurs in the Senate civil rights bill."

The bill would outlaw discrimination in the sale or rental of 68 per cent of the nation's housing.

Martin Luther King Jr.: Leader of Millions in Nonviolent Drive for Racial Justice

CAREER A SYMBOL OF INTEGRATION

Nobel Winner Was Attacked by Both Negro Militants and White Extremists

By MURRAY SCHUMACH

To many millions of American Negroes, the Rev. Dr. Martin Luther King Jr. was the prophet of their crusade for racial equality. He was their voice of anguish, their eloquence in humiliation, their battle cry for human dignity. He forged for them the weapons of nonviolence that withstood and blunted the ferocity of segregation.

And to many millions of American whites, he was one of a group of Negroes who preserved the bridge of communication between races when racial warfare threatened the United States in the nineteen-sixties, as Negroes sought the full emancipation pledged to them a century before by Abraham Lincoln.

To the world Dr. King had the stature that accrued to a winner of the Nobel Peace Prize; a man with access to the White House and the Vatican; a veritable hero in the African states that were just emerging from colonialism.

Between Extremes

In his dedication to nonviolence, Dr. King was caught between white and Negro extremists as racial tensions erupted into arson, gunfire and looting in many of the nation's cities during the summer of 1967.

Militant Negroes, with the cry of, "burn, baby burn," argued that only by violence and segregation could the Negro attain self-respect, dignity and real equality in the United States.

Floyd B. McKissick, when director of the Congress of Racial Equality, declared in August of that year that it was a "foolish assumption to try to sell nonviolence to the ghettos."

And white extremists, not bothering to make distinctions between degrees of Negro militancy, looked upon Dr. King as one of their chief enemies.

At times in recent months, efforts by Dr. King to utilize nonviolent methods exploded into violence.

Violence in Memphis

Last week, when he led a protest march through downtown Memphis, Tenn., in support of the city's striking sanitation workers, a group of Negro youths suddenly began breaking store windows and looting, and one Negro was shot to death.

Two days later, however, Dr. King said he would stage another demonstration and attributed the violence to his own "miscalculation."

At the time he was assassinated in Memphis, Dr. King was involved in one of his greatest plans to dramatize the plight of the poor and stir Congress to help Negroes.

He called this venture the "Poor People's Campaign." It was to be a huge "camp-in" either in Washington or in Chicago during the Democratic National Convention.

In one of his last public pronouncements before the shooting, Dr. King told an audience in a Harlem church on March 26:

"We need an alternative to riots and to timid supplication. Nonviolence is our most potent weapon."

His strong beliefs in civil rights and nonviolence made him one of the leading opponents of American participation in the war in Vietnam. To him the war was unjust, diverting vast sums away from programs to alleviate the condition of the Negro poor in this country. He called the conflict "one of history's most cruel and senseless wars." Last January he said:

"We need to make clear in this political year, to Congressmen on both sides of the aisle and to the President of the United States that we will no longer vote for men who continue to see the killing of Vietnamese and Americans as the best way of advancing the goals of freedom and self-determination in Southeast Asia."

Object of Many Attacks

Inevitably, as a symbol of integration, he became the object of unrelenting attacks and vilification. His home was bombed. He was spat upon and mocked. He was struck and kicked. He was stabbed, almost fatally, by a deranged Negro woman. He was frequently thrown into jail. Threats became so commonplace that his wife could ignore burning crosses on the lawn and ominous phone calls. Through it all he adhered to the creed of passive disobedience that infuriated segregationists.

The adulation that was heaped upon him eventually irritated even some Negroes in the civil rights movement who worked hard, but in relative obscurity. They pointed out—and Dr. King admitted — that he was a poor administrator. Sometimes, with sarcasm, they referred to him, privately, as "De Lawd." They noted that Dr. King's successes were built on the labors of many who had gone before him, the noncoms and privates of the civil rights army who fought without benefit of headlines and television cameras.

The Negro extremists he criticized were contemptuous of Dr. King. They dismissed his passion for nonviolence as another form of servility to white people. They called him an "Uncle Tom," and charged that he was hindering the Negro struggle for equality.

Dr. King's belief in nonviolence was subjected to intense pressure in 1966, when some Negro groups adopted the slogan "black power" in the aftermath of civil rights marches into Mississippi and race riots in Northern cities. He rejected the idea, saying:

"The Negro needs the white man to free him from his fears. The white man needs the Negro to free him from his guilt. A doctrine of black supremacy is as evil as a doctrine of white supremacy."

The doctrine of "black power" threatened to split the Negro civil rights movement and antagonize white liberals who had been supporting Negro causes, and Dr. King suggested "militant nonviolence" as a formula for progress with peace.

At the root of his civil rights convictions was an even more profound faith in the basic goodness of man and the great potential of American democracy. These beliefs gave to his speeches a fervor that could not be stilled by criticism.

Associated Press

ALABAMA—1956: Dr. King, seated behind the Rev. Ralph D. Abernathy, rides a forward seat in a Montgomery bus after the Supreme Court's desegregation order. Next to him is the Rev. Glenn Smiley of New York; woman next to Dr. Abernathy was not identified.

Scores of millions of Americans — white as well as Negro — who sat before television sets in the summer of 1963 to watch the awesome march of some 200,000 Negroes on Washington were deeply stirred when Dr. King, in the shadow of the Lincoln Memorial, said:

"Even though we face the difficulties of today and tomorrow, I still have a dream. I have a dream that one day this nation will rise up and live out the true meaning of its creed: 'We hold these truths to be self-evident, that all men are created equal.'"

And all over the world, men were moved as they read his words of Dec. 10, 1964, when he became the third member of his race to receive the Nobel Peace Prize.

Insistent on Man's Destiny

"I refuse to accept the idea that man is mere flotsam and jetsam in the river of life which surrounds him," he said. "I refuse to accept the view that mankind is so tragically bound to the starless midnight of racism and war that the bright daybreak of peace and brotherhood can never become a reality.

"I refuse to accept the cynical notion that nation after nation must spiral down a militaristic stairway into the hell of thermonuclear destruction. I believe that unarmed truth and unconditional love will have the final word in reality. This is why right, temporarily defeated, is stronger than evil triumphant."

For the poor and unlettered of his own race, Dr. King spoke differently. There he embraced the rhythm and passion of the revivalist and evangelist. Some observers of Dr. King's technique said that others in the movement were more effective in this respect. But Dr. King had the touch, as he illustrated in a church in Albany, Ga., in 1962:

"So listen to me, children: Put on your marching shoes; don'cha get weary; though the path ahead may be dark and dreary; we're walking for freedom, children."

Or there was the meeting in Gadsden, Ala., late in 1963, when he displayed another side of his ability before an audience of poor Negroes. It went as follows:

King: I hear they are beating you.

Audience: Yes, yes.

King: I hear they are cursing you.

Audience: Yes, yes.

King: I hear they are going into your homes and doing nasty things and beating you.

Audience: Yes, yes.

King: Some of you have knives, and I ask you to put them up. Some of you have arms, and I ask you to put them up. Get the weapon of nonviolence, the breastplate of righteousness, the armor of truth, and just keep marching."

It was said that so devoted was his vast following that even among illiterates he could, by calm discussion of Platonic dogma, evoke deep cries of "Amen."

Dr. King also had a way of reducing complex issues to terms that anyone could understand. Thus, in the summer of 1965, when there was widespread discontent among Negroes about their struggle for equality of employment, he declared:

"What good does it do to be able to eat at a lunch counter if you can't buy a hamburger."

The enormous impact of Dr. King's words was one of the reasons he was in the President's Room in the Capitol on Aug. 6, 1965, when President Johnson signed the Voting Rights Act that struck down literacy tests, provided Federal registrars to assure the ballot to unregistered Negroes and marked the growth of the Negro as a political force in the South.

Backed by Organization

Dr. King's effectiveness was enhanced and given continuity by the fact that he had an organization behind him. Formed in 1960, with headquarters in Atlanta, it was called the Southern Christian Leadership Conference, familiarly known as SLICK. Allied with it was another organization formed under Dr. King's sponsorship, the Student Nonviolent Coordinating Committee, often referred to as SNICK.

These two organizations reached the country, though their basic strength was in the South. They brought together Negro clergymen, businessmen, professional men and students. They raised the money and planned the sit-ins, the campaigns for Negro vote registration, the demonstrations by which Negroes hacked away at segregationist resistance, lowering the barriers against Negroes in the political, economic and social life of the nation.

This minister, who became the most famous spokesman for Negro rights since Booker T. Washington, was not particularly impressive in appearance. About 5 feet 8 inches tall, he had an oval face with almond-shaped eyes that looked almost dreamy when he was off the platform. His neck and shoulders were heavily muscled, but his hands were almost delicate.

Speaker of Few Gestures

There was little of the rabblerouser in his oratory. He was not prone to extravagant gestures or loud peroration. His baritone voice, though vibrant, was not that of a spellbinder. Occasionally, after a particularly telling sentence, he would tilt his head a bit and fall silent as though waiting for the echoes of his thought to spread through the hall, church or street.

In private gatherings, Dr. King lacked the laughing gregariousness that often makes for popularity. Some thought he was without a sense of humor. He was not a gifted raconteur. He did not have the flamboyance of a Representative Adam Clayton Powell Jr. or the cool strategic brilliance of Roy Wilkins, head of the National Association for the

(continued)

Advancement of Colored People.

What Dr. King did have was an instinct for the right moment to make his moves. Some critics looked upon this as pure opportunism. Nevertheless, it was this sense of timing that raised him in 1955, from a newly arrived minister in Montgomery, Ala., with his first church, to a figure of national prominence.

Bus Boycott in Progress

Negroes in that city had begun a boycott of buses to win the right to sit where they pleased instead of being forced to move to the rear of buses, in Southern tradition or to surrunder seats to white people when a bus was crowded.

Negroes in that city had begun a boycott of buses to win the right to sit where they pleased instead of being forced to move to the rear f buses, in Southern tradition or to surrunder seats to white people when a bus was crowded.

The 381-day boycott by Negroes was already under way when the young pastor was placed in charge of the campaign. It has been said that one of the reasons he got the job was because he was so new in the area he had not antagonized any of the Negro factions. Even while the boycott was under way, a board of directors handled the bulk of administrative work.

However, it was Dr. King who dramatized the boycott with his decision to make it the testing ground, before the eyes of the nation, of his belief in the civil disobedience teachings of Thoreau and Gandhi. When he was arrested during the Montgomery boycott, he said:

"If we are arrested every day, if we are exploited every day, if we are trampled over every day, don't ever let anyone pull you so low as to hate them. We must use the weapon of love. We must have compassion and understanding for those who hate us. We must realize so many people are taught to hate us that they are not totally responsible for their hate. But we stand in life at midnight; we are always on the threshold of a new dawn."

Home Bombed in Absence

Even more dramatic, in some ways, was his reaction to the bombing of his home during the boycott. He was away at the time and rushed back fearful for his wife and children. They were not injured. But when he reached the modest house, more than a thousand Negroes had already gathered and were in an ugly mood, seeking revenge against the white people. The police were jittery. Quickly, Dr. King pacified the crowd and there was no trouble.

Dr. King was even more impressive during the "big push" in Birmingham, which began in April, 1963. With the minister in the limelight, Negroes there began a campaign of sit-ins at lunch counters, picketing and protest marches. Hundreds of children, used in the campaign, were jailed.

The entire world was stirred when the police turned dogs on the demonstrators. Dr. King was jailed for five days. While he was in prison he issued a 9,000-word letter that created considerable controversy among white people, alienating some sympathizers who thought Dr. King was being too aggressive.

Moderates Called Obstacles

In the letter he wrote:

"I have almost reached the regrettable conclusion that the Negro's great stumbling block in the stride toward freedom is not the White Citizens Counciler or the Ku Klux Klanner, but the white moderate who is more devoted to order than to justice; who prefers a negative peace, which is the absence of tension, to a positive peace, which is the presence of justice."

Some critics of Dr. King said that one reason for this letter was to answer Negro intellectuals, such as the writer James Baldwin, who were impatient with Dr. King's belief in brotherhood. Whatever the reasons, the role of Dr. King in Birmingham added to his stature and showed that his enormous following was deeply devoted to him.

He demonstrated this in a threatening situation in Albany, Ga., after four Negro girls were killed in the bombing of a church. Dr. King said at the funeral:

"In spite of the darkness of this hour, we must not despair. We must not lose faith in our white brothers."

As Dr. King's words grew more potent and he was invited to the White House by Presidents Kennedy and Johnson, some critics — Negroes as well as white — noted that sometimes, despite all the publicity he attracted, he left campaigns unfinished or else failed to attain his goals.

Dr. King was aware of this. But he pointed out, in 1964, in St. Augustine, Fla., one of the toughest civil rights battlegrounds, that there were important intangibles.

"Even if we do not get all we should," he said, "movements such as this tend more and more to give a Negro the sense of self-respect that he needs. It tends to generate courage in Negroes outside the movement. It brings intangible results outside the community where it is carried out. There is a hardening of attitudes in situations like this. But other cities see and say: "We don't want to be another Albany or Birmingham,' and they make changes. Some communities, like this one, had to bear the cross."

It was in this city that Negroes marched into the fists of the mob singing: "We love everybody."

Conscious of Leading Role

There was no false modesty in Dr. King's self-appraisal of his role in the civil rights movement.

"History," he said, "has thrust me into this position. It would be both immoral and a sign of ingratitude if I did not face my moral responsibility to do what I can in this struggle."

Another time he compared himself to Socrates as one of "the creative gadflies of society."

At times he addressed himself deliberately to the white people of the nation. Once, he said:

"We will match your capacity to inflict suffering with our capacity to endure suffering. We will meet your physical force with soul force. We will not hate you, but we cannot in all good conscience obey your unjust laws . . . We will soon wear you down by our capacity to suffer. And in winning our freedom we will so appeal to your heart and conscience that we will win you in the process."

The enormous influence of Dr. King's voice in the turbulent racial conflict reached into New York in 1964. In the summer of that year racial rioting exploded in New York and in other Northern cities with large Negro populations. There was widespread fear that the disorders, particularly in Harlem, might set off unprecedented racial violence.

At this point Dr. King became one of the major intermediaries in restoring order. He conferred with Mayor Robert F. Wagner and with Negro leaders. A statement was issued, of which he was one of the signers, calling for "a broad curtailment if not total moratorium on mass demonstrations until after Presidential elections."

The following year, Dr. King was once more in the headlines and on television — this time leading a drive for Negro voter registration in Selma, Ala. Negroes were arrested by the hundreds. Dr. King was punched and kicked by a white man when, during this period of protest, he became the first Negro to register at a century-old hotel in Selma.

Martin Luther King Jr. was born Jan. 15, 1929, in Atlanta on Auburn Avenue. As a child his name was Michael Luther King and so was his father's. His father changed both their names legally to Martin Luther King in honor of the Protestant reformer.

Auburn Avenue is one of the nation's most widely known Negro sections. Many successful Negro business or professional men have lived there. The Rev. Martin Luther King Sr. was pastor of the Ebenezer Baptist Church at Jackson Street and Auburn Avenue.

Young Martin went to Atlanta's Morehouse College, a Negro institution whose students acquired what was sometimes called the "Morehouse swank." The president of Morehouse, Dr. B. E. Mays, took a special interest in Martin, who had decided, in his junior year, to be a clergyman.

He was ordained a minister in his father's church in 1947. It was in this church he was to say, some years later:

"America, you've strayed away. You've trampled over 19 million of your brethren. All men are created equal. Not some men. Not white men. All men. America, rise up and come home."

Before Dr. King had his own church he pursued his studies in the integrated Crozier Theological Seminary, in Chester, Pa. He was one of six Negroes in a student body of about a hundred. He became the first Negro class president. He was named the outstanding student and won a fellowship to study for a doctorate at the school of his choice. The young man enrolled at Boston College in 1951.

For his doctoral thesis he sought to resolve the differences between the Harvard theologian Paul Tillich and the neo-naturalist philosopher Henry Nelson Wieman. During this period he took courses at Harvard, as well.

Dr. King 3d Negro to Get Nobel Prize

The Rev. Dr. Martin Luther King Jr. was the 14th American, the 3d Negro, and the youngest man to win the Nobel Peace Prize.

When he accepted the prize in Oslo, Norway, on Dec. 10, 1964, on behalf of the civil rights movement he said he was doing so for "all men who love peace and brotherhood."

At the presentation ceremony at Oslo University, Dr. King, then 35 years old, said that the award had come "at a moment when 22 million Negroes of the United States are engaged in a creative battle to end the long night of racial injustice."

Dr. Alfred B. Nobel, the Swedish inventor of dynamite, who established the prizes, stipulated in his will that one of the prizes to be awarded annually in his name should go to:

"The person who shall have done most to promote the fraternity of nations and the abolition or diminution of standing armies and the formation or increase of peace congresses."

However, the Nobel Peace Prize has taken on a broader interpretation of "peace" since the first one was awarded in 1901.

Emphasis in recent years has been placed upon brotherhood.

Was Deeply Moved

When it was announced on Oct. 14, 1964, in Oslo that Dr. King would be awarded the prize, the civil rights leader said in Atlanta that he was deeply moved by the honor. He also said then that "every penny" of the prize money, about $54,000, would be given to the civil rights movement.

Associated Press

Dr. King being congratulated by King Olav V of Norway after the presentation of the peace prize in Oslo, 1964.

Among those who were present at the presentation ceremony three months later were King Olav V of Norway, Government and diplomatic leaders, members of Dr. King's family and his associates in the civil rights movement. The ceremony was televised throughout Europe.

Dr. King was hailed at the time by Dr. Gunnar Jahn, the chairman of the Norwegian Parliament's Nobel Committee, as an "undaunted champion of peace" and the "first person in the Western world to have shown us that a struggle can be waged without violence."

The two Negroes to previously receive the award were Dr. Ralph J. Bunche, who was awarded the prize in 1950 for his work as Under Secretary of the United Nations, and Zulu Chief Albert J. Luthuli of South Africa, who in 1960 received the award for advocating nonviolence in the solution of apartheid, South Africa's policy of racial segregation.

While he was working on his doctorate he met Coretta Scott, a graduate of Antioch College, who was doing graduate work in music. He married the singer in 1953. They had four children, Yolanda, Martin Luther King 3d, Dexter Scott and Bernice.

In 1954, Dr. King became pastor of the Dexter Avenue Baptist Church in Montgomery, Ala. At that time few of Montgomery's white residents saw any reason for a major dispute with the city's 50,000 Negroes. They did not seem to realize how deeply the Negroes resented segregated seating on buses, for instance.

Revolt Begun by Woman

On Dec. 1, 1955, they learned, almost by accident. Mrs. Rosa Parks, a Negro seamstress, refused to comply with a bus driver's order to give up her seat to a white passenger. She was tired, she said. Her feet hurt from a day of shopping.

Mrs. Parks had been a local secretary for the National Association for the Advancement of Colored People. She was arrested, convicted of refusing to obey the bus conductor and fined $10 and costs, a total of $14. Almost as spontaneous as Mrs. Parks's act was the rallying of many Negro leaders in the city to help her.

From a protest begun over a Negro woman's tired feet Dr. King began his public career.

In 1959 Dr. King and his family moved back to Atlanta, where he became a co-pastor, with his father, of the Ebenezer Baptist Church.

As his fame increased, public interest in his beliefs led him to write books. It was while he was autographing one of these books, "Stride Toward Freedom," in a Harlem department store that he was stabbed by a Negro woman.

It was in these books that he summarized, in detail, his beliefs as well as his career. Thus, in "Why We Can't Wait," he wrote:

"The Negro knows he is right. He has not organized for conquest or to gain spoils or to enslave those who have injured him. His goal is not to capture that which belongs to someone else. He merely wants, and will have, what is honorably his."

The posibility that he might someday be assassinated was considered by Dr. King on June 5, 1964, when he reported, in St. Augustine, Fla., that his life had been threatend. He said:

"Well, if physical death is the price that I must pay to free my white brothers and sisters from a permanent death of the spirit, then nothing can be more redemptive."

KING CITED THREAT DAY BEFORE DEATH

Told 2,000 Supporters He Had Seen Promised Land

MEMPHIS, April 4 (AP)—"It really doesn't matter what happens now. I've been to the mountaintop."

The speaker was the Rev. Dr. Martin Luther King Jr. His audience was a cheering crowd of some 2,000 supporters. It was last night.

Dr. King said last night that he was aware that threats had been made on his life. But he said he had seen the fulfillment of his goals of nonviolence, and did not worry about the future.

He said that his flight to Memphis from Atlanta Tuesday had been delayed because of a baggage search that airlines officials had said resulted from threats to him.

"And there have been some threats around here," he said.

"We've got some difficult days ahead, but it really doesn't matter now," Dr. King said. "Because I've been to the mountain top."

"All the News That's Fit to Print."

The New York Times.

LATE CITY EDITION
POSTSCRIPT
Rain or snow today, colder at night. Tomorrow generally fair and colder.
Temperatures Yesterday—Max., 37; Min., 26

Copyright, 1936, by The New York Times Company.

VOL. LXXXV.....No. 28,483. Entered as Second-Class Matter, Postoffice, New York, N. Y. NEW YORK, SATURDAY, JANUARY 18, 1936. P TWO CENTS In New York City. | THREE CENTS Within 200 Miles | FOUR CENTS Elsewhere Except in 7th and 8th Postal Zones.

GLASS ASSAILS NYE ON WILSON CHARGE; MAY BLOCK INQUIRY

Word 'Coward' Used as Virginian Tells Senate Only Rules Curb His Vocabulary.

SPEECH STIRS HIS HEARERS

He Pounds Desk Until Knuckles Bleed as He Emphasizes Wilson's High Aims.

OTHERS JOIN HIM IN ATTACK

North Dakotan Reiterates Accusation That War President 'Falsified' on Pacts.

Text of Senator Glass's speech appears on Page 4.

By TURNER CATLEDGE.
Special to THE NEW YORK TIMES.

WASHINGTON, Jan. 17.—One of the bitterest personal attacks heard in the Senate in recent years was loosed today by Senator Glass against Senator Nye, chairman of the Munitions Investigation Committee, for his recent assertion, repeated today on the floor, that President Wilson and former Secretary of State Lansing "falsified" as to their knowledge of wartime secret treaties.

Beating his desk until his knuckles bled, his voice first shaking with emotion, then rasping in anger, the Virginian opened wide his noteworthy vocabulary to characterize one whom he said had made a "shocking assault" upon the character of Woodrow Wilson, expressing regret that the Senate rules kept him from using the word "coward" in describing the man, and "mendacious" in describing his attack.

Senator Glass took the floor just after Senator Nye, answering a like attack made upon him yesterday by Senator Connally, had reiterated his statement about President Wilson and Mr. Lansing, and at the same time had declared his intentions to proceed with the munitions inquiry along the lines already laid.

Nye Refers to Records.

Mr. Nye read from or referred to voluminous records in support of his charge that the United States entered the World War "knowing that the spoils had already been agreed upon." He deprecated the "gutter English" which he said his opponents were using in an attempt to discredit his inquiry into the munitions industry.

Mr. Nye's defense of his course, Senator Glass's castigation of the "dirt-daubing" of the sepulchre of Woodrow Wilson, another attack on the committee by Senator Connally and interpolations by Senators Robinson and Byrnes furnished another chapter in the sudden intra-Senatorial opposition to the munitions inquiry.

Out of it all came the clear indications that old-line Democrats, the lovers of Woodrow Wilson, may seek to cut the investigation short by refusing further funds after the pittance it has left is gone.

Senator Glass said that he, as chairman of the Appropriations Committee, would not vote "another dollar" to the committee, while Senators Robinson and Byrnes, both becoming incensed at the disclosure that relief workers had been put at the disposal of the committee for clerical help, indicated that they, too, would oppose any further funds.

Silent Crowd Hears Glass.

A silent and crowded Senate heard Mr. Glass's attack upon the man who had attacked his wartime chieftain. Before he arose to speak reports had passed about the Capitol that he would take the floor as soon as Senator Nye had finished his remarks.

From the challenging tone of the North Dakotan's speech it was readily concluded that some Democrat would answer, and when it was found that Mr. Glass was to take the responsibility himself, persons accustomed to following the doings of Congress knew that fur was soon to fly.

A quorum call brought Senators from the cloakrooms and lobbies. Word passed to the House brought a large number of members from that body. The galleries already were filled with spectators, largely veterans and others who had assembled to hear the debate on the Bonus Bill.

Every seat on the Democratic side was filled as the Virginian began.

Senator Nye sat through about half of the speech, then left the chamber. Occasionally he scribbled a note on a pad before him, but did not rise at any point to answer or to ask Senator Glass to yield.

He had used time earlier, however, to express his views. Answering then the sharp attack made upon him yesterday by Senator Con-

Continued on Page Four.

King Has Heart Ailment, Causing Concern in Britain

'Cardiac Weakness' Aggravates Bronchial Catarrh, Say Physicians—Oxygen Is Administered to the Sovereign.

Special Cable to THE NEW YORK TIMES.

LONDON, Saturday, Jan. 18.—A bulletin regarding the health of King George V caused anxiety here last night when it was broadcast. It was issued from Sandringham, the King's present residence, as follows:

The bronchial catarrh from which His Majesty the King is suffering is not severe, but there have appeared signs of cardiac weakness which must be regarded with some disquiet.

It was signed by three doctors, Lord Dawson of Penn, Sir Frederic Jeune Willans and Sir Stanley Hewett. Lord Dawson went to Sandringham yesterday and stayed for the night.

It was stated that oxygen had been administered as part of the modern method of treating bronchial catarrh when accompanied by cardiac trouble, but that this action did not indicate necessarily that the patient was gravely ill.

A telephone message from Sandringham after midnight said the King was then sleeping peacefully.

At 7:45 A. M. [2:45 A. M. Eastern Standard time] it was announced that there had been no change in the King's condition.

Sir Maurice Alan Cassidy, noted heart specialist and physician extraordinary to the King, was summoned to Sandringham early this morning.

The Prince of Wales left London for Sandringham yesterday, but it was emphasized that his visit was "just an ordinary one." Later it was said he would return to London today.

Two trained nurses have arrived at Sandringham. The King, who is in his seventy-first year, was last seen in public Wednesday, when he was out riding his white pony.

News of his illness was broadcast shortly before the conclusion of tonight's radio program of the British Broadcasting Company. Dance music was faded out and the bulletin read.

At Sandringham weather conditions are the worst possible for a bronchial patient. A keen easterly wind has followed a snowstorm, and the thermometer is falling.

Nursing Sister Agnes Black, who

Continued on Page Three.

HOFFMAN DEFENDS GRANTING REPRIEVE

Holds Murder Was Not One-Man Job—Defies Demand for Impeachment.

TO DETAIL REASONS LATER

Questions the Truthfulness and Mentality of Some of the State's Witnesses.

By CRAIG THOMPSON.
Special to THE NEW YORK TIMES.

TRENTON, N. J., Jan. 17.—Declaring that he doubted some parts of the State's case against Bruno Richard Hauptmann, Governor Harold G. Hoffman defended himself today against critics who had demanded his impeachment.

The demand was made in an editorial in The Trenton Times. For the first time Governor Hoffman made his position plain. He doubts the responsibility of some of the witnesses. He does not think Hauptmann was alone in the crime. And, he added, he "will not run away" from an investigation of his conduct.

Meanwhile Dr. John F. Condon, the Jafsie of the ransom negotiations for the return of Charles A. Lindbergh Jr., was advised by Attorney General David T. Wilentz to continue his vacation in Panama. "There is no need to change your plans," the Attorney General cabled after Dr. Condon had sent a telegraphic offer to return immediately. The Governor had said earlier that he wished to question Dr. Condon.

Wilentz Regrets Reprieve.

Using the telegram to Dr. Condon, which he made public, as an opportunity for expressing his opinion, Mr. Wilentz declared:

"I regret the course taken by the Governor only because it may be construed as a reflection upon the State, the State's witnesses, the police authorities of the several States of the nation who participated."

Meanwhile it was learned that death and kidnapping threats have begun to pour upon the Governor, who so far has paid no attention to them.

Threats have also been received by Mr. Wilentz and Anthony M. Hauck, Hunterdon County prosecutor, who participated in the case.

The Trenton Times printed the impeachment demand on the front page of the same issue that carried the reprieve announcement.

There is little likelihood, however, that impeachment proceedings will be started in the Legislature, according to persons well informed politically.

The Democratic leaders of the State, it was learned, are eager to keep clear of the Hauptmann case. They feel that the criticism that has already been made of the Governor has served their political purpose without starting an action which could not be successful without the aid of members of his own party in the Legislature.

There were, however, reports that a group of taxpayers who have not yet decided to identify themselves publicly were planning a mandamus action against Colonel Mark O. Kimberling, principal keeper of the New Jersey State Prison. Under this action Colonel Kimberling

Continued on Page Two.

GOEBBELS DEMANDS COLONIES FOR REICH

Tells 18,000 Time Will Come When It Must Claim Them as He Sympathizes With Italy.

SAYS 'BOILER WILL BURST'

Nation Can Do Without Butter if Need Be but Not Without Cannon, He Declares.

Wireless to THE NEW YORK TIMES.

BERLIN, Jan. 17.—Dr. Joseph Goebbels, the Minister of Propaganda, in a fiery address in the new Deutschland Hall tonight thunderously applauded by 18,000 of the National Socialist party rank and file, declared uncompromisingly that the time was coming when Germany must demand colonies.

"The German people, compared to other peoples, are a truly poor nation," he said. "We have no colonies and no raw materials. We must make our way through life the best we can.

"But the time will come when we must demand colonies from the world. In the long run it will be impossible for us to continue to vegetate as we are now doing. The rest of the world is drowned in excess and we have nothing.

"We have done all we can to improve our position through internal measures. But it is not enough. Every reasonable being in the world must see, therefore, that we need colonies. Others took our colonies away from us once upon a time and now they do not know what to do with them.

Sympathizes With Italians.

"We in our position can sympathize with the fact that people such as the Italians need room in which to live. When one does not know how a nation is to be nourished in the long run that fact becomes eventually a threat to the whole world."

Turning to immediate difficulties, Dr. Goebbels made no secret of the increase of 500,000 in unemployment during December but assured his audience that by February and March re-employment would set in. He laid the increase in the jobless to seasonal factors and the shortage of foreign raw materials.

In this connection he also referred to the coming necessity for demanding colonies and to the army's increasing need of copper, wool and other standard raw products that were either not produced at all in Germany or in insufficient quantities to keep the new military establishment equipped.

"We can get along, if it is essential, without butter, but never without cannon," the Propaganda Minister declared. "If we were to be attacked we could not defend ourselves with butter but only with cannon and rifles.

"Perhaps we should consider whether the League of Nations cannot guarantee peace through its moral authority. But such theoretical exercises are not calculated to relieve us of the necessity for owning cannon. The more irons in the fire the better."

Germany's workers were warned by Dr. Goebbels in this same connection not to expect any general rise in wages.

"National discipline means that we must recognize that at present no general increase in wages is

Continued on Page Nine.

RUDYARD KIPLING DIES AT AGE OF 70; CONSCIOUS AT END

Wife and Daughter Are With Him at Death Resulting From Peritonitis After Operation.

RULERS SHOWED CONCERN

Author's Works a Saga of the Glory of the Empire—Stirred Many Controversies.

Special Cable to THE NEW YORK TIMES.

LONDON, Saturday, Jan. 18.—Rudyard Kipling, one of Britain's greatest men of letters, died at 12:10 o'clock this morning, five days after he had undergone an emergency operation for a perforated stomach ulcer. He was 70 years old.

The author, who won fame for his picturesque tales and ballads about India and for his ardent imperialism, had lapsed into a coma early yesterday morning. At his bedside in the Middlesex Hospital here at the end were his American-born wife and their daughter, Mrs. George Bambridge.

Oxygen and infusions were used yesterday in a futile effort to keep up Kipling's waning strength.

[Dr. A. E. Webb-Johnson, who was attending Mr. Kipling, said after his death, according to The Associated Press: "Mr. Kipling's end was very peaceful—it came very suddenly. His wife and daughter were with him. He put up a splendid fight and remained conscious all the time."]

Snow Deadens City's Roar.

A light fall of snow had whitened the somber buildings around Middlesex Hospital—itself a gloomy pile standing almost within a stone's throw of busy Oxford Street—and to some extent had deadened the roar of London's traffic, when, about 11 P. M., a matron quietly roused Mrs. Kipling and her daughter, both of whom had been resting in a near-by room.

"We fear the end is near," she said.

Dr. A. E. Webb-Johnson, Mr. Kipling's physician, who had behind him all the science and skill that London could provide, was standing at the bedside as they entered. He was watching the effect of the last blood transfusion and of an infusion of saline. But Kipling was beyond aid and the end came soon.

Mrs. Kipling and her daughter, who had kept their vigil for more than forty-eight hours, were physically worn out. They were gently led away to rest.

Then down a long corridor in the silent building came an official with a paper in his hand.

"Mr. Kipling is dead," he told the waiting newspaper men. And out into the snowy streets they took the news that will sadden hearts wherever English is read.

Was on Way to South France.

Kipling was in London en route to the south of France for a Winter vacation with Mrs. Kipling when he was suddenly stricken last Sunday night. He was taken to the hospital in an ambulance Monday morning and his illness was diagnosed as the most serious form of gastric ulcer formation.

Kipling rallied well after the operation and Mrs. Kipling was allowed to sit at his bedside. Then, after he had rested quietly for more than twenty-four hours, peritonitis set in.

The author's tenacity, however, brought another rally, and early Thursday a bulletin from the hos-

Continued on Page Seven.

Nine Stavisky Aides Sentenced to Prison; Wife of Swindler Among Eleven Acquitted

Wireless to THE NEW YORK TIMES.

PARIS, Jan. 17.—Nine persons were convicted and eleven acquitted when after two years of political discord which have shaken the foundations of the French Republic a verdict finally was delivered today in the Stavisky case.

Mrs. Arlette Stavisky, widow of the swindler, was among those acquitted, and the heaviest penalty imposed was that of seven years at hard labor upon Gustave Tissier, former director of the Bayonne municipal pawnshop.

There was a huge throng both in the courtroom and outside but the calm with which the verdict was received contrasted strongly with violent passions which were aroused by the disclosure of the scandal and which resulted in rioting and bloodshed in the Place de la Concorde.

The curtain was rung down with a feeling of general relief but it was realized that the conclusion was being written not to the Stavisky case but to the Bayonne pawnshop scandal.

When the trial started fifty-four days ago, however, the names of the accused persons indicated that this trial would not touch any of those important personalities against whom charges so freely had been bandied.

The case had been reduced to its lowest terms as a vulgar financial fraud case. Two deputies, Joseph Garat and Gaston Bonnaure, were among those sentenced today. Bonnaure received a suspended sentence. Others were minor characters in the affair and they received terms from one to five years in jail.

Most of the accused have already served nearly two years of their sentences, and the same is true of those who were acquitted. Among the latter was Mrs. Stavisky, who was imprisoned many months and who said tonight her only desire now is to escape the limelight and obtain an obscure situation, preferably abroad, which would permit her to support her children.

There were also two prominent newspaper men, Camille Aymard, former editorial writer for Liberté, and Albert Du Barry, former director of Volonte, among those who were released. They were cheered and received the congratulations of many friends as they left the Palais de Justice.

PRESIDENT HOLDS SOIL ACT IS BASIS OF LONG RANGE AAA

It Makes Possible the Permanent Program Outlined on Oct. 25, He Tells the Press.

SILENT ON RAISING FUNDS

Paramount Agricultural Problem Is to Maintain Fertility of the Land, He Asserts.

Special to THE NEW YORK TIMES.

WASHINGTON, Jan. 17.—Assuming personal leadership of the new program to substitute the half-forgotten Soil Conservation Act of 1935 for the Agricultural Adjustment Act, President Roosevelt today not only endorsed such a course but went to some lengths in a White House press conference to explain that the shift in method of crop adjustments necessitated by a Supreme Court decision follows a program he laid down on Oct. 25.

Meanwhile, legislative draftsmen of the committees on agriculture of the House and Senate were working on amendments to the Soil Conservation Act in cooperation with legal and commodity experts of the Department of Agriculture.

In general the amendments would declare it to be the intention of Congress to maintain farm income at a level reasonably commensurate with that of industrial workers, and would make clear that farmers should be rewarded for maintaining "soil fertility" as distinguished from the prevention of "soil erosion."

Through the amendments it would be possible for the Department of Agriculture to broaden vastly the present soil conservation program by concentrating as much upon the upbuilding of quality as on the prevention of wastage.

Thus it would be made the permanent policy of the Federal Government to reward farmers for conserving soil resources. It is expected that the Department of Agriculture, in giving effect to the new program, will give due emphasis to patriotic motives in its appeal that the basic farm plant should be left unimpaired for posterity.

Not a Reply to Hoover Speech.

The President cautioned reporters not to interpret his remarks as a reply to the speech delivered yesterday by former President Hoover, saying that he had not read the speech.

Mr. Roosevelt did not claim credit for the substitution of the conservation method of crop control for the government-farmer contract method, an action he approved at a conference of officials at the White House yesterday, but he showed by his cheerful manner that he considered this a most happy solution of the problem.

He was unable to say at this time, he remarked in response to questions, where or how the government would raise the funds necessary for continued expenditures in the form of payments on leases as a means of withdrawing surplus and submarginal land from production and, in fact, was careful to keep talk of finance separate from discussion of the operation of the conservation program.

On the other hand, he said that the Conservation Act, with a few simple amendments which he was not ready to describe, would carry out exactly the program he laid down in a public statement on Oct. 25, in which he defined the admin-

Continued on Page Five.

ELLSWORTH TELLS THE STORY OF FLIGHT ACROSS ANTARCTIC; BATTLED A RAGING BLIZZARD

Byrd Hails Exploit of Ellsworth and Aide; Explorers Here and Abroad Add Praise

By Rear Admiral R. E. BYRD.
Special to THE NEW YORK TIMES.

PORTLAND, Ore., Jan. 17.—Your wire received and thank you for the opportunity to express my opinion of Lincoln Ellsworth's flight.

In the first place he showed supreme courage; in the second it was a wonderful job of navigating, unsurpassed I believe; thirdly it must have been very productive and important from a geographical standpoint.

It will in my opinion take rank in history with the greatest flights. Ellsworth and Hollick-Kenyon have given us, who have been in the Antarctic, reason to take our hats off.

Special Cable to THE NEW YORK TIMES.

LONDON, Jan. 17.—Admiral Sir William Goodenough, past president of the Royal Geographical Society, expressed delight today with the news that Lincoln Ellsworth and Herbert Hollick-Kenyon were safe.

"It is great," he said. "It shows what enterprise can do when carried out with forethought. The whole world will rejoice on knowing these two brave men have come through safely."

"It is the best news I could have heard," said Dr. Hugh Robert Mill, geographer and meteorologist. "It is an extraordinary coincidence that the Discovery II should have been instrumental in finding them, especially at this time. It was exactly two years ago when the Discovery went to rescue Rear Admiral Byrd by getting a doctor to him from New Zealand. Now she has been able to save the lives of another American explorer and his English companion.

"It is good to know the Discovery's time has not been wasted. It will now be quite impossible for her to carry out the scientific investigations for which she was sent out, as the channel is only navigable for a month or two at most each year.

Continued on Page Three.

NOW ABOARD RESCUE SHIP

Forced to Land 4 Times on Trip to Little America, Once for Week.

GALE LASTED THREE DAYS

Finally Gasoline Gave Out and He and Hollick-Kenyon Could Not Power Radio.

WALKED THEN TO BYRD BASE

They Found Shack in Good Condition and Lived Comfortably There Until Rescued.

By LINCOLN ELLSWORTH.
Copyright, 1936, by The New York Times Company and NANA, Inc.
Wireless to THE NEW YORK TIMES.

ABOARD THE DISCOVERY II, in the Bay of Whales, Antarctica, Jan. 17.—At last the transantarctic flight has been accomplished, but not without some difficulty. We were forced to land four times on the way and we were held up once for seven days, for three days of which a blizzard raged. On a previous landing we had been delayed for two days by bad visibility and snowstorms.

Finally our fuel gave out at Lat. 78 degrees 45 minutes S. and Long. 163 degrees 36 minutes W., which is about twenty-five miles from Little America. We remained for four days with the plane, doing our best to get in communication with the outside world, but our trail radio set proved ineffective and we had no more gas with which to run either the plane engine or the emergency engine for the radio.

Walked to Little America.

Failing to receive a response from our signals, we packed our sledge, hauled it to Little America and there found the radio shack in first-class conditon, and in it we lived comfortably until yesterday, when the roar of an airplane overhead let us know that our lonely wait was over.

We realized that our plane radio set had failed shortly after 4:15 P. M. [all times given are Greenwich Mean] on the day we started, but there was nothing we could do about it in the air and all we could do was to continue.

Shortly after passing the plateau beyond the Hearst Land coastal range we crossed another range, which extended for seventy-five miles and the peaks on it ranged to 13,000 feet.

Beyond that to Little America we were above an enormous fairly level plateau.

We found our food and equipment excellent. The Polar Star performed wonderfully well and Hollick-Kenyon [Herbert Hollick-Kenyon, his co-pilot] and I, except for a slight cold I picked up a few days ago, are in excellent health and are looking forward to joining the Wyatt Earp [Ellsworth's supply ship] on Sunday.

Flew Over High Plateau.

After passing the mountains of Hearst Land on our flight on Nov. 23 we flew at an altitude of 10,000 feet over a high plateau with isolated mountains at intervals. Then these gave way to an unbroken plateau.

At 4:15 P. M. we found that the radio transmitter failed to work, and later we discovered that the switch and the antennae lead were defective.

At 5:45 P. M. I dropped the Stars and Stripes on hitherto unclaimed territory. At that time we were near another mountain range. At 7:35 we were right opposite the mountains, which seemed to extend for at least seventy-five miles and some of the peaks were 13,000 feet in altitude. The visibility so far on the flight was excellent and we could see for about 130 miles.

At 9:05 P. M. we ran into bad visibility and went down to 6,400 feet, then lower, and at last we were forced to land. Our position was then latitude 79 degrees 12 minutes south, longitude 104 degrees 10 minutes west.

After some time the weather seemed to clear and on the 24th, at

Continued on Page Three.

T. J. COOLIDGE QUITS HIS TREASURY POST

Under-Secretary Pictured by Friends as Opposing More Spending by Government.

L. W. ROBERT JR. ALSO GOES

Assistant Secretary Returns to Private Business—All Exchange Cordial Letters.

Special to THE NEW YORK TIMES.

WASHINGTON, Jan. 17.—T. Jefferson Coolidge, Under-Secretary of the Treasury, sent his resignation to President Roosevelt today, because, his friends said, he felt that he could not give 100 per cent support to the administration, and disapproved the continuation of an emergency spending policy by the government at a time when business was showing signs of improvement.

Neither Secretary Morgenthau nor Mr. Coolidge would discuss the resignation, but there was every evidence of sincere regret on their part that the break had come. This feeling was expressed by President Roosevelt. The President and Mr. Morgenthau sent Mr. Coolidge letters in which he was addressed affectionately as "My Dear Jeff" and thanked him for the service he had given his country. The resignation was accepted as of Feb. 15.

President Roosevelt today also received and accepted, as of Feb. 15, the resignation of L. W. Robert Jr. as Assistant Secretary of the Treasury. Mr. Robert for some time has been planning to return to private business. There was an interchange of cordial communications in which Mr. Robert thanked the President for the opportunity to "serve my day and generation in your great and forward-looking administration," and Mr. Roosevelt replied with a characteristic letter addressed to "Dear Chip."

Thinks Emergency Is Over.

There have been rumors from time to time that Mr. Coolidge might retire, but they were denied, and his action came as a surprise to all but a few of his intimate friends.

The most authoritative explanation obtainable, in the silence of Mr. Coolidge himself, was that while in March, 1934, when he first went to the Treasury as a special assistant to the Secretary, he felt that an emergency existed which called for carrying through many of the New Deal policies temporarily, he had reached the conclusion that the emergency had ended.

As to fiscal policies, Mr. Coolidge was said to have had little faith in the administration's silver program, or the large outlays of money which delayed the day when a balanced budget could be reached and more orthodox methods revived.

This being an election year, if Mr. Coolidge had remained in the Treasury post it would have been tantamount, his friends said, to endorsement of policies affecting the Treasury with which he was not in accord.

Information from one source also was that Mr. Coolidge was concerned with the question of Federal versus State rights involved in

Continued on Page Six.

SENATE BONUS VOTE DELAYED TILL TODAY

Harrison Predicts Bond Bill Will Become Law Whether or Not Roosevelt Signs It.

'BEST FOR ALL,' HE SAYS

Thomas, Urging Payment by Currency Issue, Warns of 4 Billion Cost in 1945.

Special to THE NEW YORK TIMES.

WASHINGTON, Jan. 17.—Following a prediction of Senator Harrison that whether the Bond Bonus Bill was signed by the President or not, it would become law, the Senate tonight unanimously agreed to limit debate of each Senator to fifteen minutes after 2 o'clock tomorrow afternoon, in the hope of passing the measure before adjournment.

The House will not be in session tomorrow, so the bill will lay over until next week before final action is taken and the measure is sent to the White House.

But for another acrimonious debate concerning the activities of the Senate Munitions Investigation Committee, in which Senators Nye, Glass, Connally, Robinson and Byrnes took part, the bonus probably would have been approved before recess tonight. The unexpected flare-up delayed discussion of the bill for more than three hours.

Senator Harrison spent forty minutes explaining the differences between the Senate Bond Bill and the House cash payment plan before Senator Nye interrupted bonus debate.

"I have worked hard to get a bill that would be passed," Senator Harrison told the Senate. "I want to get it out of the way and I do not think this should be a political issue. It crops up every year and it is best for everybody that it be passed. I do not know whether the President will sign it or not.

"There is a great difference between this bill and the one sent to him last year and which he vetoed.

"Senator Robinson and I have tramped our way to the White House and to the offices of Senators in an effort to reach an agreement on the bill. But I will say, whether it is signed by the President or not, it will become law because it is the best way out of the situation, and because it is lighter and easier on the government."

Just before he concluded, he said in reply to Senator Couzens:

"I think he (the President) may easily sign the bill and I hope he will sign it."

For more than one hour late today Senator Elmer Thomas presented figures on the total bonus cost, in an effort to convince the Senate that his amendment providing for issuance of currency against the gold and silver reserve would be the cheapest method of financing the measure.

Mr. Thomas said that 495,000 veterans had not yet borrowed and so probably would carry their bonds until 1945, and that about 250,000 who had borrowed, but were not now in distress, would not cash the remainder due them. This would involve about $600,000,000.

But the other 2,768,191 veterans, he said, "will cash the bonds as

Continued on Page Six.

RUDYARD KIPLING DIES AT AGE OF 70

Continued From Page One.

pital announced that he was maintaining progress, with a slight improvement in his condition. Thursday evening, however, his condition was termed "extremely grave." From then on it became steadily worse, and Dr. Webb-Johnson was at his bedside constantly.

Since the World War, in which his son was killed, the author had been virtually a recluse at Burwash, Sussex, where he lived in a medieval house surrounded by a moat and an eight-foot hedge. One of the last times he was seen in public was at the King's Jubilee Garden Party at Buckingham Palace last Summer.

During his final illness King George and Queen Mary were frequently informed of his condition.

KIPLING A CHAMPION OF IMPERIAL GLORY

His Fame Is Expected to Rest on Vivid Tales of British in a Vast, Mysterious India.

STIRRED MANY DISPUTES

'Slight' to Victoria Closed the Laureateship to Him—Was 'Dated' in Recent Years.

Rudyard Kipling was beyond question one of the most fabulous figures of his generation. In a field for which he was uniquely and opulently endowed, Kipling produced an amazing series of masterpieces in both poetry and prose.

He made the world gasp with the freshness, vividness and vigor of his first writings out of India. He swept powerfully and turbulently across international public consciousness as a story-teller, a novelist, a poet of exceptional compulsion.

At the peak of his fame he represented probably better than any other the spirit of his land. He was a tremendous voice hailing the empire on which the sun never set; a storming prophet of its expanding greatness. He twisted the vague concept of imperialism into the striking image of the "White Man's Burden" and he culled from the scrubby borderline between the British Tommy and the native water-boy the touching legend of Gunga Din.

Offended Queen Victoria.

Kipling was a disciple of strength, of forthright expression, of color, movement, achievement. Vortex of scores of whirling controversies, he offended from royalty down; and for his reference to Queen Victoria in "The Widow at Windsor," he was believed to have doomed all hope for the Poet Laureateship. He did win the Nobel Prize for Literature in 1907 and was the first Englishman so honored.

But when that is forgotten, together with the suspicion of lèse majesté, it is likely that Kipling will live as a laureate in his own right. He combined startling talent as writer and propagandist, a true champion of Britain. The principles with which he girded his work began to crack and crumble long before he died; his voice was ignored in some quarters and somewhat ridiculed in others. But he remained Rudyard Kipling.

The author was generally considered best in his portrayals of the India of the native. These included "Soldiers Three," "The Gadsbys," "The Man Who Would Be King," "Without Benefit of Clergy," and especially, "Kim," frequently looked upon as his finest single book, embodying a vibrant panorama of the many-hued vastness of the peninsula.

He was a master of style. He had an unerring sense of balance of the right word. He knew the brutal small-talk of the barracks, whose tenants in India he did more to immortalize than any of their officers, and he was capable of the loftiness of "The Recessional." In verse he was a splendid workman, with a wide range of meters within easy command. It was the perfect lilt of many of his poems, as well as their dramatic qualities, that led to their widespread repetition as recitation pieces.

Kipling's works, begun in 1886 with a compilation of his verse first published in the Lahore Civil and Military Gazette, are now represented in more than fifty volumes, which have been published in virtually every country boasting printing presses.

Advice to the Empire.

During the past twenty-five years he had not written so much nor so well, but he remained a figure not only in literature but also as a propagandist and even, in a minor way, a politician. He often and vehemently gave Great Britain advice on the subject of the colonies, on expansion, on the Boer War, against Canadian reciprocity, on the Irish question, on woman suffrage —the world still quotes his line "the female of the species is more deadly than the male," which showed how he regarded feminism—and there were reports that he advised his cousin, Stanley Baldwin, during his second incumbency of the Premiership, on the ways the empire should go.

Once, in 1912, he made a stump speech for the Liberal Unionists, but it was not considered a success, and two years later when the Bordesley Liberal Unionist Association asked him to stand for Parliament he refused.

Earlier, in 1911, after he had collaborated in a "History of England," he was criticized twice in the House of Commons for what were described as "libels on the Irish" in the book, for Kipling was a violent Ulsterite; and in 1912, on the eve of the presentation of a Home Rule Bill, he issued some verses entitled "Ulster" which aroused Irishmen to bitter anger.

Some Called Him "Scold."

Writings such as these detracted somewhat from the esteem in which he was held for his earlier work. He was called a "scold," but his pen and his voice became valued and valuable again when he urged and glorified the task that was Britain's in the World War, in which he lost his only son, John.

But it is on his work on India that Kipling's fame is expected to rest. No one had told of such an India before he appeared with that first slim volume, "Departmental Ditties," and told the British of their Tommy following it with "Plain Tales From the Hills" and six short stories. These gave the world fascinating pictures of a land it did not know, just as for the first time Bret Harte gave it images of picturesque California and Mark Twain of a picturesque Mississippi Valley.

Kipling wrote of India in such a way that no man who has written of it since has been able to make his words memorable to the public, but no one, perhaps, knew India as Kipling knew it. He was born there Dec. 30, 1865, the son of John Lockwood Kipling and Alice MacDonald, each the child of a Wesleyan preacher, who had married in Staffordshire, England, early in the same year, and gone to Bombay, where Mr. Kipling had obtained a post as Professor of Architectural Sculpture in the British School of Art.

Early Life in England and India.

The boy was named Rudyard after a lake in Staffordshire where the artist John Kipling met and courted Alice MacDonald. To this lake Rudyard Kipling was brought by his mother when he was 3 years old, and there, in 1868, his sister was born. In the following year the mother and the two children returned to Bombay, remaining there until 1871, when the family returned for a while to England, leaving the children there for schooling.

Rudyard, a precocious, studious, energetic child, was taught first by relatives at home, but ever he roamed far afield and supplemented

Associated Press Photo.

One of the last photographs of Rudyard Kipling as he approached his seventieth birthday, last Dec. 30.

his studies by reading, so much so that at 10 years of age he wore double-lensed spectacles and was dubbed "Beetle" because he stumbled when he walked.

The future author was disclosed first at school, in the United Services College at Westward Ho in North Devon, where so many Anglo-Indian families sent their youngsters for schooling. Kipling then was 13 years old, still precocious, imaginative and, it has been written, already strong-willed. He wrote much for the school paper, which he eventually edited, and for The Bideford Journal, a newspaper in the school town. Here he remained until 1882, when he was 17 years old, and then he went back to India, where already he had been promised a place as a reporter on the Lahore Civil and Military Gazette, the most influential newspaper in Northwest India.

First Work of His Genius.

In Lahore, in addition to all the multitudinous and drudging details that fall to a cub reporter, young Kipling, goggle-eyed, industrious and painstaking, wrote verse and stories with such a flair for the picturesque, the glamorous, the sentimental and the salty details of Indian life that the contributions, published in The Gazette, were commented upon everywhere the British Tommy was stationed; and the sun did not set on British dominions. Orders for old numbers of the newspaper containing the verses of the young writer encouraged Kipling to compile a volume of them. He set most of the type himself in the composing room of The Gazette and did his own binding and called the volume "Departmental Ditties." They appeared in 1886, when the author was not yet 21 years old, and he described the volume's appearance later as a "sort of lean, oblong docket, wire-stitched to imitate a D. O. Government envelope printed on one side only and secured with a red tape."

Next he followed the practice of Walt Whitman and marketed the volume without aid. He printed postcards, containing order blanks, requesting remittance with order, and mailed them to the newspaper's readers everywhere. The profit, as he wrote later, was so good it "has since prevented my injuring my health sympathizing with publishers who talk of their risks and the cost of their advertisements."

In the following year, after nearly five years' service on The Gazette, Kipling was sent to Allahabad to work on The Pioneer, which was controlled by the same persons who published The Gazette, and there, too, his contributions were esteemed. So the next year, 1888, he published at Calcutta "Plain Tales From the Hills," which was an instantaneous success, and it was followed quickly in the same year with six green-covered pamphlets, which, although sold mostly at the railroad stations, were to make him famous. They were later translated into nearly every foreign language, and the original editions a few years later, during the height of the Kipling craze, were worth almost their weight in gold to collectors. These six pamphlets were "Soldiers Three," "The Gadsbys," "In Black and White," "Under the Deodars," "The Phantom Rickshaw" and "Wee Willie Winkie."

But the young writer was not to have an unbroken career of success. In 1890 he started on a tour of the world, going first to Japan and then the United States, hoping to make his living by writing, and then he suffered his first bad fortune. Publishers here neglected him. In London a year later he said he toured the United States from coast to coast in search of newspaper work without getting a chance even to state his qualifications.

Popular Phrases Taken From Kipling's Works

Among the most popular of the scores of phrases by Rudyard Kipling that became familiar in every-day conversation — often without the speakers knowing who had originated them and often in corrupted form—were the following:

"East is East and West is West, and never the twain shall meet. . . ."

"A rag and a bone and a hank of hair. . . ."

"You're a better man than I am, Gunga Din!"

"I've taken my fun where I've found it. . . ."

"The tumult and the shouting dies. . . ."

"The White Man's burden. . . ."

"The female of the species is more deadly than the male."

"An' I learned about women from 'er!"

"For the colonel's lady an' Judy O'Grady

"Are sisters under their skins!"

"There's no discharge in the war!"

Lived in a London Garret.

However, even London was little more hospitable to the newcomer at first; for, it has been recorded, he had to live meagerly in a garret, and when he had finished two or three stories he sold them; but the writer who later asked and got the highest prices paid an author, even, it was said, a dollar a word, sold these first two or three stories for $15.

In 1892 he came to the United States again after a visit to South Africa, Australia and Ceylon, and in New York that year he married Miss Caroline Starr Balestier, a daughter of H. Wolcott Balestier, whom he had met the previous year in London while collaborating with her brother, Walcott, in writing "The Naulahka."

Mr. and Mrs. Kipling went first for a wedding trip to Japan and returned to live here at Brattleboro, Vt., where, in the shadow of the Green Mountains, he built a home and worked until 1896, writing "Barrack Room Ballads," "The Seven Seas" (poems), "Many Inventions" and the two Jungle Books. They went to England in 1897, when he wrote "The Recessional" for Queen Victoria's Diamond Jubilee.

Serious Illness in New York.

They returned to New York in 1899. Here on Feb. 22, 1899, he suffered an attack of pneumonia which affected both lungs. He lay near death in his apartment at the Hotel Grenoble and for a while his life was despaired of. Interest in his condition was intense throughout the nation, hundreds of messages of sympathy being sent to Mrs. Kipling and their three children.

Then, as Mr. Kipling's rugged constitution began to assert itself, and it was seen he would recover, his daughters, Josephine, 6 years old, and Elsie, 3 years old, became ill with pneumonia at the home of Miss Julia De Forest, a friend of the family, at 121 East Twenty-fifth Street. Josephine died on March 6 and her father was not told until several weeks later, because it was feared the shock might cause a relapse. Elsie later married Captain George Bambridge.

The Kiplings returned to England in June, taking their daughter's ashes with them in a porphyry urn, which Mrs. Kipling carried in a black traveling case. The ashes were buried in the family plot at Rottingdean, and the Kiplings never returned to this country.

Rudyard Kipling's work was prodigious, even though he worked most slowly, and threw away, it was said, six stories for every one published. Four-fifths of his work, critics have said, was good, some of it excellent, and the remainder has been called bad. His earlier works have pleased most generally. "The Light That Failed" (1891), his first long novel, was his answer to critics who said he could write only in flashes of short narrative. "The Brushwood Boy" (1895) added to the merit of his fame. "The Seven Seas" (1896) showed even the most carping of his critics that he was a real poet.

In the following year Kipling wrote "The Recessional," which was a prayer for humility in the breasts of Britons:

God of our fathers, known of old,
  Lord of our far-flung battle-line,
Beneath whose awful Hand we hold
  Dominion over palm and pine—
Lord God of Hosts, be with us yet,
Lest we forget—lest we forget!

The tumult and the shouting dies;
  The captains and the kings depart;
Still stands Thine ancient sacrifice,
  An humble and a contrite heart.
Lord God of Hosts, be with us yet,
Lest we forget—lest we forget!

Far-called, our navies melt away;
  On dune and headland sinks the fire;
Lo, all our pomp of yesterday
  Is one with Nineveh and Tyre!
Judge of the Nations, spare us yet,
Lest we forget—lest we forget!

If, drunk with sight of power, we loose
  Wild tongues that have not Thee in awe,
Such Boastings as the Gentiles use,
  Or lesser breeds without the Law—
Lord God of Hosts, be with us yet,
Lest we forget—lest we forget!

For heathen heart that puts her trust
  In reeking tube and iron shard,
All valiant dust that builds on dust,
  And guarding, calls not Thee to guard.
For frantic boast and foolish word—
Thy Mercy on Thy People, Lord!

Turning Point in His Career.

All the English-speaking world was moved by the lines, but Kipling, who wrote them, seemed to forget them later when he rebuked as "flanneled fools" the Britons who were squeamish about the Boer War, the "Little Englanders"

(continued)

who were about to persuade other Britons to forget the rude strength, firm purpose, steady courage and hardy enterprise with which Britannia ruled the waves and kept intact her empire.

In 1897, too, he wrote another novel, "Captains Courageous," also successful, and in 1898 he published "The Day's Work," in which he showed a new side, that of the mechanical engineer.

The turning point in his literary career, it has been said, came in the year of his illness. After that he was more the imperialist and the mechanic than the poet and story teller, although he wrote in 1901 "Kim," one of his best known works and which, it has been said, no other man could have written.

Everywhere he was honored. He received honorary degrees from McGill University, Durham, Oxford, Cambridge and the University of Paris, and St. Andrews University made him a rector to succeed Sir James Barrie.

In 1920 he published "Letters of Travel," made up of observations of trips he had made in various parts of the world. Then, in 1923, he published a "History of the Irish Guards in the Great War," the story of the regiment in which his son, John, had been a Lieutenant.

Yet, despite the quality of his early work and the enthusiasm it aroused throughout the English-speaking world, there were critics who ridiculed it. One, James K. Stephen, who was widely quoted, linked Kipling's work with Rider Haggard's, which critics had generally scorned.

Again Attacked by Pneumonia.

In December, 1925, Kipling suffered another attack of pneumonia, from which, as in 1899, he recovered after doctors had virtually given up hope of saving him.

A year later his fiftieth book was published, a collection of poems and short stories called "Debits and Credits." While it added nothing to his literary reputation, a storm of protest was aroused in America because of a poem it contained, called "The Vineyard," casting what was considered a slur on America's part in the World War.

The high opinion Kipling enjoyed among littérateurs was demonstrated by the prices early editions of his books brought at an auction held in New York Jan. 17 and 18, 1928—a total of about 400 items—a copy of the first edition of "Letters of Marque" bringing $10,900. Several months before that the Rosenbach Company had paid $14,000 for a copy of "The Smith Administration," said to be the highest price ever paid up to that time for a book by a living writer.

Controversy in Recent Years.

The last decade was not free of controversy involving Kipling, although it saw the growth of a generation to whom the writer was more generally a dated prophet of empire than a national hero. In May, 1928, his "Hymn Before Action" was chosen as a test piece for a musical competition at Brighton. The choir of Union Church there promptly withdrew its secretary, declaring:

"In the mouths of troops of savages bent on slaughter and calling on the tribal deity, such words might be appropriate enough, but they present a primitive, unworthy conception of the Deity and are unfit to be sung by a choir in a Christian church."

In September, 1928, wide interest was aroused in the announcement that Kipling had arrived at Balmoral Castle as guest of the King and Queen. It was widely interpreted as indicating the lifting after nearly twoscore years of the unofficial "ban" said to have been incurred by "The Widow at Windsor."

He visited Jerusalem in the Spring of 1929. That Fall a poem appeared evidencing the poet's interest in the new phase of aviation—the transoceanic flight. It was called "Hymn of the Triumphant Airman." Addressing schoolboys a month later, he asserted that "there is not much justice in your present world."

Laureateship Missed Again.

He was in Bermuda in 1930 when the death of Robert Bridges left the first possibility for his elevation to the laureateship since 1913. It was recalled that the alleged taboo on Kipling was ended; but it was also pointed out that certain attitudes of the writer who conceived the "Bear that walks like a man" might eventually make his selection internationally embarrassing. John Masefield was chosen.

Times Wide World Photo.

The Kipling home at Burwash in Sussex.

Times Wide World Photo.

Mrs. Kipling.

Times Wide World Photo.

His daughter, Elsie.

From Bermuda, Kipling went to Canada, remarking, before he left, that writing was "an awful trade—I mean it." Back in England, he stirred a minor tempest with "Memories," a poem steeped in bitterness at the Labor Government's proposal to lessen the frequency of official wreath-laying at the tombs of Unknown Soldiers.

Early in 1933 Kipling was widely quoted when he declared:

"In a certain measure I am remarkably like the rest of the English. First I convince myself that a thing is not going to happen, and when it does happen I say perhaps something will turn up. When it continues to happen I sit down and say, 'Well, I don't see what can be done; let us go for a walk.' I believe in hope. I don't know that I believe much in principles, in politics."

Named to French Academy.

He was named to the French Academy shortly afterward. On July 12 his agent in London revealed that the swastika would not appear on the cover of Kipling's next book. It had been carried previously on all of them, but Adolf Hitler had become German Chancellor a few months before. The agent said no explanation had been given by the writer.

Heard here over the radio for the first time that same July, Kipling, speaking from London, ended with the observation that "one's own heart is the best place in which to store the few things of life that really matter."

In December, 1933, he composed a toast to the empire for Christmas: "Our Empire: Her peace, her power, her security." Eleven months later he paid tribute to the valor of Australians in the World War in an ode written for the Victoria Centennial Celebration. It was read for the first time when the Duke of Gloucester dedicated the Shrine of Remembrance in Melbourne before 300,000 persons.

New Poems in 1934.

Two new poems were heard at the opening of the great Pageant of Parliament at Albert Hall, London, on June 29, 1934. The last stanza of a poem that appeared in a technical publication in March, 1935, was particularly powerful. It read:

Veiled and secret Power
  Whose paths we search in vain,
Be with us in our hour
  Of overthrow and pain;
That we—by which sure token
  We know Thy ways are true—
In spite of being broken—
Because of being broken—
  May rise and build anew,
  Stand up and build anew.

In 1935 "The Light That Failed" went toward the movies, with Sidney Howard doing the adaptation. Kipling himself touched up the script; one change, according to a film official, involved the line, "How could you?" Kipling made it read: "How the hell could you, you ass?"

"Review of the Fleet by the King," a dramatic descriptive poem, appeared July 16, 1935. Like many other Kipling poems, it was widely transmitted by cable; he was one of the very few poets whose work was regarded as important enough to be worth cable tolls.

Big Sale for Anthology.

"Kipling Week" was widely observed in connection with the author's seventieth birthday Dec. 30. The last of his works published here was "A Kipling Pageant," containing excerpts from prose and poetry and a few selections in full. It appeared on Nov. 29. The publishers announced recently that 60,000 copies had been sold.

That the prolific genius who created Kim slipped gradually from a peak of world acclaim that has seldom been matched will probably not be denied by his stanchest admirers. In a sober, precise sense, it will be difficult for those admirers to refute the charge that their old idol became dated, outlived his own improbable and fantastic glory.

But it will be even more difficult for those most relentless in their depreciation of Kipling as the prophet of a broken-down ideal to minimize his stature as a Titan in the world of the written word.

MASEFIELD VOICES PRAISE OF KIPLING

He Was 'Best of the English Imperial Poets,' the British Laureate Says in the West.

WALPOLE ADDS TRIBUTE

Novelist Extols Fellow-Author's Artistry, but Holds His Ideas Are 'Old Fashioned' Now.

LOS ANGELES, Jan. 17 (AP).—John Masefield, Poet Laureate of England, paid tribute to the memory of Rudyard Kipling tonight.

"Kipling was undoubtedly the best of the English imperial poets who helped to celebrate the achievements of the great reign of Queen Victoria," he said. "He was a story writer of genius, whose works have been a delight to many millions all over the world.

"To myself, who did not know his recent poetry, he is a Victorian poet whose best poems are not yet as well known as they should be. The great popularity of many of his ballads has tended to hide the merits of much work deeply felt and weightily told.

"When he rose first into fame the class which most loved him often used the phrase 'the white man's burden,' which was, I believe, his invention. He was the voice of that imperialism which was the main religion of the upper middle classes of the late nineteenth century.

"He is still widely read and admired. 'If' is probably the most popular poem now in the world. His short stories for the young and for the old have not yet been matched."

Walpole Pays Tribute.

Hugh Walpole, British novelist, said:

"Had Rudyard Kipling died forty years ago, it is no exaggeration to say that the civilized world would have been shaken from end to end by the news. When he was ill of pneumonia [at that time] both the Kaiser and the King of England sent telegrams to inquire of his progress.

"Now it is not so. He has had the luck, or the misfortune, to live on into a world to which he did not really belong. But that makes no difference in the final estimate of a great artist—for a great artist he was.

"He wrote prose so electrically exciting, so rich in its choice of words and rhythm of sentences that to read them will always be for any one who loves literature a marvelous experience.

"His ideas seem old-fashioned today and in their immediate imperial implication they are old-fashioned. But the philosophy of his books is based on fidelity, courage, humor and tolerance and those things will never be old-fashioned."

"Stalky" Eulogizes Kipling.

Special Cable to THE NEW YORK TIMES.

LONDON, Saturday, Jan. 18.—Major Gen. Lionel Charles Dunsterville, original of Rudyard Kipling's character "Stalky," eulogized the author today at Crowborough, Sussex.

Speaking of that immortal trio—Beetle, Stalky and McTurk—General Dunsterville said that their exploits as recounted by Kipling were based on actual incidents, embellished with "pure fiction."

In its comment on the death of Kipling The Daily Telegraph said that "Kipling roused a spirit in Britain which had long lain dormant beneath the current of insincerities of that period."

"Rhodes and Kipling," it added, "were protagonists of the new imperialism."

The Daily Mail said:

"He taught England the meaning of Empire and the Empire the meaning of England."

The Daily Express declared that "to strengthen our will and lift up our hearts that we might be fitter to discharge our heritage—this is what Kipling did for Britain."

The Morning Post said:

"He did not believe there would be an end to war nor that the empire could rest on any other foundation than the valor to defend and the wisdom to maintain it. This ardent patriotism, this scorn of democracy made him a byword of the Fabian and Liberal politician, but his shafts pointed with truth and feathered with music, struck the marks at which they shot. He gave youth a new and more robust faith. He was loved and his lines and characters have passed into the usage of our common intercourse."

KIPLING IS MOURNED; PRAISE WORLD-WIDE

Body, Which Will Be Cremated, Lies Before Altar in Hospital Where He Died.

QUEEN EXPRESSES GRIEF

Messages From All Parts of Globe and All Classes Are Received by Widow.

By FREDERICK T. BIRCHALL.

Special Cable to THE NEW YORK TIMES.

LONDON, Jan. 18.—The body of Rudyard Kipling, poet laureate of the British Empire by popular acclaim, lies tonight in the chapel of Middlesex Hospital, where he passed away, while from every place where the English language is spoken or read there pour in to the family, to newspapers and to public institutions tributes of his greatness, his inspiration and his skill as a master craftsman in literature.

His coffin lies on a bier before a modest altar, for the hospital is

(continued)

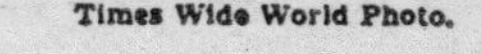

no show place—merely a quiet sanctuary built in memory of those who have died in the hospital's service. The coffin is covered by the Union Jack as fitting for a writer whose every effort was given in its service, and on it lies a bunch of violets sent by Mrs. Stanley Baldwin, wife of Kipling's cousin, the Prime Minister.

The soft light from the altar shines over the bier, and a privileged few paid tribute there today.

Body to Be Cremated.

It has been made known that the body will be cremated in accordance with a wish expressed by Kipling, but no details of this last rite or of the memorial service that certainly will be held have yet been arranged.

The death of one of the greatest personalities in English literature is a fact that has been to some extent obscured by British concern over the illness of King George. And that again is probably as Kipling himself would have had it.

It is notable, however, that thus far no suggestion has been heard that he should lie or some memento of him should be placed in Westminster Abbey, which he glorified so often in his writings and where so many of those great in English literature rest now. It seems as if he would pass as modestly as he lived, honored only by that great public that chooses its own heroes and is unmoved by titles and decorations, which he himself scorned.

However, the Queen, despite her great anxiety today over the menace of death in the royal household itself, was moved to send this message to Mrs. Kipling:

"The King and I are grieved to hear of the death this morning of Mr. Kipling. We shall mourn him not only as a great national poet but as a personal friend of many years. Please accept our heartfelt sympathy. MARY R."

In the course of the day there came to light an interesting memorial gift. The British Museum placed on view for the first time in Grenville Library the original manuscript of "Kim," together with the manuscript of a volume of Kipling's poems. They had been presented to the museum by the author in 1925 on condition that the gift should not be made known during his lifetime and that they should not be used for "collation or reproduction." A notice to that effect was placed beneath the manuscripts.

The conditions attached to the gift are characteristic of the giver, whose personal modesty—and irascibility when it was disregarded by infringement of what he considered his privacy—were well known. Kipling was subjected to plagues of popularity more than most men. At one time he had to cease paying his bills by check; autograph hunters bought up his checks from tradesmen in his village.

An Annoyance Doubled.

A new story was current today regarding this side of Kipling's existence. In the days when he lived at Rottingdean, Sussex, there was a bus driver who used to point out Kipling to his fares with a flourish of his whip. Kipling wrote a letter of protest to the bus proprietor. There was no answer. Kipling wrote again and yet again. Then he called. The bus proprietor received him all smiles.

"I wish you would write me a letter every day, Mr. Kipling," said he; "it's better than the bus business."

Tributes to the dead writer are coming from every part of the globe and from every class of men. One from United States Ambassador Robert W. Bingham was among the earliest.

"I feel that my rating of Kipling is representative of all Americans," said the Ambassador. "He was a great poet, a great prose writer and one of the supreme masters of the English tongue. In the United States he was read and admired throughout the entire country."

Rabindranath Tagore, Indian poet, grieves that "the voice which added new power to the English language is hushed in silence; I among the others who love the great literature of England mourn Kipling's passing."

Alfred Noyes's comment is that it is "only when great landmarks have disappeared that their loss is fully recognized." "Kipling," Mr. Noyes said, "will be read and remembered by generations as far removed from our own as our own is from that of Chaucer."

"Never Grew Up," Says Shaw.

George Bernard Shaw calls him benevolently "a great storyteller who never grew up." "He achieved greatness in his youth; he reached the climax of his career before he had grown up," Mr. Shaw commented.

But perhaps one of the most interesting tributes is one raked up from the past. In a letter to Henry James in December, 1890, Robert Louis Stevenson wrote:

"He amazes me. Certainly he has **the gifts; the fairy godmothers at his christening were all tipsy."**

From India are coming many reminiscences of Kipling's early life there. One of them shows how humble were the beginnings of his literary career. Sir Edward Buck, who knew him when he was a subeditor in Lahore, told a correspondent in Delhi:

"Mrs. Kipling, Senior, wrote me in Simla begging me to try and sell some copies of Rudyard's publication, "Plain Tales From the Hills." I sold seven at 1 rupee each, purchased five myself and remitted her the amount. Her letter of thanks and the five copies, alas, were never preserved, for it happened fifty years ago."

Mahatma Gandhi, who has been ill recently in Bombay, was asked by a news agency correspondent for comment, but unfortunately he was unable to make any because he had just had two more teeth removed. But all of Bombay who remembered **Kipling's boyhood there were anxious to talk of the precocious lad he was.**

Bungalow Birthplace Still Stands.

The bungalow in which he was born seventy years ago still stands, large, roomy and spacious, with the cool, wide verandas characteristic of that pre-refrigerator age. It is in the compound of the Bombay School of Art, where his father was a professor, and already there is a tablet on it, beneath which today are many memorial wreaths.

From the press of all countries but especially the press of France and Belgium, whose cause Kipling so warmly upheld throughout the war, are coming to London genuine expressions of sorrow over his passing and of appreciation of his genius. **Belgium has a lasting memorial of him, for at the Menin Gate, inscribed with the names of thousands of British soldiers who died in the surrounding battlefields, a bugler nightly at sunset sounds "Last Post." He is paid by a fund established by Kipling in memory of his own son, who was among those who fell there.**

PORT OF SPAIN, Trinidad, Jan. 18 (Canadian Press)—**"Kipling's exotic stories will carry him down to posterity," Somerset Maugham, British author, said today on his arrival here for a vacation that had been suggested by Kipling himself, who visited the West Indies several times in search of material for his tales.**

Mr. Maugham said he had been shocked to learn of the death of his intimate friend.

MAGIC OF KIPLING'S WORDS

His Imagination Ranged Afar and He Molded The Thoughts of a Host of Engishmen

By H. I. BROCK.

The death of Rudyard Kipling early yesterday morning, just past 70 years of age, removed from the world's stage not a mere poet and teller of tales but a monumental figure of the late nineteenth century with a powerful projection into the twentieth—in a very real sense the last of the Victorians and the first of the moderns among Englishmen.

Looking back over half a century it is easy to see that no single writer has contributed so much as he to mold the attitude toward life and form the ideals of the generation of English-speaking people that the World War found just turned 40 or even a little bit younger. This is true especially of the users of the language outside the British Isles, from North America to Australia and from the Cape of Good Hope to any of those "isles aside" that Kipling thanked God had escaped being his birthplace.

It was just fifty years ago that "Departmental Ditties" were published. "Plain Tales From the Hills" followed one year later. And for two decades and more afterward the new Kipling book was for most of us the literary event of every year. A Briton born in Bombay ("no mean city," as he has said, but a far cry from the white cliffs of Dover and the green hedgerows haunted by Puck of Pook's Hill), he was a brother to all the men and women of British stock whose nativity lay a long journey from the breeding place of that stock.

Struck a Responsive Note.

So that the passion of pride in the race and the soil of old England which breathed through all that Kipling wrote—grave or gay, prose or poetry—struck a note with a wide responsive echo. He smote his bloomin' lyre and drew together scattered nations that had almost forgotten their common kinship and all but lost the feeling of England as the home country of long ago.

A great story-teller from the beginning was this beetle-browed little man who began his literary career on an Indian newspaper on the other side of the world just about the time we here in New York were founding our Metropolitan Opera and opening our miraculous suspension bridge to Brooklyn. His was the magic that gives the written word power to people the imagination with creatures more vividly alive than any of those we meet daily in the street or encounter in the camp and in the wilderness or even going down to the sea in ships.

He had a feeling for old things and for new things. He could summon from the dim past the long dead garrisons of Roman walls and the crews of oar-driven galleys and make meaningful again to common coat-and-suit clothed mortals the lusty fellows that built the ancient empires and carried abroad their cultures, their commerce and their inventions.

Magic of His Words.

From the East to the West (though never the twain might meet) he could flash a sense of the strain in the dwelling together of alien races, white and brown and black and yellow. He could set you Tommy Atkins doing sentry-go among the heathen in their blindness, yet full of ancient wisdom and equipped with guile far beyond Tommy's understanding—or ours. He had a magic which made even the animals of the jungle talk to city-bred humans. And that is a very old magic indeed.

And then he could take MacAndrew's engines and make them sing the hymn of the new age that had yet in those days to produce either skyscrapers or airplanes, the radio or the movies. **He could send the Night Air Mail across the Atlantic before the Wrights flew at Kitty Hawk. Steamships and turbines and gas motors and submarines and aircraft took to themselves souls in his philosophy as at once instruments and symbols of the mechanic phase of the human drama which sets modern men matching their brains and courage against the secret powers that guard the riddle of the universe.**

The Little People that fancy finds still in moonlit shadows and who came into the world before ever the race of Adam arrived, these were real to Kipling. The master of the dynamo was not less real—or more. His wanderings over, and his experience as a resident of the United States of America relegated to the past (though it had given him an American wife in Caroline Balestier), he settled down in an ancient stone house in the heart of Southern England, the seat of an iron master who may have furnished the ore for swords and plowshares in the days before Elizabeth's admirals crushed the Spanish Armada.

The New and the Old.

But he was one of the very first men in all the British Isles to get a motor car. And it was his delight to think that the airmen, on the cross-Channel flight between Croydon and Le Bourget, swung down in thick weather to catch the sure landmark furnished by the mirrors turned to the sky by the still water of the round pond and the square pond in a garden set with the yew trees and hedges—the garden which lay beside that old stone house of his, with its clustered chimneys.

It was a mighty comfort to Kipling, as master of this house called Bateman's, to remember not only that the Romans and Duke William's men had marched along an ancient track not far from his gate, but that the motor cars still used it as the stage coaches had used to do, and that the air route between England and the Continent of Europe lay right overhead.

In the garden under a yew tree the bard of the far-flung British Empire—who was never to be poet laureate of little England—used to play with a little dog, belonging to his son, John, then a boy at school, but destined to serve in the Irish Guards and perish in the great war.

The war rent Europe asunder and left Kipling not much changed to the outward eye—though the boy and the dog were gone. But the eyebrows which had furnished the name "Beetle" to Stalky & Co. had grown more and more shaggy.

Naturally things—especially since the war—did not always suit the author of the Kipling tradition. He delivered his mind sharply from time to time both in prose and in verse. But even in the "Recessional" the prophet spoke warningly to his chosen people. And these later years have forgotten much that is mighty important in any vision of the world which distills from the past so religiously as does the vision which was Kipling's.

KIPLING

Sir Wm. Rothenstein Drawing.

Associated Press Photo.

Accompanying King George on an inspection trip of the British graves in Belgium during the war.

Scott, Poet, Adds Praise.

OTTAWA, Jan. 17 (Canadian Press).—"The verse of Kipling came like a breeze of fresh air. His stories revolutionized the art of short story writing." Thus Duncan Campbell Scott, famous Canadian poet, spoke tonight of the effect Rudyard Kipling had on young Canadian writers.

It is difficult, he said, for the present generation to understand exactly how Kipling impressed those who were beginning to write at about the same time as the British poet and story teller.

Kipling Fortune Believed To Total About £750,000

By The Associated Press.

LONDON, Jan. 18.—The fortune of the late Rudyard Kipling was estimated at £750,000 tonight by The Sunday Express.

"The Jungle Books" alone brought him an income of more than £10,000 annually, the paper said.

Kiplings's American royalties alone are estimated to have been nearly $1,750,000. More than 3,500,000 copies of his books have been sold by his official American publishers in the last forty years.

NRA U.S. WE DO OUR PART

"All the News That's Fit to Print."

The New York Times.

LATE CITY EDITION
WEATHER—Fair today, moderate temperature; tomorrow rain.
Temperatures yesterday—Max., [illegible]; min., 46.

Section 1

VOL. LXXXIV....No. 28,239. Entered as Second-Class Matter, Postoffice, New York, N. Y. NEW YORK, SUNDAY, MAY 19, 1935. Including Rotogravure Picture, Magazine and Book Sections. PPP TEN CENTS | TWELVE CENTS Beyond 200 Miles Except in 7th and 8th Postal Zones

BONUS CHIEFS FEAR ROOSEVELT SPEECH; PLAN NEW TACTICS

Patman Group Arranges for Last-Minute Appeal to the President Tomorrow.

LINES BELIEVED WAVERING

Swaying of House Votes to Sustain Veto Seen as Recheck Shows Senate Holds Firm.

INFLATIONISTS RESENTFUL

They Talk of 1936 Issue—Radio Will Broadcast Executive's Message to the Country.

Special to THE NEW YORK TIMES.

WASHINGTON, May 18.—President Roosevelt's decision to deliver in person his message vetoing the Patman Soldiers' Bonus Bill, now tentatively scheduled for Wednesday before a joint session of the Senate and House, caused expressions of resentment today from currency inflationists in Congress.

Taking for granted that the President would attack the measure's method of financing as threatening a further budgetary deficit through a currency issue, implied in the Patman bill provision for issuing $2,000,000,000 in United States notes with which to pay the veterans, the currency expansionists, as they prefer to be called, asked why they should be picked on for such a rebuke.

Arguments for President.

The House bonus steering committee made known late today through Representative Patman of Texas, author of the bill, that it had arranged for an appointment with the President for 10:30 A. M. Monday for a last effort to win him over.

"We will advance some arguments in favor of the bill that we do not think can be answered," Mr. Patman said.

Meanwhile Mr. Roosevelt polished his message while cruising on the yacht Sequoia over the week-end. Last night he had worked on it at the White House until after midnight.

Speaker Byrns said today that tentative arrangements for delivery of the President's message called for a radio broadcast to the nation over both the National Broadcasting Company and Columbia networks.

The President's personal appearance was expected to sway some House members who voted for passage of the Patman bill under pressure from home, but who could explain all to their constituents by saying that they "voted for Roosevelt" on the veto issue. These would be insufficient, however, to uphold the President's action, leaders believed.

In the Senate, the original Patman bill vote showed enough Senators opposed to any kind of bonus legislation to uphold the veto, and their strength appeared to be confirmed today in a re-check.

While Senator McCarran, a bonus backer, predicted that the personally delivered message would not sway a single vote in the Senate, others voiced the conviction that the President's visit would strengthen any wavering spines.

Heavy Vote Due in the House.

The most optimistic estimate heard in the House gave 125 as the number of votes that would be cast to uphold the President. This is well short of the theoretical 144 that would constitute the one-third necessary to block final passage of the measure.

The membership of the House is now 432 (there are three vacancies), but at least two members are expected to be kept away by illness. These are Representatives Bankhead of Alabama, the Democratic leader, and Peyser of New York. If all the remaining 430 were present and voting, it would need 144 ballots to sustain the veto.

An almost complete vote is expected on the issue, as every member wants to be on record on one side or the other. On final passage of the Patnam bill, the House polled 408 votes, and the President's personal appearance for the first veto message ever so delivered will undoubtedly attract a full attendance.

In the Senate, administration forces were counting on a minimum strength of the thirty-three Senators who voted against the Patman bill on its final passage to hold firm. If they do, they would sustain the veto even if the possible vote of 96 were cast.

To the fifty-five Senators who voted for the measure when it passed, Senator Thomas and other bonus leaders added the name of

Continued on Page Thirty.

Lawrence Dies of Crash Injuries After a Six-Day Fight by Doctors

Leader of Revolt in Arabia Was Unconscious Since Accident in Dorset in Which He Swerved Motorcycle to Save Boy—Called One of Britain's Greatest Heroes.

Wireless to THE NEW YORK TIMES.

WOOL, Dorset, England, Sunday, May 19.—After an amazing struggle for life Colonel T. E. Lawrence, "Lawrence of Arabia," succumbed this morning to the severe injuries he had suffered last Monday in an accident on his motor cycle.

For almost six days since the accident the 46-year-old steel-nerved leader of the Arab revolt in the World War had lain unconscious in the little military hospital at Bovington Camp, his life hanging by a thread. Noted specialists and a group of special nurses had done all that their skill could do for him, but from the first the odds were against him.

The physicians resorted to artificial feeding in an effort to maintain his strength, but the prolonged unconsciousness gradually sapped it. A close watch had been kept on him in the event that he might regain consciousness.

At 1 o'clock this morning Sir Faruhar Buzzard, the King's physician, arrived at his bedside after having driven from Oxford. He was immediately joined by other physicians, including Dr. H. W. B. Cairns, brain specialist, who made a dramatic dash, motoring the 100 miles from Arundel upon receiving an urgent call and reaching the hospital at 12:20 A. M.

Dr. A. Hope Gosse, London lung specialist, arrived at the hospital at 2:20 A. M. by auto and immediately went into consultation with Captain C. P. Allen, the hospital surgeon, and the specialist. Colonel Lawrence's relatives, summoned last night, were still maintaining an anxious vigil.

At 3 A. M. it was reported that there had been some failure of Colonel Lawrence's heart action.

"The outlook becomes much less favorable as a consequence of progressive congestion of one lung," the bulletin added.

Colonel Lawrence suddenly took a turn for the worse last night and relatives and close friends were hastily summoned.

The first indication of the extreme gravity of the patient's condition came at 6:45 P. M. when Captain Allen, who had been fighting throughout the week to save

Continued on Page Thirty-four.

VICE PROSECUTOR ASKED OF LEHMAN

Dodge Has Proved Inefficient or Worse, the City Affairs Committee Charges.

VISIONS VAST CRIME RING

City-Wide Organization Said to Run Rackets and Gambling as 'Big Business.'

The City Affairs Committee sent a telegram last night to Governor Lehman demanding that he supersede District Attorney William C. Dodge with a special prosecutor to take charge of the "vice and crime situation."

The committee also issued a statement saying that it would ask Mayor La Guardia to "undertake a thorough-going public investigation" of crime in the city, which it declared to be more prevalent than at any time since the days of District Attorney William Travers Jerome.

The statement, picturing the city as in the grip of a "trinity of social evils, prostitution, gambling and racketeering," declared that District Attorney Dodge had "proved himself inefficient or worse."

The District Attorney has been publicly "discredited" by the failure of the current grand jury investigation, the statement asserted.

Holds Lehman Responsible.

The statement, issued over the names of John Haynes Holmes, chairman of the City Affairs Committee; Rabbi Stephen S. Wise, vice chairman, and Frederick L. Guggenheimer, executive director, declared that "Governor Lehman cannot escape responsibility" for Mr. Dodge's conduct. Mayor La Guardia, the statement predicted, will welcome the suggestion of an investigation, as crime conditions, while "largely inherited from the past" are now "definitely on his hands."

Prostitution is rife in an organized and commercialized system, entering even into the public schools; gambling is fostered by business as well as criminal interests, and racketeering has invaded every private business and every public enterprise, the statement asserted. The committee declared that an "indignant public opinion" would be necessary to make any drive on crime successful.

Statement of Committee.

The statement, authorized by the directors of the City Affairs Committee, follows:

"The grand jury investigation, now drawing to a close, has revealed one fact at least with perfect clearness, and that is the tragic plight of the District Attorney of New York County. Mr. Dodge stands before his fellow-citizens discredited.

"As an official charged by the law with responsibility for the protection of the community from crime, he has proved himself inefficient, or worse. In spite of able and courageous grand juries and an aroused public opinion, there can be little done so long as this man occupies an office which he uses only to cheer himself and to jeer his critics.

"Meanwhile, vice and crime in this community remain what the City Affairs Committee and other civic bodies have described and de-

Continued on Page Fourteen.

LOUIS A. CUVILLIER DIES OF PNEUMONIA

Oldest Member of Assembly in Years of Service Led in Fight on Prohibition.

BECAME HIS PARTY'S WHIP

Hofstadter Committee Member Had Turbulent Career in Democratic Ranks.

Louis A. Cuvillier, veteran Democratic representative of the Twentieth Assembly District, who was the oldest member of the Assembly in years of service, died at 7:30 o'clock yesterday morning of bronchial pneumonia at the home of his sister, Mrs. Alice Cooley of 1,120 Bryant Avenue, the Bronx. He was 64 years old. Friends were inclined to believe yesterday that his strength had been seriously weakened by his exertions during the last session of the Legislature, and by the strain of the exciting final night.

The near relatives who survive, in addition to Mrs. Cooley, are his daughter, Mrs. Madeleine McCarten of Darien, Conn., and a grandson, Louis A. Cuvillier McCarten. His wife, the former Margaret Dufry, died four years ago. A high mass of requiem will be celebrated Tuesday morning in St. Paul's Church, 117th Street, near Park Avenue. Burial will take place in Arlington Cemetery.

A Veteran in the Assembly.

One of the veterans of the Legislature, Louis A. Cuvillier was regarded as the most independent member of the Assembly. He served during the years 1907-13 inclusive. Several factors, among them his opposition to woman suffrage, brought about his defeat in 1913. He was re-elected to the Assembly in 1919 and had been there ever since, except for a year's absence following his defeat in 1933. Although the Democratic leader could usually count upon Mr. Cuvillier's vote on a purely party measure, his independence in voicing his opinions frequently caused embarrassment to his Democratic colleagues.

Mr. Cuvillier was credited with knowing more about the State Government and parliamentary procedure than almost any other Democratic member of the Legislature in recent years. He did not use that knowledge always to expedite the Assembly's business. The general opinion regarding him is fairly expressed by the following report of the Citizens Union:

"Louis Cuvillier—Experienced and eccentric member; one of the most attentive; usually bothersome, but frequently useful."

Ardent Worker for Repeal.

In recent years Mr. Cuvillier had been an outstanding opponent of prohibition. He was chairman of the Constitutional Liberty League, which sought to bring about the repeal of the Eighteenth Amendment by a constitutional convention.

In the Assembly Mr. Cuvillier introduced many anti-prohibition measures. One of these, which failed of passage in the Senate, was a resolution to put the Legislature on record in favor of repeal. Another measure, which also failed, was for a referendum on repeal. Mr. Cuvillier's opposition to prohibition began even before the adoption of the Eighteenth Amendment. After the adoption of prohibition besides ad-

Continued on Page Thirty-two.

MUNICH NAZIS BEAT CATHOLICS IN RIOTS; END CHARITY DRIVE

People Flee Into Churches for Refuge as Collectors and Priests Are Mobbed.

POLICE FAIL TO INTERVENE

Troopers Tear Fund Badges From Contributors' Coats—Resentment Is Intense.

Wireless to THE NEW YORK TIMES.

MUNICH, May 18.—Nazi bands broke up a Catholic charity drive here today, finally staging city-wide anti-Catholic riots. Catholics fled to their churches for refuge while the Nazis marched through the streets and tore from the coats of contributors to the Catholic fund the badges that had been given to them.

The police made no effort to interfere and the Munich authorities at 3 o'clock this afternoon issued an order prohibiting the Catholic collectors from remaining on the streets. The money collected was temporarily confiscated.

Last year Caritas, the Catholic Charities Association, was not allowed to hold its annual drive in Bavaria, but it reported larger returns than the Nazi charity organizations in many other parts of Germany. This year the Catholic charities received official permission to carry on a two-day street campaign in Munich.

This morning 4,000 voluntary solicitors appeared in the vicinity of the churches and busy corners. At first they were successful and crowds of people put coins in their boxes.

Storm Troopers Appear.

Within half an hour, however, organized groups of Storm Troopers in civilian clothes and other Nazi party members appeared waving copies of the morning's edition of the Voelkischer Beobachter containing the report from Berlin of the sentencing of a nun to five years' penal servitude yesterday on the charge of exchange smuggling.

"Not a penny for smugglers! Don't give to black-frocked traitors!" cried the demonstrators in unison.

The Nazis gathered in groups in order to intimidate would-be contributors, brandishing their newspapers in the faces of pedestrians and shouting, "Don't give to traitors!"

Before long crowds of Catholic laity gathered to protest against the demonstrators. Immediately detachments of Brown Shirts and black-coated troopers in uniform appeared and drove the Catholics away.

Later several collectors were assaulted. The police arrested the victims "to secure their safety." The Nazis who had beaten them were left undisturbed or requested to move on.

After the police order appeared calling on the solicitors to withdraw, Storm Trooper bands began to patrol the sidewalks and proceeded to make insulting remarks to men and women pedestrians. At this stage uniformed Storm Troopers joined the groups in civilian clothing and began picking quarrels and jostling passers-by.

As the police did not interfere ordinary citizens streamed into the churches and the altars were sur-

Continued on Page Twenty-six.

LEHMAN REBUFFS FARLEY'S DEMAND FOR EXTRA SESSION

Governor Will Not Call Legislature Unless Reapportionment Can Be Passed.

NEEDED VOTES UNASSURED

Efforts of Postmaster General to Win Tammany to His Program Still Futile.

Special to THE NEW YORK TIMES.

ALBANY, May 18.—Governor Lehman declared today that he would not issue a call for an extraordinary session of the Legislature to consider reapportionment of the State Senate and Assembly districts and of the State's seats in Congress unless he was assured that there would be enough votes to pass measures providing for a change in the present set-up. Thus far, he has no such assurance.

The Governor made his views known in a chat today after cleaning up yesterday the last of the thirty-day bills left behind by the Legislature at its regular session. At that session Tammany Hall successfully blocked passage in the Assembly of bills reapportioning the State Senate, Assembly and Congressional districts.

Farley Wants Measure.

"I have no intention," said the Governor, "of calling a special session on reapportionment until I am absolutely certain there are enough Republican and Democratic votes to pass the bills. I do not propose to spend the taxpayers' money under any circumstances."

The Governor's stand is a blow to the Postmaster General of the United States, James A. Farley, who is also the chairman of the National and State Democratic Committees. Mr. Farley, who used all his influence in vain at the regular session to have passed a reapportionment bill which would reduce the representation of Tammany Hall in the State Legislature and Congress, believes such a measure could be forced through in a special session. He says the legislation he advocates would go a long way toward cementing the hold of the party on the State.

During the regular legislative session this year the Tammany leaders defied James J. Dooling, leader of the Hall, on the reapportionment measures, and it is understood their mood has not changed, despite the urgings of Mr. Farley. Originally Mr. Dooling consented to passage of the bill for State redistricting, but announced that he was not in a position to bind his local leaders.

Under the bills introduced at the regular session of the Legislature, Tammany Hall would lose three Representatives in Congress, three State Senators and seven Assemblymen.

The chief factor, however, in cementing the opposition of the Hall was that under the measure providing for legislative reapportionment, the present Assembly district boundaries which serve as a basis for district leadership, would be changed, throwing the already turbulent situation within the Democratic party in New York County into even greater confusion.

Since the adjournment of the regular session, Mr. Farley has

Continued on Page Thirty-one.

Epstein Calls Royal Academy 'Climbers'; President Refused to Defend Artist's Nudes

Special Cable to THE NEW YORK TIMES.

LONDON, May 18.—Jacob Epstein, American-born sculptor, has written to the Royal Academy asking that his name be withdrawn from the list of candidates for membership.

Sir William Llewellyn, president of the academy, had declined to sign an appeal for preservation of the eighteen nude statues by Epstein on the British Medical Association's former building, now the premises of the Rhodesian Government, which regards the statues as "unsuitable" and intends to remove them. Sir William is reported to have said: "It is not an academy affair."

"Not their affair!" exclaimed Mr. Epstein. "Then what on earth is the affair of the Royal Academy of Arts? Is it not their duty to prevent artists from being insulted and their works from being defiled?

"The Royal Academy is simply a smug company of business men. Membership is just a step toward social position. I want no association with such a company of social climbers. They are completely out of touch with artists."

Jacob Epstein's denunciation of the Royal Academy was based on a decision of the Rhodesian Mission in London to remove eighteen nude figures on which passers-by in the Strand have gazed for twenty-seven years.

When he was first starting on his stormy career of pioneering in sculpture Mr. Epstein, in 1907, got a commission for seven heroic figures to decorate the outside of the Medical Association building. They were daring nudes, seven feet high, intended to symbolize the life of man in various stages.

When they were unveiled an outcry was raised against them and police action was demanded by the National Vigilance Society and other bodies.

The Medical Association refused to remove them and the government decided not to act against it. Consequently the statues remained while one controversy after another developed over Mr. Epstein's succession of figures. The most recent of these was over his supposed representation of Christ, which has been called blasphemous.

The latest controversy arose after the Medical Association turned its building over to the Rhodesian Mission and that body decided the nudes were not suitable for a government building. It wants to sell the figures to galleries, but Mr. Epstein has insisted they shall not be moved.

SOVIET'S BIG PLANE CRASHES, WRECKED BY STUNTING CRAFT; 49 KILLED IN TWO MACHINES

Tomlinson Sets Three World Speed Records With Loaded Plane on 1,244-Mile Flight

By REGINALD M. CLEVELAND.

Slipping down out of the sunset sky at Floyd Bennett Field yesterday, Lieut. Commander D. W. Tomlinson added three new world's records for speed with load for land planes and two new American records to the fourteen he set on Thursday. In addition, he bettered all the marks he had made in the same TWA flying laboratory, the Douglas DC-1, for distances up to 2,000 kilometers.

In all he and his two co-pilots, Joseph Bartles of the same airline and the speedy gyro pilot, which he said handled the plane 90 per cent of the time, have returned eight world records to the United States and established or broken eleven American records.

The score in world's records in aviation now stands: France 40, United States 39, Italy 21, Germany 8, Poland 1 and Austria 1. As soon as Hamilton constant-speed propellers, the gear-shifts of the air, can be adjusted to the two 715-horsepower Wright Cyclone engines of the Douglas, Commander Tomlinson said last night, he will try to bring back to the United States two altitude records for loaded land planes now held abroad.

Apprised of the success of the flight in which the former navy sea hawk sent his big low wing monoplane hurtling around the 621 miles course for two laps or a total of 1,244 miles at an average speed of 190.906 miles an hour, Senator William G. McAdoo, president of the National Aeronautic Association, sent a telegram from Washington to Jack Frye, president of TWA, at Kansas City which read:

"Telegram received. Congratulate you heartily on your fine performance."

As she was during the long grind of Thursday in which her husband flew five laps of the course from Floyd Bennett to Bolling Field to Willoughby Spit, Va., and return, Mrs. Tomlinson was an interested but calm observer during yesterday's run. Most of the time she spent in the control tower of the administration building at the field, where the officials of the N. A. A. and the two-way radio apparatus

Continued on Page Two.

COLLISION NEAR MOSCOW

3 on Ground Reported Killed in the Fall of Largest Land Plane.

NONE ON BOARD SURVIVES

Eight Women and 6 Children, the Relatives of Aviation Workers, Are Victims.

CRAFT FALLS APART IN AIR

Pilot of Small Plane That Struck the Maxim Gorky Blamed in Disaster.

By HAROLD DENNY.

Special Cable to THE NEW YORK TIMES.

MOSCOW, May 18.—The airplane Maxim Gorky, the world's largest land plane and the pride of the Soviet Union, crashed in complete destruction near here today, killing forty-eight persons, every soul aboard it. The pilot of another plane, which collided with the Maxim Gorky in midair and caused the disaster, also was killed. In addition, three persons were reported killed on the ground by falling wreckage.

Most of the victims were engineers, technicians, shock-workers and their families, the men being members of the Central Aerodynamic Institute here, where the Maxim Gorky was designed. They were being taken on a sightseeing flight over the city as a reward for faithful work.

There were thirty-seven passengers, including eight women and six children, and eleven members of the crew aboard the Maxim Gorky.

Stunting Plane Hits Big Craft.

The plane that caused the disaster was a small training plane of the institute. It had been sent aloft to emphasize the Maxim Gorky's size by contrast while a motion picture of the Maxim Gorky in flight was being taken from a third plane.

The pilot of the small plane, Nikolai Blagin, had been specifically told not to stunt, it was announced officially tonight, but he engaged in acrobatics near the Maxim Gorky to entertain a young guest aboard the latter. In the midst of a loop a heavy gust of wind blew his plane into the Maxim Gorky's wing, and the small plane was wedged between two of the Maxim Gorky's powerful engines.

Locked together, both planes dropped sharply. The Maxim Gorky's two crack pilots, Nikolai Juroff and Ivan Mykhayeff, got it back under control, cut the ignition switches and tried to glide back to the field.

Horrified watchers on the ground—they included thirty-two other workers of the institute awaiting their turn to go up—saw fragments of the Maxim Gorky fall away, and then a dense cloud of smoke billowed from the huge dismembered craft. Although it was said officially that there was no explosion, some force rent the giant plane asunder in midair.

Spilling its human cargo from a height of 2,300 feet, the Maxim Gorky fell in a score of great twisted fragments over an area a half mile in diameter, centring in the village of Sokol, on the outskirts of Moscow.

The fuselage cut the whole roof off a house. Two engines buried themselves in the ground across the street. Another fragment, villagers said, killed a man on a bicycle.

Immediately after the crash, which occurred at 12:45 o'clock this afternoon, large police detachments established a cordon around the scene, and aviation chiefs and experts began an investigation of the catastrophe.

Awards for Bereaved.

The dead will be buried at the State's expense Monday, it was announced tonight. The government will give each bereaved family 10,000 rubles and will award to them higher than normal pensions.

Not only was the crash the greatest airplane disaster in history but all the circumstances made it doubly tragic. The only crumb of comfort was that the accident was due to no fault either of structure or operation of the Maxim Gorky plane, of which the Russians had

Continued on Page Three.

LITHUANIA SPARES LIVES OF 4 NAZIS

President Smetona Commutes Death Sentences to Life Imprisonment in Kaunas.

GERMANY IS NOT SATISFIED

Berlin Spokesman Asserts the Decision Does Not Correct 'Injustice' of the Cases.

By The Associated Press.

KAUNAS, Lithuania, May 18.—The threat of grave complications between Lithuania and Germany was partly removed today when President Anatanas Smetona saved from a firing squad four Nazis convicted of plotting Memel's return to the Reich. President Smetona commuted the death sentences, which legally would have been carried out today, to life imprisonment.

Although the Supreme Court yesterday upheld the death penalties, the Nazis, with the prospect of less than twenty-four hours to live, steadfastly refused to appeal to the President, their only hope. Their lawyers, however, asked for clemency, and although the request had no legal validity it was granted.

Property Confiscated.

The decree removed the men's citizenship and confiscated their property. They will receive cells in the Kaunas jail, while eighty-three other prisoners convicted with them will serve terms of from six months to eighteen years imprisonment in provincial prisons.

Police reinforcements patroled the Memel territory to prevent anti-government demonstrations, and strong forces were held on duty in Kaunas.

The government charges the four Nazis who received clemency killed a colleague because he confessed the Memel plot to Lithuanian authorities.

To Protest to Germany.

Special Cable to THE NEW YORK TIMES.

KAUNAS, Lithuania, May 18.—The Lithuanian Government decided today to protest to Germany against the Koenigsberg demonstrations and others yesterday at Tilsit. It is reported that at Tilsit windows of the Lithuanian Consulate were broken by stones and a Lithuanian servant injured.

Germany Not Appeased.

BERLIN, May 18 (AP).—The action of Lithuania's President in commuting the death sentences of four Nazis today failed to create a favorable official reaction in Germany. A spokesman for the Propaganda Ministry expressed the opinion that "the President's decision did not correct the injustice."

"Lithuania," he said, "was warned by one of the signatories [of the treaty governing supervision of the Memel territory]. This was obviously induced by a wish to avoid further tension in the general European situation."

German newspapers unanimously defined the clemency decision as dictated "by reasons of political expediency."

PLANE DIVE KILLS 3 AT MICHIGAN FIELD

Pilot and 2 Passengers Are Victims, 2 Others Injured During Airport Dedication.

DIES HONORING PILSUDSKI

Hausner, Who Twice Tried to Fly to Poland, Crashes Over Detroit Church.

By The Associated Press.

FLINT, Mich., May 18.—A pilot and two passengers were killed and eight other occupants of a tri-motored plane were injured, two seriously, here today when the plane plunged to the ground while a new airport was being dedicated.

The Dead.

THEODORE KNOWLES of Detroit, the pilot.

Mrs. MARY RUSHLOW, aged 34, of Flint.

CONRAD RUSHLOW, 7, her son.

Clement D. Rushlow, husband of the woman killed, and a daughter, 3 years old, were taken to a hospital in a serious condition.

Knowles's plane, in which he had been carrying passengers throughout the day, fell as he attempted to take off from the field with ten passengers. At an altitude of less than 200 feet both wing motors failed, witnesses said, and the pilot barely slipped his craft past a group of tents occupied by a Selfridge Field ground crew. An instant later the ship struck the ground and nosed over.

Twenty-one army planes had come here to take part in the dedication of Bishop Airport. The officers immediately called into service their own ambulances and trucks and conveyed the injured persons five miles to a hospital.

Knowles was buried beneath the wreckage and was dead when rescuers reached the spot. The plane broke in two pieces as it struck, spilling the passengers to the ground. Mrs. Rushlow died soon after she was taken to the hospital and her son died an hour later.

No Fuel in Plane's Tanks.

Army fliers who saw the crash said Knowles apparently made a desperate effort to land his plane and still clear the tents, in which he knew soldiers were quartered. He landed the plane in the only clear space in the area, barely grazing one tent as he came down.

The others injured were Joseph Setzer, aged 13; Mrs. Marbelle Hardwick, superintendent of a children's home here; Mildred Anderson, Alfred Anderson, 33, a letter carrier; Dewitt Elwood and Minnie Ann Griese. Elwood suffered a leg fracture and both Anderson and his wife were said to have possible fractures.

An inspection of the plane by Colonel Floyd Evans, State aeronautical director, revealed that there was no fuel in the tanks after the crash. Colonel Evans said Knowles

Continued on Page Two.

Scorn for Honors Marked Romantic Career of Lawrence, Hero of Arabia

LAWRENCE A HERO OF EPIC STATURE

Made Desert Kingdoms, Then Scorned Honors and Riches as Arabs Were Rebuffed.

LED NOMADS TO VICTORY

Was an Archaeologist Before He Gained World War Fame, Aircraftsman Afterward.

Personality, circumstance and destiny contrive to meet at a single time and place but seldom in the course of history. When they do, a hero emerges and legends grow up about him until they reach the dimensions of a Homeric epic. Such a hero was Thomas Edward Lawrence, who, having created kingdoms, scorned honors and riches, died, after his brief hour, in dramatic, self-imposed simplicity.

His was a story of dazzling intrigue and adventure, with the vast tapestry of the World War its background and romantically mysterious Arabia its setting. He was at once the most striking individual leader and the most puzzling enigma cast up by the Great War.

It seems almost as if fate had been preparing him all his life for the great rôle he was to play in the small but important theatre of war from Mecca north to Damascus through Transjordan. When Great Britain's hour of need struck he was ready, and when the need had passed he sought nothing for his services except justice as he saw it for the Arabs, whom he had won to her cause with promises of independence.

Wrote of Part He Played.

Of the part he played in the destruction of the Turkish Empire he himself has written in "Revolt in the Desert," an abridged version of "The Seven Pillars of Wisdom."

Others have retold the story, but neither he nor they nor his official biographer, Robert Graves, has quite succeeded in explaining the raison d'être of one of the most fascinating characters of this century.

It is not easy to understand how the fair-haired Lawrence, a youth of 26, could win the trust and faith of warring Bedouin chieftains who did not trust each other. It is not a simple task either to explain why one who could have been an Emperor chose to give up all rank, or why one who roused a nation to war afterward felt guilty for having done so. Nor is it easy to understand, much less portray, a man whose almost every action was a paradox.

Yet such a man was Lawrence, who remarked a sort of racial schizophrenia in his own personality. In "Revolt in the Desert" he said that he sometimes felt himself possessed of an Eastern and a Western self and wrote:

"Sometimes these two selves would converse in the void; and then madness was very near, as I believe it would be near the man who could see things through two veils at once, of two customs, two educations, two environments."

A Lifelong Individualist.

A lifelong individualist, Lawrence balked at routine and discipline, eating and sleeping when bodily needs overcame him rather than at regular intervals. Yet when his war service was over he submerged himself in the routine of life as an aircraftsman in the Royal Air Force. It was as if, realizing that the rest of his life was destined to be an anticlimax, he deliberately set out to achieve the dramatic effect of the utmost in anticlimaxes.

His biographer suggested that for him the air service represented the modern counterpart of the monastic life.

Lawrence sought sensation in driving his racing motorcycle at breakneck speed along the quiet highways of England but abstained from tobacco and liquor, explaining that he feared a taste for the latter would diminish his enjoyment of water. Disliking to be touched, he seldom shook hands if he could avoid it, never looked at the person with whom he was talking and often passed friends and acquaintances without revealing the slightest trace of recognition.

His Physical Appearance.

Something of the paradox of the man was reflected in his physical appearance as it was described by Mr. Graves in "Lawrence and the Arabian Adventure." The English poet-biographer wrote:

"He is short (five feet, five and a half inches), with his body long, I should judge, in proportion to his legs, for he is more impressive seated than standing. He has a big head of the Morse type, rising steeply at the back. His hair is fair (not blond) and rather fine; his complexion is fair and he could go unshaved longer than most men without showing it.

"The upper part of his face is kindly, almost maternal; and the lower part is severe, almost cruel. His eyes are blue-gray and constantly in motion. His hands and feet are small. He is, or was, of great physical strength."

This was the man who in the keffiyeh and burnoose of the Bedouin led his Arab horde in countless raids against the Turk; who with dynamite concealed in tulips blew up seventy-nine troop trains, and who at last led his guerrilla warriors on camelback into Damascus as conquerors.

The crowds that lined the streets of that ancient city on that day acclaimed their own leaders in a mighty chant, but with these Semitic names they linked Lawrence's transmogrified British surname:

"Feisal, Nasir Shukri Urens!"

26 When the War Began.

When the war broke out in 1914 Lawrence, who was to become an Emir and a Prince of Mecca and who alone among Europeans was to win the right to wear the curved gold sword of a direct descendant of Mohammed, was 26 years old and an obscure member of a British archaeological party seeking relics of the Hittites in the Valley of the Euphrates.

Years of roaming on foot through Syria and Arabia had given him a knowledge of the customs and language of the land such as few Europeans possessed. Some peculiar affinity for the desert and its people already had made it possible for him to meet Bedouin chieftains on terms of friendship and equality. Yet his hour had not struck and he returned to England to join Kitchener's army.

He failed, however, to meet the physical requirements for active service. Instead he was commissioned a second lieutenant and assigned to the map department of General Headquarters in Cairo, where his eccentricities and dislike of military formalities quickly made him unpopular with the staff officers, who readily consented to his making what even he regarded as a junket.

At that time the Sherif of Mecca, who later became King Hussein of Hejaz, had started the Arab revolt against Turkish rule, and Ronald Storrs, Oriental Secretary to the British High Commissioner for Egypt, had been ordered to Jeddah to present his compliments to the rebel leader. Lawrence obtained permission to accompany him.

Becomes Feisal's Adviser.

In Jeddah Lawrence heard of a young Arab prince, Feisal, who was besieging the Turkish garrison at Medina and went into the interior to meet him. From the moment of their meeting Lawrence became Feisal's adviser and the brains and driving force of the Arab revolt. He made the cause of Arab independence so completely his own that for the time he was more Arab than British.

Describing his meeting with Feisal, whom he later helped place upon the throne of Iraq under a British mandate, Lawrence wrote in "Revolt in the Desert":

"I felt at first glance that this was the man I had come to Arabia to seek—the leader who would bring the Arab revolt to full glory. Feisal looked very tall and pillar-like, very slender in his long white robes and his brown headcloth bound with a brilliant scarlet and gold cord. * * * One never asked if he were scrupulous, but later he showed that he could return trust for trust, suspicion for suspicion."

Feisal, who had commanded Turkish troops in the field, knew Turkish military tactics perfectly, and he also knew the Bedouin tribesmen. With Lawrence as the guiding spirit, the two enlisted all the surrounding tribes under their own chieftains and made them forget their blood feuds and hatreds for the first time in six centuries.

By the force of his personality and earnestness Lawrence led the revolt behind its nominal head with such success and acumen that the British authorities soon gave him all possible support. He spoke the native dialects, dressed as an Arab, lived as a Bedouin and transformed himself into one of the desert nomads who have changed scarcely at all since Abraham's time and who still speak of the lands of Edom, Ammon and Moab, as in biblical times.

Noted Raider Enlisted.

His army strengthened and reorganized, Feisal moved northward, threatening the communications of Medina by attacking the Hejaz Railway. Lawrence meanwhile rode off into the interior to bring more tribes into the fold, raising the northern hordes in revolt and so extending the area to be snatched from Turkish rule and defended against it.

He pushed forward to and beyond Baalbek, behind the enemy lines in Syria, and on his return picked up a Huweitat force under Auda Abu Tayyi, a noted raider, who became henceforth one of the revolt's most powerful allies. The campaign that was to sweep the Turks from a thousand miles of territory between Mecca and Damascus was under way at last.

With Auda Abu Tayyi, Lawrence routed a Turkish battalion near Maan and forced a passage to Aqaba, which was occupied for the revolting forces in August, 1917. This exploit was so conspicuous that Lawrence was promoted to the rank of lieutenant colonel and was cited for both British and French decorations, which, however, he refused.

Lawrence and his nominal leaders faced what appeared to be a completely hopeless task at first. They had no funds with which to finance the revolt, no means of transportation except a few camels and no means of communication except a handful of camel-riders. They had to raise and equip an army in a country of no manufacturing interests, in a terrain that produces little food and even less water. In many parts of the country over which they fought and rode the water holes were five days apart by camel trek.

Men Suffered in Winter.

Winter in the desert was no less dreadful than the blistering heat of Summer. The men in their loose, flowing garments withered under the unexpected icy blasts that swept down out of the highlands. Often they baked by day and froze by night. It was a biblical war with all the aboriginal hardships, plus high explosives and modern field pieces.

As the revolt progressed, the British fleet cooperated by bringing much-needed supplies and ammunition, the ships acting as depots and throwing terror into the hearts of the Turks. Lawrence began blowing up trains and bridges of the Hejaz Railway, cutting communication lines and leading small bands of his Bedouins in guerrilla raids.

When the campaign began to show signs of great promise Lord Allenby, subsequently the conqueror of Jerusalem, then in command of the British Near East forces, sent for Lawrence. Blistered red by the terrific heat, barefooted and silk-skirted, Lawrence promised to cripple the enemy if entrusted with arms and provisions and a fund of £200,000 to "convince and control" his converts. Allenby agreed.

Finally there came the day late in 1918 when Allenby broke through the Turkish front on the coast in Palestine. Simultaneously along the desert's rim in the interior Lawrence led his Bedouins on their last dash to the north, riding over the routed, disorganized Turkish armies into Damascus, where Feisal was enthroned.

Disillusioned at Parley.

That was the time of victory and of rejoicing. Disillusionment came later when Lawrence took Feisal to Paris and tried to win the peace conference to Arab independence. The British Foreign Office was bound to France by a secret treaty that had parceled out Syria long before it was won from the Turks and Lawrence knew what he had long suspected—that he had been binding the Arab chieftains to the allied cause with promises that could not be kept.

Feisal, however, retained his faith in the promises that had been made to him and refused to attack the French when they were weak, although urged by his tribesmen to do so. In 1920, however, he wearied of waiting and proclaimed himself King of Syria, but soon afterward it was mandated to the French and General Gouraud forced Feisal to relinquish his throne.

The star of the desert chieftain seemed to have set when he was forced from his throne and driven into exile in England, but Colonel Lawrence as an adviser in the British Foreign Office was still working to obtain recognition for his country's valuable wartime ally.

Mesopotamia had been partitioned, but Iraq was set up as a British mandate and, with the approval of the British and a vote of the Arabs, Feisal was made King of this new domain of 140,000 square miles and about 3,000,000 inhabitants. He was enthroned in ancient Baghdad on Aug. 23, 1921.

Refused Honors From King.

The treatment accorded Feisal and his followers left a bitter taste in the mouth of Lawrence. He refused the honors with which King George sought to reward him for his services in the desert with the remark that when a man who has served two masters must offend one of them it is better for him to offend the more powerful.

One of the puzzles that the story of Lawrence leaves unanswered is why he consented to carry on with his desert campaign knowing that the promises he was making on behalf of his sovereign could not be kept. His biographer hints at the answer by telling that two of Lawrence's brothers were killed on the western front in the early days of the war.

His eagerness for revenge, however, was cooled just before his triumphal entry into Damascus, his biographer suggests, when he saw German units standing firm in defeat amid a routed, panicky Turkish army. It was his first glimpse of German troops in action.

The full story of his adventure in Arabia was written by Colonel Lawrence soon after his return to Europe. The revised manuscript and photographs were lost at a railway station, but he wrote the story again from memory and a few stray notes. The work turned out to be 400,000 words long when in 1922 he induced a newspaper press in Oxford to print eight copies for private distribution. Three of these were destroyed or lost.

A Costly Publication.

"The Seven Pillars of Wisdom," as the work subsequently appeared in 1927, was probably the most costly publication of modern times. It was illustrated by famous artists and printed on special paper. Only 110 copies were printed in England, for sale to a few of the author's friends at $156 a copy.

In order to protect his copyright and prevent pirating, Lawrence consented to the publication of an American edition of twenty-two copies, of which only ten were available for public sale. These were quoted at the time of publication at $20,000 apiece.

It was to make up the deficits incurred in these sumptuous experiments in publishing that Lawrence agreed to issue his "Revolt in the Desert," an abridged version of "The Seven Pillars of Wisdom," for public sale. The book had a phenomenal sale both here and in England. When the author's deficit had been wiped out he ordered publication stopped.

Efforts were made from time to time by enemies of Lawrence to show that in his book he had sought to credit himself for all the accomplishments to which others had contributed as much as he, but his fame lived on and the legend about him continued to grow in glamour.

This year it was revealed that he had designated "Revolt in the Desert" as "a dishonest thing" in a letter that had come into the possession of the Hoover War Memorial Library at Stanford University. This statement had been made to a friend whom he addressed as "Dear P."

George H. Doran, his publisher, explained the statement by saying that Lawrence never had been satisfied with the account of his experiences written after the original manuscript had been lost.

Never Quite Satisfied With It.

"The rewritten book," with which Lawrence himself was never quite satisfied, was a purely personal record. His impregnable spirit, however, had been broken down to the extent of allowing a lengthy abridgement for publication by a "friendly man of letters."

It has been calculated that more than 30,000 copies of "Revolt in the Desert" were sold to the public. The author designated it as a "dishonest thing," the publishers indicated, merely because he distrusted his superb memory by which it had been written, for his notes with the manuscript of the original had disappeared at the Reading railway station and he could not check up the events it narrated.

For this reason, apparently, he refused to sign a copy of "this rotten little book" sent to his friend "P." He added in the letter that the book had been allowed to be published to "pay my overdraft"; in other words, to reimburse his friends who had subscribed for the original edition.

Long before publication of his book Lawrence, finding the notoriety that was his both irksome and unpleasant, had renounced his rank and even his name to enlist in the Royal Air Force as a mechanic at 80 cents a day. This was in August, 1922, when he was 34 years old.

He had adopted the name of Shaw—because it was his mother's name, according to some versions of the story, and, according to others, because he had once been mistaken for a son of George Bernard Shaw while calling on the author.

Disguise Soon Penetrated.

Whatever his reason for changing his name, his disguise was soon penetrated and the "uncrowned King of Arabia" became the "most famous private soldier in the world." He then adopted the name of Ross temporarily and served for nearly two years near Dorchester in the Royal Tank Corps, to re-enter the air service again in 1925 as "Aircraftsman Shaw."

Subsequently he was sent to India, but publicity once more sought him out and he was recalled to England after it was reported that he was conducting an anti-Bolshevist campaign along the Afghan-Soviet border. Such rumors were constantly recurrent after the story of the Arabian adventure had been told.

In August, 1930, Lawrence was reported captured while escaping from Kurdistan, but the prisoner turned out to be a German newspaper correspondent.

Instead of stirring up revolts and carrying on the tradition of "Lawrence of Arabia," Aircraftsman Shaw was apparently engaged in quite other pursuits, for late in December, 1932, he completed a new English translation of the Odyssey of Homer in which such phrases as "What means the wanderer thereby?" were rendered as "What ails the tramp?"

Aircraftsman Shaw remained in His Majesty's service until February, 1935, when he retired to a cottage near Moreton, in Dorset, silent regarding his future plans. For four months prior to his retirement from the service he had been in Bridlington working on bombing-target boats. He journeyed from his Bridlington lodgings to his Dorsetshire home astride the motor cycle from which he was thrown some six weeks later in trying to avoid a collision.

Was Born in North Wales.

Lawrence, or Shaw, for that was his legal name when he died, was born in Tremadoc, North Wales, in August, 1888. Of his ancestry B. H. Liddell Hart, author of "Colonel Lawrence, the Man Behind the Legend," has this to say:

"He was of mixed race. His father's family were Elizabethan settlers from England, favored in gaining land in County Meath [Ireland] by Walter Raleigh. * * * They never married into Ireland but chose their wives from intruders such as themselves from England, from Holland even. His mother was island Scottish in feeling and education, but her parentage was part English, part Scandinavian. The sympathy of his home was Irish, but he was born in Wales."

For a few years Lawrence and his family lived on the Isle of Jersey. When he was 10 they moved to Northern Scotland, where they remained for three years. Moving next to France, Lawrence attended a Jesuit school for a short time, although his family were not Catholics.

Later the family returned to England and Lawrence passed his examinations for entrance to Oxford, matriculating at Jesus College, where as a Welshman he received a special rate.

At Oxford, Lawrence, who disliked organized games, lived a solitary but not lonely life. In childhood he had taken to hunting for fragments of Roman and medieval pottery, and in France he had developed a passionate interest in the architecture of famous cathedrals and castles and the fortifications around them. For his thesis at Oxford he chose to write on "The Influence of the Crusades on the Medieval Architecture of Europe."

While still a student he urged his parents to let him go to the Near East to pursue his studies further. His family finally gave him permission and about $500, thinking that he would spend it on a flying tour of Asia Minor, Syria and Palestine.

But he had other plans. Arriving in Syria, he adopted the native costume and tramped hundreds of miles over desert country, living with the Bedouin tribes and studying the manners and customs of all that complicated mosaic of peoples who dwell in the ancient corridor between Mesopotamia and the valley of the Nile.

When finally he returned home to complete his studies he still had about $250 of the original sum his family had given him. He remained home just long enough to complete his studies.

In 1908 an Oxford expedition had begun excavations in the Euphrates Valley in search of Hittite relics. Because of Lawrence's first-hand knowledge of tribal ways, he was invited to join the expedition and take charge of the Kurds, Turkomans, Armenians and Arabs employed in the digging.

Probably Lawrence never dreamed when he was studying Hittite ruins that it was his destiny to help change the map of the modern world instead of merely to piece together for a scholar's thesis the fragments of a dead and buried kingdom. Yet the work he did then helped to prepare him for the task that awaited him.

THE "MYSTERY MAN" OF THE WORLD WAR IN SOME OF HIS ROLES.

Times Wide World Photo.

"Lawrence of Arabia" as he appeared when he went into Damascus.

Associated Press Photo.

Colonel Thomas E. Lawrence astride his motor cycle which he was wont to ride through the countryside at terrific speed and on which he met with an accident that caused his death.

Times Wide World Photo.

"Aircraftsman Shaw" leaving a naval launch at Plymouth after it was secretly sent by the government to take him off a liner returning from the East in 1929.

Lowell Thomas Describes Meeting With British 'Blue-Eyed Bedouin'

Lawrence, Reading Monograph on Archaeology, Winced When He Was Introduced as 'Uncrowned King of Arabia'—Called One of Greatest Men in Empire's History.

The author of "With Lawrence in Arabia" tells here his first-hand impressions of the man who became the uncrowned King of the Arabs during the World War.

By LOWELL THOMAS.

The first time I saw T. E. Lawrence was in Jerusalem soon after its capture by General Allenby. Strolling past the bazaars on Christian Street I had observed a Bedouin arrayed in the agal, keffiyeh and aba worn only by the princes of the desert. And in his belt was the short gold sword of a descendant of the prophet Mohammed.

But a second look convinced me that he was anything but a Bedouin Prince. He was blond as a viking and had the most piercing blue eyes you ever saw. Moreover, he was clean-shaven, whereas all Bedouins have beards as long as they can grow them—they swear by their beards, literally.

For all his short stature, he carried himself with all the dignity of a true Arabian shereef, but on his face was an expression of serenity that gave him the air of an early Christian saint, strolling through Jerusalem, lost in religious meditation.

Later in the day I asked General Ronald Storrs who the youth might be. "Ronnie" Storrs had the office once held by Pontius Pilate; he was the new Governor of Jerusalem. In answer to my question he threw open the door of an adjoining room. There, seated at a table, reading a monograph on archaeology, was the blue-eyed Bedouin. And General Storrs said:

"Let me introduce you to Colonel Lawrence, the uncrowned King of Arabia."

The young man winced at the description and shook hands shyly and almost without a word. He obviously resented the interruption.

I had first heard of this desert man of mystery on my way from Italy to Egypt to join Allenby. Fantastic tales were being told about his exploits, but always in hushed tones, because they were being kept secret for political reasons.

Thus I became acquainted with the most extraordinary individual I ever met. Surely there never was a man with more contradictory characteristics than T. E. Lawrence. A scholar and a man of action, an archaeologist and an intrepid fighter, a poet-dreamer and a first-rate mechanic, a statesman with a morbid, almost pathological aversion to publicity.

He had at times an excruciating, biting humor, especially when describing the pompous stuffed shirts of officialdom. Yet his sense of humor was not adequate to accepting with a shrug and a smile the inevitable celebrity that followed his accomplishments. And it was this, really, that was the indirect cause of his accident. Two books had just been published in England attacking him. As a result he became once more the target for reporters and camera men, and it was in an effort to escape them that he crashed.

Through the war in the desert young Lawrence carried Doughty's "Arabia Deserta" as his bible and military textbook. For light reading he had the plays of Aristophanes, in the original. These he would read on the march, perched on the back of a camel. He also took the Oxford Book of English Verse and Malory's "Morte d'Arthur."

But he was no owlish scholar, and he took glee in telling me that a barber used to visit No. 10 Downing Street every day—to dress Lloyd George's hair! Of Lord Curzon, "that most superior purzon," he said:

"Lord Curzon divides all the inhabitants of this earth into two groups, the masses and the classes. The classes are Lord Curzon and the King. Everybody else belongs to the masses."

When Lawrence went to the Foreign Office the haughty proconsul remarked to one of his retainers: "I say, who is this person Lawrence? See that he is brought into our presence." When Lawrence was ushered into the presence Curzon patronizingly waved his diminutive visitor to a chair and started to deliver a lecture on the Near East. Lawrence stood it as long as he could, then quietly said to His Britannic Majesty's ex-Viceroy of India:

"But, my dear man, you don't know what you are talking about."

I suppose my greatest stroke of luck came when Lord Allenby gave me permission to join the Arab army led by Lawrence, the army in which every man considered himself a general. On one occasion we were attending a conference of Arab sheiks. Everybody had a different plan of campaign. Lawrence heard every one patiently, criticized nobody and seemed to approve of every idea in turn. When the consultation was over it was Lawrence's plan that was adopted—without any one's realizing it.

"In the British Army," said Lawrence, "a general is allowed to make a mess of things all by himself, whereas here in Arabia every man wants a hand in making the mess complete."

One evening we were discussing the ancient civilization of the Hittites. In the middle of a sentence Lawrence broke off with the remark: "Do you know, one of the most glorious sights I have ever seen is a trainload of Turkish soldiers ascending skyward after the explosion of a 'tulip'!" He seemed to take an unholy joy in blowing up Turkish trains, but not through any desire to kill.

Whenever his force ran out of provisions or luxuries Lawrence would plant one of his dynamite "tulips," a train would be wrecked and his Bedouins would swoop down with yells and begin looting. General Allenby assured me that "Lawrence has made the dynamiting of trains the national sport of Arabia."

Lawrence's aversion to publicity was equaled only by his shrinking from honors, titles, medals. The governments of all the allied nations tried to confer decorations upon him. Only a shy, timid British schoolboy temperament could go to the extreme of rushing to an airport in Cairo and flying back to Arabia in order to duck the ceremonies essential to an investiture. And his tentmate once discovered in an old chocolate tin the Croix de Guerre with two palms.

There were British officers who sneered at what they called Lawrence's theatricalism, his arraying himself in princely Arabian robes. Some of these criticisms were animated by jealousy, some by a genuine insular disapproval.

Actually T. E. did it for reasons of policy. The secret of Lawrence's success was his profound knowledge of intricate Arab customs, respect for their ideas. Like Bertram Thomas, who crossed the Rub 'al Khali, he admired the Arab, he liked the Bedouins as people. His magnificent Bedouin clothes were part of a carefully designed plan to gain the confidence and sympathy of the Arabs. "If you wear Arab dress," he told me, "you should always wear the best."

No picture of Lawrence would be complete that did not convey his almost incomparable unselfishness. I should say selflessness, but for his morbidity about publicity. As any newspaper man knows, a few concessions to journalism would have made him immune from what he considered persecution. His quest of obscurity only made him a more vulnerable target.

Most important of all, it was his complete unselfishness and lack of ambition that enabled him to make three kings. Had Lawrence been ambitious for himself, he never would have made three reigning monarchs in Asia Minor.

A great man, this. One of the greatest in the history of the British Empire. A scholar, a poet, a philosopher and a man of action. We shall not look upon his like in our lifetime.

T. E. LAWRENCE DIES OF CRASH INJURIES

Continued From Page One.

his life, came out to the waiting newspaper men.

"I'm afraid I have bad news for you tonight," he said, and then read this bulletin:

"The condition of T. E. Shaw [the name Colonel Lawrence assumed when he entered the Royal Air Force as a private after his Arabian adventures] has taken a sudden change. Condition is now very grave."

Shortly before 6 o'clock a motor cycle driven by Pat Knowles, Colonel Lawrence's orderly and close friend, with the colonel's brother, A. W. Lawrence, on the pillion seat, dashed up to the hospital. The colonel's brother and his wife arranged to remain at the hospital throughout the night.

Oxygen Is Brought.

At 7:30 a soldier raced from the hospital for a supply of adrenalin that had been ordered held ready, and an ambulance brought two cylinders of oxygen. The oxygen was administered and at 11 P. M. Colonel Lawrence's condition was very critical. X-ray photographs were sent for and carefully studied by the medical experts.

Anxiety had grown throughout the day following the morning's bulletin reporting some congestion in Colonel Lawrence's right lung, for which reason a specialist was summoned.

News of the gravity of Colonel Lawrence's condition spread rapidly in the little village of Bovington. Shopkeepers stood outside their doors with groups of tank corps soldiers discussing the situation, and every one coming from the hospital was asked, "How is he getting on?"

The military authorities, anxious to dispel the mystery clinging to the accident—there have been stories that it was the work of foreign agents—yesterday permitted 14-year-old Frand Fletcher, son of a bandsman, to tell his story. He said he was bicycling with Albert Hargreaves, son of another soldier, on a bird's nesting expedition; Colonel Lawrence came up behind them and there was a crash. Hargreaves, who is in the same hospital, is making good progress.

Swerved to Save a Boy.

Colonel Lawrence suffered a compound fracture of the skull, hemorrhage of the brain, a broken leg and other injuries in the motor cycle accident last Monday at Cloud's Hill, about a mile from the tiny Dorsetshire cottage in which he had been living since his retirement from the Royal Air Force, in which he had served as "Aircraftsman Shaw."

While speeding along a peaceful country road Colonel Lawrence swerved sharply to avoid hitting a boy on a butcher's delivery bicycle. The lad was thrown to the roadway but only slightly hurt.

It was believed that Colonel Lawrence must have been traveling at high speed at the time. He was known as a daredevil rider who thought nothing of hurtling over long straight roads at 100 miles an hour.

Immediately after the accident he was rushed to the Bovington Camp hospital, where the military authorities posted special guards with strict orders to scrutinize the credentials of all who came to see him. At the same time telegrams flashed the tragic news to his family. His parents sped to the hospital from London in a specially chartered airplane.

From the first his physicians had held only faint hope of his recovery. As the days passed bulletins announced that he was still unconscious, but holding his strength well.

The tragedy of his death was heightened by the fact that he was about to come back into active life after his self-imposed seclusion of more than fifteen years. No one knew in what direction his return would have taken.

"All the News That's Fit to Print"

The New York Times

LATE CITY EDITION

Weather: Sunny, warm today; fair tonight. Mostly fair tomorrow. Temp. range: today 89-66; Wed. 83-65. Temp.-Hum. Index yesterday 74. Complete U.S. report on Page 94.

VOL. CXVIII ... No. 40,682 NEW YORK, THURSDAY, JUNE 12, 1969 — 10 CENTS

NIXON'S DECISION TO END SPACE LAB LAID TO CONGRESS

Rising Pressure by Critics of Military Costs Termed Key in Intense Struggle

BLOW TO AIR FORCE SEEN

Bureau of Budget Reported Scoring a Rare Triumph in Debate With Pentagon

By JOHN W. FINNEY
Special to The New York Times

WASHINGTON, June 11—The White House ordered the cancellation of the manned orbiting laboratory program—the military's most ambitious space project—over the objections of the Defense Department and the Air Force, Congressional sources reported today.

While the cancellation was a blow to Air Force aspirations in space, the Administration decision is taking on a larger symbolic significance in the Congressional debate over the military budget.

The manned orbiting laboratory program was the first major military project to be canceled by the Administration. The White House, in turn, was driven to the decision by the mounting Congressional pressures to hold down spending, particularly by the military.

While the cancellation of the program, announced yesterday by the Pentagon, seemed abrupt, an intense struggle over the $3-billion project had been going on for several weeks within the Administration.

The Sides Form

The argument, basically between the Budget Bureau and the Pentagon, pitted the budgetary pressures on the Administration against military justifications that the United States "must maintain superiority in space"—the rationale offered for the MOL project since it was conceived by the Air Force six years ago.

For the first time in a long time, the Budget Bureau, as an arm of the White House, challenged a major Defense Department project and won.

The cancellation also was a major victory for military economizers in Congress. Even before the Pentagon decision, Senator Thomas J. McIntyre, Democrat of New Hampshire, chairman of the Senate Armed Services Subcommittee on Research and Development, had been zeroing in on the MOL project and was prepared to recommend to the full committee that it be scrapped.

Yesterday before a private meeting of the Senate Democratic Policy Committee, Charles L. Schultze, former Budget Bureau director, explained that in the past the bureau had made no real attempt to fight Pentagon programs because "it would have been like tilting at windmills."

To some leaders in the Congressional economy force, the cancellation of the MOL project was proof of how the increasingly critical mood in Congress was giving the executive branch, and the [illegible]

Continued on Page 28, Column 1

John L. Lewis Dies; Led Miners' Union In Years of Battle

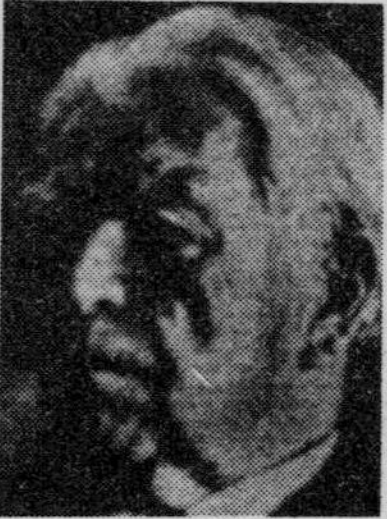

Associated Press

John L. Lewis

By The Associated Press

WASHINGTON, June 11—John L. Lewis, a giant of the American labor movement and for decades a top figure on the American scene, died tonight at Doctors Hospital, where he was admitted Sunday night suffering from internal bleeding.

The president emeritus of the powerful United Mine Workers Union was 89 years old. Mr. Lewis, who waged notable battles with the

Continued on Page 34, Column 1

LATIN GRIEVANCES AGAINST THE U.S. HANDED TO NIXON

Chilean Presents Report for 21 Countries—President Pledges Serious Study

By BENJAMIN WELLES
Special to The New York Times

WASHINGTON, June 11—Foreign Minister Gabriel Valdés of Chile, presenting President Nixon with a list of Latin America's complaints about United States trade and aid policies, asserted today that Latin America was "conscious of the deep crisis" in hemisphere relations.

On behalf of 21 governments, he warned of "growing and harmful resentment" against United States policies throughout Latin America. He charged that United States aid tended more toward the growth of affluent areas than toward assisting the poorer nations.

Dr. Valdés handed Mr. Nixon the 6,000-word report drawn up at a meeting of Latin-American representatives two weeks ago in Viña del Mar, Chile.

Nixon to See Rockefeller

The President said that he would give it serious consideration. He observed that it would complement the report that Governor Rockefeller is due to make to him after the Governor's series of four fact-finding trips in Latin America.

Mr. Rockefeller is to confer with the President tomorrow before setting out on the third leg of the tour.

The Viña del Mar document called for more effective inter-American cooperation and for the curtailment or elimination of many United States barriers to Latin-American exports to the United States. It also deplored the existence of "political and military conditions" for United States aid.

'Operative Measures' Asked

The report also urged the United States to adopt "operative measures" to assist hemispheric development in such fields as international trade, financing, investment, transportation and scientific and technological development.

Dr. Valdés said today: "Private investments have meant, and mean today, for Latin America that the amounts that leave our continent are many times higher than those that are invested in it. Latin-American leaders are convinced that Latin America gives more than it receives."

He added that "no solidarity can be based upon these realities."

White House sources said that neither Mr. Nixon nor Dr. Valdés had alluded to Chile's

Continued on Page 16, Column 3

United Press International

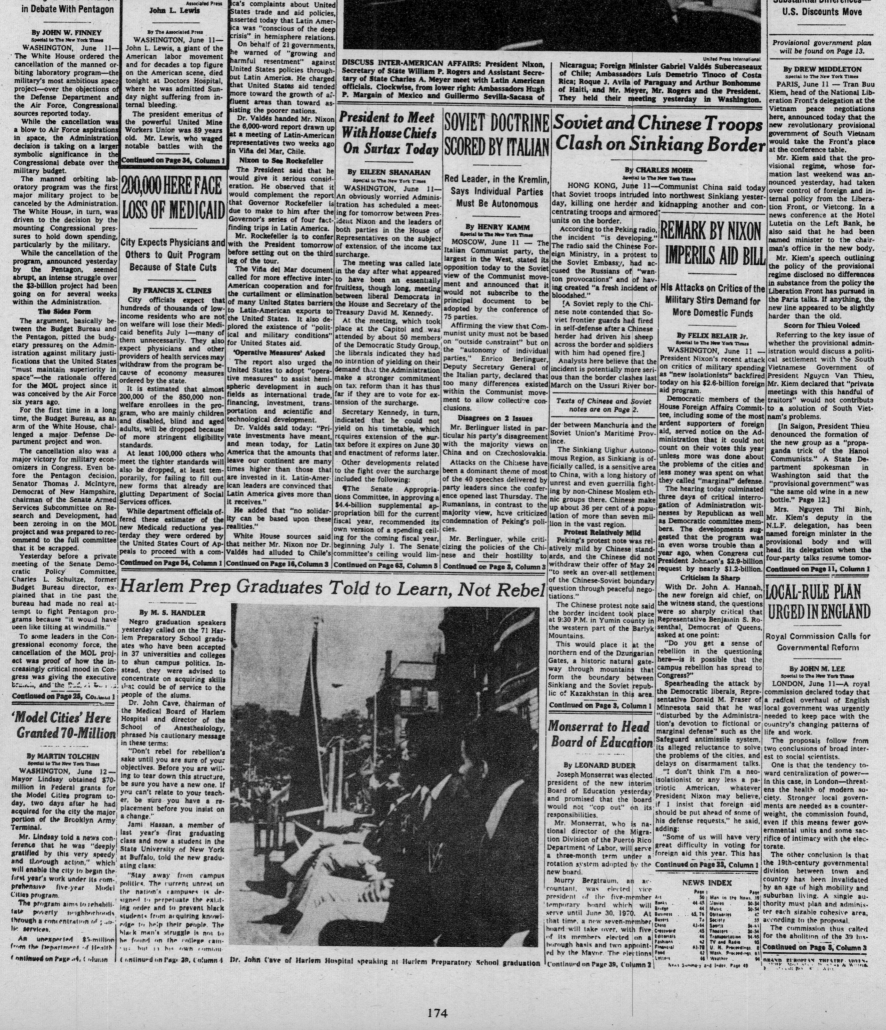

DISCUSS INTER-AMERICAN AFFAIRS: President Nixon, Secretary of State William P. Rogers and Assistant Secretary of State Charles A. Meyer meet with Latin American officials. Clockwise, from lower right: Ambassadors Hugh P. Margain of Mexico and Guillermo Sevilla-Sacasa of Nicaragua; Foreign Minister Gabriel Valdés Subercaseaux of Chile; Ambassadors Luis Demetrio Tinoco of Costa Rica; Roque J. Avila of Paraguay and Arthur Bonhomme of Haiti, and Mr. Meyer, Mr. Rogers and the President. They held their meeting yesterday in Washington.

President to Meet With House Chiefs On Surtax Today

By EILEEN SHANAHAN
Special to The New York Times

WASHINGTON, June 11—An obviously worried Administration has scheduled a meeting for tomorrow between President Nixon and the leaders of both parties in the House of Representatives on the subject of extension of the income tax surcharge.

The meeting was called late in the day after what appeared to have been an essentially fruitless, though long, meeting between liberal Democrats in the House and Secretary of the Treasury David M. Kennedy.

At the meeting, which took place at the Capitol and was attended by about 50 members of the Democratic Study Group, the liberals indicated they had no intention of yielding on their demand that the Administration make a stronger commitment on tax reform than it has thus far if they are to vote for extension of the surcharge.

Secretary Kennedy, in turn, indicated that he could not yield on his timetable, which requires extension of the surtax before it expires on June 30 and enactment of reforms later.

Other developments related to the fight over the surcharge included the following:

¶The Senate Appropriations Committee, in approving a $4.4-billion supplemental appropriation bill for the current fiscal year, recommended its own version of a spending ceiling for the coming fiscal year, beginning July 1. The Senate committee's ceiling would lim-

Continued on Page 63, Column 5

SOVIET DOCTRINE SCORED BY ITALIAN

Red Leader, in the Kremlin, Says Individual Parties Must Be Autonomous

By HENRY KAMM
Special to The New York Times

MOSCOW, June 11 — The Italian Communist party, the largest in the West, stated its opposition today to the Soviet view of the Communist movement and announced that it would not subscribe to the principal document to be adopted by the conference of 75 parties.

Affirming the view that Communist unity must not be based on "outside constraint" but on the "autonomy of individual parties," Enrico Berlinguer, Deputy Secretary General of the Italian party, declared that too many differences existed within the Communist movement to allow collective conclusions.

Disagrees on 2 Issues

Mr. Berlinguer listed in particular his party's disagreement with the majority views on China and on Czechoslovakia.

Attacks on the Chinese have been a dominant theme of most of the 40 speeches delivered by party leaders since the conference opened last Thursday. The Rumanians, in contrast to the majority view, have criticized condemnation of Peking's policies.

Mr. Berlinguer, while criticizing the policies of the Chinese and their hostility to

Continued on Page 3, Column 3

Soviet and Chinese Troops Clash on Sinkiang Border

By CHARLES MOHR

HONG KONG, June 11—Communist China said today that Soviet troops intruded into northwest Sinkiang yesterday, killing one herder and kidnapping another and concentrating troops and armored units on the border.

According to the Peking radio, the incident "is developing." The radio said the Chinese Foreign Ministry, in a protest to the Soviet Embassy, had accused the Russians of "wanton provocations" and of having created "a fresh incident of bloodshed."

[A Soviet reply to the Chinese note contended that Soviet frontier guards had fired in self-defense after a Chinese herder had driven his sheep across the border and soldiers with him had opened fire.]

Analysts here believe that the incident is potentially more serious than the border clashes last March on the Ussuri River border between Manchuria and the Soviet Union's Maritime Province.

Texts of Chinese and Soviet notes are on Page 2.

The Sinkiang Uighur Autonomous Region, as Sinkiang is officially called, is a sensitive area to China, with a long history of unrest and even guerrilla fighting by non-Chinese Moslem ethnic groups there. Chinese make up about 36 per cent of a population of more than seven million in the vast region.

Protest Relatively Mild

Peking's protest note was relatively mild by Chinese standards, and the Chinese did not withdraw their offer of May 24 "to seek an over-all settlement of the Chinese-Soviet boundary question through peaceful negotiations."

The Chinese protest note said the border incident took place at 9:30 P.M. in Yumin county in the western part of the Barlyk Mountains.

This would place it at the northern end of the Dzungarian Gates, a historic natural gateway through mountains that form the boundary between Sinkiang and the Soviet republic of Kazakhstan in this area.

Continued on Page 3, Column 1

REMARK BY NIXON IMPERILS AID BILL

His Attacks on Critics of the Military Stirs Demand for More Domestic Funds

By FELIX BELAIR Jr.
Special to The New York Times

WASHINGTON, June 11 — President Nixon's recent attack on critics of military spending as "new isolationists" backfired today on his $2.6-billion foreign aid program.

Democratic members of the House Foreign Affairs Committee, including some of the most ardent supporters of foreign aid, served notice on the Administration that it could not count on their votes this year unless more was done about the problems of the cities and less money was spent on what they called "marginal" defense.

The hearing today culminated three days of critical interrogation of Administration witnesses by Republican as well as Democratic committee members. The developments suggested that the program was in even worse trouble than a year ago, when Congress cut President Johnson's $2.9-billion request by nearly $1.2-billion.

Criticism Is Sharp

With Dr. John A. Hannah, the new foreign aid chief, on the witness stand, the questions were so sharply critical that Representative Benjamin S. Rosenthal, Democrat of Queens, asked at one point:

"Do you get a sense of rebellion in the questioning here—is it possible that the campus rebellion has spread to Congress?"

Spearheading the attack by the Democratic liberals, Representative Donald M. Fraser of Minnesota said that he was "disturbed by the Administration's devotion to fictional or marginal defense" such as the Safeguard antimissile system, its alleged reluctance to solve the problems of the cities, and delays on disarmament talks.

"I don't think I'm a neo-isolationist or any less a patriotic American, whatever President Nixon may believe, if I insist that foreign aid should be put ahead of some of his defense requests," he said, adding:

"Some of us will have very great difficulty in voting for foreign aid this year. This has

Continued on Page 23, Column 1

NEW 'GOVERNMENT' IS REPLACING N.L.F. AT TALKS IN PARIS

Front's Delegate Says Group Formed by Vietcong Has Assumed All Functions

LITTLE POLICY CHANGE

Kiem's Statement Shows No Substantial Differences—U.S. Discounts Move

Provisional government plan will be found on Page 13.

By DREW MIDDLETON
Special to The New York Times

PARIS, June 11 — Tran Buu Kiem, head of the National Liberation Front's delegation at the Vietnam peace negotiations here, announced today that the new revolutionary provisional government of South Vietnam would take the Front's place at the conference table.

Mr. Kiem said that the provisional regime, whose formation last weekend was announced yesterday, had taken over control of foreign and internal policy from the Liberation Front, or Vietcong. In a news conference at the Hotel Lutetia on the Left Bank, he also said that he had been named minister to the chairman's office in the new body.

Mr. Kiem's speech outlining the policy of the provisional regime disclosed no differences in substance from the policy the Liberation Front has pursued in the Paris talks. If anything, the new line appeared to be slightly harder than the old.

Scorn for Thieu Voiced

Referring to the key issue of whether the provisional administration would discuss a political settlement with the South Vietnamese Government of President Nguyen Van Thieu, Mr. Kiem declared that "private meetings with this handful of traitors" would not contribute to a solution of South Vietnam's problems.

[In Saigon, President Thieu denounced the formation of the new group as a "propaganda trick of the Hanoi Communists." A State Department spokesman in Washington said that the "provisional government" was "the same old wine in a new bottle." Page 12.]

Mrs. Nguyen Thi Binh, Mr. Kiem's deputy in the N.L.F. delegation, has been named foreign minister in the provisional body and will head its delegation when the four-party talks resume tomor-

Continued on Page 11, Column 1

200,000 HERE FACE LOSS OF MEDICAID

City Expects Physicians and Others to Quit Program Because of State Cuts

By FRANCIS X. CLINES

City officials expect that hundreds of thousands of low-income residents who are not on welfare will lose their Medicaid benefits July 1—many of them unnecessarily. They also expect physicians and other providers of health services may withdraw from the program because of economy measures ordered by the state.

It is estimated that almost 200,000 of the 850,000 non-welfare enrollees in the program, who are mainly children and disabled, blind and aged adults, will be dropped because of more stringent eligibility standards.

At least 100,000 others who meet the tighter standards will also be dropped, at least temporarily, for failing to fill out new forms that already are glutting Department of Social Services offices.

While department officials offered these estimates of the new Medicaid reductions yesterday they were ordered by the United States Court of Appeals to proceed with a com-

Continued on Page 54, Column 1

Harlem Prep Graduates Told to Learn, Not Rebel

By M. S. HANDLER

Negro graduation speakers yesterday called on the 71 Harlem Preparatory School graduates who have been accepted in 37 universities and colleges to shun campus politics. Instead, they were advised to concentrate on acquiring skills that could be of service to the people of the slums.

Dr. John Cave, chairman of the Medical Board of Harlem Hospital and director of the School of Anesthesiology, phrased his cautionary message in these terms:

"Don't rebel for rebellion's sake until you are sure of your objectives. Before you are willing to tear down this structure, be sure you have a new one. If you can't relate to your teacher, be sure you have a replacement before you insist on a change."

Jami Hassan, a member of last year's first graduating class and now a student in the State University of New York at Buffalo, told the new graduating class:

"Stay away from campus politics. The current unrest on the nation's campuses is designed to perpetuate the existing order and to prevent black students from acquiring knowledge to help their people. The black man's struggle is not to be found on the college campus but in his own commun-

Continued on Page 39, Column 4

Dr. John Cave of Harlem Hospital speaking at Harlem Preparatory School graduation

'Model Cities' Here Granted 70-Million

By MARTIN TOLCHIN
Special to The New York Times

WASHINGTON, June 12—Mayor Lindsay obtained $70-million in Federal grants for the Model Cities program today, two days after he had acquired for the city the major portion of the Brooklyn Army Terminal.

Mr. Lindsay told a news conference that he was "deeply gratified by this very speedy and thorough action," which will enable the city to begin the first year's work under its comprehensive five-year Model Cities program.

The program aims to rehabilitate poverty neighborhoods through a concentration of public services.

An unexpected $[illegible]-million from the Department of Health

Continued on Page ?4, Column [illegible]

Monserrat to Head Board of Education

By LEONARD BUDER

Joseph Monserrat was elected president of the new interim Board of Education yesterday and promised that the board would not "cop out" on its responsibilities.

Mr. Monserrat, who is national director of the Migration Division of the Puerto Rico Department of Labor, will serve a three-month term under a rotation system adopted by the new board.

Murry Bergtraum, an accountant, was elected vice president of the five-member temporary board which will serve until June 30, 1970. At that time, a new seven-member board will take over, with five of its members elected on a borough basis and two appointed by the Mayor. The elections

Continued on Page 39, Column 2

LOCAL-RULE PLAN URGED IN ENGLAND

Royal Commission Calls for Governmental Reform

By JOHN M. LEE
Special to The New York Times

LONDON, June 11—A royal commission declared today that a radical overhaul of English local government was urgently needed to keep pace with the country's changing patterns of life and work.

The proposals follow from two conclusions of broad interest to social scientists.

One is that the tendency toward centralization of power—in this case, in London—threatens the health of modern society. Stronger local governments are needed as a counterweight, the commission found, even if this means fewer governmental units and some sacrifice of intimacy with the electorate.

The other conclusion is that the 19th-century governmental division between town and country has been invalidated by an age of high mobility and suburban living. A single authority must plan and administer each sizable cohesive area, according to the proposal.

The commission thus called for the abolition of the 39 his-

Continued on Page 5, Column 3

NEWS INDEX

John L. Lewis, Labor's Thunderer, Led Mine Union and Helped Found the C.I.O.

Continued From Page 1, Col. 2

White House and the coal industry as the miners' leader, served in recent years as trustee of the union's multi-million-dollar health and welfare fund.

He was president of the mine workers for 40 years until his retirement in 1960. In the years after 1920 he headed its frequently bloody organizing battles and strikes over the next three decades.

Through the nineteen-thirties and nineteen-forties there were few names more frequently in headlines than Mr. Lewis's.

With the exception of President Franklin D. Roosevelt, there were few in those years who exerted more influence in shaping the economic face of the United States.

Through formation of the Committee for Industrial Organization he changed the structure and orientation of the labor movement. His influence helped fashion much of the labor legislation enacted by Congress.

Of little formal education, Mr. Lewis was a Shakespeare student and a truly self-educated man, sharp of wit and tongue.

Mr. Lewis's wife, Myrta, died in 1942 and he lived with a chauffeur in suburban Alexandria, Va., in the boyhood home of Robert E. Lee. A daughter, Kathryn, died in 1962. A son, John L. Lewis Jr., is a psychiatrist in Milwaukee.

There will be no public funeral service. A memorial service will be held at a date to be announced. Burial will be in Springfield, Ill.

A Fighting Leader

By ALDEN WHITMAN

For 40 years, and especially during the turbulent nineteen-thirties, forties and early fifties, John Llewellyn Lewis, a pugnacious man of righteous wrath and rococo rhetoric, was a dominant figure in the American labor movement. He aspired to national political and economic power, but they both eluded his grasp except for fleeting moments. He nudged greatness as a labor leader only to end in isolation from the mainstream of trade unionism.

But in his headline years Mr. Lewis, with his black leonine mane, his snaggly reddish eyebrows and his outthrust-jaw stubbornness, was an idol without peer to millions of workers and the symbol of blackest malevolence to millions in the middle and upper classes.

Gruff and unsmiling in public, his broad-brimmed fedora tilted over his eyes, he reveled in the dramatic tensions he helped to create, and he sparkled whether he was in center stage or whether he was the deep stentorian voice from the wings. As the thunderer for labor he was unexcelled.

MOVER AND SHAKER: A superb orator, John L. Lewis made full use of his dramatic powers in pursuing his labor goals. He is shown in 1938 addressing the first constitutional convention of the Congress of Industrial Organizations, which began as a committee that he helped form after a dispute within the American Federation of Labor. The group elected him as its first president.

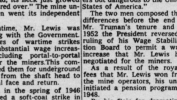

The New York Times

Hutton in The Philadelphia Inquirer

Werner in The Indianapolis Star

Robinson in The Indianapolis News

Seibel in The Richmond Times-Dispatch

Crawford in The Newark News

AS THE CARTOONISTS SAW HIM: Impressions of the bushy-browed labor leader

Starting in 1935, when coal was the country's kingpin fuel and he was president of the United Mine Workers of America, Mr. Lewis shattered the complacent craft-union American Federation of Labor by setting up the Committee for Industrial Organization to organize workers into single unions for each big industry.

He went on to lead convulsive sitdown strikes, to humble the auto industry and Big Steel, to endorse and then to break bitterly with President Franklin D. Roosevelt, to defy the Government in coal-mine disputes in World War II, to battle with President Harry S. Truman in two coal strikes in which he was twice held in contempt of Federal court and fined.

In the course of tumultuous labor politics, Mr. Lewis's wealthy and influential union left the American Federation of Labor and then rejoined it after leaving the Congress of Industrial Organizations. Finally, Mr. Lewis took his union out of the A.F.L. in the late nineteen-forties and went it alone. Although he wrote history for all labor, and with seldom a dull line, the mine union, which he ruled with a fierce pride, held his steadiest focus.

Addressing the miners, he summed up his efforts in their behalf:

"I have never faltered or failed to present the cause or plead the case of the mine workers of this country. I have pleaded your case not in the quavering tones of a mendicant asking alms, but in the thundering voice of the captain of a mighty host, demanding the rights to which free men are entitled."

Soot-smirched miners heeded Mr. Lewis without question. If he called for a shutdown, the pits were deserted. If he wanted the mines run on a three-day week, as he did during contract talks in 1949-50, that was the way they were operated. For their unswerving loyalty the miners received periodic wage increases, vacation pay, pensions at age 60, pay for underground travel time, improved mine safety and many other benefits.

In the larger context of American life, Mr. Lewis, by force of personality, was able to bend public officials to his will. Perhaps the most notable instance of this occurred during the C.I.O. sitdown strike in 1937 in General Motors plants in Flint, Mich. The strikers had ignored an injunction to leave the factories and Gov. Frank Murphy was about to declare a state of insurrection and order the National Guard to evict the workers. The Governor took a copy of his order to Mr. Lewis in his Detroit hotel in an 11th-hour effort to get him to end the strike.

After Mr. Lewis had refused, Governor Murphy asked him what he would do if the Guard were called out. Mr. Lewis replied:

"You want my answer, sir? I give it to you. Tomorrow morning, I shall personally enter General Motors plant Chevrolet No. 4. I shall order the men to disregard your order. I shall then walk up to the largest window in the plant, open it, divest myself of my outer raiment, remove my shirt and bare my bosom. Then when you order your troops to fire, mine will be the first breast those bullets will strike.

"And as my body falls from that window to the ground, you listen to the voice of your grandfather [he had been hanged in Ireland by the British for rebellion] as he whispers in your ear, 'Frank, are you sure you are doing the right thing?'"

Associated Press

AT MINE DISASTER: Mr. Lewis after inspecting scene of a 1951 explosion in West Frankfort, Ill., that killed 119 miners. He led the fight for Federal mine-safety laws.

Color draining from his face and his body quivering, the Governor left the room. The order was not issued.

Mr. Lewis was also the master of the oblique approach, which he demonstrated in dealings with Myron Taylor, chairman of the United States Steel Corporation, in 1937. He charmed the industrialist by chatting with him in his Fifth Avenue mansion about gothic tapestries and statuary. He flattered Mrs. Taylor. He also convinced Mr. Taylor, in a series of conversations, that Big Steel would be wise to recognized the Steel Workers Organizing Committee of the C.I.O. Mr. Taylor, in turn, persuaded other steelmen to deal with Mr. Lewis. The result was a stunning victory for the C.I.O.

A superb orator with a bass-baritone that could shake an auditorium without electrical amplification or that could be muted to a whisper audible in the last rows, Mr. Lewis swayed thousands of emotion-hungry audiences.

With mine operators in wage negotiations Mr. Lewis was equally effective. C. L. Sulzberger, in his book "Sit Down With John L. Lewis," related this episode from contract talks in the early thirties:

"Lewis began to walk up and down. Back and forth he went, deftly, stolidly, with a peculiar, light-footed stride, throwing his chest forward. He stuck a cigar in his mouth, folded his nubby hands behind him.

"'Gentlemen,' he said, speaking in a slow, tricky way. 'Gentlemen, I speak to you for my people. I speak to you for the miners' families in the broad Ohio Valley, the Pennsylvania mountains and the black West Virginia hills.

"'There, the shanties lean over as if intoxicated by the smoke fumes of the mine dumps. But the more pretentious ones boast a porch, with the banisters broken here and there, presenting the aspect of a snaggly-tooth child. Some of the windows are wide open to flies, which can feast near by on garbage and answer the family dinner call in double quick time.

"'But there is no dinner call. The little children are gathered around a bare table without anything to eat. Their mothers are saying, 'We want bread.'

"They are not asking for more than a little. They are not asking for a $100,000 yacht like yours, Mr.——,' suddenly pointing his threatening cigar, 'or for a Rolls-Royce limousine like yours, Mr. ——,' transfixing him with his beetle-browed gaze. 'A slim crust of bread . . .'"

The operators, according to Mr. Sulzberger's book, squirmed, and one of them muttered, "Tell him to stop. Tell him we'll settle."

On other contract occasions he could be more blunt. In 1949 talks, A. H. Raskin of The Times reported, Mr. Lewis intransigently told the chief negotiator for the operators:

"You need men and I have all the men and they are in the palm of my hand; and now I ask, 'What am I bid?'"

Many thought Mr. Lewis merely theatrical. In a sense he was, for his histrionics were in the grand manner; but when he was speaking from a position of strength there was nothing hollow about his acting. On the other hand, when he lacked public sympathy — as in his court battles in the late forties — he tended to bombast.

Those who crossed Mr. Lewis discovered there was sting to his tongue. When, in 1939, John Nance Garner, then the Vice President, took exception to some of the labor leader's views, Mr. Lewis called him "a labor-baiting, poker-playing, whisky-drinking, evil old man."

Of William Green, president of the A.F.L., he once said:

"I have done a lot of exploring of Bill's mind and I give you my word there is nothing there."

He characterized Walter Reuther, head of the United Automobile Workers Union, as "an earnest Marxist chronically inebriated, I think, by the exuberance of his own verbosity."

George Meany, president of the A.F.L.-C.I.O., was dismissed as "an honest plumber trying to abolish sin in the labor movement."

Mr. Lewis's showmanship sometimes tended to obscure his matchless fund of knowledge about coal production and marketing. In appearances before Congressional committees he was the professor lecturing sophomores on fuel economics.

He was also exceedingly well read in the classics of English literature, in the Bible, in Napoleonic lore, in American history and in labor-industry problems. His talk was laced with literary allusions.

Mr. Lewis was often pictured as a radical, especially by those who opposed his type of trade unionism. Basically, however, Mr. Lewis's economic and political views tended to be conservative. A Republican in the twenties, he was twice considered for appointment as Secretary of Labor. He supported President Roosevelt in 1936 and was on close personal terms with him until the outbreak of World War II in Europe in 1939, when, fearing American involvement, he switched to Wendell L. Willkie, the Republican leader. He later fell out with President Truman, and, although he never again became an ardent Republican, neither was he a stanch Democrat.

Although much of the public may have equated Mr. Lewis with bellicosity, he was actually an amiable and courtly person, possessed of a nimble wit and a pleasant laugh. In private he was also gracious and conciliatory, and he was hospitable, even to those with whom he disagreed.

"I am not disappointed about anything," he remarked toward the close of his active union leadership, when it was suggested that he had failed to exercise enduring labor and political influence. "When you see those editorials about me being a bitter, disappointed old man, just remember that I do my laughing in private."

Mr. Lewis, whose salary rose over the years to $50,000 a year plus expenses, was not a flashy liver. He had a modest, book-lined house on a quiet street in Alexandria, Va., and shunned most Washington parties.

Fastidious about the trim of his hair and his sartorial appearance, he had a fondness for well-tailored suits and excellent shirts and ties. He liked to travel in high-powered cars and he liked to lunch at the Sheraton-Carlton in Washington. But he passed up gourmet viands for meals of steak or roast beef and potatoes, topped off with banana cream pie, which accounted for his weight of 230 pounds in his earlier years. He occasionally sipped a glass of sherry or a weak highball for sociability's sake. He smoked Havana cigars, or sometimes chewed them unlighted.

John Lewis was born to the coal mines and to unionism. His father was Thomas Lewis, a miner who had emigrated from Wales to Lucas, Iowa. His mother, Louisa Watkins Lewis, was also Welsh and the daughter of a miner. John, their first child — there were in all six sons and two daughters — was born Feb. 12, 1880, in Lucas.

For his role in a Knights of Labor strike Thomas Lewis was blacklisted for several years, and talk of militant trade unionism and of the miners' hazardous lot filled John's childhood.

The youngster left school after the seventh grade and was toiling in the mines at 15. In his leisure time he organized both a debating and a baseball team. And he read, at first planlessly and then guided by Myrta Bell, the daughter of a Lucas physician who became his wife in 1907.

But before that, when John was 21, he left Lucas and wandered the West as a casual laborer for five years. He mined copper in Montana, silver in Utah, coal in Colorado, gold in Arizona.

Returning to Lucas and a mine job, he was elected a delegate to the national convention of the United Mine Workers, which traced its history to 1849. It was his first step to union leadership. The next was to move to Panama, Ill., with his five brothers, and in a year he was president of the local mine union.

Shortly he became Illinois lobbyist for the union and, in 1911, he was named general field agent for the A.F.L. by Samuel Gompers, then its president. This gave him a chance to travel widely and to get to know the ins and outs of labor politics. One result was that Mr. Lewis built a large personal following in the mine union, for which he became chief statistician in 1917 and later that year vice president. In 1920 he became president, an office he did not relinquish for 40 years.

Role in Defense Council

In World War I he sat on the National Defense Council, where he successfully opposed proposals for Government operation of the mines. His first major confrontation with the Government occurred in 1919 in a strike of 400,000 miners. It was denounced by President Woodrow Wilson and Mr. Lewis sent his men back to the pits after the Government had obtained an injunction.

All through the twenties Mr. Lewis worked to consolidate his power in the union and to enlarge its membership. He fought the operators on the one hand and the Communists on the other. He earned a reputation as a Red-baiter and for his imagination for "Moscow plots." He purged his union opponents from time to time on, it was said, flimsy charges.

His attitude toward the Communists softened in the thirties, when party members were among the most active organizers of the C.I.O. Chided, he retorted:

"Industry should not complain if we allow Communists in our organization. Industry employs them."

The genesis of the C.I.O. was in the plague years of the Depression when unemployment mounted to 15 million workers. Union working and wage standards were toppled, and the A.F.L. lost thousands of members, and with them its effectiveness. The mine union itself dropped to 100,000 members.

At the same time it became evident that organization of workers by skilled crafts, which was the basis of the A.F.L., was unrealistic in most major industries, where unskilled or semiskilled workers constituted the bulk of employes. This situation lead to the C.I.O.'s efforts to organize the unorganized.

That was made possible in part by Section 7A of the National Industrial Recovery Act, adopted in 1933 as part of President Roosevelt's attempt to reverse the Depression. Section 7A, often called "Labor's Magna Carta," gave workers the right to organize and bargain collectively through representatives of their choice. It was Mr. Lewis who was chiefly instrumental in getting the section into the N.I.R.A.

Organizers Sent Out

With its adoption he sent scores of organizers into the coal fields with the cry, "The President wants you to join the union," and in two years membership rose to 400,000.

The C.I.O. came into being after the A.F.L. convention of 1935 in which tensions between industrial and craft unions erupted in a fist fight between William Hutcheson of the Carpenters Union and Mr. Lewis. When the convention adjourned, Mr. Lewis met to form the C.I.O. with, among others, Charles P. Howard of the International Typographical Union; David Dubinsky of the International Ladies Garment Workers; Thomas McMahon of the Textile Workers; and Sidney Hillman of the Amalgamated Clothing Workers.

Subsequently these and other unions backing the C.I.O. were expelled from the A.F.L., but it was an empty gesture for, virtually from the outset, workers responded to the C.I.O. campaigns in the basic industries. First autos capitulated, then Big Steel, then others, until four million workers were enrolled in C.I.O. unions. But the steady procession of successes was interrupted in late 1937 by Little Steel, the smaller fabricators, and especially by Tom Girdler of Republic Steel.

The Little Steel strike, an old-fashioned walkout, was marked by violence. In Chicago on Memorial Day the police shot and killed 10 strikers and sympathizers, and there was sporadic shooting elsewhere. In the course of the strike, which was lost, President Roosevelt was asked what he thought of the dispute. "A plague on both your houses," he replied, a remark that enraged Mr. Lewis, whose union had contributed $500,000 — $120,000 as an outright gift — to the President's 1936 campaign. His retort was:

"It ill behooves one who has supped at labor's table and who has been sheltered in labor's house to curse with equal fervor and fine impartiality both labor and its adversaries when they become locked in deadly embrace."

Mr. Lewis followed this excoriation with others equally acerbic in the campaign of 1940, in which he sought to rally organized labor against the Roosevelt third-term bid. "Sustain me now, or repudiate me," he said in accusing the President of Caesarism. After Mr. Roosevelt won the election he resigned as head of what was then the Congress of Industrial Organizations, and Philip Murray, a Lewis lieutenant, took over. In 1942, however, Mr. Lewis broke with Mr. Murray, his "former friend," and the mine union left the C.I.O.

Harris & Ewing

GUILTY OF CONTEMPT: The mine workers' chief leaving court in Washington in 1948 after his second conviction for contempt of court in not obeying orders to halt a walkout. Mr. Lewis and his union were both fined.

Mr. Lewis's period of greatest national influence, waning since 1940, concluded at that point. But from 1935 to 1942, when he symbolized the C.I.O., his name brought millions into the ranks of organized labor. Its magical incantation seemed to these workers to offer the promise of higher wages, better working conditions, union recognition. The name stirred hopes among those who toiled in textile mills, in rubber and tire factories, on the docks, in brass foundries, in shipbuilding, in glass works, in garment and glove shops, and even on the farms.

Mr. Lewis, at that time, was larger than life. But his charisma was diminished after he quit the C.I.O.

Four years later he and his union were back in the A.F.L., but their stay lasted less than two years. Again there was a battle of words, this time over a provision of the Taft-Hartley Act requiring union officials to swear they were not Communists. The A.F.L. was willing to comply with the act, Mr. Lewis was not. To him the law was "damnable, vicious, unwholesome and a slave statute." As for the A.F.L., it had "no head, its neck just growed and haired over." The mine union then went its independent way.

Meantime, Mr. Lewis was tangling with the Government. A series of wartime strikes won substantial wage increases, including portal-to-portal pay for the miners. This compensated them for underground travel, from the shaft head to the coal face and return.

Then in the spring of 1946 he called a soft-coal strike in a bid for royalties on each ton of coal mined, the money to go into the union's health and welfare fund. President Truman ordered the mines seized and the strike ended on May 29 with a wage increase and a royalty arrangement. A hard-coal strike followed almost immediately, but it ended quickly on just about the same terms as were obtained in the bituminous fields.

Peace, however, was short-lived. In November Mr. Lewis denounced the contract under which the Government had been running the mines. Quickly, on motion of the Government, Federal Judge T. Alan Goldsborough issued an order restraining Mr. Lewis from maintaining the contract-termination notice. President Truman ordered the Justice Department to seek a contempt citation if Mr. Lewis disobeyed the court. And when the union chief made no move to halt the walkout, the judge found him and the union guilty of civil and criminal contempt. A fine of $10,000 was imposed on Mr. Lewis and $3.5-million on the union.

Three days later, Mr. Lewis sent the miners back to work pending appeal of the contempt ruling to the Supreme Court. In a 7-2 decision in March, 1947, that tribunal upheld the contempt judgment and the fine against Mr. Lewis. The fine against the union was reduced, however, to $700,000, with $2.8-million more to be assessed if a strike occurred during the Government's operation of the mines. Mr. Lewis complied with the court and purged himself and the union of contempt.

In 1948, after the Government had returned the mines to the operators, Mr. Lewis was once again in court. The miners were idle in a pension dispute, and Judge Goldsborough ordered Mr. Lewis and the union to end the walkout. He declined and was fined $20,000 and the union $1.4-million. The fines were eventually paid.

At the mine union convention in 1948 Mr. Lewis stormed against Mr. Truman for persecuting the union.

"He is a man totally unfitted for the position," Mr. Lewis said of the President. "His principles are elastic. He is careless with the truth. He is a malignant, scheming sort of individual who is dangerous not only to the United Mine Workers but dangerous to the United States of America."

The two men composed their differences before the end of Mr. Truman's tenure and in 1952 the President reversed a ruling of his Wage Stabilization Board to permit a wage increase that Mr. Lewis had negotiated for the miners.

As a result of the royalty fees that Mr. Lewis won from the mine operators, his union initiated a pension program in 1948.

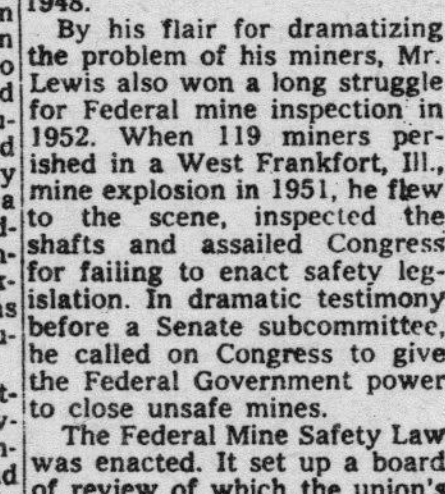

By his flair for dramatizing the problem of his miners, Mr. Lewis also won a long struggle for Federal mine inspection in 1952. When 119 miners perished in a West Frankfort, Ill., mine explosion in 1951, he flew to the scene, inspected the shafts and assailed Congress for failing to enact safety legislation. In dramatic testimony before a Senate subcommittee, he called on Congress to give the Federal Government power to close unsafe mines.

The Federal Mine Safety Law was enacted. It set up a board of review of which the union's safety director was a member. To insure its passage, Mr. Lewis called a 10-day "memorial" stoppage.

In the fifties coal lost its dominance as a fuel. Oil and gas became competitive. To meet the crisis Mr. Lewis cooperated with the mine operators in introducing mechanization into coal production. This made it possible in 1952, for example, for 375,000 bituminous mines to produce more coal than double that number could have dug 30 years before.

Million Aided by Fund

He also convinced the operators that it was wise to close uneconomic mines and pay high wages in the efficient ones. This was done quietly, in contrast to his former tactics, and by 1955 the miners' daily scale was $20.25 — well above the standard in other mass industries. When he stepped down as union chief in 1960, the scale was $24.25 a day. By that time the welfare and pension fund had collected $1.3-billion, had a reserve of $130-million and had aided more than a million persons. Miners were enabled to retire at 60 with a pension of $100 a month. In 1960, a total of 70,000 were receiving these retirement benefits.

In the last years of the fifties Mr. Lewis clamped down on unauthorized strikes. Laying down the law at the union convention in 1956, he warned fractious miners that "you'll be fully conscious that I'm breathing down your necks" if they struck.

When he announced late in 1959 that he was preparing to retire, the operators expressed regret. They praised him both for his "outstanding ability" and as "an extraordinarily fine person."

In his farewell address to his union he said:

"The years have been long and the individual burdens oppressive, yet progress has been great.

"At first, your wages were low, your hours long, your labor perilous, your health disregarded, your children without opportunity, your union weak, your fellow citizens and public representatives indifferent to your wrongs.

"Today, because of your fortitude and your deep loyalty to your union, your wages are the highest in the land, your working hours the lowest, your safety more assured, your health more guarded, your old age protected, your children equal in opportunity with their generation and your union strong with material resources."

He retired on an annual pension of $50,000 and was voted the title of president emeritus.

Associated Press

BEFORE THE BREAK: Mr. Lewis with President Franklin D. Roosevelt during the 1936 campaign. Mr. Lewis supported the President that year but later broke with him and sought to rally labor against his bid for a third term.

"All the News That's Fit to Print"

The New York Times

LATE CITY EDITION

Weather: Chance of showers today, tonight. Partly cloudy tomorrow. Temp. range: today 68-83; Monday 68-75. Highest Temp.-Hum. Index yesterday: 71. Details on Page 65.

VOL. CXXIII..No. 42,584 | NEW YORK, TUESDAY, AUGUST 27, 1974 | 20¢ beyond 50-mile radius of New York City, except Long Island. Higher in air delivery cities. | 15 CENTS

Lindbergh Dies of Cancer in Hawaii at the Age of 72

The New York Times/Jack Manning

Charles A. Lindbergh

W. C. Persons

Mr. Lindbergh and his plane before 1927 flight to Paris

Special to The New York Times

KIPAHULU, Maui, Hawaii, Aug. 26—Charles A. Lindbergh, the first man to fly the Atlantic solo nonstop, died this morning at his simple seaside home here. He was 72 years old.

The cause of death was cancer of the lymphatic system, according to Dr. Milton Howell,

An obituary article appears on Pages 18 and 19.

a longtime friend. With him when he died at 7:15 A.M. local time were his wife, Anne Morrow Lindbergh, the writer, and Land, one of his three sons.

Mr. Lindbergh was buried about three hours later in the cemetery adjoining the tiny Kipahulu church. He was dressed in simple work clothing and his body was placed in a coffin built by cowboys employed on cattle ranches in the nearby town of Hana. Dr. Howell said that the aviator had spent the last weeks of his life planning his funeral.

In a tribute this evening to Mr. Lindbergh, President Ford said the courage and daring of his Atlantic flight would never be forgotten. He said the selfless, sincere man himself would be remembered as one of America's all-time heroes and a great pioneer of the air age that changed the world.

Mr. Lindbergh arrived here eight days ago after a 26-day stay in Columbia-Presbyterian Medical Center in New York for treatment of his illness. He was flown to Honolulu on a United Airlines flight on Aug. 17 and then was brought to this island by small plane. The trip had been kept secret at his request.

"When he knew that he would not recover, Mr. Lindbergh requested that he be taken here from Columbia so he could die," Dr. Howell said. "He had made his vacation home here for many years and he wanted to die here."

Mr. Lindbergh, whose New York-to-Paris flight in 1927 in the monoplane Spirit of St. Louis brought him lasting celebrity, built an A-frame cottage here in 1971. It looked out on

Continued on Page 17, Column 1

WALDHEIM MEETS CYPRUS LEADERS; ARRANGES TALKS

U.N. Chief Brings Together Heads of the Greek and Turkish Communities

By JAMES F. CLARITY
Special to The New York Times

NICOSIA, Cyprus, Aug. 26—Secretary General Waldheim of the United Nations and the heads of the Greek and Turkish Cypriote administrations conferred here today and said afterward they had achieved some progress toward an eventual solution of the crisis on the island.

After separate meetings with President Glafkos Clerides, the Greek Cypriote leader, and Rauf Denktash, the chief Turkish Cypriote official, the Secretary General brought the two men face to face for the first time since the Geneva conference on the Cyprus crisis collapsed two weeks ago.

It was the collapse of the talks that led to the Turkish Army's advances until it held about 40 per cent of the island.

'Very Encouraging Sign'

Secretary General Waldheim, who spent 18 hours in Nicosia on his way from Greece to Turkey, said before boarding a helicopter at Nicosia's airport that the meeting of the two leaders and an agreement by them to confer weekly from now on was "a very hopeful development."

"I leave the island in hope that we have made a step forward," Mr. Waldheim said. "A limited step, but the fact that the leaders have agreed to direct talks is a very encouraging sign for the future."

Mr. Clerides and Mr. Denktash, who met with Mr. Waldheim and each other in a corrugated metal barracks of the United Nations forces in Nicosia, agreed that the meetings had been useful. The Cypriote leaders emphasized, however, that their forthcoming meetings would be to discuss "humanitarian issues."

No Dramatic Promises

Both leaders indicated clearly that they were approaching the talks gingerly. There were no promises of dramatic or imminent political solutions.

Mr. Waldheim said that the talks today had been "constructive" and that they had included the possibility of "resuming the negotiations for a lasting peace in Cyprus."

If progress can be made by the Cypriote leaders on humanitarian matters such as the treatment of war refugees, he added, then "we have a better chance to solve political problems."

"This is a very important de-

Continued on Page 3, Column 1

President Selects 5 Goals For 2-Day Inflation Talks

Sept. 27-28 Summit Conference Would Try to Identify Causes and Develop Policies to Deal With the Economy

By PHILIP SHABECOFF
Special to The New York Times

WASHINGTON, Aug. 26 — President Ford's "summit conference" on inflation will be held here Sept. 27 and 28 and will be preceded by a series of preliminary meetings between the Administration and leaders of individual sectors of the nation's economy.

The White House press secretary, J. F. terHorst, announced today that the President had set five goals for the summit conference but added, "It would not be realistic to expect President Ford to achieve a miracle."

At a meeting with his Cabinet this morning, Mr. Ford said that the summit meeting, which he intends to preside over, must consider "new and realistic" policies to cope with inflation, Mr. terHorst reported at a news briefing.

The following are the goals of the conference as set forth by the President:

1. To clarify the nation's present economic condition.
2. To identify the causes of inflation.
3. To develop a consensus on basic policies to deal with inflation.
4. To consider new and realistic approaches to the inflation problem.
5. To define hardship areas requiring immediate action.

Mr. terHorst and other White House officials did not mention any specific areas that might require immediate action. However, the President has already received recommendations for dealing with specific problems, including the construction industry's decline, the hardships being faced by citizens living on fixed incomes and the rising unemployment rate.

President Ford will act as chairman of two of the preliminary meetings as well as spending as much time as possible presiding over the Sept. 27-28 summit conference, Mr. terHorst said. All meetings will be open to news coverage, including live television.

The President, the press secretary said, wants to involve "every one in the country—every part of America"—in the effort to come to grips with inflation.

"The last thing he wants is a cosmetic treatment of this issue," Mr. terHorst declared.

Later in the day, the executive director of the steering committee for the summit meeting, L. William Seidman, said

Continued on Page 16, Column 3

BUTZ SEES NO NEED FOR PANIC ON FOOD THIS YEAR OR NEXT

Ample Beef, Less Pork and Fewer Broiler Chickens Are Predicted by Panel

RISE IN PRICES IS LIKELY

Farmers Are Urged to Plan Full Use of Their Acreage During Coming Year

By WILLIAM ROBBINS
Special to The New York Times

WASHINGTON, Aug. 26—The United States will have plenty of beef in the coming year despite disappointing fall crops of livestock-feed grains, but lower supplies of pork and broiler chickens will be available, a panel of administrators led by Secretary of Agriculture Earl L. Butz said today.

At the same time the panel predicted that, although food prices would continue rising, reduced foreign demand would ease the impact of the recent drought on supplies of corn and other livestock-feed grains.

"In spite of the disappointing prospect of farm crops this fall, there is absolutely no basis for panic on the food supply in the United States this year or in 1975," Secretary Butz said in opening a briefing session for newsmen, called in an effort to put the United States production situation into perspective with regard to national needs and the world outlook.

'Task Force' on Meats

Dr. Butz urged farmers to plan for all-out production next year, saying no acreage would be set aside in idle reserves, and his special "task force" on meats offered recommendations for price-restraining economies in the distribution system.

A department economist, Terry Barr, who is the Agriculture Department's chief analyst on demand and prices, predicted in line with earlier forecasts that food prices over all would rise about 3 per cent in this year's third quarter and a little more in the fourth quarter.

The Weather Factor

But Mr. Barr said weather affecting crops and harvests could still cause variations of as much as 2 per cent, either upward or downward, in the price outlook. Recent rains are expected to improve the prospects for soybeans but to have little effect on the hard-hit corn crop.

The panel accompanying Dr. Butz made these other predictions:

¶United States agricultural exports in the 1974-75 fiscal year will fall substantially below last year's volume but, because of higher prices, the dollar value will be nearly equal. In the fiscal year ended June 30, the total was $21.3-billion.

¶World wheat exports will decline about 5 per cent, and the record United States crop will permit a slight build-up in reserve supplies.

¶Reserves of livestock-feed grains will decline, but because of increased production abroad and reduced demand, the Unit-

Continued on Page 12, Column 3

Convict Killed, 2 Seized As Texas Manhunt Ends

By The Associated Press

STEPHENVILLE, Tex., Tuesday, Aug. 27—Three escaped convicts who had terrorized the Texas ranch country were cornered by police last night. One convict was killed and the others were captured.

The state police said three officers saw the silhouettes of three men near a farm road and started shooting when the men refused to halt.

"We had some dogs with us," said Jim Elmore of the Mineral Wells Police Department. "The dogs barked. We threw the light at them and we saw the silhouettes. We hollered for them to stop. They did not and then started running and we started firing."

The three policemen had joined 200 other local officers, sheriff's deputies and state troopers in the two-day search in the rugged, mesquite-covered ranchlands near Stephenville.

The police identified the dead convict as Richard Mangum, 22 years old, and said he was shot in the face, arms and body.

A convicted murderer, Jerry Ulmer, 22, suffered a sprained ankle. The third convict, Dalton Williams, 29, was not hurt.

Erath County District Attorney Bob Glasgow said Mr. Ulmer and Mr. Williams would be charged with the murder of Mrs. Ray Ott. Mr. Glasgow said he expected other charges to be filed later.

The three men escaped from the Colorado State Prison last Thursday and headed south on a mission of revenge against the people who had helped send them to prison.

Two Killed, Five Wounded

A man and a woman were killed and five persons were wounded. Two young women were abducted and raped. Family dogs were shot, and a roadside cafe was fired upon for no apparent reason.

After Saturday's shooting wave, the hunters became the hunted. For the next two days they eluded a massive police manhunt. Yesterday morning, a policeman spotted them through binoculars while they walked along a creek, but authorities were unable to catch up with the fugitives.

The sighting caused a massive police response. Some officers brought bloodhounds, others arrived on horseback. Troopers lined Texas Highway 108 to prevent it from being used as an escape route. More than 60

Continued on Page 24, Column 6

SOVIET LAUNCHES 2 ON SPACECRAFT

Soyuz 15 Is Placed in Orbit —Astronaut Is First Grandfather in Space

By CHRISTOPHER WREN
Special to The New York Times

MOSCOW, Tuesday, Aug. 27—The Soviet Union has launched a new two-man spacecraft into orbit around the earth, the official press agency Tass announced early today.

The spacecraft, Soyuz 15, was launched at 3:58 P.M. Eastern daylight time yesterday, but the details were released today by Tass. The Soviet Union does not report such launchings until it knows that they have been successful.

Soyuz 15 was the second such spacecraft to be launched in less than two months. The last, Soyuz 14, was sent up on July 3, the day that President Nixon ended his summit visit here.

Mission Described

Tass reported that the Soyuz 15 spacecraft had been launched "to continue the scientific research and experiments in space" begun by the previous Soyuz 14 crew on the Salyut 3 space station, suggesting that the astronauts might attempt to link up with and live in the space station, which was recently reported to be still functioning in earth orbit.

The commander of the new spacecraft was identified as Lieut. Col. Gennady Sarafanov, who is 32 years old and a native of Saratov in the Lower Volga region. The flight engineer is Lev Demin, a 48-year-old civilian from Moscow.

Tass noted that Mr. Demin is the first astronaut to be a grandfather. His daughter Natasha has

Continued on Page 14, Column 1

Portuguese Guinea Wins Independence

Pact Signed in Algiers Takes Effect Sept. 10

Special to The New York Times

ALGIERS, Aug. 26—Portugal today began the dissolution of her colonial empire in Africa with the signing of an agreement granting independence to Portuguese Guinea on Sept. 10.

The accord, signed here with the guerrilla movement of the West African territory, formally ended more than 11 years of fighting. However, a de facto cease-fire has existed in Portuguese Guinea since shortly after the military coup in Lisbon that toppled the authoritarian Government of Premier Marcello Caetano on April 25.

With the agreement, which was worked out here and in London, beginning last May, the Portuguese Government of President António de Spínola pledged to remove all troops from the territory by Oct. 31. A troop airlift has already begun.

The accord contained one surprise—a provision for a referendum to be held at some unspecified date on the future of the Cape Verde Islands, which have been administered as part of Portuguese Guinea.

The guerrilla movement, the African Party for the Independence of Guinea and the Cape Verde Islands, had demanded that Portugal renounce sovereignty over the islands at the same time and that they be part of the new republic of Guinea-Bissau. But Portugal refused, largely because the islands, 300 to 400 miles off West Africa, are considered of strategic value to the North Atlantic Treaty Organization, to which she belongs.

The solution, a referendum, opened the way to the agreement signed here today in the People's Palace.

The agreement to end five

The New York Times/Aug. 27, 1974

Referendum Planned on Cape Verde Islands

centuries of colonial rule in Portuguese Guinea is the first of three steps to dissolution of the rebellious African empire. However, difficult negotiations are still ahead with the nationalists of the West African territory of Angola and the East African territory of Mozambique.

Last Sept. 24, the guerrilla movement of Portuguese Guinea proclaimed the republic of Guinea-Bissau in a liberated part of the Portuguese territory, and more than 100 countries have recognized it.

The first president of the republic is Luis Cabral, brother of Amilcar Cabral, founder and leader of the independence movement, who was assassinated early in 1973.

The signing of the agreement took place here today in the presence of the Algerian Government, headed by President Houari Boumediene, who is reported to have played a role in bringing the two sides together. Also on hand were the diplomatic corps and the representatives of the various liberation movements that have

Continued on Page 2, Column 4

G.M.'s Price Increases Range Up to $1,316

Special to The New York Times

DETROIT, Aug. 26—The General Motors Corporation disclosed today that it was raising prices of some of its 1975 models hundreds of dollars more than the average $426 increase it announced last week for its new cars and trucks.

In several cases the company is also adding new, more expensive models to the top of its lines, a familiar pricing device in the auto industry.

G.M. released today its detailed list of 1975 prices for the Chevrolet, Buick, Oldsmobile, Pontiac and Cadillac lines.

Price changes range from a decline of $37 for two Oldsmobile models to an increase of $1,316 on a Cadillac limousine.

The company said prices of 144 models were increased while those of five were lowered. G.M. has added 27 new models and discontinued nine. It said it would offer 176 models for 1975, compared with 158 this year

A G.M. spokesman said that the price list was "in keeping with the announced $54 decrease in average prices" announced last week. The company said then it was cutting its planned average price increase from 9.5 per cent to 8.5 per cent—from $480 to $426.

G.M. rolled back part of its increase after President Ford said he was "very disappointed" at the size of the rise and the new Administration hoped the company would reconsider. G.M. followed by reducing the average price increase by one percentage point.

The G.M. spokesman said that this was a sales-weighted average based on the past experience of retail cars and trucks delivered and equipment ordered for them by customers. He said the price list adheres strictly to the average increase announced last week.

But a customer who wants a particular car may find it has gone up by a larger amount.

General Motors provided a comparison of price figures on a Chevrolet Nova compact car equipped with power steering, power brakes, AM radio, automatic transmission, air-conditioning and white sidewalls.

The price now, including all that equipment, is $4,174. This is an increase of $443, or 11.8 per cent, from the final 1974 price of $3,731 for a comparably equipped car. Moreover, it is $827, or 24.7 per cent, above the original 1974 price of the car, which was $3,347.

In addition, the shipping

Continued on Page 44, Column 2

Fire 'Hero' Seized at City Hall For Questioning in Fatal Arson

By JOSEPH B. TREASTER

Wilberto Diaz went to City Hall yesterday morning to be honored for rescuing four children from a burning tenement, but instead of shaking hands with the Mayor, he was handcuffed and taken into custody for questioning about a fire five hours earlier in which one man was killed.

The police said that witnesses had reported seeing Mr. Diaz, who is 18, and three other men running from a six-story building at 234 East Third Street shortly before it burst into flames at about 5:30 A.M.

Mr. Diaz, who lives at 46-48 Avenue B, and a friend who was not implicated in the fire yesterday morning, Angel Jiminez, 20, were to have received citations from Mayor Beame for their "unusual heroism" and "selfless action" in hoisting four youngsters to safety from the top floor of a Lower East Side building that was badly damaged by flames last Monday.

The two had told newsmen it was the third time in a year and a half that they had rescued people from fires in the neighborhood.

Minutes before the awards were to have been made at 10:30 A.M., Detective John O'Kane called City Hall to say he had information that Mr. Diaz had been involved in the latest fire.

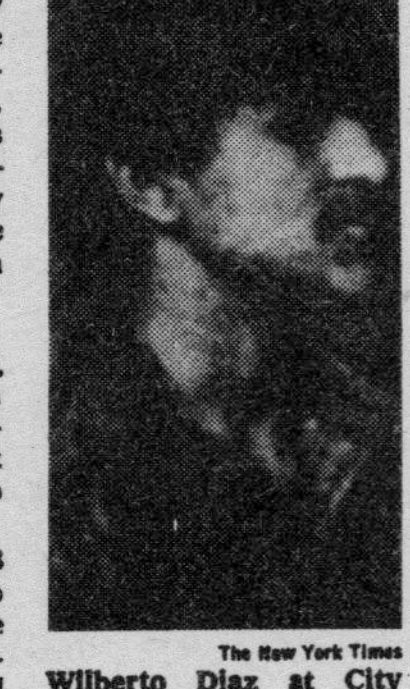

The New York Times

Wilberto Diaz at City Hall yesterday morning.

The youths were escorted to Fire Department headquarters a few blocks from City Hall, and a short time later Mr. Diaz was taken into custody.

At the Ninth Precinct station at 321 East Fifth Street, Mr. Diaz and the three others were booked for burglary.

The police said that as they had poked through the burned-out building, they had found that a ground-floor office building had been broken into and that some tools and plumbing materials had been taken.

Both firemen and the police

Continued on Page 30, Column 6

Revenue Sharing Target Of New General Scrutiny

By WILLIAM E. FARRELL
Special to The New York Times

WASHINGTON—For nearly two years, one of the smallest Federal bureaucracies in Washington has been quietly mailing out checks—reaching a total of $14.3-billion—to thousands of units of state and local government.

The Federal largesse, disbursed under terms of the General Revenue Sharing Act, has been a success among governors, mayors, county officials and others associated with state and municipal government throughout the country.

These officials, many of whom lobbied for passage of the Revenue Sharing Act, clearly like having Federal money to spend with a minimum of Federal restrictions on how they should spend it.

President Ford has just told urban leaders that he supports general revenue sharing and wants to see it renewed. The program expires at the end of 1976.

Meanwhile, some members of the House and Senate are beginning to re-evaluate the law with an eye toward possible amendments. And civic, watchdog and minority groups have become unhappy with various aspects of it.

The groups are critical of the low level of community participation in determining how the Federal dollars should be spent, they question whether anti-

Continued on Page 52, Column 5

NEWS INDEX

Lindbergh Dies of Cancer at Age of 72

Continued From Page 1, Col. 2

the Pacific, and it was the place where he had hoped to retire after years of restless global wanderings as a consultant for Pan-American World Airways. He had hoped to write a long-postponed book outlining his philosophical and conservationist views.

Mr. Lindbergh slipped into a coma late last night, Dr. Howell said, but until then he had been fully alert and aware of his surroundings. The aviator made no final statement, according to the physician, who said Mr. Lindbergh's "final theme was that he would like for his actions in coming to Maui in having a simple funeral to be—in itself—a constructive act.

Mr. Lindbergh's whole life centered on aviation, but in recent years he developed an active concern with conservation. This interest brought him into the news after a quarter-century of self-imposed obscurity. One of his last public appearances occurred last summer in Little Falls, Minn., where he was born, to dedicate a public park in honor of his father, C. A. Lindbergh Sr., a former United States Representative.

Before Mr. Lindbergh left New York, he talked with his two other sons, Scott of Paris and Jon of Seattle. He also saw his daughters, Anne and Reeve. Anne, who also lives in Paris, was visiting her parents at their home in Darien, Conn.

Mr. Lindbergh was ill last fall, suffering from what was then diagnosed as shingles. He lost about 20 pounds, but by last spring he had managed to regain about 10 of them. Just before he entered the hospital he came down with what was officially described as influenza.

But when his temperature rose to 104 degrees, his physicians admitted him to Columbia-Presbyterian. About three weeks ago his wife said that he had perceptibly improved and that she expected him to be discharged shortly. He took a turn for the worse, however, and his condition was diagnosed as lymphatic cancer.

In addition to his widow and five children, Mr. Lindbergh is survived by 10 grandchildren.

The New York Times

Mr. Lindbergh and his wife, Anne Morrow Lindbergh, at the dinner of the National Institute of Social Sciences here on Nov. 21, 1968. They were honored — he for conservation and she for literature — with gold medals.

Among the tributes to Charles A. Lindbergh were the following:

PRESIDENT FORD: From the moment that the Spirit of St. Louis landed in Paris on May 21, 1927, Charles A. Lindbergh had earned a place in history. For a generation of Americans, and for millions of other people around the world, the "Lone Eagle" represented all that was best in our country—honesty, courage and the will to greatness. In later years, his life was darkened by tragedy, and colored by political controversy. But, in both public and private life, General Lindbergh always remained a brave, sincere patriot. Nearly a half century has passed since his courageous flight across the Atlantic, but the courage and daring of his feat will never be forgotten.

CLARENCE CHAMBERLIN, pioneer aviator who crossed the Atlantic 10 days after Mr. Lindbergh: He was a great pilot. He sort of sparked everything. After he went to Paris, people began to think aviation. He did it—he started the ball rolling.

HOWARD HUGHES, in a telegram to Mrs. Lindbergh: It was with a great sense of sadness and reawakened appreciation that I learned of your husband's passing. He was a pioneer in the conquest of the impossible. May the knowledge of his contributions sustain and comfort you. The courage and example of your lives, together with the accomplishment and vision which marked his career, have been a source of encouragement and hope to all of us.

LAURANCE S. ROCKEFELLER, who was active with Mr. Lindbergh in conservation projects: The loss of Charles Lindbergh leaves America and the world bereft of one of the most dedicated and eloquent spokesman of man's concern for the preservation of his natural environment. This role was probably the greatest of his many achievements. He will be sorely missed.

MAYOR BEAME: New Yorkers will always remember Charles Lindbergh as an authentic hero. His memorable trans-Atlantic journey was an inspiring achievement for Americans and Europeans alike. When "Lucky Lindy" returned from Paris, thousands of New Yorkers welcomed him home with a ticker-tape parade and a celebration perhaps never equaled in the city's history. Lindbergh's solo flight was more than an act of individual bravery. It was an early landmark of the revolution in transportation and communications that has dramatically reshaped our world.

LOWELL THOMAS, the radio commentator and a longtime friend: He was one of the three real heroes of our time—the others being Capt. Eddie Rickenbacker and Jimmy Doolittle. We all know about his shyness—something that was ingrown in him even before the tragedy. I admired his spirit, what he did for his country.

Daring Lindbergh Attained the Unattainable With Historic Flight Across Atlantic

By ALDEN WHITMAN

In Paris at 10:22 P.M. on May 21, 1927, Charles Augustus Lindbergh, a one-time Central Minnesota farm boy, became an international celebrity. A fame enveloped the 25-year-old American that was to last him for the remainder of his life, transforming him in a frenzied instant from an obscure aviator into a historical figure.

The consequences of this fame were to exhilarate him, to involve him in profound grief, to engage him in fierce controversy, to turn him into an embittered fugitive from the public, to accentuate his individualism to the point where he became a loner, to give him a special sense of his own importance, to allow him to play an enormous role in the growth of commercial aviation as well as to be a figure in missile and space technology, to give him influence in military affairs, and to raise a significant voice for conservation, a concern that marked his older years.

All these things were touched off when a former stunt flier and airmail pilot touched down the wheels of his small and delicate monoplane, the Spirit of St. Louis, on the tarmac of Le Bourget 33½ hours after having lifted the craft off Roosevelt Field on Long Island. Thousands—no one knows how many—trampled through fences and over guards to surround the silvery plane and to acclaim, in a wild outburst of emotion, the first man to fly the Atlantic solo nonstop from the United States to Europe—a feat that was equivalent in the public mind then to the first human step on the moon 42 years later. Icarus had at last succeeded, a daring man alone had attained the unattainable.

What enhanced the feat for many was that Lindbergh was a tall, handsome bachelor with a becoming smile, an errant lock of blond hair over his forehead and a pleasing outward modesty and guilelessness. He was the flawless El Cid, the gleaming Galahad, Frank Merriwell in the flesh.

The delirium that engulfed Paris swirled out over the civilized world. Banner headlines heralded the event. Medals galore were bestowed on Lindbergh. He was gushed over, adulated, worshiped, feted in France, Belgium and Britain. President Calvin Coolidge sent the cruiser Memphis, flagship of the United States European Fleet, to bring him and the Spirit of St. Louis back to the United States and later awarded him the Medal of Honor, previously reserved only for military heroes. And already a captain in the United States Officers Reserve Corps, Lindbergh was jumped to a full colonel.

As the cruiser steamed up Chesapeake Bay, she was met by four destroyers, two Army blimps and 40 airplanes from the Army, Navy and Marine Corps. Debarking at Washington in a civilian's blue serge suit, Lindbergh was glorified by the President, who said that the trans-Atlantic flight was "the same story of valor and victory by a son of the people that shines through every page of American history."

The panoplied Washington reception, which was topped by an award—the first in the nation's history—of the Distinguished Flying Cross, was followed by an even noisier outpouring in New York, where four million people spilled into the streets. Ticker tape and confetti rained on the Broadway parade, and the day was climaxed by a banquet for 4,000 guests. "We measure heroes as we do ships, by their displacement," the bewhiskered Charles Evans Hughes told the multitude. "Colonel Lindbergh has displaced everything."

And then there were triumphal parades and receptions, seemingly endless, in other cities. Lindbergh eventually flew the Spirit of St. Louis to every state in the Union. Everywhere he went a throng collected. Even a supposedly private visit to Orville Wright, co-inventor of the airplane, was noised about, and crowds appeared.

Lindbergh, at one point, was "so filled up with listening to this hero guff that I was ready to shout murder."

What the parades, the pandemonium, the oratory, the hero worship obscured was that Lindbergh's epic flight was a most minutely planned venture by a professional flier with 2,000 air hours amassed over five years. "Why shouldn't I fly from New York to Paris?" he had asked himself in September, 1926. "I have more than four years of aviation behind me. I've barnstormed over half of the 48 states. I've flown my mail through the worst of nights."

There had been two previous Atlantic flights—both in 1919, the first when one of three Navy craft flew from Newfoundland to the Azores; and the second when John Alcock and Arthur Brown made it from Newfoundland to Ireland. But no one had made the crossing alone, or from continent to continent.

Once he conceived the notion of the flight, Lindbergh, with characteristic energy, began to elaborate the details. He helped design the plane to his specifications, calculating every ounce that went into it. He laid out his route. Every

(continued)

The New York Times

The aviator was awarded the Medal of Honor and the nation's first Distinguished Flying Cross. Here he was with President Calvin Coolidge in 1928.

foreseeable circumstance was checked out.

Two elements could not be figured: the weather and his ability to stay awake. With the weather he took a calculated risk. Fighting off sleep proved a problem, and only his indomitable determination overcame that, although he conceded there were moments of touch-and-go.

One of the attractions for the Paris flight was a $25,000 prize, for which there were several competitors, among them Clarence Chamberlin and Adm. Richard E. Byrd. Lindbergh, though, was confident he could be first and be successful. He was motivated, he told this writer in later years, by a desire to improve his standing as a pilot as well as by an eagerness to win the prize. And although there was great interest in him before take-off time (his hope and that of his rivals to fly the Atlantic had excited wide newspaper coverage), Lindbergh had not calculated the response to his achievement, the degree to which he would be lionized or the extent to which he would be regarded as public property, especially by reporters and photographers, whom he came quickly to detest.

'Extraordinary Situation'

"The situation I encountered was extraordinary in the extreme, and often fantastic," he recalled, and cited, as an example, a woman who "wanted to rent the hotel room I was leaving so she could take a bath in the same tub."

Overwhelmed, without precedents to guide him, pressed by dizzying demands on his time, Lindbergh was happy to accept an invitation from Harry Guggenheim, a very rich and very conservative financier who was connected with the Daniel Guggenheim Fund for the Promotion of Aeronautics, to escape for a while to his Long Island estate. The invitation was at the suggestion of Dwight Morrow, the Morgan banker, who told Mr. Guggenheim, "Harry, almost everyone in the country is after this young fellow, trying to exploit him. Isn't there something you and the fund can do to save him from the wolves?"

At Falaise, the Guggenheim castle, which was perhaps the most opulent private home he had stayed in, the aviator was able to catch his breath for three weeks and rewrite the ghost-written manuscript that became the book "We." He also retained Henry Breckinridge, a conservative Wall Street lawyer, to help handle his affairs. Many of his new associates held conservative views, which his father, a neo-Populist Republican, spent 20 years fighting.

Lindbergh was not conceived of then as a possible political figure, but rather as a nice young man, perhaps a little unpolished socially, who deserved the best that could be provided. His new friends were considerate of his strong individualism. They did not impose flattery, they were respectful and, above all, helpful. The income from "We" and from his flight articles in The New York Times made him a millionaire—a considerable eminence for a man accustomed to thinking hard before he spent $5. His friends helped him invest his fortune.

And after Lindbergh made his good-will flights around the country and to Latin America in the Spirit of St. Louis, his friends saw to it that he got a job in keeping with his interest in aviation and his status. The position was as an adviser in both Pan American World Airways and the predecessor of Trans World Airlines in laying out trans-Atlantic, transcontinental and Caribbean air routes for the commercial aviation that his Paris flight had done so much to popularize.

The conservative views that Lindbergh later articulated, the remarks about Jews that proved so startling when he was opposing American entry into World War II, his adverse opinion of the Soviet Union, his belief in Western civilization — these were all a reflection of a world view prevalent among his friends, which he absorbed over the years.. An engineer and aviator of genius, he was, however, not an intellectual, nor a consistent reader, nor a social analyst.

The assumption of this élitism accounted for his conviction that "America should lead the world in the development of flight," that "a conflict between English and German groups of nations would [be] a fratricidal war," that race was a valid judgmental concept and that to accomplish an objective one should deal with "the top people." It also accounted for what many people thought was his anti-Semitism.

Lindbergh did not regard himself as an anti-Semite. Indeed, he was shocked a couple of years ago when this writer put the question to him. "Good God, no," he responded, citing his fondness for Jews he had known or dealt with. Nor did he condone the Nazi treatment of German Jews, much less Hitler's genocidal policies. On the other hand, he accepted as fact that American Jewish groups were among those promoting United States involvement in World War II.

He voiced these views in a speech in Des Moines, Iowa, on Sept. 11, 1941. After asserting that those groups responsible for seeking American "entanglement in European affairs" were "the British, the Jewish and the Roosevelt Administration," he went on to say:

"It is not difficult to understand why Jewish people desire the overthrow of Nazi Germany. The persecution they suffered in Germany would be sufficient to make bitter enemies of any race. No person with a sense of the dignity of mankind can condone the persecution the Jewish race suffered in Germany.

"But no person of honesty and vision can look on their prowar policy here today without seeing the dangers involved in such a policy, both for us and for them.

"Instead of agitating for war, the Jewish groups in this country should be opposing it in every possible way, for they will be among the first to feel its consequences. Tolerance is a virtue that depends upon peace and strength. A few far-sighted Jewish people realize this and stand opposed to intervention. But the majority still do not. Their greatest danger to their country lies in their large ownership and influence in our motion pictures, our press, our radio and our government."

The speech evoked a nationwide outcry. Lindbergh, it was said, had not only impugned the patriotism of American Jews, but also had used the word "race," a word many Jews considered both pejorative and inaccurate. Lindbergh never withdrew his remarks, which he considered statements of "obvious fact." "The violence of the reaction to my naming these groups was significant and extremely interesting," he said 25 years later. "In hindsight, I would not change my action."

Lindbergh's attitude toward the Jews was matched by an adamantine stubbornness on other matters. These together sometimes cast him in an unfavorable public light.

One example of his unwillingness to concede that he might have acted unwisely involved the Service Cross of the German Eagle, a civilian medal that was awarded him in 1938 by Hermann Goering, the Nazi leader, "at the direction" of Hitler. The presentation, a surprise to Lindbergh, was made at a stag dinner in the home of the American Ambassador to Berlin and was, he was told, in recognition of his services to aviation, especially his 1927 flight.

The award was reported briefly in the newspapers and stirred little criticism. However, the night of the award Mrs. Lindbergh told her husband that it was "the albatross," and she urged him to return it. Lindbergh took the position then and later that to do so would affront the Ambassador and Goering, as well, who was technically his host in Germany.

Although he never wore the medal (he gave it to the Lindbergh collection of the Missouri Historical Society in St. Louis, along with other awards and trophies), it became an issue when he opposed American war involvement. It led, among other things, to his being called a Fascist sympathizer, particularly when he declined a suggestion in 1942 to repudiate it; and the medal plagued his reputation for the rest of his life.

He disdained the criticism, however, saying:

"Personally, I am not at all concerned about any damage that may have been done to my reputation by the presentation of the medal.

"I felt the throwing back of the medal was like taking part in a child's spitting contest. If I must fight, I'll fight; but I prefer not to spit at my enemy beforehand. Also, I felt Goering had given me the medal with good intent and in friendship. Regardless of how much I disagreed with him about other things, or later on, I did not want to throw it back in his face."

Lindbergh's life, like his personality, was full of shadows and enigmas. Born Feb. 4, 1902, in Detroit, he was the son of C. A. Lindbergh, a prosperous Little Falls, Minn., lawyer and land speculator, and his second wife, Evangeline Lodge Land. The elder Lindbergh's first wife had died, leaving him two daughters. Charles Augustus Lindbergh Jr. was born in Detroit because his mother's uncle was a physician there. He was returned to Little Falls six weeks later and lived in that small town, the center of a farming and timbering community, with few interruptions until he was 18.

His paternal antecedents were Swedes, who changed their name from Mansons to Lindbergh when they emigrated from Sweden in 1860. They had a history of independence and vigor. The Lands, of Irish and English background, arrived in the United States shortly after 1812. Lindbergh's maternal grandfather was C. H. Land, a dentist and inventor. Both Dr. Land and C. A. Lindbergh were strong advocates of free inquiry and individual initiative, and both impressed on young Charles the merits of personal independence.

Charles's world was jolted when his father was elected to the House of Representatives, where he served from 1907 to 1917. He went to Washington, his first venture into a metropolis, and disliked it. About that time, his mother and father ceased living together, although for appearance's sake there was no legal separation and both parents took care to give the child a sense of security.

Apart from saying that the separation was "a tragic situation" for his parents, Lindbergh shut his lips about the situation and shied from talking about the psychic hurts that he bore. He was equally taciturn on other personal matters.

The future aviator's interest in flying was sparked in 1908 or '09, when, one day, he heard a buzzing in the sky and climbed out of a dormer window onto the roof of his home to witness a frail biplane skimming through the clouds.

The Fun of Flying

"Afterward, I remember lying in the grass and looking up at the clouds and thinking how much fun it would be to fly up there among those clouds," he recalled in later years, adding:

"I didn't think of the hazards—I was just interested in getting up there in the clouds."

But he was torn for a time by a strong yearning to go to Alaska, a land pictured as a wild frontier and the source of mythic Gold Rush tales. For him Alaska was also the scene of Robert W. Service's verse, some of which he memorized so thoroughly that he could recite it faultlessly in old age.

Although Lindbergh Sr. led an active and exciting political life as a maverick Republican who battled (and helped to overthrow) the entrenched Establishment in the House, led an assault on "the money trust" and voted against American entry into World War I, his son was bored by politics and all the speeches. The issue that his father espoused in Congress and later as a Farmer-Laborite supporter of Robert LaFollette failed, so the son said, to make any impressions on him. His mother, too, eschewed political thinking.

In World War I, Lindbergh operated the family farm, leaving it in the fall of 1920 to study engineering at the University of Wisconsin. His grades were poor and he left after a year and a half, but not before learning how to shoot quarters out of the outstretched fingers of his friends at 50 feet with a rifle.

From Wisconsin, he motorcycled to the Nebraska Aircraft Corporation in Lincoln, which was then producing an airplane and giving flying lessons to promote the product. "I can still smell the odor of dope [cellulose acetate or nitrate] that permeated each breath," he said years later in recalling his first close-up view of an aircraft.

Lindbergh took his first flight April 9, 1922. In succeeding months he learned to fly, to wing-walk and to parachute. Of equal importance, he absorbed all there was to know about the planes of that day and the various styles of flying. And he made friends with fliers who passed through Lincoln and with Harlan A. (Bud) Gurney, with whom, among others, he barnstormed over the Midwest. Called Slim by his friends because of his lithe, gangling body and 6-foot-2½-inch height, Lindbergh was billed to the public as "Daredevil Lindbergh" for his stunt feats.

However, he did not solo until April, 1923, when he purchased his first plane, a Jenny, in Georgia. Shortly afterward he began to earn his living as a flier by taking up passengers in various towns at $5 a ride. It was all seat-of-the-pants flying and Lindbergh gloried in it; but he gave it up to enlist in the Army in March, 1924, so he could attend the Army flying school at Brooks Field, San Antonio, Tex. For the first time, he found some joy in textbooks and classes.

Chief Pilot on Mail Run

Indeed, he was graduated as the top man in his class, and was commissioned a second lieutenant in the Army Air Service Reserve in March, 1925. He was by this time an experienced flier. He spent some time as an air circus stunt flier at county fairs and the like before being hired by the Robertson Aircraft Company of St. Louis as the chief pilot on the mail run to Chicago. He made the first run in April, 1926. It was the only paycheck job in the normal sense of the word that he ever held.

Meantime, he had made a further commitment to the military by joining the Missouri National Guard, where he taught other pilots and became a first lieutenant.

On one of his flights to Chicago in September, 1926, he was musing about the possibilities of long-distance trips, and he "startled" himself by thinking "I could fly nonstop between New York and Paris."

In many ways, Lindbergh's life was a series of responses to imperatives. When he became convinced that he "ought" to do something—he ought to oppose entry into World War II, he ought to speak out for conservation—he reacted with vigor and dispatch. And virtually immediately he began to plan the details of the trip—getting financial backing, getting a specially designed plane, mapping the route, seeking to eliminate any chance of failure.

Ultimately, he persuaded a group of St. Louis businessmen to put up $15,000, which was one reason why the plane was called the Spirit of St. Louis. After many racking incidents, the Ryan Company, with Lindbergh's help, designed and built a craft tailored for him and the Wright Company built an engine of 223 horsepower to accommodate the plane.

For several years after the Paris flight, Lindbergh lived in the glare of publicity and popping camera flashbulbs. The public would not let him alone. "I recall stepping out of a building on Wall Street, and having almost everyone on the street turn and follow me," he said. He was regarded as a sort of oracle, and his opinion was solicited on every conceivable subject.

He was, moreover, linked falsely in the press with a number of girls. His interest, however, was in Anne Spencer Morrow, the beautiful blue-eyed daughter of Dwight Morrow, then Ambassador to Mexico. The couple met in Mexico City at Christmastime in 1927, when Miss Morrow, then a Smith student, went there for the holidays. They were married in a private ceremony in the Morrow home in New Jersey on May 27, 1929.

The marriage was a union of opposites. Sensitive, retiring, a poet, Mrs. Lindbergh wanted nothing so much as a life of peace and quiet. Seldom coddling her, her husband proved hyperactive, happy as a nomad who was rarely at home for long periods. Yet despite some moments of tension, the marriage was an enduring and affectionate one.

For a while Mrs. Lindbergh accompanied her husband on many of his trips—to the Caribbean, where he was laying out air routes; to Europe and to Asia. He had taught her to fly, and she learned to navigate and to operate a Morse Code radio. "North to the Orient" is her chronicle of one of these flights.

Their first child, Charles Augustus 3d, was born June 24, 1930. Twenty months later, when Mrs. Lindbergh was pregnant with her second child, the baby was kidnapped from his nursery crib in his parents' home in Hopewell, N. J. The date was March 1, 1932. On May 12 the baby's body was found in a shallow grave not far from the house.

In between, there was a bizarre hunt for the child that included payment of a $50,000 ransom at a cemetery in the Bronx and a cast of characters that ranged from Dr. John F. (Jafsie) Condon, a school principal, to Gaston B. Means, a swindler. There were false leads and sensations galore, through all of which Lindbergh bore himself with great public stoicism.

His private emotions were never disclosed, and about the only references that he made in later years to the kidnapping and murder were fleeting mentions of "that New Jersey business."

If public attention glared on Lindbergh during the hunt for his son, it positively poured down on him with the arrest and trial of Bruno Richard Hauptmann, a Bronx carpenter, in 1934.

(continued)

The trial, which Lindbergh attended daily, was reported with diligence and sensationalism. Lindbergh received up to 100,000 letters a week, and the Hopewell estate, which he had long since left, was overrun with curiosity seekers, one of whom dug up and lugged off the earth where the baby was found buried.

A Move to England

After a six-week trial, in which a web of circumstantial evidence was woven about Hauptmann, he was found guilty and executed. Although there were doubts (Hauptmann, the German-born father of a son about the age of Lindbergh's son, denied he was guilty), Lindbergh was satisfied that "Hauptmann did the thing."

Meantime, there were new threats to kidnap Lindbergh's second son, Jon, and the family was living an abnormal existence. Lindbergh was telling friends that Americans exhibited "a morbid curiosity over crimes and murder trials" and lacked "respect for law, or the rights of others." Against this background, Lindbergh took his family to England to seek a safe, secluded residence away from "the tremendous public hysteria" that surrounded him in the United States.

One result of the case was passage of the so-called Lindbergh law, which made kidnapping a Federal crime. Part of the statute was ruled unconstitutional in 1967.

Before departing, Lindbergh completed a scientific project on which he had been working with dedication and enthusiasm since 1930. It was the design and building of a tissue-perfusion apparatus at Rockefeller Institute (now University) in New York. He was introduced to the project by Dr. Alexis Carrel, who had won the Nobel Prize for physiology and medicine in 1912 for development of blood vessel transplant procedures. The French-born Carrel was interested in the thirties in living organs outside the body, and the problem was to devise an instrument to perfuse these organs and keep them alive.

"For me," Lindbergh recalled, "that began an association with an extraordinarily great man. To me, his true greatness lay in the unlimited penetration, curiosity and scope of his mind, in his fearlessness of opinion, in his deep concerns about the trends of modern civilization and their effect on his fellow man."

In addition to perfecting a pump—an important breakthrough in its time — Lindbergh invented a quick way of separating serum from whole blood by means of a centrifuge. The Lindbergh-Carrel friendship lasted for 14 years, until the scientist's death in 1944.

A brilliant investigator, Carrel tinkered with philosophy and other matters; and his thoughts in these areas were sometimes quirky. He believed, for example, in extrasensory perception. He also spoke against "industrial civilization" and suggested that "we ought to try to produce a certain number of individuals above the mental stature we observe in the best." He said, moreover, that "only the élite make the progress of the masses possible."

Some of these notions rubbed off on Lindbergh and were reflected in his little-known book, "Of Flight and Life," in which he inveighed against "scientific materialism." In this 1948 book, he said, "I believe the values we are creating and the standards we are now following will lead to the end of our civilization, and that if we do not control our science by a higher moral force, it will destroy us with its materialistic values."

In his plea for the recognition of metaphysical values, Lindbergh wrote: "To progress, even to survive, we must learn to apply the truths of God to the actions and relationships of men, to the direction of our science. We must learn from the sermons of Christ, the wisdom of Laotzu, the teachings of Buddha."

But Lindbergh, in this book, also espoused a doctrine of American superiority in the world. "For Americans, the doctrine of universal equality is a doctrine of death," he wrote. "If we ever become an equal people among other peoples of the world, our civilization will fall."

When Lindbergh went abroad to live, first in Britain and then in France, he was 33 years old. He was immediately treated with courtesy and respect—and given the privacy he so much desired. His new friends were in the upper reaches of British society and Tory politics.

Moreover, as a distinguished aviator, he was invited to visit airplane factories in France by the French Air Ministry. He was also invited by the German Government to inspect the Luftwaffe and warplane factories in the Reich. He received red-carpet treatment, visited many factories and was told repeatedly that the Nazis were eager "to create an air force second to none." He visited Germany several times before 1938 and was increasingly impressed with the quality of the air force.

It seemed to him all the more fearsome by comparison with the air arm in Britain, France and the Soviet Union. By 1939 he had concluded that the power of the Luftwaffe was overwhelming, and that the air forces of other European countries were comparatively insignificant. In off-the-record conversations with the leaders of these countries, the Soviet Union excepted, he sought to warn them of the perils they were facing.

Neither then nor later did Lindbergh, according to his journals, believe that German air power would be the decisive factor in a war so much as it would be an essential element. And he sought to impress on France, Britain and the United States the need to bestir themselves.

Lindbergh and his family returned to the United States in 1939 shortly before World War II broke out. He felt he ought to do all he could to prevent American involvement. Not a pacifist nor an isolationist, he was a noninterventionist.

"My opposition to World War II resulted from the growing conviction that such a war would probably devastate Europe, kill millions of men and possibly result in the end of Western civilization," he told this writer a few years ago, adding:

"Under the circumstances of prewar Europe, I concluded that Germany could not be defeated without the active intervention of the United States. I doubted that Germany could be defeated even with American intervention.

"Obviously this depended a great deal on the relationship between Germany and Russia. But if Germany were defeated, it seemed to me almost certain that Russia would be the real victor and that a Stalin-dominated Europe would be even worse than a Hitler-dominated Europe.

"I felt that the wisest policy for Western powers would be to arm, stay neutral and let Germany and Russia clash—and thereafter to feel their way according to changing circumstances. I still think this would have been the wisest policy."

Lindbergh made his first antiwar speech—a radio talk—on Sept. 17, 1939. It was arranged by Fulton Lewis, a well-known conservative commentator.

In the months that followed, he made other radio speeches and worked actively with other antiwar personalities in public and private life, including Senator Burton K. Wheeler of Montana; Senator Harry F. Byrd of Virginia; former President Herbert Hoover; Senator William Borah of Idaho; Henry Ford; Merwin K. Hart, an avowed right-winger; William Castle, a diplomat; Dean Carl Ackerman of the Columbia Journalism School; Theodore Roosevelt Jr.; and James E. Van Zandt, head of the American Legion.

Lindbergh spoke and worked under his own auspices until April, 1941, when he joined the national board of the America First Committee, the country's principal antiwar group. Although its membership was heterogeneous, its effective leadership rested with Robert E. Wood, board chairman of Sears, Roebuck & Co., and Robert R. McCormick, publisher of The Chicago Tribune. Both were archconservatives and zealous haters of President Franklin D. Roosevelt.

America First was strongest in the Midwest, the traditional seat of the nation's isolationist attitudes; but it was also a powerful force in New York and Boston. Popular support for its antiwar objectives was widespread, and Lindbergh epitomized that support. He rallied millions to the cause with such effectiveness that Roosevelt considered him a major threat.

The President vented his anger at a news conference in April, 1941. Roosevelt was asked why he did not call Lindbergh, an Army officer, into uniform. The reason, he replied, was that Lindbergh was a defeatist, and he went on to compare him with Representative Clement L. Vallandigham, a Civil War Congressman from Ohio, the chief spokesman of a group called the Copperheads, who said the North could never win. Roosevelt's attack was perhaps set off by a Lindbergh magazine article that declared, "While our leaders have shouted for peace, they have consistently directed us toward war."

Irving Haberman

Returning from residence abroad as World War II approached, Lindbergh advocated U.S. nonintervention and rallied support for antiwar stance. He spoke to an America First rally, above, in Madison Square Garden in 1941.

'Insult From Roosevelt'

Considering his honor impugned, Lindbergh resigned his commission. "If I did not tender my resignation," he said in the published version of his "Wartime Journals," "I would lose something in my own character that means even more to me than my commission in the Air Corps.

"No one else would know it, but I would. And if I take this insult from Roosevelt, more, and worse, will be probably be forthcoming."

Thirty years later Lindbergh still felt wronged by the President, and professed not to see that he himself had questioned Roosevelt's integrity.

With Pearl Harbor, America First collapsed and Lindbergh sought to join the armed forces. "Now that we are at war I want to contribute as best I can to my country's war effort," he wrote. "It is vital for us to carry on this war as intelligently, as constructively, and as successfully as we can, and I want to do my part."

His bid to soldier was rebuffed, however, an action for which he blamed Roosevelt personally. Lindbergh, then 39, joined the Ford Motor Company as a consultant, working at the Willow Run plant in Michigan, which was producing bombers. Later he was a consultant to the United Aircraft Corporation, attached chiefly to its Vought-Sikorsky Division in Stratford, Conn. Vought was producing the Navy Corsair F4U. As part of his job, he traveled to the Pacific war area in 1944 to study the Corsair under service conditions, and, as a civilian, flew 50 missions against the Japanese.

The flier had at least one very close brush with death in a dogfight near Biak Island. He described this and other episodes in "The Wartime Journals," and they constitute the best writing in the book.

After the war, Lindbergh went to Germany for the Naval Technical Mission in Europe to study developments in Nazi aircraft and missiles. He had been interested in rocketry since 1929, when he sought out Dr. Robert Goddard, then an obscure physics professor at Clark University in Worcester, Mass. (Goddard, who had been ridiculed for his ideas, has since been recognized as a space flight pioneer.)

Lindbergh was always proud of his association with Goddard and of having raised money to fund his experiments. For 16 years until his death in 1945, Goddard, also a loner, received Lindbergh's help and encouragement; and Goddard's basic rocketry patents were used in the development of United States missiles after the war. The aviator's crucial assistance to Goddard did not become well known until Goddard's biography was published in 1963, a book for which Lindbergh wrote an introduction.

For more than 15 years after the war Lindbergh virtually disappeared from the news. He was a member of Army Ordnance's CHORE project at the University of Chicago; he was consultant to the Secretary of the Air Force; he took part in the reorganization of the Strategic Air Command; and he was a member of scientific ballistic-missile committees of the Air Force and the Defense Department. In 1954, he was commissioned a brigadier general in the Air Force Reserve.

Much of the aviator's work in these years dealt with security-classified projects; but it is believed that he was active in rocketry and space flight programs, where his technical expertise was valuable. He enjoyed top-secret clearance, and spoke of his tasks as having to do with security.

In this period, Lindbergh completed his autobiographical account of his 1927 flight, which had been written in bits and pieces in various parts of the world over 14 years. "The Spirit of St. Louis," published in 1953, won the Pulitzer Prize for biography in 1954 and was made into a movie three years later, with James Stewart as the lead. The book was intended to supersede "We," which, written in haste, had never satisfied the aviator as an accurate account of his flight.

Starting sometime after the war, he rejoined Pan American as a consultant for the nominal fee of $600 a month. The job, which eventually led to his working on the design specifications for the Boeing 747, allowed him great freedom to travel and to develop any interest he chose. And travel he did, seemingly having no settled abode.

In Africa, in 1964, he found an interest that was to occupy his last years and to bring him out of his public reticence and reclusiveness. The issue was conservation.

"Lying under an acacia tree with the sounds of the dawn around me," he recalled, "I realized more clearly the facts that man should never overlook: that the construction of an airplane, for instance, is simple when compared to the evolutionary achievement of a bird; that airplanes depend on an advanced civilization, and that where civilization is most advanced few birds exist.

"I realized that if I had to choose, I would rather have birds than airplanes."

He concluded, he said, "that I ought to do something."

Concern for Environment

That imperative, which unfolded slowly, led him to activity in conservation organizations, to having a large hand in saving the humpback and the blue whales, to concern for endangered species and to public advocacy of steps to save the world's environment.

He made his first public speech in 1968—the first since 1941—to the Alaska Legislature. The following year he granted what amounted to his first newspaper interview in 35 years. This was to The New York Times and this writer, the occasion being his conservation activity in the Philippines. There was another interview in 1970, again in the Philippines, but centering on his concern for primitive peoples. And again in 1971, he took this writer with him on a long American conservation tour, which was also a journey backward in time to his boyhood home in Minnesota.

Lindbergh said that he had unveiled himself because he thought the cause of conservation so urgent. "I have had enough publicity for 15 lives," he said, "and I seek no more of it, but where I can accomplish a purpose I will do things I otherwise abhor."

There was no doubt that his leadership was effective.

Even though he was talking to a generation born long after his Paris flight, his person and his name evoked a tangible response. He did not pretend to be an expert, but had a singular ability to stir response and activity to enunciate general principles and to cheer people on.

It did not appear to matter that he had published his bulky "Wartime Journals" in 1970 to general critical dispraise. What seemed to count was that he was Charles Augustus Lindbergh, the hero still of 1927, whose smile was engaging, whose words were straightforward, whose manner was simple and whose message was forceful.

This was, perhaps, the ultimate enigma of his life; for beneath his outer coating was a man who kept more to himself (and perhaps to his wife) than he ever gave to the public.

"All the News That's Fit to Print"

The New York Times

LATE CITY EDITION

Weather: Showers and thunderstorms likely today, tonight. Sunny tomorrow. Temp. range: today 82-70; Thurs. 77-64. Full U.S. report on Page 56.

VOL. CXIX ... No. 41,131 | NEW YORK, FRIDAY, SEPTEMBER 4, 1970 | 15 CENTS

Delegates Welcome Governor at A.F.L.-C.I.O. Parley

The New York Times

Governor Rockefeller—and his wife, just visible behind him—at Kiamesha Lake, N. Y.

Labor Convention Backs Rockefeller After Battle

By DAMON STETSON

Special to The New York Times

KIAMESHA LAKE, N. Y., Sept. 3—Delegates to the New York State A.F.L.-C.I.O. convention here endorsed Governor Rockefeller for re-election tonight after a bitter and raucous debate. The standing vote was judged by Raymond R. Corbett, president of the federation, to be in favor of the endorsement, which had been recommended to the 1,500 delegates and alternates by the executive council.

The session was then quickly adjourned in turmoil, amid angry shouts by supporters of Arthur J. Goldberg, Mr. Rockefeller's Democratic-Liberal opponent, that they had been tricked.

The endorsement was the first ever given by the federation to a Republican candidate for Governor. It created the paradox of a millionaire Republican triumphing at a labor convention over a man with a long record of labor credentials.

Mr. Goldberg has been counsel for the United Steelworkers of America and other unions, as well as Secretary of Labor.

Cheering for Governor

The cheering, whistling, table-pounding welcome given to Mr. Rockefeller as he entered the convention hall of the Concord Hotel here foreshadowed his victory, though Goldberg supporters insisted before the voting that the Governor's strength was exaggerated.

The Goldberg supporters contended that no one really knew how the votes would add up until lists of delegates and their respective voting strengths—based on per-capita dues payments for their unions—were made available.

The battle was described by veterans of federation conventions as the most bitter and angry in the history of the organization. The heckling and shouting by rival sides was strident and sometimes personal. Speakers were often drowned out by shouts and boos.

At one point as he sought to speak, Jerry Wurf, presi-

Continued on Page 14, Column 1

M'CORMACK AIDE IS GIVEN 2½ YEARS

Sweig Also Gets $2,000 Fine for Perjury in Testimony on Use of Influence

By CRAIG R. WHITNEY

Dr. Martin Sweig, who was the principal aide of Speaker of the House John W. McCormack until Sweig was charged last year with defrauding the Government, was sentenced yesterday to two and a half years in prison and a $2,000 fine for lying to a grand jury.

Sweig was convicted July 9, after a three-week trial, of perjury in denying that he knew or had interceded with Government agencies on behalf of Gary Roth, a Long Island serviceman who wanted a hardship discharge from the Army.

Before Federal Judge Marvin E. Frankel sentenced him yesterday, Sweig stood up in the oak-paneled courtroom above Foley Square and said:

"I am bewildered by all this. I never had occasion to be before a grand jury before in my life. If I have done wrong I certainly did not mean to, or to cause harm to anyone."

Judge Frankel then told him: "I am of the view that I would be derelict if I did not impose a substantial prison sentence in this case, and I will." He was doing so, he said, because Sweig's actions presented "a picture of corruption of a very profound kind."

United States Attorney Whitney North Seymour Jr., who prosecuted the case with Richard Ben-Veniste, told the court: "We do not have the com-

Continued on Page 36, Column 5

CITY FACING LOSS OF 2 HOUSE SEATS

District Merger Is Possible in Manhattan—Brooklyn May Lose One of Six

By PETER KIHSS

Manhattan faces the loss of one of its four members of Congress as a result of the new census returns, and the likely solution may be a merger of districts now represented by William F. Ryan and Leonard Farbstein, both Democrats.

The Farbstein seat is being contested this fall by Bella S. Abzug, Democrat; Barry Farber, Republican-Liberal, and Salvatore Lodico, Conservative. The second Congressional seat being lost by the state—to reduce its total from 41 to 39—may be one of Brooklyn's six.

Political analyses of the still-preliminary census returns, which will lead to required reapportioning of Congressional and legislative districts, showed strength shifting to the suburbs. Forecasts at this stage were as follows yesterday:

¶Suffolk County will be entitled to two Congressional seats and part of a third, instead of the present one of its own and another shared with Nassau County. It has had the state's largest county increase in population, up 441,002, or 66.1 per cent, over 1960 to 1,107,786.

¶The Buffalo seat now held by Representative Richard Max McCarthy, Democrat, may be swallowed by four neighboring areas.

¶In the 150-member Assembly,

Continued on Page 15, Column 1

ARMS TALKS CLOSE AS VOTE SUPPORTS TREATY ON SEABED

U.S.-Soviet Plan Forbidding Atom Weapons Is Said to Win in Geneva, 24-1

By THOMAS J. HAMILTON

Special to The New York Times

GENEVA, Sept. 3—The disarmament conference ended its 1970 session today after achieving near unanimity on a draft treaty to prohibit the emplacement of nuclear weapons or launching platforms on the seabed outside the 12-mile limit.

According to reliable sources, 24 members—all except Mexico—gave their approval to the joint United States-Soviet text, and its endorsement this fall by the United Nations General Assembly appears assured. Upon endorsement by the Assembly, the pact would come into force after 22 governments have ratified it. The draft says that certain unidentified governments must be among the 22.

U. S. Plan Is the Basis

Most provisions are the same as those in the original United States proposal, submitted to the conference in the spring of 1969. It was slightly modified when the Soviet Union, which had proposed a prohibition on all military uses, dropped the fight last October and joined the United States in submitting the first of four versions to the conference.

Many changes sought by rank-and-file members were accepted by the two sponsors.

Henri F. Eschauzier, the Dutch representative, told a correspondent that the 1970 conference had constituted real negotiation. Canada led the successful fight for stronger means of verifying compliance with the treaty, including inspection and the right to request United Nations assistance.

Proposal Was Limited

The United States originally proposed that surface ships observe objects on the seabed. The Soviet proposal was limited to mutual inspection of seabed objects by parties to the treaty.

Mexico's unwillingness to accept the draft is based on the contention that a phrase in it would permit an outside state to install nuclear weapons in the 12-mile coastal zone of another state.

That "allied option," Mexico maintains, would allow the United States to install nuclear weapons on the seabed off the Dutch coast, for example, if The Hague requested it, and would permit the Soviet Union to do the same off the Polish coast.

United States and Soviet

Continued on Page 4, Column 6

Bruce and Thuy Meet at Paris Talks for the First Time

David K. E. Bruce of U.S. arrives for session

Associated Press

Xuan Thuy of North Vietnam ends boycott

HANOI'S DELEGATE IS BACK AT PARLEY

Thuy Ends 9-Month Boycott in Paris, but No Change Is Seen in Positions

Special to The New York Times

PARIS, Sept. 3—North Vietnam's chief negotiator, Xuan Thuy, ended his nine-month boycott of the Paris peace talks today. But he declared that the United States position had not changed in that time, and he made it plain that the Communist bargaining position had not changed either.

He repeated the two conditions set by the Communists when the talks began nearly 20 months ago: The United States must agree to withdraw from Vietnam unconditionally and must "renounce" the Saigon Government of President Nguyen Van Thieu.

Mr. Thuy and David K. E. Bruce, the United States chief delegate, each told reporters after today's session, the 82d of the series, that the other side had presented nothing new.

Mr. Thuy described as "very flexible and generous" his side's proposal to support a coalition government of "all political tendencies in South Vietnam that stand for peace, independence and neutrality, including those who for political reasons have to live abroad." At a news conference, a Vietcong spokesman twice emphasized that "even within the Government of Saigon" there

Continued on Page 3, Column 1

Mrs. Meir Pressing U.S. To Cancel Egypt's Gains

By PETER GROSE

Special to The New York Times

JERUSALEM, Sept. 3 — Premier Golda Meir today welcomed Washington's acknowledgment of an Egyptian missile build-up in violation of the three-week-old Middle East cease-fire. But she pressed for further United States action to demand that the Soviet Union act to cancel Egypt's new military gains.

A "difficult debate" between Israel and the United States is over, Mrs. Meir said at a meeting of the Israel Labor party.

Mrs. Meir spoke after qualified sources indicated that the Cabinet had finally overcome bitter divisions on Washington's stand. The reported compromise would give the United States time for quiet diplomacy with the United Arab Republic and the Soviet Union aimed at preserving the peace talks that began at the United Nations on Aug. 25 under Dr Gunnar V. Jarring, Secretary General Thant's special representative for the Middle East.

Defense Minister Moshe Dayan, confirmed his concurrence in the compromise, saying in a radio interview that "what has been decided today will not lead me to leave the Government."

There had been widespread reports that he was threatening to resign if immediate steps were not taken to destroy the missile sites that Israel says Egypt has constructed in the cease-fire zone—32 miles on either side of the Suez Canal—since the truce came into effect on Aug. 7.

The reported decision, accepted by all Cabinet factions, holds that the Nixon Administration finally realizes the danger of the Egyptian missile

Continued on Page 6, Column 4

U.S. Acts Against Whites In Alabama School Sit-In

By JON NORDHEIMER

Special to The New York Times

BIRMINGHAM, Ala., Sept. 3 The Justice Department took action today in Federal court to block a group of white parents in a rural Alabama school district from interfering with court-ordered desegregation there.

It was the first major case entered by the Government since the massive round of desegregation now under way in Southern schools began, according to a Justice Department spokesman

The role of the Justice Department in the South has been clouded by the political reverberations that greeted Attorney General John N. Mitchell's announcement last summer—since rescinded—that 100 lawyers would be sent into the South at the opening of school to monitor the progress of desegregation.

Last week the Justice Department entered a motion involving extra-curricular activities in a small Georgia school district, but the legal steps taken today represent the first move against significant opposition to a court order.

The case grew out of an attempt earlier this week by a group of white parents in Talladega County to occupy classrooms in schools where they insisted on sending their children in defiance of a court plan that assigned them to formerly all-black schools in the district.

District Judge H. Hobart Grooms ordered nine of the parents to appear in his court in Birmingham tomorrow to show cause why they should not be enjoined from further interference with the plan.

In an affidavit filed by the

Continued on Page 11, Column 1

U.S. BIDS SOVIET AND EGYPT AVOID NEW VIOLATIONS

Asks Immediate Resumption of Peace Talks at U.N. to Preserve Cease-Fire

ISRAEL IS DISSATISFIED

She Is Believed Distressed Over Reported Failure to Get Additional Arms

By TAD SZULC

Special to The New York Times

WASHINGTON, Sept. 3—The United States appealed to the Soviet Union and the United Arab Republic today to refrain from further violations of the tenuous cease-fire in the Middle East and urged an immediate resumption of the peace talks at the United Nations.

But Israel immediately made it clear to the Nixon Administration that despite a new American pledge to guarantee her military security, her negotiators would not return to the peace talks until Egypt removed the newly introduced antiaircraft missiles from the Suez Canal cease-fire zone.

The talks were initiated on Aug. 25 by Dr. Gunnar V. Jarring, Secretary General Thant's special representative for the Middle East.

Israeli Unhappiness Noted

Israel was also said to have conveyed her unhappiness over the reported refusal of the United States to increase the current shipment of arms, including deliveries of replacements for Phantom fighter-bombers lost in action before the cease-fire.

In recent pronouncements, Administration leaders, notably Secretary of Defense Melvin R. Laird, have given the impression that the United States would not allow the balance of power in the Middle East to be tipped against Israel.

The announcement of the appeal for the observance of the truce and the resumption of the peace talks, as well as the latest military assurances to Israel, were contained in a brief statement issued by the State Department, which also acknowledged officially for the first time that the cease-fire had been violated by the deployment of Soviet-made missile batteries.

McCloskey Reads Statement

The statement read by Robert J. McCloskey, the department's spokesman, said:

"Our latest evidence confirms that there have been violations of the cease-fire-standstill agreement. We are not going into details. We are taking up this matter both with the United Arab Republic and Soviet Union through diplomatic channels.

"We are continuing to watch the balance closely and, as we previously stated, have no intention of permitting Israel's security to be adversely affected. In the meantime, we believe it is of the utmost importance that the talks between the parties under Ambassador

Continued on Page 6, Column 7

Vince Lombardi, Football Coach, Dies

Robert Riger

Vince Lombardi discussing play. He once said, "Coaches who can outline plays on a blackboard are a dime a dozen. The ones who win get inside their players and motivate them."

By WILLIAM N. WALLACE

Vince Lombardi, the professional football coach who symbolized toughness and dedication in sports, died of intestinal cancer yesterday in Georgetown Hospital in Washington. His age was 57.

His wife of 30 years, Marie, and his son, Vincent, were at the bedside.

Lombardi, who guided the Green Bay Packers to the premier position in the National Football League in the nineteen-sixties was seeking to do the same with the Washington Redskins in the nineteen-seventies.

The Redskins had long been losers. But Vincent Thomas Lombardi had never associated with losers in his 31 years as a football coach.

Last year, his first in Washington, the Redskins had their first winning record in 14 seasons.

"Winning isn't everything," Lombardi once insisted. "It is the only thing."

Under his direction the Green Bay Packers won six division titles and five national Football League championships in nine seasons between 1959 and 1967. This was professional football's best winning record and Lombardi was acclaimed as the sport's best coach.

He retired from coaching after the 1967 season, when he was 53 years old. But his wife and his close friends wondered how long he could stay away from the sidelines. The answer: one year. Most pro football games are played on Sunday afternoons and during the season that Lombardi confined himself to the duties of the Packers' general manager he said, "I miss the fire on

Continued on Page 24, Column 1

West Point Cadet Loses Fight In Court for Objector Discharge

A West Point senior who had been denied a discharge from the Army as a conscientious objector failed yesterday to get a court order directing the Army to release him, as he wished.

With the rejection of his suit, the cadet, 20-year-old Cary E. Donham of New Baden, Ill., faces one of three prospects: He can resign from the United States Military Academy, be dismissed for lack of military aptitude, or appeal to a higher court.

The academy has said it would accept his resignation, but whether it does that or dismisses him, Cadet Donham would be liable to further military service as an enlisted man in the Army Reserve.

His lawyers, Rabinowitz, Boudin & Standard, said yesterday that they were not sure what they would do next. Two weeks ago Federal Judge Marvin E. Frankel, who decided against Cadet Donham yesterday, ordered the Army to give the youth enough time to resign before it tried to do anything else with him.

The cadet is believed to be the first student at West Point who has ever filed for conscientious-objector status, although Lieut. Louis P. Font, a West Point graduate, did it six months ago and was turned down.

Cadet Donham's application was denied last July 21 by an Army conscientious objector review board, which found that he lacked the requisite "depth of sincerity."

He then tried to get a Fed-

Continued on Page 4, Column 7

Lawyer Teams to Observe Demonstrations Here

By DAVID BURNHAM

An experimental group of neutral observers has been organized by the Association of the Bar of the City of New York in an effort to reduce violence at mass demonstrations.

Edwin J. Wesely, chairman of the special eight-man committee established by the association to initiate the experimental observer program, said yesterday, "We contemplate having from two to 12 specially trained lawyers at all demonstrations at which there might be trouble."

"Our men will not be there as marshals or demonstrators, but just to observe and report." Mr. Wesely continued. "We will try to report on all aspects of a demonstration—the demonstrators, the counter-demonstrators, the Police Department and the bystanders."

The existence of the legal observer experiment, requested by Mayor Lindsay the day after the May 15 demonstrations by construction workers got out of hand at City Hall, became known yesterday in a brief Police Department order sent to all major commands.

The New York Civil Liberties Union and the Police Department's Civilian Complaint Review Board both have strongly recommended the establishment of a regular team of trained observers at demonstrations. The review board made its suggestion in a report several months ago that said a failure of police leadership was an important factor in the violence at Columbia University in the spring of 1968.

Aryeh Neier, executive director of the New York Civil Liberties Union, said last night that the presence of neutral observers would reduce violence at demonstrations by making the police "conscious that they are to be accountable for their actions" and by giving demonstrators "confidence that if there is abuse directed against them it will not pass unrecorded."

The observers probably would not deter provocateurs among the demonstrators, but provocations would be "less likely to attract the support of other demonstrators" with

Continued on Page 12, Column 6

NEWS INDEX

Vince Lombardi, Pro Football Coach, Is Dead at 57

Continued From Page 1, Col.

Sunday." Edward Bennett Wilianms, president of the Redskins,early in 1969 offered Lombardi a position as coach, general manager and owner of 5 per cent of the team's stock, and the offer was quickly accepted.

"Everyone wants to own something sometime. Isn't that right?" asked Lombardi in explaining why he resigned the Packer post with five years remaining on his contract.

Lombardi was a symbol of authority.

"When he says 'Sit down,' I don't even bother to look for a chair," one of the Packer players explained.

"He's fair. He treats us all the same—like dogs," said Henry Jordan, another Packer.

"He coaches through fear," said Bill Curry, a sensitive player Lombardi let go.

Most of his athletes accepted his demanding ways and biting criticisms. His primary target was a player named Marvin Fleming, who said in reflection, "I didn't mind. When I came to him I didn't have anything. He taught me how to be a winner."

Another Packer, Jerry Kramer, said, "His whippings, his cussings and his driving all fade; his good qualities endure."

'It's for Them'

Lombardi admitted that his scoldings sometimes were merely for effect. During his last season at Green Bay, when he was goading an aging team to another championship, he said, "I have to go on that field every day and whip people. It's for them, not just me. I'm getting to be an animal."

Lombardi was always a hard man when it came to football. In college, at Fordham where he graduated with honors in 1937, he played guard on a famous line called the Seven Blocks of Granite. He was the smallest of the group at 5 feet 8 inches and 175 pounds. "But he hit like 250," a teammate said.

The son of an immigrant Italian butcher, Lombardi was born June 11, 1913, and grew up in the Sheepshead Bay section of Brooklyn. He went to Cathedral High School and St. Francis Preparatory School before Fordham. He had ambitions to study for the Roman Catholic priesthood for a while, but after graduation he went to law school for a year.

He supported himself by playing for a minor league football team, the Brooklyn Eagles, and serving as an insurance investigator. But a coaching career was calling and in 1939 he joined the faculty at St. Cecelia High School in Englewood, N. J. For an annual salary of $1,700 he was an assistant football coach and a teacher of physics, chemistry, algebra and Latin.

36 Victories in Row

Lombardi stayed at St. Cecilia for seven years. He soon was head coach of the football, basketball and baseball squads. His football teams won six state championships and had a string of 36 victories in a row.

He returned to Fordham to coach the freshmen in 1947 and served as an assistant in 1948. When Ed Danowski was reappointed head coach for the 1949 season, Lombardi left and joined Col. Earl Blaik's staff at the United States Military Academy.

Life at West Point suited Lombardi and he was strongly influenced by Colonel Blaik, who had his own hero, Gen. Douglas MacArthur. Lombardi, too, became a disciple of General MacArthur and in ensuing years he attempted to inspire his teams by quoting one or the other of the military men with sayings such as, "If you can walk, you can run."

The New York Times (by Mike Lien)

Vince Lombardi demonstrating a pitchout to quarterbacks at training session in Washington. Last year, his first with Redskins, the team had its first winning season in 14 years. He was coach, general manager and part owner.

Pro football beckoned in 1954 when the New York Giants put together a new coaching staff under Jim Lee Howell, who delegated the offense to Lombardi.

"Vince didn't understand our game," said Frank Gifford, one of his stars. "At first we players were showing him. But by the end of the season he was showing us."

Green Bay's Offer

Lombardi's opportunity to be a head coach did not come until 1959, when he was 46, which is considered old in that line of work. The Green Bay Packers, a community-owned team in a city of only 70,000, were losers and troubled financially.

The directors offered Lombardi the job as coach and general manager. He insisted upon full authority and they gave it to him. The prior coach, Ray McLean, had a team that won only one game in 12. With a nucleus of the same players, Lombardi's first Packer team won seven of 12 games and tied for third place in the western division of the N.F.L.

The next season they were first but lost the league championship to the Philadelphia Eagles. Then the parade began, with league titles in 1961, 1962, 1965, 1966 and 1967, plus Super Bowl victories over the American League champion in 1967 and 1968.

During his span of nine seasons as head coach, Lombardi saw his teams win 141 games, lose 39 and tie four. He insisted that the Packers never lost. Time merely ran out on them.

Avenue Named for Him

Green Bay, the smallest city in the league, became nationally known, and the citizens adulated Lombardi. They named the street outside the stadium Lombardi Avenue.

One year when the Los Angeles Rams were striving to woo him away, the directors gave Lombardi 320 acres of apple orchards in nearby Door County.

Under the rules of their incorporation, the Packers could not pay their 1,700 stockholders any dividends. The money piled up and Lombardi spent it in enlarging the stadium and building a magnificent field house. After the winning of the first championship, he bought the players' wives mink stoles.

To keep a touted rookie from Texas, Donny Anderson, from signing with the rival American League, Lombardi agreed to pay the young man the highest bonus in pro football's history, $600,000.

Lombardi, who had a keen appreciation for money, related winning to business success in pro football. "The teams that win the most make the most money," he said.

Although the Packers had annual profits as high as $800,000, Lombardi insisted upon keeping players' salaries "in line." Jim Ringo, a center who once played a game for Lombardi with 14 painful boils, held out for more money one season. He was traded the next.

The Packer fullback star, Jim Taylor, exercised the option clause in his contract and became a free agent, so he could sign for more money with another team. The other running star, Paul Hornung, retired the same year. "We'll miss Hornung," Lombardi said. "The other fellow we'll replace."

Hornung, like Gifford, was a favorite of the coach. Lombardi was deeply hurt when Hornung was suspended for the 1963 season for gambling in violation of his contract, but Lombardi quickly forgave him.

The Catholic and military influences upon Lombardi were strong. After the assassination of Senator Robert F. Kennedy, whom he knew, Lombardi said, "What's the matter with the world? There has been a complete breakdown of mental discipline."

In speaking before an audience of businessmen, Lombardi said, "There is an abuse of freedom in our society—freedom without responsibility."

He deplored the long hair, the sideburns and mustaches of youth. He told a Redskin rookie, Trenton Jackson, "You could run faster if you didn't have that thing on your lip." Jackson shaved off the mustache at lunchtime.

No Mystery, He Said

Lombardi maintained there was no mystery to the Packer success. "Coaches who can outline plays on a blackboard are a dime a dozen," he once said. "The ones who win get inside their players and motivate them."

Perhaps there was no mystery. But the Packers had a losing record the first season after he retired as coach.

Lombardi believed in attacking strength. "Hit them at their strongest point," he said. Before their first regular season game in his first year at Green Bay, Lombardi told the Packers in the locker room, "Go through that door and bring back victory."

Bill Forester, a tackle, said, "I jumped up and hit my arm on my locker. It was the worst injury I had all year."

Lombardi loved to laugh, and his friends delighted in his company. But he put off strangers, and the public regarded him with both awe and fear.

René Carpenter, the former wife of the astronaut Scott Carpenter, described a reception held for Lombardi when he first came to Washington. "All of a sudden my skirt was too short and my back too bare," she said. "We were reduced to feeling like children."

Underwent Surgery Twice

Although the seriousness of Lombardi's condition had been known to close friends, no public announcement on his condition was made until Wednesday when Mrs. Lombardi authorized a statement describing him as suffering from "an extraordinarily virulent form of cancer."

He underwent two operations. After the first, on June 27, he appeared to be recovering and was released on July 14. However, his condition deteriorated and he had to be operated on a second time, on July 27.

In addition to his wife, the former Marie Planitz, and son, the coach leaves a daughter, Mrs. Susan Bickham of Green Bay, Wis.; his parents, Mr. and Mrs. Harry Lombardi of Brooklyn; two brothers, Joseph of Englewood, N. J., and Harold, of San Rafael, Calif.; a sister, Mrs. Claire Brandshagen of Hazlett, N. J., and six grandchildren.

The body will lie at Joseph Gawler's Sons' Funeral Home, Wisconsin Avenue and Harrison Street, N.W., in Washington, on Friday after 2 P.M. and on Saturday and Sunday, from 10 A.M. to 10 P.M. at The Abbey, 888 Lexington Avenue, at 66th Street in New York.

A mass will be celebrated at St. Patrick's Cathedral on Monday at 11 A.M. by Terence Cardinal Cooke, Archbishop of the Diocese of New York, described by a Redskins' spokesman as "a great admirer and old friend."

President Leads Tributes

Many notables paid tribute yesterday to Vince Lombardi, the pro football coach. Following are some of the comments:

PRESIDENT NIXON — When I think of Vince Lombardi, I think of him standing at the side of a football field, his attention focused sharply on his team. He was an imposing figure—and an inspiring one. On the field and off, his very presence was commanding. As I think of him that way, I know that he will always hold a commanding place in the memory of this nation.

Like the power sweep which became his trademark, the power of Vince Lombardi's personality swept the world of sports and made a lasting impact on the life of all it touched. He asked a great deal of his players and his associates. But he never asked more of any man than he asked of himself. The lesson all Americans can learn from Coach Lombardi is that a man can become a star when, above all, he becomes an apostle of teamwork.

GOVERNOR ROCKEFELLER— Vince was more than a giant in the world of athletics. He was a leader in every sense of the word. His unrelenting demands on himself and on his players for the best efforts always are a matter of record and legand.

GEORGE HALAS, owner of the Chicago Bears—All too few men are around to match his forceful leadership and competitive qualities. I regret that I really came close to Vince only within the last five years—all too short a time to enjoy and admire his unforgettable personality. We understood each other. I loved him as a friend and a man. I am sure Vince would have been a leader in any field and in any era.

THE REV. MICHAEL P. WALSH, S. J., president of Fordham University—Vince Lombardi's players often said, "He made us better than we were." Many of us at Fordham who knew him as a magna cum laude undergraduate, as a brilliant assistant football coach, as a loyal alumnus and devoted trustee, could say much the same thing. His education, self-discipline, and love of God and his fellow man inspired many of us when our spirits flagged. The public side of Vince Lombardi was well publicized. But there was another—the private side—that his innate shyness often offered. This was a gentle, compassionate family man with deep religious convictions and steadfast loyalty to his alma mater and to his friends.

"All the News That's Fit to Print"

The New York Times.

LATE CITY EDITION
U. S. Weather Bureau Report (Page 61) forecasts: Variable cloudiness today; chance of rain tonight. Clearing tomorrow.
Temp. Range: 55—39; yesterday: 51—29.

VOL. CXIII . No. 38,789. NEW YORK, MONDAY, APRIL 6, 1964. TEN CENTS

THOUSANDS HELD IN BRAZIL'S DRIVE TO ROOT OUT REDS

Fears of Reversal of Coup by Leftist Supporters Lead to Wide Arrests

CACHES OF ARMS SEIZED

Military and Press Charge That Purge Is Not Being Pushed Hard Enough

By EDWARD C. BURKS
Special to The New York Times

RIO DE JANEIRO, April 5—Several thousand persons were reported today to have been arrested throughout Brazil in the drive by the Government against Communists and suspected Communists.

A number of those arrested were being held on a ship in the Bay of Guanabara outside Rio de Janeiro.

Some of the pro-Goulart people were reported in hiding in the State of Rio de Janeiro waiting for the opportunity to strike back.

Meanwhile, there were complaints in military and civilian circles that not enough was being done to purge Communists from the Government, the military forces and unions.

Anti-Communist newspapers warned that there was a danger the revolution would be lost.

Brazil's military leaders, backed by 10 state governments, overthrew President João Goulart early Thursday on the ground that he was leading the country toward an extreme leftist dictatorship.

Arms Caches Reported

In the drive against the Communists, the police reported finding several Communist cells in the rural area with arms, propaganda and large sums in dollars. Among those in the police net were eight Chinese Communists and at least one Cuban.

The Soviet Embassy was burning documents to such an extent that the neighbors complained of the smoke.

[In exile in Uruguay, Mr. Goulart declared "Everyone knows I have never been a Communist" and said he expected to remain active in politics.]

Seven of the country's governors, including those from the four most influential states, called on Congress to elect the army chief of staff, Gen. Humberto Castelo Branco, as President to fill out Mr. Goulart's

Continued on Page 10, Column 3

United Press International Radiophoto
IN URUGUAY: João Goulart with son at news conference

Khrushchev Calls Attack By Chinese Reds 'Crazy'

By PAUL UNDERWOOD
Special to The New York Times

MISKOLC, Hungary, April 5 — Premier Khrushchev strongly defended today his policy of seeking to improve the living standards of the Soviet people. Alluding to the Chinese Communists, the Soviet leader said criticism of this aim as "degenerate" was "crazy."

In another allusion to Peking, which defends Stalin's dictatorial and aggressive policies, Mr. Khrushchev said: "Anyone who loves Stalin can take him if they like the smell of corpses."

The Soviet Premier spoke to a crowd of about 80,000 gathered to welcome him to Miskolc, a manufacturing center in northeastern Hungary that is the country's second most important industrial city.

He Praises Hungarians

Mr. Khrushchev, who has been in Hungary on an official visit since last Tuesday, traveled to Miskolc by special train with the Hungarian Premier, Janos Kadar, and other figures of the Hungarian Communist party and Government.

In a 20-minute talk, the Soviet leader hailed the "correct teaching" of the Hungarian Communist party, which he said "reflects the interests of the peasants, workers and office employes."

"This is not the teaching of the people who want to bring Stalin's corpse back to life, who do not rely on the ideas of Marxism-Leninism, who want to rely on the ax and the knife," he added.

Mr. Khrushchev began his speech quietly, but as he warmed up his voice rose. He began to shout and wave his

Continued on Page 3, Column 1

TURKS SAY CYPRUS CAN'T END TREATY

Deny Makarios Can Cancel Right of Troops on Isle—Cypriotes Seize Britons

Special to The New York Times

ISTANBUL, Turkey, April 5—The Turkish Government rejected today a move by the Cypriote President, Archbishop Makarios, to terminate the Cyprus Treaty of Alliance. It called such a move "completely worthless, both legally and effectively."

The position was made known following a three-hour Cabinet meeting under the chairmanship of President Cemal Gursel. The meeting was attended by top military leaders, including the Chief of the General Staff, Gen. Cevdet Sunay.

After the meeting, Premier Ismet Inonu said: "This, of course, is another attempt of Makarios to abrogate the treaty unilaterally. He has tried before, and this attempt will fail exactly as have his previous attempts."

Treaty for Defense

The Treaty of Alliance binds Greece, Turkey and Cyprus together for their common defense. It gives Turkey the right to keep 650 troops in Cyprus and Greece 950 troops.

[In Cyprus, Greek Cypriotes held 20 British soldiers of the United Nations force at gunpoint for three hours before releasing them. The Associated Press reported from Nicosia that a Greek Cypriote was shot dead at a Turkish Cypriote barricade.]

The Turkish Foreign Minister, Feridun C. Erkin, said tonight: "Turkey refuses to accept such an illegal abrogation. There is no provision in the

Continued on Page 8, Column 3

FULBRIGHT SCORES 'MORBID' CONCERN OVER U.S. SECURITY

Says It Induces Blind Faith in Military and Diverts the Country's Energies

Excerpts from Fulbright talk will be found on Page 16.

By MAX FRANKEL
Special to The New York Times

CHAPEL HILL, N. C., April 5 — Senator J. W. Fulbright said tonight that the cold war had become "an excuse as well as a genuine cause" for the diversion of national energies and resources.

The Arkansas Democrat, who last week kindled a controversy in Washington with a speech about what he called myths and realities in American foreign policy, expressed similar complaints about national priorities in domestic affairs.

He complained about "morbid" preoccupation with the dangers of Communist aggression abroad and subversion at home. That preoccupation, he said, did not end with the McCarthy era of a decade ago.

Defense Budget Cited

The overriding concern with security, Senator Fulbright asserted, produced a blind faith in the military, an inclination to permit the vast military establishment to run itself, a refusal in Congress to supervise and even debate the defense budget properly and a "splendid indifference" to the size and content of that budget.

All this is going on, Mr. Fulbright declared, while the nation's human resources are "being extravagantly wasted and neglected."

Mr. Fulbright, who is chairman of the Senate Foreign Relations Committee, delivered the address that opened a week-long symposium at the University of North Carolina. The symposium's subject is "Arms and the Man: National Security and the Aims of a Free Society." About 1,700 people heard Mr. Fulbright's speech.

Wide Public Approval

It was the Senator's first venture out of Washington since his controversial address about the "myths" that govern discussions of foreign policy in the United States. Newspapers have been divided for and against that address in the Senate, but a public response of more than 3,000 letters and telegrams has been running about 4 to 1 in approval.

In tonight's address, titled "Individual Freedom and Collective Security," Mr. Fulbright conceded that the cold war had had some beneficial results in stimulating intellectual and scientific achievement and in breaking the shell of American isolationism.

But the country has paid a

Continued on Page 16, Column 4

GROSS WILL MEET RIGHTS LEADERS AT PARLEY TODAY

School Superintendent Says He Called Conference to Help Clear the Air

By JOSEPH LELYVELD

Dr. Calvin E. Gross, the city's Superintendent of Schools, has taken the initiative in the school integration controversy by inviting civil rights leaders to confer with him today.

An announcement from the Superintendent's office yestersay said that the meeting "might help clear the air" and uncover a "new common basis for progress."

At his home yesterday Dr. Gross said that he had called the meeting because he thought it was "a constructive step to take." He said he had not consulted the board's president, James B. Donovan, who has been the school system's main spokesman on racial matters in recent months.

Although Dr. Gross has sat in on meetings with civil rights leaders called by Mr. Donovan, he has not attempted to take the initiative since last August, when he submitted his preliminary plan on school integration to the State Commission of Education.

Had No Part in Board Plan

It is understood that the Superintendent had no hand in the drawing up of the preliminary integration plan announced by the board last Jan. 29. Dr. Gross was in California during January, recuperating from an illness. He returned to his desk on Feb. 2, the day before the first citywide school boycott was held in protest against the board's plan.

The board was to have offered its final integration plan on March 16, the date that was later chosen for the second boycott. The plan was delayed to permit meetings with local school boards.

In recent weeks, amid widespread reports that the plan was being weakened, the board has been working overtime to put it in publishable form. It is understood that Dr. Gross has not taken a prominent role in this effort.

Meeting to Be Small

The meeting, which was called on Friday, will be held this afternoon at the Roosevelt Hotel. Dr. Gross, who will complete his first year in office next week, said it would be "a fairly small meeting." He declined to say who had been invited.

According to one source, the invitation list includes representatives from the National Association for the Advancement of Colored People, the Congress of Racial Equality, the Urban League of Greater New York and the Citywide Committee for Integrated Schools, which is headed by the Rev. Dr. Milton

Continued on Page 17, Column 1

The New York Times
GENERAL OF THE ARMY DOUGLAS MacARTHUR

Urban Renewal Reviving Centers of Nation's Cities

By WILL LISSNER

Urban renewal programs, often involving controversy and changes of plan, are beginning to transform the slum-ridden downtown sections of the nation's larger cities into sleek new inner cores of rejuvenated urban areas.

The problems and the prospects of urban renewal are being studied and debated in Boston this week at the annual conference of the American Society of Planning Officials. The nearly 1,000 planning and city officials at the sessions include many who carry responsibility for such programs.

The shabby, obsolescent downtown sections of many cities have been the urban renewal movement's biggest challenge. Often these sections included important commercial investments. Usually they represented an important source of their city's taxes.

Successes and Failures

Is downtown undergoing successful renewal?

Correspondents of The New York Times in a dozen cities have sought answers to this question. In some cities there have been notable successes, in others conspicuous failures.

In a few cities only time will tell whether the efforts have succeeded.

But in all cities except a very few, one fact stands out. Downtown, which has been largely a Skid Row in many communities, is being transformed into an important part of the sprawling urban complex, performing vital services for the burgeoning metropolitan area.

The United States' experience in redeveloping the centers of its cities has yielded many les-

Continued on Page 22, Column 1

RIGHTS BILL FOES MAY ALLOW VOTES

Russell Expects Balloting on Amendments to Start Within Two Weeks

Special to The New York Times

WASHINGTON, April 5 — Senator Richard B. Russell of Georgia, who leads the Southern forces against the civil rights bill, said today that voting on amendments to the bill might begin in a week or two.

The Senate has been talking about civil rights since March 9. No votes will be possible unless the Southern opponents permit them or two-thirds of the members agree to limit debate by imposing closure.

There is no possibility of obtaining enough support for closure until the debate has run many weeks more. The chances of any preliminary voting therefore, depend on Southern sufferance.

Bill's Aims Debated

At the moment, the Northern forces favoring the bill are in the middle of a broad exposition of its purposes. They expect to take several more days, possibly the rest of this week.

Then, Senator Russell said in an interview, the Southerners will want a week to answer them. At that point, he indicated, some amendments might be put to a vote.

First up may be the changes proposed by Senator Everett McKinley Dirksen, Illinois Republican, in the fair employment title. Leaders of the civil rights forces have indicated that they may accept these as not affecting the substance of the title.

The backers of the legislation were encouraged by a letter received from 22 leading

Continued on Page 16, Column 8

M'ARTHUR IS DEAD; LED ALLIED FORCE IN JAPAN'S DEFEAT

General of Army, 84, Also Commanded U.N. Troops in the Korean Conflict

JOHNSON LAUDS SOLDIER

Death, After 3 Operations, Is Attributed to Failure of Liver and Kidneys

By JACK RAYMOND
Special to The New York Times

WASHINGTON, April 5 — General of the Army Douglas MacArthur died today after a determined fight for life. He was 84 years old.

The general, who led the Allied victory over Japan in World War II and commanded the United Nations forces in the Korean War, died at 2:39 P.M. at the Walter Reed Army Medical Center, where he had been a patient since March 2. Death was attributed to acute kidney and liver failure.

Life had ebbed slowly. The general had undergone three operations to relieve common duct obstruction, esophageal bleeding and intestinal obstruction with perforation.

Despite the operations, blood transfusions and artificial assistance for vital internal functions, he had regaled hospital attendants and visitors with reminiscences until Friday night, when he sank into a "peaceful coma."

Johnson Praises General

The general's wife, Jean; their only child, Arthur, 26; and his wartime aide and principal assistant, Maj. Gen. Courtney Whitney, were at the hospital at the end.

President Johnson, leading the nation in mourning, said:

"One of America's greatest heroes is dead. General of the Army Douglas MacArthur fought his last fight with all the valor that distinguished him in war and peace."

Tributes to the general poured in from around the globe.

Mr. Johnson ordered that American flags be flown at half-staff around the world until after the burial next Saturday in the General Douglas MacArthur Memorial in Norfolk, Va.

The body of General MacArthur was taken to New York City, where it will lie in repose Tuesday. On Wednesday, it will be returned to Washington, to lie in state in the Capitol Ro-

Continued on Page 25, Column 1

CONGOLESE CLASH WITH U.N. ENVOYS

Rift Considered a Danger as Withdrawal Date Nears

By J. ANTHONY LUKAS
Special to The New York Times

LEOPOLDVILLE, the Congo, April 5 — Relations between high United Nations and Congolese officials have broken down in bitterness and misunderstanding.

For more than two months, Premier Cyrille Adoula has persistently refused to receive Max H. Dorsinville of Haiti, officer in charge of the United Nations operation here.

Mr. Adoula and other leading Congolese officials have openly snubbed Mr. Dorsinville at diplomatic receptions.

Refused to Receive Aide

Until recently Mr. Adoula also refused to receive Mr. Dorsinville's second in command, Bibiano Osorio-Tafall of Mexico, who is chief of the United Nations civil operation here.

He has still not officially recognized Mr. Osorio-Tafall as resident representative of the United Nations Technical Assistance Board here, although he is now reported prepared to do so.

Relations have been strained between Maj. Gen. Joseph D. Mobutu, commander of Congolese armed forces, and Gen. J. T. U. Aguiyi-Ironsi of Nigeria, the United Nations force commander.

This situation is causing deep concern to Western diplomats here because it seriously ham-

Continued on Page 7, Column 3

Premier of Bhutan Killed by Assassin

By The Associated Press

GANGTOK, Sikkim, Monday, April 6—The Premier of the Himalayan kingdom of Bhutan, Jigme P. Dorji, was shot dead by an unidentified assailant last night at Phunchholing on the Bhutan-India border, officials announced here.

The assassin fired through a window at a traveler's bungalow where the 45-year-old Premier was staying with his wife and his younger brother. The bullet struck him in the back. The assailant escaped.

According to meager reports available in this capital of the adjoining kingdom of Sikkim, the shooting occurred after Mr. Dorji had bade farewell to an Indian political officer, R. Avtar Singh, at Samchi, a Bhutanese

Continued on Page 8, Column 4

Flushing Meadow Is Fair Game for Sunday Afternoon Sightseers

The New York Times
Throngs of sightseers and would-be World's Fair visitors mill about along 111th Street fence near Top of the Fair

By MARTIN TOLCHIN

Scores of wishful gate-crashers resorted to ingenious but ill-fated ruses yesterday to gain a premature glimpse of the World's Fair, which opens April 22. Sneaking into the fair has become a fashionable way to spend a sunny Sunday afternoon, and yesterday's clear skies and balmy temperature whetted the curiosity of 10,000 hopeful sightseers. Most were content to crane at the pavilions from behind wire fences. And in midafternoon, many were allowed to enter the patio of the Port Authority building, from which they could see the U.S. Rubber ferris wheel, the Sinclair Oil dinosaurs and the huge Chrysler engine. They also saw close-ups of unpaved streets, unfinished pavilions and unplanted trees whose

Continued on Page 64, Column 3

Roving TV 'Radar' Checks on Audience

By JACK GOULD
Special to The New York Times

CHICAGO, April 5—Television viewers may soon be unable to keep their program choices a secret.

A device exhibited here today can count how many TV sets in a household are turned on and determine to which channels they are tuned. The viewers in the house would not even know that the tabulation had been made.

A truck containing a device much like radar would roam the streets and pick up tiny signals radiated by all TV sets. The signals indicate the number of the channel to which a receiver is tuned.

The device is part of the engineering exhibit at the annual convention of the National

Continued on Page 63, Column 1

GENERAL'S BODY WILL LIE IN CITY

Coffin Will Also Be Seen in Washington and Norfolk

By RICHARD J. H. JOHNSTON

Funeral rites for General of the Army Douglas MacArthur will be held in New York, Washington and Norfolk, Va.

The body will lie in repose tomorrow at the Seventh Regiment Armory, Park Avenue and 66th Street. The doors will be opened to the public at 10 A. M. and will close at approximately 10 P. M.

Later the body will lie in state in the Rotunda of the Capitol in Washington and in the new MacArthur Memorial in Norfolk, Va., the city General MacArthur chose as his "home by choice."

After services in historic St. Paul's Episcopal Church in Norfolk, the body will be entombed in the memorial's rotunda.

Army spokesmen said the coffin would be closed throughout all ceremonies, according to military tradition. But they said that this decision could be changed by members of the general's family.

President Johnson has or-

Continued on Page 25, Column 3

NEWS INDEX

General MacArthur Is Dead at 84; Commanded Allied Troops in Defeat of Japan

LED U.N. FORCES IN WAR IN KOREA

Death, After 3 Operations, Is Attributed to Failure of Liver and Kidneys

Continued From Page 1, Col. 8

tunda until Thursday noon.

Nineteen-gun salutes will be fired at noon tomorrow and on Saturday at military installations in the United States and in the Pacific area.

General MacArthur, one of the most decorated as well as one of the most controversial American military leaders, was the senior five-star officer at the time of his death.

Born on an Army frontier post in Indian territory, near Little Rock, Ark., on Jan. 26, 1880, General MacArthur had an active military service that spanned nearly half a century before his forced retirement in 1951.

Since his retirement, General MacArthur had served first as chairman of the board of Remington Rand, Inc., and then of the Sperry Rand Corporation.

Won Medal of Honor

He had won the Medal of Honor in World War I, served as Chief of Staff of the Army, commanded Allied forces in the Pacific in World War II and the Korean War and headed the occupation forces in Japan.

In the Korean War, however, President Harry S. Truman removed General MacArthur for publicly disputing the war strategy approved by the Joint Chiefs of Staff.

The general, who was at times considered an active candidate for the Republican Presidential nomination, left active service April 12, 1951. In a farewell speech to a joint session of Congress, he observed that "old soldiers never die — they just fade away."

His final battle with death appeared to bear out this self-characterization.

M'ARTHUR VOICED BELIEF IN DESTINY

Confident He Had a Role in History—Served as Army Chief of Staff, 1930-35

GUIDED MANILA TROOPS

Builder of Islands' Defenses Kept Vow and Returned to Liberate the Philippines

General of the Army Douglas MacArthur served his country as a soldier for more than 60 years. He achieved the highest acclaim for his exploits as a grand strategist in World War II and in Korea and then held the center stage in one of the bitterest civil versus military controversies in the history of the nation.

Virtually every military honor was bestowed upon him, yet his active career ended in bitterness and recrimination when he was relieved of his command in the midst of a war by his Commander in Chief.

His life was marked by no struggle against poverty or lack of privilege. His rise to prominence was unmarred by temporary setbacks or misfortune. Even the final, discordant note of his career — his removal from command — left him serenely confident in his judgment, outwardly unmoved by the events that swirled about him.

Believed in Destiny

General MacArthur's evaluation of his role in history was probably most succinctly and characteristically voiced by him in 1950 in a protracted conversation with a newspaper correspondent who had known him for many years.

Asked if he could explain his success, he puffed slowly at his corncob pipe, looked out the window of his Tokyo office across a moat at the Imperial Palace ground and said:

"I believe it was destiny."

Douglas MacArthur was born Jan. 26, 1880, in a section of the armory building at Fort Dodge, Little Rock, Ark., that had been set aside as the post hospital. He was the third of three sons born to Capt. Arthur MacArthur and his Virginia-born wife, the former Mary Pinkney Hardy.

His eldest brother was Arthur, born in 1876, who graduated from the United States Naval Academy in 1896, had a distinguished naval career in the Spanish-American War, the Boxer Rebellion in China and as commander of the light cruiser U.S.S. Chattanooga in World War I. Arthur died of a ruptured appendix in 1923.

The second brother was Malcolm, born 1878, who died at the age of 5.

Of the older brother's death, General MacArthur wrote 40 years later, "His premature death left a gap in my life which has never been filled."

General MacArthur's father was the son of Arthur MacArthur, a descendant of the MacArtair branch of the Clan Campbell. The MacArtairs had their seat near Glasgow, Scotland. General MacArthur's grandfather, with his widowed mother, came to this country in 1825 and settled in Chicopee Falls, Mass. He became a lawyer.

Recollections of Grandfather

General MacArthur's recollections of his grandfather remained, he said, vivid in his memory. In his memoirs to be published next fall by McGraw-Hill, he told the story of a court case presided over by his grandfather. One of the contending lawyers appeared to have overstated his case and lost the suit. He recounted the episode to his grandson Douglas:

"My grandfather," he wrote, "thus illustrated a lesson, which, unhappily, I have not always kept in mind: Never talk more than is necessary."

General MacArthur's father was destined for West Point, but in August, 1862, a little more than a year after the outbreak of the Civil War, he joined the 24th Wisconsin Volunteer Infantry. He rose through the ranks, won the Medal of Honor in the Battle of Missionary Ridge in November, 1863, and was known as "the boy colonel." The war over, he left the Army to study law, was recalled to the ranks and fought against the Indians in the West. While he was on duty at Fort Dodge, his third son was born.

Associated Press

CADET: Douglas MacArthur graduated from U. S. Military Academy in 1903. He was first in his class.

Associated Press

WAR—EUROPE: As a brigadier general he served with Rainbow Division in World War I in France.

In 1898, the elder MacArthur was ordered to the Philippines where, following the capitulation of Spain, he fought against Emilio Aguinaldo's revolutionaries, including Manuel Quezon. The elder MacArthur rose to major general commanding the Army of the Philippines, and retired as a lieutenant general.

During these years Douglas MacArthur and his mother remained in the United States, while he prepared for entry into West Point.

The MacArthurs had established their home in Milwaukee. It was there in 1898 that he took the competitive examinations for the United States Military Academy.

"Always before me," he wrote many years after, "was the vision of West Point, that greatest military institution in the world. To join the Long Gray Line had been the lodestar of all my hopes since the sound of bugles had ushered me into the world."

He passed the examination with high marks and entered West Point in June, 1899. Much has been written of his West Point military and academic record. In the four undergraduate years he attained a scholastic record not equaled in the previous 25 years. He recalled that there were others in his class smarter than he, but said that his achievement resulted, perhaps, from having "a somewhat clearer perspective of events—a better realization that first things come first. Or, perhaps, it was just luck."

If his military, scholastic and athletic records were outstanding as a cadet, his tutelage was among the strangest ever noted on the Plains of West Point.

Mother Lived Near Academy

His mother established a residence just off the West Point reservation. Her son visited her every day of his cadet life.

Recalling a crisis in his cadet career when he was summoned to a hearing on the question of hazing at the academy and faced the challenge of being ordered to disclose the names of culprits involved, General MacArthur told of his mother's stanch support of his decision to remain silent on pain of dismissal.

He wrote that his mother "sensed the struggle raging in my soul," and composed an inspirational poem urging him to stand fast.

"I knew then what to do," he wrote.

He remained in the academy and graduated first in his class with many honors in 1903. He chose the Corps of Engineers, he recalled, because chances of promotion were good in that branch.

Much of General MacArthur's success as a cadet has been credited, by him and associates of the period, to his mother, the indomitable "Pinky" MacArthur. With his father serving in the Army 10,000 miles away in that critical period of his life, the young cadet drew from the aristocratic, forceful woman the inspiration and strength that sometimes come from both parents.

To her, throughout his life, General MacArthur attributed his sense of rectitude and "destiny" that was to move his admirers to boundless praise and annoy those who thought him an egocentric.

As a newly commissioned second lieutenant he was posted to the Philippines and was involved in surveying the islands where, although the insurrection had been put down, skirmishes with Moro dissidents were not uncommon and survey parties were ambushed from time to time. There, for the first time, he heard shots fired in anger. And, as a prelude to many escapes on many other battlefields, he once had his hat shot off.

In the years before World War I, General MacArthur saw service in Mexico, once disguising himself as a drifter to lead a raiding party, an early evidence of his proclivity for independent action. As a captain, he served in the expeditionary forces at Veracruz.

The ascendance of his military star began with the outbreak of World War I. He helped to organize the 42d (Rainbow) Division and went to France as commander of one of its brigades.

Exhibiting daring and dash —frequently to the annoyance of his superiors—he savored the excitement of war and the dangers of combat. Moreover, he displayed the detached self-confidence that marked his career through nearly a half-century as an active soldier.

Competition for Sedan

As a brigade commander with the temporary rank of brigadier general, he directed actions that sometimes ran counter to grand strategy. On one occasion, with the capture of the French city of Sedan assigned to the French Army, he entered into competition with the French to be first in the town.

The prize was of particular significance to the French because it was the site of the surrender of the French to the Germans in 1870.

Orders for the operation had been drawn up by Col. George C. Marshall, an operations officer at the headquarters of the American Expeditionary Force. General MacArthur acted on his own interpretation of the orders. History recorded conflicting accounts of which forces first entered Sedan, but the French were listed officially as the first.

Thirty-three years later George C. Marshall, then Secretary of Defense, drew up another set of orders to which there was no opportunity for General MacArthur to apply a dissenting interpretation. They were the orders in 1951, relieving General MacArthur of his Far East commands during the Korean conflict.

Having once said to General MacArthur, "Young man, I do not like your attitude," Gen. John J. Pershing, commanding the American Expeditionary Force in France, nevertheless, pinned the Distinguished Service Cross and the Distinguished Service Medal on the bold young officer.

In 1919, General MacArthur returned to the United States and was appointed Superintendent of the United States Military Academy. He was credited with broadening the curriculum and raising the status of the Army's "trade school" to academic levels equal to those of nonmilitary colleges and universities.

Encouraged Athletics

A former varsity football and baseball player, General MacArthur encouraged intramural athletics and wrote the motto that now stands in bronze on the inner wall of West Point's new gymnasium:

"Upon the fields of friendly strife are sown the seeds that, upon other fields, on other days, will bear the fruits of victory."

Sinking into peacetime doldrums and sagging appropriations from Congress and public unconcern with military might in a world that had just won democracy's "ultimate" triumph over tyranny, the Army offered only routine duties at routine stations for its professionals.

General MacArthur filled a number of these assignments at home and in the Philippines. He became involved routinely in a lively controversy as a member of the court in the court-martial of Brig. Gen. William B. Mitchell in 1926. Billy Mitchell was an enthusiastic champion of the airplane as an instrument of war. After having publicly charged the Government with having failed to recognize the validity of his position, he was court-martialed.

The court ruled the charges against him "proved" and he

(continued)

resigned from the Army. For decades rumors, neither confirmed nor denied by General MacArthur, said that General MacArthur had cast a dissenting vote. The actual vote was never disclosed.

General MacArthur achieved his fourth star in 1930, when he was named Chief of Staff of the Army by President Herbert Hoover.

It was in this post, during the Depression, that he came into sharp contact with the realities of the disarray in the nation's economic life. In the summer of 1932, several thousand unemployed men, many of them veterans of World War I, gathered in Washington to demand immediate payment of war bonuses. They camped in squalor on Washington's Anacostia Flats amid widespread sympathy for their plight, but to the vast embarrassment of the Hoover Administration.

Eisenhower an Aide

On July 29, President Hoover issued written orders to Chief of Staff MacArthur to clear and destroy the camp. The task was accomplished. With Maj. Dwight D. Eisenhower, an assistant executive officer to the Assistant Secretary of War, at his side, General MacArthur directed the operation of the scene. In some newspapers General MacArthur was pictured as a beribboned military dandy directing his troops to shoot down hungry former soldiers.

When President Franklin D. Roosevelt succeeded Mr. Hoover, General MacArthur was reappointed Chief of Staff of the Army. He held the post until 1935, longer than any predecessor.

There have been charges by General MacArthur's critics that with the war in Europe only four years away, he was no more aware, despite his position as Chief of Staff, of the strides Germany and Japan were making toward waging a modern war than other top officers in the United States military establishment.

He was credited, however, in the face of penurious appropriations, with having effected a minor modernization of the Army. In his friendly biography of General MacArthur, "The Untold Story of Douglas MacArthur," Frazier Hunt discussed at length the general's dispute with President Roosevelt over the President's attempts to reduce military appropriations. Mr. Hunt wrote that General MacArthur had threatened to resign and take his case to the people unless the President dropped plans for certain drastic reductions in military budgets.

It was not the first, nor was it to be the last, time General MacArthur showed himself to be recalcitrant to higher authority. It was noted by observers of the proud and stiff professional soldier as another of those curious stances he took that appeared to belie the very essence of his training and profession—discipline and compliance with orders from above. The man who demanded and got complete obedience to his orders on the part of subordinates did not always apply the military golden rule to himself.

In such moments he explained himself as being "animated by the sole desire to help restore, preserve and advance those great American principles and ideals of which we have been beneficiaries ourselves and are now trustees for future generations."

Used Words As Weapons

Throughout his career he used words as weapons, often soaring to heights of grandiloquence in search of a phrase, inspirational in content, sonorous in tone and evocative of his call to "destiny."

No rapport ever developed between President Roosevelt and General MacArthur. Each had his "style." As in his relations with all Commanders in Chief during his active military service, General MacArthur appeared unable to acknowledge that a civilian whose trade was politics could be the repository of ultimate wisdom. Among his statements and writings, references to a President as the "Commander in Chief" are sparse.

President Roosevelt relieved General MacArthur as Chief of Staff on Oct. 3, 1935, and named Gen. Malin Craig as his successor. Resuming his permanent rank of major general, General MacArthur was sent to the Philippines as military adviser to the commonwealth.

For two years he worked at building a military force in the Philippines that might ultimately be capable of defending the islands with American help.

On Aug. 6, 1937, he was notified that he would be returned shortly for duty in the United States. Stating that his task in the Philippines was not yet completed, he abruptly terminated 34 years of uninterrupted service by applying for retirement from the Army.

In a message addressing him as "Dear Douglas," President Rooosevelt notified him that his retirement had been granted. The President wrote:

"Your record in war as in peace is a brilliant chapter of American history."

Manuel Quezon, the Philippines Commonwealth President, then appointed him Field Marshal of the Philippines. He was the only American to hold such a rank. It was then, exercising the privileges of that exalted rank, that General MacArthur designed the gold leaf-encrusted garrison cap that, along with sunglasses and a corncob pipe, was to become his trademark.

The Philippines Government paid the commander a salary of $25,000 a year and provided him with a penthouse atop the Manila Hotel. Other emoluments were provided, making it possible for him to live, as he did later in Tokyo and in the Waldorf Towers, a simple life amid luxurious surroundings.

It was noted during his service to the Philippines Government that General MacArthur was the highest paid military officer in recent history. His considerable investments, both in the Philippines and in this country, were the basis of frequent conjecture, but their extent and nature were never disclosed. His mode of living after achieving top rank was such that he seldom opened a door, drove an automobile or had to perform the myriad personal tasks of ordinary persons.

Spare and just short of 6 feet tall, General MacArthur maintained a deceptively jaunty air that the unsuspecting thought invited familiarity, which was swiftly and coolly spurned. Save for his battered, braid-encrusted campaign cap, his military dress was simplicity itself. Almost ostentatiously, he wore no ribbons, insignia or braid other than the tiny circlet of five stars on his right collar tabs.

As the possibility of war grew, the Philippine Army was merged with the United States Army under the command of General MacArthur, who was restored to duty with the American forces as a lieutenant general on July 27, 1941. In December he was made a full general 11 days after the Japanese attack on Pearl Harbor.

That attack was followed on the same day by a Japanese attack on military installations in the Philippines where General MacArthur's forces were caught completely by surprise. His air arm was virtually destroyed. His air command later explained that it was caught at Clark Field simply because there were no other airfields capable of receiving it.

Now began the greatest fighting retreat of General MacArthur's life. A hardened, well-equipped Japanese force landed on Luzon and struck toward the fortified United States military base on Bataan Peninsula into which MacArthur had drawn his forces.

Government of the Philippines

WAR—THE PACIFIC: General MacArthur led the way ashore from a landing craft in the invasion of Leyte in Philippines on Oct. 30, 1944, a little more than two and one-half years after he left the Philippines and stated: "I shall return." U. S. and Philippine troops he led when World War II began had been overwhelmed by the Japanese.

With the opening of the battle on Dec. 10, General MacArthur commanded 12,000 Philippine scouts and 19,000 United States troops. Added to this force were about 100,000 partly equipped Filipinos. The Japanese rolled the American forces into the Bataan Peninsula where it was hoped they could hold out for 14 months.

Roosevelt Reported Incensed

General MacArthur assured his troops that this aid would be forthcoming, although he had been given no assurances by Washington that reinforcements would come.

His assurances to his troops reached President Roosevelt and, it was reported, the President was incensed by General MacArthur's statements.

An entry in the diary of William Hassett, a White House aide, published in 1953, disclosed that the President had said it had been "criminal for General MacArthur to raise false hopes among his men."

Meanwhile, the highly trained Japanese forces tightened the noose around Bataan, forcing the American and Filipino troops toward the tip of the peninsula, setting the stage for the final battle for Corregidor.

As General MacArthur directed the defense from the labyrinthine, underground fortifications of Corregidor, orders came to him on Feb. 22 to leave his command in the hands of Lieut. Gen. Jonathan (Skinny) Wainwright and proceed to Australia to take command of the newly created Southwest Pacific Area.

Bidding farewell to his men and their Filipino comrades, General MacArthur uttered a phrase that was to be added to his trademarks.

"I shall return," he said.

With his wife and their 4-year-old son, Arthur, and a Chinese amah, or nursemaid, General MacArthur was taken off Corregidor by a PT boat in a dramatic dash.

Learned of Allies' Plight

Arriving in Melbourne, the general learned in full detail the plight of the retreating Allies from the Philippines to Southeast Asia.

He began agitating Washington with demands for more men and equipment, seeming not to comprehend or not to want to understand that the war in Europe held first priority for the time being. In addition, he expressed bitter disappointment that the area of his command had been limited.

He dreamed of relieving Corregidor up to the very moment of its capitulation to the Japanese on May 5, 1942.

Until this time, United States strategy in the Pacific was wholly defensive. But with the increase in Allied strength, the initiative passed from the Japanese, and on Aug. 7, 1942, Marines landed at Guadalcanal.

A prolonged struggle took place, and it was not until early in February, 1943, that the Japanese were forced to evacuate Guadalcanal. It was General MacArthur's belief, and that of the Navy, that the Bismarcks Barrier had to be broken.

The MacArthur-Navy agreement on this point, however, did not extend to the over-all strategy of defeating Japan. In fact, the views of the general and those of Admiral Chester W. Nimitz, United States Commander in the Pacific, were to be opposed until the middle of 1944.

General MacArthur favored moving up on Japan through the Solomons and Bismarcks by what he called the New Guinea-Mindanao Axis. He wanted to have the entire fleet and amphibious forces under his command to liberate the Philippines before advancing on Japan itself.

The Navy plan, which the general opposed as too long a route, was for an advance through the Pacific, taking key points in the Gilbert, Marshall and Caroline Islands on the way, then to the Marianas, to Taiwan and finally to the coast of China to establish a base for the assault on Japan.

The plan that was adopted in May, 1943, was a combination of the two, but pointing toward China as the invasion base for Japan, a move later abandoned in deference to General MacArthur.

In June, General MacArthur's forces, supported by the Navy, began the slow, grinding process of leapfrogging their way through the Japanese-held islands.

By the end of February, 1944, the Gilbert and Marshall Islands had been secured and the Bismarcks Barrier had been broken. From then on, General MacArthur's forces advanced steadily, taking the Admiralties at the same time as Admiral Nimitz's forces drove into the Marianas, Tinian and Guam.

During the months that followed, it was left open whether the general would try to liberate all or part of the Philippines or go straight from Mindanao and the Marianas into Taiwan. The Navy wanted to go directly into Taiwan from Saipan and Mindanao, bypassing the other Philippine islands.

General MacArthur was still intent on liberating all of the Philippines and using Luzon as the springboard to Japan. He made a strong emotional appeal, backed up by strategic arguments, that the United States was honor-bound to liberate the Philippines.

At a conference in Pearl Harbor in July, 1944, he convinced both President Roosevelt and Admiral Nimitz to liberate the Philippines first.

On Oct. 30, 1944, two and a half years after he had vowed to return to the Philippines, General MacArthur waded ashore at Leyte and proclaimed:

"I have returned. By the grace of Almighty God, our forces stand again on Philippine soil."

On Dec. 18, 1944, he was promoted to the newly created rank of General of the Army. His forces went on to Manila, which fell Feb. 25, 1945.

By this time, Okinawa had been chosen as a substitute for Taiwan or China as the last stop before Japan. Okinawa fell in July.

The next month, the doom of Japan was sealed with the dropping of the first atomic bombs used in warfare, on Nagasaki and Hiroshima.

The long-expected bloody assault on the Japanese home islands were a nightmare that never happened. The destroyed empire was reduced to a shattered, charred and bewildered collection of islands that had never known a conqueror's boot.

Unconditional Surrender

In a career studded with military triumphs, the greatest of these for General MacArthur came on Sept. 2, 1945, when Japanese representatives boarded the battleship U.S.S. Missouri in Tokyo Bay to sign the unconditional surrender documents under his gaze.

Representing Emperor Hirohito, Mamoru Shigemitsu, attired in morning coat and top hat, clumped to the document table on his one sound and one artificial leg. It appeared that the Japanese representative intended to read the surrender document before signing it.

"Show him where to sign, Sutherland," the General ordered Lieut. Gen. Richard K. Sutherland, his Chief of Staff.

(continued)

Without further hesitation the Foreign Minister signed his name. The Japanese Empire was ended.

A few years later General MacArthur assayed his role as Supreme Commander of the Occupation of Japan as follows:

"If the historian of the future should deem my service worthy of some slight reference, it would be my hope that he mention me not as a commander engaged in campaigns and battles, even though victorious to American arms, but rather as that one whose sacred duty it became, once the guns were silenced, to carry to the land of our vanquished foe the solace and hope and faith of Christian morals.

"Could I have but a line a century hence crediting a contribution to the advance of peace, I would yield every honor which has been accorded by war."

The occupation of a proud nation, prostrate, bewildered and hated, was to prove a phenomenon in the history of defeat and conquest.

The remnants of its military establishment were dismantled. Its military leaders were imprisoned, tried and punished as war criminals. Its vast industrial complex was in ruins and its people were fearful and uncertain of the future. In swift strokes, the occupation stripped the Emperor of his divinity, dismantled the Zaibatsu (an informal but all-powerful industrial hierarchy based on family ties) and instituted reforms that shook the roots of an ancient class society.

Sitting remotely and serenely atop the occupation was the architect of the defeat of the Japanese, the symbol of their conquest, whose power over them exceeded that of the now powerless Emperor. Rightly or wrongly, this was the Japanese view of General MacArthur in September, 1945.

With the beginning of the occupation of Japan, the extent to which the Soviet Union would share it had not been decided on the highest levels. Taking advantage of this, General MacArthur rode roughshod over Soviet efforts to get a foot in the door.

It quickly became a standing joke in Tokyo that the ranking representative of the Soviet Union in Japan, Lieut. Gen. Kuzma Nikolayevich Derevyanko, spent more time in General MacArthur's outer office awaiting audiences that never took place than anyone else in the country.

General Derevyanko, who had signed the surrender for his country aboard the Missouri, sought General MacArthur's ear for a discussion of the Soviet role in the occupation, but the Russians never obtained one. General Derevyanko went home in the first week of October, 1945, and the occupation remained an American affair.

The occupation moved along through five years during which General MacArthur, remote but omnipresent, moved between his office in the downtown Dai Ichi Building and his residence in the sprawling, white stone-and-concrete United States Embassy.

Traditionalists Were Appalled

Thousands of Japanese lined the streets and sidewalks to watch him pass in a long, black car four times a day. All precedent was shattered and Japanese traditionalists were appalled when, early in the occupation, the Emperor called on him at his home. The Tenno (Emperor), believed by Japanese to be a descendant of the Sun Goddess, went, as did many others of high station from many nations, to pay his respects to the American general.

Two slightly irreverent American newspaper correspondents published a book, "The Star-Spangled Mikado," which, translated into Japanese, had a wide circulation.

Of the occupation, General MacArthur made this observation:

"The pages of history in recording America's 20th-century contributions may, perchance, pass over lightly the wars we have fought. But, I believe they will not fail to record the influence for good upon Asia which will inevitably follow the spiritual regeneration of Japan."

The serenity of Asia was shattered at dawn on the morning of June 25, 1950, when North Korean troops who had been trained and equipped by Russians swept southward across the 38th parallel in a lightning effort to overwhelm the inadequate South Korean forces, who were being trained under the direction of a United States military advisory team of fewer than 1,000 men and officers.

Technically, General MacArthur was not responsible for the protection of South Korea, but the fate of the military advisory group, their families and several thousand other Americans in the country was in doubt.

Step-by-Step Decisions

President Truman ordered General MacArthur to take whatever steps he thought necessary to evacuate the Americans from South Korea. The civilians were evacuated by sea and air. The advisory troops remained with the Korean units.

Then General MacArthur informed Gen. Lawton Collins, Chief of Staff, that the South Koreans, in all probability, could not defend themselves successfully. In Washington decisions were being made hourly as a result of which the United States became, step by step, involved in the struggle.

The Fifth Air Force, initially assigned to protect the evacuation, began to try to support the rapidly retreating South Korean forces. President Truman decided to act on General MacArthur's recommendation to send United States troops in Japan and Okinawa into the struggle to stem the Communist tide.

The unequal struggle between the highly trained North Korean Communist Army of 500,000 and the ill-prepared South Korean Army of slightly more than 100,000 men soon involved scattered units of American troops, swept up hastily from scattered bases in the Far East and thrown into the conflict.

If equal in spirit to the challenge, the young, postwar G.I.'s had little training and less ability to stem the Communist tide, sweeping under Soviet-prepared battle plans down the mountain valleys and into the rice bowl of South Korea.

The United States appealed to the United Nations to join the struggle against armed aggression. Since the Soviet Union was at that moment boycotting the Security Council for other reasons and was not present to use its veto, the United Nations decided to join forces with the South Koreans and the United States in the struggle.

Meanwhile, one of General MacArthur's most trusted and competent officers, Lieut. Gen. Walton H. Walker, commanding the United States Eighth Army, was given the task of halting the aggressor.

Several factors were in General Walker's favor as he sought to build up his forces while fighting bitter rear-guard actions against the invader. The North Korean air arm was negligible, its naval forces were nonexistent; General Walker's Fifth Air Force support was on constant increase, his seaborne supply lines were unhampered. He took his stand on the Naktong perimeter in August, protecting the vital supply port of Pusan and ground down the enemy by repulsing, with costly casualties, its assaults on the defenses.

On Sept. 12, 1950, General MacArthur executed a daring and massive strike from the sea on the North Korean rear and flank with an amphibious landing at the western port of Inchon.

North Korea's defense broke and the remnants of its army fled in disorder across the 38th parallel. General MacArthur announced that for all practical purposes the war had ended, except for the need to pursue the enemy to the Yalu River, the border between Communist China and North Korea.

Near the end of September, mopping-up operations of North Korean Communist forces south of the 38th parallel continued while some United Nations units, their areas cleared of the enemy, marked time.

The taste of victory sent the enthusiasm of United Nations forces soaring. Unit commanders were in favor of pursuing the enemy northward without delay. However, orders were held in abeyance as word came that there was grave consternation at United Nations headquarters as to whether the intent of the combined effort had been to repel the invaders or rid the entire peninsula of Communist military forces.

Seated in his Tokyo office-command post in the Dai Ichi Building, General MacArthur marshaled his arguments in support of the pursuit plan.

For more than three months he had directed the affairs of Japan with one hand, and conducted the grand strategy of the war with the other.

Deep within his all-but-impenetrable office, surrounded by a staff that guarded his time and presence with zeal, he read the daily and sometimes hourly battlefront reports.

On fewer than a dozen occasions he motored to Haneda or Tachikawa Airports outside Tokyo, boarded his luxuriously appointed four-engine personal transport plane, the Bataan, for a visit to Korea and talks with his field commanders.

Except for frequent teletype and telephone conversations with his field commanders, General MacArthur's routine of five years was not visibly affected. He came and went between office and residence with the same clockwork regularity while Japanese and G. I.'s alike gawked at the detached splendor of his passings.

On Oct. 10, President Truman flew to Wake Island for a meeting with General MacArthur. The President appeared to be concerned with the General's propensity for independent action.

At Wake Island, General MacArthur was understood to have expressed great optimism about the Korean situation. He told the President there was "very little" chance that the Chinese Communists or the Soviet Union would react to a venture into North Korea.

General MacArthur returned to Tokyo and began to "close out" the Korean War. Near the end of October a regimental airborne combat unit was employed in the war's only paratroop operation. United States paratroopers were dropped at two points just north of the North Korean capital of Pyongyang to cut off fleeing and disorganized Communist units. At the same time United Nations ground troops slashed across the 38th parallel in a dash to the Yalu River, Korea's northern boundary with China.

But elements identified as Chinese Communist troops were found south of the 38th parallel in the central and east coast sectors at about the same time—the end of October. They had crossed the Yalu about Oct. 16. General MacArthur's intelligence officers, however, apparently failed to attach any significance to the reports of their presence.

Second Phase of War

First Cavalry Division units reached the river, but within hours the Chinese Communist Army struck across the border and the second phase of the Korean struggle was under way. By the second week in November full-scale warfare had begun and the United Nations forces were giving ground at a speed that, in many instances, amounted to a rout.

Once again, at the 38th parallel, the United Nations forces regrouped and stood their ground for a time. Later, however, Seoul, the South Korean capital, fell to the Communists for the second time.

What General MacArthur had called "a new war" went on through the winter and into the spring. He became restive and wanted to strike at Chinese depots and supply lines within Chinese territory.

He let it be known that he was displeased with high decisions to refrain from attacking outside Korea lest the war spread. In a message to the American Legion, he reiterated his views and, in a reply to a request from Representative Joseph W. Martin Jr., the Massachusetts Republican, he set down a position that Washington did not believe consonant with its views. In the message, he said:

"There is no substitute for victory."

In April, 1951, he was relieved of his commands in the Far East by President Truman.

In his book, "MacArthur, His Rendezvous with History," the General's long-time friend and senior aide, Maj. Gen. Courtney Whitney, recalled the moment General MacArthur received the fateful order:

"MacArthur's face froze. Not a flicker of emotion crossed it. For a moment, while his luncheon guests puzzled on what was happening, he was stonily silent. Then he looked up at his wife, who still stood with her hand on his shoulder. In a gentle voice, audible to all present, he said: 'Jeannie, we're going home at last.'"

In the message that accompanied his order relieving General MacArthur, President Truman said:

"Full and vigorous debate on matters of national policy is a vital element in the constitutional system of our free democracy. It is fundamental, however, that military commanders must be governed by the policies and directives issued to them in the manner prescribed by our laws and Constitution. In time of crises this consideration is particularly compelling.

"General MacArthur's place in history as one of our greatest commanders is fully established. The nation owes him a debt of gratitude for the distinguished and exceptional service which he has rendered his country in posts of great responsibility. For that reason I repeat my regret at the necessity for the action I feel compelled to take in this case."

On April 17, the general, his wife and son arrived in San Francisco. His return was that of a conquering hero as city after city feted him with parades.

Beginning May 3 he testified for three days before the Armed Services and Foreign Relations Committees of the Senate, insisting he could have won the Korean conflict if he had been given a free hand. He addressed the joint houses of Congress on April 19, creating a deep impression by the moderation of his speech and the dignity of its presentation.

He ended with a quotation from an old Army song — "Old soldiers never die — they just fade away."

He did not fade away, however. He continued to make speeches and pronouncements. His name was brought up before the 1952 Republican National Convention as a possible Presidential nominee. He was the keynote speaker, but the nomination went to General Eisenhower.

Of the United Nations he once said:

"It represents perhaps the noblest effort man has yet made to evolve a universal code based upon the highest of moral precepts. It became the keystone to an arch of universal hope."

General MacArthur and his wife settled in a 37th floor suite of the Waldorf Towers, high above Park Avenue. On Aug. 1, 1952, he was named chairman of the board of Remington Rand Inc. (now Sperry-Rand), manufacturers of electrical equipment and business machines. General Whitney remained his inseparable companion and confidant.

With the death in 1959 of Gen. George C. Marshall, General MacArthur became the senior officer of the United States Army in the rank of General of the Army. He remained on active duty without assignment, entitled to a small staff and pay and allowances amounting to $20,543 a year.

In July, 1961, General MacArthur, accompanied by his wife, made a sentimental journey to the Philippines, his only trip abroad following his return to the United States in 1951. Additional honors were bestowed upon him by the Government there.

Yearly, on Jan. 26, his birthday, he joined old comrades at a private dinner in the Waldorf to reminisce about the campaigns they had been through. Delegations of West Point cadets called each year to serenade him.

His only previous serious illness struck him in January, 1960, when he underwent surgery for a prostate condition. He recovered from the ordeal despite his 80 years.

Associated Press

SETBACK: He bade farewell to Japan in 1951 after he was relieved of his commands by order of President Truman.

"All the News That's Fit to Print"

The New York Times

LATE CITY EDITION

Weather: Showers likely today and tonight. Partly cloudy tomorrow. Temperature range: today 63-73; Thursday 60-79. Details, page D17.

VOL. CXXV .... No. 43,329

NEW YORK, FRIDAY, SEPTEMBER 10, 1976

25 cents beyond 50-mile zone from New York City, except Long Island. Higher in air delivery cities.

20 CENTS

MAO TSE-TUNG DIES IN PEKING AT 82; LEADER OF RED CHINA REVOLUTION; CHOICE OF SUCCESSOR IS UNCERTAIN

The Pattern of Partisan Support for Ford and Carter

FORD CARTER SUPPORTERS

40% 30 20 10 0

Republicans | Independents (Leaning Republican) | Independents | Independents (Leaning Democratic) | Democrats

The New York Times/Sept. 10, 1976

This chart shows that President Ford's support is predominant among Republicans and that Jimmy Carter's support rises steadily along the Democratic end of the spectrum. For example, 22 percent called themselves Republicans. Among these Ford had roughly a seven-to-one advantage.

Poll Shows Ford Trailing in Bid For 2 Voter Groups G.O.P. Needs

By R. W. APPLE Jr.

President Ford is trailing Jimmy Carter among self-described independents and moderates, the two elements of the electorate without whose strong support Republican nominees have been unable to win Presidential elections in the post-World War II era.

With less than two months remaining until Election Day, the President's strength is concentrated in groups that lack the voting power to elect a President—the well-to-do, the Republicans, the white Protestants, the conservatives. In almost every other segment of the electorate, Mr. Ford is running well behind his Democratic opponent, Mr. Carter.

Those are two of the central conclusions that emerge from the first national poll taken by The New York Times and CBS News since the two party conventions—a survey of 1,703 registered voters, selected at random, who were interviewed by telephone during the week that ended Sept. 5, immediately before the formal start of the general election campaign on Labor Day.

The New York Times/CBS News poll was not designed to predict the outcome of the election but to analyze the thinking of the electorate as it stood early this month. Nonetheless it reflected the same over-all standing of the candidates as recent surveys by the Gallup and Harris organizations, with Mr. Carter leading the President by a margin of roughly 4 to 3.

Insofar as issues determine how people cast their votes for President, the poll indicated, President Ford is suffering from the continuing deep divisions in the country over two issues he inherited from his discredited predecessor — the

Continued on Page A19, Col. 3

AGREEMENT REACHED ON TAX REVISION BILL

Conferees Adopt First Reform of Estate Levies in 35 Years

By EDWIN L. DALE Jr.

Special to The New York Times

WASHINGTON, Sept. 9 — House and Senate conferees agreed tonight on all provisions of the sweeping tax revision bill after adopting the first major reform of the nation's system of estate taxes in 35 years.

The final version of the bill, it was estimated, would give the Treasury $1.6 billion more in revenues in the fiscal year 1977, thus meeting the demands of the new Congressional budget control process and greatly augmenting the bill's chances for passage.

The revenue increase would rise to $2.4 billion five years from now, offset in part by revenue losses from the new estate tax reform.

The bill has hundreds of provisions, among them a significant increase in taxes on wealthy taxpayers who avail themselves of various tax "shelters."

It also would impose tax penalties on United States companies complying with the Arab boycott of Israel.

The estate tax reform would provide

Continued on Page D17, Col. 5

Ford Asserts Rival Would Create Peril To Defense of U.S.

By JAMES M. NAUGHTON

Special to The New York Times

WASHINGTON, Sept. 9—President Ford said today that Jimmy Carter's plans to reduce Pentagon spending and troop levels overseas would make it "impossible to have a defense adequate to maintain our freedom and the freedom of our friends."

Addressing the national convention of B'nai B'rith one day after Mr. Carter did, the President departed from a prepared text to read notes sharply critical of the national security positions of his Democratic challenger.

Says Carter Invites Crisis

Mr. Ford contended that the former Georgia Governor's proposals would, among other things, require the United States to rely on "a nuclear strategy of massive retaliation" and thus "invite a major crisis with our allies, including Israel."

Mr. Carter, meanwhile, took issue with Mr. Ford's remarks yesterday, in which the President embraced proposals for a constitutional amendment to limit abortions. The Democratic nominee said that he thought the sensitive abortion issue could backfire on any Presidential candidate who attempted to exploit it.

Even Mr. Ford's running mate, Senator

Continued on Page A21, Col. 1

Radar Images From Venus Depict Vast Area of Possible Lava Flow

By JOHN NOBLE WILFORD

American astronomers who have obtained the first detailed radar images of a large portion of the surface of Venus say they reveal a possible lava flow the size of Oklahoma, an impact basin much like those on the moon and evidence of mountain-building processes similar to those that have shaped the Earth.

Since Venus is completely enveloped by thick clouds, the radar images represent the first relatively clear picture of what the planet's surface looks like. The images covered an area of about four million square miles in the northern latitudes of Venus.

The most distinctive feature in the north of Venus, as shown by the radar, is a very bright Oklahoma size area that the scientists said looked like a broad lava field. It appears to be a sharply defined feature overlaying an older surface.

The scientists said that the area did not have a shape that might have been created by the impact of a meteorite, but instead seemed to be a result of processes internal to Venus, such as a volcanic eruption of lava. The feature has been tentatively named Maxwell, for James Clerk Maxwell, the 19th-century Scottish physicist.

Maxwell's surface appears extremely rough and apparently contains long paral-

Continued on Page A18, Col. 5

KISSINGER IS CAUTIOUS

Discerns No Setback for U.S. Relations With China, but Sees Hazards in a Change

By BERNARD GWERTZMAN

Special to The New York Times

WASHINGTON, Sept. 9—Secretary of State Henry A. Kissinger said today that he did not think Mao Tse-tung's death would set back Chinese-American relations, but he cautioned that "when any historical figure disappears it is extremely difficult to predict everything his successor will do."

At a brief news conference Mr. Kissinger reflected Washington's uncertainty about the future in light of Mao's death. Officially, Secretary Kissinger and President Ford expressed confidence that the trend toward improved relations started by the Chinese leader and President Richard M. Nixon in 1972 would continue.

[In Moscow, diplomatic observers said the death of Chairman Mao raised the possibility of a relaxation of tensions between the Soviet Union and China. Page A17.]

Kissinger Met Mao Five Times

The Secretary of State, who has met Mao five times since 1971, tempered the official optimism with the caution that because China was probably on the verge of major changes, the eventual trend of its policy could not be predicted with assurance.

"We have to remember that when a towering figure disappears from the scene, not even his successors can know exactly what the shape of events will be and it is premature to speculate as to what the future evolution should be," he said in answer to a question.

Mr. Kissinger, in a signal to Chinese leaders, said that since the opening to China, it and the United States had "created a durable relationship based on mutual confidence and perception of common interests."

Pledge to Adhere to Communiqué

"We for our part will continue to cement our ties with the People's Republic of China in accordance with the Shanghai Communiqué issued at the end of Mr. Nixon's visit and calling for normalization of relations.

Earlier in the day the Secretary told newsmen that "we consider our opening to the People's Republic of China one of the most important foreign policy actions of the recent period and we don't really expect any change on the Chinese side, but the methods and the nuances

Continued on Page A17, Col. 6

United Press International

Mao Tse-tung is shown in 1969 at the Ninth Party Congress, proclaiming the triumph of his Cultural Revolution over disgraced President Liu Shao-chi.

Political Uncertainty in China

Natural Disasters and Reports of Indiscipline Leave Analysts Fearful of Forecasting Events

By FOX BUTTERFIELD

Special to The New York Times

HONG KONG, Sept. 9—The death today of Chairman Mao Tse-tung comes at a time when China's political situation seems more uncertain than at any point since the end of the Cultural Revolution.

News Analysis

Over the last 18 months four other members of the nine-man standing Committee of the party's Politburo, China's highest decision-making body, have died, including Prime Minister Chou En-lai. Since last winter Peking has been preoccupied wtih a divisive political campaign, there have been growing reports of a breakdown in public discipline, and there have even been some isolated incidents of violent conflict.

There have also been other misfortunes for China. Last July parts of Northern China were devastated by the world's worst earthquake in a decade, and both northeast and southwest China have recently been hit by strong tremors.

No analysts here believe that the Communist regime is likely to be seriously jeopardized by these troubles. But few of them would dare to forecast the shape of events.

The most likely course of events in China after the funeral, some analysts believe, is that a transitional collective leadership, following current party ranking, will emerge centered on the new Prime Minister, Hua Kuo-feng.

The tall, burly, crewcut Mr. Hua, a career party administrator, seems to have swiftly strengthened his grip on the levers of leadership in Peking. He headed relief efforts after July's earthquake and last week, in a major speech, he called for the strict restoration of law and order against "class enemies."

Background and Philosophy Cloudy

Little is known about Mr. Hua's personal background or political philosophy. But judging from his few public statements, he seems to share the pragmatism of his late predecessor, Chou, and yet to be keenly aware of the need to use some of the language of Chairman Mao's more radical followers, lest the party be further split.

Whoever emerges as the dominant figure, if anyone, it is possible Peking may not actually fill Mao's place as party chairman in the immediate future. For one thing, it would be a symbolic recognition that no one was capable of succeeding Mao. North Vietnam has never filled Ho Chi Minh's post as party chairman.

Moreover, Peking's leaders may find it

Continued on Page A16, Col. 3

Panel on Paperwork Assembling A Litany of Constant Redundancy

The New York Times/Neal Boenzi

The Commission on Federal Paperwork at the World Trade Center yesterday with a 45-foot string of forms that represents one year's paperwork on a single child on Aid to Dependent Children.

By MOLLY IVINS

The Commission on Federal Paperwork convened in New York City yesterday to communicate on the feasibility of implementing a restriction in the ongoing paperflow.

The commission, which reports to both the Congress and the President, has been assigned the almost insuperable task of doing something about the sea of forms, applications and reports that threatens to engulf everyone.

The members of the commission seem almost awed by the dimensions of the paperwork problem: They estimate that paperwork and red tape cost the nation's economy $40 billion a year, not counting paper clips. But they are making inroads on the problem.

They have a way to go, as was shown by Philip Toia, Commissioner of New York State's Department of Social Services, who arrived trailing a 45-foot-long string of forms—the result of one year's paperwork on a single child in the program of aid to dependent children.

Clients Ping-Ponged

The commission has been holding a series of hearings around the country, and this one focused on the paperwork in income maintenance programs.

James Reed, director of the Monroe County Department of Social Services, explained his department's procedure for Supplemental Security Income recipients. It was a five-minute litany of recipients getting ping-ponged between agencies, punctuated by requirements to fill out 22-page forms.

Tales of the labyrinthine inner workings of assorted New York welfare de-

Continued on Page B18, Col. 1

PARTY IN UNITY PLEA

Appeal to People Is Coupled With Delayed Disclosure of Chairman's Death

By Reuters

PEKING, Sept. 9—Mao Tse-tung, the pre-eminent figure of the Chinese Communist revolution and the leader of his country since 1949, died today at the age of 82.

His death, at 12:10 A.M. after a long illness, left uncertain the question of who

Obituary article appears on pages A13-15; text of announcement, page A16.

was to succeed him. There is no designated heir, nor is there anyone among his subordinates who commands the awe and reverence with which he was regarded among the 800 million Chinese.

The party leadership delayed the announcement of Chairman Mao's death for about 16 hours until 4 P.M. [4 A.M. Thursday New York Time]. The announcement included an appeal to the people to uphold the unity of the party that he had headed.

Plea to Follow Mao's Policies

It said China must "continue to carry out Chairman Mao's revolutionary line and policies in foreign affairs resolutely."

It urged the people to "deepen the criticism" of former Deputy Prime Minister Teng Hsiao-ping, who was toppled in the power struggle that followed the death in January of Mao's closest comrade in arms, Prime Minister Chou En-lai.

After the disgrace of Mr. Teng, Hua Kuo-feng, regarded as a centrist, was made Prime Minister and First Deputy Chairman of the party.

Funeral music followed today's announcement broadcast over the Peking radio, and 2,000 people gathered in the vast Tien An Men Square, many wearing black armbands, some weeping. Flags fluttered at half staff.

'Internationale' Heard Across City

"The Internationale," the world Socialist anthem, echoed over the city from loudspeakers at dusk as bicyclists made their way home from work.

Eight days of memorial ceremonies were scheduled to begin Saturday and end Sept. 18 with the entire nation standing in silent tribute for three minutes but with trains, ships and factories sounding sirens.

The announcement said that no foreign leaders would be invited to Peking during the period of mourning.

Chinese embassies abroad, it said, would express gratitude to foreigners wishing to come, but would "inform them of the decision of the Central Committee of our party and the Government of our country not to invite foreign governments, fraternal parties or friendly personages."

It was believed the actual cremation or burial would be attended only by the

Continued on Page A16, Col. 1

Borman Son Denies Bribe at West Point

By CHARLES KAISER

Special to The New York Times

WEST POINT, N. Y., Sept. 9—Lieut. Frederick P. Borman, a 1974 West Point graduate, categorically denied tonight that he had received $1,200 to change his vote on an honor-code board.

"It's completely false," Lieutenant Borman said of the allegation, part of an affidavit sworn to by two cadets who had been accused of cheating at the United States Military Academy here.

[Lieutenant Borman's father, Frank Borman, the former astronaut who is president of Eastern Airlines, said in an interview with The Associated Press that he had no intention of stepping down as chairman of a five-member special West Point review panel appointed by the Secretary of the Army.

[Robert K. Koster, another cadet accused of cheating in affidavits signed by other cadets, said he had resigned from the Academy. He is the son of Maj. Gen. Samuel W. Koster, a former West Point superintendent who stepped down from his position after charges that, when he commanded the Americal Division in Vietnam, he had helped to cover up the alleged massacre by American soldiers at My Lai.]

Lieutenant Borman said that he had

Continued on Page A11, Col. 1

INSIDE

Spending Limit Voted

Congress has voted to limit spending to about $413 billion, $13 billion more than President Ford has projected, in the fiscal year 1977. Page A18.

British Strike Threat

The British Government and its allies in the labor movement held meetings in an effort to prevent a strike that could damage the economy. Page D1.

Medicaid Law

A new state law intended to prohibit kickbacks by clinical laboratories may actually have legalized the practice, city health officials said. Page B2.

News Summary and Index, Page B1

Mao Tse-tung Dies in Peking at 82; Leader of Red China's Revolution

Continued From Page A1

Chairman's family and top members of the party, the Government and other organizations.

Peking Radio and Hsinhua, the Chinese press agency, said Mao's body would lie in state in the Great Hall of the People.

The radio announcement of Mao's death was a simple one. It said: "Mao Tse-tung passed away at 0010 hours on Sept. 9 (12:10 P.M. Wednesday, New York time) because of the worsening of his illness and despite all treatment, although meticulous medical care was given him in every way after he fell ill."

Parkinson's Disease Indicated

While the announcement did not specify the illness, which had kept Mao out of the public eye for months, it was widely believed that the chairman had been suffering from Parkinson's disease, which causes progressive rigidity of the body's muscles.

It had been known for some time that Mao was approaching the end. Meetings with visiting statesmen had been cut to 15 to 20 minutes. Official photographs showed him seated, his head back against the top of his chair.

Mao last appeared in public on May Day 1971. For just a few minutes he sat on a rostrum overlooking Tien An Men Square to watch a fireworks display. A sea of faces sought a glimpse of him, but most of the time he stayed out of sight, sipping tea behind a parapet.

The last foreign leader to see him was Prime Minister Zulfikar Ali Bhutto of Pakistan on May 29. He said that Mao had a bad cold and was frail, but that he "was very quick on the uptake and grasped everything."

President Ford visited him last December.

The announcement of Chairman Mao's death was preceded by warnings over the radio that an important broadcast would be made at 4 P.M.

The announcement was addressed to "The whole party, the whole army and people of all nationalities throughout the country."

It was given out by the Central Committee of the Communist Party of China, the Standing Committee of the National People's Congress of the People's Republic of China and the Military Commission of the Central Committee of the Communist Party of China.

"All victories of the Chinese people were achieved under the leadership of Chairman Mao," the statement said in eulogizing the man who led the Communist takeover in 1949 and then dominated the nation as he guided it from backward isolation to the status of a nuclear power with a burgeoning industrial base, purging rivals, defying Soviet ideological leadership, opening a relationship with the United States and winning a seat in the United Nations.

In factories, shops and apartment houses, residents gathered around their sets.

The faces of the comparatively few people on the streets were grim; some were close to tears.

Hundreds of people gathered in the clusters in the center of the city. One crowd heard a man on a stepladder make a speech honoring Mao.

Traffic seemed to have thinned out. Although a few cars and bicycles were on the streets, it seemed that many people had rushed indoors to hear the news.

Hugues Vassal/Liaison

Chairman Mao Tse-Tung

Political Uncertainty in China Leaves the Analysts Fearful of Forecasts

Continued From Page A1

impossible to call the Central Committee meeting or Party Congress that such an important move would require without touching off a violent power struggle.

Certainly no Chinese leader can really take Mao's place as China's predominant figure—a master military strategist, a consummate political tactician, a charismatic evangelist, a sentimental poet. He was the energetic force that led the Chinese Revolution to victory in 1949, restored China to its rightful place as a great nation, and sometimes sent it into political convulsions in quest of his search for revolutionary purity.

Succeeded Ousted Teng

How closely Mr. Hua and the others will hew to Chairman Mao's rigorous insistence on class struggle, mass enthusiasm and strict egalitarianism is open to question.

Mr. Hua was named Prime Minister and more important, first Vice Chairman of the Communist Party last April after the unexpected ouster of Teng Hsiao-ping, who had seemed in line to succeed Mao.

Some Chinese leaders, like Mr. Teng, who was also purged during the Cultural Revolution in the late 1960's, have reportedly long argued in private that the Chairman's ideas were outdated, no more applicable to an industrialized society than, say, the myth of the lone American cowboy.

In today's official announcement of Chairman Mao's death carried by Hsinhua, the Chinese press agency, the party's Central Committee invoked the Chairman's ideological legacy and called on China's 800 million people to "carry on the cause left behind by Chairman Mao."

His legacy, of course, is subject to different interpretations, and the announcement seemed to stress the need for unity.

In keeping with a moderately worded editorial this week in the Communist Party newspaper, Jenmin Jih Pao, today's death notice made only passing reference to earlier, more inflamed calls for attacking rightists and "the bourgeoisie within the party."

The editorial, entitled "Grasp criticism of Teng Hsiao-ping and promote production," appeared to be a deliberate attempt to turn the current antirightist campaign into a drive for increased production.

Analysts here were wary of drawing too much significance from the editorial and the death notice, since a call for unity could probably be expected anyway, given Chairman Mao's death. But the two documents struck a different tone from the more strident rhetoric of only a month ago, and suggested that whoever is in control in Peking may now be trying to de-emphasize the campaign.

How Mao's passing will affect China's foreign policy is a subject diplomats here have debated for years with little consensus.

Peking's dispute with Moscow seems too deep-seated to resolve easily, based as it has been partly on ideological disputes, partly on national differences and partly on Mao's own fights with Stalin and other Russians during his rise to power in the 1920's and 1930's.

In China itself there has been little visible controversy over foreign policy in recent years. But there have been growing signs of impatience with the United States over Taiwan, and it should be remembered that it was Chairman Mao who charted China's momentous split with tht Soviet Union and who initiated the invitation to President Richard M. Nixon.

How much control or influence Mao exerted in his last months is unknown, though it seems unlikely that the antirightist campaign mounted this year could have succeeded in toppling Mr. Teng so swiftly without the Chairman's strong backing.

With Mao's departure, the factions into which analysts generally divide Peking's leaders seem nearly evenly balanced, at least on the Politburo. Roughly six of the surviving 16 members of the 21-member Politburo are grouped as "moderates," or pragmatic administrators concerned with orderly government and economic development.

These include Mr. Yeh Hien-ying, the 78-year-old Minister of Defense, Chen Hsi-lien, the powerful commander of the Peking military region and the party's highest-ranking army man, and Li Hsien-nien, China's chief economic planner.

Six others are often classified as "radicals," or ideologues who have associated themselves with Mao and the reforms he instituted to try to preserve China's revolutionary purity. The most prominent among them are the Chairman's wife, Chiang Ching, an outspoken, energetic woman unpopular with many Chinese, Yao Wen-yuan, a Shanghai polemicist, and Wang Hung-wen a youthful leftist from Shanghai.

In the announcement today of the funeral committee for Chairman Mao, Mr. Hua's name was listed first, as due his official position.

Chang Rated Major Contender

The three other surviving members of the nine-man Standing Committee of the Politburo named in 1973 were listed next: Mr. Wang, who gained prominence during the Cultural Revolution but who has been an enigma over the past year, Mr. Yeh, and Chang Chun-chiao, the smooth, capable former Shanghai party organizer who is now senior Deputy Prime Minister and head of the general political department of the armed forces.

Of these three, Mr. Yeh seems too old and Mr. Wang too young to assume real leadership now. But Mr. Chang, who is thought to be in his early 60's, could be a major contestant for power. Although Mr. Chang was once regarded as a leftist because of his actions during the Cultural Revolution, some analysts think he may have shifted to a more centrist stance.

In the view of some analysts, the balance of power on the Politburo may well be held by Mr. Hua and another shadowy but important figure, Wu Teh, the Mayor of Peking. Both have been career party administrators, both would seem to have logical ties to the "moderates," but both rose to power in the Cultural Revolution or its aftermath and apparently get along well with their more ideologically fervent colleagues.

Of course, the definitions of radicals and moderates are oversimplified and many Chinese may not fit neatly into either category. In recent times, personal rivalries and petty jealousies seem to have played as important a role as deep-seated ideological differences.

At the same time, however, very real issues are involved and a major debate is likely to continue over how faithfully to preserve the political legacy that Mao fought for so many years to create.

During the Cultural revolution, for example, to prevent China from slipping into "revisionism," Mao instituted a series of sweeping reforms, known as the "Socialist newborn things," which some more moderate party leaders have branded as impractical.

To check the growth of incipient capitalism, he curtailed bonuses and wage raises. To narrow the gap between city and country, he required urban school graduates to be sent to live with the peasants. To equalize education opportunities, he revamped the school system to place a student's political background ahead of his academic record. And to prevent the growth of a new elite, he ordered party cadres and scientists alike to spend more time at manual labor.

Without the Chairman's awesome presence, it is hard not to imagine some slippage here.

(continued)

After all, that is what Mr. Teng was accused of trying to do last year, emphasizing production, technology and orderly conventional approaches to achieve Chou's goal of making China a "powerful, modern Socialist state by the turn of the century."

Mr. Hua has carefully echoed official rhetoric since he assumed office last spring, but he has shied away from the strong calls for attacks on the "bourgeoisie within the party" that are sometimes found in more radical articles.

With Peking preoccupied over the next few months, or possibly years, with this ideological conflict and the question of succession, more power may devolve on the powerful party and military commanders in China's provinces. Some of the provinces, like Szechwan, with a population of over 80 million, are bigger than most Western European nations.

To some extent this transfer of power seems to have begun already, with the provincial party leaders, most of whom are pragmatists and old party administrators, interpreting the antirightist campaign to suit their own purposes. But China's 2,000-year tradition of unity is too strong to imagine the country really splitting into what the Chinese Communists call "mountaintop kingdoms."

CHINA MAY BECOME MORE BUREAUCRATIC

U.S. Scholars Expect a Push for Modernization Without Maoist Efforts to Arouse Masses

By JOSEPH LELYVELD

Special to The New York Times

WASHINGTON, Sept. 9—China without Mao Tse-tung is likely to become a more coercive and bureaucratic state, heavily committed to the modernization of its economy but less intent on arousing the rural masses to take part in the country's political life.

That was the tentative conclusion of American scholars today as they attempted to look beyond the uncertainties of the moment and define the enduring elements of the Maoist legacy.

None of the scholars doubted that the Chinese leadership would continue to invoke Chairman Mao's teachings to justify the claims of competing factions or new directions in policy.

"It's sort of like the Gospel," said Edward Rise of the Center for Chinese Studies at the University of California. "It's subject to reinterpretation when necessary."

But there was considerable doubt as to whether the successors would have either the desire or the ability to resort to the kind of revivalist campaign that Chairman Mao repeatedly instigated in order to give China's millions a sense of direct involvement in politics.

"I recognize Mao's guile and, in some ways, cruelty and arrogance in the use of power," said Prof Michael Oksenberg of the University of Michigan. "But I don't think it's strange to say that he introduced humane nations.

Technocrats May Gain

"The successor is not going to have the moral authority the Chairman had," he continued. "Lacking that, what can he have but the carrot and the stick? And how much carrot will he be able to offer in view of China's developmental problems?"

It remained an open question, Professor Oksenberg said, whether Chairman Moa's strong commitment to the rural masses would survive him in the Chinase leadership, or whether his successors would share his determination to reduce the gap in living standards between the cities and the countryside.

"The commitment will have to be there," he said, "but it may not be as intensely held."

Prof. Benjamin Schwartz of Harvard saw no possibility of "a return to a complete Stalinist orientation," but he speculated that technocrats would have enhanced status and influence in China. "Maybe there will be a tendency to pay more attention to what the experts have to say about the requirements of their expertise," he said.

Text of the Announcement Issued by Peking Reporting Death of Chairman Mao

Special to The New York Times

HONG KONG, Sept. 9 (Reuters)—Following is the text of the announcement on the death of Chairman Mao Tse-tung issued by Hsinhua, the Chinese press agency:

The Central Committee of the Communist Party of China, the Standing Committee of the National People's Congress of the People's Republic of China, the State Council of the People's Republic of China and the Military Commission of the Central Committee of the Communist Party of China announce with deepest grief to the whole party, the whole army and the people of all nationalities throughout the country:

Comrade Mao Tse-tung, the esteemed and beloved great leader of our party, our army and the people of all nationalities of our country, the great teacher of the international proletariat and the oppressed nations and oppressed people, Chairman of the Central Committee of the Communist Party of China, Chairman of the Military Commission of the Central Committee of the Communist Party of China, and Honorary Chairman of the National Committee of the Chinese People's Political Consultative Conference, passed away at 00:10 hours, Sept. 9, 1976, in Peking, [12:10 P.M. Wednesday, New York time] because of the worsening of his illness and despite all treatment, although meticulous medical care was given him in every way after he fell ill.

Founder and Leader of Party

Chairman Mao Tse-tung was the founder and wise leader of the Communist Party of China, the Chinese People's Liberation Army and the People's Republic of China. Chairman Mao led our party in waging a protracted, acute and complex struggle against the right and left opportunist lines in the party, defeating the opportunist lines pursued by Chen Tu-hsiu, Chu Chiu-pai, Li Li-san, Lo Chang-lung, Wang Ming, Chang Kuo-tao, Kao Kang, Jao Shu-shih and Peng Teh-huai and again, during the great proletarian Cultural Revolution, triumphing over the counterrevolutionary revisionist line of Liu Shao-chi, Lin Piao and Teng Hsiao-ping, thus enabling our party to develop and grow in strength steadily in class struggle and the struggle between the two lines.

Led by Chairman Mao, the Communist Party of China has developed through a tortuous path into a great, glorious and correct Marxist-Leninist party which is today exercising leadership over the People's Republic of China.

During the period of the new democratic revolution, Chairman Mao, in accordance with the universal truth of Marxism-Leninism and by combining it with the concrete practice of the Chinese revolution, creatively laid down the general line and general policy of the new democratic revolution, founded the Chinese People's Liberation Army and pointed out that the seizure of political power by armed force in China could be achieved only by following the road of building rural base areas, using the countryside to encircle the cities and finally seizing the cities, and not by any other road.

He led our party, our army and the people of our country in using people's war to overthrow the reactionary rule of imperialism, feudalism and bureaucrat capitalism, winning the great victory of the new democratic revolution and founding the People's Republic of China.

The victory of the Chinese people's revolution led by Chairman Mao changed the situation in the East and the world and blazed a new trail for the cause of liberation of the oppressed nations and oppressed people.

In the period of the Socialist revolution, Chairman Mao comprehensively summed up the positive as well as the negative experience of the international Communist movement, penetratingly analyzed the class relations in Socialist society and, for the first time in the history of the development of Marxism, unequivocally pointed out that there are still classes and class struggle after the Socialist transformation of the ownership of the means of production has in the main been completed, drew the scientific conclusion that the bourgeoisie is right in the Communist Party, put forth the great theory of continuing the revolution under the dictatorship of the proletariat, and laid down the party's basic line for the entire historical period of socialism.

All the victories of the Chinese people were achieved under the leadership of Chairman Mao; they are all great victories for Mao Tse-tung thought.

The radiance of Mao Tse-tung thought will forever illuminate the road of advance of the Chinese people.

Enriched Treasury of Marxism

Chairman Mao Tse-tung summed up the revolutionary practice in the international Communist movement, put forward a series of scientific theses, enriched the theoretical treasury of Marxism and indicated the orientation of struggle for the Chinese people and the revolutionary people throughout the world.

With the great boldness and vision of a proletarian revolutionary, he initiated in the international Communist movement the great struggle to criticize modern revisionism with the Soviet revisionist renegade clique at the core, promoted the vigorous development of the cause of the world proletarian revolution and the cause of all the people of all countries against imperialism and hegemonism, and pushed the history of mankind forward.

Chairman Mao Tse-tung was the greatest Marxist of the contemporary era. In the past half century and more, basing himself on the principle of integrating the universal truth of Marxism-Leninism with the concrete practice of the revolution, he inherited, defended and developed Marxism-Leninism in the protracted struggle against the class enemies at home and abroad, both inside and outside the party, and wrote a most brilliant chapter in the history of the movement of proletarian revolution.

He dedicated all his energies throughout his life to the liberation of the Chinese people, to the emancipation of the oppressed nations and oppressed people the world over, and to the cause of communism. With the great resolve of a proletarian revolutiontionary, he waged a tenacious struggle against his illness, continued to lead the work of the whole party, and the whole army and the whole nation during his illness and fought till his last breath.

The magnificent contributions he made for the Chinese people, the international proletariat and the revolutionary people of the whole world are immortal. The Chinese people and the revolutionary people the world over love him from the bottom of their hearts and have boundless admiration and respect for him.

Guided by Chairman Mao's proletarian revolutionary line, our party, our army and the people of our country continued their triumphant advance and seized great victories in the Socialist revolution and Socialist construction, particularly in the great proletarian Cultural Revolution, in criticizing Lin Piao and Confucius and in criticizing Teng Hsiao-ping and repulsing the right deviationist attempt at reversing correct verdicts. Upholding socialism and consolidating the dictatorship of the proletariat in the People's Republic of China, a country with a vast expanse and a large population, is a great contribution of world historic significance which Chairman Mao Tse-tung made to the present era; at the same time, it has provided fresh experience for the international Communist movement in combating and preventing revisionism, consolidating the dictatorship of the proletariat, preventing capitalist restoration and building socialism.

Grief for All Revolutionaries

The passing away of Chairman Mao Tse-tung is an inestimable loss to our party, our army and the people of all the nationalities of our country, to the international proletariat and the revolutionary people of all countries and to the international Communist movement. His passing away is bound to evoke immense grief in the hearts of the people of our country and the revolutionary people of all countries.

The Central Committee of the Communist Party of China calls on the whole party, the whole army and the people of all nationalities throughout the country to turn their grief into strength with determination:

We must carry on the cause left behind by Chairman Mao and persist in taking class struggle as the key link, keep to the party's basic line and persevere in continuing the revolution under the dictatorship of the proletariat.

We must carry on the cause left behind by Chairman Mao and strengthen the centralized leadership of the party, resolutely uphold the unity and unification of the party and closely rally round the party central committee.

We must strengthen the building of the party ideologically and organizationally in the course of the struggle between the two lines and resolutely implement the principle of the three-in-one combination of the old, middle-aged and young in accordance with the five requirements for bringing up successors to the cause of the proletarian revolution.

We must carry on the cause left behind by Chairman Mao and consolidate the great unity of the people of all nationalities under the leadership of the working class and based on the worker-peasant alliance, deepen the criticism of Teng Hsiao-ping, continue the struggle to repulse the right deviationist attempt at reversing correct verdicts, consolidate and develop the victories of the great proletarian Cultural Revolution, enthusiastically support the new socialist things, restrict bourgeois right and further consolidate the dictatorship of the proletariat in our country.

We should continue to unfold the three great revolutionary movements of class struggle, the struggle for production and scientific experiment, build our country independently and with the initiative in our own hands, through self-reliance, hard struggle, diligence and thrift, and go all out, aim high and achieve greater, faster, better and more economical results in building socialism.

We must carry on the cause left behind by Chairman Mao and resolutely implement his line on army building, strengthen the building of the army, strengthen the building of the militia, strengthen preparedness against war, heighten our vigilance, and be ready at all times to wipe out any enemy that dares to intrude. We are determined to liberate Taiwan.

We must carry on the cause left behind by Chairman Mao and continue to carry out Chairman Mao's revolutionary line and policies in foreign affairs resolutely.

We must adhere to proletarian internationalism, strengthen the unity between our party and the genuine Marxist-Leninist parties and organizations all over the world, strengthen the unity between the people of our country and the people of all other countries, especially those of the third-world countries, unite with all the forces in the world that can be knitted, and carry the struggle against imperialism, social-imperialism and modern revisionism through to the end.

We will never seek hegemony and will never be a superpower.

We must carry on the cause left behind by Chairman Mao and assiduously study Marxism-Leninism-Mao Tse-tung thought, apply ourselves to the study of works by Marx, Engels, Lenin and Stalin and works by Chairman Mao, fight for the complete overthrow of the bourgeoisie and all other exploiting classes, for the establishment of the dictatorship of the proletariat in place of the dictatorship of the bourgeoisie and for the triumph of socialism over capitalism, and strive to build our country into a powerful socialist state, make a still greater contribution to humanity and realize the ultimate goal of communism.

Long live invincible Marxism-Leninism-Mao Tse-tung thought!

Long live the great, glorious and correct Communist Party of China!

Eternal glory to our great leader and teacher Chairman Mao Tse-tung!

MAO TSE-TUNG: FATHER OF CHINESE REVOLUTION

By FOX BUTTERFIELD

Special to The New York Times

HONG KONG, Sept. 9—Mao Tse-tung, who began as an obscure peasant, died one of history's great revolutionary figures.

Born at a time when China was wracked by civil strife, beset with terrible poverty and encroached on by more advanced foreign powers, he lived to fulfill his boyhood dream of restoring it to its traditional place as a great nation. In Chinese terms, he ranked with Chin Shih-huang, the first Emperor, who unified China in 221 B.C., and was the man Chairman Mao most liked to compare himself to.

With incredible perseverance and consummately conceived strategy, he harnessed the forces of agrarian discontent and nationalism to turn a tiny band of peasants into an army of millions, which he led to victory throughout China in 1949 after 20 years of fighting. Along the way the army fought battles as big as Stalingrad and suffered through a heroic march as long as Alexander's.

Then, after establishing the Chinese People's Republic, Mao launched a series of sweeping, sometimes convulsive campaigns to transform a semifeudal, largely illiterate and predominantly agricultural country encompassing almost four million square miles and a fifth of the world's population into a modern, industrialized socialist state. By the time of his death China had manufactured its own nuclear bombs and guided missiles and had become a major oil producer.

With China's resurgence, Mao also charted a new course in foreign affairs, putting an end to a century of humiliation under the "unequal treaties" imposed by the West and winning new recognition and respect. Finally, in 1972, even the United States abandoned its 20 years of implacable hostility when President Richard M. Nixon journeyed to Peking, where he was received by a smiling Mao.

At the same time he brooked no opposition to his control. To consolidate his new regime in the early 50's he launched a campaign in which hundreds of thousands were executed. In the late 50's, despite criticism from other party leaders, he ordered the Great Leap Forward, ultimately causing widespread disruption and food shortages. Throughout his years in power he toppled one of his rivals after another in the party. In the Cultural Revolution he risked throwing the country into chaos.

While China achieved enormous economic prograss under Mao, some critics felt his constant political campaigns and his emphasis on conformity finally reduced many Chinese to a dispirited, anxious mass ready to go along with the latest shift in the political wind.

Complex Figure

One of the most remarkable personalities of the 20th century, Mao was an infinitely complex man—by turns shrewd and realistic, then impatient and a romantic dreamer, an individualist but also a strict disciplinarian. His motives seemed a mixture of the humanitarian and the totalitarian. He himself once commented that he was "part monkey, part tiger," and perhaps after all he was riven with the same contradictions he was fond of analyzing in the world around him.

A Chinese patriot, a combative revolutionary, a fervent evangelist, a Marxist theorist, a soldier, a statesman and poet, above all Mao was a moralist who deeply believed, as have Chinese since Confucius, that man's goodness must come ahead of his mere economic progress. Like many Chinese of the past 100 years, angered by the insults of imperialism, he wanted to tear China down to make it stronger. He envisioned creating in China an egalitarian, revolutionary utopia in which mass enthusiasm provided the motive force.

"I have witnessed the tremendous energy of the masses," Mao wrote in 1958 in the midst of the Great Leap Forward, one of his biggest but ultimately most disruptive campaigns. "On this foundation it is possible to accomplish any task whatsoever." The two sentences are a striking summary of his thought.

Unlike many great leaders, Mao never exercised, or sought, absolute control over day-to-day affairs. But the man who rose from humble beginnings in a Hunan village became virtually sovereign, if not a living god, to the 800 million Chinese. His very words were the doctrine of the state. Printed in millions of little red plastic-bound books as "Quotations from Chairman Mao Tse-tung," they were taken to possess invincible magic properties.

Power, Prestige and Anxieties

Although Mao was a devoted Leninist who, like his Russian predecessor, stressed the need for a tightly organized and disciplined party, he came to cast himself above his party and sought to replace it with a personal cult when it thwarted him.

Despite awesome power and prestige, in the later years of his life—from about 1960 onward—he seemed obsessed by anxieties that the Chinese revolution was in danger of slipping back into the old elitism and bureaucratic ways of imperial China. This danger appeared all the greater, in his eyes, because of the concurrent development in the Soviet Union of what he termed "revisionism." In Mao's view, Nikita S. Khrushchev's emphasis on material incentives to increase consumer-oriented production and the clear emergence of a privileged party elite were anathema. Looking at the problems in China, Mao complained in 1964, with perhaps characteristic exaggeration, "You can buy a branch secretary for a few packs of cigarettes, not to mention marrying a daughter to him."

To revitalize China, to cleanse the party and to insure that the revolution survived him, Mao launched the Great Proletarian Cultural Revolution in 1966. As he conceded later, it had consequences even he did not foresee.

Party Unity Undermined

Hundreds of thousands of youngsters were mobilized as Red Guards. Often unruly, given to fighting among themselves, they roamed the country and humiliated and chastised Mao's opponents in the party after his call to "bombard the headquarters." After two years of turmoil, economic disruption and even bloodshed, order was finally restored, with help from the increasingly powerful army under Lin Piao, then Minister of Defense, and some surviving party leaders of a less radical bent such as Prime Minister Chou En-lai.

But Mao had severely undermined the critical and long-standing unity of the party, forged in the 1930's during the epochal Long March—an anabasis of 6,000 miles that took the fledgling army over mountains, rivers and wastelands from Kiangsi, in South China, to Shensi, in the northwest. Foremost among those purged in the Cultural Revolution were Liu Shao-chi, head of state, and Teng Hsiao-ping, the Secretary General of the party, who were labeled "capitalist roaders." Mr. Liu, for years one of Mao's closest associates, had served as head of state since 1959, when Mao relinquished the post in order to give his potential successors more experience. Mao's only official post after that was Chairman of the Chinese Communist Party's Central Committee.

Marshal Lin, for his role in keeping the army behind Mao and his constant and fulsome praise, was termed "Comrade Mao Tse-tung's close comrade in arms and successor" and his inheritance was engraved in the 1969 party constitution. But Marshal Lin lasted only two years; according to the official version, he died in a plane crash in Mongolia in 1971 after trying to escape to the Soviet Union when his plot to kill Mao was discovered. Even more bizarre, Mao insisted in letters and speeches that have since reached the outside world that he had been suspicious of Marshal Lin as early as 1966 and had used him only to help get rid of Mr. Liu.

For several years after Marshal Lin's death, the redoubtable Mr. Chou, a master administrator and conciliator, helped the visibly aging Mao lead the country and embark on what seemed a sustained period of economic growth. But Mr. Chou's death from cancer in January 1976 left the daily leadership in the hands of Mr. Teng, the former party Secretary General, whom Mr. Chou resurrected in 1973, evidently with Mao's approval, and installed as senior Deputy Prime Minister and likely successor.

An Even Quicker Fall

Mr. Teng then fell victim to Mao's suspicions even more quickly than had Mr. Liu and Marshal Lin. Only three months after Mr. Chou's demise, Mr. Teng was stripped of his posts, castigated once again as a "capitalist-roader within the party" and accused by Mao of misinterpreting his personal directives by overstressing economic development.

In these later years there were some who thought that Mao appeared as an aging autocrat, given more and more to whim. His invitation last winter to Mr. Nixon to revisit Peking, the scene of his greatest triumph as President, was viewed as a possible sign of a man becoming divorced from reality, though it was understandable in Chinese terms as a kind gesture to a good friend.

Mao made his last public appearance in 1971; in published photographs since then he often looked like a sick man. His apparent difficulty in controlling the movement of his hands and face and his slurred speech stirred speculation that he had suffered a stroke or had Parkinson's disease.

Yet he continued to receive a succession of foreign visitors in his book-lined study, sitting slouched down in a tartan-covered chair, and he apparently remained active in the political conflict that divided Peking. One of his last acts, it was said, was to select a final successor, Hua Kuo-feng, a relative unknown who had spent his early party career in Mao's home district, Hsiangtan, in Hunan. Whether the two men had a close personal relationship was not clear.

Rift With Moscow

In recent years Mao had also been preoccupied with China's monumental quarrel with the Soviet Union, one of the pivotal developments of the postwar world. From the Chinese side the conflict was partly doctrinal, over Mao's concern that Soviet revisionism was a dangerous heresy that threatened to subvert the Chinese revolution. It was partly political and military, concerned with Mao's effort first to resist Moscow's domination of the Chinese party and later to defend against Soviet troops on China's border. It was partly territorial, over Peking's contention that Czarist Russia had annexed Chinese territory.

Although few outsiders perceived it until the quarrel surfaced in the early 1960's, it is clear now that the trouble had its origin in the earliest contact between the Chinese Communists and the Russians in the 1920's. It was a period when Mao and others in the newly organized Chinese party were groping for a way to power, and Stalin, from the distance of Moscow gave them orders that repeatedly led them into disaster.

Stalin and his representatives from the Communist International who served as advisers in China—Mao dubbed them "imperial envoys"—first directed the Communists to ally with Chiang Kai-shek's Nationalists. Then, after Generalissimo Chiang turned on the Communists in 1927, massacring thousands, Stalin ordered the party to anticipate a "revolutionary upsurge" in the cities by the (largely nonexistent) proletariat.

Mao was shorn of his posts and power in the early 1930's as a result of direct Soviet interference. It was only after the Communists were forced to begin the Long March in 1934, after more errors in strategy, that Mao won command because of his genius for organizing and leading peasant guerrillas in a revolution in the countryside.

His First Journey Abroad

When Mao traveled triumphantly to Moscow—it was his first journey abroad—at the end of 1949, soon after setting up his government, he immediately ran into the first foreign policy crisis of the People's Republic of China in the form of a two-month argument with Stalin over terms of an aid agreement and Soviet concessions. Although Mao was to try the Soviet model of economic development, with its emphasis on heavy industry, for a few years, by the mid-1950's he came to have doubts about it, both for its utility in a basically agricultural country such as China and because of the bureaucratic, elitist and capitalistic tendencies — material incentives—it brought with it.

A series of events in the mid- and late-1950's turned this history of uneasy relations into bitter wrangling and eventually open armed clashes. First among these was Nikita S. Khrushchev's speech in 1956 denouncing Stalin for his brutality and personality cult. Mao, who by then envisioned himself as the world's major Marxist-Leninist thinker and revolutionary, was caught by surprise. He resented not being consulted, and he was put in an awkward position by revelations by Mr. Khrushchev, then the party leader.

There followed in rapid succession the evident Soviet complicity in the affair of Peng Teh-huai, the Chinese Defense Minister who was purged in 1959 after criticizing Mao for the chaos of the Great Leap Forward; Moscow's failure to support Peking in a border clash with India, the offshore islands crisis with Taiwan and Washington, and finally the abrupt withdrawal of all Soviet technicians in July 1960, canceling hundreds of agreements to build factories and other installations.

At the same time Mr. Khrushchev labeled the Chinese leaders as madmen in a speech to the Rumanian Party congress, and Mao was soon to tell his colleagues that "the party and state leadership of the Soviet Union have been usurped by revisionists."

The conflict reached its climax in the winter of 1969, when Soviet and Chinese patrols clashed along the frozen banks of the Ussuri River.

China Pictorial

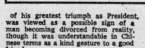

Mao reviewing troops of Eighth Route Army in Yenan, his base in northwest China after the epic Long March that took more than a year, starting in 1934, and covered 6,000 miles of the most difficult terrain. It became a national legend.

Some Quotations From Chairman Mao

A man's head is not like a scallion, which will grow again if you cut it off; if you cut it off wrongly, then even if you want to correct your error, there is no way of doing it. (1956)

•

Our nation will never again be an insulted nation. We have stood up. (1949)

•

The Red Army is like a furnace in which all captured soldiers are melted down and transformed the moment they come over. In China not only the masses of workers and peasants need democracy, but the army needs it even more urgently. (1928)

•

The popular masses are like water, and the army is like a fish. How then can it be said that when there is water, a fish will have difficulty in preserving its existence? An army which fails to maintain good discipline gets into opposition with the popular masses, and thus by its own action dries up the water. (1938)

•

Every Communist must understand this truth: Political power grows out of the barrel of a gun. Our principle is that the party commands the gun; the gun shall never be allowed to command the party. (1938)

•

Within the ranks of our people, democracy stands in relation to centralism, and freedom to discipline. They are two conflicting aspects of a single entity, contradictory as well as united, and we should not one-sidedly emphasize one to the detriment of the other. Within the ranks of the people, we cannot do without freedom, nor can we do without discipline. All this is well understood by the masses of the people. (1937)

•

In a big country such as ours, it is nothing to get alarmed about if small numbers of people create disturbances; rather we should turn such things to advantage to help us get rid of bureaucratism. (1957)

•

We are not only good at destroying the old world, we are also good at building the new. (1949)

Thereafter the Russians continued to build up their army, navy and air force along the Chinese frontier until a fourth of their troops were stationed in the area.

Mao spent hours lecturing every visiting head of state on the danger of Soviet expansionism—hegemonism, as he termed it. His belief that Soviet "social-imperialism" was the greatest threat to peace enabled him to take a more sanguine view of the United States and helped bring about the gradual improvement in relations after 1972.

An Austere Style

Although Mao commanded enormous authority—in 1955, in a casual talk with local officials, he overturned the provisions of the five-year plan fixed only a day before by the National People's Congress—he shunned the trappings of might. He seldom appeared in public, perhaps to preserve a sense of awe and mystery, and he eschewed fancy dress or medals, in conformity with the simple standard he himself had set during his guerrilla days. Whatever the occasion, he wore only a plain gray tunic buttoned to the neck and trousers to match that came to be called a Mao suit in the West and for a period in the 1970's became a fashion craze.

Edgar Snow, the American journalist who in 1936 became the first Westerner to meet Mao, felt that his style owed much to the simplicity, if not roughness and crudeness, of his peasant upbringing. He had the "personal habits of a peasant, plain speaking and plain living," Mr. Snow reported after a visit to the Communists' guerrilla headquarters in Shensi, near Yenan. Mao was completely indifferent to personal appearance; he lived in a two-room cave like other peasants "with bare, poor, map-covered walls." His chief luxury was a mosquito net, Mr. Snow found, and he owned only his blankets and two cotton uniforms.

"Mao's food was the same as everybody's, but being a Hunanese he had the southerner's ai-la, or love of pepper." Mr. Snow wrote. "He even had pepper cooked into his bread. Except for this passion, he scarcely seemed to notice what he ate."

In the classic "Red Star Over China," the first public account of Mao, Mr. Snow wrote that he found Mao, "a gaunt, rather Lincolnesque figure, above average height for a Chinese, somewhat stooped, with a head of thick black hair grown very long, and with large searching eyes, a high-bridged nose and prominent cheekbones." The account continued: "My fleeting impression was of an intellectual face of great shrewdness."

"He appears to be quite free from symptoms of megalomania," Mr. Snow said—the cult of Mao would not begin until the first "rectification" campaign in 1942. But, Mr. Snow added, "he has a deep sense of personal dignity, and something about him suggests a power of ruthless decision."

Seeming Reserve and Aloofness

Agnes Smedley, another journalist who encountered Mao in Yenan at that time, felt that though he could communicate intensely with a few intimate friends, he remained on the whole reserved and aloof. "The sinister quality I had at first felt so strongly in him proved to be a spiritual isolation," she related. "As Chu Teh [the military commander] of the Red Army was loved, Mao Tse-tung was respected. The few who came to know him best had affection for him, but his spirit dwelt within himself, isolating him."

Other American visitors—diplomats, army officers and journalists—who trooped to Yenan in the 1940's during an optimistic interlude when Washington hoped to bring Mao and Chiang together to fight the Japanese, inevitably were impressed by Mao's obvious earnestness and by his willingness to sacrifice personal comfort for the pursuit of an ideal. In these he contrasted all too clearly with the corruption and indifference of most Nationalist leaders.

Some of Mao's dedication, toughness and reserve may also have been the product of his bitter personal experiences along the road to power. His sister and his second wife, Yang Kai-hui, were executed in 1930 by General Chiang; a younger brother was killed fighting a rear-guard action during the Long March; another younger brother was executed in 1943 in Sinkiang, and Mao's eldest son was killed in the Korean War. Another son, according to Red Guard sources during the Cultural Revolution, was said to have gone mad because of the way he was brought up by a "bourgeois" family after his mother was executed.

Mao also had several close brushes with death. In 1927, when he was organizing peasants and workers in Hunan, he was captured by local pro-Kuomintang—that is, pro-Nationalist—militiamen, who marched him back to their headquarters to be shot. Just in sight of their office, Mao broke loose and fled into a nearby field, where he hid in tall grass until sunset.

"The soldiers pursued me, and forced some peasants to help them search for me," he related to Mr. Snow. "Many times they came very near, once or twice so close that I could almost have touched them, but somehow I escaped discovery. At last when it was dusk they abandoned the search."

Mindful of Cost to Family

He was certainly mindful of the cost of the revolution to his family and friends. In a talk in 1964 with Mao Yuan-hsin, the son of his executed brother, Mao recalled: "Very many members of our family have given their lives, killed by the Kuomintang and the American imperialists. You grew up eating honey, and thus far you have never known suffering. In the future, if you do not become a rightist, but rather a centrist, I shall be satisfied. You have never suffered—how can you be a leftist?"

Perhaps his losses contributed to Mao's attitude toward his enemies. Unlike Stalin, Mao never sought to put vast numbers of his opponents in the party to death. Instead, in a very Chinese, even Confucian, way, he believed in the power of education to reform them and sent them off to labor camps or the countryside for reindoctrination and redemption.

However, he did not cavil at killing those whom he considered true counterrevolutionaries. One of the first instances of this occurred in late 1930 in the small town of Futien, in the Communists' base area, which Mao had built up since 1927. In putting down a revolt by soldiers who challenged his rule, Mao had 2,000 to 3,000 officers and men executed. In the early 1950's, to consolidate the Communists' power, Mao launched a violent campaign against counterrevolutionaires. According to an estimate accepted by Stuart Schram, Mao's most careful and sensitive biographer, from a million to three million people, including landlords, nationalist agents and others suspected of being "class enemies," were executed.

"There is no evidence whatever," Mr. Schram wrote, that Mao "took pleasure in killing or torturing. But he has never hesitated to employ violence whenever he believed it necessary. No doubt, Mao regarded it all as a natural part of revolutionary struggle. He gave no quarter, and he asked for none."

As Mao himself put it, in one of the most celebrated passages in his writing, his 1927 "report of an investigation into the peasant movement":

"A revolution is not the same as inviting people to dinner or writing an essay or painting a picture or embroidering a flower; it cannot be anything so refined, so calm and gentle, or so 'mild, kind, courteous, restrained and magnanimous' [the virtues of Confucius as described by a disciple]. A revolution is an uprising, an act of violence whereby one class overthrows the authority of another. To put it bluntly, it was necessary to bring about a brief reign of terror in every rural area."

Little is known about Mao's personal life or habits, which he kept sheltered from the glare of publicity. He was an inordinate cigarette smoker, and during the Long March, when cut off from regular sources of supply, is said to have experimented by smoking various leaves. Perhaps because of his habit, his voice was husky and he coughed a good deal in later life.

He apparently liked to work 13 or 14 hours a day, and Mr. Snow found that he frequently stayed up until 2 or 3 in the morning reading and going over reports. Despite infirmity in his last years, Mao had an iron constitution that he consciously developed as a student in Changsha, the provincial capital of Hunan.

'No Time for Love or Romance'

In this Mao and his student friends—"a serious-minded little group" that "had no time for love or romance," Mao recalled —were trying to overcome the traditional Chinese prejudice that any physical labor or exercise was lower class. Mao himself was so much a product of this tradition that when the Chinese revolution of 1911 broke out and he joined the army for a few months in a burst of enthusiasm, he spent much of his salary of $7 a month to pay carriers to fetch his water since intellectuals did not do that kind of work.

Physical strength, courage and military prowess remained a basic theme of Mao's life. Even his first published writing, an essay written in 1917, was a plea that Chinese exercise more. "Our nation is wanting in strength," it began. "The military spirit has not been encouraged."

Whether, in another period—July 1966—Mao actually took his widely publicized swim in the Yangtze for 65 minutes is perhaps more a matter of legend than of fact. But his approach to swimming typified his dogged pursuit of an objective.

"I say that if you are resolved to do it, you can certainly learn, whether you are young or old," Mao once advised his principal military officers in discussing the need to improve themselves. "I will give you an example. I really learned to swim well only in 1954; previously I had not mastered it. In 1954, there was an indoor pool at Tsinghua University [in Peking]. I went there every day with my bag, changed my clothes, and for three months without interruption I studied the nature of water. Water doesn't drown people. Water is afraid of people."

Wide and Voracious Reader

A voracious reader, Mao enjoyed both the Chinese classics and novels he had devoured as a boy, and Western history, literature and philosophy, which he read in translation. He often impressed his visitors with an apt allusion to literature or a salty proverb, but he could be remarkably offhand and whimsical for the leader of a country. In the 1950's, when he was still head of state, he once greeted a particularly tall Western diplomat with the exclamation: "My God! As tall as that!"

Mao's informal style, his pithy and frequent use of Chinese metaphors and his transcendent charisma made him a natural leader for the masses of peasants. A Chinese writer observed that "Mao Tse-tung is fundamentally a character from a Chinese novel or opera."

In his later years Mao spent most of his time in his simple, yellowish residence inside Peking's Forbidden City, cut off from all but a small group of people. Some of these were female nurses who helped him walk; others were the three women interpreters who usually translated for him when there were foreign visitors. Given his difficult Hunan accent and speech problem, one of the women had to translate his

Continued on Following Page

The Globe and Mail, Toronto/John F. Burns

Chiang Ching, Mao's widow, was a one-time film actress who met him in Yenan. She has become major party leader.

Leader of Long March Based Power on Discontent of Peasants

Continued from Preceding Page

words into comprehensible Mandarin Chinese.

Assigned to do that was Wang Hai-jung, whom some believed was his niece but others thought was the daughter of one of his favorite teachers. In any event, in the spring of 1976, after the downfall of Teng Hsiao-ping, Miss Wang and the two others were suddenly replaced without an announcement, stirring speculation that someone else in the entourage was jealous of their position.

In Classical Vein

For all the overwhelming changes Mao brought to China, the drama of how he and others at the top of the Communist hierarchy reached decisions seemed a tale from the Ming Dynasty court.

Who Mao's aides were, for example, who arranged his appointments, prepared documents for him to read and sign in his study behind the red velvet drapes, or carry his orders to the Central Committee—all this is not known outside China. One key figure in the mystery was certainly Chiang Ching, his fourth wife, an outspoken, sometimes vitriolic woman who claimed the mantle of his most faithful disciple.

Mao considered that he had been married only three times—his first wife was a peasant girl whom his parents married him to when he was only 14 and she was 20. He never lived with her, and as he told Mr. Snow, "I did not consider her my wife and at this time gave little thought to her."

His second wife, Yang Kai-hui, the woman executed in 1930, was the daughter of one of Mao's most influential teachers in Changsha, Yang Chang-chi, a professor of ethics. Professor Yang was to introduce the young Mao to Li Ta-chao, a brilliant nationalistic intellectual and writer in Peking who was one of the founders of the Communist movement in China.

Although Mao has sometimes been adjudged an ascetic man, bent only on the pursuit of revolution and power, he evidently could also be sentimental and romantic. In 1937, in reply to a commemorative poem written by a woman whose husband was a Communist leader killed in battle, Mao composed the following verse:

I lost my proud poplar, and you your willow,
Poplar and willow soar lightly to the heaven of heavens.
Wu Kang, asked what he has to offer,
Presents them respectfully with cassia wine.
The lonely goddess in the moon spreads her ample sleeves
To dance for these faithful souls in the endless sky.
Of a sudden comes word of the tiger's defeat on earth,
And they break into tears of torrential rain.

The Poplar and the Willow

The official interpretation accompanying a later collection of Mao's poems points out that his second wife's surname means "poplar" while the name of the man killed in battle means "willow."

According to an ancient legend, Wu Kang, mentioned in the third line, had committed certain crimes in his search for immortality and was condemned to cut down a cassia tree on the moon. Each time he raises his ax the tree becomes whole again, and thus he must go on felling it for eternity. The tiger in the seventh line refers to the Kuomintang regime Mao was fighting, and, hence, the last couplet describes the emotion of Mao's lost companion at the final triumph of the revolution. The official interpretation found that the poem contained a "large element of revolutionary romanticism."

In 1928, while Mao's second wife was still alive and he was 35, he began living with an 18-year-old, Ho Tzu-chen. By some accounts she was a forceful character and a commander of a woman's regiment; she was also said to have been the daughter of a landlord. In any case she married Mao in 1930, after Miss Yang was executed, and later accompanied him on the perilous and exhausting Long March, one of the few women to take part. One of the five children she bore Mao was born on the march.

The rigors evidently broke her health, and not long after reaching the Communists' new base area in Yenan, in the northwest, she was sent to the Soviet Union for medical treatment. While she was away, there arrived in Yenan a minor movie actress from Shanghai, Lan Ping, who, in contrast to the plain-living and isolated Communists, must have seemed glamorous and attractive. According to one version, she came to Mao's notice after ostentatiously sitting in the front row at one of his lectures and clapping loudly. It was apparently love at first sight for Mao, and Miss Lan—with her name changed to Chiang Ching—was soon living in Mao's cave house.

Their affair reportedly angered some of Mao's colleagues, who felt that he had betrayed his faithful companion of the Long March, Miss Ho, a genuine Communist, for the seductive Miss Chiang. To win approval for their marriage Mao is said to have pledged that Miss Chiang would stay out of politics. This may have been the origin of the widespread suspicion of and distaste for her among party leaders that have dogged her since.

Cultural Revolution

Miss Chiang did keep a low profile for much of the next three decades, but in 1964, when Mao grew dissatisfied with the party and prepared to launch the Cultural Revolution, he turned to her as one of the few people he could trust.

She undertook a vigorous reform of the popular traditional opera and the movies, demanding that they inject heavy doses of "class struggle" into every performance and paint all heroes in the whitest whites and villains in the blackest blacks. She also lined up a leftist literary critic in Shanghai, Yao Wen-yuan, who was willing to write a scathing attack on a play, "Hai Jui Dismissed from Office," that was an allegorical criticism of Mao. The publication of the article in November 1965 in Shanghai—Mao could not get it printed in Peking, where his opponents were in control—signaled the start of the Cultural Revolution.

Miss Chiang was soon promoted to a commanding position in the group Mao established to direct the Cultural Revolution, and she vastly increased her unpopularity by making stinging personal attacks on many leading officials.

When the Cultural Revolution subsided Miss Chiang's authority was reduced, but in the following years she continued to try to exert her influence. She may have been instrumental in the downfall of Mr. Teng early in 1976. He was accused among other crimes of failing to attend any of her model operas and of trying to cut off a state subsidy to her pet production brigade near Tientsin.

Not Even a Telephone Call

How Mao regarded his controversial wife is difficult to say. She once indicated to an American scholar, Roxane Witke, that she and Mao were not always close personally. In 1957, when Mao made his second trip to Moscow she happened to be there in the hospital but he neither stopped in to see her nor phoned, she related. Later, at the start of the Curltural Revolution, Mao wrote her a letter that is often cited by her detractors in the party.

"I think you also ought to pay attention to this problem," he wrote. "Don't be obsessed by victory. It is necessary to constantly remind ourselves of our own weaknesses, deficiencies and mistakes. I have on countless occasions reminded you of this. The last time was in April in Shanghai."

Although Miss Chiang had a reputation among Chinese for being rancorous and spiteful, Americans who met her during the visits to Peking by Presidents Nixon and Ford found her gay and vivacious. Miss Witke was impressed with her evident devotion to Mao's cause and felt she had suffered from being a woman in a world where men predominated.

Mao's apparent fondness for women and the checkered pattern of his married life contrasted sharply with the monotonous austerity and Puritanism he enforced since 1949. Romance is now frowned on as a decadent bourgeois idea and the age when women may marry has been pushed back to 25 and for men to 28.

Marriage was not the only instance of a certain willingness on Mao's part to bend the rules for himself. Though he insisted that all plays, novels, poems and paintings follow the often-stultifying code of socialist realism—"So far as we are concerned, art and literature are intended for the people," he said in talks at Yenan in 1942 that became the basis of a rigid artistic canon—he continued to write poetry as he chose, much of it in difficult classical forms with obscure allusions to the now-discredited Chinese classics. This contradiction, Mr. Schram, his biographer, noted, "seems to fill him with a mixture of embarrassment and pride."

Chinese Patriot

Looking into Mao's endlessly complex character, Mr. Schram concluded that he was fundamentally a Chinese patriot. Mao dated his attainment of "a certain amount of political consciousness" from the reading of a pamphlet in 1909, when he was 16, that deplored China's "loss" of Korea, Taiwan, Indochina, Burma and other tributary states. In 1936, speaking with Mr. Snow, Mao still recalled the opening sentence of the pamphlet: "Alas, China will be subjugated."

In Mao's case his native xenophobia was to be reinforced by his discovery of Leninism, in which imperialism was blamed for the backwardness of countries like China. But, Mr. Schram wrote, while Mao became "a deeply convinced Leninist revolutionary, and while the categories in which he reasons are Marxist categories, the deepest springs of his personality are, to a large extent, to be found in the Chinese tradition, and China's glory is at least as important to him as is world revolution."

Mr. Schram noted that in the closing

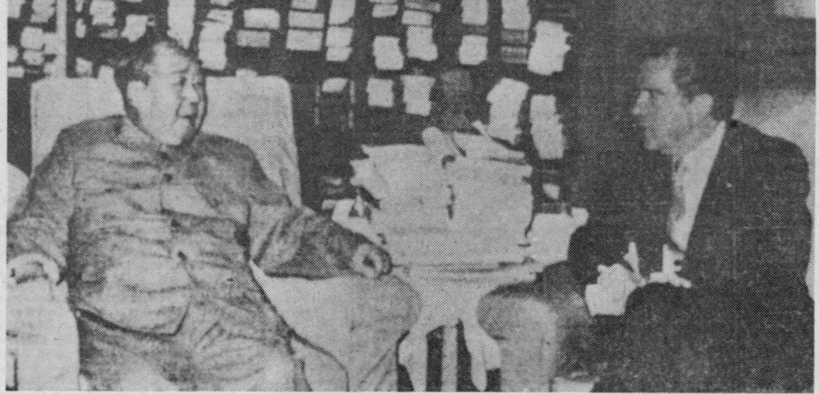

United Press International

He welcomed President Richard M. Nixon to Peking in February 1972. The visit of state of the President of the United States signaled a new era in relations between the two countries.

Magnum/Brian Brake

Chairman Mao outside his residence in Peking in the 1950's. He made his last public appearance in 1971, as his health declined, but he continued to receive many visitors from abroad.

years of Mao's life, he went so far as to subtly play down the importance of Marxism-Leninism in the Chinese revolution, envisioning it only as a storehouse of political techniques. This was in some ways a throwback to the views of 19th-century conservative Chinese imperial officials who wanted to strengthen China against the West but insisted that it borrow only Western "techniques" like gunboats and parliaments without bringing in "Western learning," which might subvert the Chinese essence. As Mao put it in 1965, consciously referring to the 19th-century formulation: "We cannot adopt Western learning as the substance. We can only use Western technology."

'Proletarian' Consciousness

Mao's contribution to Marxism-Leninism lay not in his theoretical writings, which were often plodding and in which he showed little interest himself, but in his Sinification of Marxism. When the Chinese Communists were floundering and faced extinction because of their orthodox concentration on the cities and the proletariat, Mao discovered the peasantry. He succeeded in imposing a party organized along tight Leninist lines and, animated by certain basic Marxist tenets, on a largely peasant base.

With suitable indoctrination, as Mao saw it, both the Chinese peasantry and Chinese intellectuals, who made up much of the party's leadership, could develop a "proletarian" consciousness. As Prof. Benjamin I. Schwartz of Harvard wrote in his pioneering study, "Chinese Communism and the Rise of Mao," it was "a heresy in act never made explicit in theory."

The other basic element in Mao's approach to revolution was his inordinate belief in the power of the human will to overcome material obstacles and his conception that the necessary energy to propel the revolution lay stored among the masses. The potential energy of the peasantry was borne home to him with sudden force in 1927, when he embarked on the investigation of the peasant movement in his home province that formed the basis of his famous report. The liberation Mao found at work in village after village, with peasants overthrowing their landlords, had an enormous impact on him.

Beginning with these two basic insights—the importance of the peasantry to revolution in China and the power the human will—Mao went on to elaborate the strategy and tactics for the entire revolution. First, he recognized the importance of winning the support of the people, who were, as he put it in his widely quoted formulation, like the ocean in which the guerrillas must swim like fish. Talking with André Malraux in 1964, Mao related: "You must realize that before us, among the masses, no one had addressed themselves to women or to the young. Nor, of course, to the peasants. For the first time in their lives, every one of them felt involved."

Careful Rules of Behavior

Similarly, to keep the allegiance of his guerrilla fighters, who received no pay and often inadequate food and weapons, Mao developed careful rules of behavior.

"The reason why the Red Army has been able to carry on in spite of such poor material conditions and such frequent engagements," he wrote, "is its practice of democracy. The officers do not beat the men; officers and men receive equal treatment; soldiers are free to hold meetings and to speak out; trivial formalities have been done away with: and the accounts are open for all to inspect. The soldiers handle the mess arrangements. All this gives great satisfaction to the soldiers."

For military tactics Mao drew on his boyhood reading of China's classic swashbuckling novels such as "The Romance of the Three Kingdoms" and "The Water Margin," which described in vivid detail the exploits and strategems of ancient warriors and bandits. Not surprisingly Mao's military tactics—which were to an important role in Vietnam—bore a close resemblance to those of Sun Tzu, the military writer of the fifth century B.C.

The basic problem was to find a way for a guerrilla force to overcome General Chiang's much larger and better equipped army. To this end Mao revised two principles—concentration of force so that he attacked only when he had a numerical advantage, and surprise.

"We use the few to defeat the many. That is no longer a secret, and in general the enemy is now well acquainted with our method. But he can neither prevent our victories nor avoid his own losses, because he does not know when and where we shall act. This we keep secret. The Red Army generally operates by surprise attacks."

Slogan for the Troops

Mao's military precepts were summed up in a four-line slogan his troops memorized:

"The enemy advances; we retreat.
"The enemy camps; we harass.
"The enemy tires; we attack.
"The enemy retreats; we pursue."

To these Mao was to add the concept of a base area where his guerrillas could rest and replenish their supplies, and from which, over time, they could expand. In the end, this strategy led to victory.

The Moment of Victory

The supreme moment came on Oct. 1, 1949, when Mao, at age 54, stood on the high balcony of Tien An Men, the Gate of Heavenly Peace in Peking through which tribute-bearers had once come to prostrate themselves before the emperors, and proclaimed the People's Republic of China.

Processions had filled the square in front of the scarlet brass-studded gate. The air was chilly with the wind from the Gobi. Mao, wearing a drab cloth cap and a worn tunic and trousers, had Mr. Chou and Marshal Chu with him. Below them the immense throng shouted: "May Mao Tse-tung live 10,000 years!"

Suddenly there came a hush. Sliding up the immense white staff in the square was a small bundle that cracked open as it neared the top to reveal a flag 30 feet broad, blood red, with five yellow stars in the upper left quadrant. Guns roared in salute. On cue the crowd broke out in the new national anthem, and Mao stepped to the microphone amid more cheers.

"The Central Governing Council of the People's Republic of China today assumes power in Peking," he announced. A week before, speaking to the Chinese People's Political Consultative Conference, he said: "Our nation will never again be an insulted nation. We have stood up. Let the domestic and foreign reactionaries tremble before us."

His words came 28 years after he and 11 others founded the Chinese Communist Party in Shanghai. Its membership then was 52. "A small spark can start a prairie fire," Mao once said. It had.

Peasant Origins

Mao Tse-tung was born in a tile-roofed house surrounded by rice fields and low hills in Shaoshan, a village in Hunan Province, in central China, on Dec. 26, 1893. His father, Mao Jen-sheng, was a tall, sturdily built peasant, industrious and thrifty, despotic and high-handed. Through hard work, saving and some small trading he raised himself from being a landless former soldier to what his son later described as the status of a "rich peasant," though in the China of those days that hardly meant being wealthy.

Mao's mother, Wen Chi-mei, was a hardy woman who worked in the house and fields. A Buddhist, she exhibited a warm-hearted kindness toward her children much in contrast to her husband's patriarchal sterness. During famines, when her husband—he disapproved of charity—was not watching, she would give food to the poor who came begging.

The China into which Mao was born was a restive empire on the point of its final breakup, which came in 1911. Since the middle of the 19th century the ruling Ching Dynasty had been beset by rural uprisings, most notably the Taiping revolt in the 1860's, and by the encroachments of foreign powers that challenged China's traditional belief in its superiority.

The mandarins who governed on behalf of the emperor in Peking seemed helpless to stop either the internal decay or the foreign incursions. Corrupt, smug, the product of a rarified examination system based on the Confucian classics, they procrastinated. China had no industry, and its peasants, 85 percent of the population, were mired in poverty and ignorance, subject to the constant threat of starvation and extortionate demands by landlords.

In the Fields at Age 6

At age 6 Mao was set to work in the rice fields by his father, but because he wanted the youngster to learn enough characters to keep the family's accounts, he also sent him to the village primary school. The curriculum was the Confucian Analects, learned by rote in the old style. Mao preferred Chinese novels, "especially stories of rebellions," he later recalled, which he used to read in school, "covering them up with a classic when the teacher walked past."

At 13 Mao left the school, working long hours on the farm during the day and keeping the accounts at night. His father frequently beat Mao and his two younger brothers and gave them only the most meager food, never meat or eggs.

At this point there occurred an incident that Western writers have seized on as a seminal clue to Mao's later life. During a reception Mao's father began to berate him for being lazy and useless. Infuriated, he fled to a nearby pond, threatening to jump in. Eventually the quarrel was resolved by compromise when Mao agreed to kowtow—on one knee only—in exchange for his father's promise to stop the beatings. "Thus the war ended," Mao recalled, "and from it I learned that when I defended my rights by open rebellion my father relented, but when I remained meek and submissive he only cursed and beat me the more."

Some scholars have also noted the possible influence on Mao of growing up in Hunan. A subtropical region, its many rivers and mountains made it a favorite haunt for bandits and secret societies. Hunanese are also famed for their vigorous personalities and their political talents as well as their love of red pepper, and they have produced a disproportionate number of leaders in the 19th and 20th centuries.

Going to Another School

Although out of school, Mao retained his passion for reading in his spare time, and at 16, over his father's opposition, enrolled in a modern higher primary school nearby. It was at this school, in a busy market town, that Mao's real intellectual and political development began. In newspapers a cousin sent him he learned of the nationalistic late 19th-century reformers, and in a book. "Great Heroes of the World," he read about Washington and Napoleon (from his earliest days Mao was fascinated by martial exploits).

Most of his fellow students were sons of landlords, expensively dressed and genteel in manner. Mao had only one decent suit and generally went about in an old, frayed coat and trousers. Moreover, because he had been forced to interrupt his education for several years, he was much older than the others and towered above them. As a result this tall, ragged, uncouth "new boy" met with a mixture of ridicule and hostility. The experience may also have left its mark in his attitude toward the landlord class.

After a year wanderlust took Mao off to the provincial capital, Changsha, where he entered a junior high school. The year was 1911, the time of the overthrow of the Manchu Dynasty, and he was caught up in the political turmoil that swept the country. He cut off his pigtail, a rebellious act, and it was then that he joined a local army unit. After several more months of drifting and scanning classified ads in the press for opportunities, he spent half a year in the provincial library, where he read translations of Adam Smith's "Wealth of Nations," Darwin's "On the Origin of Species" and Rousseau's "Social Contract." He also saw a map of the world for the first time.

In 1913 Mao enrolled in ghe provincial normal school in Changsha, where he received his last five years of formal education. Although it was really only a high school, its standards were high, and Mao was particularly influenced by his ethics teacher, Prof. Yang Chang-chi, whose daughter he was later to marry. Professor Yang who had studied in Japan and Europe, advocated combining Western and Chinese ideas to prod China back to life. Through him Mao soon found himself in touch with the mainstream of intellectual life, which was then caught up in what was called the May 4th Movement, an explosive nationalistic effort to modernize Chinese culture.

His First Published Writing

It was at this time that Mao published his first writing, an article for the popular Peking Magazine Hsin Ching Nien, or New Youth, on the need for physical fitness to build military strength. He also began to display his genius for leadership, setting up a radical student group.

Having graduated from the normal school in 1918, Mao set off that fall for Peking. The timing was critical. It was a period when intellectuals were turning from one Western "ism" to another in search of the latest and most potent elixir to revive their nation In Mao's case, as he later wrote, he arrived just when "the salvos of the October Revolution" in Russia were bringing Marxism to China.

Mao secured a menial job as a library assistant at Peking University under Li Ta-chao, who had published an influential article "The Victory of Bolshevism," and who had just founded the first Marxist study society in China. Mao was still somewhat "confused, looking for a road," but he was becoming "more and more radical."

Early the next spring he left Peking for Shanghai, where he saw off some friends on their way to study in France; he was reluctant to go because of his lack of ability in foreign languages. Over the next two years he moved between Shanghai, Peking and Changsha, teaching part of the time and throwing himself into organizing radical student groups and editing two popular journals that were suppressed by the local warlord government.

A Tendency Toward Populisim

One article he published at the time, "The Great Union of the Popular Masses," which held that the vast majority of Chinese were progressive and constituted a mighty force for change, reflected what Mr. Schram has called Mao's populist tendency. In the biographer's opinion, "this idea can be regarded as the bridge which led him from the relatively conservative and traditionalist nationalism of 1917 to a genuinely Marxist viewpoint."

In the fall of 1920 Mao copied the example of his former boss in Peking, Mr. Li, who had just established a small Communist group there, and formed one in Changsha. The following July Mao and the 11 other delegates met in Shanghai to form the Chinese party.

The first congress was forced by a police raid to flee from its original meeting place in a girls' school to a holiday boat on a nearby lake. Filled with a new sense of zeal, Mao returned to Hunan, where, in orthodox Marxist fashion, he set about organizing labor

Continued on Following Page

China's Path Zigzagged as Mao Tried to Spur Economic Change

NYT Pictures/Audrey Topping

Thousands of Chinese students and gymnasts displaying flash cards of Mao as the helmsman of the country, during a national sports festival in Peking in 1975. Such a demonstration was typical of mass ideological adulation of Mao.

Continued from Preceding Page

unions and strikes. He had found his true vocation as a revolutionary.

The embryonic party fell heavily under the influence of the Russians, who helped engineer an alliance between the Chinese Communists, and the much stronger Nationalists of Sun Yat-sen. Stalin's goals in this, as in all his later moves in China, did not necessarily coincide with those of the Chinese Communists, and herein lay the source of much of the later friction.

Stalin wanted first to secure a friendly buffer on his eastern flank, so had to avoid any upheaval that would invite Western intervention. Second, he sought control over the Chinese party. His policy of alliance worked well enough for the first few years, giving the Communists a chance to expand, but in 1927 it suddenly became a disaster when General Chiang, who had succeeded to leadership of the Nationalists in 1925, turned on the Communists and carried out his massacre.

Patriotism Near the Surface

Perhaps because of Mao's populism and his highly nationalistic feelings, he was one of the most enthusiastic supporters of the alliance. His patriotism was always near the surface.

Criticism of his dual role had a fortuitous result, eventually making him uncomfortable enough so that in 1925 he returned to his native village for a rest and, in the process, encountered a wave of peasant unrest. "Formerly I had not fully realized the degree of class among the peasantry," he told Edgar Snow. From this time on Mao was to take a major interest in the peasantry—first lecturing at the Kuomintang's Peasant Movement training Institute in Canton in 1926, then in early 1927 making his renowned inspection of the Hunanese countryside, and finally in the fall of 1927, after the Communists split with general Chiang, he led his small surviving band of supporters up into the Chingkangshan Mountains to start the search for power all over again—on his terms.

Party Wrangling

The period from 1927 to 1935, when Mao finally won command of the party, was filled with complex wrangling over leadership and policy. The principal figures in the party, who remained in the security of the international settlement in Shanghai, and Stalin kept looking for a "revolutionary upsurge," and in accordance with conventional Marxist dogma planned attacks on cities. Mao, cut off in the countryside, was condemned for his peasant "deviation," though he was not often informed of the latest shifts in line or of his demotions until much later. Twice in 1927 and 1930, he was directed to lead attacks on cities, both ending in catastrophic defeats. Mao was to recall, "Long ago the Chinese Communists had first-hand experience of some of Stalin's mistakes."

The Chingkangshan area where Mao gradually worked out his own strategy was a storybook setting; a range of precipitous mountains on the border between Kiangsi and Hunan, it was an almost impregnable vastness populated only by a few simple villages and groups of bandits. By allying with these bandits and drawing on the peasants, whom he rewarded by reducing rents, Mao built his band of 1,000 soldiers into 100,000 by 1934. A capital was declared at Juichin, in southern Kiangsi.

Mao's very success proved his undoing. In 1931 the party Central Committee moved up to Kiangsi from Shanghai and proceeded to strip him of his posts in the party and army, with Mr. Chou replacing him as chief commissar in 1933. One of Mao's few steadfast supporters at this time was Mr. Teng, whom he was to oust from high position in 1976.

The loss of control was doubly grave because it coincided with the fifth of General Chiang's, encirclement campaigns to wipe out the Communists. The previous efforts had failed in the face of Mao's tactics, withdrawing when outnumbered and then launching surprise attacks in overwhelming force on isolated units. Now the other Communist leaders tried the Nationalists head on, but General Chiang had 700,000 men—a seven-to-one advantage—and on the advice of a Nazi general, Hans von Steeckt, slowly strangled the Communists with a ring of barbed wire and machine-gun emplacements.

Flight Was the Only Answer

The only answer was flight. On Oct. 15, 1934, the main body of the Communist army broke through the Nationalist lines and headed southwest, beginning the Long March. Neither their destination nor their purpose was clear. Some thought of finding a new base area; others, including Mao, spoke of going north to fight the Japanese, who had been expanding farther and farther into China since 1931.

Of the 90,000 Communists who broke out, only 20,000 would eventually reach the new base area in Shensi, in the northwest, over a year and 6,000 miles later. For all its hardships, the Long March both saved and strengthened the Communists, giving them a legend of invincibility, a guerrilla ethic, a firm discipline and unity, and a new leader—Mao. He was finally given command, after several more blunders along the march, when the army stopped at the remote town of Tsunyi, in Kweichow Province, in January 1935. Tsunyi had been captured without firing a shot by using a ruse straight out of The "Romance of the Three Kingdoms," involving captured Kuomintang uniforms and banners.

A New Party and a New State

In Yenan, just below the Great Wall, the area where Chinese civilization originally developed over 3,000 years before, Mao proceeded to build a new party and state fully in his own image. This was a critical period, for the ideas he worked out in Yenan he would turn back to nostalgically in the late 1950's and 60's, when he launched the Great Leap Forward and the Cultural Revolution. Among them were the sending of party cadres down to the countryside for ideological remolding and the stress on self-reliance, mutual aid teams on farms and popularized education.

His mood at this time was perhaps best suggested by his poem "Snow," written in February 1936 shortly after his arrival in the northwest. A ringing affirmation of his links with China's glorious past and his love for the land, it reads:

This is the scene in that northern land;
A hundred leagues are sealed with ice,
A thousand leagues of whirling snow.
On either side of the Great Wall
One vastness is all you see.
From end to end of the great river
The rushing torrent is frozen and lost
The mountains dance like silver snakes.
The highlands roll like waxen elephants,
As if they sought to vie in height
with the Lord of heaven,
And on a sunny day
See how the white-robed beauty
is adorned with rouge, enchantment
beyond compare.
Lured by such great beauty in our landscape
Innumerable heroes have rivaled
one another to bow in homage.
But alas, Chin Shin-huang and Han Wu-ti
were rather lacking in culture,
Tang Tai-tsung and Sung Tai-tsu
had little taste for poetry,
And Genghis Khan,
the favorite son of heaven for a day,
knew only how to bend his bow
to shoot great vultures.
Now they are all past and gone.
To find heroes in the grand manner,
We must look rather in the present.

Incarnation of Resistance

The most decisive stroke by Mao at this time was his genius in making the Communists the incarnation of Chinese resistance to the Japanese. The Japanese invasion, which began in 1931 in Manchuria and culminated in full-scale war in 1937, had provoked an enormous wave of popular resentment.

In the face of this, General Chiang continued to insist that his army would fight the Communists first and deal with the Japanese later. This strategy backfired in December 1936, when pro-Nationalist troops under Chang Hsueh-liang, the young warlord whom the Japanese had driven from Manchuria, kidnapped General Chiang at Sian, near the Communists' base area. He was released only after agreeing to a second united front with the Communists to fight the Japanese.

Although frictions were obvious from the start, the agreement gave Mao a badly needed breathing spell and the chance to expand Communist areas across the whole of North China under the guise of fighting the Japanese. For this the Communists were well prepared by their guerrilla training. By the end of the war in 1945, Communist troops, renamed the Eighth Route Army, had increased to a formidable force of a million men covering an area inhabited by 100 million people.

By an accident of history the Japanese invasion was to prove "perhaps the most important single factor in Mao's rise to power," Mr. Schram concluded in his biography.

Using this time of relative stability to read and write broadly, Mao systematized his thought. Several of his most important books and speeches were produced in the Yenan period, including "On Protracted War," "The Chinese Revolution and the Chinese Communist Party," "On New Democracy," and "On Practice" and "On Contradiction."

'Out of Barrel of a Gun'

One of his most-quoted speeches came in 1938:

"Every Communist must grasp the truth: 'Political power grows out of the barrel of a gun.' Our principle is that the party commands the gun, and the gun will never be allowed to command the party. But it is also true that with guns at our disposal we can really build up the party organization."

In 1942, to discipline the thousands of new officials the party was enrolling and to insure their fidelity to his thought, Mao launched the first rectification campaign. It was the beginning of thought reform, and it was also the start of the cult of Mao. He lent the cult a hand by ordering the study of his works. (In the Cultural Revolution he would promote an article praising his thought that he had helped compose.)

The rectification campaign had another purpose — to end what Mao saw as overreliance on Soviet guidance: "There is no such thing as abstract Marxism, but only concrete Marxism. What we call concrete Marxism is Marxism that has taken on a national form. Consequently the Sinification of Marxism—that is to say, making certain that in all of its manifestations it is imbued with Chinese peculiarities—becomes a problem that must be understood and solved by the whole party." It was a call for independence from Moscow.

For a brief time in 1944-45 Mao and Americans had a short-lived courtship. American diplomats and journalists who were allowed into Yenan at this time, when Washington hoped to bring the Communists and Nationalists together against the Japanese, were invariably impressed by Mao and his army's accomplishments. Mao, for his part, looked to the possibility of winning some of the United States aid that was flowing to General Chiang for use against Tokyo.

"The work which we Communists are carrying on today is the very same work which was carried on earlier in America by Washington, Jefferson and Lincoln," said an encouraging editorial in the official party newspaper on July 4, 1944. But General Chiang's intransigence blocked all efforts in this direction.

When the war ended in 1945, Washington endeavored to play a dual role. On the one hand it helped General Chiang by continuing aid to him and airlifting thousands of his troops to occupy Japanese positions in Manchuria ahead of the advancing Communists. On the other hand it sponsored negotiations for a coalition government. At the urging of the Americans Mao flew to Chungking—his first airplane flight—where he held 43 days of ultimately futile talks with General Chiang. In November 1945 President Harry S. Truman dispatched Gen. George C. Marshall to China as his special envoy; he would continue trying to arrange a cease-fire and coalition government until January 1947, but full-scale civil war had broken out early in 1946.

General Chiang was vastly overconfident. He had American backing, apparent neutrality on the part of Stalin, who was not eager to see Mao win, and a four-to-one numerical advantage. But his army was racked by corruption, punishing inflation and an incompetent officer corps in which promotion was based entirely on loyalty. The general war-weariness and hostility of the populace to the Nationalists also played a role.

By the middle of 1947 the Nationalists' advantage had been reduced to two to one, and by mid-1948 the two sides were almost even. Nationalist generals began surrendering in packs, and within a year it was all over.

In Soviet Path

Over the next five years much of China's development followed the orthodox Soviet model. Mao had proclaimed in 1949 that henceforth China would "lean to one side" in cooperation with the Soviet Union, and so it seemed. The first five-year plan (1953-57) placed emphasis on heavy industry, centralized planning, technical expertise and a large defense buildup in the Soviet pattern. Several technical schools required courses in ballroom dancing, as the Russians had done since Peter the Great.

Part of this may have been the result of what Mao later maintained was his decision in 1949 to retreat to a "second line" and leave "day to-day work" to others. He did this, he said, "out of concern for state security and in view of the lessons of Stalin in the Soviet Union." "Many things are left to other people, so that other people's prestige is built up, and when I go to see God there won't be such a big upheaval in the state," he wrote. "It seems there are some things which the comrades in the first line have not managed too well."

Whatever the case, China was disrupted in 1950 by the Korean War. Although its exact origins are still obscure and controversial, the weight of evidence seems to indicate that it was basically a Soviet initiative and that Mao was not consulted. The war had terrible consequences for the new state. It prompted President Truman to order the defense of Taiwan, which General Chiang had retreated to in 1949; it froze Mao's relations with Washington for two decades; it cost tens of thousands of Chinese lives and funds urgently needed for reconstruction.

The war over, Mao began to grow impatient with the speed of China's development and the way socialism was being introduced. In 1955 he ordered an acceleration in the tempo of collectivization in the countryside. In a speech that July he seemed to be returning to his belief in the power of the human will to overcome material obstacles; it was a precursor of things to come:

"In China 1955 was the year of decision in the struggle between socialism and capitalism. The first half of 1955 was murky and obscured by dark clouds. But in the second half the atmosphere changed completely. Tens of millions of peasant households swung into action. It is as if a ranging tidal wave has swept away all the demons and ghosts."

Mao Shifting His Gears

If over the succeeding years China often appeared to follow a zigzag course, it must have been more than in part a result of shifting of gears as Mao alternated between his warlike, utopian outlook and his more prudent realism in the face of obvious economic difficulties.

In 1956, following Mr. Khrushchev's revelations of Stalin's excesses, the riots in Poland and the uprising in Hungary, Mao took a new tack and proclaimed the policy of "let a hundred flowers bloom." He hoped that some relaxation of tight controls would bring forth useful but limited criticism of the party to avert similar problems in China and at the same time encourage Chinese intellectuals to become good Communists. But he did not intend full-scale liberalization.

In a speech "On the Correct Handling of Contradictions Among the People," in February 1957, Mao outlined his own typically two-sided or contradictory rationale for this. China should have both more freedom and more discipline, an impossibility in Western eyes but not to Mao who saw similar contradictions or dichotomies everywhere. He said, "If there were no contradictions and no struggle, there would be no world, no progress, no life, and there would be nothing at all."

The trick lay in analyzing contradictions correctly. As he put in in 1957: "Within the ranks of our people democracy stands in relation to centralism and freedom to discipline. They are two conflicting aspects of a single entity, contradictory as well as united, and we should not one-sidely emphasize one to the detriment of the other."

Mao's tendency to reason in this fashion owed much to the dialectics of Marxism, but it may also have had its origin in the Chinese theory of yin and yang, the two great alternating forces, which Mao absorbed as a boy.

Vast Outpouring of Criticism

When, contrary to Mao's expectation, the hundred flowers policy led to a vast outpouring of criticism that called the Communist Party itself into question, he quickly switched to the other side of his formula—discipline—and instituted a tough rectification campaign.

It was at this time that he made his second trip to Moscow, in November 1957, and created a sensation by declaring that there was no need to fear nuclear war. "It said that if the worse came to the worst and half of mankind died, the other half would remain, while imperialism would be razed to the ground, and the whole world would become socialist: in a number of years there would be 2.7 billion people again and definitely more."

This accorded with his deeply held belief that men, not machines or weapons, were the decisive factor. In 1947, in an interview, he had declared: "The atom bomb is a paper tiger used by the U.S. reactionaries to scare people. It looks terrible, but in fact it isn't. Of course, the atom bomb is a weapon of mass slaughter, but the outcome of a war is decided by people, not by one or two new types of weapon." It was a guerrrilla's view.

In Mao's recollection, this period, the winter of 1957-58, marked a great watershed in China. His misgivings about the Soviet Union had reached the breaking point, and he resolved to put an end to copying the Russians. He reached back to the wellsprings of his experience in Kiangsi and Yenan, re-emphasizing the countryside and the potential energy of the peasantry to overcome material obstacles. China was to make "a great leap forward." By reorganizing the peasants into communes, Mao would release their energy, vastly increase agricultural production and catch up with the West overnight. It was a vision, not a plan.

As Mao described it: "China's 600 million people have two remarkable peculiarities; they are, first of all, poor, and secondly blank. That may seem like a bad thing, but it is really a good thing. Poor people want change, want to do things, want revolution. A clean sheet of peaper has no blotches, and so the newest and most beautiful words can be written on it."

All China went to work at a fever pitch. Peasants set up backyard blast furnaces to make their own steel, the symbol of industrialization. Cadres became dizzy with success and reported a 100 percent jump in agricultural production in a single year. A jingle by peasants in Hunan caught the mood:

"Setting up a people's commune is like going to heaven. The achievements of a single night surpass those of several millennia."

It was not so easy. Terrible dislocations ensued, food grew scarce and there was even some starvation. It took three years to restore the economy.

Leader Attacked

These steps led to the first serious challenge to Mao's leadership since the early 1930's. At a Central Committee meeting in the summer of 1959 at the mountain resort of Lushan, he was boldly criticized by Peng Teh-huai, then Minister of Defense. Under the impact of Mr. Peng's attacks, Mao became tense and irritable. "Now that you have said so much, let me say something, will you," he finally told the group. "I have taken sleeping pills three times, but I cannot to seep."

Candidly accepting some of the onus for the disaster, he declared: "The chaos was in a grand scale, and I take responsibility. I am a complete outsider when it comes to economic construction, and I understand nothing about industrial planning."

But with devasting tactical skill Mao also counterattacked and ousted Mr. Peng from his post. This done, Mao was satisfied to leave the running of China to others, and over the next few years concentrated on foreign affairs, particularly the growing quarrel with Moscow.

Foreign policy often seemed to swing almost as wildly as domestic political campaigns; from intervention in Korea to the Bandung (Indonesia) conference and the five principles of peaceful coexistence, from calls for world revolution to President Nixon's trip and the Shanghai communiqué. Behind these shifts, scholars agree, it was Mao himself who made all the fundamental decisions, even if Mr. Chou was often China's ambassador to the world.

Moreover, underneath these swings Mao adhered to several deeply held ideas.

First, China would pursue a strictly defensive policy; it would not, for example, intervene in Vietnam. "Others may come and attack us, but we shall not fight outside our borders," Mao told the Central Committee, "I say we will not be provoked."

Helping Third World Revolts

Second, he was committed to supporting revolutionary movements in the third world. But with his penchant for reasoning in contradictions, he worked out a way of conducting correct diplomatic relations with a government at the same time as he aided Communist guerrillas dedicated to overthrowing it.

Third, Mao was dedicated to making China a great power again, and he recognized early that only by building it up economically and militarily would the imperialists, led by the United States, come to accept it. Time proved him right. In the mid-1970's, after the thaw in relations with the United States, China's formerly hostile neighbors in Southeast Asia followed suit.

At the same time Mao became increasingly obsessed with the Soviet Union, both as an external threat and as a heretical internal system that might subvert the Chinese revolution. After the 1959 encounter with Mr. Peng, Mao may have already felt that the party had betrayed him and was in the hands of the bureaucrats who wanted to follow the Soviet example of gradual growth based on a party elite, material incentives and heavy industry. In addition, Mao came to have doubts about China's youth; as he told Mr. Malraux in August 1965, "This youth is showing dangerous tendencies."

"Humanity left to its own does not necessarily re-establish capitalism, but it does re-establish inequality," he said. "The forces tending toward the creation of new classes are powerful."

"Revolution and children have to be trained if they are to be properly brought up," he added. "Youth must be put to the test."

The Test: Cultural Revolution

The test, which Mao launched that fall, was the Cultural Revolution. In many ways it was the longest culmination of his life, bringing together his favorite themes. "Once class struggle is grasped, miracles are possible," he remarked not long before the start of the Cultural Revolution in what might be his motto. The movement was also his ultimate revolt against the influence of the Soviet Union—its elitism and bureaucracy.

Mao remained uncertain of what would follow him. As he told Edgar Snow in 1965, in 1,000 years even Marx and Lenin might "appear rather ridiculous."

Last year, in a poem addressed to the dying Chou En-lai, he put it more poignantly:

Loyal parents who sacrificed so much for
the nation
Never feared the ultimate fate.
Now that the country has become red,
who will be its guardian?
Our mission, unfinished,
may take a thousand years
The struggle tires us, and our hair is gray.

The poem concludes: "You and I, old friends, can we just watch our efforts be washed away?"

United Press International

The chairman welcoming Prime Minister Chou En-lai on return from a diplomatic mission to the Soviet Union in 1964. Mao, the party ideologue, worked intimately with Chou, the practical statesman, who died last January.

"All the News That's Fit to Print."

The New York Times.

LATE CITY EDITION
POSTSCRIPT
Cloudy, little change in temperature today.
Temperatures Yesterday—Max., 83; Min., 66.

VOL. LXXXVI.....No. 29,032. Entered as Second-Class Matter, Postoffice, New York, N. Y. NEW YORK, TUESDAY, JULY 20, 1937. TWO CENTS in New York City. | THREE CENTS Within 200 Miles. | FOUR CENTS Elsewhere Except in 7th and 8th Postal Zones.

LEHMAN CALLS COURT PLAN DANGEROUS AND ASKS WAGNER TO VOTE AGAINST IT; PROPONENTS, RESENTFUL, PRESS FIGHT

ROOSEVELT IS FIRM

He Maintains Silence on Position Taken by the Governor

'STAB IN BACK,' SAYS AIDE

Meanwhile Steps Are Mapped to Meet Senate Show-Down on Recommitting the Bill

PARLEY AT WHITE HOUSE

Keenan Flies Back to Capital Ahead of Robinson Train and Delivers an Envelope

Special to THE NEW YORK TIMES.

WASHINGTON, July 19.—Facing a crucial test of its strength and, possibly, an irreparable party breach in the bitter fight over the Judiciary Reorganization Bill, the administration was determined tonight to fight to the last ditch to prevent an effort to kill the measure for this session by having it recommitted to the Judiciary Committee for further consideration. Events today indicated that the administration considers such an attempt by opponents of the bill inevitable.

The decision to pit its full strength against such a move appeared to be the only tangible result of a conference on legislative plans at the White House. Present with Mr. Roosevelt were Attorney General Cummings and Senator Hugo Black of Alabama.

With Senate leaders in the fight on their way back to the capital for resumption of debate on the issue tomorrow, the President gave over most of the afternoon to study of the factors involved.

As to Gov. Lehman's Stand

The administration was represented as feeling "deep resentment" over the position taken by Governor Lehman of New York in opposition to the court reorganization bill. An official high in the administration, who had talked with Mr. Roosevelt during the day, but who would not be quoted, declared that the Governor's letter to Senator Wagner was "a stab in the back" for the administration.

Officially, the White House and other quarters in the executive branch followed the policy of ignoring the incident. At the White House Stephen T. Early, one of the President's secretaries, announced that there would be "no comment."

Asked whether the White House might make public the President's reply to the letter which Governor Lehman said he had sent to Mr. Roosevelt some time ago, Mr. Early said there had been no reply so far as he was aware, and that if there had been, it probably was in the form of a personal note to the Governor.

Senator Copeland of New York commented:

"I'm glad to hear it. Governor Lehman is a patriot and a good American and would be against anything that would be a blot on our national life."

Representative Fish, Republican of New York, observed that "the Governor has driven another nail in the coffin of the President's plan."

After being closeted with Mr.

Continued on Page Two

Gov. Lehman's Letter

Special to THE NEW YORK TIMES.

ALBANY, July 19.—Governor Lehman's letter to Senator Wagner, stating his opposition to the President's Court Reorganization Bill and urging him to vote against it, read as follows:

Honorable Robert F. Wagner, the Senate, Washington, D. C.

My dear Senator Wagner:

I am writing to you as a citizen of the State of New York, which you represent in the United States Senate, to voice my opposition to the Court Bill and to express the hope that you will vote against it.

The President is already familiar with my views with regard to the bill. Several months ago I wrote to him that I believe its enactment would not be in the best interest of the country. In the months that have passed since then my convictions have become strengthened.

Like many others I have frequently felt keen disappointment that important legislative measures have been declared unconstitutional by a slim and unconvincing margin in the Supreme Court. And yet I believe that the orderly and deliberate processes of government should not be sacrificed merely to meet an immediate situation.

From the broad standpoint of the public interest whatever immediate gain might be achieved through the proposed change in the court would, in my opinion, be far more than offset by a loss of confidence in the independence of the courts and in governmental procedure.

I have whole-heartedly supported most of the President's social program both while he was Governor of New York and since he became President of the United States. His program taken as a whole has in my opinion represented the greatest step forward in social reform that any nation has undertaken for many years. I look forward to the opportunity of continuing to support his courageous leadership in matters that are in the interest of the social well-being of our people.

This bill, however, I believe to be contrary to their interest. Its enactment would create a greatly dangerous precedent which could be availed of by future less well-intentioned administrations for the purpose of oppression or for the curtailment of the constitutional rights of our citizens.

Very sincerely yours,
HERBERT H. LEHMAN.

LETTER IS SURPRISE

Governor as a 'Citizen' Takes Stand Opposing Old Friend and Ally

FEARS FUTURE OPPRESSION

'Orderly Processes' Should Not Be 'Sacrificed' to Meet an Immediate Need

MANY CONGRATULATE HIM

Messages Pour Into Albany, Some Acclaiming His 'Courage' —Senate Foes Cheered

Special to THE NEW YORK TIMES.

ALBANY, July 19.—Governor Lehman came out today in opposition to the Supreme Court Reorganization Bill of his close personal and political friend, President Roosevelt. He urged Senator Wagner to vote against the measure, which he felt would create a "greatly dangerous precedent."

The Governor stated his views in a letter to Senator Wagner, which was made public at the executive office here after being telephoned from Hot Springs, Va., where Mr. Lehman is passing a vacation.

"The President is already familiar with my views in regard to the bill," the Governor wrote. "Several months ago I wrote to him that I believe its enactment would not be in the best interests of the country. In the months that have passed since then my convictions have become strengthened."

Holds Courts Would Lose

Mr. Lehman took the stand that "whatever immediate gain might be achieved" through the Court Bill would be "far more than offset by a loss of confidence in the independence of the courts and in governmental procedure."

The Governor restated his belief that President Roosevelt's broad, general program "represented the greatest step forward in social reform that any nation has undertaken in many years." He added:

"I look forward to the opportunity of continuing to support his courageous leadership in matters that are in the interest of the social well-being of our people.

"This bill, however, I believe to be contrary to their interests. Its enactment would create a greatly dangerous precedent which could be availed of by future less well-intentioned administrations for the purpose of oppression or for the curtailment of the constitutional rights of our citizens."

The Governor's letter came as a distinct surprise, and according to word received here may have a profound impact on the fate of the Court Bill, now facing an early vote in the Senate.

Opponents of the proposal hailed the letter as a sharp blow to the President's plan to force it through.

Many Commend His Action

"Scores" of congratulatory telegrams poured into the Executive offices, according to the Governor's secretary, Walter T. Brown.

Oswald D. Heck, Speaker of the Assembly, the only Republican here who would discuss the Governor's action, said:

"I am surprised. I am pleased that one of the closest friends of the President felt called upon to oppose the President in this most important legislation."

The action of Governor Lehman in making public the letter on the Court Bill constituted his first opposition to any major proposal in President Roosevelt's program since their personal and political friendship began in 1928.

The two men have traveled down the same political path together since they were elected Governor and Lieutenant Governor, and they kept to the same path when Mr. Roosevelt went on to the White House and Mr. Lehman moved into the executive office.

Had Not Confided in Friends

Governor Lehman had given no hint of his plan to take a public stand. He is known to have had strong doubts of the wisdom of the President's policy ever since the original plan was broached. Persons who talked with him in private quickly became aware of that.

He kept his peace, however, as far as public statements went, for he was said to have been conscious as Governor of the effect public

Continued on Page Three

NANKING RECEIVES A 'FINAL WARNING' FROM TOKYO ARMY

Japanese General Leaves After Demand That China's Troops Retreat to Stations

CHIANG IS READY FOR WAR

Leader Urges 'Fight to the Bitter End' Against Seizure of More Territory

OFFICIALS BEGIN PARLEY

Chinese Note Suggests Peace Efforts Through the Usual Diplomatic Channels

The Chinese Situation

NANKING—The Chinese Foreign Minister and Japanese Ambassador conferred after the Japanese Army had issued a "last warning" that Chinese troops must be withdrawn in the north. China in a note proposed settlement by diplomatic procedure. Page 1.

SHANGHAI — Generalissimo Chiang Kai-shek informed the Chinese nation that it must not accept the Japanese demands even if forced into a defensive war. He said if hostilities began "we must fight to the bitter end." Page 16.

TIENTSIN—China continued to send troops northward and more Japanese arrived. Well-informed circles believed the Japanese Army was protracting negotiations until it got ready to strike. Page 16.

TOKYO—War was seen unless China abandoned her policy of obstruction. It was believed that the Chinese Army was ready to fight. Page 15.

'Last Warning' From Japanese

By The Associated Press.

NANKING, Tuesday, July 20.—A meeting was arranged today between the Chinese Foreign Minister, Dr. Wang Chung-hui, and Shinrokuro Hidaka, the Japanese Chargé d'Affaires, in a new effort to find a peace formula in North China.

Their conference was called under the pressure of what the Japanese Domei news agency said was the Japanese Army's "last warning" that the hostilities in the Tientsin-Peiping area must be ended on Tokyo's terms.

Chinese commanders were warned by the virtual ultimatum of Major Gen. Seiichi Kita, the Japanese military attaché in China, the news agency said, that they must "disregard minor differences" and "save the situation by the prompt withdrawal of Central Government troops and air forces to their original stations."

Previously Mr. Hidaka had been reported, apparently without basis, as having demanded Chinese acceptance of Japan's terms by last midnight.

Chinese Note to Japan

The Chinese Foreign Office disclosed the contents of a note Dr. Wang sent to the Japanese Embassy. It was said to have been written in part by Generalissimo Chiang Kai-shek, head of the Central Government, who has remained at Kuling, a Summer resort on the Yangtse River. The note follows:

Since the outbreak of the Wanping incident [the first clash west of Peiping July 7] China, desirous of not aggravating the situation or provoking conflict with Japan, repeatedly has declared its readiness to seek a settlement by peaceful means.

The Japanese, while professing anxiety not to see the situation aggravated, at the same time have dispatched large numbers of troops into Hopei. The movements of Japanese troops, which have not ceased, indicate the clear intention of Japan to resort to force.

Circumstances have forced China to take precautionary measures of self-defense, but the National Government has not relaxed its efforts for peace.

On July 12 Foreign Minister Wang Chung-hui proposed to the Japanese a mutual cessation of military movements and withdrawal of the troops of both sides to their original positions. It is regretted that no reply to this proposal has been received.

China wishes to reiterate its desire for a peaceful settlement. It is therefore proposed that the two parties jointly fix a date on which both sides simultaneously shall cease military movements and withdraw their respective armed forces to the positions occupied prior to the incident.

In view of the peaceful aspirations the Japanese Government has voiced, China trusts this proposal will be acceptable.

Regarding the procedure to be

Continued on Page Sixteen

Eden Warns Italy of War In a Mediterranean Row

Asserts Britain Would Fight to Defend Her Interests—He Is Firm on Spain—Clamor in Commons on Guns Facing Gibraltar

By FERDINAND KUHN Jr.

Special Cable to THE NEW YORK TIMES.

LONDON, July 19.—In more forthright language than he has ever used officially before, Foreign Secretary Anthony Eden warned Italy in the House of Commons today that Britain would fight, if necessary, to defend her interests in the Mediterranean Sea and along the road to India.

The warning was unmistakable, although Mr. Eden was careful not to be provocative in his words or in his manner. Britain has no thought of challenging the interests of other powers, he said, and she believes in keeping the Mediterranean highway open to all.

"The word 'vendetta' has no English equivalent," he declared, and since the word is Italian, it was obvious that he intended that his reassurance be heard in Rome.

But his speech underlined every warning that had gone from London since the start of Anglo-Italian tension in 1935. It went further, in fact, for it served notice for the first time that Britain would not tolerate Italian domination over any part of the Arabian peninsula.

"It has always been and it is today a major British interest," Mr. Eden said, "that no great power should establish itself on the eastern shore of the Red Sea. I need hardly add that this applies to ourselves no less than to others."

Official sources explained later that this passage had been included in Mr. Eden's speech at the direct request of King Ibn Saud of Saudi Arabia, who has been increasingly uneasy in recent weeks over apparent Italian efforts to establish a protectorate over Yemen, just across the Red Sea from Italy's new empire in Africa.

But apart from the reference to the Red Sea, there was immense conjecture at Westminster tonight over the reasons behind Mr. Eden's new show of firmness toward Rome. What had induced it, all of a sudden? His own Foreign Office has kept anxious eyes upon

Continued on Page Seventeen

MARCONI IS DEAD OF HEART ATTACK

Wireless Inventor Succumbs at His Home in Rome at the Age of 63

HIS CAREER STARTED AT 21

He Patented His System in 1896 and Then Went From Success to Success

By The Associated Press.

ROME, Tuesday, July 20.—Guglielmo Marconi, inventor of the wireless, died unexpectedly last night of a heart attack at his home here. He was 63 years old.

At 21 Took Up Wireless.

Guglielmo Marconi's father wanted him to study music in Bologna after he was graduated from the university there in 1895, but the young man had grown interested in the practical possibilities of certain invisible electric waves. He had seen them demonstrated in the physics laboratory as the latest scientific curiosity. They passed through free space and acted on a detector at the other side of the room.

He was then 21, and was convinced that these waves which had been discovered seven years previously by Heinrich Hertz, thirty-one years after Clerk Maxwell had predicted them mathematically, could be used to transmit telegraphic dots and dashes over a distance without the use of wires.

He was right from the very beginning.

In 1895, with a spark coil as a sender of Hertzian waves and with a receiver invented some years previously by Edouard Branley of France and known as a coherer, he established the first radio station in his father's home in Pontecchio, near Bologna, and sent telegraphic messages more than a mile without wires.

He patented his system next year in London and demonstrated it for the British Postoffice Department over distances up to nine miles. He had no difficulty in finding backers in London, who organized Marconi's Wireless Telegraph Company, Ltd., in 1897.

The backers regarded it as an opportunity such as had not appeared since the American inventor, Samuel F. B. Morse, with a similar practical turn of mind, had taken the electromagnet out of the physics laboratory and given the world a telegraph and cable system of communications.

From Success to Success.

With the backing of his company, Marconi's development of wireless telegraphy proceeded from success to success. In 1898 he established wireless communication across the English Channel with France; the wireless was used in naval manoeuvres over distances up to seventy-four miles; and it had its first application in the sending of a rescue call at sea when the English lightship East Goodwin was run down by a liner. The lightship, which had been equipped with an experimental wireless set to communicate with the South Foreland Lighthouse, was able to send a wireless message for help to the lighthouse in time to have lifeboats sent to the rescue.

Marconi's results so far had been

Continued on Page Eleven

SCOTTSBORO TRIAL DROPS DEATH PLEA

State Changes Front for the First Time in 6½-Year History of Cases

LENIENCY FOR ALL HINTED

But No Assurance Is Given That It Will Go Beyond Present Defendant

By F. RAYMOND DANIELL

Special to THE NEW YORK TIMES.

DECATUR, Ala., July 19.—The first sign of a let-up in the prosecution of nine Negroes arrested six and a half years ago on a charge of attacking two white girls on a Southern Railway freight train came today in Morgan County Court when the State agreed to waive the death penalty in the case of Andy Wright.

Thus Wright, being retried as a sequel to the United States Supreme Court order setting aside the verdict of a Jackson County jury condemning him to death, became the first of the nine defendants to face a jury without having his life placed in jeopardy under the Alabama statute which permits juries to determine whether the penalty for the type of crime involved in these cases be prison for ten years or the electric chair.

Wright, sitting with his back against the wall behind the table at which sat his chief counsel, Samuel Leibowitz of New York, heard the news of the State's change of front without a flicker of expression. Only last week a fellow-defendant, Clarence Norris, was convicted and sentenced to death. Ninety miles away in Birmingham, Heywood Patterson, saved from death three times by reversals of jury verdicts, waits in jail for his lawyers to appeal from his most recent sentence of seventy-five years' imprisonment.

Quest for Jury Is Begun

Mr. Leibowitz and the attorneys for the State, Thomas S. Lawson, Assistant Attorney General; Melvin C. Hutson, the Circuit Solicitor here, and H. C. Bailey, prosecutor of the original trials at Scottsboro, in Jackson County, refused to comment when asked if the attitude taken today should be considered as precedent for the six cases still awaiting trial.

They proceeded with the selection of a jury, with the defense exercising the same meticulous care as if this were still a capital case.

Once the State had consented to waive the death penalty in Wright's case, however, Mr. Leibowitz agreed to the dismissal of a special venire of sixty-five Morgan County citizens called to supplement the regular panel of thirty-five. Many of this panel of thirty-five were absent today, probably because of the heavy thunderstorms which struck Northern Alabama last night and this morning, turning roads into muddy swamps but lowering the torrid temperatures.

When Judge W. W. Callahan recessed court until 9 A. M. tomorrow, progress in the selection of the jury had been halted by challenges for cause which left the panel of veniremen short of the required thirty. The hour was too late for the Sheriff to round up the additional ten veniremen deemed necessary by Judge Callahan to conform with the letter of the law.

"It's all right with me," Mr.

Continued on Page Twenty-four

REBELS MASS MEN TO WEST OF MADRID TO INTENSIFY DRIVE

Franco Estimated to Have 42,000 in the Lines and 84,000 in Reserve

LOYALISTS WARY OF TRAP

Guard Against Circling Move as Insurgents Shell Towns North, South and East of Brunete

The Spanish Situation

MADRID—The Insurgents massed heavy forces for a new assault. They were reported to have 42,000 in the lines and 84,000 in reserve. Loyalist lines were severely shelled in preparation. Page 1.

SALAMANCA—General Franco, celebrating "a year of triumphs," spoke of a restoration of the monarchy with Don Juan as king. He said the Loyalist offensive at Madrid had "collapsed." Page 13.

BERLIN—A series of trade agreements has been completed between General Franco and Germany. The Reich will be able to get immediate deliveries of iron and copper ores, of which she is in urgent need. Page 13.

Rebels Gather Big Army

By HERBERT L. MATTHEWS

Wireless to THE NEW YORK TIMES.

MADRID, July 19.—After yesterday's fierce fighting, which has had no equal in Spain's civil war, both sides struggled with less energy today as they gathered strength for the crucial activity of the next few days. All the effort the Insurgents expended against the government lines in the salient occupied last week has gained them nothing, for tonight the lines remained unchanged.

Although negative in its results, the Loyalists' accomplishment in withstanding thus far this greatest of all attacks has been highly significant. Just to hold what has been gained would represent a considerable victory.

Today was one chiefly of artillery fire on the part of the Insurgents, who in that way covered the absence of pressure by their troops. Even in the air action was relatively tame, for there was only one small combat in which an Insurgent pursuit plane was shot down. Observers outside this city saw a Rebel bomber brought down by anti-aircraft guns, but for some reason it has not been included in the Air Ministry's communiqué.

Air Losses Revised

Although it may seem strange to say so after the figures given out yesterday, it is true that the Loyalist general staff and air command are leaning over backward to make no claims that have not been carefully checked. This correspondent has tried to do some checking today on yesterday's great aerial combat, which will certainly take its place among the most significant events of this war. I gave the most conservative figures obtainable—twenty-three Rebel planes lost to the government's four. Now there seems to be no doubt that twenty-six to twenty-eight Rebel planes were shot down while the Loyalists lost only one.

The Rebels were flying their newest model planes, which none of the government's pilots had ever seen before. Some of the Loyalist pilots were Spaniards who had just completed training and were getting their baptism of fire.

Aviators here can hardly talk coherently about the great day yesterday. Most of the speculation centers on the reasons for it. Some think the Insurgents made a great tactical error in breaking formation early in the fight. Others be-

Continued on Page Twelve

Building Strike Threatens on Federal Jobs To Back Union Painters' Walk-Out in Capital

Special to THE NEW YORK TIMES.

WASHINGTON, July 19.—A strike of the more than 5,000 building trades workers now employed on Federal construction in this city appeared a possibility tonight as members of the local painters' union began to walk out on projects handled by the procurement division of the Treasury, in sympathy with painters who struck at Internal Revenue buildings.

The trouble started in the morning, when a score of painters at the Internal Revenue building went on strike, charging that William Wilson & Sons of Atlanta, painting and plastering contractor, gave preference to non-union painters in picking men.

Work had not started on the City Postoffice building, but it was stated that Coones & Raptis, New York firm having the painting contract on that building, intended to use non-union labor.

Union spokesmen threatened a general strike on all Federal projects unless the contractors on the Internal Revenue and City Postoffice jobs were required to use union labor.

A major strike on District of Columbia school construction, involving $850,000 of work, was blocked in the afternoon, when Dan I. Sultan, District engineer commissioner, ordered work stopped on two schools where non-union labor was being employed.

Upon this order, union officials agreed to send their men back to work on three other school jobs where the union men went out in protest. The commissioner acted under the Bacon-Davis act, which requires that workers be employed at the prevailing wage scale.

C. I. O. VOTE BARRED IN 2 B. M. T. UNITS

Labor Board Rules Motormen and Signalmen Already Have Proper Representation

STRIKE DANGER AVERTED

Union Accepts Principle of the Decision Putting Burden of Proof of Fitness on It

Acting as delegate with full powers of the State Labor Relations Board under the Doyle-Neustein act, the City Industrial Relations Board ruled yesterday against the Transport Workers Union, C. I. O. affiliate, when it decided that the 1,200 motormen and signalmen employed by the B. M. T. shall be excluded from an election of the company's employes. The balloting will be held under the auspices of the State board to determine the collective bargaining agent or agents for the employes.

The election, in which more than 10,000 B. M. T. employes will participate, will be held next week. The exact date will be set as soon as other arrangements are completed. The voting will be probably in a city armory.

Union Accepts Decision

Although the Transport Workers Union had insisted that the motormen and signalmen be included in the poll, it accepted the board's decision. By this action the union removed all possibility of a strike on the B. M. T. subway and elevated lines arising from the question of union representation.

The B. M. T. motormen and signalmen, who are affiliated, respectively, with the Brotherhood of Locomotive Engineers and the Brotherhood of Railway Signalmen, had threatened "to resist to the last" any effort to include them in the proposed election.

Their contention was that the brotherhoods were their bona-fide collective bargaining agents, through whom they had made contracts with the company. The contracts have fifteen months still to run. The Transport Workers Union attempted to challenge the validity of these contracts.

In its decision, made known by Professor Carl L. Llewellyn of Columbia University, chairman, the City Industrial Board found that the contracts were properly drawn in accordance with union procedure and the brotherhood constitutions, and declared them valid. The board ruled also that the Transport Workers Union had failed to produce prima facie evidence that the majority of the motormen and signalmen desire to displace the brotherhoods as their representatives. An important statement in the board's ruling was that duly chosen representatives to be effective "must at the minimum be protected from challenge based on any but major doubts."

The board's decision was regarded as important in that it circumscribed the possibility of challenge by another organization without

Continued on Page Six

TAMMANY LEADERS SEEK TO END SPLIT

Hines and 2 Others Reported on Visit to Dooling to Warn Him of Ouster Move

COPELAND TO STAY IN RACE

Four County Chiefs Designate Taylor and Max Schneider to Fill Out Ticket

Members of the Tammany Hall executive committee held several conferences yesterday on means of averting what many of the district leaders believe will be a disastrous primary fight, if James J. Dooling, Tammany leader, insists on supporting Senator Royal S. Copeland for the Democratic Mayoralty nomination.

Several leaders declared that no solution of the problem had been reached, but it was reliably reported that James J. Hines, Charles W. Culkin and William P. Kenneally, the chairman of the executive committee, left one of the meetings to go to Mr. Dooling's home at Belle Harbor for a show-down.

It was said that Mr. Hines, one of the most powerful leaders in Tammany Hall and an original supporter of Grover A. Whalen for Mayor, intended to demand that Mr. Dooling withdraw Senator Copeland, if that was possible, or else face an ouster move at the meeting of the Tammany executive committee Thursday night. Mr. Hines and his friends up to yesterday had been supporting Mr. Dooling's leadership in preference to permitting Christopher D. Sullivan and his friends to gain control of the Hall.

Dooling's Friends Silent

Friends of Mr. Dooling declined to comment on the report last night, and neither Mr. Hines, Mr. Culkin nor Mr. Kenneally had been reached up to last evening. The results of the meeting are scheduled to be reported to the district leaders today.

The leaders left before Senator Copeland in Washington announced that he was in the race to stay and that he would enter the Republican primaries as well as the Democratic, if the Republican leaders desired to nominate him. They left also before Governor Lehman's message to Senator Wagner on the Court Bill was made public. District leaders who had hoped that Mr. Copeland would withdraw from the race were confused, Tammany appeared to be in a turmoil, and none ventured to say what connection the Lehman statement might have with the city fight.

The Lehman letter was regarded as certain to have some effect on the local situation, confusing the New Deal and anti-New Deal issues, and making it impossible for politicians and observers alike to forecast with any degree of certainty the eventual line-up in the local battle.

Friends of Mr. Dooling, replying to the contention of Bronx County

Continued on Page Ten

MARCONI IS DEAD OF HEART ATTACK

Continued From Page One

regarded by scientists as interesting, but not surprising. To them Marconi was and always remained simply an engineer making practical use of electrical science. To engineers, on the other hand, Marconi in 1900 seemed to have reached the effective limit of wireless when he telegraphed without wires through a distance of 150 miles.

Since his Hertzian waves traveled at the speed of light, they were assumed to have the characteristics of light, which could not be sent over the horizon to reach a receiver on the other side of the world.

Nevertheless the Marconi Company built for him a powerful station at Poldhu in Cornwall in 1900, and Marconi crossed the ocean to St. John's, Nfld., in 1901 to listen for the first transatlantic wireless message.

Not Bound by Theory.

His attitude toward theorists who were sure they knew what could not be done practically with a natural phenomenon was expressed then and re-stated at various times during his life. "I do not think it wise to believe in the limitations indicated by purely theoretical considerations or even by calculations," he said. "As we have learned from experience, they are often based on insufficient knowledge of all the relevant factors. I believe, in spite of adverse forecasts, in trying new lines of research, however unpromising they may seem at first."

He was 27 when he established himself with his receiving apparatus and two technical assistants, G. S. Kent and P. W. Paget, on top of Signal Hill outside St. John's Harbor, and cabled to his operator at Poldhu to start sending a set of signals according to a prearranged program at 11:30 A. M. and 2:30 P. M., Newfoundland time.

The signal was to be the letter "S," which in Marconi's code is made by three dots; and it was to be sent in a definite time pattern to avoid mistaking any electrical disturbance for the signals.

In a howling gale on Dec. 12, 1901, Marconi sent up a kite which raised 400 feet of bare copper wire into the air as the antenna to intercept the message which other engineers said he could not send around the curved earth, across 1,700 miles of ocean.

Transatlantic Attempt Wins.

The first attempt was a complete success. There was no doubt about it. But Marconi waited until the next day and repeated the test, with the same success, before announcing to the world that transatlantic wireless communication had come into existence.

On both sides of the Atlantic the general public accepted the announcement with little excitement, under the apparent impression that the transmission of signals not confined to wires, but broadcast to the infinite, would have little or no effect on their lives.

Since then the date of this first transatlantic message has been elevated into the opening of a new epoch in human history, in which the world has been brought within the instant sound of a man's voice, whether it be a King, a Pope, a President, a dictator or an explorer flying over the Pole.

The development was rapid. The first ocean daily newspaper which is now a regular equipment of all liners was published on the Campania in 1904. When Marconi in 1907 announced that he was ready to establish commercial wireless between America and Europe, there was a sharp drop in cable shares. In 1910 Congress ordered all vessels of more than fifty passengers to carry wireless apparatus for sending distress calls.

Meanwhile, electrical engineers were rapidly filling in the technical apparatus of radio communication, and with the development of the radio tube, wireless messages which had been confined to the dots and dashes of the telegraphic code, became commercial telephone conversations about 1912, and broadcasting took its start experimentally with the World War.

Thirty years after the first transatlantic message, the Pope, in February, 1931, addressed a broadcast message in Latin and Italian to the entire world.

Even before the World War, radio was a new world industry, and the courts of every nation were busy deciding patent suits and complaints of investors who felt they had suffered in some way or other during the radio boom.

Marconi, however, remained personally absorbed in the engineering side of radio, proceeding like his friend Edison to deal with the broad problems still to be solved or the advances to be made, such as static and short-wave transmission, with the help of the technical resources of the world in which radio engineering had become a separate profession.

In 1930 he was responsible for directing the attention of radio engineers to the use of ultra-short waves, which had been neglected on the ground that they were too close to light and could not travel around the horizon. Within a few years he had demonstrated that they could be transmitted five times further than might be assumed with light waves, and were little affected by fading and static.

Most of his work was done on his floating laboratory, the steam yacht Elettra, on which he could place himself on the face of the ocean in experimental positions with respect to land stations terrestrial obstruction, fogs or whatever he was attacking.

He remained an optimist about what could be done with radio. His prediction of transatlantic telephony was thirteen years ahead of the accomplishment. He expected television by 1926, and he expected that power would be transmitted eventually by a directed radio beam.

Promised New Surprise.

In April, 1934, he startled his associates in London with an unexplained promise: "I hope to surprise you in a year or two as I surprised you by transmission across the ocean in 1901."

Honors were heaped on him beyond enumeration during his lifetime. In 1909 the Nobel Prize in Physics was awarded to him, as well as the Albert Medal of the Royal Society of Arts, and in the United States, the Franklin Medal.

In 1914 the King of Italy appointed him a Senator, an honor reserved by his country for the highest achievement.

In 1931, fourteen nations of the world joined in a broadcast celebration of the thirtieth anniversary of the new epoch which began with his first transatlantic message.

Marconi's life was devoted to radio. According to his own explanation in 1934, he took everything else on faith.

"There is no doubt," he said then, "that from the time humanity began to think, it has occupied itself with its origin and its future, which undoubtedly is the problem of life. The inability of science to solve it is absolute. That would be terribly frightening were it not for faith."

Although he was born in Italy, at Bologna, on April 25, 1874, he was a citizen of the world through his travels. His father was an Italian banker and his mother was Anna Jameson, an Irish woman. He spoke English as perfectly as Italian.

In 1906 he married the Hon. Beatrice O'Brien in London, and in 1924 was divorced by her under the laws of Fiume. He had the marriage annulled in 1927 by the Rota of the Roman Catholic Church and immediately married Countess Marie Bezzi Scali. At this ceremony his best man was Mussolini.

Times Studio

FAMOUS INVENTOR WHO IS DEAD
Guglielmo Marconi

SCIENTISTS PRAISE MARCONI'S WORKS

Heads of Radio Industry Also Pay Tributes to the Inventor for Vast Help to World

STRESS PERSONAL CHARM

Broadcasting Systems Point to the Social Debt of the Listening Millions

The expressions of regret at the death of Guglielmo Marconi yesterday were as widespread as the radio structure that has been built on his practical pioneer work.

Scientists whose researches have developed radio from the uncertain dot-dash telegraph of forty years ago to the present prospect of television paid tribute to Marconi's continuing contributions in the field which he dramatically opened.

Heads of the radio industry, which has risen on his work to a capital investment of hundreds of millions of dollars in the United States alone, paid tribute to him likewise as an industrial scientist.

From radio broadcasting systems came acknowledgments of the social debt of listening millions to whom Marconi's belief that messages could be sent without wires brought a fuller life of entertainment and enlightenment through the dials.

Some of the tributes follow:

DAVID SARNOFF, President Radio Corporation of America—In the swiftly moving decades since destiny selected him, a youth of 22, as its agency for revealing in nature's treasure chest the phenomenon of radio, Marconi has remained in the vanguard of radio progress. His outlook continued as youthful as the art he created, which has become a symbol of the modern spirit. His scientific interest was very alert. Not content with undying fame already won, he continued his research and his valuable discoveries until his death. His visits to the United States have given Americans an opportunity to know of him not only as a great scientist but also as a man of rugged character and extraordinary personal charm. America joins the world in the deep sense of loss which his death brings. It was my great privilege to have known Marconi personally since I was a boy. For more than thirty years I regarded him as an inspiring teacher and a loyal friend. The world has lost a great man. Science has lost a great genius. And I have lost a great friend.

FRANK B. JEWETT, President and Director of the Bell Telephone Laboratories and one of the foremost American authorities on electrical communications — To those of us who have spent our lives in the work of developing electrical communications and are approximately his contemporaries in age, the basis for Marconi's standing is clear. It is not merely to the fact that Marconi, in his early experiments, did an astounding piece of work, at a time when such things were less common than at present, that his permanent standing is due. His work has always been well done, and his ability to present it graphically has been outstanding. These characteristics, coupled with the fact that he has never been diverted from the general field of his first achievement, have been sufficient to maintain his position in the science and art which long ago ceased to be dominated by the organizations which grew up around his personal work. In the field of electrical communications, Marconi's name will be permanently impaneled with those of Morse and Bell.

LENOX H. LOHR, President National Broadcasting Company—In the death of Guglielmo Marconi radio has lost its greatest engineer, and the listening millions of the world will mourn a great benefactor. Marconi's genius is reflected today in the fact that the peoples of all nations will hear tributes paid to the inventor through the vast instrument of communication which was born of his inspiration. The entire world is immeasurably richer for the culture, enlightenment and entertainment that broadcasting carries to homes everywhere. On the high seas radio guards the passage of ships. On the air radio guides the flight of airplanes. For these things civilization owes a debt to Guglielmo Marconi which must place his name high among history's roster of those who have served mankind.

WILLIAM S. PALEY, President Columbia Broadcasting System—In every epoch it is given to a few men to look further ahead than their contemporaries may see and to gauge their lives, not so much toward the end of personal fulfillment, as toward the end of a fuller life for all mankind. Such a man was Guglielmo Marconi. At 21, Marconi's destiny as world benefactor was sealed as he watched in a physics laboratory a demonstration which convinced him — and him alone — that electrical impulses flashing through space could carry human communication around the globe at the speed of light. From that day Marconi allowed nothing to deter him from his goal of uniting the world with a medium for instantaneous communication.

OWEN D. YOUNG, Chairman General Electric Company—The death of Guglielmo Marconi takes from us the most productive contributor to the radio art and a great adventurer in the vast and little-known area of the air. Like all great men devoted to science, Marconi was modest, even overmodest, in the appraisal of his own contributions and very generous to his associates and coworkers, with the result that they ungrudgingly yielded him the credit he so richly deserved.

Mayor FIORELLO LA GUARDIA—It is a great loss to the entire world. His contributions to science will last to the end of the world. Like all great men, he was kindly, modest and a warm friend. I had the privilege of spending a great deal of time in his company during the World War. He was the most lovable man I ever met.

Signor Marconi is seen with the apparatus he was using in the late 1890s on ships and at shore stations.

"All the News That's Fit to Print"

The New York Times.

LATE CITY EDITION
Cloudy with rain today. Fair, continued cold tomorrow.
Temperature Range Today—Max., 48; Min., 43
Temperature Yesterday—Max., 49; Min., 40
Full U. S. Weather Bureau Report, Page 45

VOL. CIV...No. 35,349. Entered as Second-Class Matter. Post Office, New York, N. Y. NEW YORK, FRIDAY, NOVEMBER 5, 1954. Times Square, New York 36, N. Y. Telephone LAckawanna 4-1000 FIVE CENTS

NEW 5-POWER BID ON ARMS IS VOTED BY U. N. ASSEMBLY

Action Revives Subcommittee to Study Proposals for Cuts and Nuclear Ban

VAN KLEFFENS HOPEFUL

Calls Action 'Important Step' —Wadsworth of U. S. Sees 'Long, Rocky Road Ahead'

By THOMAS J. HAMILTON

Special to The New York Times.

UNITED NATIONS, N. Y., Nov. 4—The United Nations General Assembly asked the five leading atomic powers today to make a new attempt behind closed doors to reach agreement on disarmament and the prohibition of nuclear weapons.

The Assembly, in a resolution adopted unanimously, asked the United Nations Disarmament Commission to revive a subcommittee that met in London last summer. The subcommittee was composed of the United States, the Soviet Union, Britain, France and Canada. These are the five states that sponsored the proposal for a new start.

The unanimous vote recalled the high hopes that prevailed in January, 1946, when the Assembly, in another unanimous vote, created the Atomic Energy Commission. In December, 1946, another unanimous vote brought about the establishment of the commission on conventional or non-atomic armaments.

Dr. Eelco N. Van Kleffens, president of the Assembly, announced after the vote that the resolution constituted "an important step forward," and that it carried with it the possibility of making progress. So far, he said, "our organization can hardly be said to have made real progress in the field of disarmament."

Gap Is Still 'Wide and Deep'

Paul Martin, Canadian Minister of National Health and Welfare, who submitted the original resolution, told the Assembly the gap between the positions of the principal atomic powers had narrowed in the past year but that it remained "wide and deep."

James J. Wadsworth of the United States said that "a long and rocky road" lay ahead, and gave a pledge that the United States would continue its efforts to achieve the common goal. In similar language, Andrei Y. Vishinsky of the Soviet Union declared that "a host of difficulties" remained, and declared that the Soviet Union was determined to surmount them.

However, Mr. Vishinsky added that recently the Soviet Union had adjusted its position on "a number of issues" in an attempt to reach agreement—he did not say what they were—and that it was now up to the Western powers to do the same on the disarmament question.

Sir Pierson Dixon, the British representative, emphasized that agreement on disarmament and the prohibition of nuclear weapons was by no means "just around the corner," but Jules Moch of France appeared to be more optimistic about the results to be expected from the revival of the negotiations.

M. Moch emphasized the importance of Mr. Vishinsky's speech to the Assembly Sept. 30, in

Continued on Page 2, Column 6

Adenauer Confirms Breach In His Coalition Over Saar

Two Minor Government Parties Inform Chancellor Accord Is Unsatisfactory, Joining Free Democrats in Opposition

By M. S. HANDLER

Special to The New York Times.

BONN, Germany, Nov. 4—Chancellor Konrad Adenauer said tonight the Government coalition was in serious disagreement on the acceptability of the Saar settlement.

In a tired and dispirited voice he said in a broadcast:

"When I returned to Bonn [from the United States] I found some strange confusions. I felt during the talks I had today that the election campaigns [for the State Parliaments] in Hesse and Bavaria must be blamed for a good part of the confusion.

"I regret to have to state that a number of politicians are not correctly estimating the over-all world political situation on which Germany also depends. The elections in Hesse and Bavaria [scheduled Nov. 28] are not the yardsticks with which one should measure one's policy.

"I think that the first duty of anyone who must deal with public affairs is to evaluate everything with a cool head. I have been asked about the Saar. I do not want to go into detailed explanations now. The agreement will be presented to the Bundestag but I do want to say this:

"All parties have been asking for years for the restoration of the political freedoms in the Saar. Well, this agreement will guarantee these freedoms. The Saar people can freely decide on what the peace treaty should contain as regards the Saar. He who wants the Saar people to freely voice their opinions should welcome this agreement * * *."

Under the Saar settlement it was agreed that the existing

Continued on Page 3, Column 2

DEMOCRATS OFFER HARMONY IN RULE OF 84TH CONGRESS

Capture House by Margin of 29 Seats and Senate Probably by One Vote

By WILLIAM S. WHITE

Special to The New York Times.

WASHINGTON, Nov. 4—A coalition Government, with the Democrats in narrow command of its legislative arm, is in prospect from Tuesday's bitterly contested Congressional elections.

The Democrats captured the House of Representatives by a margin of twenty-nine seats in a total of 435, results showed today.

They took the Senate as well—though by a single vote—barring some overturn in Oregon of Richard L. Neuberger's thin apparent victory over Senator Guy Cordon, the Republican incumbent, which would send to the Senate the first Democrat from Oregon in forty years.

Assuming that Mr. Neuberger's success survives a recount, and the apparent victory in New Jersey of the liberal Republican, Clifford P. Case, does likewise, the Senate in the Eighty-fourth Congress meeting in January will be thus divided:

Democrats	48
Republicans	47

Independent, 1, Senator Wayne Morse of Oregon.

Senator Morse has said he would vote with the Democrats on organization of the Senate.

The old division had been:

Republicans	49
Democrats	46
Independent	1

Line-Up in the House

The new House stands:

Democrats	232
Republicans	203

The old House had stood on election morning:

Republicans, 218, one Republican vacancy; Democrats, 212, three Democratic vacancies; one Independent.

In Oregon complete but unofficial returns from 2,499 precincts gave Neuberger 284,378, Cordon 282,212, according to The United Press.

In New Jersey the latest figures on a recheck, which was still in progress, gave Mr. Case a plurality of 3,308.

The atmosphere here among powerful Congressional politicians in general was one of tolerance and rather good feeling, though this was more marked in the Senate than in the House.

There had been no outright recriminations in the most important Republican circles.

The Republican Senate floor leader, William F. Knowland of California, criticized President Eisenhower by implication, however, for not having been more active in the campaign.

Senator Knowland also declared that Vice President Richard M. Nixon, who was the operating head of the Republican campaign and took the lead in stressing the theme of alleged Democratic "softness" toward communism, had been "helpful" to the Republicans generally.

This had been true, Mr. Knowland said, "particularly in those areas where there may have been some Republican apathy."

While he remarked that Presi-

Continued on Page 9, Column 2

SUPPORTERS LAUD DIXON-YATES PACT AS HEARINGS OPEN

Administration Asks Action on Power Contract Before New Congress Convenes

DEMOCRATS WANT DELAY

Anderson Criticizes Plan—Strauss, Hughes Defend It as Needed, Economical

By WILLIAM M. BLAIR

Special to The New York Times.

WASHINGTON, Nov. 4—Administration leaders said today that the Dixon-Yates contract was in the public interest.

They testified before the Joint Congressional Committee on Atomic Energy on the Administration's proposal to feed private power into the Tennessee Valley Authority's electric transmission grid.

The spokesmen described the contract as a good example of how free enterprise works and said that it would strengthen the T. V. A. system and that it was "entirely fair as a business proposition for the Government."

Under this contract Middle South Utilities, Inc., and the Southern Company would build a $107,000,000 plant at West Memphis, Ark., to supply power to the T. V. A. to replace power it furnishes to the Atomic Energy Commission. The Government's contractor would be the A. E. C.

The Administration has asked the joint committee to waive the statutory requirement that the proposal lay before the committee for thirty days while Congress is in session.

Democrats, armed with probable control of the next Congress, questioned the urging of the Administration officials for quick action to get a start on the private power plant called for in the contract and avoid a power shortage.

Brownell Upholds Legality

The first day of the joint committee's hearings developed these highlights:

¶Attorney General Herbert Brownell Jr. held in a formal opinion that the authority of the Atomic Energy Commission to execute the twenty-five year contract "cannot be questioned." His opinion was based on amendments to atomic energy law.

¶Mr. Brownell was backed up by Acting Controller General Frank Weitzel, who also asserted that revision of atomic law authorized the Dixon-Yates arrangement on a negotiated basis. Democrats called for competitive bidding.

¶Rear Admiral Lewis L. Strauss, A. E. C. Chairman, said the contract had been negotiated at "arm's length" and that he had "never done any business of any nature directly or indirectly" with the private companies or their principal officers. He asserted "there was no guarantee of any percentage return on the equity" of the investors.

¶Rowland R. Hughes, Director of the Bureau of the Budget, said the contract had developed from a desire to assure T. V. A. of an adequate supply of power to meet increasing demands and give the Administration time for further study to avoid committing "us to a policy of establishing a nation-wide Federal power monopoly."

¶Senator Clinton P. Anderson, New Mexico Democrat who won re-election, charged a "loophole" in the contract would permit two private southern utilities to get the proposed plant constructed without "putting up one thin dime." The Dixon-Yates group, he said, could reclaim its $5,500,000 investment by making a cost-plus contract with a subsidiary for constructing the plant and retiring the investment from the profits. Senator Anderson may be the new committee chairman under Democratic control of Congress.

¶Senator John O. Pastore, Rhode Island Democrat, suggested that Congress might well review the contract for thirty days after it reconvenes on Jan. 5.

The Dixon-Yates plan was developed by the Administration as an alternative to a T. V. A. plan to build a $100,000,000 steam plant at Fulton, Tenn.

The proposal takes its name from Edgar H. Dixon, president of Middle South, and Eugene Yates, chairman of the Southern Company. Both attended the hearing but did not testify.

The Administration made public for the first time the proposed

Continued on Page 8, Column 3

Associated Press Wirephoto

THEY SEEK POWER CONTRACT: Edgar H. Dixon, left, and Eugene A. Yates, officials of private utility companies, outside hearing room as Congressional inquiry started.

Low-Tariff Prospects Gain Under Democratic Congress

By JOHN D. MORRIS

Special to The New York Times.

WASHINGTON, Nov. 4—Prospects for favorable action on President Eisenhower's liberal foreign trade program have been decisively enhanced by the Democratic Congressional victory. Whatever effects the party's victories may have on relations between Congress and the Republican Administration in other fields, it was clear today that foreign economic policy is the major issue holding the greatest hope for harmonious cooperation.

European diplomats in Washington were reporting to their capitals that the elections would result in smoother relations within the Western alliance.

The prospective Democratic chairmen of House and Senate committees having jurisdiction are strong advocates of the lower tariff program laid down by the President last March 30.

They reflect the Democratic party's traditional position in a struggle that has divided the nation since before the turn of the century. Traditionally, the Republicans have been on the side of a high protective tariff.

Early Consideration Likely

The President's recommendations are likely to be the first order of business in the House Ways and Means Committee when the Democrats take over in January.

"I would think they should have early consideration," said Representative Jere Cooper of Tennessee, who will become chairman. "I have always strongly supported the reciprocal trade program and all Democratic members of the committee have also done so."

Mr. Cooper, a quiet but effective legislator of the New Deal-Fair Deal school, succeeds Representative Daniel A. Reed of upstate New York as head of the important committee, which also has initial jurisdiction over tax legislation.

Mr. Reed, through the years,

Continued on Page 8, Column 4

FRENCH ARMY HITS REBELS IN ALGERIA

Armored Units Attack Knot of Terrorists in the East as Arrests Continue

Special to The New York Times.

PARIS, Nov. 4—Strong French armored forces today attacked terrorist bands in the mountainous Aurès region of eastern Algeria.

While in the remainder of the French territory the calm that followed the sudden violence early Monday morning continued, the French made strenuous efforts to rid themselves of a hard and dangerous knot of resistance formed by about 1,000 nationalist rebels apparently recruited in Algeria and in neighboring Tunisia.

According to French officials, the terrorist campaign in Algeria was coordinated and encouraged by Arab elements in Cairo. Protests to the Egyptian Government, particularly against Arab League radio broadcasts, have been to no avail.

Egypt is also accused of harboring training camps for Arab "commandos," who later slip into Tunisia through Libya and into French Morocco from the Spanish zone.

Cabinet Meets Today

The Cabinet, which meets tomorrow, is expected to discuss the Algerian situation and the future of diplomatic relations with Egypt. Particular bitterness is felt over the Arab attacks because Algeria is considered here to be as much a part of France as Brittany or Normandy.

The Government of Premier Pierre Mendès-France must also face a hardening of opposition to its policy of appeasement of nationalist movements in Tunisia and Morocco from French political groups here and in North Africa.

Christian Fouchet, Minister of Tunisian and Moroccan Affairs, declared tonight that the Government intended to continue its announced policy in Tunisia. He said that if the policy of reaching agreement with the nationalists on internal autonomy and protection of French rights had been applied sooner it would have avoided many incidents and that it was necessary for Tunisia's peaceful future.

M. Fouchet promised that in the same spirit the Government would take up the Moroccan question "in the near future."

Meanwhile, the Government has reacted energetically to the attacks in Algeria and a large number of reinforcements have already been sent there.

This morning at dawn two French columns left Batna and Khenchela, two major centers of the Aurès area, and met about forty miles to the south at Foum Toub, which has been under fire from rebels in the surrounding mountains. While armored cars

Continued on Page 2, Column 5

CASE'S LEAD RISES; RECOUNT WEIGHED

Democrats Refuse to Concede —Senate Group to Make a Survey Tomorrow

By GEORGE CABLE WRIGHT

Clifford P. Case, Republican candidate for United States Senator from New Jersey, held a lead last night of 3,308 over his Democratic opponent, Representative Charles R. Howell.

His lead had increased slowly but steadily during the day as county clerks throughout the state continued to recanvass the results of Tuesday's balloting.

However, because all absentee ballots had not been tallied, and because unofficial and official results have varied widely in past years, the outcome of the race was still uncertain. Indications were that the victor might not be known until Nov. 30 when the official totals are released by the State Board of Canvassers.

The count last night stood 861,181 for Case and 857,873 for Howell.

Meanwhile, although Republican leaders jubilantly acclaimed Mr. Case the winner, Democratic leaders refused to concede. They made it clear that a recount probably would be sought, saying the Democratic National Committee had agreed to underwrite part of the cost if that step was decided upon.

Party officials held a closed meeting in Princeton on Wednesday night, and early yesterday began their own recheck. Last night they said their canvass of county totals would not be completed until sometime today, but that it already had reduced Mr. Case's plurality to about 1,500.

Seeks Bi-partisan Action

Democratic State Chairman George E. Brunner then reported he had invited Republican State Chairman Samuel L. Bodine to join him in a "bi-partisan move" to impound ballot boxes and voting machines throughout the state pending a possible recount.

Mr. Brunner said he had acted in the interest of "a fair and honest election."

"We are not impugning anyone's motives," he said, "or accusing anyone of trying to steal the election, but certain ugly rumors have arisen which cast shadows over our reputation as a state.

"Tuesday the citizens of New Jersey elected a new United States Senator. We want to be sure they are not cheated, whether the victor be Mr. Case or Mr. Howell."

At his Flemington home, Mr. Bodine said he would not comment on Mr. Brunner's proposal until he had discussed it with other Republican leaders. He added that he would probably take it up with them today.

Earlier in the day, Senator Robert C. Hendrickson said he had asked the Senate subcommittee on privileges and elections to survey the New Jersey results in view of the close finish. Senator Frank Barrett, Republican of Wyoming, chairman of the subcommittee, later announced in Cheyenne the committee would convene in Trenton tomorrow at

Continued on Page 7, Column 5

State Recanvass Under Way; Vote Fraud Inquiry Begins

Official recanvasses of the vote cast in Tuesday's state election were under way yesterday in a dozen or more upstate counties. Others, including the one in New York City, are to start next week. The outcome of these official counts will determine whether the shaky 9,657-vote margin given to Averell Harriman, the Democratic-Liberal candidate for Governor, in unofficial tabulations will stand up.

In a special broadcast from Amsterdam, N. Y., last night Mr. Harriman said he was not at all worried that the recanvass might upset his apparent victory.

"As it continues my margin will go up," he predicted confidently.

Mr. Harriman was interviewed by telephone from his country home in Harriman, N. Y., by Garrison Dillon, an announcer on the local station. The questions and answers were broadcast.

Won't Cut Aid to Education

Replying to other questions, Mr. Harriman said he would urge a state appropriation to promote the sale of fluid milk and that he would not "be a party to taking any educational aid away from any community in the state, whether it is rural or urban."

Attorney General Nathaniel L. Goldstein, a Republican, opened, meantime, a "big-scale" investigation into alleged voting irregularities in Tuesday's election. The result of this inquiry could also affect the final decision in the contest for Governor.

Counties known to have started their recanvassing already are Lewis, Cortland, Ulster, Oswego and Onondaga. Officials reported that recounting was also under way in at least ten others.

A special meeting of the New York City Board of Elections has been called for this morning to arrange, in consultations with representatives of the major political parties, the procedure to be followed in the New York City recanvass, which will start next Tuesday. Mr. Goldstein is scheduled to announce details of his

Continued on Page 7, Column 7

3 FIRE AIDES HERE ACCUSED OF GRAFT

Battalion Chiefs Suspended on Charge of Taking Bribes From Demolition Concern

Three battalion chiefs of the Fire Department were suspended last night by Fire Commissioner Edward F. Cavanagh Jr. on charges of taking $100 bribes.

They were accused of accepting the money from Atlas Demolitions, Inc., of 646 Lorimer Street, Brooklyn.

While the exact basis for the charges was withheld by the department pending further inquiry, it was indicated that two of the chiefs had been lax in the number, types and supervision of builders' demolition fires set in downtown Brooklyn.

Demolition fires for the burning of debris are authorized under permits issued by the Fire Department to wreckers tearing down buildings. The purpose is to hasten the job of demolition. The fires are, as a matter of policy, strictly limited in crowded areas.

The two charged with laxity were Battalion Chiefs Daniel M. Regan and Joseph A. Massano of the Thirty-first Battalion at 365 Jay Street, Brooklyn. The third man accused was Acting Battalion Chief Edward T. Heeg, in charge of the department's Brooklyn office of Fire Prevention and Combustibles.

Chief Heeg, it was charged, failed to block permits, approved by the other two accused chiefs, that did not properly enforce re-

Continued on Page 46, Column 2

Queen Mother Guest Of the Eisenhowers

By EDITH EVANS ASBURY

Special to The New York Times.

WASHINGTON, Nov. 4—Queen Mother Elizabeth of Britain arrived this afternoon for a week's visit in Washington. She last saw the capital in 1939, when she and her husband, the late King George VI, were the first ruling monarchs to stay in the White House.

The visit of the Queen Mother to this country has been continuously described as an unofficial one, and it was characterized by a certain amount of informal sightseeing and shopping during her nine days in New York. Tonight, however, an official state dinner was given for her, and she and her party will stay at the White House until Saturday. On that day, she will move to the British Embassy for the remainder of her visit here.

Three Republican Roosevelts

Continued on Page 3, Column 3

Art World Mourns Henri Matisse, Dead at Home in Nice at Age of 84

First Scorned as 'Wild Beast' for Paintings, He Became One of Top Modernists

Special to The New York Times.

PARIS, Nov. 4—The world of art today mourned Henri Matisse, one of France's greatest painters, who died in his apartment in Nice yesterday afternoon of a heart attack. He was 84 years old.

Death came swiftly to the aged artist, who had been a semi-invalid since undergoing a serious operation in 1940. At his bedside were his daughter, Mme. Marguerite Duthite; his physician, a nurse and his secretary. Mme. Duthite had arrived in Nice from Paris a few days ago to visit her father.

Jean Cassou, director of the Museum of Modern Art in Paris, recalled that Matisse, bedridden much of the time after his operation, continued to work from his room.

"Henri Matisse is one of the last representatives of French genius," he said. "If the title of master suits any artist it certainly suited him. All men deserving of this name, all men who

Henri Matisse

think, can consider themselves as his disciples. His thinking has illuminated our era."

André Bertheim, Minister of National Education, in a statement on the death of the artist, said that the "world will mourn" with France.

"His was the most French of palettes. Intelligence, reason and the alliance of a sense of finesse

Continued on Page 15, Column 2

East 59th Street I. R. T. Station To Be Express Stop in 2 Years

By LEONARD INGALLS

A Fifty-ninth Street stop for express trains of the Lexington Avenue I. R. T. subway was approved yesterday by the Transit Authority.

The agency also awarded a contract for installation of a conveyor belt system to replace the shuttle trains between Grand Central and Times Square, and agreed to a joint committee with the Transport Workers Union, C. I. O., to work out the problem of possible lay-offs in connection with transit economies.

The new express station was proposed by Sidney H. Bingham, executive director of the authority, to provide a better connection between the East Side line and the B. M. T. line to and from Queens at Sixtieth Street.

It is expected that conversion of the Fifty-ninth Street station from its present use as a local stop to one that would serve both local and express trains will take two years and cost $5,000,000. The Board of Estimate will be asked to include the funds in the city's 1955 capital budget.

By enabling passengers to transfer to express trains at Fifty-ninth Street, Mr. Bingham explained, some of the pressure would be taken off the I. R. T. station at Grand Central, the busiest subway stop in the city. The new facility, he said, is dictated by the rapid development of the East Side at midtown.

Funds already have been requested by the authority in next year's capital budget for conversion of the Fifty-ninth Street station on the West Side I. R. T. line to an express stop. This would cost an estimated $5,500,000. The expanded station would serve the new Coliseum at Columbus Circle.

In proposing the East Side im-

Continued on Page 15, Column 4

MATISSE MOURNED BY WORLD OF ART

Continued From Page 1

and of simplifying geometry gave to all he painted the rare virtue of being truly French." M. Berthoin said.

Matisse's two sons, Jean, a Paris sculptor, and Pierre, a New York art dealer, arrived in Nice tonight to attend the funeral.

While the date and type of service have not yet been set, it was understood from Matisse's daughter that the painter had often requested a simple service with burial somewhere on the Riviera, where the artist had lived since 1939.

Variety in His Approach

Henri Matisse, leader of young rebel artists who brought the modern art movement into being in Paris a half century ago, was a master of color, a supreme draftsman who imbued a relatively small range of subject matter with constant variety.

The artist's long career, begun with years of academic schooling, became set in its brilliant revolutionary course in 1905, when, in company with Rouault, Derain, Dufy, Vlaminck and a few others, Matisse set Paris on its ears in the Autumn Salon. The painters were excoriated as fauves—wild beasts—and their pictures, flaming defiant canvases, were condemned as impossible.

On June 25, 1951, thousands of tourists and natives crowded the small village of Vence in south France to see the Bishop bless what Matisse had called his "masterpiece"—a chapel on which he had started work four years before.

Ailing and bedridden through much of this period, Matisse serenely progressed with his decorations for the chapel, drawing his designs with a long charcoal-tipped stick on the walls of his bedroom, later copying them on tiles and transferring them to stained glass. This was his last work, he announced: "My bags are packed."

Matisse held no common ground with those who considered modern art as a new mode. He once said that every art is a logical reflection of the time in which it is produced—an orderly and rational development of what had gone before.

Ruled Out Reproduction

Representation to him was a means to an end and not the end itself. On a visit to the United States in 1930, he answered the challengers of new art forms by saying, "By mechanical means an image is now fixed on a photographic plate in a few seconds—an image more precise and exact than it is humanly possible to draw. And so, with the advent of photography disappeared the necessity for exact reproduction in art. Cezanne no longer painted one individual apple; he painted all apples. Van Gogh's 'Postman' is a portion of humanity."

The artist was born on Dec. 31, 1869, the son of a grain merchant in Le Cateau in Picardy. The law had been chosen as his profession, and it took some persuasion over parental objections for Matisse to begin the art studies he yearned for. In Paris he studied under Gustave Moreau, and from 1893 to 1896 he produced sober still lifes and other quiet pictures influenced by Chardin and Corot. He copied old masters in the Louvre, earning his way through his schooling. In later years, telling about it, he said, "One must learn to walk firmly on the ground before one tries the tightrope."

In 1893 he married Amélie Moellie Parayre. The family was supported through the sale of all the painter's still lifes to a dealer who paid 400 francs apiece for them.

Matisse narrated later: "One day I had just finished one of my pictures. It was quite as good as the previous one and very much like it, and I knew that on its delivery I would get the money which I sorely needed. I looked at it, and then and there a feeling came over me that it was not I, that it did not express me or express what I felt." The artist destroyed the picture, counting his emanicipation from that day.

Opinions on the art of Matisse from the beginning of his emancipation through the tide of impressionism, post-impressionism and fauvism, varied considerably during the 1912 exhibition in London of modern French painters' work.

Matisse emerged as an artist of great powers, but sections of the academic world called his work "not art, but a dangerous and infectious disease." In 1908, excited comment had followed an exhibition of Matisse's paintings in the Stieglitz Gallery of New York; in 1913, at the famed Armory Show, the artist was the center of stormy debate.

Through the years that have seen his pictures become prized pieces in public and private collections in all parts of the world, the artist grew in stature. He never left his explorations, and age only increased his daring as a colorist and his brilliance and gaiety. A few have complained that his work of recent years "complacently repeated," but numbers of authoritative writers on Matisse and leading connoisseurs regard him as the foremost painter of the day.

Self-portrait

Matisse established himself permanently in Nice in 1917. When World War II started, the artist was in Paris. He made his way in stages by taxi and train back to Nice.

In 1941, his son Pierre, reported that Matisse had undergone a serious operation. Friends tried to persuade the aging artist to leave France, but Matisse said, "If all the talented people left France, the country would be much poorer. I began an artist's life very poor, and I am not afraid to be poor again. . . . Art has its value; it is a search after truth and truth is all that counts.

The artist's birthdays during his last years usually found him working on a limited schedule, with congratulatory messages coming in from all over the world. At 83 he donated 100 of his works—valued at up to $14,000,000—to his home town of Le Cateau.

And at about the same time, in a piece he wrote for the United Nations Educational, Scientific and Cultural Organization, Matisse told a little more of his theory of art.

"An artist has to look at life without prejudices, as he did when he was a child," he wrote. "If he loses that faculty, he cannot express himself in an original, that is, in a personal way."

By way of illustration he said there was nothing more difficult for a truly creative painter than to paint a rose.

"Because before he can do so," explained the artist, "he has first of all to forget all the roses that were ever painted."

Collection of Mrs. Maurice Newton

"Michaela" was done in 1943 after the painter, ill, had moved to Nice in southern France

Museum of Modern Art

Henri Matisse painted "The Bather" in oil in 1909. During that period he was known as the King of the Fauves, or wild beasts, as the young artists were called who brought forth modern art movement in 1905 at the Autumn Salon in Paris.

Helene Adant

He considered his masterpiece to be the Chapel of the Rosary of the Dominican Nuns of Vence, a small town on the French Riviera. M. Matisse designed the structure and all its appointments, including this altar, with its crucifix and candles, and the stained-glass window. Painted by the artist on white tile is the figure of St. Dominic, the order's patron.

"All the News That's Fit to Print"

The New York Times.

LATE CITY EDITION
U. S. Weather Bureau Report (Page 94) forecast:
Light rain and snow, then clearing today; becoming cloudy tomorrow.
Temp. range: 46—37; yesterday: 48—42.

VOL. CXV..No. 39,408. NEW YORK, THURSDAY, DECEMBER 16, 1965. TEN CENTS

TWO GEMINIS FLY 6 TO 10 FEET APART IN MAN'S FIRST SPACE RENDEZVOUS; CREWS, FACE TO FACE, TALK BY RADIO

U.S. JETS SMASH BIG POWER PLANT OUTSIDE HAIPHONG

Cut Nation's Current 15% —Generators Supported Industries in Hanoi

By NEIL SHEEHAN
Special to The New York Times

SAIGON, South Vietnam, Dec. 15—United States jet fighter-bombers destroyed a large power plant today 14 miles from Haiphong, North Vietnam's chief port, in the first American air strike against a North Vietnamese target of major industrial importance.

A military spokesman said the planes, flown by Air Force pilots, had struck the Uongbi thermal power plant, northeast of Haiphong. The plant has a capacity of 24,000 kilowatts, about 15 per cent of North Vietnam's total electric-power output. It supplies some of the power needs of both Hanoi and Haiphong.

The center of the plant, housing steam turbines, generators and other sensitive equipment, was smashed at 11 A.M. with 12 tons of 3,000-pound bombs. A single flight of F-105 Thunderchief fighter-bombers—apparently four to six craft—made the raid.

Secondary Blasts Sighted

A spokesman said that the pilots had encountered bad weather and heavy antiaircraft fire but reported having destroyed the plant. Several secondary explosions—detonations of explosives on the ground—were observed during the raid.

This was the first time United States aircraft had struck so close to North Vietnam's two major cities—Hanoi and Haiphong. The closest previous strike was a recent raid against a firing site for Soviet-made surface-to-air missiles, 22 miles from Hanoi.

[Secretary of Defense McNamara, who arrived back in Washington shortly after midnight from the North Atlantic Alliance meeting in Paris, said the bombing of the power plant near Haiphong "is representative of the type of attack we have carried out and will continue to carry out," The Associated Press reported Thursday. Page 3.]

Many Homes Darkened

According to military spokesmen here, the destruction of the power plant was certain to affect North Vietnamese civilians much more directly than have previous strikes, almost all of which have been aimed at road, rail and river networks and military installations.

The power-station raid will probably cut off electricity in large numbers of civilian homes as well as significantly reduce the amount of power available for industries in the Hai-

Continued on Page 3, Column 1

U.S. Said to Caution Latins on Moscow

By HENRY RAYMONT
Special to The New York Times

MONTEVIDEO, Uruguay, Dec. 15—The United States is warning Uruguay and other Latin-American countries against underestimating the continued aggressiveness and subversive potential of Soviet Communism, qualified sources said today.

The diplomatic initiative is directed against what United States authorities consider to be undue complacency among Latin-American leaders.

These authorities think that the split between Moscow and Peking has led to the assumption among Latins that pro-Soviet Communists no longer threaten republican institutions in the Western Hemisphere.

According to United States officials, this assumption ignores the deterioration in East-West

Continued on Page 17, Column 1

Gemini 7 Crew

Lieut. Col. Frank Borman

Comdr. James A. Lovell Jr.

Major Steps From Launching to Rendezvous

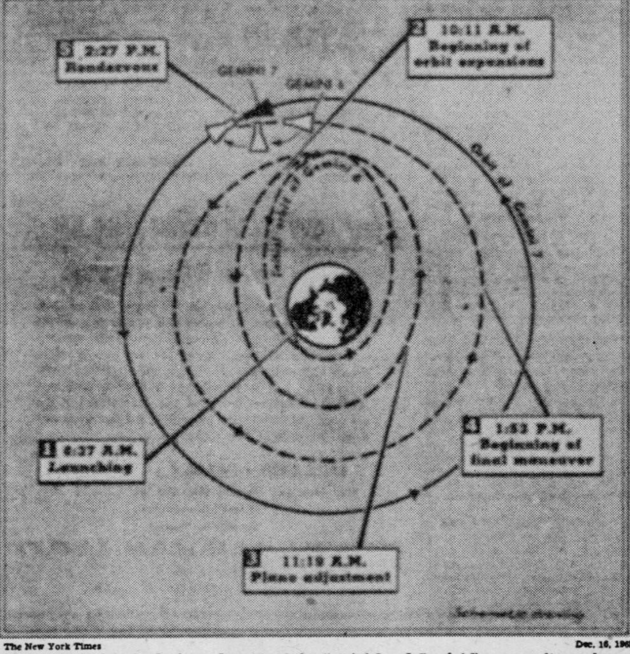

The New York Times Dec. 16, 1965
Major steps of yesterday's rendezvous of the Gemini 6 and Gemini 7 spacecraft are shown, from the launching of Gemini 6 to its meeting with Gemini 7, orbiting about 185 miles above the earth. At rendezvous two craft were nose to nose within 10 feet of each other.

Gemini 6 Crew

Capt. Walter M. Schirra Jr.

Maj. Thomas P. Stafford

Craft in Formation Orbit 185 Miles Up

Officials of Space Agency Are Jubilant at Success—Maneuver Is Vital to a Manned Landing on Moon

By JOHN NOBLE WILFORD
Special to The New York Times

HOUSTON, Dec. 15—Four American astronauts steered Gemini 6 and Gemini 7 today to man's first rendezvous in the vastness of outer space.

In a spectacular performance of space navigation, the astronauts brought their craft within six to ten feet of each other about 185 miles above the earth. The two capsules then circled the earth nearly two times on a four-hour formation flight before Gemini 6 broke away to a lower orbit.

The pilots of the pursuing Gemini 6 were Capt. Walter M. Schirra Jr. of the Navy and Maj. Thomas P. Stafford of the Air Force. Pilots of the Gemini 7 target ship were Lieut. Col. Frank Borman of the Air Force and Comdr. James A. Lovell Jr. of the Navy.

The crews came close enough to see into each other's cabins, trade gibes and inspect details on the exteriors of their funnel-shaped spacecraft. The Gemini 6 astronauts could see Commander Lovell's beard and could tell that Colonel Borman was chewing gum.

"We have company tonight!" radioed Colonel Borman from Gemini 7, which has been in orbit 11 days of its record 14-day mission. Gemini 6, launched from Cape Kennedy at 8:37 A.M., Eastern standard time, today, is expected to splash down near the Bahamas at 10:29 A.M. tomorrow.

Officials Jubilant

The success of the mission brought jubilation at the space center here.

"It's the biggest milestone since the flight of John Glenn," Christopher C. Kraft Jr., the flight director, said.

Colonel Glenn's Mercury flight, on Feb. 20, 1962, was the first orbital mission by an American.

The two Geminis today proved that two spacecraft can find each other, rendezvous and presumably link up.

Such a maneuver is necessary if astronauts are to land on the moon and then return to their mother ship, which would be circling in a lunar orbit. Space officials are aiming for such a manned landing in 1969.

Today's rendezvous also opens the way to operations in which men and supplies can be ferried out to orbiting stations, such as the Air Force's planned Manned Orbiting Laboratory.

'Made It Look Easy'

"These crews made it look easy," said Dr. Robert Gilruth, director of the Manned Spacecraft Center here, praising all those who had made the mission a success.

Just before final rendezvous, there was an anxious moment of silence. Radio contact between the craft and the ground was lost. Then a relay tracking station off Hawaii reported in. The two Gemini had drawn within 120 feet of each other.

"There just seems to be a lot of traffic up here," Captain Schirra commented.

"Call a policeman," Colonel

Continued on Page 28, Column 1

McNamara Warns NATO Of Chinese Atom Threat

By PETER BRAESTRUP
Special to The New York Times

PARIS, Dec. 15—Defense Secretary Robert S. McNamara urged the United States' Western European allies today to start worrying now about the threat posed by Communist China's growing nuclear strength.

At the same time, he pledged that the mounting United States effort in Vietnam would not require the withdrawal of "major combat units" from American forces in Western Europe.

Mr. McNamara addressed ministers of the 15-nation North Atlantic Treaty Organization in their year-end meeting, which began yesterday.

Behind Closed Doors

The Defense Secretary spoke behind closed doors. His remarks, like those of other speakers, were summarized by a delegation spokesman.

Mr. McNamara said that the Chinese Communists, having already detonated two test nuclear devices, would produce enough fissionable material in the next two years to start a small stockpile of atomic weapons.

Moreover, he continued, the Chinese, despite a "near-famine" economy, are spending 10 per cent of their gross national product on defense.

He said Peking's new mili-

Continued on Page 8, Column 3

JOHNSON AND AYUB CALL PEACE VITAL

Say Dispute With India Must Cease So Efforts Can Be Turned to Key Problems

By JOHN D. POMFRET
Special to The New York Times

WASHINGTON, Dec. 15—President Johnson and President Mohammad Ayub Khan of Pakistan said today that they agreed on the need for a peaceful resolution of all outstanding differences between India and Pakistan.

This is necessary, they said, "so that the energies and resources of the peoples of the subcontinent would not be wastefully diverted from their efforts to meet their vitally important social and economic problems."

The two leaders issued a joint communiqué at the conclusion of two days of meetings at the White House. It described the discussions as "frank, wide-ranging and productive."

Kashmir Main Issue

The main dispute between India and Pakistan is over Kashmir. This dispute led to a short war last summer.

There was no expressed agreement between the two Presidents on the specific lines along which the dispute over Kashmir should be settled.

They both were said to believe that the working out of such specific arrangements must await the outcome of further conferences that already have been scheduled.

President Ayub and India's Prime Minister, Lal Bahadur Shastri, are to meet Jan. 4 at the invitation of the Soviet Union to discuss their differences. They will confer at the Soviet Central Asian city of Tashkent.

Prime Minister Shastri and President Johnson will meet in Washington Feb. 1 and 2.

The United States cut off military aid and new economic

Continued on Page 6, Column 8

47-CENT FARE SEEN IN QUILL DEMANDS

Transit Authority Warns It Would Be Needed to Meet Union Pay Proposals

By EMANUEL PERLMUTTER

The Transit Authority said yesterday that if it granted the contract demands of its unions it would have to raise the 15-cent fare to 47 cents.

It asserted that a fare increase that great would lead to such a loss of riders that "the reduced use of the system would be financially catastrophic."

The authority has estimated that demands of the Transport Workers Union would cost it $680 million in a two-year contract.

"Adding an increased labor cost of $340 million annually to the T.A. budget would, in the absence of other sources of revenue, increase the present 3-cent deficit incurred for each passenger carried by 19 cents, creating a 22-cent operating deficit per ride," the authority asserted. "The fare would have to be increased to not less than 47 cents."

The authority said that granting the demands would also result in increasing the "basic wage rate per hour alone

Continued on Page 58, Column 4

Staggered Working Hours Urged to Cut Transit Jam

By JOSEPH C. INGRAHAM

The chronic morning and evening subway crushes can be eliminated by staggering working hours, according to a plan made public by Mayor Wagner yesterday. The success of the proposal hinges on whether employers and employes can be persuaded to alter their traditional 9-to-5 work pattern, the Mayor said.

Only the conclusions of the eight-volume, 200,000-word report, based on a six-year study that cost $200,000, were released by the Mayor. The study was directed by Prof. Lawrence B. Cohen of the department of industrial engineering of Columbia University.

Principal Finding

The principal finding was that "work staggering is a feasible way of relieving subway congestion into and out of Manhattan's central business district during the rush hours so that standing passengers might be reasonably comfortable."

Professor Cohen held that the idea was technically and economically feasible and, within limits, which he defined very generally, was sociologically acceptable to management and labor.

In Professor Cohen's view, rush-hour crowding would be markedly alleviated if a 25 per cent spread of the peak loads

Continued on Page 58, Column 3

Somerset Maugham Is Dead at 91

Novelist, Short Story Writer, Playwright Succumbs in Nice

By The Associated Press

NICE, France, Thursday, Dec. 16—W. Somerset Maugham died early today at his Riviera villa, La Mauresque. The world-famous novelist, playwright and short-story writer was 91 years old.

Maugham fell last Friday and then suffered a stroke. He was taken to the British-American Hospital Saturday. After a medical consultation on Sunday, physicians gave him only hours to live.

He rallied slightly but weakened yesterday. When all hope was gone, he was taken from the hospital to die in his Moorish-style villa at nearby Cap Ferrat, his secretary and companion of many years, Alan Searle, said in announcing Maugham's death.

A prolific author, Maugham turned out 30 plays, 21 novels and 120 short stories. His masterpiece was "Of Human Bondage," published in 1915 when he was 41 years old. It centered

Continued on Page 50, Column 1

Pictorial Parade
W. Somerset Maugham

NASA CUTS BACK SCIENCE PROGRAM

Orbiting Solar Observatory Canceled in Move to Hold Down Expanding Budget

Special to The New York Times

WASHINGTON, Dec. 15—The National Aeronautics and Space Administration, caught in a tight budgetary squeeze, canceled today one of its most ambitious scientific projects.

"Budgetary considerations" were cited by the agency in explaining a halt in further work on the Advanced Orbiting Solar Observatory. The observatory, capable of making detailed observations of the sun, had been planned for launching in 1969.

Behind the cryptic explanation was the deliberately unpublicized fact that the agency was faced with a budgetary dilemma. It has been attempting to finance its expanding program and still heed White House directives to hold down nonmilitary spending.

Some Delays Foreseen

The present expectation is that the civilian space budget for the fiscal year 1967, beginning next July 1, will be held by the White House to about $5.17 billion, equal to the appropriation for this year, and perhaps even less. This would be about $500 million less than the space agency considered necessary to maintain the momentum of its expanding program and sought from the White House.

Enough money will be provided in the budget next year to keep Project Apollo on its schedule of landing a manned expedition on the moon before 1970. But to keep within the budgetary confines imposed by the White House, there will have to be some curtailment in the

Continued on Page 30, Column 4

AT LAST, GEMINI 6 HAS A PERFECT DAY

Even Sun Comes Out in Time to Dispel Last Doubt of Jubilant Ground Staff

By EVERT CLARK
Special to The New York Times

CAPE KENNEDY, Fla., Dec. 15—After twice having had its wings clipped by failure, the Gemini 6 finally climbed to its space rendezvous today in a most spectacular way.

For 15 years, missiles have flown from this sandy point of land. But no one today could recall a flight of greater beauty.

It left behind a sense of exhilaration missing since Mercury capsules took the first American astronauts into space four years ago.

On top of the triumph, plans were quickly made to have Gemini 6 splash down about 800 miles east of here at 10:29 o'clock tomorrow morning. The pilots will return here on Friday for the first of many days of debriefings.

A splendid sunrise had created the perfect backdrop and set the mood for the day. It dispelled a worrisome ground fog that had clung to the scrubby palmetto like the doubts that had hung over Gemini 6 in recent days.

Attitude Was Cautious

Through last night the memory of two recent false starts was so fresh that the attitude was one of caution and crossed fingers.

Yet today, from the beginning, a cockiness and almost a jubilance seemed to run through the pilots, the overworked ground crews and official observers.

It was typified by the reaction of James S. McDonnell, the 67-year-old engineer whose factory in Missouri makes the Gemini capsules.

He overslept. Awakened at 6:30 A.M., as the sun began to turn the high, scattered clouds the color of a tea rose, he looked at the sky and cried out:

"You see! I told them I'd bring them good weather from St. Louis!"

It became a day for enthusiasm.

"She looks like a dream," Navy Capt. Walter M. Schirra

Continued on Page 28, Column 8

Johnson Calls Feat Step Toward Moon

By JACK RAYMOND
Special to The New York Times

WASHINGTON, Dec. 15—President Johnson hailed the Gemini satellite rendezvous today as a step toward the moon.

The President congratulated the astronauts and all those who had anything to do with the space feat.

"You have all moved us one step higher on the stairway to the moon," he said exuberantly.

The President conveyed his feelings in a message to James E. Webb, administrator of the National Aeronautics and Space Administration. He had watched the progress of the launching and flight anxiously throughout the day.

Bill D. Moyers, the President's press secretary, said Mr. Johnson watched the Gemini 8 launching over his bedroom television set. Then, throughout the

Continued on Page 29, Column 4

NEWS INDEX

W. Somerset Maugham, a Major Literary Craftsman of the Century, Dies at 91

PROLIFIC AUTHOR OF STORIES, PLAYS

Best Known for 'Of Human Bondage,' 'Miss Thompson' and 'Moon and Sixpence'

Continued From Page 1, Col. 5

on a club-footed medical student's painful romance with a slatternly waitress.

Among Maugham's most powerful pieces was the short story "Miss Thompson," which—as a play called "Rain"—became one of the theater's perennial hits.

Maugham abandoned a medical career to become a globe-trotting author. For decades he cast a clinical eye on human behavior and turned out works that made him a fortune few writers have equaled.

"Most of my life," he once said, "I've written for money, written what people want to read." Hollywood adapted many of his works for the screen.

Maugham died without any apparent change in the view expressed last year to a friend and biographer, Wilmon Menard: "I have not uncovered any evidence in my ecclesiastical researches to cause me to change my agnostic views. I still neither believe in the existence of God nor in the immortality of the soul."

He said he wanted no funeral, no "holy Harry" delivering a eulogy following what he called the "hellishly boresome experience" of dying.

Cremation Tomorrow

NICE, France, Thursday, Dec. 16 (Reuters)—Alan Searle said today that Maugham had expressed a wish to be cremated and that his ashes be taken back to England.

"The cremation will probably take place tomorrow, it will have to be fairly soon," Mr. Searle said. "The ashes will probably not go to England before Christmas."

Mr. Searle added that he did not think any of Maugham's family would come to France for the cremation.

Writing Made Him Wealthy

"The day broke gray and dull. The clouds hung heavily, and there was a rawness in the air that suggested snow."

From its opening words, the novel, "Of Human Bondage," was a terse, controlled and vivid work. It captured and audience slowly and earned little money at first, but it became the cornerstone in the career of one of the major literary craftsmen of the 20th century — William Somerset Maugham.

For nearly 50 years, Somerset Maugham wrote a stream of novels, plays, short stories and reminiscences that made him one of the richest authors in the world.

His style was neat and simple; his stories were sharply defined, with a clear beginning, middle and end; his characters were a fascinating spectrum of humanity, from dukes to hucksters, from princesses to prostitutes, from governors general to lackeys. His audience was vast.

Critics have tended to place him among the highly professional craftsmen of his time, rather than among the major creative artists, such as Henry James, Thomas Hardy or James Joyce. But Maugham accepted the judgment of critics dryly.

"In my twenties the critics said I was brutal," he wrote in his autobiography, "The Summing Up." "In my thirties they said I was flippant, in my forties they said I was cynical, in my fifties they said I was competent, and in my sixties they say I am superficial."

Breath of the Past

At the end of his life, Somerset Maugham sat in the living room of his Villa la Mauresque in Cap Ferrat, France, speaking softly, craning to hear. Even in his final days, however, a glimmer of Edwardian and Georgian London clung to the author.

He was small and walked with the shuffling, hesitant step of the aged. His neck was thinning, his skin sallow and his lips rather thin and curved downward. And yet, despite his years, he maintained a casual elegance of dress that gave him the appearance of a retired English officer or colonial official or, perhaps, a character in a Somerset Maugham novel.

For Maugham was almost the sum of what he had created. He was the shy and tortured youth in "Of Human Bondage." He was the promising young author who carries the story forward in "The Moon and Sixpence." He was one of the lovers of Rosie in "Cakes and Ale."

"I was born to write," Somerset Maugham said. "I took to writing as a newborn child takes to breathing."

At another point, he said: "I am almost inclined to say that I could not spend an hour in anyone's company without getting the material to write at least a readable story about him."

In his novels and short stories, in locales as varied as China, Burma, France, England and the United States, Maugham's hallmark was a cool, detached—some said cynical—attitude. One critic wrote that Maugham was "an aloof, sardonic clinician who expects little from existence is surprised at nothing, is skeptical of aspirations and amused by the follies of mankind."

Another critic wrote that despite Maugham's range of scene and character "he has treated it as though it was there to be observed from a club window, from the cafe chair of the man of the world, who can be unperturbed even by the most shocking things, because he does not have to share the life that produced them."

Maugham himself said that he "painted easel pictures, not frescoes," that the story was the thing and that he was satisfied to be taken as an entertainer.

"At his (Maugham's) best," wrote the British critic, Walter Allen, in The New York Times Book Review in 1964, "he is much more than a 'mere' teller of stories, a 'mere' entertainer. Maugham is the last survivor of a vanished age, an age which had not divorced, as ours has largely done, the idea of entertainment from the idea of art."

"In Maugham we have our one serious craftsman who has not gone to pieces in his great success, but who has maintained his standards," wrote another critic, V. S. Pritchett. "He insists on the professional discipline of literature. He knows very well his own limitations."

Mr. Pritchett continued: "He conducts no propaganda, and perhaps because he sees people isolated from society, its past and its future, his work seems almost puritanically private. In Malaya, for example, before the war, he saw little but love affairs and solitude; none of the framework of that precarious scene.

"Yet, as a dossier of upper middle-class life, its illusions, daydreams, desires, conventions, and rebellions, Maugham's work is a complete exposure. He could not have warned more completely had he been a prophet. The man of the world now seems to us an archaic figure, but the world of the man of the world found in Maugham its most accomplished, assiduous and various investigator."

Like his work, Somerset Maugham appeared at times vaguely contradictory, a curious mélange of fiction and reality. He was called by some bitter, cruel and cynical. Others said he was charitable and humane. "I cannot imagine anyone really knowing him," said a friend once. "He lives behind walls—a wall of reserve, a wall of gentlemanliness, a wall of exquisite good manners. No one has ever breached these defenses."

Another old acquaintance remarked: "I always have the feeling that Willie is wearing a mask. And not once, in all the years that I've known him, have I seen the mask drop. He's on guard all the time, alert as a hawk, watching everything he does and says."

"There are very few people who know anything about me," Maugham once said. "And even they do not know as much as they imagine."

For most of his career, Maugham was a symbol of a glittering, perhaps anachronistic sophistication, unrelated to writing or art. He traveled extensively, lived in a Riviera villa surrounded by priceless paintings, and appeared not infrequently in gossip columns.

"Do you have many visitors here?" an interviewer asked in 1961.

"Oh, yes," Maugham replied. "Jean Cocteau, who is a good friend of mine, comes often. Adlai Stevenson was here. Also, Cecil Beaton, Marc Chagall, S. J. Perelman, Art Buchwald and Christopher Isherwood."

Yet despite the parties in France, and the card games with Elsa Maxwell in New York and bridge with the Queen of Spain, a more serious vein was revealed in his work.

The Value of Suffering

On the one hand he gazed skeptically at his characters, looking at them with amusement or disdain or tolerance. On the other hand, a recurring theme suggested that isolation, suffering and renunciation bring their rewards in art and in a spiritual life.

In "The Moon and Sixpence," a novel suggested by the painter, Gauguin, a man renounces his business and his wife in order to devote himself to art. In "The Painted Veil," a jealous husband takes his adulterous wife into a region where cholera is raging. She meets a community of Catholic nuns and sees the value of a life of renunciation. In "The Razor's Edge," an American airman, shocked at the death of his fellow officers, renounces his rich family and attempts to become a mystic.

"When we read 'Of Human Bondage,'" writes V. S. Pritchett, "we have the whole of Maugham in our hands—all his merits and all his defects, all of the many strands of his talent.

"We strike, above all, that other strain in him, which is as important as his preoccupation with the idea of the gentleman or the man of the world. This other strain is the ascetic. It is the 'human bondage of the flesh' that preoccupies the writer who is so much concerned, even obsessed, by the sexual act which is fundamentally disassociated in his mind from love. The ascetic strain is the disturbing element in his talent."

Born in Paris

William Somerset Maugham was born in the British Embassy in Paris on Jan. 25, 1874. His father was Robert Ormond Maugham, a solicitor in the Embassy, and his mother, Edith Mary, was a daughter of Major Charles Snell of the Indian Army.

"My mother was consumptive and her sister had died of the complaint," Maugham wrote in a memoir, "Looking Back," published in Show Magazine in 1962. "At that time doctors held the theory that it was good for a woman who was thus affected to have a baby. That is how it came about that I was born six years after the birth of my youngest brother."

Before he was six his mother died of tuberculosis, and his father died of cancer when he was 10. He was sent to live with a paternal uncle, Henry McDonald Maugham, Vicar of Whitstable in Kent, six miles from Canterbury.

As a child, Maugham was almost pathologically shy. His painful childhood experiences—a pronounced stammer, incipient tuberculosis, a stiff relationship with his uncle—were documented later in "Of Human Bondage."

Maugham's stammer—in the novel, Philip Carey, the hero, had a clubfoot—plagued him at the King's School in Canterbury. Later, he spent two successive winters on the French Riviera because of his health and studied there under an English tutor.

Studied Medicine

After attending lectures at the University of Heidelberg, he returned to Kent at the age of 18 and after briefly studying accountancy, moved to London in the autumn of 1892. He enrolled as a medical student at St. Thomas's Hospital, but spent most of the time reading and writing in his notebooks.

"Willie," as his friends called him, was dazzled by London. His recollections in his memoirs of his early years there are frank — detailing his first sexual experience (resulting in gonorrhea) and a later affair with a married woman.

In his third year as an intern, young Maugham came into contact with the sick of Lambeth, a London slum. Almost a transcript of one of his cases, his first published novel, "Liza of Lambeth" (1897), told the story of the last year in the life of a young factory girl.

At the end of five years, Maugham qualified in medicine, but left for Spain to devote full time to writing. "At one time, I had so many stories I wanted to tell that I could barely wait to finish one before starting another," he said many years later.

Quickly Maugham wrote a series of short stories, novels and sketches. He lived in Spain, London and Paris, writing continually, but producing only one moderate success, "Mrs. Craddock," a novel, in 1902.

Young Maugham, to some extent, suffered financially in his first 10 years as a writer. He never earned more than £100 a year and this was supplemented by only a small inheritance. There were, even then, however, a growing number of dinner parties and luncheons.

"I came to know a number of persons in the world of fashion," he recalled. "I have often wondered why these rich and worldly people bothered about me. I had precious little to offer. I was poor and shy; I stammered; and I knew nothing about the sort of things they talked about. Many, many years later I asked one of the hostesses of my youth what she and others had seen in me that they were so kind to me.

"'You were different from other young men,' she said. 'Though quiet and silent, you had a sort of restless vitality that was intriguing.'"

Becomes a Playwright

Turning to the theater, young Maugham wrote several plays of which one, "A Man of Honour," was briefly performed in 1903.

Four years later, Maugham's comedy of manners, "Lady Frederick," opened and became a smash hit. From then on, he was a continual financial success as a writer.

"I had no notion of living on a crust in a garret if I could help it," he wrote. "I found out that money was like a sixth sense without which you could not make the most of the other five."

One year after "Lady Frederick" opened, four of Maugham's plays were running simultaneously on London's Strand. In all, he wrote 30 plays—though he later called playwrighting "one of the lesser arts, like wood-carving and dancing."

In 1913, Maugham met Mrs. Syrie Barnardo Wellcome, then separated from her husband. "She had lovely brown eyes and a beautiful skin," the writer recalled. "She was very nicely dressed in the height of fashion and wore on her fingers large cabochon emeralds. I did not know then they were false."

Maugham began seeing her regularly. When her husband, Wisconsin-born Henry Wellcome, later Sir Henry Wellcome, divorced his wife in 1915, after she had given birth to a child, he named Maugham as co-respondent. Mrs. Wellcome was married to the writer in 1917. They were divorced 10 years later, partially because of the travels that Maugham began. She died in London in 1955.

'Human Bondage' Emerges

Meantime, Maugham had been engaged for several years with a novel, first called "The Artistic Temperament of Stephen Carey." When a publisher refused to give him a £100 advance royalty, he laid the book aside, but only temporarily.

"I could not forget the people, the incidents, the emotions," Maugham wrote. "Certain of my recollections were so insistent that, waking or sleeping, I could not escape from them. My memories would not let me be. They became such a torment that I determined at last (in 1912) to have done with the theatre till I had released myself from them."

Maugham corrected the proofs of the book—whose title changed to "Beauty From Ashes" and then "Of Human Bondage," — by a flickering candle while working in a Red Cross ambulance unit in Ypres, after the outbreak of World War I.

The book appeared in 1915 and received a cool reception. One critic condemned it for being sordid; another said it left a feeling akin to nausea. But Theodore Dreiser was ecstatic. "It sings, it has rapture, it has color," he cried. And Heywood Broun and Carl Van Doren created enough attention to help develop a large American market for the novel.

As a study of a youth's search for meaning and truth in a world of cruelty and deceit, "Of Human Bondage" stands apart from the remainder of Mr. Maugham's work for, among other things, its brutal honesty. The character of Philip was so close to Maugham that he was unable to read the novel after it was published. On one occasion, when he began to read it for the first time in 30 years, he found himself unable to continue beyond the opening paragraph.

"I choked up and then, to my utter humiliation, I broke down and cried," Maugham said.

After "Of Human Bondage," the publication of several novels by Maugham disappointed critics, some of whom said that he had denigrated his talents for money.

One critic wrote that Maugham had "lost the two qualities which determine greatness: his fire and his wings."

What followed was a series of novels and short stories, many of which were sold to the movies. "The Moon and Sixpence" was published in 1919, followed three years later by a collection of short stories, "The Trembling of a Leaf." One of these stories was "Miss Thompson," which later enjoyed a long Broadway run as a play, "Rain," with Jeanne Eagels as Sadie Thompson.

In a two-part article published by Show magazine in 1962, Maugham told how he had come to write of Sadie Thompson:

"I had gone to Honolulu with the intention of taking a ship that would land me at Tahiti. I wanted to go there because I had long had the idea of writing a novel based on the life of Gauguin, of whom I had heard a good deal during the year 1905, which I spent in Paris, and I hoped to find in Tahiti matter that would be useful to me.

"For some reason which I have forgotten there was no ship to take me there and it appeared I could do nothing but wait for one that put in at Honolulu on the way to New Zealand and stopped to put off passengers at Pago Pago. There I could get a schooner that would take me on.

"When the ship I was waiting for arrived at Honolulu I booked my passage. The night before this the red-light district of Honolulu, called Iwelei, to the general excitement had been raided by the police. A few minutes before my ship sailed a young woman hurried on board.

"As we came to know later, she was a prostitute escaping from the law. The other passengers were a doctor and his wife and a missionary with his. When we arrived at Pago Pago, we learned that there was an epidemic of measles there, often a fatal disease among the Kanakas, and telegraphic instructions had been received from Apia to say that the schooner, we—the missionaries, the doctor and his wife, and I—would not be allowed to enter the harbor till it was certain that no member of the crew was affected.

"We were obliged to stay at Pago Pago till further notice. The delay gave me the opportunity to write the story I wrote. It was given me by pure chance."

In 1930 Maugham's favorite novel, "Cakes and Ale," was published. The book, a satire on the English literary scene, included what many believed to be an acid portrait of Thomas Hardy in the character of Edward Driffield, the "Grand Old Man of English Letters." Maugham, however, denied that Driffield was modeled upon Hardy.

Perhaps the most dramatic episodes of Maugham's life occurred in World War I when, after serving with the ambulance unit, he spent a year in Switzerland as a British intelligence agent. Posing, at times, as a novelist seeking to escape the war so that he might finish a book, Maugham fulfilled several secret missions — experiences that were detailed in "Ashenden, or the British Agent." (1928).

Maugham's older brother, Frederick Herbert Maugham, had also served with the government. He became Lord High Chancellor in the Cabinet of Prime Minister Neville Chamberlin. In 1939 he was elevated to the peerage and eventually became a viscount. He died in 1958.

Takes to Travel

After a bout with tuberculosis, the writer set out in the 1920's to travel extensively, to "enlarge my experience. I did." The travels to such spots as the South Seas, Malaya and China became the basis for numerous short stories and the Maugham legend.

"I journeyed over a dozen seas, in liners, in tramps, in schooners," he wrote in "The Summing Up." "I went by train, by car, by chair, on foot or on horseback. I kept my eyes open for character, oddness and personality. I learnt very quickly when a place promised me something and then I waited till I had got it. Otherwise I passed on. I accepted every experience that came my way."

Critics have pointed out that many of the women Maugham created — regardless of their social standing — are cold and dominating. Others were pitiable or lonely and only a few are pleasing. These include the good-natured Rosie, of course, in "Cakes and Ale," and Ata, the gentle Polynesian heroine in "The Moon and Sixpence," and Suzanne, the French model in "The Razor's Edge."

Maugham frankly admitted that he never quite recovered from the hurt caused by his mother's death. His relationship with a young woman, upon whom Rosie was based, ended after eight years, when he finally proposed marriage and she rejected him.

Of the end of his marriage to Mrs. Syrie Barnardo Wellcome, he wrote in "The Summing Up": "My peace of mind shattered through my own foolishness and vanity by occurrences upon which I need not dwell." He later documented the arguments and misunderstandings of that marriage in what Glenway Westcott, the writer and critic, called "the strange memoir of his extreme old age, 'Looking Backward'" (1962).

"In the second half of his life," wrote Mr. Westcott last year in an introduction to a paperback issue of "The Summing Up," "no woman has meant as much to him, for weal or woe, as his good Rosie and his beautiful wife had meant."

"To oversimplify the pattern somewhat," Mr. Westcott added, "in the twenties and thereafter the great vacancies of human nature, the needs and wishes to which even the most independent and disciplined creative worker is subject, often increasingly so as the years go by, were chiefly filled and provided for by his two secretarial employes, first an American named Gerald Haxton, until he died, and a Londoner named Alan Searle ever since—very suitable, loyal, able, and in some ways remarkable, literature-loving men."

Legal Dispute Over Paintings

Mr. Searle, together with Maugham and the author's daughter, Lady John Hope, were involved in a tangled and highly publicized legal fight that began in 1962. At the time, a lawyer for Maugham announced that the author had adopted Mr. Searle as his son and that Maugham was planning court action for the return of gifts worth $2 million given to his daughter, on the grounds of "ingratitude and illegitimacy." These gifts included valuable art and controlling shares in a company that owned Maugham's villa, estimated to be worth nearly $1 million.

In July, 1963, a Nice court nullified the adoption and declared that Lady John Hope, whose husband was a former British Minister of Works, was legally Maugham's daughter. The writer said he would appeal.

On Jan. 22, however, a few days before his 90th birthday, the writer settled his two-year-old difference with his daughter. Lady John Hope confirmed that she would receive $280,000 from the sale of nine pictures, including a two-sided Picasso. The auction at Sotheby's in 1962 netted the equivalent of $642,000.

The nine pictures were part of a collection of 35 sold for a total of $1,466,000. (At the time, Maugham remarked: "That's rather a lot of money for a single gentleman to get.") Presumably, with Maugham's death, the villa will go to Lady John Hope.

Purchased in 1928, the villa was, like its owner, elegant and vaguely mysterious. At one time a staff of 13, including 5 gardeners, were employed. Planted oleanders, camellias and avocado trees from California grew in the garden. Parties were frequent, the meals were perfect, the service was superb. His glassware and fine linens were marked, however, with a typical Maugham touch—a symbol that he explained was the Berber sign to ward off the evil eye.

Attitude Toward Religion

Maugham was intrigued by the mystical, the exotic. In his story "The Pool" he has one of the characters remark what he may have felt of the Far East: "It was a more natural life than any he had known; it was nearer to the friendly, fertile earth; civilization repelled him and by mere contact with these creatures of a more primitive nature he felt a greater freedom."

Maugham had no conventional religious beliefs. "For my own part the best answer I know is that given by Fray Luis de Leon [a 16th-century mystic and lyric poet]," he wrote at the close of "The Summing Up." "The beauty of life, he says, is nothing but this, that each should act in conformity with his nature and his business."

Even during World War II, which Maugham spent mostly in the United States, his working routine was constant. He awoke early, had coffee and toast, then did some "serious" reading until 10 A.M., when he went into his writing room. He wrote with a fountain pen, and frequently rewrote a sentence or a page 10 or 15 times.

"One fusses about style," he once said. "One tries to write better. One aims at balance and rhythm. One sweats one's guts out. And yet the fact remains that the four greatest novelists the world has ever known—Balzac, Dickens, Tolstoi and Dostoyevski—wrote their respective languages very badly. It proves that if you can tell stories, create characters, devise incidents, and have sincerity and passion, it doesn't matter a damn how you write."

Shortly before 1 P.M., Maugham emerged from his writing room and had a gimlet. Then lunch, a nap, the mail, a ride or a walk and tea. He permitted himself only a few cigarettes and two cigars a day, one after lunch and one after dinner.

Near the close of his life, Maugham had stopped writing. He read and played bridge and traveled a bit and lived on the earnings of an enormously successful career—a career in which more than 80 million copies of his books had been sold around the world. He wrote 21 novels, and 26 volumes of his short stories were published, though many of the volumes repeated stories. He also wrote a variety of autobiographical works.

"I am like a passenger waiting for his ship at a wartime port," he wrote at the end of "A Writer's Notebook." "I do not know which day it will sail, but I am ready to embark at a moment's notice. I read the papers and flip the pages of a magazine, but when someone offers to lend me a book I refuse because I may not have time to finish it, and in any case with this journey before me I am not of a mind to interest myself in it. I strike up acquaintances at the bar or the card table, but I do not try to make friends with people from whom I shall so soon be parted. I am on the wing."

Taking note of this passage, W. H. Auden wrote: "We can only answer: 'We shall miss you. Of course we shall find new writers to read, but art, like friendship, is personal — that is, unique—and no writer is replaceable by or even comparable with another. Thank you for having given us so much pleasure for so long, for having never been tedious'—and so wish him godspeed."

W. Somerset Maugham in 1911, as he was painted by Sir Gerald Kelly. They shared an apartment in Montmartre.

Always True to Himself

Maugham Had Bad Word for Everyone But He Cared for Literary Reputation

By DREW MIDDLETON

A Memoir

One of the first things one learned about Somerset Maugham in London was that no one liked him very much. He, in turn, cared much for what posterity would think of his work and little for the opinion of a world he had described with infinite craftsmanship. Willie Maugham, as he was known, was respected. By some it was because of his industry, his prodigious output of plays, novels and short stories. By others it was because of the quality of his best work. Publishers and businessmen admired the manner in which Maugham had won lucrative contracts and invested wisely. The former, fortunately for them, encountered few writers with his shrewd eye for pounds, shilling and pence. Amateurs of the arts praised his sophisticated taste in painting and furniture.

Yet he was not personally popular. Some of the reasons were trivial. He was slow to buy a drink, he did not suffer fools gladly and his comments were wounding. He was kind to young writers but there was a vein of almost feminine maliciousness in his remarks about his contemporaries.

Hugh Walpole had been a popular man in London literary circles. Few of his friends ever forgave Willie Maugham the brilliant and destructive lampooning of Walpole as Alroy Kear in "Cakes and Ale."

Angered Old Friends

In his last years few of Maugham's old colleagues remained. Those who lived on remembered and resented the way he had treated his wife, Syrie. They were angered anew when the author agreed to the publication by the Beaverbrook Press's Sunday Express of sections from his autobiography. These were cruel to his wife and wounding to his daughter.

"Willie's been true to himself," one publisher said, "he's had a bad word for everybody."

The author was not an impressive-looking man. He was short with a large, heavy head sparsely covered by thinning brown hair. On the Riviera he dressed with a certain gaiety. In London, it was usually a well-worn gray flannel suit and scuffed suede shoes. As he grew older his neck thinned and his collars gaped. The tie's knot was usually very large.

His routine in London was well established. One, possibly two, dry martinis in front of the fire in the lounge of his club, usually the Garrick. Luncheon at the head of the long table flanked by old cronies from the card room. Some days he was animated, talkative. Other times he sat almost in silence: his eyes reproving those bridge partners who lingered over their food.

Maugham's homosexuality was well known but excited little comment in the tolerant literary world of London. Certainly, there were no outward signs of it except, perhaps, a certain waspishness about women. But as a craftsman, and he was always that, he was always ready to respect women who were competent in the arts.

Once when a group had been talking about a rather lackluster British Broadcasting Corporation play based on his short story "The Letter," someone remarked that Celia Johnson had been very good.

"But, of course, of course," the old man said, "she's a very fine actress, very fine indeed."

For a large part of his life Somerset Maugham was a wealthy writer respected by the British Establishment as much, perhaps, for his success as for his writing. But it was evident from what he wrote and said that, with a few exceptions (Winston Churchill was one) he had little use for the class he had depicted in so many short stories, novels and plays.

Maugham had not gone to one of the big public schools but to King's School, Canterbury; the Tercanbury of his novels.

Whatever the reason he held the public schools and their products in low esteem, arguing that they had contributed much to the loss of Britain's empire. He was a man who saw historical developments in terms of people rather than of great historical movements.

He liked to remark that Henry James had turned his back on one of the great adventures of the 19th century, the rise of the United States, to report the tittle tattle of London tea parties. But Maugham, if not interested in tittle tattle, was interested in the people at those tea parties.

Admired Common Man

Beneath the cold, cynical surface there lodged a genuine affection and respect for the ordinary people of Britain. No government was so bad, he remarked once, that it could entirely quench the energies of the British. To him the shopkeepers and postmen and bank clerks were the true stuff of the country. They got his courtesy; the rudeness was reserved for dukes.

Certainly there was a strain of patriotism in his singular character. He was an able intelligence officer in World War I. Characteristically he once said, that if he didn't get a decoration he at least got a very good book out of the conflict. He referred to "Ashenden."

Was there a great love in his life? An elderly publisher said there certainly had been.

"She was Rosie, you know, Rosie, the barmaid in 'Cakes and Ale,'" he said. "There's also someone like her near the end of 'Of Human Bondage.' I don't know who she was but she did exist. Whatever happened, I don't know. But after that he never cared tuppence for another woman."

Toward the end he cared most for his literary reputation. Just before his 90th birthday he remarked that his greatest, indeed his only consolation, was the letters that came to him every day from young people all over the world. They were still reading him, he said with a touch of pride.

The day broke gray and dull. The clouds hung heavily & there was a rawness in the air that suggested snow. A servant came into a bedroom in which a child was sleeping & drew the curtains. She glanced mechanically at the house opposite, a small stucco house with a portico, & went to the child's bed.

First lines of the novel "Of Human Bondage" as they appeared in original manuscript by Maugham. The work, which was published in 1915, became cornerstone of his career.

Posthumous Publication Barred By Maugham, Executor Reports

By HARRY GILROY

W. Somerset Maugham instructed his literary executor, Alexander S. Frere, that no unpublished writing of his should be printed after his death. The author himself staged a "holocaust" of his notebooks and works in progress about five years ago at his Mediterranean home, the Villa Mauresque.

Mr. Frere revealed Maugham's instructions last Tuesday during a visit here. As president of William Heinemann, Ltd., he was Maugham's English publisher until 1962.

The publisher and the author were close friends. They had last met six weeks ago at lunch in the Villa Mauresque. Mr. Frere said that the author had been feeble, almost blind and "stone deaf" but still sticking to his routine of "a very dry martini" and a proper lunch.

Mr. Frere expressed regret that Maugham's determination to be known only by the work he published in books had weakened when "he wrote that last biographical piece, 'Looking Back,' in which he cast doubt on the legitimacy of his daughter." The article appeared in the London Express and in Show Magazine in New York.

He said that "Willy" Maugham was a kindly man "who loved his daughter," and that the article was "so out of character."

"It was a very sad thing," he continued, "to see a finely balanced mind, a real critical intelligence, going off the rails. H. G. Wells once described such a state as that of a mind at the end of its tether."

Mr. Frere said he had been named in Maugham's will as an executor—not just literary executor — along with Alan Searle, Maugham's secretary. He added: "I don't know if that is still the case, as Mr. Maugham has made some changes in his will in recent years, but he has never notified me of any change."

He indicated that Maugham had a considerable estate. His books and plays earned "millions of pounds, literally," Mr. Frere said. Royalties still pour in. The Villa Mauresque, which "Willy bought for about $150,000, is now worth $2.5 million," Mr. Frere said. He told also of Maugham's American investments.

"Once in San Francisco, on his way to Tahiti, where he got the material for 'Rain' and other stories, he met a San Francisco stockbroker, Bert Alanson, and gave him a thousand pounds to invest, and the broker turned that into a million dollars—stocks and bonds, nothing to do with writing," Mr. Frere said.

The publisher said that he had never met anyone "more completely a novelist and an imaginative writer than Willy was." He added: "He was like blotting paper. He took in everything and all of it came out as fiction treated with superlative skill."

Maugham was "not impressed with his own writing," the publisher said. He would turn in a perfect manuscript, ask for no opinion on it, correct proofs with professional expertness and then expect no further word until a finished book was put in his hands. "He could not bear to talk about his own writing," Mr. Frere said.

MAURICE P. KOHL

Special to The New York Times

CLEVELAND, Dec. 15—Maurice P. Kohl, Ohio distributor for Charles Meyers & Co., trouser manufacturers of St. Louis, died of a heart ailment in Mount Sinai Hospital today. He was 61 years old and lived in Shaker Heights.

Mr. Kohl, who changed his name from Koshetz, is survived by his widow, Mrs. Eve Katz Kohl; a son, Ronald; a daughter, Karen; two brothers, Herbert Koshetz, assistant to the financial-business news editor of The New York Times, and Herman Kohl; four sisters, Mrs. Yetta Nisenbaum, Mrs. Rose Racher, Mrs. Emma Ball and Mrs. Gertrude Greenberg, and a granddaughter.

WILLIAM W. SKINNER

Special to The New York Times

MONTCLAIR, N. J., Dec. 15—William W. Skinner, a former investment officer and director of the St. Paul Fire & Marine Insurance Company of St. Paul, died yesterday at Mountainside Hospital here. He was 77 years old and lived at 54 Melrose Place.

Mr. Skinner, who retired in 1946, was a graduate of the Sheffield Scientific School of Yale University and was a former trustee of the Montclair Art Museum.

"All the News That's Fit to Print"

The New York Times

LATE CITY EDITION

Weather: Partly sunny today; rain tonight. Becoming fair tomorrow. Temperature range: today 58-77; yesterday 59-76. Details, page 44.

VOL.CXXVI...No.43,673 · © 1977 The New York Times Company · NEW YORK, SATURDAY, AUGUST 20, 1977 · 25 cents beyond 50-mile zone from New York City. Higher in air delivery cities. · 20 CENTS

The New York Times

CARRYING A MESSAGE: The Voyager spacecraft being lifted onto the Titan-Centaur booster rocket in preparation for today's launching to outer planets of solar system. Craft will carry recorded message from earth. Page 8.

IDEOLOGICAL SHIFT CONSIDERED LIKELY AT PEKING MEETING

Communist Party's 11th Congress Expected to Drop Radicalism, Adopt Pragmatic Policies

By Reuters

PEKING, Aug. 19—A mass meeting, apparently the 11th Congress of the Chinese Communist Party, was under way in the Great Hall of the People late tonight amid reports that a major shift in the official ideology from revolutionary radicalism to more down-to-earth policies would be announced within 24 hours.

Reliable sources said today that the announcement would come by tomorrow and that the congress, the first since Mao Tse-tung's death, was ending.

[In Washington, United States officials, on the eve of Secretary of State Cyrus R. Vance's visit to China, went out of their way to stress that relations will not be normalized with China if this required even the appearance of abandoning Taiwan. Page 3.]

Careful Preparation

The expected announcement in Peking seemed to be receiving careful preparation. Cars and buses were parked neatly outside the lit-up building, and several hundred Chinese waited across the road on the Square of Heavenly Peace.

The main evening radio news contained no mention of the congress but there were signs that Peking was gearing up to celebrate the event. Firecrackers exploded occasionally and in the back alleys people were making paper flags.

The sources said the key address to the congress, the political report, was read by Mao's successor, Chairman Hua Kuo-feng. A second major speech on revision of the party constitution was delivered by the aged Deputy Chairman, Yeh Chien-ying, they added.

As soon as the congress ends, a full session of the newly elected Central Committee will be held, the sources said.

Emphasis on Order Expected

The congress's political report is expected to emphasize the "order and economic development" program that China has pursued since the radical leaders were driven out in disgrace last October.

The press has recently been emphasizing the trend, stressing ideology less and adopting a practical approach to the task of modernization.

Besides approving the political report and new party constitution, the congress, which is believed to have opened last week, discussed filling many vacancies in the party and state leadership.

Speculation that a new Prime Minister would be named to replace Chairman Hua, who has continued to fill the post since becoming party chairman, has centered on Deputy Prime Minister Teng Hsiao-ping, a moderate who was purged last year in a campaign led by the since-disgraced radical faction head by Mao's wife, Chiang Ching, but who won back all his former titles four weeks ago.

Earthquake Strikes Indian Ocean; It May Be the Strongest on Record

Epicenter of Shock Is Between Australia and Indonesia

By The Associated Press

JAKARTA, Indonesia, Aug. 19 — A powerful earthquake, possibly the strongest ever recorded, struck the eastern Indian Ocean between Australia and Indonesia today, rattling tall buildings as far away as Perth, Australia, 1,000 miles to the south.

There were no immediate reports of injuries, but the Indonesian islands closest to the quake's epicenter are relatively isolated and reports from the area were delayed.

Earthquake monitoring stations around the world reported the strength of the tremor at between 7.7 and 8.9 on the Richter scale. Vienna seismologists who reported the 8.9 reading said energy waves might have distorted their reading, but that the quake was "one of the strongest in recorded history."

No Indication of Sea Wave

There was no immediate indication whether the earthquake had set off a sea wave. Such waves are often the most devastating effect of quakes in this part of the world.

The Indonesian Meteorology Department said the epicenter was in the ocean 931 miles southeast of Jakarta. It said the quake struck at 1:11 P.M. Jakarta time and that tremors and aftershocks lasted for more than an hour.

The closest major land area to the epicenter was the Indonesian island of Sumba, about 200 miles to the north. About 25,000 people live on the mountainous island, most of them farmers and breeders of horses and other livestock.

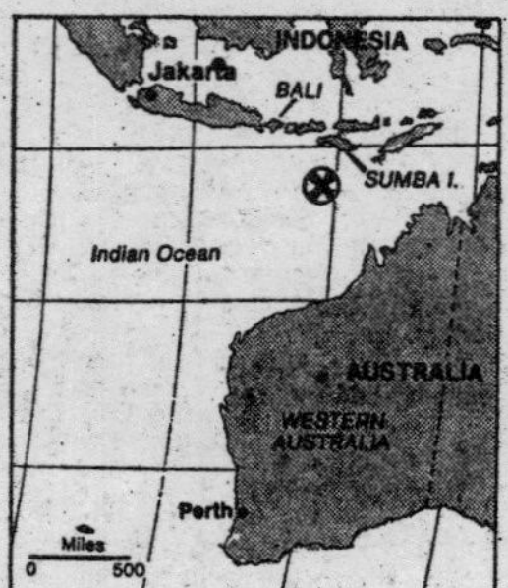

The New York Times/Aug. 20, 1977

Cross indicates epicenter of quake

Tremors were felt along the 2,400-mile coast of Western Australia.

In Perth, Western Australia's major city, hundreds of frightened workers fled from tall office buildings as windows and venetian blinds rattled and chairs slid across floors. Many refused to return to work.

Seismologists in Honolulu recorded the quake at 7.7 on the Richter scale, and the Uppsala Seismological Institute in Sweden reported it at 8.3.

The Vienna Institute for Meteorology and Geodynamics recorded 8.9, noting the energy waves had knocked its equipment "out of scale."

An institute spokesman added that a less sensitive seismograph in a nearby city registered the tremor at 8.25. "This suggests the actual strength was well beyond the eight-point mark," he said.

The catastrophic earthquake that struck northeastern China last year registered between 7.6 and 8.2 on various seismographs and has generally been regarded as the strongest tremor of recent history.

CONSUMER PRICE RISE 0.4% FOR LAST MONTH, SMALLEST THIS YEAR

CHEAPER GROCERIES A FACTOR

Government Economists Pleased by Decline, but Others Predict More Inflation Problems

By CLYDE H. FARNSWORTH

Special to The New York Times

WASHINGTON, Aug. 19—Consumer prices rose four-tenths of 1 percent in July, the smallest monthly increase of the year, thanks in large measure to a decline in grocery food prices, the Labor Department's Consumer Price Index showed today.

Government economists said that they were encouraged by the indicator, which they cited as further evidence that the rise in the inflation rate in the first quarter of the year to 10 percent and more was an aberration.

But some private economists suggested that troubles would reoccur, citing Government policies in energy, agriculture, Social Security and environmental quality as some of the factors that could contribute to future price increases.

Below May and June Rises

The July increase was below the rises of six-tenths of 1 percent in each of the two preceding months and brought the rise in the index over the last 12 months to 6.4 percent. The indicator further showed that it cost $182.60 last month to buy what could have been purchased for $100 in 1967.

The price of food purchased in grocery stores declined one-tenth of 1 percent in July. The drop, which is the first since last November, reflected lower prices for beef, poultry, pork, fresh fruits and vegetables, sugar and ground coffee. But prices continued to rise for other foods, such as dairy products, cereal and bakery products, fats and oil products and processed fruits and vegetables.

However, the drop in food prices is hurting incomes in the farm belt and has already spurred efforts both to peg farm prices at higher levels and to curb production. Most economists felt that grocery store prices would inevitably start easing after the 10 percent slide over the last three months in the prices farmers have been receiving for their crops.

Inflation Matching Wage Rises

Adding restaurant and snack bar prices, however, the total food price index actually rose by one-tenth of 1 percent in July.

Meanwhile, the prime lending rate rose today, and Jack Carlson, chief economist of the Chamber of Commerce of the United States, said this reflected "apprehension that the rate of inflation has only temporarily moderated." Several major

Continued on Page 44, Column 3

Madison Square Garden Corp. Taken Over by Gulf & Western

By PAUL L. MONTGOMERY

Special to The New York Times

WESTBURY, L.I., Aug. 19—Gulf and Western Industries completed its eight-year campaign to absorb the Madison Square Garden Corporation and its sports holdings this morning after a hectic final stockholders' meeting at Roosevelt Raceway.

The 32-1 margin in the vote for merger was a foregone conclusion because Gulf and Western owned 81 percent of Madison Square Garden stock when the meeting started and 100 percent when it ended. The Garden corporation thus became a wholly owned subsidiary of G. & W., and the Garden holdings—which include the Garden itself and the adjacent 29-story office tower, Roosevelt Raceway, the Knicks, the Rangers and the international Holiday on Ice troupes, Arlington and Washington Parks and the O'Hare Hilton Hotel in Chicago, and real estate in Long Island, Manhattan and Chicago—were dispersed in the vast G. & W. empire.

Alan N. Cohen, president of the old corporation, said he did not expect the merger to have any day-to-day effect on the Garden's many operations, even though most of the top executives in the company are excluded from the new board of directors.

As nearly as can be determined, G.& W. spent about $55 million to acquire the Garden stock and also assumed the corporation's $130 million in long-term debt. The conglomerate began its acquisition of the corporation in 1969 and started buying stock in earnest in 1973 with the first in a flurry of tender offers. Garden stock traded as high as $70 a share in the 1967 bull market and fell as low as $3.25 in 1974.

Gulf and Western's last tender offer was $10 a share, and that is the price the few remaining stockholders will receive following today's merger.

The $10-a-share price was unilaterally determined by Gulf and Western. The Garden was a Michigan corporation, and under Michigan law the

Continued on Page 14, Column 1

Lance Issue Prompts Wide Inquiry Into Comptroller Office Standards

By JUDITH MILLER

Special to The New York Times

WASHINGTON, Aug. 19—The inquiry into the financial activities of Budget Director Bert Lance has touched off a full-scale examination of the standards and methods used by the Office of the Comptroller of the Currency in regulating the nation's banks, well-placed officials said today.

According to the sources, three senior officials in the Comptroller's office are under scrutiny by the Internal Revenue Service for their roles in an earlier examination of Mr. Lance's banking and personal finances.

While it had been reported earlier by The New York Times that the Comptroller's office was being investigated by the Inspection Division of the I.R.S., the officials said today that the scope of the inquiry was much more serious than had been thought at first.

These officials said the handling of the Lance matter by the Comptroller's office had raised broader questions, which will now be examined, of whether the agency's staff had been overly lenient in its supervision of the national banks it is charged with regulating. One official said the investigation so far seemed to indicate that some of the agency's staff had been "co-opted" by the banking system they supervise.

"Heads will roll," one senior official said when asked about the investigation.

Meanwhile, the White House disclosed today that President Carter had made two campaign trips aboard a corporate aircraft belonging to Mr. Lance's Georgia bank, and the President's records were being checked to see if the bank had been reimbursed. [Page 9.]

In a letter accompanying a report on Mr. Lance issued yesterday, Comptroller

Continued on Page 9, Column 5

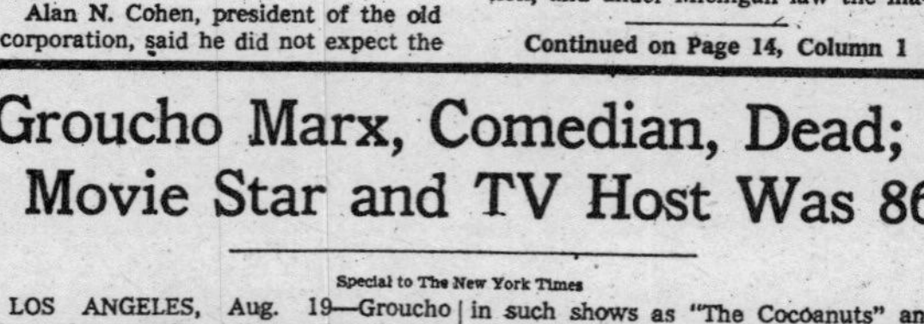

Groucho Marx, Comedian, Dead; Movie Star and TV Host Was 86

Special to The New York Times

LOS ANGELES, Aug. 19—Groucho Marx, the comedian, died tonight at the Cedar Sinai Medical Center here after failing to recover from a respiratory ailment that hospitalized him June 22. He was 86 years old.

Marx, whose entertainment career began almost 70 years ago and ranged from vaudeville to television, slumped into semiconsciousness late last night and failed quickly, the doctors said.

His death was attributed to pneumonia.

Marx, with his brothers Chico, Harpo, Gummo and Zeppo, conquered Broadway in such shows as "The Cocoanuts" and "Animal Crackers," and then moved to Hollywood where they started an almost legendary series of movies, highlighted by such pictures as "A Night at the Opera" and "A Day at the Races."

At Groucho's death, Zeppo became the only survivor of the five brothers.

Groucho first entered the hospital in March, suffering from a hip ailment. Following surgery to repair a damaged hip joint, he was released in late March. Subsequently he reinjured his hip and returned for more surgery.

He stayed 11 days, was released, and was readmitted after only one day, suffering from a respiratory condition. He did not leave the hospital again. During his hospitalization, he was not made aware of a bitter court battle over the stewardship of his estate.

With him when he died were his son, Arthur; Arthur's wife, Lois, and Groucho's grandson, Andrew.

A hospital spokesmen said no funeral arrangements had been made as of tonight.

Associated Press

Groucho Marx

Master of the Insult

By ALBIN KREBS

Effrontery, of the most lunatic, unsquelchable sort, was the chief stock in trade of Groucho Marx. As the key man in the most celebrated brother act in motion pictures, he developed the insult into an art form. And he used the insult, delivered with maniacal glee, to shatter the

Continued on Page 7, Column 1

The New York Times/Neal Boenzi

REWARD FOR DILIGENCE: Five of 25 policemen who were promoted yesterday for their work in .44-caliber-killer case saluting during national anthem at Police Headquarters. From left: Timothy Dowd, Joseph Borrelli, George C. Hambrecht, James Chillis and Michael Cataneo Jr. Page 10.

INSIDE

F.B.I. Case Is Dropped

The Justice Department has decided not to prosecute an F.B.I. official who was in charge of a New York unit accused of illegal wiretapping. Page 45.

Airport Ordered Closed

Beame banned all landings at Flushing Airport, but the airport stayed open and its management said it would go to court to test legality. Page 44.

South Africa Is Planning a Wider Role for Minorities

By JOHN F. BURNS

Special to The New York Times

JOHANNESBURG, Aug. 19—The South African Government, under growing pressure to abandon exclusively white rule, is reported to have completed a constitutional review and to have settled on a system that would allow Asians and those of mixed race, but not blacks, to share political power.

Under a system that will be laid before a caucus of the ruling National Party in Cape Town tomorrow, the existing parliamentary system would be scrapped and replaced by a presidential system loosely based on the French model. The first president is almost certain to be the current Prime Minister, John Vorster.

Press reports of the plan, although unconfirmed by the Government, tally closely with hints that cabinet members have been giving for some time. After winning the ruling party's approval, the new system is expected to go before the Parliament next year, with the president possibly assuming his office as early as 1979.

The new plan follows months of intensive debate among the 2.4 million whites who rule this racially divided country. The failure to offer a larger political role to the country's 18.6 million blacks is a sharp disappointment for Afrikaner intellectuals who have argued that only by giving the majority group a wider role could the whites hope to preserve a future for themselves here.

Present indications are that the ruling party is unlikely to go much beyond the current proposal, even if Mr. Vorster steps down. The debate within the party has shown that the conservatives enjoy overwhelming support at the grassroots level.

The new plan, devised by a cabinet committee that has been studying the matter for 18 months, would not disturb the existing realities of power in the country. Whites, through the presidency, would remain in ultimate control, while the other two racial groups would be given a minority voice in national affairs through a multiracial council.

The blacks would gain nothing. They would be allowed political rights only in the nine tribal homelands—underdeveloped areas that account for 13 percent of the country's area. The 10 million blacks living outside the homelands, mostly in the black townships outside

Continued on Page 8, Column 3

Groucho Marx, Film Comedian and Host of 'You Bet Your Life,' Dies

Continued From Page 1

than life. He was the gruesomely stooped man in the swallowtail coat who took great loping steps across the stage or screen, holding a long, plump cigar behind him. His seemingly depraved eyes rolled and leered from behind steel-rimmed glasses. Below his large nose a smudge of black greasepaint passed for a mustache.

His humor was based on the improbable, the unexpected, the outrageous. In a Marx Brothers play he would interrupt a scene by stepping to the footlights to inquire urgently, "Is there a doctor in the house?" When an unsuspecting physician rose, he would demand to know: "If you're a doctor, why aren't you at the hospital making your patients miserable, instead of wasting your time here with that blonde?" And during one of his television quiz shows, which were immensely popular in the 1950's, when a contestant was asked her age and said she was "approaching 40," he replied, "From which direction?"

Aimed at Deflation

But Groucho's expertly delivered, rapid-fire insults were more mad than maddening; they really weren't unkind, for they evolved from his interest in humor that deflated rather than annihilated. This quality was, in fact, the distinguishing mark of the comedy so richly dispensed by Groucho Marx, his brothers and their great contemporaries, such as Charles Chaplin, W. C. Fields and Buster Keaton.

"It was the type of humor that made people laugh at themselves," Groucho said in 1968, "rather than the sort that prevails today—the sick, black, merely smart-aleck stuff designed to evoke malicious laughter at the other fellow."

Throughout his hectic life the comedian remained able to laugh at himself. He even appeared not to take seriously the fact that his early years were passed in extreme poverty. For example, when it was suggested that his rags-to-riches rise bore Lincolnesque overtones, he said, "There weren't any rails to split in the neighborhood around 93d Street and Third Avenue. Just the third rail on the el, and there wasn't much of a future in fooling around with that."

United Press International

Groucho Marx

Julius Henry Marx was born Oct. 2, 1890, in a tenement on East 93d Street. His Alsatian-born father, Samuel Marx, was an unsuccessful tailor; his mother, the former Minnie Schoenberg, was the stage-struck sister of Al Shean, of the comedy team of Gallagher and Shean.

Mrs. Marx pushed all five of her sons into show business, partly because she was the embodiment of the "stage mother," but also because every member of the family had to be a breadwinner. At 10, Groucho was singing soprano with the Gus Edwards vaudeville troupe, and at 14 he completed his formal education by quitting P.S. 86. "If I intended to eat, I would have to scratch for it," he wrote years later.

Mother Assembled Act

Still in his teens, Groucho got a $4-a-week job with the Le May Trio, an act that broke up in Denver, leaving him penniless. He worked in a grocery store long enough to earn train fare back to New York, where his mother was putting together an act called the Six Musical Mascots.

It consisted of Groucho and two of his brothers, Adolph (later Harpo) and Milton (Gummo), an attractive soprano named Janie O'Riley, Mrs. Marx and her sister Hannah. Mrs. Marx soon realized that she and her sister were so bad that the act was doomed unless they left it. They retired from show business.

What was left was The Four Nightingales, an act that, in the course of its travels through whistle-stop towns, in the South and Midwest, changed its name to The Marx Brothers and Co. Harmony singing, popular on the vaudeville circuit at the time, was the basis of the act before the brothers fairly stumbled onto the format that was to make them famous.

They did so when they played a seedy little theater in Nacogdoches, Tex., in 1914.

"Our act was so lousy," Groucho said, "that when word passed through the audience of numbskull Texans that a mule had run away, they got up en masse to go out and see something livelier. We were accustomed to heckling and insults, but that made us furious, so when those guys wearing ten-gallon hats over pint-size brains came back, we let them have it. It wasn't the best line I ever ad-libbed, but I recall I told them 'Nacogdoches—is full of roaches.' And —ultimate insult —I called those Texans 'damn yankees.'"

The audience loved the insults and the ad-libs, and from that point on, the Marxes sang less and worked in more jokes, puns and one-liners. They used carefully plotted sketches, but never hesitated to throw in topical ad-libs.

Hobby of Nicknames

The Marx Brothers perfected their style and characterizations over several years of one-night stands. They got their nutty names from Art Fisher, a monologuist whose hobby was making up nicknames. Harpo's name came from the instrument he played, Gummo's from his gumshoes, Chico's from his reputation as a lady-killer, and Zeppo's from Zippo, star of a chimpanzee act. Because of his saturnine disposition, Groucho's name was a natural.

Groucho first wore his famous frock coat in a sketch called "Fun in Hi Skule," in which he played the professor. He adopted the omnipresent cigar because he liked to smoke cigars in the first place, and they served as useful props. "If you forget a line," he said, "all you have to do is stick the cigar in your mouth and puff on it until you think of what you've forgotten."

The painted-on mustache, which was Groucho's chief trademark for 30 years, until he grew a real one, resulted from a dispute with the manager of the Fifth Avenue Theater. One night he arrived too late to put on his paste-on mustache. Instead he drew one on with greasepaint. After the show the manager demanded "the same mustache you gave 'em at the Palace," so Groucho handed him the fake mustache. The greasepaint smear was thenceforward substituted.

The Marxes' first Broadway hit was "I'll Say She Is," in 1924. It was a success largely on the strength of a rhapsodic review in The New Yorker by Alexander Woollcott, who spent the rest of his life pouring praise upon the brothers, Groucho in particular.

In 1929 Groucho very nearly suffered a nervous breakdown. He and his brothers filmed "The Cocoanuts," which had been their second Broadway hit, on Long Island during the day, and appeared nightly in the stage version of "Animal Crackers" (which was committed to film in 1930). He had invested all his savings, $240,000, in the stock market, and lost it all in the crash. Under the strain of too much work and worry over finances, he developed insomnia, which plagued him the rest of his life.

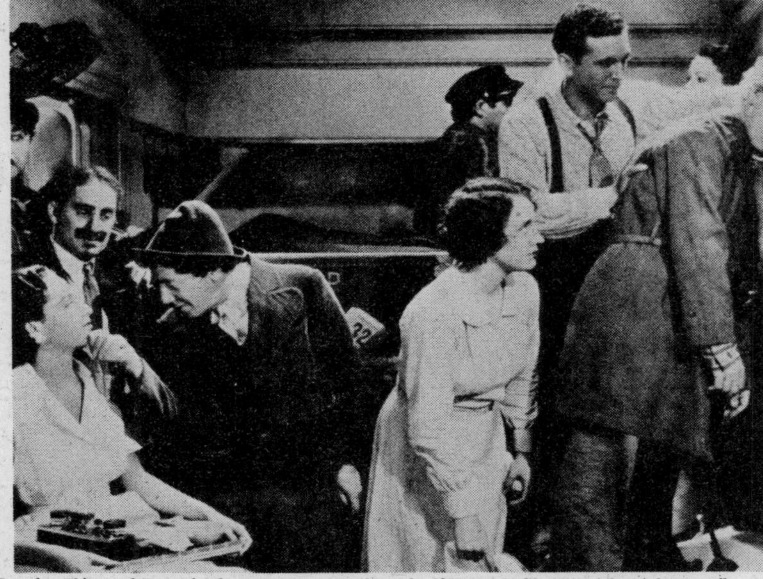

Groucho, Chico and Harpo in the stateroom scene from the 1935 M-G-M film, "A Night at the Opera"

A Favorite of Fans

"Animal Crackers" gave Groucho his most celebrated character, Capt. Jeffrey T. Spaulding, the bumbling African explorer, as well as a monologue that Groucho aficionados have loved over the years. The monologue depended heavily for its humor on Groucho's wildly comic delivery, but even in print, it suggests the outrageousness of the Marx manner.

The monologue is a lampoon of the African adventure saga, delivered by Groucho (Spaulding) before guests at a rich woman's soiree. "Africa is God's country, and He can have it," Groucho begins. "Well, sir, we left New York drunk and early on the morning of Feb. 2. After 15 days on the water and six on the boat, we finally arrived on the shores of Africa. . . . One morning I shot an elephant in my pajamas. How he got in my pajamas, I don't know. . . . But that's entirely irrelephant. . . ." And so on.

Groucho, the master of the ad-lib, refused to follow the scripts of his plays and movies, although some of them were turned out by such masters of comedy writing as George S. Kaufman, Morrie Ryskind and S. J. Perelman. Some of his ad-libs worked so well that they were incorporated into the script. For example, in "Horse Feathers" (1932), an actor said to Groucho, "Jennings has been waiting for an hour and he is waxing wroth," to which Groucho replied, "Tell Roth to wax Jennings for a change." The line went into the script.

In "Animal Crackers," as well as eight other Marx Brothers pictures, Groucho's long-suffering comic foil was Margaret Dumont, whose haughty demeanor suggested the epitome of the grande dame. In their scenes, Groucho was invariably the mangy lover intent on fleecing the rich society matron of her last cent, while at the same time hurling at her the most ungentlemanly insults.

"You're the most beautiful woman I've ever seen, which doesn't say much for you," he ardently told Miss Dumont in "Animal Crackers." In "Duck Soup" (1933), as he, Chico and Harpo fended off Miss Dumont's enemies, he said of her, "Remember, we're fighting for her honor—which is probably more than she ever did."

Surprise for Thalberg

The most popular of the Marx movies was "A Night at the Opera" (1935), produced for Metro-Goldwyn-Mayer by Irving Thalberg, who quickly learned he was dealing with zanies. After he kept the Marxes waiting in his office for more than two hours, Groucho instructed his brothers to disrobe. When Mr. Thalberg finally came out to greet them, he found Groucho, Chico and Harpo before the fireplace, roasting marshmallows in the nude.

Groucho was the quack Dr. Hackenbush in "A Day at the Races" (1937). It was his favorite role because, he said, "It tickled up the medical profession, and I think it can stand a bit of lampooning now and then."

By 1939, with the release of "The Marx Brothers at the Circus," he and his brothers were tiring of making movies. "I continued to appear in them" he said, "but the fun had gone out of picture-making. I was like an old pug, still going through the motions, but now doing it solely for the money."

The Marx Brothers wound up their M-G-M contract with "Go West" (1940) and "The Big Store" (1941). They were idle until 1946, when they made "A Night in Casablanca," and broke up the brother act for good in 1949 with "Love Happy."

(Gummo had left the act many years previously, even before the brothers made their Broadway debut, to become a theatrical agent. Zeppo quit the act after "Duck Soup" in 1933, also to become an agent. Chico died in 1961, Harpo three years later.)

Career on His Own

With "You Bet Your Life," a radio-television quiz show that began in 1947 and lasted a decade, Groucho forged a new career for himself as a single. The program, at one time the highest-rated TV show in the country and the winner of several broadcasting awards, featured the quizmaster's irreverent insult humor rather than jackpot cash awards.

On one program, when a contestant developed mike-fright and was unable to utter a word, Groucho said, "Either this man is dead, or my watch is stopped." Interviewing a tree surgeon, he asked, "Have you ever fallen out of any of your patients?"

Groucho's eccentric antics carried over into his private life. He kept an air rifle beside his bed, and when he heard a howling dog, he would bound to the window to shoot at it. He drove his family to distraction, according to his son Arthur, by practicing on the guitar for stretches of six hours, or playing Gilbert and Sullivan recordings into the wee hours.

He tried to master golf, with results so unsatisfactory that on one occasion, while playing on a course overlooking the Pacific, he walked to a cliff, dropped his golf balls one by one into the sea and then tossed his bagful of clubs after them. "He turned away with a benignly happy look on his face," a fellow player reported.

A Chaotic Ceremony

The comedian married his first wife, the former Ruth Johnson, in 1920, not long after he and his brothers opened in an act called "Home Again" at the Palace Theater—and landed at last in the big time. The wedding ceremony was as chaotic as Marx Brothers routine. While Chico and Harpo skittered about the room carrying potted palms, Groucho harangued the minister with remarks such as, "Why are you going so fast? This is a five-buck ceremony. Aren't we entitled to at least five minutes of your time?" The marriage, which produced two children, Miriam and Arthur, lasted until 1942.

In 1945 he married the former Catherine Gorcey and they had a daughter, Melinda, of whom he was inordinately proud. When Melinda was prevented from swimming with friends in the pool at a country club that excluded Jews, her father wrote the club president an indignant, highly publicized letter in which he said, "Since my little daughter is only half-Jewish, would it be all right if she went in the pool only up to her waist?"

His second marriage ended in divorce in 1950. He married a former model, Eden Hartford, in 1953, when he was past 60 and she was 24.

That marriage broke up in 1969, and Groucho did not marry again. Still, for a number of years, he sought to maintain his image as a leering satyr and seldom let himself be seen in public without the company of a young and beautiful woman.

In 1972, when he returned to the New York stage for the first time in 43 years to give a one-man, one-performance show at Carnegie Hall, he was accompanied by Erin Fleming. Miss Fleming had been his "secretary-companion," as she was described then, since his third divorce.

By the time of the Carnegie concert, Groucho, who had shaved four years off his actual age for decades, was no longer lying about the fact that he was past 80. He looked it, too. His voice was feeble and he could hardly hear, even with his hearing aid, but his eyes were still merrily bright.

Battle Over Estate

Last November, he was to have been lionized in Washington, where he intended to present Marxian memorabilia, including the pith helmet he wore as Captain Spaulding in "Animal Crackers," to the Smithsonian Institution. But the trip was canceled at the last minute, ostensibly because Miss Fleming had the flu and he would not go anywhere without her.

Groucho went to the hospital for an operation on his hip last March. As he was recuperating, confined to his Beverly Hills home, an unpleasant court battle went on over the management of his estate, which was estimated at $2.5 million at the time he divorced his third wife.

Three years ago, Miss Fleming was appointed his guardian. She also was temporary conservator for the estate and Groucho's son, Arthur Marx, sought to replace her in that position. According to the testimony, Miss Fleming, now 37, had exerted a baneful influence over Groucho, even threatening his well-being, though others declared that she was the only reason he was clinging to life then.

The court compromised by appointing Groucho's friend of 45 years, Nat Perrin, the screen writer, as temporary conservator pending a final decision.

Early in 1973, Groucho's son, Arthur, published "Son of Groucho," a memoir. In it, he recalled his father as a singularly penurious man who, when going out to dine in an expensive Hollywood restaurant, would park blocks away to save a parking fee.

His stinginess notwithstanding, and despite the pains he took to make himself financially secure, Groucho, his son reported, was not terribly well off in his old age, chiefly because of the expensive alimony and property settlements resulting from his three divorces.

Groucho's irresponsibility in his personal dealings was legendary. It was not unusual for him to call a friend in the middle of the night—this was one of his ways of taking the boredom out of his insomnia—and launch into a barrage of abuse:

"This is Professor Waldemar Strumbelknauff. Aren't you ashamed of yourself, beating your children that way? If you were a man you'd come over here and knock my teeth out. If you were half a man you'd knock half my teeth out. . . . This is Groucho. How are you? As if I really care." And then he'd hang up.

Shunner of Parties

He grew to hate New York, because he was expected to wear a tie when he went out. He was so addicted to informal wear that he shunned parties, developing, immediately upon being told he was expected to go to one, "a grippey feeling." When he himself entertained, he often took leave of his guests at an early hour, telling them to "go ahead and get drunk on my booze and make fools of yourselves—I don't care because I'm going to bed."

The comedian, who supplemented his meager formal education by reading omnivorously, greatly admired writers. He considered George Bernard Shaw's observation that "Groucho Marx is the world's greatest living actor" as the compliment of his lifetime. For some years he carried on a correspondence with T. S. Eliot, and in 1965 was invited to speak at a memorial service for the poet. Typically, he used the occasion to say something outrageous: "Apparently Mr. Eliot was a great admirer of mine—and I don't blame him."

He was a compulsive letter writer. In 1964 he wrote Gov. William Scranton of Pennsylvania to tell him he had heard him, during a broadcast, mispronounce a Yiddish term. "If you are going to campaign in Jewish neighborhoods," he counseled the Governor, "rhyme mish-mash with slosh."

A collection of his correspondence was published as "The Groucho Letters." The Library of Congress asked him for his letters and papers, which included the manuscripts of two books he wrote, "Groucho and Me" and "Memoirs of a Mangy Lover."

Groucho Marx was actually a moody man, those who knew him best said. They insisted that beneath his brash, fast-talking exterior, he was thoughtful, shy and kindhearted. His longtime friend, the songwriter Harry Ruby, said, "The guy doesn't mean to be insulting; it's an involuntary notion with him, like a compulsion neurosis." And to his son, Arthur, Groucho was "a sentimentalist, but he'd rather be found dead than have you know it."

Groucho himself admitted that "my trouble is that I don't like to let just everybody get in a word edgewise, and can't stand anyone else having the last word." To make sure this wouldn't happen to him ultimately, he took the precaution of writing his epitaph in advance: "I hope they buried me near a straight man."

Mr. Marx with a contestant on his quiz show, "You Bet Your Life"

Lucille Ball and the Marx Brothers in *Room Service.*

A Sampler of Groucho Marx Wit

Groucho: Oscar [Levant], you look tired. Why don't you come to my house for dinner? I've got the most wonderful cook in town, I've saved a steak four inches thick and we'll have a dessert that's out of this world.

Levant: What's your address?

Groucho: Wouldn't you like to know!

•

To a dinner of screenwriters: We in the industry know that behind every successful screenwriter stands a woman. And behind her stands his wife.

Edgar Allen Poe created deathless prose in a drafty garret. Shakespeare wrote "Hamlet" on a crust of bread—didn't even have paper. And Balzac, the greatest French novelist of all time, forced himself to write all night by chaining himself to his bedpost. But he got the maid in trouble anyway. And so I say to you writers, keep your imagination in the stars, your prose in the heavens and your price in the gutter. I thank you—Balzac thanks you —and the maid thanks Balzac.

•

Overseas entertaining troops for the U.S.O., Groucho finds himself in a general's headquarters. A Signal Corps phone rings and Groucho grabs it:

"World War Two-oo."

•

Straight man: Stop at a Western Union office. I want to wire my father.

Groucho: What's the matter? Can't he stand up by himself?

•

From "Monkey Business": "Afraid? Me? A man who's licked his weight in wild caterpillars? Afraid? You bet I'm afraid."

•

Zeppo: The garbage man is here.

Groucho: Tell him we don't want any.

•

Chico: I would like to say goodbye to your wife.

Groucho: Who wouldn't?

•

From an interview: I always wanted to be rich. I still want to be rich. Why, years ago I came to Los Angeles without a nickel in my pocket. Now I *have* a nickel in my pocket. Unfortunately, the nickel today isn't worth what it used to be. Do you know what this country needs? A seven-cent nickel. We've been using the five-cent nickel since 1492. So why not give the seven-cent nickel a chance? If that works out, next year we could have an eight-cent nickel. And so on.

•

I wouldn't belong to any club that would have me for a member.

•

Groucho: Have you got any stewed prunes?

Waitress: Yes.

Groucho: Well, give 'em some black coffee. That'll sober 'em up.

•

I have no advice to give young actors. To young, struggling actresses, my advice is to keep struggling. If you struggle long enough, you will never get in trouble, and if you never get in trouble you will never be much of an actress.

•

From "Horsefeathers": I'd horsewhip you if I had a horse.

•

A man who has just introduced his wife to Groucho: Matilda's just dying for you to say something insulting to her.

Groucho: You ought to be ashamed of yourself. With a wife like that, it should be easy to think of your own insults.

•

Woman: I'm from South Wales.

Groucho: Did you ever meet a fellow named Jonah? He lived in whales for a while.

•

Frankie Avalon: I'm a singer.

Groucho: You mean you're a sewing machine?

•

Interviewer: Will there always be a Groucho?

Groucho: There'll always be a Groucho, just as there will always be an England—although lately, England hasn't been doing so well.

"All the News That's Fit to Print"

The New York Times.

LATE CITY EDITION
U. S. Weather Bureau Report (Page 42) forecasts: Mostly fair, warm and humid today, tonight and tomorrow.
Temp. range: 86—69; yesterday: 85—65. Temp.-Hum. Index: 76; yesterday: 78.

VOL. CXI..No. 38,180. | NEW YORK, MONDAY, AUGUST 6, 1962. | 10 cents beyond 50-mile zone from New York City except on Long Island. Higher in air delivery cities. | FIVE CENTS

COMMON MARKET AND BRITISH VOICE HOPES IN IMPASSE

Both Sides Say Gains Were Made on Role for London Before Session Ended

OCTOBER MEETING SET

Failure to Settle Question of Commonwealth Exports Is Blow to Macmillan

By EDWIN L. DALE Jr.
Special to The New York Times.

BRUSSELS, Belgium, Aug. 5—Representatives of Britain and the European Economic Community expressed disappointment and some bitterness but no discouragement today over their failure to reach full agreement on the basis for British membership in the Community.

They stressed that substantial progress had been made on major issues.

The protracted negotiations, the present session of which lasted four days, will resume early in October.

After nearly twenty-two hours of continuous effort, the negotiators gave up this morning on the key matter still impeding agreement: Britain's effort to assure markets for the agricultural imports she receives from Canada, Australia and New Zealand.

New Tariff to Be Imposed

At the end, only a few points were still unsettled in a Common Market plan designed to give some assurance to the three Commonwealth countries. Their exports, now in large part duty-free in the British market, will be subject to a new common tariff and a variable levy system for farm products if Britain joins the six-nation Community.

The plan includes world commodity agreements, a pledge of a "reasonable" farm price policy aimed at preventing overproduction and a detailed arrangement to maintain preferential treatment for all British Commonwealth countries during a transition period up to 1970.

[The inconclusiveness of the negotiations was viewed in Britain as a setback for Prime Minister Macmillan. It is believed he will now find it more difficult to hold doubtful Conservatives in line and to get an unqualified reaction from the Commonwealth Prime Ministers when they meet next month.]

Key to the Failure

The key to the failure to conclude the matter appears to have been the last-minute introduction by France of a highly complex financial issue. While hundreds of millions of dollars are potentially involved, the issue has no connection with the Commonwealth. The French made agreement on the point a condition for an over-all settlement.

The result of the work of the last four days is that the British will have the "major part" of the terms of their entry to present to the Commonwealth Prime Ministers when they meet in London Sept. 10, but not a full outline, as had been wished.

The British Government must deal with the political as well as the economic consequences

Continued on Page 4, Column 5

Marilyn Monroe Dead, Pills Near

Star's Body Is Found in Bedroom of Her Home on Coast

Police Say She Left No Notes—Official Verdict Delayed

Special to The New York Times.

HOLLYWOOD, Calif., Aug. 5—Marilyn Monroe, one of the most famous stars in Hollywood's history, was found dead early today in the bedroom of her home in the Brentwood section of Los Angeles. She was 36 years old.

Beside the bed was an empty bottle that had contained sleeping pills. Fourteen other bottles of medicines and tablets were on the night stand.

The impact of Miss Monroe's death was international. Her fame was greater than her contributions as an actress.

As a woman she was considered a sex symbol. Her marriages to and divorces from Joe DiMaggio, the former Yankee baseball star, and Arthur Miller, the Pulitzer Prize playwright, were accepted by millions as the prerogatives of this contemporary Venus.

The events leading to her death were in tragic contrast to the comic talent and zest for life that had helped to make "Seven Year Itch" and "Some Like It Hot" smash hits all over the world.

Associated Press
Marilyn Monroe

Miss Monroe's physician had prescribed sleeping pills for her for three days. Ordinarily the bottle would have contained forty to fifty pills.

The actress had also been under the care of a psychoanalyst for a year, and had called him to her home last night. He had suggested she take a drive and relax. She remained home, however.

After an autopsy the Los Angeles coroner reported that Miss Monroe's "was not a natural death." He attributed it to a drug. He added that a toxicological study, to be completed within forty-eight hours, should yield more detailed information. He refused, until then, to list the death as a suicide.

Pending a more positive verdict by Dr. Theodore J. Curphey, the coroner, the Los Angeles police refused to call the death a suicide. They said they had no idea how many pills the actress might have taken, or whether any overdose might have been accidental. Miss Monroe left no notes, according to the police.

In addition to a physical autopsy, Los Angeles has a "psychological" autopsy. Two experts will look into the psychological history of Miss Monroe.

However, the non-physical

Continued on Page 13, Column 6

PRESIDENT NAMES DEAN AT COLUMBIA TO POST ON A. E. C.

John G. Palfrey Is Second Lawyer Picked for Agency in Resolution of Dispute

Special to The New York Times.

HYANNIS PORT, Mass., Aug. 5 — President Kennedy announced today his intention to appoint John G. Palfrey, dean of Columbia College, New York, as a member of the Atomic Energy Commission.

He also announced his selection, reported yesterday, of James T. Ramey, executive director of the Congressional Joint Committee on Atomic Energy, to fill another vacancy on the A. E. C. Mr. Palfrey will succeed Loren K. Olson. Mr. Ramey will succeed John S. Graham.

Mr. Palfrey and Mr. Ramey are lawyers.

Mr. Palfrey, who has done research work on the political and legal aspects of atomic energy, served three years on the staff of the office of the general counsel of the A. E. C.

Dispute Over Posts

Since the resignations of Mr. Olson and Mr. Graham July 1, the Administration and some influential members of the Joint Committee on Atomic Energy have been arguing behind the scenes over candidates for the two $22,000-a-year posts.

Some Executive Branch officials, particularly in the Atomic Energy Commission itself, had rejected candidates, including Mr. Ramey, who had been put forward by the Democrats on the Congressional committee. The Democrats then refused to accept Administration candidates.

The resolution of the dispute was regarded as a compromise. The committee Democrats got Mr. Ramey, one of "their boys." The A. E. C. got Mr. Palfrey, who had been in the office of the general counsel of the commission from 1947 to 1950.

May Serve Short Terms

Besides settling the differences between the two parties, the Administration also had to find two men who would be willing to serve as short a term as one year.

Mr. Palfrey's term officially runs to July 30, 1967, and Mr. Ramey's to June 30, 1964. But it is understood that the Administration is planning to ask Congress next year to replace the commission with a single administrator.

The selection of Mr. Palfrey and Mr. Ramey presumably will satisfy fears expressed by some members of the Joint Committee that the commission was falling into the hands of scientists.

The present three members of

Continued on Page 2, Column 4

The New York Times Aug. 6, 1962

BLAST IN THE ARCTIC: The Soviet Union resumed tests of nuclear weapons in the air over Novaya Zemlya (cross).

RUSSIANS RESUME A-TESTING IN AIR; BLAST 2D BIGGEST

Explosion at High Altitude Over Arctic Island Is Put in 40-Megaton Range

U. S. DEPLORES ACTION

But Voices Hope Soviet Will Still Work for a Treaty—Stresses Pending Offer

By TAD SZULC
Special to The New York Times.

WASHINGTON, Aug. 5 — The Soviet Union resumed its nuclear tests in the atmosphere early today with a powerful high-altitude blast believed to have been in the forty-megaton range.

The blast, over Novaya Zemlya, in the Arctic, appeared to have been the second most potent nuclear explosion ever achieved. The record is held by the Soviet Union, which detonated last Oct. 30 a nuclear device with an explosive force estimated at the equivalent of fifty-eight megatons of TNT. A megaton is 1,000,000 tons.

The United States Government called the resumption a "somber episode," but expressed the hope that Moscow would nonetheless cooperate in working for an effective treaty prohibiting all tests of nuclear weapons.

This morning's test, at 5:08 A. M., Eastern daylight time, was first reported by Swedish and Japanese scientists. It was later confirmed, without details, by the Atomic Energy Commission here. News of the test was withheld from the Soviet people.

Issue Before Geneva Parley

The start of the Soviet test series, forecast by Moscow two weeks ago, came on the eve of the expected presentation before the seventeen-nation disarmament conference in Geneva of new and simplified United States proposals for a test ban treaty.

Moscow broke a three-year-old moratorium on nuclear testing last fall. The United States followed with an extensive series of tests underground and in the atmosphere.

In a statement made public this morning, the State Department commented that, "despite its resumption of atmospheric nuclear testing, we hope the Soviet Union will match our efforts to negotiate an effective nuclear test ban treaty."

It said that "the Soviet Union's initiation of yet another series of atmospheric tests — the second such series in less than a year—can only be regarded as a somber episode."

The statement stressed that "the series was started even as

Continued on Page 3, Column 5

Ben Bella Ally Is Named Chief of Political Bureau

By HENRY TANNER
Special to The New York Times.

ALGIERS, Aug. 5—Mohammed Khider, Mohammed Ben Bella's closest ally, was named today as Secretary General of the powerful Political Bureau. The position is the key post on the seven-man organ of the Algerian National Liberation Front.

Mr. Khider, envoy of Mr. Ben Bella in the negotiations last week that ended a month-long crisis in the nationalist leadership, was also given charge of financial affairs and information.

Hadj Ben Alla, another close collaborator of Mr. Ben Bella, was given control of military affairs.

Mr. Ben Bella himself was put in charge of "coordination of interior affairs" with the Transitional Executive. This, too, is regarded as a key position.

Executive Has Little Power

The Transitional Executive theoretically has responsibility for the country's administration under the cease-fire agreement signed in March with France. But it has no real power of its own and is taking instructions from nationalist leaders.

Mr. Ben Bella apparently will be the man through whom the Transitional Executive will have to work in the future. Some observers said he would act as Algeria's Interior Minister until the Constituent Assembly election set for Sept. 2.

Mohammed Boudiaf, one of Mr. Ben Bella's most determined opponents, was given charge of "guidance and external affairs." He is one of the principal ideologists of the nationalist movement.

The Political Bureau is the policy-making body of the National Liberation Front, the

Continued on Page 8, Column 6

SOVIET TEST STIRS REGRET AT GENEVA

Negotiators for Ban Hope New Series Will be Last —Dean and Zorin Meet

Special to The New York Times.

GENEVA, Aug. 5 — Western and neutralist delegates at the seventeen-nation disarmament conference here expressed regrets today that the Soviet Union had renewed nuclear tests. The test renewal had long been accepted here as inevitable.

Arthur H. Dean of the United States commented that the new round of testing begun by the Soviet Union was "particularly regrettable when we are trying our best to work out a test ban treaty."

"It makes our work all the more complicated," the United States negotiator said.

Arthur S. Lall of India said India was "against tests by anyone, anywhere, any time."

Renewed Effort Urged

"Although both sides are now testing," the Indian delegate said, "this should not be allowed to interfere with the efforts to get a test ban treaty. On the contrary, efforts must be redoubled because of the greater urgency of the problem."

Mr. Dean held an "inconclusive" discussion today on the test ban issue with Valerian A. Zorin, a Deputy Foreign Minister, who is Moscow's delegate at the talks.

Mr. Dean was understood to have emphasized that Moscow must agree to on-site inspections if Washington makes concessions on the controls to guarantee the observance of the projected treaty to end testing.

No arrangements were made during their ninety-minute private talk for a formal discussion of the test ban problem in full conference here.

Meeting Inconclusive

Mr. Dean and Mr. Zorin, who are co-chairmen of the conference, also failed to set a meeting of the three-power subcommittee in which the United States, Britain and the Soviet Union conduct negotiations for a treaty to outlaw atomic tests.

They met at the Soviet delegation's headquarters. No Soviet comment was immediately available. United States sources described the session as "inconclusive."

The hope among the neutralists in particular is that once the United States and the Soviet Union have completed their current tests they will consider their defense requirements satisfied and will be better prepared to compromise on a test

Continued on Page 3, Column 2

N.A.A.C.P. to Ask Courts To End Union Racial Bars

By JOHN D. POMFRET
Special to The New York Times.

WASHINGTON, Aug. 5—The National Association for the Advancement of Colored People is planning a major legal assault on discrimination against Negroes by labor unions. The new effort is to begin in early fall. The aim will be to create a body of judge-made law equal to that now found in the field of public education.

The N. A. A. C. P. was instrumental in creating these laws following the 1954 Supreme Court decision outlawing segregation in public schools.

Much as the association attacked the doctrine of "separate but equal" in the school segregation case, its lawyers are preparing to make the doctrine of "voluntary association" a main target in the union field.

This doctrine holds that private voluntary groups have the right to decide whom they will admit. It has been advanced by some unions as a defense against legal efforts to compel them to take in Negroes.

Role of Unions Cited

The association will argue that the doctrine does not apply to unions because they are not voluntary associations. Their certification by the National Labor Relations Board as exclusive bargaining agents, their role in collective bargaining and their control in some situations of access to jobs distinguish them from social or fraternal groups, the association will contend.

Herbert Hill, the association's labor secretary, said that the N. A. A. C. P. was going into court as a "last resort." In the seven years since it was established, he declared, the merged labor federation has been "either unwilling or unable to eliminate racial discrimination" by its affiliated unions.

Mr. Hill asserted that the American Federation of Labor and Congress of Industrial Organizations had given the elimination of racial discrimination by affiliated unions "a low level of priority."

"They have no understanding of the problem," Mr. Hill said. "What is progress for them is not progress for us."

A federation spokesman said that the federation "has made progress in the fight against discrimination."

"We will not be satisfied until discrimination is completely eliminated and we will continue to make progress in a trade union way undeterred by outsiders," he asserted.

Animosity between the association and the federation dates from early 1959 when the association concluded that the federation was not going to move vigorously enough to end discrimination against Negroes.

Since then, the association has assisted in building Negro caucuses inside unions to exert internal pressure and has filed complaints with Federal and state anti-discrimination agencies against unions. The legal effort now in preparation is an extension of these efforts into a new field.

The first case, according to Mr. Hill, will begin as a petition to the National Labor Relations Board to decertify a union on

Continued on Page 22, Column 8

CITY ACTS TO PAY ITS BILLS FASTER

Economies Are Expected—Tenney Says Poor Liaison Is a Cause of Delays

By PAUL CROWELL

Steps are being taken to have the city pay its bills more quickly, city Administrator Charles H. Tenney reported yesterday.

Mr. Tenney said that delays were a result, in part, of inadequate liaison between the office of the Controller and the management offices of other city agencies.

His report was based on a study requested in January by Controller Abraham D. Beame. Mr. Beame said at the time that he was convinced many individuals and companies were reluctant to bid for city business only because there were long delays in the payment of bills.

Changes Already Made

More bidders, Mr. Beame said, would mean more competition and, probably, lower prices and savings for the city.

The Tenney study, in which Mr. Beame's office took part, found that the procedures of the Controller's office in processing venders', suppliers' and contractors' bills were "basically sound."

Mr. Tenney reported that bookkeeping and record-keeping changes had already been made to shorten and simplify the handling of bills in the office of the Controller.

Mr. Tenney, who sent copies of his report to Mayor Wagner and Mr. Beame, said he would

Continued on Page 10, Column 3

KENNEDY PRESSES FOR SAFER DRUGS

Asks Senate to Stiffen Bill to Improve Quality and Combat Health Hazard

By ALVIN SHUSTER
Special to The New York Times

HYANNIS PORT, Mass., Aug. 5—President Kennedy asked the Senate today to strengthen its pending new drug law to insure "safer and better" drugs for the American consumer.

The President proposed a series of "essential" amendments to the Senate bill. One would enable the Government to move faster to remove from the prescription market any new drug suspected of being a hazard to public health.

Safety Goal Stressed

The proposals were substantially the same as those requested in a special message the President sent to Congress earlier this year. They were renewed today in a letter to Senator James O. Eastland, Democrat of Mississippi, who is chairman of the Senate Judiciary Committee.

Last month the committee approved a bill embodying many of the earlier proposals. But, as the President told his news conference last week, it did "not go far enough."

Accordingly, he asked Senator Eastland to amend the bill to make sure the American people were protected "against

Continued on Page 28, Column 1

TRIBES REASSERT POWER IN CONGO

Aim Is to Revise Provinces to Follow Ethnic Lines

By DAVID HALBERSTAM
Special to The New York Times.

LEOPOLDVILLE, the Congo, Aug. 5 — Tribal political power is reasserting itself strongly in the Congo. It is manifest in the powerful desire of the Congolese to form new provinces along basically tribal lines.

When the Congo won independence from Belgium on June 30, 1960, there were only six major provinces in this huge country. With the sanction of Parliament, seven new provinces have been approved. A total of nineteen provinces is foreseen shortly.

Observers view the trend as essentially federalist and traditionalist and thus anti-national and against the mainstream of pan-African political development. It marks, in effect, these observers believe, the failure of the late Patrice Lumumba and his nationalist movement to make any deep inroads into the traditional tribal alignment in the Congo.

There are, the observers note, about forty ethnic groups in the Congo, of which about twenty are major groups. The new provinces are generally being developed along major ethnic lines.

The new province of South Kasai, for example, is essentially a Baluba tribal area,

Continued on Page 8, Column 4

Jamaica Now Independent After Long British Rule

Associated Press Radiophoto

Prime Minister Sir Alexander Bustamante with Princess Margaret at National Stadium

By R. HART PHILLIPS
Special to The New York Times.

KINGSTON, Jamaica, Monday, Aug. 6—Jamaica became an independent nation within the British Commonwealth today. Princess Margaret as representative of her sister, Queen Elizabeth II, witnessed the end of the 307 years of British colonial status. About 30,000 Jamaicans jammed the big new National Stadium and cheered the raising of the new flag. On the stroke of midnight, the huge spotlights were turned off and in silence and darkness, the British flag that had flown over the island was hauled down and the green, gold and black

Continued on Page 6, Column 2

Charter Change Urged to Keep Fiscal Power of Estimate Board

The Citizens Budget Commission urged yesterday an early revision of the new City Charter to preserve the Board of Estimate's authority to control capital projects from the time a site is chosen through the appropriation of funds.

The present Charter gives the board this authority. In exercising it the board has followed a time-consuming procedure of holding public hearings on each aspect of a given capital project, from the planning stage on.

The Citizens Budget Commission recommended a single public hearing on each project, covering all its phases. It proposed that the Mayor should not initiate any project unless the Board of Estimate then approved it.

The civic organization pointed out that the new Charter, which becomes effective Jan. 1, provides for a public hearing by the Board of Estimate on all capital projects before the Mayor initiates them, but gives the board no power to disapprove them since the hearing would be held after the budget was approved.

The public hearing, the civic group contended, would therefore be "farcical and deceptive."

It proposed that the Charter be revised through a local law giving the Board of Estimate authority to approve "the site, final plans, cost estimates, major construction contracts, proposed bond issues and necessary appropriations."

As it now stands, the new Charter provides for appropriation of funds for all projects in the city's capital budget when the budget is adopted by the Board of Estimate and the City Council. The Citizens Budget Commission contended this would leave actual initiation of any project listed in

Continued on Page 10, Column 6

NEWS INDEX

MARILYN MONROE DEAD, PILLS NEAR

Continued From Page 1, Col. 4

study will reach no conclusions as to whether she committed suicide. Nor will it have a bearing on the toxicological tests.

During the last few years Miss Monroe had suffered severe setbacks. Her last two films, "Let's Make Love," and "The Misfits," were box-office disappointments. After completion of "The Misfits," written by Mr. Miller, she was divorced from him.

On June 8 Miss Monroe was dismissed by Twentieth-Century-Fox for unjustifiable absenses during the filming of "Something's Got to Give," in which she was starred. Filming on the picture has not resumed.

Shortly before she was dismissed, Miss Monroe angrily protested to a reporter about attacks on stars. She said she had never wanted to do "Something's Got to Give."

"We're what's O.K. with the movie business," she asserted. "Management is what's wrong with the business. To blame the troubles of Hollywood on stars is stupid. These executives should not knock their assets around."

But a few weeks later, during which a $500,000 suit had been filed against her, Miss Monroe pleaded with Fox to let her return to work on the picture.

In low spirits she withdrew to her one-story stucco house in an upper middle-class section, which was far different from the lavish suites of the Beverly Hills Hotel that had been more typical of her. She died in the house at 12305 Fifth Helena Drive.

Housekeeper Last to See Her

The last person to see her alive was her housekeeper, Mrs. Eunice Murray, who had lived with her. Mrs. Murray told the police that Miss Monroe retired to her bedroom about 8 P. M. yesterday.

About 3:25 A.M. today, the housekeeper noticed a light under Miss Monroe's door. She called to the actress, but received no answer. She tried the bedroom door. It was locked.

Mrs. Murray went outside and peered into the bedroom through the closed French windows. Miss Monroe, she later told the police, looked "peculiar." An arm was stretched across the bed and a hand hung limp on a telephone, she said.

The housekeeper rushed back into the house and telephoned Miss Monroe's analyst, Dr. Ralph R. Greenson. When he arrived a short time later, he broke a pane of the French window and opened it.

He quickly examined the star. She was dead. He phoned Miss Monroe's personal physician, Dr. Hyman Engelberg. After his arrival, the police were called. This was at 4:20, almost an hour after the housekeeper had called Dr. Greenson.

Inspector Edward Walker of the Los Angeles police was asked if he regarded such a delay in calling the police as unusual. He said he did not think so.

"So far as the doctors were concerned, there was no evidence of crime, and the first doctor already knew she was dead," he said. "I have no criticism to make of them."

Two radio patrolmen and a sergeant were the first policemen to arrive in the tree-lined neighborhood. Shortly afterward the case was taken over by Detective Sgt. R. E. Byron.

Room Simply Furnished

Sergeant Byron said Miss Monroe's bedroom was neat, but sparsely furnished. He estimated it at fifteen feet square.

"All she had in the room, so far as I can recall, was the bed, a little dressing table and the night table. And the telephone that she pulled on the bed."

After the police had completed their investigation, Miss Monroe's body was removed to the Westwood Village Mortuary. The house was sealed and placed under guard.

The body was later taken to the county morgue for the autopsy, which was performed by Dr. Tsunetomi Noguchi, a pathologist.

In the last two years Miss Monroe had become the subject of considerable controversy in Hollywood. Some persons gibed at her aspirations as a serious actress. They considered it ridiculous that she should have gone to New York to study under Lee Strasberg.

Miss Monroe's defenders, however, asserted that her talents had been underestimated by those who thought her appeal to movie audiences was solely sexual.

The disagreement about Miss Monroe took another form. One group contended she was typical of stars who had abused their privileges on sets.

An opposite group argued that Miss Monroe was an outstanding example of how Hollywood wanted to treat talent as just another commodity.

Peter G. Levathes, executive vice president of Fox, said the suit would not be pressed against her estate.

Miss Monroe wound up as a virtual recluse.

This was the portrait drawn by neighbors hours after the death of the actress.

Hardly any of her neighbors had seen her more than once or twice in the six months since she had moved into her two-bedroom bungalow, which is modest by Hollywood standards.

Marilyn Monroe with her second husband Joe DiMaggio at their wedding in 1954.

FIRST SCENE PUT HER IN LIMELIGHT

Actress Enjoyed Immense Popularity but Said She Was Seldom Happy

The life of Marilyn Monroe, the golden girl of the movies, ended as it began, in misery and tragedy.

Her death at the age of 36 closed an incredibly glamorous career and capped a series of somber events that began with her birth as an unwanted, illegitimate baby and went on and on, illuminated during the last dozen years by the lightning of fame.

Her public life was in dazzling contrast to her private life.

The first man to see her on the screen, the man who made her screen test, felt the almost universal reaction as he ran the wordless scene. In it, she walked, sat down and lit a cigarette.

Recalled 'Lush Stars'

"I got a cold chill," he said. "This girl had something I hadn't seen since silent pictures. This is the first girl who looked like one of those lush stars of the silent era. Every frame of the test radiated sex."

Billy Wilder, the director, called it "flesh impact."

"Flesh impact is rare," he said. "Three I remember who had it were Clara Bow, Jean Harlow and Rita Hayworth. Such girls have flesh which photographs like flesh. You feel you can reach out and touch it."

Fans paid $200,000,000 to see her project this quality. No sex symbol of the era other than Brigitte Bardot could match her popularity. Toward the end, she also convinced critics and the public that she could act.

During the years of her greatest success, she saw two of her marriages end in divorce. She suffered at least two miscarriages and was never able to have a child. Her emotional insecurity deepened; her many illnesses came upon her more frequently.

Dismissed From Picture

In 1961, she was twice admitted to hospitals in New York for psychiatric observation and rest. She was dismissed in June by Twentieth Century-Fox after being absent all but five days during seven weeks of shooting "Something's Got to Give."

"It's something that Marilyn no longer can control," one of her studio chiefs confided. "Sure she's sick. She believes she's sick. She may even have a fever, but it's a sickness of the mind. Only a psychiatrist can help her now."

In her last interview, published in the Aug. 3 issue of Life magazine, she told Richard Meryman, an associate editor:

"I was never used to being happy, so that wasn't something I ever took for granted."

Considering her background, this was a statement of exquisite restraint.

She was born in Los Angeles on June 1, 1926. The name on the birth record is Norma Jean Mortenson, the surname of the man who fathered her, then abandoned her mother. She later took her mother's last name, Baker.

Family Tragedies

Both her maternal grandparents and her mother were committed to mental institutions. Her uncle killed himself. Her father died in a motorcycle accident three years after her birth.

Her childhood has been described as "Oliver Twist in girl's clothing."

During her mother's stays in asylums, she was farmed out to twelve sets of foster parents. Two families were religious fanatics; one gave her empty whisky bottles to play with instead of dolls.

At another stage, she lived in a drought area with a family of seven. She spent two years in a Los Angeles orphanage, wearing a uniform she detested.

By the time she was 9 years old, Norma Jean had begun to stammer—an affliction rare among females.

Her dream since childhood had been to be a movie star, and she succeeded beyond her wildest imaginings. The conviction of her mother's best friend was borne out; she had told the little girl, day after day:

"Don't worry. You're going to be a beautiful girl when you get big. You're going to be a movie star. Oh, I feel it in my bones."

Nunnally Johnson, the producer and writer, understood that Miss Monroe was something special. Marilyn, he said, was "a phenomenon of nature, like Niagara Falls and the Grand Canyon.

"You can't talk to it. It can't talk to you. All you can do is stand back and be awed by it," he said.

This figure in the minds of millions was difficult to analyze statistically. Her dimensions—37-23-37—were voluptuous but not extraordinary.

She stood 5 feet 5½ inches tall. She had soft blonde hair, wide, dreamy, gray-blue eyes. She spoke in a high baby voice that was little more than a breathless whisper.

Heavy Fan Mail

Fans wrote her 5,000 letters a week, at least a dozen of them proposing marriage. The Communists denounced her as a capitalist trick to make the American people forget how miserable they were. In Turkey a young man took leave of his senses while watching "How to Marry a Millionaire" and slashed his wrists.

There were other symbols of success. She married two American male idols—one an athlete, one an intellectual.

Her second husband was Joe DiMaggio, the baseball player. Her third and last was the Pulitzer-prize winning playwright, Arthur Miller.

She was 16 when she married for the first time. The bridegroom was James Dougherty, 21, an aircraft worker.

Mr. Dougherty said after their divorce four years later, in 1946, that she had been a "wonderful" housekeeper.

Her two successive divorces came in 1954, when she split with Mr. DiMaggio after only nine months, and in 1960, after a four-year marriage to Mr. Miller.

She became famous with her first featured role of any prominence, in "The Asphalt Jungle," issued in 1950.

Her appearance was brief but unforgettable. From the instant she moved onto the screen with that extraordinary walk of hers, people asked themselves: "Who's that blonde?"

In 1952 it was revealed that Miss Monroe had been the subject of a widely distributed nude calendar photograph shot while she was a notably unsuccessful starlet.

Revealed Her Wit

It created a scandal, but it was her reaction to the scandal that was remembered. She told interviewers that she was not ashamed and had needed the money to pay her rent.

She also revealed her sense of humor. When asked by a woman journalist, "You mean you didn't have anything on?" she replied breathlessly:

"Oh yes, I had the radio on."

One of her most exasperating quirks was her tardiness. She was, during the years of her fame, anywhere from one to twenty-four hours late for appointments. Until lately, she managed to get away with it.

Her dilatory nature and sicknesses added nearly **$1,000,000** to the budget of "Let's Make Love." The late Jerry Wald, **head** of her studio, simply commented:

"True, she's not punctual. She can't help it, but I'm not sad about it," he said. "I can get a dozen beautiful blondes who will show up promptly in make-up at 4 A. M. each morning, but they are not Marilyn Monroe."

The tardiness, the lack of responsibility and the fears began to show more and more through the glamorous patina as Miss Monroe's career waxed.

Speaking of her career and her fame in the Life interview, she said, wistfully:

"It might be kind of a relief to be finished. It's sort of like I don't know what kind of a yard dash you're running, but then you're at the finish line and you sort of sigh—you've made it! But you never have—you have to start all over again."

Marilyn Monroe and Clark Gable in *The Misfits.*

"All the News That's Fit to Print"

The New York Times.

LATE CITY EDITION
U.S. Weather Bureau Report (Page 89) forecasts: Showers late today and tonight; fair and mild tomorrow.
Temp. range: 58—48; yesterday: 54—50.

VOL. CXIV..No. 39,176. © 1965 by The New York Times Company Times Square, New York, N.Y. 10036 | NEW YORK, WEDNESDAY, APRIL 28, 1965. | TEN CENTS

PRESIDENT SAYS FEDERAL DEFICIT DROPS A BILLION

Spending Cut and Revenue Rise Combine to Reduce Figure to $5.3 Billion

STEEL ACCORD IS HAILED

Johnson Calls Interim Pact 'Statesmanlike'—Notes Wage-Price Stability

By JOHN D. POMFRET
Special to The New York Times

WASHINGTON, April 27—President Johnson said today that the Federal budget deficit this fiscal year would be at least $1 billion below the January estimate.

Half the estimated drop results from decreased Government expenditures and half from increased revenues, the President told a news conference. [Opening statement, Page 16.]

The new estimate of the deficit for the year ending June 30 is $5.3 billion—the difference between $97 billion in expenditures and $91.7 billion in receipts.

Mr. Johnson attributed the drop in expenditures to "our continuing drive to hold down Government spending." The Bureau of the Budget said the spending decrease was in the Department of Defense and a number of other agencies.

The President also congratulated negotiators for the steel industry and the United Steelworkers of America for having reached a "statesmanlike" interim labor agreement putting off the earliest possible strike date to Sept. 1.

Sees 'Responsible' Pact

"I think we can be confident that the final settlement will be a responsible one which fully considers not only the interests of the immediate parties but also the larger public interest," Mr. Johnson said.

The President apparently was expressing hope that the final settlement, which the negotiators will begin discussing in mid-May, would not only be peaceful but would not be inflationary as well.

Mr. Johnson said that "so far in 1965 our record of wage-price stability remains intact."

Negotiated wage increases this year are running at about the same level as last year's, he asserted, and "a number of important settlements were at approximately the level of our guideposts."

The general guidepost for noninflationary labor settlements set forth by the President's Council of Economic Advisers says that the annual increase in total employe compensation, including fringe benefits, should equal the national trend of increase in output per man-hour. This is about 3.2 per cent a year. Mr. Johnson de-

Continued on Page 17, Column 2

CAVANAGH DENIES JAIL IS 'SNAKE PIT'

Report to Wagner Defends City Prison for Women

By WILLIAM E. FARRELL

Deputy Mayor Edward F. Cavanagh Jr. said yesterday that an investigation of charges of "snake-pit" conditions at the Women's House of Detention "were without substance."

Mr. Cavanagh's nine-page report to Mayor Wagner was released at a news conference at City Hall. The report disputed a number of allegations made by a former inmate, Mrs. Irene Perry, 39 years old, in sworn testimony before the chairman of the Assembly's Committee on Penal Institutions, which is investigating the women's prison.

Reached in Albany, Assemblyman Joseph Kottler, the chairman of the committee, termed the report a "completely and totally inadequate investigation of Mrs. Perry's charges."

The report declared that for the first time in more than 30 years there were fewer inmates at the House of Detention than

Continued on Page 50, Column 5

Tax Benefit Upheld For Business Sold To a Foundation

Special to The New York Times

WASHINGTON, April 27—The Supreme Court held today that a businessman may sell his company to a tax-exempt organization, continue to operate it and pay capital-gains tax rates on the profits up to the amount of the sales price.

The Court by a 6-to-3 vote approved an elaborate transaction involving Clay B. Brown, owner of a lumber concern near Fortuna, Calif. Mr. Brown contracted in 1952 to sell his business to the Institute for Cancer Research for $1.3 million.

He retained control of the company as manager of Fortuna, a new corporation that leased the assets from the institute. Mr. Brown's lawyers were directors of Fortuna.

Fortuna paid the institute 80 per cent of its pretax profits as rent. The institute, in turn, paid 90 per cent of this back to Mr. Brown and the

Continued on Page 24, Column 3

HIGH COURT VOIDS A STATE VOTE CURB

Calls Virginia's Residence Law a Poll-Tax Substitute —24th Amendment Cited

By FRED P. GRAHAM
Special to The New York Times

WASHINGTON, April 27—A unanimous Supreme Court held today that a Virginia law requiring voters in Federal elections to file a residence certificate is a substitute for a poll tax and therefore unconstitutional.

In the first decision involving the 24th Amendment, the Court struck down the law, which allows the voter to pay the state poll tax in lieu of filing the residence certificate. It said the statute imposes a penalty on the right to cast the Federal ballot.

The law was passed by the Virginia Legislature in 1963 in anticipation of the ratification of the 24th Amendment on Feb. 4, 1964. The amendment declares that the right of a citizen to vote in Federal elections "shall not be denied or abridged" by failure to pay a Federal or state poll tax.

Certificate Is Required

The Virginia Legislature retained its poll tax for state elections but added the statute requiring that a voter for Federal elections must file a witnessed or notarized residence certificate at least six months prior to the date of an election in order to vote. This requirement was excused if the person's state poll taxes had been paid.

The original suit contesting the residence certificate law was brought by Horace E. Henderson of McLean, Va., former state Republican chairman, and Lars Forssenius, a Young Republican official of Roanoke.

Another aspect of poll taxes came up at President Johnson's news conference today. The President indicated that he would have liked a flat ban on them in the pending voting-rights bill but had deferred to legal advice that this might raise a constitutional problem. [Question 8, Page 16.]

Today was the first day on which the Supreme Court broke from a century-old tradition of issuing opinions only one day a week—almost invariably on Mondays. Under its new procedures, it may issue opinions on any day that it is sitting—usually Mondays through Thursdays.

A Price for Privilege

In an opinion by Chief Justice Earl Warren, the Court held that the Virginia voting requirement is an illegal abridgement of the right to vote in Federal elections because it "exacted a price for the privilege of exercising the franchise."

The Court said Congress had approved the amendment to eliminate the price on the right to vote and the requirement that the tax be paid months in advance. It said that Congress had also meant to curb the opportunity the state requirement gave for fraudulent block voting by political machines that could pay the tax and its use to discourage voting by Negroes.

All these voting restrictions, the Court declared, were retained to a certain extent by the optional system, making

Continued on Page 24, Column 5

DOMINICAN REVOLT FAILS AFTER A DAY OF SAVAGE BATTLE

Hundreds Believed Killed—Accord Calls for a Junta to Rule Till Election

By TAD SZULC
Special to The New York Times

SAN JUAN, P. R., April 27—The military-civilian revolt aimed at restoring former President Juan Bosch to power in the Dominican Republic collapsed tonight at the end of a day of savage fighting in which hundreds may have been killed.

The rebels surrendered after they had controlled Santo Domingo, the country's capital, for three days. Their capitulation came in dramatic negotiations conducted at the United States Embassy and with the active assistance of United States diplomats.

The tacit agreement on which the surrender was based calls for the formation of a military junta and the holding of elections, probably in September.

The junta had not yet been formed and the Dominican Republic in effect had no Government. The Presidential Palace was empty and splintered glass from windows smashed in air attacks covered the grounds and hallways.

Martial Law Proclaimed

The victorious forces, a coalition of the air force, the navy and part of the army, proclaimed martial law as rearguard fighting continued in Santo Domingo late in the evening with heavy sniper action by armed civilians.

There also were indications that some rebel troop units were not willing to capitulate and continued fighting was considered possible.

Earlier in the day a United States Navy task force swiftly evacuated 1,172 Americans from Santo Domingo by ship and helicopter.

Seven helicopters were left behind at the Hotel Embajador in Santo Domingo in case more Americans wished to be evacuated and the task force, headed by the U.S.S. Boxer, stood offshore.

Acting Chief Flees

In the wake of the rebels' surrender, José Rafael Molina Ureña, who had served as the Acting President since last Sunday, fled to asylum at the Colombian Embassy in Santo Domingo.

The fate of his military and civilian associates was not immediately known.

Dr. Bosch, who had hoped to fly to Santo Domingo to resume the Presidency, from which he was ousted by the military 19 months ago, canceled a planned television appearance and went into seclusion at his home in San Juan after he had received word of the rebellion's collapse.

In an attempt to restore Dr. Bosch to office, a group of young army officers and civilians, in a swift uprising over the weekend, ousted the civilian junta that succeeded Dr. Bosch. That junta, headed by Donald Reid Cabral, was originally supported by all the armed forces.

Although all the army units in Santo Domingo, the police and thousands of armed civilians stood behind the Bosch cause, the revolution finally collapsed because of the adamant opposition of Brig. Gen. Elias Wessin y Wessin, com-

Continued on Page 3, Column 1

Head of Howard U. Warns Communists

By BEN A. FRANKLIN
Special to The New York Times

WASHINGTON, April 27—Dr. James M. Nabrit Jr., president of Howard University, said today that Communists had joined a student protest group on the campus of the predominantly Negro college here in an effort to "disrupt our fight for justice."

He said that in the interests of "freedom of speech and academic freedom" they would be tolerated "as long as they do not break the rules."

But he warned that attempts to interfere with the "normal operations" of the university would not be tolerated.

He was plainly issuing a warning to civil rights groups on the campus that radicals of the extreme left were seeking to "cloak themselves in the mantle of civil righters and plot

Continued on Page 28, Column 5

Associated Press Wirephoto

THE PRESIDENT GOES BEFORE THE NATION: President Johnson arriving in the East Room of the White House yesterday to begin televised news conference. He discussed many problems, particularly the war in Vietnam.

Subways Will Limit Entrances at Night In Fight on Crime

By MARTIN GANSBERG

The Transit Authority announced yesterday that it would close at least one entrance at 175 of the city's 481 subway stations from 8 P.M. to 4 A.M. in its campaign against crime.

Joseph E. O'Grady chairman of the three-man authority, said the stations had been selected on the basis of police reports that showed they were in areas of high crime incidence. Eight entrances to seven stations in Manhattan, Brooklyn and the Bronx already are closed, he said.

"Our efforts to police the subways and stations are meeting with success," Mr. O'Grady declared. "We're going to do even better by limiting the area that our police will have to cover."

Police Patrol Subways

Policemen have been riding trains and patrolling every station after 8 P. M. since April 7, when Mayor Wagner announced an intensive program to combat crime in the subways.

The policing area will be reduced because passengers will be restricted to a single approach to a station. If a station runs two city blocks and has entrances at each end, those at one end will be shut.

Mr. O'Grady said it would take several months to complete the closings because maintenance men had to build and install wooden barriers.

"The public should not be surprised," he declared, "because

Continued on Page 31, Column 5

PRESIDENT NAMES AIR AGENCY HEADS

8 Top Federal Posts Filled—Boyd, Head of C.A.B., Gets Transport Job

By WILLIAM M. BLAIR
Special to The New York Times

WASHINGTON, April 27—Eight major appointments, including a change in the heads of the Government's aviation agencies, were announced by President Johnson today.

Alan S. Boyd, who is 42 years old, was shifted from chairman of the Civil Aeronautics Board to Under Secretary of Commerce for Transportation.

The President announced at his new conference that he had chosen Charles S. Murphy, 55, who has been Under Secretary of Agriculture since 1961 and is a former special assistant to President Harry S. Truman, to succeed Mr. Boyd at the C.A.B. [Opening statement, Page 16.]

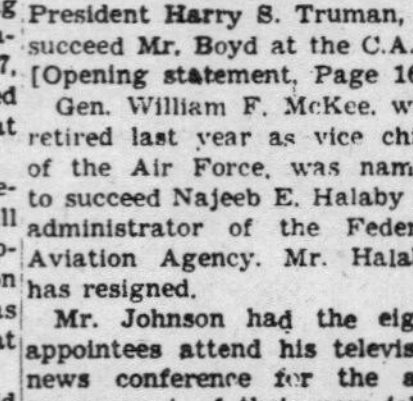

Gen. William F. McKee, who retired last year as vice chief of the Air Force, was named to succeed Najeeb E. Halaby as administrator of the Federal Aviation Agency. Mr. Halaby has resigned.

Mr. Johnson had the eight appointees attend his televised news conference for the announcement of their new jobs. Each stood as the President named him. Mr. Johnson followed a similar procedure at an earlier news conference at his Texas ranch.

The appointments require

Continued on Page 16, Column 7

Edward R. Murrow, Broadcaster And Ex-Chief of U.S.I.A., Dies

War Reporter From London and TV Commentator, 57, Succumbs to Cancer

Edward R. Murrow, whose independence and incisive reporting brought heightened journalistic stature to radio and television, died yesterday at his home in Pawling, N. Y., at the age of 57.

The former head of the United States Information Agency had been battling cancer since October, 1963. He had been in and out of the hospital ever since, and death came three weeks after he was discharged from New York Hospital for the last time.

The ever-present cigarette (he smoked 60 to 70 a day), the matter-of-fact baritone voice and the high-domed, worried, lopsided face were the trademarks of the radio reporter who became internationally famous during World War II with broadcasts that started, "This . . . is London."

Later, on television, his series of news documentaries, "See It Now," on the Columbia Broadcasting System from 1951 to 1958, set the standard for all television documentaries on all networks.

President Johnson, on learning of Mr. Murrow's death, said that

The New York Times

Edward R. Murrow

all Americans "feel a sense of loss in the death of Edward R. Murrow."

He was, the President said, a "gallant fighter" who had "dedicated his life as a newsman and as a public official to the unrelenting search for truth."

Mr. Murrow died at his home on the rolling hills of his 280-acre Pawling farm shortly before noon.

He is survived by his widow, the former Janet Huntington Brewster; a son, Charles Casey Murrow, a freshman at Yale University; and two brothers, L. V. Murrow of Washington and

Continued on Page 43, Column 1

De Gaulle Voices Concern Over 'Spreading' Asia War

By HENRY GINIGER
Special to The New York Times

PARIS, April 27—President de Gaulle declared tonight that he strongly disapproved of "the war in Asia, which is spreading more and more each day." The French leader made plain his opposition to United States bombings of North Vietnam in a radio and television speech that stressed French independence of the United States but affirmed friendship with it.

An assertion in the speech of French refusal to accept United States leadership came while important talks were in progress here with the Soviet Union.

Foreign Minister Andrei A. Gromyko had a "cordial" meeting with President de Gaulle for more than an hour in the afternoon and was believed to have renewed a standing invitation to the President to visit Moscow.

Support for Parley Reported

French diplomatic sources reported that Mr. Gromyko had also backed a French proposal for a disarmament conference of the five countries that have atomic weapons — the United States, Britain, France, the Soviet Union and Communist China.

The President recorded his 17-minute speech this morning before he met Mr. Gromyko. The Soviet Minister began his talks with French officials yesterday.

Appearing somewhat thinner but as forceful as ever, the President looked back over his seven years in power and said that the "capital fact" was that France had resisted the "siren calls of abandonment" to outside direction and had "chosen independence."

He said that France had regained her "faculty of judgment and action" and that this seemed sometimes "to offend a state that might think itself, because of its power, to be

Continued on Page 14, Column 2

Morhouse Invokes The Fifth 30 Times

By The Associated Press

ROCHESTER, April 27—Former Republican State Chairman L. Judson Morhouse invoked the Fifth Amendment of the United States Constitution about 30 times today to avoid answering questions at a Federal hearing into alleged bribery at the Finger Lakes Race Track.

"I decline to answer, based on my rights under the New York Constitution and the Fifth Amendment to the Federal Constitution, on grounds that the answers might tend to incriminate me," Mr. Morhouse told a court-appointed trustee for the bankrupt track.

Francis J. D'Amanda of Rochester, the trustee, is trying to learn whether there was anything illegal about the award of the license and concession contracts for the thoroughbred

Continued on Page 83, Column 4

SOVIET HESITATES ON CAMBODIA TALK

Sihanouk's Opposition Cited—Peking Says Moscow Is Collaborating With U.S.

By HENRY TANNER
Special to The New York Times

MOSCOW, April 27—The Soviet Government was reported today to be reluctant to act quickly on its own proposal for a conference on Cambodia.

Such a meeting has been under consideration as a possible back door for arriving at negotiations to end the war in Vietnam. As co-chairmen of the 1954 Geneva conference on Indochina, Britain and the Soviet Union must act jointly to convene any talks on Cambodia.

The expression of Soviet hesitation came a day after Britain had formally endorsed the proposal and two days after the United States had expressed interest in it.

[Communist China accused the Soviet Union of collaboration with the United States to defeat the Vietcong. Analysts in Hong Kong said the timing of the denunciation suggested that it was aimed at dissuading North Vietnam from accepting any Soviet peace-talk proposal. Page 14.]

New Situation Is Seen

Acting Foreign Minister Vasily V. Kuznetsov, in talks with Western diplomats today, was understood to have voiced concern over the fact that Prince Sihanouk, the Cambodian chief of state, had declared himself opposed to the conference proposal in a recent statement.

According to informed sources, Mr. Kuznetsov indicated the Soviet Government felt that the statement of the Prince had created a new situation and that it had to be studied carefully.

He gave the impression that the Soviet Government had not yet reached a decision on whether it was advisable immediately to issue invitations for the conference, the informants said.

Mr. Kuznetsov, a First Deputy Foreign Minister, is in charge in the absence of For-

Continued on Page 14, Column 4

NEWS INDEX

JOHNSON RENEWS BID ON VIETNAM; DEFENDS BOMBING

Repeats His Offer to Confer With Any Government Without Conditions

PEACE HOPES STRESSED

But President, in Televised News Conference, Says Air Strikes Must Continue

Transcript of news conference and summary, Page 16.

By MAX FRANKEL
Special to The New York Times

WASHINGTON, April 27 — President Johnson renewed today his offer to talk with any government, without any conditions, about ways of ending the war in Vietnam.

Emphasizing the "utmost restraint" of his Administration in the war, the President defended the bombing of North Vietnam as necessary to hamper the Communists' military effort and to demonstrate United States firmness. The bombing will continue, he said at a news conference, as long as North Vietnam's aggression continues. [Opening statement and Question 9, Page 16.]

At the same time, Mr. Johnson stressed his hope for a peace conference and his resolve to do everything "within reason" to hold down the war's cost in lives. [Questions 4 and 13.]

The President's discussion of Vietnam, which dominated his televised news conference in the East Room of the White House, capped a major effort by the Administration to explain and defend United States involvement in the war.

No Major Change Indicated

Mr. Johnson's formal opening statement, read from a prompting device, and his answers to questions suggested no major changes in either diplomatic or military tactics at this stage.

As in his policy address on Vietnam in Baltimore three weeks ago, the President was careful to offer "unconditional discussions" only to governments, thus apparently excluding direct talks at this time with the Vietcong rebels or their political organization, the National Liberation Front.

Officials here refer to the rebels as agents of North Vietnam, but the Communist nations have proclaimed the front to be the "only legitimate representative" of the people of South Vietnam.

Although the President said last month that he was ready to go anywhere, any time to meet with anyone, he substituted "any government" for "anyone" today.

"And if any doubt our sincerity," he added, "let them test us."

His offer may be rejected, as

Continued on Page 14, Column 5

CAIRO WITHDRAWS ENVOY IN TUNISIA

Attack on U.A.R. Embassy Over Israel Issue Blamed

By HEDRICK SMITH
Special to The New York Times

CAIRO, April 27—The United Arab Republic announced tonight that it had withdrawn its Ambassador from Tunisia in the wake of a reported attack on its embassy by Tunisian crowds. The Government also denounced any attempt by President Habib Bourguiba of Tunisia to be an intermediary between the Arabs and Israel.

"This is a case in which there can be no intermediary, no negotiation nor compromise," Foreign Minister Mahmoud Riad told National Assembly members tonight.

It was the first official Egyptian comment on Mr. Bourguiba's proposal for Arab recognition of Israel and negotiation on repatriating Palestine refugees.

"The United Arab Republic rejects" these proposals and "strongly denounces the issuance of such a proposal from the head of an Arab state," Mr. Riad declared.

Mr. Bourguiba's statement came under fire from the chairman of the National Assembly's Arab Affairs Committee, who said there was no reason for

Continued on Page 11, Column 1

Edward R. Murrow, Broadcaster and Ex-U.S.I.A. Chief, Dead

Continued From Page 1, Col. 5

Dewey Murrow of Spokane, Wash.

A funeral service will be held on Friday at 2 P.M. at St. James Episcopal Church, 865 Madison Avenue, between 71st and 72d Streets. Burial is to be announced.

In many years of receiving honors and tributes, the most recent was conferred on Mr. Murrow on March 5, 1965, by Queen Elizabeth II, who named him an Honorary Knight Commander of the Order of the British Empire.

On September, 14, 1964, President Johnson awarded him the Medal of Freedom, the highest civilian honor a President can confer on an American citizen.

Mr. Murrow's career with the Columbia Broadcasting Company spanned 25 years. It ended in January, 1961, when President Kennedy named him head of the United States Information Agency.

In October, 1963, a malignant tumor made the removal of his left lung necessary, and three months later he resigned as head of the agency. Last November, Mr. Murrow again underwent surgery.

Brought Controversy Into Homes

Mr. Murrow achieved international distinction in broadcasting, first as a radio correspondent reporting from London in World War II and then as a pioneer television journalist opening the home screen to the stimulus of controversy. No other figure in broadcast news left such a strong stamp on both media.

In an industry often given to rule by committee. Mr. Murrow was always recognized as an individual, whether in the front lines of the war, in the executive conferences of a network or, in what he enjoyed most, in planning his next story. His independence was reflected in doing what he thought had to be done on the air and worrying later about the repercussions among sponsors, viewers and individual stations. The fruits of his determination are shared today by newsmen at all networks; they enjoy a freedom and latitude not yet won by others working in the medium.

Mr. Murrow was a realist about fame. He could not walk a block in New York without pedestrians turning for a look or someone trying to strike up a conversation. But in the context of television he knew the value of adulation. "It can get a lot of things done," he once remarked. That was his concern.

In the last war, Mr. Murrow conveyed the facts with a compelling precision. But he went beyond the reporting of the facts. By describing what he saw in visual detail, he sought to convey the moods and feelings of war.

Had a London street just been bombed out? The young correspondent was soon there in helmet, gray flannel trousers and sport coat, quietly describing everything he saw against the urgent sound patterns of rescue operations.

Or he would be in a plane on a combat mission, broadcasting live on the return leg and describing the bombing he had watched as "orchestrated hell."

He flew 25 missions in the war, despite the opposition of top executives of the Columbia Broadcasting System in New York, who regarded him as too valuable to be so regularly risked. In the endless German air raids on London, his office was bombed out three times but he escaped injury.

Mr. Murrow, never fevered or high-blown, had the gift of dramatizing whatever he reported. He did so by understatement and by a calm, terse, highly descriptive radio style. Sometimes there was a sort of metallic poetry in his words.

In one memorable broadcast he said that as he "walked home at 7 in the morning, the windows in the West End were red with reflected fire, and the raindrops were like blood on the panes."

For a dozen years, as radio's highest paid newscaster, he was known by voice alone to millions of his countrymen. "This . . . is London," was his matter-of-fact salutation, delivered in a baritone voice tinged with an echo of doom. Later it was, "This . . . is the news."

Then television added to the distinctive voice an equally distinctive face, with high-domed forehead and deep-set, serious eyes. Mr. Murrow's casual television manner was superimposed on a quite obvious native tension.

As the armchair interviewer on "Person to Person," Mr. Murrow carried out a gentlemanly electronic invasion of the homes of scores of celebrities in the nineteen-fifties from Sophie Tucker through the evangelist Billy Graham.

The darkly handsome Mr. Murrow, his brow knotted and two fingers holding his ever-present cigarette, sat in the studio facing a greatly magnified television image of his subjects at home. He would make what one writer called "urbane small talk" with them, generously admiring their children and perhaps inquiring exactly where that handsome vase on the side table had been acquired. It was not momentous, but it was interesting.

Series of Documentaries

From 1951 to 1958 Mr. Murrow also did a series of news documentaries under the title "See It Now." In the 1953-54 season the telecast studied the various aspects of the impact of the emotional and political phenomenon known as "McCarthyism."

Senator Joseph R. McCarthy, Republican of Wisconsin, was then conducting his crusade against alleged Communist influence. Some regarded it as a hard, honest search for subversives by a zealous patriot; others saw it as a demagogic opportunism, the exploitation of a real issue for the purpose of gaining political infuence by intimidation.

The debate over Senator McCarthy was supercharged with emotion and fervent belief. Since commercial television thrives by giving little offense, the medium had given the matter gingerly treatment.

Mr. Murrow and his long-time co-editor, Fred W. Friendly, broke this pattern decisively on Tuesday evening, March 9, 1954. Using film clips that showed the Senator to no good advantage, the two men offered a provocative examination of the man and his methods.

The program, many thought, had a devastating effect. "McCarthyism" did lose public force in succeeding months. "The timing was right and the instrument powerful," Mr. Murrow said of the telecast later.

Decided to Go Ahead

Jack Gould, television critic of The New York Times, wrote that "Mr. Murrow decided to go ahead with the program at a time when passions in the broadcasting industry were running wild on the issue of Communist sympathizers and dupes. It was the autonomy of the Murrow-Friendly operation, often the source of internal controversy within C.B.S., that got the vital show on the air."

That autonomy was a singular thing in network broadcasting. It was based on Mr. Murrow's immense prestige, initially gained when he became one of the first radio war correspondents and built a superb news staff for C.B.S. in Europe.

Mr. Murrow, one writer said, "has achieved a position at C.B.S. that is outside, and basically antithetical to, the corporate structure of authority" and he thereby enjoyed a large measure of "freedom from authority of all kinds." He ran his own news island within the network for many years.

"See It Now" employed five full-time camera crews and they went anywhere in the world. A sponsor paid $57,000 a week for the show, but Mr. Murrow did not limit himself to that if he thought a better show could be done for more. The network paid the difference.

"They come to me, the vice presidents, and say, 'Look, there's so much going out of this spout and only so much coming in.' And I say, 'If that's the way you want to do it, you'd better get yourselves another boy,' Mr. Murrow once said.

Reduction in Authority

When "See It Now" became "C.B.S. Reports" in 1958-59, the network diffused the responsibility for documentary telecasts and Mr. Murrow's authority was reduced. "He was blocked," one friend wrote, "in his raging desire to get the network he loved onto new paths of glory."

On "Small World," from the fall of 1958 to 1960, he brought top world figures together by remote telecasting and moderated their continent-spanning discussions. But it was known that he was not very happy at the network then.

Egbert Roscoe Murrow was born on April 25, 1908, at Pole Cat Creek, N. C., a "mixture of English, Scotch, Irish and German" descent. He changed his first name to Edward in his second year at college.

His father, a tenant farmer, moved to Blanchard, Wash., where his son grew up in the great Northwest and worked on a survey gang in the timberlands during summer vacations.

In 1930 he graduated from Washington State College with a Phi Beta Kappa key. He became president of the National Student Federation that year, a job that paid $25 a week with a basement office in New York.

In 1932 he became assistant director of the Institute of International Education. He met Janet Huntington Brewster, a Mount Holyoke graduate, on a train that year and two years later they were married in the bride's hometown, Middletown, Conn.

In 1935, Mr. Murrow was employed by C.B.S. as director of talks and education. Part of his work was to address important groups on the potential of radio as a medium of education.

He was in New Orleans in 1937, attending a meeting of the National Education Association, when he received an unexpected call from headquarters asking if he would go to Europe.

His answer—"yes"—was the decisive turn of his career. He later said that it had led to his having "a front row seat for some of the greatest news events of history."

The young man, then 29, became the network's one-man staff in Europe, a pleasant life. He arranged cultural programs and interviewed leaders. Though his office was in London, he traveled extensively, typically visiting Rome for a week to arrange a Vatican choir broadcast.

As war began to seem inevitable he hired William L. Shirer, a newspaper man, to cover the Continent. Both he and Mr. Shirer were arranging musical broadcasts when Hitler marched into Austria.

Mr. Murrow flew to Berlin and chartered a Lufthansa transport to Vienna for $1,000. He rode a streetcar into the city in time to watch the arrival of goose-stepping German troops.

For 10 days he was allowed to broadcast, and he described the nation's swift transition to a subject state. Life changed drastically for the young newsman. At home, millions hung on his and Shirer's words.

He Hired the Staff

As news chief for C.B.S. in Europe he hired the men who were to become the network's famous roster of war correspondents—among them Eric Sevareid, Charles Collingwood, Howard K. Smith, Richard Hottelet, Cecil Brown and Larry LeSueur.

"I'm hiring reporters, not announcers," Mr. Murrow told "the shop" (as he usually called New York headquarters) when C.B.S. executives complained that he was hiring men who sounded "terrible" on the air. Their on-the-scene reports reached into farm and city homes from New England to the Pacific states, bringing the realities of war close.

One former staff member recalled the instruction Mr. Murrow gave to his newsmen.

The reporter must never sound excited even if bombs are falling outside, Mr. Murrow said.

Rather, the reporter should imagine that he has just returned to his hometown and that the local editor has asked him to dinner with, for example, a banker and a professor.

"After dinner," Mr. Murrow counseled, "your host asks you 'Well, what was it like?' As you talk, the maid is passing the coffee and her boyfriend, a truck driver, is waiting for her in the kitchen and listening. You are supposed to describe things in terms that make sense to the truck driver without insulting the intelligence of the professor."

Mr. Murrow's wartime broadcasts from Britain, North Africa and finally the Continent gripped listeners by their firm, spare authority; nicely timed pauses; and Mr. Murrow's calm, grave delivery. One observer wrote that his voice always "conveyed the impression that he knows the worst."

He was the first allied correspondent inside the Nazi concentration camp at Buchenwald. Near 300 bodies, he saw a mound of men's, women's and children's shoes.

"I regarded that broadcast as a failure," he said. "I could have described three pairs of those shoes—but hundreds of them! I couldn't. The tragedy of it simply overwhelmed me."

Returning to the United States in 1946 after nine years overseas, he became a vice president of C.B.S. in news operations. He soon found executive tasks—in and out baskets, memos, conferences and the rest—wearisome. He was away from the microphone for 18 months. "I wanted to be a reporter again because I needed the dignity and satisfaction of being a reporter," he said.

On Sept. 29, the former war correspondent went on the air with his evening radio report, "Edward R. Murrow With the News." It was carried by 125 network stations to an audience of several million people nightly except weekends for 13 years.

Unlike most news commentators, Mr. Murrow did not allow his sponsor to break into the news with a middle commercial. When he had finished giving the news and doing what he called the "end piece"—the graceful essays that caused him to be regarded as "the social philosopher of radio correspondents"—the closing commercial would be read. To hold the audience, Mr. Murrow would then come back with a brief "Word for Today," usually a quotation appropriate to the news that had gone before.

His sign-off on both radio and television was a crisp "Good night, and good luck."

By 1949 Mr. Murrow was earning $112,000 a year, which jumped to about $240,000 when he became the only major radio news personality to make a full successful switch to television. "Hear It Now," the radio historical documentary series he started in 1948, also made the transition to television, becoming "See It Now," which ran for seven years.

Mr. Murrow and his wife occupied a 10th-floor apartment at 580 Park Avenue and a log house in Pawling, N. Y., with acres thick with pheasant and ducks, a trout stream and 9 holes of golf nearby.

Off-camera Mr. Murrow was a convivial companion, given to a whisky sour at lunch, a relish of journalistic shoptalk and amusement and exasperation over the ways of the television business. He appreciated humor if it had style and from years on the air instinctively leaned to the short sentence. On hazardous missions overseas he was usually the coolest passenger.

If Mr. Murrow had one private concern about his professional life it was that he might slip into the role of the television news prima donna reading the words of some anonymous rewrite man.

An often chaotic schedule necessitated some measure of assistance in script preparation, but he felt it was his obligation to be in the field more often than not. His restlessness was always in evidence.

Won Four Peabodys

Mr. Murrow won the Peabody Award for excellence in broadcasting in 1943, 1949, 1951 and 1954. William S. Paley, then president of C.B.S., called him "a man fitted for his time and task—a student, a philosopher, at heart a poet of mankind and, therefore, a great reporter."

Mr. Murrow became the nation's chief tactician in the propaganda war when President Kennedy chose him as director of the United States Information Agency in January, 1961.

The appointment ended a 25-year association with C.B.S.—he had been a member of its board of directors from 1947 to 1956—and removed Mr. Murrow from the domestic broadcasting scene. His salary was $21,000 a year.

From Washington, he directed the output of prodigious amounts of news and propaganda, sending the nation's message in manifold forms to all the nations of the earth. He emphasized plain speaking and straightforward reporting in 789 weekly hours of broadcasting and in the daily 10,000-word wireless file of news to newspapers in 100 cities overseas.

Mr. Murrow aimed at putting a more professional emphasis on Voice of America broadcasts, with shorter, crisper reports. Because he believed that explained verity was more persuasive than sheer propaganda, he told agency writers to report the facts in perspective, the bad as well as the good.

He defended the agency's policy of distributing news of racial flareups in this country, saying such events could not be kept a secret and arguing that there was no choice but to present the facts with balanced interpretation.

"We cannot make good news out of bad practice," he said with typical pith when Senators criticized his staff for not depicting things as generally rosy.

At one point, Murrow the reporter came into a singular conflict with Murrow the propagandist. Before joining the agency, he had narrated the telecast "Harvest of Shame," a chilling documentary on the exploitation of migrant farm laborers in the United States.

The British Broadcasting Corporation bought the film from C.B.S. In an unusual intervention by a Government official, Mr. Murrow telephoned the B.B.C. and asked that the film not be used.

The B.B.C. announced that it had bought the film in good faith and added, with what must have seemed stunning irrelevancy to Mr. Murrow, that it had "the greatest faith in Murrow," meaning the reporter.

As the nation's best-known chain smoker—he smoked 60 to 70 cigarettes a day—Mr. Murrow once sat through a half hour televised round-table discussion without lighting a single cigarette. A reporter called the U.S.I.A. to see if he had quit smoking. "His ashtrays are still full," he was assured.

Mr. Murrow was frequently mentioned in 1962 as a possible Democratic candidate for the United States Senate, but he said that he had never "had a horizon of more than 90 days."

"All the News That's Fit to Print"

The New York Times.

LATE CITY EDITION
Partly cloudy today. Mostly clear and warmer tomorrow.
Temperatures Yesterday—Max., 63; Min., 41
Sunrise today, 5:57 A. M.; Sunset, 7:59 P. M.

VOL. XCIV..No. 31,873. Entered as Second-Class Matter, Postoffice, New York, N. Y. NEW YORK, MONDAY, APRIL 30, 1945. THREE CENTS IN NEW YORK CITY

U.S. 7TH IN MUNICH, BRITISH PUSH ON BALTIC; RUSSIANS TIGHTEN RING ON BERLIN'S HEART; MILAN AND VENICE WON; MUSSOLINI KILLED

BIG POWERS SCAN 4 OAKS CHANGES PROPOSED BY U. S.

Revising of Charter by Later Parley and Wider Scope for Assembly Are Emphasized

LEAGUE FUNCTIONS KEPT

Soviet-Latin Trade on Bids to Argentina and Lublin Reported Sought

By JAMES B. RESTON

Special to THE NEW YORK TIMES.

SAN FRANCISCO, April 29—Delegates of the big four nations at the San Francisco Conference began exchanging views on amending of the Dumbarton Oaks proposals this weekend, but the question of bringing Argentina and Poland into the United Nations Conference on International Organization continued to hamper progress on this important subject.

There were several private meetings among various members of the sponsor nations yesterday and today. In one of these it was apparently decided that White Russia and the Ukraine should be brought into the conference this week, but when the question of inviting Argentina was raised the Russian Foreign Commissar, Vyacheslaff M. Molotoff, again proposed inviting representatives of the Polish government in Warsaw.

This suggestion, which had been defeated in the steering committee, was again opposed in the firmest manner by the American Secretary of State and the British Foreign Secretary, and it now is likely that the Russians will not insist on forcing the Polish issue to a vote, although they are clearly not yet happy about inviting Argentina.

Four Changes Offered

The United States suggested to the other sponsor powers that four changes be made in the Dumbarton Oaks proposals. These changes would provide:

First, that the charter to be written at this conference be subject to revision in a United Nations constitutional convention at a future date. The principle of writing a temporary rather than a permanent charter has been accepted by all members of the American delegation and is supported by the British, but the amendment as it now stands does not stipulate when the constitutional convention would be held and some members of the delegation think that it should. This will be discussed when the conference commissions are set up this week and the subject will be followed up in the commissions by Comdr. Harold E. Stassen.

Second, that all members obligate themselves to settle disputes in accordance with justice and fundamental human rights, and specifically to adhere to the principles of the Atlantic Charter.

Third, that the assembly have the right to recommend the revision of treaties and the removal of conditions that might lead to a breach of international peace and security.

Fourth, that the charter make provision for taking over responsibility of the functions of the old League of Nations, including responsibilty for the League mandates, and also provde for a system of trusteeship over colonial areas.

Some Vandenberg Points Fail

In the final meetings here among members of the American delegation on the Dumbarton Oaks proposals, several specific proposals by various members of the delegation were rejected. Although Senator Arthur H. Vandenberg, Republican, of Michigan, put in several amendments that were accepted in the points listed above, two of his proposals dealing with the rights of the General Assembly were rejected.

One of these was that the General Assembly should—contrary to the Dumbarton Oaks proposals—be authorized to make recom-

Continued on Page 10, Column 4

Moscow Blackout Ends for May Day

By Wireless to THE NEW YORK TIMES.

MOSCOW, April 29—Moscow's stifling blackout ends tomorrow after almost four years of war. For some weeks now, increasing numbers of street lamps have been turned on, but the obscuring of lights in homes remained rigidly enforced.

The removal of this confounded nuisance will add to the general festivities accompanying the May Day holiday and the imminent fall of Berlin and the end of the European conflict. Workmen on scaffolds have been putting light bulbs back into the huge stars on the Kremlin's towers.

CARRIER ROOSEVELT IS CHRISTENED HERE

Widow Speaks at Floating of $90,000,000 Ship—Forrestal Reveals Navy's Strength

As gray sea water lapped at her keel in building dock 5 of the New York Navy Yard in Brooklyn, a gigantic new aircraft carrier was christened the Franklin D. Roosevelt in impressive ceremonies yesterday morning. The 45,000-ton vessel, built at a cost of $90,000,000, is one of a class of three ships described by the Navy as the largest warships afloat and the biggest ships of any type ever built in this country.

At the ceremony Mrs. Franklin D. Roosevelt, clad in deepest mourning, made her first public appearance since her husband's funeral. In a brief, unscheduled address she expressed her gratitude that the Navy had given her husband's name to the new carrier, previously scheduled to be called the U. S. S. Coral Sea, and voiced a prayer that the ship would bring her officers and men home safe and victorious.

James V. Forrestal, Secretary of the Navy, who made the principal address, revealed some hitherto secret figures about the present size of the United States Fleet. He said that it now consisted of twenty-three battleships, twenty-six combat aircraft carriers, sixty-five escort carriers, sixty-seven cruisers, 386 destroyers, 368 destroyer escorts, and 240 submarines.

For Strong Naval Force

Secretary Forrestal warned those at the ceremony that the United States must retain the military ability "for swift and effective application of force" if peace is to be maintained in future years. He said that the retention of force by the United States would not conflict with her aspirations at the San Francisco Conference, but was essential for realizing the aims sought there.

Unlike the previous 45,000-ton ships built at the New York Navy Yard, the battleships Iowa and Missouri, the Franklin D. Roosevelt was not launched in the traditional fashion down greased building ways into the East River.

Continued on Page 32, Column 2

SLAIN BY PARTISANS

Italy's Former Dictator Shot After Trial—Other Fascists Executed

SEIZED AS HE FLED

OnetimePremierBegged for Life—Bodies on Display in Milan

By MILTON BRACKER

By Wireless to THE NEW YORK TIMES.

MILAN, April 29—Benito Mussolini came back last night to the city where his fascism was born. He came back on the floor of a closed moving van, his dead body flung on the bodies of his mistress and twelve men shot with him. All were executed yesterday by Italian Partisans. The story of his final downfall, his flight, his capture and his execution is not pretty, and its epilogue in the Piazza Loretto here this morning was its ugliest part. It will go down in history as a finish to tyranny as horrible as any ever visited on a tyrant.

At 9:30 A. M. today, Mussolini's body lay on the rim of the mass of corpses, while all around surged a growing mob wild with the desire to have a last look at the man who once was a Socialist editor in this same city. The throng pushed and yelled. Partisans strove to keep them back but largely in vain. Even a series of shots in the air did not dissuade them.

Bullet Hole in Head

Mussolini had changed in death, but not enough to be any one else. His closely shaved head and his bull neck were unmistakable. His body seemed small and a little shrunken, but he was never a tall man. At least one bullet had passed through his head. It had emerged some three inches behind his right ear. There was another small hole nearer his forehead where another bullet seemed to have gone in.

As if he were not dead or dishonored enough, at least two young men in the crowd broke through and aimed kicks at his skull. One glanced off. But the other landed full on his right jaw and there was a hideous crunch that wholly disfigured the once-proud face.

Mussolini wore the uniform of a squadrist militiaman. It comprised a gray-brown jacket and gray trousers with red and black stripes down the sides. He wore black boots, badly soiled, and the left one hung half off as if his foot were broken. His small eyes were open and it was perhaps a final irony that this man who had thrust his chin forward for so many official photographs had to have his yellowing face propped up with a rifle-butt to turn it into the sun for the only two Allied cameramen on the scene.

When the butt was removed the face flopped back over to the left. Meanwhile I crouched over the body to the left in order not to

Continued on Page 7, Column 1

THE INGLORIOUS END OF A DICTATOR

Benito Mussolini in Milan's Piazza Loretto after his execution by Italian Partisans. Also seen is the body of Clara Petacci

The New York Times Radiophoto

5TH SEIZES MILAN, FASCISM'S CRADLE

Americans Surge On to Como—8th Army Takes Venice and Cuts Adige Line

By VIRGINIA LEE WARREN

By Wireless to THE NEW YORK TIMES.

ADVANCED ALLIED FIELD HEADQUARTERS, Italy, April 29—United States Fifth Army troops today entered Milan, Italy's largest, wealthiest and most politically conscious city, where the history of

Continued on Page 3, Column 4

Nazis in Berlin Compressed Into 18-Square-Mile Pocket

By C. L. SULZBERGER

By Wireless to THE NEW YORK TIMES.

MOSCOW, Monday, April 30—Determined Russian troops drove deeper into the heart of Berlin's wreckage yesterday, nearing the hastily fortified Tiergarten from two sides and edging to within a mile of the Reichstag as division after division gave itself up to the Red Army. Within the past forty-eight hours the First White Russian Army and the First Ukrainian Army have captured more than 50,000 prisoners in and around the burning capital.

Southeast of the city, in the

Continued on Page 4, Column 5

War News Summarized

MONDAY, APRIL 30, 1945

Munich, birthplace of nazism, and Milan, cradle of fascism, were entered by American troops yesterday while the world waited for further word on what Himmler was going to do about the Allied demand that Germany surrender unconditionally to Great Britain, the United States and the Soviet Union. Count Bernadotte, who carried the Nazi's proposal to give up to the western Allies only, was returning from seeing Himmler again, presumably with a reply to the Allied ultimatum. [1:7.]

It was the United States Seventh Army that smashed into Munich after a twenty-mile advance. Opposition was light, and the Americans were soon in occupation of that beer cellar from which Hitler launched his ill-fated revolt in 1923. Front reports said Munich had been captured. The Third Army was advancing on Berchtesgaden and Salzburg, while in the center the Ninth burst from its Elbe River bridgehead toward the Russians in the Wittenberg area. To the north the British Second Army crossed the Elbe southeast of Hamburg, and the Canadians progressed along the coast. The French First Army was twelve miles from Austria in the Alps. [1:8; map P. 3.]

Milan was taken by the United States Fifth Army, which also reached Como and the north end of Lake Garda. The British Eighth Army captured Venice and seized Mestre, eighty-five miles from Trieste. The Brazilian Expeditionary Force compelled a German division to surrender. The captured Marshal Graziani was arranging for the surrender of his Fascist Ligurian army. [1:4; map, P. 3.]

Mussolini's body was dumped from a moving van into a Milan square, where it received the scornful attention of the residents. He, his mistress and more than a dozen other Fascists had been executed by Partisans near Como. [1:3.]

Berlin's last-ditch defenders were squeezed into an eighteen square mile area in the center of the city, and Russian troops were within half a mile of Hitler's ruined chancellery. A German pocket southeast of the city was liquidated, while in the north two Soviet armies joined forces and swept toward Rostock and Swinemuende. [1:5-6, maps P. 4.] A wave of suicides was said to be sweeping Berlin. [4:1.]

Washington and London learned from Moscow that a provisional anti-fascist government had been set up in Austria headed by Dr. Karl Renner, former Chancellor and last president of the free Assembly. [1:6.]

A marked trend toward the Left was shown in early returns from France's first elections since 1937. Communists jumped into the lead in Paris. [1:6-7.]

A clearly marked Navy hospital ship was attacked off Okinawa by a Japanese plane, which killed twenty-nine and injured thirty-three; one man was missing. Some 200 other enemy planes kept the Pacific Fleet under prolonged attack, damaging some light units; 104 of the enemy aircraft were destroyed. On shore, troops captured the northern half of Machinato airfield in a general advance. [1:2-3.]

Americans on Mindanao seized the Padada airfield along Davao Gulf and advanced up to seventeen miles in the center. [8:5.] Japanese resistance slowed the British drive on Rangoon, in Burma. [8:7.]

Enemy Suicide Pilot Dives Plane On U. S. Hospital Ship Off Okinawa

By W. H. LAWRENCE

By Wireless to THE NEW YORK TIMES.

ABOARD AMPHIBIOUS FLAGSHIP, off Okinawa, April 28 (Delayed)—A Japanese "suicide" pilot machine-gunned and then crashed his bomb-laden plane squarely into the well-lighted, unarmed United States naval hospital ship Comfort fully loaded with casualties from Okinawa in clear weather about sixty miles southeast of here at 8:58 o'clock tonight.

Twenty-nine were killed by the exploding airplane, which apparently struck the surgery section of the hospital ship as she was bearing wounded toward rear area hospitals.

Although first reports from the ship indicated that it would be necessary to abandon ship, it later was found that the damage was not as heavy as it seemed, and the vessel was able to continue under her own power.

Tempers ran high in naval circles at this premeditated and cold-blooded attack upon the hospital ship, which was proceeding alone with full illumination, including powerful searchlights that lighted up huge red crosses painted on the sides, superstructure and stack.

It was the first time that the Japanese had been known to attack an American hospital ship deliberately, although two other hospital ships were menaced during the Okinawa operation. Until tonight's incident, naval men had been inclined charitably to attribute these attacks to mistakes.

But there was no possibility of mistake about tonight's attack. There was a full moon and the sky was clear. The Japanese plane, one of several in the area, swept in

Continued on Page 3, Column 3

AUSTRIA CREATES INTERIM REGIME

Moscow Announces Renner Is Premier—Britain and U. S. Not Consulted

By Wireless to THE NEW YORK TIMES.

MOSCOW, April 29—An Austrian Provisional Government, the first independent authority in that German-speaking country since the Nazi annexation of more than seven years ago, has been created in Vienna under the leadership of Dr. Karl Renner, 74, a Social Democrat.

His Cabinet of thirteen men includes three non-party representatives, three Social Democrats, four Christian Socialists and three Communists. The Communists hold the key posts of the Interior and Education Ministries as well as one of the three seats on the political

Continued on Page 4, Column 7

NEW NAZI PROFFER ON PEACE AWAITED

Stalin Note to Truman and Churchill Said to Spurn Himmler's Proposals

By CLIFTON DANIEL

By Wireless to THE NEW YORK TIMES.

LONDON, Monday, April 30—London took Saturday night's "peace scare" calmly and yesterday confidently marked time in anticipation of an actual capitulation by Germany and peace in Europe within a matter of days. Amid reports about negotiations with Heinrich Himmler and a variety of rumors of the death of Adolf Hitler, official quarters here quietly awaited a Nazi reply to the British and American Governments' statement that unconditional surrender could be accepted only by all three major Allies.

Opinion was strong that Himmler's offer of surrender would be extended to the Russians—an opinion based on the belief that the Gestapo chief, now evidently ruler of the Reich, would never have made his proposal if Germany's situation had not been so desperate as to preclude further resistance.

[Reuter reported that Premier Stalin in a note to President Truman and Prime Minister Churchill has urged rejection of Himmler's proposals. Mr. Church-

Continued on Page 3, Column 2

Communists Take Lead in Paris As France Holds First Elections

By The Associated Press.

PARIS, April 29—Communist candidates for municipal office in Paris held a commanding lead on the basis of almost complete returns today.

Election returns from other metropolitan centers indicated that their voters, too, had supported candidates of the leftist parties in contests for municipal offices, the only ones at stake in today's voting. Only a few returns had been received from traditionally conservative country districts.

In Paris and other principal cities the Communists' lead seemed to be safe, while Socialists and Radicals ran well ahead of center parties and rightists. Political observers speculated that eleventh-hour Communist demands for the quick trial and conviction of Marshal Henri-Philippe Pétain had drawn support to the party candidates, including many voters unaffiliated with any party.

André Mornet, Attorney General, who will conduct the case against Pétain, was returned to office with a heavy plurality. Edouard Herriot, former President of the Chamber of Deputies, who has just reached Switzerland from a German prison camp, was elected to the Municipal Council of Lyon by a 4-to-1 margin. Six members of the Cabinet who ran for city offices were also elected.

Joseph Paul-Boncour, a member of the French delegation to the San Francisco Conference, was also elected by a big margin.

Not only was this the first election that France had held since her fall to the Germans but it was the first time that women were al-

Continued on Page 5, Column 6

3 DIVISIONS ENTER

Americans Roll Into Nazi Birthplace Without Meeting Opposition

ITS FALL IS REPORTED

British Cross the Elbe and Drive Northeast to Cut Off Denmark

By DREW MIDDLETON

By Wireless to THE NEW YORK TIMES.

PARIS, April 29—American and British Armies dealt shattering blows to waning German hopes of holding out in the southern and northern redoubts today.

Troops of the United States Seventh Army crashed into Munich, birthplace of the Nazi party and the principal enemy stronghold barring the roads to the redoubt in the Austrian Tyrol while Tommies of the British Second Army smashed over the Elbe southeast of Hamburg.

Elements of the Twelfth Armored and Forty-second Infantry Divisions entered Munich at 4 o'clock this afternoon, meeting only light resistance, according to reports from the front. Later the Twentieth Armored Division rolled in.

Beer Cellar Occupied

Reports from the front line tonight said that Munich had fallen. There was no confirmation of these reports, either at Supreme Headquarters or at any Army group, but in view of the slackening resistance all over Germany and the failure of the enemy to attack the first troops entering the city, it is entirely possible that Munich has been taken.

Munich was reached after a twenty-mile advance by Seventh Army columns. According to reports from the front the Americans hold the beer cellar where Hitler planned his premature putsch of 1923 and where he addressed Nazi leaders yearly. The cellar was partly destroyed by a bomb in the autumn of 1939.

The infamous concentration camp at Dachau is believed to have been overrun in the advance to the city.

Push on Redoubt Gains

The thrust into Munich was accompanied by a general advance to the south and southeast toward the northern face of the redoubt by the United States Third and Seventh Armies, while on the right flank of the Seventh Army infantry felt its way southeastward into the redoubt, pushing toward Innsbruck and the valley of the Inn River, the most important, indeed the only communications system within the redoubt.

The thrust over the Elbe by the Fifteenth Scottish Division and the British First Commando Brigade to the north followed a bombardment in typical Montgomery fashion in which more than 400 guns were employed. It was accompanied by heavy blows on the German line west and east of the Weser and the flattening of an enemy salient northeast of Bremen.

The Ninth Army front, long dormant, awoke today when Lieut. Gen. William H. Simpson's troops suddenly attacked out of their bridgehead over the Elbe, capturing the towns of Zerbst, Jutrichau and Bias and advancing northeast and southeast of the towns. This attack was described here as a "local attack."

Four divisions, the Twelfth and Twentieth Armored and the Third and Forty-second Infantry Divisions, moved on Munich this morning. The Twentieth is a new division, fed into the battle yesterday by Lieut. Gen. Alexander M. Patch.

Between Munich and the Austrian frontier around Fuessen, other armored, cavalry and infantry units of the Seventh Army drove on toward the southeast, crossing the Lech River in force.

The Forty-fourth Infantry Division, which is moving methodically

Continued on Page 3, Column 6

MUSSOLINI KILLED IN NORTHERN ITALY

Continued From Page 1

cut off the sun from his turned face. A group of us had been thrust by the enthusiastic Milanese, who had not yet seen any Americans, right into the circle of death. It was naturally one of the grimmest moments of our lives, but it will at least serve to give absolutely authentic eyewitness accounts.

Mistress Shot With Him

Mussolini lay with his head on the breast of his mistress, Clara Petacci, who had sought to rise to movie fame through him. Younger even than his daughter, she had been executed with him in a suburb of the village of Como on the shore of Lake Como, and now she lay in a ruffled white blouse, her dark hair curly and her relative youth apparent even now.

The other bodies lying in a semicircle, only a few kilometers from the Piazza San Sepolcro, where fascism actually began, included those of Alessandro Pavolini, Mussolini's Secretary of State; Francesco Barracu, vice chairman of the Cabinet; Paolo Zerbini, Minister of the Interior, and Goffredo Coppola, rector of the University of Bologna, who had fled ten days before the Allies' entry.

Others whose bodies are on exhibit were Fernando Mezzasoma, Minister of Propaganda; Ruggero Romano, Minister of Public Works; Augusto Liverani, Minister of Communications; Paolo Porta, a party inspector; Luigi Gatti, a Prefect; Ernesto Daquanno, editor of Stefani; Mario Nudi, president of the Fascist Agricultural Association, and Nicola Bombacci, a former Communist.

The last chapter in the life of the man who led a phony March on Rome in October, 1922, began last Wednesday, when, after a transport workers' strike on the previous Sunday, a general strike of all Milanese workers tied up the whole city of more than 1,000,000 people. Mussolini was still chief of the puppet Fascist Republican Government. He appealed to Ildefonso Cardinal Schuster to act as intermediary at a meeting with the leaders of the Committee of National Liberation. This took place at the archiepiscopal residence just off the Piazza Fontana.

At this meeting Mussolini appeared more tractable than Marshal Rodolfo Graziani. Told that the Germans in Milan had already indicated a desire to surrender to the Allies, however, Mussolini turned on his Axis partners and declared that they had "betrayed" him.

According to the Popolo of Milan, he went on: "They have treated us as servants, and harshly—for many, far too many years. Now we have had enough."

Rejects Terms

Returning to his quarters after having asked an hour's leave to discuss the terms, Mussolini then sent word that the terms were not acceptable and he would leave. He arrived in Como at 10 P. M. on Wednesday and made efforts throughout the night to arrange passage across the Swiss frontier. The first reports said that his wife, Rachele was with him but it would appear now that it was not she but Signorina Petacci.

Some time on Thursday morning, in a caravan of some thirty cars, Mussolini headed north up the west shore of Lake Como. He was wearing a black coat over his uniform. Near Dongo, a sheltered village about three-quarters of the way up the shore, a Partisan named Urbano Lazari spotted him. Like the fleeing Marie Antoinette, he was made to alight and temporarily sheltered in a cottage in the tiny hamlet of Giulino di Mezzegre, near Dongo. Signorina Petacci was with him but the others in the caravan were held separately. After a brief trial they were sentenced and executed.

From this point the details came from a Committee of National Liberation leader in this area known only as Eduardo. When word of the arrest reached him, he sent ten men from Milan with an unnamed colonel from the Milan area of the Italian Command. The colonel handled the details of the trial and sentence, but for the moment, at least, this phase of the story is unascertainable. Eduardo's men brought back the bodies last night and they gave this version through him.

When Mussolini first saw the Italian officer with the group from Milan, he sought to embrace them, thinking that they were Fascists and his friends. Disabused, he was shocked and later, after the trial and the death sentence, he said within the hearing of one Partisan known as Piero: "Lasciatemi salvare la vita e vi daroó un impero [Let me save my life and I will give you an empire]." But this incredible plea was vain and the execution was carried out at 4:10 P. M. yesterday.

Eduardo's men said that Mussolini had died badly. He yelled: "No! No!" as his very last words. He wore no blindfold. The order to fire was given by Riccardo, a 40-year-old veteran of the Spanish Civil War who led Eduardo's ten men under the general command of the colonel.

The others, except Signorina Petacci, were shot elsewhere. Pavolini was said to have died bravely, proclaiming: "Viva l'Italia"! Barracu wore a high military decoration; he died saying: "Do not hit the medal."

Signorina Petacci's brother, Marcello, tried to flee but was shot. Possibly his was one of the otherwise unidentified "extra bodies" in the piazza this morning.

All the corpses were loaded into the moving van, which started down twenty-five miles of the superb autostrada after dark. The bodies were dumped in the Piazza Loretto because recently fifteen patriots were executed there. In fact, the name of the piazza has been changed to Piazza Quindici Martiri. The bodies arrived much later than scheduled because the van was repeatedly stopped en route by heavily armed Partisans who wanted to make sure that the driver was not a Fascist trying to take the bodies to honorable burial. This doubt grew so serious at one point that the driver and the men with him were actually lined up for execution and it took an hour's argument to persuade the Partisans to let the truck proceed. The bodies were dumped without ceremony and the truck rolled away. Word that they were there did not get around generally until this morning, when the papers carried last-minute make-over stories. The effect on the city was obvious.

There is no way of telling how long the gruesome show will go on. But if many more misguided young men leap through the circle aiming their boots at what is left of Mussolini there will be hardly enough left for burial.

Mistress 25 Years Old

ROME, April 29 (U.P.)—Signorina Petacci was about 25 years old. She was the daughter of a Rome doctor. Mussolini met her on a beach in 1939 and built a large villa for her outside Rome and, with his influence, tried to make her a motion picture star but she failed in that venture. The mistress was arrested after Mussolini was ousted as Premier in July, 1943, but the Germans rescued her and she joined Mussolini in northern Italy.

Vatican's Feelings Mixed

ROME, April 29 (U.P.)—The Roman public and the Government, including Premier Ivanoe Bonomi, hailed the news of Mussolini's execution with satisfaction tonight but it was understood that the news was received by Vatican City with mixed feelings.

The United Press learned from unimpeachable Vatican sources that the Holy See believed that a more formal procedure should have been adopted for the trial and execution of Mussolini and his henchmen. There was no belief in the Vatican that their lives should have been spared, but it was stated that the procedure should have been more orderly. Vatican circles were also greatly displeased by the fact that the corpses were more or less maltreated and reviled during their public display in Milan.

Mussolini with King Victor Emmanuel of Italy in 1936.

Mussolini with his staff.

Mussolini with Hitler.

GRAZIANI REPORTED TRIED, EXECUTED

Slaying of Mussolini Sets Off Purge in North but Allies Order It Stopped

VATICAN PAPER CRITICAL

Dissents Sharply From Official and Roman Press Opinion on Partisans' Actions

MILAN, April 30 (AP)—Marshal Rodolfo Graziani, ruthless conqueror of Libya and former Chief of Staff of the Italian Army, was reported tonight to have been tried and executed by Partisans in a purge of Fascists touched off by the execution of Benito Mussolini. There was no immediate official confirmation.

[Graziani was turned over to Col. Norman Fiske of the Allied Military Government, who took him to the American Fourth Corps headquarters outside Milan, where he was held for trial as a war criminal, The United Press reported.]

Tonight Mussolini's body lay in a half-open white wooden coffin in Milan. Next to it, in another crude coffin was the body of his mistress; scattered throughout the room were dozens of bodies of men executed by the Partisans. They were labeled "unknown."

Graziani, who was also captured by the Partisans in northern Italy, was reported to have gone on trial this morning a few hours after the bodies of Mussolini and his followers had been removed from the Piazza Quindici Martiri, where they had been displayed publicly since Saturday night. At headquarters of the Committee of National Liberation it was said unofficially that Graziani had been convicted and quickly executed.

Bodies Hung Up by Feet

By Wireless to THE NEW YORK TIMES.

MILAN, April 29 (Delayed)—The degradation to which the bodies of Mussolini, his mistress, Clara Petacci, and his fascist followers were subjected this morning did not end in the muddy gutter.

Soon after 10 A. M., six of the corpses, including Mussolini's and Signorina Petacci's, were hung by the feet with wire from an exposed steel girder of a former gasoline station a few yards from the original dumping point. Black-lettered white signs bearing their names were plastered above them. Later the bodies were cut down and taken to the morgue, where a crowd gathered all over again, and men, women and children climbed fences to get a final look.

An inspection of the bodies revealed a delicate square gold locket that Signorina Petacci had worn. Outside, in the lower right corner, it bore initials and the inscription: "Clara—io sono te, tu sei me [Clara—I am you, you are me]." It was signed "Ben" and dated April 4, 1939, and April 4, 1941—presumably when Mussolini met Signorina Petacci and when he gave her the locket.

No funeral plans had been set tonight and there was some talk of an autopsy on what was left of the dictator. Frankly, it was not much, for the crowd had kicked his face out of shape.

Vatican Paper Disapproves

ROME, April 30 (AP)—The Vatican daily, the Osservatore Romano, dissented today from a chorus of official and press approval of Mussolini's execution and deplored "impetuous violence and macabre manifestations" in dealing out justice.

The Milan radio broadcast a statement tonight by the prefect of Milan that "in virtue of the powers today entrusted to me by the Allied military command for Lombardy, I order the immediate suspension of summary trials held by formations of volunteers or people styling themselves as such." The broadcast warned that "Italian authorities and the Allied Military Government will take measures of extreme severity against all those who infringe this order."

The Vatican newspaper's deploring attitude contrasted with an official endorsement of Mussolini's execution from Mario Berlinguer, High Commissioner for the Punishment of Fascist Crimes, and unanimous expressions of satisfaction from Rome's many newspapers, which held that Fascist violence had simply reaped its own harvest. Signor Berlinguer said that the Northern Committee of National Liberation had Government authority to seize and try Fascists and that Mussolini's execution "was only fair." He added: "It is true that a writ for his arrest had been prepared for some months."

Mussolini's Widow Held

LONDON, April 30 (Reuter) — Donna Rachele Mussolini, the dictator's widow, and her two youngest children have been arrested at Como, the Swiss radio reported tonight.

MUSSOLINI FIRST OF FOES TO FALL

Exemplar of Modern Dictators Rose From Obscurity to Leadership of Italy

Benito Mussolini, founder of Fascism and for more than twenty years the ruler of Italy in all but name, was the first of the modern totalitarian dictators to achieve power, as he was the first of them to lose it.

His career, from its beginnings in obscurity to its end, was unfailingly colorful and dramatic. Never was this more true than in his downfall, which served to provide one of the great turning points of the World War for which he bore such a heavy burden of responsibility.

Although the Fascist regime had been badly shaken by the Axis defeats in North Africa and the loss of the Italian Empire on that continent, it was the invasion of Sicily by the Anglo-American forces under Gen. Dwight D. Eisenhower that set in motion the chain of events that culminated in the overthrow of Il Duce.

Within a week after the Allied landings Mussolini asked Hitler for a conference, which was held at Feltre, in north Italy, from July 17 to 19, 1943. At this conference the Italian General Staff asked for forty-nine divisions and 3,000 planes to help defend the Italian mainland. The Germans were supposed to have replied that they had not more than two divisions and 300 planes to reinforce the forces already in Italy.

Hitler, according to the reports that leaked out long afterward, prevailed upon Mussolini to accept a strategic policy calling for the abandonment of southern Italy and the holding of a strong natural defensive position from the vicinity of La Spezia to the region around Rimini. Mussolini returned to Rome determined to adhere to this plan.

He found the Italian capital, which had just been bombed by Allied planes for the first time, in a state of great confusion. His colleagues in the Government were dismayed by the decision to abandon the southern part of the country, and the dictator found himself forced to convene the Fascist Grand Council, which had not met since 1939.

When the gathering met, on the evening of July 24, Mussolini made a forceful address outlining the plans decided upon at the Feltre conference. Count Dino Grandi, however, accused Mussolini of having given a false account of what had taken place at that meeting. He claimed that he had been hiding at a point from which he could hear Hitler and Mussolini, and read from notes he claimed to have taken on their conversation.

A general uproar followed and, after a long and heated debate, the Council voted, 19 to 6, against Mussolini, who thereupon withdrew. The Council continued its meeting and decided to overthrow the dictator and seek peace with the Allies. Mussolini, meanwhile, was unaware of these decisions and believed that he had been able to ride out the storm.

About 4 P. M. on July 25 King Victor Emmanuel sent for the Premier, who was surprised, on his arrival at the Quirinal Palace, to find Count Grandi there. The King accused Mussolini of having made a false official report, and told him his usefulness was at an end. He handed Il Duce a prepared letter of resignation, which the dictator refused to sign. The King thereupon told him it was accepted, regardless whether it was signed.

Became a Prisoner

As he started to leave the palace, a general of the Carabinieri led him to a waiting ambulance instead of to his own automobile. He realized that he was being made prisoner, and had to be overpowered by the guards. He was taken to Gaeta, then transferred to Ponza by ship. Several weeks later he was transferred to the Gran Sasso Hotel, near Lake Bracciano, about seventy-five miles north of Rome.

On Sept. 12, four days after the announcement of the armistice, Mussolini was rescued from the hotel, where he was still being held by the Badoglio regime. Prime Minister Churchill later absolved the Badoglio government of bad faith in his escape, explaining that it had not foreseen the audacious attempt to rescue him.

Three days after his rescue, German and north Italian radio stations carried an announcement that Mussolini had organized a new government of "Fascist Republican Italy" and had declared the King dethroned for his part in the plot to oust the dictator. On Sept. 18 Mussolini's own voice, according to persons familiar with it, was heard calling upon all Italians to take up arms once more by the side of Germany and Japan.

The government of which he was the nominal head succeeded, by the aid of German arms, in making good its temporary hold over the cities of northern Italy, where it took over complete control of all vital economic concerns, including those providing essential raw material supplies, power and other indispensable services.

Mussolini was born on July 29, 1883, in the hamlet of Dovia, Province of Forli. His parents were miserably poor. His mother was a school teacher; his father was a blacksmith and Socialist agitator, who named him Benito Juarez after the Mexican revolutionary who overthrew the Emperor Maximilian.

(continued)

As a boy he was unruly, turbulent and aggressive. On completing his elementary education he became a teacher, but soon tired of this life. He wandered through Switzerland, Germany, France and Austria, working as a bricklayer, station porter, weaver and butcher's boy. In the evenings he attended various universities, or studied alone.

Returning to Italy he became prominent as a Socialist agitator in Forli, serving a prison sentence for his part in an agricultural strike. It was in this period that he married and his eldest child, Edda, who later married Count Ciano, was born. In Forli he founded the newspaper Lotta di Classe—Class Struggle—which became the local Socialist organ.

A bitter opponent of the Italo-Turkish War, which he considered a useless shedding of blood, Mussolini stood trial for his active stand against the war, but was acquitted. His oration in his own defense helped win him national recognition as the leader of the left wing of the Socialist party, the place he held when the first World War broke out.

Denounced by Socialists

Within a few months he swung violently away from his radical and pacifist position to one of active championing of Italian entry into the war on the side of the Allies. For this he was denounced as a traitor by his former Socialist comrades, who contended, probably truly, that he had been subsidized by Allied propagandists.

In January, 1915, he founded the Fasci of Revolutionary Action, whose purpose was to bring about Italian participation in the war. He actively pushed the same cause at public meetings, often tumultuous, held all over Italy. During the same period he fought a number of political duels. When Italy declared war on May 23, Mussolini immediately volunteered for active service, but was not called until the following September.

Assigned to the Bersaglieri, he made an exemplary soldier, although he was never promoted past the rank of sergeant, because his past political record was against him. But he was wounded several times and repeatedly mentioned in dispatches.

After the war Mussolini secretly allied himself with the most reactionary elements. He founded the Fasci di Combattimento in Milan in March, 1919, for the avowed purpose of fighting the widespread unrest. The progress of the movement was slow at first, but it received a great impetus when the Italian Government sent Italian troops to fire upon Gabriel d'Annunzio and his followers in Fiume.

This move sent thousands of volunteers flocking to the standards of Fascismo. When the anarcho-syndicalists, with some help from the Communists, occupied a number of Italian factories, the Fascisti turned on them fiercely, and when the strike collapsed quickly set up a fanfare about how they had saved Italy from a Red revolution. Actually, some historians believe the alleged strikes were deliberately fomented by a provocateur.

By the autumn of 1922 the Fascist party claimed more than 1,000,000 members, of whom 500,000 youths were organized in its militant section. At the party convention held in Naples on Oct. 24 of that year, Mussolini issued this ultimatum to the Government:

"Either the government of the country is handed to us peaceably or we shall take it by force, marching on Rome and engaging in a struggle to the death with the politicians now in power."

Four days later the black-shirted legions began the march on Rome from their headquarters in Milan, discreetly followed by Mussolini in a sleeping car. The Cabinet declared martial law, but King Victor Emmanuel refused to sign the decree. The Cabinet thereupon resigned and the King asked Mussolini to form a government.

He first formed a coalition Cabinet, in which the Liberal, Conservative and Catholic parties were represented, although the Fascists were, of course, dominant. He himself took the posts of Minister of War and Minister of the Interior, and demanded a grant of extraordinary power from the Chamber of Deputies to balance the budget, solve the labor problem and revise Italy's foreign policy.

Within a month he used these powers to make himself dictator. He began a drastic overhaul of the entire governmental machinery, displacing old government employes by members of his own black-shirted militia. He boasted that he would make Italy powerful, prosperous and efficient and would make the dreams of Mazzini and Garibaldi come true by reviving and extending the spirit of nationalism.

He met with strong opposition in the early years of Fascism from the remnants of the Republicans, Socialists, Communists and Free Masons. He and his unruly young Blackshirts were ruthless in grinding down these opponents, raiding political meetings and newspapers, burning buildings, disciplining obstreperous opponents with beatings and forced doses of castor oil.

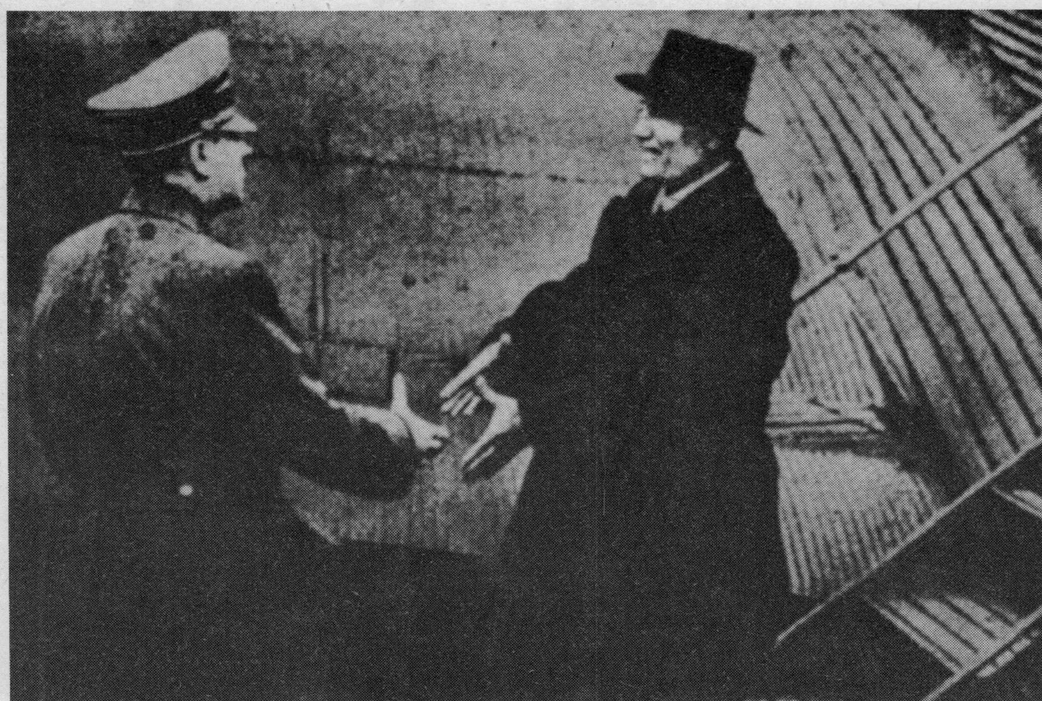

In 1943 Hitler welcomed the former Duce to German territory after he was liberated by the Fuehrer's paratroopers from a hotel in Italy.

Associated Press

The fascist leader when he was speaking of his empire

The New York Times

Mussolini and his regime met its first great crisis in June, 1924, when Giacomo Matteotti, leader of the Socialist party and the only outstanding politician who continued publicly to defy the dictator within Italy, disappeared. Well-known Fascists were arrested as his kidnappers. When Matteotti's murdered body was found later in the summer, a world-wide storm of indignation broke.

His Power Consolidated

For a time Mussolini seemed in danger of falling, but he used the crisis ruthlessly as a means of extending his power. He abandoned all pretense of a coalition government and substituted one that was frankly Fascist, driving all who were not loyal to that party completely out of public life.

Under fascism the Government regimented every aspect of the life of the Italian people and their industry. The Government took complete control of all capital and labor relations. It limited profits, fixed wages and hours, prohibited strikes and lockouts, regulated working conditions, made arbitration of labor disputes compulsory and set up special labor courts to deal with such cases. Professional and agricultural workers as well as factory and office employes were brought under the Fascist codes.

Although Mussolini did not regard himself as a "good" Catholic, he looked upon religion as a necessary moral force and as a bulwark against communism. Consequently he was careful to make enough concessions to the Roman Catholic Church to keep it friendly toward him. He settled the long-standing quarrel between Church and State in Italy by the Lateran accord of 1929, by which he recognized the sovereignty of Vatican City.

Mussolini's foreign policy was ultra-nationalistic and ultra-militaristic. As early as 1923, in the Corfu incident, he sent the Italian fleet to bombard the Greek island of Corfu in a dispute over the murder of four Italian commissioners. Greece appealed to the League of Nations, but Mussolini refused to recognize the right of the League to interfere. He won his point, even though for a time his policy threatened to bring on a war with Great Britain.

More than a decade later he again defied the League and risked war with Great Britain when, after long, secret preparations, he began the carefully planned conquest of Ethiopia. In the interim he had tried to pose as the savior of the peace of Europe through the Four-Power Pact of 1933, in which Great Britain, France, Germany and Italy undertook to guarantee the peace of Europe for ten years. The pact fell to pieces when his designs against Ethiopia became apparent.

Disregarding the opposition in Great Britain, which saw in his plans a threat to the Empire's communications as well as a breach of the obligations of the League of Nations, Mussolini took advantage of border clashes between his troops and the Ethiopians as a pretext for the invasion, which began on Oct. 2, 1935. The Ethiopians fought bravely but were eventually overwhelmed.

In May, 1936, the Council of the League of Nations refused Mussolini's request to drop the sanctions that it had imposed, whereupon the Italian delegation walked out of the council chamber. Friction continued between the British and Italian Governments and the British Home and Orient fleets were stationed in the Mediterranean. After several weeks' tension, however, the British withdrew their ships. Later the League of Nations likewise dropped its sanctions.

Hardly had this dispute been settled when the Spanish Civil War broke out. Although Italy joined the other western European powers in a non-intervention pact, Mussolini at first covertly and later openly sent men, arms and money to aid the rebel forces.

The hatred of Britain that Mussolini felt as the result of the sanctions policy was ameliorated little if at all by the effort at appeasement that followed the advent of Neville Chamberlain to power. This led eventually to the outstanding event of Italian foreign policy under Mussolini—the formation of the celebrated Axis with Germany, at first a secret and then an avowed declaration of solidarity by the totalitarian powers against the democracies of western Europe.

The first important fruit of that agreement was the occupation of Austria by German troops in March, 1938. After the occupation was successfully completed, Mussolini exchanged telegrams pledging continued friendship with Hitler.

In the succeeding crisis over Czechoslovakia, which agitated Europe to its depths in the early autumn of 1938, Mussolini and Hitler were again found side by side. During the days of greatest tension Mussolini, in a series of speeches, urged the partition of Czechoslovakia and called upon France and England to abandon the smaller democracy.

Despite his truculence, Prime Minister Chamberlain of Great Britain turned to Mussolini in his efforts at appeasement. On Sept. 28 he sent an appeal to Mussolini to use his good offices to keep Hitler from marching into the territory of the Sudeten Germans. Mussolini telephoned Hitler and persuaded him to meet Mr. Chamberlain and Premier Daladier at the Munich conference, at which Czechoslovakia was partitioned.

In the year between Munich and the outbreak of the war, Mussolini took a more and more pronounced pro-Nazi attitude. In the Chamber of Deputies his henchmen set up a cry for Corsica and Tunisia, French possessions with large Italian populations. He introduced a series of anti-Semitic measures into Italy and speeded up preparations for the war that seemed inevitable.

When it actually came, with the German invasion of Poland on Sept. 1, 1939, Mussolini was silent. It was not until Sept. 23 that he declared his intention of maintaining Italy's neutrality. This position he maintained, although with marked indications of pro-German sympathy, until the German onslaught crushed the French Army.

Mussolini took his country into the war on June 10, 1940, two days before the Germans reached Paris. Mr. Churchill likened his action to that of a jackal, while President Roosevelt, speaking at Charlottesville, Va., used almost equally strong language.

"On this tenth day of June, 1940, the hand that held the dagger has struck it into the back of its neighbor," the President solemnly declared.

Began Invasion of Greece

The course of the war soon showed that Mussolini had gravely miscalculated. Although he shared in the quick and easy triumph over France, he received little of the spoils he had anticipated. In the autumn Italian armies began an invasion of Greece and suffered such heavy reverses that in the spring Germany had to come to their assistance.

In North Africa, meanwhile, his forces were surprised and shattered by numerically inferior British armies. Italian air power likewise proved unequal to the tasks that were placed upon it, while the vaunted Italian Navy, which Mussolini had boasted would make the Mediterranean "Mare Nostrum," was rudely handled by the British Mediterranean fleet, far inferior to it on paper.

In June, 1941, Mussolini obediently followed the Fuehrer into war against Russia, and on Dec. 11 of that year declared war on the United States.

As defeat followed defeat for Italian arms in the year and a half that followed, Mussolini appeared less and less often on his favorite balcony. The terrific blow dealt his troops by the British Eighth Army at El Alamein; the heavy bombings of Italian industrial cities by the Royal Air Force, and the American landings in North Africa in November, 1942, combined to crush the spirits of his followers.

Mussolini was a prolific writer. Besides innumerable political pamphlets and speeches, he wrote several plays and novels. Among his more important works were the following: "The Trentino Seen by a Socialist," 1909; "The Cardinal's Mistress"; "Political Speeches," 1921; "My War Diary," 1923; "Diuturna," a collection of political writings, 1924; "Ancient Rome on the Sea," 1926; "Journalistic Battle," 1927, and "My Autobiography," 1928.

"All the News That's Fit to Print"

The New York Times

LATE CITY EDITION

Weather: Sunny, cool today; clear, cool tonight. Fair, mild tomorrow. Temp. range: today 60-48; Monday 66-52. Full U.S. report on Page 85.

VOL. CXX.. No. 41,156

NEW YORK, TUESDAY, SEPTEMBER 29, 1970

15 CENTS

NASSER DIES OF HEART ATTACK; BLOW TO PEACE EFFORTS SEEN; NIXON CANCELS FLEET EXERCISE

United Press International

VATICAN CITY: President Nixon with Pope Paul VI during special audience yesterday. Later, he flew by helicopter to U.S.S. Saratoga, with Sixth Fleet in the Mediterranean.

A GESTURE BY U.S.

President Terms Loss Tragic—He Joins Fleet Off Italy

By Reuters

ABOARD U.S.S. SARATOGA, in the Mediterranean, Tuesday, Sept. 29—President Nixon last night ordered cancellation of today's exercises of the United States Sixth Fleet in the Mediterranean because of the death of President Gamal Abdel Nasser of Egypt.

The President, who arrived aboard this aircraft carrier last night, had planned to watch a demonstration of Sixth Fleet firepower, including the launching and recovery of aircraft.

Officials said: "Upon hearing of the death of President Nasser, the President ordered the cancellation of the firepower demonstrations, which were to be held in conjunction with his visit to the Sixth Fleet."

They said that Mr. Nixon's conferences with Sixth Fleet commanders aboard the flagship Springfield would go on as scheduled.

The President flew to this carrier off the coast of Italy by helicopter after a day in which he had conferred in Rome with the President and the Premier of Italy and with Pope Paul VI.

'Tragic Loss'

The President in a statement said that the death of President Nasser was a tragic loss of an outstanding Arab leader.

"I was shocked to hear of the sudden death of President Nasser," Mr. Nixon said. "The world has lost an outstanding leader who tirelessly and devotedly served the causes of his countrymen and the Arab world.

"This tragic loss requires that all nations, and particularly those in the Middle East, renew their efforts to calm passions, reach for mutual understanding and build lasting peace.

"On behalf of the American people I extended deep sympathy to his family and to his people."

Stresses Role of Fleet

Earlier Mr. Nixon had told the men of the Saratoga that never had American military and diplomatic power been used more effectively than in the latest Middle East crisis.

Chatting with sailors who greeted his helicopter on the flight deck, Mr. Nixon spoke of "a hard two or three weeks," which he said had been capped by success. He referred to the Jordanian truce and recovery of the hostages from the hijacked airliners.

"The fact that we were successful is the fact that you were there," he told the sailors. He mentioned their

Continued on Page 19, Column 1

United Press International

President Gamal Abdel Nasser bidding good-by to King Hussein of Jordan after meeting in Cairo yesterday. From ceremony, he returned home where he died of heart attack.

ARAB-WORLD HERO

Vice President Sadat Takes Over as the Interim Leader

Obituary article will be found on Page 16.

By RAYMOND H. ANDERSON

Special to The New York Times

CAIRO, Tuesday, Sept. 29—President Gamal Abdel Nasser, leader of Egypt for 18 years and hero of much of the Arab world, died here yesterday.

The Government radio said the 52-year-old President was the victim of a heart attack.

The death was announced on Cairo's television and radio stations shortly before 11 P.M. by Vice President Anwar Sadat. An hour earlier, regular programs on television and radio were abruptly suspended and replaced with chanting of verses from the Koran. Official mourning was proclaimed for 40 days.

The President suffered the heart attack at 3 P.M. and died three hours later.

No obvious successor to Mr. Nasser was in sight, and no Egyptian seemed in a mood tonight to speculate about the matter.

Funeral Will Be Thursday

Vice President Sadat took over as interim ruler. He reported that emergency meetings had been held by the higher executive committee of the Arab Socialist Union, the political organization created by Mr. Nasser, and the Council of Ministers.

President Nasser's funeral will be held Thursday.

The impact of Mr. Nasser's death will be felt throughout the Arab world. Despite controversies and rivalries during his long years of power, he was the strongest figure of leadership among the Arabs.

Since the battlefield defeat of three Arab armies by Israel in June, 1967, Mr. Nasser was the leader who rallied the Arabs to rebuild their forces for a war of liberation if other means to recover the lands failed.

Favored Political Solution

But he repeatedly emphasized that he favored a political solution of the conflict with Israel if one could be achieved.

Although Mr. Nasser gained a reputation in his early years in power as a fire-breathing radical, in recent years he had become a force for moderation and pragmatism.

Even on the emotional issue of Israel, he was able to swing much of the Arab world behind his acceptance in July of a United States initiative for a cease-fire and he revived efforts for a negotiated settlement. The outlook for pursuing

Continued on Page 17, Column 1

50,000 FLEE BLAZE IN SAN DIEGO AREA

Brush Fire, 30 Miles Long, Is California's Biggest Yet —5 Die in Copter Crash

By United Press International

LOS ANGELES, Sept. 28—The largest brush fire in California history raged today through mountain canyons near the Mexican border, driving thousands of persons from their homes as the flames advanced.

In the San Gabriel Mountains to the north, a helicopter being used by the United States Forest Service to fight another fire crashed late today, killing the five persons aboard.

More than 50,000 persons were evacuated from small communities in San Diego County. The 200-acre fire there erupted in the Cleveland National Forest on Saturday when a falling tree severed a power line. At least 250 structures have been destroyed.

Decreasing winds tonight and a forecast of scattered showers in mountain areas raised hopes that the blaze could be contained tomorrow.

Arson Arrests Made

The enormous blaze, 30 miles from tip to tip, eclipsed in size the Matailaja fire of 1930, which burned 125,000 acres in Kern and Los Angeles Counties.

"We've barely kept up with the situation," said Arlen B. Cartwright of the State Division of Forestry. "The problem seems to come from the fact that fire nuts run around and see flames and smoke and this makes them want to set more fires—which they do."

Arson was suspected in two other major blazes in San Diego County, and five arrests were made in Los Angeles County.

More than 5,000 men worked 36-hour shifts on the fire lines and the neighboring county of San Bernardino was stripped of all but five of its fire engines.

Continued on Page 10, Column 2

Intrepid Wins Series, 4-1, And Keeps America's Cup

By STEVE CADY

Special to The New York Times

NEWPORT, R.I., Sept. 28—The longest series in 100 years of America's Cup challenges came to a desperately dramatic close today with Intrepid completing a 4-1 conquest of Gretel II.

Once again, the defender of yachting's most famous prize had to fight off almost constant pressure by the chunky Australian challenger.

Until a wind shift put Intrepid in clover starting the final leg of the 24.3-mile race, the action had been about as close as a boat race can produce. The cynics say watching two yachts is like watching grass grow, but the grass was on fire again today, as it was so often during this controversial series.

Stage Set for Upset

When Gretel II closed to within two boat lengths at the fifth mark, the stage was set for another upset of the kind the Australian sloop brought off last Thursday. Then the wind shifted from north to east, Intrepid hit it on the right tack and the suspense evaporated.

With the final windward leg turned into a race, the redesigned 1967 defender opened up and came home safely, 1 minute 44 seconds ahead.

As Intrepid swept majestically across the line about 250 yards ahead of her dangerous rival, the familiar dream of another successful Cup defense began unfolding. Horns, whistles and sirens aboard some 150 spectator boats and Coast Guard patrol vessels cut loose with a noisy salute to the American yacht—the second ever to defend the Cup twice.

A Triumphant Allusion

Bill Ficker, the 42-year-old Californian with the bald head and the bold starting-line maneuvers, shook hands with his young crew. They, in turn, hoisted a "Ficker Is Quicker" flag to the top of Intrepid's mast, a triumphant allusion to the tactical swiftness of their skipper.

In today's race, Ficker and his young stalwarts had to be quicker. Jim Hardy gave Gretel II a slight lead at the start but Ficker took it away early on the opening windward leg. He spent the rest of a cold, overcast afternoon desperately keeping the Aussies from breaking through in the fluky

Continued on Page 53, Column 1

U.S. Officials See Period Of Instability in Mideast

By TERENCE SMITH

Special to The New York Times

WASHINGTON, Sept. 28—United States officials, startled by the death of Gamal Abdel Nasser, tended to view it today as a blow to peace-making efforts in the Middle East.

A ranking State Department official described the Egyptian President's death as a "critical loss at a decisive moment in history."

The immediate reaction of officials here was that it would bring a period of instability in the Arab world and would therefore reduce the already-thin prospects for negotiating an early resolution of the Arab-Israeli dispute.

[In Moscow, Western diplomats expected the Soviet leaders to assure the United Arab Republic that President Nasser's death would not affect Soviet support for the Arab cause. Page 17.]

An hour before the Cairo radio announcement, a cable from Donald C. Bergus, the senior United States representative in Cairo, reported a rumor that the Egyptian leader was critically ill or perhaps dead. The message was being decoded as the public announcement came.

Six hours earlier Rodger P. Davies, the Acting Assistant Secretary of State for Near Eastern and South Asian Affairs, had told a closed session of the House Foreign Affairs Committee that the Nixon Administration was "leaning toward optimism" about the prospects of getting the United States-sponsored peace initiative in the Middle East back on the track.

The Senate was informed of the news by Senator John C. Stennis, Democrat of Mississippi, who interrupted a debate on election reform. He described Mr. Nasser, the leader in Cairo since 1952, as "superior to most anyone who might have been in power."

"I hope his death does not mean upheaval and turmoil in

Continued on Page 19, Column 1

THE ARAB WORLD IS GRIEF-STRICKEN

Moslems Fire Rifles Into Air as Sign of Mourning —Koran Read on Radio

By JOHN L. HESS

Special to The New York Times

BEIRUT, Lebanon, Sept. 28—The Arab world went into mourning tonight over the loss of its major international figure. Arab distress was heightened by the fear that instability would increase in the area and diminish the already slender prospect of peace.

Television stations went off the air and radio programs were replaced by chants and readings from the Koran. In Beirut, Moslems fired thousands of shots into the air as a sign of emotion for the loss of Gamal Abdel Nasser. Men walked in the streets in impromptu procession declaiming "Allah Akbar!"—"God is great."

Security forces raced to thwart rioting of the kind that followed President Nasser's offer of resignation after the six-day war of June, 1967.

Youths started bonfires of automobile tires and a crowd began collecting outside the United States Embassy.

[A senior Cabinet minister in Israel said that the Israelis now appeared to face an indefinite stalemate on peace negotiations. Page 18.]

Observers here said that President Nasser was the only Arab

Continued on Page 17, Column 7

John Dos Passos Is Dead at 74; Acclaimed for 'U.S.A.' Trilogy

Special to The New York Times

BALTIMORE, Sept. 28—John Dos Passos, the novelist of the post-World War I generation who wrote more than 30 books, including the trilogy "U.S.A.," died today in his apartment.

Mr. Dos Passos, who was 74 years old, had been troubled by a heart ailment in recent years and was released only Saturday from Good Samaritan Hospital. When not away on his extensive travels, he divided his time between his apartment here and a home in Westmoreland, Va.

Mr. Dos Passos is survived by his widow, the former Elizabeth Hamlin Holdridge; their daughter, Lucy, and a stepson, Christopher Holdridge.

A funeral service will be held Thursday at 10 A.M. at the William Cook-Brooks Funeral Home in the nearby town of Towson, Md.

Gil Friedberg-Pix

John Dos Passos

Fame From Early Books

By ALDEN WHITMAN

The life and writings of John Dos Passos were marked by a progression from left to right. "Every day I become more Red," he said in his youth. "My one ambition is to be able to sing 'The International.'" But in middle and old age, he turned against his former ideas, berating liberals, Socialists and Communists with zeal. The onetime writer for The New Masses became a contributor to The National Review; the friend of Ernest Hemingway became that of William F. Buckley Jr.; and the supporter of William Z. Foster turned into the backer of Barry Goldwater.

His novels, too, marched rightward. The trilogy "U.S.A.," completed in 1936 and generally recognized as one of the hinges of modern fiction, was a painstakingly detailed and angry portrait of industrial America between 1898 and 1929. It concluded with the heroine's joining the Communist party in revulsion over what she believed were the injustices of the Sacco-Vanzetti case.

His subsequent trilogy, "District of Columbia," completed in 1949, acerbically chronicled what the author clearly viewed as the failure of the New Deal

Continued on Page 47, Column 1

Malpractice Suits Reported Soaring

By LAWRENCE K. ALTMAN

Witnesses at a State Senate public hearing testified here yesterday that a steep rise in medical malpractice suits was forcing physicians to practice "defensive medicine," shirk hazardous modes of treatment that could be of benefit to patients, and pass along the costs of skyrocketing insurance premiums to patients.

"One physician of every six has been sued for malpractice," State Senator Norman F. Lent told the hearing. And more than 10,000 Americans will initiate medical malpractice suits this year, Senator Lent, who is chairman of the Senate Committee on Health, added.

Because some insurance companies find medical malpractice insurance unprofitable, wit-

Continued on Page 32, Column 1

Anti-Arab Jet Plot Laid to Seized Pair

By MORRIS KAPLAN

An Israeli Army veteran and his wife, accused of trying to board a London-bound plane here with a live hand grenade and four loaded guns hidden in their clothing, were reported yesterday to have planned to hijack an Arab airliner and take it to Israel.

Law-enforcement sources said that the couple reportedly had planned to board a United Arab Airlines plane bound for Cairo at the London airport and divert the flight to Israel "in retaliation" for a recent attempted hijacking of an El Al airliner in London.

The sources said that the veteran, Avraham Hershkovitz, had worked as a "manager" here for the Jewish Defense

Continued on Page 12, Column 3

Arab Truce Observers Arrive In Generally Peaceful Amman

By ERIC PACE

Special to The New York Times

AMMAN, Jordan, Sept. 28—One hundred foreign Arab officers arrived here today to serve on the peace-keeping observer teams that will be deployed in Amman under the agreement reached yesterday in Cairo to end hostilities between the Jordanian Government and the Palestinian commandos.

The cease-fire instituted last Friday after nine days of civil war seemed generally effective this morning. There were no fires along the capital's skyline, although a few bursts of firing resounded in the center of Amman and on Jebel Luweibida and Jebel Amman, two of the city's seven hills.

Text of Cairo agreement is printed on Page 18.

Western diplomats also reported that shelling or shooting was continuing in part of the Palestinians' Ashrafiyeh quarter, where many of the airline hostages had been held.

There was no sign that either the army or the commandos had abandoned their positions in Amman, as the Cairo agreement called for. The guerrillas are entrenched in a populous area around the Hussein Mosque at the heart of the city, where gunfire was occasionally heard during the day.

Despite a further provision of the Cairo agreement for a release of detainees, scores were still visible this morning at the army prison camp on the way to the airport. As their women peered in through the barbed-wire fence, they were seated in orderly rows, apparently being indoctrinated by their Jordanian Army captors.

The army appeared yesterday to be trying to finish its clean-up of Ashrafiyeh, once a commando stronghold. Aside from that, no wide-scale military operations were known to be under way. The general calm this morning followed radio broadcasts of the 14-point agreement signed by King Hus-

Continued on Page 18, Column 5

Fourth Group of Hostages Here After Seeing President in Rome

By ROBERT D. McFADDEN

Thirty-three travel-weary Americans, whose ordinary lives became the focus of international concern during three harrowing weeks while they were hostages in Jordan, arrived at Kennedy International Airport last night and were met by loved ones, friends and a clamoring throng of newsmen.

The passengers—26 men, 6 women and an infant—were the fourth group of Americans brought home safely from an ordeal that began with multiple hijackings Sept. 6. All but two of the 33 were released in Amman over the weekend and were flown home through Nicosia, Cyprus, and Rome.

Their faces were haggard but smiling and their clothes rumpled after a 12-hour flight from Rome, where they met briefly with President Nixon in the morning. They stepped off a chartered flight at the Trans World Airlines terminal shortly after 6 P.M. They were ushered quickly through Customs and led into a private room for a reunion with 175 relatives.

Nearly 1,000 friends greeted them in the corridors and public waiting rooms as they emerged.

Six Americans are still being held of the original group on three hijacked planes. They are someplace in Jordan.

Contrary to the confused reports at three previous returning flights, passengers who were reluctant to talk were not besieged by newsmen thrusting cameras and microphones into

Continued on Page 18, Column 2

NEWS INDEX

John Dos Passos Is Dead at 74

Continued From Page 1, Col. 3

the despotism of central government and the catastrophe of World War II. The villain was a recognizable composite of Henry A. Wallace and Harry Hopkins. Twelve years later came "Midcentury," a 496-page novel that most critics perceived as a one-sided attack on trade unions.

Mr. Dos Passos' reputation was founded on his early novels — "Three Soldiers," "Manhattan Transfer" and "U.S.A." Charles Poore, writing of "U.S.A." in The New York Times, echoed the feelings of many critics when he called its publication "a literary event of importance in this Republic." He declared that Mr. Dos Passos had produced a "major work of considerable stature," and added that although no one could get the whole of the United States into a work, "I think no modern novelist has got so much of it into a book as has John Dos Passos."

Ranked High in 1930's

Indeed, in the twenties and thirties Mr. Dos Passos was ranked as a writer with Hemingway, F. Scott Fitzgerald and William Faulkner. Jean-Paul Sartre even thought him "the best novelist of our time." But the novels published from the forties onward disappointed many critics. Commenting on "District of Columbia," for example, Maxwell Geismar said:

"One can only regret that an accomplished literary technique is accompanied by such a narrow view of life, and that this bright star in the great literary constellation of the nineteen-twenties should now sparkle so dimly."

The reviewer for Newsweek, commenting on "Midcentury," asserted:

"What [Mr. Dos Passos] means to say about the midcentury scene all comes down to a single, not very inspired sentence near the end of the book: 'So long as a man got his handout, who cared?'

"Painstakingly unsnarled, the novel amounts to a ranting, disapproving history of the rise of American labor. Dos Passos, once the great proletarian propagandist, is now out to show that 'it's mass organization which turns man into a louse.'"

Despite the decline in Mr. Dos Passos' creative powers after "U.S.A.," some critics discerned a connective thread in his fiction, and that was an intense distaste for institutional authority of any kind as being inimical to personal liberty. Clive James, the British critic, put it this way:

"The preoccupation of 'U.S.A.' is with the overwhelming power of impersonal forces. 'U.S.A.' is really a set of parables which show men trying to retain their individuality before these forces. But the awkward fact, for those radicals who consider the early Dos Passos their champion, is that this preoccupation will do as well for the right as for the left: the individual resistance to central pressure is what the American right considers itself to be all about and the reason why it is able to document itself so well constitutionally."

This was an appraisal that Mr. Dos Passos himself seemed to share. "I don't think I've changed as much as people make out," he remarked a couple of years ago. "I was never that much involved in ideologies. I put them in only because they're part of the scene."

In agreement, Robert Gornam Davis, the critic, once remarked that Mr. Dos Passos wrote "social novels without sociology." Another critic, Robie Macauley, pointed out his essential antihumanism. "He sees things with the clarity and coolness of the camera's eye, which accounts for one of his faults," the critic said. "His two-dimensional vision tends to create types."

A Similar View

Edmund Wilson expressed a similar attitude in the thirties, commenting that Mr. Dos Passos' "disapproval of capitalistic society seems to imply a distaste for all the beings who go to compose it."

As a historical, or topical, novelist, Mr. Dos Passos was a sort of Kilroy who went everywhere, did everything and met everybody. He was a passionate traveler and observer, with an eye for sensory detail and an ear for the subtleties of speech.

His travels began almost from birth. Born in Chicago Jan. 14, 1896, John Roderigo Dos Passos was the son of John R. Dos Passos and Lucy Addison Sprigg. His father, of Portuguese descent, was a prosperous corporation lawyer who was in his 50's when his son was born. His mother, of Southern stock, bore her son at the age of 48.

John's parents traveled a good deal and as a boy he lived in Mexico, Belgium, Britain, Washington, D.C., and Westmoreland County, Virginia. From reading the novels of Frederick Marryat, he acquired a love of the sea and for a time had his heart set on attending Annapolis.

But the dream faded, and the youth studied at the Choate School and at Harvard, from which he was graduated in 1916. He wrote poetry and painted watercolors and acquired the nick-name of Dos. He also developed a liking for the prose of John Reed, whose impressionistic style — a combination of the factual and the personal — he incorporated into his own pungent brand of topical reportage.

Drove Ambulance in War

After college he was a "gentleman volunteer" ambulance driver with the Norton-Harjes unit in France, and he later served in the United States Army's Medical Corps. In those days he was saying, "I've decided my only hope is in revolution — in wholesale assassination of all statesmen, capitalists, warmongers, jingoists, inventors, scientists." He was also saying, "Organization is death."

Mr. Dos Passos came out of the war with a mission, he said, "to put the acid test to existing institutions, to strip them of their veils." His first novel, "One Man's Initiation —1917," was, however, a quite pallid evocation of his ambulance-driving experiences. But his second novel, "Three Soldiers," published in 1921, touched off a storm of controversy. It was a bitter condemnation of war and the aura of glory that surrounds it. Such an attack was new at the time, and it drew attention to the young author.

Meantime, Mr. Dos Passos wandered about Spain, Mexico and the Middle East as a newspaper correspondent and freelance writer, and, of course, he got to Paris, where he consorted with the big fish and the little fish: E. E. Cummings, Robert Hillyer, Edmund Wilson, Fitzgerald, Hemingway, James Joyce, the Gerald Murphys, Léger, von Sternberg, Marlene Dietrich, Blaise Cendrars and Eisenstein.

In "The Best Times," an informal memoir, Mr. Dos Passos recalled how "Hem read me 'The Torrents of Spring,'" at the Closerie des Lilas in Paris; and how he met and mingled with celebrities among the avant-garde and expatriates.

A Gracious Manner

"I used to meet Dos Passos occasionally during the twenties in Paris and New York," Matthew Josephson, the social historian, wrote, "and I remember him as a tall young man with a round, thinly covered head and near-sighted gaze. In manner he was uncommonly gracious, with an air both shy and eager to please."

His standing in literary circles was enormously enhanced in 1925 with publication of "Manhattan Transfer," a *roman fleuve* influenced by Joyce that was a portrait of New York. The book marked the beginnings of Mr. Dos Passos' distinctive style; and it was also contemporary history with the author displaying a dazzling capacity for describing the day-to-day living of ordinary people.

In the next few years Mr. Dos Passos became involved directly in social struggles. He was twice jailed for picketing during the Sacco-Vanzetti agitation; he visited the Soviet Union; he went into the coal fields of Kentucky to help the miners during a strike, for which he was indicted for criminal syndicalism. And he wrote articles and plays of social protest, including "Airways" for the New Playwrights Theater. His friends became Michael Gold and John Howard Lawson and Theodore Dreiser; and with them, and others, he endorsed the Communist Presidential ticket in 1932, headed by William Z. Foster.

Meanwhile, in 1930, "The 42nd Parallel," the first volume of "U.S.A.," was published, a stunning literary event of the year.

In this book, as in the two succeeding ones, Mr. Dos Passos employed three techniques that gave his work a sense of commitment and immediacy. He inserted biographical sketches of significant Americans of the period — among them Woodrow Wilson, Eugene Victor Debs, Frank Lloyd Wright and Henry Ford — etching his portraits in "swift, stinging rhythms." He developed sections called the Newsreel that quoted newspaper headlines, portions of news articles and popular songs. And in the Camera Eye he gave an impressionistic record of the narrator's experiences in a Joycean manner.

The other novels in the trilogy were "1919" and "The Big Money." To many readers they constituted a sympathetic account of the ordinary working man and his struggles for economic and political justice in the early years of this century. One character, Mac, was a Wobbly, or member of the Industrial Workers of the World.

Mr. Dos Passos' break with his Communist friends began in 1934 and culminated in 1937-38, when he returned disenchanted from a look at the Spanish Civil War. He published articles criticizing the Communist International and defended the Spanish anarchists. Ultimately, he was read out of the proletarian pantheon by Mike Gold, The New Masses critic, who said, "Like the Frenchman [Louis-Ferdinand]Céline, Dos Passos hates Communists because organically he hates the human race."

Sympathies Described

For himself Mr. Dos Passos wrote in 1939:

"My sympathies lie with the private in the front line against the brass hat; with the hod-carrier against the strawboss, or the walking delegate for that matter; with the laboratory worker against the stuffed shirt in a mortarboard; with the criminal against the cop."

In the forties and fifties Mr. Dos Passos pursued his passion for travel while maintaining a weatherbeaten Cape Cod house at Provincetown, Mass. His neighbors knew him as a shy man, who spoke up occasionally at town meetings. He planted a few radishes and beans and went swimming when the words would not flow easily into his typewriter. At other times he tried his hand at water-colors and chalk drawings, which were good enough to be exhibited in New York galleries.

The author worked closely with his first wife, Katherine Smith, also a writer. She was killed in an automobile accident in 1947, in which her husband lost his left eye.

Two years later the author remarried. He took his wife, Elizabeth Hamlin Holdridge, to live on a fragment of his father's old farm in Virginia.

But the Virginia house, as well as his apartment in Baltimore, was only a temporary resting place between travels, about which he wrote for magazines. He also produced some books that combined history, another of his interests, with his journeyings, including "The Portugal Story." As a historical writer, he did books on Thomas Jefferson and World War I.

In 1957 Mr. Dos Passos received the Gold Medal for Fiction of the National Institute of Arts and Letters, of which he was a member. He was also a member of the American Academy of Arts and Letters. In 1967 he received the Feltrinelli prize, worth $32,000, from the Italian Academia Nazionale dei Lincei.

A spokesman for Doubleday & Co. said yesterday that Mr. Dos Passos had completed "Easter Island: The Island of Enigmas," based on a trip he made there last year, and it will be published next March. At his death he was "going along very well" on a novel, "The 13th Chronicle," according to a spokesman for its intended publisher, the Houghton Mifflin Company.

By 1960 Mr. Dos Passos had aligned himself with the conservative forces in the United States. He appeared, for example, at a Madison Square Garden rally in 1962, sponsored by Young Americans for Freedom, that paid tribute to Moise Tshombe of Katanga, former President Herbert Hoover and Charles Edison, a former New Jersey Governor.

In recent years Mr. Dos Passos became something of a country squire — he liked to wear a sports jacket and dark shirt and tie. He was courtly to visitors, and his voice, which was reedy, was tinged with Southern softness. He chain-smoked cigars as he wrote, with one finger on a portable typewriter.

Early in 1960, the writer was pessimistic about his country. "I think the American people's distaste for Communism is nothing but a surface reaction," he told an interviewer. "After all, what the Russians are spreading is nothing but a less plausible version of what we already have here. Add a secret police to the combined A.F.L.-C.I.O. and you couldn't tell the difference."

As the decade drew to a close, he was sunnier. "I'm rather optimistic about the United States," he confessed in 1968. "We are going through our toughest period since the Civil War. I have occasion to travel a lot through the nation and I find tremendous energy and a great deal of life in our people. I don't need to go to Australia yet."

And asked about retiring, Mr. Dos Passos fixed the time as "when the undertaker comes through the door."

Nasser Dies at 52 After a Heart Attack

Continued From Page 1, Col. 8

a peaceful solution of the Arab-Israeli conflict is seriously clouded.

The Egyptian leader's death came only one day after a triumph of patient negotiation in which he overcame deep hostilities and achieved an agreement to end fighting between the Jordanian Army and Palestinian Guerrillas.

In recent years, President Nasser had been suffering from diabetes. He underwent treatment at a spa in the Soviet Union two years ago but appeared in good health in recent months.

Mr. Sadat said that Mr. Nasser was stricken shortly after having returned home from the closing ceremonies of the Arab leadership conference that signed the agreement on the crisis in Jordan.

Treated by 5 Doctors

The President was reported to have felt the first symptoms of the heart attack at the Cairo airport during farewell ceremonies for the Emir of Kuwait, Sabah al-Sabah, who took part in the Arab meeting on Jordan. Mr. Nasser was taken to his residence in Manshiet el Bakri, a northeastern suburb of Cairo, and was under treatment by five doctors when he died.

The body was later taken to Kubbeh Palace, the Government's executive office. People from throughout Cairo converged on the palace, in some cases commandeering buses. Sobbing, screams and shouts "Nasser! you are in our hearts!" echoed through the streets.

In his broadcast, Vice President Sadat said: "The United Arab Republic, the Arab nation and all mankind have lost one of the most precious men, most courageous and most sincere men, President Gamal Abdel Nasser, who passed away at 6:15 this evening while he was standing on the field of struggle, striving for the unity of the Arab nation and for the day of victory."

Led Group of Officers

Mr. Sadat paid tribute to Mr. Nasser as a leader "whose memory will remain immortal in the hearts of the Arab nation and all mankind."

The broadcast, which lasted 50 minutes, added:

"Gamal Abdel Nasser was more than words. He is more immortal than any words. Nothing can describe him except his record in the service of his people, nation and humanity: a struggler for freedom, for humanity, a struggler for truth and justice, a fighter for honor to the last moment of life.

"No words are sufficient to express condolences for Gamal Abdel Nasser. The only thing that can be commensurate with his righteousness and esteem is that the entire Arab nation should stand patient, steadfast, —a steadfast, solid, heroic, and able stand so that it can realize the victory for which the great son of Egypt and the hero of this nation, its man and leader, had lived and was martyred."

For 18 Years Nasser Had Almost Hypnotic Power in His Leadership of Egyptians

"Nas-ser! Nas-ser!," Cairo crowds cried out in anguish on the June night in 1967 when Gamal Abdel Nasser announced that, after 15 years in power, he had decided to resign as President of the United Arab Republic.

No sooner had he spoken, over the Cairo radio, than workingmen wept, women wailed and gangs of youths streamed through the streets shouting pleas for him to stay in office.

Coming on the heels of Egypt's catastrophic defeat by Israel, the Cairenes' cries of support for Mr. Nasser were proof of the almost hypnotic power of leadership that he had built up in the proud aftermath of the ouster of King Farouk.

But the events of that turbulent night also underscored Mr. Nasser's defects as a leader. Errors in his judgment — notably overconfidence in his pampered armed forces — had helped pave the way for Israel's swift victory, which in turn prompted the announcement of his resignation.

And as the dark hours passed, Mr. Nasser's political organizers skillfully set about arranging even larger mass demonstrations of support. These were crowned a few hours later with the announcement that he would stay in office after all.

Compared to Saladin

Proud, imprudent, wily, Mr. Nasser's personal style was in many ways that of the typical Arab — but on a scale larger than life. It made him the most respected leader within the Arab world. He was compared sometimes to Saladin, the 12th-century Sultan of Egypt who was famous for his victories over the Crusaders. Mr. Nasser's revolutionary Government put Saladin's device, the eagle, in its coat of arms.

Although military glory escaped him, Mr. Nasser nourished the average Egyptian's pride by breaking the power of the land-owning aristocracy, taking over the Suez Canal, building the Aswan High Dam and providing the opportunity for education and social advancement to almost every Egyptian child.

He became thereby a hero to radicals in many parts of the Arab world. Posters picturing his face with its blazing eyes and smile, its strongly molded nose and jaw, hung even in hovels in remote corners of the Arabian Peninsula.

Over the years Mr. Nasser's imprudence cost him some, though not all, of that admiration and brought him criticism from abroad. His prestige was battered when he sent a costly expeditionary force to shore up the revolutionary regime in Yemen, but failed to break the will of royalist insurgents seeking to bring it down. The Egyptians' reported use of poison gas in the Yemen — consistently denied in Cairo — was widely denounced as cynical and inhumane.

Similarly, Mr. Nasser's headlong efforts to industrialize Egypt, even to start an aircraft industry in a society in which men were still sometimes harnessed to the plow, were in large part unsuccessful for lack of skilled workers, realistic planning and foreign exchange.

Population Problem

And in his rush to improve his people's lot, he gave scant attention to Egypt's central economic problem, the population's precipitate increase. A growth rate of almost 3 per cent a year glutted schools, exacerbated unemployment and made the country dependent on wheat imports from foreign countries to feed the teeming cities.

Delmas-Pix

Gamal Abdel Nasser

The President's fledgling birth-control program floundered, undermanned and underfinanced, while he tried to bolster the country in other ways after the Arab-Israeli war of 1967.

Mr. Nasser helped to bring about Israel's June offensive by a series of rash moves. He abruptly deployed more than 80,000 Egyptian troops on the Sinai Peninsula opposite the Israeli border. He demanded the dissolution of the United Nations peace-keeping force along that border and goaded the Israelis further by declaring a blockade of the Strait of Tiran, the gateway to the Israeli port of Elath.

The disastrously poor performance of the Egyptian armed forces after Israel attacked demonstrated how imprudent Mr. Nasser had been to entrust their direction to Field Marshal Abdel Hakim Amer, an old and trusted friend who was more distinguished by his supposed loyalty than by military skill.

Dismissed after the defeat, Marshal Amer staged an abortive plot against the Nasser Government, which was a police and military dictatorship resting on a balance between subordinates competing for influence.

Shortly after the plot was discovered and broken up, the marshal was officially reported to have committed suicide.

The same shrewd talent for manipulation that enabled Mr. Nasser to help bring down King Farouk in 1952 through a military conspiracy helped him to retain his power after the June war and the Amer plot.

By mass dismissals and transfers he broke up potential centers of dissidence within the armed forces, which were bitter and bewildered in defeat. He sought to soothe fractious students with promises of changes in the Egyptian political system that would make it appear more liberal without undercutting his own control. And he tried to rally the population as a whole with talk of further battles with Israel, and of reconquering the Israeli-occupied Sinai Peninsula "inch by inch" if necessary.

At the same time, however, Mr. Nasser became humiliatingly dependent on the Soviet Union and the East bloc in general for arms to rebuild his shattered military forces, for economic aid and for wheat. This dependence gave a hollow ring to Cairo's customary declarations of independence from the East as well as the West bloc.

Nonalignment had long been a source of pride to Mr. Nasser and a cornerstone of his prestige in the "third world," and indeed he was zealous in his final years in rejecting any intimacy with the United States.

But while nationalistic Cairo intellectuals grumbled about the presence in the United Arab Republic of more than a thousand Soviet military advisers, the Soviet Ambassador in Cairo, Serge, Vinogradov, became a continual visitor at the sprawling Kubbeh Palace, the Egyptian equivalent of the White House.

A Subdued Figure

There Mr. Nasser, who had long since dropped his military title of colonel, cut a subdued figure in his somber business suit, more grizzled than he was in his early days of revolutionary glory.

He made few public appearances except for occasional visits to Cairo mosques. Many of his speeches were to small, restricted audiences or simply before the microphone of Cairo radio and television.

In the speeches, after the war as before, Mr Nasser was sometimes blunt and sometimes vague. He generally used simple Arabic in his efforts to sustain the loyalty and enthusiasm of his populace and to articulate its hopes. A pained, almost defensive note crept into some of his discourses, however, as evidence of student and worker dissidence mounted after the June war. He castigated criticism of his Government as the work of "counterrevolutionaries."

Unending hostility to Israel was a perennial theme of his speeches, although many foreign and not a few Arab observers felt that Egypt would have been better served if he had concentrated his efforts on domestic affairs.

After the June war his speeches against Israel focused on her occupation of the Sinai Peninsula. In March, 1968, he brought cheers from an audience of workers by affirming that "our mission must be to liberate this land; this is what we promise Allah and ourselves."

But he did not specify when he thought the U.A.R. would be ready to enter into such a war with any assurance of victory, and Western military analysts felt that the Egyptian armed forces remained inferior to those of Israel, despite their stepped-up training and large quantities of Soviet arms.

Another perennial Nasser theme was anti-Americanism. It struck a responsive chord among Arabs resentful of American sympathy for Israel and of Western influence in the Middle East and underdeveloped countries in general.

In another speech in the spring of 1968, Mr. Nasser said the United States "attempts to humiliate us and wants to put us in a position of defeat so that we surrender to Israel's wishes."

In recent speeches dealing with domestic issues, Mr. Nasser liked to stress that he was not a "professional politician." He said he prayed to Allah that the nation be saved from "despotism." After the June war, he played on antimilitary feeling among the civilian populace by criticizing unspecified "military elements" who, he said, "felt they had inherited power in this country." He said the United Arab Republic, should have a permanent constitution — which it did not have — providing "full guarantees to insure individual liberty and security under all circumstances."

Autocratic Rule

This was an indirect response to a growing dissatisfaction among Cairo's middle classes with Mr. Nasser's autocratic methods of rule. As President, he was empowered to name the Cabinet. The National Assembly, composed exclusively of members of the Socialist Union, his political organization, was subservient to his wish.

Such criticism, though muted, became widespread in the winter after the June defeat. In earlier years the public had largely been dazzled by Mr. Nasser's success in uprooting the old monarchic system and in making himself and Egypt a power in the world.

After he first took power, the Egyptian people came to revere Mr. Nasser as their champion against colonialism and poverty.

Within a few years he was acknowledged leader of a pan-Arabism that was expanding to menacing proportions in the Middle East and North Africa. Early in 1958 he merged the Republic of Syria with Egypt to form the United Arab Republic.

In Iraq, in July of that year, a pro-Nasser coup replaced the monarchy with a republic. Fear that Colonel Nasser might try to take over the Kingdom of Jordan, and perhaps the oil-rich shiekdoms of the Arabian Peninsula as well, led the United States to land 15,000 troops in revolution-torn Lebanon while the British sent about 1,000 paratroops to Amman, capital of Jordan.

Egypt in Strategic Position

Much of President Nasser's power lay in the fact that Egypt was at the strategic crossroads of the world. When he announced the nationalization of the Suez Canal in July, 1956, he posed a problem of world-shaking importance. A large part of the economy of Western Europe depended upon the Middle East oil that reached the West mainly by pipeline and through the canal.

Nobody knew exactly how powerful President Nasser was in the concert of world powers, in the Arab world, in the Mediterranean or indeed in the hectic political affairs of his own country. The fact was that during and after the Suez Canal crisis he became one of the world's most dour and foreboding figures.

Whether he was pro-Communist or whether he found it to his country's advantage to play the Western powers and the Soviet Union off against each other was a question with many answers.

Mr. Nasser edged his way to power in a country totally without a log-cabin-to-success tradition. Like Mustafa Kemal Ataturk of Turkey, who was probably the only Moslem dictator of modern times to create of stir, he decided as a boy to become a professional army officer.

To his people he seemed honest. soldierly and unpretentious. His enemies admitted that therein lay much of his political allure.

When President Nasser reached the front rank of newspaper space fillers in 1956, the world saw a tall, hefty Egyptian of 38 who carried his compact 200 pounds with ease. He had brown eyes and closely cropped hair just beginning to be tinged with gray, and his big, slightly hooked nose and gleaming array of teeth were the delight of cartoonists around the world.

He spoke quietly and seldom displayed anything but smiling self-assurance. As shrewd and experienced a diplomat as Jefferson Caffrey, former United States Ambassador to Egypt, called him one of the greatest conspirators of his day.

His followers, however, believed that he was a devoted family man with all the traditional Egyptian family virtues, and he was often photographed with his wife, an upper-middle-class woman of property, and their two sons and two daughters.

Gamal Abdel Nasser was born on Jan. 15, 1918, in Alexandria, but grew up in the small town of Beni Mor in Upper Egypt. His father was a minor postal official and his mother, who was of pure Arabian blood, was a daughter of an Alexandria building contractor.

As a boy, he displayed an indiscriminate passion for American motion pictures and a somewhat excessive unruliness.

Dislike for British Army

The youth developed an early and powerful dislike for the British Army, whose officers, with their gleaming Sam Browne belts and chilly man-

(continued)

ners, seemed such a permanent and exasperating feature of Cairo life.

At 20 he was graduated from the Royal Military Academy and within a short time was involved with a grass-roots revolutionary movement in the Egyptian Army.

In 1948 he was a lieutenant colonel of infantry at the front during the Arab-Israeli war and was wounded. He and a group of his brother officers were infuriated and humiliated when Egypt and her allies were defeated by smaller but better equipped and led Israeli forces. They formed the Committee of Free Officers to overthrow the Government.

A respected senior officer was needed for this enterprise and Colonel Nasser and his fellow conspirators selected Maj. Gen. Mohammed Naguib, a dignified but not very inspiring leader who was the nearest thing that Egypt had to a war hero. It was Colonel Nasser who masterminded the revolt.

At dawn on July 23, 1952, Egyptian troops of the Revolutionary Command Council surrounded the palace of King Farouk, handed him an ultimatum to renounce the throne, gave him time to put on a naval officer's uniform, put him on his yacht, saved his face by firing a 21-gun salute for him and packed him off to Italy.

Regency Council Formed

A Regency Council was formed, Ali Maher Pasha became Premier and General Naguib was endowed with the titles of President and commander of the armed forces. After Ali Maher resigned, he became Premier. But by Nov. 14, 1954, Colonel Nasser had contrived to kick General Naguib upstairs into virtual retirement and began his administration in the name of the Regency Council.

He briskly nipped several small army mutinies and hanged a number of pro-British officials, together with several leaders of the Moslem Brotherhood, a fanatical Islamic fraternity that he accused of "installing a state within a state."

Colonel Nasser instituted sweeping domestic reforms. On Sept. 8, 1952, at his instigation, a decree of agrarian reform was promulgated limiting maximum land holdings to about 208 acres and providing for distribution of surplus properties to needy peasants. Strong laws were introduced protecting labor, and studies were instituted to increase the cultivable area of Egyptian land. Right of foreigners to control enterprises was protected in order to attract capital.

High Dam at Aswan

President Nasser's boldest domestic development enterprise was the scheme for the High Dam south of Aswan. Egypt could not finance this project, and he placed himself in a position of playing the Soviet Union and the United States off against each other to get the necessary funds.

Great as was the desire of both of these powers to win a position of influence in Egyptian affairs, by mid-1956 neither had made any definite commitment for financing the dam, which the Egyptian leader had made one of the major projects of his domestic policy.

In foreign affairs, President Nasser's foreign policy could boast two important achievements in the first two years of his Government. The problem of the Anglo-Egyptian condominium of the Sudan was resolved, at least, temporarily, and — biggest of all his coups — Britain agreed to turn the Suez Canal over to Egypt.

On July 27,1954, a pact was signed calling for the evacuation of British troops from the canal within 20 months. It also provided for continuous maintenance of the canal by British civilian technicians under the sovereign control of Egypt. It seemed that a reasonable settlement had been reached in this irritating affair.

In the fall of 1954, an attempt was made on the President's life during a speech given in Alexandria. Eight pistol shots were fired at Mr. Nasser, but none hit their target.

The nagging, festering trouble between Egypt and Israel periodically posed a threat of war in the Middle East. The Egyptian hatred for Israel was fanned by Mr. Nasser and was soon extended to include the United States, which was considered one of the sponsors of Israel.

Having failed to purchase arms from Britain and the United States in the summer of 1955, the Egyptian leader turned toward the Soviet bloc. In a barter deal with Communist Czechoslovakia, he arranged the exchange of Egyptian cotton for an undisclosed quantity of heavy military equipment and munitions. The United States and her Western allies became alarmed at an obvious drift in the direction of war.

By July, 1956, Egypt had begun to press the United States for a definite reply on whether American financial assistance for the Aswan High Dam could be given. In an abrupt move, Secretary of State John Foster Dulles announced that the United States would not participate in the project.

Nationalized Suez

The announcement caused consternation and resentment in Cairo, where the United States long had given the impression that Washington financing for the dam was likely. The United States decision was a heavy blow for President Nasser, and his chagrin was increased by the revelation, soon after the Washington announcement, that the Soviet Union was not planning to give financial help for the dam.

On July 26, he suddenly proclaimed to the world that he was nationalizing the international company that had operated the Suez Canal for nearly a century.

Egypt herself, he said, would operate the canal, keeping it open to all nations, and revenues would be used to build the Aswan High Dam.

Egypt's move provoked a bitter and hostile reaction in many Western nations, particularly in Britain and France. France saw Mr. Nasser's prestige enhanced and his menace to France's colonial control of Algeria increased. Britain, principal beneficiary of Suez Canal commerce, was shaken by the prospect of his being able, at any time, to shut off free transit through the canal.

Britain and France took the lead in demanding a return to international control and threatened to attack Egypt if Cairo refused to concede such an arrangement.

President Nasser resisted British and French pressures. The United States attempted to play a mediatory role at international conferences of canal users called to work out new schemes for operating the waterway.

By November, no agreement satisfactory to Britain and France had been reached on the canal issue with Egypt. Forces of the two powers attacked Egypt by land and air, beginning their assault shortly after Israel had begun an invasion of the Sinai Peninsula and Egypt had rejected a British-French ultimatum that Egyptian forces be withdrawn from the Suez Canal zone.

Port Said Captured

British and French forces captured Port Said but halted operations aimed at occupying the canal when faced with decisive opposition against them in the United Nations. Both Russia and the United States took stands against the aggression of the three attackers.

Having occupied the entire Sinai Peninsula, Israel halted her attacks simultaneously with the cease-fire by the British and French.

The destruction of a large part of his ground and air forces by the attacking powers hurt Mr. Nasser's prestige somewhat both in Egypt and in other Arab lands. Anti-Communist Middle East and Western powers were alarmed at the amount of Soviet bloc military material and influence the attacks had revealed in Egypt.

However, the fact that the attacks were halted short of any decisive result left him still strongly in power. He insisted on a full withdrawal of foreign forces before permitting a reopening of the canal, which the Egyptians had blocked by sinking many ships along it.

When President Nasser brought about the union of Egypt and Syria in 1958 to form the United Arab Republic he added more than 72,000 square miles and a population of more than 3,000,000 people to Egypt. Syria had been subjected to strong Communist influences before the merger.

Later that year, a pro-Nasser coup overthrew the pro-Western Government of Iraq. The action resulted in the death of King Faisal II. President Eisenhower accused pro-Egyptian plotters of murder and of driving the Iraqi Government from office.

President Nasser disclaimed any responsibility for rioting in Lebanon. During the succeeding weeks he made a secret trip to the Soviet Union, his second visit in two months.

As time went on, relations improved with Lebanon and Jordan. President Nasser exchanged friendly messages with the Government of Lebanon. A short time later, he and King Hussein were addressing each other as "dear brother" and had made a bid for closer cooperation.

Construction of Dam Begun

In 1960, construction on the Aswan High Dam got under way. It was completed in July, 1970. At a dedication ceremony in 1960, President Nasser thanked the Soviet Union for its financial aid. He said he bore the Russians no rancor, despite the fact that two years earlier he sharply attacked the Communists for their opposition to Arab unity.

In the fall of 1960, President Nasser visited the United States for a meeting of the United Nations General Assembly. He was one of the most active participants at the session in a bid by the neutralists to ease world tensions.

In September, 1961, Syria seceded from the United Arab Republic following an army revolt. For the first time, the revolution of President Nasser began to suffer setbacks and the crisis began to show in the face of its leader.

President Nasser, observers said, began to look grimmer. His smile disappeared and his face was drawn. Associates said his temper was shorter.

As a result of the loss of Syria, President Nasser increased his emphasis on domestic reforms. Land holdings were reduced and most of the nation's industry was placed under Government control. He began to add new and eager men to his staff.

After the 1967 war, Mr. Nasser was preoccupied with revenge against the Israelis. Within weeks of his military debacle, he had negotiated with the Russians to replace nearly all of the arms Egypt lost in the war.

Last July, at the conclusion of a 19-day visit to Moscow, he began an intensive drive to guide his Arab allies toward a political settlement in the Middle East through implementation of a November, 1967, Security Council resolution.

It was Mr Nasser who took the lead in accepting a United States proposal for a settlement of the Middle East conflict. Jordan and Lebanon quickly went along, but Iraq and Syria were angry holdouts. Finally, however, with Israel's acceptance of the plan, a cease-fire and the beginning of negotiations at the Uited Nations began on Aug. 7.

The peace offensive was almost immediately endangered by the hijacking of airliners by Palestinian guerrillas who destroyed one of them in Egypt and three in Jordan. The hijacking crisis was followed by a war between Jordan and the guerrillas. A cease-fire was arranged in Cairo last Sunday, with Mr. Nasser one of the signers of the accord that proclaimed the support of the Arab world for the guerrillas in their fight against the "aggressive Israeli enemy."

Mr. Nasser no doubt played a major part in arranging an end to the fighting that had so divided the Arab world. It was actions such as this that made him a revered figure throughout that world and idolized in his own country.

"Everything in this country is in doubt, exept the people's devotion to Nasser," it was said of the charismatic Mr. Nasser in Cairo not long ago. "Egypt is like a hard-pressed family that has closed ranks behind its father."

Symbol of the Dream

By HEDRICK SMITH

Special to The New York Times

WASHINGTON, Sept. 28—To millions of Arabs from Morocco to the Persian Gulf, Gamal Abdel Nasser was the symbol of the lost dream of Arab greatness, a proud challenger to the Goliaths of the West.

His durability and political success in the face of many setbacks not only frustrated policymakers in Washington, London and Tel Aviv, but also baffled them: he seemed to defy the political laws of gravity. The answer to this riddle lay in his connection to the nationalist yearnings of the Arab masses after World War II.

News Analysis

His military ventures against Israel and Arab rivals consistently ended in failure, and yet millions of Egyptians and other Arabs clung to him as a promise of ultimate victory. Although he never won back an inch of lost Palestine, the refugees long cherished him as their one real hope for regaining their homeland He was a commanding figure, the most natural leader of the dozen military plotters who overthrew the Egyptian monarchy in 1952.

Known for His Rhetoric

He was known in the West for his biting, often belligerent rhetoric, and yet he was privately regarded by many specialists as the one Arab leader politically strong enough to risk a political settlement with Israel. No wonder then that his death was taken as a setback to chances for Arab-Israeli negotiations.

In the middle nineteen-fifties Mr. Nasser made his reputation as the savior of Egyptian independence when he ousted British troops and nationalized the Suez Canal. Yet, at his death, he left not only a great economic and political debt to the Soviet Union, but also a large Soviet military presence that will weigh heavily in the inevitable struggle for power to succeed him.

To the Soviet Union, he provided the first real opening into the Arab world, the chance to leapfrog the Western defense system in Turkey.

The real test of his long-term value for the Soviet Union comes now that he is gone, and Moscow must learn whether it can maintain the foothold he allowed.

The United States, like Israel, could never come to terms with Mr. Nasser's brand of Arab nationalism. Although few Americans seem aware of it, in his early years in power he turned first to the United States—not to the Soviet Union—for military assistance and was rebuffed. But the real break came in July, 1956, when Secretary of State John Foster Dulles withdrew the American offer to help finance Mr. Nasser's dream—the Aswan High Dam. That move, and the continuing tension over American support for Israel, prevented any genuine accord.

In the Arab world, President Nasser proclaimed the goal of Arab unity but he spent more time battling rival Arab leaders—the conservative Kings of Saudi Arabia or the Baathist militants of Syria—than he did fighting the Israelis.

His most ambitious attempt at unity with Syria in 1958 collapsed in disaster three years later. His military campaign in 1962 to bring Yemen under Cairo's wing ended in bloody defeat. Yet, before his death, he spawned a new alliance with left-wing regimes in the Sudan and Libya, a sign that he remained a potent symbol of Arab unity.

The Real Challenge

But the real challenge to his hegemony in the Arab world arose after the Arab-Israel war in 1967. Palestine, the sacred Arab cause, was no longer his monopoly. Palestinian commando groups gained prominence with a militancy that was more than rhetoric and by promising a more violent, perhaps more glamorous way of regaining the homeland.

This July, when the commando groups criticized his acceptance of the United States proposal for peace talks with Israel, Mr. Nasser ended their programs on the Cairo radio and ousted some of them from Egypt. But when King Hussein of Jordan launched a bloody crackdown against the Palestinians two weeks ago, Mr. Nasser felt that it was too harsh a repression, and he turned against the king. He may have been hedging his bets, uncertain who would win the Jordanian civil war.

For Egyptians as well as for foreigners, Gamal Abdel Nasser's career was full of paradoxes. He said he was the champion of socialist revolution, yet in his last few years his regime had become a tired, middle-aged, top-heavy bureaucratic state. Still, it had its achievements.

Egyptian finances were perennially in trouble during his 18 years of rule, and yet he succeeded in bringing schools, health clinics, fresh drinking water—the basic elements of modern life—to millions of desperately poor peasants whose lives had been unchanged for hundreds of years.

Yet the profound support he won from his people rested on something much more basic to Arab psychology than economic achievements. And never was it more dramatically demonstrated than on June 9, 1967, in the wake of Israel's shattering defeat of the Arabs, when masses of Arabs demonstrated against his planned resignation.

Such a crushing setback would have ended a leader's career in almost any other country. But the Egyptian people demonstrated, and so did thousands of Arabs in other countries, because in their bleak moment of defeat they felt they could not give up Mr. Nasser. With his charismatic nationalism, he had come to personify their search for dignity and a place on the world stage.

"All the News That's Fit to Print."

The New York Times.

LATE CITY EDITION
WEATHER—Rain and sleet today; tomorrow cloudy, warmer.
Temperatures Yesterday—Max., 45; min., 37.

VOL. LXXXIV....No. 28,199. Entered as Second-Class Matter, Postoffice, New York, N. Y. NEW YORK, TUESDAY, APRIL 9, 1935. P TWO CENTS In New York City. | THREE CENTS Within 200 Miles | FOUR CENTS Elsewhere Except in 7th and 8th Postal Zones.

Adolph S. Ochs Dead at 77; Publisher of Times Since 1896

Adolph S. Ochs
1858-1935

Special to THE NEW YORK TIMES.

CHATTANOOGA, Tenn., April 8.—Adolph S. Ochs, publisher of THE NEW YORK TIMES, died here at 4:10 o'clock this afternoon amid the scenes of his first venture in publishing and of his first professional triumphs. He was 77 years old.

Mr. Ochs suffered a cerebral hemorrhage at 1:45 P. M., while at lunch in a Chattanooga restaurant. So quietly as to be unobserved by his companions he passed into unconsciousness from which he did not rally. He was taken to the Newell Sanitarium here, where he died.

The end of the publisher's long and active career, in which for fifty-seven years he was able to put to the test a philosophy of journalism evolved from his first days as a "printer's devil," came after he had opportunity once more to visit his associates of the staff of The Chattanooga Times, whose success under his direction made that of THE NEW YORK TIMES possible. Because of illness he had not been able to visit Chattanooga during the past three years.

Had Spent Morning With Old Friends.

Apparently in renewed health and in splendid spirits, Mr. Ochs visited the office of The Chattanooga Times during the morning. He greeted the personnel in each department, lingering to chat happily with some who had been with the newspaper thirty-nine years ago when he left Chattanooga to risk his all on the extension of his editorial and business principles to New York.

Active to the last, after he had visited with his friends and associates on the paper, he went to the office of his nephew, Adolph Shelby Ochs, general manager of The Chattanooga Times. They became immersed in a discussion of details of the paper's affairs and Mr. Ochs was so interested that he allowed his luncheon hour to slip past. It was about 1 o'clock before he ended the discussion to start for lunch.

With his brother, Colonel Milton B. Ochs, and Miss Cunningham, a nurse, Mr. Ochs set out for a restaurant, stopping on the way to enter the office of R. E. Walker, editor of The Chattanooga Times, whom he asked to be a member of the little luncheon party. Mr. Walker joined them.

Chatting pleasantly, the group took their seats in the restaurant and there was no indication of illness on the part of the host until the menu cards were brought. Colonel Ochs asked his brother what he intended to eat. He received no reply. Colonel Ochs raised his voice.

Then the others became aware that, without having uttered a sound, the publisher had suffered a stroke that had rendered him unconscious. Miss Cunningham administered a hypodermic injection. Colonel Ochs and Mr. Walker hurriedly summoned physicians and an ambulance, which carried Mr. Ochs to the sanitarium.

Oxygen Fails to Revive Him.

Dr. Edward T. Newell, Dr. Charles Roberts Thomas, a specialist, and several other physicians were called in to attend him. Oxygen treatment was applied but every effort at resuscitation failed and he died without having regained consciousness. The physicians said that the stroke had been one from which he could never have recovered his physical strength, even if medical treatment had succeeded in prolonging life.

At Mr. Ochs's bedside when he died were Colonel Ochs and Mrs. Milton B. Ochs; his sister, Mrs. Harry C. Adler, and Mr. Adler; his granddaughter, Miss Marian Sulzberger of New York, who made the trip from New York with him; his nephew, Adolph Shelby Ochs, and Mrs. Ochs; Rabbi Abraham Feinstein of Julius and Bertha Ochs Memorial Temple, and his nurse, Miss Cunningham.

Arriving in Chattanooga last night, Mr. Ochs spent the night at

Continued on Page Two.

The obituary of Mr. Ochs will be found on Pages 20 and 21.

DANZIG VOTE HELD BLOW TO NAZISM; NEW POLL SOUGHT

Hitlerites Glum as Failure Is Regarded as Sure to Affect Three-Power Talks.

FOES CHARGE ILLEGALITIES

Three Groups Plan to Demand League Action May 18—Two Hurt in New Clash.

M'DONALD TO GO TO STRESA

France Uncertain of Policy—Baldwin Warns Nations Are on Road to War.

The European Arms Situation.

DANZIG—The results of the Volkstag election were regarded as a severe blow to Nazism, certain to have a bearing on the Stresa conference. Opposition parties in Danzig planned to demand of the League of Nations a new vote, charging the Nazis with illegalities.

LONDON—Prime Minister MacDonald will go to the Stresa three-power arms conference with Sir John Simon, the Foreign Secretary. He will replace Anthony Eden, the Lord Privy Seal, who is ill. Stanley Baldwin, in a speech, said the nations were walking on "the dangerous roads leading to war."

PARIS—France was uncertain on her policy at the Stresa conference, with unanimity lacking in government circles. The French view was that Premier Flandin should attend the conference in view of Prime Minister MacDonald's presence, which, it was held, would add to complications facing talks.

MOSCOW—Pessimism prevailed as a result of a report that the Stresa conferees would drop the "Eastern Locarno" in favor of a general European security pact.

Danzig Nazis Dismayed.

By OTTO D. TOLISCHUS.

Wireless to THE NEW YORK TIMES.

DANZIG, April 8.—The defeat of the National Socialist effort to obtain a two-thirds majority in yesterday's Volkstag election as a preliminary to elimination of all other parties and establishment of a totalitarian State in Danzig has thrown the National Socialists into confusion, brought joy to their opponents and created a profound impression in international circles in this Free City.

Some were already inclined to liken "the battle of Danzig" not to Waterloo, but to the Battle of Moscow, which marked the turn of the Napoleonic tide. It was believed inevitable that this failure would have important repercussions on both Germany and Europe.

Blow to Totalitarianism.

For, as seen from here, the Danzig vote has been a body blow to the totalitarian pretensions of the National Socialist party, which, by virtue of 80 and 90 per cent majorities in recent elections in Germany and the Saar, had claimed the right to be sole ruler of the State. Danzig is so typically German that, in the view of neutral observers here, an election in Germany, carried out even under the same high pressure conditions as in Danzig and with the same handicaps to the opposition, would produce a similar result, provided the opposition was permitted to exist at all. The National Socialist party would still have a majority, but a 60 per cent majority such as was obtained in Danzig reduces it from the one party to just a party, which means the death of party autocracy.

Nobody has any illusions that the National Socialists will permit such an election to take place in Germany while they hold the power to prevent it. But international quarters here take into consideration that the statesmen of other powers must reckon not only with existing governments but also with the popular backing that these governments command. In this respect the Danzig election has been particularly enlightening and is accepted to have an important bearing on any decisions reached at Stresa.

Count Is Completed.

Meanwhile, the count of the ballots, completed today, confirmed that if the Danzig Constitution as guaranteed by the League of Nations is observed Danzig is destined to remain a kind of national park reserve of German democracy. The final count, though still declared to be preliminary, showed the following results, compared with the election of May, 1933:

	1935.	1933.	New Seats.
National Socialists	139,043	109,029	44
Socialists	38,015	37,882	12
Catholic Centrists	31,525	31,336	9
German Nationalists	9,691	13,596	3
Communists	7,990	14,566	2
Poles	8,310	6,743	2

The National Socialists gained

Continued on Page Thirteen.

400-YEAR-OLD RECORDS ARE LOST IN PARIS FIRE

By The Associated Press.

PARIS, April 8.—Some of the 400-year-old records of the central Paris court house were destroyed by a fire which raged more than an hour in ancient St. Louis Tower today before firemen brought it under control.

Police said the blaze started from a spark blown from a chimney near by to the wooden shingles on the conical roof of the stone tower.

The fire-fighters had to reach the blaze by climbing extension ladders to a point 150 feet above the ground. They were endangered by a heavy weather vane, which swayed threateningly as most of the supports underneath burned away.

LINK ALUMINUM CO. TO FOREIGN CARTEL

Researchers Report to NIRA That Mellon Company Is Connected by Canadian Unit.

AMERICAN PRICES DICTATED

Record Shows Concern Offered Fabricated Material for Less Than Raw Material Cost.

Special to THE NEW YORK TIMES.

WASHINGTON, April 8.—Connection between the Aluminum Company of America and the International Aluminum Cartel was shown today in a report on the aluminum industry, submitted to the National Industrial Relations Board by Lon Henderson, director of the NRA Research and Planning Division. The report also said that the Aluminum Company also dominated all aluminum prices.

The report pointed out that prior to 1928 the aluminum-making facilities of Canada were owned by the Aluminum Company of America, a Mellon-controlled corporation, but in the latter year a separate corporation, Aluminium, Ltd., was set up, while the control remained in the same hands as previously.

A chart in the appendix showed that the family and associates of Andrew W. Mellon, former Secretary of the Treasury, controlled 1,023,100 shares of the stock of the American concern, or 69.2 per cent of the total issued, and 433,078 shares, or 73.3 per cent, of the stock of Aluminium, Ltd.

"Accordingly, it is not surprising that, although Canada is the world's largest aluminum exporter, this country has never competed in the United States market with domestic aluminum," the report adds. "Practically all of the Canadian aluminum that has come to the United States has been handled by the Aluminum Company of America.

Production Equally Divided.

"Approximately equal amounts of aluminum are produced on the North American continent and in Europe. The European aluminum producing companies can be divided into two groups, viz.: members of the international cartel and non-member countries.

"The aluminum-making facilities of the latter group are, however with one small and insignificant exception, financially controlled by the members of the cartel. The actual result is that the international cartel, which is identical with the Alliance Aluminum Compagnie in Switzerland, is a dominant factor in the formation of business policies for all European aluminum makers.

"This situation gains increased significance for the United States on the basis of the fact that Canada, which is so closely tied to the American aluminum company, became a member of the international cartel late in 1931.

Cartel Contains Curbs.

"As the cartel contract has not been made public there is some doubt as to how far the cartel regulation of the industry goes. It is certain that the cartel fixed the raw aluminum price for European markets and prescribes a mandatory rate of curtailment of production if markets are in a depressed state.

"Compliance of members to cartel edicts is made most effective by a provision which authorizes the above-mentioned Alliance Aluminum Compagnie to finance distressed stocks of aluminum, but makes such financing contingent on the adherence to the curtailment of production program."

The report considers the various charges made by independents against the Aluminum Company of America, especially those relating to alleged monopoly price, and points out, as previous reports have, that the Aluminum Company has predominant control of raw materials and 100 per cent control of the production of domestic virgin ingot.

In the fabricating field, the report states that the company "no doubt enjoys the advantages which are

Continued on Page Six.

LEADERS' TRIBUTES MOURN PUBLIC LOSS

President Roosevelt, Members of Cabinet and Governors Grieve for Mr. Ochs.

Leaders in the affairs of the nation, State and city joined yesterday with those of many foreign countries in paying tribute to Adolph S. Ochs.

The tributes and expressions of condolence received by THE NEW YORK TIMES and Mr. Ochs's family follow:

PRESIDENT FRANKLIN D. ROOSEVELT—I am deeply distressed to learn of the passing of my old friend. His great contribution to journalism and to good citizenship will always be remembered. Please accept my sincere sympathy.

PRESIDENT CARLOS MENDIETA of Cuba—The death of the illustrious president of THE NEW YORK TIMES is not only a loss for the great daily, an example of a moral and constructive press, but for the United States and for all American countries, whose interest THE NEW YORK TIMES has loyally and disinterestedly furthered. I join with THE NEW YORK TIMES in mourning his loss.

GOVERNOR LEHMAN—I am terrifically shocked and grieved to hear of the death of Adolph S. Ochs. I knew Mr. Ochs from my earliest boyhood days, and I have always had the greatest admiration and affection for him. I have looked upon him as one of the truly great men of our generation. He was broadly intelligent, courageous, public spirited and militantly loyal to his country and to his faith. Few men have wielded so wide an influence or used it so devotedly in the public good. And with it all he was one of the kindliest and most simple of men. His death is a great loss to the nation, and New York State mourns the passing of one of its most distinguished sons. Mrs. Lehman joins me in deep sympathy to his family.

GOVERNOR HILL McALISTER of Tennessee—I have learned tonight with the deepest sorrow of the

Continued on Page Two.

MR. OCHS'S CAREER MARKED BY HONORS

Degrees Were Bestowed by Six Universities in Recognition of Services to Nation.

Six universities conferred honorary degrees upon Adolph S. Ochs; and in doing so emphasized that these honors were in recognition of the service rendered to the nation and the contribution made to education by the high character of journalism for which Mr. Ochs stood as publisher of THE NEW YORK TIMES. Mr. Ochs believed in the educational value of a newspaper which gave complete, accurate, nonpartisan news of events of interest to intelligent readers. What was said by the presidents of the universities in conferring the honorary degrees constitutes an appraisal of the educational worth of the newspaper Mr. Ochs directed and is here reprinted.

In addition Mr. Ochs received the Gold Medal of the National Institute of Social Sciences in 1927; and in 1929 he was cited by the Chamber of Commerce of the State of New York as one of the "distinguished living men in various lines of endeavor who have been notably engaged in matters of benefit to the entire community." THE NEW YORK TIMES also received in June, 1918, the first Pulitzer Gold Medal in Journalism awarded by the Trustees of Columbia University; and the first of the series of annual awards by the School of Journalism of the University of Missouri was presented to THE NEW YORK TIMES in May, 1930.

Gold Medal in Journalism.

The Pulitzer Gold Medal in Journalism was awarded to THE NEW YORK TIMES in 1918, in the words of the notification:

> For the most disinterested and meritorious public service rendered by any American newspaper during the year was awarded to THE NEW YORK TIMES for its service in publishing in full so many official reports, documents and speeches by European statesmen relating to the progress and conduct of the war.

In conferring on Mr. Ochs the honorary degree of Master of Arts

Continued on Page Five.

SNOW MAROONS AUTOS IN PENNSYLVANIA HILLS

By The Associated Press.

BEDFORD, Pa., April 8.—More than 350 automobiles, many of them bearing returning visitors from Washington's cherry-blossom show, were marooned overnight on the mountainous Lincoln Highway near here by the Spring snowstorm which struck Western Pennsylvania.

Fog, sleet, snow and icy roads combined to force the motorists to find temporary haven until highway crews could cinder the roads. Most of them spent the night at Grandview Inn on the mountain above Fishertown.

The storm had ceased at daylight, and with the highway cindered most of the wayfarers were able to proceed.

ALDERMEN TO PUSH INQUIRY ON RELIEF

Spurn Plea of Deutsch to Leave Knauth Untrammeled in Reorganizing Bureau.

DIRECTOR IS INDUCTED

Asks Wilgus to Stay as Head of Works Division—Mayor Gives Post to Critic.

Overriding the plan of Bernard S. Deutsch, President of the Board of Aldermen, to abandon the Aldermen's investigation of relief because of the appointment of Oswald W. Knauth as the new head of relief administration, the inquiry committee voted yesterday to resume its sessions in City Hall at 10 A. M. today.

Mr. Deutsch said early in the day that the inquiry should be dropped, but later joined members of the committee which he heads in voting to continue it. He explained that the committee would proceed until it knew Mr. Knauth's wishes. He has an appointment for 1 o'clock this afternoon with the new relief head, at which the inquiry will be discussed.

Announcement that the inquiry would be halted aroused members of the committee and its counsel, Lloyd Paul Stryker. Mr. Stryker said the investigation would go on, declaring that he was working for the committee "and not for Mr. Deutsch." Alderman Joseph E. Kinsley, vice chairman of the committee, was equally insistent on going ahead.

Gives Post to Opponent.

Striking back at his critics, Mayor La Guardia named Alderman Kinsley last night as a member of the Mayor's Complaint Bureau, which handles relief complaints. He replaces Mrs. Rose Miller of Mr. Deutsch's staff, who resigned last week with the complaint that access to the committee's files had been denied her.

"In naming Mr. Kinsley I am picking an outspoken critic of relief," the Mayor said. "I think that's the best answer to any charge that the Mayor's Complaint Bureau intends to whitewash relief administration. Police Inspector Louis Costuma, head of the bureau, will receive formal notice of Mr. Kinsley's appointment tomorrow."

"I accept the appointment," said Mr. Kinsley, "because I want to show that I can cooperate as well as criticize. I intend to do everything I can to improve relief administration here and rid it of the chiselers that are costing the city $24,000,000 a year."

Professor Raymond Moley, formerly one of President Roosevelt's chief advisers, will attack the relief critics in a radio speech over WMCA from 10 to 10:15 this evening. The title of his address is "Relief Is No Laughing Matter." He is expected to mince no words in dealing with those who have made fun of white-collar projects here It was learned that he will make the speech in a personal capacity, rather than as a representative of the Federal administration.

Today's session of the investigating committee will deal with the personnel employed on relief projects. Mr. Kinsley said there would be none of the levity that characterized last week's hearings. Mr. Knauth, who said he pronounced his name "K'nowt," declared that he had no opinion on the continuance of the inquiry, except that he would welcome any information of practical value that it might develop.

Knauth Formally Inducted.

He added that his sole objection would be tactics that would harm relief administration. Mr. Knauth arrived at City Hall early yesterday morning to be appointed as chairman of the Emergency Relief Bureau. He supplants Welfare Commissioner William Hodson in that post and Mr. Hodson henceforth will confine himself to running the Department of Public Welfare. Members of the Emergency Relief Bureau elected Mr. Knauth director

Continued on Page Seven.

ROOSEVELT SIGNS WORK RELIEF BILL; BEGINS ALLOCATING

Acting on Train Bound Here, He Allots $155,842,000 for Emergency Outlays.

REMARKS SENATE DELAY

President Peruses Measure Three Hours and Approves It on Advice of Experts.

A 4-POINT SPENDING PLAN

Washington Looks for Water, Land and Mineral Projects With Related Works.

Start of National Works.

On a train bound here, President Roosevelt signed the $4,880,000,000 work relief resolution, after a three-hour perusal, largely on the recommendation of departmental experts.

Making a start in carrying out the measure, the President immediately allocated $125,000,000 for continuing emergency relief, $30,000,000 for the Civilian Conservation Corps and $842,000 for conservation work in Indian reservations.

A four-point program of land, water and mineral projects, with related public works, forms the basis of spending policies to be followed under the big Relief Act.

Meanwhile a legislative snarl in both houses of Congress forced shelving for the present of the Copeland Pure Food and Drug Bill in the Senate and impelled House leaders to await the personal aid of President Roosevelt before putting the social security program to a vote.

Work Relief Bill Approved.

By CHARLES W. HURD.

Special to THE NEW YORK TIMES.

ON BOARD PRESIDENT ROOSEVELT'S SPECIAL TRAIN, April 8.—The $4,880,000,000 work relief resolution was signed by President Roosevelt today as his first official act after his thirteen-day fishing cruise.

The President received the bill in the sitting room of his car on a special train which awaited him at Jacksonville and is taking him northward tonight to attend in New York tomorrow the funeral of Warren D. Robbins, Minister to Canada and a first cousin of the President.

The train was traversing South Carolina when the President affixed his signature following a three-hour perusal of the measure.

Upon approving the measure, which carries the largest single appropriation in the nation's history, the President announced the immediate allocation of $125,000,000 for continuing emergency relief; $30,000,000 for continuance of the Civilian Conservation Corps, and $842,000 for similar work on Indian reservations.

Delay on Bill Laid to Senate.

Mr. Roosevelt remarked that he had had time only to give the bill a cursory review, but that, despite new questions raised by amendments, he had approved it on the recommendation of experts who had given it careful study.

Approval of the bill had become an emergency action by the time Mr. Roosevelt landed because the FERA not only had exhausted all of its own funds provided for the care of an estimated 21,000,000 persons without other means of support, but also had drawn on funds provided for permanent works to such an extent that the latter were jeopardized.

A statement issued on behalf of President Roosevelt attributed this delay to the long time taken by the Senate in completing its share of the work on the work-relief measure.

The bill, as finally agreed upon, was delivered by airplane to the temporary White House office at Miami last night, and then taken to Jacksonville by Marvin H. McIntyre, assistant secretary to the President.

Statement on Approving Bill.

In approving the Works Relief Bill the President authorized the following statement:

"The joint resolution making appropriations for relief purposes was finally passed last Friday. On Saturday and Sunday the resolution, including all the amendments finally agreed on, was examined by the departments and agencies concerned and sent to Jacksonville by plane and received by the President at 1 P. M.

"While a number of new questions are presented by recent amendments, those who have studied the joint resolution have recommended its approval and the President has affixed his signature to it after further study at 4 P. M.

"Immediately thereafter the Pres-

Continued on Page Eight.

Adolph S. Ochs Dies at 77; Times Publisher Since 1896

Continued From Page One.

the home of Mr. and Mrs. Adler at Fifth and Cedar Streets. He arose this morning apparently in full strength and ate his usual breakfast.

Mr. Ochs had looked forward for weeks to a visit to the offices of The Chattanooga Times, his interest in which never diminished. His family and friends had been apprehensive over his ability to withstand the railroad trip from New York, but he seemed to be in good physical condition when he reached this city. He greeted members of his family circle with enthusiasm, giving no indication of dangerous weariness. To expressions of surprise and pleasure over his seeming hearty appearance, he replied throughout the morning with cheerful repartee reminiscent of his younger days.

Mr. Ochs's body was taken to the home of Mr. and Mrs. Adler, which he and Mrs. Ochs had occupied during their long residence in Chattanooga. It will lie in state at the Julius and Bertha Ochs Memorial Temple here, which he erected in memory of his parents, from 2 until 5 o'clock tomorrow afternoon. A funeral service will be held at the memorial temple at 9:30 o'clock Wednesday morning, at which Rabbi Feinstein and the Rev. Dr. T. S. McCallie, pastor of the Central Presbyterian Church, will officiate. Afterward the body will be taken to New York on the 11 A. M. train.

Mr. Ochs is survived by Mrs. Ochs; by a daughter, Mrs. Arthur Hays Sulzberger; a brother, Milton B. Ochs of Chattanooga; three sisters, Miss Nannie Ochs of New York, Mrs. Harry C. Adler of Chattanooga and Mrs. Bernard Talimer of Philadelphia, and four grandchildren, Marian, Ruth, Judith and Arthur Ochs Sulzberger.

Funeral Services in New York on Friday.

Funeral services for Mr. Ochs will be held at 10:30 o'clock Friday morning at Temple Emanu-El, Fifth Avenue at Sixty-fifth Street, New York. Burial will be in Mount Hope, N. Y.

Mr. and Mrs. Adolph S. Ochs
On the Fiftieth Anniversary of Their Wedding, Feb. 28, 1933.

MR. OCHS'S CAREER MARKED BY HONORS

Continued From Page One.

in 1922, President James Rowland Angell of Yale University said:

In recognition of the service rendered the nation by great journalism, which strives to print the truth and to discuss it with insight, intelligence and impartiality, and for your achievement as a representative of such journalism in the upbuilding of a great newspaper enjoying wide public confidence, we confer upon you the degree of Master of Arts and admit you to all its rights and privileges.

When Columbia University conferred the honorary degree of Doctor of Laws upon Mr. Ochs in 1924, Dr. Nicholas Murray Butler, president, said:

The master mind of the outstanding triumph of modern journalism in any land; building on the firm foundation of sound principle and large vision a great organ of public education and public opinion, which now has no equal in influence, which sets the standard of excellence for newspaper service and the fair and adequate treatment of the world's news, and which faithfully represents the United States to the world and the world to the United States. I gladly admit you to the degree of Doctor of Laws.

"A Directing Genius."

The University of Chattanooga made Mr. Ochs a Doctor of Letters in 1925. In conferring the degree Dr. Arlo A. Brown, president, said:

Adolph S. Ochs, directing genius of the greatest newspaper in the world, this college honors itself in honoring you today. Classrooms, libraries and laboratories are not the only distinguishing features of an educational institution. In a very real sense the reporters who send to your office news from the ends of the earth, the editors who organize and present the material to the public, and all of the skillful men and women who help with the mechanical features of a newspaper are truly workers in a great educational organization.

You and your colleagues have been creators of educational values. Your slogan, "All the News That's Fit to Print," has set a standard which every newspaper should adopt. Your insistence that the interpretation of news shall not be controlled by advertisers or other powerful groups has shown your moral courage as well as your love for truth. Thoughtful men may differ with you, but they will always respect and honor you.

Your love for humanity at home and across the seas, your ideas of community service, evidenced so often by your leadership in difficult undertakings, your joy in bringing benefits to others, have endeared you to multitudes who do not know you. But today you are with your personal friends, in the presence of men and women who admired you in your early struggles and have rejoiced in your great achievements. You are also in the presence of a younger generation which has been inspired by your sterling virtues, the success which they have brought to you, and by the modesty with which you have carried your honors.

In conferring this degree the University of Chattanooga is acting in behalf of your neighbors and fellow-townsmen. If they had higher honors in their power to bestow they would award them. Hence, by virture of the authority vested in me by the Faculty and Trustees of the University of Chattanooga, I hereby confer upon you, Adolph S. Ochs, the honorary degree of Doctor of Letters.

In 1926 New York University conferred the degree of Doctor of Letters upon Mr. Ochs. The Chancellor, Dr. Elmer Ellsworth Brown, said:

Adolph Simon Ochs, man of power in the world of journalism, you who have won your power by sheer ability, ideals and industry, and who made use of your power not only to the end of extraordinary achievement in journalism, but in the fostering of cognate undertakings for the spread of knowledge and information, honored citizen of America, and of the crowning City of New York, as Chancellor of New York University I welcome you to the degree of Doctor of Letters, with all the rights and privileges thereunto appertaining; in evidence whereof you will receive this diploma and the insignia appropriate to this degree.

The Gold Medal of the National Institute of Social Sciences was awarded to Mr. Ochs in 1927 in recognition of his service to society in promoting and maintaining high standards of journalism. The presentation speech was made by Frank B. Noyes, president of The Associated Press, who said:

No great institution that I know of, and no one man can so completely be identified as creation and creator as is the case with THE TIMES and Mr. Ochs, and this is so, although since the day that he acquired control of the paper—then a fast-sinking property—he has sought for and gained the association with it of very able and strong men, to whom he has generously and justly given full credit for very notable work.

The fact that this medal is being awarded to Mr. Ochs is proof that I can add nothing to what you already know of THE TIMES, and I realize that I am only lamely giving voice to the general recognition of a very great newspaper, the greatest, in my opinion; of a very great journalist and of a very great citizen.

It is pleasant to remember that Mr. Ochs has met with extraordinary material success and at the same time printed a newspaper that has been a source of pride to the newspaper men of America. Most of his profits have been plowed back into the paper, for no expenditure has seemed prodigal to him that made THE TIMES better and more complete.

As examples of unexploited expenditures which it has seemed to him fitting for THE TIMES to make, I may mention two which have come to my knowledge and which should appeal especially to this gathering. One was the underwriting of the American Year Book for five years. The guarantee of 1926 was to meet the expenses of that year up to $20,000. The second was the agreement of THE TIMES to advance a total of $500,000 for the preparation of the manuscript of the Dictionary of American Biography, a monumental work sponsored by the American Council of Learned Societies Devoted to Humanistic Studies.

I think, however, the benevolence from which Mr. Ochs gets the most pride and satisfaction is the fund that the readers of THE TIMES subscribe to each year for the benefit of the "Hundred Neediest" and which has increased year by year from $3,650 in 1912 to $280,000 in 1926.

For more than a quarter of a century I have been most intimately associated with Mr. Ochs in our common work in The Associated Press, and have come to really know his high ideals and keen intelligence, his absolute justness.

On his personal side, I love the man, his tolerance, his generosity, his kindly humor.

"Pre-eminence in Journalism."

The degree of Doctor of Humane Letters was conferred upon Mr. Ochs by Lincoln Memorial University, Cumberland Gap, Tenn., in 1928. The Chancellor, Dr. John Wesley Hill, said in his citation:

In recognition of his pre-eminence in journalism, evinced in his control of the greatest newspaper in the world—stamped with rare editorial genius, its news universal in variety and discriminating in character, unique in its purity, moral, economic and social idealism; and in recognition of his leadership in social and industrial justice; his mastery of literature, art and political science, his devotion to the ideals of Abraham Lincoln and his patronage of higher education, Lincoln Memorial University confers upon Adolph S. Ochs the degree of Doctor of Humane Letters, with all the privileges, responsibilities and honors appertaining thereto.

Dartmouth College conferred the degree of Doctor of Laws upon Mr. Ochs in 1932. Dr. Ernest Martin Hopkins, president, said of Mr. Ochs:

Adolph Simon Ochs, publisher of THE NEW YORK TIMES—the path of whose achievement stretches from newsboy in a Southern city to leadership in metropolitan journalism and to proprietorship of one of the world's greatest newspapers—it is the manner not less than the scope of your accomplishment that commands recognition of the American college. Capturing the vision of your early years, cumulatively capitalizing the experience which you have avidly sought, and tenaciously holding to your carefully conceived conceptions of what makes for trustworthy and comprehensive presentation of the news, you have rendered acceptable service to an appreciative public and you have created a fount of knowledge from which day by day flows more abundantly than has ever been known before the fundamental data significant to understanding of the world's affairs. Estimable as a citizen, generous and intelligent in public service, talented to the point of genius in your field of specialized effort, I confer upon you the honorary degree of Doctor of Laws.

LEADERS' TRIBUTES MOURN PUBLIC LOSS

Continued From Page One.

death of Mr. Ochs. His native State has taken the deepest pride in her contribution to his long useful life to American journalism. It is difficult to estimate the profound influence which he exercised upon the men and women of his time.

Mayor F. H. LA GUARDIA—I am indeed sorry to hear of the death of Mr. Ochs. His passing will be a great loss to the city. As a publisher, he kept in very close contact with the affairs of this city through his newspaper. He was a man of great ideals. It is a real personal loss to me.

DR. NICHOLAS MURRAY BUTLER, President of Columbia University—It is hard for me to speak calmly of Mr. Ochs. I enjoyed his friendship for many years and had the greatest admiration for his public service and his lofty conception of journalism. In a few short years he made THE TIMES a newspaper which for dignity, for fairness, for elevation of tone and for avoidance of the vulgar, the nasty and the crudely

(continued)

sensational, was a model to the whole world. He was a true leader and a builder in the great field of human institutions. When conscienceless seekers after advertising and circulation left no disgusting tastes untouched, Mr. Ochs showed how to gain a large and influential circulation for his newspaper among refined and cultivated men and women whose support really counts. He was a truly great and highly influential figure in our nation's life.

OTHERS VOICE SORROW.

Leaders in the Professions and Civic Activities Mourn.

BERNARD M. BARUCH—Just learned with deepest regret of the death of Mr. Ochs and hasten to extend to you my heartfelt sympathy.

SAMUEL UNTERMYER—I am inexpressibly shocked and saddened. He was one of my oldest and dearest friends. Our country has lost one of its greatest citizens. He was a tremendous force and will be sadly missed.

PAUL D. CRAVATH—New York has suffered an irreparable loss in the death of Mr. Ochs. He was one of New York's great citizens and will be missed by a host of friends. The great newspaper which he built up will be a monument to his genius.

GIULIO GATTI-CASAZZA, General Manager, Metropolitan Opera Association—It is with deep sorrow that I hear of the death of Adolph S. Ochs. American journalism has lost in him one of its most eminent and vital personalities. THE NEW YORK TIMES a genius of organization and a leader of idealistic and unique qualities, the art of music a genial connoisseur, and the Metropolitan an illustrious and sympathetic friend.

LEE SHUBERT—The death of Mr. Ochs is a great loss to journalism and to his many friends. He stood for nothing but the finest and he was a friend to everybody who knew him.

GEORGE M. COHAN—Mr. Adolph S. Ochs was the outstanding newspaper mind of this country. His death is a terrible loss to all America. I treasured his friendship and feel terribly upset at the sad news.

Mme. FRANCES ALDA—Mr. Ochs was one of the greatest men I ever met, an intimate friend and a great gentleman. His death is a great loss.

JOHN SLOAN—As a citizen, an artist and an ex-newspaper man, I feel that not only New York journalism but all the United States have lost the highest example of a newspaper publisher that we have ever had. THE NEW YORK TIMES remains his memorial, and I hope they will keep up the standards that he set up for it.

JOSEPHUS DANIELS, Ambassador to Mexico—The death of no private citizen of America would distress the world so much as that of Mr. Ochs. He found THE TIMES, with an honorable record, a moribund journal. His genius converted it into an institution invaluable to students, publicists and business men in every part of the world. He made it truly a vade mecum. He put his life into it and had the wisdom to collaborate with men who shared his views of the peculiar place THE TIMES ought to occupy. He will be missed, but I doubt not he has provided for the institution he created to carry on along the large lines to which he gave it impetus. He brought honor and distinction to my profession, and I was always proud that a fellow-Southerner had won high place with the noblest of journalists.

ARTHUR WILLIAMS—May I express my deepest sympathy to THE NEW YORK TIMES in the passing of one of the nation's greatest personalities, Mr. Adolph S. Ochs. To his constructive vision and genius the nation will be forever indebted. His friendship, enjoyed for many years, was one of my dearest possessions.

LOUIS SCHLESINGER, Philanthropist—Inexpressibly shocked at the passing away of Mr. Adolph S. Ochs, whom I have known for over twenty years and considered him one of the outstanding men in the world. My expression of profound sympathy to Mrs. Ochs and the executives of THE NEW YORK TIMES.

Former Senator FREDERICK W. KAVANAUGH of Waterford—The country loses its great outstanding editor and newspaper man. We have been friends for a great many years. He was one of the most human, kind-hearted and thoughtful men that I have ever come in contact with. He and I have visited together at his home and mine for years and years back, and he was beloved by all of the people from one end of Lake George to the other. He was a very liberal contributor to everything that was for the best interest and the good of all people at Lake George.

CHARLES A. OBERWAGER, Former Magistrate—Shocked beyond expression by the sad news of the death of Adolph S. Ochs, I hasten to express my deep sorrow and sympathy to the family. He was one of America's foremost molders of public opinion, linking the entire world by news, preaching the doctrine of peace and enlightenment, always deeply interested in human affairs, seeking a better understanding of all peoples in an effort to create harmonious relations. His death is an indescribable loss to the nation.

MEN IN HIS OWN PROFESSION.

Newspaper Leaders Throughout the Nation Pay Tribute.

OGDEN REID, Publisher of The New York Herald Tribune—When one has known, liked and admired a man for a quarter of a century it is not possible to state in a few minutes what one thinks of him. The first impression is a shock at the loss of a friend. The second is the realization that somehow we must get along without him. Mr. Ochs has made a definite impression on modern journalism. Like other good executives he picked good assistants and he gave them an opportunity to produce. His judgment of men was good and his venture was a success. He had high principles and he instilled them into the people whom he had selected to carry out his ideas. Adolph Ochs understood the newspaper business before he came to New York and he applied his knowledge, his energy and his imagination to the task. The result has been a very fine newspaper devoted to the interests of the nation and the community in which he lived. Mr. Ochs had very definite ideas as to what he would and would not do. He turned down plans that might have meant circulation but were below his standards. He also worked assiduously on what seemed to him to be sound, though others in his organization disagreed with him. In both cases he displayed what are the most essential qualities of a great publisher, courage and character.

FRANK B. NOYES, President of The Associated Press—The death of Adolph Ochs comes to me as a shock that words cannot express. My feeling as to his preeminence in journalism has been often expressed. THE TIMES is his monument, and no one in our profession could have a greater one than is found in the newspaper which he created, for THE NEW YORK TIMES of today is of his creation. His service to The Associated Press from the start of the Illinois corporation which preceded the present organization has been of an inestimable value and is an example to self-respecting journalism, is a heritage which we must cherish. For myself I have lost a very dear friend of nearly half a century and I am in sorrow.

KENT COOPER, General Manager of The Associated Press—I can think of no one whose passing must mean a greater loss both to journalism and to those who knew him than that of Mr. Ochs. Words are not to be found that would properly record appraisal of his sterling worth and his monumental contribution to the newspaper profession. Personally, there never will be another who will be more to me as mentor, guide and friend. Those he loved who have been engaged with him in the publication of THE NEW YORK TIMES will miss him in its affairs as I will in the affairs of The Associated Press, which he also loved so much; but from the strength of his character, from the admirable qualities of his genius, will arise new determination to carry onward and upward upon the high principles of the profession which were his throughout his long life.

WILLIAM RANDOLPH HEARST—By the death of Mr. Ochs, the nation has lost one of its greatest newspaper geniuses and one of its most magnificently loyal and devoted citizens. It is a matter of great grief to all his fellow-citizens that the country should have lost this intellectual leader in these fateful times. His conservative and constructive leadership will be deeply missed at a time when he is needed most. His great paper, solidly built on firm foundations, will remain a national institution; but the guidance of his loyal and liberal mind in public affairs will be gone. The personal loss in his death, to his many friends and admirers, will be irreparable.

[Mr. Hearst directed that his statement be printed in all his newspapers.]

RALPH PULITZER—Adolph Ochs was a great and upright man, a good and useful citizen and an admirable journalist who built THE TIMES up to its present wonderful success by his unfaltering conviction that the life-blood of a newspaper is the news. His death is both a personal and a public loss which I feel very deeply.

NOTABLES ABROAD MOURN MR. OCHS

Special Cable to THE NEW YORK TIMES.

LONDON, April 8.—Lady Astor, who learned of the death of Adolph S. Ochs when she returned to her home in St. James Square from the House of Commons tonight, expressed for herself and Viscount Astor regret at the loss of a personal friend and their appreciation of his qualities as a great journalist and as a citizen of the world.

"We first knew him in England in the war days," Lady Astor said. "He has lived a full and splendid life. The qualities which impressed me through the nearly score of years I knew him were his extraordinary fairness and his real desire to do what was best for the world at large. He had neither pride nor prejudice nor partial affections and his courage in backing the Allied cause was magnificent.

"He saw what was right and did it when it was unpopular, regardless of any adverse effect it might have on him or his newspaper. His death means a great loss not only to America but to the whole world, now more than ever."

In its introduction to a long obituary of Mr. Ochs The Times points to the growth and influence of THE NEW YORK TIMES since 1896, and adds:

"Its success and influence were due mainly to the industry, farsightedness and wise leadership of Mr. Ochs, who, though seldom openly or forcibly exerting his authority, was always felt to be the molding and guiding power in the organization and production of his paper."

The Times also says that "Mr. Ochs always was a loyal friend of Great Britain, and under him the paper labored more than any other in the United States for better understanding between the two countries."

United States Ambassador Robert W. Bingham said in mourning the death that "Mr. Ochs set the highest mark in the newspaper world by publishing a newspaper that contained all the news from all sides and without color."

"His death is a sad loss to me," Mr. Bingham declared, "for when I saw him last he was undoubtedly at the full height of his powers. He was an amazing man. His career was most interesting to me because he started on The Louisville Courier-Journal, the paper I now own. I think he would have been successful in any walk of life. He was successful in journalism because he won the confidence of every one with whom he came into contact—those able men he got around him and the readers of his publications."

Adolph S. Ochs

The story of Adolph S. Ochs is one of a career which, in poverty and wealth, in obscurity and eminence, was all of one piece. The qualities that his employers and associates noted when he began his newspaper career as office boy and printer's devil in Knoxville, Tenn., were the qualities he manifested throughout his life. The principles he announced and put into practice when at the age of 20 he took charge of a bankrupt small-town newspaper were the principles he announced and put into practice eighteen years later when he took charge of the bankrupt NEW YORK TIMES and carried it to influence and prosperity. He knew how to publish, he believed in publishing, only one single kind of paper; and his great achievement was the proof that the publishing of that kind of paper—"clean, dignified, trustworthy and impartial," as he phrased it in his announcement in THE TIMES on Aug. 18, 1896—was practically possible; was not an exercise in altruism, but could be made economically as well as ethically successful.

That he made it successful was due no doubt to native ability, to a mind which, strong in its grasp of organization, also was unusually intuitional and, in flashes of inspiration, covered in an instant ground that slow-thinking men might labor over for months; but also very largely to the fact that he learned the newspaper business from the ground up, was in it all his life, and never wasted his time or his ambitions on outside enterprises or on the political aspirations that have proved a curse to so many other newspaper makers (not least to his predecessor, Henry J. Raymond, founder of THE NEW YORK TIMES). The poverty of his parents cut short his formal schooling; but, as he told the National Editorial Association in its convention of 1916, the printing office was his high school and university, and something of the impress of the old-time printing shop and of that unique and salty breed, the old-school printers, stayed with him all his life.

Principles Learned at Home.

But the principles were his before he learned how to put them into practice; he learned them at home. He was born in Cincinnati, March 12, 1858, eldest of the six children of Julius and Bertha Levy Ochs. Both his parents belonged to the group of German liberals and intellectuals who had been driven from home by the repressive measures of autocratic governments, against which the revolution of 1848 was an ineffectual protest. Julius Ochs, born in Furth, Bavaria, in 1826, came to the United States at the age of 18, possessor of an excellent education and fluent in six languages—German, French, English, Spanish, Italian and Hebrew. He taught languages in various Southern schools, a career only briefly interrupted by his volunteering for the Mexican War, as his regiment was never called into active service. In Natchez, in 1853, he met Miss Levy, and they were married in Nashville two years later. Adolph Ochs's mother, born in Rhenish Bavaria of a family with distinguished connections in France and Alsace, had had to leave Germany in haste in 1848 to escape arrest for her connection with revolutionary committees. She traveled by sailing ship to New Orleans, where an uncle lived. The influence of this brilliant and cultured woman on her son was immense and lasting. At the age of 70 his telegram of congratulation to Alfred E. Smith on his nomination to the Presidency took this characteristic form:

"Every good mother's son is inspired and encouraged by this well-earned climax to an extraordinary career."

Until she moved to Cincinnati after her marriage Mrs. Ochs's American residence had been in the South; her sympathies were with the South in the Civil War that presently broke out, and her brother served in the Confederate Army. Julius Ochs, however, despite his Southern connections and his residence in Kentucky and Tennessee, was a Union man; he enlisted in an Ohio regiment in 1861 and served throughout the war, rising to the rank of Captain. The division in politics did not affect the harmony of the family; but when Captain Ochs died in Chattanooga in 1888 the Grand Army of the Republic was prominent at his funeral; when his wife died in New York in 1910 a similar part was played by the Daughters of the Confederacy.

Family Moves to Knoxville.

After the war Captain Ochs found himself in the position of a good many demobilized soldiers; he had to start again from the beginning. With his growing family he moved to Knoxville, Tenn., a town that had been somewhat battered in the war but seemed to have bright prospects for future growth. That expectation was justified; but Julius Ochs, scholar and idealist, lacked the talent for material success that would have enabled him to share in the town's prosperity. He served as Justice of the Peace and United States Commissioner, and later for a short time as Probate Judge; his continuing enthusiasm for clean and progressive politics, in an age when such ideas had fallen out of favor, carried him as a delegate to the Liberal Republican Convention which nominated Greeley in Cincinnati in 1872. Active in lodge work, he was universally popular and respected; deeply pious and a student of the religious writings of the Hebrew faith, he served his unorganized co-religionists in Knoxville as what one of his Tennessee friends later called "a first-class emergency rabbi." But his material fortunes did not prosper, and his sons grew up in the realization that as soon as possible they must begin to contribute to the family income.

Adolph, the oldest boy, went to work at the age of 11 as office boy to Captain William Rule, editor of The Knoxville Chronicle. This Republican paper, successor of Parson Brownlow's Knoxville Whig of pre-war days, never succeeded in winning its newest employe to its politics; Adolph Ochs grew up in sympathy with the conservative Democrats of the Reconstruction period. But Captain Rule became one of the determining influences of his life, and inspired a loyalty and affection that were enduring. Fifty two years later, when all Knoxville declared a holiday to celebrate the eighty-second birthday of Captain Rule—then, and until his death in his ninetieth year, still in active service as an editor—the publisher of THE NEW YORK TIMES was a sort of secondary guest of honor; and Captain Rule recalled that "he swept my sanctum and cleaned up the papers and trash so methodically that he was promoted to delivery boy," getting up long before dawn to deposit The Chronicle on the doorsteps of subscribers, for $1.50 a week.

After a year or so of this the family decided that the boy might have a better chance in a larger city, so he was sent to Providence, R. I., where his mother's two brothers had a grocery in which he worked as cash boy. But the next year he was back in Knoxville, working in a local drug store, where (tradition has it) he lost his job some six months later

(continued)

by selling a customer borax in mistake for sal soda. Early in 1872 he returned to The Chronicle, this time as printer's devil—the old-time printer's term for the boy who did the odd jobs and dirty work about the composing room; and this established him in the newspaper business, where he was to remain for the rest of his life.

Keen in Quest of Knowledge.

In the chaotic conditions of a town recovering from the Civil War through the handicaps of reconstruction, it would be hard to say whether a boy worked outside of school hours or went to school outside of working hours. Adolph Ochs had got the beginnings of his school education at Bradford's Hampden - Sydney Academy, a Knoxville day school, and during his next three years in The Chronicle composing room he attended classes when he could in the preparatory department of the East Tennessee University (now the University of Tennessee), where he impressed his teachers, as he impressed his employers, with his diligence and quickness. The few years he actually spent in a schoolroom might not have amounted to much, however, had it not been for what he learned outside; as an office boy, a carrier, a grocery or drug store clerk, he was always asking questions—an acquaintance of those days described him as "a human interrogation point"; and the deficiencies of his formal education were compensated by the advantages of a cultured home and the private tuition of a scholarly father.

There remained the printing office, his high school and university, as he later described it; but the thorough grounding in the newspaper business which he got in The Knoxville Chronicle shop came to him largely by accident. When the 13-year-old boy became a printer's devil he still had no idea of making the newspaper business his life work; he went after the job because he needed the money, and was hired because his services as office boy and carrier had impressed the editor of The Chronicle with his trustworthiness.

Now it happened that the printer's devil had to work at night, and that his duties were finished earlier than those of the journeyman printers, who were the aristocracy of the composing room. He had to go home alone, and the way home, along unpaved, poorly lighted streets, led past the graveyard of the First Presbyterian Church. A boy of 13 who had grown up in a town where there were plenty of superstitious residents, both white and colored, might be excused for sometimes forgetting the information he had no doubt received at home, that a graveyard was nothing to be afraid of. He hated to go home alone in the dark; and because the foreman of the composing room, Henry C. Collins, lived near him, little Adolph Ochs used to stay in the shop after his own day's work was over till Mr. Collins had finished and could walk home with him.

Staying in the shop, he had to occupy his time, and the natural way to do it was by learning more about the printing trade than would come the way even of an alert and observant printer's devil during his ordinary and well-filled working hours. He learned and he learned fast; and in later years the proprietor of THE NEW YORK TIMES was not ashamed to admit that what really made a newspaper man of him was the need of company when he walked past the graveyard late at night. Half a century later, when Mr. Ochs returned to Knoxville for the Rule celebration, he and Mr. Collins went over that route again. Most of the landmarks had vanished, but the friendship that sprang up in the composing room still endured.

Those years as devil and later apprentice were busy ones for young Adolph Ochs; learning his trade in the printing office, going to school as he found opportunity, and acting as usher, with his younger brothers George and Milton, in Mayor Peter Staub's Opera House, where traveling companies played "The Two Orphans," "Monte Cristo" and "Hazel Kirke," and ushers picked up a little extra money by selling candy between the acts.

Starts Out in Wider Field.

And so it went till October, 1875, when Adolph Ochs, 17 years old, decided to go out and see what he could do in a larger field. There is a tradition that he had some idea of settling, eventually, in California, but his immediate objective was Louisville; and the letters of recommendation that he took with him when he left his home town were considered more than perfunctory discharges of obligation; they were curiously prophetic. Captain Rule, the editor of The Chronicle, wrote that he had found him "honest, zealous, reliable and trustworthy * * * quick to comprehend and faithful to execute," and "endowed with an intellect capable of reaching the highest point of mental achievement." Collins, his foreman, said that "He is to a foreman what money is to a miser—a necessity, hard to part with." His associates in the composing room presented him with a volume of Hood's poems—he kept it all his life—with an inscription on the flyleaf over all their signatures expressing the hope that "some day we shall be able to note you among the nation's honored sons." And Mayor Staub, losing a valuable usher from his opera house, chose to speak in his civic rather than his private capacity: "For the Mayor of any city such a loss as your departure, my young and worthy friend, is quite serious."

Armed with these testimonials, the young printer went to Louisville and found work in the job printing department of The Courier Journal. But six months later he was back in Knoxville; and as Edward H. Edwards, a printer who worked with him there, has put it, "if there ever was a turning point in the life of Adolph S. Ochs it was when, having gone out from his father's roof to seek his fortune, he so sorely felt the loss of family ties and the personal contact of those near and dear to him that he was impelled to return home." Ambition as well as homesickness was a motive, however; a new paper, The Tribune, had just been established in Knoxville, and it offered perhaps a better opportunity to a boy who was indeed trusted and admired by his old employers on The Chronicle, but might never have lived down the fact that he started at the very bottom, might never have seemed to them any more than Adolph the office boy grown up.

Attracted by Chattanooga.

His year and a half on The Tribune gave him a more varied experience. He worked at first in the composing room, then as a reporter, and was presently made assistant to the business manager, Franc M. Paul—a rehearsal in each of the three departments of newspaper-making which he was soon to find invaluable. For already his ambitions, and those of some of his associates on The Tribune, were looking southward to Chattanooga. The strategic importance of this city, so great in the military operations of the Civil War, had not yet been appreciated commercially; the centre of a number of railroads, with rich mineral deposits lying in the mountains roundabout, Chattanooga had only some 12,000 people and was still in spirit a small town. Yet there were a few persons, including Adolph Ochs, who realized its possibilities; and this town of promise was served by only a single newspaper, The Times, an organ miserably inadequate from every point of view which was living from hand to mouth. Young Ochs and Colonel J. E. MacGowan, an editorial writer on The Knoxville Tribune, were planning to establish a new paper in competition with The Chattanooga Times when they discovered that their colleague Franc Paul had anticipated them and started The Chattanooga Dispatch, to which he brought them both in the Fall of 1877, Colonel MacGowan as editor and Adolph Ochs as advertising solicitor.

But The Chattanooga Times, feeble as it was, refused to fold up in the face of competition. The outcome has been succinctly described by William M. Stone, a Chattanooga printer who was afterward for many years on Mr. Ochs's staff:

"In less than six months The Dispatch, despite Paul's planting and Adolph's watering, proved a hopeless failure. But this, unfortunate as it seemed at the time, proved a great blessing to Chattanooga, as it left Adolph so poor that he could not leave town."

Paul went back to Knoxville, Colonel MacGowan stayed in Chattanooga and got another job, and Adolph Ochs was made receiver of The Dispatch, and eventually managed to liquidate its debts. But meanwhile he had to eat; and discovering that Chattanooga had no city directory, he set to work on this his first publication. He himself did all the work on it but the binding; he got the information, wrote it, set it up in type, read the proof and printed it on a hand press. And this directory had two consequences besides the urgent and immediate one of enabling its publisher to eat—it gave him a comprehensive and thorough acquaintance with all the population and all the business of Chattanooga, and it awakened the citizens to the realization that their town had possibilities that they had overlooked, but which were plain to the eyes of an observant (and hungry) young immigrant from Knoxville.

Takes Over the Local Times.

The directory not only made Ochs acquainted with Chattanooga, but made Chattanooga acquainted with Ochs. The Times had been able to outlast the competition of The Dispatch; but it was about ready to give up the ghost, and its editor offered to sell it to Mr. Ochs for $800, provided he would assume the paper's debts, amounting to $1,500 more. The young man from Knoxville would have been glad to accept the offer, but for one insuperable difficulty: he did not have $800. Indeed, he had almost nothing; but he had made acquaintances and established his personal standing in Chattanooga, and after further negotiations he discovered that he could borrow $250. With that borrowed $250 he bought a half interest in The Chattanooga Times, stipulating that his half should carry with it the control of the paper; he assumed the paper's $1,500 debt in addition to the $250 he had borrowed to buy it; and with his own private fortune of $37.50 as working capital he became publisher of The Chattanooga Times on July 2, 1878.

The salutatory of the new publisher announced the theme around which his whole life was to be woven. The Times intended to become "the indispensable organ of the business, commercial and productive, of Chattanooga, and of the mineral and agricultural districts" surrounding the town; it would get all the news it could, at home and abroad (the earlier Times had had no telegraph news at all), and would support conservative Democratic principles while reserving independence in State politics, "being cognizant of the need of and the strongly expressed desire for such a newspaper in Chattanooga as the above outline indicates The Times to be, we have taken the people at their word and shall give them a chance to support that which they have been asking for."

But, it was added, "in this matter of patronage we shall make no appeals, but rely upon that sense of propriety and justice which must teach every intelligent citizen that the obligation between himself and the paper is a mutual one, ours to print and circulate such a journal as we have described, his to see that he contributes his share, in proportion to the benefits such a paper confers on him as a citizen, the means to sustain it and promote its growth. * * * In short, we shall conduct our business on business principles, neither seeking nor giving sops and donations."

Task a Formidable One.

Chattanooga knew what this meant. The Chattanooga Times before Mr. Ochs's day had, in the words of Henry M. Wiltse, "dragged itself from pillar to post, and had to lean heavily against the one or the other whenever it desired to cast a shadow or take a long breath."

It was a failing not uncommon in the small-town journalism of the seventies, a precarious trade whose practitioners, unless they were unusually able or unusually lucky, were likely to find that they could keep afloat only by giving sops to local interests, or by accepting donations of one sort or another which were rarely disinterested.

The young man who had turned his back on this sort of thing, who had announced that he would give Chattanooga what he thought it needed and would accept from it only what he thought he had earned, had nothing behind him but his abilities and his knowledge of his trade. He had been a resident of the town for less than a year; despite the mustache which he then wore to give himself an air of maturity, he could hardly conceal from his fellow-citizens that he was not yet old enough to vote. He had a newspaper plant fit for hardly anything but the junk heap, publishing a four-page paper with a circulation of 250; he owed $1,750 and his working capital amounted to just about 2 per cent of his debts. Yet from that slender beginning came not only The Chattanooga Times, but THE NEW YORK TIMES of today.

Colonel MacGowan, another immigrant from Knoxville left behind after the collapse of The Dispatch, was hired to serve as editor of The Times in such time as he could spare from his other **job, at a salary of a dollar a day. There was one reporter and a business office staff of one; five men in the composing room, besides a foreman who also acted as proofreader and pressman; and the proprietor and publisher, besides being general editorial supervisor, was also business manager and advertising solicitor. The payroll even of this modest force, even in those times, was somewhat over $100 a week, without allowing any compensation for the publisher; and the problem of meeting the payroll in the first year was often an acute one. But it was always met, and met without any compromise with the principles announced by the new publisher in his first issue. His first year with The Chattanooga Times was perhaps the hardest, certainly the most critical, in Mr. Ochs's whole career; but the end of the year saw him on the road to success.**

Profits Put Into Business.

His total receipts that year were $12,000; but his expenses were only $10,000, including $900 withdrawn for his own living, and the profit was plowed back into the business. From the first he had given The Times the telegraph service of the old Western Associated Press; this was expanded as rapidly as possible, and Colonel MacGowan was soon engaged as full-time editor, a post he held until his death twenty-five years later. When it became apparent that the new venture was going to be successful the publisher brought his family down from Knoxville, and his brothers George and Milton presently took their turn as reporters on The Times, thus beginning newspaper careers that were later to bring distinction to both. Two years

(continued)

The Chattanooga Times when Mr. Ochs bought it in 1878.

after he had bought the control of The Times Mr. Ochs was able to buy the other half interest in the paper that had been beyond his reach in 1878. At that time he could have bought it for $400, or probably even less; by 1880 he had to pay $5,500 for it, every cent of the increment in value being the result of his own success with the paper.

The newspaper which was thus succeeding was fulfilling its promise of impartiality and disinterestedness. To L. G. Walker, on his appointment as editor of The Chattanooga Times years later, Mr. Ochs said: "Your only policy is to have no policy—no policy that is, except to be right." It was on that principle that The Times was conducted from the very first, in a day when newspapers, especially in the smaller cities, were far more likely to be affected by outside influence than they are at present; and it was that same principle that Mr. Ochs later put into practice in New York. But it never meant a weak policy or an absence of policy. It meant independence and a sense of civic duty. The Chattanooga paper prospered and the town prospered with it. In the language of William M. Stone. Mr. Ochs "took the dirty, poverty-stricken village by the nape of the neck and by sheer force of magnetic optimism and courageous enterprise lifted it to where it is today." One of his own contributions to the upbuilding of the city was the erection, in 1892, of the substantial building of The Chattanooga Times.

Captain Rule, years before had noted that his young employe was not only honest but zealous; and it was that zeal that Chattanooga was feeling now—the zeal of a young man who had picked out a town that he thought had a future, and was resolved to make that future a pleasant reality. There was no civic improvement of those years in Chattanooga that The Times did not promote—indeed often it started them—the opera house, the firemen's fountain, the dredging of a channel in the Tennessee River. More important, perhaps, was the Chickamauga National Park, of which Mr. Ochs was one of the originators, and which served to get him started in the park movement which was to prove one of the great interests of his life.

His Only Public Office.

It was perhaps this zeal for promotion of his home town that led him to accept the only public office he ever held in his life—membership on the Chattanooga School Board in 1884 and 1885.

Mr. Ochs's leadership in the boosting of his home town had a number of consequences, one of which was not altogether pleasant. Chattanooga was flourishing, largely because of the vigorous work of The Times; and in 1888 the town paid the inevitable penalty of a real estate boom. The publisher of The Times later admitted that he ran wild like everybody else and bought up a lot of land which for years afterward ate its head off in taxes; but the boom turned out to be only an anticipation of values that were really there, and ultimately Mr. Ochs lost no money by this demonstration of his faith in Chattanooga.

Another by-product of Mr. Ochs's civic leadership had more agreeable and, as it turned out, more fruitful consequences. By common consent the publisher of The Times, young, affable and abundantly enthusiastic, was accepted as the unofficial reception and entertainment committee for distinguished visitors to the town. He was the better able to discharge this function since he had been married in Cincinnati on Feb. 28, 1883, to Miss Effie Miriam Wise, daughter of the Rev. Dr. Isaac M. Wise, founder of the Hebrew Union College and the Union of American Hebrew Congregations. Marriage brought him not only an invaluable helpmate but a brilliant connection. In the early days when the whole Ochs family was collaborating in getting out The Chattanooga Times, Mrs. Ochs did her part as book reviewer and dramatic critic, besides presiding over the household at which eminent visitors to Chattanooga were entertained. To this union was born some years later a daughter, Iphigene Bertha, who was married in 1917 to Arthur Hays Sulzberger.

All sorts of people passed through Chattanooga in the later eighties and earlier nineties, and the publisher of The Times met most of them. There was President Cleveland; there were Governors, Senators, bankers, Bishops and railroad presidents. A young Republican editor from Ohio named Warren G. Harding came to town on his honeymoon, and confessed to the publisher of The Times that he wasn't satisfied with his prospects back home and had some idea of starting a Republican paper in Chattanooga. This notion was promptly dropped when Mr. Ochs pointed out to him that the only Republicans in Chattanooga were colored people, few of whom in those days could read.

Casual Remark Prophetic.

Another caller, in 1890, was Harry Alloway, a Wall Street reporter for THE NEW YORK TIMES, who was writing a series of articles on the industrial development of the South, to whom Mr. Ochs remarked casually that he thought THE TIMES, then in the beginnings of decay, offered the greatest opportunity in American journalism. This remark was forgotten by the young publisher; but Harry Alloway remembered it, and the rehabilitation of THE NEW YORK TIMES was the fruit of that passing comment.

The outcome of all this entertainment of distinguished visitors, unintended but inevitable, was that the publisher of The Chattanooga Times was acquiring a national acquaintance far larger than falls to most small-city publishers, and the time was at hand when he would find it useful. In his trade, too, he was becoming widely and favorably known. Invited to address the meeting of the National Editorial Association at St. Paul in 1891, he put his finger on the great change American journalism was undergoing at the time and foretold th tendency of the future. Through the mid-nineteenth century the great papers had been essentially political and essentially personal; they were the platforms on which great editors could display their personal brilliance and the news columns were usually as biased and argumentative as the editorial page. But Mr. Ochs told the assembled editors at St. Paul: "The day of the organ, if not past, is rapidly passing. A journal conducted as a newspaper (with the emphasis on the news) is the newspaper of the future."

Many newspapers of the South, The Chattanooga Times included, were at that time getting their telegraph news from the old Associated Press, an Illinois corporation composed chiefly of Middle Western newspapers, with The New York World as its principal Eastern member. In opposition, the other New York papers were maintaining, at heavy cost, the old United Press. Southern papers were not altogether satisfied with the service they were getting, and in 1891 Mr. Ochs, as secretary of the Southern Press Association, called a meeting which organized The Southern Associated Press, of which he became general manager and later chairman of the executive committee. But the division of newspaper territory among three competing organizations did not prove successful; in 1894 the majority of Southern papers threw in their lot with The United Press. Mr Ochs thought that the Western organization had a better

THE PUBLISHER OF THE TIMES IN 1896.

Mr. Ochs when he came to New York from Chattanooga to enter the metropolitan newspaper field.

prospect of surviving the struggle than the Eastern; The Chattanooga Times went into The Associated Press, and the connections there formed were presently to prove of immense value to its publisher and to the greater enterprise which he was about to undertake, as well as The Associated Press itself.

His First Call to New York.

Early in 1896 Mr. Ochs received a telegram from a friend in New York—Leopold Wallach, a lawyer—informing him that "the opportunity of your life lies before you." To an ambitious young mar of 38 who had already explored and realized on about all the opportunities that were offered in Chattanooga the information was too alluring to be overlooked; Mr. Ochs went to New York to see what it was all about.

The reality was disillusioning. This great opportunity was only the business managership of The New York Mercury, a small paper dealing chiefly in theatrical and sporting news, which a group of politicians who favored free silver were planning to buy in order to give New York a silver newspaper in the Presidential campaign of 1896, in which it was already evident that the currency issue would play a large part. Mr. Ochs, however, was a believer in the gold standard, which The Chattanooga Times was valiantly supporting, even though the majority of Southern Democrats had abandoned it. With the management of a silver paper, in New York or elsewhere, he would have nothing to do; but when the silver group presently gave up its plan to buy The Mercury the owner of that paper, anxious to get rid of it before it died on his hands, offered to sell it to Mr. Ochs direct.

This was rather more of a temptation. Mr. Ochs believed that in New York at the time there was an opening for a compact paper devoting itself strictly to the presentation of news and selling at 1 cent, a price then represented in New York only by the flamboyant "yellow" papers of the time, The World and The Journal. The paper he envisioned was very much the sort of thing that another ambitious young man, Alfred Harmsworth, was just then beginning to publish in London; and it was Mr. Ochs's notion that The Mercury could be developed into what he had in mind. But all depended on The Mercury continuing to receive, as it was then receiving, the service of The United Press, and when he found that its owner could give him no assurance of that Mr. Ochs returned to Chattanooga.

Hardly had he reached home before he had a telegram—on his thirty-eighth birthday, as it happened—from that Harry Alloway of THE NEW YORK TIMES to whom he had remarked six years before that THE TIMES offered the greatest opportunity in American journalism. Since 1890 THE TIMES had sadly declined, there was talk of an imminent reorganization and Alloway—purely on his own account, and without any authority—wired to Mr. Ochs that if he were interested in THE TIMES it could probably be bought cheap. In Mr. Ochs's early years in New York rumor kept insisting that he had been brought to town by various personages, from President Cleveland on down, to rehabilitate THE TIMES; but the fact is that the only man who "brought him to town" was THE TIMES reporter who wanted to see the paper set on its feet, and believed that the Chattanooga publisher had the ability to do it.

At the moment Mr. Ochs did not take the idea very seriously; but it happened that the next day business took him to Chicago. There, at lunch, he mentioned the matter to his friend Herman Kohlsaat, publisher of The Chicago Times-Herald, who exclaimed, "Ochs, there's your opportunity." "But," Mr. Ochs protested, "I don't believe I'm a big enough man for the job." This argument failed to impress Mr. Kohlsaat. "Don't tell anybody," he advised, "and they'll never find it out."

Becomes Interested in The Times.

Thus encouraged, Mr. Ochs went to New York and began to investigate the situation, which was to prove not only his opportunity but THE TIMES's, too.

George Jones, who had joined with Henry J. Raymond in founding THE NEW YORK TIMES in 1851 and had conducted it since Raymond's death, had died in 1891. The antiquated organism, which he knew how to operate, his children were unable to conduct successfully, and within two years of his death his heirs were prepared to save themselves further losses by selling THE TIMES to anybody who would pay the price. As it turned out, only one purchaser was willing to pay the $1,000,000 they asked for nothing but the paper's name and good-will—a company hastily organized by the editors of the paper, with all the money they had themselves and all they could get from their friends, to prevent an institution of great and honorable tradition from falling into unworthy hands. The company thus established, under the presidency of Charles R. Miller, editor of THE TIMES since 1883, never had a fair chance to get started. Almost at once the panic of 1893 struck a paper which had no working capital, and the only marvel is that the organization managed to keep going for three years longer.

By the Spring of 1896 the circulation of THE TIMES had dwindled to 9,000 (the paper was printing 19,000 copies a day, but more than one-half of them were coming back unsold); it had outstanding obligations of $300,000, and was losing $1,000 a day. Mr. Miller, a brilliant scholar, thinker and stylist, but no business man, who would never have tried to be anything but an editor except under the pressure of necessity, had endeavored to interest other New York editors and newspaper managers in the rescue of THE TIMES, but these men who were on the spot, who knew all the details of the situation, were of the unanimous opinion that it could not be done. A plan of reorganization—involving, of course, the raising of more money to be thrown into what began to look like a bottomless pit—was being formulated by Charles R. Flint and Spencer Trask, already heavily involved in the Times Company; but it was generally recognized that what the plan needed was a man to work it, and every man in New York who might have been supposed to see in THE TIMES the opportunity of his life had declared the thing was impossible.

A Momentous Interview.

In this situation the young publisher from Chattanooga came to town, and through Alloway arranged an interview with the editor and president of THE TIMES. Mr. Miller, hard driven and worried, had so little hope of finding a solution for his troubles in this encounter that he arranged for a meeting at his home, and decided to squeeze it in between dinner and a trip to the theatre on which he had promised to take his wife and children to forget the troubles that THE TIMES had brought down on their heads. But it needed only a few minutes to make it clear to the editor that, as Fraser Bond puts it in his life of Miller, this small-town newspaper man had forgotten more about the business than most metropolitan executives ever knew. Theatre time arrived and Mr. Miller told his family to go on, that he would join them later. But he never did join them; they came home after the play to find him still deep in discussion with Mr. Ochs; and when the two men parted after midnight Mr. Miller was convinced that THE TIMES had found the man.

Meeting Mr. Flint and Mr. Trask the next day, Mr. Ochs impressed them so favorably that he was invited to join their syndicate. He was compelled to decline, for their plan would have required him to invest more money than he had or would have cared to try to borrow. Mr. Flint then proposed that if the plan were carried out Mr. Ochs should become the manager of the paper. He mentioned a salary of

(continued)

$50,000 a year—a staggering amount for a man from Chattanooga. But Mr. Ochs had decided that he could not rescue THE TIMES unless he owned and controlled it. The Flint-Trask project thereupon collapsed, and another group of stockholders came forward with a proposal to consolidate THE TIMES with The Recorder, another daily newspaper then also in difficulties and which went out of existence the same year. But Mr. Miller and his associate editor, Edward Cary, felt sure that Mr. Ochs could save the paper as an independent publication if he only had a little time. They therefore obtained the appointment of a receiver, who kept THE TIMES going while Mr. Ochs worked out his own plan, obtained the approval of stockholders and creditors and raised the needed funds.

Takes Over The Times.

Now at last his service as greeter and entertainer of distinguished visitors to Chattanooga bore fruit. An unknown young man from a small city, however sound his plans and heartening his enthusiasm, might have had some trouble persuading wary creditors that he could do what all the newspaper executives in New York had pronounced impossible. But, headed by a letter from President Cleveland, the Chattanooga publisher was able to produce a mass of recommendations from men whose names meant something in New York. President Cleveland's letter, in his own handwriting, said of Mr. Ochs:

* * * "In your management of The Chattanooga Times you have demonstrated such a faithful adherence to Democratic principles and have so bravely supported the ideas and policies which tend to the safety of our country as well as our party, that I should be glad to see you in a larger sphere of usefulness."

With such references behind him, and with the soundness of his own ideas to prove that the testimonials were not perfunctory, Mr. Ochs managed to gain acceptance of his own plan for the reorganization of THE TIMES, which was transferred to him on Aug. 18, 1896.

The new plan was briefly this: The New York Times Company was organized with 10,000 shares of capital stock and a bond issue of $500,000. Two thousand shares of stock were exchanged for the shares of the old company on a one-for-five basis; holders of the old company's notes received in exchange bonds of the new company, dollar for dollar, and $200,000 worth of bonds were sold at par to provide working capital. (The new publisher discovered when he took charge that the paper had about $100,000 worth of unfunded obligations, so half of that working capital was eaten up before Mr. Ochs got started.) As a needed incentive, each purchaser of a thousand-dollar bond got fifteen shares of stock with it; and Mr. Ochs himself, with all the money he had and all he could borrow—most of it was borrowed—bought $75,000 worth of bonds, carrying with them 1,125 shares of stock. Of the rest of the stock, 3,876 shares, just enough to make an absolute majority, were put into escrow, to be delivered to the publisher whenever the paper had paid its way for three consecutive years. His control, however, was to be absolute from the first.

This, of course, was a gigantic gamble: but it was a gamble in which nobody but the purchasers of bonds for cash stood to lose anything which was not hopelessly lost already; and of these bonds the new publisher had bought nearly half. The rest were purchased mainly by capitalists who considered them a good if speculative investment, but would not have been seriously discommoded if the venture had failed. Almost the only man who stood to lose much, in other words, was Adolph S. Ochs. He had mortgaged his achievements of the past and his prospects of the future; but if he won, everybody else would win with him.

Competes With Yellow Press.

At the moment it seemed almost incredible that he could win; he had bought THE TIMES with $75,000 and his abilities, but all he had bought was a great name (of late somewhat shopworn) and a deficit. Dominating New York journalism of the period were The Herald, The World and The (morning) Journal, now The American; the former with an excellent and costly foreign service which THE TIMES could not hope to rival for years, the latter two wildly sensational, according to the ideas of that day, with immense circulations built up at a price of 1 cent, while the other morning papers, THE TIMES included, sold for 3 cents.

It is evident in retrospect, as it was clear to Mr. Ochs at the time, that to have imitated any of these successful competitors would have been suicidal; but he would not have done it anyway. There was only one sort of paper that he knew how to or cared to publish, the sort of paper The Chattanooga Times had been ever since he took it over, and the sort of paper THE NEW YORK TIMES had been in the best days of Raymond and Jones. His salutatory announcement on Aug. 19, 1896 (published in full elsewhere in this issue), promised "to conduct a high-standard newspaper, clean, dignified and trustworthy," for "thoughtful, pure-minded people." Impartial news was promised and the opening of a forum for opinion; and the continuation of the editorial policies which the paper had previously advocated, with Mr. Miller still in the editor's chair. Despite the prosperity of the "yellows" Mr. Ochs believed that there was still a public for the sort of paper THE TIMES had been in its best days, and he meant to seek that public out.

His influence was instantly apparent in the news columns of THE TIMES, which in the late unhappy days had made room for items that were free publicity rather than news, and had injected some editorial bias into news reporting, which the new publisher promptly stopped. Columns of dull matter left in from mere tradition were dropped from the paper, and the policy of printing news for "thoughtful, pure-minded people" was emphasized, as against the sensationalism of The World and The Journal, by the adoption on Oct. 25, 1896, of the motto "All the News That's Fit to Print," which THE TIMES carries to this day. This definition of THE TIMES's purpose was Mr. Ochs's own; it has been much criticized, but the criticisms deal usually with the phraseology rather than with its practical interpretation, and the phraseology was simply an emphatic announcement that THE TIMES was not and would not be what the nineties called a yellow newspaper. In place of the comic supplements of the yellows THE TIMES soon offered a pictorial Sunday magazine; and a few months after Mr. Ochs took charge the Saturday Review of Books, later shifted to the Sunday issue, became a permanent feature of the paper. Letters to the editor controverting the paper's editorial policy were admitted to the rejuvenated TIMES on a scale not previously known. THE TIMES of 1896, smaller and simpler, as was necessitated by its constricted resources and by the less advanced newspaper technology of the period, was essentially THE TIMES of today.

Road to Success a Hard One.

The new paper found favor; in the first year of Mr. Ochs's proprietorship the circulation more than doubled, and the deficit, which had been $1,000 a day when he took charge, averaged less than a fifth of that at the end of the year. But there was still a deficit; and after the years of prosperity in Chattanooga the publisher had been suddenly flung back to the conditions of his beginnings as a newspaper proprietor when each week's payroll was a problem. All the other prominent papers in New York had millions behind them; Mr. Ochs had nothing, and his personal credit had been strained to what seemed at the time the uttermost in obtaining the money to buy the paper. It turned out to be capable of extensions, because there were men in New York who began to realize what he was doing with THE TIMES, and to see that the paper was a good commercial risk. But it was years before that problem was definitely a thing of the past; and it was years before some of the men whose investments in THE TIMES, old and new, Mr. Ochs was saving for them began to realize how fully he deserved their trust.

Some of them knew it from the first; the faith inspired in Mr. Miller at that first interview endured, and personal friendship came to reinforce it. Another man whose confidence in and affection for the new publisher proved of immense value was Colonel Marcellus Hartley, a member of the reorganization committee, who did perhaps more than any one else to teach the young man from Tennessee his way around New York and the technique of dealing with New Yorkers.

If Mr. Ochs's way was pretty hard in the first years, it was made hard partly by his own principles. The volume of advertising in THE TIMES did not increase as fast as the increase in circulation warranted, because the new publisher had brought to New York not only some novel ideas about the treatment of news but an unusually rigorous conscience about advertising. Certain types of objectionable advertising that were commonly carried in the papers of the nineties were excluded from THE TIMES from the first, and a censorship system was established to investigate all offered advertising in which there was suspicion of fraud and to exclude questionable matter. In Mr. Ochs's opinion all good and honest advertising was in its way news, and he regarded his paper—editorial columns, news columns, advertising columns—as all of one piece.

Big Tammany Offer Rejected.

Furthermore, he was alert from the first to reject advertising which seemed to have strings to it. A notable instance occurred in his first year in New York when the city government (then as usual under Tammany control) offered all its regular advertising to THE TIMES. This amounted to $150,000 a year—a sum sufficient to insure success to Mr. Ochs's venture, at a time when it seemed highly probable that otherwise it would end in disaster. Furthermore, THE TIMES was assured that the offer was not expected by the Tammany leaders to change THE TIMES's customary attitude toward that organization; it was made simply because they felt that it was a good idea to support a conservative Democratic paper in New York in the general interest of the party.

Nevertheless, the offer was refused. It was Mr. Ochs's opinion that regardless of the effect such a contribution to a paper of small circulation and dubious stability might have on the staff, it would be taken by the general public as proof that THE TIMES had been bought by Tammany, and that the paper could not afford for a moment to let that belief, however unfounded, be spread abroad. Moreover, he wished to avoid that subtle and almost unrealized influence which Tammany might wield by the mere threat of withdrawing its advertising once the paper had adjusted itself to that much-needed revenue. A similar feeling led him four years later to reject the proposal of the Republican National Committee to buy a million copies (at a time when the paper's circulation was little more than 80,000) of an issue containing an especially cogent editorial supporting the Republicans on the national issues of 1900.

The early years were frequently enlivened by controversies with advertisers who thought they were buying more than advertising space. To one such gentleman, who wanted certain guarantees from the management of THE TIMES about its advertising policies, Mr. Ochs wrote:

"You must excuse me from discussing with you the policy of THE NEW YORK TIMES. That is a subject we do not care to discuss with an advertiser. * * * We are seeking to secure the good-will and confidence of intelligent, discriminating newspaper readers. The advertiser is a secondary consideration. * * * If your advertisement remains out of THE NEW YORK TIMES until you have some assurance, other than the paper as it appears every day, as to the policy of the publisher, THE TIMES so long as it is under its present management will endeavor to get along without your business."

In the course of time the advertiser in question discovered, as did others who raised similar issues, that THE TIMES could get along without him better than he could get along without THE TIMES, and he returned with the understanding that what he bought was space in the paper and no more. These advertising policies, like the policy in treating news which Mr. Ochs announced in 1896 and followed ever afterward, are now the commonplace practice of all respectable newspapers. But in the nineties they were not commonplace, and newspapers then and now counted respectable did not always adhere to them—until Mr. Ochs had demonstrated that it was possible to publish a paper of those principles, and make it pay.

Two Alarming Setbacks.

Despite what many practical newspaper men of the nineties must have regarded as the handicaps of honesty and dignity, THE TIMES was steadily, though slowly, going ahead in circulation and advertising. But in Mr. Ochs's first two years came two external calamities, each of which in turn all but ruined the new venture before it was fairly started. In 1897 the old United Press, which most of the New York papers had been supporting at heavy cost, collapsed. Mr. Ochs, whose Chattanooga Times was a member of The Western Associated Press, immediately applied for membership in that organization for THE NEW YORK TIMES, as did the other New York papers. The World had previously been the only member of The Associated Press in New York, and Joseph Pulitzer had the power of veto over new applicants in the city. He readily agreed to admit The Sun, The Herald and The Tribune; but at first he would not have The Associated Press service extended to THE TIMES. The paper was dying, he said, and there was no use in prolonging the agony. Refusal of Associated Press service at a period when THE TIMES could afford very little special correspondence would have ruined the paper; but eventually Mr. Pulitzer was persuaded to let it come into The Associated Press with a Class B non-voting membership which, though it carried a derogatory implication with it, did give THE TIMES The Associated Press news.

A few years later The Associated Press had to be reorganized under a New York charter; and Mr. Ochs, whose paper could no longer be stigmatized as "moribund," became a full member, a director and member of the executive committee. He held these offices for the rest of his life, and was one of the three or four men who practically made The Associated Press of today.

The second and more disastrous external event was the war with Spain. It was largely made by the newspapers, and was perhaps the greatest opportunity for newspaper showmanship that has ever been offered. The immense expenditures for staff writers, staff artists, special dispatch boats and cable tolls in which the other New York papers competed were beyond the capacity of THE TIMES; it had to be content with The Associated Press news, supplemented by a little mail correspondence, and consequently could not hope to share in the fantastic rise in circulation which partially compensated some of its more prosperous rivals for the money they poured out. But, inevitably, THE TIMES lost advertising when the other papers did; and a loss that the Hearst, Pulitzer, Reid and Bennett fortunes could bear threatened to be fatal to the publisher of THE TIMES, who had used up his meager working capital and had absolutely nothing else.

The deficit in Mr. Ochs's second year was $78,000—larger than in the first year; the circulation had been pushed up to 25,000, but the advertising linage of 1898 showed only a 10 per cent gain over 1896. Something had to be done. Mr. Ochs was advised to raise the price of the paper from 3 cents to 5 cents a copy, on the theory that people who wanted his kind of paper would as soon pay 5 cents for it as 3. To the astonishment of every one, Mr. Ochs proposed instead to cut the price to 1 cent.

Faith in Public Vindicated.

This was to prove one of the most brilliant of his inspirations; but it had behind it the solid faith of a lifetime—the faith that there was a public for the only kind of paper Mr. Ochs could or would publish, and a larger public than THE TIMES then enjoyed. Mr. Ochs believed that there were many people in the city who bought the "yellow journals" only because they cost a third as much as the other papers, and that they would buy a different sort of paper if they could get it for the same price. He was well aware that the 1-cent price was regarded as the badge of the yellow press, and that some people would suppose, when THE TIMES went to that price, that it was going to that manner, too; he knew that there would be—as indeed at first there were—suspicions that some outside interest had subsidized the paper. His only defense against these suspicions would have to be the paper as it appeared every day; and he had faith that people who could now get for 1 cent the same kind of paper that they had formerly paid 3 cents for would realize that the suspicions were baseless.

They did. Despite the universal belief among New York newspaper men (outside THE TIMES) that the cut in price was the beginning of the end, it was in fact the beginning of victory. The circulation of the paper instantly began to leap; the public for that kind of paper at a lower price, which Mr. Ochs alone had discerned, was actually there. A year after the change the circulation of THE TIMES had trebled, rising from 25,000 to 76,000, and except for a brief recession after the World War it has been rising ever since, even though in 1918, when all newspapers had to face increased production costs, the price per copy was raised to 2 cents. Mr. Ochs's third year as publisher showed a profit of $50,000, and from then on the success of THE TIMES was assured. So obvious was this that the reorganization committee of 1896, which was to continue until the paper was firmly on its feet, was dissolved at the end of the sec-

(continued)

ond year. The original agreement had stipulated that the 3,876 shares held in escrow should be turned over to Mr. Ochs when he had made the paper pay for three successive years. On July 1, 1900, he had fulfilled this condition and became the owner of a majority stock interest in THE TIMES, which he retained ever afterward, with some increase.

Growth Financed With Profits.

The great fight of Mr. Ochs's life was won, therefore, by 1900, and he won it by himself. Other men, before and afterward, made great contributions to the paper, the value of which he was always the first to acknowledge. But he was the man who (as E. A. Bradford, a veteran of the editorial staff, put it) "found the paper on the rocks and turned them into foundation stones." Another editorial veteran, F. J. Mortimer, amplified this a little:

"The rest of the paper, plant and men, was just the same the day before he took command and the day afterward. He was the only difference; and from the moment he came in, a paper that had been steadily going down turned right around and started going up."

That it kept on going up was due very largely, in Mr. Ochs's opinion, to the fact that most of the profits were plowed back into the business—plowed back, needless to say, in a wise and productive fashion. THE TIMES paid its way out of its own earnings. On Mr. Ochs's twenty-fifth anniversary, Aug. 18, 1921, he announced that the gross income of the paper for that quarter century had been about $100,000,000, of which only $3,750,000—an average of $125,000 a year—had been withdrawn as dividends. The rest of the profits had gone into financing the growth of the paper.

The story of Adolph S. Ochs during those years was the story of THE NEW YORK TIMES. The two are inseparably woven. He had already laid down his fundamental code of integrity, soundness and completeness, and from this he never varied. But new inventions, new ideas and the broadening horizon of world events made necessary a constantly widening interpretation of "All the News That's Fit to Print." As THE TIMES grew, Mr. Ochs grew with it, seizing upon every improvement in technique that would enable his paper to get the news more quickly and more fully and to print it and get it to the reader in the best possible form and with the least possible lapse of time. The development of THE TIMES carried the double threads of constantly improved newspaper making and of world-shaking events which put an unprecedented strain upon every facility a newspaper had.

An account of the mechanical improvements in the production of THE TIMES since Mr. Ochs took over the paper would be a long story in itself. In 1896 THE TIMES was still being published on Park Row, in a building which at its completion eight years earlier had been regarded as the last word in newspaper housing. With the paper's growing prosperity this building became too small. Realizing the northward drift of business and population, Mr. Ochs resolved to build in what is now known as Times Square, then a decidedly second-rate neighborhood. The design chosen for this structure, which is still one of New York's landmarks, was derived from the celebrated Giotto Campanile at Florence, and it was regarded as one of the architectural triumphs of its decade. Pressrooms and editorial rooms were newly equipped and enlarged, and in January, 1905, the paper was moved uptown without missing an edition.

New Quarters Soon Outgrown.

Perhaps nothing so dramatically indicates the growth of THE TIMES during this period as does the fact that this spacious building, planned with all the foresight that proprietor, architect and staff possessed, became too small in exactly seven years. THE TIMES grew out of its quarters, then and afterward, somewhat as a healthy boy grows out of his clothes. From the Times Building, which still bears that name, the paper migrated, in 1913, to the Times Annex at 229 West Forty-third Street, just off the square. In 1924 and again in 1931 additions had to be made to the Annex. In each case Mr. Ochs took pride in erecting a dignified, appropriate and beautiful building.

Meanwhile the development of rotogravure made necessary a separate plant for that process, constructed at 636 West Forty-fourth Street in 1925. A new building was erected in Brooklyn in 1931 to print the paper's Brooklyn and Queens edition. The processes of setting type, of stereotyping and of printing were continually being improved, and THE TIMES, under Mr. Ochs's direction, never lagged in taking advantage of each new improvement. Mr. Ochs, who had set type by hand and had done some of his first printing on a hand-operated press, took a personal interest in each forward step in the mechanical department. In becoming a newspaper proprietor he took pride in not ceasing to be a printer—and a good one.

In 1926 he found it necessary to become, by proxy, a papermaker as well as a printer. In that year THE TIMES became a large stockholder in the Spruce Falls Power and Paper Company, with holdings of approximately 5,000 square miles of timber rights in Northern Ontario, and subsequently one of the greatest papermaking plants in the world was erected by the company at Kapuskasing, Ont. From this mighty plant comes now all of the newsprint used by THE TIMES.

The mechanics of communication were always important in Mr. Ochs's eyes. He was early interested in Marconi's experiments with the wireless, and arranged with Marconi, in cooperation with The London Times, for the first regular transatlantic wireless news service in 1907. For a time most of THE TIMES's European news was transmitted in this fashion. Mr. Ochs was also a pioneer enthusiast for aviation, encouraged some of the first cross-country flights and made use of airplanes for carrying photographs and delivering papers.

He saw, too, that improved means of communication and higher speed presses would be of little value without a well-organized world-wide news service, and this he set out to get, just as he had earlier done on a smaller scale in Chattanooga. In 1901 he arranged with The London Times for an exchange of services which gave him the dispatches of that paper from all parts of the earth. It was this cooperation that gave THE TIMES the first wireless account of a naval battle—that sent by Captain Lionel James from a dispatch boat 150 miles at sea during the encounter between the Russian and Japanese fleets in 1904. Mr. Ochs had a keen interest in exploration, both for its own sake and for its value as news, and showed it in practically every expedition of importance from Peary's journey to the North Pole to Admiral Byrd's flight over the South Pole and afterward. He realized, too, the value of scientific news of all kinds, and THE TIMES gave much space to it, especially after the World War. But complete presentation of all news worth printing, whether routine or otherwise, continued to be his ideal.

The World War was a severe test not only of a paper's ability to get and print the news, but of its editorial soundness and of the impartiality of its news columns. Editorially, THE TIMES decided that the German Government was in the wrong. In the news columns and in the Sunday editions it aimed to present not only all the actual events of the war without bias, but also to give every point of view a chance for expression. Mr. Ochs took it as a tribute to the success of this latter policy that THE TIMES was accused by German sympathizers of favoring the Allies and by allied sympathizers of favoring Germany. THE TIMES organized its European news service so thoroughly that it sometimes published more special foreign dispatches than all other American newspapers combined. Of particular value to students of the war was its practice of printing all important documents in full, no matter what their length.

At the end of the war Mr. Ochs had the satisfaction of knowing that his newspaper had reached a peak of prestige and prosperity which in the earlier years he had hardly dared dream of. In June, 1918 THE TIMES had received the first award of the Pulitzer Gold Medal for "disinterested and meritorious service" for publishing in full so many official reports, documents and speeches by European statesmen relating to the progress and conduct of the war. Advertising, circulation and the size of the paper had expanded greatly, though the records of 1918 were to be far surpassed in later years. Mr. Ochs was not the man to take this success as a purely personal triumph, and he was generous in his appreciation of the men who had worked with him to bring it about. His material success probably meant less to him than the demonstration that his ideals of journalism and his faith in the fundamental decency of human nature were sound.

In Fight for World Peace.

The post-war period did nothing to shake either his ideals or his faith, though it culminated in the depression of 1929. Editorially THE TIMES threw itself into the fight to bring about world peace through the League of Nations just as it had fought for the same end in a different way during the war. The post-war news was just as important and almost as exciting as that of the war itself, and THE TIMES expanded its news-gathering network in Europe and all over the world. It continued to print important documents in full, beginning with the full text of the Versailles treaty, which it was the first paper in the world to publish completely. It retained its interest in science and exploration.

It adhered to its old policy of presenting the news without bias. Its success in this field was illustrated in 1932 when Walter Duranty, THE TIMES correspondent in Moscow, received the Pulitzer Prize. Editorially THE TIMES had as little sympathy as a newspaper could have with the ideas and policies of the Soviet Government, yet it was able, through Mr. Duranty, to give the news of the Communist experiment so impartially that it gained the confidence of readers of all shades of opinion. In May, 1930, THE TIMES received the first award of the medal of the University of Missouri School of Journalism "for distinguished service in journalism."

The success of THE TIMES might have suggested to another man than Mr. Ochs the possibility of a chain of newspapers based on the same idea, which, as it always seemed to him, would work not only in Chattanooga and New York but in any other American city. In 1899 Mr. Ochs did contemplate buying The New York Telegram, then owned by James Gordon Bennett. Later, in 1901 and 1902, he bought The Philadelphia Times and Ledger and amalgamated them, his brother, the late George W. Ochs Oakes (who took the added name of Oakes in 1917), becoming editor. In 1913 Mr. Ochs sold The Ledger to Cyrus H. K. Curtis. In 1918 he had almost completed arrangements to buy The Herald and The Telegram when the death of Mr. Bennett put an end to the negotiations. In the end Mr. Ochs came to regard the management of THE NEW YORK TIMES, with its growing circulation, not only in New York but throughout the world, as a big enough job for any man. As related but independent enterprises, however, he established The Annalist, a weekly financial review; Current History, a monthly survey of world affairs, long edited by George W. Ochs Oakes, and the Midweek Pictorial, an illustrated review of the week's news. As component parts of THE TIMES he developed the weekly Book Review, THE TIMES Magazine and the Sunday feature section.

Steady Rise in Circulation.

The steady growth of the paper is reflected in the circulation statistics over a period of years. The figures by two-year periods from 1896 to 1934 are as follows:

	Weekday.	Sunday.
1896	21,516	22,000
1898	25,726	34,041
1900	82,106	39,204
1902	100,738	48,354
1904	109,770	46,991
1906	124,267	59,511
1908	158,692	86,779
1910	178,708	113,325
1912	220,139	158,539
1914	270,113	231,409
1916*	327,711	376,933
1918*	339,238	434,157
1920*	327,275	499,924
1922*	344,596	542,039
1924*	345,149	576,321
1926*	356,471	610,041
1928*	405,707	700,925
1930*	437,577	757,028
1932*	467,296	780,470
1934*	466,470	716,135

*Averages as reported to Postoffice Department.

Mr. Ochs often spoke of this circulation growth as "a vindication of the newspaper reader," in that it proved that there was a public interested in a clean, dignified newspaper. There was nothing perfunctory in his relation to anything that THE TIMES did. He was interested in every activity as an exemplification of the ideals that he, as a publisher, was trying to carry out. He took a similar interest in the business policies of the paper, a field in which he was just as much at home as in the news and editorial departments. In his eyes THE TIMES was a unified enterprise, with operating distinctions between the different departments, but with no difference as to fundamental principles among them. Truth in advertising was as important to him as truth in the news columns and integrity in the editorial columns, as he proved again and again, at whatever sacrifice of revenue. THE TIMES's censorship of advertising set a standard for American journalism. In the field of circulation Mr. Ochs never had any sympathy with artificial devices to bring in new readers. He relied on the paper itself to be its own circulation-getter, and the circulation department did its work without any offer of premiums or other special inducements.

Mr. Ochs made much of his conception of THE NEW YORK TIMES as the accepted newspaper of record. It was the obligation of a newspaper, he thought, to present a complete record of its time. An important and logical part of this conception was the inauguration, in 1913, of THE NEW YORK TIMES INDEX, listing and cross-referencing every news item in THE TIMES's columns. In 1927, to make the record in its files imperishable, THE TIMES began printing each day a limited edition upon pure rag paper stock for indefinite preservation in bound files.

The personality of Mr. Ochs dominated his newspaper. Probably few other journals have ever reflected the personality of their publishers more definitely and completely than THE TIMES has Mr. Ochs's—but in a different way from that generally associated with such a reflection. He placed an imprint of character upon the organization. He did not permit THE TIMES to exploit himself, his personal interests, antipathies or likes, or to swerve in the slightest degree because of his own opinions from the balance of impartial news presentation. His name rarely appeared in its columns.

Mr. Ochs believed that a single authority should control and direct a newspaper. He thought that committee management was fatal, ineffective. But though he was supreme he welcomed the frank expression of opinions contrary to his own. He once said that one of the most valuable men on his staff was one who rarely agreed with him. Mr. Ochs always could count upon this man for a strong, reasoned statement of the other point of view.

Pioneer in Many Ways.

Mr. Ochs's eager, active mind, devoting itself constantly to THE TIMES, was generally so far in advance of others that some of his associates felt their task was to serve as a brake upon his audacity.

Generally he was looked upon as a conservative. Yet it was he who pioneered in many fields of newspaper building. He was the first to bring rotogravure printing for newspaper picture sections to the United States. He looked upon this beautiful process of printing as the best means of presenting news in pictures to readers. THE TIMES rotogravure section has not shown oddities and notorious persons, but has accepted its task as gathering the important news of the world in pictures. THE TIMES's own Wide World Photo Service, with bureaus and correspondents all over the world, for the purpose of assembling the best news pictures, was Mr. Ochs's idea of what such a department of a newspaper should be.

Again Mr. Ochs was a pioneer in the improvement of newspaper printing. He developed the idea of THE TIMES's typographical standards, which forbade display advertisements to use unlimited areas of crude blacks in type or illustration of bizarre arrangements of type—a forward step now adopted by more than a score of other important newspapers.

Mr. Ochs had a habit of making friendly and unostentatious tours of the building, often with some distinguished visitor. His use of power had nothing of arbitrariness; rather was it exerted as an influence. The editorial page, for instance, commanded his keenest interest, and when at the office he was accustomed to interrupt his executive duties at noon each day to preside over the editorial conference which argued out and decided on the editorials for the following issue. In consonance with his general theory of newspaper policy he believed that an editorial page should be temperate in statement and should recognize that there is usually something to be said on both sides of a question. Coming up from Chattanooga he had described himself as a conservative Democrat, a term which had some meaning in Grover Cleveland's day. Mr. Ochs had a whole-hearted admiration for Woodrow Wilson, as he had had for Cleveland. But his Democratic principles did not prevent him giving support to the President of whatever political faith so long as the administration policies warranted it.

Consistently Broad-Minded.

In this and other matters of policy the editorial page was a reflection of Mr. Ochs's personality. Naturally he did not bring to THE TIMES editorial writers who were not in sympathy with its general principles; he did not believe that it would be fair to the writers or to THE TIMES to do so. Yet

(continued)

THE TIMES editorial staff under Mr. Ochs's direction had room not only for the full freedom of the individual writer's conscience, but for a considerable variety of temperament and opinion. On points not involving his fundamental principles Mr. Ochs was always ready to listen to argument; in fact, he enjoyed the clash of opinions. On certain issues which he felt keenly he did not yield, but even then no man ever had to write against his own convictions. The power of Adolph S. Ochs was not that of the money which had come to him, but of his personality and his ideas. To THE TIMES he was more than a proprietor; he was what he had been to Foreman Collins of The Knoxville Chronicle—"a necessity, hard to part with."

The least pretentious of men, he refused to make a mystery of his own success. The principles he had followed seemed to him self-evident, and he believed that they would have the same results if they were followed anywhere else. To a newspaper man who observed in later years that Mr. Ochs had come to New York and taught New York journalists something new he remarked that he had only reminded them of something they had forgotten. Speaking at the convention of the National Editorial Association in 1916 he said that he had practiced no new journalism in New York—only the old journalism, the kind that succeeded best in small towns. The policy of having no policy except to be as right as you know how—this had been his sole admonition to a new editor of his Chattanooga paper—was what he had followed in Chattanooga and in New York as well. It means that clear, honest thinking, not expediency or partisanship, dictated the editorial decisions.

He seemed hardly aware that high principles, though they make success a public good instead of a public evil, do not guarantee success; and that his own achievement was due not only to the ideas and ideals which he cherished, but to his boundless energy, his supreme confidence, his willingness to stake everything on what he believed to be right and sound, and the confidence he inspired in other men. He had the qualities of a born leader. He had the rare ability, as he showed in 1896, to win victories with a defeated and discouraged army.

Paper's Leader to the End.

Mr. Ochs continued to direct THE TIMES all his life, keeping in close touch by telephone or cable whenever he was away from the office. As one of his subordinates testified before a Senate committee which once had some suspicions of absentee influence on THE TIMES, he was, when in town, "there every day." His town house was for many years at 308 West Seventy-fifth Street, until in the Fall of 1931 he bought an estate in White Plains. During the war Mr. Ochs purchased the country seat of George Foster Peabody, Abenia, on Lake George, and there used to spend his Summers in a colony where he had many friendships and where he could enjoy a daily game of not very laborious or too serious golf; but even during the Summer absences at the lake he was in communication with THE TIMES by telephone, morning, afternoon and evening. In his later years he traveled in Europe more frequently than he had done before the war, became acquainted with virtually all the leaders of politics and public opinion, and devoted himself with all his private energies as well as those of his paper to the endeavor to smooth out misunderstandings and promote a better relation between Europe and the United States.

The publishing of THE TIMES was his avocation and his hobby as well as his vocation. He put into it the best that he had to give to his fellow-men, with a high seriousness and an unremitting sense of responsibility. He was a religious man in his daily work as well as outside of it, and many of his statements bore testimony thereto. Not only by tradition but by conviction he was a firm adherent of the reformed Jewish faith. He said at the Cleveland convention of the Union of American Hebrew Congregations, in January, 1927:

"What we as a religious people have preserved through centuries of oppression is rapidly becoming the accepted concept of the fatherhood of God and the brotherhood of man. It is called Modernism, but it harks back to the underlying faith of an ancient people, who gave to civilization the Ten Commandments, the prophets and the Psalms."

It was in keeping with his conception of his faith and of his people's place in history that he was opposed to Zionism. In a statement in The American Israelite in 1922 he said that "the greatest heritage of the Jew is his religion. * * * As a distinctive race the Jews need no place in modern civilization." Nevertheless, he was open-minded enough to be immensely impressed, during his travels in Palestine, by the achievements and the spirit of the Zionist pioneers, however much he questioned the ultimate validity of their objective.

Active in Well-Doing.

For many years he was a trustee of Temple Emanu-El in New York, and in 1924 he gave to the congregation in Chattanooga a new building which was named, in honor of his parents, the Julius and Bertha Ochs Memorial Temple. In 1926 he undertook the chairmanship of the committee which succeeded in raising more than $4,000,000 for the Hebrew Union College, which his father-in-law had founded.

One of the principal interests of his later years was the park movement, in which he had been active long before as one of the advocates of the proposal for the Chickamauga National Park, near Chattanooga. It was due chiefly to him that the Lookout Mountain National Park was later instituted to preserve this historic battlefield nearer the city; he was active also in the organization which preserved the battlefield of Saratoga. THE TIMES's consistent endeavors to protect New York City parks against encroachment is, of course, well known. In recognition of this stand the Park Association of New York City awarded its medal to Mr. Ochs in 1931.

Of his contributions to public causes, perhaps the most notable was the gift of $500,000 which he caused THE NEW YORK TIMES to make to finance the preparation of the manuscript of the Dictionary of American Biography, whose successive volumes have met a need of American scholarship which had long been felt. THE NEW YORK TIMES also began in 1928 the preparation and publication of The American Year Book.

Of the numerous foreign decorations which he might have had Mr. Ochs accepted only one—membership in the French Legion of Honor, in which he was later promoted to be Commander. He made an exception of the Legion because it was so universally looked upon as being free from political significance. To the acceptance of academic honors, fittingly bestowed on a publisher who had done his best to make his paper an educational institution, he was more hospitable. He was made an honorary Master of Arts by Yale in 1922, and in subsequent years received honorary doctorates from Columbia University, the University of Chattanooga, New York University, Dartmouth and Lincoln University. In 1927 he received the gold medal of the National Institute of Social Sciences, in 1929 he was one of seven citizens of New York cited for distinguished service by the Chamber of Commerce, and in 1931 he became a member of the American Philosophical Society.

No honor gratified him more, however, than the title of Citizen Emeritus of Chattanooga, which was formally conferred on him in July 1928, at the conclusion of a three-day celebration of his semicentennial as proprietor of The Chattanooga Times. This celebration was organized by the city and county governments and attended by deputations from The Associated Press, the American Newspaper Publishers' Association, the newspaper publishers and the Advertising Club of New York City and the Chamber of Commerce of the State of New York. He always retained an affection for Chattanooga and an interest in its affairs, and the friendships which he had made there as a struggling young man were broken only by death.

Mr. Ochs on a Visit to the Late Thomas A. Edison.

Welfare of the Staff.

Of the welfare of the army of employes required to get out THE TIMES Mr. Ochs was always solicitous. On March 12, 1918, he celebrated his sixtieth birthday by the establishment of group insurance for all employes, increasing the maximum amount on later anniversaries. His quarter-centennial as publisher of THE TIMES was marked by the institution of a system of sick benefits and a retirement pension fund. For Mr. Ochs's unusual thoughtfulness and generosity in individual instances hundreds of THE TIMES staff in both important and humble positions had cause to be grateful. An incident illustrates his unvarying thoughtfulness. Junior employes of THE TIMES receiving less than $18 weekly have a lunch card which permits them to purchase a complete 50-cent lunch for 10 cents. When The Times Annex was enlarged in 1931 it was necessary to close the restaurant for two weeks, and due notice was given. Upon the reopening of the restaurant every employe having a lunch card was surprised to receive, at Mr. Ochs's orders, a check to cover the extra cost of their lunches for the period of closing.

The Hundred Neediest Cases.

A charity which came close to Mr. Ochs's heart and engaged his warm personal interest was the collection of funds, each year at the Christmas season, for "The Hundred Neediest Cases." This feature was inaugurated by him in 1912, when a fund of $3,630 was collected, to be distributed to persons in direst need chosen from lists furnished by the leading charitable organizations of the city. The appeal was and still is made solely through the publication of brief individual narratives in THE TIMES. In this way Mr. Ochs tried to bring home to his readers the poignant facts of destitution and to enlist their cooperation in relieving it. There was no personal solicitation; the contributions were wholly spontaneous, sometimes coming from readers who did not even give their names; and every cent collected went to relieve want, the expense of administration being met by the charitable organizations sending in the lists of cases and the other expenses by THE TIMES. No feature of the paper had more importance in Mr. Ochs's eyes during the Christmas season than this. He followed the campaign closely, even in its details, and rejoiced as the totals mounted.

The number of cases relieved during the first twenty years totaled more than 5,000 and the number of individuals nearly 18,000. For the Christmas season of 1930 the total of gifts was $345,790. In many instances contributions came from persons who were themselves out of work and limited as to funds. Trust funds, gifts given in memory of the dead and repeated contributions from readers who took pride in keeping up the annual totals made "The Hundred Neediest Cases" a notable institution, and its success was a source of real joy to Mr. Ochs.

Monuments He Leaves.

Mr. Ochs leaves behind him two newspapers—he retained his controlling interest in The Chattanooga Times—the building of which occupied nearly all his energies for nearly all the working years of his life. Both were close to his heart. He could not have existed without intimate daily contact with their affairs. Each was created out of next to nothing by his personal efforts, in the face of discouragements which would have defeated most men and of obstacles which seemed insuperable. These newspapers are his monuments, and he would now be willing to be judged by them.

But his greatest monument is invisible—the principle of clean, temperate and impartial presentation of news and of higher standards in advertising. These are now such commonplaces of decent newspaper practice that many newspaper men of today may think they have obtained from time immemorial. But they did not secure a foothold easily or automatically; they did not prevail in New York City until Adolph S. Ochs came to town from Chattanooga and risked everything he had on his faith that not only could such a newspaper be published but that there was a public which wanted it.

Mr. Ochs was more than a publisher. He was a man who had faith in humanity and who backed that faith by all the intelligence, all the energy and all the fighting spirit that was in him.

His Views on Life's Meaning.

In October, 1931, Will Durant, in preparing his book "On the Meaning of Life," asked Mr. Ochs for his views. The following paragraphs are quoted from that book:

Evidently religion does not die; in the vast majority of men it is still a living force for good and ill. I find a sincere note of it in the reply of Adolph Ochs, publisher of that finest achievement in modern journalism, THE NEW YORK TIMES; by this letter I am better able to understand the solid, quiet success of this man in making his paper the most respected and most influential in America without ever catering to the mob.

"New York, Oct. 22, 1931.

"Dear Mr. Durant:

"* * * You ask me what meaning life has for me, what help—if any—religion gives me, what keeps me going, what are the sources of my inspiration and my energy, what is the goal or motive-force of my toil, where I find my consolation and my happiness, where in the last resort my treasure lies.

"To make myself clearly understood, if I were able to do so, would take more time and thought than I can give the matter now. Suffice it for me to say that I inherited good health and sound moral principles; I found pleasure in work that came to my hand and in doing it conscientiously; I found joy and satisfaction in being helpful to my parents and others, and in thus making my life worth while found happiness and consolation. My Jewish home life and religion gave me a spiritual uplift and a sense of responsibility to my subconscious better self—which I think is the God within me, the Unknowable, the Inexplicable. This makes me believe I am more than an animal, and that this life cannot be the end of our spiritual nature.

"Yours faithfully,

"ADOLPH S. OCHS."

More and more it stands out that a man must combine action with thought in order to lead a life that shall have unity and significance. Surely a monument like THE TIMES is meaning enough for one life!

ADOLPH S. OCHS.

Proud Chattanooga's flag has he unfurled
High 'mid the city-banners of the world:
A bit of blue above the crimson dawn
A single star—when all the rest have gone—
Staying to welcome through the Eastern gate
The best that is to be, for his loved State;
A flag upon faith's Lookout Mount to scan
The wider destiny of Western man—
That signals to the youth, below, the way
From out the dark despairs of yesterday
Up past the Smoky Altars, toward the West
In never-halting, never-aging quest.

"All the News That's Fit to Print"

The New York Times

LATE CITY EDITION

Weather: Sunny, mild today. Fair, milder tonight through tomorrow. Temp. range: today 54-33; Saturday 50-31. Full U.S. report on Page 91.

SECTION ONE

VOL. CXIX ... No. 40,986

NEW YORK, SUNDAY, APRIL 12, 1970

60c beyond 50-mile zone from New York City, except Long Island. 75c beyond 200-mile radius. Higher in air delivery cities.

50 CENTS

U.S. RIGHTS PANEL CRITICIZES NIXON ON SCHOOL POLICY

Commission Says His Recent Statement on Integration May Signal a Retreat

A UNANIMOUS REBUTTAL

Study Implies That President Has Not Given Example of 'Courageous Leadership'

By JACK ROSENTHAL
Special to The New York Times

WASHINGTON, April 11—The President's recent policy statement on school desegregation is inadequate, over-cautious and may even signal a major retreat, the Commission on Civil Rights declared today.

In a formal, unanimous rebuttal to the President, the commission said what is needed above all is "the continuing example of courageous moral leadership from the President of the United States."

The report strongly suggested that the commission believes Mr. Nixon has not provided such leadership.

The commission is a six-member independent Federal agency. It has no enforcement powers but has frequently played an outspoken gadfly role and provides a rallying point for civil rights advocates.

Of the six members, who serve at the pleasure of the President, three are Republicans and two are Democrats. The Rev. Thomas M. Hesburgh, president of the University of Notre Dame, an independent, is chairman.

'More Is Necessary'

The commission spoke out today in a 27-page analysis of the complex Presidential statement issued March 24. The commission's language is moderate, but unmistakably critical of most of the statement.

"The President has made it clear to all that his Administration intends to carry out the Supreme Court's mandate of an immediate end to legally sanctioned dual school systems," the commission report said.

"Much more, however, is necessary. The problems of racial isolation in the nation's schools cannot be resolved solely through cautious adherence to a narrow construction of existing case law.

"The commission fears that the President's statement well may have the net effect, though unintentional, of signaling a major departure from the policy of moving toward integrated schools and that open society of which he spoke so well in his statement."

The report disputed the President essentially on three major points—his sharp distinction between de facto and de jure

Continued on Page 27, Column 1

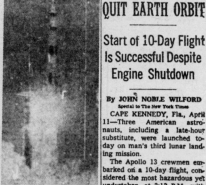

RALLY IN PNOMPENH: Young Cambodians with signs in Khmer, their language, and French, marching yesterday

Associated Press

Judge Bids Defiant Kirk Pay $10,000-a-Day Fine

By MARTIN WALDRON
Special to The New York Times

TAMPA, Fla., April 11—Federal District Judge Ben Krentzman ordered Gov. Claude R. Kirk Jr. today to stop disobeying his school desegregation orders or pay a fine of $10,000 a day.

The judge found the Republican Governor guilty of contempt of court and directed him to begin Monday morning to implement a court-ordered integration plan for the Manatee County public schools.

If the Governor, who has used armed guards to hold physical control of the Manatee school system since Wednesday, certifies by noon Monday that he is complying with the court's orders, no fine will be collected, the judge said. Otherwise, the daily fines will begin, retroactive to today.

Judge Krentzman also found two of Governor Kirk's administrative assistants in contempt and ordered them to pay fines of $1,000 a day under provisions similar to those applying to Mr. Kirk. The two assistants are Lloyd Hagaman, 42 years old, and Robert D. Hoffman, 40.

Both men testified last night that they would obey the Governor rather than the Federal court.

C. A. Butler of Washington, chief of field operations of the United States Marshal Service, said that the judge's orders would soon be served on Governor Kirk in Tallahassee, the state capital.

"The fun and games is over," Mr. Butler said.

The Governor could not be reached for comment. Earlier, he had said he would pay no attention to the judge's findings.

"If he holds me in contempt, he need not plan on collecting any fines. I won't sign the checks," Mr. Kirk said in an interview Thursday.

Last night the Governor and his 70 armed guards vacated the school administration building in Bradenton, county seat of Manatee, but late today, at least one guard was inside the building. He refused to say who he was or whom he worked for.

Judge Krentzman dismissed

Continued on Page 31, Column 1

BUSINESS RENT TAX URGED BY LINDSAY

New Proposal Would Raise $40-Million in Revenue, City Advisers Say

By MAURICE CARROLL

Another tax increase—restructuring the tax on commercial rents to increase city revenue by $40-million—was suggested yesterday by Mayor Lindsay.

Doling out more information from the continuing private discussions in which city and state officials are trying to find money to fill a massive gap in next year's city budget, the Mayor's men disclosed the third Lindsay tax package in three days.

"Our motto is 'A tax a day keeps the doctor away,'" one mayoral aide muttered before officials disclosed the new one.

The latest proposal would make the rates of the commercial occupancy tax more progressive so that those paying rents of $4,000 a year or more would have a sharp increase

Continued on Page 35, Column 1

Cambodians Stage Nationalistic Rally With Martial Tone

By HENRY KAMM
Special to The New York Times

PNOMPENH, Cambodia, April 11—The new leaders of Cambodia staged their first mass rally today in an atmosphere of intense nationalism and martial resolution. The accent was on youth, and the tone was military.

The marching contingents from colleges, schools, ministries and state-owned enterprises carried belligerent posters as they trooped approximately in step into the vast National Stadium and many also carried clubs.

Meanwhile, in the Vietnamese section of floating houses on the Tonle Sap River, residents remained indoors. They would have done so even if the Government had not put them under a 6 P.M.-to-6 A.M. curfew as of last night.

Casualties Listed

Most did not know yet about the curfew, which the Government in an announcement today attributed to an increase in subversive activities by Vietcong sympathizers in Pnompenh, and none seemed to know that at least 89 Vietnamese civilians were killed Thursday night in what was described as a cross-fire occasioned by a Vietcong attack on the vilage of Prasot near the border.

The Government announced today that Vietcong and North Vietnamese forces attacked the village and were repulsed. It listed the casualties as 20

Continued on Page 4, Column 1

U.S. to Tighten Surveillance of Radicals

By JAMES M. NAUGHTON
Special to The New York Times

WASHINGTON, April 11—The Nixon Administration, alarmed by what it regards as a rising tide of radical extremism, is planning to step up surveillance of militant left-wing groups and individuals.

The objective, according to White House officials, is to find out who the potential bomb planters and snipers may be before they endanger others.

Preparations for expanding and improving the domestic intelligence apparatus—informers, undercover agents, wiretaps—were disclosed in a series of interviews with key officials, who requested anonymity.

According to these officials, President Nixon is disturbed by the rash of bombings and bomb scares, courtroom disruptions and reports of small but growing numbers of young people who feel alienated from the American system.

Parallels Are Drawn

On March 12, the same day that bombs exploded in three Manhattan office buildings, Mr. Nixon met over dinner in the White House with Irving Kristol, professor of urban values at New York University.

One aide who attended the dinner said the discussion included attempts to draw parallels between young, middle-class, white Americans who are resorting to violence and the Narodniki—children of the mid-19th century Russian aristocracy who murdered Czar Alexander II, and between militant black nationalists here and Algerian revolutionaries.

Mr. Kristol told the President it was not unrealistic to expect the Latin American resort to political kidnappings to spread soon to Washington. Mr. Kristol confirmed the dinner meeting and commented, "Some of these kids don't know what country this is. They think it's Bolivia.

Some, but not all, of Mr. Nixon's domestic advisers are convinced that the situation is critical. One of the more conservative aides contended, "We are facing the most severe internal security threat this country has seen since the Depression."

The officials have concluded that attempts to bring militants back into society's mainstream are as futile, as one stated it, "as turning off the radio in the middle of a ball game to try to change the score."

The official view is that extreme radicals cannot be won over with welfare, electoral or draft reforms or by White House appeals. "It wouldn't make a bit of difference if the war and racism ended overnight," said a highly placed Nixon assistant. "We're dealing with the criminal mind, with people who have snapped for

Continued on Page 69, Column 1

Truman Greets Guests 25 Years After He Took Over Presidency

By FELIX BELAIR Jr.
Special to The New York Times

INDEPENDENCE, Mo., April 11—Harry S Truman sat in the front parlor of his white Victorian mansion on North Delaware Street today and extended his hand, his wit and his thanks to a dozen distinguished visitors from out of the past.

They came through the wrought-iron gate and up the short walk singly and in pairs—former Ambassador W. Averell Harriman, former Secretary of State Dean Acheson, former Chief Justice Earl Warren, former Treasury Secretary John W. Snyder, former White House Counselor Charles S. Murphy, and others.

They came to pay tribute to the 85-year-old irascible, indomitable man from Independence on the 25th anniversary of his succession to the Presidency. The anniversary is tomorrow.

And from all accounts, they found him full of bounce and good humor, his memory of men and events and his penchant for blunt talk undulled by the passage of time.

The former President rose easily from his upholstered Queen Anne chair to greet each visitor and, preferring to reminisce about old times and politics, he made little of the afflictions of old age.

"My only trouble," he remarked, "is that I've been chased for years by a woman named Anno Domini. But now that the weather is turning warm, I'll be getting back to the morning walks that have

Continued on Page 74, Column 1

NIXON SAID TO CUT HIGH COURT LIST TO THREE JUDGES

Minnesotan Called Leading Candidate—A Nomination Is Expected This Week

By DAVID E. ROSENBAUM
Special to The New York Times

WASHINGTON, April 11—A high Administration official said today that President Nixon had narrowed his search for a new Supreme Court Justice to three Federal judges—Harry A. Blackmun of Minnesota, Edward T. Gignoux of Maine and Alfred T. Goodwin of Oregon.

The source, who has been involved in the decision-making process and who asked that he not be identified, indicated that Judge Blackmun appeared to have the best chance to be nominated. Judge Blackmun was in Washington yesterday.

Other sources said Mr. Nixon planned to disclose his choice by the middle of next week.

'Under Consideration'

At the White House, Ronald L. Ziegler, Mr. Nixon's press secretary, said that "a number of people are under consideration."

Asked specifically about Judge Blackmun, Mr. Ziegler said: "It would be folly for me [to] imply that Judge Blackmun is not under consideration."

Mr. Nixon's first two nominees for the seat left vacant by the resignation of Justice Abe Fortas last year, Judge Clement F. Haynsworth Jr. of South Carolina and Judge G. Harrold Carswell of Florida, were rejected by the Senate.

After Judge Carswell's defeat this week, Mr. Nixon said he would not name another Southerner to the position.

Strict Constructionists

Judge Blackmun sits on the United States Court of Appeals for the Eighth Circuit. Mr. Gignoux and Mr. Goodwin are Federal district judges. Legal experts said here today that each had a record as a "strict constructionist," but that none appeared to be as conservative as Judge Haynsworth or Judge Carswell.

None of the three could be reached for comment today. Judge Goodwin told United Press International last night: "If there is any speculation at all, it is going on somewhere else. But they would have to do a lot of screening of names before anyone was notified."

This week, Federal Bureau of Investigation agents were in the three judges' home cities, apparently checking on their backgrounds.

Indications that Judge Blackmun was the top candidate included his presence in Wash-

Continued on Page 38, Column 1

ASTRONAUTS OFF ON 3D MOON TRIP; LAND WEDNESDAY

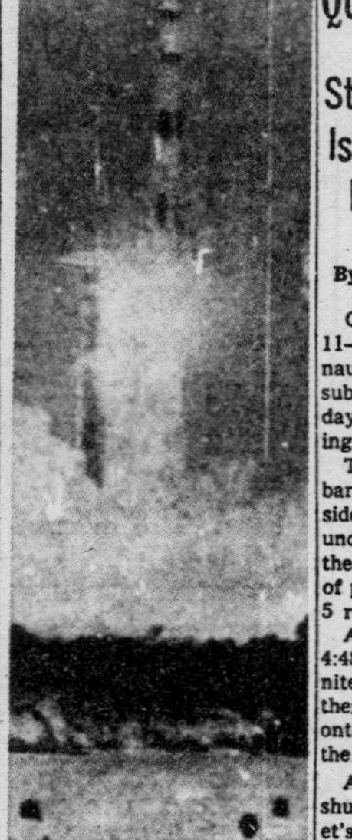

Associated Press

LIFT-OFF: The Saturn 5 rocket carrying the Apollo 13 spacecraft yesterday.

QUIT EARTH ORBIT

Start of 10-Day Flight Is Successful Despite Engine Shutdown

By JOHN NOBLE WILFORD
Special to The New York Times

CAPE KENNEDY, Fla., April 11—Three American astronauts, including a late-hour substitute, were launched today on man's third lunar landing mission.

The Apollo 13 crewmen embarked on a 10-day flight, considered the most hazardous yet undertaken, at 2:13 P.M., with the fiery and thunderous thrust of power from the giant Saturn 5 rocket.

After orbiting earth until 4:48 P.M., the astronauts reignited a rocket engine to boost them out of earth orbit and onto an accurate course toward the moon, 246,500 miles away.

An early and unexplained shutdown of one of the rocket's second-stage engines did not deter the spaceship and its crew—Capt. James A. Lovell Jr. of the Navy, and Fred W. Haise Jr. and John L. Swigert Jr., both civilian astronauts.

Mr. Swigert, a 38-year-old rookie astronaut, was named to the crew a day before the launching, replacing Lieut. Comdr. Thomas K. Mattingly, 2d., who is threatened with the German measles.

Brandt Watches Lift-Off

Captain Lovell, the 42-year-old commander, is making his fourth and final space flight. He and the 36-year-old Mr. Haise plan to land on the ancient hills of Fra Mauro on Wednesday.

"It looks good to be up here again," Captain Lovell said as he looked back at the earth he just left.

Tomorrow, the astronauts are expected to spend a quiet day coasting toward the moon. A 30-minute television transmission from Apollo 13 is scheduled at 8:28 P.M.

Apollo 13 is aiming for a touchdown in a narrow valley on the eastern shore of the moon's Ocean of Storms. The area's rocks and hills are believed to be some of the oldest on the moon, bearing possible clues to the origin of the earth's only natural satellite.

Lift-off came on schedule after a smooth countdown. The skies were clear, and thousands of visitors, including Vice

Continued on Page 61, Column 2

John O'Hara Dead; Novelist Dissected Small-Town Mores

By PAUL L. MONTGOMERY

John O'Hara, the prolific American novelist who took the public poses and the private hells of the small-town rich as his theme, died of a heart attack yesterday morning in his sleep at his country home in Princeton, N. J. He was 65 years old.

Mr. O'Hara died at the secluded French manor house in the woods where he had lived and written since 1953. He spent his days as a country squire, his nights toiling in his study to add to the remarkably long list of hard-boiled stories and novels that began in 1934 with "Appointment in Samarra."

He had recently completed another novel, "The Ewings," scheduled for publication in February, 1971, and was working on a sequel to it. At his death, he had completed 70 pages.

The novelist is survived by

Continued on Page 88, Column 1

Associated Press

ON THEIR WAY: Apollo 13 crew leaving quarters at Cape Kennedy, Fla., yesterday are, from left, Capt. James A. Lovell Jr., commander; John L. Swigert Jr., who replaced Lieut. Comdr. Thomas K. Mattingly 2d, and Fred W. Haise Jr.

Today's Sections

Index to Subjects

John O'Hara, the Novelist, Dies in His Sleep at 65

Continued From Page 1, Col. 7

his third wife, the former Katherine Barnes Bryan; a daughter, Mrs. Dennis J. Holahan of New York; two sisters, Mary O'Hara and Mrs. Robert Fuldner; five brothers, Martin, Eugene, James, Joseph and Thomas, and two grandchildren.

John Henry O'Hara was once asked what he would write about himself if he were a critic. This was his reply:

"Better than anyone else, he told the truth about his time, the first half of the 20th century. He was a professional. He wrote honestly and well."

His novels and stories were part social commentary, part fast-moving fiction, part catalogue of the men and mores of the small, grimy town—his native Pottsville, Pa., in real life, "Gibbsville" in his stories—that was at the center of his work.

Mr. O'Hara was often called the Boswell of the post-Fitzgerald generation, but he disdained scholarly views of his work. "Being a cheap, ordinary guy, I have an instinct for what an ordinary guy likes," he said.

Novels Sold Well

His novels were always successful sellers, and in his later years he made a very good income from his work—estimated at more than $100,000 a year, including rights for many movie and theater adaptions. Except for an 11-year gap when drinking and success kept him from writing any novels at all, he worked steadily and painstakingly on the body of work that reached 36 books at his death.

Mr. O'Hara was born in Pottsville (Pop. 25,000) on Jan. 31, 1905, the oldest of eight children of Dr. Patrick Henry O'Hara and Katherine Delaney. His father was a leading surgeon in the community, and the boy had all the prerequisites of well-off small-town youth.

The boy was brought up as a Roman Catholic. He attended the Fordham Preparatory School and the Keystone State Normal School, and was expelled from both for indiscipline. In 1924, he was graduated from the Niagara Preparatory School in Niagara, N. Y. He had already passed his college entrance examinations.

However, when Dr. O'Hara died, the family fortunes swiftly changed. The prospects of fast cars and chic girls and college at Yale or Princeton were gone. The boy, who had always thought he would be a writer, worked for a time on the local newspaper and then traveled. "I went on the bum," he recalled much later. "I traveled out West, worked on a steamer, took a job in an amusement park."

The thought of writing was always on his mind. He admired the small-town stories of Owen Johnson and Booth Tarkington, and was devoted to the work of F. Scott Fitzgerald. "I was fascinated by the small-town boy in the Ivy League world," he said.

Eventually, Mr. O'Hara came to New York to work on newspapers and magazines, including Time, The New Yorker, and The New York Herald Tribune. He was variously rewrite man, football writer, drama critic and religion reporter. His first short story in The New Yorker appeared in 1928. Mr. O'Hara recalled those days as hard-drinking periods when midnight often mingled imperceptibly with dawn in the speakeasys of the age.

In 1933, he decided to find out if novels were really his calling. He took a room in a Manhattan hotel and, using the

The New York Times

John O'Hara in the study of his home in Princeton, N. J.

bed as a desk, write all night, slept all day, and in the evenings drank coffee in his old barroom haunts. He always said he could not write with liquor in him.

"When I got down to my last $3 I wrote to Harcourt, Brace," he recalled. "They liked the chapters I sent them and paid me $50 a week for six months until I finished it."

The book was "Appointment in Samarra," an instant success when it was published in 1934. The mordant novel, tightly constructed and fast paced, detailed the three-day slide to self-destruction of a young man named Julian English. With tough language and a touch of snobbishness, the work told of the family life and social life, the drinking habits and the sexual habits of Gibbsville's upper-class.

Mr. O'Hara was a meticulous craftsman. He would pore over old newspapers and magazines in search of realistic touches, such as the real estate prices and skirt lengths of the time.

His style was taut and simple, preferring the Anglo-Saxon to the Latinate. His working habits were nocturnal. In his later years in Princeton he would watch a late television movie until 1 A.M., then settle down at the Remington typewriter in his study. He wrote cleanly and rapidly, limiting himself to a single draft without carbon that he sent to his publishers with few changes.

Mr. O'Hara was a broad, gregarious 6-footer, a welcome visitor at any bar. Some of his bouts with liquor are legendary. He began to taper off in 1945, after the death of his friend, the humorist Robert Benchley, and stopped drinking after he suffered a massive stomach hemorrhage in 1953.

After his success with "Appointment in Samarra," Mr. O'Hara fell easily into the life of a bon vivant and Hollywood screen writer. He kept a duplex apartment in New York near "21," his favorite restaurant, and favored fast cars. Out of those experiences came "Pal Joey," a series of sketches about a ne'er-do-well hoofer, and "Butterfield 8," a novel about the seamier side of New York's flashy life.

During the 30's, however, he wrote little except stories of the slick, quick New Yorker variety. In World War II he went off to the Pacific as a war correspondent.

The tide turned again in 1948, when "Rage to Live" was published. He returned once again to the small-town life that had got him started. From that time the output of his typewriter was a torrent, averaging a book a year until his death.

Mr. O'Hara was sensitive about the paucity of awards given to his work, the exceptions being a National Book Award for "Ten North Frederick," an award for his musical play "Pal Joey," and a gold medal of merit from the American Academy of Arts and Letters in 1964.

"It used to hurt never winning an award, but I've never been the pet of intellectuals, the eggheads," he said. "I'm an extremely conscientious writer and I know my trade. When I write a novel, I do a lot of digging. I was okay for good notices when a book came out, but not good enough for an award. It used to hurt quite a bit."

As sensitive as he was to criticism of himself, Mr. O'Hara was not above excoriating his contemporaries in the writing craft. One exception was Ernest Hemingway. On Sept. 10, 1950, The New York Times Book Review published on its first page a review by Mr. O'Hara of the newest Hemingway novel, "Across the River and Into the Trees."

While sparing in his praise of the book—which was roundly rejected by most critics—Mr. O'Hara was unstinting in his praise of Mr. Hemingway as a writer and a man. "The outstanding author since the death of Shakespeare," Mr. O'Hara wrote, "the most important, the outstanding author out of the millions of writers who have lived since 1616."

The review touched off a storm of protest including one letter to The Times in which one writer said: "I assume that the second most 'outstading author since Shakespeare' is John O'Hara."

Mr. O'Hara was married three times. His first marriage, to Helen Ritchio Petit, ended after two years. In 1937, he married Belle Wylie, the mother of his daughter. She died in 1953, and the next year he married Katherine Barnes Bryan.

At his home in North Brooklin, Me., yesterday, E. B. White, the author and long-time writer for The New Yorker, paid tribute to Mr. O'Hara's "terrifically good ear, his gift for the language, his eye for details and his great love for accuracy."

Albert Erskine, a vice president of Random House and Mr. O'Hara's editor since 1955, said:

"I have lost a friend. John O'Hara achieved great popularity but not the honor he deserved. For a long time he had been eligible for all the literary prizes that are available but he received few of them. Some reviewers were always lying in wait for O'Hara. He was a hot-tempered man who would snap back. But the more you got to know him the more you got to like him."

In Beverly Hills, Calif., Bennett Cerf, the co-founder and chairman of Random House, recalled his long association with the novelist. Random House was Mr. O'Hara's publisher for all his books except the first.

"He was one of the most underrated authors in America," said Mr. Cerf. "He belongs right up there with William Faulkner and Ernest Hemingway. I really believe this and have said it over and over."

"John was a thorny guy," the publisher went on. "You never knew when you were offending him. We would fight about something but a few weeks later would forget all about it."

Mr. Cerf recalled that last year, on his 70th birthday, he had a few friends at his home in Mount Kisco, N. Y. "John was very huffy because I didn't invite him," the publisher said. "I told him I didn't want him to go to all the trouble of the trip from Princeton. The next day I received 70 American Beauty roses, one for each year, and I cried with pleasure. That was John O'Hara, and we won't see his like for a long, long time."

Prober of a Town's Soul

O'Hara Cast Cool Eye on Gibbsville, Heartland of His 36 Years of Fiction

By CHRISTOPHER LEHMANN-HAUPT

An Appraisal

To serious-minded critics — few of whom John O'Hara would have counted among his friends—the verdict was in long ago: He would never fulfill the high promise of his first novel, "Appointment in Samarra." What had seemed at first to be a penetrating eye and an uncanny way with fictional dialogue that would carry him to any fictional heights he chose to scale, gradually turned out to be a habit, an easy trick that no one could quite imitate, but which O'Hara himself did not choose to develop profoundly.

But he seemed not to mind. Nor did his audience. For 36 years after the publication of that first book, he churned out novels and short stories as steadily as the seasons changed. And his reading public snatched them up and onto the best-seller list just as regularly. The fictional town of Gibbsville, Pa.—where "Samarra" was set and to which O'Hara returned whenever he was not up in New York with "Pal Joey" or the people of "Butterfield 8"—came to seem as real and familiar as one's own hometown. And if O'Hara's people were too worried about money and sex and status—if the author himself seemed permanently stuck in a small corner of Hemingway country — why that was all right. O'Hara believed in old-fashioned fiction; he told a good story; and his people appealed to the secret snobs and tough guys and social climbers in all of us.

For John O'Hara the act of writing was not the agonizing search for new perceptions or novel modes of reality. It was getting down on paper what he knew best as clearly and economically as he knew how. And doing it was simply part of his day, as routine as the arrival of the commuter train and the highballs before dinner. But there are those who have observed that the writers whose work endures are not the pathfinders and experimenters, but rather those who stake out their own territories and draw them so accurately as to give them lives of their own. If that is so, then John O'Hara's huge body of work may be around much longer than we had predicted.

O'Hara's Published Works

"Appointment in Samarra" (novel), 1934.
"Butterfield 8" (novel), 1935.
"The Doctor's Son, and Other Stories," 1935.
"Hope of Heaven" (stories), 1938.
"Files on Parade," 1939.
"Pal Joey" (novel), 1940.
"Pipe Night" (stories), 1945.
"Here's O'Hara" (3 novels, 20 stories), 1946.
"Hellbox" (stories), 1947.
"Stories of Venial Sin," from "Pipe Night," 1947.
"A Rage to Live" (novel), 1949.
"The Farmers Hotel" (novel), 1951.
"Sweet and Sour" (nonfiction), 1954.
"Ten North Frederick" (novel), 1955.
"The Great Short Stories of John O'Hara," 1956.
"A Family Party" (novella), 1956.
"Selected Short Stories," 1956.
"Three Views of the Novel" (with Irving Stone and MacKinlay Kantor), 1957.
"From the Terrace" (novel), 1958.
"Sermons and Soda-Water," three volumes, 1960.
"Ourselves to Know" (novel), 1960.
"Five Plays," 1961.
"Assembly" (stories), 1961.
"The Cape Cod Lighter" (stories), 1962.
"The Big Laugh" (novel), 1962.
"Elizabeth Appleton" (novel), 1963.
"The Hat on the Bed" (stories), 1963.
"49 Stories," 1963.
"The Horse Knows the Way" (stories), 1964.
"The Lockwood Concern" (novel), 1965.
"My Turn" (newspaper columns), 1966.
"Waiting for Winter" (stories), 1967.
"The Instrument" (novel), 1967.
"And Other Stories," 1968.

"All the News That's Fit to Print"

The New York Times

LATE CITY EDITION

Weather: Fair, very cold today and tonight. Chance of snow tomorrow. Temp. range: today 24-14; Sunday 33-26. Full U.S. report on Page 30.

VOL. CXXIV..No. 42,785

NEW YORK, SUNDAY, MARCH 16, 1975

$1.00 beyond 50-mile zone from New York City, except Long Island. Higher in air delivery cities.

60 CENTS

Portugal's Regime Nationalizes Insurance Companies

Measure Comes 2 Days After Military Ordered Take-Over of Banks

By HENRY GINIGER
Special to The New York Times

LISBON, March 15—Within the last two days, Portugal's new High Council of the Revolution has seized the great bulk of the country's financial power.

It nationalized all insurance companies today, following up the nationalization of banks Thursday.

The council, formed Tuesday night after the failure of what was described as an attempted coup by rightists, continued the country's leftward impetus with a statement declaring that it had been "urgent" to seize control of the country's 35 insurance companies because they controlled huge sums of money that were being used "not for the benefit of the working class but to augment still further the profits of a privileged minority."

[Portugal is considering granting fueling facilities to the Soviet Union's merchant fleet on the island of Madeira, an Information Ministry announcement said.]

Although foreign banks were not included in Thursday's nationalization measure, insurance companies with foreign participation did come under today's decision. However, a distinction was made in the type of control. Administrative commissions were named for

Continued on Page 13, Column 1

United Press International
Antiaircraft guns set up inside presidential palace in Lisbon in wake of coup attempt

Spinola May Have Aided Left With Coup Attempt

Special to The New York Times

LISBON, March 15—Former President António de Spínola, a stanch opponent of the Communists, may have inadvertently bolstered their political fortunes in Portugal, according to an account of an abortive coup attempt last Tuesday.

Leftist officers supported by the Communists are now in control and have nationalized the banks and insurance companies.

Yet, according to the most plausible account now available, they came close to losing power on Tuesday and were saved by premature action of General Spínola that may have defeated the cause of moderation in Portugal. The general fled and is now in South America. [Brazil on Saturday granted him political asylum. Page 12.]

For weeks, a moderate, anti-Communist reaction had been spreading within the armed forces, some of it in favor of General Spínola, some of it in favor of President Francisco da Costa Gomes, and all of it against the far left.

Within the military, a center-right trend was perceived as a reaction to Communist successes in gaining power in various sectors of national life and as a reaction to disorders reportedly provoked by the extreme left.

The moderate trend was also

Continued on Page 11, Column 1

CAREY PROPOSES STRONGER AGENCY TO HELP CONSUMER

Calls 'Caveat Emptor' Creed Long Dead—Fines of Up to $5,000 in Program

By FRANCIS X. CLINES
Special to The New York Times

ALBANY, March 15—Governor Carey submitted his consumer program to the Legislature today, proposing a stronger government agency to specialize in the field, greater authority for consumers to instigate lawsuits and a variety of protective measures covering such matters as credit cards, traffic tickets and apples.

The principal proposal is for the scrapping of the present Consumer Protection Board, which has been much criticized by consumer groups, and for the formation of a Division of Consumer Affairs.

The new agency would have the power to subpoena witnesses before hearings, to serve as a consumer advocate before regulatory bodies and to issue regulations carrying civil penalties of up to $5,000. The enforcement of the regulations, however, would rest not with the division but with the State Attorney General's office.

"We have long passed the day when caveat emptor is an acceptable standard for business dealings," the Governor declared in his message to the Legislature.

Points of Program

The Governor's program includes the following proposals:

¶The new consumer division, to be headed by Commissioner Rosemary Pooler, now head of the Consumer Protection Board, with powers to intervene in class action suits, receive and refer consumer complaints and list deceptive and unconscionable business practices subject to penalties.

¶The option for enforcement power to be assumed by a local government's consumer affairs agency, if a local law is passed.

¶A bolstering of consumers' court powers by creating "a private right of action" through which consumers would be entitled to sue to recover damages from violators of division regulations.

¶An enlargement of the realm of small-claims courts, in which individuals can bring suits on their own without hiring a lawyer, so that the present limit of jurisdiction, claims

Continued on Page 25, Column 1

Aristotle Onassis Is Dead Of Pneumonia in France

Amassed a $500-Million Fortune in Shipping—Wed Mrs. Kennedy

Special to The New York Times

PARIS, March 15—Aristotle Onassis, the Greek shipping magnate, died today at the American Hospital in nearby Neuilly-sur-Seine.

Mr. Onassis was taken to the hospital by special plane from Athens last Feb. 7 and underwent an operation to remove his gall bladder two days later. Although the operation was successful, he was also suffering from myasthenia gravis, a debilitating neurological disease, which had affected his heart.

Dr. Maurice Mercadier, one of his physicians, said death was due to bronchial pneumonia, which "resisted all antibiotics." Mr. Onassis had been receiving cortisone treatment, which, the doctor said, lowered his resistance to infection and made the pneumonia "uncontrollable."

Mrs. Onassis, the former Jacqueline Kennedy, was in New York today, but left for here by air in the evening. Mr. Onassis had not left the hospital since he arrived five weeks ago, and his wife had taken to commuting between Paris and New York.

Associated Press
Aristotle Onassis

Christina Onassis, the shipowner's daughter by his first marriage, was at the hospital with her father today.

His son, Alexander, died in an airplane crash in Greece two years ago.

Burial on Skorpios

By United Press International

ATHENS, March 15—Aristotle Onassis will be buried on his private island of Skorpios next to his son, Alexander, family

Continued on Page 54, Column 3

PRESIDENT WEIGHS ACCORD TO LIMIT FEDERAL SPENDING

Would Permit Tax Cut Up to $30-Billion and Increase in Deficit to $70-Billion

AIDES PONDER STRATEGY

Changes May Be Offered in Return for a Pledge of Restraint by Congress

By PHILIP SHABECOFF
Special to The New York Times

WASHINGTON, March 15—The Ford Administration is considering an offer of major concessions on the President's economic program in return for a commitment of Congressional restraint on spending.

The possible offer of substantial changes, disclosed privately today by White House officials, would be made in the light of Administration fears of an uncontrolled spending spree by Congress.

The Administration is reported now to be willing to accept a tax cut of as much as $30-billion and a budget deficit of $70-billion or more in the fiscal year starting this July.

This would be an increase from the $16-billion tax cut and a budget deficit of $52-billion that the President proposed in January as the core of his program to fight the recession.

Decisions for Future

In return, the Administration would expect some kind of pledge from Congress to keep its "stimulative package"—its combined tax cut and new spending—below a specified level.

Although no decisions have been reached yet, and the details of the Administration offer are still to be worked out, the White House is reported to hope to keep the budget deficit from sailing out of the $70-to-$80-billion range.

The original White House calculation of next year's budget deficit included the President's proposed $16-billion tax cut. But the House approved in late February a $19.9-billion tax reduction, and yesterday the Senate Finance Committee

Continued on Page 18, Column 1

Rockefeller C.I.A. Inquiry To Touch on Plots Abroad

By NICHOLAS M. HORROCK
Special to The New York Times

WASHINGTON, March 15—The Rockefeller commission will investigate allegations of Central Intelligence Agency complicity in assassination plots against leaders of foreign Governments, reliable White House sources have confirmed.

The investigation, an outgrowth of the panel's inquiry into C.I.A. domestic intelligence-gathering, is being instituted because of President Ford's growing concern over news reports linking the C.I.A. to several assassination plots over the last two decades. One senior White House aide said that Mr. Ford's knowledge of any C.I.A. involvement in the cases about which there is speculation was "very, very cursory" and that it had been a "dilemma" to the White House as to how to deal with rising number of questions.

Mandate Is Take-Off

The commission is expected to request an additional 30 days of life to complete its inquiry and report. Vice President Rockefeller originally hoped to finish in 90 days, but, commission sources said, 30 days were used up "just getting our staff together" and additional time will be needed.

The commission, the White House sources said, will use its mandate to investigate alleged domestic violations by the C.I.A. as a springboard to look into the allegations about plots for assassinations overseas. For instance, one source said, the commission will follow up on a given case where the allegation indicates the plotting of an assassination took place in the United States.

This criterion could be expected to lead the commission into an inquiry into an alleged plot to assassinate Cuban Premier Fidel Castro because the reports now circulating involve American citizens and activities in Washington and Miami.

Another source, familiar with the investigation, said the criterion taken on "face value" could lead the commission "wherever it wants to go." "No plot to assassinate a foreign leader was ever hatched and executed with C.I.A. ap-

Continued on Page 21, Column 1

Cambodia Takes Key Town Near Capital

By DAVID A. ANDELMAN
Special to The New York Times

PHNOM PENH, Cambodia, March 15—Government forces today retook the strategic town of Tuol Leap—a Communist firing site for rocket attacks on the capital's airport—in the first major advance by Government troops since the start of the insurgent offensive this year.

At the same time, however, at least nine rockets landed in the vicinity of the United States Embassy in downown Phnom Penh. Two of them struck a Buddhist pagoda less than 100 yards away, killing four persons and wounding 20, including the monk who heads the pagoda.

Government forces have been trying for nearly three weeks to retake Tuol Leap. They lost the area during a major move against rocket emplacements northeast of the village.

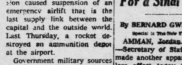

Since then, the Communist forces have reportedly moved in more rockets and 105-mm. howitzers, which are far more accurate than their 107-mm. rockets, for the daily attacks on Pochentong Airport.

The rockets and artillery bombardments have on occasion caused suspension of an emergency airlift that is the last supply link between the capital and the outside world. Last Thursday, a rocket destroyed an ammunition depot at the airport.

Government military sources said that the troops reoccupied Tuol Leap about 5 P.M. today, after having inflicted heavy casualties on the Khmer Rouge troops. There was no mention of the extent of Government casualties in the assault.

Possibly one measure of the troop advance in the area, eight miles west of the capital, was that only seven rockets landed on the airport today compared with as many as 65 on earlier days.

The Government forces have been able to halt or slow enemy

Continued on Page 6, Column 1

Prek Phnoeu
Tonle Sap
Prek Luong
Phnom Penh
POCHENTONG
Neak Luong
CAMBODIA
Bassac
Mekong R.
Takeo
0 Miles 20

The New York Times/March 16, 1975

Syria Is Said to Balk At Kissinger's Plea For a Sinai Accord

By BERNARD GWERTZMAN
Special to The New York Times

AMMAN, Jordan, March 15—Secretary of State Kissinger made another apparently fruitless effort today in Syria to persuade President Hafez al-Assad to at least go along with the quest for a new Egyptian-Israeli agreement in the Sinai Peninsula.

But after five hours of talks with Mr. Assad, Mr. Kissinger flew to the Jordanian capital without any apparent sign that the Syrian leader had altered his opposition to the Egyptians' negotiating with the Israelis alone.

As he did eight days ago in his first session with Mr. Assad on his current Middle Eastern visit, Mr. Kissinger held open a possibility that once there was an Egyptian-Israeli accord, Israel and Syria might hold talks of their own—something that American officials acknowledge is only a distant hope.

Aboard Mr. Kissinger's Air Force jet, reporters were told that the Secretary did not exclude Syrian-Israeli talks.

At the airport Mr. Kissinger said he would return again to

Continued on Page 16, Column 5

Mental Hospital Safety

Dr. Lawrence C. Kolb, new Commissioner of the State Department of Mental Hygiene, said security at state mental institutions had been tightened, with violent patients segregated from the nonviolent. Page 50.

Saigon Police Kill French Newsman

By JAMES M. MARKHAM
Special to The New York Times

SAIGON, South Vietnam, March 15—The police last night shot and killed a French journalist who had been summoned earlier in the day by the authorities about a dispatch he had written about the battle for Ban Me Thuot.

According to a police statement, Paul Leandri, a 37-year-old correspondent of Agence France-Presse, was accidentally killed when he drove away from police headquarters in his Peugeot automobile and refused to heed warning shots and cries for him to stop. The statement said a patrolman had fired three times at the tires of the vehicle to stop it and that one shot killed Mr. Leandri.

According to doctors at the French-staffed Grall Hospital, one bullet struck Mr. Leandri on the left side of his head and lodged in his skull, apparently killing him instantly. One hospital source said the bullet appeared to have been fired from a distance of about 30 feet

A French diplomat reportedly found the Peugeot crashed against a pillar at the main gate of police headquarters with Mr. Leandri's body slumped against the steering wheel. The car was said to have bullet holes in its front and rear and in its windshield.

French and South Vietnamese officials opened separate investigations of the incident. Mr. Leandri's German-born wife, Hansi, who is pregnant, was described by close friends as being in shock.

Mr. Leandri, a Corsican, had been summoned by the police

Continued on Page 4, Column 1

Church Groups See Danger In Child-Care Bias Lawsuit

By RICHARD SEVERO

A little-noticed lawsuit called Wilder v. Sugarman is forcing some of the city's Roman Catholic, Jewish and Protestant leaders and their lawyers into a series of intense negotiations to combat what they see as a direct threat to the traditional role of religious groups in caring for children who are neglected, abandoned, unwanted and abused.

There are about 28,500 such children in New York City who are now living in foster homes or treatment centers. Of these, the city cares for only about 3,800, the rest are the responsibility of agencies affiliated with one of the three major religious groups.

The reason for the concentration of children in the voluntary agencies is historic: a 19th-century Protestant concern for the welfare of foundlings was passed on to Catholics and Jews who also wanted to take care of their own children and to propagate their own faith and culture.

Discrimination Is Charged

But what started as an expression of charity has become for some the focus of acrimony. For the plaintiffs in Wilder v. Sugarman are charging that the dominance of the system by agencies affiliated with the three religions has meant discrimination against black children, who now make up more than half of all the unwanted youngsters needing help here.

In assigning help to neglected or abandoned children, the city's Bureau of Child Welfare routinely classifies most black children as Protestants and refers them to Protestant-affiliated agencies. But facilities for Protestants are lacking and the Catholic and Jewish agencies, even though they take care of large numbers of blacks, insist that they first take care of the children of their own faiths. As a result, the plaintiffs note, of 3,839 children that must be directly supervised by the city, 3,074 are black.

The voluntary agencies receive anywhere from 70 per cent to 95 per cent of their funds from the Federal and state government. The Wilder

Continued on Page 44, Column 3

Long-Range Plans to Feed World Are Moving Ahead

By BOYCE RENSBERGER

In the four months since the World Food Conference ended in Rome amid criticism of its failure to provide immediate famine relief, several of the meeting's long-range proposals for preventing famines have been moving toward realization at a promising pace, according to experts on the world food situation.

This is another in a series of articles, appearing from time to time, on the world food situation.

Although there have been interagency disputes, clashes of personal and political philosophies, delays on short-range proposals, and other stumbling blocks, many of those familiar with the traditional complexities of international organizations say these are par for the course. They say it is already evident that the conference marked a significant beginning in the world's efforts to prevent famine.

Beyond the creation of several new international agencies, the conference has also been credited with helping to foster a new awareness of the importance of improving agriculture in poor countries.

"The Rome conference and the follow-up have accomplished more than anybody had a right to expect," said James P. Grant, president of the Overseas Development Council, a private study group that has been concentrating on the food situation.

"In coming years," Mr. Grant

Continued on Page 28, Column 1

The New York Times/John Sotomayor
Divers searching near marker buoy for bodies of two who drove off the Staten Island ferry at slip in St. George, S.I.

Mother and Son in an Auto Plunge to Their Death From S.I. Ferryboat

By MURRAY ILLSON

As dozens of passengers watched, a car containing the wife and son of a Staten Island surgeon crashed through the retaining barriers of a ferryboat moored to a slip in St. George, S.I. yesterday afternoon and plunged both to their death in the murky waters off the terminal.

The incident occurred shortly before 1:30 P.M. as the ferryboat, the American Legion, was taking on passengers and cars for its half hour trip to Manhattan. The victims, Thelma Masella, 54 years old of 25 Windy Hollow Way, S.I., and her son, Francis, 23, had been the first to move from the dock onto the boat.

Victor F. Rossi, director of the city-run ferry operation, said ferry employes reported that the small blue convertible "never stopped," but rode over the wheel chocks they had placed near the bow, passed under a steel retaining cable and crashed through a metal fence before hurtling over the side. According to an earlier account by the police, the car had stopped near the bow, then

Continued on Page 41, Column 3

Today's Sections

Index to Subjects

Aristotle Onassis Dies of Pneumonia at American Hospital in Paris

Continued From Page 1, Col. 7

friends said today.

Prof. Ioanis Georgakis, a close associate and legal adviser to the multimillionaire, had already left here for the island to make the arrangements, the sources said.

They said that details of the funeral would be announced tomorrow.

Skorpios is a 350-acre, pine-covered island off the west coast of Greece in the Ionian Sea.

Shrewd and Adventurous

By ALBIN KREBS

A shrewd and adventurous businessman who amassed a fortune estimated at more than $500-million, Aristotle Socrates Onassis knew the uses of money and the power that came with it.

He was said to have used these, often, to move quietly and with secrecy into positions of influence in the international shipping and petroleum industries and in high finance. He also knew how to use his influence with political leaders in his native Greece.

Known to both admirers and detractors as "the Golden Greek," the oil-tanker magnate professed to despise publicity, but loved spending lavishly at nightclubs and for many years carried on an internationally headlined romance with Maria Callas, the soprano.

Despite his oft-repeated protestations against press attention, he attracted it more than ever after 1968, when he married one of the most famous women of her time, Jacqueline Bouvier Kennedy, widow of President Kennedy.

Mrs. Kennedy's surprise choice of Mr. Onassis for a husband took his name off the shipping, financial and society pages of newspapers around the world and put it on Page One.

Gave Varying Birthdates

At the time of their marriage on Oct. 20, 1968, Mr. Onassis was, depending on which of his birthdates he gave at various times, 29 or 23 years older than his 39-year-old bride. He maintained that he was 62, but an Argentine passport issued to him in 1927 gave his birthdate as Sept. 21, 1900, and World War II draft board reports indicated that at one time he had sworn he was born in 1900. But he later said the year was 1906, contending that he had had to falsify his age because Argentina would take in no immigrants below the age of 22.

He was born in Smyrna, now Izmir, a Turkish city on the Aegean with a large Greek colony, to Greek parents, Socrates Onassis, a tobacco merchant, and Penelope Dologlu Onassis. Greece won the city for its part in World War I, but it was recaptured in 1922 by Kemal Ataturk's troops, who herded Greek males between the ages of 16 and 40 into concentration camps.

Mr. Onassis said that one of his uncles had been lynched before his eyes, but that he himself managed to flee with the rest of the family to Greece. In 1923 he boarded a freighter at Piraeus bound for Argentina. He arrived there with about $60 in his pocket.

Working for 25 cents an hour, Mr. Onassis served as a lineman and operator for the United River Plate Telephone Company in Buenos Aires. He listened in on overseas calls to learn several languages.

Gradually, Mr. Onassis worked himself into the tobacco import business, taking advantage of an Argentine fondness for Turkish and Bulgarian tobaccos, which had recently been introduced there. In two years he had made more than $100,000, and by 1930 was a millionaire.

For a time during the nineteen-twenties, Mr. Onassis, who held Greek and Argentine passports, served as Greek consul in Buenos Aires. It was a job that required his dealing with many Greek freighter captains, and it was during this period that he became interested in ships.

Bought Ships for $20,000

In London, in 1930, Mr. Onassis learned that the Depression had forced the laying up of ships around the world. "You could pick up a ship for the same price as a Rolls-Royce," he later recalled.

At $20,000 each, Mr. Onassis bought six freighters — which had cost $2-million each to build in 1920 — from the Canadian National Railway. In the decade that followed, he added more freighters and tankers to his fleet, and when World War II came, he owned many of the precious tankers in Allied waters.

The war, followed by the Marshall Plan, the Korean war, the Indochina war, the Suez crises and the Vietnam war, gave the shipping industry its golden age of growth and profits. By 1968, Mr. Onassis, using shipping as a base but dabbling in other interests, had amassed an estimated total of $500-million.

As the controlling figure in about 100 companies in a dozen countries, Mr. Onassis operated a fleet of about five million tons displacement under "flags of convenience." His holdings included hotels (a quarter interest in the Pierre in New York, for example), banks, pier facilities and real estate, as well as Olympic Airways, the Greek national airline, for which he obtained from the Greek Government a concession set for expiration in the year 2006.

But by late last year, the airline's fortunes had declined, and Mr. Onassis canceled his contract. The Greek Government then began proceedings to take over the airline.

By that time, too, his multimillion-dollar Olympic Towers, a New York building planned to include offices as well as condominium apartments, was nearing completion at Fifth Avenue and 50th Street.

The yacht he had ordered, in 1970, as a 41st-birthday present for Jacqueline Onassis, was still being built late last year and the couple were still using the yacht Christina, which had been Mr. Onassis's floating home for years.

Mr. Onassis also owned a house in Athens, a villa in Monte Carlo, a hacienda near Montevideo, Uruguay; a Paris penthouse filled with 18th-century paneling and Louis XV furniture, and the island of Skorpios in the Ionian Sea. He and Mrs. Kennedy were married in the island's chapel in Greek Orthodox ceremonies.

Increased Tanker Size

Before Mr. Onassis got into the oil-tanker business, the largest tankers built were about 12,000 tons. "It doesn't take a genius to realize that the bigger the vehicle the lower the cost of transportation," he said, and acting on that premise, he built a 20,000-ton tanker.

In the middle nineteen-fifties he ordered five 28,500-ton tankers at a cost of $35-million. A decade later he and other shipowners were building 250,000-tonners.

Mr. Onassis had been told that such supertankers would never make money, as they could not negotiate the Suez Canal. The closing of the canal in 1956 by President Gamal Abdel Nasser of the United Arab Republic was a stroke of luck for Mr. Onassis, who made millions with his speedy supertanker hauls around the Cape of Good Hope. And when the 1967 Arab-Israeli war again closed the canal, the freight rate on oil soared from $5 to $18 a ton. By 1974, with the advent of the oil crisis, the price had almost doubled.

The international nature of Mr. Onassis's operations was reflected in the history of the Tina Onassis, a 45,000-ton tanker. The ship was built in Germany, mortgaged in the United States, insured in London, financially controlled from Monaco and manned by Greeks. It flew the flag of Liberia.

"My favorite country," Mr. Onassis once said, "is the one that grants maximum immunity from taxes, trade restrictions and unreasonable regulations."

Indicted in U. S.

Mr. Onassis's wheelings and dealings got him into trouble with several countries, notably the United States, which indicted him on civil and criminal conspiracy charges under the Shipping Act of 1916.

Mr. Onassis had bought 20 surplus Liberty ships after World War II, at cut-rate prices, with the understanding that they would be operated by American-controlled companies. But the Government charged that he controlled the companies in fact, if not in name. Ultimately, the criminal charges were dropped and the civil suit was settled for $7-million.

When he first met with Justice Department officials to arrange the civil settlement, Mr. Onassis grinned and asked one of them, "Well, what is the ransom?" Later, at a Congressional hearing, he was asked what he meant by the remark. "Ransom means recapture of your freedom," he answered smoothly. "It used to happen among the best people. Kings used to take kings and pay ransom."

In 1954, just after some of Mr. Onassis's tankers were seized by the Federal Government as a down payment on the settlement, the rest of his tanker fleet was boycotted by the big oil companies when it was revealed that he had made a deal to monopolize the oil-carrying market of Saudi Arabia. Mr. Onassis knuckled under to the oil producers, and the Saudi Arabian deal was called off.

He also took a loss in his dealings with Prince Rainier of Monaco. In 1952, wanting to rent office space in Monte Carlo, he approached the Société des Bains de Mer, the corporation that controls the gambling concession and the major hotels and clubs in the principality. His suggestion that he be rented space in the unused Winter Sporting Club was ignored.

Secretly, Mr. Onassis, through the 49 Panamanian companies he then controlled, started buying the Monaco corporation's shares on the Paris stock market, at about $5 a share.

He soon gained a majority interest and became known as "the man who didn't break, but bought, the bank at Monte Carlo."

Aristotle Onassis with his wife, Jacqueline.

For some time afterward, Mr. Onassis got along well with Prince Rainier, who appreciated the fact that when it became known the shipowner was injecting capital into the Monaco corporation, its shares doubled in value. The tourist business started booming, too.

Rift With Rainier

But Mr. Onassis had a basic dislike for gambling, Monaco's chief attraction for tourists. When he pushed the idea of tearing down tourist hotels and clubs and building office buildings in their place, he and Prince Rainier reached a parting of the ways.

In 1967, Mr. Onassis finally bowed to the Prince and sold his shares back to the corporation for $10-million. He said the shares were worth "six or seven times what they paid me." Despite the break, Mr. Onassis continued to operate several of his corporations from Monaco, taking advantage of the principality's tax laws.

In running his vast complex of business enterprises, the peripatetic Mr. Onassis caromed from one major city to another, usually carrying only a small briefcase. He maintained duplicate wardrobes in his various homes and in leased hotel suites in a dozen countries, and thus seldom needed luggage.

Mr. Onassis's social headquarters for many years was the Christina, formerly the Canadian frigate Stormont, which he bought in 1954. He spent $2.5-million converting it into a floating palace with vast staterooms, baths of Siena marble with gold fixtures, lapis lazuli fireplaces, a mosaic dance floor that drops to become a swimming pool, and its own amphibian plane.

A 50-man crew tended the Christina, whether she was anchored in the harbor at Monte Carlo or on one of the many cruises of the Mediterranean, Aegean and Caribbean on which Mr. Onassis took his friends.

End of First Marriage

It was during one such cruise, in 1959, that Mr. Onassis and his first wife decided to end their marriage, and another cruise, in 1963, that he met his second wife, Mrs. John F. Kennedy.

In 1946 Mr. Onassis had married Athina Livanos, daughter of Stavros Livanos, an even wealthier Greek-born shipping magnate than Mr. Onassis or Stavros Niarchos, also a shipping multimillionaire, who married another Livanos daughter, Eugenie. Tina Onassis and her husband had two children, Alexander, born in 1948, and Christina — for whom the yacht was named — born in 1950.

On the Christina's summer cruise in 1959 were, among others, Sir Winston Churchill and his wife and daughter Diana; Battista Meneghini, a Milan industrialist, and Mr. Meneghini's wife, the soprano Maria Callas. Mr. Onassis had met Miss Callas in 1956, and despite his evident dislike for opera—he was known, later, to be subject to snoring in his box during a Callas performance — they became extremely close. By the time the 1959 cruise began, gossip columns had begun linking them romantically. By the time it ended, it was evident the Onassis and Meneghini marriages would also end.

The Onassises were divorced in 1960, the same year the Meneghinis were legally separated. Mr. Onassis and Miss Callas remained close until 1968, although they never married. She maintained apartments in the same hotels he did in Paris and Monte Carlo. In 1968, Mr. Onassis told his semiofficial biographer, Willi Frischauer: "There was an affinity between us. No more than a friendship. . . ."

Meeting Mrs. Kennedy

Mr. Onassis met his second wife in the fall of 1963, when Mrs. Kennedy was on holiday in Greece after the birth and death of her second son, Patrick Bouvier Kennedy. With her was her sister, Princess Lee Radziwill, an old Onassis friend. Mr. Onassis brought them aboard the Christina for one of his standard tours of the Aegean, which included a stopover on Skorpios. After President Kennedy's assassination later that year, Mr. Onassis often visited the Kennedy family in Hyannis Port, Mass.

But there were few, if any, rumors of a romance developing between the shipowner and the President's widow and so, when it was announced that they would be married in October, 1968, the news created shocked—and sometimes incredulous — headlines in the United States and abroad. "Jackie, How Could You?" was the headline in Expressen, of Stockholm.

The furor was probably a result of the fact that at home, the much admired, elegant widow of a President had been put on a pedestal, while abroad she had virtually been enthroned. And she was marrying a much older man, a self-made, mostly unschooled, tough, high-living businessman and playboy.

"All the News That's Fit to Print"

The New York Times.

LATE CITY EDITION
Partly cloudy and cool today.
Fair, cool tomorrow.
Temperature Range Today—Max., 43; Min., 32
Temperatures Yesterday—Max., 43; Min., 35
Full U. S. Weather Bureau Report, Page 31

VOL. CIII....No. 35,007. Entered as Second-Class Matter. Post Office, New York, N. Y. NEW YORK, SATURDAY, NOVEMBER 28, 1953. Times Square, New York 36, N. Y. Telephone Lackawanna 4-1000 FIVE CENTS

25% RISE IN FARES FOR L. I. COMMUTERS URGED BY I.C.C. AIDE

Examiner Says Increase Would Not Cover $5.9 Million Loss Service by Line Incurs

NASSAU WILL FIGHT MOVE

State Commission and Rider Groups Protest That Federal Agency Lacks Jurisdiction

Special to The New York Times.

WASHINGTON, Nov. ‾ —An increase of 25 per cent in the commutation fares of the Long Island Rail Road was recommended today by an Interstate Commerce Commission examiner, Charles B. Gray.

The report said the $4,061,875 in added annual revenue from the increase would not cover the deficit of $5,900,000 a year incurred by the Long Island from furnishing commuter services.

Parties to the proceedings will have thirty days in which to file exceptions to Mr. Gray's report, after which proponents and opponents of the rate rises may file briefs. In the normal course, it is expected that final action by the commission on Mr. Gray's recommendations probably will not be taken in less than three months. The proceedings might take twice as long.

[Determined opposition to Federal action on local transportation rates was voiced in Mineola by A. Holly Patterson, county executive of Nassau County, where a large part of the Long Island's patrons reside. He said the county would ask the Interstate Commerce Commission to reject the examiner's findings, and would take the matter to court if the commission fails to do so.]

P. R. R. Plan Considered

The examiner's proposal comes during a pause in the Long Island reorganization proceeding now pending before the commission. Hearings were held last week here, and were then adjourned to Dec. 8. Under consideration is a plan proposed by the Pennsylvania Railroad, owner of 94 per cent of the stock of the Long Island. The subsidiary railroad is also heavily indebted to the Pennsylvania for advances.

Mr. Gray's recommendations followed hearings on a complaint filed by the Pennsylvania that the present commutation fares of the Long Island placed a burden on other traffic and on interstate commerce because they did not produce sufficient revenue.

The Pennsylvania filed its complaint when the Long Island trustee, William Wyer, held off requesting major increases in commutation fares until he explored all other possibilities of increasing the revenues of the Long Island.

The New York State Public Service Commission and various commuter groups have protested that the I. C. C. is without jurisdiction in the case. However, the examiners suggested that the Federal regulatory body did not have to wait until every possible remedy before the state commission had been exhausted.

Every type of commuter ticket is involved in the proposals of the Pennsylvania, which Mr. Gray says should be approved.

He pointed out that commutation traffic constituted the largest part of the Long Island's total business, producing 70 per cent of the total passenger-miles, and producing more revenue than any

Continued on Page 18, Column 8

NOTICE

The Photo-Engravers Union Local #1 has called a strike against a majority of New York newspapers represented by the Publishers Association of New York City. A contract between the two groups expired Oct. 31 last and work on a new agreement has been in progress since Sept. 23. Yesterday the Union rejected the offer of arbitration that the Publishers had made.

Newspapers can publish without the aid of photo-engravers, whose primary occupation is making "cuts" for the reproduction of illustrations. In consequence, all newspapers will make an earnest effort to appear as best they can without the help of this particular union and they anticipate little difficulty if the other unions with whom they deal observe the contracts now existing. Should, however, their agreements be violated, the strike will become general; and in strikes as in war the innocent and the guilty suffer alike.

In that event the affected newspapers have arranged to purchase space in the New York Herald Tribune of next Monday and will run their news as advertising. The Herald Tribune is not presently involved in the dispute by reason of the fact that it has no contract with this union but has its photo-engraving done for it by a commercial shop. To avoid duplication the newspapers have allocated segments of the news among themselves and thus will endeavor to cover all facets of the days' report.

We regret the hardship and inconvenience that this arrangement forces upon our employes, our readers, and our advertisers.

As much as possible of The Sunday Times, including those sections published in advance, will be distributed.

The New York Times

AUTHORITY TO MEET QUILL ON NEW PACT

Grants Request for Parleys, Starting Thursday, on His $50,000,000 Demands

By LEONARD INGALLS

The Transit Authority granted a request by Michael J. Quill yesterday to meet with him and other officers of the Transport Workers Union, C. I. O., next Thursday.

They are to discuss the union's demand for $50,000,000 in higher pay and working improvements for the 44,000 employes of the city-owned lines.

As international president of the union, Mr. Quill had complained frequently that since the authority assumed management of the city lines last June he could never get to meet officially the full board of five members.

Thus far the authority has been firm in its dealings with the union, and there was no indication yesterday that it would change its attitude. Maj. Gen. Hugh J. Casey, authority chairman, said the meeting on Thursday would be held at authority headquarters, 370 Jay Street, Brooklyn, starting at 9:30 A. M. The session, he said, will be devoted to "setting up machinery for negotiations."

The present memorandum of understanding covering wages and working conditions for transit workers will expire Dec. 31. It provides for the opening of discussions on a new memorandum, a month in advance of the expiration date.

Union Officials Invited

Invited to the meeting, in addition to Mr. Quill, were Gustav Faber, secretary-treasurer of the T. W. U.; Matthew Guinan, president of New York Local 100, and Ellis Van Riper, secretary-treasurer of Local 100.

In a letter to the authority on Monday, the union urged that an "eleventh-hour struggle" be avoided. It outlined the fifteen proposed contract improvements, including a 25-cent hourly pay raise and additional vacation, holiday, pension and grievance improvements.

The authority said, after its regular meeting yesterday, that it was considering a re-identification of the transit lines as the red, green or blue line instead of the B. M. T., I. R. T. and IND. It was explained that the purpose of the change would be to assist the public in finding the right trains. No decision has been reached on such a change in identification.

The letter designations, abbreviations for the two private companies and the city line that were unified in 1940 under city management, have continued as a matter of convenience. B. M. T. stood for Brooklyn-Manhattan Transit Corporation, I. R. T. was the abbreviation for Interborough Rapid Transit Company, and IND stood for the Independent line.

Thought also is being given to placing timetables in stations and at bus stops after reductions in non-rush hour service go into effect in the next two months. Trains and buses will run at intervals up to half an hour after midnight.

The authority authorized an out-

Continued on Page 32, Column 2

STRIKE DUE TODAY AT 6 PAPERS HERE

Photo-Engravers Reject Offer to Arbitrate—Other Unions May Respect Picket Lines

Texts of statements concerning strike appear on Page 32.

Photo-engravers on six major New York City newspapers decided yesterday to go on strike today for higher pay and other contract improvements.

The decision to strike followed rejection of a proposal by the Publishers Association of New York City that all issues be referred to arbitration. The vote rejecting arbitration was 207 to 147.

After the vote was announced at a meeting at Manhattan Center, Denis M. Burke, president of Local 1, International Photo-Engravers Union, A. F. L., told the engravers to be ready for picket duty at the six shops at 5 A. M. today. He said, however, that picketing would not begin officially until 9 A. M., when the last part of the night shift completes its work.

Mr. Burke said he believed some 20,000 other union employes on the six newspapers would refuse to cross picket lines. During the strike by the New York Newspaper Guild, C. I. O., against The World-Telegram and The Sun in 1950 mechanical workers honored Guild picket lines and the newspaper was unable to publish.

The union said the newspapers that would be affected by today's scheduled walkout were: The New York Times, The Daily News, The Daily Mirror, The New York Journal-American, The New York Post and The New York World-Telegram and The Sun. The New York

Continued on Page 32, Column 2

U. N. PREPARES PLAN NEARER RED TERMS ON A PEACE PARLEY

Dean's Korea Conference Items Put Soviet on Foe's Side and Define Non-Voting Neutrals

By ROBERT ALDEN

Special to The New York Times.

PANMUNJOM, Korea, Saturday, Nov. 28—The United Nations representative, Arthur H. Dean, is prepared to make today a counter-proposal on the composition of the Korean peace conference. He hopes his suggestions will lead to a successful conclusion of the preliminary talks here.

Mr. Dean's plan will embrace much of the original Communist proposal, including the allowing of neutrals as non voting observers at the peace conference.

Some of his modifications of the Communists' plan were outlined by Mr. Dean at yesterday's meeting here of the main subcommittee of Allied and Communist diplomats, as he tried to define in exact terms just how that plan would work.

Mr. Dean apparently has enough data on the Communists' plan from what they have said at the meetings, to report back to the United Nations member nations and the Republic of Korea and win their approval of the counter-proposal he is prepared to set forth.

Chairmanship Hazard

Whether or no Mr. Dean manages to present his proposal today depends on the way this morning's meeting proceeds. Since there is no chairman at these negotiations, the first one to speak after the delegates walk in is the one who has the floor. Should a Communist representative speak first and ask some extraneous questions, Mr. Dean may not get an immediate chance to set forth his plan.

Here are points in Mr. Dean's definition of the Communist proposal as he found them yesterday, on which both sides are expected to be able to reach an agreement, if additional matters can be negotiated satisfactorily:

¶The peace conference shall take the form of a meeting on equal footing of the two sides.

¶The United Nations side shall consist of representatives of the R. O. K. and the United States and the fifteen other members of the United Nations contributing armed forces to the United Nations Command. The Communist side shall consist of representatives of the People's Republics of China and of Korea and, at their invitation, the Soviet Union.

¶All decisions of the conference shall be by unanimous agreement of the two sides and the decisions shall be binding on all signatories, including the Soviet Union.

¶Any item shall be adopted only if it receives the approval of both sides and the Soviet Union (under this interpretation the Soviet Union's role will be as a full participant and not as a "neutral," as the Communists had proposed).

¶Each side shall vote as a unit.

¶The neutrals, whom Mr. Dean called "non-voting observers," if invited, will be entitled to speak at a meeting only on an item on the agenda and only "at such times, places, meetings and in such manner as are agreed upon unanimously by both sides and only upon topics as they are scheduled at the conference by the two sides.

¶These neutrals, if invited, will

Continued on Page 2, Column 2

Rhee-Chiang Talks in Taipei Said to Hint at Alliance

Associated Press Wirephoto via Radio from Taipei

Dr. Syngman Rhee, right, President of the Republic of Korea, as he was welcomed yesterday at the airport at Taipei, Formosa, by Generalissimo Chiang Kai-shek, President of Nationalist China. Between them is Kim Hong Il, South Korean Ambassador to Nationalist China.

By The Associated Press.

TAIPEI, Formosa, Saturday, Nov. 28—The Communist-hating Presidents of Nationalist China and South Korea conferred anew today after a dinner last night at which their champagne toasts strengthened signs of an anti-Red alliance. President Chiang Kai-shek told Dr. Syngman Rhee it was his "sincere hope that the Republics of China and Korea will closely cooperate in a common effort to eliminate communism and the Russian invader." His words tied in with speculation that Nationalist Chinese troops might be sent to Korea if the war there with the Commu-

Continued on Page 2, Column 2

U. S. WOULD ACCEPT A FREE PUERTO RICO

Lodge Tells U. N. President Would Agree if the Island Asked Full Self-Rule

Special to The New York Times.

UNITED NATIONS, N. Y., Nov. 27—The United States told the United Nations today that President Eisenhower would support full independence for Puerto Rico if the Puerto Rican Government asked for it.

Shortly after the announcement was made by Henry Cabot Lodge Jr., chief United States delegate, the General Assembly recognized by vote that Puerto Rico was a self-governing territory.

"I am authorized to say on behalf of the President," Mr. Lodge told the Assembly, "that if at any time the Legislative Assembly of Puerto Rico adopts a resolution in favor of more complete or even absolute independence, he will immediately thereafter recommend to Congress that such independence be granted. The President also wishes me to say that in this event he would welcome Puerto Rico's adherence to the Rio [de Janeiro] pact and the United Nations Charter."

The Rio pact is an agreement among twenty-one American nations calling for mutual aid for hemispheric defense. It was adopted at the inter-American defense conference at Petropolis, near Rio de Janeiro, Aug. 30, 1947.

Constitutional Status Found

By a vote of 26 to 16 with 18 abstentions the Assembly later adopted a resolution declaring that the people of Puerto Rico "by expressing their will in a free and democratic way have achieved a new constitutional status" and have shown that they have "effectively exercised their right to self-determination."

The resolution then asserted that the United States no longer had to give the United Nations information on conditions in Puerto Rico. According to the United Nations declaration on non-self-governing territories, the nations that administer them must present to the United Nations reports showing that conditions in those areas are such as to leave the road open for eventual self-government.

In spite of the tone of the resolution, the United States was not completely in favor of it, although it did vote for it. The position of the United States is that it is not the United Nations business to decide whether or not a territory is self-governing. Throughout a lengthy procedural dispute the United States firmly stood behind efforts to impose the two-thirds majority rule, although this would have meant the defeat of the pro-United States resolution.

Although the Assembly affirmed that Puerto Rico was self-govern-

Continued on Page 3, Column 5

Laniel Wins Vote, 275-244, As Gaullist Deputies Abstain

By LANSING WARREN

Special to The New York Times.

PARIS, Nov. 27—Premier Joseph Laniel won a vote of confidence from the French National Assembly today to carry on "with the creation of a united Europe." The vote was 275 to 244.

The wording of the motion of the Assembly after long debate on foreign affairs was so ambiguous, however, that it could not be construed as an endorsement for the Eurpean army treaty or for any one of the many types of European integration that have been proposed.

In fact, the Government was on the verge of a defeat and would have been in the minority if Gaullist opponents of the supranational six-nation European Defense Community treaty had not decided to abstain. They felt that the international situation was too serious to let the Cabinet fall.

Jacques Chabandelmas, spokesman of the Gaullists, said they would let the Cabinet stay in office so that France might be represented at the closing session of the current six-power conference of foreign ministers at The Hague and so that Premier Laniel could go to Bermuda to confer with President Eisenhower and Prime Minister Churchill next week.

Although M. Laniel's Cabinet will have only three more weeks of active life until it resigns at the Presidential election Dec. 17, it will suffice for the Premier to go to Bermuda and present the case of France. He said in the Assembly that he would ask help to end the war in Indo-China and would seek a promise that Britain and the United States would maintain troops on the European Continent.

He said that he would also try

Continued on Page 4, Column 3

BRITISH WILL PRESS FOR 4-POWER TALKS

Churchill Is Expected to Urge Such a Parley in Bermuda—Discord With U. S. Expected

By DREW MIDDLETON

Special to The New York Times.

LONDON, Nov. 27—The British Government delegation will go to the Bermuda conference with the United States and France intent on arranging the foreign ministers' meeting with the Soviet Union suggested in the Soviet Government's latest note.

It is felt here that this Soviet message is an unconditional proposal for talks, representing a considerable modification of Soviet tactics, but no change in over-all policy.

Manifold difficulties and obstacles are expected to arise in arranging the meeting. Nevertheless, when President Eisenhower, Prime Minister Churchill and Premier Joseph Laniel meet in Bermuda the British leader will try to arrange a meeting.

The Conservative Government still favors the Prime Minister's proposal for a high-level meeting between Georgi M. Malenkov, So-

Continued on Page 6, Column 3

Pier Board Bars 255 From Jobs Pending Crime Record Hearings

The Waterfront Commission of the New York Harbor announced yesterday that the right to work on the waterfront after Monday had been denied for the time being to 187 longshoremen, twenty-four hiring bosses, four pier superintendents and forty port watchmen.

Lawrence E. Walsh, executive director of the New York-New Jersey agency set up to wipe out racketeering on the New York harbor piers, said working permits and licenses had been withheld from the 255 men because of criminal records. Whether the right to work on the docks will be restored will depend on decisions of the commission after individual hearings.

The commission, meanwhile, has mailed out work permits to 23,997 longshoremen and has issued temporary licenses to 550 hiring bosses, 384 pier superintendents and 2,257 watchmen.

Other developments in the waterfront situation yesterday were these:

¶Chief Inspector Conrad Rothengast of the Police Department ordered 624 officers and men assigned to duty at ten employment information centers the Waterfront Commission will operate here when its powers over employment on the piers become fully effective Tuesday.

¶The new International Longshoremen's Union, affiliated with the American Federation of Labor, sought to show at a National Labor Relations Board hearing that the independent International Longshoremen's Association should be barred from an election to establish collective bargaining rights. The new union argued that the officials of old I. L. A., which was expelled from the A. F. L. last September, also were officers of employer groups.

A conflict appeared between the

Continued on Page 31, Column 4

U.S. REACTS COOLLY ON RUSSIAN OFFER TO MEET IN BERLIN

Says Note Is 'Disappointing' Reiteration of Conditions That Are 'Unacceptable'

TWO ALLIES DISPUTE VIEW

Britain and France Consider Moscow Stand Acceptance of Proposals by West

Unofficial text of Soviet's note to United States, Page 6.

By WALTER H. WAGGONER

Special to The New York Times.

WASHINGTON, Nov. 27—The State Department responded coolly but inconclusively today to the Soviet Union's counter-proposal for a four-power foreign ministers' conference on world tensions.

In a statement drafted at the highest levels of the department, Henry Suydam, its news chief, described the Soviet reply to the Western Big Three communication of Nov. 16 as "disappointing," a reiteration of "unacceptable" Soviet positions, and "another effort to gloss over the uncompromising nature" of Kremlin policy.

For the most part, the latest Soviet communication set down again Moscow's basic objections to the free world's foreign policy and programs for security. But it concluded with a proposal that the foreign ministers of the United States, Britain, France, and the Soviet Union meet in Berlin at an unspecified date and there discuss the question of holding a five-power meeting, which would include Communist China, "in the near future."

Allies Differ in Reaction

The State Department's negative response to the new Soviet note, received by the Western powers late last night, was in sharp contrast to the favorable reaction it received in London and Paris. In those capitals the Soviet communication was regarded substantially as an acceptance of the standing Western Big Three proposal for a four-power conference of foreign ministers, and as a basis for prompt and positive action.

This difference of opinion between the United States and its allies, of major importance to their efforts for reaffirming Western unity toward the new Soviet regime, promised to give the heads of those three governments a topic for some intense conversation when they meet in Bermuda a week from today.

Despite indications from Paris that the French felt that a reply to the Soviet note could be made without delay, the State Department made it clear that an answer could not be expected before President Eisenhower, Sir Winston Churchill and Joseph Laniel, French Premier, found a unified position at their Bermuda rendezvous.

Privately, United States officials expressed the view that while the Soviet's note restated its familiar objections to Western defense efforts and other elements of free world policy, it nevertheless appeared to abandon certain conditions for Moscow's acceptance of a four-power foreign ministers meeting.

Basis for Parley Is Noted

Some observers felt this change could provide the basis for eventual agreement between the Western Big Three and the Soviet Union on the terms for a four-power conference.

The inconclusive nature of the State Department response to the Soviet proposal was made clear in the statement that the note, while "disappointing," would "continue to receive the most serious study and consideration by this Government."

This left room for either rejection or acceptance in the future, but the feeling of encouragement that ran so strong in London and Paris appeared to weigh in favor of at least a qualified acceptance.

The note would appear "to represent another Soviet effort to impede progress" on the formation of the European defense community and "other efforts toward greater European unity and strength," the State Department said.

Other points made by the State Department were as follows:

¶The note was an attempt to "gloss over the uncompromising nature of Soviet policy" as revealed in the previous Soviet communication. The Nov. 3 notes "shocked the world" by showing that the Soviet Government was unwilling to "seek a relaxing of tensions" unless the Western powers abandoned in advance their

Continued on Page 6, Column 4

Eugene O'Neill Dies of Pneumonia; Playwright, 65, Won Nobel Prize

He Also Took Pulitzer Award for Drama Three Times—Ill for Several Years

Special to The New York Times.

BOSTON, Nov. 27—Eugene O'Neill, noted American playwright whose prolific talents had brought to him both Nobel and Pulitzer Prizes, died today of bronchial pneumonia. His age was 65.

The announcement of the death was made by Dr. Harry L. Kozol of Boston. Mr. O'Neill had been ill for several years with Parkinson's disease, a form of palsy that made writing virtually impossible.

The writer had been in and out of various hospitals in eastern Massachusetts in recent years, but had sought to keep the visits unpublicized.

Mr. O'Neill died in a Boston apartment where he had been living recently. His third wife, Carlotta Monterey, and Dr. Kozol were at the bedside.

He also leave a daughter, Oona O'Neill, who resides with her husband, Charles Chaplin, the actor, in Lucerne, Switzerland, and London. The funeral will be private.

Eugene O'Neill

Eugene Gladstone O'Neill was generally regarded as the foremost American playwright, his achieve-

Continued on Page 22, Column 3

Bank Hold-Up Foiled On Governors Island

An audacious attempt to rob a small bank branch on Governors Island and escape by ferryboat to Manhattan failed yesterday for two young civilians from Miami Beach, Fla.

The attempt was thwarted about 1:45 P. M. when outcries of the branch's sole teller alerted two military policemen stationed about thirty feet away in the same building.

The prisoners were identified by the Army as Stuart Deutch, 27 years old, a television repair man who, until January, had been a soldier on the base, and Paul Goldnagen, 21, a student of the University of Miami.

Deutch, using his knowledge of the base, gained their admittance to the island as visitors. Also by subterfuge—a request to buy travelers checks—they were admitted by the teller behind the

Continued on Page 10, Column 6

EUGENE O'NEILL, 65, DIES OF PNEUMONIA

Continued From Page 1

ments in the theatre overwhelming those of his ablest contemporaries. Whatever judgment posterity may make, the history of the stage will have to find an important niche for him, for he came upon the scene at an opportune moment and remained active long after the American theatre had come of age.

In the words of Brooks Atkinson of The New York Times, Mr. O'Neill broke a number of old molds, shook up the drama as well as audiences and helped to transform the theatre into an art seriously related to life. The genius of Mr. O'Neill lay in raw boldness, in the elemental strength of his attack upon outworn concepts of destiny.

The playwright received the Pulitzer Prize on three occasions and was the second citizen of this country to win the Nobel Prize for Literature.

The author of some thirty-eight plays, most of them grim dramas in which murder, disease, suicide and insanity are recurring themes, Mr. O'Neill was in recent years too wracked by illness to write and lived a secluded life in a little house by the sea with his third wife, a former actress.

But the decline of his fortunes saw no loss of public interest in his works. His plays continued to be produced to acclaim here and abroad and the fall of 1951 saw a real O'Neill "revival" on Broadway. The American National Theatre and Academy scheduled his "Desire Under the Elms" to launch its new season and the Craftsmen, a small dramatic group, produced the same play at the Barbizon-Plaza Theatre. In addition, the New York City Theatre Company picked "Anna Christie" as the second offering of its winter season.

A revival of "Ah, Wilderness!," the playwright's nostalgic comedy of first love, found its way to the television screen when the Celanese Theatre offered it, with Thomas Mitchell in the role originated by the late George M. Cohan.

Had International Audience

Actually, no modern playwright except the late George Bernard Shaw had been more widely produced than Mr. O'Neill. He was as well known in Stockholm, Buenos Aires, Vienna, Mexico City, Calcutta and Budapest as in New York.

There was as much color and excitement in his early life as there was in his plays. Indeed, much of his success was attributable to the fact that he had lived in and seen the very world from which he drew his dramatic material.

As a young man he spent his days as a common sailor and his nights in dives that lined the water's edge. Out of these experiences came such plays as "The Hairy Ape," "Anna Christie" and "Beyond the Horizon," all of which **have had a lasting life in the theatre.**

Mr. O'Neill was born on Oct. 16, 1888, in a third-floor room of the Barrett House, a family hotel that used to stand at Forty-third Street and Broadway. His father was the James O'Neill who starred for so many years in "The Count of Monte Cristo." His mother was the former Ellen Quinlan, who was born in New Haven but was reared in the Middle West. The first seven years of Eugene's life were spent trouping up and down the country with his actor-father and housewife-mother.

The boy's days as a theatrical camp follower ended at his eighth birthday, when he was enrolled in a Roman Catholic boarding school on the Hudson. In 1902, when he was 13, he entered Betts Academy in Stamford, Conn., considered at the time one of the leading boys' schools in New England.

He was graduated in 1906 and went to Princeton. After ten months at the university, he was expelled for heaving a brick through a window of the local stationmaster's house. It marked the end of his formal education.

The youth got a job as a secretary in a New York supply company business but quit after a few months to go to Honduras with a young mining engineer named Stevens. The two spent several months exploring the country's endless jungles and tried their hand at prospecting for gold. The venture ended after Mr. O'Neill became ill with fever and was shipped home by a kindly consul.

A recent photograph of Eugene O'Neill.

Worked for His Father

For a time the young man worked as an assistant stage manager for his father, who was touring in a play called "The White Sister." But he soon succumbed to the lure of far-off places and shipped as an ordinary seaman on a Norwegian freighter bound for Buenos Aires. This began his acquaintance with the forecastle that was to stand him in good dramatic stead later on.

In Buenos Aires he took such jobs as came his way. Tiring of that, he shipped again, this time for Portuguese East Africa. From there he sailed right back to Buenos Aires, then worked his way to New York on an American ship.

In New York he lived at a waterfront dive known as "Jimmy the Priest's," and incidentally acquired the locale for "Anna Christie." For a time he joined his father's troupe as an actor of bit parts. Later he turned up at his father's summer place in New London, Conn. In August, 1912, he went to work as a reporter on The New London Telegraph. His newspaper career lasted for four months, because, as he readily admitted, he was more interested in writing verse, swimming and sunbathing than in gathering news.

Just before Christmas in 1912 he developed a mild case of tuberculosis and was sent to the Gaylord Farm Sanitarium at Wallingford, Conn. He spent five months there and was to say later that it was while at the sanitarium that his mind got a chance to "establish itself, to digest and to evaluate the impressions of many past years in which one experience had crowded on another with never a second's reflection."

At Gaylord, too, he began to read Strindberg. "It was reading his plays," Mr. O'Neill later recalled, "that, above all else, first gave me the vision of what modern drama could be, and first inspired me with the urge to write for the theatre myself."

After his discharge from the sanitarium he boarded with a private family in New London for fifteen months. During this period he wrote eleven one-act plays and two long ones. He tore up all but six of the one-acters. His father paid to have five of the six short plays printed in a volume called "Thirst," published in 1914 and now a collector's item.

The elder O'Neill also paid a year's tuition for his son at Prof. George Baker's famous playwriting course at Harvard. The year over, Mr. O'Neill returned to New York and settled down in a Greenwich Village rooming house. The young man proceeded to soak up more "local color" at various Village dives, among them a saloon known as "The Working Girls' Home," where John Masefield, the British poet, was for a time a bartender.

Mr. O'Neill lived in the Village until 1916, when he moved to Provincetown, Mass., and fell in with a group conducting a summer theatrical stock company known as the Wharf Theatre. He hauled out a sizable collection of unproduced and unpublished plays and one of them, a one-acter called "Bound East for Cardiff," was put into rehearsal. It marked Mr. O'Neill's debut as a dramatist.

The Wharf Theatre did not go out of business at summer's end but set up shop in New York and called itself the Provincetown Players, a name that was to become famous. The company produced more of Mr. O'Neill's plays and the budding playwright began to be talked about in theatrical circles farther afield. At about the same time, as well, three of his one-act plays, "The Long Voyage Home," "Ile" and "The Moon of the Carribbees," were published in the magazine Smart Set.

In 1918 Mr. O'Neill went to Cape Cod to live, occupying a former Coast Guard station on a lonely spit of land three miles from Provincetown. He started working on longer plays and, in 1920, had his first big year when he won the first of his three Pulitzer Prizes for "Beyond the Horizon." The play marked Mr. O'Neill's first appearance on Broadway. The other prize winners were "Anna Christie" in 1922 and "Strange Interlude" in 1928.

Ranked as Money Maker

"Beyond the Horizon" established Mr. O'Neill not only as a ranking playwright but as a money maker. **The play ran for 111 performances and grossed $117,071. Mr. O'Neill needed the royalties badly; he had to use the $1,000 Pulitzer Prize money to pay off some debts.**

The Theatre Guild began producing his plays with "Marco Millions" in 1927 and staged all his plays thereafter. At least three of the plays, "Mourning Becomes Electra," "Strange Interlude" and "The Iceman Cometh," marked a new departure—they ran from four to five hours in length, requiring odd curtain and intermission times.

Mr. O'Neill's dramas ranged from simple realism to the most abstruse symbolism but one play —"Ah, Wilderness!"—was more in the tradition of straight entertainment and was interspersed with sentiment usually lacking in his introspective analyses of human emotions. The play ran for 289 performances.

Mr. O'Neill did not always meet with approval. At times, even, he was the object of bitter denunciation, especially from persons who believed his works smacked of immorality. By his choice of themes he several times stirred up storms that swept his plays into the courts.

"All God's Chillun Got Wings," which figured in the headlines for weeks, was fought by New York authorities on the ground that it might lead to race riots. "Desire Under the Elms" kicked up a big fuss in New York and almost was closed in the face of mounting protests. It never did open in Boston. The play was permitted to go on in Los Angeles, but after a few performances the police arrested everybody in the cast.

"The Hairy Ape," which starred Louis Wolheim in the role of Yank, a powerful, primitive stoker, was one of the dramatist's most popular works. The play ran for ten weeks, went on the road for a long tour and later was popular abroad.

"Electra" Highly Rated

Many critics felt that "Mourning Becomes Electra," which opened on Oct. 26, 1931, and had fourteen acts, was Mr. O'Neill's greatest masterpiece. Mr. Atkinson called it "heroically thought out and magnificently wrought in style and structure." John Mason Brown said that it was "an achievement which restores the theatre to its highest state" and Joseph Wood Krutch observed that "it may turn out to be the only permanent contribution yet made by the twentieth century to dramatic literature."

After "Days Without End" was produced in 1934—a play that received scant praise and lasted only fifty-seven performances — Mr. O'Neill was not represented on Broadway again until 1946, when "The Iceman Cometh" was staged.

In the intervening years, he settled in California and began the most ambitious project of his life —a cycle of nine related plays dealing with the rise and fall of an American family from 1775 to 1932. The venture never came off. In 1936, he won the Nobel Prize **but could not go to Stockholm to receive it because of an appendicitis operation.**

In a letter to the prize committee, Mr. O'Neill said:

"This highest of distinctions is all the more grateful to me because I feel so deeply that it is not only my work which is being honored but the work of all my colleagues in America — that the Nobel Prize is a symbol of the coming of age of the American theatre.

"For my plays are merely, through luck of time and circumstance, the most widely known examples of the work done by American playwrights in the year since the World War—work that has finally made modern American drama, in its finest aspects, an achievement of which Americans can be justly proud."

Play About His Family

After "The Iceman Cometh," Mr. O'Neill wrote a play called "Long Day's Journey Into Night," which will not be produced until twenty-five years after his death. He refused to talk about it but he had shown the manuscript to a few friends, and it was reported that the play deals with his own family life.

Mr. O'Neill was stricken with Parkinson's Disease, a palsy, about 1947. The disease caused his hands to jerk convulsively, making it impossible for him to write in longhand. He tried to compose a play by dictation but discovered he could not work that way. Despite the infirmity, he remained in good spirts and displayed evidences of his wit when friends dropped in.

The dramatist married the former Kathleen Jenkins in 1909, who bore him a son, Eugene O'Neill Jr. The son, who became a noted Greek scholar, committed suicide at Woodstock, N. Y., on Sept. 25, 1950. The first marriage ended in divorce in 1912, and six years later, Mr. O'Neill married the former Agnes Boulton. They were divorced in 1929. A son Shane, and Oona were born to this marriage. Mr. O'Neill married Miss Monterey on July 22, 1929.

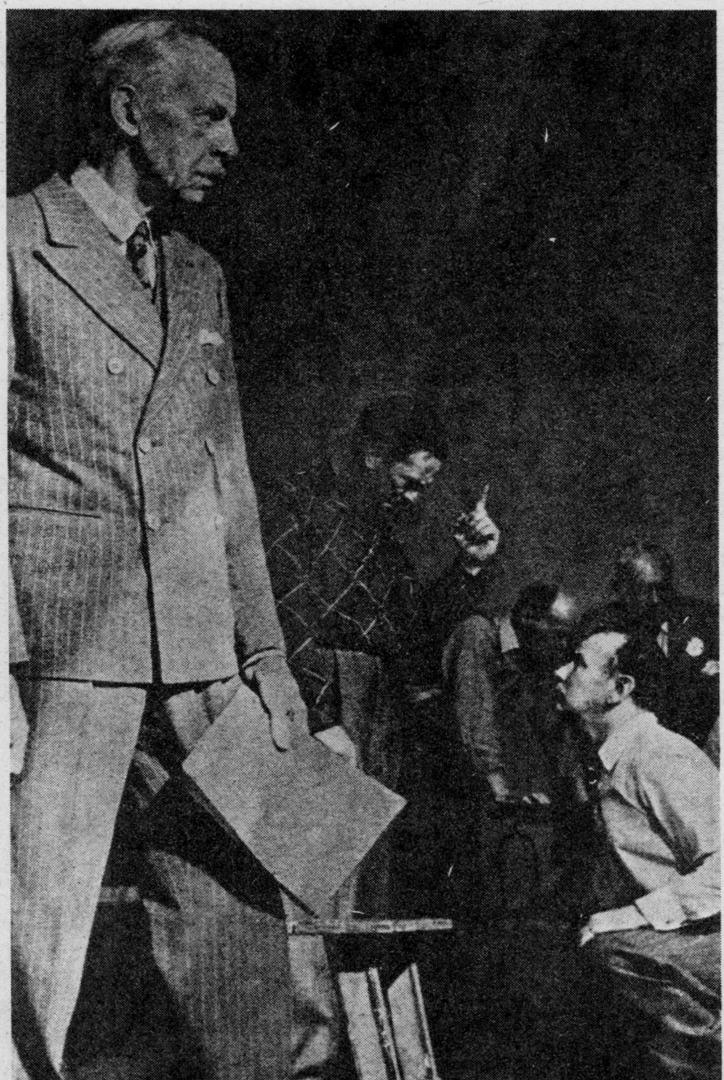

Eugene O'Neill at a rehearsal of the original Broadway production of *The Iceman Cometh*, 1946.

"All the News That's Fit to Print"

The New York Times

LATE CITY EDITION

Weather: Cloudy today, becoming fair tonight through tomorrow. Temp. range: today 54-44; Friday 52-47. Full U.S. report on Page 60.

VOL. CXVI. No. 39,947 NEW YORK, THURSDAY, JUNE 8, 1967 10 CENTS

ISRAELIS ROUT THE ARABS, APPROACH SUEZ, BREAK BLOCKADE, OCCUPY OLD JERUSALEM; AGREE TO U.N. CEASE-FIRE; U.A.R. REJECTS IT

JOHNSON WILL USE CABINET TO COURT STATES' OFFICIALS

Aides Will Seek to Tighten Ties Between Governors and the White House

By WARREN WEAVER Jr.
Special to The New York Times

WASHINGTON, June 7—President Johnson has decided to use the members of his Cabinet as diplomatic agents in his campaign to improve relations between the Administration and state governments.

The President has approved a plan under which each member of the Cabinet would be assigned four or five states as his personal responsibility, with instructions to maintain personal contact between the Governors and the White House.

As part of the same effort, each of the 50 states will be given a "day" in Washington next fall and winter, when a planeload of its key officials will fly here to hold conferences all over the capital, capped by a meeting of the Governors with the President.

Bryant's Work Continued

Both projects reflect Mr. Johnson's continuing determination to build domestic as well as foreign bridges by working to sort out the tangled Federal-state relations that have been increasingly complicated by the administration of the Great Society programs.

Both are attempts to give some permanency to the contacts established during the last four months by Farris Bryant, the President's envoy to the states, on visits to 40 capitals with a squad of Federal experts.

Mr. Bryant, a former Governor of Florida who is now the director of the Office of Emergency Planning, plans to leave his White House post this summer, possibly to return to politics in his home state, and he is eager to help establish more permanent lines of communication before his departure.

As now envisioned, each Cabinet officer would visit all of

Continued on Page 29, Column 2

Rise in Debt Ceiling Rejected in House; Johnson Rebuffed

Special to The New York Times

WASHINGTON, June 7—The House of Representatives dealt the Johnson Administration a sharp setback today by rejecting a bill to increase the ceiling on the national debt $29-billion, to $365-billion.

The vote against passage was 210 to 197, with Republicans voting solidly to kill the bill. Enough Democrats, mostly Southerners, voted with them to turn the tide.

About six Northern Democratic "doves"—opponents of the war in Vietnam—also joined the opposition.

In all, 34 Democrats joined with 176 Republicans to defeat the measure.

Today's action raised the possibility — though a slim one—of financial chaos after June 30. At that time the debt limit reverts to its "permanent" ceiling of $285-billion, though the debt, at $330-billion, is already far above that level. The legal authority of the Treasury to pay its bills would be in doubt.

However, the Ways and

Continued on Page 30, Column 4

U.S. VOWS TO SEEK A DURABLE PEACE

Johnson Recalls Bundy for New Mideast Planning Unit—'Real Chance' Is Seen

By MAX FRANKEL
Special to The New York Times

WASHINGTON, June 7 — President Johnson pledged today to do his best to help translate the new Middle Eastern situation into a more lasting settlement between Israel and her Arab neighbors.

Apparently hoping to exploit Israel's lightning military success—which has surprised but not displeased the White House—Mr. Johnson ordered the drafting of special policies for a "new peace" and set up new machinery to deal with the situation.

The President said that the United States, which had worked hard to avoid the war, felt that "there is now a real chance" to turn from "the frustrations of the past to the hopes of a peaceful future."

But Mr. Johnson said the handling of the crisis and the preparations for a lasting settlement would require the most careful consideration in the United States Government. To organize that effort he recalled McGeorge Bundy to temporary duty at the White House as executive secretary to a special subcommittee of the National Security Council.

Mr. Bundy will seek a temporary leave from the presidency of the Ford Foundation, which he assumed last year after serving as special assistant for

Continued on Page 19, Column 1

EBAN SEES THANT

Says Acceptance Is Based on Enemy's Reciprocal Action

Excerpts from debate at U.N. are printed on Page 18.

By DREW MIDDLETON
Special to The New York Times

UNITED NATIONS, N. Y., June 7—The Security Council unanimously adopted a Soviet resolution today calling on the combatants in the Middle East to "cease fire and all military activities" at 4 P.M., New York time today.

The Government of Israel shortly thereafter announced that she had accepted the call of the Council for a cease-fire, provided her Arab foes agreed.

In the evening, reports from the Middle East indicated rejection of the call by the United Arab Republic, Syria, Iraq, Saudi Arabia, Algeria and Kuwait. Jordan told Secretary General Thant that she would abide by the cease-fire, except in self-defense.

Says It's in Effect

Abba Eban, the Foreign Minister of Israel, told the Secretary General that a cease-fire was already in effect between Jordan and Israel.

In presenting the resolution, the Soviet delegate, Nikolai T. Fedorenko, made it clear that if Israel failed to heed the Security Council's demands, Moscow would consider severing diplomatic relations. The original Security Council resolution, adopted yesterday, simply called for a cease-fire.

But the reports from the Arab capitals indicate, diplomatic sources here said, that military operations will continue.

According to diplomats, the best hope lies in a draft resolution presented by George Ignatieff, the Canadian delegate. This proposes that the President of the Security Council and the Secretary General take measures to insure compliance with the resolutions.

Today's resolution demanded that the combatants "cease fire and all military activities on 7 June 1967 by 2000 hours Greenwich mean time." The resolution was adopted less than an hour before this time, which is 4 P.M. New York time, 10 P.M. in Jordan and Israel and 11 P.M. in the United Arab Republic and Syria.

The Council adjourned without voting on the Canadian draft largely because Milko Ta-

Continued on Page 18, Column 2

CONFEREES BLOCK A DRAFT LOTTERY

Compromise Bill Continues Deferment of Students

By United Press International

WASHINGTON, June 7 — Senate and House negotiators reached agreement today on a new military draft bill that rules out, for the present, any lottery-like random selection system to determine the order of induction.

The bill was a compromise of differing bills that the Senate and House had passed. It would guarantee the continuance of educational deferments for college undergraduates and students enrolled in apprentice and job training programs.

Senator Richard B. Russell Democrat of Georgia, who is chairman of the Senate conferees, said the Senate might act on the four-year draft extension bill tomorrow. House action must await approval by the Senate.

Congressional action will clear the way for President Johnson, under current discretionary powers, to reverse the order of induction and take 19-year-olds first from the Selec-

Continued on Page 8, Column 1

NEWS INDEX

Dorothy Parker, 73, Literary Wit, Dies

By ALDEN WHITMAN

Dorothy Parker, the sardonic humorist who purveyed her wit in conversation, short stories, verse and criticism, died of a heart attack yesterday afternoon in her suite at the Volney Hotel, 23 East 74th Street. She was 73 years old and had been in frail health in recent years.

In print and in person, Miss Parker sparkled with a word or a phrase, for she honed her humor to its most economical size. Her rapier wit, much of it spontaneous, gained its early renown from her membership in the Algonquin Round Table, an informal luncheon club at the Algonquin Hotel in the nineteen-twenties, where some of

Continued on Page 38, Column 1

OLD JERUSALEM IS NOW IN ISRAELI HANDS: Israeli soldiers in prayer at the Wailing Wall yesterday

United Press International Radiophoto

Major Mideast Developments

On the Battlefronts

Israel claimed victory in the Sinai Desert after three days of fighting. Sharm el Sheik, guarding the entrance to the Gulf of Aqaba, fell after a paratroop attack, and the Israelis said the blockade of the gulf was broken. Other Israeli units were within 20 miles of the Suez Canal, and one Israeli report placed them in the eastern section of Ismailia, on the canal itself.

In Jerusalem, for the first time in 19 years, Israeli Jews prayed at the Wailing Wall as their troops occupied the Old City. Israeli troops captured Jericho, in Jordan, and sped northward to take Nablus, giving them control of the west bank of the Jordan.

The Egyptian High Command reported that its forces had fallen back from first-line positions in the Sinai Peninsula and were fighting fiercely from unspecified secondary positions. It announced that Egyptian troops had pulled back from Sharm el Sheik to join main defense units.

In the Capitals

In the United Nations, Israel accepted the call for a cease-fire, provided the Arabs complied. Jordan announced that she would accept and ordered her troops to fire only in self-defense. But Baghdad declared that Iraq had refused. There were indications that Syria, Algeria and Kuwait were also opposed.

In Cairo, an Egyptian official said the United Arab Republic would fight on.

In Moscow, the Soviet Union threatened to break diplomatic relations with Israel if she did not observe the cease-fire.

In Paris, the French proposed an international agreement for free passage in the Gulf of Aqaba similar to the one governing the Dardanelles in Turkey.

In Washington, President Johnson promised to seek a settlement that would assure lasting peace in the Mideast.

In London, the British urged the Israelis to halt before they aroused more turmoil in the Arab world and diminished the chances for a settlement.

Israelis Weep and Pray Beside the Wailing Wall

By TERENCE SMITH
Special to The New York Times

JERUSALEM, June 7—Israeli troops wept and prayed today at the foot of the Wailing Wall—the last remnant of Solomon's Second Temple and the object of pilgrimage by Jews through the centuries.

In battle dress and still carrying their weapons, they gathered at the base of the sand-colored wall and sang Hallel, a series of prayers reserved for occasions of great joy.

They were repeating a tradition that goes back 2,000 years but has been denied Israeli Jews since 1948, when the first of three wars with the Arabs ended in this area.

The wall is all that remains of the Second Temple, built in the 10th century before Christ and destroyed by the Romans in A.D. 70.

The Israelis, trembling with emotion, bowed vigorously from the waist as they chanted psalms in a lusty chorus. Most had submachine guns slung over their shoulders and several held bazookas as they prayed.

Among the leaders to pray at the wall was Maj. Gen. Moshe Dayan, the new Defense Minister. He told the troops:

"We have returned to the holiest of our holy places, never to depart from it again."

General Dayan, who was ap-

Continued on Page 17, Column 1

CAIRO ANNOUNCES A SINAI PULLBACK

Blames Foreign Aid to Foe, but Says Troops Fight On in Secondary Positions

By ERIC PACE
Special to The New York Times

CAIRO, June 7—An Egyptian military communiqué reported today that forces of the United Arab Republic had fallen back from some first-line positions on the Sinai Peninsula and were engaged in fierce fighting against Israeli troops from secondary positions.

Another statement of the High Command, broadcast four hours later by the Cairo radio, said Egyptian troops at Sharm el Sheik, guarding the entrance to the Gulf of Aqaba, had joined other Egyptian forces "now concentrated in the Sinai Peninsula."

There was no elaboration, but the communiqué, broadcast about 5:30 P.M., appeared to confirm Israeli reports that the Egyptians had been forced to retreat from Sharm el Sheik.

At night, the High Command reported that Israeli paratroops had dropped over the "second-line Egyptian front" but had been "completely wiped out."

The communiqué also said the Israelis had tried another drop at Sharm el Sheik after the

Continued on Page 17, Column 6

AQABA GULF OPEN

Dayan Asserts Israel Does Not Intend to Capture the Canal

By The Associated Press

TEL AVIV, June 7—Israel proclaimed victory tonight in the Sinai Peninsula campaign against the United Arab Republic. On the eastern front, both the Old City of Jerusalem and Bethlehem were captured from the Jordanians.

"The Egyptians are defeated," said Maj. Gen. Itzhak Rabin, the Israeli Chief of Staff. "All their efforts are aimed at withdrawing behind the Suez Canal, and we are taking care of that. The whole area is in our hands. The main effort of the Egyptians is to save themselves."

Israel Losses 'Not Great'

Describing the developments through the third day of this third Arab-Israeli war in 19 years, General Rabin made these claims:

¶Sinai, the Egyptian territory between Israel's Negev Desert and the Suez Canal, is taken.

¶Most of the Jordanian territory on the west bank of the Jordan River, including Jericho, is in Israeli hands, and most of Jordan's army has been captured.

¶Relative to what was done, the number of Israelis casualties was "not great."

The Israelis were reported to have swept to the Suez Canal.

[An Israeli delegation source at the United Nations said Israeli troops had seized that part of the canal city of Ismailia that is on the eastern side of the waterway. But this was denied by an army source in Tel Aviv, who said, according to Reuters, that the Israelis had not taken any point along the canal.

[Maj. Gen. Moshe Dayan, the Israeli Defense Minister, declared that there was "no intention" of taking the canal, United Press International reported.]

'Never to Depart'

After the fall of the Old City of Jerusalem, Defense Minister Moshe Dayan said there that the Israelis had reunited their capital and would never "depart from it again."

Israel reported that paratroops aided by naval units had captured Sharm el Sheik, commanding the entrance to the Gulf of Aqaba, and said the blockade that the Egyptians had mounted from that position had been broken.

"The Strait of Tiran is now open," General Rabin said.

Israel's chief of staff said his men had taken on the United Arab Republic, Jordan, Syria and Iraq, knocked out their air forces and overrun their armor and infantry.

"All this the armed forces of Israel did alone," he declared.

The general then turned over the briefing to Brig. Mordechai Hod, commander of the air force, who announced 441 Arab

Continued on Page 16, Column 1

Pentagon Believes Israeli Jets Struck From Sea, Eluded Radar

By WILLIAM BEECHER
Special to The New York Times

WASHINGTON, June 7 — At least a part of the Israeli Air Force that caught large numbers of Egyptian aircraft on the ground in the early hours of the war may have slipped through gaps in the United Arab Republic's radar net by flying in over the Mediterranean.

This possibility was raised today by Pentagon analysts. If correct, it would help to explain how Israeli pilots were able to surprise so many Egyptian jets before they could get into the air.

It might also serve to provide part of the explanation behind insistent Arab assertions that carrier-based United States and British jets participated in the raids.

The early blows to Arab, and especially Egyptian, air strength is credited by most military analysts as having been a decisive factor in the Israeli successes on land that followed.

"We know that some of the Israeli planes returned to their bases by way of the sea," one ranking officer said, "and we assume they may have approached from the seaward too."

The officer said it was obvious that Israel had excellent intelligence on weaknesses in the Egyptian radar system and exploited them.

Shortly after the raids, he went on, the Jordanian radio charged that Jordanian radar

Continued on Page 18, Column 8

The New York Times June 8, 1967

CONQUEST IN THE MIDEAST: Israeli troops took Sharm el Sheik (1), drove on to the Suez Canal (2) and seized control of the Old City in Jerusalem (3). Photo was taken in September, 1966, during the flight of Gemini II.

Dorothy Parker, Short-Story Writer, Poet, Literary Wit, Dies at Age 73

Continued From Page 1, Col. 2

the city's most sedulous framers of bon mots gathered.

Franklin P. Adams, the somewhat informal elder statesman of the group, printed Miss Parker's remarks in his "Conning Tower" column, and fame was quickly rapping on her door.

Miss Parker was a little woman with a dollish face and basset-hound eyes, in whose mouth butter hardly ever melted. It was a case, as Alexander Woollcott once put it, of "so odd a blend of Little Nell and Lady Macbeth."

Many of Miss Parker's writings appeared in The New Yorker magazine, to which she was a contributor from its second issue, Feb. 28, 1925, until Dec. 14, 1957. In paying tribute to her last night, William Shawn, the magazine's editor, said:

"Miss Parker, along with Robert Benchley, E. B. White, James Thurber, Frank Sullivan, Ogden Nash and Peter Arno, was one of the original group of contributors to The New Yorker who, under Harold Ross's guidance, set the magazine's general tone and direction in its early years."

The humorist's personal and literary style, Mr. Shawn added, "were not only highly characteristic of the twenties, but also had an influence on the character of the twenties—at least that particular nonserious, unsolemn sophisticated literary circle she was an important part of in New York City."

Sentimentalist at Heart

Her lifelong reputation as a glittering, annihilating humorist in poetry, essays, short stories and in conversation was compiled and sustained brickbat by brickbat. One of her quips could make a fool a celebrity, and vice versa. She was, however, at bottom a disillusioned romantic, all the fiercer because the world spun against her sentimental nature. She truly loved flowers, dogs and a good cry; and it was this fundamental sadness and shyness that gave her humor its extraordinary bite and intensity.

When the mood was on her, Miss Parker's conversation was like a Fourth of July sparkler; but humor did not come easily to her pen. "I can't write five words but that I change seven," she once confessed.

The best of Miss Parker's humor was wry and dry, antic and offbeat, even that about herself. For her epitaph she suggested "Excuse My Dust," and of her poetry she said, "I was following in the exquisite footsteps of Miss Edna St. Vincent Millay, unhappily in my own horrible sneakers."

Barred Glasses in Public

She took seriously her couplet about women and glasses: Men seldom make passes/At girls who wear glasses. Although she was quite nearsighted, she refrained from wearing her horn-rimmed spectacles in public, or when men were present: She much preferred to blink her luminous hazel-green eyes.

"Deceptively sweet" was the phrase her friends most often applied to her. And indeed she looked it, for she was elfin, with a warm smile and perfect manners and a short-stepped, ladylike walk. She had a mass of dark hair that, toward middle age, she cut off and wore in bangs.

She was "the verray parfit, gentil knight" of the squelch, which she delivered deadpan in a clear, mellow, lamblike voice. Informed that Clare Boothe Luce was invariably kind to her inferiors, Miss Parker remarked, "And where does she find them?" Of a well-known author, "The only 'ism' she believes in is plagiarism."

Associated Press

Dorothy Parker

And of a cocky friend, "His body has gone to his head."

Miss Parker's background was not literary. She was born on Aug. 22, 1893, in West End, N. J. Her father, J. Henry Rothschild, was a New Yorker of means; her mother, the former Eliza Marston, was of Scottish descent. She attended Miss Dana's School at Morristown, N. J., and the Sacred Heart Convent in New York.

She was, she recalled, "a plain disagreeable child with stringy hair and a yen to write poetry."

After she had by chance sent some of her verses to Vogue magazine, she was hired at $10 a week to write picture captions. At the same time, Mr. Adams, who was generally known by his initials of F.P.A., published some of her poetry in his column, then appearing in The Daily Mail.

Miss Parker worked for Vogue for two years, 1916 and 1917, and in the latter year was married to Edwin Pond Parker 2d. The marriage was terminated by divorce in 1928, but she retained Parker as her professional name.

After her marriage, Miss Parker became drama critic for Vanity Fair from 1917 to 1920, when, during an office reorganization, she resigned. It was during the following five years that she attained her celebrity for sizzling, off-the-cuff wit from her repartee at the Algonquin Round Table.

Miss Parker, Mr. Benchley and Robert E. Sherwood were the founders of the group when they all worked at Vanity Fair, which had offices at 19 West 44th Street. The group got going because the Algonquin was nearby on 44th Street, and the three could not bear to suspend their office conversations.

The group rapidly expanded, and Frank Case, the hotel's proprietor, provided a round table for it. The group, usually about 10 a day, lunched together for about a decade. At one time or another it included George S. Kaufman, Harold Ross, Donald Ogden Stewart, Russel Crouse, Edna Ferber, Heywood Brown, Ruth Gordon, and, of course, F.P.A., and the three founders.

Miss Parker was one of the luminaries, but she later took a down view of the Round Table. "People romanticize it," she said. "This was no Mermaid Tavern. These were no giants. Think of who was writing in those days — Lardner, Fitzgerald, Faulkner and Hemingway. Those were the real giants. The Round Table was just a lot of people telling jokes and telling each other how good they were.

"At first I was in awe of them because they were being published. But then I came to realize I wasn't hearing anything very stimulating.

"I remember hearing Woollcott say, reading Proust is like lying in someone else's dirty bath water. And then he'd go into ecstasy about something called 'Valiant Is the Word for Carrie,' and I knew I had enough of the Round Table.

"The one man of real stature who ever went there was Heywood Broun. He and Robert Benchley were the only people who took any cognizance of the world around them. George Kaufman was a nuisance and rather disagreeable. Harold Ross, The New Yorker editor, was a complete lunatic; I suppose he was a good editor, but his ignorance was profound."

As one result of her poems and stories, Miss Parker was pointed out at parties and literary gatherings, not always to her amusement.

"Are you Dorothy Parker?" a woman at one party inquired. "Yes, do you mind?" the humorist retorted.

On another occasion, assured by a drunk who accosted her that he was really a nice person and a man of talent, Miss Parker replied:

"Look at him, a rhinestone in the rough."

"This reputation for homicidal humor," Miss Parker recalled in after years, "used to make me feel like a fool. At parties, fresh young gents would come up defiantly and demand I say something funny and nasty. I was prepared to do it with selected groups, but with others I'd slink away."

An Admirer Disappointed

At one party a man followed her around all evening waiting for a bright remark. He finally apologized, saying, "You're not at all the way I thought you'd be. I'm sorry."

"That's all right," Miss Parker rejoined. "But do me a favor. When you get home, throw your mother a bone."

Miss Parker herself understood the ephemerality of conversational humor. "Wit has truth in it," she said. "Wisecracking is simply calisthenics with words."

Nonetheless, it was the sort of gymnastics at which she could be very good indeed. At a party where she was seated with Somerset Maugham, the author asked if she would write a poem for him. "I will if you like," Miss Parker said, and scribbled out:

Higgledy Piggledy, my white hen;
She lays eggs for gentlemen.

"Yes, I've always liked those lines," Mr. Maugham commented.

Miss Parker bestowed a cool smile and without an instant's hesitation added:

You cannot persuade her with gun or lariat
To come across for the proletariat.

Miss Parker laced her wit with heady truth as a book reviewer, first for The New Yorker as Constant Reader and then for Esquire as book review editor for many years. Her notices were written with a chatty trenchancy, as though she were talking informally to the reader; but she could (and did) impale authors who displeased her, either by synopsizing a pompous plot in all its ludicrousness or by pulverizing the book with a phrase.

Book Briefly Dismissed

She reduced A. A. Milne's sugary "The House at Pooh Corner" to water by remarking that "Tonstant Weader Fwowed up" after reading one too many of the word "tummy."

Her verdict on Edith Wharton's autobiography was equally to the point: "Edie was a lady." Edward W. Bok, the prestigious editor of The Ladies Home Journal, was left in tatters with Miss Parker's summary of him as "the Eddie Guest of prose."

"Inseparable my nose and thumb," she once wrote, and she delighted in wiggling her fingers at folk gods. "'In the Service of the King' has caused an upset in my long-established valuations," she wrote. "With the publication of this, her book, Aimee Semple McPherson has replaced Elsie Dinsmore as my favorite character in fiction."

Miss Parker was not entirely negative, however. She praised F. Scott Fitzgerald, the early Ernest Hemingway, some of Sinclair Lewis, James Baldwin and Edward Albee.

Miss Parker's reputation for light poetry was based on four books of verse: "Enough Rope" (1926), "Sunset Gun" (1928), "Death and Taxes" (1931) and "Not Deep as a Well" (1936). On the surface the poems were a blend of the cynical and the sentimental — just right for the sweet-winning generation of the late nineteen-twenties and early thirties.

If there was a touch of Miss Millay in them, there was also an overtone from Housman, as in "Pictures in the Smoke:"

Oh, gallant was the first love, and glittering and fine;
The second love was water, in a clear white cup;
The third love was his, and the fourth was mine;
And after that, I always get them all mixed up.

In Miss Parker's evocation of heartburn, there was, too, a bit of Donne and a hint of La Rochefoucauld, as in "Words of Comfort to Be Scratched on a Mirror:"

Helen of Troy has a wandering glance;
Sappho's restriction was only the sky;
Ninon was ever the chatter of France;
But oh, what a good girl am I!

Miss Parker wrote her last published poem in 1944, and then gave up the craft. "Let's face it, honey," she explained, "my verse is terribly dated."

But her final poem, "War Song," was her favorite. It is quintessentially Miss Parker, and it reads:

Soldier, in a curious land
All across a swaying sea,
Take her smile and lift her hand—
Have no guilt of me.
Soldier, when were soldiers true?
If she's kind and sweet and gay,
Use the wish I send to you—
Lie not alone until day.
Only, for the nights that were,
Soldier, and the dawns that came,
When in sleep you turn to her
Call her by my name.

As a short-story writer, Miss Parker produced several that were more than merely excellent: "Big Blonde," which won the O. Henry Memorial Award in 1929; "Telephone Call"; "Soldiers of the Republic" and "Arrangement in Black and White."

The latter is a particularly mordant satire of a woman explaining her own and her husband's attitude toward Negroes. Its most memorable passage reads:

"But I must say for Burton, he's heaps broader-minded than lots of these Southerners. He's really fond of colored people. Why, he says himself he wouldn't have white servants."

In 1933 Miss Parker was married to Alan Campbell, an actor. They were divorced in 1947 and remarried three years later. The Campbells went to Hollywood and collaborated on a number of motion picture scenarios; between times Miss Parker wrote short stories and book notices. Mr. Campbell died in California in June 1963, and Miss Parker, already ill, moved back to New York.

Writing Always Careful

Miss Parker, for all her mercury-quick mind, was a careful, even painful, craftsman.

"To say that Miss Parker writes well," Ogden Nash once remarked, "is as fatuous as proclaiming that Cellini was clever with his hands."

She had her own definition of humor, and it demanded lonely, perfectionist writing to make the truly funny seem casual and uncontrived.

"Humor to me, Heaven help me, takes in many things," she said. "There must be courage; there must be no awe. There must be criticism, for humor, to my mind, is encapsulated in criticism. There must be a disciplined eye and a wild mind. There must be a magnificent disregard of your reader, for if he cannot follow you, there is nothing you can do about it."

Toward the close of her life Miss Parker was convinced that humor had fallen on evil days.

"There just aren't any humorists today," she said on her 70th birthday in 1963. "I don't know why. I don't suppose there is much demand for humor. S. J. Perelman is about the only one working at it, and he's rewriting himself."

From the late nineteen-twenties, when Miss Parker was fined $5 for "sauntering" in a Boston demonstration against the execution of Nicola Sacco and Bartolomeo Vanzetti, she was active in liberal causes. In the Spanish Civil War and afterward, she was national chairman of the Joint Anti-Fascist Refugee Committee and active in its behalf.

Faced House Committee

This had repercussions in 1951 when she was cited, by the House Un-American Activities Committee, with 300 other writers, professors, actors and artists, for affiliation with what the committee designated as "Communist-front" organizations. One committee witness identified her as a member of the Communist party, an accusation she persistently denied.

In her final illness Miss Parker was melancholy about her life's accomplishments. She wanted to write again, especially short stories, but she lacked the strength.

The summing up came from Edmund Wilson, the critic, who wrote:

"She is not Emily Brontë or Jane Austen, but she has been at some pains to write well, and she has put into what she has written a voice, a state of mind, an era, a few moments of human experience that nobody else has conveyed."

Examples of Saucy Wit

Following is a sampling of Dorothy Parker's comments in essays, book reviews, short stories, in conversation and in poetry:

NEWS ITEM

Men seldom make passes
At girls who wear glasses.

*

A girl's best friend is her mutter.

*

The only thing I ever learned [in school] that did me any good in after life was that if you spit on a pencil eraser, it will erase ink.

*

Brevity is the soul of lingerie—as the Petticoat said to the Chemise.

*

THE FLAW IN PAGANISM

Drink and dance and laugh and die,
Love, the reeling midnight through,
For tomorrow we shall die!
(But, alas, we never do.)

CONJECTURE

Into Love and out again—
So I went, and thus I go.
Spare your voice and hold your pen—
Well and bitterly I know
All the songs were ever sung,
All the words were ever said.
Can it be, when I was young,
Some one dropped me on my head?

*

Salary is no object; I want only enough to keep body and soul apart.

*

As far as I am concerned, the most beautiful word in English is cellar-door.

*

Most good women are hidden treasures who are only safe because nobody looks for them.

"All the News That's Fit to Print."

The New York Times.

LATE CITY EDITION

Copyright, 1945, by The New York Times Company.

VOL. XCV..No. 32,109. Entered as Second-Class Matter, Postoffice, New York, N. Y. NEW YORK, SATURDAY, DECEMBER 22, 1945. THREE CENTS NEW YORK CITY

GEN. PATTON DIES QUIETLY IN SLEEP; BURIAL IN EUROPE

BLOOD CLOT FATAL

He Succumbs to a Lung Congestion 2 Weeks After Auto Crash

FUNERAL MONDAY LIKELY

Burial Site Expected to Be on Road That He and Third Army Blazed to Berlin

By KATHLEEN McLAUGHLIN

By Cable to The New York Times.

FRANKFORT ON THE MAIN, Germany, Dec. 21—Gen. George S. Patton Jr. is dead. One of the most vivid figures among Allied combat leaders in World War II succumbed at 5:50 P. M. (11:50 A. M., Eastern standard time) to a lung congestion that probably would not have resulted fatally except for complications brought on by his paralysis of the chest, the result of his auto accident two weeks ago.

The failure of his heart functions, in consequence of his inability to obtain normal relief by coughing, and the ensuing cardiac pressure, had heightened the gravity of the condition of the former United States Third Army commander for more than twenty-four hours before the end came ar he was sleeping. He was 60 years old.

The starkly simple sick room in the 130th Station Hospital at Seventh Army Headquarters in Heidelberg was the scene of his passing. Army men who knew him best acknowledged that he would have found a grim sort of satisfaction in the knowledge, if it could have been brought to his attention, that the setting for this final phase in the great soldier's life so perfectly fitted his background.

Will Be Buried in Europe

The building had been a German cavalry barracks before it was pressed into service as an emergency military hospital by the German Army in the final stages of the war. And it was retained in that capacity by the United States forces as they swept across this area in their drive to Berlin.

By the decision of Mrs. Patton, and with the concurrence of the War Department, received here this evening, General Patton will be buried abroad. The site has not been chosen, but it will without doubt be selected from the strategic territory of northwest Europe over which his troops blazed their trail to victory in the sweep toward Germany.

The time of the funeral service likewise is not known yet, but it is regarded as probable that Monday will be the date. Transportation will be provided overseas for those of his family who will attend.

McNarney Issues Tribute

The news was given to the press in a brief announcement by Brig. Gen. John M. Willems, Chief of Staff of the Seventh Army, who said merely that General Patton had "died peacefully."

Shortly after, Lieut. Gen. Joseph T. McNarney, Chief of Staff of the United States Forces in the European Theatre, released the following:

It is my painful duty to announce the death of a great fighter and a great man.

Gen. George S. Patton Jr. died peacefully at seventeen fifty hours this afternoon in the 130th Station Hospital of injuries received in an automobile accident of Dec. 9. His injuries were grave, but his fight to overcome them was gallant. He went down fighting. General Patton would have died in no other way.

And now, for those of us over here who loved him, and for all the world who applauded his bravery, there is a sudden, empty feeling. He brought a large share of our magnificent victory, and this, too well known to need description, belongs to history.

The world tonight is a poorer place without the fighting heart of George Patton.

Lieut. Gen. Lucian K. Truscott, successor to General Patton both as commander of the Third Army and as Military Governor of Bavaria, notified all military installations under his supervision that memorial services for

Continued on Page 5, Column 3

BIG 3 CONFEREES MAKING PROGRESS, MOSCOW ASSERTS

Parley Reported in 'Positive' Stage but News to Support Optimism Is Lacking

EARLY FINISH IS SURMISED

Accord Believed Near Without Recourse to Economic Deals —Four-Hour Talk Held

By BROOKS ATKINSON

By Cable to The New York Times.

MOSCOW, Dec. 21—The proceedings of the conference of Soviet, United States and British foreign secretaries have reached a positive stage, according to information received today. Nothing was revealed to explain this improvement in attitude over the neutral tone that prevailed yesterday.

The fifth session of the conference was held yesterday for two hours before the reception for the Moscow diplomatic corps, given between 6 and 8 o'clock, by Foreign Commissar and Mrs. Vyacheslaff M. Molotoff. In the circumstances it seems reasonable to suppose that one or more of the proposals submitted at the preceding sessions proved to be generally acceptable thereafter.

Although it is not known what proposals are being currently discussed, the conference has had adequate time to exchange preliminary views on atomic energy. From the atmosphere prevailing today correspondents were guessing that this was not going to be a long conference, in fact that it might be over within a few days and that the prospect for resuming close collaboration between the Big Three was good.

Horse-Trading Minimized

There are a great many problems to be discussed by the Foreign Ministers, but efforts were being made to deal with each on its merits and with no trading or economic favors for political agreement.

The conference continued to be workmanlike and sparingly social. Secretary of State James F. Byrnes has been too busy studying telegrams from the United States and the business of the conference to leave Spasso House, where he is staying, except for yesterday's parley in Spirodonovka House and the Molotoffs' reception. The Chinese Ambassador, Foo Ping-sheung, called at Spasso House.

Mr. Bevin was likewise engrossed in business in the British Embassy. It is understood that the French and Chinese Ambassadors are being informed of the proceedings of the conference that concern their Governments.

It is considered that it would prejudice the work of the United Nations Organization if, for example, the Big Three attended the first session of the UNO without a fundamental understanding or policy on atomic energy. In time, it is hoped, the affairs of the world will be in such a state that the UNO will be able to assume full control and responsibility for the future peace and security of the world.

Meanwhile the Big Three want to try to avoid dumping on the new organization problems that they consider trilateral. The Council of Foreign Ministers of the United States, Britain, the Soviet Union, France and China, whose London conference broke up on

Continued on Page 6, Column 3

Iran Crisis Deepens; Minister Hangs On

By The Associated Press.

TEHERAN, Iran, Dec. 21—Khalil Fahimi refused today to accept dismissal from his post as Minister of the Interior in Iran's political crisis caused by the splitting off of Soviet-occupied Azerbaijan Province as an autonomous State.

Mr. Fahimi said in a statement that under the constitution he could not be replaced unless he resigned. The appointment of Allahy Saleh, former Embassy employe in Washington, in his place had been announced by Premier Ebraham Hakimi.

The political import of the controversy was expected to become plainer when Parliament convened tomorrow. Premier Hakimi's supporters yesterday shouted down a proposal for changes in the constitution to permit social reforms and negotiations with the Azerbaijan regime. The proposal in effect would have recognized the autonomy of Azerbaijan.

M'ARTHUR GUIDANCE NEARLY COMPLETE

He Asserts New Orders Will Probably Be Supplements to Those Issued in Japan

By LINDESAY PARROTT

By Wireless to The New York Times.

TOKYO, Dec. 21—The Supreme Allied Command has virtually completed the program for the disarmament and reform of Japan under the terms of the Potsdam agreement, a statement from Gen. Douglas MacArthur's headquarters indicated today.

The announcement declared that with the issuance of last week's directive banning the State Shinto religion "the final impetus has been given to the form the new Government shall take" and added that further directives probably will be limited to those necessary to supplement orders previously issued.

The statement, which comes only four months after the first American troops landed in Japan, pointed out that the Supreme Commander already has "issued directives to remove all of the bars that directly or indirectly could influence the Japanese people" to resume tendencies that led them toward war and defeat.

The statement ranks among the most important documents of the occupation. It tells the harassed and confused Japanese public that no sweeping measures opening new fields of reform are in prospect and that the empire can now settle down to establishment of the best methods for carrying out orders already given.

The statement is calculated to set at rest one of the principle objections of the Japanese to the occupation program, that it has gone so fast and entered so many

Continued on Page 8, Column 5

Turks' Refusal to Cede Land Affirmed by Foreign Chief

General Pledges Fight if Russia Insists on Territory—Calls Kars Nation's Backbone —Ankara Irked by Bid to Armenians

By C. L. SULZBERGER

By Cable to The New York Times.

LONDON, Dec. 21—Assertions by the Turkish Foreign Minister, Hassan Saka, and by one of the country's most respected generals, that Turkey would oppose with force, if necessary, any Soviet attempts to alter her present frontiers became known tonight in delayed dispatches from Ankara.

Mr. Saka, addressing the National Assembly yesterday, declared Turkey would continue her policy of requesting nothing of anybody and giving "nothing to anybody."

At the same time Gen. Kiazim Karabenkir, commander of the Turkish army on the Caucasian front during the war of independence, said Turkey would have no alternative but to fight if the Soviet Union insisted on its demands. He said that two areas allegedly coveted by the Soviet Union were "the throat of the Turkish nation" [the Dardanelles and Bosporus] and "its backbone" [the Kars Plateau].

The Assembly debate took place before the latest and wider Soviet demands had become known in Turkey, demands by which the controlled Soviet press staked out a claim for a huge chunk of territory in what is obviously a planned Moscow effort to carve a firm foothold in the Middle East by the pressure of diplomacy.

[Efforts to induce Armenians in Turkey to migrate to Soviet Armenia have been bitterly criticized by the Turkish press, according to an Ankara dispatch.]

Meanwhile pro-Soviet troops in Iranian Azerbaijan mopped up resistance centers, and southeastern Turkey is to all intents cut off

Continued on Page 6, Column 5

KIMMEL HAD 'MAGIC,' WAS STARK'S BELIEF

Turner Also Asserts Fleet Was Based at Hawaii to Fight and Not for Its Security

By WILLIAM S. WHITE

Special to The New York Times.

WASHINGTON, Dec. 21—A misconception among senior Naval officers for nearly a year before Pearl Harbor left Admiral Harold R. Stark, then Chief of Naval Operations, under the erroneous impression that the Hawaiian Command had facilities for breaking the highest Japanese code and possessed vital information as to Japan's intentions, Admiral Richmond Kelly Turner asserted today.

In his third day before the Congressional Pearl Harbor Investigating Committee, Admiral Turner also disclosed that in July, 1941, nearly six months before the sneak attack, he had declared to Kichisaburo Nomura, Japanese Ambassador in Washington, as the then Chief War Plans officer of the Navy, his opinion that a Japanese invasion of British or Dutch territory in the Pacific would cause President Roosevelt to ask Congress for a declaration of war.

After the Admiral ended his testimony, the committee recessed until Dec. 31.

Concerning the disaster of Dec.

Continued on Page 9, Column 3

CONGRESS CLOSES; RECORD IS HAILED

Rayburn Voices Pride and Taft Stresses Bills That Failed—New Session Jan 14

Special to The New York Times.

WASHINGTON, Dec. 21—The first session of the Seventy-ninth Congress, which saw the end of the World War and functioned under the recommendations of two Presidents, ended quietly today after almost continuous work, except for a summer respite cut short by the unsolved problems of peace, since January. The second session will convene Jan. 14.

Neither house had a quorum. A threatened quorum call in the Senate was resisted successfully by the leaders. When the House adjourned at 2:11 P. M. seven Republicans and nine Democrats were in their seats.

Before adjourning at 3:47 P. M. the Senate acted on secondary legislation, debated and blocked a move looking to the prompt release of more than 1,000,000 fathers from the armed services, and received notice that early in the new session the bill to create a permanent Fair Employment Practices Commission would be called up for a test.

The reaction among some Southern Senators was that if this were

Continued on Page 22, Column 3

PRIORITIES ORDERED ON 400,000 HOUSES FOR VETERANS IN '46

Small, Head of CPA, Tells Plan to Control Ten Materials for Moderate-Priced Buildings

COST LIMIT PUT AT $10,000

Preference Will Go to Veterans Both in Buying or Renting—Area Quotas Are Possible

By SAMUEL A. TOWER

Special to The New York Times.

WASHINGTON, Dec. 21—The Administration's program to provide next year at least 400,000 houses of moderate cost for veterans of the second World War through a system of priorities for critical building materials will get under way on Jan. 15, J. D. Small, head of the Civilian Production Administration, disclosed today.

On that date fifty-two field officers of the Federal Housing Administration will begin the issuance of certificates entitling veterans, or builders giving preference to veterans, to obtain priorities for specific percentages of ten construction materials which are in short supply. Power to award the preference ratings has been delegated to FHA by CPA.

The assistance is confined to the construction of homes costing not more than $10,000, including land and improvements, or to structures renting for not more than $80 a month.

In outlining the program, Mr. Small told a news conference that he expected "a substantial proportion" of the new houses to cost far below the established maximum, adding that, with a flow of materials assured, he had received many pledges from builders to undertake housing in the lower-cost brackets.

Quotas May Be Established

"If we find," he declared, "that a preponderance of priorities applications are for homes to sell at the $10,000 ceiling, we will establish quotas to see that a fair share of the homes are built in lower-price ranges," adding that "we won't stand for 100 per cent $10,000 houses."

Mr. Small indicated that his agency was prepared also to establish a system of geographic quotas if applications came in to an "overwhelming" degree, but expressed the hope that contractors would not "try to gobble up" more materials than they could use.

The prices at which the new houses will be sold will be checked by the FHA through a procedure by which applicants for priorities will submit to the agency the specifications for their proposed construction and the selling price or rental at which it will be made available to veterans. The FHA will not grant ratings to applicants whose prices were far out of line, it was stated.

Officials of both OPA and FHA indicated, however, that there would not be a rigid control over prices.

"The FHA must be satisfied that the proposed price or rent is reasonably related to the proposed accommodations," said Mr. Small, while Raymond Foley, FHA commissioner, who sat in on the news conference, stated:

"There is no intention to make this a price-fixing measure. FHA will determine only if prices bear a

Continued on Page 2, Column 3

FACT-FINDERS ASK NEW BARGAINING IN GM, OIL CASES

OIL PEACE IS LIKELY

But GM Officials Are Noncommittal as Case Is Put Over to Dec. 28

'ABILITY TO PAY' RULE SET

If a Firm Refuses Evidence, Panel May Take Union Data or Draw Own 'Inferences'

By LOUIS STARK

Special to The New York Times.

WASHINGTON, Dec. 21—Governmental fact-finding boards considering the General Motors Corporation employes' strike and the oil workers dispute today turned these cases back to the parties involved for further collective bargaining with the proviso that if direct negotiations fail they will return to this city for the next step, namely, investigation of the necessary facts preliminary to recommendations for settlement.

The parties in the oil industry dispute were requested by the board, of which Dr. Frank P. Graham is chairman, to return on Jan. 7 if necessary, and those involved in the automobile workers strike were asked to appear on Dec. 28.

Extreme confidence prevailed among those affected by the oil workers' dispute. They felt that collective bargaining would be successful and "the Government will not hear from us again."

General Motors Noncommittal

No such confidence was expressed by the General Motors Corporation or the United Automobile Workers-CIO.

Walter P. Reuther, vice president of the union, said his organization would continue to cooperate with the fact-finding board named by President Truman, headed by Lloyd K. Garrison.

The General Motors officials, however, did not commit themselves to abide by the fact-finding procedure as set forth by President Truman yesterday when he issued a statement declaring that fact-finding boards must examine employers' books since ability to pay was always relevant to an increase in wages.

The position of General Motors with respect to the procedure outlined to its officials by the Garrison fact-finding board for several hours today was that it would hold its final reply in abeyance.

This board said that ability to pay would be regarded as one of the relevant factors but not the only one in determining the "fair" wage adjustment.

But the board did not go so far as the implication in the President's statement in so far as the production of books was concerned. It merely said that whether it would call for the books, in accordance with the President's statements, "will be determined by the future developments in the case."

Schwellenbach Gives Rules

A spokesman for the company said that it could not believe that the Garrison board, in view of this statement would seek to build up a higher wage structure in one manufacturing unit than in another.

The rules applying to all fact-finding boards were given in a statement by Secretary Schwellenbach today. In these rules, the Secretary, implementing President Truman's policy, announced yesterday, set forth how a fact-finding panel might recommend a wage increase, depending on whether such payments might be made without price increases or could be used as the basis for requesting price increases.

This document, although made public this morning at the oil case hearing, was not put before the General Motors officials, who spent several hours this afternoon with the Garrison board discussing the latter's "rules of the game."

The Garrison board's rules were somewhat milder, but nevertheless, in the corporation's opinion, contained certain provisions that they questioned as feasible or desirable.

However, these officials did not hesitate to say that had they been told that their case was to be considered under the "drastic" rules

Continued on Page 2, Column 5

Ezra Pound Insane; Unfit to Be Tried

By The United Press.

WASHINGTON, Dec. 21—Ezra Pound, 60-year-old poet accused of treason, was adjudged insane today and mentally unfit for trial.

The ruling was made by District Judge Bolitha J. Laws on the basis of a report by four psychiatrists. The poet was committed to St. Elizabeth's Federal Hospital for observation and treatment.

The treason charge was based on allegedly pro-Axis radio broadcasts while he was in Italy.

The psychiatrists said that Pound's personality had been abnormal for many years. They added that it "has undergone further distortion to the extent that he is now suffering from a paranoid state which renders him mentally unfit to advise properly with counsel or to participate intelligently and reasonably in his own defense."

"He insists that his broadcasts were not treasonable, that all of his radio activities stemmed from a self-appointed mission to 'save the Constitution,'" the psychiatrists said.

GE PAY RISE OFFER REJECTED BY UNION

10% Increase Counters $2-a-Day Demand—Company Cites Request by Truman

A union demand for $2 daily wage increases was countered yesterday by the General Electric Corporation with an offer of 10 per cent, which Charles E. Wilson, president of the corporation, declared was not warranted under present operating conditions but was made in view of the recent statements of President Truman on the need for higher wages.

The offer, however, was immediately rejected by the United Electrical, Radio and Machine Workers of America, Congress of Industrial Organizations, which charged in a letter to E. D. Spicer, vice president of the corporation in charge of employe relations, that GE was still refusing to "bargain in good faith."

Speed-Up Is Feared

The union letter, signed by Joseph Dermody, international representative, asserted that the offer was inadequate to meet the needs of GE employes, whose wages have been cut more than 50 per cent and was less than the 13.5 cent hourly increase offered by the General Motors, which the union has turned down.

The union also said the corporation had served notice of cancellation of its contract and accused it of seeking arbitrary hiring and firing powers and the right to unlimited speed-up.

Electrical workers voted Dec. 13

Continued on Page 2, Column 6

World News Summarized

SATURDAY, DECEMBER 22, 1945

The Moscow conference of the Big Three Foreign Ministers appeared to be going well as informed sources reported that the talks had reached a "positive stage" and that the prospects for close collaboration of the three powers were good. [1:3.]

Turkey will yield "nothing to anybody," Foreign Minister Saka told the Turkish National Assembly following Russian demands on Turkish territory. Another Turkish leader, General Karabenkir, described the Dardanelles as "the throat of the Turkish nation" and the Kars plateau, claimed by Soviet Armenia, as "its backbone." [1:4-5.]

The Allied Reparations Conference announced that, after Russia and Poland had received 25 per cent of the reparations from western Germany, Britain would get 28 per cent of what was left, the United States and France 20 per cent each, the remainder being divided among the other nations. [7:1.]

General Patton died in his sleep, twelve days after the automobile accident that paralyzed him, as a result of complications that affected his lungs and heart. The former commander of the American Third Army, which spearheaded the Allied offensive from the Normandy beachheads through France and into Germany, will be buried in Europe. [1:1.]

Four months after the American occupation of Japan, virtual completion of the plan for that nation's disarmament and reform under the Potsdam agreement was indicated by General MacArthur's headquarters. [1:3.]

General Marshall was greeted by Generalissimo Chiang Kai-shek in person upon his arrival in Nanking and soon afterward the two began their conferences on bringing peace to strife-torn China. [1:2-3.]

Britain launched a drive for a UNO location on the Atlantic seaboard as a subcommittee decided to ballot today on holding a vote between the western or eastern United States for the organization's headquarters. [6:2.]

The Pearl Harbor inquiry was informed that senior naval officers in Washington had been under the erroneous impression for nearly a year before the Japanese attack that the Hawaiian command had facilities for breaking the highest Japanese code. [1:4.]

Federal fact-finding boards recommitted the General Motors strike and the oil workers' dispute for further collective bargaining and told both sides that if these direct negotiations failed they must return to Washington to submit to investigation preliminary to recommendations for settlement. [1:8.]

The FHA will begin Jan. 15 to issue priority certificates for the construction of at least 400,000 moderate-priced homes in 1946 for war veterans. [1:6.]

Hundreds of millions of dollars' worth of surplus supplies will be made available by the Federal Government to the nation's schools and colleges at 40 per cent of the "fair value" of the equipment. [22:2.]

President Truman sent a Christmas message to the members of the armed services in which he said that "our prayer this day is that our youth may now find a true and lasting fellowship of peace." [12:2.] Congress adjourned for a three-week holiday. [1:5.]

Marshall Is Welcomed by Chiang; Nanking Talks Begin Immediately

By The Associated Press.

NANKING, Dec. 21—Gen. George C. Marshall arrived here today by plane from Shanghai and was warmly greeted at the airport by Generalissimo Chiang Kai-shek, who cast protocol aside to welcome the special American envoy.

The two men and Mme. Chiang left at once for the generalissimo's official residence to begin talks that may vitally influence strife-torn China's hopes of internal peace and unity.

They clasped hands on Nanking's dusty, windswept airfield at a moment when all China and a large part of the Orient watched tensely for signs that General Marshall's mission might bring an end to the country's undeclared civil war.

Generalissimo Chiang's presence at the airport was regarded as a significant gesture of friendship for the United States. According to protocol in such matters the generalissimo would have awaited General Marshall in his official residence inside the walled city.

"Tell him I am deeply honored," General Marshall said to the Generalissimo's Chief of Staff, Gen. Shang Chen, who was serving as interpreter. The generalissimo replied: "I welcome you to Nanking."

The two men met for the first time since the Cairo conference in 1943. Their talks are expected to cover a wide range of topics, the most pressing of which are the halting of internal hostilities and the possible formation of a coalition government taking in all major political groups.

The American envoy's plane was trailed out of Shanghai by a transport carrying more than thirty correspondents and photographers.

An Associated Press correspondent reported from Shanghai that the lull in the North China military situation was regarded as at least partly attributable to General Marshall's arrival. The conflicting factions seem to be marking time, he said, while waiting to see what the American envoy accomplishes.

In Chungking a Chinese Com-

Continued on Page 5, Column 5

Major Fabbricatore Convicted; Gets 3 Years for Army Frauds

Special to The New York Times.

MITCHEL FIELD, L. I., Dec. 21—The meteoric Army career of 27-year-old Alphonse J. Fabbricatore, which saw him rise from private to major, came to an inglorious end today as a general court-martial board of ten officers found him guilty of seventeen of nineteen specifications involving fraudulent transfers and discharges of enlisted men at the Army Air Forces base here.

He was at once sentenced to dismissal from the service, forfeiture of pay and allowances, and three years at hard labor. The verdict of the board and the sentence was announced by Brig. Gen. John R. Hawkins, commanding general of the First Fighter Command, based at the field, president of the board.

Standing at rigid attention before the board, Major Fabbricatore declared:

"In spite of these findings, I still say that my conscience is free."

He asked for and received permission to telephone his wife at their home, 255 Cedar Street, Hempstead. To reporters he said: "Considering the length of the trial and the number of specifications, I do not consider that a severe sentence." He was composed throughout the trial, which covered a full two weeks, and showed no emotion when the sentence was read.

Minutes of the trial will be reviewed by Maj. Gen. Robert W. Douglass Jr., commanding general of the First Air Force, who may decrease but not add to the sentence. Successively the case will go to the Board of Review of the Judge Advocate General's office and then to the Board of Review recently set up by President Truman. The entire procedure is expected to consume from six weeks to six months.

Pending the various reviews the Major will be relieved of his rank and turned over to military police for confinement at this field.

The board deliberated two hours before reaching a verdict in secret.

Continued on Page 20, Column 3

GEN. GEORGE S. PATTON JR. Associated Press, 1945

Gen. Patton Dies Quietly in Sleep; Burial in Europe Decided Upon

Continued From Page 1

their former chief would be held within the next few days.

"I personally have lost a great friend; the country a great citizen and soldier; his family a true and devoted husband and father," he added. "Every American will join with his friends, his comrades of the Third Army who fought with him, and with his family in mourning his death."

Mrs. Patton, who arrived in Heidelberg more than a week ago and had been the guest of Lieut. Gen. Geoffrey Keyes, commander of the Seventh Army, was not present as death claimed her husband. When his condition became alarming she moved to the hospital and was occupying a room arranged for her a short distance down the hall. Capt. William Duane Jr., one of three physicians in charge of the case, summoned her promptly when his patient suffered a sinking spell, but he had breathed his last before she reached the bedside.

Lieut. Margery Rundell of Ashland, Wis., Army nurse who was on duty at the time, was the only other person present.

PATTON'S CAREER A BRILLIANT ONE

Germans Admitted He Was the American Field Commander Whom They Feared Most

Gen. George Smith Patton Jr. was one of the most brilliant soldiers in American history. Audacious, unorthodox and inspiring, he led his troops to great victories in North Africa, Sicily and on the Western Front. Nazi generals admitted that of all American field commanders he was the one they most feared. To Americans he was a worthy successor of such hard-bitten cavalrymen as Philip Sheridan, J. E. B. Stuart and Nathan Bedford Forrest.

His great soldierly qualities were matched by one of the most colorful personalties of his period. About him countless legends clustered—some true, some untrue, but all testifying to the firm hold he had upon the imaginations of his men. He went into action with two pearl-handled revolvers in holsters on his hips. He was the master of an unprintable brand of eloquence, yet at times he coined phrases that will live in the American Army's traditions.

"We shall attack and attack until we are exhausted, and then we shall attack again," he told his troops before the initial landings in North Africa, thereby summarizing the military creed that won victory after victory along the long road that led from Casablanca to the heart of Germany.

At El Guettar in March of 1943 he won the first major American victory over Nazi arms. In July of that year he leaped from a landing barge and waded ashore to the beachhead at Gela, Sicily, thus beginning a campaign that, as he himself observed, out-blitzed the inventors of Blitzkreig. In just thirty-eight days the American Seventh Army, under his leadership, and the British Eighth Army, under Gen. Sir Bernard Montgomery, conquered all of Sicily.

But it was as the leader of his beloved Third Army on the Western Front that General Patton staked out his strongest claims to military greatness. In ten months his armor and infantry roared through six countries—France, Belgium, Luxembourg, Germany, Czechoslovakia and Austria. It crossed the Seine, the Loire, the Moselle, the Saar, the Rhine, the Danube and a score of lesser rivers; captured more than 750,000 Nazis, and killed or disabled 500,000 others.

There were times, in those great days when the tank spearheads of the Third were racing across France with almost unbelievable speed and again when they were cutting the dying Nazi armies to pieces in the final spring of the war, that not even Supreme Headquarters itself knew where his vanguards were. Driven by his iron will, his advanced units had to be supplied with gasoline and maps dropped by air.

About such a leader it was inevitable that heroic myths grew up. One eager war correspondent wrote that he jumped onto the Normandy beachhead waving a $1,000 bill and offering to bet it that he would beat Marshal Montgomery to Berlin. When the tale caught up with him, he pithily remarked that he had never seen a bill of that denomination.

One of his men brought back the story that he swam the icy, 150-foot Sauer River in January, 1945, under machine gun and artillery fire, to inspire the men of the Third to follow him. That, too, General Patton denied, but the extent to which the story was believed was eloquent testimony to General Patton's habit of being where the fighting was fiercest.

His best-known nickname—"Old Blood and Guts"—was one that he detested, but his men loved. "His guts and my blood," his wounded veterans used to say when they were flown back here for hospitalization. His explosive wrath and lurid vocabulary became legendary wherever American soldiers fought.

General Patton had a softer side to his nature, too. He composed two volumes of poetry, which he stipulated were not to be published until after his death. He was an intensely religious man, who liked to sing in church and who knew the Episcopal Order of Morning Prayer by heart.

He seemed fated to be the center of controversy. Again and again, when his fame and popularity were at their height, some rash statement or ill-considered deed precipitated a storm about his head. **The most celebrated of these incidents, of course, was the slapping of a soldier whom he took to be a malingerer but who was actually suffering from battle fatigue in a hospital during the Sicilian campaign.**

This episode resulted in widespread demands for his removal from the command of American soldiers, in Congress and in the press, and caused the Senate to delay his confirmation to the permanent rank of major general for almost a year. General Eisenhower sharply rebuked him, but insisted that his military qualifications, loyalty and tenacity made him invaluable in the field.

The turmoil over this incident had hardly died away when he caused another stir by a speech at the opening of a club for American soldiers in London. The original version of his remarks there quoted him as saying that the British and American peoples were destined to rule the world, but after this had evoked an outburst of criticism Army press relations officers insisted that he had actually said that "we British, American and, of course, the Russian people" were destined to rule.

He raised another brief teapot tempest when he came home in June, 1945, and told a Sunday school class that its members would be the officers and nurses of the next war. But this was nothing compared to the furore he caused by an interview he granted American correspondents after his return to Germany. Discussing conditions in Bavaria, where the military government was under his command, he asserted that too much fuss was being made over denazification and compared the Nazi party to the losers in an election between Democrats and Republicans back home.

General Eisenhower promptly called him on the carpet for these remarks. General Patton promised that he would be loyal to General Eisenhower's orders and to the Potsdam agreements prescribing the complete and ruthless elimination of all elements of nazism from German life, but ten days later, on Oct. 2, 1945, he was removed from the command of his beloved Third Army.

Although reports were current that he might retire, General Patton took his transfer in soldierly silence. He assumed command of the American Fifteenth Army, a paper organization devoted to a study of the tactical lessons to be learned from the war just completed, and told friends that this was in line with what had been his favorite mental occupation since he was 7 years old: the study of war.

Although he customarily signed himself George Smith Patton Jr., General Patton was actually the third in line of his family to bear that name. The original George Smith Patton, his grandfather, was a graduate of Virginia Military Institute, and became a colonel in the Confederate Army. He was killed in action at the battle of Cedar Creek.

Expert Horseman From Childhood

General Patton's father went through V. M. I., then studied law, and moved west. He married a daughter of Benjamin Wilson, who was the first Mayor of Los Angeles, and for whom Mount Wilson was named. The future general was born on the family ranch at San Gabriel, Calif., on Nov. 11, 1885, and from childhood was an expert horseman.

At the age of 18 he came east and entered V. M. I., but after a year there he entered West Point with the class of 1909. There is a legend at the academy that he boasted at his entrance that he would be cadet captain, the highest post in the cadet corps, and that he would also be the first member of his class to become a general. Actually, he was cadet adjutant, the second highest post, and was the second member of the class to become a general.

He was a poor student—throughout his life he remained remarkably deficient in spelling—but an outstanding athlete at the Point. He excelled as a sprinter on the track team, and was also an expert fencer, swimmer, rider and shot. He continued his interest in sports and athletics after his graduation as a second lieutenant of cavalry.

In 1912 he represented the United States at the Olympic Games in Stockholm, Sweden, competing in the modern pentathlon, a contest which up to that time had been almost monopolized by Swedish Army officers. He finished fifth among more than thirty contestants, immediately after four Swedes. Of the five events, swimming, riding, fencing, running and shooting, he made his poorest showing in the pistol marksmanship competition, but he subsequently practiced until he overcame this weakness.

Early in his Army career he established himself as a hell-for-leather cavalry man. His first post was at Fort Sheridan, Ill., but in December, 1911, he was transferred to Fort Myer, Va., where he was detailed to design a new cavalry saber. In 1913 he went to France to study French saber methods, and on his return was made Master of the Sword at the Mounted Service School, Fort Riley, Kan.

He accompanied Gen. John J. Pershing as his aide on the punitive expedition into Mexico after the bandit, Pancho Villa, in 1916, and the next year he went to France with the general as a member of his staff. He attended the French Tank School and then saw action at the battle of Cambrai, where the British first used tanks on a large scale.

The new weapon was one to gladden the heart of a cavalryman, and from that time on his service was closely connected with tanks. He was assigned to organize and direct the American Tank Center at Langres. **For his service in that capacity he was subsequently awarded the Distinguished Service Medal. But he was not satisfied with a training command, and sought action.**

He took command of the 304th Brigade of the Tank Corps and distinguished himself by his leadership of it in the St. Mihiel offensive in September, 1918. Later that autumn, during the Meuse-Argonne offensive, he was severely wounded in the left leg while charging a pillbox, after 40 per cent of the tanks in his command had been disabled.

His life was saved by Pvt. Joseph T. Angelo of Camden, N. J., who dragged him to safety in a shell hole.

After the first World War he served with tank units and then with the cavalry at various posts in the United States. He was graduated from the Cavalry School, the Command and General Staff School and the Army War College. While on duty in the office of the Chief of Cavalry in Washington, he was detailed as aide to the Prince of Wales on one of his visits to this country. He told the Prince that a game called "craps" was very popular in this country, and taught him to play it.

A Colonel in 1940

When this country began to rearm in the summer of 1940 Patton was a colonel. He was sent to Fort Benning, Ga., for duty as commander of a brigade of the Second Armored Division, then being formed. In April, 1941, he became its commanding officer and made the division famous as a tough and rough-and-ready outfit. Promoted to corps commander, he organized the Desert Training Center in California.

When the North African invasion was planned, General Patton was placed in command of the American forces scheduled to land on the Atlantic coast of Morocco. One of the closest of the many narrow escapes for which he was noted came when a landing boat into which he was about to step was sunk. But he got ashore and after a brief but fierce fight took his objectives.

During the Tunisian campaign that followed, General Patton became celebrated for the strictness of his discipline. He punished men who failed to wear their helmets, even in back areas.

After the American reverse at Kasserine Pass in February, General Patton took command of the Second United States Corps, which forced the Nazis back into a narrow corridor between the mountains and the sea, up which the British Eighth Army under General Montgomery pursued them. He won the battle of El Guettar in March, but not long thereafter disappeared from the public eye. On April 16 Gen. Omar Bradley succeeded him in command of the Second Corps.

The reason for the shift was not made known at the time and there were rumors that General Patton had fallen into disfavor. Actually, General Eisenhower had withdrawn him from action in order to prepare the American Seventh Army for the invasion of Sicily in July. The invasion was brilliantly successful, and General Patton's troops cut clear across the island to Palermo; then fought their way along the north coast to Messina.

This magnificent feat of arms was marred, however, by the slapping episode, which did not become generally known to the public until the following November. General Patton, who drove himself as hard as he drove his men, visited a hospital not far from the front lines at a time when he had been under prolonged strain and was in an overwrought condition.

There he encountered two men who showed no signs of visible wounds, but who had been diagnosed by medical authorities as suffering from battle neurosis. Losing his temper, General Patton called them "yellow bellies" and other unprintable epithets, and struck one of them so that his helmet liner flew off and rolled on the ground.

General Eisenhower made an investigation and sharply castigated General Patton, although he did not formally reprimand him. General Patton made personal apologies to all those present at the time of the episode, and later sent public apologies to each division of the Seventh Army.

General Patton did not appear during the campaign on the Italian mainland that followed, and some observers thought he had been relegated to a secondary role because of the storm of criticism that his action had caused in this country. Actually, however, General Eisenhower had picked him for a key role in the invasion of Western Europe, and he was then in England preparing for it.

Whereabouts a Mystery

For almost two months after D-Day, June 6, 1944, General Patton's whereabouts remained a mystery. The fact that he was in England, at the head of an army, was well known, and the inability of the Nazi intelligence to locate him forced their High Command to retain the German Fifteenth Army in the Pas de Calais area, far from the Normandy beachhead, lest he head a landing there.

Instead, the Third Army landed on the beachhead in great secrecy, and deployed behind the First Army. When the First Army broke the German lines between St. Lo and the sea on July 25, the Third Army poured through the breach to exploit it. The opportunity was ideal for a dashing, driving leader of General Patton's talents. His spearheads roared clear across the base of the Breton Peninsula, then turned east toward Paris.

"All the News That's Fit to Print."

The New York Times.

THE WEATHER
Slightly warmer today; Sunday rain or snow.
For weather report see next to last page.

VOL. LXIX...No. 22,673 • • • NEW YORK, SATURDAY, FEBRUARY 21, 1920. TWO CENTS Metropolitan District 50 Mile Radius | THREE CENTS Within 200 Miles | FOUR CENTS Elsewhere

REPUBLICANS ISSUE 'MODEL' PLATFORM; WOMEN RESENTFUL

Convention Demands Immediate Treaty Ratification with Senate Reservations.

DELEGATE SLATE INDORSED

National Affairs Covered in the Hope That Chicago Convention May Follow Lead.

MISS HAY STILL INSURGENT

Mrs. Knapp and Her Friends Charge That She Was Used as a Pawn by Chairman Glynn.

The program prepared by the Republican leaders for the unofficial State Convention at Carnegie Hall went through yesterday without a snarl. After a platform, which dealt mostly with national affairs, had been adopted and the four delegates and alternates at large for the National Convention in Chicago in June had been selected, the convention adjourned, with no attempt by the women to resent their being unrepresented by a delegate. While the women made no open manifestation of displeasure, many of them are nursing grudges.

Miss Mary Garrett Hay, who heads a faction opposed to the renomination of Senator James W. Wadsworth, Jr., and whose friends propagated a boom for her for delegate at large, said she had never objected to courtesy being extended to Senator Wadsworth, and that she was in no way opposed to Mrs. Arthur L. Livermore's going to the convention as alternate at large, but she knew it would be a disappointment to thousands of women "that the Empire State has not seen fit to recognize the new electorate by sending some woman as delegate and not merely as alternate."

At the same time Mrs. Florence Knapp of Syracuse and her friends considered that they had been badly treated by Chairman George A. Glynn and other leaders. They said it had been solemnly promised that Mrs. Knapp was to be one of the "Big Four," and that it looked very much as if she had been used by the men leaders as a pawn on the chessboard. They promised to let the State Committee hear from them later.

The Republican leaders figured that they had put out a very able document in their platform. As the platform deals almost entirely with national issues, the leaders hope it will be made the basis for the platform to be adopted at the National Convention.

The Platform in Brief.

The salient points of the platform are:

Immediate ratification of the treaty of peace with the Senate reservations, retaining for the United States its right to withdraw from the League of Nations on proper notice.

A declaration against Article X. in its present form and demanding protection for the Monroe Doctrine "in letter and spirit."

Establishment of an international high court of justice to decide disputes among nations and an international conference to promote and revise international law.

Speedy ratification of the woman suffrage amendment by State Legislatures so women may vote for President and Congressmen in November.

Vigorous measures to prevent the spread of radicalism.

Establishment of a commission on industrial relations to make strikes increasingly unnecessary and infrequent, with the right given to labor to share in determining the circumstances under which it shall be employed.

Reduction of public expenditures, with revision of taxation and business regulations to promote rather than to prevent enterprise and production.

Prompt legislation to authorize a national budget.

Retention of the "principles of protection" as a national policy to "insure the nation's economic independence."

Opposition to Government ownership of railroads and the Plumb plan.

A merchant marine flying the American flag and owned by private capital.

Reorganization of the Federal Trade Commission, which is charged with having "prostituted its proper functions."

A small standing army with a trained citizen reserve "subject to call for service only in case of declaration of war by Congress."

Enforcement of the immigration laws.

A constructive policy of co-operation for the prevention of war and the reduction of armaments "without sacrificing love of country and the American ideals to a false and harmful form of internationalism."

Sweet's Opinion.

Dr. Nicholas Murray Butler, himself a candidate for the nomination for President, was Chairman of the Committee on Resolutions, which drew up the platform, and Speaker Thaddeus C. Sweet of the Assembly was a member.

"It is a clean-cut declaration of the present-day aims and purposes of the party," commented Mr. Sweet. "It is both retrospective and prospective. It points out the existing dangers and suggests the remedy. It proposes to restore a republican form of government and put an end to autocracy and dictatorship; it points the way to the read-

Continued on Page Three.

Thousands Return to Europe, Blaming Prohibition Here

GENEVA, Feb. 19.—Thousands of Poles, Czechoslovaks and Jugoslavs, mostly of the middle and working classes, who made small fortunes in America, arrived in Switzerland recently on the way to their own countries, where their incomes will be increased by the rate of exchange some 60 to 80 per cent.

Some of them are returning through patriotism or homesickness, and others for gain, but fully three-fifths because, they declare, America has gone dry, which they consider tyranny, holding that after ten or twelve hours of work a workman should be permitted to buy his beer or other drink.

Thousands of the immigrants are awaiting trains at Basle, Constance and Buchs, which, owing to the lack of coal, are infrequent. Meantime the Swiss cafeterias are mixing a mild concoction labeled as whisky which is being sold to the exiles at a high price.

NAME MASTER MIND IN GREAT BOND PLOT

Court Petition Calls "Nicky" Arnstein Head of Plan to Steal $5,000,000 in Wall Street.

ONE OF THE GONDORF GANG

Surety Co. Seeks to Seize Money Gained by Thefts of $1,500,000 from Messengers.

Through the filing of an involuntary petition in bankruptcy yesterday the identity of the man the police allege to be the "master mind" in the recent plot to steal $5,000,000 worth of securities from brokerage houses and banks in the financial district was revealed.

According to the petition, which was filed by Paul S. Meyers, attorney for the National Surety Company at 115 Broadway, the man is Nicholas Arnstein, better known in the "white light" district as "Nicky" Arnstein, who also is alleged in the petition to be known internationally as a criminal, having been arrested in Paris, London and Monte Carlo at various times in the last ten years on swindling charges.

The petition of the surety company also says that Arnstein, who also is identified under half a dozen aliases which he gave to the police of this country and Europe when arrested at various times, is the man who received from criminals who robbed messengers in the financial district securities valued at $1,500,000. William A. Thompson, a Vice President of the surety company, declared after Judge A. N. Hand had appointed Edwards H. Child of 59 Wall Street receiver in the bankruptcy proceeding, that the assertion that the bankrupt was "Nicky" Arnstein was based on a confession recently made to Richard C. Murphy, Assistant District Attorney, by Joseph Gluck, one of seven men arrested ten days ago by Detectives Brown, Mayer and Mindheim in connection with the plot to steal $5,000,000 worth of securities.

Mr. Thompson also said that Gluck told Mr. Murphy and the detectives that about $1,500,000 which he and his brother, Irving Gluck, had stolen from messengers in the financial district had been turned over by him to "Nicky" Arnstein, who had disposed of most of them through crooked brokerage houses in this and other cities. The petition filed by the National Surety Company alleges that Arnstein, using the name J. W. Arnold, recently deposited in the Pacific Bank of this city $16,000, and Mr. Thompson asserted that the money was part of a payment "Nicky" Arnstein received from a brokerage house in this city for stolen securities placed with it.

Seeks Reimbursement.

The surety company says in its petition that the bankruptcy proceeding was instituted because the company, having issued what it called "blanket bonds" to members of the New York Stock Exchange, investment houses and banks in the financial district that have in the last six months lost more than $1,500,000 through thefts of securities from messengers employed by them, has been forced to reimburse those firms and banks for their losses.

It is also asserted in the petition that "Nicky" Arnstein has assets consisting of many thousands of dollars, the proceeds of the sale of stolen securities delivered to him by Gluck and others who have been operating in the Wall Street district. The petition also avers that Arnstein recently transferred large sums of money he had on deposit in banks in this city to "Nick Cohen and wife," which Mr. Thompson declared to be another alias assumed by Arnstein.

When the detectives recently arrested the Gluck brothers and "Big Bill" Furey, also well known in the "white light" region, on the charge of stealing $2,500 worth of securities from Murray Abramowitz, a messenger employed by Parrish & Co., brokers, at 115 Broadway, they revealed that they had uncovered a plot to steal $5,000,000 in securities from brokerage houses. Furey and the Gluck brothers were arrested in front of the Woolworth Building at Broadway and Park Place just after Joseph Gluck had taken the securities owned by Parrish & Co., from young Abramowitz's pocket.

The detectives said that for more than two months they had been on the trail of an organized band of criminals who were robbing brokerage houses in the financial district, and that the arrest of the Gluck brothers and "Big Bill" Furey was the result of a trap set by the police with the aid of young Abram-

Continued on Page Two.

ADMIRAL R. E. PEARY, POLE DISCOVERER, DIES AT CAPITAL

Arctic Explorer Succumbs to Pernicious Anemia After Two Years' Illness.

EIGHT ATTEMPTS AT POLE

Reached His Goal of Farthest North in 1909 After Leading Seven Previous Expeditions.

FRIENDS PAY HIM TRIBUTE

Foremost Northern Venturer, Says Stefansson—Burial at Arlington Likely.

Special to The New York Times.

WASHINGTON, Feb. 20.—Rear Admiral Robert Edwin Peary, United States Navy (Retired), the discoverer of the North Pole, died at 1:28 o'clock this morning at his residence in this city, 1,831 Wyoming Avenue. With him when the end came were Mrs. Peary, who was Miss Josephine Diebitsch of Washington; their son-in-law and daughter, Mr. and Mrs. Edward Stafford, and Miss Madge Diebitsch, a niece of Mrs. Peary. Admiral Peary was 64 years old. He probably will be buried at Arlington with full naval honors of his rank.

Admiral Peary's death was due to pernicious anemia. He was first found to be suffering from this disease about two years ago when he returned to Washington on a lecture tour in the interest of aerial military preparedness. His physicians decided that the only remedy for the disease lay in blood transfusion. Since then, according to a statement made today by the attending physician, Dr. H. F. Strine, Admiral Perry had undergone thirty-five transfusions of blood.

Two days ago the last transfusion operation was performed at the United States Naval Hospital. It was reported that Admiral Peary's condition had been improved and he was taken back to his home. Yesterday afternoon he suffered a relapse and failed to rally.

Since his return to the United States about ten years ago, after his discovery of the North Pole, Admiral Peary had divided his time between Washington and his Summer residence at Eagle Harbor, Me. His daughter, now Mrs. Stafford, was widely known as the "snow baby," from the fact that she was born in the arctic regions during one of the explorer's early expeditions. She has the distinction of having been born further north than any white child. Her husband is the son of Justice Stafford of the Supreme Court of the District of Columbia.

Furthered Aerial Navigation.

Admiral Peary devoted the last years of his life to furthering the cause of aerial navigation. He particularly advocated the establishment of a coast patrol by aircraft, and was actively engaged during American participation in the World War in the effort to have this policy carried out. Admiral Peary was a member of the Board of Governors of the Aero Club of America and was President of the Aerial League of America. Early this year it was announced that he had been elected President of the Aero Cruiser Corporation, which plans to build airships capable of crossing the ocean.

Daniels Pays Navy's Tribute.

WASHINGTON, Feb. 20.—Tribute to the achievements of Admiral Peary was paid by Secretary Daniels today in the following message of sympathy to Mrs. Peary:

"Voicing the sentiments of the whole navy, I desire to express deep sympathy in your bereavement. If any earthly comfort can help you in this hour, it must be the assurance that the whole country sorrows with you and that all over the world there will be profound regret at the death of your distinguished husband.

"He had the honor to accomplish the realization of a great ambition and to receive the plaudits of all nations. His great achievement brought particular distinction to the American Navy, of which he was an honored and distinguished officer."

Robert Peary, son of the Admiral, also was at the bedside of the famous explorer when he died.

LIFE OF EXPLORER FILLED WITH ACTIVITY

He Paid a Heavy Price for Fame as Foremost of Arctic Voyagers.

On the afternoon of Sept. 6, 1909, while the world was hailing Dr. Frederick A. Cook as the discoverer of the north pole, THE NEW YORK TIMES received the following message:

> Indian Harbor, via Cape Ray, N. F., Sept. 6, The New York Times, New York:
>
> I have the pole, April sixth. Expect arrive Chateau Bay, September seventh. Secure wire control for me there and arrange expedite transmission big story. PEARY.

Following the receipt of this message, other telegrams were received in this city to the same effect. Soon afterward

Continued on Page Four.

Air Traffic Convention Signed by British, French and Swiss

BERNE, Feb. 20.—Switzerland signed a provisional convention with France and Great Britain dealing with air traffic, which comes into force March 1. Each country agrees to grant free passage over its territories and territorial waters during peacetime to registered aircraft which comply with the conditions of the convention.

Air machines must not carry wireless without special licenses from their States, according to the agreement, and must cross frontiers only at certain points which are to be specified. Each of the States will name one or more airdromes on its territory which must be used for the arrival and departure of machines.

WILSON DENIES SHIP DEAL WITH BRITISH

But Gives Senate Copy of Proposed Compact to Credit Germany with Excess Over Losses.

SUBJECT TO CONGRESS WILL

Would Not Affect Our Title to Seized Vessels—Some Officials Place Cost to Us at $30,000,000

Special to The New York Times.

WASHINGTON, Feb. 20.—President Wilson in an official communication to the Senate today denied that there was or had been any agreement with officials of Great Britain concerning the sale of ex-German ships in the possession of the United States. Mr. Wilson's statement, which was in reply to a resolution by Senator Brandegee, Republican, of Connecticut, adopted by the Senate, adds, "nor is there any agreement or understanding with respect to what disposition shall be made of those ships by the United States."

The President at the same time, however, "in order that the Senate may be in possession of all the information there is in any way relating to the vessels in question" submitted to the Senate a copy of a proposed agreement signed by him and Lloyd George in Paris in May, 1919, on the stipulation that it meet the wishes of Congress. Under this Germany would eventually be credited by the Reparations Commission with the excess of the valuation of the seized ships over the total merchant tonnage lost by the United States in the war. But he made it clear that the proposed agreement does not affect the title to the ships.

This tentative agreement, Mr. Wilson said, he intended to submit to Congress at the proper time, when the Versailles Treaty had been ratified.

The tentative agreement covers all ships captured, seized or retained by any of the Allied or Associated Governments, and Shipping Board officials pointed out that it was signed after the controversy between the British Premier and Mr. Wilson in which Lloyd George's proposal that all the ships captured, seized or detained be pooled and allotted on the basis of losses was opposed by the President.

Chairman Payne of the Shipping Board said tonight that an appraisal of the ex-German ships, made at the direction of the President, and taking into account the damage done to the ships by the crews, placed the value of the ninety-five ships at $34,193,190. The aggregate tonnage of the seized vessels is placed at 630,000 tons, and American losses through war causes are estimated at 362,751 tons.

"We take the ships absolutely, title free," said Chairman Payne, "and when we come to settle with Germany we put in the common pool the difference between our losses and the appraised value of the ships."

Some officials in Washington estimated that were the agreement to become effective it might lead to the United States having to credit Germany with about $30,000,000 before the Reparations Commission.

Text of President's Message.

The President's message to the Senate was as follows:

"I have the honor to acknowledge the receipt of a resolution passed by the Senate on Feb. 14 requesting the President to inform that body 'whether any, and if so what, agreement or understanding exists between him and officials of Great Britain concerning the disposition by the United States of America of the German ships which the Shipping Board is proposing to sell, or which were acquired by the United States after the termination of hostilities between said United States and the Central European Teutonic powers.'

"The ships for the purchase of which bids have been asked by the Shipping Board were taken over by Executive orders issued pursuant to the joint resolution of Congress of May 12, 1917, authorizing the President to take over for the United States the possession and title of any vessel within its jurisdiction under enemy ownership or under the registry of an enemy country. The Government of the United States is not in possession of any ex-German vessels except those taken over under this resolution. Under an armistice agreement between the German Government and the allied and associated powers, certain German vessels were taken over, primarily for the transport of food to Europe, including Germany, and for

Continued on Page Eight.

SEE CLOSE VOTE ON RAILWAY BILL IN HOUSE TODAY

Advocates of Conference Report Expect Its Adoption by a Small Majority.

LABOR OPPONENTS ACTIVE

Their Threat to Prevent Reelection Turns Some Wavering Members Against Measure.

FARMERS ALSO OPPOSING

Both Sides Marshal Their Forces as Debate on the Bill Proceeds.

Special to The New York Times.

WASHINGTON, Feb. 20.—Opposition by organized labor to the adoption of the conference report on the Railroad bill by the House, it is asserted, has greatly weakened the support claimed by advocates of the measure. Republican leaders admit tonight that the declaration by organized labor leaders that they intend to organize a campaign to defeat those who vote for the report has caused wavering members to inform their colleagues they cannot afford to stand against the dictates of labor.

Throughout the day Republican and Democratic leaders were most active in checking up their canvass. Telegrams were sent to absent members and every effort was employed to have a full attendance tomorrow when the House, after a five hours' debate, will vote on the adoption of the conference report. It was announced by Republican leaders tonight that if all those who had promised support carried out their promises the bill would be adopted by a majority ranging from 20 to 40. Indications are that the drive now being made against the bill by organized labor and the Farmers' National Council will reduce the vote to a narrow majority.

La Follette to Lead Senate Opposition.

Senator La Follette of Wisconsin, it was announced today, will return to lead the Senate fight against the adoption of the report. He admitted in discussing the outlook with labor representatives that there was no real hope of defeating the bill, as the country insisted upon the return of the railroads to their owners and legislation which would assure an adequate return to the carriers.

In the opinion of those in charge of the railroad legislation, both houses will adopt the conference report and send the bill to the President early next week, so that the railroads will be returned on March 1, with legislation to protect their interests, provided the President approves the bill.

While the conference report was not taken up in the House today, it was referred to at considerable length by three Democratic members—Representatives Blanton of Texas, Rayburn of Texas and Huddleston of Alabama.

Mr. Huddleston told the House that passage of the Railroad bill would assure the defeat for re-election of any member who voted for it.

Forty Democrats Opposed.

Representative Rayburn, who is a Democratic member of the Interstate Commerce Committee, which prepared the Railroad bill, pleaded with his colleagues to get behind the measure. He said such legislation was necessary, and, while he did not agree with all the features of the bill, yet, on the whole, it represented wise and progressive legislation.

These speeches of Messrs. Blanton and Rayburn strengthened the Democrats to some extent, but it was reported that forty Democrats would not support the bill.

Mr. Rayburn said he could not agree with the bill as a whole, but he intended to take what he believed to be the right course, regardless of threats which might come from the outside or from any organization, whether of owners or employes of the carriers. Mr. Rayburn insisted that action must be taken before March 1, or chaos and bankruptcy would result, and for that reason, as well as the fact that he supported many provisions of the bill, he would vote for the report.

"Every man who knows the situation knows that it is not the labor provision to which Mr. Gompers and his organization objects," said Mr. Rayburn. "No man or set of men in America can write a bill for return of the railroads that Gompers and his crowd will indorse. They want the Plumb plan; they want two years extension of Government control. These men know that if the situation goes on and the railroads are held for two years longer, it means what they are after, which is Government ownership, and that only. The fear that would come to me would be to vote against the bill and for the rate of expenditures to go on for two years longer. The issues will be joined pretty soon."

George P. Hampton, Managing Director of the Farmers' National Council, made public tonight a letter written to members of Congress opposing the railroad bill, and asking them to work for the two-year extension of Government operation of the roads. Mr. Hampton said nearly every national farmers' organization of any size, regardless of its position on the return of the railroads, had opposed the Government guarantee of dividends and a Government subsidy, which was specifically provided in the bill, which instructed the Interstate Commerce Commission to fix rates which would yield 5½ per cent. on the aggregate value of the railroads and permit them to add not to exceed one-half of 1 per cent. of such aggregate value as a guaranteed dividend.

WILSON DEMANDS ADRIATIC SETTLEMENT ON THE BASIS OF DECEMBER AGREEMENT; WASHINGTON WANTS NOTES MADE PUBLIC

Forecast of President Wilson's Note to Premiers Covering Disputed Points of Adriatic Settlement

Special to The New York Times.

WASHINGTON, Feb. 20.—As nearly as the President's note to the allied powers on the Adriatic settlement can be forecast tonight, in the light of the best obtainable information, it will cover these points:

1—He cannot accept those changes made by the Anglo-Franco-Italian accord of January in the Anglo-Franco-American accord of December, which he regards as vital. He would point out that the United States was not consulted in the making of these changes, and explains why he could not have accepted those of them which he considers basic, even if he had been consulted.

2—That he cannot accept, in particular, that change in the Anglo-Franco-American accord of December which provided for the cession to Italy of control over the Volosca strip running around the shore line from Fiume, through territory inhabited by the Croats, to connect with Istria Italiana.

3—That all questions relative to the future status of Dalmatia should be determined by negotiation through diplomatic channels. He also desires that the United States should be considered in the proposed changes in the boundaries of Albania.

4—That he is unalterably opposed to the application of the Treaty of London, of April 26, 1915, either as an alternative for failure to effect an Adriatic settlement, or otherwise.

5—The note will set forth, in careful detail, the ground of the objections of the President to the modified plan of settlement and his reasons for opposing the enforcement of the Treaty of London.

CHANCE FOR CLASH ON TURKISH POLICY

Wilson's Opposition to Secret Treaties May Affect Near Eastern Settlement.

SECRET SESSION ON SULTAN

Prospect of His Stay in Constantinople Excites Bitter Comment in British Press.

By EDWIN L. JAMES.

Special Cable to THE NEW YORK TIMES.

PARIS, Feb. 19.—The importance of the pending differences between the American Government and the Governments of the allied nations reaches far beyond the Adriatic problem. Much more than the Adriatic does Turkey hold possibilities of clashes between American ideas and ideals of peacemaking and European ideas and ideals. Just as the secret agreement of London complicates Adriatic adjustments, so another secret agreement affects the Turkish settlements.

Today's dispatches from London say that the allied Premiers have determined to allow the Greeks to hold Smyrna and a certain amount of the hinterland. The secret treaty of 1917, signed by England, France, Italy and Greece, promised Smyrna to Greece. The ideas of Premier Venizelos and those of President Wilson as to how the boundary line should run in the Smyrna district are miles and miles apart.

Furthermore, it is most likely that the progress of the Turkish discussions will reveal other promises which the Allies have made one another, as, for instance, regarding Italy's claims in Anatolia, those of France in Syria, or England's in Mesopotamia. President Wilson is bitterly opposed to the Treaty of London. He is probably no less opposed to the secret treaties affecting Turkey. On the other hand, Premiers Millerand, Lloyd George and Nitti, as well as Premier Venizelos, contend that they are bound by those agreements.

Council Considers the Turkish Treaty.

LONDON, Feb. 20.—Some of the less important phases of the Turkish Peace Treaty were discussed by the Allied Supreme Council at its one brief session today. The particular points taken up, however, were not revealed.

It is believed the Turkish question has reached a stage where the council must await the reports of the several commissions it has created to consider various ends of the subject. It is desired also to have Premier Millerand of France with the council when the more important questions are being considered. The French Prime Minister is expected to be present on Monday.

An interesting sidelight on the Turkish situation appeared yesterday afternoon, when it was announced arrangements had been made to publish officially throughout India the allied decision that the Sultan is to remain in Constantinople. Opposition among Indian Moslems to the removal of the head of the Church from the spiritual capital has given cause for much anxiety.

Special Cable to THE NEW YORK TIMES.

LONDON, Feb. 19.—Although assenting today to Premier Lloyd George's plea for adjournment of debate on Turkey, the Liberals are greatly disturbed over what has already been done. Bonar Law the other day was questioned by Lord Robert Cecil about the future of Constantinople. He refused to tell the Commons anything, and a few hours

Continued on Page Two.

SUPREME COUNCIL ACTS TO END LEAKS

Bald Communique Now the Only Information Given to Press in London.

NEW PROTESTS AT SECRECY

Failure to Publish Adriatic Correspondence Censured by Two London Journals.

Special Cable to THE NEW YORK TIMES.

LONDON, Feb. 19.—The lid has been shut down with a snap on the proceedings of the Supreme Council. When the representatives of British and American newspapers gathered at the Foreign Office at the appointed hour tonight to learn what progress had been made during the day all they received was a short communiqué announcing the hour the statesmen met, the hour they adjourned, and the fact that they filled the interval by chatting about Russia.

The sudden resort to the communiqué form of giving out news is regarded as a deliberate snub to the British press. When the conference adjourned to London it was arranged that Lord Riddell, as head of the Newspaper Proprietors' Association, was to be the channel of communication between the statesmen and the press. He was to visit 10 Downing Street twice daily and learn what had been accomplished and would then hold conferences at the Foreign Office with the newspaper men and satisfy their curiosity as well as he could.

To these gatherings the American correspondents have been kindly admitted. A similar arrangement was made by the French correspondents, their source of information, however, being the French Embassy. It appeared very soon, however, that the French had the best of the bargain. Whatever might be the understanding as to the news to be published, the French Press Bureau worked much more freely than the British. All kinds of news kept a deep secret at the Foreign Office seemed commonplaces at the French Embassy, and after Pertinax had published the news of the Wilson note and the Matin had made the statement that Greece was to get Smyrna people began to look for cables from Paris, and not to the columns of home news to find out what was taking place in Downing Street.

So the members of the Newspaper Proprietors' Association met yesterday and solemnly considered the situation. They passed resolutions protesting against the facilities granted to the French press and called upon the conference to "take immediate and effective steps to insure the prompt, systematic and simultaneous issue" of the news to the press of all countries. The Supreme Council responded so far as to "take immediate and effective steps," but in place of letting British newspaper men know all the interesting items their French colleagues had been enjoying, refused to tell anything of value to anybody.

It is, of course, presumed that Pertinax and all the other French correspondents are tonight getting nothing but the communiqué; but every London newspaper man will read the telegrams from Paris before he accepts the supposition as a fact.

The Daily Mail, protesting against the official reticence displayed by the British Government in announcing the decisions reached by the Supreme Council, says that he crops of rumors regarding President Wilson's note and the allied reply is a striking example of the evil of partial disclosures.

"One of the cardinal rules laid down by President Wilson for the Peace Con-

Continued on Page Two.

NEW NOTE IS VERY POSITIVE

Rejects Treaty of London and Last Compromise but Leaves Door Open.

WILL PROBABLY GO TODAY

This Statement Expected to End Argument, but Situation Is Not Regarded as Acute.

FULL PUBLICITY FAVORED

Washington Officials Desire to Give Out All Documents When Latest Note Is Delivered.

Our Aid in Turkish Settlement Now Asked; Wilson May Refuse

Special to The New York Times.

WASHINGTON, Feb. 20.—President Wilson has been invited to send a plenipotentiary to the allied conference in Paris on March 10 to deal with questions involved in arranging the Turkish settlement, preliminary to the actual peace treaty with Turkey. No decision has been reached by the President, but present indications are that no American plenipotentiary will participate in the conference.

This is not to be interpreted as meaning that President Wilson is not concerned about the settlement to be made with Turkey. It is understood that he hopes that the Turkish treaty will be framed on the same principles of a new order of right and justice for which he fought in framing the German, Austrian, Bulgarian and Hungarian treaties and that he stands ready to submit his views, if sought, through regular diplomatic channels.

When in Paris he outlined to the allied Premiers his views respecting the Turkish problem.

Special to The New York Times.

WASHINGTON, Feb. 20.—President Wilson's reply to the allied note on the Adriatic settlement will probably be ready in its final form to be cabled to London tomorrow. It did not go forward today because, as drafted yesterday by the President and turned over to the State Department, it had to be put in shape by the State Department officials. There has been no delay in the preparation of the note. It was understood yesterday that it probably could not be a complete document inside of forty-eight hours. As the arguments advanced by the Allies are being dealt with and answered categorically, time is required for the State Department's part of the work. The course followed in the preparation of diplomatic notes during the war is being observed in this case.

There has been no change in the President's attitude. He is standing firm on the Anglo-Franco-American accord on the Adriatic problem as embraced in the joint proposal to which these nations agreed in writing at Paris on Dec. 9. His position is today the same as when that agreement was reached. He is emphatically opposed to the Anglo-Franco-Italian accord of Jan. 9 (so-called compromise of Jan. 20), involving a modification, without consulting the United States, of a plan to which we had already become a party. This modification would have imposed upon the United States certain vital responsibilities, too important, in the President's settled opinion, to be disregarded by this country, both from the viewpoint of what has taken place under the Anglo-Franco-Italian plan of settlement, and its bearing on our proposed participation in the general peace settlement under the League of Nations and in connection with the application of the Treaties of Versaillics, St. Germain and Neuilly.

Note a Positive Statement.

The statement in THE NEW YORK TIMES this morning that the President is "standing pat" in his opposition to the project of the Allied Powers can be reiterated in the light of what has been learned today. It can be asserted very positively that the position of the Government of the United States is being so directly, firmly and unequivocally stated in the reply now being drafted that it will leave no doubt in the minds of the Allied Premiers as to the attitude of the President in rigid opposition to the Anglo-Franco-Italian accord, the "secret" Treaty of London and the communication of these to the Government of Jugoslavia as alternatives which must be accepted as an ultimatum.

President Wilson is not disposed to engage in further argument over the matter with the Allies. His reply will virtually permit no discussion of his reasons for rejecting both the Anglo-Franco-Italian accord of January and its alternative—the enforcement of the pact of London. The President has endeavored in the note now receiving its finishing touches to meet the allied argument with a clear statement of his position on each point raised by the communication from the powers. He has undertaken to make it perfectly

EXPLORER'S LIFE FILLED WITH ACTION

Continued from Page 1, Column 3.

The Associated Press received the following:

Indian Harbor, via Cap Ray, N. F., Sept. 6:

Stars and Stripes nailed to the pole.
PEARY.

These messages, flashed from the coast of Labrador to New York and thence to the four corners of the globe while Dr. Cook was being acclaimed by the crowned heads of Europe and the world at large as the discoverer of the north pole, added a remarkable chapter to the story of an alleged achievement which had held the civilized world up to the highest pitch of interest since April 1 of that year, when Dr. Cook's claim to having reached "the top of the world" was telegraphed from the Shetland Islands.

Controversy with Dr. Cook.

With the message from the then Commander Peary there arose one of the greatest controversies of all the ages over the honor of the first discovery.

Commander Peary's assertions were not seriously questioned, but among newspaper readers there came to be two great camps, for and against Cook. There was instant acceptance among the geographers in Washington of the assertion of Peary in his laconic message, and there was ready rejoicing, for Peary was popular with scientific men in the capital and they were ready to take his word at its face value without examination or delay.

There was a sharp contrast in the attitude of the same men toward the announcement from Dr. Cook. At first they were disposed to accept Cook's assertion and announced their belief that Dr. Cook really did reach the north pole in April, 1908—nearly a year ahead of Peary. The latter, it was felt certain, would be able to produce documentary evidence that would be not only complete but unquestionable. Not so with Dr. Cook. On him was imposed the necessity of producing the records which later failed to constitute the authority of his claim.

Behind Peary was the record of seven successful voyages to the arctic, his official standing in the United States Navy and in scientific circles, and thus he easily held the commanding position in the controversy. Scientists in European capitals at once hailed Peary, as before they believed Cook, but, as in Washington and New York, there was the belief that both men had reached the pole—Cook ahead of Peary. But it was only after the scientific bodies, one by one, had sifted the evidence and pronounced Cook's claims unfounded that Peary's title as the discoverer of the north pole was really won.

The Price Peary Paid for Fame.

This episode, with its bitterness, was only one item in the price which Peary paid for the immortal fame that is now acknowledged to be his. He spent practically all he had in money, gave all that was in him for hard work, and suffered all that the human frame could endure from hunger, cold, and disappointment. He made eight journeys to the arctic, spent upward of half a million dollars, and several times barely escaped the death which in various forms had been the fate of more than 700 explorers before him.

Dr. Cook had been the surgeon of the Peary expedition to the arctic in 1891-2, and since 1909 had been on several trips of exploration in many parts of the world. Before he made the arctic trip, which brought him sudden fame and as sudden condemnation as a "monumental faker," "monster of duplicity," and "intrepid liar"—some of the epithets which have been applied to him—he had laid claim to having reached the top of Mount McKinley. This, too, he is alleged to have "dreamed."

He still claims, however, that he is the discoverer of the north pole, and several years sought to have this title bestowed on him by Congress.

Dr. Cook Repudiated.

Dr. Cook was repudiated by the tribunal of his own choosing, the Danish Geographical Society, Copenhagen University, and other institutions in Denmark. Rear Admiral Peary's evidence, on the other hand, was sustained by the National Geographical Society and many similar organizations, and Denmark approved the American experts' findings. Philip Gibbs, whose dispatches from the British battlefront are received by The New York Times, in a dispatch from Copenhagen to The London Chronicle and The New York Times on Sept. 7, 1909, said:

"Dr. Frederick A. Cook's lecture tonight before the King of Denmark and a great audience at the Geographical Society proves conclusively that his claim to have reached the north pole belongs to the realm of fairy tales.

"It was all so very quick. In his own phrase he 'climbed the ladder of latitude with lightning rapidity,' although on the downward journey he beat about ice floes in a bewildered way, and put up for months in Winter quarters, in spite of the daily risk of starvation, for his provisions would have been exhausted months before but for the convenient mirables of magic bears and birds. They appeared on the ice and he was able to kill them with slings. In the same way the magic boat appeared. We never heard of that boat before.

"His way back was like a delirious dream of an arctic explorer, zigzagging and returning constantly upon his own path. The great audience which was anxious to hear about the north pole remained at that spot exactly two minutes on this personally conducted tour, and knew little more than what the map and geography primers had taught them as children. But they were solaced with Dr. Cook's last words, that if they desired further knowledge they would be able to buy his book, which would be published shortly.

"There were many awkward pauses, and Dr. Cook stumbled badly over figures. His face was flushed, his forehead beaded with perspiration. He had the grim look of a man determined to be believed as he drove that 'big nail' home with unconvincing, flashy phrases. I am in a position to state that the Danish Geographical Society, in limiting the lecture to an hour, asked Dr. Cook to dilate especially on his travels near the pole and what Eskimos said and did on that April day. He did not do so tonight."

REAR ADMIRAL ROBERT E. PEARY.

Further, in 1917, Donald McMillan, the explorer, retraced the route Dr. Cook took in his journey toward the north pole, accompanied by an Eskimo who had traveled with Dr. Cook, and he interviewed other Eskimos who were in Cook's party. He found that the physician's "furthest north" was far short of the pole.

The first step that led Peary toward the pole was taken in Washington one day, when he walked into a book store and picked up a fugitive account of Greenland. He became an insatiable reader on the subject of the arctic.

Began Career as Draftsman.

Robert Edwin Peary was born at Cresson, Penn., May 6, 1856, the son of Charles N. and Mary Wily Peary. His father died when he was 3 years old, and his mother took him to Portland, Me., where he spent his boyhood, roaming about Casco Bay. He went to Bowdoin College, won fame there as a runner and jumper, and stood in the honor column of scholarship. It was a little later that he went to Washington to work as a draftsman in the Coast and Geodetic Survey offices. He spent his entire time studying civil engineering, and passed in that branch into the naval service. He became Lieutenant Peary, U. S. N.

His first assignment was to the tropics. He was the leader of the surveying for the Nicaragua Canal route. It was when he returned to Washington that he fell upon the book about Greenland, and thereafter virtually consecrated himself to polar exploration.

Obtaining leave from the naval service, he led an expedition into Greenland to determine the extent of this mysterious land. He determined its insularity, discovered and named many arctic points which today are familiar names, such as Independence Bay, Melville Island, and Heilprin Land, and in one of his voyages he discovered the famous meteorites, which he brought back to civilization. One of them, weighing 80 tons, is the wonder of visitors to the Museum of Natural History in this city. Between voyages Peary resorted to the lecture platform to raise funds for further exploration. In one instance he delivered 168 lectures in ninety-six days, raising $13,000. For determining the insularity of Greenland, Rear Admiral Peary received the Cullum Medal of the American Geographical Society, the Patron's Medal of the Royal Geographical Society of London, and the Medal of the Royal Scottish Geographical Society at Edinburgh.

He made another Arctic voyage, lasting from 1893-1895, during which he made a thorough study of the little tribe of Arctic Highlanders. In 1894 he discovered the famous Iron Mountain, first heard of from Ross in 1818, which proved to be three meteorites. One of them, weighing ninety tons, is the largest known to exist. He brought the Cape York meteorites during Summer voyages in 1896 and 1897. From 1898 until 1892 he commanded the expedition to the Arctic under the auspices of the Peary Arctic Club of New York, rounding the northern extremity of the Greenland Archipelago, the last of the great groups. He named the Northern cape, the most northerly land in the world, (eighty-three degrees, thirty-nine minutes north latitude,) Cape Morris K. Jesup, and attained the highest north in the Western Hemisphere, (eighty-four degrees, seventeen minutes north latitude.)

In July, 1905, he sailed north again, in a vessel especially built by the Peary Arctic Club and named The Roosevelt, and returned in October, 1906, having reached the "highest north."

After he had discovered the northernmost tip of land he was still in great despair. He wrote this in his diary:

"The game is off. My dream of sixteen years is ended. I have made the best fight I knew. I believe it was a good one. But I cannot accomplish the impossible."

His Eighth Invasion.

By the time Peary had reached civilization after his sixth trip he decided on still another voyage. With the especially designed ship, The Roosevelt, he drove further into the frozen ocean than navigator had ever been before. On foot he advanced until his record for this seventh trip stood at 86.6, where starvation and cold again checked the party. The explorer was 52 years old, when in July, 1908, he set out on his eighth and successful invasion of the polar region. Captain Bartlett, the veteran navigator for Peary, shouted to Colonel Roosevelt as the ship was leaving its wharf here:

"It's the pole or bust this time, Mr. President."

The method of attacking the pole was in five different detachments, pushing north in the manner of a telescope and planned with the precision of a military campaign. At the eighty-eighth parallel Peary parted with Captain Bartlett, in charge of the fourth detachment, and he, with another member of his crew and four Eskimos made the final dash. They covered 135 miles in five days.

"At this time," he said in his book, "The North Pole," "it may be appropriate to say a word regarding my reasons for selecting Henson [Matthew A. Henson, an assistant,] as my fellow-traveler to the pole itself. In this selection I acted exactly as I have done on all my expeditions for the last fifteen years. He had in those years always been with me at my point farthest north. Moreover, Henson was the best man I had with me for this kind of work, with the exception of the Eskimos, who, with their racial inheritance of ice technic and their ability to handle sledges and dogs, were more necessary to me, as members of my own individual party than any white man could have been. Of course they could not lead, but they could follow and drive dogs better than any white man.

"Henson, with his years of arctic experience, was almost as skillful at this work as an Eskimo. He could handle dogs and sledges. He was a part of the traveling machine. Had I taken any other member of the expedition he would have been a passenger, necessitating the carrying of extra rations and other impedimenta. It would have amounted to an additional load on the sledges, while the taking of Henson was in the interest of economy of weight."

Describes March to the Pole.

He then went on to describe the march that began on a clear sunlit morning, with a temperature of minus 25 degrees, with the wind of the last few days subsided to a thin breeze. With each passing day, he said, the Eskimos were becoming eager and interested, notwithstanding the fatigue of the long marches. They would climb to some pinnacle of ice and strain their eyes to the north, wondering if the pole was in sight, for they were certain that the party should get there this time.

Peary's last march northward ended at 10 o'clock on the forenoon of April 6. After the usual arrangements for going into camp he made the final observation, indicating that his position was then 89 degrees 57 minutes.

"Yet, with the pole actually in sight, I was too weary to take the last few steps. The accumulated weariness of all those days and nights of forced marches and insufficient sleep, constant peril and anxiety, seemed to roll across me all at once. I was actually too exhausted to realize at the moment that my life's purpose had been achieved. But, weary as I was, I could not sleep long. It was, therefore, only a few hours later when I awoke. The first thing I did after awaking was to write these words in my diary:

"The pole at last. The prize of three centuries. My dream and goal for twenty years. Mine at last! I cannot bring myself to realize it. It seems all so simple and commonplace."

Quickly Leaves His Life's Goal.

Observations which were later registered at the United States Coast and Geodetic Survey, in Washington, were made, and the return trip made in all haste. Though conscious that he was leaving, said Peary, he did not wait for any lingering farewell to his life's goal, as four hundred and thirteen nautical miles of ice floes and possibly open leads still lay between the party and the north coast of Grant Land.

"I gave one backward glance and then turned my face south and toward the future," he said.

He had spent thirty hours from April 6 to April 7 around the pole, a great tract of frozen sea—none of the land which Dr. Cook reported. The weather was cloudless and flawless. The temperature ranged from 33 below to 12 below. Where open places permitted soundings 9,000 feet of wire, which was all Peary had, failed to touch the bottom.

When he got back to civilization Peary was surprised to find such a fierce controversy raging over him and his rival, Dr. Cook, but he easily established his claim before scientific bodies throughout the United States. He was raised to the rank of Rear Admiral of the United States Navy and retired on pay. Congress voted him its thanks in a special act, and gold medals, decorations, and honors of many kinds were showered upon him.

A scientific and popular narrative of his success he wove into a book called "The North Pole," which has been quoted here, while his other expeditions are described in detail in his "Northward Over the Great Ice" and "Nearest the Pole."

Peary's closing years were spent in a well-earned rest, living for a large part of the time with his family of three, wife, daughter and a son, on Eagle Island, off the coast of Portland, Me. Mrs. Peary was formerly Miss Josephine Debitsch of Washington, D. C., marrying the explorer in 1888. She frequently accompanied her husband on his northward journeys and on one of these trips Marie Ahnighite Peary was born and bears the distinction of having been born further north than any other white child in the world. She was popularly known as "The Snow Baby." She was married to Captain E. Stafford on Oct. 7, 1917.

In recent years Rear Admiral Peary had become interested in aviation and was prominently identified with the aeronautic preparedness movement. He was a member of the Royal Geographic Society of London, the Philadelphia Geographic Society, the Peary Arctic Club, the Aero Club of America, and the Explorers' Club. He received the Hubbard Gold Medal by the National Geographic Society, the Culver Gold medal by the Chicago Geographic Society, the Kane Gold Medal by the Philadelphia organization, as well as the Daly and Cullum Gold Medals by the National Geographic Society. Rear Admiral Peary also received medals from the German, Austrian, and Hungarian societies and the Royal, Royal Scottish, Italian, and Belgian Geographic Societies. He was President of the Eighth Geographic Congress held in Washington in 1904; Honorary Vice President of the Ninth Geographic Congress, at Geneva, 1908, and the tenth, at Rome, in 1913, the year he was made an officer of the Legion of Honor of France.

He was a member of all the principal home and foreign geographical societies, the American Alpine Club, the Museum of Natural History, the New York Chamber of Commerce, Phi Beta Kappa, and Delta Kappa Epsilon fraternities.

ADMIRAL PEARY.

The passing of Robert E. Peary brings to mind, as if it were yesterday, that electrifying dispatch from Indian Harbor on Sept. 6, 1909, to The New York Times, which had faith in the explorer and was interested in his quest: "I have the Pole, April 6." And later on the same day came the triumphant message to The Associated Press: "Stars and Stripes nailed to the Pole." This was not as figurative as it seemed. Peary had marked with the national colors the spot on the vast field of ice where was the top of the world. There they rose and fell in the winds that might come from every quarter and not come far, after the indomitable American and his companions had turned their faces south, weary in body but victorious in soul, the Eskimos as joyous as Peary and Matthew Henson.

The memorable dispatch may fittingly be termed electrifying, since it cleared the air of the fog made by the fictions of the unashamed Cook. Robert E. Peary's announcement arrived about the time that Cook—was it not on the very day?—appeared before the King of Denmark and the Geographical Society at Copenhagen in the attempt to make good his claim to the satisfaction of men of science that he had attained the Pole "a year ahead of Peary." Philip Gibbs, reporting the ordeal of the adventurer who previously had not climbed Mount McKinley, wrote that his lecture "proves conclusively that "his claim to have reached the North "Pole belongs to the realm of fairy "tales." The doctor faced his critics not at all like a heroic explorer who had a solid hold upon immortality. He "stumbled badly over figures, his face "was flushed, his forehead beaded "with perspiration." Still there were many of the unscientific sort who clung to the cause of Cook with a blind and desperate loyalty, unwilling to acknowledge that they had been hoodwinked. But there could be no doubting the accomplished officer and gentleman Robert E. Peary, who had devoted his life to polar exploration and had headed eight hazardous enterprises to nail the Stars and Stripes to the Pole. He could not stumble over his figures, for he knew how to make the calculations himself. He had cheerfully failed seven times, and when he declared that the eighth time success had been won men threw their hats into the air for the American who would not be denied. The incarnation of a fixed idea, he had made it prevail over all the obstructive powers of the Arctic. Immediately the fog in men's minds began to clear away. The Indian Harbor dispatch completed Cook's confusion at Copenhagen.

Peary's hold upon immortality is secure. The mention of his name will always suggest one of the most remarkable achievements of the human mind and the human frame. Hundreds of stout and brave men had gone before him to unlock the mystery of the North. Many had died on the long trail, the place of their sepulture to be always unknown. Peary himself, after reaching the "highest north" in 1906, despaired in a moment of depression. "I have made the best fight I knew," he wrote in his diary; "I believe it was a good "one. But I cannot accomplish the "impossible." But scarcely had he rested when he fared forth again, at a time of life when most men are done with hazards and resigned to glorious failure. Peary's story of his march to the Pole in five dashes is one of the most absorbing, one of the most thrilling, in the literature of exploration, and what a touch of realism there is in that entry in his diary when the "top of the world" was "in sight":

> The Pole at last. The prize of three centuries. My dream and goal for twenty years. Mine at last! I cannot bring myself to realize it. It seems all so simple and commonplace.

It was halcyon weather in the very furthest north, winds light, temperature clement for the Arctic, level fields of ice on every side. Peary has been criticised for preferring his faithful Henson, the negro, to Robert A. Bartlett, the rugged Captain of the Roosevelt, when the homestretch lay before the party. The Admiral was honest about his selection of Henson, the exclusion of Bartlett, if you please. Henson was a better man on the ice and the way promised to be extra dangerous, requiring more skill in ice work than Bartlett was master of—the Eskimos could not, of course, be spared in such an emergency, for they were native with the bear and the walrus. Moreover, Peary, who had given his active life up to the quest, thought it no reflection upon his patriotism and his manhood to desire that an American should be the discoverer of the Pole. He explained, too, that Bartlett was the best man to lead the fourth group in blazing the way, and there was honor in that. Nothing became the brave Nova Scotian more than the manner of his yielding to the wishes of his chief. His heart on fire for the adventure, he bowed his head and stepped aside for Peary's fame, content in the line of duty that a man born under the British flag should not share it.

There may be differences of opinion about Peary's action, but he was commander, the responsibility was his, he faced the extreme hazards of the unknown, and if there was a flaw in his armor in the supreme moment it was a defect of those robust and masterful qualities without which he could never have won his goal after years of indefatigable effort.

"All the News That's Fit to Print"

The New York Times

LATE CITY EDITION

Weather: Partly cloudy today; cool cloudy tonight, showers tomorrow. Temp. range: today 30-48; Sunday 33-44. Full U.S. report on Page 74.

VOL. CXXII ... No. 42,079

NEW YORK, MONDAY, APRIL 9, 1973

15 CENTS

5 SHIPS OF CONVOY WITH FUEL REACH CAMBODIA CAPITAL

13 Vessels Turn Back as Communist Fire Along the Mekong Proves Intense

ONLY 6-DAY OIL SUPPLY

But Food Is Sufficient for a 3 to 4-Week Blockade—U.S. Bombing Continues

By JOSEPH B. TREASTER

Special to The New York Times

PHNOM PENH, Cambodia, April 8—Three tankers and two cargo ships from an embattled convoy of 18 vessels reached this besieged capital late today with the first fuel that the city has received in two weeks.

The shell-pocked tankers brought just enough fuel to last for six days in this city of 1.5 million. Government officials had said that nine tankers were needed to ease the critical fuel shortage that began to grip Phnom Penh last week as Communist troops cut all the roads to the capital and blocked traffic on the Mekong River.

Thousands of Cambodians lined the banks of the Mekong late this afternoon as the first ship in the convoy, a flat-bottomed freighter, the Lucky Star, turned into the harbor.

Most Ships Turned Back

The convoy had begun with 18 ships. But after a series of delays caused by a lack of security on the river that resulted in an attack near the convoy's staging area in South Vietnam, most of the ships turned back.

To clear the way, American B-52's and smaller fighter-bombers had pounded the banks of the river for several days. When the remaining ships started their run this morning at the Cambodian border, the American planes were continuing their attacks, and olive-colored patrol boats sped close to the shore firing bursts of machine gun bullets.

Nevertheless, the ships came under fire several times, according to Capt. Si Chung Lo of Hong Kong, the skipper of the Lucky Star.

[One of the vessels, the Taiwanese freighter Ally, was sunk, and another, the Filipino tanker Mekong, was set afire and left burning, The Associated Press reported.]

Hit Three Times

Captain Lo said the Lucky Star was hit three times—twice by recoilless-rifle fire and once with a rocket—and that "the tankers got more."

"Everytime we slowed down," the skipper continued, "we got shot at." He added that of the 10 trips he had made to Phnom Penh, "this one was the worst." No one was wounded, however.

For the last month, the American planes, operating from bases in Thailand and Guam, have been trying to stop the advancing Communist forces with large-scale air raids throughout Cambodia. Despite the bombers, however, the Communists have persisted, and in addition, thousands of Cambodian peasants have started streaming into the towns to escape the destruction in the countryside.

With the situation worsening late last week, United States officials started planning an airlift to relieve the city, and the White House sent Gen.

Continued on Page 6, Column 1

Picasso Is Dead in France at 91

Pablo Picasso in 1966 — Brassal

Special to The New York Times

MOUGINS, France, April 8—Pablo Picasso, the titan of 20th-century art, died this morning at his hilltop villa of Notre Dame de Vie here. He was 91 years old.

The death of the Spanish-born artist was attributed to pulmonary edema, fluid in the lungs, by Dr. Jean-Claude Rance, a local physician who was summoned to the 35-room mansion by the family. Dr. Rance said that Picasso had been ill for several weeks.

With him when he died was his second wife, the 47-year-old Jacqueline Roque, whom he married in 1961. In the last few years, Picasso rarely left his 17-acre estate, which was surrounded by barbed wire. He had been in exile from his native land since 1939, when Generalissimo Francisco Franco defeated the Republican Government of Spain in the three-year Civil War.

About 10 days ago, Picasso was helping to assemble 201 of his paintings for exhibition at the Avignon Arts Festival, which will open in that city May 23 at the Palais des Papes. According to Paul Puaux, the festival director who had visited the artist at his home on the Riviera above Cannes, these canvases covered the artist's output from October, 1970 to the close of 1972.

"There was something com-

Continued on Page 47, Column 1

M'CORD REPORTED LINKING PAYOFFS TO A G.O.P. LAWYER

Says He Believes Parkinson Paid Bugging Defendants —Attorney Denies It

By SEYMOUR M. HERSH

Special to The New York Times

WASHINGTON, April 8 — James W. McCord Jr. has told a Federal grand jury that he believes that Kenneth W. Parkinson, an attorney for the Committee for the Re-election of the President, channeled cash payments to the Watergate defendants in return for silence after their arrest inside Democratic headquarters last June 17, sources close to the case said today.

The sources said that McCord, one of seven men sentenced to prison for their role in the break-in, further testified that he believed that Mr. Parkinson was responsible for "applying the pressure" on the defendants to plead guilty shortly before the trial began in January. Five of the seven did so plead and the two others were convicted.

McCord subsequently confirmed his testimony in a telephone interview with The New York Times, but refused to provide further details.

Some Hearsay Evidence

The sources noted, however, that McCord had based much of his grand jury testimony on hearsay evidence. For example, they said, he acknowledged that his basic information about Mr. Parkinson's alleged role in funneling money and advice to the men had been told to him by Mrs. Dorothy Hunt, the deceased wife of a convicted Watergate participant, E. Howard Hunt Jr. He named Mrs. Hunt as the conduit for the money.

Today's disclosure marked the first time that the name of Mr. Parkinson or that of any member or employe of the Republican re-election committee had been linked to the cash payments made to the Watergate defendants after their arrest, although the existence of such payments was reported three months ago.

Mr. Parkinson, a member of the Washington law firm of Jackson, Gray & Laskey, categorically denied making any cash payments to Mrs. Hunt.

Denies Money Role

"That's absolutely false," he said during a telephone interview. "I've never met Mr. Hunt or Mrs. Hunt and I've never met any of the other defendants. I've never handled any money myself."

The lawyer said that he had not been connected with the Republican re-election campaign in any way until a few days after the Watergate break-in, when he was retained to represent the Republicans in a civil lawsuit filed by Lawrence F. O'Brien, then chairman of the Democratic National Committee.

A number of Justice Depart-

Continued on Page 26, Column 1

The New York Times

Mayor Lindsay reading his statement critical of Governor Rockefeller yesterday. In background is a studio mural showing twin towers of the World Trade Center.

LINDSAY CHARGES GOVERNOR HARRIES CITY GOVERNMENT

He Asserts That Attacks Are Political and Scores Rockefeller's Record

STATEMENT IS LENGTHY

A Spokesman for the State Accuses the Mayor of Mismanagement

By MAURICE CARROLL

Mayor Lindsay accused Governor Rockefeller yesterday of politically motivated "harassment" of the city government and of "callous indifference to sound management" in the way the Governor runs the state.

With the length, detail and marshaled argument of a lawyer's brief or a formal government paper, the Mayor summed up in one major statement all of the various skirmishes and hit-and-run confrontations of his long personal and political feud with the Governor.

Text of the Lindsay statement is printed on Page 52.

He said that efforts to aid the city's economy were "seriously undermined by senseless attacks" from the Governor. He cited a familiar series of claims and statistics on city achievements and attacked Mr. Rockefeller for failing to reform the state courts, which Mr. Lindsay called "the major bottleneck" in law enforcement; for trying to take over the city-run Offtrack Betting Corporation, for "trying desperately to kill two of the mainstays of New York City's middle class—rent control and a tuition-free City University."

Governor's Office Comments

Mr. Rockefeller did not reply directly. A spokesman issued a two-sentence comment saying that Mr. Lindsay's "disastrous mismanagement" of the city had been "headline news day after day."

Mr. Lindsay noted in his statement that he had decided not to seek a third term. But a politician scanning it said, "Uh, oh. There's his first campaign paper for 1974."

The Mayor is thought to be planning to run next year, perhaps for Senator, perhaps for the Governor's job, a circumstance that lends a certain edge to his relationship with Mr. Rockefeller.

Three days after returning from a Colorado vacation where he had seethed over telephoned reports about the Governor's statement last week on the "crisis" that New York City was in under the Lindsay administration, the Mayor met with his top assistants at Gracie Mansion to draft a detailed, formal reply.

Takes 13 Minutes

Last night, he read it — seven and a half pages of double-spaced text — on his weekly television program on WPIX. It took 13 minutes.

"The Mayor just felt this thing had gone on long enough," said Deputy Mayor Edward K. Hamilton, one of the participants in the writing session on Saturday.

Robert Laird, deputy press

Continued on Page 52, Column 1

VIETCONG ADMIT DOWNING COPTER

6 From Truce Commissions and 3 U.S. Crewmen Killed in 'Regrettable Accident'

By FOX BUTTERFIELD

Special to The New York Times

SAIGON, South Vietnam, Monday, April 9—Six representatives of the two peace-keeping commissions, including two Vietcong officers, were killed when their helicopter was shot down by a Communist missile Saturday, a Vietcong spokesman said last night. The three crewmen of the helicopter also died. Two were Americans and one was believed to have been a Filipino.

The Vietcong spokesman termed the incident a "regrettable accident." He said the dead were one Canadian, one Indonesian and two Hungarians, all members of the International Commission of Control and Supervision, the two Vietcong men, and crewmen of Air America, the charter airline used by the international commission.

Communist forces fired on two more helicopters this morning in the Mekong delta, hitting one that belonged to the military commission and forcing it to make a crash landing in Chuong Thien Province, officials of the international commission said. There were no reports of casualties. An officer of the Inter-

Continued on Page 7, Column 1

Environmental Movement Registers Gains in 3 Years

By GLADWIN HILL

Three years ago millions of Americans interrupted their usual pursuits to observe Earth Day, an interlude of contemplation of the nation's deteriorating environment and of resolve to rehabilitate and protect it.

The third anniversary of the occasion, extended to a full week by proclamation of President Nixon and other public officials, begins today across a nation profoundly altered by what is being widely called the Environmental Revolution.

This movement has yielded, among other things, important new legislation, major changes in government, and legal and educational innovations. In addition, the environment issue has become a growing factor in politics, both domestic and international, and has challenged traditional cultural values.

Physically the nation does not yet seem too different. Air pollution and water pollution are, with a few notable exceptions, substantially undiminished. Mountains of solid waste continue to pile up. Airplanes, traffic and jackhammers keep up a nerve-jangling cacophony around cities.

And no one denies the exist-

Continued on Page 28, Column 1

Floodway Opened to Ease A Threat to New Orleans

By United Press International

A spillway 25 miles from New Orleans was opened yesterday in an attempt to divert floodwaters from the Mississippi River, which is building toward its highest New Orleans crest in 23 years after almost incessant rains the last two weeks.

In Mississippi, the Army Corps of Engineers poured tons of crushed rock in the Eagle Lake area to bolster a dam in danger of giving way.

The Army engineers in New Orleans said the Bonnet Carre Floodway would reduce the water level at New Orleans by directing some of the Mississippi's waters through lakes and canals around the city.

While Louisiana struggled with floods, New Yorkers yesterday encountered a touch of snow mixed with the more usual April showers. The rain, which started Saturday night, amounted to 0.86 inches by the time it ended yesterday afternoon.

The Bonnet Carre Floodway is just south of the little community of Montz, La., where 44 families had to abandon their homes because the swift river

Continued on Page 23, Column 2

Investigators' Study Finds State's Drug Courts Fail

By DAVID BURNHAM

The State Commission of Investigation said yesterday that it had concluded that a major program initiated by Governor Rockefeller and supported by President Nixon to toughen the prosecution of narcotics dealers in New York City had not been successful.

In an unusually outspoken report, the commission said the federally financed system of special narcotics courts here had "failed to bring about any significant improvements in the administration of justice in connection with narcotics felony cases."

The commission said there were "two major causes of this failure."

"First," it said, "the special narcotics parts are not operating effectively, and second, the judges assigned to these parts are not imposing appropriate substantial prison sentences."

The charges of failure were denied by the assistant district attorney in charge of the program and by a spokesman for Governor Rockefeller.

The Governor had first promised an improved enforcement of the drug laws through special narcotics courts during his campaign for re-election in the fall of 1970. In June 1971, the Governor and President Nixon announced in Washington that the Federal Government would support the program with a $7.5-million grant.

Two weeks after getting the Federal money, Governor Rockefeller signed state legislation authorizing the new courts. He released a statement asserting that "the efficient and skillful prosecution of felony narcotic cases will help remove more narcotics peddlers from our streets, deter professional drug traffickers and stem the flow of drugs into our communities."

The sharp criticism of the effectiveness of Governor Rockefeller's narcotics court program was made by the State Commission of Investigation as the Legislature was considering another controversial Rockefeller proposal: mandatory life imprisonment for all sellers of

Continued on Page 15, Column 1

U.S. and Jersey Investigate Cahill's Top Fund-Raisers

By RONALD SULLIVAN

Special to The New York Times

TRENTON, April 8 — The separate bank deposits of the State Republican Finance Committee and Governor Cahill's principal political fund-raisers in New Jersey have been subpoenaed in Federal and state investigations of Republican campaign funds, authoritative sources reported here tonight.

According to state officials, the separate but parallel investigations have implicated a number of top Republican leaders in New Jersey, including former State Treasurer Joseph M. McCrane Jr.

According to another report, the Federal investigation also involves charges that checks for a portion of several $100,000 contributions collected by Cahill fund-raisers ended up being cashed at the pari-mutuel windows at Garden State Park, a race track in Cherry Hill. The track is owned by Eugene Mori, Mr. McCrane's father-in-law.

Mr. McCrane was president and general manager of the race track until being named State Treasurer after Mr. Cahill was elected.

According to sources here, the state investigation also involves charges that contractors attempted to write off campaign contributions as business expenses. In one case, it was said that funds were funneled into a public relations company by a contractor who wrote the money off on his income tax return as a company expense even though the funds were diverted into a political campaign, this in violation of Federal and state laws dealing with campaign expenditures.

Republican leaders warned that the new charges could have a disastrous impact on Governor Cahill's campaign for renomination in the Republican gubernatorial primary in which his opponent, Representative Charles W. Sandman Jr., has

Continued on Page 41, Column 5

Many Finding Inflation No Bar to the Good Life

By WAYNE KING

Millions of American housewives bypassed the meat counter last week, but many Americans were not letting inflation stand in the way of the good life.

They proved it where it counted—at the cash register.

"Doing things first class is a matter of having developed a taste for good things," says Sepy Dobronyi, a Miami sculptor and photographer. "I'd rather pay $15 for a good steak than $5 for a mediocre one."

It's a sentiment millions of Americans seem to share, if not for steaks, certainly for other items. There is no index of the national willingness to pay premium prices for the privilege of "going first class," but a sampling of some items indicates that while buyers are inflation-conscious to a painful degree, they aren't forgoing convenience, or even luxury, as a result.

There is no doubt that the soaring prices of meat brought inflation home to the American public. The nation's women protested meat prices almost as angrily as if actual hunger faced them.

The boycott ended at midnight Saturday and beginning today in supermarkets and all but the smallest grocery stores

Continued on Page 31, Column 1

Knicks Go Into Final

The New York Knicks defeated the Baltimore Bullets, 109-99, yesterday at Madison Square Garden and advanced to the Eastern Conference final of the National Basketball Association playoffs. The Knicks now meet the winner of the Boston-Atlanta series. Details are on Page 53.

NEWS INDEX

Associated Press

The Bonnet Carre spillway, just south of Montz, La., being opened yesterday by the Army Corps of Engineers

Picasso Dies at His Villa in Southern France at 91

Continued From Page 1, Col. 4

pletely different, something less tortured in certain paintings," Mr. Puaux said today in Paris. He added:

"You feel there is a change, a new period. There is much less eroticism and much more softness. His wife told me that he was working much more slowly, more deliberately now, searching and dogging into each canvas."

The main subject of the 201 works, Mr. Puaux said, "is man, as always — children, a number of mothers with child —but also musical instruments, trumpets and flutes, birds and one very, very beautiful landscape, which is rather unusual for Picasso."

The dominant color of the canvases is bistre, a warm, brownish black, Mr. Puaux said.

Three years ago, in 1970, 165 of Picasso's paintings and 45 drawings were shown in the Palais des Papes. They constituted Picasso's production from January, 1969, through January, 1970. The pictures were mostly of vibrant men and women, often in close embrace. There were also dozens of goateed, lusty figures, which the artist's friends called "the musketeers."

In 1971, on the occasion of Picasso's 90th birthday, the Museum of Modern Art in New York, which has the world's largest public collection of his works, put on a special exhibition. At the same time, the French Government displayed some Picassos in the grand gallery of the Louvre, the first time the museum had ever exhibited work by a living artist.

As for Picasso, he ignored his birthday, shutting himself up in his villa, even refusing to receive a delegation from the French Communist party, of which he was a member. The group included his old friend, Louis Aragon, the poet.

Why He Was a Communist

The artist had a succinct reply to those who asked him why he was a Communist. "When I was a boy in Spain, I was very poor and very aware of how poor people had to live," he told a journalist in 1947, adding:

"I learned that the Communists were for the poor people. That was enough to know. So I became for the Communists."

Sometimes, however, Picasso was an embarrassment to his party. A portrait he did of Stalin on the Soviet leader's death in 1953 caused a furor in the party leadership. Earlier, the Soviet Government had locked its collection of Picasso's early works in the basement of Leningrad's Hermitage Museum.

Publicly, Picasso displayed amusement at the Soviet Union's banishment of his paintings. Everybody had a right to react to his work as it affected them, he said.

Although the artist passionately detested Franco, he admired his fellow countrymen. One expression of his feelings came in the spring of 1970, when he decided to give 800 to 900 of his early works to Barcelona. These were said to be the best of his output up to 1917.

Earlier, in 1963, Picasso's close friend, the late Jaime Sabartés, had donated his Picasso collection of some 400 works to the city of Barcelona, and the Palacio Aguilar was then renamed the Picasso Museum. However, the Franco regime covertly opposed the museum, and the artist's name was not on the door.

A Paris friend credited Picasso's gift to Barcelona to his sense of irony. "He liked putting an important Picasso collection right in the middle of Barcelona when there was unrest in Spain and Franco was on his way out," the friend explained.

Picasso's works fetched enormous prices at auction, in the hundreds of thousands of dollars. By sales through his dealers, the artist himself became wealthy, although the precise size of his estate was not known.

In addition to his wife, Picasso leaves four children, a son, Paulo, born to his late first wife, the dancer Olga Khokova; a daughter, Mrs. Pierre Widmaier, born to his mistress Marie-Thérèse Walter, and a son, Claude, and a daughter, Paloma, both the children of Françoise Gilot, another mistress, now the wife of the biologist Dr. Jonas Salk.

Funeral plans were incomplete last night.

Picasso: Protean and Prodigious, the Greatest Single Force in 70 Years of Art

By ALDEN WHITMAN

There was Picasso the neoclassicist; Picasso the cubist; Picasso the surrealist; Picasso the modernist; Picasso the ceramist; Picasso the lithographer; Picasso the sculptor; Picasso the superb draftsman; Picasso the effervescent and exuberant; Picasso the saturnine and surly; Picasso the faithful and faithless lover; Picasso the cunning financial man; Picasso the publicity seeker; Picasso the smoldering Spaniard; Picasso the joker and performer of charades; Picasso the generous; Picasso the Scrooge; even Picasso the playwright.

A genius for the ages, a man who played wonderful yet sometimes outrageous changes with art, Pablo Picasso remains without doubt the most original, the most protean and the most forceful personality in the visual arts in the first three-quarters of this century. He took a prodigious gift and with it transformed the universe of art.

Henri Matisse and Georges Braque, two painters with assured stature in modern art and both his close friends, were also original; but both developed a style and stuck pretty much to it, whereas Picasso, with a feverish creativity and lavish talent lasting into old age, was a man of many styles whose artistic life revealed a continuous process of exploration. He created his own universe, investing it with his own human beings and his own forms of beasts and myths.

"For me, a picture is neither an end nor an achievement but rather a lucky chance and an experience," he once explained. "I try to represent what I have found, not what I am seeking. I do not seek — I find."

'One Step on a Long Road'

On another occasion, however, he saw his work in a different light. "Everything I do," he remarked at 76, "is only one step on a long road. It is a preliminary process that may be achieved much later. Therefore my works must be seen in relation to one another, keeping in mind what I have already done and what I will do."

For all his guises, or disguises, Picasso had an amazing fecundity of imagination that permitted him to metamorphize a mood or an idea into a work of art with bewildering quickness. He was, in André Malraux's phrase, "the archwizard of modern art," a man who, as a painter alone, produced well over 6,000 pictures. Some he splashed off in a few hours; others took weeks.

In 1969, his 88th year, he produced out of his volcanic energy a total of 165 paintings and 45 drawings, which were exhibited at the Palace of the Popes in Avignon, France. Crowding the walls of that venerable structure, the Picasso array drew exclamatory throngs and moved Emily Genauer, the critic, to say, "I think Picasso's new pictures are the fire of heaven."

Explaining the source of this energy, Picasso said as he neared 90, "Everyone is the age he has decided on, and I have decided to remain 30."

The painter was so much known for works that blurred or obliterated conventional distinctions between beauty and ugliness and for depersonalized forms that he was accused of being an antihumanist. That appraisal disturbed him, for he regarded himself, with all his vagaries, as having created new insights into a seen and unseen world in which fragmentation of form was the basis for a new synthesis.

A Bull From a Bicycle Seat

"What is art?" a visitor once asked him. "What is not?" he replied. And he substantiated this point once by combining a bicycle seat and a pair of handlebars to make a bull's head.

"Whatever the source of the emotion that drives me to create, I want to give it a form that has some connection with the visible world, even if it is only to wage war on that world," he explained to Françoise Gilot, who was one of his mistresses and herself a painter.

"Otherwise," he continued, "a painting is just an old grab bag for everyone to reach into and pull out what he himself has put in. I want my paintings to be able to defend themselves, to resist the invader, just as though there were razor blades on all surfaces so no one could touch them without cutting his hands. A painting isn't a market basket or a woman's handbag, full of combs, hairpins, lipstick, old love letters and keys to the garage.

"Valéry [Paul Valéry, the French poet] used to say, 'I write half the poem. The reader writes the other half.' That's all right for him, maybe, but I don't want there to be three or four thousand possibilities of interpreting my canvas. I want there to be only one and in that one to some extent the possibility of recognizing nature, even distorted nature, which is, after all, a kind of struggle between my interior life and the external world as it exists for most people.

"As I've often said, I don't try to express nature; rather, as the Chinese put it, to work like nature. And I want that internal surge — my creative dynamism — to propose itself to the viewer in the form of traditional painting violated."

In the long course of upending traditionalism, Picasso became a one-man history of modern are. In every phase of its turbulent (and often violent) development he was either a daring pioneer or a gifted practitioner. The sheer variousness of his creations reflected his probings of modern art for ways to communicate the multiplicity of its expressions; and so Picasso could not be categorized as belonging to this or that school, for he opened and tried virtually all of them.

In his peripateticism he worked in oils, water-colors, pastels, gouaches, pencil and ink drawings and aquatints; he etched, made lithographs, sculptured, fashioned ceramics, put together mosaics and constructed murals.

Collection of Mr. and Mrs. John Hay Whitney

SELF-PORTRAIT, 1901, dates from period when Picasso, still under Spanish influences, began to immerse himself in modern French painting. (He first visited Paris in 1900 and moved there in 1904.) Portrait reflects his first absorption of post-impressionist painting before developing own style.

One of his masterpieces was "Guernica," painted in 1937 and on loan for many years to the Museum of Modern Art in New York. An oil on canvas 11¼ feet high and 25½ feet long, it is a majestic, stirring indictment of the destructiveness of modern war. By contrast, another masterpiece was a simply and perfectly drawn white pigeon, "The Dove," which was disseminated around the world as a symbol of peace. But masterpiece or something not so exalted, virtually all Picasso were interesting and provocative. Praised or reviled, his work never evoked quiet judgments.

A Different View

The artist, however, held a different view. "There is no such thing as a bad Picasso," he said, "some are less good than others."

Exhibitions of his work, especially in his later years, were sure-fire attractions. The mention of his name was sufficient to lure thousands, many of them only barely acquainted with any art, to museums and galleries and benefits. Reproductions and prints were nailed up in homes all over the Western world, a certain mark of the owner's claim to culture. Originals were widely dispersed, both in museums and in the hands of collectors wealthy enough to meet Picasso's prices. And they were steep. In 1965 he charged London's Tate Gallery $168,000 for "Les Trois Danseuses," a painting he did in 1925. For a current painting, private collectors felt that $20,000 was a steal and $35,000 not too much.

For the last 50 years there has been no such thing as a cheap Picasso. Indeed, Leo and Gertrude Stein and Ambroise Vollard, a Paris dealer, may have been the last to get a Picasso for $30, and that was in 1906 and 1907.

Income Grew With Fame

As Picasso's fame grew, so did his income until it got so that he could manufacture money by sketching a few lines on a piece of paper and tacking on his dramatic signature. He was probably the world's highest paid pieceworker, and there were many years in which he garnered more than $1-million.

"I am rich enough to throw away a thousand dollars," he told a friend with some glee.

The artist, however, was canny about money, driving hard bargains with his dealers and keeping the bulk of his work off the market. He released for sale about 40 of his paintings a year out of a production of hundreds, so that the market for his work was never glutted. What he did not sell (and he said that many of these constituted the best from his palette) he squirreled away in bank vaults, studios, in a castle not far from the Riviera and in empty rooms in his villa near Cannes. Picasso did not exactly hide his collection, for on occasion he permitted special friends to see it, to photograph it and to publish the results.

Toward the close of his life he donated 800 to 900 of his finest early works to a Barcelona museum. Worth a multimillion-dollar fortune, his works represented his Spanish period and were given in memory of Jaime Sabartés, his longtime secretary. In 1971 he gave an early constructed sculpture, "Guitar," to the Museum of Modern Art in New York.

Mostly, though, Picasso took a merchant's delight in acquiring his money. "Art is a salable commodity," he once observed. "If I want as much money as I can get for my art, it is because I know what I want to do with it." But just what that was only a few intimates knew. He is said to have owned a great deal of real estate in France and to have made some excellent stock investments.

Contrary to Miss Gilot's suggestion that Picasso was tightfisted, he gave large sums to the Republican side in the Spanish Civil War and then to refugee groups that cared for the defeated Republicans who had fled to France.

All his studios and homes—even the 18-room rambling La Californie at Cannes — were crammed and cluttered with junk—pebbles, rocks, pieces of glass, a hollow elephant's foot, a bird cage, African drums, wooden crocodiles, parts

Continued on Following Page

of old bicycles, ancient newspapers, broken crockery, bullfight posters, old hats, weird ceramics. Picasso was a compulsive collector of oddments, and he never threw any of them away, or permitted anyone to move any object once he had dropped it, tossed it or placed it somewhere.

To compound the chaos inside La Californie, the villa's lawn was home to clucking chickens, pigeons, at least one goat, dogs and children. They all disported among bronze owls, fountains and statuary scattered about the grounds. Freedom for animals and children was a cardinal belief.

He always had several projects in hand at the same time, and to each he seemed equally lavish with his talent. "Painting is my hobby," he said. "When I am finished painting, I paint again for relaxation."

"He used no palette," Miss Gilot wrote of his working habits. "At his right [as he addressed his easel] was a small table covered with newspapers and three or four large cans filled with brushes standing in turpentine.

"Every time he took a brush he wiped it off on the newspapers, which were a jungle of colored smudges and slashes. Whenever he wanted pure color, he squeezed some from a tube onto the newspaper. At his feet and around the base of the easel were cans — mostly tomato cans of various sizes—that held gray and neutral tones and other colors that he had previously mixed.

Stood for Several Hours

"He stood before the canvas for three or four hours at a stretch. He made almost no superfluous gestures. I asked him if it didn't tire him to stand so long in one spot. He shook his head.

"'No,' he said. 'That is why painters live so long. While I work I leave my body outside the door, the way Moslems take off their shoes before entering the mosque.'"

"Occasionally he walked to the other end of the atelier and sat in a wicker armchair. He would cross his legs, plant one elbow on his knee and, resting his chin on his fist, would stay there studying the painting without speaking for as long as an hour.

"After that he would generally go back to work on the portrait. Sometimes he would say, 'I can't carry that plastic idea any further today,' and then begin to work on another painting. He always had several half-dry unfinished canvases to choose from.

"There was total silence in the atelier, broken only by Pablo's monologues or an occasional conversation; never an interruption from the world outside. When daylight began to fade from the canvas he switched on two spotlights and everything but the picture surface fell away into the shadows.

"'There must be darkness everywhere except on the canvas, so that the painter becomes hypnotized by his own work and paints almost as though he were in a trance,' he said. 'He must stay as close as possible to his own inner world if he wants to transcend the limitations his reason is always trying to impose on him.'"

Mood was a vital ingredient of Picasso. Everything he saw, felt or did was for him an incomplete experience until it had been released and recorded. Once he was lunching on sole and happened to hold up the skeleton so that it caught his glance. He got up from the table and returned almost immediately with a tray of clay in which he made an imprint of the skeleton. After lunch he drew colorful designs around the filigree of the bones, and the eventual result was one of his most beautiful plates.

Here, as in other art areas, when the inspiration was upon him he worked ceaselessly and with such concentration that he could, for example, paint a good-sized picture in three hours.

Scores of Close Friends

Although whim at times governed whom he would see and for how long, Picasso was generally a hospitable host in the Spanish manner. He had scores of close friends—Mr. Kahnweiler, Jean Cocteau, Paul Eluard and Louis Aragon among many others.

However, as with most illustrious men, Picasso attracted gushing admirers and sycophants. Some called him "maestro" and fawned on him for the subsidiary fame that came from standing in his light. He was not above their company; and, indeed, he seemed to have relished some who gave him favorable publicity.

Women were one of Picasso's most persistent preoccupations. Apart from fleeting affairs, there were seven women significant in his personal and artistic life. He married two of them, but his relationships with the five others were well recognized and generally respected. Two of his companions bore three of his four children.

The artist's wives and mistresses served as his models, organized the domestic aspects of his household so far as that was possible, petted him, suffered his mercurial moods and greeted his friends.

In Picasso's early days in Paris, his mistress was Miss Olivier, a young painter and teacher, who lived, as he did, in the Bateau-Lavoir—a Montmartre building called that by the poet and painter Max Jacob because it swayed like a creaky Seine laundry boat.

"I met Picasso as I was coming home one stormy evening," Miss Olivier recalled. "He had a tiny kitten in his arms, which he laughingly offered me, at the same time blocking my path. I laughed with him. He invited me to his studio."

Their liaison lasted until 1912, when Picasso met Marcelle Humbert, the mistress of a sculptor friend. The two ran off together, and there followed a series of superb canvases expressing the artist's happiness. He called Miss Humbert "Eva" and signed two of his works "J'aime Eva." Miss Humbert died in 1914.

In Rome, early in 1917, he met Olga Khoklova, a ballerina with Sergei Diaghilev's Ballets Russes. He painted her in a Spanish mantilla, and he and Olga were married in 1918. Three years later a son, Paolo—Italian for Pablo or Paul—was born.

Separated for 20 Years

The mariage broke up in 1935, and Olga died in southern France 20 years later. The couple were never divorced. One reason, it is said, was that they had been married under a community property arrangement that would have obliged Picasso to divide his fortune with her.

At the time of the separation Picasso's mistress was his blond model, Marie-Thérèse Walter. In 1935 she bore him a daughter, Marie de la Concepcion. A portrait of the girl, known as Maïa, was one of Picasso's most fetching naturalist studies.

Dora Maar, a young Yugoslav photographer, was the painter's next mistress. Their companionship lasted until 1944.

The same year, when Picasso was 62, he began an 11-year liaison with Miss Gilot. Their children were Claude, born in 1947, and Paloma, born in 1949. In 1970 Miss Gilot was married to Dr. Jonas E. Salk, the polio-vaccine developer.

Picasso's final attachment was to Jacqueline Roque, who became his mistress in 1955, and his wife in 1961, when she was 35 and he was 79. Miss Roque had a rather wry sense of her role in the painter's life. A member of a movie crew that was making a picture at their home asked her quite innocently who she was. "Me, I'm the new Egeria," she replied; and from all accounts she was happy in devoting her life to her husband's.

Amid the Bohemian clutter in which he lived and thrived, despite the concomitant disarray of his personal affairs, Picasso maintained a strong, consistent and lasting emotional bond to the country of his birth. This bond influenced his painting and, after 1936 and the Spanish Civil War, propelled him for the first time into politics. His attachment to Spain was romantic and passionate; and the fact that he shunned Generalissimo Francisco Franco's Spain yet kept his Spanish nationality was an expression of his umbilical feeling for the country.

There were two principal consequences of this bond: One was "Guernica" and the other was his membership in the French Communist party, which he joined in 1944. "Up to the time of the Spanish Civil War, Picasso was completely apolitical," Mr. Kahnweiler, his agent, recalled. "He did not even know the names of the different parties. The Civil War changed all that."

Previously, Picasso's insurgency had been that of every artist against the constrictions of conventional life. But with the outbreak of conflict in his homeland, Picasso became instinctively an aroused partisan of the Republican Government.

In January, 1937, he began etching the two large plates of "Sueño y Mentira de Franco" (The Dream and Lie of Franco). These showed the rebel leader as a perpetrator of symbolic horrors —himself ultimately transformed into a centaur and gored to death by a bull. Countless copies of these etchings were dropped like propaganda leaflets over Franco territory.

Museum of Modern Art

'LES DEMOISELLES D'AVIGNON,' Picasso's landmark canvas of 1907, started the movement known as cubism, called the greatest revolution in painting since the Renaissance. In reducing the appearance of objects to what he considered their significant forms, he broke up the canvas into geometric planes and angles. Though distorted, the figures on the left still refer to the nudes of ancient art. The two on the right, with their grotesquely dislocated bodies and masklike faces that show the influence of African sculpture, represent a complete break with the past. The squatting figure is seen from several different angles simultaneously. With "Les Demoiselles d'Avignon," painting was liberated from its fidelity to surface appearance.

But it took the bombing of the Basque town of Guernica y Luno on April 26, 1937, to drive Picasso to the heights of his genius. At 4:30 on that cloudless Monday afternoon, German airmen, who had been provided to Franco by Adolf Hitler, descended on Guernica, a town of no military importance, in a test of the joint effect of explosive and incendiary bombs on civilians. The carnage was enormous, and news of it appalled the civilized world.

At the time Picasso had been engaged by the Loyalist Government to do a mural for its pavilion at a Paris fair later that year. The outrage at Guernica gave him his subject and in a month of furious and volcanic work he completed his great and stunning painting.

In Trust for the Nation

The monochromatic mural, stark in black, gray and white, was retained by the artist in trust for the Spanish nation. It was to be given to the nation when it became a republic again.

Assessing the picture's searing impact on viewers over the years, Roland Penrose wrote:

"It is the simplicity of 'Guernica' that makes it a picture which can be readily understood. The forms are divested of all complications which would distract from their meaning. The flames that rise from the burning house and flicker on the dress of the fallen woman are described by signs as unmistakable as those used by primitive artists.

"The nail-studded hoof, the hand with deeply furrowed palm and the sun illuminated with an electric-light bulb are drawn with a childlike simplicity, startling in its directness."

"Guernica" was responsible for one of Picasso's most noteworthy ripostes. During the Nazi occupation of France in World War II, a German officer visited the artist's studio, where a large reproduction of the mural was on display.

"Ah, so it was you who did that," the German said.

"No," snapped Picasso. "You did it!"

Picasso painted two other major historical pictures, "The Korean Massacres" and "War and Peace." The two large compositions are in an old chapel in Vallauris, France. Both were intended to arouse the conscience of mankind to the horrors of war.

Toward the close of World War II the artist joined the Communist party, and L'Humanité, the party daily, marked the occasion by publishing almost a full-page photograph of him. Although his decision seemed clearly motivated by the Spanish War and the ensuing World War, there were many who thought at first that the action was another of Picasso's caprices.

He responded to such charges with a statement published in Les Lettres Françaises, which said in part:

"What do you think an artist is? An imbecile who has only his eyes if he is a painter, or his ears if a musician, or a lyre at every level of his heart if he is a poet, or, if he is merely a boxer, only his muscles?

"On the contrary, he is at the same time a political being, constantly alert to the heart-rending, burning, or happy events in the world, molding himself in their likeness.

"How could it be possible to feel no interest in other people and, because of an ivory-tower indifference, detach yourself from the life they bring with such open hands?

"No, painting is not made to decorate apartments. It is an instrument of war, for attack and defense against the enemy."

Denounced by Soviet Critic

But Picasso's brand of Communism was not Moscow's, at least in the Kremlin's Stalinist period. In 1948, his works were denounced by Vladimir Kemenov, a Soviet art critic, as an "apology for capitalistic esthetics that provokes the indignation of the simple people, if not the bourgeoisie."

"His pathology has created repugnant monstrosities," Mr. Kemenov went on. "In his 'Guernica' he portrayed not the Spanish Republic but monsters. He treads the path of cosmopolitanism, of empty geometric forms. His every canvas deforms man—his body and his face."

Picasso was pained but unmoved by the attack. "I don't try to advise the Russians on economics. Why should they tell me how to paint?" he remarked to a friend.

Continued on Following Page

About that time, according to one account, an orthodox Soviet painter said to Picasso on being introduced, "I have known of you for some time as a good Communist, but I'm afraid I don't like your painting."

"I can say the same about you, comrade," Picasso shot back.

After Mr. Kemenov's appraisal, Moscow's attitude to the artist fluctuated. "The Dove" helped, quite unintentionally, to create a thaw, and it came about this way:

One day in 1949 Matisse came to visit Picasso, bringing a white fantail pigeon for his friend's cote. Virtually on the spot, Picasso made a naturalistic lithograph of the newcomer; and Louis Aragon, the Communist poet and novelist, who saw it shortly afterward, realized its possibilities at once.

The lithograph, signed by the artist, was first used as a poster at a World Peace Conference. And from that introduction it flew around the world, reproduced in all sizes and in all media as a peace symbol.

Picasso got into Communist hot water again, however, in 1953. This time the attack came from his French comrades. The occasion was Stalin's death and a crayon portrait that the artist sketched. The imaginative likeness of Stalin as a young man stirred up the working-class members of the French party. Mr. Aragon, who had published it, felt obliged to recant in public, and Picasso was not amused.

"When you send a funeral wreath, the family customarily doesn't criticize your choice of flowers," he said.

Nevertheless, in 1954 Moscow appeared to relent, for it took out of hiding its 37 precious early Picassos (they had never been shown to the Soviet public) and lent them to a Paris exhibition. And two years later the Soviet Union marked the painter's 75th birthday by showing a large number of his pictures and ceramics to the public.

Picasso's distortions of reality, to which Mr. Kemenov objected, also baffled less political critics who were unaccustomed to the artist's private language and private mythology or who did not appreciate the esthetics of plane and solid geometry and of Mercator-like projections of the human face and form.

Born on Spain's South Coast

The man who so largely created the special esthetic of modern art was born on the night of Oct. 25, 1881, in Málaga, on Spain's south coast.

Picasso's father was José Ruiz, an Andalusian who taught for small pay in the local school of arts and crafts. His mother was Maria Picasso, a Majorcan. Pablo could draw as soon as he could grasp a pencil, but as a pupil in the ordinary sense he preferred looking at the clock to doing sums and reading. Save for art, he managed to avoid all but the rudiments of formal schooling. He was obstinate about this, as in other matters.

As a child, Picasso often accompanied his father to the bullfights. These made an indelible impression, for throughout his life bullring scenes and variations on them were a significant part of his work, recurring more persistently than any other single symbol. His first oil, at the age of 9, was of the bullring.

In 1895 the family moved to Barcelona, where Pablo's father taught at the School of Fine Arts. By that time the youngster's talent was truly Mozartean, so obviously so that his father solemnly presented him with his own palette and brushes. This confidence was justified when Pablo, at 15, competed for admission to the art school. A month was ordinarily allowed, but he completed his picture, a male nude, in a single day and was admitted to classes in 1896.

He remained there for a year before going to Madrid for further study. During an illness he lived among the peasants of Catalonia, the poverty and barrenness of whose lives appalled him. From them and from the countryside, he said later, he learned "everything I know."

Dropped Father's Name

Late in 1898, the young artist dropped his father's name from the signature "P. Ruiz Picasso" for reasons that have never been made clear. (His full baptismal name had been Pablo Diego José Francisco de Paula Nepomuceno Paria de los Remedios de la Santísima Trinidad Ruiz Picasso.)

Picasso paid his first visit to Paris in 1900 and after three more visits settled in Paris in 1904. On one of these visits he met Max Jacob, who was, next to Pierre Reverdy, his most appreciative friend until his death in a Nazi concentration camp. Picasso also became acquainted with Berthe Weill, the art dealer, who purchased some of his paintings, and Petrus Manach, another dealer, who was to support him briefly at the rate of $37.50 a month.

Meanwhile, Picasso's "blue" pictures had established him as an artist with a personal voice. This period, ending about 1904, was characterized by his use of the color blue to depict fatalistically the haunting melancholy of dying clowns, most of them in catatonic states, and agonized acrobats. "La Mort d'Arlequin" is one of the most widely known of these.

When the artist moved into the Bateau-Lavoir, his rickety and drafty studio became an important meeting and talking place for persons later to be famous in arts and letters. In addition to Mr. Jacob there were Guillaume Apollinaire, the poet; André Salmon, the writer; Matisse; Braque; Le Douanier Rousseau; Juan Gris, the Spanish painter; Cocteau, Dufy, Gertrude and Leo Stein, Utrillo, Lipschitz and Marcoussis. Apollinaire, Picasso's spiritual guide in those days, introduced him to the public with a long article in a Paris review in 1905.

One of Picasso's lifelong habits, painting at night, started during this time, and for the simple reason that his day was frequently absorbed by friends and visitors. It was also the time of his two-year "rose period," generally dated from 1904 to 1906, so-called because hues of that color dominated his pictures.

Near the rose period's close, he was taken up by the Steins, American expatriates in Paris. Leo and Gertrude did not so much discover the painter as popularize him. He, in turn, did a portrait of Gertrude with a face far from representational. When Miss Stein protested that she didn't look like that, Picasso replied, "But you will," and, indeed, in her old age Miss Stein came to resemble her picture.

The year 1907, the end of a very brief "Negroid" or "African period," was a milestone for the painter, for it marked the birth of cubism in an oil of five distorted nudes called "Les Demoiselles d'Avignon."

With cubism, Picasso—along with Braque—rejected light and perspective, painting not what he saw, but what he represented to himself through analysis. (The name "cubism" was coined afterward, and it was based on the cube forms into which Picasso and Braque tended to break up the external world.)

"When we painted as we did," Picasso said later, "we had no intention of creating cubism, but only of expressing what was inside us.

"Cubism is neither a seed nor a fetus, but an art which is primarily concerned with form, and, once a form has been created, then it exists and goes on living its own life."

This was also the case when Picasso added a new dimension to cubism in 1911 or 1912 by inventing the collage by gluing a piece of imitation chair caning to a still life. Later he went on to an even less academic cubism, sometimes called rococo cubism.

Invention of the Collage

These expressions in the cubist manner were not Picasso's total expression in the years from 1907 to 1917, for at the same time he was painting realistically.

His first substantial recognition came in this period through an exhibition in New York in 1911 and one in London in 1912. His pictures began to fetch high prices—almost $3,000 for "Acrobats" in 1914.

With the war and his marriage to a ballerina, Picasso was a costume designer and scenery painter for the Ballets Russes up to about 1925, all the while painting for himself, mostly in a neoclassic and romantic manner. "The Woman in White" is among the best-known of these naturalistic pictures.

With the advent of the surrealist movement in the middle twenties, the artist's work turned to the grotesque. Some of his figures were endowed with several heads, displaced noses, mouths and eyes, overenlarged limbs. Turbulence and violence seemed to be at the bottom of his feelings.

Then, in 1929, Picasso returned somewhat abruptly to sculpture, of which he had done little for 15 years. But again it was not a full preoccupation, and he was soon attacking his easel, this time with variations within a distinctive generally surrealistic framework. One typical picture was "Young Woman With a Looking-glass," painted in 1932.

With these and other pictures of a similar genre, the artist's renown and income reached new heights. Life was also quieter for him, especially after 1935 when Dora Maar helped put routine into his daily existence. She was also the model for a notable series of portraits in which the Mercator projection principle was applied to the human face.

Serenity, or as much of it as ever was possible for Picasso, persisted until the fall of Paris in 1940. He rejected an opportunity to escape to the United States, and, instead, remained in Paris throughout the war, painting industriously amid considerable personal hardship and the prying of Nazi soldiers. It was forbidden to exhibit his pictures or to print his name in the newspapers.

After the war, Picasso became enchanted by lithography, which he taught himself. In a short period he turned out more than 200 lithographs. He was at the same time painting, in Paris and in Antibes, and restlessly investigating pottery. Ceramics entranced him, and his work with clay created an industry for the town of Vallauris, not far from the Riviera. In a single year he made and decorated 600 figures and vessels, all different.

Toward the close of his life he also produced a number of seascapes and paintings as a composer would write variations on another's theme. Among Picasso's more notable variations were 10 on Cranach's "David and Bathsheba," 15 on Delacroix's "Femmes d'Alger" and 44 on Velázquez's "Las Meninas."

He also painted scores of portraits of his wife in a variety of poses—on a bed fondling a cat, seated nude in his studio, reading. They were portraits only in the sense that they were vaguely representational of Jacqueline Roque, for the figure and the face were almost always distorted.

Many of these pictures were published in "The Artist and His Model." They gave the impression of a man of unlimited vitality in a perpetual state of creation. As if in confirmation of this, Picasso told a visitor who admired the vigor of the works:

"A painter never finishes. There's never a moment when you can say, 'I've worked well and tomorrow is Sunday.' As soon as you stop, it's because you've started again. You can put a picture aside and say you won't touch it again. But you can never write THE END."

Acclaim Mounted With Age

Popular acclaim for Picasso seemed to mount with his age. In 1967, when he was 86, "Homage to Picasso," an exhibition of some of his works, drew throngs to museums here and abroad. His sculpture was given a special exhibition at the Museum of Modern Art in New York. One example of his sculpture, "Bust of Sylvette," is a 60-ton, sand-blasted work that rests in University Plaza, in downtown New York.

A Picasso play also attracted attention, not to say notoriety. It was "Desire Caught by the Tail," which he had written in three days on a sickbed in 1941. It was produced privately in Paris three years later with a cast that included the playwright, Simone de Beauvoir, Valentine Hugo, Albert Camus, Raymond Queneau and Jean-Paul Sartre. The main prop was a big black box that served as a bed, bathtub and coffin for the two principal characters, Fat Anxiety and Thin Anxiety. The play's action was earthy.

When "Desire" was commercially staged in St. Tropez in 1967, it aroused protests even in that resort town's atmosphere of tolerance. The objection was that some of the characters were expected to urinate on stage. Although this did not take place, the play was thought overly suggestive.

Picasso wrote a second play, "The Four Girls," in 1965, but it was not produced.

The painter did not venture to St. Tropez for his play, nor did he often leave his hilltop villa in his last years. He seemed to feel the world slipping away from him, especially when his old friends died one after another. He shut himself up, refusing to answer the telephone, for example, to mourn Ilya Ehrenburg in September, 1967.

But for the most part he painted. Rather than stand, he sat down, bending almost in half over his canvas. Age lines in his face underscored an intensity of purpose hardly abated by time. And as he painted his nostrils flared, his eyes widened, he frowned and all the while his hand was never still.

He was, in the words of a friend, "like a sturdy old oaken tub brimful of the wine of life."

"You would think," another friend said, "he is trying to do a few more centuries of work in what he has left to live."

Museum of Modern Art

'THREE MUSICIANS,' produced by Picasso in 1921 during his last phase of cubism. Pierrot (left) and Harlequin (center) are the summation of a long series of figures from the Italian comedy. Although rendered entirely in paint, the flat, colored shapes derive from the collage techniques developed earlier by Picasso and Bracque, in which thicknesses of cut-out paper and other materials gave the canvas a three-dimensional effect without the use of perspective. The shapes anticipate some of the metal sculptures Picasso was to make in the next decade. In the painting here, Pierrot plays a clarinet and Harlequin strums a guitar while another mummer, costumed as a monk, holds a musical score.

"All the News That's Fit to Print"

The New York Times

LATE CITY EDITION

Weather: Rain likely today; mild tonight. Sunny, warm tomorrow. Temperature range: today 71-85; yesterday 68-79. Details, page D19.

VOL. CXXVI .... No. 43,670 · NEW YORK, WEDNESDAY, AUGUST 17, 1977 · 20 CENTS

25 cents beyond 50-mile zone from New York City. Higher in air delivery cities.

Gary Null/NBC

Elvis Presley as he appeared on a special television program in 1973

ELVIS PRESLEY DIES; ROCK SINGER WAS 42

Heart Failure Cited by Coroner —Acclaim Followed Scorn

By MOLLY IVINS

Elvis Presley, the first and greatest American rock-and-roll star, has died at the age of 42. Mr. Presley, whose throaty baritone and blatant sexuality redefined popular music, was found unconscious in the bedroom of his home, called Graceland, in Memphis yesterday at 2:30 P.M.

He was pronounced dead an hour later at Baptist Memorial Hospital, after doctors failed to revive him.

Dr. Jerry Francisco, the Shelby County coroner, who conducted a two-hour examination of the body, said "preliminary autopsy findings" indicated that the cause of death was "cardiac arrhythmia," which a hospital spokesman defined as "an irregular and ineffective heart beat." The coroner was not immediately able to determine the cause of the "cardiac arrhythmia."

Mr. Presley was once the object of such adulation that teen-age girls screamed and fainted at the sight of him. He was also denounced for what was considered sexually suggestive conduct on stage. Preachers inveighed against him in sermons and parents forbade their children to watch him on television. In his first television appearance on the Ed Sullivan show, his act, which might be thought of as tame by today's standards, was con-

Continued on Page D18, Col. 1

Presley Gave Rock Its Style

He Didn't Invent Form, But Did Bestow Image

By JOHN ROCKWELL

An Appraisal

For most people, Elvis Presley was rock-and-roll. And they were right. Bill Haley may have made the first massive rock hit, and people such as Chuck Berry and Little Richard may have had an equally important creative impact on this raucous new American art form. But it was Elvis who defined the style and gave it an indelible image. The songs were tough and driving in a time, 20 years ago, when American popular music was still based on Tin Pan Alley tune-smithing. And the image was of a working-class rebel, pushing sex into the nation's consciousness long before the "sexual revolution." With his ominous, greasy, swirling locks, his leather jacket and his aggressive undulations, Elvis was a performer whom parents abhorred, young women adored and young men instantly imitated.

Presley's national impact began in the spring of 1956, after he had signed with RCA Victor; in that year alone, he had such hits as "Heartbreak Hotel" (the first), "Don't Be Cruel" and "Hound Dog" (a double-sided hit), "Blue Suede Shoes" and "Love Me Tender."

But before that Presley had forged his style in Sam Phillips's Sun Records studio in Memphis. Although he was not a song-

Continued on Page D18, Col. 1

FORD GIVES SUPPORT TO NEW AGREEMENT ON PANAMA CANAL

Ex-President Calls Pact 'Important Step Forward' and Suggests Prompt Senate Approval

By The Associated Press

VAIL, Colo., Aug. 16—Former President Gerald R. Ford today threw his support behind the Panama Canal agreement announced by the Carter Administration. Mr. Ford labeled the pact "an important step forward" and called for prompt Senate approval.

After a briefing at his vacation retreat, Mr. Ford said he was "absolutely convinced it's in the national interest of the United States that the treaty be approved."

The agreement, which would cede control of the canal to the Panamanian Government at the end of this century although insuring continued neutrality, was announced last week after 16 years of negotiations.

Carter Faces Uphill Struggle

Mr. Ford's backing was important to the Carter Administration, which faces an uphill struggle to get the agreement approved over the objections of conservative senators.

Ambassador Sol M. Linowitz, who took part in the final negotiations, and Gen. George S. Brown, Chairman of the Joint Chiefs of Staff, flew to Vail earlier in the day and spent about 90 minutes at Mr. Ford's vacation home.

Asked whether he would try to put pressure on conservative Republicans to support the measure, Mr. Ford said he would do what he could and expressed the "hope that his endorsement would be helpful.

Ford Calls for Support

His support followed by one day a White House meeting between Henry A. Kissinger, who was Secretary of State under Mr. Ford, and President Carter. Mr. Kissinger said then that if later briefings upheld his first impression, he would support the pact in testimony before the Senate.

Mr. Ford said the agreement "follows the guidelines of my Administration," and he called on Americans to support it. "I hope I speak for the vast majority of Americans," the former President said

Continued on Page A5, Col. 1

Associated Press

President Tito with Leonid I. Brezhnev after the Yugoslav leader arrived in the Soviet Union for official talks.

Catholic Prelates Organizing a Drive Against Abortions

By KENNETH A. BRIGGS

Archbishop Joseph L. Bernardin, president of the National Conference of Catholic Bishops, signaled the start of a major new church drive against abortion last night, coupling it with proposals for a church-led campaign against social ills that cause women to seek abortions.

In a speech to a Knights of Columbus gathering in Indianapolis, he set forth the most comprehensive antiabortion program yet proposed by the American hierarchy. But in doing so, he called for church initiatives in the fields of employment, housing, health care and welfare reform as "an concrete test of the seriousness of our commitment to the basic human right to life."

Archbishop Bernardin emphasized that the recent Supreme Court decision upholding the right of states to withhold public funds for abortions should "not

Continued on Page B20, Col. 1

U.S. JUDGE IS CHOICE AS NEW F.B.I. DIRECTOR

Frank Johnson of Alabama Expected to Be Named Today by Carter

By ANTHONY MARRO

Special to The New York Times

WASHINGTON, Aug. 16—Frank M. Johnson Jr. of Alabama, a Federal District Court judge who gained a national reputation in the late 1950's and early 1960's because of decisions that advanced the cause of civil rights, has been selected to be the new director of the Federal Bureau of Investigation, Administration sources said today.

The sources said that the decision is expected to be announced tomorrow at 2:30 P.M., at a White House briefing by Attorney General Griffin B. Bell.

If formally nominated and confirmed, Judge Johnson will become the third full-time director in the history of the bureau, which in recent years has been accused of abuses ranging from harassment of political dissidents to illegal break-ins, wiretaps and mail opening.

Offers Previously Refused

Before selecting Judge Johnson, President Carter and Mr. Bell apparently rejected five candidates proposed by a so-called "search committee" which they had created to find a new director.

The judge, a Republican who lives in Montgomery, was reliably reported to have been offered, and to have refused, both the F.B.I. post and the No. 2 post in the Justice Department earlier this year.

Mr. Thornburgh, who also is a Republican, had actively sought the job but had not been recommended by the search committee. He recently returned to Pittsburgh, where he has resumed the practice of law, and where he is considering a

Continued on Page A22, Col. 1

Sitting During Flag Pledge Upheld

By ROBERT HANLEY

Special to The New York Times

NEWARK, Aug. 16—A state law requiring all public school students in New Jersey to at least stand at attention during the pledge of allegiance to the American flag was overturned as unconstitutional today in Federal District Court.

Judge H. Curtis Meanor ruled that the standing mandated by the State Education Law illegally compelled "symbolic speech" and violated students' First Amendment rights of freedom of expression and speech.

The New Jersey statute stipulates that the pledge be recited and a flag salute rendered by all children in public schools, except for the children of foreign diplomats or for youngsters with "conscientious scruples" against the acts.

But the law requires that the exempt pupils "be required to show full respect to the flag while the pledge is being given merely by standing at attention." Judge Meanor objected to the "mandatory language" of that section of the law.

He said pupils opposed to the patriotic exercise could remain seated while their classmates voluntarily saluted and recited the pledge as long as the seated pupils did not "whistle, drum, tap dance, or otherwise be disruptive."

The successful challenge to the part

Continued on Page B3, Col. 5

BREZHNEV DEPICTS CARTER'S OVERTURE AS A POSITIVE MOVE

SAYS HE'LL LOOK AT AN INITIATIVE

Soviet Leader, at Dinner for Tito, Stops Short of Specific Ideas for Mending Relations With U.S.

By CHRISTOPHER S. WREN

Special to The New York Times

MOSCOW, Aug. 16—Leonid I. Brezhnev indicated today that he welcomed President Carter's latest efforts to mend Soviet-American relations and pledged that the Soviet Union would respond to any practical measures to resolve the current differences.

The Soviet leader's remarks, at a dinner for President Tito of Yugoslavia, were phrased circumspectly and stopped short of specific proposals. They did not prevent Mr. Brezhnev from criticizing Washington's allocation of funds for the neutron bomb.

But the response was the most positive public signal to the United States since relations began deteriorating earlier this year.

Carter's Statements Welcomed

"We are all familiar with the latest statements by President Carter," Mr. Brezhnev was quoted by the press agency Tass as having told President Tito. "He speaks in particular about the desirability of developing Soviet-United States relations in the interests of strengthening universal peace.

"Compared with the previous moves by the United States Administration, these statements sound positive. If there is a wish to translate them into the language of practical deeds, we will willingly look for mutually acceptable solutions."

Mr. Brezhnev seemed to be alluding to a foreign policy speech made last month by Mr. Carter in Charleston, S.C. Since the Soviet leader left on vacation before the speech, today's dinner gave him the first public occasion to make his comments.

Strategic Arms Pact the Key Issue

Relations between Washington and Moscow have suffered mainly from lack of progress toward a strategic arms limitation. But relations have also been affected by Mr. Carter's outspokenness on human rights and by the lack of movement in Washington toward easing restrictive trade legislation.

Mr. Brezhnev alluded to some of these frictions when he said that "a hostile propaganda campaign against the socialist countries" on the human rights issue "was being used as a smokescreen for another round of the arms race."

"This connection has become particularly obvious after the United States adopted a decision to develop the cruise missile and allocate funds for the neutron bomb," Mr. Brezhnev said.

He expressed regret that "the pace of the most important talks, on limitation of the arms race, has slowed down." But he went on to declare that "if a good initiative appears anywhere, we are always ready to respond to it."

Most of the speech underscored interests and responsibilities shared by the Soviet Union and Yugoslavia. Mr. Brezhnev said he and President Tito had developed good relations because of mutual

Continued on Page A6, Col. 1

S.E.C. Seeking to Salvage Report, Called Inadequate, on City's Crisis

By MICHAEL C. JENSEN

Special to The New York Times

WASHINGTON, Aug. 16—Ranking officials of the Securities and Exchange Commission's enforcement staff are personally directing an intensive effort to salvage what regulatory sources close to the investigation describe as an inadequate report on New York City's financial crisis.

Because of persistent speculation that the report will criticize Mayor Beame and Comptroller Harrison J. Goldin, the S.E.C. has come under increasing pressure to issue its investigative findings before the mayoral primary on Sept. 8. Yesterday in Manhattan the regulatory agency's ranking attorney told reporters that it "hopes to be in a position to issue a report by the end of next week."

Harvey Pitt, the S.E.C.'s general counsel, disclosed its target date after a hearing before a Federal appeals court considering a lawsuit filed on June 27 by Joel Harnett, a mayoral candidate, to compel the commission to release its report to the public. The three-judge appeals panel issued no decision yesterday.

Specific details of the draft report's reported inadequacies could not be obtained. The lengthy initial investigation was conducted by the S.E.C.'s New York regional office, which also prepared the draft report. The New York staff effort was described by the regulatory sources as poorly investigated and badly written.

The rescue team of top officials that early last week set up temporary headquarters in New York was said to include Stanley Sporkin, the S.E.C.'s director of enforcement; Wallace Timmeny, the division's associate director, and Alfred E. T. Rusch and Theodore A. Levine, both as-

Continued on Page D3, Col. 1

INSIDE

Rome-Bonn Ties Strained

A meeting between Italian and West German leaders was postponed as relations were strained because of the escape of a Nazi war criminal. Page A9.

Berkowitz Enters Plea

David R. Berkowitz, the alleged .44-caliber killer, pleaded not guilty to murdering Stacy Moskowitz and said he would plead insanity if tried. Page B2.

Ruling for Renee Richards

Dr. Renee Richards, the transsexual tennis player, won a preliminary injunction in her effort to qualify for the United States Open. Page B7.

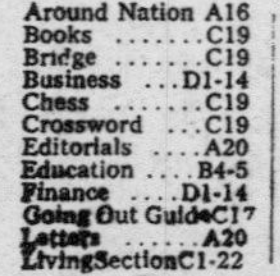

United Press International

SEEKING ASYLUM: Haitian refugees crowded into a small boat being towed to Miami by the Coast Guard late Monday. The 61 persons on the leaky craft said they had been at sea for 30 days and had lost their way. Yesterday, 17 more Haitians arrived. All 78 were given medical examinations and turned over to immigration officials.

Carey Kills Bill On Assailants Of the Elderly

By RICHARD J. MEISLIN

Special to The New York Times

ALBANY, Aug. 16—Governor Carey today announced his veto of a bill that would have increased penalties for crimes against the elderly or disabled. He asserted that its provisions were "inconsistent" with the state's criminal laws and that it "would not be effective in achieving its stated goals."

The Governor, in a lengthy memorandum, said that, "while I share the deep concern of those in the Legislature who supported the bill," he believed that "the wisdom and usefulness of creating separate categories of crimes based on one characteristic is open to serious question."

The veto drew immediate criticism from a "disappointed and saddened" Assembly Speaker Stanley Steingut, Democrat of Brooklyn, and an "outraged" Senator Ralph J. Marino, Republican of Nassau County and chairman of the Senate Crime and Correction Committee. They were the chief sponsors of the compromise measure that was the Legislature's response to the public outcry over violent crime against the aged.

Mr. Marino accused the Governor of "insensitivity," declaring that "his program on crime, in substance, amounted

Continued on Page B4, Col. 5

Elvis Presley, Rock-and-Roll Singer, Is Dead at 42; Object of Teen-Age Adulation and Adult Ire in 50's

Continued From Page A1

sidered by the broadcasters to be so scandalous that the cameras showed him only from the waist up, lest his wiggling hips show.

Mr. Presley's early hit songs are an indelible part of the memories of anyone who grew up in the 50's. "Hound Dog," "Heartbreak Hotel" and "Blue Suede Shoes" were teen-age anthems. Like Frank Sinatra in the decade before and the Beatles a decade later, Mr. Presley was more than a singer—he was a phenomenon.

Mr. Presley was a show-business legend before he was 25 years old. At the age of 30 he was the highest-paid performer in the history of the business. He made 28 films, virtually every one of them frivolous personality vehicles and nearly all of them second-rate at best but they grossed millions.

In recent years, Mr. Presley, who used to carry about 175 pounds on a 6-foot frame, had been plagued with overweight. A recently published book called "Elvis, What Happened?" by three of his former bodyguards alleged that the singer was given to using amphetamines.

History of Mild Hypertension

Dr. Francisco said yesterday that Mr. Presley had a history of mild hypertension and that he had found evidence of coronary artery disease. Both of these, the coroner said, could have been "contributing causes" in Mr. Presley's death.

"But the specific cause may not be known for a week or two pending lab studies," he said, adding, "It is possible in cases like this that the specific cause will never be known."

A hospital spokesman said that the coroner is required by law to conduct an examination of death is not immediately apparent.

Responding to repeated questions about whether the autopsy had revealed any signs of drug abuse, the coroner said the only drugs he had detected were those that had been prescribed by Mr. Presley's personal physician for hypertension and a blockage of the colon, for which he had been hospitalized twice in 1975.

Elvis Aron Presley was born in a two-room house in Tupelo, Miss., on Jan. 8, 1935. During his childhood, he appeared with his parents, Gladys and Vernon Presley, as a popular singing trio at camp meetings, revivals and church conventions.

The family moved to Memphis when Mr. Presley was 13. He attended L. C. Humes High School and worked as an usher in a movie theater. After graduation, he got a job driving a truck for $35 a week. In 1953, Mr. Presley recorded his first song and paid $4 for he privilege; he took the one copy home and played it over and over.

A shrewed song promoter called "Colonel" Thomas A. Parker was impressed by the early records and took over the management of Mr. Presley's career. Mr. Presley toured in rural areas under the sobriquet "The Hill Billy Cat." Colonel Parker, a character of P. T. Barnum proportions, followed the credo, "Don't explain it, just sell it." He once observed, "I consider it my patriotic duty to keep Elvis up in the 90 percent tax bracket."

When Colonel Parker went to negotiate with 20th Century-Fox on a film deal that would be Mr. Presley's screen debut, the studio executives dwelled on the singer's youth and inexperience. "Would $25,000 be all right?" one executive finally asked. Colonel Parker replied: "That's fine for me. Now, how about the boy?"

"Heartbreak Hotel," Mr. Presley's first song hit, was released by RCA in January 1956. A blood-stirring dirge about love and loneliness, it burned up the jukeboxes and eventually sold two million copies.

A phenomenal string of hit songs followed, and Elvis Presley fan clubs sprouted all over the world; membership at one time numbered 400,000.

In 1957, he went to Hollywood to make his first film, "Love Me Tender." It opened to unanimous jeers from the critics and grossed between five and six times what it cost to make.

His later films were considered equally obnoxious by cineastes. One critic remarked of "Jailhouse Rock" that Mr. Presley had been "sensitively cast as a slob." Mr. Presley responded, "That's the way the mop flops."

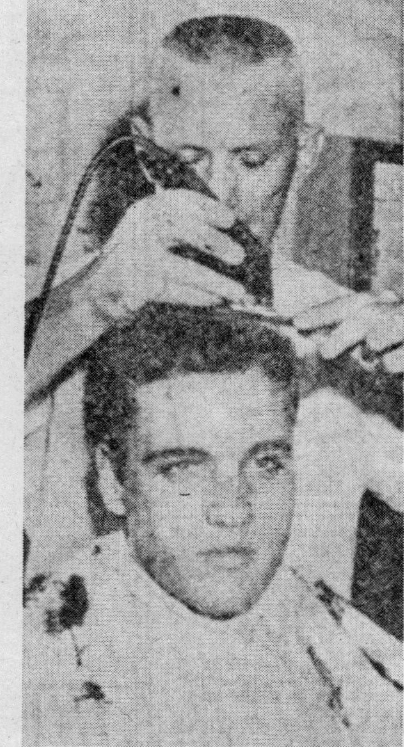

Associated Press

After he was drafted in 1958, Elvis Presley lost his locks to the Army barber at Fort Chaffee, Ark.

Drafted Into the Army

In the spring of 1958, Mr. Presley was drafted into the Army as a private, an event that caused as much stir as an average Super Bowl. "The Pelvis," as he many was known, was stationed in West Germany for two years and was given an ecstatic welcome home by his fans.

In 1967, Mr. Presley married Priscilla Beaulieu, the daughter of an Air Force colonel. They met during his military service, and had a daughter named Lisa Marie, born on Feb. 1, 1968. Although concrete details of their private life remained sketchy through his deliberate design, the fan magazines were full of reports of marital difficulties, and the couple separated in February, 1972. They were divorced in Santa Monica, Calif., in 1973.

Mr. Presley was said to have been a shy person, and rarely granted interviews. He seems to have been scarred by some of the early heavy publicity, and returned from his stint in the Army more withdrawn than he had been.

Generous and Sentimental

In the early 60's he made no personal or even television appearances, but made $5 million a year simply by cutting a few records and making three movies a year. He made a picture called "Harem Holiday" in 18 days and was paid $1 million.

In the 70's Mr. Presley appeared with some frequency in Las Vegas, Nev., nightclubs. Although he sometimes appeared bloated, he was still an excellent showman and audiences always loved him.

In his nightclub act, he would occasionally parody himself. "This lip used to curl easier," he joked, referring to his one-time trademark of singing with a sneer.

It was believed that Mr. Presley neither smoked nor drank, but according to the book by his former aides, he depended heavily on stimulant and depressant drugs. He is also said to have been depressed by the book's "iconoclastic treatment of him.

He was a generous and often sentimental man. He deeply mourned the death of his mother, and kept a suite for his grandmother, Minnie Presley, at his home in Memphis.

The house, Graceland, was an 18-room $1 million mansion with a jukebox at the poolside. Mr. Presley surrounded himself with a retinue of young men called the Memphis Mafia, who served as bodyguards, valets and travel agents. He had a passion for cars, especially Cadillacs, which he tended to acquire in multiples.

Preferred Night Hours

Mr. Presley also gave Cadillacs away with startling frequency. He would from time to time see some stranger, nose pressed against a car-showroom window, and invite the person to go inside and pick out the color he or she liked best. Mr. Presley would then pay the entire cost of purchase on the spot.

Mr. Presley was a nocturnal person who thrived when most others were asleep.

Maurice Elliott, a vcie president and spokesman for Baptist Hospital, said Mr. Presley had gone to sleep yesterday morning at 6 A.M. Some time during the evening or early mornin ghours, Mr. Elliott said, Mr. Presley visited a dentist. Then, between 4 A.M. and 5:30 A.M. he played racket ball on the court of his mansion, the hospital official reported.

When Mr. Presley was a patient in the hospital, Mr. Elliott recalled, "he would put tin foil over the windows. He would normally not get up until noon or thereafter, and not go to bed until 2, 3, 4 A.M."

Mr. Presley's movie career ended in 1970, and in that year he made a successful television special. Critics remarked on how little he had aged. He kept in shape for years with karate, in which he had a black belt. But his penchant for peanut butter and banana sandwiches washed down with soda finally caught up. In one of his last appearances, his trademark skintight pants split open.

Although he reportedly fretted about becoming fat and middle-aged, Mr. Presley was taken more seriously as a musician toward the end of his career. He was sometimes called the "grandfather" of big-time rock-and-roll, and serious rock stations held special programs by and about him.

After his death became known yesterday, radio stations around the country began playing nothing but old Presley records. Mr. Presley recorded about 40 albums, many of them soundtracks of his films. They include "Loving You," "King Creole," "Frankie and Johnny," "Paradise, Hawaiian Style," "Clambake" and "Speedway."

At his death, Mr. Presley had been an indelible part of the nation's musical consciousness for 20 years.

The funeral is being handled by the Memphis Funeral Home. A spokesman said late yesterday that arrangements had not been completed.

Mr. Presley is survived by his 9-year-old daughter, father and grandmother. His father and his daughter were reportedly at Graceland at the time of his death.

Presley Didn't Invent Rock, Gave the Form Its Image and Style

Continued From Page A1

writer, Presley still deserves more credit than he is generally accorded for the creation of his style. Early rock-and-roll derived from a blend of white rockabilly and black rhythm-and-blues. Elvis was not an ignorant country boy who stumbled into the style or who followed the orders of wiser mentors. The by-now-legendary "Sun sessions" of 1954 and 1955, which produced his greatest recorded work and which were recently reissued on an RCA LP, saw Presley carefully working and reworking the songs, evolving his craft on the spot.

Elvis's first national impact—the "Elvis the Pelvis" days—saw the greatest eruption of hysteria about a singer since the days of the young Frank Sinatra. He was mobbed and idolized, even as he was denounced as the devil's tool. Presley became the focus for a new kind of youth music, one that swept aside the gentilities of the adult-oriented pop of previous decades and reflected the swelling youth market of the postwar baby boom.

By the late 1950's however, Presley's image began to change. He went into the Army, and by the time he returned to performing, his main impact was felt in the films he had begun to make soon after his initial success. There were rocking moments in them, to be sure; "Jailhouse Rock," from his second film, was one of his greatest hits. But in most of his movies he became a sultry Lothario, crooning ballads like "Love Me," his first hit of this sort.

By the mid-60's, following the Beatles and the so-called British Invasion, Presley's career had reached its nadir. He still made films and records, and they still sold respectably. But he was no longer a creative force in popular music. In that context his appearance in Las Vegas in 1969, and a subsequent television special and album consituted a genuine comeback.

From then on, the Presley career took an erratic course. At his best—and he was capable of his best right up to the end—he could reach back and deliver his uptempo songs with passion and power. He no longer topped the charts, and he no longer affected people except as an icon, but he could give surprisingly profound musical pleasure.

But Presley appearances in recent years had long since transcended the category of concerts and become ritual celebrations. He didn't sell millions of records, but he sold out sports arenas with monotonous regularity. And the audiences at those concerts were something to behold. Elvis would come on, overweight but regally commanding, and thousands of Instamatics would light up like rippling waves of fireflies wherever he turned. Grown people would cry unashamedly in their seats, and renditions of appalling indifference would be cheered as lustily as were the occasional really brilliant efforts.

Others Indebted

The inconsistencies and irrelevancies of Presley's later career don't dim his earlier achievements. Rock is even more a youthful art form than Romantic poetry, after all; in both, the brightest creativity comes early, and successful artists tend to live out their lives on their youthful reputations.

Elvis will remain the founder of rock-and-roll in most people's minds, and every rock singer owes something to him in matters of inflection and visual style. The Beatles and Bob Dylan brought the music closer to art as it has been traditionally defined. But Elvis was and remained a working-class hero, a man who arose from obscurity and transformed American popular art in answer to his own needs—and who may possibly have been destroyed by the isolation that being an American celebrity sometimes entails. He was as much a metaphor as a maker of music, and one of telling power and poignancy.

Elvis Presley in *Jailhouse Rock.*

"All the News That's Fit to Print"

The New York Times

LATE CITY EDITION

Weather: Sunny, warm today; mild tonight. Partly cloudy tomorrow. Temp. range: today 64-83; Monday 68-86. Temp.-Hum. Index yesterday 77. Full U.S. report on Page 70.

VOL. CXXII . . No. 42,185 NEW YORK, TUESDAY, JULY 24, 1973 — 15 CENTS

PRESIDENT REFUSES TO RELEASE TAPES; SENATE UNIT AND COX SERVE SUBPOENAS; WHITE HOUSE EXPECTED TO IGNORE THEM

COURT TEST SEEN

Separation-of-Powers Doctrine Is the Basis of Nixon's Stand

By R. W. APPLE Jr.

Special to The New York Times

WASHINGTON, July 23—President Nixon refused today to release tape recordings of his conversation about the Watergate case. Both his special prosecutor and the Senate Watergate committee moved at once to subpoena the tapes.

Three subpoenas—one each from the prosecutor, Archibald Cox, and the Senate committee covering the tapes and one from the committee covering other documents—were served shortly after 6 P.M. They were accepted by Leonard Garment, the acting White House counsel, and J. Fred Buzhardt, a special counsel.

Texts of Nixon's letter and replies are on Page 19.

Gerald L. Warren, the deputy Presidential press secretary, said that he could not predict whether they would be honored or not, but other White House officials said that the decision had already been made to ignore them, thus implicitly inviting a test in the Federal courts.

Response Sought Thursday

The subpoenas call for a response on Thursday.

And so the constitutional struggle between the President and those charged with investigating the Watergate and allied scandals was finally joined, more than 13 months after the break-in at the Democratic National Committee.

Mr. Nixon took his firm stand behind the doctrine of separation of powers, despite the prevailing view among politicians outside the White House that to do so would convince the public that he had something to hide.

He also took the risk that the battle could result in his being the first President to be impeached—put on trial before the Senate—since Andrew Johnson in 1868. But the White House inner circle believes, and many Senators and Representatives agree, that the Congress will hesitate before forcing the issue to that extreme.

Letter to Ervin

In a letter to Senator Sam J. Ervin Jr., Democrat of North Carolina, the Senate committee chairman, the President argued that "the tapes are entirely consistent with what I know to be the truth and what I have stated to be the truth." But he insisted that "the tapes would not finally settle" the question of his involvement.

"As in any verbatim recording of informal conversations," Mr. Nixon added, "they contain comments that persons with different perspectives and motivations would inevitably interpret in different ways."

"If you will notice," Sen-

Continued on Page 18, Column 3

Stolen Jet Reported Blown Up, 141 Safe

By Reuters

CAIRO, Tuesday, July 24—A hijacked Japanese airliner was blown up at Benghazi airport, Libya, this morning, the Middle East News Agency reported here.

The agency that reported the plane was blown up after the evacuation of all passengers.

Earlier Details

A hijacked Japanese jumbo jet, parked since Saturday on a desert airfield in the Persian Gulf sheikdom of Dubai, took off with 141 hostages early today, flew to Damascus, Syria, and took off again and was reported headed toward Benghazi, Lybia.

The plane was spotted over Beirut, Lebanon, and flew over Cyprus. It entered Greek airspace and then departed after having asked for a route and reports of weather over southern Greece.

The Athens airport gave the requested information and asked for the plane's destination. "They did not answer," a spokesman for the Athens airport said.

Lybia is ruled by a revolutionary regime that supports the Palestinian guerrillas.

Airport officials at Damascus said that the plane landed there at 2:35 A.M. Tuesday (7:35 P.M. Monday, New York time) and took off 3 hours and 20 minutes later.

High-ranking Syrian Government officials and the Japanese chargé d'affaires at Damascus were on hand when the jet came in, according to news-agency dispatches.

An airport spokesman said

Continued on Page 8, Column 3

116 Reported Dead In Two Air Crashes

A Pan American jet bound from Tahiti to California with 69 passengers and 10 crewmen crashed in the Pacific just after take-off yesterday. There was only one known survivor.

In St. Louis, an Ozark Air Lines turbojet carrying 42 passengers and three crewmen crashed into a suburban residential area. County officials said there were 38 dead. No fatalities were reported on the ground.

Details on Page 31.

FOOD-PRICE RISES ARE SHARP HERE; MORE PREDICTED

Increases Mark Beginning of the 'Bulge' Expected From End of Freeze

By GERALD GOLD

The beginning of what has been widely predicted as a "bulge" or "peak" in food prices following the lifting of the Government's freeze became evident yesterday, as price increases—some of them extraordinary—went into effect at the wholesale and retail levels.

The Geo. A. Hormel Company, for example, told wholesalers in a letter that the price of a 12-ounce can of Spam as of 4 P.M. last Wednesday, the day the freeze ended, was 16 cents higher. The current retail price of Spam, a pork-based luncheon meat, is about 61 cents, and under the Phase 4 guidelines, the 16-cent increase now can be passed on to consumers.

Warning Is Issued

Prices for some basic items in the nation's food supply rose in the Chicago grain markets. All wheat deliveries rose 10 cents a bushel, the daily permissible limit. Some corn was also up as much as 10 cents, and some oats rose as much as the limit of 6 cents. Soybeans also showed a sharp increase.

As expected, eggs were up sharply in retail stores, as high as $1.19 a dozen at a small corner grocery, but around 89 cents to 92 cents at supermarkets. Last week, eggs at supermarkets were selling at about 73 cents to 83 cents. Pork and chicken prices were also up.

Sam Dumbrov, head buyer for Krasdale Foods, a wholesaler, commented as he reviewed the first notifications, "The

Continued on Page 53, Column 3

Aqueduct Shut Today

There will be no racing at Aqueduct today because of a strike called last night by Local 15B of the International Union of Operating Engineers. Details, Page 23.

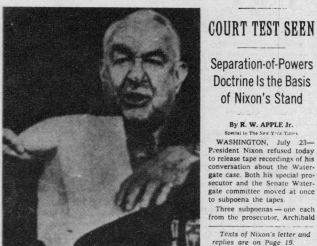

The New York Times/George Tames

Rufus L. Edmisten, left, deputy counsel, and Terry F. Lenzner, assistant chief counsel, delivering the Watergate committee subpoenas to Executive Office Building.

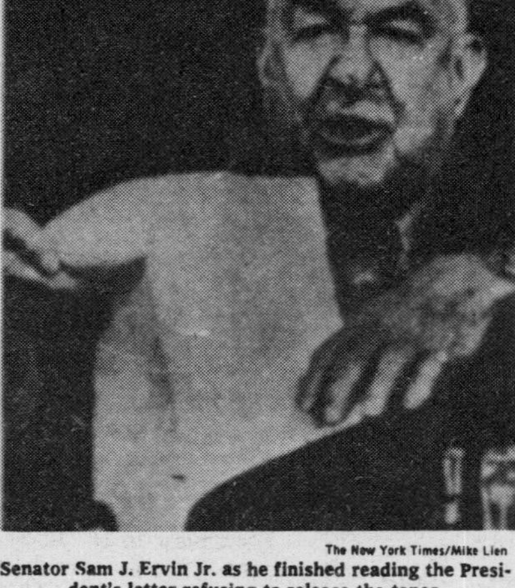

The New York Times/Mike Lien

Senator Sam J. Ervin Jr. as he finished reading the President's letter refusing to release the tapes.

Intruder in Police Station Shoots 2 Officers. Is Slain

By ROBERT D. McFADDEN

An apparently deranged young man with two fire bombs and a revolver in a brown paper bag walked into the 19th Precinct police station on East 67th Street last night and shot a sergeant and a lieutenant before being killed in a fusillade of police bullets.

Deputy Inspector Daniel J. McGowan, the 48-year-old commander of the station house at 153 East 67th Street, and one of his patrolmen set up the crossfire that cut the intruder down and ended a minute of terror as abruptly as it had begun.

The wounded men, Lieut. Frank DarConte, 41, who was shot in the left abdomen, and Sgt. Daniel Brennan, 38, who was shot in the right collarbone, were rushed to nearby Lenox Hill Hospital. Both were described as being in good condition after emergency treatment.

The assailant was tentatively identified from social security and veteran's papers in his possession as Victor Lewis Camacho-Rivera, 25 years old. The papers listed addresses in Puerto Rico and in Bridgeport, Conn., but gave no local address.

Mayor Lindsay and Police Commissioner Donald F. Cawley visited the station and the hospital last night and both took the occasion to denounce cheap handguns, such as the

Continued on Page 27, Column 1

Governor Proposes Flexibility in Ceiling On Mortgage Rates

By FRANCIS X. CLINES

Governor Rockefeller yesterday proposed giving the State Banking Board the power to set home mortgage loan rates at whatever ceiling it judges necessary for changing market conditions.

The proposal, which will be submitted to the special session of the Legislature opening tomorrow, would give the board the flexibility to raise the ceiling from its present 7½ per cent to the 8 per cent that a number of states have set lately, or higher if it were deemed necessary, or lower if the lending market should ease.

Mr. Rockefeller had sought this authority for the Banking Board in past sessions, most recently last spring, and had been rebuffed, with the Legislature choosing to set the ceiling itself.

The Senate Democratic minority leader, Joseph Zaretzki of Manhattan, said the Democrats would oppose the bill again because "we don't think the banking board is a borrower's agency." His contention was that the board would protect the banking industry

Continued on Page 70, Column 5

CONGRESS IS WARY ON NIXON DECISION

Let's Wait and See' Appears to Be View—but Many Think President Errs

By MARJORIE HUNTER

Special to The New York Times

WASHINGTON, July 23—Members of Congress reacted cautiously today to President Nixon's refusal to supply tape recordings of his personal conversations to Watergate investigators.

Many Democrats and Republicans said privately that they felt the President had made a grave political mistake. But there appeared to be no genuine move toward impeachment—nor even more than a scattering of support for a proposed House study of whether the House should begin impeachment proceedings.

The watchword around Congress, today as in past weeks, is "Let's wait and see."

Yet, there appeared to be concern in some quarters that the President's action would make it increasingly difficult for Senate and House leaders of both parties to continue to

Continued on Page 18, Column 1

Strachan Sure Haldeman Wanted Files Destroyed

By DAVID E. ROSENBAUM

Special to The New York Times

WASHINGTON, July 23—Gordon C. Strachan, a former aide to H. R. Haldeman, testified today that three days after the Watergate break-in, under what he believed to be orders from Mr. Haldeman, he destroyed documents indicating that Mr. Haldeman knew that G. Gordon Liddy was conducting a political intelligence operation with a sizable budget.

Mr. Strachan, who was Mr. Haldeman's political assistant until early this year, told the Senate Watergate committee that Mr. Haldeman, then the White House chief of staff, had instructed him, after the burglary at Democratic national headquarters on June 17, 1972, to "make sure our files are clean."

Excerpts from testimony on Watergate, Pages 19 and 20.

He said that he had no doubt then and none now that his boss was telling him to destroy papers showing that Mr. Haldeman knew of the intelligence-gathering scheme, and Mr. Strachan testified that he did put such material through a paper shredder.

When he reported to Mr. Haldeman later that he had shredded the documents, he recalled, Mr. Haldeman did not express surprise.

In his public statements, in a civil deposition and in his interviews with the staff of the Watergate committee, Mr. Haldeman has denied any foreknowledge of the burglary and any participation in efforts to cover up the scandal.

Mr. Strachan also said that as early as April 4, 1972, Mr. Haldeman, who was the White House staff member

Continued on Page 20, Column 5

President Based Decision On Two Legal Doctrines

By WARREN WEAVER Jr.

Special to The New York Times

WASHINGTON, July 23—President Nixon based his refusal today to furnish the White House tapes to the Senate Watergate committee on the intertwined legal doctrines of separation of powers and executive privilege.

Neither of these principles has been tested in the courts in anything resembling the current Watergate context, but the President's action seemed certain to precipitate such a test, one that could reach the Supreme Court in a matter of months.

The separation of powers involves the doctrine that the executive, legislative and judicial branches of the Government, established separately by the Constitution, do not have the power to encroach on each other's jurisdictional territory, to maintain a balance of authority among them.

Executive privilege is the rationale invoked by Presidents when they refuse to divulge to Congress or the courts private internal communications between the President and his aides or among those aides, on the theory that some preliminary confidentiality is essential to any government.

In his letter to Senator Sam J. Ervin Jr. of North Carolina, the committee chairman, President Nixon did not cite executive privilege as such, but he argued that the tapes contained "a great many very frank and

Continued on Page 21, Column 1

Capt. Eddie Rickenbacker Is Dead at 82

Eddie Rickenbacker, a leading fighter ace in World War I and retired chairman of Eastern Air Lines, died early yesterday in a Zurich hospital.

He was 82 years old. His health had been failing since he suffered a stroke in Miami last October, but had improved enough to permit the trip to Switzerland. He was admitted to Neumuenster Hospital with a heart ailment on July 15, four days after his arrival.

His wife said the body would be cremated privately and the ashes flown to his birthplace, Columbus, Ohio, for burial.

Edward Vernon Rickenbacker was a man whose delight in turning the tables on seemingly hopeless odds took him to the top in three distinct fields.

In the daredevil pre-World War I days of automobile racing he became one of this country's leading drivers, although he had a profound dislike for taking unnecessary risks. He had entered the auto industry as a trainee mechanic and made his first mark servicing the cranky machines of that day.

In World War I he became the nation's "Ace of Aces" as a military aviator despite the fact that he had joined the Army as a sergeant-driver on Gen. John J. Pershing's staff.

He was named by Gen. William Mitchell to be chief engineering officer of the fledgling

Continued on Page 38, Column 1

Associated Press

Capt. Eddie Rickenbacker, as a World War I ace, by his Spad, which carries the insignia of the 94th Squadron.

Boy, 16, Is Slain for $1 While on Park Pool Job

By EMANUEL PERLMUTTER

A 16-year-old boy who got his first job two weeks ago as a Parks Department summer worker was robbed of $1 and stabbed to death yesterday morning in the maintenance building of a Lower East Side park swimming pool.

The Hamilton Fish Pool at East Houston and Pitt Streets where Gary Caserta was murdered was described later by the Parks Department Administrator, Richard M. Clurman, as "among our worst problem areas."

"A number of our employes have been threatened, attacked and injured during the season at this site," he said. "We find it hard to get anyone to work there."

The murdered boy was a student at the George Westinghouse Vocational and Technical High School in Brooklyn.

The slain youth worked from midnight to 8 A.M. in the filter room and was driven to the pool every night from his home at 6014 Fifth Avenue, Brooklyn, by his father, Sylvester, a Sanitation Department employe.

Mr. Caserta told the police that he drove his son to work because he didn't want him riding the subways at midnight. He said that when he left the boy Sunday night, the young-

Continued on Page 42, Column 1

NEWS INDEX

Symington Doubts Validity of Raid Fund

Special to The New York Times

WASHINGTON, July 23—Senator Stuart Symington, acting chairman of the Armed Services Committee, declared today that $145-million appropriated by Congress to pay for the secret B-52 bombing of Cambodia may have been obtained under "false pretenses."

A majority of the Armed Services Committee members "didn't know" that the funds appropriated for defense needs would be used to subsidize secret air raids in 1969 and 1970, he said. "Inasmuch as they didn't know, that money must have been obtained under what could be known as false pretenses."

The Missouri Democrat spoke with newsmen after a two-hour secret committee hearing with Jerry W. Friedheim, the ranking Pentagon spokesman, as the only witness. It was Mr. Friedheim who admitted last week that the Defense Department had sent falsified classified material to the Armed Services Committee in 1971 and again earlier this year. After today's meeting, however, committee members refused to say whether Mr. Friedheim had named the official who authorized him to do so.

Committee sources said that the Friedheim testimony marked the beginning of what could be extensive hearings into the over-all conduct of the Vietnam air war.

Other scheduled witnesses, the sources said, will include Gen. John D. Ryan, the Air Force Chief of Staff who retires next week; Adm. Thomas H. Moorer, Chairman of the Joint Chiefs of Staff; retired Gen. Earle G. Wheeler, who was Chairman of the Joint Chiefs at the time the Cambodian bombing was authorized, and William P. Clements Jr., Deputy Secretary of Defense, who, some say, was involved in the decision to withhold some of

Continued on Page 5, Column 1

Rickenbacker, Ace of World War I, Is Dead

Continued From Page 1, Col. 1

Army Air Corps. His transfer to actual combat flying—in which he shot down 22 German planes and four observation balloons—was complicated not only by his being two years over the pilot age limit of 25, but also because he was neither a college man nor a "gentleman" such as then made up the aristocratic fighter squadrons of the air service.

In the highly competitive airline business, Mr. Rickenbacker was the first man to prove that airlines could be made profitable, and then the first to prove that they could be run without a Government subsidy and kept profitable. This, despite a previous venture in the automobile manufacturing business that fell victim to the competition of bigger companies and failed.

While his successes came in fields that were developed in the 20th century, his philosophy seemed to many a carryover from the 19th century.

Opposed to Interference

Mr. Rickenbacker, or Captain Eddie as he preferred to be known (he was a colonel in the reserve but insisted that the title of captain was the only one he had earned), was an individualist of the old empire-building school. In any kind of fight he neither asked for nor gave quarter. His opposition to Government "interference" was widely known, as were his outspoken objections to subsidies for industries or individuals. He was also an intransigent foe of trade unionism and liberal democratic concepts.

Mr. Rickenbacker was fond of saying that the greatest privilege this country had to offer was the "freedom to go broke," and that "a chance" was the only "favor" needed to succeed in the United States.

In recent years, he had identified himself more and more closely with ultra-conservative and right-wing causes. In 1963, when he retired as board chairman of Eastern Air Lines he announced that he would devote himself to "awakening the American public to the grave problems facing them."

In frequent speeches during the years that followed, Mr. Rickenbacker predicted that the American people someday would erect a monument to the memory of Senator Joseph R. McCarthy, and he urged United States withdrawal from the United Nations, the severance of diplomatic relations with the Soviet Union and repeal of the 16th Amendment, which authorized a personal income tax.

"I am going to expand my crusade to save the American way of life for future generations," he wrote in his letter of resignation from Eastern Air Lines, "as I want our children, our grandchildren, and those who follow them to enjoy the American opportunities which have been mine for 73 years."

A self-made man whose formal education ended with the sixth grade, Mr. Rickenbacker was a driving leader. He put the stamp of his dominant personality on everything he touched. His relations with his employes were on a personal basis that was heavily larded with paternalism. He frequently referred to his employes as "the boys and girls," but he devoted much of his time to pushing, prodding and cajoling them into making the same efforts to rise that he had made.

But in the long run it will not be his material successes that will be remembered. Rather, he will be recalled as a larger-than-life figure cast in the same mold as legendary folk heroes of the past.

Part of this heroism was in the military field. When he was given command of a fighter squadron on Sept. 24, 1918, he wrote in his diary:

"Just been promoted to command of 94th Squadron. I shall never ask any pilot to go on a mission that I won't go on. I must work now harder than than I did before."

He did not delay suiting action to the words. The next day, while leading a patrol before breakfast, he spotted a flight of five German Fokker pursuit planes escorting two observation craft near Billy, France. He slammed his Spad fighter into a power dive, coming down out of the sun onto the unsuspecting enemy. Closing fast, he fired a long burst and saw one of the Fokkers fall away and crash.

Taking advantage of the momentary confusion of the German fighter pilots, he plunged through their formation and went after the two-seater observation planes, which were then streaking back toward enemy territory. He made several unsuccessful passes at the heavier craft while their rear gunners were firing at him and the entire dogfight moved behind the German lines.

When he saw that the Fokkers had regrouped and were closing fast at higher altitude, he decided to make one final try. Sideslipping his Spad between the two observation planes, which were flying about 50 feet apart, he sent one down in flames before streaking for home.

This double-header, as he called it, earned him the Medal of Honor, but at the time Mr. Rickenbacker had other things on his mind. "I was glad it had come this morning for the good effect it would have on the other pilots," he said.

His determination to set a good example did not end with the twin killing. He went on to achieve 18 of his 26 victories between taking command of the Squadron and the end of the war—a matter of 48 days in all. Much of his combat was against the "flying circus" of Baron Manfred von Richthofen, the "Red Baron."

For 41 years, Mr. Rickenbacker was officially credited with shooting down 21 planes and four balloons, although he maintained he had downed 22 planes and four balloons. In 1960, the Air Force approved his request for correction of the official record and granted him his 26th kill.

While Mr. Rickenbacker's wartime exploits may have been the result of what he described as "planned recklessness" and "taking all the breaks," he was later to exhibit courage of a steelier kind.

B-17 Crash-Landed

On a foggy night in February, 1941, one of his own Eastern Air Lines planes, on which he was a passenger, crashed into a hill as it approached Atlanta. Although he was pinned to the body of a dead steward by the wreckage and had a shattered pelvic bone, half a dozen broken ribs, a broken leg and one eyelid torn away, he remained conscious for nine hours until he was taken to a hospital.

During that time he took command of the plane. He reassured survivors, sent some of the walking injured for help and shouted warnings against lighting matches in the gasoline-filled cabin.

Associated Press

Capt. Edward V. Rickenbacker in 1970 with model of a World War I Spad.

Sixteen months later, fully recovered except for a limp, he was to have a still greater test of his courage.

That came when a B-17, on which he was making an inspection tour of World War II bases in the Pacific, had to make a crash landing in the ocean, 12 hours out from Honolulu. In minutes the plane sank and its eight passengers and crewman took to rubber rafts.

For the next 22 days, Mr. Rickenbacker, the only civilian in the group, gave the orders. He divided the four oranges that made up the initial food supply. When a seagull landed on his head, he captured the bird smoothly. Then, when fish were caught, he divided the catch. After eight days it rained and he took charge of the water distribution.

Cursing one man who prayed for death, dragging back another who tried to drown himself to make more room for the others, the grim, indomitable figure taunted his comrades to stay alive. Hating him every minute, six of these seven survived to be rescued by a patrolling plane that found them almost by chance. Most of them came to believe that they owed their lives to Mr. Rickenbacker's iron will.

As for the commander of the rafts, he continued his trip after two weeks of rest. He was then 52 years old.

Mr. Rickenbacker was born of a German-Swiss father and a French-Swiss mother in Columbus, Ohio, on Oct. 8, 1890. His name originally was Edward Reichenbacher, but he modified the spelling of the family name during World War I to make it less Germanic, and added the middle name Vernon for a touch of "class."

His father, a construction contractor of moderate circumstances, died when Mr. Rickenbacker was 12. The boy, who was the third of eight children, quit school and went to work. After a series of jobs, he entered the automobile industry as an unpaid porter in the Frayer-Miller Company in Columbus.

Took Engineering Course

He received a job for wages when Lee Frayer, head of the company, learned that his voluntary helper had taken a correspondence course in mechanical engineering. When Mr. Frayer moved a short time later to the Columbus Buggy Company, just beginning the manufacture of automobiles, Mr. Rickenbacker was taken along.

The young man, then 16 and a crack mechanic, developed a local reputation as a driver—although he never held a driver's license nor did he ever obtain a pilot's license. Mr. Frayer, who advertised his cars by racing them, gave his aide his next chance by making him a combination racing driver-salesman. For the next six years he traveled all over the country, racing cars one day and selling them the next.

In 1912, when he was 22, Mr. Rickenbacker dropped the dual role and devoted his full time to racing. It was a hard, dangerous life, but he had less than his share of accidents and walked away from those he had.

He said of this phase of his life that it taught him to "scheme."

"You didn't win races because you had more guts. You won because you knew how to take the turns and baby your engine. It wasn't all just shut your eyes and grit your teeth."

The "scheming" paid off. Mr. Rickenbacker set a world record of 134 miles an hour in a Blitzen-Benz at Daytona Beach, Fla., and in 1916, the last full year of his active racing career, he earned $80,000.

He was in England in 1917, buying motors for a racing team, when the United States entered the war. He hurried home and tried to interest the War Department in organizing an air squadron of former racing drivers. Failing this, he enlisted on May 27, 1917, as a sergeant in the Signal Corps and sailed for France as General Pershing's chauffeur.

Transferred to the Air Corps shortly afterward, he was made a first lieutenant on Aug. 20 and put in charge of engineering of the American air training center at Issoudon.

Attended Gunnery School

Transferred again at his own request, he attended gunnery school and then was assigned to French units for flight training.

His assignment to the 94th Squadron was not pleasing to the other airmen of the unit. They resented his civilian fame and his undeniable cockiness about it. In addition, he was regarded as uncouth, domineering and profane. To top it off, he insisted on checking his plane engine before every flight and personally supervised the loading of machine-gun bullets in his ammunition belts, instead of relying on the fortunes of war as gallantry dictated.

The first Rickenbacker victory came on April 29, 1918, while on a patrol with the squadron commander, the late Capt. James Norman Hall, who later wrote "Mutiny on the Bounty" with Charles Nordhoff. He dired hs Nieuport to within 150 yards of a German Albatross before opening fire.

His squadron mates, whose earlier iciness slowly changed to respect and then fondness, have said that he was never a fancy flier, but always a ferocious fighter. And when Captain Hall was shot down and captured by the Germans, Captain Rickenbacker, who by then was an ace with seven confirmed kills, was promoted to command the 94th.

After the war, he went on a lecture tour, but turned down an offer to appear in a movie. Instead, in 1922, he accepted the proposal of a group of financiers to lend his name and talents to the manufacture of an automobile.

The Rickenbacker Motor Company, which produced the first car with four-wheel brakes in this country, failed in 1927, leaving Mr. Rickenbacker $200,000 in debt and with no job.

He said subsequently, the business had failed because he had forgotten the importance of proper timing in making his moves. "We were just too early with four-wheel brakes," he said of the equipment that is now standard on all American cars. He kept as prized souvenirs the advertisements of rival concerns of the time that scored the four-wheel brakes as un-

He resolved to pay off the big debt, and then raised $700,000 more. With this he bought the Indianapolis Speedway, which he ran until 1945, when he sold out to devote his full time to aviation.

In 1928 Mr. Rickenbacker became a $12,000-a-year assistant sales manager of the Cadillac division of the General Motors Corporation. He then was transferred to the big company's various aviation divisions.

In 1934 he was sent as a trouble-shooter to salvage what he could of General Motors' Eastern Air Transport Division, which then owned Eastern Air Lines jointly with North American Aviation.

The companies had sunk about $6-million into Eastern, but while the line had little competition on its choice New York-Miami routes, it was called the ugly duckling of an industry not then notable for successes. Mr. Rickenbacker's job was to shore up the failing line so the owners could sell it for their $1-million asking price.

In its first year under his management, Eastern turned in a net gain of $350,000—the first profit in the history of the airline industry. The second year he doubled the profits. By the third year, when the Government ordered G. M. to sell its airlines or get out of aircraft manufacturing, a banking syndicate offered more than $3-million for Eastern.

Mr. Rickenbacker pleaded with his employers for an equal chance to "save the airline for the boys and girls who helped build it." He received 60 days to raise the money and was told the company would be his for $3.5-million. The night before the option expired he got his final commitment, and the next day, March 2, 1938, he owned Eastern Air Lines.

Mr. Rickenbacker ran his company in much the same manner he had commanded the 94th Squadron in World War I. He set impossible goals, and then went out and achieved them himself before complaints got out of hand. He also applied other early lessons to the airlines. He was never the first to buy a new plane. Only when other companies had tested a new type and proved it satisfactory did he place his order.

He had homes in New York and Key Biscayne, Fla.

Under Mr. Rickenbacher's dominance, Eastern was considered an efficient and profitable airline, but somewhat austere compared with many of its competitors. In the eyes om many travelers, its lack of emphasis on in-flight service and other frills gave it a spartan image.

Nevertheless, the airline prospered. For 25 years under Mr. Rickenbacker's guidance—from 1935 to 1960—it earned a profit every year. Then, along with many other lines that were jolted by the financial headwinds accompanying the introduction of jet airliners, it experienced losses during the early sixties.

In 1959, Mr. Rickenbacker resigned as president of Eastern, and four years later, on Dec. 31, 1963, he retired as director and chairman of the board.

"All the News That's Fit to Print"

The New York Times

LATE CITY EDITION

Weather: Mostly sunny, cool today; clear, cool tonight. Fair tomorrow. Temp. range: today 51-62; Tuesday 58-74. Full U.S. report on Page 93.

VOL. CXXII ... No. 41,913 NEW YORK, WEDNESDAY, OCTOBER 25, 1972 15 CENTS

THIEU ASSAILS PEACE-PLAN TERMS, ASKS GUARANTEE, HANOI PULLOUT; U.S. LIMITS NORTH VIETNAM RAIDS

SIGNAL TO ENEMY

Bombing Curb Called Act of Appreciation for Concessions

By WILLIAM BEECHER

Special to The New York Times

WASHINGTON, Oct. 24—The White House has ordered a temporary cessation of all bombing north of the 20th parallel in North Vietnam, Administration sources disclosed today.

They said, without elaboration, that North Vietnam had made some concessions in recent secret negotiations. The curtailment of bombing, the sources declared, was ordered last weekend as a signal to the leadership in Hanoi that Washington appreciates the concessions and that the principal stumbling block to an Indochina cease-fire at this point lies in Saigon.

No Announcement Seen

But the restriction of bombing to the panhandle region of North Vietnam, officials said, probably will not be announced for the following two reasons:

First, if President Nixon publicly announced a partial bombing halt as President Johnson did in March, 1968, the United States would lose the threat of resuming air strikes in the far north if this should appear valuable in some future stage of negotiations.

Second, if the North Vietnamese should take advantage of the curtailment to pour tanks, artillery and surface-to-air missiles from China into the Hanoi-Haiphong area, the United States wants to remain free to resume bombing against the two rail lines from China and against supply depots in the northern half of North Vietnam.

Thieu Has Reservations

Officials here said the signal to Hanoi also should not be lost on the South Vietnamese President, Nguyen Van Thieu.

Henry A. Kissinger, the President's adviser on national security, returned last night after five days of talks with Mr. Thieu on what the officials described as tentative arrangements hammered out between the United States and North Vietnam in Paris. But President Thieu had some strong reservations to portions of the proposed arrangement, the officials said, without going into specifics.

The bombing limitation, Ad-

Continued on Page 18, Column 3

DISCUSSING PEACE PLAN: President Nixon with Henry A. Kissinger at the White House. Details, Page 16.

Associated Press

SPEECH IN SAIGON

Cease-Fire Obstacles Seen, but President Expects Agreement

By CRAIG R. WHITNEY

Special to The New York Times

SAIGON, South Vietnam, Oct. 24 — President Nguyen Van Thieu said tonight that all the peace proposals discussed by Henry A. Kissinger and the North Vietnamese in Paris so far were unacceptable, and, in an ambiguous statement, he asserted that there were great difficulties in the way of a cease-fire.

In a nationwide broadcast, President Thieu said on the other hand that a cease-fire could come "very soon" but

Excerpts from Thieu's speech will be found on Page 17.

emphasized that the South Vietnamese could not agree to the Communist proposal for a cease-fire in place before a political settlement.

A cease-fire would be acceptable, he added, only if it was Indochina-wide, guaranteed and involved the withdrawal from the South of all North Vietnamese troops.

Stand Termed Unshakable

"Whether there is a cease-fire now, before the United States election, or one month, two months, three months, or four or five months after the election, our position will remain the same," he said.

What he appeared to do in his speech was to leave the Americans in the position of being able to offer only an undefined cease-fire with no guarantee that they could convince the South Vietnamese to accept a compromise political settlement — something the North Vietnamese, at least in public, have insisted must accompany the silencing of the guns.

"The Communists could only hope to win if our allies betray us and sells us out," Mr. Thieu said, "but our main ally will never betray us. He has invested so much blood and money."

In detailing his objections to several aspects of the current Communist proposals, Mr. Thieu asserted: "I have always said we are not afraid of a cease-fire, but our stance is that if there is a cease-fire it must go along with a political settlement."

"Our position," he added, "has been put forward with the purpose of guaranteeing a just and lasting peace. But this stance is that if they want U. S. troops to withdraw their troops back to the North."

Geneva Accords Recalled

At another point he said: "Today I would like to reaffirm our standpoint in this way: To restore peace we first must use the 1954 Geneva accords as a basis. This means that North Vietnam is North Vietnam and South Vietnam is South Vietnam. For the time being one must accept the two Vietnams, and neither side can invade the other."

"I say that a cease-fire will have a chance to be augured soon," he added, "if such a cease-fire is guaranteed and internationally supervised ... proposed by ... and our American ..."

Mr. Thieu's broadcast was not announced until just after he arrived at the studio at 7:30 P.M. United States Embassy officials declined to comment un-

Continued on Page 16, Column 7

U.S. Pushing Retraining Of Saigon's Entire Army

By JOSEPH B. TREASTER

Special to The New York Times

SAIGON, South Vietnam, Oct. 24—United States Army instructors are putting the entire South Vietnamese Army through a brief but intensive retraining program in a tacit acknowledgment that Vietnamization has not worked as American officials had hoped.

Most of the instruction in the course, which runs 14 days, is elementary, beginning with how to aim and fire the M-16 rifle, the basic weapon for most regular South Vietnamese units since late 1968.

Senior American officers try to gloss over the shortcomings of the South Vietnamese soldiers, but the junior officers and sergeants who are doing the training—mainly men with Special Forces experience and previous tours in Vietnam—readily concede that there is a wide range of basic and critical deficiencies.

Deficiencies Cited

In general, according to the instructors, the deficiencies are these:

¶The troops do not know how to shoot accurately and they drain off ammunition at a dangerously high rate.

¶They seem to have virtually no concept of even the simplest infantry tactics.

¶They do not know how to use their mortars and recoilless rifles.

¶They cannot maintain their

Continued on Page 16, Column 2

M'GOVERN LINKS NIXON TO 'HAWKS'

Says President Needlessly Prolonged Vietnam War to Satisfy Right Wing

By DOUGLAS E. KNEELAND

Special to The New York Times

MILWAUKEE, Oct. 24—Senator George McGovern accused President Nixon today of having needlessly prolonged the war in Vietnam to satisfy "right-wing war hawks."

The Democratic Presidential nominee made the charge on a nationwide television program in New York this morning. He concluded the day here with the fourth in a series of 10 telethons, in which he has been answering questions from callers.

In this morning's interview on the Columbia Broadcasting System's "Morning News" show, Senator McGovern declared that the terms under which the Nixon Administration might be able to settle the war now "appear to be exactly the same terms that the war could have been ended on four years ago."

"It appears to me," he went on, "that, if the President should end the war before we count the votes here on Nov. 7, he has run it for another four years purely to avoid criticism from the right-wing war

Continued on Page 32, Column 4

Nixon Outlay Tops McGovern by 2 to 1

By BEN A. FRANKLIN

Special to The New York Times

WASHINGTON, Oct. 24—President Nixon's main national campaign organization has outspent Senator George McGovern's by about 2 to 1 in the Presidential campaign, official campaign financial statements disclosed today.

The comparison does not include the period of the Democratic primary campaigns but does include that of the Republican primaries, in which Mr. Nixon did not participate.

In the reporting period from Sept. 1 to Oct. 16, for which mandatory financial disclosures were made today by both parties, the principal Nixon campaign committees reported

Continued on Page 33, Column 1

PARENTS SCUFFLE AT SCHOOL DOORS BARRED TO BLACKS

Canarsie Protesters Seek to Register 29 Pupils in Defiance of Edict

SCRIBNER IS CRITICIZED

His Reversal of Decision on Tilden House Youths Is Termed a 'Sellout'

By RONALD SMOTHERS

The parents of 29 black children unsuccessfully tried to push their way past policemen and barricades yesterday to register their children at Canarsie's John Wilson Junior High School 211 in defiance of an order by Chancellor Harvey B. Schribner, who reversed an earlier directive and barred the students from entry.

The parents demonstrated outside the Brooklyn school for two hours, embittered by the Chancellor's reversal Monday of an Oct. 11 order that they be admitted to John Wilson School and further angered by the issuance of a new directive assigning the students to Isaac Bildersee Junior High School 68.

Denouncing the Chancellor and charging that his reversal was a "sellout and a pacifier" to white parents who had occupied the school last week in protest of the earlier order, the black parents, all of whom live in Brownsville's Samuel J. Tilden Houses, rejected the new assignments.

Parents Give Views

The white parents contended that the school, with an enrollment of 70 per cent whites and 30 per cent blacks, was "naturally" integrated and there was no need to bring in students from outside its area.

The protest yesterday at the Wilson school, at Avenue J and East 100th Street, was the latest in the five-week controversy over integration of the Tilden Houses Pupils into three predominantly white schools of District 18 in the Canarsie and East Flatbush sections.

The black pupils assigned to Wilson have not attended school at all this year. The dispute has led to demonstrations by black parents, the three-day occupation last week of Wilson by white parents and the assignment of the black youths to two—and with this new order—finally a third school in the district.

Students are Screened

Parents of the Tilden pupils, insisting that they would not send their children to the 97 per cent white Bildersee School, alternately tried to push past four policemen who stood in the narrow gateway to Wilson or tried to sneak their children past the assistant principals screening every student entering the school.

Dr. Scribner's new order caused a wave of criticism and reaction among educators, civil rights leaders and educational associations around the city as well as in other parts of the district.

Parents and staff members

Continued on Page 25, Column 1

The New York Times/Barton Silverman

A scene outside John Wilson Junior High School yesterday in Canarsie, Brooklyn

3 Teachers and 3 Parents Held Up in Queens School

By MICHAEL KNIGHT

Three youths walked unchallenged into a quiet elementary school in Forest Hills, Queens, yesterday morning and robbed three teachers and three parents, saying that they were armed with guns.

A few hours later a youth walked into a first-grade classroom at Public School 26 in the University Heights section of the Bronx, seized a teacher's pocketbook and threatened to "blow the kids' heads off" if the teacher resisted.

The two robberies were the latest in a recent rash of incidents involving teachers. They bring to 16 the number of teachers and parents robbed in schools or in front of classes this month.

Board of Education officials had no explanation for the robberies which at first glance appear to have sprung up suddenly.

2 Robberies Last Month

Comparative figures for September and for last March, when a new incident-reporting system went into effect, show two robberies of teachers in those months.

Meanwhile, tightened security measures were put into effect and others were debated in a number of schools where teachers were assaulted last week.

In the Bronx incident, the police said that a youth about 19 years old walked into the first-floor classroom of Harriet Gittler at P.S. 26, at 1930 Andrews Avenue near University Avenue, at 1:55 P.M.

The teacher's pocketbook containing $80 was lying on her desk, the police said, and the youth quickly grabbed it, delaying a moment only to

Continued on Page 26, Column 3

EX-POLICE OFFICER HELD AS 'BAG MAN'

Seized After Brooklyn Chase —2 Detectives Arrested in Mafia Inquiry

A retired police lieutenant accused of being "a bag man and connection between gamblers and the police" was arrested in Brooklyn last night after he allegedly passed more than $5,000 to an undercover police agent.

Earlier yesterday, two Brooklyn police detectives were arrested and accused of having arranged for the dismissal of a criminal case against four persons linked to a Canarsie junkyard trailer that was named by Brooklyn District Attorney Eugene Gold as a Mafia meeting place.

The detectives' arrest was unrelated to last night's apprehension of the retired police lieutenant, which stemmed from a Staten Island investigation.

Last night's arrest followed a high-speed chase through the streets of the Bay Ridge section when the former lieutenant tried to outrun several police cars, according to a police official.

The official, Deputy Police Commissioner William P. McCarthy, head of the Police Department's Organized Crime Control Bureau, described the former lieutenant's arrest in an unusual news conference at the 68th Precinct station at 12:30 this morning.

Commissioner McCarthy identified the arrested former officer as James E. McDermott, 52 years old, who retired from the force Aug. 3, 1971.

His last assignment, Mr.

Continued on Page 29, Column 3

WORKER FOR G.O.P. RECALLS SABOTAGE

Secretary Asserts She Was Part of Anti-Muskie Plot in Florida's Primary

By MARTIN WALDRON

Special to The New York Times

TAMPA, Fla., Oct. 24—A 26-year-old Tampa secretary has said that she was part of a Republican scheme to sabotage the Presidential campaign of Senator Edmund S. Muskie in Florida last winter.

The secretary, Miss Patricia E. Griffin, who said she had served as a Muskie volunteer to carry out the anti-Muskie effort, told a Tampa newspaperman that she had been recruited by Robert Benz in Tampa. She said that Mr. Benz had told her he worked for Donald H. Segretti of California.

There have been a number of reports linking Mr. Segretti to political sabotage efforts financed by the Committee for the Re-Election of the President, and alleging that he was paid by a special campaign fund. The New York Times has learned that a number of telephone calls, made from Mr. Segretti's phone or charged to his credit card, were placed to the White House and to the home of Dwight L. Chapin, an assistant to President Nixon.

But Miss Griffin's admission is the first direct evidence of actual Republican sabotage against Democrats. Previous reports said that Mr. Segretti had attempted to recruit a number of persons to engage in such activity, but none said that any such efforts had actually taken place.

None of the allegations con-

Continued on Page 32, Column 1

Jackie Robinson, First Black in Major Leagues, Dies

By DAVE ANDERSON

Jackie Robinson, who made history in 1947 by becoming the first black baseball player in the major leagues, suffered a heart attack in his home in Stamford, Conn., yesterday morning and died at Stamford Hospital at 7:10 A.M. He was 53 years old.

As an all-round athlete in college and later the star infielder of the Brooklyn Dodgers, he became the pioneer for a generation of blacks in the major professional sports after World War II.

Mr. Robinson, who was honored at the World Series in Cincinnati a week ago Sunday, had been in failing health for several years. He recovered from a heart attack in 1968 but then lost the sight of one eye and the partial sight of the other as a result of diabetes.

He remained active, though, in national campaigns against drug addiction—from which his son, Jackie Jr., had been recovering before he was killed in 1971 in an automobile accident. In fact, Mr. Robinson planned to attend a drug symposium yesterday sponsored by the business community in Washington.

When he was stricken at home, an emergency call was made to the Stamford police by his wife, Rachel, who is an associate professor of psychiatric nursing at the Yale School of Medicine. They applied external massage and oxygen before a Fire Department ambulance took him to the hospital.

For sociological impact, Jack Roosevelt Robinson was perhaps America's most significant athlete.

As the first black player in major-league baseball, he was a pioneer. His skill and accom-

Continued on Page 56, Column 1

Nimo Yakubu/Nancy Palmer Agency

Jackie Robinson in New Jersey office last week.

The New York Times

Robinson stealing home against the Cubs in 1952 with the bases loaded. He excelled in the daring plays.

Grand Jury Finds No Evidence In Its Inquiry on Newark Official

By RICHARD PHALON

Special to The New York Times

NEWARK, Oct. 24—An Essex County grand jury found "without substance" today allegations that the appointment of Robert Notte as executive director of the Newark Housing Authority had been supported by organized crime.

Superior Court Judge James R. Giuliano, who released the presentment today, also freed Peter J. Bridge, a former reporter for The Evening News of Newark, who was serving his 20th day in the Essex County Jail.

Mr. Bridge was sentenced for contempt for the life of the grand jury, which is expected to come to its formal end tomorrow, after refusing to go beyond the details of a story that appeared in the now-defunct newspaper last May 2.

The article quoted Mrs. Pearl Beatty, a member of the Housing Commission, as having said that she had been offered $10,000 by an unidentified man for control of her vote on the appointment of a new executive director of the authority.

In a 30-page presentment, the grand jury found no cause for indictment in allegations that Mr. Notte's appointment had been marked by attempted bribery, intimidation, harassment and the prospect of political payoffs held out by Mayor Kenneth A. Gibson to Assemblyman Anthony Imperiale.

Most of the allegations were

Continued on Page 51, Column 7

NEWS INDEX

Jackie Robinson, First Black Major Leaguer, Dies at 53

Dodger Star, in Hall of Fame, Began in '47

Continued From Page 1, Col. 4

plishments resulted in the acceptance of blacks in other major sports, notably professional football and professional basketball. In later years, while a prosperous New York businessman, he emerged as an influential member of the Republican party.

His dominant characteristic, as an athlete and as a black man, was a competitive flame. Outspoken, controversial, combative, he created critics as well as loyalists. But he never deviated from his opinions.

Commented on Debut

In his autobiography, "I Never Had It Made," to be published next month by G. P. Putnam's, he recalled the scene in 1947 when he stood for the National Anthem at his debut with the Brooklyn Dodgers. He wrote:

". . . but as I write these words now I cannot stand and sing the National Anthem. I have learned that I remain a black in a white world."

Describing his struggle, he wrote:

"I had to fight hard against loneliness, abuse and the knowledge that any mistake I made would be magnified because I was the only black man out there. Many people resented my

Mr. Robinson in uniform before joining Montreal.

impatience and honesty, but I never cared about acceptance as much as I cared about respect."

His belligerence flared throughout his career in baseball, business and politics.

"I was told that it would cost me some awards," he said last year. "But if I had to keep quiet to get an award, it wasn't worth it. Awards are great, but if I got one for being a nice kid, what good is it?"

To other black ballplayers, though, he was most often saluted as the first to run the gantlet. Monte Irvin, who played for the New York Giants while Robinson was with the Dodgers and who now is an assistant to the commissioner of baseball, said yesterday:

"Jackie Robinson opened the door of baseball to all men. He was the first to get the opportunity, but if he had not done such a great job, the path would have been so much more difficult.

"Bill Russell says if it hadn't been for Jackie, he might not ever have become a professional basketball player. Jack was the trail-blazer, and we are all deeply grateful. We say, thank you, Jackie; it was a job well done."

"He meant everything to a black ballplayer," said Elston Howard, the first black member of the New York Yankees, who is now on the coaching staff. "I don't think the young players would go through what he did. He did it for all of us, for Willie Mays, Henry Aaron, Maury Wills, myself.

"Jack said he hoped someday to see a black manager in baseball. Now I hope some of the owners will see how important that would be as the next step."

Elected to Hall of Fame

After a versatile career as a clutch hitter and daring baserunner while playing first base, second base, third base and left field at various stages of his 10 seasons with the Brooklyn Dodgers, he was elected to baseball's Hall of Fame in 1962, his first year of eligibility for the Cooperstown, N.Y., shrine.

Despite his success, he minimized himself as an "instrument, a tool." He credited Branch Rickey, the Brooklyn Dodger owner who broke professional baseball's color line. Mr. Rickey signed him for the 1946 season, which he spent with the Dodgers' leading farm, the Montreal Royals of the International League.

"I think the Rickey Experiment, as I call it, the original idea, would not have come about as successfully with anybody other than Mr. Rickey," he often said. "The most important results of it are that it produced understanding among whites and it gave black people the idea that if I could do it, they could do it, too, that blackness wasn't subservient to anything."

Among his disappointments was the fact that he never was afforded an opportunity to be a major-league manager.

"I had no future with the Dodgers because I was too closely identified with Branch Rickey," he once said. "After the club was taken over by Walter O'Malley, you couldn't even mention Mr. Rickey's name in front of him. I considered Mr. Rickey the greatest human being I had ever known."

Robinson kept baseball in perspective. Ebbets Field, the Brooklyn ballpark that was the stage for his drama, was leveled shortly after Mr. O'Malley moved the Dodger franchise to Los Angeles in 1958. Apartment houses replaced it. Years later, asked what he felt about Ebbets Field, he replied:

"I don't feel anything. They need those apartments more than they need a monument to the memory of baseball. I've had my thrills."

He also had his heartbreak His older son, Jackie Jr., died in 1971 at the age of 24 in an automobile accident on the Merritt Parkway, not far from the family's home in Stamford.

Son Became Drug Addict

Three years earlier, Jackie Jr. had been arrested for heroin possession. His addiction had begun while he served in the Army in Vietnam, where he was wounded. He was convicted and ordered to undergo treatment at the Daytop drug abuse center in Seymour, Conn. Cured, he worked at Daytop, helping other addicts, until his fatal accident.

Robinson and his wife, Rachel, had two other children—David and Sharon.

"You don't know what it's like," Robinson said at the time, "to lose a son, find him, and lose him again. My problem was my inability to spend much time at home. I thought my family was secure, so I went running around everyplace else. I guess I had more of an effect on other people's kids than I did on my own."

With the Dodgers, he had other problems. His arrival in 1947 prompted racial insults from some opponents, an aborted strike by the St. Louis Cardinals, an alleged deliberate spiking by Enos Slaughter of the Cardinals and stiffness from a few teammates, notably Fred (Dixie) Walker, a popular star from Georgia.

"Dixie was very difficult at the start," Robinson acknowledged, "but he was the first guy on the ballclub to come to me with advice and help for my hitting. I knew why—if I helped the ballclub, it put money in his pocket. I knew he didn't like me any more in those few short months, but he did come forward."

A Cautioning by Rickey

As a rookie, Robinson had been warned by Mr. Rickey of the insults that would occur. He also was urged by Mr. Rickey to hold his temper. He complied. But the following season, as an established player, he began to argue with the umpires and duel verbally with opponents in the traditional give-and-take of baseball.

As the years passed, Robinson developed a close relationship with many teammates.

"After the game we went our separate ways," he explained. "But on the field, there was that understanding. No one can convince me that the things that happened on the ballclub didn't affect people. The old Dodgers were something special but of my teammates, overall, there was nobody like Pee Wee Reese for me."

In Boston once, some Braves' players were taunting Robinson during infield practice. Reese, the popular shortstop, who came from Louisville, moved to the rescue.

"Pee Wee walked over and put his arm on my shoulder, as if to say, 'This is my teammate, whether you like it or not,'" Robinson said. "Another time, all our white players got letters, saying if they don't do something, the whole team will be black and they'll lose their jobs. On the bus to the ballpark that night, Pee Wee brought it up and we discussed it. Pretty soon, we were all laughing about it."

In clubhouse debates, Robinson's voice had a sharp, angry tone that rose with his emotional involvement.

"Robinson," he once was told by Don Newcombe, a star pitcher, who was also black, "not only are you wrong, you're loud wrong."

As a competitor, Robinson was the Dodgers' leader. In his 10 seasons, they won six National League pennants—1947, 1949, 1952, 1953, 1955 and 1956. They lost another in the 1951 playoff with the New York Giants, and another to the Philadelphia Phillies on the last day of the 1950 season.

In 1949, when he batted .342 to win the league title and drove in 124 runs, he was voted the league's Most Valuable Player Award In 1947, he had been voted the rookie of the year.

"The only way to beat the Dodgers," said Warren Giles, then the president of the Cincinnati Reds, later the National League president, "is to keep Robinson off the bases."

He had a career batting average of .311. Primarily a line-drive hitter, he accumulated only 137 home runs, with a high of 19 in both 1951 and 1952.

But on a team with such famous sluggers as Duke Snider, Gil Hodges and Roy Campanella, who was also black, he was the cleanup hitter, fourth in the batting order, a tribute to his ability to move along teammates on base.

But his personality flared best as a baserunner. He had a total of 197 stolen bases. He stole home 11 times, the most by any player in the post-World War II era.

Ran Like Football Player

"I think the most symbolic part of Jackie Robinson, ballplayer," he once reflected, "was making the pitcher believe he was going to the next base. I think he enjoyed that the most, too. I think my value to the Dodgers was disruption — making the pitcher concentrate on me instead of on my teammate who was at bat at the time."

In the 1955 World Series, he stole home against the New York Yankees in the opening game of Brooklyn's only World Series triumph.

Pigeon-toed and muscular, wearing No. 42, he ran aggressively, typical of his college football training as a star runner and passer at the University of California at Los Angeles in 1939 and 1940. He ranked second in the Pacific Coast Conference in total offense in 1940 with 875 yards—440 rushing and 435 passing.

Born in Cairo, Ga., on Jan. 31, 1919, he was soon taken to Pasadena, Calif., by his mother with her four other children after his father had deserted them. He developed into an all-round athlete, competing in basketball and track in addition to baseball and football. After attending U.C.L.A., he entered the Army.

He was commissioned a second lieutenant. After his discharge, he joined the Kansas City Monarchs of the Negro National League as a shortstop.

"But if Mr. Rickey hadn't signed me, I wouldn't have played another year in the black league," he said. "It was too difficult. The travel was brutal. Financially, there was no reward. It took everything you made to live off."

If he had quit the black leagues without having been signed by Mr. Rickey, what would he have done?

"I more than likely would have gone to coach baseball at Sam Houston College. My minister had gone down there to Texas as president of the college. That was about the only thing a black athlete had left then, a chance to coach somewhere at a small black college."

Instead, his presence turned the Dodgers into the favorite of black people throughout the nation.

"They picked up 20 million fans instantly," said Bill Russell, the famous center of the Boston Celtics who was professional basketball's first black coach. "But to most black people, Jackie was a man, not a ballplayer. He did more for baseball than baseball did for him. He was someone that young black athletes could look up to."

As the Dodgers toured the National League, they set attendance records. But the essence of Robinson's competitive fury occurred in a 1954 game at Ebbets Field with the rival Giants.

Sal Maglie, the Giants' ace who was known as "The Barber" because of his tendency to "shave" a batter's head with his fast ball and sharp-breaking curve, was intimidating the Dodger hitters. In the Dodger dugout, Reese, the team captain, spoke to the 6-foot, 195-pound Robinson.

"Jack," said Reese "we got to do something about this."

Robinson soon was kneeling in the on-deck circle as the next Dodger batter. With him was Charlie DiGiovanna, the team's adult batboy who was a confidant of the players.

"Let somebody else do it, Jack," DiGiovanna implored. "Everytime something comes up, they call on you."

Robinson agreed, but once in the batter's box, he changed his mind. Hoping to draw Maglie toward the first-base line, Robinson bunted. The ball was fielded by Whitey Lockman, the first baseman, but Maglie didn't move off the mound. Davey Williams, the second baseman, covered the base for Lockman's throw.

Knocked Over Williams

"Maglie wouldn't cover," Robinson recalled. "Williams got in the way. He had a chance to get out of the way but he just stood there right on the base. It was just too bad, but I knocked him over. He had a Giant uniform on. That's what happens."

In the collision, Williams suffered a spinal injury that virtually ended his career. Two innings later, Alvin Dark, the Giants' captain and shortstop, retaliated by trying to stretch a double into a third-base collision with Robinson.

Realizing that Dark hoped to avenge the Williams incident, Robinson stepped aside and tagged him in the face. But his grip on the ball wasn't secure. The ball bounced away. Dark was safe.

"I would've torn his face up," Robinson once recalled. "But as it turned out, I'm glad it didn't happen that way. I admired Al for what he did after I had run down Williams. I've always admired Al, despite his racial stands. I think he really believed that white people were put on this earth to take care of black people."

Ironically, after the 1956 season, Robinson was traded to the rival Giants, but he announced his retirement in Look magazine. Any chance of his changing his mind ended when Emil (Buzzy) Bavasi, then a Dodger vice president, implied that after Robinson had been paid for the by-line article, he would accept the Giants' offer.

"After Buzzy said that," Robinson later acknowledged, "there was no way I'd ever play again."

He joined Chock Full O'Nuts, the lunch-counter chain, as an executive. He later had a succession of executive posts with an insurance firm, a food-franchising firm and an interracial construction firm. He also was chairman of the board of the Freedom National Bank in Harlem and a member of the New York State Athletic Commission.

In politics Mr. Robinson remained outspoken. He supported Richard M. Nixon in the 1960 Presidential election. When Mr. Nixon and Spiro T. Agnew formed the 1968 Presidential ticket, however, he resigned from Governor Rockefeller's staff, where he was a Special Assistant for Community Affairs, to campaign for Hubert H. Humphrey, the Democratic nominee.

Mr. Robinson's niche American history is secure — his struggle predated the emergence of "the first black who" in many areas of the American society. Even though he understandably needed a Branch Rickey to open the door for him, Branch Rickey needed a Jackie Robinson to lead other blacks through that door.

"All the News That's Fit to Print."

The New York Times.

LATE CITY EDITION

THE WEATHER—Rain today; tomorrow fair, not much change in temperature.
Temperatures yesterday—Max. 40, min. 37
U. S. Weather Forecast—For details see Page 14.

Copyright, 1931, by The New York Times Company.

VOL. LXXX....No. 26,730. **** + NEW YORK, WEDNESDAY, APRIL 1, 1931. TWO CENTS in Greater New York | THREE CENTS Within 200 Miles | FOUR CENTS Elsewhere Except 7th and 8th Postal Zones

MANAGUA IS DESTROYED, 1,100 REPORTED KILLED, THOUSANDS INJURED IN EARTHQUAKE AND FIRE; MANY AMERICAN CASUALTIES; HOOVER RUSHES AID

PRESIDENT DECLARES AGAINST A TAX RISE; ASKS PEOPLE TO AID

Increase Can Be Avoided if Congress Will Follow Budget Figures, He Asserts.

GROUP DEMANDS TO WAIT

Restraint by the Public Is Called For to Make the Economy Program Effective.

HELP PLEDGED BY WATSON

Senator Favors Short-Term Borrowing to Meet Deficit—Collections Continue to Decline.

Special to The New York Times.

WASHINGTON, March 31.—President Hoover declared today that there would be no increase in taxes next year if Congress would keep appropriations within budget recommendations and sectional and group demands for Federal assistance were postponed.

Republican Senators, including Senator Watson, the floor leader, and Senator Jones of Washington, chairman of the Appropriations Committee, immediately pledged their efforts to keep taxes down, and declared that by cooperation between Congress and the President new taxation can be avoided. Short-term borrowing can be resorted to to tide over in an emergency, the Senators said.

After a Cabinet discussion of fiscal conditions and a conference with Senator Watson, President Hoover issued an appeal for the cooperation of the people in withholding sectional and group demands. The President's statement follows:

"There will be no increase in taxes if the next Congress imposes no increases upon the budget or other expenditure proposals which the administration will present. But for Congress to do this, the people must cooperate to effectively discourage and postpone consideration of the demands of sectional and group interests."

Tax Collections Still Decline.

The deficit this year is likely to be greater than estimated, because of the great decline in income tax collections, which for twenty-eight days in March have amounted only to $230,741,000, a reduction of $222,000,000 from the same period last year.

The President's statement, in the opinion of Republican leaders, defines the policy that the party will follow in Congress, and sets at rest predictions that new taxation will be imposed to meet the deficit.

Democratic Congressional leaders are reported to be disposed to accept the administration's fiscal plans, and indications are that no attempts will be made to pass new revenue measures in the next Congress, in which the Republicans will have only nominal control.

The administration, in deciding that the deficit can be handled without imposing new taxes, did so in the belief that an upturn in business will increase revenues. Treasury experts have reported that the government can carry on without any embarrassment by borrowing, and by reducing the amount applied to reduction of the national debt.

Rely on Pick-up in Business.

At the treasury it was pointed out that during a period when business is slack it would appear to be better policy to increase the public debt than to raise taxes. While another deficit is probable in 1932, it is generally believed that business will have recovered so much that government receipts again will start upward, permitting the usual reductions in the public debt as required by statute.

Senator Borah said that, of course, there would be no increase in taxation until after the Presidential election.

"Congress kept below the budget estimates in the two last sessions," he said, "and yet the deficits increased, due, among other things, to a reduction in the taxes last year."

Since taxes were reduced when a surplus existed, they should be increased when the necessity arises for additional revenues, Senator Borah added. The surtaxes should be raised, he declared.

During March the government has suffered the severest drop in revenue in any year since the World War. For the fiscal year, through March 28, income tax collections were $1,502,172,000, a decline of $303,000,000 from the same period a year ago.

Final figures for March will be available Thursday. They will show losses in all receipts for the nine months of the fiscal year of more than $500,000,000, including, besides income taxes, a drop of more than $129,600,000 in customs revenue and $40,000,000 in miscellaneous internal revenue receipts.

For the nine months total expendi-

Continued on Page Seventeen.

Single, Widowed and Divorced Must Pay Heavy Rumanian Tax

Wireless to THE NEW YORK TIMES.

BUCHAREST, March 31.—A bill was introduced in the Rumanian Parliament yesterday to provide heavy taxation for unmarried persons.

The bill, contrary to most proposals of the same type, is not a tax merely on bachelors, but provides for complete equality of sexes. All unmarried persons between the ages of 30 and 65 will have to pay an additional 20 per cent on his or her income tax with a further charge varying from 200 to 500 lei.

Those who have lost their spouses by death or in the divorce courts will have to pay the same taxes unless they remedy the loss within two years.

INQUIRY COMMITTEE TO BE NAMED AT ONCE

Macy Goes to Albany to Speed Action After Seabury Objects to Waiting Until April 10.

MAYOR RETURNING TO FIGHT

Clark Prepares for First Crain Hearing Wednesday—Bastress Indicted for Bribery.

Developments yesterday in the investigations into city affairs were:

W. Kingsland Macy left for Albany to speed the naming of the legislative committee.

Mayor Walker started home to reply to charges.

Samuel Seabury, pushing Crain inquiry, won access to Federal grand jury records.

Rollin C. Bastress, former Building Inspector for Manhattan, was indicted on bribe charges.

COMMITTEE TO BE SPEEDED.

Speedy appointment of the legislative committee to investigate the city administration was expected yesterday as Mayor Walker started back from California to answer his accusers and rally his followers for the stiffest fight Tammany has faced in more than three decades.

W. Kingsland Macy, Republican State Chairman, went to Albany to advise legislative leaders that they must lose no time in setting up the machinery of the investigation which he was successful in obtaining after a long and bitter fight. He was to tell them also that Samuel Seabury, who now is investigating magistrate's courts and the District Attorney's office would serve them as counsel provided he got a free hand.

Macy and Seabury Confer.

Mr. Macy, who conferred with Mr. Seabury before starting for Albany, ascertained that the prospective counsel was not interested in the personnel of the committee so long as it agreed in advance not to hamper his inquiry with political considerations. Mr. Macy, on the other hand, promised there would be no interference.

As a consequence it was predicted that the committee would be named within a few days with Senator Samuel H. Hofstadter, sponsor of the empowering resolution in the upper house, as chairman. Three of the committee's members are to be named by Senator John Knight, president pro tem of the Senate, and four by Speaker Joseph A. McGinnies of the Assembly. Before the Legislature adjourns April 10, it was said, the committee would hold its first meeting to offer the post of counsel formally to Mr. Seabury, and promise him it would not interfere with the investigation.

It had been understood that the committee would not be appointed or hold a meeting until after the adjournment of the Legislature. The decision to speed up the program was attributed to Mr. Seabury's belief that the investigation, to be effective must start with as little delay as possible.

Fund Feared Inadequate.

As preparations were made for beginning the inquiry into city scandals in all five boroughs, fear was expressed in some quarters that the $250,000 appropriation in the resolution authorizing the investigation would prove inadequate for the task ahead of Mr. Seabury. One eminent member of the bar familiar with investigations predicted that unless Mr. Seabury obtained many volunteers to serve without pay on his legal staff, the funds would be exhausted within a few months.

Meanwhile Mr. Seabury, in his dual capacity of investigator of the lower courts for the Appellate Division and of District Attorney Crain as Commissioner for Governor Roosevelt, hastened to conclude those tasks before assuming the larger one ahead. He is to preside today at a public hearing on magistrates while John

Continued on Page Twenty-two.

KNUTE ROCKNE DIES WITH SEVEN OTHERS IN MAIL PLANE DIVE

Ship's Engine Fails Above the Clouds, Wing Rips Off, Craft Falls on Kansas Farm.

ALL OCCUPANTS FOUND DEAD

Football Leaders of the Country Pay Tribute to Great Coach's Qualities.

CONSUMMATE IN STRATEGY

His Skill Raised Football Technique to Great Heights in His Notre Dame Teams.

Special to The New York Times.

WICHITA, Kan., March 31.—Knute Rockne, Notre Dame football coach, and seven others, were killed at 11 o'clock this morning when a ten-passenger Trans-Continental & Western Airways plane dived into a pasture in the Flint Hills cattle country near Bazaar in Southeastern Kansas.

Besides Rockne the dead were:

CHRISTEN, H. J., Chicago.
HAPPER, J. H., Chicago.
MILLER, W. B., Hartford, Conn.
GOLDTHWAITE, SPENCER G., New York City.
ROBRECHE, C. A., Wheeling, W. Va.
FRYE, ROBERT, pilot.
MATHIAS, JESS, pilot.

Radio Communication Ceases.

In a hazy drizzle which gave poor flying visibility the tri-motored Fokker left Kansas City at 9:15, three-quarters of an hour late after waiting for mail connections. It was due in Wichita at 10:25 under the regular schedule.

Flying above the clouds the big transport maintained radio communications with the Kansas City Airport until it sighted Cassoday, southwest of Bazaar. It asked for weather conditions at Wichita and then radio communication ceased, apparently at about the scene of the crash.

Witnesses heard the drone of the motors above the clouds, heard them sputter and stop and soon saw the big craft flash down through the cloud bank with a trail of smoke fluttering out behind.

A wing tore loose and swirled away like a falling leaf, to land half a mile from where the plane plowed itself into the soft earth of the pasture of S. H. Baker. One of the three motors was completely buried by the impact. All on board the plane were dead when witnesses arrived.

Four bodies were thrown clear, Baker said. He was feeding cattle when he heard the plane strike the earth. He telephoned to Cottonwood Falls, fifteen miles north, for ambulances.

Flying in a Dangerous District.

Bazaar is an isolated village in a section particularly treacherous for aviators. The hills provide bumpy air conditions.

Clarence McCracken, a farmhand on the Seward ranch, who also saw the plane fall, helped Baker and others to free the bodies. All were taken to a morgue at Cottonwood Falls over fifteen miles of muddy road, which impeded progress.

Identification was difficult, but was finally established by means of bill folds and luggage. W. L. White, son of William Allen White of The Emporia Gazette, confirmed the identification of Rockne's body, although for a time there was doubt whether he had been aboard the plane. Four of the eight bodies were identified at the scene of the crash and the others later at Cottonwood Falls.

Two hours after the accident Department of Commerce officials from Wichita and Kansas City were on their way to Bazaar to conduct an

Continued on Page Twenty-four.

Quake a Blow at Canal Plans, Engineers in Panama Suggest

Special Cable to THE NEW YORK TIMES.

BALBOA, C. Z., March 31.—There is much discussion here among canal officials as to whether the Managua earthquake will end the project of constructing a new canal through Nicaragua.

Noting the severity of the shock, it is said by engineers here that any canal in the vicinity would have suffered enormous damage.

This may settle definitely the question of constructing a secondary canal.

ROOSEVELT SIGNS CUVILLIER WET BILL

Approves Appeal to Congress for Constitutional Convention on Repeal.

BUT CALLS REQUEST FUTILE

Medical Liquor Measure Passed—Provision for State Sale Is Killed.

By W. A. WARN.

Special to The New York Times.

ALBANY, March 31.—Governor Roosevelt today approved the bill of Assemblyman A. Cuvillier, wet leader in the Legislature, placing the lawmaking body on record as petitioning Congress to call a national constitutional convention for the repeal of the Eighteenth Amendment.

In a memorandum announcing his action, the Governor stated that he felt it his duty to sign the measure because of an overwhelming demand throughout the State for "some immediate action to change the Eighteenth Amendment" and also because by a veto he would deny to the Legislature a constitutional right.

In his opinion, he said, the sentiment in favor of repealing or changing the Eighteenth Amendment was based on "two righteous and sane objectives." One was to eliminate the source of organized crime and the other to promote temperance.

"To this policy, as I have repeatedly stated, I subscribe," Governor Roosevelt said.

Medical Liquor Bill Passed.

This action by Governor Roosevelt was only one of the day's developments concerning prohibition. The Assembly passed the Hastings medical liquor bill, which now goes to the Governor, having been adopted by the Senate.

The bill creates a new division in the Department of Education, charged with dispensing medicinal liquor to physicians, subject only to rules and regulations established by the department itself. For the cost of administration $250,000 is provided.

The Senate, regarded as normally wet, by a vote of 25 to 24 defeated the Feld-Post bill. Favorably acted on by the Assembly, providing for the appointment by the Governor of a commission of five to report a plan for the manufacture, sale, transportation and distribution of alcoholic beverages by the State.

All the Democrats voted for the bill, but all the Republicans, with the exception of Senator Hofstadter of

Continued on Page Eighteen.

Thousands See Two Geysers in Times Square As 20-Inch High-Pressure Steam Main Bursts

A huge steam conduit of the New York Steam Corporation burst in two places in Forty-third Street, between Sixth Avenue and Broadway, early this morning, blowing manhole covers high into the air, sending up two geysers of steam more than five stories high and attracting an early morning crowd of 2,000 spectators. No one was injured. Several passing taxicabs escaped undamaged.

The two pillars of steam showered a heavy mist and rain for more than a block in all directions, soaking policemen, firemen and onlookers. A leakage from a cold water pipe, causing cold water to flow to the twenty-inch steam conduit, which had a steam pressure of eighty pounds per square inch, was blamed for both explosions.

The conduit first broke at a point about ten feet east of Times Square about 2 A. M. Before the arrival of emergency crews from the steam company with tools for shutting off the conduit another explosion occurred in the same pipe about fifty feet further east on Forty-third Street.

As soon as the first explosion occurred, calls were sent in for police and fire crews and for emergency crews from the steam company. The crowd of spectators, thinking at first that an explosion had occurred in the Times Square subway station, gathered quickly, but they were kept at a distance of more than 200 feet from the scene, fascinated by the spectacle.

With the second explosion tongues of steam began shooting out of other manholes, the covers of which were hastily removed to relieve the pressure underground. Cracks in the street paving added to the weirdness of the scene.

The main that exploded furnished heat and power for hotels and other buildings in the Times Square area.

Telephone service on the Medallion exchange was disrupted, presumably because of water flooding into the telephone conduits. The water also flowed into the cellars of near-by buildings and into the Times Square subway station.

QUICK ACTION BY HOOVER

President Takes Personal Charge, Ordering Army and Navy to Aid.

SHIPS AND PLANES SENT

Red Cross Official Leaves for Nicaragua to Direct Work—$10,000 Cabled Envoy.

PHYSICIANS UNDER ORDERS

They Will Fly From the Canal Zone—Naval Vessels Are on the Way.

Special to The New York Times.

WASHINGTON, March 31.—President Hoover had no sooner been informed of the disaster at Managua than he took personal charge of relief measures. This was right in line with his experience in relieving distress in Belgium, Russia and other countries in Europe and in the flood-stricken area of the Mississippi Valley. Within a few minutes after word came that the Nicaraguan capital had been destroyed by earthquake, the machinery of the government and the American Red Cross was in operation.

It was through a brief bulletin of The Associated Press from Panama City that the President was notified that a major catastrophe had taken place at Managua. That was soon after 11 o'clock this morning, and not long afterward came official confirmation from Major Gen. Preston Brown, commanding the United States Army forces in the Panama Canal Zone.

Hears 500 to 1,000 Are Dead.

Reports received by the War Department tonight from the Canal Zone estimated deaths in Managua at from 500 to 1,000, and 1,000 injured, with fire destroying those buildings that were not leveled by the quake. The American and British Legations, after surviving the quake, were on fire.

A report to the State Department from Willard L. Beaulac, Chargé d'Affaires of the American Legation at Managua, said he and the other officers of the legation were safe. Matthew E. Hanna, the American Minister, and Mrs. Hanna were believed to be in Guatemala, he reported.

The War Department also was told tonight that no member of the battalion of army engineers making a survey of a route for the proposed ship canal across Nicaragua had been injured. A surgeon and a detachment of engineers were sent to Managua with medical and other supplies.

Central Committee Formed.

By direction of the President, a meeting was held in the Red Cross building this afternoon, attended by officials of the State, War and Navy Departments and the Red Cross. High ranking officers of the government were present.

After the exchange of views, based on the information then at hand, a central relief committee was organized to operate from Washington.

Before this organization meeting has been held, measures of relief, upon the orders of the President, had already begun to take shape. Ernest J. Swift, acting director of the Division of Foreign and Insular Affairs of the Red Cross, was instructed to proceed immediately to Managua to assume charge of the relief organization on the ground.

It was planned that he leave Washington this afternoon by a naval airplane, but when word came from the Naval Observatory that a wind of hurricane force threatened the coasts of North and South Carolina it was decided that Mr. Swift should take a train for Miami and, if more favorable weather reports were received, the naval plane could follow and pick him up along the route and transport him direct to Managua.

A quick survey of facilities at hand showed that the Red Cross was amply supplied with relief material while the army and the navy had supplies of tents, cots, blankets, medical stores and food which could be transported to Nicaragua from the United States and the Panama Canal Zone.

Radio messages from various gov-

Continued on Page Two.

The Map Shows the Location of Managua, Stricken Capital of Nicaragua, and the Proposed Route of the Nicaragua Canal.

2,500 AMERICANS ARE IN NICARAGUA

Of These, 900 Are Estimated to Be in the Vicinity of Managua Alone.

MARINES PLACED AT 1,440

Most of Them Camp in Tents on Outskirts of Capital—845 Civilians.

Special to The New York Times.

WASHINGTON, March 31.—The number of Americans in the earthquake-stricken area of Managua and its immediate vicinity was estimated by officials today as more than 900, while the number in all Nicaragua was placed at more than 2,500.

The estimates included 1,440 marines, seventy-five navy medical officers, 148 army engineers, ten diplomatic officers and 845 civilians in the country. In Managua and its environs latest reports showed 550 marines, five diplomatic officers and 355 civilians.

The marines and medical officers constitute the American force of occupation, those in Managua being for the most part camped on the outskirts of the city in tents.

The army engineers have their headquarters at Granada, twenty-three miles southeast of Managua, and are occupied with the survey of the projected transoceanic Nicaraguan canal, a task which scatters them from one coast to the other. The diplomatic officers include Matthew E. Hanna, the American Minister, and his assistants, who reside in Managua.

155 Located in Corinto.

The civilians are in various business pursuits, their number of 845 being an estimate of the State Department today based upon its records. The department records showed that on Jan. 1, 1931, there were 155 American civilians in Corinto, and reports as of February, 1929, the latest available for Managua, showed 355 there at that time.

The staff of the American Legation at Managua consists of:

Mr. Hanna, Ohio, Envoy Extraordinary and Minister Plenipotentiary.

Willard L. Beaulac, Rhode Island, Second Secretary.

Roger Sumner, Massachusetts, Third Secretary.

Marion P. Hoover, Osborn, Ohio, clerk.

Ellis M. Stevens, Jenkintown, Pa., and Bangor, Me., clerk.

The following are assigned to the legation, but as they are also assigned to legations in other Central American countries it is not known at the State Department whether they are in Managua at the present time.

Major Fred T. Cruse, Military Attaché.

Major Peter C. Geyer, Naval Attaché.

George C. Peck, Commercial Attaché.

Girvan Teall of New York is Vice Consul at Corinto.

John A. Willey of California is Consular Agent at Matagalpa.

Engineer Officers Number 23.

The latest report received in the War Department from the United States Army engineer battalion in Nicaragua, which is conducting the Nicaraguan Canal survey, shows twenty-three officers and 125 enlisted men on duty.

The roster of the officers is as follows:

Lieut. Col. Dan I. Sultan, commanding officer.

Major Charles P. Gross, Corps of Engineers.

Continued on Page Two.

AVIATOR DESCRIBES HORROR AT MANAGUA

Marine Says Buildings Fell on the Dead and Injured, Causing Panic.

PRISON TRAPS ITS INMATES

Flier Gets Aid in Corinto—American Women and Children to Be Evacuated by Air.

From the radio operator on Motor Ship City of Panama, at Corinto.

Wireless to THE NEW YORK TIMES.

ABOARD MOTOR SHIP CITY OF PANAMA, AT CORINTO, Nicaragua, March 31.—Hoke Palmer, an aviator of the United States Marine Corps at Managua, was the first eyewitness to reach here today from the stricken capital. He came to obtain medical supplies from this ship. Mr. Palmer said:

"The entire town of Managua is in ruins. There is not a building left standing. Hundreds of bodies are entombed in the ruins, including many Americans. Fire is raging among the wreckage.

The greatest number of deaths occurred in the penitentiary, which crumbled to powder. Panic followed the earthquake and martial law was immediately declared.

"We shall evacuate all surviving American women and children as soon as possible by air. The railroad is destroyed, all wires are down, and there is no way at present to communicate with the outside world except by airplane to Corinto and then by radio from the motor ship City of Panama.

Rescue Work Well Under Way.

"Rescue work in charge of the United States marines was well under way when I left Managua.

"Among the dead are Lieut. Commander Baske, U. S. N.; Mrs. Murray, wife of Major Murray."

A special train has left Corinto for Managua, but it is believed it will be unable to reach Managua, due to the railroad tracks being torn up within a radius of ten miles around the city.

Martial law is enforced by the marines, as it is feared the bandits who have been causing so much trouble in the past will make a raid on the burning city.

Medical supplies of all kinds are being rushed to Managua from other cities and towns in the vicinity.

The earthquake was entirely centred within a ten-mile radius around Managua. Every effort is being made to rescue those buried by falling buildings. Rescue parties have been organized, and the marines are in full action.

Navy Sending Plane Down.

Special to The New York Times.

PHILADELPHIA, March 31.—A tri-motored Fokker plane, probably in charge of Lieutenant Christian F. Schilt, holder of a Congressional Medal of Honor for bravery in Nicaragua, will start from the Philadelphia Navy Yard tomorrow for Managua.

Orders for the flight were received this afternoon from Washington and a plane was tested immediately. Lieutenant Schilt, who recently flew to Nicaragua with Captain Ralph D. Weyerbacher, former commandant of the naval aircraft factory here, expects to complete the flight in two days if he is assigned as pilot.

Plane Line Helps in Emergency.

Emergency measures were taken yesterday afternoon by Pan-American Airways, it was announced at its offices in New York, to establish adequate communication facili-

Continued on Page Three.

CITY RAZED IN SIX SECONDS

Flames Start at Market, Where 35 Burn to Death—Water Cut Off.

MARTIAL LAW IS DECLARED

Marines Fight Holocaust With Dynamite—Snatch Bodies From Menaced Ruins.

REFUGEES AT MARINE CAMP

Roads Cleared for Ambulances—Only One Hospital Left—Loss Put at $30,000,000.

DEAD MAY TOTAL 2,500.

Special Cable to THE NEW YORK TIMES.

BALBOA, C. Z., March 31.—Eleven hundred dead already have been located in Managua and the toll of dead may reach 2,500, according to radio reports received here.

By S. H. MOORE.

Special Correspondent of The New York Times. Via Tropical Radio to The New York Times.

MANAGUA, Nicaragua, March 31.—An earthquake destroyed Managua at 10:10 A. M. today (11:10 in New York).

The dead were estimated tonight at 1,000 and the injured at several thousand.

The tremor lasted only six seconds, but it razed nearly every building in the business district. Fire which started in the central market raged through the section, completing the devastation. Marines are fighting the fire, dynamiting where possible to check its spread.

The market was crowded with women and children, and thirty-five of them were burned to death when its walls collapsed.

Martial law has been declared and United States Marines and Nicaraguan National Guardsmen are enforcing it.

The first contingent of marines had expected to leave Managua tomorrow in accordance with the recently announced withdrwal plan, but because of the emergency the order for embarkation has been cancelled and the marines will remain to aid.

Among the known American casualties are:

THE DEAD.

Lieut. Commander HUGO F. A. BASKE, a doctor in the Nicaraguan National Guard.

Mrs. JOSEPH D. MURRAY, wife of Captain Murray, U. S. M. C.

Two United States officers in the Nicaraguan National Guard.

Two wives of National Guard officers.

Chauffeur for Irving W. Lindberg, Collector General of Customs.

THE INJURED.

IRVING W. LINDBERG, Collector General of Customs; leg injury.

Lieut. Col. FREDERIC BRADMAN, commander of the marines; slight head injury.

Chief Quartermaster Clerk JAMES F. DICKEY of Vallejo, Cal.; severe internal injuries, buried debris national penitentiary. Nearest relative, Lillian R. Dickey, wife, same address.

Gunnery Sergeant LOUIS ROSSICK of Detroit; severe scalp wounds and internal injuries. Nearest relative, B. N. Rossick, brother, same address.

Mrs. LOUIS ROSSICK, Sergeant Rossick's wife; fractured skull, eyes possibly destroyed.

First Sergeant ROBERT G. CRAWFORD of Summerville, Ga.; severe internal injuries. Father, George H. Crawford, same address.

Mrs. R. G. CRAWFORD, Sergeant Crawford's wife, slightly injured.

Major ROBERT L. DENIG of Sandusky, Ohio; fractured right leg below knee. Mother, Mrs. Robert G. Denig, same address.

Gunnery Sergeant GEORGE OCCHIONERO of Brainerd, Minn.; severe scalp wounds, severe injury right hip. Wife, Mrs. Gertrude Occhionero, same address.

First Lieut. JAMES L. DENHAM of Chevy Chase, Md.; scalp wound, not serious. Wife, same address.

Sergeant HUGO A. MAKUS of Parr, Ind.; bad body bruises. Wife, same address.

First Sergeant CHARLES DAVIS of Buffalo; contusions left foot. Wife, Mrs. Marie A. Davis, same address.

Mrs. BUCKNER, wife of Gunnery Sergeant Buckner; slightly injured.

Line Sergeant HODSKIN, scalp and face injuries.

The marine camp is a place of refuge for all injured and as many

ROCKNE DIES WITH 7 IN MAIL PLANE FALL

Continued from Page One.

investigation. Reports as to what happened were indefinite. All actual witnesses agreed that a wing ripped loose before the plane hit the ground. Baker said he heard only the noise of the fall. McCracken said the only warning came from the sputter of the engine. Both said the plane was above the clouds, probably at about 2,000 feet.

Rockne was on his way to Los Angeles, where he was to make a talking picture at Hollywood. He had waited at Kansas City for a chat with his sons, Billy Rockne, 11 years old, and Knute Rockne Jr., 14 years old, but missed them by minutes because he had to leave the railroad station before they arrived in order to get to the airport on time. Then the plane delayed its departure. They arrived twenty minutes after their father had left.

The boys, who had been visiting their mother at Coral Gables, Fla., were returning to Pembroke School, Kansas City. When news of the accident came, Dr. D. M. Nigro got into telephone communication with Mrs. Rockne, who remained at Coral Gables, and she asked him to take charge of the body. He brought the sons here by automobile tonight. The news was told to them only after their arrival. They showed the strength of their father in bearing the blow.

Dr. Jacob Hinden, coroner at Cottonwood Falls, inspected the wreckage of the airplane. He said that, contrary to early reports, there had been no fire, indicating that the pilot, fighting to control the ship, had foreseen the crash and cut his ignition before it hit.

A theory was put forward to the Coroner by H. G. Edgerton of Wichita, district passenger agent of the line, that ice had formed on the wing of the plane and broken it. The temperature on the ground was above the freezing point.

Some witnesses told of a gust of wind coming down sharply on a nearby hilltop soon after the plane fell.

New York Times Studio.

KNUTE ROCKNE.

ROCKNE A PIONEER ON FOOTBALL FIELD

Perfected Forward Pass and Shift Play and Taught Scoring From Any Position.

HAD FIVE UNBEATEN TEAMS

Made Them Work Closely Together on Simple Lines and Frowned on Tricks.

DEVELOPED MANY COACHES

A Keen Student of Psychology, He Knew When to Keep His Sharp Tongue in Leash.

By ROBERT F. KELLEY.

From his days as a player Knute Rockne made his influence felt on the trend of football. As captain of the 1913 Notre Dame team, he figured at end in the most successful exhibition of forward passing the game had seen up to that time; and from that date on the forward pass grew steadily to its present importance in the game.

As a coach he brought the shift play to its highest state of perfection and made it such an important factor in offensive football that the rules committee finally passed legislation designed to take some of its power away.

That shift development, the back field hop, was the most important of his contributions to the coaching of the game, but he added others, notably the reshaping of the line. Prior to Rockne, linemen were big men inevitably. Rockne brought the idea of using linemen, particularly guards, in interference, and demonstrated that the small, fast lineman could hold his own with the big man and outplay him where the big man was not as fast.

Changed Strategy of Touchdown.

He worked for the perfection of a team as a whole and his last two teams won game after game through the successful application of what came to be called "the perfect plays." In these every individual carried out a part of the blocking, and when no man failed to carry out his job the play often went for a touchdown.

This perfect play did a great deal to wipe away the idea of aiming first for scoring territory and then the score. Rockne always said that every play, if perfectly carried out, would go for a touchdown from wherever it was started. His last two teams usually started their scoring with long runs from scrimmage.

In coaching he tried always for perfection and spent hours in teaching the art of blocking. Simple plays, well executed, were his idea of the way to win football games. He had small use for any so-called trick plays. There were only seven places in a line to send a man with a ball, he said, and there ought not to be many more than seven plays.

Hard work was another of his slogans. "The best thing I ever learned in life," he said last June during a visit to Poughkeepsie for the intercollegiate boat race there, "was that things have to be worked for. A lot of people seem to think there is some sort of magic in making a winning football team. There isn't, but there's plenty of work."

Suddenly Developed the Pass.

As a player and captain of the 1913 Notre Dame team, the first to ever beat the Army, Rockne began his shaping of football's destinies by bringing the forward pass suddenly and dramatically into the front of the game. Army that season had scheduled Notre Dame as a "breather" game on its schedule. Only a small crowd turned out, and they stood amazed as Notre Dame defeated Army, 35 to 13. Gus Dorais, now coach at Detroit, threw seventeen passes in that game and thirteen were completed, and a great majority of these went to the short, chunky end, Knute Rockne.

The forward pass had been more or less of a haphazard thing until that time. The success of this Western team with it amazed the football world. Dorais and Rockne remained behind at West Point for a few days after that game to show the Army how its was done. One of the results of that was the famous Pritchard to Merrillat combination of Army teams.

In that first success was an indication of the capacity for taking pains which Rockne owned. That game was the direct result of the Summer before. Dorais and Rockne had obtained vacation jobs together at a mid-West beach and included a football in their baggage. All that Summer they got out on the beach and threw passes. The success against Army was no accident. It had been carefully planned.

Remarkable Record as Coach.

As a coach, of course, Rockne's record is one of the most remarkable that any coach of any sport has ever piled up. Nearly all of his teams have been in the front rank of the game, despite the fact that they always played hard schedules. Five of them were undefeated. Taking over the head coach job, after helping instruct in the chemistry department of Notre Dame, in 1918, Rockne had almost immediate success. His 1919 team was undefeated and his 1920 team was one of the greatest that he had.

To the game in general Rockne brought the high development of the backfield shift and a new conception of line play. He never claimed the invention of the shift play. But there can be small argument with the idea that under him Notre Dame's players brought it to its highest perfection.

So successful were his teams with the shift that three years ago the football rules committee, fearing the offense of the game would overbalance the defense, began ruling against it and this last year finally insisted that a full second, in which an official might count five, must come between the close of the shift and the start of the ball.

Rockne never was reconciled to this and never lost an opportunity to defend his favorite style of play. Legislating against the shift, he said, was like taking the feinting out of boxing and leaving in only the slugging.

Rockne organized coaching schools in which coaches might gather during the off seasons and study the methods of others. He assisted with Summer schools all over the country and in 1928 even conducted one at sea when he chartered a ship and took a party of coaches and athletes to the Olympic Games of that year.

Developed Famous Players.

Perhaps his greatest teams came in 1920, 1924, 1929 and 1930. On the first was George Gipp, who was named by Rockne as the greatest player he ever had. The coach told the story of seeing Gipp, who was not trying for the team, throwing a ball and kicking on the campus and of inducing him to join the squad. Gipp died a few weeks after the close of the 1920 season of a throat infection, with Rockne at his bedside.

The 1924 team was the one of the famous Four Horsemen, Harry Stuhldreher, Jimmy Crowley, Don Miller and Elmer Layden. As a combination, they have not been excelled in modern back fields and they had a great line in front of them, led by the famous Adam Walsh at centre, who is now assisting with the coaching at Yale. That team of the Four Horsemen won all over the country, beating Princeton at Princeton with a temperature of 10 above zero, and several weeks later journeying to the Coast to defeat Stanford in a temperature of 70 degrees.

The records and names of the members of the two recent teams are still fresh in memory, Frank Carideo, Marchmont Schwartz, Marty Brill, Joe Savoldi, Bucky O'Connor, Moon Mullins. And the 1930 team came very near to being the best. Northwestern, Army and Southern California were played on successive Saturdays. One Saturday, in Chicago, Army was turned back in ice and cold rain and the following week the highly regarded Southern California team was badly beaten on the Coast.

If there were any doubt of the influence of Rockne on football, the list of head coaches for the past year might remove it. There were, throughout the country, North, South, East and West, twenty-three head coaches of football from Notre Dame without naming the assistants here and there. Notable among them are Walsh and Rip Miller, who has this year been elevated to head coach at Navy.

The mere record of his work fails to bring out for those who did not know him the biting, incisive, clear-cut character and personality of the man. Dramatic in everything he did, even to his death, Rockne became a sort of god to the boys who played for him. A great talker, a keen wit, he had a balanced, sane philosophy of life and a keen knowledge of psychology.

There are numerous instances in the near legends which have sprung up about him of his use of the latter element in dealing with his boys. The year that Army and Navy played in Chicago, in 1926, he went to Chicago to watch the game, confident his strong team would beat Carnegie Tech without too much trouble in his absence. They did not.

Used the Delayed Criticism.

The coach returned to South Bend. The next week the team was to play on the Pacific Coast. All week, Rockne coached without mentioning the defeat. The players kept waiting for him to say something. He did not. But when they boarded the train and opened their baggage, each player found a carefully clipped account of the lost game in his baggage. They won on the Coast.

This year, before the Army game, Rockne sat in the dressing room with his players, waiting for the time to go out on the field. The players sat silently, waiting for him to say something. The minutes ticked off in the quiet room, and finally an official came to tell them to come out. Rockne nodded, stood up and said, "Come on, boys." That was all.

He has given words to the vocabulary of the sport as well, some of which fit exactly the army of people who criticize the players and coaches after a defeat, waiting until the day after to display their wisdom. "Sunday morning coaches" was Rockne's name for this class.

A polished story-teller and a constantly interesting companion, Rockne made friends wherever he went, and was almost as much at home at the colleges he played against on his numerous visits as he was at his own. At these places he will be greatly missed as a friend.

Rockne's Sons "Take It Like Sports."

COTTONWOOD FALLS, Kan., March 31 (AP).—Dr. D. M. Nigro, president of the Notre Dame Club of Kansas City, and a close friend of Knute Rockne, broke the news of the coach's death to his two young sons here tonight. He had brought them from Kansas City. After identifying the body and calling up Mrs. Rockne in Florida, he told the boys.

They sobbed for a few minutes on his shoulder, but he comforted them, and they fought back the tears and became more composed when asked to "take it like sports—the sons of a great man."

"I'm going to be a coach like my father," Knute, Jr., said.

Rockne Had Double Mission.

Special to The New York Times.

LOS ANGELES, March 31.—Knute Rockne was en route to Los Angeles on combined business with motion picture interests and the Studebaker Corporation, according to General Manager Earl R. Carpenter of the Paul G. Hoffman Company, Studebaker agents here. Due to arrive tonight, he was to have appeared at the Los Angeles Breakfast Club tomorrow and to have spent Wednesday and Thursday at Universal studios in connection with a football picture in which he was to appear.

He was expected to hold a sales promotion meeting for local Studebaker salesmen Friday, as he recently signed a contract as sales promotion manager of that concern, agreeing to devote available time outside his football work to it.

"Just a moment after hearing of the fatal air crash," Carpenter said, "I received a telegram from the head office asking me to get in touch with Rockne here and arrange a sales meeting Friday."

Horace M. Hanshue, president of Transcontinental and Western Airways, late today issued this statement:

"Until we have obtained and analyzed accurate reports on the conditions of the wrecked plane and all of the provable circumstances incidental to the crash it is useless to speculate on the cause of the tragedy. Needless to say every one connected with Transcontinental and Western, Inc., grieves with those bereaved by the accident."

MRS. ROCKNE TOLD OF DEATH.

At First Refuses to Believe It, Then Prepares for Journey.

CORAL GABLES, Fla., March 31 (AP).—Shocked by news of the death of her husband, Mrs. Knute Rockne bravely helped members of her household here pack for their departure for South Bend tonight.

She was with Mr. and Mrs. Thomas O'Neil of Akron, old friends of the family, on a shopping tour today when a filling-station attendant called Mr. O'Neil aside and told him of the accident.

Mr. O'Neil immediately took Mrs. Rockne to his Miami Beach home and summoned the Rev. Father David Garry of Miami Beach. They then informed Mrs. Rockne of her husband's death. Mrs. Rockne at first refused to believe it, but when she was convinced asked to be taken home in order to prepare for her trip North.

WORKED SIX YEARS TO GET TO COLLEGE

Rockne While at Notre Dame Was an Instructor in Chemistry —Native of Norway.

When Knute Rockne first went to Notre Dame as a freshman in 1910, he explained later, he was "looking only for an education—to my mind, college players were supermen to whose heights I could never aspire."

He had been about six years getting to the college at South Bend, Ind., after he was graduated from the Northwestern Division High School (now Tully) in Chicago. He had to earn the money first. By working as a railroad brakeman and later as a mail clerk in Chicago he accumulated $1,000 and reached the age of 22.

His original intention was to go to the University of Illinois when he had saved this much, but two of his friends were going to Notre Dame at the time and they urged him to go with them. According to his own explanation of his decision, the chief inducement was the possibility of living more cheaply at South End.

Since his father brought him to this country at the age of 6 from Voss, Norway, where he was born, the cost of living was the chief thing that affected Knute Rockne's life.

Notre Dame made him a chemist, good enough to be an instructor during his last undergraduate year, and it also made him an end and captain of the football team who made forward-passing history in the combination of Dorais to Rockne on the plains of West Point.

After his graduation in 1914 Rockne remained at Notre Dame to teach the young men, not chemistry, but football. He did it with such success that the public in Chicago has paid as much as $400,000 at the gate in recent years to see Notre Dame in one of its big games. Last year, as a physical indication of Rockne's influence on the corporate fortunes of the college, Notre Dame opened a $750,000 stadium in South Bend, Ind.

After he was graduated from Notre Dame in 1914, Rockne returned there that Fall as assistant football coach. He became head coach in the Fall, 1918, succeeding Jesse C. Harper.

His tenure at South Bend was uncertain only once, in 1925, when J. R. Knapp, chairman of the Columbia football committee, obtained his agreement to come to New York if a release could be secured from Notre Dame on a ten-year contract which Rockne had signed the previous year. His salary would have gone from $10,000 a year to $25,000.

Premature publicity disturbed the negotiations, and Rockne traveled back from New York to South Bend, wondering publicly if he still had a job. In testimonial of the undiminished esteem of Notre Dame, a group of alumni in Chicago collected $2,000 and bought him a new automobile.

Rockne was born in 1889. He is survived by his wife, Bonnie Skiles Rockne of Kenton, Ohio, whom he married in 1914, and by their four children, William D., Knute Jr., Mary Jean and John V. The two older boys have already begun to play midget football.

NEWS OF ROCKNE'S END STUNS NOTRE DAME

University to Hold Mass Today —Group Will Bring the Body There Tomorrow.

Special to The New York Times.

SOUTH BEND, Ind., March 31.—News of the death of Knute Rockne came as a stunning blow to Notre Dame University and to all of South Bend. Flags throughout the city are at half staff. Men, women and children who knew the famous coach seem to be dazed by the sudden passing.

A solemn requiem mass will be said for the noted coach at the Sacred Heart Church on Notre Dame campus tomorrow morning. The entire university is in mourning; but semester examinations will be completed, as the Easter recess starts tomorrow noon.

The Rev. Michael Mulcaire, vice president of the university; Heartly Anderson and Jack Chevigny, assistant coaches, and Howard Edward, South Bend manufacturer, a close friend of Rockne and captain of the Notre Dame football team in 1910, left in the afternoon for Kansas City to bring the body of Rockne back to this city.

At the same time the Rev. Charles L. O'Donnell, C. S. C., president of the university, talked with Mrs. Bonnie Rockne, widow, at Miami, Fla., over the telephone and was informed that she was leaving at once with their two youngest children, Jackie and Mary Jean, for South Bend.

When the Notre Dame group arrives in Kansas City it will be met by Dr. Michael Nigro, a Notre Dame graduate and friend of the coach, who will accompany the body to South Bend. It is probable that Jesse Harper, former coach and tutor of Rockne in football, also will return with the body. He was located by telephone at his ranch at Sitka, Kan.

"All the News That's Fit to Print."

The New York Times.

LATE CITY EDITION
WEATHER—Fair, continued warm today; tomorrow cloudy, showers.
Temperatures Yesterday—Max., 86; Min., 72

Copyright, 1935, by The New York Times Company.

VOL. LXXXIV....No. 28,329. Entered as Second-Class Matter, Postoffice, New York, N. Y. NEW YORK, SATURDAY, AUGUST 17, 1935. P TWO CENTS In New York City. | THREE CENTS Within 200 Miles | FOUR CENTS Elsewhere Except in 7th and 8th Postal Zones.

ROOSEVELT CALLS CHIEFS TO ARRANGE CONGRESS WIND-UP

Conference Tomorrow Is Expected to Set Program for Adjournment Thursday.

FIVE MAJOR BILLS FAVORED

Wealth Tax, Banking, Coal, Alcohol Control and Gold Ban Measures Slated to Pass.

UTILITY DEADLOCK HOLDS

Holding Company Curb and Other Major Bills Likely to Wait Till Next Session.

By The Associated Press.

WASHINGTON, Aug. 16.—A semi-final conference of Democratic leaders to make arrangements for a prompt adjournment of Congress was called tonight by President Roosevelt for Sunday night.

The expectation of some of the party chiefs was that at that meeting the President would disclose which measures he was willing for Congress to drop and which he wanted enacted before adjournment.

Among those invited to the conference, beginning at 8:30, were: Vice President Garner, Speaker Byrns, Senator Robinson of Arkansas, the Democratic leader; Chairman O'Connor of the House Rules Committee, Chairman Harrison of the Senate Finance Committee and Chairman Doughton of the House Ways and Means Committee.

It was indicated by one of the conferees that any agreement reached Sunday night, however, would be subject to possible modification if particular pressure developed for the enactment of any measure.

Conjecture on Program.

From what they already had heard directly and indirectly from the President, some of the conferees, talking privately, said the meeting made more clear the possibilities of an end to the present session by the end of next week at the latest.

Some were talking about an adjournment Tuesday, or Thursday. Most agreed that it probably would be the latter part of next week before everything could be wound up to their satisfaction or to that of the President.

The expectation of some of the conferees was that the President would renew his insistence upon enactment of:

1. The Guffey Coal Stabilization Bill, which proponents and some opponents say will pass the House Monday and be approved by the Senate early next week;
2. The Federal alcohol control plan.
3. The $250,000,000 Tax Bill.
4. The Omnibus Banking Bill, on which conferees reached an agreement late today.
5. The measure forbidding suits for gold payments on government contracts.

Six Bills May Be Shelved.

Their belief was that unless action was hastened the following would be left behind when this session ended, with their present status remaining the same until the next session:

1. The Utilities Bill;
2. The rivers and harbors legislation;
3. The measure expanding Federal control over food and drugs;
4. Railroad reorganization;
5. General oil regulation;
6. The Ship Subsidy Bill.

Leaders said the Utilities Bill probably would be left behind, not because the President did not want the legislation, but because the conference deadlock could not be broken.

A possibility was seen by some that the Rivers and Harbors Bill might be insisted upon because it would legalize the millions already spent by the Federal Government on a number of projects, such as the Parker Dam. And they added that they had but scant doubt that before Congress had adjourned it would ratify the oil compacts entered into in Dallas last February.

House Tax Conferees Named.

Special to The New York Times.

WASHINGTON, Aug. 16.—A determined drive to adjourn Congress by Tuesday night, with Thursday as the latest alternate date, was started today following formal commitment of the Wealth-Tax Bill to conference and a conference agreement on the Eccles Banking Bill.

The promise of Tuesday adjournment was held out by Senator Robinson as the Senate voted to take a recess until Monday. Early in the day he had informed the Senate of his desire to quit at that time and in so doing issued a warning

Continued on Page Fourteen.

Davey Sets Ohio Vote for 1936, Defying Opponents of New Deal

Governor, Here, Denies Delaying Test on Advice of Roosevelt Forces, Gives Economy as Reason—He and President Are Accused of 'Conspiracy' by Republican Leader.

Governor Martin L. Davey of Ohio moved formally yesterday to defy Republican demands for a special State-wide election this year for Representative at Large to test New Deal sentiment in the State.

The Governor was visiting New York City during the day and telephoned his office in Columbus to frame an order in legal form setting the election for next year. All that remains to put the order into effect is the signature of the Governor, which he said he would affix when he reached Ohio tomorrow.

With the Republican national leaders, heartened by a victory in the Rhode Island Congressional elections, demanding that Ohio vote this November to fill the vacancy caused by the death of Representative Charles V. Truax, the Governor insisted that the election should be held next year to avoid imposition of from $500,000 to $600,000 special election costs on hard-pressed taxpayers of the State.

He ridiculed the charge made by his political adversaries that the election was being postponed until next year, apparently under advice from the Roosevelt forces at Washington, to prevent an early test of the New Deal in such a key State as Ohio.

"There is no moral justification of loading that extra cost for a special election on the units of the State," Governor Davey said at the Hotel Biltmore. "The good and ample reason for this order is that a recent referendum reducing the tax limit from 15 mills to 10 mills on the dollar has, with the aid of the depression, depleted the treasuries of the counties and the cities so badly that they could not well stand the expense of a special election.

"Now I want to point out that no district in Ohio will be without representation meanwhile, since this post is that of a Representative at Large. I have an excellent precedent for this action, since the same course was followed in my

Continued on Page Seven.

ROOSEVELT RESTS AT HYDE PARK HOME

Joins Family on Two-Day Visit to Celebrate 21st Birthday of Franklin Jr.

AVOIDS ISSUE ON HOOVER

President Intercedes for Man Caught at Baltimore While Stealing Ride on His Train.

From a Staff Correspondent.

HYDE PARK, N. Y., Aug. 16.—President Roosevelt returned to Hyde Park House today for a brief period of quiet contemplation before undertaking the direction of strategy designed to bring the current session of Congress to a satisfactory conclusion from the administration standpoint.

He came here overnight aboard a special train which arrived at 8:30 o'clock this morning for the announced purpose of attending a family party tomorrow in celebration of the twenty-first birthday anniversary of Franklin D. Roosevelt Jr., his third son.

However, an impromptu "press conference" held by Mr. Roosevelt while he sat in an automobile for the ride from the train to his mother's estate overlooking the Hudson River gave ample indication of the many problems awaiting a directing hand, if not a definite solution, by the President.

These problems he plans to tackle actively on Sunday, when he will return to the White House for a long series of conferences with the individuals and groups representing the administration leadership on Capitol Hill.

A cheery confidence was radiated by Mr. Roosevelt today as he was subjected to a barrage of questions by reporters who clustered around his automobile in the bright morning sunlight.

Questioned on Utility Bill.

The questions dealt principally with the Utility Holding Company Bill, which has been deadlocked in conference between the House and Senate for some time, and the Tax Bill which was sent to conference yesterday after the Senate had approved a measure considerably different than the House bill.

Asked if he expected enactment of the Utility Bill this session, Mr. Roosevelt replied smilingly that he hoped so, with an inflection in his voice which some reporters interpreted as indicating that he intended to have this done.

Would he be willing, he then was asked, to accept the House bill, which differs from the Senate bill and administration recommendations in its omission of the celebrated "death sentence" section? At this question, Mr. Roosevelt smiled and closed the topic with the assertion that he could not comment on details.

A request for comment on the action of the Senate in passing the Tax Bill in changed form brought the rejoinder from the President that the Tax Bill had not been finally passed by Congress yet; that it was still an open question.

Renewed efforts by correspondents to get specific comment from the President on the recent statement by former President Hoover requesting Mr. Roosevelt to set forth definitely his plans regarding possible changes in the Constitution, elicited from the President only the reply that he had read Mr. Hoover's statement very hurriedly and therefore was in no position to comment.

Aside from the conferences Mr.

Continued on Page Fourteen.

CONFEREES AGREE ON BANK MEASURE

Glass and His Senators Win on Nearly All Points, Ending Long Battle on Bill.

ONE VICTORY FOR HOUSE

Effort to Force State Banks Into Reserve Is Put Off—Swift Finish Planned.

Special to The New York Times.

WASHINGTON, Aug. 16.—Unanimous agreement on every feature of the hotly contested bill to change the nation's banking laws was reached by Senate and House conferees late today and arrangements were made to hurry this highly important measure through both branches of Congress early next week.

Senator Glass and his conservative colleagues of the Senate conferees won a smashing victory over Representatives Steagall and Goldsborough of the House conferees in almost every particular, but the two House liberals succeeded in postponing efforts to force State banks into the Federal Reserve System.

Senator Glass was delighted by the outcome. He and the other members of the conference asserted that the bill would go through both branches with ease.

Action will be taken on the conference report in the House Monday. The conferees arranged to file formal reports to both branches tomorrow.

The end of the conference marks a long and bitter fight over the policies of Marriner S. Eccles, governor of the Federal Reserve Board, as expressed in the bill passed by the House, and the views of the Glass group as set forth in the Senate bill.

Opinion tonight was that Mr. Glass, veteran banking legislator, had once more come out the victor.

Reserve Board Is Increased.

He and the other Senate conferees succeeded in carrying out their views on the open market committee, particularly in the aspect that government securities must be purchased on the open market and not direct from the Treasury.

Likewise, Senate conferees prevailed in their insistence that the Federal Reserve Board must be increased from the present six to seven members, with the Secretary of the Treasury and the Controller of the Currency eliminated as members ex officio.

The suggested permission of the Senate bill for banks of deposit to underwrite securities was stricken out at the request of President Roosevelt, Senator Glass stated.

The provision of the Senate bill that bankers may serve on not more than two bank boards simultaneously was retained but made subject to the discretion of the Reserve Board, however.

A big feature of the bill is the arrangement for the open market committee, which would be composed of seven Reserve Board members and five representatives of the twelve regional Reserve Banks. This committee would have power to influence the flow of credit by purchase and sale of government bonds by the Reserve Banks.

Policy Is Mandatory.

The policy laid down by the committee would be mandatory upon the Reserve Banks.

Following the view of Mr. Eccles, the House gave complete voting control of open market operations entirely to the Reserve Board, with

Continued on Page Fourteen.

HOPSON ADMITS TRYING TO CONTROL PRESS WITH ADS

He Also Tells Senators He Urged Move to Kill Utility Bill in Conference.

ATTACK ON TIMES RENEWED

House Committee Told That His 1934 Income Was Between $300,000 and $500,000.

Special to The New York Times.

WASHINGTON, Aug. 16.—Howard C. Hopson, who now admits that he was the guiding influence of the $900,000 lobby that the Associated Gas and Electric Company waged against the Wheeler-Rayburn bill, was forced to state before the Senate lobby inquiry committee today that the company had not hesitated to use the advertising columns of newspapers as a club to minimize unfavorable publicity.

He also said he had suggested to another high utility holding company official that a campaign be waged to kill the administration's utility program in conference of the two branches of Congress. As matters stand tonight every indication is that the Wheeler-Rayburn bill will die in conference, where for more than a month the conferees of the Senate and House have been deadlocked. All hope had not been given up by the measure's advocates, however.

Earlier in the day, before the House investigating committee, Mr. Hopson for the first time gave figures on his income last year. He said he had received "some three or four or five hundred thousand dollars" from his private companies.

Admits Borrowing Millions.

He also said that the A. G. E. had borrowed several million dollars since the first of the year, and that had it not been for the Wheeler-Rayburn bill the borrowings might have been a million dollars less.

He was directed to supply the names of the banks from which the money was borrowed, and said he would do so.

Before the Senate committee Mr. Hopson again made charges involving The New York Times. He asserted that the newspaper was under "the strong influence" of the Morgan and Carlisle interests, and that because of this alleged influence the A. G. E. should expect at "more or less frequent intervals" more "unpleasant attacks from that quarter."

The charges were made in a telegram to the H. C. Hopson Company, New York, which was signed by Duncan Robertson, Mr. Hopson's private secretary.

The telegram was in fact his own, said Mr. Hopson, explaining that it was his custom to have Mr. Robertson sign practically all of his messages to his New York office.

Messages to Hearst Admitted.

William Randolph Hearst was pictured before the committee as the writer of an editorial printed in the Hearst newspapers Sunday, June 2, which Senator Black asserted was strikingly along lines suggested by Mr. Hopson in a telegram to Mr. Hearst dated May 31.

Mr. Hopson admitted sending frequent messages to Mr. Hearst, who was dubbed by Senator Minton "the sage of San Simeon," but insisted that he had no reason to believe his messages inspired editorials or news articles in the Hearst papers.

Arthur Brisbane, Hearst writer, was pilloried, however, and documents placed in evidence showed

Continued on Page Twenty-six.

COAL BILL SPLITS HOUSE DEMOCRATS; PASSAGE HELD SURE

Widest Party Schism Since 'Death Sentence' Marks 'Must' Measure Debate.

VICTORY BY 30 CLAIMED

Administration Leaders Are Confident Despite Attacks as Unconstitutional.

Special to The New York Times.

WASHINGTON, Aug. 16.—In the face of the most serious party schism which has yet confronted any of President Roosevelt's projects for industrial reform, the Guffey-Snyder Coal Bill was manoeuvred by House leaders tonight into a position for final action on Monday.

With general debate on the measure concluded, they planned to carry it through the amending stage tomorrow and adjourn before the vote on passage.

Not since the vote on the President's demand for the "death sentence" for utility holding companies has the rank and file of the Democratic majority been so thoroughly split as on the merits of the Guffey-Snyder measure, and leaders were working overtime to make good their prediction that the bill would pass by about thirty votes.

Although they conceded that the final count would be close, all said enough votes had been obtained to assure passage of the administration "must" measure. Their estimate of thirty votes was verified by Republican leaders.

"Stalwarts" Oppose Measure.

Shouts of "unconstitutional," "communism," and "regimentation" from some of those who have been among the stanchest supporters of the administration on some other reform programs marked consideration of the bill on the floor today.

The opposition among Democrats was so strong that Republicans either sat back to watch them denounce the measure or left the floor entirely.

Emphasizing the broad difference of opinion on the constitutionality of the measure was the performance of such Ways and Means Committee "stalwarts" as Representatives McCormack of Massachusetts, Cooper of Tennessee and Fuller of Arkansas, all of whom took the floor to oppose it, and sometimes on Republican time. The bill had been reported favorably by the committee by a vote of 12 to 11.

The special rule for consideration of the bill was adopted 241 to 94, after a perfunctory debate. Representative McCormack, one of the two Democrats on the Ways and Means Committee who abstained from voting on reporting out the measure, said that he would vote for the rule but against the bill.

He told other members that there would be no inconsistency in such a position, and that he thought the bill should have a chance for consideration on the floor.

Representative Fuller of Arkansas called Speaker Byrns's attention to the distribution by pages in the hall of copies of the bill bearing typewritten slips which said:

"Bituminous Coal Bill as amended and reprinted. Controversial propaganda largely eliminated. Two-thirds of tonnage output operators favored bill and more than 95 per cent of labor."

Representative Snyder of Pennsylvania, co-author of the bill, said that he had pasted the slips on the measure and had instructed the

Continued on Page Seven.

Lawyer Charges Judge Downs Beat Him; Sues for $50,000 in Contempt Case Row

County Judge Thomas Downs of Queens was sued in the New York Supreme Court yesterday by Lorenzo C. Carlino, a lawyer, for $50,000 damages. The lawyer charged that Judge Downs, after finding him guilty of contempt of court in a trial, and fining him $250, had knocked him down and kicked him at the St. Albans Golf Club in Queens.

Mr. Carlino alleges that his appeal from the contempt order was based on the ground that it was a violation of the section of the Judiciary Act which requires that a contempt order cite the specific facts upon which it is based. The lawyer further asserts that he got an order from the Appellate Division restraining Judge Downs from making any change in the order pending the appeal.

Mr. Carlino served the order on Judge Downs at the golf club on May 7 last, he alleges, when the jurist was about to step into his car. He says that as soon as he showed a signature of Presiding Justice Lazansky on an injunction order, "the defendant, Thomas Downs, struck the plaintiff, knocked him down, then kicked him while on the ground and trampled upon the order which was served upon him. Defendant called plaintiff vile, filthy names and otherwise used vile and filthy language."

In addition to the suit against Judge Downs the lawyer asks $25,000 damages from Sheriff Peter J. McGarry of Queens for brutal treatment when he was arrested on the contempt order, which was later set aside by the Appellate Division.

Judge Downs denied last night he had assaulted Mr. Carlino.

"I was getting into my automobile parked in front of the clubhouse about 10 o'clock one night more than three months ago," the judge explained, "when a man I did not recognize in the darkness rushed out at me from some shrubbery. I was all alone and had received only a few days before an anonymous threat against my life. I hit the man at once. He fell down and a paper dropped to the ground. The man picked up the paper and ran away."

WILL ROGERS, WILEY POST DIE IN AIRPLANE CRASH IN ALASKA; NATION SHOCKED BY TRAGEDY

Sergeant Morgan's Report of the Death Of Rogers and Post as Seen by Natives

Special to The New York Times.

SEATTLE, Wash., Aug. 16.—The radio message sent by relays from Point Barrow, Alaska, to Seattle, in which Staff Sergeant Stanley R. Morgan informed the world of the tragic death of Will Rogers and Wiley Post, read as follows:

"Ten P. M. native runner reported plane crashed fifteen miles south of Barrow.

"Immediately hired fast launch, proceeded to scene.

"Found plane complete wreck, partly submerged, two feet water.

"Recovered body Rogers, then necessary tear plane apart extract body of Post from water.

"Brought bodies Barrow. Turned over Dr. Greist.

"Also salvaged personal effects, which am holding. Advise relatives and instruct this station fully as to procedure.

"Natives camping small river fifteen miles south here claim Post, Rogers landed and asked way to Barrow.

"Taking off, engine misfired on right bank while only fifty feet off water.

"Plane, out of control, crashed nose on, tearing right wing off and nosing over, forcing engine back through body of plane.

"Both apparently killed instantly.

"Both bodies bruised.

"Post's wrist watch broken, stopped 8:18 P. M."

The message was received by Colonel George E. Kumpe, in charge of the army signal corps headquarters here. It had been relayed through two radio stations and took about two hours to reach Seattle.

Sergeant Morgan won fame last Spring when he stayed at his post through a severe influenza epidemic while others, including his wife and 2-year-old son, Barrow, lay seriously ill. Sergeant Morgan and Dr. Henry W. Greist, the Presbyterian medical missionary, waged a bitter fight against the epidemic. While Dr. Greist ministered to the sick, Sergeant Morgan radioed for the aid which finally defeated the epidemic.

10-MINUTE HOP THEIR LAST

Engine Fails on a Take-Off for Final 15 Miles to Point Barrow.

LANDED TO GET BEARINGS

Startled Eskimos See Huge Bird Plunge to River Bank From 50 Feet Above Water.

ONE RUNS 3 HOURS TO TELL

Humorist Revealed as Financing a Trip Around the World With Famous Pilot.

(Copyright, 1935, by The Associated Press.)

POINT BARROW, Alaska, Aug. 16.—Will Rogers, beloved humorist, and Wiley Post, master aviator, were crushed to death last night when a shiny, new airplane motor faltered and became an engine of tragedy near this outpost of civilization.

Both were killed when their red Arctic sky cruiser, slipped and fell fifty feet head-on into a river bank. The 550-horse-power motor, driven back into the fuselage, snuffed out the lives of the two men instantly.

A native runner raced to Point Barrow with word of a plane crash. Sergeant Stanley R. Morgan of the Army Signal Corps dashed to the scene to learn the full significance of the tragedy.

First he took the body of Rogers from the cabin. Then he was forced to tear the plane apart to recover that of the flier who twice had flown around the globe—once alone.

Bodies Are Taken to Barrow.

The bodies were brought here and given to the care of Dr. Henry W. Greist, a Presbyterian medical missionary.

It was a trifling ten-minute flight that ended the careers of two famous figures long accustomed to flying. Although Rogers—gentle master of the "wise crack"—never became a pilot, he was perhaps the world's foremost airplane passenger.

Resuming a happy-go-lucky aerial tour of Alaska, a prelude to a flight to Siberia and on to Moscow, the noted travelers left Fairbanks late yesterday for a 500-mile hop to Point Barrow, northernmost white settlement in America.

Fifty miles out they encountered fog. Post "sat down" on Harding Lake for a while, but resumed the journey soon.

Apparently uncertain of his bearings, he again brought his pontooned plane to the surface of a shallow river fifteen miles southwest of here to ask natives the way to Point Barrow.

Rogers chatted with the Eskimos. Post tinkered with the plane during the brief stop. Soon after 5 P. M. (11 P. M. Eastern daylight time) they took off for the last little hop.

Motor Misfires on Take-Off.

The natives told the story to Sergeant Morgan. They said the motor of Post's new specially built plane misfired soon after it rose. The pilot quickly banked to the right; then the ship plummeted nose first, out of control. It dived into the edge of the stream, where the water was only two feet deep.

When Sergeant Morgan arrived at the scene by launch, he said today, "he found the monoplane a complete wreck, partly submerged. The right wing was broken off.

The soldier said Post's watch had stopped at 8:18 P. M., apparently the time of the accident. [The difference in time indicated by the aviator's watch and that reported by the natives probably is accounted for by the time zones through which he had flown.]

The runner arrived here at 10 P. M. with word of the tragedy. Recovering the flier's personal effects, Sergeant Morgan turned them over to Dr. Greist, awaiting instructions from Mrs. Rogers and Mrs. Post and from Morgan's superior, Colonel George E. Kumpe at Seattle.

The unrelenting Arctic, grave of other such noted fliers as Carl Ben Eielson and Frank Dorbandt, played a leading part in this new tragedy.

Rogers and Post had left Fairbanks in the face of poor flying conditions. The stop at Harding Lake enabled them to await the

Continued on Page Four.

ETHIOPIANS OFFER ITALY GUARANTEES

Bar Military Occupation, but Propose Mine, Rail, Trade and Settlement Rights.

ASK ROME TO STATE CASE

Britain and France Hold That Frank Presentation of Demands Is Essential.

By FREDERICK T. BIRCHALL.

Wireless to The New York Times.

PARIS, Aug. 16.—Throughout the day and until late this evening, with only an interval for luncheon, Premier Pierre Laval, Anthony Eden of Great Britain and Baron Pompeo Aloisi of Italy have been in conference at the Quai d'Orsay over the Italo-Ethiopian problem in an effort to avert a war, with its resultant repercussions in Europe.

The first day's deliberations closed tonight with one definite, positive step taken toward results. The British and French have made a joint formal request to the Italians to state fully and frankly their complaints against Ethiopia and their consequent claims upon her.

From a British source it is learned that the Ethiopian Government, which is not represented at this conference, has shown a disposition to concede several points that may go far toward satisfying the Italian claims when these are made.

Offers Security Guarantees.

The Addis Ababa government, for instance, has expressed willingness to provide the most complete guarantees of security from Ethiopian aggression for the present Italian colonies and such economic concessions as may be agreed upon, provided the guarantees expected fall short of military occupation.

Emperor Haile Selassie is willing to grant reasonable rights for developing mineral and commercial possibilities within the Ethiopian territory, specific concessions to Italy being made in both fields.

He is further willing to consider granting some rights to Europeans to settle in Ethiopian territory and develop it while maintaining their original nationality. This last point would go a long way toward compliance with the Italian wishes.

Finally, he is willing to renew and even extend by making further concessions the old understanding with Italy, giving her permission to undertake a certain amount of commercial road and railroad construction in this country. This again anticipates an obvious Italian demand.

No answer to the Franco-British query was forthcoming from Rome tonight. Indeed, an immediate response was not expected. Baron Aloisi agreed to submit the request to Rome and to report the result as soon as possible. He received assurance from the others that if Italy would comply with this re-

Continued on Page Three.

CAPITAL SADDENED BY ROGERS DEATH

Both House and Senate Halt Business for Tribute to the Humorist and to Post.

GARNER DEEPLY AFFECTED

Robinson Hails 'Best Loved Citizen'—Deaths 'Real Loss,' Speaker Byrns Says.

Special to The New York Times.

WASHINGTON, Aug. 16.—The death of Will Rogers and Wiley Post shocked and saddened the capital, which knew Rogers as a frequent visitor and liked him as an amiable "josher" of politicians.

Legislative machinery stopped briefly in tribute. The Senate dropped other business to honor the humorist, a friend of Presidents, diplomats and political leaders. The House also listened to a speech of eulogy, while from all quarters came expressions of sorrow over his death.

As soon as the Senate convened, Senator Robinson, the Democratic leader, took the floor and said:

"Probably the most widely known private citizen in the United States and certainly the best beloved met his death some hours ago in a lonely, far-away place.

"We pause for a moment in the midst of our duties to pay brief tribute to his memory and to that of his gallant companion, Wiley Post.

"I do not think of Will Rogers as dead. I shall remember him always as a sensible, courageous, loyal friend, possessed of unusual and notable talents.

"He made fun for all mankind. In nothing that he ever said was there an intentional sting. He was kind, generous, patriotic.

"His companion was a courageous representative of a gallant group who, on wings of adventure, sought remote places and conquered long distances."

News Saddens McNary.

Senator McNary, the Republican leader, said:

"Mr. Rogers has brought happiness, joy and good feeling to the hearts of millions of Americans. In common with all his fellow-citizens, I regret his tragic end and that of his doughty and valiant companion."

Vice President Garner, a friend of long standing, who shared the humorist's dislike of ceremonial attire, could only say, when informed of his death:

"Awful bad! Awful bad!"

Mr. Rogers had boomed Mr. Garner for the Presidency three years ago, and the two had a gay time together Jan. 17 when the Vice President entertained for President Roosevelt.

Speaker Byrns, addressing the House, mentioned Mr. Rogers's in-

Continued on Page Four.

ROGERS AND POST KILLED IN PLANE

Continued From Page One.

lifting of fog there. Then they encountered it again as they streaked further on toward the Pole.

They sighted the Eskimo camp southwest of here, an area described by Andrew Bahr, the reindeer driver, as one of the most desolate places in the world.

Obtaining directions, they set out on the little hop to Barrow. Here Rogers wanted to visit Charles Brower, known as "the King of the Arctic." Brower has lived in the Arctic fifty-one years. He is a trader and operates a whaling station near by.

The tragedy occurred during the height of the short Arctic Summer. Barrow is more than 300 miles inside the Arctic Circle, at the end of Alaska's northernmost point. Even yet its "harbor" is open only at intervals to shipping, and the Coast Guard cutter Northland is held in the icepack off Wainwright, seventy-five miles southwest of here, after her annual visit here.

Crosson Funeral Plane Pilot.

The bodies rested tonight in the Presbyterian Mission warehouse here, to be flown to Fairbanks by the flying friend of both men, Pilot Joe Crosson, who had advised them against taking off from Fairbanks because of bad weather.

Flying from Fairbanks, accompanied by Robert Gleason, local radio chief of Pan American Airways, Pilot Crosson arrived here this evening and planned to take off with the bodies on his return trip some time tonight.

Dr. Greist said the rescue party reported that "the plane débris was readily removed, as it was torn and broken to fragments by the plunge."

"The bodies," he said, "were dressed by Charles Brower, whom Rogers was flying to see; Sergeant Stanley R. Morgan of the United States Army Signal Corps, and myself."

As Dr. Greist understood the stories of the accident, Rogers and Post had landed on the river when the Arctic fog made them uncertain of their bearings on a 500-mile flight from Fairbanks to Point Barrow.

An Eskimo pointed out the way. A few seconds after the take-off the plane's engine spluttered. The ship dropped into the river, striking first on its right wing and then nosing into the bank head on.

"The Eskimo said he ran to the water's edge and called, but there was no answer," said Dr. Greist.

"Alarmed, he turned and ran to Barrow and informed Sergeant Morgan."

Ran 15 Miles With News of Crash.

The Eskimo was three hours running the fifteen miles to Barrow over the rough tundra, with many small lakes to encircle and many streams to cross.

"The native runner," Dr. Greist went on, "in his excitement on first arriving here, mumbled in his dialect of a red plane 'blowing up' close to his little camp.

"Sergeant Morgan immediately set out in a whale boat for the scene, but darkness and ice made progress slow.

"The bodies of the two men and their effects were placed in a skin boat and towed back here."

Post and Rogers had left Fairbanks in the face of a report that there was a dense fog along the route and the thermometer registered 45 degrees.

Friends quoted Post as saying, "I think we might as well go, anyway."

Rogers, they said, agreed, declaring, "There's lots of lakes we can land on."

Cutter Northland Delayed.

The Northland radioed that the time of her arrival at Barrow was "very indefinite because conditions are unfavorable."

"Only feasible method of quick removal of bodies is by airplane," the Northland advised.

Behind the fliers when their dash to the top of Alaska ended in the shallow Arctic stream lay miles upon miles of barren, treeless tundra traversed by the Colville River and its few and winding tributaries.

Barrow itself is a tiny spot on the end of Point Barrow. It is inhabited by about a dozen white persons and several hundred natives.

The visit to Alaska was the jovial philosopher-comedian's first. Post is well known here. Everywhere at their stops along the way crowds flocked to cheer them and to shake their hands.

Rogers would flash the grin known round the world.

"Me and Wiley," he said once, "are just a couple of Oklahoma boys trying to get along."

In a transport plane they flew over the government's Matanuska Valley colonization project yesterday. Rogers had said he wanted to organize a polo team there.

It was the first extended flight for Post's new monoplane, aside from a Southwestern hunting trip on which Rogers and Mrs. Post accompanied him.

Post shelved his famed world-girdling Winnie Mae, in which he twice circled the globe, after his attempts to span the continent in the substratosphere.

Alaska first saw the aviator in the Summer of 1931 when he and Harold Gatty made a record-breaking flight around the world. Two years later, however, Post, flying solo, bettered the time by nearly a day, and Alaska again saw him as he streaked across the Territory, although he had a minor crash at Flat.

Army Signal Corps Notified.

Special to THE NEW YORK TIMES.

SEATTLE, Aug. 16.—Will Rogers and Wiley Post were killed last night when the motor of their plane failed and the craft plunged into a small stream fifteen miles south of Point Barrow, Alaska, the office of the Army Signal Corps, which maintains the only system of communication with Barrow, was notified today.

Messages did not give the name of the river, but there are several streams close to Barrow which do not bear names on the maps.

Rogers and Post left here Wednesday morning, Aug. 7. They took off from Lake Washington, at the Renton Airport, and flew to Juneau.

Post had arrived here several days before to supervise installation of pontoons on his plane. His wife accompanied him.

Rogers arrived by airplane on Aug. 5.

Mrs. Post was planning to accompany the famous pair on their northern flight, but changed her plans and returned to California by plane after her husband and Rogers departed.

At all times here Rogers was the wise-cracking, carefree humorist endeared to millions, but he maintained silence as to the real plans of his flight. The revelation that he intended to fly to Siberia was made by W. W. Conner, Pacific Coast vice president of the National Aeronautic Association. Mr. Conner, who was with the two men much of the time they were in Seattle, said:

"Mr. Rogers didn't say anything about it, because he and Mr. Post liked to keep things a mystery, but he had made up his mind to go on to Siberia."

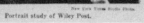

New York Times Studio Photo.

Portrait study of Wiley Post.

New York Times Studio Photo.

Portrait study of Will Rogers.

CAPITAL SADDENED BY ROGERS DEATH

Continued From Page One.

fluence on American politics and the American people.

"Will Rogers had the ear of the public as few in this country did," he said. "Everybody read what he had to say in his quaint way. His death is a real loss, and Post's is, too."

Representative Will Rogers of Oklahoma, who ran for Congress because of his name, though not related to the comedian, declared:

"Oklahoma has lost its greatest son."

He estimated that the fact his namesake endorsed him for Congress won him 50,000 votes.

Senator Ashurst, himself a former cowboy, remarked that "the shocking news of the tragic death of Will Rogers and Wiley Post saddens all hearts."

Jesse H. Jones, chairman of the Reconstruction Finance Corporation, declared:

"In the passing of Will Rogers the world has lost its most unique character, our country an invaluable citizen that cannot be replaced. We are sad today, millions of us."

Patrick J. Hurley, former Secretary of War, proposed immediately that Rogers's name be perpetuated in the Congressional Hall of Fame.

AIRPLANE IS SENT TO BRING BODIES

Lindbergh and Pan American Officials Offer Aid to Widows of Rogers and Post

GOVERNMENT IS ASSISTING

But Coast Guard Cutter Northland Is Unable to Reach Point Barrow Because of Ice.

Both Colonel Charles A. Lindbergh, technical adviser to the line, who is in Maine, and local officials of Pan American Airways were in touch yesterday with Mrs. Will Rogers and Mrs. Wiley Post to offer the facilities of Pacific Alaska Airways, a subsidiary, Juan T. Trippe, president of the parent company, said last night. He said that the bodies of the two fliers would be brought by plane from Point Barrow by way of Juneau.

"At the request of both Mrs. Rogers and Mrs. Post," he said, "arrangements have been made to dispatch a seaplane from Fairbanks to return the bodies to Juneau. Although this is the saddest of missions, we are glad to be of service to the families of those two outstanding Americans who have done so much for aviation.

"No one in America has done so much to encourage advancement of modern air transportation as has Will Rogers—no one has meant quite so much to American aviation or to those engaged in the industry. Wiley Post, who has contributed so importantly to the advancement of American aviation within the past few years, was distinguished among the world's great pilots."

Mr. Trippe explained that in carrying out the wishes of Mrs. Rogers and Mrs. Post arrangements for the return of the bodies were coordinated with various government departments, which had all been anxious to be of any possible service. The Treasury Department, in particular, he said, had ordered the Coast Guard cutter Northland to return to Barrow should any aid be required of it.

Government Agencies Help.

Special to THE NEW YORK TIMES.

WASHINGTON, Aug. 16.—Government officials today immediately announced readiness to render any assistance in bringing the bodies of Will Rogers and Wiley Post from Point Barrow, Alaska. After a request by Mrs. Rogers and Mrs. Post that they be returned by air, Assistant Secretary Gibbons of the Treasury Department, which has supervision over the Coast Guard, announced late today that the bodies would be flown in a Pacific Alaska Airways plane to Fairbanks, preparatory to returning them to the United States.

The Coast Guard cutter Northland, now in the vicinity of Point Barrow, but prevented by ice from entering the roadstead, will stand by to give any possible assistance, and Major Gen. Paul B. Malone, commander of the Ninth Corps Area, which has jurisdiction over Alaska, has been ordered by the War Department to help in bringing back the bodies.

The Northland reported that "the only feasible method of getting the bodies out now is by plane."

Fog and other hazards make the effort difficult. Only a light plane with soft rubber tires can land in the vicinity, it was said.

The Department of Commerce ordered an inspector in Alaska to proceed immediately to the scene of the disaster to make the investigation required by law.

FLIERS DIED AT LAND'S END

WASHINGTON, Aug. 16 (AP).—Point Barrow, near where the Post-Rogers plane fell in Alaska, is the most Northern point on the North American continent, corresponding in latitude to the North Cape of Norway.

It is 600 miles east of Bering Strait, and was named by the explorer Beechey in 1826.

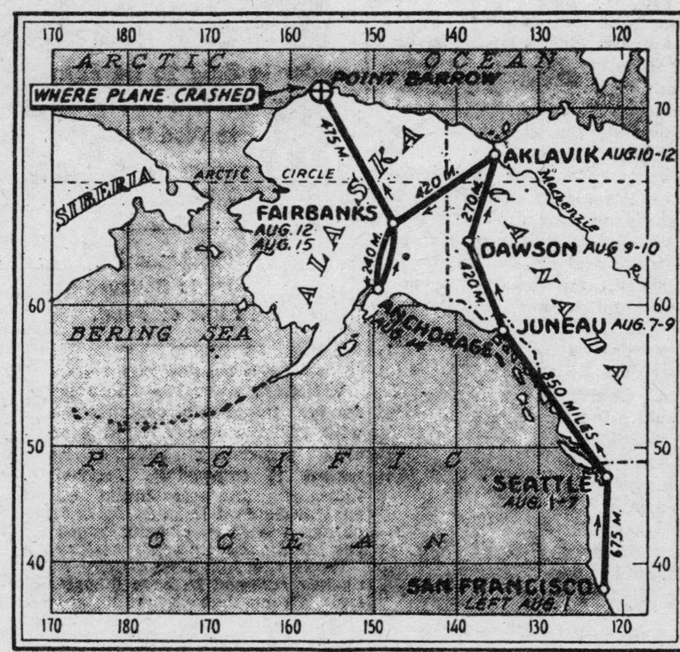

ROUTE OF THE ROGERS-POST FLIGHT.

The black line shows the areas covered, from Seattle to Point Barrow, on the fatal holiday jaunt.

Daily Rogers 'Box' Started With a Cable Sent 'Collect' to the Editor of The Times

On the night of July 29, 1926, THE NEW YORK TIMES received a query from Will Rogers, who was then in London as an unofficial ambassador of good-will, asking if the newspaper would pay the cable tolls on a brief message.

He was informed that the tolls would be paid, and a little later the following message addressed to the editor trickled across the Atlantic:

Nancy Astor, which is the nom de plume of Lady Astor, is arriving on your side about now. She is the best friend America has here. Please ask my friend Jimmy Walker to have New York take good care of her. She is the only one over here that don't throw rocks at American tourists.

Yours respectfully,
WILL ROGERS.

While the message was addressed as a letter to the editor and normally would have found a place on the editorial page, the late Joseph Tebeau, then night managing editor, ordered it published on the first page of the second section.

Without any further arrangements being made, each day brought a new message collect from Will Rogers. That practice continued until the Rogers "box" had achieved a pre-emptive right to its position in the newspaper.

Until Oct. 15, 1926, when Mr. Rogers returned from abroad, he received no remuneration for his daily comment. On that date, however, THE NEW YORK TIMES arranged to buy the daily feature from the McNaught Syndicate. Such was the origin of one of the most widely syndicated newspaper features.

Occasionally, Rogers's comments brought a storm of protest from readers. This was especially true in November, 1932, when he undertook to express his opinion on the war debt situation. On that occasion The Times reproved him gently in an editorial.

On Dec. 8, the following retort from Mr. Rogers was printed in the space which had become his:

"Beverly Hills, Cal., Dec. 7.—I would like to state to the readers of the New York Times that I am in no way responsible for the editorial or political policy of this paper.

"I allow them free reign as to their opinion, so long as it is within the bounds of good subscription gathering.

"But I want it distinctly understood that their policy may be in direct contrast to mine.

"Their ediorials may be put in purely for humor, or just to fill space.

"Every paper must have its various entertaining features, and their editorials are not always to be taken seriously, and never to be construed as my policy.

"Yours,
"WILL ROGERS."

The retort was reminiscent of the manner in which Rogers explained his mimicking of President Coolidge on the radio so effectively that many listeners thought it was the President speaking.

He didn't want to insult the American sense of humor, he said on that occasion, by explaining that the "nonsense" to which they had been listening emanated from him and not from the President.

ADVENTURE MARKED LIFE OF HUMORIST

Born in Indian Territory on Nov. 4, 1879, He Rose to Become 'Envoy of World.'

OFTEN ACCLAIMED ABROAD

Became a Familiar Figure to Broadway at Hammerstein's and the Follies.

Will Rogers had what it takes to tickle the national funny bone. His wry countenance, with its occasionally wistful expression, was comical to see, and his consciously cultivated drawl lent a rustic savor to his sophisticated quips. Most important of all, he had the knack of translating into trenchant phrases the inchoate thoughts of masses of "average" Americans.

He razzed Congress unmercifully, twitted Presidents and Kings, kidded the American public for falling for the blandishments of European borrowers, and he echoed the generally held impression that politicians should do more and talk less. He could be serious, too—putting into words the national pride that was stirred by the Paris flight of Colonel Charles A. Lindbergh and the public indignation that was felt over the murder of the aviator's infant son. Characteristically, a few years ago he suggested the following epitaph for his tombstone:

"I joked about every prominent man in my lifetime, but I never met one I didn't like."

Follows Own Advice.

America's foremost comedian, he had become, in recent years, one of its leading boosters of air travel. He wrote thousands of words in defense of the argument that it was safer to travel by plane than by train and demonstrated that he meant it by following his own advice.

As a passenger he flew back and forth across the continent, covered most of South America and got a birds-eye view of Europe and some of Asia. It has been estimated by aviation experts that he flew more than 500,000 miles in the past seven years.

He was in one crack-up before the one in which he lost his life, but that did not diminish his enthusiasm for the new means of transportation. The accident occurred at Las Vegas in June, 1928, when the rope-twirling raconteur was en route to the Republican National Convention. Rogers told the story of the crash in one of the brief dispatches he sent daily to THE NEW YORK TIMES.

"Wheel broke when she come down and turned over and lit on her head," he wrote. "Am the first candidate to land on his head, but being a candidate it didn't hurt the head."

William Penn Adair Rogers—to use all of it—has been called the lineal descendant of Artemus Ward. For years he watched the shifting American scene, noting its movements with flippancy and wisdom. While it is easy to call a spade a spade, he did so and yet made the spade like it—which is something else. His comments on life were widely followed and almost universally quoted. One of the most used American expressions was "Did you see what Will Rogers said?"

Before settling down as a philosophic jester, he had been almost everything else. He was a cowboy, a circus performer and an actor. Sometimes he denied this last, on the ground that he was "not smart enough to act." He starred in vaudeville and on the stage and in the movies after they became vocal. His attempts with the screen before it became audible were not overly successful. Finally, he was a lecturer and a writer, having to his credit an enormous output of pithy comment on the daily events.

Times Wide World Photo.

Mrs. Rogers with her husband.

He was once Mayor of Beverly Hills, Acting Mayor of New Orleans and Ambassador to the World—the last without portfolio. His name was mentioned for the Governorship of Oklahoma and for the Presidency of the United States a couple of times. Voting for Will Rogers became a habit with people; it was one of the best ways to file a protest without going Socialist.

Amassed Wealth in Work.

He had a tremendous financial success, and never mentioned it. When his friend, Fred Stone, was injured some years ago he dropped all his contracts—totaling some half-million dollars—in order to take his place until Stone recovered. He toured the country raising money for drought and flood relief and took part in hundreds of benefits. In his quiet way, he gave thousands of dollars of his private fortune to charity.

He was born at Oolagah, in Indian Territory, on Nov. 4, 1879, but he called Claremore, Okla., his "home town." He had some Indian blood, and one of his more famous remarks came when, in a discussion of ancestry, he remarked that his ancestors had not come over in the Mayflower; they had "met the boat." He went to school at the Willow Hassell School at Neosho, Mo., and Kemper Military Academy at Booneville.

Difficult to interview at all times, he once replied to a question about education by saying: "I studied the Fourth Reader for ten years." At all events, his mother saw in him a Methodist preacher, but she saw that quite alone. Will Rogers developed a passion for horses and he learned the use of the lariat. The chewing gum came later, when he was established. Talking about the days that followed the death of the Methodist dream, he once said:

"I was a kid in Oklahoma and had me a buddy and a little cattle ranch and I sold my cows for about $7,000 and took my buddy and went to New Orleans, figuring on catching a boat for the Argentine, because I had seen a map or read a dime novel or something. Well, there weren't any boats, so we took a boat for New York, figuring to catch one there.

"But New York didn't have any Argentine line either, so my buddy said I ought go to England; and we went to England and caught a boat there, and by the time we got to Rio I was just about broke and my buddy was homesick, so I paid his way back and got me a job on a ranch, thinkin' I could rope.

"Well, those gauchos down there taught me different, swishin' a lasso over my head from twenty feet behind and downin' a cow better than I can shoot a guy with a Winchester. So I worked awhile and then worked my way to South Africa on a cattle boat, and there I joined up with a little Wild West show, doing a roping act.

"From South Africa I went to Australia, where I worked with the Wirth shows, owned by Mae Wirth's daddy. Then I went to Japan and China, and then to San Francisco, and from there I bummed my way back home, and a feller told my dad he didn't think I had done so well because he heard I came home wearing overalls for underdrawers.

"Well, that only goes to show the success magazines are full of bunk when they write about a fellow winning fame and fortune by working hard and sticking to one job. All of you know, as well as I do, it was some accident started you off on the right track, but you ain't going to tell the reporters that, the next time they interview you."

How He Won First Fame.

The "accident" seems to have been a cow. The tradition is that one day, while Mr. Rogers was playing in the Wild West show in New York, one of the animals got free. He captured it with the rope, got into the public eye and so was hired for a turn on the Hammerstein Roof. This was in 1905. He went from the roof to vaudeville, back to the roof and then to Ziegfeld, and was there almost ever after, at least as long as he remained on Broadway.

A legend has grown up on Broadway about the transition from pantomime to monologue in the early Rogers vaudeville act. One of his most difficult tricks was the double lassoing of a horse and rider. Two ropes and a good deal of concentration and hope were required, but the finer nuances of the job were lost on the drug store cowboys in the balcony.

He Finds His Voice.

Some one told Rogers that he ought to explain what he was getting at. He did and these are handed down as the first words ever spoken by the national commentator before an audience:

"Ladies and gentlemen, I want to call your sho nuff attention to this next little stunt I'm agoing to pull on you, as I am going to throw these two ropes at once, catching the horse with one and the rider with the other. I don't have any idea that I'll get it, but here goes."

The audience laughed and Rogers was angry. He had not meant to be funny. He was just being himself. For a long time afterward he could not be induced to say another word, but finally he did, and he said later it was "the luckiest thing" he ever did. For a while he confined himself to comments on the other acts in the show, but finally he began searching for other material.

He turned naturally to the newspapers, scanning the late editions of the evening papers and sometimes the early editions of the morning papers just before going on for his act, often managing to get off a pithy comment on some occurrence in the day's news before his audience knew of the event itself. This was the origin of one of his first widely quoted wisecracks:

"All I know is what I read in the papers."

In a little while Rogers was twirling his rope and amusing the patrons at Hammerstein's Roof with his comments on personalities and events. He appeared in Ziegfeld's "Follies" and the "Frolics" for more than six years and at the opening of one of them remarked:

"Yes, a first night at the Follies is quite a function. Every one brings his new wife to see the old one act."

Made Many Silent Films.

In 1919 Will Rogers abandoned the stage and went to Hollywood to make some silent pictures. Not unqualified successes, some of them were: "Two Wagons, Both Covered," "Doubling for Romeo," "Boys Will Be Boys," "Family Fits," "Jubilo," "Our Congressman," "Going to Congress," "Gee Whiz, Genevieve" and a series of shorts called "Strolling Through Europe With Will Rogers." In 1922 he returned to the "Follies" and remained on Broadway until the talkies came. Then he made "They Had to See Paris."

When Fred Stone was hurt, Mr. Rogers took his friend's place in "Three Cheers." Charles Dillingham, its producer, used to send the comedian his salary in the form of a signed check, permitting Mr. Rogers to fill in the amount. When the show went on the road he returned to Hollywood and appeared in "So This Is London," "Lightnin'," "A Connecticut Yankee," "Ambassador Bill," "Young as You Feel," "Business and Pleasure" and other pictures.

Other items, besides the usual collection of stories about him, were various. He was married in 1908 to Betty Blake of Oolagah and they had three children. Will Rogers got up a family polo team which did pretty well for a time. "Had to give it up," he said finally. "Mary [a daughter] went society on us." And then there was the undoubted fact that in Claremore is a hotel—"with more bathrooms than Buckingham Palace"—called The Will Rogers.

When he went to Hollywood his studio built him a place. There was a garden and adobe hut and cactus and an electric stove. He looked in, said it was "swell" and never went back until former President Coolidge and Mrs. Coolidge came later in the year to call. "Well," he explained after he had seen them there, "they had to sit somewhere, didn't they?" He played dangerous polo, "because you couldn't make my mug look any worse no matter how much I hurt it." He owned a hurdy-gurdy, the only instrument he could play.

In 1927 Mr. Rogers went to Mexico at the same time as Colonel Lindbergh and was the guest of Ambassador Dwight Morrow. When the drought struck the West in 1931 he started a campaign for money and barnstormed over the country raising it. It was he who in 1930 made the suggestion that a silver cup be awarded by the American people to the "world's most cheerful loser," Sir Thomas Lipton. This last was done. He went to Europe at least a half dozen times, receiving the welcome accorded mostly to crowned heads.

He contributed widely to magazines and newspapers and the "box" published daily in THE NEW YORK TIMES was syndicated to about 500 newspapers in the United States and Canada, as was a weekly article of comment. He wrote several books, among them, "Rogerisms," a collection of his wisecracks; "The Cowboy Philosopher on Prohibition, 1919," "The Cowboy Philosopher on the Peace Conference," and "What We Laugh At, 1920." In 1924 his "Illiterate Digest" was greeted as one of the funniest books of the year.

Once an interviewer asked him for his recipe for humor and Rogers replied:

"A gag to be any good has to be fashioned about some truth. The rest you get by your slant on it and perhaps by a wee bit of exaggeration, so's people won't miss the point."

A few years ago Mr. Rogers came one evening to THE TIMES office and was shown around by the publisher. They reached the composing room, where the comedian was recognized. A small crowd grouped around. Suddenly taking his hat in his hand and waving it, he yelled: "We want more pay and less work!"

It was that sort of scene he did best.

Times Wide World Photo.

Will Rogers broadcasting.

ROGERS AND POST HONORED ABROAD

Leaders in London Join Press in Paying Tribute to the Actor and Aviator.

Special Cable to THE NEW YORK TIMES.

LONDON, Aug. 16.—The popularity which Will Rogers enjoyed in Great Britain may be measured to some extent by the way the news of his death and that of his companion Wiley Post swept all other news off the front pages of London's evening papers, but still more so by the depth of feeling shown in the tributes of his many friends here.

He probably was best known to the British public for appearances in the movies, but, as Charles B. Cochran recalls, he scored a tremendous success in "Cochran's Revue" nine years ago at London Pavilion, where he played during one of his periodical vacations here.

"His most important asset," Cochran said, "was his real grasp of the topics of the day and his wonderful wit. His loss is irreparable."

The London Times, which reprints Mr. Rogers's last letter to THE NEW YORK TIMES to be received here up to Aug. 8, remarks that Mr. Rogers was one of the very few American humorists who won an international reputation through three different channels—stage, screen and newspaper.

"His death robbed American life of something which not only enlivened but illustrated it. In him the eccentric individualism of the 'open spaces,' where he was born, had been wedded to the sophistication of the East and he was as much at home on the pavement as he was on the prairie."

HONOR MEDAL FOR ROGERS

ST. LOUIS, Aug. 16 (AP).—Will Rogers will receive posthumously a medal the Society of American Engineers intended to bestow personally because of the humorist's contribution to the cause of aviation.

James Doolittle, St. Louis flier and secretary of the Spirit of St. Louis Medal Board of Awards of the American Society of Mechanical Engineers, made the announcement today.

The Spirit of St. Louis medal was to have been given to Rogers here during a meeting of the aeronautic division of the society in October. The posthumous presentation will be made at a banquet of the organization on Oct. 10.

POST SURMOUNTED MANY OBSTACLES

Loss of an Eye in an Accident Failed to Shake His Hope of a Flying Career.

NOTED PARACHUTE JUMPER

He Financed His Earlier Air Adventures by Laboring in Oklahoma Oil Fields.

Wiley Post literally climbed to the heights of international fame from the comparative obscurity of the barren plains of Texas and Oklahoma. He overcame many obstacles, physical and financial, before he emerged, like a character from a Jules Verne fantasy, as one of the great aerial pioneers of the world.

His exploits were varied. His record of twenty-five hours and forty-five minutes from New York to Berlin, made, incidentally, as part of his record-breaking flight around the world in 1933, still stands as the greatest and most accurate flight to date. His adventures into the substratosphere stand out as having provided highly important information now being used by aeronautical engineers as the bases for the design of future aircraft.

Throughout his career the flier retained a reputation as among the most modest of all pilots. Never hard to find, he nevertheless became reticent when asked for dramatic impressions on his breathtaking experiences.

Despite the loss of an eye in an oil-field accident when a boy, Post struggled through the early stages of training as a pilot and finally convinced Federal officials that he was entitled to a transport pilot's license. He was forced by the injury to fly many more hours than is customary for other candidates who pass strict physical examinations. Throughout the early stages of his flying career he financed himself by working in the oil fields.

First Became Prominent in 1930.

He first came into prominence as a cross-country flier in 1930. To the amazement of veteran pilots, he led the fastest airplanes in the country in the Los Angeles-Chicago Derby of the 1930 National Air Races. His plane, the Winnie Mae of Oklahoma, was owned by F. C. Hall, an Oklahoma oil man, and in it the flier made most of his subsequent records.

Wiley Post was born in Grand Saline, Texas, Nov. 22, 1899. His father was of Scotch descent and his mother Irish. He was the fourth son of six children. His only sister, Mary, is now Mrs. L. A. Junnel, and lives in Dallas, Texas.

As a youth he was subjected to the gradual mechanization of Western farm life and developed a keen mechanical sense. For some years he was the neighborhood handy man.

His first interest in aviation came in 1913 when he visited the county fair in Lawton, Okla., and saw his first airplane. It was an old Curtiss "pusher," flown by Art Smith, then one of the veterans. The Post family at that time had moved to Chickasha, Okla.

In Signal Corps During War.

During the war Post enlisted in the radio school of the Signal Corps and on his discharge obtained work in an automobile repair shop. A few months later he became a "roughneck" in the oil fields of his own State, Oklahoma. He said of that part of his life:

"We got $7 a day, but the work was hard and dirty. Sometimes I fed boilers, sometimes I had to climb the derrick to thread pulleys, and at other times I drove cars. The gambling fever of the oil fields hit me hard. My first stake went into a wildcat scheme, but I went back to work as a driller and made another at $25 a day."

It was in the Summer of 1919 that Post took his first ride in an airplane. He paid $25 for the ride and was flown by a man he never further identified than as "Captain Zimmerman." Four and a half years later he embarked on the aviation career which terminated yesterday.

At Wewoka, Okla., a flying circus was stationed and after much persuasion Post obtained one assignment as a parachute jumper. Berl Tibbs, an old barnstormer, was the pilot. His first parachute landing nearly ended in disaster. With some practice, however, Post became proficient at jumping and put in two years, during which he took his first dual instruction from one of the pilots, Sam Bartel.

Described His First Solo Flight.

It was 1926 before he made his first solo flight, of which he said:

"It wasn't until I had wobbled down the rough ground and cleared the fence that I realized I was alone in the plane. For the first time in my life I was almost frightened. I climbed to where I felt comfortable and flew around until I was sufficiently sure of myself to attempt a landing. I forgot to clear the motor out and nearly ended in a forced landing. I discovered later that I barely missed a tree with the right wing before I pulled the ship up again and slipped in over the fence a bit high. I got the thing down without breaking anything and called it a day."

Lack of business in aviation sent the flier back to the oil fields in December, 1925. His first day on the field lost him his eye and apparently blasted his hopes of becoming an airplane pilot. A "roughneck," driving an iron bolt through the derrick, chipped a piece from his sledge which flew into Post's left eyeball. The eye had to be removed when an infection set in.

Post related recently how he took the $1,800 compensation for his eye, practiced depth perception with his other eye until his sight was superior to that of his two eyes, and bought his first airplane. In it on June 27, 1927, he eloped from Sweetwater, Texas, with Miss Mae Laine. In the getaway in the airplane he had a forced landing in a cornfield.

Struggle to Get Air License.

Next year he took a place as personal pilot to F. C. Hall. The first ship he flew was a Travelair open-cockpit machine, which he used for a year. Then his employer bought a cabin plane and he spent another year in that.

With the cabin plane his employer insisted that Post conform to the regulations of the Department of Commerce and take out a license. He could not pass the eye examinations, of course, and it was only after he had piled up 700 hours of flying the machine that the government officials finally granted him his ticket. He completed the 700 hours in eight months.

Depression then set into the oil industry, and Post obtained a place with the Lockheed Aircraft Corporation as a test pilot. He went on demonstration tours, competed in the 1929 National Reliability Tour for the Edsel Ford Trophy, and did experimental work, which later stood him in good stead in his own record making flights. He also spent some time flying between El Paso and Brownsville, Texas, and Mazatlan, Mexico.

In 1930 his former employer decided to buy another plane and Post was assigned to supervise its construction. That plane was the now famous "Winnie Mae," which carried him to all of his records. In it he won the classic of the 1930 National Air Races at Chicago and came into national prominence as a pilot.

Flight Around the World.

On June 23, 1931, he and Harold Gatty, a navigator, took off from Roosevelt Field, L. I., and started around the world.

With stops at Harbor Grace, N. F.; Chester, England; Berlin, Moscow, Novo-Sibirsk, Irkutsk, Blagoveshchensk and Khabarovsk, Siberia, Solomon Beach in Alaska, Edmonton in Alberta, and Cleveland, they arrived back at Roosevel. Field in exactly 8 days, 15 hours and 51 minutes in the most dramatic flight in history up to that time.

Gatty became navigation instructor to the Army Air Corps as a result of that flight. Post resumed his duties as a pilot after purchasing the "Winnie Mae" from his employer. He held an agency for airplane distribution in the Southwest and then began new experiments.

He equipped his plane with a robot pilot and in July, 1933, repeated his flight around the world. It was in the course of that flight that he established the record to Berlin. His record around the world he lowered to 7 days, 18 hours and 49 minutes.

Last year he had designed and appeared in his familiar "Man From Mars" flying suit. It was of rubber and capable of inflation to make possible constant pressures at high altitudes. He had his airplane engine specially supercharged and began a series of assaults on the altitude records. In one of his flights he claimed an altitude of more than 49,000 feet but trouble with the barograph prevented his record from becoming official.

Tests in the Substratosphere.

His altitude experiments were merely incidental to his real purpose in exploring the substratosphere as a medium to high speed transport, however, and he abandoned them in favor of cross-country flights at high levels.

Four times he was thwarted by mechanical failures in trying to lower the transcontinental record. Each time he took off from Los Angeles and dropped the landing gear of his plane to lessen the wind resistance. Once he was forced down on a dried lake in the Mojave Desert, another time he came down in Lafayette, Ind.; a third time in Cleveland and the last time at Wichita, Kan., on June 15 of this year. His plane, "Winnie Mae," was about worn out and ready to retire.

Returning to California, he ordered the plane in which he so suddenly met death Thursday night. He planned a vacation in a leisurely jaunt backward over his route from Moscow. He planned to stop off in Alaska, fly out over Kamchatka to Siberia and revisit some of the people who had aided him on his two former globe-circling flights.

Will Rogers accompanied him as far as Alaska as a close personal friend, a fellow-Oklahoman and an aviation enthusiast. When Post chronicled his experiences with Gatty in 1931, Mr. Rogers wrote an introduction to the book.

The pilot is survived by his wife, his parents, now living in Oklahoma, and his sister and four brothers.

One brother, Byron Post, is a private pilot and the only other member of the Post family who has taken up aeronautics as a vocation.

TRAGEDY IS SHOCK TO LEADERS HERE

Public Officials, Figures in Aviation and on Stage Express Grief Over Deaths.

WORLD LOSS, SAYS MAYOR

Many Messages of Condolence Are Sent to the Widows of Rogers and Post.

At the news of the death of Will Rogers and Wiley Post, shocked expressions of grief and appreciation came yesterday from men in public life, leaders in aviation and men connected with the stage. At a press conference at City Hall, Mayor La Guardia said:

"I am deeply shocked by this double tragedy. The loss is not only a national one; it will be felt throughout the world. We have lost a great and courageous flier, another martyr to the progress of aviation development. The tragic death of my friend Will Rogers grieves me beyond expression, a distinct loss to the country. Rogers's humorous philosophy developed into a distinct school of thought. Rogers Says Today started conversation at the breakfast table of millions of American families.

"Perhaps one of the most forceful and accurate interpreters of American public opinion, he never exploited his influence. How he will be missed! Every good American will feel a personal loss in the sudden passing of these two beloved characters."

Bernard S. Deutsch, President of the Board of Aldermen, said:

"Death has taken its toll of America's modern Autocrat of the Breakfast Table, Will Rogers. Those Americans who, even in these trying times, have retained their sense of humor, will miss Will Rogers's splendid contribution. It is too bad, indeed, that the progress of modern science in aviation should, at one fell stroke, have deprived us of the splendid personality of Will Rogers and daring and intrepid Wiley Post."

"The news comes as a distinct shock," said former Governor Alfred E. Smith when he learned of the crash. "They were two great Americans who will be missed by everybody."

Among men of the aviation industry there was a numbed sense of grief at the loss of two pioneers, one of whom they considered as among the world's leading pilots and the other one of the greatest friends that flying ever had. Thomas A. Morgan, president of the Aeronautical Chamber of Commerce of America, sent the following telegram to Mrs. Rogers:

"On behalf of the industry, the Aeronautical Chamber of Commerce of America extends to you and family sincere sympathy for your loss. We mourn the loss of Will Rogers as a great American and an aviation enthusiast who had made scores of long trips on scheduled air lines without undue incident. We deeply regret the tragic fate that awaited him and Wiley Post on their adventurous flight to the Far North."

To Mrs. Post he telegraphed in the name of the chamber:

"Your loss is ours. Wiley Post repeatedly distinguished himself by exploits of flying demanding the utmost in energy, courage and resourcefulness. His adventurous spirit made him a true pioneer, ever seeking new paths over barren wastes. We cannot find words to convey our sorrow that his last great adventure in the northern wilderness should have had such a tragic ending."

Both Called Pioneers.

Captain E. V. Rickenbacker, general manager of Eastern Air Lines, also stressed the fact that Will Rogers was, on his last flight, not an air traveler but a pioneer.

"Both Rogers and Post have been pioneers with new equipment over uncharted skyways," he said. "Will Rogers was not a passenger but an adventurer with Wiley."

Commander Frank Hawks said:

"America has lost a great person in Will Rogers and a great flier in Wiley Post."

Clyde Pangborn, conqueror of the Pacific and himself preparing for a round-the-world flight, exclaimed:

"The worst tragedy since the Knute Rockne crash, from a public viewpoint."

Major Alford J. Williams, former navy speed pilot, said at Roosevelt Field:

"This is a real loss to aviation; Wiley Post, our leading American long-distance and stratosphere research pilot, a real pioneer in aeronautics, and Will Rogers, aviation's best salesman."

Sanford L. Willits, chief inspector in this district for the Bureau of Air Commerce, said:

"A very regrettable accident and a great loss to aviation."

Jack Frye, president of TWA, said:

"Air transport today has lost two of its principal characters. That they were killed far from established airways and therefore removed from the aids to air navigation which our airways know so well merely goes to prove the interest which each held in the furtherance of the cause of flight. Will Rogers was considered America's No. 1 air traveler. Wiley Post has added much to the technical knowledge which we seek in scheduled high altitude flying."

Gen. Johnson Lauds Rogers.

General Hugh S. Johnson, director here of the Works Progress Administration, said:

"I knew Will Rogers as a boy, but it was not until after the World War that we became close personal friends. He had been a personal and dear friend for many years. The loss to me is both personal and poignant. I did not know Wiley Post personally, but, with the rest of the world, I admired him greatly. It's a terrible loss."

Mr. and Mrs. Post.

Rogers Gave an Epitaph For Gravestone in 1930

By The Associated Press.

BOSTON, Aug. 16.—The death of Will Rogers recalled remarks he made in a speech here in 1930 concerning the epitaph to be placed on his grave.

"When I die, my epitaph, or whatever you call those signs on gravestones, is going to read: 'I joke about every prominent man of my time, but I never met a man I didn't like.'

"I am proud of that," Mr. Rogers added. "I can hardly wait to die so it can be carved. And when you come around to my grave, you'll probably find me sitting there proudly reading it."

"All the News That's Fit to Print"

The New York Times.

LATE CITY EDITION

U. S. Weather Bureau Report (Page 77) forecast: Chance of early showers, then cloudy today and tonight. Rain tomorrow. Temp. range: 54–40; yesterday: 51–41

VOL. CXII.. No. 38,274. NEW YORK, THURSDAY, NOVEMBER 8, 1962. FIVE CENTS

10 cents beyond 50-mile zone from New York City except on Long Island. Higher in air delivery cities.

GAIN FOR KENNEDY PROGRAM SEEN IN RESULTS OF CONGRESS ELECTION; NIXON BITTER IN CONCEDING DEFEAT

U.S. WILL VERIFY MISSILE REMOVAL BY CHECK AT SEA

Agreement With Soviet Said to Call for a Count of Crates Leaving Cuba

DETAILS REMAIN SECRET

Washington Declines to Tell if Americans Will Board the Russian Vessels

By E. W. KENWORTHY

Special to The New York Times

WASHINGTON, Nov. 7 — The United States and the Soviet Union have reached an agreement under which United States naval vessels will make contact with Soviet ships and count missiles being removed from Cuba.

The agreement was reached by United States and Soviet representatives today at the United Nations and announced by the Defense Department here just before 6 P.M.

The terse announcement, which left many questions unanswered, was read by Arthur Sylvester, Assistant Secretary of Defense for Public Affairs. It said:

"The Soviet Union has reported ships are leaving Cuba with missiles aboard. Arrangements are being made with Soviet representatives for contact with these ships by United States naval vessels and for counting the missiles being shipped out."

Navy to Count Crates

According to officials, the agreed procedure calls for a Navy vessel to pull alongside the outbound Soviet ship. The missiles will be crated in large boxes stored on deck. Presumably the accosting ship would make a count of the visible crates.

Officials declined to say whether United States officers would go aboard the Soviet vessels or whether the count would simply be made from a position alongside.

Nor did these officials say how, under such an inspection system, there could be absolute certainty of what was in the crates.

Officials declined to say for security reasons how many Soviet missiles—both of medium and intermediate range—were known or estimated to be in Cuba. In Moscow today, Premier Khrushchev put the figure at 40.

Officials also refused to respond to questions whether the United States intended to insist that international observers—either under United Nations auspices or through some other

Continued on Page 3, Column 1

ALL ROCKETS OUT, KHRUSHCHEV SAYS

He Asserts That Missiles in Cuba Totaled 40

By SEYMOUR TOPPING

Special to The New York Times

MOSCOW, Nov. 7 — Premier Khrushchev declared tonight that the Soviet Union had taken its rockets out of Cuba.

In an impromptu toast at a Kremlin reception celebrating the 45th anniversary of the Bolshevik Revolution, Mr. Khrushchev said that 40 Soviet rockets had been emplaced on the Caribbean island.

"We have taken our rockets out and they probably are on the way," he added. The remarks of the Premier seemed to indicate that the missile bases had been dismantled and the equipment was being loaded aboard Soviet ships.

The reception, which took place after the traditional military parade in Red Square, was marked by repeated declarations by Mr. Khrushchev about the need for peaceful coexistence, compromise and mutual concessions in East-West relations.

The Russian leader, talking to newsmen, said that the importance of obtaining a Berlin settlement had become even more acute, but that he saw no necessity at the present for a summit meeting.

The Premier added that the tension over Cuba had not completely eased. He recalled solemnly that during the crisis "we

Continued on Page 2, Column 3

Mrs. Roosevelt Dies at 78 After Illness of Six Weeks

Mrs. Franklin D. Roosevelt

Mrs. Franklin D. Roosevelt died last night.

The former First Lady, famous as the wife and widow of the 32d President of the United States and an international figure in her own right, died at 6:15 P.M. in her home at 55 East 74th Street. She was 78 years old.

Reaction to Mrs. Roosevelt's death was quick and deep.

The woman who was a noted humanitarian, author and columnist, delegate to the United Nations and active force in the Democratic party was mourned by people over the world.

President Kennedy called her "one of the great ladies in the history of this country." The President and former President Harry S. Truman announced they planned to attend Mrs. Roosevelt's funeral.

Mayor Wagner ordered flags on city buildings flown at half-staff.

Mrs. Roosevelt succumbed

Continued on Page 34, Column 1

MENON IS OUSTED FROM CABINET JOB

Nehru Yields to Pressure—U. S., Britain and Canada Study Joint Arms Aid

By A. M. ROSENTHAL

Special to The New York Times

NEW DELHI, Nov. 7—Indian politicians cheered today as Prime Minister Jawaharlal Nehru announced the acceptance of the resignation of V. K. Krishna Menon from the Cabinet.

A power in India and in international diplomacy for more than a decade, Mr. Menon sat hunched and silent as Mr. Nehru made his announcement in a New Delhi caucus room.

[The United States, Britain and Canada are drafting a broad new program of military aid for India, a dispatch from Washington said.]

Two hours earlier the Indian Government announced that the Chinese Communists, whose attack led to Mr. Menon's fall from power, were building up their strength in northern India and were preparing for new attacks.

The Government, which says it is becoming more convinced that it faces a long struggle, ordered the arrest here of 17 Indian Communists and of others elsewhere in the country. They are suspected of sympathizing with Peking and were members of a "China lobby"

Continued on Page 9, Column 1

Estes Found Guilty; 8-Year Term Set By Jury in Texas

By United Press International

TYLER, Tex., Nov. 7 — A jury of 11 men and one woman found Billie Sol Estes guilty today of swindling a Pecos, Tex., farmer, T. J. Wilson, on a mortgage deal. They set a sentence for the 37-year-old Estes of eight years in state prison.

The jury deliberated two hours and seven minutes before reaching its verdict. It asked District Judge Otis T. Dunagan three times to send various records of the mortgage transaction into the jury chamber.

The jury fixes the sentence in Texas. The judge does the formal sentencing but must follow the jury's decision. The defense has 15 days to file appeal for a new trial.

Appeal to Be Made

A defense attorney, John D. Cofer, said he would file a motion for a new trial, a legal procedure that will clear the way, if refused, for an appeal to the Court of Criminal Appeals.

Estes was permitted to remain free on his current $5,000 bond, pending the judge's action on the defense motion for a new trial. If the motion is refused, the judge then will pass formal sentence.

Estes' attorneys did not ask the jury for a suspended sentence. The case went to the panel with a passionate plea for acquittal.

The defendant was impassive during the reading of the verdict. He sagged momentarily

Continued on Page 56, Column 8

SCHOOLS IN CITY SCORED AS WEAK IN STATE REPORT

'Bleak' Future Is Predicted Unless Teaching System Undergoes Revamping

Excerpts from report on city schools appear on Page 44.

By LEONARD BUDER

A state report declared yesterday that "serious deficiencies" and "alarming weakness" existed in the instructional program of the city school system.

The report, based on a year-long study by the State Education Department, said that the system was staggering "under its immense problems." Unless these problems can be met, it declared, the future will be "a bleak one" for the city.

Although highly critical in tone, the report noted that there also was much to commend in the city system.

"The schools have moved mountains, because there are mountains to be moved," it said. "The fact that they have not moved them far enough or fast enough is a measure of the staggering problems they face, not of ineptitude, dereliction or irresponsibility on the part of teachers, principals and officials."

Findings Are Listed

These were some of the findings:

¶Major improvements are needed in the curriculums offered at all levels of the system, particularly in the elementary and junior high schools.

¶Although many city teachers and supervisors are competent and dedicated, many others are poorly prepared, are unable to meet regular standards, are assigned to teach unfamiliar subjects and generally are unable to provide high-caliber instruction.

¶Classes are generally too large and teachers are burdened by the heavy pupil loads. The effectiveness of even good teachers and supervisors is limited by too many clerical and housekeeping chores.

¶The achievement of the city's elementary pupils is generally below that of children in other schools of the state. A large proportion of high school students cannot even meet minimum standards in reading.

¶Children in schools in underprivileged areas, who need the best teachers because of their special problems, often have the poorest and most inexperienced teachers.

¶Although newer city school buildings have fine facilities, many older buildings provide sub-standard environments for learning. Some of the schools visited were dirty and unsanitary.

¶Guidance, social work, attendance and health and psychological services offered by the system are inadequate.

¶The procedure of the system's Board of Examiners "needs to be replaced with less time-consuming methods of teacher selection." Principals and other supervisors must as-

Continued on page 44, Column 1

ACKNOWLEDGES DEFEAT: Richard M. Nixon talking to reporters yesterday after losing in California gubernatorial race. "This is my last press conference," he told them.

Associated Press Wirephoto

PRESIDENT ELATED

Prestige Is Heightened By His Success in Midterm Voting

By TOM WICKER

Democrats have scored a remarkable midterm election success. The outcome of Tuesday's election demonstrated support for President Kennedy's Cuban policies and warded off a Republican threat to his legislative strength.

In California, in the most closely watched election of the year, Gov. Edmund G. Brown defeated Mr. Kennedy's rival for the Presidency in 1960, Richard M. Nixon—probably ending the latter's political career.

In what amounted to a victory statement, Mr. Kennedy made no mention of the California triumph but said he was "heartened" by the national returns.

A White House statement added that analysis showed "a clear net gain in support of the President's program" in the House of Representatives.

The ultimate impact of the Democratic gains of four seats in the Senate and minimal Democratic losses in the House might well bear out that claim and improve prospects for New Frontier legislation

Campaigning Cut Short

The President emerged with increased prestige and political strength from an election in which he had first gone all out for his party, but from which he withdrew completely when the Cuban crisis erupted in mid-October.

His party will apparently have perhaps four fewer seats in the House of Representatives in the 88th Congress, but the losses were primarily among Southern Democrats who had been antipathetic to the Administration.

Unofficial returns from the 39 Senate races resulted in a Democratic gain from 64 to 68, reducing the Republican minority from 36 seats to 32.

In the House contests, 257 Democrats and 176 Republicans were elected, with two undecided contests in Alaska and California in which Democrats were leading.

But recounts were assured in

Continued on Page 16, Column 3

ROCKEFELLER EDGE SPURS '64 HOPES

Despite Lower Margin, He Is Still Rated High as a Presidential Contender

By LEO EGAN

Governor Rockefeller remains in the front rank of contenders for the Republican Presidential nomination after his 518,218-vote victory over Robert M. Morgenthau, the Democratic-Liberal candidate in Tuesday's election.

But the national effects of his victory were offset by several factors: His margin was the lowest of any statewide Republican winner, and it was more than 55,000 short of his plurality in 1958, when he defeated Gov. W. Averell Harriman.

Senator Jacob K. Javits won re-election over James B. Donovan, his Democratic-Liberal opponent, by a margin of 975,366. Attorney General Louis J. Lefkowitz defeated Manhattan Borough President Edward R. Dudley, the Democratic-Liberal candidate for Attorney General, by 646,813 votes.

State Controller Arthur Levitt, running as a Democrat-Liberal, defeated John P. Lo-

Continued on Page 23, Column 1

Capehart Unseated As Bayh of Indiana Confounds Experts

Special to The New York Times

INDIANAPOLIS, Nov. 7—In one of the most stunning upsets of yesterday's election, Birch E. Bayh Jr., a 34-year-old Democrat, unseated Senator Homer E. Capehart, Republican of Indiana.

Mr. Capehart, who at 65 has served in the Senate longer than any other man in modern Indiana history, had sought a fourth consecutive term.

With only 10 of 4,380 precincts to be counted, Mr. Bayh led Senator Capehart by almost 10,000 votes. Mr. Bayh had 902,123 votes, Mr. Capehart 829,180.

The Senator conceded at a news conference at noon today. He said he would never again seek public office.

This was the closest Indiana Senate race since 1938. The turnout set an off-year record.

Experts Are Shocked

Mr. Bayh, a lawyer and farmer, shocked political experts by running as strong in predominantly Republican rural areas as in the big-city Democratic strongholds.

He had waged a strenuous campaign but was all but counted out of the race when President Kennedy ordered a quarantine of Cuba. Senator Capehart had been advocating a blockade for several months.

President Kennedy visited Indiana Oct. 13 and gave Mr. Bayh a strong endorsement. Mr. Bayh continued his vigorous campaign and refused to listen to predictions that he could not possibly win.

Mr. Bayh has served four

Continued on Page 31, Column 1

NIXON DENOUNCES PRESS AS BIASED

In 'Last' News Conference, He Attributes His Defeat to Crisis Over Cuba

Transcript of Nixon press conference is on Page 20.

BY GLADWIN HILL

Special to The New York Times

BEVERLY HILLS, Calif., Nov. 7—Richard M. Nixon conceded defeat today. He later devoted what many observers regard as the possible valedictory of his national political career to a bitter denunciation of the press.

He also made some acid remarks about his victorious gubernatorial opponent, Gov. Edmund G. Brown, in a statement to about 100 newsmen at the Beverly Hilton Hotel here. The statement was his first public utterance since the election yesterday, which dashed the former Vice President's hopes of a political comeback.

A failure to win his native state had been widely assessed before the election as impairing, probably irreparably, the 49-year-old Republican's viability in national politics.

His defeat came by a vote margin six times as large as the margin by which he carried California in 1960, when he lost the Presidential election to John F. Kennedy. The virtually unanimous opinion of political observers was that the defeat had obliterated the lingering possibility, despite his disclaim-

Continued on Page 18, Column 1

A.F.L.-C.I.O. FACES ITS DEEPEST SPLIT

Reuther Could Quit Council or Pull Auto Union Out

By JOHN D. POMFRET

Special to The New York Times

WASHINGTON, Nov. 7 — The American Federation of Labor and Congress of Industrial Organizations is facing its most severe internal crisis since its founding in 1955.

Walter P. Reuther has set the stage either to resign from the organization's executive council when it meets here next week or to take the more drastic step of pulling the United Automobile Workers of America out of the merged labor federation.

The auto union's executive board will meet here simultaneously with the council session Monday and Tuesday, so Mr. Reuther will have the leaders of the union he heads on hand to approve whatever move he decides to make.

In addition, the auto union has allowed its dues payments to the parent organization to lag as far behind as possible. Its July per capita payment to the federation of about $69,000 was made Oct. 15. Had it been made a day later the union would have faced suspension.

These preparations, coupled with the absence of any softening of the intense dislike between Mr. Reuther and George Meany, president of the A.F.L.-C.I.O., have led some well-informed union aides to conclude that the federation is closer to

Continued on Page 48, Column 4

Soviet Shows New Missile Said to Be Capable of Undersea Firing

United Press International Radiophoto

The naval rocket being displayed yesterday in the Moscow parade marking anniversary of the Bolshevik Revolution

Special to The New York Times

MOSCOW, Nov. 7 — The Soviet Union displayed today a 50-foot naval rocket described by Izvestia, the Government newspaper, as a missile of great accuracy that could be launched from a submarine under water. The newspaper report was one of the first indications that the Soviet Navy might have developed a missile similar to the Polaris employed by the United States Navy. The rocket was the only new piece of equipment shown in a 45-minute military parade in Red Square marking the 45th anniversary of the Bolshevik Revolution. The dark green rocket, mounted on a six-wheel trailer, was pulled quickly past the reviewing stand by a tracked personnel carrier. A crew of 16 sailors rode in the open personnel carrier in addition to the drivers in the cab. At the rear of the missile was a cluster of what appeared to be

Continued on Page 4, Column 3

Grumman to Build Lunar Craft; Project Will Spur L. I. Economy

By JOHN W. FINNEY

Special to The New York Times

WASHINGTON, Nov. 7—The space agency selected the Grumman Aircraft Engineering Corporation of Bethpage, L. I., today to build the lunar excursion "bug" that is designed to land two American astronauts on the moon.

The contract is expected to have a major economic impact on Long Island, making the area one of the principal industrial centers in the rapidly expanding space program.

The National Aeronautics and Space Administration said that the contract, still to be negotiated with Grumman, was expected to be worth around $350,000,000. But industry officials believe that before the project is completed the contract could reach $500,000,000 to $1,000,000,000.

With the award, the space agency has placed under contract the last major part of its Apollo program—the high-priority project to land a manned expedition on the moon before the end of the nineteen-

Continued on Page 56, Column 7

NEWS INDEX

Mrs. Roosevelt Dies Here at 78 After an Illness of Six Weeks

Continued From Page 1, Col. 3

four weeks after her birthday, which was Oct. 11, and six weeks after she entered a hospital with anemia and a lung infection.

Her family announced that a private funeral service would be held at St. James's Protestant Episcopal Church in Hyde Park, N. Y., at 2 P. M. Saturday.

The family said that the service would be attended by representatives of the United States Government and the United Nations, New York officials and close friends.

There will also be a memorial service at the Cathedral Church of St. John the Divine within two weeks. The time and date will be announced.

Mrs. Roosevelt will be buried next to her husband, who died on April 12, 1945. There is a tombstone over his grave, in the rose garden of the Hyde Park home, which contains his name, the year of his birth and the year of his death. Also carved into the stone are the name Anna Eleanor Roosevelt and the year of her birth.

It was Mrs. Roosevelt's specific request that no flowers be sent. It was her hope, the family said, that those who wished would send contributions to the Wiltwyck School at 260 Park Avenue South, to the Eleanor Roosevelt Cancer Foundation at 521 West 57th Street or to the American Association for the United Nations at 345 East 46th Street.

Family With Her

Physicians and some members of Mrs. Roosevelt's family were with her when she died. Mrs. Anna Roosevelt Halsted, her daughter, who had been staying with Mrs. Roosevelt during her illness, said that doctors were present because of "indications of cardiac failure."

Shortly after the first signs of illness, she went to the Columbia-Presbyterian Medical Center, on Sept. 26. She marked her 78th birthday in the hospital and, it was learned last night, began pressing to be released so that she could convalesce at home.

Physicians were reported to have preferred that Mrs. Roosevelt remain in the hospital, but she persuaded her family to back up her wishes, and she went home on Oct. 18.

Three of Mrs. Roosevelt's children were at the apartment last night. In addition to Mrs. Halsted, wife of Dr. James A. Halsted, there were Franklin D. Roosevelt Jr. and John. The two other sons took planes to come here. Elliott was flying from Miami and James arrived early today by plane from California, where he won re-election to the House of Representatives in Tuesday's elections.

The following statement concerning Mrs. Roosevelt's illness was issued by her family:

"Two and one-half years ago it was found that Mrs. Roosevelt was suffering from a complicated type of anemia. Treatment was instituted and she responded fairly satisfactorily to the extent that she could continue with her many activities.

"In September, 1961, Mrs. Roosevelt was hospitalized at the Columbia-Presbyterian Medical Center for a medical checkup, which was satisfactory. In July of 1962 her anemia worsened and she was hospitalized for a series of tests and X-rays. On leaving the hospital she went to Hyde Park for a rest and visited the family's old home on Campobello Island for a week. She appeared to be improving slowly but fairly satisfactorily.

"About the middle of September she started running a slight fever for a few hours each day. Treatment was started in an effort to cure the infection, which was obscure. Because the fever persisted she was hospitalized again at the Columbia-Presbyterian Medical Center in the Harkness Pavilion, where she could be treated while further tests were undertaken."

Physicians Accede

The statement continued:

"After three weeks the attending physicians felt they could accede to her request to return to her home. This occurred on Oct. 18. The contentment which she experienced in being among her own surroundings and with her family was of great importance during the last days of her life, and the same treatment which she had in the hospital was continued.

"Her illness was complex from the start. It is known that she had a plastic anemia, for which she was treated. Complicating this was the infection, producing considerable fever. Tuberculosis was suspected, but not proven until Oct. 25 when a culture proved that this was the cause of her fever.

"Vigorous anti - tuberculosis treatment had been started shortly after her admission to the hospital in September. The tuberculosis was noncontagious in form.

"Mrs. Roosevelt responded partially to the treatment and had occasional days without fever. Her general condition, however, gradually worsened during the last few weeks of her life.

"The family will always be grateful for the excellent and thoughtful care which she received at the hospital and for the devotion of her attending physicians and nurses."

Mrs. Roosevelt's body was taken last night from the five-story building where she had occupied the second and third floors, placed in an unmarked hearse at 8:25 o'clock and taken to the Columbia-Presbyterian Medical Center for an autopsy.

During her illness, Mrs. Roosevelt had only one visitor who was not a member of the family—Adlai E. Stevenson, the United States representative at the United Nations. Mrs. Roosevelt had worked closely with Mr. Stevenson in the United Nations for many years, and she had asked him to talk with her about the Cuban crisis.

The family announced shortly after Mrs. Roosevelt's death that no one would be permitted inside the house here, but an exception was quickly made for Mr. Stevenson. He stayed five minutes.

Besides her five children, Mrs. Roosevelt is survived by 19 grandchildren and 15 great-grandchildren.

President Kennedy Leads Nation in Expressing Sorrow at Death of Mrs. Roosevelt

FARLEY, JOHNSON ALSO MOURN LOSS

President Kennedy led the nation last night in expressing grief at the death of Mrs. Franklin D. Roosevelt. He called her "one of the great ladies in the history of this country."

The President received the news at the White House in a telephone call from Mrs. Roosevelt's son James, a member of Congress from California.

Mr. Kennedy issued the following statement:

"One of the great ladies in the history of this country has passed from the scene. Her loss will be deeply felt by all those who admired her tireless idealism or benefitted from her good works and wise counsel.

"Since the day I entered this office, she has been both an inspiration and a friend, and my wife and I always looked forward to her visits to the White House, to which she always lent such grace and vitality.

"Our condolences go to all the members of her family, whose grief at the death of this extraordinary woman can be tempered by the knowledge that her memory and spirit will long endure among those who labor for great causes around the world."

Adlai E. Stevenson, United States representative to the United Nations, said:

"Like so many others, I have lost more than a beloved friend. I have lost an inspiration. She would rather light a candle than curse the darkness, and her glow has warmed the world."

Vice President Lyndon B. Johnson said:

"I am deeply grieved to learn of the passing of a great lady who impressed upon our country her warm philosophy of helping those who needed help. Our people will mourn as they grieved at the death of her husband. This is a different world because of the Roosevelts, and they will never be forgotten."

Secretary of State Dean Rusk said:

"Her untiring work at the United Nations in support of human rights is a monument to her whole life's work. Her memory will sustain all other champions of human brotherhood who follow in her steps."

James A. Farley, former Postmaster General and longtime political aide of Franklin D. Roosevelt said:

"Her devotion to duty was truly unselfish, and as long as the memory of an American woman is recorded in our country's annals, the name of Anna Eleanor Roosevelt will be enshrined."

Former Gov. Herbert H. Lehman, a friend of Mrs. Roosevelt for more than four decades and an associate in many causes, said:

"Her place can never be filled in the hearts of countless people whom she has befriended and helped over a life of unfailing service and selfless devotion. The world is much poorer for her going."

Former President Herbert Hoover said:

"Mrs. Roosevelt was a lady of fine courage and great devotion to her country."

Senator Jacob K. Javits said:

"The life of a historic and beloved American lady has ended. All in the world with a heart will mourn her loss."

Mayor Wagner issued the following statement:

"In the death of Eleanor Roosevelt, we have lost the greatest woman of our time, one of the greatest of any time.

"She was so grand a woman, so rare a person, so pure a spirit, that to judge our loss at this moment is impossible. Her personal goodness affected the entire climate of her age and we live surrounded by the concepts of generous and compassionate behaviour which she along with her great husband—brought into the public life of our nation.

"The world has suffered a loss. New York has suffered a loss. I—we all have suffered a loss, too deep to weigh or to measure.

"A light has gone out of our lives, something has died for each and every one of us."

Mrs. Roosevelt with John F. Kennedy for whom she campaigned in the 1960 election.

Mrs. Roosevelt, First Lady 12 Years, Often Called 'World's Most Admired Woman'

SHE WON ACCLAIM IN HER OWN RIGHT

President's Widow Served in U.N., Wrote Newspaper Column, Traveled Widely

Mrs. Franklin D. Roosevelt was more involved in the minds and hearts and aspirations of people than any other First Lady in history. By the end of her life she was one of the most esteemed women in the world.

During her 12 years in the White House she was sometimes laughed at and sometimes bitterly resented. But during her last years she became the object of almost universal respect.

Again and again, she was voted "the world's most admired woman" in international polls. When she entered the halls of the United Nations, representatives from all countries rose to honor her. She had become not only the wife and widow of a towering President but a noble personality in herself.

In the White House and for some time thereafter, no First Lady could touch Mrs. Roosevelt for causes espoused, opinions expressed, distances spanned, people spoken to, words printed, precedents shattered, honors conferred, degrees garnered.

She was as indigenous to America as palms to a Florida coastline, and as the nation's most peripatetic woman, she brought her warmth, sincerity, zeal and patience to every corner of the land and to much of the world.

Her seemingly ceaseless activity and energy provoked both a kind of dazzled admiration and numberless "Eleanor" jokes, particularly in the nineteen-thirties and forties. The derision fell away at the end; the admiration deepened.

Held in High Esteem

After her husband's death and a career as mistress of the White House that shattered precedents with a regularity never approached by Abigail Adams and Dolley Madison, President Harry S. Truman appointed Mrs. Roosevelt in 1945 a delegate to the General Assembly.

The esteem in which Mrs. Roosevelt was held in this country was immense, despite intense criticism that some observers held stemmed from persons who differed politically and ideologically with her husband. She was accused of stimulating racial prejudices, of meddling in politics, talking too much, traveling too much, being too informal and espousing causes critics felt a mistress of the White House should have left alone. She even became what she called a "phony issue" in her husband's campaigns for re-election.

On the other hand, she was hailed by countless numbers as their personal champion in a world first depression-ridden, then war-torn and finally maladjusted in the postwar years. She was a symbol of the new role women were to play in the world. As a result of her work in the United Nations, particularly in behalf of the little peoples of the world, this esteem soon transcended national barriers to become virtually worldwide.

Although she was no longer First Lady, her influence had diminished but little.

A typical example of the kind of enthusiasm she could arouse abroad, one among many examples, occurred during Mrs. Roosevelt's visit to Luxembourg in 1950. Perle Mesta was then American Minister to that country.

One of Mrs. Roosevelt's first acts was to call upon the Grand Duchess in her palace—a long call. To catch just a glimpse of her, thousands of Luxembourgers stood outside for hours in an unrelenting rain, calling again and again: "Mees-ees Roose-velt! Mees-ees Roose-velt!"

Thousands more turned out later throughout the tiny country in villages gay with banners and flowers and smiling faces. In her distinctive warbling falsetto, she thanked as many as she could.

Mrs. Roosevelt was an enthusiastic airplane traveler. She went down into the mines. She wandered throughout the world with little ostentation. She maintained a prodigious correspondence.

Her Influence Questioned

The more important chroniclers of Mr. Roosevelt's days in the White House have noted few instances in which it could be established that her counsels were of first importance in changing the tide of affairs. Nor did President Roosevelt always confide in his wife where matters of state were concerned. For example, he did not tell her that he was going to Newfoundland to confer with Prime Minister Winston Churchill of Britain on matters concerning the war. He merely told her that he was "going on a trip through the Cape Cod Canal."

There were, however, many known incidents in which Mrs. Roosevelt was able to direct the President's attention to such matters as injustices done to racial or religious minorities in the armed services or elsewhere in the Government.

With characteristic feminine candor, Mrs. Roosevelt always insisted that she had to do what she felt was right. As a result, injustice and inequality, whether manifested by such diverse agencies as the State Department or the Russians, evoked a strong reaction.

Mrs. Roosevelt got along well with the State Department until the Palestine issue arose. In February and March of 1948 she publicly opposed American policy, which maintained an arms embargo on shipment of arms to Israelis. She also came out in favor of partitioning Palestine into Jewish and Arab states.

While often critical of Soviet tactics, Mrs. Roosevelt consistently urged the United States to continue efforts to end the cold war by negotiation. She also advocated the abandonment of nuclear weapons tests and called for United States recognition of Red China.

Some of the most serious criticism leveled at Mrs. Roosevelt followed her support and sponsorship of a number of groups in which Communists and "fellow-travelers" were active. She often pointed out that she recognized a person's right to be a Communist, provided he did not deny this affiliation. Later, however, she pointed out that experience had taught her that it was impossible to work with Communist-dominated groups.

Took Stand in Column

Her break with groups she once stanchly defended came as the war approached and as she found that several of them were opposed to national defense, lend-lease and the national draft. In August, 1942, after the United States had become an ally of Russia in the war, she made her position even clearer by formally repudiating the left wing of the American Labor party and by supporting the right wing in a primary fight.

Mrs. Roosevelt addressing the Democratic National Convention in 1940.

In 1949 Mrs. Roosevelt became embroiled in a bitter controversy with Cardinal Spellman, Roman Catholic Archbishop of New York. It followed some remarks she had made against use of Federal funds for parochial schools.

In discussing a measure for aid to education then before Congress, Mrs. Roosevelt wrote in her "My Day" column that "those of us who believe in the right of any human being to belong to whatever church he sees fit, and to worship God in his own way, cannot be accused of prejudice when we do not want to see public education connected with religious control of the schools, which are paid for by taxpayers' money."

The Cardinal accused Mrs. Roosevelt of ignorance and prejudice and called her columns "documents of discrimination unworthy of an American mother."

The dispute was ultimately resolved amicably, but not before it was waged by leading members of the clergy and became an issue in the 1948 campaign as political figures aligned themselves for and against Mrs. Roosevelt. It ended in August of that year when Cardinal Spellman called on Mrs. Roosevelt at her Hyde Park home and both issued statements clarifying what they said had been a "misunderstanding."

Her service as a delegate to the United Nations began under President Truman in 1947 and ended, temporarily, in 1952. In 1961, President Kennedy appointed her as one of five members of the United States delegation to the 15th session of the General Assembly.

In the intervening years, Mrs. Roosevelt devoted herself to her syndicated newspaper column and to the American Association for the United Nations. When leading Democrats formed the National Issues Committee in an effort to restore Democratic control of the Federal Government, she accepted its national chairmanship.

Mrs. Roosevelt never lost interest in the Democratic party. She addressed its national convention in 1952 and 1956, and both years campaigned for Adlai E. Stevenson. At the 1960 convention in Los Angeles, she pressed for a Stevenson-Kennedy ticket and seconded Mr. Stevenson's nomination.

Throughout her years of association with the party, Mrs. Roosevelt had been identified with its liberal wing. In 1959, speaking at a dinner in honor of her 75th birthday, she took sharp issue with former President Truman, who also addressed the dinner. Mr. Truman lashed out at "hot-house liberals" whom he accused of hurting the cause of liberalism and inviting the way for reaction. Mrs. Roosevelt replied, saying: "I know we need a united party. But it cannot be a united party

(continued)

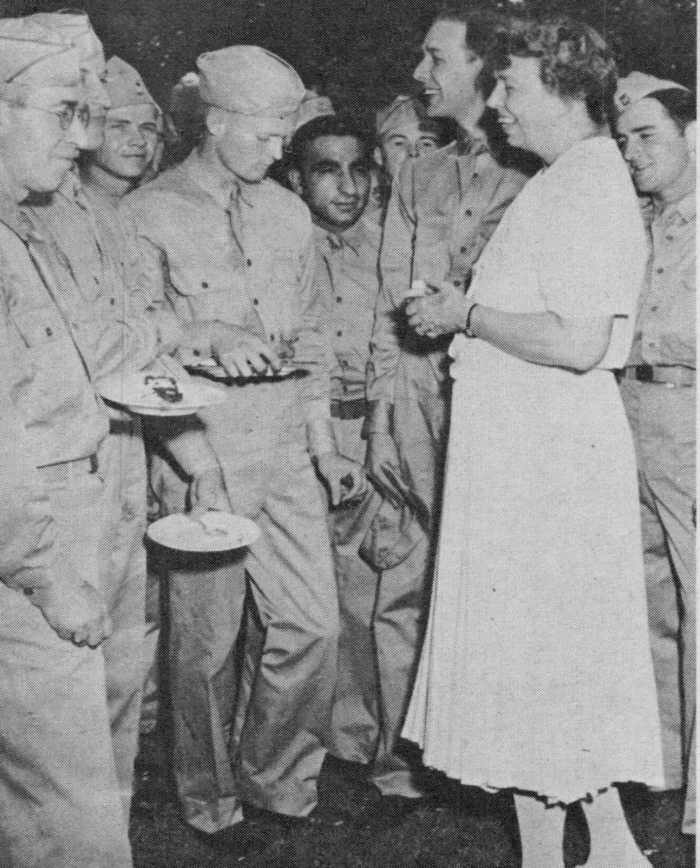

Mrs. Roosevelt visits the troops in the South Pacific during World War II.

that gives up its principles."

The same year she joined with former Senator Herbert H. Lehman in a drive to consolidate the Democratic reform movement in New York City to oust Carmine G. De Sapio, leader of Tammany Hall.

The next year she again aligned herself with the reform group and stumped for Senator John F. Kennedy. Her most recent political activity was as a leader, with Mr. Lehman, of the reform faction during the 1961 mayorality race in New York and during the 1962 primaries. Her candidate in 1961, Mayor Wagner, won re-election by more than 400,000 votes.

Theodore Roosevelt's Niece

Anna Eleanor Roosevelt was born to Elliott and Anna Hall Roosevelt in New York on Oct. 11, 1884. Theodore Roosevelt, the 25th President, was her uncle. The families of both her parents were prominent socially, the Roosevelts a wealthy family of Dutch descent and the Halls of the same family as Philip Livingston, the English-descended signer of the Declaration of Independence.

Mrs. Roosevelt's father was known as a sportsman and big-game hunter, and her mother was a noted beauty of the day. When Eleanor was 8 her mother died, and the young girl went to live with her maternal grandmother, Mrs. Valentine G. Hall, at Tivoli, N. Y., not far from Poughkeepsie. Her father died a year and a half later.

She was taught at home by tutors for the most part, and she recalled later in her autobiography, "This Is My Story," that her real education did not begin until she went abroad at the age of 15.

As a child she worried becausse her mother and other members of her family were somewhat disappointed in young Eleanor's appearance. When she was 15 the family decided that it would be better to supplement her social chances by a finishing trip abroad. In 1899 she was taken to England and placed in Allenswood, a school conducted by a Miss Souvestre, whom her grandmother remembered as a stimulating and cultured lady who had instructed her in her own youth.

She remained abroad for three years, studying languages, literature and history under Miss Souvestre, perfecting her French and Italian, and spending her vacations traveling on the Continent and absorbing European culture. She was drilled in the French system of acquiring and repeating precise judgments on everything.

At the age of 18 she was brought back to New York for her debut. "It was simply awful," she said in a public discussion once. "It was a beautiful party, of course, but I was so unhappy, because a girl who comes out is so utterly miserable if she does not know all the young people. Of course I had been so long abroad that I had lost touch with all the girls I used to know in New York. I was miserable through all that."

She was relieved of her misery within two years by meeting Franklin Delano Roosevelt, who had graduated from Harvard in 1904 and had come to New York to attend the Columbia Law School. He was serious-minded and intent on a career. He found Miss Roosevelt good company.

Besides, the two Roosevelts were distant cousins; they had met first when he was 4 years old and she 2; and they got along easily together. Their relatives approved so highly that the marriage followed naturally. President Roosevelt came from the White House to New York on March 17, 1905, to give the bride in marriage.

After the wedding, a brilliant social event in New York, Mrs. Roosevelt passed into domesticity and maternity for a score of years. The couple's first child, Anna, was born in 1906. Eighteen months later a son, James was born. A second son, named Franklin D. Jr., died three months after birth. Three more sons, Elliott, another Franklin D. Jr. and John Aspinwall, were born during the first 11 years of marriage.

Eleanor Roosevelt at the age of 6, is seen with her father.

Eleanor and Franklin D. Roosevelt, 1920.

Mrs. Roosevelt had her first brush with politics and government in 1911 after Mr. Roosevelt had been elected a State Senator and the family moved to Albany. In 1913 the Roosevelts went to Washington when the future President was appointed Assistant Secretary of the Navy in the Wilson Administration. In 1920 she saw more of the political scene when her husband was a candidate for the Vice Presidency on the Democratic ticket with James M. Cox, who ran for President against Warren G. Harding.

The next year poliomyelitis struck her husband, and Mrs. Roosevelt attended him and encouraged him for three years until it was evident that any further recovery would come slowly through the remainder of his life.

It was at this point that Mrs. Roosevelt emerged seriously in search of a career. Friends of the family and Mr. Roosevelt's physicians urged Mrs. Roosevelt to work with her husband in an effort to rekindle his interests. Some observers felt that shortly thereafter her determined introduction of activity after activity into her own life and his was a deliberate maneuver to rescue him from his invalidism, and force him to resume his former interest in affairs of the outside world.

Began Political Activity

She took part in political discussion with other women after several years of suffrage, and pointed out in those early years, prophetically perhaps, that "women were not utilizing their opportunity to elevate politics." She joined the board of the League of Women Voters, took part in work of the Women's Trade Union League, and beginning in 1924 took an active role in the state and national committees of the Democratic party.

Mrs. Roosevelt continued to increase her activity with lectures, parties and speeches in the interest of popular political enlightenment, education and welfare. In 1926, with Marion Dickerman, she founded the Valkill Shop, a nonprofit furniture factory near the Roosevelt home in Hyde Park, to give employment to disabled men in the manufacture of early American furniture. A year later, with Miss Dickerman and Nancy Cook, she bought the Todhunter School, a New York private school for girls, and Mrs Roosevelt became director and teacher of classes in modern history and current events.

She withdrew from politics with the election of her husband as Governor of New York in 1928, but despite this withdrawal she enlarged her interests. She was busier than ever acquiring ideas and spreading them. She became a director of the Foreign Policy Association and of the City Housing Corporation. In addition, she became a syndicated newspaper columnist, edited a magazine and judged contests.

On March 4, 1933, her husband was inaugurated as the 32d President, and Eleanor Roosevelt began her 12 years as the First Lady. At the White House she established a weekly conference with the press, the first of its kind ever held by a First Lady, and attended only by women journalists.

The White House became a somewhat different place under the influence of Mrs. Roosevelt. Except for the formal occasions and official events, there was a gay informality about it, with grandchildren and an odd assortment of dogs scampering through its halls. Visitors were frequent and, Mrs. Roosevelt once laughingly remarked, "We call it a hotel."

Broadened Her Writings

In 1939 the nation noted a change in Mrs. Roosevelt's newspaper writings. Until then she had devoted the bulk of her space to women. In 1939 her columns began discussing the Works Progress Administration, United States neutrality and other current topics, with the result that political observers noted that what she had to say either anticipated or supplemented the President's statements. Concomitantly, she found herself more and more in the field of controversy.

The same year Mrs. Roosevelt announced in her column her resignation from the Daughters of the American Revolution because the society had refused the use of Constitution Hall in Washington for a concert by Marian Anderson, the Negro contralto.

As the war came she saw her four sons go into the service. She was an active interventionist even before Pearl Harbor. In 1941 she took her first "government job," as assistant director of civilian defense, with the late Mayor Fiorello H. La Guardia of New York as director. It was not a happy experience.

In its early stages, the civilian defense effort was chaotic, and whether the responsibility lay with the directors was never established. Mrs. Roosevelt resigned in February, 1942, after a storm arose over her appointment of Mayris Chaney, a dancer and protégée of hers, to a post with the Office of Civil Defense.

Flew to Visit England

Mrs. Roosevelt flew to England in October, 1942, becoming the first First Lady who had ever gone abroad alone and also the first First Lady to fly the Atlantic.

On her English visit she toured training camps of American troops and was greeted with shouts of "Hi, Eleanor!" She saw several of the many orphaned children she adopted for the duration of the war, was a guest at Buckingham Palace and visited widely.

Mrs. Roosevelt was the author of numerous children's books and records. She also published "India and the Awakening East," "You Learn by Living" and two volumes of autobiography, "This I Remember" and "On My Own."

She had just passed her 78th birthday—and had just left the hospital—when her last book was published. Entitled "Eleanor Roosevelt's Book of Common Sense Etiquette," it held that true good manners consist of sincere goodwill and of being oneself.

Mrs. Roosevelt held honorary degrees from Russell Sage College, the John Marshall College of Law and Oxford University. She was an honorary member of Phi Beta Kappa.

She also received many awards, including the 1939 award from the Humanitarians, the 1939 Churchman's Award, the first annual Nation Award in 1940 and the first annual Franklin Delano Roosevelt Brotherhood Award in 1946.

Others were the Award of Merit of the New York City Federation of Women's Clubs in 1948, the Four Freedoms Award in 1950, the Prince Carl Medal (Sweden) in 1950 and the Irving Geist Foundation Award in 1950.

As First Lady, Mrs. Roosevelt played an active role. Here she is seen wearing a miner's cap on a visit to a coal mine in 1933.

"All the News That's Fit to Print"

The New York Times.

LATE CITY EDITION
Clearing and warm today.
Fair, continued warm tomorrow.
Temperatures Yesterday—Max., 74; Min., 54
Sunrise today, 6:21 A. M.; Sunset, 7:32 P. M.

VOL. XCIV...No. 31,856. Entered as Second-Class Matter, Postoffice, New York, N. Y. NEW YORK, FRIDAY, APRIL 13, 1945. THREE CENTS IN NEW YORK CITY

PRESIDENT ROOSEVELT IS DEAD; TRUMAN TO CONTINUE POLICIES; 9TH CROSSES ELBE, NEARS BERLIN

U. S. AND RED ARMIES DRIVE TO MEET

Americans Across the Elbe in Strength Race Toward Russians Who Have Opened Offensive From Oder

WEIMAR TAKEN, RUHR POCKET SLASHED

Third Army Reported 19 Miles From Czechoslovak Border—British Drive Deeper in the North, Seizing Celle—Canadians Freeing Holland

By DREW MIDDLETON
By Wireless to THE NEW YORK TIMES.

PARIS, April 12—Thousands of tanks and a half million doughboys of the United States First, Third and Ninth Armies are racing through the heart of the Reich on a front of 150 miles, threatening Berlin, Leipzig and the last citadels of the Nazi power.

The Second Armored Division of the Ninth Army has crossed the Elbe River in force and is striking eastward toward Berlin, whose outskirts lie less than sixty miles to the east, according to reports from the front. [A report quoted by The United Press placed the Americans less than fifty miles from the capital.] Beyond Berlin the First White Russian Army has crossed the Oder on a wide front and a junction between the western and eastern Allies is not far off.

[The Moscow radio reported that heavy battles were raging west of the Oder before Berlin, indicating that Marshal Gregory K. Zhukoff had launched his drive toward the Reich's capital. The Soviet communiqué announced further progress by the Red Army forces in and around Vienna.]

Paris is wild with excitement tonight. A special edition of the newspaper France-Soir carries a report by the radio station "Voice of America" that places American forces fifteen and five-eighths miles from Berlin after an airborne landing that had linked up with Lieut. Gen. William H. Simpson's forces advancing eastward from the Elbe. This would put American forces only seventy-five miles from the Red Army vanguard.

No Confirmation at Headquarters

There was no confirmation of this report at Allied Supreme Headquarters, which by its own admission was thirty-six hours behind developments on some sectors of the front.

Resistance was continuing only on the northern and southern flanks. The center had burst wide open. Weimar fell to Lieut. Gen. George S. Patton's infantry, and reports from the front said Erfurt also had been cleared. Schweinfurt and Heilbronn, two German bastions on the south, had fallen to United States Seventh Army forces, who were driving on Bamberg, while farther north Third Army forces were about thirty-five miles from the Czechoslovak frontier in the area east of Coburg.

[The German radio reported American Third Army forces at Lichtenberg, nineteen miles from the Czechoslovak border, The United Press said.]

The offensives to liberate the Netherlands and reduce the Ruhr

Continued on Page 12, Column 2

OUR OKINAWA GUNS DOWN 118 PLANES

Japanese Fliers Start 'Suicide' Attacks on Fleet, Sink a Destroyer, Hit Other Ships

By W. H. LAWRENCE
By Wireless to THE NEW YORK TIMES.

GUAM, Friday, April 13—Japanese attempting to halt the American march to Tokyo, have started "desperate, suicidal" aerial attacks upon our ships and men in the Okinawa area, losing 118 planes on Thursday alone, Fleet Admiral Chester W. Nimitz announced today.

The Japanese succeeded in sinking a destroyer and damaging several other surface units, the communiqué said. All of the damaged vessels remained in action.

It was the first time that the Navy had revealed the suicidal nature of the Japanese air missions against our ships and men. The Japanese radio has been saying that this type of assault was being carried on by a "special attack corps" known in Japanese as "kamakazi," which, translated literally, means "divine wind."

Attack at Low Levels

The Japanese fliers launched their attacks upon our ships and men at a high speed and from low levels, diving directly into a ship or troop concentration to explode their bombs as they crashed.

There was no official estimate of the total number of enemy aircraft engaged in the Okinawa area attack other than the report of the 118 enemy planes destroyed.

Admiral Nimitz reported that the attacks began early on April 12 (Eastern Longitude time) with seven enemy planes shot down during the morning in the vicinity of the Hagushi beaches.

The tempo of the attack was stepped up in the afternoon as the Japanese bore in on our ships in wave after wave. Admiral Nimitz said that ships' guns, carrier aircraft and shore-based anti-aircraft shot down 111 of the attackers.

The revelation of the suicidal Japanese air attacks was the highlight of Admiral Nimitz' regular morning communiqué, which also disclosed the identity of two Marine and two Army divisions that have gone into action on Okinawa. These included the Twenty-seventh Army Division, formed from New York National Guard units, which are seeing action for the first time since the Saipan campaign and previously had engaged in the Gilbert Islands assault. It is com-

Continued on Page 13, Column 2

Army Leaders See Reich End at Hand

By The Associated Press.

WASHINGTON, April 12—High Army officials told Senators today that the end of organized fighting in Germany probably would come within a few days.

Describing the pell-mell dash of American Armies across Germany, General Staff officers expressed the opinion to members of the Senate Military Committee that a collapse of German arms was imminent.

Those who attended said the army chiefs declared that they were so sure of the results that orders had been drawn for a drastic reduction in shipments of durable equipment to Europe.

Franklin Delano Roosevelt
1882-1945

SECURITY PARLEY WON'T BE DELAYED

State Department Urges That World Be Shown We Plan No Changes in Policy

By JAMES B. RESTON
Special to THE NEW YORK TIMES.

WASHINGTON, April 12—The United Nations Security Conference will open in San Francisco on April 25, despite the death of President Roosevelt, Secretary of State Edward R. Stettinius Jr. announced tonight.

Mr. Stettinius said that he had been authorized by President Harry Truman to make this announcement after a meeting of the Cabinet at the White House.

Most of the overseas delegations to the San Francisco conference have either arrived in this country or are now on their way, but while this was said to have been a factor in the decision to proceed with the conference, State Department officials urged that every attempt be made to give immediate evidence to the world that President Roosevelt's foreign policy would be sustained by the new Administration.

President Roosevelt had planned to address the San Francisco conference. His interest in an international organization of nations to maintain peace and security had gone back to his service in the Wilson Administration, when he sat in the gallery of the Senate and listened to the debate that resulted in the rejection of the League of Nations Covenant. He had expressed to friends his desire to participate in the San Francisco conference and to see the United States enter the new league during his term in office.

The sudden elevation of Presi-

Continued on Page 2, Column 1

War News Summarized

FRIDAY, APRIL 13, 1945

President Roosevelt died yesterday afternoon, suddenly and unexpectedly. He was stricken with a massive cerebral hemorrhage at Warm Springs, Ga., on the eve of his greatest military and diplomatic successes—the impending fall of Berlin and the opening of the San Francisco Conference to set up a World Security Organization that would make the world free from martial and economic strife [1:7-8.]

Mr. Roosevelt had been sitting in front of the fireplace of his Little White House, having gone to Warm Springs on March 30 for a three-week rest. About 2:15 Eastern war time he said, "I have a terrific headache," lost consciousness in a few moments and died at 4:35. He was 63 years old. [1:6.]

The tragic word spread quickly around the world. Expressions of sorrow poured in from all sections. [4:5.] American soldiers and sailors refused to believe the reports until there was no longer doubt that their Commander in Chief had gone. [4:2-3.]

Harry S. Truman was sworn in as President at 7:09 o'clock last night, and a few minutes later Mrs. Roosevelt left for Warm Springs. [1:7.] The new President immediately called a Cabinet meeting and declared that Mr. Roosevelt's policies would be continued, that the war would be carried on until Germany and Japan surrendered unconditionally and that the San Francisco Conference would open April 25 as scheduled. [1:3.]

Some 500,000 American soldiers of the Third and Ninth Armies, and thousands of tanks, sped along a 150-mile front toward Berlin and Leipzig. The Ninth, surging across the Elbe, according to delayed reports was less than fifty miles from the German capital and 115 from the Russians along the Oder. The Third Army captured Weimar, home of the late German Republic, and was twenty-three miles below Leipzig, with the First closing a pincers from the north. [1:1-2; map P. 2.]

The Moscow radio reported that the Red Army was waging fierce battles east of Berlin, indicating resumption of the drive on that city. Elsewhere Russian troops scored wide gains and cut the last escape railroad from Vienna. [13:1.]

Open cities were ruled out and every German was ordered by Himmler to fight to the death, although Goebbels said "the war cannot last much longer." [12:6-7.]

The Ninth Air Force destroyed at least 117 more German planes yesterday. [11:8.]

In Italy the Eighth Army advanced along a thirty-mile front toward Bologna and the Po Valley; the Fifth Army also made good gains and was eleven miles from La Spezia. [13:8, with map.]

Japanese planes resumed their suicide attacks on American ships off Okinawa, sinking a destroyer and damaging several other vessels. One hundred and eighteen enemy planes were shot down. [1:2.] The Americal Division invaded Bohol, last of the enemy-held central Philippines. [18:6.] The B-29 attack on Koriyama, 110 miles north of Tokyo, set a new Superfortress distance record. [18:2.]

Secretary of State Stettinius and Secretary of War Stimson, denouncing Germany's "steadily increasing" mistreatment of American prisoners, said those responsible would be brought to justice. [13:6-7.]

Clashes between Right and Left wing elements in Iran were reported from Moscow. [13:2.]

LAST WORDS: 'I HAVE TERRIFIC HEADACHE'

Roosevelt Was Posing for Artist When Hemorrhage Struck—He Died in Bedroom

By The Associated Press.

WARM SPRINGS, Ga., April 12—President Franklin D. Roosevelt's last words were:

"I have a terrific headache."

He spoke them to Comdr. Howard G. Bruenn, naval physician.

Mr. Roosevelt was sitting in front of a fireplace in the Little White House here atop Pine Mountain when what was described as a massive cerebral hemorrhage struck him.

The President's Negro valet, Arthur Prettyman, and a Filipino messboy carried him to his bedroom. He was unconscious at the end. It came without pain.

Dr. Bruenn said that he saw the President this morning and he was in excellent spirits at 9:30 A. M.

"At 1 o'clock," Dr. Bruenn added, "he was sitting in a chair while sketches were being made of him by an artist. He suddenly complained of a very severe occipital headache (back of the head).

"Within a very few minutes he lost consciousness. He was seen by me at 1:30 P. M., fifteen minutes after the episode had started.

"He did not regain consciousness, and he died at 3:35 P. M. (Georgia time)."

The artist sketching Mr. Roosevelt was N. Robbins of 520 West 139th Street, New York.

Only others present in the cottage were Comdr. George Fox, White House pharmacist and long an attendant on the President; William D. Hassett, Presidential secretary; Miss Grace Tully, con-

Continued on Page 4, Column 3

END COMES SUDDENLY AT WARM SPRINGS

Even His Family Unaware of Condition as Cerebral Stroke Brings Death to Nation's Leader at 63

ALL CABINET MEMBERS TO KEEP POSTS

Funeral to Be at White House Tomorrow, With Burial at Hyde Park Home—Impact of News Tremendous

By ARTHUR KROCK
Special to THE NEW YORK TIMES.

WASHINGTON, April 12—Franklin Delano Roosevelt, War President of the United States and the only Chief Executive in history who was chosen for more than two terms, died suddenly and unexpectedly at 4:35 P. M. today at Warm Springs, Ga., and the White House announced his death at 5:48 o'clock. He was 63.

The President, stricken by a cerebral hemorrhage, passed from unconsciousness to death on the eighty-third day of his fourth term and in an hour of high triumph. The armies and fleets under his direction as Commander in Chief were at the gates of Berlin and the shores of Japan's home islands as Mr. Roosevelt died, and the cause he represented and led was nearing the conclusive phase of success.

Less than two hours after the official announcement, Harry S. Truman of Missouri, the Vice President, took the oath as the thirty-second President. The oath was administered by the Chief Justice of the United States, Harlan F. Stone, in a one-minute ceremony at the White House. Mr. Truman immediately let it be known that Mr. Roosevelt's Cabinet is remaining in office at his request, and that he had authorized Secretary of State Edward R. Stettinius Jr. to proceed with plans for the United Nations Conference on international organization at San Francisco, scheduled to begin April 25. A report was circulated that he leans somewhat to the idea of a coalition Cabinet, but this is unsubstantiated.

Funeral Tomorrow Afternoon

It was disclosed by the White House that funeral services for Mr. Roosevelt would take place at 4 P. M. (E. W. T.) Saturday in the East Room of the Executive Mansion. The Rev. Angus Dun, Episcopal Bishop of Washington; the Rev. Howard S. Wilkinson of St. Thomas's Church in Washington and the Rev. John G. McGee of St. John's in Washington will conduct the services.

The body will be interred at Hyde Park, N. Y., Sunday, with the Rev. George W. Anthony of St. James Church officiating. The time has not yet been fixed.

Jonathan Daniels, White House secretary, said Mr. Roosevelt's body would not lie in state. He added that, in view of the limited size of the East Room, which holds only about 200 persons, the list of those attending the funeral services would be limited to high Government officials, representatives of the membership of both

Continued on Page 3, Column 3

TRUMAN IS SWORN IN THE WHITE HOUSE

Members of Cabinet on Hand as Chief Justice Stone Administers the Oath

By C. P. TRUSSELL
Special to THE NEW YORK TIMES.

WASHINGTON, April 12—Vice President Harry S. Truman of Missouri, standing erect, with his sharp features taut and looking straight ahead through his large, round glasses, became the thirty-second President of the United States in a ceremony lasting not more than a minute in the Cabinet Room of the White House at 7:09 o'clock tonight.

The oath was administered by Chief Justice Harlan F. Stone two hours and thirty-four minutes after the sudden death of President Roosevelt at Warm Springs. Mr. Truman had picked up a Bible from the end of the big Cabinet conference table, held it with his left hand and placed his right hand upon the upper cover. After repeating the oath, he bowed his head, lifted the Bible to his lips and kissed it.

Even before he had taken the oath Mr. Truman had asked President Roosevelt's Cabinet to continue in service. He also authorized Edward R. Stettinius Jr., Secretary of State, to announce that the United Nations Conference for International Organization would go on as scheduled.

To the newsmen at the White House he sent this word, through Stephen Early, press secretary:

"For the time being I prefer not to hold a press conference. It will be my effort to carry on as I believe the President would have done, and to that end I have asked the Cabinet to stay on with me."

Soon after he became President, Mr. Truman left the White House for the five-room Connecticut Avenue apartment where he has resided with Mrs. Truman and their 20-year-old daughter, Mary Margaret, for four years. He said he was "going home, to bed."

It was shortly after he had finished presiding over the Senate debate on the United States-Mexican Water Treaty late this afternoon that Mr. Truman received word from the White House of President Roosevelt's death. This was at about 5:15 P. M., a half hour before the news was made public. Reaching for his hat, he dashed out of the office, calling back to his staff that he was going to the White House.

Arriving at the White House, the

Continued on Page 3, Column 6

Byrnes May Take Post With Truman

Special to THE NEW YORK TIMES.

WASHINGTON, April 12—James F. Byrnes, recently resigned as Director of War Mobilization and Reconversion, known to be one of President Truman's warmest friends in official Washington, is expected to be called to the White House for consultation, and possibly to take an important post in the Cabinet, in the immediate future.

President Truman's admiration of former Justice Byrnes is well known here. He undoubtedly would have been Mr. Truman's choice as a successor to Cordell Hull as Secretary of State.

ROOSEVELT IS DEAD; TRUMAN PRESIDENT

Continued From Page 1

houses of Congress, heads of foreign missions, and friends of the family.

President Truman, in his first official pronouncement, pledged prosecution of the war to a successful conclusion. His statement, issued for him at the White House by press secretary Jonathan Daniels, said:

"The world may be sure that we will prosecute the war on both fronts, East and West, with all the vigor we possess to a successful conclusion."

News of Death Stuns Capital

The impact of the news of the President's death on the capital was tremendous. Although rumor and a marked change in Mr. Roosevelt's appearance and manner had brought anxiety to many regarding his health, and there had been increasing speculation as to the effects his death would have on the national and world situation, the fact stunned the Government and the citizens of the capital.

It was not long, however, before the wheels of Government began once more to turn. Mr. Stettinius, the first of the late President's Ministers to arrive at the White House, summoned the Cabinet to meet at once. Mr. Truman, his face gray and drawn, responded to the first summons given to any outside Mr. Roosevelt's family and official intimates by rushing from the Capitol.

Mrs. Roosevelt had immediately given voice to the spirit that animated the entire Government, once the first shock of the news had passed. She cabled to her four sons, all on active service:

"He did his job to the end as he would want you to do. Bless you all and all our love. Mother."

Those who have served with the late President in peace and in war accepted that as their obligation. The comment of members of Congress unanimously reflected this spirit. Those who supported or opposed Mr. Roosevelt during his long and controversial years as President did not deviate in this. And all hailed him as the greatest leader of his time.

FAMILY OF WEALTH GAVE ADVANTAGES

Roosevelt at Age of 3 Began to Travel Abroad—'Gold Coast' Man at College

INSURGENT IN LEGISLATURE

Defeat for the Vice Presidency in 1920 Followed by Attack of Infantile Paralysis

The early life of Franklin Delano Roosevelt was typical of a member of a family of wealth and assured social position—an aristocratic family, as aristocracy is measured on this side of the Atlantic.

His birthplace was a stately mansion on the Roosevelt estate, overlooking the Hudson River and set in the midst of broad acres near Hyde Park. The property had been in the possession of his family for a hundred years.

He was born on Jan. 30, 1882, the only child of James and Sara Delano Roosevelt. His father's family was of Dutch descent and made its first appearance in America in 1654. The Delanos, from whom his mother sprung, were of Flemish origin and had followed a migratory group into Massachusetts even earlier than the Roosevelts came to New York.

The god-father of Mr. Roosevelt when he was christened in the St. James Episcopal Church at Hyde Park was Elliott Roosevelt, only brother of the elder Theodore Roosevelt. His father was a fourth cousin of the elder T. R.

The family, when Franklin Delano Roosevelt was born, was moderately wealthy. James Roosevelt, his father, had been president of the Louisville & New Albany Railroad and was vice president of the Delaware & Hudson. He had inherited some wealth. His health was not of the best, he had little taste for business and retired rather early to lead the life of a country gentleman on the family estate. Like Franklin D., his father and grandfather before him had been Democrats.

Early Education at Home

He received his early education at home from tutors and was said to have mastered French, German and Spanish. At 14 he entered Groton to prepare for Harvard. He was 18 when he entered that ancient university and became one of the envied dwellers on the "Gold Coast."

At Harvard Franklin D. Roosevelt became a member of the select clubs, including the Hasty Pudding. In Greek fraternities he qualified for Alpha Delta Phi and by the time he was graduated he had won the coveted key of Phi Beta Kappa. In his last year at Harvard he was president and editor of The Harvard Crimson. He was graduated in 1904.

Turning his back on Annapolis and a prospective naval career, he entered the Columbia Law School, completed his studies and passed his bar examination in 1907. He went to work as a clerk in the law firm of Carter, Ledyard & Milburn, later establishing a law partnership of his own. He did not stay long at the practice of law, however.

Married While Law Student

While still a student of law at Columbia, Franklin D. Roosevelt married his sixth cousin. Miss Anna Eleanor Roosevelt was the daughter of Elliott Roosevelt, who was the godfather of Franklin D. She was the favorite niece of the elder Theodore Roosevelt, who, President of the United States at the time, gave the bride in marriage. The wedding was in this city on March 17, 1905. They had five children: James, Anna, who became Mrs. Curtis B. Dall of New York and later Mrs. John Boettiger; Elliott, Franklin D. Jr. and John A. Roosevelt.

The year 1910 was a turning point in politics in this State, when after a generation of Republican rule at the Capitol the Democrats took over control of both the executive branch of the State Government and the legislative. The period found the youthful Roosevelt, then only 28, running for State Senator from his home district, made up of the counties of Dutchess, where the Roosevelts lived, Columbia and Putnam. Normally a strongly Republican district, Mr. Roosevelt carried it. Two years later he was re-elected by an even more substantial majority.

When the time had come to stand for re-election, Mr. Roosevelt was confined to a sickbed and the fight was made for him by the late Col. Henry McHenry Howe. Colonel Howe who became secretary to the President when Mr. Roosevelt assumed office, was largely instrumental, through management of the pre-convention campaign activities, in obtaining for his chief the Presidential nomination in 1932. Colonel Howe died in 1935.

Leads Insurgent Group

Almost unknown outside the district, the young Democratic Senator from Dutchess went to Albany to take his seat soon after Jan. 1, 1911. Before many days he had attracted nation-wide attention by assuming the leadership of a group of insurgents in the Legislature which he had mustered and which revolted against Tammany Hall and its leader, Charles F. Murphy, then at the heyday of his power, over a Tammany proposal to send William F. (Blue-eyed Billy) Sheehan to the United States Senate.

It was the last time a United States Senator was elected in this State by joint ballot of the Legislature. The Republicans, in a minority, were pledged to the re-election of Chauncey M. Depew. At its beginning the fight started by young Roosevelt seemed a forlorn hope. The insurgent group was in a small minority and with the caucus resorted to, the election of Mr. Sheehan seemed certain, despite a State-wide wave of protest against his election on the ground that he was too close to Mr. Murphy and, indeed, to the Tammany organization.

FDR with his mother at age 11.

But prior to the caucus the nineteen Democratic legislators of the insurgent group bound themselves to oppose the election of Mr. Sheehan to the end. They held the balance of power on a joint ballot. They remained out of the caucus. Nothing that Mr. Murphy could do or say made any difference to Mr. Roosevelt and his insurgent flock. For sixty ballots and almost three months the conflict raged.

The insurgents had a candidate of their own, Edward M. Shepard. With Mr. Sheehan he was killed off in the contest, which ended in an honorable compromise with the election of James A. O'Gorman on the sixty-fourth ballot. From this period dated the first acquaintance of Franklin D. Roosevelt and Alfred E. Smith, who was Democratic floor leader and later became speaker of the Assembly.

Fought Tammany as Senator

All through his service in the State Senate Franklin D. Roosevelt fought Tammany, then firmly in control of both branches of the Legislature. He voted for a direct primary bill, although it was but a half-way measure, grudgingly supported by Tammany. He opposed a number of Tammany grab bills.

Tammany Hall was opposed to the nomination of Woodrow Wilson for President and the delegation from this State was lined up for Champ Clark, then speaker of the House of Representatives. Anti-Tammany Democrats throughout the State, however, favored Mr. Wilson, and Franklin D. Roosevelt took his stand with this group.

At Baltimore, where the 1912 Democratic National Convention was held, Mr. Roosevelt, although not a delegate, was active in behalf of Mr. Wilson, who was nominated and elected in that year of the Bull Moose exodus from the Republican party led by another Roosevelt. His reward, after Woodrow Wilson had taken office, was the appointment to be Assistant Secretary of the Navy.

The World War broke out in 1914, about fifteen months after Mr. Roosevelt had become Assistant Secretary of the Navy. But in advance of hostilities in Europe and the entry of the United States into the great conflict, the Wilson Democrats in this State had a score to settle with Tammany Hall.

He was the candidate of the anti-Tammany wing for United States Senator in the Democratic primary, held Sept. 28, 1914, but was defeated by James W. Gerard, later Ambassador to Germany.

Sought to Sway Hoover

In Washington during the years that followed he was drawn into close and friendly relations with Herbert Hoover, who was to be an opponent in the 1932 fight over the Presidency. Mr. Roosevelt sought to prevail upon Mr. Hoover to become a Democrat with a view to grooming him for the Democratic nomination for President in 1924, and actually thought he had succeeded when Republicans of prominence managed to persuade Mr. Hoover that he would profit politically by becoming a Republican. The rest is history.

Came 1920 and another Presidential contest. The Democrats nominated Gov. James M. Cox of Ohio for first place on their ticket. Mr. Roosevelt drew second place. The campaign that followed was fought on the Wilson record during his two administrations and on the League of Nations, the Republicans having taken their stand definitely against the United States joining the League.

A keen believer in the Wilson policies and the peace mission of the League, Mr. Roosevelt took up the party fight. He toured the country in a special train and kept up the fighting until the eve of the election. Friends of Mr. Roosevelt gave him credit for something like 1,000 speeches, short and long, in the course of his campaign for the Vice Presidency.

The Republican landslide marked Mr. Roosevelt's second defeat for public office. He had won two. With five children to rear, Mr. Roosevelt returned to the practice of law, resuming a partnership with the firm of Emmet, Marvin & Roosevelt. He also accepted a position as vice president with the Fidelity and Deposit Company of Maryland. At about that time, too, he was elected an overseer at Harvard. He also undertook the task of reorganizing the Boy Scout organization in the country, and he became chairman of a committee created to raise funds for the Woodrow Wilson Foundation.

Stricken by Paralysis

Then, in August, 1921, came his tragic illness of infantile paralysis, which at first threatened to end his career and possibly even his life, **but which later came to be regarded as the turning point from which began his upward climb to the White House.** With members of his family he was swimming near his summer home at Campobello, N. B., when he was stricken. The next day he felt a stiffness, as if a cold were coming on. On the second morning he could not get out of bed. His leg muscles were paralyzed.

The attack was serious. It was with extreme difficulty that he was brought back to New York, where he could receive the most skillful medical treatment obtainable. For months his life was despaired of, then the progress of the dread disease was arrested. After a truly epic fight for health he began to recover. The optimism which was a cardinal trait in his make-up, his patience and his courage were powerful allies in the battle. He was paralyzed from the waist down. It was almost a year before he could move about at all with the aid of crutches. But he never gave in. To a man in love with outdoor life, swimming, sailing, tennis and riding, the ordeal was doubly trying.

It was at this time that he "discovered" Warm Springs, Ga., and the health-giving qualities of its waters in cases such as his. He went to Warm Springs and spent much time swimming in the pool. Gradually he regained in part the use of his legs. He discarded his crutches and was able to move about with the aid of canes and steel braces which had been fitted to his lower limbs. The process of recovery, however, took years.

RISE TO PRESIDENCY FOLLOWED ILLNESS

Political Activities Maintained Through Convalescence—Pioneered for Smith

The foundations of his political career were laid by Franklin Delano Roosevelt while he convalesced from infantile paralysis and in the three years he was absent from the public scene, from 1921 to 1924, he maintained close contact with the key figures in the Democratic party.

Among the first to advance the name of Alfred E. Smith as a Presidential possibility, Mr. Roosevelt seconded his nomintaion in 1920 at the Democratic convention in San Francisco, and four years later he was carried into Madison Square Garden to bring his name before that convention. His polished and telling speeches and his appealing manner brought Mr. Roosevelt thunderous ovations. In 1928, when Mr. Smith finally won the Democratic nomination at Houston, it again was Mr. Roosevelt who placed his name before the delegates.

After the Houston convention Mr. Roosevelt spent some time over important work at the eastern headquarters of the Democratic National Committee in New York, but in September he went to Warm Springs for rest and to promote recovery. He was there when the Democratic State Convention was held. There were a number of aspirants for the Governorship nomination. On one ground or another they were all found wanting and in turn eliminated.

The name of Franklin D. Roosevelt had been in the minds of all the party leaders, but he had made it known to them that he would not under any circumstances enter the field. Finally Alfred E. Smith got on the long-distance telephone and, on the plea that his candidacy would greatly strengthen the national ticket, wrung from him a reluctant consent to run for Governor.

Elected Governor of New York

Mr. Roosevelt was nominated. He did not permit his physical handicap to stand in the way of vigorous campaigning. He toured the State from end to end, by train and by automobile. On Election Day he carried the State by a plurality of a little more than 25,000, while Governor Smith lost his own State to Hoover by an adverse plurality of more than 103,000.

When he took office as Governor Mr. Roosevelt found himself, as had Governor Smith before him, with a Republican Legislature on his hands. A Republican Legislature had proved a foil and a great help to Governor Smith in advancing his political fortunes. It was destined to be of equal service to Governor Roosevelt.

Much of his legislative program during his first term in office consisted of unfinished business from the three preceding Smith administrations. But he initiated many measures of importance and some of these he forced through the Legislature.

He submitted in a revamped form to the Legislature the Smith proposal for development and operation under State auspices of a water power plant on the St. Lawrence River and before his first term was over had received legislative sanction for a commission of his own choice to investigate the subject and recommend a plan. This was followed during his second term with a further concession which made possible the creation of the St. Lawrence Power Authority, which, before Mr Roosevelt left Albany to step into the Presidency, already was engaged in preliminary negotiations and other labors for the realization of the huge State power project. This was a victory which his resourceful predecessor had not been able to wrest from a hostile Republican Legislature.

Mr. Roosevelt had not been long in office before he demonstrated his huge capacity for work and his consummate skill as a politician. He set himself at once to the upbuilding of the Democratic party in the State, outside the City of New York, a field that Mr. Smith, astute politician that he was, had refused to cultivate, preferring to depend upon his huge vote in the cities for successive victories.

Mr. Roosevelt wooed the farmer, backbone of the Republican political strength in the State, by an extensive program for farm relief. He reaped a rich reward in votes when he ran for Governor the second time in 1930, receiving a huge plurality of 725,000 votes, of which almost 175,000 was supplied by voters outside of New York City, an unparalleled feat.

(continued)

Mr. Roosevelt's greatest triumph during his two terms as Governor undoubtedly was his victory in the long drawn out controversy over water power. In many of the reforms he recommended he was blocked by hostile Legislatures. But a long list of measures to his credit made his service in the Governor's office one of notable achievement, although it left a big hole in the State treasury. His successor, Gov. Herbert H. Lehman, was called upon to wipe out an inherited deficit of more than $100,000,000 when he took office in 1933.

Mr. Roosevelt faced a delicate situation as Governor in connection with disclosures of corruption in the New York City government, dominated by Tammany Hall, which were made in the winter of 1931. The Republicans in the Legislature by concurrent resolution created an investigating committee, of which Senator Samuel H. Hofstadter, New York City Republican, became chairman and Samuel Seabury, former judge of the Court of Appeals and an anti-Tammany Democrat, became counsel.

In the face of an insistent clamor for action by reform elements and the press, Mr. Roosevelt for a time remained silent and inactive. But when charges of official dereliction were presented to him against Thomas C. T. Crain, the Tammany-sponsored District Attorney of New York County, he appointed ex-Judge Seabury to sit as a commissioner, review the evidence and make a report. This did not recommend the removal from office of Mr. Crain, although it censured his administration of the prosecutor's office.

And when as the result of disclosures by the Hofstadter committee a demand was made for the removal of Sheriff Thomas M. Farley, another Tammany office holder, and finally of Mayor James J. Walker, Governor Roosevelt himself sat and heard the evidence, ordering the removal of the Sheriff, while Mayor Walker anticipated an adverse decision from the Governor by resigning his office.

The Walker hearing was not held until after Mr. Roosevelt had received the Democratic nomination for President, with Tammany's delegation and that of John H. McCooey from Kings voting against him on every ballot. In the Farley case Mr. Roosevelt delivered an opinion that holders of office should properly be held to a higher standard of conduct in relation to their financial affairs than was required by law from the private citizen. Friends of good government hailed this opinion as of the utmost value as a precedent.

Less cordial relations between Governor Roosevelt and Alfred E. Smith had existed ever since Mr. Roosevelt won his first victory as a candidate for Governor, even though it was at Mr. Smith's urgent request that Mr. Roosevelt made the run.

Friends of both men, realizing their different outlook on life and on many public questions and the different environment from which they had sprung, had marveled at how they could be drawn very closely together. As a matter of fact the depth or warmth of the feeling they entertained for each other had never been subjected to an acid test. The demonstrations of friendship had been mostly on public occasions of political portent, when such a display might have been a matter of expediency to one or both.

In 1924, when Mr. Roosevelt was head and front of the pre-convention movement for the nomination of Mr. Smith, he was not ready to make a drive for the nomination himself. Nor was he in 1928. The crushing defeat sustained by Mr. Smith in that campaign, with loss of half of the electoral vote from the South, did not come as a surprise to Mr. Roosevelt. The defeat of Mr. Smith and his own victory as a candidate for Governor in that year in effect opened the way for him to the White House four years later. Mr. Smith, following these development, sensed in Mr. Roosevelt a rival for the high honor he had not then as yet lost hope of winning for himself.

Mr. Smith for months held back and it was not until late in the campaign that he consented to make some speeches for Mr. Roosevelt. He became active only after their common interest in the nomination and election of Herbert H. Lehman as Governor had brought them together in a concerted move at the Democratic State Convention in 1932 to outflank Tammany and its allies, who had taken a stand in opposition to the nomination of Mr. Lehman.

At the Democratic National Convention in Chicago some months earlier Mr. Smith made a fight for the nomination against Mr. Roosevelt which was fraught with bitterness on both sides. And after Mr. Roosevelt on the fourth ballot had received 945 votes in the convention out of a total of 1,154 and was declared the nominee, no motion came from Mr. Smith, who had the next largest vote, 190½, to make the vote unanimous.

Immediately after his nomination, Mr. Roosevelt shattered precedent by proceeding with Mrs. Roosevelt and some other members of his family by air to Chicago, where he was received with tumultuous enthusiasm when he appeared at the Stadium before the delegates who had nominated him and made his speech of acceptance.

In this address he sounded what subsequent utterances demonstrated to be the keynote of his campaign. He came out in full acceptance of his party's national platform, was more outspoken on the question of prohibition than at any time before and declared that he was not a worshiper of precedent or "foolish" tradition if they stood in the way of social and economic reconstruction of the country. He again sprang to the defense of his "forgotten man."

Carries Forty-two States

At the close of the Presidential contest Mr. Roosevelt carried forty-two States. The remaining six, Connecticut, Delaware, Maine, New Hampshire, Pennsylvania and Vermont, gave their electoral votes to Mr. Hoover.

The months that intervened between Mr. Roosevelt's election and his inauguration were occupied by an intensive study of national and international problems, and a preparation of remedial measures for meeting the critical situation. In this study Mr. Roosevelt was assisted by a group of advisers popularly nicknamed the "Brain Trust," composed of college professors and technical experts in various fields of government.

Prominent in this group of advisers were three former Columbia professors, Raymond Moley, Rexford G. Tugwell and A. A. Berle Jr.; Dr. Mordecai Ezekiel, vice president of the American Statistical Society, and William C. Bullitt, a writer who as far back as during the Wilson Administration at Washington had figured in confidential foreign missions.

About three weeks before his inauguration, on Feb. 15, 1933, Mr. Roosevelt had a narrow and miraculous escape from death at the hand of an assassin. This was at Miami, Fla. Mr. Roosevelt was returning from a pleasure cruise in West Indian waters aboard Vincent Astor's yacht, the Nourmahal. He had landed and was on his way to board a train to carry him north, when he stopped to deliver an open-air address at Bay Front Park, in acknowledgment of a continuous ovation that he had received while motoring to the railroad station.

During the address the would-be assassin fired several shots into the multitude, with the design to kill the President-elect. The wielder of the deadly weapon, Giuseppe Zangara of Hackensack, N. J., was prevented from accomplishing what he had set out to do only because a woman in the crowd seized him by the arm and deflected his aim. The next moment a Miami policeman pounced on him and felled him. He was arrested.

On investigation he proved to be an anarchist and a man crazed by bodily pain. Several persons were wounded; Anton Cermak, the Democratic Mayor of Chicago, who had been standing by the side of Mr. Roosevelt, fatally. Zangara within the month was tried, convicted and executed.

Mr. Roosevelt in this crucial test showed the greatest coolness and courage, both during and after the shooting, driving at once to the hospital where the victims of the assassin had been taken for treatment.

Conferred Twice With Hoover

Momentous events occurred between Mr. Roosevelt's election and his inauguration on March 4. Although Mr. Roosevelt's term as Governor of New York State did not expire until Dec. 31, 1932, on Nov. 12 President Hoover addressed a communication to him at Albany reporting the request of foreign Governments for suspension of their war debt payments. The President also invited the President-elect with "any of the Democratic Congressional leaders" to confer at the White House on the foreign debt situation and other phases of the general economic situation, which was becoming acute.

Mr. Roosevelt had two conferences with President Hoover, one on Nov. 22 and another on Jan. 20. He declined, however, to join President Hoover in a joint statement calling upon the country to remain calm in the crisis. Mr. Roosevelt explained later that he did not consent to such joint action because he was a private citizen without any authority in the nation's affairs At the time many of his supporters believed that he declined because he saw no reason why he should assume responsibility for a situation that he believed was due in part to the acts or omissions of President Hoover.

Between Jan. 1, 1930, and March 3, 1933, the day before Mr. Roosevelt became President, 5,504 banks, with a total of deposits of $3,432,000,000 had closed their doors. The country was in the grip of fear bordering on panic.

COUNTRY REVIVED BY FIRST INAUGURAL

'Only Thing We Have to Fear Is Fear Itself' Set Pattern for Fight on Depression

In his first inaugural address, directed to a nation racked and ravaged by the greatest depression in history, President Roosevelt demonstrated that he had a considered plan for the nation's recovery. His outstanding declaration was that "the only thing we have to fear is fear itself."

That memorable address, delivered in fighting words on March 4, 1933, set the pattern for most of the accomplishments of his first term, and also for many of the events in later administrations. In it, he intimated that if remedial legislation enacted by Congress should prove inadequate to the occasion he would ask that he be vested with executive power as broad as if the country were at war.

He attacked the selfish interests, "the unscrupulous money changers," to whom he attributed the economic depression. He asserted that these interests having "fled from their high seats in the temple of our administration," there was no recourse other than to have the Government assume the task of putting men to work, by direct recruiting if necessary. He dedicated the nation to a world "good-neighbor" policy.

With this revolutionary address behind him, he lost no time in calling the Congress into extraordinary session on March 9 and, within the next one hundred days, the Congress, at his urging, enacted more legislation than in any like period in American history. Much of it was in fulfillment of pledges made in the Democratic national platform.

Legislation Enacted

This legislation included:

Ratification by Congress of all the steps taken by the President in proclamations dealing with the banking crisis, before the special session was convened, including the ending of gold as a medium of exchange, and later steps taking the country off the gold standard, plus emergency control of virtually all banking transactions.

An economy bill, cutting governmental expenses and veterans' benefits, most of the economies of which were later dissipated, either by Congressional action or by the President's switch to a spending policy to get the nation's unemployment problem solved.

Legalization of 3.2 per cent beer, before the repeal of the Eighteenth Amendment. In this connection it might be noted that the President was credited, in the months that followed, with having been the only man who could have obtained ratification of the repealer amendment, the Twenty-first, as speedily as it was done. Passed by Congress on Feb. 20, 1933, the repeal amendment became effective on Dec. 5 of the same year.

The first Federal farm-subsidy measure, under which the Agricultural Adjustment Administration was set up, giving the Government the right to pay subsidies to farmers for not producing, plus a law for the refinancing of farm mortgages with Federal aid.

The Civilian Conservation Corps law, one of the most successful of the New Deal experiments, in which the younger generation of the unemployed were set up in camps throughout the country and employed in forestry and conservation work.

The Tennessee Valley Authority, under which the vast potential of water-power in the Tennessee Valley was developed as a governmental enterprise.

The first Securities and Exchange Commission law, under which the issuance of securities by corporations became subject to governmental regulation.

The Home Owners Loan Corporation Act, under which hundreds of thousands of private homes were saved for their owners by the Government taking over and refinancing the mortgages at a low rate of interest, and over a twenty-year period. This law created the then new type of mortgage under which equal payments took care of interest and principal until both obligations were wiped out.

Expansion of the activities of the Reconstruction Finance Corporation, set up under the Hoover Administration, so that it could be used to finance a large number of present and future governmental activities by special corporations.

Cancellation of the gold clause in both public and private obligations.

The National Recovery Administration, most short-lived of the emergency legislation, designed to permit industries to govern themselves, and prevent ruinous competition, with Government aid, so that higher wages could be paid and some profits kept. While it had wide public support at the time, it failed to work, and finally was thrown out as unconstitutional by the Supreme Court.

The President also launched the AAA, with Secretary of Agriculture Henry A. Wallace as administrator, in an effort to raise agricultural purchasing power to provide a market for industry. The President began by issuing a decree fixing a processing tax of 4.2 cents a pound on cotton as the first step of his comprehensive farm program. Processing taxes later were placed on other farm staples, such as wheat and corn, in order to pay the expenses of that part of the plan which called for the payment of Federal bounties to farmers signing contracts to restrict production. The purpose was to get rid of surpluses and raise prices. In the fall he authorized the AAA to purchase food and clothing for 3,500,000 families on relief rolls, partly to provide relief and partly to diminish surplus commodity stocks, particularly cotton and pork, which still depressed farm prices.

The President announced in October his plan to buy gold in order to depreciate the value of the dollar and so decrease unemployment in both industry and agriculture, keep commodity prices stable in terms of a managed currency, and make possible the payment of debts at or near the price levels at which they were contracted. He also embarked on a silver purchase program.

Work Relief Is Begun

During the winter of 1933 President Roosevelt started his first national work relief program, headed by Harry L. Hopkins, Federal Emergency Relief Administrator, with a credit of $400,000,000, for the purpose of transferring 4,000,000 needy unemployed from direct relief to work relief. This was known as the Civil Works Administration, with relief as its main purpose, to distinguish it from the Public Works Administration, under Secretary of the Interior Harold L. Ickes, which made relief secondary to the construction of large-scale public works.

The "hundred days" of Congress rounded out a program which vested in a President for the first time in a period of peace powers virtually dictatorial in essence and broad in scope, which wrought changes of a fundamental and revolutionary character in the American plan of government. But the President himself and his political advisers were at pains to emphasize that the grant of power was delegated and strictly within constitutional lines. What Congress had given, Congress could take away. The first measures proposed to Congress were passed by practically unanimous vote. Party lines for the moment seemed forgotten as Mr. Roosevelt's venturesome policies won widespread approval throughout the country. His willingness to assume responsibility, his exhibition of unflinching and unprecedented courage in high office at a time of grave crisis, compelled universal admiration and was reflected in a revival of hope and confidence, at the same time producing a rise in the price of securities on the exchanges.

The first inauguration of Franklin Delano Roosevelt, 32nd President.

Emergency Powers Used to Combat The Depression by Planned Economy

After the adoption of the new legislation, President Roosevelt began to put the New Deal into effect, using his emergency powers to meet the crisis with great vigor, in a broad attempt to defeat the depression by means of a planned economy, and at the same time institute social reforms.

He appointed the dynamic Gen. Hugh A. Johnson as Administrator of NRA, the core of the New Deal.

While the NRA codes for specific industries were being formulated, the President issued decrees providing for a blanket code to raise wages and shorten hours of work, and called on the nation to support NRA in order to obviate strikes and lockouts. The year ended with the President's popularity undiminished.

There was concern over the delegation of "dictatorial" power to the Executive by Congress, but it was generally believed that this was necessary in view of the prompt action needed to combat the emergency on many fronts.

In his message to the first regular session of the Seventy-third Congress on Jan. 3, 1934, President Roosevelt outlined his program of social and economic reforms as well as recovery measures. Two weeks later, in a special message, he asked authority to devaluate the dollar at some point between 50 and 60 per cent of the existing gold standard, to create a stabilization fund of $2,000,000,000 with the profits thus accruing to the Government, in order to protect the dollar in foreign exchange, and to transfer gold holdings from the Federal Reserve Banks to the Treasury. Congress immediately passed a monetary bill granting this authority, and he fixed $35 an ounce as the price of Treasury gold, thus devaluing the gold dollar to $0.5906. The bill also abandoned gold coinage.

Congress also passed a bill recommended by the President authorizing him to purchase silver at not more than 50 cents an ounce and to nationalize silver whenever he should deem it wise, with the purpose of establishing an ultimate monetary base of 25 per cent silver and 75 per cent gold under international agreements to coordinate the double standard.

Following a decision in February to discontinue the civil works program, the President announced a widespread program for relief of distressed families in rural areas, stranded populations in places where there was little or no hope for future re-employment, and the masses of unemployed in large cities. A little later he sent a special message to Congress asking an appropriation of $1,322,000,000 to carry on relief work in the fiscal year beginning July 1. He also advocated social security and housing programs, urged the further development of Government power projects, and attacked business and industrial leaders on the grounds of seeking excessive profits at the expense of public welfare and of refusing to study the problem of national economic planning seriously.

The President pressed both NRA and AAA throughout the year. He announced his intention of trying to make NRA a permanent part of the Government machinery, especially with respect to the principle of collective bargaining contained in Section 7a, the maintenance of minimum wages and maximum hours, and the ban against child labor. He extended the scope of AAA by signing the Bankhead Cotton Bill for compulsory control of cotton production, by bringing sugar under the AAA, and by setting up a quota system for both domestic and foreign sugar producers in the American market.

After getting legislation from Congress permitting the Federal authorities to take action, President Roosevelt through the Department of Justice instituted a war on criminal gangs which had waxed powerful during prohibition, and which after repeal had turned to kidnappings, bank robberies and other crimes.

The President again demonstrated his political leadership during the 1934 meeting of Congress, and was able to push through most of his program. However, it became clear that the fears of "dictatorship" under the extraordinary powers Congress had granted to him were unfounded. He was badly beaten on economy legislation, Congress restoring the pension cuts for veterans and pay cuts of Government employes made in 1933 and passing this measure over the President's veto. Congress also defeated an Administration proposal for ratification of the St. Lawrence waterway. He was also forced by Congress to compromise on the silver issue. Bills providing for the control of crops, the Stock Exchange and currency were modified to meet Congressional criticism.

Where the President won out in the 1934 session was in the adoption of Administration bills for large spending of public funds, especially for relief; the reciprocal tariffs, bank deposit insurance and the regulation of the Stock Exchange, security sales and public utilities. The power of patronage, represented especially in the thousands of new Federal jobs created outside of civil service by the emergency legislation, enabled the President to maintain his leadership on most questions, although not on all.

The President made an extended trip on the naval cruiser Houston in the summer of 1934, becoming the first President to pass through the Panama Canal and to visit Hawaii.

Endorsed by Voters in 1934

During 1934 criticism of the New Deal grew slowly, although there was little criticism of the President himself. Even the objections to the New Deal were confined largely to financial and business circles, and were centered around farm "regimentation" and "collectivism," governmental interference with business, especially in NRA and in labor matters; the unbalanced budget and the big spending program. President Roosevelt's personal popularity continued unabated, and the New Deal also remained popular with the masses of voters. This was shown by the Congressional elections in November, in which the Democrats gained in both the Senate and the House of Representatives.

The year marked the beginning of cleavage between Mr. Roosevelt and the New Dealers on one side and certain conservative Democratic leaders on the other hand. The big spending program caused a break between the President and Lewis W. Douglas, Director of the Budget, who resigned after failing to persuade the President in favor of Government economies and prompt balancing of the budget.

Stronger opposition to the New Deal arose in Congress, including the conservative wing of the Democratic party, during the 1935 session, but the President, with his large majorities, succeeded in completing his legislative program in virtual entirety, although with some modifications.

He staggered the country with a demand, which Congress granted, for an appropriation of $4,880,000,000 for unemployment relief, chiefly for a Federal work program, in which the Works Progress Administration, headed by Mr. Hopkins, was the central part. This took care of about 3,500,000 employable unemployed during the fiscal year 1935-36, while responsibility for unemployables was returned to the States and localities.

Youth Administration Set Up

Under the work program, the President established a National Youth Administration to provide financial aid for needy school and college students, continued and expanded the program of the Civilian Conservation Corps, one of the most popular New Deal activities, and established a Rural Resettlement Administration under Assistant Secretary of Agriculture Rexford G. Tugwell, in an effort to settle city dwellers on farms and move farmers from barren to fertile lands.

The President also got his social security program through Congress, providing for old-age benefits, unemployment insurance, and for aid to maternal and child welfare and public health. This he presented as an essential part of the Government's future unemployment policy, as it would not only protect future needs, but prevent any future Government from going heavily into debt to furnish relief.

President Roosevelt found strong opposition in Congress to his request to extend the NRA for two years when it should expire on June 16, 1935, as NRA's unpopularity was growing, but in the midst of the controversy the Supreme Court unanimously held the NRA to be unconstitutional. This resulted in the President's famous "horse-and-buggy" interview, in which he expressed bitter disappointment, held that it raised the issue whether the Government should have any right to control national economic or social problems, and that it relegated the country to the "horse-and-buggy" age.

Coal Bill Supported by the President Overruled by the Supreme Court

Because of the critical situation in the bituminous coal industry, the President strongly supported the Guffey Coal Bill, sometimes called a "Little NRA," and asked Congress to pass it in spite of doubts as to its constitutionality. This was done. The Supreme Court declared it unconstitutional in 1936.

President Roosevelt then advanced the idea that the AAA should be evolved into a permanent farm program after the existing emergency. He obtained the adoption of AAA amendments designed to meet the challenge to its constitutionality which had been raised in the courts.

A storm of controversy was aroused by the President when he recommended a "tax the wealth" revenue bill.

He asked Congress to impose inheritance taxes in addition to the existing estate taxes, and also gift taxes to prevent evasion of the inheritance tax. He also urged increases in the tax on large individual incomes and the substitution of a corporation income tax graduated according to the size of the corporation income in place of the existing uniform tax. Congress enacted most of the President's bill, but left out the inheritance taxes while increasing estate and gift levies.

Bitter controversy also followed the President's demand for strict regulation of utilities, especially holding companies, but here again he won most of his demands.

President Roosevelt vetoed a bonus bill passed by the 1935 session, and his veto was upheld.

Features of the President's program enacted into law by Congress in 1935 were:

Alcohol Control Act, creating an Alcohol Control Administration to control the liquor traffic.

Air-Mail Act, empowering the Interstate Commerce Commission to investigate rates, fix routes and establish contract terms.

Banking Act of 1935, strengthening Federal control over money and credit.

Gold Clause Act, prohibiting citizens after Jan. 1, 1936, from suing the Government for damages arising from dollar devaluation.

Labor Disputes Act, establishing a National Labor Relations Board to promote equality of bargaining between employers and employes.

Motor Carriers—Bus and truck lines put under regulation of Interstate Commerce Commission.

National Defense—Nearly $1,000,000,000 appropriated to strengthen the Army and Navy.

Petroleum Act, partly regulating interstate and foreign commerce in petroleum and its products.

Railroad Pension Act, establishing retirement annuities for railroad workers.

Railroad Reorganization Act, simplifying and improving procedure for financial reorganization of railroads.

Tennessee Valley Act, sanctioning TVA sale of surplus power, building of additional dams, and acquisition of electric facilities.

It was in the Supreme Court that the President met his great reverses. After decisions in his favor in the gold cases, the Supreme Court handed down a steady line of adverse decisions on New Deal legislation, including the unanimous NRA decision. The Railroad Retirement Act, the Frazier-Lemke Farm Mortgage Act and the "Hot Oil" Act also were held unconstitutional. The court held that Congress had illegally delegated powers to the Executive in certain emergency legislation, that it had tried to exercise powers it did not possess in regulating commerce, and that it had deprived individuals of their rights under the due process clause.

Personal Popularity Retained

It was quite clear that the New Deal had lost more popularity than the President himself. Although there was a bitter personal tone in criticisms of the President in financial and business circles, he retained personal popularity elsewhere, especially among the masses.

In the summer of 1935 the President made a trip to California by rail, reviewed the fleet off the Pacific Coast and visited the Panama Canal Zone.

Late in the year the President announced that the peak of the depression had passed, that business recovery was coming fast, and that Federal deficits would decrease. He said that in the spring of 1933 leading bankers had estimated to him that the country could stand a national debt of $55,000,000,000 to $70,000,000,000.

When the 1936 session of Congress was opened on Jan. 3 everyone expected a short session, and the President said in his annual message that no new taxes would be necessary, based on existing laws. This plan was upset by two events—the passage of the Bonus Bill over the President's veto and the invalidation of AAA and its processing taxes by the Supreme Court.

The result was a long and bitter debate in Congress over the President's demand for a new and heavy tax on the undivided profits of corporations. The differences were finally ironed out in conference, and Congress adjourned late in June.

On Saturday, June 27, 1936, at the Democratic National Convention at Philadelphia, Mr. Roosevelt was renominated by acclamation for the Presidency. That night he traveled from Washington, following the precedent he had set four years earlier, and delivered his acceptance speech before a crowd of 105,000 persons at Franklin Field, Philadelphia. The keynote of his address was that, as the fathers of the Republic had achieved political freedom from the eighteenth-century royalists, Americans today are struggling for economic freedom from the "economic royalists" and "princes of privileges" who ruled the country before his election and were now trying to return to power.

The President made it clear that he intended to make his own personality and record in office the main issue of the campaign, and to continue to steer a course "a little left of center," which he said means progress, if re-elected.

During the year the reaction against the President's policies had increased in financial and business circles, and among conservative Democrats as well as Republicans. Former Gov. Alfred E. Smith attacked the New Deal in a speech before the American Liberty League early in the year in which he threatened to "take a walk" from the party, and joined Bainbridge Colby, James A. Reed, Joseph B. Ely and Daniel F. Cohalan in an appeal to the Democratic convention to repudiate the New Deal and nominate "a genuine Democrat."

At the same time Mr. Roosevelt's strength grew among the masses, especially of organized labor. John L. Lewis, head of the United Mine Workers, and other prominent labor leaders organized a nonpartisan labor league which promised to produce millions of votes for the President. The great battlegrounds of the campaign, it appeared, would be among the middle-class economic groups.

Bitter Campaign Waged

The campaign itself was bitter, with the Republicans focusing their attack on the WPA. They attacked the entire program as "boondoggling," a tag pinned on the agency's work by Western ranch hands employed under it during idle winter months. The anti-Roosevelt newspapers seized on this term, too, one of them printing a box each day titled the "daily boondoggle." The Republicans further sought to discredit the WPA by accusing the administrative heads of herding their project workers into the Roosevelt camp under threat of dismissal.

They further charged that Postmaster General James A. Farley was bludgeoning the nation's political leaders into line for the President by threatening to cut off Federal patronage.

The nation finally went to the polls on Nov. 3 after more than $13,000,000 had been spent by all parties in the campaign. When the results were in President Roosevelt and Vice President John Nance Garner had been re-elected in the greatest sweep ever to hit the nation, carrying every State in the union except Maine and Vermont. Of all political prognosticators, only Postmaster General Farley had been brash enough to predict such an enormous victory. He called the turn to the exact dot, naming even the two States that would go to Mr. Landon.

Campaigning for re-election in 1936.

POLICIES EXPANDED BY WORLD CRISES

Domestic Problems Thrust Aside in Later Years of Roosevelt's Tenure

As the overshadowing world crisis developed, President Franklin D. Roosevelt turned his attention more and more from domestic social and economic reforms to the great problems of international affairs. Although he came to office two months after Adolf Hitler had seized the reins of power in Germany, foreign policy was so little in the minds of the new President and his fellow-countrymen that it was the subject of only a single paragraph in his first inaugural address.

Even before his tenure of office was half over, however, the perilous state of the nation's foreign affairs was demanding the major share of the President's thought and energies, and the time eventually came when he urged the country to cease identifying his administration with the New Deal.

Earliest among his international undertakings, and perhaps one that cast an unfavorable augury for the diplomacy of his administration, was Mr. Roosevelt's message of 1933 wrecking the London Economic Conference, convoked largely at the instance of the United States.

Quarantine of Nations

This was followed, however, by two developments of 1934, each destined to be of long-lasting effect. One was the Congressional enactment empowering the President to negotiate reciprocal trade agreements with other nations. The other was Mr. Roosevelt's action, taken to implement his "Good-Neighbor" policy toward the world in general and Latin America in particular. Specific steps were the abrogation of the Platt Amendment, which had given the United States the right to intervene in Cuba, the withdrawal of American marines from Haiti, and the signing of a bill guaranteeing ultimate independence to the Philippines.

Through the immediately following years the pyramiding uncertainties of the future of Europe necessarily came more and more to the attention of the President, but in his public pronouncements at least foreign policy remained subordinated to domestic questions until, in one bold speech delivered at Chicago in October, 1937, he called for the quarantine of aggressor nations. Public reaction to the address was not entirely favorable; as a consequence the President "went slow" for a time, but did not thereafter deviate from the line of action he had suggested to the country.

As the war clouds grew blacker over Europe Mr. Roosevelt did what he could to dispel them. In August, 1938, he made it known that the United States would not "stand idly by" if Canada should be attacked. Four days before Munich he appealed to the Czechs and the Germans alike to reach a peaceful settlement of their difficulties over the Sudetenland. On Nov. 14, as a gesture of protest against widespread anti-Jewish rioting in Germany, he called the American Ambassador home from Berlin.

Appealed to Hitler

In the following spring, on April 15, the President addressed an appeal to Chancellor Hitler and Premier Mussolini asking them to pledge their nations to ten years of peace, and promising to use his own good offices to bring about economic adjustments that might be necessary. When this move failed, and a few months later the long-dreaded war broke out, Mr. Roosevelt promised that all his efforts would be devoted to keeping this nation at peace.

His first step in fulfillment of that purpose was to call a special session of Congress for amendment of the Neutrality Act. He argued that by repealing the arms embargo and substituting for it a "cash and carry" provision for the sale of American arms to the nations defending themselves this country could keep the war far from its shores. He succeeded in winning Congressional approval for his policy. Meanwhile he sought to foster the unity of the nations of the two Americas for hemisphere defense.

When, after a period of somnolence and of charges that it was "phony," the war leaped into sudden flame in April, 1940, with the German invasion of Denmark and Norway, Mr. Roosevelt denounced the Nazis in unmeasured terms. The following month, when the German armies swiftly overran the Low Countries and France, he called upon the United States to embark upon a defense program of unprecedented magnitude.

Defense Program Outlined

In quick succession he called for 50,000 war planes, a two-ocean Navy, the enactment of a selective service law and the building up of the nation's defenses on a scale so great that the appropriations and authorizations entailed eventually mounted to $28,500,000,000. Asserting that the nation was facing a grave emergency, he persuaded two prominent Republicans, Henry L. Stimson and Col. Frank Knox, to enter his Cabinet as Secretary of War and Secretary of the Navy, respectively.

Meanwhile he sought to extend to the faltering French nation, and, after its defeat, to the imperiled British, every assistance that lay within his power. Out of surplus Army stocks left over from World War days he rushed to the British, in the days following Dunkerque, vast quantities of arms and munitions, including more than 80,000 machine guns and almost 1,000,000 rifles. He arranged a trade of fifty over-age American destroyers to Britain in return for the right to lease a series of air and naval bases on British possessions from Newfoundland to British Guinea.

Soon after his third election, Mr. Roosevelt arranged an American loan of $100,000,000 to China to stiffen resistance against Japan, and early in December, 1940, he assured the Greek Government, then at grips with Italy, that the United States would supply aid, in accordance with a "settled policy" of assisting peoples to defend themselves against aggression.

These steps, however, were mere preliminaries to his announcement of his "lease-lend" plan, which, first foreshadowed at a press conference on Dec. 16, was explained in more detail to the people of the United States in a radio fireside chat on Dec. 30, and was outlined in detail in a message to Congress on Jan. 5, 1941. He asked Congress for authority and funds with which to aid the victims of aggression and said that the most useful role for the United States was to act as an "arsenal" for the democracies.

Row Over Power to Aid

A bill to confer upon the President practically unlimited power to place American war equipment, new and old, at the disposal of the nations fighting the Axis powers was introduced into Congress on Jan. 10 and immediately began a bitter controversy. Opponents of the bill charged that it would give Mr. Roosevelt dictatorial powers, and one of them, Senator Burton K. Wheeler of Montana, leader of the fight against the President's Supreme Court bill, went so far as to charge that it represented "another New Deal triple A foreign policy—plow under every fourth American boy." The President promptly retorted that the charge was "rotten" and "dastardly."

Whether Mr. Roosevelt really believed at this time that America could give "all aid short of war" to those opposing the Axis powers without actually getting into the war may never be known. It is probable that the President regarded our entrance into the conflict as inevitable and was working to stymie the up-to-then successful Axis technique of taking on its eventual opponents one at a time.

For certainly, with the passage of the Lend-Lease Act, the United States became committed to war, regardless of the words of the moment.

The "isolationists" of the day waged their bitterest battle against lend-lease, but it passed Congress by a substantial margin, was signed by the President on March 11, and the President immediately set up a seven-billion-dollar fund to implement the new policy. In the interim, at his third inaugural, on Jan. 16, he told the American people that "in this day the task of the people is to save the nation and its institutions from disruption without," and that "we do not retreat, we are not content to stand still. As Americans we go forward in the service of our country, by the will of God." He emphasized the importance of the coming struggle a few days after he signed the Lend-Lease Bill by telling the country that "the impact of this gigantic effort will be felt by Americans in every walk of life."

Alliance With England Nearer

In April we moved a step closer to actual alliance with England when the President removed the Red Sea from a previously designated combat zone which American ships were not allowed to enter. It meant that, with the recently established English control of those waters, we intended to use our ships to supply their new bases. In May he publicly defied the Nazi-proclaimed blockade, appealed to the French over the head of their nominal government not to support Pétain's policy of collaboration with Germany, and finally proclaimed a state of unlimited national emergency in this country, thereby vastly increasing his own powers in connection with the war and the home front.

This came right after he had struck a blow at one of America's leading isolationists, Charles A. Lindbergh. The President likened him to Vallandigham, Civil War Copperhead, precipitating another of the storms which were typical of the period.

June saw the President freezing, by executive order, the assets of Germany and Italy in this country—to be followed the next month by a reciprocal closing of consulates—as well as a declaration by the President branding Germany as an "international outlaw," engaged in "piracy," due to Germany's sinking American ships. It was also the month that saw Hitler make his first major error, the invasion of Russia. Sentiment against Russia was strong in this country up to then, due to Communist-inspired strikes and general tactics designed to delay or hamper our defense effort, and it was three full days after the invasion before the President pledged the nation to give "all possible aid" to Stalin and his compatriots. Winston Churchill had given it for England when the invasion was only hours old, declaring, in a broadcast which reached around the world, that anyone who fought nazism was going to get British help.

Still the trend continued toward our entrance. We took over Iceland in July, with the consent of invaded Denmark, we froze Japan's assets in this country, and the President asked Congress, which consented, to let him hold selectees under the first draft, and National Guardsmen as well, in service for longer than the year originally scheduled.

In rapid succession, through the waning summer and then the fall, as a result of the sending of supplies by us to England, and to a smaller extent to Russia, and the attacks on some of them by U-boats, there came orders to the Navy to shoot at sight any submarines entering "waters the protection of which is necessary for American defense," a declaration that a "shooting war" had actually started and revision of the old Neutrality Act to permit our ships to sail any sea.

A feature of Mr. Roosevelt's foreign policy throughout all these years was his insistence upon being his own spokesman, and to a great extent the active negotiator in his dealings with other nations. In his first term, even though engrossed principally with domestic problems, he found time to hold lengthy, intimate and secluded conferences with statesmen representing the great powers of the earth, including Ramsay MacDonald, the British Premier; Edouard Herriot, who, at the President's invitation, was sent as the emissary of France; Prime Minister R. B. Bennett of Canada, and high spokesmen for Italy, Germany and Japan. War debts, tariffs, stabilization of currencies, trade relations, were among the topics at these international conversations.

The President, in addition, took advantage of them to make known his deep appreciation of the interdependence among modern nations and his desire for the end of trade wars, as well as the conflicts fought upon the battlefield.

It was in furtherance of these aims that Mr. Roosevelt did an unprecedented thing when, on May 16, 1933, discarding the diplomatic practice of international communication through the Foreign Offices of the nations concerned, he addressed a message directly to the heads of fifty-four nations that were to participate in the General Disarmament Conference at Geneva and the World Monetary and Economic Conference in London, strongly urging that "wise and considered" international action be taken to supplement domestic programs for economic recovery and that practical measures of disarmament be evolved to lessen the peril of armed conflict.

Other examples of the President's policy of giving his direct attention to affairs of state occurred in 1935, when, in connection with the passage of the Neutrality Bill of that year, he strongly advocated "taking the profits out of war," and in November of the following year, when he attended the Inter-American Conference at Buenos Aires. Other instances of this dealing personally with the welter of foreign problems preceding actual American participation in the war marked the following years.

In September, 1938, he sent personal messages to Hitler, Chamberlain, Daladier and Benes, urging peaceful settlement of the Sudeten crisis in Czechoslovakia, and calling upon Mussolini to intercede with Hitler to avert war. After Munich he denounced the methods of the dictators, with the result that the Government-controlled press of Germany singled him out for bitter attacks. Meanwhile, the President pressed for an even greater rearmament effort in the United States, and in successive steps recalled the American Ambassador to Germany as a protest against Nazi persecution of the Jews and the use of force as an instrument of national policy, and made personal appeals to Germany, Italy and Soviet Russia. In the latter case he asked the Soviet Government to moderate its demands upon Finland.

After the German-Russian pact and the invasion of Poland he reconvened Congress in special session and obtained eventually a modification of the Neutrality Act, permitting sale to the Allies of war materials on a cash-and-carry basis.

Welles 'Scouted' for Peace

Again, in a characteristically bold stroke early in 1940, he sent Sumner Welles, Under-Secretary of State, on a European "scouting" expedition to discover the prospects of peace. Shortly afterward the President broke another precedent by appointing Myron C. Taylor, former head of the United States Steel Corporation, as his personal representative at the Vatican, with special reference to the possibility of restoring peace. The President cruised to the Pacific Ocean via the Panama Canal and on his return sought appropriations to strengthen the isthmian defenses.

As the previously quiescent war flamed into activity in the spring and summer of 1940 Mr. Roosevelt sought an increased defense program, and with the fall of France in June sought to extend every aid to the stricken republic. It was in connection with the entrance of Italy into the war at this time that he interpolated into a prepared speech delivered at the University of Virginia:

"On this tenth day of June, 1940, the hand that held the dagger has struck it into the back of its neighbor."

In rapid succession thereafter the President established an export license system for petroleum products and scrap metal and obtained from Congress the power to call the National Guard and the organized reserves for a year of military training.

ONE OF 'BIG THREE' IN WORLD CONFLICT

Roosevelt Brought Prestige That Helped Maintain the Morale of Our Allies

One of the Big Three of the second World War—the triumvirate of Churchill, Roosevelt and Stalin, which was a parallel to the Wilson, Clemenceau and Lloyd George team in the first world conflict—President Roosevelt brought to his war leadership a tremendous prestige in Great Britain and on the Continent.

This prestige was an aid in maintaining the morale of our allies during the long period of preparation for vital military operations, and it was a powerful weapon when Mr. Roosevelt appealed to the people in the occupied and enemy countries over the heads of their leaders. At home, while on non-war matters there was no political truce, the President as war leader received the unified support of political friend and foe.

He was on a vacation in Warm Springs when Japan was massing forces for an attack in the East. Where the new act of Japanese aggression would occur no one knew. Thailand, a base for further expansion south, seemed likely.

Plea to Hirohito, Dec. 7

The crisis was grave enough to bring the President rushing back from Warm Springs to issue secret orders for a constant alert by our forces in Hawaii and the Philippines. The morning of Dec. 7, 1941, American newspapers carried the story of a personal appeal by the President to Emperor Hirohito for peace.

Whether the appeal was delivered before the blow was struck was not known, but the Japanese carriers that blasted Pearl Harbor that Sunday morning had started for their destination days, maybe weeks, earlier.

That same Sunday the President, grave and tense, heard the news—"all bad," he remarked of it—and called a special session of Congress for the next day. When Congress assembled, the President told the members that Dec. 7 was "a day that will live in infamy," and that "with confidence in our armed forces, with the unbounding determination of our people, we will gain the inevitable triumph, so help us God."

Congress declared war on Japan and followed this action the next day with war on Germany and Italy, which already had recognized that a state of war existed. America's war effort then really began.

Prime Minister Churchill came to this country on a battleship on Dec. 22 and flew home on Jan. 14, 1942. While here he discussed war plans with Mr. Roosevelt. The Japanese sped their aggression with a great southward drive in the Pacific, and the Philippines, Malaya and the Dutch East Indies fell to their superior forces. The President pledged the eventual liberation of these lands.

Troops and equipment were shipped to England and the invasion of North Africa prepared. This blow, the first taste the Axis had of the combined military might of Britain and the United States, was dealt with great secrecy and it caught the Germans off guard. Meanwhile, Mr. Roosevelt was losing prestige at home as the public became restive over what seemed to be a lack of action.

The invasion of North Africa was welcomed by the public as a turning point in the war, and Presidential popularity rose again.

For "Unconditional Surrender"

Early in 1943 the President visited Churchill at Casablanca, in North Africa, to lay down the "un-

(continued)

conditional surrender" terms to the Axis powers. He stopped off, on the way back, to visit Liberia, Brazil and Trinidad, to lift his travel mark to 200,000 miles while in office up to that point.

America, under the President's leadership, and also as a result of Red Army successes, was drawing closer to a better understanding with Russia. In the spring of 1943 Joseph E. Davies was sent on a "mission to Moscow" with a secret letter from the President to Marshal Joseph Stalin, Premier of the Soviet Union. Stalin replied and the President was able to report to the public that the understanding and accord between the two was "excellent." When Stalin soon thereafter dissolved the Comintern, international revolutionary organization sponsored by the Russian Government, much of the old fear of Russia and communism ceased to be publicly expressed.

Despite the domestic situation, and the increasing food shortage, the Gallup poll was able to report in June, 1943, that 56 per cent of the voters would be for President Roosevelt for a fourth term. Tunisia had surrendered, the Allies controlled the Mediterranean, Pantelleria had been taken and the President was able to invite the Italians to kick out their fascist rulers and their German "visitors" and make a separate peace—a gesture of military success at the time.

Churchill in Washington

Winston Churchill had come to Washington for conferences on the war in the Pacific, and he and Mr. Roosevelt allayed the then-existing fears on the part of some that we were fighting too much of the war in Europe and not enough in the Pacific. It was argued that Japan had been the first to attack us, and that our natural theatre of war was the Pacific. Mr. Churchill pledged every British ship and British plane to help us in the Pacific, as soon as Hitler and Mussolini had been disposed of in the other principal theatre of the global war.

Up to this time, apart from the Atlantic Charter in 1941, the President had given no blueprint of any post-war plans. In March, 1943, he had endorsed the broad principles of a Senate resolution (Ball-Burton-Hill-Hatch) pledging international cooperational to maintain peace after the war, but he implied that the time was not ripe for a detailed statement of the organization.

Yet, international cooperation among the United Nations was under way, with the President as a directing force. He had named his old associate, Herbert H. Lehman, as Director of Foreign Relief and Rehabilitation, and when the Lehman organization began functioning in Africa, in the spring of 1943, as additional territory was reconquered, it was made clear that this help was to be on the basis of international cooperation, not just "hand-outs" from the United States.

An international food conference was held at Hot Springs, Va., with forty-four nations represented, and plans were laid down for future cooperation on the world-wide food problem, both during and after the war.

To aid the prosecution of the war, the President and Mr. Churchill, with their chiefs of staff and many other advisers, held an Anglo-American conference in Quebec. Mr. Roosevelt was there from Aug. 17 to 24, 1943. It was mainly a military conference, but Anthony Eden, British Foreign Secretary, was there, with Secretary Hull, Secretary of War Stimson and Secretary of Navy Knox arriving before the close. Dr. T. V. Soong, Chinese Foreign Minister, attended for two days.

One result of the Quebec conference was that both the American and British Governments announced a qualified recognition of the French Committee of National Liberation as the administrative authority over French colonies in its control.

Meanwhile, in the Mediterranean area, Sicily had been invaded and taken; on Sept. 3, Allied troops had landed on the Italian mainland across from Sicily. In the Pacific, the capture of Kiska Island and the withdrawal of the Japanese from the Aleutians, was followed on Sept. 6 with Gen. Douglas MacArthur opening an offensive on New Guinea to isolate the Lae-Salamaua area.

Italy's unconditional surrender on Sept. 8 was characterized by the President as a great victory for the Allied nations and for the Italian people. No commitments were made to the Badoglio Government. Italy's declaration of war against Germany was announced jointly on Oct. 13 by Roosevelt, Churchill and Stalin.

Joint Communiqué on Cairo

In the diplomatic field, a conference in Moscow of Secretary Hull and Foreign Ministers Eden and Molotoff in November preceded the long-wished-for conference between Mr. Roosevelt, Mr. Churchill and Mr. Stalin. Their historic conference at Teheran, the capital of Iran, came immediately after Mr. Roosevelt, Mr. Churchill and Generalissimo Chiang Kai-shek had conferred outside Cairo from Nov. 22 through Nov. 26.

First news of the Cairo conference was flashed to the world from Lisbon, Portugal, by Reuter, British news agency. This premature announcement brought a protest from Elmer Davis, head of the Office of War Information, but Mr. Davis was forced to make a similar protest a few days later when the Moscow radio broadcast the first definite announcements of the Teheran meeting.

While Mr. Roosevelt and Mr. Churchill were secretly at Teheran with Marshal Stalin, a joint communiqué on the Cairo conference was announced on Dec. 1. The three great powers, the United States, Britain and China, it said, had reached full agreement to press unrelenting war against their brutal enemies by land, sea and air: to renounce all territorial gains for themselves and to strip the Japanese of all Pacific islands seized since 1914; to restore to China the lost lands of Manchuria, Formosa and the Pescadores; to expel Japan from all other territories she had taken by violence and greed; to guarantee the future independence of enslaved Korea, and to persevere in the serious and prolonged operations necessary to procure the unconditional surrender of Japan.

The closely guarded conferences were held at the Mena House, a luxury hotel five miles outside Cairo. It was the first meeting for Generalissimo Chiang with either President Roosevelt or Prime Minister Churchill. The President made the trip by plane, as did the Generalissimo, who was accompanied by Mme. Chiang. The Prime Minister went by ship.

The Teheran conference lasted from Nov. 28 through Dec. 1 and was held at the Russian Embassy in the Iranian capital. Mr. Roosevelt was a guest of Marshal Stalin. It was said to be the first time the marshal had left the Soviet Union since the revolution in 1917. Mr. Churchill stayed at the British Embassy near the Russian Embassy. It was the first meeting between Mr. Roosevelt and Marshal Stalin.

Out of this dramatic meeting came a declaration of the three leaders expressing "our determination that our nations shall work together in the war and in the peace that will follow," and asserting that final plans had been made for the destruction of the German forces. Declaring the attacks would be relentless and increasing, they said that "no power on earth can prevent our destroying the German armies by land, their U-boats by sea and their war plants from the air."

Asserting confidence in "an enduring peace," they said: "We recognize fully the supreme responsibility resting upon us and all the nations to make a peace which will command good-will from the overwhelming masses of the peoples of the world and banish the scourge and terror of war for many generations." They said they would welcome the cooperation of all nations seeking to eliminate tyranny and oppression: "We will welcome them as they may choose to come into the world family of democratic nations."

After Teheran, Mr. Roosevelt and Mr. Churchill conferred with President Ismet Inonu of Turkey at Cairo. The three issued a declaration saying that "the closest unity existed between the United States of America, Turkey and Great Britain in their attitude to the world situation." But no change resulted in the Turkish foreign policy.

The President returned to the United States on Dec. 16, having traveled an estimated 25,000 miles since his departure on Nov. 11. He said the conferences had been a success in every way. In a Christmas Eve broadcast he said the four powers had agreed to use force to maintain peace after victory.

Turned to Post-War

Throughout 1944 and the early part of 1945, as American and Allied forces swept through to victory after victory in both Europe and the Pacific, invading France, crossing the Rhine on one side of the world, while carrying the war to Japan's doorstep on the other side, President Roosevelt turned more and more to the diplomacy of the post-war world. Seeing that the second World War was fast approaching its end, at least in its European phase, he began to work out plans to prevent a third world war through international cooperation and collective security in both the political and economic spheres.

Following up the United Nations conferences on world food supplies and on the relief and rehabilitation of liberated areas, which were held in 1943 at Hot Springs, Va., and Atlantic City, N. J., President Roosevelt assumed the leadership in calling the nations of the world together for the United Nations Monetary and Financial Conference at Bretton Woods, N. H., in the summer of 1944, and the International Civil Aviation Conference at Chicago in November and December of the same year.

Whereas the United Nations Relief and Rehabilitation Administration, organized in Atlantic City, undertook the short-range task of feeding and clothing those war-ravaged peoples who were unable to take care of themselves, and helping them restore their devastated industrial and agricultural plant so that they could support themselves as quickly as possible, the International Monetary Fund and the International Bank for Reconstruction and Development, blueprinted at Breton Woods, were designed to stabilize world currencies and provide guaranteed loans for long-range reconstruction of world production and the international exchange of goods in the interests of world-wide prosperity.

The aviation conference aimed at world agreement to promote the coming of the future Air Age in a manner to promote the welfare of all countries and minimize the danger of economic rivalries that might threaten the peace of the world in the future. Similar international conferences have been proposed to deal with the problems of world shipping, telecommunications, and foreign trade in general, for the same purposes.

Dumbarton Oaks Parley

The most ambitious of President Roosevelt's post-war projects—to create a world organization to maintain peace and security in place of the League of Nations, and without the mistakes which kept this country out of the League and weakened its influence in the rest of the world—began to take shape when the Dumbarton Oaks conference was held in Washington, D. C., in October, 1944. At this conference the United States, Great Britain, Russia and China drafted proposals for the establishment of a general international organization to maintain peace and security, including a general Assembly, a Security Council, a Court of International Justice and an Economic and Social Council.

Mr. Roosevelt then held the last and most famous of his series of conferences with Prime Minister Churchill and Marshal Stalin—the meeting at Yalta from which emerged the fateful Crimea Declaration of Feb. 11, 1945.

The Crimea Declaration reaffirmed the pledge of the Atlantic Charter for a free world, the Casablanca demand for unconditional surrender by the Axis, and the Teheran strategy of coordinated war against Germany on all fronts.

"It is our inflexible purpose to destroy German militarism and nazism and to insure that Germany will never again be able to disturb the peace of the world," the declaration read.

It was decided that the United States, Great Britain, France and Russia would occupy four separate parts of Germany and that each would be responsible for German disarmament and the control of German military and industrial potential in its own area, through an interallied control commission to be located in Berlin.

The big three agreed at Yalta on new boundaries for Poland, giving Russia all Polish territory east of the Curzon Line, compensating Poland with part of East Prussia, other German territory and an outlet to the sea, and providing for a transfer of population. They also agreed on the reconstitution of the Russian-backed Lublin Government with new "democratic" representatives of Poles in exile and at home, and on later free elections to permit the Poles to have a Government of their own choice.

Finally, it was decided to call a United Nations security organization at San Francisco on April 25, 1945, at which the charter of the new world organization would be drawn up along the lines agreed upon at Dumbarton Oaks. France was invited to join the United States, Great Britain, China and Russia in sponsoring the San Francisco Conference, but General de Gaulle, head of the provisional French Government, declined this invitation, and also rejected a bid to meet President Roosevelt at Algiers on the latter's homeward trip. Paris reports indicated the French were irked at having been left out of the Yalta Conference.

Yalta Decision Revealed

Some time after President Roosevelt's return to this country it was revealed that the Yalta Conference had agreed to a proposal by the President on voting procedure in the Security Council, which had been left open at Dumbarton Oaks. It had been provided at Dumbarton Oaks that the Security Council should include eleven seats, of which five should be permanent places for the largest powers—the United States, Russia, Great Britain, France and China.

The Yalta decision was that in all pacific settlements no nation could vote in a dispute to which it was a party, but that in all cases that involved the use of military or economic sanctions against an aggressor no action could be taken without unanimous agreement of all permanent members of the council.

This limited veto for the big powers caused considerable criticism among the smaller and middle-sized nations, but President Roosevelt and his colleagues indicated that it was necessary at this time in order to attain united action by the big powers, without which no plan for world organization was held to be practical.

If he had lived, President Roosevelt would have journeyed to San Francisco to preside at the formal opening of the world security conference.

The last meeting of the Big Three. Prime Minister Churchill, President Roosevelt and Premier Stalin at Yalta.

VICTORY IN SIGHT WHEN DEATH CAME

In a simple ceremony on the south portico of the White House Franklin D. Roosevelt on Jan. 20 last was inaugurated the country's first fourth term President, the fifth wartime President of the United States.

President Roosevelt began his fourth term just after the start of the Russian campaign against Germany in the East. Death ended it with American, British and Canadian armies in the West and Russian armies in the East pressing hard toward Berlin and with complete defeat of the Wehrmacht in sight, with the Philippines regained and with American naval and military forces closing in on Japan.

President Roosevelt also came to the premature end of his fourth term with every prospect that the United States would abandon its traditional policy of isolationism and join with other allied nations in formation of an international organization to maintain peace after victory. He expressed this hope in his last inaugural address, in which he said:

"We have learned that we cannot live alone, at peace; that our own well-being is dependent upon the well-being of other nations. We have learned that we must live as men, and not as ostriches, nor as dogs in the manger.

"We have learned to be citizens of the world, members of the human community. We have learned the simple truth, as Emerson said, that 'the only way to have a friend is to be one.'"

"All the News That's Fit to Print"

The New York Times.

LATE CITY EDITION
Partly cloudy and warm today. Scattered showers tomorrow.
Temperature Range Today—Max.,84; Min.,70
Temperature Yesterday—Max.,82; Min.,70
Full U. S. Weather Bureau Report, Page 43

VOL. XCVII...No. 33,078. Entered as Second-Class Matter. Postoffice, New York, N. Y. NEW YORK, TUESDAY, AUGUST 17, 1948. Times Square, New York 18, N. Y. Telephone LAckawanna 4-1000 THREE CENTS IN NEW YORK CITY

CITY POLICE REJECT RUSSIANS' VERSION IN KOSENKINA CASE

State Department Gets Report Holding Their Kidnapping Charge Is 'Unfounded'

LOMAKIN RENEWS ATTACK

Consulate Statement Admits Leap Was Suicide Attempt, Laying It to U. S. Harassing

Text of the statement by Consul General Lomakin, Page 3.

By ALEXANDER FEINBERG

An exhaustive report by the Police Department, made to Mayor O'Dwyer and turned over by him to prosecuting agencies, says flatly that the Soviet charges that Mrs. Oksana Stepanova Kosenkina was kidnapped are "unfounded."

This was learned last night from trustworthy sources as Consul General Jacob M. Lomakin was restating these charges and giving to the American press the official Soviet version of the Russian teacher's leap from a window of the Soviet consulate last Thursday.

For the first time Soviet officials admitted in a formal statement that Mrs. Kosenkina's fall was not an accident but that she had jumped from a third-story window in an attempt at suicide. He attributed the attempt to a breakdown brought on by harassment from American sources.

The police report, the contents of which have been kept secret, has been in the offices of District Attorney Frank Hogan and United States Attorney John F. X. McGohey since late Saturday. A copy has been forwarded to Attorney General Tom Clark in Washington and a copy of the confidential document was received yesterday by the State Department.

It is on this that the State Department will rely for the answer of the United States Government to the formal protests made in Moscow by Soviet Foreign Minister Molotov and in Washington by Ambassador Alexander S. Panyushkin.

Teacher's Statement Included

It contains, it was learned, a complete stenographic statement from Mrs. Kosenkina, given to police in question and answer form through a competent interpreter. In her story she denies to ranking police officials that she was kidnapped and declares that she jumped from the consulate window to effect her escape from confinement in the building.

Mrs. Kosenkina refutes in her statement the declaration by the consul that she had jumped after listening to radio accounts of her "drugging" and "kidnapping" by "White Russian bandits" and her subsequent "rescue," by Mr. Lomakin and members of his staff, from the Reed Farm at Valley Cottage, N. Y., operated by the Tolstoy Foundation, Inc.

The Soviet teacher, who sought a haven here after determining not to be sent back to Russia with the other teachers of a now closed Soviet school for children in New York, says that she had a radio in her room at the consulate but that she heard her case discussed only once. That was on Wednesday, the day before her leap.

At that time, she says, she heard her name mentioned along with that of Mikhail Ivanovitch Samarin, the other teacher who refused to return to Russia and who is now in hiding, but she told her questioners that she was unable to understand the broadcast because of her imperfect knowledge of the English language.

The day she jumped, she says, she did not have the radio turned on.

Investigation Termed Thorough

The report, which originated from a complaint by the Consul General addressed to Police Commissioner Arthur W. Wallander, who is now recovering from an operation, closes with the considered police opinion that "the charge of kidnapping is unfounded." The investigation was said to be one of the most thorough and exhaustive ever made by the department.

At no time has the complaint by Mr. Lomakin been listed as a kidnapping. It was placed in the classification of "investigation." Completion of the investigation, it was pointed out, does not automatically place the case in the category of those listed as "case

Continued on Page 3, Column 2

4 More Olympic Men Refuse to Go Home

By The Associated Press.

LONDON, Aug. 16 — Four more Czech Olympic athletes decided today against returning to Communist-ruled Czechoslovakia.

Their decision brought to at least eight the number of Olympic competitors refusing to go back to Communist homelands. Two Czechs and three Hungarians disclosed yesterday that they intended to stay in England, but one of the Hungarians later went back to Budapest.

The Czech Committee for Political Refugees, which announced the action of the athletes, withheld the names. A spokesman said:

"Six Czech athletes who came here for the Olympic Games definitely have decided against returning. Two of the athletes are swimmers. The other four were on the rowing team."

ALGER HISS TO FACE CHAMBERS AUG. 25

'Confrontation Day' Set in Spy Inquiry After Ex-Official Is Questioned in Secret

By C. P. TRUSSELL
Special to THE NEW YORK TIMES.

WASHINGTON, Aug. 16—Three hours of closed-session questioning of Alger Hiss, former State Department official, left the House Committee on un-American Activities admittedly unable tonight to determine whether he or Whittaker Chambers, who accused him of leadership in an "elite" pre-war Communist "underground," was telling the truth.

At the committee's open hearings Mr. Hiss had denied, sweepingly and categorically, the charges by Mr. Chambers, a senior editor of Time magazine. He asked an opportunity to confront his accuser, declaring that he never had known him and never had seen him.

Mr Chambers swore that, while serving as a courier for the alleged "underground," he had known Mr. Hiss well and went to his home later and urged him to break away from the Communists.

Mr. Hiss repeated today his previous denials and made new denials, it was reported, as new questions were flung at him. These new questions arose, it was understood, from a second questioning of Mr. Chambers behind closed doors in New York last week.

"Confrontation Day" Set

After today's session the committee set "a confrontation day," Aug. 25, when Mr. Hiss and Mr. Chambers will face each other before the investigating body.

Mr. Hiss left the committee room this evening refusing to comment on his long session with the committee. Representative J. Parnell Thomas, committee chairman, issued a statement in which he said:

"From the testimony of the two witnesses it is impossible at this point to tell which one is telling the truth. The committee is taking every step to determine the true facts."

Mr. Thomas declared that transcripts of the closed session interrogations of Mr. Hiss and Mr. Chambers would be sent to George Morris Fay, United States attorney for the District of Columbia. Last week Mr. Fay asked for complete record of the committee's investigation into spy rings. He indicated

Continued on Page 3, Column 6

3 WESTERN ENVOYS AND MOLOTOV MEET IN LONGEST PARLEY

Sixth Kremlin Session Lasts 3 Hours 40 Minutes—Word on Further Talks Lacking

NEW BERLIN RULE LOOMS

Three-Power Kommandatura Studied—2 Russian Fighters Buzz British Passenger Plane

By The Associated Press.

MOSCOW, Aug. 16—Envoys of the United States, Great Britain and France met with Soviet Foreign Minister Molotov again tonight in the negotiations seeking to settle East-West differences in Berlin and Germany.

The meeting in the Kremlin was the longest since the negotiations began July 31, lasting three hours and forty minutes. None of the Western diplomats would comment as they left the Kremlin; they refused even to say whether they thought there would be another meeting.

[In Berlin, the three Western Powers were considering establishing a tripartite Kommandatura as a first line of defense against Soviet claims to supreme authority over all of Berlin, it was learned authoritatively. Two Russian Yak fighters buzzed a British passenger plane en route from Berlin to Hamburg, evoking a strong protest from the British. Gen. Lucius D. Clay, United States Military Governor, said he knew of no plans for a change in United States policy but that if there were a shift it did not mean he intended to resign.]

United States Ambassador Walter Bedell Smith and French Ambassador Yves Chataigneau went immediately from the Kremlin to the British Embassy with Britain's special envoy, Frank Roberts, for a conference.

Smith in Good Spirits

General Smith seemed in good spirits as he sent his chauffeur to get something to eat. But the envoys themselves went right into the meeting without stopping for food.

[A responsible diplomatic informant in London said Mr. Molotov was to have given Russia's reply to the Western proposals for a Berlin settlement at this meeting. The informant said the Western proposals had been "rehashed but not modified" and added that this talk might be the climax of the eighteen-day discussions.]

Tonight's conference was the sixth with Mr. Molotov. The Western envoys met with the Soviet Foreign Minister July 31. He also was present at the Aug. 2 meeting with Premier Stalin, which was followed by meetings with Mr. Molotov on Aug. 6, Aug. 9 and Aug. 12.

The three Western diplomats met among themselves at the British Embassy before they left for the Kremlin.

There has been no indication in Moscow as to how the talks are going: the Western diplomats have been silent on their progress. Most Moscow observers were of the opinion, however, that today's talks were crucial for the further

Continued on Page 2, Column 2

Israel Issues Own Currency Today; New Pound Is Convertible at $4

By GENE CURRIVAN
Special to THE NEW YORK TIMES.

TEL AVIV, Israel, Aug. 16—The Provisional Government of Israel issued tonight a declaration of monetary independence. Beginning tomorrow, there will be Israeli currency completely divorced from British sterling or Palestinian pounds.

The notes will be backed up to 60 per cent with dollars, gold and sterling balances for the main part, and their convertibility will be at the present rate of a trifle over $4 to the pound. There will be exceptions as there are now, with pounds being exchanged for $3 in foreign trade with dollar countries and at that rate for gift dollars such as those received by the Jewish Agency for Palestine.

[An Israeli communiqué said that Arab riflemen had resumed sniping at highway traffic.]

The announcement was made by Eliezer Kaplan, Israeli Finance Minister and treasurer of the Jewish National Council, who said that the Council would effect necessary legislation tonight.

He declared that about £75,000,000 ($300,000,000) of Palestinian funds was held in Britain. He added that he was not worried about it because "Great Britain had clearly undertaken the legal obligation to make funds available in sterling on the basis of one pound sterling for one pound Palestinian." He declared: "It is clearly impossible that an independent state should leave control of its currency in the hands of a foreign government."

"The Israeli pound," Mr. Kaplan said, "which will take the place of the Palestinian pound, will be equal to it and to the pound sterling. Bank notes in Israeli pound denominations will be issued by the Anglo-Palestine Bank of Tel Aviv, which has at all times served as the Jewish national bank and at present acts as banker to the Government.

"The bank will for this purpose open an issue department. This

Continued on Page 6, Column 3

Babe Ruth, Baseball Idol, Dies At 53 After Lingering Illness

GEORGE HERMAN (BABE) RUTH

The home-run king, in the uniform of the New York Yankees, when he was the mightiest hitter in the game's history.

The New York Times

Famous Diamond Star Fought Losing Battle Against Cancer for 2 Years—End Comes Suddenly After Encouraging Rally

By MURRAY SCHUMACH

Babe Ruth died last night. The 53-year-old baseball idol succumbed to cancer of the throat at Memorial Hospital at 8 o'clock, less than two hours after a special bulletin had announced he was "sinking rapidly."

The home-run king's death came five days after he had been placed on the critical list. It ended nearly two years of fighting against a disease that had sent him repeatedly to hospitals.

About a half hour before his death the famous Yankee slugger said a prayer. Last rites of the Roman Catholic Church had been administered on July 21.

After his death, the Rev. Thomas H. Kaufman of Providence College, Providence, R. I., who had blessed him shortly before death, said: "The Babe died a beautiful death. He said his prayers and lapsed into a sleep. He died in his sleep."

At the deathbed, besides the priest, were the Babe's wife, Claire, his two adopted daughters, Mrs. Daniel Sullivan and Mrs. Richard Flanders; his sister, Mrs. Wilbur Moberly; his doctor, his lawyer, and a few of his closest friends.

There was a hush around the hospital when the end came. The groups of youngsters who had gathered about the red-brick hospital since Wednesday when the name of George Herman Ruth first

Continued on Page 15, Column 5

World News Summarized

TUESDAY, AUGUST 17, 1948

President Truman signed yesterday the anti-inflation measure tightening consumer and bank credit that was adopted by the recent special session of Congress. He accompanied his signature with a bitter attack upon Republican Congressional leadership. [1:8.]

While Senator McGrath, Democratic National Chairman, put out a statement of the accomplishments of the Roosevelt-Truman Administrations as the basis for the Democrats' campaign [11:1], it was agreed in the Republican camp that Governor Warren would be used extensively in campaigning and that both he and Governor Dewey would make coast-to-coast trips. [1:6.]

The House Committee on Un-American Activities questioned Alger Hiss, former State Department official, in a three-hour closed session, but reached no conclusion. Mr. Hiss will confront his accuser Whittaker Chambers, on Aug. 25. [1:2.]

Five days after Mrs. Kosenkina's leap from a window of the Soviet Consulate in New York, the Consulate reversed its version of the incident and said that she had attempted suicide. An official police report on the case, which has been sent to the State Department, rejects the Russian story of the kidnapping of the teacher. [1:1.]

Attorney General Clark announced that an American-born Japanese girl, known as Tokyo Rose, would be brought to this country to face a treason charge. [1:6-7.]

In Moscow, the three Western envoys again conferred with Foreign Minister Molotov. It was reported in London that he was to give Russia's reply to the Western proposals on Berlin at this meeting. [1:3.] In Berlin, the three Western powers considered the possible establishment of a tripartite Kommandatura as a defense against Russian claims to supreme authority over the whole city. [2:2.]

In the Soviet sector of the city and in the Soviet occupation zone, a vigorous purge of the Socialist Unity party was being carried out to reduce it to purely Communist elements. [2:4.]

General Clay stated that he did not expect to resign as Military Governor even if United States policy on Western Germany were changed, which he thought unlikely. [2:8.]

Russian occupation authorities in Austria banned from the Soviet zone, on the charge of warmongering, seven newspapers published in the Western zones. [4:5.]

The Government of Israel announced that it would begin the circulation of new currency today and that the currency would become the sole legal tender in the country on Sept. 15. [1:2-3.] An Israeli communiqué said that Arab riflemen had resumed highway sniping. Israeli forces and Arabs engaged in a pre-dawn artillery duel. [6:6.]

Count Bernadotte reported to the United Nations that 330,000 Arab and Israeli refugees were in grave danger and need. [6:3.] The United Nations Children's Emergency Fund will spend $400,000 to feed displaced Arab mothers and children. [6:4-5.]

Babe Ruth died in a New York hospital at 8 o'clock last night. [1:4-5.]

BIG CAMPAIGN ROLE SET UP FOR WARREN AT DEWEY MEETING

Brownell Reveals Conference Assigns California Governor to Coast to Coast Tours

SENATE VOTES AT STAKE

Candidates and Managers Will Devote Attention to Contests Where Seats Appear Close

By LEO EGAN
Special to THE NEW YORK TIMES.

ALBANY, Aug. 16—Gov. Earl Warren of California, the Republican candidate for Vice President, will receive a major role in the campaign to win votes for the party's national ticket headed by Gov. Thomas E. Dewey of New York, the candidate for President.

This was disclosed this afternoon by Herbert Brownell Jr., campaing manager for the Dewey-Warren ticket, during a top level Republican strategy conference in Governor Dewey's office in which the two candidates appeared.

Meeting with reporters, Mr. Brownell said also that the candidates and the campaign managers would devote "plenty of attention" to those states where contests for United States Senate seats appeared close. There are eleven in this category, seven of which are now held by Republicans and four by Democrats.

Senate Situation Main Topic

The Senate situation was a major topic today as the two candidates and their advisers mapped plans for the campaign and talked over routes that each will follow. Governor Dewey regards retaining Republican control of the Senate as a major goal in the coming campaign.

Because of the location of seats to be filled this year, some observers regard it as possible that Republicans could win control of the White House and lose the Senate.

Setting at rest reports that Governor Warren would be used chiefly on the West Coast, where he is best known, Mr. Brownell said that both Governors would make coast to coast tours. They are working out itineraries to "reach a maximum number of voters and satisfy a goodly number of the invitations that have poured into national headquarters since their nominations," he said.

Mr. Brownell said he was unable to state at this time when or where they would begin their tours or what mode of travel they will use.

Candidates to Visit Same States

It is probable, he said, that Governor Dewey and Governor Warren will visit some of the same states in the course of the campaign but unlikely they will be in the same state at the same time.

Mr. Brownell's reference to their desire to reach "the maximum number of voters" was taken as an indication they will devote a major part of their time to large metropolitan centers where the Republican Party has been notably weak since the late President Roosevelt was first elected in 1932.

Hickman Powell, free lance writer and a researcher and political adviser of Governor Dewey for the last six years, may be assigned to accompany Governor Warren

Continued on Page 12, Column 3

5,792 Miles Flown By Loaded Bomber

By The United Press.

WASHINGTON, Aug. 16—The Strategic Air Command announced today that a B-29 carrying a simulated bomb load of more than 10,000 pounds set a record last week-end by flying 5,792 miles non-stop from Florida to the West Coast and back in 23 hours and 30 minutes.

Leaving MacDill Air Force Base at Tampa, the B-29 flew to the West Coast, dropped its "bombs" in the Pacific and returned to its base with 317 gallons of gasoline left in its tanks—enough for about another hour of flying

The Strategic Air Command said the return flight was made at an altitude of more than 25,000 feet. The plane and crew are from the Eighth Air Force 509th Bomb Group, stationed at Walker Air Force Base, N. M.

CUT RATES PLANNED AT BATTERY GARAGE

Ground Is Broken for Building to Park 1,500 Autos—First in City Publicly Owned

As ground was broken yesterday for the city's first publicly owned garage at the Manhattan approach to the Brooklyn-Battery Tunnel it was made known that the rates would be substantially under the tariffs exacted by private garages and parking lots.

The ceremony, at the site of what is to be a 1,050 or 1,500 car facility, was brief. At a signal from Mayor O'Dwyer, a huge crane operated by Ben Griff dropped its clam-shell scoop into the stony soil soon after noon and construction of the $3,500,000 project started officially.

Looking on were Robert Moses, chairman of the Triborough Bridge and Tunnel Authority, the agency that is building the structure; Peter Eller, president of Thompson-Starrett Company, Inc., the contractors, and several high city officials involved in the undertaking.

The garage will rise seven stories on land provided by the city. The plot was assessed at $800,000 and taken by condemnation at $1,000,000. The building will be constructed of reinforced concrete and cars will move from floor to floor by a circular ramp. There also will be space for parking on the roof.

The ramp design was copied from one developed by a private operator in Detroit, Mr. Moses said. While the garage has been laid out for 1,050 cars on the basis of self-parking, with elevators for persons parking their own vehicles, its capacity can be increased to 1,500 cars if attendants do the parking. That will be determined after the building is in operation and depends upon "economic feasibility," Mr. Moses said.

The Authority plans to lease the building to a private operator who will guarantee to meet all amortization and interest charges as well as reimburse the Authority for its supervisory expenses. In addition, the Authority has agreed to pay the city $23,600 a year in lieu of taxes out of any net earnings from the garage in excess of all operating expenses, Mr. Moses reported.

Provision also is being made for servicing cars and the sale of automobile accessories. The first floor

Continued on Page 23, Column 3

Arrest of 'Tokyo Rose' Ordered; San Francisco Jury to Sift Case

By JAY WALZ
Special to THE NEW YORK TIMES.

WASHINGTON, Aug. 16—The only American-born girl to whom American troops in the Pacific are believed to have applied the name "Tokyo Rose" will be brought to this country to face a treason charge, Attorney General Tom Clark announced today.

The Department of Justice chief asked the Army to arrest Iva Toguri d'Aquino and transport her as quickly as possible to San Francisco where a grand jury will be convened to determine if she should be tried.

Mrs. d'Aquino is only one of a half dozen women who took part in Tokyo broadcasts beamed to United States soldiers while they were stationed on islands across the Pacific. The idea of the programs was to instill war-weariness in our fighting men. In sweet-toned chit-chat the various Tokyo Roses talked to their American listeners as "forgotten men," and made frequent mention of wayward wives and sweethearts back home.

It is in connection with such broadcasts that Mrs. d'Aquino, a native of Los Angeles who once attended the University of California, will be prosecuted. When first seized by the Army shortly after the war, Mrs. d'Aquino explained that her part in the wartime Tokyo broadcasts was simply to announce phonograph recordings. She said she never attempted propaganda for American fighting men.

She also contended that her marriage a few months before the end of the war to Philip d'Aquino, a Portuguese employe of Domei, Japanese news agency, made her a citizen of Portugal as well as of the United States.

She was arrested after the Japanese surrender, but was released a year ago when no charge was made. She said she applied for a passport to return to the United

Continued on Page 9, Column 5

SIGNING CREDIT BILL, TRUMAN DENOUNCES 'AID TO PRIVILEGED'

He Deplores Fighting Inflation 'by Putting Average Family Through the Wringer'

ECONOMIC CRASH FEARED

Congress Failed U. S. as Whole, He Says, Comparing Aid to Aged With Business Profits

Text of President's statement on anti-inflation bill, Page 11.

By FELIX BELAIR Jr.
Special to THE NEW YORK TIMES.

WASHINGTON, Aug. 16—President Truman signed today the extra-session measure tightening consumer and bank credit and in doing so asserted that Republican leaders of the Eightieth Congress had served the ends of special privilege rather than the welfare of the whole nation.

The final proof of this, the President maintained, was the refusal of the Republican leaders to consider his anti-inflation program.

He termed the enacted measure a "tiny fraction of what we need" and "feeble response" from Congress to the popular demand for relief from exorbitant prices and for strong safeguards against inflationary threats to our prosperity.

He did not believe the nation should fight inflation by putting the average American family "through the wringer," he declared.

All Credit Affected

In addition to reviving wartime consumer-credit controls, the new law will tighten bank credit by authorizing increased reserve requirements behind bank notes and deposits. Both moves were intended to make it more difficult for individuals and business to get credit and thus to lessen the amount of money available for spending on short supplies.

President Truman's allegations brought a quick response from Senator Eugene D. Millikin, Republican, of Colorado, chairman of the Finance Committee and president of the Senate Republican Conference.

"The Congress did not give the President the right to reimpose allocations, rationing, inventory and price control and excess-profits taxes," Senator Millikin said. "This parcel of egregious error was misdirected to a peacetime America devoted to its economic and political freedom. Therefore it was rejected by the special session of the Congress.

"Even if said controls were solutions, the administration of them could not be entrusted to the present Executive Department."

President Truman asserted that while the Republican majority had no anti-inflation program of its own, it had turned a deaf ear to his proposals.

Fears Worse Conditions

"Unless inflation is checked, the situation will get even worse, and we shall invite economic collapse," he added.

The President said that the nation had the resources and the ingenuity to maintain good farm prices, good wages, full employment and maximum production and that all these could be accomplished "if we have faith and act together."

But he said it could not be done by turning our backs on common problems and ignoring the lessons of our recent economic history.

"Unfortunately for all of us, this Congress has failed to heed those lessons of the immediate past," he said.

Mr. Truman noted that the same people who opposed as inflationary his proposals for a higher minimum wage, increased Social Security benefits and Federal aid to education "refuse to do anything about the excessive profits of giant corporations."

He assailed "these same men" who protested as inflationary a $19.50-a-month increase in old-age benefits while remaining silent about the inflationary consequences of reducing the taxes of a couple with an income of $100,000 so that they had $16,725 more a year to spend.

Still directing his remarks to Republican Congressional leaders, the President recalled how "these same men" argued that we could end inflation by letting wages fall behind prices, withdrawing farm price supports, creating large-scale unemployment and bring on a recession.

The President said there was a

Continued on Page 11, Column 8

BABE RUTH, 53, DIES AFTER LONG ILLNESS

Continued From Page 1

appeared on the critical list, were home having dinner.

In the marble lobby, where late last week groups of boys had occasionally tarried, sometimes leaving flowers for the great right fielder, there were just a handful of adults, all of them waiting to see other patients.

On the ninth floor, where the Babe had spent his final illness, nurses and doctors talked in whispers. Those who had seen him had been shocked at the cnange since the days of his baseball prime.

The powerful six-footer who had once electrified Americans with sixty homers in a season, had wasted away. The famous round face had become so hollowed that his snub nose looked long. The once black hair so often seen when the Babe doffed his cap rounding the bases, was almost white.

Deeply moved, Father Kaufman said little as he left after having been with the Babe most of the day. Others in the party were just as uncommunicative and hastened past the dozens of youngsters who quickly gathered in East Sixty-eighth Street outside the hospital.

The Babe's death brought tributes from men equally famous in other fields. Among those who sent messages were President Truman and former President Herbert Hoover. Included in the many tributes from baseball figures were those from Will Harridge, president of the American League, and Ford Frick, head of the National League.

Members of the Ruth family said that although funeral plans had not yet been completed, it had been arranged tentatively that a mass would be sung in St. Patrick's Cathedral at 11 A. M. Thursday. Meanwhile the body was to be taken to the Universal Funeral Chapel, 595 Lexington Avenue.

Relapse Comes Suddenly

Though the public had been aware for several days of the baseball idol's grave condition, his relapse yesterday was surprising because he had shown steady improvement over the week-end. On Sunday he had left his bed for twenty minutes.

Even yesterday morning, the first bulletin, issued at 10:20 o'clock, showed a continuation of this trend. It said the former Yankee slugger had spent a comfortable night and was "holding his own." "There has been no significant change," the announcement said.

In the next few hours, however, the patient's temperature began to rise. Early in the afternoon his condition was obviously worse. At 2:20 P. M. the second hospital bulletin noted that pulmonary complications that had not been present the previous day had returned in "moderate" degree. At the same time the Babe showed difficulty in taking nourishment.

But the full extent of his relapse did not become evident until nearly three hours later. In a special bulletin at 5:10 P. M.—ordinarily hospital authorities would have waited until 9 P. M. for the next report—it was announced:

"Pulmonary complications have become worse since this morning. Condition considered more critical."

Even then, however, visitors to the hospital were unaware that anything unusual was taking place. The groups of youngsters that on previous days had gathered outside the twelve-story building were missing. There was no excitement in the lobby, and most of the green chairs were unoccupied.

At 6:25 o'clock the second special bulletin was issued. As the word passed down from the patient's room on the ninth floor to the lobby, photographers began testing their equipment.

Within five minutes, a flurry of telephone calls that set switchboard lights flashing made it apparent that news of the Babe's extremely critical condition had spread beyond the hospital.

From the moment it became known last Wednesday that Babe Ruth was critically ill, his condition became a matter of nation-wide concern exceeding that usually accorded to the country's most important public officials, industrialists and princes of the church.

Headed by President Truman and Cardinal Spellman American leaders in many fields inquired about his health and wished him recovery. By last night more than 15,000 messages had been received at the hospital from all over the United States and Canada.

The range of greetings to the ailing man, who was more famous in his heyday than Presidents, showed how strong a hold he still had on the people.

On the one hand, Mayor James M. Curley of Boston set aside Friday in his city as "Babe Ruth Day," thus following the precedent established in New York on July 26. At the other extreme, hundreds of youngsters huddled outside the hospital or drifted into the lobby for a few moments.

Though many persons had long been aware that the famous slugger was very ill, the first announcement of his critical condition on Wednesday came as a shock. He had entered Memorial Hospital on June 24, presumably for observation and rest.

Last Monday, when it became known that he had a cold, the situation was not considered alarming by the public, particularly when, the next day, his condition was reported improved. The Babe had been in and out of hospitals since Nov. 26, 1946, when he was admitted to French Hospital.

On Wednesday, however, it was obvious that this illness might be Ruth's last. Only his wife, immediate relatives and closest friends were allowed to see him. He was running a high temperature, hospital officials said then, and there were pulmonary complications. Police Headquarters added telephone operators because of the surge of public interest.

The next day, though the Babe improved slightly, his condition was still critical. That evening, his personal physician conferred with Dr. George Baehr, president of the New York Academy of Medicine.

By Friday, the hospital was issuing its reports only three times a day and the patient was reported to be continuing his recovery. His temperature went down and he began taking nourishment. However, he was still on the critical list.

That night, at the Yankee Stadiium, more than 60,000 fans stood for a minute in silent prayer for the man whose bat had furnished so much baseball drama.

Over the week-end the patient's improvement continued. His temperature went down and he took more nourishment. On Sunday he even left his bed for twenty minutes after spending what the hospital bulletin called "the most restful night of the past ten days."

The Bambino addressing crowd at ceremony marking "Babe Ruth Day" at the Yankee Stadium on April 27, 1947. Standing behind are (left to right): Ford Frick, president of the National League; an unidentified technician; Mel Allen, radio announcer; Francis Cardinal Spellman and A. B. Chandler, baseball commissioner.

NATION'S LEADERS MOURN BABE RUTH

Truman Joins With Others in Expressing Sorrow Over Death of Baseball Star

President Truman joined with leaders in the sports world and in other fields throughout the nation last night in expressing sorrow at the passing of Babe Ruth. Charles G. Ross, White House press secretary, said the President was informed of the baseball star's death soon after it was announced and arranged to send a message of condolence to Mrs. Ruth.

The White House had called the Memorial Hospital here last week at Mr. Truman's request to inquire about the Babe's condition.

Former President Herbert Hoover said in a statement here: "He was a great sportsman in the very best sense of the term."

Mr. Hoover recalled that when a small boy asked him for his autograph during a public gathering in Los Angeles, the lad requested and received three copies "because it takes two of yours to trade for one of Babe Ruth's."

Word of Babe Ruth's death reached Governor Dewey and Gov. Earl Warren of California while the Republican standard bearers were conferring at Albany on campaign plans, according to The Associated Press. They issued the following statements:

Governor Dewey: "George Herman Ruth was the idol of millions of sports-loving Americans. A spectacular baseball player whose equal may never be reached, Babe Ruth was above all a great American. An inspiration to generations of youth all over the country, he typified the fair play, honesty and clean sportsmanship that exemplified American sport. An ambassador of good-will, he took these American sports ideals to the four corners of the earth. In his passing, I have lost a good friend. He will be greatly missed by the many millions of his fans who knew and loved him."

Governor Warren: "A great American has passed on. Few men in American history have been a greater inspiration to the youth of our land. Throughout his life he played the game fair and hard and never gave up to the very end. Those of us who not only admired him, but who knew him feel a deep sense of personal loss in his passing."

Chandler Pays Tribute

Baseball Commissioner A. B. (Happy) Chandler, said:

"His was the American story, the boy who came up from obscurity to learn the people's game and go on to be a great national hero. His deeds will be an inspiration for the children of the world who will try to emulate him."

Will Harridge, president of the American League, said: "Babe Ruth was the greatest single figure and personality in the history of baseball. The indomitable sportsmanship and courage he displayed so many years on the playing field, which he showed through his long illness, stands as a part of a glorious Ruth legend that will live on always in the annals of our national sport and be an inspiration to youth forever."

Ford Frick, president of the National League:

"Babe Ruth needed every inch of that big chest of his to protect the world's largest heart. I knew the Babe well when I traveled with the Yankees as a baseball writer, and I never saw a man with more heart—and you can interpret that as meaning both courage on the field and consideration for others."

Edward G. Barrow, former president of the New York Yankees, who converted Babe Ruth from a southpaw pitcher into an outfielder who became the all-time home-run king, almost collapsed when he received the news at his home in Larchmont.

"Oh, my God," he said. "I just can't believe it. I am terribly shocked and terribly sorry. He was certainly the greatest player of them all. This is a tremendous personal loss to me and an even greater loss for all America."

Last Reunion On June 13

Barrow's last reunion with Ruth was on June 13 at the Yankee Stadium when the players of the 1923 world championship Yankees gathered for their silver anniversary. Both broke into tears when they embraced on the diamond. Mr. Barrow, who now is more than 80 years old, had many differences with Ruth, mostly in regard to the star's fabulous salary and his indifference to training rules, but beneath it all there existed a warm friendship.

Other tributes were:

BURT SHOTTON, Manager Brooklyn Dodgers—All of us in baseball mourn the passing of a great and courageous fellow. But today's players in particular owe a debt of gratitude to Babe Ruth. His spectacular feats on the diamond widened interest in the game, drew record crowds and enabled club owners to double and even treble the capacity of big-league parks.

GEORGE WEISS, general manager of the Yankees—The Yankee organization deeply mourns the passing of Babe Ruth. He will always be the outstanding symbol of Yankee baseball.

EMIL FUCHS, once president and for a brief period manager of the Boston Braves, who hired Ruth as a player and "assistant manager" after the Babe drew his release from the Yankees—Ruth was a great figure in the game and but for certain circumstances would probably still be alive and here at Braves Field today. He was a colorful figure —how colorful we will realize when today's big attendances return to normal.

BILLY SOUTHWORTH, manager of Boston Braves — In all the years that I have been associated with baseball I cannot recall any one event which has saddened so many ball players as the news that Babe Ruth had passed away.

LEO DUROCHER, Giants manager, who played on one of the Ruth clubs—I am shocked at the news. Somehow I thought he would pull through. Babe was a great competitor. His passing is a loss not only to baseball but to sports generally.

7TH OF '27 YANKEES TO DIE

Six Who Preceded Ruth Were Members of Famous Team

Babe Ruth became the seventh member of the famous Yankee team of 1927 to die. This was the team that swept easily to a pennant with its "Murderers Row" and fine pitching.

Among those who played prominent roles with that club and have since died were Lou Gehrig, first baseman; Tony Lazzeri, second baseman; Herb Pennock, pitcher; Urban Shocker, pitcher; John Grabowski, catcher, and Miller Huggins, manager.

Shocker died in 1928, after he had passed his prime. A year later, Huggins, who had fined the Babe $5,000, died at his peak. Gehrig's death came in 1940, and last year Lazzeri died.

Grabowski was killed in a fire the next month, and early this year Pennock, one of the great southpaws of his day, died of a cerebral hemorrhage.

Babe Ruth, Baseball's Great Star and Idol of Children, Had a Career Both Dramatic and Bizarre

WORLD-WIDE FAME WON ON DIAMOND

Even in Lands Where Game Is Unknown, Baseball's Star Player Was Admired

SET HOME RUN MARK IN '27

First a Talented Pitcher, Then Foremost Batter, He Drew Highest Pay of His Time

Probably nowhere in all the imaginative field of fiction could one find a career more dramatic and bizarre than that portrayed in real life by George Herman Ruth. Known the world over, even in foreign lands where baseball is never played, as the Babe, he was the boy who rose from the obscurity of a charitable institution in Baltimore to a position as the leading figure in professional baseball. He was also its greatest drawing-card, its highest salaried performer—at least of his day—and the idol of millions of youngstehs throughout the land.

A creation of the times, he seemed to embody all the qualities that a sport-loving nation demanded of its outstanding hero. For it has always been debatable whether Ruth owed his fame and the vast fortune it made for him more to his ability to smash home runs in greater quantity than any other player in the history of the game or to a strange personality that at all times was intensely real and "regular," which was the one fixed code by which he lived.

He made friends by the thousands and rarely, if ever, lost any of them. Affable, boisterous and good-natured to a fault, he was always as accessible to the newsboy on the corner as to the most dignified personage in worldly affairs. More, he could be very much at ease with both.

He could scarcely recall a name, even of certain intimates with whom he frequently came in contact, but this at no time interfered with the sincerity of his greeting. Indeed, by a singular display of craft, he overcame this slight deficiency with consummate skill. If you looked under 40 it was "Hello, kid, how are you?" And if you appeared above that line of demarcation it was "Hello, doc, how's everything going?"

How Ruth Aided Small Boy

The story is told of the case of Johnny Sylvester, a youngster whose life doctors had despaired of unless something unusual happened to shock him out of a peculiar malady. The boy's uncle, recalling how fond he always had been of baseball, conceived the idea of sending word to Babe Ruth and asking his aid.

The next day the Babe, armed with bat, glove and half a dozen signed baseballs, made one of his frequent pilgrimages to a hospital. The boy, unexpectedly meeting his idol face to face, was so overjoyed that he was cured—almost miraculously.

A year later an elderly man accosted the Babe in a hotel lobby and, after receiving the customary whole-hearted greeting of "Hello, doc," said:

"Babe, I don't know whether you remember me, but I'm Johnny Sylvester's uncle and I want to tell you the family will never forget what you did for us. Johnny is getting along fine."

"That's great," replied the Babe. "Sure, I remember you. Glad to hear Johnny is doing so well. Bring him around some time."

After a few more words they parted and no sooner had the man removed himself from earshot than the Babe turned to a baseball writer at his elbow and asked:

"Now, who the devil was Johnny Sylvester?"

Never Lost Carefree Spirit

Nor must this be mistaken for affectation, for there was never a doubt that the Babe at all times was tremendously sincere in his desire to appear on friendly terms with all the world. And though in later years he acquired a certain polish which he lacked utterly in his early career, he never lost his natural self nor his flamboyant, carefree mannerisms, which at all times made him a show apart from the ball field.

Single-handed, he tore the final game of the 1928 world's series in St. Louis to shreds with his mighty bat by hitting three home runs over the right-field pavilion. That night, returning to New York, he went on a boisterous rampage and no one on the train got any sleep, including his employer, the late Colonel Jacob Ruppert.

Such was the blending of qualities that made Babe Ruth a figure unprecedented in American life. A born showman off the field and a marvelous performer on it, he had an amazing flair for doing the spectacular at the most dramatic moment.

Of his early days in Baltimore even Babe himself was, or pretended to be, somewhat vague during his major league baseball career. Thus various versions of his childhood were printed over the years with neither denial nor confirmation from Ruth as to their accuracy.

However, the following account of his boyhood years appeared in a national magazine under Ruth's own "by-line:"

"In the first place I was not an orphan. * * * My mother, whose maiden name was Schanberg, lived until I was 13. My father, George Herman Ruth, lived until my second year in the majors. Few fathers ever looked more like their sons than my pop and I. My mother was mainly Irish, and was called Kate. My father was of German extraction. It is not true that our family name was Erhardt, as has been repeatedly written. Or Ehrhardt, or Gearhardt.

"But I hardly knew my parents. I don't want to make any excuses or place the blame for my shortcomings as a kid completely on persons or places. * * * Yet I probably was a victim of circumstances. I spent most of the first seven years of my life living over my father's saloon at 426 West Camden Street, Baltimore. * * *

"On June 13, 1902, when I was 7 years old my father and mother placed me in St. Mary's Industrial School in Baltimore. It has since been called an orphanage and a reform school. It was, in fact, a training school for orphans, incorrigibles, delinquents, boys whose homes had been broken by divorce, runaways picked up on the streets of Baltimore and children of poor parents who had no other means of providing an education for them.

"I was listed as an incorrigible, and I guess I was. * * * I chewed tobacco when I was 7, not that I enjoyed it especially, but, from my observation around the saloon it seemed the normal thing to do.

Gaps in School Life

"I was released from St. Mary's in July, 1902, but my parents returned me there in November of the same year. My people moved to a new neighborhood just before Christmas, 1902, and I was released to them again. This time I stayed 'out' until 1904, but then they put me back again and I was not released again until 1908. Shortly after my mother died I was returned to St. Mary's once more by my father. He took me back home in 1911 and returned me in 1912. I stayed in school—learning to be a tailor and shirtmaker—until Feb. 27, 1914. The last item on my 'record' at St. Mary's was a single sentence, written in the flowing hand of one of the teachers. It read:

" 'He is going to join the Balt. Baseball Team.' "

In Hollywood, where he was portraying himself in a motion picture dealing with the life of his team-mate, the late Lou Gehrig, played by Gary Cooper (right).

Associated Press

Ruth said he played in the band at St. Mary's and always pointed with pride to this accomplishment, frequently reminding friends that he also was a musician as well as a ball player. Curiously enough, however, no one ever discovered what instrument the Babe played, although he always stoutly denied that it was the bass drum.

But baseball captivated his fancy most and now began a train of circumstances that was to carry this black-haired, raw-boned youngster to fame and a fortune that has been estimated as close to $1,000,000. It also happened that Brother Benedict, one of the instructors at St. Mary's, was a great lover of the national pastime.

Using baseball, therefore, as the most plausible means to a laudable end in keeping the Babe out of mischief as much as possible, the good Brother encouraged the youngster to play as much as he could. The Babe scarcely needed encouragement. Every hour he was allowed to spare from his classrooms found him on the ball field.

He batted left-handed and threw left-handed. He played on his school team, also on a semi-professional team. He also played pretty nearly every position on the field. At the age of 19 he astounded even his sponsor, Brother Benedict, who now saw a real means of livelihood ahead for the young man, though little dreaming at the time to what heights he would soar.

He recommended the Babe to his friend, the late Jack Dunn, then owner of the Baltimore Orioles of the International League, and Ruth received a trial, alternating in the outfield and in the pitcher's box. That was in 1914. The same summer he was sold to the Boston Red Sox for $2,900, and after a brief period of farming out with Providence was recalled to become a regular.

Under the direction of Bill Carrigan, then manager of the Red Sox, Ruth rapidly developed into one of the most talented left-handed pitchers ever in the majors. He had tremendous speed and a baffling cross-fire curve, which greatly impressed Ed Barrow, later to become associated with Colonel Ruppert as general manager of the Yankees. Barrow became the leader of the Red Sox in 1918 and gave much time to Ruth's development.

But even then he also displayed unmistakable talent for batting a ball with tremendous power and with unusual frequency, and Barrow, one of baseball's greatest men of vision, decided to convert Ruth permanently into an outfielder on the theory that a great hitter could be built into a greater attraction than a great pitcher.

It was quite a momentous decision, for in the 1918 world's series against the Cubs Ruth had turned in two masterful performances on the mound for the Red Sox, winning both his games. He had also turned in one victory for the Red Sox against Brooklyn in the world's series of 1916.

But Barrow had also seen Ruth, in 1918, hit eleven home runs, an astonishing number for that era, particularly for a pitcher, and his mind was made up.

The next year—1919—Ruth, pitching only occasionally, now and then helping out at first base, but performing mostly in the outfield, cracked twenty-nine home runs and the baseball world began to buzz as it hadn't since the advent of Ty Cobb and the immortal Christy Mathewson. This total surpassed by four the then accepted major league record for home runs in a season, set by Buck Freeman with the Washington Club in 1899.

But it was the following year—1920—that was to mark the turning point, not only in Babe Ruth's career but in the entire course of organized baseball. Indeed, baseball men are almost in accord in the belief that Babe Ruth, more than any individual, and practically single-handed, rescued the game from what threatened to be one of its darkest periods. Not only rescued it, but diverted it into new channels that in the next decade were to reap an unprecedented golden harvest.

The first sensation came early that winter when Ruth was sold by the late Harry Frazee, then owner of the Red Sox, to the Yankees, owned jointly by the two Colonels, Jacob Ruppert and Tillinghast L'Hommedieu Huston, for a reported price of $125,000. It may even have been more, for in making the purchase the Yankee owners also assumed numerous financial obligations then harassing the Boston owner, and the matter was very involved. But whatever the price, it was a record sum, and New York prepared to welcome its latest hero prospect.

The Babe did not disappoint. The Yankees were then playing their home games at the Polo Grounds, home of the Giants, and before the close of the 1920 season they were already giving their more affluent rivals and landlords a stiff run for the city's baseball patronage.

Ruth surpassed all expectations by crashing out the unheard-of total of fifty-four home runs and crowds which hitherto had lavished their attention on the Giants now jammed the historic Polo Grounds to see the marvelous Bambino hit a homer.

Crisis in History of Game

But scarcely had the echoes from the thunderous roars that greeted the Ruthian batting feats subsided than another explosion was touched off that rattled the entire structure of baseball down to its sub-cellar. The scandal of the world's series of 1919 broke into print and through the winter of 1920-21 the "throwing" of that series by certain White Sox players to the Reds was on every tongue.

The baseball owners of both major leagues were in a panic, fearful that the public's confidence in what they had so proudly called America's national pastime had been shaken beyond repair. True, they had induced the late Kenesaw Mountain Landis, a Federal judge, to assume the position of High Commissioner with unlimited powers to safeguard against a repetition of such a calamity, but they feared it was not enough.

With considerable misgivings they saw the 1921 season get under way and then, as the popular song of the day ran, "Along Came Ruth."

Inside of a fortnight the fandom of the nation had forgotten all about the Black Sox, as they had come to be called, as its attention became centered in an even greater demonstration of superlative batting skill by the amazing Babe Ruth. Home runs began to scale off his bat in droves, crowds jammed ball parks in every city in which he appeared and when he

(continued)

closed the season with a total of fifty-nine circuit clouts, surpassing by five his own record of the year before, the baseball world lay at his feet.

In addition to that, the Yankees that year captured the first pennant ever won by New York in the American League, and Ruth was now fairly launched upon the first chapter of the golden harvest. With the help of his towering war club, the Yankees won again in 1922 and repeated in 1923, in addition to winning the world's championship that year.

Also in 1923 came into being the "House That Ruth Built," meaning the great Yankee Stadium with its seating capacity of more than 70,000, which Colonel Ruppert decided to erect the year previous in order to make himself clear and independent of the Giants, whose tenant he had been at the Polo Grounds. The right-field bleachers became "Ruthville." Homers soared into them in great abundance and the exploitation of Babe Ruth, the greatest slugger of all times, was at its height.

Spent Earnings Freely

But now there crept in a dark episode, decidedly less glamorous, though spectacular enough, and which must be chronicled in order to appreciate more fully the second chapter of the golden harvest. Money was now pouring upon the Babe and was being poured out as speedily. In 1921 he had drawn $20,000 and the following season he signed a five-year contract at $52,000 a season. In addition to this he was collecting royalties on all sorts of ventures.

But money meant nothing to the Babe, except as a convenient means for lavish entertainment. He gambled recklessly, lost and laughed uproariously. The Ruthian waistline began to assume alarming proportions. He still took his baseball seriously enough on the field, but training had become a horrible bore.

Of such phenomenal strength, there seemed to be no limits to his vitality or stamina. It was no trick at all for him to spend an evening roistering with convivial companions right through sun-up and until game time the next afternoon and then pound a home run.

Along in the 1924 season Colonel Ruppert began to fear he had made a mistake in having signed the Babe to that long-term contract at $52,000 per season which ran from 1922 to 1926 inclusive. The Yankees lost the pennant that year and there came ominous rumblings that Miller Huggins, the mite manager who had just piloted the Yankees through three successful pennant years, was not in harmony with the Babe at all.

There even had been trouble back in 1921 when Ruth openly flouted Commissioner Landis by playing on a barnstorming tour that fall after the limit date set by the commissioner. The following spring Landis, in order to demonstrate his authority, suspended Ruth for thirty days from the opening of the season.

But it was not until 1925 that the real crash came and high living proved as exacting in collecting its toll as the high commissioner. Coming north at the end of the training season Ruth collapsed at the railroad station at Asheville, N. C., from a complication of ailments.

He was helped aboard the train, carried off on a stretcher on the team's arrival in New York and spent weeks in a hospital. He did not appear again in a Yankee lineup until June 1.

Nor had all the lesson been yet fully learned. Later in the same campaign Huggins, exasperated beyond all measure at the Babe's wayward way of deporting himself, slapped a $5,000 fine on him for "misconduct off the ball field." It was the highest fine ever imposed on a ball player, and Ruth at first took it as a joke. But Huggins stuck by his guns, received the backing of Colonel Ruppert, who was now the sole owner of the club, and the fine came from the Babe's pay check.

Now the lesson was learned and another startling change came over the Babe. He became, almost overnight, one of Miller Huggins' stanchest supporters. He trained faithfully in 1926, hammered forty-seven homers as against a meager twenty-five in 1925, and started the Yankees on another pennant-winning era. Sixty homers, a new record sailed off his bat in 1927, and Ruth was a greater figure in baseball than ever.

Another pennant followed that year and still another in 1928, on top of which the Yankees swept through two world series triumphs in those two years without the loss of a single game.

Became Good Business Man

In the Spring of 1929, several months after his first wife, from whom he had been estranged for a number of years, died in a fire in Boston, the Babe married Mrs. Claire Hodgson, formerly an actress, and to her also is given a deal of credit for the complete reformation of the Babe, who in the closing years of his baseball activities trained as faithfully to fulfill what he considered his obligation to his public as it was humanly possible.

Simultaneously with this Ruth suddenly became a shrewd business man with an eye to the future. Giving heed to the advice of Colonel Ruppert and Ed Barrow, the Babe invested his earnings carefully. In 1927 he became the highest salaried player of his time with a three-year contract at $70,000 a year. In 1930 he signed a two-year contract at $80,000 per season, but in 1932 acceding to economic pressure of the times, accepted a $75,000 stipend for one season.

That proved an excellent investment, for the Yankees won another pennant that year and defeated the Cubs in four straight games, Ruth causing a sensation by indicating to the spectators in Chicago where he meant to hit the ball when he made two home runs in the third game of the series for the championship. The next year saw a further decline in the salary of the star to $52,000, and in 1934 he signed for $35,000.

At the close of his baseball career it was estimated that in his twenty-two years in the major leagues he had earned in salaries $896,000, plus $41,445 as his share of world series receipts. In addition, he was reputed to have made $1,000,000 from endorsements, barnstorming tours, movies and radio appearances.

As a consequence, when he retired the Babe was able to live in comfort, maintaining a large apartment on New York's West Side. For, despite his earlier extravagances, he later invested so well he was able to realize a monthly income of $2,500 by the time he had reached 45.

In addition to the great crowds he had drawn steadily to major league parks, he also brought vast sums into the Yankee coffers from spring exhibition tours. In 1929 and 1930 the Yanks booked two tours through Texas and the Middle West on their way north from the training camp in Florida and played to record-smashing crowds that stormed hotel lobbies and blocked traffic in all directions to get a glimpse of baseball's most famous character.

And through all this new homage showered upon him, he steadfastly remained the same Babe, more serious-minded, but as cordial and affable as ever. The youngsters he worshiped possibly as much as they worshiped him. In Waco, Tex., he broke up an exhibition game by inviting some of the kids to come out on the field and roll around on the grass. They poured out of the stands by the thousands, overran the field, swamped the local police and ended the game.

Ruth came to the parting of the ways with the Yankees after the 1934 season. He had always aspired to be a manager, and that Winter he asked Colonel Ruppert, with his accustomed bluntness, to make him leader of the New York team. Ruppert was satisfied with the results obtained by Joe McCarthy in winning the 1962 world series after coming from the Cubs in 1931 and refused. However, he said that he would not stand in the way of Ruth if the latter could find a place as manager.

The opening came in the spring of 1935, when Judge Emil Fuchs, then president of the Boston National League Club, offered Ruth a contract as a player at $25,000 a year, with a percentage from exhibition games and a percentage of the gain in the earnings of the club, together with a promise of becoming manager the following season. Ruppert gave Ruth his release and he joined the National League team at its training camp in St. Petersburg, Fla., that spring.

Ruth never was a success with the Braves. He was his old self as a batsman and player only in spots and the team sank into the National League cellar. On May 25, 1935, in Pittsburgh he showed the last flash of his former greatness when he batted three home runs in consecutive times at bat at Forbes Field, but a week later, on June 2, after a dispute with Fuchs he asked for and received his release. He had several offers from minor league teams after that, but refused them all.

It was not until June 17, 1938, that his chance came to re-enter the big leagues. Then he was named coach of the Dodgers. Burleigh Grimes, the manager of the team, recommending the move, said "you can't keep a man like that out of baseball." Although the team was a loser, Ruth entered into the work of upbuilding enthusiastically and was hailed with the usual acclaim around the circuit and in towns where he played in exhibition games.

Although Ruth's continued popularity helped the Dodgers to draw additional fans through their turnstiles, a service for which the club paid him a $15,000 salary, he was not re-engaged as coach at the close of the 1938 season.

It was then that Leo Durocher was appointed manager to succeed Grimes. Ruth, taking his dismissal in good spirit, explained that a new manager necessarily would want to make his own choice for the coaching jobs, and he wished the Dodgers good luck.

The Bambino once again became the retired business man, and as he returned to the role of "baseball's forgotten man," he increased his activities on the links. His name soon became associated with some of golf's leading players, while his scores consistently ran in the low 70's.

At World's Fair Baseball School

However, he never overlooked lending a hand to his first love wherever baseball offered him some opportunity for showing himself. During 1939 he appeared at the World's Fair baseball school in the role of instructor, took part in the old-timers' game in the baseball centennial celebration at Cooperstown, played a prominent role in the Lou Gehrig appreciation day ceremonies and in the spring of 1940 appeared for a time with a baseball training school at Palatka, Fla.

During 1941, Ruth, principally through the medium of his golfing prowess, stayed in the public eye. During the summer he engaged in a series of matches with his old diamond rival, Cobb, the proceeds going to the British War Relief Fund and the United Service Organizations. Cobb, victor in the first match in Boston, 3 and 2, lost the second match at Fresh Meadow, New York, 1 up on the nineteenth hole, but came back to defeat the Babe in the deciding tilt in Detroit, 3 and 2.

Later in the year Ruth signed a contract to appear in the Samuel Goldwyn motion picture based on the life of his famous team-mate, Lou Gehrig, with the Babe appearing as himself.

The Babe hit the headlines and frightened his friends before 1942 scarcely had begun. On the morning of Jan. 3 he was removed to a hospital in an ambulance, the reason being "an upset nervous condition," partly brought on by an automobile accident in which he was involved.

But three weeks later Ruth was off on a hunting trip in up-State New York and by February was in Hollywood, teaching Gary Cooper (who was to portray Gehrig) how to bat left-handed and signing autographs for screen stars.

On April 9 Ruth went to the Hollywood Hospital suffering from pneumonia and described by his doctor as "a border line case," but two days later the Babe's countless friends and well-wishers were cheered by the same physician's statement: "I believe he is over the hump." Ruth was out of the hospital by April 22 and back on the movie lot to complete his work in the Gehrig film.

During that and succeeding war years Ruth answered any and all demands for his appearance at war bond rallies and charity enterprises. He played in golf tournaments, went bowling and sold bonds. On Aug. 23, 1942, he paired with the late Walter Johnson, another of baseball's immortals, at the Yankee Stadium to aid in a benefit show for two war services.

With Johnson pitching, the Babe came through, as he always had, by hitting a "home run" into the right field seats and "rounding the bases" via a short cut from first to third base. That was his final homer.

Late in 1943 Ruth proved a bad prophet when he predicted that major league baseball would become a war casualty in 1944, "if not sooner." His prophesying was as wholehearted as his ball playing had been, for he said: "It's a cinch they won't open the ball parks next year."

Although never realizing an ambition to manage a major league club, Ruth became manager for a day in mid-July of 1943, when he piloted a team of all-stars, including such players as Ted Williams and Dom DiMaggio, to a triumph over the Boston Braves as part of a charity field-day program in Boston. A dozen days later he filled the same role in a similar game at Yankee Stadium.

Ruth's activity in aiding war causes increased in 1944 and it was in March of that year that he was the subject of one of the oddest dispatches of the conflict. It came from Cape Gloucester, New Britain, where United States Marines were fighting the Japanese and recounted that when the little men charged the Marine lines their battle cry was:

"To hell with Babe Ruth!"

Babe's rumbling comment to that was:

"I hope every Jap that mentions my name gets shot—and to hell with all Japs anyway!"

The Babe didn't know, or care, that nine years before the Japanese sounded that battle cry a Japanese publisher had been assassinated by a Japanese fanatic and that Ruth was partly blamed for it. The assassin had said the publisher's crime was in sponsoring the Japanese tour of a group of American ball players, headed by Babe Ruth.

In June of 1944 Ruth went into the hospital once more, this time to have a cartilage removed from his knee. Reports immediately followed that he might try to play ball again as a pinch-hitter.

Early in 1946 Ruth took a trip to Mexico as a guest of the fabulous Pasquel brothers, "raiders" of American organized baseball. This resulted in a rumor that he would become commissioner of the Mexican National League, the Pasquel loop, but as usual nothing came of it.

On his return to New York Ruth disclosed that he had sought the manager's berth with the Newark club, owned by the Yankees, but that "all I got was a good pushing around" by Larry MacPhail. The Babe also praised the Pasquels and at the same time revealed that he had turned down an offer of $20,000 from the Federal League while getting $600 a season from Baltimore.

"I turned it down because we were told by organized baseball that if we jumped we would be barred for life. But nobody was barred for life and I just got jobbed out of $20,000 without a thank-you from anybody."

There was scarcely room for real bitterness in the expansive and warm Ruthian temperament, but the big fellow undoubtedly did feel at times a resentment against the owners in major league baseball because no place in it ever was found for him. And whatever slight flame of resentment may have lighted in him was frequently fanned by many writers who openly chided the baseball moguls for sidestepping the great Bambino.

Through the unhappy medium of a protracted illness and a serious neck operation that kept him hospitalized from late November 1946, to mid-February, 1947, Ruth came back into the public eye. Recurrent reports that his condition was critical resulted in a deluge of messages from sympathetic well-wishers.

There was general rejoicing among his legions of followers when he was sufficiently recovered to leave the hospital. That this feeling was shared in official baseball circles was promptly indicated when Baseball Commissioner A.B. (Happy) Chandler paid unprecedented tribute to the Sultan of Swat by designating April 27, 1947 as "Babe Ruth Day."

All organized baseball joined on this date in honoring the man who contributed so much to the game. Ruth himself was present at the Yankee Stadium, where a crowd of 58,339 turned out for ceremonies that were broadcast over the world and piped into the other major league ballparks.

Extremely conscious of his debt to the "kids of America," to whose loyal support he attributed his success, Ruth identified himself with welfare programs after his discharge from the hospital. He was engaged by the Ford Motor Company as a consultant in connection with its participation in the American Legion junior baseball program and he was named by Mayor William O'Dwyer of New York as permanent honorary chairman of the Police Athletic League.

In May, 1947, he established and made the first contribution to the Babe Ruth Foundation, Inc., an organization whose resources were to be devoted to the interests of underprivileged youth.

Although the ravages of his illness left little of his once robust physique, the Babe, now gaunt and bent and his once resonant voice reduced to a rasping whisper, continued to astound his physicians by tackling his new job with all his oldtime vigor. Throughout the summer he made innumerable public appearances all over the country.

On Sunday, Sept. 28, the final day of the 1947 championship season, he returned to the Yankee Stadium to receive another thunderous ovation. On this day, under the direction of MacPhail, a galaxy of more than forty stars of former Yankee and other American League world championship teams, assembled to engage in an Oldtimers Day.

Ruth continued his role as consultant, making appearances all over the country. He went to Hollywood to help with the filming of his life story. While there, the Babe was informed that the Yankees were planning to celebrate the twenty-fifth anniversary of the Yankee Stadium. He readily agreed to participate in the ceremonies. He accepted the managership of the 1923 Yankees, who were to play an abbreviated exhibition game against later-year Yankees, to be piloted by Barrow.

June 13, 1948, was the date set for "Silver Anniversary Day." It turned out to be a memorable day, one that Ruth, despite his physical condition, would not have missed for anything. Despite a wretched day—rain, fog, etc.—the Babe donned his old uniform with the No. 3 on the back. When he was introduced and walked slowly to home plate, a thunderous ovation from 49,641 men, women and children greeted him.

Many in the gathering wept as Ruth, in a raspy voice, told how happy he was to have hit the first homer ever achieved in the Stadium; how proud he was to have been associated with such fine players and how glad he was to be back with them, even if only for a day.

It was the last time that No. 3 was worn by a Yankee player. For, the Babe turned his uniform over to the Hall of Fame, retired for all time. It was sent to the baseball shrine at Cooperstown, N. Y., where it was placed among the Ruth collection there.

Ruth's team scored a 2-0, two-inning victory that day and the man to whom a big-league manager's job was never given managed a winner in the "House That Ruth Built."

"All the News That's Fit to Print"

The New York Times

LATE CITY EDITION

Weather: Fair, hot and humid today, tonight and tomorrow. Temp.-range: today 90-68. Saturday 81-65. Temp.-Hum. Index 75. Saturday 76. Full U.S. report on Page 63.

SECTION ONE

VOL. CXVI..No. 39,992

NEW YORK, SUNDAY, JULY 23, 1967

60c beyond 50-mile zone from New York City, except Long Island. Higher in air delivery cities. 40 CENTS

HOUSE UNIT BACKS RISE IN TAX RATES ON AGED BENEFITS

Ways and Means Panel Cuts Social Security Payments Proposed by Johnson

MEDICARE COSTS CITED

Present Plan Would Set Top Taxable Pay at $7,800—Final Approval Near

By JOHN D. MORRIS

Special to The New York Times

WASHINGTON, July 22 — The House Ways and Means Committee is striving to complete work, possibly next week, on a scaled-down version of the Administration's Social Security bill.

While trimming major provisions for increases in benefits, the committee has tentatively agreed that Social Security tax rates must be raised beyond Administration recommendations to allow for underestimates of Medicare costs.

The committee still plans, however, to put a $7,800 limit on the amount of annual pay to which the payroll taxes apply. The present taxable base is $6,600. The bill, as introduced, called for increases to $7,800 next year, to $9,000 in 1971 and to $10,800 in 1974.

Rise Varies by Income

The net effect of the committee plan would be a larger increase than the Administration proposed for workers earning less than $7,800 and a smaller one, in the long run, for those earning more than $7,800.

As the bill now stands, cash benefits under the Old Age, Survivors and Disability Insurance program would be raised across-the-board by 13 per cent instead of by 15 per cent as recommended by the Administration.

Members said this might be scaled down further—perhaps to 11 or 12 per cent—before the measure emerged from committee.

Monthly Minimum Up

A provision to raise the minimum monthly benefit from $44 to $70 has also been modified in an effort to reduce the bill's prospective cost. Committee members said the new minimum would be no higher than $60 and might be as low as $50. A tentative decision to make it $60 is now being reconsidered.

In addition, the committee has reconsidered an earlier decision to accept without change a provision for Medicare benefits to persons under 65 who receive cash disability payments under the Old Age, Survivors and Disability Insurance program.

The present Medicare law limits the coverage of hospital and voluntary medical insurance to persons over 65. The original Administration bill would have extended the cov-

Continued on Page 40, Column 1

Fred Stein

Carl Sandburg

Carl Sandburg, 89, Poet And Biographer, Is Dead

Health Poor Since '65

Special to The New York Times

FLAT ROCK, N.C., July 22—Carl Sandburg, the snowy-haired poet, folk singer and biographer of Lincoln, died here today at his 240-acre goat ranch. He was 89 years old.

The Pulitzer Prize winner had been in poor health since hospitalization in 1965 for an intestinal infection.

Six weeks ago, in his house of hand-hewn timbers dating from the Civil War, he suffered a heart attack. About a week ago, he had another. He spent his last weeks looking out from his bed at the pine trees and mountains he had come to love in his 22 years here. His wife, Lillian Paula, said this afternoon:

"It was a wonderful way to pass away. No pain at all. At midnight yesterday, I looked in on him—he had his nurses around the clock. He brightened and said, 'Paula.' This morning he

Continued on Page 62, Column 1

The American Bard

By THOMAS LASK

Carl Sandburg was more than a poet, biographer, spinner of tales and wandering minstrel—he was the American bard.

The sense of being American informed everything he wrote. In his poetry, Wichita, Omaha and Buffalo were names as rich and flavorsome as Siena, Padua and Ravenna. It was Sandburg,

An Appraisal

writing of Monte Cristo in "The People, Yes," who said that he was "on a par with Frankie who shot Johnnie," and that though Cristo put on a good show, "Jesse James beat his record."

Discussing his poetic practice, he once remarked, "I searched for picture words as the Indians and Chinese have them." The use of picture words was scarcely restricted to Sandburg. Pound (to take an obvious case) made much of its use. But while

Continued on Page 62, Column 2

GROMYKO BLAMES U.S. FOR IMPASSE IN U.N. ON MIDEAST

On Way Home, He Decries Assembly Failure to Call for Israeli Withdrawal

By DREW MIDDLETON

Special to The New York Times

UNITED NATIONS, N. Y., July 22—Foreign Minister Andrei A. Gromyko said today that the United States was mainly to blame for the failure of the General Assembly in its emergency session to demand the immediate withdrawal of Israeli forces from conquered territory in three Arab states.

Mr. Gromyko made this charge, on which he did not elaborate, at Kennedy International Airport shortly before his departure by air for Moscow. The Assembly session, which Moscow had requested, ended last night without achievement of the Soviet delegation's central aim.

The Russians had hoped to get an Assembly demand for the withdrawal of Israeli troops from occupied areas in the United Arab Republic, Syria and Jordan, as well as an Assembly condemnation of Israeli aggression.

Help Sought From U.S.

Before the session closed, Mr. Gromyko had asked and obtained the help of Arthur J. Goldberg, the United States representative, in drafting a milder compromise resolution calling for an Israeli pullback, but this was rejected by the Arabs.

Israeli withdrawal, the Foreign Minister insisted today, is "the most immediate and most acute" question in the Middle East.

Mr. Gromyko said the positive side of the session's work had been that most delegations "in one form or another condemned the aggressive actions of Israel." The Soviet attempt to obtain a formal condemnation was rejected by the Assembly on July 4.

"The negative side," the foreign minister said, "is that, mainly because of the position of the United States Government, the General Assembly was not able at this stage to pass a recommendation for the immediate withdrawal of Israeli troops."

Eban Renews Plea

Abba Eban, Israel's Foreign Minister, who also departed today, renewed his plea for negotiations between Israel and the Arab states.

Referring in an airport statement to the Assembly's failure to achieve progress on peacemaking, Mr. Eban said, "The solution cannot be found in parliamentary terms" but must be found by the Arab states themselves.

"The United Nations cannot solve problems for nations that do not want to solve them," he declared, and the Arab countries, he added, cannot solve their problems "without contact with Israel."

Leaders of the Arab states vowed today they would have the Assembly reconvened when the need arose and warned that they might take such action if Israel continued to ignore two resolutions demanding she halt the unification of Jerusalem. This was in line with the words

Continued on Page 16, Column 3

RETURNS TO MOSCOW: Soviet Foreign Minister Andrei A. Gromyko at Kennedy International Airport here yesterday. Seeing him off are Ambassador Anatoly F. Dobrynin, at center, and Nikolai T. Fedorenko, the Soviet representative at the United Nations.

U.S. IS PLANNING RISE IN ADVISERS FOR SAIGON UNITS

50 Per Cent Increase Likely—Goal Is a Step-Up in Combat Effectiveness

OTHER MOVES WEIGHED

South Vietnamese May Get a Request to Expand Their Local Forces by a Third

By WILLIAM BEECHER

Special to The New York Times

WASHINGTON, July 22—The Johnson Administration is planning a 50 per cent increase in the number of American advisers assigned to South Vietnamese combat units.

This is among a number of moves designed to achieve major increases in combat efficiency through relatively modest adjustments in present force levels.

The plans were worked out in the recent White House meetings of President Johnson with Gen. William C. Westmoreland, commander of United States forces in Vietnam, and Secretary of Defense Robert S. McNamara. There are now about 465,000 American troops in Vietnam.

Provide Guard for Villages

According to top defense planners, the Administration will also ask South Vietnam to increase by 30 per cent the size of its Popular Forces, as they are called, the primary mission of which is to guard villages and hamlets against guerrilla assault.

There are now about 5,200 Army men working as advisers with Saigon's regular army, with the regional forces which operate in provinces under the province chiefs, and with the Popular Force units.

Officials say this adviser total will be increased by more than 2,600, most of the men destined to advise South Vietnamese Popular Force troops in local defense missions.

May Lower the Draft Age

South Vietnam's Popular Forces now number about 145,000. About 50,000 will be added, according to present plans. This may require lowering the South Vietnamese draft age from 20 to 18, they say.

Other components of the South Vietnamese armed forces are the regular army of about 320,000, in which an increase of about 13,000 is planned, and the Regional Forces of about 145,000. Thus the projected total for Saigon's armed forces is in the neighborhood of 675,000.

Officials say the final shape of several of the actions approved at the White House review of Vietnam policy last week will not become fixed for some time. For example, they point out that inflation fears prompted Washington

Continued on Page 3, Column 1

Hanoi's 'Hero' Stirs Propaganda War

By BERNARD WEINRAUB

Special to The New York Times

SAIGON, July 21—A frail 21-year-old peasant is the focus of an intense psychological-warfare duel between the North Vietnamese, who contend he is dead, and United States officials, who insist he is alive.

The youth, a former Vietcong ammunition carrier, Nguyen Van Be, has been proclaimed a national hero by the Vietcong and the North Vietnamese. They say he sacrificed his life last May by seizing a mine in his hands and smashing the detonator against an armored vehicle, killing "69 American aggressors and puppet troops."

But the United States officials say that he was captured by South Vietnamese troops and is in custody in Saigon. They believe that the North Vietnamese actually thought the youth was dead. When he showed up in prison, the officials say, the North Vietnamese refused to concede that they had made an error and stepped up their drive to make him a hero.

"I am still alive," a youth identified as Nguyen Van Be said today in an interview. "Why do they use my name? Why do they use this story?"

"I am frightened," the youth went on, nervously lighting a cigarette. "People say I'm a hero and I cannot be alive. How can a hero be alive? People say they will certainly kill me. They cannot afford to have a live hero, can they?"

The American officials say the North Vietnamese and the Vietcong had two choices when confronted with the photographs and news conference statements of Nguyen Van Be.

"They could have dropped the whole thing and forgotten about it or they could have ignored us and turned up the volume," said Donald Rochlen, the officer for special projects in psychological warfare at the Joint United States Public Affairs Office. "They turned up the volume."

At the moment, four million young men and women are taking a six-week course in North Vietnam on the exploits of Nguyen Van Be. United States officials estimate that 4,000 teachers and

Continued on Page 3, Column 4

ARMS SALES FACING CONGRESS INQUIRY

Role of Export-Import Bank in Financing Deals Stirs Concern in Both Houses

By E. W. KENWORTHY

Special to The New York Times

WASHINGTON, July 22—Both the Senate and the House are now expected to delay action to extend the life and lending authority of the Export-Import Bank until a thorough investigation has been made of the bank's financing of arms sales to foreign nations.

Representative William B. Widnall of New Jersey, the ranking Republican on the House Banking and Currency Committee, noted today that in the last two fiscal years more than 39 per cent of the bank's loans had been for arms purchases. And these "arms credits," he said, "amounted to nearly $1.5-billion, as compared to $2.3-billion in credits for peaceful goods."

"Once again," Mr. Widnall said, "I call upon the Congress

Continued on Page 12, Column 1

50 Turkish Towns Jolted by a Quake; Casualties Heavy

Special to The New York Times

ISTANBUL, Turkey, July 22—Hundreds of casualties were reported over a wide area about 20 miles east of Istanbul tonight after an earthquake caused heavy damage and spread panic in about 50 towns and villages.

The center of the quake appeared to be in Adapazari, a city of 80,000 almost due east of Istanbul. The semiofficial Anatolia News Agency reported that 60 people had been killed and 200 injured in Adapazari and nearby villages.

Twenty deaths and 140 injuries were reported from Sakarya, south of Adapazari. Ambulances, doctors, nurses and medical supplies have been sent to both towns from Istanbul, and Turkish Army units were sent from a garrison at Izmit, 30 miles west of Adapazari.

The Ankara-Istanbul railway line was cut, and rail traffic halted. Highway policemen were turning back civilian automobiles on the Istanbul

Continued on Page 2, Column 4

FIGHTING RENEWED NEAR BUFFER ZONE

9 Marines Killed in 5-Hour Action Near Khesanh After a 2-Week Lull

By TOM BUCKLEY

Special to The New York Times

SAIGON, South Vietnam, July 22—A North Vietnamese battalion attacked a Marine platoon just below the demilitarized zone, bombarding it with 120 rounds of mortar fire, as action flared for the first time in two weeks in the area, a high command spokesman said today.

Nine marines were killed and 30 wounded in the five-hour encounter, which took place yesterday eight miles northeast of a defensive position at Khesanh and about two miles south of the buffer zone along the border between North Vietnam and South Vietnam. Twenty-four enemy soldiers were reported killed.

Clash Near Khesanh

The marines were members of a special landing force of the Third Regiment that is stationed aboard a helicopter carrier in the Gulf of Tonkin. They were sweeping along Highway 9 from Camp Carroll, an artillery base, when the attack occurred.

A Marine spokesman at Danang said that battle was broken off by the North Vietnamese at 9 o'clock last night after the marines were reinforced and were given air and artillery support.

In the hills six miles northwest of Khesanh, near the Laotian border yesterday, five marines of the 26th Regiment were killed and nine wounded in a one-hour clash between their company and what was called a North Vietnamese force of unknown size.

The marines fought a bitter two-week battle in late April and early May for the possession of the hills that dominate Khesanh. The objective of the present sweeps to the north,

Continued on Page 4, Column 1

VIOLENCE AFFLICTS ENGLEWOOD AGAIN

Gunfire by Snipers Reported as Well as Looting and Two Supermarket Fires

By MARTIN GANSBERG

Special to The New York Times

ENGLEWOOD, N. J., Sunday, July 23 — Sporadic gunfire by snipers beginning soon after 9 o'clock last night was reported by the police here today as racial disturbances broke out for the second night in this city of 30,000.

The shooting was limited to a one-block area in the predominantly Negro Fourth Ward, according to the police. Snipers were firing along William Street, a north-south thoroughfare, from Linden Avenue to Jay Street.

No injuries were reported, but the police said they had arrested eight persons, including one woman. This raised the two-day total to 13 persons.

There also were reports that fires had been started in two supermarkets and that at least one tavern, the Blue Moon, had been hit by a Molotov cocktail. The outbreak was at the intersection of Jay and William Streets, where store windows were broken and bottles and stones thrown at police cars Friday night and last night.

At 12:30 this morning, Mayor Austin N. Volk, after a tour of the city, said that "everything is completely peaceful and normal."

He said he had toured the city two or three times and found that the situation was calm.

"There is no comparison with

Continued on Page 26, Column 1

Puerto Rico to Vote On Its Status Today; No Change Is Likely

By HENRY GINIGER

Special to The New York Times

SAN JUAN, P.R., July 22—A majority of Puerto Rico's voters are expected tomorrow to choose to keep their island as an autonomous commonwealth within the United States orbit, rejecting either independence or statehood.

For the first time since the United States took possession of Puerto Rico from Spain in 1898, Puerto Ricans are being given an opportunity to choose their political status by referendum. Of the 1,067,000 island residents over the age of 21, between 700,000 and 800,000 voters are expected to seize the chance to make their wishes known. Puerto Ricans living in the United States will not vote.

At the end of a frenetic and

Continued on Page 63, Column 4

Sports News

THOROUGHBRED RACING

Hobeau Farm's Handsome Boy, ridden by Eddie Belmonte, upset Buckpasser, the 7-10 favorite, in the $106,700 Brooklyn Handicap yesterday at Aqueduct. Buckpasser, Ogden Phipps's 4-year-old colt, who was trying for a sweep of the handicap triple crown, found the impost of 136 pounds too great and finished second in the 1¼-mile race. At Monmouth Park, Mrs. Frances Genter's In Reality won the $55,500 Choice Stakes.

BASEBALL

The Chicago Cubs rallied for two runs in the last of the ninth inning to edge the San Francisco Giants, 6-5, and tie the St. Louis Cardinals for first place in the National League. The Cards bowed in 13 innings to the Atlanta Braves, 5-4.

After trading Ken Boyer, a third baseman, to the Chicago White Sox, the Mets bowed to the Dodgers, 4-3, last night. The Yankees, despite home runs by Mickey Mantle and Steve Whitaker, lost to the Detroit Tigers, 11-4, and dropped to 10th place.

Details in Section 5

After Year and a Half, Copter Critics Are Quieter

By SYDNEY H. SCHANBERG

"We are trapped by noise. We cannot open our windows. This is a disgraceful way to spend one's summer," says Mrs. Richard Tully, who lives at 2 Tudor City Place, near the United Nations.

"I think it's an excellent thing. It takes traffic off the roads and it's also a glamorous, exciting part of living in New York," says Charles G. Leedham, the city's deputy commissioner of marine and aviation.

Both Mrs. Tully and Mr. Leedham were talking about the same thing—the 50 helicopter flights a day to and from the roof of the Pan Am Building that link the congested midtown area by air to Kennedy International Airport (7 minutes) and Teterboro Airport in Bergen County, N. J. (5 minutes).

New York Airways began helicopter passenger service from the 808-foot-high pad just before Christmas, 1965, after more than two years of controversy in which the skyscraper heliport was hailed by its proponents as a forerunner of the future in urban travel and denounced by its critics as a noise nuisance and a safety hazard.

Now, a year and a half later, the protesters are still vocal from time to time. But the intensity of their campaign has waned out of discouragement, mostly because they now grudgingly recognize that the Pan Am heliport is a fait accompli that has won the approval of all the necessary government agencies and is not likely to lose that approval.

In that year and a half, New York Airways has increased its flights, worked many kinks out of its system, and altered its flight routes and hours—at the city's suggestion—to meet the objections of the noise protesters. But it is still a losing operation financially and likely to remain so for the next few years at least.

The line, which used to be subsidized by the Federal Government, is now subsidized by Pan American World Airways and Trans World Airlines. The two overseas airlines pick up the bill for the annual losses, which in 1966 were $161,106. Prospects for this year are not much better.

New York Airways not only flies the service to and from the Pan Am Building, which is at 200 Park Avenue, just north of Grand Central Terminal, but also an entirely separate service, on which it does its biggest business. This is the shuttle linking the three area airports—Kennedy, LaGuardia and Newark—and the Wall Street Heliport, at Pier 6 on the East River. There is also a service between Kennedy and the Westchester County Airport, which like the Teterboro route, opened last March.

New York Airways' annual report for 1966 talks repeatedly of the "pressing need" to expand its operations in order to pay off its loans ($1.8-million outstanding) and

Continued on Page 42, Column 1

Today's Sections

Index to Subjects

Carl Sandburg, Poet, Folk Singer and Biographer of Lincoln, Dies in South at 89

PRESIDENT LEADS NATION'S TRIBUTE

He Eulogizes Pulitzer Prize Winner as 'Chronicler of Truth and Beauty'

Continued From Page 1, Col. 2

was barely conscious. He was breathing with difficulty. The nurses gave him artificial respiration, and we called Dr. [D. I. Campbell] King. He slowly breathed away shortly after 9 o'clock this morning."

President Johnson was among the first to pay tribute. He said:

"The road has come to an end for Carl Sandburg, my friend and the good companion of millions whose own life journeys have been ennobled and enriched by his poetry.

"But there is no end to the legacy he leaves us.

"Carl Sandburg was more than the voice of America, more than the poet of its strength and genius. He was America. We knew and cherished him as the bard of democracy, the echo of the people, our conscience and chronicler of truth and beauty and purpose.

"Carl Sandburg needs no epitaph. It is written for all time in the fields, the cities, the face and heart of the land he loved and the people he celebrated and inspired.

"With the world, we mourn his passing. It is our special pride and fortune as Americans that we will always hear Carl Sandburg's voice within ourselves. For he gave us the truest and most enduring vision of our own greatness."

Mrs. Sandburg, sister of the photographer Edward Steichen, said a funeral service would be held here Monday afternoon at the interdenominational church of St. John's in the Wilderness.

"It will be just for the family," she said.

Also surviving are the couple's three daughters, Margaret and Janet Sandburg, and Mrs. George Crile, and two grandchildren, Karlen Paula and John Carl.

Prairie-Haunted Figure

Carl Sandburg was a poet whose lines could be read as prose and the writer of a classic biography shot through with poetry.

He was a figure as prairie-haunted, as rough-hewn as the Lincoln he had memorialized in six volumes. He was as American as the Chicago he had hailed in irregular stanzas that somehow caught the beat and throb and shrug and hiss and clatter of the city.

Mr. Sandburg worked at a hundred jobs and sang a thousand songs strumming a guitar. He was the son of a poor immigrant, but he came to know Presidents and the King of Sweden, his ancestral land. He swayed politicians ritually assembled, and ordinary people sprawled on grass or sitting around a fire. He had a manner, a voice and a long lock of silver-gray hair as free as his spirit.

But as a writer, he had his own fierce discipline. "The War Years," the last four volumes of his monumental biography of Lincoln, took [illegible]6 years. Its 1,175,000 words made it a quarter-million words longer than the Bible, 150,000 longer than all the known works of Shakespeare.

Mr. Sandburg won one Pulitzer Prize for prose ("The War Years," 1940) and one for poetry ("Complete Poems," 1950.) It will take time to determine which contribution was the more lasting. (His Who's Who in America sketch used "writer," not "poet," like Robert Frost's.) But in the writer's lifetime more controversy eddied about his verse, as such, than about his biography.

This was dramatized to some extent by the fact that he and Frost were contemporaries. Frost was not yet 4 years old when Mr. Sandburg was born in 1878. Eight decades later, both were literary titans, honored on all levels. And each had a granite face, a marvelously gripping patina of age, like a preservative of essential character.

Difference in Technique

The difference was in the technique of their poetry. Frost was no slave to rhyme, but he generally employed it, and with marvelous skill. And one of his most familiar aphorisms was that free verse was like tennis without a net.

Mr. Sandburg, on the other hand, rarely, if ever, used rhyme, and his rhythms were unfettered by any regular scheme. Critics, even those who acknowledged the "feeling" of poetry in his lines, often pointed out that if they had been written as prose no one would have known the difference: the "illusion" of poetry in them was based more on the arrangement of the lines than on the lines themselves.

Mr. Sandburg was fully aware of this criticism. In "Notes for a Preface," opening the "Complete Poems," he had his say on the subject:

"There is a formal poetry only in form, all dressed up and nowhere to go. The number of syllables, the designated and required stresses of accent, the rhymes if wanted—they all come off with the skill of a solved crossword puzzle. Yet its animation and connotation are less than that of 'a dead mackerel in the moonshine,' the latter, even as an extinct form, reporting that once it was a living fish a-swim in bright waters."

He went on to quote Oliver Wendell Holmes on the absurdity to which the need for finding a rhyme for "stars" might force a poet: "Can there be imagined a more certain process for breaking up all continuity of thought," the quotation asked, "than this miserable subjugation of intellect to the clink of well- or ill-matched syllables?"

Then, Mr. Sandburg concluded:

"The fact is ironic. A proficient and sometimes exquisite performer in rhymed verse goes out of his way to register the point that the more rhyme there is in poetry the more danger of its tricking the writer into something other than the urge in the beginning."

The key words were the last five. Mr. Sandburg wrote most of his poetry on "the urge in the beginning."

(Once, in Stockholm, he did what Frost would not conceivably have done: dictated upon request six lines of a "poem" about Stockholm that were taken down by the wife of a publisher who wanted them for a book about the city.)

Many poems were written while Mr. Sandburg was waiting around. And one, composed while he was sitting in the anteroom of a juvenile-court judge whom he was to interview, became one of his most quoted, and a great favorite with children, who found it easy to memorize.

Called "Fog," it runs:

The fog comes
on little cat feet.
It sits looking
over harbor and city
on silent haunches
and then moves on.

Obviously the short lines could have been written straight out, as two prose sentences embodying a "poetic" image: the fog as a cat. Thus besides being famous in its own right, the poem re-posed the old question: Was Mr. Sandburg's poetry in the substance or in the arrangement of the lines?

The other most quoted piece of his verse was unquestionably the first five lines of "Chicago," a roaring hymn to the city with which he was most closely identified:

Hog Butcher for the World,
Tool Maker, Stacker of Wheat,
Player with Railroads and the Nation's Freight Handler;
Stormy, husky, brawling, City of the Big Shoulders.

In "The Prairie Years," the first two volumes of the Lincoln biography, Mr. Sandburg was able to get touches of perhaps a purer, because less self-conscious, poetry into his prose descriptions of the young Lincoln. For instance:

"He lived with trees, with the bush wet with shining raindrops, with the burning bush of autumn, with the lone wild ducks riding a north wind and crying down on a line north and south, the faces of open sky and weather."

A Final Cadence

Such a passage, of course, might have been written in Mr. Sandburg's own autobiography, he had lived with the wet bush and the lone wild ducks; he knew the "faces of open sky and weather."

The Sandburg poetry glinted also in "The War Years," although only — perhaps deliberately so—in the very last lines of the final volume. Here was no experience Mr. Sandburg had shared with Lincoln; he was describing not what he had seen or felt but a national emotion at the time it became history:

And the night came with great quiet.
And there was rest.
The prairie years, the war years were over.

So was an American masterpiece.

Carl Sandburg was born in Galesburg, a prairie town in western Illinois, on Jan. 6, 1878, in the 13th year after the death of Abraham Lincoln. His father, August, whose schooling in his native Sweden had been rudimentary, became a blacksmith in the Galesburg railroad shops. The older Sandburg, who called his son "Sharley," endorsed his pay checks with X—his mark.

Years later, when someone remarked that the Lincoln biography was "so very American," the poet commented (according to Karl Detzer's "Carl Sandburg"):

"Yes. It's a book about a man whose mother could not sign her name, written by a man whose father could not sign his. Perhaps that could happen only in America."

As schoolboys, he and his younger brother, Martin, helped their father build a house. Mr. Detzer suggests that some of the solid perfection of Mr. Sandburg's work on Lincoln stems from the patience and pride of craft he learned from his father's painstaking carpentry. After 50 years the house stood, its frame sound, its lines true.

At 17, Carl Sandburg embarked on a hobo period. He rode boxcars; in Keokuk he fried eggs at a lunch counter; at Bean Lake, near Atchison, Kan., he worked as a section hand. He blacked stoves, dug potatoes, washed windows, threshed wheat. And in the spring of 1898, he enlisted for the Spanish-American War in Company C, Sixth Illinois Volunteer Infantry.

He served for eight months in Puerto Rico. His letters to The Galesburg Evening Mail were published as war correspondence; they were his first published works.

Back in Galesburg, he put part of his $122 discharge money into books and equipment for study at Lombard University, a tiny institution with 125 students. While there, Mr. Sandburg absorbed some campus atmosphere and cultural programs at a larger local college, Knox.

In his freshman year at Lombard, he also took entrance examinations for the United States Military Academy. Deficiency in arithmetic barred his entry.

Jailed in Pittsburgh

He was at Lombard four years, but he did not graduate. He renewed his wandering. En route from Philadelphia to Wisconsin, he was among eight freight riders arrested at McKee's Rocks, Pa. He spent 10 days in the county jail in Pittsburgh.

Finally, he reached Milwaukee. It was a time of great social ferment, and Milwaukee was a capital of liberal ideas. Mr. Sandburg worked as a reporter and editorial writer; he went from The News to The Sentinel to The Journal to The Leader. He read, wrote and spoke. He was active at headquarters of the Social Democratic party. In 1910, he was named secretary to Emil Seidel, the city's Socialist Mayor, and he held the post for two years.

One day at Social Democratic headquarters in Milwaukee, Mr. Sandburg met a party worker, on vacation from her job as Latin teacher in the high school at Princeton, Ill. They were married on June 15, 1908.

The girl was Lillian Paula Steichen, sister of Edward Steichen, a native of Luxembourg, who was to become one of the greatest of modern photographers.

Mr. Sandburg went to Chicago in 1912. The move was prompted by a newspaper strike there: only The Chicago Daily Socialist was not affected. Its circulation soared; it needed men. Mr. Sandburg and several others on The Milwaukee Leader responded. When the strike ended, they were quickly out of jobs. But Chicago and Mr. Sandburg were natural comrades, and the young man stayed in town.

By this time, he had already written a lot of poetry, none of which had been sold. But the breakthrough came in Poetry magazine, edited by Harriet Monroe. In 1914, Mr. Sandburg won his first award, the $200 Levinson prize. It was for a series of pieces including "Chicago."

At last his voice had been heard.

Journalistic Handyman

Meanwhile, he worked for trade publications, reviewed motion pictures and wrote a column. His journalistic career tended to flower on The Chicago Daily News. These were the golden days under Henry Justin Smith, a managing editor who was also a kind of "principal" in the "Chicago school" of writers. Mr. Sandburg's poetry was not stifled by his daily chores; it was encouraged.

His work was published regularly, and increasingly it shone with his indignation at the plight of the many and at man's inhumanity to man.

Steeped in the border atmosphere that had nurtured Lincoln, Mr. Sandburg was also shaped by the American Socialist influence of such men as Victor Berger and Eugene V. Debs. He was always interested in (and identified with) the handicaps and aspirations of common men. In this, as in poetic technique, he differed significantly from the New England individualism of Robert Frost. Clearly in style, and to some extent in substance, he was much closer to Walt Whitman; he had lectured on "Leaves of Grass" and given readings from it.

In 1918, Mr. Sandburg went to Stockholm as a correspondent for the Newspaper Enterprise Association. He became a good friend of Per Albin Hanson, then managing editor of a newspaper and later Sweden's Premier. Returning to Chicago and The Daily News, Mr. Sandburg was given increased freedom. The Lincoln material he had been collecting since his days in Galesburg began to suggest a pattern.

While pursuing every scrap of information about Lincoln he could lay his hand on, Mr. Sandburg traveled about the country carrying a guitar. He read his own poetry and sang folk songs. His figure became familiar, almost symbolic: the tall, lean and stooped minstrel, his hair parted in the middle, and hanging low toward his temples. He had a good baritone voice, and he had a touch of showmanship.

Most of the actual writing of the biography was done at the author's home on the Lake Michigan dunes near Herbert, Mich., 60 miles from Chicago. The place was transformed into a combination library and newspaper "morgue." With space at a premium, Mr. Sandburg would cut and rebind the essential nonduplicating chapters of books on Lincoln. When it came to writing, he sometimes sat on a cracker box, evoking, while he typed, the boxes on which Lincoln had sat in crossroad stores.

Labor of Love and Genius

It was a colossal task; a labor of love and genius. Some critics hailed the finished work as surpassing all competitors in detail, fidelity and sweep.

"That son-of-a-gun Lincoln grows on you," Mr. Sandburg remarked as he neared the midpoint on his biography. One measure of that growth was the clear, homely, often loving style in which the book came to be written—a style that echoed Lincoln's in its moving simplicity.

The demands of research and writing were heavy, and partly to pace himself, partly to support the project and partly to visit private Lincoln collections and libraries, Mr. Sandburg traveled the country in the winters.

He invariably took along one of his guitars, and sang folk songs and gave readings from his poetry wherever he went. Many of the ditties and ballads were collected in "The American Songbag" (1927) and in "New American Songbag" (1950).

Mr. Sandburg possessed a sweet baritone, and he sang in a lilting, dreamy style and frequently moved his listeners to tears. Sitting on a stool at these folk-music concerts, he seemed as authentic as the lonesome ballads he offered, an impression accentuated by the silver hair that fell over his eyes and the wide grin that creased his face.

'Wanderin'' Was a Favorite

There were many favorites among Mr. Sandburg's repertory and one of them was "Wanderin'":

My daddy is an engineer,
My brother drives a hack,
My sister takes in washin'
An' the baby balls the jack,
An' it looks like
I'm never gonna cease my wanderin'

I been a wanderin'
Early and late,
New York City
To the Golden Gate
An' it looks like
I'm never gonna cease my wanderin'

Been a-workin' in the army
Workin' on a farm,
All I got to show for it
Is the muscle in my arm.
An' it looks like
I'm never gonna cease my wanderin'

This, and similar songs, helped to nurture the popularity of folk music and country music. And until late in life Mr. Sandburg was a folk minstrel, appearing before staid audiences and college groups, at hootenanies, and chanting to groups that visited him at his North Carolina home.

Not until he was well into his Lincoln project did Mr. Sandburg begin to attain financial security, although he had had occasional wealthy periods. In 1928, he was invited to be the Phi Beta Kappa poet at Harvard. The work he read, "Good Morning," was bought by a women's magazine for $1,000.

And when success came, Mr. Sandburg enjoyed it. During World War II, he served on relief committees and often spoke for liberal causes. His convictions had not changed; he simply had a larger audience. He was respected for his work, and, wherever he went, recognized for his highly individualized Americanism.

"Always the Young Strangers," a glowing autobiography of his first 21 years, appeared in 1953. Robert E. Sherwood, whose three Pulitzer Prizes for drama included one in 1939 for "Abe Lincoln in Illinois," said Mr. Sandburg's work was the "best autobiography ever written by an American."

Awed the Capitol

But it was less by knowledge and scholarship than by personality and mastery of the language that Mr. Sandburg earned one of the most notable public triumphs of his later career.

This was on Feb. 12, 1959. The occasion was a joint session of Congress to mark the 150th anniversary of Lincoln's birth. Rarely patient with Presidents, no less poets, the legislators were first hushed, then transfixed, as the Illinoisan began his Lincoln tribute:

"Not often in the story of mankind does a man arrive on earth who is both steel and velvet, who is as hard as rock and soft as drifting fog, who holds in his heart and mind the paradox of terrible storm and peace unspeakable and perfect."

A few months later, Mr. Sandburg was honored in Sweden by King Gustav VI Adolf. On that trip, he visited Appuna and Asbo, where his parents had grown up. He found nine cousins, and spoke to them in Swedish recollected from his boyhood.

A cast including Bette Davis explored "The World of Carl Sandburg" at Henry Miller's Theater in 1960. And in June, 1962, Galesburg High School decided that Mr. Sandburg would finally get his diploma—on Jan. 6, 1963, his 85th birthday. He had entered Lombard University on the basis of a special qualifying examination, not with benefit of high-school diploma.

By that time, of course, he already held honorary doctorates from a dozen institutions, including Harvard, Yale and Dartmouth.

POET: Carl Sandburg, son of Swedish immigrants, was as much in the American grain as the prairie town of Galesburg, Ill., where he was born Jan. 6, 1878, or Chicago, which he immortalized in verse. Picture was taken by his brother-in-law, Edward Steichen.

The American Bard

Continued From Page 1, Col. 3

others acknowledged what they owed to the Chinese, Sandburg mentioned what he owed to the American Indian.

It was impossible, for example, to think of Sandburg as an expatriate, knocking on the doors of the British Establishment for admittance, or counting out francs in some seedy bistro in a murky dawn. Sandburg would never have asked, "Why should the aged eagle stretch its wings?" His eagle—fierce, taloned, gimlet-eyed and cruel perhaps — had a sovereign's view of America: Oklahoma badlands and Kansas wheat fields, skyscraper and bean row, Ty Cobb and a wandering dynamiter, and "the Jew fish crier down on Maxwell Street."

There was also in his work a strong note of social protest, also in the American grain. His lines lash out against the confidence men, the bunkshooters, the grafters, the mighty captains and mercantile lords. But Sandburg was no doctrinaire radical. His lines are a cry from the heart against the injustices he saw about him.

Dedicated Scholarship

The massive six-volume life of Lincoln was as much a work of dedication as of scholarship. More than the ordering of such a mass of material, more than the labors of writing it, was the spirit of the writer that hovered over it. What was there about Lincoln, Sandburg wondered, that appealed both to the stolid conservative burghers in Galesburg and the socialist workers in Milwaukee. In trying to explain Lincoln, Sandburg hoped to explain America itself.

This was true, too, of "Remembrance Rock," written when Sandburg was 70. It is not so much a novel as a long ruminative essay on the "American Dream." He wanted to record "the costly toil and bloody struggles that have gone to keep alive and carry further that Dream." His almost instinctive spirit of independence also conditioned the writing of the "Roottabaga" Stories for children: "I wanted something more in the American lingo. I was tired of princes and princesses and I sought the American equivalent of elves and gnomes. I knew that American children would respond, so I wrote nonsense tales with American fooling in them."

As a poet, Sandburg came at a time when the frontier had run out, when the prairie, turning back on itself, met the metropolis. It is to Sandburg's lasting merit that he synthesized both worlds in his mind. Though he knew the coarseness and brutality of city life, he knew also its vigor and excitement. And just as he could understand the limited horizons and incessant labor of those mortgaged to farm and field, he knew also the sweetness of their lives and their sense of permanency.

His mind was not divided: "I was born on the prairie and the milk of its wheat, the red of its clover, the eyes of its women gave me a song and slogan." But he could also write in "Prayers of Steel":

Lay me on an anvil, O God.
Beat me and hammer me into a steel spike.
Drive me into girders that hold a skyscraper together.

Had Model in Whitman

Although he had his model in Whitman, Sandburg did as much as any poet to destroy the genteel tradition in American verse; not only in subject matter but in language and stanzaic form. The language he used was more than mere colloquial speech. It was the argot, the slang, the street cries of his day. There was for him no special poeticizing language. Like the poetry, it had its roots in the tumble of life. When Sandburg wrote about hod-carriers, ice handlers, dockers, hoboes and jailbirds he was not slumming.

The body of his poetry was substantial. (The "Collected Poems" contains more than 800 items.) Perhaps he should have been more selective. He could also repeat himself. Sometimes he never fully worked out his feelings in poetic terms. This and the passage of time ("Chicago Poems" came out in 1916), have taken away some of the excitement and some of the force of his work.

He was always at his best in shorter forms. Paul Rosenfeld said many years ago that Sandburg's poems were "a series of lyrical starts" and that even his long poems were a collection of short ones. "Fog," probably his best-known poem, is made up of only 21 words. But Sandburg caught in his pages a certain moment and certain place in our history. Anyone who would know them must consider him part of the permanent record.

A Sandburg Sampler

Following are excerpts from Carl Sandburg's poetry, taken from "Complete Poems" by Carl Sandburg, published in 1950 by Harcourt, Brace & Co.:

The people is Everyman, everybody.
Everybody is you and me and all others.
What everybody says is what we all say.

(From "The People, Yes")

* * *

Hope is a tattered flag and a dream out of time.
Hope is a heartspun word, the rainbow, the shadblow in white,
The evening star inviolable over the coal mines,
The shimmer of northern lights across a bitter winter night,
The blue hills beyond the smoke of the steel works,
The birds who go on singing to their mates in peace, war, peace,
The ten-cent crocus bulb blooming in a used-car salesroom,
The horseshoe over the door, the luckpiece in the pocket,
The kiss and the comforting laugh and resolve—
Hope is an echo, hope ties itself yonder, yonder.

(From "The People, Yes")

* * *

The people, yes,
Out of what is their change
from chaos to order
and chaos again?
"Yours till the hangman doth us do part,"
Don Magregor ended his letters.
"It annoys me to die,"
said a philosopher.
"I should like to see what follows."
To those who had ordered them to death,
one of them said:
"We die because the people are asleep
and you will die because the people will awaken."
Greek met Greek when Phocion and Democritus spoke.
"You will drive the Athenians mad some day and they will kill you."
"Yes, me when they go mad, and as sure as they get sane again, you."

(From "The People, Yes")

* * *

TRINITY PLACE

The grave of Alexander Hamilton is in Trinity yard at the end of Wall Street.
The grave of Robert Fulton likewise is in Trinity yard where Wall Street stops.
And in this yard stenogs, bundle boys, scrubwomen, sit on the tombstones, and walk on the grass of graves, speaking of war and weather, of babies, wages and love.
And iron picket fence . . . and streaming thousands along Broadway sidewalks . . . straw hats, faces, legs . . . a singing, talking, hustling river . . . down the great street that ends with a Sea.
. . . easy is the sleep of Alexander Hamilton.
. . . easy is the sleep of Robert Fulton.
. . . easy are the great governments and the great steamboats.

(From "Smoke and Steel")

* * *

NIGHT MOVEMENT—NEW YORK

In the night, when the sea-winds take the city in their arms,
And cool the loud streets that kept their dust noon and afternoon;
In the night, when the sea-birds call to the lights of the city,
The lights that cut on the skyline their name of a city;
In the night, when the trains and wagons start from a long way off
For the city where the people ask bread and want letters;
In the night the city lives too—the day is not all.
In the night there are dancers dancing and singers singing,
And the sailors and soldiers look for numbers on doors.
In the night the sea-winds take the city in their arms.

(From "Smoke and Steel")

* * *

THE WINDY CITY

It is easy to come here a stranger and show the whole works, write a book, fix it all up—it is easy to come and go away a muddle-headed pig, a bum and a bag of wind.

Go to it and remember this city fished from its depths a text: "Independent as a hog on ice."

Venice is a dream of soft waters, Vienna and Bagdad recollections of dark spears and wild turbans; Paris is a thought in Monet gray on scabbards, fabrics, facades; London is a fact in a fog filled with the moaning of transatlantic whistles; Berlin sits amid white scrubbed quadrangles and torn arithmetics and testaments; Moscow brandishes a flag and repeats a dance figure of a man who walks like a bear.

Chicago fished from its depths a text: Independent as a hog on ice.

(From "Slabs of the Sunburnt West")

Photographs by Ann Zane Shanks, George Tames; cartoon by Fitzpatrick

THE SENSE OF BEING AMERICAN: During the Lincoln years he began to roam the country with his guitar, reading his poetry and singing folk songs. Looking and sounding as authentic as the ballads, he nurtured interest in folk music. Fame did not affect his instinctively independent spirit; he gained a wider audience for his record of "the costly toil and bloody struggles that have gone to keep alive and carry further the American dream."

"All the News That's Fit to Print"

The New York Times.

LATE CITY EDITION

U. S. Weather Bureau Report (Page 30) forecasts: Fair today, tonight and tomorrow. Temp. Range: 74—58; yesterday: 74—57. Temp.-Hum. Index: near 69; yesterday: 70.

VOL. CXIV—No. 39,307. NEW YORK, MONDAY, SEPTEMBER 6, 1965. TEN CENTS

UNION RATIFIES NEW STEEL PACT COVERING 3 YEARS

Action Taken in Pittsburgh by Wage Policy Committee After 2½-Hour Meeting

FORMAL SIGNING TODAY

Contract Provides Pay Rise and Improved Benefits—Pattern for Industry

By DAVID R. JONES
Special to The New York Times

PITTSBURGH, Sept. 5—The United Steelworkers of America ratified today a new contract that assures labor peace in the basic steel industry for nearly 35 months.

I. W. Abel, the union president, announced the action at a news conference here following a 2½-hour meeting of the union's Wage Policy Committee. The agreement has already been accepted by 10 major steel companies.

The new contract will provide 350,000 workers at the 10 steel companies with improved wages, pensions, insurance and other benefits valued by the union at 47.3 cents an hour by the time all the benefits are in effect, Mr. Abel said. It is expected to serve as the pattern for settlement with smaller steel companies and fabricators employing 100,000 more workers.

Johnson Suggests Terms

Union officials said the 47.3-cent figure consisted of a 16.2-cent average wage increase in the first year, a 17.6-cent increase in pension costs during the second year, and an 8.5-cent wage rise and 5-cent insurance cost increase in the third year of the contract.

The union and industry reached agreement in principle on a new contract Friday in Washington after President Johnson had suggested terms for resolving their remaining differences. Mr. Abel said today that efforts were being made to prepare contracts for formal signing by midnight tomorrow.

The union president said that any contract or local issues not resolved by then would be left standing. He said, however, that he did not expect any local strikes to result from these outstanding issues.

Some Members Complain

The Wage Policy Committee's approval of the contract proved a political triumph for Mr. Abel and his fellow union leaders, who took over the reins of the 1.1-million-member union in June from David J. McDonald.

Some committee members complained that the leadership had not delivered on its promise to give more attention to local issues. But the agreement was ratified without much commotion.

The union's cost estimate indicates that the agreement could cost the industry more than 3.5 per cent annually in increased labor costs in the 35 months from last Wednesday until its expiration on Aug. 1, 1968. The industry estimates the cost of the agreement at more than 46 cents an hour beyond present average wage-benefit costs of $4.40 hourly. Mr.

Continued on Page 6, Column 3

Associated Press Wirephoto
AFTER STEEL ACCORD: I. W. Abel, head of United Steelworkers of America, leaves Pittsburgh meeting.

Throng Spends Sunday at the Fair

Aerial view of Avenue of Commerce. Tower of Light is at upper left, General Electric Pavilion at the upper right.

Attendance at Fair Sets 2-Year Mark of 317,310

By ROBERT ALDEN

Yesterday was the biggest day in the two-year history of the New York World's Fair. With the weather ideal and six weeks left before the final closing, the old attendance mark of 265,560 set last Memorial Day was surpassed at 4 P.M. By closing time, 317,310 had paid their way onto the grounds.

Huge traffic jams developed on the Grand Central Parkway and the Van Wyck Expressway at the approaches to the fair. Cars overheated and stalled, aggravating an already aggravated situation.

By noon the main parking lots serving the fair were filled. Auxiliary parking fields, never used for the public this season, were opened. They, too, were quickly filled to capacity.

The police estimated that tens of thousands who tried to get to the fair by auto abandoned their efforts.

The weather was a factor in the new attendance mark. It was sunny, clear and not overly hot. As a result many families decided to head for the fair and not for the beach. There were only 75,000 persons at Jones Beach, compared with 160,000 on Sunday of the Labor Day weekend last year. And only 50,000 persons showed up at Coney Island. More than 10.000 at-

Continued on Page 20, Column 3

INCREASE IN JOBS IS REPORTED HERE

Employment Up 13,600 to 3,554,000—Major Gain Next Year Forecast

By EMANUEL PERLMUTTER

An optimistic report on jobs in New York was given yesterday by James J. McFadden, Acting City Labor Commissioner.

He reported an increase of 13.600 in the number of employed persons here in the first six months of this year, compared with the same period in 1964. And he predicted that "next year will witness the greatest rise in employment in New York in many years."

Mr. McFadden said 3,554,000 persons were employed here in the first six months of 1965, compared with 3,540,400 at that time last year.

He also reported the unemployment rate for the six months ended in July had dropped to 5.3 per cent from 5.7 per cent last year. An average of 226,300 persons were out of jobs this year, he said, compared with 241,900 in 1965, a decrease of 15,600 jobless.

The Change Is Gradual

Although the city unemployment rate was higher than the national average of about 4.7 per cent, Mr. McFadden said New York did not experience sharp cyclical rises and declines in jobs like cities that were dependent on one or two industries. Hence the decrease in unemployment took place slowly, he explained.

Discussing the city's job future on the WNBC-TV "Direct Line" program and in a lengthy interview later, Commissioner McFadden said he expected 30,000 more persons would find work here in 1966.

"The recently enacted medi-

Continued on Page 5, Column 5

Labor Day

Following is a list of services and facilities that are affected today:

Banks, stock and commodity exchanges—Closed.

Department stores and retail business in the city and suburban areas — Most closed.

Post Offices—No postal deliveries except for special delivery mail and perishables.

Parking—Alternate side rules suspended; Sunday rules in effect.

Sanitation—No refuse collection.

RISE IN ECONOMY SPURS REVENUES BEYOND ESTIMATE

Treasury Collection Up 10% in 2 Months of Fiscal '66—No Deficit Growth Seen

By EDWIN L. DALE Jr.
Special to The New York Times

WASHINGTON, Sept. 5 — With the current fiscal year only two months old, the Treasury's receipts are already soaring far above expectations.

The sharp rise in receipts, reported today by informed sources, promises to make the economic and financial aspects of the war in Vietnam easier to handle and to make unlikely any large increase in the budget deficit.

The main reason for the unexpected performance of receipts, as nearly as Government officials can tell, is the continuing strong expansion of the national economy — an expansion more vigorous than even the Government had foreseen — but there may be other reasons as well.

In the first two months of the fiscal year 1966, which started July 1, total cash receipts of the Treasury were $18.5 billion, up $1.7 billion, or 10 per cent, from the same two months a year ago, according to figures in the regular daily Treasury statement.

Revenues Going Up

While this "raw" growth of receipts alone is regarded as impressive, even more important in the view of officials is how the revenue collections compared with projections.

According to reliable information, the collection of withheld income taxes and Social Security taxes alone in the two months ran at a rate that, if continued for the entire fiscal year, would produce $2 billion more in revenues than had been projected for the year. For the two months, the excess over projections was nearly $200 million.

This figure does not include revenues from many other sources, such as corporation taxes. With profits at record levels, collections from this source are also likely to exceed expectations.

Job Rate Grows

The original projections had been based on a strong performance of the economy, but employment and payrolls have risen even more sharply than expected, automatically producing more revenue.

Government economists have consistently maintained that, as long as there is unemployment and idle plant capacity in the economy, actions by the Government to spur expansion will produce more revenue. This applies even to tax cuts. In the last fiscal year, collections rose even though income tax rates were sharply reduced by the big tax cut.

It is now widely assumed both inside and outside the Govern-

Continued on Page 4, Column 6

U.S. SURVEY FINDS NO ECONOMIC PERIL IN ARMS CUTBACK

Presidential Panel Asserts Even Full Disarmament Could Be Dealt With

By JOHN D. POMFRET
Special to The New York Times

AUSTIN, Tex., Sept. 5 — A committee of Government experts said today that neither a gradual reduction in defense expenditures nor a shift from one kind of defense outlay to another would present major problems for the economy.

"Even general and complete disarmament would pose no insuperable problems; indeed, it would mainly afford opportunities for a better life for our citizens," the committee said in a 92-page report released by the White House.

President Johnson said that what he found most encouraging in the report was the conclusion that the current heavy commitment to defense was not a bar to rapid progress toward disarmament.

Servant of People

In a letter to Gardner Ackley, chairman of the committee and of the President's Council of Economic Advisers, Mr. Johnson declared:

"The American people will continue to be determined that our great industrial effort for the national defense is their servant and not their master. This is the tradition of the armed forces themselves, and it is the conviction, I am sure, of those who serve in the national defense industries, too.

"This country will therefore go forward with renewed courage and conviction to provide the defenses that freedom demands and at the same time to press along the hard road toward disarmament mankind must have."

Senior Officials Members

The 13-member group that reported today is called the Committee on the Economic Impact of Defense and Disarmament.

It was established Dec. 21, 1963, by President Johnson and is composed of senior officials of Government departments and agencies most involved in making defense expenditures and working out ways of easing the potentially disturbing economic impact of changes in the size or type of defense spending.

The committee expressed confidence that national economic growth and prosperity could be maintained with the fiscal and monetary tools now at the Government's disposal.

Apart from any consideration of the impact of disarmament, the committee said, major decisions relating to government tax, expenditure and credit policies are going to be required in the next few years to sustain rapid growth and general prosperity.

This is because of the enormous increase in Federal rev-

Continued on Page 4, Column 7

Nixon Bids U.S. Press for Victory

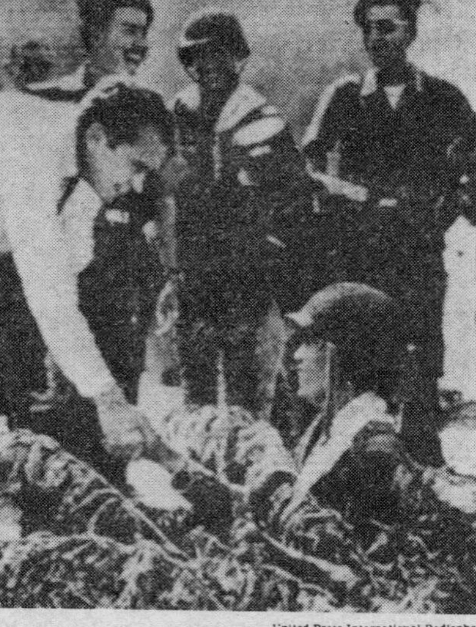

United Press International Radiophoto
Richard M. Nixon visits Vietnamese soldier. Behind him is Brig. Gen. Nguyen Chanh Thi, I Corps commander.

By NEIL SHEEHAN
Special to The New York Times

SAIGON, South Vietnam, Sept. 5 — Richard M. Nixon said today that he opposed any negotiations on Vietnam unless the North Vietnamese were prepared to withdraw their forces from the South and to cease aggression. "I do not feel that negotiations at this time would serve any useful purpose," the former Vice President declared. Mr. Nixon expressed his views in a news conference shortly before leaving for Bangkok after a three-day visit to South Vietnam. He is touring Asia on what is described as a pri-

Continued on Page 2, Column 6

Marines Shut Sea-Air Trap On a Company of Vietcong

By CHARLES MOHR
Special to The New York Times

SAIGON, South Vietnam, Monday, Sept. 6—A force of United States Marines, numbering more than two companies, closed in by sea and by air early yesterday on a company of the Vietcong and smashed the guerrilla unit in a sharp engagement.

A United States military spokesman said that the marines killed 25 Vietcong and captured three others in the fight. The action was near Quinhon, on the Central Vietnam coast about 260 miles north of Saigon.

After the fighting, the spokesman said, the marines collected about 150 war refugees from villages in the area and were feeding and caring for them.

[Early Monday, the big United States B-52 jets again bombed suspected Vietcong positions in Zone D, 30 miles north of Saigon, said The Associated Press.]

One section of the marines stormed ashore from amphibious assault vehicles on a small peninsula about 10 miles north of the town of Quinhon in Binhdinh Province shortly before dawn yesterday. Meanwhile a second element landed from helicopters a mile to the rear.

By 10 A.M., the marines made contact with the company

Continued on Page 2, Column 7

INDIAN ARMY GRIM AS FOE DRIVES ON

'We'll Hold,' Officer Vows, but Superior Equipment Propels Pakistanis

By J. ANTHONY LUKAS
Special to The New York Times

WITH INDIAN FORCES, in Kashmir, Sept. 5 — India's troops are battling to halt a Pakistani attack that has gained at least 12 miles in the last two days.

Twenty-five-pound field guns and medium artillery, hidden in the elephant grass, have pounded away at the Pakistani Army's Patton and Sherman tanks rolling across sugar-cane fields a few thousand yards away.

From a forward command post on a hillside, the "crump-crump" of Indian artillery can be heard, and then the hiss of the shells as they hurtle overhead, followed by the booming of the Pakistani 80-pound guns.

Indians in Retreat

Pointing over the rise, an Indian staff officer said the fighting was going on around the village of Jaurian, 3,000 yards up the winding macadam road.

The officer conceded that the Indian forces had fallen back repeatedly before the strong Pakistani attack, which he said was spearheaded by 100 American-supplied Patton and Sherman tanks and supported by American-supplied F-86 and F-104 jets.

But he said grimly, "We are going to hold them now."

The heavy price of the Indian defense lay steaming in the midday sun: seven charred and twisted hulls of trucks that were hit by rockets from a flight of 12 Pakistani jets yesterday afternoon.

The officer said the trucks had been empty at the time they were hit, returning in a convoy to Jammu for more men and supplies. The drivers and several other men were

Continued on Page 2, Column 2

NEWS INDEX

INDIAN ARMY UNITS GO INTO PAKISTAN IN AREA OF LAHORE

Invasion From Punjab Called Move to Protect Border—Parliament Cheers

AIR CONFLICT SPREADS

New Delhi Says Foe Raided a Big Base Near Amritsar—Pakistan Denies It

By Reuters

NEW DELHI, Monday, Sept. 6—Indian troops in the Punjab have moved across the border with Pakistan in the vicinity of Lahore "for the protection of the Indian border," India's Defense Minister, Yashwantrao Chavan, told the House of the People (lower house) here today.

[Indian Air Force planes carried out a bombing attack on the Lahore area of Pakistan early Monday, according to The Associated Press of Pakistan news agency.]

Mr. Chavan also told a wildly cheering Parliament:

"Our aircraft carried out a number of sorties over West Pakistan this morning and attacked a number of military installations, including a goods train carrying stores.

"They inflicted considerable damage. All our aircraft returned safely."

Pakistanis in Thrust

By JACQUES NEVARD
Special to The New York Times

KARACHI, Pakistan, Sept. 5 — Pakistani forces have smashed within a few miles of the key Indian crossroad town of Akhnur in fierce Kashmir fighting, a Pakistani spokesman said tonight.

The thrust threatens the Indian Army's main line of communications with the villages of Napshera, Jhangar, Rajaori, Mendhar and Punch in the Indian-held part of Kashmir.

[New Delhi charged that Pakistani jet planes had for the first time invaded Indian airspace outside Kashmir and had fired rockets at an air base at Amritsar, a major city. Pakistan denied the charge. In Paris, according to The Associated Press, the Pakistani Embassy said it had asked President de Gaulle for his good offices to try to end the conflict. Page 2.]

Ayub Commends Troops

The Pakistani advance earned for the troops a commendation from Field Marshal Mohammad Ayub Khan, the President. And Gen. Mohammad Musa, Commander in Chief of the Pakistani Army, sent his forces a message exhorting them to maintain pressure on the Indian Army:

"You have got your teeth into him. Bite deeper and deeper until he is destroyed. And destroy him you will, God willing."

According to Pakistani officials, the heavily defended Indian position of Jaurian was captured at 8 A.M. as Pakistani advance elements reached 18 miles east of the 1949 United Nations cease-fire line.

Pakistan's advance in the Bhimbar-Chhamb area came

Continued on Page 2, Column 1

Associated Press Cablephoto
PATROL IN KASHMIR: Indian troops move through town near Haji Pir Pass in advance on Pakistanis.

Albert Schweitzer, 90, Dies at His Hospital

Doctor Won Nobel Peace Prize for Work in Africa

By Reuters

LAMBARENE, Gabon, Sept. 5 — Albert Schweitzer died last night in his jungle hospital here. He was 90 years old.

Schweitzer's death was kept secret through the night because of a request he had made to give his daughter time to send telegrams to relatives. He died at 11:30 P.M. (6:30 P.M. New York time).

His death was attributed to circulatory trouble brought on by his advanced age.

He was buried in a brief and simple ceremony early this afternoon next to an urn containing the ashes of his wife, Héléne, who died in Europe in 1957. The grave, on the banks of the Ogooué River, is marked by a cross he made himself.

Hospital workers, lepers, cripples and other patients gathered in the jungle heat as the body of the noted physician, scholar, philosopher and musician was lowered into the ground.

Direction of the Lambaréné hospital has been handed over to Schweitzer's assistant, Dr. Walter Munz. Schweitzer's only daughter, Mrs. Rhena Eckert, will be its administrator.

Lambaréné was where Schweitzer chose to die. "I feel at home here. I belong to you until my dying breath," he told co-workers at the sprawling hospital on his 90th birthday Jan. 14.

He fell ill from exhaustion on Aug. 28 and his condition worsened steadily.

The family and close friends were prepared for the end. In a telegram that Mrs. Eckert sent to them from here Saturday, she said: "He is dying, inevitably and soon. He goes quietly, in peace and dignity."

His brother, Dr. Paul Schweitzer, 83, was not able to be with him. He is suffering from a heart ailment.

Reverence for Life

Man's ultimate redemption through beneficent activity — the theme of Part II of Goethe's

Gaby-Pix
Dr. Albert Schweitzer

He Was Also Noted as Musician and Theologian

"Faust," a metaphysical poem much admired by Albert Schweitzer — threads through this extraordinary man's long, complex and sometimes curious life. With Faust himself he could join in saying:

. . . This sphere of earthly soil
Still gives us room for lofty doing.
Astounding plans e'en now are brewing:
I feel new strength for bolder toil . . .
The Deed is everything, the Glory naught.

"You must give some time to your fellow man," Schweitzer counseled in paraphrase. "Even if it's a little thing, do something for those who have need of a man's help, something for which you get no pay but the privilege of doing it."

Also like Goethe, on whose life and works he was expert, Schweitzer came near to being a comprehensive man. He was theologian, musicologist, organ technician, physician and surgeon, missionary, philosopher of ethics, lecturer, writer and the builder and chief force of the famous hospital at Lam-

Continued on Page 16, Column 1

Albert Schweitzer, Felled by Exhaustion, Dies at His Jungle Hospital in Gabon

DOCTOR DEDICATED LIFE TO HUMANITY

Alsatian, Expert on Goethe, Also Drew Deeply on Kant and Bach

Continued From Page 1, Col. 6

baréné, in Gabon, the former French Equatorial Africa.

To a marked degree, Schweitzer was an eclectic. Franco-German yet cosmopolitan in culture, he drew deeply from the music and philosophy of the 18th century, especially Bach, Goethe and Kant. At the same time, he was a child of the 19th century, accepting its creature comforts yet rejecting its complacent attitudes toward progress. In line with the 20th century he sought to put religion on a rational footing and to accept the advances of science; yet he was a foe to materialism and to the century's criteria for personal success.

As a person, Schweitzer was a curious mixture. Widely honored with degrees, citations, scrolls, medals, special stamps, even the Nobel Prize for Peace in 1952, he seemed oblivious to panoply. He did not preen himself, nor did he utter cosmic statements at the drop of a cause. Instead, he seemed to many observers to be a simple, almost rustic man, who dressed in rumpled clothing, suffered fools gladly, stated fundamental verities patiently and paternally and worked unobtrusively. In this respect, he was undoubtedly made more of by cultists than he was willing to make of himself, although he was by no means a man with a weak ego.

Some of his more ardent admirers insisted that he was a jungle saint, even a modern Christ. But Schweitzer rejected such adulation; he held that his own spiritual life was its own reward and that works redeemed him.

In World and in God

He took the search for the good life seriously. For him it had profound religious implications. "Anyone can rescue his human life," he once said, "who seizes every opportunity of being a man by means of personal action, however unpretending, for the good of fellow men who need the help of a fellow man." He sought to exemplify the idea that man, through good works, can be in the world and in God at one and the same time.

For all his self-abnegation, Schweitzer had a bristly character, at least in his later years, a formidable sense of his own importance to Lambaréné and a do-good paternalism toward Africans that smacked more of the 19th than the 20th century.

For example, John Gunther got a dressing-down from Schweitzer for writing that he resembled Buffalo Bill and also, perhaps, for implying that he did not know what was going on in nationalist Africa.

If Schweitzer was thin-skinned to criticism from irreverent journalists, he heard little of it at Lambaréné, where his proprietorship was unquestioned. Not only did he design the station, but he also helped build it with his own hands. His co-workers were quite familiar with the businesslike and sometimes grumpy and brusque Schweitzer in a solar hat who hurried along the construction of a building by gingering up the native craftsmen with a sharp:

"Allez-vous OPP! Allez-vous OPP-opp. Hupp. upp. OPP!"

When Schweitzer was in residence at Lambaréné, virtually nothing was done without consulting him. Once, for instance, he all but halted the station's work when he received a letter from a Norwegian child seeking a feather from Parsifal, his pet pelican. He insisted on seeing personally that the youngster got a prompt and touching reply from his own pen before work was permitted to resume. His autocracy, was more noticeable as his years advanced and as his medical assistants grew less awesome of him.

Schweitzer regarded most native Africans as children, as primitives. It was said that he had scarcely ever talked with an adult African on adult terms. He had little but contempt for the nationalist movement, for his attitudes were firmly grounded in 19th-century benevolence. Although thousands of Africans called him "le grand docteur," others plastered his village with signs, "Schweitzer, Go Home!"

Needs Held Elementary

"At this stage," Schweitzer said in 1963, "Africans have little need for advanced training. They need very elementary schools run along the old missionary plan, with the Africans going to school for a few hours every day and then going back to the fields. Agriculture, not science or industrialization, is their greatest need."

His attitude was sharply expressed in a story he liked to tell of his orange trees. "I let the Africans pick all the fruit they want," he said. "You see, the good Lord has protected the trees. He made the Africans too lazy to pick them bare."

Although Schweitzer's views on Africa were out of date, he did what no man had done before him—he healed thousands and he welded world attention on Africa's many plights. A jungle saint he may not have been; a jungle pioneer he surely was.

Whatever Schweitzer's idiosyncrasies, he constructed a profound and enduring ethical system expressed in the principle Ehrfurcht vor dem Leben, or Reverence for Life. It is conceivably the only formal philosophical concept ever to spring to life amid a herd of hippopotamuses.

As Schweitzer recounted this climactic incident, he had been baffled in getting an answer to the question: Is it at all possible to find a real and permanent foundation in thought for a theory of the universe that shall be both ethical and affirmative of the world and life? The answer came in a flash of mystic illumination in September, 1915, as he was steaming up the Ogooué River in Africa.

Late in the third day of his journey he was on deck thinking and writing. "At the very moment when, at sunset, we were making our way through a herd of hippopotamuses, there flashed upon my mind, unforeseen and unsought, the phrase 'Reverence for Life.'"

"The iron door had yielded," he went on, "the path in the thicket had become visible. Now I had my way to the idea in which world [affirmation] and life-affirmation and ethics are contained side by side! Now I knew that the world-view of ethical world-and-life-affirmation, together with its ideal of civilization, is founded in thought."

Schweitzer's ethical system, elucidated at length in "The Philosophy of Civilization," is boundless in its domain and in its demands. He summarized it once by saying:

"A man is ethical only when life, as such, is sacred to him, that of plants and animals as that of his fellow men, and when he devotes himself helpfully to all life that is in need of help."

"Let me give you a definition of ethics," he wrote on another occasion. "It is good to maintain and further life; it is bad to damage and destroy life. And this ethic, profound, universal, has the significance of a religion. It is religion."

Called upon to be specific about Reverence for Life, he explained that the concept "does not allow the scholar to live for science alone, even if he is very useful to the community in so doing."

"It does not permit the artist," he continued, "to exist only for his art, even if it gives the inspiration to many by its means. It refuses to let the businessman imagine that he fulfills all legitimate demands in the course of his business activity. It demands from all that they should sacrifice a portion of their own lives for others."

A Guide to Action

Schweitzer earnestly sought to live his philosophy, which for him was a creedal guide to action. He was genuinely proud of his medical and missionary station at Lambaréné. He had scratched it out from the jungle beginning in 1913; he had designed it; he had worked as an artisan in constructing many of its buildings; and, although the station was many times beset by adversities that would have discouraged a less dedicated man, it had grown at his death to more than 70 buildings, 350 beds and a leper village of 200.

The compound was staffed by 5 unpaid physicians, 7 nurses and 13 volunteer helpers. Visitors who equated cleanliness, tidiness and medicine were horrified by the station, for every patient was encouraged to bring one or two members of his family to cook for him in the ditches beside the wards. Babies, even in the leper enclave, dropped toys into the dust of the unpaved streets and then popped them into their mouths. Noisome animals wandered in and out, including Schweitzer's pet parrot (which was not taught to talk because that would lower its dignity) and a hippopotamus that once invaded the vegetable garden.

Lambaréné resembled not so much a hospital as a native village where physicians cared for the sick. Actually, Schweitzer preferred (and planned) it in this fashion on the ground that the natives would shun an elaborate, shiny and impersonal institution.

The compound even lacked electricity, except for the operating and dental rooms, and members of the staff read by kerosene lamp. Of course, it had no telephone, radio or airstrip.

Schweitzer's view that "simple people need simple healing methods," however it might have outraged medical sophisticates, won for Lambaréné a tremendous measure of native confidence. Thousands flocked there, and thousands responded to Schweitzer's sermons as well as to his scalpel, for he believed that the good shepherd saves not only the animal but also his soul.

Lambaréné was suffused with Reverence for Life to what some critics thought was an exaggerated degree. Mosquitoes were not swatted, nor pests and insects doused with chemicals; they were left alone, and humans put up with them. Indeed, building was often brought to a halt lest nests of ants be killed or disturbed. On the other hand, patients received splendid medical care and few seemed to suffer greatly from the compound's lack of polish.

Critic's Accolade

Schweitzer's accomplishments are recognized even by his most caustic critics. One of them, Gerald McKnight, wrote in his book "Verdict on Schweitzer":

"The temptation for Schweitzer to see Lambaréné as a place cut off from the world, in which he can preserve its original forms and so reject any theory of treatment or life other than his own, is understandable when one considers the enormous achievement he has attained in his own lifetime. He came to the Ogooué in 1913 when horses drew the buses of London and leprosy was considered an incurable scourge. Housed originally in the grounds of a mission, he chose to leave this comparative sanctuary for the unknown and forbidding regions of the jungle nearby.

"No doubt a wish to have absolute dominion over his hospital drove him to this course, linked with the inner purpose which had brought him to Africa, but it was nonetheless heroic. Today, the hospital has grown, entirely under his hand and direction, into a sizable colony where between 500 and 600 people live in reasonable comfort. No greater tribute to his abilities as a conqueror of the jungle need be cited than the fact--regarded locally as something of a miracle—of his own survival."

Schweitzer came to French Equatorial Africa as a tall, handsome, broadly powerful, young man with a shock of rich, black hair, an enormous mustache and a look of piercing determination in his bold eyes. The years thinned and grayed his hair (without making it less unruly); age seamed his face, shrunk his frame, made him appear bandy-legged; time softened his eyes and made them less severe. But determination to make his life an "argument" for his ethical creed was as firm at 90 as it was on his 30th birthday, the day he decided to devote the rest of his life to the natives of Africa as a physician.

Schweitzer's arrival at this decision was calculated, a step in a quest for a faith to live by. It was a search that had haunted him, driven him, since childhood.

Albert Schweitzer was born at Kaystersberg, Haute Alsace (now Haut-Rhin), Jan. 14, 1875, just two months after Germany had annexed the province from war-prostrate France. During that year, his father, a Lutheran pastor, moved with his wife and eldest son to the neighboring village of Günsbach amid the foothills of the Vosges. It was to this picture-book Franco-German village and its vineyards that Schweitzer was invariably to return between periods of self-imposed exile in Africa.

A Musical Prodigy

As a child, he was frail and an indifferent student in everything but music, for which he showed the interest of a prodigy. He began to play the church organ at 8, when his feet barely reached the pedals. At the age of 18 he entered the University of Strasbourg as a student in theology, philosophy and musical theory. By this time he had also studied the organ briefly in Paris under the legendary Charles Marie Widor, who was so impressed with Schweitzer's talents that he taught him then and later without fee. Indeed, Schweitzer became a notable organist, especially in the works of Bach.

Schweitzer's university life was interrupted by a year of compulsory military service in 1894, a period that proved crucial to his religious thinking and to his life's vocation. The moment of awakening came as he was reading Matthew x and xi in Greek, chapters that contain Jesus' injunctions to His apostles, among them the one that commands, "Heal the sick, cleanse the lepers, raise the dead, cast out devils: freely ye have received, freely give"; and the verse that urges men, "Take my yoke upon you, and learn from me; for I am meek and lowly in heart: and ye shall find rest unto your souls."

Why Jesus Cried Out

Schweitzer was not only struck by the application of these verses to himself, but even more by the over-all content of the two chapters as expressed in Jesus' assertion that "the kingdom of heaven is at hand." These chapters started a chain of thought that resulted in "The Quest for the Historical Jesus." Published in 1910, it at once established Schweitzer as an eminent, if controversial, theologian whose explosive ideas had a profound influence on contemporary religious thinking.

Schweitzer depicted Jesus as a child of his times who shared the eschatological ideas of late Judaism and who looked for an immediate end of the world. Jesus, Schweitzer contended, believed himself the Messiah who would rule in a new kingdom of God when the end came; at first Jesus believed that his Messianic reign would begin before his disciples returned from the teaching mission commanded of them in the Gospel according to St. Matthew. When the world's end did not occur, according to Schweitzer's view, Jesus decided that He must undergo an atoning sacrifice, and that the great transformation would take place on the cross. This, too, failed, Schweitzer argued, hence the despairing cry, "My God, My God, why hast Thou forsaken Me?"

"The Jesus of Nazareth . . . who founded the kingdom of Heaven upon earth, and died to give his work the final consecration, never had any existence," Schweitzer wrote. "He is a figure designed by rationalism, endowed with life by liberalism and clothed by modern theology in an historical garb."

Schweitzer maintained, nonetheless, that Jesus' concepts were eternal. "In reality, that which is eternal in the words of Jesus is due to the very fact that they are based on an eschatological world-view, and contain the expression of a mind for which the contemporary world with its historical and social circumstances no longer had any existence.

"They are appropriate, therefore, to any world for in every world they raise the man who dares to meet their challenge, and does not turn them and twist them into meaninglessness, above his world and time, making him inwardly free, so that he is fitted to be, in his own world and in his own time, a simple channel of the power of Jesus."

Meantime, as these beliefs were maturing in Schweitzer's mind, he continued his student life at Strasbourg and fixed with great precision the course of his future. In 1896, at the age of 21, he pledged himself that he would give the following nine years to science and art and then devote himself to the service of suffering humanity.

Wrote on Kant

In those years he completed his doctoral thesis in philosophy, a study of Imanuel Kant's views on religion; studied the organ, again with Widor in Paris; won his doctorate in theology; was ordained a curate; taught theology and became principal of the faculty at Strasbourg; wrote "The Mystery of the Kingdom of God"; and, at Widor's urging, completed a study of the life and art of Johann Sebastian Bach.

The English version, "J. S. Bach," is a two-volume translation of the German text, itself an entire reworking of the first version written in French. It approaches Bach as a musician-poet and concentrates on his chorales, cantatas and Passion music. Schweitzer presents Bach as a religious mystic, as cosmic as the forces of nature. Bach, he said, was chiefly a church composer. As such, and as a Lutheran, "it is precisely to the chorale that the work of Bach owes its greatness."

"The chorale not only puts in his possession the treasury of Protestant music," Schweitzer wrote, "but also opens to him the riches of the Middle Ages and of the sacred Latin music from which the chorale itself came.

"From whatever direction he is considered, Bach is, then, the last word in an artistic evolution which was prepared in the Middle Ages, freed and activated by the Reformation and arrives at its full expression in the 18th century."

Turning to Bach's nonchurch music, Schweitzer said:

"The Brandenburg concertos are the purest product of Bach's polyphonic style. We really seem to see before us what the philosophy of all ages conceives as the fundamental mystery of things — that of self-unfolding of the idea in which it creates its own opposite in order to overcome it, and so on and on until it finally returns to itself, having meanwhile traversed the whole of existence."

Bach's "Well-Tempered Clavier" also drew Schweitzer's warmest praise.

Schweitzer's probing conception of Bach created a sensation in its time, and it still remains a classic study, not only for the detailed instructions it provides for the playing of Bach but also for its challenging esthetic.

True to his pledge, Schweitzer turned from music and theology to service to others. On Oct. 13, 1905, he posted letters from Paris to his parents and friends saying that at the start of the winter term he would become a medical student to prepare himself for the life of a physician in French Equatorial Africa.

This decision, protested vigorously by his friends, was, like so many others in his life, the product of religious meditation. He had pondered the meaning of the parable of Dives and Lazarus and its application to his times, and he had concluded that Dives represented opulent Europe, and Lazarus, with his open sores, the sick and helpless of Africa.

Explaining his decision later in more mundane terms, Schweitzer said:

"I wanted to be a doctor that I might be able to work without having to talk. For years I had been giving myself out in words. This new form of activity I could not represent to myself as talking about the religion of love, but only as an actual putting it into practice."

Studied Medicine 7 Years

For seven years, from 1906 until he received his M.D. degree in February, 1913, Schweitzer studied medicine, but he did not entirely cut himself off from his other worlds. Attending the University of Strasbourg, he served as curate at St. Nicholas, gave concerts on the organ, conducted a heavy correspondence and examined Pauline ideas, especially that of dying and being born again "in Jesus Christ." It resulted in a book, "Paul and His Interpreters," published in English in 1912.

That same year he resigned his curateship and his posts at the university and married Hélène Bresslau, the daughter of a well-known Strasbourg historian. A scholar herself, she became a trained nurse in order to share her husband's life in Africa.

On Good Friday, 1913, the couple set sail from Bordeaux for Africa, where Schweitzer established a hospital on the grounds of the Lambaréné station of the Paris Missionary Society. The society, wary of Schweitzer's unorthodox religious views, had barred him from preaching at the station, but agreed to accept his medical skills.

Lambaréné, on the Ogooué River a few miles from the Equator, is in the steaming jungle. Its climate is among the world's worst, with fiercely hot days, clammy nights and seasonal torrents of rain. The natives have all the usual diseases, plus Hansen's disease (leprosy), dysentery, elephantiasis, sleeping sickness, malaria, yellow fever and animal wounds.

From the first, when Schweitzer's hospital was a broken-down hen coop, natives flocked by foot, by improvised stretcher, by dugout canoe to Lambaréné for medical attention.

He had barely started to clear the jungle when World War I broke out. He and his wife (they were German citizens) were interned as prisoners of war for four months, then released to continue the work of the hospital. In this time and the succeeding months he started to write the two-volume "The Philosophy of Civilization," his masterwork in ethics that was published in 1923. It is a historical review of ethical thought leading to his own original contribution of Reverence for Life as an effective basis for a civilized world.

Schweitzer's book (and other writings as well) disputed the theory that human progress toward civilization was inevitable. He disagreed sharply with Aristotle's view that man's knowledge of right and wrong would surely lead him to make the right choices. He maintained, instead, that man must rationally formulate an ethical creed and then strive to put it into practice. In Reverence for Life, he concluded, "knowledge passes over into experience."

In 1917 the Schweitzers were returned to France and later to Alsace. To support himself and to carry on the work at Lambaréné, Schweitzer joined the medical staff of the Strasbourg Hospital, preached, gave lectures and organ recitals, traveled and wrote. He returned to Africa alone in 1925, his wife and daughter, Rhena, who was born in 1919, remaining in Europe.

In the almost eight years of his absence, the jungle had reclaimed the hospital grounds, and the buildings had to be rebuilt. This was no sooner under way than Schweitzer fell ill, an epidemic of dysentery broke out and a famine set in. The epidemic prompted Schweitzer to move his hospital to a larger site two miles up the Ogooué, where expansion was possible and where gardens and orchards could be planted.

Two physicians had arrived from Europe, and to them and to two nurses he turned over all medical responsibilities for a year and a half while he supervised (and helped) to fell trees, clear ground and construct buildings. The main hospital room and the dispensary were complete when he departed for Europe in midsummer 1927.

He returned to Lambaréné in 1929 and remained for two years, establishing a pattern of work in Africa and sojourns in Europe during which he lectured, wrote and concertized to raise funds for his hospital. On one of these occasions, in 1949, he visited the United States and lectured on Goethe at a conference in Aspen, Colo.

Le Mot Juste

Hundreds flocked to hear him and to importune him. On one occasion a group of tourists pulled him away from the dinner table to get an explanation of his ethics. He responded with remarkable courtesy for about 20 minutes until one questioner prodded him for a specific application of Reverence for Life. "Reverence for Life," Schweitzer replied, "means my answering your kind inquiries; it also means your reverence for my dinner hour." The tourists got the point and he returned to his meal.

On his trips to Europe, Schweitzer invariably made his headquarters at his home in Günsbach, which was expanded until it was also a leave and rest center for the hospital staff. Of an afternoon, Schweitzer could often be seen leaving his home to slip over to the church to play Bach. (He played Bach at Lambaréné, too, on pianos especially lined with zinc to prevent rot.) He not only played throughout Europe, but he also repaired church organs and kept up a ceaseless study of music.

Schweitzer received many honorary degrees and recognition from a number of governments and learned societies. He was made an honorary member of the British Order of Merit in 1955. He was elected to the French Academy in 1951.

After his wife died in 1957, Schweitzer was almost continuously in Lambaréné. He celebrated his 90th birthday there as hundreds of Africans, Europeans and Americans gathered to wish him well. Among the messages he received was one from President Johnson. "In your commitment to truth and service," the President cabled, "you have touched and deepened the lives of millions you have never met."

Camera Press-Pix

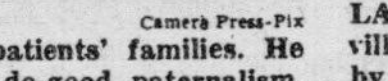

'LE GRAND DOCTEUR': Dr. Schweitzer acknowledging gifts brought to his hospital by patients' families. He regarded most native Africans as children and was criticized for his 19th-century kind of do-good paternalism.

Dalmas-Pix

LAMBARENE: Dr. Schweitzer's jungle hospital complex in Gabon is more like a native village than a hospital. Those who equate cleanliness with medicine have been shocked by conditions at Lambaréné, where animals and insects mingle freely with the patients.

Associated Press Radiophoto

FUNERAL: Dr. Schweitzer's coffin being borne to grave on the bank of the river near his hospital yesterday.

MUSICOLOGIST: Dr. Schweitzer, musicologist and organ technician as well as missionary, physician and theologian, was inspired by life and art of Johann Sebastian Bach.

Patients Paid for Care, If Only a Pig or an Egg

A standing rule at the Lambaréné jungle hospital required that every patient contribute something in return for its services—often a chicken, a pig or an egg.

Medical and other supplies used by the compound were purchased with funds contributed by persons throughout the world.

Dr. Schweitzer raised money by giving concerts in Europe, and he turned over his $33,840 Nobel Peace Prize check to the hospital.

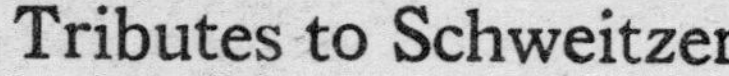

Tributes to Schweitzer

Following are tributes to Albert Schweitzer:

PRESIDENT JOHNSON: The world has lost a truly universal figure. His message and his example, which have lightened the darkest years of this century, will continue to strengthen all those who strive to create a world living in peace and brotherhood.

QUEEN ELIZABETH II in a letter to Schweitzer's daughter: I and my husband were so sorry to hear of the death of your father, Albert Schweitzer. His great work in so many fields will long be remembered and his humanity will inspire this and future generations.

CHANCELLOR LUDWIG ERHARD, of West Germany: A great human being, theologian, philosopher and musician has been called from this life. In this true world citizen beat the heart of a benefactor of humanity. With the founding of the jungle hospital in Lambaréné he created two generations ago the shining example of what is known today as development aid, and which has found its echo in our land and in the entire world.

WALTER ULBRICHT, head of East Germany's Communist party: Albert Schweitzer enjoyed throughout the world the reputation of an outstanding physician, musicologist and theologian, who with his impassioned appeal stanchly supported general and complete disarmament and a ban on all nuclear weapons. The death of Albert Schweitzer is a painful loss for the world-wide peace movement.

GIUSEPPE SARAGAT, President of Italy: The death of Prof. Albert Schweitzer constitutes a serious mourning for the entire world which recognized in him the highest expression of human brotherhood.

RAYMOND MARCELLIN, French Minister of Health: In fighting against epidemics, sickness and suffering with uncommon energy and faith, Dr. Schweitzer has merited public gratitude.

ARTHUR M. RAMSEY, Archbishop of Canterbury: Albert Schweitzer was one of the great Christians of our time, or of any time.

BERTRAND RUSSELL: Genuinely good and dedicated men are uncommon. Our age is hardly fit to understand them. It certainly does not deserve them. Dr. Schweitzer was both a good and dedicated man.

MOSCOW RADIO: Dr. Schweitzer was one of the first scientists in the West to demand a ban on atomic weapons. He responded energetically to the Soviet proposals for general and complete disarmament and repeatedly underlined their importance in his speeches.

"All the News That's Fit to Print"

The New York Times.

LATE CITY EDITION
Cloudy today and rain tonight. Fair and colder tomorrow.
Temperature Range Today—Max.,53; Min.,36
Temperatures Yesterday—Max.,40; Min.,21
Full U. S. Weather Bureau Report Page 51

VOL. C..No. 33,885. Entered as Second-Class Matter. Post Office, New York, N. Y. NEW YORK, THURSDAY, NOVEMBER 2, 1950. Times Square, New York 18, N. Y. Telephone LAckawanna 4-1000 FIVE CENTS

ASSASSINATION OF TRUMAN FOILED IN GUN FIGHT OUTSIDE BLAIR HOUSE; PUERTO RICAN PLOTTER, GUARD DIE

KOREAN REDS HIT U. S. UNIT; NOW USE JETS

REGIMENT TRAPPED

Foe Employing Rockets Against First Cavalry Division at Unsan

U. N. TROOPS FORCED BACK

Only 24th Division Makes Gain and Then It Is Told to Halt Its Advance

By LINDESAY PARROTT
Special to THE NEW YORK TIMES.

TOKYO, Thursday, Nov. 2—North Korean Communists, reinforced by troops of the Chinese Red Army, savagely attacked today advance guards of the United States First Cavalry Division thrown into action near the west coast of Korea to reinforce the weakening South Korean troops.

The attack made north and west of Unsan, where the Communists had concentrated their strength during the last few days and had driven back South Korean spearheads by as much as thirty miles in some sectors. Using tanks, artillery and heavy mortar fire, the North Koreans cut off one regiment of the United States Cavalry Division. Other units of the division were reported to be attempting to fight their way through to reach the isolated troops.

The fighting was in progress between Unsan and Taechon, but a spokesman for the United States First Corps said the situation was too vague and confused to locate the positions to which the United States troops had been forced to retreat.

Admits Chinese Are Fighting

For the first time a corps spokesman officially admitted that "Chinese troops" were launching an assault.

"We don't know whether they represent the Chinese Government," he said, and added that it also was unknown whether or not Chinese reinforcements made up the bulk of the new strength that had enabled the shattered North Korean Army to take the offensive again—at least locally—against the United Nations move toward the Manchurian border.

The Communists launched their attack in the morning. According to reports from Korea, they used heavy rocket bombardment for the first time in the war. The latest accounts said the enemy had overrun several First Cavalry positions, capturing weapons and turning them against Americans who had been hurriedly brought up to the combat line after all but one United States division—the Twenty-fourth Infantry, farther to the west—had been out of the contact with the enemy and behind the Korean Republican spearheads driven in by the enemy counter-attack.

This morning the North Koreans were reported to be within one half mile of Unsan.

Rockets Launched on Ground

The use of the rockets, fired from launchers on the ground, represented the second new weapon introduced on the North Korean side within the last two days. Yesterday for the first time the enemy flung jet-propelled fighter planes into combat.

Meanwhile, the ground advance of the Allied forces halted at Chongko, where the United States Twenty-fourth Infantry Division stood within eighteen miles of the border city of Sinuiju, reported to be the new capital of the North Korean Communist Government.

All along the rest of the front South Korean divisions were in retreat or on the defensive against enemy attacks strengthened by contingents of Chinese Communist soldiers trained in the Chinese Red Army.

Six enemy jet fighters made their appearance yesterday over Sonchon on the west coast, fought a brief dogfight with Mustangs of the United States Fifth Air Force and then flashed back toward the Manchurian border without casualties on either side. Observers said the jet-propelled planes resembled the Soviet model MIG-15, with swept back wings and a speed of 600 miles an hour. On the previous occasion jet planes were believed to have been seen over North Korea, but this was the

Continued on Page 3, Column 1

PLAYWRIGHT DIES

George Bernard Shaw
The New York Times

BERNARD SHAW, 94, DIES IN HIS HOME

Famous Irish Wit Had Been in Coma for Day—Broken Thigh Led to Final Illness

By The Associated Press.

AYOT ST. LAWRENCE, England, Thursday, Nov. 2—George Bernard Shaw, one of the modern age's greatest dramatists and its most caustic critic, died today at the age of 94. The white-bearded Irish-born sage, whose wit was renowned throughout the world for half a century, succumbed at 4:59 A. M. (11:59 P. M. Wednesday, Eastern standard time).

His death was announced to newsmen by his housekeeper, Mrs. Alice Laden. Wearing black, she appeared at the gates of the cottage, Shaw's Corner, and told the reporters: "Mr. Shaw is dead."

A few minutes after her announcement, Dr. Thomas Probyn, Shaw's physician, hurried into the house. Twenty minutes later, Shaw's longtime biographer, F. E. Loewenstein, told newsmen that the playwright died peacefully without regaining consciousness. Only two nurses were with him when death came.

The famed dramatist, who professed himself both a Communist and an atheist, was visited in his last hours by an Anglican clergyman, who said final prayers for the old sage's soul.

"It is wrong to say that he was an atheist," said the minister, the Rev. R. G. Davies. "He believed in God."

Shaw lapsed into his final coma yesterday morning at 3 o'clock (10 P. M. Tuesday, Eastern standard time) and never regained consciousness. Operated on seven weeks ago for a broken thigh suffered when he slipped and fell in his garden, he grew steadily weaker. A bladder ailment aggravated his condition.

Lights burned for two nights in Shaw's Corner, the red brick

Continued on Page 28, Column 2

LIE TERM EXTENDED AS U. N. SECRETARY FOR 3 YEARS, 46 TO 5

Assembly Vote Continues Him in Office Despite Bitter Attacks by Russians

ARAB BLOC, CHINA ABSTAIN

Australia Also Shuns Support—Final Move by Vishinsky to Block Step Fails

The text of Secretary Lie's address is printed on Page 3.

By THOMAS J. HAMILTON

Overriding last-ditch Soviet opposition, the General Assembly yesterday extended the term of Trygve Lie as Secretary General of the United Nations for another three years. The vote was 46 to 5, with only the five members of the Soviet bloc opposed.

However, Australia, Nationalist China and six members of the Arab bloc—Egypt, Iraq, Lebanon, Saudi Arabia, Syria and Yemen—abstained. Haiti was absent.

Mr. Lie, whose present five-year term will expire next Feb. 2, told the Assembly when it reconvened for the afternoon session that he interpreted the extension of his term as a vote of confidence and a reaffirmation of the independence and integrity of the position.

Mr. Lie did not refer to his stand in favor of United Nations action for the defense of South Korea, which had led the Soviet Union to veto his re-election. But he said that he had worked hard for the past five years to reconcile "the conflicting interests that divide the world" and that he would continue to do so.

Iraq Explains Abstention

Immediately after the vote Dr. Fadhil Jamali of Iraq explained that he had not been able to vote for the extension of Mr. Lie's term because he felt that, despite Mr. Lie's "many fine qualities," he had not been "entirely impartial" on the Palestine question. He added that "Mr. Lie did not react toward recent Jewish aggressions in Palestine with anything like the zeal which he displayed on the question of Korea."

"With due respect to Mr. Lie, we do not believe that he helped enough to make the United Nations bring about peace and justice to the Arabs of Palestine," Dr. Jamali said.

Nasrollah Entezam of Iran, President of the Assembly, who had given Dr. Jamali the floor to explain his vote, then pounded his gavel, declaring that this was not an explanation, and that Dr. Jamali could not "continue this way in attacking a person who is not present here and who has received the confidence of the General Assembly by forty-six votes in his favor."

Dr. Jamali then stepped down from the rostrum with the statement that "it would certainly have been a betrayal of Arab public opinion and sentiment if we had not abstained."

Sir Keith Officer, who then was recognized to explain Australia's abstention, said that Australia shared the view that Mr. Lie must not be punished for doing "his clear duty as regards the action of the United Nations in Korea," but that Australia had "genuine doubts" about the legality of the extension of Mr. Lie's term, which

Continued on Page 3, Column 5

CAPITAL STARTLED

Police Swiftly Cordon Blair House as Shots Attract Big Crowds

PHOTOGRAPHERS NEAR BY

Leap From Their Auto, Halted by Traffic Light, Into Action—Passers-by See Fight

By PAUL P. KENNEDY
Special to THE NEW YORK TIMES.

WASHINGTON, Nov. 1—This city, which has heard the sound of assassins' guns before, reacted with electric suddenness today as shots exploded before the front door of President Truman's own residence.

Within a few moments after the firing had stopped in front of Blair House hundreds of spectators were straining at police cordons almost magically thrown up at the intersecting streets bounding the block in which the President's temporary residence is situated.

Street cars, which run along Pennsylvania Avenue in front of the White House and Blair House, were backed up three blocks from Jackson Place, which bounds the Blair House block on the east, and for as many blocks from Seventeenth Street, which bounds Blair House block on the west.

Automobile traffic snarls blocked the approach of a number of ambulances and police squad cars, and wailing sirens heightened the confusion.

Approaching the scene of the shooting from the outer fringe of the crowd, one picked up at least a dozen accounts of what had happened. The accounts grew less lurid toward the core of the trouble.

Rumors Fly Among Throngs

These reports were received from spectators, at least a half block from the Blair House, and from newspaper men scurrying from the scene to the nearest telephones. On the outer reaches of the crowd the rumor was that two or three persons had entered Blair House with submachine guns firing and that the President had been assassinated or wounded.

Even among the reporters and photographers directly in front of the Blair House, the early accounts were confusing. It was not until fully fifteen minutes after the firing that it was clearly estab-

Continued on Page 16, Column 6

WOULD-BE ASSASSIN OF PRESIDENT SHOT DOWN

Oscar Collazo lying at the bottom of the steps to the Blair-Lee House as White House guard is putting his revolver back in his holster. This picture was made by a photographer of The New York Times, who was waiting to accompany Mr. Truman to a dedication ceremony at Arlington Cemetery.
The New York Times (by Bruce Hoertel)

PUERTO RICO'S HEAD LINKS TWO ATTACKS

Governor Says Nationalist Forces Sparked by Reds Shot at Truman, Himself

By The United Press.

SAN JUAN, Puerto Rico, Nov. 1—Gov. Luis Muñoz Marin said tonight that Puerto Rican Nationalists were being used by the Communists both in the attempt to assassinate President Truman and in the abortive revolt here, in which he also was a target.

"This further crime—the Washington attempt—further confirms me in my conviction that the Nationalists are having their lunacy, fanaticism and irresponsibility manipulated for the benefit of Communist propaganda and strategy," the Governor said.

"We all feel deeply relieved that no tragic consequences resulted from this criminal action.

"The people are profoundly

Continued on Page 19, Column 2

Assassins' Kin and Friends Are Rounded Up in Bronx

By MEYER BERGER

Thirteen Puerto Ricans—six women and seven men—were taken to the offices of the United States Secret Service at 90 Church Street last night for questioning about the attempt yesterday on President Truman's life in Washington.

Policemen said they were the families and friends of the two assassins. Unofficially, Oscar Collazo of 173 Brook Avenue, the Bronx, one of the men who fired a gun at Blair House, was described as treasurer of the New York City branch of the Puerto Rican Nationalists, bitter enemies of the United States.

Collazo, wounded, is in the Emergency Hospital in Washington. The second gunman, tentatively identified by Secret Service men as Griselio Torresola of 1259 Ward Avenue in the East Bronx, was killed by police bullets.

Mrs. Rose Collazo, 42 years old, the wounded man's wife, was one of those taken into custody. She was arraigned at 2 o'clock this morning in Federal Court before United States Commissioner Edward M. McDonald on a charge of having conspired with the two assassins and two unnamed persons to harm a member of the Government. Commissioner McDonald held her in $50,000 bail for a hearing next Thursday.

Following the arraignment Secret Service men took her to the Federal House of Detention.

At the request of Assistant United States Attorney Irving H. Saypol, Commisisoner McDonald issued John Doe warrants for the two unidentified persons named in the conspiracy complaint.

Earlier Mrs. Collazo had told officials and newspaper men:

"I am Oscar Collazo's wife. He

Continued on Page 18, Column 3

PRESIDENT IS CALM AT DILL DEDICATION

Speaks, After Attempt to Kill Him, at Unveiling of Statue of British Field Marshal

By The Associated Press.

WASHINGTON, Nov. 1—Less than an hour after an attempt had been made to assassinate him, President Truman calmly dedicated a memorial to Britain's Field Marshal Sir John Dill at Arlington National Cemetery today.

"It is important to the peace of the world that peoples understand each other and have full faith in each other's sincerity," he said.

He made no reference to the gunfight in front of his Blair House residence. Many of the 600 dignitaries present at the unveiling wondered why Mr. Truman was surrounded by such an unusually heavy guard of Secret Service men.

The President in his address said that he welcomed "this opportunity to remind my countrymen that the maintenance of a perfect understanding between the people of Great Britain and the United States is of great impor-

Continued on Page 17, Column 2

PRESIDENT RESTING

Awakened by Shots, He Sees Battle in Which Three Are Wounded

HE KEEPS APPOINTMENTS

Documents Link 2 Assassins, Who Lived Here, to Puerto Rican Extremist Leader

By ANTHONY LEVIERO
Special to THE NEW YORK TIMES.

WASHINGTON, Nov. 1—Quick-shooting White House guards cut down two assassins this afternoon when they attempted to invade Blair House in a Puerto Rican Nationalist plot to assassinate President Truman.

Tonight one assassin and one policeman were dead, and two policemen were wounded, one critically. The other assassin, seriously wounded, told the United States Secret Service that he and his companion had come down from New York two days ago to kill Mr. Truman.

On the body of the dead assassin Secret Service agents found a letter and a "memorandum," both cryptic but indicative of conspiracy. The missives were in the same handwriting and on the same stationery. They bore in the form of a signature, the name of Pedro Albizu Campos, leader of the Puerto Rican Nationalist extremists who carried out the uprising in Puerto Rico Monday.

U. E. Baughman, chief of the Secret Service, cautioned reporters, however, that he had no proof that Albizu Campos was the author of the two documents.

THE DEAD

COFFELT, Pvt. Leslie, of Arlington, Va., White House guard.

TORRESOLA, Griselio, of 1259 Ward Avenue, New York, assassin.

THE INJURED

COLLAZO, Oscar, of 173 Brook Avenue, New York, assassin; shot in the chest.

DOWNS, Pvt. Joseph, of Silver Spring, Md., White House guard, in critical condition with multiple wounds.

BIRDZELL, Pvt. Donald T., of Washington, White House guard; in "fair" condition with knees shattered by bullets.

All three wounded are expected to recover.

Taking his usual afternoon nap and roused by a fury of shooting, Mr. Truman looked down from an upstairs bedroom of Blair House. In the bright sun of Pennsylvania Avenue was terror and confusion. At the foot of the stoop leading into Blair House lay one of the assassins, alive, blood flowing from the middle of his chest and staining his blue shirt.

"A President has to expect those things," Mr. Truman said, later.

Truman Keeps to Schedule

Serene, a man of good conscience, for he had told the people of Puerto Rico unequivocally that they were free to work out their own political destiny, Mr. Truman punctiliously kept his remaining appointments of the day.

The outrage, however, made the Federal police agencies increasingly alert, and new safeguards were put around the President and his family. Meanwhile, the Secret Service began to trace back the plot through New York, to its apparent source in the island possession in the Caribbean, which is

Continued on Page 16, Column 2

Pope Affirms Dogma of Assumption Of Mary to Heaven 'Body and Soul'

By CAMILLE M. CIANFARRA
Special to THE NEW YORK TIMES.

ROME, Nov. 1—Pope Pius proclaimed today the dogma of the Assumption into heaven of the Virgin Mary.

"We pronounce, declare and define to be a dogma revealed by God that the Immaculate Mother of God, Mary, ever virgin, when the course of her life on earth was finished was taken up body and soul into heaven," the Pope declared.

The Pontiff spoke ex cathedra as supreme pastor of the church and teacher of Roman Catholic doctrine during an open air ceremony of pomp and magnificence to an audience of thirty-six Cardinals and 480 Archbishops and Bishops in the grandiose setting of St. Peter's Square.

A throng of 200,000 faithful, including Holy Year pilgrims from so many countries that they could be said truly to represent the whole Catholic world, packed every inch of space of the oval-shaped square that had been transformed for the occasion into a vast Christian temple.

Beginning today 400,000,000 members of the Catholic religion must believe explicitly and without reservation—otherwise they will incur excommunication as heretics—the Catholic tradition of the Assumption now defined as a dogma or an article of faith. The Catholic Church holds that dogmas are truths revealed directly by God or through the apostles and contained in the two sole fonts of Catholic doctrine—the Bible and tradition.

As such they are irrevocably binding on all Catholics and may be defined by the Pope either alone as today or jointly with the Bishops in the Ecumenical Council repre-

Continued on Page 13, Column 1

Vatican texts on dogma and speech by Pope are on Page 12.

World News Summarized

THURSDAY, NOVEMBER 2, 1950

Two assassins, identified as Puerto Rican Nationalists, attempted to kill President Truman yesterday while he was taking an afternoon nap in Blair House. One assailant was killed and the other badly wounded in a gun fight outside the house with guards, one of whom died. Two policemen were seriously wounded. The President went to the window to see what had happened and was shooed to safety by alert agents. [1:8.] Later he dedicated a memorial in Arlington Cemetery honoring Sir John Dill, British Field Marshal. [1:7.]

Secret Service agents listed the two Puerto Ricans as Bronx residents, and last night six women and five men were taken to 90 Church Street for questioning. [1:6-7.] An hour before the Blair House attack an unidentified man threw two bottles of ignited gasoline into the Puerto Rican labor office in this city, but they did not explode. [17:7.] In Puerto Rico, which has been torn by Nationalist uprisings, the Government spurred its hunt for revolutionary leaders. [1:5.]

Washington, electrified by the attack, the sixth attempt on a President's life [16:2], crowded to the scene. Eyewitness reports were confusing and conflicting. [1:4]. An ironic twist to the assassination attempt was the fact that President Truman was a strong advocate of Puerto Rican independence. [16:1.]

Chinese and North Korean troops, using rockets and heavy guns, drove back United States troops in the Unsan area, trapping one regiment. Other United States forces were ordered to halt their advance 18 miles from the border. [1:1; map Page 2.]

India expressed "keen disappointment" in answering Communist China's rejection of her concern over the invasion of Tibet. [9:2.]

The United Nations General Assembly, 46 to 5, extended the term of Secretary General Lie for three years. Only the Soviet bloc voted no, while Australia, Nationalist China and the Arab states abstained. [1:3.]

France is ready to contribute half of forty divisions planned for Western Europe by 1953, Defense Minister Moch said. Secretary Acheson declared it was agreed there should be no German general staff, national army or war industries. [8:3.]

Pope Pius proclaimed as dogma the Assumption of the Virgin Mary into heaven. [1:2-3.]

George Bernard Shaw died at his home in England. He was 94 years old. [1:2.]

Theodore Roosevelt, Woodrow Wilson, Alexander Graham Bell, Dr. William C. Gorgas, Josiah Willard Gibbs and Susan B. Anthony were elected to the Hall of Fame. [34:3.]

The City Planning Commission approved a record $478,761,756 capital budget for 1951 and a $1,235,850,237 five-year program. [33:1.]

Index to other news appears on Page 32.

November Heat Record of 81° Set; Zoo and Parks Draw Big Crowds

By IRA HENRY FREEMAN

November came in like a lamb yesterday, a spring lamb.

On the fourth day of an unseasonably warm wave extending over the eastern third of the country, the temperature in this city climbed to 81 degrees at 1:15 P. M. It dropped one degree for an hour, but at 2:15 again reached 81, and the latter time was officially accepted as the record.

This was not only the warmest for any Nov. 1 but also higher than ever reached in November since the Weather Bureau began keeping records here in 1871. The previous record for Nov. 1 was 70 degrees in 1946, while the previous high for any November day was 80 on Nov. 6, 1948.

The coolest it got during the day was 59 degrees from 6 to 7 o'clock in the morning. That was two degrees above the normal maximum for Nov. 1, Col. James W. Osmun, chief assistant meteorologist in charge of the New York Weather Bureau, pointed out.

During the luncheon period when the mercury was rising 4 and 5 degrees an hour, throngs of office workers and shoppers on the midtown streets were uncomfortably warm. In Bryant Park the benches were jammed with men in shirt sleeves and girls in summer blouses.

Some air-cooled restaurants and offices turned the refrigeration back on temporarily. Women shoppers in Fifth Avenue and Fifty-seventh Street strolled along with their suit jackets over their arms. The retail clothing business, incidentally, was slackened temporarily by the weather, Thomas A. Terry, executive vice president of the Fifth Avenue Association, reported.

The brass Prometheus bringing

Continued on Page 22, Column 1

Campos Captured In San Juan Home

By The United Press.

SAN JUAN, Puerto Rico, Thursday, Nov. 2—National policemen poured five heavy volleys of rifle and pistol fire into the home of Pedro Albizu Campos early today and captured the Nationalist party leader when he fled into the street.

The Puerto Rican Governor, Luis Muñoz Marin, earlier had accused the Nationalist extremist leader of responsibility for the assassination attempt made against President Truman yesterday. The would-be assassins were said to be members of the Nationalist party.

George Bernard Shaw, Dubliner Who Mocked Man's Works, Rose From Poverty

THOSE HE PILLORIED FLOCKED TO DRAMAS

Playwright, a Master in Aiming Attacks at Dogma, Lived a Conventional Life

EARLY WRITING REJECTED

Tangles With British Censors Followed First Successes in Long Theatrical Career

Goaded by the voice of Henry George and guided by the hand of Karl Marx, George Bernard Shaw stepped from the poverty of Dublin to flit across the Western World, the flaming, mocking, deadly serious messenger boy of the "new age." Tossing off sparks of wit and satire as his heels clicked against the pavement of conservatism, thumbing his nose at the smug and censorious, urging the world to read his books and reform, he never stopped his capers even when his red hair had turned white and his Mephistophelian eyebrows drooped with age.

He criticized the best-loved institutions of mankind — and "got away with it" because he was a supreme wit. Nothing escaped him, and those he pilloried the most flocked by the thousands to see his plays and helped make him rich by buying his books.

Mr. Shaw's was a life of contradictions. One of the best descriptions of him is by William Archer, who tells that the first time he saw Shaw the Irishman was sitting in the British Museum, alternately studying the French translation of "Das Kapital" and the score of "Tristan und Isolde." Shaw himself once said "Karl Marx made a man of me."

His huge energy and mental agility had made him an early controversialist. He moved from the benches of debating halls to the platform after being fired by the eloquence of Henry George.

"George switched me over to economics," he said. "I became very excited about his 'Progress and Poverty.'" Told that no one was qualified to discuss George until he read Karl Marx, the 26-year-old Shaw hied to the British Museum to read "Das Kapital." That, he told a biographer, "was the turning point in my career. Marx was a revelation. His abstract economics, I discovered later, were wrong, but he rent the veil."

"Das Kapital" converted Mr. Shaw to socialism, transformed him into a political agitator and a revolutionary writer, even gave him a religion.

A "Social Evolutionist"

An extreme individualist, he called himself a social evolutionist during most of his life, and his was the self-assumer task of saying that only when the world espoused socialism would it be worth living in and there would be no further need of Shaw. In the nineteenth century he turned his withering satire upon thoughts and ideals long held sacred. But in the twentieth, he himself had become an institution.

Mr. Shaw was the greatest master of paradox as a destroyer of dogma, but he was one of the most dogmatic men anywhere in the expression of his ideas. Happily married for many years, he enjoyed nothing better than to sit comfortably by his snug hearth and ridicule home and marriage as institutions. Shy and gentle by nature, he donned the protective mask of a clown and delighted in shocking and annoying any who displeased him.

Ever since the turn of the century critics have been writing about and disagreeing over Mr. Shaw. To some his appellation of journalist was final. By journalist, of course, they took him to mean propagandist for a new social order. They quoted him: "Every play or preface I wrote contains a message. I am the messenger boy of the new age." Other critics found him above all else a comedian. Archibald Henderson, his official biographer, has stoutly maintained (and scanned his prose to prove his point) that he was, more than anything, a poet.

The critics could not agree. But the Shaw who let Karl Marx mold him as a man, who let Ibsen make him a dramatist, and who never lacked courage to say his piece on any topic under the sun and claim that he was right in what he said, made all the world read his words.

It was as a dramatist that he did his greatest work. He taught himself to write by laboriously constructing five novels, not one of which is considered to have lasting worth. He earned a living, and made himself known by scribbling criticism on art and music for the daily press.

Devoted Himself to Plays

Then, out of what he had learned about "the importance of the economic basis" from his own poverty and the pages of Marx, he wrought the first of his great plays, and from then on he devoted himself mainly to this medium.

Mr. Shaw was born in Dublin on July 26, 1856. He was the third child and only son of George Carr Shaw, an impecunious civil servant, and of Lucinda Elizabeth Shaw, daughter of Walter Bagenal Gurley, a County Carlow landowner.

The Shaw family traced its pedigree to Capt. William Shaw, a Hampshire gentleman of Scottish descent, who went to Ireland with William III in 1689. George Bernard Shaw's grandfather was Bernard Shaw, High Sheriff of Kilkenny, whose first cousin, Robert Shaw, was created a baronet in 1812.

From his father, Mr. Shaw inherited his Irish gayety, wit and humor, but little else. A few years before the son's birth the father's public post had been abolished, and he had compounded his pension in a lump sum to engage in business as a corn merchant. He failed to make a go of it. Consequently, the family life of the Shaws was one of shabby gentility, of the kind familiar to readers of nineteenth-century British novels.

One of Mr. Shaw's pronounced traits can be traced to his father. It was his abhorrence of alcohol. The young Shaw learned about alcohol in a manner that taught him an early moral lesson. His father professed to the boy such a horror of alcohol that Mr. Shaw decided to become a convinced teetotaler. Soon the young Shaw discovered that "the governor" was a steady drinker.

"Now, a convivial drunkard," he told a biographer later, "may be exhilarating in convivial company. Even a quarrelsome or boastful drunkard may be found entertaining by people who are not particular. But a miserable drunkard—and my father, in theory a teetotaler, was racked with shame and remorse even in his cups—is unbearable." The family, he said, was dropped socially through his father's drinking.

His Mother Was a Singer

Mr. Shaw's mother was a singer who took part in amateur operatic performances in Dublin. Through her interests and associates, the Shaw children acquired a culture in music, drama and painting which laid the groundwork for Mr. Shaw's career.

His formal education was extremely limited. After receiving private lessons in Latin grammar from the Rev. William George Carroll, vicar of St. Bride's, Dublin, an uncle reputed to be the first Irish person to espouse Home Rule, he was sent to the Wesleyan Connexional School, later known as Wesley College, in Dublin. Pride was mixed with poverty in the Shaw family, and the embryo dramatist was brought up, as he put it, "to believe that there was an inborn virtue of gentility in all Shaws, since they revolved impecuniously in a sort of vague second-cousinship round a baronetcy."

Against this sort of snobbishness Mr. Shaw revolted, as he did against the Irish Protestant tradition of his family, in which he saw a combination of hypocrisy and mock gentility resulting in a stultification of the life around him.

Mr. Shaw was employed for five years in the office of a Dublin land agent, at a salary which ranged from the equivalent of about $90 to $240 a year. This work was irksome to one of his temperament, and in 1876, at the age of 20, he threw it up and fled to London to take up a literary career. There he joined his mother, who had left her alcoholic husband and was earning her own living in that city as a professional music teacher.

Early Career Precarious

It was at first a poverty-stricken existence, for in nine years he was able to earn no more than the equivalent of about $30 with his pen. Of that sum, about $25 came from an advertisement he wrote for a patent medicine.

During this period he was supported by pittances which his father sent him from his unsuccessful corn business in Dublin, and which his mother supplied from her likewise meager earnings.

Beginning three years after his arrival in London, Mr. Shaw made an effort to become a novelist.

The first of his novels was called, "with merciless fitness," as Shaw put it, "Immaturity." George Meredith, as reader for a publishing firm, rejected it with an emphatic "No!" Another novel was "Cashel Byron's Profession," in which the late Jim Corbett appeared some years later in the rôle of the pugilist in the dramatized version.

The others in this series were "The Irrational Knot," which reflected Shaw's admiration for Ibsen; "Love Among the Artists," a criticism of shallowness in art and in family relations, and "An Unsocial Socialist," which has been described as "the first genuine blast of the Shavian gale."

"Unsocial Socialist" was his fifth and last novel. None had been successful. Altogether he garnered about sixty rejections from American and English publishers. Later, when his fame mounted, American magazines pirated them.

In 1884 Mr. Shaw joined the Fabian Society of moderate Socialists, founded in that year, and became widely acquainted among such advanced thinkers as Sidney and Beatrice Webb, Annie Besant, Edward Carpenter, William Morris, James Leigh Joynes, Sydney Olivier (later Lord Olivier), Keir Hardie, Ramsay MacDonald, and others. He became an ardent pamphleteer and a lecturer for the cause of socialism.

THROUGH THE YEARS WITH THE WORLD-FAMOUS AUTHOR AND PLAYWRIGHT

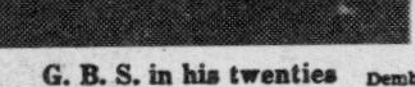

G. B. S. in his twenties — Dembitz

In 1898 at 42

Busy at the typewriter — Pix

Dressed in a Chinese robe and using some feathers as a fan, he entertained Sir Robert Ho-Tung, a Hong Kong industrialist, at his home a few days before his 93d birthday. — The New York Times

Averaged 3 Talks a Week

For twelve years Mr. Shaw spoke at street corners, in parks, in halls in London and halls in the country, averaging three talks a week. He took no money for his efforts. Preaching his Fabian-adapted Marxism and considered a dangerous revolutionary, he frequently conducted his harangues under police surveillance. On two occasions he volunteered for prison martyrdom on the issue of free speech but his challenges were not taken up.

At about the same time, he embarked upon a notable career in London journalism. Through the influence of William Archer, critic and dramatist, Mr. Shaw became art critic of The World in 1885, when he was 29 years old. He also wrote on books for The Pall Mall Gazette and on music for The Star under the pseudonym of "Corno di Bassetto." Later, he became music critic for The World, where the initials "G. B. S." became famous, and drama critic for The Saturday Review.

Mr. Shaw as a critic was a sympathetic interpreter and an ardent champion of Ibsen at a time when that great dramatist was regarded as dangerously modernistic. He wrote "The Quintessence of Ibsenism" in 1891, which was regarded by many as the most profound of all his essays in criticism. In music he was an equally devoted follower of Wagner, and wrote "The Perfect Wagnerite," which appeared in 1898.

While still engaged in journalism, Mr. Shaw began his career as a dramatist, but for several years he was unable to get his plays produced in any of the regular theatres in London. They were produced in small "independent" theatres only, but their author, with his indomitable energy and resourcefulness, hit upon the plan, then an innovation in London, of having them published for general reading. With them were published lengthy and brilliant prefaces on social, political and economic subjects, sometimes entirely independent of the plays they accompanied.

Mr. Shaw's popularity as an active dramatist began in New York and Germany in the middle Nineties, several years before his plays came to be the vogue in the London commercial theatre.

He began his first play in collaboration with William Archer in 1885, but the collaboration lagged and Mr. Shaw completed the play alone seven years later. It was "Widower's Houses," an attack on slum landlordism and a direct outgrowth of his Fabian activities. In the next year, Shaw wrote "The Philanderer," a commentary on Ibsenism and the "new woman," for the same theatre.

License Refused for Play

Mr. Shaw wrote "Mrs. Warren's Profession," at the suggestion of Mrs. Sidney Webb, as a treatise on prostitution in its relation to the existing social order, in 1894. Under the British Censorship Law the Lord Chamberlain refused a license for the performance of the play, and it was not produced until 1902, when it was privately performed by the Stage Society. In 1905, when Arnold Daly's repertoire company played it in New York, the actors were arrested and prosecuted.

"Arms and the Man," Mr. Shaw's satire on romanticism and the "false glory" of war, was produced in 1894 by Richard Mansfield at the Herald Square Theatre in New York and at an independent experimental theatre in London. "Candida," a vindication of the woman in the home, was written in the same year.

Mr. Shaw suffered a breakdown from overwork in 1898, at the age of 42. This caused him to abandon journalism and most of his platform activities, and to devote himself entirely to the stage. In the same year he married Miss Charlotte Frances Payne-Townshend, of County Cork, a wealthy Irish woman who shared his interest in social reform and the theatre and was a sister of Lady Cholmondeley. She had nursed him back to health after his illness.

Mr. Shaw finally came into his own with the London playgoing public in 1905, when his "Man and Superman" was produced at the Royal Court Theatre under the management of T. E. Vedrenne and Harley Granville-Barker, with Granville-Barker in the role of John Tanner, author of the "Revolutionist's Handbook and Pocket Companion." This led to a long association between Shaw and Granville-Barker in prompting the "new theatre."

"Man and Superman" definitely established Mr. Shaw's fame with the general public and, together with a group of revivals, led to a collective reconsideration of his earlier work. What he was really driving at became clear to thousands who had not hitherto troubled to think of him otherwise than as a political fanatic or a buffoon. The doctrine of "creative evolution" which underlay this play was seen as the guiding social philosophy of all his work.

With his position in the theatre thoroughly established, Mr. Shaw also began turning out new plays which were produced by the same management. "John Bull's Other Island," a satire on the land problem in Ireland before autonomy, was a great success. Then came "How He Lied to Her Husband," "Major Barbara," and "Captain Brassbound's Conversion."

Wrote Farce for Cyril Maude

Mr. Shaw wrote "You Never Can Tell," a farce designed primarily to entertain, for Cyril Maude. This was hailed as a supreme example of dramatic criticism of manners. At this period Shaw also wrote "Caesar and Cleopatra" for Forbes-Robertson, "The Man of Destiny" and "The Devil's Disciple."

In 1906 came "The Doctor's Dilemma." In 1907 "The Showing Up of Blanco Posnet," was banned by the censor. "Getting Married" came in 1908, "Press Cuttings," also banned by the censor, in 1909; "The Dark Lady of the Sonnets" in 1910, "Fanny's First Play" in 1911; "Overruled" in 1912, "Androcles and the Lion," a brilliant intellectual farce and a great entertainment, in 1913, and "Pygmalion," in which Mrs. Patrick Campbell appeared, a pioneer play in the daring use of "barrack room" language on the stage, in 1914.

During the war Mr. Shaw's popularity was temporarily eclipsed because of his pacifist attitude. Within a few months of the outbreak of hostilities, he wrote an anti-war pamphlet, "Common Sense and the War," in which he outraged the sensibilities of thousands of Englishmen by his bitter attack upon "British Junkerism," although at the same time he invested $100,000 in British war loans and insisted that the war must continue until Germany was defeated, thereby offending the pacifists as much as the patriots.

Toward the end of the war he wrote "Heartbreak House," a philosophical and religious treatise. After the war, when England "went pacifist," his popularity leaped back to its old heights with one bound.

The war and the destruction of life and of civilized standards which accompanied and followed it made a profound impression upon Mr. Shaw. On one side, he returned to his old rôle as a pamphleteer. On the other side, he wrote fewer plays, and in them dealt with even more profound subjects than before, becoming more and more preoccupied with religious and philosophical themes.

"Hans Herzenleid," a mystifying interlude which no one could understand, had a poor reception when produced in New York and Vienna in 1920, but in the next year Mr. Shaw published one of his greatest plays, "Back to Methuselah." Although it had to wait two years for its first English production, it created a remarkable impression throughout the world.

This gigantic work, comprising five plays grouped under a single title and centered in a single theme, was recognized everywhere as an important contribution to modern thought, expressing the idea that mankind, through creative evolution, may reach a state of longevity which resembles eternal life.

Next came his great historical chronicle, "Saint Joan," which was produced by the Theatre Guild in New York late in 1923 and at the New Theatre in London the next spring. It was a great dramatic spectacle in which the author dug for truth beneath the traditional crust of history, and succeeded in creating on the stage a masterly living portrait of a woman.

"Heartbreak House," "Back to Methuselah" and "Saint Joan" were accepted by the critics as formulating a Shavian philosophy in which the dramatist attempted to voice his gropings after a religious purpose in life. According to St. John Ervine, the leading British authority on Shaw, this philosophy is based upon the idea that the Life Force (God) is an imperfect power striving to become perfect. All existence has been occupied in this struggle for perfection, in which various instruments that have been found useless or no longer helpful toward this end have been scrapped. But man is still on probation, and will be scrapped as the mammoth beasts were if he fails to achieve God's purpose.

Won Nobel Prize in 1925

In 1925 Mr. Shaw received the Nobel Prize for Literature. He turned it down, remarking that since he had written nothing in the previous year he took it to be "a token of gratitude for a sense of world relief." Under pressure he accepted the prize momentarily, just long enough to turn the £7,000 over to the Anglo-Swedish Literary Alliance. The money, he snapped, was "a lifebelt thrown to a swimmer who has already reached the shore in safety."

A long pause in his output followed, explained in 1928 by the publication of a socialistic tract, "The Intelligent Woman's Guide to Socialism and Capitalism," a voluminous restatement of his social doctrine and a plea for universal equality of income.

In 1929 began what was virtually a new phase of his career. "The Apple Cart," "Too True to Be Good" and "On the Rocks" were three plays which showed Mr. Shaw responding to the wide movement against the confusions of parliamentary government. King Magnus in "The Apple Cart" said farewell to the old forms of democracy and Fabian socialism. In a preface to "Too True to Be Good" Mr. Shaw proclaimed the world's need for new affirmations to replace what he termed the impossible negativism of old faiths decayed. "On the Rocks" revealed him as flirting with the ideas of dictatorship and universal conscription.

Read in conjunction with "The Adventures of the Black Girl in Her Search for God," a satirical novel published in 1933, the three plays of this final period disclosed Mr. Shaw as having broken with the constitutional Socialists and as having accepted for the first time the principle of revolutionary collectivism.

Mr. Shaw visited Russia in 1931 with a party of distinguished Britons, including Lord and Lady Astor and the Marquess of Lothian.

Until 1933 Mr. Shaw consistently refused all invitations to visit the United States. He habitually ridiculed and scoffed at Americans.

In that year he made a world tour with Mrs. Shaw on the steamship Empress of Britain. He made two American stops, at San Francisco and New York. While on the Pacific Coast, he visited the San Simeon (Calif.) ranch of William Randolph Hearst, who had syndicated some of his later writings.

Arriving in New York on April 11, 1933, he stayed only twenty-six hours, just long enough to make an incognito sight-seeing tour and to deliver his only American lecture before a crowded audience at the Metropolitan Opera House. In a speech of 16,000 words, he advised the United States to scrap its Constitution, nationalize its banks, destroy the power of financiers and cancel all war indebtedness.

The speech failed to make a good impression.

For many years he would have no more to do with the movies or the radio than with the United States, and once refused an offer of $1,000,000 for exclusive movie rights to his works, but he finally succumbed. Late in life he talked frequently over the radio, including international hook-ups, posed and talked for news reels, and in 1930 sold the movie rights to his plays.

No Aversion to Royalties

No reliable estimates exist on Mr. Shaw's fortune, though it was considerable. He was, some one once remarked, a Socialist who had no aversion to fat royalties. Typically, he complained about money. After the second World War, praising the value of friendship, he said that it was all he had left. "War taxation has left me little more than that, although you all think I'm a very rich man. Still, I have nothing to complain of."

Theatrical people who had to deal with Mr. Shaw knew him to be a shrewd bargainer.

During the early Thirties, a sensation was created by the publication in book form of some 300 letters which had passed between Mr. Shaw and Ellen Terry, the celebrated actress, for whom he had written the leading rôle in "Captain Brassbound's Conversion." The letters covered the period from 1892 to 1928, and those of 1896 and 1897, just before Shaw's marriage, were passionate love letters in form. There was another sensation, typically Shavian in its paradoxical nature, when it was disclosed that the love affair was an entirely platonic one, and that Shaw and Miss Terry never met until 1905, except publicly in the theatre. For years they purposely refrained from meeting lest it spoil their correspondence and end their "delicious flirtation."

Of this correspondence Mr. Shaw made a characteristic remark in which was hidden a great deal of his own intellectual approach to life. Several of his critics insisted he always wrote far more from the mind than he did from the heart or the emotions. He said: "Let those who may complain that it was all on paper remember that only on paper has humanity yet achieved glory, beauty, truth, knowledge, virtue and abiding love."

"Confession" of Love Life

About the same time as this correspondence was published, there appeared a biography of Mr. Shaw by Frank Harris, who as a literary editor in earlier days had greatly assisted Shaw's journalistic career. This volume contained several contributions from Mr. Shaw, including a letter in which he had written a "confession" of his love life.

The "confessional" letter was written after much prompting by Harris, who twitted Mr. Shaw on his well-known abstemious habits, declaring that they extended to the point of making him unduly shy in his relations with the opposite sex.

Mr. Shaw was a vegetarian and also abstained all his life from liquor and tobacco, which he often made the subject of attack in his plays and other writings. He was a vigorous opponent of vivisection and vaccination.

Mr. Shaw took good care of his health. In London, where he had an apartment in historic Adelphi Terrace, just off the Strand and overlooking the Thames, with Sir James Barrie as a neighbor, and later in Whitehall Court, also on the Thames embankment, with H. G. Wells and Sir Gilbert Parker as neighbors, he walked a great deal.

In later years he lived most of the time at Ayot, St. Lawrence, in a twelve-room, three-story house set on a few acres of ground.

In the winter he usually visited Antibes on the French Riviera. He believed in sunlight, and his tall, bearded figure could be seen lying almost nude on the beach or on a raft for hours at a time. Reading, talking, swimming and watching prize fights were among his recreations.

A feature of his home in England was his working shop, called The Shelter. Mounted on a swivel, the hut was rotated during the day to admit as much sunlight as possible.

"Consultant to Mankind"

Throughout the second World War Mr. Shaw maintained his lifelong role of "general consultant to mankind," still unable to stay out of any controversy. In 1941 he had protested the threatened bombing of Rome. He protested the closing of British theatres, and excoriated the British Government for dawdling, denouncing the party system of government, and, while steadfastly maintaining his love for democracy, found it, as practiced, a fraud on the people.

He was fatalistic about the prospect of peace under the benevolent guidance of an iron-fisted, powerful Big Four. Far from believing they could bring the world to peace, he even doubted if they could stick together. "We must still live dangerously, whether we like it or not," he said, refusing to celebrate V-E Day. He added: "The worst is yet to come."

His mordant wit, seemingly undulled, turned to any public question. He scoffed at projected war-guilt trials. He sent his japeries across the seas to America, which, he said, would soon lose Shaw and would then be in a devil of a fix.

Always disdainful of birthday celebrations, he tried to ignore his reaching the 90-mark in July, 1946. People tried to visit him at his home at Ayot, St. Lawrence. Mr. Shaw snorted: "They've come to see the animal just because he's 90."

He also said he intended to have nothing to do with a gala dinner organized in New York to honor him on the eve of his birthday. At the last minute, he broadcast a message in which he declared that "it's pleasant to be among friends." The message covered a range of subjects, from his own beginnings as a writer, to advice to parents on bringing up children.

"I assure you," he said, "that the only fun of my birthday is yours. It's the people who celebrate me who have the fun." He had had all the hard work, he added, "and I'm half dead by the experience."

Compendium Published at 90

The ninetieth birthday was also marked by the publication of a compendium entitled "G.B.S. 90" to which a group of authors contributed in a many-sided assessment of Mr. Shaw's life and work.

On his ninety-fourth birthday, Mr. Shaw showed signs of getting modest. He told his domestic staff that "no birthday is to be mentioned in this house," adding that he wanted "to see no birthday cards—they will all be thrown out on arrival."

He wrote a letter to W. D. Chase of Flint, Mich., organizer of the United States branch of the Shaw Society, in which he said:

"The utmost I can claim for myself in my best days is that I was one of the 100 best playwrights in the world, which is hardly a supreme distinction."

Not so many years before, he had toasted himself as the greatest playwright and political thinker of his time.

In September, 1950, a theatre full of newspaper critics in London, trying hard to be kind, gently but almost unanimously turned thumbs down on a presentation of Mr. Shaw's "Far-Fetched Fables." The six little stories, played like charades without a curtain were described by The Daily Telegraph's reviewer as "an absurd parody of Shaw's 'Back to Methuselah' without its wit."

His Place in History

Many have tried to anticipate the judgment of history upon the question whether Mr. Shaw is to take his place among the true geniuses of the world. Frank Harris, his close friend, thought he would not as an artist, but would as a personality. According to Mr. Harris, Mr. Shaw would survive like Dr. Johnson and Samuel Pepys, "two men in English literature whose personalities also were bigger than their works." To Prof. Archibald Henderson, the American who became Mr. Shaw's official biographer, and to St. John Ervine there was no question as to his genius. Others held many different views, including the extreme opposite one that Mr. Shaw was just a charlatan, a mountebank, a buffoon, who was not to be taken seriously at all.

Whether he was genius or charlatan, Mr. Shaw's age did not know. It hated him, but it laughed at him and with him; it tried to stop him, but he wouldn't be stopped. He confounded his critics, both those who admired him and those who derided him. The newspaper men continued to seek him out for interviews when on his cruises or in his quiet flat. He would not give up the world. He grew old and was the last of his generation. If nothing else, he had made it think and had given it a good time; and if the "messenger boy of the new age" never found what he thought he was looking for, he and his thousands of admirers in two hemispheres lost nothing by reason of his long, tumultuous search.

AS GEORGE BERNARD SHAW ADDRESSED HIS NEIGHBORS

He made one of his rare public appearances last year at the demolished abbey near his home at Ayot St. Lawrence when a gate was presented to the parish. — Associated Press

George Bernard Shaw Dies at 94; Broken Thigh Led to Final Illness

Continued From Page 1

house where he made his home, while his whole staff kept vigil.

The reedy sage of Ayot St. Lawrence, never noted for modesty, proclaimed himself "the dramatic emperor of Europe," and many conceded him the title. He was the author of more than fifty plays. Many, like "Pygmalion," "Candida" and "Major Barbara," are world famous. Indeed, Shaw considered himself the rightful successor and perhaps the superior of Shakespeare. He was working on a light comedy, "Why She Would Not," when he fell in his garden on Sept. 10.

Shaw ate only vegetables but spoke as if he fed only on raw meat. He gloried in his reputation as acknowledged world master of the studied insult. Even as death approached he continued to shoot vitriol-dipped barbs at the notions and foibles of his contemporaries.

Insisted He Was Communist

To the end he insisted he was a Communist. If he was, he was the most unorthodox Communist in the world. He professed admiration of the Russian Communist experiment, but he snorted at Karl Marx, the prophet of communism, as a ponderous and unreadable fuddy-duddy. He tossed off major heresies which would have meant Siberia in the country he professed to admire.

While describing himself as an "old skeleton" just before his ninety-fourth birthday, Shaw led an active life, rising before 8 daily and not retiring until midnight. When he wasn't writing, he was playing the piano, and sometimes even singing in a croaking but enthusiastic voice. His diet was mostly soup—vegetable—and great quantities of fruit and vegetable juices.

The tall, gray pundit was cantankerous with the physicians and nurses who attended him after his fall. He refused—and raged in anger—when doctors suggested sniping his famous beard so that he might more easily be given an anesthetic. It had to be taped down, instead. He curtly told his doctors it would be ill luck for them if he did not die on their hands, because, he said, doctors are noted mostly for the eminent men they lose.

Kidney Infection Blamed

AYOT ST. LAWRENCE, England, Thursday, Nov. 2 (UP)—Ironically, it was not the thigh fracture that caused Shaw's death. Astounding his doctors, Shaw's "brittle bones," as he called them, knit perfectly after the operation in September despite his great age.

But the shock of his fall stirred into fatal activity a latent kidney bladder infection that might otherwise have lain dormant for years.

On Sept. 11, Shaw was taken from this tiny village—where he wrote many of the plays, essays and ideas that stirred the whole world—to Luton Dustable Hospital. After an operation on his thigh, he underwent two operations for his kidney bladder. With the infection and its discomfort went much of the indomitable will to live that carried Shaw through the earlier crises in his career.

Although he was never told, he knew even in the hospital that he could exist only as an invalid, unable to walk. He complained to visitors, among them Lady Astor, that he would rather die than have to be carried about his beloved Hertfordshire countryside.

"All the News That's Fit to Print"

The New York Times.

LATE CITY EDITION
Fair, little temperature change today. Mostly fair tomorrow.
Temperature Range Today—Max., 42; Min., 29
Temperature Yesterday—Max., 44; Min., 33
Full U. S. Weather Bureau Report, Page 47

VOL. CII..No. 34,740. Entered as Second-Class Matter, Post Office, New York, N. Y. NEW YORK, FRIDAY, MARCH 6, 1953. Times Square, New York 36, N. Y. Telephone LAckawanna 4-1000 FIVE CENTS

STALIN DIES AFTER 29-YEAR RULE; HIS SUCCESSOR NOT ANNOUNCED; U.S. WATCHFUL, EISENHOWER SAYS

WORST CITY CRISIS SINCE 1933 IS SEEN IN STATE TAX PLAN

Moore and McGovern Demand Payroll Levy and Transit Unit Mandated to Raise Fares

MAYOR CALLS DEMOCRATS

Estimate Board to Get Report on Views of County Leaders —Bus Reduction Directed

By PAUL CROWELL

The city Government is facing the most serious financial and political crisis to confront any Administration since 1933, when leading banking houses rescued a Democratic regime from fiscal disaster.

This was the consensus last night of top city officials to whom Lieut. Gov. Frank C. Moore and State Controller J. Raymond McGovern had indicated earlier in the day that a sound fiscal program for 1953-54 and succeeding years should include both a city payroll tax and a transit authority with a duty to increase fares to meet operating deficits of the municipal lines.

That the city Administration realized the political dangers inherent in the adoption of the suggested fiscal program was indicated later in the day when Mayor Impellitteri, without consulting the Board of Estimate, asked the five Democratic county leaders to confer with him at noon today at City Hall. Among those invited was Tammany leader Carmine G. DeSapio, the only member of the group who is at loggerheads with the Mayor on matters of patronage.

Leaders' Views Important

After a two-hour conference with Mr. Moore and Mr. McGovern at Mr. McGovern's office, 270 Broadway, the Mayor and Board of Estimate held an even longer closed meeting at City Hall, which will be resumed at 3 o'clock this afternoon. At today's session an important factor will be the attitude of the five Democratic county leaders, as reported by the Mayor, toward the proposals upon which the two state officials apparently are insisting.

In another municipal development, the Mayor's Transit Advisory Commission demanded that the eight privately owned bus companies involved in the recent bus strike and Michael J. Quill's Transport Workers Union, C. I. O., take immediate steps to wipe out excess bus lines and to reduce the number of buses on lines that were needed. City tax relief was made dependent on such action.

The conference with Mr. Moore and Mr. McGovern was a continuation of last Monday's talks at Albany on the city's $218,700,000 fiscal program, which in effect already had been rejected by the two state officials in their joint memorandum of Feb. 22.

At the outset of the meeting the

Continued on Page 19, Column 1

F.B.I. Agents Depict Rebuff by Monaghan

By LUTHER A. HUSTON
Special to THE NEW YORK TIMES

WASHINGTON, March 5—Leland V. Boardman, special agent in charge of the New York office of the Federal Bureau of Investigation, asserted today that Police Commissioner George P. Monaghan had notified him that he would not make New York City policemen available to any Federal law enforcement agency for questioning and that they would respond only to summonses from a Federal grand jury.

This policy, Mr. Boardman said, was founded upon a purported agreement between the New York Police Department and the Criminal Division of the Department of Justice to block out F. B. I. investigators from cases involving police brutality in civil rights cases.

Another agent quoted Commis-

Continued on Page 16, Column 3

Eisenhower Plans to Pare Policy-Level Civil Service

Directive Will Repeal 2 That Truman Issued Anchoring Some Democrats in Their Jobs —Organization of Administration Object

By PAUL P. KENNEDY
Special to THE NEW YORK TIMES.

WASHINGTON, March 5—Several hundred persons face the possibility of losing Civil Service status and probably their Government jobs under an Executive Order to be issued by President Eisenhower next week.

In announcing the forthcoming order, James C. Hagerty, White House press secretary, said that all those affected would not necessarily lose their jobs. The announcement was generally interpreted, however, to mean that the Administration was preparing to clear out holdover Democrats in high policy-making and administrative positions in order to replace them with personnel of the Administration's own choosing.

President Eisenhower's order, which he directed to be drafted immediately, will repeal two Executive Orders of former President Truman in 1947 and 1948 in which certain persons on Schedule A of Civil Service rules would receive Civil Service protection against separation from the Government.

The President's order will emphasize that the rights of veterans, specified in the Veterans Preference Act of 1944 would be respected.

Schedule A is a list of positions to which appointments may be made without reference to Civil Service rules or regulations. The appointees may assume their positions without Civil Service examinations and their classifications are not subject to review by Civil Service Boards.

Mr. Hagerty said the "several hundred" persons to be affected by the order were employed in all departments and agencies of the Government. The order, he said, applied to people who had been put under Civil Service in the last twenty years.

The new Administration, since coming into office Jan. 20, Mr.

Continued on Page 15, Column 2

President May Take a Hand If Inquiries Imperil Amity

By C. P. TRUSSELL
Special to THE NEW YORK TIMES.

WASHINGTON, March 5—President Eisenhower indicated today that if the Senate investigation into the Voice of America, being conducted by Senator Joseph R. McCarthy, or other Congressional inquiries, reached a point of inviting international misunderstandings and difficulties he might intervene.

This, he emphasized at a news conference, would mean that he would have to desert his long-held conviction that the Congress had an inherent right to investigate as it pleased. He was still hoping, he said, to avoid a situation in which a spokesman for the Executive Branch of the Government would have to take issue with actions of the coordinate Legislative Branch.

The question that prompted these responses was based upon the hearings being conducted, largely before television, by the Judiciary subcommittee headed by Senator McCarthy, Republican of Wisconsin.

The group is inquiring into the management and personnel of the Voice, the Government's radio program for telling the story of America. Broadcasts are beamed to eighty-seven countries in nearly forty languages.

At yesterday's hearing Reed Harris, deputy director of the State

Continued on Page 14, Column 6

EISENHOWER PRAISES RESTRAINT IN PRICES

Asserts There Has Been Little Evidence of Gouging—More Controls Are Removed

By CHARLES E. EGAN
Special to THE NEW YORK TIMES.

WASHINGTON, March 5—President Eisenhower today complimented business for what he termed the admirable restraint it had shown in pricing policies since the removal of most price controls.

General Eisenhower said at his news conference that since the program of removing major segments of the economy from price regulation got under way Feb. 6, there had been little discernible evidence of attempts to gouge consumers.

The President's observations came immediately before an announcement from the Office of Price Stabilization that it had removed price ceilings on another wide range of items, including bread and bakery products, new and used cars, major household appliances, dry cleaning and diaper services.

Hopes for a New Climate

Another development was a Senate committee hearing at which Charles R. Sligh Jr., president of the National Association of Manufacturers, attacked proposals to establish stand-by controls authority. With such authority, the President could declare a ninety-day "freeze" of all prices and wages in event of all-out war or other critical emergency.

About the only major price increase that has occurred since the Office of Price Stabilization began implementing his orders for relaxation of price ceilings, the President said, has been an expected rise of 6 to 7 cents a pound in copper.

The absence of price gouging, the President added, confirms his belief that the American people are ready to be considerate and moderate. He added that he hoped a climate might be established—in labor-management relations, for instance—that would minimize harmful pressures on the economy

Continued on Page 15, Column 3

VISHINSKY LEAVING

Foreign Minister Called to Moscow to Report —Will Sail Today

U. N. TO LOWER FLAG

Lie Praises Premier as Statesman—Pearson Hails Fight on Nazis

By THOMAS J. HAMILTON
Special to THE NEW YORK TIMES.

UNITED NATIONS, N. Y., March 5—Soviet Foreign Minister Andrei Y. Vishinsky, who was reported to have been informed of the death of Premier Stalin before the public announcement by the Moscow radio, plans to leave for Moscow tomorrow.

Mr. Vishinsky and a party of Soviet officials are scheduled to sail aboard the French liner Liberté tomorrow at 4 P. M. Plans for the sailing were disclosed at Police Headquarters. The police said they had been informed that the party would travel in seven automobiles from Glen Cove, L. I., where the Soviet delegation to the United Nations has headquarters, to Pier 88, Hudson River at Forty-eighth Street. The liner will call at Plymouth and Le Havre.

Mr. Vishinsky has a heart condition and therefore avoids air travel whenever possible.

Valerian A. Zorin, Soviet representative to the United Nations, revealed this afternoon Mr. Vishinsky's plans to leave tomorrow. Mr. Vishinsky's decision was taken after he had received a telephone call from Moscow earlier in the day.

Disclosure by Consulate

There was no indication whether this telephone call had given any indication of Mr. Stalin's death. The news that Mr. Vishinsky had been informed prior to the public announcement came from a telephone inquiry at the Soviet Consulate at 680 Park Avenue.

Earlier inquiries at the headquarters of the Soviet delegation to the United Nations had brought repeated denials that Mr. Vishinsky was there. The consulate revealed, however, not only that Mr. Vishinsky was actually at the delegation headquarters but also that he had been informed of the news earlier.

According to United Nations protocol, the only flag that will fly at the United Nations flagpole tomorrow is the banner of the United Nations itself, and it will be at half-staff. The same procedure will be followed during the day of the funeral of Premier Stalin.

Informed of the death of Mr.

Continued on Page 13, Column 2

CONDOLENCES SENT

President Orders Terse Formal Note on Stalin Dispatched to Soviet

TRIBUTE IS OMITTED

Eisenhower Still Ready to Confer on Peace With the Kremlin

By JAMES RESTON
Special to THE NEW YORK TIMES.

WASHINGTON, March 5—President Eisenhower authorized John Foster Dulles, Secretary of State, tonight to send the United States' "official condolences" to the Soviet Government on the death of Premier Stalin.

Earlier the President had told reporters at his press conference that he could not tell what effect the illness of the Premier would have on the "cold war." A definite watchfulness is our policy for the moment, the President added.

The President announced the statement of condolences less than an hour after he had been informed of Mr. Stalin's death by James C. Hagerty, press secretary, at 3:25 P. M. The statement was as follows:

> The President authorized the Secretary of State to send the following message to the American Embassy in Moscow: The Government of the United States tenders its official condolences to the Government of the Union of Socialist Soviet Republics on the death of Generalissimo Joseph Stalin, Prime Minister of the Soviet Union.

Dulles Informed by Hagerty

Mr. Hagerty notified Mr. Dulles, who was a guest at the British Embassy, immediately after the President had been informed.

The press secretary said the President's message would be transmitted to the Soviet Government by Jacob D. Beam, Chargé d'Affaires in Moscow.

The terse wording of the message was noted here, especially the phrase "official condolences." Diplomatic circles suggested that the wording was about as brief and formal as possible under diplomatic protocol.

They recalled, however, that the President previously had expressed condolences. In the first White House statement issued after word had been received of the serious illness of Mr. Stalin, General Eisenhower directed his words to the Soviet people rather than the Premier or the Government.

Indications were that the President's official condolences would stand in so far as the Government

Continued on Page 12, Column 5

PREMIER JOSEPH STALIN
A portrait released by Sovfoto, Soviet picture agency

Soviet Fear of an Eruption Discerned in Call for Unity

By HARRY SCHWARTZ

The fact that appeals for "monolithic unity" and "vigilance" have now become the main theme of Soviet domestic propaganda appears to be a clear indication that the present Soviet rulers fear Premier Stalin's death may result in an explosive resolution of the major tensions now repressed in the Soviet Union.

The unity theme dominates the official announcement of Stalin's death. It was first voiced in the initial communiqué regarding Stalin's illness issued by the highest Government and Communist party authorities. Unity and vigilance were the central ideas in the long leading editorials that appeared yesterday morning on the front pages of both Pravda and Izvestia.

Yesterday's Pravda editorial may also have given the first hint that Georgi M. Malenkov is leading in the succession race, but this hint seemed far from conclusive. The editorial mentioned by name only Lenin, Premier Stalin, and Mr. Malenkov, quoting the latter's speech last October when he said, "The prospects and ways of our progress are based on the laws of the national economy, on the science of the Communist social structure which have been evolved by Comrade Stalin."

The fact that Moscow has announced that Nikita S. Khrushchev will head the committee preparing

Continued on Page 12, Column 2

AMMUNITION SHORT, VAN FLEET ASSERTS

He Affirms Scarcity in Korea and Byrd Writes to Wilson Demanding Explanation

By HAROLD B. HINTON
Special to THE NEW YORK TIMES.

WASHINGTON, March 5—Gen. James A. Van Fleet, former Commander of United Nations ground forces in Korea, told the Senate Armed Services Committee today that he had been handicapped during the entire twenty-two months he had had the command by shortages of ammunition and manpower. He specified hand grenades, and mentioned "other types" of ammunition as having been seriously short all the time and critically short on occasions.

The apparent contradiction of the General's testimony today with that of yesterday, in which he indicated there were no serious shortages of anything in Korea, was unexplained, except for the interpretation that yesterday he had been speaking for the present, whereas today he had been speaking for the past.

Praised by Symington

So much the general said before a public meeting of the committee. Senator Stuart Symington, Democrat of Missouri and former Secretary of the Air Force, praised General Van Fleet for his intelligence and courage in reporting these matters to the public. If other military figures would emulate the example, he declared, "we won't send our youth out to fight with these shortages, even if we have fewer television sets."

[In the Korean war action, Air Force Thunderjet fighter-bombers made a record 1,000-mile raid on a Communist industrial center on the northeast coast sixty miles from Siberia. Navy carrier bombers made heavy attacks in North Korea. Ground action was light.]

In a later closed session with the committee, General Van Fleet apparently amplified his discussion of the shortages. The amplification prompted Senator Harry F. Byrd, Democrat of Virginia, to write a letter to Charles E. Wil-

Continued on Page 2, Column 5

PREMIER ILL 4 DAYS

Announcement of Death Made by Top Soviet and Party Chiefs

STROKE PROVES FATAL

Leaders Issue an Appeal to People for Unity and Vigilance

Text of official announcement of Stalin's death, Page 8.

By HARRISON E. SALISBURY
Special to THE NEW YORK TIMES.

MOSCOW, Friday, March 6—Premier Joseph Stalin died at 9:50 P. M. yesterday [1:50 P. M. Thursday, Eastern standard time] in the Kremlin at the age of 73, it was announced officially this morning. He had been in power twenty-nine years.

The announcement was made in the name of the Central Committee of the Communist party, the Council of Ministers and the Presidium of the Supreme Soviet.

Calling on the Soviet people to rally firmly around the party and the Government, the announcement asked them to display unity and the highest political vigilance "in the struggle against internal and external foes." [No announcement was made of a successor to Premier Stalin.]

The Soviet leader's death from general circulatory and respiratory deficiency occurred just short of four days after he had been stricken with a brain hemorrhage in his Kremlin apartment.

Accompanying the death announcement was a final medical certificate issued by a group of ten physicians, headed by Health Minister A. F. Tretyakov, who cared for Mr. Stalin in his last illness under the direct and closest supervision of the Central Committee and the Council of Ministers.

Pulse Rate Was High

The medical certificate revealed that in the last hours Mr. Stalin's condition grew worse rapidly, with repeated heavy and sharp circulatory and heart collapses. His breathing grew superficial and sharply irregular. His pulse rate rose to 140 to 150 a minute and at 9:50 P. M., "because of a growing circulatory and respiratory insufficiency, J. V. Stalin died."

[The news of Mr. Stalin's death was withheld by Soviet officials for more than six hours.]

Pravda appeared this morning with broad black borders around its front page, which was devoted entirely to Mr. Stalin. The layout included a large photograph of the Premier, the announcement by the Government, the medical bulletins and the announcement of the formation of a funeral commission

Continued on Page 8, Column 2

Treaties Manifesto Shelved in Congress

By WILLIAM S. WHITE
Special to THE NEW YORK TIMES.

WASHINGTON, March 5—President Eisenhower's proposed United States declaration against "perversion" of the wartime Yalta and Potsdam agreements into instruments for enslaving peoples was put on the shelf in Congress today.

The announced Congressional reason was that the manifesto would be inopportune now in view of Premier Stalin's fatal illness, though the President himself indicated at his news conference that he thought this need not delay action. The Congressional developments came before the announcement of Mr. Stalin's death.

The Republican leaders in Congress could not take the resolution to the floor of either house

Continued on Page 6, Column 5

Pole Flies to Denmark in First Intact Russian MIG-15 to Reach West

Associated Press Radiophoto

A young Polish pilot seeking political asylum flew this Soviet-made MIG-15 into a Danish airport at Bornholm yesterday, making it the first fighter plane of its type acquired undamaged by the West. Name of pilot (center figure) was withheld.

Special to THE NEW YORK TIMES.

COPENHAGEN, Denmark, March 5—The first intact Russian-built MIG-15 jet fighter—the newest known type of Russian jet fighter—to land west of the Iron Curtain came down this morning at Roenne Airport on the Danish island of Bornholm. It came from a Polish Baltic base.

The 21-year-old Polish lieutenant who fled with the fighter gave himself up to Danish authorities as a political refugee and asked for asylum. Very little is known about his story. Danish authorities are keeping it secret for the time being.

The young Pole performed a fantastic maneuver in landing the jet fighter on the grass-covered airstrip at Roenne, only 1,200 meters (3,937 feet) long. Jet fighters normally require a 3,000-meter (9,843 feet) concrete runway to start and land.

At the farther end of the air-

Continued on Page 3, Column 2

STALIN SUCCUMBS; 29 YEARS IN POWER

Continued From Page 1

headed by Nikita S. Khruschchev, secretary of the Central Committee of the party.

Other members of the commission are Lazar M. Kaganovich, Premier Stalin's brother-in-law; Nikolai M. Shvernik, President of the Soviet Union; Alexander M. Vasilevsky, War Minister; N. U. Pegov, an alternate member of the Presidium; P. A. Artemyev, commander of the Moscow military district, and M. A. Yasnov, chairman of the city of Moscow.

Pravda's announcement said Mr. Stalin's body would lie in state in the Hall of Columns.

His death brought to an end the career of one of the great figures of modern times—a man whose name stands second to none as the organizer and builder of the great state structure the world knows as the Soviet Union.

[The United Press said members of Mr. Stalin's family and his closest associates in the Presidium and Central Committee were at his bedside.]

The Soviet leader began his life in the simple mountain village of Gori deep in poverty-stricken Georgia. He rose to head the greatest Russian state that has ever existed. For nearly thirty years, Mr. Stalin was at the helm of the country. No other statesman of modern times has led his nation for a longer period.

This morning's official announcement declared that the Government and party would strengthen "the defense, capacity and might of the Soviet state" in every manner, and in "every way" strengthen the Soviet Army, Navy and organs of intelligence "with a view to constantly raising our preparedness for a decisive rebuff to any aggressor."

The declaration comprised an important statement of policy, both external and internal. With regard to foreign relations, it declared that the party and Government stood by an inflexible policy of securing and strengthening peace, of struggle against the preparation and unleashing of a new war, and for a policy of "international collaboration and development of businesslike connections with all countries."

Friendship for China Cited

The second foreign policy point was the declaration of firm support for "proletarian internationalism," for the development of brotherly friendship with [Communist] China, with the workers of all countries of the "people's democracy" and with the workers of capitalist and colonial countries fighting "for peace, democracy and socialism."

The announcement of Mr. Stalin's death was made to the Soviet people by radio early this morning. The announcement was early enough so that persons going to work had heard the news before leaving their homes.

This correspondent circled the Kremlin several times during the evening and early morning. The great red flag flew as usual over the Supreme Soviet Presidium building behind Lenin's Tomb.

Lights blazed late as they always do in many Kremlin office buildings. Sentry guards paced their posts at the Great Kremlin Gate.

The city was quiet and sleeping, and in Red Square all was serene. The guards stood their duty at Lenin's Tomb, but otherwise the great central square was deserted, as it always is in the hours just before daylight.

The last medical bulletin before the announcement of Mr. Stalin's death was issued shortly before 9 o'clock last night, reporting his condition as of 4 P. M. yesterday. It said his condition had grown worse despite every method of therapy employed by Soviet physicians.

The bulletin revealed that, at 8 o'clock yesterday morning, there occurred a sharp heart circulatory collapse, which was corrected by "extraordinary curative measures."

A second "heavy collapse" occurred at 11:30 A. M., which "was eliminated with difficulty."

Pravda, organ of the Central Committee of the Communist party, and Izvestia, organ of the Soviet Government, called on the Soviet people yesterday to rally around the party and the Government in "these difficult days" and to display what Izvestia characterized as "heightened revolutionary vigilance." Pravda also demanded from all Soviet citizens "stanchness of spirit and vigilance."

Pravda's editorial appeal to the populace was read repeatedly over the radio. It was also read and discussed in factories shops and offices throughout the country. Pravda had clearly sounded the theme of the day—vigilance and unity.

Last night's medical bulletin on the Premier's condition declared that an electrocardiogram taken at 11 A. M., showed "sharp disturbances in blood circulation in the coronary arteries of the heart with lesions in the back wall of the heart." An electrocardiogram taken on Monday had not established these changes, the bulletin said.

After measures taken to liquidate the 11:30 A. M. collapse, the condition was eased to some extent, although the "patient's general condition continued extremely grave," the bulletin asserted.

At 4 P. M., Mr. Stalin's blood pressure stood at 160 over 120, the bulletin said, with his pulse rate 120 a minute and his respiration 36 times a minute. His temperature stood at 37.6 centigrade (99.68 degrees Fahrenheit), slightly lower than in a 2 A. M. bulletin.

The bulletin noted that the white blood corpuscle count stood at 21,000. At 2 A. M. the white blood corpuscle count was 17,000.

The bulletin said the principal objective of the struggle now being waged with Mr. Stalin's illness was an effort to curb the interruptions in respiration and in blood circulation, particularly coronary circulation.

Every device and treatment known to modern medicine was employed by a team of ten top Soviet specialists, headed by the country's new Health Minister, A. F. Tretyakov, and directed closely by the highest bodies of the party and Government—the Central Committee and the Council of Ministers.

The medical bulletin issued at 7 o'clock yesterday morning, giving his condition as of 2 A. M., was the second issued since Mr. Stalin's stroke Sunday night. It carried a most detailed account of the progress of the illness and the measures taken to combat it. The communiqué showed that, despite every treatment thus far employed, Mr. Stalin's breathing and heart functions continued to be sharply impaired. He lay unconscious.

Penicillin had been administered to Mr. Stalin. Other treatments mentioned in the communiqué were directly concerned with the fight to maintain and regularize his breathing and heart functions. These included the use of oxygen to supplement his oxygen deficiency, and camphor and caffeine to stimulate the heart. Strophantine and glucose also were introduced, and medical leeches applied as a means of bringing down his blood pressure.

In its call to the people to rally in unity and in vigilance around the party and Government, Pravda declared that the qualities now needed were "unity and cohesion, stanchness of spirit and vigilance," and called on all citizens to stand firm behind Mr. Stalin's goal—"building communism in our country."

Pravda called its editorial "Great Unity of the Party and People." Izvestia called its editorial "Unity and Solidarity of the Soviet People."

Izvestia said that in these times "there is no doubt" that all citizens will "multiply their strength in the struggle for a successful fulfillment of the tasks of Communist construction and will ceaselessly raise their revolutionary vigilance and even more closely rally their ranks around the Central Committee of the party and the Soviet Government."

Throngs of Muscovites made their way to Red Square this morning and stood in silent tribute to their lost leader.

The Hall of Columns where Mr. Stalin's body will lie in state is one of the most beautiful buildings in Moscow and one of the architectural jewels of Europe.

The building is ordinarily used as the house of Soviet trade unions, but is often employed for important state functions. It was here that Lenin's body lay in state in January, 1924, and it is here that many great thinkers of the Soviet world have lain in the last hours before their burial.

The central hall of the building is dominated by twenty-four beautiful marble columns reaching three stories to the ceiling. The room is hung with great chrystal chandeliers.

The Hall of Columns was erected in the mid-nineteenth century as a club for Moscow noblemen.

The outside of the hall, which is located in the heart of the city only a few hundred yards from Red Square, was decorated just after dawn today with heavy black-bordered red Soviet flags, which are used here as a symbol of mourning.

A great forty-foot portrait of Mr. Stalin in his gray generalissimo's uniform was erected on the front of the building. It was framed in heavy gilt.

In this famous hall Mr. Stalin's body will lie in state so that millions of Soviet citizens can throng past the bier and pay their last respects.

STALIN'S STRATEGY BROKE NAZI ARMY

He Was Considered a Master Military Planner Who Did His Work Behind Scenes

Joseph Stalin was considered a master military strategist who worked quietly behind the scenes, sifting campaign details with special emphasis on logistics but never losing his perspective on the over-all political aspects of the situation.

He was not the type of commander who led his men into battle, but those who did the leading had a Stalin blueprint that had been carefully worked out beforehand. While the final and crucial decisions were invariably Stalin's his generals received considerable leeway in the exercise of judgment in the field and in most cases were consulted when the blueprints were on the drafting board.

There is little doubt among historians that Stalin's planning helped break the German Army siege around Moscow in the winter of 1941 or that he masterminded the 1943 Stalingrad fight.

Although the Moscow episode had all the dramatic qualities of a Tolstoy masterpiece, the Stalingrad debacle was the more spectacular and had greater military repercussions. It resulted in the decimation of a German army of more than 300,000 men and came at the strategic moment when the alliance of England, Russia and the United States needed victory as a morale booster. It was the turning point of the war and never again did the armies of Hitler attain real land supremacy.

Order for the Counter-Offensive

The Reich forces were fighting a house-to-house battle in the streets of Stalingrad when Stalin ordered the historic counter-offensive on Nov. 19, 1943. He ordered three armies from the north, northwest and south to strike concentric blows at the besiegers' rear while at the same time bringing in his air force to keep the corridors open. By the end of December the main German force had been thrown back 120 miles and three Nazi generals had surrendered with their troops.

He had hoped early in July, 1942, that his Allies would open a second front to relieve the pressure on both Stalingrad and Moscow but was informed by Winston Churchill that current plans called for an invasion of Sicily instead. It was then that he gave his famous order to the Stalingrad garrison, "Not a step back." He was reported to have visited the Rostov front at that time.

One of Stalin's so-called master strokes of strategy took place on Dec. 6, 1941, when he was holed up in the Kremlin with some of his general staff. His Government had already fled to Kuibyshev on the Volga, and Hitler's forces were at the gates of Moscow.

Whether it was intuition, fifth column information or outright military genius, the generalissimo anticipated Hitler's suspension of winter activities by two days. Just before the Germans started to settle in for the winter within sight of Moscow, Stalin ordered the counter-offensive that drove them into costly retreat over barren land that had been stripped by a Stalin-ordered scorched-earth policy. Hitler faded away as Napoleon had.

Plans Made Far Ahead

Throughout the Moscow siege Stalin was busy laying plans for the future. Visiting statesmen who found him working on military strategy heard his demands from Britain and the United States for tanks and planes that he felt would bring victory if properly coordinated. The aid eventually came and with it victory.

The advent of lend-lease brought Stalin closer to the Western powers. After conferences with President Roosevelt, Mr. Churchill or their emissaries, the joint military effort broadened to the point where the defeat of Germany was the prime objective. Stalin launched a land offensive in conjunction with the West and when the forces joined, Germany was crushed in the vise.

Three months later the Red Army was in the war against Japan, fulwilling a promise he had made at one of the conferences.

Moscow Chief's Wide Knowledge Impressed Visitors From Abroad

Outside World Found the Stalin Personality of Continued Interest—Bedell Smith Said It Was 'Not Unattractive'

The little that the outside world ever learned about Joseph Stalin as a personality, as distinct from Joseph Stalin the dictator, came mainly from accounts by foreigners of their meetings with him.

During his lifetime Stalin rarely left Russa, but he met hundreds of foreigners of many types: writers such as H. G. Wells and Emil Ludwig, statesmen such as Franklin D. Roosevelt and Winston Churchill, Moscow correspondents for foreign newspapers and many others.

There can be little doubt that Stalin was very interested in making the proper impression on the foreigners he met. During high level negotiations with President Roosevelt, Prime Minister Churchill and others he was often charming, so much so that he earned the sobriquet of "Uncle Joe" for a time in Western diplomatic circles.

Stalin's interest in what foreigners thought, said, or wrote about him was illustrated by the experience of one American correspondent. That correspondent had been one of the few who in the early Nineteen Hundred and Twenties had thought Stalin had a chance to succeed Lenin and had labeled him "the dark horse" of the succession race. Almost a decade later, after the correspondent had concluded a long interview with him, Stalin called him back and with a smile said: "Well, the dark horse won after all, didn't he?"

The accounts of Stalin by foreigners who met him usually stressed his industry, his wide range of knowledge on many topics, and his awareness of his absolute power.

Gen. Walter Bedell Smith, former United States Ambassador to the Soviet Union, described the Soviet ruler in these terms:

"Met face to face, Stalin is not by any means the unattractive personality which some writers have depicted. Indeed, he has genuine charm when he chooses to exercise it. While not tall, he is square and erect, giving the impression of great strength. * * * I scarcely noticed the pockmarks which some American writers have emphasized. The most attractive feature of Stalin's face is his fine dark eyes, which light up when he is interested."

Harry Hopkins recorded his impression of Stalin thus:

"An austere, rugged, determined figure in boots that shone like mirrors, stout baggy trousers, and snug-fitting blouse. * * * He's built close to the ground, like a football coach's dream of a tackle. He's about five feet six, about a hundred and ninety pounds. His hands are huge, as hard as his mind. His voice is harsh but ever under control. What he says is all the accent and inflection his words need. * * * If he is always as I heard him, he never wastes a syllable."

In his memoirs, Mr. Churchill recounts that Stalin often used the term "God" in his speech. When Mr. Churchill, for example, described plans for the invasion of the Mediterranean coast of Europe from Africa, Stalin's reply was, "May God prosper this mission."

At a conference in Moscow in 1941 Lord Beaverbrook got a chance to look at Stalin's doodling during a meeting. He found that Stalin busied himself during translations by drawing many pictures of wolves on the paper in front of him, filling in the background in red.

Mr. Churchill visited Stalin's private apartment in the Kremlin and found him to be an affectionate father, proud of his pretty, red-haired daughter, who joined the two there. Mr. Churchill describes Stalin's apartment as simple, consisting of four moderate-sized rooms, a bedroom, a dining room, a working room, and a large bathroom.

At a dinner with Stalin, Mr. Churchill jokingly remarked that Vyacheslav M. Molotov's delayed return from his wartime visit to Washington had been caused by his going off on his own, probably to New York. Stalin's face became very merry at this and he replied: "It was not to New York he went. He went to Chicago, where the other gangsters live."

PRAYER URGED FOR STALIN

Vatican Holds the Premier's Soul Was 'Redeemed by Christ'

ROME, March 5 (UP)—The Vatican radio has urged Roman Catholics to pray for the soul of Soviet Premier Stalin.

The appeal was made in the course of a broadcast last night by the Rev. Antonio Ferri.

Father Ferri said Premier Stalin had personified the present-day phenomenon of world communism—"a phenomenon of no small responsibility and one whose attitude toward religion is known to all."

The Vatican broadcast added: "For Catholics, this is the moment to regard the chief of the Soviet state as a soul, like all others, redeemed by Christ, and therefore in the sense of universal and supranatural Christian charity, object of the prayers that Catholics raise to infinitely merciful God."

Vishinsky Asserts Name Of Stalin Is Immortal

GLEN COVE, L. I., March 5 (AP)—Soviet Foreign Minister Andrei Y. Vishinsky said tonight that the death of Premier Stalin was a blow to all humanity.

Reached by telephone at his country retreat on Long Island, the Kremlin's diplomatic chief at the United Nations said:

"With great sorrow I confirm the death of Premier Stalin. It is a great blow to all of the Soviet people and to all humanity. The name of Stalin is immortal."

Stalin Rose From Czarist Oppression to Transform Russia Into Mighty Socialist State

DICTATOR RUTHLESS IN MOVING TO GOALS

He Furthered Socialization and Industrialization of World's First Marxist Nation

LED WORLD WAR II EFFORT

Hard, Mysterious, Aloof, Rude, He Outlasted the Dreamers and Solidified Power

Joseph Stalin became the most important figure in the political direction of one-third of the people of the world. He was one of a group of hard revolutionaries that established the first important Marxist state and, as its dictator, he carried forward its socialization and industrialization with vigor and ruthlessness.

During the second World War, Stalin personally led his country's vast armed forces to victory. When Germany was defeated, he pushed his country's frontiers to their greatest extent and fostered the creation of a buffer belt of Marxist-oriented satellite states from Korea across Eurasia to the Baltic Sea. Probably no other man ever exercised so much influence over so wide a region.

In the late Nineteen Forties, when an alarmed world, predominantly non-Communist, saw no end to the rapid advance of the Soviet Union and her satellites, there was a hasty and frightened grouping of forces to form a battle line against the Marxist advance. Stalin stood on the Elbe in Europe and on the Yalu in Asia. Opposed to him stood the United States, keystone in the arch of non-Marxist states.

Stalin took and kept the power in his country through a mixture of character, guile and good luck. He outlasted his country's intellectuals, if indeed, he did not contrive to have them shot, and he wore down the theoreticians and dreamers. He could exercise great charm when he wanted to. President Harry Truman once said in an unguarded moment:

"I like old Joe. Joe is a decent fellow, but he is a prisoner of the Politburo."

But the Stalin that the world knew best was hard, mysterious, aloof and rude. He had a large element of the Oriental in him; he was once called "Ghengis Khan with a telephone" and he spent much of his life nurturing the conspiracies that brought him to power and kept him there.

Opinion of Leon Trotsky

Leon Trotsky, Stalin's brilliant and defeated adversary, regarded him as an intellectual nonentity who personified "the spirit of mediocrity" that impregnated the Soviet bureaucracy. Lenin, who valued Stalin highly as a party stalwart, characterized him as "crude" and "rough" and as a "cook who will prepare only peppery dishes."

But those who survived the purges hailed Stalin as a supreme genius.

Although he remained an enigma to the outside world to the very end of his days, Stalin's role as Russia's leader in the war brought him the admiration and high praise of Allied leaders, including President Roosevelt and Winston Churchill. And, indeed, only a man of iron will and determination like Stalin's could have held together his shattered country during that period of the war when German armies had overrun huge portions of Russian territory and swept to the gates of Moscow, Leningrad and the Caucasus. Like Churchill in England, Stalin never faltered, not even at moments when everything seemed lost.

When most of the Government machinery and the diplomatic corps were moved to Kuibyshev in December, 1941, in expectation of the imminent capture of Moscow, Stalin remained in the Kremlin to direct the operations that finally hurled the Nazi hordes from the frontyard of the capital. His battle orders and exhortations to the Russian armies and people to persevere in the fight contributed immensely to final victory. Repeatedly, Churchill referred to him in Parliament as Russia's "great warrior."

War Role Paramount

With the turn of the tide against the Germans, Stalin proclaimed himself marshal of the Soviet Union and later generalissimo. Surrounded by a galaxy of brilliant generals, whose names will go down in history as among the greatest of Russia's military leaders, Stalin was portrayed in the Soviet and foreign press as the supreme commander responsible for over-all strategy. To what extent this was true will have to be determined by the future historian, but that his role in the conduct of the war was paramount is undeniable.

The energy and will power he displayed both before and during the war confirmed the justification for his name, for Stalin in Russian means "man of steel," a nom de guerre he adopted early in his revolutionary career. Long before he dreamed of becoming the supreme autocrat of Russia he had displayed the steel in his character as a political prisoner under the Czarist regime. A fellow prisoner of that period gave an illustration of Stalin's grit. This was in 1909, in the prison at Baku. In punishment of rioting by the prisoners, the authorities ordered that they be marched in single file between two lines of soldiers who proceeded to shower blows upon them with rifle butts. With head high, a book under his arm, Stalin walked the gantlet without a whimper, his face and head bleeding, his eyes flashing defiance. It was the kind of grit he demanded from others, the kind that helped save Russia from Nazi conquest and domination. His experience under the Czarist regime and his Asiatic character taught him how to treat political opponents.

In his relations with the Allied powers during the war and in his diplomacy before and after the war Stalin won the reputation of a grim realist.

Joseph Vissarionovich Djugashvili, later to become famous under his revolutionary name of Joseph Stalin, was born in the Georgian village of Gori Dec. 21, 1879.

His father was an impoverished and drunken shoemaker who made him sullen and resentful by regular beatings. His mother, Ekaterina, a peasant's daughter, was a woman of singular sweetness, patience and strength of character who exercised great influence on her son. She called him Soso (Little Joe) and lived to see him dictator of the world's largest empire.

Attended a Seminary

When he was 6 or 7, young Stalin contracted smallpox, which left him pock-marked for life. Through the efforts of his mother, who worked as a part-time laundress, Stalin entered a church school at 9. He was remembered there as a bright, self-assertive boy who loved argument and who flew into a fury with those who did not agree with him. He remained in this school from 1888 to 1893.

By heroic exertions, Stalin's mother obtained for him a scholarship in the Theological Seminary at Tiflis, where he studied from October, 1894, to May, 1899. The seminary was a gloomy institution—a cross between a barracks and a monastery—where the students attended endless lectures on theology and spent their few spare moments plotting to obtain forbidden books from the outside.

Stalin was among the worst offenders. An entry against him in the seminary's book of discipline has been preserved:

"At 11 A. M. I took away from Joseph Djugashvili Letourneau's 'Literary Evolution of the Nations.' * * * Djugashvili was discovered reading the said book on the chapel stairs. This is the thirteenth time this student has been discovered reading books borrowed from the Cheap Library. * * *"

The official reason for Stalin's expulsion was that for "unknown reasons" he failed to attend examinations. He declared he was expelled for "propagating Marxism."

Stalin as a student at Tiflis Theological Seminary in 1894.

Stalin in 1927.

To support himself he obtained a temporary job as night attendant in the Tiflis Observatory, but he was more concerned with his observations at meetings of Tiflis railway workers during the day than of the stars at night. His revolutionary apprenticeship was served as an organizer of the Tiflis transportation workers. He helped stage street demonstrations and distribute revolutionary leaflets.

In April, 1899, he received his first baptism of fire at a demonstration he helped organize in the heart of the city. The demonstration was drowned in blood by Cossacks, and he went into hiding for a year to escape the police. At this time he assumed the nickname of "Koba," after a hero in Georgian mythology.

On Nov. 11, 1901, he was elected a member of the Tiflis Committee of the Russian Social Democratic Labor party, in his native Georgia. A few weeks later he was deputized to go to Batum, a thriving industrial and commercial center, to direct revolutionary activity. In March of that year he led a strike of oil workers in that city.

In April, 1902, he was arrested and lodged in the Batum prison, from which he was transferred to Kutais. While in prison he learned of the meeting in London, in 1903, of the second congress of the Russian Social Democratic party, at which the party split into Bolsheviks and Mensheviks—extremists and moderates — an event that subsequently determined the entire course of the Russian Revolution. Stalin allied himself with Nikolai Lenin, leader of the Bolsheviks. Trotsky was against Lenin, although in 1917, after the revolution, he joined Lenin and became his principal lieutenant in the October Revolution and in the establishment of the Soviet regime.

On July 9, 1903, while in prison in Kutais, Stalin was sentenced to three years of exile to Siberia, and in November of that year he was transferred to the bleak, remote village of Novaya Uda. There he received his first letter from Lenin in response to one posing certain questions concerning Bolshevist policy and tactics. The letter confirmed him in his adherence to Lenin, whom he glorified as "Mountain Eagle." Determined to escape, Stalin made his way safely to Irkutsk at the end of the year. From there he proceeded to Baku, in the Caucasus, where he experienced his second baptism of fire as leader of a strike of oil workers. It was part of a wave of strikes that swept Russia with her defeat by Japan, a wave that was the harbinger of the Revolution of 1905.

Shortly after the outbreak of the general strike, which was the key element in the revolution of 1905, Stalin met Lenin for the first time at a party conference in Tammerfors, Finland.

From the Tammerfors conference Stalin returned to his activity in the Caucasus, where on June 26, 1907, on Erivan Square in Tiflis, he directed the celebrated "expropriation" which netted the Bolshevik party 340,000 rubles. There had been other such "expropriations," but this was the biggest and most dramatic. Formally, Lenin and his associates had frowned upon these acts, but they, nevertheless, accepted the proceeds to help finance the party's work. In the Erivan Square affair a band of revolutionists directed by "Koba" fell upon

(continued)

Molotov signs the Nazi-Soviet Pact (1939) as Ribbentrop (L) and Stalin look on.

a convoy of two carriages carrying Government funds fron. the railway station to the state bank, and after bombing the Cossack guard escaped with the money, which was sent to Lenin.

Following the "expropriation," Stalin was arrested and lodged in Bailov fortress, in Baku, where the incident of his running the gantlet of rifle butts took place. Soon thereafter he was exiled for the second time to Solvychegodsk, in Siberia, from which he escaped on June 24, 1909. He returned to Baku to resume his revolutionary activity, but remained at liberty only eight months, when he was again arrested and sent back to Solvychegodsk. From that place he conducted a secret correspondence with Lenin and his staff at Bolshevik headquarters in Cracow.

Eager to attend a party conference in Prague, Stalin again escaped and made his way to St. Petersburg, where he was arrested and exiled to Vologda. Once more he escaped and reached St. Petersburg on the day of the notorious massacre of workers in the Lena goldfields in Siberia. In St. Petersburg he helped found Pravda, the official organ of the Bolshevik party, but on the day of its first issue he was arrested and exiled to Narym, in the Urals. On Sept. 1 1912, he escaped and returned to St. Petersburg to resume the editorship of Pravda. This time he was betrayed by the agent provocateur Malinovsky, who had him arrested together with Jacob Sverdlov, the future first President of the Soviet Union, at a concert given for the benefit of Pravda. Stalin and Sverdlov were exiled to Turuchansk, in Siberia, from which they were taken to the outlying settlement of Kureika, 800 miles north of the Trans-Siberian Railway. After twenty years of revolutionary activity and repeated imprisonments and exilings, Stalin found himself at a dead end. Letters arrived from Lenin, but they seemed very remote and futile. Then came the news of the first World War in 1914, the war that Lenin predicted would bring the downfall of the Russian autocracy and world revolution.

Stalin was transferred to Atchinsk, on the Trans-Siberian Railway, and it was there he first received word of the revolution of March 12, 1917. Almost the very first act of the Provisional Revolutionary Government, in which Alexander Kerensky was at first Minister of Justice and later Premier, was to order the release of all political prisoners. Among the many thousands who profited by this decree signed by Kerensky was Joseph Stalin. He made his way speedily to Petrograd.

On his arrival in Petrograd in March, 1917, Stalin went directly to the office of Pravda, where he was met by V. M. Molotov and Leo Kamenev. Lenin and most of his staff were in Zurich, Switzerland. It was not until April 16, 1917, that Lenin arrived in Petrograd after his famous journey through Germany in a sealed car provided by the German General Staff. The journey led across Germany to Stockholm and through Finland. A month later Trotsky arrived from America.

Upon his arrival in Petrograd in May, 1917, from the United States, where he had lived for several months, Trotsky lost no time in associating himself with Lenin in his demand for the overthrow of the Provisional Government, conclusion of an immediate peace, a sweeping Socialist program and advocacy of world revolution. From the very beginning of this development Trotsky completely overshadowed Stalin and all others among Lenin's lieutenants. He became Lenin's "big stick."

In the first Council of Commissars, formed upon the formation of the Soviet Government, Stalin was given the modest, obscure post of Commissar of Nationalities. Nevertheless, that post in the hands of Stalin became symbolic and significant, for it was under Stalin as supreme dictator that the Soviet Union, conceived as a multiple state of nationalities, achieved its greatest expansion, territorially and politically.

In the October Revolution Stalin took a relatively modest part. Although his admirers picture him as taking the initiative with Lenin in planning and executing that historic upheaval against the opposition of Trotsky and others in Lenin's immediate entourage, the minutes of the Central Committee of the party for Oct. 23, two days before the coup d'état, show clearly that Lenin and Trotsky took the lead in demanding approval of the uprising, while others were either opposed or hesitant. Stalin supported Lenin. On that occasion, the minutes attest, Lenin, angry and defiant over the refusal of his collaborators to approve the plans for the uprising, rose and, pointing to Trotsky, shouted, "Very well, then, he and I will go to the Kronstadt sailors," meaning that he would summon the sailors of the Baltic Fleet to rise in rebellion against the Kerensky regime. The Baltic Fleet played a leading role in the uprising. Later these same sailors, who had been glorified by Trotsky as "the pride and beauty of the Russian Revolution," were shot down en masse by Trotsky in their revolt against the Soviet regime in March, 1921.

During the civil war after the Bolshevik revolution Stalin and Trotsky were at loggerheads. This was particularly true during the fighting on the Tsaritsin and Perm fronts. Repeatedly Trotsky called him to order and on various occasions Lenin had to intervene to make peace between them. The enmity and hatred between Trotsky and Stalin dated from that period.

Already during Lenin's illness, which lasted about two years, Stalin began preparing for his future leadership of the party and of the Government. This he ultimately achieved by utilizing his new position as general secretary

Stalin, Roosevelt and Churchill at the Teheran Conference, 1943.

of the party in building a party machine loyal to him.

Member of Triumvirate

After Lenin's death, authority was vested by the party in the hands of a triumvirate, consisting of Stalin, Zinoviev and Kamenev. There were three principal factions in the party, the left, represented by Zinoviev; the right, headed by Rykov and Bukharin, and the center, of which Stalin was regarded as the spokesman. Trotsky, who was ill a good part of the time, so much so that he had been unable to attend Lenin's funeral, had plans of his own. He felt that ultimately, as Lenin's chief collaborator, he would inherit Lenin's mantle.

In the bitter factional polemics that ensued, Stalin played the left against the right and vice versa, and eventually defeated both, as well as Trotsky.

In 1936, during the period of purges, Stalin proclaimed a new Constitution for Russia, with promises of universal secret suffrage, freedom of the press, speech and assembly. It was interpreted to maintain the dictatorship and to stabilize the revolution.

Not since the days of Peter the Great, who sought to westernize Russia by force, had the country witnessed so violent a transformation. In fact, nothing in the history of revolutions could compare with the gigantic social and economic upheaval brought about under Stalin. Profound as was the

In 1929 Stalin began predicting a second world war and avowed that his purpose was to keep Russia clear of the conflict. Despite this policy, with the advent of Hitler to power he joined in collective security measures. He abruptly abandoned his advocacy of collective security in 1939, when he about-faced and signed a mutual nonaggression pact with Nazi Germany.

It led to World War II, into which Russia later was drawn by Hitler's attack on her. This onslaught forged a Soviet alliance with the West, an alliance that ultimately enlarged the Soviet sphere.

70th Birthday Celebrated

Stalin's fiftieth and sixtieth birthdays were celebrated, but the press prepared the Soviet public on his sixty-ninth anniversary for the grim reality that years had left their impress even on "the teacher and inspirer of the world proletariat." Pictures were published showing that Stalin's hair had whitened. Then on his seventieth birthday in 1949 his anniversary was celebrated in grand fashion.

It was the first occasion in which Stalin had permitted public participation in his private life, and hence little was known about his personal affairs. He married twice. His first wife was Ekaterina Svanidze, who died after a long illness in 1907. They had a son, Jacob whose fate has been unknown since he became a German prisoner during World War II. In 1919 the Premier married Nadya Alliluyeva, the 17-year-old daughter of his old revolutionary crony, Sergei Alliluyev. She died in 1932 under mysterious circumstances. They had a daughter and a son. The latter, Vassily, is now a lieutenant-general in the Soviet Air Force. All that became known of the daughter was her name, Svetlana, and her intellectual interests.

PURGES SOLIDIFIED DICTATOR'S POWER

Stalin Pressed On After Exile of Trotsky With Ouster of His Rival's Old Guard

MURDER OF KIROV A SPUR

After his defeat of Leon Trotsky for control of Soviet power, Joseph Stalin solidified that control through the historic and dramatic purges of the nineteen thirties.

By 1928 Trotsky stood alone and was exiled to Alma Ata, in Siberia. Two years later he was driven from Russia on Stalin's orders. With the launching of the first five-year plan at the end of 1928 Stalin was supreme, although it took several years longer before he was able to consolidate the power and embark upon the purging of Lenin's old guard. In launching the program of forced industrialization and collectivization, Stalin took over the basic ideas advocated by Trotsky.

Not until 1936 did Stalin venture upon the task of exterminating virtually all his opponents among Lenin's old guard. The immediate impulse for this fantastic phase of the Bolshevik regime was given by the assassination in Petrograd in December, 1934, of Sergei Kirov, a Stalin partisan, who had succeeded Zinoviev as head of the Northern Commune, a region of which the former capital was the center. In the series of purge trials that began in 1935 and ended in 1937, most of the leaders who had been Lenin's principal lieutenants for decades—the organizers, propagandists, high officials, diplomats and apostles of the revolution—were accused of treason, of collaboration with Nazi Germany and Japan in plans against Soviet Russia, of conspiring to restore capitalism in Russia. The Kirov assassination was pictured as having had a relation to these alleged crimes. From the indictments in the trials and the "confessions" of the accused it appeared that the Bolshevik Revolution led by Lenin and Trotsky, who was tried and condemned in absentia as the chief culprit, was carried out and the Soviet regime established with the aid of traitors guilty of the blackest crimes. Stalin's opponents denounced the trials as frame-ups. In this country, Prof. John Dewey headed a commission of inquiry which, after study of the trials, characterized them as such.

Among the most startling of the trials was that of Marshal Tuchachevsky and a galaxy of Russia's leading generals. They were accused of treason, of conspiracy with Hitler, and executed. Executed later were also the majority of generals who had constituted the court that condemned Tuchachevsky and his colleagues. The trials of Tuchachevsky and his group as well as of their judges were held in camera.

The purges described here were accompanied by a nation-wide shake-up of the party and governmental machine, involving the imprisonment of thousands of army officers and the removal or exile of hundreds of thousands of Government officials and party members.

Internationally there were defections from Stalin's rule after World War II. His most important ideological defeat of the post-war period came in 1948 when Marshal Tito broke with the Cominform after he had refused to subordinate Yugoslavia's interests to those of the Kremlin. The Yugoslav Premier soon became the No. 1 devil of Stalinism.

To forestall similar defections in other countries Stalin moved in the years that followed to purge top leaders in other satellite Communist parties, including Gomulka in Poland, Rajk in Hungary, Slansky in Czechoslovakia, Kostov in Bulgaria and Ana Pauker in Rumania.

Churchill, Truman and Stalin at Potsdam, July 1945.

"All the News That's Fit to Print"

The New York Times

LATE CITY EDITION

Weather: Mostly sunny today; clear and cold tonight. Fair tomorrow. Temp. range: today 45-30; Friday 46-34. Full U.S. report on Page 73.

VOL. CXVIII . No. 40,509 NEW YORK, SATURDAY, DECEMBER 21, 1968 — 10 CENTS

DE SAPIO INDICTED BY U.S. IN A PLOT TO BRIBE MARCUS

Accused Also of Conspiring to Shake Down Con Edison for Construction Jobs

CORALLO IS NAMED, TOO

A Co-defendant With Fried —Charges 'Entirely False,' Ex-Tammany Head Says

By EDWARD RANZAL

Carmine G. De Sapio was indicted yesterday by a Federal grand jury on charges of conspiring to bribe former Water Commissioner James L. Marcus and to shake down Consolidated Edison for construction contracts.

Several hours later, Mr. De Sapio pleaded not guilty and was released without bail by Federal Judge Edward Weinfeld.

Of the charges, the tall, immaculately groomed former Tammany Hall boss, wearing the familiar dark-tinted glasses would say only:

"The charges are entirely false, and I have every confidence that the trial will establish this."

Corallo and Fried Named

Named in the four-count indictment with Mr. De Sapio were Antonio (Tony Ducks) Corallo, 55 years old, of 13-61 144th Place, Whitestone, Queens, a powerful Mafia leader, and Henry Fried, 69, of Mount Kisco, N. Y., a wealthy contractor. They will plead to the indictment on Monday.

Mr. De Sapio, who is 59, lives at 11 Fifth Avenue.

Last June, Corallo and Fried were convicted of conspiring to bribe Marcus to obtain a city contract for Fried's company for the rehabilitation of the Jerome Park Reservoir in the Bronx. Corallo was sentenced to three years and Fried to two. Both are free on bail pending appeal.

Marcus, who was also named in the reservoir indictment, pleaded guilty before trial, testified for the Government, and was later sentenced to 15 months in prison.

Another defendant was Herbert Itkin, a labor lawyer who said he was a Federal Bureau of Investigation informer. Itkin,

Continued on Page 25, Column 1

Ex-Tammany Leader at Courthouse

The New York Times

Carmine G. De Sapio talking with reporters before he pleaded not guilty to an indictment in Federal Court.

'Mafia Pressure' Charge Sworn To by Jersey Aide

By RONALD SULLIVAN
Special to The New York Times

HACKENSACK, N. J., Dec. 20—An aide to a State Senate crime committee who had charged that an Assembly committee chairman told her he was under "pressure" from a Mafia leader told her story tonight to a representative of the State Attorney General's office.

Mrs. Claire Curran Johnson, an aide to Senator Joseph C. Woodcock Jr., a Bergen County Republican and chairman of the Senate Committee on Law and Public Safety, gave a written, notarized statement in the Senator's law office here.

Neither the representative—Martin Greenberg, a detective from the office of Arthur J. Sills, the State Attorney General—nor Mrs. Johnson would comment later.

"I'm prepared," she said, "to appear under subpoena or on call before any proper investigatory body."

Wary on Witness Role

Nevertheless, Mrs. Johnson, a plump, middle-aged woman with closely cut hair, conceded that she was extremely wary of being placed in the role of a state witness.

"I don't want to get dramatic," she said, "but do you remember what happened to Victor Riesel? I love my baby blue eyes."

Mr. Riesel, the labor columnist, was blinded, apparently in retaliation for articles he wrote exposing the corruption of labor unions by organized crime.

This evening's meeting between Mrs. Johnson—who as Claire Curran was for years The New York Daily Mirror's New Jersey correspondent—and a state investigator was arranged yesterday by Senator Woodcock and the first assistant state attorney general, Joseph A. Hoffman.

Mr. Woodcock was the chairman of the Senate hearings last September that heard New Jersey described as the most politically corrupt state in the

Continued on Page 28, Column 1

STATE WILL STUDY SCHOOL PRESSURES

Governor to Join Regents in Bid to Solve Problems of Cities and Financing

By SYDNEY H. SCHANBERG

The Board of Regents and Governor Rockkefeller have decided to undertake a "major examination" of the quality, cost and financing of the state's public school system.

The goal is to develop a financing plan to remove the "gross inequities" from district to district that now exist and to make the system more relevant to new educational pressures such as special urban problems, racial imbalance and district consolidation in non-urban areas.

One of the major results of such a study could be more money for city schools, especially in slum areas.

Governor Sets Conditions

The study was proposed to the Governor by the Regents, the governing body for education in the state, in a letter earlier this week and in a meeting with him Thursday in Albany.

Although he agreed to join the Regents in naming a "high-level committee of specialists in education, finance and taxation" to make the study, he first insisted that the inquiry be broadened to include, not only the state's role in financing the public schools, but also the Federal role.

He also insisted that the educational cost structure be examined thoroughly with a view to finding and eliminating areas of waste and duplication.

The Regents and their administrative head, State Education Commissioner James E. Allen Jr., agreed to the Governor's suggestions and are in-

Continued on Page 30, Column 2

Youth Corps Thefts Stir Insurance Fight

By RICHARD SEVERO

The Neighborhood Youth Corps, which has lost an estimated total of $2-million through thefts and embezzlements, has been informed that it is not insured for such losses.

The city has expressed its strong opposition to the stance of the insurer, the United States Fidelity & Bonding Company, which made its position known in a letter to the Human Resources Administration, the parent organization of the Youth Corps.

The insurer's letter charges that the administration was less than candid with the company when the bonding agreement was signed last July 17.

The letter, dated Nov. 12 and sent to Robert C. Flick, an attorney in the general

Continued on Page 16, Column 3

OIL TO BE RUSHED TO SERIOUSLY ILL

Emergency Fuel Deliveries Planned for Apartments

By DAMON STETSON

The city set up an emergency procedure yesterday to facilitate fuel oil deliveries to heatless apartment buildings where there are occupants who are seriously ill.

Deputy Mayor Timothy W. Costello announced the new plan, aimed at alleviating "life and death" situations, as hundreds of additional houses and apartment buildings ran out of fuel.

Marvin Gersten, Commissioner of Purchase, reported that deliveries of fuel to the city's hospitals were now proceeding smoothly, with more than 80 hospitals serviced yesterday.

Despite a tentative agreement in the five-day-old walkout of fuel oil truck drivers, shortages of oil continued in thousands of homes and apartment buildings as the strikers held off deliveries to private dwellings—except in emergency situations certified by the City Health Department.

The 2,800 striking members of Local 553 of the Teamsters Union are scheduled to vote on ratification of the new agreement between 8 A.M. and 1 P.M. tomorrow at two sites—Roosevelt Auditorium, 100 East 17th Street, and a hall at 101-49 Woodhaven Boulevard, Ozone Park, Queens.

The strikers rejected a tentative contract last Sunday that would have given them a $20-

Continued on Page 45, Column 4

NIXON PICKS YOST AS U.N. DELEGATE IN SURPRISE MOVE

Retired Career Diplomat Is Named After Talks With Shriver Break Down

By R. W. APPLE Jr.

President-elect Richard M. Nixon yesterday named Charles W. Yost, a 61-year-old retired career diplomat, as chief United States representative at the United Nations.

Mr. Nixon turned to Mr. Yost, who has had wide experience in the Middle East and at the world organization, after negotiations with Sargent Shriver, the present Ambassador to France, broke down early this week.

But the President-elect also announced that Mr. Shriver, a brother-in-law of John, Robert and Edward Kennedy, had agreed to remain as the envoy at Paris under the new Administration.

In choosing the slight, soft-spoken Mr. Yost, Mr. Nixon broke with the tradition of sending a political figure of world stature to the United Nations—a tradition that had put such men as Henry Cabot Lodge, Adlai E. Stevenson and Arthur J. Goldberg in the position.

Worked for Humphrey

But he held to his promise of appointing a Democrat, partly to offset the all-Republican complexion of his Cabinet. Mr. Yost not only voted for Vice President Humphrey, the Democratic nominee, but also headed his study group on international organizations and peace keeping.

The President-elect introduced Mr. Yost at a news conference at the Pierre Hotel, describing him as "probably one of the best appointments I have made."

"I think there have been times," Mr. Nixon said, "when the role of Ambassador to the U. N. was better filled by a political personage with a world reputation. It is my belief that at this particular time we need the kind of Ambassador Mr. Yost will be: a highly skilled negotiator, a man who knows the U. N. and is deeply dedicated to seeing it strengthened."

He noted with some emphasis that Mr. Yost had agreed to serve "for the duration"—as long as the Nixon Administration is in office. That was believed to have been a major factor in the President-elect's ultimate choice.

Mr. Nixon also said that Mr. Yost, who served as a deputy under both Mr. Stevenson and Mr. Goldberg, would sit with the National Security Council and the Cabinet when matters affecting the United Nations were on the agenda.

But he hedged on a major question—the issue of whether

Continued on Page 18, Column 1

Astronauts Who Will Leave Earth on Space Journey

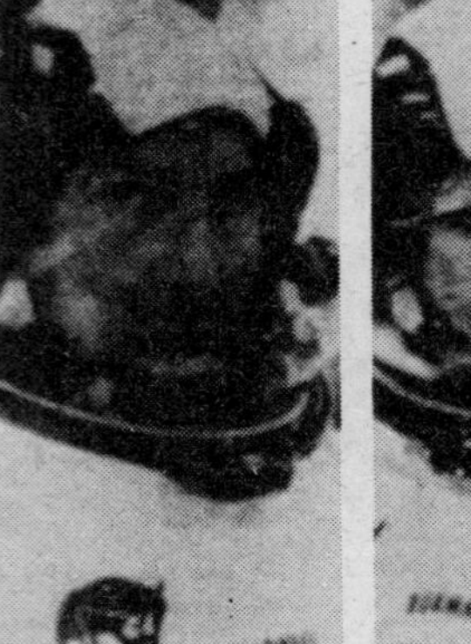

NASA

Capt. James A. Lovell Jr.

Col. Frank Borman

United Press International

Maj. William A. Anders

Kidnapped Girl, Buried Alive, Is Freed

Parents Pay $500,000 —Coed Kept in Box for About 80 Hours

By The Associated Press

MIAMI, Dec. 20 — Barbara Jane Mackle, who was kidnapped Tuesday and buried in a box for 80 hours, was found in a Georgia woodland today by agents of the Federal Bureau of Investigation after her parents paid $500,000 ransom, J. Edgar Hoover, F.B.I. director, said tonight.

The coffinlike box in which the 20-year-old Emory University junior was buried held an air pump, food, water and a battery-powered light that failed just hours before she was located, Mr. Hoover said.

Miss Mackle still wore the red-and-white-checkered flannel nightgown she had on when she was kidnapped at gunpoint from her sickbed in a suburban Atlanta motel.

Mr. Hoover passed the word of the girl's safety to her father, Robert F. Mackle, millionaire land developer. The father immediately flew to Atlanta to join his daughter.

Earlier in the day Mr. Hoover announced that an escaped convict and a woman biology researcher had been charged with the kidnapping.

The box was buried 18 inches underground, the F.B.I. said. Agents found the macabre subterranean prison in an isolated, heavily wooded rural area some 20 miles northeast of Atlanta, Mr. Hoover said.

The agents who found the girl said she apparently had been in the box about 80 hours. The top of the box had been fastened with screws and the box contained a small battery unit and fan and two flexible vent pipes that protruded just above the ground.

Negotiations for the girl's release began just hours after she was taken at gunpoint from a motel in suburban Atlanta. The Mackle family placed a classified ad in Wednesday morning's Miami Herald to let the kidnappers know they would meet the terms.

The ad said: "LOVED ONE—please come home. We will pay all expense and meet you anywhere at any time. Your Family."

Early today — shortly after midnight and only a few hours after the kidnappers renewed contact with the parents—the suitcase crammed with $500,000 in $20 bills was left near the Coral Park Shopping Center at Southwest 97th Avenue and Tamiami Trail, about five miles northwest of the Mackles' home.

A pre-dawn attempt yesterday by the girl's father, Robert F. Mackle, to hand over the ransom was foiled when the police happened on two persons

Continued on Page 43, Column 3

Strike by Dockers Ties Up All Ports On the East Coast

By GEORGE HORNE

Longshoremen from Maine to Texas went on strike last night as Federal mediation efforts failed.

The strike was a resumption of a walkout that began Oct. 1 and was halted the next day for an 80-day cooling-off period under provisions of the Taft-Hartley Act.

The injunction expired at 7:05 P.M. yesterday, but the collapse of talks and the official strike call were announced earlier—at 4:20 P.M.

The talks collapsed on disagreement over containerized cargo. Wages and pensions were not at issue.

As the deadlock came, it was apparent that efforts for a settlement were hopeless and that a multimillion-dollar industry employing 75,000 dock-

Continued on Page 73, Column 6

U.S. ENDS ITS CURB ON SOVIET ARTISTS

Moscow Symphony to Visit —Ban Imposed Following Czechoslovak Invasion

By BERNARD GWERTZMAN
Special to The New York Times

WASHINGTON, Dec. 20—The United States has told the Soviet Union that it has lifted the suspension of official cultural exchanges imposed after the Soviet-led invasion of Czechoslovakia in August.

The State Department announced today that as a result the Moscow State Symphony Orchestra would make a tour of the United States beginning in February.

Officials said discussions would begin soon between the United States and the Soviet Union on carrying out other parts of the 1968-69 cultural agreement, which virtually came to a halt after the invasion.

Under the agreement, each side is to send three major performing arts groups to the other's country and each side is

Continued on Page 8, Column 5

Nigerians Declare Dec. 24-25 Truce; Britons See Break

By Reuters

LAGOS, Nigeria, Dec. 20—Maj. Gen. Yakubu Gowon, head of the federal Nigerian Government, today ordered a two-day Christmas truce in the 18-month civil war with secessionist Biafra.

The order followed talks in Lagos during the day between General Gowon and two Labor party members of the British Parliament, Lord Brockway and James Griffiths, a former Secretary for Commonwealth Relations, who are taking an independent peace initiative in the Nigerian political crisis. The truce will cover Dec. 24 and 25.

[In Ethiopia Emperor Haile Selassie appealed to both sides to observe a one-week truce during Christmas and Moslem holidays, Agence-France-Presse said. President Johnson was reported planning to support his appeal.]

Lord Brockway, reporting on British peace efforts, said it was up to the Biafran leader, Lieut. Col. Odumegwu Ojukwu, "to accept the truce which we

Continued on Page 13, Column 1

APOLLO CREW SET FOR START TODAY OF MOON VOYAGE

7:51 A.M. Launching Slated for First Manned Flight Toward Lunar Orbit

6-DAY TRIP IS PLANNED

Borman, Lovell and Anders Retire Early as Saturn 5 Spacecraft is Fueled

By JOHN NOBLE WILFORD
Special to The New York Times

CAPE KENNEDY, Fla., Saturday, Dec. 21—Three American astronauts, anticipating the greatest of space-age adventures but mindful of the risks, were poised to embark early this morning on man's most far-reaching voyage of exploration, his first flight around the moon.

As the pale moon beckoned 220,000 miles away, technicians raced the countdown clock, fueling the rocket and overcoming equipment problems, to be ready to get the six-day Apollo 8 mission off on time at 7:51 A.M.

The astronauts — Col. Frank Borman of the Air Force, Capt. James A. Lovell Jr. of the Navy and Maj. William A. Anders of the Air Force — went to bed early after eating a steak dinner and learning from space officials that the countdown was proceeding smoothly.

Skies Watched Closely

"We are 'go' for the Apollo mission," a spokesman for the National Aeronautics and Space Administration said.

Launching crews, however, kept a watchful eye on the cloudy skies, lest they close in on the space center here and prevent adequate visibility during liftoff. Space officials want to be able to track the rocket for the first 2,000 feet to be sure it is on a safe course away from land.

And into the night their computerized inspection system checked and double-checked to see that the Saturn 5 rocket, the most powerful ever flown, was up to its historic task.

Along the beaches and in the neighboring towns, thousands upon thousands of Government officials, foreign dignitaries, aerospace executives and engineers, newsmen and tourists waited anxiously as the moment drew near. It was said to be the largest gathering here since Col. John H. Glenn Jr. made the nation's first manned earth-orbiting flight in 1962.

Most Critical Test

For Apollo 8 promised to be the most critical test thus far in the seven and a half years since President Kennedy initiated the $24-billion Apollo project to land men on the moon and bring them back to earth in this decade.

American astronauts have flown 15 missions around earth, but never ventured farther out than 850 miles. American robot spacecraft have crashed into the moon, landed on it and circled it; they have photographed it in detail, picked at

Continued on Page 22, Column 4

John Steinbeck Dies Here at 66

By ALDEN WHITMAN

John Steinbeck, one of six Americans to have won the Nobel Prize for literature, died late yesterday afternoon of severe coronary and valvular heart disease at his home, 190 East 72d Street. He was 66 years old.

Mr. Steinbeck, who had been in failing health since Memorial Day, had moved into the city at that time from his country home in Sag Harbor, L. I.

Of Mr. Steinbeck's 24 works of fiction, one novel, "The Grapes of Wrath," was the anchor of his fame. A compassionate, realistic and deeply emotional account of a farm family's forced migration from the Depression dustbowl of Oklahoma to the exploitive migrant labor camps of California, the book, published in 1939, brought its 37-year-old author overnight praise and denunciation.

The New York Times

John Steinbeck

The acclaim was for the novel's lucid and powerful narrative of the Joads and their fellow Okies and migrants, whose human frailties made more poignant their desperate struggle to survive. Their survival was not a triumph of heroic individualism but the result of a painfully learned lesson in the importance of cooperation to achieve a common purpose. This was a story—and a theme—that was especially congenial to Depression-era readers, many of whom had jettisoned the concept of rugged individualism.

The criticism was for Mr. Steinbeck's apparent attack on capitalism and his suggestion that it could produce the poverty and the dislocation that all but swept the Okies under. Many of these critics were certain that the writer was a Communist (he was not), and his book was banned as subversive by a number of libraries. Actually, "The Grapes of Wrath"

Continued on Page 31, Column 1

Pope Voices Pessimism in Christmas Message

He Mourns Decline in Values but Sees Hope for Man in Renewal of Christianity

By ROBERT C. DOTY
Special to The New York Times

ROME, Dec. 20—Pope Paul VI tonight delivered a Christmas message of deep pessimism over the temporal prospects of man, urging a renewal of Christianity as "the true and the highest hope" for salvation.

Excerpts from Pope's message are printed on Page 41.

In one passage, the Pontiff even saw a possibility of the use of nuclear weapons as a consequence of causes that "neither science nor technique can, of themselves, dominate."

"Our presumptuous struggle to save ourselves only serves, finally, to underline the conviction of our radical incapability," the Pontiff said in his message, which was broadcast to the world from his study in the Vatican.

He showed no sign of strain or concern over the crisis of dissidence and contesting of his authority that has arisen in the Roman Catholic Church from his disputed encyclical renewing the Catholic ban on artificial means of contraception and from Vatican efforts to check powerful currents of progressive theology.

The Pontiff deplored the decline of traditional moral and social values, the "murderous forces" man commands, the depersonalization produced by industrial society, the maldistribution of its wealth and the anarchic, violent protests of those who grope for change without moral, religious absolutes to guide them.

He balanced this assessment, however, with a firm reaffirmation of his faith that the Christian message would produce revival, "slow but sure, toilsome but triumphant, ancient but thrillingly new."

"We have need of Christ," he said. "It is necessary that we have divine power, because no other power can overcome our ills."

There is no lack of hope in the temporal world, the Pope said. Indeed, it is "the interior mainspring of modern dynamism." But it is the "hope in

Continued on Page 40, Column 6

NEWS INDEX

John Steinbeck, Nobel-Prize Winning Novelist, Is Dead

'GRAPES OF WRATH' WON '40 PULITZER

Continued From Page 1, Col. 5

contains a specific defense of private property and private enterprise, although this was overshadowed by the book's denunciation of big business as irresponsible.

Whatever the author's ideology, however, his novel touched off a national explosion of protest and indignation over the plight of the dispossessed. "No novel of our day has been written out of a more genuine humanity, and none, I think, is better calculated to arouse the humanity of others," was how Louis Kronenberger expressed it in The Nation. The book was read and debated less as a novel than as a sociological document, so much so that it was compared, in its impact on the public, to Harriet Beecher Stowe's "Uncle Tom's Cabin."

Although the comparison turned out to be facile—Mr. Steinbeck was not nearly so radical as Mrs. Stowe—"The Grapes of Wrath" became a classic because its drama of humanity dealt with real people in real situations. It won a Pulitzer Prize in 1940 and was made into a memorable movie of social protest that starred Henry Fonda and Jane Darwell. The book has sold over three million copies in various American editions, and has long been required reading in scores of colleges and universities.

"The Grapes of Wrath" made its California author an unwilling celebrity, a condition he resisted all his life. "I am not neurotic about personal publicity," he said. "I just think it's foolish. The fact that I have housemaid's knees or fear of yellow gloves has little to do with the books I write."

He shunned award ceremonies; dodged interviews and declined as often as he could to pose for photographs. "They ain't going to lionize me," he told a friend in 1940.

Zealously guarding his privacy, Mr. Steinbeck took little part in the public literary life of his time. He rarely served on committees, signed appeals, attended parties, lectured at colleges or commented on the work of other writers. He lived simply, inconspicuously and off the beaten track—in a ranch house in California, in a cottage at Sag Harbor, L. I., in a nondescript brownstone on New York's Upper East Side.

Because Mr. Steinbeck isolated himself so much, he was considered reserved and difficult to get to know really well. "John always seemed occupied with his inner thoughts," an acquaintance of many years said recently. "He had a way of putting you off if you tried to probe him and a way of making you feel as if you were being observed under his microscope."

In another view, Mr. Steinbeck was accounted a delightful companion in a small circle of intimates that include Nathaniel Benchley, Elia Kazan, Arthur Miller, Edward Albee, Abe Burrows, John Huston and Thomas Guinzburg, his publisher.

"John was a very soft man, once you got to know him," Mr. Guinzburg said. "He was wonderfully kind. He was pleased by small things, just like a big kid."

Mr. Steinbeck felt very much at home with people of no pretension — the Okies among whom he lived and worked for a while, workers in a fish-canning factory, ranch hands, apple pickers and paisanos. He delighted to talk with them, drink with them and worry over their day-to-day problems. And for their speech he developed a marvelously accurate ear and for their ways a keen eye.

Preferred Sweaters to Suits

A husky six-footer with brown hair that turned to gray with age, the writer was ill at ease in conventional attire. He preferred sweaters, baggy trousers and battered shoes to sack suits, and for years he did not own a dinner jacket.

Early in his adulthood he grew a mustache and, later, a beard. Over the years this underwent a number of changes in style, but it seemed to be fixed in his last years as a short Vandyke, which gave his face a Mephistophelean cast.

At Sag Harbor, he wrote in a small building apart from his cottage, to which he retired for a few hours every day. He wrote in pencil on yellow lined paper, and his manuscripts were transcribed by a typist at Viking Press, his publisher. His novels, according to Mr. Guinzburg, required only light editing.

Mr. Steinbeck liked to putter and to do things with his hands. In time he acquired considerable skill in woodworking, and, in proof of his talent, delivered the manuscript of "East of Eden" in a handcrafted box of complicated design.

The simple, even casual, life was part of John Ernst Steinbeck Jr.'s California heritage. He was born Feb. 27, 1902, in the town of Salinas of German, Irish and New England extraction. He was the only son of a miller who was once treasurer of Monterey County. His mother was Olive Hamilton Steinbeck, a teacher in the Salinas Valley schools. As a youth John played basketball and excelled at track, but he spent much of his spare time in the out-of-doors and in reading. His fare was Malory's "Morte d'Arthur," Milton's "Paradise Lost," the Bible, Hardy's "The Return of the Native."

From this reading sprang a lifelong absorption in allegory, a form around which most of his fiction is built. His reading also turned him toward mythopoetic expression, which is also intricately woven into the fabric of his novels.

After his high school years, young Steinbeck entered Stanford University, which he treated as an academic adventure. He tasted the curriculum, taking courses in literature, science and writing; and he wrote poems and comic satires for college publications.

Restless and seemingly undirected, he worked as a ranch hand and toiled on a road-building gang and in a sugar-beet factory. He left Stanford in 1925 without a degree, but with a passion to write and went to New York to establish himself. He worked briefly as a reporter for The New York American (facts eluded his grasp and he was dismissed) and as a hodcarrier in the construction of Madison Square Garden.

When a publisher rejected Mr. Steinbeck's manuscript, a collection of stories, he returned to California, where he took a job as a lodge caretaker at Lake Tahoe in the Sierras. There in loneliness he created his first novel, "Cup of Gold," a historical extravaganza about Sir Henry Morgan, a 17th-century Caribbean pirate.

Containing strong hints of its source in the Arthurian quest for the Holy Grail, the novel is an allegory designed to convey the notion that swashbuckling heroes are out of place in the modern world, that civilization destroys innocence.

The book, appearing in 1929, sold about 1,500 copies and excited no critical interest. Undiscouraged, Mr. Steinbeck married Carol Henning and moved to Pacific Grove on a monthly allowance of $25 from his family. He tried to sell short stories, fashioned a new novel and formed a fast friendship with Edward Ricketts, a marine biologist.

Mr. Steinbeck told the story of his profound intellectual and emotional debt to this man in "About Ed Ricketts," a memoir issued in 1948 after his death. Mr. Ricketts gave coherence to the writer's philosophical attitudes, providing him with the arguments for a biological view of man that infuses his novels.

This view — that man must adapt to his environment if he is to survive — was presented in "The Grapes of Wrath" and in "Cannery Row," where it is suggested that men should accept themselves as they are and stop persecuting others for being different from them.

Mr. Ricketts, in addition to being the writer's mentor, was his closest drinking and talking companion. Slightly disguised, the biologist appeared in three of his friend's novels —"In Dubious Battle," "Cannery Row" and "Sweet Thursday."

'Tortilla Flat' Acclaimed

Mr. Steinbeck's second novel, "The Pastures of Heaven," came out in 1932, followed a year later by "To a God Unknown." The former was a satire of mediocrity, the latter an allegory about the breakdown of a family. Although neither was a popular success, each stirred the interest of a Chicago bookseller who, in turn, insisted that Pascal Covici, the publisher, read them. He was impressed sufficiently to publish "Tortilla Flat," Mr. Steinbeck's next book and the one that earned his first critical huzzas.

"Tortilla Flat" was at once a pointed satire of middle-class values and a tragic story of a man who fails while trying to achieve greatness. The people of the novel were a group of paisanos, a band of idlers who shunned the amenities of civilization and pursued their own eccentric moralities.

Warm, sentimental, off-beat, the novel quickly became a best seller and was purchased by Hollywood — but not filmed for 10 years (and then badly). With the money from the book, Mr. Steinbeck had his first taste of affluence and the heady experience of being in demand as a writer.

He followed his success with "In Dubious Battle," the story of an apple-pickers' strike that attacked both insensitive employers and militant strike leaders. Although the author's sympathies were clearly with the strikers — "the working stiffs"—he pictured them as exploited both by the capitalists and the Communists.

On the strength of the book, Mr. Steinbeck was hired by The San Francisco News to write about California's migrant labor camps, and from this searing experience came the idea for "The Grapes of Wrath." Meantime, however, he wrote "Of Mice and Men," a tragic fable of the strong and the weak, published in 1937. The book introduced Mr. Steinbeck to Broadway, where "Of Mice and Men" was converted into a play with George S. Kaufman's help. Although the play barely missed winning the Pulitzer Prize, it did take the New York Drama Critics Circle award and went on to become a movie.

The night the play opened, its author was in a migrant camp, having traveled to California from Oklahoma with some of its inhabitants. All the pathos of these uprooted people was translated into "The Grapes of Wrath," which made its author a national figure in spite of himself. To escape, he and Mr. Ricketts journeyed to the Gulf of California. Their adventure is described in "Sea of Cortez," a semitravel book.

Moved to New York

Shortly afterward Mr. Steinbeck went to Mexico to make "The Forgotten Village," a notable documentary film about the introduction of modern medicine to a backward village.

Restless, he took to traveling, which over the years became virtually a way of life for him. These trips caused his wife to divorce him in 1942. She received a $220,000 settlement.

The following year, with Paul de Kruif, the medical writer, serving as best man, he married Gwyndolen Conger, who became the mother of his two children, Thom and John. This marriage lasted until 1948. His third marriage, which was said to be happier, came in 1950, when he wed Elaine Scott, divorced wife of Zachary Scott, the movie actor.

With his second marriage, Mr. Steinbeck moved to New York, a change of milieu that, in the opinion of many critics, adversely affected the quality of his fiction.

After the high point of "The Grapes of Wrath," his next novel, "The Moon Is Down," an abstract account of the German occupation of a Scandinavian country, was coolly received. More enthusiasm greeted his film script for "Lifeboat," an allegory about a world adrift that starred Tallulah Bankhead. The movie was a hit on its release in 1944.

Mr. Steinbeck's first postwar novel, "Cannery Row," returned to the scene of his earlier triumphs. A story of the denizens of Monterey's Cannery Row, it described the destructive force of respectability. Two years later, in 1947, he published "The Wayward Bus," a semiphilosophical examination of a group of stranded bus riders. It failed to attract much attention, as did "A Russian Journal," an account of a trip to the Soviet Union with Robert Capa, the photographer.

The novelist turned again to the movies, working on the script for Marlon Brando's "Viva Zapata!" in 1950. The same year his play "Burning Bright" failed on Broadway after 13 performances.

Wrote for Magazines

Mr. Steinbeck's literary (or at least popular) stock rose markedly in 1952 with "East of Eden," a lusty family chronicle that developed into an intricate gloss on the Cain-and-Abel theme. Although critics tended to disparage it as rambling, the book sold well, and Elia Kazan transmuted part of it into a movie in which James Dean made his screen debut.

Nonetheless, "Sweet Thursday" was only indifferently received in 1954, as was "Pipe Dream," the musical comedy version of the book. In those years Mr. Steinbeck wrote for magazines, including Holiday and Saturday Review, and did an introduction to the collected campaign speeches of Adlai E. Stevenson. Warren French, a sympathetic critic, called most of the writer's output during the nineteen-fifties "superficial journalism."

Mr. Steinbeck made a comeback of sorts in 1961 with "The Winter of Our Discontent," an inversion of the Gospel story in modern dress that portrayed the decline of moral standards in the United States. But to many it seemed more of a sermon than a novel, and it did not do very well for all its articulateness.

Although Mr. Steinbeck had been mentioned years earlier as a possible Nobelist, the awarding of the prize to him in 1962 was a surprise. The citation, calling attention to his "sympathetic humor and social perception," implied that it was his sociological fiction that had captivated the judges. At the same time, it was said that the jury had also liked "The Winter of Our Discontent" because of its "instinct for what is genuinely American, be it good or bad."

Mr. Steinbeck was one of six Americans who won the Nobel Prize for literature since the prizes were instituted in 1901. The others were Ernest Hemingway, William Faulkner, Pearl Buck, Eugene O'Neill and Sinclair Lewis.

With the prize Mr. Steinbeck appeared to have lost his fictive voice altogether. "The prize did terrible things to John's ability to create fiction," Mr. Guinzburg said. "He felt vastly frustrated and he wouldn't fool around with an entertainment, or something light, to break the tension."

The year of the Nobel Prize Mr. Steinbeck published "Travels With Charley," a whimsical chronicle of a trip across the United States with his poodle. The book affirmed his attachment to America as well as his fondness for, and rapport with, simple people.

"I began to feel that Americans exist, that they really do have generalized characteristics regardless of their states, their social and financial status, their education, their religious and their political conviction," he wrote, adding cryptically:

"But the more I inspected this American image, the less sure I became of what it is."

In the middle sixties, Mr. Steinbeck talked from time to time of writing a "big" novel, but seemed unable to put it together. His most recent book, "America and Americans," was a collection of thoughts on the United States that accompanied 105 photographs of the national scene.

In the Vietnam war he dismayed and puzzled his friends in the intellectual community, most of whom opposed the war. Mr. Steinbeck, who took a trip to South Vietnam, aired his hawkish views in columns he wrote for Newsday, the Long Island newspaper. These were titled "Letters to Alicia," the reference being to Alicia Patterson, the paper's founder, who had died several years before the columns appeared.

He was also censured in a poem by Yevgeny Yevtushenko, the Soviet writer, as "betraying" his principles. Mr. Steinbeck, who maintained that the Vietnam conflict was "a Chinese-inspired war" that the United States must win, replied to the Soviet poet. He challenged Soviet authorities to print his tart letter, which accused them of perpetuating the war. The challenge was accepted, and the letter appeared on the front page of a Moscow newspaper.

In recent years, Mr. Steinbeck secluded himself in his Sag Harbor home. He declined to see interviewers, although he was available, as always, to his close friends.

"All the News That's Fit to Print"

The New York Times.

LATE CITY EDITION

U.S. Weather Bureau Report (Page 58) forecasts: Clearing, warm and humid today; fair tonight. Sunny tomorrow.
Temp. Range: 8[illegible]—72; yesterday: 93—71.
Temp.-Hum. Index: mid-70s; yesterday: 82.

VOL. CXIV . No. 39,254. | NEW YORK, THURSDAY, JULY 15, 1965. | TEN CENTS

M'NAMARA HINTS AT EARLY CALL-UP OF RESERVE UNITS

Bolsters Johnson Remark on Need for 'New and Serious Decisions' on Vietnam

LARGER DRAFT IS SEEN

Secretary, Before Departing for Saigon, Predicts Rise in Guerrilla Operations

By MAX FRANKEL
Special to The New York Times

WASHINGTON, July 14—The Johnson Administration hinted even more strongly today that the war in Vietnam would probably soon require the mobilization of reserves, larger draft calls and the extension of enlistments for men on active duty.

At a news conference before his departure for Vietnam, Secretary of Defense Robert S. McNamara said he expected further increases in Vietcong operations, leading to a further build-up of United States forces. The Secretary left for Saigon tonight.

His comments, following President Johnson's public anticipation yesterday of "new and serious decisions," made it clear that the Administration was now preparing public opinion for a major manpower expansion.

Formal decisions will await Mr. McNamara's return, officials reiterated, but they acknowledged that plans to provide for reserves of men and equipment were in preparation.

Budget to Increase

An increase in the size of United States forces in Southeast Asia—which is now being taken for granted here—will "almost surely" require additions to the military budget, Mr. McNamara said. It is "reasonable to assume," he added, that such an increase will make it necessary to consider calls for more civilians and the retention of men in service.

The Secretary said a call for reserves would yield far more active and combat-ready units than the call-up of 1961. He thus indicated that the Army, which would issue the largest call, would look first at the eight National Guard divisions upon which it has lavished the most money and equipment in recent years.

Six 'Priority' Divisions

These are six so-called "high-priority" divisions—the 42d Infantry of New York, the 50th Armored of New Jersey, the 28th Infantry of Pennsylvania, the 26th Infantry of Massachusetts, the 30th Infantry of North Carolina and the 30th Armored of Tennessee. Also, there are two "special-mission" divisions—the 38th Infantry of Indiana and the 47th Infantry of Minnesota.

High-priority divisions have been furnished with the most up-to-date equipment and training for modern warfare. The special-mission units have, in addition, been trained and equipped for special tasks.

Of the six Army Reserve divisions and the 23 National Guard divisions in the nation, the eight special ones would be most likely to provide the best-trained units or full-strength divisions, informed

Continued on Page 8, Column 1

U.S. Jets Strike a Target 40 Miles From Red China

Raid Is Called Farthest North in Vietnam—2 Marines Killed

By The Associated Press

SAIGON, South Vietnam, Thursday, July 15—United States jet fighter-bombers yesterday made their deepest officially announced strike into North Vietnam, ranging to a point less than 40 miles from Communist China's frontier in one of a series of raids.

A spokesman said four United States Air Force F-105 Thunderchiefs had heavily damaged two trucks they spotted 37 miles north-northeast of Dienbienphu, the onetime French stronghold that is 75 miles from the Chinese border.

The planes hit the target "at a point farther north of Hanoi than any other target previously hit by United States aircraft," he said.

This backed up the Pentagon's denial of reports broadcast by Hanoi and Peking that United States jets bombed the border town of Laokay, 160 miles northwest of Hanoi, last Sunday, and flew over the neighboring Chinese town of Hokow.

The New York Times July 15, 1965

U.S. planes struck north of Dienbienphu (1) and south of the Danang air base (2).

The deepest raid previously announced here was a four-plane attack last Saturday on an ammunition dump 85 miles northwest of Hanoi. Dienbienphu is 210 miles west-northwest

Continued on Page 2, Column 5

JOHNSON ORDERS PANEL TO ASSESS WATER SHORTAGE

Calls for Udall to Report in Week on Problem Along the Eastern Seaboard

Special to The New York Times

WASHINGTON, July 14 — President Johnson asked today that a report be submitted to him within a week on how the Federal Government could help alleviate the "urgent water problem" in the New England and Middle Atlantic States.

The President instructed Interior Secretary Stewart L. Udall to call the Ad Hoc Water Resources Council together immediately to study the question.

The council is made up of Government officials whose departments deal with water problems. An Interior Department spokesman said that Mr. Udall hoped to call a meeting not later than Friday.

Mr. Johnson said that the council would assess what further actions might be taken to assist the states in meeting the water problems now confronting the two regions.

May Transport Water

Some of the possibilities expected to be considered by the council are the use of flood control dams to create reservoirs, civilian use of reservoir systems at abandoned military installations, and transporting water supplies by tank car to emergency areas.

Mr. Johnson met on the water problem with Buford Ellington, head of the Office of Emergency Planning and the President's liaison man with the state Governors.

The White House said that the President had asked Mr. Ellington to move ahead "as rapidly and efficiently as possible" with mobilizing the resources of the Federal Government to help the states involved cope with the water shortage.

Ellington Is Coordinator

Mr. Ellington will work with the Water Resources Council and will coordinate Federal and state activities to deal with the situation.

[In New York, water conservation programs for the metropolitan area of 14 million population were stepped up and officials looked for ways to avoid further shortages. Page 59.]

Mr. Johnson said it would require imaginative planning, a willingness to cooperate and some sacrifices if the nation was to make the best use of its water resources.

"We must move quickly and firmly to preserve what we have and what we receive," he said. "An abundance of water is critical for the present generation of Americans and a vital legacy for the next."

Mr. Johnson said that the

Continued on Page 59, Column 2

DEMOCRATS MAKE NEW BID TO STAY ELECTION IN FALL

Legislative Leaders File 2d Petition With Harlan Despite U.S. Ruling

By SIDNEY E. ZION

The Democratic leadership in the Legislature filed a new petition with United States Supreme Court Justice John M. Harlan yesterday seeking a stay of Tuesday's Federal court order requiring a state election in November.

It was the second such motion this week by the Democrats in their continuing efforts to block a special legislative election under a Republican reapportionment proposal known as Plan A. The new application was necessitated by Tuesday's Federal court ruling.

While that ruling barred all persons "forever" from interfering with the election, a specific exception was made for an appeal to the Supreme Court.

Court Conflict Kept Alive

The move yesterday kept alive the confrontation of state and Federal judicial power set off last week when the New York Court of Appeals, the state's highest court, ordered cancellation of the election after a three-judge Federal court on May 24 had ordered the balloting. That action had placed matters at an impasse until the Federal court, on Tuesday, reaffirmed its May order.

Only a stay of that order by Justice Harlan can prevent a November election.

But in view of a June 1 ruling by the full Supreme Court denying an identical petition, few believed that a stay would be granted.

However, some Democrats spotted a glimmer of hope in the fact that Justice Harlan was the one member of the court who favored the stay and that he had expressed himself strongly on it.

"It's a thin reed," said one lawyer, "but why not try?"

Fleming Is Pessimistic

Prof. Robert B. Fleming of the Buffalo University Law School, who won the short-lived victory in the Court of Appeals last week, was pessimistic.

"It was fun while it lasted," he said.

In any event, the issue has served to spotlight the growing uneasiness of many state judges over what they consider to be an unjust intrusion on their jurisdiction by Federal courts.

Once confined to the South, in race cases, this sensitivity has spread across the country in recent years and now encompasses a wide range of issues, the basic ones being reapportionment and criminal law.

What has happened, according to legal authorities, is that a libertarian Supreme Court, under Chief Justice Earl Warren, has extended the Bill of Rights to a degree heretofore undreamed of.

Lawyers noted that this did not require Federal courts to move into state areas since the state courts, after all, are empowered to interpret the Federal Constitution. But, they said, the fact is that state judges have generally been conservative and out-of-step with the Supreme Court's broaden-

Continued on Page 19, Column 5

ADLAI STEVENSON DIES IN LONDON STREET AT 65; JOHNSON LEADS TRIBUTE

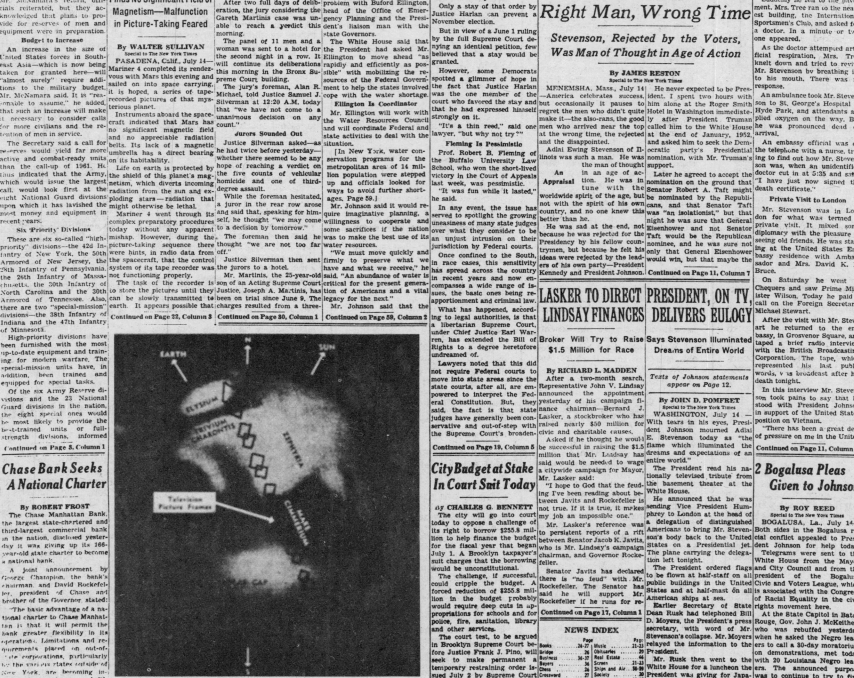

Associated Press Cablephoto

ADLAI E. STEVENSON

Mr. Stevenson outside the American Embassy in London yesterday shortly before he collapsed and died in the street.

ENVOY ON STROLL

Mrs. Tree, With Him, Gets Help but Fails in Revival Effort

By ANTHONY LEWIS
Special to The New York Times

LONDON, July 14—Adlai E. Stevenson collapsed on a London street today and died.

The United States representative at the United Nations, twice Democratic candidate for President, was 65 years old. He had been in London since Saturday and had seemed in good health and good spirits.

Doctors declined to state the cause of death until a coroner's report was filed. The general assumption was that it was a heart attack.

Mr. Stevenson was walking along Upper Grosvenor Street, about 50 yards from the United States Embassy, at 5:10 on a warm, sunny afternoon. Mrs. Marietta P. Tree, his old friend and fellow member of the American delegation at the United Nations, was with him.

Falls to Pavement

Suddenly he fell to the pavement. Mrs. Tree ran to the nearest building, the International Sportsmen's Club, and asked for a doctor. In a minute or two one appeared.

As the doctor attempted artificial respiration, Mrs. Tree knelt down and tried to revive Mr. Stevenson by breathing in to his mouth. There was no response.

An ambulance took Mr. Stevenson to St. George's Hospital at Hyde Park, and attendants applied oxygen on the way. But he was pronounced dead on arrival.

An embassy official was on the telephone with a nurse, trying to find out how Mr. Stevenson was, when an unidentified doctor cut in at 5:35 and said: "I have just now signed the death certificate."

Private Visit to London

Mr. Stevenson was in London for what was termed a private visit. It mixed some diplomacy with the pleasure of seeing old friends. He was staying at the United States Embassy residence with Ambassador and Mrs. David K. E. Bruce.

On Saturday he went to Chequers and saw Prime Minister Wilson. Today he paid a call on the Foreign Secretary, Michael Stewart.

After the visit with Mr. Stewart he returned to the embassy, in Grosvenor Square, and taped a brief radio interview with the British Broadcasting Corporation. The tape, which represented his last public words, was broadcast after his death tonight.

In this interview Mr. Stevenson took pains to say that he stood with President Johnson in support of the United States position on Vietnam.

"There has been a great deal of pressure on me in the United

Continued on Page 11, Column 1

Right Man, Wrong Time

Stevenson, Rejected by the Voters, Was Man of Thought in Age of Action

By JAMES RESTON
Special to The New York Times

MENEMSHA, Mass., July 14—America celebrates success, but occasionally it pauses to regret the men who didn't quite make it—the also-rans, the good men who arrived near the top at the wrong time, the rejected and the disappointed.

An Appraisal

Adlai Ewing Stevenson of Illinois was such a man. He was the man of thought in an age of action. He was in tune with the worldwide spirit of the age, but not with the spirit of his own country, and no one knew this better than he.

He was sad at the end, not because he was rejected for the Presidency by his fellow countrymen, but because he felt his ideas were rejected by the leaders of his own party—President Kennedy and President Johnson.

He never expected to be President. I spent two hours with him alone at the Roger Smith Hotel in Washington immediately after President Truman called him to the White House at the end of January, 1952, and asked him to seek the Democratic party's Presidential nomination, with Mr. Truman's support.

Later he agreed to accept the nomination on the ground that Senator Robert A. Taft might be nominated by the Republicans, and that Senator Taft was "an isolationist," but that night he was sure that General Eisenhower and not Senator Taft would be the Republican nominee, and he was sure not only that General Eisenhower would win, but that maybe the

Continued on Page 11, Column 7

MARINER 4 MAKES FLIGHT PAST MARS

Finds No Significant Field of Magnetism—Malfunction in Picture-Taking Feared

By WALTER SULLIVAN
Special to The New York Times

PASADENA, Calif., July 14—Mariner 4 completed its rendezvous with Mars this evening and sailed on into space carrying, it is hoped, a series of tape-recorded pictures of that mysterious planet.

Instruments aboard the spacecraft indicated that Mars has no significant magnetic field and no appreciable radiation belts. Its lack of a magnetic umbrella has a direct bearing on its habitability.

Life on earth is protected by the shield of this planet's magnetism, which diverts incoming radiation from the sun and exploding stars—radiation that might otherwise be lethal.

Mariner 4 went through its complex preparatory procedures today without any apparent mishap. However, during the picture-taking sequence there were hints, in radio data from the spacecraft, that the control system of its tape recorder was not functioning properly.

The task of the recorder is to store the pictures until they can be slowly transmitted to earth. It appears possible that

Continued on Page 22, Column 3

Martinis Jurors, Closer to Verdict, Locked Up Again

By EDITH EVANS ASBURY

After two full days of deliberation, the jury considering the Gareth Martinis case was unable to reach a verdict this morning.

The panel of 11 men and a woman was sent to a hotel for the second night in a row. It will continue its deliberations this morning in the Bronx Supreme Court building.

The jury's foreman, Alan R. Michael, told Justice Samuel J. Silverman at 12:20 A.M. today that "we have not come to a unanimous decision on any count."

Jurors Sounded Out

Justice Silverman asked—as he had twice before yesterday—whether there seemed to be any hope of reaching a verdict on the five counts of vehicular homicide and one of third-degree assault.

While the foreman hesitated, a juror in the rear row arose and said that, speaking for himself, he thought "we may come to a decision by tomorrow."

The foreman then said he thought "we are not too far off."

Justice Silverman then sent the jurors to a hotel.

Mr. Martinis, the 25-year-old son of an Acting Supreme Court Justice, Joseph A. Martinis, has been on trial since June 9. The charges resulted from a three-

Continued on Page 30, Column 1

Jet Propulsion Laboratory—The New York Times July 15, 1965

RENDEZVOUS IN SPACE: Mariner flew past Mars last night in mankind's first attempt to take close-up pictures of the planet. Rectangles mark the approximate areas of 17 of the 21 pictures planned as the spacecraft moved southward above Martian surface. First attempt to transmit pictures to earth was set for 8:41 A.M. today, New York time.

Chase Bank Seeks A National Charter

By ROBERT FROST

The Chase Manhattan Bank, the largest state-chartered and third-largest commercial bank in the nation, disclosed yesterday it was giving up its 166-year-old state charter to become a national bank.

A joint announcement by George Champion, the bank's chairman, and David Rockefeller, president of Chase and brother of the Governor, stated:

"The basic advantage of a national charter to Chase Manhattan is that it will permit the bank greater flexibility in its operations. Limitations and requirements placed on out-of-state corporations, particularly by the various states outside of New York, are becoming increasingly troublesome and difficult."

The change in status will not affect the bank's present opera-

Continued on Page 39, Column 1

City Budget at Stake In Court Suit Today

By CHARLES G. BENNETT

The city will go into court today to oppose a challenge of its right to borrow $255.8 million to help finance the budget for the fiscal year that began July 1. A Brooklyn taxpayer's suit charges that the borrowing would be unconstitutional.

The challenge, if successful, could cripple the budget. A forced reduction of $255.8 million in the budget probably would require deep cuts in appropriations for schools and for police, fire, sanitation, library and other services.

The court test, to be argued in Brooklyn Supreme Court before Justice Frank J. Pino, will seek to make permanent a temporary restraining order issued July 2 by Supreme Court Justice Mark A. Costantino prohibiting the city from borrowing the budget-balancing funds.

The borrowing is being chal-

Continued on Page 24, Column 1

LASKER TO DIRECT LINDSAY FINANCES

Broker Will Try to Raise $1.5 Million for Race

By RICHARD L. MADDEN

After a two-month search, Representative John V. Lindsay announced the appointment yesterday of his campaign finance chairman—Bernard J. Lasker, a stockbroker who has raised nearly $50 million for civic and charitable causes.

Asked if he thought he would be successful in raising the $1.5 million that Mr. Lindsay has said would be needed to wage a citywide campaign for Mayor, Mr. Lasker said:

"I hope to God that the feuding I've been reading about between Javits and Rockefeller is not true. If it is true, it makes my job an impossible one."

Mr. Lasker's reference was to persistent reports of a rift between Senator Jacob K. Javits, who is Mr. Lindsay's campaign chairman, and Governor Rockefeller.

Senator Javits has declared there is "no feud" with Mr. Rockefeller. The Senator has said he will support Mr. Rockefeller if he runs for re-

Continued on Page 17, Column 1

NEWS INDEX

PRESIDENT, ON TV, DELIVERS EULOGY

Says Stevenson Illuminated Dreams of Entire World

Texts of Johnson statements appear on Page 12.

By JOHN D. POMFRET
Special to The New York Times

WASHINGTON, July 14 — With tears in his eyes, President Johnson mourned Adlai E. Stevenson today as "the flame which illuminated the dreams and expectations of an entire world."

The President read his nationally televised tribute from the basement theater at the White House.

He announced that he was sending Vice President Humphrey to London at the head of a delegation of distinguished Americans to bring Mr. Stevenson's body back to the United States on a Presidential jet. The plane carrying the delegation left tonight.

The President ordered flags to be flown at half-staff on all public buildings in the United States and at half-mast on all American ships at sea.

Earlier Secretary of State Dean Rusk had telephoned Bill D. Moyers, the President's press secretary, with word of Mr. Stevenson's collapse. Mr. Moyers relayed the information to the President.

Mr. Rusk then went to the White House for a luncheon the President was giving for Japanese Cabinet members here to discuss trade and other economic problems with United States officials. The Secretary

Continued on Page 12, Column 4

2 Bogalusa Pleas Given to Johnson

By ROY REED
Special to The New York Times

BOGALUSA, La., July 14—Both sides in the Bogalusa racial conflict appealed to President Johnson for help today.

Telegrams were sent to the White House from the Mayor and City Council and from the president of the Bogalusa Civic and Voters League, which is associated with the Congress of Racial Equality in the civil rights movement here.

At the State Capitol in Baton Rouge, Gov. John J. McKeithen, who was rebuffed yesterday when he asked the Negro leaders to call a 30-day moratorium on demonstrations, met today with 20 Louisiana Negro leaders. The announced purpose was to continue to try to find a solution to Bogalusa's racial problems.

The state government started a program of riot-control train-

Continued on Page 26, Column 3

Stevenson Dies at 65 in London

2 FAIL IN ATTEMPT AT RESUSCITATION

Mrs. Tree, Walking With Him, Gets Doctor—Heart Attack Assumed Cause of Death

Continued From Page 1, Col. 8

States from many sources to take a public position inconsistent with that of my Government," he said.

"Actually," he went on, "I don't agree with those protestants. My hope in Vietnam is that resistance there may establish the fact that changes in Asia are not to be precipitated by outside force."

Last Monday Mr. Stevenson talked with British and American journalists for more than an hour. To some there seemed to be in him an undertone of unhappiness about aspects of American foreign policy, perhaps especially over the Dominion affair. But he said nothing directly critical of the President or his policy.

High-Spirited at Party

At a party last night in the embassy he was as gay as ever, and he looked a little leaner and more fit, if anything, than in recent years. At a dinner party afterward, one person said "He went up the stairs like a bird."

The embassy affair was a reception given by Mr. and Mrs. Bruce for Robert G. Kaiser, who married Hannah Joplin this morning. Mr. Kaiser is the son of Philip M. Kaiser, the American Minister here and a friend of Mr. Stevenson.

A rumor last week had it that he was thinking of remarrying. Asked about that, he called the story a "happy exaggeration" and said he intended to keep his marital status unchanged.

His humor, which helped win him a strong personal following in the United States among those he christened "eggheads," also endeared him to the British.

They loved the skepticism and self-doubt that hurt him politically at home. They took to him right away in his first try for the Presidency, in 1952, and could never really understand why so intelligent and sympathetic a man was not elected.

Tonight the Foreign Secretary issued an official statement expressing the Government's sympathy. It spoke of Mr. Stevenson's "liberality of mind and lucidity of expression."

Remembered for His Qualities

"He will be remembered not only for what he did and what he stood for," the statement said, "but for the tolerant, humane way he acted.

"He will never be forgotten as a man because he was so much an individual, so humorous, so considerate and so firm and yet so gentle."

The Times of London, in an editorial, appraised the place of Mr. Stevenson in broader terms. It called him a "tragic figure" in American history "who was a prophet before his time, who received honor but not power" and who "died full of disappointments."

"Yet his life has left a mark that will not be eradicated," the editorial said. "Abroad he came to represent that aspect of his country that most sustains foreign confidence in the fundamental virtue of its intentions even when its actions seem wrong."

"Through all the placid confidence of the Eisenhower era and the clumsy crusades of Mr. Dulles, he reminded the world that there was another America — sensitive, self-critical, thoughtful and visionary. At home he kept the light of intellect burning through a period when it was not fashionable to think," The Times of London said.

Near the embassy this evening small groups of Americans stood talking dazedly about Mr. Stevenson. Within the embassy there were some tears.

For a candidate twice badly defeated for the Presidency, this reaction emphasized that he was a man with unusual appeal. He had had a significant effect on the Democratic party, bringing into it a new breed of postwar, middle-class liberal.

His national following arose suddenly in 1952. It really began with the extraordinarily literate welcoming speech he made, as Governor of Illinois, to the Democratic convention in Chicago.

As a candidate he said he would "talk sense to the American people." He warned that there was "no easy road."

In defeat he struck sympathetic chords again. He said on election night in 1952 that he was reminded of the Lincoln story about the boy who stubbed his toe — "He said he was too old to cry, but it hurt too much to laugh."

Then, at length, the self-doubt that won him intellectual hearts helped cost him power. At the 1960 convention in Los Angeles his failure to make up his mind whether to be a candidate hurt him badly. The transition of the Democratic party was over, and it moved on to the more affirmative style of another skeptic, John F. Kennedy.

In a message to President Johnson Prime Minister Wilson said: "I should like to send you this personal message to say how much we have been shocked at the sudden death of Adlai Stevenson. He was a personal friend of mine over many years and I never visited the United States without going to see him."

An unconfirmed medical report was that Mr. Stevenson had suffered a coronary thrombosis, a massive blockage of the arteries near the heart. Friends said that he had had no history of heart defect.

The body was expected to remain at the hospital tonight. An embassy spokesman said no plans would be made until the delegation sent by President Johnson arrives tomorrow.

Mr. Stevenson is survived by three sons, Adlai E. 3d, of Chicago; Borden, of New York; and John Fell, of San Francisco; a sister, Mrs. Ernest Ives of Bloomington, Ill., and five grandchildren. The grandchildren are the four children of Adlai 3d — Adlai 4th, Lucy Wallace, Katherine Randolph and Warwick Lewis Stevenson —and John Fell Jr., born last Feb. 9.

A Wish by Stevenson To Retire Is Reported

A television newsman who chatted privately with Adlai E. Stevenson two days before his death said yesterday that the United States representative at the United Nations wanted to quit his post but was not sure how or when to tell President Johnson.

Eric Sevareid, a correspondent for the Columbia Broadcasting System, said on a broadcast that on the same night he and Mr. Stevenson talked at the United States Embassy.

"He grew visibly tired during the conversation, not all of which I feel at liberty to repeat," Mr. Sevareid said. "What was important was that he wanted to resign from the U.N. post. He thought he had had it long enough.

He did not wish to take another Government job, Mr. Sevareid added.

Right Man, Wrong Time

Continued From Page 1, Col. 7

General should win. Was it not time, he asked, for the Republicans to come to power after 20 years of Democratic rule? Was it not true that the absence of power, as well as the exercise of power, tended to corrupt?

Would not General Eisenhower finally lead his party away from its isolationist tradition, and was this not good for the country?

Later he changed, but this objective quality of mind in Mr. Stevenson was precisely why he was so respected by the intellectual and diplomatic communities, and why at the same time he was so unpopular with the most political elements of his own party.

His disappointments came later. He wanted to be Secretary of State more than he expected to be President, but both Mr. Kennedy and Mr. Johnson passed him over for the job, and while they listened politely and often reluctantly to his advice, they did not follow it—or at least, he died believing that they were more interested in power and politics and did not agree with him about Vietnam, or the Dominican Republic, or the importance of the spirit of the United Nations.

Talked About Resigning

He talked many times about resigning, from the Bay of Pigs to the bombardment of North Vietnam, but at the same time he loved the stir and prominence of public life, he hated "scenes," and could not quite bring himself to the point of getting out.

Mr. Stevenson was not bitter about not being President or Secretary of State. He was too full of self-doubt and even self-mockery for that. It was not his ambition but his pride that was affronted by what he thought was the rejection of his advice to rely more on United States moral than military power.

For example, he wanted President Johnson to reassure the United Nations that the United States wanted to end the legal dispute over financing the United Nations, but the President rejected his advice only a few days ago and exhorted the United Nations merely to follow American policy.

The tragedy of Adlai Stevenson, however, is not that the United States has lost a representative at the United Nations, but that the Western world has lost another of its few eloquent men.

Language is power, and in the last few years the West has lost most of the men who could define its purposes—Churchill and Gaitskell in Britain, Kennedy in the United States, Hammarskjold at the United Nations, Nehru in India, not to mention those spokesmen of the Western literary world, Frost, Faulkner and T. S. Eliot.

Maybe Mr. Stevenson's critics were right—he may have been primarily a writer and a public speaker, rather than a political leader.

But as Churchill proved, speaking and writing are important in politics, and the only one now left with the gift of articulation in the West is de Gaulle, who is using his eloquence, not on behalf of Western civilization, but on behalf of the French alone.

Even after he was nominated for the Presidency at the Democratic convention in Chicago in 1952, his doubts and his eloquence were apparent:

"I would not seek your nomination for the Presidency," he said, "because the burdens of the office stagger the imagination. Its potential for good or evil now and in the years of our lives, smothers exultation and converts vanity to prayer.

"I have asked the Merciful Father—the Father of us all—to let this cup pass from me. But from such dread responsibilities one does not shrink in fear, in self-interest, or in false humility.

"So, if this cup may not pass from me, except I drink it, Thy Will be done."

Power of Expression

Yet at that same convention, he startled the delegates by his power of expression in his welcome to Chicago:

"Here on the prairies of the Middle West," he said, "we can see a long way in all directions. We look to east, to west, to north and south. Our commerce, our ideas, come and go in all directions. Here there are no barriers, no defenses to ideas and aspirations. We want no shackles on the mind or the spirit, no rigid pattern of thought, no iron conformity. We want only the faith and conviction that triumph in free and fair contests."

When he was defeated he summed up the spirit that endeared him to the people he admired the most in these words:

"Looking back, I am content. Win or lose I have told you the truth, as I see it. I have said what I meant and meant what I said. I have not done as well as I should like to have done, but I have done my best, frankly and forthrightly; no man can do more and you are entitled to no less."

Adlai Ewing Stevenson: An Urbane, Witty, Articulate Politician and Diplomat

2 DEFEATS SERVED TO ADD TO STATURE

He Won World-Wide Praise in 4 Years at the U.N. as Debater and Negotiator

Adlai Ewing Stevenson was a rarity in American public life, a cultivated, urbane, witty, articulate politician whose popularity was untarnished by defeat and whose stature grew in diplomacy.

He graced the Presidential campaigns of 1952 and 1956, and his eloquence and his wit won him the devoted admiration of millions of Americans.

In more than four years as the nation's chief spokesman at the United Nations, he gained the same sort of admiration from the world statesmen for his ready tongue, his sharp mind and his patience in dealing with the grave issues that confronted the world organization.

As chief United States delegate, with the rank of Ambassador, Mr. Stevenson was in the thick of debate and negotiations during the Bay of Pigs and Cuban missile crises, disarmament talks, upheavals in the Congo, the war in South Vietnam and the revolt in Santa Domingo.

One of Mr. Stevenson's greatest satisfactions was the signing in 1963 of the treaty banning all but underground testing of nuclear devices. He was a member of the United States delegation that traveled to Moscow to sign the document.

When he ran for the Presidency in 1956, Mr. Stevenson suggested a world agreement to ban the testing of hydrogen bombs. It was attacked by the Republicans at the time as visionary, and it may have hurt his campaign.

TV Would Show Him Intent During Council Sessions

During television coverage of Security Council debates, Mr. Stevenson's tanned, freckled and balding head was a familiar sight as he sat at the Council's horseshoe-shaped table. He looked intent as he crouched over the table to listen to the remarks of another delegate.

But he relaxed when it came his turn to speak. His words flowed easily and steadily in a voice that, for its precision and diction, reminded some of Ronald Coleman, the movie actor.

His logic and his words could be corruscating, as when he was disputing Soviet spokesmen or they could take wings of idealism, as when he was expounding the importance of the United Nations as the keeper of the world's peace.

However much Mr. Stevenson might berate the Soviet Union at the council table, he refrained from banal personalities. The result was that he was on good social terms with the Soviet diplomats, as he was with those of other countries whose views he found more congenial.

Mr. Stevenson was appointed to his United Nations post in 1961 by President Kennedy and reconfirmed in the job by President Johnson. The appointment came in response not only to Mr. Stevenson's deep knowledge of foreign affairs but also to the pressure from influential Democrats who had backed Mr. Stevenson for the Presidential nomination in 1960.

Mr. Stevenson held Cabinet rank, but there were indications that his role as a policy-maker was limited. In the Bay of Pigs crisis in 1961 he suffered grave embarrassment in Security Council debates because the White House had not briefed him truthfully on the United States involvement in the invasion of Cuba by Cuban exiles. It was a measure of his popularity in the diplomatic community that he recovered from that incident with little loss of prestige.

There was some hint that Mr. Stevenson was less than ecstatic about his United Nations re-

(continued)

sponsibilities.

"This job has been a terrible drill," he told Martin Mayer in an interview earlier this year for an article in The New York Times Magazine.

"In my own life I've been accustomed to making policy," he continued. "I've sometimes been a little restless in this role of executing and articulating the policies of others.

"There is a disadvantage in being anywhere other than the seat of power. And every issue that comes to the U. N. has its antecedents before it gets here. The State Department has been involved in the negotiations, and now the situation has become insoluable, so it gets dumped onto us."

Mr. Stevenson also expressed the belief that he had become "an old and familiar face" at the United Nations headquarters building in New York.

"You take on the coloration of your country, your country's face, and you become predictable," he said adding:

"You lose some of the rosy glow you brought with you. Apart from my taste for creative aspects, the time comes when you should bring in a fresh face and a new outlook."

Despite these reservations, M Stevenson, with his Hamlet-like ability to state another proposition, said that "it's easy to reconcile a sense of duty with this job." He conceded that his decisions had "always come about more by circumstances and events than by conscious calculation."

As a diplomat, Mr. Stevenson put in punishing hours. Most days he was on the go from an appointment at 8:15 A. M. to well after midnight.

After an official working day, he would go on the cocktail-party-and-dinner circuit for the rest of the evening—social duties that his post required of him. In these he had a truly awesome stamina, for he was as eruditely charming late at night as he had been at breakfast.

A good part of Mr. Stevenson's charm rested in his ability to discuss himself without pomposity. Although he was badly beaten for the Presidency by Dwight D. Eisenhower in 1952 and 1956, he was not bitter. Talking to a group of volunteers after his defeat in 1956, he said:

"To you who are disappointed tonight, let me confess that I am too. . . . Be of good cheer and remember, my dear friends, that a wise man said: 'A merry heart doeth good like a medicine but a broken spirit dryeth the bones.'"

Mr. Stevenson, although he dressed well, was not happy as a fashion plate. As Governor of Illinois he preferred to work in his office in a brown tweed sports jacket, odd trousers and a striped shirt. His favorite footgear then was a pair of old golf shoes with the spikes removed.

His predeliction for informal attire was not only a matter of personal comfort, but also an expression of the fact that, although he was well-to-do, he was not a conspicuous spender.

During his gubernatorial term, which began in 1949, he purchased only one new suit. A hole in his shoe, which was a trademark of his White House campaign in 1952, was another example of his frugality.

After his defeat in 1956 Mr. Stevenson practiced law and traveled extensively on business, visiting more than 30 countries. On one trip he spent three weeks in the Soviet Union and had a long conversation with the then Premier, Nikita S. Khrushchev.

Although Mr. Stevenson had chided General Eisenhower in 1956 as "a part-time President", and had been critical of the Eisenhower foreign policy, the President appointed him consultant to the Secretary of State in preparation for a meeting of the North Atlantic Treaty Organization's council in Paris.

In 1960 many liberals and intellectuals in the Democratic party urged him to seek the Presidential nomination. He was then, as he had been in 1952 and 1956, the idol of the eggheads, men and women who were not ashamed to confess to a college education and to ideas more profound than those ordinarily passed at the bridge table.

Stevenson with his grandfather, Adlai E. Stevenson, after whom he was named, when the latter was running unsuccessfully for the Vice Presidency on the ticket headed by William Jennings Bryan.

Adlai, foreground, poses with his father Lewis G. Stevenson and his sister Elizabeth.

Professional politicians, however, were less enthusiastic, because he seemed reluctant to work with them and because they thought he talked over the heads of his audiences.

Mr. Stevenson vacillated, and it was not until the last minute that he agreed to let his name be placed before the convention. By then, it was too late. He got the applause of the gallery while Mr. Kennedy reaped the delegates' votes.

Some of Mr. Stevenson's ambivalence toward politics sprang from a feeling that gladhanding was a species of hokum. He expressed this sentiment to an old friend after one hard day of handshaking in the 1952 campaign in these words:

"Perhaps the saddest part of all this is that a candidate must reach into a sea of hands, grasp one, not knowing whose it is, and say, 'I'm glad to meet you,' realizing that he hasn't and probably never will meet that man."

When he went into the 1952 campaign, Mr. Stevenson was virtually unknown nationally, but in the election he polled more than 27 million votes, a surprising figure. However, this won him only 89 electoral votes as General Eisenhower swamped him with nearly 34 million popular votes and 442 in the Electoral College.

The Democratic candidate emerged from the campaign with the grudging respect of many Republicans for the quality of his speeches—he wrote most of them himself—and for his good manners.

For all his politeness and his patrician birth and education, Mr. Stevenson became, after 1952, one of the hardest-hitting adversaries of the late Senator Joseph R. McCarthy, Republican of Wisconsin, a notable exponent of jugular-vein politics.

Moreover, Mr. Stevenson turned into an articulate spokesman for internationalism and an active titular leader of his party.

To the shallowness of practical politics, he added a philosophy of liberalism that was almost Jeffersonian in its literate defense of the rights of the individual, its educated revulsion against mob-inflaming demagoguery.

"When demagoguery and deceit become a national political movement," he asserted, "we Americans are in trouble; not just Democrats, but all of us."

Genial, with a touch of shyness, this product of Princeton, Harvard and Northwestern University seemed so out of place in practical politics that a more seasoned politician tutoring him for active campaigning recalled, "Godawmighty, we almost had to tear off the starched dickeys and the Homburg hat he used to wear."

Trained to the law and diplomacy, he was a realist at dealing with essential political compromise. But when moved deeply by principle he risked political sabotage and personal obloquy for his convictions.

Thus, during 1952, when he was asked why, in 1949, he had signed an affidavit speaking well of the reputation of Alger Hiss, later convicted of perjury, Mr. Stevenson replied:

"I am a lawyer. I think that one of the most fundamental responsibilities, not only of every citizen, but particularly of lawyers, is to give testimony in a court of law, to give it honestly and willingly, and it will be a very unhappy day for Anglo-Saxon justice when a man, even a man in public life, is too timid to state what he knows and what he has heard about a defendant in a criminal trial for fear that defendant might be convicted. That would to me be the ultimate timidity."

On July 25, 1952, what was described as the first "open" Democratic National Convention in 20 years nominated Mr. Stevenson as its Presidential candidate and Senator John J. Sparkman of Alabama as his running mate. They opposed General Eisenhower and the then Senator Richard M. Nixon of California.

Mr. Stevenson, then Governor of Illinois had insisted repeatedly that he would "rather not" be President. He was quoted as having said that he was not fitted mentally, temperamentally or physically for the office.

The Stevenson boom began in the spring of 1952, after he had visited President Truman in Washington. But keeping outwardly aloof from the scramble for convention delegates, he refused to identify himself as a candidate down to the moment the voting began.

In his acceptance speech to the convention the candidate told the cheering delegates:

"Sacrifice, patience, understanding and implacable purpose may be our lot for years to come. Let's face it. Let's talk sense to the American people."

His candor cost him many votes. On the question of who should receive the benefit of royalties from offshore oil deposits, he took his stand with President Truman that the Federal Government had "paramount rights" in the deposits. This cost him much support in Texas, Florida and Virginia.

He refused to take a stand in favor of continuing discrimination against Negro citizens, which antagonized "white supremacy" elements in the Democratic party in the South. At the same time his firm belief in states' rights and responsibilities cost him some Negro votes.

Among other issues that influenced the vote substantially were corruption in Washington, Communist infiltration, the Korean war, high taxes and the high cost of living, fear of inflation and the growth of Federal centralism. These were pressed by Republican campaigners.

But the greatest obstacle to Mr. Stevenson's success was the popularity of his opponent.

Analyses of the vote indicated that although labor had gone solidly for Mr. Stevenson and although he had retained much of the farm vote, he had lost the support of women voters and particularly the so-called independent voters of both sexes.

But the strength of Mr. Stevenson's candidacy was shown in the fact that under circumstances that should have produced an overwhelming Republican landslide—a popular candidate, popular issues and an incumbent Administration whose party had been in power for 20 years—the Democratic candidate rolled up 3,000,000 more votes than were received by President Truman in 1948 in his victory over Thomas E. Dewey.

With the 1952 election over, Mr. Stevenson took the role of Opposition leader, although he admitted that he envied one man the Governor of Illinois.

His first speech and a four-day visit to Washington rallied nearly all Democrats to his side. He received such an admiring welcome from the jubilant Republicans at the capital that political opponents jested that he could not have been feted more if his candidacy had been successful.

Part of the tribute arose because he took immediate steps to heal the wounds of the bitter phases of the campaign and did

(continued)

Stevenson and his sons (left to right) Adlai Ewing III, John Fell and Borden in 1950.

what he could to rally his fellow Democrats behind the incoming President.

During the visit, Mr. Stevenson met with Democratic leaders and mapped plans to unite the party in opposition. He also conferred with leaders of the Republican Administration about his plans for a nonpolitical world tour, covering particularly the Far East.

On the five-month tour he talked with leading figures and studied conditions in Korea, Malaya, Burma, India and the then Indochina, as well as in various European countries. He said the real purpose of his tour had been self-education.

Mr. Stevenson underwent a kidney stone operation in Chicago in April, 195[illegible]. A month later it was reported that he had completely recovered.

Taking a vigorous part in the bitter Congressional election campaign of 1954, he hammered in his speeches at the three principal issues of foreign policy, domestic economy and internal security. This confirmed him as his party's chief national spokesman. The Democratic victory in the elections made him the leading contender for the 1956 Presidential nomination.

He Said Republican Party Was 'Half McCarthy'

His attacks on the Republicans concentrated on the influence of Senator McCarthy. The Republican party, he charged, had become "half McCarthy and half Eisenhower" and Vice President Nixon the principal Republican campaigner he accused of preaching "McCarthyism in a white collar."

Mr. Nixon declared that Mr. Stevenson had "not changed since he testified for Alger Hiss," and he accused Mr. Stevenson of unconsciously having spread Communist propaganda.

After the election of 1954 Mr. Stevenson announced that he was returning to the private practice of law in Chicago. "I have done what I could for the Democratic party for the past two years," he said, "and now I shall have to be less active and give more attention to my own affairs."

Mr. Stevenson was admitted to practice before the United States Supreme Court and was engaged by the Radio Corporation of America to defend it in a $16,000,000 antitrust suit. He lost the first two legal skirmishes of the case.

He still kept in touch with political and foreign affairs, however. In April, 1955, after a long Democratic silence, he made a national radio address opposing the defense of the Chinese Nationalist islands of Quemoy and Matsu. He also called for a joint declaration by the United States and its Allies pledging united defense of Taiwan pending its final disposition.

Although Mr. Stevenson repeatedly refused to say whether he would be a candidate for the Presidential nomination in 1956, he had won the support of the party's most influential leaders. However, many in the South who had opposed him in 1952 still did so.

In sharp contrast with his preconvention attitude of indifference toward the 1952 nomination, Mr. Stevenson quickly jumped into the fight for the 1956 nomination. He formally announced his candidacy on Nov. 15, 1955.

Moderation was the keynote of his campaign, particularly with respect to enforcement of the Supreme Court's decision abolishing racial segregation in public schools, but generally with respect to all issues, foreign and domestic.

Mr. Stevenson took an early lead in the race for the nomination. The support of political organizations in large-population states gave him an imposing list of delegate strength. However, he suffered setbacks in early 1956 state primaries, where Senator Estes Kefauver of Tennessee showed surprising popular support.

These reverses stimulated Mr. Stevenson to more aggressive tactics. Instead of holding aloof from the crowds, he began to make hand-shaking tours asking the voters for support. As the primaries continued, he began to fare better, and by May the political observers seemed to agree that he had reversed th tide, which then appeared to be running in his direction.

Mr. Stevenson's campaign managers from the beginning claimed victory for him. They asserted that more delegates had been pledged to him than the majority necessary to nominate at the Democratic National Convention.

In 1952 Mr. Stevenson had surrounded himself largely with "amateurs," but in the 1956 campaign he put more emphasis on practical politics in choosing top aides at his Chicago campaign headquarters.

He pitched his early campaign speeches to a vigorous attack on President Eisenhower's foreign policy. Whenever possible he ignored his Democratic opponents for the nomination, and sought to draw the issue from the beginning as Stevenson versus Eisenhower.

In the election, he was defeated by a greater margin than in 1952, polling 26 million popular votes to more than 35.5 million by President Eisenhower. The Electoral College figures were 73 to 457.

His Father Was Executive Of Hearst Enterprises

Mr. Stevenson was born on Feb. 5, 1900, in Los Angeles, where his father, Lewis Green Stevenson, was at the time an executive of Hearst newspapers, mining and ranching properties. His family roots went back to the pre-Revolutionary War period.

He was a grandson and namesake of a Vice President of the United States—the Adlai Stevenson who held the office in the second term of Grover Cleveland's Administration. Through his mother, he was a fifth-generation Illinoisan, a grandson of Jesse Fell, who was the first to propose Abraham Lincoln for the Presidency.

When Adlai was 6 years old, the family moved back to their home town of Bloomington, Ill., where Mrs. Stevenson's family owned The Daily Pantagraph. Adlai's father later became State Secretary for Illinois and, from 1914 to 1917, served as chairman of the State Board of Pardons.

Mr. Stevenson went to the Choate Preparatory School, Wallingford, Conn., and Princeton University, from which he was graduated in 1922. He was managing editor of The Daily Princetonian.

After leaving Princeton, Mr. Stevenson went to Harvard Law School for two years. He got passing marks but was disinterested in his studies.

A legal case that evolved from the death of an uncle redistributed shares in The Pantagraph between members of the family. As a result Mr. Stevenson and his cousin, Davis C. Merwin, decided they would learn the newspaper business.

Mr. Stevenson spent a couple of years on the paper in various editorial posts, but by the time the courts had ruled that the Stevenson and Merwin families should have equal shares of ownership, his interest in becoming a newspaper editor had waned.

He decided to finish his law course and, having fallen a year behind his classmates, who already had been graduated from Harvard, he entered the law school of Northwestern University. He received his law degree in 1926.

Soon after his graduation, he settled in Chicago to practice law.

In December, 1928, Mr. Stevenson married Ellen Borden of Chicago. Her father, a socialite and financier who made the first of several fortunes as a colleague of John Hertz in the Yellow Cab Company, later became active in mining in St. Louis.

The Stevensons were divorced in 1949. His wife was said to abhor politics and to have wished to devote herself to the world of art and literature. No other person and no scandal were involved in the legal proceedings, held in Las Vegas, Nev.

The couple had three sons, Adlai Ewing III, Borden and John Fell.

Soon after the 1952 Presidential boom started for Mr. Stevenson, he was approached by a would-be biographer. The man told the Governor he was going to write a book about him.

"I don't see how you are going to do it," Mr. Stevenson said. "My life has been hopelessly undramatic. I wasn't born in a log cabin. I didn't work my way through school nor did I rise from rags to riches, and there's no use trying to pretend I did. I'm not a Wilkie and I don't claim to be a simple, barefoot La Salle Street lawyer. You might be able to write about some of my ancestors. They accomplished quite a lot at one time or another but you can't do anything much about me. At least, I'd hate to have to try it."

Mr. Stevenson had laid the groundwork for his political career by public service that began in 1933, when he first went to Washington as one of the many bright young lawyers President Franklin D. Roosevelt had summoned to help formulate the New Deal.

For two years, Mr. Stevenson was special counsel to the Agricultural Adjustment Administration, touring the country, holding hearings and advising regional groups of farmers, ranchers, orchardists and dairymen how to utilize the measure and then returning to Washington to try to work out marketing agreements.

At the end of the two years he went back to private law practice in Chicago. He served as president for one term of the Chicago Council on Foreign Relations—a post in which he got considerable experience as an after-dinner speaker—and he also became Chicago chairman of the William Allen White Committee to Defend America by Aiding the Allies.

Mr. Stevenson brought people like Wendell Willkie, Carl Sandburg and Dorothy Thompson to address meetings, one of which, in 1941, filled the Chicago Stadium. In the summer of that years the late Frank Knox, then Secretary of the Navy and a close friend of Mr. Stevenson's, telephoned.

Mr. Stevenson later quoted Mr. Knox as saying, "Everyone else around Washington has a lawyer and I guess I ought to have one too."

He was in Washington within a few days, starting to prepare legal machinery whereby the Navy, in case it became necessary, could take over the strike-bound Kearny shipyards in New Jersey, then building essential warships. He continued to do similar legal work for the Navy Department until 1943, when he led a mission to Italy to plan occupation policies.

Later he served as an assistant to Secretaries of State Edward Stettinius and James Byrnes. He also was a representative to the San Francisco United Nations Conference, and then was an aide to the United States delegation in the United Nations General Assembly.

At the meeting of the General Assembly held in London in January, 1946, Mr. Stevenson was senior adviser to the American delegation. He resigned after the session ended in March, but President Truman appointed him alternate delegate to the second session that fall.

Mr. Stevenson returned to Chicago in 1947. His friends backed him as a "clean-up" candidate against the Republican administration of Gov. Dwight W. Green,

Winning the backing of Jacob M. Arvey, chairman of the Cook County Democratic Committee, Mr. Stevenson was nominated for Governor. Paul Douglas, then Professor of Economics at Chicago University, was named for Senator.

The Democratic "clean-up," team swept into office, Mr. Stevenson defeating Mr. Green by 572,000 votes, while President Truman was nosing out Thomas E. Dewey in Illinois by a mere 34,000. The self-styled "amateur" in politics consecrated his Government in an inaugural address to "plain talk, hard work and prairie horse sense."

Drive on Gambling Listed Among Acts as Governor

During his term in office Mr. Stevenson was credited with the following accomplishments:

¶He sent state policemen to stamp out commercial gambling downstate when local officials failed to act.

¶He lopped off 1,300 non-working politicians from the state payroll.

¶He set up a merit system in the state police force that ended the system of politically preferential appointments.

¶He increased state aid to school districts.

¶He started a broad road improvement program that included enforcement of truck-weight limits, a higher gasoline tax and increased truck licenses to pay construction costs.

¶He overhauled the state's welfare program, placing it on a merit basis and forcing financially able relatives to pay for the care of patients.

¶He streamlined the state Government by pushing through 78 reform measures.

Stevenson addressing the UN General Assembly in 1961.

Stevenson with Eleanor Roosevelt during the 1956 presidential campaign.

"All the News That's Fit to Print"

The New York Times.

LATE CITY EDITION

U. S. Weather Bureau Report (Page 69) forecasts: Partly cloudy, milder today; chance of rain tonight or tomorrow. Temp. range: 68—52; yesterday: 58—41.

VOL. CXI . No. 37,904. NEW YORK, FRIDAY, NOVEMBER 3, 1961. 10 cents beyond 50-mile zone from New York City except on Long Island. Higher in air delivery cities. FIVE CENTS

PRESIDENT TAKES STEPS TO PREPARE FOR TESTING IN AIR

Says He Will Approve Atom Blasts if Needed to Hold U. S. Lead in Weapons

MOSCOW IS DENOUNCED

Kennedy Terms Resumption of Program 'Irresponsible' —Truman at Meeting

Text of President's statement will be found on Page 2.

By JOHN W. FINNEY
Special to The New York Times.

WASHINGTON, Nov. 2—President Kennedy ordered today that preparations be made for the resumption of atmospheric atomic tests that might be found necessary to maintain United States superiority in nuclear weapons.

However, the President did not give approval at this time on conducting tests in the atmosphere. Such approval, he said, will be given only if an evaluation of the latest Soviet test series shows that the United States must conduct some tests in the atmosphere "to maintain our responsibilities to free world security."

[The Political Committee of the United Nations General Assembly approved a resolution asking the atomic powers to refrain from nuclear testing. The measure was opposed by the United States, Britain and the Soviet Union.]

U. S. 'Prudence' Stressed

"As a matter of prudence," the President said, "the United States will make the necessary preparations for atmospheric tests so as to be ready in case it becomes necessary to conduct them."

Although the evaluation of the Soviet tests has not been completed, the President emphasized that the United States held a superior position on defense.

"In terms of total military strength," he said, "the United States would not trade places with any nation on earth. We have taken major steps in the past year to maintain our lead —and we do not propose to lose it.

"It is essential to the defense of the free world that we maintain this relative position," President Kennedy said. It was for this reason, he said, that he was ordering advance preparations for atmospheric tests. A

Continued on Page 2, Column 2

TRADERS FORESEE BATTLE ON TARIFF

Plans for a Freer Policy Get Wide Support Here

By BRENDAN M. JONES

A difficult time in Congress was forecast by foreign traders here yesterday for the Administration's new trade policy proposals.

The plan was outlined in a speech here Wednesday by George W. Ball, Under Secretary of State for Economic Affairs. Under it, the President would be given broad powers to reduce and eliminate trade barriers, thus curbing the controls exercised by Congress and the Tariff Commission.

This would virtually end the traditional methods by which protectionists have promoted tariff restrictions—lobbying and appeals to the commission.

Mr. Ball noted that with the broad new reciprocal tariff reductions desired by the Administration a comprehensive program of Federal aid to domestic industry was contemplated.

This would include assistance and funds for channeling production into new lines, retraining and relocating workers, faster write-offs for obsolete equipment and credits for plant modernization.

Mr. Ball's presentation of Administration trade-policy proposals was made at a final dinner session of the forty-eighth National Foreign Trade Convention at the Waldorf-Astoria Hotel.

He stressed that the rapid economic expansion of the European Common Market as a free-trading and powerfully competi-

Continued on Page 18, Column 5

Congo Says Invaders Gain 35 Miles in Katanga Drive

Mobutu Reports Towns and Missions Occupied —Resistance Light

By DAVID HALBERSTAM
Special to The New York Times.

LEOPOLDVILLE, the Congo, Nov. 2—Maj. Gen. Joseph D. Mobutu, commander in chief of the Congo Army, said today that his troops had begun a general offensive against Katanga Province along a wide stretch of the Kasai-Katanga border.

He said the troops had penetrated as far as thirty-five miles into Katanga and had occupied villages and mission stations.

The troops, he said, are receiving a joyous reception from the people and are not meeting any stiff resistance. They crossed the border at several points, he added.

General Mobutu, just back from the border area, made the statements at a news conference here today. He parried one crucial question—whether this was an all-out invasion with the capture of Elisabethville as its goal.

Western observers here, are inclined to think that the Congolese are more serious about this foray into secessionist Katanga Province than about others before. But whether it can actually succeed and whether the Congolese leaders themselves really are counting on its success are different matters.

The Congolese soldiers, General Mobutu said, are planting the Congolese flag wherever they go.

The military commander reported that the troops had

Continued on Page 14, Column 4

[Map] Stanleyville · REPUBLIC OF THE CONGO · RUANDA-URUNDI · KIVU · KASAI · Luluabourg · Kongolo · Albertville · Kaniama · Kamina · KATANGA · Lake Mweru · Jadotville · ANGOLA · Elisabethville · Ndola · NORTHERN RHODESIA

The New York Times Nov. 3, 1961
Site of fighting (cross)

U.N. to Elect Thant Today To Hammarskjold's Post

By THOMAS J. HAMILTON
Special to The New York Times.

UNITED NATIONS, N. Y., Nov. 2—U Thant of Burma will be elected Acting Secretary General of the United Nations tomorrow to fill the unexpired term of the late Dag Hammarskjold. The term expires April 10, 1963.

The Security Council will meet in closed session at 11 A. M. to recommend the election of Mr. Thant.

His election by the General Assembly, which will meet at 3 P. M., will follow under arrangements completed tonight by Valerian A. Zorin, a Soviet Deputy Foreign Minister and President of the Security Council for November, and Adlai E. Stevenson, chief United States representative.

The resolution recommending the election of Mr. Thant will be introduced jointly by the United States, the Soviet Union, Ceylon, Liberia and the United Arab Republic.

Western Powers Agree

Mr. Thant met this morning with Mr. Zorin, Mr. Stevenson, Sir Patrick Dean of Britain and Armand Bérard of France to give them copies of the declaration he will make to the Assembly announcing that he will work in "a spirit of mutual understanding" with a limited number of officials, who will be his principal assistants.

These arrangements were accepted on the spot by the three Western delegates, who agreed yesterday to leave to Mr. Thant the decision on the one issue still in dispute—the number of Assistant Secretaries General

Continued on Page 6, Column 3

PARIS URGES PACT FOR WEST EUROPE

France's Partners Studying Treaty on Closer Political Ties in Common Market

By EDWIN L. DALE Jr.
Special to The New York Times.

PARIS, Oct. 31—A draft statute or treaty for a closer political union of the six nations of the European Common Market has been proposed by France and is being studied in the capitals of the five other member nations.

The proposal has not been announced and its details are still secret. It is known, however, that the aim of the plan would not be a "United States of Europe" but rather an organized system of close cooperation, particularly on foreign affairs, among sovereign nations. Nevertheless, its adoption would mark an important step toward European unity.

France, it is understood, would like to present Britain with a political "accomplished fact"—that is, to have the political aspect of the European Economic Community, or Common Market, settled before rather than after Britain joins the grouping. Britain's application for membership was submitted recently.

The French proposal is the outcome of a decision in principle by the heads of government of the six nations last summer to "give form and body to the will for political unity" already expressed in the economic treaties that join them. The other nations are West Germany, Italy, Belgium, the

Continued on Page 18, Column 3

Roa's Sister-in-Law Seeks U. S. Asylum

Special to The New York Times.

WASHINGTON, Nov. 2—Sara Kouri Barreto, sister-in-law of Dr. Raul Roa, Cuban Foreign Minister, requested political asylum in the United States today.

The 25-year-old Señorita Kouri had served since Aug. 9 as the secretary of Carlos M. Lechuga, the Cuban representative in the Organization of American States in Washington. From September, 1959, until she came here early in August, she was the private secretary of Dr. Roa at the Foreign Ministry in Havana.

Señorita Kouri has been living in the Cuban Embassy building on Sixteenth Street here. She left the premises yesterday morning despite urgings by Cuban diplomats that she reconsider her decision.

In the last few days Dr. Roa

Continued on Page 11, Column 4

James Thurber Is Dead at 66; Writer Was Also Comic Artist

Created Walter Mitty—His Stories and Drawings Long Appeared in New Yorker

James Thurber, the writer and humorist, died of pneumonia yesterday afternoon at Doctors Hospital, where he had undergone surgery a month ago for a blood clot on the brain. His age was 66.

The blind author took a turn for the worse yesterday morning and went into a coma, a hospital spokesman said.

Mr. Thurber will be best remembered for his hilarious tales, his indescribable dogs and his unforgettable character, Walter Mitty.

His tales were mingled with the exploits of unicorns, enraged wives, stupid athletes and excitable relatives. His drawings of dogs, which he produced with abundance on the backs of envelopes, in telephone books and on tablecloths, had a quality that seemed to link them with no other beast on earth.

When the late Harold Ross, editor of The New Yorker magazine, was criticized for keeping on his staff "a fifth-rate artist like Thurber," he replied loyally:

"You're wrong; Thurber is a third-rate artist."

William Shawn, editor of The

The New York Times
James Thurber

New Yorker, yesterday called Mr. Thurber "a master among comic artists, one of the great American writers of our time, and one of the few great humorists in all literary history."

"By the time he died," Mr. Shawn said, "his writings and drawings were loved by millions of people throughout the world."

Walter Mitty, of course, towered above all others in the Thurber carnival. The story,

Continued on Page 35, Column 2

MAYOR PROMISES TO PROTECT FLOW OF MILK INTO CITY

Says Municipal Trucks May Be Used—He Will Conduct Negotiations Personally

By STANLEY LEVEY

Mayor Wagner announced last night that the city would guarantee that properly inspected milk could be brought into New York—with police protection if necessary.

In a firm, almost grim, ten-minute television talk the Mayor said the strike by three locals of the International Brotherhood of Teamsters against several hundred dealers here and on Long Island "must be settled with dispatch."

At 2:35 A. M. today he said he had called both (sides) to a negotiating session for 10 A. M.

"I will direct the meeting," Mr. Wagner said angrily, "and they will stay there until I let them out."

Mr. Wagner said the employers would offer new proposals.

Impact Lessens

The Mayor made his TV talk on the ninth day of the walkout, whose impact has gradually lessened. Yesterday, in fact, an industry spokesman estimated the city was getting 20 per cent of its normal daily supply and that Long Island was receiving better than a third.

Mr. Wagner reported he had instructed the Department of Health "to arrange to inspect milk at plants outside the city of New York at whatever locations may be necessary to facilitate the flow of milk into New York."

The Mayor, who left his room at the Delmonico Hotel, where negotiations are taking place, to announce today's nonstop session, also amplified his earlier television statement on bringing milk into the city if the strike continues.

"We would be willing to supply city vehicles if we have to," the Mayor said," and we'll guarantee that they'll get through."

Unionists Send Wire

In a significant development last night a rank and file section in Local 584, the key union group in the strike, sent a telegram to the Mayor indicating it would be willing to negotiate the time-clock issue and assuring him the membership would accept the principle of an "honest count" of overtime.

The wire was regarded as important because it came from Terry Boyle, who ran for president of the local last December and was defeated by thirty-four votes.

His group, in opposition to the local leadership, headed by John Kelly, president, had demanded the inclusion of a time-clock clause in any new contract. Observers believed the development would go a long way toward opening the deadlocked negotiations on the question.

Samuel J. Cohen, counsel for Locals 584, 602 and 607 of the

Continued on Page 20, Column 3

Democratic Candidates Get Backing of President

The New York Times
President Kennedy with Mayor Wagner outside of Carlyle Hotel yesterday afternoon

United Press International Telephoto
At airport near Trenton, Mr. Kennedy is met by Gov. Robert B. Meyner, left, and Richard J. Hughes, candidate for Governor of New Jersey. Mr. Kennedy spoke at party rally.

WALKER RESIGNS FROM THE ARMY

Tells Senators He Will Push Anti-Communist Drive—May Enter Politics

Excerpts from Gen. Walker's statement are on Page 22.

By JACK RAYMOND
Special to The New York Times.

WASHINGTON, Nov. 2—Maj. Gen. Edwin A. Walker made known today his decision to resign from the Army.

He gave his reasons and assailed his critics in a written statement to the Senate Preparedness subcommittee, which has been holding hearings on Defense Department limitations upon public statements by men in uniform.

The subcommittee is scheduled to begin investigating his case Nov. 27.

The general was formally admonished and removed from command of the Twenty-fourth Infantry Division in Europe last April on charges that he had engaged in partisan political activity.

An inspector general's report said he attempted to influence the voting of his troops in the elections of 1960 through anti-Communist troop-indoctrination courses.

In his statement to the subcommittee, General Walker said his career had been destroyed.

"I must be free from the

Continued on Page 22, Column 5

Crisis on Cabinet In Bonn Worsens

By SYDNEY GRUSON
Special to The New York Times.

BONN, Germany, Nov. 2—The West German Government crisis was intensified tonight.

The Free Democratic party balked at suggested changes in the agreement for a coalition previously reached with Chancellor Adenauer, leader of the Christian Democratic Union.

The new snag, involving differences on social and economic questions, came after a day of dramatic developments. They included bitter protests by the Berlin Christian Democratic Deputies against the choice of Dr. Gernard Schroeder to succeed Dr. Heinrich von Brentano as Foreign Minister.

The Berlin members charged that Dr. Schroeder, the Minister of the Interior in the outgoing Government, was "soft" on the Berlin question and withdrew

Continued on Page 4, Column 1

De Sapio Refuses To Back Wagner; Levitt for Mayor

By RUSSELL PORTER

Carmine G. De Sapio, former leader of Tammany Hall, announced yesterday that he would not vote for Mayor Wagner next Tuesday, but would vote for other Democratic candidates.

He was opposed in his stand by Representative Charles A. Buckley, Democratic leader of the Bronx, and State Controller Arthur Levitt, the organization candidate whom Mayor Wagner defeated in the Democratic primary in September.

Both Mr. Buckley and Mr. Levitt said they would vote for the Mayor. Mr. Levitt thus reversed a position he had taken in the primary campaign when he said he would not support the Mayor if the latter won the nomination.

Mr. De Sapio, who lost control of the New York County Democratic organization in the primary, did not say which candidate for Mayor he would vote for, if any.

Charges 'Desertion'

He charged Mayor Wagner, among other things, with "deserting" the Democratic party and recommending Liberal party candidates against Democrats.

Mr. Wagner has the Liberal party as well as the Democratic party nomination for Mayor.

The Mayor has urged the election of Emilio Nunez and Gustave G. Rosenberg, both Democrats who were refused the Democratic party nominations and then were nominated by the Liberal party as candidates for Supreme Court Justice in Manhattan and the Bronx.

Michael H. Prendergast, the Democratic state chairman, issued a statement Wednesday urging the election of City Controller Lawrence E. Gerosa as Mayor. Mr. Gerosa, a Democrat, is running as an independent candidate on the Citizens party ticket.

Mr. Wagner predicted that Mr. Prendergast's support of Mr. Gerosa would have "no effect at all" on the election.

Regarding Mr. De Sapio's statement, the Mayor said:

"That's the best news I've had

Continued on Page 23, Column 1

NEWS INDEX

News Summary and Index, Page 37

PRESIDENT HAILS HUGHES IN JERSEY

Tells Rally That Candidate and He Are Committed to 'the Same Program'

Text of Kennedy's address is printed on Page 26.

By CLAYTON KNOWLES
Special to The New York Times.

TRENTON, Nov. 2—President Kennedy told an enthusiastic Democratic rally here tonight that he was proud to come to New Jersey to urge the election of Richard J. Hughes as Governor.

In his first campaign speech since he entered the White House, the President maintained that the Democratic nominee was "committed to the same progress for the United States" that he was.

"I am delighted to join him in asking support for the things in which he believes and I believe," the President said.

"And that is, the states of the Union moving with the country, year in and year out, building here at home so that we can maintain our position abroad until that day comes when the powerful forces of freedom in every man, as well as every nation, ultimately bring about liberty here and around the world."

The President, acting in his role as political leader of the Democratic party, spoke to a

Continued on Page 26, Column 6

3 Scientists Given Nobel Prizes for '61

By WERNER WISKARI
Special to The New York Times.

STOCKHOLM, Nov. 2 — Nobel prizes in science for 1961 were awarded today to a chemist and a physicist from the United States and a physicist from West Germany, now in the United States.

The chemistry prize was won by Prof. Melvin Calvin, 50 years old, of the University of California at Berkeley.

He was cited for his establishment of the sequence of chemical reactions involved when a plant assimilates carbon dioxide. His prize money amounts to about $48,300.

The physics prize, awarded to two physicists, recognizes separately made contributions to man's knowledge about the nucleus of the atom. Half the prize money will be given to Prof. Robert Hofstadter, 46, of Stan-

Continued on Page 24, Column 3

KENNEDY, IN CITY, SUPPORTS WAGNER IN STRONG TERMS

President Says Re-election of the Mayor Will Further Administration Aims

MOTORCADE IS CHEERED

Crowds Along Route Greet Both Men—Running Mates Share the Limelight

By DOUGLAS DALES

President Kennedy strongly endorsed Mayor Wagner yesterday for a third term.

On his arrival at La Guardia Airport for an afternoon in the city, Mr. Kennedy released a statement voicing "with the utmost conviction my whole-hearted support for the re-election of Mayor Robert F. Wagner."

The President described the Mayor as a man with unmatched experience in coping with city problems, and declared it was important to the success of his own program to have a Mayor in New York City who shared his convictions.

Then, in further aid to the Democratic candidate, Mr. Kennedy, with Mayor Wagner at his side in an open car, rode on a ten-mile route to the Carlyle Hotel, Madison Avenue and Seventy-sixth Street.

Escorted By Motorcycles

Moderately large crowds greeted the President and the Mayor as the motorcade of thirty vehicles, escorted by sixty-five motorcycle policemen, traveled across 125th Street from the Triborough Bridge, then down Broadway to Fifty-seventh Street and on to the hotel.

At several intersections on 125th Street in Harlem crowds stood two or three deep in the bright autumn sunshine. With the temperature just a shade under 60 degrees, the weather was ideal.

Other moderately large crowds were on hand as the motorcade, traveling between twenty and thirty miles an hour, passed Columbia University and Barnard College on Broadway, between 118th and 116th Streets. Other crowds of 1,000 or more were at Broadway and Fifty-seventh Street and at Fifth Avenue.

The President and the Mayor acknowledged cheers and applause with waves.

Mr. Kennedy stood up only once, at Seventy-second Street.

Continued on Page 26, Column 2

CHRYSLER ACCORD ENDS STRIKE PERIL

3-Year Contract Is Reached Before Union's Deadline

By DAMON STETSON
Special to The New York Times.

DETROIT, Nov. 2 — The Chrysler Corporation and the United Automobile Workers reached an agreement tonight on a new three-year contract covering 60,000 workers.

Walter P. Reuther, union president, emerged from the bargaining room at 11:10 P. M. to announce that a national agreement covering economic and non-economic matters had been reached.

He said a few details still had to be worked out on the national contract, and the negotiators would stay in session two more hours.

John D. Leary, Chrysler vice president for personnel, said he hoped the new contract could be signed soon.

Mr. Reuther said several local unions, which had not reached agreements, would continue working until midnight. But he said he felt that the new national agreement would avert a strike.

The pact was reached after a day of negotiations aimed at averting a walkout that had been called for midnight.

The pact provides wage increases and improved benefits similar to those in contracts recently negotiated with the General Motors Corporation and the Ford Motor Company.

The settlement is expected to give Chrysler a period of labor peace as the company attempts a comeback with its 1962 model cars after a disappointing year.

A strike at this time would

Continued on Page 27, Column 5

James Thurber, Writer and Humorist, Is Dead

Continued From Page 1, Col. 4

"The Secret Life of Walter Mitty," which describes the valorous daydreams of an unimportant little man who sees himself doing heroic deeds, begins:

"'We're going through!' The commander's voice was like thin ice breaking. He wore his full-dress uniform with the heavily braided cap pulled down rakishly over one cold, gray eye.

"We can't make it, sir. It's spoiling for a hurricane if you ask me.'

"'I'm not asking you, Lieutenant Berg,' said the commander. 'Throw on the power lights! Rev her up to 8,500! We're going through!'

"The pounding of the cylinders increased: ta-pocketa-pocketa-pocketa-pocketa....

"'Not so fast! You're driving too fast!" said Mrs. Mitty. 'What are you driving so fast for?'

"'Hummm?' said Walter Mitty. He looked at his wife, in the seat beside him, with shocked astonishment...."

Millions of men have seen themselves, or have been referred to by others, as "Walter Mitty types," and one of Britain's most learned medical journals, The Lancet, has referred to the "Walter Mitty Syndrome."

'Versatile and Zany'

E. B. White, a New Yorker colleague of Mr. Thurber, wrote of him:

"Most writers would be glad to settle for any one of ten of Thurber's accomplishments. He has written the funniest memoirs, fables, reports, satires, fantasies, complaints, fairy tales and sketches of the last twenty years, has gone into the drama and the cinema, and on top of that has littered the world with thousands of drawings. Most writers and artists can be compared fairly easily with contemporaries. Thurber inhabits a world of his own."

All of Mr. Thurber's associates tried to account for the zany quality of his mental processes. Mr. White wrote:

"His thoughts have always been a tangle of baseball scores, Civil War tactical problems, Henry James, personal maladjustment, terrier puppies, literary tide rips, ancient myths and modern apprehensions. Through this jungle stalk the unpredictable ghosts of his relatives in Columbus, Ohio."

The late Wolcott Gibbs, another associate on The New Yorker, wrote that "Thurber has a firm grasp on confusion."

The Thurber family was a closely knit unit in the Midwest. When James was a boy the Civil War was still much talked about. In later years he could name about thirty Union generals, complete with middle initials, or the same number of Confederate generals, in about fifteen minutes.

James Grover Thurber was born in Columbus, Dec. 8, 1894. His father, Charles Leander Thurber, was a tall, thin man who usually wore a derby and who had been unsuccessful in politics.

Mamie Thurber, James Thurber's mother, was a vigorous woman who had at one time considered becoming an actress. When she was past 80 she never wore black because she thought it made her look old.

When James Thurber was 6 he lost his left eye when one of his brothers accidentally shot him with an arrow. For the next thirty-five years his right eye did double duty, but a cataract developed, and gradually he became totally blind.

Joked About Eyesight

Mr. Thurber ignored his impaired eyesight as much as possible, but he received many bruises from bumping into doors and tables. Making a mild joke about his sight, he said that he planned to entitle his memoirs, "Long Time No See."

He entered Ohio State University at Columbus in 1913. He was remembered there as a tall, gangling young man with a squint and a great shock of hair that, as one contemporary put it, "gave him the air of an emaciated sheepdog."

When he wrote a clever English theme satirizing the dime novel, he gained the friendship of Elliott Nugent, future actor and producer, who was a campus "wheel" at Ohio State. He made young Thurber buy a suit, get a haircut, speak to the right people and join one of the more elite fraternities, Phi Kappa Psi. Mr. Thurber and Mr. Nugent were later associated in writing plays and in other literary ventures.

An active army buff, Mr. Thurber was unhappy at being barred from service in World War I because of his eyesight. But he got to France a few weeks after the war's end as a code clerk for the State Department.

Returning to Columbus in 1922, Mr. Thurber worked for three years as a reporter for The Columbus Dispatch.

Marriage and Paris

In 1922, Mr. Thurber married Miss Althea Adams, the daughter of an Army surgeon. Miss Adams was studying at Ohio State to be a domestic-science teacher. Both wanted to go to Europe, and after they had saved $125 they went to Paris, where Mr. Thurber got a job on the Paris edition of The Chicago Tribune at $12 a week. The Thurbers had pretty thin going for a time.

After another period—thinner still—of doing society news on speculation for The Paris Herald, the Thurbers made their way back to New York, where Mr. Thurber got a job with The Evening Post. He had discovered The New Yorker and was sending them pieces without much success. In fact he sent them twenty pieces before he sold one.

In 1927, Mr. Thurber met E. B. White at a Greenwich Village party. Mr. White was doing the "Notes and Comments" for the "Talk of the Town" section of The New Yorker, and he agreed to get him on the staff.

When Mr. Thurber settled down in his office at The New Yorker, he found out that he was the magazine's managing editor.

Disliking administrative work, Mr. Thurber soon contrived to get himself shifted to the "Talk of the Town" department, where Mr. White presided. With only one reporter as a staff, they turned out a weekly collection of odd incidents and comments.

This column was fresh and odd-ball in the magazine journalism of the Nineteen Twenties, but many observers have regarded it as being responsible for the early success of The New Yorker.

When the first of the Thurber drawings were published in The New Yorker they were an immediate success. They had an other-world quality about them that was like nothing else. Soon improbable bipeds and other animals joined the standard Thurber dogs, and the humorist began to illustrate his theory of the importance of the constant battling between the sexes.

Mr. Thurber left The New Yorker in 1933 but continued as a contributor for many years. Many of his books appeared in part as articles in The New Yorker.

'Male Animal' a Success

"The Male Animal," a play by Mr. Thurber and Mr. Nugent, was a success on the stage and on the screen. It teased the somewhat pompous side of university administration and the rah-rah aspects of college football. It was said that the play was not entirely popular at Ohio State, which Mr. Thurber had attended but from which he had not graduated.

Mr. Thurber added still another accomplishment — acting —when he stepped into the cast of his "A Thurber Carnival" for the final two months of its nine-month run on Broadway last year. Reviews of his work, both as playwright and performer, were complimentary and affectionate.

Mr. Thurber's writing and drawing brought him wealth. He and Mrs. Thurber lived in a twelve-room ninety-year-old house on sixty-five acres of land in West Cornwall, Conn.

His last book of essays, "Lanterns and Lances," was published in April of this year.

One child, Rosemary, was born to the Thurbers. She is now Mrs. Frederick Savers of Chicago and the mother of three children. Mr. and Mrs. Thurber were divorced in 1935.

Mr. Thurber's second wife, who was sometimes called his seeing-eye wife, was Helen Wismer. A Mount Holyoke graduate, she had been editor of several pulp magazines before her marriage to Mr. Thurber.

He is survived also by two brothers, William and Robert Thurber.

© 1932 James Thurber

"All right, have it your way—you heard a seal bark!"

This cartoon was one of the most famous by James Thurber.

James Thurber in 1934.

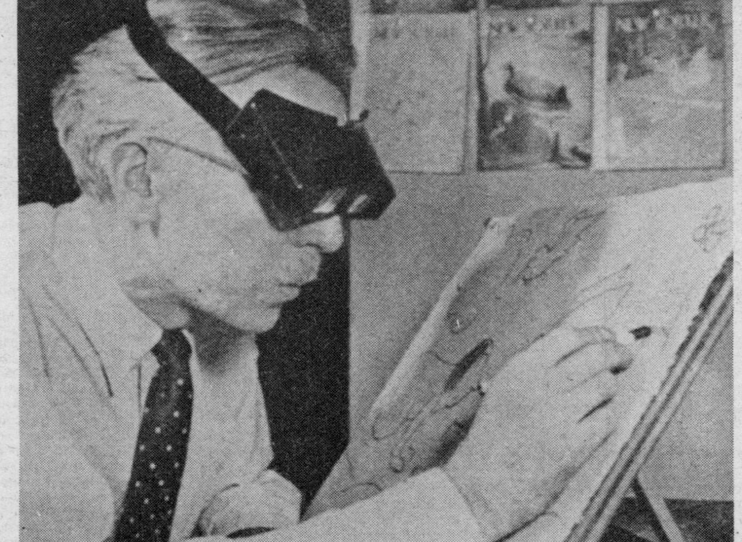

Thurber at work.

Self-portrait

"All the News That's Fit to Print"

The New York Times.

LATE CITY EDITION
Condensation of U.S. Weather Bureau forecast:
Increasing cloudiness and cold today. Clearing, cold tomorrow.
Temperature range today: 22—13
Temperature range yesterday: 27.3—13.9
Full U. S. Weather Bureau Report, Page 58.

VOL. CVI . No. 36,153. Entered as Second-Class Matter, Post Office, New York, N. Y. NEW YORK, THURSDAY, JANUARY 17, 1957. Times Square, New York 36, N. Y. Telephone Lackawanna 4-1000 FIVE CENTS

PRESIDENT ASKS 71.8 BILLION BUDGET, A PEACETIME HIGH; TAX CUT OPPOSED; HUMPHREY IS CRITICAL OF SPENDING

WEST WANTS U. N. TO CONTROL GAZA AND AQABA AREAS

Would Station Forces There Pending Reaching of More Permanent Settlements

COMMON POLICY GAINING

Hammarskjold Terms Israeli Withdrawal to Armistice Lines Essential to Peace

Text of Hammarskjold note will be found on Page 4.

By JAMES RESTON
Special to The New York Times.

WASHINGTON, Jan. 16—Substantial progress has been made in the last few days toward working out a common Western policy for the highly inflammable situation around the Gulf of Aqaba and the Gaza Strip.

[At the United Nations, the delegations of the United States, Canada, Norway, and some Latin-American countries were discussing a resolution based on this common policy. Secretary General Dag Hammarskjold said in a report to the Assembly that Israeli withdrawal behind the armistice lines was essential to peace.]

West in Accord on Aims

It is understood that there is now general agreement among the Western powers on these objectives in the dispute between the Arab states and Israel:

¶The United Nations Emergency Force should occupy the extreme southeastern strip of the Sinai Peninsula along the Strait of Tiran and the island of Tiran until a new agreement is reached guaranteeing freedom of transit for all nations through the Gulf of Aqaba and the Strait of Tiran.

¶The United Nations Emergency Force should also assume control of the Gaza Strip pending a more permanent settlement of the issues there.

¶Israeli troops should withdraw from both these areas on the understanding that United Nations forces would remain there long enough to enable a negotiated settlement of the Gulf of Aqaba and Gaza Strip problems.

¶Meanwhile, the United States, Britain and France, together with Canada, which is continuing to try to work out compromise solutions of these problems at the United Nations, should oppose any efforts to force Israel, by resolutions and economic pressure, back into the position that existed before the outbreak of the war in Egypt.

Delay of Decision Favored

Washington does not want to press for agreement on these questions in the United Nations this week. It is opposed to the idea of trying to return to the status quo that prevailed before the Israeli invasion of Egypt, which some members of the African and Asian bloc are trying to force through a resolution directed against Israel at the United Nations.

However, officials here want to give Mr. Hammarskjold time to work toward a compromise solution, and hope he will be able to make progress toward the objectives defined in the foregoing.

It is recognized here that the Gaza Strip problem is more complicated than anything else, and

Continued on Page 5. Column 1

Toscanini, 89, Dies at Home In Riverdale After a Stroke

Associated Press
Arturo Toscanini conducting N. B. C. Symphony Orchestra

Arturo Toscanini died yesterday morning in his sleep at his home in Riverdale, the Bronx. He would have been 90 years old March 25.

His son Walter said the world-famed conductor had suffered a stroke on New Year's Day and had not recovered. At his bedside when Toscanini died were his son and his daughters, Countess Wally Castelbarco and Mrs. Vladimir Horowitz. The Maestro is survived also by three grandchildren. His wife Carla died in 1951.

Toscanini's body was taken to the Frank E. Campbell Funeral Home at Madison Avenue and Eighty-first Street. It will lie in state for public viewing today after 1:30 P. M. until Saturday morning at 9 o'clock. At 10 A. M. Saturday a solemn re-

Continued on Page 22. Column 2

INQUIRY IS SOUGHT BY STATE SENATOR ON 'TRANSIT MESS'

Mitchell Wants Spending of Half-Billion Subway Bonds and Other Issues Sifted

By LEO EGAN
Special to The New York Times

ALBANY, Jan. 16—State Senator MacNeil Mitchell, Manhattan Republican, proposed today a legislative inquiry into the New York City transit system.

In a resolution submitted to the Senate, Mr. Mitchell suggested the following specific questions for study:

¶What has happened to the $500,000,000 bond issue approved in 1951 for the announced purpose of building a Second Avenue subway?

¶Are expenditures being made for rehabilitation of the transit system's obsolete power-generating plants justified?

¶Why has the Transit Authority failed to carry out a legislative mandate to sell its bus lines, most of which are big money-losers?

¶What is wrong with the Transit Authority's labor relations practices?

Mitchell Discusses Project

Mr. Mitchell explained that the resolution was introduced to fulfill a campaign promise made when he sought re-election last fall.

If the resolution is approved, the investigation would be conducted by the Senate Committee on the Affairs of New York City, of which Mr. Mitchell is chairman. An appropriation of $5,000 would be made to finance the inquiry.

[In New York, the Transit Authority released figures showing that $392,265,730 of the $500,000,000 bond issue had been spent to rehabilitate and modernize the existing transit system. Chairman Charles L. Patterson said the agency would "cooperate fully" in any investigation.]

Director Already Chosen

Anticipating that the resolution will be approved, Mr. Mitchell announced that he had arranged to have Dr. Martin P. Catherwood direct the inquiry. Dr. Catherwood is the dean of the State College of Industrial and Labor Relations at Cornell University. He was state Commissioner of Commerce from 1941 to 1947.

Explaining his proposal, Senator Mitchell said today:

"The concept of this investigation is a four-pronged approach to what has been termed the 'transit mess' in New York City.

"The people have a right to know what has happened to the $500,000,000 bond issue. Nearly $400,000,000 of the sum approved by the voters of the

Continued on Page 23, Column 4

CONGRESS IS SPLIT

Some Members Seek Spending Drop but Chances Are Slim

By JOHN D. MORRIS
Special to The New York Times

WASHINGTON, Jan. 16 — President Eisenhower's budget stirred demands today for cuts by some Republicans as well as Democrats.

Realistic legislators, however, looked for few significant reductions in the $71,807,000,000 spending program for the fiscal year starting July 1.

"In times like these we don't usually cut budgets very much," Representative Sam Rayburn, Democrat of Texas and Speaker of the House of Representatives observed.

Similarly, the Senate Democratic leader, Lyndon B. Johnson, also of Texas, took a neutral view. For a budget of "such huge proportions," he said, it will take Congress considerable time "to go through all of the items and determine whether the type of spending requested is necessary, wise and adapted to our needs."

Republican leaders found ground for praise in the fact that projected revenues would exceed expenditures for the third successive year despite record peacetime outlays.

Martin Is Confident

The House Republican leader, Representative Joseph W. Martin Jr. of Massachusetts, voiced confidence that Congress would vote appropriations "substantially" as recommended by the President.

"With the Government to operate in the black for the third year in a row," he remarked, "the groundwork can be laid for further general tax cuts as soon as our defense needs will permit."

But criticism of the budget came from some powerful Republicans just below the official leadership level. They included Representatives John Taber and Daniel A. Reed, both of upstate New York. Mr. Taber is the senior Republican member of the House Appropriations Committee. Mr. Reed holds the same rank on the tax-writing Ways and Means Committee.

In addition, Senator Styles Bridges, Republican of New Hampshire, promised to make "every effort to pare it down in every place possible." He is the

Continued on Page 19, Column 8

Secretary Warns Outlays And Taxes Must Decrease

Defends Budget but Believes It Can Be Trimmed—Says He Opposes Several Programs—Fears Incurring Deficits

Special to The New York Times.

WASHINGTON, Jan. 16—The Secretary of the Treasury is dissatisfied with the rising trend of Federal spending as reflected in the budget.

George M. Humphrey warned at a news conference it was imperative that expenditures be curbed and taxes cut in the future.

Although saying he was "opposed" to several Government programs, Mr. Humphrey discounted a suggestion that he was at odds with the rest of the Administration on spending. He defended the budget as the best possible in the circumstances.

However, the Secretary said he thought "there are a lot of places in this budget that can be cut."

He was asked if he wished to encourage Congress to "cut this budget quite a lot."

He replied that he would be glad to see cuts "if Congress can find ways to cut and still do a proper job with respect to our security and with respect to the proper service to the public."

The news conference was held yesterday. The Secretary's remarks were made public with the issuance of the budget today.

He emphasized his hope that, through Government economy, spending in the next fiscal year would be below the estimated total of $71,800,000,000. In each of the last two years, however,

Continued on Page 20. Column 3

MESSAGE IS SENT

Receipts Are Estimated at $73,620,000,000 —Arms Costs Rise

Text of Budget Message is on Pages 15, 16, 17, 18 and 19.

By EDWIN L. DALE Jr.
Special to The New York Times.

WASHINGTON, Jan. 16—President Eisenhower sent to Congress today a record peacetime budget. It estimated that the expenditures of the Federal Government would be $71,807,000,000 for the 1958 fiscal year, which begins next July 1.

The President estimated that receipts would be $73,620,000,000, a record sum. Thus he could report that he expected a surplus of $1,813,000,000. However, he firmly opposed a general tax reduction on the basis of a surplus of such modest size.

Several aspects of the budget, including a third successive annual increase in appropriations requested from Congress, indicated still higher spending next year. This cast doubt on the prospect of a tax cut even next year, though the booming economy continues to swell revenues.

Highlights of Budget

These were the highlights of the budget:

¶Spending: $71,800,000,000, up $2,900,000,000 from the latest estimate for the current fiscal year, now half completed. Most of the increase was in defense and related national security programs, which will take 63 cents out of every dollar spent.

¶Receipts: $73,600,000,000, up $3,000,000,000 from the latest estimate for the current year. The reason for this estimated increase is an official Government prediction that general prosperity will continue and expand over the next year.

¶New obligational authority (mostly new appropriations): $73,300,000,000, up $2,800,000,000 over the amount granted by Congress last year. It also is up $16,200,000,000 over the recent low of the fiscal year of 1955, the President's first budget. This figure tends to influence future spending, since in many programs money is spent a year or more after it is appropriated.

Special Trust Funds

These figures for the regular budget do not include several major programs such as Social Security, unemployment compensation and the new highway program. These programs are handled through special trust funds and collect their own income.

When these programs are included, the total estimated Federal outlays come to a post-war high of $82,900,000,000 and total receipts to $85,900,000,000. The resulting "cash" surplus of $3,000,000,000 indicates that total Federal operations will have a mildly anti-inflationary impact on the economy during the 1958 fiscal year.

The President told Congress that his basic budget policy was to help restrain inflationary pressures. The prospective surplus, he said, will reinforce monetary and credit restraint toward this end. The basic policy required, he said, "that less pressing expenditure programs must be held back and some meritorious proposals postponed."

Aid to Small Business

The President asked, as expected, that present rates on corporation taxes and certain excises, due to decline April 1, be extended by Congress. He opposed all tax measures that would reduce revenues "substantially." However, he did favor minor changes in taxation affecting small business and a tax change designed to spur overseas investment.

George M. Humphrey, Secretary of the Treasury, made plain, however, that the small business tax changes would not include relief through lowering the present corporate tax rates on small profits, as recommended by a special Cabinet committee.

Mr. Humphrey also indicated that a surplus of $3,000,000,000 to $5,000,000,000 would be needed next year before he would favor tax cuts. He said that the

Continued on Page 14, Column 2

RAYBURN BACKING PLAN ON MIDEAST

He Favors Military Aspects of President's Proposal— Wavers on Aid Fund

By WILLIAM S. WHITE
Special to The New York Times.

WASHINGTON, Jan. 16 — Speaker Sam Rayburn has passed the word that Congress should quickly and decisively grant President Eisenhower's request for stand-by authority to use troops in the Mideast.

Mr. Rayburn's influence has been put into play against all proposals to modify Congressional backing for this aspect of the President's plan.

The Speaker has not been convinced, however, that Congress necessarily should accompany this action with immediate approval of the second part of the program.

In this part the President seeks authorization for free use of $200,000,000 in existing economic aid funds in the Mideast. Future Administration requests for an additional $400,000,000 are contemplated, but are not at issue.

Urgency Is in Doubt

Mr. Rayburn said publicly today that he did not regard it as especially important for Congress to move at once on the economic section of the Administration's resolution.

He thus gave some support to a widening Congressional movement to delay the issue of special economic assistance at least until the coming regular foreign aid bill is brought up at the Capitol.

It may be stated, however, that he has not closed his mind on the question of immediate action on the economic section. His ultimate decision might not necessarily be unfavorable to that course.

His concern now is to have the Democratic Eighty-fifth Congress support the President without the shadow of reservation on the one point that the Speaker regards as transcendental—backing for the use of troops.

Specifically, he has made it known that he wants and expects the House to adopt a resolution with the full force of law, and not one merely expressing Congressional opinion, that the President should feel free to move militarily against any Communist lunge.

A Resolution Is Opposed

Thus, he has informed his associates that he would regard as inadequate what is called a concurrent resolution—meaning one that would be passed by both houses but would not go to the President for his signature. This concurrent approach is being considered by many in Congress.

Mr. Rayburn has said, instead, that he wants what the Administration wants—a joint resolution—a paper that would go to the White House for the

Continued on Page 2. Column 4

Export of Cottons Limited by Japan In Pact With U.S.

Special to The New York Times.

WASHINGTON, Jan. 16—Japan notified the United States today she would impose a ceiling of 235,000,000 square yards annually on cotton-textile exports to this country.

The quota, worked out in talks between the two Governments in Tokyo, was hailed by the State Department as "a major step forward in the development of orderly and mutually beneficial trade" between the two nations.

It will remain in effect for five years, though it is subject to review annually. It outlines a program of textile exports to the United States that would be equitably spread through the year and would guarantee a broad diversification of products flowing to the American market.

[In New York, spokesmen for textile mills greeted the new quotas without enthusiasm. They seemed disposed to accept the over-all figure, but some indicated they might protest the allocations in some sectors, such as ginghams.

[However, industry leaders meeting in Charlotte, N. C., said the plan "should dissolve promptly the cloud of doubt and uncertainty which has disrupted United States textile markets. * * * We believe the plan deserves a fair trial."]

Tokyo Sets Quotas

Under the over-all export ceiling, Tokyo set up ceilings on major types of textiles and, under these, ceilings on specific categories.

In addition, it provided that exports from Japan should be distributed equally through the year's quarters "as far as practicable and as necessary to meet seasonal demands."

Two major categories in which Japanese exports will be sharply reduced are ginghams and velveteens. Both these cotton cloths

Continued on Page 41, Column 2

Record 5 Billions Asked for Farms As Crisis Is Cited

By WILLIAM M. BLAIR
Special to The New York Times.

WASHINGTON, Jan. 16—The Administration put itself deeper into the farm business today despite an avowed desire to get out. It proposed a record budget for agriculture.

Plagued by continuing farm surpluses and drought, plus political pressure to do more for farmers, President Eisenhower put up to Congress an agricultural budget of nearly $5,000,000,000. This was $2,000,000,000 higher than the budget covering the last full year of the Truman Administration.

The President also proposed direct subsidy payments to farmers of $1,600,000,000. Most of these payments would come from the soil bank plan to get farmers to retire surplus-producing land. The Administration hopes to get 40,000,000 acres, or about 12 per cent of the country's crop land, out of production.

The peak Federal spending, the President asserted, was necessary to bring about adjust-

Continued on Page 20, Column 6

6 NEW ATOM UNITS TO AID U. S. ALLIES

A Record 38 Billion Defense Figure Set—Eisenhower Lists Strategy Changes

By JACK RAYMOND
Special to The New York Times.

WASHINGTON, Jan. 16 — President Eisenhower announced today that six "atomic support commands" would be created to bolster the defense forces of other nations in the free world.

He disclosed also new concepts of the nation's military strategy, tactics and organization for possible nuclear warfare. These presaged reductions in the size and number of some military units, particularly the Air Force.

In his budget message to Congress, the President referred to "events in recent months," which he said dramatized the need for collective security. He then offered this reminder:

"We shall continue to expand our nuclear arsenal until an agreement has been reached for reduction and regulation of armaments under safeguarded guarantees."

Despite military reorganization and emphasis on economy, the over-all defense expenditure estimate rose by nearly $2,000,000,000. It reached a record peacetime spending figure of $38,000,000,000 for the 1958 fiscal year, which begins July 1.

The President's spending estimate indicated that 53 cents of each budget dollar would go for defense. Related security items would add 10 cents to this cost. The 53 cents would provide for the maintenance of 2,800,000 men under arms, about the same as at present, despite earlier plans to reduce the number.

The prototype for the new atomic support commands is the American-manned South Europe

Continued on Page 19, Column 5

Cold Due to Continue, Prolonging Peril of Ice and Slush

The New York Times
Ankle-deep slush, like this at Broadway and Forty-third Street, flooded many city corners

The cold weather, which was accompanied yesterday by snow, is expected to continue at least until the week-end. Ernest J. Christie, meteorologist in charge of the New York Weather Bureau, said last night that he saw no prospect of any break before Saturday, and even that was uncertain. He predicted temperatures of 16 to 18 degrees this morning, nothing higher than 20 to 25 today, and readings tonight similar to those of last night. The outlook for continued cold threatened to prolong some of the driving hazards as created by yesterday's snowstorm. The snow covered an area from New England southward to Vir-

Continued on Page 25, Column 2

Chou Accord Halts Isolation of Poland

By SYDNEY GRUSON
Special to The New York Times.

WARSAW, Jan. 16—Poland and Communist China signed a joint declaration today that in effect halted Poland's growing isolation from the family circle of Communist nations.

The declaration summed up five days of discussions between the Polish leaders and Premier Chou En-lai. The Chinese gave a brief press conference after signing and then left for Budapest in a Soviet jet airliner.

The Poles surrendered ground on two positions they had held tenaciously since their October revolution won them a measure of independence from Soviet control. But they did not give up the positions entirely nor yield as much ground as they feared would be necessary before the discussions began.

The Poles accepted "proletari-

Continued on Page 6, Column 3

Pakistan Urges U.N. Rush Kashmir Force

By MICHAEL JAMES
Special to The New York Times.

UNITED NATIONS, N. Y., Jan. 16—Pakistan asked the Security Council today to send a United Nations force to Kashmir "at once." She also requested that India be ordered to agree to a plebiscite in the mountainous state at an early date.

Malik Firoz Khan Noon, Foreign Minister of Pakistan, presented his nation's case. He warned that unless the United Nations took immediate steps, "I fear that war might break out."

Mr. Noon said he had just received reports of a massing of Indian troops on Pakistan's frontiers. There is also imminent danger of revolt by the Kashmiris "if the United Nations does not deliver them

Continued on Page 10, Column 3

U. S. Aids Afghans, Countering Moscow

Special to The New York Times.

WASHINGTON, Jan. 16—The United States is beginning development of Afghanistan's civil airline and airports as one phase of economic aid intended to counter Soviet penetration.

Another phase is to start tomorrow when engineering concerns will be invited to bid on the job of surveying transportation problems between Afghanistan and Pakistan.

A third phase, consisting of irrigation projects, is recommended in a report written by former Gov. Len Jordan of Idaho. The report is expected to reach the Afghan Government tomorrow.

With these operations, United States officials think, they can hope to compete with the Russians as Afghanistan

Continued on Page 3. Column 2

Tributes to Toscanini Offered by President, Mayor and Leaders in the Music World

MAESTRO IS CITED AS BEST MUSICIAN

Many Messages Come From Conductors, Singers and Officials Here and Abroad

President Eisenhower expressed his sorrow yesterday at the death of Arturo Toscanini.

"I have learned with deep regret of the death of Arturo Toscanini," the President's statement said. "As man and as musician he gained the admiration of the world. He spoke in the universal language of music, but he also spoke in the language of free men everywhere. The music he created and the hatred of tyranny that was his are part of the legacy of our time."

Other tributes to Toscanini were received yesterday from leaders in all walks of life.

Among the messages of condolence to the Toscanini family were:

MAYOR WAGNER—In behalf of all the citizens of New York I extend my deepest sympathy to you and your family in the death of our beloved Maestro and patriarch, Arturo Toscanini, the world's outstanding conductor, whose music was universal in concept and acceptance.

ROBERT W. SARNOFF, president of the National Broadcasting Company—The Maestro's genius will live on in the hearts of those who knew him and in the hearts of future generations through the recorded works he left us.

RUDOLF BING, general manager of the Metropolitan Opera—We are deeply moved by the loss of the Maestro, who first came to this country with the Metropolitan and who has already gone into history as the outstanding musician of our time.

DAVID M. KEISER, president of the Philharmonic-Symphony—The Philharmonic-Symphony Society's pride in the brilliant years of its association with Arturo Toscanini is now equaled by its sorrow at the death of the man who, perhaps more than any other person in our time, has symbolized the supreme peak in musical perfection.

DIMITRI MITROPOULOS, musical director of the Philharmonic-Symphony—The death of my beloved colleague means to the world the loss of a magnificent interpreter, and a man whose spirit has been an inspiring force for all serious artists.

BRUNO WALTER, conductor—In him was greatness, and I am sure the memory of his glorious activities in the fields of dramatic and absolute music will live on in the hearts of us all.

LEONARD BERNSTEIN, conductor-composer—I have no words to express the enormity of the loss. The world of music will never be the same.

EUGENE ORMANDY, conductor of the Philadelphia Orchestra—He was a perfectionist who would never accept mediocrity and who inspired everyone.

PIERRE MONTEUX, conductor—The world has lost its greatest conductor.

JAMES C. PETRILLO, president of the American Federation of Musicians—The death of the great Toscanini deprives the music world of an irreplaceable genius.

LOTTE LEHMANN, soprano—One of the greatest artists of all time has gone away.

LAURITZ MELCHIOR, tenor—Anybody who worked with Toscanini has had an enormous amount of development in himself through that association.

BENIAMINO GIGLI, tenor—The death of the maestro is an immense loss to the world of music.

SIR ARTHUR BLISS, British composer—Toscanini's nobility as a man, his humility toward the great classics and his idealistic standards in the performance of fine music secure him a place among the legendary musical figures of all time.

HENRI SAUGUET, French composer—One of the highest and most brilliant stars in the musical sky was extinguished today.

FREDERIC R. MANN and SAMUEL RUBIN of the American Fund for Israel Institutions—With the passing of Arturo Toscanini the world loses the greatness of a man who combined supreme artistic talent with the highest degree of humanitarianism. We shall always be indebted to him for his inspiring assistance in the founding of the Israel Philharmonic.

SIR ADRIAN BOULT, conductor—Toscanini was supreme as an interpreter not only among conductors but among all musicians.

BOYD NEEL, dean of the Royal Conservatory in Toronto—He was probably the outstanding conductor of all time—a unique man.

VIRGILIO FERRARI, Mayor of Milan—Toscanini was the greatest among conductors of all time.

ILDEBRANDO PIZZETTI, Italian composer—With Toscanini we have lost the musical interpreter whom for sixty years all the world has looked upon as the greatest.

GEORGES HIRSH, administrator of the Paris Opéra—It is a world loss. Toscanini was the greatest orchestral conductor.

JOACHIM TIBERTIUS, city councilor for culture in West Berlin—Toscanini was a man before whose temperament and sovereign interpretation we all have to bow our heads.

Associated Press

CONDUCTOR AT LA SCALA: Arturo Toscanini and son, Walter, in 1903, at time he conducted at Milan opera house.

Associated Press

WITH FAMILY IN TURIN: The Maestro was photographed in the Italian city in 1911 with wife and daughter Wally.

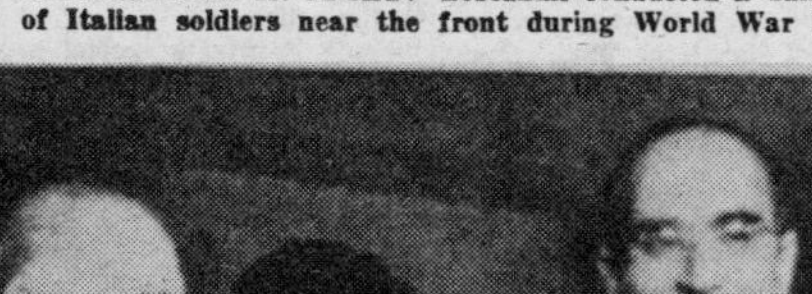

N. B. C.

BANDMASTER IN ITALY: Toscanini conducted a band of Italian soldiers near the front during World War I.

Arturo Toscanini Is Dead at 89; Suffered Stroke New Year's Day

Continued From Page 1

quiem mass will be offered in St. Patrick's Cathedral.

For more than half a century, Toscanini was one of the dominating figures in the world's musical life. Both as an operatic and symphonic conductor, he achieved a stature no other conductor before him had attained.

When Toscanini conducted he was, in a sense, the whole show. This was not because he sought the limelight—all through his long career he did just the opposite—but because of universal respect for his judgment, experience, vast musical knowledge, uncompromising standards and the touch of incandescent brilliance he infused into every performance he conducted.

Bursting With Energy

Toscanini, on or off the podium, was a striking figure. Short of stature, he was trim, erect and bursting with energy. In his eighties, he ran upstairs two at a time.

His white hair, which he wore long, was trimmed by his wife or daughters rather than a barber. His eyes were a piercing dark brown under shaggy eyebrows. His voice, from years of shouting at orchestra rehearsals, was permanently husky.

Observers were astonished by the almost girlish smoothness of his unwrinkled face. The Maestro prosaically attributed this to the profuseness with which he perspired during concerts. Off the podium, his usual dress was a short morning-coat, wing collar with Ascot tie, and striped trousers.

As a musician, Toscanini represented absolute, uncompromising integrity. He strove earnestly to realize as exactly as possible the composer's intentions as printed in the musical score. To achieve perfection he drove musicians relentlessly, himself hardest of all.

Because of his weak eyesight and because, as he put it, "the conductor should have the score in his head rather than his head in the score," Toscanini memorized every work he conducted. From memory he was able to correct any error made by the musicians, even in a full orchestra altutti.

Despite his encyclopedic memory he was constantly restudying works he had been conducting for years. The Maestro suffered from insomnia, and a pile of orchestral scores always lay on his bedside table.

Was a Conductor at 19

Toscanini was 19 when he made his first appearance as a conductor. The opera was "Aida," which later served as his first opera at the Metropolitan in 1908, and the theatre was in Rio de Janeiro. The young, dark-eyed, handsome boy had gone to the Brazilian capital to play the 'cello in the opera. The conductor of that opera company went from bad to worse and finally he had to be dismissed. The impresario looked around for a new conductor. Some of the men in the orchestra suggested that young Toscanini might be able to do the job. For want of anyone better, the impresario gave Toscanini a chance.

The young 'cellist took his place on the podium that night. He knew the score thoroughly and conducted it from memory. He gave a striking performance, and his success was electric. The unknown 'cellist had suddenly become a maestro.

His phenomenal memory, which allowed him to conduct hundreds of operas, symphonies and concertos without a score, gave him full scope to utilize his talents. In practically no time he memorized the most intricate scores, conducting with a sureness that inspired the members of the orchestras that he led.

Toscanini returned to Italy shortly after that and made a name for himself as a conductor at Turin, Treviso, Bologna and Genoa.

Twelve years after his triumph in Rio de Janeiro Toscanini had reached that goal of all conductors—the leadership of La Scala at Milan. He was then only 31 years old.

Toscanini conducted La Scala for nineteen years, but at different times.

It was after his first period at La Scala that Toscanini came to New York in 1908 and conducted for seven years in the Metropolitan Opera House, where his genius found its fullest expression.

Toscanini's success in New York was instantaneous. Whether it was opera or symphony orchestra it was one triumph after another. The culmination came when he made his celebrated tour of European cities as conductor of the Philharmonic-Symphony Orchestra of New York in 1930. Toscanini received ovation after ovation. Royalty patronized the concerts wherever royalty still existed. No conductor had ever risen to greater fame.

Toscanini was born at Parma, Italy, the son of Claudio and Paolina Toscanini. He became a pupil in the Parma Conservatory when he was 9 years old and when he was 17 he conducted one of his own compositions before a private audience in the conservatory.

Not long after that, having won high honors in piano and 'cello studies, he became a 'cellist and played in various orchestras.

It was characteristic of Toscanini that he hated affectation and exaggerated applause. New York audiences have often seen him leave angrily after too many demands for encores. From boyhood he shrank from facile applause and praise. At the Parma Conservatory his fellow-students nicknamed him Il Genietto, the little genius, and he was almost boorish in his resentment.

While Toscanini was generally composed while conducting concerts, he often became unnerved while directing rehearsals. It was told of him that on one occasion he fell to his knees, folded his hands as in prayer and, turning a pleading face to the musicians, cried "pianissimo, please! pianissimo." Then he straightened up and dropped his handkerchief.

"Like this the music should be," he said. "Just like this handkerchief falling down."

Directed Opera Premières Here

At the Metropolitan here Toscanini directed the premières of Puccini's "Fanciulla del West," Giordano's "Madame Sans-Gêne," as well as the first rendering in the United States of many other works.

When he arrived in New York the first time he came with Giulio Gatti-Casazza, the new general manager of the Metropolitan Opera House. They quarreled in 1915 and were not reconciled until seventeen years later.

While he was emphatically against the intrusion of politics into art, it cannot be said that Toscanini was not a patriot. He gave a fine demonstration of that in 1917 and was decorated for bravery for leading an army band on the heights of Monte Santo during an Italian attack against the Austrians.

From 1916 to 1918 Toscanini had plenty to do leading concerts on behalf of welfare work. He contributed his great talents in times when suffering was great.

He visited the United States, however, and he was the conductor of the Philharmonic from 1926 to 1936.

In the winter of 1934 there was talk of merging the orchestra with the Metropolitan Opera in the interest of economy. Toscanini put an end to this, however, when he vigorously asserted that such a merger would add luster to the artistic merits of neither the orchestra nor the opera.

Rumors of his resignation from the Philharmonic had been rife in the fall of 1935. The day that they first took printed form

Associated Press

PORTRAIT of him in 1950

in New York, he heatedly denied them in Paris. When he arrived in this country he created a scene on the steamer as he madly dashed down the stairway to his stateroom with his wife and his famous poodle following in his wake, and a group of baffled reporters bringing up the rear. The Philharmonic - Symphony announced his resignation "with regrets" in February and he conducted what was announced as his final concert under the society's aegis at Carnegie Hall on the evening of April 29, 1936.

Thousands of persons were turned away and sixty mounted and foot policemen had difficulty holding them back. Some even attempted to get in by scaling the fire-escapes, only to be hauled down by the officers.

At the end of the concert, while Toscanini was modestly receiving the ovation of the packed hall, a photographer elbowed his way to the foot of the platform, raised his camera and set off a flash. Bewildered, Toscanini threw his arms over his never-strong eyes, gasped and then turned and stumbled blindly from the stage. The photographer barely escaped unscathed amid the hisses and jeers of the 3,000 witnesses.

Toscanini left America shortly thereafter for a summer at the Salzburg Festival and later in 1936 went to Palestine to direct the new Palestine Symphony Orchestra at Tel Aviv, which he did with notable success.

In the next year, the National Broadcasting Company commissioned Samuel Chotzinoff, then music critic of The New York Post and a close friend of the Maestro, to persuade Toscanini to lead an orchestra especially created for him.

With some trepidation Mr. Chotzinoff went to Milan, where the Maestro was living in retirement. Mr. Chotzinoff cautiously brought up the subject of the N. B. C. Symphony Orchestra and the Maestro, after some persuasion, consented to direct it.

He was reported to have been paid $40,000 for his services in leading this orchestra, the first of its kind subsidized by a broadcasting corporation. Fears that this would detract from the popularity and success of the Philharmonic were expressed, but they proved groundless.

On Dec. 25, 1937, Toscanini directed the first of his concerts with the N. B. C. Symphony in Radio City. For the occasion he had chosen a program consisting of the Vivaldi Concerto in D minor, Mozart's Symphony in G minor, and the First Symphony of Brahms. The concert was attended by some 1,400 persons, as many as could be packed into an auditorium into which about 3,500 had exerted every possible influence to enter.

At 9 P. M., one hour before the concert began, the 1,000 unreserved seats on the main floor were already filled. The reserved section in the balcony, seating 400, was filled by 9:30 P. M., twenty minutes before the doors were closed.

When Toscanini's contract expired at the end of the first season, it was renewed for three years. In addition to the regular concerts, he gave several benefit programs with the orchestra, and conducted it in several neighboring cities.

During the years he was making his annual visits to this country to lead his N. B. C. Symphony series he found time to carry on his musical activities abroad. In May and June of 1937 he directed six concerts of the B. B. C. Symphony Orchestra in London, and in 1938 returned to Palestine to direct the Palestine Symphony.

In June, 1940, Toscanini embarked, with the 102-piece N.B.C. Symphony Orchestra, for South America. He directed in Rio de Janeiro, which he had not visited in fifty-four years, and also in São Paulo, Buenos Aires and Montevideo. The tour was a series of triumphs.

After an absence of six years Toscanini returned to lead the New York Philharmonic-Symphony in the spring of 1942. His six concerts at that time were a post-season series and crowned the celebration of the orchestra's centennial season.

He appeared in later years as guest conductor with the Philadelphia Orchestra and conducted the Chicago, Los Angeles and Cincinnati Symphonies in guest appearances.

During the war Toscanini conducted a special series of concerts under the auspices of the Treasury Department as part of a war bond drive. He also conducted special concerts for the benefit of the Red Cross, including a tremendous one at Madison Square Garden in which the N. B. C. Symphony was joined by the New York Philharmonic - Symphony. After the war there were frequent benefits for worthy causes.

In 1950, after he had passed his eighty-third birthday, Toscanini set out on an undertaking that some of his admirers feared would be too much for him. He led the N. B. C. Symphony Orchestra in a transcontinental tour that covered twenty cities from coast to coast in six weeks.

The orchestra traveled on a special train dubbed the "Toscanini Special," and he had a private car for himself. That train was received with affection wherever it stopped, not merely in cities where concerts were scheduled but also in hamlets throughout the United States. Seldom in the history of America had a musician received such warm and widespread veneration.

The Maestro was in fine fettle on this trip. His concerts had the ardor that only he seemed to know how to retain from his young manhood, and they had a deep spirituality as well.

Relished the Journey

Away from music, Toscanini relished the journey. It gave him pleasure to revisit cities where he had been before and he attacked with enormous zest the discovery of new places.

In New Orleans, while driving on a sightseeing tour, he had his car pause in front of a hot-jazz spot so that he might better hear the popular music.

When his special train stopped in northern California at Mount Shasta, standing majestically snow-capped in the distance, the conductor said not a word but brought his hands together to applaud the mountain and its beauty.

On a day spent in picnicking with the orchestra at Sun Valley, Idaho, the Maestro went up on the ski tow with the vivacity of a young blood and then conducted a make-shift band that included washboards and metal pots.

In Washington he had former President Harry S. Truman as a visitor backstage at Constitution Hall before the concert and the two men spoke about their mutual interest—music.

During the 1950-51 season the conductor's knee, injured in a fall, gave him serious trouble, and he was obliged to reduce all his commitments. He conducted only a couple of concerts with the N. B. C. Symphony, and he canceled his engagement to conduct the opening concerts of the Festival of Britain in London's new Festival Hall.

It was predicted gloomily that these cancellations were the beginning of the end. There were some who said that Toscanini would not conduct again.

But he was back full of vigor and authority for the 1951-52 season, conducting all twelve concerts he had engaged to do with the N. B. C. Symphony Orchestra. In his enthusiasm he did more recording than at any other time in his career. He directed nearly thirty recording sessions. On three different occasions he conducted sessions in the afternoon and again right after midnight in the same twenty-four hour period. The men in the orchestra were dead-tired, but Toscanini was ready for more work.

When a close friend was asked whether the Maestro was now recording so much because he wanted to leave as many of his performances as possible for posterity, the answer was, "Not at all, he just wants to work."

Toscanini spent the summer of 1953 with members of his family and friends at his island villa in Lago Maggiore. While there he told a correspondent that his 1953-54 season with the N. B. C. Symphony would be his "last" appearance on the concert platform.

The Maestro once told a friend: "Quando in mano mi trema la bacchietta, non farò piu il direttore." ("When the baton trembles in my hand, I shall conduct no more.") That sad occasion came on April 4, 1954, at Carnegie Hall, when Toscanini led his farewell concert with the N. B. C. Symphony.

Toscanini according to those who knew him well, was overcome with emotion at the thought of leaving his orchestra. At one point he stopped conducting altogether. Alarmed N. B. C. officials cut off the broadcast, substituting a recording by Toscanini. When the concert was finished Toscanini dropped his baton, walked off the stage and did not return.

The New York Times

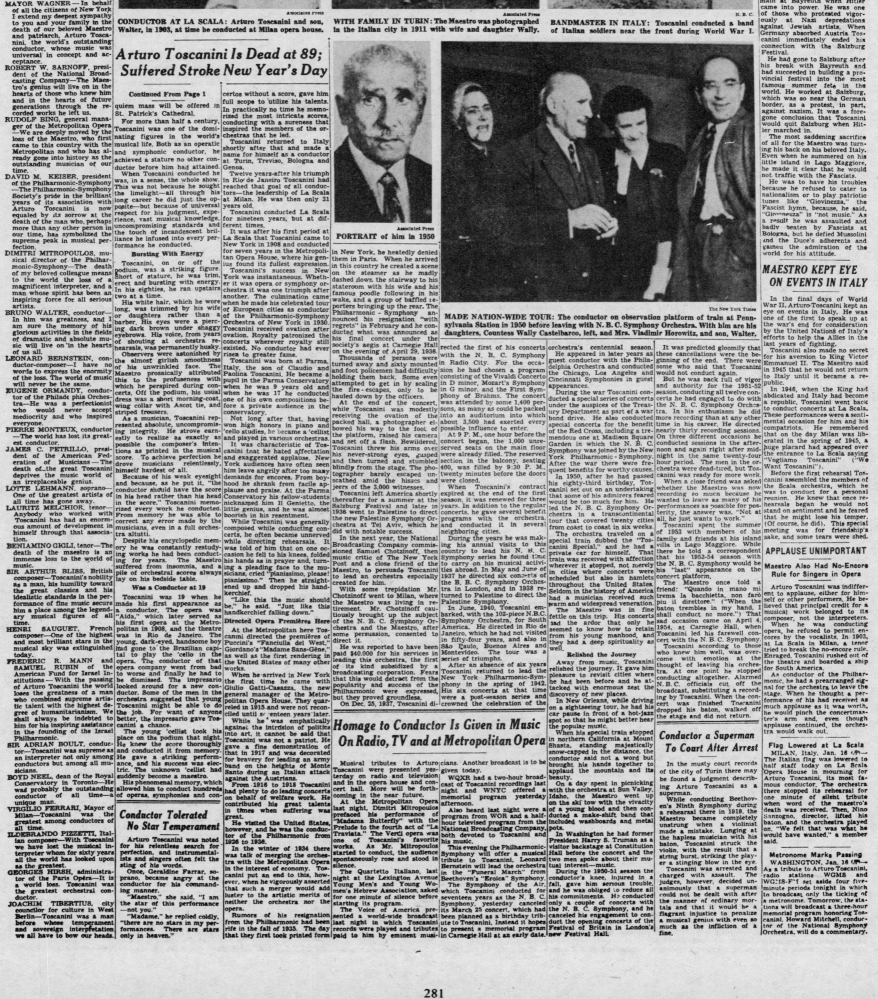

MADE NATION-WIDE TOUR: The conductor on observation platform of train at Pennsylvania Station in 1950 before leaving with N. B. C. Symphony Orchestra. With him are his daughters, Countess Wally Castelbarco, left, and Mrs. Vladimir Horowitz, and son, Walter.

Conductor Tolerated No Star Temperament

Arturo Toscanini was noted for his relentless search for perfection, and instrumentalists and singers often felt the sting of his words.

Once, Geraldine Farrar, soprano, became angry at the conductor for his commanding manner.

"Maestro," she said, "I am the star of this performance—not you."

"Madame," he replied coldly, "there are no stars in my performances. There are stars only in heaven."

Homage to Conductor Is Given in Music On Radio, TV and at Metropolitan Opera

Musical tributes to Arturo Toscanini were presented yesterday on radio and television and in the opera house and concert hall. More will be forthcoming in the near future.

At the Metropolitan Opera last night, Dimitri Mitropoulos prefaced his performance of "Madama Butterfly" with the Prelude to the fourth act of "La Traviata." The Verdi opera was one of Toscanini's favorite works. As Mr. Mitropoulos started to conduct, the audience spontaneously rose and stood in silence.

The Quartetto Italiano, last night at the Lexington Avenue Young Men's and Young Women's Hebrew Association, asked for one minute of silence before starting its program.

The Voice of America presented a world-wide broadcast last night in which Toscanini records were played and tributes paid to him by eminent musicians. Another broadcast is to be given today.

WQXR had a two-hour broadcast of Toscanini recordings last night and WNYC offered a memorial program yesterday afternoon.

Also heard last night were a program from WOR and a half-hour televised program from the National Broadcasting Company, both devoted to Toscanini and his music.

This evening the Philharmonic-Symphony will offer a musical tribute to Toscanini. Leonard Bernstein will lead the orchestra in the "Funeral March" from Beethoven's "Eroica" Symphony.

The Symphony of the Air, which Toscanini conducted for seventeen years as the N. B. C. Symphony, yesterday canceled its March 25 concert, which had been planned as a birthday tribute to Toscanini. Instead it hopes to present a memorial program in Carnegie Hall at an early date.

Conductor a Superman To Court After Arrest

In the musty court records of the city of Turin there may be found a judgment describing Arturo Toscanini as a superman.

While conducting Beethoven's Ninth Symphony during a rehearsal there in 1919, the Maestro became completely unstrung when a violinist made a mistake. Lunging at the hapless musician with his baton, Toscanini struck the violin, with the result that a string burst, striking the player a stinging blow in the eye.

Toscanini was arrested and charged with assault. The judges, however, decided unanimously that a superman could not be dealt with after the manner of ordinary mortals and that it would be a flagrant injustice to penalize a musical genius with even so much as the infliction of a fine.

TOSCANINI FOUGHT AGAINST FASCISM

Beaten for Refusal to Play Mussolini's Song, He Won World's Praise for Stand

A fine musician, Toscanini was also a human being of profound sensibilities who did not hesitate to take a stand on the side of what he considered the right. As a result he became one of the stanchest foes of nazism and fascism.

The Maestro gave proof to the entire world of how he felt about Fascist Italy when he performed Verdi's "Hymn of the Nations" over a national network on Jan. 31, 1943. In his own handwriting he changed the words, "Italia, patria mia," to "Italia tradita ("Italy betrayed"). This was his denunciation, through the medium of music and in his own tongue of the tyranny he hated.

Toscanini willingly gave up things that he treasured when his conscience was outraged. He felt that his complete fulfillment as an artist had taken place at Bayreuth at the annual Wagner festivals, but he did not remain at Bayreuth when Hitler came into power. He was one of those who protested vigorously at Nazi depredations against Jewish artists. When Germany absorbed Austria Toscanini immediately ended his connection with the Salzburg Festival.

He had gone to Salzburg after his break with Bayreuth and had succeeded in building a provincial festival into the most famous summer fete in the world. He worked at Salzburg, which was so near the German border, as a protest, in part, against nazism. It was a foregone conclusion that Toscanini would quit Salzburg when Hitler marched in.

The most saddening sacrifice of all for the Maestro was turning his back on his beloved Italy. Even when he summered on his little island in Lago Maggiore, he made it clear that he would not traffic with the Fascists.

He was to have his troubles because he refused to cater to nationalism or to play patriotic tunes like "Giovinezza," the Fascist hymn, because, he said, "Giovinezza" is "not music." As a result he was assaulted and badly beaten by Fascists at Bologna, but he defied Mussolini and the Duce's adherents and gained the admiration of the world for his attitude.

MAESTRO KEPT EYE ON EVENTS IN ITALY

In the final days of World War II, Arturo Toscanini kept an eye on events in Italy. He was one of the first to speak up at the war's end for consideration by the United Nations of Italy's efforts to help the Allies in the last years of fighting.

Toscanini also made no secret for his aversion to King Victor Emmanuel II. The Maestro said in 1945 that he would not return to Italy until it became a republic.

In 1946, when the King had abdicated and Italy had become a republic, Toscanini went back to conduct concerts at La Scala. These performances were a sentimental occasion for him and his compatriots. He remembered that on the day Milan was liberated in the spring of 1945, a huge placard had appeared over the entrance to La Scala saying "Vogliamo Toscanini" ("We Want Toscanini").

Before the first rehearsal Toscanini assembled the members of the Scala orchestra, which he was to conduct for a personal reunion. He knew that once rehearsals began he would not stand on sentiment and he feared that he might lose his temper. (Of course, he did). This special meeting was for friendship's sake, and some tears were shed.

APPLAUSE UNIMPORTANT

Maestro Also Had No-Encore Rule for Singers in Opera

Arturo Toscanini was indifferent to applause, either for himself or other performers. He believed that principal credit for a musical work belonged to its composer, not the interpreters.

When he was conducting opera, he refused to permit encores by the vocalists. In 1903, at La Scala in Milan, a tenor tried to break the no-encore rule. Enraged, Toscanini rushed out of the theatre and boarded a ship for South America.

As conductor of the Philharmonic, he had a prearranged signal for the orchestra to leave the stage. When he thought a performance of his had received as much applause as it was worth, he would pinch the concertmaster's arm and, even though applause continued, the orchestra would walk out.

Flag Lowered at La Scala

MILAN, Italy, Jan. 16 (AP)—The Italian flag was lowered to half staff today on La Scala Opera House in mourning for Arturo Toscanini, its most famous conductor. The orchestra there stopped its rehearsal for one minute of silent tribute when word of the maestro's death was received. Then, Nino Sanzogno, director, lifted his baton, and the orchestra played on. "We felt that was what he would have wanted," a member said.

Metronome Marks Passing

WASHINGTON, Jan. 16 (AP)—As a tribute to Arturo Toscanini, radio stations WGMS and WGMS-FM set aside four five-minute periods tonight in which to broadcast only the ticking of a metronome. Tomorrow, the stations will broadcast a three-hour memorial program honoring Toscanini. Howard Mitchell, conductor of the National Symphony Orchestra, will do a commentary.

"All the News That's Fit to Print"

The New York Times

LATE CITY EDITION

Weather: Mostly cloudy, seasonably cold today, tonight and tomorrow. Temp. range: today 34-42; Tuesday 37-42. Full U.S. report on Page 78.

VOL. CXXII . . . No. 41,976 — NEW YORK, WEDNESDAY, DECEMBER 27, 1972 — 15 CENTS

TRUMAN, 33D PRESIDENT, IS DEAD; SERVED IN TIME OF FIRST A-BOMB, MARSHALL PLAN, NATO AND KOREA

HARRY S. TRUMAN, 1884-1972

Funeral to Be Tomorrow In Independence Library

By B. DRUMMOND AYRES Jr.
Special to The New York Times

KANSAS CITY, Mo., Dec. 26—Harry S. Truman, the 33d President of the United States, died this morning. He was 88 years old.

Mr. Truman, an outspoken and decisive Missouri Democrat who served in the White House from 1945 to 1953, succumbed at 7:50 A.M., central standard time, in Kansas City's Research Hospital and Medical Center.

He had been a patient there for the last 22 days, struggling against lung congestion, heart irregularity, kidney blockages, failure of the digestive system and the afflictions of old age.

In the more than seven years he was President, from the time Franklin Delano Roosevelt's death suddenly elevated him from the Vice-Presidency until he himself was succeeded by Dwight David Eisenhower, Mr. Truman left a major mark as a world leader.

He brought mankind face to face with the age of holocaust by ordering atomic bombs dropped on Japan, sent American troops into Korea to halt Communist aggression in Asia, helped contain Communism in Europe by forming the North Atlantic Treaty Organization and speeded the postwar recovery of Europe through the Marshall Plan.

His domestic record was somewhat less dramatic, for his proposals and ideas were often premature. He ended up on the losing side of fights other Presidents later won — Federal health care, equal rights legislation, low income housing.

His other legacies were perhaps less tangible but no less remembered — the morning walk, the "give 'em hell" campaign that nipped Thomas E. Dewey at the wire, the desk plaque that proclaimed "The buck stops here!" and the word to the timid and indecisive: "If you can't stand the heat, you better get out of the kitchen."

An obituary article appears on Pages 46-49. An appraisal by the late Dean Acheson, written in 1964, will be found on Page 45.

Toward the end of his struggle for life, the former President weakened steadily. Early yesterday, his doctors warned that death might come "within hours."

When it came, the doctors announced that the cause was "a complexity of organic failures causing a collapse of the cardiovascular system."

A state funeral will be held Thursday in nearby Independence, Mr. Truman's home

Continued on Page 44, Column 1

United Press International
The Truman home in Independence, Mo., yesterday

National Day of Mourning Proclaimed by President

By JACK ROSENTHAL
Special to The New York Times

WASHINGTON, Dec. 26—President Nixon today declared Thursday a national day of mourning for former President Harry S. Truman and made plans to pay his personal respects tomorrow in Independence, Mo.

In a proclamation issued before leaving the vacation White House in Key Biscayne, Mr. Nixon ordered all Federal offices to close Thursday and urged that the nation pay homage to the late President in worship services.

Text of Nixon's proclamation will be found on Page 44.

As he returned to Washington, Mr. Nixon announced that he and Mrs. Nixon would fly to Independence tomorrow to lay a wreath at the Truman Presidential Library, where Mr. Truman's body will lie in state. Officials said that the Nixons hoped to have the opportunity to offer their condolences in person to Mrs. Truman.

The Nixons plan to return to Washington after the wreath-laying, indicating that they will not attend the funeral in Independence on Thursday.

The reason, it appeared, was the desire of the Truman family to have a private funeral.

It was announced in Austin, Tex., that former President and Mrs. Lyndon B. Johnson and members of their family would also go to Independence tomorrow to pay their final respects. They planned to return to Texas in the late afternoon.

All stock exchanges will be closed Thursday. Most banks, with the exception of those in Connecticut, will be open. Post offices will be closed, and there will be no regular delivery of mail. [Details on Page 59].

A memorial service for Mr. Truman here will be held in the Washington Cathedral, for Federal and foreign dignitaries. No date has been set, but the State Department said it would be within two weeks.

As a Senator and as Vice-Presidential candidate in 1952, Mr. Nixon had been bitterly critical of Mr. Truman, but today, the President voiced warm and unstinting praise.

In a statement issued an hour after word of Mr. Truman's death reached the vacation White House in Florida, Mr. Nixon said:

"Harry S. Truman will be remembered as one of the most courageous Presidents in our history, who led the nation and the world through a critical period with exceptional vision

Continued on Page 44, Column 2

U.S. SAYS BOMBING IS BACK AT LEVEL PRECEDING PAUSE

Warplanes From Thailand, Guam and Carriers Take Off for North Vietnam

HALT LASTED 36 HOURS

Hanoi Reports 8 B-52's Shot Down in Day—Pentagon Calls Loss Rate Normal

By JOSEPH B. TREASTER
Special to The New York Times

SAIGON, South Vietnam, Wednesday, Dec. 27—With its 36-hour pause in the bombing of North Vietnam ended, the United States command said yesterday that the planes were once again operating as they had last week, when the raids were the heaviest of the war.

Maj. Jere K. Forbus, a spokesman for the command, announced yesterday afternoon that the Christmas pause in bombing had ended three hours earlier, at 1 P.M. (midnight Monday, New York time). At that time, warplanes started taking off from aircraft carriers in the South China Sea and from bases in Thailand and Guam.

Informed officers had said before the pause that about 100 B-52's and several hundred smaller fighter-bombers had been participating in the attacks.

57 Listed as Missing

Many officers in Saigon said yesterday that despite denials from the Pentagon, B-52 losses since the raids began Dec. 18 have been much higher than had been expected.

As of last evening the command had acknowledged having lost 11 of the heavy eight-engine bombers, which each carry more than 24 tons of bombs and which usually fly in formations of three. The command has also reported six fighter-bombers down.

Altogether, the command says, 57 American airmen are missing in action. Hanoi says it has captured more than 100.

The Hanoi radio said today that eight more B-52's and an F-4 Phantom fighter-bomber were shot down yesterday. The North Vietnamese now maintain that they have destroyed a total of 62 American aircraft, including 26 of the heavy bombers, which are valued at $8-million each, since the raids began Dec. 18.

[The Pentagon had no comment on the Hanoi radio report, but it said earlier that the loss rate of B-52's was not materially greater than in raids last spring though now "there are more B-52's involved."]

'Brutal and Barbaric Act'

In a statement condemning the resumption of the bombing, the North Vietnamese Foreign Ministry said over the Hanoi radio this morning that many B-52's and "scores of other aircraft" struck urban and suburban areas in Hanoi, Haiphong, Thai Nguyen — the site of the nation's principal steel mill—and other cities last night.

"This is a brutal and barbaric act aimed at killing civilians, an act that surpasses Hitler's war crimes in scope and intensity," the Foreign Ministry

Continued on Page 10, Column 1

Jury Begins Investigation Into Drug Losses by Police

Judge Threatens Murphy With Contempt for Refusal to Cooperate in Inquiry as Two Officers Fail to Appear

By EMANUEL PERLMUTTER

A grand jury began taking testimony yesterday in the recently disclosed theft of 300 pounds of heroin and cocaine from the Police Department, and a judge threatened Police Commissioner Patrick V. Murphy and two of his aides with contempt for refusing to cooperate with the jury.

Gene L. Grupposo, the police property clerk, testified before the jurors in the morning in the Manhattan Criminal Court Building. However, Assistant Chief Inspector John Guido, who is in charge of the inspection division, and Inspector Howard A. Metzdorff of the internal affairs division, were not present to testify when their names were called.

The subpoenaing of the policemen by the grand jury was a rebuff to Maurice H. Nadjari, the special state prosecutor, and to Governor Rockefeller. Last October, the Governor had directed Commissioner Murphy to send information about possible criminal-justice corruption only to Mr. Nadjari. The city's District Attorneys and Mr. Nadjari are fighting over who should investigate the narcotics thefts.

A subpoena had been served on Commissioner Murphy last Friday, calling for the three witnesses to appear before the grand jury yesterday. Mr. Murphy was also directed to turn over to the jurors department records on the stolen narcotics that had been held as evidence by the police.

Frank Rogers, a special assistant district attorney who is in charge of prosecution in the 12 narcotics courts in the city, is supervising the citywide grand jury that is investigating the drug thefts as well as other narcotics cases.

At the request of Mr. Rogers, Supreme Court Justice Sidney A. Fine issued the subpoenas last week.

In a hearing yesterday before Justice Fine, Mr. Rogers contended that the grand jury

Continued on Page 25, Column 6

School Board Plans Offer To Buy Scribner Contract

By GENE I. MAEROFF

The Board of Education was drafting a letter yesterday that it intends to send to School Chancellor Harvey B. Scribner, outlining a proposal to buy up his contract. A board member, who declined to be identified, said that there "had been no dissent" at a meeting Friday at which the five members decided to offer to pay Dr. Scribner for the remaining six months of his three-year contract and relieve him of his $53,000-a-year post.

Dr. Scribner, who was reported to be out of town and unavailable for comment, announced at a news conference Thursday that he intended to leave his post June 30. He blamed his decision on a "confidence gap" that he said had developed between him and the Board of Education.

The names of possible successors have not been mentioned by the board, but speculation centered on Irving Anker, the deputy chancellor.

Once Headed System

Mr. Anker headed the 1.1-million-pupil New York City school system on an interim basis in 1970, before Dr. Scribner assumed the job. Mr. Anker is seen as someone who could again serve on an acting basis until a permanent chancellor is named.

Should Dr. Scribner refuse to accept a settlement, the board—if it continues to seek his removal—would have to bring departmental charges against him, which is regarded as an unlikely possibility.

"We would rather not have to think about this aspect," one board member said yesterday.

Prior to his announcement last week, Dr. Scribner's reappointment was by no means assured, but he was regarded as still being in contention.

However, he apparently

Continued on Page 27, Column 3

GRAND JURY GETS POLICE SHOOTING

Defendant Is Central Figure in $500 Bail Dispute Involving Two Judges

By RALPH BLUMENTHAL

A grand jury here began an investigation yesterday of the holdup shooting of a patrolman—a case that has stirred controversy because of the release of the suspect in $500 cash bail.

Among the first to testify was another man shot in the holdup. He said he had told the grand jury he could identify the holdup man.

The witness, Edward M. Blagden, then returned to his hospital bed, from where he made public an open letter berating Criminal Court Judge Bruce McMarion Wright for having released the suspect in $500 cash bail.

Judge Wright indicated yesterday that the case was under review by the Appellate Division and a spokesman said the judge was under the division's orders not to discuss the matter publicly.

Other judicial authorities, meanwhile, said they had no jurisdiction and indicated they were not now preparing any

Continued on Page 25, Column 1

Appraisal of the Arts

The second half of an assessment of the year in art and culture by nine critics for The New York Times appears on Page 29.

CITY AIDES TO LOSE APPROVAL POWER ON NEW BUILDING

Owners to Be Responsible Under Antigraft Plan—Delays Seen Curbed

By ROBERT E. TOMASSON

In a major move aimed at reducing "graft-inducing situations" in the construction industry, the city will shift authority for initial building approval next month from its 75 plan examiners to individual owners, architects and engineers.

The "sharp departure from tradition" was announced by Joseph Stein, Commissioner of the Department of Buildings, who said the move was taken in response to the industry's complaint of excessive delays in obtaining building permits that "created graft-inducing situations to obtain expeditious approval."

Instead of the months that were often required to obtain the necessary building permits, they will be issued within days under the new system, Commissioner Stein said.

Builder Cites 'Ways'

Owners will still be held accountable for meeting requirements of the building code, Mr. Stein said, but will no longer have to suffer delays because of objections raised by individual examiners.

Building plans have often had to be submitted several times before their approval, and there has been widespread talk in the industry that there "were ways," as one major builder phrased it yesterday, to expedite approval.

One alleged widespread abuse was the consideration of plans out of sequence in which they were submitted.

In a series of articles in The New York Times last summer, it was estimated that the construction industry paid out at least $25-million in bribes annually to officials and others in connection with virtually every phase of building.

Rise of the 'Expediter'

The complexity of the city's 371-page building code has given rise to creation of the position of men known in the trade as "expediters" whose essential function is to cultivate plan examiners.

One chief executive of a large construction firm here said yesterday that plan approval was often obtained "on what amounts to a scale system, with so much graft for each apartment" in a proposed project.

John Tudda, an architect whose firm has functioned as a consultant to expedite city approval on projects including the Ruppert Brewery Urban Renewal site in the Yorkville area of Manhattan and Lincoln

Continued on Page 18, Column 4

Study Finds Incomes More Unequal

By PHILIP SHABECOFF
Special to The New York Times

WASHINGTON, Dec. 26—A changing population and a changing industrial structure are producing a persistent trend toward inequality in the distribution of income among wage and salary earners in the United States, a study published by the Labor Department has found.

The trend is toward a concentration of an increasingly large share of average wage and salary income among people in jobs and professions that already bring higher pay, and it is likely to continue for some time, Peter Henle, author of the study, says.

The study, in the department's current Monthly Labor Review, departs from the widely accepted view that there has been little change in the distribution of income in America since World War II.

Most studies of income distribution examine family incomes, which include such nonearned incomes as welfare and Social Security payments. Family incomes also reflect the growing trend toward more than one wage earner per family.

The study by Mr. Henle, senior specialist on labor for the Library of Congress, examines only the money earnings, wages and salaries of male workers, so as to obtain a view of shifts in the distribution of payments for work performed.

Male Workers Studied

In the period examined, 1958-1972, average earned income was steadily rising throughout the economy as a whole. But in the distribution of that income Mr. Henle found "a slight persistent trend toward inequality." This trend toward inequality was found between various occupations and industries and was also found within several occupations and industries.

For example, using unpublished data from the Bureau of the Census, Mr. Henle found that from 1958 to 1970 the share of aggregate wage and salary income earned by the lowest fifth of male workers declined to 4.60 per cent from 5.10. At the same time, the share of the highest fifth of male wage and salary earners rose to 40.55 per cent from 38.15.

This trend did not necessarily affect the very highest-paid and lowest-paid workers on the earned income scale, Mr. Henle said. For example, he noted that, while there had been a marked increase in the number of professionals earning $40,000 to $50,000 a year, there had been little change in the number of executives earning $200,000 or more.

Denies 'Scheme Against Poor'

In a telephone interview, he stressed that the inequality in income distribution was not caused by any "nefarious scheme against poor people." Rather, the trend reflects a tendency in the economy to produce more higher-paying jobs without reducing the number of lower-paid workers, he said.

One reason has been a heavy flow of young people into the labor force as a result of the

Continued on Page 22, Column 4

NEWS INDEX

Tug of War Strains West Side Housing

By DEIRDRE CARMODY

An empty brick-strewn lot on the Upper West Side, first scheduled for middle-income housing and now slated for low-income housing, has become the symbol of controversy between groups in the neighborhood that are dedicated to preserving the ethnic and economic mix in the area but that cannot agree on how to do it.

The site, on Columbus Avenue between 90th and 91st Streets, is also a symbol of the pitfalls of the ambitious West Side Urban Renewal Project, which celebrates its 10th anniversary next month.

It is caught in a tug-of-war between those who believe there is an urgent need for middle-income housing to keep the area from becoming a slum and those who say that the urgent need is for low-income housing to relocate the hundreds of residents who have been uprooted by the urban-renewal project.

One of the major complainants about the housing change from middle-income to low-income is Trinity School, which is directly across 91st Street from the lot. The private coeducational school, which has been on its present site since 1893, has filed suit against the city in Federal Court for allegedly having reneged on an agreement with the school that provided for a middle-income apartment house on the site across the street.

According to school officials, Trinity has long considered moving the entire institution to Pawling, N. Y., where it owned land. As the area around the school became shabbier and increasingly less attractive to prospective parents (who today pay from $1,600 for a first-grader to $2,500 for a 12th-grader), the decision to move became more imminent.

By the mid-nineteen sixties the area, in the words of the lawsuit, was "deteriorated, substandard unsanitary" with "delapidated and crumbling structures" and a high incidence of crime.

At this time, however, the city was completing its fourth revision of the West Side Urban Renewal Project, which envisioned the refurbishing of the area from 87th Street to

Continued on Page 16, Column 4

Navy Buys $1.7-Million in Stock Of Ailing Defense Plant on L.I.

By DAVID A. ANDELMAN
Special to The New York Times

HAUPPAUGE, L.I., Dec. 26—The Navy has purchased all 17,414 shares of preferred stock in the Gap Instrument Corporation here as a means of helping the company, which has been experiencing heavy cost overruns. This has made the Department of Defense the largest single stockholder in the company.

The arrangement, believed to mark the first time that the Department of Defense has purchased stock in a private corporation, provides that no dividends be paid on the $1.7-million in nonvoting, nonconvertible shares and that the stock be redeemed beginning in 1976 but only out of the company's after-tax profits.

The company has not shown a profit in the last four years, and in 1968 showed a profit of only $10,700.

Last week, Senator William Proxmire criticized the Navy for acting as "Grumman's banker" because the Navy delivered a $26-million loan at 6⅞ per cent interest to that aerospace company for the F-14, a plane that has also experienced cost overruns.

Gap first ran into trouble nearly three years ago on a contract to manufacture 31 fire-control consoles for Navy destroyers. The company had

Continued on Page 20, Column 4

Truman, 33d President, Is Dead at 88

HE ASSUMED POST IN CRITICAL PERIOD

Marshall Plan, NATO and Korean War Highlighted Fight on Communism

Continued From Page 1, Col. 8

town, to mark his passing. Much of the ceremony will be subdued and private at the family's request.

State funerals are conducted only for former commanders in chief, although the President can direct that a state funeral be held for an individual. Modifications in state funerals, which usually cover four or five days with considerable ceremony, are made at the request of the family, as in this case.

President Nixon has declared the day of burial, Thursday, to be a day of national mourning. The American flag is to be flown at half-staff for 30 days.

The former President's body will lie in state in the Truman library in Independence from 1:35 P.M. tomorrow until 11 A.M. Thursday. Burial will follow on the library grounds at a spot chosen by Mr. Truman himself.

President Nixon will fly to Kansas City tomorrow afternoon, then go to the library to lay a wreath at the base of Mr. Truman's coffin. Although it was understood that the President's name appeared on the official list of persons invited to attend the funeral, it was expected that, in keeping with the subdued and private nature of the ceremony, he would not stay overnight for the funeral service and burial.

Tomorrow morning the coffin will be transported to the library in a motorcade that will pass the Victorian Truman home on the way from the Carson funeral home a few blocks away.

The service, scheduled to begin at 2 P.M. Thursday, will be held in the library's 250-seat auditorium. Attendance will be by invitation. Burial will follow immediately.

A memorial service for Mr. Truman here will be held in the National Cathedral in Washington for Federal and foreign dignitaries. No date has been set, but the State Department said it would be within two weeks.

Mrs. Truman at Home

The Truman family has asked that, in lieu of flowers, friends make donations to the library or charities.

At the time of his death, Mr. Truman's wife, Bess, 87, was at their home in Independence, having spent most of yesterday at the hospital. She was told of her husband's passing by his personal physician and long-time friend, Dr. Wallace Graham.

Mr. Truman's only child, Mrs. Clifton Daniel of New York, also was at the home. She flew to Kansas City last night for a brief visit with her father.

Today, Mr. Daniel, an associate editor of The New York Times, was met at the Kansas City airport by his wife and Mrs. Truman. The four Daniel boys—Thomas Washington, 4; Harrison Gates, 7; William Wallace, 11, and Clifton Truman, 13—are to arrive tomorrow.

The only other immediate Truman survivor is the former President's 83-year-old sister, Miss Mary Jane Truman of Grandview, a town southeast of Kansas City. She has been a patient in Research Hospital since suffering a fall several weeks ago and was notified of her brother's death in a nearby room within minutes.

The hospital announcement of Mr. Truman's death was released at 8:10 A.M. by Wayne E. Conery, an assistant administrator. It was the 80th bulletin concerning the former President's last illness and stated:

"The Hon. Harry S. Truman, 33d President of the United States, died at 7:50 A.M. at Research Hospital and Medical Center.

"The cause of death has not been determined. Dr. Wallace Graham was present.

"Mrs. Truman and Mrs. Clifton Daniel were notified at 7:52 A.M.

"Funeral arrangements have not been finalized. It is the wish of the family that in lieu of flowers, friends make memorial donations to the Harry S. Truman Library Institute, Independence, Mo. or to the charities of their choice."

Eighth Illness

Mr. Truman's final illness was the eighth to put him in Research Hospital in the post-Washington days. The others involved four cases of intestinal infection, a broken rib, a hernia and appendicitis.

The final period of illness began in late November as a case of minor lung congestion. Doctors initially treated Mr. Truman at home.

But they ordered him hospitalized on Dec. 5 when the congestion grew worse and his heart, already weakened by a long struggle with hardening of the arteries, began to beat irregularly under the strain.

At the time he was admitted to Research, Mr. Truman's condition was termed "fair." The next night, however, he became critically ill when his blood pressure dropped to 80/60, his pulse soared to 120 beats a minute, his temperature rose to 102.83 degrees and his breathing became labored.

But the former President fought back and was moved up to the "serious" list near the end of his first week of hospitalization. Asked how he felt, he told a doctor, "Better."

A few days later, just as his heart and lung condition seemed to be stabilizing, his kidneys began to fail under the strain of prolonged illness. His condition was described as "very serious" as impurities began to build in his blood.

But again he fought back, telling his doctors near the end of his second week of hospitalization that he felt "all right," even though they had ruled out the use of a kidney machine because of his hardened arteries. Mrs. Daniel returned to New York.

At that point, Mr. Truman's doctors began feeding him a special solution designed to reduce the impurities that were still building in his blood. There was an immediate reduction and a hospital bulletin reported:

"President Truman is showing remarkable strength and tenacious physiological reactions, which are a reflection of his attitudes toward life. We believe that we have begun a favorable trend."

But the trend was not to last.

At daybreak on the 18th day of his hospitalization, Mr. Truman went through what doctors termed a "dangerous period" as his blood pressure dropped and his temperature rose.

Mr. Truman's condition was changed from "very serious" to "critical" and his doctors and nurses began to monitor him almost constantly, particularly as his breathing became labored, his kidney output decreased, fluid built in his lungs and his heart began to flutter.

On Christmas morning, the former President was so weak that his doctors said death could come "within hours."

Today, it finally came.

The room in which the former President died is on the sixth floor of Research Hospital, a 500-bed facility he helped dedicate in 1963. Two red and green Christmas bells hang in the window, which looks east toward Independence and the recently completed baseball and football stadium of the Harry S. Truman sports complex.

The room cost $59.50 a day. In Mr. Truman's case it was paid for by private medical insurance and Medicare.

Long an advocate of Federal health plans, Mr. Truman held Medicare Card No. 1. He had not been able to push such a plan through during his own Presidency, but Lyndon B. Johnson was more successful and came to Independence in 1965 to sign the Medicare act in the Truman Library, enrolling the former President as the first member.

It was a final political victory for Harry S. Truman.

National Day of Mourning Proclaimed

Continued From Page 1, Col. 8

and determination. Our hopes today for a generation of peace rest in large measure on the firm foundation that he laid."

"He was a fighter, who was at his best when the going was toughest." Mr. Nixon continued. And then, making tacit reference to his own criticisms, Mr. Nixon said that Mr. Truman's friends and opponents alike "recognized and admired him—in a description he himself might have appreciated the most—as a man with 'guts'."

While Mr. Truman was embroiled in controversy during his Presidency, his "stature in the eyes of history has risen steadily ever since." Mr. Nixon said. "He did what had to be done, when it had to be done, and because he did the world today is a better and safer place—and generations to come will be in his debt," the President went on.

The statement was the second of four to come out of Key Biscayne today as Mr. Nixon prepared to return to Washington after a six-day Christmas holiday. The first was a personal message of condolence from the Nixons to Mr. Truman's widow. The contents of the note were not disclosed.

A third statement was a proclamation declaring the day of mourning and directing that flags be displayed at half-staff for 30 days. While this was largely a formal document, it also included expressions of high praise.

Mr. Truman, it said, "gave himself unstintingly to the duties of the Presidency while he held it, and in the years afterward he honorably supported and counseled each of his successors."

Nixon Leads Truman Tributes From U.S. and World Leaders

Following are tributes to former President Harry S. Truman that were expressed yesterday:

PRESIDENT NIXON—Harry S. Truman will be remembered as one of the most courageous Presidents in our history, who led the nation and the world through a critical period with exceptional vision and determination.

Our hopes today for a generation of peace rest in large measure on the firm foundation that he laid.

Recognizing the new threat to peace that had emerged from the ashes of war, he stood boldly against it with his extension of aid to Greece and Turkey in 1947—and the Truman Doctrine thus established was crucial to the defense of liberty in Europe and the world. In launching the Marshall Plan, he began the most far-sighted and most generous act of international rebuilding ever undertaken. With his characteristically decisive action in Korea, he made possible the defense of peace and freedom in Asia.

He was a fighter, who was at his best when the going was toughest. Like all political leaders, he had his friends and his opponents. But friends and opponents alike were unanimous in respecting him for his enormous courage, and for the spirit that saw him through whatever the odds. Whether in a political campaign or making the great decisions in foreign policy, they recognized and admired him—in a description he himself might have appreciated the most—as a man with "guts."

Embroiled in controversy during his Presidency, his stature in the eyes of history has risen steadily ever since. He did what had to be done, when it had to be done, and because he did the world today is a better and safer place—and generations to come will be in his debt.

It is with affection and respect that a grateful nation now says farewell to "the man from Independence"—to its 33d President, Harry S. Truman.

FORMER PRESIDENT LYNDON B. JOHNSON — A 20th-century giant is gone. Few men of any times ever shaped the world as did the man from Independence. President Truman presided over the destiny of this country during one of its most turbulent eras, never flinching in the face of events throughout the world.

When I last visited President Truman in Independence, I reminded him that it was his vision which led to much of the progress America has made in health care, aid to education, human rights and so many other programs he urged when they were not nearly so popular.

I told him that many of these became our laws, but they were his dreams. Because he championed the cause of the people, he had his critics and detractors, but history is just and Harry Truman will live on in the memory of free people as one of the greatest men to lead freedom's cause.

Harry Truman was my friend before he was President. He continued as friend and counselor, guide and inspiration after he left the Presidency.

When the burdens of that office fell upon me, he was one of the first to call and come to my side offering his support and strength. I shall miss him in a most personal and private way and I shall be grateful all my days for the privilege of having known so great a man.

QUEEN ELIZABETH II (in a message to President Nixon) —The people of Britain will long remember him warmly for his great personal and public qualities, and he will always be remembered with gratitude for his part in the creation of the Marshall Plan, which did so much to help Britain and the rest of Europe to recover from the ravages of war.

PRESIDENT POMPIDOU (in cables addressed both to President Nixon and to Mrs. Truman)—His name will forever be linked to the restoration of peace to the world and particularly to Europe following the Allied victory.

PRESIDENT PARK CHUNG HEE (in messages to President Nixon and to Mrs. Truman)—His name has become so dear to the Korean people and will continue to occupy the warmest spot in the thoughts of the Korean people. We are saddened at the loss of the distinguished world statesman whose heroic leadership and decisions during World War II and in the nineteen-fifties to save freedom and liberty in Korea and elsewhere will continue to be remembered with a sense of abiding appreciation.

SECRETARY GENERAL WALDHEIM (in a message to Mrs. Truman)—I wish to convey to you my deepest sympathy on the death of your most distinguished husband. We in the United Nations have special reason to hold President Harry S. Truman in high esteem. He personally attended the San Francisco conference which led to the creation of the charter and the establishment of the United Nations. He is thus truly one of our founding fathers.

His country and the world have lost a unique and courageous leader and we in the United Nations mourn the passing of a very warm and human friend. I extend to you and your family my deepest condolences.

PRIME MINISTER PIERRE ELLIOTT TRUDEAU in a letter to President Nixon—President Truman was well known to Canadians, and we recall with affection his visit to Ottawa in 1947. He exemplified to Canadians American warm-heartedness and close family life. In addition, we recall the courage and effectiveness with which he discharged the burdens of his high office at the close of the second World War and his great efforts for peace and postwar reconstruction.

HARRY S. TRUMAN: DECISIVE PRESIDENT

'The Lightning' Strikes in War

By ALDEN WHITMAN

AT 7:09 P.M. on April 12, 1945, Harry S. Truman, the Vice President of the United States, was elevated by the sudden death of Franklin D. Roosevelt to the Presidency of the United States. He lacked a month of being 61 years old, and he had been Vice President for only 83 days when Chief Justice Harlan F. Stone administered the oath in the White House Cabinet Room.

It was the third time since 1900 that a President had died in office, but it was the first wartime accession. For Truman, a hitherto minor national figure with a pedestrian background as a Senator from Missouri, the awesome moment came without his having intimate knowledge of the nation's tremendously intricate war and foreign policies. These he had to become acquainted with and to deal with instantly, for on him alone, a former haberdasher and politician of unspectacular scale, devolved the Executive power of one of the world's mightiest nations.

"But now the lightning had struck, and events beyond anyone's control had taken command," Truman wrote later.

These events, over which he presided and on which he placed his indelible imprint, were among the most momentous in national and world history, for they took place in the shadow and the hope of the Atomic Age, whose beginning coincided with Truman's accession. And during his eight years in office, the outlines of the cold war were fashioned.

In war-ravaged Europe in those years, Truman and the United States established peace and held back Soviet expansion and built economic and political stability through the Truman Doctrine, the Marshall Plan and the North Atlantic Treaty Organization. In the Mideast he recognized the State of Israel. In the Far East the President imposed peace and constitutional democracy on the Japanese enemy, tried valiantly to save China from Communism and chose to wage war in Korea to halt aggression. In the United States, Truman led the nation's conversion from war to peace, while maintaining a stable and prosperous economy.

Truman was sworn in as President by Chief Justice Harlan Fiske Stone at 7:09 P.M. on April 12, 1945.

Summons to Leadership

The drama and significance of these accomplishments were, of course, not readily predictable when Truman took office April 12, 1945, as the 33d President, but there was an element of theatricality in the way he was notified that the burden had fallen on him.

Two hours before Truman stood, Bible in hand, before the Chief Justice that misty Thursday, he had entered the office of Speaker Sam Rayburn in the House wing of the Capitol for a chat. Writing to his mother and sister a few days later, he said: ". . . as soon as I came into the room Sam told me that Steve Early, the President's confidential press secretary, wanted to talk with me. I called the White House, and Steve told me to come to the White House '*as quickly* and as quietly' as I could.

"I ran all the way to my office in the Senate by way of the unfrequented corridors in the Capitol, told my office force that I'd been summoned to the White House and to say nothing about it. . . ."

He arrived there at 5:25 P.M. and was taken by elevator to Mrs. Franklin D. Roosevelt's study on the second floor. As he emerged, Mrs. Roosevelt stepped forward and put her arm across his shoulders.

"Harry," she said quietly, "the President is dead."

For a minute Truman was too stunned to speak. Then, fighting off tears, he asked, "Is there anything I can do for you?"

With her characteristic empathy, Mrs. Roosevelt replied, "Is there anything *we* can do for *you*? For you are the one in trouble now."

In the next hour and a half Truman learned the details of Roosevelt's death at Warm Springs, Ga., gathered his composure and prepared to take the oath in the presence of Congressional leaders, Cabinet members, his wife, Bess, and their daughter, Margaret.

The person on whom the Executive power of the United States was so abruptly thrust was, in appearance, not distinctive. He stood 5 feet 8 inches tall. He had broad, square shoulders, an erect carriage, a round, apple-cheeked face, a long, sharp nose, deep blue eyes that peered through steel-rimmed glasses, and thin gray-white hair that was neatly parted and carefully brushed.

Apart from the plain eyeglasses, the most catching feature of Truman's face were his thin lips, which could be clamped in grimness or parted, over even teeth, in an engaging smile.

Dressed in a conservative double-breasted suit, with a 35th Infantry Division insigne in the left lapel and a white handkerchief peeping out of the breast pocket, Truman looked neat and plain. His only jewelry was a double-band gold Masonic ring on the little finger of his left hand. Aside from his speech—its flat, clipped, slightly nasal quality pegged him as a Middle Westerner—he seemed a typical small-city businessman, pleasant and substantial more at home on Main Street than on Pennsylvania Avenue.

Certainly he could not have been typecast as a Senator. He was not an orator, nor even a frequent speaker, in his 10 years as a Democratic Senator from Missouri. But when he did speak, he was listened to closely, for his remarks were coherent, forceful and usually brief.

He was industrious on Senate committees, and he served with distinction and fairness as chairman of the Special Committee to Investigate the National Defense Program. He was popular ("Harry" to everyone) and a member of the Senate's inner circle. He was known for his informal geniality, his homely language and also, on occasion, for his irascibility and brusqueness.

Unlike most of his fellow legislators, Truman did not have a college degree or a fixed profession. His formal education had ended with high school, and he had been in business from time to time, but mostly he had been in politics. He was a county official from 1922 until his election to the Senate in 1934.

An inquisitive and retentive mind helped to compensate for Truman's lack of schooling, and he employed it in prodigious, if haphazard, reading, especially in American political history.

Although he had been Roosevelt's choice as a ticket mate in 1944 and although the two men were on good terms, Truman was not, even as Vice President, a White House intimate, closely informed on the progress of the war. He had supported Roosevelt at home and abroad, but his personal inclinations were more conservative.

His private attitude toward Roosevelt was astringent, according to Margaret Truman Daniel's "Harry S. Truman," published this year. His daughter's book quoted a desk-pad memo of 1948 that said "I don't believe the USA wants any more fakers—Teddy and Franklin are enough. So I'm going to make a common-sense, intellectually honest campaign."

From the very first, Truman had to exercise his new authority from minute to minute, while his advisers briefed him as swiftly as they could. "I did more reading than I ever thought I could," he said after his first full day in office. But he was aware of his inadequacies.

"Boys," he told a group of reporters in those first days, "if you ever pray, pray for me now. . . . I've got the most terribly responsible job a man ever had."

Truman's first decision was routine. The question: Should the San Francisco conference on the United Nations meet April 25, as scheduled? "I did not hesitate a second" in giving an affirmative response, he recalled.

His second decision—to meet with the Cabinet and ask its members to remain on—was also easy. But most of the judgments that followed (including Cabinet dismissals) were not.

"I felt as if I had lived five lifetimes in those first days as President," he said of his "mighty leap" into the White House and global politics.

'The Buck Stops Here'

In creating and carrying out his policies, Truman built a reputation for decisiveness and courage. He did not fret once his mind was made up.

"I made it clear [to the first Cabinet session] that I would be President in my own right," Truman said, "and that I would assume full responsibility for such decisions as had to be made."

Expressing the same thought, a sign on his desk read: "The buck stops here."

With the war in Europe near its triumphant end, Truman had immediately to deal with Soviet intentions to impose Communist regimes in Eastern Europe and possibly to exploit the economic breakdown in Western Europe. Simultaneously he had to seek military and political solutions in the war against Japan. Both situations involved Soviet-American relations, and both gave initial shape to decades of strife and conflict between the world's two major powers.

Whereas Roosevelt tended to be flexible in coping with the Russians, Truman held sterner views. "If we see that Germany is winning the war, we ought to help Russia; and if that Russia is winning, we ought to help Germany, and in that way let them kill as many as possible. . . ." he said as a Senator in 1941. This basic attitude prepared him to adopt, from the start of his Presidency, a firm policy.

Showdown With Molotov

The Polish question epitomized his approach. This thorny matter arose from the Yalta agreements of February, 1945, when the Red Army had driven the Nazis from the plains of Poland. The accord, calling for a broadly based Polish regime and eventual free elections, was fuzzily worded. The Russians took it to mean a pro-Moscow Government; Truman read it to require a Western style of government.

"I was not afraid of the Russians and . . . I intended to be firm," he said. "I would be fair, of course, and anyway the Russians needed us more than we needed them."

Determined to push his point on Poland as a symbol of Soviet-American relations, Truman had his first personal exchange, tart and brusque, with Vyacheslav M. Molotov, the Soviet Foreign Minister, in Washington on April 22 and 23, 1945. The President used "words of one syllable" to convey his insistence that Poland be "free and independent."

"I have never been talked to like that in my life," Molotov complained.

"Carry out your agreements, and you won't get talked to like that," his host retorted.

After much pulling and hauling, Poland got a regime that the United States recognized, but not before Truman's dislike of Russian diplomatic in-fighting had hardened.

"Force is the only thing the Russians understand," he concluded, and force in one guise or another was to underlay his subsequent dealings with Moscow and the Communist bloc.

Even so, Truman got along rather well with Josef Stalin, the Soviet dictator, whom he met for the first time at the Potsdam Conference in July, 1945. "I liked him a lot," Truman said, adding that, of course, "Uncle Joe" (as he called Stalin behind his back) "didn't mean what he said" and consistently broke his word.

In the foreground of Truman's dealings with Stalin at Potsdam and afterward was the atomic-bomb project. Started in the deepest secrecy in the early days of World War II, it was on the verge of producing its first explosive when Truman became President.

Although project scientists, some people in the military and a few civilians were aware of the incalculable world importance of an atomic bomb, the President himself had been told nothing. Not only had the project been kept secret from him as a Senator and as Vice President, but also the immense scientific, military, civilian and moral implications of atomic fission had not been presented to him.

Atomic Power Unchained

Thus Truman was unprepared when Secretary of War Henry L. Stimson explained the atomic project to him on April 25, 1945—13 days after he had become President—and told him of the then presumed fantastic power of an atomic bomb. Apart from its staggering military potential, what impressed the President almost immediately were its implications for American diplomacy and world peace.

"If it explodes, as I think it will, I'll certainly have a hammer on those boys," he said, alluding to the Russians.

At the same time it was assumed by Truman and Stimson and virtually everyone connected with the atomic project that the bomb would be employed as a matter of course to shorten the Japanese war. The moral implications of its use and the total effect of atomics on United States-Soviet relations, later topics of vigorous debate, were not then publicly raised or widely appreciated.

Nevertheless, once an atomic device was tested and its destructiveness confirmed, Truman said in an interview in 1966 for this article that he had given the matter of actually using the bomb "long and careful thought."

"I did not like the weapon," he said, "but I had no qualms, if in the long run millions of lives could be saved."

Against his critics—and there were many in after years—he took the responsibility for the atomic havoc inflicted on Hiroshima and Nagasaki. The bombs, he maintained, did shorten the war and did save millions of American and Japanese battlefield casualties.

With the unconditional surrender of Germany on May 8, 1945, a meeting of Truman, Stalin and Winston Churchill, the British Prime Minister, became necessary to consider Europe's problems and to prepare, in accordance with Yalta, for Soviet entry into the Pacific war. Twice delayed by Truman pending the plutonium-bomb test at Alamogordo, N. M., the conference at Potsdam began July 17—the day Truman learned the bomb was a success—and lasted through Aug. 1. It was the President's only meeting with Stalin and his first with Church-

(continued)

President Truman joined Churchill and Stalin at Potsdam after Nazi Germany collapsed in May 1945.

ill, with whom he formed a lasting friendship.

For all the popular hope that was invested in Potsdam and for all the grinding hours that the statesmen and their aides conferred, few European disputes were settled. Stalin pledged, however, to invade Japanese-held Manchuria early in August, and he subscribed to a surrender appeal to Japan that implied she could retain a constitutional Emperor.

Amid the Potsdam wrangles, Truman, by arrangement with Churchill, offhandedly informed Stalin of the bomb, but not that it was atomic.

"On July 24 I casually mentioned to Stalin that we had a new weapon of unusual destructive force," Truman recalled. "The Russian Premier showed no special interest. All he said was that he was glad to hear it and hoped we would make 'good use of it against the Japanese.'"

Tottering since June, Japan surrendered Aug. 14, 1945, after the atomic-bomb toll at Hiroshima and Nagasaki had exceeded a total of 100,000 lives and after the Russians had stormed into Manchuria. The victory was sealed on the battleship Missouri, in Tokyo Harbor, when Gen. Douglas MacArthur, the United States commander, accepted the capitulation of the Japanese. The global war, in which the United States had been engaged since 1941, was ended, and a new and different era was emerging.

In the war's course the United States created an industrial plant of unrivaled productivity, with a Gross National Product that soared from $101-billion in 1941 to $125-billion in 1945. Its citizens, meanwhile, accumulated millions in unspent cash. How to handle this new affluence without touching off a perilous inflation was the major concern of reconversion.

Program for Prosperity

The Truman program, given to Congress on Sept. 6, 1945, called for full employment, increased minimum wages, private and public housing programs, a national health program, aid to education, Negro job rights, higher farm prices and continuation of key wartime economic controls.

A President generally friendly to labor (he vetoed the Taft-Hartley bill in 1947), Truman stoutly refused what he considered exorbitant pay goals. In April, 1946, he seized the coal mines when John L. Lewis's 400,000 miners struck for more money. And in another strike that November, Lewis and his union were fined.

The contest between Truman and Lewis, both stubborn men, captured the headlines, with Lewis insisting that mine seizure by troops was a hollow gesture, because "you can't mine coal with bayonets," and with Truman appealing to the miners' patriotism. It was Lewis who yielded, as did the railway unions when the President seized the carriers in May, 1946, to avert a walkout.

If Truman turned out to be not a pet of labor, neither was he a darling to business and industry. He lifted price and profit controls gingerly, vetoed a $4-billion tax cut in 1947, seized steel plants in a labor-and-price dispute in 1952 and increased the Federal budget.

Fair Deal programs met a mixed reaction in Congress, especially after the midterm elections of 1946 gave the Republicans a majority in both the House and the Senate. Truman proposals for broadening civil rights and for Medicare were shunned. In both areas he was in advance of his time, but he lived to see himself vindicated.

In 1965, when Congress passed the Medicare bill, President Johnson journeyed to Missouri to sign the measure in Truman's presence. The Civil Rights Act of 1964 reflected many of Truman's aspirations for Negro equality.

President Truman fared better on unification of the armed forces into a Department of Defense and on establishment of an Atomic Energy Commission. On taxes, price controls and union regulation, his relations with Congress were not uniformly smooth.

"I discovered that being President is like riding a tiger," he remarked afterward. "A man has to keep on riding or be swallowed."

Truman's individuality was also reflected in Cabinet changes. The Roosevelt Cabinet, save for James V. Forrestal as Secretary of Defense, was dismembered by 1948. Some departures were summary, as with Treasury Secretary Henry Morgenthau Jr. and Commerce Secretary Henry A. Wallace.

Wallace was discharged in the fall of 1946 in an uproar over a speech that seemed to contradict the President's hard Soviet policy. Wallace had thought his remarks were approved by the White House, but it turned out that Truman had only glanced at the text.

Other appointments brought Gen. George C. Marshall, whom Truman revered, into the Cabinet as Secretary of State and Secretary of Defense; Dean Acheson, whose intellect Truman admired, as Secretary of State; and John C. Snyder, whose financial acumen the President respected, as Treasury Secretary. James F. Byrnes served briefly as Secretary of State and was dropped in a personality clash.

Truman's foreign program was to combat Communist expansion and to strengthen what he called the free world. Supported by Senator Arthur H. Vandenberg and other leading Republicans, this policy became bipartisan in its major aspects. Backed by American economic and atomic power, it was remarkably successful. In China, however, the Nationalist Government collapsed despite American exertions, and the Communists took over in 1949.

But in the Middle East the Soviet was obliged to withdraw from Iran. In Yugoslavia a non-Stalinist regime developed. There was outstanding success in Europe, thanks to the Truman Doctrine, inaugurated in 1947.

In that year Britain, for lack of money, had to halt her subventions to Greece and Turkey, nations under heavy Communist pressure. With great dispatch, Truman convinced Congress it should extend cash help. This historic action, he said later, was "the turning point" in damming Soviet expansion in Europe, because it "put the world on notice that it would be our policy to support the cause of freedom wherever it was threatened."

The President's doughty action kept Greece and Turkey in the Western orbit, and the Truman Doctrine was the logical base for the Marshall Plan, enunciated by Secretary of State Marshall in the summer of 1947. Under it, the United States invited all European nations to cooperate in their economic recovery, with billions of dollars in American backing.

Western Europe, on the brink of economic disaster, responded favorably, achieving stability and eventually a new prosperity. The Marshall Plan, or the European Recovery Plan as it was formally named, "helped save Europe from economic disaster and lifted it from the shadow of enslavement by Russian Communism," Truman said.

Truman's leadership of the non-Communist world was reflected in vigorous support of the United Nations. Through its mechanism he hoped to keep world peace by positive actions, as well as by thwarting Soviet power plays and intrigues. Moscow, for its part, appeared bent on trouble-making both in the United Nations and out of it.

The Soviet strategy of trying to humble the United States had a crucial test in 1948, when the Russians blockaded Berlin by land in an effort to force the United States to quit the city. Truman resisted, and under his direction an American airlift was organized to fly food and medicines into that beleaguered city. The airlift, in which hundreds of planes participated over many months, forced the Russians to back down.

Soviet-American clashes intruded into domestic politics, especially after the Soviet Union exploded its first atomic device in 1949. A vocal segment of public opinion asserted that the Russians could only have mastered atomics by stealing American secrets. Outcries led to heated charges of Communist infiltration in high Government places. In time a loyalty-security program was set up for Government employes and defense workers.

But disquiet, fear and suspicion spread in the land. In vain Truman sought to establish calm and a sense of perspective that could be gained through judicial proceedings against suspected spies and disloyal persons.

As Truman's first term came to a close, he was accounted successful in foreign affairs and beset by domestic ones.

He had won recognition as a person in his own right, but there was dispute over the degree to which the country liked what he had become—dogged, scrappy, "right in the big things, but wrong in the small ones," as House Speaker Sam Rayburn phrased it.

From Missouri Farm to Fame

"MY first memory is that of chasing a frog around the backyard in Cass County, Missouri. Grandmother Young watched the performance and thought it very funny that a 2-year-old could slap his knee and laugh so loudly at a jumping frog."

Harry S. Truman was 68 when he wrote that recollection of his carefree farm childhood, so secure in strong, affectionate family bonds.

A product of the Middle Border and of hardy farming stock with frontier traditions, Truman was born at 4 P.M. May 8, 1884, in a small frame house at Lamar, Mo. He was the first-born of John Anderson Truman and Mary Ellen Young Truman. The initial 'S' was a compromise between Shippe and Solomon, both kinsman's names.

Within the year the family moved to a farm near Harrisonville, Mo., where another son, Vivian, was born in 1886. A year later the Trumans were living on a Jackson County farm, near what was to be Grandview. There, Mary Jane, the third child, was born.

"Those were wonderful days and great adventures," Truman said of his growing up on 600 stretching acres. "My father bought me a beautiful black Shetland pony and the grandest saddle to ride him with I ever saw." When Harry was 6, the family moved once more, to Independence, a Kansas City suburb, but John Truman remained a farmer and took up the buying and selling of cattle, sheep and hogs.

The Girl With Golden Curls

It was in Independence that Harry, whose mother had taught him his letters by 5, went to school. He made friends, one in particular. "She had golden curls . . . and the most beautiful blue eyes," he said of Bess Wallace, the childhood sweetheart who was to become his wife. Harry was a shy boy with weak eyes, who wore glasses from the age of 8. Shunning rough-and-tumble sports, he read fast and furiously. By 14 he "had read all the books in the Independence Public Library, and our big old Bible three times through."

Poor eyesight barred him from the United States Military Academy (to which he had an appointment) when he was graduated from high school in 1901; and, since the family lacked the money to send him to college, he turned to a variety of jobs. He worked as a drugstore clerk, timekeeper on a railroad construction project, in a mailroom, in a bank. He speculated in zinc and oil. And he toiled on the family farm. Meantime, he joined Battery B of the National Guard in 1905 and became a member of the Masonic Order in 1909.

When the United States entered World War I, Truman, then 32, was a farmer. He left the soil to help organize the 129th Field Artillery, and he became commander of its Battery D. He led it into action at St. Mihiel, in the Meuse-Argonne offensive in France, and again at Verdun, gaining the respect and affection of his men. (At convivial reunions later, "Captain Harry" used to play the piano—he had learned as a youth, at his mother's insistence—while his comrades sang.)

Mustered out in 1919, he returned to Independence and married Miss Wallace on June 28. Then 35 and without a firm station in civilian life, he opened a haberdashery shop in Kansas City in association with Edward Jacobson, an Army buddy. At the start, business was excellent, but the postwar depression changed all that, and Truman & Jacobson were obliged to close. Jacobson went through bankruptcy proceedings; Truman did not, and he was still paying off his creditors (the total was $28,000) 10 years later when he was a Senator.

Truman's entry into politics was fortuitous. It occurred in 1921, when James Pendergast, an Army friend, introduced Truman to his father, Mike Pendergast, who, with his brother, Thomas J., ran Democratic politics in western Missouri. A veteran, a Baptist, a Mason, the personable Truman was adjudged a likely officeholder, and in 1922 he was elected a judge of the Jackson County Court. The post, a nonjudicial one, had juris-

(continued)

diction over the building and upkeep of the county roads and public buildings.

Truman was conscientious, vigorous and industrious, both as a campaigner and as an administrator. He was defeated, however, in 1924. But in 1926 he was elected presiding judge and again in 1930, both times with the help of the Pendergast organization. In 1934 Truman wanted to run for the House of Representatives, but the Pendergasts put him up for the Senate instead. Running on a pro-Roosevelt program in a strenuous campaign, he won with a majority of more than 250,000 votes. His record of probity as a county official and his Masonic connections helped him.

Although Truman never disavowed his close friendship with Thomas Pendergast, the leader of the party machine, he made it clear in the Senate and elsewhere that he was not "Pendergast's messenger boy." There was never any tarnish on his reputation for personal integrity.

Truman was nearly 51 when he took his Senate seat. But "I was as timid as a country boy arriving on the campus of a great university for his first year," he recalled. "I had a prayer in my heart for wisdom to serve the people acceptably."

First Lieutenant Truman who served overseas during World War I.

'Plain Folks' in Capital

In Washington, Senator and Mrs. Truman lived simply in an apartment with their daughter and only child, Mary Margaret, who was born Feb. 17, 1924. The family was "plain folks," with Truman coming home in the evening to talk to Margie, as he called his daughter, and to recount the day's happenings to his wife, whom he called "The Boss." The Trumans were little evident on the social and cocktail circuit. Mrs. Truman was popular with the Congressional wives and her husband with his colleagues. For relaxation, he liked to sip bourbon and water (but never in the presence of women, not even his wife) and to play a bit of poker. Otherwise he worked; there were documents and books and reports to read, committee duties to fulfill, constituents to see and do favors for, Senate sessions to attend.

The years Truman spent in the Senate he recalled as "the happiest 10 years of my life." He found his fellow Senators "some of the finest men I have ever known," and he used the word "cherish" to describe his friendship for them. He was a member of two important committees—Appropriations and Interstate Commerce—to whose work he devoted himself with diligence. He read voluminously from the Library of Congress, but he spoke seldom on the Senate floor, and then simply, briefly, without ostentation. His voting record was New Deal, which earned him the opposition of the big Missouri papers.

Truman was re-elected in 1940, but only after a hard and close Democratic primary race. Harry Vaughan, later to be a White House crony, and Robert Hannegan, later to be Postmaster General, worked hard for Truman, and to them, as to other friends, he was unswervingly loyal. It was part of his creed of "doing right."

Defense Waste Exposed

When Truman was sworn for his second term in 1941, the nation was preparing for war, and the letting of defense contracts was surrounded with rumors of favoritism and influence. Deeply concerned, Truman got into his automobile for a 30,000-mile tour of major defense plants and projects.

"The trip was an eye-opener, and I came back to Washington convinced that something needed to be done fast," he said. "I had seen at first hand that grounds existed for a good many of the rumors . . . concerning the letting of contracts and the concentration of defense industries in big cities."

The result was the Special Committee to Investigate the National Defense Program, soon shortened to the Truman Committee after the name of its chairman. It saved the country many millions of dollars by curbing waste and discouraging graft. And it made Truman a minor national figure, conspicuous for his firmness and his fairness.

Truman prepared his investigation by making a thorough study of similar committees in the past, especially of the records of the Joint Committee on the Conduct of the War Between the States. Defining his approach, the Senator said:

"The thing to do is to dig up the stuff now and correct it. If we run the war program efficiently, there won't be an opportunity to undertake a lot of investigations after the war and cause a wave of revulsion that will start off the country on the downhill road to unpreparedness and put us in another war in 20 years."

The committee got under way slowly, with $15,000 appropriated for its tasks. Truman invested $9,000 of this in the salary of Hugh Fulton the group's investigator and counsel. The committee quickly turned up disquieting evidence of waste in military-camp construction and equipment. And once its first reports—sober, factual and damning—were issued, more money for its operations was forthcoming.

The dollar-a-year man came under its scrutiny, and the committee was able to produce evidence that between June 1, 1940 and April 30, 1941, Army and Navy contracts totaling almost $3-billion had gone to 65 companies whose officials or former officials were serving in Washington and elsewhere as unpaid advisers to Federal agencies.

Truman also inquired into aluminum production, the automobile industry, the aviation program, copper, lead, zinc and steel; into labor, plant financing, defense housing, lobbying, ordnance plants, small business and Government contracts. Scarcely any aspect of procurement escaped his attention. The committee's hearings were orderly, remarkably free of partisanship, but they produced news and, more important, correction of the abuses that the Senators had brought to light.

Truman was as unsparing of industrialists as he was of union leaders. He criticized William S. Knudsen, director of the Office of Production Management, for "bungling"; he was just as harsh with Sidney Hillman, the union leader, who was associate director of the office.

The Senator was himself a zestful investigator and a keen questioner. He said later that the committee's watchdog role "was responsible for savings not only in dollars and precious time but in actual lives" on the battlefield.

Mr. Truman (L) was a partner in a Kansas City haberdashery from 1919 to 1922.

In the course of the committee's work, Truman was in touch with President Roosevelt, but there was no immediate serious thought of him as Vice-Presidential material. When early in 1944 some friends mentioned the possibility to him, Truman "brushed it aside."

"I was doing the job I wanted to do; it was the one I liked, and I had no desire to interrupt my career in the Senate," he said.

Indeed, Truman had so far removed himself from consideration that he had agreed in July, on the eve of the Democratic Convention in Chicago, to nominate James F. Byrnes for Vice President, after Byrnes told him that Roosevelt had given him the nod. Meantime Roosevelt had decided to drop Vice President Henry A. Wallace and also, it turned out, to pass over Byrnes.

The choice fell on Truman. He was not so closely identified with labor as Wallace, although he was acceptable, nor was he a Southern conservative, as was Byrnes. He was without fierce enemies, had an excellent reputation, was moderate on civil rights and was a Midwesterner. Truman, however, was almost the last to know of Roosevelt's decision.

"On Tuesday evening of convention week," he recalled, "National Chairman Bob Hannegan came to see me and told me unequivocally that President Roosevelt wanted me to run with him on the ticket. This astonished me greatly, but I was still not convinced. Even when Hannegan showed me a longhand note written on a scratch pad from the President's desk which said, 'Bob, it's Truman. F.D.R.,' I still could not be sure that this was Roosevelt's intent."

It took a long-distance call to Roosevelt, then on the West Coast, to convince Truman.

"Bob," Roosevelt said, "have you got that fellow lined up yet?"

"No," Hannegan replied. "He's the contrariest Missouri mule I've ever dealt with."

"Well, you tell him," Truman heard the President say, "if he wants to break up the Democratic party in the middle of a war, that's his responsibility."

"I was completely stunned," Truman remarked afterward. After walking around the hotel room, he said, "Well, if that is the situation, I'll have to say yes, but why the hell didn't he tell me in the first place?"

Following the nomination, Truman stumped the nation for Roosevelt and himself; for the President campaigned almost not at all. The Roosevelt-Truman slate won with ease over Gov. Thomas E. Dewey of New York and Senator John W. Bricker of Ohio, the Republican choices for President and Vice President. The popular vote was 25,602,555 to 22,006,278. and the Electoral College tally was 432 to 99.

On Jan. 20, 1945, a snowy Saturday, Harry S. Truman stood on the South Portico of the White House and was inaugurated. The man he was about to displace, Vice President Henry A. Wallace, administered the oath.

The Glorious Comeback of 1948

"A GONE GOOSE" was how Clare Boothe Luce described Harry S. Truman in 1948. With that Republican assessment of the President's chances for election on his own, many Democrats agreed—Frank Hague of Jersey City and Mayor William O'Dwyer of New York among them. Truman had his own views.

"There was no doubt of the course I had to take," he said. "I felt it my duty to get into the fight and help stem the tide of reaction, if I could, until the basic aims of the New Deal and the Fair Deal could be adopted, tried and proved."

The Republicans' exultancy and the Democrats' pessimism seemed well founded. Early in 1948 Truman, who had always opposed discrimination, submitted to Congress a series of moderate civil rights proposals that included antilynching and antisegregation measures. Southern Democrats were disconcerted. They organized a States Rights party, with Senator J. Strom Thurmond of South Carolina as its Presidential candidate, to sunder the Democrats' traditional Solid South.

At the other end of the political spectrum, pacifist and leftist groups, alarmed over the Cold War with the Soviet Union, and dissident labor groups rallied around Henry A. Wallace and formed a Progressive party to challenge the Democrats in the big Northern and Western cities.

Added to those seemingly fatal Democratic rifts was a generalized voter discontent over inflation, high taxes, the presence of Truman's Missouri friends in the White House and in preferred administrative jobs.

Furthermore, some sophisticates thought ill of a President who relaxed at Key West, Fla., in brightly hued sports shirts, whose words lacked scholarly elegance and who was inclined to be snappish with his Republican Congress.

Truman himself conceded the dismal outlook for his fortunes. "Almost unanimously the polls taken before the 1948 Democratic Convention showed my popularity with the American people to have hit an all-time low," he said.

He was convinced nonetheless that this "resulted from the efforts made by the American press to misrepresent me and to make my program, policies and staff appear in the worst possible light." His complaint had some merit: most publishers were stanchly Republican, and frequently their news columns gave more space to Truman's opponents than to his defenders.

"I knew I had to do something," the President recalled, and that "something" was to "go directly to the people in all parts of the country with a personal message."

The consequence was a "nonpolitical" train trip in May to the West Coast and back. On it Truman delivered 76 speeches, many at whistle stops, and the bulk of them extemporaneously. They were plain, earnest talks that expounded his domestic and foreign program, and they created a favorable impression. Indeed, even those Democrats who were considering drafting Gen. Dwight D. Eisenhower, because of his aura as a war leader, now warmed up to Truman.

He was thereupon nominated with ease, and selected to run with him was Senator Alben W. Barkley of the border state of Kentucky.

Earlier, expectant Republicans had chosen Gov. Thomas E. Dewey of New York as their Presidential candidate and Gov. Earl Warren of California as his ticket mate. Their platform emphasized that "it is time for a change," and it pledged action to halt rising prices, meet the housing shortage, promote civil rights and aid education. The party exuded confidence; the campaign appeared to be little more than a formal prelude to inauguration.

Truman, however, took the offensive, starting with his acceptance speech before the Democratic Convention. It was a rousing talk given from notes, and it foreshadowed his campaign strategy and his style.

"I made a tough, fighting speech," he recalled. "I recited the benefits that had been won by the Democratic Administrations for the people."

He singled out farmers and workers, telling them that "if they don't do their duty by the Democratic party, they are the most ungrateful people in the world."

Then, to use his words, he "tore into the 80th Congress" and the Republican party, building to his climax—an announcement that he would recall the Congress into special summer session to

(continued)

enact the recently adopted Republican platform.

It was a masterly tactic, for the special session accomplished nothing. Its Republican leaders were awaiting what seemed to them an assured Dewey victory in November, and they had no desire to give Truman credit for legislation that might better go to Dewey. In the meantime Truman took himself to the country.

"I am going to fight hard; I am going to give them hell," he assured Barkley as he prepared to denounce again and again "that no-good, do-nothing 80th Congress."

The Long Campaign Trail

His campaign covered 31,700 miles, and it included 256 speeches—16 in one day once. More than 12 million people turned out to see him. "I simply told the people in my own language," he said later, "that they had better wake up to the fact that it was their fight."

He appealed to farmers not to jeopardize their prosperity. To labor he vowed a fight to repeal the Taft-Hartley Act. To Negroes he promised more civil rights. And to everyone he said he would carry on his domestic program "for the benefit of all the people."

The response, mild at first, grew in late September and October, and at the end, wherever he appeared, the crowds were large and friendly, and there were yells of "Give 'em hell, Harry," and the throngs applauded and cheered when he did just that. Owing to bipartisanship, however, foreign policy was not an active issue; the concentration was on domestic affairs.

Dewey, for his part, was speaking in polished and euphonious generalities, virtually ignoring his opponent. He pleaded for "unity" among the voters, much like a man who had already won an election. The polls and the commentators all predicted he would win, and he did not see how he could lose.

But Truman sensed something else. A homespun man without guile, he believed that he had touched the common man with simple, hortatory speeches, whose theme was, "Help me."

Dewey 'Election' Reversed

Election eve, Truman was in Missouri. He took a Turkish bath, ate a ham sandwich, drank a glass of milk and went to bed. He awoke twice during the night, both times to listen to Hans von Kaltenborn's clipped, slightly Teutonic-voiced radio analyses of the returns. These showed Truman ahead in the popular vote—but he couldn't possibly win, the commentator insisted. (For years afterward Truman delighted in imitating Kaltenborn's remarks that night, just as he enjoyed poking fun at The Chicago Tribune, which "elected" Dewey in its early-edition headline.)

At 6 A.M. on Nov. 3, when the California vote came in, Truman was elected in what many experts called a stunning upset. The tally gave him 24,105,695 votes to Dewey's 21,969,170; in the Electoral College the vote was Truman, 303; Dewey, 189, and Thurmond, 39. Wallace received no electoral votes, though his popular vote, a little more than a million, equaled Thurmond's.

"I was happy and pleased," the President said, not only for himself but also for the Democratic Congress that was elected with him.

The President opened his new term with characteristic audacity, by using his Inaugural Address on Jan. 20, 1949, to call for fulfillment of his domestic plans and to urge reinforcement of the Western alliance against Soviet power.

But the high spot of his foreign program was a proposal that the United States share its tremendous scientific and industrial experience with nations emerging from colonialism into freedom. He summed up the plan (quickly shortened to Point Four, because it was the fourth point in the foreign program) in these words:

"I believe we should make available to peace-loving people the benefits of our store of technical knowledge, in order to help them realize their aspirations for a better life."

Help to Weaker Nations

Point Four captured the imagination of the peoples in the underdeveloped world, and more than 34 nations eventually signed up for technical assistance. By 1953 Truman was able to report that the program "had relieved famine measurably in many portions of the world, had reduced the incidence of diseases that keep many areas poverty-stricken, and had set many nations on the path of rising living standards by their own efforts and by the work of their own nationals."

Truman detailed his domestic proposals in a State of the Union message. These included controls on prices, credit, wages and rents to fight inflation; priorities and allocations of essential materials; new civil-rights laws; a 75-cent-an-hour basic wage; health insurance; expanded Social Security; low-cost housing and a tax increase.

"Every segment of our population and every individual has the right to expect from our Government a fair deal," he declared. The "fair deal" phrase was picked up and became the shorthand name for his program.

Meanwhile the President was confronted with a fearful and insecure Europe, uncertain anew of the extent of Soviet bellicosity after the Communist take-over of Czechoslovakia in 1948. The response Truman framed was military: the mutual security system of the North Atlantic Treaty Organization. The treaty embracing Western Europe and the United States was signed April 4, 1949, and ratified Aug. 14 by the Senate.

The pact, which placed this country's allies under its military umbrella, was a milestone in American foreign relations, for it dramatized United States determination to block any Soviet westward thrust by force of arms.

To head the NATO command, Truman had one man in mind—Dwight D. Eisenhower, whose organizational skills the President admired. With the general in charge, NATO quickly shaped common defense measures for Europe, and by early 1950 its nations were receiving the first of many hundreds of shipments of American arms. Military might was reinforcing the economic recovery fostered through the Marshall Plan and the Truman Doctrine.

Domestically business slumped in 1949, swelling the jobless rolls to 3.7 million and creating a Federal deficit of $3.7-billion. Despite vigorous prodding from the White House, Congress was not, on the whole, responsive to appeals for social legislation or economic pump-priming; nor did it repeal the Taft-Hartley Act, as Truman had urged. Much of its mind, instead, was on the loyalty of Federal employes, a question raised acutely by the Soviet explosion of an atomic device in 1949 and by revelations in the Alger Hiss case.

A former high State Department officer, Hiss was convicted of perjury in 1949. Testimony at his trial alleged that he had been involved in giving classified information to Soviet agents. This, and similar charges involving other former and current Federal employes, aroused demands for a finer screening of Government workers and for restraint of Communist and leftist groups.

Although Truman objected pungently to what he termed "the witch-hunting tactics" of Congressional inquiries, and although he stoutly defended witness invocations of the Fifth Amendment, he did tighten loyalty-security procedures in an effort to bar Communists and subversives from Federal jobs.

Nonetheless he was never entirely convinced that these programs were in the American tradition, because, he argued, virtually any such program gave "Government officials vast powers to harass all of our citizens in the exercise of their right of free speech."

"There is no more fundamental axiom of American freedom," he declared at the time, "than the familiar statement: 'In a free country, we punish men for the crimes they commit but never for the opinions they have.' "

It was in that vein that the President vetoed the Internal Security Act of 1950—a law designed to curb and punish "subversive" political expression. It was a courageous move, but an ineffective one, for Congress overrode the veto within 24 hours.

Internal security problems preoccupied legislators and the public for the remainder of Truman's term, becoming acute when Senator Joseph R. McCarthy, Republican of Wisconsin, began to accuse the State Department of harboring Communists and to charge that the Administration was "soft" on party members and sympathizers.

Truman, of course, was not "soft" on Communists, but neither was he "soft" on McCarthy, whom he scorned as a demagogue. He was especially bitter about McCarthy's attacks on Marshall and the imputation that the general, who had headed a mission to China, was responsible for the Nationalist débâcle there. Later the President condemned Eisenhower for his failure, in 1952, to disavow McCarthy publicly for having criticized Marshall.

Beset on the home front, Truman was soon fatefully involved again in the Far East. As one result of the peace settlement there, Japan was obliged to give up her 40-year suzerainty over Korea. The peninsula was divided for occupation purposes between the United States and the Soviet Union, with American forces supervising the area south of the 38th Parallel.

Shortly, however, a Communist regime was established in the Soviet zone, and it became North Korea. In the American zone a government headed by Syngman Rhee had been set up in 1948, after elec-

(continued)

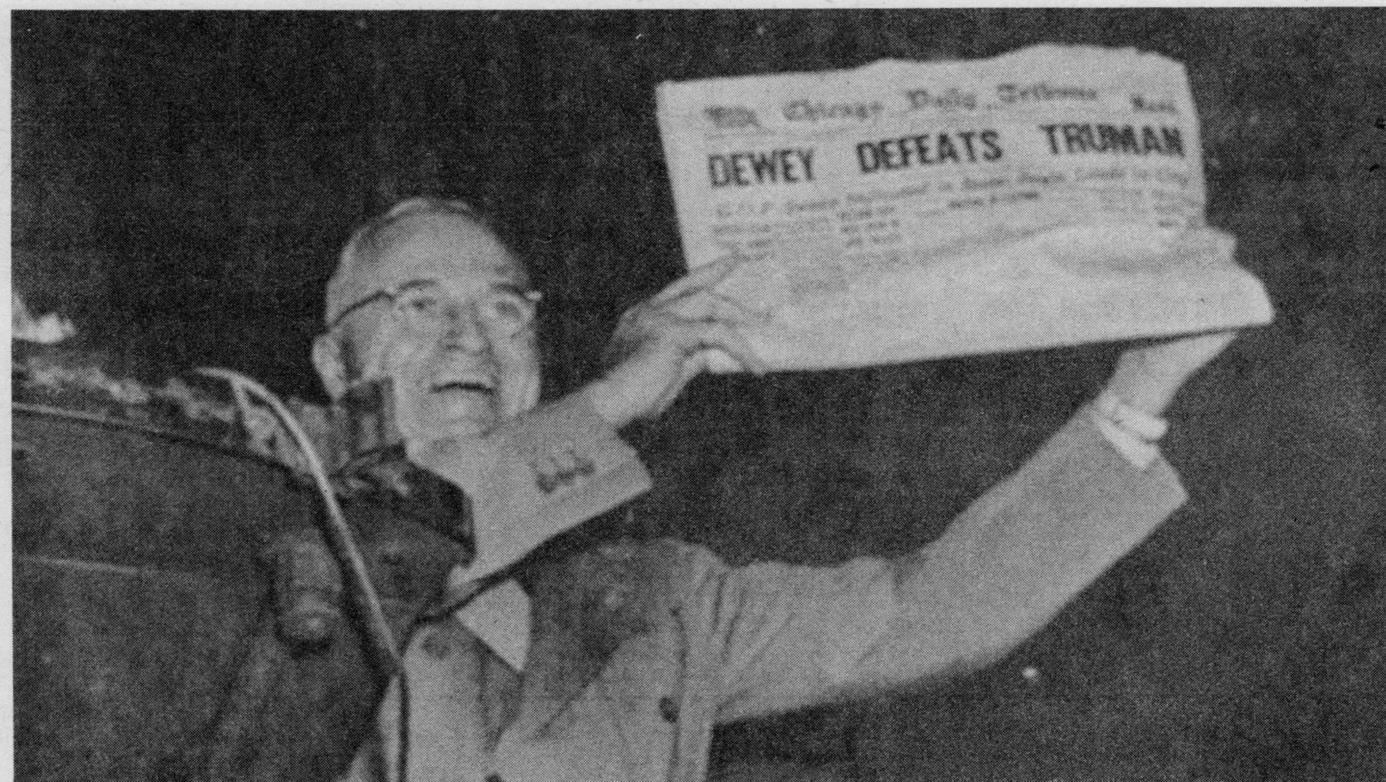

President Truman was amused by the premature headline in *The Chicago Tribune* after he defeated Gov. Thomas E. Dewey of New York, the favorite in the 1948 campaign.

President Truman relieved Douglas MacArthur in 1951 as U.S. and U.N. Korean Commander. They are seen here in 1950.

tions watched over by a United Nations commission. To this new republic the United States extended military and economic aid.

Nonetheless pockets of discontent persisted in South Korea, and these were exploited by Communists in the North. By 1950 it seemed to North Korea that the Republic of Korea could be readily obliterated and the peninsula united in a single Communist regime.

The War in Korea

Throughout the spring Central Intelligence Agency reports indicated to Truman that the North Koreans might attack, but these reports, the President noted later, were vague on timing. Besides, he said, "these same reports also told me repeatedly that there were any number of other spots in the world where the Russians 'possessed the capability' to attack." Moreover, at that time, America's first-line defense perimeter did not include Korea, as Secretary of State Dean Acheson had made clear.

So it was that on Saturday, June 24, 1950, the President was in Independence, Mo., on a family visit. "It was a little about 10 in the evening, and we were sitting in the library of our home on North Delaware Street, when the telephone rang," he recalled. "It was the Secretary of State calling from his home in Maryland. 'Mr. President,' said Dean Acheson, 'I have very serious news. The North Koreans have invaded South Korea.'"

Truman's reaction was swift: to request an immediate special meeting of the United Nations Security Council and to seek from it a declaration that the invasion was an act of aggression under the United Nations Charter.

The next day Truman flew back to Washington for a Blair House conference with his diplomatic and military advisers. As they were meeting, the Security Council (which the Soviet Union was boycotting at the moment) approved, 9 to 0, a resolution ordering the North Koreans to halt their invasion and to withdraw their forces. (Yugoslavia abstained on the roll-call.)

"As we continued our discussion," Truman wrote later, "I stated that I did not expect the North Koreans to pay any attention to the United Nations. This, I said, would mean that the United Nations would have to apply force if it wanted its order obeyed.

"Gen. [Omar] Bradley said we would have to draw the line somewhere. Russia, he thought, was not yet ready for war, but in Korea they were obviously testing us, and the line ought to be drawn now.

"I said most emphatically I thought the line would have to be drawn."

With North Korean forces rapidly penetrating southward, the President ordered Gen. Douglas MacArthur, in Tokyo, to use American air and naval forces to aid the South Koreans. Simultaneously, with United States backing, the Security Council called on all members of the United Nations to help South Korea.

Within the next few days, under nominal United Nations command, American ground troops entered the conflict. This decision to intervene, Truman said later, "was probably the most important of all" that he made in his years of office.

In succeeding weeks Truman was immersed in the conflict and its incessant demands for decisions that only he could make. From the start, he did not regard the United Nations effort as a war but rather as a "police action" to punish aggression; as an armed struggle with clearly limited objectives.

"Every decision I made in connection with the Korean conflict," he said, "had this one aim in mind: to prevent a third World War. . . . This meant that we should not do anything that would provide the excuse to the Soviets and plunge the free nations into full-scale, all-out war."

On the battleground itself, the North Koreans pushed the battered South Koreans and American forces into a pocket, and disaster seemed imminent until MacArthur, in a brilliant maneuver, landed troops at Inchon, behind the North Korean lines. Slowly the American forces regained the initiative. In October American troops were sweeping up the neck of the peninsula, deep into North Korea.

In Washington the President explained his objectives in Korea to Congressional leaders and to Dewey, as the titular head of the Republican party, and received their support. Then he set about to put the nation on a semiwar footing.

He asked Congress to remove limitations on the size of the armed forces, authorize priorities and allocation of materials to prevent hoarding, raise taxes, restrict consumer credit and add $10-billion for armaments. The proposals, most of which were adopted, gave rise to grumbling later on, in 1952, when the conflict became stalemated.

Early in the conflict there were two developments that, as they matured, deeply affected the fighting and brought Truman into collision with MacArthur. These were indications that the Communist People's Republic of China might intervene in North Korea and that the general was not hewing to the Truman policy that called for a neutral Taiwan.

(MacArthur doubted the likelihood of Red Chinese intervention, and he wanted to bring Chiang Kai-shek into the fighting. His public disagreement with Truman on that point almost cost him his command in August, 1950.)

Truman decided that the best way to handle his differences with MacArthur was in a face-to-face talk. "Events since June had shown me that MacArthur had lost some of his contacts with the country and its people in the many years of his absence," the President wrote. "He had been in the Orient for nearly 14 years then. . . . I had made efforts through [W. Averell] Harriman and others to let him see the worldwide picture as we saw it in Washington, but I felt that we had little success. I thought he might adjust more easily if he heard it from me directly."

The two men met for the first time on Wake Island in the Pacific on Oct. 15, 1950. The general was optimistic: The Chinese Communists would not enter Korea and the fighting would end by Thanksgiving, he predicted. Truman was pleased, and again he emphasized that the "police action" had strictly limited objectives, a prime one being the containment of the fighting to Korea.

Strategists differ as to what prompted the action, but on Oct. 25 the Chinese did enter the conflict, sending thousands of "volunteers" across the Yalu River into North Korea. Thus reinforced, the Communist forces eventually beat back the American and United Nations troops to the 38th Parallel, where a front was established that lasted until the truce of 1953.

Truman's policy in the face of the Chinese intervention was to continue to confine the fighting to Korea, to avoid escalation, a policy in which other members of the United Nations concurred. MacArthur, on the other hand, wanted to strike directly at the Chinese by air action in Manchuria across the Yalu River.

Matters came to a head in March, 1951, when MacArthur wrote to Representative Joseph W. Martin Jr., the House Republican leader, criticizing the President's policy. Truman believed that he had no choice but to relieve the general of his command.

"If there is one basic element in our Constitution, it is civilian control of the military," he explained. "Policies are to be made by elected political officials, not by generals or admirals. Yet time and again General MacArthur had shown that he was unwilling to accept the policies of the Administration. By his repeated public statements, he was not only confusing our allies . . . but, in fact, was also setting his policy against the President's."

Amid mounting public speculation, Truman acted dramatically on April 10, 1951. In a concise order he discharged MacArthur for insubordination. To the American public, MacArthur was an almost legendary figure as a result of his Pacific War exploits — a general with superb aplomb who had turned the tide against Japan—and it was difficult at first to accept the possibility that he had overstepped the bounds of his role in Korea. It seemed logical, after all, for a general to want to win a clear-cut victory, and it was obvious to many that it must be frustrating for him to be forbidden the means to do it.

Realizing this, the President went on the radio to explain his action. The United States and the United Nations, he said, could not permit the Korean conflict to become a general war. Bringing China into that conflict directly, he warned, might unleash a third World War.

"That war can come if the Communist leaders want it to come," he said. "But this nation and its allies will not be responsible for its coming."

The deposed MacArthur returned to the United States, and to triumphal adulation. It appeared for a time that Truman, the Commander in Chief, was about to be outflanked by MacArthur, the dismissed general. Senate hearings were called in an air of expectancy, but after a few weeks the furor subsided, and the validity of Truman's step was generally accepted.

Assassination Foiled

In the midst of the Korean conflict there was a crude attempt to assassinate the President. It occurred Nov. 1, 1950, when the Trumans were living in Blair House while the White House was under repair.

On the street below the President's window, guards kept vigil. At 2 P.M., as Truman was napping, a taxicab stopped nearby, and two men got out and walked toward Blair House. Suddenly one drew a pistol and fired at a guard. The other ran toward the front door of Blair House.

The guards sprang into action, and when the shooting ceased in a few minutes, Griselio Torresola, a Puerto Rican extremist, lay dead, and Leslie Coffelt, a guard, was mortally wounded.

The second would-be assassin, Oscar Collazo, was shot in the chest. He was subsequently convicted of murder and sentenced to die, but the President commuted the penalty in 1952 to life imprisonment.

Truman's second term, like his first, was marked by greater harmony on foreign policy — especially economic and military aid to Europe—than on domestic affairs. He found Congress reasonably willing to spend on foreign aid but reluctant to provide for social welfare, housing and education. This, in part, stemmed from home-front discontent over dislocations—taxes and a rise in living costs—caused by the Korean fighting.

Truman strove to keep the economy stable, a determination that he dramatized by seizing the steel industry on April 8, 1952, to avert a strike and a price rise in that basic commodity. Invoking his Korean conflict emergency powers, he put the industry under Government operation. The stunning move aroused the ire of the business community, but the President was prepared with an explanation.

"If we give in to the steel companies on this issue," he said, "you could just say goodbye to stabilization. If we knuckled under to the steel industry, the lid would be off, prices would start jumping all around us — not just the prices of things using steel but prices of many other things we buy, including milk and groceries and meat."

Steel challenged the seizure and was upheld by the Supreme Court on the ground the President had exceeded his authority. He was obliged to approve a price rise. He always insisted, however, that the seizure was justified and legal.

As far back as 1949 Truman had decided not to run for election in 1952, and as that year drew near, he cast about for a suitable candidate. Once, in 1945, he had impulsively told Eisenhower he would back him in 1948, but by 1952 the general had been courted by the Republicans.

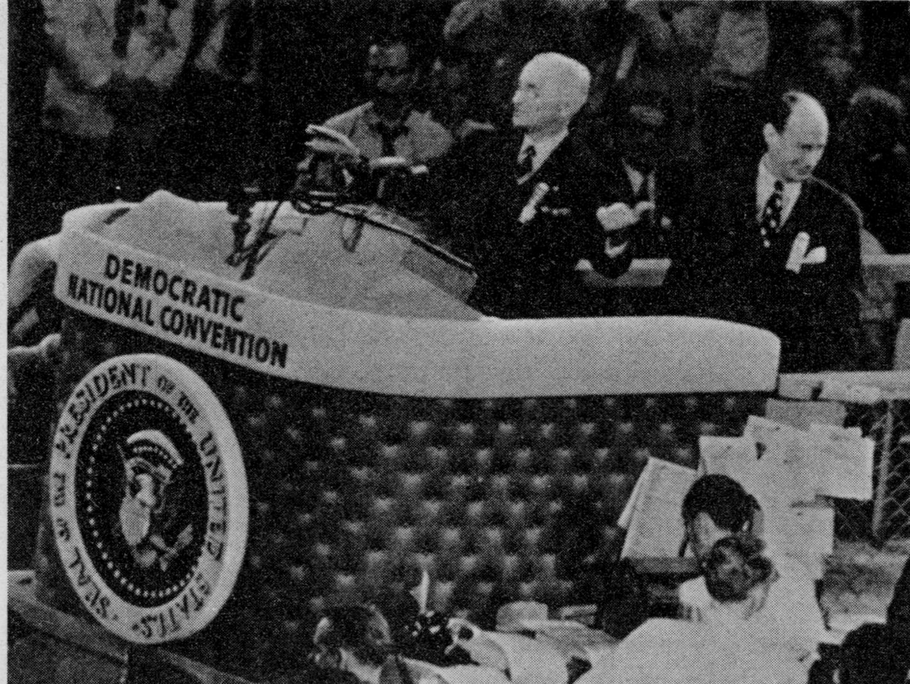

Declining a third-term attempt, Truman favored Adlai E. Stevenson as the Democratic Party's 1952 Presidential candidate.

Support for Stevenson

Truman's initial choice for 1952 was Chief Justice Fred M. Vinson, but the latter declined on grounds of health in the fall of 1951. The President then turned to Gov. Adlai E. Stevenson of Illinois, who had been elected in 1948 by an impressively large vote. Stevenson rejected Truman's proffer at least twice. Then, after almost six months of uncertainty, he decided to seek the nomination.

Truman, always a loyal party man, helped him get the nomination and stumped for him vigorously. The President, however, did not like Stevenson's campaign tactics, and he was not greatly astonished when Eisenhower won.

Afterward Truman made elaborate arrangements to acquaint the President-elect with pending problems, but the White House meeting was stiff and unproductive. Truman felt that the general was still smarting from the partisanship of the campaign.

Truman's intimates and advisers, who had watched him mature in office, praised him above all for his forthrightness. He himself, reviewing his actions in December, 1952, said:

"The Presidents who have done things, who were not afraid to act, have been the most abused . . . and I have topped them all in the amount of abuse I have received."

If he had to do it all over again, he went on, he would not change anything.

On another occasion, he was more poignant. He said:

"I have tried my best to give the nation everything I had in me. There are probably a million people who could have done the job better than I did, but I had the job, and I always quote an epitaph on a tombstone in a cemetery in Tombstone, Arizona: 'Here lies Jack Williams. He done his damndest.'"

Home Again To Independence

THE pomp of the Presidency, the incessant blaring of "Hail to the Chief," the constant pressure at the center of attention left remarkably few imprints on Harry S. Truman. He escaped, he once said, acquiring an "'importance' complex"; so when he returned to his 14-room Victorian home in Independence, Mo., to live until his death, he was still a man of simple tastes and uninflated ambitions. He was prepared to make an easy transition to private life.

He quickly discovered, however, that a former President is a considerable object of curiosity and that he could not just become Citizen Truman. Visitors came to gape at his stately white house and to finger the iron picket fence that surrounded it; to watch him take his customary early-morning stroll; to look as he ate luncheon in Kansas City; to visit the nearby Harry S. Truman Library in hope of catching a glimpse of him. He was sought out to run for the Senate, to speak at Democratic party rallies, to receive plaques and scrolls and degrees, to endorse candidates, to write of his experiences.

"When you're elected President, you're elected for life," he mused to one visitor. He was nearing 82 at the time, and he sat in front of a stack of letters that asked his autograph or a signed picture or an inscription in his books.

His was a busy retirement, and until the frailties of age intervened, he seldom spent a day of complete inactivity. When he was in Independence, he worked in

(continued)

his library office every weekday, starting at 8 o'clock in the morning, and sometimes on Saturday and Sunday. He took short trips, especially between 1953 and 1964, and wherever he went crowds sprang up to greet him. They called him "Harry" for the most part, sometimes "Mr. President." Whatever the appellation, it was uttered with affection, for however much Truman had been criticized in the White House, he was much admired as a person, and this esteem grew in his retirement.

Strong Sense of Family

Among the qualities that endeared Truman to the public was his strong sense of family. He was extraordinarily close to his mother, Martha Ellen. Even in his busiest years in Washington he wrote her a weekly letter in his clear and angular hand. "Dear Mamma and Mary," these letters began (the 'Mary" was his younger sister, who lived with his mother in Missouri), and in unaffected sentences they recounted his activities, news of his wife and daughter, and family chitchat.

His mother was a cover-to-cover reader of The Congressional Record, with fixed likes and dislikes of members of Congress. In 1947, just before her death at the age of 94, she discussed political figures with her son, mentioning her distaste for Senator Robert A. Taft, the Ohio Republican.

"Is Taft going to be nominated?" she asked.

"He might be," Truman replied.

"Harry, are you going to run?"

"I don't know, mamma."

"Don't you think it's about time you made up your mind?" Mrs. Truman said, as if talking to a small boy. Her death in July, 1947, overwhelmed her son.

Truman's hearty and unabashed affection for his wife, Bess, charmed most Americans. He was accustomed to confide in Mrs. Truman, for whose judgment he had enormous respect. They talked over each day's events, with Mrs. Truman offering her comments, political and personal. Except at campaign time, Mrs. Truman remained in the political background. Her husband wanted it that way, for he was convinced that womanhood was a state apart and that Bess was not fair political game.

The quickest way to arouse Truman's ire was to cast a slur on his wife. On the ground that they had maligned her, two members of Congress were barred from the White House, as was Clare Boothe Luce, the wife of the publisher. According to Harry Vaughan, the President's aide and confidant, Henry Luce inquired about the ban.

"Mr. Luce," the President replied, according to Vaughan, "you've asked a fair question, and I'll give you a fair answer. "I've been in politics 35 years, and everything that could be said about a human being has been said about me. But my wife has never been in politics. She has always conducted herself in a circumspect manner, and no one has a right to make derogatory remarks about her. Now, your wife has said many unkind and untrue things about Mrs. Truman. And as long as I am in residence here, she'll not be a guest in the White House."

In Truman's retirement "The Boss" or "The Boss Lady" (as he referred to his wife) also remained out of the spotlight. Nonetheless, she exercised a veto over his tendency to be too active and too gregarious. Her tug at his sleeve was sufficient to bring an end to a conversation or to quiet him down.

Of his daughter, Margaret, Truman was aggressively proud. At one point when her father was in the White House Miss Truman made her bow in Washington as a professional singer. Paul Hume, music critic of The Washington Post, reviewed her voice unenthusiastically. Truman read the notice, reached for his pen and dashed off a salty note in which he promised to punch the critic in the nose. Margaret was embarrassed, and Truman apologized for his outburst, but the episode added to his luster as a family man.

In later years Truman was an appreciative fan of his daughter's roles as an actress and television personality.

The former President had four grandchildren—Clifton, William, Harrison and Thomas, sons of Miss Truman's marriage in April, 1956, to Clifton Daniel, now associate editor of The New York Times. Truman proved to be a doting grandfather, visiting the children and their parents frequently in New York and being host to them in Missouri.

Interest in the welfare of young people occupied much of his attention as a private citizen. Before he left the White House he had decided, he said, that "the rest of my life was to be spent in large measure teaching young people the meaning of democracy as exemplified in the Republic of the United States."

For several years he was what he called "a kind of roving teacher." He would talk or lecture at colleges and universities and then reply to student questions. "To me," he said, "there is nothing more rewarding than to stand before young people and find them so vitally interested in everything pertaining to the affairs of the country and the world." His aim was to pass along both his experiences in government and his fund of information on American political history.

He strove to encourage study of the Presidency. He helped set up the Harry S. Truman Library Institute for National and International Affairs, to which he contributed his lecture fees and other monies. The institute is designed to help young scholars who are investigating the Presidency and the Truman years. "The library," he told one visitor with pride, "aims to be a storehouse for the history of the Presidency, and I want to see it used that way."

Besides talking to older students, Truman took great delight in chatting with groups of schoolchildren who visited the library after it was opened in 1957. Once or twice a week, as long as he was at the library, the former President talked to these groups. Standing at a lectern, he was a relaxed and informal schoolteacher as he solicited and answered questions from the floor. Aides, anxious about his health, tried to restrain him, but he enjoyed the sessions so much that they gave up.

The library was very much the focus of the former President's life. Built by private subscription, it was given to the Government and administered by the National Archives and Records Service. In addition to museum-like exhibits dealing with Truman's life and the Presidency, it houses Truman's public and private papers and a large collection of books. His office in the library occupied one wing of the horseshoe-shaped structure.

When he returned to Independence in 1953, he was restless without a fixed daily routine. Most days he would go to a temporary office in Kansas City, 10 miles away, but by noon he was eager for companionship. Tom Evans, a businessman and a friend of 40 years, took to inviting him to lunch at the 822 Club in the Kansas City Club, where, after the dishes were cleared, there followed a few hours of poker (being too inquisitive, he was not a good player), a nap and the return to Independence. He was bored. Apart from walking, he had no athletic diversions. He shunned household chores. Despite his years as a farmer, he disliked to garden or mow the lawn.

In the early days of his retirement, his wife, perhaps to tease him, pressed him to do something about the lawn, but he devised a canny plan.

"So I waited until Sunday morning," he recalled, "just as our neighbors were beginning to pass on their way to church, and I took out the lawn mower and started to cut the grass. Mrs. Truman, preparing to leave for church, was horrified to see me cutting the lawn.

"'What are you doing on Sunday?' she asked.

"'I'm doing what you asked me to do,' I replied.

"Meanwhile the neighbors continued to pass by the house. Their glances were not lost on Mrs. Truman. She never asked me to mow the lawn again."

Being aware of Truman's hopes for a library dating from the White House years, Evans and a few other close friends stepped up fund-raising for the project. Land was given by Independence, and the completed building was dedicated with a speech by Chief Justice Earl Warren, whom Truman held in high esteem. Thereafter the former President organized his time around the library, where he worked and received visitors with warmth and in simple dignity.

There, in a book-lined office, he worked behind a trinket-strewn desk. Facing him on one wall were paintings of Andrew Jackson and Sam Rayburn. The Presidential flag stood in a standard beside a leather couch. Over the bookcases on other walls were pictures of his wife, his daughter, his grandchildren and his ancestors.

In one bookcase was a thumbed four-volume set of "Great Men and Famous Women," which had been published in 1894. It was a reminder of his youth and his first vision of the world beyond Jackson County, Mo.; for from these biographies Truman had drawn his early inspiration and his first criteria of public greatness.

Memoirs Published

Shortly after leaving the Presidency, Truman sold the rights to his memoirs for $600,000. The two volumes—"Year of Decisions" and "Years of Trial and Hope"—took about two years to prepare. The books, which were best-sellers, were published by Doubleday. He also wrote "Mr. Citizen," published in 1960 by Bernard Geis Associates. It was a collection of articles on his role as a private citizen that included a suggestion that former Presidents sit in Congress, with a voice but no vote.

Truman's views on public issues were much sought after, and he became the master of the walking news conference. These took place mostly in large cities when reporters accompanied him on his 120-paces-a-minute prebreakfast hikes. He was a familiar sight in New York as, walking stick in hand, he strode the Upper East Side at the head of a covey of panting newsmen. He could usually be depended upon for a peppery remark or two about current politics.

From time to time Truman also wrote on public issues for the North American Newspaper Alliance. These were reflective statements in which he concerned himself with principles rather than with personalities. In the same vein, he appeared on a television series, "Years of Decision," that dealt with world events. His written and televised remarks displayed a strong sense of history, and his desire to expound it without flourish.

His version of postwar events and of his Presidency was strongly challenged by some historians who believed that his hard-line anti-Sovietism, which set the tone of the cold war, was a serious misreading of Russian and Chinese ambitions. In this view, a policy of peaceful coexistence might have been evolved between 1945 and 1953, had Truman exhibited more flexibility in his world outlook. These historians argued that his division of the globe between the Free and the Communist Worlds was ultimately counterproductive.

As much as the former President liked the comfortable outlines of life in Independence and the tree-shaded quiet of its residential area, he was also drawn to occasional travel. He preferred casual trips similar to the one that he and his wife took in 1953, when they drove from Missouri to Washington and New York. More often, though, because of the crowds he collected, he was obliged to travel by train and plane. He used the train as often as he could, because his wife and his family abhorred air travel.

In 1956 the Trumans visited Western Europe for seven weeks and were received by Queen Elizabeth II in Britain and King Baudouin in Belgium. There was also a private audience with Pope Pius XII and an honorary degree at Oxford. But the former President didn't really enjoy himself he confessed later, because the trip was too ceremonial.

Out of office, Truman was not out of Democratic politics, for he was a lifelong politicker. But his force in party councils diminished over the years. He handpicked Gov. Adlai E. Stevenson of Illinois to head the ticket in 1952. Afterward he was critical of the candidate, asserting that Stevenson "didn't understand people" and had "conducted a campaign that was not in support of the Democratic program of President Roosevelt and myself." In 1956 he backed W. Averell Harriman of New York for the nomination, but he stumped for Stevenson when the latter again carried the convention.

"I was just as unsparing of myself as if I were campaigning for myself," Truman said. He took especial pride in his party loyalty. "This is the way I think a man must act in politics," he said. "He must close ranks and forget personalities."

He exemplified this in 1960. After boycotting the Democratic convention on the ground that it had been rigged to produce the nomination of John F. Kennedy, he made his peace with Kennedy and campaigned for him. He was far happier with the nomination in 1964 of Lyndon B. Johnson, whose legislative and executive skills he esteemed. And he backed Hubert H. Humphrey in 1968.

Truman lived to witness the realization of at least four programs close to his heart. They were Medicare, low-income housing, broadened civil rights and a peace center in Israel. Medicare, which he proposed in principle in 1945, was enacted in 1965, and the bill was signed in his presence. He was acclaimed by President Johnson as "the real daddy of Medicare" when he received his Government enrollment card.

Peace Center Set Up

In the crucial confrontations of clashing national ambitions in the postwar years, Truman acted, according to his lights, to preserve peace and to uphold freedom. This aspect of his career was recognized in 1966, when the Harry S. Truman Center for the Advancement of Peace was set up by private subscription at Hebrew University in Jerusalem. On his doctor's advice, Truman did not attend the ceremonies in Israel in July, but he sent a vigorous call for a "fresh start" on solving the world's peace problems.

"When it is time to close the book of my life," he said earlier, "I will be comforted by the hope that this center will become a major source of light and reason toward the achievement of eternal peace."

A nonsmoker and a daily exerciser, Truman enjoyed robust health for most of his life. "My only trouble is that I've been chased for years by a woman named Anno Domini," he remarked in the spring of 1970 as he approached his 86th birthday. The occasion was the 25th anniversary of his accession to the Presidency, when a number of old friends including Dean Acheson, W. Averell Harriman and Earl Warren visited him at his home.

Sitting in a Queen Anne chair with a mahogany cane nearby, he reminisced about his Washington years with bounce and good humor. When it was remarked that "Harry's become a little hard of hearing," he retorted, "No problem—I can hear anything I want to hear, and nearing 86 I guess I've heard about enough anyway."

Although he liked to chat about the careers of others, the former President found it difficult to reflect on his own long climb from farm boy to the pinnacle of power. "I've never liked to go back and retrace my steps," he told this reporter a few years ago. "I find it hard to talk about myself. I did what I had to do, and that is that."

President and Mrs. Truman with their daughter Margaret in 1956.

"All the News That's Fit to Print."

The New York Times.

THE WEATHER
Showers today; tomorrow fair, slight change in temperature.
Temperature Yesterday—Max. 73; Min. 65.
For weather report see Page 42.

VOL. LXXV....No. 25,049. NEW YORK, TUESDAY, AUGUST 24, 1926. TWO CENTS in Greater New York | THREE CENTS Within 200 Miles | FOUR CENTS Elsewhere in the U. S.

PEACE HOPE FADES AS MEXICAN BISHOPS REJECT COMPROMISE

Prelates Refuse to Negotiate Further Till Calles Suspends Religious Regulations.

WON'T RESUME SERVICES

Boycott Will Continue to Be Pressed, Says Bishop Diaz, as Catholics' Legal Right.

DOUBLE-DEALING CHARGED

President Is Accused of Altering the Episcopate's Statement and Shifting on Registry of Priests.

Special Cable to THE NEW YORK TIMES.

MEXICO CITY, Aug. 23.—Unless the Mexican Government suspends all regulations of the penal code affecting religion and the order for the registration of the priests, the Episcopate will not continue negotiations for an adjustment of the controversy between the Church and the State.

This position was taken by the prelates today when they rejected the formula for a compromise advanced in the conference of their delegates with President Calles late Saturday night.

The President, they said at the time, had assured them that the registration of the priests was entirely administrative in purpose, but later they discovered that he gave out a statement to a newspaper saying that returning priests would be "subject to the laws." The Bishops also charged that the statement which they issued after the conference, at the President's request, had been altered in its wording at the Chapultepec Palace.

As a result of the breakdown in negotiations, the Episcopate has dropped its tentatively considered project for resuming services in the churches.

Episcopate Decides to Fight On.

The Episcopate held a meeting tonight and unanimously decided to carry out the orders first issued when the Calles decrees were published, suspending all church services. It was decided that further conferences were useless as the prelates were convinced that the present Government was playing for time and was unwilling to suspend the penal regulations and the order requiring the registration of priests.

The bishops are confident that four weeks more of the boycott will bring the Government to terms, as Catholics in all parts of the republic report that the whole country is showing the effects.

Bishop Diaz Explains Situation.

Bishop Pascual Diaz of the State of Tabasco, who as Secretary of the Episcopate is the spokesman of the Church in Mexico, explained to THE NEW YORK TIMES correspondent today the reasons for the conference with President Calles and the significance of the result.

Moved by a desire to place themselves on record as having protested against the religious regulations in person to President Calles, he said, a committee of the episcopate, comprising Archbishop Leopoldo Ruiz y Flores of Michoacan and Bishop Diaz, readily accepted the invitations extended by Eduardo Mestro to meet the President.

Bishop Diaz added that the episcopate always had been ready and anxious to accept mediation in a form that would satisfy the Catholics and would permit the renewal of religious worship.

The members of the episcopate were consulted, and after a discussion it was agreed that Archbishop Ruiz and Bishop Diaz should explain to President Calles the exact position of the Church, and, if possible, arrive at a conclusion that would permit the faithful to use the churches and at the same time settle once for all the difficulties under which the Catholic Church had been working for many years. It was believed that through personal contact with President Calles the Catholic questions would be placed before the Chief Magistrate in such a form that an agreement would soon be reached.

Calles's Power to Act at Issue.

When ushered into the presence of the President in the Chapultepec Palace, Bishop Diaz found him in unusually good humor. The conference began immediately. During the conversation, which lasted for two and a half hours, no decision was reached, as both sides continued firm in their positions.

Archbishop Ruiz, presenting the Church side of the problem, told the President that if Señor Calles, in the exercise of his extraordinary powers which were granted by Congress and through which he issued the penal decrees and the order for all priests to register, would suspend the regulations, the prelates would immediately reopen the churches, resume services and use their personal influence with the faithful to end the present agitation.

President Calles in reply said that he personally could not use these same powers, as Congress would be in session within the next few days.

Bishop Diaz then pointed out that as Congress did not meet until Sept. 6 President Calles still enjoyed the usage of these privileges and that it was an easy matter for the President to suspend the regulations until Congress could find time to study the question and through the proper legal channels amend the articles to which the majority of Mexicans objected.

Dependence on Rome's Consent.

Bishop Diaz further informed the President that unless the regulations were suspended church service could not be resumed, at least until consent

Continued on Page Four.

Callizo, French Flier, Rises 41,811 Feet, World's Record

BUC, Versailles, France, Aug. 23 (AP).—M. Callizo is reported to have broken the world's altitude record today, reaching a height of 12,800 metres (41,811 feet). The record had stood at 12,066 metres (39,576 feet) a mark made by the same aviator. Callizo took off at the airdrome at 5 o'clock this afternoon and landed at Le Bourget two hours and twenty-five minutes later.

His instruments will be officially tested by the Air Ministry tomorrow, but experts here are confident that the record will stand. The mark he set is approximately eight miles.

Lieutenant John A. Macready holds the American altitude record, 38,704 feet, made on Jan. 19. He attempted to break Callizo's record March 13, but reached only 37,575 feet.

PANGALOS CAUGHT; PRISONER IN ATHENS

Destroyer on Which He Was Fleeing Quit When Threatened With Destruction.

TWO AIDS ARE ALSO TAKEN

Attempt to Hide in Wireless Turret Has Brought Ridicule on Former Dictator.

Special Cable to THE NEW YORK TIMES.

ATHENS, Greece, Aug. 23.—The destroyer Leon, which had been sent by the new Condylis régime to prevent the escape of General Pangalos, deposed President, found the destroyer Pergamos, on which he was fleeing, near Cape Matapan last night. The Pergamos refused to heave to at first, but after warning shots had been fired she surrendered. The crew of the Pergamos intended to surprise the Leon by using hand grenades until they saw from the first fusillade that resistance was impossible.

General Pangalos was found hiding on board in spite of the commander's denials. The warships returned here about 6:30 o'clock this morning. Pangalos is now confined under close guard in the military hospital here.

General Condylis, leader of the revolution, addressed a popular demonstration yesterday which was called to celebrate the suppression of General Pangalos's "tyrannical rule." He was repeatedly interrupted by the crowd, which demanded immediate formation of a coalition Government and announcement of a general election. This General Condylis promised to do. He declared that those who had been responsible for the tyranny now suppressed must be held fully responsible for their action and that their punishment was a duty to the nation.

Demand Punishment as Example.

A similar demonstration held in Saloniki demanded that the army return to its work and that exemplary punishment be meted to those responsible for the Pangalos Government as an example for posterity and as the end of all dictatorships.

General Condylis today called a conference of party leaders to discuss formation of a new coalition Cabinet, but it probably will not be held until tomorrow, to give the parties time for discussion.

Admiral Conduriotis was expected to return this evening to take up his duties as President of the republic.

General Pangalos will be put on trial before the High Court of Justice with the other deposed Ministers. While a prisoner on board the Pergamos he was interviewed by Representative Elefteros Typos, who once supported him. Pangalos expressed sorrow and surprise because his former friends and supporters had betrayed him and encompassed his downfall. He said he had had definite plans to bring about normal conditions and to announce holding elections. He said he had a clear conscience and had done his duty

Continued on Page Five.

HALL SUSPECTS STAY IN JAIL AS BAIL PLEA IS SHIFTED BY COURT

Justice Gummere Refuses to Act, Holding Case Is One for Justice Parker.

HEARING LIKELY THURSDAY

Two Now Balk at Signing Their Testimony, but Revisions Won't Be Allowed.

ONE TOLD OF FINDING CLUB

Charlotte Mills Said to Have Given New Clue—More Evidence in Abeyance, Beggans Says.

Henry de la Bruyere Carpender and Willie Stevens, who are charged with the murder of the Rev. Dr. Edward W. Hall and Mrs. Eleanor R. Mills four years ago near New Brunswick, N. J., did not win freedom on bail yesterday. Chief Justice William S. Gummere, before whom applicatiton was made in Newark, refused to act. He said that his colleague, Supreme Court Justice Charles W. Parker, whose judicial district includes the place of the crime, had volunteered to cut short his vacation in order to hear the bail application.

Justice Parker is at Northeast Harbor, Me. Robert H. McCarter, counsel for the accused men, who have been in jail twelve days, telephoned and telegraphed to the Justice, seeking a date for a hearing. Senator Alexander Simpson, in charge of the Hall-Mills investigation, did likewise.

At Northeast Harbor, Me., it was said last night that Justice Parker had started back.

The hearing before Justice Parker probably will be held in Somerville on Thursday, according to the understanding last night of Mr. McCarter.

Court Hearing in Newark.

Application to the Chief Justice was made in the Newark Court House. After several routine motions in other litigation had been disposed of, but before all the motions awaiting ruling had been presented, Senator Simpson broke in to bring up the Hall-Mills case.

"If the Conrt pleases," he said, "I am here in response to a telegram signed Robert H. McCarter. I had no formal notice of motion and I am wondering whether they are going to make a motion. I have had no formal notice and I have been sitting here for an hour waiting for themto make the application.

"This is a criminal matte and I understood that your Honor would hear criminal matters in the beginning of the litigated motions. So I would like to know whether they are going to make the motion."

Former Attorney General McCarter, leader of the defense, was obviously surprised by the action of the special prosecutor. He explained to the Chief Justice that he had been merely awaiting the convenience of the Court.

"What is your application?" said the Chief Justice.

"Our application is to admit to bail Mr. Henry Carpender and Mr. William C. Stevens, who are incarcerated in the Somerset County Jail because of the charge of murder on Sept. 14, 1922."

Asks Why They Come to Him.

"Why do you make the application to me?" asked the Court.

"Because Justice Parker, who sits in that circuit, is away and will not return until September, I understand, and also because Judge Cleary, the local Judge, has no jurisdiction to hear such an application."

Justice Gummere paused, and then said:

"I heard an application some two weeks ago to release Mrs. Hall on bail, probably connected with the same crime, according to the theory of the State. I had no knowledge of the application going to be made until it was made.

"Justice Parker, having observed in the newspapers—there has been some little notoriety given to this case in the newspapers now and then—wrote telling me that if at any time before his normal period of return any matter

Continued on Page Eight.

Vault Built to Withstand Mobs and Bombs To Hold State's $200,000,000 in New Building

Special to The New York Times.

ALBANY, Aug. 23.—A most modern vault for holding $200,000,000 in cash and gilt-edged securities owned by the State will be built in the new twenty-six-story office building which the State is to erect just west of the Capitol. In case of fire it can be flooded with water. State Architect Sullivan W. Jones declared today it would be the safest vault that human ingenuity could devise. It will contain alarms connected with sirens outside the building and also with Albany Police Headquarters and the bankers' protective system.

Plans for the vault are being drawn by the State Architect's force. Its proposed location is being kept a secret and the specifications and details of the construction are confidential. It will measure approximately 50 by 50 feet.

On Wednesday Governor Smith and members of the State Building Commission will open bids for the wrecking of the buildings that now occupy the site where the new office building is to be built. By Jan. 1 next it is proposed to have the site cleared, test borings completed and the final program for construction ready for presentation to the Legislature.

Departments of the State Government that now have large sums on hand or hold large blocks of securities hire strong boxes at the local banks, but when the new building is ready and all the State departments are housed under one roof this will not be necessary.

While the State carries no insurance, the new vault will be so designed and built that it would take the lowest insurance rate. It will be fire and burglar proof and as near drill proof as it can be made, and will offer the greatest resistance to bombs and explosives or to mob attack.

The walls, floors and roof will be of flint concrete forty-eight inches in thickness, reinforced by an armor mat of high grade cold-drawn steel fabric. The doors will be of the circular type, two feet in thickness, with a time lock opened and closed with a concealed electric engine.

The day gate will be of hardened steel, equipped with a spring-bolt cylinder lock. A corridor will run all around it and mirrors will enable guards to see all sides. Three shifts of armed guards will be on duty every minute of the day and night. The expectation is that they will be former service men, former policemen and detectives.

Only accredited representatives of State departments will have access to the vault, and they will be triply identified by photographs, signatures and fingerprints. State troopers, it is expected, will provide additional guards.

Small vaults will be built into the structure for the use of departments such as the Controller's, Banking and Insurance.

Berry Ousts Two Chief Aids, Tammany Men; General Shake-Up of His Office Forecast

A general shake-up of the higher officials of the city's Finance Department was forecast yesterday when it became known that Deputy Controller John J. Sullivan and Hans P. Freece, chief of the Bureau of Law and Adjustment, had resigned at the request of Controller Charles W. Berry. Both are residents of Manhattan and Tammany men. The salary of the Deputy Controller is $10,000 a year and that of the place held by Mr. Freece $7,500.

"There is no scandal of any sort," General Berry said. "We had many differences of opinion regarding the conduct of the department. That is all. I thought that it would be better to release the two officials and fill their places with appointees with whom I can work in harmony."

Another Finance Department official who is prominent in Tammany denied that the requests for the resignations of the two men were aimed at Tammany or was due to the recent differences of opinion between the Controller and Mayor Walker over transit and bus policies.

Mr. Sullivan entered the employ of the Finance Department in 1924. He was chief of the Law and Adjustment Bureau until last January, when he was promoted to Deputy Controller by General Berry on recommendation of Tammany. The Law and Adjustment Bureau is considered one of the most important in the department. It handles negligence claims against the city and the cla'ms of contractors, these claims amounting to millions of dollars annually.

General Berry said he was not ready to announce the successors to Messrs. Sullivan and Freece. Robert B. Jordan of 123 Cambridge Place has been put in Mr. Freece's place and it was said he might obtain a permanent appointment.

U. S. TO PAY FOR TIPS TRAPPING RUM BOATS

Clause of Tariff Act Allowing Percentage of Proceeds Up to $50,000 Is Invoked.

NEW SQUADS PATROL RIVERS

Forty Customs Inspectors on Prohibition Duty in Three Eight-Hour Shifts.

The Federal Government is prepared to pay tipsters for information leading to the seizure of rum boats. This was announced yesterday by Deputy Surveyor of Customs John McGill, who is in charge of the new harbor patrol of forty customs inspectors who were sworn in on Saturday as prohibition agents in General Lincoln C. Andrews's latest drive to dry up New York.

These inspector-agents who began patrolling the East, North and Harlem Rivers yesterday in three converted rum-runners which they will use until the arrival of eight specially built speed boats ordered from Detroit, retain their customs rank, although they are on the payroll of the prohibition department, and with it the right of search and seizure.

The patrol will work in three shifts of eight hours each and will devote its attention principally to attempts to land liquor from liners. While customs officials said yesterday that they were satisfied that no legitimate steamship company was helping in the work of unloading liquor at this port, they said a good sized rum traffic was being carried on by individual firemen and other men of the crews of various vessels. Already several seizures of considerable size have been made, the liquor in such cases usually being hidden beneath coal in the bunkers of liners. "And we will get more," Mr. McGill said yesterday.

Rewards Under Tariff Act.

In announcing that the Government was prepared to reward persons giving information leading to the seizure of rum boats, Mr. McGill said a similar practice had long been in effect in regard to gems and other things being smuggled into the country. The clause in the Tariff act of 1922 makes provision for such things, he said, and he quoted Section 619 under the heading "Awards and Compensations," which reads:

"Any person not an officer of the United States who detects or seizes any vessel, vehicle, merchandise or baggage subject to seizure and forfeiture under the customs laws and reports the same to an officer of the customs or who furnishes to a District Attorney, to the Secretary of the Treasury, or to any customs officer original information concerning any fraud upon the customs revenue, or a violation of the customs laws perpetrated or contemplated, which detection and seizure or information leads to a recovery of any duties withheld, or of any fine, penalty or forfeiture incurred, may be awarded and paid by the Secretary of the Treasury a compensation of 25 per centum of a net amount recovered, but not to exceed $50,000, which shall be paid out of the moneys appropriated for that purpose. For the purpose of this section any amount recovered under a bail bond shall be deemed a recovery of a fine incurred."

Old Rum-Runner in Use.

Among the converted rum-runners doing service with the new patrol is the Cigarette, formerly one of the fastest and most elusive of the craft carrying liquor into this port. The auxiliary schooner U. S. Customs 417 is doing duty as mother ship for the new fleet and will serve as a headquarters and repair base.

United States Attorney William A. De Groot in Brooklyn filed padlock proceedings yesterday for violation of the Volstead act against five former saloons and two restaurants. The saloons are at 3,902 Fort Hamilton Parkway, 1,420 Neck Road, 2,117 Utica Avenue, 122 Troy Avenue and 176 Richards Street. The restaurants are at 2,937 West Eighth Street, Coney Island, and 170 Hamilton Avenue.

Jean Schulman, 18 years old, a blond typist of 996 Herkimer Street, Brooklyn, was yesterday arraigned in the United States District Court in Brooklyn and charged with selling a bottle of home-made liquor to Patrolman Nicholas Gaffney for $1 on July 19. She pleaded guilty and was fined $200, which her mother paid. Gaffney said he made the arrest after he had received complaints that the tailor shop owned by Miss Schulman's father was a "speakeasy."

DEMANDS $45,000,000 IN ALUMINUM SUIT

G. D. Haskell Names Directors and J. B. Duke's Executors in Anti-Trust Action.

R. B. MELLON A DEFENDANT

Deal With Duke to Bar Plaintiff and Keep American Co. as a Monopoly Is Charged.

A suit for $45,000,000 against the Aluminum Company of America of Pittsburgh, seven members of its directorate and the executors of the estate of the late James B. Duke was filed here yesterday in the United States District Court by George D. Haskell of Springfield, Mass., President and director of the Bausch Machine and Tool Company.

Mr. Haskell alleges that the Aluminum Company of America now owns or controls substantially all the deposits of bauxite, the ore from which aluminum is manufactured, in this country, and that it also owns or controls large deposits in foreign countries.

He further charges that the defendant company has for many years maintained, and now maintains, a monopoly in trade and commerce in crude or semi-finished aluminum in the United States and that it is operating in restraint of trade in violation of the Sherman Anti-Trust law.

Cites Agreement With Duke.

The bill of complaint sets forth that the plaintiff entered into an agreement with the late James B. Duke in 1924 by which they were to undertake the manufacture of aluminum in competition with the Aluminum Company of America.

Prior to this time, the complaint states, Mr. Duke had about completed a water-power development on the Saguenay River in the Province of Quebec. The plant cost $40,000,000 and generated 600,000 horsepower per annum.

The plaintiff says that for many years he had been preparing to enter into the manufacture and sale of aluminum and had ascertained facts regarding the existence of bauxite deposits in foreign countries which had not been acquired by the Aluminum Company of America. Water power in large quantity being necessary to the manufacture of aluminum, he says he ascertained the existence of and had under consideration large water-power developments in various parts of the country.

He asserts he had entered into tentative arrangements with capitalists for furnishing the funds for the acquisition of water power and bauxite deposits sufficient for the profitable manufacture of aluminum when, in 1924, he learned of Mr. Duke's Saguenay River development and began negotiations with him for sufficient water power for his proposed enterprise.

Mr. Duke, the plaintiff says, was then offering the water power of his development at $12 per horsepower per annum, "a rate at which commercial production of aluminum and its importation and sale in and among the several States of the United States in competition with the defendant Aluminum Company of America was not only possible but carried with it a suggestion of great profits."

While these negotiations were being carried on, the plaintiff says, Mr. Duke was advised of the use the plaintiff planned to make of the water power and all the material facts with regard to the plaintiff's undertaking in the manufacture of aluminum.

Planned Saguenay Plant.

"Thereupon," the complaint says, "as the result of negotiations, an agreement was reached between the plaintiff and said James B. Duke that they should jointly undertake the establishment of an aluminum manufacturing business on the Saguenay River; the said James B. Duke to furnish said enterprise the water power at $12 per horsepower per annum and to assist in financing the enterprise; the plaintiff, on the other hand, to contribute to the joint enterprise his knowledge of the aluminum business, its processes of manufacture, location and availability of bauxite beds, and other facts which had resulted from the plaintiff's study covering a period of several years.

"The business itself, the object of their joint undertaking, was to be the manufacture of aluminum and its sale in commerce among the States of the United States and with foreign nations, and in competition with the business of defendant Aluminum Company of America.

"In pursuance of said joint venture and as instrumentality in carrying it out, said James B. Duke caused the Quebec Company, Ltd., to be organized with a capital stock temporarily fixed at $1,000,000."

The complaint then says that the plaintiff has at all times fulfilled the

Continued on Page Nine.

VALENTINO PASSES WITH NO KIN AT SIDE; THRONGS IN STREET

Three Doctors and Two Nurses See "Film's Greatest Lover" Die After Long Coma.

MANAGER WEEPS IN HALL

Crowds Blocking Traffic, Held Back by Police Reserves, Rush to Funeral Church.

ASSOCIATES PAY TRIBUTES

Actor Dead at 31 Left Little of Huge Earnings—Arrangements for Funeral Yet Unmade.

Rudolph Valentino, motion picture actor, died at 12:10, yesterday afternoon, at the Polyclinic Hospital where he had undergone a double operation for acute appendicitis and gastric ulcers on Aug. 15. He was thirty-one. His youthfulness and rugged constitution aided him in making a valiant fight even after his five doctors had given up hope. Peritonitis and septic endocarditis, an affection of the heart tissues, were the immediate causes of death.

When the end came, the street in front of the Polyclinic Hospital was blocked by thousands of the actor's admirers and the curious, awaiting the latest bulletins from his bedside. The hospital switchboard was swamped by endless calls from persons anxious for the latest news.

Valentino lost consciousness several hours before he died. Shortly before the end came, a priest was called and administered the last rites of the Roman Catholic Church.

Last Words Gave Cheer.

The actor closed his thoughts against death, almost to the end. His last rational words were spoken to Joseph M. Schenck, Chairman of the Board of Directors of the United Artists Corporation, who was at his bedside at 6 A. M.

"Don't worry, Chief," said Valentino. "I will be all right."

Dr. Harold G. Meeker, who operated upon Valentino, said that the actor never gave up his thoughts of a vacation, so sure was he that he would conquer the complications which followed the operation.

"He passed peacefully," said Dr. Meeker. "He didn't know he was going. At 3:30 this morning, he turned to me and said cheerily:

" 'Doctor, do you know the greatest thing I am looking forward to?'

" 'What is it?' I asked.

"Valentino smiled and said: 'I am looking forward to going fishing with you next month. I hope you have plenty of fishing rods. Mine are in California.' "

Valentino left no fortune from his very large earnings. Mr. Schenck said the actor had spent practically all of his last year's income, which totaled close to $1,000,000. It is not yet known whether he left a will. His life insurance, totaling $200,000, goes to the United Artists Corporation as beneficiary. Reports that Valentino's insurance amounted to $1,000,000 were erroneous.

No Relatives at His Side.

Despite the fact that Valentino had been cited as an illustration of the fact that "all the world loves a lover," he died alone save for his three doctors and two nurses. His brother and sister are in Europe. His first wife, Jean Acker, remained in New York in order to be in constant communication with the sick bed, but was not at the hospital when Valentino died. His second wife, the former Winifred Hudnut, known on the stage as Natcha Rambova, is in Europe.

Pola Negri, who recently had been reported engaged to Valentino, is in California. By long distance telephone she had made many inquiries concerning his condition. Her last call to the Polyclinic Hospital was at 4:25 A. M. yesterday. She tried to get the actor's manager, S. George Ulmann, and failing in that, tried to communicate with others near Valentino for the latest information concerning him.

Unnerved by his long and patient vigil, Mr. Ulmann was unable to remain in the sickroom before the end came. He had not slept for four nights and four days. He stood just outside the door so as to be near Valentino while the actor's life ebbed away. Mr. Ulmann broke down when he was informed that Valentino was dead. Doctors ordered him to bed. Before withdrawing, he expressed appreciation of the solicitude shown for Valentino. He said:

"Mr. Valentino was greatly cheered during his last days by the thousands of messages sent him by his friends and motion picture admirers, and while he was too weak to read all of them, it was a great comfort to him

Continued on Page Three.

Berlins Plan Start for New York Tonight By Train, Mrs. Berlin Dreading Motor Ride

Special to The New York Times.

ALEXANDRIA BAY, N. Y., Aug. 23.—Irving Berlin, composer of jazz music, and Mrs. Berlin, the former Ellin Mackay, daughter of Clarence Mackay, who are sojourning in St. Lawrence Park, the guest of Mr. and Mrs. Max Winslow of New York, passed a quiet day. It is understood that they expect to leave by train tomorrow night for New York, taking a sleeper at Watertown or Syracuse. They motored to Alexandria Bay from Quebec. Mrs. Berlin remained indoors today, but Mr. Berlin, with Mr. Winslow, played nine holes of golf on the Municipal Links, and went shopping in the village. Mr. Berlin, wearing white flannels and a silk shirt, turned in at the neck, said:

"We had a wonderful trip over on the ship. We are seeking now a rest and a little vacation. I am at peace with the world and I hope everybody is as happy as we are. We only want a chance to be happy and to be left alone."

Mr. Berlin said he had to get back to Broadway soon to begin work on a new musical piece. Mrs. Berlin is so weary from the long motor ride from Quebec that they shrink from going by motor to New York.

At Mr. Berlin's apartment at 29 West Forty-sixth Street it was said yesterday that no word had been received from him, and at the music publishing house the same information was given.

Friend Says Valentino Had Premonition of Dying Young

LOS ANGELES, Cal., Aug. 23 (AP).—Rudolph Valentino, who died today in New York, had a premonition of an early death and welcomed it in preference to living to a decrepit old age, it was revealed here today by John W. Considine, producer of his pictures.

Considine said: "Valentino several times remarked to me, 'I shall die young. I know it, and I shall not be sorry. I would hate to live to be an old man.'

"Valentino's prophecy has been fulfilled, but it has been a terrific blow to his friends. I found Rudolph a man of great courage and unquenchable spirit. He will be greatly missed."

COURT FINDING HALTS VOTE MACHINES HERE

Their Use in Fall Elections Is Doubtful, Knapp Contract Being Held Illegal.

ONLY HOPE LIES IN APPEAL

Justice Crain Finds Secretary of State Violated Charter in Acting as City's Agent.

Unless a decision by Supreme Court Justice Crain, handed down yesterday, is reversed by the higher courts before the November election, no voting machines paid for by the city's funds will be used here during the Fall balloting. This is the result of a ruling that the contract made by Secretary of State Florence E. S. Knapp, in behalf of the city, with the Automatic Registering Company of Jamestown, N. Y., is in violation of the city charter and constitutes a waste of city funds.

The contract called for the installation of about 3,000 machines, to cost $848.65 each, in the voting precincts of New York City over a period of three years.

Justice Crain grants an injunction in the suit of Adolph Hill, a taxpayer, who alleged waste of city funds amounting to about $200 on each machine because of the manner in which the contract was let. The Court upholds this contention and finds that under the requirements for the purchase of city property the machines could have been bought for less money.

City's Opposition Lethargic.

Although the question was taken before the court in the guise of a taxpayer's action and it was made evident that it was in behalf of the Shoup Voting Machine Company, an unsuccessful bidder on the voting machine contract, who asserted that the terms were so drawn that only the Automatic Company's machine fulfilled the requirements, the members of the Tammany City Administration involved were not active in opposing it.

Controller Berry, as disbursing officer of the city's funds, was made a main defendant with the Secretary of State, but the argument before Justice Crain was made by Deputy Attorney General Obermeier in behalf of the Secretary of State.

Temporary Victory for City.

The result of the suit is a temporary victory for the city officials in opposing action by the State Legislature to compel the installation of voting machines in New York City. The bill requiring the city to buy and use them was passed four years ago, and contained a provision that if the city officials did not act the Secretary of State had authority to do so.

During the Hylan régime Commissioner of Accounts Hirshfield declared that the cost of the Jamestown machines was excessive by $200, and the Administration refused to buy.

Justice Crain's decision is based upon his findings that, although the Legislature succeeded in one respect in circumventing the New York City charter in empowering the Secretary of State to buy supplies for the city, by making ineffective the charter provisions as to the purchase of "patenter articles," the lawmakers failed to overcome other requirements as to making contracts for city supplies. Justice Crain accordingly said:

"It is conceded that the provisions of the charter were ignored by the Secretary of State in the making of the contract. She did that which the applicable charter provisions did not permit her to do, and omitted to do that which the applicable charter provisions required her to do. Her action was illegal and it will incidentally involve an outlay of money in excess of that which the city would have been called upon to make had the charter provisions been followed.

"The Secretary of State's motives for doing what she did are not involved

Continued on Page Two.

REPUBLICAN CHIEFS WILL CONFER TODAY ON GOVERNORSHIP

Wadsworth, Koenig and Morris to Discuss Candidates at Meeting in Saratoga.

KOENIG CONSULTS COOLIDGE

County Chairman Lays the New York Political Situation Before the President.

CROPSEY MEN RENEW HOPE

Leaders at Work Up-State to Win Convention Delegates Who Will Be "Harmonious."

Special to The New York Times.

PAUL SMITH'S, N. Y., Aug. 23.—Samuel S. Koenig, Chairman of the New York County Republican Committee, conferred with President Coolidge today on State politics, but their discussion did not result in determining who should be the party nominee for Governor this Fall.

Mr. Koenig left this afternoon for Saratoga, where he will meet tomorrow Senator Wadsworth and Chairman Morris of the Republican State Committee. The conference of these party leaders is expected to lead to more positive results on the Governorship.

The conferences held here with President Coolidge have been intended only to demonstrate that the President is vitally interested in New York State affairs, and to help soften, if possible, the opposition of the drys, among whom the President is strong.

Cropsey and Hilles Lead List.

After today's conference between the President and Mr. Koenig Supreme Court Justice Charles J. Cropsey and Charles D. Hilles appeared to be leading the list from which the nominee for Governor will be selected. It was indicated that Justice Cropsey seemed to satisfy more sections of the State than others who had been considered, and that he would be acceptable to the party leaders if he agreed to enter the race.

In his half-hour conference with the President, who is greatly interested in the New York situation because of the national politics involved, Mr. Koenig told him that the Republicans would gain four members of Congress in Greater New York and the party would control the next delegation from the State.

Mr. Koenig also assured Mr. Coolidge that prosperity was going to be a big asset favoring Senator Wadsworth's re-election, assuring him support from Democrats sufficient, in his opinion, to overcome the loss from up-State Republican drys.

Mr. Coolidge is not interfering in any way in New York politics, Mr. Koenig made it clear after the conference, but is interested in seeing that the Republicans increase their hold in Congress and retain the Wadsworth seat in the Senate. He will make no speeches in New York and do nothing to aid the party here, except what he may do before the November election in the way of a general statement on the trend of politics.

Mr. Koenig declined to commit himself on the Governorship, but admitted that Justice Cropsey seemed to be coming to the front. He said he felt that Cropsey, Attorney General Ottinger or Charles D. Hilles would make a strong standard-bearer in the State fight.

As to what the candidate would represent as between the wets and drys, Mr. Koenig declared he would not be a wet.

Suggests Campaign Issues.

"The issue of the Republican candidate for Governor will be the extravagance of the Smith Administration and the splendid record the Republican Legislature made last year," he said.

"The wet issue will figure only incidentally, but still as a live and vital question. There will be other economic matters that are going to appeal to the voters, and, as the situation now stands, the Republicans enter the field with excellent chances.

"As for Senator Wadsworth, he will present the business prosperity brought about by the Republican Administration and stand on the accomplishments of the party. His chief appeal will not be modification of the Volstead amendment, but that and more far-reaching issues.

"I see no reason to feel that Mr. Wadsworth will be defeated. He is going to get a large vote in New York, much larger than the normal Republican vote. It will come from Democrats and ought to be large enough to overbalance his losses to the dry candidate for the Senate. There are thousands of dry Republicans, Democrats and independents who will vote for him to sustain the National Administration; then, too, the referendum will bring to his support wets who have been generally aligned against the Republican Party on State issues.

"The Republicans will not wage their campaign on the sole issue of prohibition. Senator Wadsworth will discuss national issues, and the candidate for Governor will stress the failures of the Smith Administration and the work done by the last Legislature.

Won't Be "Tool of the Drys."

"This is the first election in years that the Republican organization has not had to carry the load of being the tool of the drys. The agitation against Senator Wadsworth up-State is going to help him in New York City. The more the drys declare they are going to beat him, the greater his strength will become among the wets, with a consequent weakening of the Democratic candidate for the Senate."

It became known after Mr. Koenig's visit that there is a well organized movement under way to defeat Representative LaGuardia of New York,

VALENTINO PASSES WITH NO KIN AT SIDE

Continued from Page 1, Column 6.

to know that so many friends were interested and sympathetic. I know he would want me to express the gratitude he felt. Personally I want to thank the physicians and nurses and the hospital attaches who worked so hard and conscientiously to save his life. Everything humanly possible was done for him."

Throughout the night a watch at the bedside of the patient was maintained by Dr. Meeker and Dr. William Bryant Rawls, house physician of the Polyclinic Hospital, and two nurses, Pearl Franks, who had been in attendance upon Valentino from the second day that he was in the hospital, and Jean Littlefield, who was called in on the case Sunday, after Valentino had taken a second turn for the worse.

At 3:30 A. M. the doctors gave the patient a hypodermic to induce sleep. Valentino slept until about 6 o'clock. Soon afterward Mr. Schenck and Mr. Ulmann entered the sick room. When Mr. Ulmann started to lower the window shade, Valentino objected, saying: "Don't pull down the shade. I am feeling fine."

Valentino's condition remained virtually as it was on Sunday, but at 9 A. M. there was a slight rise in temperature to 104.5, according to Mr. Ulmann. At that time his pulse was 105 and his respiration 30.

The last rites of the Catholic Church were administered to the dying actor at 10 o'clock by Father Joseph M. Cangedo of the Church of the Sacred Heart of Jesus and Mary. Father Cangedo came to America from the little town in Italy where Valentino was born. He had known Valentino since the actor's boyhood. Father Cangedo had heard Valentino's confession and granted him absolution on Sunday, after the screen star's condition had taken a sharp turn for the worse.

Two Priests Summoned.

When the surgeons saw that Valentino was sinking rapidly they called, in addition to Father Cangedo, Father Edward F. Leonard of St. Malachi's Roman Catholic Church. After the last rites had been administered, Father Leonard and Father Cangedo left, thinking that the actor's death might be delayed. When Father Leonard was called a second time, he arrived just after Valentino had passed away.

According to Dr. Meeker, Valentino did not speak a word in English after 6:30 o'clock. At intervals he cried out in Italian which no one at his bedside understood. At 8 o'clock he went into a coma. Death, according to Dr. Meeker, was directly due to peritonitis and septic endocarditis. Peritonitis was caused by ulcers of the stomach and endocarditis followed the development of pleurisy in the left chest on Saturday.

Dr. Meeker said when Valentino suffered an attack of stomach trouble six weeks ago, he had not considered the trouble as serious. The gastric ulcers which brought on the operation and resulted in death were probably manifesting themselves at the time of that attack, the doctor said.

Mr. Schenck said he believed that Valentino's appeal to women motion-picture fans was to be explained by a personality which typified most women's ideal of romance.

Mr. Schenck said that Valentino had left no fortune out of the large amounts of money he had made in motion pictures. He said that Valentino was a mere boy in money matters, and spent as fast as he earned. In explaining how Valentino's earnings in 1925 totaled about $1,000,000, he said they included $200,000 a picture and 50 per cent. of the profits on three pictures he made for United Artists, and $200,000 which he was paid by J. D. Williams for "Cobra."

Valentino's 1926 contract with United Artists Corporation provided for a payment of $200,000 a picture and 25 per cent. of the profits.

Mr. Schenck said that Valentino spent a large amount of money when he visited Europe last year. He toured the shops of art and antique collectors and bought a large collection for his home in Beverly Hills, Los Angeles.

Mr. Ulmann, Mr. Schenck, and Father Leonard departed from the hospital soon after Valentino died. The two nurses left the death bed, and preparations were made to take the body to the Campbell Funeral Parlors, Broadway and Sixty-sixth Street.

Crowds Block Traffic.

News of Valentino's death spread through the hospital and to the streets with amazing rapidity. The crowds outside the hospital building continued to grow until it blocked traffic. The hospital authorities called up the West Forty-seventh Street Police Station, and requested the police to take charge of the situation. Not until the police arrived was traffic resumed through West Fiftieth Street between Eighth and Ninth Avenues. Many of the curious adopted all kinds of ruses to get into the hospital, but they were turned out as fast as they got through the entrance.

The body of Valentino was placed in a plain wicker basket, covered with cloth of gold, and taken to Campbell parlors. The crowds remained in front of the hospital, hoping in vain to see the removal of the body, which was taken from the building through a private entrance on West Fifty-first Street.

After the body was taken to the undertaking establishment, the crowds began to collect there in such numbers that a guard had to be posted by the police. No plans for the funeral have been made. Friends of Valentino are awaiting instructions from his brother, Alberto Guglielmi.

Mr. Schenck cabled Mr. Guglielmi in Paris on Sunday that Valentino was dying, and received a cablegram that the actor's brother would sail for New York on the first ship. Mr. Schenck said last evening that he had heard nothing further from him. Valentino's sister, who was in Turin, also was advised by cable of the star's approaching end.

No word has been received from her.

The Valentino death certificate was filed with the Board of Health at 3:50 in the afternoon. It gave "ruptured gastric ulcer and general peritonitis" as the cause of death, and specified "septic pneumonia and septic endocarditis" as contributing causes. Valentino's name, "Rudolfo Guglielmi" was entered upon the death certificate, and his age was given as 31. A slight delay in filing the certificate was occasioned by difficulty in getting data as to his age.

One of the first persons who tried to view Valentino's body at the undertaking rooms gave his name as Camillo Santomero, 210 Stanton Street, and described himself as a traveling salesman and a cousin of the dead actor. He had failed in repeated attempts to get into the Polyclinic Hospital, and pleaded to get into the undertaker's by saying he had not seen Valentino for five years. He asserted that his mother was a sister. He was accompanied by Guido Valenti, who claimed to have been a boyhood friend of Valentino.

Body May Lie in State.

In response to constant inquiries, employes of the establishment announced that no definite information as to whether the body would be permitted to lie in state could be given.

© Wide World.

Photograph of Screen Star Taken in The Times Studio a Few Weeks Before His Death.

Valentino as He Appeared in "The Son of the Sheik," His Latest Picture on Broadway, a Sequel to the Film in Which He Scored His Greatest Success.

VALENTINO'S FAME A TRIUMPH OF YOUTH

Actor Wanted to Be a Gardener and Went to California to Get Work on a Farm.

Rudolph Valentino was born on May 6, 1895, in Tastelameta, Italy, the son of Giovanni Gugliemi, a veterinary doctor. After taking an "agriculturalist's" diploma from the Royal School of Agriculture in Genoa, Italy, he came to this country in December of 1913 to seek work as a gardener.

He did not find what he wanted, he said later, although it is understood he worked a while on the Long Island estate of Cornelius Bliss Jr. His next position was as an apprentice landscape gardener in Central Park. He found something much more attractive to him in the dance halls and cafés of the city, and in them picked up the accomplishment of dancing. For some time he was practically penniless, accepting such odd jobs as shining brass on automobiles, sweeping and the like.

The head waiter at Maxim's first employed him as a dancer, and thus began his professional career. As dancing partner of Bonnie Glass, and later to Joan Sawyer, he attained some reputation. But at that time he still was bent on farming, and his fruitful journey to California, he told friends, was made with the idea of becoming a farmer there. He reached the Coast by joining a musical comedy troupe, which stranded him in San Francisco.

Valentino was advised by a friend he had known in the East, Norman Kerry, to try motion pictures, and on the bounty of Kerry he traveled to Los Angeles. He obtained only occasional jobs as an extra about the movie lots of Hollywood until June Mathis selected him for the rôle of Julio in "The Four Horsemen of the Apocalypse." In that he made his first triumph. That was in 1921. A feature of the picture was the Argentine tango as danced by Valentino, for the tango was then enjoying some of the popularity that has since been accorded the Charleston.

He gained his nickname from "The Sheik," a screen version of another best-seller. One of his earlier pictures was "Camille" in which he played opposite Nazimova. Official stardom came to him after "Beyond the Rocks," a Paramount picture from the story of Elinor Glyn in which he appeared with Gloria Swanson, "Blood and Sand" was his first starring vehicle—hitherto he had been a featured player only.

Valentino's last film was "The Son of the Sheik," which opened in New York on July 25 of this year.

Trouble Over Divorce.

The screen idol's marital difficulties brought him into the public eye almost as much as did his pictures. In 1919, when he was still a struggling and often hungry young film aspirant, he married Jean Acker, an actress who, although not a star, had met with some success. Miss Acker obtained an interlocutory decree of divorce from him in January of 1922.

Valentino waited only a few months before slipping across the Mexican border at Tia Juana to marry Miss Winifred Hudnut, stepdaughter of Richard Hudnut, millionaire manufacturer of perfumes. Miss Hudnut was also known as Natacha Rambova, Winifred de Wolf and Winifred Shaughnessy. It was while playing Armand in "Camille" that Valentino met Miss Hudnut. She was at that time working for Nazimova, and had designed the settings for the younger Dumas' melodrama.

Valentino came back to California with his bride, only to learn that he faced a charge of bigamy. The "divorce" won by his first wife, Miss Acker, would not be complete, according to law, until a year from the granting of the interlocutory decree.

The film star was freed of the bigamy charge in a preliminary hearing, and a Grand Jury that investigated it later dropped it with no action. The couple were remarried at Crown Point, Ind., on march 15 of the following year after the interlocutory decree had became absolute.

In January, 1926, Miss Hudnut obtained a final divorce decree from Valentino in Paris, and since then rumors have been current that Rudolph was going to wed Pola Negri.

Challenged Editorial Writer.

A month ago the "Shiek" became indignant over an editorial appearing in The Chicago Tribune entitled "Pink Powder Puffs." He resented the imputation that he was the cause of American men using face powder, and issued a challenge to the author of the editorial.

When the Chicago editorial writer would not reveal himself, Valentino said he considered the silence vindication.

After the war Valentino heard from a brother that he was rated a "slacker" in Taranto, Italy, because he had not fought for the United States. As a matter of fact, his services were refused on account of poor eyesight. He waited until he had cleared his name in Italy before taking out first citizenship papers in New York in November, 1925.

In 1922 and 1923 Valentino became involved in a dispute with his employers, Famous Players-Lasky Corporation. He broke with the company but patched things up soon afterward.

When Valentino became famous in "The Four Horsemen," many stories began to circulate about his early life. It was popularly supposed that he had supported himself after his arrival in America by working as a bus boy, a dish washer, and even a barber. All of which Valentino rose to deny.

He had, he said, been educated at Dante Alighieri College at Tarento, Italy, and at the military college della Sapienza in Perugia. He tried to enter the Government Naval Academy, but failed to pass the tests owing to a chest that was an inch short of the required measurement. After attending the agricultural school, he came to New York as a first-class passenger on the S. S. Cleveland of the Hamburg-American line.

He knew nothing of the language, and, failing to get work as a gardener, he became the dancing partner of Bonnie Glass and Joan Sawyer. He even appeared on the legitimate stage in minor rôles. His acting in "The Eyes of Youth," a C. K. Young production, attracted the attention of June Mathis, who had just finished her adaptation for the screen of "The Four Horsemen." She decided that Valentino was just the type to play Julio Desnoyers, and with his engagement for the rôle he leaped from obscurity to fame almost overnight.

Wrote Book of Poems.

Besides his better known successes, Valentino appeared on the screen in "Passion's Playground," "The Wonderful Chance," "Moran of the Lady Letty," "The Young Rajah," "Frivolous Wives," "A Rogue's Romance," "Monsieur Beaucaire" and "A Sainted Devil."

In 1924 Rudolph evinced activity in another sphere: he published a book of verse. "Day Dreams" was the title and it was brought out by MacFadden Publications. The poems were described as "jig-saw" verses on love, passion, kisses and kindred topics.

Some of Valentino's pictures were great money-makers. "The Four Horsemen of the Apocalypse" is said to have earned more than $2,000,000 and "The Sheik" more than $1,000,000. Valentino always insisted "The Sheik" was his idea of a poor performance.

"All the News That's Fit to Print."

The New York Times.

THE WEATHER
Rain Monday; fair and colder Tuesday; fresh south, shifting to west, winds.
For full weather report see Page 17.

VOL. LXV...NO. 21,114. ... NEW YORK, MONDAY, NOVEMBER 15, 1915.—EIGHTEEN PAGES. ONE CENT In Greater New York, Jersey City and Newark. | Elsewhere TWO CENTS.

NINE AMERICANS LOST ON THE ANCONA; AUSTRIA SAYS LINER TRIED TO FLEE; ITALY SENDS PROTEST TO ALL NEUTRALS

FRENCH OPEN FIRE FOR NEW ASSAULT

Big Guns Again Battering the German Lines in Artois.

FOE NOW ON LAST RIDGE

Clinging to Vimy—With That Retaken, French Will Move on Lille.

FAITH IN FOCH'S GENIUS

Times Correspondent Finds Strong Belief That Famous Strategist Will Break Enemy's Line.

From a Staff Correspondent.
Special Cable to THE NEW YORK TIMES.

PARIS, Nov. 14.—Fuller knowledge of why it is taking so long to drive the Germans out of France, clearer insight into why the recent general offensive resulted in such an apparently insignificant advance, and at the same time better belief that the war will actually end some time with a French victory has been furnished me during a trip to the front in Artois, from which I have just returned.

This was my third visit to that particular "sector north of Arras," as it has so often been named in the official communications.

The first was last February, when the definite trench lines, formed after the battle of the Marne, were comparatively new, and the preparations for the first general offensive of last Spring were just becoming evident. The second trip was at the end of May, a few days after Carency fell, when I was the only neutral observer permitted actually to see the battle of the Labyrinth. Therefore, with the second general offensive only six weeks passed, when the War Office decided that correspondents should be allowed to see the new lines, I was included in the party for the purpose of making a comparison with the situation [illegible].

From this Artois front as it now exists it is possible for the actual observer to get a clearer understanding of the entire western battle front than even in the Champagne where the gains were greater, but not a bit more important from the viewpoint of French strategists. The fact that that master strategist, General Foch, whom I was permitted to meet on this trip, has never been changed from command of the northern group of armies is sufficient evidence to cause the belief that the break-up of Germany's still resisting wall is quite as likely to begin there as where the more sensational part of the recent general offensive was launched.

Writing under the direction of a personal censor—a Captain of the General Staff, who accompanied the party—it is impossible for me to give complete information which might plainly prove all three of the assertions with which I have commenced this story. I may not quote the words that have been spoken and the figures that have been shown that would positively indicate my meaning. And more jealously than ever are guarded the names of the points upon which the French are hammering day and night in ceaseless preparation for what, in my mind, will be the final offensive through that famous territory, every yard of which already has been stained with both French and German blood.

The Vital Positions.

On my first trip in Artois the German lines were too far advanced for an observer to get a real understanding of the country necessary to realize why it is considered so vitally important. From a distant range of hills I then looked upon Bois de Bouvigny and Mont Saint Eloi. Carency, Ablain, and Neuville Saint Vaast were only vague distances directed to my mind by the pointing finger of the officer conducting the party. On my second trip I walked through former German trenches into Carency and repeatedly lost myself in the tortuous twistings of the trenches of La Targette and the Labyrinth. Still the necessary geography of the country was not impressed upon me.

On my third trip all this was changed. This time I walked through the ruins of Ablain into the trenches leading to Souchez and rode openly in an automobile over an entire countryside from Arras nearly to Bethune on roads where had a similar trip been attempted last May our car would have been blown to pieces before we could travel a hundred yards. On this trip I enjoyed the spectacle of standing openly on a hillside and watching French shells breaking in constant clouds over the crest of Vimy, which is the last range of hills shutting the plateau of Artois from the great Plain of Douai. The crest of Vimy, flanked by strong positions in Givenchy and behind Arras, is the last battle line of Germany in Artois.

"They Must Keep on Going Away."

In quaint English an officer who accompanied us said:

"When we take any of those positions the Germans must go away. They will have no place to go but into the Plain of Douai. When they get into the Plain of Douai they must keep on going away."

Except for this Crest of Vimy, which is a freakish formation of hills rising from the valley at the extreme eastern side, the plateau of Artois may be compared in shape to the fingers of a human hand with the knuckles slightly raised and the fingers slightly apart and sloping to the valley before the Vimy Heights. It is a vast succession of hill ranges and valleys running hori-

Continued on Page 2.

VATICAN SAYS KAISER SENT NO TRUCE PLEA

None of the Belligerents Has Made Peace Representations to the Pope.

ROME, Nov. 13, (via Paris, Nov. 14.)—The assertion made in various quarters recently that Emperor William had written to Pope Benedict asking the Pope to obtain a truce from the Allies was emphatically denied at the Vatican today.

Officials there declared that neither side had made any representations to the Pontiff looking for peace.

They added that no negotiations for peace were taking place and that there was no probability that pourparlers for peace would be started.

A dispatch from Rome last Monday credited the Giornale d'Italia with the statement that a mysterious envoy from the ruler of one of the belligerent nations was in Rome. His mission, it was added, had not been accomplished, and it was not known whether he was awaiting a reply from the Vatican or orders from his chief.

SAYS THE POPE LEFT VATICAN'S PRECINCTS

Traditional Imprisonment Disregarded by Benedict XV., Reports Rome Paper.

ROME, Nov. 14.—Pope Benedict has made an important departure from the custom of the Pontiffs by visiting the Church of Saint Anna, adjoining the Apostolic Palace, and thus going outside the Vatican precincts, according to the Giornale d'Italia.

Since the end of the Popes' temporal power one form of Papal protest against the new order of things has been the seclusion of the Pontiffs in the Vatican.

In January of this year it was reported from Rome that Pope Benedict XV. in visiting the Santa Marta Hospital, had disregarded the traditional imprisonment of the Pope, always observed by Popes Pius IX., Leo XIII., and Pius X. after the end of the temporal power of the Papacy, but this was denied. It was explained that Pope Benedict has passed through the Apostolic Palace inside of St. Peter's, reaching the hospital without touching Italian soil, and that his predecessor in the same way had visited the wounded in the Santa Marta Hospital after the earthquake in Messina.

It is probable that a similar explanation may apply to this case, as the proximity of the Church of Saint Anna to the Apostolic Palace suggests that the visit may have been made without traversing what is technically Italian soil. Italians often refer to the Pope as [illegible]

CHURCHILL'S OLD FOES NOW CORDIAL TO HIM

Editorial Writers Hint That His Plans Failed Through Others' Mismanagement.

LONDON, Monday, Nov. 15, 3:06 A. M.—Laudatory editorials appear in some of the London morning papers, justifying Winston Spencer Churchill in quitting the Cabinet under the circumstances he has already indicated.

The Daily Mail asks whether Mr. Churchill was really responsible for the "unfortunate Dardanelles miscarriage," and says that he leaves office with the good wishes of every one in the country.

Other papers, not friendly toward Mr. Churchill, are also asking whether Mr. Churchill's plans in the Dardanelles and the other undertakings for which he was supposed to be responsible failed of their object through delays or mismanagement in their execution on account of other personages in the Government or Administration.

Lord Rosebery writes to The Times, advocating that the Government take advantage of Mr. Churchill's "regrettable resignation" to add to the Cabinet some non-political man of business, "if only for the purposes of retrenchment and to supply sorely needed new blood."

The Morning Post strongly advocates the formation of an official Opposition in Parliament to force upon the Government improvement in the conduct of affairs.

CANNON STRICKEN IN CHURCH PULPIT

Ex-Senator Is Attacked by Heart Trouble in Lecture on Mormonism.

Ex-United States Senator Frank J. Cannon of Utah, who now lives in Denver, Col., was taken ill last night while speaking on "Mormonism vs. Americanism" in the pulpit of the Rutgers Presbyterian Church, Broadway and Seventy-third Street. He was assisted to one of the church parlors, where two physicians were called to attend him. After the pastor, the Rev. Dr. Russell, had been assured by the physicians that Mr. Cannon would soon recover, he made this announcement to the congregation:

"Mr. Cannon had been indisposed throughout the day, and the exertion and emotion with which he addressed us has overtaxed his strength and has brought on a slight attack of heart failure. The physicians assure me that he will soon recover."

The ex-Senator had been speaking forty-five minutes probably, and had just quoted a section from the book of the Mormon doctrine to illustrate one of his statements, when he was seen to falter. He laid the book upon the pulpit and turned toward a chair back of the pulpit, which he managed to reach unassisted. He became pale and showed evidence of suffering, but struggled against it until his condition was observed by Trustee Henry D. Brewster and the pastor and others, who assisted him to the church rooms.

Mrs. J. H. Radley of 112 West Seventy-first Street, and W. A. Silver, who is one of the elders of the church, and were in the congregation, hurried to his aid. Soon afterward he recovered from the attack, and with his wife and several of the church members he was taken in an automobile to the Hotel Collingwood, at 45 West Thirty-fifth Street.

FAY TO NAME ALL IN SHIP BOMB PLOT

Active Head of Teutonic Conspirators Offers to Turn State's Evidence.

DESERTED BY HIS BACKERS

District Attorney Marshall Will Hear His Story of Great Spy Ring Today.

INDICTMENTS FOR TWO MORE

American Secret Agents in Europe Barp Prisoner's Career—Scholz May Confess

"Lieutenant" Robert Fay, active head of the German conspiracy in this country to destroy ships carrying munitions of war to the Allies, and now under indictment, with five other alleged conspirators, for that crime, which is a felony under the piracy laws of the United States, has agreed to turn State's evidence.

His change of front followed a long talk with William J. Flynn, Chief of the United States Secret Service, yesterday afternoon. This morning Fay will be taken to the Federal Building, where he is expected to lay bare the conspiracy in all of its details.

Whether the Government will accept Fay's offer to turn State's evidence will be determined after his talk with District Attorney Marshall. If Mr. Marshall accepts Fay as a witness, it is considered certain that Walter Scholz, who is in the Tombs in default of bail and is Fay's brother-in-law, also will offer to testify for the prosecution.

No One to be Shielded.

Chief Flynn and District Attorney Marshall arrived here from Washington yesterday morning. They came back, so it was generally understood, with authorization to go ahead and get at the bottom of the alien conspiracies in this country, and to dig deeply, regardless of whom they hit.

Flynn had not seen back many hours before he appeared at the Tombs. It was said that Fay had sent for him. Fay was taken into the room reserved for lawyers consulting their clients, and for more than an hour remained with the Secret Service Chief. What Fay told him and whether his disclosures involved the men "higher up" could not be ascertained. Chief Flynn refused to discuss the case from any angle, and when efforts were made to get a note to Fay in the Tombs the Warden informed reporters that the orders were to take no notes to the prisoner.

It is now understood that the investigation of Fay's story by agents of the Secret Service in Europe was completed several days ago, and that they traced his career for the last sixteen years, or back to the time when he was a boy in his teens, gifted with an unusual knowledge of mechanics. This investigation is said to have proved that Fay's story of having conferred with a high official of the German Secret Service before coming to this country was true, and that he did receive funds from that official before embarking under the name of "J. J. Kearling" on the Rotterdam at Rotterdam.

Verified Fay's Story.

Other details of the story told by Fay immediately following his arrest are said to have been checked up in Europe and to have been found to be generally true.

Fay is the man's right name; he did fight in the German Army, and he was in Brussels on the day on which he says he met the German Secret Service official there. In his statement at the time of his arrest Fay said he had been promoted to a Lieutenancy in the army, and that as such he received a furlough to visit the United States. The Secret Service official in Brussels, he added, gave him $4,000 for expenses. He also asserted he received instructions as to what he was to do in this country.

The German Secret Service agent, according to Fay, showed him a letter written by Dr. Herbert Kienzle, another of the indicted men, to his [Kienzle's] father, which gave the names of various ships engaged in the munition trade out of New York, and specified certain railroads which were transporting ammunition for the Allies to New York and other American ports. The New York Central and the New York, New Haven & Hartford were two of the roads named. The letter also mentioned several firms engaged in munition work. The Secret Service official, Fay said, told him to memorize the names and to use the information to identify himself when he arrived in New York.

As soon as he landed in New York, Fay continued, he sought out Dr. Kienzle and proved his trustworthiness by quoting from the letter he had seen in Brussels. Later, he said, he called on Captain Boy-Ed, Naval Attaché, and Captain von Papen, Military Attaché, both of the German Embassy in Washington, but he added that both of those men told him that he must not in any circumstances tamper with ships in New York Harbor. Fay declared he received also letters to certain other men, some of them prominent, and all of pronounced German sympathies. Whether he disclosed the names yesterday afternoon Chief Flynn refused to tell.

Chief Flynn Reticent.

The Chief, always reticent, was especially uncommunicative yesterday following his talk with Fay. He did not deny that Fay had agreed to be a

Continued on Page 3.

Austrian Aeroplanes Shell Verona: Kill 30 and Wound 49 Civilians

ROME, Nov. 14, (via Paris.)—Thirty persons are dead in Verona as a result of three Austrian aeroplanes dropping bombs on the city. Thirty other persons were seriously and nineteen slightly injured.

The bombs of the aircraft found most of their victims in the principal square of the city, where citizens and peasants from the outlying districts were attending the market. Nineteen persons were killed by one bomb.

The aeroplanes visited various parts of the city, but none of the missiles dropped by them fell near any of the military buildings.

This is the second time Austro-Hungarian aeroplanes have made a raid on the fortified city of Verona. Last July an Austrian machine dropped about a dozen bombs on the city and then escaped, notwithstanding a fire directed at it by the forts defending the city.

Verona is the scene of Shakespeare's tragedy, "Romeo and Juliet," and his comedy, "Two Gentlemen of Verona." Hundreds of American tourists visit the city in normal times to see the reputed tomb of Juliet and the house where her parents, the Capulets, are said to have lived.

There are several fine churches in the city, some of which date back to the early part of the twelfth century. Among them is the famous Church of San Zeno Maggiore, which contains one of Titian's masterpieces. Verona, with its ancient churches and palaces, is still one of the most picturesque cities of Italy, and has not been much affected by the commercial expansion of Padua and Mantua, which are within a radius of twenty-five miles.

When the last census of Verona was taken in 1901 the city had a population of 74,271.

DR. B. T. WASHINGTON, NEGRO LEADER, DEAD

Founder of the Tuskegee Institute Expires of Hardening of Arteries After Brief Illness.

TAKEN TO HIS HOME TO DIE

Seth Low and W. J. Willcox Persuaded Him to Consult Specialists, Who Told Him He Was Doomed.

TUSKEGEE, Ala., Nov. 14.—Booker T. Washington, foremost teacher and leader of the negro race, died early today at his home here, near the Tuskegee Institute, which he founded and of which he was President. Hardening of the arteries, following a nervous breakdown, caused his death four hours after Dr. Washington arrived from New York.

Although he had been in failing health for several months, the negro leader's condition became serious only last week while he was in the East. He then realized the end was near, but was determined to make the last long trip South. He said often: "I was born in the South, have lived all my life in the South, and expect to die and be buried in the South."

Accompanied by his wife, his secretary, and a physician, Dr. Washington left New York for Tuskegee at 4 o'clock on Friday afternoon. He reached home last midnight, and died at 4:40 o'clock this morning. His last public appearance was at the national conference of Congregational churches in New York, where he delivered a lecture on Oct. 25. The funeral will be held at Tuskegee Institute on Wednesday morning at 10 o'clock.

Dr. Washington's Career.

No one knows the day, nor even with certainty the year, of the birth of Booker T. Washington; but the day of his death was announced by telegraph and cable to many parts of the world.

He began life as "just another little nigger" on a plantation of a family named Burrows in Hale's Ford, Va. The month and year of his birth were probably April, 1858, although Dr. Washington himself was not sure of this. In the biographical paragraph under his name in "Who's Who in America," it is said that he was born "about 185[illegible]." The only certain fact is that he was born into slavery when negro mothers made no record of nor long remembered the date of a child's birth.

Soon after the close of the civil war the little negro boy went with his stepmother to Malden, West Va., where he worked in salt furnaces for nine months in the year and attended school for three months. After several years of such life the boy obtained work in the kitchen of Mrs. Viola Ruffner, a New England woman who had married a Southerner. Mrs. Ruffner soon recognized the boy's eagerness and ability to advance himself, so she taught him the elementary subjects. Booker Washington felt grateful to her to the end of his life, because she really gave him his start.

He heard of the Hampton Institute, for negroes, in 1871, when he was about thirteen years old, and he decided at once to attend it. So, with the little money he had been able to save from his wages of $6 a week, he set out for Richmond, Va., hoping to earn enough there to enable him to go on to Hampton, which is near Norfolk. This was in 1871. Dr. Washington founded the Tuskegee Institute just ten years later. He was admitted to the institute and was graduated at the head of his class in 1875, after working his way through the school.

After graduation Dr. Washington returned to Malden and taught school until he had earned enough to enable him to go to the Wayland Seminary in Washington, D. C., where he studied until 1879, when he was called to Hampton as a teacher in the institute. After he had taught for two years, in 1881 the State of Alabama voted to found an industrial institute for negroes similar to that at Hampton, and, after searching for a negro qualified to head the proposed institution, Dr. Washington was selected. This was his entrance into the "black belt" of the South, a chance which he had long desired, and when he assumed charge of the institute at Tuskegee, Ala., his real life's work began.

The Start of Tuskegee.

The State had appropriated $2,000 a year, and it was the task of the negro to organize the school. How well he did this is shown by a comparison of statistics. The institute opened on July 4, 1881, with one teacher and thirty pupils. At that time it had neither land nor buildings, nothing but the $2,000 a year granted by the Alabama Legislature.

When the institute celebrated its twenty-fifth anniversary it owned 2,000 acres of land and eighty-three large and small buildings, which, with its equipment of live stock, stock in trade, and other personal property, were valued at $831,895. This did not include 22,000 acres of public land remaining unsold from the 25,000 acres granted by Congress, valued at $135,000, nor the endowment fund, which was $1,275,644. During the year there were more than 1,500 students enrolled in the school, more than 1,000 young men, and more than 500 young women. The students were trained in thirty-seven industries.

It was on the opening day of the Atlanta Exposition in 1895 that Dr. Washington became a national character. On that day he delivered an address that was heard by thousands and read by other thousands in far-away places with wonder that a man so wise and clear-seeing should arise from among his people to lead them upward. For it was because Dr. Washington stood out as a negro striving in a sensible and sincere

Continued on Page 5.

SAYS PROPAGANDA COST FORTY MILLIONS

Bernstorff and Albert in Last Four Months Got $10,000,000, Providence Journal Avers.

REMITTANCES BY WIRELESS

Von Nuber's Circular Letter "Demanding" That Workers Quit and Implying Compensation.

Special to The New York Times.

PROVIDENCE, R. I., Nov. 14.—That between $35,000,000 and $40,000,000 has been spent in this country in the last four months for propaganda work against the Allies, under the immediate supervision of Count von Bernstorff, the German Ambassador, and Dr. Heinrich Albert, German Privy Counselor, who describes himself as a fiscal agent of his Government, is asserted in an article to be published in The Providence Journal tomorrow morning.

The Journal says it has a positive record of the receipt by Ambassador von Bernstorff and Dr. Albert of at least $10,000,000 in the time mentioned. A great deal of this money, it is asserted, has come through the Guaranty Trust Company of New York, and most of it has been immediately transferred to the Chase National Bank and other banks in which Dr. Albert and Ambassador von Bernstorff keep a joint account.

The Journal charges that not one dollar of this money has been spent for legitimate purposes, that all of it is going for propaganda work of the most vicious description.

"One item alone," says the newspaper, "the maintenance of bureaus for dragging men out of munition factories, amounts to many millions of dollars. The cost of sustenance of the consular service of Germany and the expenses of the Embassy reach the various officials through regular channels which are in no way connected with the fund referred to. It is believed that the entire cost of propaganda work conducted by Austrian Consuls and Consuls General is financed from this German fund."

The article in The Journal continues:

Interview with Dr. Albert.

Dr. Albert was interviewed in his office, Room 74 of the Hamburg-American Building, New York City, last Friday by a Journal representative, and was asked point blank to state whether the financial transactions in which he had been recently involved covered legitimate operations, the character of which he could explain in general to the public. Dr. Albert immediately called in a secretary as a witness to the conversation and then replied:

"I am fiscal agent of my Government in this country, and I am handling certain sums of money."

"Will you tell us," he was asked, "if you and the German Ambassador have joint funds in the Chase National Bank and a number of other banks in this country?"

"What is your purpose in asking me that question?" he asked. He was told the only purpose was to have him state, if he would so state, that, whatever joint funds he and the Ambassador were carrying and however great the sum total of these funds was, they were being expended for lawful purposes.

Dr. Albert refused to make any statement whatever in regard to this matter. He was then asked if he would deny that he had received personally over $5,000,000 from his Government in the past two months, and if he did not on Sept. 5 receive, through the Guaranty Trust Company, the sum of $2,000,000 for "accordonica" work.

At this question Dr. Albert was visibly thrown off his balance. The question was based on a wireless dispatch received by the Guaranty Trust Company on Sept. 5, through Sayville, purporting to come from the Litmus Company of Berlin, really the Berlin Foreign Office, and which read as follows:

"Accordonica—Pap on application to Geheimrat Heinrich Albert, New York, $2,000,000. Notify him. Let us know by wire when part of payment is done. Cable receipt of telegram."

"What do you mean by asking me a question like that?" Dr. Albert said finally.

"We mean," said The Journal representative, "that 'accordonica' is a code word used by both the German Ambassador and yourself in communicating with Berlin and that it designates the particular account for which the money is to be expended."

Dr. Albert said: "I refuse to make any statement whatever to The Providence Journal or to anybody else. I will make no statement, no matter what you print."

It was immediately after the exposure of the contents of Dr. Albert's portfolio on Aug. 15 that he began to receive these great sums of money. Up to that time most of the peremptory demands for large sums from the Foreign Office had gone from Count von Bernstorff, who, within a period of a week, just before the breaking up of the Huerta plot, got over $3,500,000. The Government has in its possession evidence of these large transfers.

Dumba's Appeal for $611,246.

The Journal says that on Sept. 22 Dr. Dumba "was also violently affected with a distressing financial shortage" and sent the following wireless message to the Minister of Foreign Affairs in Vienna, from Lenox, Mass.:

Wiederholung Telegrammes vom fuenfzehnten wenn ich bis zum sech-

Continued on Page 3.

List of Americans Who Were Lost on the Ancona; Only Two Out of the Eleven Aboard Were Saved

ROME, Nov. 14, (via Paris.)—So far as Thomas Nelson Page, the American Ambassador, has been able to ascertain from the official reports received through the Italian Government and from the British consuls at Bizerta and Tunis, the following American citizens were lost on the Ancona:

ALEXANDER PATATIVO and his wife and four children.
Mrs. FRANCESCO MASCOLO LAMURA.
PASQUALE LAURINO.
Mrs. GIUSEPPE TORRISI.

Two other American citizens on board—Dr. Cecile L. Greil and Giuseppe Torrisi—were saved.

BRITAIN'S ONLY TERMS OF PEACE

Dismemberment of Germany, Austria, and Turkey Forecast by Masterman.

GERMAN FLEET ABOLISHED

Huge Indemnities to Belgium and Serbia—Nothing for Greece or Rumania Unless They Fight.

Special Cable to THE NEW YORK TIMES.

LONDON, Monday, Nov. 15.—The Right Honorable C. F. G. Masterman, in an article entitled "The Only Possible Peace Terms," published in The Daily Chronicle, quotes Premier Asquith's statement, "We shall never sheath the sword, which we have not lightly drawn, until Belgium recovers in full measure all, and more than all, that she sacrificed; until France is adequately secured against menace of aggression; until the rights of the smaller nationalities of Europe are placed upon an unassailable foundation, and until the military domination of Prussia is wholly and finally destroyed. That is a great task worthy of a great nation." Mr. Masterman, who is believed to represent the Government's views, then proceeds:

"The minimum of so inspiring and righteous an ideal has been interpreted non-officially to me by some such scheme as follows:

"Belgium will be restored to complete independence with an indemnity paid by Germany adequate to the rebuilding of her ruined cities and villages and the revival of her destroyed industries, and full compensation for her disabled and her dead.

"France will receive Alsace and Lorraine and an indemnity for all the damage done in the present conquered provinces, but also a natural and defensive boundary. The natural boundary which would render Germany's attack forever unrepeatable alike upon Belgium and France is the boundary of the Rhine. Let Germany remain there, for the Rhine is its natural boundary.

"Denmark shall receive Schleswig, which is purely Danish.

"German, Austrian and Russian Poland shall be united under the Czar or a King appointed by him.

"Italy would receive the Trentino and the whole of Italy Irredenta.

"The Turkish Empire would be torn to fragments, and Armenia, Syria, Palestine, Mesopotamia, and Thrace divided amongst those who would develop and revive these once fair places now desolated under alien rule. The Turks would generally be penned up in Central Anatolia, where they would be compelled to learn to work instead of massacre.

"Serbia will be restored with heavy indemnity from Austria-Hungary to repair the vast damage done. She will receive Bosnia and Herzegovnia, full and adequate access to the Adriatic and all of Austria that is Serb.

"A united Rumania, a united Greece, is possible, if these nations can rise to the height of their opportunity. If Greece or Rumania consider Greece irredenta or Transylvania not worth fighting for, they will never receive them in the end, for a government and nation which will not risk its life for its enslaved brethren is a government and nation unfit by such cowardice to be given the privilege of ruling over them, even if liberated by other hands.

"The German fleet should be surrendered and either sunk or divided up among the Allies. All Zeppelin or Zeppelin hangars should be burnt. German colonies worthless in themselves must remain as trophies for the nations who conquered them—South Africa, India, Australia, and New Zealand.

"On some such basis European peace might be secured. The terms may seem unduly favorable to Germany, but no German would be left ruled by or subjected to another race, and no other race would be ruled by a German. Nationality would be vindicated and only by nationality being vindicated is there hope of peace."

RUSSIAN THREAT TO GREECE.

Papers Hint at Resort to Force to Make Her Join Allies.

LONDON, Monday, Nov. 15.—A dispatch to The Times from Petrograd says the Russian press is hinting at the use of forcible means, if other methods fail, for inducing Greece to join the Entente Allies.

SERBIANS CHECK BULGAR ADVANCE

But the Main Body Falls Back Before the Austro-German Attacks in the North.

FRENCH EXTEND THEIR LINE

Italians Join in Operations with Warship Attack on the Port of Dedeaghatch.

LONDON, Monday, Nov. 15.—The Serbians are falling back from mountain range to mountain range before the advance of the Austro-German forces, which report the capture of a thousand or more prisoners daily, a few guns and quantities of stores. They are fighting continuously, however, and are inflicting considerable losses on their pursuers.

Along the eastern front the Serbians appear to be holding their own against the Bulgarians, and are making a stand on the western bank of the Morava River. So stubborn has been their resistance that the Bulgarians have had to call for assistance from the Austro-German artillery in their effort to drive the defenders out of Katchanik Pass. Thus far they have been unsuccessful.

On Saturday a battalion of Serbians recaptured the town of Tetovo, with one gun and a quantity of stores, but the place later was taken again by the Bulgarians, who outnumbered the Serbians two to one. A Bulgarian attack on the left bank of the Ornaya River was repulsed with considerable loss to the invaders.

Allied Troops Active.

The British and French troops, which are receiving reinforcements, besides repulsing Bulgarian attacks have undertaken small offensive movements with good results. The Athens correspondent of the Paris Havas Agency, in a dispatch dated Saturday, says that news from a private source reported that the French were within twelve kilometers of Veles.

Military officers at Salonjki have taken stringent measures to assure secrecy regarding the operations and movements of the troops of the Entente Allies, according to a dispatch from Greece to the Paris Temps. All suspects, including a number of irregular troops and merchants, have been expelled from the military zone.

For the moment the political situation is graver than the military. The Central Powers have again protested to Greece against the landing of allied troops at Saloniki. King Constantine is reported to have replied that as Saloniki is an open port there has been no infringement of Greek rights in the landing, and that Greece will remain neutral until one of the belligerents has transgressed against those rights. France and Italy, who has now joined her allies by sending a warship to Saloniki, are particularly anxious as to the attitude of Greece.

The London Times correspondent, wiring from Athens on Saturday, however, says:

"It now seems certain that the Greek Government has defined the attitude which it will adopt if the allied troops should be forced out of Serbian territory across the Greek frontier.

"The Entente powers have been assured that Greece has no intention of departing from her attitude of cordial friendliness or of giving any cause for offense. There are indications that the Entente powers consider these declarations adequate."

An Athens dispatch to the Exchange Telegraph Company says:

"The possible retreat of the Serbian forces over Greek territory is causing no disquietude in official circles, according to the newspaper Embros, as such an event would be unlikely to strain the relations existing between Greece and the Entente powers. At the present time the movements of the Serbian Army do not indicate that such an eventuality is close at hand."

The Italian warship which has joined in the operations is the cruiser Piemonte, and on Friday she bombarded and destroyed the railroad station at Dedeaghatch, Bulgaria, together with two trains made up of eighty cars loaded with war munitions, according to a dispatch from Saloniki.

Official Reports of Operations.

Berlin's official report of the operations issued yesterday, says:

The armies of Generals Koevess and Gallwitz, after tenacious battles, have again thrown back the Serbians along the whole front. Thirteen officers and

Continued on Page 2.

DEATH ROLL NUMBERS 208

Only Two Americans Among the Saved on the Ancona.

AUSTRIA ACCUSES CREW

Says 45 Minutes Was Allowed for Escape, but Some Boats Were Not Lowered.

DENIES SHELLING SURVIVORS

Washington, Confronted by a Serious Problem, Still Awaits Report from Page.

BERLIN, Nov. 14, (by Wireless to Sayville.)—The Austro-Hungarian Admiralty today officially announced that the Italian steamship Ancona attempted to escape at full speed after a warning shot had been fired across her bow, and that the vessel only stopped after being shelled several times by an Austrian submarine, says the Overseas News Agency.

The submarine commander, it is further asserted, allowed the Ancona's passengers and crew forty-five minutes to abandon the ship, after which the vessel was torpedoed, sinking three-quarters of an hour later. The report that the submarine fired on the lifeboats is denied.

The statement issued by the Austro-Hungarian Admiralty, after declaring that the foreign press had spread false rumors regarding the Ancona incident, says the sinking took place as follows:

"The submarine fired one shot in front of the Ancona's prow, whereupon the steamer fled at full speed, in accordance with the order issued by the Italian authorities, which instructs ship commanders to flee or to sink the submarine. The submarine pursued the steamer and continued firing, but the vessel stopped only after being hit several times.

"The submarine allowed forty-five minutes for the passengers and crew to abandon the steamer, on board of which panic reigned, but only a small number of boats were lowered, and these were occupied principally by the crew.

"A great number of boats, probably sufficient to save all the passengers, remained unoccupied.

"After a period of fifty minutes, as another steamer was approaching, the submarine submerged and torpedoed the Ancona, which sank after an additional forty-five minutes.

"If any of the passengers lost their lives this was due to the fault of the crew, because the steamer tried to escape after it had received orders to stop, and then the crew only saved themselves and not the passengers.

"Reports published in the foreign press that the submarine fired on the Ancona's lifeboats are mendacious inventions. When the steamer stopped the submarine ceased firing."

Italy Appeals to Neutrals.

ROME, Monday, Nov. 15, (via London.)—The Italian Government has sent an official communication to the neutral Governments, dealing with the sinking of the Italian liner Ancona. The note denies that the Ancona carried any arms or contraband or persons in belligerent military service, or that there were any circumstances justifying such an attack as a necessity of war.

The note declares that the submarine began to cannonade the Ancona without any previous warning or a blank shot, and fired without respite at the wireless apparatus, the decks, and even at the boats in which passengers were attempting to escape.

"Many of these," adds the note, "were killed or wounded, while many who approached the submarine were driven off with jeers. Thus nearly 200 people were drowned."

Another estimate gives the number of dead as 209.

The opinion is expressed here that it was the same submarine, proceeding from Gibraltar or from the Aegean Sea, which first sank the Ancona and then the steamer Firenze. All the reports agree that the submarine was a very large one—about 200 feet long.

It has been decided that the survivors of the disaster will be sent back to Italy by the Italian Consuls at Bizerta, Tunis, and Malta when vessels for their transportation are available.

PRESENTS TANGLED PROBLEM.

Washington Faces an Odd Situation in Austrian Report on Ancona.

Special to The New York Times.

WASHINGTON, Nov. 14.—The official Austro-Hungarian version of the submarine attack upon the Ancona was made public here tonight by the Embassy of Austria-Hungary, which gave out the text of a radiogram received by the embassy from the Admiralty at Vienna. The dispatch contains the only statement of the circumstances surrounding the sinking of the Ancona that has yet reached Washington.

Neither from American Ambassador Thomas Nelson Page at Rome nor from any American Consulate, nor from the

DR. B. T. WASHINGTON, NEGRO LEADER, DEAD

Continued from Page 1.

way to help negroes that he commanded attention on that day in Atlanta.

His subject was "The New Negro," and white men saw in what he said a sane hope for the negro race and a real solution of the vexing "negro problem."

The character and difficulties of Dr. Washington's work are told in a magazine article written by him. When elected to organize the Tuskegee Institute, he traveled through the "black belt" in order to become acquainted with the people whom he was to teach.

"In the plantation districts," he wrote later, "I found large families, including visitors when any appeared, living and sleeping in a single room. I found them living on fat pork and corn bread, and yet not infrequently I discovered in these cabins sewing machines which no one knew how to use, which had cost as much as $60, or showy clocks which had cost as much as $10 or $12, but which never told the time. I remember a cabin where there was but one fork on the table for the use of five members of the family and myself, while in the opposite corner was an organ for which the family was paying $60 in monthly installments. The truth that forced itself upon me was that these people needed not only book learning, but knowledge of how to live; they needed to know how to cultivate the soil, to husband their resources, to buy land and build houses, and make the most of their opportunities."

Men of Affairs Come to His Aid.

Word of his aims, advertised to the world in the Atlanta speech, spread all over the country, and soon men and women of means began to want to assist Dr. Washington. Chief among these was Andrew Carnegie, who began by giving a $20,000 library to the institute, which he followed with a regular contribution of $10,000 a year. The climax of Mr. Carnegie's generosity toward the institute was reached in 1903, when he gave $600,000 to the endowment fund.

Among those who indorsed and supported Dr. Washington by act and speech were Presidents McKinley, Roosevelt, Taft, and Wilson; the officials of many States, and the heads of many institutions of learning. Though he never seemed to seek them, honors of all kinds were bestowed upon the negro. The degree of M. A. was conferred upon him by Harvard in 1896, and LL. D. by Dartmouth in 1901. In 1910, when Dr. Washington was in Europe, he was received by the King of Denmark, addressed the National Liberal Club in London, and visited Mr. Carnegie in Skibo Castle.

Among those who gave the most effectual assistance to Dr. Washington in his work was Robert Curtis Ogden, who died in Maine on Aug. 6, 1913. Mr. Ogden became itnerested in negro educational work through his association with General Samuel Chapman Armstrong, the founder of the Hampton Institute, and as the President of the Southern Educational Board he did much to overcome southern prejudice against the education of negroes and spread the knowledge of Hampton and Tuskegee among both the white and black people.

An incident of Dr. Washington's life that stirred up a controversy throughout the country was the occasion of his dining at the White House with President Roosevelt on Oct. 16, 1901. Dr. Washington went to the White House at the invitation of the President, and, when the news was spread abroad, thousands, both North and South, who were moved by race prejudice or by a belief that social equality between blacks and whites had been encouraged, became angry. Most of the criticism fell upon Colonel Roosevelt, but the incident served also to injure Dr. Washington's work in some parts of the South.

In addition to his work at Tuskegee and upon the lecture platform, Dr. Washington wrote a number of books and pamphlets upon the negro question. Chief among his works were: "Sowing and Reaping," 1900; "Up from Slavery," 1901; "Future of the American Negro," 1899; "Character Building," 1902; "The Story of My Life and Work," 1903; "Working with Hands," 1904; "Tuskegee and Its People," 1905; "Putting the Most Into Life," 1906; "Life of Frederick Douglass," 1907; "The Negro in Business," 1907; "The Story of the Negro," 1909; "My Larger Education," 1911. and "The Man Farthest Down," 1912.

Dr. Washington was married three times, and is survived by his third wife, two sons and a daughter.

COL. ROOSEVELT GRIEVED.

Says One of the Most Useful Citizens of the Land Has Gone.

OYSTER BAY, N. Y., Nov. 14.—Colonel Theodore Roosevelt, when told of the death of Booker T. Washington, said:

"I am deeply shocked and grieved at the death of Dr. Washington. He was one of the distinguished citizens of the United States, a man who rendered greater service to his race than had ever been rendered by any one else, and who, in so doing, also rendered great service to the whole country. mourn his loss, and feel that one of the most useful citizens of our land has gone."

Julius Rosenwald of Chicago, an admirer of Booker T. Washington, who aided him in his work by contributions to Tuskegee Institute, who has just returned from Tuskegee and is at the Hotel St. Regis, commenting on the educator's death last night, said:

"In the death of Booker T. Washington this country has lost one of its foremost educators. By emphasizing the dignity of labor he has rendered a great service not only to his own race but to the white race as well. I know no nobler character than he possessed. The injustices he was made to suffer never embittered him. Those who knew him best were proudest of his friendship. His life enriched not only this country but the entire world."

LEARNED HIS DOOM HERE.

Dr. Washington Taken. Dying, from Hospital to His Home.

While Booker T. Washington was in New York about two weeks ago his friends realized that something serious was causing the poor health which he had suffered for some time. Accordingly Seth Low and William G. Willcox, two of his warmest friends and supporters, insisted that he go to Dr. W. A. Bastede of 57 West Fifty-eighth Street, for a diagnosis. Dr. Bastede found the patient suffering from Bright's disease, and he astounded Mr. Low and Mr. Willcox by reporting to them that the length of Dr. Washington's life was only a question of days.

Hoping still that Dr. Washington might be saved, his friends sent him to the hospital of the Rockefeller Institute, where Dr. Lucas G. Cole made another diagnosis. It agreed with that of Dr. Bastede. On the advice of the two surgeons, however, Dr. Washington was sent to St. Luke's Hospital so that a desperate effort might be made to save his life. Mr Willcox obtained one of the best private rooms in the hospital for him and Dr. Bastede began treatment.

The case was hopeless, though and soon Dr Washington's wife was notified. She came from Tuskegee with the patient's family physician, Dr. John A. Kenny, a negro, and when she learned that there was no chance for her husband to recover, she expressed the wish, in which he concurred, that he might die in Tuskegee. He was taken from the hospital therefore, on Friday afternoon and put aboard the train which arrived in Tuskegee late on Saturday night, his wife and physician accompanying him. His son, Ernest David Washington, who had been in Vermont lecturing in the interest of the institute, passed through New York last night on his way to the family home.

DR. WASHINGTON BURIED.

Plantation Melodies Sung as Part of Funeral Service.

TUSKEGEE, Ala., Nov. 17.—Simplicity marked the funeral of Booker T. Washington, the negro educator, race leader, and author, which took place this morning at Tuskegee Institute, which he made famous and which has taken such an important part in the elevation of the negro race. Fully 8,000 persons came to Tuskegee to pay their last respects to Dr. Washington, only 2,500 of whom could get into the chapel.

A procession formed in front of the administration building and marched to the chapel. It was headed by the Board of Trustees, and included William G. Willcox of New York, W. W. Campbell and Charles W. Hare, Tuskegee; A. J. Wilborn, William J. Schieffelin, New York; Belton Gilreath, Birmingham, Ala.; Frank Trumbull, New York; Warren Logan, Tuskegee Institute; Victor H. Tulane, Montgomery, Ala., and William H. Baldwin, 3d, New York. Members of the Faculty, the Executive Council of the school, and distinguished visitors, educators, and students followed.

The simple Episcopal burial service was read and many old plantation songs which Dr. Washington loved so well were sung.

A few of the thousands of telegrams of condolence from all parts of the country were read. Prominent men from all walks of life, whites as well as negroes, attended the services. Burial was in the institute grounds.

WASHINGTON LIKE MOSES.

Jacob H. Schiff Compares Negro Educator to Israel's Leader.

Memorial services for Booker T. Washington were held yesterday afternoon at the Bethel African Methodist Episcopal Church, 52 West 132d Street. Negroes from all parts of the city and vicinity attended and listened to speeches by the Rev. B. W. Arnett, the pastor; Acting Mayor George McAneny, President Thomas W. Churchill of the Board of Education, Jacob H. Schiff, Henry Clews, and others.

The band of the Hebrew Orphan Asylum was sent to the church for the service and, between the speeches, played "Lead, Kindly Light" and other hymns. The band opened the service with "Nearer, My God, to Thee." The bugler closed it with "Taps." After the congregation had sung "America" J. Frank Wheaton, the negro lawyer, presided.

Booker Taliaferro Washington, 1906

Mr. McAneny said he was a director of Tuskegee and that he had known Dr. Washington twenty years. No man, he declared, had done so much for his race, and few had done more for the South. No man had done more to bring the blacks and the whites to a mutual understanding. His creed was the application of common sense to great problems. He felt sure, he said, that a leader and funds would be found to carry on the work left by Dr. Washington.

Mr. Schiff said the educator was the Moses of his race. Like Moses, he had led his race to the boundary of the promised land, but had not been allowed to enter it himself.

"But he showed the way," declared Mr. Schiff, "to the time when there will be no distinctions made because of color, race, or creed. Such a time must come. As the decades and the centuries roll by he will rise higher and higher in the memory of his race and of all mankind.

Major Reginald Foster, who attended the meeting with Major A. L. Reagan, both of the Governor's Staff, told the audience of Governor Whitman's sympathy with the race in its bereavement, and expressed his high appreciation of Dr. Washington as a man and an educator.

HIS VIEW OF SLAVE TRADE.

Booker T. Washington Realized That Good Came From It.

Special Cable to THE NEW YORK TIMES.

LONDON, Friday, Nov. 19.—Professor Fisher, Vice Chancellor of Sheffield University, writes to The Times:

"I once asked Booker T. Washington whether he regretted the slave trade. He paused for a moment to reflect, and then answered slowly as follows:

"'No, I do not regret the slave trade. I have traveled in Africa, and can compare the lot of the African race on both sides of the Atlantic. The slave trade was accompanied by terrible cruelties, but through it part of my race was forced into association with white men and has so been enabled to reach a higher level of civilization.'"

WISE EULOGIZES WASHINGTON.

Says Negroes as a Race Must Take Their Former Leader's Place.

Dr. Stephen S. Wise, rabbi of the Free Synagogue, in Carnegie Hall yesterday eulogized the character of Booker T. Washington, saying the negro as an educator, a statesman, and a public servant was one of the greatest Americans of his generation. "It may be that the newly freed race leaned too heavily upon Washington," said the speaker, "but now the race must take the place left by its leader or that place will remain vacant. The world does not adjudge the negro race by Booker T. Washington, but the whole race may be misjudged by the misconduct of a few of its wretches."

The speaker said that in some parts of the world, particularly in Russia, the Jew had to bear the same ill-will, displeasure, and malice that the negro had to bear in the South. He expressed the hope that the race would cling to its burdens, and not try to slip them off, and quoted the remark of Washington: "No one can insult us but ourselves."

There are two memorials to Washington for his work in bringing the negro race closer to the white race, and for teaching the negro that freedom is not a thing of proclamation, but a thing wrought from his own soul, said the speaker. Dr. Wise said that the outward memorials to Washington were the institutes, Tuskegee and Hampton, and that the inward memorial was the "heretofore untried justness of attitude in remembering that the negro is not a problem, but a man."

LAUDS BOOKER WASHINGTON

Roosevelt Pays Tribute to Educator at Memorial Exercises.

TUSKEGEE, Ala., Dec. 12.—Ex-President Roosevelt, addressing a large gathering at Tuskegee Institute here tonight, paid tribute to the memory of Booker T. Washington, negro educator, author, and publicist, who died on Nov. 14. Some of the foremost citizens of the State and nation attended the memorial services. Seth Low, former Mayor of New York and President of the Board of Trustees of Tuskegee Institute.

Mr. Low, Julius Rosenwald of Chicago, Frank Trumbull of New York, W. W. Campbell of Tuskegee, and Isaac Fisher, President of the Tuskegee Alumni Association, also spoke.

Colonel Roosevelt said Dr. Washington directed his life work toward making Tuskegee Institute, which he founded, an asset to the State and nation. He also asserted that, when he was in the White House, Dr. Washington was one of the few men to whom he turned for advice because he "knew that he would not give me one word based on a selfish motive, but because he would state what in his best judgment was for the best interests of the people of the entire country."

"Booker T. Washington," Colonel Roosevelt continued, "did justice, loved mercy, and walked humbly. His every step helped others. His monument lies in the minds and memories of those whom he has served and uplifted.

"The nation profited by Dr. Washington's work because he believed economic fitness was the greatest asset that can be possessed by the negro race. He taught honesty, cleanliness, and efficiency."

"All the News That's Fit to Print"

The New York Times

LATE CITY EDITION

Weather: Cloudy and cold today; chance of snow tonight, tomorrow. Temp. range: today 8-24; Sunday 10-26. Full U.S. report on Page 53.

VOL. CXXI . . No. 41,666

NEW YORK, MONDAY, FEBRUARY 21, 1972

15 CENTS

PRESIDENT LEANS TO AN AMENDMENT ON PUPIL BUSING

Regards It as 'Live' Option in Slowing Courts, Despite Misgivings of Aides

3 OTHER WAYS STUDIED

Nixon Is Viewed as Seeking to Defuse Issue Before Schools Open in Fall

By ROBERT B. SEMPLE Jr.

Special to The New York Times

WASHINGTON, Feb. 20—Despite the misgivings of some of his own staff and Cabinet officers, President Nixon is still "very strongly interested" in a constitutional amendment to halt busing aimed at achieving racial balance in the schools.

In an interview yesterday, a senior White House official said that several influential members of the White House staff supported such an amendment and that Mr. Nixon himself, while not foreclosing other means of responding to the busing issue, regarded a constitutional amendment as a "live" option in his search for some way to slow the courts, protect his own political flanks, and defuse what he feels is a dangerous and divisive public issue.

Accordingly, the official said, a proposed constitutional amendment would be included in the "option papers" on the busing issue that will be presented to Mr. Nixon for decision after he returns from his China trip.

2 Expressed Doubts

In statements last week that were taken to reflect White House attitudes, Vice President Agnew and the Secretary of Health, Education and Welfare, Elliot L. Richardson, both expressed doubts about the wisdom of a constitutional amendment. But the official said these statements did not reflect President Nixon's present thoughts.

Shortly before he left for Peking, the aide said, Mr. Nixon was told by his advisers that in two solid days of effort they had been able to construct an amendment that, they felt, would effectively restrain the courts from ordering busing without at the same time repudiating other constitutional guarantees and rolling back 17 years of desegregation already achieved.

Yet they also told him that the amendment, as written, was extraordinarily cumbersome and "almost as long as the Constitution itself." Mr. Nixon said

Continued on Page 20, Column 4

Cahill Declares President Neglects the Urban States

By RONALD SULLIVAN

Special to The New York Times

TRENTON, Feb. 20—Gov. William T. Cahill, expressing bitterness at what he sees as the Federal Administration's failure to help urban states, like New Jersey, believes that President Nixon "doesn't relate to the average guy in the street."

At the same time a Republican party leader in New Jersey reported this weekend that despite recent mutual and public efforts to gloss over their past political differences, Mr. Nixon and United States Senator Clifford P. Case had had "violent disagreements" and were still politically and personally cool to each other.

The criticism and the reported differences, involving as they do New Jersey's two top Republicans, may spell political trouble for Mr. Nixon's Presidential drive to capture the 17 electoral votes of New Jersey.

Senator Case is running for a fourth term as a United States Senator from New Jersey this year on the Republican ticket headed by Mr. Nixon. Governor Cahill is the unchallenged leader of New Jersey's Republican party. Both are independent liberals and both have won election by landslide pluralities.

Mr. Cahill said in an interview that he would be willing to serve as Mr. Nixon's campaign chairman in New Jersey—in part as payment for the President's campaign appearance for him in 1969. But he is unwilling to volunteer for the appointment, as have Governor Rockefeller in New York and Gov. Ronald Reagan in California.

"I have a lot of other things

Continued on Page 22, Column 1

The New York Times

Gov. William T. Cahill

United Press International

Senator Clifford P. Case

Mujib Says He Would Let Biharis Leave for Pakistan

By C. L. SULZBERGER

Special to The New York Times

DACCA, Bangladesh, Feb. 15—Sheik Mujibur Rahman, Prime Minister of the enormous new state of Bangladesh, said in an interview today that he would welcome an internationally arranged population exchange with Pakistan, enabling non-Bengalis now living in this fledgling country to depart.

Such a step, he said, would facilitate the return here of Bengalis now in the Islamic nation that, as West Pakistan, controlled this country until the independence struggle and the Indian invasion in December.

Sheik Mujib estimated that the minority of non-Bengalis who would wish to be transferred out of Bangladesh amounted to 750,000 people.

The general belief is that there are perhaps two million Biharis in Bangladesh in a population of 75 million. The Biharis — Bihari is the general term to denote non-Bengali Moslems — are widely detested. They contributed much active support for, and collaborated with, the Pakistani military and civilian authorities in the bloody campaign against the Bengalis' autonomy movement.

The Prime Minister said that he thought the United Nations was the proper authority to administer such a population exchange and that he would enthusiastically welcome it. Nevertheless, he took pains to insist that the minority here was being treated tolerantly by the majority despite recent horrors.

Notwithstanding Sheik Mujib's assurances, it is known that the Biharis live in great fear and that some have been badly treated since independence.

Sheik Mujib is an unusual

Continued on Page 4, Column 3

FUNDING NEAR END FOR U.S. STATIONS AIMED AT RED BLOC

Cutoff Tomorrow for Radio Free Europe and 2d Outlet Unless Congress Acts

By BERNARD GWERTZMAN

Special to The New York Times

WASHINGTON, Feb. 20—Radio Free Europe and Radio Liberty, the American-run stations born of the cold war and secretly financed for more than 20 years by the Central Intelligence Agency, will lose their Government funding Tuesday and are struggling desperately to stay alive.

If Senator J. W. Fulbright, Democrat of Arkansas, has his way, the funding will not be renewed.

"These radios should be given an opportunity to take their rightful place in the graveyard of cold war relics," Mr. Fulbright, the chairman of the Foreign Relations Committee, told the Senate on Thursday.

Future Seems Bleak

But even if a compromise is reached in Congress to provide additional funds at least through the end of the current fiscal year, which ends June 30, the future of the organizations seems bleak, even to their most ardent supporters.

Through the years the C.I.A. provided about a half billion dollars to the two stations, which broadcast to the Soviet Union and Eastern Europe.

Radio Free Europe, with 1,600 employes, was founded in 1950. It broadcasts in native languages to Bulgaria, Czechoslovakia, Hungary, Poland and Rumania. Radio Liberty, with about 1,000 employes, was founded in 1951, and broadcasts to the Soviet Union in Russian and other Soviet languages.

Nonprofit Operation Sought

Because the stations often broadcast mater:. . not available in the controlled Communist media, the Soviet Union and its allies have long sought to still them. They are both based in Munich and the Communist governments have put pressure on West Germany to revoke their authority to operate, a move up to now resisted by Bonn.

The C.I.A. financing for the stations — about $36-million yearly—came to an end last year after Senator Clifford P. Case, Republican of New Jersey, disclosed the extent of the secret funding.

The Nixon Administration, seeking to keep the organizations alive through direct Congressional funding, sought a bill to set up a nonprofit organization independent of the Govern-

Continued on Page 5, Column 1

NIXON ARRIVES IN PEKING TO BEGIN AN 8-DAY VISIT; MET BY CHOU AT AIRPORT

HISTORIC HANDSHAKE: President Nixon being welcomed by Premier Chou En-lai. At the left is Mrs. Nixon.

United Press International

HONOR GUARD REVIEWED: Mr. Nixon and Mr. Chou passing part of 500-man contingent

A QUIET GREETING

No Airport Speeches —Plane Stops in Shanghai an Hour

By MAX FRANKEL

Special to The New York Times

PEKING, Monday, Feb. 21—President Nixon arrived in Peking this morning to mark the end of a generation of hostility between the United States and China and to begin a new but still undefined relationship between the most powerful and the most populous of nations.

The President received a studiously correct but minimal official welcome as he began his eight-day visit to China—the tribute due a chief of state but without any acclaim for a Government that still does not officially recognize the People's Republic of China.

Besides foreign correspondents and their interpreters and a few dozen Chinese officials, the Americans were met at Peking airport by a 500-man military honor guard. Two flags, one Chinese, one American, were raised a few minutes before Mr. Nixon's arrival, but there were no special decorations visible in this city, nor were any crowds of citizens, farmers or school children assembled for the welcome, as there usually are for visiting foreign dignitaries who are on good terms with the Chinese.

Overnight Stop in Guam

Mr. and Mrs. Nixon, leading an official party of 15 but a total contingent of more than 300 Americans, flew in from the Pacific across the muddy mouth of the Yangtze River and touched down at Shanghai's Hung Chiao Airport just before 9 A.M. (8:00 P.M. Sunday New York time). The President's plane had taken off three hours and 45 minutes earlier from Guam, where Mr. Nixon made a last overnight stopover on the long journey from Washington, which began Thursday.

After having tea and soup with officials and eating a tangerine at the terminal in Shanghai during a one-hour stay, the President and his party flew on, with a Chinese navigator aboard the plane, across the wintry North China plain and landed in Peking just before 11:30 A.M. (10:30 P.M. Sunday New York time).

Premier Chou En-lai led the reception committee at the airport. His handshake symbolized the end of American ostracism of his Communist Government. Mr. Nixon grasped the hand

Continued on Page 12, Column 1

David Dubinsky Mugged on 'Village' Street

Union Statesman, 79, Is Robbed of $90

By LAURIE JOHNSTON

David Dubinsky, the labor statesman whose 80th birthday is tomorrow, traded punches Saturday night with a strapping young holdup man who shoved him on a snowy sidewalk a block from his home on lower Fifth Avenue.

The honorary president of the International Ladies Garment Workers Union was on his way to buy a quart of milk in a Greenwich Village delicatessen when he was robbed of his wallet containing $90. He went on, undeterred, and bought the milk on credit.

Yesterday, waving his ever-present cigar, he made light of an inch-long cut beneath his shock of white hair. But he confessed that he had spent a sleepless night, "agitated" by the event and critical of his own performance.

"I couldn't forgive myself for not putting up a better fight, even if I'd been hurt," said the 5-foot 4-inch Mr. Dubinsky.

"He gave me a punch and I gave him one back. But I was in a bad position—I was nearly down and he was practically on top of me."

Vowing that "I will not walk these streets alone any more," Mr. Dubinsky shook his head and said: "That it should happen to me! I thought I was an exception."

He would not predict what the incident would do to his two-hour Sunday bicycle trips to Central Park in good weather. Wearing his familiar beret, he ventures "as far as 100th Street" on his 10-speed English racing model that is a rich, candy-colored luminescent purple.

"The fifth bike I've had since

Continued on Page 54, Column 3

The New York Times/John Soto

David Dubinsky in his apartment on lower Fifth Avenue

NEWS INDEX

5 Arrested in Bronx as a Mobile Gang

By RALPH BLUMENTHAL

Three students and two young men with steady jobs, said by the police to have been operating as a mobile mugging gang in the Bronx by using a panel truck to stalk their victims, were arrested early yesterday morning.

The arrests came minutes after the suspects allegedly robbed three men at knifepoint in three separate incidents.

The police of the 50th Precinct, who arrested the five in the truck after a three-block chase in the Riverdale section, said they were investigating the possibility that the group might have been involved in as many as 40 similar robberies in the Bronx in the last two months.

According to the police at the station house at 3101 Kingsbridge Terrace, one of the prisoners, Walter Sanders, a 23-year-old gas station attendant, his wrists handcuffed behind him, leaped head first through a window in an attempt to escape.

Apparently unaware that the building sits on a hill and that the ground floor rises a full story above the street in the rear, the prisoner fell 10 feet to the ground and was recaptured,

Continued on Page 54, Column 3

Walter Winchell Is Dead on Coast at 74

United Press International

Walter Winchell in 1967

By The Associated Press

LOS ANGELES, Feb. 20—Walter Winchell, the fast-talking song-and-dance man who became a newspaper columnist and popular newscaster on radio, died today at the age of 74.

The cause of death was given as cancer of the prostate.

Mr. Winchell died at the University of California at Los Angeles Medical Center, where he had been confined since Nov. 19. A hospital spokesman said the columnist had been in the hospital several times in the last few years. He underwent surgery for a growth two years ago, but said he had recovered.

By ALDEN WHITMAN

"Other columnists may print it—I make it public," said Walter Winchell, the creator of modern gossip writing. His self-description, typical of his brash, egotistical manner, was remarkably accurate, for in the 20 years of his heyday, from 1930 to 1950, he was the country's best-known and most widely read journalist as well as among its most influential.

Millions read "On Broadway," his daily column that appeared locally in the old Daily Mirror and was syndicated nationally. And more millions listened to his weekly radio broadcasts that he addressed to "Mr. and Mrs. America—and all the ships at sea."

"WW," as he often styled himself, or "Mrs. Winchell's little boy, Walter," purveyed a mélange of intimate news about personalities, mostly in

Continued on Page 31, Column 1

Walter Winchell Is Dead on Coast at 74

Continued From Page 1, Col. 7

show business and politics; "inside" items about business and finance; bits and pieces about the underworld; denunciations of Italian and German Fascism; diatribes against Communism; puffs for people, stocks and events that pleased him, and a large smattering of innuendoes.

Although Mr. Winchell was often demonstrably inaccurate or hyperbolic, he was implicitly believed by many of his readers and auditors. In clumsier hands, his "news" might not have had much impact, but he imparted a certain urgency and importance to what he wrote and said by the frenetic and almost breathless style of his presentation. His column items were usually short and separated by dots and cast in breezy neologisms, while his broadcasts, delivered in a barking voice at the rate of 227 words a minute, sounded as compelling as the clicking telegraph key that accompanied them.

Devised a Language

Not only did Mr. Winchell contrive the modern gossip column, but also he devised a language to go with it. "Inasmuch as he is chiefly concerned with the life of Broadway and its circumambient night life, his inventions have largely to do with the technics and hazards of its ethnology," H. L. Mencken reported in "The American Language."

Thus, in Winchellese, a person could start life as "a bundle from Heaven," attend "moom pitchers" in his youth, then be "on the merge" or "on fire" and "middle-aisle it' or be "welded" to a "squaw." Later on, the couple might "infanticipate" and be "storked" and perhaps have a "dotter," which could be the occasion for imbibing "giggle-water" along the "Bulb Belt." Still later, the couple's "pash" could dim and they would "phewd," "phfft" and employ "profanuage." Ultimately, they would be "Renovated," but if they were sophisticated they still might attend a "revusical" together and gaze at is "terpsichorines" and their comely "shafts."

Although Mr. Winchell was often thought lacking in taste, he had friends in high and low places. Among those in exalted places were President Franklin D. Roosevelt and J. Edgar Hoover, director of the Federal Bureau of Investigation. From the outset of the New Deal, the columnist was a fervent backer of Mr. Roosevelt, and early in his second term Mr. Winchell was invited to the White House for the first of several private conversations. At one press conference, the President made his feelings evident. "Walter, I've got an item for you—stick around," he said.

Gave Roosevelt Jokes

Mr. Winchell kept the President supplied with the latest Broadway jokes, and Mr. Roosevelt countered with news tidbits and encouragement for the columnist's vitriolic attacks on the "Ratskis," his name for the German Nazis and their American followers. These attacks, incidentally, infuriated the Nazis, who publicly excoriated their author as "a new hater of the New Germany." They also disquieted William Randolph Hearst, a Hitler admirer and Mr. Winchell's boss, who ordered his editors "to leave out any dangerous or disagreeable paragraphs."

Mr. Hoover, another top-level friend, was chronicled admiringly in the column, and he and Mr. Winchell were frequent companions at Sherman Billingsley's Stork Club, a restaurant the columnist single-handedly made famous. Mr. Winchell's praise for Mr. Hoover (and his agents) developed into an enduring relationship. "Dear Walter," the F.B.I. chief wrote in one letter that was signed "John," "Just a note to say hello. Do take good care of yourself and don't overdo because you are far too valuable to the country."

In 1939, in one of the most spectacular episodes of his career, Mr. Winchell was able to arrange the surrender of Louis (Lepke) Buchalter, a New York gangster, to Mr. Hoover. The hoodlum was wanted in New York on capital charges and by the Federal Government for narcotics smuggling. He telephoned Mr. Winchell, offering to give himself up to Mr. Hoover if the columnist were present.

Escorted Gangster to F.B.I.

The result was that Mr. Winchell picked up the gangster on a Manhattan street corner and delivered him to Mr. Hoover a few blocks away.

"Mr. Hoover," said the columnist, "this is Lepke."

"How do you do," said Mr. Hoover.

"Glad to meet you," said the hoodlum.

In his prime years as a columnist, Mr. Winchell made the rounds of Broadway on the prowl for news. Of medium height, he was carefully tailored, and his cherubic face and blue eyes were set off by a snap-brim fedora that was his newspaperman's trademark. He loved to respond to police and fire calls (he had a police-band radio in his car), often arriving at the scene first. His car, courtesy of the police, was outfitted with a siren and a red light.

At a crime, according to Bob Thomas's authoritative "Winchell," he "interviewed victims and interrogated suspects, some of whom spilled out confessions because of awe over meeting" the columnist.

Mr. Winchell hustled for many of his items, but as time went on he came to rely more and more on press agents, some of whom were employed for their known or presumed ability to get their client's name in the column. These press agents came to Table 50 in the Stork Club's Cub Room — Mr. Winchell's throne — to pay homage.

Reward for a Word

Press agents were rewarded for their gossips or their printable jokes or their suggestions by plugs for their clients. To one press agent who invented the word "neWWsboy," the columnist said in thanks, "I owe you five plugs."

But press agents whose items proved unreliable or who in others crossed Mr. Winchell were placed on his "DD," or drop dead list, and were curtly banished from his presence (and his column) for varying periods. It was a dread experience.

Two press agents were enormously helpful to Mr. Winchell. One of them, Irving Hoffman, contributed what Mr. Thomas called "large portions" of the column while receiving film studio retainers for his ability to inspire Mr. Winchell's "orchids," or praise, for certain movies. Ernest Cuneo, a lawyer with connections in Washington, reportedly prepared a number of Winchell columns about public affairs. Some of the columns entitled "Things I Never Knew Till Now" were supplied by press agents, one of whom, Herman Kerfeld, was on the columnist's payroll, according to Mr. Thomas. And many of the cloying verses that appeared over the signature of "Don Wahn" were spun from the pen of Philip Stack, a clerk at the Brooklyn Edison Company.

With the exception of the poems, most Winchell columns bore his imprint, for he did edit, to a greater or lesser degree, the submissions of others.

Secretary's Column Was His

Contrary to a widespread belief, the "My Girl Friday," one of the most popular of the regular columns, was Mr. Winchell's and not that of either Ruth Cambridge, his first secretary, or Rose Bigman, who succeeded her in 1935. The column was a potpourri of his secretary's notes to him and it contained occasional apologies and retractions.

Mr. Winchell lived and worked in a free-spending atmosphere to which he himself was immune. Save for a Westchester house he bought to please his wife, "he lavished money on nothing," Mr. Thomas reported, adding:

"He hadn't the slightest inclination to art and other possessions. He owned eight suits, no more. He lived with utmost simplicity in an apartment which was useful only for sleeping. Every restaurant and nightclub owner in New York was eager to entertain him."

He kept his money in cash in bank vaults. On becoming a millionaire in 1937, he had the Colony Club cater him an elegant meal, which he ate alone.

Born into Poor Family

The plates and napery of that lunch were far removed from the poverty in which the columnist was reared. Born April 7, 1897, near the corner of Madison Avenue and 116th Street, Walter Winchell was the elder son of Jacob and Janette Bakst Winchel—the son later added a second "l" to the name. Jacob left the family when Walter was young, and the boy was obliged to learn the lessons of survival early.

He picked up his first money as a street-corner newsboy. When he was 12 he made his debut in the entertainment world. George Jessel's mother urged the manager of the Imperial Theater to hire her son and Walter as ushers, but the boys persuaded the manager to try them out as singers. Their success was only middling, but it was sufficient for Walter to quit P.S. 184 in the sixth grade, which was the total of his formal education.

That was an era of child performers, and Gus Edwards added the boys and Jack Wiener, another youngster, to his "Song Revue," billing them as the Imperial Trio. Walter toured the country for two years with the Edwards revues in company with young Jessel, Eddie Cantor, Lila Lee and Georgie Price. It was not an easy life, and Walter received a thorough knockabout education in the petty chicaneries of show business.

In 1915, Walter teamed in a vaudeville act with Rita Green, an act that once played for a week at the American Roof in New York. There was time out for World War I, in which Mr. Winchell, a volunteer in the Navy, served as an admiral's receptionist in New York. Returning to second-rate vaudeville after the war, Mr. Winchell began his column in embryo. He was with a Pantages road show in 1919, and he began typing and posting a bulletin that contained the gossip of the troupe. It was called "Newsense."

Column Drew Attention

Mr. Winchell and Miss Green were married in 1920—the union lasted two years—and he began to submit show business gossip columns to Billboard, an entertainment weekly, and later to The Vaudeville News, for which he went to work in 1922 as a combined reporter and advertising salesman. His column, "Stage Whispers," attracted attention, and he himself became known around Broadway as a bright and eager and very brash hustler, who took notes with a left-handed scrawl.

In his rounds, he met June Magee, a red-haired dancer, whom he married in 1923. She died in 1970, reunited with her husband after a long estrangement.

After about two years on The Vaudeville News, Mr. Winchell's energy demanded a larger field. He managed an introduction to Fulton Oursler of The Evening Graphic, a bizarre tabloid that had been founded in 1924 by Bernarr Macfadden, an eccentric millionaire, food faddist and physical culture advocate. Mr. Winchell was hired to write a column and play reviews and to serve as drama editor, amusement editor and ad solicitor. His pay was $100 a week.

The Graphic was a free-wheeling paper, but at first Mr. Winchell's column (it was then weekly) was curiously staid in the midst of its surrounding sensationalism. One day in 1925, with no jokes or poems for his column, he sat down and typed out a clutch of gossip notes he had acquired on his theatrical beat. The first few items read:

"Helen Eby Brooks, widow of William Rock, has been plunging in Miami real estate. . . . It's a girl at the Carter de Havens. . . . Lenore Ulric paid $7 income tax . . . Fanny Brice is betting on the horses at Belmont . . . S. Jay Kaufman sails on the 16th via the Berengaria to be hitched to a Hungarian . . . Report has it that Lillian Lorraine has taken a husband again . . ."

Backbone of Circulation

It was the prototype of Winchell columns for almost 40 years. Shortly "Your Broadway and Mine," the column's title then, was the backbone of The Graphic's circulation.

There had been columnists before Mr. Winchell, notably Col. William d'Alton Mann, who wrote about society personalities for the weekly Town Topics. But none indulged in saucy gossip, nor wrote with piquancy. These were Mr. Winchell's contributions to the genre. Others sought to emulate him in New York and other cities, but none managed to capture his special flavor. For this reason, "making Winchell" — being mentioned in his column—was a badge of almost unbearable distinction.

Mr. Winchell's years at The Graphic—they ended in 1929—were filled with tensions. He and Emile Gauvreau, the hard-driving managing editor, frequently exchanged shouted abuse in the city room. At The Graphic, the columnist also began his long feud with Ed Sullivan, a fellow reporter. Its origins were trivial, but its proportions and its vituperativeness grew with years as Mr. Sullivan and Mr. Winchell became rival columnists. Their differences were ultimately patched up after Mr. Winchell had retired.

Leaving The Graphic after an explosive display of temper and invective, Mr. Winchell transferred himself and his column to The Mirror. His first column appeared there June 10, 1929, and he was paid $500 a week.

In those years, when gangsters were a recognized feature of New York, Mr. Winchell was on good terms with many of them — Owney Madden and Dutch Schultz among others. At one point in the liquor-gang wars, Mr. Winchell was guarded by two of Madden's best gunmen.

Angered Many People

During his years with The Mirror, Mr. Winchell made a number of enemies apart from mobsters. He angered Earl Carroll, the producer, by panning his shows. (Mr. Winchell quoted Groucho Marx as saying of one of these shows, "I saw it at a disadvantage—the curtain was up.") He offended Marlen Pew of Editor & Publisher; O. O. McIntyre, another columnist; the Shuberts, theater owners and producers; Westbrook Pegler, the sportswriter and columnist; and Mrs. Eleanor (Cissie) Patterson, owner of The Washington Times-Herald.

Anti-Winchell sentiments were expressed by, among others, Representatives Carl Vinson, John E. Rankin and Martin Dies and Senators Burton K. Wheeler, Theodore Bilbo and Champ Clark—all of whom smarted from Mr. Winchell's columnar barbs.

Mr. Winchell had few close friends, but among them was Damon Runyon, the legendary Broadway writer. The two spent many evenings together in an amity unusual for the columnist, for Mr. Runyon was one of the very few persons who could tease him and get away with it. On Mr. Runyon's death of cancer in 1946, his friend established a cancer research fund. By 1970 the Damon Runyon Memorial Fund for Cancer Research had collected and disbursed $32-million, with no expenses for administration.

The awesome power and influence of Mr. Winchell's column (he could make a book a best seller and a movie a hit) started to wane in the late forties. He did not hit it off with President Truman, and after a time anti-Truman items began to appear in the column.

Turned Right Politically

These were the start of a political turnabout that took the columnist to the far right. He became a champion of Senator Joseph R. McCarthy and his investigations; he wrote screeching anti-Communist columns; he was unkind to Adlai E. Stevenson; he countenanced an instance of discrimination against Josephine Baker, the black entertainer, and wrote column items disparaging to her; he got into trouble with Mrs. Dorothy Schiff, publisher of The New York Post, as well as with Leonard Lyons, one of its columnists.

Moreover, appearing on television, Mr. Winchell dealt in horse tips, as he had formerly, over the radio, and touted stocks. Communications executives became wary of him also because he devoted so much of his time to his feuds and vendettas. His column slipped from 800 papers to 175, and it virtually disappeared with the demise in 1963 of The Mirror, whose circulation he had sustained for many years. For a while he saw print one day a week in The World Journal Tribune, but that paper, too, folded.

He tried syndication himself without much luck. The king of the columnists was now a commoner, a victim of his own excesses and of changing public taste.

"Let's face it," said Robert Sylvester, a New York Daily News columnist, in 1967, "the decline of Broadway meant the decline of the Broadway column. Broadway was once a great, glamorous street. Now look at it. It's shoddy. You can't be the historian of something that no longer exists."

"All the News That's Fit to Print"

The New York Times

LATE CITY EDITION

Weather: Sunny, warm today; fair and mild tonight. Warm tomorrow. Temp. range: today 58-85; Sunday 53-81. Full U.S. report on Page 34.

VOL. CXXI ... No. 41,764

NEW YORK, MONDAY, MAY 29, 1972

15 CENTS

McGovern and Humphrey Clash on War and Relief

The New York Times

Senators George McGovern and Hubert H. Humphrey, below, before televised California confrontation.

Rivals, in Debate, Differ on Spending Plans

By WALLACE TURNER

Special to The New York Times

LOS ANGELES, May 28—Senator Hubert H. Humphrey and Senator George McGovern, treating the California primary as if it was the Presidential election itself, repeatedly stung each other in cold anger in their first television confrontation today.

Mr. Humphrey attacked Mr. McGovern's welfare program and plans to cut the defense budget. Mr. McGovern attacked Mr. Humphrey's assertion that the Minnesotan had opposed the war in Vietnam in terms similar to those of Mr. McGovern.

The testiness of the exchanges is illustrated by Mr. McGovern's recollection that, as late as October, 1967, "Senator Humphrey was saying Vietnam is our greatest adventure and a wonderful one it is."

Dispute Over Defense

Mr. Humphrey raised the threat of Soviet diplomacy turning the United States into a second-class power, which he said he would oppose, and then added, "Nor am I going to let Senator McGovern's defense proposals make America into a second-class power."

Mr. McGovern, who had been growing impatient to speak, finally interrupted to say, "After all, I have known something about war at first-hand. I saw a good many of my friends die right in front of my eyes because we weren't adequately defended."

Those who know both men recognized this as a reference to Mr. McGovern's World War II service as a bomber pilot and the fact that Senator Humphrey did not see military service in that war.

Under the format of the

Continued on Page 18, Column 2

The New York Times

ABDICATION, 1936: The Duke of Windsor during radio broadcast on Dec. 11 announcing act of abdication.

Duke of Windsor Dies

Special to The New York Times

LONDON, May 28—The Duke of Windsor, who gave up the throne of England to marry the American woman he loved, died early today at his home in Paris in the Bois de Boulogne. He was 77 years old.

The body of the Duke will lie in state for two days this week and be buried near Windsor Castle, a royal residence for seven centuries.

Buckingham Palace, which announced the plans for the former King's funeral, said his body would be flown to England on Wednesday.

It will lie in state Friday and Saturday in St. George's Chapel at Windsor Castle. A private burial will take place next Monday in the tiny cemetery at Frogmore, less than a mile from the castle.

Palace sources said the arrangements for the funeral were made long ago by the Duke and King George VI, his younger brother who succeeded him to the throne and died in 1952. The Duke abdicated on Dec. 11, 1936, to marry Mrs. Wallis Warfield Simpson, a twice-divorced American.

The Duke's widow, the Duchess of Windsor, will accompany the body to Britain in a Royal Air Force plane. The Windsors were childless.

The palace said that the Duchess had accepted Queen Elizabeth's invitation to stay at Buckingham Palace.

Messages of tribute and sympathy were sent to the Duchess today from all parts of the world. Queen Elizabeth, who visited the Duke and Duchess in Paris 10 days ago, said she was grieved to hear of the death of her uncle.

"I know that my people will always remember him with gratitude and great affection and that his services to them in peace and war will never be forgotten," she said in a telegram.

Prime Minister Heath expressed Britain's "deep feelings of gratitude" for the Duke's "service to the nation."

A statement from 10 Down-

Continued on Page 7, Column 5

SAIGON IS STALLED IN DRIVES TO OPEN ROADS TO 2 TOWNS

Highways to Besieged Anloc and Kontum in Highlands Remain Blocked by Foe

By MALCOLM W. BROWNE

Special to The New York Times

SAIGON, South Vietnam, Monday, May 29—The war continued to produce casualties on both sides yesterday, but there was little change in the over-all situation, with many opposing units dug into strong positions on South Vietnam's three most active fronts.

For Government forces, the most dangerous immediate situation remained the siege of Kontum in the Central Highlands, where North Vietnamese forces were holding several pockets of the city proper.

In fighting in and around Kontum yesterday, Government forces reported killing 155 enemy troops with a loss of only six killed. A spokesman said Saigon troops drove enemy demolition teams out of a school and an orphanage they had occupied.

Major Drive Expected

Communist attacks on Kontum so far are regarded by some high military sources as only a preliminary to the main drive yet to come.

The campaign by Saigon troops to push up Route 13 to the town of Anloc, 60 miles north of the capital, was at a dead stop.

A military source said yesterday that of 6,000 Govern-

Six Days in Anloc

A downed American pilot spent six days recently in the beleaguered South Vietnamese city of Anloc. An account of his experience is on Page 2.

ment troops moved into the town when the siege began nearly two months ago, only 3,500 under arms remained. The losses have been caused by the daily drain of casualties, sometimes as many as 50 a day, from nearly incessant enemy shelling.

Little Action Near Hue

Along the Mychann line 25 miles north of Hue in the northern part of the country, where enemy troops attacked several times Saturday, no major new action was reported yesterday. A Government spokesman said that 172 North Vietnamese were killed and four enemy tanks destroyed in Saturday's fighting in the area.

For the Government, stalled campaigns to open two key roads remained a major concern.

Despite continuing intense air and artillery bombardment, the North Vietnamese strongpoint on Chupao mountain, which overlooks Route 14 between Kontum and Pleiku 25 miles to the south, was still preventing movement along the road.

The problem of supplying Kontum is expected to become

Continued on Page 2, Column 2

INTO SOVIET HOMES: President Nixon being watched by a Muscovite as he delivered speech from the Kremlin.

United Press International

AFTER SERVICE: The Nixons leaving Moscow's only Baptist church. Sign says "All-Union Moscow Council of the Community of Evangelist Christian Baptists."

NIXON TALKS ON TV TO SOVIET PEOPLE AND HAILS ACCORD

Says the Wartime Alliance Can Be Inspiration for Renewed Cooperation

SPEAKS FROM KREMLIN

Kosygin and Rogers Meet to Work Out an Agenda for Extended Trade Talks

By THEODORE SHABAD

Special to The New York Times

MOSCOW, May 28 — President Nixon told the Soviet people in a televised speech today that the memory of the wartime alliance between the United States and the Soviet Union "can serve as inspiration for renewal of cooperation in the nineteen-seventies."

He declared that agreements reached in the summit meeting with the Soviet leaders had helped to reduce the risk of war between the two countries and improved prospects for a peaceful world.

"As great powers, we shall sometimes be competitors, but

Text of President's speech is printed on Page 3.

we need never be enemies." Mr. Nixon said.

His 20-minute address, telecast live from the Kremlin and transmitted by satellite to the United States, gave the citizens of this vast nation their first good look at the President, who has been carefully shielded from contact with the public during his visit.

Phrases in Russian

Audience rating surveys are not practiced in the Soviet Union, but the national television network is theoretically capable of reaching 140 million of the population of 247 million.

During the day, Secretary of State William P. Rogers and Premier Aleksei N. Kosygin met for an hour to summarize their differences and work out an agenda for extended trade talks. United States officials said that the chances for specific agreements on new trade arrangements remained dim.

Mr. Nixon opened and closed his speech with Russian phrases, made a few folksy remarks and used proverbs and aphorisms, always dear to every Russian's heart.

Following Soviet television practice, the President's reading of his text was accompanied by a simultaneous translation, with the Russian superimposed on the tuned-down, but still audible English voice.

The initial reaction of a few Soviet listeners who were questioned after the broadcast was favorable, but some appeared puzzled that the President had not used the opportunity to explain his policy in Vietnam. The war in Vietnam was not

Continued on Page 3, Column 7

6 Killed by Bomb in Belfast Include 3 I.R.A. Members

Special to The New York Times

BELFAST, Northern Ireland, May 28 — Six people were killed early today in a big bomb explosion in Short Strand, a Roman Catholic section of Belfast.

Three of the dead, all men, were identified later as members of the Irish Republican Army. Security forces said that they believed the bomb blew up accidentally while being taken to another part of the city.

One of the dead was identified as a well-known I.R.A. explosives expert who had been high on the British Army's wanted list for some time. The three other victims, two men and a woman, could not be identified immediately.

Seventeen persons, including several children, were injured by the explosion, and 20 houses in the narrow street were so badly damaged that they will have to be demolished.

British Army officers regard it as significant that soldiers making emergency repairs were treated to crates of beer by the people of the area.

Tension in the Catholic areas remained high after yesterday's show of strength by the 10,000-strong Ulster Defense Association—commonly regarded as the Protestants' answer to the Irish Republican Army.

The men who marched through the city center in combat jackets, caps and masks broke a law against the wearing of paramilitary uniform, but it would be difficult to prosecute one group while proceedings are impossible against the I.R.A. in areas where it is in command.

There was more shooting between Protestant and Catholic districts in Belfast last night

Continued on Page 4, Column 8

Critics Forcing Changes in Master Plan

By RALPH BLUMENTHAL

A deluge of community criticism of the city's proposed Master Plan will bring major changes in some neighborhood projects, according to Donald H. Elliott, chairman of the City Planning Commission.

However, he said, critics who have denounced the plan as merely an inventory of possibilities and existing facilities, instead of a blueprint for action, have misunderstood its function as a guideline. The concept of the massive document itself will not be changed, he added.

Revisions to Be Asked

The Planning Commission ended last week two years of hearings on the plan in 67 communities. Mr. Elliott said in an interview that among the significant revisions that he was prepared to seek, in light of the widespread complaints, were the following:

¶Demolition as soon as possible of the decaying third Avenue elevated line in the Bronx.

¶Redesign of traffic and development patterns in the congested Fordham Road shopping hub in the Bronx.

¶A change in priorities from industrial to residential development for parts of the northern shore of Staten Island.

¶A shift in focus in Bensonhurst, Brooklyn, from housing for the elderly to housing for newer immigrant groups, such as Haitians and Dominicans.

¶The development, particularly in Manhattan, of new types of accommodations to replace single-room occupancy units without toilets and kitchens that now house the poor and elderly. These units will be eliminated by a state law in the next several years.

¶Restudy of a plan to move Manhattan's flower market from the upper 20's and lower 30's on the West Side to Hunt's Point in the Bronx.

Such changes and others in the master plan, should a majority of the Planning Commission agree in deliberations over coming months, would not

Continued on Page 34, Column 1

The New York Times

Donald H. Elliott

U.S. Auto Makers Begin To Stem the Import Tide

By JERRY M. FLINT

Special to The New York Times

DETROIT, May 28 — The counterattack from Detroit and Washington against foreign-made cars is starting to succeed.

Fewer Americans are buying the little German Volkswagen and Japanese Datsun; instead, they are going for American mini and compact models. The sellers of foreign cars, with their merchandise piling up, are cutting prices. Paradoxically, this may hurt the imports even more.

The retreat is just starting. Import car sales are still high; probably 1.4 million vehicles, most from Japan and Germany, will be sold in the United States this year. But the invading importers, who captured nearly 1.6 million American customers in 1971 and were taking almost one in five new car sales last summer, are falling back.

The trend is significant for the following reasons:

¶After years in which foreign manufacturers captured or made serious inroads in market after market in the United States — steel, clothing, radios and the like — an American industry has shown that its products may be able to hold their own with effective Government help.

¶A serious threat to the jobs of hundreds of thousands of workers in the automobile industry is beginning to be eased.

¶In the long run, the situation could help the nation's trade deficit. In April, the deficit was \$699-million, the second largest in history. This year's deficit is expected to be larger than the \$2-billion deficit in 1971.

Part of the American counterattack originated in Washington. After President Nixon announced his economic controls program, the Federal Government lowered the size of the allowable price increases for

Continued on Page 34, Column 1

4 Years of Sea Drilling Yields Vast Lore

By WALTER SULLIVAN

After four years of drilling into the ocean floor, the Glomar Challenger, an ungainly vessel with a giant drilling derrick amidships, has produced a vast treasure of important new information on the history of the earth.

Some of the findings are so revolutionary that there are scientists who still find them incredible. Much of the material, extracted from more than 350 holes bored deep into the sediments that have accumulated at the bottom of the sea for tens of millions of years, remains to be studied.

The saga of the drill ship—the stepchild of the ill-fated Mohole Project of the mid-nineteen-sixties — has been marked by dramatic encounters with fog-shrouded icebergs and storms, including a typhoon. There have also been bizarre mishaps, as when the ship-control computer ran amok.

But it is primarily a tale of discoveries, some probably of historic magnitude. Because they were made in remote areas and because the ship is almost constantly on the move, many of these findings have not until now been made public.

While some of the first drill holes confirmed the theory that sea floors are slowly but steadily moving away from the mid-ocean ridges, the more recent drilling has shown that the history of this activity is extremely complex. When that history is reconstructed, it should explain why the mountain ranges of the world formed where they did—and when they did.

The voyages of the Glomar Challenger, known as the Deep Sea Drilling Project, are financed by the National Science Foundation and are administered by the Scripps Institution of Oceanography. Interviews with participants and a study of the reports, published and unpublished, have brought to light, among others, the following discoveries and conclusions:

¶Although man is descended from creatures that lived in the sea, all of the oceans inhabited by his ancestors have vanished. None of the major ocean basins of today existed when the mammals began to evolve from certain reptilian species about 180 million years ago. The geography of the oceans has, so to speak, been completely recycled.

¶Some 5.5 million years

Continued on Page 36, Column 1

NEWS INDEX

Associated Press

ANDERSON STREET, BELFAST: Baby carriage is among debris after bomb blast in the Catholic section yesterday

Duke of Windsor Dies at 77 at His Home in Paris

Continued From Page 1, Col. 4

ing Street said the Duke "in all he did sought to make monarchy less remote and more in tune with the needs and aspiration of his time." He "made monarchy a living reality," Mr. Heath said.

In Paris, a Rolls-Royce with British license plates briefly entered the mansion grounds early this morning. Then a stream of visitors came to present condolences to the Duchess or to leave cards or flowers. Among early callers were former King Umberto of Italy; Achille Peretti, president of the National Assembly, and a number of Paris socialites.

The Queen, her husband, the Duke of Edinburgh, and their son, Prince Charles, the Duke's successor as Prince of Wales, called on the Windsor during the royal visit to France. Illness had confined the Duke to an upstairs sitting room in the mansion, which was rented from the city of Paris.

The announcement of his death came at 6 A.M. in a statement from Buckingham Palace. It said

"It is announced with deep regret that His Royal Highness, the Duke of Windsor, has died at his home in Paris at 2:25 today, Sunday, May 28, 1972." It was 9:25 P.M. Saturday night in New York.

The Duke, who reigned for less than a year as King Edward VIII, had been in ill health for some time. He was known to have suffered from cancer of the throat. He underwent a hernia operation in Paris last February.

His general condition deteriorated sharply in the last month, and the Duke ended his evening walks with his dogs, his only recent outings.

In announcing the funeral plans, Buckingham Palace said that a period of court mourning would extend until June 5, the day of burial. Some royal engagements would be canceled and flags would fly at half-staff on government buildings.

The burial site at Frogmore is across a lake from Frogmore House, a colonnaded, Georgian mansion in Windsor Park. As a young boy, the Duke sailed model ships and fished with his brother, Bertie, who later became his successor as King George VI.

According to palace sources, the Duchess of Windsor will be the sole heir in the Duke's will. It was understood, however, that the will provides for several individual bequests to friends, members of his personal staff, servants and others.

A Tribute by Nixon

MOSCOW, May 28 (UPI) —President Nixon today called the Duke of Windsor a man of "noble spirit and high ideals" who was respected by millions of Americans.

"Mrs. Nixon and I are both deeply saddened by the death of the Duke of Windsor," the President said in a statement released here.

"He was a man of noble spirit and high ideals, for whom millions of Americans felt deep respect and affection.

"We join in extending our profound sympathy to the Duchess and to the many others who will mourn his passing."

The Life of Edward—as Prince, King and Duke

By ROBERT ALDEN

In a Paris restaurant some years ago, a 6-year-old American boy, impressed by the attention that was being paid to a slight, white-haired man with a tanned, deeply lined face, approached the man and asked for his autograph.

The man obliged.

"But who are you?" the little boy asked.

The man smiled down at the little boy.

"Well, I could not possibly expect you to remember," he said. "But I was once a King."

Indeed, the man—the Duke of Windsor—had been King Edward VIII of England. He also was the first monarch in the thousand-year history of the British crown to give up his throne of his own free will.

And, in the manner of a storybook monarch, Edward VIII gave up his throne—for love.

Eleven months after he had become King, Edward VIII abdicated on Dec. 10, 1936, to marry Wallis Warfield Simpson, an American woman who had been twice divorced.

In a voice palpably tremulous with sadness he spoke over the radio to his subjects:

"But you must believe me when I tell you that I have found it impossible to carry the heavy burden of responsibility and to discharge my duties as King, as I would wish to do, without the help and support of the woman I love."

In 1930 the Prince met Mrs. Ernest Simpson. Mr. Simpson, a moderately prosperous maritime broker, was Mrs. Simpson's second husband. Her marriage to E. Winfield Spencer, a United States Navy officer, had ended in divorce.

Disappointing Topic

It was a grim, cold winter's day at Melton Mowbray, where Edward had gone for fox hunting. Mr. and Mrs. Simpson were guests in the same house. Mrs. Simpson was suffering from a head cold and since she was an American, the Prince tried to strike up a conversation on the lack of central heating in Britain.

As recalled by the Duke of Windsor in his memoirs:

"'I am sorry, Sir,' she said, 'but you have disappointed me.'

"'In what way?'

"'Every American woman who comes to your country is always asked that same question. I had hoped for something more original from the Prince of Wales.'"

Later the Duke wrote:

"In character, Wallis was, and still remains, complex and elusive, and from the first I looked upon her as the most independent woman I had ever met. This refreshing trait I was inclined to put down as one of the happier outcomes of the events of 1776."

Often Edward was a guest at the Simpsons' apartment in Bryanston Court. The place was small but beautifully furnished and Mrs. Simpson kept it filled with flowers. The food was good, the conversation stimulating. Mrs. Simpson received neither bores nor bohemians.

A Genuine Interest

As for Mrs. Simpson herself, she had the ability to take an exclusive and genuine interest in the conversation of the person to whom she talked. Edward had his troubles. The duties of the Prince of Wales were burdensome and he shared them with a sympathetic Mrs. Simpson.

The friendship of the pair ripened over the years and grew into love. The Prince of Wales found that he wanted to marry Mrs. Simpson after she obtained a divorce that had been contemplated for some time.

Britain knew nothing of all of this. But pictures of the Prince and Mrs. Simpson began appearing in American publications.

It was at this point, on Jan. 20, 1936, that the Prince's father, George V, died.

In the words of the Duke of Windsor:

"All was still as we—his wife and children — stood together by my father's bedside waiting for life to be extinguished. Death came to him five minutes before midnight. And while my mind was still trying to comprehend the profound event that had in that instant occurred my mother did an unexpected thing.

"She took my hand in hers and kissed it; before I could stop him my brother George stepped forward and followed her example.

"I knew, of course, that this form of homage was by custom my due. But, like my father, the action embarrassed me. I could not bring myself to believe that members of my own family, or indeed anyone else, should be expected to humble themselves before me in this way.

"Nevertheless, these two spontaneous gestures served to remind me, however needlessly, that I was now King."

Two days later Edward VIII heard himself publicly proclaimed King of the Garter King of Arms in Friary Court at St. James's Palace and as he heard the words proclaimed over the heralding trumpets they "seemed to tell me that my relations with Wallis had suddenly entered a more significant stage."

As ruling monarch, Edward fretted under the restraints of office. At times he covertly, if not openly, rebelled. As an instance, in his first broadcast to his people—March 1, 1936—he included at the end a thought that he felt was purely personal and that he would not, therefore, submit to the Home Office for advance approval.

The thought was indicative of the kind of monarch he was during his 11 months on the throne:

"I am better known to you as Prince of Wales—as a man who, during the war and since, has had the opportunity of getting to know the people of nearly every country of the world, under all conditions and circumstances.

"And, although I now speak to you as King, I am still that same man who has had that experience and whose constant effort it will be to continue to promote the well-being of his fellow men."

During his reign, Britain passed through the first of the crises that in the end resulted in World War II. Hitler reoccupied the Rhineland.

"Intuitively I felt," Windsor later wrote, "that another great war in Europe was all too probable; and I saw all too clearly that it could only bring needless human suffering and a resurgent Bolshevism pouring into the vacuum

(continued)

INSTRUMENT OF ABDICATION

I, Edward the Eighth, of Great Britain, Ireland, and the British Dominions beyond the Seas, King, Emperor of India, do hereby declare My irrevocable determination to renounce the Throne for Myself and for My descendants, and My desire that effect should be given to this Instrument of Abdication immediately.

In token whereof I have hereunto set My hand this tenth day of December, nineteen hundred and thirty six, in the presence of the witnesses whose signatures are subscribed.

SIGNED AT FORT BELVEDERE IN THE PRESENCE OF

Edward RI

Albert

Henry.

George.

Combine

The King's Instrument of Abdication was signed on Dec. 10, 1936, and witnessed by his brothers. The next day Edward made a farewell broadcast and left the country.

Associated Press

The Duke of Windsor and Mrs. Wallis Warfield Simpson, an American, after wedding in June 3, 1937, at Chateau de Cande at Monts, near Tours. They were wed 35 years.

of a ravaged and exhausted Continent. . . . I turned back to my routine work gravely troubled in spirit."

On Oct. 27, Mrs. Simpson received a preliminary divorce decree on the ground of adultery. (Mr. Simpson died in 1947.) She and an aunt, Mrs. D. Buchanan Merryman, went to live at Edward's residence of Fort Belvedere in Windsor Great Park.

Prime Minister Stanley Baldwin gave an early warning to the new monarch of future difficulties if gossip about him and Mrs. Simpson continued. On Nov. 16, after consulting with his Cabinet colleagues, Mr. Baldwin had an audience of King Edward and was told:

"I am going to marry Mrs. Simpson and I am prepared to go."

Mr. Baldwin replied: "Sir, that is most grievous news, and it is impossible for me to make any comment on that today."

Compromise Rejected

Two weeks later, the impasse over Mrs. Simpson finally was published in the long-silent British press. Of the leading newspapers, only The Daily Express sided with the monarch. A compromise suggested by the King — a morganatic marriage in which his wife would not be queen—was also rejected by Mr. Baldwin.

When the crisis was debated in the House of Commons, both the Government and the Labor opposition led by Clement R. Attlee, later Earl Attlee, overwhelmingly backed Mr. Baldwin's refusal to introduce legislation permitting such a marriage.

Winston Churchill asked the Commons to make it possible for the King to have more time to consider. Edward later wrote:

"He [Churchill] strode into the House of Commons . . . undaunted and quite alone, to launch his attack. Hardly was he on his feet before hostility smote him like a great wave.

"The memorable scene of Mr. Churchill being howled down has often been described . . . I am proud . . . that of all Englishmen it was Mr. Churchill who spoke up to the last for the King, his friend."

So it was that before his coronation, King Edward VIII abdicated his throne and was succeeded by his brother, the Duke of York, who became King George VI.

"I now quit altogether public affairs, and I lay down my burden," Edward said in the broadcast after the act of abdication was signed.

"And now we all have a new King. I wish him and you, his people, happiness and prosperity with all my heart. God bless you all. God save the King."

Married in June

At 2 o'clock on the morning of Dec. 12, 1936, H.M.S. Fury slid silently and unescorted out of Portsmouth Harbor carrying His Royal Highness Prince Edward, as he had identified himself at the time of his broadcast speech. One of the new King's first acts was to create his brother Duke of Windsor. When Mrs. Simpson's divorce decree became final, she and the Duke were married on June 3, 1937, at the Chateau de Candé at Monts, near Tours, in France.

The Duke believed that the majority of the British people would have rallied to him had he chosen to make an issue of his right to marry Mrs. Simpson. But, as he explained:

"I reject the notion put forward by some that, faced with a choice between love and duty, I chose love. I certainly married because I chose the path of love. But I abdicated because I chose the path of duty.

"I did not value the crown so lightly that I gave it away hastily. I valued it so deeply that I surrendered it, rather than risk any impairment of its prestige."

Edward VIII had been a King of great popularity. The abdication that caused a worldwide sensation visibly distressed his subjects.

In the years that followed, the Duke, who as Prince of Wales had been a romantic and carefree Prince Charming blessed with the common touch, became a rootless wanderer, an ornament of international society, a former monarch whose life lacked visible purpose.

As he puttered in the garden at his home in the Bois de Boulogne on the edge of Paris in his 70's, visitors noted a look of melancholy in his eyes.

But those who knew the Duke well said that even as the young and debonair Prince of Wales, that haunted look of wistful sadness was there. Even when he was a boy it could be noticed.

"That look of melancholy in the Prince's eye is something which I cannot trace to any ancestor of the House of Hanover," Lord Esher, a courtier of the royal household, remarked 50 years ago.

In his 25 years as Prince of Wales, heir apparent to the British throne, and his short reign as King, Edward was a figure of moment in the history of this era.

His travels in the years between the World Wars embraced the globe. The Prince of Wales was as a goodwill ambassador for the Court of St. James's extraordinarily successful both among those peoples within the British Empire and those without.

Unorthodox Approach

Everyone said of the young Prince that he always tried to do the right thing. He had a fresh, unorthodox approach, a touch of the common not associated with British royalty.

The Prince of Wales expressed an open interest in the social problems of a country deeply hurt by its grave losses during World War I. On a visit to Welsh miners, he said grimly that something must be done to improve conditions. Many applauded his daring.

In his memoirs, "A King's Story," published in 1947, the Duke of Windsor wrote with some overtones of bitterness of the royal status that he defined as "duty without responsibility, pomp without power."

But the period in which he lived was so charged with social change and destructive war that even though every effort was made to keep the British royal family above the play and counterplay of the flow of world events, Windsor, justly or unjustly, became linked with current happenings.

Oft-Repeated Story

The one often repeated story that clouded the career of the King who gave up his throne was that he was involved in clandestine dealings with Nazi Germany. The charge was flatly denied by both the Duke and the British Government.

After the fall of France, the Germans did plot to try to keep Windsor in Britain rather than accept the post of Governor in the Bahamas.

The New York Times

The future Queen Elizabeth II with her favorite uncle in 1933. They were riding to Balmoral Castle in Scotland.

He was to be used as a pivot to bring about a negotiated peace between Britain and Germany on Hitler's terms. In return, the Duke and Duchess would have been allowed to assume the throne.

The British Foreign Office agreed that heavy pressure had been put on the Duke, but "at no time" did he "ever have any thought of complying." He assumed his wartime post in the Bahamas, never wavering "in the loyalty of the British cause."

The Duke said that he had treated the suggestions of the Nazis "with contempt."

There were other reports that as King, Edward sought to curry favor with Hitler. These reports were termed "absurd" by the Duke.

Nonetheless, the Duke had been indiscreet in criticizing the Treaty of Versailles and in suggesting that Nazi aspirations for the Polish Corridor might be considered. He also paid a visit to Adolf Hitler and Hermann Goering, the Nazi leaders, in the years before the start of World War II. The visit itself was thought improper and his flattering remarks about his hosts enhanced an impression that the Duke has found them congenial. The Duke always insisted that his visit and his words were misconstrued.

From the vantage point of history it can be seen that the 77 years of the Duke's life spanned an era that wrought a particularly profound change in the world. Through it all Edward was, in one way or another, ever in the public eye.

During those years, the two most destructive wars in history were fought. Between the wars there was a period of chaos in Europe. Then a deep economic depression gripped the world. Those years saw the dissolution of the British Empire and the emergence of the Commonwealth.

Quarter of the Globe

On June 23, 1894, the day of Edward's birth, his great-grandmother, Queen Victoria, 75 years old, was in the 57th year of her reign. The British Empire embraced a quarter of the earth's surface and nearly a quarter of the world population. British sea power and commercial influence were supreme in the world.

Queen Victoria's children and grandchildren ruled the courts of Europe. The Dowager German Empress Victoria was her eldest daughter; Kaiser Wilhelm II of Germany was her grandson; the Czar of all the Russias, Nicholas II, was a nephew of her eldest son's wife.

Victoria had 9 children, 40 grandchildren and countless nieces and cousins by marriage, all of them princes and princesses of the British Empire or Hohenzollerns, Hesses, Romanoffs, Coburgs, Battenbergs or collateral relatives in the royal houses of Belgium, Holland, Scandinavia and the Balkan countries.

Edward, the latest of these, was born at 10 o'clock on that June evening at White Lodge, Richmond Park, Surrey, 10 miles outside London, to the former Princess Victoria Mary of Teck, later to be Queen Mary.

The boy's father was the Duke of York, later to become King George V. His grandfather was Albert Edward, Prince of Wales, who was to become King Edward VII.

The youngster was christened Edward Albert Christian George Andrew Patrick David of the House of Saxe-Coburg-Gotha. (George V. on July 17, 1917, renounced the German name of the royal house and proclaimed it the House of Windsor.)

The name Edward had already been borne by six British Kings; Albert was in deference to Victoria's desire that all her descendants should bear the name of her husband, Albert of Saxe-Coburg; the name Christian was given out of respect for King Christian IX of Denmark, the father of the newborn Prince's grandmother, Alexandra; George, Andrew, Patrick and David are respectively the names of the patron saints of England, Scotland, Ireland and Wales.

The royal family always referred to the boy as David, the last of his given names.

Edward passed much of his childhood at Sandringham in Norfolk, a big red-brick building with a gray slate roof, which Edward, his brothers and a sister all knew as "The Big House."

The brothers and the sister were born there—Albert (Bertie), who was to become George VI; Mary, the Princess Royal; Henry, Duke of Gloucester; George, Duke of Kent, and Prince John, who died at the age of 14.

Relations With Father

Edward's relations with his father were difficult, although in his memoirs the Duke of Windsor contended that the two truly loved each other. His father had a mariner's beard and a voice that, because of an eardrum injured in gunnery practice, seemed geared to the tempest.

"In my father's rigorous schedule we children occupied small, fixed niches," the Duke of Windsor wrote. "He and my mother always popped into the nursery to say goodnight while on their way to dinner. My father, never demonstrative, would peer down at us gravely, in the dim light, perhaps touch the covers gently, and then slip quietly out of the room.

"I have often thought that my father liked children only in the abstract."

"We were, in fact, figuratively speaking," Edward later wrote, "always on parade, a fact that he would never allow us to forget. If we appeared before him with our navy lanyards a fraction of an inch out of place, or with our dirks or sporrans awry, there would be an outburst worthy of the quarter-deck of a warship.

"Constriction was the order of our schoolroom costume. We had a buttoned-up childhood, in every sense of the phrase. Starched Eton collars invariably encircled our necks and, when old and frayed, cut into our skin like saws.

"The idea of a boy in shirt-sleeves and an open-necked collar was unthinkable."

Sir Harold Nicolson in his book "King George V" wrote of Edward's father:

"How came it that a man, who was by temperament so utterly domestic, who was so considerate to his dependents and the members of his household, who was so unalarming to small children and humble people, should have inspired his sons with feelings of awe, amounting at times to nervous trepidation?"

An Inheritance of Fright

In the book by Randolph Churchill on the 17th Earl of Derby, a close friend of George V, it is recorded that Lord Derby was distressed

(continued)

by the way the King bullied his children. When he raised the subject George V was silent for a moment and then said:

"My father was frightened of his mother [Victoria]; I was frightened of my father [Edward VII]; and I am damned well going to see to it that my children are frightened of me."

On Feb. 18, 1907, at the age of 12, Edward, in accordance with his father's wishes, entered the Royal Naval College at Osborne on the Isle of Wight, where the discipline was most rigorous. On one occasion the future King Edward VIII was made to stand to attention while red ink was poured over his head by senior students.

On another occasion, as Edward recalled, "an empty classroom window was raised far enough to push my head through and then banged down on my neck, a crude reminder of the sad fate of Charles I and the British capacity to deal with royalty who displeased."

Edward VII died on May 6, 1910. George V succeeded to the throne. Since Edward was now Prince of Wales, the heir apparent, it was decided that his education should be broadened from one suiting him only for a naval career. He was sent to Magdalen College at Oxford.

Perferred the Banjo

Edward did not excel academically. He proved more interested in his banjo than in his books.

"He will never be a British Solomon," the president of the college said, even as he granted the future monarch a privilege never granted a student at Magdalen before—the right to a private bedroom.

Between his banjo and his dancing Edward did manage to have some fun before the outbreak of World War I.

Edward's diary contains such entries during this period as ". . . my dancing is improving, I got in at 4," and ". . . I have had not more than eight hours' sleep in the last 72 hours!!"

The war changed everything.

In July, 1914, a month before the beginning of World War I, Edward was a subaltern with the First Life Guards. When the war came he was transferred to the Grenadier Guards, a 5-foot-7-inch stripling amid the hulking guardsmen. As color ensign, he learned to carry the regimental colors while doing the slow-step prance of the British infantry at the changing of the guard.

Many of Edward's friends in the Guards Brigade were soon fighting in France. Edward did everything he could to join them. But Lord Kitchener, the War Secretary, was adamant.

"What difference is it if I am killed? The King has four other sons," Edward said in exasperation.

Lord Kitchener replied:

"If I were certain you would be killed, Sir, I don't know whether I should be right to restrain you. What I cannot permit is the chance of the enemy securing you as his prisoner."

Served in France

Edward's persistence finally got him to France as a member of the staff of Sir John French, commander of the British Expeditionary Force. The Prince of Wales served for four years and, although never permitted in the front lines for long, he was under fire several times and performed his duty well.

By letter he was chastised by his father for not wearing decorations given him by the French and Russian Governments. Edward replied:

"My dearest Papa:

"First I must apologize. I think you know how distasteful it is to me to wear these two war decorations, having never done any fighting and having always been kept well out of danger! I feel so ashamed to wear medals which I only have because of my position, where there are so many thousands of gallant officers, who lead a terrible existence in the trenches and who have been in battles of the fiercest kind (many severely wounded or sick as a result) who have not been decorated. No doubt I look at this thing from a wrong and foolish point of view. But this is the view I take."

Royal Tours Followed War

At the close of the war the Prince of Wales embarked on the first of a series of royal tours that were to take him the equivalent of six times around the world.

Seldom has princely progress been attended with such lavish pomp. On Nov. 18, 1919, H.M.S. Renown brought him to New York for his first visit to this city. He was accorded a thunderous welcome.

Then, as well as on his later visits to the United States, socially prominent persons competed vigorously for the privilege of providing his private entertainment.

As a bachelor, the Prince's name had been linked at one time or another with the names of most of the world's eligible princesses. But in the United States nobody bothered about princesses. Whoever Edward happened to dance with was worth a spectacular headline.

A pretty newspaper reporter, assigned to cover the Prince, spent a few pleasant hours dining and dancing with him. When she returned to her office she burst into tears and told her astonished editor: "It was all too sacred; I could never write about it."

Once as he was leaving the United States on one of his visits, the question was shouted at him as to whether he would consider marrying an American. His prophetic reply, all but lost in the hubbub, was that he would, "if I loved her."

Wherever the bachelor Prince traveled he was at the center of attention. A slightly built young man with straw-colored hair and good features, he had a shyness of manner that was most ingratiating.

His genuine friendliness allowed him to mingle with all kinds of people. He really liked them, and it was recognized early that he would prove a most popular King.

Edward was also an excellent horseman. He took chances and pictures were often printed of him hurtling over the head of his falling mount. He was badly shaken up a few times. But his courage to remount was irrepressible.

Four Voyages

Speaking in his memoirs of the four voyages that he had made about the world between the ages of 25 and 31, Edward called them "my principal occupation." He said:

"They took me into 45 different countries and colonies and carried me a total distance of 150,000 miles. In this age of air travel such mileage spread over a period of six years may not seem impressive.

"But when I had finished poking into the corners of the world, I could have qualified as a self-contained encyclopedia on railroad gauges, national anthems, statistics, local customs and dishes and the political affiliations of a hundred mayors.

"I knew the gold output of the Rand, the storage capacity of the grain elevators at Winnipeg, and the wool export of Australia; and I even have held my own on the subject of the chilled-beef trade of the Argentine.

"The number of memorial trees I planted, if they have survived the vicissitudes of climate and the depredations of man, must today constitute a substantial forest. And the number of public buildings and institutions whose cornerstones I laid would comprise, could they be put together, a sizable city."

Edward had his own word for these activities—"princing."

Busy traveler and sportsman that he was in the nineteen-twenties, the Prince also led a private life of greater domesticity than might have been supposed. His liaisons were well known and accepted in British social circles, although there was, of course, no publicity about them. One of the Prince's friends, a woman of great charm, was an American, Thelma, Lady Furness.

Would 'Do It Again'

In the years after his abdication in 1936, the Windsors became familiar fixtures in International Society, and the Duke always insisted that he would "do it all over again."

His widowed mother, Queen Mary, was deeply hurt by Edward's abdication and never overcame her grief. Eighteen months after the abdication, she wrote him:

"You will remember how miserable I was when you informed me of your intended marriage and abdication and how I implored you not to do so for our sake and the sake of the country. You did not seem able to take in any point of view but your own.

"I do not think you ever realized the shock which the attitude you took up caused your family and the whole nation. It seemed inconceivable to those who had made such sacrifices during the war that you, as their King, refused a lesser sacrifice. . .

"My feelings for you as your Mother remain the same, and our being parted and the cause of it grieve me beyond words. After all, all my life I have put my country before everything else, and I simply cannot change now."

The new Duchess of Windsor was not received by the royal family and was not entitled to be addressed as "Your Royal Highness," as were the wives of the other royal princes.

Even the Rev. Robert Jardine of Darlington, Yorkshire, who performed the religious ceremony of the marriage in France, was ostracized by the Church of England.

When Elizabeth II came to the throne it was thought that she might receive the wife of her Uncle David, her favorite uncle, but the period of formal social ostracism for the Duchess did not end until June, 1967. At that time, the Duke and Duchess joined the Queen and other members of the royal family at the unveiling of a memorial plaque to his mother, Queen Mary, outside Marlborough House near Buckingham Palace.

Queen Met Duchess

A step toward ending the alienation had been taken in March, 1965, when Queen Elizabeth, by arrangement, twice met the Duchess at the bedside of the Duke while he was in London for a series of eye operations.

Eleven days ago, as the Duke lay half-blind and dying, the Queen visited her favorite uncle, going to the bedroom of the Windsors' home in Paris. There is no clue as to what occurred during that final meeting.

In those last months the Duke and Duchess had not been much in the news, a sharp contrast to the first years of their marriage, when they were ever in the limelight. Then they were regularly interviewed wherever they appeared with their dogs and their mountains and mountains of luggage. They shuttled back and forth between Paris and the Riviera, and from time to time came to New York to live in a suite reserved for them in the Waldorf Towers.

The Duke's last official duties were performed in World War II, when he was appointed Governor and commander in chief of the Bahamas. The Duchess described the years in Nassau as "happy and imbued with a sense of purpose that we were sorry to lose."

She appeared clearly to recognize the Duke's frustration because of the general purposelessness of their lives as part of a kind of international cafe society, after all his years of preparation for the crown.

But through the years the Duke maintained that he had done the right thing.

But the aura of sadness about the former King persisted.

A friend said of the Windsors, "They have elevated the art of doing nothing into a ceremonial for princes."

So the Duke, who had once been a Prince and a King, became a figure half-forgotten, a man of another era, a relic of history. A British writer said of him, "He was a King that got away."

In the man's life the sense of promise unfulfilled was strong.

© Henry Grossman

The Duke and Duchess of Windsor in a portrait taken in 1967. Couple lived on edge of Paris in Bois de Boulogne.

"All the News That's Fit to Print"

The New York Times.

LATE CITY EDITION
U. S. Weather Bureau Report (Page 60) forecasts:
Partly cloudy and mild today.
Increasing cloudiness tomorrow.
Temp. range: 62—52. Yesterday: 73.9—54.1.

VOL. CVIII..No. 36,966. | NEW YORK, FRIDAY, APRIL 10, 1959. | 10 cents beyond 50-mile zone from New York City except on Long Island. Higher in air delivery cities. | FIVE CENTS

CITY VOTE BACKS A BAN ON TRAFFIC IN WASHINGTON SQ.

Buses Will Be Rerouted and Only Emergency Vehicles Permitted in Park

JULY START IS POSSIBLE

Board Delays Action on Big Slum Project to Weigh Attacks on Sponsor

By CHARLES G. BENNETT

A statement of policy prohibiting the use of Washington Square Park to all but emergency traffic was approved by the Board of Estimate last night.

Even buses would be excluded. About July 1 the Board of Estimate will receive from the Bureau of Franchises and Traffic Commissioner T. T. Wiley a plan for rerouting the buses. Until that time the buses will operate in the park.

The board expects to act on the report soon after it is received. Borough President Hulan E. Jack of Manhattan said after last night's action that John E. McCarthy, president of the Fifth Avenue Coach Company, was "cooperating to the fullest."

Mr. McCarthy's company operates the buses in the park. Since last Nov. 1 in an experimental closing the park has been barred to regular traffic, but buses have been permitted to operate.

Wiley Sought Delay

Mr. Wiley said in a report two weeks ago that the experiment had been "inconclusive." He asked that the experiment be continued eight months, during which the buses would have tried alternate routes.

Last night's decision apparently doomed previous proposals that either a thirty-six or forty-eight-foot roadway be constructed through the park for general traffic.

A campaign by Greenwich Village groups, aided by Carmine G. De Sapio, New York County Democratic leader, among others, to close the park to all traffic grew out of their fight against the widened roadway proposals.

The Board of Estimate's action last night was hailed by Raymond S. Rubinow, chairman of the Joint Emergency Committee to Close Washington Square Park.

Honor for Jack Urged

Mr. Rubinow thanked Mr. Jack, Mr. De Sapio and others and said he would propose that the space in the park from which the buses would be cleared be named "Hulan E. Jack Plaza."

The Board of Estimate reached its decision during a forty-minute executive session. After the session Mr. Jack, on the board's behalf, read the following statement:

"That the Traffic Commissioner and the Director of Franchises are hereby requested to conclude negotiations with the Fifth Avenue Coach Company for the rerouting of buses to avoid using Washington Square Park, such negotiations to be concluded no later than July 1, 1959, or thereabout.

"That on whatever date the

Continued on Page 19, Column 1

Frank Lloyd Wright Dies; Famed Architect Was 89

Leader in Modern U. S. Style of Building—Stirred Controversy

Special to The New York Times.

PHOENIX, Ariz., April 9—Frank Lloyd Wright, regarded by many as the greatest architect of the twentieth century, died early today in St. Joseph's Hospital. He was 89 years old.

Mr. Wright, who had considered himself to be "the greatest living architect," was admitted to the hospital Monday night for emergency surgery to remove an intestinal obstruction. His physician said he was "getting along satisfactorily and then suddenly died."

From his estate, Taliesin West, northeast of Phoenix, Mr. Wright designed a new Capitol for Arizona. He proposed an "oasis in the desert, its fountains and greenery contrasting with the sand and rocks around it." The plan created a controversy, but was rejected.

When a group of architects proposed a skyscraper type of building for a Capitol, Mr. Wright looked at the drawing and described it as "a sidewalk-happy chimneypot with a derby hat on top, a poor version of a poor original—the

The New York Times (by Sam Falk)
Frank Lloyd Wright

United Nations Building in New York."

This was typical of Mr. Wright's comments, for which he was almost as well known as

Continued on Page 26, Column 1

7 NAMED AS PILOTS FOR SPACE FLIGHTS SCHEDULED IN 1961

One Will Be Aboard Nation's First Manned Satellite—Rigid Training Ahead

By JOHN W. FINNEY
Special to The New York Times.

WASHINGTON, April 9—Seven young military test pilots were presented today as the nation's future pioneers in space.

With a dramatic flourish, the National Aeronautics and Space Administration named the seven men who had been selected, after rigorous and extensive examinations, to undergo training as the first astronauts.

To one of these volunteers, some two years from now, will go the risky honor and distinction of being picked to ride the nation's first manned satellite into space.

On this flight, the Senate Space subcommittee was told today, the astronaut will circle the earth two or three times in his one-ton space capsule at an altitude of about 125 miles before returning for a splash landing in the Atlantic Ocean.

All Are in Their 30's

The seven men chosen as astronauts for the project, known as Mercury, are:

Navy Lieut. Malcolm S. Carpenter, 33 years old, of Boulder, Colo.

Air Force Capt. Leroy G. Cooper Jr., 32, of Carbondale, Colo.

Marine Lieut. Col. John H. Glenn Jr., 37, of New Concord, Ohio.

Air Force Capt. Virgil I. Grissom, 33, of Mitchell, Ind.

Navy Lieut. Comdr. Walter M. Schirra Jr., 36, of Hackensack, N. J.

Navy Lieut. Comdr. Alan B. Shepard Jr., 35, of East Derry, N. H.

Air Force Capt. Donald K. Slayton, 35, of Sparta, Wis.

The seven, who will henceforth be known as Mercury Astronauts, were presented at a news conference by Dr. T. Keith Glennan, director of the Space Administration.

Space Program Outlined

For an hour and a half they faced the ordeal—the worst, one pilot confessed, in weeks of exhaustive examinations—of being ordered around by photographers and of having their personal lives and beliefs laid bare by reporters.

A few hours before the astronauts made their debut, scientists of the Space Administration were telling the Senate Space subcommittee how they planned to hurl the young men into space and the new horizons in space travel that they would open.

The first Mercury flights will be short, probably only a few hours, but then they will gradually be extended to last twenty-four hours, the scientists said. Following the Mercury flights, which were described as the "simplest" form of orbital

Continued on Page 3, Column 1

Akihito Weds a Commoner in Colorful Japanese Rites

Michiko Shoda leaving home for the wedding rites. Behind her are her brother Osamu, right, and unidentified man.

Associated Press Radiophotos
Crown Prince Akihito as he left home for the ceremony.

By ROBERT TRUMBULL
Special to The New York Times.

TOKYO, Friday, April 10—Crown Prince Akihito and Michiko Shoda were married in brief but very colorful Shinto rites this morning. The young couple, in brilliant court robes of a past era, entered the sacred palace shrine together promptly at 10 A. M. (8 P. M. Thursday, Eastern standard time). They emerged married, exactly eleven minutes later in a solemn procession with priests, chamberlains and ladies-in-waiting. Sips of wine taken in turn had formalized the marriage. The brief ceremony changed the 2,619-year-old history of perhaps the world's oldest throne by placing one of the common people in line to be Empress for the first time. Thousands of cheering well-wishers, many waving tiny rising sun flags, had watched

Continued on Page 7, Column 2

U. S. SEEKS TO END BONN-LONDON RIFT ON GERMAN POLICY

Drafts Plan of Unification and Arms Reduction for Talks With Soviet

SPLIT CAUSES CONCERN

Adenauer's Resentment at British Is Said to Date From 1945 Incident

By DANA ADAMS SCHMIDT
Special to The New York Times.

WASHINGTON, April 9—The State Department is moving into the breach between West Germany and Britain with a set of principles for European security and German unification.

American officials hope their formula for parallel steps toward a security system and unification will satisfy the British and Chancellor Konrad Adenauer's requirements as well.

The principles will be put before a group of United States, British, French and West German diplomats who will meet in London tomorrow to resume efforts to work out common strategy for a conference with the Soviet Union.

They are understood to call for gradual reunification of East and West Germany, beginning with expanded economic and cultural relations and formation of non-governmental joint commissions.

Party Rights Would Follow

Further stages would provide for permission for all political parties to work throughout Germany, formation of a joint committee of East and West Germans to prepare an election and, finally, actual reunification and conclusion of a peace treaty.

Accompanying each stage would be steps toward disarmament and an eventual East-West treaty that would guarantee all participants against aggression.

But key United States and foreign diplomats were not confident that technical agreement on such a formula would get at the real causes of tension between Bonn and London.

Chancellor Adenauer's criticism of Britain yesterday did not take Washington by surprise. The West Germans had already voiced their complaints through diplomatic channels. The only surprise was that the Chancellor felt so strongly as to put his feelings on public record.

Ouster by British Recalled

These feelings are thought to have their origins back in early 1945 when the British removed Dr. Adenauer as Mayor of Cologne on the ground of incompetence. This gave Dr. Adenauer his opportunity to start his larger political career. But, according to Germans who have observed him for more than a decade, he never quite forgave the British.

Most recently, these sources report, his suspicion of the British has been brought to a feverish pitch by three developments:

First, press reports of what Prime Minister Harold Macmillan said to President Eisenhower at Camp David convinced the Chancellor that the Prime Minister had not, during his visit to Bonn, told Dr. Adenauer what

Continued on Page 2, Column 5

MAYOR SEES HOPE FOR FEWER TAXES

Hints It May Be Possible to Avoid Some of New Levies Authorized by Albany

By PAUL CROWELL

Mayor Wagner hinted last night that the city might try to balance its 1959-60 expense budget of $2,173,113,999 without imposing all of the new or increased special taxes authorized by the 1959 Legislature.

The hint was dropped in a recorded radio talk on city finances over WMGM.

"We are going to have to impose virtually all of the new taxes the Legislature gave us the right to impose this year," the Mayor said, "and we're going to have to do that just to get by."

Inquiry about the reason for the Mayor's use of the word "virtually" disclosed that serious consideration was being given to not imposing the proposed tax on cigars and tobacco products at this time.

The annual yield from this levy has been estimated at $500,000 to $1,000,000. The city's 30,000 retail tobacco dealers have registered strong protests against the tax, predicting that it would cause many of their customers to make their purchases in Connecticut and New Jersey or in Nassau and Westchester.

The broadcast was the first of five planned by the Mayor before public hearings on his

Continued on Page 19, Column 3

14 Maritime Unions Act to Cooperate On Land and Sea

By JACQUES NEVARD

A far-reaching proposal to promote unity among seafaring, waterfront and associated unions was enthusiastically received here yesterday by officials of fourteen labor organizations.

The proposal was to set up a steering committee to foster "coordinated cooperation." The step was hailed by one of the leaders as "the most all-inclusive effort ever made by marine workers in history."

Officials denied it was a step toward a council or confederation of transport unions such as has long been urged by James R. Hoffa, president of the International Brotherhood of Teamsters.

Hoffa Backs Plan

But Mr. Hoffa was present at the meeting and gave his backing to the proposal. This was viewed as surety that any joint effort launched by the maritime workers would probably have the support of the powerful teamster union.

The steering committee proposal was made jointly by Paul Hall, president of the Seafarers International Union, and Joseph Curran, president of the National Maritime Union.

The immediate objective of the unity move, according to the two sponsors, was to rally support for continuing a fight against "runaway" or "flag-of-convenience ships."

Mr. Hall and Mr. Curran, long-time enemies, buried their

Continued on Page 21, Column 2

STEWART HEARING OPENS IN A CLASH

Senators Wrangle Over Right to Question Justice on Integration Ruling

By ANTHONY LEWIS
Special to The New York Times.

WASHINGTON, April 9—Justice Potter Stewart of the Supreme Court came under a barrage of critical questions from Southern Senators today as the long-delayed hearings on his confirmation began.

In two hours before the Senate Judiciary Committee he was asked whether he was a "creative judge," whether the Constitution meant what it did in 1787 and whether he agreed with the "reasoning" of the Supreme Court decision in 1954 declaring school segregation unconstitutional.

Inquiry about school segregation set off a lengthy committee wrangle about the propriety of the question. Justice Stewart finally said he could not appropriately answer yes or no. But he said to the questioner, Senator John L. McClellan, Demo-

Continued on Page 14, Column 4

Tibetan Tribesmen Reported Carrying Fighting Into China

By The Associated Press.

NEW DELHI, India, April 9—Fighting has broken out between Tibetan rebels and Chinese Communist forces in Tsinghai Province and the Sikang area, both in China, press reports said today.

The Times of India said rebels had cut off Chamdo, on the main supply road between China proper and Lhasa, the Tibetan captal.

"Chamdo is like an island protected by the Chinese garrison," said The Times' correspondent in Gangtok, capital of the princely state of Sikkim between India and Tibet.

Huge Forces Reported

He said rebels also were fighting Chinese in the Amdo area of Tsinghai Province, birthplace of Tibet's self-exiled Dalai Lama.

Authoritative sources in Taiwan estimated that 200,000 tribesmen were fighting the Chinese Communists in Sikang and Szechwan Provinces.

"Reports of vast troop movements in central Tibet reach here almost daily," the Gangtok reporter wrote. He added that, in addition to calling up reinforcements, the Chinese were trying to draft Tibetans into the battle against the rebels.

The reporter said the Chinese were using spotter planes against the rebels and had sent in jet fighters to guard against attempts by Nationalist Chinese planes to drop weapons and supplies to the rebels.

The Times said most of the

Continued on Page 6, Column 5

MOSCOW ASSAILS EISENHOWER TALK

Khrushchev Says Gettysburg Speech Raises Tension—Pravda Prints Text

By Reuters.

LONDON, Friday, April 10—Premier Nikita S. Khrushchev accused President Eisenhower today of "making a definite contribution" to attempts to raise tension, the Soviet agency Tass reported.

The Soviet Premier was commenting in an interview with the Communist party newspaper Pravda on President Eisenhower's speech at Gettysburg College in Pennsylvania on April 4, Tass said.

In the Gettysburg speech President Eisenhower warned against appeasement of the Soviet Union over Berlin as "dishonorable and most dangerous."

"The Gettysburg speech could not but occasion surprise," Mr. Khrushchev declared in the Pravda interview.

"People everywhere learned with joy that agreement had been reached among states to call a meeting of ministers and a meeting at the summit for the solution of pressing international problems.

Sees Hopefulness Opposed

"As a result everybody felt a definite improvement in the international climate. There appeared a hope that statesmen would be able to reach agreement and that it would be possible to insure peace.

"But, on the face of it, this does not suit some people. Attempts are being made to play on people's nerves, to raise tension. It should be said that President Eisenhower, too, is making a definite contribution to this."

Mr. Khrushchev said the President had repeated almost all the basic propositions concerning the Soviet Union that had been advanced repeatedly by the most rabid proponents of the policy of "brinkmanship."

Answering President Eisenhower's allegation of a "Communist conspiracy to attain world domination," Mr. Khrushchev said: "The Soviet state has never had and never will

Continued on Page 2, Column 7

Blouse Case Stirs Major Trust Fight

By A. H. RASKIN

Government efforts to use the antitrust laws to upset the complex labor-management structure in the garment industry seemed likely yesterday to touch off a legal battle as bitter as that involved in the famous Danbury Hatters case a half-century ago.

The importance of the current fight was underscored by an announcement that the legal staff representing the International Ladies Garment Workers Union would be headed by Adlai E. Stevenson, twice the Democratic candidate for President, and former Federal Judge Simon H. Rifkind.

One of the three employer associations awaiting trial with Local 25 of the I. L. G. W. U. in an alleged conspiracy to monopolize trade in the manu-

Continued on Page 21, Column 6

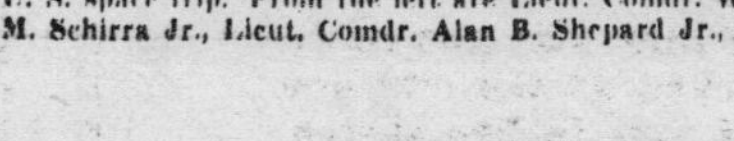

Associated Press Wirephoto

CANDIDATES FOR SPACE FLIGHT: These seven military pilots have been chosen for training for first U. S. space trip. From the left are Lieut. Comdr. Walter M. Schirra Jr., Lieut. Comdr. Alan B. Shepard Jr., Capt. Virgil I. Grissom, Capt. Donald K. Slayton, Lieut. Col. John H. Glenn Jr., Lieut. Malcolm S. Carpenter and Capt. Leroy G. Cooper Jr. The selection of men was announced by the National Aeronautics and Space Administration.

U. S. Rubber Plants Struck in 11 States

A spokesman for the United States Rubber Company said that 25,000 workers at eighteen plants in eleven states began a strike at 12:01 A. M. today.

The spokesman said the workers struck after negotiations here had failed to reach agreement on union demands for improvements in fringe benefits. The proposals took in pensions, insurance, severance pay and a supplemental unemployment benefit plan.

The company's 2,500 employes at its Passaic, N. J., plant were among the strikers. Pickets appeared before the plant at midnight.

Wages were not an issue. They normally are negotiated during the summer in the United States Rubber Company, as well as in other major producers in the rubber industry.

Continued on Page 14, Column 7

NEWS INDEX

Drastic Change Set In French Theatre

By HENRY GINIGER
Special to The New York Times.

PARIS, April 9—French youth is thirsting for culture and France's new republic is out to satisfy its thirst.

This was stated today by André Malraux, Minister of State for Cultural Affairs, who is also a leading novelist and art philosopher.

Some 200 reporters gathered to hear M. Malraux' long-heralded plans to shake up the nationally run dramatic and lyric theatres. They got the shake-up all right—even the Opéra-Comique's dust-laden "Carmen" will not escape. They also got an outline of the Gaullist regime's ambitious plan to form French youth's taste for the higher things of life, at least theatrically.

The plan is to revolutionize the theatre-going public as well

Continued on Page 8, Column 6

Frank Lloyd Wright, Dies in Phoenix

ICONOCLAST NOTED FOR STRONG IDEAS

Believed Form in Building Should Follow Function—Once Foe of Skyscrapers

Continued From Page 1, Col. 3

his buildings. He condemned retiring at 60 as a "murderous custom" and pleaded for a curb to America's "lust for ugliness."

A gradual change in the architect's fame, fortune and attitude might have been marked on May 28, 1953, when he received the Gold Medal Award of the National Institute of Arts and Letters. He then said:

"A shadow falls; I feel coming on me a strange disease—humility."

From Radical to Leader

During his lifetime Mr. Wright was in turn the great radical of American architecture and the acknowledged leader of a flourishing modern school of building.

This change in status of the white-haired iconoclast of American architecture did not evolve through any relaxation of his uncompromising theory that form in building should follow function, but rather in the public's gradual acceptance of his doctrine and deviations.

Hailed in Europe in his early years as the creator of an American architecture, he did not so readily gain acceptance in his own country, where the skyscraper was king. Although trained by Louis Sullivan, who was known as the "father of the skyscraper," Mr. Wright was strong in his condemnation of that peculiarly American architectural phenomenon.

Mr. Wright scathingly condemned the topless towers of New York. He had no use for the great steel and stone cities; he denounced the "box" house in this country, declaring that "a box is more of a coffin for the human spirit than an inspiration."

His own philosophy of architecture was enunciated in low terrain-conforming homes that became known as "prairie architecture"; in functional office buildings of modest height utilizing such materials as concrete slabs, glass bricks and tubing; in such monumental structures as the Imperial Hotel in Tokyo that withstood the great earthquake of 1923.

Native of Wisconsin

Mr. Wright was born on June 8, 1869, at Richland Center, Wis., the son of William Cary Wright and the former Anna Lloyd-Jones. His family was intensely religious. His father became a minister, and gave Mr. Wright a religious training. From his mother, who was a school teacher, it was said that he developed the idea of being an architect. From both parents he developed a strong individuality and the rebellious quality that characterized him and his work.

As a boy he attended public school in Wisconsin and then was sent to the University of Wisconsin to study civil engineering. Deciding he wanted to be an architect, Mr. Wright left college in his last year and headed not for Paris and the Ecole des Beaux Arts, but, with his typical indiduality, for Chicago.

There he found work in the drafting room of Mr. Sullivan, the French-Irish Bostonian who had rebelled against classic architecture taught in France and at Massachusetts Institute of Technology. Although he and Mr. Sullivan were inevitably to disagree, they had in common an opposition against the classic form.

Mr. Sullivan taught the young apprentice the ground rules of architecture and instilled in him his ideas for radical design. After four years they quarreled and Mr. Wright set up his own office. But throughout his life he referred to Mr. Sullivan, who died in 1927, as "der Meister" and freely acknowedged his great debt to the man who built the famed Wainwright Building in St. Louis and the Chicago Auditorium.

Trip to Germany

Mr. Wright naturally took to rebellion. From the very beginning his designs were different from anything that had been built before—"designed-for-living" bungalows. He built the first one for himself. It was the home for his bride, the former Catherine Tobin, whom he married when he was 21. She was 19. They met at a church social, married and went to live at Oak Park, a Chicago suburb noted for its many churches. There the Wrights's six children were born: Lloyd and John, who became architects; Catherine, David, Frances and Llewellyn.

The architect's Oak Park houses were low bungalows, free of fancy woodwork, dormer windows, corner towers or towering chimneys. The horizontal planes of the structures were accentuated. They "hugged the earth."

Among architects the houses created a sensation. Soon Mr. Wright's designs became known in this country as "prairie architecture" because they fitted so snugly into the flat landscape for which they were made. In Europe they were widely hailed and in Germany several books were written about them and a portfolio of them was published. America, for the most part, still chose to ignore both the builder and his creations.

Suddenly Mr. Wright gained fame, not through his already substantial contribution to modern American architecture, but through scandal and tragedy. In 1909 he went to Germany to arrange for publication of the portfolio of his work and some essays on architecture he had written. A short time before, he had built a house for E. H. Cheney, a neighbor at Oak Park. When the architect sailed for Germany, Mrs. Cheney went with him.

When they returned, Mr. Wright built perhaps his most famous structure, his own home, Taliesin ("Shining brow" in his ancestral Welsh), in Spring Green, Wis. He built his country home on a commanding site overlooking the Wisconsin River. It was to be a "refuge" for Mrs. Cheney, whose husband had divorced her.

On Aug. 15, 1914, tragedy struck Taliesin. Mrs. Cheney, her two children and four other persons were killed by a crazed servant, who also burned the house to the ground. Mr. Wright later rebuilt Taliesin, determined, as he said "to wipe the scar from the hill."

Meanwhile, publication in Germany of Mr. Wright's work had come to the attention of the Emperor of Japan, who, in the fall of 1915 sent a delegation of officials and architects to see him and to ask him to submit plans for a $4,500,000 hotel the Emperor hoped to build in Tokyo. The architect made sketches, which were accepted, and he went to Japan to superintend the building of the hotel.

His greatest problem was to foil the earthquakes that periodically brought destruction and death to Japan. The brilliance with which he solved his problem was demonstrated twice—once before the hotel was completed, when a minor quake shook Tokyo, and again when it had been up for two years.

The Imperial Hotel was an elastic structure, the walls and floors having a sliding quality never before attained. Its plumbing was designed so that pipes would not break and the electric wiring was placed so that temblors would not cause short circuits and charge the building with high-voltage death.

It was completed in 1922. A year later fierce quakes rocked Tokyo and Yokohama. Nearly 100,000 persons died under collapsing walls and falling roofs or were burned to death in the holocaust that followed. Days later, when communication between Tokyo and the outside world was re-established, word went out that the Imperial Hotel was the only large structure that had survived the disaster.

In the next few years domestic trouble continued to harass the architect. He had been estranged from his first wife, who finally consented to divorce him after his return from Tokyo. His second marriage, to Miriam Noel, a sculptor, was brief. They were married in 1923 and divorced in 1927. The next year Mr. Wright married Olga Lazovich. They had a daughter, Iovanna.

In 1927, when he lost Taliesin by foreclosure of a mortgage, Mr. Wright called in his friends, many of them wealthy business men, and incorporated himself under Wisconsin laws, selling stock on his earning power.

He regained Taliesin, built several houses and planned extensive projects, most of which were too "visionary" and did not materialize. In 1929 he incorporated himself again and established the Taliesin Fellowship Foundation, where he trained many apprentice architects.

Through controversy and criticism the architect rose steadily while his critics declared he was not only ahead of his time, but also ahead of all time, and his disciples and admirers made extravagant claims for his work. In 1940, when a comprehensive exhibition of Mr. Wright's work was shown in New York, he was reckoned as a great force in American architecture, but not as the last word.

Gradually he began to gain vogue and commissions. Among the structures for which the architect became famous were the Midway Gardens in Chicago, the Larkin Company administration building in Buffalo, the S. C. Johnson Company building at Racine, Wis.; the Falling Water House of Edgar J. Kaufmann at Bear Run, Pa., which he built above a waterfall, and the Price Tower at Bartlesville, Okla.

There also was the circular Friedman house near Pleasantville, N. Y., in a cooperative development known as Usonia Houses. Usonia was the descriptive word used by Mr. Wright to typify what he considered to be the ideal American architectural style.

He added Taliesin West, his own home in Phoenix, Ariz., to the rapidly growing list of Wright showplaces throughout the nation. This home, situated in Paradise Valley, he used as he did Taliesin East, as headquarters for his foundation teaching program. Approximately forty young apprentice architects yearly spent the term from April through November in the Wisconsin Taliesin and from December through March in the Arizona home.

One of Mr. Wright's largest commissions was the $10,000,000 campus of Florida Southern College in Lakewood. The project was begun in 1936 and sixteen structures were to be completed by 1960. Again Mr. Wright received mixed reactions for one of the edifices—a modern chapel building.

Even as an octogenarian who had received many prizes and honors, including election to the American Academy of Art and Letters, the white-haired individualist was still capable of stirring up the critics.

Mr. Wright was the author of many books, including "Modern Architecture" and "Two Lectures on Architecture," 1931; "An Autobiography," and "The Disappearing City," 1932; "An Organic Architecture," 1939; "When Democracy Builds," 1945; "Genius and Mobocracy," 1949; "An American Architecture," 1955, and "A Testament," 1957.

He received the Royal Gold Medal for Architecture from King George VI in 1941, the Gold Medal of the American Institute of Architects in 1949, the Italian Star of Solidarity in 1951 and the Gold Medal of the City of Florence in 1951. Mr. Wright held honorary degrees from Wesleyan, Princeton University, the University of Venice and Florida Southern.

He was an honorary member of the Academie Royale des Beaux Arts of Antwerp, the Akademie der Kunst of Berlin, the Royal Institute of British Architects and of the National Academies and architectural societies in Mexico, Portugal, Uruguay, Cuba, Brazil and Finland. He was a member of the National Academy of Design, the American Institute of Decorators and Phi Delta Theta.

Rejections were still possible even to the famous octogenarian. His plans for a building in Yosemite National Park were rejected ("politics," he snorted); and Venice turned down his plans for a glass and marble palace on the Grand Canal ("the tourists have won," he said).

Mr. Wright opened fire on plans for the Air Force Academy in Colorado, dubbed it a "factory for birdmen." He built a skyscraper in a small Midwest town; was commissioned to do a million-dollar synagogue in Philadelphia and a $45,000,000 cultural center in Baghdad; planned a mile-high building for Chicago's lakefront; designed prefabricated houses.

And so he continued to live his later years, much as the earlier ones, hard at work and deep in discussion with his fellowman. At 89 he continued his teaching at Taliesin with sixty-five architectural students. Working a full day, he emerged often to make a public appearance in flowing tie, white hair under porkpie hat, and to make a characteristic utterance.

Besides his wife and children, Mr. Wright leaves a sister, Mrs. Maginel Wright Barney of New York; nine grandchildren and eight great-grandchildren. His daughter Frances died last February. One of his grandchildren is Anne Baxter, the film actress.

"FALLING WATER," 1936: The Edgar J. Kaufmann house at Bear Run, Pa., was cantilevered over a waterfall by the architect. Mr. Wright said he looked at the site and went home to make a drawing. The house that resulted was almost exactly like sketch.

Museum Opens Tribute To the Architect Today

Photographs of buildings designed by Frank Lloyd Wright and a tribute to the architect will be on view today at the Museum of Modern Art, 11 West Fifty-third Street.

The small show includes the Johnson's Wax Building in Racine, Wis., the Robie House in Chicago, the dwelling, Falling Water, at Bear Run, Pa., and the uncompleted Guggenheim Museum on upper Fifth Avenue.

"All the News That's Fit to Print"

The New York Times.

LATE CITY EDITION
Increasing cloudiness, cold today. Snow, not so cold tomorrow.
Temperature Range Today—Max.,18; Min.,6
Temperatures Yesterday—Max.,24; Min.,5.5
Full U. S. Weather Bureau Report, Page 31

Copyright, 1948, by The New York Times Company.

VOL. XCVII No. 32,879. Entered as Second-Class Matter. Postoffice, New York, N. Y. NEW YORK, SATURDAY, JANUARY 31, 1948. THREE CENTS NEW YORK CITY

MANY HOMES WITHOUT HEAT AS ZERO COLD IS DUE HERE; U. S. CUTS OIL EXPORTS 18½%

FUEL CRISIS GROWS

Hundreds of Families Reported Suffering in City Area

BAY STATE SEIZES PLANT

Bradford Acts When Walkout Threatens Boston Gas—Oil Diversion Denied Here

By WILL LISSNER

Hundreds of families in the city were reported by their landlords to be in cold homes for lack of fuel oil last night as temperatures dropped toward zero in Manhattan and toward subzero levels in the suburbs.

At 3 A. M. today the temperature dropped to 2.2 degrees, establishing a new low record for the season. The previous record was 5 degrees, registered last Saturday.

The winter's coldest weather gripped not only New York but the whole Northwest. The Midwest and South, however, got some relief yesterday from the protracted cold spell. The fuel situation was reported acute in many cities throughout the East.

Temperatures, after falling to points between zero and 5 degrees above in Manhattan and zero and 10 degrees below in the suburbs, are expected to rise today to 20 degrees. The cold is due to continue, according to the United States Weather Bureau, but whereas yesterday was sunny, increasing cloudiness was expected today. More snow is threatened tomorrow. The lowest temperature yesterday was 5.5 degrees at 9:50 A. M.

Yesterday's hourly temperatures were:

1 A. M.	23	2 P. M.	12
2 A. M.	23	3 P. M.	15
3 A. M.	22	4 P. M.	14
4 A. M.	18	5 P. M.	12
5 A. M.	13	6 P. M.	12
6 A. M.	9	7 P. M.	11
7 A. M.	8	8 P. M.	9
8 A. M.	7	9 P. M.	8
9 A. M.	6	10 P. M.	7
9:50 A. M.	5.5	11 P. M.	7
10 A. M.	6	12 M.	6
11 A. M.	7	1 A. M.	5
Noon	9	2 A. M.	4
1 P. M.	10	3 A. M.	2.2

Petroleum Exports Cut

As the fuel shortage produced critical conditions for many apartment and home owners in this and other cities, officials took steps to relieve the situation.

The Commerce Department announced in Washington that it had ordered exports of petroleum products cut 18½ per cent from 11,850,000 to 9,650,000 barrels during the first quarter of the year. Oil exports to Japan and the Ryukyus were cut from 1,600,000 barrels to 100,000. Exports will be allowed only from areas where fuel can be spared best, the department said.

In Massachusetts Gov. Robert F. Bradford ordered the seizure of a gas plant in Everett where a walkout of 900 workers was threatened that would have affected service to sixty-four hospitals and 1,500,000 residents of Greater Boston. After seizure and issuance of a temporary injunction, union leaders ordered their followers to remain at work.

In Tennessee, Governor James McCord proclaimed a state of emergency and announced a voluntary fuel conservation program.

In Rochester, Sheriff's deputies and city policemen were organized to make emergency deliveries of fuel oil in extreme cases.

In Endicott, Mayor E. Raymond Lee declared an emergency due to the gas shortage and urged residents to conserve fuel. Many homes there and in Binghamton and Johnson City were without heat and residents sought emergency shelter.

Philadelphians Warned

Residents of Philadelphia were warned of a gas shortage caused by the oil shortage and were urged to restrict use of gas to the absolute minimum.

Police Commissioner Arthur W. Wallander of this city, regional fuel coordinator, sent telegrams asking eighty-six terminal dealers here to remain open today and tomorrow, because of the expected severe cold, to supp fuel oil to hardship cases.

Mayor O'Dwyer declared during the afternoon that it was not necessary at this time to proclaim a state of emergency and to divert

Continued on Page 12, Column 5

Petroleum Shipment Abroad Is Curbed to Ease Shortage

Department of Commerce Orders Quotas Reduced From 11,850,000 to 9,650,000 Barrels for Quarter—Slashes Japan

Special to THE NEW YORK TIMES.

WASHINGTON, Jan. 30—The Department of Commerce announced today that "in view of the serious shortage of fuel oils," in this country it had ordered an 18½ per cent cut in exports of petroleum products during the first quarter of this year. Its action will reduce from 11,850,000 to 9,650,000 the barrels of petroleum designated for overseas.

The Department also announced that it would limit licenses for export of petroleum products to shipments for those areas of the United States where the fuel can best be spared during the emergency.

In addition, it was disclosed that a separate quota of gas oil and distillate fuel oil had been established for the first quarter for shipments to Japan and the Ryukyus, drastically cutting their supply from 1,600,000 barrels to 100,000. The Department said that the difference would be met from oil producing areas outside the United States.

Proposals had been made in Congress to stop all shipments abroad except those going to American military forces. Bills designed to accomplish this end have been introduced in the House and the Senate.

Walter S. Hallanan, chairman of the National Petroleum Council, said today that the petroleum industry had taken "prompt and forthright action to alleviate the shortages of some petroleum products which have been rendered acute in certain sections by the severe cold weather." The industry "takes pride in the fact that it was the first to develop a voluntary agreement under the recent authorization of Congress," he added.

Canada Is Not Affected

WASHINGTON, Jan. 30 (AP)—The action today of the Depart-

Continued on Page 11, Column 4

Hope Wanes in Sea Search For 28 Aboard Lost Airliner

By FREDERICK GRAHAM

The Atlantic area northeast of Bermuda was being searched last night for survivors of a British South American Airways plane that disappeared in the area early yesterday morning with a crew of six and at least twenty-two passengers, but hope had almost been abandoned.

The thirty-two-passenger plane, which listed among those aboard Air Marshal Sir Arthur Coningham, Royal Air Force, who commanded the Second Tactical Air Force of the Allies at the invasion of Normandy, was out of London and on the Azores-to-Bermuda leg of the flight when last heard from about 1 A. M. (EST) yesterday.

At least fifteen United States Air Force, Navy and Coast Guard planes plus three Coast Guard cutters, two commercial steamers and a British South American Airways plane worked over a large area about 400 miles northeast of Bermuda without success. More aircraft are scheduled to continue the search today.

The plane, a converted Lancaster bomber of the type used by the RAF for saturation bombing of Germany, had stopped in Santa Maria in the Azores to refuel. An Associated Press dispatch from Bermuda said the plane, believed to have been commanded by Capt. David Colby, radioed to Bermuda that it would arrive there at midnight Thursday, an hour and a half late. One hour later it reported to Bermuda again, saying it was 440 miles northeast of Bermuda, that there was a moderate sea swell and that it was bucking strong headwinds. Nothing more has been heard from the plane.

The only other report that might

Continued on Page 10, Column 2

ORVILLE WRIGHT, 76, IS DEAD IN DAYTON

Co-Inventor With His Brother, Wilbur, of the Airplane Was Pilot in First Flight

Special to THE NEW YORK TIMES

DAYTON, Ohio, Jan. 30—Orville Wright, who with his brother, the late Wilbur Wright, invented the airplane, died here tonight at 10:40 in Miami Valley Hospital. He was 76 years old.

Mr. Wright, who had been confined to a hospital in October, collapsed in his office on Tuesday. He was suffering from lung congestion and coronary arteriosclerosis.

At the bedside when Mr. Wright died were Horace A. Wright, a nephew; Mrs. H. S. Miller, a niece, and Delyle Myers, a nurse.

The announcement of his death was made by Dr. A. B. Brower, family physician.

Engrossing Amusement

In the early fall of 1900 fishermen and Coast Guardsmen dwelling on that lonely and desolated spot of sand dividing Albemarle Sound from the Atlantic Ocean on the coast of North Carolina called

Continued on Page 12, Column 2

Arms Get Atomic Energy Priority In Policy Set by Congress Group

By WILLIAM S. WHITE
Special to THE NEW YORK TIMES.

WASHINGTON, Jan. 30—The Joint Committee on Atomic Energy laid down today a firm policy that the production of atomic weapons, rather than work on peacetime applications of atomic energy, must be the "vital business" of the United States for the foreseeable future.

It declared also that "uninterrupted operation" of the "critical," or military, facilities of the Atomic Energy Commission was so essential to national security that an investigation was in motion to find a formula to assure "continuity of work" under all labor eventualities.

In its first report to Congress, the committee indicated some dissatisfaction "in a number of cases" with certain aspects of the handling of internal security within the personnel of the Atomic Energy Commission.

"In certain of these cases," the report went on, "the committee has requested that the commission outline in detail its security policy as applied to these specific instances."

"In the majority of these cases," it was added, the men in question had been employed while atomic energy still was under Army control.

As to the essential policy to be followed in atomic development, the committee declared:

"Until such time as an effective, enforceable and reliable program for the international control of atomic energy is in successful operation, the most vital business of the Atomic Energy Commission must be the meeting of the atomic requirements of national defense.

"The joint committee has been assured that those charged with these responsibilities are keenly aware thereof. This phase of the atomic energy program is of para-

Continued on Page 7, Column 5

Record 799-Million Budget Is Asked by Dewey for State

He Estimates Actual Outlay at 753 Millions for Next Fiscal Year, but Says No Rise in Taxes Is Needed—Warns on Inflation

By LEO EGAN
Special to THE NEW YORK TIMES.

ALBANY, Jan. 30—Governor Dewey submitted another record-breaking budget to the Legislature tonight, calling for appropriations of $799,600,000, including deficiencies for the current year, but estimating expenditures in the new budget year at a figure of $753,500,000. The Governor regards the lower figure as his "budget" total.

Appropriations recommended are $128,200,000 higher than those carried in last year's budget message but, because of supplemental grants for teacher pay, veterans' housing, college housing, central schools and rent control, only $53,400,000 higher than actual appropriations, which were $746,200,000.

The expenditures of $753,500,000 contemplated in Mr. Dewey's message compare with an actual total of $707,500,000 in the current year, according to revised estimates. The revised figure reflects increased relief contributions and higher food prices for inmates of state institutions which are being provided for in deficiency appropriations.

Allowing for continuance of the reductions made in 1946, which he recommended, the Governor estimated that existing regular taxes would produce $758,600,000 in the new budget year, enough to balance expenditures and leave a $5,000,000 surplus.

The regular tax structure does not include the additional one-cent-a-package levy on cigarettes or the 20 per cent increase in existing income tax rates which were voted to finance the $400,000,000 veterans' bonus. If the present return from these special levies continued, Mr. Dewey said, the bonus bonds might be retired in eight or

Continued on Page 9, Column 1

Text of Gov. Dewey's budget message will be found on pages 8 and 9.

REALTY VALUATIONS RISE $745,775,468 IN CITY FOR 1948-49

Higher Accrued Value Is Chief Factor in $17,684,240,921 Total, Biggest Since '33

By LEE E. COOPER

New York's land and buildings, regarded as the richest segment of real estate in the world, have risen in value to $17,684,240,921 on the city's tax books for the coming fiscal year.

Municipal assessors have chalked up a tentative increase of $745,775,468 over current figures on taxable properties for the year beginning July 1, 1948, to carry the aggregate valuations to the highest level since 1933.

A report submitted to Mayor O'Dwyer yesterday by Harry B. Chambers, president of the Tax Commission, showed an average rise of about 4⅓ per cent for the five boroughs, accounted for largely by an upswing in "accrued value" rather than by addition of new construction to the assessment rolls.

The report set the following ten-

Continued on Page 11, Column 3

GOP GROUP SHAPES SHARP ERP REVISION WITH FUND REDUCED

A Proposal to Sell U. S. Goods to Latin America for Food for Europe Wins Favor

By FELIX BELAIR Jr.
Special to THE NEW YORK TIMES.

WASHINGTON, Jan. 30—A fighting nucleus of eighteen Senate Republicans agreed late tonight to press for important changes in the Administration's European Recovery Program as the party's legislative leaders brushed aside President Truman's demand for approval of the full $6,800,000,000 asked for the first fifteen months of operations.

The group of eighteen Senators, in which Westerners predominated, called for a complete shift in emphasis of the Marshall Plan "from the underwriting of trade deficits to the support of specific production programs" in which financial aid would be contingent on increased output of food, coal, steel and transportation facilities.

Senator Joseph H. Ball of Minnesota said the principles agreed

Continued on Page 6, Column 2

World News Summarized

SATURDAY, JANUARY 31, 1948

Mohandas K. Gandhi, 78-year-old spiritual leader of hundreds of millions of Indians, was shot in New Delhi yesterday as he walked toward a pergola to lead 1,000 of his followers in evening prayer. He died twenty-five minutes later. His assassin, a Hindu, was seized after he had fired three quick shots into the frail leader, who only recently had ended a hunger strike in protest against communal strife. [1:8.]

News of the tragedy shocked the world. In Bombay, it ignited a new outburst of rioting. [2:3.] United Nations officials at Lake Success feared this might be the beginning of a new wave of violence throughout India. [2:4-5.] President Truman said the whole world would mourn and expressed hope that the assassination would "not retard the peace of India and the world." [2:1.] Similar expressions of regret were voiced in London, where the King and the Queen and Prime Minister Attlee were among the many leaders to pay tribute to Mr. Gandhi. [1:6-7.]

The French National Assembly approved, 308 to 242, the Government's program to establish a free gold market and to allow Frenchmen to repatriate foreign assets by paying a tax. The Socialists reversed their previous stand and voted for the program. [1:6-7.]

Two recent Russian notes protesting the reopening for American use of an airfield in Tripolitania and the presence of American naval craft in Italian ports will be rejected by the State Department. [8:5.] The Navy announced that another 1,000 marines would go to the Mediterranean soon to replace an equal number now serving in that area. [6:4-5.]

The United States consulate in Jerusalem declared American citizens participating in the fighting would lose their passports and right to protection. [1:7.] Britain announced at Lake Success before the Palestine Commission that she could not allow the formation of any armed militia in Palestine before her mandate ends. [4:3.]

In Washington a group of eighteen Senate Republicans urged a change in the European Recovery Program to support specific production goals and brushed aside the Administration's request for approval of the full initial fund of $6,800,000,000. [1:5.]

An 18½ per cent reduction in exports of petroleum products was ordered by the Commerce Department "in view of the serious shortage" of oil in this country. [1:2-3.]

Also in Washington, the Joint Committee on Atomic Energy declared this nation must concentrate for the foreseeable future on the "uninterrupted" production of atomic weapons in preference to the peaceful utilization of atomic energy. [1:2-3.]

Governor Dewey asked the Legislature to appropriate $799,600,000 as he submitted another record-breaking budget. Appropriations last year totaled $746,200,000. [1:4-5.]

Winter's coldest weather hit the metropolitan area, with the thermometer hovering near zero in the city. In the suburbs the temperature was expected to fall to sub-zero levels during the night. Some homes suffered from a shortage of fuel oil. [1:1.]

A thirty-two passenger British plane was feared lost on its way to Bermuda. [1:2-3.]

Orville Wright, air pioneer, died in Dayton, Ohio, at 76. [1:2.]

GANDHI IS KILLED BY A HINDU; INDIA SHAKEN, WORLD MOURNS; 15 DIE IN RIOTING IN BOMBAY

MOHANDAS K. GANDHI
The New York Times

THREE SHOTS FIRED

Slayer Is Seized, Beaten After Felling Victim on Way to Prayer

DOMINION IS BEWILDERED

Nehru Appeals to the Nation to Keep Peace—U. S. Consul Assisted in Capture

By ROBERT TRUMBULL
Special to THE NEW YORK TIMES.

NEW DELHI, India, Jan. 30—Mohandas K. Gandhi was killed by an assassin's bullet today. The assassin was a Hindu who fired three shots from a pistol at a range of three feet.

The 78-year-old Gandhi, who was the one person who held discordant elements together and kept some sort of unity in this turbulent land, was shot down at 5:15 P. M. as he was proceeding through the Birla House gardens to the pergola from which he was to deliver his daily prayer meeting message.

The assassin was immediately seized.

He later identified himself as Nathuran Vinayak Godse, 36, a Hindu of the Mahratta tribes in Poona. This has been a center of resistance to Gandhi's ideology.

Mr. Gandhi died twenty-five minutes later. His death left all India stunned and bewildered as to the direction that this newly independent nation would take without its "Mahatma" (Great Teacher).

The loss of Mr. Gandhi brings this country of 300,000,000 abruptly to a crossroads. Mingled with the sadness in this capital tonight was an undercurrent of fear and uncertainty, for now the strongest influence for peace in India that this generation has known is gone.

[Communal riots quickly swept Bombay when news of Mr. Gandhi's death was received. The Associated Press reported that fifteen persons were killed and more than fifty injured before an uneasy peace was established.]

Appeal Made By Nehru

Prime Minister Pandit Jawaharlal Nehru, in a voice choked with emotion, appealed in a radio address tonight for a sane approach to the future. He asked that India's path be turned away from violence in memory of the great peacemaker who had departed.

Mr. Gandhi's body will be cremated in the orthodox Hindu fashion according to his often expressed wishes. His body will be carried from his New Delhi residence on a simple wooden cot covered with a sheet at 11:30 tomorrow morning. The funeral procession will wind through every principal street of the two cities of New and Old Delhi and reach the burning ghats on the bank of the sacred Jumna River at about 4 P. M. There the remains of the greatest Indian since Gautama Buddha will be wrapped in a sheet, laid on a pyre of wood and burned. His ashes will be scattered on the Jumna's waters, eventually to mingle with the Ganges where the two holy rivers meet at the temple city of Allahabad.

These simple ceremonies were announced tonight by Pandit Nehru in respect to Mr. Gandhi's wishes, although many of the leaders desired that his body be embalmed and exhibited in state. India will see the last of Mr. Gandhi as it saw him when he lived—a humble and unassuming Hindu.

News Spreads Quickly

News of the assassination of Mr. Gandhi—only a few days after he had finished a five-day fast to bring about communal friendship—spread quickly through New Delhi. Immediately there was spontaneous movement of thousands to Birla House, home of G. D. Birla, the millionaire industrialist, where Mr. Gandhi and his six secretaries had been guests since he came to New Delhi in the midst of the disturbances in India's capital.

While walking through the gardens to this evening's prayer meeting Mr. Gandhi had just reached the top of a short flight of brick steps, his slender brown arms

Continued on Page 2, Column 6

All Britain Honors Gandhi; Truman Deplores Tragedy

By HERBERT L. MATTHEWS
Special to THE NEW YORK TIMES.

LONDON, Jan. 30—Mohandas K. Gandhi, in death, has won the unanimous tribute of Britons—something he never hoped for or expected during his life. Nowhere outside of India has the shock of his assassination contained the feelings and emotions evident here today because Britain and Mr. Gandhi have been linked for good or evil over the last forty years.

In a special broadcast to the British people tonight the Prime Minister said:

"The voice which pleaded for peace and brotherhood has been silenced, but I am certain that his spirit will continue to animate his fellow countrymen and will plead for peace and concord."

[President Truman and Secretary Marshall expressed their grief and condolences in messages to India. Members of Congress were apprehensive. Leaders of many other lands joined in paying tribute and in deploring the manner of Mr. Gandhi's death.]

The sincerity of today's expressions of regret, which came from the King and Queen, the Prime Minister, the political parties—even the Communist—and from many humble Londoners who filed silently into India House this afternoon to pay tribute, cannot be doubted.

Those many quarrels when Mr. Gandhi fought with his passive resistance against the imperial power of Britain are truly things of the past. Mr. Gandhi himself paid high tribute to Britain for her policy of freeing India and of trying to help to keep the two dominions at peace with each other.

The British, on their side, have

Continued on Page 2, Column 2

U. S. WARNS CITIZENS IN PALESTINE FIGHT

Consulate General Says They Face Loss of Passports and All Protective Rights

By SAM POPE BREWER
Special to THE NEW YORK TIMES.

JERUSALEM, Jan. 30—United States citizens fighting in the armed services of the Jews or the Arabs will lose their passports and their right to protection, the United States Consulate General warned Americans in Palestine tonight. Furthermore, naturalized citizens, it was said, would lose their American nationality if they fought for a foreign power.

[Zionist hopes for getting United Nations help in arming a Jewish militia in Palestine were dimmed by the statement of Sir Alexander Cadogan, chief British representative, that the British Government would not allow formation of such forces before the end of the mandate.]

The consular warning is being twisted by Arab sources into a promise that those fighting for the Jews may have their passports back when the fighting ends. The relevant passage reads: "American passports valid only for direct

Continued on Page 4, Column 4

France Votes Free Gold Market, Legalizes Hidden Assets by a Tax

By HAROLD CALLENDER
Special to THE NEW YORK TIMES.

PARIS, Jan. 30—Parliamentary sanction was given today for the Government's devaluation of the franc and its accompanying monetary policy.

By a vote of 308 to 242, the National Assembly passed the Government's bill to create a free gold market and to legalize the hitherto illegal possession of foreign securities held by Frenchmen, if those assets were repatriated and the owners paid a special tax of 25 per cent of the assets' value.

As a comparatively free market in dollars had already been established by decree—although its opening was delayed by the freezing of bank notes of 5,000 francs—today's vote by the Assembly completed the series of measures framed by the Government to derive maximum benefit from devaluation by getting possession of privately owned foreign securities and hoarded gold.

Estimates of the total of these illegal securities have been in the neighborhood of $300,000,000 in the United States alone, while official guesses have placed the value of the hidden gold in France at $2,000,000,000.

Apparently placated by the freezing of the bank notes, the Socialists once again switched their position and voted today for the gold market bill, which they had opposed bitterly Wednesday, although their Ministers had apparently accepted it in the Cabinet meeting last Saturday. They were not reluctant to switch, for they did not desire to upset the Government and wreck the "Third Force," hostile though they were to the Government's departure from a planned economy.

The freezing measure, taken when the Socialists had precipitated a Cabinet crisis by balking at the gold market, was considered mainly a political move. But René Mayer, Finance Minister, told the

Continued on Page 5, Column 2

ORVILLE WRIGHT, 76, IS DEAD IN DAYTON

Continued From Page 1

Kitty Hawk discovered a new and engrossing amusement. Whenever they usually had the time — and they usually had plenty of it — they would trudge through the deep sand and beach grass to the side of the cone-shaped twin dunes known as the Kill Devil Hills and watch two young men from Ohio try to break their necks.

Taking turns, these young men would launch themselves from the steep side of one of the hills lying flat down on the lower panel of what appeared to be a huge box-kite. His companion at one wing and a volunteer helper at the other would run and help the kite into the air. Then for perhaps fifty feet and sometimes much farther the kite would fly while the bird-man turned his body this way and that to help it maintain balance.

This was interesting, but the real fun came when the kite would suddenly nose down and plow into the sand, perhaps at the very start of the flight, while the operator would hurtle out the front doubled up into a ball and roll in a cloud of sand and dust down the side of the hill until all momentum had been lost.

Beginnings of Aviation

Cap'n Bill Tate and his companions did not know it, but they were witnesses at the birth of aviation, and the two who provided them with so much entertainment were Orville Wright, the first man to fly a heavier-than-air machine, and his brother, Wilbur.

Twelve years later, in the midst of what at times was a bitter struggle against rivals who sought to take the fruit of their labors, both in this country and abroad, Wilbur died of typhoid fever, leaving Orville to carry on the mission they had set themselves, the conquest of the air.

After the 1900 visit to Kitty Hawk it took three years more to experiment with gliders before the Wright brothers were actually to fly in a powered machine, three years of research and pure discovery in the unknown realm of aerodynamics and hundreds of bruising tumbles and daring flights in the frail gliders, and it took another six years before the United States Government officially recognized in a substantial manner the existence of the airplane.

It is difficult to tell the story of one brother without that of the other, so closely were their lives and work linked. Orville was born at Dayton on Aug. 19, 1871, four years after the birth of Wilbur, the son of Bishop Milton Wright, a militant pastor and publicist of the United Brethren Church. There were seven children in this minister's family, but only two others, Lorin and a sister, Katherine, were especially concerned with the development of aviation.

Before he was through high school Orville built a printing press and published The West Side News, with Wilbur as chief editorial writer. Their father encouraged these little ventures and apparently let the boys have a free reign.

First Interested in Problem in 1896

As early as 1891 they had read of the experiments of Otto Lilienthal and other glider pioneers, but it was not until Lilienthal's death in 1896 in a glider accident that they took a definite interest in the problems of flight. Orville at that time was recovering from a bout with typhoid fever and Wilbur read aloud to him. From Lilienthal they went to Samuel P. Langley and his experiments. They read Marey on animal mechanism and by 1899 had progressed through the records of Octave Chanute and a list of works which they had obtained through the Smithsonian Institution.

From Lilienthal and Chanute they got the enthusiasm that decided them to attempt gliding, and during Orville's convalescence they settled to serious study. They sent for Langley's tables and Lilienthal's and watched the progress of Sir Hiram Maxim's experiments. Langley and Maxim represented the school of scientific research and Chanute and Lilienthal were the experimenters actually trying their wings and the two young men of Dayton were drawn to the fliers rather than the mathematicians and physicists.

The Wrights then combined the methods of both schools. Through gliders and a study of wind currents and painful experiments they learned to fly. Through careful and scientific research they built up their own equations and tables of aerodynamics and established as fact beyond doubt the principles upon which every airplane is built and flown today.

Using the tables of Lilienthal and Langley, they went to work and constructed a series of gliders. The gliders did not function and so the Wrights changed them, still following the tables of their predecessors. Then, regretfully but finally, they decided that something was wrong with the tables.

Begin Kitty Hawk Flights

Among other things they found that concave wing surface produced a resultant force when air passed across it utterly at variance with the theory of Langley and Lilienthal. Equipped with their new tables they made a second trip to Kitty Hawk. They had been contented before 1900 with wind currents on the comparatively flat Ohio terrain. They knew that for the best results they must find steady, even winds blowing up over smooth hills. With characteristic zeal and thoroughness they sought the aid of the United States Weather Bureau and thus discovered Kitty Hawk.

While hundreds of attempts to "mount the machine" were made on the first Kitty Hawk visit, the brothers flew only a few minutes altogether. They returned to their home to study and make plans for the summer of 1901. In this period they had the benefit of visits and advice from Chanute, who had given up practical experiment himself. On the second Kitty Hawk expedition in the summer of 1901 Chanute visited their camp. The second glider they took to Kitty Hawk was better than the first, but they were not satisfied. Again they returned to Dayton and this second winter they carried on their wind tunnel experiments, developing the new tables. In the autumn of 1902 they were ready with a new machine, a biplane with the adjustable trailing edges on the wings, exemplifying the principle of the aileron which in later years they were to debate through the courts with Glenn H. Curtiss and others, the horizontal elevator and the vertical rudder. They connected all these to a single set of controls—the first time anything of the sort had been done—and with this machine they made 700 flights in less than three weeks.

In 1903 they returned to Kitty Hawk and on this occasion they sent out special invitations to the natives to be present as witnesses. They were not experimenting now. They knew they were going to fly. From late in September until December they worked on the ma-

(continued)

The Wright Brothers experimenting with gliders at Kitty Hawk, North Carolina, in 1902.

Orville Wright

chine in a shed which nearly blew away, airplane and all, during a hurricane. Even after they were ready, bad weather set in again and they had strong winds day after day.

During the enforced idleness they invented and constructed an air-speed indicator and a device for actually measuring the distance flown in respect to the moving air itself. Finally a good day came. The two brothers flipped a coin to decide who should be the first and Wilbur won. The engine was started and the machine lifted after a short run along the track they had built for its skids. But immediately one wing dipped. It stalled and was on the ground again after being in the air for three seconds. Pleased with the result, the brothers were still not willing to call it a flight. A skid was broken in the attempt and two days were consumed in fixing it. Finally on the evening of Dec. 16 everything was again ready and the flight was set for next morning. It was Orville's turn.

Guardsmen from the life saving station and one or two others were on hand to watch. The wind was blowing twenty-seven miles an hour. Orville said that years later after having made thousands of flights he would never have attempted a first flight in an untried machine in such a wind. Into the teeth of this wind the plane was pointed. Orville released the wire that connected it to the track and it started so slowly that Wilbur was able to keep pace alongside, clinging to one wing to help steady the frail craft. Orville, lying flat on the lower wing face down, opened the engine wide. The plane speeded up and lifted clear.

It rose about ten feet suddenly and then as suddenly darted toward the ground. A sudden dive 120 feet from the point it rose into the air brought it to earth again and man's first flight in a powered heavier-than-air machine was over. It had lasted twelve seconds, and allowing for the wind, it had made a forward speed through the air of more than thirty-three miles an hour. Three more flights were made that day, with Wilbur up twice and Orville once, and on the fourth trial Wilbur flew fifty-nine seconds, covered 852 feet over the ground and made an air distance of more than half a mile.

In July, 1909, Orville, with Lieut. Benjamin D. Foulois as passenger, won the first big Government contract here by attaining a speed of forty-two miles an hour, winning $30,000. His contract called for a plane that could make forty miles an hour and the Government offered a bonus for speeds above that limit.

Manufacturing on a large scale soon began at Dayton, and a third brother, Lorin, was placed in charge of the factory. Soon the Wrights had orders for sixty planes and were operating a thriving flying school. This period also was marked by the beginning of a series of famous patent fights, in which the Smithsonian Institution became indirectly involved. Glenn Curtiss was starting his experiments at Hammondsport and adapted principles which the courts finally ruled were the property of the Wright brothers. During the protracted litigation Mr. Curtiss obtained the ill-fated Langley machine from the Smithsonian Institution, and after alterations flew it successfully at Hammondsport. It was argued and is still maintained in some quarters that the Langley machine's flights at Hammondsport proved that Samuel Pierpont Langley's plane was the first successful man-carrying heavier-than-air machine. The Wrights, however, won on their patents and their victory was hailed with approval by aeronautical enthusiasts all over the world. The Langley machine was flown in 1914 and a year later Orville sold his rights and retired from active manufacturing to experiment.

Others were manufacturing, and aviation, although still experimental, was coming to be accepted as an accomplished fact. Orville, except for visits to Washington, occasional attendance at the meetings of scientific organizations and regular visits to the Langley memorial laboratories at Langley Field, Virginia, worked on quietly at Dayton. The death of Wilbur in 1912 left him very much alone. He did not want for money and he had had his fill of fame. Although friendly and generally accessible to visitors he sedulously avoided the spotlight.

Wilbur Wright flying at Pau, France.

The Wright Brothers airplane factory in Dayton, Ohio.

WILBUR WRIGHT DIES OF TYPHOID FEVER

Ill More Than Three Weeks, the End Came at 3:15 o'Clock Thursday Morning.

WON SUCCESS WITH BROTHER

President Taft and Others Pay High Tributes—Wilbur's Flights Abroad—A Sister's Timely Aid.

DAYTON, Ohio., May 30.—Following a sinking spell that developed soon after midnight, Wilbur Wright, aviator and aeroplane builder, died of typhoid fever at 3:15 A. M. to-day. Wright had been lingering for many days and though his condition from time to time gave some hopes to members of his family, the attending physicians, Drs. D. B. Conklin and Levi Spitler, maintained throughout the latter part of his sickness that he could not recover.

When the patient succumbed to the burning fever that had been racking his body for days and nights, he was surrounded by the members of his family, which included his aged father, Bishop Milton Wright, Miss Catherine Wright, Orville, the co-inventor of the aeroplane; Reuchlin Wright and Lorin Wright. All of the family reside in this city, except Reuchlin, who lives in Kansas.

The most alarming symptoms in Wright's sickness developed yesterday, shortly before noon, when his fever suddenly mounted from 104 up to 106 and then quickly subsided to its former stage. At this juncture of the crisis, the patient was seized with chills and the attending physicians were baffled by the turn of events.

The condition of the aviator remained unchanged throughout the rest of the day, and there was no improvement until last midnight. Then Wright began to show an improvement and the watchers at his bedside were reassured, but soon after midnight the patient suddenly became worse and Dr. D. B. Conklin was called. The doctor arrived at 3:25 and learned that Wright had breathed his last a few minutes before.

Wilbur Wright was seized with typhoid on May 4 while on a business trip in the East. On that day he returned to Dayton from Boston and consulted Dr. Conklin, the family physician. He took to his bed almost immediately, and it was several days before his case was definitely diagnosed as typhoid. Throughout the early part of his illness Wright attributed his sickness to some fish that he had eaten at a Boston hotel. He explained to his physician, however, that he had no particular reason to believe that the disease originated from this source.

Wilbur Wright's Career.

The place of Wilbur Wright's birth was a matter of dispute for several years after his reputation was made in aviation. Most people said he was born in Dayton. But Indiana set up a counter-claim, holding that Bishop Milton Wright was a well-known citizen of that State for years before he went to Ohio, and that when he moved he took with him two Indiana boys in the persons of Wilbur and Orville.

The persistent reticence and uncommunicativeness of the two aviators was responsible for the fact that the controversy was able to rage along the Ohio border for many months. Then an editor of "Who's Who" demanded exact data, and it was shown that both sides in part were winners. Indiana made good its claim in the case of Wilbur, who was born near the Town of Dune Park in that State on April 16, 1867, while Ohio triumphed as to Orville, since he was born four years later after the family had removed to Dayton.

The article in "Who's Who" concerning Wilbur Wright is typical of him throughout his career. It is the briefest biography of any of the sixteen Wrights who receive recognition in the international edition. Its most emphatic statement is that he was an aeronaut "with his brother Orville." Wilbur in every interview emphasized his younger brother's association with him, and never neglected an opportunity to praise him. Instead of referring to any achievement as his own he invariably referred to it as coming from "the Wright brothers." Wilbur and Orville were seen flying together in the same machine when the now well-remembered band of "war correspondents" secreted themselves in the Kill Devil Hills in North Carolina and peered at them through field glasses before flashing the news to a doubting world that it was really true, and men were flying through the air above the sand dunes just like the birds.

Wilbur and Orville stood together to receive the salutations of President Taft upon their triumphant return from Europe in 1908, when they were awarded the medal of the Aero Club of America, on which their portraits were placed together. On the day when Dayton outdid itself to welcome them home they again stood together. Into the life of neither brother did any romance enter, other than that associated with aeroplanes. Neither married. Mrs. Frank Coffyn, wife of one of Wilbur Wright's first pupils, declared that it was common talk in the Wright household that the only woman Wilbur ever truly loved was Miss Liberty, upon whom he used to delight to call via aeroplane at her island home in New York Harbor.

In the days of their humble beginnings Wilbur and Orville repaired bicycles together in their Dayton shop. They pulled on the same kite string that flew their first aeroplane after it had refused to leave the ground with a man aboard, and in the days of their first glory they received identical honorary degrees from the same European and American schools. The only other person who entered the close fellowship of the brothers was their sister Katherine. The brothers had her join them in Europe in time to receive the congratulations of King Alfonso in 1908, after Wilbur's flying had electrified Spain, and Miss Wright remained with them throughout their early trials at Fort Myer. When the first fatal accident occurred, in which Orville was seriously injured, his sister, a trained nurse, became his constant hospital attendant.

The brothers had brought into the world something entirely new, with whose principles the world was not at all familiar. Aviators sprang up in all parts of the world, suddenly gaining more of the world's attention than either of the Dayton brothers. The world was slow to comprehend that they were attempting to steal by early appropriation the fruits of the brothers' labor. All the world cheered Delagrange as he skimmed a few feet above the earth in 1908. Wilbur and Orville Wright for five years had flown constantly, making more than 100 flights in 1904 alone on the outskirts of Dayton, and had never received a single write-up in the papers, except jocular ones. Once, when their sister Katherine invited one of her fellow-teachers in a Dayton school to come out to the flying grounds, the teacher burst into tears and sobbed, "And you, too, poor girl!"

They knew that these unheralded, unnoticed flights had gone vastly further in achievement than any of the French flights that were stirring the world. They knew that they had achieved a speed of forty miles an hour, had carried a weight of 750 pounds, and had flown twenty miles over a straightaway cross-country course in 1904.

In 1906, after all persons to whom the Wrights had applied for funds had turned a deaf ear, they heard that the French Government had become interested in their experiments, and that a commission, representing a powerful French syndicate, was coming over to investigate their claims. At that time all the machines they had used in experimenting were broken, and they had come to the end of their cash resources.

Katherine Saves the Day.

Katherine Wright came forward with her savings as a school teacher and furnished the money with which to build an aeroplane to exhibit before the Frenchmen, who were delighted. They were the first men really to honor the Wrights, and asked for an option on the French patent rights and made glowing promises as to the reports that they would make to their backers.

Meantime Octave Chanute had gone to France with a magic-lantern lecture meant to attract attention to the World's Fair, then being planned for St. Louis. Among his pictures were many scenes of the Wright brothers in flight. They showed everything about the machine that a picture could show, and Chanute described in his lecture the manner in which the boys controlled their machine in the air and told how successful they were with it.

The lecture was innocent enough in purpose, but it was perhaps the most disastrous thing with which the Wrights had to contend. When it came, years later, to a test of the Wright patents before the officials of the German Patent Office they were able to sweep aside with the greatest ease all claims of various "fathers of flight" whom the German airmen had brought forward to prove that their "experiments" were founded upon the work of predecessors in Germany. But they failed to sweep aside proofs that Chanute had described the Wright inventions.

The Patent Office officials called to their assistance an old law that declared no patent valid for any device whose nature had been made public by the inventor, or had become public in any manner, before the application for a patent. And on that slender ground the Wrights were ruled out and forced to appeal to the higher courts, where their claims now await adjudication.

On the Wright finances the Chanute lecture had a blighting effect: The Frenchmen cut off all negotiations and allowed their option on the Wright patents to run out.

Wilbur then went to France. The French fliers were tipping over at every flight and smashing their machines.

Wilbur in France and Orville in America made flights in the same week. Orville won permission to make tests at Fort Myer, under the army's supervision. Wilbur gained a hearing from the French and pitched his camp at Auvours. Orville fell and young Selfridge was killed.

Four days after Orville fell at Fort Myer Wilbur took the air in France and circled the field for ninety-one minutes. Before half the flight was done, with its series of long glides and dips and figure eights, the Frenchmen were in a frenzy of delight. Here was something compelling to them, and they yielded the first full public adulation the Wrights had ever received.

The French company decided that after all there was a good deal more in the Wright machines than had been divulged through the photographs. They offered again the price for paptent rights that had been allowed to lapse the year before and Wilbur received a sum sufficient to put the Wrights on a safe operative basis.

In 1909 the tide turned toward the Wrights. Orville made a conquest of Germany as marked as had been Wilbur's conquest of France. Orville, in Germany, rose 750 feet in the air. Katherine, who had gone abroad with him, became the world's first air woman, and for a long time the holder of the world's record for continuous experience as a passenger, although Mrs. Hart O. Berg of Paris was the first woman to ascend in a Wright machine.

On May 13, 1909, the Wright brothers returned to this country. The Aero Club had a medal struck off, and on June 11 President Taft presented it at a White House function in the presence of many noted Americans and the members of the Diplomatic Corps. "Perhaps I do this at a delayed hour," declared the President in bringing forward the medal as the first American recognition.

In the Autumn of 1909 the Hudson-Fulton celebration was scheduled here, and Wilbur was much attracted by the poetic and historic possibility of a flight from New York to Albany up the Hudson River. He arrived at Governors Island simultaneously with Glenn H. Curtiss, who was fresh from winning laurels at the Rheims meet, his machine having come off victorious in contests with the foreign rigid types.

Wright and Curtiss had hangars adjoining each other, and while Curtiss greeted reporters with a smile Wright had the guards force them away with fixed bayonets. He had not yet forgotten his experience in France and in Dayton. Curtiss made no flights as the winds continued high, but Wilbur flew to Grant's Tomb and made several flights to the Statue of Liberty. On the bottom of his machine was attached a small river canoe, purchased in a Broadway store.

During Wilbur's stay in New York a stranger approached him one day on a ferryboat, presented his card, and asked the price of a Wright machine. Wilbur was hardly patient enough to be courteous. He turned to a friend and remarked as the man walked away:

"I hope I can make my living without murdering people. I am working out an aeroplane idea. I haven't it worked out yet. I need the money, but I won't make it murdering people with a half developed machine."

The reporters, who eagerly sought some word from Wilbur's hangar, one day saw some little boys from the garrison on Governors Island approach the guards. The newspaper men expected to see the children rebuffed as the reporters had been. They saw instead a kindly smile on Wilbur's face, and saw him welcome them, and through the open doors watched as he explained every detail of the machine. An aged officer in an invalid's chair was wheeled to the hangar. He, too, was welcomed and the machine fully explained to him. The first descriptions printed hereabouts were gathered by the reporters from the children who had composed Wilbur's little party.

Wilbur ceased flying in public in 1910 and gave his entire attention to experimental work and to suits over patents against Curtiss in this country and flyers in Germany and France. He came here recently to see Frank Coffyn while he was a patient in the Presbyterian Hospital, following an automobile accident in Central Park. He said to a friend during that visit that he was convinced there was a greater job ahead of him than developing the aeroplane. It was, he said, to carry on a fight for a revision of the patent law until a patent should become something more than a delusion and a snare to its holder. He said that should he undertake such a fight he would be prepared to show that under the present laws an inventor might easily bring into the world the greatest idea of its history and yet be wholly cheated out of the proceeds of his invention. For his rigid attitude of hostility to other flyers who had not recognized his patent rights, Wilbur was often severely criticised. He always insisted that he aimed at no control of the market whatever, and that if flyers came out honorably and admitted their obligations to the Wrights he would permit them to proceed under nominal patent fees.

From the invention of the aeroplane Wilbur Wright received his first material rewards in France where in many flights for prizes in 1908 he won the first returns from his eight years of experimentation.

The principal sums received by the Wright Brothers, were these:

From a French syndicate for control of their French patents	$50,000
From various European prizes	100,000
From the United States Government for the first aeroplane turned over to it	30,000
From the Hudson-Fulton Celebration Commission for flights at Governors Island	15,000
Total	$195,000

WILBUR WRIGHT

NOTABLE FLIGHTS BY WILBUR WRIGHT.

1903, Dec. 17.—At Kittyhawk, jump from the ground of 12 seconds in 27-mile wind on second trial of the machine, Orville having made the first trial. Neither jump demonstrated power control.

Dec. 17.—At Kittyhawk, flight of 852 feet in 59 seconds, on fourth trial, this being the first real flight by man in an aeroplane.

1904, August-December.—At Dayton, flight of 1 minute, in August, followed by constant experiments which produced 105 flights before December, the best flight being 5 minutes in duration.

1905, Sept. 26.—At Dayton, flight of 11.125 miles in 38 minutes 3 seconds, the flight being longer than all previous flights added together. In all 49 flights were made by Wilbur and Orville during the year.

1906, 1907.—No flights occurred, the Wrights giving their time to seeking backers and building machines with which to make demonstrations.

1908, May 11.—At Kittykawk, flight of 1.855 miles in 2 minutes 28 seconds, this flight being the first to be observed and reported by newspaper correspondents.

1908, Aug. 8.—At Le Mans, France, flight of 1 minute 47 seconds, followed by short flights until Aug. 12, when a flight of 4 miles stirred all France with spontaneous approval of Wilbur Wright. During September Wilbur made frequent flights, one on Sept. 21 of 1 hour 31 minutes 21 4-5 seconds. The distance was 41 miles.

Dec. 31.—At Le Mans, flight to celebrate passing of the year. Duration, 2 hours 20 minutes 23 seconds. Distance, 77 miles.

1909, March-May.—At Pau, France, and Rome, Italy, he made many flights, taking up passengers.

Oct. 4.—At Governors Island, flight of 33 minutes 33 seconds, to Grant's Tomb and back, covering a distance of 21 miles, the flight followed by others to the Statue of Liberty during the Hudson-Fulton Celebration.

1910, January-June.—At Dayton, frequent flights in teaching first aviation pupils, after whose graduation Wilbur Wright ceased public flying, although he occasionally went up as a passenger in 1911, and privately for his own pleasure.